Twentieth-Century Literary Criticism

Guide to Gale Literary Criticism Series

When you need to review criticism of literary works, these are the Gale series to use:

If the author's death date is:	You should turn to:
After Dec. 31, 1959 (or author is still living)	*CONTEMPORARY LITERARY CRITICISM* for example: Jorge Luis Borges, Anthony Burgess, William Faulkner, Mary Gordon, Ernest Hemingway, Iris Murdoch
1900 through 1959	*TWENTIETH-CENTURY LITERARY CRITICISM* for example: Willa Cather, F. Scott Fitzgerald, Henry James, Mark Twain, Virginia Woolf
1800 through 1899	*NINETEENTH-CENTURY LITERATURE CRITICISM* for example: Fedor Dostoevski, George Sand, Gerard Manley Hopkins, Emily Dickinson
1400 through 1799	*LITERATURE CRITICISM FROM 1400 TO 1800 (excluding Shakespeare)* for example: Anne Bradstreet, Pierre Corneille, Daniel Defoe, Alexander Pope, Jonathan Swift, Phillis Wheatley
	SHAKESPEAREAN CRITICISM Shakespeare's plays and poetry

Gale also publishes related criticism series:

CONTEMPORARY ISSUES CRITICISM

Presents criticism on contemporary authors writing on current issues. Topics covered include the social sciences, philosophy, economics, natural science, law, and related areas.

CHILDREN'S LITERATURE REVIEW

Covers authors of all eras. Presents criticism on authors and author/illustrators who write for the preschool to junior-high audience.

ISSN 0276-8178

Volume 13

Twentieth-Century Literary Criticism

Excerpts from Criticism of the Works of Novelists, Poets, Playwrights, Short Story Writers, and Other Creative Writers Who Died between 1900 and 1960, from the First Published Critical Appraisals to Current Evaluations

Dennis Poupard
James E. Person, Jr.
Editors

Thomas Ligotti
Associate Editor

Gale Research Company
Book Tower
Detroit, Michigan 48226

STAFF

Dennis Poupard, James E. Person, Jr., *Editors*

Thomas Ligotti, *Associate Editor*

Denise B. Grove, Marie Lazzari, *Senior Assistant Editors*

Earlene M. Alber, Lee Fournier, Sandra Giraud,
Sandra Liddell, Serita Lanette Lockard, Jay P. Pederson, *Assistant Editors*

Sharon K. Hall, *Contributing Editor*

Robert J. Elster, Jr., *Production Supervisor*
Lizbeth A. Purdy, *Production Coordinator*
Denise Michlewicz, *Assistant Production Coordinator*
Eric Berger, Paula J. DiSante, Amy Marcaccio, *Editorial Assistants*

Karen Rae Forsyth, *Research Coordinator*
Jeannine Schiffman Davidson, *Assistant Research Coordinator*
Kevin John Campbell, Victoria B. Cariappa, Robert J. Hill, Harry N. Kronick,
Rebecca Nicholaides, Leslie Kyle Schell, Valerie J. Webster, *Research Assistants*

Linda M. Pugliese, *Manuscript Coordinator*
Donna Craft, *Assistant Manuscript Coordinator*
Colleen M. Crane, Maureen A. Puhl, Rosetta Irene Carr, *Manuscript Assistants*

L. Elizabeth Hardin, *Permissions Supervisor*
Filomena Sgambati, *Permissions Associate*
Janice M. Mach, *Permissions Coordinator*
Patricia A. Seefelt, *Assistant Permissions Coordinator, Illustrations*
Susan D. Nobles, *Senior Permissions Assistant*
Margaret A. Chamberlain, Mary M. Matuz, Joan B. Weber, *Permissions Assistants*
Dorothy J. Fowler, Kathy J. Grell, Diana M. Platzke, Mabel C. Schoening, *Permissions Clerks*
Margaret Mary Missar, Audrey B. Wharton, *Photo Research*

Frederick G. Ruffner, *Publisher*

James M. Ethridge, *Executive Vice President/Editorial*

Dedria Bryfonski, *Editorial Director*

Christine Nasso, *Director, Literature Division*

Laurie Lanzen Harris, *Senior Editor, Literary Criticism Series*

Library of Congress Catalog Card Number 76-46132
ISBN 0-8103-0224-1
ISSN 0276-8178

Contents

Preface 5

Authors to Be Featured in *TCLC,* Volumes 14 and 15 9

Additional Authors to Appear in Future Volumes 10

Appendix 499

Cumulative Index to Authors 511

Cumulative Index to Nationalities 551

Cumulative Index to Critics 553

Isaac Babel 1894-1941 11

Bertolt Brecht 1898-1956 42

Saratchandra Chatterji 1876-1938 71

Anthony Comstock 1844-1915 85

Joseph Conrad 1857-1924 98

Géza Csáth 1887-1919 145

Alfred Döblin 1878-1957 156

Édouard Dujardin 1861-1949 182

Hector Saint-Denys Garneau 1912-1943 193

Emma Goldman 1869-1940 ... 206

William Hope Hodgson 1877-1918 228

Ricarda Huch 1864-1947 239

Franz Kafka 1883-1924 255

Giuseppe Tomasi di Lampedusa 1896-1957 290

Sinclair Lewis 1885-1951 323

H. L. Mencken 1880-1956 355

Marcel Proust 1871-1922..... 399

Rudolf Steiner 1861-1925..... 433

Thomas Wolfe 1900-1938..... 465

Preface

It is impossible to overvalue the importance of literature in the intellectual, emotional, and spiritual evolution of humanity. Literature is that which both lifts us out of everyday life and helps us to better understand it. Through the fictive lives of such characters as Anna Karenin, Lambert Strether, or Leopold Bloom, our perceptions of the human condition are enlarged, and we are enriched.

Literary criticism can also give us insight into the human condition, as well as into the specific moral and intellectual atmosphere of an era, for the criteria by which a work of art is judged reflects contemporary philosophical and social attitudes. Literary criticism takes many forms: the traditional essay, the book or play review, even the parodic poem. Criticism can also be of several kinds: normative, descriptive, interpretive, textual, appreciative, generic. Collectively, the range of critical response helps us to understand a work of art, an author, an era.

Scope of the Series

Twentieth-Century Literary Criticism (TCLC) is designed to serve as an introduction for the student of twentieth-century literature to the authors of the period 1900 to 1960 and to the most significant commentators on these authors. The great poets, novelists, short story writers, playwrights, and philosophers of this period are by far the most popular writers for study in high school and college literature courses. Since contemporary critics continue to analyze the work of this period—both in its own right and in relation to today's tastes and standards—a vast amount of relevant critical material confronts the student. To aid students in their location and selection of criticism written on works of authors who died between 1900 and 1960, *TCLC* presents significant passages from the most important published criticism on those authors.

The need for *TCLC* was suggested by the usefulness of the Gale series *Contemporary Literary Criticism (CLC),* which excerpts criticism on current writing. Because of the difference in time span under consideration *(CLC* considers authors who were still living after 1959), there is no duplication of material between *CLC* and *TCLC.* For further information about *CLC* and Gale's other criticism series, users should consult the Guide to Gale Literary Criticism Series preceding the title page in this volume.

Each volume of *TCLC* is carefully compiled to include authors who represent a variety of genres and nationalities and who are currently regarded as the most important writers of their era. In addition to major authors, *TCLC* also presents criticism on lesser known writers whose significant contributions to literary history are important to the study of twentieth-century literature.

Each author entry in *TCLC* is intended to provide a definitive overview of criticism on an author. Therefore, the editors include approximately twenty authors in each 600-page volume (compared with approximately sixty authors in a *CLC* volume of similar size) so that more attention may be given to an author. Each author entry represents a historical survey of the critical response to that author's work: some early criticism is presented to indicate initial reactions, later criticism is selected to represent any rise or decline in the author's reputation, and current retrospective analyses provide students with a modern view. The length of an author entry is intended to reflect the amount of critical attention the author has received from critics writing in English, and from foreign criticism in translation. Critical articles and books that have not been translated into English are excluded. Every attempt has been made to identify and include excerpts from the seminal essays on each author's work. Additionally, as space permits, especially insightful essays of a more limited scope are included.

An author may appear more than once in the series because of the great quantity of critical material available, or because of a resurgence of criticism generated by events such as an author's centennial or anniversary celebration, the republication of an author's works, or publication of a newly translated work or volume of letters. Beginning with Volume 13, several author entries in each volume of *TCLC* will feature criticism on single works by major authors who have appeared previously in the series. Only those individual works that have been the subjects of vast amounts of criticism and are widely studied in literature classes will be selected for this in-depth treatment. Joseph Conrad's *Heart of Darkness* and Franz Kafka's *The Metamorphosis* are examples of such entries in *TCLC,* Volume 13.

Organization of the Book

An author entry consists of the following elements: author heading, biographical and critical introduction, principal works, excerpts of criticism (each followed by a bibliographical citation), and an additional bibliography for further reading.

- The *author heading* consists of the author's full name, followed by birth and death dates. The unbracketed portion of the name denotes the form under which the author most commonly wrote. If an author wrote consistently under a pseudonym, the pseudonym will be listed in the author heading and the real name given in parentheses on the first line of the biographical and critical introduction. Also located at the beginning of the introduction to the author entry are any name variations under which an author wrote, including transliterated forms for authors whose languages use nonroman alphabets. Uncertainty as to a birth or death date is indicated by a question mark.

- The *biographical and critical introduction* contains background information designed to introduce the reader to an author and to the critical debate surrounding his or her work. Parenthetical material following many of the introductions provides references to biographical and critical reference series published by Gale. These include *Contemporary Authors, Dictionary of Literary Biography, Something about the Author,* and past volumes of *TCLC.*

- The *list of principal works* is chronological by date of first book publication and identifies the genre of each work. In the case of foreign authors where there are both foreign language publications and English translations, the title and date of the first English-language edition are given in brackets. Unless otherwise indicated, dramas are dated by first performance, not first publication.

- *Criticism* is arranged chronologically in each author entry to provide a useful perspective on changes in critical evaluation over the years. All titles by the author featured in the critical entry are printed in boldface type to enable the user to ascertain without difficulty the works being discussed. Also for purposes of easier identification, the critic's name and the publication date of the essay are given at the beginning of each piece of criticism. Unsigned criticism is preceded by the title of the journal in which it appeared. When an anonymous essay is later attributed to a critic, the critic's name appears in brackets at the beginning of the excerpt and in the bibliographical citation.

- Important critical essays are prefaced by *explanatory notes* as an additional aid to students using *TCLC.* The explanatory notes provide several types of useful information, including: the reputation of a critic; the importance of a work of criticism; the specific type of criticism (biographical, psychoanalytic, structuralist, etc.); a synopsis of the criticism; and the growth of critical controversy or changes in critical trends regarding an author's work. In many cases, these notes cross-reference the work of critics who agree or disagree with each other. Dates in parentheses within the explanatory notes refer to a book publication date when they follow a book title and to an essay date when they follow a critic's name.

- A complete *bibliographical citation* designed to facilitate location of the original essay or book by the interested reader follows each piece of criticism. An asterisk (*) at the end of a citation indicates that the essay is on more than one author.

- Most *TCLC* entries include *illustrations* of the author. Beginning with Volume 13, many entries will also contain illustrations of materials pertinent to an author's career, including holographs of manuscript pages, title pages, dust jackets, letters, or representations of important people and events in an author's life.

- The *additional bibliography* appearing at the end of each author entry suggests further reading on the author. In some cases it includes essays for which the editors could not obtain reprint rights. An asterisk (*) at the end of a citation indicates that the essay is on more than one author.

An appendix lists the sources from which material in each volume has been reprinted. It does not, however, list every book or periodical consulted in the preparation of the volume.

Cumulative Indexes

Each volume of *TCLC* includes a cumulative index to authors listing all the authors who have appeared in *Contemporary Literary Criticism, Twentieth-Century Literary Criticism, Nineteenth-Century Literature Criticism,* and *Literature Criticism from 1400 to 1800,* along with cross-references to the Gale series *Children's Literature Review, Authors in the News, Contemporary Authors, Dictionary of Literary Biography, Something about the Author,* and *Yesterday's Authors of Books for Children.* Users will welcome this cumulated author index as a useful tool for locating an author within the various series. The index, which lists birth and death dates when available, will be particularly valuable for those authors who are identified with a certain period but whose death date causes them to be placed in another, or for those authors whose careers span two periods. For example, F. Scott Fitzgerald is found in *TCLC,* yet a writer often associated with him, Ernest Hemingway, is found in *CLC.*

Each volume of *TCLC* also includes a cumulative nationality index. Author names are arranged alphabetically under their respective nationalities and followed by the volume numbers in which they appear.

A cumulative index to critics is another useful feature in *TCLC*. Under each critic's name are listed the authors on whom the critic has written and the volume and page where the criticism may be found.

Acknowledgments

No work of this scope can be accomplished without the cooperation of many people. The editors especially wish to thank the copyright holders of the excerpted criticism included in this volume, the permission managers of many book and magazine publishing companies for assisting us in securing reprint rights, and Jeri Yaryan for assistance with copyright research. We are also grateful to the staffs of the Detroit Public Library, University of Detroit Library, University of Michigan Library, and Wayne State University Library for making their resources available to us. The editors wish particularly to thank Bernard Garber for his assistance with the entry devoted to Rudolf Steiner.

Suggestions Are Welcome

In response to various suggestions, several features have been added to *TCLC* since the series began. Recently introduced features include explanatory notes to excerpted criticism that provide important information regarding critics and their work, a cumulative author index listing authors in all Gale literary criticism series, entries devoted to criticism on a single work by a major author, and more extensive illustrations.

If readers wish to suggest authors they would like to have covered in future volumes, or if they have other suggestions, they are cordially invited to write the editors.

Authors to Be Featured in *TCLC,* Volumes 14 and 15

Innokenty Annensky (Russian poet and critic)—One of the most important Russian literary theorists of the early twentieth century. Annensky's work profoundly influenced the generation of Russian writers that included Anna Akhamatova and Osip Mandelstam.

Charles A. Beard (American historian)—An important historian who examined the influence of economics on all aspects of American history, including the drafting of the U.S. Constitution.

Kate Chopin (American novelist)—Her novel *The Awakening* is often described as the first novel to examine honestly the plight of women in American society. Chopin has been the subject of a great deal of critical comment during the past decade.

Havelock Ellis (English psychologist and literary critic)—A pioneering researcher in the field of human sexuality, Ellis is largely responsible for the liberalization of British and American attitudes regarding human sexuality. His theories had a wide-ranging effect on twentieth-century literature.

F. Scott Fitzgerald (American novelist)—Fitzgerald's *The Great Gatsby* is one of the masterpieces of twentieth-century literature. In an entry devoted solely to that work, *TCLC* will present major critical essays examining every aspect of the novel.

Ford Madox Ford (English novelist)—A major novelist of manners, Ford has been the subject of a critical revival in recent years.

Henrik Ibsen (Norwegian dramatist)—Ibsen's *The Wild Duck* is one of the major works of the twentieth-century stage. *TCLC* will devote an entire entry to critical discussions of this important drama.

William James (American philosopher)—The foremost philosopher America has produced, James examined the metaphysical dilemmas of modern life. *TCLC* will present a summary and explanation of his thought as well as critical reactions to his work.

James Joyce (Irish novelist)—Joyce's *A Portrait of the Artist as a Young Man* examines the nature of youthful idealism and the role of the artist in modern society. In an entry devoted solely to that work, *TCLC* will present the major critical essays on the novel.

Vladislav Khodasevich (Russian poet)—Called the greatest Russian poet of the twentieth century by Vladimir Nabokov, Khodasevich has been the subject of recent critical interest in the United States.

Ring Lardner (American short story writer)—One of America's greatest humorists, Lardner examined small-town Midwestern life and American provincialism.

David Lindsay (English novelist)—An important writer in the genre of fantasy, Lindsay addressed metaphysical and spiritual questions in novels that strongly influenced the works of C.S. Lewis and J.R.R. Tolkien.

Liu E (Chinese novelist)—His *Travels of Lao Ts'an* is one of the most important Chinese novels of the twentieth century.

Jack London (American novelist)—Although often considered an adventure writer, London examined issues of social equality and personal morality in his fiction. Recent years have witnessed greatly renewed interest in his works.

Thomas Mann (German novelist)—His *Death in Venice* examines the decay of early twentieth-century European civilization and the nature of human passions. *TCLC* will devote an entire entry to critical discussions of this novella.

Émile Nelligan (Canadian poet)—He is often called the Canadian Rimbaud for the intensity of his lyric verse and the tortured quality of his life.

Mori Ogai (Japanese novelist)—An author crucial to an understanding of modern Japan, Ogai examined in his novels the effects of Western influences on traditional Japanese culture.

George Orwell (English novelist and essayist)—During the past two years, his novel *Nineteen Eighty-Four* has been more widely discussed than at any other time since its initial publication. *TCLC* will present the critical history of the work and an extensive survey of recent criticism on *Nineteen Eighty-Four* in 1984.

Leo Tolstoy (Russian novelist)—His *Anna Karenin* is considered one of the greatest novels in world literature. *TCLC* will devote an entire entry to the critical history of this work.

Paul Valéry (French poet)—Valéry is widely recognized as one of France's outstanding poets and literary theoreticians. His work bridges the movements of nineteenth-century Symbolism and twentieth-century Modernism.

Additional Authors to Appear in Future Volumes

Abercrombie, Lascelles 1881-1938
Adamic, Louis 1898-1951
Ade, George 1866-1944
Agustini, Delmira 1886-1914
Aldanov, Mark 1886-1957
Aldrich, Thomas Bailey 1836-1907
Allen, Hervey 1889-1949
Archer, William 1856-1924
Arlen, Michael 1895-1956
Austin, Mary 1868-1934
Babits, Miholy 1888-1941
Bahr, Hermann 1863-1934
Barea, Arturo 1897-1957
Benét, William Rose 1886-1950
Benjamin, Walter 1892-1940
Benson, E(dward) F(rederic) 1867-1940
Benson, Stella 1892-1933
Berdyaev, Nikolai Aleksandrovich 1874-1948
Bergson, Henri 1859-1941
Binyon, Laurence 1869-1943
Bishop, John Peale 1892-1944
Blackmore, R(ichard) D(oddridge) 1825-1900
Blum, Leon 1872-1950
Bodenheim, Maxwell 1892-1954
Bosschere, Jean de 1878-1953
Bourne, Randolph 1886-1918
Broch, Hermann 1886-1951
Campana, Dina 1885-1932
Cannan, Gilbert 1884-1955
Chand, Prem 1880-1936
Churchill, Winston 1871-1947
Corelli, Marie 1855-1924
Croce, Benedetto 1866-1952
Daumal, René 1908-1944
Davidson, John 1857-1909
Day, Clarence 1874-1935
Delafield, E.M. (Edme Elizabeth Monica de la Pasture) 1890-1943
DeVoto, Bernard 1897-1955
Douglas, (George) Norman 1868-1952
Douglas, Lloyd C(assel) 1877-1951
Dovzhenko, Alexander 1894-1956
Drinkwater, John 1882-1937
Durkheim, Émile 1858-1917
Duun, Olav 1876-1939
Fadeyev, Alexander 1901-1956
Feydeau, Georges 1862-1921
Field, Rachel 1894-1924
Flecker, James Elroy 1884-1915
Fletcher, John Gould 1886-1950
Frank, Bruno 1886-1945
Frazer, (Sir) George 1854-1941
Freud, Sigmund 1853-1939
Fuller, Henry Blake 1857-1929
Futrelle, Jacques 1875-1912
Gladkov, Fydor Vasilyevich 1883-1958
Glyn, Elinor 1864-1943
Gogarty, Oliver St. John 1878-1957
Golding, Louis 1895-1958
Gosse, Edmund 1849-1928
Gourmont, Remy de 1858-1915
Gray, John 1866-1934
Gumilyov, Nikolay 1886-1921
Hale, Edward Everett 1822-1909
Harper, Frances Ellen Watkins 1825-1911
Harris, Frank 1856-1931
Hawthorne, Julian 1846-1934
Hernandez, Miguel 1910-1942
Hewlett, Maurice 1861-1923
Heyward, DuBose 1885-1940
Hilton, James 1900-1954
Hope, Anthony 1863-1933
Howe, Julia Ward 1819-1910
Hudson, W(illiam) H(enry) 1841-1922
Hulme, Thomas Ernest 1883-1917
Ishikawa Takuboku 1885-1912
Ivanov, Vyacheslav Ivanovich 1866-1949
Jacobs, W(illiam) W(ymark) 1863-1943
James, Will 1892-1942
Jerome, Jerome K(lapka) 1859-1927
Kaye-Smith, Sheila 1887-1956
King, Grace 1851-1932
Korolenko, Vladimir 1853-1921
Kuzmin, Mikhail Alexseyevich 1875-1936
Lang, Andrew 1844-1912
Lawson, Henry 1867-1922
Leverson, Ada 1862-1933
Lewisohn, Ludwig 1883-1955
Liliencron, Detlev von 1844-1909
Lindsay, (Nicholas) Vachel 1879-1931
Long, Frank Belknap 1903-1959
Louÿs, Pierre 1870-1925
Lucas, E(dward) V(errall) 1868-1938
Lugones, Leopoldo 1874-1938
Manning, Frederic 1887-1935
Maragall, Joan 1860-1911
Martin du Gard, Roger 1881-1958
Masaryk, Tomas 1850-1939
McCoy, Horace 1897-1955
Meredith, George 1828-1909
Mirbeau, Octave 1850-1917
Mistral, Frederic 1830-1914
Monro, Harold 1879-1932
Moore, Thomas Sturge 1870-1944
Morley, Christopher 1890-1957
Murray, (George) Gilbert 1866-1957
Murry, J. Middleton 1889-1957
Nathan, George Jean 1882-1958
Nordhoff, Charles 1887-1947
Norris, Frank 1870-1902
Ophuls, Max 1902-1957
Parrington, Vernon L. 1871-1929
Pickthall, Marjorie 1883-1922
Pinero, Arthur Wing 1855-1934
Platonov, Andrei 1899-1951
Pontoppidan, Henrik 1857-1943
Porter, Gene(va) Stratton 1886-1924
Prévost, Marcel 1862-1941
Quiller-Couch, Arthur 1863-1944
Rappoport, Solomon 1863-1944
Riley, James Whitcomb 1849-1916
Rinehart, Mary Roberts 1876-1958
Rohmer, Sax 1883-1959
Rolland, Romain 1866-1944
Rőlvaag, O(le) E(dvart) 1876-1931
Romero, José Rubén 1890-1952
Roussel, Raymond 1877-1933
Ruskin, John 1819-1900
Sabatini, Rafael 1875-1950
Saintsbury, George 1845-1933
Santayana, George 1863-1952
Sardou, Victorien 1831-1908
Service, Robert 1874-1958
Seton, Ernest Thompson 1860-1946
Shestov, Lev 1866-1938
Solovyov, Vladimir 1853-1900
Squire, J(ohn) C(ollings) 1884-1958
Stockton, Frank R. 1834-1902
Sudermann, Hermann 1857-1938
Sully-Prudhomme, René 1839-1907
Summers, Montague 1880-1948
Tey, Josephine (Elizabeth Mackintosh) 1897-1952
Tolstoy, Alexei 1882-1945
Turner, W(alter) J(ames) R(edfern) 1889-1946
Vachell, Horace Annesley 1861-1955
Van Dine, S.S. (William H. Wright) 1888-1939
Van Doren, Carl 1885-1950
Veblen, Thorstein 1857-1929
Wallace, Edgar 1874-1932
Wallace, Lewis 1827-1905
Walser, Robert 1878-1956
Webster, Jean 1876-1916
White, Walter Francis 1893-1955
Wister, Owen 1860-1938
Wren, P(ercival) C(hristopher) 1885-1941
Yonge, Charlotte Mary 1823-1901
Zangwill, Israel 1864-1926
Zoshchenko, Mikhail 1895-1958
Zweig, Stefan 1881-1942

Readers are cordially invited to suggest additional authors to the editors.

Isaac (Emmanuilovich) Babel

1894-1941

(Also transliterated as Isaak, Izaak; also Emanuilovich; also Babel'; also wrote under pseudonym of Kiril Liutov) Russian short story writer, dramatist, screenwriter, essayist, journalist, editor, autobiographer, and translator.

Babel is considered Russia's most gifted short story writer of the post-Revolutionary era. His highly compressed, anecdotal fiction makes consistent use of contrast and paradox to emphasize the opposition between violence and passivity, romanticism and primitivism, hero and antihero, and, most importantly, the tension between a traditional Jewish ethos in a non-Jewish environment. The pathetic war sketches of *Konarmiia (Red Cavalry)* and the picaresque stories of *Odesskie rasskazy (The Odessa Tales),* Babel's two most important collections, are praised for their emotional depth and have earned him a prominent reputation as both a brilliant stylist and as a sophisticated observer of human nature.

Ardis Publishers

Born in the Jewish ghetto of Odessa, Babel was the son of a middle-class merchant family. His early education consisted of studies in a local business school and traditional Judaic studies in Hebrew, the Bible, and the Talmud. In his formative years Babel witnessed the full force of anti-Semitism during the pogroms of 1905. The pogroms, which were massive riots led by Cossack horsemen and sanctioned by government authorities, resulted in brutal assaults on Jewish citizens and the devastation of Jewish communities. These ruthless demonstrations fostered Babel's concurrent horror of and fascination with the violent Cossack existence and formed the basis for some of his finest works, including the highly acclaimed autobiographical tales "I storiya mori golubyatnei" ("The Story of My Dovecote") and "Pervaya lyubov" ("First Love"). In 1915, after graduation from Kiev Institute of Finance and Business Studies, Babel moved to Petrograd (formerly St. Petersburg, later Leningrad) with the hope of publishing the few stories he had written in school. While in Petrograd he was greatly encouraged when a fortuitous meeting with the Russian proletarian writer Maxim Gorky resulted in the publication of two of his stories in Gorky's magazine *Letopis'*. Recognizing Babel's raw talent, Gorky advised him to gather more first-hand experiences in order to enhance his future literary works. Babel readily agreed and enlisted in the Russian army, serving during World War I at the Romanian front until he was stricken with malaria. After his military service, he claimed to have worked for a short time in Petrograd with the Cheka, a political police force designated to identify and eliminate counterrevolutionary or anti-Communist groups, and a forerunner to the Soviet Union's present-day KGB. However, Babel's daughter, as well as many critics, have disputed this claim, and the extent of Babel's involvement with the Cheka is still undetermined. Throughout this period he continued to write, publishing several short stories in local journals and newspapers.

His major literary development came in 1919 as a war correspondent with the Red Army. Under the command of Semyon Budyonny, Babel rode with the Cossack cavalry against the Poles and Czarist White forces, and many commentators have found it ironic, if not incredible that these soldiers, who had been the source of the destruction Babel witnessed in his youth, became the inspiration for his most important literary achievements. Some critics observe that this incongruity was made possible by Babel's infatuation with the primitivism of the "noble savage" epitomized by the Cossacks, while others believe that Cossack life offered him a welcome escape from the religious and moral orthodoxy of his youth. The sketches recorded in Babel's diary during his attachment to the Red Army were developed into the stories of *Red Cavalry,* now considered by most critics to be his masterpiece. During the 1920s, Babel received considerable literary recognition for these sketches, and for the heroic tales of the Jewish gangster Benya Krik which were later collected in *The Odessa Tales*. Eventually Babel's works were censored by the Soviet regime for their erotic detail and lack of commitment to proletarian causes. Thereafter Babel, who refused to write political propaganda, voluntarily restricted publication of his work. In 1934 Babel remarked on his self-censorship when he declared himself to be "master of a new literary genre, the genre of silence." He was arrested in 1939 after subtly criticizing the Stalinist regime in a screenplay he was writing. It is believed that Babel died while in prison in 1941.

Critics generally focus their discussions of Babel's work on his major collection of stories, *Red Cavalry*. While the impressionistic sketches within the work are diverse in subject matter,

they are linked by the first-person narration of Babel's alter ego Kiril Liutov, by the doleful images of the Revolution, and by Babel's overriding concern with violence. The protagonists of *Red Cavalry* are usually illiterate Cossack soldiers who live by their primitive instincts and find self-esteem in direct proportion to their ability to brutalize for the good of the Revolution. Most critics observe that the major tension throughout *Red Cavalry* is the narrator's subliminal Jewish morality contrasted with the more violent Cossack ethos, and his desire to be no longer alienated from the Cossacks as a "bespectacled intellectual." Lionel Trilling notes: "The stories of *Red Cavalry* have as their principle of coherence what I have called the anomaly, or the joke of a Jew who is a member of a Cossack regiment." Thus, in the story "Moi pervy gus" ("My First Goose"), Liutov is morally unable to take a human life, but still wins the esteem of the Cossack force by ruthlessly murdering an old woman's goose. In addition to this contrast between the narrator and his barbaric comrades, Babel employs exacting detail and laconic prose to facilitate the skillful ironic twists characteristic of most of his stories, reminiscent in technique of the works of Guy de Maupassant. For example, in "Pis' mo" ("The Letter") a son boasts to his mother how he tortured and murdered his father who was on the opposite side of the Revolution; in "Pan Apolek" an itinerant Polish artist who reverently paints local citizens as biblical characters is received as a genuine Christian of true faith until, to the delight of Liutov, he relates a vulgar tale about a marriage between Jesus and the Jewess Deborah. Critics praise the distinctive style of *Red Cavalry,* and although the episodes comprising this work are essentially plotless and anecdotal, they are considered among the finest short stories in Russian literature.

For the most part, the stories of Babel's second major work, *The Odessa Tales,* were written during the same period as the stories of *Red Cavalry*. However, with *The Odessa Tales* Babel turned to the ghetto of his childhood to create a legendary world of Jewish gangsters and racketeers. Benya Krik, the central character in several of these tales, is an elusive criminal who menaces the wealthy Jews of the community. Many critics note that, for Babel, Benya Krik represented a romantic reversal of the downtrodden Jew—an identification Babel tried to abandon in his *Red Cavalry* stories. *The Odessa Tales* are rich in the culture and heritage that he regarded so ambivalently in the works of *Red Cavalry*. Throughout the stories, Babel employed many of the same themes and stylistic elements as in his master work, but critics note that *The Odessa Tales* are primarily based on traditionally romantic and humorous situations, and lack the depth of the more contemporary *Red Cavalry* stories. Of the differences between Babel's two major works, Simon Markish has observed that "despite their stunning stylistic discoveries and innovations, despite their nostalgia for a recent but already irrevocable past, despite the utterly new and unexpected appearance of a bandit-hero in Russian-Jewish literature, the *Odessa Tales* continue and perhaps crown the pre-revolutionary tradition of social observation in this literature, whereas *Red Cavalry* opens a new period and establishes a new tradition."

Babel's works were suppressed in the Soviet Union from the time of his arrest in 1939 until 1954, when the death of Joseph Stalin and the rise to power of Nikita Khrushchev initiated a new freedom in literature and the arts. Babel and many other writers who had been incarcerated for slandering the "image" of Stalin, were posthumously rehabilitated into Soviet culture. Thereafter his stories and some of his previously unpublished works were collected and translated into English. Although Babel produced a relatively small body of work, his fiction has been widely praised by Western readers and critics, and today he is recognized as one of the masters of the Russian short story.

(See also *TCLC,* Vol. 2 and *Contemporary Authors,* Vol. 104.)

PRINCIPAL WORKS

Konarmiia (short stories) 1923
[*Red Cavalry,* 1929]
Rasskazy (short stories) 1925
Istoriia moei golubiatni (short stories) 1926
Zakat (drama) 1927
[*Sunset* published in journal *Noonday,* 1960]
Odesskie rasskazy (short stories) 1931
[*The Odessa Tales* published in *The Collected Stories,* 1955]
Mariia [first publication] (drama) 1935
[*Maria* published in *Three Soviet Plays,* 1966]
Benya Krik, the Gangster, and Other Stories (short stories) 1948
The Collected Stories (short stories) 1955
Isaac Babel: The Lonely Years, 1925-1939 (short stories, letters, essays, and speeches) 1964
I. Babel: Izbrannoe (short stories, dramas, autobiography, letters, and speeches) 1966
You Must Know Everything: Stories 1915-1937 (short stories) 1969
The Forgotten Prose (short stories and diary excerpts) 1978

ALEKSANDR VORONSKIJ (essay date 1925)

[*A Russian critic, Vornskij was appointed editor of the first Soviet literary journal* Krasnaya Nov' *in 1921. He was a conservative Marxist, and, as such, he judged literature according to its literary significance rather than by its adherence to the political ideology of proletarian art, a method which contrasted with the Marxist belief that literature should present an accurate depiction of objective social reality. For his uncompromising critical method, Voronskij was removed as editor of* Krasnaya Nov' *in 1927 and expelled from the Communist party. A year later he was readmitted to the party only to disappear shortly thereafter. In the following excerpt, Voronskij provides an early assessment of Babel's work. He focuses on Babel as an accomplished miniaturist whose epic style captured the essence of an era in the throes of political and social transformation.*]

There is still no collected works of Babel, but the 100 to 200 pages he has published thus far mark him as a writer of unmistakable maturity. This is not to say that his job is done, that he has fully expressed himself. On the contrary, there is still much to come including his most important work. Babel has not yet realized his full creative potential. Not all his works are at the same artistic level, but his prose already shows firmness, maturity, self-assurance and craftsmanship—testimony to sustained, assiduous effort. Babel has his own voice, his own style, but he takes hold not only because he speaks from "the gut," but also because of his intelligence and his capacity for hard work. This is apparent in almost all his miniatures [vignettes]. Clearly he has been to a workshop. He has culture, and this is his crucial advantage over the bulk of Soviet fiction writers who are trying to make it on their "guts" and on the sheer wealth of their observations and who consider study and hard work a tedious bourgeois prejudice. That is why it so often happens in our country that after a debut, an artist begins to peter out and go downhill: his first or second appearance has made an impact because he expressed himself so fully and directly that formal lapses either were not noticed by the reader or were forgiven as a warrant of the author's sincerity. To make predictions about writers is an idle pastime, but it is proper to take note of Babel's culture, his intelligence, and the firmness of his talent. These qualities give one the right to hope that Babel will not deteriorate and will not go the way of several of his young confreres.

Babel is miles away from naturalism or flatly descriptive realism, but he is also a far cry from Andrej Belyj. He has something in common with Maupassant, with Chekhov and with Gorky, yet he cannot be bracketed with them either. Maupassant is a skeptic, Chekhov is sad, Gorky is a romantic, and all this is reflected in each one's style. Babel's manner is epic, at times biblically epic. (pp. 182-83)

In his miniatures Babel is impassive, calm, slow. He does not hurry, nor does he hurry the reader. He draws out deliberately his spare, weighty, carefully chosen words. He is epic, even in those instances when he becomes lyrical. But Babel's epic is not the kind that is indifferent to good and evil on the assumption that the past has long become ancient history, the topical has evaporated, and all the passions have died out. Babel tries to be epic in his tales about Budënnyj's Red Cavalry. . . . He writes about the stuff of yesterday, follows in the fresh tracks of recent experience; in essence he is writing about the present. His epic is like a campfire that has just gone out: beneath the ashes hot coals are still glowing. Babel's epic quality is *sui generis;* it is an artistic device, calculated and deliberate. (p. 183)

Actually Babel is not at all impassive, indifferent to good and evil, or calm. He has his own point of view; he has a definite attitude toward the epoch, the people, the events, but he has got a grip on himself as an artist. He speaks simply, without unnecessary verbiage, just as we have become accustomed to living simply and without unnecessary verbiage in the midst of the unusual and unprecedented. More important, he understands that the true artist's task does not lie in hitting the nerves harder, but in touching up the canvas "just a bit," as Lev Tolstoy put it—in singling out unerringly whatever reveals the essence of an object, a person, an episode. (p. 184)

Babel has a way of coupling adjectives with nouns that is startling and apt. "Flaming cloaks," "passionate rags," "a dusty wire of curls," "the thick expanses of the night," "a raspberry-colored wart," "powerful evenings," "the deathly aroma of brocade," "the smoke of a secret murder," "the cool depth of the night," "the orange battles of sunset," "the stuffy air turned sour," "the sparkling sky, inexpressibly empty as always during hours of danger," and so on. Perhaps it is this proclivity for epithets that contributes in part to the slowness, the leisureliness, the expressive, flowing quality of his narration.

Babel is also a lyricist. His lyricism is somewhat dreamy, indolent, cool; it does not hold the reader back, nor does it disturb the rhythm of the narrative. The presence of lyricism, incidentally, exposes the precariousness of his epic manner. Babel plays sly games with the reader; he is not a chronicler, but our passionate contemporary.

Babel is cementing the bond between literature and the Republic of the Soviets and the Communist Party. He is close to us and has a firm sense of what our life and our era are about. One can say without exaggeration that Babel is a new landmark on contemporary literature's tortuous, complex road toward Communism. Though some people fail to see this, the content of Babel's works is absolutely unequivocal. (p. 185)

Aleksandr Voronskij, "Isaac Babel," translated by James Karambelas (originally published under a different title in Literaturnye tipy *by Aleksandr Voronskij, 1925), in* Twentieth-Century Russian Literary Criticism, *edited by Victor Erlich (copyright © 1975 by Yale University), Yale University Press, 1975, pp. 182-97.*

PRINCE D. S. MIRSKY (essay date 1926)

[Mirsky was a Russian prince who fled his country after the Bolshevik Revolution and settled in London. While in England, he wrote two important and comprehensive histories of Russian literature, Contemporary Russian Literature *(1926) and* A History of Russian Literature (1927). *In 1932, having reconciled himself to the Soviet regime, Mirsky returned to the U.S.S.R. He continued to write literary criticism, but his work eventually ran afoul of Soviet censors and he was exiled to Siberia. He disappeared in 1937. In the following excerpt Mirsky examines the art of Babel's collection of stories,* Rasskazy. *He finds that Babel combines Russian dialect with a terse, personal form of "journalese" to produce a lively and provocative language that is artistically appealing.]*

Babel, this time is not the great and wicked city of the Bible, but merely a young Russian author of Jewish origin, who has written some short stories of considerable merit [called **"Rasskazy" ("Tales")**]. (p. 581)

Babel's stories are the nearest approach, in contemporary Russian prose, to perfection of form, and to what I venture to call "pure art." "Pure art," in the sense I use it here, is that kind of art where the process of "transforming" the "original experience" into artistic values has been completed, and has left no undistilled residue of "human significance," no "ragged edges" of untransformed "emotion." The distinction between pure and alloyed art, in this sense, has, I think, nothing to do with the now much-discussed distinction of Classic and Romantic: it has nothing to do with the quality of the "original experience," but only with the transforming process. The result of "pure art" is that in a work of this description all the human, psychological, or emotional elements possess no significance apart from their *context* to the whole fabric. The examples that come most readily to my mind are (outside pure poetry) Pushkin's "Queen of Spades" and [Synge's] "The Playboy of the Western World." Babel has another point in common with Synge, and that is his language. All his best things are in dialect, and in a dialect spoken by men not originally of Russian speech—consequently full of "solecisms" and offences against the very spirit of standard Russian. The two dialects he uses with best effect are the Russian Jewish jargon of Odessa and the Russian of the (originally Ukranian-speaking) Cossacks of the Kuban, as modified by badly digested Red journalese. I have, myself, a certain familiarity with the latter form of speech and can testify to Babel's extraordinarily truthful rendering of it. His aim, however, is not to phonograph curious dialect, but to put it to the best artistic use, to open up all its latent possibilities of vocabulary and syntax—in short to make "language" of it. His dialectical style, like Synge's, has that tightness, that inevitable fullness and saturatedness, that approach it to the language of poetry. There are no "empty" words in Babel's Odessite or Kuban Russian—each single word has its necessary place and is made to contribute to the effect of the whole. Compared to the splendour of his dialectal passages (which are placed in the mouth of his characters), Babel's own "author's" Russian is strikingly different. It possesses a certain vividness, but no distinction. It is a hardly glorified form of the semi-impressionistic journalese that has been worn to rags by Russian journalists within the last twenty or twenty-five years. Babel is fully aware of this limitation. To transcend it is evidently beyond his power, but he exploits it very cleverly, and in some of his best stories plays it off against the glorious speech of his characters to emphasize his own wretched intellectualdom—an object of contempt for the rough-and-ready "Red Fighters" of Comrade Budenny's famous Army. This power of irony at his own (or rather "the narrator's") expense is a very prominent feature in Babel, and it redeems, or even annuls, much that otherwise would have to be considered very serious blemishes. And at times these blemishes remain unredeemed, and make some of his stories little better than clever (always that), but rather tasteless journalism. An instance of this kind is the shrewd, but cheap, skit of Kerensky called **"Colour and Line,"** where that politician's statesmanship is explained by his shortsightedness, which allows him to see, in a crowd, only its colour, but not its outlines.

For a writer who has such a sense of economy and concentration, and who has approached so near to absolute perfection, Babel is curiously uneven. He has a peculiar limitation which seems to be an inability to invent his plots. This would explain why some of his stories are so good, and others so indifferent, or even positively bad. The former are evidently those in which he took a good subject "from life"—the latter those in which he was left to shift for himself. Of the ten stories contained in the little volume before me (the only one so far published, except for a small pamphlet of thirty-two pages), three are as good stories as I have read. The others are either not stories at all or very bad stories. In the former case they are sometimes supremely good journalism, and sometimes first-rate narrative *material* without a narrative skeleton to hold it together.

The three good stories all belong to one of two cycles. The first turns on the person of a famous Jewish bandit of Odessa, Benya (=Ben) Krik, surnamed the King—who I am told by Odessites is a real character, and was called in real life Misha Yaponshik (Mike the Jap). The other cycle relates to the exploits of the Red Fighters of the famous cavalry army of Budenny in the Civil and Polish Wars. The word "cycle" is not irrelevantly reminiscent of things heroic and Homeric. Babel's stories are distinctly heroic in tone, in spite of the slangy dialect used by the heroes, and in spite of a rather extreme form of realism in dealing with previously tabooed subjects and objects. But this mixture of outspoken (*very* outspoken) realism and of heroic romance is seasoned by a zest for shrewd irony—the whole making a mixture of very complex, original, and piquant flavour. In this mixture even Babel's own second-rate journalese, when he speaks in the first person, contributes to complicate the whole and introduce a new and necessary note. From the point of view of extreme complexity of tone (only an advertising agent to some "new and piquant sauce" would be able to find adequate words to describe it), the most remarkable of Babel's stories is **"The King,"** relating to one of the greatest exploits of that great hero. What gives the story its unique flavour is that "the King's" most heroic stroke of cunning against the police has as a background the wedding of his middle-aged and deformed sister to a young man whom he had bought with money—the produce of his robberies. The story ends on this note of sordid but spectacular realism. When in the early morning Benya returns home after assisting with mock sympathy at the fire he had arranged at the police-station, he finds all the wedding guests either gone or asleep.

> Only Droyra [the bride] was not thinking of sleep. With both hands she was pushing her discouraged bridegroom towards the doors of the nuptial chamber, looking at him the while, greedily, like a cat who has the mouse in her mouth, and is slightly trying it in her teeth.

The other two first-rate stories, **"A Letter"** and **"Salt,"** are of the Budenny cycle. Here Babel's manner is to treat the worst horrors and cruelties as a matter of course, a manner common to many of the young writers, but in which no one, not even Vsevolod Ivanov, can rival Babel. In both these stories he uses the form of a letter written by a semi-literate (or dictated by an illiterate) Red Trooper. This gives full scope to his masterly command of language. For the Russian reader these two stories are the daintiest delights in all modern literature. They have the verbal concentration of poetry, they can be learned by heart (several persons of my acquaintance know **"Salt"** practically by heart). **"A Letter"** is a terrible story—a father who is a sergeant-major in the White Army kills his elder son, who is a Red soldier—and for this he is tortured to death by his second son, also a Bolshevik; the story is told in a letter to his mother by the youngest son. The subject of **"Salt"** (which is only a few hundred words long) cannot be summarized, so wonderful is the concentration of the story: it takes the form of a letter of a Red Corporal to the Editor of a Red Front newspaper. It is a joy for ever, a real jewel—in spite of the crass and casual horror of the details. For the horror and filth are without residue distilled into what I cannot call anything but poetry.

To translate Babel quite adequately is, of course, impossible, considering what I have said of his language. But his best stories have sufficient narrative backbone and sufficient art in them to make such a (necessarily inadequate) translation worth the while. (pp. 581-82)

Prince D. S. Mirsky, "Babel," in The Nation and the Athenaeum, *Vol. XXXVIII, No. 17, January 23, 1926, pp. 581-82.*

S[EMYON] BUDYONNY (letter date 1928)

[*Budyonny was the commander of the First Cavalry Army to which Babel was assigned as a newspaper correspondent during the Russian Civil War in 1919. It is Budyonny and his regiment who are depicted throughout Babel's* Red Cavalry. *When the stories were first published in newspapers and magazines in 1923 and 1924 Budyonny was outraged, and in 1924 he wrote a deprecating letter to the editors of* Krasnaya Nov' *expressing his disapproval of Babel's work. In 1928, in the newspaper* Pravda, *Maxim Gorky wrote an essay entitled "To Rural and War Correspondents—How I Learnt to Write" in which he notes his approval of Babel's portrayal of Budyonny and the Cossacks in* Red Cavalry. *The following excerpted letter is Budyonny's public reply to Gorky's essay and his explanation of his distaste for Babel's stories. For Gorky's reply to Budyonny, see the excerpt below, 1928.*]

Dear Alexei Maximovich,

Our national dailies, *Pravda* and *Izvestia,* on September 30 carried an excerpt from your pamphlet "To Rural and War Correspondents—How I Learnt to Write."

In that piece, in discussing the main trends in literature—Romanticism and Realism—you state the following: . . .

> Comrade Budyonny has pounced upon Babel's ***Red Cavalry*** and I don't believe he should have, because Budyonny himself likes to embellish the outside not only of his men, but of his horses too. Babel, on the other hand, embellished his men on the inside, which, in my opinion, is better and more truthful than what Gogol did for his Zaporozhe Cossacks.
>
> Man is still a beast in many respects and, culturally, he is only an adolescent. It is always useful to embellish and to praise him.

Although it is very difficult for me to argue with you on literary matters, nevertheless, since ***Red Cavalry*** has come up as a subject of discussion once again, I must say that I cannot agree with you, Alexei Maximovich, despite all my respect for you, and I will try to explain why I criticized ***Red Cavalry*** and why I think I did so with good reason.

To start with, I believe [a writer] should know his source material and I dare say Babel was never and could never have been a genuine, active combat soldier in the First Cavalry. I know that he hung around with some unit deep in the rear, one of those units that, to our misfortune, were always a drag upon our fighting men. To be precise, Babel was in the backwaters of our First Cavalry.

What does Babel write about that gives him the right to use such a broad title as ***Red Cavalry***?

Babel indulges in old women's gossip, digs into old women's garbage, and tells with horror about some Red Army man taking a loaf of bread and a chicken somewhere. He invents things that never happened, slings dirt at our best Communist commanders, lets his imagination run wild, simply lies . . .

The subject matter of Babel's stories is distorted by the impressions of an erotomanic author. His topics range from the ravings of a mad Jew to the looting of a Catholic church, to the thrashing the cavalrymen give to their own foot soldiers, to the portrayal of a syphilitic Red Army man and end with a display of the author's scientific curiosity, when he wishes to see what a Jewish woman raped by about ten Makhno men looks like. Just as he looks upon life as a sunny meadow in May with mares and stallions on it, so he also views the operations of the Red Cavalry and he sees them through the prism of eroticism.

I happen to know for certain that while Babel saw women's breasts and bare legs around the army's field kitchens, Pani Eliza's servants' quarters, in the middle of the forest, awake and asleep, in various combinations, there were a few other things the First Cavalry was doing that Babel did not see.

And that's quite natural and understandable. How could Babel possibly have seen from the deep rear the spots where the fate of the workers and peasants was being decided. He just couldn't have.

I believe that if Babel wanted to give a title which would correspond to his genre of writing, he should have called his book *In the Backwaters of the Red Cavalry*. That would have been more accurate.

Now I ask: did the author maintain even the most elementary truthfulness, the least respect for historical perspective that is a must for realistic art? He didn't and it is the more shocking in that he is dealing with men of whom some are still alive and with facts familiar to every Red Army man. Alas, Alexei Maximovich, there is not the least concern for truthfulness in it.

I believe, Alexei Maximovich, that you will agree with me that to describe the heroic class struggle, a struggle unprecedented in the history of mankind, it is necessary before anything else to grasp the nature of those classes, i.e., to at least be partly familiar with Marxist dialectics. And it so happens that Babel doesn't qualify by those standards. And that is why his attempt to depict the life and the traditions of the First Cavalry reads like a lampoon and is permeated by a petty-bourgeois outlook.

Of course, the heroic fighters of the First Cavalry are simple, plain, often almost illiterate, men, but "pieces of art" like this one, appearing at a moment when we are witnessing decisive battles between labor and capital, are not only unwelcome, but, I believe, outright harmful.

That is why I have criticized Babel's ***Red Cavalry.*** And I am not the only one to do so, for all the revolutionary masses with whom we are building socialism before your eyes are on my side.

How can one say, in view of all this, that Babel depicted his Red Cavalrymen better and more truthfully than Gogol did his Zaporozhe Cossacks? Is it possible that a sensitive person like you, Alexei Maximovich, has failed to feel that, even when he gave us his "beautiful untruth" about the Zaporozhe Cossacks, Gogol, being a great artist, avoided a sordid tone, while Babel, the alleged realist, has so embellished his fighting men from inside that, to this day, I keep receiving letters protesting against his crude, deliberate and arrogant slander of the First Red Cavalry.

For a long time, we have considered Babel's book as a lampoon, and I wouldn't have mentioned it again if it hadn't been mentioned by you, Alexei Maximovich, just when you were telling our new proletarian rural and war correspondents how to write.

I do not think that they should describe the inspiration of our days the way Babel did. (pp. 384-87)

S[emyon] Budyonny, in a letter to Maxim Gorky, translated by Andrew R. MacAndrew (originally published in Krasnaya Gazeta, *October 26, 1928), in* Isaac Babel: The Lonely Years 1925-1939 *by Isaac Babel, edited by Nathalie Babel, translated by Andrew R. MacAndrew and Max Hayward (reprinted by permission of Farrar, Straus and Giroux, Inc.; copyright © 1964 by Farrar, Straus and Company, Inc.), Farrar, Straus and Giroux, 1964, pp. 384-87.*

M[AXIM] GORKY (letter date 1928)

[A Russian novelist and critic, Gorky is recognized as one of the earliest and foremost exponents of socialist realism in literature. A Marxist theory, socialist realism demands of all the arts an accurate, realistic representation of the evolution of the socialist state. Adhering to this aesthetic principle, Gorky's brutal, yet romantic portraits of the working class had an inspirational effect

on the oppressed people of his native land. From 1920 until his death in 1936, he was considered Russia's greatest living writer; today Gorky is acclaimed in the Soviet Union as the voice of the proletariat and a model for all socialist writers. The following excerpt is Gorky's reply to Semyon Budyonny's attack on Babel's works (see excerpt above, 1928).]

Dear Comrade Budyonny,

I cannot agree with your opinion of Babel's ***Red Cavalry*** and I firmly protest your evaluation of that talented writer.

You say that Babel "hung around with some unit deep in the rear." That cannot take anything away either from Babel or his book. In order to make soup the cook does not have to sit in the pot. The author of *War and Peace* never took part in the fighting against Napoleon, and Gogol was not a Zaporozhe Cossack.

You talk about Babel's erotomania. I have just re-read Babel's book and I found no symptoms of that disease in it, although, of course, I do not wish to deny the presence of certain erotic details in his stories. And this is as it should be. War always awakens an enraged eroticism. And that is something you can learn from any war, from the behavior of the Germans in Belgium, as well as from the behavior of the Russians in East Prussia. I am inclined to consider it a natural although abnormal heightening of the instinct for the preservation of the species, an instinct common in people who are facing death.

I am a careful reader but I didn't find in Babel's book anything that suggests a "lampoon." On the contrary, his book awakened love and respect in me for the fighting men of the Red Cavalry by showing them to me as real heroes—they are fearless and they feel deeply the greatness of their cause. I cannot think of another such colorful, lively portrayal of individual fighting men, another such description of the psychology of the mass of the Red Army that would have helped me to understand the strength that enabled it to accomplish that extraordinary campaign; it has no parallel in Russian literature.

The attack of the French cavalry in Zola's *La Débâcle* shows only the mechanical movement of the mass of fighters and their mechanical clash.

Nor can I agree with you that our fighting men are "simple plain men." I wouldn't have thought they were even without Babel, who with such talent has supplemented my understanding of the heroism of an army which is the first in history to know what it is fighting for and what it is going to go on fighting for.

Allow me to tell you, Comrade Budyonny, that the abrupt and unjustified tone of your letter visits an undeserved insult on a young writer.

Our writers live in a moment of transition under the complex conditions of a country in which there are at least 20,000,000 individual owners and only 2,000,000 Marxists, of whom almost half mouth Marxist precepts about as intelligently as parrots repeat human words. It is impossible under these conditions to make very strict demands of ideological consistency upon these writers. Our life is contradictory and it is not at all as didactic as the past, which can easily teach us whom to love and whom to hate. A writer is a man who lives by the truth, using the color of imagination in order to generate in his reader a reaction of active love or active hatred. You must not forget that people have been brought up with religious views on own-

Cover of Red Cavalry, *the first volume of Babel's* Collected Works *(1928).*

ership and that all the misfortunes, all the tragedies of life, all its nasty sides, are rooted in the proprietary instinct which from ancient times has been celebrated as the foundation of the state and the main source of private happiness.

It is impossible to re-educate in ten years people who have been brought up for thousands of years to worship gold and money. But we, in our own interest, must make allowances for and treat carefully every man who can help us in our struggle against the decaying but still strong props of the disgraceful past. Babel is a talented man. There are not so many of us that we can afford to spurn talented and useful men. You are not right, Comrade Budyonny! You are mistaken, and you have forgotten that scores of thousands of your fighting men heed your judgments. To be correct and useful a critic must be objective and considerate of our young literary forces. (pp. 387-89)

M[axim] Gorky, in a letter to Semyon Budyonny, translated by Andrew R. MacAndrew (originally published in Pravda, *November 27, 1928), in* Isaac Babel: The Lonely Years 1925-1939 *by Isaac Babel, edited by Nathalie Babel, translated by Andrew R. MacAndrew and Max Hayward (reprinted by permission of Farrar, Straus and Giroux, Inc.; copyright © 1964, by Farrar, Straus and Company, Inc.), Farrar, Straus and Giroux, 1964, pp. 387-89.*

ISAAC BABEL (essay date 1934)

[*In 1934 Babel spoke at the Writer's Congress, a party sanctioned literary organization. In his speech, excerpted below, he professed his allegiance to the Soviet state then attempted to explain his lack of published work during the 1930s by declaring that he lacked talent and chose to be silent rather than produce inferior work. However, Babel ironically implies that the inferior work he could not bring himself to produce was political propaganda. In his introduction to Babel's* Collected Works, *Lionel Trilling (see Additional Bibliography) notes of Babel's speech: "Yet beneath the orthodoxy of this speech there lies some hidden intention. One feels this is the sad vestiges of the humanistic mode that wryly manifest themselves. It is as if the humor, which is often of a whimsical kind, as if the irony and the studied self-depreciation, were forlorn affirmations of freedom and selfhood. . . ."*]

Marx once said that the important thing was not to describe the world but to transform it. In one sixth of the globe great changes have taken place and now we must attack our themes in a new way. We must have a new style. And we won't learn that new style from old books.

We must learn. But where?

Speaking of the use of words, I must mention a man who doesn't have any special professional dealings with words. Nevertheless, look how Stalin hammers out his speeches, how his words are wrought of iron, how terse they are, how muscular, how much respect they show for the reader. (Applause) I don't suggest here that we should all write like Stalin, but I do say that we must all work at our words as he does. (Applause)

I have spoken about the respect due to the reader. Well, the reader, nowadays, is really giving us plenty of trouble. To borrow Zoshchenko's expression, he's a regular drainpipe. (Laughter)

Now, foreign authors tell us that they search for their readers with a flashlight in broad daylight. But in our land it is the readers who march at us in closed formation. It's a real cavalry attack. They rush at us with their hands extended and you'd better think twice before you put a stone in that hand—what they are after is artistic bread.

Of course, we must come to an agreement with our readers. They demand it, sometimes with touching directness. And so we'd better warn the reader. Bread—that we'll be able to put into his outstretched hand, but when it comes to the shape of the loaf or the quality, that's quite another matter and he'd better take a good look at it himself.

Some readers naively make a demand: "All right, describe me." And the writer thinks: "All right, I'll give him that description and make it true and honest." But that won't do. Into a description of Ivan Ivanovich there must be injected a philosophical view, some lofty ideas. For without ideas, there can be no literature.

Respect for the reader. I am suffering from a hypertrophy of that feeling. I respect the reader so much that it makes me numb and I fall silent. And so I keep silence. (Laughter)

And when I think of an audience of 500 readers consisting of Party district committee secretaries, people who know ten times more than all the writers put together about bee-keeping, farming and how to build gigantic steel plants, who have been all over the country and who, just like us, are "engineers of human souls," I realize that I cannot get away with empty talk and school-kid stuff. If one says something, it has to be something serious and to the point.

Now, speaking of silence, I cannot avoid talking about myself, the past master of that art. (Laughter) I must admit that if I lived in a capitalist country, I would have long since croaked from starvation and no one would have cared whether, as Ehrenburg puts it, I was a rabbit or a she-elephant. My capitalist publisher would have forced me to be a rabbit and as such he would have forced me to leap around, and if I hadn't leapt, he would have forced me to become a grocer's assistant.

But in our country people take into consideration whether you are a rabbit or a she-elephant. They don't push you in the belly if you have something inside there and they don't insist too much on whether the baby will be a redhead, just light brown, or very dark, on what sort of things he'll have to say.

I am not happy about my silence. Indeed, it saddens me. But perhaps this is one more proof of the attitude toward the writer in this country.

I think that, as Gorky said yesterday, Sobolev's words, "We have everything" should be written on our flag. The Party and the government have given us everything, depriving us only of one privilege—that of writing badly.

It must be said frankly, without false modesty: it is a very important privilege that has been taken away from us and we took full advantage of it. And so, Comrades, we declare at this writers' congress: Let us renounce completely that old privilege. (pp. 398-400)

Isaac Babel, "'Our Great Enemy—Trite Vulgarity'," translated by Andrew R. MacAndrew (originally published in Pravda, *August 25, 1934), in his* Isaac Babel: The Lonely Years 1925-1939, *edited by Nathalie Babel, translated by Andrew R. MacAndrew and Max Hayward (reprinted by permission of Farrar, Straus and Giroux, Inc.; copyright © 1964 by Farrar, Straus and Company, Inc.), Farrar, Straus and Giroux, 1964, pp. 396-400.*

RAYMOND ROSENTHAL (essay date 1947)

[*In the following excerpt Rosenthal discusses Babel as a writer whose works are informed by an artistic detachment, but also by an ingrained Jewish ethos.*]

In Babel's epic-like chronicle of the Civil War, ***Red Cavalry,*** nature, seen through the new eyes of a Jew, takes on the stylized perfection of a Byzantine mosaic: rivers, plains, and trees become the richly brocaded background for the crudest deeds of war. The coarse dialect of Budenny's Cossacks, newly encrusted with the jargon invented by the Revolution, and the liturgical eloquence of the Hasidic Jews, sound to him like the words of some ancient folk song. Certainly James Joyce's dictum that genius turns its very handicaps into "the portals of discovery" is wonderfully illustrated by Babel: he converted his very rootlessness into the organizing principle of a fresh perception of reality.

Red Cavalry is undoubtedly Babel's masterpiece. So far it is the only complete book of his to have been translated into English. The book purports to be a series of disconnected sketches, but actually it is a subtly counterpointed saga. When Sherwood Anderson said that he thought "the true history of life is but a history of moments," he was describing perfectly the aesthetic approach of Babel's concentrated *nouvelles,* which depend for their impact on the flash-like capture of a passionate moment. In one of his autobiographical stories, **"Maupassant,"** Babel also testifies to the profound influence that French writers, especially Flaubert and Maupassant, had on his sense of form. "A phrase," he says, "is born into the world both good and bad at the same time. The secret consists in a barely perceptible turn. The lever must be held and warmed in the hand, and must be turned once, and not twice."

Reason never speaks in Babel's work. Never is an attempt made at logical analysis or persuasion. Few writers have so completely depended on the immediate flow of sensible reality for their total effect. Overwhelmed by sensations, immersed in atmospheres, colors, voices, we are in contact with a universe that, grasped wholly by the senses, never requires the intervention of the reasoning intellect to explain it. Babel's mastery of the primitive and unthinkable joy of sensuous delight has secular affiliations with the Hasidic literature, but in him it is the ecstasy of experience as such, stripped of the religious logic of the Hasidim.

Equipped so bizarrely, Babel went out into the Civil War, in Heine's phrase, "like God's spy," and with great detachment recorded the brutal episodes of the Red Army's Polish campaign of 1921. At the center of his canvas stands the familiar figure of the alienated Jewish intellectual—the sceptical, ironic observer "with spectacles on his nose and autumn in his heart"—obviously Babel himself. He is in love with the Cossack's primitive directness of instinct, but he is also fascinated by the Hasidic Jew—the war is being fought on the traditional ground of the Jewish Pale—and holds him up as a counter-hero of the spirit to offset the Cossack's primitiveness. Babel identifies himself with a Cossack commander who, as he says, "looked on the world as a meadow in May—a meadow crossed by women and horses." But he is drawn to the Jews, too. Ghedali, the Jewish antique dealer, voices Babel's own discontent when he cries out: "Where is the joy-giving Revolution?" For moments, in certain of these stories, Babel's subtle shuttling back and forth between the two opposing groups of Cossacks and Jews seems designed to call up from all the disorder and bloodshed the image of a totally *new man* who would contain in himself the traits that attracted Babel in both Jew and Cossack. Not the natural savage of Rousseau, nor the Talmudic genius of ingrown religiosity, but the new and more rounded man that the social upheaval might produce, fills Babel with the longing that underlies his ***Red Cavalry*** stories.

The mood of elation that flares up so often in these stories reflects the dominant feeling of the Russian Jew immediately after the October insurrection. At one stroke he had been freed from the Czarist prison and had attained—so it appeared to him—the open arena of unlimited social possibility. From his own experience, the Jew knew the violent contrasts, the dizzying velocity of the transformation, more completely than anyone else in Russia. Compared with the 19th-century German emancipation, which had unfolded in organic fashion, permitting the Jews over a long period of years to infiltrate slowly into the bourgeois setup, the Russian liberation took place overnight. No wonder that it raised such intense hopes—above all in the Jew.

Soon after his success with ***Red Cavalry,*** Babel wrote the ***Odessa Tales,*** a group of exotic sketches about the ghetto of his youth. Here the hero is the fabulous Jewish gangster Benia Krik. Having found his true voice in the Civil War, Babel had returned to the streets and docks of Odessa to fashion a Jewish Cossack. These stories are based to a large extent on fact; Odessa provided fertile material, being more akin to Marseilles or Naples than to the ghetto towns of the Pale.

Odessa Tales was also the final symbolic action of Babel's creative life. His next stories are written in a pared, elegantly simple style that departs from his usual manner by going in for psychological investigation. They deal exclusively with reminiscences, not with contemporary events—as if Babel were impelled not only by a state censorship, but also by his own curiosity, to retrace the trajectory of his flight from the ghetto. (pp. 128-29)

Although Babel's attitude towards art borrows dark overtones from romantic literature, it is still an intuitively keen analysis of the roots of his own alienation. For Babel was unquestionably an alienated artist. **"Maupassant"** is not simply a casual story, but contains a retrospective summing-up of his whole career, a kind of parable of what happened to his art. Yet to plaster the term alienation on Babel and imagine we have dealt deeply with him would be a grave mistake. For the artist is always a special case; it is in his very nature to be detached. He transforms his aloofness from life into a valid and functioning value, a movement of the nerves prior to any rupture occasioned by society.

Thinking of the process of alienation in this special sense, Henri Bergson regarded all artists as the fortunate products of a profound detachment. "Now and then," he declares in his book *The Creative Mind,* "by a lucky accident, men arise whose senses are less adherent to life. When they look at a thing, they see it for itself, not for themselves. They do not perceive simply with a view to action; they perceive in order to perceive—for nothing, for the pleasure of doing so. In regard to a certain aspect of their nature, whether it be their consciousness or one of their senses, they are born detached. . . ."

Surely Babel was such a "lucky accident." But to "perceive for nothing, for the pleasure of doing so"—precisely this had implications that eventually led to his opposition to traditional Jewish life. Even in the semi-cosmopolitan seaport of Odessa, the ghetto remained a village, with its strict ethical system, its own customs and rituals as a protection against the alien surrounding world. Any interest in the world, in sexual love for its own sake, in the uneconomic activity of art, in pleasure, was anathema to its code. At this point, when Babel was forced to break with Jewish life in order to become an artist, the process of alienation, a process already begun in his nerves, acquires a sociological meaning. Yet one can readily see that this is a peculiar alienation which has as its chief characteristic not sickly and introverted self-regard, but an outgoing and eager interest in the world. Isaak Babel was that rare figure in Jewish-nurtured literature, a Jew who found his purpose in enjoying the world.

Always ready for the "mystic" experience that the world might offer, Babel yet suffered from a flaw inside himself, an inherited sense of the ethical. In his most ecstatic passages, one can hear its harsh undernote. Like the Hasidic rabbis of modern times, he had learned all the prayers, but the miracle of complete possession which should have accompanied them never occurred. And only the "miracle" of revolutionary events brought his art to its highest achievement in ***Red Cavalry.*** But this was an external event, and the artist, in the long run, depends only on his own powers.

In the end, one recalls the final story in ***Red Cavalry,*** the one in which Babel presents the portrait of Ilya, "the last, cursed and unruly son" of the Hasidic prince, Rabbi Motaley Bratslavsky. Using a technique that reminds one of Eisenstein's montage effects, Babel compresses the whole history of Jewish participation in the revolutionary movement into one brief sketch.

Ilya has become a Bolshevik and a Red Army soldier, and now he lies on the dirty floor of the retreating troop train dying of typhus, surrounded by the lyrical disorder of this life. In elegiac tones Babel fondly enumerates the items, the images of Ilya's torn existence: ". . . the mandates of the propagandist and the memorandum books of the Jewish poet; the portraits of Lenin and Maimonides lay side by side; the knotted iron of Lenin's skull beside the dull silk of the portrait of Maimonides. A lock of woman's hair lay in a book, and the Resolutions of the Party's Sixth Congress, and the margins of Communist leaflets were crowded with the crooked lines of Hebrew verse. They fell in a mean and depressing rain—pages of the Song of Songs and those revolver cartridges. . . ."

And while Ilya, last prince of an aborted Hasidic destiny, waits for his death, "a monstrous and inconceivable Russia" tramps in bast shoes alongside the train. All the despair and confusion of military defeat sigh enormously over Ilya's dying body. "And I," cries Babel, "who can scarce contain the tempests of my imagination within this primeval body of mine, was there beside my brother when he died." Reading this story now, with Babel's real fate in mind, one thinks of him as he thought of Ilya—as the last of those joy-possessed Hasidic princes who rose out of the submerged but deeply spiritual ghetto world. And his lamentation for Ilya becomes his own lament for the loss of that hope of the marvelous, that perfection of joy which animated his entire life's search. (pp. 130-31)

Raymond Rosenthal, "The Fate of Isaak Babel: 'A Child of the Russian Emancipation'," in Commentary, *Vol. 3, No. 2, February, 1947, pp. 126-31.*

IRVING HOWE (essay date 1949)

[A longtime editor of the leftist magazine Dissent *and a regular contributor to* The New Republic, *Howe is one of America's most highly respected literary critics and social historians. He has been a socialist since the 1930s, and his criticism is frequently informed by a liberal social viewpoint. Howe is widely praised for what F. R. Dulles has termed his "knowledgeable understanding, critical acumen and forthright candor." Howe has written: "My work has fallen into two fields: social history and literary criticism. I have tried to strike a balance between the social and the literary; to fructify one with the other; yet not to confuse one with the other. Though I believe in the social approach to literature, it seems to me peculiarly open to misuse; it requires particular delicacy and care." In the following excerpt, Howe praises Babel as a genius of the picaresque tale who draws upon Russian and Yiddish culture to enhance his stories.]*

The name of Isaac Babel is virtually unknown in this country, which is something of a pity since he is one of the few genuinely important writers of post-Chekhov Russia. (p. 149)

The two main cultural sources on which Babel drew, Russian and Yiddish literature, flourished most in the 50-75 years directly before his birth; by the turn of the century both had begun to decline. Babel was one of those remarkable writers who spring up at the end of such a creative period and absorb its energies as if they were still at their fullest. The Chekhov strain in Russian literature, which winds like a placid valley between the peaks of Tolstoy and Dostoevski, is strongly evident in Babel, with all its characteristic pathos, warm skepticism, and tender lovingness. One also finds strong influences of Yiddish literary tradition: the powerful comic grasp of social relationships, the sardonic arguing with God, the attraction to the absurd undersides of history that can be found in Sholom Aleichem, the great Yiddish humorist. Compare Babel's bitter wit with Sholom Aleichem's impudent reverence in writing about Jewish fate. Babel: "But wasn't it a mistake on God's part to settle the Jews in Russia, where they've had to suffer the tortures of Hell? Would it be bad if the Jews lived in Switzerland, where they'd be surrounded by first-class lakes, mountain air and nothing but Frenchmen? Everybody makes mistakes, even God." Sholom Aleichem: "Apparently if He wants it that way, that's the way it ought to be. Can't you see? If it should have been different it would have been. And yet, what would have been wrong to have it different?"

I should be doing Babel's potential readers a disservice if I were to imply that the quality of his work can be grasped merely by imagining a blend of Chekhov and Sholom Aleichem. Like all true artists he transcended his influences. He is one of the very few Russian or Yiddish writers who had a native genius for the picaresque story. In both literatures it is difficult to find specimens of the picaresque, for the good reason that only a society acclimated to the idea of individual adventure and feeling secure against any possible enroachments by the adventurer will take to the story of the rogue. But in nineteenth-century Russia there was no such social ease and confidence—and as for the Jews, how could they know what it meant to move freely and boldly from place to place or from one forbidden social level to another?

Yet in his stories about Benya Krik, the gangster [***Benya Krik, the Gangster, and Other Stories***] Babel created genuine picaresque tales: wild, racy, very funny, soaked in the atmospheres of cosmopolitan Odessa. What is more (this is a kind of miracle) Benya is a Jew who creeps out of the ghetto to terrorize policemen. It is not hard to imagine the emotional impulsion behind such stories: how pleasant to see this young scoundrel pummel the city officials, how convenient, too, that he robs only wealthy Jews. The picaresque hero becomes a racial Robin Hood, foreshadowing the revolution which for Babel is more a matter of enthusiasm and fraternity than organized politics.

In a different vein, **"The History of My Dovecot"** is a story worthy of Chekhov. It begins in idyllic tones, with happy and simple phrases of recollection: a Jewish boy, loving pigeons, finally has enough money to buy a dovecot. As he wanders through his town, pressing the pigeons to his body with delight, he is astonished to see the streets overrun with people frantically carrying off looted articles. The puzzled boy stops before a crippled beggar, who is wailing over his inability to join in the looting: "Is it that God has elected me? . . . Am I then the son of man?" In a fury at being left out of the fun, the beggar grabs one of the boy's pigeons and smashes it against his face. "I lay on the ground and the entrails of the crushed bird trickled down my temple. . . . A tender bluish gut of the pigeon crept down my forehead, and I shut the eye which could still see, so as not to behold the world spread out before me." Stumbling away past enflamed mobs, the boy searches for his father, at last educated in the meaning of a pogrom.

In this story, narrative, prose, and symbol work together toward a final emotional impact. The boy's innocence moves charmingly from the story's beginning while the terror of the pogrom seems, as it were, to come forward from the story's end; midway they clash and the shock of knowledge is delivered to the boy in a superbly executed symbolic act: the crushing of the innocent pigeon against his eyes. The ironic sub-note of having the blow delivered by a cripple who bemoans *his* unhappy status is especially praiseworthy. As a study in innocence and evil, this story is a masterpiece.

The final group of stories is least substantial, though its theme is fascinating: the uneasy collision and partial merger of Judaism and the revolution. **"The Rabbi's Son"** is a tender sketch of a Red Army soldier, son of a rabbi and a convinced Marxist, on whose Communist pamphlets the margins are lined with Hebrew verse. "Portraits of Lenin and Maimonides lay side by side: the gnarled iron of Lenin's skull and the dull silk of Maimonides' likeness."

Babel is a writer of bold effects: alternately turbulent and elegiac, he delights in human vigor and mourns over its decline. Sometimes the richness of emotion may seem strange to a Western reader, as in the story **"In the Basement"** which portrays a boy's suicide attempt (a shameful act in the Jewish mores) and the extraordinary vulgar-loving rebuke of his grandfather: "My grandson . . . I'm taking a dose of castor oil, so as to have something to place on your grave. . . ."

Babel seems to have been born with the storyteller's gift, the resourcefulness of the bardic spieler who instinctively builds incidents into myths. As a boy, he recalls, he would invent stories about Spinoza: "Spinoza's death, that free, lonely death of his, I pictured as a battle. The Sanhedrin urged the dying man to repent, but he was adamant. I even brought Rubens into the picture. I had Rubens standing at the head of the bed, making a death mask." His imagination blossomed and, until it was silenced or driven to prefer silence by powers beyond its control, became a source of splendid stories—stories in which one finds that most admirable quality of Russian writing: the liberating tone of secured love, never stated or analyzed, always imbedded and felt. (pp. 150-52)

Irving Howe, "Tone in the Short Story," in The Sewanee Review *(reprinted by permission of the editor; © 1949, renewed 1976, by The University of the South), Vol. LVII, No. 1, Winter, 1949, pp. 141-52.**

STEVEN MARCUS (essay date 1955)

[In the following excerpt Marcus offers a balanced assessment of Babel's works, focusing on the use and significance of violence in Babel's stories.]

Babel's writing is most refreshing in its quality of directness—the style in which he addressed himself to experience and to his readers was calculated to be blunt in its effect of reality. Babel made only perfunctory gestures toward the contrivances of fiction; his stories are simply about himself—his experiences and his response to the experiences of others. Whenever he did write a conventional story the familiar, invented devices of the form plainly distracted him from exploiting his skill and intelligence. It was his great good fortune to discover at the outset of his career that his powers of observation accommodated all his other faculties to them; the brilliance of his registering eye made his use of any of the simpler literary means seem opaque, pallid and superimposed. Indeed, he was vexed by a self-consciousness of his superb aptitude as a witness, and he suffered Reb Arye-Leib's chastening without reply: "'You have spectacles on your nose and autumn in your heart'"—not until his art reached an autumnal maturity could he bring himself to acknowledge with any satisfaction the handicaps of being an observer. His stories emanate a rare salubrity, the influence of a cultivated, self-possessed talent coming directly to holds with the trials of its experience. The canon of Babel's work is the story of his life, and because he could look at his life without being embarrassed by the very fact of his looking at it we are not embarrassed either, as we so often are by other contemporary writers who dissimulate their passions about themselves in the transparent formalities of "literature."

In another way, however, Babel is one of the most indirect and elusive of writers—no recent writer, not even Joyce, has managed a more thorough impersonality. Babel rendered his impersonalness by means of a pervasive and extremely wrought irony. Irony, we all know, is an instrument of the intellect, and many of us seem to believe that it is virtually the intellect itself. That is probably because we do not often meet with an ironist so accomplished that he can deploy his irony against his intelligence. Babel's virtuosity in manipulating ironies was such that he frequently used it to fend off a warranted decisiveness, to blur a genuine distinction or to restrain himself from saying what he apparently had an impulse to say. For though he was a passionate man he severely mistrusted his passions, and in ***Red Cavalry,*** his most impressive and most flawed work, his irony served to neutralize their impact and to excuse him from moving in the direction of their prodding. He undercut himself consistently, finding, it would almost seem, a grim pleasure in self-contradiction, in the subversion of a story's design.

"Pan Apolek," one of the ***Red Cavalry*** stories, is an example of this unfortunate habit. During one of the movements of the campaign of 1920 Babel finds himself in "the ruins of a town swiftly brought to confusion." He billets in a church which possesses a set of remarkable frescoes and icons, the work of one Pan Apolek, an itinerant painter who, in the company of a blind accordion player, roams the countryside in "a state of blissful intoxication, with two white mice in his bosom and in his pocket a collection of the finest brushes"—the portrait naturally alludes to the culture and ideals of the Gospels. Apolek contracts to decorate a local church and becomes its rustic Michelangelo. "For five months Apolek, confined in his wooden seat, crept along the walls, around the dome and the choir." At the unveiling of his work the people of the town recognize themselves in the characters of the sacred paintings. "The eminent citizens who had been invited by the priest recognized Yanek, the lame convert, in St. Paul, and in Mary Magdalene a Jewish girl named Elka, daughter of unknown parents and mother of numerous waifs and strays. The eminent citizens ordered the sacrilegious portraits to be covered up. The priest hurled threats upon the blasphemer." But the common people of the town defend him even before the derision of their furious Vicar who insists that "'He has surrounded you with the ineffable attributes of holiness, you who have thrice fallen into the sin of disobedience, distillers of brandy in secret, merciless usurers, makers of false weights, and dealers in your own daughters' innocence.'" Apolek, we are led to believe, is the genuine Christian of untroubled spirit and primitive faith. And then Babel pulls the rug out from under us by having Apolek relate his fantasy of the marriage of Jesus and Deborah, a maid betrothed to "a young Israelite who traded in elephants' tusks." When Deborah's bridegroom approaches her "a hiccough distended her throat, and she vomited forth all she had eaten at the wedding feast." Shame overcomes her and her family and she is mocked by her husband. Then Jesus, pitying her anguish and shame, "placed upon Himself the bridegroom's apparel and, full of compassion, was joined with Deborah, who lay in her vomit," and Deborah bears his child. With this account,

Babel has cleverly diverted the drift of his story. Apolek suddenly appears as a disgusting clod, and his literalistic faith a grotesque vulgarity. Whatever may have provoked this twist—his anticlericalism, his dislike of the passive or submissive character—Babel abruptly suspends his original affection and respect for Apolek; that affection and respect are, presumably, to be remembered as subsidiary ironies in the newer, more "complex" pattern of the story. It is as if he were on the verge of an experience very much like that which Kafka describes in "In the Penal Colony," and then quickly turns and walks away. Like the explorer in Kafka's tale he is too discomposed by his revulsion to allow it to soften itself in disillusion, but unlike him, he cannot even allow his revulsion to act itself out. Nor should we mistake Babel's vulgarization of Christianity for the kind of naiveté of taste we find in *The Man Who Died*. The quality of **"Pan Apolek"** was deliberate and reasoned; it was a vulgarity itself, albeit an elegant one—an unwillingness to allow certain sentiments to suggest their own kind of justification.

Associated with this restricting, deflecting irony was Babel's reluctance to extend a story beyond the slightest possible duration; his finest effects are hit off with the shortest strokes. Like many first-rate short story writers he was possessed with the search for the single right word or phrase. "The secret lies in a slight, an almost invisible twist. The lever should rest in your hand, getting warm, and you can only turn it once, not twice." Only the unquestionable trenchancy of his insights justifies the brevity of his best work. "No iron can stab the heart with such force as a period put just at the right place," he wrote, alluding to that paragon of ironists, the writer of *Proverbs:* "Iron sharpeneth iron: so a man sharpeneth the countenance of his friend." And yet he frequently applied his ability to compress and foreshorten as he applied his ironic skill, to deflect and dissipate his passions. To the young Babel, literature sometimes seemed a deadly serious game which was played by hiding one's hand, by holding back secrets from one's audience and probably oneself. He negotiated this sophisticated coyness with the same facility with which he turned his irony, and his stories were damaged by it in the same way—it was a genuine embarrassment of riches.

Red Cavalry, in which all these faults are most obtrusive, is, nevertheless, a modern classic, quite in the category of excellence of *Dubliners* and *In Our Time*. In 1920 Babel served in the Polish campaigns of Budenny's Cavalry, troops of horse recruited principally from the Cossacks. Many of the sketches and stories of ***Red Cavalry*** were committed to writing in the midst of the campaign, Babel's powers of contemplation being so mercurial that he could sometimes transform experience into literature almost without a pause.

Red Cavalry is concerned with an appropriate response to the life of the times—this straightforward moral inquiry underrode all Babel's complexity of treatment. He found that the Cossacks' response was appropriate and because it was appropriate admired and cherished them. Babel conceived the times as substantially Hobbes' state of nature, where each man's hand was ready to be turned against his brother and where if one's life and death were not gallant and glorious they would be poor, nasty, brutish and short. In **"A Letter,"** Babel records with tacit approval how a Cossack father and his sons, on opposite sides of the Revolution, methodically and remorselessly proceed to torture and kill each other, communicating his sense of the propriety that lay within the necessity of terror. The Cossacks had been made for this epoch of carnage, and they surmounted it with "the masterful indifference of a Tartar Khan." Like Tolstoy, he saw in the Cossacks a conjunction of beauty and fierceness, in which their athleticism gave grace to their aggressiveness. "And he swung his well-proportioned athlete's body skilfully out of the saddle. Straightening his perfect legs, caught at the knee with a small strap, he went with circus agility over to the moribund animal." This appears in **"The Remount Officer,"** where Dyakov has just had his horse collapse beneath him. The story continues:

> It fixed wide, deep eyes on Dyakov and licked from his ruddy palm a sort of imperceptible injunction. Immediately the exhausted beast felt a dexterous strength flowing from the bald and vigorous Romeo in the prime of life. Straightening its head and slithering on its staggering legs at the impatient and imperious flicking of the whip on its belly, the jade got up, slowly and warily.
>
> Then we saw a delicate wrist in a wide, flowing sleeve patting the dirty mane, and perceived how the whip cracked whining against the bloodstained flanks. Her whole body trembling, the jade stood on her legs, her doglike eyes, filled with love and fear, never for an instant leaving Dyakov's face.

This episode may call to mind similar ones in *Crime and Punishment, Hard Times* or *St. Mawr,* and it does not take much to discern in it a moral inclination at odds with them. Familiars of "Spotted Horses," however, will at once notice a likeness of account.

Babel and Faulkner resemble each other remarkably, especially in their understanding of that state in which men are possessed by a passion so huge and immolating that they are turned dispassionate in consummating it. In **"Prischepa's Vengeance"** Babel describes a "tireless ruffian who had been turned out of the Communist Party, a future rag-and-bone man, a carefree syphilitic, and a happy-go-lucky fraud," one of his characteristically gay destroyers. Prischepa's parents were killed by the Whites, and he returns to his village for revenge. "Prischepa went from neighbor to neighbor, leaving behind him the trail of his blood-stained footprints. In the huts where he found gear that had belonged to his mother, a pipe that had been his father's, he left old women stabbed through and through, dogs hung above the wells, icons defiled with excrement. . . . The young Cossacks were scattered over the steppe, keeping the score." After the massacre "he sent for vodka, and shutting himself up in the hut, he drank for two whole days and nights, singing, weeping, and hewing the furniture with his Circassian saber." For Babel as for Faulkner, violence was the great cathartic and revenge its sweetest and most corrupting form. But the butchery of Babel's Cossacks is not the despairing, forlorn and solitary mayhem of Faulkner's Southerners. They spread their carnage gayly, for they were born to this existence not driven to it. They are as much like Faulkner's Indians as they are like his Southerners—atavistic, immune to guilt, untrammelled in their celebration of the momentous circumstances of life. Writing of the burial of Squadron Commander Trunov, Babel wants us to recall the Homeric funeral games and to esteem the Cossacks as if they were Achaeans. "The whole squadron leaped into the saddle and fired a volley in the air, and our old three-incher champed forth a second time. Then we sent three Cossacks to fetch a wreath. They dash off, firing, at full gallop, dropping out of their saddles and performing all sorts of Cossack tricks; and returned bringing whole armfuls of red flowers. Pugachov scattered them on the coffin and we began to move up to Trunov for the last kiss." Before Trunov died he had murdered a defenseless prisoner, an old man, cutting his throat with a sword and then riding away. "The sun came out of the clouds at that moment and impetuously surrounded Andie's horse, its lively pace, and the devil-may-care swing of its docked tail." Babel would like us to believe that the universe conspires with joy in the Cossacks' bright brutality. And here, in his exaltation of violence, Babel departs from Faulkner who is as concerned with it as Babel, but for different reasons. Faulkner's violence mourns the death of traditions and institutions which he loved. Babel's rejoices in the death of traditions and institutions which he had come to hate.

Precisely because the Cossacks were innocent of the traditional institutions of Russian society, Babel admired them. Having no piety toward the stations and duties of the old rotted society—existing, indeed, almost without any preconceptions about the virtue of society at all—they were delivered from any compunction about destroying it or whatever defended and represented it. For Babel they became the ironic embodiment of the Revolutionary ideal, the irresistible, anarchic simplicity that would execute the catastrophe of war and survive it as the first and finest fruits of the new society; for he had few expectations of industrial greatness or educated masses—the true revolution would create something like the Cossacks. He was more right than he knew.

In comparison with the Cossacks, however, Babel found himself miserably inadequate. As a Jew, an intellectual, a revolutionary, he was unable to meet the violent requirements of the revolution. When he is called upon to kill a wounded Cossack to prevent his falling into the hands of the Poles, he cannot. When he borrows a Cossack's horse he promptly afflicts the beast with saddle-sores. He wanders through a battle with an unloaded pistol, and convicts himself of lacking "the simplest of proficiencies—the ability to kill my fellow-men." The Cossacks, apprehending Babel's peculiar unfitness for his work, reproached him: "'You're trying to live without enemies.'" Such, he confesses, is the fate of a man with spectacles on his nose.

But Babel did not castigate himself with any lasting bitterness for this failing. He realized that his time was unable to respond to him; it could not gratify his vagrant impulses of love. **"Gedali,"** one of his finest stories, expresses this dilemma beautifully. (pp. 400-05)

Babel respected the Jews only when they answered the violence done to them with violence of their own—a Polish woman cries out "with sudden and terrible violence" over the body of her murdered father, or the Jews of Volhynia and Galicia who "moved perkily, in an uncontrolled and uncouth way, but their capacity for suffering was full of a somber greatness, and their unvoiced contempt for the Polish gentry unbounded." Benya Krik, the hero of ***Tales of Odessa,*** was the kind of Jew Babel could admire unreservedly. "Gangster and kind of gangsters" in the Odessa ghetto, Benya "could spend the night with a Russian woman, and satisfy her," was able together with his brother Lyovka to cripple his father, received a proposal of marriage while he was in bed with a prostitute, and was a man whom nothing could dismay or deceive. He was, in other words, a kind of Cossack. These stories of Odessa seem to me unpalatable. Aside from their moral dubiousness, they affect a folksy amiability and relaxation which are not appropriate to their intense violence and chicanery. Unlike the stories of ***Red Cavalry*** they seem to have been "gotten up" into literature, but Babel's deliberation over them was unproductive of finer or more humane judgments.

The trouble lies, I think, in the fact that the young Babel made a too sizable investment in violence. . . . ***Red Cavalry*** is a discussion of the multifarious ways of destruction, and it is not even so much a discussion as it is an exposition, for, unfortunately, nearly all of Babel's reservations about violence were *merely* ironic. In **"Berestechko"** the Cossacks commit one of their senseless murders. "Kudrya of the machine gun section took hold of his head and tucked it under his arm. The Jew stopped screaming and straddled his legs. Kudrya drew out his dagger with his right hand and carefully, without splashing himself, cut the old man's throat." . . . In another story he writes, unforgivably, and without a shred of irony, "Then I stamped on my master Nikitinsky, trampled on him for an hour or maybe more. And in that time I got to know life through and through. With shooting . . . you only get rid of a chap. Shooting's letting him off, and too damn easy for yourself. With shooting you'll never get at the soul. . . . But I don't spare myself, and I've more than once trampled an enemy for over an hour. You see, I want to get to know what life really is, what life's like down our way." Here at its worst Babel's style was bloated with gore, "horribly stuff'd with epithets of war."

Babel's overinvestment in violence led him into active personal brutality. **"My First Goose"** records how he gruesomely slaughtered a bird and upbraided a harmless old peasant woman in order to feel potent and mature and accepted by the Cossacks. Nor should we neglect the fact that Babel later became a member of the Cheka—though no information is available about what he did for it—and that he went along on the infamous grain-collecting expeditions of 1917-1918: on three separate occasions he was somehow associated with the dirtiest work of the Revolution. . . . Babel's frequent and ingenious juxtapositions seem deliberate and contrived enough, I think, to warrant the supposition that he sensed his overcommitment to the way of violence; and so he called upon objects and sentiments which would have the appearance of compromising his rancor and destructiveness—he sought a dialectic, but this search was essentially strategic. The young Babel was inspired by the negating passions; his one powerful benign impulse was the will to record and understand and convey. This impulse fortified his sense of the need for a dialectic, but it could not alone supply him with one. I do not mean to imply that Babel had no strong affections—indeed he did; nor do I wish to maintain that his use of irony is altogether spurious. But what may appear to be a dialectic in this respect, is, I think, more accurately a duality, in which the spiritual and the fleshly find it politic to appear together in print—like two enemies compelled to associate in public. Actually, I find, Babel's ironies and contradictions often tend to destroy, rather than create, each other.

Babel's affinity for destruction and cruelty may be understood though not condoned through his early life. In two sketches of 1925, **"The Story of My Dovecot"** and **"First Love,"** he describes the most important day of his life—on October 20, 1905 there was a pogrom in Odessa. Babel's grandfather was killed, his father, "his soft red hair fluttering, his paper dickey askew and fastened to the wrong button," humiliated, and Babel himself crushed and terrified into a nervous disorder. He saw his father pleading on his knees before a Cossack officer who "rode as though through a mountain pass, where one can only look ahead." And he, young Isaac, who had just been allowed to buy some pigeons as a reward for his assiduous scholarship, saw his pigeons mangled in front of him. . . . In one day the male line of his family was disgraced and emasculated. Babel accommodated himself to these scarifying hours by coming to idealize the Cossacks and dislike the Jews. By living as a Cossack, immersing himself in brutality, he hoped to cleanse himself and his country of the filthy past. ***Red Cavalry*** is his great effort in that direction. Several of the stories reflect the effort literally—**"My First Goose,"** in which he tears apart a bird himself, is one. In another story he stands by while a Cossack shoots a Polish boy "and bits of brain dripped over my hands." And in a third he exacts retribution by urinating into the mouth of a Polish corpse: "It was pouring out of his mouth, bubbling between his teeth, gathered in his empty eye-sockets." In ***Red Cavalry*** he tried to rid himself of the past, and the final story ends in a hopeful self-deception. "Months passed, and my dream came true. The Cossacks stopped watching me and my horse."

As the years passed he continued to scrutinize his notions of the Revolution and of his Jewishness; he began to realize that he had deceived and indulged himself. Hesitantly, sorrowfully, he came to be critical of the unremitting violence of Soviet life, and as his trust in violence wavered he became increasingly involved in reminiscences of his childhood and lenient in his judgment of it. As his energy for carnage declined, he gradually ceased to disparage his Jewish endowments—curiosity, the love of irony, the love of ideas. He even asserted, once, that his savagery was an inherited gift too, a wistful and quickly abandoned illusion. And he perceived that the life of art had its own kind of violence, a self-inflicted sort, and reflecting upon Maupassant's final years his "heart contracted as the foreboding of some essential truth touched me with light fingers."

Caricature of Boris Efimov, based on Babel's story "My First Goose."

He was a wiser and a gentler man, but his art had faltered. He picked at his Jewishness laboriously; it was not an immediate actuality but a sequence of memories and ideas upon which he ruminated and by which he tried to reveal himself anew. These later stories are the work of a fatigued and burdened talent—they took a long time to write, and Babel, unable to obey his own dictates about style, was forced to "turn the lever" more than once. Nor could he ever be at ease with the milder, retrospective sentiments; he tricked out his nostalgia in pseudo-ironic pathos, he recreated his memories and his Jewishness primarily in order to keep on writing about something. As he learned more about himself his subject-matter trickled away from him; his special talent did not thrive on the wisdom that comes with resignation. He had met life a ferocious young observer, and his best work was volatile, predatory and imperfect—with all its immoralities ***Red Cavalry*** is his enduring achievement. When his passion for "the state of nature" waned, his art, which in its way was a state of nature too, waned with it.

Before Babel silenced his own voice, however, he wrote one great story, **"Di Grasso,"** which along with **"Gedali"** is his finest work. It tells of an Italian troupe of players that stopped at Odessa one year; Di Grasso, the star performer in a rustic Sicilian melodrama, portrays a jealous shepherd who avenges himself on Giovanni, the city slicker that has stolen his love. "The shepherd . . . stood there lost in thought; then he gave a smile, soared into the air, sailed across the stage, plunged down on Giovanni's shoulders, and having bitten through the latter's throat, began, growling and squinting, to suck blood from the wound." This beautiful, savage leap has a profound effect on Babel, and on all the Odessans who witness it. Somehow it gets at the heart of Babel's greatest and truest appreciation of violence in a way that ***Red Cavalry*** never did. Perhaps the most significant reason for this is the fact that it takes place through the agency of art: it is art Babel is witnessing here, not life. And when he says of Di Grasso's performances that they confirm "with every word and gesture that there is more justice in outbursts of noble passion than in all the joyless rules that run the world," one wonders if he does not now have in mind the violence that only art can properly represent, and that only art, by its peculiar magic, can cause to vitalize our moral beings. One wonders also if he does not now have a deeper sense of what constitutes a noble passion, and a noble violence. Certainly it seems so to me, for his description of the humanizing influence of the performance upon even the "tricky customer" Nick Schwarz, to whom Babel had pawned his father's watch, and upon Nick's grenadier-like wife, is an indication that he senses where the real nobility and justice in violence lies: in its power to evoke the non-violent affections, to evoke love, even to evoke guilt, and always to evoke our moral humanity. After the play, Madame Schwarz says, "Now you see what love means," and with tears in her fishlike eyes she suddenly demands that her husband return Babel's watch to him—which he does, albeit with a "vicious pinch." Thus saved from his father's anger, Babel turns into Pushkin Street and "saw for the first time the things surrounding me as they really were: frozen in silence and ineffably beautiful." The violence of ***Red Cavalry***—which was the violence of life itself—has passed. The violence of **"Di Grasso"**—which is the violence of art—has taken its place. And it is in the latter that we find the nobility and justice Babel sought. I think **"Di Grasso"** ought to be read after the stories of ***Red Cavalry,*** for then it would serve to instruct those of us who are so familiar with the literary modes of violence that we are inclined to forget what a monstrous actuality the thing in itself really is. (pp. 407-11)

Steven Marcus, "The Stories of Isaac Babel" (copyright © 1955 by Partisan Review; *reprinted by permission of* Partisan Review *and the author), in* Partisan Review, *Vol. XXII, No. 3, Summer, 1955, pp. 400-11.*

ANDREY SINYAVSKY (essay date 1964)

[*A highly respected Russian novelist, short story writer, essayist, and critic, Sinyavsky was arrested in 1965 for publishing work outside of the Soviet Union under the pseudonym Abram Tertz. His monumental* A Voice from the Chorus (1976) *is comprised of notes and letters that Sinyavsky mailed to his wife while he was incarcerated. Within the work, interspersed with his philosophical and literary meditations, are comments from other prisoners, or the "chorus." The bitter, satirical tone of the writing reveals a highly refined intelligence and wit, as well as a deep compassion and understanding for the Russian condition. In the following excerpt from an earlier study, Sinyavsky discusses Babel's literary style in* Red Cavalry *and* The Odessa Tales.]

What strikes one first of all in Babel is the variety of characters, of situations, and of styles. A sublime pathos appears alongside images of the most brutal reality, painted with the precision of a naturalist. Light and shadow, the beautiful and the hideous, are juxtaposed in combinations that are unexpected and often bizarre. The law of contrasts directs the development of subjects, the selection of details, the juxtaposition of words. The choice of heroes in Babel's narratives, of the characters that people ***Red Cavalry,*** is very significant in this regard. In their psychology good and evil rub elbows and interpenetrate, and in one and the same character, traits cohabit that at first sight seem irreconcilable: cruelty and magnanimity, brutality and tenderness, infamy and innocence. Even the appearance of Babel's heroes is often paradoxical: "'Warsaw is ours' howled the Cossack in bast shoes and a derby hat. . . ." Such also is the language of the illiterate mass who rise above their ignorance, the common but salty language of disheveled revolutionaries. Political slogans mingle with a frequently obscene argot, journalistic clichés with coarse oaths: "Let's die for pickled cucumbers and the world revolution!"—here is an example of language that is as expressive and as contradictory as the character of the men who use it.

Babel has taken for the material of his tales impressions gathered in 1920 during the Polish campaign for the First Cavalry Army. But this has nothing to do with a chronicle of military history. He is careful to avoid copying events "in their raw grandeur." Deliberately, he condenses colors, alters proportions, creates confrontations between extremes in the life and the consciousness of his heroes. His whole effort is centered on the rough-hewn man of the masses, loaded with defects and vices, but compelling admiration by his courage, even his heroism. Far from idealizing his characters, Babel carries the play of black-and-white to grotesque lengths, accentuating and exaggerating at will, and makes us see in his Red Cavalry the moral and esthetic greatness of these men, even though they are stained with blood and mire.

Several tales, developing an argument which is essential for anyone who wants to grasp the main idea of ***Red Cavalry,*** present two different points of view: the dream of a good-natured and harmless revolution, without bloodshed, to which is opposed the author's conviction: "It's impossible not to shoot, because it's revolution."

The idea of virile humanism is embodied in the soldiers and the officers of ***Red Cavalry,*** who chide the narrator for his softness, his poor adjustment to the rigors of military life. One of the basic points of Babel's style is that the narrator is not necessarily the spokesman of the author and cannot be identified with the real "I" of the writer, which is hidden, camouflaged under the twists and turns of the action. Constantly ironic in regard to his autobiographical hero, Babel takes pleasure in uncrowning, even humiliating him. Their contrast with this pleasantly scatterbrained intellectual makes even more striking the heroic traits of the combatants of the Red Cavalry.

The depiction of characters and the artistic weaving of plot in ***Red Cavalry*** reveal to us the two sides of the work of Babel. The lucidity of the realist does not chill the impetuous temperament of the romantic. His heroes of flesh and blood bathe "in torrents of luxury and power," in a climate of the marvelous and the extraordinary. Handsome, gaudily clothed, camped in a rich setting, they often seem to us like figures in an epic, whose very appearance compels wonder. (pp. 301-02)

Babel is prodigal of bright colors, of resplendent, glistening garments. We find "the pearly mist of birches," "clouds sailing like swans," blood flowing "like a brook with coral foam," in short, all the battle gear of romantic literature. The tone rises readily to the emphatic and the sublime. The author can't resist uttering sentiments which suffuse his book with waves of emotion that sometimes seems affected. But this sentimentality is only the canvas for scenes and personages conceived in a quite different register, rigorous and stripped-down to the point of asceticism.

Babel—like his heroes—does what one least expects at any given moment. At points of extreme dramatic tension, these characters manifest a remarkable calm. On the other hand, they sob, tear their garments, pass from despair to jubilation, for reasons which may seem to us very trifling. One of these heroes, Afonka Bida, weeps hot tears on learning of the discharge of his commanding officer, but remains unmoved when it is a question of carrying out the last wish of a mortally wounded comrade. "You must waste a cartridge on me. . . . Those Polish bastards will be coming, they'll make sport of me." In Babel, emotional reaction is in inverse proportion to the event that excited it.

Babel's restraint is extreme. As soon as a heroic exploit or a tragic event comes up, he affects impassivity, letting the action speak for him. His characters die and kill with simplicity, without self-serving poses, without impressive eloquence. All the more moving are those scenes whose very bareness creates their horror and their majesty. (p. 303)

The lack of agreement between the form and the content of a remark, between the meaning of a sentence and its intonation or its vocabulary, is customary in Babel. The terrifying is told gently, the sublime, coarsely. Tragic events are related to us with the vulgar awkwardness of an illiterate, bordering on burlesque. The purpose of this is to deflate solemn bombast, to bring the story down to earth.

The same is true in the brutally physiological descriptions he uses to tell about the habits and the characters of the heroes of ***Red Cavalry.*** Taboo topics, ultrarealistic images, fill Babel's tales, contrasting violently with the most exalted romanticism. They serve as dissonances in this verbal symphony with its many expressive elements and insert themselves in the romantic context like deep shadow next to brilliant light.

The presence and the interaction in Babel of such different elements (the fantastic and the documentary, the sparkling metaphor and the trivial statement, the lyric flight and the unemotional recital) gives to his images and his language an unequaled power of expression. Neutral and colorless phrases are almost totally absent from his texts. The language is laden with sensibility and creates images that are almost physically perceptible, almost dazzling: "The barn was crammed with new-mown hay, as exciting as perfume"; "an odor of lilies pure and strong as alcohol." Supersaturating his style, Babel pushes to the extreme the materiality of the world and the clarity of the image of it that he offers.

The laconic style in which our author excels goes along with this intensity of verbal expression. It is not just a question of the art of brevity in writing. Revealing to us in one of his tales his most cherished thoughts about style, Babel credits his brevity with enormous expressive power:

> . . . I am speaking of style, of the army of words, of an army in which all the arms are in movement. No metal can pierce the human heart with such paralyzing violence as a period placed at just the right spot.

It is the quest for the greatest possible expressiveness that motivates Babel's laconic style. The more confined the verbal space, the weightier the significance of each word that penetrates our consciousness like the point of a lance, provoking an explosive reaction. The prose of ***Red Cavalry*** would be unsuitable for a novel of large dimension: it is made to deliver quick blows, and the violent effects the author is fond of would be weakened if used over too long a space. The style of our epoch, said Babel, consists "in courage, in restraint, and it is full of fire, of passion, of power, and of gaiety."

The maturity and extraordinary originality of Babel's talent are fully manifested in ***Red Cavalry.*** This said, one may observe how the most unexpected artistic traditions meet and intermingle in his work.

Maxim Gorky played an exceptionally important role in Babel's literary career. Like many other Soviet writers, Babel passed through the school of Gorky. To him he owed his literary debut. It was Gorky who in 1916 published in his review *Chronicle* the first stories of Babel. In them the author of ***Red Cavalry*** can be only dimly discerned. The tone of the narration is dull, lacking in expression and poetry. This was chiefly the result of the paltry inner experience of the young writer, freshly arrived in Petrograd after a period in a commercial school. In the time that followed, Babel temporarily abandoned literature. He took off on long travels, took part in grain requisitioning campaigns, fought with the Army of the North and in the First Cavalry Army. After these experiences he undertook again the craft of writing. Having plunged, on the advice of Gorky, into the whirlwinds of revolutionary reality, he had not only stored up experiences and impressions, but he had also found his place in the struggles of his times and had taken a position on both the artistic and the ideological level. Such was the road that led him to ***Red Cavalry,*** which introduced a new stage in his life and his work. Very significantly, the gestation of this book was likewise linked with the name of Gorky. Babel sent him his new stories and Gorky replied that "he might begin now." Understandably Babel considered Gorky "his first and principal teacher."

But along with this his style indicated predilections that were quite foreign to Gorky. One must cite to this effect Babel's piece ***Odessa*** . . . , his first attempt at an esthetic program. Russian literature, Babel affirms, developed till now under the sign of Petersburg, grey, morose, and crepuscular, to which must be opposed another symbol of faith—Odessa, city of the sea and of the sun, blossoming in a perpetual climate of festival and of light.

This sunlit esthetic, proclaimed from the writer's earliest youth, is masterfully embodied in the ***Tales of Odessa,*** published at the same time as ***Red Cavalry.*** . . . The Odessa cycle is distinguished not only by a heady "local color," but also by esthetic principles that are clearly new. The talent of Babel appears in a novel light.

It is a gush of gaiety, of joy, of light. The humor of Babel, purposely suppressed in the accounts of the war, where it served mainly to accentuate the atrocious and the tragic, gives itself free rein here and becomes the preponderant element. The mischievous smile of the author of the ***Tales of Odessa*** is a sign of exuberance, of energy, of joie de vivre. This laughter is born of youth and health, of the fullness of physical and moral vigor, of a happy springtime acceptance of life. "The boys dragged the girls behind hedges, and the sound of kisses rose over the tombstones."

Descriptions of customs (weddings, burials, marriage proposals, and so forth) occupy the first level of ***Tales of Odessa.*** But these are fantastic pictures which seduce precisely by their unusual character, the brilliance of their exotic colors. Babel's Odessa is a fairyland where local images and national traits are surrounded by a halo of legend. At Odessa the power of His Imperial Majesty ends, and there begins the realm of Benya Krik, the gentleman-burglar, king of the bandits of Odessa. Here ragged Jews perform prodigies of valor, defy the police, and terrorize the rich. The women have Titanic strength, unheard-of-height, and stentorian voices. The beggars drink Jamaica rum and smoke cigars which have come straight from the plantations of John Pierpont Morgan.

Here everything is excessive. "Odessa had never seen and the whole world never will see such a funeral." And so on—up to the drunken workman who sprawls "right in the middle of the universe" and not just in the gutter. Odessa is promoted to the rank of center of the world, it comes to be administered by marvelous laws and traditions. The image of the real city is enriched by the dream of the famished barefoot beggar. And precisely because most of these pictures exist only in the imagination of Odessans, the exaggeration, the bragging became an unending source of comedy. Just the opposite of ***Red Cavalry,*** the romanticism of ***Tales of Odessa*** is subordinated to the humor, and performs the function of a conventional device, purposely exaggerated by the author. What in ***Red Cavalry*** borders on the sublime here provokes hilarity. In ***Tales of Odessa*** the most prosaic things take on the air of an epic. At a wedding celebration the wine brings forth "belches as loud as a battle trumpet.'' The account teems with amusing incongruities, absurd comparisons, exaggeration, and droll fakery.

Babel worked very strenuously on the cycles which compose ***Red Cavalry*** and ***Tales of Odessa.*** In each of these collections the tales are linked by subject, by material, by theme, and by style. (pp. 304-07)

Publishing only the works about which he felt completely confident, Babel wrote much more than he published and didn't like to divulge his literary projects, his conceptions of art. We can, however, judge of his esthetic ideas, of his searches and his meditations, as indicated in several stories dealing with the theme of art, and chiefly in his autobiographical writings of the years 1925-30. These evocations of the years of childhood came, in order of importance, immediately after ***Red Cavalry*** and ***Tales of Odessa.*** A direct line of descent links them to the autobiographical accounts of Gorky. Moreover, the first of these pieces, ***The Story of My Dovecote (Istoriya moei golubyatnei),*** was dedicated to Gorky. Babel here in his way replies to the famous question of Gorky: Why did you begin to write, and what childhood impressions inclined you to your vocation? The emphasis is placed on problems that are of capital importance for Babel: the romantic and the realistic vision of the world, dream and reality, the truth of fact and the truth of fiction. Thus, while recounting his childhood, he analyzes his evolution as a writer and defines his conception of literary creation.

In this connection one must examine the story ***My First Honorarium (Pervy gonorar).*** In order to understand it correctly, one must consider the particular characteristics of Babel's style: the nonconformity of content and form, the tendency to ''debasement'' through contrast, and to mystification which creates the illusion of the documentary exactness of an autobiographical account when it's really a matter of pure fiction. Whether they were founded on fiction or on authentic fact, the works of Babel should always be viewed in the perspective of art and analyzed according to the logic of art and not of life.

In the story in question, ***My First Honorarium,*** the artist's noble role is degraded to the contrivance of a hoax calculated to shock the conventional taste. His first honorarium, the author says, was the money which, when he was young, a prostitute refused, touched by a story—which was itself shocking enough—that he had reeled off to her. In this pseudoautobiographical form, in this crude representation of the most sordid venal love, Babel offers moral and esthetic ideas rich in exalted poetry and philosophic profundity. The young hero of ***My First Honorarium,*** devoured by the passion to write, and by love for the one who sees in him only a client among many others, tells her a fanciful story of his unhappy childhood. This story, a real work of art, moves the girl to the point where she repays him with a sincere and honest love, really his ''first honorarium,'' and the only thing capable of repaying the torment and the illumination of artistic creation.

The narrative of the hero, presented as a worthy model of the literary craft, is at the same time so unconventional and so simple that the most audacious fiction takes on the force of complete authenticity.

In a general way, the problem of truth and fiction has always obsessed Babel, especially in that new, transitory period of his career as a writer, when his style was changing and when the realistic vision of the world was taking the upper hand. But for Babel, fiction was not the opposite of reality. The truth of fiction helped to penetrate the truth of life and to recreate it much more compellingly than a vulgar copy could. ''To invent'' is not ''to deceive,'' but neither is it to copy facts just as they were or ''are ordinarily.'' Art is the quest for the unexpected, the unaccustomed, the unique, themselves the source of veracity, for real experience always contains new elements and assumes discovery, creation, and not the repetition of what is already known.

In his speech at the First Congress of Soviet Writers, in 1934 [see excerpt above, 1934], Babel said: ''Without elevated thought, without philosophy, there is no literature.'' His work corroborates this profession of faith. It bears the imprint of noble thought and perfect form. During his lifetime, criticism did not always pay homage to this philosophical aspect of the narratives of Babel. Fascinated by his skilled craftsmanship, it hardly looked beyond the beauties of his style. All the more because the author purposely disguised his thought, refused to impose it, or to present it circumstantially in grandiloquent and ostentatious declarations. In Babel, thought always fosters concrete images which speak by themselves, which form the inner content of a work intended for an attentive and thoughtful reader. (pp. 307-09)

Andrey Sinyavsky, ''Isaac Babel,'' translated by Catherine Brown (originally published under a different title in Oeuvres et opinions, *No. 8, August, 1964), in* Major Soviet Writers: Essays in Criticism, *edited by Edward J. Brown (copyright © 1973 by Oxford University Press, Inc.; reprinted by permission, Oxford University Press, New York, 1973, pp. 301-09.*

THE TIMES LITERARY SUPPLEMENT (essay date 1967)

[In the following excerpt the critic offers an appraisal of Babel's talent.]

Red Cavalry and ***Tales of Odessa*** are written in an overlush, heavily metaphorical style. Some of Babel's figures are acceptably inventive: ''The dying sun, round and yellow as a pumpkin'', ''The moon hung above the yard like a cheap earring''; elsewhere, though, one finds that the sunset's ''foaming rivers flowed along the embroidered napkins of peasant fields'', and that the sky was ''like an accordion with lots of keyboards''. By 1925, after finishing ***Red Cavalry*** and ***Tales of Odessa,*** Babel began to shed this kind of mannerism. Magnificent stories like **''The Awakening'', ''Dante Street'', ''The Kiss'',** reveal a wholly different, superior talent. The themes are often the same, but the style is simple, unadorned, flippantly exact. These stories give one an idea of the excellence Soviet literature was deprived of with Babel's death.

''Commentary: Babel in the Theatre,'' in The Times Literary Supplement *(© Times Newspapers Ltd. (London) 1967; reproduced from* The Times Literary Supplement *by permission), No. 3426, October 26, 1967, p. 1015.*

V. S. PRITCHETT (essay date 1969)

[Pritchett is a highly esteemed English novelist, short story writer, and critic. He is considered one of the modern masters of the short story, and his work is a subtle blend of realistic detail and psychological revelation. Pritchett is also considered one of the world's most respected and well-read literary critics. He writes in the conversational tone of the familiar essay, a method by which he approaches literature from the viewpoint of a lettered but not overly scholarly reader. A twentieth-century successor to

such early nineteenth-century essayist-critics as William Hazlitt and Charles Lamb, Pritchett employs much the same critical method: his own experience, judgment, and sense of literary art, as opposed to a codified critical doctrine derived from a school of psychological or philosophical speculation. His criticism is often described as fair, reliable, and insightful. In the following excerpt, Pritchett discusses Babel's artistry as a short story writer.]

Isaac Babel was the most *telling* writer of abrupt stories to come out of the Russian revolution. This gentle Jew was a man who hit one in the belly. More important he had—what is indispensable to short stories—a distinct voice. . . .

The subjects of a very large number of Babel's stories are primitive and direct. The war and the expropriations have turned the peasants on the Asiatic border into murderers, looters, and bandits; the new government forces were as ruthless in getting a new regime set up. Babel's prose is sharp and laconic. There is little comment. And yet within the fatalism of the tales there is the unmistakable Jewish humanity, sometimes the Jewish humor and fantasy—what one can only call the irony of recognition: the recognition of the manly or womanly essence of each briefly elicited character. Babel had a master in Gorki, but his deeper masters were Gogol and Maupassant: Gogol for the imaginative richness, Maupassant for detachment, economy, and devilish skill. Eventually Babel was to find Maupassant cold. What I think Babel meant was that the Frenchman was *outside,* whereas all Babel's characters carry some grain of the presence of Russia, the self being a fragment of the land's fatality. One says, as one sees the Kulak kill his horse rather than let it go to the Cheka people when he is turned out, when one sees him become a legend as a bandit, and when he is run to earth and killed in a pit: "Yes, that is how it was. It was the end of an epoch, dreadful." One has seen the rage of a lifetime.

As an artist, Babel describes himself in ***My First Fee:***

> From childhood all the strength of my being had been devoted to the invention of tales, plays and stories—thousands of them. They lay in my heart like toads on a stone. I was possessed by devilish pride and did not want to write them down prematurely.

His early idea was to "dress them up in beautiful clothes" and he could write, for example:

> The flowering acacias along the street began to moan in a low, faltering voice.

Later, in his innumerable re-writings (so that one very short tale might be drained from dozens of versions as long as a novel) his aim was to cut and cut and cut. He was tormented by the amount of words and inventions inside himself.

Sometimes he cut too severely. ***My First Fee*** has an early laconic version called ***Answer to an Inquiry,*** which contains one of those brief asides which are a remarkable but traditional part of his art—an item in a prostitute's room:

> In a small glass bowl of milky liquid flies were dying—each in his own way.

and, although the end is sharper in the first version, the second and longer one is richer. The boy's lying tale is now really fantastic; and the symbol for describing the sexual act is more truthful than anything by contemporary masturbators:

> Now tell me, I should like to ask you: have you ever seen a village carpenter helping his mate to build a house? Have you seen how thick and fast and gaily the shavings fly as they plane a beam together? That night this thirty year old woman taught me all the tricks of her trade.

In story after story Babel worked until he hit upon the symbol that turns it from anecdote into five minutes of life. He was not a novelist. By 1937 he was being semi-officially questioned about not writing on a large scale like Tolstoy or the very *bien vue* Sholokhov. It was being insinuated that he was idle and not pulling his weight. Poor devil! Short story writers are poets. Babel could not but be opposed to the clichés of Socialist Realism and particularly to the rhetorical magazine prose it had led to. He was also asked why he wrote of the exceptional rather than the typical, and one knows what Stalinism meant by typical: the middlebrow ideal. He replied with Goethe's simple definition of the *novella:* it is a story about an unusual occurrence. . . . He was opposed to the short story as a condensed novel. The short story is an insight.

V. S. Pritchett, "Five Minutes of Life," in The New York Review of Books *(reprinted with permission from* The New York Review of Books; *copyright © 1969 Nyrev, Inc.), Vol. XIII, No. 2, July 31, 1969, p. 3.*

GLEB STRUVE (essay date 1971)

[*A Russian-born educator, Struve is internationally known for his critical studies of Slavic literature. In the following excerpt, Struve comments on Babel's use of contrast and paradox to create the striking, pathetic effects of his stories.*]

The ***Red Cavalry*** stories brought Babel fame. Even outside Russia he began to be spoken of as the rising star of the young post-Revolutionary literature. It has been pointed out that Babel was the first among post-Revolutionary writers to revive a

Caricature of Babel by K. Rotov. The inscription on the crumbling pediment is "Bourgeois Literature."

definite literary genre—that of the pointed, short *nouvelle* (in which, incidentally, the influence of Maupassant could be easily discerned). Babel's stories, with their clear and distinct outline, their brevity, and their fastidious style, came as something new after the welter of shapeless, loose productions of the Pilnyak school and of the other "dynamic prose" writers. Yet Babel had something in common with them and differed as much as they did from the realists who were about to make their appearance and revive the traditional psychological novel. He had the same predilection for *skaz*, for ornamentalism, and for the exotic and romantic aspects of the Revolution and the same aversion to psychological analysis. But he differed from Pilnyak and his followers in his feeling for form and his concern with style. Even his *skaz* was subordinated to a deliberate stylistic design in which the element of contrast and paradox played a great part. It has been rightly said that it is style which holds his stories together, whether they be tales of the Revolution and the Civil War or pictures of Jewish life in Odessa.

Babel's attitude toward life can be described as purely sensuous and aesthetic. He is attracted by the bright, the picturesque, the unusual in life. His Jewish stories, for all their realism in the portrayal of the peculiarities of life and speech of Odessa Jews, are imbued with the same romanticism and exoticism. Instead of the familiar and traditional middle-class Jewish milieu, Babel shows us something quite out of the ordinary—the world of Jewish gangsters and bandits, who appear to us romantically glamorized and at the same time pathetic and humorous. In the center of this world stands the figure of Benya Krik, the "king" of Odessa gangsters, a character of almost legendary proportions, yet pathetically human and lovable.

In the Revolution, Babel's attention is also centered on the exotic and romantic aspects, on the unusual and paradoxical. All Babel's stories about life in Budyonny's army have this romantic streak. Babel's keen vision and great sense of line and color, combined with his extreme sensitiveness to cruelty and to all that is excessive and inordinate in life, enables him to depict graphically the Civil War in a series of Goyaesque scenes. He does this with great artistic economy and detachment. He dwells with a certain relish on scenes of plunders, riots, and executions—of senseless, instinctive, almost good-humored cruelty. It is the almost animal instinct of destruction that he shows above all in the Civil War, and this is why his ***Red Cavalry*** provoked a strong protest from Marshal Budyonny, who denounced it as a one-sided and distorted picture of his army and its exploits [see excerpt above, 1928]; Babel's stories of the Red Cavalry are not, however, realistic snapshots of its everyday life—they are full of hyperbolism, of romantic contrasts, and of a peculiar pathos wherein the cruel and the heroic merge into each other. There is in Babel a strong element of eroticism, which, despite its apparent naturalism, is also treated romantically and hyperbolically. But many readers are revolted by the crude and outspoken physiological descriptions which abound in Babel's stories.

Babel's favorite method is that of contrast and paradox. Nearly all of his stories are based on contrasts, both psychological and stylistic. Throughout ***Red Cavalry*** there runs a contrast between the cruelty, the elemental blindness and crude sensuousness of the scenes described and their perception through the spectacles of the narrator, who obviously stands for Babel himself—an educated Jew, nearsighted, physically weak, and psychologically out of tune with his surroundings and the life he is forced to share and, in addition, burdened with a skeptical attitude toward the world. Parallel with this is the contrast between Babel's poetic descriptions of nature, reminiscent of Gogol as well as of Imaginist poetry, full of color and hyperbole, and the crude physiological naturalism of many scenes. The crudeness and cruelty of human beings and their behavior are set off by this resplendent theatrical background. Babel's romanticism is tempered—one might almost say poisoned—by his irony and skepticism. (pp. 70-3)

Gleb Struve, "Prose and Poetry," in his Russian Literature under Lenin and Stalin: 1917-1953 *(copyright 1971 by the University of Oklahoma Press, Publishing Division of the University), University of Oklahoma Press, 1971, pp. 39-75.**

NORMAN DAVIES (essay date 1972)

[In the following excerpt Davies discusses the historical inaccuracy of the stories of Red Cavalry. *Although* Red Cavalry *cannot be relied on for an accurate historical picture of the Polish-Soviet war, Davies believes that the stories present an emotionally honest portrait of the dehumanizing effects of war.]*

The particular distortion of historical realities in which Babel indulged reveals much about his literary techniques. He lifted facts from their context. He changed them at a whim. He jumbled them up, and juxtaposed them for the sake of sensation. He rejected all discussion, argument or elaboration which would have rendered them intelligible. One can only say that he was practising a form of collage, where all was subordinated to the total effect, where violent contrast and shocking details were the order of the day.

Historical facts seem to have had the same function as that of the lettering devices and the printed slogans so much in vogue in the visual arts with the Cubists, Futurists and Constructivists among Babel's contemporaries. They had no meaning of their own. They were preferred because they conjured up an illusion of reality, in contrast with other vaguer elements in the composition. They were solid, precise, definite, neutral in tone, and utterly misleading. One can gain no more systematic information about the Polish-Soviet War from Babel's 'facts' than one could learn what was happening in Paris or Moscow by reading the small print on the scraps of newspapers which adorn the paintings of Braque or Goncharova.

It is almost impossible to attempt any overall assessment of Babel in competition with the aura of martyrdom which now surrounds his name, and on the basis of one work, albeit his most famous. As a writer he was obviously talented and original. His stories are vivid, but superficial. They display all the attractions and all the limitations of poster art or of a sophisticated strip-cartoon. His range of interests is narrow. In the field of Russian literature as a whole, he appears as a promising bantamweight trying his hand at a sport which is mainly intended for heavyweights.

The ***Konarmiya*** stories remain a valuable if limited asset for the historian of the period. They are the only literary product of worth from a war which all too often has been ignored for want of information. They must be read with a weather-eye open to Babel's unhistorical purposes. Despite the pitfalls which they present to any literal-minded investigator, they do convey a number of more intangible truths.

They convey the true nature of the fighting, for example, in a way that the military histories with their neat maps and generalizations can never achieve. As Pilsudski once said, the war was a sort of grand brawl. . . . It was essentially confused and fragmented. It consisted of innumerable minor skirmishes which strategists are wont to rationalize as 'advances on a broad front'. Except for the short, critical period of the Battle of Warsaw, it never assumed the characteristics of other European wars. If one were required to summarize the fighting in one paragraph, one could not do better than to turn to one of Babel's many sketches. . . . (pp. 855-56)

The stories describe the plight of the civilian population which in most of the small towns of the Borders was predominantly Jewish. They show the indiscriminate destruction visited on these centres, which provided the only targets for military operations. They show how the Jews suffered at the hands of both Poles and Russians. . . . (p. 856)

Finally, the stories [in ***Konarmiya***] reveal the predicament of an individual faced with a war he did nothing to start and surrounded by death and destruction he can do nothing to prevent. Babel, or Lyutov as he sometimes thinly disguises himself, obeys orders. He treks from place to place in a maze of half-remembered locations. He rarely thinks of politics, even though he is an intelligent man. He never questions the cause he serves, because to do so is pointless and might well be painful. He watches the thoughtless brutality of his primitive comrades, and is himself brutalized. They kill as a matter of course; he ends by killing, and advertising his viciousness, as a matter of good sense. He boasts, he lies; he gets confused; he slides off to the rear whenever he can; but he survives. He hates the enemy, the Pole, with a blind, tribal hatred, and thinks no kind thoughts until he has literally trampled on his corpse. If one really wants to know what lay in the minds of the Russians who invaded Poland in 1920, as distinct from the politicians in Moscow, the answer is here. As Gorky once said in defence of the ***Konarmiya*** stories, they are true not in the external 'but in the internal sense'. They are to a degree histories as well as stories. From the restricted vantage point of a Red Army saddle and through the highly refractive lenses of Babel's famous spectacles, they do relate certain things 'as they really happened'.

These revelations are slight enough. But anything which throws light on the state of mind of the Red Army, helps at the same time to illuminate the fears and motives of the Red Army's opponents. Anyone who has reflected for one moment about the implications of the ***Konarmiya*** stories can begin to understand why the Poles were inspired to resist so fiercely and why they inflicted the only unredeemed defeat in Soviet military history. (pp. 856-57)

Norman Davies, "Izaak Babel's 'Konarmiya' Stories, and the Polish-Soviet War" (© Modern Humanities Research Association 1972; reprinted by permission of the publisher and the author), in The Modern Language Review, *Vol. 67, No. 4, October, 1972, pp. 845-57.*

RICHARD HALLETT (essay date 1972)

[*Hallett is the author of the biographical and critical work* Isaac Babel. *In the following excerpt from that work, he provides an informative discussion of Babel's dramas and briefly explains the political circumstances which led Babel to write plays. For further discussion of Babel's dramas see the entry by Andrew Field in the Additional Bibliography.*]

Critics generally have concentrated almost exclusively on Babel the storyteller (especially on the author of ***Red Cavalry***) and given Babel the dramatist little more than a polite nod. It is true that he is known to have written only two plays. It is true also that his mastery in the short story is not matched in his writings for the stage. Further, . . . there is an almost complete absence of data concerning his theatrical credentials. Yet none of these considerations excuses the reluctance both to examine at due length Babel's stature in the Soviet theater and to consider his plays in relation to the remainder of his work.

Sunset, Babel's first play, appeared in 1928. Almost immediately it received an enthusiastic welcome from a contributor, G. A. Gukovsky, to the first book of criticism entirely concerned with Babel's art: "At this very moment, when our new and still young drama is wandering in the dark and quite often straying from the right path, a drama by a writer such as Babel cannot fail to be an event. . . ." Later in the same year Stanislavsky's Moscow Art Theater gave ***Sunset*** its Russian premiere, although it had originally been performed first in Baku and then in Odessa in October 1927. The state of the Soviet theater in 1928 was, as Gukovsky suggests, not particularly healthy. Because of the more immediate impact drama can produce upon its audience, Soviet writers were permitted less latitude when creating plays than when creating novels, poems, or short stories. Toward the end of the 1920s, moreover, the Soviet writer found his freedom of expression becoming alarmingly circumscribed. After 1917 up until approximately the mid-1920s he had enjoyed comparatively wide scope, but, as Stalin's position at the apex of power grew more secure, so his grip on the organs of opinion tightened, and the situation of the writer began rapidly to deteriorate.

Nineteen twenty-eight marked the beginning of the First Soviet Five-Year Plan. Writers were enjoined to record the nation's future hopes and present achievements. Particular pressure came to be exerted upon so-called fellow-traveling writers (Babel among them), who gave at best only tepid support to the Communist party and its ambitious program. The play, ***Sunset,*** did not, however, treat of current events. Instead it harks back to the prerevolutionary Odessa of 1913 and to the narrow world of the Moldavanka. It is instructive to observe how the short-story writer adapted his talents and compositional habits to meet the exigencies of a different medium. Of course observation is enhanced by the recent discovery of the story from which the play developed. An essential feature of Babel's style is his brevity, whether applied to sentence structure or to plot, and though **"Sunset"** almost equals **"The Story of My Dovecote"** in length, it had to be expanded before a full-length play on the same subject could result. An unusual insight offered, therefore, by a comparison between story and play is of Babel working against his natural inclinations and adding to, rather than subtracting from, a particular work.

Brevity is attained in other ways, however. The play consists of eight scenes, some extremely short and none especially long. The dialogue, moreover, reflects Babel's ingrained laconism, though with one important difference. In the story he uses dialogue more sparingly, providing most of the necessary background information through third-person narrative. A play, on the other hand, must rely almost entirely on dialogue to convey details of plot. For this reason Babel's stage characters speak at greater length, and the pithy and purposely formal-sounding witticisms of the story have to be interspersed with what, from the purely literary point of view, is rather more mundane material. As if to compensate for this dilution, Babel included detailed remarks about scenery, stage directions, and cast in the style of his short stories. It is as though he were anxious to sacrifice as little as possible of his proven technique on the altar of the theater and had determined to cater for his past readership as well as for the future playgoer.

While the plot of the drama remains fundamentally the same as in the short story, it is enriched by much that is new. Nowhere can this better be illustrated than by reference to Mendel Krik, whose characterization is deepened and whose attempts to defy his advanced years acquire additional pathos. More than before Babel isolated him within his own family. In the earlier version he could always count for support on his wife, but in the play she fulfills a smaller and more sympathetic role, resenting her husband's tyranny just as much as do her children.

Before Mendel appears on stage, the violence of the opposition to his patriarchal authority has already been demonstrated. Dvoyra, his "overripe" daughter, becomes hysterical over the disappearance of a favorite dress. She is expecting a prospective suitor, Boyarsky, but not for the first time Mendel has tried to wreck her chances of marriage, as he is too mean to supply a dowry. Both her brothers sympathize. Lyovka, the younger, voices open contempt for Mendel, while the gaudily clad Benya says little but hovers menacingly in the background.

The patriarch is introduced in person with powerful dramatic effect. He enters carrying a whip, casts it aside and sits down in silence for his wife to remove his boots. Totally ignoring Boyarsky, he questions an employee about Lyovka's impudence in giving orders without his father's permission. As a sign of displeasure he then sweeps everything off the kitchen table and declares his sole authority over the household and the business before storming out. The inevitablity of a clash between Mendel and his children is further emphasized in the following scene (which did not appear in the original story), when Benya commits the unheard of act of entering his parents' bedroom at night to complain of the noise. (pp. 66-9)

Most of the differences between the play and the story arise from the fuller characterization of Mendel. This involves in turn a wider variety of scenes and a larger cast of characters with the result that the Jewish ambience is conjured up in greater density. Basically, however, the play has much in common with the Moldavanka stories and Babel's other earlier work as regards both tone and technique. Though making unavoidable concessions to the theater medium, he succeeded in other ways already mentioned in maintaining his characteristic economy of expression. Moreover, the aura of violence pervading his Moldavanka and ***Red Cavalry*** stories is established from the very beginning of the play, and the ultimate explosion in the sixth scene is if anything excessively prepared for and delayed. As before, Babel depicted an exotic jungle of a community in which only the strong and ruthless flourish. Idiosyncratic juxtapositions are used as ever to jolt the reader. In the synagogue scene talk of moneymaking and a proposed robbery mingle with the prayers of the congregation; and Ar'ye-Leyb's instruction of a child in the scriptures precedes the decisive battle between the Kriks. Of the typically grotesque details in the play the most curious occurs when the cantor in the synagogue, finding his complaints about rats going unheeded, pulls out a revolver and shoots one during the service! Another memorably bizarre phenomenon is the choir of blind Jews that sings for Mendel in the tavern.

Apart from the bedroom scene between Marusya and Mendel there is little erotic content of the kind to be found in several earlier (and later) works. A more striking difference is the moral expounded by the rabbi at the end, which sounds strange coming as it does from an author mostly at pains to refrain from judgments of any sort. A final distinction between the play and the Moldavanka tales specifically is that the larger-than-life characters of the tales (especially Benya) assume more human proportions when appearing in the flesh and speaking for themselves. ***Sunset*** the play tends therefore to be a little less extravagant and a little more down-to-earth than **"Sunset"** the short story.

Compared with most other new plays staged in the late 1920s ***Sunset*** seemed something of an anachronism. Not only was it essentially remote from the revolution in subject and spirit, but also it did not lend itself easily to a socio-political interpretation advantageous to the Soviet régime. P. Markov, a critic respected by Babel, could view the play as an attack upon the Moldavanka way of life only by disregarding that there is no more evidence of condemnation here than in the earlier stories and that the triumphant Benya is hardly a positive hero dedicated to building socialism.

Sunset remains far superior to most other dramas of the time in the quality of its writing, though perhaps more impressive as literature to be read than a play to be performed. Babel expressed disappointment that the first production had failed to convey those subtleties he believed present beneath its surface. . . . (pp. 71-3)

Babel's second play, ***Maria,*** forsakes prerevolutionary Odessa for postrevolutionary Leningrad. The action is said to take place "during the early years of the revolution," but a reference to the likelihood of war with Poland indicates 1920. The place and period chosen offered not only rich dramatic possibilities but also ample scope for a writer with Babel's stylistic tendencies.

The year 1920 was one of political uncertainty, social transition and economic hardship. Although the Bolsheviks controlled much of the country, particularly the large cities, the civil war was by no means won and a new way of life was still emerging from the chrysalis. Babel recreated the atmosphere of the period by concentrating mainly on representatives of the old order, over whose future in a socialist society hung a disturbing question mark. Those who had decided to remain in Russia are shown adapting to radically changed circumstances in a variety of ways. A former prince, Golitsyn, literally scrapes a living by playing the cello in taverns and finds dockers most appreciative of his sad melodies. An unnamed professor is mentioned as having entered the sausage trade since the revolution. Dymshits, a Jew, smuggles in black-market goods with the aid of maimed war veterans. His girlfriend, Lyudmila Mukovnin, thinks only of having a good time and exploits her beauty to obtain it. In contrast, her elder sister, Maria, works selflessly in the political section of the Red Army and is attached to a division commanded by a former blacksmith. The fates of these and other characters are played out against a background of privation and fear, with the necessities of life in short supply and people afraid to walk in the streets at night lest they be stripped of the clothes they stand in.

The juxtaposition of old and new had been a feature of ***Red Cavalry.*** In ***Maria*** it consists in examining how former privileged persons survive at a time when their privileges have ceased and they themselves are in danger of being trampled underfoot by the class upon whose oppression their high standard of living had once depended. From their point of view the situation had the quality of a nightmare. Babel increased the general luridness by a selection of physiological details that connote decay and disintegration: the grotesquely mutilated bodies of Dymshits's accomplices; the rape of Lyudmila by Viskovsky, a former army officer; and Lyudmila's consequent venereal disease. Unfortunately, in attempting to shock, Babel veered into melodrama that is not only more acceptable in the exotic world of the Moldavanka but was also more skillfully handled for the theater in his earlier play, ***Sunset.*** For example, the shooting of Viskovsky is poorly motivated, and the writhing of General Mukovnin during a heart attack contributes little or nothing by taking place on stage. Both instances were intended as powerful dramatic situations prior to the fall of the curtain but risk arousing nervous laughter rather than horror.

Maria recalls ***Sunset*** in its length and its eight scenes. On the whole, however, it is the inferior play, as regards not only tone but also construction. The heroine, Maria, never in fact appears, and, though her expected arrival in the seventh scene does engender considerable tension, it leads also to a theatrically stagnant fifth scene devoted almost entirely to the reading aloud of a letter she has sent from the Ukrainian front. Babel here firmly established her idealism, contrasting it with the selfishness and emptiness of Lyudmila and other characters who had been nurtured by the czarist régime, but he did so in a somewhat crude literary manner and utilized none of the potentialities offered by the stage medium.

Some characters who do appear in person possess little more substance than the absent heroine. Golitsyn, the former nobleman who takes refuge in religion, remains an interesting embryonic character insufficiently developed; the depraved Viskovsky never really comes to life; and Dymshits contributes nothing new to Babel's gallery of Jewish rogues. Babel's love of brevity served him less well here than in ***Sunset,*** where the Moldavanka milieu had already become familiar through earlier stories, and the extravagant conduct of the characters was more or less acceptable in context. In setting his play in Leningrad at such a complex period of history, however, Babel needed to concentrate on fewer characters or alternatively to expand the play's length if he were to do justice to his theme.

The final scene of ***Maria,*** in which preparations are in train for a working family to move into the Mukovnins' former apartment, does not entirely succeed. Obviously such an ending aims to emphasize the rapid and radical nature of social change at the time in question, but to introduce so many new characters at such a late stage requires more theatrical expertise than Babel possessed, and the play concludes somewhat lamely in consequence. In sum, though full of interest for Babel's view of 1920, ***Maria*** does represent a technical regression by comparison with ***Sunset.***

In a letter to his mother and sister in May 1933 Babel described ***Maria*** as a herculean task that would probably bring him trouble because it did not accord with the party line. His fears proved all too justified. Though allowed to appear in print in March 1935, it incurred official displeasure and was eventually excluded from the repertory. Like ***Sunset*** in 1928, ***Maria*** may be regarded as alien to the philosophy of the epoch. In this instance Babel failed to meet the requirements of Soviet socialist realism, which commended works revealing the positive side of Russian life and deplored those featuring prominently scenes of sex and violence. The total absence of his positive heroine from the action suggests that any attempt to compromise with the new literary doctrine was at most half-hearted. On the other hand, the critic I. Lezhnev wrote, in an unenthusiastic review accompanying the original published text of the play, that it represented the first part of a trilogy and that Maria would eventually appear in person. As far as is known, however, the other two parts never materialized and Babel's career as a dramatist ended briefly and unfortunately.

In the history of the Soviet theater Babel stands out as an unusual and isolated figure. Unsurprisingly, in view of his relative lack of experience, he was not entirely at ease with the medium. Nevertheless, in only two plays he revealed unmistakable stage talent, and it is a matter for regret that he did not continue to enliven the Stalinist theater and relieve the general mediocrity of the drama it produced. (pp. 73-7)

Richard Hallett, in his Isaac Babel *(copyright © 1972, 1973 by R. W. Hallett; reprinted by permission of Basil Blackwell Publisher), Bradda, 1972 (and reprinted by Frederick Ungar Publishing Co., 1973, 118 p.).*

SIMON MARKISH (essay date 1977)

[*In the following survey of Babel's works, Markish discusses* Red Cavalry *and* The Odessa Tales *as outstanding examples of Russian-Jewish literature during the Soviet revolutionary period. He maintains that it is the conflict between Babel's Jewish ethos and his identification with the Bolsheviks that creates the tension and tragedy within his stories.*]

At the very headwaters of the Russian-Jewish literature of the Soviet period stands Isaac Babel. Or perhaps one should say that he himself was its main source—to which its peculiarities, its development, and its role within Soviet literature are in large measure traceable.

The daily life and cultural background from which Babel came played an important role in his creative life. He grew up in Odessa, in a family that was economically comfortable. (It may be pertinent to note here that many details in his quasi-autobiographical Odessa stories are invented out of whole cloth, as for example the assertion, "I come from a poverty-stricken wreck of a family.") A substantial part of the Jewish population, which in the year of Babel's birth, 1894, formed one-third, and on the eve of the revolution one-half, of the total population of Odessa, had left the old traditional and enclosed Jewish life far behind. Theirs was the path of assimilation—in the original and literal meaning of that term, "becoming like"; what they had in view was adaptation, perhaps even the first step toward integration. Despite pogroms, persecution, and discrimination, the situation in Odessa was not unlike that in America: a blending with the surrounding milieu, and at the same time a secure sense of group community, with the synagogue as spiritual and organizational (rather than purely religious) center. This situation was unique in Russia; there was nothing like it in any of the other centers of Jewish culture, neither in St. Petersburg, Kiev, nor Vilna. That the contribution of Jewish Odessa to the nascent Soviet culture proved so large was thus no accident. (p. 38)

Still, the Jewish background, Jewish traditions and emotional attachments, are not in themselves enough. The writer or artist may recall his Jewish youth with tenderness and yearning, he may prefer gefilte fish with red-hot horseradish above all other food and drink, he may indulge himself with matzot and even pop into the synagogue a couple of times a year, but none of that entitles him to a place in Jewish culture, or in a Jewish encyclopedia. This can only come when his entire creative life, or a good part of it, has taken form under the influence of Jewish self-awareness. Babel's moment of self-awareness and choice arrived rather early, and antedates his appearance in print. Two crucial pieces of work, written at the end of 1915, provide the evidence—**"Childhood II: At Grandmother's,"** and a fragment, **"Three O'Clock in the Afternoon"**—both of them entirely Jewish in theme and, more importantly, in the subjectivity that informs them.

The first is a sketch of a day spent at his grandmother's. House and grandmother together evoke this response in the boy: "Everything seemed strange to me. I wanted at the same time to run away from it all and to stay there forever." Here a familiar routine and atmosphere undergo an abrupt transformation, take on a piercing novelty, inspiring simultaneously horror (or perhaps revulsion) and a feeling for what is "one's own," ineluctable and permanent. Here we have essentially the whole Jewish Babel, the basis of his social and emotional values and the foundation of his aesthetics. Jewishness of whatever kind—the steadfastly traditional, the *shtetl*-hasidic, or the urban-emancipated—is perceived dualistically. The heritage is at once accepted and rejected, a fact which precludes simple social realism along with apologetics and denunciation—the three characteristic stances of the old Russian-Jewish literature. What appears in their stead is a fresh perspective from a new vantage point; sheer astonishment is no small part of it. Here is the source of that exoticism of the quotidian, that fantastic sharpness of line and violent emotionality which are the mark of Babel's style. But here, at the same time, is the source of his loneliness; dooming him to the role of outsider, always and with everyone.

The fragment, **"Three O'Clock in the Afternoon,"** was published in an obscure journal only in 1971, and is generally unobtainable. It has been described by a Soviet critic, however, as a combination of "plotless lyrical narration saturated with precise psychological details which constitute a second level" and a vivid story "with heightened emphasis on individual speech." Thus, long before ***Red Cavalry*** and the ***Odessa Tales,*** but at the same time when his general position had crystallized (and, obviously, as a result of that crystallization), Babel discovers, at least in principle, the expressive means and the manner which were to become his hallmark. The moment of registering this self-awareness is the moment of Babel's self-invention as a writer.

The novelty of his position involved a new approach to his subject matter. Until then it had not been possible to imagine a work of Russian-Jewish literature on a non-Jewish subject. Now the author's attitude to his material acquires greater importance: his dual vision, from within and without, deepens his imagery and gives it a dimension which it had not and could not have known before.

But if the approach "from outside" had been construed only negatively, as synonymous with "not inside," if the phrase "I wanted to run away from it all," had simply signified flight, then we would not be able to speak of the dimension that comes from binocular vision. The Bolshevik Revolution gave Babel a second vantage point, another feeling of belonging, as indisputable as the first. (pp. 39-40)

It follows that until this dual support was found, the real Babel did not exist. His first stories, published in 1916, are equally feeble, whether they have Jewish themes (**"Ilia Isaakovich and Margarita Prokofievna"**), or non-Jewish (**"Mama, Rimma, and Alla"**). His first success, ***Red Cavalry,*** was destined to prove his largest one as well—because here, as in no other work, he drew on *both* his supports with such assurance and strength.

Kirill Vasilievich Liutov, the narrator and protagonist of ***Red Cavalry,*** is not Babel, even though the writer gave him the name under which he himself had served in the First Cavalry Army as correspondent for a military newspaper. Liutov is half of him, the Jewish half that is frantically in quest of a complementary, revolutionary, Bolshevik half. "'Gedali,' I said, 'today is Friday and it's evening already. Where can I get hold of some Jewish biscuits, a Jewish glass of tea, and a bit of that pensioned-off God in the glass of tea?'" (**"Gedali"**). Jewishness gives him his bearings in the savage and bloody, longed-for and unattainable, Revolution. Thus, although the death of the hero and pillager, Trunov, is not connected with the Galician village of Sokal, except geographically, Liutov nevertheless gives a detailed (detailed, that is, for Babel—two paragraphs) account of the ancient synagogues and torn gabardines, of the noisy wrangling of the Orthodox and Hasidim, and he concludes: "Heavy-hearted because of Trunov, I too went pushing among them, shouting along with them to ease my sorrow" (**"Squadron Commander Trunov"**). The ending of the famous **"Discourse on the Tachanka,"** which appears at first glance to have no connection with the rest of the text, is in fact a most important paragraph on the Jews of Galicia and Volhynia. The son of a Zhitomir rebbe, "the last prince of the dynasty," the Red Army man Bratslavskii, a party member who had prayed in his father's synagogue because he felt unable to leave his mother, comes to understand that "in the Revolution a mother is only an episode," and, sent by his organization to take charge of a combat regiment, dies of typhus on the filthy floor of the news-correspondents' railroad car. The contents of his trunk are as mixed as those of his brief biography: "Agitator's orders and booklets of a Jewish poet, portraits of Lenin and Maimonides, pages from the Song of Songs, and bullets for his revolver." "He died, the last prince, amid verses, phylacteries, and leg windings. And I, barely able to contain the gales of my imagination within my ancient body, received the last gasp of my brother" (**"The Rebbe's Son"**).

The Red Army man Bratslavskii is more than Liutov's brother, he is his double. He sacrifices all, asking for nothing and claiming nothing, except revolutionary solidarity. Yet he dies in solitude, under the indifferent gaze of "Cossacks in red baggy trousers" and "two big-breasted typists in sailors' jackets," having been wrested by his "brother" from the mass of typhus-ridden peasants who "rolled before them the customary hump of a soldier's death" and "wheezed and scratched and flew on wordlessly." He had been alone even in that crowd; indeed, his "brother" recognizes him by his solitude: he is the only one to reach out for a pamphlet, while all the others vie with each other to grab the potatoes Liutov is scattering from the wagon. The narrative of the story is addressed to an unknown Vasilii, whose name is mentioned insistently, almost importunately, five times in two pages. This persistence rests on the opposition of brother with stranger; to the latter, no matter how hard you try and how many times you call him by name, nothing can finally be explained.

Yet the rebbe, Motele Bratslavskii, the Red Army man's father, is one of Babel's own, albeit no "brother." The dialogue between him and Liutov, in the story **"The Rebbe,"** is a conversation between people who understand each other intuitively. Joy, laughter, merriment are what Liutov craves as he wanders voluntarily through the convulsions and carnage of the class war, and the rebbe seeks the same with his pupils, as does the rag-and-bone man Gedali—which is why Gedali's praise of Hasidism has the ring of the author's own judgment. By contrast, the argument with Gedali (in **"Gedali"**), the champion of the "sweet Revolution" and the "International of good people," rings hollow. Liutov answers the ragman's "abstract humanism" with only two arguments, quite summarily presented: the Revolution "cannot help shooting, because it is the Revolution," and the International "is eaten with gunpowder and seasoned with the finest blood." In fact, these are something less than arguments. The principal refutation of Liutov's position, however, lies elsewhere: immediately after his menacing reference to gunpowder and blood comes the plaintive request, quoted above, for some Jewish biscuits and a glass of Jewish tea. "There isn't any," Gedali replies: "There isn't any. There's a tavern next door, where good people used to do business. But people don't eat there anymore, they just weep there."

Liutov has nowhere to go. The old world, from which he fled but which still retains its hold on him, has been destroyed by the new, toward which he is striving with all his heart, but which will not accept him, and repels him with its ugliness and bloodlust. The loneliness and desperation of the intellectual in the Revolution—a frequent enough literary theme in the 1920's—are compounded by the loneliness of the Jew; the Jew, moreover, being of a particular kind, split down the middle in his attitude to Jewishness, as the intellectual is split in his attitude to the Revolution. As a result, in the strength and tension of the tragic principle, the insolubility of its conflict, ***Red Cavalry*** may well take pride of place among books on the civil war.

The sharpness of the conflict is intensified by a vision so unsparing in its precision as to suggest at times the moral indifference of an aesthete:

> Right in front of my windows, some Cossacks were executing an old silver-bearded Jew for spying. The old man yelped and struggled. Then Kudrya, from the machine-gunners, tucked the old man's head under his arm. The Jew fell silent and spread his feet apart. With his right hand, Kudrya took out his knife and carefully cut the old man's throat, avoiding the spurting blood. (**"Berestechko"**)

But this precision is itself the result of a sense of apartness and alienation that often borders on active hostility. (Simple comparison for "one's own," whether in ethnic kinship or common cause, would have blurred the vision and robbed the picture of its distinctive severity.) In the same story, **"Berestechko,"** the Jewish way of life is delineated with a hostility that marks even the vocabulary ("the warm putrefaction of the old world," "the stifling decay of Hasidism," "the traditional wretchedness of this architecture," and so on); and this hostility is underlined by contrast: "The village stinks, waiting for the new era, and instead of people, it is inhabited by fading schemata of frontier misfortunes. By the end of the day I was fed up with them and I left the town, climbed the hill, and found an entry into the ruins of the Raciborski castle." Liutov is not shocked by the abomination of desolation in what was once the seat of a Polish aristocrat; his descriptive detail—the nymphs with their eyes put out, a fragment of a hundred-year old letter—sounds, rather, elegiac.

But even sharper and more merciless is the vision he turns on his comrades-in-arms. Here the alienation of an intellectual is augmented by ethnic alienation—and Liutov recoils in horror. He wants to admire and approve, and from this willed desire derive both the romantic phantasmagoria of landscapes and the infatuated portraits of his heroes, such as that of Savitskii, the divisional commander, in the opening paragraph of **"My First Goose."** But the romantic, technicolor film often snaps, and then one sees in the gaps the "raw fingers" and "fleshy, loathsome face" of another hero, another divisional commander, Pavlichenko in **"Chesniki."** The horror is even clearer in the stories told by narrators other than Liutov; between them and him lies an abyss of non-understanding and fear. With fear and bewilderment the intellectual Liutov registers the dense and savage suspiciousness of the barbarian (**"Betrayal"**); but for Liutov the Jew, much more terrible is the fanatical savagery of the *"goyim,"* trampling the enemy to death (**"The Life Story of Pavlichenko"**), ready to kill for a bag of salt (**"Salt"**), capable of parricide and the murder of a son (**"The Letter"**). It would be wrong to see Liutov's reaction to all this as reflecting only a sense of moral superiority, millennia of living with the biblical commandment, "Thou shalt not kill," for it reflects as well millennia of passive martyrdom, the heritage of discrimination and intimidation.

On the whole . . . the author of ***Red Cavalry*** stands above his hero. His dual position is stable and productive. Despite his apartness, he is still his own man in both elements, in the old and in the new, in the Jewish and in the Soviet. He is not with the Liutov who is fed up with the Jews of Berestechko, or who confesses, "I am tired of living in this Red Army of ours" (**"Evening"**). He corrects Liutov through Gedali; and he cuts short Liutov's complaining with Galin's words: "You're a ditherer, and it's our luck that we have to put up with ditherers like you. . . . We are taking the nut out of the shell for you. Soon you'll see the nut right out of its shell, then you'll stop picking your nose and start singing the praises of the new life in unusual prose. Till then, just sit quiet, you ditherer, and don't whine around our feet" (**"Evening"**).

This astonishing harmony-in-duality is what makes ***Red Cavalry*** a unique book, in Soviet as well as Russian-Jewish literature. It is Babel's best work, also his most Jewish—despite its non-Jewish subject matter—because at its center stands Jewish restlessness and yearning, gripped momentarily by the prospect of finding self-transcendence in the great common cause. That this hope was unrealizable, that the cause, "seasoned with the finest blood," would turn into an endless bloodbath, Babel did not know, and to indict him on this ground would be wrong.

Babel's works on purely Jewish subjects turn out, in a sense, to be less Jewish, precisely because in them the confidently sustained duality of position is weaker by comparison with ***Red Cavalry***—when it is not, as in the early story **"Shabbes Nakhamu"** (1918), entirely absent. The latter is a rather pallid rendering of several anecdotes, or oral tales, about Hershele Ostropolier, the Jewish variation of the trickster-hero to be found in the folklore of almost every people. Babel, however, evidently gave this experiment (which, despite its subtitle, "From the Cycle, 'Hershele,'" he never continued) special significance, for in ***Red Cavalry,*** in reply to Reb Motele's question, "What does the Jew do?," Liutov replies, "I am rendering the adventures of Hersh of Ostropol into verse."

The ***Odessa Tales*** were probably written at the same time as ***Red Cavalry.*** They are marked, however, not only by different themes: the narrator is different, as is his relation to his material. Babel writes of the gangster life of Jewish Odessa in the first person, but at one point allows the narrative to pass to the synagogue beadle (*shames*), Arye-Leib, who refers to the narrator in rather disparaging terms: "You have spectacles on your nose, and autumn in your soul." Nevertheless, the poetics and intonation, as well as the emotional background of all four tales, are identical. The narrator is as much in love with the fat, juicy, fleshy, full-blooded, expansive Odessa of robbers, rich men, and cemetery-gate beggars, as is Arye-Leib himself. Arye-Leib says of the rich man nicknamed "Jew-and-a-half": "Tartakovskii's got the soul of a murderer, but he's one of us. He started as one of us. He's our flesh and blood, just as if the same mother bore us (**"How Things Were Done in Odessa"**). *Mutatis mutandis,* Babel might have said the same thing about all of old Jewish Odessa—as old Odessa might about him. He is here at home among his own; of the urge to escape and the self-division, all that remains is the conventional pair of spectacles on the nose, contrasting with the eagle eyes of the horse-and-cart drivers, the thieves, and Tartakovskii.

None of this is intended to diminish the qualities of the ***Odessa Tales.*** I merely mean to emphasize one thing: despite their stunning stylistic discoveries and innovations, despite their nostalgia for a recent but already irrevocable past, despite the utterly new and unexpected appearance of a bandit-hero in Russian-Jewish literature, the ***Odessa Tales*** continue and perhaps crown the pre-revolutionary tradition of social observation in this literature, whereas ***Red Cavalry*** opens a new period and establishes a new tradition.

The four stories of the autobiographical cycle were written later than ***Red Cavalry*** and ***Odessa Tales.*** Two of them are dated 1925 and two 1930. These sad Jewish tales of sad Jewish childhood, with pogroms, penury, insane relatives—. . . at least half of the events and details are imaginary—would not stand out among the childhood reminiscences in which Russian-Jewish literature abounds but for the fact that here the author regards his past from a different, completely non-Jewish world. He has not broken with his former world demonstratively or noisily; he has simply left it, slipped away from it, into "nowhere," and he looks back with mixed feelings of nostalgia and fear, like the majority of children who have turned adult. Jewishness here is not the theme but the background against which the tragedies of childhood are reenacted: tragedies of love, deception, humiliation. Naturally, they are all strongly conditioned by the background, especially as, in the first two short stories, **"The Story of My Dovecote"** and **"First Love,"** the background is a pogrom, but the tragedies themselves are universal, not linked to any one place or time or people. And the heart of each tale lies precisely in these universal tragedies; perhaps that is why the narrator, in focusing on his past sufferings, renders them with Babel-like tension and insight, observing everything else—the pogrom itself, his murdered grandfather Shoil, the Cossacks and their horses, the pogromists themselves—with a gaze that is clear, calm, and at times even admiring. This contrast represents not merely the special strength of Babel's autobiographical stories, but also an innovation of the greatest significance for the modern Jewish literatures of the Diaspora.

Babel's first play, ***Sunset,*** fulfills a singular role in his fate as a writer. Written in 1926, revised and finished in 1927, it was first produced and published in 1928, on the eve of the "great breaking point." The general atmosphere of the play, as well as the characters and even the plot, had all been anticipated in the ***Odessa Tales.*** But the change of literary genre—from narrative to dramatic—in and of itself brings drastic alterations in the message. Gone is the narrator in love with his material, and what had the air of a story told with relish about big-city sharpers now takes on the oppressive seriousness of life and becomes tragedy. (pp. 40-3)

Sunset proved the beginning of Babel's own sunset. The "great breaking point" broke his backbone, too. There would still be some flights—and high ones; but there would no longer be any confident or consistent ascent. Among the chief reasons was the departure of the Jews from the Russian scene—not Mendel Krik, but the whole of that Jewry which was Babel's own. Assimilation was proceeding at breakneck speed. To the new forms of Jewish life permitted and encouraged by the authorities at the end of the 1920's and beginning of the 1930's, Babel apparently remained indifferent. As far as I am aware, he made no comment whatever on the Jewish "province" of Birobidzhan. In 1931, the Society for the Agricultural Settlement of Jewish Workers wanted to show him the new Jewish agricultural settlements in the Ukraine. He mentions this briefly in his letters, without any interest, and fails even to say whether or not he took up the invitation. He was not really interested or involved in Yiddish culture, despite his love of Sholem Aleichem, his connection with the Yiddish theater and friendship with the actor Solomon Mikhoels, and his good relations with certain Yiddish writers. The Russian-Jewish writer had had the ground cut out from under his feet.

The ascents of his last decade are, in the main, connected with the Jewish theme or with the narrator Liutov's manner of perception in ***Red Cavalry:*** the last two stories of the autobiographical cycle . . . , and the superb **"The Road"** . . . are pure Liutov. Liutov's spirit also permeates Babel's masterpiece, **"Guy de Maupassant"**—published in 1932, but, according to the author, dating from 1920-22. I am inclined to assign another remarkable story, **"Dante Street"** . . . , to this category, for its emotional key—the most important component of the story—is desperate loneliness: "There is no loneliness more desperate than loneliness in Paris." As for the ***Odessa Tales,*** their manner extends to [**"The End of the Old Folks' Home"** and **"Froim Grach"**]. . . . One can hardly call the latter an "ascent," but the two stories are linked (and detached from the ***Odessa Tales***) by the motif of departure, death, and regret for what is gone which is particularly sharp in **"Froim Grach."**

In 1935, Babel announced: "I would like to tell the world everything I know about old Odessa; after that I will be able to go on to the new Odessa." In fact he had undertaken to confront the new Odessa earlier, in 1931, when he published his story, **"Karl Yankel."** But the attempt was not a success—as Babel himself realized. In a letter written in February 1932, he expresses astonishment that the critics should pay any attention to such rubbish, and he calls the story simply bad. He cannot handle the new Odessa because he has no tender feeling for it. The scandal about the circumcision of the newborn Karl Yankel in the story of that name is inflated not merely in itself, but it is inflated and artificial for Babel, who is forcing himself and cannot disguise the fact. The same element of artificiality appears in the stereotype, Ovsei Belotserkovskii, who stockpiles farm supplies with the help of the Balta and Tiraspol district party committees. It appears in the feeding of the infant by the Kirghiz woman—a sugary vignette illustrative of the "indestructible friendship of the peoples of the USSR"—and in the pathos of the narrator's concluding exclamations. On the other hand, there is nothing false, despite some crude grotesque, in the "little operator" Naftula Gerchik; the page and a half devoted to him are Babel at his best.

Throughout the 1930's, Babel was searching for a new style. Both his letters and his public speeches are full of complaints about the agonizing difficulties of the search. He was looking not only for new expressive forms but, above all, for another atmosphere, another milieu, new ground under his feet. Beyond the bounds of Russian-Jewish literature, however, success would not favor him—even though he knew the Soviet Union very well, loved it devotedly, was himself loved and surrounded everywhere by friends. . . . [The] reasons for this are various and each has its own measure of validity; still, it would appear that the loss of his dual position, his dual vision, had a crucial effect. It is not in evidence—nor could it be—when he is regarding something entirely alien, as, for example, the high aristocracy (in the play ***Mariia***), even if by the accident of revolution a Jewish speculator has managed to worm his way into its midst. Gorky, incidentally—who justifiably disliked ***Mariia***—wrote to Babel: "I especially don't like Dymshits. . . . You make him too easy a target for the Judeophobes." I imagine such apprehensions had never occurred to Babel. The Jewish writer portrays a Jewish villain as naturally and unselfconsciously as a Russian writer would a Russian villain, and neither would worry about what the Judeophobes or the Russophobes might say. Even so, there is no dual vision when one examines a thing of one's own making: in the two surviving fragments of a lost novel about collectivization (**"Kolyvushka"** and **"Gapa Guzhva"**), Babel is truthful, that is, true to himself—but he is unable to detach himself from the material, to stand to one side, and the sharpness, clarity, and depth of his account suffer in consequence.

Babel is the most important figure in Russian-Jewish literature of the Soviet period, the model of the Jewish writer in Soviet-Russian culture. The Russian-Jewish literature that was reborn after Stalin takes its bearings from him, and is measured against him. To imitate Babel is impossibly difficult, to repeat him impossible—just as his fate is unrepeatable, just as old Odessa and turn-of-the-century Russian Jewry are beyond recall. But one can compare, assess, learn. It is unlikely that anyone today will be tempted by Babel's second standpoint, the Russian Revolution. But his feelings and views suggest the possibility of another much more attractive "bifurcation." I have in mind some such oppositions as these: insularity, rigidity, inhibition, hypertrophied rationalism—as against openness, emotional release, fullness of feeling, the joy of existence. That is what the dialogue in the bedroom of the old Kriks in ***Sunset*** is all about. Nekhama nags her husband: "Look how other people live. For supper, other people have ten pounds of meat, they make soup, they make cutlets, they make compote. The father comes home from work, everybody sits at the table, everybody eats and laughs. But what do *we* do?" And Mendel snarls back: "Pull out my teeth, Nekhama, pour some Yiddish soup into my veins, break my back. . . ." Here is the root of Babel's ill-concealed delight in his gangsters, in the violent, dangerous crank Simon-Wolf, in grandfather Levi Yitzhok, the ex-rabbi who lost his post for crooked dealing in currency, "the laughing-stock of the town, and its embellishment" (**"In the Basement," "Awakening"**). Here also is the sense of the ending of **"The Story of a Horse,"** a remarkable paragraph which has been endlessly quoted: "Khlebnikov was a quiet man, like me in character. We were both rocked by the same passions. We both looked on the world as a meadow in May, a meadow where women and horses moved about."

Not to reject tradition, not to turn away from one's own history, not to wallow either in the fruits of the Diaspora or in its rubbish, but instead, to leap into freedom, into open space, to burst free from one's chains, to know the taste, color, scent, texture of everything denied us by the ghetto wall, the Pale of Settlement, and that invisible pale which we put around ourselves and in which we suffocated for century upon century. And to find harmony in dichotomy.

This is not written in Babel's work, it is only implied. But the idea of this paradoxical harmony, which is not at all the same thing as peace and quiet and heavenly grace, comes to mind constantly when one looks at the old guard of the kibbutzim, the settlers of Palestine in the 1930's. It comes to mind with increasing frequency as one thinks of the Jews of Silence, who have now become the Jews of courage. (pp. 43-5)

Simon Markish, "The Example of Isaac Babel," translated by Donald Fanger and Harry Shukman (reprinted by permission of the publisher and the author; all rights reserved), in Commentary, *Vol. 64, No. 5, November, 1977, pp. 36-45.*

ELIAS CANETTI (essay date 1980)

[A Bulgarian-born man of letters and winner of the 1981 Nobel Prize in literature, Canetti is regarded as one of the most important intellectual figures of our era. Having fled Austria in 1938, he was deeply disturbed by the social climate in Europe before World War II, and eventually became concerned with "the conflict between culture and the mass mind." Canetti's sole novel, Auto-da Fé *(1946), is a sociopolitical satire of the greed, cruelty, and intolerance of the mass mind for the individual who is both alienated from and victimized by it. Often described as a companion piece to* Auto-da Fé, Crowds and Power *(1962) is considered his most influential work. This treatise on the psychology of the masses attempts to explain the origin, behavior, and significance of crowds as a force in society. Canetti has also achieved recognition for his autobiographical volumes* The Tongue Set Free: Remembrance of a European Childhood *(1979) and* The Torch in My Ear *(1980), which deal with family influences upon Canetti during his childhood and adolescence, and with the literary influences of his early adulthood, most notably the Austrian writers Karl Klaus and Franz Kafka. In the following excerpt from* The Torch in My Ear, *Canetti fondly recalls—as an awestruck admirer—meeting Babel during the writer's 1928 visit to Berlin.]*

I thought I would hear a great deal from [Babel] about the great Russians, but he must have taken them for granted, or maybe he found it boastful to expatiate on the literature of his own countrymen. But perhaps there was more to it; perhaps he recoiled from the inevitable shallowness of such a conversation: he himself moved in the language in which the great works of that literature were written, and I had read them at best in translations. We would not have been speaking about the same thing. He took literature so seriously that he must have hated anything vague and approximate. However, my timidity was no weaker than his; I couldn't get myself to say anything to him about ***Red Cavalry*** or ***The Odessa Tales.***

Yet in our conversations about the French, about Stendhal, Flaubert, and Maupassant, he must have sensed how important *his* stories were to me. For whenever I asked him about anything, my question secretly referred to something of his that I was focusing on. He instantly recognized the tacit reference, and his answer was simple and precise. He saw how satisfied I was; perhaps he even liked the fact that I didn't keep on asking. He spoke about Paris, where his wife, a painter, had been living for a year. I believe he had just called for her there and was already missing Paris. He preferred Maupassant to Chekhov, but when I mentioned Gogol (whom I loved more than anything), he said, to my joyful amazement: "That's one thing the French lack—they don't have Gogol." Then he reflected a bit and, to make up for what might have sounded like boasting, he added: "Do the Russians have Stendhal?"

I realize how few concrete things I have to say about Babel, and yet he meant more to me than anyone else I met in Berlin. I saw him together with everything of his that I had read—not much, but it was so concentrated that it colored every moment. And I was also present when he absorbed things in a city that was alien to him, and they were not in his language. He didn't throw around big words and he avoided drawing attention. He could *see* best if he was hidden. He accepted everything from others; he didn't reject things he didn't care for. The things that tormented him most were the things that he allowed to exert the longest effect on him. I knew all this from his Cossack stories; everyone was enthralled by their blood-filled brilliance without being intoxicated by the blood. Here, where he was confronted with the brilliance of Berlin, I could see how indifferent he was to things in which other people bathed in blabbering vanity. He disapproved of any empty reflex; instead, his thirsty eyes lapped up countless people eating their pea soup. One sensed that nothing was easy for him, even though he never said so himself. Literature was sacrosanct to him; he never spared himself and would never have *embellished* anything. Cynicism was alien to him because of his strenuous conception of literature. If he found that something was good, he could never have *used* it like other people, who, in sniffing around, implied that they regarded themselves as the culmination of the entire past. Knowing what literature was, he never felt superior to others. He was obsessed with literature, not with its honors or with what it brought in. I do not believe that I saw Babel any differently from what he was because he spoke to me. I know that Berlin would have devoured me like lye if I hadn't met him. (pp. 292-94)

Elias Canetti, "The Throng of Names," in his The Torch in My Ear, *translated by Joachim Neugroschel (reprinted by permission of Farrar, Straus and Giroux, Inc.; translation copyright © 1982 by Farrar, Straus and Giroux, Inc.; originally published as* Die Fackel im Ohr: Lebensgeschichte 1921-1931 *by Elias Canetti (copyright © 1980 by Carl Hanser Verlag), Hanser, 1980), Farrar, Straus and Giroux, 1982, pp. 265-314.**

MILTON EHRE (essay date 1981)

[*In the following excerpt Ehre examines* Red Cavalry *as a study of stylistic contrasts between that which is "epic-heroic" and that which is "pathetic."*]

The central opposition of ***Red Cavalry,*** formally that of epic and pathos, has received various thematic interpretations: the way of violence versus the way of peace, Cossack versus Jew, the new revolutionary order versus traditional society, noble savage versus civilized man, and a pair that may subsume all of these—nature versus culture. Though criticism cannot manage without such formulae, they ought not blind us to the complexities and ambiguities of a text. Not all the Cossacks are beautiful, and few, if any, are noble. Many are "solitary, poor, nasty, brutish," sprung from a Hobbesian rather than Rousseauian nature. Nor are all the Jews men of peace; some, the narrator among them, choose the way of war. What is beautiful to Babel' is the realm of heroic action. Individual Cossacks may be treated ironically, even comically. The heroic march itself is never mocked. It is always solemn.

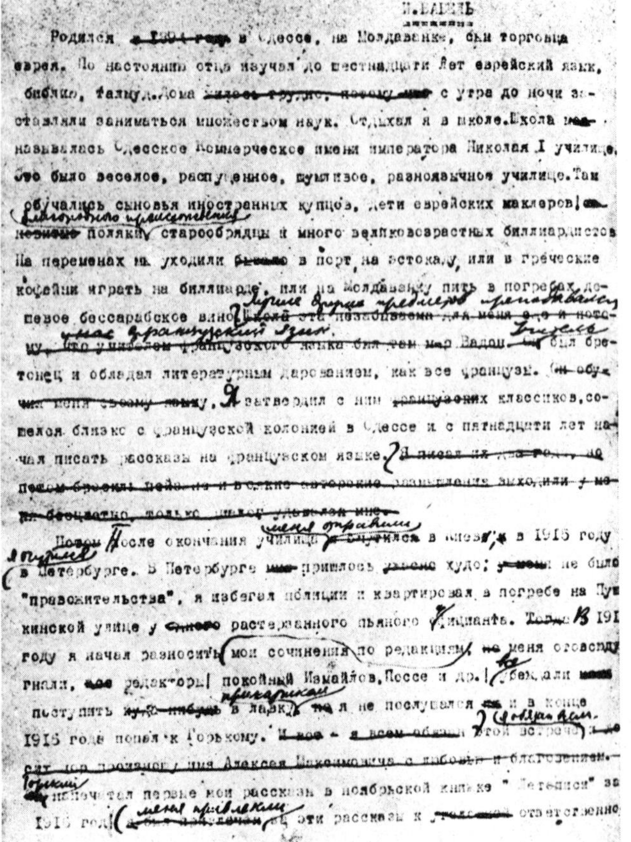
И. БАБЕЛЬ

Родился в Одессе, на Молдаванке, сын торговца еврея. По настоянию отца изучал до шестнадцати лет еврейский язык, библию, талмуд. Дома с утра до ночи заставляли заниматься множеством наук. Отдыхал я в школе. Школа называлась Одесское Коммерческое имени императора Николая I училище. Это было веселое, распущенное, шумное, разноязычное училище. Там обучались сыновья иностранных купцов, дети еврейских маклеров, благородного происхождения поляки, старообрядцы и много великовозрастных биллиардистов. На переменах мы уходили в порт, на эстокаду, или в греческие кофейни играть на биллиарде, или на Молдаванку пить в погребах дешевое бессарабское вино. Лучше других предметов преподавался у нас французский язык. Учитель был бретонец и обладал литературным дарованием, как все французы. Я затвердил с ним классиков, сошелся близко с французской колонией в Одессе и с пятнадцати лет начал писать рассказы на французском языке.

После окончания училища меня отправили в Киев, и в 1915 году я очутился в Петербурге. В Петербурге пришлось худо; не было "правожительства", я избегал полиции и квартировал в погребе на Пушкинской улице у растерзанного пьяного официанта. В 1915 году я начал разносить мои сочинения по редакциям, меня отовсюду гнали, все редакторы (покойный Измайлов, Поссе и др.) убеждали поступить в лавку, приказчиком, я не послушался и в конце 1916 года попал к Горькому. (Я обязан этой встрече) Горький напечатал первые мои рассказы в ноябрьской книжке "Летописи" за 1916 год (меня привлекали за эти рассказы к ответственно

Manuscript, with author's corrections, of Babel's autobiography.

Movement defines the epic mode. Adding history to the list of interpretive terms does not discredit previous readings but makes them more precise and adequate. Nature is necessity, what is given and not made, the weather we live in rather than the forms we create. Natural things exhibit motion; humans are capable of action—motions that result from conscious, purposive choice. As such, history in ***Red Cavalry*** is presented as a kind of natural occurrence. From the opening passage, where physical nature and human activity merge in a single awesome march, the work communicates a sense of portentous events. Armies are on the move, "striking the hammer of history upon the anvil of future ages," in the grandiloquent rhetoric of a Cossack officer. But all this movement has a formless character. It is sheer motion rather than deliberate action, an elemental "Cossack flood," whose usual expression is random and terrible violence. The future is being forged by the hammer of history, but for men like [the narrator] Liutov, compelled to act in the present, that future is obscure. On the other hand, the Cossacks, who are shaping history, seem oddly indifferent to its outcome. For them the appeal of revolution is the opportunity it gives for free exercise of their powers, which they manifest in indiscriminate violence and mindless cycles of vengeance. As in Tolstoi's *War and Peace,* history is being made by men who have no idea of what it is they are making. The eyes of the heroes of ***Red Cavalry*** are riveted to the immediate present, the act of the moment, the event as pure event. When the aged Hasidic Jew, Gedali, protests the revolution in the name of the Messianic "sweet revolution" of joy and deliverance, the narrator, speaking in the name of the actual historical Revolution, answers in a tautology: "[The Revolution] cannot help shooting . . . because it is the Revolution." The Revolution is what it is—a brute fact as ineluctable as the givens of the natural world. It will have momentous issue, but the focus of its participants, like the prose of the narrator, is on the concrete givens of immediate experience.

Brilliant and rhapsodic, the epic universe is also threatened with emptiness: "The brilliant sky loomed inexpressibly empty, as it always is in time of danger." Besides the regal standard, another recurring image for war is the desert or wasteland (*pustynia*): "Afonka . . . dragged himself to his squadron, utterly alone, in the dusty blazing desert of fields." "Beyond the window horses neighed and Cossacks shouted. The desert of war yawned beyond the window." In the desert of war, men suffer "an eternal homelessness." Some turn into beasts. Matvei Pavlichenko has a "jackal's conscience" and was "suckled by a she-wolf"; Afonka Bida roams the countryside slaughtering Poles like a "lonely wolf." When life is reduced to pure motion, empty of purpose, deprived of the nurture and restraints of culture, men turn into wild animals, or they feel themselves "utterly alone." The man without a city, Aristotle tells us, becomes either a beast or a god. What escapes him is the specifically human. The epic line of unceasing motion ultimately resolves in exhaustion. Apparently the burden of being other than human is hard. (pp. 231-32)

"Pathos" is Greek for suffering, and "passive" is from the Latin *passivus,* or capable of suffering. To suffer is to endure or bear, to be passive, not to act. In moving from the epic mode to the pathetic, ***Red Cavalry*** turns from action to passivity. The worlds of culture exist in stasis. The prose loses its dynamism, as it departs from renderings of movements to portraits of conditions. Ruined Gothic churches and deserted castles epitomize Poland in Babel''s book. . . . (p. 233)

The intransitive verbs, most of them reflexive (*mertsalo, perelivaetsia, kolvshutsia, pylaiut, valiaetsia, struitsia*), describe motions that remain frozen in place. Where the verbs depicting the epic march of the army emphasize discrete events in time—"a tender light flares," "we ford the river," "the horses enter the water"—these convey states of objects rather than events or acts. The length of the verbs, their open syllables, the profusion of liquids (not limited to the verbs) slow the tempo of the prose and contribute to its "insinuating" quality. Interspersed into the passage are verbless exclamations ("O crucifixes") that show the passage for what it is, a static evocation of a world: "Here is Poland . . . !"

This languid style and hothouse imagery of putrefaction and silky perversity are in the manner of *fin de siècle* decadence. In leaving the brilliant sunlight of war, we enter a Poland mirrored in Gothic moonlight. A sinister green hue and watery shades replace the regal purple and bright red, orange, and yellow of the heroic landscape: "The moon, green as a lizard, rose above the pond. From my window I could make out the estate of the Counts Raciborski—meadows and hopfields, hidden by the watery ribbons of twilight." (pp. 233-34)

Jewish scenes are evoked in this incantatory, quasi-liturgical style or, at other times, in a starkly naturalistic manner. Excrement is a recurring detail. Where the heroic world is expansive and sunlit, the Jewish is cramped and sunless: "At the back of the house there stretches out a shed of two, sometimes three stories. The sun never penetrates here. . . . In wartime the inhabitants seek refuge from bullets and pillage in these catacombs. Human offal and cow dung accumulate here for days. Depression and horror fill the catacombs with the corrosive and foul acidity of excrement." Babel' often portrays the Jewish Pale, as he does Catholic Poland, in the shadows of evening, but instead of the moon, a lonely star, the harbinger of the Jewish Sabbath, follows Liutov on his nighttime wanderings.

The counterpoise of Cossack vigor and Polish-Jewish decay seems to call for an obvious reading. The vital new order is hammering out the future on the battlefields of Eastern Europe; set against it is the "rot of old times" (*gnil' stariny*)—the outdated societies, transfixed in immobility, which "reek while waiting for the new era." The great watershed of the Russian Revolution made comparisons of the old and the new an obsessive preoccupation of early Soviet literature. But for complex minds like Babel''s, the schemata into which we place life are starting points and not the culmination of artistic exploration. If the epic line of the book—the movement of war and history—is vibrant and compelling, it is also barren—a desert of the heart. The old ways are in decay, but it is among them that Liutov seeks physical and spiritual nourishment. True, he occasionally finds sustenance in the form of comradeship among the Cossacks. The Cossacks are men too, and they must also take time from the incessant motion of war to look for relief in the ordinary habits of life. One of the important discoveries in Liutov's education is that the Cossacks, for all their anarchic violence, have codes of honor by which they live.

But it is usually to the wayside—to old Poland and especially the Jews—that Liutov turns for nourishment to sustain him in the desert. The taking of food is a central image of the book—one that acquires sacramental value. Evenings Liutov drinks "the wine of [the artist Pan Apolek's] conversation"; he delights in "the food of the Jesuits," though it is strange, even ominous: "These cakes . . . had an odor of crucifixes. A cunning juice was in them, together with the aromatic fierceness of the Vatican." To his fellow Jews he turns for more homely fare: "Gedali, . . . today is Friday, and it's already evening. Where are Jewish biscuits to be got, and a Jewish glass of tea, and a bit of that pensioned-off God in a glass of tea?"

The discovery of nourishment in places marked by rot and excrement marks the enigmatic and paradoxical quality of culture in ***Red Cavalry.*** Culture lies on the wayside, tangential to the highway of revolution and war. While the highway is straight and narrow and the men who pursue it single-minded, culture for Babel' is a mysterious thing. It belongs to night, the moon, and the lonely Sabbath star rather than the clear sunlight of clamorous events. Its habitats are strange Gothic churches that emanate "the breath of invisible orders," lonely aristocratic gardens where statuary of "nymphs with gouged-out eyes lead a choral dance" under the green lizard of the moon, morgue-like rooms in which motley Jews, "the possessed, liars, and idlers" await the Messiah. (pp. 234-35)

The shift from the clear sunlight and martial rhythms of the epic to the mysterious moonlit nights and evocative language of the pathetic mode marks a change in kinds of experience. Language and imagery combine to determine the book's shape of feeling. In the daylight of the epic-heroic world, in the arena of history, which is man's inescapable circumstance, action is precise, unreflective, and violent. Life admits of clearcut categorization, as humanity divides into agent and patient, actor and sufferer, forger of the future and remnant of the dying past. In the shadowy realm of human culture, where man gives himself to creation and thought instead of elemental motion, everything is hopelessly ambiguous: "I went along with [the moon], nursing unrealizable dreams and discordant songs." Here Jews wallowing in excrement proffer nourishment; the dead and blind (Gedali is blind) are possessed by visions of eternal life; decadent landscapes tempt the narrator by the beauty and power of art.

Suffering itself—the pathos that defines the wayside, particularly the life of the Jews—resists a singleness of response. The Jews are shown as wretched and impotent, grotesque figures huddled in squalid rooms, stinking of filth. But as they edge toward becoming contemptible, they suddenly surprise us with their dignity. The first story, **"Crossing into Poland,"** can serve as a paradigm of the work's contrast of Jew and Cossack. After the glorious opening march, we are introduced into a hovel with "scraps of women's fur coats on the floor, human feces, fragments of occult crockery." Jews "skip about noiselessly, like monkeys, like Japs in a circus, their necks swaying and twisting." And just when the contrast seems clear and tidy—heroic beauty and grandeur versus the ugliness of suffering—one of the pathetic victims bursts into a rhetoric of heroic stature that rivals the heroism of the Cossack warriors. . . . (pp. 235-36)

The representative figures of culture in ***Red Cavalry,*** the aged Hasid Gedali and the Polish artist Pan Apolek, embody its mystery. Jewish prophet and Polish artist and their societies—the Jewish Pale and Catholic, aristocratic Poland—seem to denote for Babel' the ethical and aesthetic imaginations, respectively. Both Gedali and Pan Apolek are incongruous and paradoxical figures, slightly comic, yet visionary. "Old Gedali, the diminutive proprietor in smoked glasses and a green frock coat down to the ground, meandered around his treasures in the roseate void of the evening. He rubbed his small white hands, plucked at his little gray beard, and listened, head bent, to the mysterious voices wafting down to him." Like Gedali, Pan Apolek is a child of evening: "On fragrant evenings the shades of old feudal Poland assembled, the mad (*iurodivoi*) artist at their head." The description of this artist, whose "wise and beautiful life" goes to Liutov's head "like an old wine," is a study in incongruity: "In his right hand Apolek carried a paintbox, and with his left he guided the blind, accordian player. The singing of their nailed German boots rang out with peace and hope. From Apolek's thin neck dangled a canary-yellow scarf. Three little chocolate-colored feathers fluttered on the blind man's Tyrolean hat. . . . It all looked as though . . . the Muses had settled . . . side by side in bright, wadded scarves and hobnailed German boots."

Incongruous in appearance, Pan Apolek leads a life and pursues an art that are exercises in paradox. He is at one and the same time a decorator of Christian churches and a heretic. His favorite story is the apocryphal tale of Jesus lying with the virgin Deborah out of pity. In the presence of his art "a portent of mystery" touches Liutov, and the mystery is of the ways the ordinary and mundane can become transfigured by art. Pan Apolek spends his life raising the poor and sinful to the condition of saints in icons of glorious color. "He has made saints of you in your lifetime," the indignant church authorities chide. His artist's vision is but another version of the Hasid Gedali's prophetic dream of the coming Revolution of Joy and the International of Good People, of a community where there are no orphans in the house and every soul is given "first-category rations." Polish village artist and Jewish shopkeeper, engulfed by brutality and violence, turn to dreams of universal compassion.

As action is the measure of man in the heroic-epic world of history, compassion is a cardinal value of culture. It provides the nourishment missing from the deserts of war. Night, which shrouds the landscapes of culture, is also a time of comfort. While the images of day are masculine—phallic standards cleaving brilliant sunlit skies—those of night are maternal: "Blue roads flowed past me like streams of milk spurting from many breasts"; "evening wrapped me in the life-giving moisture of its twilight sheets, evening laid a mother's hand upon my burning forehead"; "night comforted us in our sorrows, a light wind wafted over us like a mother's skirt."

To the oppositions of ***Red Cavalry***—epic and pathos, nature and culture, history and culture—we must add yet another: a masculine and a feminine-maternal attitude. The latter is specifically associated with Jewish values. Wrapped in "the dying evening," Gedali raises the image of the compassionate mother to a metaphysical principle. (pp. 236-37)

And at the crossroads of the book stands the narrator-protagonist Liutov, pulled one way by the claims of history and masculine action, the other by the allure of art and demands of compassion. Isaak Babel''s great book continually circles a tragic dilemma. The cultures—artistic, religious, and moral—which nurture human life are dying. The march of history leaves men famished for spiritual nourishment; yet its imperatives will not be denied or evaded. The two realms—history and culture—are never brought into harmony, but the final two stories (**"The Rabbi's Son"** and **"Argamak"**) seek out a middle ground.

We met the rebellious rabbi's son in an earlier story (**"The Rabbi"**), where he was presented as "the cursed son, the last son, the recalcitrant son." By the end of ***Red Cavalry,*** this last son of the rabbi's line has joined the Red Army, taken command of a regiment, and been mortally wounded. Like Gedali and Pan Apolek, Il'ia is an ambiguous figure. His description points to features both male and female: "a youth . . . with the powerful brow of Spinoza, with the sickly face of a nun." Liutov, while going through the dying Il'ia's belongings, discovers that he has lugged off to war emblems of all the opposites of the book: action and poetry, politics and art, things masculine and feminine.

> Everything was strewn about pell-mell—mandates of the propagandist and notes of the Jewish poet. The portraits of Lenin and Maimonides lay side by side, the knotted iron of Lenin's skull beside the dull silk of the portraits of Maimonides. A lock of woman's hair had been slipped into a volume of Resolutions of the Sixth Party Congress, and curved lines of Hebrew verse crowded the margins of Communist leaflets. They fell on me in a sparse and mournful rain—pages of the Song of Songs and revolver cartridges.

This juncture of the opposing images suggests that Il'ia has achieved a way, not to reconcile the contradictions, but to live with them. Going off to war, he takes the baggage of culture with him. The tokens of culture lie side by side with those of war and history. The two poles remain, as they have been throughout the work, discrete antinomies. A mood of elegiac melancholy sweeps over Liutov, as he once again stands face to face with the tragic incongruity of human life.

The mood is not one in which he or the rabbi's son will permit themselves to linger. Explaining to Liutov why he went to war,

Il'ia says that, though formerly he would not abandon his mother, in a revolution a mother is only "an episode." It is a pregnant remark, one that pertains at least as much to Liutov's struggle as to Il'ia's. We have seen that the opposition between action and culture also reflected the contraries of a masculine and feminine principle. On a psychological plane, the plot of ***Red Cavalry,*** its overarching action, is the story of Liutov's liberation from the maternal image—from the passive, suffering side of his nature. Evening lays "a mother's hand" upon his "burning forehead," but it also crowns him with the thorns of martyrdom. His longing for the nourishing mother inhibits him from acting in the world of men. The terrible irony is that in order to enter that world in the context of war and revolution one must learn to kill. . . . (pp. 237-38)

The maternal image and related images of nurture have been associated with culture and value. The mother, as progenitor of life and the center of the family, represents the continuity culture demands. In ***Red Cavalry,*** however, culture is also "episodic." The structures in which men and women live—family, nation, religion, art, tradition—appear to have a permanence that turns out to be illusory before the juggernaut of history. The dominant rhythm of ***Red Cavalry***—the irrevocable epic march of revolution which is sweeping traditional culture into the dustbins of history—wins out. No wonder that some critics have read the book as a renunciation of the values of culture and a celebration of primitivism.

It is a mistaken reading. Culture is ultimately not an institution but an idea. As its institutions crumble in revolution, its idea is kept alive. For Gedali, the mother, even when dead, "leaves a memory," which is "immortal." It is surely no accident that the two most visible embodiments of culture in ***Red Cavalry,*** Gedali and Pan Apolek, are marginal men—Jewish mystic and Catholic heretic. Less tied than others to temporal institutions and orthodoxies, Gedali is able to feel confidence that his values, if not yet realized as actualities, will survive as memories to stand at the "crossroads of history."

At the end of the book the rabbi's son joins them to become the third and most important of the work's bearers of culture. As Apolek offered a model of the artist to Liutov—"I vowed . . . to follow the example of Pan Apolek"—the rabbi's son gives him a model for action. Liutov feels a kinship with him stronger than any he knew before: "And I—scarcely containing the tempests of my imagination in my ancient body—I received the last breath of my brother." Brother is not a word he could have conceivably used for any of the Cossacks, perhaps not even for Gedali and Pan Apolek. He joins the Cossacks but he is too much a man of culture to go completely native. Gedali and Pan Apolek attract him by their commitment to values, both ethical and aesthetic, but they are dreamers and visionaries, too remote from the realities of history to teach him how to live in the world. The rabbi's son shows him a middle course. While participating actively in the violence, which he deems necessary, he keeps alive reminders of other ways: poetry, the thought of Maimonides, a lock of woman's hair. Choosing masculine action, he refuses to deny the feminine part of his nature. His decision is to live with the contradictions of culture and force.

These contradictions have engendered the controlling images of the book. They have become part of Liutov's experience. In riding off with the Cossack army he of necessity takes them along. We have read ***Red Cavalry*** through the filter of his consciousness, so that they have become our experience as well. What he and we have experienced is the tragic character of human life. The resolution of ***Red Cavalry*** does not lie in the triumph of any particular allegiance or in synthetic reconciliation, but in an assertion of the will to act and live in a discordant world. (pp. 239-40)

Milton Ehre, "Babel"s 'Red Cavalry': Epic and Pathos, History and Culture," in Slavic Review *(copyright ©1981 by the American Association for the Advancement of Slavic Studies, Inc.), Vol. 40, No. 2, Summer, 1981, pp. 228-40.*

EDWARD J. BROWN (essay date 1982)

[In the following excerpt Brown discusses the ironic nature of the sketches of Red Cavalry, *which grimly suggest the failure of the Bolshevik Revolution.]*

The principal work of Isaac Babel, a series of short stories concerned with incidents in the campaign of Budyonny's First Cavalry Army in Poland, is typical of [Russian] Civil War literature in the variety of its characters—Cossacks, Polish lords and peasants, Jews, and Russians—and in the cruel reality which it depicts. (p. 88)

[***Konarmia,*** usually translated as ***Red Cavalry,*** the] book on which his fame rests can best be understood if it is approached in the spirit in which it was written. ***Konarmia*** was intended as a series of anecdotes, each with an ironic twist. In the stories thoroughly absurd human beings in ridiculous situations are occupied with the slaughter of other human beings. We misread Babel if, searching for open or hidden commentary on the Revolution, or horrified by pictures of barbarism, we fail to see that each story is built around a grim incongruity. Consider these priceless anecdotes: A peasant soldier writes a letter to his mother regaling her with all the adventures of the campaign, including among them an account of how his brothers murdered their father; a Cossack remount officer reassures peasants to whom he has given worn-out nags in return for their healthy horses: "If the animal can stand up it's a horse"; a village artist offers to paint a picture of you as St. Francis and of your enemy as Judas Iscariot for a small fee; the same artist tells how Jesus lay with Deborah, a Jerusalem maid of obscure birth, and begot a son who was hidden away by the priests; a Cheka officer, sick of the Revolution and the war, asked to be reassigned to Italy where it's warm and sunny or at least to the Cheka headquarters in Odessa; the Jew Gedali wants to found an International of Good People, where every soul would get "first-category rations"; a mild intellectual assigned to a Cossack platoon earns the respect of his soldier comrades by taking and killing a goose that doesn't belong to him; the same intellectual, after spending the Sabbath with a community of Hassidic Jews, returns to his *agit-train* to finish an article for "The Red Cavalryman." After a town is taken a commissar encourages the stunned and plundered populace: "You are in power. Everything here is yours. No more Polish Pans. I now proceed to the election of the revolutionary committee." The hero is upbraided by a Cossack soldier for going into battle with no cartridges in his revolver: "You're a milk-drinking pacifist. You worship God, you traitor." A rabbi's son, who has rejected orthodoxy for the Revolution, still lives in his father's house, "because he doesn't want to leave his mother."

Ilya Ehrenburg, who wrote the Introduction to the one-volume edition of Babel's work published in the Soviet Union in 1957, claims that Babel's diary, which has not yet been published in full, contains entries proving that these sketches were based in the main on actual occurrences of the Polish campaign, and are therefore "highly realistic." It is possible to agree with Ehrenburg's statement that the sketches contain much firsthand experience, but the term realistic as applied to them is meaningless. On the other hand, Budyonny, leader of the First Cavalry Army (who appears as a character in two of the sketches), fulminated against Babel for his failure to show the heroism of the Cossack horsemen in their struggle for the Revolution [see excerpt above, 1928]. It would seem that Budyonny in rather naïve terms is criticizing the sketches for their failure as realism. But perhaps Ehrenburg and Budyonny both miss the point. The sketches do not purport to give a balanced picture of the Cavalry Army or the Polish campaign. They are a series of sketches or, as Babel called them, "miniatures" based on experiences of the author during that campaign, and held together by the deliberate injection into each one of the author's own personality. The picture of the Cossack fighters is impressionistic and subjective. We have to do with a kind of lyric apprehension of absurd violence, seen through the eyes, indeed through the spectacles, of a sensitive intellectual whose work for the Revolution has brought him into the company of innocent savages. And the Cossacks are innocent men: they shed human blood without reason but almost without malice. When the book is examined as a whole it appears that, far from offering a comprehensive treatment of Budyonny's cavalry or the Polish campaign, only a little more than half of the sketches have to do with that organization or its exploits in war. The rest tell of other things: Hassidic Jews in eastern Poland, the deserted Polish church at Novograd, an assortment of original local characters, old buildings and cemeteries, pogroms, and other matters. What is peripheral to the campaign in Poland becomes central in Babel's cycle of sketches. (pp. 89-90)

Conventional Soviet criticism is no doubt right according to its own lights in finding that Babel's work is weighted with the details of brutality, and that he has missed "the rational principle in the Civil War, and the organizing role of the Communist Party." No doubt Babel himself could have constructed a final ironic anecdote featuring the Soviet literary critics who say such things. The great virtue of his stories is precisely their lack of political color, their apparently casual and fragmented structure. Not the least of Babel's ironies is the fact that the ideals of the socialist revolution, wrapped in facile phrases, have come into the possession of Russian peasant warriors incapable of understanding or realizing them. The stories are studded with such phrases as "no more masters," "heroic revolutionary army," "all are now equal," "the teachings of Lenin," "the revolutionary consciousness of the mass," and so forth. Such ideas might have been used by another writer, Furmanov, for instance, to justify and give rational meaning to the bloodshed of the Polish campaign. But in Babel's stories they are always given in mangled, misunderstood form by a moral illiterate who has just performed some needless piece of violence, such as killing an old Jew or shooting a woman in the back. Babel's stories are reminiscent of Blok's poem *The Twelve,* where the world is at the mercy of twelve Red guards who kill and plunder to the tune of revolutionary songs and slogans. The hopes and fears of the reformers, idealists, and revolutionaries of the nineteenth century, in ***Konarmia*** as well as in *The Twelve,* find distorted utterance in brutish mouths.

The narrator of the sketches in ***Konarmia,*** whose job is political propaganda, is present in almost all of the stories, and it is his personal view of things that the reader usually becomes aware of. The fact that he is a Jew is made explicit in some of the stories, and is suggested in others by the organic hostility toward him expressed by the Cossack soldiers. He is a man of peace—the only one, if we except Sandy the Christ, a mild syphilitic moron, who travels with the Horse Army—and he finds it almost impossible to adjust to the folkways of violence. (pp. 90-1)

The trick of Babel's art is to find the stuff of life by indirection, almost by accident. The Cavalry Army itself is a kind of side issue in a world which includes a vivid array of individual peasant soldiers, plundered villages, trampled fields, and indifferent nature itself. The task of political education, of explaining what it means, is abandoned as a grim travesty. The superflux of suffering and violence seems really to serve no rational end, and, therefore, Babel takes the sensations of the moment and transforms them through art into aesthetic experience. One of the means for this transformation is an ornate and elevated style, the texture of which is variegated with elaborate and arresting metaphors: "Blue roads flowed past me like streams of milk spurting from many breasts"; "His long legs were like girls sheathed to the neck in shiny riding boots"; "And we were moving toward the sunset, whose foaming rivers flowed along the embroidered napkins of peasant fields"; "Crouching at the feet of huge estates were dead little Jewish towns"; "The orange sun rolled down the sky like a severed head"; "The deathly chill of eye-sockets filled with frozen tears"; "The stars put out by ink-swollen clouds"; "Between two and three o'clock of a spacious July day the rainbow web of heat shimmered in the air." By such lavish use of poetic language Babel screens himself and the reader from direct experience of violence. The device makes it possible to treat as matters for contemplation even Afonka Bida's empty eye socket: "In place of the left eye on his charred face there yawned horribly a monstrous pink bulge." (pp. 93-4)

Edward J. Brown, "The Intellectuals, II," in his Russian Literature Since the Revolution *(copyright © 1963, 1969, and 1982 by Edward J. Brown; excerpted by permission of the President and Fellows of Harvard College), revised edition, Cambridge, Mass.: Harvard University Press, 1982, pp. 87-104.**

ADDITIONAL BIBLIOGRAPHY

Alexandrova, Vera. "Isaac Babel (1894-1941)." In her *A History of Soviet Literature,* translated by Mirra Ginsburg, pp. 124-34. Garden City, N.Y.: Doubleday 1963.

General biographical and critical introduction to Babel's life and major works.

Andrew, J. M. "Structure and Style in the Short Story: Babel's 'My First Goose'." *The Modern Language Review* 70, No. 2 (April 1975): 366-79.

Detailed structural analysis of Babel's short story "My First Goose."

Apple, Max. "History and Case History in *Red Cavalry* and *The Day of the Locust.*" In *Nathanael West—The Cheaters and the Cheated: A Collection of Critical Essays,* edited by David Madden, pp. 235-48. Deland, Fla.: Everett/Edwards, 1973.*

Comparative study of Babel's collection of short stories *Red Cavalry* and Nathanael West's short novel *The Day of the Locust.*

Clyman, Toby W. "Babel' As Colorist." *Slavic and East European Journal* 21, No. 3 (Fall 1977): 332-43.

Focuses on the importance of color imagery in Babel's stories. Clyman believes that Babel's use of color recalls Expressionist painting.

Ehrenburg, Ilya. "A Speech at a Moscow Meeting in Honor of Babel, November 11, 1964." In *You Must Know Everything: Stories 1915-*

1937, by Isaac Babel, edited by Nathalie Babel, translated by Max Hayward, pp. 229-38. New York: Farrar, Straus and Giroux, 1969.

Encomium in honor of Babel's seventieth birthday. Ehrenburg's persistent efforts to recognize and publish Babel's works in Russia resulted in an anniversary celebration seven years after the writer's rehabilitation.

Falen, James E. "A Note on the Fate of Isaak Babel." *Slavic and East European Review* XI, No. 4 (1967): 398-404.

Discusses Babel's little known screenplay *Staraja ploščad', 4.* According to Falen, the screenplay was written in 1939 and was probably Babel's last work before his arrest. He maintains that on close analysis the screenplay assumes "the proportion of a far-reaching political allegory," and finally, after Babel's many years of artistic silence, expresses his moral indignation at the Stalin regime.

Field, Andrew. "Babel As Playwright: An Introductory Note." *Tri-Quarterly,* No. 5 (Winter 1966): 8-9.

Discusses Babel's dramas *Sunset* and *Maria.*

Freiden, Gregory. "Fat Tuesday in Odessa: Isaac Babel's 'Di Grasso' as Testament and Manifesto." *The Russian Review* 40, No. 2 (April 1981): 101-21.

Thorough analysis of Babel's 1937 story "Di Grasso." According to Friedkin, this work, written two years before Babel's arrest and disappearance, was his parting shot at the Stalin regime for its suppression of artistic works that did not wholly serve its proletarian cause.

Helstein, Nadia. "Translator's Note." In *Red Cavalry,* by I. Babel, translated by Nadia Helstein, pp. v-viii. New York: Alfred A. Knopf, 1929.

Declares that *Red Cavalry* is not concerned with the heroic deeds of an army at war, but rather with individual reactions to the mundane aspects of war.

Howe, Irving. "The Genius of Isaac Babel." *The New York Review of Books* III, No. 1 (20 August 1964): 14-15.

Laudatory critique of *Isaac Babel: The Lonely Years, 1925-39.*

Iribane, Louis. "Babel's *Red Cavalry* As a Baroque Novel." *Contemporary Literature* 14, No. 1 (Winter 1973): 58-77.

Posits that Babel originally conceived *Red Cavalry* as a novel, and that the story "Pan Apolek" serves as a unifying link between the other stories in the work. Iribane discusses the stylistic devices Babel used throughout the work and how *Red Cavalry* can be considered a novel in the baroque manner.

Lessing, Doris. "Homage for Isaac Babel." *New Statesman* LXII, No. 1605 (15 December 1961): 920, 922.

Sentimental tribute to Babel.

Lowe, David A. "A Generic Approach to Babel's *Red Cavalry.*" *Modern Fiction Studies* 28, No. 1 (Spring 1982): 69-78.

General criticism discussing *Red Cavalry* as a "cycle of stories."

Paustovsky, Konstantin. "Reminiscences of Babel." *Partisan Review* XXVIII, Nos. 3-4 (1961): 391-406.

Recollections of Babel by a contemporary. For a time Paustovsky was the managing editor of the Odessa journal *Moryak,* which published many of Babel's earliest works, including some of the Benya Krik stories.

Stroud, Nicholas. Introduction to *The Forgotten Prose,* by Isaac Babel, edited and translated by Nicholas Stroud, pp. 11-14. Ann Arbor, Mich.: Ardis, 1978.

Brief introduction to *The Forgotten Prose,* a collection of early stories which, for the most part, have been suppressed in Soviet literature.

Trilling, Lionel. Introduction to *The Collected Stories,* by Isaac Babel, edited and translated by Walter Morison, pp. 9-37. New York: Criterion Books, 1955.

Perceptive and helpful analysis concerning Babel's cultural, moral, and personal involvement with the Cossack ethos as a Jewish soldier of the regiment and as a writer.

Williams, Gareth. "Two Leitmotifs in Babel's *Konarmija.*" *Die Welt der Slaven* XVII, No. 2 (1972): 308-17.

Focuses on Babel's use of the sun and the moon as motifs in *Red Cavalry.*

Yarmolinsky, Avrahm. "Isaac Babel (1894-1941)—An Odessa Maupassant?" In his *The Russian Literary Imagination,* pp. 131-86. New York: Funk & Wagnalls, 1969.

Biographical and critical study.

(Eugen) Bertolt (Friedrich) Brecht

1898-1956

(Also wrote under pseudonym of Berthold Eugen) German dramatist, poet, critic, novelist, and short story writer.

The following entry presents criticism of Brecht's drama *Leben des Galilei (Galileo).* For a complete discussion of Brecht's career, see *TCLC,* Volumes 1 and 6.

The Granger Collection, New York

Galileo is generally considered among the masterworks of Brecht's mature drama. Like such works as Shakespeare's *Henry IV* and *Richard III, Galileo* is a chronicle play which dramatizes events revolving around a historical figure. In this drama, Brecht recounts the life of the seventeenth-century scientist Galileo, who, under the threat of physical torture, recanted his confirmation of the Copernican theory, which states that the earth revolves around the sun. Through the crisis of his hero, Brecht examines the extent of an individual's moral responsibility to society in the dissemination of truth—an ethical concern, according to Brecht, pertinent both to the seventeenth century as it teetered on the brink of a new scientific age and to the atomic age of the twentieth century.

In 1933 Brecht's Marxist politics forced him to leave fascist Germany for a self-imposed exile in Scandinavia and the United States. It was during this time that he wrote the first and second versions of *Galileo.* The first version of the drama was written in Denmark in 1938. In his personal notes regarding this early version, Brecht wrote that it was his intention to represent the new scientific age that was served by the discoveries of the Italian scientist. Never published, and produced only once in 1943, this version of *Galileo* is discussed by critics only in comparison with Brecht's subsequent rendering of the drama. The second version was written in 1945 and 1946 in collaboration with the actor Charles Laughton, while Brecht was living in the United States. Laughton translated Brecht's drama from the original German, and in the process altered, with the author's approval, the portrayal of the scientist. In the first version, Galileo is depicted as a humanitarian scientist willing to use his cunning to benefit society. Thus, his recantation in the 1938 play is viewed as a heroic ploy to avoid persecution, so that he may then surreptitiously complete the writing of his *Discorsi.* In the English version, however, the scientist is explicitly portrayed as a sensuous individual with a voracious appetite for intellectual and physical gratification. Therefore, when Galileo disavows his scientific discoveries in this rendition, the act is regarded as one of cowardice—he obliged the authorities only to assure his physical well-being. Although he clandestinely completes the manuscript of his *Discorsi,* he does so not to serve humankind but to indulge an insatiable intellectual need. Laughton and Brecht were working on this "American version" of *Galileo* when Hiroshima was destroyed by an atomic bomb, and according to Brecht "overnight the biography of the founder of the new system of physics read differently." In his assessment of the scientist, Brecht wrote: "Galileo's crime can be regarded as the 'original sin' of modern natural sciences. . . . The atom bomb is, both as a technical and as a social phenomenon, the classical end product of his contribution to science and his failure to society." Some critics believe that the relationship of Galileo's recantation to the devastation caused by the atomic bomb is an oversimplification; but others indicate that after Hiroshima, Brecht intended the drama to caution scientists about their potential power for destruction, and to remind them of their responsibility for future human welfare. In 1947 the English version of *Galileo* premiered in California with Laughton in the lead role. Though it was not successful, Laughton brought the drama to New York for six performances, where it received mixed reviews. This, however, was not to be the last version of *Galileo.* At the time of his death Brecht was occupied with still another German variation of the drama, which is regarded, as Claude Hill indicates, as the "quasi-'official' German text on which most performances throughout the world are now based." This final rendition reincorporates into the play much of what Laughton had edited. Although Galileo is still portrayed as a shrewd, often unscrupulous scientist, it is evident that he seeks to share his knowledge with society.

Criticism of *Galileo* is both varied and profuse. While some early critics maintain that Brecht manipulated historical facts to impart his Marxist ideologies, more recent commentators agree that Brecht intended to parallel the scientific era of Galileo with the present in order to dissuade the modern scientist from social alienation. Much critical discussion of *Galileo* is invariably centered around the drama's title character.

Brecht's depiction of the Italian scientist is considered one of the most complex, three-dimensional characterizations in all of his work and, as some critics suggest, in all of modern theater. Eric Bentley states: "What makes this Galileo a fascinating figure is that his goodness and badness, strength and weakness, have the same source: a big appetite and a Wildean disposition to give way to it. His appetite for knowledge is of a piece with his appetite for food, and so the same quality can appear, in different circumstances, as magnificent or as mean." Thus, in Galileo, Brecht created an ambiguous figure beset by unresolved conflicts who enlists the spectator's emotions, in direct conflict with Brecht's theory of epic theater. Much of the critical commentary is prompted by the elusive quality of Galileo's character, as critics attempt to explain his motivations and the moral and social consequences of his actions. In a concluding remark to his assessment of *Galileo,* Claude Hill notes that the "growing demands for a new morality of the scientist in our time will lead to a still greater appreciation of Brecht's magnificent *Leben des Galilei.*"

(See also *Contemporary Authors,* Vol. 104.)

KAPPO PHELAN (essay date 1947)

[The following excerpt is a review of the American production of Galileo, *which was translated from the German by Charles Laughton, revised by Laughton with Brecht, and staged by the Experimental Group Theater in New York. For other reviews of this production, see the excerpts by Irwin Shaw (1947) and George Jean Nathan (1948).]*

[There] is, I judge, so much evidence of whole growth on the part of [Bertolt Brecht] that suddenly his method has become wholly useful. I will explain this as plainly as I can, and yet it seems to me that any thoughtful explanation will depend so clearly on paradox, it may appear sophistical. But how else explain a revolutionary who has gradually acquired an appreciation of heresy? a didacticist suddenly without a program? It had better be explained at once that Brecht can no longer be spoken of as an experimentalist: his scheme is too sure. Enmeshed in Marxism in the terrible German agony after the first World War, his ideology was received, and he set himself to woo a public by every conceivable convention, invention and device. A great (I believe) if untranslatable lyricist, he has employed the simplest rhymes, borrowed the most traditional music, worked every spatial and aural dimension to lure his audience to reflection. Accompanying all this working there is a kind of strangled theory dealt out in notes and in his interpreters' desperate findings which does quite clearly exile him from our Broadway brink-stage. I think the theory is post-important; it is the practice which has told. And yet, dismayedly, I am unsure that the practice tells in the present piece [*Galileo*]. To illustrate: Brecht here posits his Galileo not only as a theological heretic, but even further as an aware scientific one. Consistently introduced to enchanting music and children's voices, this primary thinker ends only as a man, overtly interested in his supper and concerned only that his stifled disciples should be as honest. All the Shavian-Fabian mode of planned heresy is rejected in the crux scene between master and student; revolution is rejected; a scrupulous picture of the medieval church is maintained; and the man remains. But this sequence is staged necessarily as brown against brown; or, if you will, as back against ground. Earlier we have had all the orthodox colors (I speak theatrically, as I must) deliberately played. Cardinal's red, Pope's white, the people's motley. But I am not sure that the pageantry does not outweigh the sense. I am not sure that earnest people would not come away from this serious examination of tyrannies, thinking of it only as an anti-Church tract. . . . I wish that our present scientism might again engage the attention of this author. It seems to me that only his kind of serious compassion, and serious confusion, can theater the mess. And I think it had better be theatered. (pp. 255-56)

Kappo Phelan, in a review of "Galileo," in Commonweal *(copyright © 1947, copyright renewed © 1975, Commonweal Publishing Co., Inc.; reprinted by permission of Commonweal Publishing Co., Inc.), Vol. XLVII, No. 10, December 19, 1947, pp. 255-56.*

IRWIN SHAW (essay date 1947)

[Shaw is one of the best-selling contemporary American novelists. In his short review of the American production of Galileo, *excerpted below, he parallels the inquisition of Galileo with that of some journalistic practices and Congressional investigations of un-American activities that were prevalent in the 1940s.]*

Aside from [***Galileo's***] technical innovations, the story of Galileo's martyrdom by Authority is bitterly apposite for today's audiences. The heresy hunters are almost as busy today in Washington as they ever were in Florence, and recantations fill the air in a medieval blizzard of fear. *Time, Life* and Hearst have replaced the rack, and the Representative from New Jersey has donned the Inquisitor's dark satin. The sobbing "I was wrong" of the matinee idol is now to be heard, instead of the "I have sinned" of the old astronomer, but the pattern, as Brecht bleakly points out, is the same. Truth dies with conformity, this year or last. . . .

Brecht's method of saying these things, in accordance with his theories of the "Epic" theater, is abstract, cold and didactic. He assumes the air of the passionless teacher lecturing to students who are not so bright as they should be. He disdains all emotionalism; scornfully, he refuses to amuse us with the usual dramatist's tricks. His characters are symbols, not people; his action the functioning of huge forces, not the clash of human beings. The final effect is interesting, but aggravating. We get the unpleasant feeling that Brecht regards the human race, or at least that part of it which goes to the theater, as animals equipped with only the most rudimentary ability to reason. His Olympian condescension is bound to annoy us, even when we agree with him most heartily. (p. 36)

Irwin Shaw, "The Earth Stands Still," in The New Republic, *Vol. 117, No. 26, December 29, 1947, pp. 36-7.**

GEORGE JEAN NATHAN (essay date 1948)

[Nathan has been called the most learned and influential drama critic the United States has yet produced. During the early decades of the twentieth century, Nathan was greatly responsible for shifting the emphasis of the American theater from light entertainment to serious drama, introducing audiences and producers to the work of Eugene O'Neill, Henrik Ibsen, and Bernard Shaw, among others. Nathan was a contributing editor to H. L. Mencken's magazine The American Mercury *and coeditor of* The Smart Set. *With Mencken, Nathan belonged to an iconoclastic school of*

American critics who attacked the vulgarity of accepted ideas and sought to bring a new level of sophistication to American culture, which they found provincial and backward. Throughout his career, Nathan shared with Mencken a gift for stinging invective and verbal adroitness, as well as total confidence in his own judgments. In the following excerpt, Nathan provides a short critique of the American production of Galileo.]

The Brecht play [***Galileo***] . . . centers on Galileo's historic conflict with the church. Its one relative merit is that it does not, as might have been expected, take pride in drawing a parallel to truth's modern conflict with authority. Though in this instance there might have been some dramatic reasonableness, the play wisely prefers to rest in mere implication. This, surely, is a welcome change from the current tendency of our playwrights to draw parallels between the past and present which often goes to such strained lengths that, if it continues, we may anticipate plays which will demonstrate the similarity of Noah's troubles with the Ark to John Ringling North's with his circus, to say nothing, probably, of others attesting to the considerable identity of the suppression of some of Voltaire's writings and the censorship of Twentieth Century-Fox's movie, *Forever Amber*. (p. 180)

George Jean Nathan, "The Year's Productions: 'Galileo'," in his The Theatre Book of the Year, 1947-48: A Record and an Interpretation *(copyright 1948 by George Jean Nathan, and renewed 1976 by the Literary Estate of George Jean Nathan; all rights reserved; reprinted by permission of Associated University Presses, Inc., for the Estate of George Jean Nathan), Alfred A. Knopf, 1948 (and reprinted by Fairleigh Dickinson University Press, 1975, pp. 177-80).*

GÜNTER ROHRMOSER (essay date 1958)

[*In the following excerpt, Rohrmoser presents a balanced and perceptive reading of* Galileo. *In his examination of the three versions of the play, Rohrmoser focuses his discussion on whether or not the drama depicts the characteristics of a new age of reason, and how it assesses the role of individual integrity in the course of human history.*]

There are three versions of ***Galileo.*** (p. 117)

The 1938 version shows Galileo as an old man who outsmarts the Inquisition and, simulating blindness, completes his work and has the results smuggled out of the country by one of his pupils. Thus the cunning of reason triumphs also in the ethic of the scientist's political action, it is as far ahead of its century as his knowledge is, and causes a light to dawn in the darkness of his age. "I insist that this is a new age. If it looks like a blood-stained old hag, then that's what a new age looks like. The burst of light takes place in the deepest darkness." In the version of 1947 the last sentence, among others, has been deleted, just as in general the judgment upon Galileo has become harsher. Now he practices science like a vice, secretly and without any obligation to humanity. Galileo retracts his doctrines out of cowardice, and his contributions to the progress of science do not outweigh his failure to human society. Because of Galileo's failure in succumbing to sensual temptation, the new age, which emerges as a real possibility on the horizon of history, is no different from the dark ages of the past. Modern science, in itself an instrument of progress, transforms itself into a force for oppression in the hands of the rulers to whom Galileo has delivered himself.

There is no possible doubt that Brecht altered his view of Galileo and the historical importance of his scientific discoveries under the influence of the atomic bomb, which was developed and first dropped on Hiroshima during the creation of ***Galileo.*** Brecht could not ignore the fact that the atomic bomb with its fateful possibilities was a product of the science founded by Galileo at the beginning of the scientific age. In 1938-39 German physicists succeeded in splitting the uranium atom; in 1945 the atomic age began to exhibit its destructive possibilities; and in 1945 Galileo answers the question, "Do you no longer believe that a new age has begun?" this way: "Quite. Be careful when you pass through Germany with the truth in your pocket." (pp. 117-18)

It is true even in the earliest version that the perspective in which Bertolt Brecht views an event of the past is oriented to the present and its oppressive problems. But Brecht is by no means concerned with opposing to the night of barbarism threatening his own present a picture of an age in which, like the morning after a long night, an epoch of renewal and hope for mankind begins. For Brecht [writes] in his notes: "The symbols of morning and night are misleading. The fortunate ages do not come like the morning after a good night's sleep." Here Brecht is not only attacking the oversimplification of an image of history which separates epochs from one another like day and night, light and darkness, good and evil: rather he is questioning the total relevance to history of an analogy based upon a process of nature. What fascinates Brecht primarily in the historical problem of the beginning of a new age is the abstract aspect of a situation still concealing within itself all possibilities, and the courageous feeling of a man who has complete trust in the situation because he has not yet tested its strength against reality. (p. 118)

Galileo's life embraces a twofold responsibility: first to the work to be achieved, and then to the society to which this work is committed and which it seeks to serve. Can the two requirements be reconciled or do they stand in an irreconcilable contradiction to each other? If it is characteristic of a new age that society as a whole begins to move and the unquestioned oneness of the individual with its institutions begins to dissolve, then such a society offers Brecht an excellent model on which to demonstrate his basic propositions.

The shortest answer to the question of whether a new age has begun, which Brecht formulated in the [third version] Berlin text of 1955, is the one that causes the most torment and tension. It is all the more difficult to understand, as Galileo expounded shortly before the passing of judgment in his case:

> As a scientist I had an almost unique opportunity. In my day astronomy emerged in the market place. At that particular time, had one man put up a fight, it would have had wide repercussions. If only I had resisted! If only the scientists could have developed something like the Hippocratic oath of the physicians, a vow to use their knowledge for the welfare of humanity alone. As it now stands, the best one can hope for is a race of inventive dwarfs who can be hired for anything.

But how does this obviously changing interpretation in the several versions relate to the artistic and dramatic structure of the work? If it were possible to interpret the play as a revue-like, "epic" chronicle striving for colorful details, our final judgment on Galileo's life would indeed be a matter of indifference. For then the structure of the play would pursue the theatrical goal of reproducing his biography as such. The same would be true if the play were concerned with the interpretive dramatization of a complex character. Both possibilities are rejected. In turning to history Brecht is concerned in substance with the basic historical and human problem of his own age, which he is certainly correct in calling a scientific one. Galileo does not interest him as a character, but as a case, although the individual vital substance of the hero is not sacrificed to an abstract scheme to the same extent as in the plays of a Marxist cast, the didactic plays. Galileo is "shown" in the concrete detail of his daily, even intimate life, because it is just exactly here that the characteristics clearly appear which explain his behavior in the great trans-personal, historically important decisions of his life. The importance the individual physiognomy of Galileo, who cannot be reduced to a social type, acquires for the answer to the question about the beginning of a new age (from a Marxist standpoint quite questionable in its estimate of the role of the great individual for the course of history) forbids us to interpret ***Galileo*** as a drama of modern science. From this standpoint Galileo would even be morally coresponsible for the terrors of the modern atomic age.

The arrangement and execution of the play permit us to interpret Galileo's behavior in recanting under pressure from the Inquisition in the sense of a rational cunning, which accommodates itself to the powerful only formally and seemingly, in order to be able to undermine their authority more effectively. For the fact that Galileo does not fear death under all circumstances, indeed is ready to face it if the execution of his experiments requires it, is proved by his attitude during the plague: he passionately continues his experiments despite constant mortal danger. He had proved repeatedly that he only judged the forces and powers of the world functionally, insofar as they were advantageous or detrimental to his researches. Decisive however is the way in which Brecht has Galileo's inner make-up determined by a hedonistic view of life and an obsessive joy in experimentation and discovery.

The new method is made possible by Galileo's driving interest in "alienating" the world, his childish joy in removing things from their familiar, traditional explanations in an act of amazed wonder and seeing them, as though for the first time, untouched and fresh from the moment of creation. The demand Brecht made of the theater in his ***Little Organon***—namely, that the communication of the moral must give pleasure and that theater entertainment must instruct us about the methods in which the children of a scientific age acquire their sustenance—has, according to Brecht, entered history in the person of Galileo as a new possibility for the human being was realized by him. Teaching a new science in a new way, he practices a new human attitude in a world which he sees in a new way, a world which turns out to be both needful and capable of change. (pp. 119-21)

The responsibility for future, unforeseeable possibilities with which Galileo is burdened is not only historically an anachronism, but also disguises, perhaps consciously, the problem of the play. The suspense, the dramatic substance lives on the open dialectic with which the question of the beginning of a new age is put. From Brecht's humane, even radically anthropological position the question of a new age is identical with the possibility of developing a new type of human existence and establishing it in the face of the resistant tradition. Time and man stand in a dialectical union which cannot be dissolved one-sidedly in a moralistic way. If Galileo had resisted the Inquisition and had been prepared to stand up for truth with the sacrifice of his life, then he would have been able to aid progress as well as reaction. The solution to this question is dependent upon another: namely whether—and how far—the new method and attitude to things already represented an element of general social practice. If it does, then Galileo's insistence could have meant *its* final victory. If, on the other hand, the new truth had not yet entered the general consciousness, then one would have to see a meaningful action in Galileo's self-preservation. There can be no abstract yardstick here, unless one were to judge *post eventum,* which would be nothing other than making the outcome of an historical experiment the basis for its moral justification. Only the atomic bomb motivates internally the judgment which Galileo makes over himself. The suspense increasing from scene to scene is not immanent in the course of the play, but is the result of the contrast between the possibilities apparent in the described events and the actual outcome which contradicts the expectations that were called forth. The scene showing the effect of his step among his pupils allows us to recognize the method according to which the whole play is constructed. The audience knows that what Galileo does will be decisive for the fate of truth in the historical world. Truth itself is not in question, but rather the possibility of its establishing itself in the historical process. Galileo—like no one else in previous history—seems to have the chance of bringing about a turning point of epoch-making importance. By letting tense expectation, triumphant exultation, deep depression, and shocked despair among the pupils follow directly upon one another, Brecht succeeds in transforming the drama of the historical decision into a perceptible scenic movement. The "basic gestus" articulates with dialectical and most extreme intensity the meaning of this event which determines the coming centuries. No talk of epic theater ought to obscure our eye for the mastery with which Brecht forms the dialectic of thought. "Unhappy is the land that breeds no hero!" "Unhappy is the land that needs a hero!" Set up this way, the problem no longer permits of a moral solution.

Galileo cannot fulfill the historical heroic role in which his pupils would like to see him, because he is unable to transcend, and hopelessly falls victim to, the law of human frailty. He could have overcome the limitation of action forced upon him by social determinants with the sacrifice of his life. His pupils call him "winebibber" and "glutton" and fail to recognize that without the joy in good food Galileo would never have possessed the weakness of pursuing the vice of his thirst for knowledge so intemperately. That one person can at the same time discover and suppress the truth, this contradiction is grounded in the structure of a newly beginning epoch which must first establish itself against the traditions. Its knowledge does not correspond to its ability. The church, which here represents all authority but is by no means polemically presented, takes this inability into account.

One problem remains remarkably unclear in Brecht's play: the relationship of the truth of Christianity to the church which is supposed to represent truth in the scientific age, or its relationship to the truth of these sciences and especially to their intrinsic claim upon men not directly concerned in the work of science and its discoveries. The question is not one of the truth of revelation, but of the conformity of revelation to the Aristotelian view of the world and the need to secure the authority of the papal throne through this view. The historical Galileo probably used his Biblical faith in creation in his fight against the presumptions of a formal tradition; Brecht makes no use of it, because for him the refutation of Aristotelian astronomy involves a denial of the biblical faith in creation. "The heavens, it appears, are empty. People are laughing with delight because of this." For Brecht, the change in the comprehension of truth itself comes with the new method and its application, represents the newly discovered possibility of changing the sociological, historical world by means of revolutionary intervention. Since Brecht views the process from the end, backwards—from the atomic bomb, from the transformation of liberation into destruction—the reasons with which the representatives of the Church opposed the teachers of the new truth become more valid for him. The formula that the Church defended its order only for the sake of its sovereignty is too simple; instead history has taught that the Church hierarchy could be of the opinion, and not only out of self-interest, that it must protect men from the terrible possibilities to which they would be exposed on the new path. His undogmatic position permits Brecht to show masterfully a picture of the situation in which it is obvious how even the Church, in itself the force for the preservation of the old, acquires an interest in the new and cannot escape the force of the changing course of history.

A runaway monk—who, after Galileo abjures the truth, returns to the bosom of the Church—belongs to Galileo's most intimate pupils, and a cardinal favorable to the new sciences ascends the papal throne. Brecht, the epic narrator of the plot, who judges by hindsight, lets us know that at no time was Galileo's life in serious danger; bold, decisive behavior would have saved him from the torture.

What has Brecht achieved dramaturgically with this device? The event acquires the depth of tragedy in its perspective backward. Galileo's failure is based upon a false assumption; he could have avoided his renunciation of truth. If Galileo had been right, the catastrophe for which humanity was to pay with infinite suffering would not have seemed unavoidable. Brecht does not make an argument for a tragic view of history out of his insight into the objective senselessness of the situation. When he calls the attention of the audience to the fact that the tragic process taking place before its eyes would have taken another course if Galileo had been conscious of the strength of his position, he calls upon the audience to apply this consideration to the historical situation of the present. Whether or not this hope is based upon a false assumption is a matter of indifference for the effect of the play. Through the magic of the theater, the artful interplay of varying interpretations and perspectives changes the laborious profundity of speculation upon the philosophy of history into the cheerful surface of scenic and balladesque events. It is a triumph of Brecht's sovereign mastery of his means, that he does not need to interrupt the immediacy of the stage action with extraneous elements in order to make the didactic meaning transparent. The commentary has been absorbed into the text, and only the dynamic tension between the scenes produces the drama and its meaning. It would overstep the limits of our discussion if we attempted to show in detail how Brecht integrates the interpretation into the events so that the course of events becomes a commentary to what is happening. The pleasurable representation of thinking makes thinking itself a pleasure. The thesis to be demonstrated depends, to be sure, upon the premise that stupidity is the archenemy of mankind. But thinking does not take place in a vacuum that is withdrawn from history and its vicissitudes.

The abandonment of the traditional division into acts, the substitution of a loose succession of scenes which seems to be based only upon chronological order corresponds to the necessity of bringing together all the evidence which enables the audience to pass judgment on the case. The various and surprising points of view serve as an exercise in the dialectical way of looking at things which for its part determines the arrangement and construction of the scenes.

The artistic method which Brecht follows in ***Galileo*** does not develop suspense out of what is represented, but rather out of the relationship in which the mode of representation stands to the factual events. Traditional drama tends to concentrate on elements advancing the action; Brecht, however, assumes the "epic" narrative attitude of a painter of mores concerned with completeness of material. But the completeness is that of a prosecuting attorney who makes his plea for a just verdict. The oversimplified idea which people have of the founder of a new epoch and of the epoch itself is destroyed by new arguments stressing the complexity of the matter, and the members of the audience, called as witnesses, are driven to a reconsideration of the case, even seduced into it by the force of scenic suggestion.

While traditional drama developed its specifically dramatic quality out of the suspense of the process of actively and passively overcoming a given contradiction, Brecht's dramaturgy proves how impossible it is to stop the dialectic of the whole process by a one-sided solution that transcends history. It is not consistent with Marxist doctrine that Brecht permits his Galileo to be an individual, a "hero," and accords to him such a decisive role for the course of history. Rather, the part played by Marxist theory in Galileo's life is limited to the extent to which it calls attention to the truth of contradiction and its dialectical force in moving history. In the rest of Brecht's late plays, written primarily during his exile, he deals as a rule with truth as it is or ought to be, in similes disguised as parables. The playwright communicates morality didactically or narratively in such a form that the comprehended truth can intervene effectively in the world. The theme of ***Galileo*** is the process of discovering truth. (pp. 121-24)

Indeed, one can characterize the real message of the play by saying that history is basically open in its outcome and that its course is exposed to so many surprises that the activity of man is needed if the destiny of mankind is to be achieved.

Galileo's failure illustrates a fundamental failing of the Marxist historical dialectic. The materialistic view of history is in principle incapable of producing an ethic of political action. In it situations are not foreseen in which the spontaneous intervention of the individual is required in order to give to the movement of history a direction toward the human *telos*. Galileo does not betray materialism, but betrays rather his humane and social intention just because he is a consistent materialist. This is the source of the ambiguous light in which he appears in the play. It can be understood both as an accusation and as a defense. The autobiographical substance as well as the unsettled question of the extent of the individual's importance for the outcome of historical processes contribute to this ambiguity. The contradiction to the official doctrine in which Brecht finds himself in this question (it is most closely connected with the moral heritage of his late-bourgeois origins) to be sure contributes to the aesthetic quality, but on the other hand makes it almost impossible to determine the specific character of the work. It is not a tragedy, because the final result of the historical experiment still lies in the future. It cannot be interpreted as history, either, because of its forceful contemporary reference. It cannot be counted among the parable plays, because the figure of Galileo and his fate are inseparably bound to concrete history. We cannot speak at all of a "didactic play" because the "example" has a character of inimitable uniqueness which is not transferable or even applicable. In a peculiar manner the life of Galileo unites all these characteristics so that they are metamorphosed into a new form of drama. The diverging aspects are unified by the double function of the dialectic: as artistic play and as a method of overcoming the world historically.

The inconclusiveness of historical experiments transforms the dialectic into a kind of artistry; and the fate that hangs over all events calls the artist back into history, in order to use the dialectic desperately, but not without hope, in the fight for the final achievement of a free society planned for human beings and their needs. The epic elements of Brecht's theater serve to regain the original drama of a man who refuses to accept passively an uncomprehended fate. He tries to withstand it by thinking and acting. Like a second Oedipus the human being himself discovers the solution to the riddle with which the sphinx of history challenges him.

Brecht's drama communicates something of the cheerful and courageous attitude of the Enlightenment which, aware of the regressive character of one-sided progress, holds undeviatingly to progress itself and its necessity. Brecht's theater is no longer a moralistic place, but a school and courtroom in which things are accounted for: what has been gained and lost is remembered and, above all, new steps forward are practiced. Progress consists not in progress, but in progressing. This is why the Galileo of the third version is right in answering affirmatively the question about the beginning of a new age. His sensuality was not the cause of his failure—it was only a part of it—but rather a lack of knowledge concerning the importance of the demand made by the unique moment. He risked his life during the plague and endangered what he had gained by submitting to the Inquisition when history was waiting only for a sign from him.

Brecht's drama is a question which becomes a demand. Who will make up for what has been let slip? Or is it already too late? The question might be asked of Brecht whether the truth to which he refers possesses enough authority to justify the sacrifice of a human being for it. This question seems to be the inevitable result of the play and of pursuing its problems. (pp. 125-26)

Günter Rohrmoser, in an essay (reprinted by permission of Paedagogischer Verlag Schwan-Bagel GmbH and the author), in his Das deutshe Drama vom Barock bis zur Gegenwart, *edited by Benno von Wiese, August Bagel Verlag, 1958 (translated by J. F. Sammons and reprinted as "Brecht's 'Galileo'," in* Brecht: A Collection of Critical Essays, *edited by Peter Demetz, Prentice-Hall, 1962, pp. 117-26).*

ERIC BENTLEY (essay date 1961)

[*Bentley is considered one of the most erudite and innovative critics of the modern theater. He was responsible for introducing Bertolt Brecht, Luigi Pirandello, and other European playwrights to America through his studies, translations, and stage adaptations of their plays. In his critical works, Bentley concentrates on the playwright and the dramatic text, rather than on the production aspects of the play. Thus, in his first important critical study,* The Playwright As Thinker *(1946), Bentley distinguishes between "art" and "commodity" in the American theater, basing his definition of commodity on the premise that most producers are more attentive to box office receipts than to the artistic quality of a play and, as a result, the dramatist is often neglected as a true artist. Some critics consider this approach an attempt to compensate for his unwillingness to accept drama as a form of popular entertainment. Bentley's finest work,* The Life of Drama *(1964), is a comprehensive study of the development of dramatic form, specifically examining aspects of melodrama, farce, comedy, tragedy, and tragicomedy. His most recent critical works include anthologies of reviews written during his years as drama critic (1952-56) for* The New Republic, *and a collection of his essays on Brecht—*The Brecht Commentaries: 1943-80 *(1981). Bentley's association with Brecht was both personal and professional. A translator and adaptor of, and commentator on, Brecht's works, he also worked as the dramatist's assistant for the New York production of* Private Life of the Master Race *(1945) and the Munich production of* Mother Courage *(1950). In addition, Bentley is the author of* The Recantation of Galileo Galilei: Scenes from History Perhaps *(1973), which was described by John Fuegi "as a counterpart to Brecht's* Life of Galileo.*" In this excerpt, Bentley discusses the conception of* Galileo, *the drama's title character, and "*Galileo *as a portrait of the artist." For additional comments on Brecht by Bentley, see* TCLC, *Vols. 1 and 6.*]

The historical understanding played no part in the writing of ***Galileo,*** nor did Brecht pay his respects to historical accuracy except in the broad outline and in certain details. Not a great deal is known, but one can be sure that the historical Galileo was nothing like this; nor were his problems of this type; nor did his opponents resemble those whom Brecht invents for him.

Galileo is not a Marxist play either. What Marxist historian would accept the unhistorical major premise: namely, that if an Italian scientist had refused to renounce Copernicus in 1633 "an age of reason would have begun," and our age of unreason would have been avoided? What Marxist historian could accept the notion that a Catholic scientist of the seventeenth century, whose best friends were priests, who placed both his daughters in a convent as young girls, was halfway a Marxist, resented convents and churchgoing, doubted the existence of God, and regarded his tenets in physics as socially revolutionary?

But it is one of the open secrets of dramatic criticism that historical plays are unhistorical. They depend for their life on relevance to the playwright's own time—and, if he is lucky, all future times—not on their historicity.

It might, of course, be asked, why a playwright would choose historical material at all, and pretend to be limited by it. There are reasons. For one, he relies on the public's ignorance of the secrets, closed or open, of dramatic criticism. Audiences assume that most of what they see in a history play did happen, and it may be that most of the "history" in the popular mind comes from such sources. By popular, I don't mean proletarian. I met a Hollywood director at the premiere of ***Galileo*** and asked him what he thought of it. "As a play? I don't know," he answered, "but it is always thrilling to hear the truth, to see what actually happened!" Well, the joke was not on Brecht, and this incident helps to explain why historical plays are still written. (pp. 83-4)

[***Galileo***] is a play—not fact but fiction—and one of the criteria by which playwrights are judged is their ability to create characters who can, as it were, "take up their bed and walk"—who can assume the frightening autonomy of the six who once stood in the path of Pirandello. This play lives, to a large extent, by the character of the protagonist, a character which Brecht cut out of whole cloth—that is to say, created out of his own resources. What makes this Galileo a fascinating figure is that his goodness and badness, strength and weakness, have the same source: a big appetite and a Wildean disposition to give way to it. His appetite for knowledge is of a piece with his appetite for food, and so the same quality can appear, in different circumstances, as magnificent or as mean. I don't see how the theory of Epic Theater could do justice to the ambiguity here. It calls for a theory of tragedy. The problem is not social and conditioned but personal and inherent.

Whatever the theorist makes of it, that particular ambiguity is very satisfyingly presented—is perhaps the play's chief exhibit. There is another ambiguity, equally fascinating, if not equally well defined. In this work, the self-denunciatory impulse in Brecht—not to speak again of masochism—has a field day. His Galileo denounces himself twice, and the two denunciations are designed to be the twin pillars upon which the whole edifice rests. The first of them, the historic abjuration of Copernicanism, was, we may be sure, what suggested the play in the beginning. The second was Brecht's invention.

One can hardly hear either for the crackle of dialectics. The first is immediately condemned by Andrea ("Unhappy is the land that breeds no hero"), and defended in a very Brechtian proverb by Galileo ("Unhappy is the land that *needs* a hero"). Then Galileo changes his mind, and in the last scene (as performed), the argument is reversed. Andrea takes the line that the abjuration had been justified because "Science has only one commandment: contribution," Galileo having by now contributed the *Discorsi*. Thereupon Galileo whips himself up into a self-lacerating fury: "Any man who does what I have done must not be tolerated in the ranks of science!" He who had made the great False Confessions, which according to Brecht destroyed him in the eyes of the good and just, now makes the great True Confession, *which is his destruction in his own eyes—and before the eyes of the only person in the story with whom he has an emotional relationship*.

It is theater on the grandest scale, and I call the conception fascinating because it is an attempt to bring together the most widely divided sections of Brecht's own divided nature: on the one hand, the hedonist and "coward," on the other the "hero"—and masochist. It is hardly necessary to say that "no masochism was intended." Any element of masochism destroys, of course, the Marxist intention of this finale. But, once again, *Brecht is not Marxism*. Brecht is Brecht—and Galileo is *his*, not Marx's, prophet.

Here the conscious and the unconscious motives are so directly in conflict that complete clarity cannot result. What we get is an impression of improbability. We recognize that the final self-denunciation is all very moral, but we are not convinced that the old reprobate would actually make it. Such a person naturally believes, "Unhappy is the land that needs a hero." What changed his mind? There would be a drama in such a change, and one wouldn't like to miss it. When Brecht simply *announces* the change, Galileo seems only his master's voice—a very different thing from being, as he was till then, his master's embodiment.

The matter is even less clear than I make it out. It is almost possible to believe that Galileo is only scolding himself (for which we give him credit) and in general is the same man as before. In giving his ms. to Andrea he pretends he is, as usual, giving way to weakness, succumbing to temptation. The incident, particularly in the 1938-9 version, is very endearing. In this respect the man is true to character to the end, and one has to admit his character has its points. *It is possible, in the main, to stay pro-Galileo to the end*. A familiar Brechtian feature! Moral disapproval goes one way, but human sympathy goes the same way! On stage the apparatus of alienation is called into action *as a fire brigade*. (pp. 84-5)

The term "portrait of the artist"—for novelists and dramatists at least—is a relative one. A character may be three-quarters self-portrait and one-quarter a portrait of someone else or sheer invention. The proportion of self-portrayal may indeed be anything from zero to a hundred percent. There is sense in speaking of a portrait of the artist only when the relation to the artist is very marked and of special significance. In the present case, it is. (pp. 85-6)

[There] is a lot of Brecht in Baal, Kragler, and Garga. Then Brecht did not sit to himself for a long time. Which presumably means that he split himself up into *all* his characters. He often put the idealistic part of himself inside one of the young ladies with the shining eyes. He was likely to let the nonidealistic part of himself into the rogue of any play. . . .

Why Galileo Galilei? Auden says the poet cannot portray the poet, and points to Shaw's Marchbanks as an awful example. But the poet can portray the poet by pretending he is something else such as an architect (Solness) or a philosopher (Jack Tanner)—or a scientist (Galileo). Marxism considers itself scientific, which is one reason why it appealed to Brecht. Then there is the matter of History again. Whether or not the playwright is scrupulous about the historical record, a historical play carries the Idea of Fact. . . .

Getting rid of one's personality, Brecht had written at the time he gave himself to social causes, was an amusing business. If only the subjective did not exist! If only one *were* history! And science! And by the time one *is* history and science—in this play, ***Galileo***—it is interesting that one still has the same human constitution as before: one is a genius, one would like to be committed to a cause, but one is a rogue. (p. 86)

Eric Bentley, in an introduction to Seven Plays *by Bertolt Brecht, edited by Eric Bentley (reprinted by permission of Grove Press, Inc.; copyright © 1961 by Eric Bentley), Grove Press, 1961 (and reprinted as "Seven Plays ('In the Swamp', 'A Man's a Man', 'Mother Courage', 'The Caucasian Chalk Circle'), in his* The Brecht Commentaries: 1943-1980, *Grove Press, 1981, pp. 72-107).*

WALTER WEIDELI (essay date 1961)

[*In the following excerpt, Weideli comments on the complexities and contradictions within the character of Galileo, most importantly Galileo's relativistic sense of ethics. Weideli also suggests that* Galileo *contains many "autobiographical allusions," reflecting Brecht's own political and social thought.*]

In conformity to the rules of [Brecht's] epic theater, of which ***Galileo*** is the most finished example, the life of the great scientist is split into autonomous scenes. There is no center of gravity, neither is there any dramatic progression. Ascending or descending, Galileo is never the same. He is a contradictory person who, up to the last minute, is hesitating and questioning himself. "The universe," cries out the young Galileo, "has lost its center. One night is enough for it to discover an infinity of them. Each of us has become the center, each of us and yet no one." We have already encountered this assertion in ***A Man's a Man,*** but there it is colored by pessimism. Here, it expresses the joyful, careless adherence to a new ethic founded on the doubt that Galileo opposes to the congealed hierarchy of feudal values. For him everything is changing, the world and he who observes it. He is discovering space as we, today, are discovering time. To the young Sarti who objects: "But I don't perceive the earth turning," he answers: "Because you are turning with it." For one must put a distance between himself and things in order to understand them; he must exclude himself from them and cut the umbilical cord. It is an adult, scientific approach which is simultaneously accompanied by distress and pleasure.

To combat the system, Galileo needs leisure or, in other words, money. Therein lies his first contradiction. He lays claim to an absolute liberty which the system refuses him. He must then choose between two relative liberties: between Venice, which welcomes scholars but pays them badly, and Florence, which censures their writings but offers them an easy life. Galileo, between these two restrictions, chooses the one which he judges to be the lesser: he decides on the court of Florence. Is he wrong? No, for outside the system he cannot act. He can make use of it, but not escape it. The only liberty which counts in his eyes is the liberty to produce. Poverty paralyzes him. To escape from it, he perpetrates a fraud in passing himself off as the inventor of the telescope. It is true that he makes up for it immediately by discovering an unsuspected use for this stolen instrument. Thus, at the same time that he is yielding to social pressure, Galileo is liberating himself from it. We shall say then, as does Brecht, that his relation to the world is just. (pp. 109-10)

Galileo really has a *passion* for the truth, and he knows that this passion is satanic. He would deprive himself of light to know what the light is. He prefers the knowledge of things to the things themselves. "Like a lover, like a drunkard, like a traitor," he is excluded from paradise. And he who knows cannot help but disseminate his knowledge. His passion is contagious; "it is really a vice which leads to unhappiness." Thence, there is a defiance and an appeal: "How much longer shall I be able to cry out in this furnace? That is the question!"

Here we touch the heart of Brechtian tragedy. Man knows that his curiosity is accursed. And yet this demoniacal instinct for truth is so essential to him that he must obey it, even if he may die because of it. It is apparent that we are quite far from the optimism of a "progressivist" lyricism. Intelligence for Brecht is only a tiny light, storm-tossed on an ocean of shadows. It must not go out. But the effort is disproportionate to the few results. Occasionally, Brecht becomes impatient; he would like to break away from so many uncertainties, but wisdom leads him back to the common measure: "the goal is not to open the doors to an infinite truth, but to impose a limit on infinite measure."

Galileo, like Brecht, has grown older; the insolent arrogance of his youth has disappeared. He sees himself deprived little by little of the worldly harmony which had once duped him, but his humble working companions—his smelter, his glass-maker, his housekeeper—encourage him to live. Their good sense inspires him continually. It is for them that he works, writing no longer in Latin, but in the language of the people. (pp. 112-13)

Galileo's ethics are complex and vary according to his age. At fifty years, they are intransigent: "I tell you: whoever ignores the truth is an imbecile. But he who knows it and conceals it is an assassin." Ten years later they are softened and full of nuances. Galileo is, basically, a man of the flesh. "He thinks," says one of his disciples, "as he enjoys. He could no more refuse a new idea than a glass of good wine." If he takes deadly risks, it is because science is a stronger instinct in him than the instinct for self-preservation. When the attrition of old age unexpectedly arrives, intelligence is degraded and nothing remains but the elementary instincts.

Is Galileo still himself at the moment when he renounces himself? Yes and no. Yes, in his constant concern for taking instruction from even his failings. He pretends in no way to justify these failings. One day he will admit that if he were to recant, it would in no way be through ruse, but through fear of suffering. Never was Galileo more human than in this moment of admission. Through it, he shows himself to be many centuries ahead of his contemporaries. Even in his weakness, he is founding a new, realistic moral code. There is no absolute morality, only the morality of the lesser evil. "As regards obstacles," says Galileo, "the shortest distance between two points can be a curve."

This relativistic morality is scarcely understood by Galileo's disciples. In their eyes the test to which the Inquisition subjected Galileo poses a heroic dilemma. Will violence carry the day over intellect? They would have this intellect all-powerful; they are of the persuasion that Galileo will resist. (pp. 113-14)

Galileo rejects this individualistic morality in a single sentence: "Unhappy is the country that needs a hero!" It is precisely because one alone is not enough. We give too much importance to the hero; we expect too much from him. The disciples have sacrificed everything to science and now the master is renouncing it "being concerned only with saving his guts." We share their feeling of revolt, but we also admire the courage and serenity of Galileo. At this time he is gauging the limits of his liberty. It is no longer the time when the salvation of all depends on the sacrifice of one. All men depend on all other men to varying degrees. Alone, Galileo can do nothing. Yes, he is afraid of death; yes, violence finally triumphs over the intellect. But what is true for the individual is not for the species. For it converts the fear and weakness of many into courage and force.

A prisoner of the Inquisition, spied upon by his daughter, constantly watched, Galileo, a greedy, blind old man has only one ultimate concern: to transfer one last manuscript to his disciple Andrea so that he can get it into Holland. The story does not end with the death of the hero. He can very well accuse himself of having "betrayed science," but he could not set himself up as judge of his own existence. He has recognized his limits, but in recognizing them, he has surpassed himself. It is history that judges him.

Thus, the anguish of youth is converted into a serene confidence. The exiled Brecht (and who is to say that his last years too were not an exile?) continues, against all reason, instructing his son, watering trees, and writing poems. Is it the hope of despair? (pp. 114-15)

In a time hostile to the intellect, Brecht pursued "at any cost" the politics of the intellect. You can see irony in his situation. Performed in the West, ignored in the East, and badly understood everywhere, he left us a work which already begins to live with its own life. (p. 115)

Walter Weideli, in his The Art of Bertolt Brecht, *translated by Daniel Russell (reprinted by permission of New York University Press; copyright © 1963 by New York University; originally published as* Bertolt

Brecht, *Editions Universitaires, 1961), New York University Press, 1963, 145 p.*

OTTO M. SORENSEN (lecture date 1966)

[*In the following excerpt, Sorensen discusses* Galileo *as a failed drama and concludes that in the revision of the play for the American stage Brecht only half-heartedly introduced political and social issues, eventually coming up "with a hodgepodge of ideas which left his message and central character most unconvincing."*]

Leben des Galilei is perhaps the most unsatisfactory of Brecht's "maturer" works, and we can see a multitude of reasons for its failure, on both the intellectual and artistic levels of evaluation. It is a unique instance of Brecht's having left the otherwise ever-present plebeian world and entered that of thought, resulting, in the first version of the play, in an ambiguous but nevertheless comprehensible conclusion. There he remained on the level of the enlightening task of science, of progress in human thought, and dialectical behavior in the face of opposition, despite Galileo's regrets, was sustained by his pupil at play's end. It is true that the religious motive in man, by being reduced to that of superstition, is treated in an incredibly shallow fashion, but little else could be expected from our author. The possibility of a new and different religiosity in man, hinted at in Galileo's belief that God "is in us or nowhere," is but a bon mot, and the idea that acceptance of the Copernican system necessarily entails the abandonment of faith or—and this is what Brecht is really aiming at—the assumption of the atheistic posture, is whimsical.

With his political sharpening of the issues, however, the author eventually came up with a hodgepodge of ideas which left his message and central character most unconvincing. The class struggle, as it is introduced, is presented in such a half-hearted and rhetorical fashion that the viewer finds it impossible to believe the action is laid in a revolutionary setting. If anything, we are convinced of the mood of superstition, backwardness, and resignation among the "masses." The only really viable forces present are those of the reactionary upper class and the rising bourgeoisie, both of which can make use of the products of his ideas, and even some of his ideas, but not that of his belated, affixed, and artificial social utopianism. Galileo, consequently, by an act of the author's will, is to lead a revolution in a social and political vacuum, an idea preposterous to Marxists and non-Marxists alike. Realizing this, the viewer will naturally deem Galileo's self-accusations at the end of the play irrelevant to any issues at stake. His "crime" is not really a crime, since no real moral basis has been established.

Finally, Galileo's anachronistic assumption of a role as father of the atomic bomb remains most unconvincing. Out of aesthetic and political (propagandistic) motivation Brecht has piled one idea on top of another with the result being not an artistic whole—and here we have a classic example of *unwanted* atectonic play-making, but its very opposite: a fragmented conglomeration of ideas, values, and motivations with very little substance. It would be futile to ask what Brecht could have attained, had he selected ideas and motives reasonable and valid in their inception in delineating the character and significance of Galileo. We are dealing with a Bertolt Brecht not really mature in his thought and one reacting to a variety of incompatible stimuli at once. The author was simply not on top of his material. (pp. 421-22)

Otto M. Sorensen, "Brecht's 'Galileo': Its Development from Ideational into Ideological Theater" (originally a paper read before the 64th Annual Meeting of the Philological Association of the Pacific Coast, Berkeley, California, on November 26, 1966), in Modern Drama *(copyright* Modern Drama, *University of Toronto), Vol. XI, No. 4, February, 1969, pp. 410-22.*

KARL S. WEIMAR (essay date 1966)

[*In the following excerpt, Weimar discusses the unresolved conflicts within Galileo's character and demonstrates how these conflicts suggest Brecht's concern with the responsibility of science to society. For a similar discussion of Galileo's character, see the excerpt by Ernst Schumacher (1968).*]

Brecht's Galileo is a fascinating character. He is not only a hero and a criminal; he is a rational humanist, an unscrupulous inventor, a self-centered sensualist, and a dedicated scientist—in other words, a dialectic figure. Indeed, the dialectic principle informs the structure, perspective, and dialogue of the whole work. It is an aesthetic principle, however, for Brecht's delight in presenting the unresolved conflict of antithetical elements overcomes the familiar Marxist exposition of the one inevitable synthesis. Brecht's Galileo is full of the excitement of new discoveries, of new worlds. He is impatient with the restrictions of old systems and eager to explore the undiscovered, to pull away from familiar shores and sail out into the new seas. . . . He is irked with too much teaching lest it restrict his yearning to learn: "I am ignorant. I really don't know anything at all. Therefore I am compelled to fill up the holes in my knowledge. And when am I supposed to do that?" . . . He places all his faith in human reason, in his own and that of all men. He thinks in the simplest, most concrete images, as do most of Brecht's characters. When he is asked to explain what a hypothesis is, he answers:

> It's this: when someone assumes something to be probable, but has no facts. That Felice down there, for instance, in front of the basket-maker's shop, who has her child at her breast, is giving it milk and not receiving milk from it—that remains a hypothesis as long as one can't go down there and see it and prove it.
>
> (pp. 439-40)

Galileo's method is the classical one of empirical observation which he pursues with heroically unheroic ruthlessness (or perhaps it would be more accurate to say, with unheroically heroic ruthlessness) despite pestilence and death . . . , the warning of the Church, his daughter's unhappiness, recantation, and surveillance. The question of whether the ultimate nature of reality is comprehensible to man is raised only once, by a minor figure . . . , and dismissed. In the face of the danger arising from irreconcilable conflict with Church dogma, the alternative of renouncing the search for knowledge is expounded by the "Little Monk" . . . , but he too succumbs to the temptation of research. Galileo's ultimate recognition that the only goal of science is to lighten the hardships of human existence is adumbrated in his application of the telescope to practical purposes, despite his selfish and/or dishonest procedure and despite his disclaimer that he had written a book about the mechanics of the universe and did not concern himself with its social consequences. The scene immediately preceding Galileo's disclaimer makes clear that the "impulse to pursue research is a social phenomenon" and that Brecht's focal concern in the play was with a "socially oriented science." . . . In the critical Scene 14, when Galileo reveals to Andrea Sarti, his estranged disciple, that he has completed his *Dialogues* and wants him to carry the new science across the border, the young man's admiration for his teacher is restored. He hails him as the pioneer of a new ethics as well as of a new science, a hero whose recantation had stained his hands but had not emptied them, for he had gained time to serve science. But after savoring this interpretation, Galileo deflates him with the simple statement that he recanted because he feared the pain of physical torture.

Then, regrettably, the *life* of Galileo ends, and Brecht begins to speak all too clearly through his character, thus reducing the dramatic to the political dialectic. Despite the ingeniously detailed stage directions—"angry, sneering, no laughter . . . a little bit of disdain, not without ennui . . . arrogant"; "dryly, derisively, humorously" . . .—the result is an alienation effect which is quite different from the kind Brecht intentionally sought and which induces one to agree with Martin Esslin that Brecht succeeds artistically in proportion to his failure as a propagandist. Galileo concludes his speech and dismisses his disciple with the curt confession that he has betrayed his profession as a scientist, not because he called what he knew to be the truth a lie, but because he failed to apply his knowledge to the commonweal. This, of course, is hardly pertinent to the historical Galileo, but it does express Brecht's own indictment of the modern atomic physicist. In his notes to the play, Brecht boldly explains the connection between Galileo and the bomb as the beginning and the end of scientific triumph and betrayal of humanity: "The atomic bomb is technologically and socially the final product of his scientific capability and of his failure in and for society." . . . Fortunately, these sentiments, which reflect Marxist revision of history, obtrude only occasionally in the play itself. (pp. 440-41)

Karl S. Weimar, "The Scientist and Society: A Study of Three Modern Plays," in Modern Language Quarterly *(© 1966 University of Washington), Vol. XXVII, No. 4, December, 1966, pp. 431-48.**

HAROLD CLURMAN (essay date 1967)

[Highly regarded as a director, author, and long-time drama critic (1953-80) for The Nation*, Clurman was an important contributor to the development of the modern American theater. In 1931, with Lee Strasberg and Cheryl Crawford, he founded the Innovative Group Theatre, which served as an arena for the works of budding playwrights, including Clifford Odets, William Saroyan, and Elia Kazan, and as an experimental workshop for actors. Together with Strasberg, Clurman also introduced the Stanislavsky method of acting—most commonly referred to as the "Method"—to the American stage. Based on the dramatic principles of Russian actor and director Konstantin Stanislavsky, the Method seeks truthful characterization by conveying the actor's personal emotional experiences in similar situations. Clurman describes the Method as "a way of doing something with the actor . . . to enable him to use himself more consciously as an instrument for the attainment of truth on the stage." In addition, he wrote several works on the theater, including his acclaimed autobiography* All People Are Famous *(1974). Clurman was among several directors and producers eager to produce Brecht's* Galileo*. However, Brecht refused his offer, and according to Terrence Des Pres (see Additional Bibliography), it was probably one of Brecht's "saddest" mistakes. Des Pres writes: [Harold Clurman was] "a director who not only respected Brecht but whose political sense and willingness to work with experimental forms made him the perfect person to launch* Galileo *in New York. Clurman asked for the job and was turned down because Brecht saw him as a member of the Stanislavski camp. Clurman persisted, suggesting that Brecht misunderstood him. He assured Brecht that he would be happy to 'learn' the proper Brechtian principles of drama, but again no. Brecht thus spurned a talented and sympathetic man whose connections would have helped guarantee a warm reception for* Galileo*." In the following excerpt, Clurman offers his critical assessment of the production of* Galileo *by the Repertory Theater of Lincoln Center.]*

Galileo is one of the very few truly fine dramatic works of the past thirty years.

Written between 1938-39, it is a play of classic stature and ever increasing relevance. When it was first produced as part of ANTA's Experimental Season in New York in a revised version (1947), all but one of the daily reviewers treated it with indifference, if not with open disdain. There was some suspicion of Brecht on various counts: the play was "Marxist," it was rather "cold" and, though Brecht himself had supervised the production, it *was* somewhat drab. Hardly anyone referred to the play's nobility, the subtlety of its simplicity, the force of its idea.

Now once again we hear it spoken of as an "intellectual" play. For many theatregoers this spells anathema. One might as readily speak of the Parthenon or of the fugues in Bach's *Well Tempered Clavichord* as "intellectual" (not that Brecht occupies so exalted a level but the comparison makes clear the misunderstanding in the use of the word).

The play's central figure is a scientist. He is, if you like, its "anti-hero." He may be called that because he vilifies himself for having recanted his doctrine in terror and for having too late come to realize that scientific truth is not an absolute value. "I take it," Galileo says, "the interest of science is to ease human existence. If you give way to coercion, science can be crippled, and your new machines may simply suggest new drudgeries. Should you then, in time, discover all there is to be discovered your progress must become a progress away from the bulk of humanity. The gulf might even grow so wide that the sound of your cheering at some new achievement would be echoed by a universal cry of horror."

This is only part of the play's "message." But at the moment what I wish to emphasize is that calling a play "intellectual" for most of us implies that it is without "emotion." In his day, Shaw gave vent to a comic exasperation at the fact that we make dramatic heroes only out of hysterical kids like Romeo and Juliet and neurotic maniacs like Tristan and Isolde, never of men like Newton or Darwin!

This was something more than a joke. For when we speak of "emotion" in the theatre we mean visceral disturbance, passion, pathos or just tear-jerking. But there are many kinds of emotion: the grandeur of a conception may inspire the most elevated feeling, as may also the majesty of the mountain or the sea, a courageous act, the recognition of beautiful craftsmanship, the splendor of an abstract design, or what once was called "significant form."

For all its earthiness and humor—the language of the original German is simpler and more robust than the translation—***Galileo*** has a dignity, a loftiness, a purity which moves the spirit: heart and mind in unity. This quality is evident in speech after speech, in scene after scene.

Take the point at which the Little Monk, in humble compassion for his hard-worked peasant parents, speaks of the need for consolation which the Faith provides, and Galileo's deeply felt, lucid and brillant answer which ends: "I can see their divine patience, but where is their divine fury?" Consider too the scene in which the liberal and knowledgeable Pope, the naked man before he is attired in his ceremonial robes, refuses to acquiesce in the threat of torture against Galileo requested by the Cardinal Inquisitor. When finally he stands in full ecclesiastic raiment he pronounces his papal decision. "It is clearly understood: he is not to be tortured. At the very most he may be shown the instruments," to which the Inquisitor replies: "That will be adequate, Your Holiness. Mr. Galileo understands machinery." The eye instructs the mind as to the meaning.

The play is a dramatic paradigm of an idea and the trials it encounters in piercing the inertia and resistance of habit, tradition and interests of established institutions. In the scene in which Galileo is hailed as a "Bible killer," the play shows the distortion of every idea by ordinary folk who seize on its most vulgar aspect. Brecht regarded skepticism, since it counsels caution and therefore balance, as a key to wisdom. His play therefore warns us that any new idea isolated from the broadest human concerns involves us in a new danger.

No word is wasted in the play; no moment is without its contribution to the total effect. The incidental figures (priests and prelates, students, merchants, aristocrats and beggars) are colorful without caricature. A sense of humankind in its most familiar traits informs every character. Galileo—here Brecht drew on several phases of his own nature—is shown as "foxy," even opportunistic, given to creature comforts, gluttony, the ordinary man's sensuality, and the canny playfulness often found in men of common origin. All this is enacted against the pageantry of the Renaissance, all the more impressive because of the restraint with which Brecht employs it. (p. 603)

Harold Clurman, in a review of "Galileo," in The Nation *(copyright 1967* The Nation *magazine, The Nation Associates, Inc.), Vol. 204, No. 19, May 8, 1967, pp. 603-04.*

FREDERIC EWEN (essay date 1967)

[*Ewen is the author of the biographical and critical study* Bertolt Brecht: His Life, His Art, and His Times. *In the following excerpt from that work, Ewen discusses the theme and dramatic structure of* Galileo.]

In the eyes of many critics, including this one, ***The Life of Galileo*** represents the peak of Brecht's achievement. Brecht himself had many reservations about the play. He felt that like *The Rifles of Señora Carrar* it represented a culpable deflection from the epic style and was "opportunistic," that is, written for a special occasion. He had sacrificed the crucial element of "Verfremdung" ["Alienation"]. The use of factual historical material made such a transformation as, for example, occurred in ***St. Joan of the Stockyards*** impossible. ***Galileo*** does not, Brecht believed, lend itself to such devices as direct addresses to the audience or songs out of the central context. And, what probably disturbed Brecht most, it tended to provoke more empathy than the playwright could possibly desire.

It is, however, scarcely conceivable that a man of Brecht's theatrical and poetical imagination could not have solved these problems in purely epic terms if he had so desired. Actually, it seems that the material shaped itself in Brecht's imagination in the only possible way. That it at times ran counter to the theory was one of those fortunate misfortunes, just as the fact that the theory could be magnificently realized, as in ***St. Joan of the Stockyards,*** was a fortunate fortune. Each of these works has its own artistic integrity and greatness, and each is undeniably Brecht!

In fact, the play of ***Galileo*** does preserve much of the epic character: the scenes are independent, autarchic, though subtly related. Each could stand by itself as an episode. But there is a dramatic structure throughout of an architectonic impressiveness. Thus, the hymn to the new age at the beginning is balanced by the sad confessional at the end. At the midpoint we find two outstanding scenes: the conversation with the "little monk" and the robing of the Pope. The first of these again is counterbalanced by Galileo's dictation to his daughter of a letter repudiating his noble words to the "little monk," in which he had castigated oppression and injustice. It has not often been remarked how brilliantly most of the scenes end with a statement or verbal fillip that works with startling effect on the intelligence.

It is futile to attempt to charge Brecht with a violation of historical accuracy in his depiction of Galileo, as it would be to do so in the cases of Shakespeare or Schiller. It is equally naive to use the play as a gateway entitling one to enter into the innards of Brecht's unconscious "ambivalences." One reads or views the play not to obtain an apprehension of a historic past, but as a reinterpretation of such a past, and a historical figure, in the light of the present. Brecht was no more "objective" than Shakespeare; but he was no more "objective" than historians are in their treatment of history, if "objective" means the fatuous conception of absence of presuppositions or points of view. Brecht was speaking to the present, and was concerned with indicating the irreversible damage committed by an intellectual when he betrays his responsibilities to science and to the world.

But would the *Discorsi* have been written if Galileo had not recanted? Would the world have gained anything if he had been martyred? Futile questions. Brecht believed that the *Discorsi* would have been written—if not by Galileo, then by some other great scientist. Perhaps later. But what Brecht is affirming is that the recantation of a man of Galileo's stature and influence cannot but deal a serious blow to the interests of free inquiry, and, most important, the interests of the people as a whole. And in that thought Brecht was undoubtedly right.

This is not a tragedy, Brecht insisted. Nor is it the tragedy of a man. If anything, it is a study of the dire consequences of a man's actions on the better part of humanity. To that part, Galileo was intimately related: it consists of such people as Federzoni, the lens-grinder, who cannot read Latin (hence Galileo will write his works in Italian), but who understands well what Galileo is driving at; the "little monk," who is intimidated by the decree of the Church, but who cannot resist the lure of knowledge; the hard-headed iron-founder Vanni, who warns Galileo against the impending disaster; and the brilliant student Andrea Sarti; not to mention, Sarti's mother, the courageous and faithful housekeeper. They are the "people" whom Galileo betrays in betraying his science, no less than the scientists themselves who, in the wake of the recantation, shut up their writings in their desks.

For sheer brilliance there are few scenes in Brecht to match that in which Cardinal Barberini, now Pope, is being attired. The relentless and terrifying Inquisitor presses upon him the need to bring Galileo to his knees. With each garment, the

Pope yields a little, until he is persuaded that a show of instruments of torture would suffice. Outside is heard the shuffling of innumerable feet, symbolic, as one writer remarked, of the numberless generations that were to judge the actions of the Pope in the future.

So Galileo's preoccupation with his *Discorsi* at the end of his career must be viewed as evidence not of courage (as in the first version) but of a self-indulgent vice. He cannot help it any more than he can help savoring a well-cooked goose. He knows better than he does. He knows, as he says to Andrea in that last scorching confessional that it is the responsibility of the scientist to disperse the clouds of superstition and ignorance and to "lighten the drudgery of mankind." He has no use for scientists who, intimidated by authority, content themselves with "heaping up knowledge for the sake of knowledge" and so turn science into a cripple and their inventions into fresh means of oppression.

> In time [he says] you may come to discover everything that is to be discovered, and yet your progress will only be a progress away from humanity. The gulf between you and humanity can in time become so great that your triumphal cries over some new achievement could be answered by a universal scream of horror.

For himself, he continues, he had the rare opportunity—for astronomy was already reaching into the "market places." All that was needed was the "firmness, the steadfastness of one man," and these would have brought about world-shaking results. As it was, he himself stood in no immediate danger. He was strong enough at the time to have won.

> I delivered my knowledge to those in power,
> to use it, not to use it, to misuse it as suited
> their purposes.

He has betrayed his vocation, and no longer deserves to be counted in the ranks of science. Yes, a new age is coming, he admits to Andrea.

> Take good care of yourself as you pass through
> Germany, with the truth under your cloak.

Brecht is, in fact, echoing Andrea's bitter words, at the time preceding the recantation:

> So much is already won when only one man
> stands up and says, No!

In order to satisfy this passion for knowledge, Galileo has sacrificed a great deal, even his daughter's happiness. This passion, which he had epitomized in the words, *Ich muss es wissen,* he surrendered at the biddings of the flesh. He signs his own moral demise when he abandons people to exploitation by their superiors, and dictates to his daughter a letter approving the suppression of the rope-makers: "Give them more soup, but no more wages." (pp. 345-48)

Frederic Ewen, in his Bertolt Brecht: His Life, His Art, and His Times *(copyright © 1967 by Frederic Ewen), The Citadel Press, 1967, 573 p.*

ERNST SCHUMACHER (essay date 1968)

[In the following excerpt, Schumacher discusses in detail the dialectical elements of Galileo*—those unresolved conflicts of antithetical elements that are found in Galileo's character as well as the situations of the drama. For a similar discussion of Galileo's character, see the excerpts by Walter Weideli (1961) and Karl S. Weimar (1966).]*

Brecht regarded ***Galileo*** as a play with "restricted" alienation effects, but its extremely powerful dialectic shaped its internal structure, the arrangement and interrelation of the scenes, the characterization, and the language. The later theory of a "dialectical theatre" included certain ideas that had been formulated in his 1931 essay ***Dialectical Dramatics*** . . . and in his theses on ***Dialectic and Alienation*** (late 30's or early 40's)—ideas on the necessity of dialectics in modern theatre for modern purposes. ***Galileo*** reveals the great extent to which Brecht used these ideas in his art; furthermore, the play shows that the dialectic can be a major factor in the aesthetic value of any play. The over-all structure of the play demonstrates this; it expresses not only antitheses but their coherence as well. It makes possible the illustration of contradiction rather than of contrast. It is not content with merely an "either-or," but must include the "this-as-well-as-that"; not merely a "this-is-the-way," but also a "this-is-not-the-way," an "otherwise." It does not merely set negative against positive, but also shows their unity.

In ***Galileo,*** there are the antitheses of: scene 2, in which Galileo demonstrates his telescope to the Venetian Senate and is highly honored by the very men who make it impossible for him to engage in research, and scene 4, in which Galileo encounters disbelief and contempt at the very court on which he had set his hopes as a research scientist; the scene in which the Jesuits declare Galileo's theories to be correct and the scene in which the Inquisition puts the Copernican doctrine on the Index; the scene showing how Galileo's teachings spread among the common people and the (next) scene, which tells how Galileo is abandoned by the Grand Duke, on whom he relied more than on the common people. Antithesis also determines the internal composition of the scenes, and is complemented by their language. For example, the "reversal" scene in which Galileo decides to take up his research again, and the scene in which he recants. (pp. 124-25)

The theorem that a new age has dawned is integrated into the dramatic action [of ***Galileo***] as thesis/antithesis/synthesis. The new age seems agile and nimble, the old age shuffles along. And yet how weak the new age turns out to be! But the plot advances, the new age manages to survive. The discoveries have been made, the new knowledge remains, the old view of the universe will never again appear unshakeable. Reason is given a chance. Galileo seeks reason in the common people. By denying reason, he damages its chances. But even he ultimately realizes that reason is only just starting out and not ending.

The harbingers and champions of the new age have been disoriented and demoralized by their leader's betrayal. But they remain positive figures, precursors of followers capable of employing their knowledge better. (pp. 125-26)

Symmetry is an essential aspect of classical drama. In ***Galileo,*** symmetry as a dramatic structural element underlines the "conservative" nature of the play. . . . But analysis shows that it also helps express the dialectics immanent in the protagonist's life.

In the first scene, Galileo connects the new way of playing chess across the squares with the enormous perspectives made possible by new discoveries and knowledge. But when he repeats his simile to Cardinal Bellarmin's secretaries, we sense how restricted these perspectives are: the chess player's moves will be modest.

In the recantation scene, Andrea repeats the argument Galileo used with Mucius: the man who knows the truth and yet calls it a lie is a criminal. This not only ties an internal thread, it also tightens Galileo's noose, and reveals the good and bad in a single person.

The argument that one must creep into a position favorable to the dissemination of truth is used by Galileo in the third scene to rationalize his moving from Florence, and in the eighth to justify his remaining there. In both cases he has illusions: nevertheless, such "boot-licking" can be useful and necessary.

The doctrine that earthly disorder can be supported only by a metaphysical order taught by Aristotle and the Church ties together the seventh, eighth, and ninth scenes and lies at the center of the play. Yet Bellarmin, the Little Monk, and Ludovico offer it as a rationalization, while Galileo uses it as a reproach. It is an argument employed by the highest and the lowest in the social hierarchy, an ideological touchstone of decision.

The mardi gras of 1632 is a counterpart to the carnival in Bellarmin's home in 1666. But in the earlier scene, the aristocracy is amusing itself; in the later, the common people. The enjoyment is diametric. First the Inquisition refers to Galileo's support by the north Italian cities, then Vanni does—but the ultimate reversal is latent in both comments.

In the same manner the link between the first and the next-to-last scene is strengthened by events whose very similarity makes their dissimilarity apparent, as well as their intimate connection. In the opening scene, it is morning, the dawn of not only a new day but a new era, and in Galileo's room the bed is being made. In the penultimate scene, it is the evening not just of a day but of a life and its ideals, and the bed is being prepared for the night. In the first scene Galileo "sings" an "aria" to the new age. In the later scene he laboriously expresses his conviction that the new age has begun even if it looks like the old. But the theme recurs: at the end Andrea assures us that we are actually only at the beginning.

In the opening scene, Andrea is taught a lesson about nature; in the penultimate scene, a lesson on society. The teacher is the same man, yet totally different each time. The pupil has become a different person and yet remained the same.

In the second scene, Virginia asks Galileo what the night before was like. He answers, "It was bright." In the next-to-last scene, Galileo asks Virginia what the night is like. He receives the same reply. The first time, "bright" refers to nature; the second time, not only to "nature" but to the nature of mankind and history.

Thus symmetry proves crucial, an integral part of the dialectic in the composition. It is much more significant than ending each scene with a statement or an event alluding to the next scene—a practice that ***Galileo*** shares with many other Aristotelian and non-Aristotelian dramas.

Scene 13 (Galileo's recantation) shows how Brecht used images that require the spectator to compare a present event with earlier ones. Brecht doesn't bother with a sensational trial scene. Instead of letting us watch what would have been an extremely illustrative act of recantation—in church before an ecclesiastical hierarchy—he shows the event in terms of the play's basic "gesture," the scientist's responsibility to society, relating this to the internal action of the play rather than to external history. After showing, in the ninth scene, how Galileo's decision to resume research in forbidden areas affected his students, Brecht demonstrates the effect of Galileo's recantation on them. He presents substance rather than accident.

This scene (like the ninth, to which it refers) is on two levels: in the foreground, Virginia praying for her father's salvation; in the middleground, the students filled with anxiety about their master's actions. The characters all act "according to the circumstances" which have molded them. Virginia has concentrated on saving her father's soul from eternal damnation. Andrea is equally passionate about adjuring his idol and ideal. The Little Monk sustains himself with beautiful logic and the logic of beauty, the things that so greatly impressed him about his master. And Federzoni stands among them, hopeful but worried, and a realist at the very moment the others so blatantly give in to their emotions. The scene shows the students' relationship to their teacher (an important component of the plot), confronts the scientist with his daughter, and demonstrates the different meanings of the event for the various characters.

To heighten the dramatic tension, Brecht slows the tempo in two ways. First, he brings on stage the man who announces Galileo's imminent recantation and thereby precipitates Andrea's open avowal of his belief in Copernicus. Next, the author lets the fifth hour pass with no sign of recantation, so that all the students, not just an enthusiastic Andrea, say a prayer of thanksgiving for the birth of the age of knowledge. These retardations are followed by the peripetia: the tolling of bells and the public reading of the recantation formula. But the meaning, drawn from constant variations on the basic constellation—the relationship between Galileo and his pupils—would be incomplete if it were not for the dramatic confrontation between the teacher, changed beyond recognition, and the pupils, who obviously can't understand him. Now the scene reveals its true sense, shedding light on the basic problem of the play. A "final word" seems to have been spoken: "Unhappy the land that needs a hero." Yet it is final only for this scene, not for the total structure, though the scene itself can be understood only in terms of the end, whose meaning it unravels. Its power comes from the dialectical reversals, which are an image of the growth and reversals of play *in toto*. The scene is essential to clarify the theme of the scientist's responsibility in the use of knowledge for or against society.

A form of dialectic also determines ***Galileo***'s characterization; it is manifested as a relation in each person between the individual and the typical. (pp. 126-28)

Brecht's Galileo has essentially the (if not *the* essential) features of the historical figure, but includes characteristics which the author considered typical of modern-day scientists, as well as "projections" from the behavior of "ideal" scientists. These are determined by contradictions in society and in the individual: Galileo combines patience and impatience, courage and cowardice, pride and servility, sobriety and enthusiasm, acumen and narrowmindedness, affability and tactlessness, gentle humor and acerbic irony, sensuality and asceticism, commitment and cynicism, democratic ways and kowtowing to the nobles, love of truth and betrayal of truth.

Not all these traits are developed in the same way or to the same degree. Some are contradictory, some are complementary. Some seem negative but have a positive meaning. Impatience is shown by those who are no longer willing to put up with something; tactlessness can be a way of clarifying things; denial of truth can result from a love of truth. The contradictory is not necessarily antagonistic. None of these characteristics have value per se—they derive their significance from the "supreme jurisdiction" of the basic gesture, which comes from that gesture's significance for society. Not all personal qualities can be judged within a specific situation—they must be viewed in terms of the totality and the end. . . . As the kaleidoscope turns, the various fragments of the stage character finally fall into shape. Our pleasure in this picture would be incomplete if the figure did not have historical and social relevance for past, present, and future; but this enjoyment would still lack something without the idiosyncrasies which make a character the "property" of an audience and of society.

Galileo's behavior reproduces—in counterpoint, as it were—the dialectical growth of the other characters. The enthusiasm of the adult Galileo is repeated in the boy Andrea's passionate adherence to the new cause. Galileo's genius is reflected in the young initiate's intellectual maturation. Andrea's character, however, is an alternative to Galileo's, rather than simply alternating with it. Through following his master, he demonstrates consequences. Although much younger than Galileo, he seems older. Led along, he seems led astray. The result of his devotion: the prototype of a scientist prone to any recantation, denial, refusal, obedience—to whom Galileo's behavior seems natural, rather than dubious, as long as it is a contribution to science. Andrea is not only willing to learn but becomes learnèd as well. Yet while everyone else in ***Galileo*** should be seen and judged in terms of the end of the play, Andrea is to be judged in terms of his future. So he has at once the rosy bloom of youth and the grayness of old age: intellectual irresponsibility towards mankind. (pp. 128-29)

Virginia is a further example. This character is based on, but quite different from, a historical model. Her primary function is to demonstrate that the conflict between a new science and an old faith, or—speaking more generally—between social progress and reaction, penetrates the personal and family sphere. (p. 129)

Ludovico's characterization is also dialectical, although he functions primarily as a type. If he *is* an individual, then it is only despite, not because of, his class. Virginia could have been a different person, but not he. His presence is determined by what he represents, his diction by his class idiocy, his individuality by the rigidity of his caste. Although a man of the world, he is unable to cross the boundaries of his world. He has an expanded horizon—seen from a tower on his estate. When science is accepted by both Court and Church, the scientist's daughter is desirable and eligible for marriage. But the anti-Copernican decree warns him against hasty consequences. It is the father and not the daughter who must endure a period of probation; the daughter need not swear that she is pure, but the future father-in-law must promise to put an end to his impure research. . . .

But although Ludovico in this sense embodies forethought, Galileo incarnates afterthought. And that makes all the difference. Galileo may speculate correctly, but Ludovico calculates correctly. Galileo can act cold but not remain cold. Ludovico, however, can be cool, and turn icy. He is able to remain objective, while Galileo *is* an object lesson, a cause. Ludovico's profile is sharply hewn because it is so impersonal. Galileo carries out functions, but Ludovico is functionalized: a proper manor-lord. (p. 130)

Of all the characters representing the Church, the Little Monk is the most dialectical: not only a priest but an astronomer. He sees with his own two eyes that Galileo's teachings are right, yet he dare not see this because it is contrary to the Supreme Truth he has been taught. He cannot acknowledge the new knowledge because the consequences will be terrible for the simple people whose misery he is acquainted with and who—in his opinion—so as to endure their misery, need faith in a divine providence underlying the social order. His confusion is great because the contradiction is great. . . . The chasm between ideology and reality will deepen and widen. Appealed to, called upon, awoken, the "Little Monks" will bring about the victory of reason. Yet at the end of the play he has abandoned research and rests in peace in the church.

Similarly dialectical characterizations can be easily demonstrated for all the figures in the play, and in their language. The dialogue is marked by vivid imagery: the "prosaic," the penetration of new ideology and new "objective" relations on the basis of new conditions of production, is transposed into metaphor. The parabolic diction of the Bible is used verbatim in many ways, because of the very nature of the subject matter; but metaphors create the specific nature of the language, and are used by each character according to his social class and function. As for dialectics, our main concern here, the dialogue is remarkably antithetical, not only in a thesis-and-reply pattern which at times becomes stichomythic, but within individual speeches and lines. Opposing views are transcended and dissolved through gnomic maxims, contradictions resolved by "dictums" in which logic and image form a graspable unity. In this constant creation and transcendence of antitheses, a part is played by the association of images and concepts, and occasionally by the evocative use of alliteration. The syntax throughout, in coordinate and subordinate clauses, is used to develop crucial contrasts. (pp. 131-32)

The essence of drama is conflict; conflict depends on the existence of antitheses; antitheses are an essential structural element in the dramatic. ***Galileo*** is antithetical in its parts and its entirety, and these antitheses are in turn transcended through the dialectical nature of its relationships, characters, and language; yet the transcendences themselves are ephemeral. As I pointed out in the beginning, Brecht toward the end of his life came out in favor of a "dialectical theatre," of which ***Galileo***—written long before the theory—is a demonstration, not only in its technique but in its aesthetic essence. It is the "merely" narrative and "purely" demonstrative structure, as well as the appropriately "calm" production of this play, that allows us to grasp and enjoy dialectics in the theatre. (pp. 132-33)

Ernst Schumacher, "The Dialectics of Galileo," translated by Joachim Neugroschel, in The Drama Review *(copyright © 1968,* The Drama Review; *reprinted by permission of MIT Press), Vol. 12, No. 2, Winter, 1968, pp. 124-33.*

CHARLES R. LYONS (essay date 1968)

[*In the following discussion of* Galileo, *Lyons maintains that the ambiguity created by Galileo's insatiable appetite for life and his equally insatiable appetite for knowledge results in a tragic paradox that prompts Galileo's recantation and establishes the subservience of science to authority. The duality of Galileo's nature, such as his conflicting love of physical and intellectual pleasures, is also discussed in the excerpt by J. L. Styan (1981).*]

Brecht intended Galileo to be a consummate villain, and he would, in all probability have agreed with Harold Hobson's critical assertion: "As in one view humanity is saved by the grace and death of Christ, so in Brecht's, by the life and disgrace of Galileo, humanity is damned." Brecht himself considered his Galileo to be a hero-villain in the tradition of Shakespeare's evil protagonists: "He [Galileo] should be presented as a phenomenon, rather like Richard III, whereby the audience's emotional acceptance is gained through the vitality of this alien manifestation." Brecht's phrase, "the vitality of this alien manifestation," is a concise and perceptive definition of the spectator's emotional reaction to Shakespeare's villain, but while Shakespeare's characterization is complex, *Richard III* is more purely evil and less ambiguous than Brecht's ***Galileo.*** Despite the magnitude of Galileo's sin, the literal condemnation of his evil in Brecht's polemic is complicated by the fact that his insatiable appetite for life is both the source of his genius and his essential human weakness. Brecht's image of Galileo's appetite is ambiguous. In the metaphoric structure of the play, Galileo's appetite is the motive for his acquisition of scientific knowledge; in a sense, he consumes truth for the pleasure of its consumption. But his appetite for the pleasures of life, both intellectual and sensual, makes him unable to sacrifice himself to demonstrate the integrity of the truth he seeks. The tension between Galileo's hunger for life and his hunger for truth results in a tragic paradox, and Brecht's firm declaration that ***The Life of Galileo*** does not contain a tragic action does not alter the implicit tragedy of his conception of the recantation. (pp. 110-11)

In the original version of this play, which was written in 1938 and 1939, while Brecht was in exile in Denmark, Galileo is condemned as a coward in his act of recantation. However, as Gunter Rohrmoser notes [see excerpt above, 1958], in the first version there is greater emphasis upon Galileo's cleverness as he outsmarts the Inquisition and, under the guise of blindness, completes his work and smuggles it out of the country by a pupil. "Thus the cunning of reason triumphs also in the ethic of the scientist's political action, it is as far ahead of its century as his knowledge is, and causes light to dawn in the darkness of his age." However, there is evidence which would suggest that Brecht composed Galileo with the knowledge that the Nazis were exploiting the science of physics to produce the terrible atom bomb; and while Brecht and Charles Laughton were working on the English translation and revision of the play, the version this essay studies, America exploded the atomic bomb in Hiroshima. Certainly this event related to Brecht's conception of the action and its meaning, and the sin of Galileo's recantation assumes gigantic proportions in the poet's mind. (pp. 115-16)

Certainly Brecht's clearly defined purpose in the second version of ***Galileo*** is to demonstrate the scientist's sin as an historic explanation for the subjugation of science to authority. And this play existed in the playwright's mind, obviously, as a demonstration made in the terrifying context of the ultimate result of that subjugation: the already realized mass-killing of the atomic explosions in Japan and the potential annihilation ahead. This definition of Galileo's action is accomplished through the celebration of both the scientist and his discovery as the potential source of the birth of a new age, an age free from the dogmatic veneration of Rome as the focal point of the Ptolemaic universe—from the dogmatic veneration of any absolute—and through the acutely critical presentation of his failure to realize that birth. (p. 116)

In the ethical structure of ***Galileo,*** the scientist's relative truth is opposed to the absolute dogma of the church, a dogma which, significantly, is not maintained by Christian conviction but rather by the power of the capitalistic aristocracy which would collapse if dogma lost its authority. The conflict of the Copernican concept of the universe and the Christian concept of a creating God provides, in essence, only a minor aspect of the conflict of ***Galileo.*** However, it does exist at certain points; for example: after being shown the stars of Jupiter, Sagredo asks Galileo insistently, "Where is God then. . . . God? Where is God?" Galileo angrily answers: "Not there! Any more than he'd be here—if creatures of the moon came down to look for Him!" Sagredo cries: "Where is God in your system of the universe?" and Galileo's answer is significant: "Within ourselves. Or—nowhere." Even the Little Monk, in an attempt to convince Galileo and himself, does not argue from theology but from psychology, believing that the Christian conception gives meaning to his parents' otherwise pointless existence. The intellectual assumptions of Brecht's ***Galileo*** deny the existence of God; consequently, since the conflict which produced the play exists apart from a theological motive, Brecht assumes that Galileo is opposed, not from a theological motive, but from a political one. This opposition is defined in Brecht's use of Ludovico to represent Galileo's real enemy—the moneyed aristocracy. Galileo's real confrontation with the opposition comes when Ludovico forces him to decide between a commitment to scientific freedom and the compromise of silence which he has maintained for eight years. (pp. 117-18)

Brecht's attempt to define Galileo's sin explicitly is seen in the obvious structural relationship of Scenes i and xiii. In the first scene, the middle-aged Galileo enchants Andrea, the son of his housekeeper and Galileo's student, with his description of the birth of a new age in which man will break out of the Ptolemaic cage: "There was a group of masons arguing. They had to raise a block of granite. It was hot. To help matters, one of them wanted to try a new arrangement of ropes. After five minutes discussion, out went a method which had been employed for a thousand years. The millennium of faith is ended, said I, this is the millennium of doubt. And we are pulling out of that contraption." Galileo's enthusiasm for the birth of a new age predicts that science will be the possession of the common people, and the arbitrary hierarchy will disintegrate. . . . (p. 121)

In Scene xiii the birth of the new age is also discussed by Andrea and Galileo; . . . it is a discussion between an old Galileo and an adult Andrea, a confrontation of the disillusioned student and the master who betrayed his ideal by selling his science to the authorities. The implicit tension in this confrontation belies Brechtian objectivity. In his dedication to the search for knowledge, Galileo kindled a scientific idealism in his young pupil and fellow scientist. Against the standard of this idealism, a faith in the freedom of knowledge which he had inculcated, Galileo's realistic action, the compromise of his recantation, was unacceptable—a betrayal of the very freedom from dogma which his discoveries promised. In the apparent simplicity of this confrontation, a sophisticated complexity is working. When Galileo presents Andrea with the completed *Discorsi* and suggests how the mask of the faithful Christian has allowed him to complete his work, the younger man sees the value of Galileo's realism: "With the crowd at the street corners we said: 'He will die, he will never surrender.' You came back: 'I surrendered but I am alive.' We cried: 'Your hands are stained!' You say: 'Better stained than empty.' . . . You gained time to write a book that only you could write. Had you burned at the stake in a blaze of glory they would have won.'' Then Galileo, again assuming the role of teacher, attempts to counter Andrea's realism with a rekindling of the idealism he has maintained:

> The practice of science would seem to call for valor. She trades in knowledge, which is the product of doubt. And this new art of doubt has enchanted the public. The plight of the multitude is old as the rocks, and is believed to be as basic as the rocks. . . . But now they have learned to doubt. . . . As a scientist I had almost an unique opportunity. In my day astronomy emerged into the marketplace. At that particular time, had one man put up a fight, it could have had wide repercussions.

Instead, the new age, which began in the ships venturing freely from the coasts and which could have been confirmed as the "dawn of the age of reason" at the moment when Galileo refused to recant, has been transformed into the image of a "whore, spattered with blood." Rohrmoser notes a significant revision from the original text to the reworked version by Brecht and Laughton. He quotes the earlier text: "'I insist that this is a new age. If it looks like a blood-stained old hag, then that's what a new age looks like. The burst of light takes place in the deepest darkness.'" The later text, in the context of the explosion at Hiroshima, reads more ambiguously: "This age of ours turned out to be a whore, spattered with blood. Maybe, new ages look like blood-spattered whores." Brecht's later plays contain a controlled language which is in strong contrast to the richly textured imagery of the early plays and poems. The conscious deliberation of this image is, consequently, very significant. As Rohrmoser's essay on Galileo suggests, and Brecht's introductory remarks confirm [see excerpt above, 1957], the concept of the new age is a primary concern of the play. And it is vital that Galileo, who sees his own sin with such intense clarity, conceives of the new age in the image of the "blood-spattered whore"—sold and exploited. Implicit in Galileo's image is the idea that Galileo himself has sold the age, which was in his hands, which, purchased and consumed, has become the bloody whore.

The Life of Galileo is not the clear and simple defamation of Galileo's act which the isolation of these images and actions would suggest—and which, according to his own descriptions of the play, Brecht intended it to be. However, what the play loses in the explication of thesis it gains in an increasing profundity in its ambiguity—an ambiguity which sees the action in a complex of perspectives.

This ambiguity is focused in the implicit schizoid structure of its hero. Brecht uses the structural device of the split personality more obviously in a minor character than in the character of Galileo, but he uses it to define the action of compromise which anticipates Galileo's recantation. One of the most dynamic scenes of the play is that in which Barberini, being clothed in the robes of the church, moves from the identity of the Cardinal, sympathetic to science, to the identity of the Pope, opposed to the threat which science presents to dogma and papal security. (pp. 121-23)

From his Marxist perspective, surely Brecht saw Galileo's betrayal of science as an historical action which issues in the real and potential horrors of the atomic age. However, in Brecht's poetic imitation of this action, Galileo's failure becomes not exceptional but, on the contrary, essentially human; and, as the focal point of a complex of opposing motives, Galileo embodies human failure. To consume life, with all the pleasures that consumption entails, becomes a stronger motive than to maintain an abstract ideal—if forced to make a choice. And, in the central ambiguity, that ideal is generated in the very appetite for life which demands its sacrifice. The ambiguity extends to another level: while we respond to Andrea's argument that Galileo's cunning has allowed him to complete his work and make an historic gesture even more significant than his sacrifice would have been, we know that the Schweikian acquiescence which assured the continuation of his work did not derive from an abstract dedication to continue performing the birth of a new age. The suggestion of the recantation as a Schweikian trick is present in both of Brecht's major versions of ***The Life of Galileo,*** but it is not as strong an image in the second. And, it is important to realize that Galileo's continued work is accomplished itself in a compulsive joy of discovery and affirmation of hypothesis, not purely in the altruism of scientific contribution. Galileo does not plot to smuggle the *Discorsi* out of Italy; it is mere chance that Andrea comes. Surely Brecht enjoyed this final irony. . . . Brecht's Galileo has an insatiable appetite for knowledge which is only one aspect of a total appetite for life itself, an indulgence in pleasure as well as an attempt to free mankind from the prison of misconceptions in which they are bound. His work is both altruistic and essentially selfish at the same time. He is committed both to the salvation of mankind and his own indulgence in life; and when put to a decision between mankind and life, the division cannot be made—hence the tragic course. (pp. 124-26)

The primary ambiguity of ***The Life of Galileo*** finds its source in the fact that Galileo's indulgence in life's pleasures generates the appetite for knowledge and hence the knowledge itself, and simultaneously, generates the human weakness which makes him unable to say no to the threat of pain. His submission to appetite is both his strength and his weakness.

I. A. Richards considers tragedy to be "the balance or reconciliation of opposite and discordant qualities," and in ***Galileo*** we have that balance in this specific ambiguity. Galileo cannot separate the appetite for knowledge, and, consequently, the ideal of scientific freedom, from the appetite for life itself; both are the same. In Brecht's polemic, Galileo should have subordinated one appetite to the other: Galileo the scientist should have triumphed over Galileo the human being, and the ideal of scientific freedom should have been maintained. (p. 127)

Galileo is forced to choose between his indulgence in life's pleasures and the retreat from pain and the maintenance of an abstract ideal. The tragic ambiguity remains in the fact that this ideal is meaningful to Galileo only when it relates to his own personal satisfaction; his tragic course is inevitable in the terms in which Brecht has drawn his character.

The sense of tragedy in ***The Life of Galileo*** grows out of this paradox. . . . Galileo suffers acutely from the knowledge that his act of cowardice is the antecedent of terrifying destructive force. The intensity of Galileo's sensuousness, the equation of his indulgence in scientific experimentation and his indulgence in the gratification of physical pleasures, relate him to Brecht's celebration of sensuality, the grotesque Baal. However, Baal cannot comprehend an ethical concept, and Galileo is acutely aware of his ethical responsibility. Galileo experiences "THE COMPREHENSION OF THE SINGLE MAN AND THE WHOLE." However, unlike The Young Comrade in ***The Measures Taken,*** he is unable to perform the act of "cold acquiescence.'' The Young Comrade agrees to his own sacrifice with the knowledge that his death is a necessary process in the revolutionizing of the world. Galileo is unable to sacrifice his humanity, but with The Young Comrade he shares an understanding that the birth of a new age is dependent upon his acquiescence and this knowledge engenders in Galileo his painful guilt. (pp. 128-29)

The tragic nature of ***The Life of Galileo*** defeats, to a considerable degree, the explication of its didactic motive. The spectator cannot withdraw from Galileo's action and state: ''He should have been willing to sacrifice himself to pain, certainly, even death because he fully recognized the ultimate consequence of his acquiescence to the demands of authority. He should have realized that the strength of his position would have insured his safety.'' However, the perceptive spectator cannot make this judgment, because for Galileo to deny life would be for him to deny the source of scientific truth; and the Galileo trained in the denial of life could not have been the Galileo whose affirmation of life brought forth his discoveries.

Certainly Brecht's despair which informs, even directs, the early plays was not thoroughly alleviated in the Marxist solutions of the didactic plays. The unredeemed and enduring logic of exploitation, the rational maneuverings to survive, which represent Brecht's conception of human behavior are manifestations of a despair rather than affirmations of an idealistic faith in human progress. In ***Galileo,*** Brecht decries the fact that Galileo did not change the world and yet, in his fallible humanity, Galileo does not have the will to change the world. (pp. 129-30)

Charles R. Lyons, '' 'The Life of Galileo': The Focus of Ambiguity in the Villain Hero,'' in The Germanic Review *(copyright 1966 by Helen Dwight Reid Educational Foundation; reprinted by permission of Heldref Publications), Vol. XLI, No. 1, January, 1966 (and reprinted in a different version in his* Bertolt Brecht: The Despair and the Polemic, *Southern Illinois University Press, 1968, pp. 110-31).*

PETER BAULAND (essay date 1968)

[*In the following excerpt, Bauland provides interesting background information regarding Brecht's revision of* Galileo *for the American production starring Charles Laughton.*]

[Brecht's ***Leben des Galilei***] does not pretend to be historically accurate; like most of Brecht's works, it was written to prove a point and to arouse the inert to action. The Galileo of the piece is sensual, gluttonous, and unscrupulous, a man given to the easy path, one who will forsake that which is right for that which is expedient. Shown instruments of torture by the Grand Inquisitor, Galileo recants his scientific assertions to the dismay of his highly principled disciples. When his chief pupil reproaches him, ''Pity the country that has no heroes!'' Galileo replies with the most famous line in the play: ''No. Pity the country that needs heroes!'' The scientist then goes into seclusion and silence. Years later, a pupil visits the old man, now showing visible signs of his self-indulgent life. The pupil states his disgust with Galileo's cowardice, but begs forgiveness when the scientist hands him the completed manuscript of the *Discorsi,* finished in his seclusion. But after all this careful construction comes the lesson of the play: Galileo refuses to see himself as a hero; rather he considers himself a social criminal, a traitor who sold his integrity for comfort and who fears he has set a pattern for scientists to follow in the future. ''He has made science the servant of authority rather than asserting its right to transform the world for the benefit of mankind.'' This lesson is a point which Brecht actually added in a second and authorized version. The original manuscript praises Galileo's recanting as a cunning act of survival that allows him to work. Galileo is one of the protagonists Brecht conceived as he did Mother Courage and Mack the Knife—heroes who are to have little charm or appeal, who do not arouse the sympathy of the audience, and who, in fact, should evoke the viewer's indignation at the bourgeois morality displayed in their unheroic actions. In American renditions of Brecht's plays concerning ideologically detestable heroes, the protagonists are almost always played sympathetically. The possibility for such interpretation lies within the texts, so the responsibility is in part the author's, but in arousing pity for Courage, Galileo, Puntila, or Mack, a performance will undermine Brecht's very thesis. Even the *Berliner Ensemble* has played ***Galileo*** with empathetic gusto and direct, traditional audience appeal.

While Brecht was living in California, his play came to the attention of Charles Laughton, who saw not only the original genius of the playwright but also a succulent role for himself. With the assistance of Brecht and a good dictionary to supplement his admittedly weak German, Laughton translated the drama as ***Galileo*** and starred in its English premiere on July 30, 1947, at the Coronet Theatre in Beverly Hills. Audience and reviewers thought the play dull and as oppressive as the summer heat of the theatre without air conditioning. But Laughton, convinced of the value of ***Galileo,*** took it to New York, where it opened at Maxine Elliott's Theatre on December 7, 1947, under the auspices of the Experimental Theatre. The Laughton text cut Brecht's lengthy play freely, but the poet approved, for he never considered his scripts sacrosanct. The peculiar idiom of Brecht was totally lost in translation, and what the play gained in concentration by Laughton's deletions and more prosaic diction it lost in texture, wit, and gift of expression. Brecht's play itself has far fewer passages of irrelevant didacticism than do most of his other major dramas, but Laughton excised most such passages as those along with all the original's purposeful vulgarity. The result was much the same as when a play by Shaw is drastically cut. For the sake of dramatic tightness, much bright talk must be sacrificed. Furthermore, in ***Galileo,*** some of the dimension of character was lost in the interest of verbal economy. Neither in its original form nor in Laughton's version is ***Galileo*** a Marxist play. As [Eric] Bentley points out, the dialectic is hardly scientific, for who would believe that had Galileo not recanted, an age of reason would have begun and today's troubles been avoided? The tendency to read Marxism into everything Brecht wrote is dangerous, particularly when used as a weapon against his work. He always spoke for himself, never for the party with which he was always at odds. Brecht seems even more of a preacher to many than he really is for the simple reason that much of what he says appears to be patently self-evident, particularly to an audience seeing his plays as much as twenty years after they were written. Consequently, the insightful social comment of 1940 easily becomes the socio-economic cliché of 1960. Furthermore, there is an easy logical fallacy into which many fall: Brecht is didactic; Brecht was a Communist; therefore, when Brecht preaches, he is preaching communism. There is no such necessary connection between the two facts.

Despite the topical quality in the early nuclear age of the problem of the responsibility of the scientist to society, ***Galileo*** got a resounding thumping from most critics and reviewers and had no audience appeal whatsoever. It closed after six performances. The play was thought to be dull and episodic. "Even critics who rather liked ***Galileo*** had nothing to say about the form of the play except that it seemed rambling." Brecht, judged not on the basis of his goals but on the conventions of popular dramaturgy, was still completely misunderstood. Reviewers and audiences were outraged by the techniques of anti-illusionism. What was considered particularly offensive was that a very dirty Galileo destroyed all illusion by first putting on and then changing his costumes in clear view of the audience. This device was to be exactly repeated fifteen years later by the very Brechtian character, The Common Man, in Robert Bolt's *A Man for All Seasons*—the young English playwright received accolades for his inventive genius. Some of the very men who solemnly proclaim its greatness in the 1960's abhorred ***Galileo*** in 1947, almost ten years after it had been written and a decade before the American theatre would be ready for it. (pp. 164-66)

Peter Bauland, "Out of the Rubble: 1945-65," in his The Hooded Eagle: Modern German Drama on the New York Stage *(copyright © 1968 by Syracuse University Press, Syracuse, New York), Syracuse University Press, 1968, pp. 159-224.**

RUBY COHN (essay date 1969)

[In the following discussion of Galileo's character, Cohn emphasizes his heroic nature and the human weaknesses that result in his recantation.]

Though Brechtians may abhor the suggestion, Brecht's Galileo has the energy of a Claudel hero. Like *The Satin Slipper,* ***Galileo*** is set in the Renaissance. But Brecht, writing in exile in 1938, warned himself against escaping into the past, and he stresses the relevance of the stage-period for our own time. Brecht wrote three versions of ***Galileo,*** and his attitude toward the scientist grows progressively harsher. In 1938 Brecht viewed sympathetically a scientist who used his cunning to save his skin, and his first Galileo is heroic because he manages to preserve himself for science. After the atomic bomb was dropped, however, Brecht blamed a scientist who shirked political responsibility to save his skin, viewing him as a criminal. In Brecht's production notes, he emphasizes that Galileo is both a hero and a criminal, and the play dramatizes the effect of both on his people.

Brecht's Galileo has a Renaissance zest for the sensual and the intellectual, which is the source of both his heroism and his crime. Brecht's own comment is illuminating; in paragraph 63 of his ***Small Organon:*** "Isn't the pleasure of drinking and washing one with the pleasure which he [Galileo] takes in the new ideas?" (John Willet translation). Thus, we first see Brecht's Galileo half-naked, scrubbing down his gross body. His first line reveals his appetite both for food and for knowledge: "Put the milk on the table, but don't close any of my books." At the beginning of the second scene, Galileo is diminished by the projection: "Everything a great man does is not great." We have seen Galileo's physical greatness, heard of his intellectual greatness, and we will now witness how he uses his mind. Galileo's "not great" deed is to steal the idea of the telescope, and sell the instrument to the Venetians, buying free time for experimentation. Before Galileo perpetrates this "not great" trick, however, Brecht expresses Galileo's excitement about "a new time" and limitless exploration of "laughing continents." The projection connects this excitement with the Copernican theory. Galileo's delight is evident, too, at the social repercussions of his research. And yet, the double pressures of poverty and church force Galileo to sell telescopes to the Venetians. "I have no patience," he says, "with a man who doesn't use his brains to fill his belly" (Laughton translation). Galileo's trick, his "not great" deed, faintly foreshadows his recantation, where, by insincerely denying the Copernican theory, he again "fills his belly," but also satisfies his hunger for experimentation. Until the recantation, mention of Copernicus threads through the play, but Galileo does not feel threatened by Church rejection of the Danish scientist's theories, for Copernicus needed his calculations confirmed, whereas Galileo has empirical evidence—men have merely to believe what they see. Even when the advisers of the child duke Cosimo di Medici forbid him to look through the telescope, Galileo does not recognize that none are so blind as those who will not see.

Galileo's initial refusal to admit his dangerous position is paralleled by his initial courage in another dangerous position: the plague scene shows Galileo risking death from the epidemic in order not to interrupt his experiments. But, more coolly, Galileo refuses risks. In Rome he has a "friendly conversation" with two powerful cardinals; carrying their masks of lamb and dove, they advise Galileo against research that would shake the established order. Though Galileo holds his own in the dialogue, we soon learn that he spends the next eight years in piddling experiments; the recantation is foreshadowed by this subservience to church pressure. (pp. 117-18)

Brecht's play implies that the Church had good reason to fear science, for Galileo's discoveries will lead to the material and spiritual emancipation of the oppressed—to "a revolutionary twist," in Brecht's own phrase. The carnival scene colorfully stages the popular interpretations of Galileo's research. Astronomy becomes the gossip of the market-place, and the scientist is called "Galileo the Bible-killer." Brecht's production notes indicate the importance he attached to his theatricalization of Galileo's teachings, and, strategically, the carnival scene precedes the Pope's reluctant order that Galileo be forced to recant. Galileo's achievements can lead to either the confusion or the redemption of his people; only his personal sacrifice can change the course of history.

But Brecht's Galileo is incapable of martyrdom. Brecht lets us know that torture is a mere threat of the Church, but Galileo does not realize this till long afterward, and he recants off stage, to the disappointment of his co-workers, of the people in the marketplace, and of humankind. Brecht's projection reads: "A momentous date for *you and me*" (my italics). When Galileo returns after his recantation, his pupil exclaims, "Unhappy the land that breeds no hero." But Galileo closes the scene with: "Unhappy the land that needs a hero," which reflects on his own weakness and the weakness of a hero-oriented society. (pp. 118-19)

For most unprejudiced viewers of the play, there is no last word on the subject of Galileo's heroism. Galileo *does* further science through his cowardice, as he *does* stifle free inquiry through his recantation. On stage the reprehensibility of that recantation is mitigated because [we] do not see it; on the other hand, we hear it, and we cannot remain unmoved at its violent effect on Andrea. But on stage, too, Galileo attracts us by the concreteness of his mind and the saltiness of his language, for Brecht's Galileo has the kind of unified sensibility that T. S. Eliot also ascribed to the seventeenth century. Galileo's greatness and his weakness spring from his voracious appetites—mental and material. For a hero who is as whole a man as Galileo, there seems to be no simple way to redeem his people.

It is some indication of Brecht's own complexity that, though traditional heroes emerge poorly (Galileo, Caesar, Lucullus, Don Juan, Coriolanus, even St. Joan), his common man heroes seldom redeem their people. (p. 120)

Brecht's strong, anguished protagonists have influenced not only German drama but English as well. Robert Bolt's *A Man for All Seasons* and John Osborne's *Luther* descend directly from Brecht's ***Galileo.*** The first is nominally divided into two acts and the second into three, but both plays are composed of a series of Brechtian semi-independent scenes. Though both plays contain rather large casts, they center upon a towering hero who is himself aware of his own importance. Bolt acknowledges in his introduction to the play that his style is "a bastardized version of the one most recently associated with Bertolt Brecht." (p. 121)

Ruby Cohn, "The Hero and His People" in her Currents in Contemporary Drama *(copyright © 1969 by Indiana University Press), Indiana University Press, 1969, pp. 85-153.**

M. A. COHEN (essay date 1970)

[In the following excerpt, Cohen documents the various ways Brecht adhered to or altered the historical facts regarding Galileo, *and proposes that Brecht took a didactic view of history when writing the play; that is, Brecht utilized historical fact only when it suited his purposes, consistently recrafting the past as a vehicle to point morals for the present.]*

Galileo is so firmly grounded on historical re-creation that it is not always easy to separate the special pleading from the authenticity. We may agree that "it does not so very much matter whether the play is historically accurate, the moral is what counts," and yet find it difficult to isolate the moral from the history. Indeed it is arguable that the most important message of the play is essentially historical, that moral and history coincide, though what Brecht is most essentially "saying" in the play has been interpreted in a variety of ways. Whatever view we come to take, it seems likely that an analysis of the crucial manipulations of accepted fact in ***Galileo,*** of the points where Brecht most clearly exceeds his historical brief, is a useful accompaniment to an exploration of the moral. (p. 81)

Interesting though Brecht's manipulations of the facts of his hero's private life are, it is the rendering of Galileo's relationship to his society which has greater bearing on the meaning of the play. As he himself said: "It is not so much the character of Galileo that invites interest as his social role." We note first that Galileo's age is seen as one in which reason might have begun to control human affairs, a new age. In the first version of the play, Brecht had been attracted to the period as a time which, like the twentieth century, had abounded with discoveries and liberating possibilities for mankind, but which had disappointed expectations rather in the way that the twentieth century had disappointed him when the Nazis had perverted the very idea of a new age. But though the play shows the ultimate betrayal of the new age by Galileo's recantation, the initial picture of the period is idealized, the tone being set by Galileo's long speech in Scene 1, where a vision of astronomy reaching the marketplaces and the people welcoming the freedom and movement of the new world picture is painted. . . . (p. 83)

An essential strand in the play's meaning is Galileo's relationship with the people; he believes in them as the future standard-bearers of science—astronomy will be talked about in the marketplaces and will be welcomed there. Against Sagredo, who accuses him of confusing the people's "miserable cunning" with reason, Galileo invokes the everyday common sense of "the mariner who, when laying in stores, thinks of storms and calms ahead" or "the child who pulls on his cap when it is proved to him that it may rain. . . ." These are his hope because they all listen to reason (Scene 3). In Scene 9 Galileo explains why he wants to write his works in the vernacular for the people who work with their hands: "Who else wants to learn about the origins of things? Those who see only the bread on the table don't want to know how it is baked; that lot would rather thank God above than the baker. But those who make the bread will understand that nothing moves which isn't moved."

It has been pointed out that here Brecht misunderstood the significance of the new physics. The idea that nothing moves which isn't moved really belongs to "the commonsense Aristotelian theories which Galileo was in the process of superseding by groping toward the concept of inertia." Moreover, consciously or unconsciously, he gave a distorted picture of the real Galileo's relationship with the people. It corresponds to fact that the real man respected the craftsmen of his age, especially the mechanics and artisans of the Venetian Arsenal, and it is true that he was a pioneer in publishing scientific works in the vernacular. But he does not appear to have had the dramatic character's faith in the common sense of the common people in general. According to [Giorgio de] Santillana, the idea that Galileo wished to appeal to the people is a misrepresentation, for Galileo had considered it unwise to make such an appeal. (pp. 86-7)

The drama's Galileo wants more than to spread scientific knowledge to the people. He also wants to spread the spirit of doubt, and doubt appears to be the central feature of scientific thinking for Brecht. Galileo believes that such doubt, combined with the new methods of manufacturing, portends a social revolution. . . . The point is driven home in Scene 12 when the Inquisitor describes the popularity among the people of Aristotle's prophecy that "When the weaver's shuttle weaves on its own and the zither plays of itself, then the masters will need no apprentices and the rulers no servants."

It has been argued that Brecht does not in fact present Galileo himself as wanting the subversion of the cosmic order to be followed by that of the social order, but rather as a moderate who, according to his daughter Virginia in Scene 11, deplores the twist given to his astronomy by the ballad singer and the carnival crowd in the immediately previous scene, and that this is reasonably faithful to the facts about the real Galileo, who would certainly have deplored the crowd's picture of him as a "Bible Buster." Indeed, Galileo does declare himself a true son of the Church in the confrontation with Bellarmine and Barberini (Scene 7), and proves himself Barberini's match in the battle of Biblical proverbs. He also makes the essential point in the real man's case for reconciling the Bible with the new world picture: "But, gentlemen, man can misinterpret not only the movements of the stars, but the Bible too," and in Scene 14 we find him declaring his abhorrence for "cheap lucidity in sacred matters." All this is very much in historical character. The actual Galileo's letter to Castelli has been described by a Jesuit biographer as showing "an acquaintance with the Bible and the interpretation of the Fathers of the Church, especially Augustine's *De Genesi Ad Litteram,* quite extraordinary in a man whose interests lay in a very different field," and Galileo is rated as having been "better acquainted with recent commentators on the Scriptures than Bellarmine himself."

If such moments were typical of the play as a whole we should be justified in agreeing with the assertion in [Brecht's] Notes that "it corresponds to the historical truth in that the Galileo of the play never turns directly against the Church. There is not a sentence uttered by Galileo in that sense" [see excerpt above, 1957]. However, closer examination reveals that to accept Brecht's statement would be very much a case of trusting the teller rather than the tale. Scene 3 shows Galileo arguing that God is "in us or nowhere," and his reply when asked by the Little Monk to accept that the decree forbidding the propagation of the Copernican teachings showed maternal compassion toward the peasantry on the Church's part, must surely count as an attack on the institution itself. . . . (pp. 88-90)

The point at which Galileo most clearly identifies the cause of science with that of social revolution is in Scene 14. The full implications of Galileo's long speech here are seldom recognized in comments on the play. [Max] Spalter, for example, dismisses the speech as "extrinsic" to the work as a whole, on the grounds that it contradicts the characterization of Galileo which has been developed previously. (p. 90)

It is difficult to reconcile the final version of ***Galileo*** with Spalter's description. The bulk of his most interesting study is devoted to a tradition in German drama which he relates to Brecht's work, that of Lenz, Grabbe, Büchner, Wedekind, and Kraus. Brecht's early plays seem to fit in well, but it would seem that, in order to assimilate the later ones too, Spalter has, among other things, oversimplified Brecht's characterization of Galileo and perhaps underestimated the revision of the original conception by the third version of the work. In the play as Brecht left it, in *Stücke,* VIII, there is no question of the speech in Scene 14 being "extrinsic" nor of Galileo's nature being adequately defined in terms of "lust for pleasure." Galileo's sensuality, hedonism, and occasional dubious ethics (as in the matter of the telescope) are merely some facets of a many-sided character. We also meet the idealist whose faith in human reason strikes the sceptical Sagredo as naive: "I believe in mankind, and that means I believe in its commonsense. Without that belief I should not have the strength to get up from my bed in the morning." Then there is the optimistic humanist who tells the Little Monk that science and industry will provide ample substitutes for the lost faith of common people if the spirit of doubt is allowed to spread (Scene 8). Above all, there is the Galileo who affirms: "I say to you: he who does not know the truth is merely an idiot. But he who knows it and calls it a lie, is a criminal." The fact that Galileo goes on to recant his beliefs proves not his lack of an ethical imperative but his human frailty, and this is underlined in the description of his return from the Inquisition, "altered by his trial, almost to the point of being unrecognisable." Galileo's self-condemnation is a valid development of the character who has been established in the earlier stages of the play, a contradictory one it is true, but then most dramatic characterizations which go beyond the superficial encompass contradictions.

In his self-castigation, Galileo begins by arguing a view of the purpose of science to counter Andrea who, from being the first to condemn the recantation, has come to see the matter differently on discovering that Galileo has used his time under house arrest to write the *Discorsi* and to make a secret copy of it. When Galileo assures him that he recanted from fear of physical pain rather than from the calm calculation of a new ethics, he is disappointed but declares: "Science knows only one commandment: contribute to science." Galileo, however, feels that it is science which he has betrayed. He argues first that the wool merchant is concerned with both his own profits and the general health of the wool trade and, similarly, a scientist must hold himself responsible both for advancing knowledge and for promoting the development of science in the community. By science he seems to mean not only pure science but also the spirit of scepticism: "Making knowledge about everything available for everybody, science strives to make sceptics of them all." In his time the spirit of doubt had arisen for the first time among people who had been kept "in a nacreous haze of superstition and outmoded words" but who now saw hope when they turned their telescopes on their tormentors: "These selfish and violent men, who greedily exploited the fruits of science to their own use, simultaneously felt the cold eye of science turned on a thousand-year-old, but artificial misery which clearly could be eliminated by eliminating them." The clinching point in the first half of the speech comes with:

> The movements of the stars have become clearer; but to the mass of the people the movements of their masters are still incalculable. The fight over the measurability of the heavens has been won through doubt; but the fight of the Roman housewife for milk is ever and again lost through faith. Science, Sarti, is concerned with both battle-fronts.

So far from being an extrinsic attitude in the play, this is the culmination of a theme which runs through the whole work, from the first major speech with its reference to the common people's discovery that the rulers have legs like their legs, to the rejoinder made to the Little Monk in Scene 8, and later the important speech made by the Inquisitor:

> One might think: what sudden interest in such an obscure science as astronomy! Is it not all the same how these spheres move? But no one in the whole of Italy—where everyone down to the stable-boys chatters about the phases of Venus as a result of the wicked example of this Florentine—there is no one in the whole of Italy who does not think at the same time of so many things which the schools and other authorities have declared to be beyond question, and which have become a burden. What would happen if all these people, so weak in the flesh and inclined towards every excess, were to believe only in their own commonsense which this madman declares to be the sole court of appeal!

Thus Galileo's opponents also see the issue as the potential subversion of the social order by science. (pp. 90-3)

It is not uncommon for critics to represent the play's judgment on Galileo as historically simplistic: "the point of ***Galileo*** is that men do not today live in an age of reason simply because at a particular moment in the seventeenth century Galileo recanted . . ." or again, "Brecht does imply at this instant that a whole epoch of European history turns on one man's failure."

But, after all, Brecht merely speaks of an age of reason that could have *begun,* of Galileo's as only the *original* sin of modern science (and therefore, presumably, not the only one) and of the atomic bomb as the end product rather than the direct result of his action. And if he asserts that there was a setback to science as a result of the affair, he is correct, at least so far as Italy was concerned. Santillana claims that this marked the decline of the "whole scientific movement in Italy" and the vanishing of Florentine civilization from history but concludes that "as for the fate of science itself, his (Galileo's) concern was justifiably less." Of course, for Brecht, the issue was larger than an Italian one, and there was more to science than "science itself."

Ultimately, insofar as so brilliant a theatrical vehicle can be reduced to *the* point, the point is more for the present than about the past. Confronted by the drama in performance, we meet Galileo's dilemmas as our own and are not allowed to be either simply censorious or simply the reverse: "Confronted with such a situation, one can scarcely wish only to praise or only to condemn Galileo." And there is an aspect of the moral which even the bitterest opponent of Brecht's politics, or the most detached critic of his naiveté, may regard as a telling one. In Scene 14 Galileo laments his failure to help the poor in their battle for milk and cannot be consoled by his success in pure science. This is not without relevance to an age which has made great strides in the exploration of space but in which the majority go hungry. When Andrea is held up at the Italian frontier in the final scene, he finds time to obtain a jug of milk for an old woman and tries to dispel the idea that she can be a witch. As a good historical drama should, ***Galileo*** ends by leaving us at one of our own frontiers rather than in the past. (pp. 96-7)

M. A. Cohen, "History and Moral in Brecht's 'The Life of Galileo'," in Contemporary Literature *(© 1970 by the Regents of the University of Wisconsin), Vol. 11, No. 1, Winter, 1970, pp. 80-97.*

GUY STERN (essay date 1971)

[*In the following excerpt, Stern contends that* Galileo *contains a hidden, secondary theme—that of the plight of German refugees in exile.*]

Most studies of Brecht's ***Galileo Galilei,*** some at length, others in passing, have pointed out the frequent references to Brecht's own life and times in a drama based at first glance solely on the biography of a seventeenth-century scientist. [Ernst] Schumacher, for example, characterizes the drama as "related to [Brecht's] times in a complex way"; [Walter] Weideli observes: "The autobiographical elements in it seem to be numerous." Yet neither Brecht scholars nor Brecht himself, in his numerous and sometimes contradictory explanations of his drama, have commented upon a subsidiary theme in it, the plight of Germany's exiles, which at the time of the drama's genesis (1938-39) was both topical and autobiographical.

Evidence for Brecht's abiding and profound concern for the refugees from Hitler Germany emerges, of course, from other works of that period. . . . [The] dialogue ***Flüchtlingsgespräche,*** 1940-41 [***Dialogues of the Refugees***], Brecht's most extensive pronouncement on the plight of the refugees, was written only shortly after the first version of ***Galileo.*** Significantly, one of the participants of this dialogue is a physicist, an inspiration probably derived from his work on ***Galileo.*** It appears, therefore, that Brecht's own experience as an exile affected a drama based on a historical person, who was neither an exile nor a fugitive himself. Brecht, in short, accommodated a theme, the introduction of which was difficult and which occasionally seems forced.

Four aspects of the exile experience permeate the drama: the flight, economic straits, loss of identity, and intellectual suppression of the refugees. Flight, the necessity of "changing one's country more often than one's shoes," had become a way of life to Brecht; even his departure from the United States resembled one. It is therefore understandable that Brecht has his hero prepare for flight as prudently as did Brecht at various stages of his exile. In past interpretations of the play, this prudence on the part of Brecht's protagonist is often overlooked. Misled by Galileo's disclaimer, "I cannot see myself as a refugee. My comfort means too much to me," critics have explained Galilei's seeming inertia as resulting from his myopic view of danger, love of comfort, and even as a mirror of Brecht's own passivity in staying in East Berlin despite the restraints on him. [Werner] Zimmermann observes: "He [Galileo] refuses to acknowledge the immediate danger to his life and rejects an opportunity to escape, whereby [the drama] . . . does not actually make it clear whether he fails to recognize the real danger or whether he only wishes to shun the discomforts and annoyances involved in flight. . . ." And [Hans] Lucke adds: "Just as Galileo refuses to flee to Venice (scene 2), so Brecht himself, despite intellectual oppression and forced compromises, remains in East Berlin after all." But Galilei, as a close reading of the text reveals, is dissembling during his conversations with Vanni, the ironmonger. Unbeknownst even to his daughter, Virginia, to whom he feigns the same type of blind optimism, he has prepared for flight: "We are not going home from here, but to Volpi, the glass cutter. We have made arrangements that a wagon, full of empty wine-barrels, always stand ready in the adjoining courtyard of the inn, to take me out of the city." . . . Earlier in the play . . . Cardinal Barberini observes that Galilei wears no masks. Both he and Brecht's critics underestimate Galilei's ability to dissemble.

The theme of flight and emigration is struck again at the end of the drama. Andrea, Galilei's student, is preparing to emigrate to Holland (to Strassburg in the first version of the drama). A border guard challenges him:

> THE GUARD: Why are you leaving Italy?
>
> ANDREA: I am a scholar.
>
> THE GUARD to the Scribe: Enter under "Reason for leaving country": Scholar. . . .
>
> (pp. 133-34)

In addition, Brecht uses a device of the epic theater to link past and present. A transparency displayed at the beginning of the scene injects the author into the play:

> The great book o'er the border went
> And, good folk, that was the end.
> But we hope you'll keep in mind
> You and I were left behind.
> May you now guard science's light
> Keep it up and use it right
> Lest it be a flame to fall
> One day to consume us all.

Hence in one terse dialogue and a brief rhyme Brecht accuses his age and country—more so than seventeenth-century Italy—

of forcing intellectuals into exile. Being a scholar had become a reason sui generis for emigrating.

Brecht's flight from Germany brought him freedom coupled with deprivation; this was typical of the fate of the refugee. Brecht in fact felt strongly that the exile countries unconscionably made deprivation the price of freedom. In his ***Flüchtlingsgespräche*** . . . Kalle, the metal worker, is "hospitably received" in Denmark, but callously exploited as a garbage collector; later on in the work we hear of a physician, a renowned specialist in asthmatic ailments, who works in a clinic "where he was allowed to work as an orderly without pay." . . . Brecht's protest against economic exploitation in exchange for freedom carries over into ***Galileo:***

> THE CURATOR: Do not forget that while the Republic may not pay as much as certain princes, it does guarantee freedom of scientific investigation.
>
> GALILEO: Your protection of intellectual freedom is quite a lucrative business, isn't it? By pointing out that the Inquisition rules and burns in other places, you acquire excellent teachers cheaply. You compensate yourselves for the protection from the Inquisition by paying the worst salaries. . . .

It is unlikely that the historical Galilei ever made such a pronouncement. But if we substitute "National Socialism" for "Inquisition" in the passage above, Brecht's Galilei would be voicing the precise thoughts of the author and of Brecht's fellow exiles, who like him were paid considerably less than they deserved.

Brecht, in the same passage and throughout the drama, shows that even this vaunted freedom is not unalloyed—and that it is particularly precarious for foreigners. To make his point, Brecht has his protagonist recall the fate of Giordano Bruno, who was delivered up to the Inquisition by the Republic of Florence, the supposed protector of freedom. In trying to exculpate his government, the curator cites the historic "party line," that Bruno was extradited not for his heresies, but because he was a foreigner. (p. 135)

This argument is unconvincing from the start. It is furthermore demolished completely by subsequent speeches and also fails in its purpose to assuage the fears of Galileo. Hence its function within the play is difficult to fathom. But it makes perfect sense as a topical reference. In the ***Flüchtlingsgespräche*** deportation hangs heavily over the exiles: they speak with rather desperate humor of the time "when we are to be unceremoniously deported." . . . Deportation to Germany meant imprisonment and death for the exiled intellectuals as surely as extradition to Rome did, in its time, for Giordano Bruno.

Brecht, in the drama's final scene, took pains to point out the parallelism between the seventeenth and the twentieth centuries regarding thought control and flight from it. In a passage added, significantly, *after* the completion of the first draft, Galileo says: "Watch out when you travel through Germany, with the truth under your cloak." . . . This warning appears rather gratuitous, if intended for someone smuggling Galileo's *Discorsi* out of Italy; during the Thirty Years' War ownership of the manuscript would have been dangerous in some parts of Germany and not hazardous at all in others. Also this warning is inconsistent with the assertion by a reliable source—the pope himself—that Galileo, far from having to fear Catholic Germany, has powerful friends at the court of Vienna. . . . But the warning became an effective dramatic device to show the analogy between the Inquisition and the Nazis, and the necessary flight from the one as well as the other.

Finally, Brecht's use of dates referring to historical events in the seventeenth century, which are not absolutely essential to the drama of Galileo, tends to emphasize the parallelism. Dates such as 1633 and 1637 evoke the memory of events precisely 300 years later. They also evoke parallelism between the life of Brecht as an exile and that of Galileo as an intellectual exile—choosing the seventeenth-century equivalent of "inner emigration." Occasionally Brecht attributed his persecution by the Nazis in part to the Marxist tenor of his didactic plays. . . . (pp. 135-36)

The year 1932 falls into this specific period of Brecht's creativity with the completion of such works as ***Die Mutter* [*The Mother*]** and ***Kuhle Wampe.*** Brecht appears to imply that one of the factors that led to the silencing or intellectual exile of Galileo was the application of his teachings to the socioeconomic and political arena. In fact, scene 10 in ***Galileo Galilei*** is a didactic play in a nutshell proceeding from the observation of a neutral scientific fact, the earth revolving around the sun, to a utopia of the class struggle in which the master is a satellite of his servants. Brecht as the embattled and endangered writer of didactic plays joins hands across several centuries with Galileo Galilei, who inspired didactic satire, the Shrovetide Plays. Warnings of the consequences of such boldness appeared both in Brecht's life and in his fictionalized account of Galileo's. (p. 136)

The next year, or so Brecht seems to argue, both he and Galileo pay the price for carrying abstract insights to their logical conclusion. The forces that compel Brecht's involuntary emigration . . . drove Galileo into his intellectual exile. With one spatial reference that consciously or subconsciously reinforces the temporal one, Brecht drives home the parallel. In '33 both Brecht and Galileo started a prolonged residence . . . in a *Landhaus* ("country house"). To list the dates in this abbreviated and more striking form is a legitimate device because Brecht himself had recourse to this manner of emphasizing the point in one of the versions of the play. Recently a scholar has suggested that Brecht elevates his exile experience to a poetic level, which transports the trauma of the exile to the realm of the legend. As far as the relationship of these two exiles—actual or intellectual—is concerned, Galileo becomes Brecht's "legendary" alter ego. (p. 137)

The discovery of this particular hidden theme in Brecht's ***Galileo*** may, beyond its pertinence for Brecht scholarship, help solve a problem of classification in modern German literature. One of the earlier books on exile literature suggests that we will arrive at a valid typology of the genre only if we discover traces of the exile experience in works thematically divorced from it. In ***Galileo*** we have a striking example of such a transplanted exile landscape.

As far as Brecht scholarship is concerned, the theme of exile and exiles adds yet another enriching complexity to the "complex topicality" of this polychromatic work. (p. 138)

Guy Stern, "The Plight of the Exile: A Hidden Theme in Brecht's 'Galileo Galilei'," in Brecht Heute/Brecht Today *(© 1971 by Athenäum Verlag Gmbh, Frankfurt am Main; reprinted by permission), Vol. I, 1971 (and reprinted in* Exile: The Writer's Experience, *edited by John M. Spalek and Robert F. Bell, The*

University of North Carolina Press, 1982, pp. 133-38).

CLAUDE HILL (essay date 1975)

[*Hill's* Bertolt Brecht *is a comprehensive survey of Brecht's work. In the following excerpt, Hill discusses the various versions of Galileo and how Brecht's revisions affected its context. Hill concludes that the play is regarded as "one of the great plays of modern thought" because of Brecht's superb characterization of Galileo and his adventures.*]

The best way to understand and appreciate ***Leben des Galilei*** may be to shed some light on Brecht's probable intentions. A dramatist rarely if ever merely aims at total accuracy when he chooses historical material; he must be judged by other criteria. Shakespeare's *Richard III* and Schiller's *Maria Stuart* are not superb dramas because they are important chapters in the history of England but because their creators effectively used historical characters and settings for their own, quite different purposes. Brecht is not the only one who saw certain similarities between the seventeenth and twentieth centuries; we have already observed the striking parallel between Mother Courage's war and Schweyk's wars. And who will deny that the contemporaries of a Kepler, Galileo, Bacon, Descartes, and Leibnitz were as conscious of living in a "new scientific age" as Brecht claimed we are today in the era of Marx, Freud, and Einstein? . . . In short, we may almost postulate that sooner or later Brecht *had* to write a play about the greatest physicist of the seventeenth century, and that his purpose would be to show the relevance of Galileo to our time. When Brecht worked on the script, he became increasingly aware of the dangerous alienation of ever more complex modern science from ordinary man. It is no surprise, therefore, to learn from [Werner] Mittenzwei and [Ernst] Schumacher, who studied the unpublished materials in the Brecht Archives, that the playwright originally aimed at a positive folk hero who worked in close proximity to the people and who later deliberately recanted in order to get his ideas across. While I see no evidence that Brecht was motivated by Stalin's purge trials, as some critics have suggested, it seems highly likely that he was less interested in the recantation of his hero than in the fact that Galileo managed to complete his *Discorsi* under the eyes of the Inquisition. It seems to me that Brecht saw in Galileo's case a historical precedent for successfully spreading the truth despite secret police and the Gestapo. Marxist scholars are probably correct when they claim that ***Leben des Galilei*** was at first conceived as a political antifascist (i.e., anticapitalistic) play in historical disguise. It was Brecht's answer to an essay of 1934 in which he had prescribed five means for the dissemination of truth under terror: (1) the courage to write it, (2) the wisdom to recognize it, (3) the ability to use it as a weapon, (4) the proper choice of effective recipients, (5) the cunning to spread it. Thus, the Galileo of the earliest drafts was a revolutionary scientist, deeply concerned with the life of the people and their miseries, and praiseworthy, above all, for his cunning. The title of the new play was to be taken from the famous legendary (but unfounded) saying "Und sie bewegt sich doch!" (And yet it, i.e., the earth, moves!); the notes refer to a "version for workers."

It speaks for Brecht's intellectual integrity and artistic maturity that in the completed first manuscript of 1938 his Galileo had already become a more complex character and also more in line with historical truth. He is still cunning and the great, admired hero because he has deceived the authorities by pretending to be blind while he secretly continued to write; and he craftily arranges for his manuscript to be smuggled out of the country. But his recantation is no longer the result of a deliberate plan but due to his fear of death. Schumacher reports that, while an assistant of Niels Bohr, with whom Brecht discussed *The Discorsi,* approved of the recantation, "Brecht, however, was of the opinion that Galileo's recantation of his theory of the earth in 1633 represented a defeat, which was, in years to come, to lead to a serious schism between science and human society." The significant admission of the Danish physicist, "I could never understand this point of view," may well have been an additional reason why even then Brecht's Galileo became less socially conscious and more of an "intellectual" than he was intended to be in the preliminary sketches. Galileo emerges as a contradictory and ambiguous man, in some respects resembling his modern creator; and it is for this reason that malevolent critics have drawn unflattering and often foolish inferences from his dilemma. Just as the splitting of the atom by Otto Hahn in 1938 sharpened but did not precede Brecht's notion of the moral responsibility of science, so the dropping of the bomb on Hiroshima (1945), while he worked on the English translation, was only the most visible and terrifying confirmation of that "serious schism between science and human society" which the playwright had already foreseen. He did not need to drastically change Galileo's character or the structure of his drama. All that was needed was to make the great physicist somewhat more negative by presenting the completion of *The Discorsi* more as the result of habit (he was as much a compulsive researcher as he was a compulsive eater) than a deliberate act of defiance, and finally to have him condemn himself unequivocally. Most changes, therefore, occur in Scene XIV when Galileo interrupts Andrea and (quoting Brecht's own comments) "proves to him that the recantation was a crime, and not to be balanced by the work, no matter how important." Brecht added: "Should it interest anyone, this too is the opinion of the playwright." To paraphrase the change between the two versions, again in Brecht's own words: what was a "defeat" (the recantation), regrettable and to be condemned, has now become an unredeemable social "crime."

Leben des Galilei is as little a tragedy as ***Mutter Courage,*** unless we are willing to equate a scientist's thirst for knowledge and a businesswoman's greed with the tragic flaw or grain of evil of a Shakespearean hero. Brecht's Galileo is a sensuous man, and his ambiguity results from this trait. His voracious appetite is his strength and his weakness at the same time. He leaves a poorly paid but safe position in the Republic of Venice, which would have protected him from the Inquisition, for more money and more free time for research in Florence, although a friend has warned him of the greater influence of the Church there. That he is not a coward is shown in a scene, omitted in the Laughton version, in which he continues his work in the midst of a plague epidemic while everybody else flees. The Pope, who has no intention of destroying Galileo, only consents to having the instruments of torture shown to him because he knows that such a man could not stand the sight of them. In his great final speech, Galileo admits to Andrea: "I have come to believe that I was never in real danger; for some years I was as strong as the authorities, and I surrendered my knowledge to the powers that be, to use it, no, not use it, abuse it, as it suits their ends." In other words, in the last analysis Galileo recants because he misjudges the situation. When he later wrote *The Discorsi* under house arrest and defying specific orders, he simply did so because he could not help himself. His thirst for knowledge remained as insatiable as his appetite for the roasted goose we see him devouring at the end. No tragic hero he—and also, we must add, no Marxist one. Bentley put it succinctly when he wrote: "What Marxist historian would accept the notion that a Catholic scientist of the Seventeenth Century, whose best friends were priests, who placed both his daughters in a convent as young girls, was halfway a Marxist, resented convents and churchgoing, doubted the existence of God, and regarded his tenets in physics as socially revolutionary?" [see excerpt above, 1961]. However, he added just as astutely: "But it is one of the open secrets of dramatic criticism that historical plays are unhistorical. They depend for their life on relevance to the playwright's own time—and, if he is lucky, all future times—not on their historicity."

There is no question that, in the age of the hydrogen bomb, the morality of the scientist has become a theme of the greatest possible relevance, but the projection of a modern point of view and experience into a historical figure still constitutes a matter of legitimate criticism. Brecht himself was apparently never completely satisfied with ***Leben des Galilei,*** and still bothered by the recantation of his ambiguous hero when he worked over the script for a Berlin production shortly before his death. After completing the Danish version, he voiced misgivings about a certain opportunism that in his opinion had prevented "the planetary demonstration" the material demanded. His criticism then was entirely aesthetic and was directed neither against the plot nor against the characterization, but he felt that the play constituted a backward step in terms of the technical mastery of the new epic theater which he had achieved in the meantime. The fact that he compared his presumed "opportunism" with a similar one responsible for *Frau Carrars Gewehre* reminds us . . . about the relatively straightforward realism of other anti-Nazi plays such as *Furcht und Elend des Dritten Reiches* and *Die Gesichte der Simone Machard;* it tends to confirm Schumacher's and Mittenzwei's notion of ***Galilei*** as a tool originally conceived for fighting Hitler. Brecht's criticism is no longer valid because the subsequent "official" version of the play is sufficiently epic to place it in the vicinity of ***Die Mutter*** and ***Mutter Courage und ihre Kinder.*** There are recited verses and projections before and, at times, at the end of scenes; there are many passages which seem to be directed to the audience as commentaries and are not needed for the dialogue onstage; there is a whole scene interrupting the action and only serving as an alienating device for enabling the audience to gauge Galileo's standing with the common people; and there is, finally, his unhistorical self-accusation, which establishes "the planetary connection" of the play's message. In short, the final ***Leben des Galilei*** qualifies as an anti-illusionary drama for "the children of the scientific age," in Brecht's own terms; the fact that he specifically used the play to illustrate certain points of his theory in ***Kleines Organon für das Theater*** . . . proves this point. There still remains, however, the ambiguity surrounding Galileo's recantation, which in my opinion Brecht did not successfully resolve. Most readers and audiences will not agree with the playwright's stern verdict, and are likely to see only human weakness for which they can cite many mitigating circumstances. They sympathize with Galileo to the end, and disagree that they have witnessed how "a great hero" turned into "a great criminal" (Brecht's words). And this despite the fact that Brecht took great pains to emphasize Galileo's social concern and great popularity and his awareness of his own unique role in the history of science, which the full text (not the Laughton version) shows. It seems that Brecht overestimated the reasoning powers of audiences, who are supposed to see in Galileo the first physicist in history who was in a position to establish a credo for science such as Hippocrates had done for medicine, and whose betrayal must, therefore, be judged in the theological dimension of original sin. Niels Bohr's assistant who could not see Brecht's point before Hiroshima, unfortunately resembles most of his colleagues—and also government leaders—in the hydrogen era, who continue to carry on business as usual. The shrewd Hanns Eisler realistically summed up the current limitations for endowing historical figures with notions of contemporary relevance when he rejected the Galileo of the final version as superheroic and told his friend Brecht: "Let him eat at the end!"

Why then is ***Leben des Galilei*** nevertheless generally considered one of the great plays of the modern theater, even by those who have reservations about its ideological validity? To begin with, it has an overpowering impact on any audience or reader: next to Mother Courage the Italian physicist is the most convincingly three-dimensional and complex stage character Brecht created, and he dominates most scenes with his intellectual charisma as strongly as his contemporary, the sutler woman, does on an earthier level. Galileo is inquisitive, intelligent, shrewd, and not above cheating, but also capable of generosity, a born teacher inspiring admiration and unstinting loyalty, naïve to the point of acting stupidly, egotistical, filled with a love of people and especially children, compassionate and yet brutal, a man of tremendous energy, obsessed with an almost maniacal curiosity, driven by an insatiable thirst for knowledge, and endowed with a Gargantuan appetite for everything, which, in the last analysis, accounts for his glory as well as his undoing. In short, he is an actor's dream, and one can easily understand why Laughton wanted to play him. He is surrounded by an entourage of minor characters whom Brecht etched out sharply and convincingly and with admirable economy. The highest praise, however, must be reserved for the characterization of Galileo's adversaries, the dignitaries of the Church, who are not shown as mean or stupid men but as intelligent, even sympathetic representatives of the authorities of the time; they are antagonists worthy of a great opponent. Despite the play's length, each scene serves a purpose in Brecht's design. When Laughton omitted Scene V, which shows Galileo's obsession with research prevailing over his fear of the plague, and when the New York production dispensed with the procession song in Scene X, which is indispensable for revealing the link between Galileo's discoveries and their theological and political implications, the artistic quality of Brecht's masterpiece was unjustifiably and severely damaged. In terms of visual splendor and inventiveness, Scene XII, during which the new Pope, the former cardinal and mathematician Barberini, with each new garment put on him gradually yields to the Inquisition's request for having Galileo shown the instruments of torture, is dazzling in its originality and stage symbolism. The subsequent Scene XIII, in which we wait, with Galileo's disciples, for the public announcement of his recantation (and hope with them that he won't recant) until the defeated and almost unrecognizable physicist makes his entrance, is full to the brim with dramatic and emotional tension; and then there is, of course, the crucial and climactic confrontation of teacher and pupil in Scene XIV. Most of all, however, there is the brilliance of Brecht's language, at once historically accurate (he used some of Galileo's own writings, famous for their clear and simple style) and elegant in a modern sense for its sophisticated and highly ironic flavor. Brecht almost, but not quite, overcame the obstacle of transforming the inherent dryness of mathematics and astronomy into an aesthetically pleasurable theater experience. Nobody has so far done better than he in putting a convincing and historically credible scientist on the stage, and this is no mean accomplishment per se. Growing demands for a new morality of the scientist in our time will lead to a still greater appreciation of Brecht's magnificent ***Leben des Galilei.*** (pp. 114-21)

Claude Hill, in his Bertolt Brecht *(copyright ©1975 by Twayne Publishers; reprinted with the permission of Twayne Publishers, a Division of G. K. Hall & Co., Boston), Twayne, 1975, 208 p.*

RAYMOND WILLIAMS (essay date 1981)

[*An English educator, author, and critic, Williams's literary theory is informed by his socialist ideology and his belief that a reader's perception of literature is directly related to cultural attitudes, which are subject to change over the course of time. As a literary critic, Williams is best known for* Modern Tragedy *(1958), which asserts that modern tragedy derives from the inadequacies of social systems rather than weaknesses of character, as in classical tragedy, and for* Drama from Ibsen to Brecht *(1968), a study of the development of drama that utilizes his definition of tragedy to explain the development of modern drama. In the following excerpt, Williams discusses the contemporary relevance of* Galileo *and, by extension, Brecht's visions of scientific and social responsibility.*]

English Chekhov was never mere fantasy. It was a matter of playing up certain tones, playing down others. English Brecht is a similar case. The last scene of ***Galileo,*** in which the manuscript of the *Discorsi* triumphantly crosses the frontier, but in a closed coach, while the boys whom Galileo might have enlightened are still talking about witches, has only to be omitted, as has often happened in production, to tilt the play towards a quite different meaning.

Yet the problem may be deeper than that. Brecht looked for historical instances and for parables as a way of teaching us lessons, not only about history, but about the contemporary world. The method quickly engages us, but in the case of Galileo, for example, the problem now is to find anybody who doubts that the Earth moves round the Sun, or who thinks that it is socially or morally disturbing to say so. He is thus available to everyone as, in spite of everything, an intellectual hero and indeed an all-purpose liberal. Brecht's underlying argument is of course more complex. The highest value is not knowledge, or even, in that limited sense, truth. The central question is what the knowledge is used for, and Galileo's deepest betrayal, in Brecht's version, is to cut the links between knowledge and the education and welfare of the people. From this betrayal came the indifference and irresponsibility that allowed scientific research to present politicians and generals with an atomic bomb. Conclusion: Galileo was wrong, though in the immediate and local argument, about the Earth and the Sun, he is not only shown, but we know him already, to be right.

It is then necessary to distinguish between two kinds of cultural effect. English Brecht is a relatively obvious incorporation. The dialectic has been reduced to a method of open staging: as he put it himself, 'the theatre can stage anything; it theatres it all down.' But in Brecht himself there is a more difficult problem. Like most of the Left in his period, he believed in popular common sense. Yet this went along, as in orthodox Leninism, with the not readily compatible belief that intellectuals had a duty to bring the truth to the people, and to resist, in this cause, all the powers of church and state. Galileo appears to fit the model exactly: he discovered the truth but he failed to resist the authorities. But where then is popular common sense? Still talking about witches.

The difficulty lies in the initial rhetoric. It is true, as Brecht so often insisted, that real knowledge is gained by practice, and that working men, seen as merely ignorant by princes and prelates, have their own basic knowledge of the material world in which they work. But this is very different from saying that there is any comparably adequate understanding either of the material world in which they do not work and learn by observation and handling, or of the political and economic world which organises and disposes of their labour. The gap that keeps people from the first kind of knowledge can be bridged by science and education: that is the Galileo model, and in Brecht's version the measure of his failure. The gap that keeps them from the second kind of knowledge is evidently different, to be bridged only (as in Leninism and more generally in the socialist movement) by political organisation and education. Brecht's image of Galileo, in which the two kinds of gap are connected and could have been bridged in the same operation, is entirely characteristic of the socialist thought of his period, in which natural science was seen as the leading edge of a more general enlightenment and emancipation. The historical version of Galileo as scientist stays relatively close to the record. The version of Galileo as failed general emancipator is not historical, but is a projection from the later form of thought.

The screw was then turned. Fascism, not only a very brutal but a very old political philosophy, was using advanced technology. Ignorance and demonology were being diffused by powerful modern means. At the same time, natural science was reaching what could be taken as its triumphant climax: learning to control the most inward secrets of matter; splitting the atom and discovering the technology of atomic power and the atomic bomb. And meanwhile where was popular common sense? Was it a force against these new destructive powers? If it was not, there must have been a betrayal, and there he was again, Galileo, the founding figure of the default.

It is significant that Brecht turned so often to the past for what were intended to be contemporary lessons. In his own time, the intellectual Right turned regularly to identify the Renaissance and the Reformation as the beginning of the decline into modern barbarism. He did not support this, but in ***Galileo*** he went to the same historical period and drew what was apparently the opposite conclusion: it was the check of those movements, the failure to carry them through, that gave barbarism its new chance. It was a generous response, and his popular sympathies were never in doubt. But the element of projection is very obvious, and it delayed the facing of any of the harder questions.

It produced, in its way, a new demonology. There has been a very deep shift, on the left, in attitudes to natural science. From the leading edge of emancipation it has become, in some influential propaganda, at best a mixed force, at worst, as with nuclear weapons, a destroyer. To watch a production of ***Galileo*** in which, over the final scenes, there are projections of the images of Bikini Atoll and Hiroshima is a dreadful test of nerve. It is much better, of course, than the naturalised image of this engagingly greedy old man who had discovered, in spite of those silly old priests, that the Earth goes round the Sun. That is simple indulgence: the easy heroics of retrospective radicalism; the even easier conceits of retrospective truth. But from Galileo to Hiroshima is also an indulgence: an ignorant if well-meant evasion of difficulties and responsibilities. It would be much better, if we want to face the problems, to look at the dramatisations of Oppenheimer and of Sakharov, but even then we would be displacing. It is what happens when, in conceit or revulsion, any intellectual is set centre-stage. Praise or blame can be heaped on him, but while we are twisting and turning about his private conscience, the major social and historical forces are given leave of absence, or are introduced only in the convenient forms of stupid bureaucracy and generous if ignorant—or let us not quite say that, let us say 'ill-informed'—people.

Brecht fought very hard, with the weapons of his time. He remains a quite different figure from orthodox or incorporated Brechtianism. Instead of using theatre to reconcile us to failures and errors, he worked untiringly to expose error and to show that the action could be restarted, at any time, and played differently. That is still his challenge, and the only good way of responding to it is to judge everything, including his own work, in these hard and open terms. We have then to say that in his most historical plays, like ***Galileo,*** the challenge is weakened. It is only in the wildest voluntarism that we can see that action being replayed: and the false conclusion that is then waiting, in the dominant structure of feeling, is that the weight of inherited failure is just too appallingly heavy. The Brechtian exposure of error, stopped at that point, becomes a coarse acquiescence, with the talk getting rougher, for its own sake, as the sense of hopelessness settles in. An isolated colloquial vigour is then beside the point. It finds all too easy a congruence, under its label as 'popular', with the hard-pressed, resentful, cursing and cynical language of subordination. We all know what the world's like but with any luck, keeping our heads down, we'll get the occasional goose.

'Eats first, morals after.' But that savage summary of what is at once bourgeois ideology and a version of popular common sense has been stood on its head, under the polite name of the 'consumer', now the agreed point of orthodox social reference. An entire social order is organised to define this version of human destiny, and to protect its existing supplies and privileges. The morals, as indeed always, come with the eats. But then imagine a scientist who tells us untraditional truths about the limits on resources, about hunger and population, about the pollution in so much of our production and consumption. Imagine a political scientist who tells us the uncomfortable truth that these processes are locked into a social and economic order, and that this is protected by a vast system of propaganda and of weapons. Do the princes and prelates, the electoral bandwagons, listen? Does common sense listen?

Brecht defined the new drama as one in which the spectator can sit at his ease and listen—critically, of course. It is now time to shift this relationship, to move beyond this version of critical consumption, to start to see ourselves where we have always in fact been—on the stage and in the action, responsible for how it comes out. (pp. 19-20)

Raymond Williams, "English Brecht" (appears here by permission of the London Review of Books *and the author), in* London Review of Books, *July 16 to August 5, 1981, pp. 19-20.*

J. L. STYAN (essay date 1981)

[In the following excerpt, Styan examines the ambiguous nature of the character of Galileo, presented by Brecht in one instance as a great scientist and in another as a greedy sensualist. For a similar discussion of Galileo's duality see the excerpt by Charles R. Lyons (1968).]

Galileo was the most rewritten of Brecht's plays. With three versions completed over seventeen years, the revisions themselves tell the story of his development towards a dialectical drama. (p. 154)

The object of Brecht's dramaturgy in this play, and the source of the spectator's unease, is a duality in the central character. The play was written against the growing terror of atomic warfare, and Brecht was anxious that Galileo should not be the idealized scholar and scientist of history, the 'stargazer' remote from reality, but an ordinary man with earth-bound responsibilities. Indeed, Brecht chose this subject because in spite of Galileo's scientific discoveries it was hard to ignore the fact of his apparently shameful recantation when he was threatened with torture and death by the Inquisition. While it remains ambiguous whether this recantation was an act of cowardice or one of cunning, since Galileo's survival enabled him to carry on his work and smuggle a copy of the *Discorsi* out of the country, Brecht was at pains to stress that to recant was to rob science of its social importance, and permit the Church to reassert its primitive power over the people of that age. This he emphasized in revision: in the first version Galileo was shown to be carrying on his work in secret, but in the two later revisions he was represented as more and more unscrupulous, anti-social and even criminal.

The scenes in ***Galileo*** are therefore planned to secure ambivalent, dialectical, responses from the audience. Galileo is at once the great scientist, and the thief who steals the concept of the telescope from Holland. He goes to Florence to make some money 'to fill his belly', and yet while he is there he courageously defies the plague in order to continue his studies. More than this, every detail of characterization is introduced to fill out the character of Galileo as a complete human being. He is the sensualist whom we first see stripped to the waist as he enjoys his wash in cool water; it gives him pleasure to have his back rubbed. He enjoys drinking his milk, as well as his wine. As an old man he is still the glutton who greedily consumes a goose, that greasiest of birds. He shows up badly as a teacher, and when his work is interrupted by a student, he betrays his irritation. As a father, he behaves unfeelingly towards his daughter Virginia and prevents her marrying, so that we see her later as a bitter old maid, happy to spy on her father for the Inquisition. When he recants in scene 13, as Galileo [actor Charles] Laughton showed his degradation by assuming an infantile grin which indicated, in Brecht's description of the performance, 'a self-release of the lowest order'. Just as the recantation itself is not allowed to be a simple matter for praise or blame, so in such ways Galileo's contradictory personality is managed in every detail to inhibit the audience's facile reaction to him. Yet, for all the vivid realism of the action, Brecht required that the scenes should also appear like historical paintings, an effect assisted by the use of titles suspended behind the stage to lend the play the appearance of being a history lesson. (pp. 155-56)

J. L. Styan, "Epic Theatre in Germany: Later Brecht," in his Modern Drama in Theory and Practice: Expressionism and Epic Theatre, Vol. 3 *(© Cambridge University Press 1981), Cambridge University Press, 1981, pp. 150-64.*

BRUCE COOK (essay date 1983)

[Cook is an American literary journalist and the author of Brecht in Exile, *a collection of essays concerned with various aspects of*

Brecht's life in the United States. In the following excerpt, Cook explains Brecht's attempts to denigrate the character of Galileo in his successive revisions of the play and demonstrates Brecht's failure to impose his conception of his own character's cowardice upon his audiences.]

What is ***Galileo*** about? What does it say? There is, after all, reason to doubt that it actually says what Bertolt Brecht intended. In the basic sense, of course, it is about Galileo Galilei, the Italian astronomer and physicist who lived from 1564 to 1642 and challenged the prevailing notions of astronomy by suggesting that the earth was not the still center of the universe, and that the sun did not revolve around the earth but rather vice versa. In doing this, he came up against the authority of the Catholic Church, which supported the old Ptolemaic conception of the universe. Under threat of torture by the Inquisition, he recanted his position completely; but then, upon his release, he beat the ground with his foot and was heard to say, *"Eppur si muove!"* ("And yet it [the earth] moves!") In his old age, under virtual house arrest, he wrote his *Discorsi,* in which he restated and defended his views. He had them smuggled out of Italy, and they were published after his death.

Now, while Brecht altered certain historical details, he certainly remained true to the story in broad outline in the versions of the play that he wrote—although in the original (1938) text he was evidently *truer* to the facts. I say "evidently" because since this version has never been published and I was not on hand in Zurich on the only occasion when it was performed, I am relying on Eric Bentley, who has read it, probably at the Brecht Archive in East Berlin. In his excellent essay, "The Science Fiction of Bertolt Brecht" [see Additional Bibliography], Bentley contrasts the original version with the one performed by Charles Laughton in Hollywood and New York. In the earlier one he sees an "analogy between the seventeenth-century scientist's underground activities and those of twentieth-century left-wingers in Germany." He calls it "propaganda for thinking," referring directly to a line in the play, "Propaganda that stimulates thinking, in no matter what field, is useful to the cause of the oppressed." Brecht, Bentley says, so stresses the physicist's "slyness and cunning" in writing his *Discorsi* and smuggling them out for publication that he virtually excuses him for his weakness in giving in to the Church.

On the other hand, there is some evidence that even at the time that Brecht first wrote the play, he could not find it in his heart to forgive Galileo his cowardice. In researching his subject Brecht not only consulted books but also had talks with a Danish physicist, Professor C. Møller, who was a co-worker of the great Niels Bohr himself. To a German critic, Ernst Schumacher, Møller recalled his conversations with Brecht. Møller said that between them "there arose a certain difference of opinion" on a crucial point:

> Since the *Discourses* would never have been composed if Galileo had not many years before submitted to the Catholic Church, I regarded this step as justified. Only in this way could he have finally won a victory over the Inquisition. Brecht, however, was of the opinion that Galileo's recantation of his theory of the motion of the earth in 1633 represented a defeat, which was in years to come to lead to a serious schism between science and human society. I could never understand this point of view, and even today I do not understand it after reading Brecht's ***Life of Galileo,*** which does not prevent this play from affecting and impressing me deeply.

Since the ***Galileo*** that Møller read was probably the Laughton version—though it may possibly have been a third version prepared by Brecht for the Berliner Ensemble production of the play in 1953—the point is that *both* these later versions strongly stress Galileo's defeat by the Church over the later victory he won with his *Discorsi*. (pp. 175-76)

By whatever tortuous logic, Brecht came to the conclusion that if Galileo had not given in to the Pope and the Inquisition, the modern world would have been spared the horror of the atomic bomb. It could as easily be said that if **Galileo** had been more sincere in his recantation and had *not* written the *Discorsi,* Ptolemaic astronomy would have prevailed and World War II would have been fought with seventeenth-century weaponry. But that, of course, would be nonsense too.

At any rate, with the advent of the nuclear age Brecht set about with Laughton's assistance not only to translate and adapt the original text but to revise it substantially to sharpen his indictment of the physicist for his cowardice and betrayal. Most of these revisions were made in the latter part of the play. For instance, Galileo's defiant and historically verified line, *"Eppur si muove!,"* had previously seemed so important to Brecht that he used it for the title of the play's first draft—*And Yet It Moves!* It has been deleted from the second version altogether. In its place is this brilliant, if ambiguous, exchange between Galileo, who enters "changed, almost unrecognizable," from his ordeal with the Inquisition, and Andrea, his student and disciple, who looks at him in dismay, knowing he has recanted:

> ANDREA *(in the door):* Unhappy is the land that breeds no hero.
>
> GALILEO: No, Andrea: Unhappy is the land that needs a hero.

We have Professor Møller's word that Galileo's recantation deeply troubled Brecht right from the start, and so the alterations Brecht made in the text may have been something in the nature of settling an old account. Still, it must be admitted that it is a *mea culpa* that he puts in Galileo's mouth in scene 13. In good dialectical style, Brecht brings up Møller's argument that the writing of the *Discorsi* completely justified the recantation—simply so that the argument could be demolished. After many years, his former disciple, Andrea, looks in on the physicist and is asked by him to take the manuscript to Holland. Andrea is overcome. "Everything is changed!" he cries. (pp. 177-78)

In the long speech that follows, a tirade of self-loathing, Galileo sets forth Brecht's thesis that his sin was the "original sin" of science, declaring that if he had held his ground his scientific knowledge could have freed the people from their tormentors. . . . There is no rejoinder from Andrea. This is the last word on the matter and clearly what Brecht would have us also believe.

Yet this is seldom what *is* believed. For example, critics at the Coronet Theatre on opening night were full of praise for Laughton's extremely human portrayal of the scientist who, as one of them put it, is "altogether heroic while professing to be a coward." In spite of the fact that he had collaborated in the adaptation, Laughton could not help but wring sympathy from the audience for the character. The actor got deeper into his role than the playwright had intended.

But in doing this, Laughton worked no unique magic. Other actors less skilled than he have managed to do the same. Audiences and readers alike respond with sympathy to Galileo; they even see him as "heroic." Why? First of all, because Brecht could not alter the fundamental facts: even though Galileo recanted to the Inquisition, he *did* write the *Discorsi* and had them smuggled out of the country. This is certainly a case where actions speak louder than words.

But what about Brecht's words? Do they really convince? No—and the reason they don't is that by the time we hear them from Galileo we have come to know him so well and believe in him so profoundly that we cannot bring ourselves to accept the verdict against him that he himself hands down. Brecht's Galileo is one of the most fully developed characters in modern drama. No mere great man, he has such appealing, vulgar, human qualities—gluttony, greed—that his cowardice before the Inquisition (if it is that and not cunning) may be disappointing, but it is not surprising. Frankly, it would be difficult to imagine this corpulent, sensuous man stretched out on the rack, emitting agonized howls interspersed with screams of defiance to his torturers right up until that awful, final moment when his bones snap. That's not *our* Galileo. No, our Galileo might, as Andrea supposed, have given in because he knew that it was more important for him to continue his work than to die in defense of it. Or, at the very least (for the bare facts support this), he might have recanted out of fear, knowing all the while that he was right *("Eppur si muove!")*, then, after a period of years, have decided that, even though there was real risk involved, he had to set down the principles of his new physics on paper and get them published. But would he, in either case, hate himself so for not having challenged authority? He might, for in their final years men do look back upon their lives and count the missed opportunities. But the long speech of self-denunciation that Brecht puts in Galileo's mouth does *not* convince us; it does not alter appreciably the estimate of the man formed from the many scenes that preceded it. It has, rather, the effect of deepening the character, giving a hint of the tragic to a man who now yearns to be the kind of hero he never could have been.

Brecht himself must have seen that this was so, for in that third version of the play, which he prepared for production in East Berlin, he made further changes in the text, and all of them were directed toward demeaning Galileo and making the self-contempt he voices at the end more truly justified. Yet, ultimately, not even this version (available in German and English editions) manages to convince us. The historical Galileo and the character created by Brecht join forces to resist every effort by the playwright to denigrate them. We have all heard of plays that are actor-proof and director-proof; ***Galileo*** seems to be one that is playwright-proof. (pp. 178-80)

Bruce Cook, in his Brecht in Exile *(copyright ©1982 by Bruce Cook; reprinted by permission of Holt, Rinehart and Winston, Publishers), Holt, Rinehart and Winston, 1983, 237 p.*

ADDITIONAL BIBLIOGRAPHY

Benjamin, Walter. *Understanding Brecht.* Translated by Anna Bostock. London: NLB, 1973, 124 p.

Explains the theoretical concepts of Brecht's epic theater and defines the most important aspects of this theater, including a lack of sensationalism, an appeal to reason, an untragic hero, and alienation of audience sympathy with the characters through interruption of happenings. Benjamin also discusses Brecht's poetry, Brecht's own productions of his dramas, and offers reminiscences of the dramatist.

Bentley, Eric. "The Science Fiction of Bertolt Brecht." In *Galileo,* by Bertolt Brecht, edited by Eric Bentley, translated by Charles Laughton, pp. 7-42. New York: Grove Press, 1966.

Presents an interesting comparative examination of the 1938 German version of *Galileo* and the 1947 English version. Bentley is distinguished as a translator, adaptor, and critic of Brecht's works. For additional criticism of Brecht's works by Bentley see the 1961 excerpt in the entry above, TCLC, Vols. 1 and 6, and Additional Bibliography below.

———. *The Brecht Commentaries: 1943-1980.* New York: Grove Press, 1981, 320 p.

Collection of Bentley's critical essays, covering a span of almost twenty years, on Brecht's dramas and his epic theater.

Chiari, J. "Brecht." In his *Landmarks of Contemporary Drama,* pp. 161-83. London: Herbert Jenkins, 1965.

Examination of the characteristics and theories of Brecht's epic theater.

Demetz, Peter. "*Galileo* in East Berlin: Notes on the Drama in the GDR." *The German Quarterly* XXXVII, No. 3 (May 1964): 239-45.

Posits that Brecht's 1954-55 East Berlin revision of *Galileo* was written to avoid "open conflict with the German Democratic Republic." However, Demetz believes that this did not destroy *Galileo,* but rather that the drama was thus "transformed into a better play when Brecht (in 1954/55) unfolded brittle if undramatic discussions into more convincing figures and theatrical situations."

Des Pres, Terrence. "Into the Mire: The Case of Bertolt Brecht." *The Yale Review* 70, No. 4 (Summer 1981): 481-99.

Commentary on the trend of Brecht criticism over the years to assess Brecht's "art" and "life" as one.

Esslin, Martin. *Brecht: The Man and His Work.* Rev. ed. Garden City, N.Y.: Anchor Books, 1971, 379 p.

Major biographical and critical study of Brecht.

Fetscher, Iring. "Bertolt Brecht and America." In *The Legacy of the German Refugee Intellectuals,* edited by Robert Boyers, pp. 246-72. New York: Schocken Books, 1972.

Explores Brecht's artistic impressions of America, citing from some of his poetry. Fetscher finds that Brecht's initial fascination with America and praise for its modern technology changed remarkably when he examined the country from the perspective of Marxist theory, which viewed America as a "horrifying model of the capitalistic production form."

Fuegi, John. *The Essential Brecht.* Los Angeles: Hennessey & Ingalls, 1972, 343 p.

Important critical work studies Brecht's major dramas within the context of his own productions of them. Fuegi's work also includes several photos and illustrations of Brecht's plays during their various productions.

Gray, Ronald. *Brecht the Dramatist.* London: Cambridge University Press, 1976, 232 p.

Synopsis and criticism of Brecht's drama. See TCLC, Vol. 6, for a critical discussion of *Galileo.*

Haas, Willy. *Bert Brecht.* Translated by Max Knight and Joseph Fabry. New York: Frederick Ungar, 1970, 121 p.

General overview of Brecht's major dramas.

Mews, Siegfried, and Knust, Herbert, eds. *Essays on Brecht: Theater and Politics.* Chapel Hill: University of North Carolina Press, 1974, 238 p.

Collection of critical essays that focus on Brecht's theory of drama and his political ideology. This work includes essays by Siegfried Mews, Darko Suvin, Grace M. Allen, and John Fuegi, among others.

Sartre, Jean-Paul. "Brecht As a Classic." *World Theatre* VII, No. 1 (Spring 1958): 11-19.

Insightful discussion of Brecht's artistry, which equates his drama with the classics of literature. Of Brecht, Sartre states: "He has . . . this in common with our classics of old, that he possesses one general ideology, one method and one faith: like them he puts man back again in the world, that is to say—in truth."

Szczesny, Gerhard. *The Case against Bertolt Brecht: With Arguments Drawn from His "Life of Galileo."* Translated by Alexander Gode. New York: Frederick Ungar, 1967, 126 p.

Attacks the conception of Brecht as a concerned social thinker and finds *Galileo* to be insignificant as a discussion of social problems. Szczesny maintains that *Galileo* is significant only as a fair representation of Brecht's own life.

Trilling, Lionel. "Bertolt Brecht: *Galileo*." In his *Prefaces to the Experience of Literature*, pp. 56-66. New York: Harcourt Brace Jovanovich, 1979.

Explores reasons for Brecht's departure from historical actuality in *Galileo*, addressing in turn, Brecht's Marxism, his moral dictates, and his theory of epic theater.

Volker, Klaus. *Brecht Chronicle*. Translated by Fred Wieck. New York: Seabury Press, 1975, 209 p.

Chronology of important dates in Brecht's life, including a record of his theatrical productions.

White, Alfred D. "Brecht's *Leben des Galilei:* Armchair Theatre?" *German Life and Letters* n.s. XXVII, No. 2 (January 1974): 124-32.

Cites the differences between *Galileo* as it was performed in the production by the Berlin Ensemble established by Brecht in 1956 and that of the written published texts of the play. White describes the dramatic scenes that were altered or left out of the various versions and the contextual effects these alterations produced.

Saratchandra Chatterji

1876-1938

(Also transliterated as Sarat Chandra; also Chatterjee and Chattopadhyay; also wrote under pseudonyms of Surendranath Gangopadhyay and Anila Debi) Indian novelist, short story and novella writer, essayist, dramatist, poet, editor, and translator.

Drawing from a photograph; courtesy of Friends of India Society International

Chatterji is considered one of the foremost novelists in Indian literature. Following the path of Rabindranath Tagore, he contributed significantly to the modernization of Bengali literature by introducing new social and political themes to the novel and by employing Bengali dialects in his fiction. His works advocate a humanitarian attitude toward the oppressed (especially toward Hindu women, who were relegated to a lowly status in their society), and they attack British imperialism, urging freedom and the democratization of India. Moreover, Chatterji was the first Bengali writer to address the lower social classes in his fiction. Because he sought equality for the lower castes, he became one of the most beloved literary artists in his country.

Chatterji was born in Debanandapur, Bengal. His father was an unsuccessful writer and eventually the family's poor financial condition forced them to live with Chatterji's maternal grandparents in Bhagalapur. There he received a modest primary and secondary education, but was unable to afford tuition for higher studies. However, Chatterji maintained that his "true education" came from his first-hand experiences with life. During his adolescence he wandered about the Indian countryside, where he became acquainted with the Bengali peasants and where he witnessed the injustices they frequently endured from their rich landlords. He also observed the pitiable treatment of poor Hindu women within the caste society and developed a sincere compassion for the widowed women who became social outcasts upon the deaths of their husbands. These journeys, which often took him away from his studies for several days, had a profound effect in shaping his fiction. It was also during his adolescence that he developed a love of the arts; he became an accomplished vocalist, musician, actor, and painter, but ultimately turned his creative talents to writing. At seventeen, inspired by the works of Bengali writers Bankim Chandra Chatterjee and Tagore, Chatterji formed a literary coterie and contributed short stories to the group's journal, *Chhaya.* In 1903, after winning a local short story competition, he traveled to Rangoon, Burma, where he lived for over a decade before returning to his native land. During his stay in Burma he worked as an office clerk, but continued to write with the encouragement of friends. In 1907 his manuscript of *Baradidi (The Eldest Sister, and Other Stories)* was sent to the journal *Bharati.* The title novella, a love story about a widowed woman and an irresponsible man, was serialized anonymously and won a wide readership, for many believed it was written by Tagore. Chatterji did not submit any further stories for publication until five years after this initial success, but then he deluged Indian journals with his works, gaining financial success and popularity. Chatterji became the first Bengali writer to earn his living solely by writing fiction, and he continued to do so until his death.

Critics often divide Chatterji's literary career into three overlapping phases of development, placing his most important works in the middle and last phases of his career. His early works consist of experiments with the short story. Generally these works, such as "Bindur Chhele" and "Ramer Sumati," are concerned with the social problems of women in traditional Hindu society. Although they are unique in Indian literature for their compassionate consideration of women, critics usually regard these early works as overly sentimental—a common criticism of most of Chatterji's work. In the middle stage of his literary development, Chatterji candidly portrayed the social ills that plagued his country. The novels *Charitrahīn (Charitraheen)* and *Gṛhadāha (The Fire)* expose the hypocrisy of social conventions that condone marriage without love and condemn true love when it is found outside a marital union. In these works Chatterji typically extolled the intrinsic virtues of his female characters even though some of them commit moral indiscretions. While these women are socially ostracized for their behavior, the author points out society's hypocritical treatment of men who commit the same transgressions. *Pallī-Samāj* is an important novel of this period because it represents one of Chatterji's first condemnations of the exploitation of the peasantry by the wealthy. In addition to its love theme, the novel is concerned with corrupt wealth and the political powerlessness of the common people. Many critics consider

the first part of Chatterji's four part novel *Śrīkānta (Srikanta)* to be his best work. This social novel is the synthesis of all of his experiences in Rangoon. That city's cosmopolitan environment was free from the social strictures of Bengal, and while there Chatterji associated with both the Hindu emigrants who openly abandoned the proprieties of social convention and those Hindus who clandestinely discarded them only during their stay in the foreign city. Described by Humanyun Kabir as a "scathing picture of moral hypocrisy," *Srikanta* realistically depicts both the good and evil elements of life without a restrictive social code—the good manifests itself in the realization of true human value, while the evil leads to a selfish and profligate life.

The political themes which dominate the works of Chatterji's last literary phase reflect his fervent concern with home rule for India. After 1920 he was politically active in the Non-Cooperative Movement and the Civil Disobedience Movement, both of which sought India's independence from British rule. Eventually Chatterji became disappointed with the passive methods of these groups and joined those dissidents who sought India's freedom through more violent means. *Pathēr Dābī*, a bitter protest against Britain's imperialistic exploitation of India, considers the moral dilemma of choosing violent over nonviolent methods to win freedom. However, Chatterji's political ideology that "non-violence is a very noble idea, but the achievement of freedom is nobler, hundred times nobler" is evident throughout the novel. Although *Pathēr Dābī* was banned by the Bengali government, it was surreptitiously distributed and read by Indian citizens across the country, and became one of Chatterji's most popular works. Many critics agree that in *Pathēr Dābī* Chatterji sacrificed art to propaganda. However, most commentators regard the novel as an important document that records the political and economic turmoil of India, while trying to arouse the nationalistic spirit of the working class. *Śēṣ Praśna* combines Chatterji's political indictment of imperialism and oppression with the radical social and ethical themes of his earlier works. The novel depicts the human worth of a woman who is a political and social militant and who daringly chooses not to be bound by the conventions of Hindu society. Unlike his earlier works, which consistently indicate the dismal aspects of not adhering to the social structure, *Śēṣ Praśna* explains the value of allowing individuals to achieve self-realization—a humanistic ideal that serves the national good according to Chatterji. In this last major work, many critics consider the female protagonist, Kamal, to be one of Chatterji's most skillfully delineated characters.

In his literary work, Chatterji presented important social and political problems to the Bengali people through the use of simple and familiar forms of vernacular speech. Although some critics comment that his works are overly sentimental and partisan, most agree that he made a significant contribution to his country's literature with the sociopolitical statements that are at the center of his fiction and with his humanistic approach to the problems of the times. Chatterji's literary efforts were directed by his ardent belief that India would realize independence and become a part of the modern world only when its social structure changed. In a tribute to Chatterji and his work, Tagore commented that it was due to such literary concerns that Chatterji "guided Bengali novels nearer to the spirit of modern world literature."

(See also *Contemporary Authors*, Vol. 109.)

*PRINCIPAL WORKS

Baradidi (novella and short stories) 1913
[*The Eldest Sister, and Other Stories*, 1950]
Bindur Chhēlē Ō Anyānyagalpa (short stories) 1914
Pandit Maśāi (novella) 1914
Chandranāth (novella) 1916
[*Chandranath (Queen's Gambit)*, 1969]
Pallī-Samāj (novel) 1916
Charitrahīn (novel) 1917
[*Charitraheen*, 1962]
Niskrti (novella) 1917
[*The Deliverance*, 1944]
Śrīkānta, Part I (novel) 1917
[*Srikanta*, 1922]
Dattā (novel) 1918
[*The Betrothed*, 1964]
Śrīkānta, Part II (novel) 1918
Gṛhadāha (novel) 1920
[*The Fire*, 1964]
Nārīr Mūlya [as Anila Debi] (essay) 1924
Pathēr Dābī (novel) 1926
Śrīkānta, Part III (novel) 1927
***Ramā* (drama) 1928
Śēṣ Praśna (novel) 1931
Śrīkānta, Part IV (novel) 1933
Chhēlēbēlākār Galpa (short stories) 1938
Śarat Rachanābalī. 5 vols. (novels, short stories, novellas, essays, and dramas) 1976-77

*Most of Chatterji's works first appeared serially in magazines.

**This drama is an adaptation of the novel *Pallī-Samāj*.

RABINDRANATH TAGORE (essay date 1935)

[*Tagore is considered India's greatest lyric poet and the pioneer of modernism in Bengali prose literature. He was a major influence on Chatterji, whose prose works are similar to Tagore's in their protest against social domination and inequality. In the following excerpt, Tagore comments on Chatterji's role in liberating and modernizing Bengali prose.*]

The early epoch of Bengali prose suggests its parallel in the beginning of the biological age on this earth when its animal creations were cumbersome in their gait lacking in a rhythm submissive to life. Though the time is not remote yet it seems to us belonging almost to a pre-historic period of evolution when Bengali prose painfully struggled on with its adynamic grammar and a vocabulary containing words that were mostly inert and colourless. Our own growing intimacy with the modern European mind and its manner of expression reacted upon our language giving it more and more freedom of movement and the pliancy in its functions. During a remarkably rapid course of self-discovery it has developed the courage to be able to cross the orthodox enclosure of a pseudo-classical form of literature rigid in its ceremonialism. This freedom has brought our fiction close to the everyday life of the people, a large section of which was formerly shunned as untouchable in our domain of culture. The latest of the leaders who, through this path of liberation, has guided Bengali novels nearer to the spirit of modern world literature is Saratchandra Chatterji. He has imparted a new power to our language and in his stories has shed the light of a fresh vision upon the too familiar region of Bengal's heart revealing the living significance of the obscure trifles in people's personality. He has achieved the best reward of a novelist: he has completely won the hearts of Bengali readers.

Rabindranath Tagore, "Preface" (1935), in The Deliverance *by Sarat Chandra Chattopadhyaya, translated by Dilip Kumar Roy, revised edition, Vora & Co., Publishers Ltd., 1944, p. viii.*

SARATCHANDRA CHATTOPADHYAY (essay date 1938?)

[*In the following excerpt, the date of which has not been determined, Chatterji discusses his personal development and assesses his own artistic talent.*]

I was brought up in a family where poetry or fiction was considered a euphemism for immorality and music was dubbed untouchable. All its members were eager for a pass so as to qualify as lawyers. Thus passed my days in their company. But one day even this was disturbed by an unexpected turn of event. One of my relatives was a college student in the metropolis. He came home. He had a love for music and a passion for poetry. One day he called together the female inmates of the house and read out to them Tagore's *Prakrtir Pratiśōdh*. I cannot say how much of it was grasped by the listeners. But as the reader himself wept, tears also welled up in my eyes. I hurried out of the room lest my weakness should be revealed. . . . Thereafter, I found it against my grain to abide by the conservative principles of the family along with its rigid tradition of reading law. I had to return to my village home. . . .

Now came the time for me to know about the works of Bankimchandra. I could not even imagine then that there could be anything greater beyond this in fiction. I read all his novels over and over again until I almost memorised them. Perhaps this was a drawback with me. Not that I have never followed the path of blind imitation. All such attempts have proved fruitless as literary compositions; but as literary exercises they provided a profitable occupation for me as I can feel even today.

Then began the new phase of 'Bangadarsan'. Tagore's *Chōkhēr Bāli* was appearing in instalments. A fresh radiance of style and diction seemed to greet our vision. The profound and intense joy then experienced by me is unforgettable. Never before had I thought even in my dreams that things could be put in such a way and that the reader could perceive his own mind so clearly through the portraits of somebody else's imagination. At long last I came to be introduced not only to literature but to my own self as well. It is not a truth that one gets much only by reading much. (p. 408)

Am I indebted to my venerable literary predecessors alone? Do I owe any the less to those who have only made sacrifices for society but have got nothing in return, who are underprivileged, weak and oppressed, who are human beings and yet whose fellowmen have never taken account of their tears, who are doomed to spend helpless miserable lives for ever wondering why, having all, they are denied their rights in every sphere? It is the agonies of such people that have made me articulate. They it is that have briefed me to lodge a complaint on behalf of suffering humanity at the bar of human conscience. On numerous occasions have I found them victims of injustice, miscarriage of justice, and justice of a sort made intolerable by high-handedness. So my works are on these people alone. I know spring visits this world with its beauties and bounties accompanied by the cuckoo's warble and full-blown seasonal flowers along with the restless south wind redolent with their fragrance. But all these did not come within the compass in which my vision remained bound. I could not just become intimate with them. This deficiency is obvious in my writings. At the same time I had not the audacity to weave garlands of senseless but sonorous words just to show that I have attained something which, in reality, had never any access to my heart. Nor am I guilty of belittling with an air of insolent immodesty many other similar things whose significance has ever eluded my grasp. As a result, the subject-matter and theme of my literary creation are not wide and extensive, but narrow and limited. Nevertheless, it remains my claim that I have not divested them of truth by giving them colourful touches of unreality.

I do not aspire after immortality, for like many other things in life the human mind is subject to change. So what looks important today may appear insignificant some other day, and small wonder. Even if, in the long run, the major portion of my literary attainment is submerged under the neglect of unborn generations, I shall have no regrets. It remains my only hope that if there is an element of truth anywhere in it that much will survive as my contribution defying the ravages of time. It matters little if it is not abundantly rich; it is in order to pay my homage to the Muse with that humble offering that I have sacrificed my life-long labour. (p. 410)

Saratchandra Chattopadhyay, "My Life," translated by Ashim Mukhopadhyay, in The Golden Book of Saratchandra: A Centenary Commemorative Volume, *Manik Mukhopadhyay, General Editor, All Bengal Sarat Centenary Committee, 1977, pp. 407-10.*

DILIP KUMAR ROY (essay date 1944)

[*Roy was a well-known Indian musician and Chatterji's friend. In the following excerpt, he comments on the difficulties of translating Chatterji's novella* Niskrti (The Deliverance).]

The duty of a translator hardly impels him to do more than introduce his subject to foreign readers. I would only point out Sarat Chandra's fundamental kinship with two great modern writers: Dostoievsky, the interpreter of the "insulted and the injured" and Gorky, the comrade of "the outcast and the pariah." I hope some day his masterpiece **"Srikanta,"** that Saga of Indian life in all its kaleidoscopic variety, will be translated in full in its five parts if only to present him to the world as a great universalist and humanist in life and art. . . . For none has known him who has known him only as a spectator of life: he was, intrinsically, a seeker after the hidden truths that life so often hurtles past unheeding. And that is why even the insignificant things and stray waifs whom we bypass have outflowered in his art with the magic of faultless contour. This is perhaps truest in his portrayal of the vastly misunderstood womankind of India. He refused to equate those who lived under deep purdah with nonentities. In the short compass of this novelette [**"The Deliverance"**] where only a cameo corner of the feminine world is limned, a foreign reader shall see something authentic about our womankind in all their strength and weakness of love, generosity and pettiness of nature, reticence and ingenuousness of character: also something of his peerless insight into both our juvenile and adult psychology in moods of war dissolving in amity. It is a small world but a real world—a piece of moving, palpitating life of the joint-family of Bengal. (pp. xiii-xv)

Among the great Indian writers of today Sarat Chandra is probably the most difficult to render into a European tongue. The reason is that he is the most Bengali of the Bengali belletrists even as Dostoievsky is the most Russian of the Russian Romanticist realists. True, he imbibed all that is best of the Western culture, but his responses and reactions to the changing times remained, to the end, ineradicably Indian. It is this which makes his expressions, his dialogues in particular, so bafflingly untranslatable. While rendering this novelette, how often have I not regretted the elusiveness of just that quintessential savour of his, that delicate picturesqueness of his homely pathos and the humour and inbred reticence of his style which have endeared him to us, Indians. . . . But when one ventures to transplant a supreme artist of one language into the soil of another, one must not be deterred by defeatist qualms and compunctions. A Bengali proverb puts it succinctly: "A blind uncle is better than no uncle." (p. xv)

Dilip Kumar Roy, "Translator's Note" (1944), in The Deliverance *by Sarat Chandra Chattopadhyaya, edited by Sri Aurobindo, translated by Dilip Kumar Roy, revised edition, Vora & Co., Publishers Ltd., 1944, pp. ix-xvi.*

VISHWANATH S. NARAVANE (essay date 1976)

[*In his* Sarat Chandra Chatterji: An Introduction to his Life and Work, *Naravane offers a comprehensive biographical and critical examination of Chatterji and his works. The following excerpt discusses Chatterji's talent for description and character delineation.*]

The high artistic level of Sarat's stories depends mainly on his penetrating character portrayals. His descriptive passages, and the unusual situations which he often creates, cannot be appreciated in isolation from his fundamental objective of character delineation. Conversely, some of his stories appear somewhat weak because he seems to have lost his skill in making his characters come alive. Some critics have analysed the weak points in Sarat Chandra's work with reference to his occasional wordiness, his uncertain handling of adjectives, his tendency to overuse certain words and expressions like 'nevertheless', 'but enough of this', 'but that's another matter', 'without a doubt', etc. But a closer look at the passages in question will reveal that the author tends to lose his grip on the language because he is not entirely clear about his own conception of the main personalities around whom the story is woven. Such lapses, however, are very rare. Usually he is lucid about the essential nature of the human being whom he is introducing to his reader. And his language shows a corresponding clarity and ease. (pp. 154-55)

The first point which strikes us when we read his works is that he does not describe any of his main characters in a single paragraph, page or even chapter. He resists the temptation to place before the reader a complete picture of his hero or heroine all at once. He is unhurried. The man or woman is allowed to reveal various aspects of his or her nature in different contexts, in varying moods, until the total personality gradually emerges. This is, obviously, more true of his novels and novelettes than of his short stories. But even in the latter, the characters are revealed as unobtrusively as the limited compass of the story permits. Sometimes, especially in the novels, the characters are brought out not only through direct description and dialogue but also indirectly through reminiscences. These reminiscences are given sometimes by the character in question, and on other occasions by someone else who plays a minor role in the story. This method of a 'flash back' is used by Sarat Chandra very skilfully. The structure of the story is fashioned in such a manner that the situations and the sequence of events make the reminiscences look perfectly natural.

Another device which is very skilfully used for an indirect portrayal of an important character is the introduction of letters within the story. In Rabindranath's novels too this method is sometimes employed. But Sarat uses this device more frequently and with greater ingenuity. In ***Srikanta,*** the early history of Annada Didi is not revealed until she completely disappears from the scene. After bidding a final farewell to Srikanta and Indranath she writes a letter explaining her association with the snake charmer. Her suffering takes on a new dimension in this letter. And the true magnitude of her loyalty and self-sacrifice is also communicated. The character of Abhaya is also revealed in a letter which Srikanta writes to Rajalakshmi. When we first encounter Abhaya on the deck of the Rangoon-bound ship, we get glimpses of her personality only through the description of her physical appearance, actions and remarks. But the strength and rebelliousness of her temperament are fully brought out only when we read Srikanta's letter to Rajalakshmi. The correspondence between Srikanta and Rajalakshmi is, in fact, one of the most interesting features of the entire novel. In their letters they communicate their innermost feelings, longings, values and preferences in a casual, informal and spontaneous manner.

Two other examples of this kind may be mentioned. In ***Devdas,*** the two leading characters have been separated. Parvati is married and lives in her husband's home in a remote village. Devdas is sinking deeper and deeper into dissipation. During a visit to his village Devdas meets Parvati's friend, Manorama. In a letter to Parvati, Manorama gives a pathetic account of Devdas's physical and moral decline. She also mentions the rumours that she has heard about the kind of life he leads in Calcutta. This letter not only leads to an important event in the story—Parvati's visit to Devdas in Calcutta—but also completes our picture of Devdas himself. Similarly, ***Bara Didi*** opens with a brief sketch of Surendra's childlike nature. We get further insights into his characters through his strange behaviour in the house of Brajaraj Babu where he is employed as Pramila's tutor. But his personality becomes much more vivid for us when we read Bara Didi's description of Surendranath in a letter to her friend (whose name, again, is Manorama). This letter also gives an indication of the duality in Madhavi's (i.e., Bara Didi's) own attitude. She refers to Surendra as a helpless child who is unable to look after himself and needs a mother's care. But Manorama reads between the lines and knows that her friend's concern for the tutor is more than maternal, that the spark of love has been kindled. (pp. 155-56)

The popular impression that Sarat Chandra is preoccupied with the lower middle classes is only partly correct. It is true that his observation and understanding of lower middle class people in Bengal is unusually keen. But in his stories we also have characters from the landed aristocracy, the princely families and the affluent sections of Calcutta society. At the other end of the spectrum we have landless peasants, beggars, mendicants, wandering singers, fishermen, snake-charmers, prostitutes and the oppressed *shudras* who perform the most menial and degrading tasks. His range is thus much broader than one tends to expect. The impression, particularly outside Bengal, is based on the fact that most of the stories which have been translated into other languages, or taken up by film producers, deal with the conflicts and tribulations of middle class people.

In spite of this wide range, however, we rarely come across men or women who can be described as wholly evil. Sarat's concern with the tragic aspect of life sometimes creates the impression that his approach to human nature is negative. But suffering, though often the result of human frailty, need not imply any denial of the basic goodness of human nature. Sarat Chandra is fully aware of the limitations of mankind. Even in his noblest characters there is a streak of fallibility, even ignorance. His heroes are not saintly. They are merely gentler, braver or more intelligent than their fellowmen. But on the other hand none of his villains are entirely evil. One rarely encounters in Sarat's novels or stories the prototype of the 'pure villain'. (p. 157)

In ***Srikanta,*** Abhaya's husband appears before us as a disgusting specimen. He is a liar and a cheat. He beats his wife and repays her loyalty with ingratitude. But even this man cannot be regarded as a villain. He is coarse, brutish. He does not have the low cunning which one associates with a typical villain. In many of Sarat Chandra's novels we have instances of extreme selfishness and callousness. Even old women sometimes display these tendencies. Elokeshi in ***Bindur Chhele*** shields her wicked son and is a silent spectator of the tragic events that take place in Bindu's house through her son's evil influence. In ***Chandranath,*** the aunt who has barged in, and taken charge of the household, treats Chandranath's wife Sarayu, very unkindly. When Sarayu's past is revealed she does not rest content until she has driven the poor girl out of the house. But such harshness is not uncommon in Hindu families. It is one of the tragic paradoxes of Hindu society that old people can be so heartless. In ***Grihadaha,*** Suresh commits the most horrible crimes. He sets fire to the house of his dearest friend and seduces his wife. But he gives up his life in a plague-afflicted village where he uses his medical skill to tend the victims of the epidemic. Perhaps the only character who can be described as totally evil is Mathura Babu, the manager of Surendra's *zamindari,* in ***Bara Didi.*** In him we see an appalling combination of cruelty and cunning. He keeps his master preoccupied with the help of his boon companions and hangers-on. His greed leads him to accept a bribe from the man who has taken possession of Madhavi's house and farm. He squeezes the last penny out of the impoverished tenants, forges accounts, and is totally indifferent to the sufferings of a helpless widow.

But Mathura Babu is an exception. In the world of Sarat Chandra the nobler side of human nature finds expression much more vividly. It is significant that those men or women who may be described as evil usually play minor roles in Sarat's stories. The leading parts are taken up by people who are capable of self-sacrifice, fortitude, wisdom and compassion. They show us how one can retain an inward innocence in the midst of intrigue, how one can endure limitless suffering with a smile upon one's lips. A person who seems to be very complex, full of contradictions, may yet remain basically guileless. It may sound paradoxical, but psychological complexity may go hand in hand with simplicity of the heart. In Sarat's work we see a great fascination for the simple hearted. It is not surprising, therefore, that he shows a deep understanding of a child's mind. In childhood, and even in boyhood, one can be utterly self-centred without resorting to clever rationalisation or polished deceit.

The point raised above deserves a little further attention. In two of his finest stories, ***Ramer Sumati*** **('Rama's Reformation')** and ***Bindur Chhele*** **('Bindu's Son'),** we get masterly portrayals of children—not very small children, but those who are on the verge of adolescence. Ramlal in the former story, and Amulya in the latter, are both extremely mischievous. Both are deeply attached to their foster-mothers. Their pranks cause deep distress to their parents and often result in severe punishment. They are subject to fits of rage. They cannot discriminate between right and wrong. Amulya is, in fact, on the point of being completely spoilt through the bad influence of his elder cousin. But in each case we see the triumph of their essentially innocent childlike natures. In each story there is an old woman—grandmother Digambari in ***Ramer Sumati*** and aunt Elokeshi in ***Bindur Chhele***—who drives the child to despair and stubbornness through a lack of understanding. But love saves the situation.

For an even more perceptive treatment of boyhood we must turn to the first part of ***Srikanta*** and follow the career of Indranath. Indeed, Indranath is one of Sarat's finest character-creations. We see in him all the typical characteristics of a child's nature: restlessness and longing for freedom; the tendency to fantasise and live in a dream world; the ability to remain completely absorbed in a single idea for a brief period, and then forget all about it; but, in addition to these qualities Indranath has two others which few children have—boundless courage and an amazing capacity for self-sacrifice. (pp. 158-60)

Like Rabindranath, Sarat Chandra has drawn his women characters more skilfully and vividly than his men. He has not only lavished upon his women all the resources of his art but has also treated them with great tenderness and compassion. This is true even with regard to those women who play minor roles in his novels. Sarat Chandra's heroines show a good deal of diversity in their temperaments, talents, and physical appearances. But we also see in them certain common features. For one thing, most of them retain a basic honesty and candour—a 'goodness' of the heart—in spite of all their failures and faults. I have already pointed out that the 'pure villain' is practically non-existent in Sarat's world. In the portrayal of his women characters Sarat seems to have kept in mind, all the more clearly, the soul of goodness in things evil. His women often fall. They are guilty of serious errors of judgement and cause a good deal of suffering to others, including their loved ones. But they are not malicious. And they are rarely cruel. Surprisingly, when we do encounter harshness or pettiness it is in the old women—aunts, mothers-in-law, even grandmothers—rather than the young.

Another feature which is common to most of Sarat's female characters is their adherence to the religious and social traditions which they inherit. . . . Undoubtedly, his women characters are often shown as victims of the social system. They are under the pressure of forces beyond their control. But it would be a mistake to imagine that their submission is only the result of helplessness. They do not merely adapt and adjust. They also approve. This may appear strange because of the tremendous suffering which they undergo. But it should be remembered that, in India, suffering itself has never been regarded in an entirely negative light. . . . Sometimes they rebel against some particularly obnoxious aspects of tradition. But the rebellion is always partial, controlled. It is never directed against the system in its entirety. There are two ways of appraising this attitude. On the one hand it may be asserted that partial rebellion is fruitless and does not bring any tangible reward. But on the other hand, it must also be conceded that this restraint saves them from alienation, from the emptiness which results from being totally uprooted from one's moorings.

What we see in Sarat Chandra's heroines is not so much the *inability* as the *refusal* to revolt. With the single exception of Abhaya (in ***Srikanta***), they consciously remain within the framework of the world-view which, in spite of all their frustrations, they regard as the only one that can be satisfying if life is understood in its totality. They do not lack either courage or strength. Those critics who ascribe the submissiveness of Sarat's women characters to cowardice or weakness simply fail to understand the Indian point of view on this question. From the Buddha to Mahatma Gandhi it has been emphasised again and again in India that it takes tremendous courage and inner strength to accept a compromise. To be able to accept suffering without bitterness is surely the mark of self-control rather than timidity. And self-control is inconceivable without strength. Sometimes the suffering endured by the heroines in Sarat's novels reveals a grandeur which overwhelms the reader. This grandeur is not dimmed by the fact that the devotion and loyalty which lead to the suffering are directed towards men totally unworthy of such sentiments. (pp. 164-66)

[Sarat] deals with real women, with all their imperfections as well as excellences. This applies not merely to his depiction of mental or spiritual qualities but also to the physical appearances of his heroines. They have charm, graciousness, even a certain luminosity. But they are not paragons of beauty. We do not come upon any heavenly nymphs in the world of Sarat Chandra. Most of the women have dark complexions. They are, on the whole, quite typical of Bengali womanhood so far as physical appearance goes. They have long, jet-black hair. And many of them have fine expressive eyes. Their gait is rhythmical but rarely seductive. And yet, in spite of the common characteristics which they seem to share, each is unique and distinctive. Each compels attention and is beautiful in her own way. In some of his novels Sarat Chandra describes the beauty of the leading female characters in various contexts and under different circumstances so that the pictures continue to become increasingly vivid from chapter to chapter. The result is that his heroines—in their physical attractiveness no less than in other aspects of their personalities—leave the impression of being unusual, sometimes even extraordinary, but always perfectly credible. (p. 168)

Character-creation itself, in one of its important aspects, is a special form of description. It is description of the inner world, of thoughts and feelings. Let us now take a look at Sarat Chandra's art as reflected in his description of the objective world. We find two features in common between his description of the human mind and of the world in which his characters live. In the first place, we see in both types of description a combination of broad, impressionistic portrayal and minute observation of detail. Just as he can condense an entire personality in a few well-chosen words, so also can he create a vivid picture of an entire village, or forest or hermitage with a few sweeping strokes of his pen. And again, just as in his character-creation we often get striking examples of detailed analysis, so also in his description we find close attention to minute detail. The furniture in a room, the contents of a wayside shop, the costume of an actor in a folk-play, the sound of a canoe paddled in shallow water, a communal feast in a village and a fight between two canine claimants for the leavings—such small bits of life are described in a leisurely, unhurried manner. Sarat Chandra does not miss the trees for the wood.

Secondly, in his description of the external world, Sarat Chandra shows the same awareness of change and transformation which we noted in his character-creation. Nature and human life are viewed in a state of continuous flow. Through this ability to catch the fleeting, growing, changing aspects of the world, Sarat Chandra endows his descriptions with a quality of dynamism rare in modern Indian literature. He is not particularly skilful in creating images of serenity. Here and there we do get a sense of calmness in his descriptive passages. But this is not one of his strong points. It is the world of excitement, agitation and movement which seems to be of primary interest to him. (p. 175)

In view of this fascination for flux, it is not surprising that we see in Sarat's novels and stories so many people on the move. Some of his finest descriptions are of people who are travelling. And the modes of locomotion which they use are as diverse as the purposes of their travels. . . .

[Though] human life is Sarat's principal concern, he also gives us some fine descriptions of nature. Some of these show the awesome aspect of nature—the swirling current of a river in flood, the strange sounds of the jungle at night, the vultures waiting with eager anticipation on the trees of a cremation ground. But we rarely see nature 'red in tooth and claw'. Most of the pictures that linger in our minds depict the gentle, harmonious and beautiful side of nature. The river and the forest are Sarat's favourite natural phenomena. Mountains play a negligible part in his stories. Most of the time, the action takes place in the verdant river valleys of Bengal and Bihar. In his description of trees, climbers, willows, and flowering shrubs, Sarat's style acquires a poetic quality. Nature, however, is rarely seen in isolation from humanity. (p. 176)

[Sarat Chandra] was not a transcendent genius, nor was he a man of universal vision. But he was a highly talented man, and in his own chosen field of fiction he must be recognised as a great master. Some of his stories, and at least two of his novels—***Srikanta*** and ***Grihadaha***—have an unmistakably classic flavour. They will endure. His love for the common man, keenness of observation, superb character-creation, deep insight into the fundamentals of Indian life, bold realism, and the skill with which he uses his artistic talent in exposing shams and hypocrisies: these qualities have exerted a significant influence in modern Bengali literature. Some of these qualities were sorely needed at a time when many writers were groping for a synthesis between the traditional and the modern, between social involvement and recognition of the unusual and the unpredictable. (p. 178)

Vishwanath S. Naravane, in his Sarat Chandra Chatterji: An Introduction to His Life and Work *(© Vishwanath S Naravane, 1976), The Macmillan Company of India Limited, 1976, 182 p.*

SHIBDAS GHOSH (essay date 1977)

[Ghosh was a prominent Marxist philosopher. In the following excerpt, he offers an evaluation of Chatterji's literature and finds that the Indian author's work is based on a philosophy of secular humanism.]

If we want to evaluate scientifically Saratchandra's literature or, for that matter, the literary thoughts and works of any litterateur we should always keep in mind the particular time and the particular historical phase of social development, that is the particular time and social environment, in which that litterateur appeared and created his literature. We shall commit a great mistake if we try to discuss or evaluate the thoughts and the philosophy of life of any litterateur independent of his time and social environment. Because, human thoughts and ideas are conditioned by the limits of time, space and the social environment. Man's power of thinking is, no doubt, infinite and knows no bounds, but this 'boundlessness' or 'infinite power' is, in reality, limited by the limits of a given material condition or environment, that is conditioned by the given time and space. (p. 7)

Otherwise, we shall have to accept that there are some original, fundamental, unchangeable elements in human thoughts and values of life which are not subject to change with the change of time, space, environment, etc—that is not conditioned or governed by material condition—so independent of time, space, environment and hence eternal. I consider such a notion as unscientific and faulty. (p. 8)

I would say that in our country Saratchandra is the only literary personality who, in the domain of literature, most boldly and consistently held high the lofty banner of social revolution and most devotedly fought for its accomplishment. Other litterateurs talked of social revolution, no doubt, but did not perform, in the literary field, the very necessary tasks to bring it about. They could not make people unquestionably realise, through their literature, the futility of the old social order by evoking in their minds pain and anguish, sense of deprivation and longing for a better and higher social order. It was Saratchandra who alone accomplished this task quite successfully in our country. That is why Saratchandra was the main target of the most virulent attacks from the defenders of the old society. . . . The thought and literature which, with a view to bringing about a change in the mental makeup and outlook of the people, were acting against the old customs, prejudices and sense of morality of the old Hindu society, while maintaining all through the closest kinship with it, were none else than Saratchandra's literature and his thought. (p. 14)

And how strange! A critic of Bengali literature does not feel any qualm to comment that Saratchandra is a *pakshalar sahityik* [a writer whose works lack intellectual elements and are not thought-provoking]! And now-a-days our students read these types of criticisms of Saratchandra. Naturally, what else can they be other than 'big pundits'! To go by this type of critics it would seem as if Saratchandra's literature has no base conception and no well-conceived philosophy of life. It is, of course, true that in his stories and novels Saratchandra did never use high sounding phrases unintelligible to the common people. He sought to instil in the minds of the people the very essence of the higher ideas and concepts but always through the most artistic creation of *rasa*—feeling that is sublime, aesthetic and artistic—by creating compassion, pain and anguish in the minds of the readers so that it does not become imperative for one to take the aid of intellect. Those who can grasp intellectually, for them there are lots of theoretical writings on science and epistemology. Then wherein lies the utility of literature? The necessity of literature lies precisely in making a niche, even within the subtle sensibilities and delicate feelings of men, by making the realisation of truth and higher thoughts acquired through theoretical analyses sublime in the form of stories through the medium of rasa beautifully blossomed in a multitude of forms and channels with super-artistic excellence. (p. 15)

For instance, humanism once brought in its wake the concept of ethical motherhood. Saratchandra knew that all these lofty concepts were there in different books in the form of theories. But most of the people, even after studying these, often fail to grasp their essence. He sought to inscribe in the minds of the people the loftiest ideas of that age by creating and helping to realise the finest feelings of aesthetics, by awakening pathos and compassion, working upon the contradictions and conflicts that take place centring round life, the complexities that develop in human relationship and the waves and turmoils that grow in the feelings and emotions of human mind. Those who can grasp through studies and intellect, for them there is no problem. But those who cannot—the vast section of the masses—they can grasp any lofty idea if catered to them through the medium of *rasa*. (pp. 15-16)

In his literary thinking, Saratchandra was essentially a secular humanist, not a Marxist. The thoughts and ideas which we, the communists, so fondly cherish today were not reflected in Saratchandra's literature. So it is pointless to discuss, while evaluating Saratchandra's literature, whether he reflected proletarian culture and voiced the idea of working class revolution or not. Those who, off and on, raise this sort of question while evaluating Saratchandra's literature do actually muddle the whole thing by indulging in what is utterly irrelevant. Here the point is: Who had represented the most progressive trend of humanist thinking during the national independence struggle of our country? That is, in the then Indian condition, who actually reflected the most progressive thoughts and ideas of the bourgeois humanism? Were they not the petty bourgeois revolutionaries? Petty bourgeois revolutionism, in those days, was the most progressive trend of thinking in bourgeois humanism and Saratchandra in the main reflected that very trend in his literature. So, in our country it was Saratchandra's literature in which was reflected the highest standard of the most progressive thoughts and culture of the bourgeois humanism. Still then how close did he come to the working class thoughts and ideas! During the last phase of his life, working class movement had already grown in our country. So, had there been a great Marxist leader like Lenin at that time to provide correct guidelines to our literature, it would not have been altogether impossible that proletarian literature might have grown in our country through Saratchandra as was the case with Gorky in Russia. And in that case, it would have been of much higher standard because, in artistic skill, Saratchandra was undoubtedly much superior to Gorky.

In this context, I would like to cite a few illustrations from Saratchandra's literature. Whatever may be the literary value of ***Srikanta*** from the point of view of reflecting the humanist values and high cultural-ethical standard of those days, what is its worth in terms of proletarian culture? Still then we find that in the third part of ***Srikanta,*** where the construction of a railway track is described, the spontaneous indignation with which Srikanta bursts out, observing the wretched condition of the workers with whom he had to spend a night in slums, reflects not the humanist thinking, but something more—a higher thought and culture. For example, seeing the sub-human and distressed condition of the workers Srikanta says: "You, the carriers of modern civilisation, you die! Forgive not, not in the least, this cruel civilisation that has made your life such. If you are to carry it, carry it down speedily to the abysmal depth of its grave."

In ***Pather Dabi,*** too, the outlook Saratchandra expressed about labour movement, though not fully consistent with the Marxist understanding, does undoubtedly reflect a strong voice of protest against economism and reformism in labour movement. . . . Here he has clearly shown that those who organise workers' movements just for wage-increase and reforms, do greatest harm to the workers' cause under the garb of sympathy and thereby they virtually oppose the revolution itself.

In **Pather Dabi,** Saratchandra ventilated, from various angles, some aspects of his philosophical view-points. From those it appears as if he was going to supersede the limit of humanist thinking. Today the humanist values have assumed a stagnant character. Bourgeois humanism has given birth to some 'unchangeable', 'absolute' concepts about right and wrong, about ethics and aesthetics. The concepts and ideas which grew and developed out of the necessity of the bourgeois revolution to meet the needs of the revolutionary transformation of capitalist production subsequently became obsolete with the attempt of the humanists to arrest these by attributing absolute and permanent values to them. Although the Marxist concepts of ethics, morality and aesthetics have historical continuity, no doubt, with the humanist concepts of ethics, morality and aesthetics—but still then there is a break as these are two distinctly different ideological categories. According to the dialectical materialist or Marxist concept, 'necessity' does not mean pragmatic necessity, the petty interest of an individual; it grows out of objective reality, in the light of which the correctness or otherwise of any social idea, concept or ideology is determined. In **Pather Dabi** we find a trend of thinking and pattern of reasoning almost similar to this concept. It is true that the dominant thinking of Saratchandra was bourgeois revolutionism and militant humanism expressed through 'anarchism' in the then social condition of our country, but, still then, in this novel he tends even to supersede, here and there, the bourgeois humanist thinking and like startling sparks some aspects of communist thinking and ideas flashed in him. See, what Sabyasachi says in **Pather Dabi:** "There is nothing like absolute or eternal truth in this ever-changing world. It comes into being and goes out of being. With passage of time, from one age to another, it undergoes changes and assumes newer and newer forms in conformity with the changing needs of human society. The truth of the past must be adhered to in the present—such a belief is erroneus, the notion superstitious." This very concept of truth and method of reasoning of Saratchandra reveal a great deal of influence of dialectical materialism, communist thoughts and ideas and reasoning in him. (pp. 37-40)

To meet the need of the hour, if you are to give birth to the proletarian culture and proletarian literature which may be called the post-Rabindra and post-Saratchandra literature, you can do it only when you have been able to realize thoroughly and exhaust completely the most revolutionary trend of humanist literature which was reflected in Saratchandra, that is when you would be able to exhaust in the process of assimilating in you all the essence of the revolutionary humanist values reflected in Saratchandra's literature. Only then you will be able to give birth to the most advanced culture of the present era—the proletarian culture. (p. 45)

Shibdas Ghosh, in his An Evaluation of Saratchandra *(reprinted by permission of the Socialist Unity Centre of India; originally published as* Saratcandrera mūhyāyana prasaṅge*), 1977, 48 p.*

BIRENDRA KUMAR BHATTACHARYYA (essay date 1977)

[Bhattacharyya discusses Chatterji's aims and the evolution of his thought as reflected in his works.]

Saratchandra's importance as an artist lies precisely in his pioneering role in the realm of Indian social novel. He chose his raw materials from society and viewed society from the standpoint of a committed artist. He had faith in the innate wisdom of the common man and this provided the motive force of the characters in his earlier novels. However, towards the end of his career he accepted the position of a conscious artist who saw the dynamic of social change in the rise of the labouring humanity. This is clear in his later novel **Pathēr Dābī.**

He did not confine his experience in the narrow mould of a particular class, but broadened his range to include the whole gamut of social experience. He believed in change. He saw in sex relationship the essence of all human relationships and it is through depiction of contradictions within this relationship that he emphasised the necessity of social change. The structure of his best sex novels was non-cathartic; its effect on the minds of the readers was generally one of non-relief and this induced a feeling of necessity for urgent social change. This structure is met with in **Śrīkānta** and **Pallī-Samāj.** On the other hand, in his later novels like **Pathēr Dābī** and **Śēṣ Praśna** this feeling of necessity is expressed directly within a cathartic structure. **Pallī-Samāj** induces in us a feeling of social reform and a desire for better social order only indirectly. In **Śēṣ Praśna** or **Pathēr Dābī,** it is, however, explicitly stated through dialogue.

His art was dynamic. In the first half of the twentieth century, the social reform movement gradually gave way to the radical political movement for the freedom of India. In Pallī-Samāj, one feels a strong impact of the social reform movement; Ramēś believed that the rural society could be revitalised through sustained social work. It further gives us insight into the author's belief in the potency of innate wisdom of the common man. In **Śrīkānta,** too, this truth is revealed through the bold action of Abhayā in rejecting her unfaithful husband. But in **Pathēr Dābī** and **Śēṣ Praśna,** one finds that the major characters no longer stand by social reform, but advocate a revolutionary change in the basic institutions of society. Apūrba or Harēndra is as good a social worker as Ramēś, but both of them are out of tune with the revolutionary atmosphere of the two novels. Sabyasāchi no longer believes in the innate wisdom of the peasantry or the common man and their capacity for revolutionising the existing order; instead he places explicit faith in the conscious organisation of revolutionary elements. Similarly, Kamal in **Śēṣ Praśna** pleads for a conscious and fundamental change in man-woman relationship. Here Rājēn carries forward the banner of ceaseless work of social change.

As an artist, his success lies precisely in the power of harmonisation of contradictions within the social reality. He had a gift of imagination. The limited social range of the novel **Grhadāha** notwithstanding, this power of harmonisation is best expressed here. He balances here the opposed impulses of passion and convention in a fine manner. However, the aesthetic dimension here is more significant than the sociological dimension. It is essentially a middle class story of genuine passion and love, and thus expresses only an aspect of total social reality. In **Pallī-Samāj** we get an integrated picture of the rural society in transition but it is still confined to the orbit of Hindu social experience. As we move towards the worlds of **Śēṣ Praśna** and **Pathēr Dābī,** we enter into the esoteric societies far removed from the basic day-to-day reality of Bengali life from which he mainly derived his raw materials. In these novels, the desire for fundamental change is expressed mainly through dialogue and partly through idealistic action. Kamal expounds her philosophy of free love before the immigrant Bengali society of Agra, while Sabyasāchi expresses his idea of Indian revolution in the terrorist club of Rangoon. The author tried here to transcend the limits of a middle class society with an ideological sweep rare among his contemporaries. The structure of **Mahēś** is, however, such that here no resort to ideas would enable the writer to transcend the middle class world. So he uses the contradictions inherent within the casteridden rural society of Bengal to bring out the essential dynamic of social change inherent in the mind of suffering humanity. Here we get a plausible and realistic picture of the society and a suggestion for its fundamental change.

The popularity of Saratchandra is precisely due to his conscious or unconscious commitment to the basic social values. He was a pioneer among the social novelists of Bengal and has been since a source of inspiration to many.

Some critics point towards the apparent deficiencies in Saratchandra's art. But these deficiencies do not seem to be basic. Let us take some concrete examples. Gaphur of ***Mahēś*** seems to be the only major character (in the whole range of Saratchandra's literature) who belongs to the exploited labouring humanity. The story creates a closed and unified universe in which the main character survives all challenges to his existence. This world resembles the real world, but the different elements like space, time, conflict, movement of the plot, and the atmosphere get fused and unified within its contour. Oblivious of this aesthetical harmony, some may remain dissatisfied and ask for a more radical attitude or action on the part of uprooted and pauperised peasant hero. Similarly, the critics may deplore Ramā's failure to marry Ramēś in ***Pallī-Samāj.*** Others may resent Rājēn's almost inconsequential role in ***Śēṣ Praśna,*** or get hurt at Kiraṇmayī's sad fate in slipping into a state of madness. But the critics will be found wrong here, for the purpose of the writer was to use these disagreeable situations as means towards an end. Evidently, to ask these questions is to imply a direction of social change. This is the usual method with which a non-cathartic novel aims at creating a desirable effect on the reader's mind. The creative process in this type of novels involves simultaneous rejection of the hideous existence and affirmation of life at the aesthetic level. Gaphur rejects the sordid feudal world in which he lives, but accepts the continuity of life in the emerging incipient world. This is the way in which an artist expresses his spirit of rebellion. Some of the novels of Saratchandra have tragic ends, while others have either comic or idealistic ends. Whatever the ends, his novels usually affirm life and its values. Life triumphs finally over death or destruction in almost all his significant novels. (pp. 8-10)

In Saratchandra's novels, the space-time world of everyday world is not depicted beyond what is absolutely necessary, as his art is oriented towards the interior reality of the human mind. But he is too conscious and pragmatic an artist to yield to the temptation of producing a pure novel of interior reality. An analysis of his love stories shows that the bodily and mental elements in them are usually presented in a finely balanced manner. He does not aim at creating a higher form of poetic harmony after the manner of Rabindranath, nor does he degrade the unity to the lower level of an ordinary love or crime story. He avoids both the extremes and maintains an even course.

It is wrong to seek something from his work which he does not aim at creating or which is usually beyond his art. This will merely show the limitations of one's critical attitude. Judged in the light of history, his literary world-view seems to be moulded by the social reality of the first half of the twentieth century and it is based on the middle class consciousness. However, he constantly endeavoured to go beyond the ken of this middle class existence and had a wide knowledge of the rural life and culture. His women characters mostly belong to this milieu and they are typical. It would not be wrong to conclude that his experience of life was more varied and richer than those of his contemporaries.

Comparatively speaking, novel is a new genre in Indian literature. Its importance as an art form was recognised only when the pace of social change was faster. Saratchandra learnt his art from the Western masters as well as from his Indian predecessors, but he adapted it suitably to his needs. His outlook was humane, and he viewed the Indian society from the standpoint of a humanist. One of the characteristics of the Indian society is the caste system, and he was one of those writers who first drew our pointed attention to the evils associated with it. ***Bāmunēr Mēyē*** offers us a stringent criticism of these evils. A number of his characters like Nyāyaratna in ***Mahēś*** and the homicidal consort of Annadādidi in ***Śrīkānta*** are conservative, and their violence and cruelties repel us. On the other hand, Biśwēśwarī, Ramā and Rājlakṣmī, etc., retain their traditional old world virtues and humanity, despite their avowed conservative outlook. The progressive characters in his novels, similarly, are not free from foibles or contradictions. Kiraṇmayī in ***Charitrahīn*** seems to lack inherent strength to stand the strains of the new and unorthodox way of life. Kamal of ***Śēṣ Praśna*** is no doubt depicted as his alter-ego, but she lives more in the world of ideas than in the world of day-to-day reality. The author's comments on the rebellion of Bēlā against the marital injustice of her husband seem to be revealing. He opines that the divorcee is not really free as she is dependent on her former consort for her living. He was ever alert to detect the inadequacies and contradictions of the old and new living, and his specific aim in doing this was to depict the inherent conflicts in striving for a better life. His women characters reveal these conflicts in a striking manner. Saratchandra's art has thus a significance and his successors may very well learn from it the secret of selecting and using raw materials of art from the society in which they live. (p. 10)

Birendra Kumar Bhattacharyya, "Saratchandra's Art," in The Golden Book of Saratchandra: A Centenary Commemorative Volume, *Manik Mukhopadhyay, General Editor, All Bengal Sarat Centenary Committee, 1977, pp. 8-10.*

KAMALA SANKRITYAYAN (essay date 1977)

[Sankrityayan examines Chatterji's feminist concerns.]

Saratchandra has always tried to give his women characters their freedom—if not social, then at least literary freedom. His contribution in this respect is unchallenged. He puts forward in a straight, simple, clear and strong argument his thoughts on women. There is novelty in his arguing methods. Therefore, in his writing, there is to be found both social thinking as well as literary merit.

Saratchandra has created many kinds of female characters in his novels. No other writer except Saratchandra has written making women the central point of his works. Therefore, in the world of fiction, the female characters created by Saratchandra have their own place and importance. The controversial aspects of women's life, which have been narrated, receive a very sensitive expression in his fiction. It is evident that Saratchandra has made a great effort through his novels for the emancipation of women in Bengal. Future social historians will accept this truth in the coming years. The tragedy of Indian women undeniably inspired Saratchandra's art. He is always aware of and often describes so vividly the debased condition of women of his time. And so he expresses his sympathy for women through the medium of his novels.

But though Saratchandra emphasised the great importance and value of women in his essay ***Nārīr Mūlya,*** he always links women's importance with men's life. He does not talk anywhere about an independent place for women alone. Perhaps this is the reason why many of his novels are named after their heroes, for example ***Chandranāth, Bipradās, Śrīkānta, Dēbdās, Kāśīnāth,*** etc.

In all his works except ***Charitrahīn, Śrīkānta,*** and ***Grhadāha,*** Saratchandra has followed the traditional style. The writer of ***Kāśīnāth, Dēbdās, Chandranāth, Parinītā, Baṛadidi, Mējdidi, Bindur Chhēlē, Rāmēr Sumati, Birāj Bau,*** and ***Niskrti,*** has almost in all of his works written the story of the struggle within Bengali families. In some of his works he describes clearly the lack of importance for love in these loveless and strained families, and whenever love is being described, Saratchandra excellently depicts what is pure, unexpressed and untold.

A detailed study of Saratchandra's female characters is a clear introduction to his mode of thinking about women. Women and love are alter egos. There is, however, no place for sex in Saratchandra's novels. The love and affection between his male and female characters is sexless, and they live within a platonic love. Therefore, we see in Saratchandra's literature the flowing currents of love, but no unclean stream of sex.

We should here classify the female characters of Saratchandra's literature for a more detailed study:

> 1. Loving mothers who are widowed in their middle age.
>
> 2. The cruel natured women with harsh tongues.
>
> 3. The simple hearted loving women who are of three categories, that is, unmarried, married, and widowed.
>
> 4. The serious type of women who do not accept the deepness of love and who think all love a big sin.
>
> 5. Old, quarrelsome, talkative women.
>
> (pp. 130-31)

Among the first type of women, that is loving mothers, Hēmānginī of ***Mējdidī*** Bhubanēśwarī of ***Parinīta,*** Nārāyanī of ***Rāmēr Sumati*** and Dayāmayī of ***Bipradās*** are notable. All these women are, according to their nature, very soft and sentimental. Although their bodies are mortal, made up of flesh and bones, their hearts brim with unlimited affection and love. The women of this category shower their love and affection not only on their own children, but on all other children too. This affectionate nature of women is depicted with all its glory in ***Mējdidi's*** Hēmāṅginī. (p. 131)

In the second category of Saratchandra's female characters are women who are cruel and harsh voiced, their heart is full of selfishness and full of greed and cruelty. We can see in Kādambinī in ***Mējdidi*** this type of character.

We find the third category of women in all of Saratchandra's novels. They are women who are very simple, sober, with heart full of love and sincerity. Saratchandra has been idealistic in depicting this type of characters as typical of Indian women's good qualities. Some of them are married women who are symbols of virtue and purity. A woman of this kind can be found in the heroine of the novel ***Birāj Bau.*** She is a very bright character. The main sentiment of this novel is Birāj's strong character and this sentiment is betrayed in her love for her husband. She thinks herself more *satī* (chaste) than any other woman. This is her pride.

We also find some women who have been widowed since their childhood. Their existence is meaningless and they have been leading very sad lives. They are nevertheless human beings. So the fire of love is always burning in their hearts. They cannot go ahead with courage because of the fear of society. Their characters appear to us to be very weak. We can see this type of women, for example in Mādhabī of ***Baṛadidi.*** However, these women have all pure and simple hearts, and they are sentimental as they are moved by love.

Within the fourth category, we see those women who have a mysterious personality and it is very hard to define their character. Although they, too, were lovers once, their lack of simplicity makes them very hard to understand. The main strength of their character lies in their fighting against the traditional structure of life. Their character is very strong but dispassionate though there is passion hiding behind this 'dispassion'. Readers do not know when women of this type will change their minds. They are rebellious women who are indifferent towards virtue and tradition. We find this type of character in Kiraṇmayī of ***Charitrahīn.*** In ***Charitrahīn*** the writer has brought forward a kind of woman who is very different from his other female characters. The woman in Kiraṇmayī is pure in 'character'. In this character the writer does not show the woman devoted to her late husband, nor does he reveal her strong love to other people but he analyses her dispassionate heart. In this type of female characters of Saratchandra's we find wisdom as well as deep feelings towards society. The deeper we study Kiraṇmayī the closer we come to her heart's purity and sadness. (pp. 131-32)

[The] last group of women characters—those who are old, quarrelsome, talkative, harsh-voiced, those who are always free enough in their own idle lives to start fights within other people's households. This is typical of the ordinary and old Indian women. These are the women who have no creative mind but, instead, always destroy other people's happiness. They are inclined to anger and to quarrel frequently with others, especially other women. Usually brought up in an illiterate and uncultured atmosphere they are bitter characters. In this category fall the characters like Digambarī of ***Rāmēr Sumati,*** Swarṇamañjarī of ***Arakṣaṇīyā,*** and the old Baisnabi of ***Paṇḍit Maśāi.*** (p. 132)

The time when Saratchandra was writing his novels and short stories was a time of importance in the social history of Bengal. The people of Bengal during that period were much influenced by the reform movement or Renaissance. . . .

But this was not enough. The Bengali women of that period were still uneducated; although there were some facilities for obtaining an education, they were still unutilised. Child-marriage was very common at that time and the dowry system was also encouraged by society. In old Bengal, the birth of a daughter was regarded as an evil event for the family. Polygamy prevailed everywhere. A fourteen year old girl might have to marry a man of fifty or fifty-five years; this was nothing extraordinary.

During this period, Bengal came to have its first connection with the Western culture, and the struggle between two cultures intensified. The writers of that period raised their voices on seeing the pathetic plight of Bengali womanhood. But the struggle of Saratchandra was stronger than that of others, and more critical and more impressive too. He not only described the evils of his own society but also personified it in all its beauty and glory. He was no pessimist about the fate of society, and steadfastly spoke for women's rightful place in society with the help of persuasive intellectual argument. His essay on ***Nārīr Mūlya*** is the fruit of his deeper study of the thinking and the sentiment of all womanhood. He also knew how to separate good from evil and thus could accept the beauty from both old and new society.

Saratchandra has evaluated all this in his literature. The final aim of his work is to arouse the sympathy of husbands and to raise women to their rightful place in society. (p. 133)

Kamala Sankrityayan, "The Women in Saratchandra's Literature," in The Golden Book of Saratchandra: A Centenary Commemorative Volume, *Manik Mukhopadhyay, General Editor, All Bengal Sarat Centenary Committee, 1977, pp. 129-33.*

L STRIZHEVSKAYA (essay date 1977)

[*Strizhevskaya discusses* Pathēr Dābī *and* Śēṣ Praśna, *calling them two of the earliest sociopolitical novels in India. He also stresses Chatterji's concern in these works with the oppression of the working class by the bourgeoisie.*]

Along with R. Tagore, Chattopadhyay played an enormous role in creating the realistic socio-psychological novel. The leading theme in most of his works was the status of the woman. But in his first stage, the writer was only forming an idea of the problems arising out of this theme. In his second period, the suffering of those whose love turned out to be a violation of the accepted standards of conduct, became a magnifying glass, as it were, through which the writer was able to see the vices of the society of his day.

In a number of works of this second period ***(Pallī-Samāj*** and ***Bāmunēr Mēyē),*** he criticized the feudal setup and bourgeois money-grabbing ethics from far broader positions. We find in them a multifarious depiction of the village; the author likewise raises the problem of the exploitation of the peasants by the money-lenders and landlords.

Chattopadhyay's talent as a psychological genre writer was also manifested in the specific genre tales new to Bengali literature and depicting the life of the 'big family' of the middle class (***Niskrti, Bindur Chhēlē,*** and ***Rāmēr Sumati***).

In disclosing these themes, Chattopadhyay appeared as an innovator who facilitated the democratisation of Bengali literature, the awakening of interest in the life of the 'middle classes' and the peasantry, and compassion for those whom the society subjected to ostracism.

Chattopadhyay's treatment of the phenomena of life, his concepts of the human being show up the active humanism of this writer who boldly raised his voice against the grind of routine and for the triumph of the ethics.

As a rule, he limited himself to a statement of the problems, without offering any solutions to them, but, as Y. Payevskaya wrote, "even without the author's conclusions, by the realistic display of life and disclosure of its contradictions themselves" his works are "an accusation of the existing system which engenders oppression and injustice."

However, in the second period of his work there were works in which he tried to suggest his positive ideal, to find ways and means of delivering society from its evils, and of improving human relations. The novel ***Pallī-Samāj*** shows that in the matter of raising culture in the village the writer relied on the educational work of solitary intellectuals. In ***Grhadāha*** he sees the ethical ideal in the modernisation and humanisation of Hinduism.

A characteristic trait of the writer's artistic style is his deep psychological delineations. He achieves an authentic and deep conveyance of the heroes' thoughts and feelings not so much through description, as through the conduct and speech of the heroes. The dialogue invariably bears an enormous load in his works. Its important role was stipulated by the introduction into his work of the spoken language and, in some cases, of dialectical forms of speech, all of which served to democratise the language of literature.

The creation of typically national characters (in psychological makeup and outer manifestations), realistic reproduction of the general atmosphere and details of the Indian customs, posing of important problems of national life, and, lastly, close ties with the progressive social ideas of the country—these are the traits which made Chattopadhyay a deeply national writer. . . . (pp. 344-45)

Chattopadhyay approached the dividing line, which the twenties was for Bengali literature, as a writer with a well-defined creative individuality and clear-cut range of subjects. His popularity was great. And yet he was not satisfied. He felt that he had to write in a new way. The result of his quests was a greater genre diversity and extension of his theme. He wrote a number of works in a new style showing a deeper approach to social problems. Hence his realistic refined stories ***Mahēś*** and ***Abhāgīr Swarga.*** At the same time, a certain disconnectedness, inconsistency in elaborating his new artistic credo, led, at times, to the creation of rather weak works.

A special place in his works of this period was undoubtedly held by his novels ***Pathēr Dābī*** and ***Śēṣ Praśna.***

Pathēr Dābī was the first political novel in Bengali literature. It was the direct result of Chattopadhyay's adherence to the national liberation struggle and his subsequent disenchantment in the methods of non-cooperation and *satyagraha* [passive resistance]. In it, an attempt was made to supply the answer to the question of how to achieve India's independence in correspondence with the moods of the more revolutionary part of the petty bourgeois intelligentsia.

The road to independence, according to the hero of the novel, Sabyasāchī divides the political and socio-economic aims of the revolution, accepting only the first.

In the novel, the driving forces of the revolution are the intelligentsia. At the same time, the writer stresses that only a few of its representatives can sacrifice all for the sake of the idea. According to Sabyasāchī's concept, the peasantry is incapable of heroism and self-sacrifice, and therefore cannot take part in the national liberation movement. Here we can see that the writer, disappointed with the tactics and results of the national liberation movement of 1918-1922, transferred his disappointment to the masses as well, doubting whether they could hold out long.

That a certain place is relegated to the working class in the novel is, no doubt, a reflection of the fact that the working class recovered sooner than the others from the defeat of the national liberation movement. Chattopadhyay was the first in

Bengali literature to attempt to analyse the economic situation and the political role of the working class.

Comparing the chapters of the novel citing the life of the workers with M. Gorky's *Mother,* we find a certain coincidence of artistic vision. The scenes of poverty, moral depression, coarseness and hard drinking in it are akin to the description of life in the workers' district in *Mother*. Both novels show up the author's deep sympathy for the people whose lives were crippled by ruthless exploitation. The workers perceive the inhuman conditions of their life as something inevitable, and are wary of anything new and unusual, afraid that a strike may bring them nothing but suffering. Just as in Gorky's book, the enthusiasm and rightness of those who called upon the workers to resist, to fight for their rights, kindle in the hearts of the people a timid spark of protest and faith in themselves.

The arguments used by Talwārkār in addressing the workers coincide with the ideas expressed by Andrei Nakhodka in Gorky's *Mother*.

These observations cause us to believe that Chattopadhyay was familiar with Gorky's novel, and this had definitely influenced him in his treatment of the subject of the working class. (pp. 345-46)

Pathēr Dābī attracts attention first and foremost by dint of its political colouring. But it also treats of social aspects. The criticism of caste rule is here conducted from three angles: caste prejudices as a serious obstruction to personal happiness; as something contradicting the demands of modern life; and as an obstruction on the road to serving one's country.

The political and social significance of the novel can hardly be overrated.

An interesting artistic peculiarity of the novel consists in that its social problems are incarnated in images created by realistic means, and the political problems, in romantically uplifted albeit statical images (with the exception of Talwārkār). The point is that in expressing his political views, the writer proceeded not from the reality he knew, but from his ideals or 'anti-ideals' (the images of Sabyasāchī, Sumitrā and Brajēndra).

Noteworthy, also, is the fact that over a third of the novel lies beyond its seeming compositional termination. This part was necessary to the writer in order more clearly to express his views on the political problems. Everything is subordinated to this aim, and the action develops sluggishly. The artistic faults are obviously the result of the novelty of the genre, the absence of a corresponding tradition. And yet the writing of ***Pathēr Dābī*** was of enormous significance to the development of literature. The novel marked the beginning of the politicalisation of literature, paved the way to the political novel of the future.

The twenties was a time of active literary development in Bengal. The works of the young writers, at first united within the framework of the 'ati adhunik' ['ultra-modern'] trend, served as the reason for literary polemics in which R. Tagore and S. Chattopadhyay took part from diverse positions. Not only because of their different world outlooks and aesthetic ideals, but also because already then the works of the 'young' contained the rudiments of different trends. Tagore accented the 'impropriety' of replacing the ideal of beauty with ugliness, and Chattopadhyay stressed the innovatory and social role of the literature of the 'ati adhunik'. Actually, they spoke of the rudiments of different trends: modernism and progressive literature.

Both writers replied to this controversy with their work: Tagore with his novel *Śēṣēr Kabitā,* and Chattopadhyay with his ***Śēṣ Praśna.*** The main problem of the latter novel was the possibility and practical feasibility of preserving, under modern conditions, the traditional, spiritual and ethical values. Formerly often holding a dual position in this question, the writer now replies to it in the sharp negative. This position is prompted by his deep concern for the welfare of his country.

The change in the views of Chattopadhyay on religion was evident in his ***Pathēr Dābī,*** whose hero believes that religion engenders in men timidity and impotence, and obstructs the consolidation of the nation. In ***Śēṣ Praśna,*** the discrowning of the religious institutions became the leading theme. The writer depicted a heroine no longer the victim of conservatism as in his earlier works, but who actively fought against it. The moral code, free thinking and atheism of this woman were something entirely new, untypical of the times. That is probably why the author made her half-English, simultaneously stressing her Indian patriotism. Chattopadhyay endowed Kamal with broad erudition unusual in a woman of those days, and this enables her to conduct a controversy touching not only upon moral problems, but also on problems of the national life. In her arguments, she always wins out over her opponents. Presenting Kamal as a kind of ethical ideal, the writer likewise endowed her with a great many positive qualities. (pp. 346-47)

The novel also tries to show what the champion of independence ought to be like. Obviously, fearing that ***Śēṣ Praśna*** might experience the lot of ***Pathēr Dābī,*** which was censured, Chattopadhyay wrote of this problem in a veiled way. The author's 'anti-ideal' is incarnated in the depiction of 'asram'. To this is opposed the somewhat mysterious image of the revolutionary Rājēndra, a member of an underground organisation. The image of Rājēndra, like that of Sabyasāchī, is insufficiently revealed in his actions. Striving to remedy this fault, the writer here too resorts to a characterisation of Rājēndra through the opinions of the people around him, whose great respect he enjoys, regardless of whether they share his views or not, and stresses his outer likeness to Gōrā. It is noteworthy that the author places Rājēndra higher than Kamal. His image contains the revolutionary spirit of the youth. The author wishes to stress their patriotism, courage, selflessness, to call upon them to be purposeful, resolute, organised and disciplined in the cause of the struggle for independence. All these features are opposed to the qualities cultivated in the pupils of 'asram'. (pp. 347-48)

In the concept of man, as it is disclosed in the novel, the evolution of Chattopadhyay's humanism is vividly manifested, since from pity and compassion for man he progresses in his works towards the assertion of the personality of a new type actively participating in the transformation of life.

From the viewpoint of its ideological content, the novel is an exceptional phenomenon. It should be appraised as the writer's civil exploit. At the same time, ***Śēṣ Praśna*** marks the development in Bengali literature of a new genre—the publicistic social-philosophical novel. The sources of the philosophically social novel undoubtedly lie in Tagore's *Gōrā*. But *Gōrā* has been based upon historical material while ***Śēṣ Praśna,*** the first work representing this genre, is entirely devoted to the problems of vital importance for the contemporaries.

Chattopadhyay studiedly paid no attention to the development of the plot, and packed it with controversies. However, as a result, the dialogue, hardly reflecting the inner life of the characters, 'swallowed' the development of most of the characters, which renders them statical. All this, in the final analysis, is the result of posing too many problems. Nor is this a case apart in Indian literature.

In the novel, the peculiarities of educational and critical realism are interwoven. On the other hand, here, as in ***Pathēr Dābī,*** the author uses the artistic methods of romanticism.

The application by critical realism of the artistic means of romanticism and educational realism is a phenomenon fully logical in a literature which took to the path of critical realism later than in the rest of the world, and developed fast. This phenomenon is stipulated by the incompletion of the stages of romanticism and educational realism in the given literature, and the preservation of social-political conditions, whose reaction these artistic methods were.

Despite the existing opinion about the limitations of Chattopadhyay's creative diapason he is, to my mind, a versatile writer who shows a sensitive reaction to the throbbing pulse of his time. His works of different periods reveal close ties with the awakening of Bengal's and all of India's national self-consciousness. His works enable one to understand the most important problems underlying the development of the Indian society. (p. 348)

L Strizhevskaya, "The Place Held by 'Pathēr Dābī' and 'Śēṣ Praśna' in the Works of Saratchandra Chattopadhyay," in The Golden Book of Saratchandra: A Centenary Commemorative Volume, *Manik Mukhopadhyay, General Editor, All Bengal Sarat Centenary Committee, 1977, pp. 343-48.*

MANIK BANDYOPADHYAY (essay date 1977)

[*The critic examines the problems posed to the reader by* Śēṣ Praśna.]

[Among] the various adverse criticisms I have read and heard about ***Śēs Praśna,*** the one that emerges as the main is why Saratchandra wrote this novel. They do not wonder at the novelty of ***Śēs Praśna,*** but are aggrieved for not finding their familiar Saratchandra in it. This is indeed a trouble eminent writers have to face. The features which are constant in their writings, that is their literary technique, portrayal of characters, aesthetic style and such other characteristics, are indelibly imprinted upon the mind of readers. With ***Śēs Praśna*** in hand we think that we are going to read a book by Saratchandra, the writer of ***Charitrahīn*** and ***Grhadāha.*** When we go through ***Śēs Praśna,*** we keep in mind, 'we are reading a book by Saratchandra'. As this preconception is jolted page after page, our complaints against the book become countless. As against this, to write a new book of a completely new kind, changing the style, technique and such things, after following the same pattern throughout one's literary career, is a sign of great genius. In fact, I myself could not properly make out what it was about when I read ***Śēs Praśna*** in instalments in Bharatbarsa. Later, I went through the whole book at a time. I thought with wonder how did Saratchandra get the courage and daring to come out as a new writer after so much fame and esteem were heaped upon him. (p. 371)

It is not easy for all to get pleasure from the artistic restraint we find in ***Śēs Praśna.*** The book that forces tears down proves its lack of restraint in creating pathos through every drop of tear it draws. Saratchandra's love for humanity is manifest in many of his books; especially, his love for the people of this land of Bengal often supersedes art, yet, that he is not an author for whom compassion and sympathy are all, but is also very much alive to the importance of art, is proved beyond any shadow of doubt in ***Śēs Praśna.*** The aesthetics of ***Śēs Praśna*** is deep and perfectly artistic.

The characters in a novel should not proceed to a certain culmination in deference to the likings and desires of the reader; on the contrary, they should proceed independently, uninfluenced by the personality of their creator, and should unfold their own personality, I have not found this principle to be properly followed in any book other than [Knut] Hamsun's *The Growth of the Soil.* If this virtue be remarkably present in any book in Bengali literature, it is in ***Śēs Praśna.*** In this respect the excellence of ***Śēs Praśna*** cannot be denied.

It is for this virtue that Kamal is not the female counterpart of Gōrā. She has attained the bloom of her personality and has not had to depend upon the reader or the author or the technique of novel writing. She has proclaimed herself boldly from a position where she has been placed by the current of events in her life, by her accumulated wisdom, experience and prejudices. She never attempts to escape to a haven of safety making calculations if this position is dangerous for her.

The complaint heard against Kamal is that she is 'a bundle of speeches'. ***Śēs Praśna*** is alleged to be an epic of the battle between the East and the West, and Kamal fights alone for the latter. Not to say that there is not any conflict of ideals in ***Śēs Praśna,*** but that is not the dominant aspect. To go into argument is a principal trait in Kamal's character—the East-West problem is but a subject matter of her polemics. Problems throng in the mind of modern man; he has to tax his brain severely. The portrayal of a modern man is only half-complete without the revelation of his intellectual faculty. It is, therefore, not the important point whether what Kamal says is true or false. It is also no use asking why she talks so much. What is to be judged is whether her words adequately reveal to what extent intellect dominates her character.

In other words, it is not her polemics, but Kamal herself who is great. It is for this reason that Kamal has no matching opponent in ***Śēs Praśna,*** who can hold his own in arguing with her without going into antics like Akṣay. This is the reason why she practises austerity, a contradiction between her words and action which has puzzled many a critic. Otherwise, I myself would also not have believed in the poverty of a woman as beautiful and free from prejudices as Kamal.

But Saratchandra has not been forgetful of the emotions of Kamal. The inner self of Kamal, like other characters in ***Śēs Praśna,*** is properly revealed in the novel. Otherwise, the aesthetic appeal of ***Śēs Praśna*** would be wanting. I have already said that the artistic restraint in ***Śēs Praśna*** is exceptional, its aesthetic appeal has not cheapened itself through a mere exuberance of frothy emotion. (pp. 371-72)

The technique of writing, the depth of aesthetic sense of the author, his mastery over plot and characters, his style of expression—these are the marks and traits of higher literature. If a combination of all these are not discovered and appreciated in ***Śēs Praśna,*** if the criticism remains confined within baseless condemnation and irrational praise, it will be a matter of very much shame for all lovers of literature in Bengal. ***Śēs Praśna*** wields the power to withstand threadbare analysis and impartial criticism. (p. 372)

Manik Bandyopadhyay, "Śēş Praśna," translated by Manasi Bhattacharya, in The Golden Book of Saratchandra: A Centenary Commemorative Volume, *Manik Mukhopadhyay, General Editor, All Bengal Sarat Centenary Committee, 1977, pp. 371-73.*

ADDITIONAL BIBLIOGRAPHY

Gupta, Ranjit. "The Revolt of Saratchandra." *The Illustrated Weekly of India* XCVII, No. 5 (1 February 1976): 33, 35.

Discusses the theme of revolt against established Hindu society in Chatterji's *Srikanta* novels.

Kabir, Humayun. Introduction to *Green and Gold: Stories and Poems from Bengal,* edited by Humayun Kabir, pp. 1-32. London: Chapman & Hall, 1958.*

Provides a short, but balanced assessment of Chatterji's literary work. Kabir is also the author of the biographical and critical work *Sarat Chandra Chatterji.*

Mukherji, Dhurjati. "Sarat Chandra Chatterjee." *The Visva-Bharati Quarterly* 2, No. 3 (November-January 1936-1937): 61-7

Discusses aspects of Chatterji's humanism, including some of the limitations it imposed on his art.

Sengupta, S. C. *Saratchandra: Man and Artist*. New Delhi: Sahitya Akademi, 1975, 110 p.

Biographical and critical study offering a thorough discussion of Chatterji's life and writings, as well as a helpful bibliography of his works in translation.

Anthony Comstock

1844-1915

American essayist.

Comstock was one of the most prominent of the self-appointed professional censors who abounded in the United States and England during the latter part of the nineteenth century. As the founder and the most active agent of the New York Society for the Suppression of Vice, Comstock was responsible for the destruction of more than fifty tons of books and four million photographs and illustrations that had in some way outraged his sense of morality. "He was a man consumed with energy and a love of domination," his biographer Margaret Leech noted, and this need to dominate extended to the authorship of broad and severe censorship laws that remained in effect in the United States until 1973.

Born in New Canaan, Connecticut, Comstock was the son of strict, puritanical parents. His father was a wealthy farmer, but the family lived simply. Long hours of church services and morally edifying stories told by his mother were Comstock's chief entertainments as a child. When an older brother was killed during the American Civil War, Comstock left high school to fill his place in the Union army. His diary records that his initial elation at this opportunity to serve his country was dampened by the discovery that soldiers commonly drank, smoked, swore, and gambled—activities which Comstock felt imperiled the soul. Much of his free time while in the service was spent organizing prayer and temperance meetings, which were poorly attended. At the war's end Comstock worked as a clerk in a New Haven grocery store. In 1871 he moved to New York City, where he was appalled by the flourishing traffic in what he termed pornography: sexually risqué books, adventure stories for children, and tawdry pamphlets and pictures. Comstock approached Morris K. Jesup, president of the Young Men's Christian Association, with plans for an organization devoted to halting the production and sale of the cheap novels and titillating pictures. Jesup obtained the financial backing of several wealthy New York entrepreneurs, including William E. Dodge, Jr. and Samuel Colgate, and in 1872 the New York Society for the Suppression of Vice was formed, with Colgate as president and Comstock as secretary, a post he held until his death. The Society was enormously successful in conducting raids and making arrests of alleged pornographers under existing laws: in one year Comstock reported that 134,000 pounds of books, 194,000 pictures, and 60,300 rubber articles, among other items, had been seized and impounded or destroyed. Comstock, however, bitterly resented every failed prosecution, and in 1873 he lobbied successfully for the passage of a multisectioned anti-obscenity bill that he helped write. This bill prohibited the production, sale, or shipment through the mail of any "obscene, lewd, or lascivious and every filthy book, pamphlet, picture, paper, letter, writing print, or other publication of an indecent character . . . or any article, instrument, substance, drug, medicine, or thing . . . used or applied for any indecent or immoral purpose," which, Mary Alden Hopkins noted, "covers—well, everything." Hopkins found the inclusive nature of the bill "partly explains Mr. Comstock's almost uniform success in securing convictions." The various sections of the bill made

The Granger Collection, New York

the direction of interested buyers to such merchandise no less a crime than its manufacture or distribution. Birth control and abortion information were also proscribed. Possibly the most controversial aspect of what became known as the Comstock laws was the fact that entire literary works could be judged on the basis of isolated passages. Coincident with the passage of this bill was the creation of the post of Special Agent of the Postmaster General, to which Comstock was reappointed every year of his life thereafter. This position allowed Comstock to inspect anything that was passing through the United States mail system, and empowered him to make arrests without a previously obtained warrant.

Though Comstock became one of the most hated public figures of his time, at the outset of his career he received widespread approval. The scurrilous books, pamphlets, and pictures that were the vice-hunter's first targets had few defenders. However, as Leech noted, "Comstock could not discriminate between a frankly pornographic book and a sociological or medical publication of educational character," and he attacked the latter as well as the former when he found therein any reference to sexual relations. Public objection to Comstock is thought to have been occasioned by his classification of birth control information and devices as pornography. At a time when birth control measures were increasingly sought after,

the Comstock laws made it illegal to dispense or to utilize even such imperfect contraceptive techniques as were then available.

Comstock's two books, *Frauds Exposed; or, How the People are Deceived and Robbed, and Youth Corrupted* and *Traps for the Young,* are luridly written accounts of his battle against the producers and distributors of books, pictures, and other items "of indecent character." *Frauds Exposed* and *Traps for the Young* are cast almost in the form of the adventure novels that Comstock deplored, with the author himself depicted as the intrepid hero overcoming all odds to vanquish the forces of evil. These books also chronicle his lesser-known successes against illegal gambling and patent medicine advertisements placed by bogus doctors. These activities, however, did not hold for Comstock the same fascination that his vice-hunting did: as Heywood Broun wrote, "Comstock never got quite as much enjoyment out of action against gamblers as he did in the pursuit of purveyors of obscene books and pictures . . . His record in the anti-gambling crusade was an honorable one . . . In all these things he was an efficient public servant. Only when sex flew in at the window did Anthony Comstock fly off the handle." Characteristic of his approach to literary censorship was his vow to "take a hand" in the suppression of "this Irish smut dealer's books" when he learned that Bernard Shaw publicly protested the removal of his works from the open shelves of New York's public libraries; yet Comstock admitted that he had never read a book or seen a play by Shaw, or had even heard his name before the book-banning incident.

Even during his lifetime, Comstock lost a great deal of the credibility and respect he had received early in his career. With the passage of years his accusations of obscenity were dispensed with increasing irrationality. His methods of apprehending suspects began more and more to resemble entrapment. People reacted with disgust to the fact that Comstock, with grim satisfaction, listed suicides of accused criminals among the accomplishments of the Society for the Suppression of Vice. The press began to refer to those accused by Comstock as his victims. Comstock and the Society had begun to fall into disrepute at the turn of the century and there were rumors shortly before Comstock's death that the Society wished to replace him with a more moderate officer. Though he remained secretary of the Society until his death, during his last years Comstock was the object of public ridicule and opprobrium. His also is the questionable distinction of having inspired Shaw to coin the term "Comstockery" to refer to unjust and excessive censorship.

PRINCIPAL WORKS

Frauds Exposed; or, How the People Are Deceived and Robbed, and Youth Corrupted (essays) 1880
Traps for the Young (essays) 1883

D[E ROBIGNE] M[ORTIMER] BENNETT (essay date 1878)

[*Bennett was the editor of a Freethought journal called* The Truth Seeker. *On November 12, 1877 he was arrested by Anthony Comstock and charged with sending obscene and immoral material through the mail. The material in question consisted of two tracts,* "An Open Letter to Jesus Christ" *and* "How Do Marsupials Propagate Their Kind?", *which Comstock had solicited from the offices of* The Truth Seeker *by letter, under an assumed name. Though the charges against Bennett were dismissed, Comstock arrested him again the following year for sending an antimarriage tract through the mail. During the course of this case, the appellate court made the important ruling that a work could be judged by isolated passages, and that the test of obscenity would be the tendency of those isolated passages to corrupt the minds of the young and inexperienced. This ruling was widely cited in further obscenity cases to obtain convictions, and it was not until 1973 that Chief Justice Warren Burger ruled that literary works must be judged in their entirety, and not on the basis of isolated passages. In the following essay Bennett attacks Comstock, deeming him a fitting successor to the vicious inquisitors and witch-hunters of the past.*]

Comstock has evinced the same energy, the same cruelty, the same intolerance, the same hardness of heart, and the same unyielding persistence in harassing and hunting down those who presumed to differ from the orthodox standard of religious thought—and have dared to be independent in matters of theology, medicine, and the literature pertaining to them—that have marked the envenomed [religious] persecutors of the past centuries. It is the time and the advance that has been made in civilization that have made the difference. This man has evinced the disposition of hatred and cruelty that a few centuries ago would have made a first-class Torquemada, Calvin, Alva, Charles IX, or Matthew Hopkins. (p. 1009)

It is not to be denied that those bloody persecutors, commissioned by the Church to torture and slay the hapless victims who fell in their way, each possessed some good qualities and that among the heartless acts they performed, some were commendable. So it is with Anthony Comstock; he has done some good; and far is it from the writer of these pages to deny him any of the good he has performed, though the means by which he reaches his ends, and by which he brings the unfortunate to punishment, are not such as good men can approve. Among a certain class of vile publishers he has accomplished a reform that must be placed to his credit, but the system of falsehood, subterfuge, and decoy-letters that he has employed to entrap his victims and inveigle them into the commission of an offense against the laws is utterly to be condemned.

The want of discrimination which he has evinced between those who were really guilty of issuing vile publications—whose only object was to inflame the baser passions—and those who published and sold books for the purpose of educating and improving mankind, has been a serious defect with this man. While he has suppressed much that is vile, he has, to a much larger extent, infringed upon the dearest rights of the individual, thus bringing obloquy and disgrace upon those who had a good object in view. And upon those who, in a limited degree, were in fault, he has been severe and relentless to a criminal extent. He has evinced far too much pleasure in bringing his fellow-beings into the deepest sorrow and grief; and under the name of arresting publishers of, and dealers in, obscene literature, he has caused the arraignment of numerous persons who had not the slightest intention of violating the rules of propriety and morality. Could he have expended his zeal and energy only upon those who deserved punishment, and have brought them under the rule of the law by fair and honorable means, his record would stand far better than it does to-day.

In that case he would not have been compelled to make the humiliating confession which he made in a public meeting of clergymen and others in Boston, May 30, 1878, where he was endeavoring to organize a branch, auxiliary "Society for the

Suppression of Vice," the parent society of which is of Comstock's origination, and located in New York. While Comstock was addressing the meeting, the Rev. Jesse H. Jones (Congregationalist) arose, and expressed a wish to ask Mr. Comstock a few questions. He was permitted to ask three, when a disposition was manifested that the interrogatories be not continued. The questions propounded were as follow: 1. "Did you, Mr. Comstock, ever use decoy letters and false signatures? 2. Did you ever sign a woman's name to such decoy letters? 3. Did you ever try to make persons sell you forbidden wares, and then, when you had succeeded, use the evidence thus obtained to convict them?" To each of these questions Comstock answered, "Yes, I have done it.". . . It is unfortunate for the reputation of Mr. Comstock, and the society which sustains him, and in whose name he works, that the most of his business, and the larger share of his victims and arrests have been brought about by these agencies. He has simply acted the part of a despicable spy and detective. Falsehood, deception, traps, and pitfalls for the unwary have been the agencies he has employed in the prosecution of his nefarious business. It is confidently asserted that he has written thousands upon thousands of decoy letters, bearing fictitious signatures of both men and women, and written for the purpose of inducing unsuspecting persons to commit an offense against the law and to be guilty of a crime which they would not otherwise have thought of committing. It must be admitted by all honorable men that this is a contemptible course to be pursued by a society of moral, high-minded men, which was organized in the name of morality and the Christian religion. It is a question for moralists to decide whether, when a cause or a system has to be sustained by such a dishonorable course of conduct, it would not be better that the society disband and its agent resort to a more honorable means of obtaining a livelihood. (pp. 1010-12)

An honorable, good man will never willingly accept the office of a spy and informer to lie in wait and watch for the errors and weakneses of his fellow-beings and then, by decoying them on and entrapping them, use their simplicity or their confidence to throw them into prison and effect their utter ruin.

The New York Society for the Suppression of Vice was incorporated by the Legislature of New York, May 16, 1873, chiefly through the efforts of Anthony Comstock, its secretary and active agent, and the Young Men's Christian Association. He also procured the enactment by the United States Congress, and by the Legislature of New York State of a series of acts, which were placed in both the national and State statute books, and which are believed by many to be subversive of the very principles of American liberty and destructive to individual rights guaranteed by the Constitution of our country. (p. 1014)

While there are commendable features in these laws it must be confessed that [in part they] are excessively severe, besides being indefinite. When such heavy penalites are imposed, the offenses for which they are prescribed should be clearly marked out. If obscenity, indecency, and immorality are crimes to be punished by fines of $5,000 and imprisonment at hard labor for ten years, they should at least be clearly defined, so that every person can know what the law considers immoral, what indecent, and what obscene.

A learned jurist has said that "no legislative body in making laws should use language that has to be defined and construed by others. Every crime should be so clearly defined that there can be no mistaking it. . . . It is not with obscenity; the term is left to be construed by judges, lawyers, juries, and whoever chooses to decide what *is* obscene and what is *not*. . . . What is obscene to one man may be as pure as the mountain snow to another, and one man should not be empowered to decide for other men."

To procure the enactment of the foregoing laws, Comstock made frequent journeys to Washington, and he carried with him, it is said, a satchel full of lewd, filthy books, pictures, and devices which he spread out before congressmen and which he induced them to believe were being sent through the mail by scores of tons to the youth of the country and to the young school children at seminaries, boarding-schools, and so forth. After the law-makers had been regaled with a view of these unclean curiosities, they seemed to be prepared to vote, Aye, on almost any kind of laws for which their vote might be solicited. It is to be regretted that they could not have displayed better judgment than to destroy the very principles of American Liberty and Individual Freedom for the sake of protecting school children from the imaginary belief that improper mail matter was sent them. If it is true that such mail matter is sent them, how easy it would be to obviate it by having it inspected by teachers or guardians before passing it over to the children. This could be readily done without violating the Constitution of our country or crushing the rights of the entire people. (pp. 1015-17)

A very similar set of laws were, by the personal exertions of Mr. Comstock, and by a similar style of tactics, passed by the Legislature at Albany and became a part of the laws of the State of New York, and combined with the United States laws just referred to, they have proved an engine of oppression to many individuals who under them have been suddenly brought to the deepest grief. (p. 1017)

It is greatly to be regretted that in the last quarter of the nineteenth century such a base specimen of humanity as Anthony Comstock has been selected to be the protector of public morals, to be a champion of the Church, and a censor of the mails, of medical and physiological literature, and of Radical and Freethought publications. If free America is to have a censor of the press and of her mails, it would certainly be desired that a man might be selected to discharge the duties of the office who possessed some qualifications for the position, and who exhibited, at least, an average amount of morality, decency, honesty, and truthfulness. Can members of the Christian society which for years has employed this man and made him their active agent and representative, expect to add to their own credit or to that of the Christian religion by employing and sustaining such a despicable character as Anthony Comstock—the Matthew Hopkins of the nineteenth century? (p. 1091)

D[e Robigne] M[ortimer] Bennett, in his Anthony Comstock, His Career of Cruelty and Crime: A Chapter from "The Champions of the Church," *D. M. Bennett, 1878 (and reprinted by DaCapo Press, 1971), pp. 1009-119.*

J. M. BUCKLEY (essay date 1883)

[*Buckley offers a sympathetic introduction to Comstock's* Traps for the Young.]

Every new generation of youth is sent out into the world as sheep in the midst of wolves. The danger, however is not that they will be devoured by them, but that they will be transformed into wolves. Traps are laid for them in every direction,—traps which count upon their inexperience to gain the first entrance, but many of them are so ingeniously constructed, that, once in the trap, the victim will love it and press greedily forward, or even become a decoy to lead others into the same or similar meshes.

Warning, restraints, guidance and sympathy alone can save the youth. If the youth be not saved, the next generation must be corrupt. Every youth who goes astray is a man or woman lost for this world and for the next. This work lays bare these traps with a view, not of instructing youth in the wickedness of the world, but of arousing parents, teachers, and guardians to the work of saving them, and of pointing out the best means, as well as the necessity, of doing so. That such a book should be written, I have no doubt; that Mr. Comstock has had every opportunity to measure the evil and to accumulate the materials for its most striking presentation, and that he can point out what must be done, are obvious to all.

The reader will find that this work does not claim high literary merit. Its style is that of a man in earnest, who talks straight on, who tries to be understood, and to move the reader. No one but a person absorbed in a great work could write as he does. His very blemishes are an evidence of his sincerity. Without approving all that he has done, I have on various occasions commended his work in general, and gladly do so now. Let **"Traps for the Young"** be widely circulated, not among the young, but among those who have the care of them, among all Christians, patriots, and philanthropists. For to save the young is the most important and the noblest work in which either young or old can engage. (pp. 2-3)

J. M. Buckley, in an introduction to Traps for the Young *by Anthony Comstock, Funk & Wagnalls, 1883 (and reprinted in* Traps for the Young *by Anthony Comstock, edited by Robert Bremner, Cambridge, Mass.: Belknap Press, 1967), pp. 1-3.*

ANTHONY COMSTOCK (essay date 1883)

[*The following excerpt from the author's preface to* Traps for the Young *is a typical example of Comstock's prose style and his approach to the issue of censorship. The book contains numerous unsubstantiated case histories of young lives blighted by books of "questionable character" and by the lure of such "indecent" entertainments as the theater.*]

Good reading refines, elevates, ennobles, and stimulates the ambition to lofty purposes. It points upward. Evil reading debases, degrades, perverts, and turns away from lofty aims to follow examples of corruption and criminality.

This book is designed to awaken thought upon the subject of *Evil Reading,* and to expose to the minds of parents, teachers, guardians, and pastors, some of the mighty forces for evil that are to-day exerting a controlling influence over the young. There is a shameful recklessness in many homes as to what the children read.

The community is cursed by pernicious literature. Ignorance as to its debasing character in numerous instances, and an indifference that is disgraceful in others, tolerate and sanction this evil.

Parents send their beloved children to school, and text-books are placed in their hands, while lesson after lesson and precept after precept are drilled into them. But through criminal indifference to other reading for the children than their text-books, the grand possibilities locked up in the future of every child, if kept pure, and all the appetites and passions controlled, are often circumscribed and defeated at its threshold of life. This book is a plea for the moral purity of children. It is an appeal for greater watchfulness on the part of those whose duty it is to think, act, and speak for that very large portion in the community who have neither intellect nor judgment to decide what is wisest and best for themselves. It brings to parents the question of their responsibility for the future welfare of their offspring.

If a contagious disease be imported to these shores in some ship, at once the vessel and her passengers are quarantined. The port is promptly closed to the disease. The agent that brings it is estopped from entering the harbor until the contagion has been removed. It is the author's purpose to send a message in advance to parents, so that they may avert from their homes a worse evil than yellow fever or small-pox. Read the facts, and let them speak words of warning.

The author, during an experience of nearly eleven years, has seen the effects of the evils herein discussed. If strong language is used, it is because no other can do the subject justice.

This work represents facts as they are found to exist. If it shall be the means of arousing parents as to what their children read, of checking evil reading among the young, or of awakening a public sentiment against the prevailing wickedness of the day, the writer will be content.

If any one doubts the startling facts stated, let me here place on record my entire readiness to sustain my assertions with proofs.

Because men will deny, scoff, and curse is no reason why these truths should not be laid before the minds of thinking men and women. . . . For the sake of the thousands of children in the land, I appeal to every good citizen to carefully read the following pages, not to criticise, but to see what can be done to remedy the evils discussed.

Our youth are in danger; mentally and morally they are cursed by a literature that is a disgrace to the nineteenth century. The spirit of evil environs them.

Let no man be henceforth indifferent. Read, reflect, act. (pp. 5-6)

Anthony Comstock, in a preface to his Traps for the Young, *Funk & Wagnalls, 1883 (and reprinted in his* Traps for the Young, *edited by Robert Bremner, Cambridge, Mass.: Belknap Press, 1967), pp. 5-6.*

BERNARD SHAW (letter date 1905)

[*The letter excerpted below details Shaw's reaction to the news that various of his works had been removed from the open shelves of the New York Public Library in an effort to protect "the young and inexperienced" from his ideas. This may have been the first appearance in print of the term "Comstockery," which Shaw coined to characterize the activities of the era's professional censors. For Comstock's response to this letter see the 1905 excerpt below from the* New York Times.]

Dear Sir

Nobody outside of America is likely to be in the least surprised. Comstockery is the world's standing joke at the expense of the United States. Europe likes to hear of such things. It confirms the deep-seated conviction of the Old World that America is a provincial place, a second-rate country-town civilization after all. (p. 559)

THAT FERTILE IMAGINATION.

A-n-y C-m-st-k: HOLD! I ARREST YOU FOR PAINTING INDECENT PICTURES!
Artist: INDECENT! WHY THE HEAD IS THE ONLY PORTION VISIBLE.
A-n-y C-m-st-k: THAT MAKES NO DIFFERENCE. DON'T YOU SUPPOSE I CAN IMAGINE WHAT IS UNDER THE WATER?

An editorial cartoon published in Life, *January 18, 1888. Courtesy of Harvard University Press.*

It is true I shall not suffer either in reputation or pocket. Everybody knows I know better than your public library officials what is proper for people to read, whether they are young or old. Everybody knows also that if I had the misfortune to be a citizen of the United States I should probably have my property confiscated by some postal official and be myself imprisoned as a writer of 'obscene' literature.

But as I live in a comparatively free country and my word goes further than that of mere officialdom, these things do not matter. What does matter is that this incident is only a symptom of what is really a moral horror both in America and elsewhere, and that is the secret and intense resolve of the petty domesticity of the world to tolerate no criticism and suffer no invasion. (pp. 559-60)

I have honor and humanity on my side, wit in my head, skill in my hand, and a higher life for my aim. Let those who put me on their restricted lists so that they may read me themselves while keeping their children in the dark, acknowledge their allies, state their qualifications, and avow their aims, if they dare.

I hope the New York press will in common humanity to those who will now for the first time hasten to procure my books and witness the performances of my plays under the impression that they are Alsatian, warn them that nothing but the most extreme tedium and discomfort of conscience can be got by thoughtless people from my sermons, whether on the stage or in the library. (p. 560)

Pray do not suppose I am insensible of the good intentions of the leaders of the Comstockers, however corrupt and sensual may be the bigoted connubiality which provides them with the huge following that emboldens them to meddle with matters the greatest men touch with extreme diffidence. But, as I have said in 'Man and Superman,' 'All men mean well,' and 'Hell is paved with good intentions, not bad ones.' . . .

I do not say that my books and plays cannot do harm to weak or dishonest people. They can, and probably do. But if the American character cannot stand that fire even at the earliest age at which it is readable or intelligible, there is no future for America. (p. 561)

Bernard Shaw, in a letter to Robert W. Welch in September, 1905, in The New York Times *(copyright © 1905 by The New York Times Company; reprinted by permission), September 26, 1905 (and reprinted in* Bernard Shaw: Collected Letters, 1898-1910, *edited by Dan H. Laurence, Max Reinhardt, 1972, pp. 559-62).*

***THE NEW YORK TIMES* (essay date 1905)**

[The article excerpted below illuminates Comstock's lack of qualification for judging literature. He characterizes Bernard Shaw as an Irish smut dealer immediately after admitting that he has never heard of the author. Comstock's annual report to the New York Society for the Suppression of Vice for 1905 mentions that "a bold attempt was made to place the reekings of Bernard Shaw upon the public stage in this City," referring to a production of Mrs. Warren's Profession *that Comstock had closed down.]*

"George Bernard Shaw? Let's see—Shaw; who is he?" asked Anthony Comstock yesterday. . . .

"Shaw?" said Mr. Comstock reflectively. "I never heard of him in my life. Never saw one of his books, so he can't be much."

The reporter had in his pocket a copy of The New York Times in which appeared the letter [see excerpt above, 1905] written by Mr. Shaw, the author and playwright, after he had learned that his books had been removed from the "open shelves" in the New York Free Libraries. This order of removal Mr. Shaw characterized as a piece of "American Comstockery." The reporter submitted the letter, and Mr. Comstock read it carefully.

"Everybody knows," wrote Mr. Shaw, "that I know better than your public library officials what is proper for people to read, whether they are young or old."

When Mr. Comstock read that, he literally grew pale with indignation.

"Did you ever see such egotism?" he commented angrily. "I had nothing to do with removing this Irish smut dealer's books from the public library shelves, but I will take a hand in the matter now.". . .

The reporter was inclined to ask questions, but Mr. Comstock would brook no interruptions. "Take it down, son," he said, "and later we'll talk about the questions."

Then Mr. Comstock said, and the reporter wrote it down, that it was evident that "this fellow Shaw believes the proper method of curing contagious and vile diseases is to parade them in front of the public. He evidently thinks that's the way to treat obscene literature. . . .

"It matters little if the literary style is of a high order if the subject matter is bad. I had a man convicted who was printing and selling pictures of paintings hung in the Paris Salon and in the art hall at our Centennial Exposition. The only question is, 'Can this book or picture or play hurt any one morally, even the weak?' All else is of minor consequence.

"Before this, in the fight for the morals of our 35,000,000 young men and women, we have convicted Englishmen and Irishmen. I have destroyed their stuff by the tons. The English and the Irish have furnished their full quota of unfit books and pictures and plays. . . .

"I understand that the Shaw books have been put back upon the shelves from which they are said to have been taken. Before now we have routed objectionable books from library shelves where they were accessible alike to the young and old. Complaints are frequently made to me by parents concerning such books, and I have quietly had many a one withdrawn from the tables where everybody could see them. This Shaw is not outside of our rules.

"You say he has plays also and some of them have been presented and liked in New York City? Well, they will be investigated, and the plays and the playing people will be dealt with according to the law if it be found that they are such as are indicated by this Shaw himself."

"Who's Bernard Shaw? Asks Mr. Comstock," in The New York Times, *September 28, 1905, p. 9.*

MARGARET C. ANDERSON (essay date 1915)

[*Anderson was the founder and editor of the avant-garde literary magazine* The Little Review, *in which the article excerpted below appeared. In 1918 Anderson was arrested by agents of the New York Society for the Suppression of Vice under the Comstock Laws when* The Little Review *serialized James Joyce's* Ulysses.]

I want to write about so many things this time that I don't know where to begin. At first I had planned to do five or six pages on the crime of musical criticism in this country. . . . But for the moment I have found something more important to talk about: Mr. Anthony Comstock. (p. 2)

Of course there is nothing new to say about him—and nothing awful enough. The best thing I've heard lately is this: "Anthony Comstock not only doesn't know anything, but he doesn't suspect anything.". . . His latest outrage is well-known by this time—his arrest of William Sanger for giving to a Comstock detective a copy of Mrs. Sanger's pamphlet, *Family Limitation*. The charge was "circulating obscene literature." I have seen that pamphlet, read it carefully, and given it to all the people I know well enough to be sure they are not Comstock detectives. There is not an obscene word in it, naturally. Margaret Sanger couldn't be obscene—she's a gentle, serious, well-informed woman writing in a way that any high-minded physician might. I have also seen her pamphlet called *English Methods of Birth Control,* which practically duplicates the leaflet *(Hygienic Methods of Family Limitation)* adopted by the Malthusian League of England and is sent "to all persons married, or about to be married, who apply for it, in all countries of the world, except to applicants from the United States of America, where the Postal Laws will not allow of its delivery." (pp. 2-3)

I've forgotten the various steps by which "that blind, heavy, stupid thing we call government" came to its lumbering decision that she ought to spend ten or fifteen years in jail for her efforts to spread this knowledge. But Mrs. Sanger left the country—thank heaven! However, I understand that when she has finished her work of making these pamphlets known she means to come back and face the imprisonment. I pray she doesn't mean anything of the kind. Why should she go to jail for ten years because we haven't suppressed Anthony Comstock? Last year his literary supervision was given its first serious jolt when Mitchel Kennerley won the *Hager Revely* suit. But that was not nearly so important as the present issue, because *Hager Revely* was rather negative literature and birth control is one of the milestones by which civilization will measure its progress. The science of eugenics has always seemed to me fundamentally a sentimentalization—something that a man might have conceived in the frame of mind Stevenson was in when he wrote *Olalla*. Because there is no such thing, really, as the scientific restriction of love and passion. These things don't belong in the realm of science any more than one's reactions to a sunrise do. But the restriction of the birth-rate does belong there, and science should make this one of its big battles. (pp. 3-4)

Margaret C. Anderson, "Mr. Comstock and the Resourceful Police" (copyright, 1915, by Margaret C. Anderson; reprinted by permission of the Literary Estate of Margaret C. Anderson), in The Little Review, *Vol. II, No. 2, April, 1915, pp. 2-5.*

MARY ALDEN HOPKINS (essay date 1915)

[*Hopkins records an interview held with Comstock on the subject of birth control and obscene literature. In the opening passages of the following excerpt, Comstock responds to two articles on birth control published by Hopkins.*]

"Have read your articles. Self control and obedience to Nature's laws, you seem to overlook. Let men and women live a life above the level of the beasts. I see nothing in either of your articles along these lines. Existing laws are an imperative necessity in order to prevent the downfall of youths of both sex," wrote Mr. Anthony Comstock, secretary of the New York Society for the Suppression of Vice, replying to my request for an interview on the subject of Birth Control.

During the interview which he kindly allowed me, he reiterated his belief in the absolute necessity of drastic laws.

"To repeal the present laws would be a crime against society," he said, "and especially a crime against young women."

Although the name Anthony Comstock is known all over the country and over the most of the civilized world, comparatively few people know for exactly what Mr. Comstock stands and what he has accomplished. It has been the policy of those who oppose his work to speak flippantly of it and to minimize its results. The Society for the Suppression of Vice was formed to support Mr. Comstock, from the beginning he has been its driving force, and it is giving him only the credit which is due him to say that the tremendous accomplishments of the society in its fight against vicious publications for the last forty years have been in reality the accomplishments of Mr. Comstock. (p. 489)

In March, 1873, Mr. Comstock secured the passage of stringent federal laws closing the mails and the ports to this atrocious business. Two days afterwards, upon the request of certain Senators, Mr. Comstock was appointed Special Agent of the Post Office Department to enforce these laws. He now holds the position of Post Office Inspector. The federal law as it at present stands is as follows:

United States Criminal Code, Section 211.

(Act of March 4th, 1909, Chapter 321, Section 211, United States Statutes at Large, vol. 35, part 1, page 1088 et seq.)

> Every obscene, lewd, or lascivious and every filthy book, pamphlet, picture, paper, letter, writing, print, or other publication of an indecent character, and every article or thing designated, adapted or intended for preventing conception or procuring abortion, or for any indecent or immoral use; and every article, instrument, substance, drugs, medicine, or thing which is advertised or described in a manner calculated to lead another to use or apply it for preventing conception or producing abortion, or for any indecent or immoral purpose; and every written or printed card, circular, book, pamphlet, advertisement or notice or any kind giving information, directly, or indirectly, where or how, or by what means any of the hereinbefore mentioned matters, articles or things may be obtained or made, or where or by whom any act or operation of any kind for the procuring or producing of abortion will be done or performed, or how or by what means conception may be prevented or abortion produced, whether sealed or unsealed; and every letter, packet or package or other mail matter containing any filthy, vile or indecent thing, device or substance; and every paper, writing, advertisement or representation that any article, instrument, substance, drug, medicine or thing may, or can be used or applied for preventing conception or producing abortion, or for any indecent or immoral purpose; and every description calculated to induce or incite a person to so use or apply any such article, instrument, substance, drug, medicine or thing, is hereby declared to be non-mailable matter, and shall not be conveyed in the mails or delivered from any post office or by any letter carrier. Whosoever shall knowingly deposit or cause to be deposited for mailing or delivery, anything declared by this section to be non-mailable, or shall knowingly take, or cause the same to be taken, from the mails for the purpose of circulating or disposing thereof, or of aiding in the circulation or disposition of the same, shall be fined not more than $5000, or imprisoned not more than five years, or both.

Any one who has the patience to read through this carefully drawn law will see that it covers—well, everything. The detailed accuracy with which it is constructed partly explains Mr. Comstock's almost uniform success in securing convictions. One possible loophole suggested itself to me.

"Does it not," I asked, "allow the judge considerable leeway in deciding whether or not a book or a picture, is immoral?"

"No," replied Mr. Comstock, "the highest courts in Great Britain and the United States, have laid down the test in all such matters. What he has to decide is *whether or not it might arouse in young and inexperienced minds, lewd or libidinous thoughts.*"

In these words lies the motive of Mr. Comstock's work—the protection of children under twenty-one. If at times his ban seems to some to be too sweepingly applied it is because his faith looks forward to a time when there shall be in all the world not one object to awaken sensuous thoughts in the minds of young people. (pp. 489-90)

I was somewhat confused at first that Mr. Comstock should class contraceptives with pornographic objects which debauch children's fancies, for I knew that the European scientists who advocate their use have no desire at all to debauch children. When I asked Mr. Comstock about this, he replied—with scant patience of "theorizers" who do not know human nature:

"If you open the door to anything, the filth will all pour in and the degradation of youth will follow."

The federal law, which we have quoted, covers only matter sent by post. This would leave large unguarded fields were it not for the state laws. The year following the passage of the federal law, Mr. Comstock obtained the passage of drastic laws in several states, and later in all states. . . .

"Do not these laws handicap physicians?" I asked, remembering that this criticism is sometimes made.

"They do not," replied Mr. Comstock emphatically. "No reputable physician has ever been prosecuted under these laws. Have you ever known of one?" I had not, and he continued, "Only infamous doctors who advertise or send their foul matter by mail. A reputable doctor may tell his patient in his office what is necessary, and a druggist may sell on a doctor's written prescription drugs which he would not be allowed to sell otherwise."

The criticism of the laws interfering with doctors is so continuously made that I asked again:

"Do the laws never thwart the doctor's work; in cases, for instance, where pregnancy would endanger a woman's life?"

Mr. Comstock replied with the strongest emphasis:

"A doctor is allowed to bring on an abortion in cases where a woman's life is in danger. And is there anything in these laws that forbids a doctor's telling a woman that pregnancy must not occur for a certain length of time or at all? Can they not use self-control? Or must they sink to the level of the beasts?"

"But," I protested, repeating an argument often brought forward, although I felt as if my persistence was somewhat placing me in the ranks of those who desire evil rather than good, "If the parents lack that self-control, the punishment falls upon the child."

"It does not," replied Mr. Comstock. "The punishment falls upon the parents. When a man and woman marry they are responsible for their children. You can't reform a family in any of these superficial ways. You have to go deep down into their minds and souls. The prevention of conception would work the greatest demoralization. God has set certain natural barriers. If you turn lose the passions and break down the fear you bring worse disaster than the war. It would debase sacred things, break down the health of women and diseminate a greater curse than the plagues and diseases of Europe." (p. 490)

Mary Alden Hopkins, "Birth Control and Public Morals," in Harper's Weekly, *Vol. LX, No. 3048, May 22, 1915, pp. 489-90.*

H. L. MENCKEN (essay date 1917)

[*From the era of World War I until the early years of the Great Depression, Mencken was one of the most influential figures in American letters. His strongly individualistic, irreverent outlook on life and his vigorous, invective-charged writing style helped establish the iconoclastic spirit of the Jazz Age and significantly shaped the direction of American literature. As a social and literary critic—the roles for which he is best known—Mencken was the scourge of evangelical Christianity, public service organizations, literary censorship, boosterism, provincialism, democracy, all advocates of personal or social improvement, and every other facet of American life that he perceived as humbug. In his literary criticism, Mencken encouraged American writers to shun the anglophilic, moralistic bent of the nineteenth century and to practice realism, an artistic call-to-arms which is most fully developed in his essay* "Puritanism As a Literary Force," *one of the seminal essays in modern literary criticism. In the following excerpt from that essay, Mencken discusses Comstockery as a symptom of America's lingering Puritan heritage.*]

Save one turn to England or to the British colonies, it is impossible to find a parallel for the astounding absolutism of Comstock and his imitators in any civilized country. No other nation has laws which oppress the arts so ignorantly and so abominably as ours do, nor has any other nation handed over the enforcement of the statutes which exist to agencies so openly pledged to reduce all aesthetic expression to the service of a stupid and unworkable scheme of rectitude. I have before me as I write a pamphlet in explanation of his aims and principles, prepared by Comstock himself and presented to me by his successor. Its very title is a sufficient statement of the Puritan position: **"MORALS, Not Art or Literature."** The capitals are in the original. And within, as a sort of general text, the idea is amplified: "It is a question of peace, good order and morals, and not art, literature or science." Here we have a statement of principle that, at all events, is at least quite frank. There is not the slightest effort to beg the question; there is no hypocritical pretension to a desire to purify or safeguard the arts; they are dismissed at once as trivial and degrading. And jury after jury has acquiesced in this; it was old Anthony's boast, in his last days, that his percentage of convictions, in 40 years, had run to 98.5.

Comstockery is thus grounded firmly upon [a] profound national suspicion of the arts, [a] truculent and almost unanimous Philistinism. . . . It would be absurd to dismiss it as an excrescence, and untypical of the American mind. But it is typical, too, in the manner in which it has gone beyond that mere partiality to the accumulation of a definite power, and made that power irresponsible and almost irresistible. . . . [It] was Comstock who first capitalized moral endeavour like baseball or the soap business, and made himself the first of its kept professors, and erected about himself a rampart of legal and financial immunity which rid him of all fear of mistakes and their consequences, and so enabled him to pursue his jehad with all the advantages in his favour. (pp. 253-55)

In carrying on this way of extermination upon all ideas that violated their private notions of virtue and decorum, Comstock and his follwers were very greatly aided by the vagueness of the law. It prohibited the use of the mails for transporting all matter of an "obscene, lewd, lascivious . . . or filthy" character, but conveniently failed to define these adjectives. As a result, of course, it was possible to bring an accusation against practically *any* publication that aroused the comstockian blood-lust, however innocently, and to subject the persons responsible for it to costly, embarrassing and often dangerous persecution. No man, said Dr. Johnson, would care to go on trial for his life once a week, even if possessed of absolute proofs of his innocence. By the same token, no man wants to be arraigned in a criminal court, and displayed in the sensational newspapers, as a purveyor of indecency, however strong his assurance of innocence. Comstock made use of this fact in an adroit and characteristically unconscionable manner. He held the menace of prosecution over all who presumed to dispute his tyranny, and when he could not prevail by a mere threat, he did not hesitate to begin proceedings, and to carry them forward with the aid of florid proclamations to the newspapers and ill concealed intimidations of judges and juries.

The last-named business succeeded as it always does in this country, where the judiciary is quite as sensitive to the suspicion of sinfulness as the legislative arm. A glance at the decisions handed down during the forty years of Comstock's chief activity shows a truly amazing willingness to accommodate him in his pious enterprises. On the one hand, there was gradually built up a court-made definition of obscenity which eventually embraced almost every conceivable violation of Puritan prudery, and on the other hand the victim's means of defence were steadily restricted and conditioned, until in the end he had scarcely any at all. This is the state of the law today. It is held in the leading cases that anything is obscene which may excite "impure thoughts" in "the minds . . . of persons that are susceptible to impure thoughts," or which "tends to deprave the minds" of any who, because they are "young and inexperienced," are "open to such influences"—in brief, that anything is obscene that is not fit to be handed to a child just learning to read, or that may imaginably stimulate the lubricity of the most foul-minded. It is held further that words that are perfectly innocent in themselves—"words, abstractly considered, [that] may be free from vulgarism"—may yet be assumed, by a friendly jury, to be likely to "arouse a libidinous passion . . . in the mind of a modest woman." (I quote exactly! The court failed to define "modest woman.") Yet further, it is held that any book is obscene "which is unbecoming, immodest. . . ." Obviously, this last decision throws open the door to endless imbecilities, for its definition merely begs the question, and so makes a reasonable solution ten times harder. It is in such mazes that the Comstocks safely lurk. Almost any printed allusion to sex may be argued against as unbecoming in a moral republic, and once it is unbecoming it is also obscene.

In meeting such attacks the defendant must do his fighting without weapons. . . . The general character of a book is not a defence of a particular passage, however unimportant; if there is the slightest descent to what is "unbecoming," the whole may be ruthlessly condemned. (pp. 262-66)

In all this dread of free inquiry, this childish skittishness in both writers and public, this dearth of courage and even of curiosity, the influence of comstockery is undoubtedly to be detected. It constitutes a sinister and ever-present menace to all men of ideas; it affrights the publisher and paralyzes the author; no one on the outside can imagine its burden as a practical concern. I am, in moments borrowed from more palatable business, the editor of an American magazine, and I thus know at first hand what the burden is. (p. 276)

I know many other editors. All of them are in the same boat. (pp. 277-78)

But though the effects of comstockery are thus abominably insane and irritating, the fact is not to be forgotten that, after all, the thing is no more than an effect itself. The fundamental causes of all the grotesque (and often half-fabulous) phenomena flowing out of it are to be sought in the habits of mind of the American people. They are, as I have shown, besotted by moral concepts, a moral engrossment, a delusion of moral infallibility. (p. 279)

To be curious is to be lewd; to know is to yield to fornication. Here we have the mediaeval doctrine still on its legs: a chance word may arouse "a libidinous passion" in the mind of a "modest" woman. Not only youth must be safeguarded, but also the "female," the untrustworthy one, the temptress. "Modest," is a euphemism; it takes laws to keep her "pure." The "locks of chastity" rust in the Cluny Museum; in place of them we have comstockery. . . .

We have yet no delivery, but we have at least the beginnings of a revolt, or, at all events, of a protest. (p. 282)

H. L. Mencken, "Puritanism As a Literary Force," in his A Book of Prefaces *(copyright 1917 by Alfred A. Knopf, Inc. and renewed 1944 by H. L. Mencken; reprinted by permission of the publisher), Knopf, 1917 (and reprinted by Knopf, 1924), pp. 197-283.**

H. L. MENCKEN (essay date 1927)

[Writing several years after his better-known assessment of Comstock (see excerpt above, 1917), Mencken hails Comstock as the man chiefly responsible, through his excesses, for ending Puritanism in America, and dubs him the "Emperor of Wowsers." (A "wowser," by Mencken's definition, is a professional purveyor of uplift who is driven to a vituperative frenzy by the spectacle of other people enjoying life.)]

[Comstock] was, in point of fact, a man of manifold virtues, and even his faults showed a rugged, berserker quality that was sneakingly charming. It is quite impossible, at this distance, to doubt his bona fides, and almost as difficult, to question his essential sanity. Like all the rest of us in our several ways, he was simply a damned fool. Starting out in life with an idea lying well within the bounds of what most men would call the rational, he gradually pumped it up until it bulged over all four borders. But he never let go his hold upon logic. He never abandoned reason for intuition. Once his premises were granted, the only way to escape his conclusions was to forsake Aristotle for Epicurus. (pp. 1-2)

Mr. Broun, in his appendix [see Additional Bibliography], tries to find holes in Anthony's logic, but it turns out to be far from easy; what he arrives at, in the end, is mainly only proof that a logician is an immensely unpleasant fellow. Turn, for example to a typical and very familiar comstockian syllogism. First premise: The effect of sexual images, upon the young, is to induce auto-erotism. Second premise: the effect of auto-eroticism are idiocy, epilepsy and locomotor ataxia. Ergo, now is the time for all good men to put down every book or picture likely to evoke sexual images. What is wrong with all of this? Simply that Mr. Broun and you and I belong to a later generation than Anthony's and are thus skeptical to his truths. But let us not forget that they were true for him. His first premise came out of the hard, incontrovertible experience of a Puritan farm boy, His second was supported, when he was getting his education, by the almost unanimous medical opinion of Christendom. And so his conclusion was perfect. We have made no progress in logic since his time; we have simply made progress in skepticism. All his grand truths are now dubious, and most of them are laughed at even by sucklings.

I think that he himself had a great deal to do with upsetting them. The service that he performed, in his grandiose way, was no more than a magnification of the service that is performed every day by multitudes of Y.M.C.A. secretaries, evangelical clergyman and other such lowly fauna. It is their function in the world to ruin their own ideas by believing in them and living them. Striving sincerely to be patterns to the young, they suffer the ironical fate of becoming horrible examples. . . . Old Anthony, I believe, accomplished much the same thing, but on an immeasurably larger scale. He did more than any other man to ruin Puritanism in the United States. When he began his long and brilliant career of unwitting sabotage; the essential principles of comstockery were believed in by practically every reputable American. Half a century later, when he went upon the shelf, comstockery enjoyed a degree of public esteem, at least in the big cities, half way between that enjoyed by phrenology and that enjoyed by homosexuality. It was, at best, laughable. It was, at worst, revolting.

So much did one consecrated man achieve in the short span of his life, I believe, that it was no mean accomplishment. Anthony managed it, not because there was any unusual brainpower in him, but because he had a congenital talent for buffoonery. The fellow, in his way, was a sort of Barnum. A band naturally attended him, playing in time to his yells. He could not undertake even so banal a business as raiding a dealer in abortifacient pills without giving it the melodramatic air of a battle with a brontosaurus. . . .

Old Anthony was preposterous, but not dishonest. He believed in his idiotic postulates as devotedly as a Tennessee Baptist believes that a horsehair put into a bottle of water will turn into a snake. His life, as he saw it, was one of sacrifice for righteousness. Born with a natural gift for the wholesale dry-goods profession, he might have wrung a fortune from its practice, and so won an heroic equestrian statue in the Cathedral of St. John the Divine. . . .

"Your Honor, this woman gave birth to a naked child!"

An editorial cartoon by Robert Miner (1915). The Granger Collection, New York.

I confess to a great liking for the old imbecile. He is one of my favorite characters in American history, along with Frances E. Willard, Daniel Drew and Brigham Young. . . . He added a great deal to the joys of life in the Federal Republic. And, more than any other man, he liberated American letters from the blight of Puritanism. (p. 2)

H. L. Mencken, "The Emperor of Wowsers," in New York Herald Tribune Books *(© I.H.T. Corporation; reprinted by permission), March 6, 1927, pp. 1-2.*

ELMER DAVIS (essay date 1927)

[Davis's career as a journalist, radio announcer, and propagandist was marked by his liberal political views and devotion to the cause of civil liberties. In the following review of Margaret Leech's and Heywood Broun's biography Anthony Comstock: Roundsman of the Lord, *Davis discusses Comstock and judges him to be little more than a bully.]*

There will probably never be another Comstock; he was a unique and peculiar embodiment of a spirit which existed before him, and still persists, and would persist if he had never lived at all. But thanks to him that spirit is armed with a weapon of unholy power; because of his fanatical singlemindedness, his irresistible energy, his genuine conviction of what most people, even in his time, believed only perfunctorily, that one with God is a majority, each of his successors is armed for offense and defense almost as invincibly as Siegfried and Perseus. This is the burden of Anthony, the Comstock load.

The customary defense of Comstock is that all his blunders are nullified by his service in suppressing the smut pamphlets which seem to have been pretty generally on sale sixty years ago. How much harm this printed filth actually did may be open to question, but it does not appear that it ever did any good except to the people who got the money for it. Mr. Broun [in the biography *Anthony Comstock: Roundsman of the Lord*] indeed argues that such works as *Only a Boy* vaccinate impressionable youth against the undesirable glamor of sex, which may be true.But they are quite as likely to vaccinate against the desirable glamor, if one admits that there may be such a thing. No tears need be shed over this first stage of Comstock's activity, but it is going pretty far to treat it as complete justification for the later Comstock, who attacked *Mrs. Warren's Profession* and the wax figures in department store show windows with equal zeal. . . . (p. 161)

Indeed, one finishes the biography with the impression that there was a deeper irrelevance in Comstock's crusades against pornography and what he thought was pornography. His abnormal fear and hatred of sex or anything that suggested it to his superheated mind was, after all, not his dominant characteristic. Essentially he was a bully; if the human race were asexual, reproducing by fission, Comstock would still have been a nuisance. Courage he certainly had and plenty of it—but he was a large and powerful man who could reasonably count on getting the best of any physical encounter; and behind him, after the first few years, he had the Law, which in that less sophisticated day was still some protection against the knife and the gun.

Possibly the most significant sentence in the book is a quotation from Comstock's diary, occasioned by no more flagitious an occurrence than a game of croquet with his wife and a few friends: "I insisted on fair play and some thought different." There, in a line, is the biography of Anthony Comstock. Whatever he insisted on was fair play, and God help those who "thought different."

From the beginning he had much success, but the courts had an inconvenient habit of occasionally acquitting people whose guilt was clear enough to Comstock. More law was needed, then, and Comstock got it; got it by a persistent and indefatigable effort which certainly compels admiration, whatever you think of his creed and his methods. Not that there was any grave danger that legislators of the early seventies would offer open opposition to his demands; they agreed with his doctrines in theory at least, even if few of them cared enough about purity to give their time to its preservation. (pp. 161-62)

There does not seem to be much evidence that the sexual morality of the American people was materially higher in the late seventies than in the earlier seventies; but whatever the boys and girls might be doing, Comstock certainly purified the newsstands. Armed with the sword he himself had forged, he was irresistible. In a decade or so his victory over his first enemy was complete; the obscene pamphlets which had provoked him into an activity that had made him famous had been driven into a furtive obscurity from which they have never since emerged. And here was Comstock, renowned and powerful, with the laws of his own writing behind him, his own hand-made fighting machine, the Vice Society, at his command—and his occupation gone. Not unnaturally he made himself more occupations, and some of them were grotesque enough.

Some of them were worse than that. He appointed himself the champion of orthodoxy and found the free-love doctrines of earnest atheists an excuse for persecuting them less as free lovers than as atheists. He drove to suicide an unbalanced woman guilty of writing a book which endeavored, however clumsily, to make marriage more decent and beautiful—but this was only one of fifteen suicides which he was proud of having inspired, and the last one. As time passed people stopped committing suicide to gratify him; sex appeared less a peril, contributions to the Vice Society decreased, the world seemed moving away from Comstock. Desperately he tried to catch up with it, tried this and that. He spent much time attacking lotteries, and local gambling houses which were by-products of political corruption. But a short-sightedness that sprang inevitably from his temperament and upbringing confined him to accidentals; he was unable to diagnose the disease of which protected gambling and protected prostitution were symptoms, and so he missed the chance of his lifetime. (pp. 162-63)

He descended to raiding art stores, trying to suppress the catalogue of the Art Students' league, turning "September Morn" from an unimportant painting into a valuable commercial property; he essayed to abolish Bernard MacFadden and Bernard Shaw; but he seldom got anywhere.

Yet still the soldier of the Lord went on fighting, and not the Lord's battles only. More quarrelsome and ill-tempered as the years went by, he kept getting into fights, not with agents of Satan selling implements of sin, but with lawyers who dared to cross-examine him, with pedestrians who resented being knocked down because they brushed against him on crowded sidewalks. He had pampered his overbearing and bellicose disposition because he had been big enough and strong enough to get away with it; when he grew too old to win his fights, he still could not help provoking them. Here, plainly, was the ruling passion of his life; his pathological sex phobia merely happened to give it a picturesque direction.

Well, what did he accomplish? Comstock is gone but Shaw and MacFadden are still with us; and between Comstock and MacFadden it would be uncharitable to express a preference. Sex is still with us, for all Comstock's efforts; rather noticeably with us, one might say. But certainly the deliberate obscenity of our time—and without going into the question of what is and is not obscene, one may remark that obviously there is a good deal on the stage and the newsstands today which at least tries to be obscene—is more suave, less repulsive than the obscenity which Comstock drove underground. Unless you hold with Comstock that sex is sin, that improvement in taste—much room as is left for further improvement—is something gained.

But not all of that credit can be given to Comstock; it is a change in the popular temper, the popular taste; it might have happened without him. (pp. 163-64)

Comstock himself may seem to have been thrust into obscurity by this new movement, but he has played his part. We owe to him the laws which made dissemination of contraceptive information obscene by definition; we owe to him the all-embracing phraseology of the present statutes, which enables a judge to interpret them according to his own taste. An indecent play, by the New York law as it stood before amendment (and this part of course still stands), is one which "would tend to the corruption of the morals of youth, or others.". . . In other words, the diet of all of us must be that prescribed for the weakest stomach; for fear that the wicked may be still further depraved, the pervert still further perverted, the clean and intelligent must be treated as of no account.

We owe that to Comstock. He was a psychopathic case; and if you say that we all are, more or less, it must be observed that in his instance it was considerably more. In his chosen field, this foul-minded man ruled the nation for a couple of decades. It would be inexact to say that his soul goes marching on; it was a peculiar soul, hardly to be duplicated. But the weapons he invented and manufactured still arm the forces of repression; his laws are still on the books, and laws which profess to effect the moral improvement of the citizenry are rarely repealed in this virtuous nation. For a century to come, all the forces of obscurantism will have reason to be grateful to him. (pp. 164-65)

Elmer Davis, in extracts from "The Comstock Load" (originally published in its entirety in The Saturday Review of Literature, *Vol. III, No. 36, April 2, 1927), in his* By Elmer Davis, *edited by Robert Lloyd Davis (copyright © 1964 by Robert Lloyd Davis; used with permission of the publisher, The Bobbs-Merrill Company, Inc.), Bobbs-Merrill, 1964, pp. 158-65.*

ROBERT BREMNER (essay date 1967)

[*The editor of a 1967 reprint of* Traps for the Young, *Bremner offers a survey of Comstock's major writings.*]

[In June 1873 Comstock] was instrumental in the passage of a New York law, subsequently copied in other states, which increased the penalties for selling obscene matter and, as in the federal statute, lumped contraceptives and drugs and devices for inducing illegal abortion with obscenity. Meanwhile the YMCA committee which had sponsored Comstock's work since March 1872 gave way to an independent organization, the New York Society for the Suppression of Vice, whose incorporators, in addition to Jesup and Dodge, included J. P. Morgan. By the act of incorporation the organization was entitled to claim one-half the fines levied on persons brought to justice by the Society or its agents. Needless to say Comstock was its chief agent. Thus armed, Comstock began a decade of adventurous activity, whose highlights he recorded in ***Traps for the Young.*** (p. xiv)

Traps for the Young contained no hint of the economic catastrophes, social unrest, and industrial and agrarian protests of the period. Comstock's indifference to the problems which agitated some of his contemporaries is bound to strike us as peculiar because their writings have shaped our conception of the overriding concerns of the 1870's and 80's. But the neglect of social and economic issues in ***Traps for the Young*** enhances rather than lessens its value as a document. If the book tells us little about matters we have come to assume were the major problems of the time, it reminds us of other more-or-less forgotten problems which were of great import to many good and influential people of Comstock's day. It takes us into the underworld of reform, and acquaints us with the attitude of mind of inhabitants of that populous but largely unexplored region. No understanding of American reform is complete without an apprehension of the mentality and temperament depicted in ***Traps for the Young.***

Traps for the Young was Comstock's second book, a sequel to ***Frauds Exposed; or, How the People are Deceived and Robbed, and Youth Corrupted.*** . . . (pp. xiv-xv)

Like all of Comstock's writings, ***Traps for the Young*** was intended to publicize his activities and justify his methods. It

TABULAR VIEW OF RESULTS.

DESCRIPTION.	TOTAL TO 1880.
Persons arrested in U. S. Courts	205
" " " State Courts	203
Discharged by Committing Magistrates	20
" " Juries	8
Convicted or plead guilty	200
Sentenced	180
Prisoners absconded	9
" re-arrested	16
Disagreement by Juries	12
Convicted on second trial	5
Bail bonds forfeited	$38,000
Years of imprisonment imposed	yrs. mos. days. 146 0 23
Amount of fines imposed	$51,300
Convicts pardoned	17
STOCK CONFISCATED.	
Books and sheet stock seized and destroyed	24,225 lbs.
Obscene Pictures and Photo's	202,679
Microscopic Pictures for Charms, Knives, etc	7,400
Negative Plates for making Obscene Photographs	1,700
Engraved Steel and Copper Plates	352
Wood Cuts and Electro-plates	536
Stereotype Plates for printing Books, etc	14,420 lbs.
Number of different Books	165
Lithographic Stones destroyed	50
Articles for immoral use, of rubber, etc	64,094
Lead Moulds for making Obscene Matter	700 lbs.
Establishments for making same closed	5
Indecent Playing Cards destroyed	6,072
Boxes of Pills, Powders, etc., used by Abortionists	4,185
Circulars, Catalogues, Songs, Poems, etc	1,316,088
Newspapers containing unlawful Advertisements or Obscene Matter	22,354
Open letters seized in possession of persons arrested	70,280
Names of Dealers, as revealed by Account Books of Publishers	6,000
Obscene Pictures, framed on walls of Saloons	26
Figures and Images seized and destroyed	565
Letters, Packages, etc., seized in hands of Dealers, ready for mailing at the time of arrest	3,421
Names and P. O. addresses to whom Circulars, etc., may be sent, that are sold as matters of Merchandise, seized in hands of persons arrested	901,125
Obscene Plays stopped, or places of Amusement closed	4
Miles travelled by Agent outside N. Y. City	139,675

A table published by Comstock listing the results of his activities to 1880. From Frauds Exposed, *by Anthony Comstock.*

continued the account, begun in ***Frauds Exposed,*** of "devices to plunder, ruin, and debauch" whose overthrow had been his "privilege and duty." Believing his work was inspired and directed by God, Comstock did not undervalue his achievements. But his conviction of rectitude was accompanied by acute sensitivity to criticism. "It is important that a man should be right in all he does," he wrote in ***Frauds Exposed.*** "It is almost equally important that he should seem to be right, when he is right." Unfortunately, in the eyes of others, Comstock often seemed to be wrong when he was most convinced that he was right. Much of the trouble arose from the methods he employed in his war against sin. (pp. xv-xvi)

In the preface to ***Traps for the Young*** Comstock characterized the book as an alarm to alert parents and public opinion to the problem of "*Evil Reading*" [see excerpt above]. He praised "good reading" but seems to have had little interest in the subject. Comstock had the non-reader's suspicion of the reading habit and awe of the power of print. He read not for pleasure or information, but for reassurance, proof that he was right and documentation of ideas he already possessed. As a devout and orthodox Christian he took it for granted that humans had an in-born tendency toward wrong-doing which was restrained mainly by fear of the final judgment. Hence any literature which removed that fear, acted as a soporific against it, or awakened "impure thoughts," struck him as a "devil trap."

His definition of evil reading included but was not confined to obscene and impious works. As far as children were concerned evil reading encompassed nearly all light fiction and popular journalism. Comstock's abhorrence of the daydreaming and vain imaginings inspired by sentimental novels perpetuated the view firmly established—or at least often expressed—in the Connecticut of his youth that reading frivolous literature impeded the mental and moral development of children. But sentimental romances, as Comstock acknowledged, were the weakest of the devil traps. Much more dangerous were the half-dime novels and story papers examined in chapter three [of ***Traps for the Young***]. (pp. xxi-xxii)

In chapter three Comstock presented a file of youthful desperadoes of both sexes whose vexations, trials, and aggressions would have provided plots for a score of story-paper serials. Some of the delinquents, when facing arrest or imposition of sentence, or while slowly dying, put the blame for their misdeeds on evil reading; a few had story papers in their possession when apprehended; in most instances, however, there was no demonstrable connection between the crimes committed and the reading habits of the culprits. But to Comstock all the offenders were "schoolboys crazed by the accursed blood-and-thunder story papers," the increase in juvenile crime solely attributable to "recruits made by criminal reading." This view, by no means peculiar to Comstock or to Americans, prompted Gilbert K. Chesterton's derisive comment: "It is firmly fixed in the minds of most people that gutter-boys, unlike everybody else in the community, find their principle motives for conduct in printed books." In Comstock's case "evil reading" assumed the proportions of an obsession, blotting out other social or psychological causes of delinquency, and making him insensitive to crimes perpetrated on children by society. He expressed no horror in reporting the trial and conviction of a twelve-year-old child on a first-degree murder charge. He could write of the lynching of a fourteen-year-old boy without blanching, expressing indignation only at the "heartless and shameless manner" in which the boy—a confessed reader of sensational novels—awaited execution.

Comstock excluded novels by reputable authors (he cited Sir Walter Scott and George Eliot as examples) from his discussion of evil reading and did not become involved in the censorship of contemporary adult fiction until late in his career. As early as 1878, however, he assumed responsibility for suppressing new editions of the erotic literature of the past and reproductions of works of art displaying nudes. In the 1880's and thereafter these artistic and classical traps, which he denounces in chapter eleven, came to occupy an increasing share of his attention. (pp. xxiii-xxiv)

Comstock returned to the subject of artistic traps in ***Morals versus Art*. . . .** Here, as in ***Traps for the Young,*** he distinguished between original works of art, which he professed to hold in high esteem, and copies of the same which he deemed capable of mischief. In justification of a raid on the Herman Knoedler Gallery, Comstock explained that what he wanted to suppress was "not French art, but . . . cheap lewd French photographs." Declaring profound respect for the human—particularly the female—form, Comstock declared the proper place for representation of it was in museums where the display could be appreciated by "cultured minds." "Nude art" in a saloon, or store window, or any place within the reach of "the common mind" or exposed to the eyes of "the uncultured and inexperienced" was a different matter. "What would be the effect of such pictures on young men?" he asked. The question was rhetorical because Comstock knew the answer. "They appeal to passion and create impure imaginations," he said of the pictures. "To young men, cursed as thousands of the present day are with secret vices, these photographs leave impressions upon their imaginations which are a constant menace. . . . They fan the flame of secret desires." (pp. xxiv-xxv)

"It requires no expert in art or literature," Comstock gloated, "to determine whether a picture tends to awaken lewd thoughts and impure imaginations in the minds of the young." All it took was an amateur of lewd thoughts and impure imaginations. In these branches of unconscious knowledge, Comstock was without rival.

When ***Traps for the Young*** was published Comstock had not yet reached the midpoint of his career. Ahead of him stretched thirty-two more years of service to God and contest with Satan. (p. xxvi)

Ardent admirers memorialized him as a modern Galahad. According to a more sober view Comstock both embodied and caricatured the moral sense of his epoch. (p. xxxi)

Robert Bremner, in an introduction to Traps for the Young *by Anthony Comstock, edited by Robert Bremner (copyright © 1967 by the President and Fellows of Harvard College; excerpted by permission), Cambridge, Mass.: Belknap Press, 1967, pp. vii-xxxi.*

JEAN STAFFORD (essay date 1968)

[*Stafford was a critic, novelist, and Pulitzer-prize winning short story writer. In the excerpt below, she comments on the reissue of Comstock's* Traps for the Young, *edited by Robert Bremner.*]

During his reign of terror from 1872 until 1915, Anthony Comstock's name was a household word in as active currency as Mrs. Grundy's. He was a dedicated and vociferous and madly peripatetic crusader against Satan and Satan's aides—the writers and publishers of obscene literature, the manufacturers and purveyors of tobacco in all forms, pool-hall proprietors, confectioners who kept their shops open on Sunday, theater owners, champions of free love, saloon-keepers. Through these deputies, the Arch-fiend laid his traps for the young who, all too often, sickened and, if they did not die, became pariahs or incorrigible miscreants. . . . ***Traps for the Young*** . . . was a sequel to his first book ***Frauds Exposed; or How the People are Deceived and Robbed, and Youth Corrupted.*** It is a grandiloquent manual for parents whose responsibility it is to keep their lads and misses from treading the primrose path. . . .

He was a fire-breathing enemy of the policy racket (". . . that quintessence of meanness . . ."), lotteries (run by "unprincipled scamps"), prizes offered by soap companies and candy concerns, off-track betting, advertisements sent through the mail inviting the young to misbehave. All these "eye-traps . . . ear-traps and mouth-traps," destroy "nerve and tissue," to say nothing of filial devotion, and lead to "blood-shed and carnage, the natural fruitage of this planting." Fruitage is one of his favorite words and if he can get it into a sentence together with "burglarious" he is as happy as a lark.

Apart from its period prose style (he likes whited sepulchers and dungeons vile), ***Traps for the Young*** has a certain sociological interest, for, unless his case histories and statistics are altogether imaginary, it demonstrates that arsonists, train-wreckers, burglars and murderers began their careers quite as early in life as they do today—at 12 or 13—and that juvenile delinquency is no contemporary phenomenon.

Jean Stafford, "An Expert in Impure Thoughts," in Book World—The Washington Post *(© 1968 Postrib Corp. reprinted by permission of* Chicago Tribune *and* The Washington Post*), January 14, 1968, p. 12.*

JOHN DE LOSS (essay date 1968)

[*Reviewing the reissue of* Traps for the Young, *de Loss cites the book as, ironically, a useful tool in unmasking the designs of self-righteous zealotry.*]

Like it or not, part of [American] cultural history has been (and is) the effort to maintain moral standards through direct action. Critics of those who would safe-guard public morals call this process censorship; champions speak of crusade.

Anthony Comstock has the distinction of being recognized as a crusader by both camps. The only debate is over the clay on his feet. (p. 143)

At the end of the nineteenth century things were pretty rugged. Young people were assailed on every side. If they stayed home they could easily be tempted by the newspapers of the day which carried scandalous and indecent stories of the lowest members of society. Then there were the half-dime novels and story papers which were vehicles of lust pure and simple. If a young person somehow missed degradation by these means, he would most likely fall to the lure of advertising traps.

All of these terrible forces are denounced [in ***Traps for the Young***] with a vigor and force that would have done Billy Sunday proud, and with the supreme confidence that five adjectives are always better than one or two when evil is being described. (pp. 143-44)

[Comstock's] legacy includes the anti-obscenity bill of 1873. He also seems to have left us, somehow, a kind of dynamic for similar crusaders: non-discriminating, totally certain in the rightness of the cause, unmindful of the demands of freedom of expression. It is good to have this source book among us. There is much that it can teach us. It requires only a bit of reading between the lines. (p. 144)

John de Loss, "Safeguarding Morals," in Catholic World *(copyright 1968 by The Missionary Society of St. Paul the Apostle in the State of New York; used by permission), Vol. 207, No. 1239, June, 1968, pp. 143-44.*

ADDITIONAL BIBLIOGRAPHY

Blanshard, Paul. "Sex and Obscenity." In his *The Right to Read,* pp. 138-67. Boston: Beacon Press, 1955.*

Examination of the "change in American standards of literary decency" during the last three centuries, with close study of landmark obscenity trials. A section is devoted to Comstock's role in the passage of the anti-obscenity laws of the 1870s.

Broun, Heywood, and Leech, Margaret. *Anthony Comstock: Roundsman of the Lord.* New York: Boni, 1927, 285 p.

A biographical and critical examination of Comstock's career.

Mencken, H. L. "Comstockery." In his *Prejudices, fifth series,* pp. 15-21. New York: Alfred A. Knopf, 1926.

Finds that the attempt to ban sex hygiene books as obscene proved the downfall of Comstock and of other contemporaneous professional censors.

"Anthony Comstock." *The Outlook* III (29 September 1915): 246-47.

Obituary that provides a favorable assessment of Comstock's career, concluding that the "country will never know what it owes to his relentless warfare against all kinds of corruption."

Sumner, John S. "Comstock and Sumner." *Journal of Education* LXXXII, No. 17 (11 November 1915): 458-59.

Statement of the intentions of Sumner, Comstock's successor as secretary of the New York Society for the Suppression of Vice. Sumner restates Comstock's view that works must be judged as obscene "not from the point of view of a mature person" but with "the uninformed, immature, or perhaps defective intelligence and imagination" as a guideline. However, Sumner notes that "times have changed" and states that the Society will operate more quietly than in the past.

Williams, Ellen. "The Great Years of *Poetry,* 1914-1915." In her *Harriet Monroe and the Poetry Renaissance,* pp. 91-117. Urbana: University of Illinois Press, 1977.*

Briefly mentions the threat of Post Office impoundment of the November, 1914 issue of *Poetry* magazine, which contained a poem by John Russell McCarthy. Harriet Monroe, founder and editor of *Poetry,* was one of the first literary figures to join with H. L. Mencken in protesting the actions of the New York Society for the Suppression of Vice in banning James Branch Cabell's *Jurgen.* Monroe also publicly supported Margaret Anderson and *The Little Review* when the Society seized that publication for serializing James Joyce's *Ulysses.*

Joseph Conrad

1857-1924

(Born Tedor Josef Konrad Nalecz Korzeniowski) Polish born English novelist, novella and short story writer, essayist, and autobiographer.

The following entry presents criticism of Conrad's novella *Heart of Darkness*. For a complete discussion of Conrad's career, see *TCLC*, Vols. 1 and 6.

***Heart of Darkness* is considered one of the greatest short novels in the English language. On the surface it is a dreamlike tale of mystery and adventure set in central Africa; however, it is also the story of a man's symbolic journey into his own inner being. A profusion of vivid details that are significant on both literal and symbolic levels contributes to the ambiguity of Conrad's narrative and has led to conflicting interpretations of its meaning.**

Like many of Conrad's novels and short stories, *Heart of Darkness* is based in part upon the author's personal experiences. In 1890, after more than a decade as a seaman, Conrad requested the command of a Belgian steamer sailing for Africa. A diary kept during the subsequent voyage provides evidence that many of the characters, incidents, and impressions recalled in *Heart of Darkness* have factual bases. In his preface to *Youth: A Narrative, and Two Other Stories*, in which *Heart of Darkness* appeared in 1902, Conrad himself states that the story is "experience pushed a little (and only very little) beyond the actual facts of the case." Contemporary critics, however, agree that Conrad's manipulation of the African environment in the novel, and the portraits of greed, destruction, and psychological regression he creates, should be credited solely to his imaginative genius. In 1896 Conrad had written about his Congo experiences in the short story *An Outpost of Progress*, but he considered *Heart of Darkness* far superior to that apprentice work, because while the earlier story was concerned with individuals, *Heart of Darkness* examined in detail the broadest aspects of colonialism. Conrad stated that he sought to depict "the criminality of inefficiency and pure selfishness when tackling the civilizing work in Africa" and added "the subject is of our time distinctly." Ford Madox Ford, Conrad's longtime friend and collaborator, considered *Youth, Heart of Darkness*, and *The Nigger of the 'Narcissus'* the best of Conrad's works based on his sea experiences. Ford attributed the success of these works to the fact that they were written while the incidents were still fresh in Conrad's memory and the demands of his career did not interfere with leisurely rewriting.

Throughout Conrad's career *Heart of Darkness* remained one of his most popular and highly regarded works. The novella details the story of the seaman Marlow who, fresh from Europe, is sent on a boat journey up the Congo River to relieve Kurtz, the most successful trader in ivory working for the Belgian government. Prior to their personal encounter, Marlow knows and admires Kurtz through his reputation and his writings regarding the civilizing of the African continent, and sets out on the journey excited at the prospect of meeting him. However, Marlow's experience in Africa inspires revulsion at the dehumanizing effects of colonialism, a disgust that culminates when he discovers that Kurtz has degenerated from an enlightened civilizer into a vicious, power-hungry subjugator of the African natives. Marlow's journey forces him to confront not only Kurtz's corruption, but also those elements within himself which are subject to the same temptations that affected Kurtz.

The Granger Collection, New York

The relationship of Conrad to his character Marlow has been a fertile area of critical discussion. Marlow has been variously perceived as the spokesman for Conrad, a complex and separate creation, and as a combination of both. F. R. Leavis, for example, considered Marlow and the author of the story to be one and the same, and criticized Conrad's ambiguous descriptions of Kurtz and his activities in the jungle. Albert J. Guerard, however, insists that it is the created character Marlow, not Conrad, who is literally speechless when confronted with memories of Kurtz, and that the resulting ambiguity illustrates Marlow's inability or unwillingness to clearly describe the horror he discovers in the jungle. Most critics agree with Guerard that the character Marlow is a creation detached from the author, and that the story is as concerned with his development and growing perception of the horrors within human nature as it is with describing Kurtz's degeneration. For that reason Conrad deliberately limited Marlow's powers as a narrator. This is in fact accentuated by the narrative's elaborate framing device, wherein Marlow tells his

story to an unnamed narrator, who in turn comments on Marlow's method of narration.

The affinity between Marlow and Kurtz is considered the most crucial relationship between characters in the story. Two pivotal scenes in *Heart of Darkness* hint at the source of the men's bond, but the precise intention of Conrad remains ambiguous. The first of the scenes, in which Kurtz utters his famous death cry, "The horror, the horror!" is regarded by many critics as Kurtz's realization of the terrifying nature of his unrestrained behavior, a realization that is transferred to Marlow, who is allied with Kurtz through a complex mixture of repugnance and fascination. W. Y. Tindall, however, warns that Marlow contains myriad uncertainties and enigmas, and that his interpretation of Kurtz's final words as a sign of self-disgust and redemption is based on his own perceptions of life, not Kurtz's. Tindall suggests that perhaps Kurtz was lamenting his untimely and violent death, or that he found horrifying the fact that his accumulation of ivory and his godlike reign over the natives had been interrupted. Nonetheless, most critics consider the scene crucial in that Marlow glimpses the barbarous depths to which civilized man can sink, affirming a kinship between the "cultured" Europeans and the "savage" Africans in the lawless jungle. This knowledge alters Marlow's perception of the nature of truth and humanity and leads to the development of the second pivotal scene, which occurs after Marlow returns to Brussels. There, he is asked the nature of Kurtz's final words by the dead man's innocent fiancée, and he tells her that Kurtz repeated her name. Marlow's lie is a widely discussed element of the novella and is subject to many diverse interpretations. Leavis, for example, interprets the lie as Marlow's final acceptance of Kurtz as an apostle of truth who has encountered in himself the essential barbarism of humanity. Others believe that it is the act of a man creating a personal morality based on the protection of the innocent from truth that is difficult to face. Some critics, however, find that the lie weakens the final scene because Marlow's strong insistence upon the value of truth throughout the novella makes it impossible for the reader to suddenly accept falsehood as salvation. In the end, Marlow's lie reflects as much about the subjective nature of truth as it does about Marlow's character.

Many critics have commented on Conrad's evocative powers in *Heart of Darkness,* paying particular attention to his use of imagery, which manages to evoke a sinister atmosphere through the accretion of objectively described details of the African jungle and natives. The visual imagery, which heavily depends upon contrasting patterns of light and dark, contributes most appreciably to the consistently ambiguous tone of the work. To demonstrate the moral uncertainty of this world and of life in general, Conrad consistently alters common symbolic conceptions of light and dark. Thus, white is not synonymous with good, nor black with evil, but rather both symbols are interchangeable. For example, the light of civilization that Europeans bring to Africa is in fact the source of suffering and misery for the people of the continent. Similarly, ivory becomes the ultimate symbol of excess, greed, and savagery, as the Europeans systematically exploit or destroy the natives to acquire it. Throughout the novella, white and black characters are alternately examples of acute suffering, civilized dignity, moral refinement, or violent savagery, demonstrating that no race is wholly good or evil, and that all human beings are a confusing mixture of propensities for all types of behavior. While some critics consider Conrad's imagery vague and confused in a manner that does not present a clear picture of the principal characters and events, most find that the ambiguity of description lends a psychological depth to the story which demands the close attention and involvement of the reader.

The political significance of *Heart of Darkness* has also received much critical attention. C. P. Sarvan has observed that Conrad "was not entirely immune to the infection of the beliefs and attitudes of his age, but he was ahead of most in trying to break free." Social Darwinism and a strong belief in the Carlylean work ethic are two of the Victorian standards that are attacked in the novella. The first served to justify European exploitation of Africa and other areas of the world by purporting that the indigenous peoples were in need of the superior technological and religious knowledge of Europe. In *Heart of Darkness* the hypocrisy of these aims is illustrated by the all-consuming scramble for wealth by the Europeans, who destroy the land and people without remorse. Cedric Watts contends that by contrasting the harmony which exists between the native Africans, and their natural environment with the lazy, brutish grotesques that white imperialists become in Africa, Conrad proves that it is the Africans who are the fittest to survive in their native land and that Darwin's theory was in fact never intended to be applied to races or nations. In one of the work's most memorable ironic reversals of circumstance, Conrad compares the restraint practiced by a group of cannibals with the destructive greed of the European colonizers. In a similar fashion, the work ethic which Marlow seems to embrace, praising its effectiveness in keeping his mind free of undesireable thoughts, is in fact instrumental in blinding him to the events around him. The inhumanity of the work ethic as practiced in Africa is demonstrated by a company accountant who considers the use of his office as an infirmary an inconvenience: he does not care if sick Africans die or not, so long as their illnesses do not interfere with his work. Throughout the novella, Conrad's portrayal of the failure of various European ideologies in Africa suggests the consequent failure and moral bankruptcy of Europe.

Conrad's consciously ambiguous presentation of the relative nature of truth and morality, which compels the reader to take an active part in understanding the novella, is often considered a forerunner of many modernist literary techniques. For this reason Frederick R. Karl has called *Heart of Darkness* the work in which "the nineteenth century becomes the twentieth." The novella's artistic cohesion of image and theme, its intricately vivid evocation of colonial oppression, and its detailed portrait of psychological duplicity and decay have inspired critics to call *Heart of Darkness* the best short novel in the English language. As Karl notes: "It asks troublesome questions, disturbs preconceptions, forces curious confrontations, and possibly changes us."

(See also *Contemporary Authors,* Vol. 104; *Dictionary of Literary Biography,* Vol. 10: *Modern British Dramatists, 1900-1945;* and *Something about the Author,* Vol. 27.)

THE TIMES LITERARY SUPPLEMENT **(essay date 1902)**

[*The following excerpt from a review of* Youth, *a volume which contains* Heart of Darkness *and* The End of the Tether, *praises the power of Conrad's depiction of horror but disapprovingly notes the "preciousness" of Conrad's style.*]

Telling tales, just spinning yarns, has gone out of fashion since the novel has become an epitome of everything a man has to say about anything. The three stories in ***Youth*** . . . are in this reference a return to an earlier taste. The yarns are of the sea, told with an astonishing zest; and given with vivid accumulation of detail and iterative persistency of emphasis on the quality of character and scenery. The method is exactly the opposite of Mr. Kipling's. It is a little precious; one notes a tasting of the quality of phrases and an occasional indulgence in poetic rhetoric. But the effect is not unlike Mr. Kipling's. . . . The concluding scene of the **"Heart of Darkness"** is crisp and brief enough for Flaubert, but the effect—a woman's ecstatic belief in a villain's heroism—is reached by an indulgence in the picturesque horror of the villain, his work and his surroundings, which is pitiless in its insistence, and quite extravagant according to the canons of art. But the power, the success in conveying the impression vividly, without loss of energy is undoubted and is refreshing. . . . There are many readers who would not get beyond the barren and not very pretty philosophy of **"Youth"**; more who might feel they had had enough horror at the end of **"The Heart of Darkness."** But they would miss a great deal if they did not reach **"The End of the Tether."** It has this further advantage over the other two tales, that it is much less clever, much less precious.

A review of "Youth," in The Times Literary Supplement, *No. 48, December 12, 1902, p. 372.*

THE ATHENAEUM (essay date 1902)

[*The following excerpt from a review of* Youth *praises the artistry of Conrad's prose and the craft displayed in his short fiction. The critic also finds in Conrad's work an innovative ability to fully evoke the mood and atmosphere of his settings within a relatively few number of pages.*]

The art of Mr. Conrad is exquisite and very subtle. He uses the tools of his craft with the fine, thoughtful delicacy of a mediaeval clockmaker. With regard to his mastery of the *conte* [*story*] opinions are divided, and many critics will probably continue to hold that his short stories are not short stories at all, but rather concentrated novels. And the contention is not unreasonable. In more ways than one Mr. Conrad is something of a law unto himself, and creates his own forms, as he certainly has created his own methods. Putting aside all considerations of mere taste, one may say at once that Mr. Conrad's methods command and deserve the highest respect, if only by reason of their scholarly thoroughness. One feels that nothing is too minute, no process too laborious for this author. He considers not material rewards, but the dignity of his work, of all work. . . . [He] has the true worker's eye, the true artist's pitilessness, in the detection and elimination of the redundant word, the idle thought, the insincere idiom, or even for the mark of punctuation misplaced. The busy, boastful times we live in are not rich in such sterling literary merits as these; and for that reason we may be the more thankful to an author like Mr. Conrad for the loyalty which prevents his sending a scamped page to press.

A critical writer has said that all fiction may roughly be divided into two classes: that dealing with movement and adventure, and the other dealing with characterization, the analysis of the human mind. In the present, as in every one of his previous books, Mr. Conrad has stepped outside these boundaries, and made his own class of work as he has made his own methods. All his stories have movement and incident, most of them have adventure, and the motive in all has apparently been the careful analysis, the philosophic presentation, of phases of human character. His studious and minute drawing of the action of men's minds, passions, and principles forms fascinating reading. But he has another gift of which he himself may be less conscious, by means of which his other more incisive and purely intellectual message is translated for the proper understanding of simpler minds and plainer men. That gift is the power of conveying atmosphere, and in the exercise of this talent Mr. Conrad has few equals among our living writers of fiction. He presents the atmosphere in which his characters move and act with singular fidelity, by means of watchful and careful building in which the craftsman's methods are never obtrusive, and after turning the last page of one of his books we rise saturated by the very air they breathed. This is a great power, but, more or less, it is possessed by other talented writers of fiction. The rarity of it in Mr. Conrad lies in this, that he can surround both his characters and his readers with the distinctive atmosphere of a particular story within the limits of a few pages. This is an exceptional gift, and the more to be prized in Mr. Conrad for the reason that he shows some signs of growing over-subtle in his analysis of moods, temperaments, and mental idiosyncrasies. It is an extreme into which all artists whose methods are delicate, minute, and searching are apt to be led. . . . With Mr. Conrad, however, these rather dangerous intellectual refinements are illumined always by a vivid wealth of atmosphere, and translated simply by action, incident, strong light and shade, and distinctive colouring. . . . **'The Heart of Darkness'** is a big and thoughtful conception, the most important part of the book. . . .

The reviewer deliberately abstains both from quotation and from any attempt at analysis of a story like **'The Heart of Darkness.'** Any such attempt in a limited space would be a painful injustice where work of this character is concerned. Further, the reader is warned that this book cannot be read understandingly—as evening newspapers and railway novels are perused—with one mental eye closed and the other roving. Mr. Conrad himself spares no pains, and from his readers he demands thoughtful attention. He demands so much, and, where the intelligent are concerned, we think he will command it.

A review of "Youth," in The Athenaeum, *No. 3921, December 20, 1902, p. 824.*

THE NEW YORK TIMES BOOK REVIEW (essay date 1903)

[*In the following excerpt from a generally positive review of* Youth, *the critic expresses dislike for Conrad's occasionally intrusive moralizing bent.*]

The three stories by Joseph Conrad in the volume called **"Youth and Other Stories"** are all of the sea, of strange lands, and of abnormal human beings developed under abnormal conditions. The author's exceptional power is manifest in two directions: in his ability to portray extraordinary scenery and in his equal ability to impress a character upon the credulity of his readers. Although the adventures he describes are frequently little short of marvelous, and are laid among scenes wholly alien to commonplace life, they are wrought into a tissue of truth so firm and so tough as to resist the keenest skepticism. The personages who move about the ships, thread unbroken forests, establish control over swarms of savages by means of the spoken word, lie and cheat, struggle and work, make money and lose it, and talk interminably; these personages are sufficiently interesting in their various activities to lure one through many a patch of wordy underbrush to the welcome clearing where they are plainly to be seen. Their creator treats them with peculiar detachment. He wavers between the objective and the subjective method. Apparently he wishes to move swiftly along his line of adventure toward his termination, but his progress frequently is checked by the attacks of analytical meditation that overcome him at quite regular intervals. This entanglement of psychological with external phenomena is more or less wearying, as there is no very delicate adjustment between the mental and physical situations, and we are conscious sometimes of wishing that we might be allowed to supply our own moralizing. . . .

These little speeches which occur at—to the reader in quest of happenings—the most inopportune moments when a ship is burning or a man is dying, are undeniably loquacious, although usually apposite enough. They sap one's vitality of mind and cast the shadow of dullness over what otherwise would be stimulating. Nevertheless, Mr. Conrad has been amazingly successful in managing to convey a sense of solidity and veracity. Not even his Kurtz, the man of impenetrable darkness of soul, is either a bloodless or an incredible figure. Like certain caricatures that in their fidelity to the main facts make ordinary portraiture unconvincing, these grotesque figures drive home to the imagination.

"Some Stories by Joseph Conrad—Novels of Native Manufacture," in The New York Times Book Review, *April 4, 1903, p. 224.*

H. L. MENCKEN (essay date 1917)

[From the era of World War I until the early years of the Great Depression, Mencken was one of the most influential figures in American letters. His strongly individualistic, irreverent outlook on life and his vigorous, invective-charged writing style helped establish the iconoclastic spirit of the Jazz Age and significantly shaped the direction of American literature. As a social and literary critic—the roles for which he is best known—Mencken was the scourge of evangelical Christianity, public service organizations, literary censorship, boosterism, provincialism, democracy, all advocates of personal or social improvement, and every other facet of American life that he perceived as humbug. In his literary criticism, Mencken encouraged American writers to shun the anglophilic, moralistic bent of the nineteenth century and to practice realism, an artistic call-to-arms that is most fully developed in his essay "Puritanism As a Literary Force," *one of the seminal essays in modern literary criticism. A man who was widely renowned or feared during his lifetime as a would-be destroyer of established American values, Mencken wrote: "All my work, barring a few obvious burlesques, is based upon three fundamental ideas. 1. That knowledge is better than ignorance; 2. That it is better to tell the truth than to lie; 3. That it is better to be free than to be a slave." In the following discussion of* Heart of Darkness, *Mencken describes Conrad's artistic method, finding that he never defines his characters, but rather reveals aspects of their personality through his fictional situations, a method that forces the reader to suspend moral judgment and confront the basic indeterminancy and meaninglessness of life.]*

Like Dreiser, Conrad is forever fascinated by the "immense indifference of things," the tragic vanity of the blind groping that we call aspiration, the profound meaninglessness of life—fascinated, and left wondering. One looks in vain for an attempt at a solution of the riddle in the whole canon of his work. Dreiser, more than once, seems ready to take refuge behind an indeterminate sort of mysticism, even a facile supernaturalism, but Conrad, from first to last, faces squarely the massive and intolerable fact. His stories are not chronicles of men who conquer fate, nor of men who are unbent and undaunted by fate, but of men who are conquered and undone. . . . Kurtz, Lord Jim, Razumov, Nostromo, Captain Whalley, Yanko Goorall, Verloc, Heyst, Gaspar Ruiz, Almayer: one and all they are destroyed and made a mock of by the blind, incomprehensible forces that beset them. (pp. 11-12)

The exact point of the story of Kurtz, in **"Heart of Darkness,"** is that it is pointless, that Kurtz's death is as meaningless as his life, that the moral of such a sordid tragedy is a wholesale negation of all morals. (p. 16)

As for Conrad the literary craftsman, opposing him for the moment to Conrad the showman of the human comedy, the quality that all who write about him seem chiefly to mark in him is his scorn of conventional form, his tendency to approach his story from two directions at once, his frequent involvement in apparently inextricable snarls of narrative, sub-narrative and sub-sub-narrative. . . . In **"Youth"** and **"Heart of Darkness"** the chronicler and speculator is the shadowy Marlow, a "cloak to goe inbisabell" for Conrad himself. . . . Elsewhere there are hesitations, goings back, interpolations, interludes in the Socratic manner. And almost always there is heaviness in the getting under weigh. In **"Heart of Darkness"** we are on the twentieth page before we see the mouth of the great river. . . . (pp. 36-7)

In the eyes of orthodox criticism, of course, this is a grave fault. The Kipling-Wells style of swift, shouldering, buttonholing writing has accustomed readers and critics alike to a straight course and a rapid tempo. Moreover, it has accustomed them to a forthright certainty and directness of statement; they expect an author to account for his characters at once, and on grounds instantly comprehensible. . . . The discoveries that we make, about Lord Jim, about Nostromo or about Kurtz, come as fortuitously and as unexpectedly as the discoveries we make about the real figures of our world. The picture is built up bit by bit; it is never flashed suddenly and completely as by best-seller calciums; it remains a bit dim at the end. But in that very dimness, so tantalizing and yet so revealing, lies two-thirds of Conrad's art, or his craft, or his trick, or whatever you choose to call it. What he shows us is blurred at the edges, but so is life itself blurred at the edges. We see least clearly precisely what is nearest to us, and is hence most real to us. (pp. 37-9)

In the character and in its reactions, in the act and in the motive: always that tremulousness, that groping, that confession of final bewilderment. . . . One leaves **"Heart of Darkness"** in that palpitating confusion which is shot through with intense curiosity. Kurtz is at once the most abominable of rogues and the most fantastic of dreamers. It is impossible to differentiate between his vision and his crimes, though all that we look upon as order in the universe stands between them. (pp. 39-40)

Conrad's predilection for barbarous scenes and the more bald and shocking sort of drama has an obviously autobiographical basis. His own road ran into strange places in the days of his youth. . . . Some of his stories, and among them his very best, are plainly little more than transcripts of his own experience. He himself is the enchanted boy of **"Youth,"** he is the shipmaster of **"Heart of Darkness"**; he hovers in the background of all the island books and is visibly present in most of the tales of the sea. (pp. 40-1)

Whenever he turns from the starker lusts to the pale passions of man under civilization, Conrad fails. **"The Return"** is a thoroughly infirm piece of writing—a second rate magazine story. One concludes at once that the author himself does not believe in it. **"The Inheritors"** is worse; it becomes, after the first few pages, a flaccid artificiality, a bore. It is impossible to imagine the chief characters of the Conrad gallery in such scenes. (p. 42)

These things do not interest Conrad, chiefly, I suppose, because he does not understand them. His concern, one may say, is with the gross anatomy of passion, not with its histology. He seeks to depict emotion, not in its ultimate attenuation, but in its fundamental innocence and fury. Inevitably, his materials are those of what we call melodrama; he is at one, in the bare substance of his tales, with the manufacturers of the baldest shockers. But with a difference!—a difference, to wit, of approach and comprehension, a difference abysmal and revolutionary. He lifts melodrama to the dignity of an important business, and makes it a means to an end that the mere shock-monger never dreams of. (pp. 42-3)

If you want to get his measure, read **"Youth"** or **"Falk"** or **"Heart of Darkness,"** and then try to read the best of Kipling. I think you will come to some understanding, by that simple experiment, of the difference between an adroit artisan's bag of tricks and the lofty sincerity and passion of a first-rate artist. (p. 64)

H. L. Mencken, "Joseph Conrad," in his A Book of Prefaces *(copyright 1917 by Alfred A. Knopf, Inc. and renewed 1944 by H. L. Mencken; reprinted by permission of the publisher), Knopf, 1917 (and reprinted by Knopf, 1924), pp. 11-64.*

F. R. LEAVIS (essay date 1941)

[Leavis, an influential contemporary English critic, combines close textual criticism with predominantly moral, or social-moral principles of evaluation. Leavis views the writer as that social individual who represents the "most conscious point of the race" in his or her lifetime. More importantly, the writer is one who can effectively communicate this consciousness. Contrary to what these statements may suggest, Leavis is not specifically interested in the individual writer per se, but more concerned with the usefulness of his or her art in the scheme of civilization. The writer's role in this vision is to promote what Leavis calls "sincerity"—or, the realization of the individual's proper place in the human world. Literature that accomplishes this he calls "mature," and the writer's judgment within such a work he calls a "mature" moral judgment. From the foregoing comments it should be clear that Leavis is a critic concerned with the moral aspects of art, but a number of his contemporaries, most notably René Wellek, have questioned the existence of a moral system beneath such terms as "maturity" and "sincerity." Leavis's refusal to theorize or develop a systematic philosophy has alienated many critics and scholars from his work. In the following excerpt, Leavis finds that, at his best, Conrad evokes meaning through the artistry of his description; at his worst, Conrad imposes his comments or needlessly obscures the force of his story with ambiguous terminology and a failure to describe the "unspeakable," a failure that Leavis believes almost destroys the conclusion of the story. Leavis attributes this failure to Conrad's use of Marlow as a narrator. For further discussions of Conrad's treatment of the "unspeakable," see the excerpts by Thomas Moser (1957), Albert J. Guerard (1958), Marvin Mudrick (1958-59), and Frederick R. Karl (1969), and the entry by Frederick Crews in the Additional Bibliography.]

Heart of Darkness is, by common consent, one of Conrad's best things—an appropriate source for the epigraph of *The Hollow Men:* 'Mistah Kurtz, he dead'. That utterance, recalling the particularity of its immediate context, represents the strength of ***Heart of Darkness***. . . . (p. 174)

[The passage] owes its force to a whole wide context of particularities that gives the elements . . .—the pilgrims, the manager, the manager's boy, the situation—their specific values. Borrowing a phrase from Mr. Eliot's critical writings, one might say that ***Heart of Darkness*** achieves its overpowering evocation of atmosphere by means of 'objective correlatives'. The details and circumstances of the voyage to and up the Congo are present to us as if we were making the journey ourselves and (chosen for record as they are by a controlling imaginative purpose) they carry specificities of emotion and suggestion with them. There is the gunboat dropping shells into Africa. . . . There is the arrival at the Company's station. . . . There is the grove of death. . . . (pp. 174-76)

By means of this art of vivid essential record, in terms of things seen and incidents experienced by a main agent in the narrative, and particular contacts and exchanges with other human agents, the overwhelming sinister and fantastic 'atmosphere' is engendered. Ordinary greed, stupidity and moral squalor are made to look like behaviour in a lunatic asylum against the vast and oppressive mystery of the surroundings, rendered potently in terms of sensation. This mean lunacy, which we are made to feel as at the same time normal and insane, is brought out by contrast with the fantastically secure innocence of the young harlequin-costumed Russian ('son of an arch-priest . . . Government of Tambov'), the introduction to whom is by the way of that copy of Tower's (or Towson's) *Inquiry into Some Points of Seamanship,* symbol of tradition, sanity and the moral idea, found lying, an incongruous mystery, in the dark heart of Africa.

Of course, . . . the author's comment cannot be said to be wholly implicit. Nevertheless, it is not separable from the thing rendered, but seems to emerge from the vibration of this as part of the tone. At least, this is Conrad's art at its best. There are, however, places in ***Heart of Darkness*** where we become aware of comment as an interposition, and worse, as an intrusion, at times an exasperating one. Hadn't he, we find ourselves asking, overworked 'inscrutable', 'inconceivable', 'unspeakable' and that kind of word already?—yet still they recur. . . . The same vocabulary, the same adjectival insistence upon inexpressible and incomprehensible mystery, is applied to the evocation of human profundities and spiritual horrors; to magnifying a thrilled sense of the unspeakable potentialities of the human soul. The actual effect is not to magnify but rather to muffle. The essential vibration emanates from the interaction of the particular incidents, actions and perceptions that are evoked with such charged concreteness. (pp. 176-77)

[We] are given a charged sense of the monstrous hothouse efflorescences fostered in Kurtz by solitude and the wilderness. It is a matter of such things as the heads on posts—a direct significant glimpse, the innocent Russian's explanations, the incidents of the progress up the river and the moral and physical incongruities registered; in short, of the charge generated in a variety of highly specific evocations. The stalking of the moribund Kurtz, a skeleton crawling through the long grass on all fours as he makes his bolt towards the fires and the tom-toms, is a triumphant climax in the suggestion of strange and horrible perversions. But Conrad isn't satisfied with these means; he feels that there is, or ought to be, some horror, some significance he has yet to bring out. So we have an adjectival and worse than supererogatory insistence on 'unspeakable rites', 'unspeakable secrets', 'monstrous passions', 'inconceivable mystery', and so on. If it were only, as it largely is in ***Heart of Darkness,*** a matter of an occasional phrase it would still be regrettable as tending to cheapen the tone. But the actual cheapening is little short of disastrous. . . . Conrad must [in some instances] stand convicted of borrowing the arts of the magazine-writer (who has borrowed his, shall we say, from Kipling and Poe) in order to impose on his readers and on himself, for thrilled response, a 'significance' that is merely an emotional insistence on the presence of what he can't produce. The insistence betrays the absence, the willed 'intensity' the nullity. He is intent on making a virtue out of not knowing what he means. The vague and unrealizable, he asserts with a strained impressiveness, is the profoundly and tremendously significant. . . . If he cannot through the concrete presentment of incident, setting and image invest the words with the terrific something that, by themselves, they fail to convey, then no amount of adjectival and ejaculatory emphasis will do it. . . . Actually, Conrad had no need to try and inject 'significance' into his narrative in this way. What he shows himself to have successfully and significantly seen is enough to make ***Heart of Darkness*** a disturbing presentment of the kind he aimed at. By the attempt at injection he weakens, in his account of Kurtz's death, the effect of that culminating cry. . . . The 'horror' . . . has very much less force than it might have had if Conrad had strained less.

This final account of Kurtz is associated with a sardonic tone, an insistent irony that leads us on to another bad patch, the closing interview in Brussels with Kurtz's 'Intended'. . . . It is not part of Conrad's irony that there should be anything ironical in this presentment of the woman. The irony lies in the association of her innocent nobility, her purity of idealizing faith, with the unspeakable corruption of Kurtz; and it is developed (if that is the word) with a thrilled insistence that recalls the melodramatic intensities of Edgar Allan Poe. . . . (pp. 179-81)

Conrad's 'inscrutable', it is clear, associates with Woman as it does with the wilderness, and the thrilling mystery of the Intended's innocence is of the same order as the thrilling mystery of Kurtz's corruption: the profundities are complementary. It would appear that the cosmopolitan Pole, student of the French masters, who became a British master-mariner, was in some respects a simple soul. (p. 182)

F. R. Leavis, "Joseph Conrad," in Scrutiny *(reprinted by permission of Cambridge University Press), Vol. X, Nos. 1 & 2, June & October, 1941 (and reprinted in his* The Great Tradition: George Eliot, Henry James, Joseph Conrad, *New York University Press, 1963, pp. 173-226).*

ALBERT J. GUERARD (essay date 1950)

[*Guerard, an American novelist and critic, has written extensively on Conrad. His* Conrad the Novelist *(1958) is considered the standard critical interpretation of several of Conrad's works, including* Heart of Darkness. *The following excerpt is taken from an introduction to a reprint edition of* Heart of Darkness *and* The Secret Sharer; *in it Guerard finds that even though Kurtz is one of the greatest portraits of moral deterioration in literature, the principal character of* The Heart of Darkness *is Marlow, and the story is most concerned not with Kurtz's fall, but with Marlow's discovery of his own capacity for good and evil. For further discussion by Guerard of* Heart of Darkness, *see the excerpt from his* Conrad the Novelist *(1958).*]

[Conrad's] stories of adventure and romance nearly always suggest long vistas of experience beyond themselves, and their lonely heroes face no less than our common human destiny. Marlow's slow journey up the Congo into the heart of darkest Africa is a journey into the heart of man's darkness. . . . Most of Conrad's better novels thrust inward toward psychological complexity and outward toward moral symbolism. This is particularly true of the two short novels in this volume.

Conrad's long stories and short novels are far more experimental and more "modern" than his full-length novels. ***The Secret Sharer*** and ***Heart of Darkness*** are among the finest of Conrad's short novels, and among the half-dozen greatest short novels in the English language. . . . ***Heart of Darkness*** . . . is evasive in structure and even uncomfortably wordy. Words! At times Conrad and Marlow seem to want to erect (as does a psychoanalyst's patient) a screen of words between themselves and the horror of a half-remembered experience. (p. 8)

The Secret Sharer, much the more exciting and more direct of the two, is also the more difficult to analyze and understand. Both are realistic accounts of things that actually happened—of an actual tragedy at sea; of an actual expedition that Conrad made, in 1890, into the heart of Africa. But both stories are also dramas of consciousness and conscience, symbolic explorations of inward complexity. They are, like Faulkner's *The Bear,* stories of youth's initiation into manhood and knowledge, dramatized testings of personal strength and integrity, psychological studies in half-conscious *identification.* Why does Marlow seek out and remain loyal to the unspeakable and savage Kurtz in ***Heart of Darkness***? Why does the narrator (the "I") of the ***The Secret Sharer*** protect the criminally impulsive Leggatt? Both have identified themselves, temporarily, with these outcast and more primitive beings; lived vicariously in them. In the unconscious mind of each of us slumber infinite capacities for reversion and crime. And our best chance for survival, moral survival, lies in frankly recognizing these capacities. At the beginning of ***Heart of Darkness,*** Marlow does not "know himself"; at the beginning of ***The Secret Sharer,*** the narrator is naively confident of success in the sea's "untempted life." The two men must come to know themselves better than this, must recognize their own potential criminality and test their own resources, *must travel through Kurtz and Leggatt,* before they will be capable of manhood . . . manhood and "moral survival." The two novels alike exploit the ancient myth or archetypal experience of the "night journey," of a provisional descent into the primitive and unconscious sources of being. At the end of ***Heart of Darkness*** and ***The Secret Sharer,*** the two narrators are mature men. And as Marlow and the young captain both sympathize with and condemn these images or symbols of their potential selves, so too does the novelist Conrad. It is this conflict between sympathy and a cold purifying judgment that gives intensity to the stories as works of art. (pp. 8-9)

Conrad's travelogue of danger and exploitation provides one level of interest and meaning. . . . [The] megalomaniac Kurtz seems the center and "subject" of ***Heart of Darkness.*** His is one of the greatest portraits in all fiction of moral deterioration and reversion to savagery as a result of physical isolation. . . . Kurtz the shining idealist not merely exterminated some of the brutes, but put their heads on stakes around his house. He reverted to savagery himself, pretended to supernatural powers, and even "took a high seat amongst the devils of the land" . . . to be worshipped in fit religious ceremonies. Wholly claimed by the powers of darkness, he does not want to leave when the intruding whites come to get him. He returns to the moral universe only in the last hours of his life, when he judges himself succinctly: "He cried in a whisper at some image, at some vision—he cried out twice, a cry that was no more than a breath: 'The horror! The horror!'" (pp. 13-14)

But Kurtz appears on only a few of these many pages, while Marlow appears on all of them. . . . [The] final center of interest is Marlow, who has identified himself with Kurtz. . . . Marlow allies himself with Kurtz even before he has met him. What does Marlow mean when he says "that was exactly what I had been looking forward to—a talk with Kurtz"? He has been looking forward, perhaps unwittingly, to a prolonged self-examination; to "talking" to himself through the guise of another. . . . Observing Kurtz, and physically wrestling for his body and soul, Marlow can look on our original and savage nature in its nakedness. He can, that is, look into his own deepest self. This is why he ventures into the jungle without help. . . . [And] perhaps the climax of his story occurs when he confounds the beating of his heart with the beat of a savage drum. He too has taken a "night journey" into that unconscious mind which, some of the anthropologists and psychologists tell us, is the same as the primitive and prehistoric mind. Or, in Conrad's own words: "The mind of a man is capable of everything—because everything is in it, all the past as well as all the future." (p. 14)

[***Heart of Darkness*** and ***The Secret Sharer***], using slightly different symbolist techniques, are in fact the same story, and have the same mythical theme—the theme of initiation and moral education, the theme of progress through temporary reversion and achieved self-knowledge, the theme of man's exploratory descent into the primitive sources of being. Conrad believes, with the greatest moralists, that we must know evil—our own capacities for evil—before we can be capable of good; that we must descend into the pit before we can see the stars. But a price must be paid for any such perilous journeys and descents; we must atone for even temporary alliance with the powers of darkness. This, I take it, is the significance of the curious endings of these two novels. The captain of ***The Secret Sharer*** takes his ship dangerously close to the reefed shore of Koh-Ring, far closer than is necessary to permit Leggatt's escape. He must take the full risk. . . . As for Marlow, he does his penance by going to see Kurtz's fiancée, and by telling her a lie. "I laid the ghost of his gifts at last with a lie." Does telling a white lie seem a very serious penance to do? "There is a taint of death," Marlow says, "a flavor of mortality in lies . . ."

Conrad, like Marlow, had a passion for truth—including the dark truth concerning our human nature—and a hatred of complacent egoism. He was a pessimist as well as an idealist, yet his pessimism has a consoling solidity. And ***Heart of Darkness*** is the most intense expression of that mature pessimism. (p. 15)

Albert J. Guerard, "Introduction" (introduction copyright © 1950, renewed 1978, by Albert J. Guerard; reprinted by permission of the author), in "Heart of Darkness" and "The Secret Sharer" *by Joseph Conrad, The New American Library, 1950, pp. 7-15.*

HAROLD R. COLLINS (essay date 1954)

[Collins, an American author and editor, is considered an expert on African literature. In the following excerpt he contends that the cannibals and helmsman in Heart of Darkness *illustrate the contrast between the dignity of the African who still adheres to a "native" social order and those tainted by the alien influence of Westerners. Collins believes that Kurtz's behavior illustrates the same dichotomy, for Kurtz, like the helmsman and unlike the cannibals, is a man who has lost the customs and restraints of his civilization because of the influence of an alien social group. For further discussion of the role of Africans in* Heart of Darkness, *see the excerpts below by Chinua Achebe (1977), Cedric Watts (1977), Ian Watt (1979), and C. P. Sarvan (1980), and the entry by Hunt Hawkins in the Additional Bibliography.*]

We have to be very chary about pontificating on the "totality of meaning" of **"Heart of Darkness."**

Of course, wherever we look we see wonderful arrangements. Suppose we consider some humble fellows who have not received much attention in critical discussions, those cannibal crewmen and the unstable native helmsman. If we examine the episodes in which they figure and the comments Marlow makes upon their conduct we shall observe that Conrad has involved these apparently insignificant black men in the main theme.

To be sure, **"Heart of Darkness"** is primarily concerned with the moral isolation of a man much more impressive than the hungry cannibals and the flustered native helmsman. (p. 300)

Marlow's first casual mention of the cannibal crewmen associates them with the work motive, a prominent motive intimately connected with the testing of Kurtz. "More than once she [the steamboat] had to wade for a bit, with twenty cannibals splashing around and pushing. . . . Fine fellows—cannibals—in their place. They were men one could work with." This compliment ranges the man-eaters with men whom Marlow can respect, those who do real work, along with the British colonists in those dependencies marked red on the map (. . . "some real work is done in there."), the accountant who has accomplished starched collars and got-up shirt fronts and whose books are in apple-pie order, the boiler-maker who is "a good worker," that Towson whose nautical manual shows a "singleness of intention, an honest concern for the right way of going to work" which gives Marlow the impression of having come upon something "unmistakably real."

Most of the white men Marlow meets do not merit the compliment he pays the cannibals. The brickmaker at the Central Station makes no bricks. The "Pilgrims," those "greedy phantoms," spend their time backbiting and intriguing. The manager has "no genius for organizing, for initiative, for order even." The devoted band of the Eldorado Exploring Expedition led by the manager's uncle has "not an atom of foresight or of serious intention in the whole batch of them, and they did not seem aware these things are wanted for the work of the world." Even Kurtz, "the prodigy," "the emissary of pity and science and devil knows what else," is no real worker. (p. 301)

Marlow has a good deal to say about the value of work and its connection with reality. To be sure, he doesn't like work itself; he likes "what is in the work,—the chance to find yourself. Your own reality—for yourself, not for others—what no other man can ever know." When Marlow feels the "mysterious stillness" of the Congo's "inner truth" watching him at his work, his work seems mere "monkey tricks," yet he can "find himself" in those "tricks" because he does them well.

If work discloses this kind of truth to Marlow, it also, mercifully, protects him from another kind. While he worries about the elusive channel, hidden banks, sunken stones, snags, leaky pipes, and the savage fireman, the oppressive "reality" of the Congo jungle, whose stillness suggests "an implacable force brooding over an inscrutable intention," fades in his consciousness. ''The inner truth is hidden—luckily, luckily.'' He has no time for ''creepy thoughts'' about the primitive men on the shore who ''howled and leaped, and spun, and made horrid faces.'' His work gives him no time to think of his ''remote kinship with this wild and passionate uproar.''

He certainly does not imply that work means to the cannibals what it means to him, only that the man who does real work is a better man than the one who can not or will not, even though the worker is a black savage. Sham work Marlow calls ''unreal.'' He sees a good deal of such sham work in the Congo: the French war against their native ''enemies,'' the punishment of ''criminals,'' the hiring of ''workers'' by time contract, the pilgrims' ''show of work,'' Kurtz's execution of ''rebels.'' (p. 302)

When the tinpot steamer is fog-bound just below Kurtz's Inner Station and the Pilgrims are ''greatly discomposed'' at the prospect of an attack, the cannibal crewmen are calm, have ''an alert, naturally interested expression on their faces.'' Several of them grin as they haul on the anchor chain. Several exchange ''short grunting phrases which seemed to settle the matter to their satisfaction.'' Their headman coolly advises Marlow to catch some of the natives on the shore and give them to the crew, who would ''eat 'im.'' Now observe that these savages do not behave at all like such ''reclaimed'' Africans as the prisoners' guard with the unmilitary bearing and the rascally grin, the manager's boy, who announces Kurtz's death ''with scathing contempt,'' and the unstable helmsman, who conducts himself so imprudently during the attack from Kurtz's ''adorers.'' The guard, the manager's boy, and the helmsman are what the anthropologists now call ''detribalized natives''; that is, natives alienated from the old tribal life. The crewmen are still raw bush savages, the sort of Africans most white travelers and settlers prefer to more civilized Africans. Recruited from a place 800 miles from Kurtz's station at Stanley Falls . . . , they have lived a considerable distance from the coast, from which white influences radiated.

Marlow speaks of the ''dignified and profoundly pensive attitude'' of the headman who makes the cannibalistic proposal. It may seem strange, but uncivilized savages are dignified. The cannibals in **''Heart of Darkness''** seem to have the dignity and self-assurance of Africans who still have the comfortable feeling of being valued members of some native social order, who have not been in contact with the whites long enough to be troubled by the social disabilities of a civilized social order, shamed by their ignorance of European technical knowledge, confused by the conflicting moral imperatives of two cultures. They are probably sustained—as Kurtz is not—by the warm close ties of an organic society. (p. 303)

Marlow is not ''properly horrified'' by the headman's cannibalistic suggestion. Recalling that the pilgrims have thrown most of the cannibals' rotten hippo meat overboard and that their wages of brass wire have not been very useful for purchasing provisions in the riverside villages, he knows that the poor fellows must be very hungry. Indeed he wonders ''Why in the name of all the gnawing devils of hunger they didn't go for us—they were thirty to five—and have a good tuck-in for once. . . . They were big powerful men, with not much capacity to weigh the consequences. . . .'' He supposes that ''something restraining, one of those human secrets that baffle probability,'' has come into play. But what could restrain such wild men? ''Restraint! What possible restraint?'' Here we have another of the important motives of the story. Even the manager, who would be happy to hang the independent traders providing ''unfair competition,'' has his restraint: he wishes to preserve appearances. . . . [The] helmsman has no restraint, is like Kurtz in that respect. Those symbolical ornaments on Kurtz's fence signify that ''Mr. Kurtz lacked restraint in the gratification of his various lusts.''

Kurtz was on trial in the Congo. Since Marlow calls the cannibals' situation a test, ''the test of inexorable physical necessity,'' their ordeal is a significant link between the ''universal genius'' and the hungry man-eaters. . . . We might even suspect a further link between Kurtz and the cannibals in that curious cannibalistic metaphor: as that ''atrocious phantom'' is being carried out of his hut, Marlow ''saw him open his mouth wide—it gave him a weirdly voracious aspect—as though he had wanted to swallow all the air, all the earth, all the men before him.'' . . . We are tempted to try to answer Marlow's question for him: ''Was it superstition, disgust, patience, fear—or some kind of primitive honour that curbed the appetites of savages suffering the 'exasperating torment' of hunger?'' The answer might explain that ''something wanting'' in Kurtz, that ''small matter which, when the pressing need arose, could not be found under his magnificent eloquence.'' (pp. 304-05)

No matter what we may happen to know about the eating habits of Congo cannibals, no matter which tribe Conrad's cannibals belonged to . . . we must simply take Marlow's word for it: the restraint was a mystery. And wouldn't we do well to admit that the motives of human conduct are often inexplicable? As Conrad himself says in ***Personal Record,*** ''The part of the inexplicable should be allowed for in the appraising the conduct of men in a world where no explanation is final.'' The kinds of restraints that may be depended upon to keep a man within moral bounds in ordinary circumstances have not motivated these savages who have resisted the ''deviltry of lingering starvation.'' They just happen to have that ''inborn strength'' that is needed to fight hunger properly. Only such ''inborn strength'' would have saved Kurtz in his trial.

Though we may feel that Conrad might have assigned more prosaic and definite reasons for the good behavior of his cannibals, he has not idealized them; they are not Noble Savages in the manner of H. Rider Haggard. When Marlow heaves the helmsman's body overboard the hungry crewmen are as scandalized as the pilgrims ''with a better show of reason''; the second-rate helmsman is becoming a first-rate temptation.

The cannibals belong to that vengeful jungle, that darkness, that has tried Kurtz and found him wanting. While the bepatched young Russian is telling Marlow about his wonderful conversations with Kurtz (''We talked of everything. . . . Everything! . . . Of love, too.'') the crewmen are lounging near by, human illustrations of that Congo savagery from which Kurtz's conversational graces have not been able to save him. The headman turns his ''heavy and glittering eyes'' upon the young man whose mind Kurtz ''had enlarged.'' At that moment Marlow feels very keenly the power of that Congo scene which has been Kurtz's undoing. . . . If Kurtz's native mistress, ''savage and superb, wild-eyed and magnificent,'' symbolizes the fascination of the Congo scene, the cannibals symbolize its pitiless power, and its reality, which exposes Kurtz's ''noble sentiments'' as sham.

It is easy to underestimate the importance of the native helmsman in Marlow's journey to ''the farthest point of navigation and the culminating point of [his] experience.'' Does it not seem odd that he should recall this insignificant black fellow's foolish conduct in such detail, and make his death scene almost as impressive as that of Kurtz himself? When Marlow says he is not sure that the "remarkable man" was worth the life they lost in getting to him, he realizes that his listeners will "think it passing strange this regret for a savage who was no more account than a grain of sand in a black Sahara." The reasons he gives for this regret constitute a commentary on the shortcomings of Kurtz.

The helmsman "had done something, he had steered." We have the work motive again. Kurtz has not done any real work in the Congo; his methods are "no methods at all." It is questionable if he has ever done any real work. Was he a painter who wrote for the papers or a journalist who painted, or did he have any regular profession at all? Even Kurtz's cousin back in the "sepulchral city" could not tell "what he had been—exactly." A journalist in that city thinks that Kurtz ought to have been a leader of an extreme party, any extreme party, but political activity of that sort would scarcely qualify as proper work as Marlow understands it.

The helmsman has not, like Kurtz, cut himself loose from all human ties. As a "help," an "instrument," he is in a "kind of partnership" with his captain. His very deficiencies that his captain worries about create a "subtle bond" between the two of them. The "intimate profundity" of that look he gives Marlow when he dies is like a "claim of distant kinship." These human ties mean a great deal to the humble African because he is isolated from his own native society. His conduct in his work gives us the clue for understanding this isolation.

The "athletic black belonging to some coast tribe" is not a good helmsman. He is an "unstable kind of fool," steering "with no end of swagger" while his white man is at his side, but "instantly the prey of an abject funk" the moment he is alone. When Kurtz's "adorers" attack the steamer, he prances about, "stamping his feet, champing his mouth, like a reined-in horse." He leaves the wheel to open the shutter on the land side, fire off the Martini-Henry, and yell at the shore—and gets himself speared for his reckless folly.

Explaining his helmsman's fatal imprudence, Marlow anticipates his comments on the degradation of Kurtz. "Poor fool! If he had only let that shutter alone. He had no restraint, no restraint—just like Kurtz—a tree swayed in the wind." The helmsman has been tested, as the cannibals are tested, as Kurtz has been tested. The cannibals, tormented by hunger, have refrained from eating the pilgrims. Kurtz, in "utter solitude without a policeman" and "utter silence, where no warning voice of a kind neighbor can be heard," has "lacked restraint in the gratification of his various lusts," has taken a "high seat among the devils of the land." The helmsman almost wrecks the tinpot steamer, endangers the lives of the passengers, and throws his life away; when the fixed standards of conduct of his profession require steady steering, he can not resist the temptation to caper as though he were dancing an old-fashioned African war dance and to help the pilgrims squirt lead into the bush; when he should show his mettle, he merely "shows off."

The helmsman is not dignified and dependable like the cannibals, the "raw bush natives." Anyone at all familiar with modern anthropological studies of the process of "detribalization" and more recent fiction dealing with Africa will be struck by the fact that Conrad is representing "detribalized" natives in the characters of the slovenly prisoners' guard, the ill-conditioned manager's boy, and the second-rate helmsman; he is representing Africans who have been deprived of their traditional beliefs and standards of conduct without having assumed, or being able to assume, those of the white men. The manager's boy and the helmsman have come from coast tribes. Africans from the coast would be much more likely to be partially civilized, be "mission boys," in the white settlers' contemptuous phrase, than would those living upriver, for on the coast white men have long had "factories," or trading posts, and the first missions were established there. We may recall Marlow's ironical comments on these partially civilized Africans: "One of the reclaimed" (the guard), "an improved specimen" (the fireman), "an overfed young negro" (the manager's boy), "thought the world of himself" (the helmsman). In "weaning those ignorant millions from their horrid ways," the Belgian emissaries of light have produced, not dark-skinned gentlemen, but vain creatures whose ways are seldom perfectly agreeable.

Conrad understood that Africans working for white men could suffer from being deprived of the satisfactions of the old tribal life. (pp. 305-08)

Probably we would be quite safe in classing the second-rate helmsman with those Conradian characters that the critics have called "isolates." He has been deprived of the restraints and consolations of a social order, as Kurtz has been. And like Kurtz he lacks that "inner strength," that saving "definite belief" which may save the man thus deprived. (p. 309)

Conrad knew that the white men who come to Africa professing to bring progress and light to "darkest Africa," have themselves been deprived of the sanctions of their European social orders; they also have been alienated from the old tribal ways. Thrown upon their own inner spiritual resources—like detribalized natives—they may be utterly damned by their greed, their sloth, and their hypocrisy into moral insignificance, as were the pilgrims, or they may be so corrupted by their absolute power over the Africans that some Marlow will need to lay their memory among the "dead cats of civilization." (p. 310)

Harold R. Collins, "Kurtz, the Cannibals, and the Second-Rate Helmsman," in Western Humanities Review, *Vol. VIII, No. 4, Autumn, 1954, pp. 299-310.*

LILLIAN FEDER (essay date 1955)

[Feder, a literary critic with expertise in the study of classical literature and the role of myth in modern literature, compares Heart of Darkness *to the* Aeneid. *Feder finds that* Heart of Darkness *depicts Marlow's discovery of evil, a discovery precipitated by a descent into a colonial hell that mirrors the descent into Hades in the* Aeneid. *For a discussion of Feder's interpretation, see the excerpt by Robert O. Evans (1956).]*

Marlow's journey in Conrad's **"Heart of Darkness"** is usually interpreted as a study of a descent into the unconscious self. Of course, the voyage into the heart of darkness is, on one level, a symbolic representation of an exploration of the hidden self and therefore of man's capacity for evil. However, Conrad is not merely narrating a psychological experience; he is dealing with a significant moral conflict. . . . In **"Heart of Darkness,"** Conrad is depicting Marlow's discovery of evil and the responsibilities to himself and to others which this knowledge places upon him. In telling the story of Marlow's attainment of self-knowledge, Conrad does not use the language of psychology. Instead, he employs the imagery and symbolism of the traditional voyage into Hades.

By associating Marlow's journey with the descent into hell, Conrad concretizes the hidden world of the inner self. Through image and symbol, he evokes the well-known voyage of the hero who, in ancient epic, explores the lower world and, in so doing, probes the depths of his own and his nation's conscience. . . . Setting Conrad's story in relief against a background rich in associations reveals the essential unity of his political and personal themes. Moreover, such a reading shows how Conrad, by combining the traditional imagery of the epic descent with realistic details from his own experience in the Congo, created an image of hell credible to modern man.

Though Marlow's journey recalls the epic descent in general, it is most specifically related to the visit to Hades in the sixth book of the *Aeneid.* In Vergil's poem, Aeneas' descent is part of his initiation for the role of leader of the Roman people. Vergil emphasizes the fact that truth is to be found in the heart of darkness; thus, the Sibyl who, in Vergil's words, "obscuris vera involvens" (hides truth in darkness), guides Aeneas. Moreover, just as Aeneas is about to enter Hades, Vergil interrupts his narrative to ask the very elements of hell, Chaos and Phlegethon, to allow him to reveal the secrets buried in the darkness and depths of the earth. Aeneas' voyage to Hades is one means by which he learns of the tragedy implicit in the affairs of men; this is the price he pays for fulfilling his duty as founder of Rome. In the lower world he looks both into past and the future and, having observed the penalties for personal crimes, he is told of the bloodshed and cruelty which are to weigh on the conscience of his nation—the cost of Rome's imperial power. Aeneas, the pious and worthy man, learns truth through a descent into darkness.

The basic similarity between Marlow's journey and that of the epic hero, the descent to find light, is obvious. There are many close parallels between the two voyages. . . . (pp. 280-81)

At the beginning of the sixth book of the *Aeneid,* just before Aeneas descends to Hades, Vergil creates an atmosphere of pervading gloom. He speaks of the "gloomy woods," . . . and repeats the phrase "per umbram" (through the gloom). . . . Conrad too establishes this somber mood. Even before Marlow begins his story, Conrad repeats the word "gloom" continuously in his description of the friends gathered together to hear the tale. Thus, in the second paragraph of the story he mentions a "mournful gloom;" . . . in the third, "the brooding gloom;" . . . in the fourth, "the gloom to the west." . . . Marlow, sitting there like an idol, seems to have brought with him the atmosphere of the world he is about to recreate for his friends.

Just before he begins his story, Marlow, looking out at the Thames, mentions the Romans and their conquest of England. . . . He then goes on to speak of the brutality of the Romans. . . . "What redeems it is the ideal only. An idea at the back of it; not a sentimental pretence but an idea; and an unselfish belief in the idea—something you can set up, and bow down before, and offer a sacrifice to." . . . (pp. 281-82)

Implicit in Marlow's remarks is the theme of the *Aeneid,* for Vergil is concerned with this "idea," the heroic goal as justification for Rome's plunder and cruelty; moreover, Conrad, like Vergil, sees the tragic limitations of those dedicated to the heroic ideal. Thus, at the very beginning of **"Heart of Darkness,"** the Roman legend, prophesied and justified in Hades, provides an archetypal background for Kurtz's deeds and for Marlow's discovery of himself in a hell perhaps more terrible than Vergil's, but no less enlightening.

Before Marlow may descend into the heart of darkness, he must, like the epic hero, perform certain duties. His visit to the company office suggests a necessary rite performed before the fateful journey. The city itself "makes [him] think of a whited sepulcher"; the office is in "a narrow and deserted street in deep shadow," and there is "a dead silence." . . . The house itself is "as still as a house in the city of the dead." . . . Thus, Conrad creates the deathly gloom of the world Marlow is about to enter.

In the company office, two women are knitting black wool. Conrad plainly uses these women to symbolize the fates, who, like Aeneas' guide, the Sibyl of Cumae, know the secrets of the heart of darkness. Marlow feels uneasy during these "ceremonies." . . . (pp. 282-83)

He describes one of the two knitting women. . . . She seems to know everything. Marlow goes on to say, "An eerie feeling came over me. She seemed uncanny and fateful." . . . Like the Cumaean Sibyl, the two women guard the way to hell. . . . Then Marlow uses the Latin farewell, evoking its literary and legendary associations: "Ave! old knitter of black wool. *Morituri te salutant.*" . . . Conrad uses images of death, but they do not suggest actual death so much as they do the legendary world of the dead, where, paradoxically, the affairs of the living are interpreted and understood. When he is finally ready to leave, Marlow says that he feels as though "instead of going to the center of a continent," he is "about to set off for the center of the earth." . . . (p. 283)

But before he may descend into the heart of darkness, Marlow has another duty to perform. Like Aeneas, he must attend to the remains of someone who has died. Aeneas has buried Misenus, a former comrade . . . , and Marlow tries to recover the remains of Fresleven, his predecessor. Marlow feels compelled to perform this rite. (pp. 283-84)

In Marlow's first observations about the Congo, he uses the imagery of hell. Thus, the members of the "chain gang" seem to him to have a "deathlike indifference"; . . . strolling into the shade, he says, "It seemed to me that I had stepped into the gloomy circle of some inferno." . . . "Inferno," of course, suggests the Christian hell as well as the Latin "Inferna," but Conrad's development of the image is so like Vergil's description of Hades in the *Aeneid* that it seems to evoke the classical hell more readily than the Christian one. His depiction of the natives in the jungle is like Vergil's description of the tormented shades in Hades: "Black shapes crouched, lay, sat between the trees leaning against the trunks," and, like the figures at the entrance to Vergil's Hades, their very attitudes express "pain, abandonment, and despair." Like Vergil's "Diseases . . . Famine . . . and Poverty (terrible shapes to see)," . . . Conrad's figures are "nothing earthly now, nothing but black shadows of disease and starvation, lying confusedly in the greenish gloom." (p. 284)

Up to this point, Conrad has employed the associations of Hades to build up suspense, to tell the reader indirectly that this is no ordinary voyage. He has exploited the strangeness, the mystery, and the pathos of the ancient symbol of hell. Now he uses it with a new brilliance to suggest not only mystery but evil as well. Moreover, through this symbol, he suggests the tragic proportions of his theme and his characters. While he waits at the station, the wilderness surrounding it seems to Marlow "great and invincible, like evil or truth." . . . (pp. 284-85)

When Aeneas first enters Hades, Vergil compares the underworld with a forest. . . . To reach the lowest depths of Erebus, Aeneas must take a journey down the river Styx, which is surrounded by marshes. The boat seems unfit for the journey, but finally Aeneas steps out on the mud and sedge of the shore. . . . Vergil's description of this journey is brief, but he creates an atmosphere of gloom and ugliness very like that which Conrad suggests in his extended account of Marlow's voyage into the heart of darkness. Marlow too has a difficult voyage on a boat that is unsuited to the journey. He and his companions seem like "phantoms," and the earth seems "unearthly." The "black and incomprehensible frenzy" he approaches is at once the jungle, the region of "pre-historic man," and the depths of hell which Kurtz has created and in which he has been destroyed. . . . (p. 285)

When he has almost reached the heart of darkness, Marlow loses his helmsman. Here again Conrad seems to be following Vergil, for Aeneas too loses his helmsman, Palinurus, just as his ship is approaching the shore of Cumae. Palinurus loses his balance and falls overboard; when he has swum to safety, "barbarous people attack [him] with swords," and he is killed, his body floating into the sea. . . . Marlow's helmsman is killed by a native's spear, and he is buried in the sea. Both die "insontes" (guiltless), loyal to their leaders. Aeneas, meeting the shade of Palinurus in Hades, learns of the tragic sacrifice for his mission, and Marlow feels in the dying look of his helmsman a profound intimacy which he cannot forget, for it is a personal tie with one of the victims sacrificed to the "emissaries of light." Even more than the groans of the natives, the dying helmsman's last insight, innocent and profound, suggests the tragic consequences of Kurtz's betrayal. (p. 286)

Marlow is eager to deal with Kurtz, or as he refers to him, with "this shadow," and he follows him into the depths of the jungle where he is participating in his fiendish rites. In the description of their meeting, Conrad evokes again and again the associations of Hades. As Marlow approaches, Kurtz rises "unsteady, long, pale, indistinct, like a vapor exhaled by the earth, and swayed slightly, misty and silent." The setting is hell itself, with fires looming between the trees and a constant murmur of voices. A "fiend-like" figure appears. At this point Conrad refers to Kurtz as "that Shadow," this time capitalizing the initial letter, as one does in a name, for Kurtz here is a shade of hell, "this wandering and tormented thing."

Moreover, Marlow has one means of controlling Kurtz: the threat, "you will be lost, . . . utterly lost," doomed to hell entirely. These words draw Kurtz back, but even so Marlow, regarding him, says, "I before him did not know whether I stood on the ground or floated in the air," for they have not left hell. . . . Indeed, the journey next day merely reiterates the image. The crowd "flowed out of the woods again," and, like the wretched shades of Vergil's Hades watching Aeneas' boat, they stood on the shore murmuring and gesturing. . . . And the native woman, like Vergil's shades who "tendebant[que] manus" (stretched out their hands), pleading to be taken aboard, . . . "stretched tragically her bare arms after us over the somber and glittering river." . . . (pp. 287-88)

Entering the home of Kurtz's "Intended," Marlow feels that he carries with him the gloom and terror of the heart of darkness. . . .

Moreover, Kurtz's "Intended" is portrayed as no ordinary young woman; she too seems part of the lower world. She lives not in the jungle of Kurtz's hell, but in "a street as still and decorous as a well-kept alley in a cemetery," in a room whose windows are "like three luminous and bedraped columns," and whose piano is "like a somber and polished sarcophogus." This lady with her "pale head," who comes "floating" toward Marlow "in the dusk," her brow "surrounded by an ashy halo," has withdrawn from life to guard the memory of Kurtz. . . . She is given no name except the abstraction, "the Intended," for she has no existence apart from Kurtz. Through his imagery Conrad suggests that she inhabits her own section of Hades, the section devoted to the patient and disappointed shades who carry on their own "mysteries." . . . (p. 289)

Marlow's visit to this lady is the last lap of his journey to Hades. She recalls for him the "eternal darkness" despite the fact that hers is a faith with "an unearthly glow." Speaking to her, Marlow is certain that he will remember the "eloquent phantom," Kurtz, as long as he lives, and he will remember her too, a "tragic and familiar Shade, resembling," in her last traditional gesture of the longing shade, her arms stretched out, "another one, tragic also, and bedecked with powerless charms, stretching bare brown arms over the glitter of the infernal stream, the stream of darkness." . . . Through the image of the "infernal stream," Conrad unites these two shades. On each side of the stream of hell, without understanding, they devote themselves to the darkness Kurtz has created. (pp. 289-90)

It is fairly obvious that **"Heart of Darkness"** has three levels of meaning: on one level it is the story of a man's adventures; on another, of his discovery of certain political and social injustices; and on a third, it is a study of his initiation into the mysteries of his own mind. The same three levels of meaning can be found in the sixth book of Vergil's *Aeneid*. Like Aeneas, Marlow comes to understand himself, his obligations, and the tragic limitations involved in any choice through this threefold experience. Kurtz, like Aeneas, starts out as an "emissary of light," but, unlike Vergil's hero, he cannot conquer himself. Through Kurtz's experience, Marlow learns that a man is defined by his work: Kurtz's work has created a hell in the jungle, which destroys him. The symbol of the lower world suggests not only an imaginative union between the ancient world and the modern one, but a judgment on the morality of modern society. (p. 290)

Lillian Feder, "Marlow's Descent into Hell," in Nineteenth-Century Fiction *(© 1955 by The Regents of the University of California; reprinted by permission of The Regents), Vol. 9, No. 4, March, 1955, pp. 280-92.*

JEROME THALE (essay date 1955)

[Thale has written extensively on the works of nineteenth- and twentieth-century English authors. In the following excerpt, Thale finds Marlow's journey up the Congo river analogous to a quest for the grail or some other form of supreme knowledge. In this case, Marlow is the quester, Kurtz the grail, and the supreme knowledge is an understanding of the nature of evil. Thale concludes that the grail motif is linked to the pervasive imagery and symbolic use of lightness and darkness throughout the novel, the ambiguous nature of which is exemplified by the white intruders who bring darkness to Africa in the guise of enlightening culture. For further discussion of the ambiguity of the primary imagery of the novella, see the excerpts below by W. Y. Tindall (1958), Frederick R. Karl (1969), and Ian Watt (1979).]

Conrad's **"Heart of Darkness"** has all the trappings of the conventional adventure tale—mystery, exotic setting, escape, suspense, unexpected attack. These, of course, are only the vehicle of something more fundamental, and one way of getting at what they symbolize is to see the story as a grail quest. Though Conrad is sparing in his explicit use of the metaphor (''a weary pilgrimage amongst hints for nightmares''), it is implicit in the structure of the action. As in the grail quest there is the search for some object, and those who find and can see the grail receive an illumination. Marlow, the central figure, is like a knight seeking the grail, and his journey even to the end follows the archetype. His grandiose references to the dark places of the earth, his talk of the secret of a continent, the farthest point of navigation, his sudden and unwonted sense that he is off not to the centre of a continent but to the centre of the earth—these, occurring before he starts his journey, give it the atmosphere of a quest.

And in the journey itself there are the usual tests and obstacles of a quest. After Marlow passes through the bizarre company headquarters in Brussels and the inanity surrounding his voyage to the African coast, he makes a difficult and painful journey inland. At the central station he begins a seemingly routine task—going up the river to bring back a sick company agent—which will become his quest. Gradually he learns a little about Kurtz, at first a name; disgust with the manager and reports about the remarkable agent in the jungle make him increasingly eager to see the man. As Marlow's interest in Kurtz mounts, so do the trials and obstacles that are part of Marlow's test. The journey creeps on painfully in the patched ship. Near the end, just before the attack, Marlow realizes that Kurtz is the one thing he has been seeking, the ''enchanted princess'' in a ''fabulous castle,'' whose approaches are fraught with danger.

The grail motif is of course connected with the profuse—and somewhat heavy-handed—light-darkness symbolism. The grail is an effulgence of light, and it gives an illumination to those who can see it. This is the light which Marlow seeks in the heart of darkness. The grail that he finds appears an abomination and the light even deeper darkness, yet paradoxically Marlow does have an illumination: ''it threw a kind of light on everything about me.'' The manager and the others travelling with Marlow are constantly called pilgrims, ''faithless pilgrims,'' and for the faithless there can be no illumination. At the end of his quest Marlow does not find what he had expected all along, a good man in the midst of darkness and corruption. Instead he receives a terrible illumination. Such experiences are as ineffable as they are profound, and this is why the meaning of Marlow's tale must be expressed so obliquely, like the ''glow that brings out the haze.''

The nature of Marlow's illumination is determined by the remarkable man who is its occasion. And to comprehend Kurtz we must look into the reasons for Marlow's attitude towards him. Marlow is listening to the manager condemning Kurtz's methods as ''unsound.'' ''It seemed to me I had never breathed an atmosphere so vile, and I turned mentally to Kurtz for relief . . . it was something to have at least a choice of nightmares.'' Why must Marlow choose a nightmare at all? Because what he sees in one of the nightmares is so compelling that he cannot remain neutral before it. (pp. 351-52)

[Even] before meeting Kurtz Marlow finds himself on Kurtz's side. Marlow has been disgusted by everything connected with the company; he learns that the manager schemes against Kurtz, because Kurtz, like Marlow, is one of the new gang, ''the gang of virtue.'' The unseen apostle of light becomes the alternative to the cowardly plunderers. But Marlow is not trapped into an incredible allegiance; he knows what he is choosing when he later makes his real choice. Nor is it an unconsidered gesture of escape from the moral decay of the hollow men. His choice is a deliberate one.

Given Marlow's nature and his function in the story his choice must be based on something positive in Kurtz. There are strong hints in the story that Kurtz is a good man gone wrong in the jungle. But if he is merely a victim of unusual circumstances, a man to be pitied, then Marlow's choice is as sentimental as that of Kurtz's fiancée. The causes of Kurtz's tragedy are within—in his towering ambition, and his rootless idealism. Yet the jungle is important, for what happens to Kurtz can happen only under some such conditions. And what Marlow values in Kurtz is so paradoxical that it can be seen only against a dark and mysterious jungle and the corruption of colonial exploitation.

What is it in Kurtz that compels a choice and that produces such a profound change in the imperturbable Marlow? Simply that Kurtz has discovered himself, has become fully human; and Marlow's illumination, the light that is his grail, is a similar discovery about himself and all men. (p. 352)

Here self-discovery is not just the thrill of finding out what one can do, but the deeper task of finding out what one is, of coming to grips with the existence of the self. . . .

Marlow emphasizes that Kurtz is wasted and feverish from this knowledge; ''it was not disease''—only the outward manifestation of what went on in Kurtz. . . .

Existence is dangerous, menacing; too dangerous for most of us to discover. Illusion and ignorance, which Conrad treats with a mixture of indulgence and scorn, are what save most of us. ''The inner truth is hidden,—luckily, luckily.'' Women are fortunate to be out of it, living in a beautiful world that does not admit and cannot stand the light. What Marlow has learned through Kurtz he feels he must withhold from Kurtz's fiancée, for it is perilous to ''the salvation of another soul.'' ''I could not tell her,'' Marlow says, ''It would have been too dark—too dark altogether.''

For such a discovery the context of Africa is important and necessary. From the first pages this is impressed upon us. Marlow opens his tale suddenly and mysteriously, ''And this too has been one of the dark places of the earth.'' (p. 353)

The importance of this kind of milieu is developed through both symbol and statement, and Marlow seems at times to suggest that Africa had been the cause of Kurtz's destruction. ''It had caressed him . . . got into his veins, consumed his flesh, and sealed his soul to its own.'' But there can be no mistake: Kurtz is not a passive victim of Africa. Africa is like existence, is truth. In contrast to the muddle and haze of the company's operations, Africa is real. The blacks have a vitality ''that is as natural and true as the surf along the coast.'' And Marlow altogether prefers his crew of cannibals to his passengers. Ironically, what is dark in ''darkest Africa'' is not the land or the people, but the world introduced by the bringers of light and civilization.

In another sense, however, Africa seems dark. The jungle is ''a rioting invasion of soundless life, a rolling wave of plants, piled up, crested, ready to topple over the creek, to sweep every little man of us out of his little existence.'' Africa seems dark because it is the test, the condition under which one can come into contact with the self. The journey to the heart of Africa is the journey into the depths of the self: Kurtz and

Marlow travel into the heart of Africa and into the heart of man. The knowledge that is there is so terrifying that its occasion must seem sinister too.

In the depth of the jungle, Marlow tells us repeatedly, one is on one's own; there is no external restraint. "Anything can be done in this country." One feels, and Marlow says that one ought to feel, atavistic impulses, a "kinship with that wild passionate uproar." . . . It "whispered to him things about himself which he did not know, things of which he had no conception till he took counsel with this great solitude—and the whisper proved irresistibly fascinating." Outside some such context existence in its simplicity cannot be met. Too many things keep us from travelling into the interior of the self in which we exist. (pp. 353-54)

Here Kurtz is free externally and internally. In the depths of Africa Kurtz is not hampered by outside restraint. Paralleling this he has journeyed into the depths of the primal self where there are no internal checks on his freedom. The setting of the discovery is aboriginal in the anthropological sense, and, more than this, it is ab-original in a metaphysical sense. Kurtz's soul "being alone in the wilderness . . . had looked within itself, and by heavens! I tell you it had gone mad." For in the mind of man, which "contains all things," there are terrifying possibilities. (p. 355)

This radical freedom as it exists in Kurtz seems to Marlow both exalting and revolting. Exalting because it makes man human, revolting because in Kurtz it is so perverted and so absolute as to exceed all human limits and become inhuman. By distinguishing these two aspects of Marlow's response, we can make meaningful his commitment to Kurtz. To put it another way, we can sum up the two aspects of Kurtz's freedom in the phrase "I am." On the one hand, to say "I am," is to say that I exist, to say that I am free and have immense possibilities in my grasp. On the other, "I am" is the phrase which only God can utter, because only God exists simply and completely. For Kurtz to say "I am" is the ultimate and complete assertion of himself to the exclusion of all else, the assertion that he is a god.

Before Kurtz's discovery of his existence can become Marlow's illumination it has to be realized by both of them. The revelation proceeds through Kurtz to Marlow, and Marlow's full illumination, his full realization of what it means to be, must wait upon a realization in Kurtz that brings out and confirms what Marlow has already seen in him. A final awareness in Kurtz is needed to make meaningful and universalize Kurtz's experience. For Kurtz has accepted his freedom, has become human, but he has not evaluated what being human means. He must assent to the knowledge he has been trying to keep off. This realization, which must be distinguished from the agonizing discovery of his existence, can come only as its fruit. Authentic self-knowledge demands a real existent as its object. Having discovered that he can exist, Kurtz must now evaluate existence. "The horror! the horror" is this evaluation.

The most we can hope for in life, Marlow tells us, is "some knowledge of yourself—that comes too late." Marlow comes close to death and finds that he has nothing to say. Kurtz "had something to say. He said it. Since I had peeped over the edge myself, I understand better the meaning of his stare, that could not see the flame of the candle, but was wide enough to embrace the whole universe, piercing enough to penetrate all the hearts that beat in the darkness."

Only after Marlow passes his final test, his brush with death, does the full significance of Kurtz come to him. Kurtz's last cry takes us to the meaning of the whole African venture for Marlow, the illumination he receives. For Marlow sees that Kurtz's cry is more than self-knowledge, more than an insight into the depths of his own evil. It is an insight into the potentialities in all men, it gives the perspective in which we must see Kurtz's discovery of himself. . . . At the time he chooses Kurtz, Marlow declares that Kurtz is "remarkable," and to the end of the story he uses no stronger—indeed no other—epithet than this. Its occasional ironic uses only point up its understatement. And "remarkable" is Marlow's comment on Kurtz's acceptance of his freedom. (pp. 355-56)

Kurtz is the grail at the end of Marlow's quest, and of all those who come into contact with Kurtz only Marlow—the faithful pilgrim—experiences an illumination. The manager reduces Kurtz to his own terms and cannot see him. The Russian sailor, who admires Kurtz, is too much a fool—perhaps a wise fool—to recognize the challenge that Kurtz has met. The two women each see and love Kurtz, but a false Kurtz, a lie, which Marlow must meet with another lie. . . .

[Marlow] like Gulliver come back to England . . . , cannot stand the smug faces of the people walking down the streets, unaware of the challenge and the danger. Their knowledge of life seems "an irritating pretense." They do not know that they are and therefore they are not. Marlow scorns them because in the quest for Kurtz he has discovered the dreadful burden of human freedom. His full illumination, his grail, is not transcendent being but the heart of man. Yet it demands the same tests in the journey of purification and produces an illumination equally awful. (p. 358)

Jerome Thale, "Marlow's Quest," in University of Toronto Quarterly *(reprinted by permission of University of Toronto Press), Vol. XXIV, No. 4, July, 1955, pp. 351-58.*

ROBERT O. EVANS (essay date 1956)

[*Evans disagrees with Lillian Feder's assessment (1955) of* Heart of Darkness *as a reworking of the* Aeneid. *Evans, like Feder, believes that Conrad made use of the imagery of that epic, but finds the novella more closely linked, both in theme and action, to Dante's* Inferno.]

[***The Heart of Darkness***] is developed in terms of symbols, and it is, of course, not always possible to distinguish a clear separation between the symbolic and literal levels of meaning. For instance, Kurtz is plainly alive when Marlow begins his journey and still alive when Marlow reaches him, but symbolically there is no doubt that he is the arch-inhabitant of Hell or that Marlow, too, has been journeying through Hell, much as Dante did in the *Inferno*. Superficially there are differences; for example, Marlow travels alone while Dante had Virgil for his guide. But that Africa represents Hell and the great river, Acheron, Phlegethon, Styx, or all the rivers of Hell together is a traditional interpretation of the story. (p. 56)

Miss Lillian Feder [see excerpt above, 1955] has pointed out a number of significant parallels with Virgil's descent in the sixth book of the *Aeneid*, but ***The Heart of Darkness*** is more than a reworking of an old theme in modern guise. There is no question that Conrad employed epic machinery borrowed from Virgil. Essentially the story is neither a recitation of Kurtz's awful degradation nor the simple history of Marlow's enlightenment. It is a journey through the underworld, for purposes of instruction as well as entertainment, calculated to bring into focus Conrad's moral vision, as it affects the mass of humanity struggling on the brink of the "tumid river." The story is really concerned with modern ethical and spiritual values and has far more significance for the reader than any transmutation of Virgil's descent could have. Clearly it was not possible for Conrad, writing in the twentieth century, to view the world with a disregard for Christian ethics, as Virgil had to do. Accordingly one would expect Conrad to have a deeper significance than Virgil. Moreover, as one of his main themes, the descent into Hell, was not Virgil's exclusive property, it would not seem likely that Conrad should owe Virgil more than Dante, or even Milton. . . . ***The Heart of Darkness*** is not the apex of a genre but rather a special use of form towards which Conrad had been painfully working in order to express his particular, ethical view of the universe. (pp. 56-7)

From the beginning of the story there is little question where Marlow's journey will lead him, but, as Miss Feder says, the Hell into which Marlow descends is legendary rather than an actual place. This problem of how to give Hell being without the same sense of existence that Dante experienced is one of the most difficult a modern artist can face. One knows it is there, but where exactly is it? . . . Conrad solves his enigma by deft manipulation of symbols and imagery. Marlow, looking at a map of his projected journey, remarks that he is "going into the yellow—dead in the center." But as the symbolic level of meaning shifts slightly, most of the other references to Hell are described as properly black. Marlow's appointment is to replace a man who was killed in an argument over two "black hens," an image carefully related to the two females that surround Kurtz. The knitters are working "black wool." Marlow's first contact with the natives is with black men, whose loins are bound in "black rags." The single, outstanding descriptive detail about the European traders is their "black mustaches." The background of Kurtz's mysterious painting was "almost black—somber." The river is black; "there were shiny patches on the black creek." Even the natives' confidence is a "black display." Thoughts are black. And again, later, the men themselves are no more than grains of sand in a "black Sahara." Conrad colors Hell rightly but only after making it clear, partly through imagery, that it is not a literal place.

Perhaps the author's use of the *Inferno* is not quite so explicit as that of the *Aeneid,* but it is probably more important to the development of the story. In the first place, besides being shorter, Virgil's journey is ideologically simpler than Dante's, and the progression into the underworld in the sixth book of the *Aeneid* is accomplished at a fairly steady rate, while Dante's journey is interrupted; that is, he travels and then stops and comments, continues, and so on. In these respects ***The Heart of Darkness*** is more closely modelled on the Italian epic than on the Latin original. But it is the epic nature of the story that is important; throughout Conrad makes considerable use of epic machinery. (p. 57)

[The] structure of ***The Heart of Darkness,*** at least from the moment of Marlow's arrival at the first station on the African coast, closely resembles a skeletalized version of the *Inferno.* And even prior to Marlow's landing the characters in the story would appear to fit nicely into Dante's threshold to Hell. Perhaps the knitters of black wool are slightly misplaced; Dante might have introduced them earlier. The directors themselves, though they do not realize it, belong in the Vestibule, as men whose lives have warranted neither great infamy nor great praise. Seamen who have abandoned the sea, they are now businessmen. . . . But of the whole group only Marlow is shown to have adhered to the true purpose of life, the development of ethical insight, and he is the only one who still follows the sea, a distinction of symbolic importance. Actually Marlow has little space to devote to the directors; they serve as Marlow's audience, but they are not the audiences the author is trying to convince. ***The Heart of Darkness*** is not their story. They are really incapable of understanding it, as Conrad suggests when he puts in the narrator's mouth the insipid remark, "we knew we were fated . . . to hear about one of Marlow's *inconclusive* experiences" (italics mine). But at least they are capable of sensing something special about Marlow, for the same speaker relates that Marlow "had the pose of a Buddha preaching in European clothes and without a lotus flower." This is plain description of Marlow's mission.

The continentals, too, are "hollow men" living in or near the Vestibule, except perhaps for the guardians. Some, of course, are better than others. The doctor, like the narrator on the *Nellie,* has some realization of the importance of Marlow's journey, shown by his farewell, "Du calme, du calme, Adieu." The women in the story, beginning with Marlow's aunt, are not really damned but live in an unreal world of their own, incapable of understanding. Miss Feder has suggested that Kurtz's fiancee may occupy a special corner of Hades because she is related, through imagery, to Kurtz and, she says, has no separate existence apart from him. It is quite true that when the reader meets her she appears dressed in black, but I do not think the color alone enough to consign her to Hell. She is mourning for Kurtz in a mistaken, over-sentimental but not abnormal fashion. And her existence does not entirely depend on him. Conrad uses her primarily for an agent in Marlow's eventual discovery of the ethical nature of life. Structurally she is bound to Marlow. Symbolically Conrad simplified Marlow's problems until they are mostly bound in the experience of falsehood. The most distasteful action Marlow is capable of is a lie, but twice he is brought to tell one. On the first occasion he lies for practical reasons in order to obtain rivets to repair the steamer, symbolizing dishonesty in the course of the normal business of life. Of course, the lie is successful. But later, when he visits Kurtz's "Intended," Marlow tells another lie, this time with no ulterior motive, and this selfless though intrinsically sinful action, a sort of parable, completes his moral vision. Conrad needs the fiancee for Marlow far more than he does to explain Kurtz's presence in Africa. (pp. 58-9)

The close structural parallel between ***The Heart of Darkness*** and the *Inferno* is not explicit at the Vestibule stage. Moreover, Dante borrowed the Vestibule from Virgil, though Conrad's tenants resemble Dante's far more than the Latin poet's. But from the landing in Africa and Marlow's descent into Limbo the relationship becomes unmistakable. Immediately preceding the real descent, Conrad devotes several paragraphs to explanation, in symbolic terms, of his special Hades. He carefully separates Africa from modern civilization by describing machinery rusting uselessly on a hillside. (p. 59)

Next Conrad turns to Marlow's meeting with the Chief Accountant, noteworthy for his gentle annoyance at having his work disturbed by a dying man on a litter placed in the office with him. The accountant is beyond the violence and the brutality. He keeps up appearances. He does not really suffer. Accordingly, he resembles Dante's tenants who have "sinned not; yet their merit lacked its chiefest / / Fulfillment, lacking baptism, which is / / The gateway to the faith which thou believest.'' The accountant belongs in Limbo.

From the coast up the river to the second station the characters in the story closely resemble the inhabitants of Upper Hell. Conrad does not follow Dante's eschatology strictly, but certainly the ivory traders belong with the lustful, gluttonous, wrathful. The second station is the abode of the fraudulent, through which blows, appropriately, "a taint of imbecile rapacity . . . like a whiff from some corpse.'' The idea is Dante's. . . . [In] terms that would be appropriate for Dante's City of Dis, that domain in the *Inferno* of those whose aims of violence and fraud involve exercise of the will.

From the second station on, up the river to Kurtz's outpost, Conrad carefully draws his characters as if they now inhabited Nether Hell. Nevertheless there is a fundamental difference between ***The Heart of Darkness*** and the *Inferno* at this stage. The inhabitants of Conrad's City of Dis actually travel further into the underworld; Dante's damned are fixed. I think this is an essential part of Conrad's solution to the problem of making Hell real though not actual. Moreover, the geography of Hell is, naturally, somewhat altered. As Marlow travels up the river on the steam launch, the natives are literally downtrodden blacks, but they resemble those who are violent against their neighbors. In fact, violence is one of their few distinguishing characteristics. The traders, now called Pilgrims primarily because they move about in Hell, take on the attributes of the circles they have entered. They too become violent, firing wickedly if ineffectually into the underbrush. The Russian trader that Marlow and his company encounter does seem slightly out of place in terms of Dante's scheme, for he appears to be a heretic. Conrad actually calls him a "harlequin,'' a verbal resemblance that is perhaps more than coincidental. He is not himself one of the violent; his real sin is accepting Kurtz as a false god. Their relationship is also in the foreground, though Conrad does not enlarge upon it. The trader merely remarks of Kurtz, "This man has enlarged my mind,'' suggesting intellectual sin, which heresy is. Conrad leaves little doubt about their relations in the readers' minds. The trader has not meditated about his connection with Kurtz; "it came to him, and he accepted it with a sort of eager fatalism,'' Marlow explains. . . . Kurtz fits Dante's scheme perfectly, as traitor to kindred, having put behind him all relations with Europe, to country, having abandoned even the platitudinous lip-service to the civilizing ideal upheld by the others, to guests, having turned upon the trader who nursed him, to God, having set himself up as a "graven image'' in the center of Hades. In short Kurtz is the living Lucifer even without the unspeakable rites mentioned by Marlow.

His native queen, on the other hand, is an emendation to the complicated Dante-like system, though she completes Kurtz's degradation. In a sense she is not materially different from the aunt and the fiancee. In her ambitious dreams, which differ from theirs only because she is more primitive, she is out of touch with the real world. Another structural difference between the two works seems to lie in the fact that Conrad neglected the final circle of Dante's Hell, the frozen Lake of Cocytus. But Conrad's Hell is mythical. Literally Kurtz was alive when Marlow reached him. Death was still his immediate future, and perhaps he is not symbolically fixed in ice, like the Alberti brothers, because Conrad wished to suggest that evil as he was a still worse fate awaited him. His final words, "the horror, the horror,'' may not only refer back to his Satanic service but may also look ahead to an everlasting horror. (pp. 60-1)

As Marlow descends deeper into Hades, he meets characters whose sins loosely correspond with those in the Italian epic. But Conrad by no means runs through the list of the seven deadly sins with their numerous subdivisions. In fact he does not conceive evil dialectically, but he roughly follows a tripartite division of sin of his own making, materially different from but not certainly related to the commonplace medieval conception. At the first station is the accountant, doomed but not suffering, in Limbo; at the next, the City of Dis, the ivory traders much as Dante would have treated them; finally, Kurtz, Lucifer himself, taking on the attributes of all the sins in which he has participated. Such a conception would be familiar to Dante, for superimposed on the complicated structure of his Hell is the threefold machinery of Vestibule, Upper Hell, Nether Hell. Conrad's structure is epic; he was not writing the usual sort of short story. As Miss Feder recognizes, he was heroically depicting "Marlow's discovery of evil and the responsibilities to himself and to others which this knowledge places upon him.''

On the other hand, Miss Feder contends that Conrad employed the descent into Hell theme, at least to some extent, in order to "build up suspense, to tell the reader indirectly that this is no ordinary voyage.'' The voyage is certainly extraordinary, but, as I have pointed out, Conrad does not impart this information through implication. He states it so plainly and so often that the reader can scarcely mistake his meaning. Nor can I agree that the epic theme is employed to develop suspense. As I have shown, Conrad takes pains to adhere to epic structure, patterned after that of the *Inferno*. Suspense is a very slight element in both the classical epic and in Dante and of minor importance in ***The Heart of Darkness.*** Conrad's goal, as Schiller said of Homer, is "already present in every point of his progress.'' . . . The initial action is connected chronologically, through the epic list of ships, with heroic actions of the past. The Thames is geographically connected with all the other waters of the world and mythologically with the underworld. The preliminary scene, no mere enveloping action calculated to add verisimilitude, tends to do away with suspense.

In a geographical sense as well the story progresses from incident through journey to further incident, avoiding climax by diversions of great intrinsic value, much as Dante progresses through the various circles of Hell. And because of this technique few experienced readers are likely to find themselves breathless as they journey with Conrad into the dark continent. The strength of the story lies not in the suspense it develops but in the power of its clear moral insight and in the readers' realization that they, too, could perhaps follow in Marlow's footsteps. (pp. 61-2)

For the development of Conrad's purpose, the promotion of ethical insight, the reader must be left emotionally so [free] that he can judge not only Kurtz's action but Marlow's as well, and draw the right conclusions from them. I contend that Conrad was fully aware of this problem and realized that a solution in modern, prose form was extremely difficult. Throughout his career he struggled towards an answer. ***The Shadow Line*** and **"The Secret Sharer''** are attempts in the same direction, but it was only with the happy adoption of epic technique in ***The Heart of Darkness,*** based largely on the descent into Hell theme which Conrad borrowed from Dante and Virgil, that he achieved complete success. (p. 62)

Robert O. Evans, "Conrad's Underworld," in Modern Poetry Studies *(copyright 1956, by Jerome Mazzaro), Vol. II, No. 2, 1956, pp. 56-62.*

THOMAS MOSER (essay date 1957)

[In the following excerpt, Moser discusses the role of sexuality in Heart of Darkness. *Moser finds that Conrad had difficulty writing about sex or love, and that he could not create realistic dialogues between men and women. Therefore, what F. R. Leavis (1941) terms a "bad patch" of writing in the final interview between Marlow and Kurtz's Intended, Moser sees as Conrad's inability to depict a conversation between a man and a woman. Moser also discusses Marlow's lie to the Intended, concluding that it has a weakening effect on the conclusion because the importance of truth is pervasive in the novel and makes it difficult for the reader to "accept falsehood as salvation." For other interpretations of Marlow's lie, see the excerpts by F. R. Leavis (1941), W. Y. Tindall (1958), Kenneth A. Bruffee (1964), John W. Canario (1967), and Ian Watt (1979), and the entry by Frederick Crews in the Additional Bibliography.]*

There is something about the theme of love that elicits only bad writing from Conrad, something that frustrates his most strenuous efforts to create. (p. 69)

[All] the principal characters [in **"Heart of Darkness"**] are male. But Marlow, the narrator, makes some interesting comments on women; the last scene, between Marlow and Kurtz's Intended has considerable significance; and the jungle imagery raises some interesting problems. Marlow's most extended comment on women comes out apropos of his aunt's expostulations on the great missionary work of the Congo trading company. Marlow ventures to remind her that the company is run for profit, and then says in an aside to his male audience on board the yawl in the Thames estuary:

> It's queer how out of touch with truth women are. They live in a world of their own, and there has never been anything like it, and never can be. It is too beautiful altogether, and if they were to set it up it would go to pieces before the first sunset. Some confounded fact we men have been living contentedly with ever since the day of creation would start up and knock the whole thing over.

In the context of **"Heart of Darkness,"** with its theme of self-discovery, Marlow's assertion that women can take no part in the quest for truth is severe criticism indeed. Marlow says the same thing of Kurtz's Intended: "Oh, she is out of it—completely. They—the women I mean—are out of it—should be out of it. We must help them to stay in that beautiful world of their own."

Though **"Heart of Darkness"** does not hint that Marlow has any sexual interest in the Intended, their scene together at the end certainly recalls in some respects scenes between the Herveys in **"The Return"** [which depicts the menacing force of female sexuality in the eyes of an inadequate male]. For instance, though Marlow has been eager to meet her, he is filled with horror when he reaches her door. The fireplace in her drawing room has a "cold and monumental whiteness." Marlow looks at the woman and wonders what he is doing there, "with a sensation of panic in my heart as though I had blundered into a place of cruel and absurd mysteries not fit for a human being to behold." Their ensuing dialogue is halting and wooden, a "bad patch" of prose, F. R. Leavis calls it [see excerpt above, 1941]. Marlow has come there hoping to surrender to her the memory of Kurtz. She instead maneuvers him into telling her a lie: that Kurtz's last words were, not "The horror," but her name: "I heard a light sigh and then my heart stood still, stopped dead short by an exulting and terrible cry, by the cry of inconceivable triumph and of unspeakable pain." Marlow's lie certainly weakens the scene; he has made truth seem too important throughout the novel to persuade the reader now to accept falsehood as salvation.

The extended descriptions of the jungle remind us, not unnaturally, of the vegetation imagery of ***Almayer's Folly*** and ***An Outcast of the Islands.*** Here, too, the "vegetation rioted on the earth and the big trees were kings"; the reader finds himself in a "strange world of plants, water, and silence." Yet **"Heart of Darkness"** does not stress so heavily as the earlier works the strangling effects of tendrils and creepers. At one point, Marlow does mention the "living trees, lashed together by the creepers," and at another he equates vegetation with woman just as he does not only in the Malay stories but also in ***The Sisters.*** The jungle woman is, of course, Kurtz's native mistress, "savage and superb, wild-eyed and magnificent." Marlow comments:

> And in the hush that had fallen suddenly upon the whole sorrowful land, the immense wilderness, the colossal body of the fecund and mysterious life seemed to look at her, pensive, as though it had been looking at the image of its own tenebrous and passionate soul.

Any reader of **"Heart of Darkness"** must recognize that our analysis of it in terms of sexual love hardly scratches the surface. It means far more than this, and herein lies its significance. For the first time Conrad has been able to use material potentially related to sex in such a way as not to ruin his story and, in fact, in some respects to strengthen it. Our account of the imagery of the Congo jungle far from exhausts its meanings; rather, this imagery has the richness and tonality of the true symbol. The jungle stands for "truth," for an "amazing reality." Conrad equates it with the African natives who alone are full of vitality; the whites are but hollow men. Yet the jungle also means the "lurking death," "profound darkness," and "evil," which belong to the prehistoric life of man, our heritage. We cannot escape this heritage; going into the jungle seems to Marlow like traveling into one's own past, into the world of one's dreams, into the subconscious. Thus the vegetation imagery means much more than female menace; it means the truth, the darkness, the evil, the death which lie within us, which we must recognize in order to be truly alive. In the same way, while the scene between Marlow and Kurtz's Intended is imperfect, and while it does show the "inconceivable triumph" of woman over man, it has other, more important functions in the story. The scene can be read, for example, as an indictment of this woman, safe and ignorant in her complacent, Belgian bourgeois existence; she does not *deserve* to hear the truth. The scene can also be read as Marlow's reaffirmation of fellowship with Kurtz. To accept Kurtz's pronouncement, "The horror," means accepting damnation; Marlow's sin, the lie, serves to confirm this. (pp. 78-81)

[When] Conrad writes about love he does not understand his subject. Conrad is very honest in his preface to ***The Arrow of Gold:*** "what is lacking in the facts is simply what I did not know, and what is not explained is what I did not understand myself, and what seems inadequate is the fault of my imperfect insight."

Conrad differs radically from other great modern novelists in his lack of understanding, in his almost belligerent lack of genuine, dramatic interest in sexual problems. Although the Conradian villains could be labeled neurotic, exhibitionist, and unconsciously homosexual, they are really just cardboard figures plucked from nowhere and thrown up as obstacles to sexual consummation. (p. 128)

Thomas Moser, in his Joseph Conrad: Achievement and Decline *(copyright © 1957 by the President and Fellows of Harvard College; excerpted by permission), Cambridge, Mass.: Harvard University Press, 1957 (and reprinted by Archon Books, Hamden, CT, 1966), 227 p.*

ALBERT J. GUERARD (essay date 1958)

[In the following excerpt, Guerard examines in detail Marlow's growth toward self-awareness and a knowledge of evil in Heart of Darkness. *In addition to Marlow's journey of discovery, Guerard finds that a primary concern of the novel is the effect that colonialism has on the colonizers. Guerard also believes that, in Marlow's attempts to describe Kurtz and his "unspeakable" behavior, Conrad successfully illustrates the narrator's inability to describe in concrete terms the immense truths he has discovered about his own subconscious; Guerard thus concludes that Conrad chose correctly in not trying to disclose the unspeakable acts but succeeded in suggesting an indefinable capacity for evil in human beings. For contrasting interpretations of Conrad's ambiguity, see the excerpts by F. R. Leavis (1941), Thomas Moser (1957), Marvin Mudrick (1958-59), and Frederick R. Karl (1969), and the entry by Frederick Crews in the Additional Bibliography.]*

The Roi des Belges, *the ship Conrad commanded on his Congo journey. Courtesy of Thames and Hudson Ltd.*

Joseph Conrad was one of the most subjective and most personal of English novelists. And his best work makes its calculated appeal to the living sensibilities and commitments of readers; it is a deliberate invasion of our lives, and deliberately manipulates our responses. (p. 1)

[We] cannot ignore the personality and temperament that pervade the best writings (and some of the worst) and largely determine their form. For we are concerned with a style that is unmistakably a speaking voice; with a certain way of constructing novels that may derive from temperamental evasiveness; above all with an intense conflict of novelistic judgment and sympathy presumably reflecting divisions in Conrad himself. (pp. 1-2)

"Heart of Darkness" is the most famous of [Conrad's] personal short novels: a *Pilgrim's Progress* for our pessimistic and psychologizing age. . . . The living nightmare of 1890 seems to have affected Conrad quite as importantly as did Gide's Congo experience thirty-six years later. The autobiographical basis of the narrative is well known, and its introspective bias obvious; this is Conrad's longest journey into self. But it is well to remember that **"Heart of Darkness"** is also other if more superficial things: a sensitive and vivid travelogue, and a comment on "the vilest scramble for loot that ever disfigured the history of human conscience and geographical exploration." (pp. 33-4)

"Heart of Darkness" thus has its important public side, as an angry document on absurd and brutal exploitation. Marlow is treated to the spectacle of a French man-of-war shelling an unseen "enemy" village in the bush, and presently he will wander into the grove at the first company station where the starving and sick Negroes withdraw to die. It is one of the greatest of Conrad's many moments of compassionate rendering. The compassion extends even to the cannibal crew of the *Roi des Belges*. Deprived of the rotten hippo meat they had brought along for food, and paid three nine-inch pieces of brass wire a week, they appear to subsist on "lumps of some stuff like half-cooked dough, of a dirty lavender color" which they keep wrapped in leaves. Conrad here operates through ambiguous suggestion (are the lumps human flesh?) but elsewhere he wants, like Gide after him, to make his complacent European reader *see:* see, for instance, the drunken unkempt official met on the road and three miles farther on the body of the Negro with a bullet hole in his forehead. **"Heart of Darkness"** is a record of things seen and done. But also Conrad was reacting to the humanitarian pretenses of some of the looters precisely as the novelist today reacts to the moralisms of cold-war propaganda. Then it was ivory that poured from the heart of darkness; now it is uranium. Conrad shrewdly recognized—an intuition amply developed in ***Nostromo***—that deception is most sinister when it becomes self-deception, and the propagandist takes seriously his own fictions. Kurtz "could get himself to believe anything—anything." The benevolent rhetoric of his seventeen-page report for the International Society for the Suppression of Savage Customs was meant sincerely enough. But a deeper sincerity spoke through his scrawled postscript: "Exterminate all the brutes!" The conservative Conrad . . . speaks through the journalist who says that "Kurtz's proper sphere ought to have been politics 'on the popular side.'"

Conrad, again like many novelists today, was both drawn to idealism and repelled by its hypocritical abuse. "The conquest of the earth, which mostly means the taking it away from those who have a different complexion or slightly flatter noses than ourselves, is not a pretty thing when you look into it too much. What redeems it is the idea only. An idea at the back of it; not a sentimental pretence but an idea; and an unselfish belief in the idea . . ." Marlow commits himself to the yet unseen agent partly because Kurtz "had come out equipped with moral ideas of some sort." Anything would seem preferable to the demoralized greed and total cynicism of the others, "the flabby devil" of the Central Station. Later, when he discovers what has happened to Kurtz's moral ideas, he remains faithful to the "nightmare of my choice." . . . The Kurtz who had made himself literally one of the devils of the land, and who in solitude had kicked himself loose of the earth, burns while the others rot. Through violent not flabby evil he exists in the moral universe even before pronouncing judgment on himself with his dying breath. A little too much has been made, I think, of the redemptive value of those two words—"The horror!" But none of the company "pilgrims" could have uttered them.

The redemptive view is Catholic, of course, though no priest was in attendance; Kurtz can repent as the gunman of *The Power and the Glory* cannot. **"Heart of Darkness"** (still at this public and wholly conscious level) combines a Victorian ethic and late Victorian fear of the white man's deterioration with a distinctly Catholic psychology. We are protected from ourselves by society with its laws and its watchful neighbors, Marlow observes. And we are protected by work. But when the external restraints of society and work are removed, we must meet the challenge and temptation of savage reversion with our "own inborn strength. Principles won't do." This inborn strength appears to include restraint—the restraint that Kurtz lacked and the cannibal crew of the *Roi des Belges* surprisingly possessed. The hollow man, whose evil is the evil of *vacancy,* succumbs. And in their different degrees the pilgrims and Kurtz share this hollowness. (pp. 34-6)

As for Kurtz, the wilderness "echoed loudly within him because he was hollow at the core." Perhaps the chief contradiction of **"Heart of Darkness"** is that it suggests and dramatizes evil as an active energy (Kurtz and his unspeakable lusts) but defines evil as vacancy. The primitive (and here the contradiction is only verbal) is compact of passion and apathy. "I was struck by the fire of his eyes and the composed languor of his expression . . . This shadow looked satiated and calm, as though for the moment it had had its fill of all the emotions." Of the two menaces—the unspeakable desires and the apathy—apathy surely seemed the greater to Conrad. Hence we cannot quite believe the response of Marlow's heart to the beating of the tom-toms. This is, I think, the story's minor but central flaw, and the source of an unfruitful ambiguity: that it slightly overdoes the kinship with the "passionate uproar," slightly undervalues the temptation of inertia.

In any event, it is time to recognize that the story is not primarily about Kurtz or about the brutality of Belgian officials but about Marlow its narrator. (p. 37)

Substantially and in its central emphasis **"Heart of Darkness"** concerns Marlow (projection to whatever great or small degree of a more irrecoverable Conrad) and his journey toward and through certain facets or potentialities of self. F. R. Leavis [see excerpt above, 1941] seems to regard him as a narrator only, providing a "specific and concretely realized point of view." But Marlow reiterates often enough that he is recounting a spiritual voyage of self-discovery. He remarks casually but crucially that he did not know himself before setting out, and that he likes work for the chance it provides to "find yourself . . . what no other man can ever know." The Inner Station "was the farthest point of navigation and the culminating point of my experience." At a material and rather superficial level, the journey is through the temptation of atavism. It is a record of "remote kinship" with the "wild and passionate uproar," of a "trace of a response" to it, of a final rejection of the "fascination of the abomination." And why should there not be the trace of a response? "The mind of man is capable of anything—because everything is in it, all the past as well as all the future." Marlow's temptation is made concrete through his exposure to Kurtz, a white man and sometime idealist who had fully responded to the wilderness: a potential and fallen self. (p. 38)

On this literal plane, and when the events are so abstracted from the dream-sensation conveying them, it is hard to take Marlow's plight very seriously. Will he, the busy captain and moralizing narrator, also revert to savagery, go ashore for a howl and a dance, indulge unspeakable lusts? The late Victorian reader (and possibly Conrad himself) could take this more seriously than we; could literally believe not merely in a Kurtz's deterioration through months of solitude but also in the sudden reversions to the "beast" of naturalistic fiction. Insofar as Conrad does want us to take it seriously and literally, we must admit the nominal triumph of a currently accepted but false psychology over his own truer intuitions. But the triumph is only nominal. For the personal narrative is unmistakably authentic, which means that it explores something truer, more fundamental, and distinctly less material: the night journey into the unconscious, and confrontation of an entity within the self. . . . It little matters what, in terms of psychological symbolism, we call this double or say he represents: whether the Freudian id or the Jungian shadow or more vaguely the outlaw. And I am afraid it is impossible to say where Conrad's conscious understanding of his story began and ended. The important thing is that the introspective plunge and powerful dream seem true; and are therefore inevitably moving.

Certain circumstances of Marlow's voyage, looked at in these terms, take on a new importance. The true night journey can occur (except during analysis) only in sleep or in the waking dream of a profoundly intuitive mind. Marlow insists more than is necessary on the dreamlike quality of his narrative. . . . Even before leaving Brussels Marlow felt as though he "were about to set off for the center of the earth," not the center of a continent. The introspective voyager leaves his familiar rational world, is "cut off from the comprehension" of his surroundings; his steamer toils "along slowly on the edge of a black and incomprehensible frenzy." As the crisis approaches, the dreamer and his ship move through a silence that "seemed unnatural, like a state of trance"; then enter (a few miles below the Inner Station) a deep fog. "The approach to this Kurtz grubbing for ivory in the wretched bush was beset by as many dangers as though he had been an enchanted princess sleeping in a fabulous castle." Later, Marlow's task is to try "to break the spell" of the wilderness that holds Kurtz entranced.

The approach to the unconscious and primitive may be aided by a savage or half-savage guide, and may require the token removal of civilized trappings or aids. . . . In **"Heart of Darkness"** the token "relinquishment" and the death of the half-savage guide are connected. The helmsman falling at Marlow's feet casts blood on his shoes, which he is "morbidly anxious" to change and in fact throws overboard. . . . Here we have presumably entered an area of unconscious creation; the dream is true but the teller may have no idea why it is. So too, possibly, a psychic need as well as literary tact compelled Conrad to defer the meeting between Marlow and Kurtz for some three thousand words after announcing that it took place. We think we are about to meet Kurtz at last. But instead Marlow leaps ahead to his meeting with the "Intended." . . . This is the "evasive" Conrad in full play, deferring what we most want to know and see; perhaps compelled to defer climax in this way. The tactic is dramatically effective, though possibly carried to excess: we are told on the authority of completed knowledge certain things we would have found hard to believe had they been presented through a slow consecutive realistic discovery. But also it can be argued that it was psychologically impossible for Marlow to go at once to Kurtz's house with the others. The double must be brought on board the ship, and the first confrontation must occur there. (pp. 39-41)

Hence the shock Marlow experiences when he discovers that Kurtz's cabin is empty and his secret sharer gone; a part of himself has vanished. . . . And now he must risk the ultimate confrontation in a true solitude and must do so on shore. "I was anxious to deal with this shadow by myself alone—and to this day I don't know why I was so jealous of sharing with anyone the peculiar blackness of that experience." . . . We are told very little of what Kurtz said in the moments that follow; and little of his incoherent discourses after he is brought back to the ship. "His was an impenetrable darkness. I looked at him as you peer down at a man who is lying at the bottom of a precipice where the sun never shines"—a comment less vague and rhetorical, in terms of psychic geography, than it may seem at a first reading. And then Kurtz is dead, taken off the ship, his body buried in a "muddy hole." With the confrontation over, Marlow must still emerge from environing darkness, and does so through that other deep fog of sickness. The identification is not yet completely broken. "And it is not my own extremity I remember best—a vision of grayness without form filled with physical pain, and a careless contempt for the evanescence of all things—even of this pain itself. No! It is his extremity that I seem to have lived through." Only in the atonement of his lie to Kurtz's "Intended," back in the sepulchral city, does the experience come truly to an end. "I laid the ghost of his gifts at last with a lie . . ."

Such seems to be the content of the dream. If my summary has even a partial validity it should explain and to an extent justify some of the "adjectival and worse than supererogatory insistence" to which F. R. Leavis (who sees only the travelogue and the portrait of Kurtz) objects. I am willing to grant that the unspeakable rites and unspeakable secrets become wearisome, but the fact—at once literary and psychological—is that they must remain *unspoken*. A confrontation with such a double and facet of the unconscious cannot be reported through realistic dialogue; the conversations must remain as shadowy as the narrator's conversations with Leggatt. So too when Marlow finds it hard to define the moral shock he received on seeing the empty cabin, or when he says he doesn't know why he was jealous of sharing his experience, I think we can take him literally . . . and in a sense even be thankful for his uncertainty. . . . [It] may be the groping, fumbling **"Heart of Darkness"** takes us into a deeper region of the mind. If the story is not about this deeper region, and not about Marlow himself, its length is quite indefensible. But even if one were to allow that the final section is about Kurtz (which I think simply absurd), a vivid pictorial record of his unspeakable lusts and gratifications would surely have been ludicrous. I share Mr. Leavis' admiration for the heads on the stakes. But not even Kurtz could have supported many such particulars.

"I listened on the watch for the sentence, for the word, that would give me the clue to the faint uneasiness inspired by this narrative that seemed to shape itself without human lips in the heavy night air of the river." Thus one of Marlow's listeners, the original "I" who frames the story, comments on its initial effect. He has discovered how alert one must be to the ebb and flow of Marlow's narrative, and here warns the reader. But there is no single word; not even the word *trance* will do. For the shifting play of thought and feeling and image and event is very intricate. It is not vivid detail alone, the heads on stakes or the bloody shoes; nor only the dark mass of moralizing abstraction; nor the dramatized psychological intuitions apart from their context that give **"Heart of Darkness"** its brooding weight. The impressionist method—one cannot leave this story without subscribing to the obvious—finds here one of its great triumphs of tone. The random movement of the nightmare is also the controlled movement of a poem, in which a quality of feeling may be stated or suggested and only much later justified. But it is justified at last. (pp. 41-4)

[The] narrative advances and withdraws as in a succession of long dark waves borne by an incoming tide. The waves encroach fairly evenly on the shore, and presently a few more feet of sand have been won. But an occasional wave thrusts up unexpectedly, much farther than the others: even as far, say, as Kurtz and his Inner Station. Or, to take the other figure: the flashlight is held firmly; there are no whimsical jerkings from side to side. But now and then it is raised higher, and for a brief moment in a sudden clear light we discern enigmatic matters to be explored much later. Thus the movement of the story is sinuously progressive, with much incremental repetition. The intent is not to subject the reader to multiple strains and ambiguities, but rather to throw over him a brooding gloom, such a warm pall as those two Fates in the home office might knit, back in the sepulchral city.

Yet no figure can convey **"Heart of Darkness"** in all its resonance and tenebrous atmosphere. The movement is not one of penetration and withdrawal only; it is also the tracing of a large grand circle of awareness. It begins with the friends on the yacht under the dark above Gravesend and at last returns to them, to the tranquil waterway that "leading to the uttermost ends of the earth flowed sombre under an overcast sky—seemed to lead into the heart of an immense darkness." (pp. 44-5)

The travelogue as travelogue is not to be ignored. . . . Presently Marlow will discover a scar in the hillside into which drainage pipes for the settlement had been tumbled; then will walk into the grove where the Negroes are free to die in a "greenish gloom." The sharply visualized particulars suddenly intrude on the somber intellectual flow of Marlow's meditation: magnified, arresting. The boilermaker who "had to crawl in the mud under the bottom of the steamboat . . . would tie up that beard of his in a kind of white serviette he brought for the purpose. It had loops to go over his ears." The papier-maché Mephistopheles is as vivid, with his delicate hooked nose and glittering mica eyes. So too is Kurtz's harlequin companion and admirer, humbly dissociating himself from the master's lusts and gratifications. . . . And even Kurtz, shadow and symbol though he be, the man of eloquence who in this story is almost voiceless, and necessarily so—even Kurtz is sharply visualized, an "animated image of death," a skull and body emerging as from a winding sheet, "the cage of his ribs all astir, the bones of his arm waving."

This is Africa and its flabby inhabitants; Conrad did indeed have a "feel for the country." Yet the dark tonalities and final brooding impression derive as much from rhythm and rhetoric as from such visual details: derive from the high aloof ironies and from a prose that itself advances and recedes in waves. (pp. 45-6)

The insistence on darkness, finally, and quite apart from ethical or mythical overtone, seems a right one for this extremely personal statement. There is a darkness of passivity, paralysis, immobilization; it is from the state of entranced languor rather than from the monstrous desires that the double Kurtz, this shadow, must be saved. In Freudian theory, we are told, such preoccupation may indicate fear of the feminine and passive. But may it not also be connected, through one of the spirit's multiple disguises, with a radical fear of death, that other darkness? . . .

It would be folly to try to limit the menace of vegetation in the restless life of Conradian image and symbol. But [it] . . . reminds us again of the story's reflexive references, and its images of deathly immobilization in grass. Most striking are the black shadows dying in the greenish gloom of the grove at the first station. But grass sprouts between the stones of the European city, a "whited sepulcher," and on the same page Marlow anticipates coming upon the remains of his predecessor: "the grass growing through his ribs was tall enough to hide his bones." The critical meeting with Kurtz occurs on a trail through the grass. Is there not perhaps an intense horror behind the casualness with which Marlow reports his discoveries, say of the Negro with the bullet in his forehead? (p. 47)

"Heart of Darkness" . . . remains one of the great dark meditations in literature, and one of the purest expressions of a melancholy temperament. (p. 48)

Albert J. Guerard, in his Conrad the Novelist *(copyright © 1958 by the President and Fellows of Harvard College; excerpted by permission), Cambridge, Mass.: Harvard University Press, 1958 (and reprinted by Harvard University Press, 1966), 322 p.*

W. Y. TINDALL (essay date 1958)

[Tindall has written extensively on the works of twentieth-century English and Irish authors, and is a widely recognized authority on the work of James Joyce. In the following excerpt, Tindall argues that F. R. Leavis and other critics have erroneously interpreted Marlow's voice as that of Conrad. While the character and author share similar qualities, Tindall contends that Marlow is a fully autonomous character manipulated by Conrad to achieve his ends. In addition to a discussion of Marlow's character, Tindall also examines Marlow's lie to Kurtz's Intended, concluding that Marlow tells "a white lie to keep the Intended in the dark by preserving her light." Kenneth A. Bruffee (1964) sharply disagrees with this interpretation of the lie. For other discussions of Marlow's lie, see the excerpts by F. R. Leavis (1941), Thomas Moser (1957), Kenneth A. Bruffee (1964), John W. Canario (1967), and Ian Watt (1979), and the entry by Frederick Crews in the Additional Bibliography.]

The trouble with Conrad, indeed, the only trouble, says F. R. Leavis, is Marlow. **"Heart of Darkness,"** found good by some good critics, is so generally "marred" by Marlow's adjectives that it sinks into place beside ***Lord Jim*** among minor works. In **"Youth,"** a "cheap insistence" on glamor makes Conrad seem a Kipling of the South Seas, if not worse. It may be that in ***Chance*** Conrad-Marlow rises above such "shockingly bad magazine stuff" to a kind of technical respectability, but, save for that, stories in which Marlow figures cannot be counted among the major works: ***Nostromo, Under Western Eyes, The Secret Agent,*** and some others in a hierarchy of values, unsupported but proclaimed. Abandoning the "objective correlative" when Marlow is around, Leavis continues, Conrad becomes "intent on making a virtue out of not knowing what he means. The vague and unrealizable, he asserts with a strained impressiveness, is the profoundly and tremendously significant." The trouble with Leavis seems failure to read the text or else to understand it. (p. 274)

Other critics besides Leavis have confused Marlow with his creator. When Marlow speaks they think it Conrad; and one must admit some reason for this confusion. As Conrad's other writings prove, Marlow shares some of Conrad's ideas, his moral concerns, and his delight in irony. It requires little critical awareness, however, to discover that Marlow, in spite of monocle and beard (if, indeed, he wears them), is a creature distinct from his creator. Conrad, who appears at the beginning and end and sometimes in the middle of the Marlow books, listens to Marlow and tells us what he tells him. To Conrad, Marlow is the object as Jim or Kurtz seems Marlow's. Marlow may owe something to Conrad's desire for a mask in Yeats's sense of the word, but a mask is a device for achieving impersonality, drama, and distance. No longer subject but object, Marlow has been distanced to the point where Conrad can regard him as another and use him not with the warm concern we devote to ourselves but with aesthetic detachment as an artist should. Marlow is matter to be handled and shaped. Maybe his closest parallel is Stephen Dedalus, who, although resembling his creator in many ways, is nonetheless someone else. Like Stephen, Marlow often exposes his imperfections to the mocking eye. (pp. 274-75)

Conrad seems during this time to have approximated Henry James's ideas of reality. For that reason many critics have traced Marlow's origin to the master, who invented his observer several years before the emergence of Marlow. Seeing him as a development of the Jamesian observer, they have found him a kind of bearded Maisie or a monocled anticipation of Strether. Of their family maybe, Marlow differs nevertheless in so many particulars from his assumed prototype and successor that it is likely he owes Maisie no more than a possible hint. James, looking into the head of his observer, presents a selection of what goes on there. His role is that of interpreter, Conrad's of reporter. Maisie receives impressions which James attends to; Marlow, an amateur philosopher, a compulsive talker, and a kind of artist, considers, colors, and shapes his impressions by himself, while Conrad, aloof, scribbles in his notebook. Maisie's experience is immediate and current, whereas Marlow's, dependent upon memory where it receives further refraction, is distant in time and place. These differences make it clear that if, indifferent to fallacies, we allow genesis, we should look elsewhere for Marlow's.

I think that the idea of Marlow can be traced back to the inner demands of Conrad's work, immediately to ***The Nigger of the Narcissus,*** of which the Marlow stories seem natural developments—in several ways; but let us limit ourselves for the moment to . . . point of view. Since Marlow among other things is an embodied point of view, that limitation is suitable. The story of James Wait and the ship *Narcissus* is told by someone who, like the narrator of the Cyclops episode of *Ulys-*

ses, is nameless and apparently disembodied. No more than a voice, this ghostly attendant employs first person nevertheless. . . . It is plain that this concerned yet ghostly voice is an experiment, an unsuccessful experiment perhaps, marking a transition between omniscience and a personified observer. Marlow, developing from this voice, improves it. Equipped with personality, character, limits, attitude, and tone—in a word, with body—Charlie Marlow and his conspiring voice become authentic. More than observant, he not only plays his part in the action but subsumes it, leaving that ancestral voice neither here nor there.

Not Conrad's occasional description, then, but this voice determines Marlow, who, far from Polish, emerges as the Victorian gentleman, the embodiment maybe of Conrad's aspiration. . . . In love with conscious order and light, he detests disorder and darkness. Devoted to duty, fidelity, and prudence as a navigator and master must be, he observes in **"Heart of Darkness,"** at a moment of savage and commercial confusion: "I looked ahead—piloting." As he proceeds, he ruminates in the manner of the popular philosopher on the nature of things. Their nature, we discover, is not altogether different from that observed by Hardy or, indeed, by Conrad—if we may trust his letters. Marlow shares with his creator the all but existentialist conviction that however meaningless and hopeless things are, we must cherish ideals and by their aid change necessary defeat to a kind of futile victory. Such human victories, general defeats, and all things else are mixed and dubious. For this reason too Marlow is obsessed with enigmas and uncertainties. They are part of the nature of things. We can never be sure in this uncertain place, but we must try.

As for attitude: at once cynical and sentimental, Marlow is given to pity and impatience. Maybe his term "romantic" describes him best. Although he fails to define it, this term, as he uses it, seems to include imagination, illusion, anxiety, and concern with self. Marlow has little humor, though he laughs once or twice. . . . If little humor and less wit, there is plenty of irony; and that provides his common tone. Like many ironists, Marlow is committed, *engagé*. All this is apparent enough; but Marlow, changing with the years, reveals new aspects in each story. . . . (pp. 275-77)

Searching possibilities of Marlow as subject and object, Conrad followed [the] simple tale [**"Youth"**] with one of greater density or specific gravity, which may be signs or at least metaphors of value. A tale at once complex and ambiguous, **"Heart of Darkness"** is ostensibly the story of Marlow's quest for Kurtz. Actually Marlow is questing for himself: "The most you can hope," he says, "is some knowledge of yourself." While seeking assurance and knowledge, he exposes himself once more to Conrad's distant eye. But Marlow has developed. Not only a discursive commentator, he has become an imagist as well; and developing in other directions, he has acquired moral concerns. That love of mystery which appears now and again in **"Youth,"** emerges here as one of Marlow's obsessions.

"Image" and "symbol," terms used by Marlow, indicate his new method of presentation—at least in part. By "image," a term he applies to Kurtz and the wild woman, he seems to mean a significant but more or less limited concretion; and by "symbol," a term he applies to skulls on posts, he seems to mean a less definite, more generally suggestive concretion. Rusting machinery in the Belgian wasteland and the gunboat shelling the forest are images in his sense; whereas the enigmatic forest is a symbol. As if familiar with the Preface to ***The Nigger of the Narcissus*** [see *TCLC*, Vol. 6, p. 112], Marlow sometimes presents his vision in plastic, sensuous forms that seem designed to "reveal" or "disclose" embodied meaning to an audience that must take these offerings as it can. . . . We have no assurance that Marlow has read Conrad or Yeats on symbolism, but as he tells us in **"Youth,"** he has read Carlyle's *Sartor Resartus* with its famous chapter on symbol, and it seems likely from the text that he knows Baudelaire—as Conrad did. In **"Heart of Darkness"** Marlow's childish interest in the "delightful mystery" of maps and his consequent journey to the "unknown" suggest Baudelaire's "Le Voyage" as Marlow's dandy at the trading post suggests Baudelaire's ideal man. Comparing his forest to a "temple," Marlow calls to mind the forest of Baudelaire's "Correspondances," which also allows obscure, confusing intimations to emerge.

In the prelude to **"Heart of Darkness"** Conrad tells us that for Marlow "the meaning of an episode was not inside it like a kernel but outside, enveloping the tale which brought it out only as a glow brings out a haze." This "misty halo" (not unlike the white fog encountered on the Congo) seems to have little in common with the inner truth, lying deep below the surface, that Marlow seeks; but only a difference of metaphor separates these attempts to fix the meaning of symbol. Wherever its meaning lies—whether in halo, fog, or kernel—Marlow's principal symbol, aside from the forest, is the voyage. . . . (pp. 278-79)

Like Baudelaire, Marlow is seldom content to let his concretions alone. Sometimes he tries to explain them and almost always, driven by anxiety, he anticipates our reaction by stating his own. Marlow, after all, is not early T. S. Eliot. Adjectives and similes, not unlike the eager nouns by which the captain of **"The Secret Sharer"** tries to fix his delusions, are Marlow's attempts to give his response to halo or kernel and to fix his impression of the images he picks as subjective correlatives. He finds the women knitting black wool "fateful," and the "expressive and puzzling" skulls indicative of moral deficiency. Even the forest is restricted by Marlow's guesses to our primitive, repressed, and hidden desires, below "permitted aspirations." Such discursive limitations, however, are legitimate in this context; for the story is not about knitting women, forests, or even Kurtz, but about Marlow's response to them.

Trying to explain his dark forest, Marlow commonly finds it enigmatic, its darkness properly shrouded in white fog. In this respect Marlow resembles the crew of the *Narcissus,* who, like critics confronted by a text, find Wait, another dark thing, ambiguous. Far from implying certainty, Marlow's comments celebrate uncertainty, as if to support Carlyle's idea of symbol, which conceals as it reveals. The emphasis upon enigma that Leavis finds lamentable is not there to make a virtue of ignorance. Not only the heart of Marlow's darkness, it is also a consequence of his symbolist position. For romantic symbolists there can be no definite conclusions; and however certain Marlow may be about some images, his tale, as listening Conrad says, is "inconclusive."

Imagery of dark and light, by which the voice of the ***Narcissus*** expresses his uncertainties, is also useful to Marlow. Civilization is light and the forest dark; but darkness and light are always shifting and ambiguous. What seems dark may prove light and what seems light, dark; or else, mixed, they may compose the universal "grayness" that he dreads. Acclaiming light, he faces darkness; but a growing conviction that the darkness of Kurtz and the forest may be his own or that in their internal and external confusion he can no longer tell light from dark is cause for anxiety and a further cause of uncertainty. Howling natives correspond to something within himself; and at the end, still professing light, he is loyal to Kurtz's darkness.

The conflict or confusion of light and dark, inviting irony, allows morality. Marlow's moral position, though seeming plainer than it is, is emphatic. Approving fidelity, duty, discipline, and order, of which rivets, navigation, and light seem symbolic, he abhors dark disorder. Morality involves choice; Marlow's, however, is not between light and dark but between kinds of dark. Forced to choose between "nightmares," that of the rapacious Belgians and that of Kurtz, Marlow chooses the latter; for to him that ultimate exclamation seems "moral victory." Not only proving Kurtz's awareness of his "degradation," his "horror," agreeably corroborating Marlow's own convictions, seems also to imply the "immense darkness" of all things.

As for the ironies: ironic Marlow seems their main and their all but unconscious object. It is ironic that one so vocal should call Kurtz "a voice." There is irony (of which Marlow is also innocent) in his unquestioning acceptance of Kurtz's "horror" as a sign of grace and moral illumination. Marlow's character compels that view of it; but for all we know Kurtz is horrified because his rituals and ivory-gathering have been cut short—or he may be looking at Marlow. The principal irony in Marlow's interview with Kurtz's Intended does not consist, as Leavis thought, in Marlow's attitude toward her or in the discrepancy between her view of Kurtz and the actuality (whatever that is) but rather in the acceptance of darkness by an apostle of light. As Marlow, that apostle, enters the house of this lover of a darkness mistaken for light, darkness enters with him and grows deeper as he talks. His defense of Kurtz out of loyalty to what is perhaps his own mistaken idea of light amounts to defense of darkness and identification with Kurtz. Marlow tells a white lie to keep the Intended in the dark by preserving her light. But even this light is uncertain—as her black dress implies; and Marlow may be right in seeing her momentarily not as a creature of light and of his chivalric expectations but as the wild woman of the Congo. An irony of which Marlow is only half aware is the terrible confusion of light and dark that he reveals within himself. Darkness in white fog seems a fitting symbol. (pp. 280-81)

W. Y. Tindall, "Apology for Marlow" (© copyright 1958 by the University of Minnesota; reprinted by permission of the Literary Estate of W. Y. Tindall), in From Jane Austen to Joseph Conrad: Essays Collected in Memory of James T. Hillhouse, *edited by Robert C. Rathburn and Martin Steinmann, Jr., University of Minnesota Press, 1958, pp. 274-85.*

MARVIN MUDRICK (essay date 1958-59)

[In the following excerpt, Mudrick discusses Conrad's verbal and structural techniques. Mudrick considers Conrad's short works his most original, for in them he most effectively utilized what Mudrick terms the double plot, an innovative intertwining of realistic and symbolic action and description. However, Mudrick believes that Conrad is a writer with two styles, one founded upon precise description of vivid detail, the other and more inferior relying upon abstractions, partial ironies, and indirection, a style Conrad uses when he has no faith in his ability to let details and symbols suggest their intended meanings. Specifically, in the depiction of Kurtz, Mudrick contends that Conrad exploits melodrama and the stock tricks of slick magazine fiction that would be unacceptable in the work of a lesser writer. Mudrick believes that this stems from Conrad's inability to fully imagine the evil he wished to depict. For further discussion of Conrad's depiction of evil, see the excerpts by F. R. Leavis (1941), Albert J. Guerard (1958), Frederick R. Karl (1969), and the entry by Frederick Crews in the Additional Bibliography.]

Everything Conrad wrote recalls everything else he wrote, in a pervasive melancholy of outlook, a persistency of theme ("the plight of the man on whom life closes down inexorably, divesting him of the supports and illusory protection of friendship, social privilege, or love"), and a conscientious manipulation of innovational method; yet what marks Conrad as not a mere experimentalist or entertainer but a genuine innovator occurs only sporadically in his full-length novels, with discretion and sustained impulse only in several long stories or short novels: in ***The Nigger of the Narcissus,*** in ***Typhoon,*** in Part I of ***Under Western Eyes,*** and—with most impressive rich immediacy—in ***Heart of Darkness.***

Conrad's innovation—or, in any case, the fictional technique that he exploited with unprecedented thoroughness—is the double-plot: neither allegory (where surface is something teasing, to be got through), nor catch-all symbolism (where every knowing particular signifies some universal or other), but a developing order of actions so lucidly symbolic of a developing state of spirit—from moment to moment, so morally identifiable—as to suggest the conditions of allegory without forfeiting or even subordinating the realistic "superficial" claim of the actions and their actors.

Heart of Darkness—at least until we reach Kurtz and the end of the journey—is a remarkable instance of such order: details intensely present, evocatively characteristic of the situations in which they happen, and prefiguring from moment to moment an unevadable moral reality. The equatorial incubus of inefficiency, for example, is created and consolidated by a set of details memorable in their direct sensuous impact, almost farcical in the situations whose absurd disproportions they discover, and wholly dreadful as a cumulative cosmic denial of mind: the warship ("'It appears the French had one of their wars going on thereabouts'"), its men dying of fever at the rate of three a day, "'firing into a continent'"; the forsaken railway truck, looking "'as dead as the carcass of some animal,'" rusting in the grass "'on its back with its wheels in the air'"; the fat man with the moustaches trying to put out a blaze in a grass shed with a quart of water in a leaking pail; the brickmaker idling for a year with no bricks and no hope of materials for making them; the "'wanton smashup'" of drainage pipes abandoned in a ravine; burst, piled-up cases of rivets at the Outer Station, and no way of getting them to the damaged steamboat at the Central Station; the "'vast artificial hole somebody had been digging on the slope, the purpose of which I found it impossible to divine. It wasn't a quarry or a sandpit, anyhow. It was just a hole.'" . . . (pp. 545-47)

In this world of the fortuitous, acutely realized details of nightmare, such efficiency as can survive will be of a very special kind; like the accountant's—

> Hair parted, brushed, oiled, under a green-lined parasol held in a big white hand. He was amazing, and had a penholder behind his ear. . . . His appearance was certainly that of a hairdresser's dummy; but in the great demoralization of the land he kept up his appearance. That's backbone. . . .

In this climate, where life for a clot of exasperated foreigners contracts itself to the exploitation of the hopelessly alien, it is also difficult to guard against certain explicit moral errors; among them, a cruelty as ordained and unimpassioned as in "'the gloomy circle of some inferno.'" . . . (p. 547)

[Work] defines and embodies itself in its reluctant functionaries, starched accountant as well as dying natives; it has its particular countersign and gleaming talisman ("'The word "ivory" rang in the air, was whispered, was sighed. You would think they were praying to it. A taint of imbecile rapacity blew through it all, like a whiff from some corpse'"); in its tangible promise of easy gratifications, it indifferently victimizes both the unwilling natives and their incompetent overseers, it prescribes the tableau of cruelty in the grove of death, it provides its own corresponding niche for every stage of opportunism from the novice exploiter (weight 224 pounds) who keeps fainting, to the manager of the Central Station. . . . (pp. 547-48)

The general blight and demoralization are inextricable, they do not detach themselves for scrutiny, from the developing order of actions that intensely brings them to mind; they have no independent symbolic existence, nor do any other of the spreading abstractions and big ideas in the narrative. Even the journey into the heart of darkness—the more obvious broad symbolic provocations of which have given joy to so many literary amateurs—insofar as it has artistic (rather than merely psychoanalytic) force, is finely coincident with its network of details; its moral nature steadily reveals itself not in the rather predictable grand gestures of Conradian rhetoric ("'Going upriver was like going back to beginnings, when vegetation rioted and the big trees were kings'"), but in the unavoidable facts of suspense, strangeness, vigilance, danger, and fear: the difficulties of piloting the patched fragile steamer past hidden banks, snags, sunken stones upriver; the sudden "'glimpse of rush walls, of peaked grass roofs, a burst of yells, a whirl of black limbs, a mass of hands clapping, of feet stamping, of bodies swaying, of eyes rolling, under the droop of heavy and motionless foliage'"; the honest, "'unmistakably real'" book mysteriously discovered in the abandoned hut; the terrified savage tending the boiler, who "'squinted at the steam gauge with an evident effort of intrepidity'"; the arrows from nowhere; the death of the black helmsman . . . ; and, most shocking of all in its evocation of mind at an intolerable extremity, the climactic farcical detail of Marlow's panic to get rid of his shoes and socks overflowing with a dead man's blood. . . . (pp. 548-49)

When Conrad is called, with a clear confidence that the judgment is general and will not be challenged, "perhaps the finest prose stylist" among the English novelists, it is doubtless such passages as these that the critic has in mind. . . . Qualifying his account of Conrad as one of the four masters of English fiction, Dr. Leavis [see excerpt above, 1941] makes the definitive comment on this sort of thing: "Conrad must here stand convicted of borrowing the arts of the magazine-writer (who has borrowed his, shall we say, from Kipling and Poe) in order to impose on his readers and on himself, for thrilled response, a 'significance' that is merely an emotional insistence on the presence of what he can't produce. The insistence betrays the absence, the willed 'intensity' the nullity. He is intent on making a virtue out of not knowing what he means."

Qualification, however, is not enough. Conrad's lapses of this sort are not rare or incidental, they do not merely weaken his master style but schismatically parallel it in a style of their own. The "finest prose stylist" in English fiction has in fact two styles: the narrative-descriptive, in which explicit details triumphantly cohere with implicit moral moments in an accumulating point-to-point correspondence (a style whose purest, if not most imposingly complex, manifestation may be examined in ***Typhoon***); and the oracular-ruminative, which dotes on abstractions, exclamations, unexpressive indirections, pat ironies ("the arts of the magazine-writer"), a style which takes over, especially in the large-scale works, whenever Conrad loses faith in the power of his details to enforce both their own reality and the symbolic substructure whose contours they are intended to suggest—so Marlow cries out as he and his author signalize, in a joint loss of faith, their drift from master to meretricious style, "'I've been telling you what we said—repeating the phrases we pronounced—but what's the good?'"

Conrad's symbolism, and his moral imagination, are, after all, as unallegorical as possible. When they function and have effect they are severely realistic: they nourish themselves on voices heard and solid objects seen and touched in the natural world, they contract into rhetoric as soon as the voices and objects begin to appear less than independently present; when Conrad is not describing, with direct sensuous impact, a developing sequence of distinct actions, he is liable to drift into the mooning or glooming that for some critics passes as Conrad's "philosophy" and for others as his style in its full tropical luxuriance.

Moreover, to assume, as Dr. Leavis seems to assume, that all symbolism works *only* as it is anchored to a record of immediate sensations, that it must totally coincide with "the concrete presentment of incident, setting and image," is to transform Conrad's limitation (and gift) into a condition of fiction. To compare Conrad's symbolic method, his two-ply plot, with the methods of, say, Dostoievsky and Kafka is to become aware of radically different possibilities: on the one hand, Conrad's realistic mode; on the other, moral imaginations not necessarily anchored to objects and places, symbolic means capable of producing, for example, those vibrations of clairvoyant hallucination in Dostoievsky, and of meaningful enigma in Kafka, which move through and beyond immediate sensations into a world of moral meanings almost as independent as, and far more densely populated than, the other side of the mirror of traditional allegory. Of such effects, beyond the capacities of even the most evocative realism, Conrad is innocent; yet when, in ***Heart of Darkness,*** he approaches the center of a difficult moral situation (desperately more troublesome than the simple choices permitted the characters in ***Typhoon***), when facts and details begin to appear inadequate as figurations of the moral problem, it is just such effects that he is at length driven to attempt.

The problem is, of course, Kurtz. It is when we are on the verge of meeting Kurtz that Marlow's "inconceivables" and "impenetrables" begin to multiply at an alarming rate; it is when we have already met him that we are urged to observe "smiles of indefinable meaning" and to hear about "unspeakable rites" and "gratified and monstrous passions" and "subtle horrors"—words to hound the reader into a sense of enigmatic awfulness that he would somehow be the better for not trying to find a way through. . . . (pp. 549-51)

The problem, as Conrad sets it up, is to persuade the reader—by epithets, exclamations, ironies, by every technical obliquity—into an hallucinated awareness of the unplumbable depravity, the primal unanalyzable evil, implicit in Kurtz's reversion to the jungle from the high moral sentiments of his report. . . . Unhappily, though, the effect of even this minor irony is to bring to mind and penetrate Conrad's magazine-writer style as well as the hollowness of Kurtz's sentiments. Besides, Kurtz's sentiments must, to help justify the fuss Conrad makes about their author, radiate at least a rhetorical energy; yet all Conrad gives us of the report is a phrase or two of mealy-mouthed reformist exhortation that would not do credit to a Maugham missionary let alone the "extraordinary man" Kurtz is supposed by all accounts to be, so that the "irony" of the scrawled outcry at the end of the report—"Exterminate the brutes!"—is about as subtle and unexpected as the missionary's falling for the local call-girl.

In the effort to establish for Kurtz an opaque and terrifying magnitude, Conrad tends to rely more and more oppressively on these pat ironies. The very existence of the incredibly naïve young Russian is another such irony: the disciple who responds to Kurtz's abundant proofs of cruelty and mean obsession with the steadfast conviction—and no evidence for the reader—that Kurtz is a great man ("''he's enlarged my mind''"—another irony that cuts more ways than Conrad must have intended). And if the culminating irony of the narrative, Marlow's interview with Kurtz's Intended, is expertly anticipated long before . . .—it is all the more disheartening, after such anticipation, to encounter in that interview sighs, heart stoppings, chill grips in the chest, exultations, the cheaply ironic double-talk ("'She said suddenly very low, "He died as he lived." "His end," said I, with dull anger stirring in me, "was in every way worthy of his life."'") as well as the sentimental lie that provokes not only her "'cry of inconceivable triumph and of unspeakable pain'" but the final cheap irony ("'"I knew it—I was sure!" She knew. She was sure.'")—a jumble of melodramatic tricks so unabashed and so strategic that in any less reputable writer they might well be critically regarded as earning for the work an instant oblivion.

Still, in ***Heart of Darkness*** at least, Conrad is neither cynical nor laxly sentimental in his failure of imagination and corresponding failure of technique. The theme itself is too much for him, too much for perhaps any but the very greatest dramatists and novelists. The sense of evil he must somehow project exceeds his capacity for imagining it; he strains into badness while reaching for verifications of a great and somber theme that is beyond his own very considerable powers. (pp. 551-52)

[***Heart of Darkness***] is in fact one of those mixed structures whose partial success (not so neatly separable as, for example, Part I of ***Under Western Eyes***) is so profound, so unprecedented, and so strikingly irreplaceable as to survive a proportion and gravity of failure that would sink forever any other work.

It is one of the great originals of literature. After ***Heart of Darkness*** the craftsman in fiction could never again be unaware of the moral resources inherent in every recorded sensation, or insensitive to the need of making the most precise record possible of every sensation: what now appears an immemorial cliché of the craft of fiction has a date as recent as the turn of the century. If Conrad was never quite equal to his own originality, he was at least the first to designate it as a new province of possibilities for the novelist; and, in ***Heart of Darkness,*** the first to suggest, by large and compelling partial proof, the intensity of moral illumination that a devoted attention to its demands might generate. The suggestion was an historical event: for good and bad novelists alike, irreversible. After ***Heart of Darkness,*** the recorded moment—the word—was irrecoverably symbol. (p. 553)

Marvin Mudrick, "The Originality of Conrad," in The Hudson Review *(copyright © 1959 by The Hudson Review, Inc.; reprinted by permission), Vol. XI, No. 4, Winter, 1958-59, pp. 545-53.*

C. F. BURGESS (essay date 1963)

[Burgess is an English critic who has written extensively on eighteenth-century drama and dramatic criticism. In the following excerpt he disagrees with Robert O. Evans's dismissal (see excerpt dated 1956) of the role of the Russian seaman in Heart of Darkness. *Burgess believes that the character serves a dual function: to provide Marlow with information about Kurtz; and, as the fool in Kurtz's court, to give shape to Marlow's ambiguous feelings toward Kurtz, whom he feels is remarkable enough to command the loyalty of the Russian youth, yet atrocious enough to mistreat him on a whim. For another discussion of the importance of this character, see the excerpt by John W. Canario (1967).]*

The presence of the Russian, that fantastic creature of clouts and patches, in Conrad's ***Heart of Darkness*** offers certain critical difficulties. With a nervous elusiveness that is characteristic of him, he manages to baffle efforts to find a place and a function for him in the story. Robert O. Evans, for example, who finds strong overtones of the *Inferno* motif in ***Heart of Darkness,*** confesses frankly that "The Russian trader that Marlow and his company encounter does seem slightly out of place in terms of Dante's scheme, for he appears to be a heretic."

Marlow himself has some trouble coming to grips with the Russian, finding him at their first meeting, "altogether bewildering," "an insoluble problem." Ultimately, however, Marlow's bewilderment at this "phenomenon" which has burst upon him is intermixed with something akin to disgust, the disgust of the eminently practical man toward "the absolutely pure, uncalculating, unpractical spirit of adventure." This admixture of puzzled disdain reflects, it seems to me, the attitude of Polish patriot Teodor Korzenowski [Joseph Conrad's given name] who spent his early years in unhappy proximity to Russians. (p. 189)

Even so, enigmatic as he appears and artful dodger that he is, it is possible to account for the Russian in ***Heart of Darkness*** in two ways.

In the first place, on one level, the function of the Russian is a matter of technique. He is the friend of the author, much like Henry James's *ficelles.* He is there to bring the situation up to date for Marlow and the party on the steamboat. . . . It is through him that the relief party is made aware how badly the situation has deteriorated and in what peril they stand should Kurtz "not say the right thing." In effect, the Russian takes over Marlow's role as narrator, briefly, and plays a crucial part in preparing for the climactic meeting with Kurtz.

Yet it would be totally inadequate, artistically, to accept this as the sole reason for the Russian's being. Conrad is seldom obvious and in a work of enormous subtlety like ***Heart of Darkness,*** the presence of the Russian simply as a narrative expedient is scarcely to be subscribed to. There is another role the Russian plays which, while subservient to the main action, is a part of it. (p. 190)

Consider first the Russian's physical appearance. Conrad gives us several clues here. He is twice described as a "harlequin," a creature in motley, "who looked as though he had escaped from a troop of mimes." He reminds Marlow of "something funny I had seen somewhere." The over-all effect of his incredible accoutrement ("bright patches, blue, red, and yellow—patches on the back, patches on the front, patches on elbows, on knees; coloured binding round his jacket, scarlet edging on the bottom of his trousers") is somehow "extremely gay and wonderfully neat withall." In other words, all the Russian needs to make his costume complete for the role he plays is the cap and bells. With this single exception, he is perfectly drawn in the trappings of the Fool, the royal jester, the court buffoon.

He is, by his own admission, "a simple man. I have no great thoughts." He is completely adaptable, thoroughly malleable, and, as Marlow says, "uncalculating, unpractical, improbable, inexplicable." Like Marlow, he is one of those "curious men" who, Conrad tells us, "go prying into all sorts of places where they have no business." There is, in fact, a direct analogy, intentional on Conrad's part I feel certain, between the Russian's and Marlow's reasons for being in the Congo. The Russian's badgering of old Van Shuyten until "he gave me some cheap things and a few guns, and told me he hoped he would never see my face again," is reminiscent of Charlie Marlow's harrassment of his relatives on the Continent to procure for him the command of the steamboat. The difference, of course, is that Marlow has his "influential friend"—the steamboat—with him always whereas the Russian misplaces, or abandons, his hold on reality, "the simple old sailor, Towser or Towson."

The Russian's moods range from frenetic exuberance to agitated uncertainty. . . . Above all, he is completely selfless. . . . He is pathetically anxious to please, almost childlike in his desire to be understood and accepted. (pp. 190-91)

The story he tells of his relationship with Kurtz, wavering (as he speaks) between enthusiasm and bewilderment, makes the wretchedness of his state all too clear to Marlow. But the Russian gives no evidence of a psychic scar; he has rolled with the punches magnificently. His only concern is for Kurtz's reputation, which he consigns to the hands of the unwilling Marlow. He goes off, rolling his eyes characteristically at the recollection of the "delights" he has encountered and innocently grateful for the enlargement of his mind. Marlow, groggy at the impact of this *jongleur* who has tumbled across the stage before him, can only shake his head in disbelief.

The Russian, thus, is ideally equipped in appearance and in temperament for his role as Fool. But when and where does he function in this capacity? During his meeting with Marlow, the Russian is much like the performer in the dressing room. He is still in the costume of the clown, his make-up intact, but the performance is over. He has already played his role as Fool.

It has been played, of course, in the court of Kurtz—king, god, journalist, ivory hunter, hollow man, what-have-you. Kurtz had an empire, a court, a consort, why not a Fool to complete the assemblage? The Russian played his role well—the fact that he had stayed alive is perhaps the best testimony to the quality of his performance. He was available at all times, in the best tradition of the jester, to amuse Kurtz when in an expansive mood, to nurse him when ill, and to stay out of his way when dangerous. The Russian reveals the whole sordid saga to Marlow while remaining himself completely unaware of its full implications. "Very often coming to this station, I had to wait days and days before he would turn up. Ah, it was worth waiting for!—sometimes." The tentative note struck by the word "sometimes" should not be overlooked. It suggests, of course, the measure of the Russian's dependence on the capricious temperament of Kurtz. The same note, again implying the necessity for the Russian to play fool to Kurtz's fancy, is heard again. . . . One is reminded of Lear's Fool who, despite his jauntiness, is still aware of the whip.

Marlow sums up the Russian as follows: "If it had come to crawling before Mr. Kurtz, he crawled as much as the veriest savage of them all." With a kind of fascinated revulsion, Marlow now sees that Kurtz's peculiar "gifts" are fatal alike to ignorant savage and educated white man. This commingling of disgust and awe on Marlow's part toward Kurtz's treatment of the Russian prepares Marlow's final judgment of Kurtz. The Kurtz who was apparently gratified at the spectacle of the Russian playing Fool for him is indeed an "atrocious phantom." At the same time, the Kurtz who could secure the Fool's willing acquiescence is also something of a "remarkable man." (pp. 191-93)

C. F. Burgess, "Conrad's Pesky Russian," in Nineteenth-Century Fiction *(© 1963 by The Regents of the University of California; reprinted by permission of The Regents), Vol. 18, No. 2, September, 1963, pp. 189-93.*

KENNETH A. BRUFFEE (essay date 1964)

[In the following excerpt, Bruffee compares the actions of Kurtz and Marlow to those of Faust in his pursuit of forbidden knowledge. The nature of truth and the function of lies in the novel is a crucial element in Bruffee's argument. Unlike Thomas Moser (1957) and others, who view Marlow's lie to Kurtz's fiancée as a sign of his weakness, Bruffee believes that Marlow's lie functions as a godlike act in which conventional truth is sacrificed for a higher principle. Bruffee also disagrees with W. Y. Tindall (1958), who calls it a "white lie" told in inappropriate defense of the woman's illusions, an avoidance of truth that Tindall likens to Kurtz's corruption. Bruffee believes that Marlow's lie is not an evasion, but a heroic attempt to defend a weak civilization from the horrendous truth of the power of evil. For further discussions of Marlow's lie, see the excerpts by F. R. Leavis (1941), Thomas Moser (1957), John W. Canario (1967), and Ian Watt (1979), and the entry by Frederick Crews in the Additional Bibliography.]

Late in Conrad's story ***Heart of Darkness,*** Marlow expresses the belief that "some knowledge of yourself" is the only reward life offers. . . . Thus the story implies that the self-knowledge Kurtz gains—his revelation of man's deficiency—is both a reward and a penalty, although obviously a vision of horror is no reward in the usual sense of the word. Furthermore, Marlow believes that this one reward which life offers is unique for each individual, that self-knowledge is a solitary knowledge which "no other man can ever know." . . . Contrary to this belief, Marlow soon finds himself participating in Kurtz's self-revelation; and, sharing as he does in another man's experience, he is liable in some way to share the reward—and the penalty, the burden of the reward. His reward is to see and know, but not to die in terror; his penalty seems to come at the end of the story when, in telling Kurtz's Intended that the last word Kurtz spoke was her name, he sacrifices his integrity by lying.

Two paradoxes, then, seem fundamental to the story. First, a man participates in another man's self-revelation and both men profit by it. Second, the "profit" is an ironic one—that is, the original insight (Kurtz's) is both a reward of life and a terrible penalty for it, and the further insight (Marlow's), engendered by the first, is at the same time illuminating and apparently corrupting. These two paradoxes resolve themselves into one paradoxical action: a lie which establishes a condition of truth.

This paradox, too, can be resolved in several ways. The resolution I suggest here depends first of all on seeing the experience described in the story as a peculiarly twentieth-century kind of Faustian experience.

That Kurtz's experience is Faustian is quite clear. His "universal genius" . . . , his godlike power over the natives, his "forbidden knowledge" gained in the wilderness of the self—all suggest a parallel with Faust. More specifically, the wilderness of the jungle, Marlow says, had "sealed [Kurtz's] soul to its own by the inconceivable ceremonies of some devilish initiation." . . . Once initiated, Kurtz takes to calling everything his own: "'My Intended, my ivory, my station, my river, my—' everything belong to him." And yet, Marlow says, "The thing was to know what he belonged to, how many powers of darkness claimed him for their own." After establishing that Kurtz is "no fool," Marlow implies just who it is Kurtz does belong to: "I take it, no fool ever made a bargain for his soul with the devil." . . . Finally, after describing Kurtz's state of mind to be one of "exalted and incredible degradation," Marlow says, in language typical of descriptions of traditional Faustian characters, "the awakening of forgotten and brutal instincts . . . had beguiled his unlawful soul beyond the bounds of permitted aspirations." (pp. 322-23)

At the moment of self-revelation, however, Kurtz's Faustian experience initiates and begins to give way to an extension of that experience which is to be carried through and fulfilled by Marlow. It is to that extension that the story subordinates Kurtz's Faustian nature. Thus ***Heart of Darkness*** is not just a story in which a soul is sold and lost; the combined experience of Kurtz and Marlow represents a considerable departure from the "traditional" (that is, medieval and Renaissance) Faustian experience. But neither is this story one in which a soul is saved by outwitting the devil or by overcoming his evil with the powers of light. (p. 323)

Conrad's motive . . . seems to be redemption, even though he does follow the earlier tradition in that in his story the pursuit of forbidden knowledge remains an evil pursuit which does not ultimately ennoble man, but degrades him. Conrad departs from tradition in another way. Whereas Goethe and Lessing saved Faust by altering the story's assumptions, Conrad maintains the original assumptions (that there are such things in the world as forbidden knowledge and power), but alters the outcome of the experience by extending its effects. Once it is granted that the experience can be projected vicariously beyond the limits of one individual's soul to another's, it must be agreed that the benefits and penalties of the experience might project even further. Thus, through Marlow, the saving virtue brought to light by the experience he shares with Kurtz can be, and is, extended to their whole civilization—which includes, through Marlow's narration, his audience on the yawl and us, the readers. An important question arises, however, concerning the form of the extension: what, exactly, must the saving virtue be that results from their experience?

It is, of course, restraint, a virtue so simple and fundamental to humanity that the cannibal workmen on the riverboat under the pressure of extreme hunger incredibly and inexplicably exhibit it. . . . It is exactly the virtue which Kurtz lacks, but which in Marlow is reinforced by vicarious revelation of "The Horror" until it becomes the most important, conscious, and compelling force in his character.

Restraint expresses itself, however, in a most peculiar way. Marlow confesses early in the story that "there is" for him "a taint of death, a flavour of mortality in lies" which makes him "miserable and sick, like biting something rotten would do." And yet in the end, Marlow lies. The fact of the lie, it would seem, is absolutely crucial to the meaning of the story. . . . It is this [final] scene, however, which so often seems to miss being understood. (pp. 324-25)

Marlow has certainly made a kind of truth seem extremely important throughout the story. Despite this, however, the lie weakens neither the final scene nor the story. It is not that the woman does not deserve to hear the truth, but rather that she does deserve not to hear the truth. In the course of the story, Marlow's lie is inevitable once his anger—frustrations and indignation caused by the girl's persistent illusions—"subsided before a feeling of infinite pity." . . . This pity is Marlow's compassion for the fragility of the woman's illusions and the conventional "surface truth" upon which they are founded—for the fragility of the civilization, that is, however corrupt and hollow, the best of which the girl represents. Of course she is safe, complacent, and bourgeois. But she is also a "soul as translucently pure as a cliff of crystal," her "pure brow" is "illumined by the unextinguishable light of belief and love," and the "halo" she seems surrounded with, however "ashy," is still a halo. . . . To alleviate this woman's immediate grief is the first purpose of the lie. But more importantly, Marlow lies to relieve the suffering that she does not know she suffers. However hollow or dead the civilization she stands for may be, however ashy her halo, Marlow comes to believe in the last scene of the story that Kurtz's Intended is nevertheless worthy, does nevertheless deserve not to have to face the truth about Kurtz.

This conviction shows how thoroughly Marlow, in spite of himself, has become identified with Kurtz. The girl represents all the best of Kurtz's ideals—all the best of what he had "intended" for the world as well as for himself. She is the medium through which the world has seen and will see what was best in him. Since by lying Marlow protects those intentions, he thereby reaffirms his fellowship with Kurtz. But he does not thereby accept damnation; on the contrary, he rejects it. Since Kurtz has taken a step that few are willing or able to take, offering himself up to be "rent"—"For nothing can be sole or whole / That has not been rent"—his final revelation of truth, which Marlow calls "an affirmation, a moral victory paid for by innumerable defeats," . . . achieves for him at last a kind of wholeness—and after achieving this, he dies. Marlow achieves the same wholeness through self-revelation, but vicariously—and he does not die but, significantly, lives on to act upon what he has learned.

To make such an affirmation, Marlow has been thoroughly prepared. Earlier, he sided with Kurtz and was excluded from the society of pilgrims because of it. He found himself being "lumped along with Kurtz as a partisan of methods for which the time was not ripe: I was unsound! Ah! but it was something to have at least a choice of nightmares." . . . In the corruption of the "pilgrims," who represent the worst of that safe, complacent, bourgeois civilization, Marlow has found something with a stronger "flavour of mortality," something more rotten to bite into than a lie. And after having himself experienced "all the wisdom, and all truth, and all sincerity" . . . vicariously through Kurtz, when the choice comes again, he determines to choose the lesser nightmare. (pp. 325-26)

To fulfill his destiny he must act positively, because to act negatively would be to "accept damnation" passively. Marlow's positive act, then, is to place himself as an artificial barrier between the degraded and the exalted, between the degraded and the ideal (or what passes for the ideal), that is, between Kurtz and his Intended. By the end of the story, Marlow alone bears that responsibility. All that falls between these contraries is Marlow and his lie. When the lily grows on the dunghill, only illusion, appearance, artifice, that is, only the lie, keeps us from seeing the dung. Marlow's destiny is to maintain that separation just because he has seen that, in reality, no separation exists.

It may still be difficult to see how we can be persuaded "to accept falsehood as salvation," because . . . there is an insistence on truth throughout this story. Marlow, however, makes a careful distinction between "surface truth" and "inner truth." As a result, it might be expected that the story's resolution would not be in terms of mere verbal truth. Furthermore, there are distinct signs of Marlow's disillusionment with words. Words first lead him to Kurtz: "I . . . became aware," he says, "that that was exactly what I had been looking forward to—a talk with Kurtz." But in the days after the rescue, he begins to hear "more than enough" of Kurtz's talk. He becomes less and less enamored of words as the verbose Kurtz talks, contradicts, effuses, and rambles, until "the memory of that time" lingers with him "like a dying vibration of one immense jabber, silly, atrocious, sordid, savage, or simply mean, without any kind of sense." . . . After this, Marlow is only mildly astonished at the ease with which he can himself use words as the occasion demands. "It seemed to me," he says, after he lies to the girl, "that the house would collapse before I could escape, that the heavens would fall upon my head. But nothing happened." He discovers that "the heavens do not fall for such a trifle." . . . (p. 327)

Marlow has discovered, then, a larger standard of truth, a standard according to which the lie, the ethically repulsive, dishonorable act, turns out to be a kind of honorable restraint. By lying, he affirms the artificiality of restraint at the same time as he affirms the necessity of restraint in maintaining the part of civilization worth saving. Unlike Kurtz, whose mission fails as his excessive aspiration fails, Marlow, by not denying that both the light and the dark exist, but by affirming that they must be carefully distinguished, represents his, the girl's, and all society's only salvation. The story's meaning, it finally appears, is a function not of the "surface truth" of a mere articulated falsehood, but of a man's seeing beyond a conventional "principle" to a necessity which demands of him a singularly unconventional act, an "unsound" act, the time for which, however, is all too ripe. (pp. 327-28)

Analogously, Conrad's hero, after his journey into the dark regions of the mind, after his insight, after participating vicariously in a kind of Faustian experience, chooses to mock truth. Preferring artifice to veracity, he establishes an ethic of his own according to which man, having been made aware of the truth, discovers also the necessity to cloak and conceal it for the sake of humanity. The traditional Faustian experience, which itself reaches "beyond the bounds of permitted aspirations," is thus pushed even further by an act which is godlike, by a creative act which ignores conventional principles and establishes its own. (p. 329)

Kenneth A. Bruffee, "The Lesser Nightmare: Marlow's Lie in 'Heart of Darkness'," in Modern Language Quarterly *(© 1964 University of Washington), Vol. XXV, No. 3, September, 1964, pp. 322-29.*

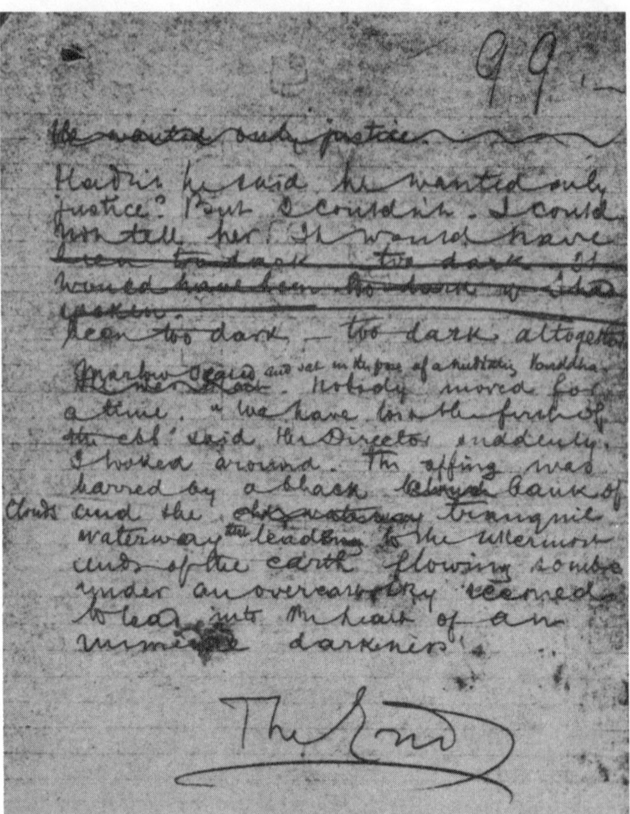

Final page of Conrad's manuscript of Heart of Darkness. *Beinecke Rare Book and Manuscript Library, Yale University.*

JOHN W. CANARIO (essay date 1967)

[Like C. F. Burgess (1963), Canario considers the role of the Russian seaman crucial to an understanding of Heart of Darkness. *As a European aborigine, the Russian is an example of innocent ignorance and primitive honor, which Conrad contrasts with the undisciplined greed and vanity of Kurtz. Canario believes that the Russian recalls for Marlow his once adventuresome, lighthearted self, forever lost after the revelations that are a result of his identification with Kurtz. Canario also offers an interesting discussion of Marlow's lie, concluding that it correctly represents to Kurtz's fiancée Kurtz's ultimate realization of his own depravity. For further discussion of Marlow's lie, see the excerpts above by F. R. Leavis (1941), Thomas Moser (1957), W. Y. Tindall (1958), Kenneth A. Bruffee (1964), and Ian Watt (1979), and the entry by Frederick Crews in the Additional Bibliography.]*

Next to Marlow and Kurtz, the most important character in Conrad's ***Heart of Darkness*** is the young Russian who meets the steamboat at Kurtz's station and soon thereafter is persuaded by Marlow to talk at some length about his life and his admiration for Kurtz. Marlow first describes this Russian as a harlequin, and he later reveals through frequent observation of harlequinesque qualities in the youth that this first impression was progressively strengthened during their conversation. Gauging the importance of the Russian's role in the novel by Marlow's description of his motley appearance, clownish mannerisms, and conspicuous gullibility, most interpreters have seen the Russian as one of several minor characters who serve chiefly to exemplify the extreme susceptibility of civilized Europeans to the corrupting influences of the Congo. However, there is considerable evidence in the story to show that this view misrepresents the Russian's thematic function. This view slights the fact that Marlow's insight into the youth's harlequinesque character moves from superficial matters to a discovery that has a crucial bearing on his initiation. The Russian, as Marlow comes to see, is not simply an irresponsible, light-headed buffoon, but rather, like the harlequin of the theatre, a modern representative of the European aborigine. When the harlequin is viewed in the light of this discovery, he assumes his true dimensions as one of the most important characters in the novel.

Although the Russian is twice mentioned by Marlow in the narrative of the journey up the river . . . , it is significant that Marlow does not meet the youth until he has traveled, figuratively speaking, back to the beginning of time. It is not until he is steering the steamboat into Kurtz's landing that Marlow sees on the river bank "'a white man under a hat like a cart-wheel beckoning persistently with his whole arm.'" . . . [The] observations of the Russian's physical appearance establish that Marlow first saw the man as simply a goodnatured but scatterbrained dunce.

That this condescending view of the Russian continues for a time to be uppermost in Marlow's mind is revealed by his comments on the childlike chatter, volatile temperament, and acrobatic agility displayed by the youth during his visit on the steamboat. Marlow notices that the Russian talks at a breathless rate, that he jumps abruptly from one subject to another, that his countenance changes mercurially "'like the autumn sky, overcast one moment and bright the next,'" . . . and that he gestures extravagantly, even leaping up at one point to grab both of his host's hands in his by way of showing gratitude for the offer of a pipeful of tobacco. (pp. 225-26)

However, despite these evidences of amused condescension in Marlow's initial impressions of the Russian, it becomes clear as Marlow continues his relation of their conversation that his opinion of his visitor grew increasingly favorable as he learned more about him. One cause of this rise in Marlow's opinion is shown to be his appreciation of the Russian's loyalty to Kurtz and of his humane concern for the safety of both the white men and the natives. Marlow is favorably impressed, for example, by the Russian's urgent assurances that the natives are simple people who can be more effectively frightened away in case of trouble by a blowing of the boat's whistle than by firing rifles at them. A second cause is shown to be Marlow's respect for the Russian's devotion to doing a good job in his regular vocation as a sailor. When Marlow returns Towson's *An Inquiry into Some Points of Seamanship* to the Russian, he perceives that the man is ecstatically happy. But a third and clearly the dominant cause of Marlow's adoption of a more favorable view of his visitor is shown to be an awakening in him of an admiration for the Russian's reckless courage and adventurous spirit.

Marlow emphasizes the moment he first began to see the harlequin in a new light by interrupting his story to describe his fresh impressions. "'I looked at him, lost in astonishment,'" Marlow exclaims. . . . He then goes on to identify the Russian as an embodiment of the "'glamour of youth,'" a person "'gallantly, thoughtlessly alive, to all appearances indestructible solely by virtue of his few years and his unreflecting audacity.'" . . . Summing up these impressions, Marlow continues, "'If the absolutely pure, uncalculating, impractical spirit of adventure had ever ruled a human being, it ruled this be-patched youth. I almost envied him the possession of this modest and clear flame.'" . . . Finally, Marlow defines a limit to this newly discovered admiration by adding, "'I did not envy him his devotion to Kurtz, though. He had not meditated over it. It came to him, and he accepted it with a sort of eager fatalism. I must say that to me it appeared about the most dangerous thing in every way he had come upon so far.'" . . .

The intensity of feeling Marlow exhibits in this reassessment of the Russian reveals that his change of attitude towards the youth was not inspired merely by a desire to correct an unfair bias in his initial judgment of him. Instead, the degree of Marlow's astonishment, his admiration, and his envy establish that the traits of character he praises in the Russian were traits that he himself possessed and valued. Thus in essence Marlow's exclamations are an expression of his surprised recognition that he and the young vagabond were much alike.

The similarity between himself and the Russian that is obviously uppermost in Marlow's mind at this juncture is that they are both persons whose lives have been directed chiefly by a reckless hunger for adventure and by a rash self-confidence in the invulnerability of their youthful vitality. For Marlow's confession of envy is a reminder that his decision to command a steamboat on the Congo River was inspired by little more than boyish curiosity and a love of adventure. But Marlow's reporting of the conversation that led up to this recognition reveals that it was not the only similarity he had become aware of. A second point of resemblance between the two men is set forth in Marlow's earlier commentary on the Russian's joy at recovering Towson's book on seamanship. The reverence that the Russian exhibits toward this technical manual calls to mind Marlow's earlier remarks on his own single-minded devotion to the mechanical problems of getting his steamboat in operating condition and safely up the river. The point suggested by the parallel is Marlow's becoming aware that both his life and the Russian's were largely confined to surface reality, to the limited aspiration of skillfully and conscientiously performing the mechanical duties of their occupation. Still a third point or resemblance that Marlow is shown to have become aware of is that both men shared a tendency to regard intellectuals with awe. Marlow conveys his recognition of this likeness between himself and the Russian in the similarity that he reveals between the youth's adulation of Kurtz and his own early development of an intense curiosity about the man.

However, at the same time that Marlow reveals that he sees something of himself in the harlequin's enthusiastic and unsophisticated outlook, he also makes it a point to introduce the reservation that he does not envy the Russian his naïve devotion to Kurtz. This reservation serves two important purposes. First, it makes absolutely clear that Marlow's attitude towards Kurtz, which was strongly inclined toward approbation when he first heard of the man, had become seriously qualified by the time he met Kurtz's disciple. Secondly, it establishes that the likenesses Marlow observes between himself and the Russian no longer existed by the time of his encounter with the youth because of the maturing effect on Marlow of his experiences in the Congo. Consequently, what Marlow is conveying in his praise of the Russian is more, finally, than the discovery that the harlequin had a youthful glamour that he admired; he is simultaneously expressing a regretful realization that his own adventures in the Congo had taught him, beyond any possibility of a return to a light-hearted view of life, a dark truth about man's potentialities for evil.

The truth that had robbed Marlow of his own harlequinesque innocence only shortly before he met the Russian is shown in his earlier descriptions of the white colonials in Africa; it is his discovery that Europeans who lack self-discipline and a strong commitment to unselfish life goals quickly degenerate to a level of brutality below that of an aborigine when their fortunes place them in an environment where there are no external checks on their behavior. . . . Marlow's reservation about the Russian's devotion to Kurtz implies that it is because Marlow had only recently learned this lesson himself that he could be both envious of the youth's innocence and apprehensive about his adulation of Kurtz.

But the growth of Marlow's insight into the harlequinesque character of the Russian does not end with his discovery that the youth personified his own lost innocence and boyish love of adventure. In his account of the remainder of his conversation with the Russian, Marlow reveals that he continued to gain new insight into the youth's character until he arrived finally at the essence of his clownlike nature. Marlow makes clear that this ultimate revelation came to him only after he at last succeeded in getting the Russian to tell him something of his life with Kurtz. In the middle of his retelling of the youth's story, Marlow digresses to comment, "'. . . never, never before, did this land, this river, this jungle, the very arch of this blazing sky, appear to me so hopeless and so dark, so impenetrable to human thought, so pitiless to human weakness.'" . . . And at the end of the story, when the youth tries to impress Marlow with a description of how the natives had to crawl when they approached Kurtz, Marlow reflects, "'I suppose that it did not occur to him that Kurtz was no idol of mine. He forgot I hadn't heard any of these splendid monologues on, what was it? on love, justice, conduct of life—or what not. If it had come to crawling before Mr. Kurtz, he crawled as much as the veriest savage of them all.'" (pp. 226-30)

In this equation of the Russian with the black followers of Kurtz, Marlow is pointing back to his own earlier reported impressions of the interior of the Congo and revealing in the light of these his discovery at the end of the youth's story of a fundamental harmony between the harlequin's character and his environment. . . . Marlow's statement equating the Russian with the savages becomes recognizable as a revelation that his curiosity about the youth led him ultimately to see that he was confronted with a white aborigine, a living example of the atavistic European from which the harlequin of the theatre evolved. (p. 230)

[It] becomes evident that Marlow's recognition that the Russian was a white aborigine brought with it a profound realization that aboriginal man possesses a capacity for humane behavior and a primitive sense of honor that makes him impervious to the greed that corrupts civilized Europeans. From the moment of this discovery onward, Marlow emphasizes by mentioning several acts of friendly assistance to the harlequin that he thereafter allied himself with the aboriginal humanity of the youth against the greed and cruelty of the company manager and the pilgrims of the Eldorado Exploring Expedition.

However, it is not the contrast between the harlequin and the pilgrims, but a contrast between the harlequin as aborigine and Kurtz as a representative of man in his most civilized state that leads Marlow to his fullest understanding of the human potential for good and evil. Marlow first suggests the importance of this contrast when he is on the threshold of describing his experiences at Kurtz's station. It is then that he makes his statement that fools and saints are impervious to the powers of darkness, but that most men do not fall into these extreme categories. (p. 232)

Through this portrayal of two men representing opposite ends of the scale of human development, Marlow makes clear that the capstone of his initiation is the realization that there are two kinds of darkness in the world: the darkness of ignorance represented by the primeval environment and aboriginal inhabitants of the Congo and a greater darkness of undisciplined greed and vanity represented by the city of the whited sepulcher in Europe.

The last section of the story reveals Marlow's belief that against these two kinds of darkness man has ultimately only the defense of a steadfast faith in the essential goodness of human nature and in the ultimate potential of civilization to make this goodness prevail. It is a recovery of this faith, objectified in the flame of a single candle produced by Marlow in an otherwise pitch-black cabin, that motivates the dying Kurtz, looking back on his corrupted life, to whisper, "The horror! The horror!" It is also Marlow's understanding that these words express Kurtz's final victory over the loss of faith that had undermined his youthful idealism that explains Marlow's lie to Kurtz's betrothed. For it is in women—in the aunt who obtained Marlow his job, in Kurtz's black mistress, and in Kurtz's betrothed—that Marlow shows the most enduring faith in man's goodness to reside. In telling the young woman that Kurtz died pronouncing her name, Marlow merely chose to adhere to vital truth rather than to literal accuracy. (pp. 232-33)

John W. Canario, "The Harlequin in 'Heart of Darkness'," in Studies in Short Fiction *(copyright 1967 by Newberry College), Vol. IV, No. 3, Spring, 1967, pp. 225-33.*

FREDERICK R. KARL (essay date 1969)

[Karl is one of the foremost authorities on Conrad. In addition to A Reader's Guide to Joseph Conrad, *from which the following excerpt is taken, Karl is also the author of* Joseph Conrad: The Three Lives, *the most thorough biography of the author. In the following excerpt Karl, who calls* Heart of Darkness *one of the world's greatest novellas, discusses the work as a quintessentially modern depiction of the absurdity of experience and equates Conrad's exploration of the mind with the work of Sigmund Freud, finding Marlow's story to be a form of self-psychoanalysis. Karl believes that this interpretation accounts for the dreamlike, existentially absurd nature of the tale as well as Marlow's inability to succinctly and straightforwardly describe anything having to do with Kurtz. For other discussions of the import of Marlow's lapses in descriptive power, see the excerpts by F. R. Leavis (1941), Albert J. Guerard (1958), and Marvin Mudrick (1958-59), and the entry by Frederick Crews in the Additional Bibliography.]*

Conrad himself recognized that [***Heart of Darkness***] penetrated to those areas of darkness, dream, indeed nightmare with which he tried to define the substance of his world. Written when he was still a fledgling novelist, ***Heart of Darkness*** helped solidify a vision that rarely wavered in Conrad's later work, and one we now accept as uniquely modern. Here he limned the images one usually encounters in dreams or in war, and here he found that discontinuous, inexplicable, existentially absurd experience which was to haunt his letters and his work.

Based on personal impressions, his own Congo journey, ***Heart of Darkness*** welled out. As he wrote apologetically and hesitatingly to Elsa Martindale (Mrs. Ford Madox Ford):

> What I distinctly admit is the fault of having made Kurtz too symbolic or rather symbolic at

all. But the story being mainly a vehicle for conveying a batch of personal impressions I gave the rein to my mental laziness and took the line of least resistance. This is then the whole Apologia pro Vita Kurtzii—or rather for the tardiness of his vitality. (unpublished letter, December 3, 1902)

The novella, then, contains a vision so powerful that Conrad excuses himself for being unable (he thought) to control it. It was also, as Freud wrote of his own *Interpretation of Dreams,* an insight that falls to one but once in a lifetime. The reference to Freud and to *Dreams* is not fortuitous. It was of course chance that Freud and Conrad were contemporaries; but chance ends when we note the extraordinary parallelism of their achievements. (pp. 136-37)

Chance is further reduced when we recognize that literature and a new style of psychological exploration have been first cousins for the last hundred years, that both Conrad and Freud were pioneers in stressing the irrational elements in man's behavior which resisted orthodox interpretation. Conrad's great contribution to political thought is his insight into the irrationality of politics, its nightmarish qualities which depend on the neurosis of a leader, in turn upon the collective neuroses of a people. Such an insight is timeless, but particularly appropriate for developments since 1900. For when has man tried so carefully to preserve life while also squandering it so carelessly? Conrad caught not only hypocrisy (an old-fashioned value), but the illogic of human behavior which tries to justify itself with precision, only to surrender to explosive inner needs. "Exterminate all the brutes," Kurtz scrawled at the bottom of his report. This is the politics of personal disintegration, uncontrollable personal needs, ultimately paranoia.

Confronting similar material, the scientist Freud was concerned with a logical analysis of seeming illogic—the apparent irrationality of dreams, on occasion of nightmares. Both he and Conrad penetrated into the darkness—when men sleep, or when their consciences sleep, when such men are free to pursue secret wishes, whether in dreams, like Freud's analysands, or in actuality, like Kurtz and his followers. The key word is darkness; the black of the jungle for Conrad is the dark of the sleeping consciousness for Freud.

In still another sense, Marlow, in his trip up the Congo, has suffered through a nightmare, an experience that sends him back a different man, now aware of depths in himself that he cannot hide. The tale he narrates on the *Nellie* is one he is unable to suppress; a modern Ancient Mariner, he has discovered a new world and must relate his story to regain stability. The account is a form of analysis—for him and for Conrad. In a way, it provides a defense against Kurtz's vision. (pp. 137-38)

[Freud's] great discovery, like Conrad's, was surely that dreams, despite the various barriers the conscious mind erects, are wish-fulfillments of the hidden self. This sense of wish-fulfillment is evidently never far from Marlow—for the very qualities in Kurtz that horrify him are those he finds masked in himself. Kurtz's great will to power, Nietzschean and ruthless in its thrust, is also Marlow's. The latter, however, can hold back, his restraint, for Conrad, a mark of his Englishness. Marlow, however, only barely restrains himself, for, irresistibly, he is drawn toward Kurtz, readily accepting the latter's ruthlessness as preferable to the bland hypocrisy of the station manager. Even Marlow is seduced—he, too, hides secret wishes and desires, his dreams curiously close to Kurtz's; and so are the dreams of us all, Conrad suggests. Kurtz's savage career is every man's wish-fulfillment, although by dying he conveniently disappears before we all become his disciples.

The secret longing, the hidden desire, the hypocritical defense, the hate covered superficially by love, the artfully contrived lie—all of these are intertwined in dreams. In this sense, Marlow's experience is a nightmare for creator, narrator, and reader. The jungle, that thick verdant cover, disguises all, but most of all hides a man's real existence from himself.

As a connoisseur of dreams, Conrad is a "dark" writer in the sense Rembrandt was a dark painter, Milton a dark poet. They begrudged the light, husbanded it, squeezed it out in minute quantities, as if it were filtered from between densely packed trees in a jungle setting. So the light in Kurtz's heart barely appears, overwhelmed as it is by the darkness of his needs, the exigencies of his situation. Light and dark, in this vision, are polarized; their antagonism runs parallel to the struggle for life in nature itself, a Darwinian battle for growth, power, supremacy.

The yellowish, wispy light, indeed the white of the ivory, later of Kurtz's very bald skull, exists against the fragmented darkness of the jungle—the contrast of colors giving Conrad a vast symbol for moral, political, and social values. And yet such is the knottiness and ambiguity of his symbol that the result is blurred, filled artfully with the illusions and deceptions that Conrad makes us accept as the pathos of existence. (pp. 138-39)

To create order from such shards of nihilism, negativism, distortion, deception, savagery, and, ultimately, fear, Conrad offered a dubious restraint. Somehow, one must find it within. It is an individual matter, and evidently either one has it or one doesn't. It is not solely a European quality by any means, since Kurtz, that pan-European, lacks it, and the Congolese tribal natives have it. Restraint—a kind of muscular courage not to do—marks the difference between civilization and capitulation to savagery. Yet where does it come from? How does one obtain it? Does the lack of it always brutalize? Such mysterious reckonings make it impossible for us to see Conrad as a meliorist. Society as constituted means little—only the responsible individual counts. Possibly one acquires restraint as the sum total of what he is. Yet decency, indeed the future of civilized society, hangs in the balance. (pp. 139-40)

[The] gnarled seaman [Marlow] is surely one of the keys to the story, and much has been written about him, including much nonsense. He is, at least here, Conrad's Everyman, Bunyan's Christian updated. What he suffers and experiences is analogous to what we as judicious democrats would feel. Conrad made Marlow sentient, somewhat intelligent, but, most of all, courageous—about himself, about life, about man's social responsibilities—yet at the same time sufficiently cynical; in brief, very much like Conrad himself. But the two are not congruent; among other things, Conrad possessed a literary intelligence that his narrator did not. He surrounds Marlow as well as enters him. But even if he is foremost a man of action, Marlow should not be taken too lightly. His intelligence is displayed in his moral sensibility. With a certain dogged charm, reminiscent of many American presidents and statesmen, he wishes to see the world based on English (or American) democracy. He accepts private enterprise—with personal restraints. He believes that imperialism must justify itself with good deeds. He expects all men to be fair and decent. Such are Marlow's preoccupations, and here Conrad demonstrated to good purpose the contradictions and rifts between modern belief and modern practice. And here also is the source of Conrad's irony—a quality that gives him considerable advantage over Marlow. (pp. 140-41)

Like Conrad, he accepts the status quo, but one maintained, he trusts, by just men. For both, this is the sole basis of the human contract—one does things in an enlightened manner and develops his moral sensibilities. This is a solid nineteenth-century philosophy, although for us somewhat naive. Marlow rarely questions whether particular work is necessary; for example, he never asks whether white men should be in the Congo—for whatever reason. Rather, he assumes they should be—since they are—but they must come as friends, as helpers, and bring enlightenment. Even while they rape, they must be benevolent. He sees them as solid, progressive Englishmen, who helped to develop countries the better to plunder them, nineteenth-century "ugly Americans." (pp. 141-42)

The long river that informs this world is described, like the Styx, in treacherous, serpentine terms—"deadly—like a snake," "resembling an immense snake uncoiled." The river is essentially a woman: dangerous, dark, mysterious, concealed, with the jungle also feminine, personified by Kurtz's savage mistress. Marlow is overwhelmed; his ideal of womanhood is clearly the girl back in Brussels, or his aunt—the brainwashed public—that naive woman who believes "the labourer is worthy of his hire." Such womanly illusions Marlow wishes to preserve. But his experience includes a treacherous, feminine river, an equally perfidious jungle that conceals its terrors, and, finally, a savage mistress—in all, an unspeakable sexual experience. Though the reticent, chivalrous Marlow never speaks directly of sex, it lies heavily on the story, in every aspect of nature—in *his* fears, in *its* demands. As much as Marlow fears the attraction of power, he shies away from the temptation of orgiastic, uncontrollable sex. He retreats into neutral shock. (pp. 142-43)

Heart of Darkness . . . is concerned with moral issues in their most troubling sense: not only as philosophical imperatives, but practically as they work out in human behavior. In a mechanical universe—"evolved out of a chaos of scraps of iron"—what is flesh? The profusion of metallic and mechanical images indicates that resistant objects have superseded softness, flexibility, humanity itself; that, clearly, one must become an object, tough and durable, in order to survive. (p. 144)

The sense of human waste that pervades the story is best unfolded in the ivory itself. It is an object for the rich—in decorations, for piano keys, for bibelots—hardly necessary for physical or mental survival. In a way, it is like art, a social luxury, and it is for art that the Congo is plundered and untold numbers slaughtered brutally, or casually. This view of ivory as art was surely part of Conrad's conception; a utilitarian object would have had its own *raison d'être*. A relatively useless item or one selective in its market only points up the horror; surely this, too, is part of Kurtz's vision. Possibly Kurtz's artistic propensities (he paints, he collects human heads, he seeks ivory) make him so contemptuous of individual lives; for art and life have always warred. In the name of art (pyramids, churches, tombs, monuments, palaces), how many have died, gone without, worked as slaves? Traditionally, beauty for the few is gained with blood of the many.

Where art rules, artifacts are a form of power. The art object takes on magical significance, becoming a kind of totem, the fairytale golden egg. Knowing this, Kurtz gains his power, indeed his identity and being, from the ivory he covets. In a world of art, the most greedy collector is often supreme; matter, not manner, counts. One source of Kurtz's fascination for Marlow is the former's will to power, Nietzschean, superhuman, and brutal. Kurtz has risen above the masses—of natives, station managers, even of directors back in Brussels. He must continue to assert himself, a megalomaniac in search of further power. Marlow has never met anyone like him, this Kurtz who represents all of Europe. The insulated Englishman now faces east, toward the continent. . . . "All Europe contributed to the making of Kurtz," we read.

He is indeed Europe, searching for power, maneuvering for advantage; and he finds the lever in the colonial adventure of ivory. No wonder, then, that his hunger for acquisition is so overwhelming. Having gratified forbidden desires, he is free of civilized taboos. In the Congo, where the white man—the civilized Belgian—ruled, he could do anything. His only prescription: produce results, send back ivory. Indeed, his very will to power, his confident brutality made him appear a kind of god—to the natives and other agents who feared him, to the Russian sailor who believed in him.

The ultimate corruption is that Kurtz can go his way without restraint. All human barriers are down. Only power counts—no matter whether political or economic. In the jungle, as in enterprise, only the strong survive, and Kurtz obviously is one of the strong. He brings European power—all of Europe—into the jungle; his weapons encompass 2000 years of western civilization. And the consequence: corruption of self and death to "inferiors" on a monumental scale.

When a journalist informs Marlow that Kurtz would have been a "splendid leader of an extreme party," Marlow understandably asks, "What party?" "Any party," his visitor answers, "he was an—an extremist." With that Conrad presents his grandest insight into the politics of our time—superficially totalitarian, but extending also to democratic powers. (pp. 144-144b)

In this conception of Kurtz, Conrad's powers as an artistic thinker were at their strongest. . . . As an artistic thinker . . . he was at once caustic, subtle, broad. His conception of Kurtz, slim on the surface, broadening beneath, is a Cassandra's view of European progress, a view both realistic and ironic. (pp. 144b-144c)

The Congo had been, since 1875, the private preserve of Leopold II of Belgium. . . . Kurtz, or his type of exploiter, was the rule, not the exception. . . . Conrad's journey, as he relates in his Congo diary, was real, Kurtz and his type prevailed, the land and the natives existed, the facts are undisputed. Even if Conrad used symbols to excess, as he feared, each symbol is solidly grounded in fact. Here is white against black, entrenched against primitive, have against have-not, machine against spear, civilization against tribe.

If Conrad's novella is to have artistic as well as political significance, it must make broad reference to human motivation and behavior. One evident part of the application comes with Kurtz's double shriek of "The horror! The horror!" The cry is far richer and more ambiguous than most readers make it. We must remember that Marlow is reporting, and Marlow has a particular view and need of Kurtz. As Marlow understands the scream, it represents a moral victory; that is, on the threshold of death, Kurtz has reviewed his life with all its horror and in some dying part of him has repented. Marlow hears the words as a victory of moral sensibility over a life of brutality and prostituted ideals. This "Christian" reading of the words is, of course, what Marlow himself wishes to hear; he is a moral man, and he believes, with this kind of bourgeois religiosity, that all men ultimately repent when confronted by the great unknown. Kurtz's cry, in this interpretation, fits in with what Marlow wants to know of human nature.

We are not all Marlows, however, and we should not be seduced into agreeing with him, even if he is partially right. More ambiguously and ironically, Kurtz's cry might be a shriek of despair that after having accomplished so little he must now perish. His horror is the anguish of one who dies with his work incomplete. In this view, Kurtz does not repent; rather, he bewails a fate which frustrates his plans. Indeed, at the very moment of death, he challenges life and death and tries to make his baffled will prevail. (pp. 144c-144d)

The irony of the story comes full turn. Returning from the world of the dead, Marlow—our twentieth-century Everyman—cannot admit the full impact of the indecency he has witnessed, of the feelings he has experienced. Even this most honest of men must disguise what he has seen and felt. Like a politician he must bed down with lies. Only Conrad, who is outside both Marlow and Kurtz, can admit the truth, can limn the lie and see it as a lie. (pp. 144d-144e)

In this and other respects, ***Heart of Darkness*** is a masterpiece of concealment. Just as Marlow has concealed from himself the true nature of his own needs, so too we can find concealment—in art, in nature, in people—in virtually every other aspect of the novella. The jungle itself, that vast protective camouflage barring the light of sun and sky, masks and hides, becoming part of the psychological as well as physical landscape. Like the dream content, it forms itself around distortion, condensation, and displacement.

Post-Darwinian and overpowering, the jungle is not Wordsworth's gentle landscape, by no means the type of nature which gives strength and support in our darkest hours. Rather, it runs parallel to our anxieties, becomes the repository of our fears. The darkness of the jungle approximates darkness everywhere, adumbrating the blackness of Conrad's humor, the despair of his irony.

The persistence of the color sets the tone and elicits our response. (p. 144e)

Kurtz's final words, his death, the report by the manager's boy, the darkness surrounding all, the frantic run out of the Congo, the meeting with Kurtz's Brussel's fiancée—connected to all such events is the shimmer and nightmare of dream, Conrad's definition of modern life. No less than Kafka, he saw existence as forms of unreality stubbled with real events. And no little part of the dream-like substance of the tale is the Russian follower of Kurtz, like Marlow a mariner. Dressed in motley, he seems a figure from another world, and yet with his ludicrous appearance he is a perfect symbol for Marlow's Congo experience. Befitting someone who worships Kurtz like a god, the Russian forgives his worst behavior and argues that a common man like himself needs someone to follow. He is persuaded that Kurtz's will to power draws in all those less capable, conveys hope and substance to them.

There is, in his view, a void in every man that only someone like Kurtz can fill. Without Kurtz, the sailor says, he is nothing. "He made me see things—things." His ordinariness is balanced by Kurtz's superiority—every disciple needs a god. Like the natives, like the superb native mistress who forgives Kurtz everything, the sailor follows power. Conrad's prescience was never more trenchant.

To Marlow's accusation that Kurtz is insane, simply mad, the Russian offers Kurtz's great intelligence, his ability to talk brilliantly, his charismatic qualities. To our objection that the sailor himself is mad, Conrad offers his influence upon Marlow—he strikes in Marlow precisely the note of love-hate that Conrad's narrator has come to feel for Kurtz. Although Marlow would like to anchor himself solidly in the Russian's sea manual and reject the vapidity of the Russian, he too is drawn into Kurtz's orbit. He senses what the sailor voices.

In this strangely insane world, all alignments defy logic. Loyalties, beliefs, love, women themselves take on new shapes and attractions. Marlow, that neuter bachelor, is fascinated by the jungle woman, by her wanton, demanding display of sex, by the "fecund and mysterious life" she embodies, by the deliberate provocation of her measured walk. He is further drawn to her sense of reality; without illusion, without question, she accepts Kurtz for what he is, as integrated with the very savagery which enfolds her.

For Marlow the pull of the primitive comes full circle. Again and again, he breaks off his narrative to assure his listeners that all this really happened. Even while he talks, this modern mariner, he must convey the depth of his experience, try to convince that it was as profound as he claims. Marlow knows what happened—yet to find the precise words is almost impossible. (pp. 144f-144h)

Possibly in some areas the language is too heavy, but to labor this point is to lose sight of the story as a whole. One might, in fact, argue the very opposite: that the words—adjectives and all—beat upon us, creating drum-like rhythms entirely appropriate to the thick texture of the jungle, a more sophisticated version of Vachel Lindsay's "Congo." When one confronts the artistry of the complete piece, Conrad's reliance on verbal embellishment appears a minor consideration.

The story in fact has form: from the opening frame, with Marlow's somewhat ingenuous listeners, to the closing sequence, with Kurtz's innocent fiancée confirming her illusions. The use of a first person narrative, through the agency of Marlow, was necessary so that Conrad could gain aesthetic distance and the reader could identify with an average man thrown into an abnormal situation. We must, Conrad realized, go through it with him and Marlow. Lacking the narrator, the story would appear too distant from the immediate experience—as though it had happened and was now over, like ancient history. (pp. 144h-144i)

So, too, in other respects did Conrad work out the shape of the story, in large and in details: through doubling of scenes and characters, through repetition, analogy, duplicating images, through difference of tone. From the beginning, when the ancient Romans on the Thames are contrasted with the modern Europeans on the Congo, Conrad used heightening and foreshortening, contrast and comparison to give the novella form. Most obviously, Marlow's peaceful setting on the *Nellie* is set off against his nightmarish Congo riverboat setting; in a different way, Kurtz's two fiancées are contrasted, each one standing for certain values, indeed for entire cultures, in conflict; further, the jungle is set off against the river, with jungle as death, river as possible relief; in another way, Kurtz is compared with other forms of evil, with the deceptive smoothness of the station manager, with the hypocrisy of the pilgrims; the pilgrims in turn are ironically compared with the savages they condemn, with the pilgrims less Christian than the pagan natives; within the natives, the tribal savages are contrasted with those exposed to civilization, detribalized as it were, the latter already full of wiles and deceit; light and dark, the painter's chiaroscuro, hover over the entire story, no less important here than in Milton's Christian epic; day dream and night dream form contrasts, worked out in the play between expectation and consequence, between professed ideals and realistic behavior, between Kurtz's humanitarianism and his barbarism, between Marlow's middle class sense of English justice and the Congo reality, between the fluctuating love-and-hate which fill both Kurtz and Marlow.

Out of the infinite possibilities facing Conrad, he chose these to give unity to his language and ideas. Such devices shape our thoughts and give form to our responses; they, too, become the substance of our awareness. (pp. 144i-144j)

What makes this story so impressive is Conrad's ability to focus on the Kurtz-Marlow polarity as a definition of our times. European history as well as the history of individual men can be read more clearly in the light of Conrad's art; for he tells us that the most dutiful of men, a Marlow, can be led to the brink of savagery and brutality if the will to power touches him; that the most idealistic of men, Kurtz, can become a sadistic murderer; that the dirty work of this world is carried out by men whose reputations are preserved by lies. Conrad's moral tale becomes, in several respects, our story, the only way we can read history and each other. (pp. 144j-144k)

Frederick R. Karl, "Early Conrad: From 'Almayer' to 'Typhoon'" (originally published in a shortened form as "Introduction to the 'Danse Macabre': Conrad's 'Heart of Darkness'," in Modern Fiction Studies, *Vol. XIV, No. 2, Summer, 1968), in his* A Reader's Guide to Joseph Conrad *(reprinted by permission of Farrar, Straus and Giroux, Inc.; copyright © 1960, 1969 by Frederick R. Karl), revised edition, Farrar, Straus and Giroux, 1969, pp. 91-144ee.*

CHINUA ACHEBE (essay date 1977)

[Achebe is a Nigerian novelist, short story writer, and poet. His first novel, Things Fall Apart *(1958) is one of the most famous works written in English by an African author. In this and his second novel,* No Longer at Ease *(1960), Achebe examined the tragic effects of colonialism on traditional African ways. In later works, including* Arrow of God *(1964) and* A Man of the People *(1966), he satirized African urbanization and political corruption, blaming the resulting problems on the indifference of the people. In the following excerpt from the transcript of a lecture, Achebe argues that Westerners have traditionally viewed Africa as a foil and antithesis for European civilization. Achebe believes that* Heart of Darkness *reflects this tradition, and he characterizes Conrad as a racist for his dehumanizing portraits of Africans. For further discussions of the role of Africans in* Heart of Darkness, *see the excerpts by Harold R. Collins (1954), Cedric Watts (1977), Ian Watt (1979), and C. P. Sarvan (1980), and the entry by Hunt Hawkins in the Additional Bibliography.]*

[It] is the desire—one might indeed say the need—in Western psychology to set Africa up as a foil to Europe, a place of negations at once remote and vaguely familiar in comparison with which Europe's own state of spiritual grace will be manifest. (p. 2)

Joseph Conrad's ***Heart of Darkness*** . . . better than any other work that I know displays that Western desire and need. . . . Of course, there are whole libraries of books devoted to the same purpose, but most of them are so obvious and so crude that few people worry about them today. Conrad, on the other hand, is undoubtedly one of the great stylists of modern fiction and a good storyteller in the bargain. His contribution, therefore, falls automatically into a different class—permanent literature—read and taught and constantly evaluated by serious academics. ***Heart of Darkness*** is indeed so secure today that a leading Conrad scholar has numbered it "among the half-dozen greatest short novels in the English language" [see excerpt above by Albert J. Guerrard, 1950]. (pp. 2-3)

Heart of Darkness projects the image of Africa as "the other world," the antithesis of Europe and therefore of civilization, a place where man's vaunted intelligence and refinement are finally mocked by triumphant bestiality. The book opens on the River Thames, tranquil, resting peacefully "at the decline of day after ages of good service done to the race that peopled its banks." But the actual story takes place on the River Congo, the very antithesis of the Thames. The River Congo is quite decidedly not a River Emeritus. It has rendered no service and enjoys no old-age pension. We are told that "going up that river was like travelling back to the earliest beginnings of the world."

Is Conrad saying, then, that these two rivers are very different, one good, the other bad? Yes, but that is not the real point. It is not the differentness that worries Conrad but the lurking hint of kinship, of common ancestry. For the Thames too "has been one of the dark places of the earth." It conquered its darkness, of course, and is now at peace. But if it were to visit its primordial relative, the Congo, it would run the terrible risk of hearing grotesque, suggestive echoes of its own forgotten darkness, and falling victim to an avenging recrudescence of the mindless frenzy of the first beginnings.

I am not going to waste your time with examples of Conrad's famed evocation of the African atmosphere in ***Heart of Darkness.*** In the final consideration it amounts to no more than a steady, ponderous, fake-ritualistic repetition of two sentences, one about silence and the other about frenzy. (p. 3)

The eagle-eyed English critic, F. R. Leavis [see excerpt above, 1941], drew attention nearly thirty years ago to Conrad's "adjectival insistence upon inexpressible and incomprehensible mystery." That insistence must not be dismissed lightly, as many Conrad critics have tended to do, as a mere stylistic flaw. For it raises serious questions of artistic good faith. When a writer while pretending to record scenes, incidents, and their impact is in reality engaged in inducing hypnotic stupor in his readers through a bombardment of emotive words and other forms of trickery, much more has to be at stake than stylistic felicity. Generally, normal readers are well armed to detect and resist such underhand activity. But Conrad chose his subject well—one which was guaranteed not to put him in conflict with the psychological predisposition of his readers or raise the need for him to contend with their resistance. He chose the role of purveyor of comforting myths.

The most interesting and revealing passages in ***Heart of Darkness*** are, however, about people. . . . Herein lies the meaning of ***Heart of Darkness*** and the fascination it holds over the Western mind: "What thrilled you was just the thought of their humanity—like yours . . . Ugly."

Having shown us Africa in the mass, Conrad then zeroes in, as you would say, half a page later, on a specific example, giving us one of his rare descriptions of an African who is not just limbs or rolling eyes:

> And between whiles I had to look after the savage who was fireman. He was an improved specimen; he could fire up a vertical boiler. He was there below me, and, upon my word, to look at him was as edifying as seeing a dog in a parody of breeches and a feather hat, walking on his hind legs. A few months of training had done for that really fine chap. He squinted at the steam gauge and at the water gauge with an evident effort of intrepidity—and he had filed his teeth, too, the poor devil, and the wool of his pate shaved into queer patterns, and three ornamental scars on each of his cheeks. . . .

As everybody knows, Conrad is a romantic on the side. He might not exactly admire savages clapping their hands and stamping their feet, but they have at least the merit of being in their place, unlike this dog in a parody of breeches. For Conrad, things being in their place is of the utmost importance.

"Fine fellows—cannibals—in their place," he tell us pointedly. Tragedy begins when things leave their accustomed place, like Europe leaving its safe stronghold between the policeman and the baker to take a peep into the heart of darkness. (pp. 3-5)

Towards the end of the story, Conrad lavishes a whole page quite unexpectedly on an African woman who has obviously been some kind of mistress to Mr. Kurtz and now presides (if I may be permitted a little imitation of Conrad) like a formidable mystery over the inexorable imminence of his departure. . . .

This Amazon is drawn in considerable detail, albeit of a predictable nature, for two reasons. First, she is in her place and so can win Conrad's special brand of approval, and, second, she fulfills a structural requirement of the story: a savage counterpart to the refined, European woman with whom the story will end. . . .

The difference in the attitude of the novelist to these two women is conveyed in too many direct and subtle ways to need elaboration. But perhaps the most significant difference is the one implied in the author's bestowal of human expression to the one and the withholding of it from the other. It is clearly not part of Conrad's purpose to confer language on the "rudimentary souls" of Africa. They only "exchanged short grunting phrases" even among themselves, but mostly they were too busy with their frenzy. There are two occasions in the book, however, when Conrad departs somewhat from his practice and confers speech, even English speech, on the savages. The first occurs when cannibalism gets the better of them:

> "Catch 'im," he snapped, with a bloodshot widening of his eyes and a flash of sharp white teeth—"catch 'im. Give 'im to us." "To you, eh?" I asked; "what would you do with them?" "Eat 'im!" he said curtly.
>
> (p. 6)

The other occasion was the famous announcement:

> Mistah Kurtz—he dead. . . .

At first sight these instances might be mistaken for unexpected acts of generosity from Conrad. In reality they constitute some of his best assaults. In the case of the cannibals the incomprehensible grunts that had thus far served them for speech suddenly proved inadequate for Conrad's purpose of letting the European glimpse the unspeakable craving in their hearts. Weighing the necessity for consistency in the portrayal of the dumb brutes against the sensational advantages of securing their conviction by clear, unambiguous evidence issuing out of their own mouth, Conrad chose the latter. As for the announcement of Mr. Kurtz's death by the "insolent black head in the doorway," what better or more appropriate *finis* could be written to the horror story of that wayward child of civilization who wilfully had given his soul to the powers of darkness and "taken a high seat amongst the devils of the land" than the proclamation of his physical death by the forces he had joined?

It might be contended, of course, that the attitude to the African in ***Heart of Darkness*** is not Conrad's but that of his fictional narrator, Marlow, and that far from endorsing it Conrad might indeed be holding it up to irony and criticism. Certainly Conrad appears to go to considerable pains to set up layers of insulation between himself and the moral universe of his story. He has, for example, a narrator behind a narrator. . . . But if Conrad's intention is to draw a *cordon sanitaire* between himself and the moral and psychological malaise of his narrator, his care seems to me totally wasted because he neglects to hint however subtly or tentatively at an alternative frame of reference by which we may judge the actions and opinions of his characters. It would not have been beyond Conrad's power to make that provision if he had thought it necessary. Marlow seems to me to enjoy Conrad's complete confidence—a feeling reinforced by the close similarities between their two careers.

Marlow comes through to us not only as a witness of truth, but one holding those advanced and humane views appropriate to the English liberal tradition which required all Englishmen of decency to be deeply shocked by atrocities in Bulgaria or the Congo of King Leopold of the Belgians or whatever. (p. 7)

The kind of liberalism espoused here by Marlow/Conrad touched all the best minds of the age in England, Europe, and America. It took different forms in the minds of different people but almost always managed to sidestep the ultimate question of equality between white people and black people. . . .

[Conrad] would not use the word brother however qualified; the farthest he would go was kinship. (p. 8)

It is important to note that Conrad, careful as ever with his words, is not talking so much about *distant kinship* as about someone *laying a claim* on it. The black man lays a claim on the white man which is well-nigh intolerable. It is the laying of this claim which frightens and at the same time fascinates Conrad, "the thought of their humanity—like yours . . . Ugly."

The point of my observations should be quite clear by now, namely that Conrad was a bloody racist. That this simple truth is glossed over in criticisms of his work is due to the fact that white racism against Africa is such a normal way of thinking that its manifestations go completely undetected. Students of ***Heart of Darkness*** will often tell you that Conrad is concerned not so much with Africa as with the deterioration of one European mind caused by solitude and sickness. They will point out to you that Conrad is, if anything, less charitable to the Europeans in the story than he is to the natives. A Conrad student told me in Scotland last year that Africa is merely a setting for the disintegration of the mind of Mr. Kurtz.

Which is partly the point. Africa as setting and backdrop which eliminates the African as human factor. Africa as a metaphysical battlefield devoid of all recognizable humanity, into which the wandering European enters at his peril. Of course, there is a preposterous and perverse kind of arrogance in thus reducing Africa to the role of props for the breakup of one petty European mind. But that is not even the point. The real question is the dehumanization of Africa and Africans which this age-long attitude has fostered and continues to foster in the world. And the question is whether a novel which celebrates this dehumanization, which depersonalizes a portion of the human race, can be called a great work of art. My answer is: No, it cannot. I would not call that man an artist, for example, who composes an eloquent instigation to one people to fall upon another and destroy them. No matter how striking his imagery or how beautiful his cadences fall, such a man is no more a great artist than another may be called a priest who reads the mass backwards or a physician who poisons his patients. (pp. 8-9)

Naturally, Conrad is a dream for psychoanalytic critics. Perhaps the most detailed study of him in this direction is by Bernard C. Meyer, M.D [see Additional Bibliography]. In his lengthy book, Dr. Meyer follows every conceivable lead (and sometimes inconceivable ones) to explain Conrad. As an example, he gives us long disquisitions on the significance of hair and haircutting in Conrad. And yet not even one word is spared for his attitude to black people. Not even the discussion of Conrad's anti-semitism was enough to spark off in Dr. Meyer's mind those other dark and explosive thoughts. Which only leads one to surmise that Western psychoanalysts must regard the kind of racism displayed by Conrad as absolutely normal despite the profoundly important work done by Frantz Fanon in the psychiatric hospitals in French Algeria. (pp. 10-11)

There are two probable grounds on which what I have said so far may be contested. The first is that it is no concern of fiction to please people about whom it is written. I will go along with that. But I am not talking about pleasing people. I am talking about a book which parades in the most vulgar fashion prejudices and insults from which a section of mankind has suffered untold agonies and atrocities in the past and continues to do so in many ways and many places today. I am talking about a story in which the very humanity of black people is called in question. It seems to me totally inconceivable that great art or even good art could possibly reside in such unwholesome surroundings.

Secondly, I may be challenged on the grounds of actuality. Conrad, after all, sailed down the Congo in 1890 when my own father was still a babe in arms, and recorded what he saw. How could I stand up in 1975, fifty years after his death, and purport to contradict him? My answer is that as a sensible man I will not accept just any traveller's tales solely on the grounds that I have not made the journey myself. I will not trust the evidence even of a man's very eyes when I suspect them to be as jaundiced as Conrad's. And we also happen to know that Conrad was, in the words of his biographer, Bernard C. Meyer, "notoriously inaccurate in the rendering of his own history."

But more important by far is the abundant testimony about Conrad's savages which we could gather if we were so inclined from other sources and which might lead us to think that these people must have had other occupations besides merging into the evil forest or materializing out of it simply to plague Marlow and his dispirited band. (pp. 11-12)

Conrad did not originate the image of Africa which we find in his book. It was and is the dominant image of Africa in the Western imagination, and Conrad merely brought the peculiar gifts of his own mind to bear on it. . . . Africa is to Europe as the picture is to Dorian Gray—a carrier onto whom the master unloads his physical and moral deformities so that he may go forward, erect and immaculate. Consequently, Africa is something to be avoided, just as the picture has to be hidden away to safeguard the man's jeopardous integrity. Keep away from Africa, or else! Mr. Kurtz of ***Heart of Darkness*** should have heeded that warning, and the prowling horror in his heart would have kept its place, chained to its lair. But he foolishly exposed himself to the wild irresistible allure of the jungle, and lo! the darkness found him out. (p. 13)

Ultimately, the abandonment of unwholesome thoughts must be its own and only reward. Although I have used the word *wilful* a few times in this talk to characterize the West's view of Africa, it may well be that what is happening at this stage is more akin to reflex action than calculated malice. Which does not make the situation more but less hopeful. . . .

[Although] the work which needs to be done may appear too daunting, I believe that it is not one day too soon to begin. (p. 14)

Chinua Achebe, "An Image of Africa," in The Massachusetts Review *(reprinted from* The Massachusetts Review, *The Massachusetts Review, Inc.; © 1977), Vol. XVIII, No. 4, Winter, 1977 (and reprinted in* Research in African Literatures, *Vol. 9, No. 1, Spring, 1978, pp. 1-15).*

CEDRIC WATTS (essay date 1977)

[Conrad's "Heart of Darkness," *from which the following excerpt is taken, is among the most important critical examinations of this work. In the following excerpt from his study, Watts demonstrates that* Heart of Darkness *anticipates the verbal and intellectual ambiguity of much twentieth-century fiction, and that the complex narrative structure furthers the pervasive sense of indeterminacy. Watts also discusses the novella as an attack on the nineteenth-century work ethic and prevailing versions of social Darwinism.*]

To begin with an immediate declaration of interest: ***Heart of Darkness*** is the best short novel I know, and in my opinion it is the finest and richest of Conrad's works. The tale is exciting and profound, lucid and bewildering; it is highly compressed, rich in texture and implication; it has a recessive adroitness, constantly ambushing the conceptualising reader; and thematically it has a remarkable range of reference to problems of politics and psychology, morality and religion, social order and evolution. In embodying a critical summary of some important nineteenth-century preoccupations, Conrad has critically anticipated some equally important twentieth-century preoccupations. Furthermore, ***Heart of Darkness*** can be related to a diversity of "traditions", generic and technical, including political satire, traveller's tale, psychological odyssey, meditated autobiography, and isolation fable; while to those readers who seek prophecies, it speaks eloquently of the brutalities and follies of subsequent history.

It has long been recognised as one of Conrad's major works, and has evoked a wealth of exegetic writing. . . . (p. 1)

One reason for [***Heart of Darkness***'s] enduring force is its critical anticipation of twentieth-century preoccupations; and one such preoccupation is ambiguity itself. . . . [In] no previous century has linguistic ambiguity as a topic approached the importance which it now holds. (p. 7)

[The] title ***Heart of Darkness*** offers not simply alternative readings in retrospect, but also, from the start, a certain disturbing mysteriousness through the immediate possibility of alternative glosses: we sense ambiguity even before consciously analysing the components of the phrase. And, throughout the tale, ambiguities proliferate in the areas of semantics (as when Marlow plays upon the different meanings of "absurd"), of association or connotation of imagery . . . , and of character, motive and action. The title thus strikes the keynote, resonant, mysterious and equivocal, for one of the most intensely orchestrated works of fiction. "Dark", "darkness": the words re-echo to the very last paragraph, in which "the tranquil waterway leading to the uttermost ends of the earth flowed sombre under an overcast sky—seemed to lead into the heart of an immense darkness".

In ***Heart of Darkness,*** corruption and evil are subversive and tentacular: they send out tentacles which entwine themselves about and amongst the seemingly sound and good. (pp. 9-10)

"Light" has the most ancient of associations with Godhead, sanctity and truth ("enlightenment"); and "darkness" has long connoted evil, death, the sinister, ignorance, error, and the oppressively mysterious. "White" has associations with holiness, purity, chastity; and "black" with evil, damnation, sin. Thus is formed a reassuringly simplistic balance of primary connotations which Conrad repeatedly evokes and upsets: upsets by intermittently exploiting secondary connotations. St. Matthew (chapter 23, verse 27) had likened hypocrites to "whited sepulchres, which indeed appear beautiful outward, but are within full of dead *men's* bones, and of all uncleanness"; and in the tale, white is the colour of Fresleven's bleached bones, of the skulls round Kurtz's hut, of Kurtz's bald head, of the ivory which elicits the pilgrims' avarice; and the city which contains the company's headquarters reminds Marlow of "a whited sepulchre". The signal examples of corruption are not among the blacks but among the white men, who are responsible for colouring-in the "white patch" that once, Marlow reminds us, filled the map of the dark continent. (p. 10)

Although "darkness" has many and varied connotations in the tale, its main connotation, gradually established, is the mysteriously or indeterminately sinister; and through repetition of the term in a variety of contexts, Conrad conveys the impression that this sinister force has an irresistible dynamism. (p. 11)

Heart of Darkness exploits the oblique narrative convention. Firstly, there is use of the familiar principle that the bizarre events recounted gain vividness through the apparently respectable and sociable normality of the contrasting outer narrative. Secondly, there is a tentacular effect: the initial impression of contrast is disturbed by the implication that there may be some complicity between the apparently respectable "outer" group [the audience of Marlow's tale] and the brutalities of the "inner" narrative [Marlow's tale itself]. Thirdly, and related to the last factor, is the handling of the convention that the characters of the outer group are known to us by vocational titles. . . . In ***Heart of Darkness*** . . . subtle use is made of the "vocational" convention, largely through its initiation of a critical discussion of the "work ethic". Fourthly, . . . the intermittent references to the outer group during the presentation of the inner narrative have incisive functions: sometimes, for example, they will be used to suggest an alarming gulf in comprehension between those who hear of nightmare and the man who has undergone it. Fifthly (and this, in turn, relates to the previous point), the handling of the inter-action between the two narratives [Marlow's narrative and the narrator's depiction of that narrative]—and between the characters of the two narrators—sometimes converts into a surprising strength that weakness noted in **'Youth',** that attraction to the incantatorily eloquent: indeed, an important thematic concern is with the blandishments of high-flown eloquence and with the value of reticence. Sixthly, Conrad now surpasses Maupassant in the ability to make the final outer scene shed a retrospectively transforming light over the preceding narrative. Finally, when a man is extemporising a yarn, the narration does naturally tend to veer about temporally and spatially, glancing ahead, darting here and there, sliding and eliding. In letting the Marlow of ***Heart of Darkness*** thus veer about, Conrad is not only developing the convention naturalistically but also increasing suspense, multiplying ironies, and offering generally a more kaleidoscopic and problematic presentation than the direct "omniscient author" technique customarily permits. (p. 27)

One important source of complexity in ***Heart of Darkness*** is that when Conrad came to analyse "the vilest scramble for loot" he was inevitably obliged to make a critical analysis of the Victorian work ethic. . . . (pp. 61-2)

Carlyle's "to let light on chaos . . . is beyond all other greatness, work for a God" has its echo in Kurtz's report: and the hubris of Carlyle's claim is exposed not only by the eventual form of Kurtz's divinity (and the worshippers of this hero include a representative of civilisation, the Russian, as well as the savages), but also by Conrad's reminder that if the light-bringing task is "work for a God", it is certainly beyond the capacities of the mass of men. The "yours not to reason why" aspect of the ethic is undermined by Conrad's emphasis on the fact that in the Congo there is ample dying but little "doing", little in the way of constructive achievement; and among the Europeans there is altogether too little "reasoning why", too little reflection about the moral implications of their actions. Where there is an appearance of collaborative endeavour among the Europeans, it is so often shown to be collaboration in a destructive, rapacious or absurd pursuit; . . . the work of the company's accountant, and even, sometimes, of Marlow himself, is presented as a refuge from moral awareness rather than as a means of moral fulfilment. (pp. 63-4)

So in ***Heart of Darkness,*** Conrad not only shows how far the company's activities fall short of the demands of the work ethic; he also looks very closely into the possible dangers of that ethic; and on the rare occasions when good work is being done, Conrad will sometimes, by psychological notation, weaken the Carlylean sense that this particularly characterises a civilised nature. He certainly amplifies the Carlylean argument that working, rather than reflecting, saves man from a paralysing sense of his littleness in the face of Nature; but while Carlyle had asserted that "Doubt, of whatever kind, can be ended by Action alone", Conrad chooses to emphasise the validity of "Doubt". Above all, . . . he intermittently but forcefully levels against the work ethic the "argument from ultimates". What, he asks, comes ultimately of any man's labours?

A critic with a literal cast of mind could find many apparent lies of omission in ***Heart of Darkness.*** He could claim that Conrad, unhistorically, takes too disparaging a view of Congolese activities by omitting any suggestion of durable and valuable achievement, any hint that the great cities and industries of modern Africa could result from the pioneering endeavours of the late nineteenth century. He could cite the researches of Norman Sherry, which show conclusively that even at the time of Conrad's journey there, trading and colonisation were far more organised than we might infer from the tale. The fictional Inner Station is a solitary decaying house; the corresponding Inner Station on Conrad's journey was Stanley Falls, a thriving settlement whose many buildings included such civilised establishments as a hospital and a stone-built prison. (p. 65)

The answer to those accusations of "lying by omission" is that ***Heart of Darkness*** is a fertile mixture of modes, among them the naturalistic, the satiric and the symbolic, and we are offered the various ways to truth which are appropriate to those modes. . . . [The] atrocities and rapacities described in the tale were historically to be found in the Congo. In terms of bricks and mortar, railways and timetables, there was more construction than the tale suggests; but given the propaganda of the time which so often exaggerated the merits of such material "progress", Conrad's partly-satiric emphasis on wasteful futility still serves the cause of truth dialectically, by offering a sceptical questioning of the inner nature and ultimate results of European imperialism. By a variety of devices, Conrad increases the range of implications of the narrative so that it offers symbolic commentary on events far beyond the local. The terrain includes the mind and the heart. (p. 67)

Conrad is Darwinian and anti-Darwinian: he uses Darwinian findings not only to combat the optimism that Darwin himself, and many of those who were later influenced by him, illicitly tried to distil from evolutionary theory, but also to combat imperialist ideologies that attempted to derive support from Darwinism.

Even when Hardy's novels are taken into account, ***Heart of Darkness*** has a more potently Darwinian atmosphere than any other major work of fiction. Insistently, Conrad raises questions about man's evolution, about the relationship between the civilised and the savage, about the relationship between the human realm and the natural environment, and about the continuity between the present age and the remote past. (p. 85)

Darwin says: "From the war of nature, from famine and death, the most exalted object which we are capable of conceiving, namely, the production of the higher animals, directly follows." . . . Whether Conrad did or did not have the ending of *The Origin of Species* specifically in mind, ***Heart of Darkness*** does in practice drive a further wedge between the confused elements by showing a "war of nature" in Africa—humans competing with each other for survival and furtherance, and competing for life with the natural environment—and by asking the reader whether that battle appears to be producing anything morally "higher". (p. 88)

In the late nineteenth century, many apologists for aggressive imperialism propped their arguments with illicit inferences from Darwinian principles—illicit, because Darwin was dealing with competition between species and species, or between species and environment, but not between nations and races. . . . [Conrad] retorts in ***Heart of Darkness*** by turning Darwinism against the political Darwinians. If a goal of the evolutionary processes is an equilibrium between the creature and its environment, that goal has in Africa been reached by the natives whom Marlow observes on the coast, who "wanted no excuse for being there" and who blend with their setting, rather than by the Europeans, who appear absurdly anomalous and perish rapidly there or survive as grotesques or brutal automata. This retort is augmented . . . by Conrad's post-Darwinian emphasis on the continuity in instincts, customs, fetishes and taboos between the savages and the Europeans. (pp. 91-2)

Cedric Watts, in his Conrad's "Heart of Darkness": A Critical and Contextual Discussion *(© U. Mursia Editore 1977), Mursia International, 1977, 171 p.*

IAN WATT (essay date 1979)

[Watt is one of the most significant contributors to the study of the novel form in the twentieth century. In his seminal work, The Rise of the Novel: Studies in Defoe, Richardson, and Fielding, *he argues that the novel is above all a realistic genre and that its unique appearance in the eighteenth century, specifically in the works of Daniel Defoe, Samuel Richardson, and Henry Fielding, was influenced by, as well as contributed to, the general movement towards "philosophical realism" in Western civilization after the Renaissance. For Watt, two characteristics define the novel in its complete form: one is "presentational realism"—the technique of rendering particular moments and events believeable to the reader; the other is what he calls "realism of assessment," which consists in the kind of moral authority and control the author exercises over his or her narrative. In the following excerpt, taken from his* Conrad in the Nineteenth Century, *the first of a two-volume biographical, historical, and interpretive study of Conrad, Watt discusses Conrad's impressionistic prose style and provides a detailed reading of* Heart of Darkness, *concentrating most forcefully on Marlow's growth to self-discovery, Kurtz's degeneration, and Marlow's lie.]*

In the tradition of what we are still calling modern literature, the classic status of ***Heart of Darkness*** probably depends less on the prophetic nature of Conrad's ideas than on its new formal elements. These new narrative elements reflect both the general ideological crisis of the late nineteenth century and the literary innovations which accompanied it; but there are other and more direct reasons for considering them. Many readers of ***Heart of Darkness*** have found it rather obscure, and in particular, obscure in its answer to questions that would have been normal to ask, and easy to answer, in the case of most nineteenth-century fiction; questions such as: What is the heart of darkness? What does Kurtz actually do and why don't we see him doing it? What does it matter to Marlow, and why doesn't he tell the Intended? These questions about ***Heart of Darkness*** all receive answers, but only in terms of its own formal presuppositions. This qualification would actually apply to almost any literary work, but the terms of ***Heart of Darkness*** are especially difficult to decipher.

Conrad provides us with very little critical guidance. This is no doubt partly because of the intuitive way he wrote. (p. 168)

Mist or haze is a very persistent image in Conrad. . . . In ***Heart of Darkness*** the fugitive nature and indefinite contours of haze are given a special significance by the primary narrator; he warns us that Marlow's tale will be not centered on, but surrounded by, its meaning; and this meaning will be only as fitfully and tenuously visible as a hitherto unnoticed presence of dust particles and water vapour in a space that normally looks dark and void. This in turn reminds us that one of the most characteristic objections to Impressionist painting was that the artist's ostensive "subject" was obscured by his representation of the atmospheric conditions through which it was observed. (p. 169)

Heart of Darkness is essentially impressionist in one very special and yet general way: it accepts, and indeed in its very form asserts, the bounded and ambiguous nature of individual understanding; and because the understanding sought is of an inward and experiential kind, we can describe the basis of its narrative method as subjective moral impressionism. Marlow's story explores how one individual's knowledge of another can mysteriously change the way in which he sees the world as a whole, and the form of ***Heart of Darkness*** proposes that so ambitious an enterprise can only be begun through one man trying to express his most inward impressions of how deeply problematic is the quest for—to use Pater's terms—"an outer world, and of other minds." . . . ***Heart of Darkness*** embodies more thoroughly than any previous fiction the posture of uncertainty and doubt; one of Marlow's functions is to represent how much a man cannot know; and he assumes that reality is essentially private and individual—work, he comments, gives you "the chance to find yourself. Your own reality—for yourself, not for others—what no other man can ever know. They can only see the mere show, and never can tell what it really means." . . . (p. 174)

The other most distinctively impressionist aspect of Conrad's narrative method concerns his approach to visual description; and this preoccupation with the problematic relation of individual sense impressions to meaning is shown most clearly in one of the minor innovations of his narrative technique.

Long before ***Heart of Darkness*** Conrad seems to have been trying to find ways of giving direct narrative expression to the way in which the consciousness elicits meaning from its perceptions. One of the devices that he hit on was to present a sense impression and to withhold naming it or explaining its meaning until later; as readers we witness every step by which the gap between the individual perception and its cause is belatedly closed within the consciousness of the protagonist. (pp. 174-75)

This narrative device may be termed delayed decoding, since it combines the forward temporal progression of the mind, as it receives messages from the outside world, with the much slower reflexive process of making out their meaning. (p. 175)

By the time Conrad came to write ***Heart of Darkness,*** then, he had developed one narrative technique which was the verbal equivalent of the impressionist painter's attempt to render visual sensation directly. Conrad presented the protagonist's immediate sensations, and thus made the reader aware of the gap between impression and understanding; the delay in bridging the gap enacts the disjunction between the event and the observer's trailing understanding of it. In ***Heart of Darkness*** Conrad uses the method for the most dramatic action of the story, when Marlow's boat is attacked, just below Kurtz's station. (pp. 176-77)

Conrad's main objective is to put us into intense sensory contact with the events; and this objective means that the physical impression must precede the understanding of cause. Literary impressionism implies a field of vision which is not merely limited to the individual observer, but is also controlled by whatever conditions—internal and external—prevail at the moment of observation. In narration the main equivalents to atmospheric interference in painting are the various factors which normally distort human perception, or which delay its recognition of what is most relevant and important. First of all, our minds are usually busy with other things—Marlow has a lot to do just then, and it is only natural that he should be annoyed by being faced with these three new interferences with his task of keeping the boat from disaster. Secondly, our interpretations of impressions are normally distorted by habitual expectations—Marlow perceives the unfamiliar arrows as familiar sticks. Lastly, we always have many more things in our range of vision than we can pay attention to, so that in a crisis we may miss the most important ones—in this case that the helmsman has been killed. Conrad's method reflects all these difficulties in translating perceptions into causal or conceptual terms. This takes us deeply into the connection between delayed decoding and impressionism: it reminds us, as Michael Levenson has said, of the precarious nature of the process of interpretation in general; and since this precariousness is particularly evident when the individual's situation or his state of mind is abnormal, the device of delayed decoding simultaneously enacts the objective and the subjective aspects of moments of crisis. The method also has the more obvious advantage of convincing us of the reality of the experience which is being described; there is nothing suspiciously selective about the way it is narrated; while we read we are, as in life, fully engaged in trying to decipher a meaning out of a random and pell-mell bombardment of sense impressions. (pp. 178-79)

Conrad's retreat from the omniscient author is applied much more radically to his characterisation and his mode of narration, and through them to the meaning of the story as a whole. As several critics have noted, Marlow's role turns ***Heart of Darkness*** into a story about—among other things—the difficulty of telling the "full story." . . . Marlow is obsessively aware of it. "No, not very clear," . . . he ruminates aloud as he begins to recall his experience, and later he is driven to conclude that it is "impossible to convey the life-sensation of any given epoch of one's existence—that which makes its truth, its meaning—its subtle and penetrating essence." . . . Marlow's ironic consciousness of how far he is from being able to tell "the full story," and the overt enactment of this within the novel, are two of the ways in which ***Heart of Darkness*** anticipates the unauthoritative, self-reflexive, and problematic nature of such later fiction as Kafka's novels and Gide's *Les Faux-Monnayeurs*.

These comparisons, however, are themselves reminders of how far scepticism is from being the only or even the main burden of meaning in ***Heart of Darkness;*** Marlow is also the means whereby Conrad incorporates three of the oldest, and predominantly affirmative, elements in storytelling: the narrator as a remembering eyewitness; the narrator as the voice of his author's opinions; and the narrator as a friendly personal presence. (pp. 210-11)

The fact that Marlow is not the primary narrator, however, has the effect of giving him an objective status that is in accord with more recent modes of storytelling. It can, indeed, be argued that retrospection does not in fact involve a breach with the relativism of the more typically impressionist modes of modern fiction. Neither the immediate verbal rendering of sense impressions, nor the later development of the stream-of-consciousness novel, has any certain basis in experience; after all, no one has ever seen an impression, let alone a stream of them, and life offers no model for putting them into words. Memory is somewhat closer to our consciousness; and the act of putting memories into words is a common and observed phenomenon. Retrospective narration, then, though one of the oldest forms of narrative, has as good a claim to represent actual experience as more modern methods; and the way Conrad uses Marlow is peculiarly adapted to showing the individual engaged in trying to understand what has happened to him.

Conrad's use of Marlow as the voice of retrospection, then, combines old and new narrative methods. Marlow's memories of his lonely experiences on the Congo, and his sense of the impossibility of fully communicating their meaning, would in themselves assign ***Heart of Darkness*** to the literature of modern solipsism; but the fact that Marlow, like Conrad, is speaking to a particular audience makes all the difference; it enacts the process whereby the solitary individual discovers a way out into the world of others. One can surmise that Conrad found the narrative posture of moral and social neutrality intolerable; and so under cover of Marlow's probing of the meaning of the past, Conrad smuggled in the ancient privilege of the narrator by the backdoor, and surreptitiously reclaimed some of the omniscient author's ancient rights to the direct expression of the wisdom of hindsight. (pp. 211-12)

Through Marlow, Conrad can unobjectionably express the sort of moral commentary on the action which had been proscribed by Flaubert and the purists of the art of the novel, and which had seemed somewhat obtrusive when Conrad did it directly, as he had occasionally in ***The Nigger of the "Narcissus"***, for instance. But Marlow is much more than a device for circumventing the modern taboo on authorial moralising; he is also a means of allowing his author to express himself more completely than ever before; through Marlow Conrad discovered a new kind of relation to his audience, and one which enabled him to be more fully himself. (p. 212)

The primary narrator first gives a low-keyed description of the *Nellie's* coming to anchor, and of the five men aboard settling down to await the ebb of the tide; then he slowly modulates into an increasingly fixed absorption on the gathering gloom and what it suggests. Almost imperceptibly, this evocation of the time and the place sets up the novel's basic symbolic dualism; the light in the sky and the luminous estuary are contrasted with the darkness along the banks of the Thames and over London. (pp. 214-15)

[Our] attention has been alerted against assuming that the narrative depends exclusively on the symbolic meanings traditionally attributed to the contrast of black as bad and white as good: for instance, the two opposites are intermingled in the case of the "torch" of civilisation, since it came from "within the land," which we have just seen as dark. . . .

Characteristically, Marlow's opening remark both reverses and expands the general meditative direction: it reverses it because Marlow is thinking, not about the light of British civilisation, but about the darkness out of which it arose; and it amplifies it because the historical perspective becomes much longer when Marlow invokes the first Roman settlers on the Thames in "very old times." This idea is developed in a long paragraph which begins by making us see civilisation, not as the established norm, but as a brief interruption of the normal order of darkness, an interruption which is as brief and unsubstantial as "a flash of lightning in the clouds."

Marlow's backward plunge into England's remoter past soon proves to be an indirect approach to a much more immediate and personal preoccupation—the moral and psychological conflict between light and darkness which goes on inside the individual. (p. 215)

The rest of the first section is mainly concerned with recounting a series of Marlow's progressive initiations. Freed from the priorities of conventional autobiography, each incident is selected and treated for its larger implications. . . . (pp. 217-18)

The four other main stages of the first section deal with Marlow's voyage out, the company station, the overland journey, and the central station. They are arranged in chronological order, with occasional flashbacks and anticipatory parentheses; and within each stage, the particular episodes which are given the greatest emphasis seem selected to amplify or complicate Marlow's internal process of moral discovery, rather than to recount his journey.

During the voyage out most of the episodes serve to reverse the conventional application of light and darkness to the colonialism-savagery dichotomy. This reversal had already been suggested when Marlow says of the unnamed city from which he sets out that it "always makes me think of a whited sepulchre." . . . So Marlow leaves a white civilisation which masks death and darkness to confront the Dark Continent; and this will bring about a complementary transvaluation of the habitual assumptions which he initially shared with his society. (p. 218)

Until now Marlow has seen the waste, ineffectiveness and cruelty of the colonial presence only at a distance, and from the outside; when he arrives at the company station he is forced to confront their human consequences at close quarters. A file of six emaciated blacks balancing baskets of earth on their heads slowly passes Marlow, "with that complete, deathlike indifference of unhappy savages." . . . (p. 219)

To shield himself from seeing any more of the lacerating results of "these high and just proceedings," of which he is "after all . . . a part," Marlow turns off the path into the shade of a grove, only to discover that "I had stepped into the gloomy circle of some Inferno." . . . As soon as his eyes have become used to the deep shade, Marlow discovers that he has taken refuge in a place "where some of the helpers had withdrawn to die." These labourers on the railway are essentially the victims, not of calculated brutality, but of the blindness to their needs of an alien and more powerful order; they have been "brought from all the recesses of the coast in all the legality of time contracts" by the rationality of a capitalist order based on legal agreements and chronometric time, an order which is wholly incomprehensible to the blacks; they are being mercilessly destroyed by a system which is administered by whites who make a point of not noticing what they are really doing. (p. 220)

By now the reversal of the symbolic associations of black and white has gone very far; it is soon given a further range of thematic complication. When Marlow gets to the company station, the first sight that meets his eye is a man who proves to be a very problematic representative of Marlow's other moral positive—work and efficiency. The "white cuffs" and "snowy trousers" of the company's chief accountant look dazzling; and Marlow at first reflects, only half ironically, that "in the great demoralization of the land he kept up his appearance. That's backbone." . . . So far, so good, perhaps; especially when it appears that the accountant is also "devoted to his books, which were in apple-pie order." This devotion, however, excludes all other human values. There is a sick company agent dying in his office, and the accountant comments: "The groans of this sick person . . . distract my attention." The cold bureaucratic attitude, Marlow later discovers, does more than atrophy natural sympathy; it incites the accountant to positive inhumanity. . . . (pp. 220-21)

The episodes of the accountant and the dying African enact a symbolic confrontation of the most absolute kind between two world views. This confrontation exists at many levels; at the most abstract of them it opposes magic to mathematics. The thematic direction of these two episodes prepares us for another metaphysical question: Can any more valid faith be found in Africa than those of the accountant and the dying black?

The overland journey to the central station supplies some negative answers. All that Marlow sees of the original native life are the deserted villages with their ruined grass walls; but he hears "the tremor of far-off drums, sinking, swelling, a tremor vast, faint; a sound weird, appealing, suggestive, and wild—and perhaps with as profound a meaning as the sound of bells in a Christian country." The meanings of the Christian conquerors, however, are only represented by a drunken white man supposed to be in charge of the upkeep of the road; when Marlow asks him why he came out, he replies scornfully: "To make money, of course. What do you think?"

When Marlow arrives at the central station he soon learns that this is indeed the only faith to be found among the colonisers. (p. 221)

Marlow has learned as many negative truths as he can bear; they add up to the discovery that the "white patch" on the map which he dreamed about as a boy has indeed become "a place of darkness," . . . and that it is his fellow whites who have made it so. (p. 223)

During the first part [the colonial theme] is developed very largely as an implicit opposition between the public pretences in Europe and the contrary realities which Marlow discovers in Africa; but then this opposition becomes part of a more general dualism of progress versus atavism, until finally both dualisms collapse when Marlow discovers that Kurtz, the highest representative of European colonial progress, has been transformed into its opposite.

Two other persistent thematic dualisms offer themselves as possible "secondary notions," although, of course, there is no reason to believe that Conrad conceived them in these abstract terms. The first of them is that of work versus words; work receives considerable emphasis in the first part, while the theme of words is developed only in the last two. As to the second dualism, that of restraint versus liberation, both ideas surface only towards the end of the second part. (pp. 224-25)

The idea of atavistic reversion emerges in Marlow's imagination at the central station; and then, as the little steamboat plunges deeper into the jungle, its manifestations find a deeper resonance as his previous assumptions about the place of man in the continuum of space and time are irresistibly undermined. . . .

As they go deeper inland Marlow gradually comes to feel "cut off for ever from everything you had known once—somewhere—far away—in another existence perhaps." . . . His old familiar world is disappearing, and Marlow contemplates the new in a spirit akin to that of Baudelaire's "Correspondences": the forest seems to have meanings and intentions; Marlow continually senses its "mysterious stillness watching me" in silent interrogation. The mute immensity of the primeval jungle makes him feel that he and his civilisation are insignificant and temporary intruders. (p. 225)

Just as the paddlers off the African coast had seemed a touchstone that exposed the unnatural and hypocritical sickness of Western civilisation, so Marlow now finds a similar appeal in his occasional glimpses of the tribal life along the river banks. Nothing he hears or sees—an occasional "roll of drums behind the curtain of trees," or "a burst of yells, a whirl of black limbs, a mass of hands clapping, of feet stamping, of bodies swaying"—has a clear meaning; he does not know if "the prehistoric man was cursing us, praying to us, welcoming us—who could tell?". . . . Still, something is communicated which is vitally human: "What thrilled you was just the thought of their humanity—like yours—the thought of your remote kinship with this wild and passionate uproar. Ugly. Yes, it was ugly enough; but if you were man enough you would admit to yourself that there was in you just the faintest trace of a response to the terrible frankness of that noise." Marlow comes to believe that his subliminal responsiveness is an echo of the primitive residues in his own being; he has a "dim suspicion" that there was "a meaning" in that noise which his listeners—"you—you so remote from the night of first ages—could comprehend. And why not? The mind of man is capable of anything—because everything is in it, all the past as well as all the future."

Kurtz's mind is to prove as capable of a fearless acting out of the whole past of human barbarism, as of propounding its verbal opposite in eloquent platitudes about boundless progress in the future.

As for Marlow, he immunises himself against both barbarism and the ugliness of progress through work, as he twice explains to his listeners. (pp. 225-26)

Marlow is implicitly dividing civilised man into three categories: those who respond to savagery and succumb, like Kurtz; those who respond but possess "a deliberate belief" which enables them to resist; and the fools who do not respond at all because they do not notice. (p. 226)

Surface truths imply deeper truths; and Marlow soons finds himself needing to posit one which introduces a new dualism. Just below Kurtz's station, when an attack is imminent, the headman of Marlow's cannibal crew puts in a claim for any edible enemy carcasses that may become available. This suddenly makes Marlow realise that, as a result of the blindness of the trading company to their needs, the crew have long been on the verge of starvation: their pay—three pieces of brass wire a week—does not buy the food it is supposed to, mainly because the villages along the river are deserted or hostile. So the cannibal crew had every reason to eat the whites on board, and being "thirty to five," . . . they could easily have done it. The crew had "no earthly reason for any kind of scruple." "What possible restraint?" then, can have checked them, Marlow wonders: "Was it superstition, disgust, patience, fear—or some kind of primitive honour?" He finds no answer, but the overwhelming fact of their restraint remains.

Restraint is tangentially related to the atavism-civilisation duality because it is a quality which is not usually needed in modern society, where all necessary sanctions on conduct are supplied externally. . . . Kurtz [is] an example of the destructive effects of first having lost inherited moral restraints through exposure to another culture, and then being removed from external restraints by circumstances. . . . (pp. 226-27)

The thematic opposite to restraint, liberation, is established as soon as the steamboat arrives off the inner station. The first man Marlow sees is not Kurtz, but the beckoning figure of the young Russian sailor, whose patched clothes make him look like a harlequin. (p. 227)

The Russian's youthful innocence is apparent from his "beardless, boyish face" with "smiles and frowns chasing each other over that open countenance like sunshine and shadow"; . . . and this betokens both the spontaneity and the self-doubt of youth, a combination which makes him the natural prey of Kurtz's malignant self-assurance. . . .

The second part ends on this note. "I tell you," the Russian cries, "this man has enlarged my mind." . . . Romantic individualism had set up the ideal of absolute liberation from religious, social, and ethical norms; and this ideal, later reinforced by many other forces of nineteenth-century history, made the spread of freedom and progress depend on the removal of all "restraints." The Russian harlequin thus represents his century's innocent but fateful surrender to that total Faustian unrestraint which believes that everything is justified if it "enlarges the mind." (p. 228)

Marlow's personal attitude to Kurtz is from the beginning largely dictated by particular external circumstances that make Kurtz seem the lesser of two evils. On his way up, Marlow has felt a growing need to dissociate himself from all the doings of his fellow whites; and at the central station this motive is reinforced when it becomes apparent both that Kurtz is the spearhead of the reform party in the trading company, and that Marlow is regarded as his ally. The obscure machinations of the manager of the central station and his cronies against Kurtz and Marlow remain vestigial as far as the plot is concerned; but they channel Marlow's disgusted bewilderment at everything he has seen into a deeper intellectual and moral identification with his imaginary picture of Kurtz. He believes, for instance, that Kurtz shares his devotion to the work ethic, because he has heard the manager talking about how Kurtz had sent back his last load of ivory with his clerk, and had then paddled back alone to his station, some three hundred miles upriver. On this Marlow comments: "I did not know the motive"; but he imagines that "perhaps [Kurtz] was just simply a fine fellow who stuck to his work for its own sake." . . . (p. 229)

It is, then, a combination of the accidents of circumstance, a reliance on out-of-date reports, and the pressures of personal need, which give Marlow a vague sense of being captured by Kurtz's mysterious power. (pp. 229-30)

Marlow's first great disillusionment comes when he arrives at the inner station and learns from the Russian that, as he surmised, the attack on the steamboat was not really an attack, or at least was only "undertaken under the stress of desperation, and in its essence was purely protective." . . . Protective of what? Of Kurtz, Marlow is surprised to discover. And why? Because, the Russian explains, they adore him, and "they don't want him to go." . . . The Russian further reveals that it was actually "Kurtz who had ordered the attack." . . . Not only is Kurtz adored; he apparently adores it.

While the Russian is still talking about Kurtz, Marlow accidentally gets visual confirmation of his tale. Being unable to go ashore, he is trying to satisfy his curiosity by looking at Kurtz's ruined house, with its fence now broken down and offering no protection from the wilderness and its denizens. Suddenly, in "a brusque movement" of Marlow's field glasses "one of the remaining posts . . . leaped up"; it bears, "black, dried, sunken, with closed eyelids,—a head that seemed to sleep at the top of that pole, and, with the shrunken dry lips showing a narrow white line of the teeth, was smiling, too." . . . Marlow discovers that there are other heads on the stakes, and that they are "turned to the house." Their function is clearly not, like those on the palisades of Arab forts, or on Traitor's Gate, to warn beholders against offending the rulers of the land; nor is their function merely aesthetic, like those which one official at Stanley Falls disposed as "a decoration around a flower bed in front of his house." In Kurtz's case the heads, as Marlow puts it, are "not ornamental but symbolic." . . . For Marlow, however, their thematic meaning is summed up in saying that "they only showed that Mr. Kurtz lacked restraint in the gratification of his various lusts."

Marlow's horror is soon turned in another direction. Kurtz's long, emaciated body is carried on board; and when Marlow hears the now triumphant manager describe Kurtz's methods as "unsound" because "the time was not ripe for vigorous action," . . . he finds it so vile in its amoral hypocrisy that, despite what he now knows, he "turn[s] mentally to Kurtz for relief." Finding a bitter comfort in the reflection that "it was something to have at least a choice of nightmares," Marlow formally aligns himself with Kurtz by refusing to discuss the matter in the manager's terms. He commits himself only to the ambiguous judgment that "Mr. Kurtz is a remarkable man"; and to appease the Russian's fear that his idol's glory will suffer if he leaves him in enemy hands, Marlow assures him that "I am Mr. Kurtz's friend—in a way," and that "Mr. Kurtz's reputation is safe with me." . . . (pp. 230-31)

That night Marlow is awakened by the sound of native drums and frenzied yells; he happens to glance casually into Kurtz's cabin; it is empty. Earlier, Kurtz's adoring tribesmen had tried to prevent his being taken away from them onto the steamboat; but now it appears that Kurtz's need for his tribesmen is equally imperious. He has gone back on his own. . . . [Marlow] quietly goes ashore to bring Kurtz back again; and he finds him crawling "on all-fours" towards the ritual fires, and the nearest black sorcerer with antelope horns on his head. Atavistic regression could hardly go further; a man crawling like an animal to be worshipped by followers in the ceremonial guise of animals.

The issue is clear. Marlow must determine whether wilderness and darkness have an invincible power over man's moral being; and so he begins to struggle for Kurtz's soul. Believing that Kurtz could only have been lured back by "the awakening of forgotten and brutal instincts, by the memory of gratified and monstrous passions," . . . Marlow tries to counter them. When he tells Kurtz that unless he comes back "You will be lost . . . utterly lost," it is "a flash of inspiration"—presumably because Kurtz cannot bear to lose the other glories that he imagines he can still win at home; and so, believing that he can still add to his triumphs, Kurtz allows himself to be supported quietly back to the steamboat. (pp. 231-32)

In addition to Kurtz's main thematic importance as the supreme exhibit of the dialectic between progress and atavism, he also represents the extreme position in several other dualities. Two have already been taken up: Kurtz stands for liberation as opposed to restraint, and for words as opposed to work. Another polarity, that which opposes belief to hollowness, is perhaps to be regarded as a corollary of the work/words dualism; in any case Kurtz is obviously intended as the climactic example of the inner moral void which Marlow has found in all the representatives of Western progress. (p. 233)

Kurtz is essentially one vast indiscriminate appetite, and his greed does not allow him to face the contradiction between the atavistic desires he has appeased in the wilderness and those with which he had set out from Europe—his dreams "of lying fame, of sham distinction, of all the appearances of success and power." . . . It is almost entirely of these last—the rewards of civilisation and progress—that Kurtz talks to Marlow. . . . Even in his final twilight Kurtz mouths the moral platitudes of his civilisation like an automaton; but they remain totally unconnected with the realities of his life. (pp. 234-35)

The final gasping anaphora of "The horror! The horror!" strains rather hard for its effect; but it embodies three effective ironies. First, that on the only occasion that Kurtz's voice loses its preternatural resonance, it should also express the truth about his deeds; second, that Kurtz should so neatly exemplify in this drastic stylistic simplification the utter contradiction between the rhetoric and the reality of progress; and lastly, that this simplification should also break so completely with the note of consolatory serenity which is traditional for deathbed utterances in fiction. (p. 236)

But the main object of Kurtz's condemnation is surely himself, and what he has done; his dying whisper pronounces rejection of the Faustian compact with the wilderness which had "sealed his soul to its own." . . . His final cry can only be judged, as Marlow judges it, "an affirmation, a moral victory," . . . if it constitutes an acknowledgment of the horror of his former deeds. Even so, that Kurtz's "judgment upon the adventures of his soul on this earth" should be presented by Marlow as a significant moral victory seems a little unconvincing today, and its force largely depends on the intellectual atmosphere of the late nineteenth century. The question had been raised, in many forms, whether the universe is, as Dostoevsky's Ivan Karamazov thinks, a fabric of meaningless cruelty in which "everything is lawful." Kurtz's whole career seemed to support this view: he acknowledged no internal or external restraint; but Marlow's worst doubts are set at rest when this "being to whom I could not appeal in the name of anything high or low" . . . makes a final judgment which is "the expression of some sort of belief"; . . . and without some ethical belief, Kurtz's judgment would have no logical basis. (pp. 236-37)

The most consistent clue to Marlow's psychological state during his journey up the river is probably the way he often recalls it in terms of dream and nightmare. The journey surely was, for Marlow as it had been for Conrad, a nightmare in a common usage of the term: an experience in which the individual's thoughts and actions are dominated by a terrifying and inexplicable sense of personal helplessness. Marlow also expresses the main content of his experience in the traditional terms of a fairy-tale hero's arduous, dangerous, and mysterious quest. . . . The analogies of nightmare and fairy tale suggest two traditional metaphors for the process whereby Marlow is unconsciously impelled to create a fantasy Kurtz: he needs a magic helper or at least a secret sharer, in any case a person who will fill the need that isolated adults as well as solitary children can feel for someone who will give them unconditional help or total personal reciprocity.

These unspoken hopes are dashed as soon as Marlow arrives at the inner station. Kurtz has not been able to deal with isolation in the wilderness; his articulateness and his claims to virtue are shams; and his behaviour to others has not been better than that of the pilgrims, but much worse. The "universal genius" has turned into an inflated version of their greedy and callous egoism. The only problem, then, is to explain why, despite his total disillusionment, Marlow's "loyalty" to Kurtz continues until, and beyond, his death.

Outwardly, Marlow's behaviour is still constrained by the fact that everyone else identifies him with Kurtz; and once he has pledged his word first to the Russian, and then to the dying man himself, he is forced to defend Kurtz's memory. His own feelings are no doubt mixed and unclear even to himself; but the evidence is consistent in showing that as soon as Marlow has come into contact with Kurtz, his behaviour can reasonably be explained primarily as the result of commitments over which he had little control. (pp. 240-41)

The Kurtz-Marlow relationship is certainly anomalous, but it is distinctly less so in the context of Conrad's own characteristics as a novelist. He usually sees relationships between individuals not as essentially personal, but as parts of a larger structure in which—as is surely true of ***Heart of Darkness***—chance, occasion, occupational activities, and general attitudes toward the physical and moral world, have enormous determining power, and allow very little autonomy to the wishes of the individual concerned. There is great psychological truth in the way that Conrad shows how the autonomy of one individual's actions can be unexpectedly, involuntarily, and yet imperatively, preempted by the contingencies imposed by the larger forces in which his personal relationships are set. This psychological truth, in turn, reflects Conrad's larger aim, which is to make Marlow enact both the ambiguities and the defeats which attend the individual's effort to build up, live by, and share with others, his vision of good and evil. . . .

After Kurtz's death, two-thirds of the way through the last section, Marlow's narrative moves very rapidly through his illness, his return to Europe, and the settling of his various affairs concerning Kurtz. Only one episode is given in any detail, that of the lie to Kurtz's Intended. It is very widely agreed that the scene is treated in a rather strained, melodramatic, and repetitive way, with little of the convincing detail which had generated the evocative power of the earlier major scenes. . . . (p. 241)

[When] Marlow finally sees the Intended, he senses her "mature capacity for fidelity, for belief, for suffering," . . . and realises once again he is being confronted with a constrained choice.

At first Marlow allows the Intended's praises of Kurtz to run on, with guarded silence or ambiguous assent his only reaction. For instance, when she says, "it was impossible to know him and not to admire him," Marlow merely answers, "unsteadily," that "he was a remarkable man." At one point the Intended's confident and self-flattering delusions about Kurtz anger Marlow, but the feeling soon subsides "before a feeling of infinite pity." . . . Finally, the Intended asks Marlow for "His last word—to live with." There is a pause, in which Marlow hears the whisper of "The horror! the horror!" ringing in his ears; and then he controls himself and slowly gives the Intended a version of Kurtz's last oral performance of the kind she expects: "The last word he pronounced was—your name." (p. 243)

There are, then, all kinds of particular pressures, none of them difficult to explain, which cause Marlow's "lie"; and he can hardly be blamed for it, especially if one considers how universally the world is pervaded by customary practices such as Marlow here follows. That they are, incidentally, practices which society has sound reason to exonerate from reprobation, is suggested by the hallowed metaphor—itself highly appropriate to Conrad's main symbolic polarity—of the white lie. (pp. 243-44)

Many other themes of ***Heart of Darkness*** are also "locked in" to the climactic scene with the Intended. Marlow, for instance, exhibits his much-taxed restraint when he masters his anger at the delusions of the Intended; hollowness is present in the Intended's posture of faithfulness to the memory of a sham whom she never really knew; and the dualism of atavism and progress is very obviously emphasised when memories of Kurtz's savage rites and his native mistress penetrate Marlow's mind while the Intended talks on "as thirsty men drink" . . . about the loss to humanity of Kurtz's "generous mind." In effect, the final scene locks in all the earlier "secondary notions" except that of work, under the large general conception of the lie. (p. 246)

He lies for many reasons: to honour his commitment to the nightmare of his choice by preserving the decency of Kurtz's memory; to spare the Intended's feelings, and therefore his own; but also because whatever system of belief he may have attained has too dubious and private a status in his own thoughts to be presented as an effective alternative to the illusions of the Intended. Marlow never feels certain that his own truth is not an illusion; and in this he reflects Conrad, who was always prone to refer to most abstract philosophical terms—like truth, ideals, principles, reality—as illusions. He used the term in a rather wide and undefined sense to assert, not so much that they are untrue as that they are unfounded, impermanent, unprovable, or uncertain. (pp. 247-48)

Conrad's frequent use of the word illusion is a sign of a philosophical scepticism which would obviously inhibit him from attempting to define the intellectual basis of his own practical human commitments; but this does not undermine, and indeed it may even strengthen, the conviction that although the sceptical mind knows that all ideological structures are really illusions, they may in practice be necessary restraints upon human egoism, laziness, or despair.

Marlow's behaviour in ***Heart of Darkness*** reflects this dual attitude. His awareness of the fragility and the intellectual hollowness of civilisation inhibits him in his dealings with others; his usual comportment is one of sceptical passivity; even his sympathy is uneasy and reserved, as in the scene with the Intended. Her grandiose illusions about Kurtz gradually force Marlow to go from taut acquiescence to more positive violation of the truth. Thus when the Intended stops her eulogy of Kurtz with "But you have heard him! You know!" . . . , Marlow replies, "Yes, I know." Then, "with something like despair in [his] heart," he bows his head before the Intended's "great and saving illusion that shone with an unearthly glow in the darkness, in the triumphant darkness from which I could not have defended her—from which I could not even defend myself."

The lie to the Intended, then, is both an appropriately ironic ending for Marlow's unhappy quest for truth, and a humane recognition of the practical aspects of the problem: we must deal gently with human fictions, as we quietly curse their folly under our breath; since no faith can be had which will move mountains, the faith which ignores them had better be cherished.

At the end of the scene we are left wondering whether it is worse that the ideals of the Intended should continue in all their flagrant untruth, or that Marlow should have been unable to invoke any faith in whose name he could feel able to challenge them. To put the alternatives in terms of the main symbolic polarity of ***Heart of Darkness*** as a whole: which perspective is more alarming? that people such as the Intended should be so blinded by their certitude of being the bearers of light that they are quite unaware of the darkness that surrounds them? or, on the other hand, that those who, like Marlow, have been initiated into the darkness, should be unable to illumine the blindness of their fellows to its omnipresence? (pp. 248-49)

Until Marlow confronts the Intended, the general development of the ramifying symbolic contrasts between light and darkness has been fairly easy to transpose into the terms which define the intellectual perspective that he has acquired as a result of his Congo experience. It can be summarised along the following lines: the physical universe began in darkness, and will end in it; the same holds for the world of human history, which is dark in the sense of being obscure, amoral, and without purpose; and so, essentially, is man. Through some fortuitous and inexplicable development, however, men have occasionally been able to bring light to this darkness in the form of civilisation—a structure of behaviour and belief which can sometimes keep the darkness at bay. But this containing action is highly precarious, because the operations of darkness are much more active, numerous, and omnipresent, both in society and in the individual, than civilised people usually suppose. They must learn that light is not only a lesser force than darkness in power, magnitude, and duration, but is in some way subordinate to it, or included within it; in short, that the darkness which Marlow discovers in the wilderness, in Kurtz and in himself, is the primary and all-encompassing reality of the universe. (pp. 249-50)

There is nothing particularly new in the idea that darkness is the primal reality to which all else in the world is posterior in origin and subordinate in power. In the Judaeo-Christian tradition, for example, the idea is embodied at the cosmic level in the book of Genesis, where "darkness was upon the face of the earth" in the beginning of things. The Western religious tradition as a whole makes light not the rule but the exception; it is the result of a beneficent divine intervention, which may be temporary and is certainly not bestowed unconditionally.

This transcendental view of the world is very difficult to embody in narrative. . . . In ***Heart of Darkness*** this quasi-transcendental perspective is most obviously apparent in its language: such words as "unspeakable," "inconceivable," "inscrutable," and "nameless" are really an attempt—on the whole unsuccessful—to make us go beyond the limits of ordinary cognition, to transcend what Conrad or anybody else really knows. The ensuing sense of rhetorical strain is particularly marked in the passages dealing with Kurtz, where Marlow uses the language of ethical absolutes, although there is no reason to believe that he accepts any conceptual structure on which they might depend. (pp. 250-51)

In the last pages of ***Heart of Darkness*** there is a final variation on the values associated with whiteness and light. . . . In the falling dusk, the Intended, all in mourning black, dedicates her soul, "as translucently pure as a cliff of crystal," . . . to the memory of Kurtz; to Marlow her "great and saving illusion" shines with "an unearthly glow"; . . . and, although the Intended is illumined by "the unextinguishable light of belief and love,'' Marlow tells us that ''with every word spoken the room was growing darker.''

Light has been degraded to a cold and artificial brightness—it can no longer combat darkness; while whiteness has become some diseased albino mutation, capable, no doubt, of producing the cold phosphorescent glow of idealism, but sick and pallid indeed. . . . We seem to have moved from a realisation of the overwhelming power of darkness in the psychological, moral, and spiritual realm, to a larger and intangible change of a metaphysical kind, in which light seems to have a peculiar affinity with unnaturalness, hypocrisy, and delusion, and to be quite as contrary to the positive values of human life as the worst manifestations conventionally attributed to darkness. (pp. 251-52)

But these negative views are surely too absolute: Marlow's tale, and the story as a whole, are not entirely, or even mainly, self-referential—its sepulchral city and its Africa are seen through Marlow's eyes, but they are places full of real horrors. What makes reading ***Heart of Darkness*** so unforgettable is surely the harrowing power with which Conrad convinces us of the essential reality of everything that Marlow sees and feels at each stage of his journey. Nor can Conrad's social and moral purport be regarded as ultimately nihilist . . . ; Marlow's positives—work and restraint, for instance—make a less impressive appearance in the narrative than do all the negatives which he discovers; but Marlow's defences are firmly present in the stubborn energy and responsibility of his daily activities. Of course, no very flattering or sanguine view of man's behaviour and prospects emerges from ***Heart of Darkness,*** and it must have seemed grotesquely pessimistic to its original readers. It surely seems a good deal less so eighty years later, except to those who have had a very blinkered view of the century's battlefields. In any case, neither Conrad nor Marlow stands for the position that darkness is irresistible; their attitude, rather, is to enjoin us to defend ourselves in full knowledge of the difficulties to which we have been blinded by the illusions of civilisation. (pp. 252-53)

Ian Watt, in his Conrad in the Nineteenth Century *(copyright © 1979 by The Regents of the University of California; reprinted by permission of the University of California Press; in Canada by the author and Chatto & Windus), University of California Press, 1979 (and reprinted by Chatto & Windus, 1980), 375 p.*

C. P. SARVAN (essay date 1980)

[*Sarvan believes that Chinua Achebe (1977) misinterpreted Conrad's intentions in the depiction of Africa and Africans in* Heart of Darkness. *In the following excerpt, Sarvan points out that any discussion of the work must take Conrad's use of irony into account and contends that Achebe erroneously confused the voice of Marlow with that of Conrad. While Sarvan concludes that Conrad was not free of the prejudices of his time, he nonetheless views* Heart of Darkness *as the earliest sincere attempt to break away from racist-imperialist beliefs. For a similar reading, see the Hunt Hawkins entry in the Additional Bibliography. The role of Africa and Africans in* Heart of Darkness *is also discussed in the excerpts by Harold R. Collins (1954), Cedric Watts (1977), and Ian Watt (1979).*]

Conrad's setting, themes, and his triumph in writing major literature in his third language, have won him a special admiration in the non-European world. . . . But African readers are also checked by, and disconcerted at, works such as ***The Nigger of the "Narcissus"*** and ***Heart of Darkness.*** The case against the latter was most strongly made by Chinua Achebe [see excerpt above, 1977]. . . . He argued that Conrad sets up Africa ''as a foil to Europe, a place of negations . . . in comparison with which Europe's own state of spiritual grace will be manifest.'' . . . Africa is ''the other world,'' ''the antithesis of Europe and therefore of civilization, a place where man's vaunted intelligence and refinement are finally mocked by triumphant bestiality.'' . . . Achebe commented on Conrad's comparison of the Congo and the Thames, and also alleged that the contrast made between the two women who loved Kurtz, one African, the other European, is highly prejudiced. Any sympathy expressed for the sufferings of the black African under colonialism, argued Achebe is a sympathy born of a kind of liberalism which whilst acknowledging distant kinship, repudiates equality. Conrad, continued Achebe, is a ''racist''—and great art can only be ''on the side of man's deliverance and not his enslavement; for the brotherhood and unity of all mankind and not for the doctrines of Hitler's master races or Conrad's 'rudimentary souls'.'' . . . Achebe concluded his attack on ***Heart of Darkness*** by describing it as ''a book which parades in the most vulgar fashion prejudices and insults from which a section of mankind has suffered untold agonies and atrocities in the past and continues to do so in many ways and many places today. I am talking about a story in which the very humanity of black people is called in question. It seems to me totally inconceivable that great art or even good art could possibly reside in such unwholesome surroundings.'' . . . (p. 6)

I shall in the following pages attempt to narrowly limit myself to an examination of the charge of racism brought against Conrad's ***Heart of Darkness.*** Let us begin with the fictional Marlow whose story was once heard and is now related by a fictional narrator. . . . Marlow's portrait is drawn with quiet irony and, at times, a mocking humor which denotes ''distance'' between creator and character. For example, he is described as resembling an idol and he sits like a European Buddha without the lotus. Marlow claims to be deeply, almost pathologically averse to telling lies but we find that he prevaricates at least twice within this tale. He condemns the Roman conquest and contrasts it with the ''superior'' European colonialism. . . . [However, the] story shows that the European colonial conquest, contrary to Marlow's claims, was much worse than that of the Romans. One remembers that harrowing description of men waiting to die. . . . Immediately after this description, Marlow meets the elegant, perfumed, ''hairdresser's dummy'' and confesses that he ''respected his collars,'' the collars of a man who comes out ''to get a breath of fresh air,'' indifferent to the despair and death by which he is surrounded. It may be argued that Marlow is here speaking with irony and the description ''hairdresser's dummy'' may appear to make Marlow's attitude to the dummy as clear and unequivocal. But Marlow continues with unmistakable admiration that ''in the great demoralization of the land he kept up his appearance. That's backbone.'' . . . He kept up *appearances,* and that points to one of the important thematic significances of this work, namely, the discrepancy between appearance and reality; between assumption and fact; between illusion and truth. Thus it is not correct to say that Marlow has Conrad's complete confidence, and even more incorrect to say that Conrad believed Europe to be in a state of grace. The glorious sailors proudly cited by Marlow were pirates and plunderers. This ironic distance between Marlow and Conrad should not be overlooked though the narrative method makes it all too easy. Nor can Conrad's very forceful criticisms of colonialism be lightly passed over as weak liberalism. What ships unload in

Africa are soldiers and customhouse clerks: the one to conquer and the other to administer and efficiently exploit. The cannon pounds a continent and "the merry dance of death and trade goes on." . . . This "rapacious and pitiless folly" attempts to pass itself off as philanthropy, and to hypocritically hide its true nature under words such as enemies, criminals, and rebels. . . . The counterparts of enemies, criminals, and rebels are the emissaries of light, such as Kurtz!

As a critic has pointed out, "Africa *per se* is not the theme of ***Heart of Darkness,*** but is used as a locale symbol for the very core of an 'accursed inheritance'." At the risk of oversimplification, the story may be seen as an allegory, the journey ending with the sombre realization of the darkness of man's heart. But it may prove emotionally difficult for some to follow the allegory when it is thought that Conrad, casting about for an external parallel, for a physical setting to match the inner darkness, chose Africa. . . . When the Romans looked down upon the people of Britain, and the Europeans upon "natives," it was because they felt they had achieved a much higher civilization than the people they were confronting and conquering. The contempt was not on grounds of race itself, and Conrad suggests that Europe's claim to be civilized and therefore superior, needs earnest reexamination. The reference in ***Heart of Darkness*** is not to a place (Africa), but to the condition of European man; not to a black people, but to colonialism. The crucial question is whether European "barbarism" is merely a thing of the historical past. Surely the contrast between savage African and "civilized" European, in the light of that greedy and inhuman colonialism, is shown to be "appearance" rather than reality. The emphasis, the present writer would suggest, is on continuity, on persistence through time and peoples, and therefore on the fundamental oneness of man and his nature. If a judgment has to be made, then uncomplicated "savagery" is better than the "subtle horrors" manifested by almost all the Europeans Marlow met on that ironic voyage of discovery. When Marlow speaks of the African in European service as one of the "reclaimed," it is grim irony for he has been reclaimed to a worse state of barbarism. Left to itself, Africa has a "greatness" that went "home to one's very heart." . . . As Marlow begins his story, the light changes as though "stricken to death by the touch of that gloom brooding over a crowd of men": . . . yet the gloom is very much over the Thames as well. The Thames as "a waterway leading to the uttermost ends of the earth" . . . is connected with and therefore a part of those uttermost ends. The river signifies what is abiding in nature, in man, and in the nature of man, even as "the sea is always the same" . . . and foreign shores and foreign faces are veiled not by mystery but by ignorance.

The immaculately dressed, fastidious, and sensitive hairdresser's dummy, a representative of civilized Europe and a part of the colonial machinery, is totally insensitive to the suffering he helps to cause and by which he is surrounded. (His extreme cleanliness is perhaps to be seen as compulsive, an attempt to keep clean in the midst of that moral dirt.) Even in the case of Kurtz, one must remember that all Europe had "contributed" to his making. . . . As for pagan rites and savage dances, the Europeans with "imbecile rapacity" were "praying" to ivory, that is, to materialism, and one red-haired man "positively danced," bloodthirsty at the thought that he and the others "must have made a glorious slaughter" of the Africans in the bush. . . . The alleged primitiveness of the boilerman only serves to show the similarity between his *appearance* and the *actions* of the "civilized."

Achebe also noted that Kurtz's African mistress is the "savage counterpart to the refined, European woman." . . . But the European woman is pale and rather anemic whilst the former, to use Conrad's words, is gorgeous, proud, superb, magnificent, tragic, fierce, and filled with sorrow. . . . She is an impressive figure and, importantly, her human feelings are not denied. The contrast, however, is not simply between these two, but between Kurtz's African mistress on the one hand, and Marlow's aunt and Kurtz's "Intended" on the other. The aunt glibly believes that he who goes to the Congo is "a lower sort of apostle." . . . The hairdresser's dummy, we recall, was first taken to be "a sort of vision." . . . The same ignorance and the same illusions are found at the end, in Kurtz's Intended. After all, he was also one of those apostles. The darkness which is often mentioned, refers not only to the darkness within man, to the mysterious and the unpredictable, but also to ignorance and illusions: it is significant that as Marlow talks with Kurtz's Intended, the "darkness deepened." . . . The African woman faces the truth and endures the pain of her dereliction, whilst the illusions of the two European women are also the fond illusions of European society.

This is not to claim that Conrad was free of all prejudice, nor to deny that he has wholly resisted the temptation to use physical appearance and setting as indicators of nonphysical qualities. Conrad reflects to some degree the attitudes of his age, and his description of the fireman as a dog in a parody of breeches, is cruel. On the one hand, in terms of technological progress, the gap between London and the Congo was immense; on the other, though it is extreme to say that Conrad called into question the very humanity of the African, one's perspective and evaluation of this work need alteration. (pp. 7-9)

Conrad too was not entirely immune to the infection of the beliefs and attitudes of his age, but he was ahead of most in trying to break free. (p. 10)

C. P. Sarvan, "Racism and the 'Heart of Darkness'," in The International Fiction Review *(© copyright 1980 International Fiction Association), Vol. 7, No. 1, Winter, 1980, pp. 6-10.*

ADDITIONAL BIBLIOGRAPHY

Baines, Jocelyn. *Joseph Conrad: A Critical Biography*. New York: McGraw-Hill Book Co., 1960, 523 p.

Biography emphasizing the ways Conrad's life affected his works. Conrad's literary aims, artistic and financial successes, family and personal problems, friends and collaborators, and the influence of these elements on his work are examined. Baines also includes many passages quoted from Conrad's letters, an appendix translating letters written in French, and passages from Conrad's diary.

Benson, Donald R. "*Heart of Darkness:* The Grounds of Civilization in an Alien Universe." *Texas Studies in Literature and Language* VII, No. 4 (Winter 1966): 339-47.

Finds that *Heart of Darkness* demonstrates a philosophy of scientific naturalism. Benson believes Conrad depicted a universe indifferent to humans, making use of evolutionary theory to account for subhuman social and biological origins as well as the brutality of a piously blind civilization that endangered itself by "assaulting" unexplored areas.

Crankshaw, Edward. *Joseph Conrad: Some Aspects of the Art of the Novel*. London: John Lane, 1936, 248 p.

Important early study of Conrad's literary artistry, treating all his novels as a unified artistic achievement. Crankshaw does not dwell upon isolated aspects of the works, but rather on the author as a craftsman. The book includes a discussion of *Heart of Darkness*.

Crews, Frederick. "The Power of Darkness." *Partisan Review* XXXIV, No. 4 (Fall 1967): 507-25.

Posits that *Heart of Darkness* is a form of dream narrative that conveys many of Conrad's deepest personal traumas and misgivings.

Curle, Richard. "Conrad's Diary." *The Yale Review* XV, No. 2 (January 1926): 254-66.

Contends that *Heart of Darkness* was inspired by the Congo experiences of Conrad. Curle, Conrad's longtime friend, introduces an extract from Conrad's diary illustrating the striking similarity between his real-life and fictional voyages.

Daleski, H. M. *Joseph Conrad: The Way of Dispossession*. New York: Holmes & Meier Publishers, 1977, 234 p.

Critical survey. The book includes a chapter on *Heart of Darkness* in which Daleski discusses Marlow as protagonist-narrator, the ambiguity of the dark and light imagery, and the meaning of Marlow's lie.

Dean, Leonard F., ed. *Joseph Conrad's "Heart of Darkness": Backgrounds and Criticisms*. Englewood Cliffs, N.J.: Prentice-Hall, 1961, 184 p.

Includes the novella, historical information, extracts from Conrad's diary, and critical interpretations.

Dudley, Edward J. "Three Patterns of Imagery in Conrad's *Heart of Darkness*." *Revue des Langues Vivantes* 31, No. 6 (1965): 568-78.

Discusses darkness, the wilderness, and death as primary images in the novel. Dudley interprets the story as a moral adventure in which each image helps convey meaning.

Follet, Wilson. *Joseph Conrad*. Garden City, N.Y.: Doubleday, Page & Co., 1915, 11 p.

Discusses the innovative nature of Conrad's works and his attitude toward his creations.

Gillon, Adam. *Joseph Conrad*. Boston: Twayne Publishers, 1982, 210 p.

Chronological survey of Conrad's career that provides thematic associations between his work and his life. The section on *Heart of Darkness* distinguishes the author's artistic method from his symbolic language.

Hawkins, Hunt. "Conrad's Critique of Imperialism in *Heart of Darkness*." *PMLA* 94, No. 2 (March 1979): 286-99.

Discussion of Conrad's ambiguity about imperialism. Hawkins concludes that Conrad was opposed to the cruelty of imperialism, but not the ideal.

———. "The Issue of Racism in *Heart of Darkness*." *Conradiana* XIV, No. 3 (1982): 163-71.

Limited agreement with Chinua Achebe and others. While Hawkins finds derogatory references to Africans in the work, he also points out instances of complimentary remarks and contends that it is the European who is treated unsympathetically. Hawkins concludes that the liberal attitudes demonstrated in the work were much ahead of their time.

Hoffman, Stanto De Voren. *Comedy and Form in the Fiction of Joseph Conrad*. The Hague: Mouton, 1969, 140 p.

Challenges the charge that Conrad's works were without humor. In the chapter "The Whole in the Bottom of the Pail: Comedy and Theme in *Heart of Darkness*," Hoffman points out absurd scenes in the midst of tragedy, likening this use of comedy to the style of burlesque and farce.

Jean-Aubry, G. "Joseph Conrad in the *Heart of Darkness*." *The Bookman*, New York LXIII, No. 4 (June 1926): 429-35.

Discusses the relationship between Conrad's artistic method and his personal recollections by an early translator of Conrad's works into French. While Jean-Aubry supplies evidence to support the contention that Conrad based *Heart of Darkness* on actual situations and people from his Congo experience, he believes that the elevation of the facts and the human insight in the story were supplied by Conrad's "individual genius."

Karl, Frederick R. *Joseph Conrad: The Three Lives, A Biography*. New York: Farrar, Straus and Giroux, 1979, 1008 p.

Detailed critical biography. This highly regarded, exhaustive study includes information regarding the milieu in which each of Conrad's works was written, the relationship between Conrad's inconsistent temperament and his production, and the influence of friends and collaborators on his production.

Kimbrough, Robert, ed. *"Heart of Darkness": An Annotated Text, Backgrounds and Sources Criticism*. Rev. ed. New York: W. W. Norton & Co., 1971, 267 p.

Includes text of *Heart of Darkness*, background information, extracts from Conrad's letters and diary that relate to the novella, a bibliography, and criticism.

Levin, Gerald. "Victorian Kurtz." *Journal of Modern Literature* 7, No. 3 (September 1979): 433-40.

Examines the degree to which Kurtz was or was not a true idealist before his Congo experience.

Lothe, Jakob. "From Conrad to Coppola and Steiner." *The Conradian* 6, No. 3 (September 1981): 10-13.

Similarities and disparities between Conrad's work and two later treatments of the same subject—Francis Ford Coppola's film *Apocalypse Now* and the novella *The Portage to San Cristobal of A.H.*, by George Steiner.

McLauchlan, Juliet. "The Value and Significance of *Heart of Darkness*." *Conradiana* XL, No. 1 (1983): 3-21.

Examines the success of the final scene of *Heart of Darkness*. McLauchlan contends that the success of the novella is dependent upon Conrad's portrayal of Marlow's meeting with Kurtz's fiancée. This essay also includes a discussion of previous interpretations of Marlow's lie and its success or failure.

Meyer, Bernard C. *Joseph Conrad: A Psychoanalytical Biography*. Princeton: Princeton University Press, 1967, 396 p.

Authoritative psychoanalytical approach to Conrad and his works. This controversial work discusses the effects of the author's physical and mental illnesses, personal relationships, and general temperament on what Meyer believes are highly autobiographical works.

Najder, Zdzislaw. *Joseph Conrad: A Chronicle*. Translated by Halina Carroll-Najder. New Brunswick, N. J.: Rutgers University Press, 1983, 647 p.

Comprehensive biography. The first Conrad biography by a Pole, the book reinterprets the myths and facts about the author and discusses his works individually, without attempting to subsume them under any single theory regarding Conrad's ideas or beliefs. It is also the first work on Conrad to succinctly examine his feelings about Poles and Poland.

Ridley, Florence H. "The Ultimate Meaning of *Heart of Darkness*." *Nineteenth-Century Fiction* 18, No. 1 (June 1963): 43-53.

Discussion of how important attention to detail is in understanding the story. Ridley examines earlier criticism and demonstrates the failure of many critics to give equal emphasis to all parts and groups of characters in *Heart of Darkness*, a technique she believes is essential to understanding the work.

Robertson, P.J.M. "*Things Fall Apart* and *Heart of Darkness*: A Creative Dialogue." *The International Fiction Review* 7, No. 2 (Summer 1980): 106-11.

Comparison of novels by Chinua Achebe and Conrad. Robertson uses the two works as a dialogue between the black African and the Westerner, and discusses Chinua Achebe's charge that Conrad was a racist (see excerpt above, 1977).

Steiner, Joan E. "Modern Pharisees and False Apostles: Ironic New Testament Parallels in Conrad's *Heart of Darkness*." *Nineteenth-Century Fiction* 37, No. 1 (June 1982): 75-96.

Discusses religious imagery in the novella. Steiner believes that Conrad was ambivalent to religion, and points out ironic and symbolic parallels with the New Testament.

Teets, Bruce E., and Gerber, Helmut E., eds. *Joseph Conrad: An Annotated Bibliography of Writings about Him*. De Kalb: Northern Illinois University Press, 1971, 671 p.

A comprehensive guide to criticism of Conrad published between 1895 and 1967.

Tessitore, John. "Freud, Conrad and *Heart of Darkness*." *College Literature* VII, No. 1 (Winter 1980): 30-40.

A psychological reading of *Heart of Darkness*. Tessitore believes that Conrad's work examines the discontent of modern civilization in a way which prefigured the work of Sigmund Freud.

Wilcox, Stewart C. "Conrad's 'Complicated Presentations' of Symbolism in *Heart of Darkness*." *Philological Quarterly* XXXIX, No. 1 (January 1960): 1-17.

Discussion of primary images and symbols of *Heart of Darkness*.

Wirth-Nesher, Hana. "The Stranger Case of *The Turn of the Screw* and *Heart of Darkness*." *Studies in Short Fiction* 16, No. 4 (Fall 1979): 317-25.

Examines similarities between the two works by Henry James and Conrad. Wirth-Nesher discusses the use of doubles, the mystery plots, the ambiguity of the endings, and other elements which make these novellas important today.

Géza Csáth

1887-1919

(Pseudonym of József Brenner) Hungarian short story writer, dramatist, critic, and essayist.

Csáth was one of a group of writers who introduced trends of European modernism into Hungarian letters. In the nineteenth century, Hungarian literature was characterized by the "popular national" school, which produced romantic works glorifying Hungary's past and which retained that culture's highly insular ideals. With the appearance in 1908 of the periodical *Nyugat,* Hungarian writers gained a forum for the exchange and dissemination of ideas relating to modern movements in European philosophy, literature, and art. The thought of Friedrich Nietzsche and Henri Bergson was widely discussed, along with theories of Naturalism in fiction and Impressionism in painting. Csáth himself was among those poets and prose writers of his country whose works reflected the influence of the nineteenth-century French Symbolist and Decadent movements. Like the fiction of Joris-Karl Huysmans and Villiers de l'Isle Adam, Csáth's stories express a sensibility alien to the values and consolations of middle-class existence. Escape into imagination, salvation through the use of intoxicants, and a perverse fascination with cruelty are the most apparent themes of Csáth's short fiction, which is represented in English by the collection *The Magician's Garden, and Other Stories.*

Csáth was born in Szabadka, a town which at the time was within the Austro-Hungarian Empire and which later became part of Yugoslavia. As a child and youth Csáth displayed exceptional talents in music, art, and literature, publishing his first story when he was sixteen years old. Though at one point he intended to pursue a career in music, he ultimately enrolled at the Budapest Medical School. He received a degree in general medicine and went on to specialize in neurology. At about this time he also began taking opium, initiating the addiction to narcotics that would last the remainder of his short life. From 1910 to 1913 Csáth worked in a research clinic and published the study "On the Psychic Mechanism of Mental Disorder." During this period he was also contributing his fiction and essays to literary journals. In 1913 Csáth married and left the clinic to become a country doctor, which also allowed him to escape the censure of his family and friends in Budapest, who disapproved of both his opium habit and his new wife. Though a confirmed addict, Csáth nevertheless served in World War I; he was discharged due to physical ailments and developing mental illness. Following an incident during which he shot his wife with a revolver, Csáth was committed to an asylum. He escaped some months later, but when he was taken into custody while attempting to reach Budapest, Csáth committed suicide by taking poison.

The brief story entitled "Opium" provides a summary of the themes of Csáth's short fiction in *The Magician's Garden*. The narrator of this piece records the suffering brought on by opium addiction while also offering a rationale for the drug's use and a general apology for escapism. Although he acknowledges the physical deterioration and premature death that accompanies his habit, he ultimately chooses the pleasures of a drug that enables him to experience "a portion of eternity's mystery and timeless wonder," and he resolves that "pleasure alone can give us knowledge of things and God's joy." The alternative to this rare experience, in his view, is a slavish and tedious life in which pleasure itself is "merely cessation of pain" and not the positive, absolute condition "which is, of course, living's whole purpose." The blatant hedonism and disdain for bourgeois existence revealed in this piece have led to comparisons of Csáth with authors of the French Decadence. In particular, Csáth's fiction has been linked with Huysmans's novel *À rebours (Against Nature),* whose protagonist, des Esseintes, seeks to escape from the routine concerns of common humanity by means of novel sensations induced through either physical or purely imaginative stimulation. The pessimistic view of life underlying the story "Opium" is reflected throughout *The Magician's Garden* in two principal ways. One is in Csáth's creation of dream worlds which harbor pleasures foreign to waking existence, private paradises that are celebrated at the expense of what is generally recognized as reality. An example of this is the placidly exotic Egyptian dream recounted by the narrator of "A Joseph in Egypt," who explains to a listener: "You couldn't begin to imagine such happiness in real life, because when you're awake there's no real freedom." The other principal manner of expression in Csáth's fiction is more objective and realistic, sometimes described as "clinical," and forms the style for a group of stories that reveal a violent, yet very ordinary world in which cruelty, madness, and lust are the ruling forces of human life. To this group belong "Black Silence," "Festal Slaughter," "Matricide," and what some critics consider Csáth's most accomplished story, "Little Emma." The title character of "Little Emma" is the victim of a children's execution "game," which is recorded in the diary of a boy who participated in the charade and who years later committed suicide. The narrator presenting the diary remarks on its "casual, and simple, directness," and it is this stylistic quality, coupled with often brutal subject matter, which suggests to critics an affinity between Csáth's fiction and the stories of Franz Kafka, especially the latter's *In der Strafkolonie (In the Penal Colony).* The overt psychosexual basis of Csáth's stories, though common to much of Decadent literature, has been interpreted as testimony of the author's use of Sigmund Freud's psychoanalytic theories, which were contemporary with both Csáth's literary and his medical career.

In world literature, as well as among authors of his own country, Csáth remains an obscure figure. Only with the recent translation into English of his short fiction has he received wider attention. In the context of both modern artistic trends and Eastern European history, Csáth's work is now seen as representative of the declining social order and disintegrating values of the early twentieth century, a period and social climate given similar literary documentation in other countries: by Robert Musil in Austria, by Bruno Schulz and Stanislaw Witkiewicz in Poland, and by Franz Kafka in Czechoslovakia. It is in this context that Joyce Carol Oates, among others, has referred to Csáth as a significant modernist author.

PRINCIPAL WORKS

Ismeretlen házban. 2 vols. (short stories, dramas, criticism, and essays) 1977
The Magician's Garden, and Other Stories (short stories) 1980; also published as *Opium, and Other Stories*, 1983

MARIANNA D. BIRNBAUM (essay date 1980)

[*In the following excerpt from her introduction to* The Magician's Garden, and Other Stories, *Birnbaum discusses the psychology of Csáth's male and female characters, the prevalence of sadism and eroticism in his stories, and the division in his fiction between narratives that are dream-like fantasies and those which are more realistic.*]

Like his life, Csáth's stories are conflicts acted out at the crossroads of sobriety and insanity, on the borderline between dream and real life. (p. 9)

Csáth was not a "fighter", nor are his male heroes. They seldom want to change the world, although most of them suffer from the constraints on their lives. When pain and humiliation create in them a thirst for something cleaner and better, they do not set out to reshape their existence; instead they attempt to escape from it in a romantic and hopeless manner by burying themselves in dreams, alcohol or opium. Some of them strike the reader as absurd, until it becomes evident that their absurdity is just a response to an absurd world they cannot fight.

The world of Csáth's women is determined by a dichotomy. The two groups can be simply divided: the world of real women and that of imaginary ones. All his real women are creatures of middle-class society at the turn of the century. Playing their prescribed roles relentlessly, they are the backbone of that shallow and empty world Csáth, as well as many of his heroes, tries so desperately to escape. None of these real women have any aspirations, none have been struck by the desire to search for a meaningful life or even to create a more meaningful environment around themselves. Their range is the narrow stage of the middle-class world, with its built-in "safe" boundaries and inherited securities. They challenge none of the accepted values because they are the prime beneficiaries of those values. None of them is creative or even a provider; all are "consumers" enjoying the fruits of their men's labor. Their ignorance about and their indifference toward their surroundings makes compassion for them difficult even when they are depicted as victims. But they are presented as "consumers" also in another sense. In their myopic existence they consume their husbands and lovers, chain them to their obligations, sexual and other, and impede them in their pursuit of ideals. This view is epitomized in Csáth's depiction of the man-woman relationship in his macabre little story **"The Pass."** Its hero, Gratian, is destroyed, engulfed by mounds of female flesh that bar his way to freedom.

Thus reduced to the role of provider and guardian of the very same life-style they want to escape, Csáth's men create their dream-women whose most important asset is that they are *undemanding*. Beyond the romanticized figures of the all-giving dead mother and grandmother, the other heroines of Csáth's dream-world also radiate ethereal kindness and understanding. The importance of the innocent first love's closing the eyes of the dying Magician should be emphasized. Among all the women surrounding him in his "death-dream" she is the only one who never wanted anything from him, and to whom therefore he can emotionally respond. Of these "dream-women," the invisible **"Young Lady"** of the hospital room is the most completely desexualized character whose role is to heal the wounds inflicted by a "real" woman. Regardless of the cause, such as the effects of opium, sexual desire and its consummation play a secondary and noticeably sublimated part in Csáth's writing. The afternoon walk in the meadows with the dead mother and the love scene in **"A Joseph in Egypt"** are essentially the same: sensual dreams with allusions to incest. A prenatal harmony and intimacy are reestablished in them, a feeling of primordial closeness is redefined. Both contacts are temporary and unattainable within the framework of daily existence, of course.

"Matricide" summarizes Csáth's basic attitudes toward women, an approach that with the writings of Strindberg became recurrent in Western literature. The "mother" and the "prostitute" of the story are equally rejected and shown to be but the reverse images of one another, playing their *roles* in the lives of men. In the romantic vein of the nineteenth century's *perdita* cult, the prostitute is still a degree "better": at least she delivers. The ambiguous relationship of the youngsters to both women is obvious to the reader. The mother is viewed as an object to be used in order to obtain the prostitute, the other object. There is no genuine sexual desire in them; their pleasure with the prostitute is rather the delight in repeating on her body some of the experiments they have conducted on animals. Neither the mother nor the prostitute assumes real, sexual qualities in the minds of the boys. Their sensual experience remains in the realm of bodiless, fluid figures floating around them, conjured up in their dreams, unreal women and much less puzzling than the ones they meet every day, who, again, do not require responses and commitment to the real world.

In a benevolent mood, influenced by Andersen who was not particularly known as a connoisseur of the female psyche, Csáth depicts woman as a fairy-tale princess under an evil spell that bars her from experiencing the deepest human emotions. Most of the time, however, his women operate in the well-defined, narrow world of tepid conventions, following the established formula of "living a life without meaning." They see everything, understand nothing, and remain forever uninitiated to the visionary world of their men. But this may be their saving grace precisely, and perhaps their lack of needing to get away from their pedestrian existence has protected them from emotional disintegration, the lot of many of Csáth's male characters. None of his women are opium addicts, anti-heroes living on the emotional fringes of society, or people whose unused energies abort in senseless brutality. Unlike their men they are at home in the world; they are the ones who belong.

Preoccupation with the role of women is manifested in Csáth's other writings. In his essay on Puccini . . . , he points out also that the composer's heroines were prostitutes or *demimondaines,* and that torture, physical and emotional, is an integral part of Puccini's operatic plots. (pp. 10-14)

Sadism, the almost orgasmic delight in causing pain or humiliation, is a central theme in many of Csáth's writings. His young heroes torture and kill for the sake of watching pain. Whether it is the tormenting of an owl or the kicking and beating of corpses, the author maintains a detached, clinical tone of narration, and by concentrating on the details and avoiding comment on the moral implication of the events, he increases the feeling of discomfort and horror in the reader. This technique is not unfamiliar, especially for those who have read

Kafka's "In the Penal Colony" and analyzed it from this point of view. Kafka, too, achieves the ultimate terror by disregarding the victim and concentrating on the instrument of torture. The dispassionate and for Kafka unusually detailed description of the machine, with only casual references to pain as if it were merely a side effect, shocks the reader who is directed to the "particulars" while in back of his mind lurks awareness of the terrifying "whole."

Besides a major difference in the symbolic use of pain and torture, Csáth's characters also differ from Kafka's in another respect. The heroes of Kafka, having faced abnormal and inhuman situations, undergo a change. Accepting or rejecting their predicament, they respond. Csáth's characters, by contrast, remain basically unaffected, even by their own violence, thereby expressing a more profound pessimism than Kafka's.

As a practicing neurologist, Csáth made belletristic use of psychiatry in quite a different way from that of those authors who also had a bent in this direction. He handles his subject as a professional, following the inner logic of the marred psyche, and he never lets the eager artist run away with the plot. The doctor, the dispassionate observer, takes the upper hand in the "clinical" stories, which are written in a dry, matter-of-fact style, resembling medical reports more than artistic creations. Their artistry lies precisely in this controlling capacity of the author, who thriftily adds just the right amount of emotional coloring, leaving the reader to generate all the compassion for the characters and their fate.

Even when it is clear that Csáth himself is the hero of the story, this essential aloofness remains, or a touch of irony appears in addition. For example, in **"The Surgeon,"** where the person of the author actually splits in two, the younger "colleague" symbolizes Csáth at the point of becoming an addict, the older representing a doctor who has already fallen victim to his mortal passion. Both sides of the "self" are treated from a third, separate point of view that distances itself from them and watches them with bemused compassion. Infrequent though it may be, this Chekhovian neutrality is broken and the world of neurotics . . . is viewed from the inside. Even there Csáth is in complete control. **"Opium"** is an example of this approach, the story in which he presents an apology for his own addiction. It was written in the year when he first started on the drug, but its hero is depicted as an addict whose intellect and sensory perception have already disintegrated. Superficially seen, the story is slavishly subordinated to the disjointed ramblings of the character. A careful reading, however, will reveal a solid inner structure. The author is able to create the effect of genuinely free-flowing associations, while the seam of the story is held firm, and his strict control contains the message within the limits of a clinical case or report. (pp. 16-18)

Most of his "clinical" stories are realistic only in the terms that they deal with "real aberrations." (p. 19)

But are his presentations really "objective," truly "clinical"? They are not, of course. His is a studied objectivity, a controlled way of narration which, with its terseness and coolness, triggers the response desired in the reader. If the heroes wail and cry, the emotional work is done by them alone. However, when the author restrains them in situations that would call for tears, the reader will respond for them. It is an old "trick of the trade," but only the very good writer can use it successfully.

Objectivity in art is, in any event, the most elusive of norms. The choice of characters and the execution of the plot subjectivizes "objective reality" while at the same time it is an arbitrary objectivization of a subjective world view imposed by the author on his medium. All the stories involving the clinic could, and indeed may well have been versions of actual events. The author has not embellished them, but by shifting pace or emphasis he removed the "plain colors" from the case histories and gave them new brilliance and sometimes even a new, lyrical depth. He was a "humanist doctor," something that he labeled jokingly in an early writing "*contradictio in adjecto.*" He also claimed that a sentimental love of mankind was a burden in the line of medical duty. Yet in his seemingly removed style he was able to convey more love and compassion for man and his plea for a humane world than even he may have wished to.

Dealing with "cases," his prose became microanalytic, almost a psychic vivisection, in the course of investigating the inner causality of things. Later, when his thinking became confused owing to opium, this tendency turns into an overwhelming compulsion. By then details become the essential, and the whole loses its significance for Csáth.

He never strove for "totality"; most of his heroes are depicted by one characteristic only. But it is the essential one, without which the person would be someone else. He is not interested in rendering a "slice of life," nor does he aim for external completeness. The *one* characteristic, however, reveals the "complete inner life" of the person, with its internal relationships to his other ontological aspects.

Thus when Csáth is called a "realist," he can only be called a "realist of the dissected soul-space."

Two of his plays, ***Janika*** **[Johnny]** and ***Ash Wednesday,*** reflect the two main directions of Csáth's writing. ***Ash Wednesday*** is a "dream-play" with the same subject as his short story **"The Magician Dies."** In the play, however, rather than really dying, the hero goes through the experience of "leave-taking" in a dream, following a night's drinking bout. He still has, therefore, a last chance of changing his ways—which the Magician is deprived of—but we all know that change he cannot and will not. Csáth had a particular affinity to this character—a kind of *alter ego*. He composed music to the piece, staged it, and while he was known usually to underestimate the value of his stories, he greatly overestimated the importance of this play. ***Janika*** is a "triangle" drama, with a tragicomic compromise solution. The aging and unattractive husband learns only after the death of his son, Janika, that the handsome subtenant, and not he, was the father of the child. He is too weak to bring the situation to a real showdown and with the grotesque satisfaction that the other has to bear the burden of paternal grief he acquiesces in the continuing of their *ménage à trois*. Thus while ***Ash Wednesday*** is in the vein of the "magic" short stories, ***Janika*** is more in line with the down-to-earth pieces in which the shallowness of life and the hypocrisy of middle-class morality are exposed. Some of Csáth's critics actually distinguish two periods in his literary career, claiming that the earlier, "vision-like" stories were replaced by pedestrian naturalism as a consequence of the dulling effect of drugs.

Rather than accepting this blanket judgment, it should be remembered that Csáth was active at a time when most artists had "split" styles, assimilating the known models and, at the same time, searching for new themes and modes of expression. This temporary coexistence of the old and the new, true for all periods, was especially true for Hungary in the years preceding World War I. Many of the important literary trends of the nineteenth century reached Hungary belatedly, and more or less simultaneously. Thus critical Realism, post-Romanticism, early Symbolism, and Secession flourished in Hungary side by side, and not only in the writings of Csáth but also in the work of most of his contemporaries. The stylistic categories of the nineteenth century remained mixed with the modernist trends of the twentieth, Naturalism surviving longest among them.

Csáth has relatively few pieces written in a truly naturalistic vein. Only a couple of his stories describe—in a seemingly naturalistic manner—the day-to-day experience of the small-town people, the actual world in which he later practiced as a doctor. Of them, **"The Musicians,"** is the only piece whose primary function is social criticism. Csáth's preoccupation is with situations that are supra-social and point to essential human relationships. Its fascinating, descriptive details notwithstanding, **"Festal Slaughter"** is an excellent example showing how the author penetrates below the surface toward the deepest stratum of human existence. A natural aspect of peasant life is that farm animals, fed and often treated like pets, are nonetheless easily slaughtered because they are food the peasant "grows," just as he grows his crop. This duality of behavior, which has long disappeared from the setting of Western city life, is brought back in **"Festal Slaughter."** Around the turn of the century even townspeople raised pigs in their backyards, and the slaughter, like a ritual sacrifice, brought the whole household out to watch. The plot of the story is decidedly simple: the pig is killed by the town's robust butcher who, after his work is done, deflowers the young servant girl in the cellar. The girl's fate can also be viewed as a second ritual, and sacrifice.

Had Csáth written a naturalistic piece, this alone would have constituted the message. He went deeper, however, and revealed a then quite new thought: the inner connection between violence and sexual desire. The act of killing—the smell of blood, the hands digging into the intestines—all whip up desire in both the butcher and the girl; the latter, viewed from this angle, is no longer a victim, but has responded to a deep human instinct.

Whether this was just a game with Csáth or whether it was owing to his work, in the course of which he had learned to expect the unexpected, he was often intrigued with the potential energy of a story, released in an unexpected, nontraditional direction. In several of his stories Csáth picked up known motifs, or entire works, and, reweaving them, changed their *topos* and *tropes* into something entirely different.

Taking the reader on a trip from the intimately known to a reshaped reality sharpens the experience, amplifies the participation. In **"Paul and Virginia,"** Csáth's model is a well-known piece of sentimental literature, the novel of Bernard de Saint-Pierre. There the background is the island of Saint-Louis where two women, a widow and a "fallen girl," raise their children in an exotic and therefore, according to the sentimental model, humane world. The children fall in love, but because of a wicked aunt, Virginia is taken away to France in order to avoid a *mésalliance* with Paul. After several years of separation she perishes at sea on her way back to Paul. He follows her in death two months later, the victim of a broken heart. In Csáth's story the young people are cousins and thus not allowed to marry until Virginia's mother, moved by their despair, confesses to adultery. Thus the lovers, no longer consanguineous, are free to marry.

> Virginia sobbed, but accepted. I believe (and there's no reason *I* should be angry at her for it) Virginia would have let her mother go to torture had her own happiness depended on it.

Csáth's variant faithfully copies the light and elegant style of sentimental prose, only to disrupt it by the shocking confession and sacrificial humiliation of the mother. Twisting around the "formula" solution of the period, according to which barred love leads to self-destruction, Csáth shows that passion is murderous and, above all, egotistic, owing no loyalty but to its own goal. (pp. 20-5)

The most masterful twist, a very elaborately camouflaged change of a traditional motif, takes place in one of Csáth's exquisitely stylized stories, **"The Magician's Garden."** Ever since the Garden of Eden, the garden has appeared in art and literature as an inner sanctuary, a separate and secluded place of joy. In a way the image of the garden was the actual model for the development of real gardens in Europe, influenced by the architectural styles of the East, perhaps through the influence of the Crusades. The monastic gardens perpetuated the idea of isolation and seclusion while the secular cultures, impressed by the tales of the Orient, emphasized more and more the garden's function as a creator and retainer of special happiness and beauty. From the gardens of Tintoretto, Veronese and Watteau, Baudelaire and Wilde, to that of the Finzi-Continis, the garden has been a place of pleasure as well as magic asylum from the harshness of reality.

There is the spell of the magic, the enchantment of the unreal also in **"The Magician's Garden,"** except that in this story the exotic, intoxicating milieu with its sensual flowers seems to be a wicked place, a trap rather than an escape. This characteristic, and the description of its dizzying beauty, reminds the reader of another bewitched garden, that of Hawthorne's tale, "Rappaccini's Daughter," "with gigantic leaves . . . and flowers gorgeously magnificent," but there the environment and its owners interact. Csáth's garden seems to be independent of its owners and onlookers; it is empty of people and is populated only by the imagination. And this garden differs herein from others in art and literature, in that while it evokes associations concerning gardens, the story is entirely symbolic, referring only to a soul state. The outside member, the observer telling the story, does not and cannot know the garden. The streets leading to it are quaint and old—because the past is being visited. And the garden, which they all see that afternoon, is the soul of the young brothers, revealed to a relative stranger. It is the dwelling-place of all the wildly rampant childhood dreams in which the character of the wicked, fairy-tale magician is mixed with the as yet indescribable, stifling eroticism of adolescent daydreams. It is a magic garden of untamed, youthful imagination, living hidden and controlled in the adult soul, and visited only occasionally, as the dead grandparents are visited in Maeterlinck's *Blue Bird*. This is why there is no "action" in **"The Magician's Garden":** its dream has already been played in the past, in childhood; now it remains, unchanged, petrified in the way it wants to be remembered, in its innocent violence.

The garden is wicked only in its potentials. To those who want more of it than an occasional visit, to those who want to return to its dreams for good, the garden is a trap—like opium; they will be lost. It is possible that Csáth was influenced by Octave Mirbeau's *The Garden of Torture*, the only contemporary work with a similar symbolism. There, the garden and its tortures allude to life itself. Mirbeau's book, though considered shocking and vulgar, was widely read throughout the Monarchy. Its possible effect also on Kafka has yet to be explored.

The dream vision, a conventional narrative form, has been used by poets ever since the Middle Ages. In its purest type the narrator falls asleep, usually in a pleasing landscape, and relates the events as he "dreams" them. In some dreams the protagonist remains alone, in others he has a companion or guide, human or in the shape of an animal. Another of the common features found in this genre is that the plots are often allegorical.

Dream visions are frequently used by Csáth, again differently from that of the conventional form. Only a few have the traditional frame of a "formula" beginning and ending (like **"An Afternoon Dream," "Meeting Mother,"** and **"A Joseph in Egypt,"** the last relating someone else's experience). **"The Black Silence"** and **"A Dream Forgotten"** start *in medias res,* increasing the suspense by pretending that the dreams are real occurrences. **"Ash Wednesday"** is a masked dream in which the dying of a symbolic *I* is experimented with: death is masked as a dream, and dream disguised as death in an ironical, tragicomic manner. A couple of stories oscillate between dreaming and being awake. In **"Toad"** the dream starts when the hero awakens, while in **"Saturday Evening"** the dream vision of the Sandman appears in the last moments before the children fall asleep. Nevertheless, with all the different approaches, Csáth uses nothing of the traditional framework of the dream vision, retaining only its allegorical, symbolic function.

The lack of utilization of this potential in creating a background for the stories might be due to Csáth's generally dispensing with detailed "surrounding." His interest always focuses on the person and the action, and in many of his stories the description of the backdrop is reduced to a few cliché opening and closing lines, often less than a paragraph. These repeatedly and almost interchangeably used sentences usually refer to the weather or to the time of the year: a "mild June afternoon," a "rainy April night," "there was May around us," or "on a September night," are often the only details, supplied *in lieu* of background. Csáth has no need for the "support" of a background; he uses and manipulates the setting as if it were the wings in a Renaissance play, deliberately diminishing the importance of a second dimension. Thus Csáth immediately transports his reader to the central point of his story, forcing him to concentrate on the inner world of heroes.

Some of Csáth's stories, especially the ones that refer to dreams, have an expressionistic quality that after a closer inspection turns out to be so only superficially. Scientific analysis of dreams and the commercial movies came about the same time. Psychoanalysis, working deductively, atomizes dreams, while films, working "forward," have the capacity of creating dreams, or dreamlike sequences, by doing away with the boundaries of time and space. Early film was fascinated by the potential of showing things in ways impossible in reality. Cause and effect could be portrayed simultaneously, various events could be superimposed and presented as parallel happenings. This presentation of reality also required a disjointed style to match it. And indeed all the above features were displayed by the Expressionists, and also by Csáth. Yet, rather than tying him to the movement, one should identify the medium of film, and not just the Expressionist films, as the common denominator to which Expressionists, or rather most modernists, were more deeply indebted than has been so far acknowledged. True, the subconscious played as important a role in Csáth's work as the "collective unconscious" with the Expressionists. Still, Csáth decidedly lacked commitment and the attitude of *engagement* which motivated his Expressionist contemporaries. Whenever a rejection of the surrounding world is expressed by Csáth, it is aimed at the *cosmic* futility of existence, rather than the social order surrounding him.

Meanwhile, it is important *not* to overlook the film-like structure of several Csáth stories. Not just the dream sequences but also some of the "realistic" stories, like **"Murder," "Festal Slaughter,"** and **"Matricide,"** unfold in a cinematic manner, reminding us of modernist trends in movie-making.

Altogether, in terms of style one cannot discern any *one* characteristic that would be identifiable as Csáth's alone. He had little pride in his linguistic devices and molded his language to his subject matter with the humility of a "translator," rather than that of an author. His "clinical" stories are bereft of ornamentation. Their style is barren, adjectives as well as other qualifying tools of the language are used thriftily. The syntax is simple, the sentences are short and formed to create the mood of the abruptness of everyday speech. Only the most necessary information is provided, thus underscoring the terseness of the story by terseness of style. In his "magic" stories, however, his wording displays the distinct features of *Art Nouveau,* or rather *Secession,* as it was referred to in the Monarchy. (pp. 26-31)

The "magic," *märchen*-like stories reveal Csáth as a poet manqué, showing an affinity to the great artistic fairy-tale writers, E.T.A. Hoffmann and Andersen, and, particularly, to Oscar Wilde in the lyric quality of some of his prose that can be conceived almost as prose poems. In terms of "message," the escapist hothouse experience of the *Jugendstil* expresses the same alienation from the stale "Realism" of his times as do his stories that focus on aberration and violence.

Csáth's desire was to know everything and to extract the maximum of joy, and—if need be—pain out of it. What Santiago Rusiñol said about his West European contemporaries also holds true for Csáth. His desire, too, was to "live on the abnormal and unheard-of . . . , sing the anguish of ultimate grief, and discover the calvaries of the earth, arrive at the tragic by way of what is mysterious; divine the unknown." Csáth chose opium to achieve this, and also because he wanted to escape something that frightened him even more than drugs: the meaninglessness and ultimate hopelessness of existence. He may have felt that his slow suicide was preferable to a quick one. He needed desperately the temporary euphoria of opium to find living bearable, and he accepted his "Faustian" pact with open eyes. His Will emphasized that side of his character that was forever engaged in searching for the profound causality of things: he requested that his brain, heart, and liver be taken to Budapest for examination. (p. 32)

Marianna D. Birnbaum, "Introduction: Géza Csáth (1887-1919)," in The Magician's Garden, and Other Stories *by Géza Csáth, edited by Marianna D. Birnbaum, translated by Jascha Kessler and Charlotte Rogers (Introduction, selection and English translation copyright © 1980 by Marianna D. Birnbaum, Jascha Kessler, and Charlotte Rogers; reprinted by permission of the publisher), Columbia University Press, 1980, pp. 7-32.*

JOYCE CAROL OATES (essay date 1980)

[Oates is an American fiction writer and critic who is perhaps best known for her novel them, *which won a National Book Award in 1970. Her fiction is noted for its exhaustive presentation of*

realistic detail as well as its striking imagination, especially in the evocation of abnormal psychological states. As a critic, Oates has written on a remarkable diversity of authors—from Shakespeare to Herman Melville to Samuel Beckett—and is appreciated for the individuality and erudition that characterizes her critical work. In the following excerpt, Oates views the stories of The Magician's Garden *as comprising an autobiographical novel reflecting the social and political decline of Central Europe in the early twentieth century. She also divides the stories into "fantasies" and "naturalistic pieces," a distinction often made by critics of Csáth's fiction.*]

In the past several years the admirable series edited by Philip Roth for Penguin Books under the title *Writers from the Other Europe* has brought to our attention superb writers virtually unknown in America, including the Kafkaesque fantasist Bruno Schulz. Now we have [***The Magician's Garden*** by] the extraordinary Hungarian modernist Géza Csáth, whose disturbing imagination evokes Kafkaesque worlds inappropriately bathed in a rapturous hedonism. If Kafka remains our touchstone, it is only a measure of our general ignorance of the kinds of writing that were being done in the first decades of the 20th century. Géza Csáth, for instance, wrote his best work between 1908 and 1912; his depiction of the collapse of Central Europe, by way of a magnification of the collapse of the individual—the magician in particular—is uncannily prophetic. (pp. 36-7)

It is a memorable volume: though uneven in tone and quality, sometimes sketchy, sometimes burdened by an excess of dream-detail, its whole far exceeds the sum of its parts both because of the excellent introduction by Marianna D. Birnbaum [see excerpt above, 1980] and because the reader, knowing beforehand the tragic pattern of Csáth's personal life, is privileged to read the heterogeneous collection as if it were an autobiographical novel. And though it is probably true that the narcissist, glorying in his insularity, would scorn the critic's predilection for seeing cultural meanings in the deliberately private and subjective, we can read Csáth's almost unrelievedly pessimistic fiction as representative of the spirit—if not the actual public voice—of a dying bourgeois order. Csáth's persona, the magician who dies young (at the age of 29) because he prefers opium to everything the world offers—even the love of a pure, sweet, selfless dream-woman—is perhaps not so private a creation as he might have thought. As we know, there are many kinds of opium—many ways of initiating a protracted suicide.

The Magician's Garden contains 24 prose pieces, some of them mere dream-sketches of little interest in themselves, since the imagery of Csáth's typical dream is far less arresting, less individual, than that of Kafka's; there is a Technicolor lushness to the opium dream that can soon become tedious. Some of them are fairly long, complex stories that exhibit a surprising range of styles—from the chillingly atonic to the mesmerizing and incantatory. . . . Though there are arresting moments in most of the fantasies, it is the naturalistic pieces—the passionate little essay **"Opium"** in particular—that are the most compelling. Csáth's exploration of his motives as a "pale greedy neurotic" who gladly surrendered decades of his life in exchange for the seductive hallucinations of opium tells us as much in three or four pages as we might get from an entire volume by a writer like Huysmans. (pp. 37-8)

The Magician's Garden, taken as a whole, as a sort of impressionistic diary of Csáth's unhappy and truncated life, does not exactly dispel the mystery of the young man's choice of what he calls a slow suicide, but it allows us to overhear him talking to himself, obsessively and defiantly, about the nature of that choice (which was wholly conscious. Csáth knew exactly what opium would do to him). Like so many gifted poets and writers of his time—of any time, no doubt—Csáth was both blessed and cursed by a sort of hyperesthesia of the spirit. He knew so much, he saw so much—how could he act? Lethargic, passive, "insolently lazy," incapable of loving anyone (he made a blatantly unwise marriage and eventually shot his wife with a revolver, in the presence of their infant daughter), he turns greedily inward, besotted with his own debilitating dreams. One thinks of Flaubert's decision for art (as an "ascetic" religion); one thinks of Max Ernst's epiphany (as he leafed idly through an advertising catalogue in 1919) in which a sudden intensification of his "visionary faculties" brought forth a sense of the absurd so violent that he immediately embarked upon a series of drawings and paintings to express it—intent only upon reproducing what seemed to "see itself in him," to use Ernst's phrase. Hallucination or vision?—art is an insatiable devourer, making no distinctions. At such moments in the individual's history and in the history of his art it is the creative impulse that seems to insist upon expression, quite empty of moral content.

In **"Opium"** Csáth explains:

> Our face in the mirror reflects mere shapeless, stiff blotchings that have nothing to do with us, obviously. Trains pull into stations and people and horse-drawn carriages trot past in the streets. How marvelous all that is, and conducive to suffering; at the same time strange, incomprehensible, leading to the conviction that in their present forms things have neither reason nor purpose. Hence one must escape. . . . Pleasure erases contours, dissolves senselessness, freeing us from the shackles of space, halting the rattling of the clock's seconds; it lifts us on its sultry undulations to the highest reaches of Life.

Though opium eventually destroys the organs and senses it is nevertheless "blessed": health, after all, is bourgeois. If one can devote 14 hours a day to opium, one should, without hesitation, for in a single day one can live thousands of years. One can transcend time—and to Csáth the passage of time is the single incontestable horror in life. Csáth's decision for opium (and slow suicide—though his own deterioration came more rapidly than he could have anticipated), so meticulously argued, is characteristic of decadent literature in general. Huysmans and Wilde, for instance, impress us with the rhetorical orderliness of their arguments for disorder. Nothing matters except interior sensation. Unless, of course, it is the verbal expression of that sensation—and some measure of fame or notoriety in the real world that is being rejected.

Still, one wants to rescue the vision itself—or at least to confirm its authenticity as an inevitable human response, necessary (so it appears) at certain moments in history. Csáth's Austro-Hungarian empire—Baudelaire's France—Wilde's England—the America of Poe: are these worlds that destroy only the weak, or is it a matter of some curious sort of strength (covert, stubborn, sly) that the "victim" defines himself triumphantly against them? Suicide is a political act, perhaps the least acknowledged of all. . . .

Géza Csáth should be recognized as one of the significant early 20th-century European modernists. (p. 38)

Joyce Carol Oates, in a review of "The Magician's Garden, and Other Stories," in The New Republic *(reprinted by permission of* The New Republic; ©

1980 The New Republic, Inc.), Vol. 182, No. 20, May 17, 1980, pp. 36-8.

IVAN SANDERS (essay date 1980)

[*Sanders distinguishes between those stories in* The Magician's Garden *which are fantasies reflecting the more exotic aspects of Decadent literature, and those which are more "clinical" and restrained in their narratives.*]

The peculiarities of a given social reality are the chief concern of most modern Hungarian writers: yet there have always been important and often neglected artists whose work reveals an entirely different orientation. In reading the stories of ***The Magician's Garden*** . . . one realizes just how unusual is the fiction of this highly gifted early-twentieth-century Hungarian writer. Géza Csáth . . . is usually classified as a decadent, and his work does reveal important affinities with that of the first generation of Hungarian modernists, especially with the early poetry and prose of Dezső Kosztolányi, who also happened to be his cousin. But in Csáth's writings—and ***The Magician's Garden*** contains a generous sampling—we often get more than voluptuous sadomasochistic fantasies, more than typical "decadent" tales of primal fears and primal desires.

Perhaps because he was also a physician, even some of Csáth's strangest, most hallucinatory narratives are notable for their restraint and clinical precision; they contain little of the decorative stylization that is so characteristic of Hungarian Secession. . . . What shows most clearly Csáth's apparent disregard for social reality—and at the same time his departure from traditional Hungarian narrative modes—is the relative dearth of physical description in his writings. As Marianna D. Birnbaum [see excerpt above, 1980] points out in her learned introduction, "Csáth has no need for the 'support' of a background; he uses and manipulates the setting as if it were the wings in a Renaissance play, deliberately diminishing the importance of a second dimension. Thus Csáth immediately transports his reader to the central point of his story, forcing him to concentrate on the inner world of heroes."

Naturally, these radical shifts in emphasis, the unconventional narrative approach, the odd choice of subject matter may seem extraordinary only in a historical context. The neurasthenic musings of turn-of-the-century decadents don't always age well. The depth-psychology strikes the modern-day reader as somewhat shallow, and the preoccupation with the perverse and the abnormal may seem quaint, even naïve, to those who have grown used to stronger stuff. Some of Csáth's opulent fantasies do appear dated: they have a surface allure but lack the inner vision that would render the exotica truly meaningful, or even relevant. The stories concentrating on aberrant human behavior ("clinical" stories, Birnbaum calls them) remain disturbing, however, mainly because morbidity in them becomes a metaphor for evil which the author accepts with equanimity.

In one of the stories two schoolboys kill their mother and present her jewelry to a prostitute; in another a man is locked in battle with a gruesome toad; in a third a son tenderly embraces the skeleton of his father. The titles alone of these stories—**"Matricide," "Toad," "Father, Son"**—suggest clinical objectivity. Yet, like the best symbolist and decadent writers, Csáth finds ways of making the aberrant beautiful. All it takes, it seems, is an equivocal detail, an odd bit of dialogue, a strategically placed description, and the most outrageous of incidents is given esthetic legitimacy. These stories prey on the mind: their effect is unnerving.

In retrospect Géza Csáth's life and work appear to be almost paradigmatic of the brilliance and dissipation of the waning years of the Austro-Hungarian monarchy. . . . One may be justified in concluding that Csáth's morbidly fascinating stories reveal more about the disintegrating world he knew than does many a conventionally realist fiction dating from this period. (pp. 673-74)

Ivan Sanders, in a review of "The Magician's Garden, and Other Stories," in World Literature Today *(copyright 1980 by the University of Oklahoma Press), Vol. 54, No. 4, Autumn, 1980, pp. 673-74.*

TIMOTHY McFARLAND (essay date 1980)

[*McFarland finds Csáth's stories in* The Magician's Garden *to be unpleasant, shallow, and badly written.*]

The steady stream of recent publications devoted to the cultural and intellectual life of the Habsburg monarchy in the early part of this century has remarkably little to tell us, by and large, about any Hungarian contribution to the scene, apart from music and some areas of academic life. Is this because Hungarian writers are linguistically inaccessible, or because they were pursuing national preoccupations which had little in common with Freud or Musil? Some limited and rather discouraging insights on this subject are provided by [Géza Csáth's ***The Magician's Garden.***] . . .

Sensational incidents, drug addiction and mental derangement are all as prominent in [Csáth's] stories as in his biography. About half of them are concerned with fantasy states, either in the form of dreams and hallucinations or as fairy-tale stories in which the first-person narrator is wafted off to Baghdad, Venice or the Nile. He is consoled by ethereal beauties in floating garments, or threatened by disconnected events, transferred identities, and by familiar people behaving strangely. Much of this material is already familiar from the nineteenth-century literature of dreams and drug-induced states from the Romantics to Huysmans and the world of *art nouveau;* only very occasionally does it support the editor's claim that these stories reveal close affinities with psychoanalysis, the early cinema, and Expressionism [see Birnbaum excerpt above, 1980]. Their mysteries are only too easy to interpret or even to predict; they offer little resistance to a critical reading and are not well enough written to be entertaining, at least in this translation, where the strain of rendering every jewel-encrusted nuance of the purple prose is very evident.

The stories dealing with real people, on the other hand, are written in a factual, unadorned style intending detached objectivity. They are nearly all very unpleasant. In **"Little Emma"** a group of schoolboys is forced to watch frequent vicious thrashings by a sadistic teacher. After a particularly brutal assault, described in great detail, they build a gallows in their attic, and proceed to execute a stray dog and, later, the prettiest girl in the school. The two boys in **"Matricide"** get their hand in by torturing and killing a captive owl before murdering their mother, in order to carry off her jewelry to the local prostitute, who had told them to bring her something pretty. The cool meticulous detail in which these and other depravities are related, often mediated through second-hand narrations, diary entries, etc., has an obsessive and at time voyeurist tone. The comparison with Kafka (especially with the atypical "In the Penal Colony", of course) is a risky one for the editor to suggest, for the distance between Csáth and Kafka's fastidious sobriety is enormous. The link with the author's medical work is obvious, but simply to equate this clinical detachment with artistic control and achieved formal perfection is a misjudgment; Csáth's narrative style is much too close to the cold curiosity of his delinquent protagonists for comfort.

It is an unrelievedly pessimistic world that his characters inhabit, impelled only by mechanisms of obsession or by a shallow *amour-propre* [''vanity'']. There is scarcely a single generous impulse or kindly action in the whole volume. His women in particular form a very uniform group of selfish bourgeois hedonists, from whom their menfolk flee to the desexualised visions of their fantasy-lives. A social dimension emerges only rarely, but where it does it generates a little warmth, as in some medical sketches and in the group portrait of Czech musicians going to seed in a philistine provincial town. They are certainly more human than any of Csáth's Magyars, and they are victims and lonely outsiders, but whether this is meant to say anything about specifically Hungarian norms of social behaviour it is difficult to judge.

Timothy McFarland, ''Strange Mentalities,'' in The Times Literary Supplement *(© Times Newspapers Ltd. (London) 1980; reproduced from* The Times Literary Supplement *by permission), No. 4044, October 3, 1980, p. 1112.*

ANGELA CARTER (essay date 1983)

[*Carter is an English fiction writer whose works, including* The Magic Toyshop *(1967),* Heroes and Villains *(1969), and* The Bloody Chamber, and Other Stories *(1979), are noted for a rich prose style and a self-conscious Gothicism reflected in their fantastic, violent, and erotic subjects. In the following excerpt from her introduction to Csáth's collection of short stories, Carter examines the Hungarian author's work in psychoanalytic terms.*]

The circumstances of Géza Csáth's brief, unhappy life are those of a child of the death throes of an empire, of a time when the public fictions that hitherto held disparate groups of people together are no longer capable of sustaining belief. At these times, a marked tendency reveals itself for the individual to look inward for sources of, shall we say, truth, because the fragmented society, like shards of a broken mirror, reflects too many possible truths. Csáth's fiction is grounded in such a sense of individual isolation, and he found the tensions inside himself, finally, too great to be borne.

The Austro-Hungarian Empire, in which Csáth was born, was a kind of dream, as all empires are, sustained by the vast bureaucracy, paranoid as a dream, that so haunted Kafka. Many of the constituent parts of that empire are now client states of another kind of imperialism; Eastern Europe is now, in its economic and political organization, as alien to the West as the other side of the moon. But the territory eventually administered by the old empire, with its complex social and ethnic groupings, its babel of tongues, its constantly shifting borders, its states that sometimes disappeared altogether, bore, in the nineteenth and early twentieth century, the same relation to the Western European imagination as Latin America does to that of the United States today. It was the location of the vague Ruritania of Edwardian romance, of innumerable operettas, perceived from the outside as exotic, and, from the inside, certainly in the fiction of Csáth, as a loveless and sinister community of small-minded individuals engaged, sometimes literally, in rending one another to pieces.

Inhabitant of a collective dream, Csáth, the opium addict and therefore a specialist in dreams, wrote short stories comfortless as bad dreams, sometimes decorating them languorously with art-nouveau impedimenta of lilies, lotuses, and sulphurous magic, at other times relating them in the cool, neutral language of the case-book. He was also a doctor. No real contradiction here; the medical profession not only offers free access to narcotics but often, since it involves considerable exposure to human suffering, implicitly invites their use.

Csáth's short stories are an extraordinary, uneasy mixture of sentimentality, sadism, and sexual repression—nasty tales, not dissimilar to some of the fictions of the contemporary United States and United Kingdom, both countries in which the collective dream has, latterly, also broken down under the impact of too much reality. During Csáth's lifetime Sigmund Freud, the scrutineer of dreams, built up the enormous hypothesis of the unconscious in Vienna, the greatest city of the empire—which encompassed Hungary, Csáth's homeland, more and more uneasily. It is difficult to read Csáth, a specialist in ''nervous disorders'' himself, without thinking of Freud's analyses of the subtexts of human experience, because Csáth was tortured by the ambiguities of that experience.

Some of Csáth's stories center on drugs and suggest he could think of no way out of the treacherous minefield of human experience; that, most of all, he wanted an end of it—but, although death is the only foolproof way of evading reality, he, a young man, full of talent, didn't want to die, yet, not quite yet. . . . So he searched, with the diligence of the obsessive, for a life drained of the necessary discomforts of actual living. Drugs! the obvious answer; ''. . . the tiny opium pipe will lead you to where we live for the sake of Life alone and nothing more.'' It's a funny kind of life, viewed from the operating end of an opium pipe or a morphine syringe; life seen as a kind of existential freedom, not to act—but to do nothing. ''I shoot up, therefore I exist.'' To exist, perhaps, but not to be. In **''Opium,''** Csáth posits life as a kind of pure distillate of inactivity, locked in the stasis induced by the drug. The drug that does not so much heal pain as freeze it, or, rather, freeze you, so you can't feel pain anymore.

The alcoholic surgeon in **''The Surgeon''** prescribes absinthe as a solvent for time; but, opium . . . ah! Opium gives the illusion of an infinitely extended duration, does not so much dissolve time as slow it down to a Jurassic pace. ''Hence in one single day I live a thousand years. . . .''

And if this sense of profoundly extensible time creates the vertigo of Andrew Marvell's ''deserts of vast eternity,'' Csáth is sufficiently seduced by the fin-de-siècle glamour of narcotics addiction to decorate those deserts with evil flowers, perfumed and lugubrious, such as blossom in **''The Magician's Garden''**—even though these flowers are, alas, already somewhat dog-eared, since they have been arranged and rearranged by a century of self-conscious decadents from Thomas De Quincey to Charles Baudelaire. It must have been this awareness of his impeccable credentials among that company of damned souls, the nineteenth-century underground with its accessories of pipe, tincture bottle, and syringe, that accounts for one of the oddest characteristics of the unnerving fiction of Csáth: its complacency. Nobody so smug as the junky, who knows quite well how daring it is to glut on the forbidden.

There is a similar sense of complacency at his own daring in the subclinical expositions of that ''real life'' he must often have visited as a stranger. Some of the finest of these stories—for Csáth's slight self-satisfaction at his own unshockableness does not prevent these stories from being very fine—depend upon the reader's presumption of the innocence of children so that Csáth can overthrow that presumption. For he likes to write about children who, on a whim, will maim and murder.

These are the truly polymorphously perverse brats of the Freudian scenario, small beings without conscience or guilt who will stop at nothing for their own gratification, products of family relationships in a state of terminal pathology, evidence in themselves of the decay of the bourgeois-liberal underpinnings of the last years of the unwieldy Hapsburg dinosaur—though this is a point Csáth makes but leaves unstressed.

Yet, cumulatively, the activities of these children of our worst fears produce an unintentionally comic effect. As Csáth's little horrors get on with their games of cutting up cats, firing houses, lynching dachshunds, and worse, the spirit of Edward Gorey seems to hover over the narratives. God help their babysitters, one thinks. But black humor is not quite Csáth's style. He perceives with atrocious clarity the monomaniacal self-centeredness of the child, any ordinary child, who, deprived of candy, cries "I'll kill you!" and means it, though he doesn't know quite what he means, only that he'd prefer the barrier to his gratification should cease to exist. After all, most of us behaved like that, once. But most of us, willy-nilly, acquire conscience and guilt through the mediation of other people. So we learn how to be human beings. But Csáth, who perceives human society as a Hobbesian nightmare of self-centeredness, must have thought that conscience was innate (although nobody who has spent much time with small children can think that for long). That conscience was innate; and the lack of it in children is a sign of—what? Evil? The inherent depravity of the human condition?

But his "little horrors," most of them just about prepubescent, appall because they continue to behave, in later childhood, with the egotistical logic of the infant—when they have the physical means to carry out their desires. They are like those children who have been stowed away in cupboards or outhouses as babies, "feral children" who have been denied access to the processes of socialization and who, therefore, become exiles from humanity. Without conscience, without guilt, they do dreadful things and there is no hope for them, none at all, and hence no hope for the world they might grow up to make. For Csáth, evidently, has no *faith* in children, and, therefore, in the future.

Since Csáth always scrupulously refrains from referring to notions of morality, there is a kind of corrupt sentimentality about his refusal to pass judgment, about the way he describes these crimes of childhood as if they *came naturally* to those who commit them. It is as though he shrugs and says: "That's how it is." Yet these stories somehow seem to mean more than they say, and this is the point at which Csáth becomes a significant writer—in those stories of his where the flesh of a cruel narrative may be seen to conceal the phosphorescent bones of certain real terrors. Where he hints at the unspeakable—certain themes for which there was no real language available to him—by means of the unmentionable—the things we don't like to talk about in polite society. Where he hints at, for example, incestuous desire for the mother, the "unspeakable" taboo, by means of a description of the murder of the mother, which, though it may be a most humanly terrible crime, does indeed happen. And **"Matricide"** might have taken its plot from any newspaper, "unmentionable" in a drawing room but not in a court of law or a forensic laboratory. (pp. 11-15)

Woman-as-mother, in Csáth, is most loved when dead, not a threat but a memory. There is less thematic difference between his dreamy, secessionist fairy tales and his "realist" narratives than might appear. The haunting **"Meeting Mother,"** which begins "My mother died giving me birth," concerns a lovely young ghost encountered in a dream after the narrator has "come back late from a woman" (presumably a prostitute). The apparition of this beloved stranger, just as she was when she died at twenty years of age, is accompanied by exquisitely symbolist music, a harp, a flute—you can almost hear them, scored by Debussy or Fauré. In his dream, the narrator covers her "girl's breasts—that had never suckled me" with lilies of the valley. The time comes to part. "I wanted to hug my lovely mother yet one last time. She looked at me with an offended expression, but then stroked my face forgivingly."

Since this dream, the narrator has abandoned all earthly women and thinks only of his mother, who "died sighing long and hard." Died sighing a sigh as of erotic satisfaction, in fact, although in the dream she has both acknowledged the existence of an incest taboo by forbidding that last embrace yet also forgiving the narrator for wanting it.

This dream consolation of the mother/not mother, who bore the narrator but did not suckle him, who is fixed as a young girl in the amber of death, adds to the already heavy burden of forbidden incestuous desire the further spiritual and psychological hazard of necrophilia. It is no wonder, given all this, that the narrator now turns away from earthly women, who represent, apart from anything else, betrayal.

Interestingly enough, Csáth's own mother died, not in his early infancy, but when he was nine years old, old enough to have acquired a cargo of authentic and hence necessarily ambivalent memory. (pp. 17-18)

Another dreamy story, actually titled **"An Afternoon Dream,"** contains a variation on the idea of the mother/not mother, a woman who can only love after she has wept over the coffin of her dead child. (In a time of high infant mortality, this idea must have seemed less deliberately perverse than it does today.) This rambling story, with its truly dreamlike incoherence and paraphernalia of magic and wizards reminiscent of the late-nineteenth-century vogue for literary fairy tales (Hans Andersen, of whom Csáth was fond; Oscar Wilde; Hugo von Hofmannsthal) weaves around this central paradox of the mother/not mother, as if in some way attempting to negate the reproductive capacity of the woman, since only this negation will permit sexual and emotional access to her. (pp. 18-19)

There is the truly strange **"Father, Son,"** told in terms of absolute realism and most strange, perhaps, because it could have sprung from a real event; it has just the quality of those macabre anecdotes beloved of medical students (as have one or two other stories, in particular **"Trepov on the Dissecting Table"**). A young man arrives at the Institute of Anatomy, looking for his father's corpse, which has been deposited there for medical research. He plans to rescue the corpse and bury it. It turns out that the Institute of Anatomy has already boiled down the corpse and reassembled it as a skeleton, for the instruction of the medical students. The son of the skeleton takes it away in his arms. "He was hurrying his strange burden off, determinedly. But averting his eyes, as if blushing for his father."

The father is, quite literally, the "skeleton in the closet" of the English idiom. The little story recalls, in a mode of grotesque irony, how Virgil's Aeneas carries his aged father on his back from the ruins of Troy. But, for Csáth, the past is not a living entity but a bundle of dry bones. To take them away for burial is an act without meaning. Indeed, it deprives the poor skeleton of any posthumous usefulness in the world—after all, the skeleton *was* performing a useful function in the Institute of Anatomy, an instructive function, which is one of the real functions of parenthood.

"Father, Son" is a tiny but perfect image of a relation to the past, to the individual's own history, that has lost any personal significance. Indeed, the father might also stand for the emperor, the father of his people, whose authority was already, in Csáth's Hungary, seen as empty form and whose rule would collapse amid a welter of corpses with the conclusion of the First World War, in which Csáth fought.

Another story, **"Railroad,"** describes the humiliation of a paterfamilias with almost gloating satisfaction, a humiliation that has all the more disastrous effect upon the poor man because, out of shame, he decides to keep it to himself. If this is a small tragedy about the deleterious effects of bourgeois manners, nevertheless here the father is incompetent, inadequate, unable to cope with the simplest operations of the reality principle.

The father in Csáth, therefore, is more of an embarrassment than a rival or a threat. (pp. 19-20)

In **"The Pass"** the lewd, unmotherly, nude bodies of women form the actual landscape of the narrative, a landscape that is inherently inimical. **"The Pass"** is written in the style of Csáth's dream visions, but, since he does not tell us that it *is* a dream, the story may be categorized in the problematic area of the "fantastic," in which the metaphor itself is the meaning.

A young man starts off on a journey and encounters first one giant, heroic, languid female nude, then another, and then another until: "they filled all the roads and the horizon, too. Awesome, a horrible and mute blockade." Finally the boy falls, "sinking into the seductive, magnetic force." The women have overwhelmed him. The (male) narrator waits for a long time, "rigid with grief," but the boy never reappears.

It is as curious an experience for a woman to read this story as it is for an African to read Conrad's "Heart of Darkness." Csáth uses the form of the fantastic as a device to extract all the reality from the idea of Woman; these women are nothing but huge objects, alien and menacing to just the degree they are beautiful and desirable. And, if objects, they are highly motivated objects. They want that boy . . . and they get him. He disappears among them as in a swamp. I'm tempted, of course, to make cheap jokes: "Can one man be so attractive to women?" And: "He should be so lucky." Since, in this way, I can evade the real hostility in Csáth's image of a fully sexualized landscape that destroys life to just the degree that this landscape is female, as if the female was somehow not natural or as if, in Baudelaire's phrase, it is abominable just because it is natural. This sexualized terrain threatens the fragile autonomy of the boy with an erotic power that must destroy him.

Best, perhaps, to murder the girl-child while she is still pubescent, as in **"Little Emma."** A group of children play at public executions with predictably disastrous consequences for "the prettiest of my kid sister Irma's friends." The child narrator himself puts the noose round Emma's neck and helps her onto the improvised scaffold: "It was the first chance I'd ever had to hold Emma in my arms." (pp. 22-3)

The tensions within Csáth, which produced these strange tales that question so much yet leave so much unquestioned, take perhaps the most disturbing form in a story of murderous children that concerns itself not with virgin girls or mothers, but with brothers, and cracks open on that gulf of darkness which is beyond questioning.

In **"The Black Silence"** the little brother grows up "between one day and another," turns overnight from a "lovely little toddler" into a ravening monster who roasts a kitten over a slow flame, robs, commits arson. Taken to a madhouse, the boy escapes, runs home. His father is powerless to deal with him; his elder brother strangles him while he sleeps. Then a transformation takes place: "A little weak child lay in the bed," changed back in death into the darling toddler he used to be.

Or, perhaps . . . always was. For this tale is told to a doctor: "Doctor, I'm writing down what this is all about"—and its teller need not necessarily be trusted. All we know for certain, all he has *really* told us, is—that he has murdered his brother. Who is the monster, here?

And with the last words of the story, in their shocking and deliberate bathos—"As a matter of fact, Doctor, I can never get a good night's sleep"—we understand we have not been reading a story about bad children, or even about sibling rivalry, a theme which makes no other appearance in Csáth, but about insanity. About that place where life is indeed lived "for the sake of Life alone," in the frozen isolation of madness. About that black silence which Csáth, the specialist in nervous disorders, must have studied with a clinical objectivity that was a defense against his own fears, the insanity that was his own melancholic fate among the final ruins of the social order in which he had all his short life found so little comfort. (pp. 24-5)

Angela Carter, "Introduction" (copyright © Angela Carter, 1983; all rights reserved; reprinted by permission of Viking Penguin Inc.), in Opium, and Other Stories *by Géza Csáth, edited by Marianna D. Birnbaum, translated by Jascha Kessler and Charlotte Rogers, Penguin Books Inc., 1983, pp. 11-25.*

PHILIP ROTH (essay date 1983)

[*Roth is an American fiction writer and critic best known for the novels* Goodbye, Columbus *(1959),* Portnoy's Complaint *(1969), and* The Ghost Writer *(1979). Critics commonly group him with the "Jewish Renaissance" writers of the 1950s and 1960s, and his works are included among the best examples of contemporary American fiction. The three most prevalent subjects of his work—sexuality, Jewish-American life, and the role of the artist in modern society—have been a source of controversy throughout Roth's career: he has been praised for the skill and insight with which he treats these subjects, as well as denounced for what some critics have perceived as gratuitous obscenity and ethnic libel. As a literary artist, Roth is esteemed for his consummate use of language for the purposes of humor and satire. However, when once asked by an interviewer if he had been influenced by the stand-up comic Lenny Bruce, with whom Roth has been compared, Roth replied: "Not really, I would say I was somewhat more strongly influenced . . . by a sit-down comic named Franz Kafka and a very funny bit he does called* The Metamorphosis.*" This reply suggests the general critical view that Roth's essential qualities—his imagination and artistry—are influenced more by literary traditions than by ethnic experience. Roth is also the author of a collection of critical essays,* Reading Myself and Others *(1975), and is the general editor of Penguin's* Writers from the Other Europe, *a series devoted to the fiction of Eastern European authors that has already reprinted the work of Bruno Schulz, Milan Kundera, and Géza Csáth. In the following excerpt, Roth comments on the frequent depictions of violence and cruelty in Csáth's fiction.*]

The twenty-four pieces in ***Opium and Other Stories*** . . . represent about a quarter of Csáth's short fiction, most of it completed during the early years of his addiction, before the outbreak of war and the political reorganization of Central Europe. In **"Matricide"**—characterizing the two sadist sons who murder their widowed mother, then steal her jewelry to present to a young whore as a gift—Csáth writes what could pass as a précis for the fiercest of the ***Opium*** stories: "Their curiosity over the mystery of pain was insatiable." The executioners in Csáth's theater of punishment—their destructive gusto, their bestial pleasure, their delirious excitement in the violent moment—lead one to comparisons with the adolescent scenarists of Musil's *Young Torless,* Gombrowicz's aging perverts in *Pornografia,* and Mishima's ghoulish fantasies in *Confessions of a Mask.* "The butcher's coming with his great big knife," chirps the coarse fifteen-year-old peasant housekeeper to the barnyard pig at the start of **"Festal Slaughter,"** and by the time he leaves he's made not only sausage out of the sow but overcome and impregnated the young girl. The brawny butcher with the bloody knife, the red-faced brute with the wild fists, the abominable lunatic and his madness—just a few of the agents of horrifying upheaval who sweep in upon Csáth's innocent sufferers and make their settled lives "a house into which Torture has moved."

"Little Emma" may be the most horrifying story, and the most teasingly allusive: "In the Penal Colony" redreamed to be performed by children—children spellbound by the spectacle of submission to violence and the weeping of the condemned broken by punishment. "The new teacher used a cane. . . . This was exciting. . . . The class would watch the beating. . . . I stood on my toes so as to miss nothing of the sight. . . ." Given the seething feelings and adrenalin addiction of the children in **"Little Emma,"** their volatile eruptions of bitterness and envy, and the fervor and confidence with which they love and quarrel, given the healthy thrill with which they hate and how brilliantly they take to playing Hangman and Judge, the surprise isn't that they build a gallows and execute a little girl—it's that they don't cut loose on a rampage that entirely destroys their world.

Philip Roth, "'Little Emma': A Story by Géza Csáth," in The New York Review of Books *(reprinted with permission from* The New York Review of Books; *copyright © 1983 Nyrev, Inc.), Vol. XXX, No. 10, June 16, 1983, p. 18.*

ADDITIONAL BIBLIOGRAPHY

Bednar, Marie. "Fiction: *The Magician's Garden, and Other Stories.*" *Library Journal* 105, No. 14 (August 1980): 1657.
Brief descriptive review.

Carter, Albert Howard, III. Reviews of *The Magician's Garden, and Other Stories,* by Géza Csáth. *Studies in Short Fiction* 18, No. 1 (Winter 1981): 91.
Brief review. The critic comments that Csáth "seems quite a mimic, able to write as a naturalist, a symbolist, a parodist, a psychological realist," and that his stories in *The Magician's Garden* are "evocative and historically interesting."

Hoberman, J. "At Home in Eastern Europe." *VLS (Village Voice Literary Supplement),* No. 21 (November 1983): 10-13.*
Discusses Csáth's short fiction and comments on its affinities with the psychoanalytic theories of Sigmund Freud.

Alfred Döblin

1878-1957

(Also wrote under pseudonyms of Alfred Börne and Linke-Poote) German novelist, novella writer, essayist, autobiographer, dramatist, and poet.

Courtesy of the German Information Center

Döblin is best known for the novel *Berlin Alexanderplatz: Die Geschichte vom Franz Biberkopf (Berlin Alexanderplatz: The Story of Franz Biberkopf)*. This was the first and has remained the only major novel in German literature to make life in a big city central to its subject. In *Berlin Alexanderplatz,* the innovative stream of consciousness technique typified by James Joyce's *Ulysses* and the "newsreel" technique of simultaneously presenting multiple events developed in John Dos Passo's *U.S.A.* trilogy appeared in a German novel for the first time. Because it introduced these elements to the German novel, *Berlin Alexanderplatz* is thought by critics to have been as influential among modern German authors as *Ulysses* has been among authors writing in English.

Döblin was born to working-class Jewish parents in the Baltic seaport of Stettin. He attended the medical schools of the universities of Berlin and Freiburg, and though he took his medical degree in 1905, with a speciality in psychiatry and neurology, he worked for the next six years as a newspaper correspondent in Regensburg. Döblin was a cofounder of *Der Sturm,* which served as a forum for writers and artists of the German Expressionist movement, and he published his first fiction in this periodical. These early novellas, later gathered in the collections *Die Erdmordung einer Butterblume* and *Die Lobensteiner reisen nach Böhmen,* are noted for both stylistic diversity and psychological depth. In 1911 Döblin moved back to Berlin to work as a psychiatrist in a lower-class neighborhood near the Alexanderplatz, a center of urban activity at the intersection of several major thoroughfares, which later furnished the setting of his most famous work. When World War I began, Döblin joined the army as a doctor and served for three years, much of the time at the front. During the course of the war he published two novels, *Wadzeks Kampf mit die Dampfturbine* and *Die schwartze Vorhang.* Following the war Döblin returned to journalistic work and began to issue political satires under the pseudonym of Linke-Poote ("Left Paw"). These satires were later published as *Der deutsche Maskenball.*

Although Döblin had never been devoutly Jewish, growing anti-Semitism in Germany, coupled with the banning of his works by the Nazis, led to his decision to leave the country in 1933. He settled first in France and took French citizenship, later living briefly in Palestine before moving with his family in 1940 to Hollywood, California. There he became a part of the German expatriate community that included Bertolt Brecht, Heinrich and Thomas Mann, Erich Maria Remarque, and Franz Werfel. During his five years in California, Döblin became a convert to Catholicism, thus resolving a longstanding intellectual and spiritual malaise which had been aggravated by the social and political cataclysms of recent German history. The steps leading to his conversion were later expounded in the philosophical and autobiographical works *Der unsterbliche Mensch; Unsere Sorge, der Mensch;* and *Schicksalreise.* Critics have found that his conversion changed Döblin's literary point of view, and that this is evident in his subsequent novels. Both the final volume of his trilogy *November 1918* and the novel *Hamlet,* which he began writing in Hollywood and completed after his return to Germany in 1945, are more involved with metaphysical than worldly concerns. In his own country Döblin was regarded chiefly as a prewar author, and despite his return immediately after World War II, his final publications and his death were little noted.

Döblin's first novel, *Die drei Sprünge des Wang-lun,* evinces the interest in oriental literature characteristic of early twentieth-century German Expressionism. Based on an historical incident, the novel relates the story of Wang-lun, a physically powerful man who belongs to a pacifist sect but is forced repeatedly into violent revolt against the militaristic society that opposes the sect. The historical novel *Wallenstein* provides a reexamination of the themes of *Die drei Sprünge des Wang-lun,* set against the background of the Thirty Years' War. Here the emperor Ferdinand II adheres to the philosophy of passive contemplation and is contrasted with the figure of the army commander Wallenstein. Throughout his literary career Döblin's primary concern was the individual in confrontation with external forces, specifically "the individual in the face of the forces and complexities of technological society that threaten to overwhelm him," as Theodore Ziolkowski has noted. Two of Döblin's novels explore the theme of humanity faced with

the complexities of a rapidly growing technology. In *Wadzeks Kampf mit die Dampfturbine* the central character, who symbolizes workers everywhere who have become obsolete, fights against the introduction of the steam turbines that have superceded his steam engines. The futuristic *Berge Meere und Giganten* is Döblin's attempt to foresee the future that might result from this tendency toward industrial growth. The novel concludes with an expression of Döblin's conviction that even the machine-augmented powers of humanity are insignificant before the powers of nature.

In his works Döblin rejected the intense individualism of many modern philosophies and concluded that the individual can find meaning only by submitting to larger forces, such as strongly felt religious or political beliefs. Döblin expanded on these ideas in his philosophical works *Das Ich über der Natur* and *Unser Dasein*. Applying his theories to fiction, Döblin attacked the trend of the modern psychological novel, which he believed erringly depicted individuals as isolated entities, noting that a more realistic fiction would focus on the portrayal of the myriad interrelationships among people. Döblin's own novels demonstrate his concern with multiple relationships and mass movements: whenever a single character is the protagonist of a novel, that character's function within the various groupings of society is of primary importance. Another recurrent concern in Döblin's novels is the conflict between decisive action and contemplative passivity, which Döblin portrays in two ways: by bringing into opposition characters of conflicting temperaments, and by studying the psychology of a single character who embodies the opposing philosophies of action and passivity and is forced into an alliance with a group that upholds one of the two philosophies.

***Berlin Alexanderplatz* is Döblin's most important work and his most successful examination of the individual within society. As the subtitle indicates, the novel tells the story of Franz Biberkopf, an urban Everyman who becomes locked in battle with the forces of life in the Alexanderplatz. He suffers a series of misfortunes until he relinquishes his efforts to singlehandedly build for himself an individual life and learns to align himself with the mass of humanity. The novel has been hailed as an exhaustive depiction of life in Berlin of the late 1920s. Utilizing narrative methods that owe a great deal to the visual arts, and especially to the early cinema, Döblin presented a verbal collage of countless facts about Biberkopf and a significant era in German history: weather reports, advertisements, popular songs, newpaper headlines, street signs, and abrupt third-person disquisitions on such diverse matters as the operation of Berlin slaughterhouses or thumbnail biographies of briefly glimpsed characters who typify particular walks of life. The novel's chaotic narrative technique was the point of departure for much early criticism of *Berlin Alexanderplatz*. Virtually all reviews of the 1931 English translation of the novel, as well as many subsequent critical studies, compare Döblin and Joyce as stylistic innovators. Döblin's narrative, however, differs from that of Joyce's *Ulysses* in a number of ways. For example, the central consciousness of the novel remains Biberkopf's throughout, rather than being distributed among several characters, and there are frequent authorial intrusions as Döblin interjects comments directed at the reader or a character, rather than maintaining the omniscient objectivity of *Ulysses*. Recently *Berlin Alexanderplatz* was adapted as a 15½ hour film by the prominent German director Rainer Werner Fassbinder.**

Although it is through *Berlin Alexanderplatz* that Döblin is chiefly known to English-language readers, the recent translation of his trilogy *November 1918* has rekindled interest in Döblin's work among English-language critics. In the first two volumes of the trilogy, Döblin presents a close, almost day-by-day examination of the events leading up to the 1918 German revolution and the overthrow of the Kaiser, and implies that the revolution failed because of inadequate leadership. The third volume, however, shifts in emphasis. In this volume Döblin reexamined the events of 1918 from his newly attained Catholic perspective, and concluded that externally imposed political revolutions are bound to fail unless they are accompanied by intrinsic change within each person. Critics have found that this concluding work, more personal than any of Döblin's previous fiction, weakens the trilogy.

It is generally agreed that among early twentieth-century German novelists, Döblin is overshadowed by the careers of his contemporaries Hermann Broch, Thomas Mann, and Robert Musil. However, Döblin is remembered within his own country as an original and innovative prose stylist, not only for his novels and novellas, but for his satires and dramas as well. And in world literature, *Berlin Alexanderplatz* is regarded as one of the greatest novels to document the conflicts and complexities within a twentieth-century metropolis.

(See also *Contemporary Authors,* Vol. 110.)

PRINCIPAL WORKS

Lydia und Mäxchen [as Alfred Börne] (drama) 1906
Die Erdmordung einer Butterblume (novellas) 1913
Die drei Sprünge des Wang-lun (novel) 1915
Die Lobensteiner reisen nach Böhmen (novellas) 1917
Wadzeks Kampf mit die Dampfturbine (novel) 1918
Wallenstein (novel) 1920
Der deutsche Maskenball [as Linke-Poot] (satire) 1921
Berge Meere und Giganten (novel) 1924; also published as *Giganten* [revised edition], 1932
Das Ich über der Natur (essay) 1927
Manas (poetry) 1927
Alfred Döblin: Im Buch, zu Haus, auf der Strasse (autobiography) 1928
Berlin Alexanderplatz: Die Geschichte vom Franz Biberkopf (novel) 1929
[*Alexanderplatz, Berlin: The Story of Franz Biberkopf,* 1931; also published as *Berlin Alexanderplatz,* 1978]
Die Ehe (drama) 1931
Unser Dasein (essay) 1933
Pardon wird nicht gegeben (novel) 1935
[*Men without Mercy,* 1937]
**Die Fahrt ins Land ohne Tod* (novel) 1937
**Die blaue Tiger* (novel) 1938
Der unsterbliche Mensch (essay) 1946
**Die neue Urwald* (novel) 1948
***November 1918*. 3 vols. (novels) 1948-50
[Published in two volumes: *A People Betrayed: November 1918, a German Revolution,* 1983; *Karland Rosa: November 1918, a German Revolution,* 1983]
Unsere Sorge, der Mensch (essay) 1948
Schicksalreise (nonfiction) 1949
Hamlet (novel) 1956

*These works are collectively referred to as either *Das Land ohne Tod* or *Amazonas*.

**This work includes the novels *Verratenes Volk, Heimkehr der Fronttrupen,* and *Karlund Rosa*.

GUSTAV JANOUCH [CONVERSATION WITH FRANZ KAFKA] (conversation date 1920?)

[*Kafka is best known as the author of* Die Verwandlund (The Metamorphosis) *and* Der Prozess (The Trial), *two seminal works of modern literature. Janouch, the son of a business associate of Kafka, met the writer when his father showed Kafka some of Janouch's poetry. Though Janouch was in his teens and Kafka in his thirties, the two became friends, and often took long walks together through Prague. Janouch made extensive notes of their conversations and later used these to write the book* Conversations with Kafka, *from which the following excerpt is taken.*]

Lydia Holzner gave me a Chinese novel, ***The Three Leaps of Wanglun,*** by Alfred Döblin. I showed it to Franz Kafka, who said:

'He has a great name among the modern German novelists. Apart from this book, his first, I only know some short stories and a strange novel about love, ***The Black Curtain.*** Döblin leaves me with the impression that he looks on the external world as something quite incomplete, to which he must give the final creative touches by his writing. That is only my impression. But if you read him attentively, you will soon notice the same thing.'

Because of Kafka's comments, I read Alfred Döblin's first novel, ***The Black Curtain,*** a novel of words and accidents.

When I spoke to him about it, he said:

'I do not understand the book. Accident is the name one gives to the coincidence of events, of which one does not know the causation. But there is no world without causation. Therefore in the world there are no accidents, but only here . . . ' Kafka touched his forehead with his left hand. 'Accidents only exist in our heads, in our limited perceptions. They are the reflection of the limits of our knowledge. The struggle against chance is always a struggle against ourselves, which we can never entirely win. But the book says nothing of all this.'

'So you are disappointed in Döblin?'

'As a matter of fact, I am only disappointed in myself. I expected from him something different from what he perhaps wished to give. But the stubbornness of my expectation blinded me so that I skipped pages and sentences and finally the whole book. So I can say nothing about the book. I am a very bad reader.'

Franz Kafka saw me with a book of Alfred Döblin's, ***Murder of a Buttercup.***

He said, 'How strange it sounds, when one takes a perfectly ordinary idea from the world of a carnivorous culture and couples it with some frail botanical name.' (pp. 92-3)

Gustav Janouch, in an excerpt from a conversaion with Franz Kafka, in his Conversations with Kafka, *translated by Goronwy Rees (all rights reserved; reprinted by permission of New Directions Publishing Corporation; in Canada by Joan Daves; originally published as his* Gesprache mit Kafka *(copyright © 1968 by Fisher Verlag GmbH, Frankfurt-am Main), S. Fisher, 1968), revised edition, New Directions, 1971, pp. 92-3.*

JULIUS BAB (essay date 1931)

[*In his review of Döblin's drama* Die Ehe, *Bab refers to Erwin Piscator, who is considered one of the most prominent directors in modern theater and who directed the works of such important German Expressionist playwrights as Georg Kaiser and Ernst Toller.*]

The authors with whom Piscator has so far worked have at best a common idea with him, but their scripts are threadbare and passe.

Indisputably new, seems Alfred Doblin's "educational" play ***Die Ehe*** **(Marriage)** produced in Munich. This most intellectually energetic of authors knows Piscator's methods and applies them, but does not present a sentimental bit of theatre which has first to be squeezed into the new mould or cut down to it. Doblin takes the mould and builds his play upon it. He takes a screen with changing pictures, moving and still, upon it; this is his background. He creates characters, not individuals but types, and moves them about to quite un-naturalistic formal rhythms, often with ghostly effectiveness. He gives them a speech where repetition heightens grotesqueness. The fact that his form stretches into an uncalled-for breadth and that a not seldom derailment into the squalid naturalism of Berlin still further injures it, must be considered a private affair for the author to settle. It is far more our concern to note that here we have been shown the beginning of a road to dramatic form of a new kind, and that is what makes this work important. As for the contents of the play itself, Doblin points with bitterness to the material factors which in the lower strata because of poverty, and in the upper because of riches, destroy the character of marriage at its source. But in his belief in the value or power of spiritual and intellectual form, he shows himself everything but a "materialist" by reason of which he is one of the communists' most unfavored artists. In the light of this, it is particularly quaint that in Munich, this play, full of the most courageous and independent-mindedness, was banned as communist propaganda! (p. 16)

Julius Bab, "Germany," in The Drama Magazine, *Vol. 21, No. 7, April, 1931, pp. 16-17.**

FLORENCE HAXTON BRITTEN (essay date 1931)

[*In a largely negative review of the first English translation of* Alexanderplatz, Berlin, *Britten notes a similarity between Döblin's style and that of James Joyce, but finds that, unlike Joyce, Döblin's narrative does not maintain a consistent point of view or a definite meaning. For other comparisons of Döblin's and Joyce's works, see the excerpts by Michael Sadleir (1931), Andrew M. McLean (1973), Robert Martin Adams (1977), and the entry in the Additional Bibliography by Breon Mitchell.*]

If your mental and emotional susceptibilities were schooled in the literary formulas of the pre-Joycean era, you cannot emerge from a reading of Alred Döblin's juggernautish **"Alexanderplatz, Berlin"** without their having suffered desperate lacerations and fatigue. Döblin is infinitely more exhausting than James Joyce, for Joyce—if you are sufficiently educated and resourceful to snare his complicated, often tenuous or abstruse allusions—unlike his German contemporary, means something definitely comprehensible in every last fragment of a line. (Or at least he did most certainly, in the days of "Ulysses" and earlier.) And, despite his perplexing shuttlings back and forth, Joyce did maintain a point of view. This last Döblin has definitely tossed into the limbo of the outworn in **"Alexanderplatz."** . . .

The epic **"Alexanderplatz"** is, as its subtitle [**"The Story of Franz Biberkopf"**] indicates, the story of a man's life. Its narrative curve is simple: it follows Franz Biberkopf's career from the moment he steps out of Tegel Prison gate, a free man terrified by his freedom, back into the underworld, until, a mere residue of his former self, beaten to a pulp by Death, he emerges strong and good, a humble workman who knows that much unhappiness comes from "walking alone." But in the interval—through some six hundred complicated pages in which everything from algebraic formulae and official weather forecasts to elaborate descriptions of the slaughter of pigs and cattle for meat, because slaughterhouses resemble life, plays its heterogeneous part in forwarding the story—Franz has been fence and crook and burglar, and homicide. (He is thus flatly spoken of in the ofttimes lewd, always harsh idiom of the novel.) But though **"Alexanderplatz"** is unmistakably Franz's intimate story, it is told neither from his point of view steadily, nor from the author's (though more often from his than from Franz's) nor from any other definitely attributable stance. Never, except when Franz is raving mad in a lunatic asylum do you get for any consecutive period of time really inside his thoughts, and this prolonged account of what an insane man thinks about is presented, one suspects, because it harmonizes so perfectly with the troubled inconsecutiveness of the whole book's method. . . .

Franz Biberkopf is, in the last analysis, a victim of the complicating effects of modern machine civilization, aggravated in his case because his place in society is the underworld. And Döblin presents him and his plight to us as if he were letting us watch an undistinguished car card reader in the subway perusing those scattered raucous claimants of his attention at the moment when the express crashes forward to a major accident. All sorts of matters which Franz most surely wots not of appear in this essentially expressionistic account of him. And the range and grotesqueness of the materials which Döblin uses make **"Alexanderplatz"** a sort of evil smelling, Gargantuan stew in which the meaty figure of a man—immortal, unique—can be unmistakably discerned. But I do not believe for one moment that the innumerable fantastic digressions which are so characteristic a part of Döblin's method have, honestly, any significant or functional place in **"The Story of Franz Biberkopf."** They are, as it were, the author's prerogative, and they must, in a modern piece like **"Alexanderplatz,"** be patiently plodded through exactly as we plodded through those tedious and discursive chapters of the Victorian novelists. And how willingly you will do that for the sake of the illumination which Döblin most certainly offers, will depend entirely, I fancy, upon how determinedly you can pursue the literary main chance in the face of the harshest vulgarities and the most mazelike interruptions.

Florence Haxton Britten, "Victim of This Civilization," in New York Herald Tribune Books *(© I.H.T. Corporation; reprinted by permission), September 13, 1931, p. 3.*

MICHAEL SADLEIR (essay date 1931)

[In a favorable review of the English translation of Alexanderplatz, Berlin, *Sadleir notes the frequent critical comparisons of Döblin's writing style with that of James Joyce in* Ulysses, *but concludes that Döblin is the superior technician of prose style. For other comparisons of Döblin's and Joyce's works, see the excerpts by Florence Haxton Britten (1931), Andrew M. McLean (1973), Robert Martin Adams (1977), and the entry in the Additional Bibliography by Breon Mitchell.]*

It is not exactly that, in order to realise ***Alexanderplatz,*** you must set yourself to learn and accept its formula; it is not exactly that the book and its method are acquired tastes, at first formidable and a little distasteful, later a delectation; it is rather that you and Herr Döblin will "click"—and remain friends for life.

Or else, of course, you will not. The alternative is undeniable; and I daresay the majority of British novel-readers—confronted with this huge work, written in an unfamiliar and at first baffling style, dealing with a city of which they know little and a social ethic for which they care less—will be tempted to throw up the job in despair and turn to more customary, less exigent, fiction for their leisure reading.

One cannot blame them. One can only appeal to them to give the book at least a fair chance; for within its covers, up and down its four hundred closely printed pages, they will find the most magnificent panorama of a post-war metropolis yet contrived; a tale of tragedy, of tenderness, and of a pathos at times unbearable; a triumphant justification of one type of modernism in literary technique; and, perhaps most unusual of all, a masterpiece of translation. For not the least remarkable feature of this English rendering of ***Alexanderplatz*** is the English into which it has been rendered. Döblin in German is tremendous and majestic, but—one would have said—impossible of translation. Mr. Eugene Jolas, editor of *transition,* has achieved the impossible.

The busy square known as the Alexanderplatz is one of the principal traffic centres of Berlin. A large and irregular open space, from which radiate several main streets, across which grind a dozen lines of tramway, above which rise the echoing viaducts and one of the chief stations of the Stadtbahn, it stands between the business and official quarters of the town and the industrial, working class and slum areas which stretch to north and east and south. (p. 788)

Alfred Döblin has done well to choose as title for his pageant of Berlin, and as centre for its massed and turbulent action, this vital point in the city's geography, this thrusting, inelegant, rather cruel Alexanderplatz, which of all traffic centres in the Prussian capital is the most characteristic and the most indigenous. He presents the passers-by, the vehicles, the police on point-duty, the shops with their signs and lettering, the hoardings, the municipal notices, the newspaper placards. These are the surface marks of Alexanderplatz. But, moving in and out of the crowds of ordinary folk or quietly sitting in two or three cafés of their own, are the sinister but unobtrusive figures of the gangsters of Berlin. For Alexanderplatz is on the edge of the crooks' quarter. . . .

The chief characters of the novel ***Alexanderplatz*** belong to this underworld; and the book's lurid but moving story is a story of gangsters' vileness, of prostitutes' fidelity and of the terrible things which befall one Franz Biberkopf, a man who has been in gaol for causing the death of a girl, who comes out of gaol bemused with fate, anxious to live straight in future, naive, credulous and penniless. He tries his hand at this job and that, resists the lure of Communism, works harder, begins to make good. Then he is cheated by a man he thought his friend, and his simple faith in his new life has its first rude shock. He drifts to a crook café on the Alex, falls in with Reinhold (surely the coldest-hearted and most loathsome villain in post-war fiction?), is once again deceived by smooth-tongued scoundrelism, joins a gang in a night burglary, realises he is to be their dupe, revolts, is thrown from a car by Reinhold and left for dead, struggles to health again but finds himself one-armed.

There follow a few months during which Biberkopf seems likely, with the help of a rival gang, to get his revenge on his betrayers. But Reinhold is in hiding and the others scattered. Franz slips lower in the scale of social decency, but finds his first real happiness with the girl Mieze, a delicate and charming figure, a flower of the streets. They live a brief idyll, which is the more moving in that it develops from an ordinary relationship of pimp and prostitute. Then Reinhold reappears. . . . Combined fear and jealousy of a man he once tried to murder decide Reinhold simultaneously to satisfy his desire for Mieze and to crush her lover. The unhappy girl is hideously sacrificed. . . .

In the end the hateful Reinhold gets some part of his deserts, and Biberkopf, after passing through the valley of the shadow and lying for weeks in a hospital asylum, achieves some measure of serenity. But he is no longer the same man. The girl who loved and slaved for him is dead; his faith in human nature is shattered; his mind is weak, his memory gone. We leave him—a creature without past or future, a sort of disembodiment of his former self—earning a humble living as a janitor, moving indifferently amid the jostle and noise and soulless scramble of the Alex.

It would be absurd to pretend that so rapid a summary as this conveys the fundamental quality of Döblin's amazing novel. No review, unless it quoted passage after passage, could present the breathlessness of style, the mixture of sly humour, simplicity, poignancy and force, with which is told the story of Biberkopf, with which around and about him is set flickering the kaleidoscope of the capital of defeated Germany. Döblin's technique has been compared to that of Joyce's *Ulysses*, but it is finer-textured, more resilient and not so harshly insolent. He runs sentences straight on, passing from a few words of narrative to a list of the stopping places on a passing tram, to mottoes on an automatic fortune-teller, to a tailor's placard, to extracts from the telephone book, to insurance advertisements, to all and any manifestation of the clamorous complexity of a huge commercial city. He breaks off to apostrophise the reader; he repeats words and phrases; he throws in a few lines of rhyme to coax a smile or change the rhythm of the reader's mind; he is demure, violent, pedantic, impressionist, frenzied, serene. There never was a book at once so tempestuous and so controlled; never a portrait of a metropolis so bewildering yet so obviously true. ***Alexanderplatz*** presents the soul of Biberkopf, the soul of the unhappy Mieze, the souls of souteneurs and criminals and paper-sellers and prostitutes—but above all the soul of post-war Berlin. (p. 789)

Michael Sadleir, "The Soul of Berlin," in The New Statesman & Nation *(© 1931 The Statesman & Nation Publishing Co. Ltd.), n.s. Vol. II, No. 43, December 19, 1931, pp. 788-89.*

FÉLIX BERTAUX (essay date 1931)

[*In his* A Panorama of German Literature: From 1871 to 1931, *Bertaux provides an overview of Döblin's major fiction up to the publication of* Alexanderplatz, Berlin.]

It is [the] . . . feeling of the flow of vital force that Alfred Döblin's novels give with unusual intensity. Döblin is a Jew, a Berliner by adoption, a practicing doctor, a psychologist, and a poet: in him a whole cataract of personalities stimulate and complement each other. He makes no effort to separate them; he lets them all burst forth at once. They fill all his books with explosive life; their combined power bursts from every smallest sentence. There is no novelist of his generation who is more variously gifted than Alfred Döblin.

He conceives of himself not merely as a writer, but as a human being whose allegiance is first to his function as a well balanced personality, then to his profession as physician, and to whom literature—being merely the supreme pleasure of expression after experience—does not come until these two are served. From the age of twenty until he was thirty-five he postponed writing for media other than the medical journals. The power that was thus dammed up within him exploded suddenly in 1915 with ***Die Drei Sprünge des Wang-Lun***, which brought him immediate fame. Döblin had written it without changing his mode of life in the least, living in the slums of Berlin, surrounded by his patients, his books, his laboratory work, and the activity before his door. For can one not make the most marvelous journey imaginable in a trolley running from the suburbs to the city, and were not ten Chinese poems, an ethnographic museum, and a miniature garden enough to evoke the tremendous swarming Asia of ***Wang-Lun***?

Döblin thinks with his imagination, which does not mean that he thinks in images, but that his thinking is fed by the imagination. For him the ear and the eye are organs of thought. The smallest fragment of life he treats like a cutting placed in the field of vision of his laboratory microscope. His eye observes something living, something swarming with a life that he can see and render, in things which would not even arrest our glance. In that swarming of life Döblin divines and brings about order. Once he finds a place for his imagination to take hold, he explores that place completely, intoxicates himself with the multiplication of surfaces and depths; and this intoxication is creative.

Döblin's danger lay in the possibility that his creative power might fail to achieve a clear orientation, might remain merely an affirmation of a prolific energy. ***Wang-Lun, Wallenstein, Berge Meere und Giganten,*** and ***Manas*** all leave the reader with an impression of a chaos in which thought is struggling toward the light like a tropical flower still tangled in a mass of overluxuriant vegetation. That vegetation combines the characteristics of the Hindu nature, the Germanic nature, and of Judaism. But the ego remains unsmothered, even by a pantheism in which Orient and Occident are mingled. Fantasy and sensibility in Döblin are allied with too strong a critical spirit and too much trenchant will, to permit him to remain permanently enslaved by the evocations of his imagination. He has an instinct which warns him that grandeur lies in order, not in mass, and in the ego which creates that order rather than in organic nature itself, which merely furnishes the elements with which the ordering ego works.

Nevertheless the myth idea exercised a powerful and primitive attraction over him. He was not merely yielding to current fashion when in the China of ***Wang-Lun*** and the India of ***Manas*** he sought the religious emotion through which the individual finds communion with the universe; he was following the tradition of the Germany of Goethe and Schopenhauer, who felt no barriers between them and the Orient. It was natural that the German spirit, irked by the machine, should once more bathe itself in the Ganges, seeking forgetfulness of an overpraised and faltering civilization. The Asia of Döblin's imagination again represented merely one Germany seeking to free itself from the other. Thirty years earlier, the naturalists, the "moderns," had set out to combat the tendency to define Germany in terms of the German past. During the years of the World War and the Revolution, the expressionists came forward in revolt against the tendency to define Germany in terms of the existing Reich. The temporal and spiritual limitations which that Germany implied were being broken. There was a growing feeling of the need to redissolve its elements in the universal flood.

The danger of this course was the possibility of falling into the undetermined, the uncertain. In his three incarnations Wang-Lun, the Chinese leader of secret societies, asks himself successively three questions. First, is violence the only means of protesting against an ill-constructed society? Second, does not the true revolution consist in non-resistance, in uncontrolled abandon to love? Finally, violence and love having both proved ineffectual, a last question: "Is it then possible not to resist, not to speak out"? Döblin anticipated what was to happen in his own country; gradually, one by one, he saw the problems that he raised arising all about him. Neither he nor anyone else found their solution. That solution is not to be found in the forgetfulness of self which Manas sought, any more than in the futuristic vision of humanity frightened by the machine but ultimately adjusting itself to it, while seeking regeneration through contact with the mountains, the sea, and the vast universe.

Gradually, yielding to the changing atmosphere about him, Döblin returned to Occidental forms of thinking. Little by little he tended to set up the ego in opposition to nature; an ego conceived as greater than nature and not to be mingled with it. A trip to Poland showed him the power of mind to liberate itself from accidental circumstance; the Jewish community had lived in Poland for many generations as a purely moral organism, without frontiers or territory or political status or social order, and yet through war and revolution and persecution had manifested an amazing grandeur of spirit. Here was an example which argued that Germany should free herself from the set of values which had held sway in the Hohenzollern era, should set spiritual values above them. By a circuitous route, Döblin was arriving at a philosophy somewhat in common with Nietzsche, George, and the Mann brothers.

Döblin's evolution is not yet complete. His recent efforts mark one phase of it—the ego raising itself above nature, with nature conceived as including the whole apparatus of modern civilization, which should be neither scorned nor overpraised. The individual is involved in the complexities of societies and cultures, Chinese, Hindu, or European; but though he may share their destiny he also has the power to undo it. The struggle for knowledge is a tragic struggle, but it leads to a progressive self-deliverance. As the individual destiny becomes more and more internal, less and less dependent on things outside itself, it reaches closer and closer harmony with the universal destiny. It need not yield to the infinite, for it is itself potentially infinite, endowed with an unlimited power of expansion. And not merely a power of expansion, but also a power of orientation. It is here, in the question of orientation, that the intervention of the lucid mind is implied; and it is for this lucidity of mind that Döblin, among others in Germany, appeals. His effort to seek contact with Mediterranean culture represents a following of the movement toward the introduction of an element of intellectualism into German thinking.

Thought must be defended against the intoxication of mass action. In his open letter to German youth, Döblin warns against the temptations of the appeal to action for action's sake—unconsidered action, a yielding to the instincts and to political passions, a blind faith in violence. Against this revival of an old German madness he sets the clarity of thought "which is itself action, the finest and most difficult kind of action." And he goes on to try to discover to what degree reason demands approval of collective forms of human activity such as have been adopted in Russia, and on the other hand to what extent we should attempt to preserve those individual values without which humanity runs the danger of becoming a mere sum of zeros; the danger of dragging civilization down to mediocrity, of stripping it of its greatest spiritual values.

Those spiritual values exist, in a latent state, within the meanest soul. It is the obligation of a democracy to extract them from the vein in which they lie. In ***Berlin—Alexanderplatz,*** thus far Döblin's greatest novel, the hero is the anonymous masses inhabiting the workmen's sections of the capital, whom the author, in his capacity as doctor to the poor, has had opportunity to examine closely in his consulting room. He has examined bodies crawling with lice and covered with ulcers, he has discovered a thousand secret sores and secret miseries. Beneath all this he finds a strong vitality, often undirected, but demanding to be delivered from evil.

The book states a moral as well as a psychological problem. Does not the lack of moral sense, the lack of *"Gewissen,"* among the poor arise from a mere lack of psychological awareness, a lack of *"Bewusstsein"*? Goethe opened this same question when he showed Gretchen turned corrupt through naïveté, love, and good will. Döblin's Franz Biberkopf steals and lets women support him, but the reason he steals is that he is tired of being a bullied bully. He is by nature a hard worker; but an ill-constructed society disgusts him with work. And, in his capacity as lover, since his women are not countesses it is explicable that he should treat them a little roughly. Unconsciously he is an apache; but though he is not aware of his strength and cannot control it, he nevertheless has his scruples. Likewise, although he cannot recognize justice beneath the green uniform of the *Schupo,* he nevertheless has a sense of equity.

Döblin's characters do not have logical minds like the characters created by the old-fashioned psychologists. They are simple, but not without emotional complexities. They are incoherent, shifting from lyricism to humor and endowed with the biting common sense of the Berliner; but their disordered existence retains an organic coherence. For the first time in Europe a novel of the masses has the true popular accent—the language of the people, reproduced with the fidelity of a phonograph recording the hum of the city crowd. Such faithful documentation, such eyewitness authenticity, make ***Berlin—Alexanderplatz*** an extremely valuable document. Apart from this, however, the book is still no more than a splendid monster in which the elements of a new esthetic are confused in the author's mind in a bubbling mass of everything from Joyce to the inspired messianism of the Old Testament. But sheer massive power gives the work value, as well as the scalpel strokes with which the author lays bare hitherto hidden fibers in the tissue of man. (pp. 186-92)

Félix Bertaux, "From Impressionism to Expressionism—The Transition between Generations," in his A Panorama of German Literature: From 1871 to 1931, *translated by John J. Trounstine (copyright, 1935, by the McGraw-Hill Book Company, Inc.; with permission of McGraw-Hill Book Co.; originally published as* Panorama de la littérature allemande contemporaine, *Éditions du Sagittaire, 1931),*

*McGraw-Hill, 1935 (and reprinted by Cooper Square Publishers, Inc., 1970), pp. 163-205.**

HARRY SLOCHOWER (essay date 1934)

[*Slochower, a certified psychologist since 1930, is the author of psychological and critical studies of Richard Dehmel, Thomas Mann, and Franz Kafka, and has served as editor of the periodicals* Guide to Psychological and Psychiatric Literature *and* American Imago. *In the following excerpt, Slochower praises Döblin's depiction of both the social and psychological forces that influence the lives of the characters in* Alexanderplatz, Berlin.]

Döblin was born in the modern, industrial city of Stettin; since boyhood he has been an inhabitant of Alexanderplatz, the proletarian quarter of Berlin, and for many years he has there been actively engaged in the practice of medicine. The grotesque experiences gathered in this life have been the constant subject-matter of Döblin's work. At the same time, a rich and boundless imagination that roams about in distant lands (never seen), that delves into the past and speculates about the future, has thrown a veil of poetry about these hard adventures. In the same way, Döblin's idiom, often brutally realistic, is also strangely unnaturalistic, suggesting the symbolic and the mythical. (p. 107)

The leading problem of Döblin's work has been, as he once expressed it the relation of the Ego to Nature. Impressed with the formative power of external forces, Döblin has sometimes denied the possibility of an isolated self. As against psychology which is concerned with separate, "dizzy" egos, Döblin has championed "metapsychology" which holds that unrelated individuality has but a ghostly existence. In his ***Wang-lun, Wallenstein,*** and ***Wadzek***, mass-movements carry the burden of the action. In the imaginative novel, ***Berge Meere und Giganten***, man of the future, in spite of great technical advances, ultimately succumbs to the outer forces of nature. This question of the relation of the individual ego to the general collective forces about it receives, however, another and more characteristic answer in Döblin's work. It is an answer which is carried by a conviction of the divinely-willed independence of every individual (***Die Drei Sprünge des Wang-lun, Reise nach Polen***). In the poem ***Manas***, the creed referred to elsewhere as "Das Ich über der Natur," assumes epic form in revealing how man's will can emerge victorious in its struggle with nature and with death. The belief that the individual ultimately possesses the power to conquer the mass-forces that surround him, finds most eloquent expression in Döblin's recent novel ***Berlin Alexanderplatz***.

Berlin has not been as fortunate in literature as Paris; it has not found its Balzac, Zola or Anatole France. Except for E. Th. A. Hoffmann, no writer of equal renown has chosen the German metropolis for the site of his major narratives. Döblin's novel fills that gap in part, in that it exhaustively dissects Alexanderplatz, that section of Berlin which is the economic and social center of its lower classes.

Alfred Döblin is, however, primarily a poet with an emphatic lyrical strain. Even his prose is carried by an intense poetical rhythm. The peculiar interest of lyrical poets has usually been the single individual in his particular uniqueness. And in the novel before us we find that it is not the mechanism of a modern city that is Döblin's sole interest. The full title of this work is ***Berlin Alexanderplatz Die Geschichte von Franz Bieberkopf***, and the precise theme of the novel is the struggle between a complex, collective organism against a simple, single individual: the struggle between Berlin Alexanderplatz and Franz Bieberkopf. (pp. 107-08)

It is the great and wonderful art of this book to picture modern city-life in all its inchoateness and diffusion; to show how the discontinuity and restlessness, the jumble and jungle of life in a modern metropolis, the infinite fragments of information that it scatters (newspaper-headlines, posters, shop-windows, street-cars, autos, passers-by, etc.), how all its endless and various impressions play on and with the individual and dismember and disperse his thoughts and acts. (And this is done without taking recourse, as in Joyce's *Ulysses* to artificial parallelisms and unnecessary obscurities of style and story.) Döblin is particularly fortunate in his presentation of the life about Alexanderplatz; he reproduces all the finer shadings of its dialect and the "Sachlichkeit" and grotesqueness of its humor. In remarkable passages (notably in the chapter on the slaughter-house), Döblin lays bare the steel-sinews by means of which the city holds and directs the life if its individual parts. Here Döblin tells the story of Berlin Alexanderplatz.

But Döblin, the poet, also tells the story of Franz Bieberkopf. And woven in with the naturalistic descriptions of Berlin's underworld are passages of a rhythmic intensity and a moving passion. In the midst of the hard, mechanical organism, Döblin hears and feels the individual soul throbbing and trembling. And it is the poet's deep conviciton that this individual soul maintains and retains its unique power, no matter how thickly woven the web is which holds it. The general, in fact, never touches the intrinsic character of the particular. What, for example, can the formula f = ma tell us about the specific force which Bieberkopf exerted to kill his girl-friend? Or can "Sunday, September 9, 1928" reveal the particular fact that on that day Bieberkopf's sweetheart was murdered? Uniqueness, particularity, individuality, "life" cannot be exhausted by or deduced from the general, the universal, the mechanical. It is from this profound insight that Döblin takes courage for his faith: if understood, the milieu can be controlled. . . . In the end, Bieberkopf learns that the world cannot be forced to fall in with the wilful biddings of the individual, learns that self-restraint, renunciation, though a form of death, is life, learns the lesson of "Stirb und Werde". And in this way Franz Bieberkopf, the factory-doorman, emerges triumphant in his long struggle with the mighty metropolis Berlin Alexanderplatz. A spiritual force: the soul of an individual, of an ordinary proletariat worker is revealed as being ultimately independent of its material environment. A rhythmic style (symbol of freedom from outer conditions) suggests an eternal, indefinable power residing in the individual, making for freedom.

Since *Der Zauberberg* [Thomas Mann's *The Magic Mountain*] no novel has appeared that offers so much in psychological depth and subtlety. With respect to its idiom, it is perhaps as significant as *A la Recherche du Temps Perdu* [Marcel Proust's *Remembrance of Things Past*], *Ulysses*, or [John Dos Passos's] *1919*. But the intellectual import of Döblin's novel is also worth careful scrutiny. It is illuminating to ask in particular what relation Alexanderplatz bears to Bieberkopf's fate. A careful reading makes it clear that the moving principle of the novel, the force emphasized as directing Bieberkopf is the collective and *mechanistic nature of city-life in general* and not the specific *economic* form that it assumes in Alexanderplatz. Bieberkopf is an individual pressed in by the mechanical forces of city-life; his status as a member of the proletariat is irrelevant to the story of his fate. In other words, Döblin treats of the physical and metaphysical problems raised by the machine-age and ignores the social and economic issues; that is, in terms of his novel he fails to do justice to the relevant implications of the social situation he chose to present. This point becomes apparent when we consider Bieberkopf's final illumination. Toward the end of the story, Bieberkopf is confronted with Reinhold, the concretion of the "evil" against which he had struggled in vain. He has the opportunity to relate incidents to the court which would precipitate Reinhold's conviction. But Bieberkopf does not tell the court of these; that is, he abandons his former practice of butting his head against the Reinholds, the symbols of the mechanistic forces. His new method is *to go out of their way*. Mechanism need not be feared provided we understand its workings and do not run up against its blind powers with our eyes shut. This insight brings about Bieberkopf's salvation. It thus appears that Bieberkopf's ailments were not due, in the last analysis, to the environment in which he moved; it appears that his difficulty was not sociological, but essentially psychological or, if one prefers, metaphysical. The lesson which he finally learns: if we are to become masters of our fate, we must view our changing situation with understanding, involves the *inner* attitude alone. (pp. 109-11)

Harry Slochower, "Frans Werfel and Alfred Döblin: The Problem of Individualism versus Collectivism in 'Barbara' and in 'Berlin Alexanderplatz'," in Journal of English and Germanic Philology *(© 1934 by the Board of Trustees of the University of Illinois), Vol. XXXIII, No. 1, January, 1934, pp. 103-12.**

CHRISTOPHER HUNTINGTON (essay date 1950)

[*Huntington provides an examination of the three autobiographical and philosophical works inspired and informed by Doblin's 1941 conversion to Christianity:* Unsere Sorge, der Mensch, Der unsterbliche Mensch, *and* Schicksalreise.]

[***Unsere Sorge, der Mensch, Der unsterbliche Mensch,*** and ***Schicksalreise***] testify, each in its own powerful way, to the grace of God; but if you read them without adverting somehow to ***Berlin Alexanderplatz,*** you will be depriving yourself of the fuller joy of seeing, as far as one may presume to, grace at work in the life of a man. "Unless a man be born again . . ." We sometimes forget that the man who is born again is still the same man; if he were not, "again" would have no meaning, and grace would annihilate instead of perfect. *Who* is it that has been born again? *What* is it in him especially that grace has perfected? We say it now: the author of ***Berlin Alexanderplatz*** was not just a brilliant, vigorous, voluble writer; he was, certainly, all of that and more—an author who *loved* his characters. He loved them not as creatures of his own imagination but as true and worthy representatives of people as they really are.

Now undeniably, ***Berlin Alexanderplatz*** abounds in episodes of the most sordid kind; but the book is written with no sordid slant. The characters treat each other at times with the utmost violence; but Döblin uses no violence upon them. Nor does he ever—and this is a great point—allow for a moment the implication that life uses violence upon them, though this is what Biberkopf, the hero, repeatedly supposes. It is not life that is violent, not even the underworld life of east Berlin; it is we ourselves. Periodically, as Biberkopf suffers the most harrowing setbacks, injuries, and betrayals, Döblin takes time out to talk directly to the reader. You think this has been bad, he says; well, it is going to get far worse; Biberkopf will be crushed utterly, yes utterly. But still I say to you, there is no reason to despair!

No reason to despair! A hair's breadth of wavering from the true inner course of this novel, and this ever recurring refrain might seem like the bitter taunt of a cynic. The lesson in store for anyone who takes it as such is Biberkopf's final awakening. He emerges from an all but mortal physical and mental illness so completely silenced by his "conversation with death" that the world considers him not to have regained his sanity. But he knows what he has learned: it will not do to make demands upon life without stopping to think what demands life has a right to make upon us; self-assertion is not everything; there is something outside us to the requirements of which we must be obedient. One might have written over this novel, in 1929, "Except the seed fall to the ground and die . . ." In 1950, one must write it. (p. 60)

No doubt all Germany, in 1933, thought it had seen the last of Alfred Döblin. He had left the country, and the Nazis had burned ***Berlin Alexanderplatz.*** The book and the man, whether you knew anything about them or not, became bywords for everything "too realistic" in literature, whether you had read it or not. A man who wrote fearlessly of Berlin lowerclass life, who had Jewish blood, who might say a good word for Freud or take an interest in communism—such a man was done for. What nobody reckoned with was that in the summer of 1941, in Hollywood, Alfred Döblin, together with his wife and youngest son, would be received into the Catholic Church. Thus did God prepare for Germany one of her biggest postwar surprises: the return of Alfred Döblin, as enterprising as ever at seventy, untiringly militant for Christ. And like Christ he has—what on the natural level is nothing for him—"compassion for the multitude.". . .

[***Unsere Sorge, der Mensch (Man, Our Worry and Concern)***] has four parts: "The Towers of Babel," "Man's Intermediate World," "The Ages of World History," and "God's Care and Concern for Man." Man as such, and twentieth century man, are exposed to full view. There are some masterly characterizations—of those, for instance, who seek their all in riches. As I see it there are three main points to the book. The first is that

> man makes his appearance as part of a system. The system involves him in tensions, and it is his greatness that he brings to these tensions. Everything that happens within us, everything we do, everything which we bury within ourselves, all starts and all completions, all actions and all results—all this is something in the world and has some significance in the system. It is, it is there, really and truly there. We are clearly told that God has counted every hair on the head of man, and this means: man not only is there, he is there in his worth and dignity, in the system of this existence.
>
> (p. 61)

The second point is that God really does care and has shown that He does by His direct intervention in our history. Beautiful use is made of the lines from the Holy Saturday *Exultet* (misprinted as *Exultas*): "It availed us nothing to be born, unless it had availed us to be redeemed."

Some will perhaps find the style too assertive. The finality, however, which Döblin allows himself is never unreferrable to that of Him Who taught "as one having authority." What gives a new stamp to the sureness of touch and adroitness of penetration which have characterized Döblin's writing from the beginning is the real discovery of the Gospel by one who—as a fortune teller once told him—is constantly on the *quivive*. The freshness and alertness are still there; so is the lesson of Biberkopf's humiliation. What is new is the Faith to which in all simplicity and directness Döblin's own humility has at last come home. There is one who was humble from the start and needed no humiliation: "Behold the handmaid of the Lord." In her humility the place of man in the system and God's care for man are brought together. So if you would strengthen your soul—and this is the third point—"make yourself gentle, make yourself small, make yourself still smaller, and in the silence you will find all that you are seeking."

In Döblin's case, this process led him to a Jesuit parish rectory in Hollywood. A few pages of ***Schicksalreise* ("Fateful Journey")** describe the well being which came over him and his wife as they sat and let themselves be told of the Faith. No perfunctory instructions these, but long and quiet conversations, prepared for and absorbed in intervals of careful thought and extensive reading. (pp. 61-2)

***Der unsterbliche Mensch* ("Immortal Man")** is remarkable above all for its patience. Patience! Patience is what it takes to proceed step by step, thought by thought, inference by inference (as, it sometimes seems, only a German can do) through the realm of reason alone, then the realm of reason and faith, into the realm of faith alone.

The book is in the form of a dialogue, with occasional monologues and interchange of letters. An older man, a believer, allows a younger man, an unbeliever, to come and converse with him about religion. Only very gradually do the younger man's eyes open to the position he must face: God is Person! Jesus of Nazareth is God!

There are many beauties to this work. The gentleness, warmth, sympathy, and—one cannot say it often enough—patience with which the whole development is handled bespeak a superlative degree of understanding of what must be expected of every apostle: a practical working knowledge of human psychology, a practical working knowledge of what it means to have to learn to think as a Catholic, and a practical working knowledge of the theology of grace. The dialogue is much more than a dressed up tract of apologetics. It is living account, in terms of intellect and will, reason and revelation, history and eternity, of a conversion—without any question, Döblin's own. (p. 62)

In one way, the last of these three books, ***Schicksalreise,*** is the least forceful; its coherence suffers inevitably from the chronological arrangement. But it is much more than a recital of the events in Döblin's life from 1940 to 1948. The substance of the book is the reliving of a whole lifetime of enthusiasms and disappointments, and each new difficulty in the path of the refugee provides a new occasion for a comprehensive retrospect. (p. 63)

Schicksalreise, while mainly an internal account, is by no means wholly so. There are some fine descriptions of scenery, no less impressive for the interpretative touch. Niagara Falls, for instance, "never heard nothing about no culture." (p. 64)

Christopher Huntington, in a review of "Unsere Sorge, der Mensch," "Der unsterbliche Mensch: Ein Religions-gespräch," and "Schicksalreise: Bericht und Bekenntnis," in Renascence *(© copyright, 1950, Marquette University Press), Vol. III, No. 1, Autumn, 1950, pp. 59-64.*

JAMES H. REID (essay date 1967-68)

[In a political interpretation of Alexanderplatz, Berlin, *Reid finds that Döblin presented the course of Franz Biberkopf's life as a parallel with the political development of Germany following the First World War.]*

In the course of Alfred Döblin's novel ***Berlin Alexanderplatz*** Franz Biberkopf receives three blows from what seems to be 'Fate': he is betrayed by his friend Lüders, he loses an arm in a quarrel with a gang of criminals, and Mieze, whom he loves, is murdered. Finally, however, the murderer is brought to justice, and Biberkopf finds employment in a factory. In the concluding pages the narrator points the moral of his story. Through his powers of reason and by uniting with the rest of humanity man can to a large extent overcome 'Fate'; if Biberkopf had realized this earlier his misfortunes might have been avoided. This epilogue has been found by many commentators to contradict the rest of the novel. . . . But if the close of the novel holds a political message, then surely the earlier political elements must take on fresh meaning. Conversely, if Biberkopf's career can be shown to be of political significance, the ending will appear consistent with the chapters which precede it.

One main objection to this interpretation must be anticipated. The 'Totentanz' passage . . . expressly relativizes all political movements, especially socialist ones. A number of historical situations portray the triumph of Death. The cries of 'Vive l'Empereur' during Napoleon's retreat from Moscow and the words of 'Die Wacht am Rhein' sung at Langemarck and the Chemin des Dames during the First World War are shown to be hollow and vain: Death is the only victor. Religious martyrdom, too, merely illustrates the triumph of Death. Finally there is a Dance of Death, in which Death is followed, not by the classes and professions as in medieval depictions of it, but by the many attempts at reforming human society: the French Revolution, the Russian Revolution, the Peasant Wars—also an abortive social revolution—and the Anabaptists, who attempted to inaugurate a form of primitive communism in Münster in 1534-35. (pp. 214-15)

It is true that death, and not a political doctrine, represents ultimate reality in the novel. Biberkopf is accused of wishing to 'preserve' himself. . . . Death is a metaphysical principle: in death Biberkopf becomes one with the universe . . . , expiating the *crimen individuationis*. But, just as the medieval Dance of Death had a social message, that of the equality of all, so death in ***Berlin Alexanderplatz*** has also a socializing function: after his symbolic death Franz re-enters society as one who will no longer insist on his individual self, but will show solidarity with his fellows. The vanity of human aspirations is not the only message of the Dance of Death—if it were, one might ask why the author should emphasize the didactic nature of the novel so strongly. Döblin insists throughout the novel—and not merely at the close . . .—that man is distinguished by his 'Vernunft', his power to analyse a situation and take steps to control it. The provocative headings of the slaughter-house descriptions . . . should not mislead one into supposing this to be Döblin's last word on the nature of man. On the contrary, these words apply only to Biberkopf, who has so far refused to use his 'Vernunft' and is accordingly incapable of avoiding the series of blows from 'Fate' . . . which the novel describes. This is made clear in the conversation with Job interpolated between the two descriptions of the slaughter-house proceedings. . . . Job wishes either to be free and all-powerful, like God, or to have no mind at all, to submit unquestioningly and unthinkingly like the beasts in the slaughterhouse. Neither of these courses is permissible: he must submit to the will of God, but *knowingly,* willing God's will from a position of understanding. . . . The hierarchy of powers . . . can be detected elsewhere in the novel. Death is the ultimate power, at whose approach even the strongest natural forces, the 'Sturmgewaltigen', are still. . . . The latter are most prominent at the scene of Mieze's death. . . . Man is weak when compared with the natural elements. But there are other spheres over which he does have control, the social and political spheres, and it is these which are Döblin's particular concern in ***Berlin Alexanderplatz.***

In the first place it is important to realize just how 'historical' ***Berlin Alexanderplatz*** is. Not only is it given an exactly identifiable place-setting . . . , but there are also exact references to the time of the action throughout. The novel, published in 1929, covers the period autumn 1927 to the spring of 1929. These are not merely abstract figures. Reference is made to historical events and figures of the time. . . . More important, however, is the historical atmosphere of the novel. Outwardly the period covered was one of relative economic and political stability. . . . Germany had regained international standing, while at home unemployment fell to 650,000 in the summer of 1928 and real wages had been rising steadily since 1925. . . . The economic situation is reflected in the novel, mainly through reference to the frenzied building activity going on at the Alexanderplatz. After four years in prison Biberkopf finds this particularly striking. . . . That unemployment is not as disastrous as it was to become is implied by the relative ease with which Biberkopf finds a job on release from prison. But Döblin's novel goes deeper than the mere outward signs of prosperity. It is obvious that there has been no social revolution. . . . But the most striking social aspect of the novel is the criminality of its characters. As far as ***Berlin Alexanderplatz*** is concerned, society consists mainly of burglars, prostitutes, souteneurs, pickpockets and armed bandits. The 'honest' people are exceptions. This in itself is a social, indeed a political comment on the Weimar Republic in 1928. . . . Not only is the criminal an ordinary member of society, but conversely the apparently honest, ordinary members of society may well be criminals. And so the 'Pums-Bande' is portrayed as a gang of criminals organized according to strict capitalist principles. . . . (pp. 215-18)

It is against the background of this society that Franz Biberkopf's career is traced. Can it, however, be claimed that this society is being criticized from a particular *political* standpoint and is this political standpoint contained in the pages of the novel itself? Only then can ***Berlin Alexanderplatz*** be justifiably called a political novel.

Initially Biberkopf is 'ein Mann anfangs 30' ['a man in his early thirties']. . . . He is old enough therefore to have taken part in the First World War. Although he blames the experience of the trenches for his impotence . . . and appears to have deserted at Arras with his Communist friend Georg Dreske out of dissatisfaction with the politics of the war . . . , he has retained much of the Prussian military code of values which can be seen to have contributed to Hitler's success in 1933 and thereafter. The keywords of his outlook are 'Haltung' ['bearing'] . . . , 'Ordnung' ['order'] . . . , 'Disziplin' ['discipline'] . . . , 'Zusammennehmen und Durchhalten' ['control'] . . . , 'Ruhe' ['peace'] . . . , and especially 'anständig' ['respectability']. . . . The first four of these terms are typically military values. No thinking is expected of the individual soldier; at best the thinking is done by the commanding officer and discipline and morale are expected to ensure automatic obedience. This mentality is criticized by Döblin, as is clear from the concluding pages of the novel. . . . (p. 218)

Biberkopf's desire for 'Ruhe', a similarly unthinking acceptance of the *status quo,* is more directly political in significance, as it is connected with the important leitmotiv of 'Die Wacht am Rhein', whose most frequently quoted line in the novel is: 'Lieb Vaterland, magst *ruhig* sein,' ['Beloved Fatherland, may you be peaceful']. . . . This patriotic song, particularly popular between 1870 and 1918—in the 'Totentanz' chapter we hear a snatch of it being sung during the First World War . . .—at once associates Biberkopf with nationalist elements in the Weimar Republic, especially those who were against the abandonment of Germany's claim to Alsace-Lorraine. Biberkopf's conception of 'Ruhe' thereby takes on a highly problematic tinge: the 'Ruhe' of 'Die Wacht am Rhein' is that imposed by a victor on a subjugated land. He sings the opening lines of it in the courtyards on his discharge from prison. . . . It reappears—ironically—during his encounter with a prostitute. . . . In an altercation with a group of Communists Biberkopf provocatively sings the first stanza . . . ; here it is directly opposed to the 'Internationale.' . . . It recurs each time after Biberkopf has suffered a blow from 'Fate': after Lüders's betrayal, when he has decided to abandon his attempt at earning an honest living . . . , and after the loss of his arm. . . . In all of these cases Biberkopf's self-assertion is involved. . . . By associating each important stage of Biberkopf's career with this nationalistic song, Döblin implies that Biberkopf's career should be interpreted allegorically in terms of the political development of Germany since the war. After four years of punishment for 'Totschlag' . . . , Germany has become strong and potentially dangerous again. The narrator's warning to all those 'denen es passiert wie diesem Franz Biberkopf, nämlich vom Leben mehr zu verlangen als das Butterbrot' ['who, like this Franz Biberkopf, ask more of life than a piece of bread and butter' (see excerpt above, 1929)] . . . , is directed at the State itself. Döblin does not, of course, mean that one should ask for no more than one's bread and butter; but once one's bread and butter is guaranteed and one is able to look further afield, one must be quite clear about what one ought to look for. People are no longer starving, but this does not justify Germany's striving to become powerful again. . . . (pp. 218-19)

The picture which emerges from a study of Biberkopf's outlook and values is that of a man essentially unpolitical, but unpolitical in a way liable to make him susceptible to nationalist and especially Nazi propaganda. This is confirmed by his development in the novel. Previously he had been a Communist, taking part in the annual pilgrimage to the graves of Karl Liebknecht and Rosa Luxemburg in the Friedrichsfelde cemetery. . . . But he has become disillusioned; the Revolution has failed in his opinion for, significantly, lack of discipline and leadership. . . . His final break with his Communist friends comes when he defiantly sings 'Die Wacht am Rhein' at them. . . . By now he has turned Nazi. . . . It cannot of course be claimed that Franz is a doctrinaire Nazi; few Germans ever were. He is basically unpolitical. . . . Although thereafter there is no mention of specific political movements in Franz's life, it is significant that he finally allies himself with the Pums gang, as we have seen, a 'capitalist' organization. . . . As criminals, feeding on the riches of others, they are as much part of the capitalist system as the stock exchange itself. The criticism that Franz's own experience could not have taught him the solidarity preached at the close is therefore invalid: he has sought it in the wrong places.

Biberkopf finally learns to abandon his unthinking, individualist self-assertion and join the working community . . . , enjoying and respecting the solidarity of the workers. . . . He suddenly develops an interest in politics. . . . As so much space is devoted to the anarchist episode . . . , we may infer that this encounter is just as important for the novel as the episodes which have been accentuated by most commentators—the conversation with Job, the slaughter-house descriptions and the story of Isaac—and that the anarchist is Döblin's mouthpiece in ***Berlin Alexanderplatz.*** The warning he gives is one of the many opportunities to 'learn and repent' . . . that Franz receives. Döblin himself was sympathetic towards anarchism. . . . He was a non-Marxist, but a member of the left-wing USPD for a time. The essay 'Kannibalisches', written shortly after the war, expresses violent opposition to the new State, which has missed the opportunity of achieving a genuine revolution; Germany is now merely a 'kaiserliche Republik', still preoccupied with upholding the State at the expense of its individual citizens. The polemic of the anarchist against the State in ***Berlin Alexanderplatz*** is very reminiscent of Döblin's earlier attacks. . . . It is therefore not fortuitous that some of the central ideas of ***Berlin Alexanderplatz*** are expressed by an anarchist.

An appreciation of the anarchist episode also throws light on the mysterious figure of Reinhold. He too had once been committed to a political cause. . . . This curious detail associates him with the figure of Paul, the leader of an anarchist group in Döblin's later novel ***Pardon wird nicht gegeben.*** But Reinhold has abandoned politics completely. He is a renegade anarchist; the fascination he holds for Franz is therefore particularly ominous. Franz tries to 'educate' him in accordance with his ideas of 'Ordnung'. . . ; the result is merely that Reinhold, whose violent impulses have been dormant since he abandoned politics, takes to drink and eventually murders Mieze. The violence which once had political meaning becomes 'die kalte Gewalt' ['cold force'] . . . amoral and unthinking.

Finally, when the anarchist episode is seen as central, the implications of the formal qualities of the novel at once become clear. The basic thesis of Döblin's **'Der Bau des epischen Werks',** published in the same year as ***Berlin Alexanderplatz,*** is that of the author's freedom to tell his story not according to previous traditions but according to the nature of what he has to tell. Just as Biberkopf learns that his conception of 'Ordnung' was an artificial one, involving discipline imposed from without, and that true social order consists in the voluntary decision of each individual to combine with his fellows, so in composing the novel Döblin rejects the traditional 'orders' of plot, characterization, a uniform narrative standpoint, even the normal conventions of syntax. At the same time . . . the chaos of the novel is only apparent. . . . The techniques of montage and association are the natural means of expression of a novel in which anarchism, but not anarchy, is the dominating principle. (pp. 220-23)

James H. Reid, "'Berlin Alexanderplatz'—A Political Novel," in German Life & Letters, *n.s. Vol. XXI, 1967-68, pp. 214-23.*

THEODORE ZIOLKOWSKI (essay date 1969)

[Kathleen Komar (see Additional Bibliography) cites Ziolkowski's study excerpted below as "a major step in the examination of" the structure of Alexanderplatz, Berlin. *Ziolkowski discerns the triadic pattern of classical tragedy in* Alexanderplatz, Berlin, *exemplified by the three great misfortunes suffered by Franz Biberkopf, each of which is brought about by Biberkopf's pride and willfulness.]*

Döblin was fascinated by facts, and facts of every conceivable kind have found their way into his novels. His narrator and characters refer to contemporary events—speeches in the Reichstag, international politics, sports events, performances in local theaters; they sing snatches of popular songs, tell current jokes, and mention familiar commercial products. And even beyond this, Döblin has incorporated great unassimilated chunks of factual matter into his text. He lists, for instance, all the stops of various streetcar lines, and his topographical data are so precise that a reader with a detailed map of Berlin can follow the action from street to street at any point in the novel. He cites birth and death statistics for 1928 as well as stock-market quotations. We catch glimpses of advertisements in shop windows, restaurant menus, and newspaper headlines. . . . And from all these facts and countless others, there emerges an immensely vivid and objective image of Berlin between the two world wars, forming the basis of what critics commonly regard as the finest metropolitan novel in German literature.

Döblin has been obsessed with facts in all his works. . . . Any reader familiar with Döblin's earlier works might have expected to find these same elements in ***Berlin Alexanderplatz*** as well. In ***The Three Leaps of Wang-Lun (Die Drei Sprünge des Wang-Lun,*** . . .), a novel dealing with a revolt in China in 1774, Döblin had copied out long lists of Chinese names, of jewels, animals, plants, cities; he had included copious excerpts from reference works on the customs, dances, and clothing of that time and place. What is new in ***Berlin Alexanderplatz*** is not the sheer obsession with facts, but their sources and the manner in which they are used.

Döblin was a prolific writer, but as a result of the great and immediate success of ***Berlin Alexanderplatz***—due in large measure to the shock value of the criminal milieu he portrayed—most people think of him as a one-book author. "People pinned me down to ***Alexanderplatz,*** which was commonly misunderstood as being nothing but a portrayal of the underworld of Berlin," Döblin later had reason to complain. This novel was the first work in a number of years in which he had treated present-day society rather than the historical past or imaginary utopias. (pp. 101-03)

In ***Berlin Alexanderplatz,*** written when he was almost fifty, Döblin turned to the city that he knew and loved so well: here the facts and documents were provided not by libraries and archives but by the city that crowded in upon him from every side. And the people in his novel were not historical or imaginary figures from remote civilizations, but gangsters, pimps, prostitutes, and the entire colorful pageant of the lower-class society with which Döblin was so intimately acquainted. . . . ***Berlin Alexanderplatz*** was written directly out of his own experience. Döblin turned to the everyday reality of contemporary Berlin with precisely the same fascination and objectivity that had motivated him when he was culling information on China and India in the reading rooms of libraries and archives. (pp. 103-04)

Döblin's earliest publications were an experimental one-act drama, **"Lydia und Mäxchen,"** . . . which bears a certain resemblance to the plays of Pirandello, and an essay entitled **"Discourses with Calypso on Music and Love."** . . . But he made his literary mark with a series of stories originally published in [Herwarth] Walden's expressionist journal *Der Sturm* and subsequently printed together under the title ***The Murder of a Marigold (Die Ermordung einer Butterblume*** . . .). But Döblin's "expressionist" phase was of no great duration. The *Sturm* group was perplexed by his first novel, ***The Three Leaps of Wang-Lun,*** and events tended to lead him away from his literary associates. (p. 105)

First there was the physical separation of the war years, which Döblin spent as a military doctor on the western front, within hearing of the cannon at Verdun. But more essentially: Döblin was not just a writer; he was a psychiatrist and neurologist with a busy practice on the proletarian east side of Berlin. Finally, like certain of his contemporaries—Gottfried Benn, Robert Musil, Hermann Broch—he was an intellectual with a serious commitment to science. . . . For Döblin this meant that the novels he turned out during these years were variations on the central theme expressed in **"The Self over Nature,"** . . . his reflections on the philosophy of nature, in which he examined the increasingly complex situation of the individual threatened by the forces of nature and society. These were problems that thrust themselves upon Döblin daily in his work with the sick and the underprivileged during the inflation years in one of the greatest urban centers of Europe. . . . These social implications are directly related to Döblin's political activity. After the revolution of 1918-1919 he left the Social Democrat Party and published a volume of political satires (***The German Masquerade Ball*** . . .), in which he pleaded for a socialism free of Marxism and communist regimentation. For Döblin was concerned—as a doctor, as a scientist, as a political being, as a writer—with the individual in the face of the forces and complexities of technological society that threaten to overwhelm him. This was nowhere more apparent than in the Berlin of the twenties. Thus Döblin became ever more firmly convinced of the social responsibility of the writer, whose obligation it is to work toward a better society by unmasking the evils that permeate the present one.

All of these elements went into ***Berlin Alexanderplatz.*** In his fascination with the city, Döblin reflected in part the trend of the times. The city had played a certain role in a few earlier works: for instance, in [Ranier Maria Rilke's] *The Notebooks of Malte Laurids Brigge,* where it catalyzed Malte's fear and his subsequent quest for meaning. But ***Berlin Alexanderplatz*** was the first, and still remains probably the greatest, evocation of the city for its own sake in German literature. The new awareness of the city as a force in the lives of men emerged largely with the artists and writers associated with *Der Sturm* and expressionism: Oskar Kokoschka, Ernst Ludwig Kirchner, George Grosz, and Max Beckmann. It is evident in Brecht's early plays (e.g., *In the Jungle of the Cities,* 1923) and in the poetry of Georg Heym. But for his own presentation of the modern urban pandemonium Döblin evolved a radically new and characteristic style.

Technically, Döblin's novel displays certain parallels with John Dos Passos' *Manhattan Transfer* (1925; German translation, 1927) and with Joyce's *Ulysses,* which Döblin read and reviewed in 1928 when he was already well along in his own novel. The techniques of montage and collage, the device of interior monologue, the concern with the struggle of man against the city, as well as other common themes and methods, put these three works into the same general category. And yet, as we shall see, there are vast differences between them as well. . . . Indeed, Döblin was more profoundly influenced by nonliterary media: by the montage effects, the short scenes, and rapid shifts of perspective of the film; by the new acoustical effects of radio, in which he was an ardent and early experimenter; and by the dadaist collages of such painters as Kurt Schwitters, which Döblin knew from the pages of *Der Sturm.*

The overwhelming impression that we receive from ***Berlin Alexanderplatz*** is one of discontinuity. The rapid shifts of focus from section to section, from paragraph to paragraph, indeed, even within the same sentence, represent an attempt to capture the full horizontal scope of the city in all its aspects and to render in its simultaneity the chaos of the city.

This horizontal thrust is complemented by a vertical element. Döblin is not only interested in conveying the simultaneity of all facets of city life; he also believes, mystically, that the present moment necessarily contains within it the past and future. . . . This accounts for such anticipations of the future as the narrator's disquisition on a fourteen-year-old boy who gets into a streetcar. The boy, we learn, will become a plumber, father seven children, and die at the age fifty-five; we are even provided with the text of the obituary notice that will appear in the newspapers some forty years hence. But more important: Döblin's sense of vertical simultaneity accounts for the frequent passages in which the past is meaningfully incorporated into the present. Thus stories from the Bible as well as from Greek myth are introduced as a specific reflection of the present action. The theme of sacrifice, which must be discussed later, first occurs in a series of sections in which the story of Job alternates with reports of activities in the slaughterhouses of Berlin.

This conception of horizontal and vertical simultaneity has important consequences for the form of the novel. In his revealing essay on **"The Structure of the Epic Work"** Döblin argues, in opposition to customary aesthetic theory, that the epic does not relate past action; rather, it represents or renders the present. In this connection the tense used is immaterial and can be varied at liberty. (Indeed, Döblin jumps easily from past to present and back in the course of a single paragraph.) The narrator must always write as though the events being portrayed were taking place at that very moment; he is not allowed the elevated standpoint of the omniscient narrator of traditional epic, who knows in advance the course of his story and how it is going to end.

This conception has radical implications for the role of the narrator as well. The novel does not have any single unified narrative point of view, but literally dozens of different narrative voices. At times the narrator withdraws behind the reporting of factual statements: weather reports, advertisements, newspaper headlines, et cetera. At other times he politely addresses the reader in standard High German, and in the next breath chats with his hero in dialect. He cites statistics at one moment and in the next parodies the tone of Old Testament lamentations or Greek tragedy. Speaking quite broadly, we can say that while Döblin knows generally what is going on in the novel as a whole, the *narrator* is never aware of anything outside the material he happens to be reporting in a given section. Or to put it another way: each section, with the language necessary for it, produces its own narrative voice. For language is in itself productive, Döblin has noted, and if properly chosen can be a stimulus to the imagination. . . . In contrast to most writers, who find a suitable narrative voice and retain it throughout, Döblin leaps from situation to situation: each is related in the language proper to it—police-court, biblical, lyrical, jargonic—and each language produces, within that particular section, its own narrative voice.

All of this means, of course, that the city presents itself to us as a chaos. It is not ordered by any authorial intelligence that relates and explains matters to us. The reality of the work is thrust upon us in its rawest form. The very language and organization of the book reflect the chaos of the city. The rationale underlying this stylistic radicality is one of inviting the reader to experience the city as it is experienced by the hero, Franz Biberkopf. We are not simply told that he feels the threat of chaos; we are given an opportunity to feel this chaos along with him.

Döblin originally entitled his book simply ***Berlin Alexanderplatz,*** but his publishers, objecting that this title was incomprehensible (since it was merely the name of a streetcar stop), insisted on the tradition of a more conventional subtitle: ***The Story of Franz Biberkopf.*** Döblin was right, of course. The title he had chosen underlines the fact that his book is a book about a collective existence, not a traditional novel about a single hero. The exemplary nature of Franz Biberkopf is repeatedly stressed, as at the beginning of Book 6: "For the man about whom I am reporting is no ordinary man, but still he's an ordinary man insofar as we understand him precisely and occasionally say: step for step, we could have done and experienced the same as he." At the same time, the full title of the work brings out the tension which keeps the novel taut, for the city exists, and is portrayed here, as Franz Biberkopf's adversary.

It is for this reason that the city must be rendered as such a vital, living force. Indeed, the chaotic, even demonic aspect under which the city is presented makes sense only if we understand that this is the way in which the city thrusts itself upon Biberkopf. A hero of different character, of greater analytical intelligence, would not experience the city in this way. . . . No, the style of the book is directly dependent upon the character of the hero, of this specific hero. This fact distinguishes Döblin's novel from those of Dos Passos, which have not one but several leading figures. Dos Passos obtains his breadth by following the various figures along their respective parallel courses through the city. In Döblin the situation is reduced to the basic conflict between Biberkopf and the city of Berlin. His novel, he once remarked, is homophonic, in contrast to Dos Passos' polyphony. (pp. 105-12)

The novel . . . presents us on various levels with the problems of man versus the city, order versus chaos, independence versus solidarity. And most of the leitmotifs and symbols of the work are related in one way or another to this network of tensions. As Franz alternates between success and failure, between the vision of paradise and one of roofs sliding from the houses, his mood shifts from happiness and confidence to despair and back again.

The novel, however, is more than a montage of elements of contemporary urban life or a symphony of symbols and leitmotifs. It is also a profound character study that reveals in amazing detail Döblin's technical mastery of the theories of his day. (pp. 116-17)

Quite early in the book the notion of classical tragedy is introduced as an ironic contrast to present-day reality. (p. 120)

The reader is amused by the juxtaposition of classical tragedy and the formulae of physics. Döblin is well aware of the humorous effects to be achieved by mixing various kinds of language and by recounting the events of one level of action in a vocabulary borrowed from another level. At the same time the reader wonders: Is it all merely parody? For this juxtaposition of ancient and modern, of tragedy and reality, occurs too often in the course of the novel to be merely gratuitous. Thus, at the beginning of Book 7, the sordid murder of a prostitute—under circumstances not unlike those in which Franz earlier murdered Ida—is explicitly called a "fate tragedy"; and the term (*Schicksalstragödie*) is intended to awaken very specific associations with a group of German romantic dramas written in accordance with an exaggerated misconception of Greek tragedy which saw the hero's downfall as being brought about by an external fate. (p. 121)

The actual movement of the action closely resembles the rhythm of tragedy. It is a tragedy which, to be sure, is disclaimed throughout by the narrator and, at the end, even by the hero. But what is disclaimed is the meaning, not the form, of tragedy. And form without meaning is form nonetheless. ***Berlin Alexanderplatz,*** I would suggest, is given its unity of action by a conscious travesty of tragedy with all its most characteristic elements. (pp. 122-23)

In all three cases, Franz's downfall is brought about by his own blindness to the character of others and by his boasting. If we return to the analogy of classical tragedy, it seems quite clear that Franz's problems are created by what Aristotle would have called his *hamartia*. The same basic situation is repeated, but with each repetition he reaches a higher peak of manic happiness and self-complacency, from which he plummets (peripeteia) to progressively deeper abysses of depression (catastrophe). In the temporal structure of the work his first recovery, after the deception by Lüders, takes only about a month (January, 1928); the second period of recovery lasts from April well into July; and the third continues from Mieze's murder at the end of August until the winter of 1928-1929.

This rhythm of development is complicated and obscured by the dual aspect of the book: the presentation of the city itself takes up roughly half the book, and the plot is constantly interrupted and loosened by the intrusion of passages not strictly related to it. As a result, it is easy to lose sight of the tragic rhythm that determines the structure of the plot. (pp. 129-30)

Biberkopf's third setback, it will be recalled, produces such severe psychic consequences that he lands in the psychiatric ward of the hospital at Buch (where Döblin served for a time as interne). As far as outer appearances are concerned, he is a textbook case of manic-depressive insanity in its severest form: for weeks he lies in a stupor, fed by a tube in his throat, incapable of communication, and a riddle to the swarm of doctors in attendance. (Döblin takes this occasion to satirize his own profession: there are the conservative old professors who take a dim view of psychogenic explanations and believe in sweatbaths as a cure for catatonic stupor, and the young internes who ascribe to the modern theories of Freudian psychiatry.) The objective description of Biberkopf's behavior and of the therapy he receives during these weeks of manic-depressive insanity is as precise as one would expect, coming as it does from an experienced neurologist who spent many years with patients suffering from the same symptoms. But the poetic rendition of the hallucinations that beset Franz is conditioned wholly by the associations with tragedy that have been gradually built up in the course of the novel. In this difficult scene, myth and psychiatry are interwoven with great virtuosity to produce a compelling and convincing image of a neurotic hallucination.

The reader will immediately note that the various images employed in these passages have been anticipated earlier in the work: for instance, the hacking of the axes was heard in the slaughterhouses, while the crash of the giant drills comes from the excavating of a new subway line on Alexanderplatz. The hallucinations are technically a masterpiece of leitmotif and collage. Before Biberkopf can experience cognition through suffering and death, his conscience must be awakened. (pp. 132-33)

These scenes can be explained most satisfactorily, I believe, if we regard them as a modern rendition of the pursuit by the Erinyes of Greek tragedy—by avenging spirits informed by twentieth-century psychiatry and drawing their imagery from the technological world of 1928, but Erinyes nonetheless. The structure of tragedy, in other words, is complete from start to finish, for it is these avenging spirits that finally succeed in making Franz accept the fact of his own guilt and responsibility, in curing him of his *hamartia*. This, in turn, casts new light on the frequent references to the Greeks and especially to the legend of Orestes. For Orestes was hounded by the Erinyes, as Döblin pointed out in the passage cited earlier; but unlike the heroes of most Greek tragedies, he lived to be redeemed and freed from the avenging spirits. Although the meaning of classical tragedy is trivialized, its form is preserved to an astonishing degree. In fact, it determines essentially the movement and imagery of the whole novel.

After he has been reduced to a trembling pulp by the pile drivers and axes of the modern Erinyes, Franz is ready for the great dialogue with Death that completes his development. . . . In a series of visions, Death now unfolds before Franz all the crucial episodes of his past, demonstrating clearly how wrong Franz has been and how foolishly he has behaved. Finally Franz acknowledges his guilt. (pp. 133-34)

One of the central symbols for the city as a menacing chaos has been the Whore of Babylon. At this point, when Franz has been redeemed, Döblin describes in a scene of vivid imagery the retreat of the Whore of Babylon before the power of Death. For now that Franz has learned to look upon the world with new eyes, he no longer regards the city with the eyes of a Greek, seeing in it a nameless destiny or threat. The last few pages of the novel recount the first steps of this "new" Biberkopf, who in distinction to his old self is now called Franz Karl Biberkopf. (pp. 134-35)

The novel, then, has revealed many dimensions of meaning. On the aesthetic level, it represents a modern "tragedy" in strict harmony with the laws of classical Greek tragedy; this determines the rhythm of the plot. On the psychological level, it shows the crisis and cure of a case of manic-depressive insanity; this determines the character of Biberkopf. On the sociological level, it depicts the rehabilitation of a criminal who ends up as gateman of a factory in the spring of 1929; this is related to Döblin's social conscience. On a political level, it represents the disenchantment of a "Deutscher Michel" with a dictatorial leader who, for a time, seems to satisfy his masochistic craving for order and obedience; this aspect, totally vitiated by history, has been most frequently attacked by critics (especially the hymn to solidarity on the last two pages of the book). And the entire human action, with its many levels of meaning, is set against a vivid montage that virtually reproduces the city of Berlin in the pages of the novel. (pp. 135-36)

Döblin . . . seeks to render totality by means of inclusion, and not by symbolic selectivity. But in order to achieve any degree of unity within this chaotic multiplicity he is compelled to erect a strong underlying structure. He therefore chooses the framework of classical tragedy to contain everything else. . . . [Döblin] has loosened the integration of the novel. He has adopted, to be sure, a broad and almost mythic framework to hold his novel together; but within that framework the individual elements are allowed to float freely and at random, as a reflection of reality itself. (p. 137)

Theodore Ziolkowski, "Alfred Döblin: 'Berlin Alexanderplatz'," in his Dimensions of the Modern Novel: German Texts and European Contexts *(copyright © 1969 by Princeton University Press; © 1979 assigned to Theodore Ziolkowski; all rights reserved; excerpts reprinted by permission of the author), Princeton University Press, 1969, pp. 99-137.*

LEON L. TITCHE, JR. (essay date 1971)

[*Titche provides an extensive comparison of* Alexanderplatz, Berlin *with the novel* Manhattan Transfer *by John Dos Passos.*]

Dos Passos' *Manhattan Transfer* (1925; German translation 1927) is the American counterpart to ***Berlin Alexanderplatz.*** It is a more traditional novel—a novel of realism, relatively uncomplicated especially in comparison with the stylistic "breakthrough" Dos Passos achieved in his *U.S.A.* trilogy. It is "uncomplicated" in the sense that it does not employ the stream of consciousness technique to the extent that Döblin does; but this does not mean that its external structure is absolutely straight. Many times in the novel two or three separate and unrelated stories appear on one page; this is also the case in ***Berlin Alexanderplatz,*** but once again it is Döblin's innovative style which makes interpretation a challenge. It is one thing to distinguish the stories from one another and place them into the novel complex; but it is an entirely different matter to have to cope with the whole range of rhetorical devices inherent in the stream of consciousness novel at the same time.

It has been said that Dos Passos tried to "encompass in fiction the whole history of his time "[Robert Gorham Davis, *John Dos Passos* (1962)]. This also applies to Döblin's works and in particular to ***Berlin Alexanderplatz.*** To best probe this "Zeitgeschichte" ["contemporary history"], what better laboratory could be found than a large city? In Manhattan and Berlin, the best monuments to man's energies, intellect, and capabilities are preserved. Here also is found the worst in man. The institutions he has founded, the laws he has established, the culture he has nurtured, and the incessant striving for wealth and power which he has accepted as part and parcel of his being are viewed on both sides of the ledger and, depending on where chance has placed him in the economic scale, he stands firmly entrenched on the inside or he waits without. There is no reconciliation or coming to terms without a complete loss of identity. It is a simple "either-or." With Döblin, the character is outside the social periphery, battering it to get in. In *Manhattan Transfer,* the characters are within, fighting to get out. (p. 126)

Franz Biberkopf experiences the first of his "rebirths" at the beginning of the novel upon his release from prison. He must now leave the ordered, rigid, safe life of the penal institution, away from the city, and take his first step into Berlin—a step he is hesitant to make because he knows only too well what awaits him. Throughout the novel, Döblin cites the vital statistics of Berlin—how many live births, how many deaths, what causes were attributed to these deaths, etc. These figures are the city, and they are presented in a matter-of-fact journalistic fashion that can only magnify the unfeeling quality of Berlin. Biberkopf, like Jimmy Herf, must accept the consequences of any struggle against this giant.

Berlin is equated with the "Hure Babylon" and slaughterhouses. . . . This is a constant motif with Döblin. The appearance of the whore of Babylon is always ominous, and it often means that Biberkopf must be faced with a terrible crisis (the numerous Biblical references, especially to Job, Jeremiah, and Ecclesiastes, point directly to him.) The symbolic presence of the city, together with the personal trials of the central character, continues throughout the novel. In this manner ***Berlin Alexanderplatz*** differs from *Manhattan Transfer*. There is no actual leitmotif in the latter; the evils of the city are depicted by Dos Passos in the encounters of the characters, in a purely descriptive and narrative manner, whereas Döblin relies heavily on symbolic and Biblical references. Not only that, but the central scene in ***Berlin Alexanderplatz***—the one which most vividly portrays the hopelessness of man in the city—is a metaphorical construction which takes place in the stockyards and slaughterhouses in Berlin. The scene is grotesque, bordering on *poésie brute,* and the sounds of the fateful hammer continue throughout the novel. (pp. 127-28)

Several "Nebenerzählungen" ["frame narratives"] are provided to show the more sordid aspects of the city, the slice of life, which makes ordinary existence a continually frightening experience. The seduction of a young girl on her way to a music lesson, glimpses at prostitution and murder—all these form isolated stories within the novel and often have nothing to do with the [principal] characters. What these scenes do reflect on the main concern of the novel is precisely that such incidents happen with great frequency in Berlin, and that to struggle against injustices is meaningless and futile; in fact, to struggle against fate itself is a deadly game. The frequent and ominous quotations from Job and Ecclesiastes, together with the reference to the slaughterhouse, are to impress this upon the reader, although they are hidden from the view of Franz Biberkopf. To a large degree the characters in *Manhattan Transfer* encounter similar situations which are, however, not as emphatically, nor as repetitiously, described. Once again the stream of consciousness technique in ***Berlin Alexanderplatz,*** especially the abundance of interior monologues, accounts for this. The reader sees how the constant bombardment of parables, sayings, proverbs and songs finds its way into the characters' psyche, never to be forgotten, yet hardly ever to be consciously realized. Dos Passos is seldom as subtle as Döblin, due to not only the different technical construction of the novels, but also to the large difference in what can be called the awareness of the characters . . . and which Dos Passos is consistent in using. A conglomeration of people together confront the huge, vast expanse which is New York, and those who remain will either continue to struggle or will merge into an animate version of the city. Franz Biberkopf has been singled out by Döblin to experience life as a representative of the neglected proletariat interests in Berlin. . . . Amid the maze of statistics, horrors and inanities which is the life-vein of Berlin, Franz wishes only to be independent and, above all, "anständig" ["decent, respectable"]. This is seen as a complete impossibility, for Franz must struggle against fate—and Berlin is the arbiter of the destiny of man. As soon as one submits oneself to it, the struggle has ended; the city emerges as judge, jury and executioner, and man's fate is sealed. This he learns after a series of misfortunes makes him temporarily insane. His therapeutic rebirth is not a product of reason, but rather of the same process of learning which makes a child realize that, after repeatedly placing its hand on a burner, fire hurts. Such is not the case in *Manhattan Transfer,* where "the value of the rational man" is affirmed. The clashes which the two central characters, Jimmy Herf and Ellen Thatcher, encounter, are shown in a rational light; whereas in ***Berlin Alexanderplatz,*** as we have seen, the opposite is true. "Within the four hundred pages of 'Manhattan Transfer'," [Maxwell] Geismar writes, "Dos Passos has recreated . . . a dozen metropolitan sagas full of fury and anguish, the distortion of being." The same is present in ***Berlin Alexanderplatz***—the "distortion of being" borders on understatement in the latter case—but the psyche of Franz is not equipped to understand either the magnitude or the meaning of his hopeless entanglements. And here is another difference in the novels. Dos Passos has many of these "sagas," most of equal importance to the novel complex; he also, as Robert Gorham Davis states, ". . . sharpens even more the sense of moment and movement—to which the whole turbulent life of the city contributes—by shifting rapidly back and forth from one group of characters to another." This technique results therefore in the presentation of isolated novels within *Manhattan Transfer,* and there is no consistent harmony or bridge from one episode to another. In ***Berlin Alexanderplatz*** the various "Nebenerzählungen," together with the leitmotific and symbolical/allegorical passages, at first glance appear to have little immediate relevance to the character of Biberkopf. Nevertheless, a closer look reveals not only a relevance, but a harmonious continuity between them. In every case, there is a thread of continuum throughout the novel, and this enables Döblin to intensify not only his central character, but the city as well.

In both novels the city is seen through many eyes; but in ***Berlin Alexanderplatz,*** as contrasted to *Manhattan Transfer,* the final focus is on one character. A further contrast resides in the epic parallel of Biberkopf with, and the irony is intended, Orestes. Indeed Döblin, in a 1932 postscript to the novel, "Mein Buch **'Berlin Alexanderplatz,'**" terms this and some of his other works, "episch ["epic"]. . . . The irony of comparing a criminal of dubious mentality and slovenly appearance with Orestes and then placing this within the framework of an epic work at first appears ludicrous. Yet, when the novel has run its course, this apparent polarization of an "ironic" and a "high mimetic" hero yields finally to a direct parallel. . . . The crimes which brought upon the curse of the House of Atreus seem lofty and, if one can use such a term in this context, noble, in comparison to the insane murder of Ida by Franz using an egg beater, his incarceration in Tegel, his relationships with prostitutes, his association with thieves, his incessant bungling and simple-mindedness. Yet he is a human being whose one hope and desire is to be "anständig," and for this yearning which is beyond his grasp he nearly loses his life. In the end both Biberkopf and Orestes become reconciled and the curse on both men is lifted. (pp. 129-31)

Biberkopf's struggles and thoughts . . . are not dependent on character or plot development. They have always been a part of him, and Döblin lets bits and pieces trickle out during the course of the work, and the reader becomes enlightened, not the character. The opposite is the case in *Manhattan Transfer*. Whereas in ***Berlin Alexanderplatz*** the constant resonance of epos pervades the work, immersing the hero more and more into the maelstrom of city and humanity while at the same time providing ironic comparison with the true epic quality of a hero which Biberkopf himself lacks, the characters in *Manhattan Transfer* are unable to find a place in humanity or society. . . . They are part of a saga of hopes broken by the force of the city. The character of Franz, on the other hand, extends far beyond this scope, by virtue of being portrayed on two levels: as a former criminal who strives vainly for "Anständigkeit," he is equivalent to one of Dos Passos' characters; as an "epic hero," he represents human nature and mankind struggling against an awesome fate. Biberkopf, it may be said, is the personification of the medieval Everyman who must be shown the "right path." In the commentaries on Job, in the pronouncements found in Ecclesiastes and so forcefully allegorized in the slaughterhouse, in the dialogues with angels and Death, in the fusion of all of these which culminates in his spiritual rebirth, Franz Biberkopf steps out of the narrow confines of individualistic consideration and into the stream of humanity. What he finds is a sudden awakening which is similar to Levin's discovery of himself at the end of *Anna Karenina*. . . . (p. 133)

In ***Berlin Alexanderplatz,*** Berlin towers over the character at the beginning of the novel. It tightens its grip on Franz as he wanders aimlessly around the Square. Each time he rises up against it, he is beaten down, but the contest does not last forever for him. There are limits, and this recognition whittles down the monolithic heights of the whore of Babylon as she meets the infinite *qua* being in Franz Biberkopf. His rebirth, a brilliant execution of a *deus ex machina* by Döblin, insures the permanence of the individual.

Both novels have raised a voice against the impending takeover of the human being by steel, concrete, and asphalt. *Manhattan Transfer* has presented much more of an overview of the city than ***Berlin Alexanderplatz***. . . . (p. 134)

Döblin . . . has as his purpose the detailed examination of a society in upheaval. Like Dos Passos, he brings in contemporary events of social and political importance and he displays with scorn the injustices and inequities which were prevalent. In some of his other novels, most notably in ***Pardon wird nicht gegeben*** and ***November 1918,*** Döblin recaptures a turbulent era in a manner comparable to Dos Passos' other works. In ***Berlin Alexanderplatz*** . . . sociological analyses never overshadow the individual, for he is the prime mover, the central figure in the city drama. The whole matter rests with him, for he alone is capable of overcoming the vicissitudes of civilization. With Döblin, Berlin is a motif within the novel complex. Dos Passos elevates Manhattan to a protagonistic level of importance. Both novels explore the city with a vindictive fervor—and at the same time with an objective view which correctly relegates them to a place of importance in the literary study of "Zeitgeschichte." (p. 135)

Leon L. Titche, Jr., "Döblin and Dos Passos: Aspects of the City Novel," in Modern Fiction Studies *(© 1971 by Purdue Research Foundation, West Lafayette, IN 47907; reprinted with permission), Vol. XVII, No. 1, Spring, 1971, pp. 125-35.**

ANDREW M. McLEAN (essay date 1973)

[*McLean compares* Alexanderplatz, Berlin *with James Joyce's* Ulysses. *Discounting the prevalent critical theory that Döblin was most heavily influenced by Joyce, McLean finds that the two novelists produced similar works because both drew from the same sources. For other comparisons of Döblin's and Joyce's works, see the excerpts by Florence Haxton Britten (1931), Michael Sadleir (1931), Robert Martin Adams (1977), and the entry in the Additional Bibliography by Breon Mitchell.*]

Döblin's influence on the modern German novel is similar to that of Joyce on the English: their writings gave a new impulse and direction to what had become a fully developed form within traditions which may have limited the novel's growth and development. . . . Critics have largely ignored an important source for the Joycean technique and innovations found in the modern European novel by failing to deal with Döblin's novel. . . . It is the technique and new structure given to the novel by Döblin which suggest the Joycean influence on his work. The use of stream-of-consciousness, interior monologue, burlesque and parody, song leitmotifs, and mythical and biblical allusions to parallel thematic development are common to both authors.

This study will suggest some similarities and parallels between two authors whose works have greatly influenced the development of the modern novel; these relationships should not be confused with labels of "influence" or "imitation." Rather, the parallels between *Ulysses* and ***Berlin Alexanderplatz*** reflect both Döblin's early involvement with German expressionism and his realization that *Ulysses* could be used as an encyclopedia of stylistic devices. The difficulty one encounters in reading these novels forces one to struggle along with the protagonist and to enter into his stream-of-consciousness. Joyce does this to effect (ultimately in Molly's "unpunctuated monologue") the fulfillment of Bloom's story and his return as a new man to Molly. Döblin, however, never allows the reader to empathize completely with Franz Biberkopf, and an authorial comment is always present to direct or to explain. Yet, both novels share a common theme. They deal with modern man's confrontation with the world about him and his struggle to find his place in it; both authors focus on the spiritual odyssey of urban man. (pp. 98-9)

Döblin's concern as he traces the wanderings of his hero through the streets of Berlin suggests the expressionists' reproach against the machine-like modern life which stifles man's freedom and limits his spiritual development. The expressionist attitude was "a radical attempt to maintain the force and validity of metaphysical aspirations in a fundamentally anti-spiritual world," and between 1900 and 1920, the German novelists share with their English counterparts a desire to redefine and shape the practice and function of narrative art. (p. 99)

Döblin presents the confusion, the ideals, the movement and the obstacles of a Germany between two world wars. Franz is a victim of three things: (1) of the organized society which he re-enters and which refuses to reclaim him; (2) of the Alexanderplatz world—the criminals, pimps, prostitutes and undesirables who are unfair to Franz; (3) of himself. It is his unconscious battle with himself and his gradual acquisition of self-knowledge that form the core of this story. Döblin interjects a host of minor characters and incidents which are woven into the plot, and stylistic variations force the reader to reflect on the action by jolting his sense of reality. For example, after describing the murder of Franz's girl Ida (the crime for which Biberkopf went to prison), Döblin enters into an elaborate scientific explanation of the murder. . . . These descriptive reports come suddenly and abruptly, standing isolated in the narration or dialogue. The function of this type of writing parallels that of the scriptural passages quoted throughout the novel and echoes one of Joyce's thematic techniques in *Ulysses*. For example, in the "The Cyclops" episode in *Ulysses* when the citizen (who has been harassing Bloom) is finally enraged by Bloom's remark that Christ was a Jew like himself, he throws a tinbox after the departing coach climaxing the funny scene with an act of violence, the report of which is reinforced by a full-page news report of earthquake tremors. . . . (pp. 100-01)

Joyce gradually introduces the stream-of-consciousness technique (first represented in full as Stephen walks along the Sandymount strand) and eventually eliminates the narrator completely (in "Penelope"), but Döblin is always present to comment and direct not only the reader, but Franz himself. Döblin's innovative style has drawn just praise, and he demonstrates an ability to heighten the dramatic tension between two characters by engaging the reader in the protagonist's struggle. . . . Döblin's omniscient narrator, aware of what is to happen, often hints at the impending action. He does so explicitly in the introduction to each of the nine chapters, summarizing the plot of each, as in the concluding chapter: "Now Franz Biberkopf's earthly journey is ended . . . He falls into the hands of . . . death . . . They settle accounts . . . The man's broken up. But a new Biberkopf will now be shown." . . . The chapters are divided into episodes, each of which is given a title indicating what is to happen: "Reinhold's Black Wednesday, but this Chapter may be Skipped," or "The Duel starts! It is rainy Weather." These titles while not revealing exactly what is to happen, serve to heighten an anticipation of the action and to maintain the reader's interest.

Döblin concentrates on the individual's mental process—on the internal aspects of his characters. In his description of Franz's thoughts while he is in the insane asylum Döblin reaches the apex of his prose writing in this novel. The tempo increases in intensity and rhythm with the increase of Franz's hysteria and mental frenzy, and then as the mental action decreases, the prose changes tone. . . . Döblin uses the interior monologue to express the confused impulses of Franz, whose sensibilities and intelligence are simpler than those of Stephen or Bloom. In this tightly packed narrative the major concerns of the novel are mentioned as they pass through Franz's mind: his loss of identity, his "friend" Reinhold who murdered Franz's sweetheart Mieze, echoes of a biblical tone recalling the biblical allusions running throughout the novel, and the inability of Franz to recognize his own situation. (pp. 102-04)

While in prison, Franz thinks only of two things: freedom and women. When released, he vows to lead a decent life, and looks forward to his freedom and women, but his tragedy is that all his attempts to keep his vow are thwarted. Seeking to understand the basic nature of Franz's tragedy, Döblin searches everywhere for symbolic explanations or interpretations to present the problem of his protagonist and to underscore his search for identity. Scriptural passages form a strong thread throughout the novel, helping the author to present his story and the reader to understand Franz's predicament. Franz is both man and symbol. He is innocence placed in the Garden; he falls and receives the curse of God. He is the afflicted Job living with the whore of Babylon (Alexanderplatz). It is to Franz that the prophet Jeremiah calls; he is called to be an obedient Abraham. The scriptural allusions comment on the plight of Franz in Alexanderplatz. Each Bible passage refers to the preceding one and foreshadows what will happen to Franz. Each also serves as a parallel allegory on Biberkopf's situation. Thus, as Franz is released from prison and returns to society, Book II opens with a descriptive passage of Adam and Eve in the Garden ("There was abiding joy the whole day long in Paradise" . . .). The "Wonderful Garden of Eden" is what Franz aspires to enter after four years of prison. For him it is his freedom and his women. But the trials ahead of him are foreshadowed by the classical allusion to Orestes who is hounded by the Furies. Franz will become a Job; he is a "criminal, an erstwhile God-accursed man." . . . (pp. 105-06)

In Book III, as Franz receives a disparaging letter from a widow he had seduced, the serpent speaks to Adam and Eve, and as the peace and contentment of Paradise fell from them, so Franz suffers his "first blow." This occurs when his friend Luders uses Franz's name as a reference for a widow whom he attempts to rape. Franz has been used by his friend and this is the start of his hardships. The world of Alexanderplatz thwarts Franz's good intentions. . . . Franz takes on the symbolic character of the suffering Job. . . . Franz fails to see the corruption about him and the injustices done to him. He had entered into criminal activities without wanting to, and now these elements press on him. Now Job is oppressed by the whore of Babylon (i.e., Alexanderplatz) as Franz becomes the victim of the "mother of abominations." Döblin jolts us when reference is made to the suffering Job and the "great mother of harlots," for the passages come abruptly within the context of the narrative or dialogue. Sometimes they are worked so smoothly into the dialogue that we are almost unaware of their presence, and a more subtle Joycean impression is made. . . . It is in the climactic scene in the insane asylum that the Job motif reaches its culmination . . . . (pp. 106-07)

Döblin clearly attempts to present the plight of Franz Biberkopf by use of these biblical and mythological allusions, but he does not attempt to present the characterization of Franz through them. Ultimately Joyce succeeds where Döblin fails in creating a masterpiece of tight, thematically interrelated prose which uses biblical references to make the meaning of the novel clear. (p. 107)

[In *Ulysses*] Bloom is the innocent lamb, the scapegoat condemned by the citizen as Christ was condemned by the citizenry of Jerusalem. Bloom is raised above the citizenry by analogy with Elijah's triumphal ascent to Heaven and the association of Bloom with Christ and Elijah transcends narrative device to become characterization—characterization which is also ironic. Joyce's use of such characterization contrasts with Döblin's more limited use of biblical parallels as narrative devices which help portray the situation of Biberkopf yet fail to penetrate his character. (p. 108)

The ethical predicament of Bloom throughout *Ulysses* is similar to the "tragedy" of Franz Biberkopf which embodies a philosophy of becoming—of becoming a reflective, decision-making, action-taking being. As Job refused to take action and suffered for his disobedience to God, Franz suffers the miseries of the "mother of abominations" until he goes through a process of humanization, a process which demands an acceptance of the reality of the human condition and necessitates reflection and decision through action. A similar situation exists with Bloom and Stephen, neither of whom is capable of action, "for action involves the assertion of the will, and it is by the will that souls are lost or saved."

Biberkopf's blindness to his situation causes his indecisiveness and inaction. This is recorded early in the novel when after being released from Tegel prison, Franz roams the streets of Berlin, delirious with joy over his return to society, and his high spirits fluctuate. (p. 109)

It is through the love and concern of the prostitute Mieze that Franz begins to find some of the peace of that Garden he sought when released from Tegel. Mieze is gentle and understanding; she is devoted to Biberkopf and he confides and trusts in her. . . . It is the shock of Mieze's murder by Reinhold that jolts Biberkopf into self-reflection and a realization that he must accept responsibility for his past actions. . . . The sensitive portrayal of her love is one of Döblin's best accomplishments in the novel. (p. 111)

Franz cannot go on being a child. In his self-pity he turns to drink, but his moment of enlightenment occurs in the insane asylum when Death accuses him of being blind. . . . The doctors have little hope for Franz but his conversation with Death forces him to exercise his will and to reflect on *la condition humaine*. . . . Franz Biberkopf has learned to think reflectively and to reason and act responsibly. He accepts the responsibility for Mieze's death, and he decides to change his way of life. This change is quickly noticed by Eva when Franz returns to Alexanderplatz. Franz has left the realm of sensual man for that of reflective man, and has become a man of action. The whore of Babylon is defeated, the suffering Job is redeemed, and Adam has found his Paradise. (p. 112)

Franz becomes worthy of God's grace through self-sacrifice and humility. What happens to Franz is basically what happens to Stephen and Bloom in *Ulysses;* they move from an inability to act and assert their wills to a moment of self-knowledge and illumination which gives their lives purpose and meaning. . . . Perhaps the morality of art is that it can lead man to a self-awareness which enables him to live more meaningfully in the world. Franz Biberkopf and Stephen Daedalus both have a myopic vision of the purpose and meaning of life; their blinders are not removed until they confront the realities of life surrounding them and ultimately confront themselves.

Franz's confrontation with Death, reminiscent of the *danse macabre* of the Middle Ages, is the highlight of a novel in which the author utilizes the inner monologue to portray the character of an entire city. Both Döblin and Joyce portray a city and the people who inhabit it, realistically presenting the action as reflected in a hero's mind which serves to mirror that city's life and action. Scientific explanations of details are effectively employed by Joyce to reveal a certain aspect of Bloom and to parody the pedantic and narrowly objective approach to life. Such parody is absent from Döblin, although his scientific interjections force the reader (as they do in Joyce) to reflect more pointedly on what is being observed or stated and often more fully impress on the reader's mind what has occurred. Perhaps such clinical objectivism is what Bertolt Brecht had in mind when he said that Döblin "sieht die Literatur mehr als Artz als Schriftsteller" ["approached literature more as a doctor than an author"]. (pp. 112-13)

Andrew M. McLean, "Joyce's 'Ulysses' and Döblin's 'Alexanderplatz Berlin'," in Comparative Literature *(© copyright 1973 by University of Oregon; reprinted by permission of* Comparative Literature*), Vol. XXV, No. 2, Spring, 1973, pp. 97-113.**

WOLFGANG KORT (essay date 1974)

[The following survey of Döblin's major fiction is taken from Kort's Alfred Döblin, *the most comprehensive biographical and critical study of Döblin in English.]*

Döblin viewed himself as a writer of extended narratives and the greater part of his works consists of lengthy novels. (p. 7)

[***Die drei Sprünge des Wang-lun*** **("The Three Leaps of Wang-lun")**] marks the breakthrough not only to a fullscale literary productivity but also to a personal style. . . .

Die drei Sprünge des Wang-lun . . . is by no means a Chinese phantasmagoria. Döblin loved facts and factual material and did intensive preparatory work for his novel. He not only gathered an enormous amount of details, but also thoroughly acquainted himself with Chinese philosophy. (p. 54)

The theme of the novel—as of all Döblin's novels—is the question of how the individual should relate to his environment. Döblin's experience and his biological and medical research seemed to demonstrate the fragility and impotence of the single being mercilessly trampled by life in its urge to preserve itself. The insignificance of man in the face of an eternal, immense nature (so vividly apparent in Japanese and Chinese color woodcuts) and in the face of suprapersonal powers in general, is one of the basic experiences conveyed by Döblin's works. . . . Wang-lun and his sect [the "Truly Weak Ones"] want to be weak and to live without resisting Tao, i.e., fate. Paradoxically, however, this very tactic challenges fate, and they are destroyed. Indeed, weakness seems to go against human nature. In an unconditional subjection, man seems to lose his dignity, so that he continually rebels against his fate, only to experience his impotence anew—an endless process. (p. 55)

[The novel's ending not only makes] clear that fate cannot be placated by nonresistance, but also that such passivity is contrary to human nature, because human nature repeatedly rebels against the fate imposed on it.

Although Döblin has left no doubt that Wang-lun is central to the novel, an interpretation concentrating on the main figures cannot do complete justice to its complexity. The many interspersed episodes, anecdotes, and parables bear witness not only to the assiduity of the author in collecting material and to his sensibility, but also unfold a picture of Chinese life in the eighteenth century in its totality. The figures of the book live only in a constant reciprocal relationship with the totality of life around them—with the countryside, the climate, society, and its culture. Everything has a place in the novel. The environment in its totality is visible. That Wang-lun is the leader of a mass could create the impression that not the individual but the mass is the "hero" of the novel. Mass scenes in such abundance and in such form—consider the attack on the Hill of Women, the festival which the Broken Melon celebrates on the barque of the goddess Kuan-yin, and the teeming masses of the great cities—were previously rare in the German novel. The influence of Futurism, especially of Marinetti's novel *Mafarka le futuriste,* is clearly evident. However, it is combined with Döblin's sociological and biological views of the insignificance of the single being—another thematic concern of the novel. The truth of existence lies, for him, basically in the masses and in anonymity, to which his heroes often return. . . . In ***Die drei Sprünge des Wang-lun,*** there is no collective hero because Wang-lun, Ma-noh, the Emperor, and their personal conflicts and decisions are too much in the center of the action.

Nonetheless, Döblin—like Kafka—uses no psychology in depicting the "individual" characters. He describes reactions, modes of behavior, moods, and movements, but he almost never intrudes upon the interior of his characters. The plasticity of his language is especially enhanced by this rejection of psychology. (pp. 63-4)

Esthetically, the novel is surely a protest against outmoded and, therefore, untrue art forms, but it is much more than that because it depicts, under the guise of a Chinese man from the age of the Manchu dynasty, the dilemma of modern man as Döblin viewed it. Modern man longs to regain the original unity of life and fate, from which he has been ejected, but the dominant powers and systems which want to manifest themselves as forces of fate make such an attitude impossible, because it places their own position in question. Even an open battle against the dominant powers proves to be hopeless. The bitter realization is that one knows the truth but cannot live it. This dilemma recurs repeatedly in Döblin's books.

Before the outbreak of World War I, Döblin had finished his second major novel, ***Wadzeks Kampf mit der Dampfturbine,*** **("Wadzek's Battle with the Steam Turbine")** which was published only in 1918. This time, he shifted the setting from distant China to his familiar Berlin. His inclination toward exact observation of detail—furthered by his own scientific endeavors and also inherited from Naturalism—and his fascination with factual material led him repeatedly to make detailed studies of his subject. The result was a method of narration that incorporated unintegrated factual material into the novel. In light of this reverence for facts, it is not surprising that Döblin made extensive studies in the Berlin factories of the *Allgemeine Elektrizitätsgesellschaft* (AEG: General Electric) for a novel set in twentieth-century Berlin. He planned a work of several volumes. A "Kampf mit dem Ölmotor" ("Battle with the Diesel Engine") was to be the sequel of the ***Kampf mit der Dampfturbine.*** This knowledge strengthened the critics in their belief that Döblin's novel deals with man's predicament in the competitive struggle of a capitalist economy and with man's self-alienation caused by the capitalistic economic system. Wadzek, with his steam engines, is pushed into the background by the steam turbines of his opponent, Rommel. He is overpowered by technological progress, and he, the man who defended himself with might and main against destruction, is marked as a helpless and powerless cretin. In his battle against Rommel, Wadzek finds an ally in Rommel's engineer Schneemann (!) ["Snowman"]. With every means at his disposal—in part even with illegal machinations—he attempts to stave off his fate, but all in vain. His fear of the loss of the basis of his existence results in inner strife and disjointedness in his life, in compulsion and in aimless walks and rides through Berlin. Certain traits of Döblin's narrative technique reminiscent of ***Berlin Alexanderplatz***—simultaneity, changing perspective, and psychic automatism—can be explained by the material and theme.

To this onset of a story that could as easily have been developed tragically, Döblin gave a grotesque twist. He gave the battle of the two "heroes" a larger dimension. Wadzek and Schneemann are no longer merely battling against the technological progress which makes their steam engines obsolete in comparison with Rommel's steam turbines, but see themselves as champions of individual freedom, of man himself, against oppression by Rommel and his ilk. Thus a revolutionary metaphor is introduced which continually underlines the discrepancy between reality and the imaginary world of Wadzek and Schneemann. The novel achieves its comic, ironic, and grotesque effects because of this intellectual contrast between mind and matter. The revolutionary pathos which carries Wadzek away is completely unsuited to the actual situation. (pp. 65-6)

In Wadzek's story, Döblin anticipated the fate of many members of the German middle class. Because of technological innovations and later because of the inflation, many experienced the collapse of their professional existence. The concomitant loss of authority in the family tempted many to flee from this unbearable reality. While the social components of the novel should not be underestimated, this theme is not sufficient to account for the whole novel in its satiric, ironic, and burlesque aspects. It should rather be viewed in relation to ***Die drei Sprünge des Wang-lun.*** Döblin himself referred to the connection in the "Epilog":

> I had to pursue these things farther. I did not
> want to be chained to ponderous and dark things.
> I did an about-face and was unintentionally,
> indeed completely against my will, drawn into
> light, fresh, and burlesque things.

These "things" which Döblin mentions here are basic to ***Wang-lun,*** the antithesis of submission to, or rebellion against, an overpowering fate. A careful study of ***Wadzek*** shows that Döblin is playing ironically with the problems of ***Wang-lun.*** Both positions—revolt against fate and appeasement of fate by submission—are presented with ironic detachment. . . .

In the second part of the novel, the transformation characteristic of all of Döblin's heroes occurs: Wadzek recognizes the hubris of his protest, the overestimation of his own person, and is ready to place himself in larger contexts and to acknowledge the interdependence of all things and events. (p. 68)

Maneuverability, adaptability, and assimilation to the ever changing situation—concepts which, as ***Das Ich über der Natur*** **["The Self over Nature"]** demonstrates, are central to Döblin's thought—are raised here to the principle of life, in an ironic fashion, admittedly. Unconditional retention of a position and rigidity in the face of life's flux are rejected. . . . (p. 69)

Döblin's next novel, written during the First World War, again turned to quite different times and settings, namely to the Thirty Year's War. . . .

As with his other two novels, Döblin had made preliminary studies and had integrated an enormous amount of factual material into his work. . . . Although the novel is entitled ***Wallenstein,*** the Emperor Ferdinand II is at least of equal importance with the great general; and Wallenstein is his contrast figure. . . . (p. 70)

Döblin's novel encompasses the time between the Battle at the White Mountain near Prague (1620) and the assassination of Wallenstein (1634) which, in the novel, coincides with the death of the Emperor Ferdinand—an historical inaccuracy because the Emperor died in 1637. Although Döblin unfolds the whole gigantic panorama of the war before our eyes, Wallenstein, and even more so Ferdinand, are the dominant figures. Other characters, such as the king of Sweden, Gustavus Adolphus (who, visualized as sailing innumerable ships across the Baltic Sea, provided Döblin with the initial stimulus for his novel) are overshadowed by these two mighty protagonists. While Wallenstein devours himself in restless activities and finally becomes the victim of his own contradictory and muddled plans, Ferdinand detaches himself increasingly from his throne and his occupation. He withdraws from politics, sinks mysteriously within himself, and returns to the mystic union of all being. Thus here again the theme of ***Wang-lun*** is sounded: the questioning of the possibility and meaning of human action, the antithesis of passivity and activity, resistance and nonresistance—now no longer centered in one person but juxtaposed in the two dominant figures. According to Döblin's own interpretation, Ferdinand chooses this path because he feels sated; and in the end he casts off everything. But, in addition, there are always signs of Ferdinand's boredom with the never-ending intrigues at court, with the endless maneuverings of the political powers—schemes and intrigues which do not bring the desired peace. (pp. 71-2)

[In ***Berge Meere und Giganten*** (**"Mountains, Seas and Giants"**) Döblin wrote] a "science fiction" novel, thus moving from the realm of history to that of prognostication. The novel is not utopian in that Döblin created no picture of an ideal world, but only attempted to describe the developments and events of the future by poetic means.

Döblin often thought about how the future would look and repeatedly attempted to sketch it. Thus, for example, in ***Der deutsche Maskenball*** [(**"The German Masquerade"**)], the dominant tendency of the age is seen as intensive industrialization, before which all differentiation becomes irrelevant. The characteristics of the coming age are the massing of mankind, the possibility of battles of the masses, the oppression of weaker groups, and the accumulation of power in the hands of the few. This will bring about the end of the industrial movement and, with it, the enervation of the technological-industrial complex. The leading role will be assigned to another group of ideas. In many respects, industry will become superfluous. . . . This evolutionary historical outline reappears in ***Berge Meere und Giganten.*** (p. 79)

In ***Berge Meere und Giganten*** . . . [Döblin] depicts the expansion of the naturalistic spirit up to its inevitable turning point in magnificent images. But how does this epoch end? Old traditions and concepts (the earth, race, blood, religion, and mysticism), from which countermovements arise, lie beneath the surface. This turn to mysticism, which always enters in Döblin's works when perception, knowledge, and technology have reached their limits, is extraordinarily characteristic of him. (pp. 80-1)

Döblin wants to portray "the development of our industrial world until about the year 2500," "a completely realistic and at the same time, completely fantastic thing; Jules Verne will turn in his grave—, but I intend something quite different from him." The question which interests Döblin is: "What will become of man if he continues to live in this way?" Technology increases the possibilities of man to an incredible point, but it leads almost to self-destruction; as in Goethe's "Zauberlehrling," man cannot contain the forces he has unleashed, and nature proves stronger than man. . . . (p. 81)

Döblin repeatedly stressed that he was especially strongly influenced by the literature of the North and of the East. His relationship to French literature was rather cool; he knew, among others, Flaubert, Balzac, Stendhal, Baudelaire, Anatole France, Romain Rolland, and Bernanos, all of whom he showed little enthusiasm for; he had also studied Proust. But . . . as an exile who made an effort to learn the language and literature of his host country, he rediscovered French literature and entered into a more productive relationship with it. He read heavily but unselectively in Pascal, Corneille, and Stendhal. (pp. 115-16)

Apparently, the novel ***Pardon wird nicht gegeben*** (**"Men without Mercy"** . . . ; 1937; literal meaning, "Pardon will not be granted"), his "family history with an autobiographical admixture," was influenced by his reading of the great French nineteenth-century novelists, for it is written in a conventional style and is diametrically opposed to Döblin's notion of an epic work. . . .

What could be more appropriate now than to see in ***Pardon wird nicht gegeben*** a retreat into his personal history. But such an interpretation surely fails to do justice to the novel. Like Edward Allison in his subsequent novel, ***Hamlet,*** Döblin is hunting for guilt, his own as well as that of society. The question of guilt would also be the point of departure for his trilogy about the unsuccessful German revolution of 1918. Thus we have only an apparent retreat into autobiography. In truth, Döblin uses autobiographical material to study the sins of the past which are responsible for the catastrophe of the present.

The autobiographical point of departure is unmistakably the collapse of Döblin's family and his move to Berlin. (p. 116)

The novel ends with a vision of the unsuccessful revolution of 1918, which was to be the subject of Döblin's longest book. . . . The novel ***Pardon wird nicht gegeben*** describes how a member of the bourgeoisie, who should have known better from his own experience, does not dare to join the revolutionary movement at the right time. Thus, half intentionally, he betrays the incipient social order to the resurrected military and noble circles. The novel converges completely with Döblin's political thinking and the description of the revolution in ***November 1918.*** (pp. 118-19)

[***November 1918***] is Döblin's longest and probably least successful work. Döblin began working on it about 1938 and finished it five years later in Hollywood. Not only his flight through France, during which he carried the manuscript with him, but also his conversion [to Catholicism] lie between the beginning and the end and were not without influence on its development.

Döblin wanted to do too much at one time and overtaxed his creative powers. He provided not only a detailed portrait of the months of revolution—December, 1918,—to January, 1919—largely a first-hand account that proceeds day by day, but also placed the German events in their international context, the peace parleys and the efforts of Woodrow Wilson. Although not the only setting, Berlin is the chief one of the trilogy. As always in his works, Döblin wanted to provide a total, comprehensive picture of this era, and thus, in addition to the chief historic actors, there are a multitude of episodes and figures: the profiteers who exploit the turbulent times, the proletarian family, Imker, and the dramatist, Stauffer, who is intended purely as a burlesque contrast figure living in his own world. Their fates move through the novel, often interrupted, in novella-like independence. As in ***Berlin Alexanderplatz,*** however, there is also a multitude of fleeting individual fates which surface in the stream of the narrative and are quickly swallowed up again. In Döblin's masterpiece, there is a definite center, the fate of Biberkopf, to which everything else can and must be related. Here, Döblin additionally aligns episodes and fates which are often too broad, even though they are intertwined with one another. What is lacking is a center of integration that would organize the massive material internally and not merely—if at all—connect it externally. Thus the fate of the central figure, Friedrich Becker, Ph.D., which, in conjunction with the history of the revolution, serves as the backbone of the plot, is only loosely connected with the portrayal of political events. The changes that occur in him are symptomatic: resignation in the face of external events and retreat into inwardness. It is characteristic of the novel that the private and public political spheres have hardly any points of contact and nearly run alongside each other without touching. But that is not all: the fate of Becker concerns, if not God himself, then at least Johannes Tauler, the mystic, who is His mouthpiece, as well as the devil in various guises. Döblin attempts to transcend the earthly sphere and to make the novel, at least in part, a Baroque *theatrum mundi*. But, as already stated, there is no internal center which—as in his other novels—could organize and connect the extremely heterogeneous parts. . . . (pp. 128-29)

Like all great political undertakings depicted in Döblin's works, the November revolution, this attempt to found a better and juster social order by a forceful change of society, also fails.

Friedrich Becker, on the other hand, wants to take the opposite tack: not the changing of society preceding the changing of men, but the alteration of man as the precondition for the alteration of society. As Döblin himself had refused, shortly before his emigration, to join one of the political parties, feeling that he could find true humanity only beyond partisanship, Becker refuses "to make a decision. He cannot choose between two and three sandbars to build his house on." That is: for him truth is not to be found in the here and now, or in party ideologies, but only in transcendence. As so often in Döblin, Becker becomes a test figure of the Christian faith, of the possibility or impossibility of being a Christian, of striving daily for God. . . . Becker follows the typical path of Döblin's heroes. Like Edward Allison in ***Hamlet,*** war and a wound put him in a profound crisis. The question of guilt leads him back to the question of the possibility of human action and issues in a desperate search for a transcendental meaning, nearly leading to insanity. The lifestyles of his friends, the political events, and party platforms, offer him no opportunity for finding the solution; his striving is directed toward the absolute. God and the devil struggle for his soul. And here it becomes clear how little Döblin's basic themes had changed despite his conversion. If in his earlier works he was concerned about the insight into the impotence of the individual, about self-abandonment, and about the conscious and voluntary alignment of the individual human being in the comprehensive context of life and the laws of nature, here he is concerned about absolute submission to God's will. But, as always in Döblin, hubris, pride, and arrogance prevent the acceptance of this insight. (pp. 132-33)

The failure of the revolution was a fact whose results Döblin had personally experienced and was still experiencing. Society here appears as corrupt. Even the positive figures, especially Becker's mother, with her affirmation of life and her readiness to help, can change it but little. His tormented search for God drives Becker into complete isolation. What remains seems to be only hope in the grace of God. A gloomy picture indeed! As Friedrich Becker, Döblin, whom one can at least partially identify with his protagonist, had reached the nadir. (p. 135)

The struggle for God and the retreat into inwardness, as reflected especially in the fate of Becker, dominate this phase of Döblin's work; the personal and confessional statement prevails. . . .

It is also evident in the treatises, mostly written in the USA but published in Germany between 1946 and 1949. (p. 136)

The two most important books expressing Döblin's world view at this time are ***Unsere Sorge, der Mensch*** (**"Man, Our Concern"**) and, above all, the dialogue on religion, ***Der unsterbliche Mensch*** (**"Immortal Man"**). Here, in a dialogue between an old man and a young one, Döblin tries to blend his philosophy of nature with the idea of a personal God and to defend his religious convictions against the purely scientific-technical orientation of the young man. The conversation is the most honest and, because of the lack of any literary trappings, the most convincing confrontation of Döblin with himself and Christianity at this time. It represents the sum of all the ideas that moved him, and since here the anonymous, suprapersonal, primeval base is identified with the personal God, the work reaches its zenith in Christian ideas. Despite all the esthetic shortcomings which pervade these writings, and ignoring the question whether Döblin's arguments convince us, his stubborn search for truth deserves our respect. He did not make it easy for himself.

This never ending search for truth is also a characteristic trait of Döblin's last novel, ***Hamlet,*** subtitled ***oder die lange Nacht nimmt ein Ende*** (**"or the Long Night Comes to an End"**). It was published one year before his death and only ten years after its completion. Many critics, probably unjustly, consider it a brilliant work of old age. In any case, it does recapture, to a great degree, the tautness and unity of composition which was only too painfully lacking in the two large trilogies. (pp. 137-38)

Like Friedrich Becker, Edward Allison returns wounded from the war and, like him, in his search for truth he also asks how such a war could come about, and who is responsible, using these questions as the point of departure. This questioning does not find its solution in politico-social circumstances; the appeal to humaneness is—as has repeatedly been shown—characteristic of the late Döblin. His old theme surfaces once more in the form of the question of whether man is a free responsible agent or a marionette ruled by anonymous powers. This is constantly discussed in the novel, whose title already indicates that Shakespeare's *Hamlet* serves as a model for the situation of the hero, Edward Allison. For, like Hamlet, Edward Allison, upon his return, finds guilt and deception in his parent's home. The fate of the two protagonists is similar, for both return home, look for the truth of human relationships in their homes, and are constantly caught in a web of truth and lies, reality and illusion. But their fates are also different, for Hamlet is destroyed, but Edward overcomes the "Hamlet ghost" . . . and regains at least the hope of a meaningful life.

Döblin typically approaches the question of the possibility of responsible action and of the essence of human existence. In the house of Edward's father, the writer Gordon Allison, stories are told to entertain the wounded son. These stories, frequently parodies of stories from world literature, correspond exactly to Döblin's ideas concerning the novella-like independence of individual parts of a novel. They have a double function. First of all, they illustrate definite views of man. Rather than doing so abstractly, the figures discuss philosophical problems with the help of illustrations in which two views of man are diametrically opposed: either man is the product of supraindividual powers which move him and act in his stead, or he is independent and thus completely responsible for his actions. Secondly—and increasingly so—the function of the stories consists in gradually unveiling the true identity of Edward's parents, and revealing the true beings behind the illusion of their masks. . . . Because the stories are open to diverse interpretations, a very complex net of relationships arises. (pp. 138-39)

The stories are intended not only to illustrate opposite points of view, but also to reveal the true identity of Gordon and Alice Allison; and this function moves more and more clearly into the foreground. (p. 140)

Edward seeks the causes of the war from which he himself has suffered and will suffer for the rest of his life. Ever more clearly he thinks that the reasons for the catastrophe lie in the nature of man. He concentrates more and more on the fate of his parents. Edward lives the Hamlet figure; thus there is no need to retell the story of the Danish prince. The parallels between

Edward and his literary model become progressively closer. The veteran tries to learn the history of his parents, which is told him partly indirectly and partly directly. . . .

Edward's penetrating search for the truth altogether destroys the apparent harmony in the Allison house. The terrible love-hate relationship of the parents comes out into the open. The ground is taken out from under the roles they had played up to now, and the whole abyss of human passions behind their apparently peaceful life opens up. (p. 141)

By his quest, Hamlet-Edward has uncovered not only the true character of his parents' marriage, but sees himself once more confronted by the experience that dark instincts beyond human reason and will seem to determine the fate of man. (p. 142)

As with Hamlet, the search for the truth in human relationships does not end in death, but with an optimistic view of life, which he begins to rediscover and in which he sees a task that is, not by chance, of a social and charitable nature. As always with Döblin, here, too, we have an open ending which does not completely satisfy us, because Edward has little basis for the optimism he shows after his experience. Thus we are confronted with a dialectic leap, something not at all unique in Döblin's works. In an earlier version of the novel, he enters a monastery to avoid life, while confronting it in the published version. These two different endings reveal, once again, the polarity of activity and passivity which permeates Döblin and his entire work. (pp. 142-43)

Döblin surely stands in the shadow of the great novelists of the first half of this century: Thomas Mann, Hermann Broch, and Robert Musil. The lack of translations of other important works besides ***Berlin Alexanderplatz*** is, as it were, the most cogent proof of this fact.

A comparison with the works of the novelists mentioned above shows at once their difference from Döblin and the specific quality of his "Döblinism." While his theory of the novel hardly sets doctrinaire limits to the form of the novel (he actually defines it as the completely free form), in his own works he prefers a language of form (*Formensprache*) which is clearly differentiated from that of the other writers. Like many of his great contemporaries, he polemicizes against psychology, causality, and erotic themes, against one-dimensional and linear plots. And he aims—in his unmistakable manner—at totality and complexity. Since the dynamics of the actions in which the individual is imbedded is most important for him, he foregoes reflective excursions and thus renounces the characteristic of the polyhistorical novel, as it occurs in Otto Flake, Broch, and Musil. Döblin wanted to be an epic writer in the original sense, rather than a novelist. He simply wanted to tell a story, not to philosophize. The proliferating narrative mood, the formlessness of many of his works, the frequently noted weaknesses of his novels' endings are only the consequences of an epic attitude which views the epic as endless and thus picks up the thread broken off in one novel in the next. Just as he always judged lyric poetry negatively, as the most esoteric of all literary forms, Döblin mistrusted a theory of the novel which, in his opinion, nearly weighed down with "culture" and knowledge, exceeded by far what he took to be the purpose of the epic: the representation of the great basic human motion in the framework of an overpowering and pervasive relationship with life and nature. The consolatory feeling of being included in this natural relationship, a basic cosmic feeling, binds him closely to the many Expressionists whom he otherwise viewed with reserve. It also contains an irrationalism pointing toward mysticism, thus creating an opposition to the intellectuality of the polyhistorical novel which, in his eyes, must per force obviate the democratization of art which he desired. Just because he consciously tried to open literature not only to the so-called educated bourgeoisie, but to all classes, he must have regretted the absence of a stronger echo.

Success came with ***Berlin Alexanderplatz,*** a work that, by no coincidence, relies on underworld motifs to a much greater degree than all his other works. Although religious themes were by no means overlooked, these motifs have contributed greatly to the popularity of the book, whose success has unfortunately overshadowed Döblin's other epic works. Nonetheless, it was ***Die Geschichte vom Franz Biberkopf*** which established the renown of its author and assured him a place in the history of world literature. Given these limitations, and with the additional limitation that only a few of his works written after 1933 have found, or will find, general favor, Döblin may be regarded as one of the great German prose writers of the first third of this century. Like hardly any other writer, he portrayed the impotence and abandonment of man, but at the same time made a postulate from this insight by describing the necessity of submission to the relationships of life and nature, to the great mass beings, while claiming that sacrifice is unavoidable. But in a dialectic turnabout, the rebellion and protest of the individual which, for its part, can lead to the (technological) hubris of man results from the insight into the impotence and the necessity of submission; and subsequently it causes another turnabout. This is an endless process, one of the essential modes of human existence which Döblin—in accordance with his concept of the epic writer—wanted to bring to light.

Thus Döblin stands in the middle of the traditional concept of a free and great personality which achieves its final peak in Nietzsche's concept of the Superman, and the total dismantling of the personality to a mere object of anonymous powers, as so frequently happens in the present. The "dialectical tension" between the two extremes is not eased in Döblin's work but continuously results in turnabouts. To have portrayed this dialectic movement in moving images is Döblin's great accomplishment. (pp. 144-46)

Wolfgang Kort, in his Alfred Döblin *(copyright © 1974 by Twayne Publishers; reprinted with the permission of Twayne Publishers, a Division of G. K. Hall & Co., Boston), Twayne, 1974, 165 p.*

A. W. RILEY (essay date 1977)

[Riley examines Döblin's treatment of a medieval legend in his final novel, Hamlet.*]*

Whereas many English-speaking readers will be familiar with Thomas Mann's version of Hartmann's 12th-century poem, *Gregorius (The Holy Sinner),* or with Hermann Hesse's novel *Narcissus and Goldmund* with its monastic setting in the Middle Ages, this is not the case with Alfred Döblin's retelling of the mediaeval legend of Jaufré Rudel in his last novel, ***Hamlet or The Long Night Comes to an End***. . . . The reasons for this are not hard to find. First, Döblin's ***Hamlet*** shared the fate of the vast majority of his works and has never been translated into English; second, his unusual sixty-page version of the story of the troubadour Jaufré Rudel and his "amor de lonh" for the Princess of Tripoli—a romantic subject which has inspired works by poets such as Uhland, Heine, Browning, Swinburne, Carducci, and Rostand—is embedded in a long *Rahmenerzäh-*

lung [''story within a story''] and is only one of a number of tales which together form the multi-hued fabric of the novel. Thus, one purpose of this essay is to draw attention to a major German author whose vast *oeuvre* has in my view been sadly neglected in the English-speaking world, and—even in his native Germany—has only been the subject of serious (and continuously growing) scholarly research for the past decade or so. (p. 132)

Döblin's ***Hamlet*** has remained, ever since it was written, a controversial, much praised and much maligned work.

Döblin's ***Hamlet*** consists of a cycle of eleven autonomous stories set within a narrative frame—the basic form of the *novella*—though of a very special kind. (p. 133)

[The individual] stories were conceived *before* the frame. Nevertheless, it would be wrong to assume that Döblin simply constructed a rough and ready framework on which he could hang the various stories he had written. Quite the opposite: each story is fitted so artistically into the frame, and indeed is so necessary for the development of the main plot, that one can justifiably speak of an inspired and unique narrative technique. Just as the tales told by the clever Scheherazade in the *Arabian Nights* serve to distract the King and prevent him from carrying out his cruel plans, the stories in ***Hamlet*** have a therapeutic purpose, though of course in a much more modern and complex sense than in the comparatively naïve world of the fabled Harounel-Raschid. The person for whose benefit the stories are told in Döblin's novel is no omnipotent and exotic potentate, but rather a very modern and even topical example—especially after the recent horrors of the Viet-Nam War—of a veteran whose case-book medical history could be found in the files of many psychiatrists today. The ''hero'' is a patient, a British soldier, who was seriously wounded in 1945 in the Pacific theatre of operations after an attack by Japanese suicide pilots on the warship which was carrying him to the Far East. At the beginning of the novel the hero, Edward Allison, has been sent back to his parents' home in England to recuperate not only physically (one of his legs had been amputated), but above all mentally. Döblin writes in his essay, ''Epilogue'':

> He lay there, sick, confused, almost deranged—it was Edward, who, returning from the war, was not able to come to terms with himself. He becomes a ''Hamlet'' who questions his surroundings. He does not wish to pass judgement, but rather to seek out the truth about a serious and urgent question: he wishes to know what has made him and the rest of mankind sick and evil.

Thus, something quite new is derived from the ''tales of distraction and diversion,'' as Döblin describes them in ''Epilogue'': not only a mosaic-like reflection of the agonizing self-doubts and self-questionings of the hero, whose quest is for truth, but of all the members of his family and beyond this—at least implicitly—of the sick, spiritually disabled members of the family of mankind in our violent century, especially in the aftermath of World War II. On the psychiatrist's couch, as it were (and it should be recalled that Döblin himself was a practising physician and neurologist from 1905 to 1931,) the shades of characters from Shakespeare's plays are conjured up, tales are told—legends from a distant mediaeval world, from the lives of the saints, from classical mythology—all of which lead step by step to the spiritual liberation of the protagonists of the novel. The therapeutic function of the tales is broadened and even reversed: not only the ''patient'' but also the ''physician'' is to be healed. But it is a healing process which gradually brings turmoil to the whole family; old wounds are opened, leading to the very depths of hatred, desire, cruelty, and finally to tragedy, accompanied by a religiously-inspired catharsis. (pp. 133-34)

[The] scope of this article is a strictly limited one: to tackle a problem which has so far been totally neglected by scholars, i.e. to discover the sources of the first, longest and perhaps the most charming story in ***Hamlet,*** the mediaeval tale of the troubadour Jaufré and his Lady of Tripoli. (p. 134)

[Edward Allison's father, Lord Crenshaw, explains] why he has retold the mediaeval tale, and why he wishes to expose, quite brutally, the true origins of the legend. . . .

> And I deliberately chose this story, with its pathetic tones, with its—forgive me—thickly cloying sentimentality (which has evidently helped the story to survive over the centuries) in order to demonstrate what reality is and what has been made out of it. No, what I want to do is precisely to discover reality.
>
> (p. 139)

[The] long literary, *i.e.* romantic, tradition of the legend . . . is present even in Heine's lyrical version, ''Geoffroy Rudèl und Melisande von Tripoli,'' despite a touch of Heinesque irony (at night in the castle of Blaye the ghosts of the dead lovers dally ''with posthumous *galanterie*'' until the dawn drives them away). Döblin/Crenshaw's version on the other hand is a radical departure from this tradition. Crenshaw's purpose, as he says, is ''carefully to remove layer upon layer of centuries-old varnish and lacquer from a genuine oil painting in order to get to the original.''. . . What he is attempting here is to ''demythologize'' and ''psychologize'' the old legend by stripping away the romantic illusions and sentimentality which have accumulated throughout the ages, and to place Jaufré Rudel firmly in the historical and social context of 12th-century Provence. The mediaeval world which generations of poets and writers (including Meller) had hitherto charmingly romanticized is ironically debunked by Crenshaw in order to prove to his son Edward that man is not a free agent, but a product of custom, society, and a prevailing *Weltanschauung, i.e.* that he is controlled by suprapersonal powers. Thus, Crenshaw's reinterpretation of the legend culminates in a reversal of the traditional, romantic view on the mediaeval code of love and chivalry. Jaufré's ''amor de lonh'' was, according to Crenshaw, not romantic at all, but rather the result of a very earthy and complicated amorous escapade with a married lady, which, as we shall see, compelled Jaufré to make a pilgrimage to Tripoli under the pretext of his declared love for a never-seen mistress, only to find there a Princess who is ancient, horribly ugly (but beautified by cosmetics and other means) and surrounded by clever advertising agents who sing her praises abroad. (Döblin's sojourn in Hollywood, where he worked for a time as a script-writer for MGM, has clearly left its mark here.) With the aid of friends, Döblin's Jaufie escapes from the clutches of the Princess (who drinks human blood—a sort of mediaeval version of live-cell rejuvenation therapy), returns to Provence, where he lives to the end of his life with his beloved Petite Lay. But the world takes no notice of this: only the legend lives on, stifling and suppressing reality. . . . Crenshaw's version of the mediaeval story has an important ''therapeutic'' function (unmasking of sentimental, romantic love, mirroring Crenshaw's own marriage, with allusions to his own relationship with his wife and son), and . . . it also is a leitmotif, which at the end of the novel undergoes a surprising religious metamorphosis, reverting, as it were, to Swinburne's traditional treatment of the legend. . . . (p. 142)

Having been dubbed Knight together with his mother Valentine (who is now a *chevalière*), Jaufie must embark on a journey throughout the land, wielding a sword and adept at song, as required by the code of troubadour-knights. This sort of vagrant life does not appeal to him, and in any case, as Döblin writes, "Jaufie was in a fix . . . for which Lady should he sing?" . . . His young mistress, Petite Lay, is out of the running, for she is of peasant stock and not a single section of the Rules for Troubadours applies to her, since these "are valid solely for noble Ladies and Knights.". . . Döblin fleshes out the bare bones of Meller's tale by having Jaufie use Petite Lay, disguised as a *jongleur,* as the go-between in his clandestine overtures to the fair Rosamunde (whom he has chosen as his Lady), wife of the boorish Robert of Artoie. (The names are to be found in Meller, but in unrelated tales.) A series of complex escapades ensues. Rosamunde falls in love with Petite Lay; the deception is uncovered; Sir Robert has Jaufie beaten by his Saracen body-guards and warns both Rosamunde and Jaufie of the terrible fate that awaits them by narrating the story of Lady Soremonda and her love for Guillem de Caberstaing, whose roasted heart she unwittingly eats when it is served to her by her cruel husband, Raymond of Castel-Rousillon. . . . The honour of both Jaufie and Robert and his wife has been seriously impugned, and the jealous husband is intent on vengeance. . . . "The custom of the age showed its strength. It was a power and had teeth and claws.". . . But help appears from an unexpected quarter: Lady Rosamunde appeals to the "Court of Love," and the Countess of Champagne and her ladies skilfully and diplomatically use various sections of the "Laws of love" to restore the honour of all concerned. . . . [Döblin bases] Jaufie's exoneration and escape from his predicament *inter alia* on Law 17: "A new love affair banishes the old one completely.". . . Prompted by the clever advice of Petite Lay, Jaufie formally declares his new love for the Princess of Tripoli, whom he has never seen but whose fabled existence provides him not only with a legal excuse to avoid the wrath of Sir Robert, but, with all parties satisfied, to embark on the pilgrimage for which he will be remembered throughout the centuries to come. Needless to say, none of this is to be found in Meller, nor indeed in any other source. Döblin's version of the Jaufré legend is his alone. (pp. 142-43)

Döblin's sly humour, his light-hearted, loving irony, his deliberate "distancing" of the mediaeval world—all are characteristic of his version of the Jaufré legend. Equally so is his humorous treatment of the theory that the whole "system" of troubadours and the Courts of Love were nothing less than a mediaeval women's liberation movement . . . , thereby creating an extremely important corner-stone on which the development of the plot of "The Princess of Tripoli" is based. (p. 145)

A. W. Riley, "Jaufré Rudel in Alfred Doblin's Last Novel 'Hamlet'" (originally published in a different form as "Jaufré Rudel und die Prinzessin von Tripoli: zur Entstehung einer Erzählung und zur Metamorphose der Legende in Alfred Döblins 'Hamlet-Roman'," in Festschrift für Friedrich Beissner, *edited by Ulrich Gaier and Werner Volke, Verlag Lothar Rotsch, 1974), in* MOSAIC: A Journal for the Comparative Study of Literature and Ideas *(copyright © 1977 by the University of Manitoba; acknowledgement of previous publication is herewith made), Vol. X, No. 2 (Winter, 1977), pp. 131-45.*

ROBERT MARTIN ADAMS (essay date 1977)

[In his AfterJoyce: Studies in Fiction after "Ulysses," *Adams demonstrates that the influence of James Joyce's novel on* Alexanderplatz, Berlin *is limited to "the counterpointed and jazzy rhythm of the background, the mechanism of city life," and that Döblin's is a "novel of pride, punishment, and personal redemption" more comparable in theme to Fedor Dostoyevski's works than to Joyce's. Adams contends that the mythological allusions in Döblin's novel serve to contrast the lives of his modern characters with figures in mythology, rather than draw parallels between them as Joyce did in* Ulysses. *For other comparisons of Döblin's and Joyce's works, see the excerpts by Florence Haxton Britten (1931), Michael Sadleir (1931), Andrew M. McLean (1973), and the entry in the Additional Bibliography by Breon Mitchell.]*

In Germany, Joyce was known early and favorably. Even where it is most obvious, however, in the work of Alfred Döblin and Hermann Broch, his influence is heavily diluted with other thematic and technical considerations; one sees it quickly, but comes almost as quickly to the end of it. ***Alexanderplatz, Berlin*** . . . by Döblin is an urban novel like *Ulysses,* though it deals with a bigger, faster, tougher city, and slices through it at a much lower social level than Joyce ever tried to penetrate. Franz Biberkopf is an earnest, inward ox of a man, determined to be good and doubly determined because, as the novel opens, he has just finished four years in the pen for killing his "fiancée," a girl (like all the girls of Franz's particular milieu) who isn't above eking out a living on the streetcorner. Franz is not only dim of brain but deeply colored by the mores of his lumpentribe. . . . (p. 134)

Unlike the narrative voice, which is consistently sardonic and wise-guy ("I've seen it all before" as from a guttersnipe Koheleth), Franz Biberkopf hardly ever gets or attempts a perspective on events—he takes the rush of them head-on, and they flow over him like a river in flood. The flotsam and jetsam of the big city are here in overwhelming quantities—gaudy storefronts, flaring ads, industrial statistics, weather reports, the sequence of stops on a subway line, fragments of popular song, unrelated episodes and fantasies involving total strangers, the random and the miscellaneous. Stitched through the thick texture of social fact are a variety of leitmotifs and persistent rhythms which convey the mood of our hero.

This is a matter of some importance because Franz Biberkopf is a manic-depressive who, in undertaking to be "good" in a milieu where practically everyone else is "bad," has assumed a superhuman task for himself. His intentions are of the best and his strength is as the strength of ten, but he is not very bright, and he blunders into one trap after another. Each successive frustration is followed by a deeper and darker fit of sulky depression. In these moods, he is prone to see his life under various mythical and legendary aspects, which are presented ambiguously at best, and sometimes in a frankly hostile light. There is a fine and funny discussion of the Furies within Franz Biberkopf that may have led him to kill Ida, as they formerly tormented Orestes for killing Clytemnestra. But the mythology breaks off into an account of the laws of physics, without knowing which we can't possibly understand how the application of a wooden cream-whipper came to fracture the seventh and eighth ribs in line with Ida's left shoulder-blade. And when we've understood these laws of physics, and Franz's application of them to Ida, we clearly don't need to consider the Furies any further. "I'm not a Greek, I'm from Berlin" is one of the leitmotifs of the novel. . . .

On the other hand, Franz Biberkopf gets into his third and deepest tangle of trouble because of a purely and obviously mythical action. His most recent and most successful affair is with a gentle and devoted little prostitute whose real name is Sonia, but whom he calls Mieze. Proud of her devotion to him, he invites sinister Reinhold to hide in the bedroom and witness their happiness. The impression is too taking; Reinhold seizes his first occasion to attack Mieze and when she resists to murder her. The entire episode is a re-enactment, of which the narrator at least is very conscious, of Herodotus's story of Gyges. Its consequences all but destroy Franz Biberkopf. As the story develops, they don't quite do so; they lead to a prolonged and terrible struggle in the depths of his catatonic psyche, from which ultimately a new Franz Biberkopf is born. The process is darkly moving. But the very fact that we are concerned on this level with the central character of the novel suggests an affinity with Dostoevsky rather than Joyce. There's little or no transparency to Franz Biberkopf, and even less sense of void; we descend into him and into the roaring traffic of his subconscious (deliberately presented in the same words as the outward traffic of Berlin, forever tearing itself up and rebuilding) as into an ultimate dark pocket. Biberkopf is Biberkopf, not Ajax or Hercules; and the battered peace he finally attains seems to encompass that crucial phrase, "I'm not a Greek, I'm from Berlin." Death, who seems to be from Berlin too (he has the accent), conveys the thought to him in a fantastic colloquy; and so Biberkopf is reborn in humility and caution—good still, as he has always been good, and strong still, but not so confident of his single strength, which has always been the serpent in his garden of Eden. To the critical eye his redemption may seem a little contrived, since it depends on his getting a modest but regular job as assistant doorman in a medium-sized factory, such as he could have had any time in the novel, at least for all we can tell. Still, these are the hazards of the novel of pride, punishment, and personal redemption; and their prominence amply emphasizes the differences of Döblin's action and emphasis from the Joycean model. What produced in the first place the impression of Joycean influence (which Döblin vigorously repudiated) was chiefly the counterpointed and jazzy rhythm of the background, the mechanism of city life. But the heart of the action was elsewhere. (pp. 136-37)

Robert Martin Adams, "Döblin, Broch," in his AfterJoyce: Studies in Fiction after "Ulysses" *(copyright © 1977 by Robert Martin Adams; reprinted by permission of Oxford University Press, Inc.), Oxford University Press, New York, 1977, pp. 134-45.**

GÜNTER GRASS (essay date 1980)

[Grass is a noted German novelist, poet, short story writer, and dramatist whose novel Die Blechtrommel (The Tin Drum) *is critically regarded as the most significant literary work to be published in Germany in the past thirty years. In the following excerpt, he acknowledges a literary debt to Döblin.]*

When people speak of Alfred Döblin nowadays, they normally speak of ***Berlin Alexanderplatz.*** There are reasons why recognition for a writer—whom I am prepared to compare and contrast with Thomas Mann, to compare and contrast with Bertolt Brecht—should be reduced exclusively to this one book. The work of a Thomas Mann, and even more so the work of a Bertolt Brecht, was consciously adapted to a classical plan shaped by its author and executed to the last detail. Both writers hewed and set stone upon stone on a clearly marked foundation, with obvious references to the classical tradition they sought to continue. (p. v)

The secondary literature dealing with either of these authors bursts bookcases. Soon Brecht, like Kafka, will be interpreted away until he is no longer ours. Döblin was spared such an abduction to Olympian fields. This anticlassicist has never had a devoted cult of followers, not even a cult of enemies. Generations grew up with Thomas Mann, familiar with every quirk of his style. The term "Kafkaesque" rolls off our tongues the moment we have difficulties with bureaucrats. And our Brechtomaniacs are recognizable by the way they toss participles about. Only Alfred Döblin has provided no impetus for symposia; only he has seldom engaged the industry of our Germanists, has seduced few readers.

I would like to be permitted to set Mann, Brecht and Kafka respectfully aside, though fully conscious of their awesome and frequently touted stature, and to express something of the gratitude a pupil feels toward his teacher. For I am greatly indebted to Alfred Döblin; what is more, I could not begin to imagine my own prose without the futuristic component in his work from ***Wang-Lun*** on through ***Wallenstein*** and ***Mountains, Sea and Giants*** and ***Berlin Alexanderplatz.*** In other words: writers do not simply appear out of the blue, they have their forebearers.

I never saw him, but this is how I picture him: small, nervous, volatile, nearsighted and as a result pressed in all too close to reality; a stenographic visionary, who is so overwhelmed by imaginative ideas that he has no time left to construct his prose periods carefully. From book to book he begins anew, contradicting himself and his continually changing theories. Manifestos, essays, books, thoughts dog each others' footsteps.

This much is certain: Döblin knew that a book must be more than its author, that the author is only a means to the goal of a book, and that an author must learn to find hiding places, which he can then leave to speak his manifestos, but which he must first search out in order to have a place to flee from his own book. Döblin proposes: "The subject of a novel is reality unchained, reality that confronts the reader completely independent of some firmly fixed course of events. It is the reader's task to judge, not the author's! To speak of a novel is to speak of layering, of piling in heaps, of wallowing, of pushing and shoving. A drama is about its poor plot, its desperately ever-present plot. In drama it is always 'forward!' But 'forward' is never the slogan of a novel." (pp. v-vi)

Döblin has never set quite right. He was too Catholic for the progressive left, too anarchistic for the Catholics; he lacked the firm theses so necessary for moralists. He was too inelegant for cultural television programs, too vulgar for educational radio.

Döblin's net worth has not as yet been fully evaluated. But one of his followers and students has converted a bit of his inheritance into fame, and it is for that reason that I am trying to repay him today with a few small coins. [It is my hope that] this testimonial . . . can at least contribute toward arousing your curiosity, toward enticing you to Döblin so that he may be read. He will unsettle you; he will trouble your dreams; you will have difficulty swallowing him; you will find him unsavory; he is indigestible, gristly. He changes his readers. The self-complacent are hereby cautioned against Döblin. (p. vi)

Günter Grass, "Günter Grass on Alfred Döblin" (reprinted by permission of the author; originally published as "Über meinen Lehrer Döblin" in his Aufsätze zur Literatur, *Luchterhand Verlag, 1980), in* A People Betrayed: November 1918, a German Revolution *by Alfred Doblin, translated by John E. Woods, Fromm International Publishing Corporation, 1983, pp. v-vi.*

ADDITIONAL BIBLIOGRAPHY

Boa, Elizabeth, and Reid, J. H. "Politics, History and Utopia." In their *Critical Strategies: German Fiction in the Twentieth Century,* pp. 129-144. London: Edward Arnold, 1972.*

Defines *Alexanderplatz, Berlin* as a political novel (see also James H. Reid excerpt above, 1967-68). The critics find that in examining the various ways Franz Biberkopf deals with his surroundings, the novel stresses the political dimension of human behavior.

Fries, Marilyn Sibley. "The City As Metaphor for the Human Condition: Alfred Döblin's *Berlin Alexanderplatz* (1929)." *Modern Fiction Studies* 24, No. 1 (Spring 1978): 41-64.

Discusses the ways in which Döblin identifies the character of Franz Biberkopf with the collective entity of Alexanderplatz, so that "On a metaphysical level . . . Biberkopf becomes a living metaphor for Alexanderplatz" while at the same time "Alexanderplatz reflects Biberkopf."

Kahn, Lothar. "Alfred Döblin: Indictment and Apostasy." In his *Mirrors of the Jewish Mind: A Gallery of Portraits of European Jewish Writers of our Time,* pp. 83-94. New York: Thomas Yoseloff, 1968.

Biographical account of the changes in Döblin's religious beliefs, examining the reasons for his growing disenchantment with Judaism that led to his conversion to Catholicism.

Komar, Kathleen. "Technique and Structure in Döblin's *Berlin Alexanderplatz.*" *The German Quarterly* LIV, No. 3 (May 1981): 318-34.

Examines the narrative elements with which Döblin reinforced the pattern of classical tragedy in *Alexanderplatz, Berlin.* This topic is also discussed by Theodore Ziolkowski (see excerpt above, 1969).

Marcuse, Ludwig. "Alfred Döblin at Seventy-Five." *Books Abroad* 28, No. 2 (Spring 1954): 179-80.

Approbatory overview of Döblin's life and career.

Mitchell, Breon. "Joyce and Alfred Döblin: Creative Catalysis." In his *James Joyce and the German Novel: 1922-1933,* pp. 131-87. Athens: Ohio University Press, 1976.

Closely examines the various extant texts of the manuscript of *Alexanderplatz, Berlin.* Mitchell determines the extent of the influence of James Joyce, and particularly of the novel *Ulysses,* upon Döblin during the writing of *Alexanderplatz, Berlin.*

Riley, A. W. "The Professing Christian and the Ironic Humanist: A Comment on the Relationship of Alfred Döblin and Thomas Mann after 1933." In *Essays on German Literature in Honour of G. Joyce Hallamore,* edited by Michael S. Batts and Marketa Goetz Stankiewicz, pp. 177-94. Toronto: University of Toronto Press, 1968.

Examines the relationship between Thomas Mann and Döblin, focusing upon the changes in their respective religious views and their bitter antagonism after Hitler came to power.

———. "The Aftermath of the First World War: Christianity and Revolution in Alfred Döblin's *November 1918.*" In *The First World War in German Narrative Prose,* edited by Charles N. Genno and Heinz Wetzel, pp. 93-117. Toronto: University of Toronto Press, 1980.

Examines *Karl und Rosa,* the second volume of Döblin's Revolution trilogy. Riley finds that only in this novel, written after Döblin's conversion to Catholicism, does Döblin come to terms with his own experiences of war.

Scherer, Herbert. "The Individual and the Collective in Döblin's *Berlin Alexanderplatz.*" In *Culture and Society in the Weimar Republic,* edited by Keith Bullivant, pp. 56-70. Manchester, England: Manchester University Press, 1977.

Interprets *Alexanderplatz, Berlin* as a departure from the traditional *Entwicklungsroman,* a novel form concerned with an individual's progress or development.

Schoonover, Henrietta S. *The Humorous and Grotesque Elements in Döblin's "Berlin Alexanderplatz."* Berne, Switzerland: Peter Lang, 1977, 280 p.

Doctoral dissertation. Schoonover examines Döblin's use of such elements as puns, authorial intrusion, and satire to introduce humor and incongruity into his work.

Édouard (Émile Louis) Dujardin

1861-1949

French novelist, critic, essayist, editor, dramatist, and poet.

Dujardin was a minor French Symbolist author who attained his greatest prominence more than thirty years after the publication of his only novel, *Les lauriers sont coupés (We'll to the Woods No More),* when James Joyce cited the work as his source for the stream of consciousness narrative technique of *Ulysses.* Subsequent critical study has revealed that *We'll to the Woods No More* is one of the earliest works of fiction in any language to be written in *le monologue intérieur,* or "inner monologue." Of Dujardin's novel, Melvin J. Friedman wrote that "the reader finds himself suspended, for probably the first time, in the consciousness of a single character through an entire novel."

Dujardin was early associated with the French Symbolist movement. He was widely known in Paris in the 1880s as the founder and editor of *La revue indépendante,* a magazine of poetry and criticism that Kenneth Cornell characterized as "a semi-official organ of symbolism." At *La revue indépendante,* Dujardin occasionally received the editorial assistance of his friends Stéphane Mallarmé and Joris-Karl Huysmans. Dujardin's critical studies of Mallarmé—*Mallarmé, par un des siens,* and *De Stéphane Mallarmé au prophète Ezéchiel, et essai d'une théorie du réalisme symbolique*—are still regarded as significant contemporary examinations of Mallarmé's work. Dujardin also founded and edited the *Revue Wagnérienne,* a periodical devoted to the study of Richard Wagner's life and works, which reflected Dujardin's lifelong enthusiasm for the music of this composer. Dujardin's admiration was further expressed in the verse dramas *Antonia, Le chevalier du passé,* and *La fin d'Antonia,* which he wrote and produced in the early 1890s, employing themes borrowed from Wagner's opera *Parsifal.* These dramas were presented as a trilogy, *La légende d'Antonia,* "which was long remembered as a spectacular flop," according to Kathleen M. McKilligan. Though Dujardin's critical faculty was acute, McKilligan has found that he was unable to draw inspiration from Wagner for an original work of his own, and thus the Wagnerian trilogy bordered on parody. Dujardin's slight fame as a novelist, editor, and dramatist receded later in his life, and until Joyce revived interest in *We'll to the Woods No More,* Dujardin was best known as a lecturer and writer on religious history. Irish novelist George Moore has noted that his lengthy discussions of religious topics with Dujardin inspired the religious themes of his own novels *The Lake* and *The Brook Kerith.*

Published in 1888, *We'll to the Woods No More* received virtually no critical attention at the time of its first appearance. Critics concur that the subject matter of *We'll to the Woods No More* is slight and, further, that Dujardin's inaugural use of the stream of consciousness technique is often awkward, even primitive. The novel chronicles six hours in the life of Daniel Prince, a Parisian dandy who hopes to be asked to spend the night with the coquettish actress whom he had been financially aiding. The entire story is related through an account of Prince's successive mental impressions during the evening. Critics have noted that in several sections of the novel Dujardin clearly steps outside the boundaries of the stream of consciousness narrative; for example, after the actress Leá postpones a rendezvous with Prince for several hours, he passes the time by rereading her letters, thus supplying an objective history of their relationship. This artificial device is often compared by critics with Molly Bloom's long monologue which concludes *Ulysses* and which provides similar flashbacks in a less contrived way. Indeed, the criticism subsequent to Joyce's revelation of indebtedness has insisted upon the enormous improvements Joyce made in the stream of consciousness technique. However, as Leon Edel has pointed out, "It is easy . . . to criticize Dujardin from our Joycean hindsight. What we must remember is the staunch, pioneer strength of *We'll to the Woods No More*" and "the beauty of certain of the writer's evocations."

ÉDOUARD DUJARDIN

LE

MONOLOGUE INTÉRIEUR

SON APPARITION

SES ORIGINES

SA PLACE DANS L'ŒUVRE DE JAMES JOYCE

Avec un index des écrivains cités

PARIS

ALBERT MESSEIN, ÉDITEUR

19, QUAI SAINT-MICHEL, 19

1931

Title page of Le monologue intérieur, *by Édouard Dujardin. Courtesy of Editions Messein S.A.R.L.*

Following Joyce's acknowledgement of Dujardin's primacy in the stream of consciousness technique, Dujardin was asked to explain his original intent and method in writing *We'll to the*

***Woods No More*. This explication, originally delivered as a lecture, was published as *Le monologue intérieur: Son apparition, ses origines, sa place dans l'oeuvre de James Joyce et dans le roman contemporain*. In this work, portions of which have been translated by Edel, Dujardin defines the inner monologue as the "unheard and unspoken speech by which a character expresses his inmost thoughts." Critics such as Edel, Lawrence E. Bowling, and Robert Humphrey, have found little relevance between *Le monologue intérieur* and the novel it purports to explain; Edel in particular wrote that *Le monologue intérieur* "reads as if Dujardin arrived at his theories from his perusal of *Ulysses,* rather than from a rereading of *Les lauriers sont coupés*." However, most critics—including Edel—have found that whether or not Dujardin arrived at his definition of inner monologue post factum, *Le monologue intérieur* is a valuable examination and definition of the stream of consciousness technique. Critics also acknowledge that with *We'll to the Woods No More* Dujardin became one of the earliest authors to present an entire fictional work in that style.**

(See also *Contemporary Authors,* Vol. 109.)

PRINCIPAL WORKS

Mallarmé, par un des siens (essays) 1887; *Mallarmé, par un des siens* [revised and enlarged edition], 1936
Les lauriers sont coupés (novel) 1888
[*We'll to the Woods No More,* 1938]
**Antonia* (drama) 1891
**Le chevalier du passé* (drama) 1892
**La fin d'Antonia* (drama) 1893
Poésies (poetry) 1913
De Stéphane Mallarmé au prophète Ezéchiel, et essai d'une théorie du réalisme symbolique (essay) 1919
Le monologue intérieur: Son apparition, ses origines, sa place dans l'oeuvre de James Joyce et dans le roman contemporain (lecture) 1931

*These works are collectively referred to as *La légende d'Antonia*.

ALFRED KAZIN (essay date 1938)

[*A highly respected American literary critic, Kazin is best known for his essay collections* The Inmost Leaf *(1955) and* Contemporaries *(1962), and particularly for* On Native Grounds *(1942), a study of American prose writing since the era of William Dean Howells. Having studied the works of "the critics who were the best writers—from Sainte-Beuve and Matthew Arnold to Edmund Wilson and Van Wyck Brooks" as an aid to his own critical understanding, Kazin has found that "criticism focussed many—if by no means all—of my own urges as a writer: to show literature as a deed in human history, and to find in each writer the uniqueness of the gift, of the essential vision, through which I hoped to penetrate into the mystery and sacredness of the individual soul." In the following review of the first English edition of* We'll to the Woods No More, *Kazin examines differences in the stream of consciousness techniques of Dujardin and James Joyce.*]

"Les Lauriers sont Coupés," which now appears for the first time in English, has enjoyed an indirect fame since the war and the advent of psycho-analysis and the stream-of-consciousness method in literature. . . . To students of James Joyce, of course the novel has long ranked as one of the principal sources of "Ulysses." . . .

Readers of Joyce and all those interested in the origins of the stream-of-consciousness method should be cautioned however, against allowing too much to Dujardin's little novel. It is surprising that Mr. James Laughlin 4th should not have done this in his otherwise helpful postscript to this edition, for there is a very radical difference between Joyce and Dujardin, a difference that goes beyond the distinction of talent and the unique circumstances of Joyce's own career. Dujardin's interior monologue is just that: it is normal and conscious speech or thought which differs from ordinary speech only in that it is not uttered aloud. Joyce's monologues spring truly from the unconscious. Broken, wayward, mischievous, the astonishing world from the depths that sprang up for the first time in the darkly lit pages of "Portrait of the Artist as a Young Man" and reached its flower in the roaring pages of "Ulysses" is in all its ramifications a world of the unknown. The difference is this: in the mind of Daniel Prince, Dujardin's hero, the words that are not spoken form coherent ideas; in the mind of Stephen Dedalus the words that cannot be spoken form sensations.

The story Dujardin has to tell is brief and fragile to an extreme, but its slight beauty and wealth of local color spring from its evocation of Paris in the nineties. . . . But the story . . . is unimportant. What has kept Dujardin's book in a state of fair preservation through the years is his use of the interior monologue.

To American readers that monologue is known through Browning more than any other. Eugene O'Neill used it with intermittent success in the less ridiculous scenes in "Strange Interlude," and it is precisely the flat, simple O'Neill style, in which one says "I love you" out loud and something else within, that one can find a more obvious correspondence to Dujardin. The parallel with Joyce, however, is less easy to see, if only because Joyce built so much upon Dujardin's experiments that the pupil (if Joyce was really that) has completely obliterated the teacher.

The effect throughout is of a soft and extremely complacent well-being. One is never conscious of Prince's strain or even of his effort; the atmosphere is all autumn leaves and gracious lamps at twilight, giggles in the dusk and healthy, fashionable youth. But in "Ulysses" (we'll leave Mrs. Bloom out of this; Molly was always a little too complete for anybody's purpose) the correspondence between what is said and what is felt is never parallel, neat, literal on the surface. What one has, instead, is a thrusting organism, aggressive and frightening, an emblem of that which lies within us, something which penetrates the things we touch and illuminates in truth the things about which we lie or remain evasive. What is even more important, of course, is that Daniel Prince is the whole of Dujardin's novel, and Daniel Prince is a cipher; while it is the richness of Stephen Dedalus's mind that makes "Ulysses" what it is.

Alfred Kazin, "Chronicle and Monologue: 'We'll to the Woods No More'," in New York Herald Tribune Books *(© I.H.T. Corporation), November 6, 1938, p. 16.*

C. D. KING (essay date 1953)

[*The excerpt below is taken from one of the most significant approbatory overviews of Dujardin's two principal works,* We'll to the Woods No More *and* Le monologue intérieur. *King's conclusions differ from those of Leon Edel (see excerpt below, 1958, and Additional Bibliography) and Lawrence C. Bowling (see Additional Bibliography), who find that* Le monologue intérieur *is more of an afterthought than a consequent to* We'll to the Woods No More. *King finds that in writing the novel "the intentions of Dujardin were new; he consciously used the form for the whole of his story," and while he "may have been influenced by afterthoughts" when he wrote* Le monologue intérieur, *this is by no means proved.*]

Les Lauriers sont Coupés is hardly a novel at all, though it calls itself one; the hundred pages which recount six hours in the life of Daniel Prince contain little more than the material of a short story. Prince, a student, is pursuing a small-part actress, Léa d'Arsay, and up to the beginning of the story he has been unsuccessful, through lack of forcefulness and experience, in obtaining the favours to which his repeated gifts of money seemed to entitle him.

While the two main characters in ***Les Lauriers sont Coupés*** are clearly defined, they lack depth. Maupassant, with the same material, might have written a cynical story a quarter of the length, starting perhaps a little before Prince's arrival in the Rue Stevens. Indeed, the story as it stands divides neatly into three in the way that some of Maupassant's more dramatic stories break up into three acts. The first, as far as Prince's rooms, deals with Prince in the present. The second largely with Léa in the past. And finally the two come together to produce the climax. In all ways Dujardin's story is carefully ordered, and shows none of that formlessness that some critics have found to be the inevitable result of using inner monologue.

But from most points of view the technique of ***Les Lauriers sont Coupés*** is the direct opposite of Maupassant's. Maupassant believed that the novelist should restrict himself to observing the observable, the visible actions and gestures which are the outward signs of an inner state. Dujardin held that what is real is the inner state. . . . And this was the principle of ***Les Lauriers sont Coupés***. . . . If Dujardin actually dedicated it 'En hommage au suprême romancier d'âmes, Racine' ['In homage to the supreme romancer of souls, Racine'], it was to show that in inventing a new technique for the novel he was conscious of making, not progress, but only change; to show his respect for Classicism; and because he was fond of the word 'âme', in one of the senses given to it by contemporary thinkers. (p. 118)

Les Lauriers sont Coupés is an illustration of the belief that only the 'âme' is real. In the words of Axël, you see the external world through your soul. This formula, used and misused by the Symbolists, is a perversion of the thought of Schopenhauer. Dujardin's novel is an experiment because, to illustrate this idea, it is written throughout in inner monologue. The whole book happens in the mind of the principal character, Prince, and is expresed by that silent voice which is a soundless reflection of the real voice, an imaginary movement of the glottis. In fact the book is a first-person narrative with the important difference that the narrator is unaware that he is narrating, that he has an audience. He is simply engaged in being himself. . . . Since the whole book is written in this way, the author has voluntarily restricted himself to one view-point, that of Prince, and to strict chronology (from which he nevertheless escapes by means of the letters), and renounced the apparent omniscience and omnipotence which the novelist normally enjoys. . . . A character presented in this way is the sum of his own past . . . , but the memory and influence of this past can be touched off only by the appropriate stimulus. It has been said that there is enough information given in *Ulysses* to provide material for a saga-type novel starting with Bloom's grandfather, and a great deal of this is actually in Bloom's monologues. In ***Les Lauriers sont Coupés*** the presence of the author is nowhere apparent; Prince holds the stage alone, while Dujardin is elsewhere. Or, in the words of Joyce, talking of lyric, epic and dramatic form, the artist, in the last of these, 'like the God of creation, remains within or behind or beyond or above his handiwork, invisible, refined out of existence, indifferent, paring his fingernails'. The mind, in inner monologue, has been dramatized. (pp. 118-19)

Whether Joyce would have written exactly the same *Ulysses* if he had never read Dujardin's novel is a matter of conjecture only and of no importance. Perhaps Joyce, when he pointed to Dujardin, was for no apparent reason joking. But at least there is no point in disputing facts, and the facts are these. Joyce reads ***Les Lauriers sont Coupés*** during his first journey to Paris in 1902. . . . And in 1929 when the French translation of *Ulysses* appeared, Joyce presented a copy to Dujardin 'annonciateur de la parole intérieure', ['forerunner of interior speech'] and signed himself 'le larron impénitent ['the impenitent thief']. . . . It is, then, no fable that Joyce read and admired Dujardin's book; and a fact that he later used the same technique.

Finally, in 1931, Dujardin published ***Le Monologue Intérieur, son apparition, ses origines, sa place dans l'oeuvre de James Joyce et dans le roman contemporain,*** in which he defines the technique as he used it and supports his claim to be the inventor. Inner monologue is not easy to define, though it is easily recognized. There is no ideal, but only examples of it. Dujardin's definition and statement of intentions appeared more than forty years after the first publication of his book, and may perhaps have been influenced by afterthoughts. But as the late eighteen-eighties were a period of theorizing, Dujardin may, indeed, have set out to write a story to order. (pp. 120-21)

The game of finding the first example of inner monologue, started by those who did not accept the claim put forward on behalf of, and later by, Dujardin, is still going on. In ***Le Monologue Intérieur*** Dujardin mentions numerous monologues of one sort and another, quoted by critics as being anterior to his own experiment, or later than ***Les Lauriers sont Coupés*** but earlier than Joyce. And there have been later suggestions. The names of Browning, Poe, Dostoevsky, Gide, Proust, Tolstoi, Stendhal, Arthur Schnitzler, Thomas Mann, Strindberg, Dickens, Fanny Burney, Fenimore Cooper, Melville, Montaigne, Amiel and Laforgue have all been put forward. This list, which could be very much lengthened, includes not only writers supposed to have written inner monologue, but some who wrote in a very similar way, and yet others who, like Stendhal (in his *Filosofia Nova*) had the idea but never carried it out. A trace of inner monologue older than any of those attributed to the above writers is seen by Jean Frappier in the thirteenth-century prose romance *La Mort le Roi Art*. . . . (p. 121)

But a study of all those authors, from Montaigne onwards, supposed by the critics to have used inner monologue before Dujardin, shows that in fact none of them wrote anything quite comparable with ***Les Lauriers sont Coupés.*** An odd sentence or paragraph here or there can hardly count, anything written in poetic form like Browning's dramatic monologues or Gide's *Bethsabée* lacks the essential naturalism, and it is not sufficient to record fast unthinking speech, as Dickens does with Jingle in the *Pickwick Papers,* or a personal history of thought and experience, like Montaigne or the writer of a *journal intime*. But some of these writers marked stages on the way to the technique. . . .

It seems necesssary, when inquiring who first wrote inner monologue, to take into account the intentions of the author.

It would be impossible to say who first noticed the existence of the silent inner voice. Socrates noticed it, and Plato described thought as a dialogue of the soul with itself. Before the end of the nineteenth century there must have been numerous instances when the idea, or something enough like it to make a comparison possible, was applied in literature. The two words 'monologue intérieur' are certainly to be found together before 1887. (p. 122)

The intentions of Dujardin were new; he consciously used the form for the whole of his story, as an end in itself. The matter of his book is, very largely, the way it is expressed, just as the matter in music is the expression. Moreover, Dujardin used the form to give a naturalistic version of the mind working in ordinary circumstances.

These points are important, because they distinguish ***Les Lauriers sont Coupés*** not only from all those writers listed above, but from another, far closer than any of them, and apparently unknown to Dujardin, the Russian author Vsevolod Garshin. . . . The work in which he uses something very like inner monologue is a story, *Four Days,* which he had composed while he was lying wounded at Kharkov, and which created a sensation when it first appeared. It is about a soldier who kills a Turk and is then himself wounded. For three and a half days he lies in a state of semi-consciousness and semi-delirium, near the rotting corpse—a period covered in thirteen pages. The whole is in the first person, but starts in the form of a recollection which changes into the dramatic present. . . . (pp. 122-23)

[Garshin's] style is very close to that of Dujardin and yet it is not quite the same. The basis of the similarity is that it treats an abnormal state—semi-delirium—and in the first person. Much inner monologue seems to present a picture of a drunken world, precisely because it recognizes that our normal mental life, if looked at dispassionately, is indeed incoherent and inorganic. If we are not normally aware of this incoherence it is because we select, suppressing those elements which do not interest us. It is presumably for this reason that Dujardin spoke of recording those thoughts which lie nearest the unconscious—but, one might object, the nearer to the unconscious they lie, the less likely they are to happen in words. Garshin used the technique as the most telling way of rendering an abnormal state, while Dujardin's character, Prince, is quite normal, and lives in normal surroundings. Indeed Dujardin was opposed to the idea of there being any intrinsic value in abnormality. (pp. 123-24)

If there is no such thing as a quite accurately defined inner monologue, there is equally no such thing as an exactly defined stream of consciousness. Valéry Larbaud was the first person to use the words 'monologue intérieur' to indicate the technique under discussion. The expression 'stream of consciousness' was introduced into the language of literary criticism by William James, who uses it in his *Principles of Psychology* (. . . 1890) in a chapter on the stream of thought. The two terms (along with other versions of the first, such as 'interior', 'internal' monologue) are now used more or less indiscriminately as synonyms; and indeed they have a lot of common ground, but it may be worth while to try to give to each its own job to do. Part of the question has been examined by Lawrence Bowling [see additional bibliography] and by Robert Humphrey. (p. 124)

Bowling finds that Dujardin makes a fundamental error in the definition and application of his method by assuming that the whole of the consciousness can be presented in the form of inner monologue, thus confusing the issue. Since one cannot determine even for oneself exactly how much thought is conducted in words, and how much in images from the senses, the answer to this objection to parts of ***Les Lauriers sont Coupés*** will have to remain a matter of opinion—as it will have to also in respect of other books. Humphrey, though he does not actually mention inner monologue, is in fact concerned with the same point. . . . And the answer to the original question, technique or genre? is that since *Ulysses, The Waves, The Sound and the Fury* (and we might add here ***Les Lauriers sont Coupés***) all use different techniques but belong recognizably to the same class of fiction, there is no such thing as a 'stream of consciousness' technique. Many different techniques may be used to present the stream of consciousness.

These conclusions are fairly acceptable, but, since psychology is, after all, a matter for psychologists, both Humphrey and Bowling might have paid more attention to the literary form they are discussing and less to what really goes on in the mind. The words 'monologue intérieur' were first given the sense they now have by Valéry Larbaud. (pp. 124-25)

Given that it is largely impossible to say what is non-language material and what is not, what is speech-level and what pre-speech level, we may adapt both Bowling and Humphrey and conclude that, since it is possible to distinguish the style of the author from that of the character, inner monologue is a consistent, naturalistic version of the thought in words of a character, and is a technique. 'Stream of consciousness', on the other hand, is the name of a phenomenon, and not, as Bowling says, of a technique. The name can, however, be used to describe the genre which is occupied with the phenomenon. And the 'stream of consciousness' may be presented by various techniques, amongst others inner monologue and what Bowling calls 'internal analysis', where the author both quotes directly and intervenes. But books are not written to fit definitions. (pp. 126-27)

Whether or not Dujardin was indebted to any specific person or work for part of the idea of the inner monologue is not a matter of very great importance. The truth is, no doubt, that the idea had a good many parents. (p. 127)

C. D. King, "Édouard Dujardin, Inner Monologue and the Stream of Consciousness," in French Studies, *Vol. VII, No. 2, April, 1953, pp. 116-28.*

LEON EDEL (essay date 1958)

[An American critic and biographer, Edel is a highly acclaimed authority on the life and work of Henry James. His five-volume biography Henry James *(1953-73) is considered the definitive life and brought Edel critical praise for his research and interpretive skill. In the following excerpt, Edel concurs with the majority of Dujardin's critics in finding that the chief importance of the narrative technique employed in* We'll to the Woods No More *is that it was noted and implemented by Joyce. Vivian Mercier (see excerpt below, 1967) found Edel's introduction to* We'll to the Woods No More *to be "admirable but faintly patronizing."]*

We'll to the Woods No More is a slender novel—its French title is ***Les Lauriers sont coupés***—written in the Paris of the 1880's and promptly forgotten, as so many books are, only to be revived in our century under strange and rather charming circumstances—and for good reason. Taken by itself, it is a minor piece of fiction; not a few readers, casting a cursory glance at it, would call it "trivial." And trivial it doubtless is, if we insist on reading only "great books"—if we think we must sojourn perpetually among the mountain-tops of literature.

Let us begin, then, by saying that ***We'll to the Woods No More*** is neither a "great book," nor a "best book," nor even a misunderstood book. It was for a long time simply a neglected book. . . . A slender novel which was neither a document nor a slice of life, which belonged to the Symbolist revolt against naturalism, could hardly expect to make an impression among more strident voices. (pp. vii-viii)

If one reads it today for "story" it proves to be an agreeable little diversion—perhaps because of the honesty with which the situation is told: a young-man-about-town wants to sleep with a Parisian actress; she puts him off, but does not hesitate to take money from him. Presently he is paying her bills. And on the one evening of the novel he thinks that perhaps, finally, she will be his. Related in this way nothing could be more banal. Yet the dew of early morning has been sprinkled over the banalities. The writing is fresh and imaginative. The book possesses, above all, a focused vividness which its early readers recognized. When we ask ourselves how a tale so hackneyed can be so vivid, we discover that our interest is held by the way in which the story is told. This is what James Joyce recognized; years later he praised the book because the reader is "from the very first line posted within the mind of the protagonist." We might add that he remains posted there to the very last line.

We'll to the Woods No More represents, thus, in its way, a small triumph of method over matter: it might be argued that the triumph is one of poetry over prose. However that may be, it is the rare and beautiful case of a minor work which launched a major movement.

For Édouard Dujardin's novel inaugurated nothing less than the era of the *monologue intérieur,* thereby altering the temporal and spatial form of the modern novel. I recognize that these are empyreal words, atmospheric and Einsteinian, and that they figure strangely in discussion of a work bounded by the boulevards and placed in the consciousness of a self-obsessed Parisian dandy. What, the reader may ask, has the chase after an actress to do with matters dimensional and horological? Certainly, Édouard Dujardin, scribbling his novel in 1887 (one imagines his pointed beard held high in the air, a flower in his buttonhole, a long-stemmed cigarette holder in his mouth), was conscious of little but the difficulties of the literary "stunt" he had set himself. He would write a novel wholly subjective. He would never go "outside" his character's mind. It would all take place in a single evening, a matter of hours—all thought and no action. The novel ran its course in the magazine [*La revue indépendante*], appeared as a volume, attracted little notice, and then faded away. A decade later Dujardin reprinted it as the title story in a collection of his prose and verse, and it was this edition, apparently, which James Joyce came upon, after the century's turn, and read during his trip from Paris to Dublin in 1902—the troubled journey commemorated in the opening pages of *Ulysses*. Twenty years later the Irish novelist still remembered the book and could pay tribute to it as the principal source for [the] stream-of-consciousness techniques in his Dublin Odyssey. (pp. ix-xi)

What was the *monologue intérieur?* How "new" was it? How was it to be defined? In due course Dujardin was invited to Germany to lecture on his "discovery." At Berlin, Marburg, Leipzig, during the dying days of the Weimar Republic, he delivered a rambling discourse, later printed, which bore the portentous title ***Le monologue intérieur, son apparition, ses origines, sa place dans l'oeuvre de James Joyce et dans le roman contemporain.*** This sounds like a formidable treatise. The title of the lecture no doubt had appeal in a country where the higher scholarship has always cultivated the higher pedantry. Dujardin, moreover, knew his Germany and may have assumed a certain Teutonic tone in his old age which his younger self would have repudiated, although he had been a "Perfect Wagnerite," in the early days of Bayreuth. It was indeed Wagner's music, so much in vogue among the Parisian Symbolists, which had suggested to him the idea for his work. In tracing his inner monologue of the Parisian dandy, Dujardin sought to capture the *leit-motifs* of consciousness, the orchestra of the inner man. The Dujardin discourse makes strange reading today. It is a farrago of self-laudation, a *potpourri* of quotations from reviewers, reminiscences, literary history, and now and again a kind of blinking search to define, in the bright light of 1930, the old candle-light intuition of 1887. The lecture reads as if Dujardin arrived at his theories from his perusal of *Ulysses,* rather than from a rereading of ***Les lauriers sont coupés.***

The most valuable part of the Dujardin lecture is his attempt to define inner monologue. The *monologue intérieur,* he says, is "in its nature on the order of poetry," by which he means that it describes reflection, abstraction, momentary impression, mood, tone, rather than narrates action; it is that "unheard and unspoken speech by which a character expresses his inmost thoughts." In this he seemed to be characterizing little more than Hamlet's soliloquies, or those passages of subjective reflection which Tolstoy brilliantly introduced in *War and Peace,* or the ruminations of Dostoevsky's driven personages. Dujardin went on to say, however, that the "inmost thoughts" have to be those "lying nearest the unconscious," and they must be recorded "without regard to logical organization." In the Dujardin theory, this can be accomplished only "by means of direct sentences reduced to syntactic minimum," set down "in such a way as to give the impression of reproducing the thoughts just as they come into the mind." Dujardin was describing what he had tried to do, what Joyce had accomplished.

Dujardin's claims failed to impress many critics. They could see no distinction between inner monologue, as he described it, and the time-tested soliloquies of the stage. Dujardin himself does not seem to have understood—as Joyce did—the new dimensions involved in his experiment. It was not only that the story was being told from the "inside out," but that from the moment this was done a significant change took place in the relationship between author and reader. For one thing, both were committed to the single "point of view" after the manner of Browning's dramatic poems or the experiments Henry James had begun to carry out in his fiction. The mind or consciousness of the protagonist was made to narrate itself, as a play does on the stage. The reader was no longer being given an organized, explained story, but by being posted in the character's mind could see, think, know only as much as was in the character's consciousness, received the sensory stimuli of that personage and was assimilated into the fictional mind, its scrambled past and present, its dislocations of time and space. The story was no longer saying "Once upon a time . . ."—it was saying "I remember the time when . . ." And the reader was present at the instant of memory.

In addition to committing the reader to a specific angle of vision and the thoughts "just as they come into the mind," this type of fiction made him aware of experience as simultaneous rather than consecutive. (pp. xi-xvi)

Mallarmé had, before Joyce, grasped the essence of Dujardin's experiment. The phrase he pronounced after reading ***Les lauriers sont coupés*** is unforgettable: *l'instant pris à la gorge.*

The moment seized by the throat! The image is as striking as it is violent. Mallarmé visioned the capture of time as a process of placing vigorous poetic hands upon the moment, if he could but get them around its elusive velvety throat. . . . Dujardin, proceeding by intuition, does not seem to have pondered the matter. He simply attacked his problem with the optimism of his youth, and the sense of an indoctrinate Symbolist convinced that words can be made to do anything:

> . . . time and place come to a point; it is the Now and Here, this hour that is striking all around me life . . .

So day-dreams Daniel Prince in the novel's opening lines and very promptly we have been placed in his world. The reader ceases to be himself. He takes over the character's thoughts; he does not receive them at second hand from the novelist. Time is present and vertical, not historical and horizontal. The intensities of feeling are no longer conveyed as of the past: *they are being experienced as they occur*. It is "the Now and Here." The sense of distance, which exists in James, which Conrad cultivated, has been completely removed.

To read Dujardin today out of his chronological place in literary history can still be an engrossing process even though we have read the works of those who learned from him. For we watch Dujardin at grips with his self-created dilemma, persisting with the determination of a pioneer. Suddenly he is floundering. He doesn't know how to graft memories of the past into the consciousness of the moment. Unable to melt his data into the inner monologue of Daniel Prince, he falls back on tried letter-diary devices and we are back in the days of Choderlos de Laclos or Samuel Richardson. Daniel Prince rereads old letters; he reads journals; the flow of the monologue is arrested for many pages while the past is reread. Yet if there has been regression, it has occurred in the interest of not betraying the experiment. We learn what has gone before. This done, we move forward again in Daniel Prince's consciousness and into the evening's denouement. Throughout the novel, however, Dujardin is struggling with still another problem. What is he to do with descriptive detail, that sense of immediate material things of which Balzac made fiction singularly aware? How describe the room, the street, the house and still remain "inside" Daniel Prince? Later writers solved this problem in many ways, but in 1887 Dujardin breathlessly moves an excessive quantity of furniture into the consciousness of his personage. (pp. xvii-xxi)

It is easy, however, to criticize Dujardin from our Joycean hindsight. What we must remember is the staunch, pioneer strength of ***We'll to the Woods No More*** and we must recognize as well, the beauty of certain of the writer's evocations. The reader who establishes rapport with Daniel Prince is in Paris in 1887. Suddenly he is aware of the soft evening, not because Dujardin has described it, but because he feels the air on his face; he is sauntering along the boulevards with top hat and gloves, or is in the carriage with Leah, or gaping at the well-dressed women, lighting a candle in his dressing room, splashing water on his face, standing on the balcony picking out the pictures of the night: the grey-black sky, the blue tiny stars "like tremulous drops of water," while all around there is the misty impressionist paleness of open sky, lighted windows, the "solid gloom of trees." Poetic fancy comes to the aid of Dujardin and he is the confirmed Symbolist: language evokes his atmosphere and it is essentially the atmosphere of the mind.

Once Dujardin had shown the way, this atmosphere was to be evoked in fiction by many writers. (pp. xxi-xxii)

How can we speak of the novel as a dying form when it is capable of such richness and refinement? How can we say that the novel has run its course when in the three-quarters of a century since Dujardin's experiment it has shown us that it is capable of evoking a whole new side of life? The century that has produced Joyce and Proust, Woolf and Faulkner, has been admirably creative and the scope of the novel has been immeasurably widened. If there has been a lag, it lies with the reader; for to read subjective fiction one must unlearn reading habits of the past. Similarly criticism has erred in discussing the novel of subjectivity in the same terms as the conventional novel. There is much to be said about the reader's problem. . . . But a discussion of this belongs to another place. What I can only add here is that in the now tolerably long history of bold and arrogant creation in our time, we must accord recognition to the precursor, to this little novel from the Symbolist workshop, with the dew sprinkled over its banalities and the fascination it offers us of reading the minor work which inaugurated a major movement. (pp. xxvi-xxvii)

Leon Edel, "Introduction" (introduction copyright © 1957 by Leon Edel; reprinted by permission of William Morris Agency on behalf of author), in We'll to the Woods No More *by Édouard Dujardin, translated by Stuart Gilbert, New Directions, 1958, pp. vii-xxvii.*

H. A. KELLY (essay date 1963)

[Kelly finds that Leon Edel's and Melvin J. Friedman's studies of the stream of consciousness technique (see Additional Bibliography) "have some interesting and enlightening things to say" but that none have added significantly to Dujardin's explication of the stream of consciousness technique in Le monologue intérieur. *Like Richard Ellmann (see Additional Bibliography), Kelly finds that Dujardin's actual use of the stream of consciousness technique is often awkward and artificial, and that Joyce improved immensely upon the technique.]*

The year 1955 marked the climax of a renewed interest in the literary technique of stream of consciousness. . . . [However], it is not apparent that any . . . attempts at analysis has succeeded in making a substantial contribution to the account of stream of consciousness given by Edouard Dujardin in 1931 in ***Le Monologue intérieur: son apparition, ses origines, sa place dans l'oeuvre de James Joyce.***

It seems to have become the fashion to look somewhat pityingly at the pretensions of the old man who was resurrected by Joyce's recognition of his work—and perhaps there is some justification for this attitude. Yet Dujardin deserves a great deal of respect, not only for producing the first systematic attempt at writing stream of consciousness, but also for having issued the most competent analysis of the technique that has appeared to this date. In fact, Dujardin's writings have had such authority that even his errors have for the most part been accepted or enlarged upon by subsequent commentators. (p. 3)

Dujardin's definition of stream of consciousness may be accepted in its main outlines. Stream of consciousness is the attempt to record the thoughts of a character directly, just as they appear in the minds, without narration, description, or editing. We may also accept Dujardin's designation of the monologues of Stephen Dedalus, Leopold Bloom, and Molly Bloom in *Ulysses* as the most expert exemplifications of this literary technique and apply them as a standard to test the other works which have claimed inclusion in the stream-of-consciousness category.

In his definition Dujardin goes on to identify unedited thought with thought that is nearest to the unconscious. This erroneous identification is the source of most of Dujardin's mistaken notions concerning the method. Following his lead, later critics have elaborated stream of consciousness into a method which supposedly concentrates upon the nonintellectual aspects of consciousness, which records chiefly "fringe consciousness" at the periphery or margin of attention, which can display before the mind's eye simultaneous levels of awareness drawn from the totality of consciousness, and which aims at reproducing the incoherency that must result when one tunes in on the private thoughts of another. A brief consideration of the nature of stream of consciousness, however, should convince us that the very opposite of all this is true. No other method has been so severely restricted to the intellectual area of consciousness, and to only one portion of this area, the "verbalizable." Far from being able to record marginal objects of attention and simultaneous awarenesses, the method is limited to displaying only one element of thought at a time, and that one element must of necessity be uppermost in consciousness and at the very center of attention. Finally, stream of consciousness aims at producing not incoherency or private code, but rather the most profound coherency, so that the reader will be able to reproduce the thoughts in his own mind as intelligibly as they appear in the mind of the character himself.

To begin with, the writer can use only words. Therefore, in a strictly realistic method of this sort, he can employ with impunity only that portion of the intelligible or conceptual order of consciousness which can be put into words. That is to say, the writer is limited to recording the mental comment that a character makes upon the objects which he is aware of at any given time. The sound of a bell, for example, or the memory of a bell ringing, is not verbalizable. (pp. 3-4)

When using conventional methods of writing, he can simply describe sensations, emotions, and actions, or have one of the characters narrate this kind of nonverbalized material. When Edouard Dujardin composed his revolutionary novel, ***Les Lauriers sont coupés,*** he made the mistake of having the character whose mind was on display become his own narrator from time to time, with a result that is highly unrealistic. For example, while indulging in a fish dinner, Daniel Prince is represented as having these thoughts: "Confound these bones! All bones this sole is; but the flavor's good. There, that's enough, leave the rest. I lean back now. . . ." Dujardin allowed us to infer that Prince laid down his knife and fork when he recorded his mental comment: "There, that's enough, leave the rest." But he should have given us a similar mental comment to let us know that he was leaning back in his chair, such as, "These chairs have almost no back at all." Ordinarily, a man simply does not tell himself he is going out the door.

Dujardin's attempt makes one thing clear: when an author is limited to the mere recording of the mental comments his character is likely to make at a given moment, it is almost impossible to convey to the reader an adequate account of external events. Joyce found one way out of this dilemma by placing Molly Bloom in a situation where there is almost no external activity. Molly does not narrate a single line, and she does not need to. She communes with no one but herself, as she tries to go to sleep in a darkened room. (pp. 4-5)

Dujardin attempted to free himself from the restrictions of stream of consciousness by a stratagem which Lawrence Bowling has called "sensory impression" [see additional bibliography]. When using this device, the author simply lists the objects of sensation, imagination, or memory as the character becomes aware of them, with nouns signifying motionless objects, and participles added to indicate action. There is an example of sensory impression on page 86 of ***We'll to the Woods No More:*** "Lighted windows in the houses; opposite me white curtains of a café, transparent; an omnibus rumbling past; a girl, pink face, dark blue dress; the crowd; the boulevard. . . ." But such a "stream" is obviously nothing more than truncated description, and as such strikes the reader as highly artificial and contrived. These words would certainly not be in Daniel Prince's mind, although the sights and sounds which they describe would be present.

Joyce did not follow Dujardin's lead in the matter; I think that it can be asserted as a general rule that Joyce never uses the sensory-impression device to convey external sensations. (p. 6)

H. A. Kelly, "Consciousness in the Monologues of 'Ulysses'," in Modern Language Quarterly *(© 1963 University of Washington), Vol. XXIV, No. 1, March, 1963, pp. 3-12.**

VIVIAN MERCIER (essay date 1967)

[*Mercier, an advisory editor of* The James Joyce Quarterly, *has written extensively on Irish and French literature—most notably on the work of Samuel Beckett and Joyce. Unlike most scholars, Mercier believes Dujardin quickly grasped many of the aspects and "incidental possibilities" of the stream of consciousness technique, "though he did not choose to exploit them with Joycean thoroughness." Dujardin is most often portrayed as a less skilled writer, who made an awkward attempt at the technique that Joyce later developed; for examples of this interpretation, see the excerpts by Alfred Kazin (1938), Leon Edel (1958), and H. A. Kelley (1963).*]

I don't seriously stand behind the rather melodramatic title of this article; indeed, some readers will feel that Joyce was overly generous in acknowledging the indebtedness of *Ulysses* to Dujardin's ***Les lauriers sont coupés*** . . . , by now accepted widely as the first novel ever written entirely in stream-of-consciousness style. Yet I do feel that Stuart Gilbert's translation, ***We'll to the Woods No More*** . . . in places does less than justice to the poetic qualities and the pioneering courage of its original. Furthermore, I suspect that Leon Edel's admirable but faintly patronizing introduction [see excerpt above] . . . is based upon a reading of the English translation, and that he would have been a shade more respectful if he had looked again at the original French. (p. 209)

Stuart Gilbert's translation adheres to the definitive edition with reasonable faithfulness, but there are moments . . . when it becomes too Joycean, even to the extent of introducing verbal reminiscences of *Ulysses*. The danger here is that someone unable to consult the French may suspect Dujardin of "faking" in his last revision, after Joyce's acknowledgments resuscitated the brief novel that had been moribund for a generation. Actually, if some unconscious faking has occurred, the sole culprit is Gilbert. (p. 210)

Once Dujardin had hit upon the stream-of-consciousness technique, he was shrewd enough to become aware of many of its incidental possibilities, though he did not choose to exploit them with Joycean thoroughness. For example, any uninterrupted presentation of the stream of consciousness must perforce accompany the "viewpoint" character during his excretory functions. Dujardin presents only one such scene, whereas Joyce has several in *Ulysses*. Another aspect of the new technique that Dujardin quickly grasped was the possibility of error on the part of the central consciousness. He gives at least two examples of this, though in each case Daniel is represented as quickly seeing his own error. . . . These remind us of many of Bloom's fumbling efforts at calculating mentally or recalling scientific formulae, besides being the forerunners of countless similar passages in Beckett and the *nouveau roman*.

Dujardin, as he made abundantly clear in ***Le Monologue intérieur*** . . . , regarded ***Les lauriers sont coupés*** as an organic development from his career as a *Symboliste* poet. Indeed, he viewed the stream-of-consciousness technique as a logical, almost inevitable outgrowth of the poetic "*mouvement de 1885.*" . . . ***Les lauriers sont coupés,*** for all its surface triviality, is a sustained poem in prose, "undertaken with the mad ambition of transposing Wagner's methods into the literary domain." . . . Like all poetry, then, it is in the last analysis untranslatable. Despite the gallant efforts of that seasoned translator Stuart Gilbert, those who possess sufficient French should make a point of reading the first stream-of-consciousness novel in its original tongue. (pp. 212-13)

Vivian Mercier, "Justice for Édouard Dujardin," in James Joyce Quarterly *(copyright, 1967, The University of Tulsa), Vol. 4, No. 3, Spring, 1967, pp. 209-13.*

MELVIN J. FRIEDMAN (essay date 1974)

[Friedman, a former associate editor of Yale French Studies *and former editor of* Comparative Literature Studies *and* Wisconsin Studies in Contemporary Literature, *is Professor of Comparative Literature and English at the University of Wisconsin-Milwaukee. He was a Visiting Senior Fellow at the University of East Anglia in 1972, and Fulbright Senior Lecturer at the University of Antwerp in 1976. Friedman is the author or editor of some dozen books, the most recent of which include* The Added Dimension: The Art and Mind of Flannery O'Connor *(2nd edition, 1977) and* The Two Faces of Ionesco *(with Rosetta C. Lamont, 1978). He is also the author of* Stream of Consciousness: A Study in Literary Method *(see Additional Bibliography). In the following excerpted essay, Friedman cites similarities between the characters Daniel Prince of* We'll to the Woods No More *and Leopold Bloom of* Ulysses.*]*

Leopold Bloom has decided affinities with Dujardin's Daniel Prince. When he hums bits and pieces from *Don Giovanni* we are not far from Prince's refrain—'*le vin, l'amour et le tabac*'—and both threads run insistently through the characters' thoughts. Bloom and Prince both suffer keenly from unrequited sexual needs, memories and hopes, in something of the same comic way. Prince despairs of his chaste liaison with Léa; Bloom, compensating for his current unsatisfactory relations with Molly, carries on his pen-pal flirtation with Martha Clifford. The associations with Dujardin's book are particularly close in the 'Lestrygonians' chapter of *Ulysses,* where Bloom's sexual and culinary needs reach a crescendo; we watch his intense search for a 'moral pub' to satisfy his hunger for food, when it appears unlikely he can satisfy the other hunger, and his temporary haven at Davy Byrne's resembles that Daniel Prince found in the more exotic '*Café Oriental, restaurant*'. Bloom's Lestrygonian movements from one to two p.m. are a daytime equivalent of Prince's nocturnal wanderings; the settings are different, but the sensibilities not. (p. 457)

Melvin J. Friedman, "The Symbolist Novel: Huysmans to Malraux" (copyright © Penguin Books, 1976, 1978; reprinted by permission of the author), in Modernism: 1890-1930, *edited by Malcolm Bradbury and James McFarlane, Penguin Books Limited, 1974 (and reprinted by The Harvester Press, 1978, pp. 453-66).**

K. M. McKILLIGAN (essay date 1979-80)

[McKilligan examines the extent of Wagner's influence upon Dujardin's unsuccessful verse trilogy La légende d'Antonia, *citing many similarities between Dujardin's dramas and Wagner's opera* Parsifal. *McKilligan concludes, however, that Dujardin could not differentiate between "inspired transformation" and "straightforward borrowing" and that therefore the* Antonia *plays sometimes resemble parodies of Wagner's dramas.]*

Nowadays when the name of Edouard Dujardin is heard, as often as not it is in connection with the stream-of-consciousness novel, thanks to James Joyce who brought Dujardin's experimental novel . . . , ***Les Lauriers sont coupés,*** to public notice in the 1920's by mentioning it as a predecessor of *Ulysses.* At the turn of the century, however, Dujardin was best known in Paris as an editor and dramatist: he published two influential Symbolist journals, the *Revue wagnérienne* and the *Revue indépendante,* between 1885 and 1888, and from 1891 to 1893 he staged a dramatic trilogy, ***La Légende d'Antonia,*** which was long remembered as a spectacular flop, sometimes even referred to as the *Cid* or the *Hernani* of the Symbolist movement. While the serious pioneering efforts of the *Revue wagnérienne* and the flamboyant, rather eccentric performances of ***La Légende d'Antonia*** may at first sight appear to have little in common, in fact ***La Lègende d'Antonia*** and the *Revue wagnérienne* derive from the same source, the single-minded devotion which Dujardin had for the work of Richard Wagner. But just how Wagnerian were the plays of ***La Légende d'Antonia?*** This is a question which has never been considered, for while those who have studied Wagner's influence in France have invariably mentioned Dujardin's plays in passing . . . the actual nature of the 'Wagnerian' epithet attached to them has never been investigated.

The actual substance of ***La Légende d'Antonia*** is very thin, in fact quite inadequate to sustain a three-part exposition as in Dujardin's trilogy. Nothing could be further from the complex plots of the bourgeois drama to which theatre audiences had become accustomed in nineteenth-century France than the stark simplicity of the tale of Antonia. The first play presents us with two lovers, named only as L'Amant and L'Amante, who clearly symbolize the destiny of humanity as seen by Dujardin, with the woman bringing misery to herself and her lover through her infidelity. At first sight it appears that the second play, ***Le Chevalier du passé,*** digresses slightly, showing us a courtesan in all her glory. Suddenly, however, she is redeemed from her sin by the *chevalier du passé* himself, and it becomes evident that she is no other than the fallen Eve of ***Antonia.*** Finally, in ***La Fin d'Antonia,*** after attempting in vain to escape her destiny by committing suicide, Antonia or 'la femme éternelle' is prevailed upon to accept the traditional female role of matrimony and motherhood. (pp. 283-84)

Why . . . does ***La Légende d'Antonia*** merit its undisputed place in the annals of French Symbolism? The answer lies in its presentation: thanks to the memorable stage production of the trilogy, in three successive years, ***La Légende d'Antonia*** was in no danger of sinking into oblivion as had ***Les Lauriers sont coupés.*** The first play, ***Antonia,*** was actually staged comparatively quietly. . . . Dujardin himself played L'Amant—a comment in the *Mercure de France* suggests that his acting left something to be desired—while students took the other roles. It was only after this that Dujardin set about writing the next play in the series, ***Le Chevalier du passé,*** which was produced with much greater ostentation. . . . The guests—entrance was once again by invitation only—arrived to find a gold and red canopy over the door, while free programs were distributed inside the flower-decked auditorium. Whereas ***Antonia*** had been staged with a minimum of scenery, this time there were striking sets . . . and delightful costumes. . . . (p. 285)

What really made ***Le Chevalier du passé*** unforgettable, however, was the audience's reaction: although the play was billed as a tragedy and there was nothing intentionally comic in the first act, part of the audience could hardly suppress its laughter. . . . Clearly offended by such a reaction, Dujardin came on stage when the curtain fell on the first act to suggest that if his guests were not prepared to give his play a courteous hearing, they would do better to leave. (pp. 285-86)

Disastrous though such productions may seem by normal standards, they undoubtedly served to make ***La Légende d'Antonia*** and its author widely known. To Dujardin's contemporaries, almost equally notable was the Wagnerian nature of his trilogy. Although the first play attracted comparatively little attention, its Wagnerian characteristics—or intentions—did not go unnoticed. . . . But it was only with the production of ***Le Chevalier du passé*** that the Wagnerian nature of Dujardin's work was widely remarked upon. While Henri de Régnier, expressing a largely favorable opinion of the play, described it as having "de solides bases wagnériennes," Pierre Veber saw it more as a pathetic imitation, calling it a "tragédie moderne en trois actes [the subtitle], par MM. Edouard Dujardin et Richard Wagner." . . . In all, it is quite untrue to say, as does A. G. Lehmann, that "the servile copying of Wagnerian themes by Dujardin . . . passed unnoticed."

What was it about ***Le Chevalier du passé***—oddly enough the one play of the three that had no overt dedication to Wagner—that made the Wagnerian comparison inevitable? The play has very little action: in the first act the heroine, presented in general terms as "La Courtisane," offers her customary solaces to weary travellers who land on her island, but she feels strangely dissatisfied afterwards. The crisis comes in Act II, when the Courtisane evokes her lost past, and her deceased lover, the *chevalier du passé* of the title, appears in a vision to recall her from her life of debauchery. Act III serves merely as a protracted conclusion, which from the dramatic point of view has little purpose. Yet such action as there is is heavily derivative. The Courtisane appears not alone, but surrounded by four handmaidens dressed in pastel shades. With the rather naïve abruptness typical of Dujardin's manner of introducing his characters, they leave us in no doubt as to their functions: "Nous sommes les Floramyes." . . . These Floramyes are one of the most obvious borrowings from Wagner in the whole Antonia trilogy, and they do indeed bear a considerable resemblance to the maidens at Klingsor's command in *Parsifal.* In 1892, only ten years after the first performance of *Parsifal,* the resemblance was no doubt far more obvious than it is today. (pp. 287-88)

"Floramyes" was in fact a name fairly commonly used in talking of the beautiful girls, referred to in Wagner's original text as "Klingsors Zaubermädchen," whose temptations Parsifal so nobly resists. . . . Dujardin's Floramyes did, in 1892, recall the girls Wagner had used in *Parsifal,* especially in view of their similar function as subordinates to one supreme seductress. This particular Wagnerian borrowing proved Dujardin's undoing, for despite the fact that the only apparent purpose of the first act of ***Le Chevalier du passé*** is to set the scene, it is in fact the longest of the play's three acts and, as already mentioned, was found intolerably tedious by the invited audience. Most of the first scene, of over 120 lines, is filled with short exchanges by the Floramyes, never exceeding three lines each, relieved only by two fourteen-line speeches by the Courtisane.

The turning-point of the action hangs upon the other major Wagnerian borrowing, for the Courtisane's whole life is changed by a single kiss, just as the one kiss Parsifal receives from Kundry reveals to him simultaneously her nature and his own destiny. The Chevalier du passé also shares Parsifal's role of redeemer, and once the woman confesses that she has become a prostitute, he makes clear that he is really the voice of her conscience, summoned in order to reorientate her life by the appeal she had made to her past. . . . This predestination of Antonia, fated like Parsifal to carry out a mission which at first she knows not, becomes the whole meaning of the third play of the trilogy, which bears the double-edged title ***La Fin d'Antonia,*** where *fin* is clearly to be interpreted as "destiny," "purpose," as well as in its more common sense of "end." Like Parsifal, Antonia has done wrong through her innocence: the fatal wound her fiancé receives in the first play in his combat with that symbol of unauthorized love, Pâris, results directly from her thoughtless infidelity to him. She succumbed to the temptation of someone new and different, in much the same way that the sight of some knights in shining armor has led Parsifal to forsake his mother Herzeleide, causing her to die of grief. Here, of course, is where Dujardin's heroine falls short of the mark, for while Parsifal is endowed by centuries of legend with a sacred mission, handed down to him by his peculiar family circumstances, Dujardin's Antonia is rarely more than a wayward fallen woman. That she should be raised to heroic status, and worshipped in the end in terms which suggest close parallels with the Virgin Mary, is a self-indulgence on the author's part, quite unjustified by anything we have heard of Antonia's past in the first play.

Yet to some extent Dujardin had indeed tried, from the start, to endow Antonia with religious significance. While ***Le Chevalier du passé*** stands out as the most Wagnerian of the three plays, the first and the last are linked by a strong reliance on religious symbolism. The circumstances in which the two lovers first meet, for example, with the man, who is tired and far from his native land, being offered a drink from the well by a girl from the nearby village, recall the episode in Genesis 24.10-21 in which Abraham's servant, sent to Mesopotamia in search of a wife for Isaac, decides that the girl who offers water to him and his camels will be the wife chosen by God. In the next act, just before the young couple dedicate themselves to one another, they are united by a vision of the cross of Christ, and in prophetic ecstasy the man recalls a dream in which he had seen "la première femme"—Antonia has just stressed the permanent threat of temptation posed by woman since the fall of Eve . . .—while an archangel had foretold how this woman would cause his downfall, in a clear parallel with the Crucifixion. . . . The same images reappear in the last scene of the play, where the man is seen dying as a result of a wound received in combat with Pâris, the new arrival who has succeeded in enticing Antonia away from him. In the course of an extremely long monologue, lasting nearly five hundred lines, he speaks of his misery once more in terms of the Crucifixion. . . . The real sorrow of his death, however, seems to lie for him in the knowledge that their love can never be fulfilled, for the real significance of their union would have been to have taken part in the eternal cycle of perpetuating the human race. . . . In this theme of procreation ***Antonia*** is closely linked with ***La Fin d'Antonia,*** in which the heroine finally discovers maternity to be her destiny in life. The third play of the trilogy introduces this theme from the start, for it opens with two woodcutters discussing the purpose of life. (pp. 288-91)

Yet once again an apparently simple underlying theme is endowed by Dujardin with supernatural significance, for in Act III of ***La Fin d'Antonia,*** the climax of the whole trilogy, there arrive on stage three characters named Melchior, Gaspard, and Balthazar who have, somewhat predictably, been guided to the spot by an extraordinarily bright light after a night of strange and terrible happenings. Typically, the Christian parallel is only partial: the three men turn out to be shepherds, and their function is to worship a future mother as the symbol of the continuing human race, rather than as mother of a child of any particular individual importance. Antonia has grown in stature through acceptance of the reality of the world, by overcoming her desire to annihilate herself since she cannot find the ideal of life for which she has sought. Just as she evaded the husband offered in the first play, so she thinks to escape spiritually unscathed from the determined shepherd who pursues her in the last, but the latter's conviction that to renounce life is impossible has proved correct. Solitude and self-absorption are denied Antonia, and her suicide attempt fails, but her eventual acceptance of life as it is, including her role in the world, has wider significance in terms of Dujardin's analogy. . . . This analogy is reinforced by the "Finale" which ends the play, in which Melchior and his companions present the mother-to-be with gifts of gold, frankincense, and myrrh.

Clearly, one intended function of such religious parallels is to add an aura of distinction to otherwise ordinary events. The suppressed mirth reported among the spectators, however, testifies amply to the lack of success achieved by such vague religiosity. Although in middle age Dujardin was to become an expert in comparative religion—even lecturing on the subject at the École Pratique des Hautes Études in Paris—his other early works show not the slightest interest in religion. Why then did he choose to endow the characters of his trilogy with pseudo-Christian behavior and expression? . . . Given the patent borrowings from *Parsifal,* it does seem likely that it was the experience of Wagnerian drama that inspired Dujardin to attempt the creation of some similar dramatic monument, relying on religious symbolism to support his theme. It is also quite possible that Dujardin was influenced by the ideas of his other idol, Mallarmé, in this respect, for as readers will recollect Mallarmé enjoyed stressing the analogies between stage drama and the rituals of religious celebration. . . . [In] ***La Légende d'Antonia*** . . . , Antonia's submission to destiny is seen very much as part of the eternal, inevitable cycle of nature.

The only real clue we have to Dujardin's intentions when he embarked upon his trilogy is in the epigram he attached to *Antonia* in 1891, "Ich sah Ihn und lachte ["I saw him and laughed"]. This line, spoken by Kundry at the end of Act II of *Parsifal* when she is explaining to Parsifal how she was condemned to wander the world, eternally laughing but unable to cry, for having laughed at Christ as he struggled under the weight of the Cross, is a sentence which seems to have caught Dujardin's imagination, for he quoted it twice in the lengthy article called "Considérations sur l'art wagnérien" which he published in his own *Revue wagnérienne* . . . some three years before writing ***Antonia.*** The interpretation Dujardin offers of *Parsifal* in the climax to this article is of considerable interest for the study of his plays, for by his comments on certain aspects of *Parsifal* Dujardin provides us almost with an advance defence against some of the criticisms levelled at his plays. In fact, as Dujardin frequently projects his own ideas onto Wagner in discussing the composer's aims, what we have here is not so much an objective analysis of *Parsifal* as a highly subjective interpretation based on Dujardin's own theories of artistic creation. Dujardin certainly knew *Parsifal* well. . . . (pp. 291-93)

Interestingly, much as critics dismissed the subject-matter of the ***Antonia*** plays as trivial, Dujardin starts his discussions by unequivocally condemning the subject of *Parsifal*. . . . He asks if the dramatic value lies instead in the psychology of the characters, but this is not the case either. . . . Such remarks might well be made of ***La Légende d'Antonia,*** where there is no depth of characterization whatever. . . . (p. 294)

[Until Antonia] finds and accepts her predestined role, there can be no peace for her in the world. The parallel with Parsifal and his mission is clear. Any feeling we might have that Antonia's search is scarcely of the value of Parsifal's is countered by the pseudo-religious aura which surrounds her in the final play, which attempts to endow her with something of the universal significance of the Virgin Mary. That the trilogy is ambiguous and inconsistent in its attitude towards Antonia is deliberate, for it is evident that Dujardin believed in fluidity of interpretation, or in what would nowadays be termed multiple meaning. (pp. 294-95)

Undoubtedly Dujardin bends Wagner's text to suit him. . . . The parallel with the Crucifixion in the final act of ***Antonia*** is easier to understand when we see how Dujardin could weave this fantasy development around the action of *Parsifal*. (pp. 295-96)

While such interpretations are clearly highly idiosyncratic, Dujardin's attitude in broad outline is in fact not entirely out of keeping with the French view of Wagnerian drama at the time. . . . [A] form of drama, capable of interpretation on two levels, is clearly what we have in Dujardin's ***Antonia*** plays, for the conflicting reactions of the spectators make it plain that the trilogy was seen on the one hand as a rather boring tale of a reformed prostitute and on the other as a fairly laudable attempt at "l'art pur." (p. 296)

Returning to our original question of how Wagnerian Dujardin's trilogy really was, we see that in the strict sense of the adjective there is less in the plays to merit such description than might be supposed. While it would be misleading to suggest that Wagner's influence on ***La Légende d'Antonia*** was merely a matter of isolated borrowings, of what Grange Woolley described as "bric-à-brac wagnérien," Dujardin's interpretation of Wagner is sufficiently flexible to allow him considerable freedom in his own creation. At the same time, although it is hard to pinpoint specifically Mallarmean influences, Mallarmé's ideas on the symbolic, ritualistic functions of the drama may well have been instrumental in forming Dujardin's notions about religion and drama. . . . It was unfortunate that, in his grandiose attempt to express the meaning of human existence, Dujardin did not realize the difference between inspired transformation of religious themes, such as the redemption theme in *Parsifal,* and straightforward borrowing, which can all too easily resemble parody. (p. 297)

K. M. McKilligan, "Theory and Practice in French Wagnerian Drama: Édouard Dujardin and 'La Légende d'Antonia'," in Comparative Drama *(© copyright 1980, by the Editors of* Comparative Drama*), Vol. 13, No. 4, Winter, 1979-80, pp. 283-99.*

ADDITIONAL BIBLIOGRAPHY

Alexander, Theodor W., and Alexander, Beatrice W. "Schnitzler's *Leutnant Gustl* and Dujardin's *Les lauriers sont coupés.*" *Modern Austrian Literature* 2, No. 2 (Summer 1969): 7-15.*

Comparative study of the two works, noting Arthur Schnitzler's admission of indebtedness to Dujardin's inner monologue technique.

Bickerton, Derek. "James Joyce and the Development of Interior Monologue." *Essays in Criticism* XVIII, No. 1 (January 1968): 32-46.*

Examines, in part, the extent that Joyce was influenced by Dujardin's use of the stream of consciousness technique.

Bowling, Lawrence Edward. "What is the Stream of Consciousness Technique?" *PMLA* LXV, No. 4 (June 1950): 333-45.*

Discussion of Dujardin's explication of *le monologue intérieur* and its use in *We'll to the Woods No More*. Bowling concurs with Leon Edel (see excerpt above, 1958, and Additional Bibliography) that Dujardin apparently formulated his definition of the inner monologue "more upon the basis of Joyce's work than upon his own." Works by Honoré de Balzac, Fedor Dostoevsky, Ernest Hemingway, William Faulkner, Virginia Woolf, and Dorothy Richardson that employ this technique are also discussed.

Budgen, Frank. "Chapter V." In his *James Joyce and the Making of "Ulysses,"* pp. 73-106. Bloomington: Indiana University Press, 1960.*

Recounts a conversation in which Joyce acknowledged that he "took" the method of portraying "the unspoken, unacted thoughts of people" from Dujardin's novel.

Colum, Mary. "Life in Paris." In her *Life and the Dream,* pp. 377-98. Garden City, N.Y.: Doubleday & Co., 1947.*

Colum theorizes that Joyce's attribution of the stream of consciousness technique to Dujardin was a vast literary practical joke, believing instead that Joyce owes the technique to his knowledge of Freudian and Jungian psychology.

Cordasco, Francesco. "George Moore and Édouard Dujardin." *Modern Language Notes* LXII, No. 4 (April 1947): 244-51.*

Examination of Dujardin's influence upon two of Moore's novels, *The Lake* and *The Brook Kerith*. Cordasco finds that the character of Ralph Ellis from *The Lake* is based upon Dujardin, and that "Dujardin furnished the raw material for *The Brook Kerith*" during many long discussions that he had with Moore about biblical study.

Cornell, Kenneth. *The Symbolist Movement*. New Haven: Yale University Press, 1951, 217 p.*

Includes several references to Dujardin's contributions to French Symbolism. The magazine *La revue indépendante,* which Dujardin established, is cited as "a semi-official organ of symbolism," particularly during the years 1887-1888. Cornell also briefly mentions Dujardin's unsuccessful verse drama trilogy *Antonia*.

Edel, Leon. *The Modern Psychological Novel*. Rev. ed. New York: Grosset & Dunlap, 1961, 210 p.*

Establishes that *We'll to the Woods No More* "is without a doubt the first consistently sustained (even though technically primitive) stream-of-consciousness novel to have been published." Chapter V, "A Symbolist Experiment," is devoted to a study of the novel, and contains Edel's translations of some salient passages from Dujardin's *Le monologue intérieur*.

Ellmann, Richard. *James Joyce*. Rev. ed. New York: Oxford University Press, 1983, 887 p.*

Frequently mentions Dujardin and the stream of consciousness technique. Ellmann concludes that Joyce was given the idea for the stream of consciousness technique from his reading of Dujardin's novel; however, the method "was of consequence only because Joyce saw what could be done with it." Ellmann also discusses Joyce's efforts, together with Valéry Larbaud, to obtain recognition of Dujardin's pioneering accomplishment in writing the first such novel.

Friedman, Melvin. "Édouard Dujardin and Valéry Larbaud: The Use of Interior Monologue." In his *Stream of Consciousness: A Study in Literary Method,* pp. 139-77. London: Oxford University Press, 1955.*

Acknowledges the great originality of the conception of the narrative technique of *We'll to the Woods No More,* stating that the novel "has no exact literary ancestry."

Heppenstall, Rayner. "Streams of Consciousness." In his *The Fourfold Tradition: Notes on the French and English Literatures, with Some Ethnological and Historical Asides,* pp. 132-59. Norfolk, Conn.: New Directions Books, 1961.*

Finds that "the desirability of a continuous narrative viewpoint" was perhaps the most significant element assimilated by Joyce through his reading of *We'll to the Woods No More*.

King, C. D. "Édouard Dujardin and the Genesis of the Inner Monologue." *French Studies* IX, No. 2 (April 1955): 101-15.

Discussion of Dujardin's attempts to arrive at a definition of inner monologue. This study is largely inaccessible to English-language readers because lengthy quotations from Dujardin's *Le monologue intérieur* are untranslated.

Kumar, Shiv. Introduction to his *Bergson and the Stream of Consciousness Novel,* pp. 1-16. New York: New York University Press, 1963.*

Credits Dujardin with having popularized in literary criticism the term *le monologue intérieur*. Though Dujardin himself believed that the term was first used by Valéry Larbaud in 1882, Kumar finds Victor Eggar's 1881 treatise *La parole intérieur* to contain the first literary application of the term.

Laughlin, James, IV. "Dujardin's New Direction." In *We'll to the Woods No More,* by Édouard Dujardin, pp. 149-57. Cambridge, Mass.: New Directions, 1938.

Brief account of the publication history of Dujardin's novel. Laughlin also provides a summary of *Le monologue intérieur,* and states that *We'll to the Woods No More* is not only "a very fine piece of writing, a nearly perfect recreation of the atmosphere of a time and place," but is also "the first novel to be written entirely in the interior monologue."

McKilligan, Kathleen M. *Édouard Dujardin: "Les lauriers sont coupés" and the Interior Monologue*. Occasional Papers in Modern Languages, no. 13. Hull, England: University of Hull, 1977, 108 p.

Historical study of Dujardin's novel, asserting that Dujardin created the interior monologue technique.

Staley, Thomas F. "James Joyce and One of His Ghosts: Édouard Dujardin." *Renascence* XXXV, No. 2 (Winter 1983): 85-95.*

Provides an elaboration upon what is known about Joyce's involvement with Dujardin's career, based upon four recently discovered letters from Dujardin to Joyce's literary agent. Staley is the author of numerous critical studies of Joyce.

Struve, Gleb. "Monologue Intérieur: The Origins of the Formula and the First Statement of Its Possibilities." *PMLA* LXIX, No. 5 (December 1954): 1101-111.*

Discussion of the first applications of the inner monologue as a literary technique. Struve traces the literary use of the term inner monologue to the Russian author Nikolay Gavrilovich Chernyshevsky.

Hector (de) Saint-Denys Garneau

1912-1943

Canadian poet, diarist, essayist, and critic.

Reproduced by permission of Les Editions Fides

Although there has been serious debate concerning the merits of Garneau, both as a poet and as the troubled personality revealed in his journal, he is generally considered one of the most significant figures in French-Canadian literature. For many critics and readers, the achievement that most justifies Garneau's important place among French-Canadian writers is his powerful articulation of the repressive parochial atmosphere of Quebec society that existed in the poet's lifetime and that, in the opinion of some critics, continues to exist in the form of French-Canadian nationalism. To a large extent, the social and political environment of nineteenth-century Quebec was determined by a strong bond between the provincial government and the Catholic Church. Termed a "theocratic establishment," this alliance of power very effectively circumscribed acceptable attitudes and forms of behavior well into the twentieth century, fostering that sense of desperation and solitude that critics find reflected in much French-Canadian writing. It is exactly this characteristic mood of introversion, especially as exacerbated by religious and sexual anxieties, that epitomizes Garneau's poetry and informs his journal.

Garneau was born in Montreal to a wealthy aristocratic family whose ancestors had distinguished themselves by their literary, military, and social accomplishments. His great-grandfather was Francois-Xavier Garneau, an early historian of French Canada, and his grandfather was the poet Alfred Garneau. From Montreal the Garneau family moved to Sainte-Catherine-de-Fossambault, a town north of Quebec city, where Garneau spent his childhood. In 1923 the family returned to Montreal, and there Garneau briefly attended the Jesuit College Sainte-Marie. He later enrolled in the École de Beaux Arts to study painting, an interest that in his later writing appears in the form of art criticism. In 1928 Garneau suffered rheumatic fever, a malady that left him with a permanently damaged heart, and in 1933 a related illness caused him to abandon his formal education. However, he continued to paint—an exhibition of his work was shown the next year at the Montreal Art Gallery—and helped found the art magazine *La relève*. During this period from 1935 to 1937, Garneau associated with a prominent circle of Montreal writers and artists which included the poet and essayist Jean Le Moyne, who later became the editor of Garneau's posthumous *Poésies complètes (Complete Poems of Saint-Denys Garneau)*. In these few years Garneau also wrote most of his poetry and published *Regards et jeux dans l'espace,* the only collection to appear in his lifetime. Although the book received little notice, and the few reviews of it that did appear were not especially strong in either praise or criticism, Garneau suffered a sense of disgrace and exposure following its publication. Believing that his poems revealed both an artistic and a spiritual insufficiency, Garneau wrote in his journal: "I feared only one thing: not to be misunderstood, not to be rejected, but to be discovered." A gradual lapse began in his contact with society, and the course of this estrangement is preserved in his journal—"that terrible record of neurosis, guilt, and despair," in the words of Garneau's translator John Glassco. While it is known that Garneau started an earlier journal, the work published as *Journal (The Journal of Saint-Denys Garneau)* begins in the year 1935 and extant entries cease with January 1939, though there is speculation that there was also a later journal which was lost or destroyed. Garneau eventually left Montreal and spent his last years in the family home at Sainte-Catherine-de-Fossambault, where he led a reclusive existence until suffering a fatal heart attack at the age of thirty-one.

One of the poems in Garneau's collection *Regards et jeux dans l'espace* (which can be translated as "Visions and Games in Space") is addressed to a group of children and includes the lines "You do not know how to play with space," and "The city cuts off your vision at the start." This poem, "Spectacle of the Dance," indicates what many critics view as the shaping influence on both Garneau and his poetry, and what Jean Le Moyne has described as the "ghastly cultural vacuum of Montreal in the early thirties." Much of Garneau's poetry has been discussed as the artistic product of a highly introspective personality whose tendency for self-doubt and deprecation was intensified by a puritanical society that restricted individual expression. The resulting themes of alienation, guilt, and disintegration of personal identity are visible throughout Garneau's poetry, culminating in his famous poetic statement: "It is they who killed me." But while Garneau's sense of isolation is often viewed by critics as instrumental to his profound un-

happiness, the strongly inward quality of his work has contributed to his achievement as a poet who, in John Glassco's phrase, "transcends nationality." With the exception of a few literary figures, such as Émile Nelligan, French-Canadian poetry before Garneau's time consisted largely of provincial themes and subject matter concerned with a limited sphere of traditions and cultural experience, and these limitations have resulted in neglect by modern critics and readers. By contrast, the intimate, psychically extreme experiences that Garneau made the basis of his poetry have proven to be those which are best transmitted in an artistically effective way to modern readers unfamiliar with French-Canadian traditions. As is evident from the "Notes on Nationalism" in his journal, Garneau found the truest function of literature to lie in concerns that are essentially separate from their cultural significance, though conceivably the examination of these concerns could aid a culture in achieving self-understanding. While Garneau believed that it made no sense "to 'form' French-Canadians, that is to say to make them conscious of themselves as such," he also spoke optimistically of "the creator, the poet who will give the French-Canadian people their own true image."

That Garneau did not believe himself the fulfillment of his vision of a French-Canadian poet-creator is strongly supported by his journal, a document that consists of reflections on literature, philosophy, music, and art, and contains Garneau's unsparing analysis of himself and his poetry. While he believed some of his poems possessed a certain value, Garneau dismissed much of his writing in emphatic terms, describing one poem as "unreadable" and another as a "vile piece of padding." The basis of these stern criticisms was something that Garneau viewed as integral to his own character—the lack of authenticity. "Authenticity," by his definition, "means inalienable, incorruptible," attributes he felt were denied him. Repeatedly Garneau insisted on the emptiness of his nature, his nonexistence as a human being, and on his unreality. He wrote: "But when I consider the life of others, no matter whose, how full of reality it is compared to mine!" This self-abnegation later inspired French-Canadian writers who were more concerned with positive self-definition to reject Garneau's work. For example, the French-Canadian essayist Robert Vigneault has noted Garneau's "strong aversion to reality" and has condemned him as a "poet of nothingness." As elaborated in his journal, the principal values of Garneau's life derived from art, religion, and love, though each of these was the occasion for what Garneau described as his "vain habit of self-analysis" and a consequent feeling of self-disgust. An unwavering Christian from childhood, Garneau frequently denounced himself for falling short of a whole-hearted spiritual vocation, a life in which romantic love would be elevated beyond what he considered the encumbrances of sexuality.

Both Garneau's poetry and his journal have been viewed as attempts to exorcise an array of essentially personal troubles that nevertheless were unique neither to himself nor to the particular society in which he lived. In his essay on Garneau, Le Moyne wrote: "Better than anyone else he described all that had been done to him and what, at the same time, threatens all of us." The works that resulted from this effort have been recognized as among the most important in French-Canadian literature.

(See also *Contemporary Authors,* Vol. 111.)

PRINCIPAL WORKS

Regards et jeux dans l'espace (poetry) 1937
Poésies complètes (poetry) 1949
[*Complete Poems of Saint-Denys Garneau,* 1975]
Journal (journal) 1954
[*The Journal of Saint-Denys Garneau,* 1962]
Lettres à ses amis (letters) 1967
Oeuvres (poetry, journal, essays, criticism, and letters) 1971

SAINT-DENYS GARNEAU (journal date 1937)

[*In the following excerpt from his* Journal, *Garneau articulates his severely critical estimate of the poems in* Regards et jeux dans l'espace.]

Then, that evening at R—'s, F— spoke of a writer who had to withdraw a book he wrote. "It's too bad, isn't it?" he says with an irony aimed I know not where but which strikes me to the heart. I see: "He didn't like my book [***Regards et jeux dans l'espace***]." At one stroke my book and I are destroyed. And over that I torment myself. We are listening to music. At certain moments I am sensitive to music in spite of the paralysis F— always induces in me when we are listening to it. I analyse my sensations. By dint of making material approximations, craftily and carefully, I have been able to teach my nerves and my senses to recognize harmony and to taste it mendaciously, for it is a thing of the spirit. In fact, deep within me, I am as dumb as matter confronted with spirit: I do not exist. (This moment I have the notion of an autobiographical novel, whose hero discovers his falsity and his nothingness and goes to his death in a brothel, thinking to find there a real contact with life, an ultimate and true consciousness of his existence, but finding nothing there, only the same vain despairing labour of impotence, the bitter insufficiency.)

This reduction, this kind of brutal and excruciating spoliation which numbs the pain of my agony, gives me the upper hand of my despair, because my being is so superficial and affords no lasting or deep hold to despair itself. Then at the end of the evening I question F— directly and he tells me that he liked my book, some things in it very much and others, which were too facile, less. This cheers me, it is like a refreshing bath, a light of hope. I do not altogether relinquish the conclusions I have just arrived at, but I ascribe a greater part of them to my physiological condition. My book rises in my estimation.

Then my experience at M—'s. I had no existence, I had nothing to say: and what I could have said was untruth. My book and my article on the French painters. I was shown up there, in a boundless humiliation, in ridiculous and horrible misery. A blend of the tragic, the contemptible and the absurd.

The other night, at J—'s. I asked F— if he had seen a certain page of cartoons. "Yes," he answers, and he quotes, "'I used to do the new paint-jobs on stolen jalopies.'" It struck home like a shaft.

And then, ever since my book was published, but especially the other day—that is, in a more open and less guarded way—I studied the newspapers anxiously, read the reviews of my book anxiously, like a wanted criminal. At first I tried to believe I was doing this out of eagerness to know how it was being received. But I had a strong suspicion, and lately have admitted, that it was out of a desperate concern lest I be *"dis-*

covered." With a badly-assumed air of reserve, of semi-indifference and detached curiosity, I read the articles with great uneasiness, great apprehension, and just the other day in a positive fever. I was glad when the reviewers did not understand me, when they rejected me without understanding, or when they accepted me under my disguise (am I being extravagant?), when they accepted what I had tried to evoke, to provoke, to call forth in myself, the appeals I had made to myself through my poems and which received only this quivering response, this shallow quiver on the surface of my soul. I feared only one thing: not to be misunderstood, not to be rejected, but to be discovered. It must be, then, that there is something false in my book, something dishonest and lying, a swindle, a cheat, an imposture. As for those who accepted my poems, didn't I have the feeling that I had robbed them, deceived them, cheated them? Just as it would seem to me dishonest to be loved and esteemed by a stranger in my present state: there must have been some cheat in it, I must have appealed to him by some deceptive promise, false pretence, bluff, fanciful suggestion, because I am not one to be loved, because I barely exist and so can possess nothing, give nothing, receive nothing (except from God, of course). Being is the central point of all things.

Thus my book cannot exist, since I do not exist. It cannot, unless it lies, possess either greatness or originality. Otherwise it appears to be what it is, so feeble that it is nothing: it is not poetry. Or else it has the semblance of existing, of possessing a poetic and human reality, and then it proceeds from the same illusion, from the same lie which gives me myself only the semblance of having existed, loved, etc. It puts the world on the false scent of nothingness. It imposes an attitude on me, something I can bear no longer; the attitude of a being who exists in himself, who has distinction, clarity, grace, kindness, vision. And the same for my painting, my criticism.

Can I determine the principle and the course of this fatal illusion, this false construction, this imposture? I think it can be traced back to a missed, rejected vocation, to the misuse of grace, of a knowledge of grace and purity which were given me for another purpose, a supernatural one. There could also be an inability to take part in the life of joy, the careless, "happy" life (lack of abundance, generosity, trust) aggravated by lack of sexual satisfaction. Having rejected the sacrifice for the Good, and all the sacrifices that follow, and as man cannot live without giving himself, I had to give myself in that way (that is, through poetry), led by my mean capacities and that aptitude for grace which was perverted to my worldly advantage and then to my damnation and death. (pp. 58-60)

Saint-Denys Garneau, in a journal entry in 1937, in his Journal, *translated by John Glassco (© McClelland and Stewart Limited, 1962; copyright, Canada, 1962 by McClelland and Stewart Limited; used by permission of Librairie Beauchemin Ltee and The Canadian Publishers, McClelland and Stewart Limited, Toronto; originally published as* Journal, *Beauchemin, 1962), McClelland and Stewart, 1962, pp. 53-61.*

SAINT-DENYS GARNEAU (journal date 1938)

[*In the following excerpt from his* Journal, *Garneau reveals misgivings about his life and his poetry following the publication of* Regards et jeux dans l'espace.]

One can bring to one's reading, one's writing, etc., a habit of excess more culpable than fleshly excess. One can bring to it an illicit gluttony. The measure of evil comprised in these actions lies in a certain determination, whether avowed or not, to enjoy and to profit. (Not as a healthy body profits by healthy food, but in the sense of an exploitation for profit.) This determination may reach the point of vice (which point would be a craving, a hunger without a corresponding power of assimilation by the whole creature. This suggests to me a certain geometric figure: a sphere traversed by a straight line or rather by a current. The sphere represents the being with respect to itself, or rather such a being in itself, in accord with the balance between what it receives and what it can assimilate. A natural balance. A disproportion between the hunger and the faculty of assimilation, between the culture and the creature, between "being" and "wish to have," destroys the perfect form of the sphere, overthrows it, dissolves it: vice. The current stands for love, the gift which should quicken the whole interior of the sphere and transcend it, and engage it. This figure applies equally well to the kind of being which is comprised in a work of art, complete and rounded in itself but traversed by a current. All this is incomplete . . .)—may reach the point of vice, where a being is wilfully bent on possession and enjoyment, on unearthing all the being it can compass, and more, and still more.

How large a part this wilfulness has played in my alleged art! In all I have written, what really needed to be said?

For original reality: ***Spleen, Accompagnement, Cage d'oiseau,*** the unfinished poem beginning,

Un bon coup de guillotine
Pour accentuer les distances . . .

[One good stroke of the guillotine
To emphasize the space between]

The two lines,

Dans ma main
Le bout cassé de tous les chemins . . .

[In my hand
The shattered stump of all the roads]

Perhaps

Le souvenir qui nous a déchiré jusqu'ici
De cette espèce d'entrevue avec la Promise.

[Like a distant memory tearing us till now
This bridal pledge and kind of parley with a bride]

And ***Enfants.***

Perhaps none of this is interesting work, being wanting in intensity, in continuity of inspiration and in quality of brilliance (in itself, I mean, not in the words which I can easily make brilliant, even false). Yet each of those images has or has had a certain real existence in myself, a certain fairly permanent inner demand.

And as songs: ***Portrait, Paysage II,*** certain parts of ***Tu croyais tout tranquille*** . . . and what else?

All the rest is spurious and verbose *pompage,* and most of the time meretricious, overweening. The first part of my book [***Regards et jeux dans l'espace***] has no genuine correspondence with my own reality: it is a kind of touched-up portrait. ***On a décidé de faire la nuit*** is full of a tragic romanticism which can perhaps only fool whoever wants to be fooled. ***Fièvre*** is unreadable. ***Qu'est-ce qu'on peut pour*** . . . is a vile piece of padding. ***Mains*** the same: the exploitation of a minor sensation. In all these I was parading in borrowed peacock's feathers; I was covering up my tracks, an absolute emptiness clothed in brilliancy. All this springs simply from the itch to write, the desire to be a poet, competent or incompetent.

And even the few allegedly genuine poems I have just listed are characterized to a certain extent by this undercurrent, this proud, vain and lying intent. Perhaps, at bottom, their success was only a matter of luck. I ought to have confined myself to them alone. But then would I have ever written them? There are so many accidental factors involved. And after all, would my conscience be easy, even then, faced with those few lines? (pp. 108-10)

Saint-Denys Garneau, in a journal entry on February 15, 1938, in his Journal, *translated by John Glassco (© McClelland and Stewart Limited, 1962; copyright, Canada, 1962 by McClelland and Stewart Limited; used by permission of Librairie Beauchemin Ltee and The Canadian Publishers, McClelland and Stewart Limited, Toronto; originally published as* Journal, *Beauchemin, 1962), McClelland and Stewart, 1962, pp. 107-27.*

W. E. COLLIN (essay date 1955)

[In the following excerpt Collin discusses Garneau's conceptions of good, evil, and God. For a further discussion of the religious conflicts that preoccupied Garneau, see the excerpt below by Gilles Marcotte (1962).]

An important event in the world of poetry was the publication of Saint-Denys-Garneau's ***Journal***. . . . It covers the years 1935 to 1939. Garneau died in 1943, having spent the last few years of his life at the home of his parents at Saint-Catherine, resigned to silence and solitude. The central fact about him is the split in his psyche, the dualism, the play of two contradictory forces in his soul, which reduced him to loneliness and impotence and almost drove him mad. One such experience of impotence, he says, happened to him in February, 1935:

> Last week I experienced a feeling of helplessness, humiliation, solitude. I thanked God for not giving me foresight, for if my imagination had prolonged this condition of extreme tension together with this feeling of precariousness, uselessness, and impotence, it would have led me to a kind of hopeless folly and delivered all my being to a blinding darkness which I have felt threatening me especially since last autumn. . . . I remember that for a long time states of exaltation, a sort of flight outside of myself and beyond the control of my will, had troubled me. But at that time, the violent inner separation from which I suffer was not so accentuated, as my physical being was more robust and my lucidity less acute.

During that period he was "visited by God's Grace," "strangely illuminated in the necessity of holiness" and brought so decisively face to face with "the dilemma of good and evil" that it was "impossible to choose evil." "I am terrified of evil," the journal continues. "To do evil is an irrevocable act, a total refusal of God, a conscious rebellion, a total acceptance of pride and of sin altogether and of despair, down to the depths, which can only end in madness."

Turning from a world of power and gladness into himself he may have found, as he says of Beethoven, "the great inner isolation where a man can no longer be touched, or cast down; the cell whose only window opens towards God." Yet in his inner sanctuary he felt oppressed by impotence, weariness, spiritual drought, the source of which is not hard to find. "Here I am," he says, "with my load of original sin, without the possibility of a single resting-place in the good-nature of the flesh." An ingrained habit of associating the flesh with the idea of sin, and the consequent impossibility of conceiving a pure love, are traits which make Garneau a representative of his generation. He notes: "All my life, the impression that innocence was repressed more and more from bottom to top. At the same time a desire to have nothing to do with the corrupt part, the part without light. . . . So that, during adolescence, a sort of wish that my body might end at my waist." "Baudelaire, that tragic figure, cast on evil a pitiless light, a lucidity which still makes the world shiver." He was a Jansenist, says Garneau; he associated love with the idea of sin. It is against a long tradition of Jansenism that Garneau rebels. "Jansenism demands too much of man; it will not compromise with the actual state of man; and because it wants man as without original sin, it incessantly sticks to that original sin and cannot get beyond it." It is the Jansenism in Mauriac that revolts Garneau. "His thinking always smells of a mouldy and most despondent Jansenism, his inquietude is darkened so that it horrifies you and it seems to border on heresy by that Jansenism." And Garneau wonders how the artist can become so detached from the man as to reach the grandeur of *Le Baiser au Lépreux* and the transparent serenity of *Le Noeud de Vipères*. "Very dangerous inner vices," he believes, "are at work in this complexion. It is not at all balanced. The thought contains stubborn errors and the feeling is falsified in a way that recalls another age; a state of mind long since left behind. Mauriac is behind the times." Garneau's lucid awareness of the split in his own personality made him readily detect a similar malady in others.

He may keep his window open towards God, he may feel that a man who says that "the pleasure of love resides in the consciousness of committing evil" is preferring himself to God, yet he knows that the very thought of preference is occasioned by the split in his psyche, by the dissociation of spirit and flesh. In despair of the purity of love, Garneau goes to meet the woman on the street. Unlike Baudelaire he finds no pleasure in her. Like Lemelin, like Elie, Garneau is hounded by the idea of guilt. And he knows the reason. "The cause lies in a spiritual and emotional complex, as far as I can see, a complete poisoning of the whole personality." He experienced positive anguish when he saw anything beautiful, a beautiful sunset, for example.

> I am so broken and reduced to such a contemptible dough that I don't know why or in what to hope. Reduced as I am, what can I become? What is going to become of me? I cannot peacefully look at trees or animals, my sick vision splits and suffers wherever it strikes, finding everywhere my emptiness, my lie, my impotence, my baseness, my nothingness, my complete poverty. Inside me, I find nothing but desert and nothingness.

As a literary man he sensed that it was a creative moment. "The idea came to me," he says, "of writing an autobiographical novel the hero of which discovers his lie and his nothingness and goes to die in a brothel believing that he has found there a real contact with life, a final and real consciousness of his existence, actually finding the same useless, depressing work of impotence and bitter dissatisfaction."

Indeed it is to the inner split that we owe Garneau's creative visions. The idea of the bones, for example: "This idea of the bones consisted in stripping oneself of one's flesh in which one can never trust, of this mask which does not stop deceiving us at the moment we least expect it." The joy of our body is destroyed by the slightest shock, the slightest fear, desire, or feeling of impotence. Therefore, "it would be better to strip oneself of this cumbersome appearance and be reduced to the simple hardness of the bones, to the silence of the bones." In the same order is the impression of the tree with its branches lopped off: "That my vertebral column is a trunk, from which the branches are lopped off by clean strokes of an axe. They are my ribs. Also, that little creatures in my back are driving a wedge between my ribs and separating them. Not a painful impression, almost a relief, rather."

Not unconnected with his revulsion against the self is Garneau's critique of nationalism: "Every movement in the direction of self is sterile. . . . All this retroactive mysticism seems to me against nature, sterile and sterilizing. . . . Culture is something essentially human. It intends to make men and not French Canadians." In this shift of emphasis from the national to the human, Garneau anticipated the present current of neo-humanist criticism. (pp. 321-23)

W. E. Collin, "Letters in Canada: 1954—Publications in French," in University of Toronto Quarterly *(reprinted by permission of University of Toronto Press), Vol. XXIV, No. 3, April, 1955, pp. 306-34.**

JEAN LE MOYNE (essay date 1961)

[*Le Moyne is a Canadian poet and essayist who, along with Garneau, helped found the journal* La rèleve. *In his essay* "Saint-Denys Garneau's Testimony to His Times," *excerpted below, Le Moyne writes of his friendship with Garneau and explains the moral and cultural climate of Quebec during the 1930s. Le Moyne believes that Quebec was in a state of "poisonous confusion" that he considers responsible for much of the emotional suffering expressed in Garneau's work.*]

I cannot speak of Saint-Denys-Garneau without anger. Because they killed him. His death was an assassination prepared over a long time. I will not call it premeditated because I refuse to credit those who choked his life with so fine a thing as conscience. Who were in fact, his closest enemies? The half-dead, victims themselves, diminished and sick with a miserable fear which, unluckily, was only strong in its power of contagion. One cannot get angry with mindless creatures, though one cannot help resenting the spirit that animates mindlessness. . . .

I go back in memory to the first years of our friendship. Those were the days when he was one of the group who, in 1934, were to found the review *La Relève*. The preoccupations of the group were such that, when their first essays were published, certain of us were taken to be members of the priesthood. As for Saint-Denys-Garneau, since his death and the appearance of his ***Poésies Complètes*** and his ***Journal,*** he has been surrounded by an aura of tragic gravity. But we were never a chapter meeting or a committee. We were just friends around a table whose only programme and intention was a quest for the absolute, solidly motivated despite the incoherency of our enthusiasm. There was no order of the day, only the disorder of the evening meetings, especially on Sunday evenings when we exchanged heated and tumbling accounts of what we had done during the week, during those weeks so full of discoveries and excitement, shot through with ecstatic perspectives and darkened with anguish. Among these friends Saint-Denys-Garneau was one of those who was most fully present, one of the most gifted, one of the gayest. And he was the subtlest and the wittiest. His liveliness was that of one who is intoxicated with life and who could expect a liberal and exquisite share of it, generously divided between love, art and thought. When I now hear, clear in my memory, through the murmur of those distant conversations, a phrase thrown out by one of us with a kind of anxious conviction, something like: "Gentlemen, it is absolutely essential to restore to sin its proper grandeur and dignity," I tremble for him in retrospect. Not for the others; for them it was a password to salvation. Such a statement was an obscure but valuable claim to an indispensable autonomy. It was a refusal to accept that the question should be raised in a spirit of fear or that judgment should be passed under the rule of any illusion. It was a key for the liberation that was to come. And, as far as the other members of those reunions are concerned, they are all still alive. But as for him, it was already too late. I shudder, in retrospect, at the thought that already he did not dare assert his instinctive hold on life, that already he was on the verge of committing the irreparable error of mistaking his healthy uncertainty for the sign of an interdiction, an interdiction that was to be studded with false crosses. And I firmly believe that this confusion was the cause of his death, and that it has killed others before and after him, and that it goes on killing today. I assert that it paralyses and sterilizes and prevents and misguides many, and that this poisonous confusion is the most damnable of our official impositions.

I could almost recapture the moment when the balance of forces in Saint-Denys-Garneau began to swing over towards absence and death. . . .

Why death for him, why life for the others? The question of relative merits has, of course, no bearing. Psychologically his disorder was in no way exceptional. The same degree of morbidity is quite common with us. Not to admit that is to understand nothing of our society: a certain neurotic quality is part of our cultural heritage. Saint-Denys-Garneau had then, as they say, problems. Moreover he was gifted with an extreme delicacy of conscience and was possessed by a need to be fully present in whatever he did, which prevented him from paying himself out in mixed doses, from compensating, as many do, for hindrance in one direction by increased activity in another, for uneasiness in one matter by a carefree attitude in others. In other words, the Christian humanist in him could accept no local solution. He was made for total presence.

Physically, his constitution was rather weak, and he certainly lacked that brute energy which might have been, despite himself, his saving grace. He did not have the strength that would have let him disobey those imperatives, true and false, which were then so inextricably intermingled in him. He lacked the strength that might have let him override them, roughshod, that sly and ruthless perseverance of an animal fighting for life. His body was thin, his heart weak, his walk faltering. But from time to time he would get his teeth into something and tear it to pieces without a second thought. And occasionally he would surprise us by getting hold of something big and, whether it resisted or not, would devour it with a savagery that was absolved by his hunger. . . .

If we go back to the year 1935, we find Saint-Denys-Garneau working on the poems that were to make up the collection ***Regards et jeux,*** published two years later. It is also in 1935 that he began his ***Journal.*** This is the period when he began his decisive self-interrogation and his definitive life's work. For us it marks the start of an irrefutable testimony.

His solitude as a poet was complete. It is scarcely necessary for me to say that he took our Canadian rhymesters for what they are: exactly nothing. As far as his own poetic genesis was concerned, his parentage was purely French. Verlaine and Baudelaire were his breviary: he used them constantly, absorbed them and passed beyond. Though he was very fond of Pierre Jean Jouve, Reverdy and Nerval, they left no discernable mark on his work. He admired Claudel but was on his guard against the overpowering old man. Supervielle perhaps helped him to develop certain formal elements. But on the whole ***Regards et jeux*** stands out in our literature as the first product of an authentic necessity. It is the first work to come from so pure, personal and highly aware a source.

In evaluating the substance and the amount of concentration and effort required to produce ***Regards et jeux*** one should not forget the ghastly cultural vacuum of Montreal in the early thirties. Today one can contract heavy debts of humanity in this city, dispersed throughout a society that is relatively rich and diversified, but in those days it was inconceivable to owe anything to more than a few friends. Strictly speaking Saint-Denys-Garneau's intellectual and religious milieu was made up of four or five intimate friends.

"I will feed these musings on my own marrow", he wrote. This is the ultimate material of every artist, and studying his use of it one can only have admiration to express if he succeeds, and nothing at all to say if he fails.

The incredible poverty of his milieu forced Saint-Denys-Garneau to draw doubly on his own resources to nourish his work. If only he had been free to spend his gifts without keeping track of how much he had exhausted. But such was not his case. He had to compensate for what he called a loss in volume. Working against the clock he had to make up for a permanent leaking away of life and energy. It is this feeling of ineluctable loss, of ever increasing deficit, that he expresses in the extraordinary parable of the beggar who carried all his possessions in a sack with a hole in it, and by the terrifying image of the corpse that becomes his double. . . .

The irreparable loss of inner content, the rupture of temporal ties, the invasion of the living being by its own death, these are some of the most common and original themes. There is another that he has not treated explicitly in his work but which was the subject of countless discussions among us, the theme of general misunderstanding.

By the idea that sin had been deprived of its grandeur and dignity, I think we expressed, without knowing it, the depths of our alienation. Not entirely aware of this, we conscientiously sought to assume a just degree of responsibility. The unlimited extension of guilt revolted us but, on the other hand, the only logical and effective absolution—total self denial—seemed inhuman to us, despite the seductions of the cloth. Seriously afflicted by this sickness, the part of us that remained healthy protested that there was a total misunderstanding. How we struggled with those exhausting and ridiculous anxieties! But in as much as our protests were real, our anxiety bore fruit and became fruitful question. And obscurely a decision was taken in favour of life at any cost.

It was then that I had the feeling that our friend was separating himself from us. Not because of any loss of contact, but because he accepted the equivocal terms at the heart of this misunderstanding as the expression of an ultimate reality. There was some immediate proof of this, and two years later, in 1937, I had come to the heart-rending certainty that we were losing him, that he was lost to life. That does not mean that as early as 1935 the debate was closed in his mind, but that, badly begun, it had taken a fatal turning. . . .

Labouring under the terrible suspicion that he had been robbed of it, he brooded over his lost joy. . . .

In his desolation he saw himself blocked off from any avenue to the outside and questioned where and when the roads had been cut or had run astray. . . .

Then, faced with the scandalous and all-pervading menace, he began a meticulous examination, making an inventory of his limbs and articulations, of all his energies and faculties. . . .

But he could not find the defective, the missing part, and in his ***Journal*** the theme of the inventory ended up as the mutilation of the poor, as reduction to the very lowest terms, to the vertebral column, symbol of the last vital obstinacy, symbol of the last evidence of being, of a man from whom everything had been taken, everything stolen, to the point where he judged, in all sincerity, that nothing good had ever belonged to him, and accused himself of having been one of the unworthy poor.

Nonetheless, in a flash of anger the poet identified his immediate enemies—who are also ours—and called down a terrible accusation on them:

> It is they who killed me
> Fell on my back with their weapons, killed me
> Fell on my heart with their hate, killed me
> Fell on my nerves with their shouts, killed me
> It is they in an avalanche who crushed me
> Broke me into splinters like wood . . .

When there was coincidence between his servitude and his own springs of life, Saint-Denys-Garneau grasped reality with great lucidity and judged it with an impeccable objectivity. The same internal juxtaposition of forces which allowed him suddenly, and with such energy, to name his enemies led him to attribute French-Canadian lack of good taste to the absence of any positive tastes whatsoever, and by going on to show that taste is a matter of being and loving, he uncovered one of the major features of our alienation. The same clearsightedness illumines his reflections on nationalism, which he denounced as a usurper of first things. It is true that human factors take precedence over national ones, and that these fortuitous and secondary national interests become nothing but tools of alienation if they claim the right to prevent us from risking our essential humanity. Nationalism has been a favourite tool of the forces of alienation in this country and, despite various corruptions of that fact, we are not ready to forget it. One could find many other moments of similar ease and assurance in Saint-Denys-Garneau's thought, but unfortunately they are only moments and his analysis never goes to the root cause of the alienation. Instead, his powers of penetration tended to turn inward, to work against him, to attack him on all sides, to strip him of everything. His analytical drive led him to undervalue the worth of his own talent and work, to accuse himself of being an imposter, to sentence himself morally and spiritually with extreme severity, even to deny the presence of desire in himself and, the supreme error, led him to the conclusion that he lacked existence, that his own identity was too weak to justify its external reality. . . .

So we begin to see in what way Saint-Denys-Garneau is a witness for his time and his society. He is so by merit of the crucifying scope of his suffering and because he gave such an exhaustive account of it, transposing it into poetry, into critical reflection, into the dialogue of his correspondence and the self-examination of his ***Journal.*** Better than anyone before or since he described all that had been done to him and what, at the same time, threatens all of us. But he did not explain it. His mind did not dominate it. And, paradoxically, it is due to this deficiency that his testimony is so complete, so indisputable. By laying himself bare in this unjust fashion, until the tragic twistings of his thought finally led him back to bear against his own identity, he warns us of the dangerous reach of the alienation that is our constant menace. Saint-Denys-Garneau became exemplary through self-negation. . . .

Jean Le Moyne, "Saint-Denys-Garneau's Testimony to His Times," in his Convergence: Essays from Quebec, *translated by Philip Stratford (reprinted by permission of Philip Stratford; originally published as* Convergence *by Jean Le Moyne, Editions HMH, 1962), Ryerson Press, 1966.*

GILLES MARCOTTE (essay date 1962)

[*Marcotte is a Canadian novelist and literary critic noted for his insightful observations on French-Canadian literature. In his introduction to the English translation of Garneau's* Journal, *Marcotte discusses the significance of this work for both French-Canadian literature and for Canadian literature in general. He also examines the religious questions and conflicts that were among Garneau's deepest preoccupations and that are important to any understanding of his life and work. For another discussion of Garneau's conceptions of religion, see the excerpt above by W. E. Collin (1955).*]

[The] translation of Saint-Denys-Garneau's ***Journal*** is a notable event, not only insofar as it involves the wider diffusion of a literary work which well deserves to be known outside the sphere of its origin, but still more because it marks a new stage in the intellectual relations between English and French Canada. (p. 9)

[The] difficulties of such a work seem to me of less moment than its importance and significance in the cultural framework in which we are living. Here is a book which appears before the Anglo-Canadian public with none of the advantages of a foreign setting, with a true local colour. It is the record of a spiritual process which, even so, might have taken place in any country in the world. (When it appeared in 1954 a French critic could discover striking similarities between the tragedy of Saint-Denys-Garneau and the experience of Rimbaud.) If it illustrates the French-Canadian position, it does so at a new and unaccustomed level, as far removed from the commonplaces of regionalism as of sociological analysis. The ***Journal*** of Saint-Denys-Garneau reveals its author, it reveals his background, but *from within,* with none of the outward signs which conveniently define a situation, a way of behaving, an attitude. It would certainly be wrong to expect to find in it any sound, perfectly rational elucidation of what is called "the French-Canadian problem." This book must be approached with an open mind, with no other purpose than to encounter a man.

By a strange coincidence, moreover, this translation appears at the precise moment when the representative value of the work itself has been most violently called in question in French Canada. In the Preface to the original French edition I wrote, "Saint-Denys-Garneau, whether tender consciences like it or not, represents us. He assumed, to the furthest extent of which he was capable, the burden of isolation which is implied and inherent in all our previous literature and which is powerfully emphasized in the most significant work of the present time." I still affirm this statement today. The work of Saint-Denys-Garneau is beyond doubt one of the pivotal works, the key works, of French Canada. More deeply than anyone else, he has expressed the spiritual ordeal we have gone through in the difficult position in which history has placed us. But I would be no less in agreement with those who refuse to see in this ***Journal*** any definitive statement of the French-Canadian tragedy. *We are no longer living in the day and age of Saint-Denys-Garneau.* Many of the problems he faced no longer confront us, at least in the particular form they assumed for him. One has only to read contemporary French-Canadian poetry to realize that our *ways of existing* have been diversified and transformed. The consciousness of guilt which informs the ***Journal*** and the poetry of Saint-Denys-Garneau has not been dispelled all at once, but it must be allowed that the present generation has weapons against it which the poet of ***Regards et jeux dans l'espace*** did not possess. (pp. 9-10)

The ***Journal*** was begun at the same time as the poems forming the collection ***Regards et jeux dans l'espace.*** (Here it must be emphasized that the ***Journal*** can only be fully understood in conjunction with Saint-Denys-Garneau's poetry itself. It is the same story unfolding throughout, told in different but complementary ways.) This journal was not the first which he kept. He began an early one in 1927, another in 1929, and later on a third containing only three entries of which one alone bears a date, that of January 24, 1935. The ***Journal*** we are here concerned with was begun a few days later in the same year. In the following August he wrote his first really original poems, the **"Esquisses en plein air"** of ***Regards et jeux dans l'espace.*** At the age of twenty-two Saint-Denys-Garneau had found himself, had come to grips with the essential element in himself, and the next nine years of his life—the last nine—were occupied only in familiar converse with a few friends and in the feverish search after a truth within the span of time still left him. He had abandoned his studies without any hope of resuming them, and had no outside occupation to distract him from his search. He led, without excess, the *vie de bohême* of a middle-class young man: most of his poems and at least some of the pages of the ***Journal*** were written in restaurants where he retreated for hours on end, coming home only in the early morning. This was the period of the happy, enthusiastic meetings with the group of his friends who soon founded the magazine *La Relève;* but there was also emerging in him, even then, a sense of isolation which only increased, until the decisive retreat to Ste-Catherine where Saint-Denys-Garneau was to die, alone, one autumn evening. . . .

This sense of isolation, the menace of an isolation which is not a contraction of the self or a concentration of one's strength, but an inability to marshal the faculties and to communicate, is apparent from the very beginning of the ***Journal.*** On February 5, 1935, he wrote, "Last week I went through an inner experience of abandonment, humiliation, isolation. I thanked God for not making me prescient, for the thought of enduring for any length of time that state of extreme tension as well as that feeling of precariousness, futility and helplessness, would have driven me to a kind of madness of despair. . . ." He speaks again of an "excessive inner dislocation"—that is, an internal splitting, and an inability to reintegrate himself—which comprises the essential drama from which the ***Journal*** and the poems were to spring. . . . When Saint-Denys-Garneau began to write it was in answer to this threat of an "inner dislocation" which, in its final signification for him, bore the name of death, and whose true countenance was soon to be revealed to him. From the outset he faced the most fundamental of human questions. His daily meditations, his efforts at poetic creation, are set down in an urgent search after unity. He had to find the *centre,* or perish. To this centre Saint-Denys-Garneau had already given a name: it was Christ, the charity of Christ. One will understand nothing of his experience if one makes light of this spiritual attraction and of the religious disposition by which it was coloured. Saint-Denys-Garneau was Christian, profoundly so, and from beginning to end his quest is for a salvation not only human but supernatural. That he may have been the victim of certain distortions of Christian thought, we freely admit. But it was in the context of faith that he waged his combat, and it would be a mistake to see in that combat only a simple projection of the anguish of a man threatened in his carnal being.

At this point, it is not irrelevant to recall just what *La Relève* was. The magazine, founded in 1934 by a number of friends—Robert Charbonneau, Paul Beaulieu, Claude Hurtubise, Jean Le Moyne, Robert Elie, Saint-Denys-Garneau—had its roots in a common spiritual disquiet. It took part in that revival of the Christian intellect whose pioneers in France were—to mention only three names—Gabriel Marcel, Charles du Bos and Jacques Maritain. Maritain, exiled by the war, was often in Montreal during those years, and his contacts with the group of *La Relève* were numerous and fruitful. Saint-Denys-Garneau had nothing of the philosopher about him, although the ***Journal*** contains many allusions to the work of Maritain, Aimé Forest and Gabriel Marcel, as well as critical analyses of great penetration. He was above all a poet, and it was as a poet that he received Maritain's message. Everything seems to indicate that his encounter with this man, for whom Being and Christ are a constantly renewed interrogation, played no small part in the crisis which Saint-Denys-Garneau was going through. The demands of being and the passion for truth which appear everywhere in the ***Journal*** echo, but in a wholly personal and private manner, some of the fundamental theses of the French philosopher. In this respect Saint-Denys-Garneau's work unmistakably transcends, even while it comprehends, the psychological and social conditions of his own surroundings. When in the latter part of the ***Journal*** he resolves his inner contradictions within the Communion of the Saints, in an eminently Catholic notion of human communion, he does more than respond to the demand of his personal destiny; he reaches the crux of that common spiritual participation in which the Christian image of our time is formed.

Need we inquire more closely into this internal crisis, this "experience of abandonment, of humiliation," which stands at the threshold of Saint-Denys-Garneau's creative period? We have already pointed out that his health had been shattered; no doubt this is a principal factor in any explanation, and the most apparent. One might also borrow the language of psychoanalysis and speak of psychological imbalance, of neurosis. Saint-Denys-Garneau himself had not ignored this point of view. "The cause [of my sickness]," he wrote in the ***Journal,*** "lies therefore in a complex of sensibility and spirit, so far as I can see, a complete poison spread through the whole personality." But with all due regard to the physical and psychological circumstances of which Saint-Denys-Garneau was the victim, the fact remains that he underwent his experience with a man's undivided consciousness. Cardiac, neurotic: these are categories a little too simple for the man who wrote ***Regards et jeux dans l'espace, Les Solitudes*** and the ***Journal.*** We must look further, deeper. It seems well established that at the time he produced his work Saint-Denys-Garneau was in the grip of a great religious question. He had never been prudish, and was never to become so. But the potency of life which he carried within him, and which could have made of him a magnificent pagan, all at once found itself threatened—and at the same time curiously activated—by the ineluctable question of death and salvation. This question was no doubt presented badly, ambiguously. "Oh, the danger of happiness, of all ecstasy . . . !" Religious anxiety was felt by Saint-Denys-Garneau, as it was pretty commonly felt in his surroundings, under the guise of a feeling of guilt which denied his right to life. In the ***Journal,*** there are abundant signs of a fearful confusion between the Christian vocation—in the widest sense of the term—and the interdict laid on the instinctive manifestations of life, between the Charity which is all gift and openness, and the Jansenist temptation to reject the world. In this sense, Saint-Denys-Garneau gives evidence of an aberration which, without being peculiar to French Canada, has developed there with particular virulence and has not yet finished taking its toll of victims. His greatness lies in having faced it to its furthest reach; and in having surmounted it, if the profound expression of a malady is, in effect, a victory gained over that malady from thenceforward. Saint-Denys-Garneau staked his all in the face of death: of the physical death, naturally, whose imminence he could not but have foreseen; but also of that other death, the death of the spirit, against which he had raised the protest of a soul deeply thirsting after Charity. This ***Journal*** is perhaps, from a certain standpoint, the statement and record of a defeat. The poet did not in fact reach the self-integration, the unity he dreamed of. He seems on the contrary to have developed an ever clearer and more agonized consciousness of an inner cleavage, such as he described so exactly in the great passages of ***Le mauvais pauvre.*** But, over this species of death which he carried within him, he gained a victory: the victory of the word, of speech. A man's speech, fragile, uneven, at times awkward, but always with the accent of truth. Only let a man speak, and however desperate the message, doors open and an act of consciousness is initiated which holds out the promise of a new life. Saint-Denys-Garneau bears witness to a humanity which, faced with the most perturbing questions and with no expectation of any immediate answer, yet dares to wager, in blindness and uncertainty, on the existence of something greater than itself. (pp. 11-14)

Gilles Marcotte, in an introduction to Journal *by Saint-Denys Garneau, translated by John Glassco (© McClelland and Stewart Limited, 1962; copyright, Canada, 1962 by McClelland and Stewart Limited; used by permission of Librairie Beauchemin Ltee and The Canadian Publishers, McClelland and Stewart Limited, Toronto; originally published as* Journal, *Beauchemin, 1962), McClelland and Stewart, 1962, pp. 9-15.*

GERARD TOUGAS (essay date 1964)

[In the following excerpt, Tougas discusses the concerns and the innovative nature of Garneau's poetry.]

The poetic work of Saint-Denys-Garneau was accomplished between 1935 and 1938: ***Regards et jeux dans l'espace*** and

Solitudes, posthumous poems. A ***Journal,*** with entries from 1935 to 1939, permits us to place Saint-Denys-Garneau's poetry in relation to his intimate thoughts and fills out our picture of him.

As it has often happened in literary history, Saint-Denys-Garneau, soon after making the decision to put his thoughts down in writing, in his ***Regards et jeux dans l'espace,*** became aware that this activity was a check on his spiritual progress as well as on his weaknesses. Because he was an exceptional soul his testimony is incontestably original. In the history of French-Canadian poetry his work stands quite apart, both in material and in form. (pp. 196-97)

[Emile] Nelligan had made us feel the breath of something new at the end of the nineteenth century by his imagery, cast, it is true, in a half-Parnassian, half-Symbolist mould. Saint-Denys-Garneau, somewhat in the manner of [Charles] Péguy, puts an imprint, in lines long or short according to his inspiration, on a poetry which is the experience of the moment.

But soon he is haunted by thought of the Beyond which brings a special note to his thinking. (p. 197)

From the general scene Saint-Denys-Garneau comes to his own case. Life's melancholy becomes an existential weariness, a "grief" in a "closed house." Wasted with fever, he seems to have an obscure feeling, as Nelligan had had, that destruction is close. Death is already gnawing at him:

> Je suis une cage d'oiseau
> Une cage d'os
> Avec un oiseau
>
> L'oiseau dans sa cage d'os
> C'est la mort qui fait son nid.

> I am a bird cage, a cage of bones with a bird in it; the bird in its cage of bones is Death making its nest. [*trans.*]

He will not know the death that purifies without travelling a very difficult upward path, strewn with setbacks. With Death lying in wait, he will succumb. This temporary victory of natural instinct brings to the soul of Saint-Denys-Garneau a desperate sadness. Because he is a poet he will write ***Après les plus vieux vertiges,*** certainly one of the most beautiful poems in French-Canadian literature. Out of this deep disgust Saint-Denys-Garneau, just a short time before his death, will reach the light which takes shape in two poems unequalled by his predecessors.

Les regards et jeux dans l'espace and ***Solitudes*** raise French-Canadian literature to a pinnacle. There had to be more than a century of poetic endeavour before the birth of a work which is the expression in artistic wrapping of the drama of a true spiritual experience. It is significant that it is at a time when the French-Canadian writer is expressing himself in complete freedom that his poetic message should correspond to an act of submission, not of revolt.

How is Saint-Denys-Garneau's place to be clearly defined in relation to the contemporary poetic movement? We ask the question not so much because it seems likely to throw new light on Saint-Denys-Garneau but rather because French-Canadian criticism is faced with this inquiry.

There is no innovation, strictly speaking, in Saint-Denys-Garneau's poetry. The poet does not seem to have exerted himself to any extent to compose regular lines, like a Mallarmé, before creating his own means of expression. Between some stanzas in which the versification is traditional and others which are only prose, Saint-Denys-Garneau succeeds most often in creating poetry entirely his own and indisputably musical, which could never be reduced to rules of precise versification. It is on this score that he is completely modern. His originality began at the point where he was able successfully to fuse supple expression, which softens his verbal imperfections, with an exceptional sensitivity, which might be called anachronistic. Setting this poetry up against that of twentieth-century Europe, one runs the risk of falsifying the comparison from the beginning. Is it not more profitable simply to admit that here we are confronted with a vital personality, attesting to the strength of a young literature? (pp. 198-99)

Gerard Tougas, in an essay in his Histoire de la littérature Canadienne-Francaise *(reprinted by permission of Presses Universitaires de France), Presses Universitaires de France, 1964 (translated by Alta Lind Cook and reprinted as "The Contemporary Period,"* in History of French-Canadian Literature *by Gerard Tougas, second edition, Ryerson Press, 1966, pp. 144-250).**

Holograph copy of Garneau's poem "Que veux-tu, c'est ton sort." From Oeuvres, *edited by Jacques Brault and Benoit Lacroix. Reproduced by permission of Les Presses de l'Universite de Montreal.*

THE TIMES LITERARY SUPPLEMENT (essay date 1972)

[*The following excerpt compares Garneau to Charles Baudelaire and the French Symbolist poets and to the French-Canadian poet Émile Nelligan, who, like Garneau, is often referred to as a Canadian poète maudit.*]

Hector de Saint-Denys Garneau . . . , great-grandson of François-Xavier, is another Canadian Rimbaud, inspired by Baudelaire and European symbolism, burning himself out in three years of intense artistic activity (1935-39) in poetry and prose which fluctuates wildly in mood between extremes of ecstasy and despair. Garneau is another eternal adolescent, unable to mature for want of an acceptable adult model with which to identify, in a philistine and conformist world. Otherworldliness was encouraged in a milieu where happiness was dangerous and the flesh was sin and Garneau saw in music "une langue parfaite'' because it evoked perfectly the sense of the joy and the sadness of living which he could not or dared not formulate in words. . . .

The similarity between [Garneau's] works and the writings of Baudelaire is striking. A slim volume of published verse is supplemented with prose which is mainly art criticism, literary criticism (with a predilection for the French Catholic writers or ''âmes soeurs'' like Katherine Mansfield) and a ***Journal*** and related correspondence revealing preoccupations very similar to those of *Fusées* and *Mon coeur mis à nu*. . . .

Both [Émile] Nelligan and Saint-Denys Garneau witness eloquently, in spite of their heavy debt to European sources, to the ''difficulté d'être'' particular to the Quebec artist and to the community for which he feels and sees. Through their suffering, Quebec has discovered the painful emergence of its cultural identity from silence through to that fullness which is the harmonious blending of an expressive artistic form with an authentic human experience.

''The Quiet Revolution of Quebec,'' in The Times Literary Supplement *(© Times Newspapers Ltd. (London) 1972; reproduced from* The Times Literary Supplement *by permission), No. 3658, April 7, 1972, p. 399.**

JOHN GLASSCO (essay date 1975)

[Glassco was a Canadian novelist, poet, and translator. While he once wrote that he looked upon himself ''mainly as a pornographic novelist'' who endeavored to create ''serious and artistic works in this genre,'' Glassco is also recognized as a highly accomplished poet with strong ties to the tradition of elegaic and philosophical verse exemplified in modern literature by the poetry of Thomas Hardy and Edward Thomas. Much of Glassco's poetry, which is often remarked upon for its irony and pessimism, evokes the life and landscape of the Eastern Townships in his native Quebec. As a translator, Glassco is acclaimed for his skillful rendering of The Journal of Saint-Denys Garneau *and the* Complete Poems of Saint-Denys Garneau. *In the following excerpt from his introduction to the* Complete Poems, *Glassco discusses Garneau in the historical context of French-Canadian literature and, while acknowledging the private traumas that so strongly characterize Garneau's work, concludes that his technical innovations with poetic rhythms may be his most distinguished and enduring achievement.]*

Saint-Denys-Garneau still shares with Emile Nelligan the first place in the poetry of French Canada. The similarity of their careers—the almost overnight flowering of creativity, and its no less sudden withering away—is coincidental, and the two have nothing in common beyond being a good deal more than merely ''poets of Quebec''; and they are in fact the only poets of their nation whose accomplishment transcends nationality. But Nelligan marks the culmination of a trend: his work stands as the high-water mark of French-Canadian romanticism; while Saint-Denys-Garneau initiates a new era of both sensibility and prosody, and invokes and announces the future.

This is not to overlook the cultural importance of the third major poet of Quebec, Alain Grandbois, whom contemporary French-Canadian poets have chosen to follow on the path of an eloquence verging on fustian, a sensibility approaching sentimentality and a magnificent rejection of ideas. But while Grandbois is the poet of the splendours of the Word, who has almost singlehandedly freed French-Canadian poetry from what has been called ''the prison of the self-regarding self,'' Saint-Denys-Garneau is still the poet of the Idea, who has plumbed the depths of consciousness and conscience alike, and in doing so has, I believe, raised for himself a more lasting monument. As theoreticians of the art of poetry itself, they can of course sustain no contest: one has only to compare the luminous insights that stud Saint-Denys-Garneau's ***Journal*** with the civilized clichés of Grandbois in *Avant le chaos* and in his occasional contributions to periodicals. Their views of poetry are in fact as divergent as their practice. Both, as true poets, are spokesmen of an individual suffering and joy; but while Grandbois' ecstasy and anguish are of the flesh and the affections, Saint-Denys-Garneau's are of the soul and the intellect.

Of these three outstanding names in French-Canadian poetry, then—to which one must add those of Paul Morin, Robert Choquette and Alfred DesRochers, none of whom however, like Nelligan, has had any influence on the contemporary poetry of Quebec—Saint-Denys-Garneau remains the one who seems worthiest of a translation into English of his entire mature poetic output. (pp. 5-6)

It is some 35 years since Msgr. Camille Roy dismissed the poetry of Saint-Denys-Garneau as a ''collection of poems in the style of Valéry—that is to say, more or less incomprehensible.'' ''In these poems [he goes on] there is undoubtedly an attempt, however laboured, either at introspection or at the interpretation of the external. But this attempt all too often results in unintelligibility. For some readers, the hermetic partakes of the sublime. Here, the sublime is too closely veiled. *L'esprit français* will never lend itself to a thought it cannot perceive—the poet having hidden it under the bushel of an overly obscure symbolism. Moreover Monsieur Garneau writes without periods or commas.'' Roy seems to have missed the point entirely. Or has he? By his lights, this poetry was not ''poetry'' at all; and indeed it was not the voice of a Pamphile Lemay, a Chapman or a Nérée Beauchemin, the French-Canadian poets especially prized by this learned disciple of Brunetière. His verdict is nonetheless important, because it points up Saint-Denys-Garneau's definitive break with the past and with the worn-out body of French-Canadian literature which Roy supported with such eloquence and erudition; it marks a meeting of minds and epochs, and even raises the question of just what constitutes *l'esprit français*—something, we must note in passing, quite different from the still undetermined *esprit québecois,* which was admittedly the concern of neither writer. This ''French spirit,'' we can see now, was in fact magnificently exemplified by Saint-Denys-Garneau—by his search for new symbols and formulas of expression, his clarity of thought and command of nuance and the absolute sincerity and painstaking of his art.

As for his place in Quebec literary history, the distinguished French critic Samuel de Sacy has announced flatly, ''Insofar as any poetic tradition exists in French Canada, modern poetry, properly considered, begins with Saint-Denys-Garneau. . . . He knew not only the experience of solitude, but solitude felt as something irremediable, as a fatality, a curse, an ineluctable destiny. Thus, by assuming the whole burden of the sentence, he brought salvation to a whole generation of youth and exposed, in his poetry, its feeling of being hunted, abandoned, scorned, divided against itself and reduced to helplessness. By speaking, he exorcised.''

This was written in 1958. The generation whose demons he ''exorcised'' has now matured, and the succeeding wave of young Quebec writers have other demons, much more tangible, to fill the void and to minister to the constant need for something absolute, simple, authoritative and maternal, which is at once the spur and the crutch of *l'esprit québecois.* Mother Church has, for them, been replaced by Mother Quebec, by the incandescent ideal of an exploited and beleaguered land. In such a climate the tormented, inward-looking poetry of Saint-Denys-Garneau is now found to be unsympathetic, outmoded, almost impertinent; moreover, the cool intelligence of the **"Notes on Nationalism"** in his ***Journal*** is unacceptable to the advocates of separatism. This has inevitably led to a certain downgrading of his poetry and to a revaluation of his poetic stature, both of which are to some extent justified.

For Saint-Denys-Garneau is not a *great* poet. The very idea of being so "placed" would have horrified him. And his was no false modesty. He knew his limitations: his prophecy of the arrival of *"le créateur, le poète qui donnera au peuple canadien-français son image"* ["the creator, the poet who will give the French-Canadian people their own true image"] and who will appear "in his own good time," proves that he never thought of casting himself in such a role. It is even doubtful if he saw himself as a French-Canadian poet at all, if indeed he did not hold himself superior to the very spirit of French-Canadian poetry, or at least hold aloof from it. "I need hardly say," his friend Jean Le Moyne tells us, "that he saw our Canadian rhymesters for what they are: exactly nothing." His attitude was in this respect characteristically exclusive and fastidious; more important, his anguish was not localized in any sense of a vulgar emotional *dépaysement* ["being out of one's element"], as in a Hertel or a Miron, but in that of the universal human being.

In fact, this habit of negation had always been one of his greatest strengths. His early ability to *discard* literary influences—Maeterlinck, Henri de Régnier, Claudel—is notable. As Roland Bourneuf has pointed out, he did not read widely, doubtless following the practice of those poets who see in their own suggestibility the greatest danger to their vision and their art. His utter rejection of the fashionable surrealism of his day indicates also the sureness of his taste: the method had nothing to offer him. He was looking always inward, forging his style out of his *entrailles,* pushing back his own horizon, always exploiting his originality, to which was tragically joined the sense of his solitude. From his study of Ramuz he had grasped the principle of an absolute and rigorous sincerity: "to be simply oneself in order to be more than oneself." (pp. 7-9)

In any evaluation of the art of Saint-Denys-Garneau one must never forget that he was equally attracted by the life of religion. He was constantly tossed between the vocations of artist and ascetic, always fearful of his unfitness for either, always terrified both of the world and of hell. Out of this indecision and fear, these *balancements,* this shrinking and immoderate modesty, and out of his sense of the terrible discrepancy between life and art, and of the evanescence of both, he made his poetry. An unflinching moral dichotomist in the strictest Catholic tradition, he would compromise with no aspect of the Devil; yet, fatally attracted by the "evil" which he confronted in his own sexuality, he fell back on what seemed to him the redeeming beauty of human compassion and on the supernatural grace that somehow redeemed the carnal desire (and above all the auto-eroticism) which his ingrained Jansenism rejected and at last stifled. Overriding all these concepts is his stark terror of death and damnation; for him, the existence of a man like himself was only a way-station between nothingness and an eternity of torment, barely relieved by the fleeting beauty of nature and the forbidden ecstasy of carnal love. It was to poetry that he turned for relief. But poetry was for him communication above all things; and his anguish was thus purified by the most exhausting and consummate art, an art which became for him a quasi-religious duty. For the immediate and unrehearsed expression of his suffering he had recourse to his ***Journal,*** that terrible record of neurosis, guilt and despair.

This is not the place to discuss the ***Journal,*** except insofar as it illuminates his poetry, nor to inquire how far either of them reflected any but the most harrowing moments of his actual life—which seems indeed to have had many long periods of tranquillity and even a kind of vegetable happiness; for, like most keepers of intimate journals, he tells us nothing—no more, indeed, than Baudelaire—of his moments of joy: these moments were obviously always private, self-sufficient, craving no record. But it was only in the ***Journal*** that his ideas on poetry were clearly set forth.

These ideas are comprised in the notion, originally drawn from his own aesthetic of painting and never relinquished, that the world of apperception is only a *transparency* through which "being," or absolute reality, is grasped by means of the *signes* or symbols which the artist discerns and selects—in painting by his choice of pure colours, and in poetry by his *fresh* invention of images and rhythms. Full justice has already been done by David Hayne [see Additional Bibliography] to his "forest of symbols"—those symbols of the pruned tree, the bones, the severed head, the man full of holes, the fleshly mask of the face—which revitalized French-Canadian poetry and permanently supplanted the nightingale, church-bell, ploughshare, snowstorm and so on, which had long burdened it. But his astonishing reshaping of poetic rhythms is no less important, and was accomplished by a virtuosity in devising the most daring combinations of line lengths and stresses, by which, alternating the grave with the gay and stateliness with speed, he gave his finished poems the further dimension of the dance. One of his favourite devices was the *pair-impair* rhythm in which he sought to outdo his master Verlaine by contriving a dazzling alternation of trochees and iambs, and so broke down everything that had heretofore stood between a poetic union of sound and sense. He made the lyric dance as well as sing, thus restoring the long-lost unity of the two disciplines and even, as he suggests in his ***Journal,*** equating poetic expression with that of David dancing before the Ark. Let us take, for example, the poem **"Willows,"** the second to last of the **"Esquisses en plein air,"** which begins with a dozen short, slow, impressionistic lines, then makes a four-line pause—a calculated hesitation—and then suddenly gathers speed and breaks up into a sparkling counterpoint of reversed stresses, anapaests and syllabic pyrotechnics that resembles nothing more than the close of one of Chopin's joyous impromptus. Or look at the long untitled poem, the first in the section *Sans titre,* where for the first two thirds the alternations of lines, ranging in length from a single foot to a classic alexandrine, reproduce the tension and weight of the tormented, breathless utterance of the poem itself, and where the last third opens out into long lines of a regular, continuous, rolling suavity that enhances, like a pavane, the solemnity of an accepted despair. Again, the opening metronomic four-foot beat of the witty ***Commencement perpetuel*** reproduces to perfection the idea of *counting,* only to be followed by a conscious disordering of that simple initial rhythm, as the man who is counting, rather amusingly, loses his count. But the finest examples of this marriage of rhythm and meaning occur in the famous ***Accompagnement,*** written in a kind of brilliant dance-step further reinforced by the wry reiteration of the rhyming *joie* and *moi,* and in the still more famous ***Cage d'oiseau,*** where the desperate point is driven home, as if by the strokes of a hammer, in the recurrence of simple four-foot trochaic couplets with naive nursery-rhymes.

If undue emphasis seems to have been given here to Saint-Denys-Garneau's mastery of rhythms, it is because this may well be his highest and most lasting achievement. When his religious, neurotic and erotic agonies are forgotten, along with his often hysterical self-pity and his *bondieuserie*—that infantile, saccharine religiosity which occasionally disfigures his work—the marvellous prosody which never failed him may survive everything else: the formal *cachet* it imposed on everything he wrote was at any rate his salvation as a poet.

This technical control of image and emotion is however seen in little more than half of the 40-odd poems that he finished and approved. Much of his work, including over half of ***Regards et jeux dans l'espace,*** he either rightly repudiated in his ***Journal*** [see excerpt above, 1938] or left uncompleted in the manuscripts edited after his death by Elie and Le Moyne. And in fact all too many of the poems in ***Les solitudes*** are simply unrehearsed fragments, sometimes little more than jottings: they are often formless, at times distressingly awkward and incoherent; but there is no doubt they are, both actually and potentially, superior to the work published during his lifetime. It is impossible to appreciate his poetic stature without, for instance, the sections of ***Les solitudes*** entitled "Pouvoirs de la parole" and "La mort grandissante": these fragments, one might say, he had shored against his ruins in the final self-imposed exile at Sainte-Catherine, and though we must regret they were never brought to completion we may at least be thankful they were not lost along with the many pages of his ***Journal*** that were destroyed by his mother after his death. (pp. 12-16)

John Glassco, in an introduction to Complete Poems of Saint Denys Garneau *by Saint Denys Garneau, translated by John Glassco (copyright © 1975 by John Glassco; reprinted by permission of Oberon Press), Oberon Press, 1975, pp. 5-17.*

KATHY MEZEI (essay date 1976)

[Mezei discovers points of comparison between Garneau and his translator John Glassco, commenting that both are poets of ideas, both view poetic beauty as a quality separate from the personal motivations of the author, and both are concerned with interior, spiritual experience.]

In 1975 two brilliant translations by John Glassco appeared—*Lot's Wife* (*La Femme de Loth* by Monique Bosco) and the ***Complete Poems of Saint Denys Garneau.*** (p. 83)

What affinity has drawn Glassco to the hermetic work of Garneau, a poet tormented by the delicate balance between spirit and flesh, between aesthetics and asceticism, between silence and speech? . . .

It was out of the drama of his inner world, not his rather uneventful life, and out of his anguished attempt to come to terms with Catholicism that Garneau spun his poems. His innovative verse forms, introspective imaginings and symbolism (especially, trees, skeletons, the wind, flowers, barren winter landscapes, dead houses, the dance, the gaze) expressed the isolation and alienation of his generation, trapped by the institutions of church and state. . . .

Like Glassco, Garneau is a poet of ideas. (p. 84)

The first poems [in ***Complete Poems of Saint Denys Garneau***] are stronger because the abstract concepts and ambiguities are enclosed in concrete patterns and images whereas poems in the second part (and some of these are fragments) have not been brought into quite the order and form both poets emphasize. One also becomes impatient with such an extreme self-consciousness.

Like Glassco, Garneau is concerned with "making beautifully". His statement "Beauty. Quality of the work independent of the end pursued" (***Journal***) is echoed in the lines of Glassco's poem "The Last Word":

> The means are more important than the end,
> Ends being only an excuse for action,
> For adventures sought for their own sake alone.

Both poets seek to explore "Le terrain de l'esprit" and to reveal another "reality". For Garneau the body of the landscape, the landscape of the body and the contours of the house describe his inner anguish and division. For example,

> I think of the desolation of winter
> Through the long days of solitude
> In the dead house—
> For a house is dead when nothing is open—
> In the sealed house, ringed by woods
> **("A Sealed House")**
> (pp. 84-5)

Garneau is conscious of "correspondances" and speaks of "the poet for whom all things, all life, is a sign. And he seeks for intelligible signs, signs formed to interpret the meaning he has found." (***Journal***) (p. 85)

He also despaired of both the power and the impotence of the word. In the section titled "Pouvoirs de la parole" (Glassco retains the French in the section titles) he explores the relationship of the poet to the word. The impotence and terror that pursued the poet into his religious and sexual life is here too—"each word a sucking mouth". Since words for Garneau are an incarnation of an absolute reality, "we have no right to play a verbal game with something that is not comprised in the depth of our substance." Poetry paradoxically feeds and drains him.

His is a divided landscape in which the gaze, the two-edged blade, must penetrate as far inwards as it does outwards. Thus much of Garneau's poetry is a movement between two elements seeking an equilibrium. Until he is received and saved by God, "It is there in suspension that I am at rest". His poems reflect this duality through a deliberately ambiguous syntax and meaning. Glassco's translations are not only eloquent and sensitive but frequently clarify some of the elusiveness of Garneau without (and this is by far the most difficult test of virtuosity) losing the grace and subtlety of the French. (p. 86)

Kathy Mezei, "Like the Wind Made Visible" (reprinted by permission of the author), in Canadian Literature, *No. 71, Winter, 1976, pp. 83-7.*

ROBERT VIGNEAULT (essay date 1979)

[The following excerpt is taken from a general article examining the use of the essay form by Quebec writers. Earlier in his discussion, Vigneault defines the essay as a "piece of writing that is topical, dynamic, current, and oriented towards the future." This conception leads to criticism of Garneau's prose writings

which, Vigneault asserts, are "devoid of any real grasp of the world."]

How could we have written essays in Québec, considering that our thinking had always been riveted to pure, immobile, eternal, ideal essences? The *homo quebecensis,* whom we would one day discover with a certain surprise, had always been conceived by us as a two-footed, rational animal who regularly moved from power to action, impelled, in short, by a Prime Mover or pure Act in whom absolute perfection inhered. Besides, we had a tendency to prefer, not this philosophical man removed from the impure circumstances of time and place, but rather the being as pure being, who was finally attained at a third level of abstraction and who requited his admirers with the inoffensive joys of metaphysics. This form of thinking resolutely turned its back on existence, since existence was ultimately considered to be an accident (to which had to be added the accidents of time and space). It was a form of speculation admirably well-suited to the kind of teaching practised in those halls of disinterested intellectuality that were our classical colleges. Such institutions were fated to produce, not a Québécois, but (equipped with his general—and abstract—culture) the eternal "gentleman," utterly oblivious to the realities of life in Québec, indeed to reality altogether.

As the lucid and irritating essayist Jean Le Moyne has observed, Saint-Denys-Garneau is very much a "witness of his time" in this respect as in others. His prose writings, including selections recently published for the first time [in the 1971 edition of his complete works], clearly demonstrate the effects this kind of abstract teaching had upon him. What I find even more significant, however, is the fact that even in his imaginary world, Saint-Denys-Garneau displays an equally strong aversion to reality; for him, looking becomes the only legitimate form of contact with the world. Moreover, it is a kind of looking that denies the world its reality or tries constantly to see through it, as though its opaqueness had constantly to be purified; and yet, looking is no doubt the least active way of involving oneself in life. Garneau's looking becomes a somewhat playful activity as well, with children's games that are devoid of any real grasp of the world and therefore of any responsibility; they are games in a space that has been freed of all matter, a space of emptiness. Once the symbols have been deciphered and the ambiguities of the poetic language reduced, we are brought to realize that this poet, who has become one of our literary legends was in the last analysis a poet of nothingness! This should somewhat chill the ardour of those who stand in awe of the spiritual adventure of Saint-Denys-Garneau. . . . No doubt it was not by chance that, perceiving the frightful void of his poetic universe in a flash of unbearable lucidity, the poet reacted to this estrangement by trying to cut himself off from literature and the world, taking refuge in the false maternal security of his parents' mansion.

Saint-Denys-Garneau provides an eloquent example of this self-imposed alienation from the world since in his own way, in several of his prose writings, he was what one might call a sort of "negative image" of an essayist, turning about a secret so fearful that it could not be expressed. In fact, his secret was simply his acute and painful awareness of his own lack of presence to the world. (pp. 37-8)

Robert Vigneault, "The Quebec Essay: The Birth of Indigenous Thought," translated by Larry Shouldice, in Essays on Canadian Writing *(© Essays on Canadian Writing Ltd.), No. 15, Summer, 1979, pp. 33-50.**

ADDITIONAL BIBLIOGRAPHY

Atwood, Margaret. "The Paralyzed Artist." In her *Survival: A Thematic Guide to Canadian Literature,* pp. 177-94. Toronto: Anansi, 1972.*

Briefly compares Garneau's *Journal* with the journal *Place d'armes* by Canadian author Scott Symons, commenting that "they are both records of suffering inflicted on the individual by cultures too small for the men contained in them. Garneau is meticulous, restrained, forcing himself towards an unattainable ideal of spiritual perfection."

Fisette, Jean. "The Question of Enunciation in Poetry: Saint-Denys Garneau." *Essays on Canadian Writing,* No. 12 (Fall 1978): 216-34.

Semiotic analysis of Garneau's poem "Autrefois." The critic applies the concept of "enunciation"—the relation between writer and text—to illuminate the function of pronouns in this poem.

Hayne, David M. "A Forest of Symbols: An Introduction to Saint-Denys Garneau." *Canadian Literature,* No. 3 (Winter 1960): 5-16.

Biographical and critical essay. Coordinating excerpts from Garneau's *Journal* with quotations from his poetry, Hayne arrives at a view of Garneau as a poet who followed the literary precepts of the French Symbolists and whose work centers on four major themes: "poetic creation, solitude, authenticity, and death."

Wilson, Edmund. "Maisons Seigneuriales." In his *O Canada,* pp. 121-36. New York: Noonday Press, 1965.*

Biographical sketch. Wilson links Garneau with poet and essayist Jean Le Moyne as giving "the impression of Michels who are never to succeed in dissociating themselves from the ancient and effete tradition," and he comments that in his *Journal* Garneau writes "with a good deal of insight and eloquence" about French painters Pierre Auguste Renoir and Paul Cézanne.

Emma Goldman

1869-1940

Russian-born American autobiographer, essayist, critic, and editor.

Goldman was an outspoken libertarian and anarchist who rose to fame in the United States and Europe during the opening decades of the twentieth century. A proponent of free speech, birth control, and other individual freedoms, she addressed these issues and the need for sweeping economic, political, and social revolution in numerous speeches and articles, many of them collected in her *Anarchism, and Other Essays*. Considered for a time "the most dangerous woman in America" by FBI director J. Edgar Hoover, Goldman recounted her turbulent public and private life with such passion and candor in her autobiography, *Living My Life*, that even unsympathetic critics have been moved to appreciate her honesty and unwavering dedication to individual freedom.

Courtesy of Prints and Photographs Division, Library of Congress

Goldman was born into a lower-middle-class Jewish family in Kovno, Lithuania, in what is now a part of the Soviet Union. Early in life she realized she was unwanted: her mother, a widow who had remarried because she had two small daughters to support, considered the subsequent birth of Goldman an additional burden; her father, who could not forgive her for not being born a boy, vented his frustrations on her through violent verbal and physical abuse. Critics have cited her disturbed homelife, along with her experiences with several insensitive teachers and her awareness of Czarist atrocities, as the impetus for Goldman's later rebellion against all personal restraints and for her maternal sympathy for the downtrodden. Her family moved to the village of Popelan shortly after her birth, and later lived in Koenigsberg, Prussia, and St. Petersburg (Leningrad). These frequent moves, as well as her hostile family environment, allowed Goldman only a limited and sporadic education. Nonetheless, while in Koenigsberg she passed the entrance examination to the secondary gymnasium, which would have prepared her for college and a much desired medical degree. Her religious instructor, however, refused to grant her the necessary recommendation because of her rebellious behavior. Later, during her adolescence in St. Petersburg, she attended school for only six months before going to work at a cousin's glove factory, but during that period she became associated with nihilist and populist university students. Through them Goldman was introduced to radical ideas and literature. Soon after refusing to enter into an arranged marriage that her parents believed would "tame" her, Goldman emigrated to the United States with her older sister, Helena, and settled in Rochester, New York. She worked in garment factories in Rochester and New Haven, Connecticut, which gave her first-hand knowledge of the exploitation of immigrant workers and the need for reforms. However, it was the execution in 1887 of the Haymarket martyrs—four anarchists who many believed were falsely accused and convicted of the 1886 bombing of Haymarket Square in Chicago—which caused her to dedicate her life to anarchism. Divorcing her immigrant husband of two years, Goldman moved to New York City to seek out the country's leading anarchists.

In New York Goldman met the young anarchist Alexander Berkman, who became her lover and remained her lifelong friend. Through Berkman, Goldman met anarchist leader Johann Most, who recognized Goldman's gift of commanding speech and became her mentor, preparing her to take his place as a leader of the anarchist movement. Goldman was content in her early speeches to parrot Most's words and ideas, which aimed primarily at organizing and "liberating" the largely immigrant American labor force through anarchist means, including violence. However, Goldman soon became attracted to the ideas of Russian scientist and social philosopher Peter Kropotkin, who believed that private property, the church, and, especially the state must be abolished in favor of voluntary federations designed to supply necessary services and provisions. Larger bodies within and among countries would then be free to encourage moral, intellectual, and artistic pursuits. Most, a man of extreme loves and hatreds, considered Goldman's interest in any philosophy other than his own a personal betrayal. Despite their subsequent estrangement, Goldman remained an admirer of Most until a final and bitter break in 1892. Goldman had helped Berkman plan the murder of Homestead Steel owner Henry Clay Frick after he refused to negotiate with locked-out workers at the company's Pittsburgh plant. Frick survived the assassination attempt by Berkman, who was sentenced to twenty-two years in prison. Johann Most publicly denounced the act as foolish and wasteful, even though he had often advocated and even praised acts of violence by others as useful tools of propaganda. In her fury over his public disapproval, Goldman attended one of Most's speaking engagements, rose from her seat in the audience, and lashed him with a bullwhip. In later years, Goldman blamed their differences on age and experience; while Most tried to give his young followers the benefit of his years of suffering at the hands of the press, the government, and the penal system, Goldman and Berkman were young enthusiasts, filled with the faith of their convictions and willing to sacrifice their lives for them.

Goldman spent the year after Berkman's conviction fighting for his release. She was herself arrested and sentenced to a year's imprisonment for inciting a riot at Union Square, after she advised unemployed immigrant workers to steal bread if their demands for food remained unanswered. During the year at New York's Blackwell Island, Goldman solidified her own political philosophy, distinct from those of early, predominantly male associates. This resulted in a blend of Kropotkin's liberal, all-encompassing ideas about complete individual freedom and Goldman's innate passion for justice, no matter what philosophical or political expedience dictated—an attitude that acquaintances characterized as the protective, motherly aspect of her nature. This new philosophy included the rejection of violence, regardless of the cause. After her release she studied midwifery in Vienna, then returned to New York to practice among the poor. This experience more than any other made her aware of the need for wide dissemination of birth-control information, and reinforced her belief that marriage was based upon exploitation of the weak by the strong and only rarely upon love.

Goldman's vehement support of social revolution and her compassionate belief in individual rights and freedoms were overshadowed by press accounts of her speeches and activities, which generally characterized her as a bomb-throwing, bloodthirsty anarchist who was anti-American, anti-God, and anti-marriage. For example, when Leon Czolgosz, the convicted assassin of President William McKinley, claimed to have been inspired to his act by a Goldman speech, her name was repeatedly linked to accounts of the murder and the trial, despite the fact that Goldman rejected violence and had in fact volunteered to nurse McKinley if she was needed. In 1906 Goldman founded *Mother Earth* magazine as a forum for radical political, philosophical, and literary expression. She turned the editorship over to Berkman, who was released from prison the same year, as she continued a phenomenal schedule of nationwide lecture tours, lending her voice and reputation to such causes as free love, atheism, birth control, and free speech. Harassment by local police forces and by the United States government, which often resulted in the dispersion of assembled listeners and jail terms for Goldman, nevertheless provided constant press attention for her activities.

In 1917 Goldman's public career in America ended when she and Berkman were sentenced to two years in prison for interfering with the federal conscription act. Upon their release, they were deported to Russia along with other "undesirable aliens." Though a naturalized citizen by marriage, Goldman had been denaturalized years earlier when the U.S. government withdrew the citizenship of her missing ex-husband and intentionally concealed from her news of the hearing. Goldman welcomed the deportation as a chance to participate firsthand in the revolutionary process in Russia. However, following the government-backed massacre of unarmed sailors at Kronstradt in 1921, she denounced the Bolsheviks and their brutal tactics, accusing them of enslaving the proletariat for questionable ends. *My Disillusionment in Russia,* which chronicles Goldman's two years in that country, made her the subject of controversy in the United States once again. Most conservative critics considered her denunciation of the Communist regime proof that they were right in their opposition to it. Liberals and radicals, while not doubting Goldman's sincerity in interpreting her experiences, questioned her capacity for objectivity since all forms of state are antithetical to anarchist doctrine. Dorothy Brewster went as far as suggesting that "in the deeper layers of her consciousness she must have hated deeply the thought of Marxian success, must have longed for convincing proof of failure." Among Goldman's liberal and radical supporters, only her friend Rebecca West defended her position, pointing out the author's "proven genius for honesty and courage."

During the remainder of her life Goldman traveled throughout England and Europe. Through the efforts of writers, artists, and the American Civil Liberties Union (whose founder Goldman had inspired to his lifework by the force of a single speech), Goldman was allowed to return to the United States for a ninety-day lecture tour on literature in 1934. After the suicide of Berkman in 1936, which affected her profoundly, Goldman worked for the advance of the social revolution in Spain. While raising funds in Toronto for the then-lost cause of the Loyalists, Goldman suffered a stroke. She died three months later. Her body was returned to the country she considered her home and buried in Chicago near the graves of the Haymarket martyrs.

While Goldman was primarily a public speaker and political activist, her autobiography *Living My Life,* her essays on anarchism and on the Russian Revolution, as well as her collected letters, are considered a record of an extraordinary life and of the international political scene of her era. *Living My Life* candidly recalls Goldman's early activities and beliefs, her numerous lovers, and her assessment of the consequences of her actions. Despite the intimate experiences disclosed in the book, critics have noted the impersonal objectivity of the work. Though they acknowledge the failure of her aims, critics overwhelmingly consider the story of her life a personal triumph. To aid in writing the autobiography, Goldman requested and received thousands of letters from friends around the world. These letters provided a record of her personal thoughts and activities, placing them within a historical and political context. These, along with letters written almost daily to Berkman during their exile, display Goldman's integrity and show her to have been in private exactly what she professed to be in public, a fact that critics and biographers find remarkable considering the high standard of personal conduct her convictions demanded of her.

A self-taught intellectual and art lover, Goldman was also one of the first Americans to recognize the importance of modern English and European drama when American theater was still primarily an instrument of frivolous entertainment. In *The Social Significance of the Modern Drama,* published in 1914, Goldman examined the plays of such dramatists as Henrik Ibsen, August Strindberg, and Bernard Shaw, whose works she is sometimes credited with introducing to the American stage. Her style here, as in all her works, is appreciated most for emotional honesty and powerful persuasiveness. However, Goldman's fame does not rest upon her writings as much as it does upon her reputation as a person of integrity and high ideals. H. L. Mencken, who fought for Goldman's repatriation

despite his own political differences with her, wrote of Goldman: "I regard her as one of the most notable women now extant upon this planet," and added: "What irony in the contrast between the ideas this woman . . . has advocated in her life and the ideas she is commonly accused of advocating."

(See also *Contemporary Authors*, Vol. 110.)

PRINCIPAL WORKS

Anarchism, and Other Essays (essays) 1910
The Social Significance of the Modern Drama (criticism) 1914
**My Disillusionment in Russia* (memoirs) 1923
**My Further Disillusionment in Russia* (memoirs) 1924
Living My Life (autobiography) 1931
Red Emma Speaks: Selected Writings and Speeches (essays, lectures) 1972
Nowhere at Home: Letters from Exile of Emma Goldman and Alexander Berkman (letters) 1975

*These works were published as *My Disillusionment in Russia* in 1925.

HIPPOLYTE HAVEL (essay date 1910)

[*In the late 1890s Goldman became romantically involved with Havel, a Czech revolutionary, while she was living in London and waiting to go to Paris to study medicine. When Goldman's financial backers learned of the two lovers' anarchist activities abroad, they withdrew their support, and Goldman's dreams of becoming a doctor were destroyed. In the introduction to* Anarchism, and Other Essays, *from which the following excerpt is taken, Havel praises Goldman's bravery and her devotion to her ideals, noting that Goldman's most attractive qualities are her honesty and her sympathy for the suffering. Havel concludes that Goldman is shocking, even to radicals, because she both teaches and lives according to her convictions.*]

Among the men and women prominent in the public life of America there are but few whose names are mentioned as often as that of Emma Goldman. Yet the real Emma Goldman is almost quite unknown. The sensational press has surrounded her name with so much misrepresentation and slander, it would seem almost a miracle that, in spite of this web of calumny, the truth breaks through and a better appreciation of this much maligned idealist begins to manifest itself. (p. 5)

The mist in which the name of Emma Goldman has so long been enveloped is gradually beginning to dissipate. Her energy in the furtherance of such an unpopular idea as Anarchism, her deep earnestness, her courage and abilities, find growing understanding and admiration. (p. 7)

There are personalities who possess such a powerful individuality that by its very force they exert the most potent influence over the best representatives of their time. Michael Bakunin was such a personality. But for him, Richard Wagner had never written *Die Kunst und die Revolution*. Emma Goldman is a similar personality. She is a strong factor in the socio-political life of America. By virtue of her eloquence, energy, and brilliant mentality, she moulds the minds and hearts of thousands of her auditors.

Deep sympathy and compassion for suffering humanity, and an inexorable honesty toward herself, are the leading traits of Emma Goldman. No person, whether friend or foe, shall presume to control her goal or dictate her mode of life. She would perish rather than sacrifice her convictions, or the right of self-ownership of soul and body. Respectability could easily forgive the teaching of theoretic Anarchism; but Emma Goldman does not merely preach the new philosophy; she also persists in living it,—and that is the one supreme, unforgivable crime. Were she, like so many radicals, to consider her ideal as merely an intellectual ornament; were she to make concessions to existing society and compromise with old prejudices,—then even the most radical views could be pardoned in her. But that she takes her radicalism seriously; that it has permeated her blood and marrow to the extent where she not merely teaches but also practices her convictions—this shocks even the radical Mrs. Grundy. Emma Goldman lives her own life; she associates with publicans—hence the indignation of the Pharisees and Sadducees. (pp. 41-3)

Cowards who fear the consequences of their deeds have coined the word of philosophic Anarchism. Emma Goldman is too sincere, too defiant, to seek safety behind such paltry pleas. She is an Anarchist, pure and simple. She represents the idea of Anarchism as framed by Josiah Warren, Proudhon, Bakunin, Kropotkin, Tolstoy. Yet she also understands the psychologic causes which induce a Caserio, a Vaillant, a Bresci, a Berkman, or a Czolgosz to commit deeds of violence. To the soldier in the social struggle it is a point of honor to come in conflict with the powers of darkness and tyranny, and Emma Goldman is proud to count among her best friends and comrades men and women who bear the wounds and scars received in battle.

In the words of Voltairine de Cleyre, characterizing Emma Goldman after the latter's imprisonment in 1893: The spirit that animates Emma Goldman is the only one which will emancipate the slave from his slavery, the tyrant from his tyranny—the spirit which is willing to dare and suffer. (p. 44)

Hippolyte Havel, "Biographical Sketch," in Anarchism, and Other Essays *by Emma Goldman, Mother Earth Publishing Association, 1910 (and reprinted by Kennikat Press, 1969), pp. 5-44.*

HUTCHINS HAPGOOD (essay date 1911)

[*An American novelist and essayist, Hapgood was closely associated with the nation's various liberal social, political, and aesthetic movements during the first half of the twentieth century. He was, according to* The New York Times, *"a leader . . . in the movement which gave birth to the Greenwich Village traditions and the artists' Provincetown." The author of such realistic narratives as* The Autobiography of a Thief *(1902) and* An Anarchist Woman *(1909), Hapgood has written of himself: "My attitude of mind has consistently been what is called progressive. Sometimes I have been known as a radical, but I think those who best understand me feel that mine was a consistent effort to interpret the developing movements of all kinds." In the following excerpt, Hapgood offers a laudatory review of* Anarchism, and Other Essays, *judging the collection to be a significant contribution to the then small corpus of anarchist literature.*]

Every thoughtful person ought to read this volume of papers [***Anarchism, and Other Essays***] by the foremost American anarchist. In whatever way the book may modify or strengthen the opinions already held by its readers, there is no doubt that a careful reading of it will tend to bring about greater social sympathy. It will help the public to understand a group of serious-minded and morally strenuous individuals, and also to feel the spirit that underlies the most radical tendencies of the great labour movement of our day.

Emma Goldman is known by name to a very large number of people; but she is as yet not truthfully known to the public at large. There is probably no living man or woman who has been so thoroughly misrepresented. (p. 639)

In a brief review it is impossible to explain a philosophy and an emotional point of view which is dependent on a whole body of complex social experience new to the readers of this magazine. The point, however, at which there may be, from the very start, a meeting-ground of sympathy between the conservative world and the world which Emma Goldman tries to express is the essential idealism of anarchism. One feels this on every page of the present volume. All persons really living love poetry—fundamental poetry, whether in verse or prose. . . . When we grasp any truth profoundly it seems poetical to us.

Emma Goldman holds the opinions she has because of her idealistic passions. They are the fundamental cause of her ideas. And this is not denying her ideas truth. On the contrary, it is affirming that they possess the deepest of all truths—poetical truth. It is interesting to notice how often throughout her book she quotes, in support of her own feeling or belief, some poet or transcendental philosopher—Shelley, for instance, or Emerson.

People who are not anarchists, but who understand, would probably admit the deep ideal truth there is in the extreme individualistic, and, at the same time, the emotionally social, attitude. (pp. 639-40)

It would be unjust to suggest that general poetical truth is all there is in anarchism. Emma Goldman's book brings out many delicate psychological considerations and much specific ethical and political and economic criticism. But the general poetical truth which is an integral part of the anarchist's philosophy is the common factor between the public and the more special development of anarchistic thought. The literature of anarchism is slight and inadequate. It is difficult to appreciate what anarchists are like through their written words. But to their written words this volume of Emma Goldman's is an important contribution. (p. 640)

Hutchins Hapgood, "Emma Goldman's 'Anarchism'" (copyright, 1911, by Dodd, Mead and Company, Inc.; reprinted by permission of the Literary Estate of Hutchins Hapgood), in The Bookman, *New York, Vol. XXXII, No. 6, February, 1911, pp. 639-40.*

FLOYD DELL (essay date 1913)

[An American novelist and dramatist, Dell is best known today as the author of Moon-Calf *(1920), a novel which captures the disillusioned spirit of the Jazz Age. For several years he was a member of the Chicago Renaissance group of writers, which also included Carl Sandburg, Ben Hecht, Theodore Dreiser, and which established the American Midwest as a source of artistic material and achievement. A Marxist during his early career, Dell moved from Chicago to New York in 1914 and served as editor of* The Masses *and its successor* The Liberator *for ten years. In the following excerpt from his early study of outstanding feminist women, Dell praises Goldman as an advocate of nonviolent, libertarian social change who follows the tradition of Ralph Waldo Emerson and Henry David Thoreau.]*

There was a brief period in which Anarchists, under the influence of Johann Most, believed in (even if they did not practice) the use of dynamite. But this period was ended, in America, by the hanging of several innocent men in Chicago in 1887; which at least served the useful purpose of showing radicals that it was a bad plan even to talk of dynamite. (p. 58)

Since 1887 the Anarchists have lost influence among workingmen until they are today negligible—unless one credits them with Syndicalism—as a factor in the labor movement. The Anarchists have, in fact, left the industrial field more and more and have entered into other kinds of propaganda. They have especially "gone in for kissing games."

And Emma Goldman reflects, in her career, the change in Anarchism. She has become simply an advocate of freedom—freedom of every sort. She does not advocate violence any more than Ralph Waldo Emerson advocated violence. It is, in fact, as an essayist and speaker of the kind, if not the quality, of Emerson, Thoreau, or George Francis Train, that she is to be considered. (pp. 58-9)

She has a legitimate social function—that of holding before our eyes the ideal of freedom. She is licensed to taunt us with our moral cowardice, to plant in our souls the nettles of remorse at having acquiesced so tamely in the brutal artifice of present day society.

I submit the following passage from her writings (**"Anarchism, and Other Essays"**) as at once showing her difference from other radicals and exhibiting the nature of her appeal to her public:

> The misfortune of woman is not that she is unable to do the work of a man, but that she is wasting her life force to outdo him, with a tradition of centuries which has left her physically incapable of keeping pace with him. Oh, I know some have succeeded, but at what cost, at what terrific cost! The import is not the kind of work woman does, but rather the quality of the work she furnishes. She can give suffrage or the ballot no new quality, nor can she receive anything from it that will enhance her own quality. Her development, her freedom, her independence, must come from and through herself. First, by asserting herself as a personality, and not as a sex commodity. Second, by refusing the right to anyone over her body; by refusing to bear children unless she wants them; by refusing to be a servant to God, the State, society, the husband, the family, etc.; by making her life simpler, but deeper and richer.
>
> (pp. 60-1)

There is little in this that Ibsen would not have said amen to. But . . . Ibsen has said it already, and said it more powerfully. Emma Goldman—who (if among women anyone) should have for us a message of her own, striking to the heart—repeats, in a less effective cadence, what she has learned from him. (p. 62)

Floyd Dell, "Beatrice Webb and Emma Goldman," in his Women As World Builders: Studies in Modern Feminism *(copyright, 1913, by Forbes and Com-*

*pany; reprinted by permission of the Literary Estate of Floyd Dell), Forbes, 1913, pp. 52-64.**

MARGARET C. ANDERSON (essay date 1914)

[*Anderson was the founding editor of* The Little Review *(1914-29), one of the most important "little" magazines of the early twentieth century. Anderson defined the Chicago-based periodical's avant-garde stance as "Life for Art's sake" and wrote that* The Little Review *was published for "intelligent people whose philosophy is Applied Anarchism." A wide variety of topics, including feminism, anarchy, psychoanalysis, and modern art, were discussed in the magazine's pages, and fiction, poetry, and criticism were contributed by such noted writers as T. S. Eliot, James Joyce, Sherwood Anderson, and Ezra Pound. In the following excerpt from* The Little Review, *Anderson attempts to define Goldman's thought and motivation, using Floyd Dell's appraisal (see excerpt above, 1913) as a reference point from which to term Goldman a Nietzschean.*]

Emma Goldman preaches and practises the philosophy of freedom; she pushes through the network of a complicated society as if it were a cobweb instead of a steel structure; she brushes the cobwebs from her eyes and hair and calls back to the less daring ones that the air is more pure up there and "sunrise sometimes visible." Someone has put it this way: "Repudiating as she does practically every tenet of what the modern state holds good, she stands for some of the noblest traits in human nature." And no one who listens to her thoughtfully, whatever his opinion of her creed, will deny that she has nobility. Such qualities as courage—dauntless to the point of heartbreak; as sincerity, reverence, high-mindedness, self-reliance, helpfulness, generosity, strength, a capacity for love and work and life—all these are noble qualities, and Emma Goldman has them in the *n*th power. She has no pale traits like tact, gentleness, humility, meekness, compromise. She has "a hard, kind heart" instead of "a soft, cruel one." And she's such a splendid fighter!

What is she fighting for? For the same things, concretely, that Nietzsche and Max Stirner fought for abstractly. She has nothing to say that they have not already said, perhaps; but the fact that she says it instead of putting it into books, that she hurls it from the platform straight into the minds and hearts of the eager, bewildered, or unfriendly people who listen to her, gives her personality and her message a unique value. She says it with the same unflinching violence to an audience of capitalists as to her friends the workers. And the substance of her gospel—I speak merely from the impressions of those two lectures and the very little reading I've done of her published work—is something of this sort:

Radical changes in society, releasement from present injustices and miseries, can come about not through *reform* but through *change;* not through a patching up of the old order, but through a tearing down and a rebuilding. This process involves the repudiation of such "spooks" as Christianity, conventional morality, immortality, and all other "myths" that stand as obstacles to progress, freedom, health, truth, and beauty. One thus achieves that position beyond good and evil for which Nietzsche pleaded. (p. 6)

In his *Women as World Builders* Floyd Dell said this: "Emma Goldman has become simply an advocate of freedom of every sort. She does not advocate violence any more than Ralph Waldo Emerson advocated violence. It is, in fact, as an essayist

MOTHER EARTH

Vol. X. January, 1916 No. 11

CONTENTS

	Page
Donald Vose: The Accursed — Emma Goldman	353
Observations and Comments	358
Not Guilty — Margaret Sanger	363
Salute Mother Earth — Alexander Berkman	365
Three Hundred and Twenty-One Lectures — Ben L. Reitman, M.D.	366
The Blast — Alexander Berkman	369
Free Thought and Socialism — Walter Merchant	370
Revolt	372
Two Weeks Enlightenment For Chicago — Ben Mandell	373
Voices From the Prison — A Manifesto from Europe	376
A Brief Sojourn — Sol Davis	379
The Harbor — Lee J. Smits	382

EMMA GOLDMAN, - - Publisher and Editor
Office: 20 East 125th Street, New York City
Telephone, Harlem 6194
Price, 10 Cents per Copy One Dollar per Year

Title page to a copy of Goldman's journal Mother Earth. *Reproduced by permission of the International Institute of Social History, Amsterdam.*

and speaker of the kind, if not the quality, of Emerson, Thoreau, and George Francis Train, that she is to be considered" [see excerpt above, 1913]. I think, rather, that she is to be considered fundamentally as something more definite than that:—as a practical Nietzschean.

I am incapable of listening, unaroused, to the person who believes something intensely, and who does intensely what she believes. What more simple—or more difficult? Most of us don't know what we believe, or, if we do, we have the most extraordinary time trying to live it. Emma Goldman is so bravely consistent—which to many people is a confession of limitations. But if one is going to criticise her there are more subtle grounds to do it on. One of her frequent assertions is that she has no use for religion. That is like saying that one has no use for poetry: religion isn't merely a matter of Christianity or Catholicism or Buddhism or any other classifiable quantity. Also, if it is true that the person to be distrusted is the one who has found an answer to the riddle, then Emma Goldman is to be discounted. Her convictions are presented with a sense of definite finality. But there's something splendidly uncautious, something irresistibly stirring, about such an attitude. And whatever one believes, of one thing I'm certain: whoever means to face the world and its problems intelligently must know something about Emma Goldman. Whether her philosophy will change the face of the earth isn't the supreme issue. As the enemy of all smug contentment, of all blind acquiescence in things as they are, and as the prophet who dares to preach that our failures are not in wrong applications of values but in the values themselves, Emma Goldman is the most challenging spirit in America. (pp. 8-9)

Margaret C. Anderson, "The Challenge of Emma Goldman" (copyright, 1914, by Margaret C. Anderson; reprinted by permission of the Literary Estate of Margaret C. Anderson), in The Little Review, *Vol. I, No. 3, May, 1914, pp. 5-9.*

EMMA GOLDMAN (essay date 1914)

[*In her foreword to* The Social Significance of the Modern Drama, *Goldman details her approach to the works of such dramatists as Henrik Ibsen, August Strindberg, and Bernard Shaw, and contrasts their socially concerned works with those of the art-for-art's-sake movement. The influence of this book and the numerous lectures which inspired it are discussed in the excerpt by Van Wyck Brooks (1952) and in the entry by Joseph Ishill in the Additional Bibliography.*]

In order to understand the social and dynamic significance of modern dramatic art it is necessary, I believe, to ascertain the difference between the functions of art for art's sake and art as the mirror of life.

Art for art's sake presupposes an attitude of aloofness on the part of the artist toward the complex struggle of life: he must rise above the ebb and tide of life. He is to be merely an artistic conjurer of beautiful forms, a creator of pure fancy.

That is not the attitude of modern art, which is preëminently the reflex, the mirror of life. The artist being a part of life cannot detach himself from the events and occurrences that pass panorama-like before his eyes, impressing themselves upon his emotional and intellectual vision.

The modern artist is, in the words of August Strindberg, "a lay preacher popularizing the pressing questions of his time." Not necessarily because his aim is to proselyte, but because he can best express himself by being true to life. (p. 3)

[Any] mode of creative work, which with true perception portrays social wrongs earnestly and boldly, may be a greater menace to our social fabric and a more powerful inspiration than the wildest harangue of the soapbox orator.

Unfortunately, we in America have so far looked upon the theater as a place of amusement only, exclusive of ideas and inspiration. Because the modern drama of Europe has till recently been inaccessible in printed form to the average theatergoer in this country, he had to content himself with the interpretation, or rather misinterpretation, of our dramatic critics. As a result the social significance of the Modern Drama has well nigh been lost to the general public.

As to the native drama, America has so far produced very little worthy to be considered in a social light. Lacking the cultural and evolutionary tradition of the Old World, America has necessarily first to prepare the soil out of which sprouts creative genius. (pp. 4-5)

Therefore, America could not so far produce its own social drama. But in proportion as the crystallization progresses, and sectional and national questions become clarified as fundamentally social problems, the drama develops. Indeed, very commendable beginnings in this direction have been made within recent years, among them "The Easiest Way," by Eugene Walter, "Keeping Up Appearances," and other plays by Butler Davenport, "Nowadays" and two other volumes of one-act plays, by George Middleton,—attempts that hold out an encouraging promise for the future.

The Modern Drama, as all modern literature, mirrors the complex struggle of life,—the struggle which, whatever its individual or topical expression, ever has its roots in the depth of human nature and social environment, and hence is, to that extent, universal. Such literature, such drama, is at once the reflex and the inspiration of mankind in its eternal seeking for things higher and better. Perhaps those who learn the great truths of the social travail in the school of life, do not need the message of the drama. But there is another class whose number is legion, for whom that message is indispensable. In countries where political oppression affects all classes, the best intellectual element have made common cause with the people, have become their teachers, comrades, and spokesmen. But in America political pressure has so far affected only the "common" people. It is they who are thrown into prison; they who are persecuted and mobbed, tarred and deported. Therefore another medium is needed to arouse the intellectuals of this country, to make them realize their relation to the people, to the social unrest permeating the atmosphere.

The medium which has the power to do that is the Modern Drama, because it mirrors every phase of life and embraces every strata of society,—the Modern Drama, showing each and all caught in the throes of the tremendous changes going on, and forced either to become part of the process or be left behind.

Ibsen, Strindberg, Hauptmann, Tolstoy, Shaw, Galsworthy and the other dramatists contained in this volume represent the social iconoclasts of our time. They know that society has gone beyond the stage of patching up, and that man must throw off the dead weight of the past, with all its ghosts and spooks, if he is to go foot free to meet the future.

This is the social significance which differentiates modern dramatic art from art for art's sake. It is the dynamite which undermines superstition, shakes the social pillars, and prepares men and women for the reconstruction. (pp. 6-8)

Emma Goldman, in a foreword to her The Social Significance of the Modern Drama *(copyright, 1914, by Richard G. Badger; reprinted by permission of the Literary Estate of Emma Goldman), Badger, 1914, pp. 3-8.*

MARGARET STORM JAMESON (essay date 1916)

[*Jameson is one of England's leading writers of the "family chronicle" novel, in the tradition of John Galsworthy and Arnold Bennett. A prolific author with liberal sympathies, she is frequently concerned, in her literary criticism as in her novels, with the changes in Western mores occasioned by World War I. In the following excerpt, Jameson—though judging Goldman to be "the greatest living propagandist"—praises the cleverness rather than the substance of* Anarchism, and Other Essays, *and dismisses* The Social Significance of the Modern Drama *as the work of a critic "with an axe to grind."*]

[In ***Anarchism, and Other Essays***] the writings of Miss Goldman are as avowedly propagandist as her speeches: and they are as such more effective for her purpose as she is a much cleverer preacher than Voltairine le Cleyre. Her writing is more restrained and therefore more forceful: it is the work in fact, of the greatest living propagandist.

Yet Emma Goldman, as Voltairine le Cleyre, runs wild on approaching the question of marriage and love. There is no surer test of the intellectual quality of the "advanced"—for the most part, a pitiful crew—than the waving before them of this particular flag. The two anarchists make the usual blunder of supposing that sexual love outside marriage is a different thing from the same love in marriage; whereas there is not the slightest difference: sexual love outside marriage remains the evanescent purely animal thing that it is when sanctified by the church or legalized by the State. (pp. 135-36)

Literary criticism with an axe to grind is always bad criticism. If Miss Goldman had not been looking for anarchism [in ***The Social Significance of the Modern Drama***] she would not have suspected Sudermann of social significance, W. B. Yeats of sense, or Leonid Andreiv of honesty of purpose. Under the influence of the anarchist-complex she has produced a disingenuous criticism of a handful of European dramatists, taking them at their own valuation and making no attempt at a standard of critical values. Apparently Miss Goldman imagines Yeats and Lennox worthy of as serious consideration as Ibsen and Strindberg because they chose to write in the same form—the dramatic. We are left wondering at the childlike *naïveté* of the cultured American in the presence of so-called serious literature. (p. 136)

(Margaret) Storm Jameson, in a review of "Anarchism, and Other Essays" and "The Social Significance of the Modern Drama" (reprinted by permission of A D Peters & Co Ltd), in The Egoist, *Vol. III, No. 9, September, 1916, pp. 135-36.*

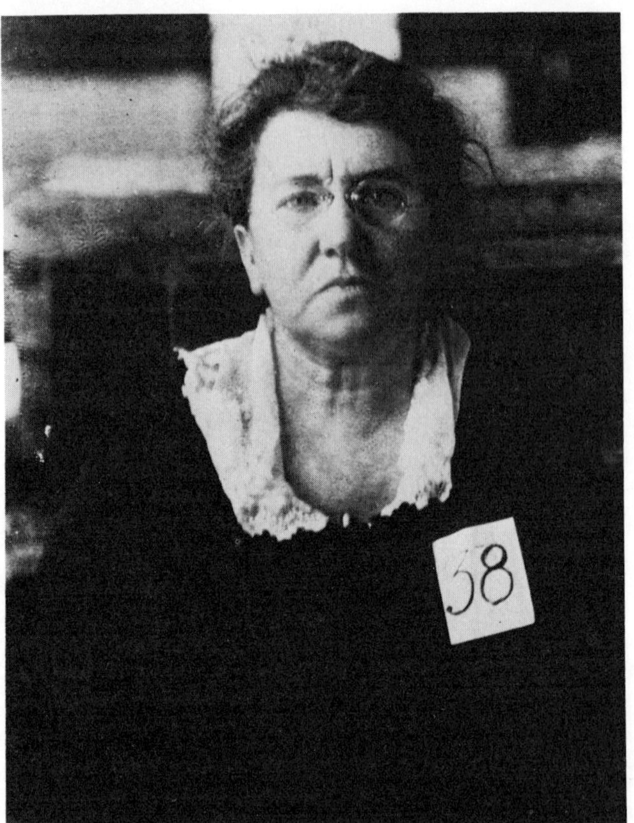

Goldman photographed at the time of her deportation from the United States. The Granger Collection, New York.

EMMA GOLDMAN (essay date 1922)

[In the following excerpt from her preface to My Disillusionment in Russia, *Goldman synopsizes her Russian experiences, which had begun on a note of hope and optimism and which had ended in horror and bitterness over the massacre of unarmed Russian sailors at the port city of Kronstadt.]*

The decision to record my experiences, observations, and reactions during my stay in Russia I had made long before I thought of leaving that country. In fact, that was my main reason for departing from that tragically heroic land.

The strongest of us are loath to give up a long-cherished dream. I had come to Russia possessed by the hope that I should find a new-born country, with its people wholly consecrated to the great, though very difficult, task of revolutionary reconstruction. And I had fervently hoped that I might become an active part of the inspiring work.

I found reality in Russia grotesque, totally unlike the great ideal that had borne me upon the crest of high hope to the land of promise. It required fifteen long months before I could get my bearings. Each day, each week, each month added new links to the fatal chain that pulled down my cherished edifice. I fought desperately against the disillusionment. For a long time I strove against the still voice within me which urged me to face the overpowering facts. I would not and could not give up.

Then came Kronstadt. It was the final wrench. It completed the terrible realization that the Russian Revolution was no more.

I saw before me the Bolshevik State, formidable, crushing every constructive revolutionary effort, suppressing, debasing, and disintegrating everything. Unable and unwilling to become a cog in that sinister machine, and aware that I could be of no practical use to Russia and her people, I decided to leave the country. Once out of it, I would relate honestly, frankly, and as objectively as humanly possible to me the story of my two years' stay in Russia. (pp. xi-xii)

I do not pretend to write a history. Removed by fifty or a hundred years from the events he is describing, the historian may seem to be objective. But real history is not a compilation of mere data. It is valueless without the human element which the historian necessarily gets from the writings of the contemporaries of the events in question. It is the personal reactions of the participants and observers which lend vitality to all history and make it vivid and alive. (p. xii)

I believed fervently that the Bolsheviki were furthering the Revolution and exerting themselves in behalf of the people. I clung to my faith and belief for more than a year after my coming to Russia.

Observation and study, extensive travel through various parts of the country, meeting with every shade of political opinion and every variety of friend and enemy of the Bolsheviki—all convinced me of the ghastly delusion which had been foisted upon the world.

I refer to these circumstances to indicate that my change of mind and heart was a painful and difficult process, and that my final decision to speak out is for the sole reason that the people everywhere may learn to differentiate between the Bolsheviki and the Russian Revolution.

The conventional conception of gratitude is that one must not be critical of those who have shown him kindness. (pp. xv-xvi)

Some people have upbraided me for my critical attitude toward the Bolsheviki. "How ungrateful to attack the Communist Government after the hospitality and kindness she enjoyed in Russia!" they indignantly exclaim. I do not mean to gainsay that I have received advantages while I was in Russia. I could have received many more had I been willing to serve the powers that be. It is that very circumstance which has made it bitterly hard for me to speak out against the evils as I saw them day by day. But finally I realized that silence is indeed a sign of consent. Not to cry out against the betrayal of the Russian Revolution would have made me a party to that betrayal. The Revolution and the welfare of the masses in and out of Russia are by far too important to me to allow any personal consideration for the Communists I have met and learned to respect to obscure my sense of justice and to cause me to refrain from giving to the world my two years' experience in Russia. (p. xvi)

Friends whose opinion I value have been good enough to suggest that my quarrel with the Bolsheviki is due to my social philosophy rather than to the failure of the Bolshevik régime. As an Anarchist, they claim, I would naturally insist on the importance of the individual and of personal liberty, but in the revolutionary period both must be subordinated to the good of the whole. Other friends point out that destruction, violence, and terrorism are inevitable factors in a revolution. As a revolutionist, they say, I cannot consistently object to the violence practised by the Bolsheviki.

Both these criticisms would be justified had I come to Russia expecting to find Anarchism realized, or if I were to maintain that revolutions can be made peacefully. Anarchism to me never was a mechanistic arrangement of social relationships to be imposed upon man by political scene-shifting or by a transfer of power from one social class to another. Anarchism to me was and is the child, not of destruction, but of construction—the result of growth and development of the conscious creative social efforts of a regenerated people. I do not therefore expect Anarchism to follow in the immediate footsteps of centuries of despotism and submission. And I certainly did not expect to see it ushered in by the Marxian theory.

I did, however, hope to find in Russia at least the beginnings of the social changes for which the Revolution had been fought. Not the fate of the individual was my main concern as a revolutionist. I should have been content if the Russian workers and peasants as a whole had derived essential social betterment as a result of the Bolshevik régime.

Two years of earnest study, investigation, and research convinced me that the great benefits brought to the Russian people by Bolshevism exist only on paper, painted in glowing colours to the masses of Europe and America by efficient Bolshevik propaganda. As advertising wizards the Bolsheviki excel anything the world had ever known before. But in reality the Russian people have gained nothing from the Bolshevik experiment. (pp. xvii-xviii)

I did find the revolutionary faith of the people broken, the spirit of solidarity crushed, the meaning of comradeship and mutual helpfulness distorted. One must have lived in Russia, close to the everyday affairs of the people; one must have seen and felt their utter disillusionment and despair to appreciate fully the disintegrating effect of the Bolshevik principle and methods—disintegrating all that was once the pride and the glory of revolutionary Russia.

The argument that destruction and terror are part of revolution I do not dispute. I know that in the past every great political and social change necessitated violence. . . . Yet it is one thing to employ violence in combat, as a means of defence. It is quite another thing to make a principle of terrorism, to institutionalize it, to assign it the most vital place in the social struggle. Such terrorism begets counter-revolution and in turn itself becomes counter-revolutionary. (pp. xviii-xix)

Till the end of my days my place shall be with the disinherited and oppressed. It is immaterial to me whether Tyranny rules in the Kremlin or in any other seat of the mighty. I could do nothing for suffering Russia while in that country. Perhaps I can do something now by pointing out the lessons of the Russian experience. Not my concern for the Russian people only has prompted the writing of this volume: it is my interest in the masses everywhere.

The masses, like the individual, may not readily learn from the experience of others. Yet those who have gained the expereince must speak out, if for no other reason than that they cannot in justice to themselves and their ideal support the great delusion revealed to them. (pp. xix-xx)

Emma Goldman, "Preface" (1922), in her My Disillusionment in Russia *(reprinted by permission of the Literary Estate of Emma Goldman), William Heinemann, 1923 (and reprinted by The C. W. Daniel Company, 1925, pp. xi-xx).*

UPTON SINCLAIR (essay date 1922)

[An American novelist, dramatist, journalist, and essayist, Sinclair was a prolific writer who is most famous for The Jungle *(1906), a novel that portrays the unjust labor practices, filth, and horrifying conditions of Chicago's meat-processing industry, and which prompted passage of the Pure Food and Drug Act of 1906. A lifelong, outspoken socialist, Sinclair addressed the excesses of capitalist society in most of his works and demanded, in his critical theory, the subservience of art to social change. Although most of his fiction is dismissed in the United States for its obtrusive didacticism, Sinclair is one of America's most-read authors outside of North America, his works being particularly popular in the Soviet Union. In the following excerpt, Sinclair comments on a series of newspaper articles written in 1922 by Goldman on her disillusionment in Russia, and takes issue with Goldman's denunciation of the Bolsheviks, which he believes proves Goldman to be inconsistent and short-sighted about the means necessary for revolution.]*

Emma Goldman has at last broken the silence of several years and is publishing all that she has to say about Soviet Russia. I know that I am going to receive a dozen or two letters from readers of this page, enclosing marked copies of Emma's articles, and asking me what I think about them; so I will save time by saying what I have to say in advance.

First, there is a very easy trade just now, at which anyone can earn a comfortable living; which trade is denouncing Soviet Russia. I could give you the names of several people who are traveling around the United States, stopping at the very best hotels, and being received in the very best society, and whose sole stock in trade is the fact that they have been inside of Soviet Russia, and didn't like it, and are willing to say so in elaborate detail. . . . I wonder how Emma Goldman will manage to stomach the chorus of applause which rises from the capitalist press of the United States as it reads her daily series of articles.

The second thing I have to say is to note the curious fact that persons who take their stand upon extreme principles, and refuse to make any compromises or concessions, are certain in a crisis or of action, to find themselves working on the side of the worst reactionaries. The Bolsheviks of Russia have had a dirty job to do, and nobody but a very foolish person would claim that they have done it perfectly. But probably they have done as well as they could under the circumstances; and in their effort to do it, they have had to meet the opposition of two groups: first, the savage and murderous reactionaries and friends of Tsardom and privilege all over the world; and second, the theorists of extreme liberty, the dogmatic libertarians and Anarchists. . . .

There was no way to save the revolution except to fight these enemies, outside and inside, and there is no way to fight and win except to have discipline; in the stage of evolution which prevails in Russia, there is no way to have discipline except by force. Emma Goldman does not believe in force—at least not governmental force—and so she says that the Bolsheviks have betrayed the revolution.

She says something else which strikes me as very comical. She says that the first great crime of the Bolsheviks was that they signed the peace of Brest-Litovsk. She denounces this action for several paragraphs, and I am wondering just how an ardent opponent of governmental wars manages to justify herself in blaming a government for making peace. I have just been reading Philip Price's detailed and convincing history of those days. It is obvious that the Bolsheviks either had to sign that peace, or else to keep on with war; and did Emma Goldman want them to keep on with war? Emma Goldman, who was deported for demanding that the United States should retire from the war!

Upton Sinclair, "Concerning Emma Goldman" (reprinted by permission of the Literary Estate of Upton Sinclair), in Appeal to Reason, *No. 1379, May 6, 1922, p. 3.*

H. L. MENCKEN (essay date 1924)

[From the era of World War I until the early years of the Great Depression, Mencken was one of the most influential figures in American letters. His strongly individualistic, irreverent outlook on life and his vigorous, invective-charged writing style helped establish the iconoclastic spirit of the Jazz Age and significantly shaped the direction of American literature. As a social and literary critic—the roles for which he is best known—Mencken was the scourge of evangelical Christianity, public service organizations, literary censorship, boosterism, provincialism, democracy, all advocates of personal or social improvement, and every other facet of American life that he perceived as humbug. In his literary criticism, Mencken encouraged American writers to shun the anglophilic, moralistic bent of the nineteenth century and to practice realism, an artistic call-to-arms which is most fully developed in his essay "Puritanism As a Literary Force," *one of the seminal essays in modern literary criticism. During the United States government's deportation proceedings against Goldman and Alexander Berkman, Mencken defended their writing talents and critical honesty as resources America could ill-afford to lose. During Goldman's exile, Mencken actively petitioned the American government and wielded his influence with congressmen in an effort to secure her reentry into the country. In the following excerpt, Mencken contrasts Goldman's* My Disillusionment in Russia *with Anna Louise Strong's* The First Time in History *(1924), a work sympathetic to the Bolshevik regime. In his defense of Goldman, Mencken finds her anarchist ideals to be indistinguishable from the tenets of the Beatitudes of Jesus' Sermon on the Mount. The critic's sympathetic equation of Goldman's doctrines with those of Jesus is interesting, for both Mencken and Goldman were Nietzscheans who frequently disparaged Christianity in their writings, with Goldman once writing: "The idea contained in the Sermon on the Mount is the greatest indictment against the teachings of Christ, because it sees in the poverty of mind and body a virtue, and because it seeks to maintain this virtue by reward and punishment."*]

Here is testimony as brilliantly conflicting as that in a divorce trial. Dr. Strong, having spent two years in Russia, comes out with the news that Bolshevist rule is a great and growing success, that the government is becoming steadily stronger and the people steadily more prosperous, that all the worst troubles of Trotsky and company are behind them. Miss Goldman, having spent almost precisely the same two years in Russia, comes out with the news that Bolshevism is a fraud and a tragedy, that the government is corrupt and liberty has been adjourned, that nothing lies ahead save inevitable disaster. Both ladies are of discreet years, and have devoted their whole lives to the uplift. Both have traveled widely and written much, and there are no flies on them. Which is to be believed? Or is it possible, after all, to reconcile them? I suspect that the answer to the last question is not an unqualified no. More than once, indeed, their statements of cold fact touch, kiss and almost coalesce. What separates them is their prejudices. Miss Goldman, for many years in active practice as an anarchist, has a violent antipathy to all forms of governmental coercion; Dr. Strong, trained under democracy and formerly a job-holder at Washington, apparently believes that the glory of the citizen is subservience to the state. So the one sees the harshness of Bolshevik rule as a violation of all the fundamental rights of man, and to the other it appears as the flower of normalcy. The result is that neither is a quite reliable witness. Miss Goldman is too indignant when she discovers that the chief Bolsheviks, like all the rest of us, are animated by intelligent self-interest—that when there is starving to be done they prefer to let the *muzhiks* do it. And Dr. Strong, I fear, permits herself to gurgle a bit when she discovers that her women friends in Russia are all getting new hats, and that the industrial system is on its legs again, and that men of enterprise are once more raking in the *mazuma*. To Miss Goldman these changes appear as surrenders to the abhorrent Wage System. To Dr. Strong they appear as subtle and occult triumphs of the New Utopia.

Of the two ladies, I prefer to admire La Goldman the more, despite the fact that my political sympathies are unfortunately against her. She writes far better than Dr. Strong, and there is behind her writing a far finer and mellower intelligence. May I be permitted to say, without risk of the hoosegow, that I regard her as one of the most notable women now extant upon this planet? If you have taken your notion of her from the harassments of the *gendarmerie* and the libels in the newspapers, then you see her very crookedly and falsely. Go read her books, if you can find them anywhere and sneak them through the mails. They reveal a woman of wide and deep culture, a graceful and urbane writer, an idealist of a rare and often singularly winning sort. A monomaniac, true enough—a naïve believer in human perfectibility, an enthusiast carried far beyond common sense, a kind of mad mullah or whirling dervish. But so was Martin Luther. So was Ignatius Loyola. So was the imaginary Abe Lincoln of the schoolbooks. What irony in the contrast between the ideas this woman, now old and worn, has advocated in her life, and the ideas she is commonly accused of advocating! Mention her name to a bank director, a realtor, a Congressman, a clergyman or any other such half-wit, and he will glide under the bed with the celerity of *Cryptobranchus alleghaniensis* on a rock. Speak it before the American Legion and you will go headlong into tar. Yet what, at bottom, is the immoral anarchism that she preaches? If you can distinguish it, even after long prayer, from the doctrines set forth in the Beatitudes, then you are a far more adept distinguisher than I am. Her plea is simply for freedom, equality, human dignity, an end of exploitation and oppression, a throwing off of all the chains that now bind poor mankind to its fears and superstitions. It is a plea as likely to be heard on this earth, now or hereafter, as a plea for common decency at a congress of Prohibition enforcement officers. But that [it] is sinful and against God I question gravely.

The Department of Justice, with characteristic intelligence, mistook La Goldman for a Bolshevik, and so deported her to Russia. It was almost as if a Baptist rector from the remote swamps of Georgia had been sent to the Vatican. She was as vastly appalled by what she found as the Hon. Charles Evans Hughes would have been. More resilient in mind than Hughes, she resolved to make the best of it—to accept the *bona fides* of the Bolsheviks and pull with them for the sake of their victims—even to give them her help. The effort, of course, came to disaster. She found that government by Lenin and Trotsky had become almost indistinguishable from government by Coolidge, Judge Gary, Daughterty, Doheny and Henry Cabot Lodge—that there was precisely the same stupidity, the same oblique self-seeking, the same exploitation of the great masses. She found the Bolshevik leaders winking at graft, oppression, and even downright murder. She found a reign of terror worse than that she had left in the United States—a bold and powerful camorra of Red Palmers and Burlesons, chiefly of the Oppressed of Israel, like herself, riding rough-shod over the millions of poor Russian peasants. So she beat a retreat, first to Riga and then to Berlin. There she now reposes, enjoying all the delights of life under a government headed by a shoemaker in tight, shiny shoes. It is a story not devoid of the grotesque, but fundamentally it seems to me to be tragic. What a head was wasted when Emma succumbed to the boozy dream of old Johann Most! What a woman she might have been if she could have stuck to earth! (pp. 122-23)

H. L. Mencken, "Two Views of Russia" (copyright 1924, copyright renewed © 1952, by American Mercury Magazine, Inc.; used by permission of The Enoch Pratt Free Library of Baltimore in accordance with the terms of the will of H. L. Mencken), in American Mercury, *Vol. II, No. 5, May, 1924, pp. 122-23.**

REBECCA WEST (essay date 1925)

[West is considered one of the foremost English novelists and critics to write during the twentieth century. Born Cecily Isabel Fairfield, she began her career as an actress—taking the name Rebecca West from the emancipated heroine of Henrik Ibsen's drama Rosmersholm—*and as a book reviewer for* The Freewoman. *Her early criticism was noted for its militantly feminist stance and its reflection of West's Fabian socialist concerns. Her first novel,* The Return of the Soldier *(1918), evidences a concern that entered into much of her later work: the psychology of the individual. West's literary criticism is noted for its wit, its aversion to cant, and its perceptiveness. Upon Goldman's arrival in England from Germany in 1924, West organized a reception in her friend's honor. One of the few friends who stood behind Goldman's attempts to form a committee for the aid of Russian political prisoners, West was virtually alone among the British liberal elite in joining Goldman's outcry against the excesses of the Bolsheviks. In her introduction to* My Disillusionment in Russia, *from which the following is excerpted, West calls Goldman "one of the great people of the world." Attacking the hypocrisy of liberals who blindly embrace the "Soviet myth" under the all-justifying rationale that their stance opposes that of conservatives, West praises Goldman for revealing "so much of the truth behind the myth."]*

[***My Disillusionment in Russia***] is a book of the first importance because of both its author and its subject. Emma Goldman is one of the great people of the world. . . . For thirty years or so she travelled round the United States saying things that struck her as being true: that free speech was a good thing; that war was a bad thing. Every now and then, people who did not like the truth hunted her out of town or put her in prison. In due course, Emma came out and said it all over again. She has a proven genius for honesty and courage.

Now, from these things it may be known that in this book Emma Goldman is telling the truth as she saw it. And that her sight was accurate enough is very likely, since for one thing she is a Russian and speaks Russian as her native language. This equipment has been felt to be in the worst possible taste by other investigators of the Russian problem who lacked it. It has been objected that her conclusions are invalidated because, being an Anarchist, and therefore against all governments, she was bound to be against the Bolshevist Government. But this is to underrate her positive qualities which made her willing all her life to work with and for non-Anarchists, provided they were on the side of liberty. It is largely through Emma Goldman's lectures that the works of George Bernard Shaw became popularly known in the United States. In point of fact her Anarchism predisposed her to admiration of the new Russia because it had the recommendation (and you may see from the afterword of this volume how very strong a recommendation that was) of having been created by a Revolution which to her Anarchist faith is *per se* a sacred thing. It cannot be doubted that all her temperamental bias was towards approval of the Bolshevist Government, and that only contact with an extremely unpleasing reality would have disenchanted her. (pp. v-vi)

But for our own sakes we must understand Bolshevist Russia; and we must not shrink if our understanding leads us to the same conclusion as the Conservative Party regarding the lack of material for admiration and imitation in the Bolshevist Government. To reject a conclusion simply because it is held by the Conservative party is to be snobbish as the suburban mistress who gives up wearing a hat or dress because her servant has one like it. And the attitude of uncritical admiration towards

Russia which is entailed by this rejection is in a fair way to rot the Socialist Movement. (p. vii)

That Tory Imperialism in its most stupid and brutal form would be openly and gleefully advocated by professed followers of the faith of liberty, equality and brotherhood, is proof enough of the mental chaos which has been created by sentimental loyalty to the Russian myth. We owe therefore a great debt of gratitude to Emma Goldman for having written this book, which tells us so much of the truth behind the myth. (p. ix)

Rebecca West, in an introduction to My Disillusionment in Russia *by Emma Goldman, The C. W. Daniel Company, 1925, pp. v-ix.*

DOROTHY BREWSTER (essay date 1925)

[In the following excerpt, Brewster argues that Goldman deluded herself when she expected to find her revolutionary ideal in Bolshevik Russia.]

The United States Government, lacking that haughty conviction of stability so marked in Jehovah, and too timid to let Miss Goldman continue her wanderings in the American wilderness, dispatched her to the Promised Land in December, 1919. She sailed to Russia in a trance of expectation: she was to behold Mother Russia, "the land freed from political and economic masters," where the peasant was raised from the dust and the worker, the modern Samson, "with a sweep of his mighty arm had pulled down the pillars of decaying society." Two years later she came out of Russia convinced that state-centralization had paralyzed individual initiative and effort; that the people were cowed into slavish submission, depraved and brutalized by organized terrorism; that every idealistic aspiration was stifled, human life cheapened, all sense of the dignity of man eliminated; that coercion had turned existence into a scheme of mutual deceit and revived the lowest and most brutal instincts of man. In brief, the Bolsheviki had not established, and were not trying to establish, the cooperative, decentralized, Anarchist commonwealth. And to Emma Goldman that is the only revolution that matters.

But how account for her intellectual or emotional somersault in accepting, even for a time, the Bolsheviki as "the symbol of the revolution"? They are Marxian Socialists, with an ideal at the opposite pole from Anarchism. A Quaker, adopting a fleet of tanks as a symbol of the brotherhood of man, would be as confusing a spectacle. It took Miss Goldman many months of bitter experience to divorce her ideal from the rashly chosen symbol. (p. 189)

Other observers of similar facts drew different inferences. There is no point at this date in rehearsing the facts. . . . Not that Miss Goldman's facts are uninteresting or unimportant. Far from it. She had excellent chances for observation over a wide area; for she had accepted a task from the Bolsheviki that she felt she could conscientiously undertake—that of collecting material for the Museum of the Revolution at Petrograd. The expedition took her in a private car from Moscow to Kiev and from Kiev to Archangel and gave her an opportunity, of which she took full advantage, to acquaint herself with all shades of disaffected opinion. But it is her inferences rather than her facts that invite comment. If one distrusts them . . . , it is for specific reasons. And the principal reason is this: violent inner conflicts are not the soil out of which sprout unbiased opinions. Miss Goldman repeatedly speaks, not merely of disappointment, but of conflict. The sufferer is not always the person who understands best the nature of his conflicts. One may be pardoned a guess about hers. She persuaded herself that she hoped to find her revolutionary ideal on the way to realization under the Bolshevik rule. But think of her deepseated antagonism, nourished for years, against the Marxians! In the deeper layers of her consciousness she must have hated intensely the thought of Marxian success, must have longed for convincing proof of failure. . . .

And one more reason for distrusting Miss Goldman's inferences. She tells how she grew up under the discipline of a German school in Königsberg, in an atmosphere of hatred to Russia; and how later her soul was completely transformed, until Russia, where she spent four years, no longer spelled evil. But one's soul does not escape so easily the effects of a rigorous childhood training, or lose the impress of a stamped-in pattern. She says many laudatory things about the Russian peasants and workers, about the revolutionary consciousness that led them to seize the land and the factories. Had they been allowed the free play of their initiative the real revolution might have come to birth. But underneath all this her distrust remains, the contempt, the unconscious Prussian attitude. It slips out unexpectedly in this rather casual comment on some peasants at a wayside station: "A peculiar people, these Russians, saint and devil in one, manifesting the highest as well as the most brutal impulses, capable of almost anything but sustained effort. I have often wondered whether this lack did not to some extent explain the disorganization of the country and the tragic condition of the revolution."

A minor satisfaction furnished by this book is that of reading quotations from *Mother Earth* and interpretations of the Anarchist ideal under the Doubleday-Page imprint. . . . Some young and plastic mind, exposed to this book, may be more impressed by the Anarchist point of view, ably expressed, than by the denunciation of Bolshevism, staled by repetition. Conservatives, now and then, appear in delightfully unexpected positions. (p. 190)

Dorothy Brewster, "Emma Goldman's Russia," in The Nation, *Vol. CXX, No. 3111, February 18, 1925, pp. 189-90.*

ROGER N. BALDWIN (essay date 1931)

[Baldwin, the Chief Probation Officer of St. Louis, reluctantly attended one of Goldman's lectures at the urging of a friend. A man whose political views were antithetic to those of Goldman, Baldwin found himself spellbound during her presentation, and he later attributed his new direction in life to her influence. After becoming involved with civil rights causes, Baldwin organized the National Civil Liberties Board, which later became the American Civil Liberties Union. In the following review of Living My Life, *Baldwin sketches Goldman's life and comments on her remarkable strength and tenacity.]*

Years ago when I was a youngster just out of Harvard, engaged in the then promising tasks of social work, Emma Goldman came to town to lecture. I was asked to hear her. I was indignant at the suggestion that I could be interested in a woman firebrand reputed to be in favor of assassination, free love, revolution and atheism; but curiosity got me there. It was the eye-opener of my life. Never before had I heard such social passion, such courageous exposure of basic evils, such electric power behind words, such a sweeping challenge to all the values I had been taught to hold highest. From that day forth I was her admirer, though often, too, her critic; I read what Harvard had never offered me; I shared from that time on, as best I could in a reformer's jobs, the struggles of the working class, to which her philosophy of anarchism was devoted.

It is as her old friend, her pupil as it were, that I read this story [***Living My Life***] of her turbulent life of struggle—a struggle finished with her successful exile from the United States, where she labored dauntlessly for thirty years, and from her native Russia, to which, deported from the United States, she returned in hope after the revolution only to be disillusioned by another tyranny. . . . Through these pages, hot with the accounts of ceaseless struggle, march all the figures of the revolutionary movements of the dramatic years before, during and since the war, in America, Russia, England. She met an incredible number of people in all classes, in all movements, for she was steadily on the go. Almost too much in detail she presents them, crowding her story with her reactions to them, but above all her reactions to the warfare of which she was the inevitable center. . . .

Her book is a great woman's story of a brave adventure into successive defeats, which read like victories. Only her indomitable will can explain how she kept on from early youth in a struggle where she met endless discouragement, colossal opposition, and such vilification from the press as has never been heaped on any radical in American life. . . .

Her part in Berkman's unsuccessful attempt on the life of Henry C. Frick she tells with a frankness and wealth of detail which reveal both the idealism and futility of three passionate young revolutionists who abandoned their profitable ice-cream parlor in Worcester, on a moment's impulse, during the Homestead strike, to do the job of "liberation." All the later events with which anarchists were identified, the assassination of McKinley, the Mooney-Billings case, "The Los Angeles Times" dynamiting case, the many strikes, she illumines with detail and comment and revelations which appear in these pages for the first time. She spares nobody, herself least of all. Everything is revealed, her personal life as well as her public; her hopes, discouragements, mistakes, failures. But behind it all glows the warmth of her love for her fellow workers; her strong attachments to people, her instant understanding of their strength and weakness. That quality always impressed me most in Emma Goldman, the warm tenderness of a mother which lay just under that defiant, unyielding public exterior.

For the cause of free speech in the United States, Emma Goldman fought battles unmatched by the labors of any organization. Wherever she was forbidden to speak she made an issue of it, going back time and again if necessary to establish her right to talk. She fought similarly for the rights of others, even of her opponents—a test of her faith. The widespread interest of middle-class intellectuals in her and their support of these efforts brought her into contact with a remarkable assortment of the leading men and women in American life. She characterizes them as she thinks they deserve, but most of them won't resent her comment, bitter as some of it is. . . .

For an understanding of thirty critical years in the United States, Emma Goldman contributes a document which could be written by no other man or woman. Though she covers the same period as Lincoln Steffens, the world she lived in was as remote from his as a far land. But far more gripping than this revelation of American life or of her later search for freedom in Russia are her revelations of the inner workings of the most challenging rebel spirit of our times in these United States, and of her philosophy of life.

Roger N. Baldwin, "A Challenging Rebel Spirit," in New York Herald Tribune Books *(© I.H.T. Corporation; reprinted by permission), October 25, 1931, p. 3.*

WALDO FRANK (essay date 1931)

[Frank was an American novelist and critic who was best known as an interpreter of contemporary civilization, particularly that of Latin America. A socialist and supporter of various radical groups in the United States, he was a founding editor of The Seven Arts *(1916-1917), a leftist,* avant-garde *magazine of literature and opinion. One of Frank's most significant works of criticism,* Our America *(1919), derides the "genteel tradition" in American letters and is considered an influential work in its support of realism in the nation's literature. In the following excerpt, Frank discusses* Living My Life *and criticizes Goldman's inability to understand what he believes is a necessary process to effect the revolutionary ends of the Bolsheviks. "Her story of a great anarchist . . ." he states, "becomes the most eloquent defense of communism." Personally, however, Frank notes Goldman's lack of self-indulgence, cowardice, and shallowness and muses "there is something about this woman that is great."]*

I hoped to glean from the autobiography of Emma Goldman [***Living My Life***] four experiences, each of them worth while: the intimate life story of a remarkable woman, the history of her ideals and thoughts as an anarchist, a portrait of toiling America during the past four decades, and an account of the years of military communism in the U.S.S.R. I got what I wanted, although in each case the net gain in light is different from what I had supposed it would be—different, I feel certain, from what Emma Goldman herself believes her book has given.

The most enlightening point, for me, in the first volume where the author describes her girlhood, her marriage, her entrance into the anarchist ranks after the Chicago executions, her love affairs, her friendships with Johann Most and Alexander Berkman, is that her narrative is almost bare of experience and ideas. The pages fly with gusto, Emma Goldman holds back nothing. But she has, rather amazingly, almost nothing inward to give! Intimately, for all her good will, she appears to remember little of her own sensations; and if there was a period of doubt and inquiry before she accepted Kropotkin and Bakunin, she takes her own thoughts for granted, giving us the bare conclusion. I had a sense of Emma Goldman writing these pages of her youth; but it was a sense of the mature woman the author, not of the young woman the subject. And this very fact: that Emma Goldman describing her loves, her factories and sweatshops, her cities, her encounters with magnates and policemen, gives no direct experience of her feelings and thoughts, helps to reveal the nature of the woman. One must make one's own deductions, as one might if one were actually speaking with the author. For Emma Goldman is a presence in her book—a deep, hearty presence. She is never the analyst or integrator of her story.

Her chief traits are goodness and energy. There is something abstract in her élan vital, since she is unaware of causes. The Freudians would doubtless call her career a flight from a cruel father (who became symbolized as authority and the state). More obviously, her life was a simple escape from the intol-

To James Colton
brave comrade
and staunch friend
Affectionately
Emma Goldman
Paris. Oct 1931

Goldman's signature from a presentation copy of her autobiography, Living My Life. *Reproduced by permission of the International Institute of Social History, Amsterdam.*

erable pain of inhibitions (personal and social) and a blind rush toward that freedom which the word "anarchism" convincingly evoked. In a life so purely dynamic, there is no pause for thought, hence her book's total lack of ideology; there is no room for emotional contemplation, hence its author's want of vivid memory. Emma Goldman cannot be said to remember her girlhood, and its record, pictorial or sensory, is absent from her pages. Which is to say, that her first thirty or forty years were lived not on an intellectual, not even on an emotional, plane; but were instinctive. Instinctive action (if I may use this obsolete term) is automatic, and leaves no memory.

But Miss Goldman's instinctivism must not be confused with that of others. It is paradoxical, being extremely good and brave. Most women who live on this level are self-indulgent, cowardly, shallow. Miss Goldman, although she seems never to have thought, has a nature both good and profound. At any moment of her youth, it is clear that she was ready to give herself to her Cause. Even her sex life, one feels, was the response of a motherly heart rather than of a lusting body. And if she followed the dictates of her body, the wonder is that even selfish impulse moved her to constant sacrifice and the acceptance of suffering.

This paradox convinces me that there are really persons in the world like the "free souls" on whose actual existence Rousseau, Proudhon and the other romantic anarchists based their theories. No wonder Emma Goldman was an anarchist—and without having to think about it. Her innocent nature predicates and incarnates the anarchist creed. Even in her appetites, she is a woman instinctively good and pure: a woman whose blithe spirit only the alien contacts of official law could poison.

The pages are, of course, full of references to anarchist comrades. Directly, she analyzes them no more than herself; but her own vitality imbues with life her portraits of men like Berkman, Reitman, Brady and Most. Like the author, these figures belong to the romantic movement. They are an issue of the same social forces which gave the Atalas, Renés, Adolphes and Werthers. The key to these characters is a deliberate return to "self"—a return which is a reaction from a system, social and intellectual, that was losing its vitality: so that the romantic return to "self" was literally the escape of "life" from the old Western order. In the profounder romantics (Rousseau, Blake, Beethoven, Stendhal, Balzac, Whitman, Nietzsche, etc.), this return to "self" was sufficiently thorough to reveal the self's cosmic implications and therewith the nucleus of a whole new social fabric. Intellectually weaker romantics did not go so far. They discovered their own yearning ego, and loved it, and regarded the world as a mere bar to its divine trajectory. Their ideas of social justice were rationalizations of their lyric need of freedom. They were the anarchists. They knew nothing of the objective world, save that it got in their way. They knew nothing even of each other, since in the last analysis they knew nothing of themselves. They were "pure being," and since "pure being" is a rationalized fantasy, their own lives have an abstract air, a lack of body and of reason.

This *unreality* of the anarchists is perfectly revealed by Emma Goldman. It is epitomized in the *attentat* on Frick by her lifelong comrade Berkman. Young Berkman (a very different man from the mature Berkman of later years) is as good as his girl friend. He *knows* nothing, either: not how to make a bomb, not how to speak English, not the crucial differences between an American magnate and the lords of Tsarist Russia; not (at the end) how to aim a pistol. His act is a "pure act" in a cruel, complex world that has thrown him off, so that he wills to destroy it. (pp. 177-80)

Volume One of Emma Goldman's story might, then, be called the premise of anarchism: there are really born in the world persons instinctively good, whom the complex tissue of laws tortures and maims. Volume Two is the conclusion of anarchism: the fate of such persons in the real world that persists. In her record of the past ten or fifteen years, the author is closer to the subject. We no longer have a woman of sixty trying to recreate a girl. We know what the young Miss Goldman was, by what she failed to record: we have the contemporary in a more positive record. For this other woman has been forced, by her frustrations, from the instinctive rush of her élan vital to the emotional plane. The natural mother blindly fighting for her children becomes the contemplative mother who can no longer wield arms, who can only suffer. The bud of the young woman's goodness blooms into a dark flower of pain. Now Emma Goldman has memory. Her last pages, in which she gives us a War America and a Russia of her own, are suffused with tragic light. (pp. 180-81)

Her bitter rejection of bolsehvism is well known. She went to Russia in 1920, ready to defend and to collaborate. A year and a half later, she and Berkman left, heartbroken by what she names the betrayal of the Cause for which she has given her life. Her record is full, and is—for reasons unknown to herself—the most significant part of her book. It is the final revelation of the utter unreality of her own kind of revolution. Emma Goldman found in Russia a ruthless state employing repression of all kinds—censorship, imprisonment, execution—in the effort to survive both the inherited chaos of the Tsarist regime and the seventeen White armies that were attacking it. This was enough for Miss Goldman: the old hated state at its old methods. She had never stopped, in her assaults on bourgeois society, to understand it; why, now, should she stop to understand the real problems of the proletarian dictatorship in Russia? Contexts are beyond Emma Goldman, whether they be White or Red. The whole activity of relations is beyond her.

Her book, in its finality, becomes the tragedy of good will and a good heart unguided by a sense of the Whole. The impulse that had made her a rebel was generous; her methods of rebellion were brave and pure. But rebellion became the automatic habit of her life; her one positive response to the objective world of men and of values. If she had *understood* the evils of bourgeois society, she would have understood the inevitability of their survival in the transition period which she witnessed in Russia. Her descriptions of what she saw are factual enough: Emma Goldman is incapable of deliberate falsehood. But she is also incapable of truth, which is the placing of facts in their vital context.

Her failure to understand Russia is the anarchist failure to understand and hence to work upon the world. Her story of a great anarchist (there is something about this woman that is great) becomes the most eloquent defense of communism. If the revolutionary impulse can go so far astray through blind emotion, become so hysterical, so impotent, so unjust, and finally so destructive, the Marxian method is imperative. (pp. 181-82)

Waldo Frank, "Elegy for Anarchism" (originally published in The New Republic, *Vol. LXIX, No. 891, December 30, 1931), in his* In the American Jungle: 1925-1936, *Farrar & Rinehart, 1937, pp. 177-83.*

LLOYD MORRIS (essay date 1947)

[Morris was an American biographer, critic, social historian, essayist, and pioneering educator who is credited with introducing contemporary literature courses to the American university system in the 1920s. In the following excerpt, he discusses conflicting tendencies in Goldman's nature and self-defeating characteristics of her thought.]

Emma Goldman loved theories with an indiscriminate ardor. The violence of her affection for ideas was equalled only by the violence of her antipathy to capitalists and reformers. As she was convinced that every attractive idea ought to be adopted, her life—except for intervals spent in prison—held few vacant moments. In the phrase of the day, she "believed in experience." So her path was littered with abandoned lovers and discarded philosophies. To all of them she had been faithful, in her fashion. Each had seemed irresistible—for a while. (p. 44)

Emma Goldman was a sentimentalist with a swollen conscience. This combination can produce a domestic nuisance, or a woman with a mission, who applies the same tactics to a larger group. Miss Goldman never doubted her mission. Indeed, she was incapable of any doubt. Humor was not her strong point. She displayed that exasperating consistency about minor matters characteristic of the genuine zealot; and, running true to form, she ignored consistency in the large. Thus, the refusal of life to be bound by the logic of the moment reduced her to permanent perplexity. There was something childlike about her persistent efforts to make it submit, to bring off the trick; and about her aggrieved surprise at having failed. It was her only perplexity. The problems raised by her industrious conscience were seldom more than rhetorical questions. She was ready with the answers even before the questions were uttered. (pp. 44-5)

Emma Goldman represented the earnest, social-minded, restless mood common to many American women in the early years of the twentieth century. Conscience, sentimentality and the new culture often conspired to make them muddleheaded, however well meaning. Emma Goldman never understood that the individualism which she professed as an ideal had produced the economic order which she hoped to see destroyed. She was contemptuous of reformers and liberals because they were not logical; and not revolutionists. She thought the settlement people—like Miss Addams—sincere but misguided idealists whose efforts, being merely palliative, only served to obstruct social change. Yet, disbelieving in reforms, she gave herself indiscriminately to all radical causes, and defended with impartial zeal all efforts to bring about the improvement of a society which she wanted to overturn. This meant only that her heart and her head did not always march in step. Her heart attached itself to all liberal—and liberating—projects. Her mind demanded the extreme, uncompromising solution. Even had she been aware of this major inconsistency, she would not have acknowledged it. Vanity would have compelled her to declare herself, as she did, a revolutionary to the very end. (p. 47)

Lloyd Morris, "The Woman Takes Over," in his Postscript to Yesterday: America, the Last Fifty Years *(copyright 1947 and renewed 1975 by Lloyd Morris; reprinted by permission of Random House, Inc.), Random House, 1947, pp. 32-63.**

VAN WYCK BROOKS (essay date 1952)

[Brooks is noted for his biographical and critical studies of such writers as Mark Twain, Henry James, and Ralph Waldo Emerson, and for his influential commentary on the history of American literature. His career can be neatly divided into two distinct periods: the first, from 1908 to 1925, dealt primarily with the negative impact of European Puritanism on the development of artistic genius in America. Brooks argued that the puritan conscience in the United States, carried over from Europe, produced an unhealthy dichotomy in American writers and resulted in a literature split between stark realism and what he called "vaporous idealism." During this early period, Brooks believed that in reality America had no culture of its own, and that American literature relied almost exclusively on its European heritage. After 1925, and his study on Emerson, Brooks radically altered his view of American literary history. He began to see much in America's past as unique and artistically valuable, and he called for a return in literary endeavors to the positive values of Emerson, as opposed to the modern pessimism of such writers as T. S. Eliot and James Joyce. Despite the radical difference in these two critical approaches, one element remains constant throughout Brooks's career, namely his concern with the reciprocal relationship between the writer and society. In an essay in The Confident Years, *from which the following is excerpted, Brooks calls* The Social Significance of the Modern Drama *the first book of its kind in the United States. Like Joseph Ishill, whose book* Emma Goldman: A Challenging Rebel *is listed in the Additional Bibliography, he praises Goldman for "introducing new ideas and fertilizing, indirectly, the American drama."]*

No one did more to spread the new ideas of literary Europe that influenced so many young people in the West as elsewhere,—at least the ideas of the dramatists on the continent and in England,—than the Russian-American Emma Goldman who established in New York, in 1906, *Mother Earth,* the anarchist magazine. Believing that the theatre, as John Galsworthy said, "should lead the social thought of the time,"—assuming that the theatre, in fact, really did lead it,—she was expressing a passionate interest that had begun in 1895, when she had gone to Vienna to study nursing. She had discovered the new dramatists there who were making literary history in Europe and awakening a social consciousness in people who might not have been reached in any other fashion, using the drama to portray the struggles of modern men and women against whatever barriers, outside or within them. . . . [Playwrights] all over Europe were presenting the conflicts of parents and children, the war between employers and workers, the rebellion of the young. . . . Bernard Shaw was discussing prostitution. There was Gorky,—like Josiah Flynt a former denizen of the underworld,—who exhibited the lives of the outcasts and tramps he had known, Ibsen who exposed the crimes committed against the unborn, Andreyev who arraigned capital punishment. Brieux agitated the frank discussion of venereal disease, and others attacked the dependence, the slavery of women and the prejudices and superstitions that underlay it. . . . [The] point about them for Emma Goldman was that they were destroying ignorance and fear and paving the way for the birth of a new free race. She had lived for a while in retirement herself after the murder of President McKinley, when anarchists were all supposed to have connived with the assassin, working as a nurse under the name "Miss Smith," continuing her studies of the "rebel artists" whose writings she had first encountered in Vienna. Later she published her ideas about them in ***The Social Significance of the Modern Drama,*** the first book of the kind to appear in English. (pp. 375-76)

There was as yet no American playwright, she was obliged to remark, who could be placed beside the great Europeans. Meanwhile, as an agitator, Emma Goldman struck one of the notes of a period when many another writer was attacking "the system," the phrase of Lincoln Steffens for the organized connection between the big-business interests and political life. (p. 378)

Van Wyck Brooks, "The Muckrakers," in his The Confident Years: 1885-1915 *(copyright, 1952, by Van Wyck Brooks; copyright renewed 1980 by Gladys Brooks; reprinted by permission of the publisher, E. P. Dutton, Inc.), Dutton, 1952, pp. 371-88.**

RICHARD DRINNON (essay date 1961)

[Drinnon, a political radical, approached with skepticism the writing of the biography from which this excerpt is taken. From Goldman's autobiography and reputation, Drinnon concluded that she was "too extraordinary a woman to be taken seriously." However, after extensive research he came to see her as a "courageous, compassionate, intelligent human being." In the following excerpt, Drinnon discusses Goldman's views on feminism, literature, freedom of speech, and other subjects.]

[When she was twelve years old, Emma Goldman] managed to secure copies of Turgenev's *Fathers and Sons,* Ivan Goncharov's *The Precipice* (1869), and Nikolai Chernyshevsky's *What Is To Be Done?* (1863). The first two of these novels, notwithstanding Goncharov's admitted caricatures of the nihilists, impressed her. But Chernyshevsky's artistically inferior novel had such a remarkable impact that a large part of her later life was consciously patterned after Vera Pavlovna, the heroine of *What Is To Be Done?*

In the novel Vera Pavlovna is converted to nihilism and therewith reborn into a world of easy comradeship of the sexes, free intellectual inquiry, and co-operative labor. She abhorrently rejects her mother's avaricious and typically Philistine aim of auctioning her off as a valuable sex-object. Instead she lives in free companionship with a poor medical student who had rescued her in the first place from intellectual death and the legal prostitution proposed by her mother. Vera also starts a co-operative sewing shop to insure her complete independence, and she seriously plans to further her development by studying medicine. Obviously more interested in equitable distribution than in maximum output, Vera longs for an ideal world of associations of producers acting freely together, unrestrained by any political bureaucracy. Once she had incorporated these views, Emma Goldman had, in embryo, her later anarchism. (pp. 9-10)

A heightened awareness of the meaning of freedom—this Emma Goldman undoubtedly gave to Agnes Inglis, Duncan, Buwalda, Baldwin, and many others, and this gave her free-speech fights a significance that should not be underestimated. If she had done nothing else than set Baldwin off on his career, her role as the woman behind the man behind the organization of the American Civil Liberties Union would have made her fights for free speech an outstanding success.

Of course, she did more. Not only did she influence other Socialists, single taxers, wobblies, social gospelers, and liberals, but she also, in the process, helped to build a bridge from immigrant radicalism to the native radical and liberal traditions. One of the most effective speakers of her time and perhaps the most accomplished woman speaker in American history, she understandably secured an audience outside anarchist circles. Since her ideas were in part merely logical extensions of the Reformation doctrine of the priesthood of all believers and of the classical liberal tradition of individual freedom and distrust of the state, liberals and radicals of other schools could be enlisted to support her views, even if they could not be persuaded to accept them. (pp. 140-41)

For years Emma Goldman had returned the conservative fire directed her way by delivering lectures which were corrosive criticisms of the institution of marriage. Then she put some of these lectures (along with others) in essay form and published them in 1911 under the title of ***Anarchism, and Other Essays.*** These essays showed that she was drawing on the same tradition of hostility to conventional marriage as had the utopian Socialists, the Anabaptists and earlier heretical Christian sects, and, to a certain extent, Plato and other Greek thinkers—all of whom, in one way or another, had rejected the exclusiveness of an institution which was anchored to private property. The essence of Emma Goldman's criticism was that marriage caused man (and woman herself) to look upon woman as an object, a thing.

Under present circumstances, Emma held, woman obviously is "being reared as a sex commodity." Since her body is capital to be exploited and manipulated, she comes to look on success as the size of her husband's income. The girl is taught to ask only this question: "Can the man make a living? . . . her dreams are not of moonlight and kisses, of laughter and tears; she dreams of shopping tours and bargain counters." The woman who enters a marriage of convenience and the prostitute are on the same level: both subordinate sexual relationships to gain. (pp. 151-52)

As an economic convenience, marriage is also productive of jealousy. This degrading phenomenon she sharply distinguished from anguish over a lost love. She argued that while the latter is virtually inevitable, jealousy is not; and she cited anthropological evidence from the writings of Lewis Henry Morgan and Elie Reclus to show that it is not inborn. It results rather, she felt, from possessiveness and bigotry. The male's conceit is hurt to realize that there are "other cocks in the barnyard"; the female's jealousy results from economic fears for herself and a petty envy of others who gain grace in the eyes of her supporter. In the final analysis, she concluded, the foundation of jealousy is marriage, for it rests on the ownership of woman—the possession of woman as a commodity or object.

She did not rule out the probability that some marriages are based on love and that in some instances love continues in married life, but she maintained "that it does so regardless of marriage and not because of it." And after all, she asked, how can love, "the defier of all laws," be coerced; "how can such an all-compelling force be synonymous with that poor little State and Church-begotten weed, marriage?" The question was rhetorical: *legitimate love,* she believed, is the final absurdity.

Emma Goldman repeatedly asserted that the tragedy of the woman's emancipation impulse was symbolized by the devout faith of women in equal suffrage. Nothing indicated any more clearly that the movement had become enmeshed in externals. Universal suffrage, she upset her feminine audiences by saying, was the modern fetish: "Life, happiness, joy, freedom, independence,—all that, and more, is to spring from suffrage." By way of answer to her sisters who expected miracles from the vote she merely asked them to look at the record of the then four states with equal suffrage. Were politics "purer" therein? As a matter of fact, she asserted, the antiequalitarianism, antagonism to labor (present from the time of Susan B. Anthony), and Puritanism of the woman suffragettes tended to make politics even more of a moral swamp than it had been.

All the narrowness of vision and inner emptiness were rooted, she thought, in modern woman's overreaction to her traditional sexual role. In some Whitmanesque lines she observed that "the great movement of *true* emancipation has not met with a great race of women who could look liberty in the face. Their narrow, Puritanical vision banished man, as a disturber and doubtful character, out of their emotional life. Man was not to be tolerated at any price, except perhaps as the father of a child, since a child could not very well come to life without a father."

Thus did Emma Goldman take issue with Charlotte Perkins Gilman, Ida Tarbell, Jane Addams, and other leaders of the woman's struggle. She felt that their emphasis was misplaced. . . . While she agreed with them in rejecting for woman the role of a mere sex commodity, she differed with them on the appropriate response of the New Woman to the problem of sex. Many of the feminist leaders joined Mrs. Gilman—whose important *Women and Economics* (1899) Emma had obviously read—in bewailing the "over-sexed" woman, in advocating the inherent value of chastity, and in holding that "excessive indulgence in sex-waste has imperiled the life of the race." On the contrary, Emma maintained, the "tragedy of the self-supporting or economically free woman does not lie in too many, but in too few experiences." In fine, she attacked not only the New Woman's fixation on the suffrage panacea, but also her epicene tendencies—her tendency to become a "compulsory vestal." (pp. 152-53)

Underlying her mimetic theory of art [in ***The Social Significance of the Modern Drama***] was a quite naïve assumption, common to the radical critics of the time, concerning "life" or "reality": reality in a capitalist society was a kickable lump of ugliness and horror. Had enough artists stumbled across this lump and depicted it realistically, then the social revolution would have been at hand. It was that simple. And after the revolution, when classes were abolished, there would be no real need for art, for life would then be in itself an all-satisfying mountain of beauty and happiness.

In truth, though she was reluctant to admit it, she evidenced more than a trace of hostility to art as an independent enterprise. There was more than a hint of fear that art acted to divert potential forces of social rebellion into "mere" aesthetic activity. Art had to get properly into harness and be true to life. (pp. 157-58)

Since these ideas led away from the rest of her thinking, her adoption of them was curious. In its formal statement her theory moved toward a mechanical realism and a totalitarian objectivism in which the artist became merely the scribe of an imperious reality. The rest of her thinking implied an organic art and a creative subjectivism in which the spontaneous artist triumphed over the constricting forces of a too narrow reality—the logical literary expression here was lyrical poetry. In a sentence, most of her ideas implied the insight that art not only reflects but also *illuminates*.

One reason for the discrepancy was that she was still under the spell of Chernyshevsky, who deprecated traditional art as "futile diversion." Too, she was influenced by the crudely instrumental theories of art held by other radicals of her day. But perhaps more important still was the unresolved tension in her thought coming from her simultaneous commitment to the mass of mankind and to a peculiar kind of elitism. Her aesthetic sentiments rested on a faith in the regenerative power of the masses. Elsewhere she lamented that the "intellectuals of America have not yet discovered their relation to the workers. . . . They seem to think that they and not the workers represent the creators of culture. But that is a disastrous mistake. Only when the intellectual forces of Europe had made common cause with the struggling masses, when they came close to the depths of society, did they give to the world a real culture." On the other hand she joined Ibsen in supporting the individual against the mass. Thus did this root tension crop up again.

No other critic ever abandoned more of his formal aesthetic theory in the practice of his craft than did Emma. In the pages of her ***Social Significance of the Modern Drama*** there was no insistence that the playwrights heed inflated *pronunciamentos* against deviating from revolutionary realism. On the contrary, like Whitman she contained multitudes and had no fear of contradicting herself. Romantics, realists, and naturalists were all grist for her mill. She wrote as sympathetically and understandingly of Edmond Rostand's romantic poetic *Chanticleer,* as of Strindberg's naturalistic prose *Countess Julia;* as enthusiastically of Hauptmann's realistic *Weavers,* as of his symbolic *Sunken Bell.* Indeed, she explicitly refused to rank her artists. . . . In practice, then, she recognized the author's right to his idiosyncratic choice of subject and style of expression. More consistently with the rest of her anarchism, she did not presume to tell the individual what he should say, or how he should say it—actually, her criticism boiled down to a socially oriented impressionism.

Notwithstanding the great improvement of her practice over her theory, her method had deep flaws from the standpoint of serious dramatic criticism. In her book . . . she tried to do too much. Within a little over three hundred pages she essayed to discuss the modern drama of Norway and Sweden, Germany, France, England, Ireland, and Russia, considering, in all, thirty-two plays by nineteen playwrights. Dizzied by such a kaleidoscopic whirl past the great names of the modern theater, the alert reader sensed that the book lacked inner unity—that the removal of its covers would have sent the chapters flying in all directions, as if they were marbles spilled from a boy's pocket.

The book did reveal Emma's ability to get inside a play and dig out the author's explicit meaning. Her summaries and description of themes were enlivened by her intense feeling about social problems; her close attention to the play itself and her exegesis of the text gave her essays a curiously modern air—though, of course, she did not have the literary training which would have enabled her to ferret out subtle and implicit meanings. But in the end her method amounted to little more than homily-hunting. (pp. 158-59)

In her haste to make her points forcibly, Emma tended to bypass ambiguities and complexities, the qualifying statement and the tentative inference. (p. 160)

Richard Drinnon, in his Rebel in Paradise: A Biography of Emma Goldman *(reprinted by permission of the author; © 1961 by The University of Chicago), University of Chicago Press, 1961, 349 p.*

KENNETH S. LYNN (essay date 1971)

[Lynn is a prominent American historian and literary critic who has written extensively on the lives and works of major American literary figures, including Mark Twain, William Dean Howells, and Theodore Dreiser. One of Lynn's primary critical concerns is the stripping away of the myths that surround America's authors, through close, unprejudiced consideration of existing biographical information. In the following excerpt, Lynn discusses Goldman's oratorical skill, her feminist theories, and the effects of her thought on modern America.]

"By what destiny or virtue," Ignazio Silone asks in *The God That Failed,* "does one, at a certain age, make the important choice, and become an 'accomplice' or 'rebel'? From what source do some people derive their spontaneous intolerance of injustice, even though the injustice affects only others?" A generation before Silone gave these haunting questions their classic statement [Emma Goldman], the author of ***Living My Life*** addressed very similar inquiries to herself, for she often was as surprised and shaken by the vehemence with which she expressed her beliefs as were the unlucky people who got in the way of her intolerance. Why, indeed, did she become so violently angry about injustices done to others? In the thousand pages of her remarkable autobiography, she was never quite able to formulate an answer. Yet the raw evidence she presents is so detailed and so brutally candid as to make it unmistakably clear that her political militancy was not only a response to objective injustices but also a subjective response to sexual exploitation. Through her defiance of the dominating and/or deceiving men whom she encountered in her childhood and young womanhood, she was psychologically prepared for participation in other rebellions. (p. 150)

The eager promise of cooperation that she made to Berkman in 1892 when he proposed to intervene in the Homestead steel strike by blowing up Henry Clay Frick was, beyond a doubt, the craziest gesture of her life. (p. 153)

Yet the Frick case catapulted Emma into celebrity and the effort to reduce Sasha's sentence of twenty-two years in prison gave her a cause. By the end of the 1890s, the speech-making of Emma Goldman was being hailed by friend and foe alike as one of the great oratorical performances of American history. She was intellectual, she was witty, and she was well organized. But what was truly stunning about her speeches was that she brought to the podium and translated to her audiences at full blast the emotional violence of her screaming, fist-swinging family combats. Speaking often without notes, her eyes in fact closed at the peaks of passion, she achieved an intensity of feeling that no other speaker of the day could match and that endowed oratory with the same sort of excitement that the highly-charged temperament of Sarah Bernhardt was currently bringing to the theater. (pp. 153-54)

If she had stuck to agitating for Berkman's release or to calling for vengeance against the capitalist executioners of the Haymarket anarchists, her impact on American life would have

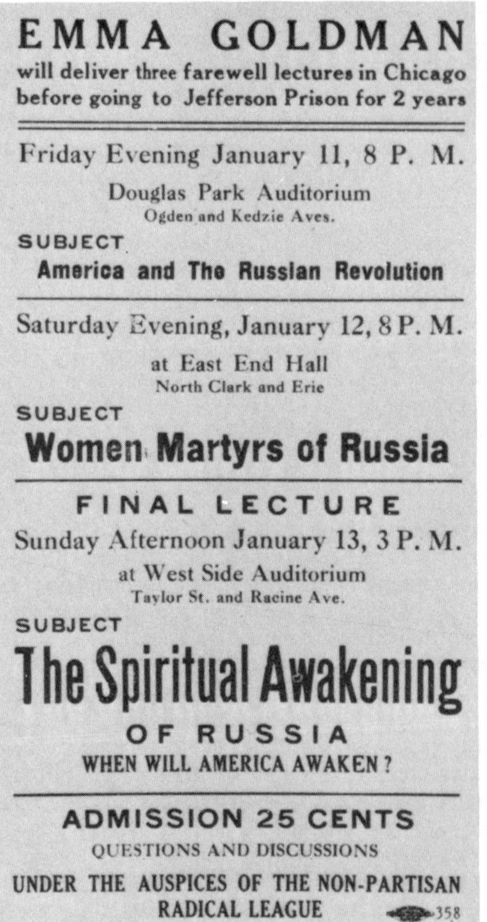

EMMA GOLDMAN
will deliver three farewell lectures in Chicago before going to Jefferson Prison for 2 years
Friday Evening January 11, 8 P. M.
Douglas Park Auditorium
Ogden and Kedzie Aves.
SUBJECT
America and The Russian Revolution
Saturday Evening, January 12, 8 P. M.
at East End Hall
North Clark and Erie
SUBJECT
Women Martyrs of Russia
FINAL LECTURE
Sunday Afternoon January 13, 3 P. M.
at West Side Auditorium
Taylor St. and Racine Ave.
SUBJECT
The Spiritual Awakening
OF RUSSIA
WHEN WILL AMERICA AWAKEN?
ADMISSION 25 CENTS
QUESTIONS AND DISCUSSIONS
UNDER THE AUSPICES OF THE NON-PARTISAN RADICAL LEAGUE

Advertisement for a lecture by Goldman. Reproduced by permission of the International Institute of Social History, Amsterdam.

been slight, no matter how pyrotechnical her oratory was. Very quickly, though, she began to expand her repertoire, until Berkman's imprisonment became not so much a subject as a metaphor of man's fate (especially woman's), and anticapitalism became only one item on an agenda, which included Ibsenism, feminism, free speech, and birth control. Through her contributions to the latter three causes, she affected the lives of every modern American. (pp. 154-55)

As a feminist, she differed from other leaders of the struggle in her refusal to believe that constitutional guarantees of equal suffrage would do very much for either the quality of politics or the happiness of women. While the attention of the other leaders was focused almost exclusively on winning independence from external tyrannies, Emma Goldman felt that internal tyrannies, sexual prudishness above all, were the most important problems facing American women. Militant feminists like Charlotte Perkins Gilman regarded excessive sexual indulgence as a threat to womanly health, but Emma Goldman insisted that the "tragedy of the self-supporting or economically free woman does not lie in too many, but in too few experiences." Inasmuch as her own love affairs never seemed to dampen her energy or damage her morale, Emma Goldman therefore became a heroine to many of the restless girls who came to Greenwich Village in the teens and who in turn inspired the flappers of the 1920s to cast loose from all bonds and assumptions and "try things out." No Americans, however, were more grateful to her for her attacks on emotional inhibition than homosexuals. Crowding up to talk with her after her unprecedented lectures in denunciation of American society's ostracism of the sexual invert, men and women across the nation confessed their anguish, their isolation, and their appreciation to her for giving them back their self-respect. (pp. 155-56)

[During] the red scare of 1919-1920, the political hysteria of the period brought the American career of Emma Goldman to a close. As her biographer, Richard Drinnon, points out, she had denounced the Spanish-American War without incident; but when she opposed the draft and other aspects of United States involvement in World War I, the government deported her. . . . In the course of her long exile, though, she recaptured her American life in one of the most revealing autobiographies of modern times. . . . (p. 156)

Kenneth S. Lynn, "Living My Life," in The New Republic *(reprinted by permission of* The New Republic; *© 1971 The New Republic, Inc.), Vol. 165, No. 22, November 27, 1971 (and reprinted in his* Visions of America: Eleven Literary Historical Essays, *Greenwood Press, Inc., 1973, pp. 149-56).*

EVA S. BALOGH (essay date 1975)

[In an essay on Nowhere at Home, *from which the following is taken, Balogh calls the collection of letters a "moving stocktaking" of the lives of Goldman and Alexander Berkman, as well as a "fascinating commentary" on history between the first and second World Wars. Balogh interprets the "idealism, integrity, and purity of heart" evinced in the letters as an inspiration to all who believe in a better world.]*

"Often I had been chided by my pal Sasha, otherwise known as Alexander Berkman . . . for my proclivity to spread myself in letters," Emma Goldman confessed in the preface to her autobiography. Nonetheless, she continued to share her deepest personal and political feelings with Berkman, a fellow anarchist who had once been her lover. ***Nowhere at Home,*** a selection from their correspondence between 1919 and 1939, is not only a moving stocktaking of their lives in exile but also a fascinating commentary on the state of the world between the two wars. It is an inspiring document: not even the worst hardened and cynical political realist can fail to admire the idealistic impulses, the courage, and the political consistency which Goldman and Berkman displayed during those difficult years when dictatorships were in the ascendancy and only a very few men and women had the moral fiber to oppose them in words and in deeds.

By the time these letters were written, the anarchist movement was dead. Gone were the days of international notoriety which had accompanied the two anarchists' activities before and during the First World War. . . . [Their] deportation from this country at the height of the Red scare put an end to their traditional life pattern. They became exiles, haunted by immigration authorities in Europe and abandoned by their liberal allies. Emma Goldman, the more optimistic of the two, came to the conclusion, bitter as it was, "that hardly anything has come of our years of effort," and Berkman, retiring and pessimistic by nature, admitted that "there is either something wrong with our ideas (maybe they don't fit life) or with our mode of propaganda for the last forty years." (pp. 139-40)

With Hitler's rise to power in Germany, their despair only deepened since Goldman and Berkman could discern little difference between the dictatorships of Stalin and Hitler. Although they conceded that Fascist and Soviet ideology and methods were at variance, they argued that the final outcome was the same: the loss of personal and political freedom and the introduction of a totalitarian regime. (p. 141)

In spite of minimal editing, ***Nowhere at Home*** is engrossing reading. It is a document of human hopes and disappointments and a tribute to two lonely persons' struggle against injustice, oppression, and corruption. Their idealism, integrity, and purity of heart, evident in every line they wrote, make the correspondence of Emma Goldman and Alexander Berkman inspiring reading for anyone who would like to believe in the possibility of a better world. (p. 143)

Eva S. Balogh, "Idealism, Integrity, Purity of Heart," in The Yale Review *(copyright 1975, by Yale University; reprinted by permission of the editors), Vol. LXV, No. 1, October, 1975, pp. 139-43.**

PAUL BERMAN (essay date 1975)

[In the following excerpt from his review of Nowhere at Home, *Berman discusses reasons for the continued public interest in Goldman's life and work.]*

More than half a century after her deportation, Goldman has acquired an attractiveness beyond any of her contemporaries, including Eugene Debs. Her works are carefully read by feminists and the libertarian left. There are any number of study and activist groups as well as a bookstore or two and a medical clinic which have taken her name. This "most dangerous woman in America," in J. Edgar Hoover's phrase, has never had more influence, and it is not hard to see why.

Her ideas have aged well, particularly because of her libertarian emphasis on the individual. She was one of the few radicals of her time who attacked not only capitalism but the power of the State, and saw the growth of government as no counterbalance to the power of capitalists; both threatened the worker and the individual. Her absolute devotion to individual liberty in the free and decentralized Communist society that she advocated—anarchist communism—got her into trouble during the early years of the Russian Revolution, because she measured the new society by a yardstick that other radicals rejected. Most of all, Goldman's feminism remains valuable because she never limited it to specific issues, not even the causes she campaigned for—birth control (for which she was jailed), or her criticisms of marriage and women's suffrage. Her idea of women's liberation was broader and more inclusive than these issues; her militancy has a modern temper because she focused on the whole texture of a woman's life.

But ultimately Emma Goldman's attractiveness today comes from something more than her ideas as a political theorist. After all, her anarchist essays don't match up to Kropotkin's, her account of the Russian revolution is less convincing than her comrade Berkman's, her feminism is overwhelmed by recent writings. Her drama criticism is tedious. She was more of a lecturer than a writer.

What makes Goldman attractive is rather the romance of her life. She was not a saint but a militant, whose politics (really, antipolitics) demanded personal freedoms as well as public ones. She lived according to her ideals and suffered much for it—independence as a woman made her notorious even beyond her defense of civil liberties and the poor, outspokenness led to persecution by the police and deportation by the federal government. But like Berkman, she was not given to compromises, even in the face of years in jail, as in their opposition to World War I. She knew that her life constituted her most important work and in fact she saw it as something of a romance. For that reason her autobiography, ***Living My Life,*** remains the most vibrant of her books. The force of her rebelliousness comes through—never cranky, sometimes arrogant and florid, but powerfully felt and perfectly fitted to her libertarian ideal. (p. 26)

Paul Berman, in a review of "Nowhere at Home: Letters from Exile of Emma Goldman and Alexander Berkman," in The New Republic *(reprinted by permission of* The New Republic; *© 1975 The New Republic, Inc.), Vol. 173, No. 19, November 8, 1975, pp. 26-7.*

ALIX KATES SHULMAN (essay date 1983)

[In the following excerpt, Schulman offers a sympathetic overview and discussion of Goldman's beliefs, noting the extremely close relationship between Goldman's anarchism and her feminism.]

Attempting to separate Emma Goldman's ideas from her deeds is a futile task, for in her the two were inextricably linked. 'Revolution is but thought carried into action,' she wrote in her essay **'Anarchism'.** She was critical of 'philosophical anarchists' and unlike many other radicals who, in the pages of leftist journals, argued endlessly over the niceties of 'correct' interpretation of events, Goldman showed at all times her determination to *do* something about them. As both an anarchist and feminist she always tried to make the revolution by inventing new ways to carry her thought into action.

Still, in her writings, as well as in some of her more imaginative actions, she did make important contributions to anarchist theory, most distinctively by her constant insistence that sexual oppression is as important as class oppression in causing human suffering, and limiting human freedom. In her analysis of society, she differed from most male anarchist intellectuals, who may have routinely acknowledged the 'Woman Question', but did not understand its pervasive and devastating effects and were themselves often blindly sexist in their dealings with women. One wonders if it is perhaps for this reason that even among anarchists Goldman is remembered hardly as a political thinker at all, despite her body of writings and her important intellectual services as an editor and lecturer. (It was she who, for example, spread the works of Ibsen and certain ideas of Freud among American audiences.) There is little doubt that since the resurgence of feminism in recent decades Goldman has returned to public consciousness as a colourful personality, but her distinctive contribution to social analysis—her expansive feminist brand of anarchism, her libertarian brand of feminism—has usually been overlooked or dismissed, both in her time and ours, even by feminists. Those who would dismiss her ideas have had ready reasons. That the movement to which she devoted her life was not the woman's movement but the anarchist movement, no less sexist than other male-dominated movements of her time, supplied motives for both anarchists and feminists to ignore her thought. Her own dismissal of the women's suffrage campaign and her bitter opposition to the social purity doctrines that inspired many feminist reformers, led her to reject for herself the label 'feminist', as it led some feminists to denounce her as 'an enemy of women's freedom' and 'a man's woman'. Nevertheless, I would like to argue that within the context of her life and work Emma Goldman was actually one of the most radical and advanced feminists of her era.

To understand Goldman's thought we must understand that feminism is not a monolith. There are and always have been different strands of feminist politics: economic issues, issues of sex and the family, legal and constitutional issues, woman-centredness; and these strands aggregate in different patterns of overlap and excusion, depending on the time and place and the individuals who embrace them. In Emma Goldman's time there were diverse forms of feminism as there are today, with the sprawling women's movement including a myriad of tendencies, including bourgeois feminism, the women's trade union movement, reform feminism or what has been referred to as social feminism, the women's club movement among others. There was the feminism that centred around social purity and there was radical feminism, a tendency surviving from an earlier time and which based its analysis of gender divisions on a radical critique of the family and often embraced the sexual radicalism of the birth control and 'free motherhood' movements.

Where did Emma Goldman's thought fit into this complex (and perhaps divisive) picture? First and most important it seems to me she was a sexual radical when it came to women. She recognised issues of sexuality and the family as absolutely basic to women's oppression. Not only economic factors, but socio-sexual issues like sexual repression, enforced childbearing, marriage, and the nature of the patriarchal family caused women's restricted life. While her contemporaries were stressing the legal and economic barriers to women's freedom, Emma Goldman was denouncing what she called the 'internal tyrants' that thwart and cripple women. Throughout her two volume autobiography runs the steady narrative of the injuries dealt her as a woman, by anarchists and others alike. She felt that almost every man she lived with tried in some way to inhibit her activities as unsuitable to her sex: they treated her—even her!—as, in her words, 'a mere female'. In speech after speech, essay after essay, she made clear that women's oppression was distinct from men's oppression, that some of the restrictions on women's liberty had different causes and consequences than the restrictions on men's liberty: women, she argued were oppressed precisely as *women,* in addition to whatever they suffered as citizens, workers or from poverty.

Professional women, 'emancipated' women, prostitutes and wives alike were all in Goldman's view victims of these forces. Even at the workplace she identified women's specific oppression as women and in the framework which we would now label sexual harassment she said, 'Nowhere is woman treated according to the merit of her work, but rather as a sex. It is therefore almost inevitable that she should pay for her right to exist, to keep a position in whatever line, with sexual favours.' . . . (pp. 222-24)

As an anarchist, naturally Goldman identified the state with its laws and the church with its morality as agents of women's oppression, but she never doubted that sexual and reproductive matters were at the very heart of women's position in society. To my mind, this uncomprising sexual radicalism, on which Emma Goldman acted repeatedly throughout her life, makes her an indisputable radical feminist, worthy of recognition. Her position went beyond the sexual radicalism of the bohemian women of her day who practised free love in Greenwich Village, for unlike them Emma Goldman was always political,

Goldman lecturing. Courtesy of Prints and Photographs Division, Library of Congress.

trying to change the social structures that restricted women instead of simply changing her own life.

Emma Goldman's major anti-feminist stand, her detractors charge, was her opposition to women's suffrage. How shall we understand this? By her time the US suffrage movement was predominantly a middle-class movement, at least one great branch of which was deeply conservative, puritanical, even racist, going so far as to propose literacy tests to keep immigrants and other poor disenfranchised. For Emma Goldman, whose life had been spent in the struggle of workers and the poor, such a movement would have to be suspect. Further, as an anarchist who opposed government in all its forms, whether elected or not, who considered all government corrupt and the state the major agent of oppression, she thought the struggle for the vote a diversion from women's real struggle and opposed it.

To Goldman it was obvious that suffrage could not do what many believed it would do. It wouldn't change women's oppression and it certainly wouldn't bring a refining or purifying element into politics. 'To assume that [woman] would succeed in purifying something which is not susceptible of purification is to credit her with supernatural powers,' wrote Goldman. . . . At best, the vote would be irrelevant for women.

Like Matilda Joslyn Gage, Emma Goldman saw the suffrage movement—which had initially been radical but had become conservative with time and the entry of such women as Frances Willard—not as a movement of liberation but as a movement towards conformism. Many of the suffragists wanted the vote, argued Goldman, in order to make woman 'a better Christian and homemaker and citizen of the state—the very Gods that woman has served from time immemorial.' . . . (pp. 224-25)

Goldman's prediction of how little benefit women would actually gain from the vote has turned out to be accurate, even to this day.

One of the main problems I see in Goldman's analysis is the credibility given to 'will' in much anarchist theory, so that a failure to change can be seen as a failure of individual will. Thus Emma Goldman sometimes seems to blame women, the victims, for their own oppression, and to attribute the absence of change in women's lives to the women themselves. Given the way Goldman changed her own life this short-sightedness is perhaps understandable.

Emma Goldman did not always identify with women in their struggles, especially middle-class women and especially wives (given her own great hostility to marriage). In her writings, as in her life, there is a peculiar mix of understanding and blame. To her the solution was in defiance and rebellion, in free love, free motherhood, without the sanction of church or state as she herself had lived. At times she almost seems to say if you suffer in marriage, then you shouldn't have married: leave your husband and be free. It was this unfeeling attitude that must have both shocked and angered many feminists, even other women anarchists. (pp. 225-26)

If Emma Goldman was impatient with middle-class and married women she did identify strongly with the needs and desires of the working-class women she helped to organise. As a trade union organiser in the tradition of bread and roses, she insisted that women ought to earn enough money so that they might be more than mere drudges, so that they might have some pleasures in life—roses, books, occasional tickets to the theatre, and of course, romantic love. Even as a young revolutionary Goldman had demanded pleasures in life: when her male comrades disapproved of her love of dancing as a frivolity unworthy of a revolutionary, she grew incensed and retorted that a revolution without dancing was not worth fighting for.

Nor did Goldman have trouble identifying with the women she met in prison, with the ghetto women she counselled on birth control as a midwife, or with the despised prostitutes. With these victims, her understanding of their plight was large, her sympathy generous. That she could not so readily identify with middle-class wives, especially those who felt personally threatened by her views, was, I think, less a failure of her feminism, than it was a function of an ordinary failure of imagination.

Insofar as feminism is more than simply a movement to help women under capitalism get ahead, Goldman's anarchism worked for, and not against her feminism. Anarchism, by definition, and radical feminism as it has evolved, share many premises, for both are fundamentally anti-hierarchical and anti-authoritarian. Both operate through loose, voluntary social organisation from the bottom up, relying on collective activity by small groups: both favour direct action to promote change. As the anarcho-feminist Lynn Farrow wrote a few years ago, 'Feminism practises what anarchism preaches.'

Emma Goldman's vision of the world was one in which everyone would be free and she was prepared to fight for the realisation of this vision. Her main quarrel with her own contemporaries was, I think, that she steadfastly refused to see women as inherently better or worse than men. If male egotism, vanity and strength operated to enslave women, it was partly, she argued, because women idolised those qualities in men, creating a self-perpetuating system. In the tradition of a long line of women from Mary Astell and Mary Wollstonecraft through to Frances Wright, Harriet Taylor, Margaret Fuller, Elizabeth Cady Stanton and Matilda Joslyn Gage, Emma Goldman argued that when women changed their consciousness, broke that circle, and freed themselves from such ill-suited ideals, they might not only liberate themselves but might also 'incidentally' help men to become free. But it was up to women to make their own revolution.

Goldman's line here between blaming the victim and recognising the necessity for a new consciousness is thin but crucial. In one of her most frequently quoted remarks—which has often been invoked in the name of consciousness raising and even of the women's liberation movement itself—she insists on complexity and struggle:

> True emancipation begins neither at the polls or in the courts. It begins in woman's soul. History tells us that every oppressed class gained true liberation from its masters through its own efforts. It is necessary that woman learn that lesson, that she realise that her freedom will reach as far as her power to achieve freedom reaches . . .
>
> (pp. 226-27)

That women were no better than men meant to Emma Goldman that women should stop trying to change (or purify) men and should start taking responsibility for their own lives and their own struggle in the quest for self-determination, in the quest for 'being considered human'. This was the essence of Emma Goldman's vision.

As is customary with most strong public women, Emma Goldman's life and work have been alternately ignored, distorted, maligned. Her strong infusion of radical feminism into anarchist theory has not received the serious treatment it deserves. In fact, Goldman has even been unfairly claimed by some radicals to belong to the anti-feminist camp. This is a gross misrepresentation of her thought. The most frequently invoked popular image of her portrays her as a joke, somewhere between a wild libertine and a bomb-throwing fanatic—perverted distortions of her undoubted strengths, vision, tenacity, integrity. Such assessments not only devalue her work but push her toward the periphery of history where neglect and then obscurity can imperceptibly enclose her.

There is only one sure antidote to neglect and misrepresentation: it is of course to study the life and work first hand and form one's own judgments. In the case of Emma Goldman, such study can be richly rewarding, for she has left behind an engrossing record of a full and vivacious life. (p. 228)

Alix Kates Shulman, "Emma Goldman: 'Anarchist Queen' (1869-1940)" (© Alix Kates Shulman, 1972, 1982, 1983; reprinted by permission of the author), in Feminist Theorists: Three Centuries of Key Women Thinkers, *edited by Dale Spender, Pantheon Books, 1983, pp. 218-28.*

ADDITIONAL BIBLIOGRAPHY

Adams, J. Donald. "Russia in the Days of the New Economic Policy." *The New York Times Book Review* (1 February 1925): 10, 26.*

Neutral review of *My Further Disillusionment in Russia.*

Beck, James M. "The Suppression of Anarchy." *American Law Review* XXXVI, No. 2 (March-April 1902): 190-203.*

Address delivered by the assistant attorney general before the New York State Bar Association. Calling anarchy and law "antipodes," Beck mentions Goldman as the instigator of President McKinley's assassination, adding that he "might never have been assassinated had the Goldman woman been deported ten years ago."

Bryant, Louise. "Emma Goldman on Trial." *The Little Review* II, No. 6 (September 1915): 25-6.

Recalls Goldman's arrest and trial in Portland, Oregon, in August 1915. Bryant recounts the circumstances by which Goldman and Ben Reitman were denied free speech under the pretext that a birth-control pamphlet, constituting "obscene literature," was distributed at one of her lectures. Bryant goes on to commend the judge who dismissed the appeal on the grounds of insufficient evidence.

Harris, Frank. "Emma Goldman, The Famous Anarchist." In his *Contemporary Portraits, fourth series,* pp. 223-51. New York: Brentano's, 1923.

Biographical sketch and quotations. Harris quotes extensively from Goldman, who tells about her early beginnings and political ideals. Calling her a "female St. Paul," Harris, a personal friend of fifteen years, describes her as one of "the three greatest women I have ever met," along with George Eliot and Olive Schreiner.

Ishill, Joseph. *Emma Goldman: A Challenging Rebel.* Berkeley Heights, N.J.: Oriole Press, 1957, 30 p.

Credits Goldman with bringing modern drama to the attention of the American public, and acknowledges her popularization of such socially conscious American writers as Ralph Waldo Emerson, Henry David Thoreau, and Walt Whitman.

Littlefield, Walter. ''Popular and Expert Evidence on Russia's Experiment.'' *The New York Times Book Review* (27 January 1924): 13, 21.*

Examines *My Disillusionment in Russia*. Comparing Goldman's personal account with Edward Alsworth Ross's scholarly *The Russian Soviet Republic,* Littlefield finds the descriptions essentially the same but the conclusions quite different and unconsciously biased. However, he believes that Goldman's retraction of her support for the Soviet system deserves sympathy if not admiration.

Mannin, Ethel. ''Russian Revolutionary Women: Emma Goldman.'' In her *Women and the Revolution,* pp. 121-41. New York: E. P. Dutton & Co., 1939.*

Offers biographical information as well as a discussion of Goldman's political philosophy within a historical context.

Shulman, Alix. *To the Barricades: The Anarchist Life of Emma Goldman*. New York: Thomas Y. Crowell Co., 1971, 255 p.

Laudatory biography with emphasis on Goldman's ''ideals and spirit.'' Included are selections from letters and manuscripts, photographs, and a selected bibliography.

Sinclair, Upton. ''Emma Goldman on Russia.'' *Appeal to Reason,* No. 1285 (17 July 1920): 3.

Discussion of Goldman's early reactions to Soviet Russia. Sinclair believes that Goldman's general objection to government prompted her negative opinion of the Bolsheviks. He, however, considers freedom incompatible to a government at war and views the government of Russia as generally ''a very determined and positive government.''

''Political: *My Disillusionment in Russia*.'' *The Times Literary Supplement,* No. 1207 (5 March 1925): 159.

Brief summary. The reviewer calls the book a most ''scathing attack upon the Soviet tyranny and its leaders,'' and praises Goldman's ''contempt for the foreign apologists of the Soviet regime.''

Wexler, Alice. ''Emma Goldman in Love.'' *Raritan* 1, No. 4 (Spring 1982): 116-45.

Draws upon letters written by Goldman to the first man who fully satisfied her sexual desires, Ben Reitman, to provide an account of Goldman's anarchist activities during her turbulent love affair. Wexler juxtaposes the rational consistency of her work with her seemingly irrational attraction to the physician known as ''the king of the hobos.''

William Hope Hodgson

1877-1918

English novelist, short story writer, poet, and essayist.

Hodgson is the author of several classics of supernatural horror and fantasy. Critics find that he possessed the rare ability to sustain a mood of horror throughout the length of a novel, and they especially praise the epic proportions and imaginative power of *The House on the Borderland* and *The Night Land*. A familiarity with the sea and with seafaring informs many of Hodgson's best-known short stories as well as his novels *The Boats of the "Glen Carrig"* and *The Ghost Pirates*. He also developed a body of horrific myth about the Sargasso Sea which is believed by some critics to be his greatest accomplishment.

Hodgson's career as a seaman began when he left home at thirteen and lied about his age to secure a shipboard position. Out of financial necessity he remained at sea for eight years, acquiring an intense dislike of the seaman's life which was later expressed in several articles in the British popular press that revealed the hard conditions under which seamen labored. He pursued two hobbies while at sea, photography and bodybuilding, both of which he later turned into successful careers. For several years he operated "W. H. Hodgson's School of Physical Culture," a health and bodybuilding club in Blackburn. Hodgson's first published works were treatises upon bodybuilding and exercise, and nonfiction essays on seafaring, illustrated with his own photographs. Hodgson spent many years lecturing on such topics as storms at sea, enhancing his presentations by showing dramatic hand-colored slides taken from his photographs. By late 1903 Hodgson had been publishing nonfiction essays regularly and abandoned his "School of Physical Culture" for a writing career. He began by writing horror and sea-adventure stories, which sold readily to British and American magazines. These works make up a large part of the later collections *Men of the Deep Waters, The Luck of the Strong,* and *Out of the Storm*. The income derived from these story sales enabled Hodgson to devote much of his time to novel-writing.

Hodgson's first novel, *The Boats of the "Glen Carrig,"* was favorably reviewed but did not sell well. Hodgson devised a scheme to sell copies from a wagon fitted out to look like a boat, and when his publisher, Chapman & Hall, dismissed the notion Hodgson took subsequent manuscripts to another firm. While seeking a publisher for his third novel, *The Ghost Pirates,* Hodgson met and became friends with Arthur St. John Adcock, an editor at the London *Bookman* magazine, who is believed to have written many of the unsigned reviews of Hodgson's books that appeared in *The Bookman* between 1909 and 1920. All of Hodgson's novels suffered the same fate as *The Boats of the "Glen Carrig":* they received excellent reviews but sold poorly. His short stories, however, garnered both critical and popular acclaim, and these provided him with an income while he worked on a final massive fantasy novel, *The Night Land*. This, too, was a critical success but a commercial failure, and Hodgson was so disappointed that he published only short stories thereafter. Hodgson was living in France when World War I began, and he returned to England to volunteer for active service. He was killed near Ypres in 1918.

Critical and popular interest in Hodgson after his death was slight until H. C. Koenig, an American fan of supernatural horror and fantasy fiction, became interested in him and began searching for his out-of-print stories and novels. As he located more and more of his works, Koenig became convinced that Hodgson was a significant author in the horror field, and wrote numerous letters attempting to interest editors and publishers in this virtually unknown author. Only a few of Hodgson's stories and novels were reprinted in magazines until 1946, when Arkham House, a specialty publisher of horror fiction, reissued four of Hodgson's novels—*The House on the Borderland, The Ghost Pirates, The Boats of the "Glen Carrig,"* and *The Night Land*—in an omnibus volume. This brought Hodgson's name to prominence, at least among readers of supernatural horror and fantasy fiction.

Although many of Hodgson's short stories are concerned with life at sea, only two of his novels, *The Boats of the "Glen Carrig"* and *The Ghost Pirates,* have an ocean setting. In *The Boats of the "Glen Carrig,"* Hodgson developed fictional details of the Sargasso Sea, a region of aquatic vegetation which he populated with carnivorous plants, amphibious "weed men," and the hulks of numerous derelict ships. Hodgson utilized the first-person viewpoint to narrate the wreck of the ship "Glen Carrig," portraying the crew's many harrowing encounters with the horrors lurking on and around a mysterious island in the Sargasso Sea, their rescue of a trapped ship, and their triumphant voyage home. Hodgson's vivid presentation of the nightmarish but corporeal plants and animals that threaten the shipwrecked sailors has been widely praised. In *The Ghost Pirates,* a haunted ship sets out on a final voyage and is eventually dragged beneath the surface of the sea by supernatural beings. Critics have noted Hodgson's ability to subtly suggest the uncanny nature of the threat which hangs over the doomed ship. Both of Hodgson's ocean novels have also been praised for their effective use of authentic maritime lore.

Critics agree that *The House on the Borderland* and *The Night Land* represent Hodgson's greatest imaginative achievements. The major portion of *The House on the Borderland* purports to be the text of a diary, and the story is framed by an introductory episode in which two travelers find the diary in the ruins of an isolated country house in Ireland. The house was apparently built on an interstice between several planes of reality and is under intermittent attack by foul pit-dwelling creatures. The diary, which was the work of the last inhabitant of the house, ends when "somethi. . ." leaves the cellar and apparently kills the writer. Time-travel episodes in *The House on the Borderland* have led critics to compare it with H. G. Wells's *The Time Machine*. *The Night Land* is generally regarded as Hodgson's finest work. An epic adventure set for the most part many centuries in the future, with the sun and the human race simultaneously waning, *The Night Land* opens with a pseudo-seventeenth century idyll of two lovers united by marriage and then separated by death. The futuristic remainder of the novel tells of the reincarnated seventeenth-century lover's trek across the blasted wastes of the dying earth in search of the reincarnation of his lost love. Critics are unan-

imous in praising Hodgson's depictions of both the dark and nearly lifeless earth and the many horrible unknown forces that threaten the few surviving humans. Critics are also united in deploring the artificiality and romantic sentimentality of the novel's opening segment, which presents the impetus for the hero's epic quest.

Hodgson's short stories, particularly his sea adventures in such collections as *Men of the Deep Waters,* have led critics Lin Carter and August Derleth to compare his short fiction with that of Herman Melville and Joseph Conrad. Hodgson's intimate familiarity with seafaring lends an air of unmistakable authenticity to these works. Probably Hodgson's best-known short story of the sea is "The Voice in the Night," which recounts the fate of two shipwreck survivors on a fungus-covered island. After eating the fungus, they find it growing on them and are ultimately consumed by the pervasive fungoid mass. This often-reprinted story is noted for its understated development of a theme of powerful horror. Unconnected with the sea are Hodgson's stories about Carnacki, an "occult detective" who investigates seemingly supernatural occurrences. The Carnacki stories follow a pattern, with a framing device similar to that of the Sherlock Holmes stories of Arthur Conan Doyle. The character of Carnacki is often compared with Holmes, as well as with Algernon Blackwood's psychic investigator John Silence and J. S. Le Fanu's Dr. Hesselius. However derivative the central character, the Carnacki stories are considered among the best of the "occult detective" series that were popular at the time. Perhaps the most innovative feature of the Carnacki stories is Hodgson's careful construction, which does not allow the reader to discover whether Carnacki has been investigating a real or a faked supernatural event until the story's end.

Although he is comparatively unknown among readers and critics of mainstream fiction, Hodgson has been called by Sam Moskowitz "the supreme master of imaginative horror in science fiction." He is equally highly regarded, on the basis of such works as *The House on the Borderland,* as a fine writer of supernatural horror, and his epic novel *The Night Land* has earned him acclaim as a superb fantasist who possessed a unique imaginative power and an ability to convey nightmare images in realistic and well-crafted prose.

(See also *Contemporary Authors,* Vol. 111.)

PRINCIPAL WORKS

The Boats of the "Glen Carrig" (novel) 1907
The House on the Borderland (novel) 1908
The Ghost Pirates (novel) 1909
Carnacki the Ghost-Finder (short stories) 1910
The Night Land (novel) 1912
Men of the Deep Waters (short stories) 1914
The Luck of the Strong (short stories) 1916
Captain Gault: Being the Exceedingly Private Log of a Sea-Captain (short stories) 1917
The Calling of the Sea (poetry) 1920
The Voice of the Ocean (poetry) 1921
Out of the Storm (short stories) 1975

THE BOOKMAN, LONDON (essay date 1908)

[*The anonymous reviewer of Hodgson's first novel,* The Boats of the "Glen Carrig", *praises Hodgson's "amazingly vivid imaginative power" and "admirably restrained" style. The critic finds, however, that the scenes of supernatural horror would have had more effect upon the reader had they been fewer.*]

Mr. Hope Hodgson writes with an amazingly vivid imaginative power, and a skill in the handling of eerie incidents, the creation of bizarre effects, and the atmosphere of nameless horror and terror, that bear comparison with the grimmest and most haunting things that even Poe accomplished. You read this strange, nightmare romance of **"The Boats of the *Glen-Carrig*"** with a keen and absorbing interest; you find it impossible to close the book till you have read to the end, yet in the latter half of it the horrors of the story are less potent in their effect upon you than were the horrors of the earlier half. They are not less forcibly or realistically imagined, nor less subtly and wonderfully described, but Mr. Hodgson has given us too much of them, we have supped so full that our palate has lost its acuteness, and though we go on swallowing, we no longer taste the full flavour of them. At the outset . . . the whole thing grips, and curiously persuades us to believe in it; the derelict ship stranded on the island, empty of all its crew, and containing fragments of writing that hint at the mysterious and unspeakable doom that had overtaken them; the clammy Something that crawls about the deck of nights, feeling with mighty, squashy hands at the door of the cabin in which the new arrivals have taken refuge; the trees from which it seems the wailings come—soft-branched trees, with grisly human heads bulging like monstrous boles among the upper boughs, pulpy, loathsome trees that bleed when the boatswain in a frenzy slashes at them with his sword: everything of this takes hold upon you, as it was meant to. But when the crew, having found a supply of water, puts out to sea again, and by-and-by comes to a vast continent of oozy, entangling weed, and land on a solid island in the thick of it, and find another derelict vessel with people aboard, and are again scared by nerve-shattering noises in the night, and attacked by men-slugs, mammoth crabs, and other unholy and unheard-of monstrosities, you begin to feel that you are not in the real world at all, but in some gruesome, wholly imaginary world, where things only seem to happen as they do in a dream. Mr. Hodgson's style is admirably restrained, but his imagination runs riot; if he had carried his shipwrecked crew through rough but possible adventures, and then dropped one or two of these creepy, weird experiences into the midst of those, they would have been immensely more effective. It is an uncommonly clever book, nevertheless, and one that augurs well for what its author will do when he has broken his imagination to harness, and has it under control.

A review of "The Boats of the 'Glen-Carrig'," in The Bookman, *London, Vol. XXXII, No. 196, January, 1908, p. 181.*

THE BOOKMAN, LONDON (essay date 1909)

[*The following excerpt is an early review discussing* The Ghost Pirates.]

There can be no need to recall to the memory two such remarkable works as Mr. Hope Hodgson's **"The Boats of the *Glen Carrig*"** and **"The House on the Borderland."** They are books of the kind that, once read, cannot easily be forgotten. **"The Ghost Pirates"** forms the last volume of the trilogy, for, as the author points out, "though very different in scope, each of the three books deals with certain conceptions that have an elemental kinship." The next sentence in his preface is a disappointment to us: "With this book the author believes that he closes the door, so far as he is concerned, on a particular phase of constructive thought." We can only hope that Mr. Hodgson may be induced to reconsider his decision, for we know of nothing like the author's previous work in the whole of present-day literature. There is no one at present writing who can thrill and horrify to quite the same effect. **"The Ghost Pirates"** does not display Mr. Hodgson's wonderful qualities of imagination to such good effect as did **"The House on the Borderland,"** nor is it so terrifying a book to read. Nevertheless, it is a very remarkable story, told in a matter-of-fact manner that materially increases its "grip." The author particularly excels in the creation of "atmosphere," but he is also possessed of a vigorous style and a wonderful ingenuity in the concoction of terrifying detail. Mr. Hodgson has his faults; his exaggerated treatment of the cockney dialect of one of the minor characters is unsatisfactory, and his punctuation is annoying. But when all is said **"The Ghost Pirates"** is a book of high literary qualities and a worthy member of a memorable trilogy.

A review of "The Ghost Pirates," in The Bookman, *London, Vol. XXXVII, No. 217, October, 1909, p. 54.*

THE BOOKMAN, LONDON (essay date 1912)

[Hodgson's fantastic novel The Night Land *is reviewed and found to be "a very original and sufficiently remarkable book."]*

You may say that in **"The Night Land"** Mr. Hope Hodgson's reach exceeds his grasp, that his story in some of its details is obscure and difficult to follow, that he tells it in a quaint, archaic language that does not make for easy reading, but at least you cannot say he has not aimed at doing a big thing. He has set himself to unfold a love tale that is not bounded by the limits of a lifetime, but continues and is renewed again at last in a strange dreamlife after many centuries. . . . Whatever Mr. Hodgson lacks it is not imagination. . . . We shall not attempt to give any full outline of Mr. Hodgson's romance; it runs to nearly six hundred pages and is crowded with incident and alive with inner significances and undercurrents of meaning. You may read it as a cloudy and elusive allegory, if you have a liking for that form of literature, but in its allegorical aspect it is not simple enough, it needs too much explaining, and you will do better perhaps to read it simply as a daringly imaginative love story, and as such you will find it a very original and sufficiently remarkable book.

A review of "The Night Land," in The Bookman, *London, Vol. XLII, No. 249, June, 1912, p. 137.*

THE BOOKMAN, LONDON (essay date 1913)

[An early reviewer offers unqualified praise for Hodgson's Carnacki stories. Most later reviewers and critics evaluate these stories negatively or praise them with severe reservations; for examples of such criticism, see the excerpts by H. P. Lovecraft (1927) and Sam Moskowitz (1973).]

Mr. Hope Hodgson's new novel [**"Carnacki the Ghost-Finder"**] comprises half-a-dozen of the "creepiest" experiences imaginable. Carnacki, the hero or victim of these experiences, narrates them to a privileged circle of friends with an artistic sense of cumulative horror calculated to create the sensation known as goose-flesh in your veriest sceptic. Whether you believe in ghosts or not, you are sure to find something to your taste in Carnacki's thrilling reports of his investigations; for in some cases the mysterious forces at work prove to be merely ingeniously contrived tricks of human origin, while in other cases strange and horrific Beings take threatening shape and have to be dealt with according to the mystic laws of supernatural "science." Read after nightfall in a dimly lighted room peopled with uneasy shadows, these tales carry with them a haunting atmosphere of terror and an ever-present sense of the unknown powers of darkness. . . . Mr. Hope Hodgson plays deftly on the strings of fear, and his new novel stamps him a fascinating panic-monger with a quick eye for all the sensational possibilities of ghost-lore.

A review of "Carnacki the Ghost-Finder," in The Bookman, *London, Vol. XLIV, No. 261, June, 1913, p. 142.*

THE BOOKMAN, LONDON (essay date 1920)

[In the following excerpt, Hodgson's first posthumously published volume of poetry, The Calling of the Sea, *is favorably reviewed.]*

It is strange that such an essentially seafaring people as the English, who have produced so many great poets, have produced so few who have written great poetry of the sea, and that most even of those few have been landsmen. However beautifully the landsman may write about it, there is usually something lacking from his verse, for it needs a sailor who has known the sea long and intimately in all its moods to interpret it aright.

That realistic truthfulness is the outstanding quality in Hope Hodgson's poems [in **"The Calling of the Sea"**]. He died, a soldier, on the fields of France; and for some ten years before the war he had lived by his pen and won a considerable reputation as a novelist; but for eight years before that he had followed the sea and gave his heart to it, and its influence is over all the best of his work. Most of his novels and short stories drew their inspiration from it, but the eeriness, the mystery, the cruelty and terror of it appealed to him more potently than did its quieter, happier aspects. He was keenly susceptible to its wonder and its beauty, but for him the wonder and the beauty often had a suggestion of something sinister underlying them. It is so in his tales, and it is so in these poems. This consistency is the natural result of his sincerity, and it is the note of sincerity that gives his poems much of their forcefulness. His passion for the sea was no pose but a real and deep emotion, as spontaneous as the verse he wrote about it. There is a bizarre imaginative power in such a blend of fantasy and realism as **"The Place of Storms"**; his descriptive pieces, such as **"Storm," "The Ship," "Down the Long Coasts,"** are etched effectively in vigorous black-and-white. He reached a higher level in his prose, but he was a true poet as he is a true novelist of the sea.

"Hope Hodgson's Poems," in The Bookman, *London, Vol. LVIII, No. 344, May, 1920, p. 81.*

A. ST. JOHN ADCOCK (essay date 1920)

[An English author of numerous works, many of which concern the city of London, Adcock served as editor of the London Bookman *from 1923 until his death in 1930. In the following excerpt, Adcock pays tribute to Hodgson as an author and as a person.]*

I first met Hope Hodgson about eleven years ago. At that date, his three best novels had been written; two of them, **"The Boats of the Glen Carrig"** and **"The House on the Border-**

land," had been published, and the third, **"The Ghost Pirates,"** was in the press. In those three stories he showed himself a writer of quite exceptional imaginative gifts, a master of the weird, the eerie, the terrible, whose strange and grim imaginings were not unworthy of comparison with the bizarre creations of Poe. He had already given himself so entirely and enthusiastically to a literary career that the talk at our first meeting was wholly of books and of his hopes as an author. He aimed high and, taking his art very seriously, had a frank, unaffected confidence in his powers which was partly the splendid arrogance of youth and partly the heritage of experience, for he had tested and proved them. (p. 3)

Only once, and then casually, he mentioned to me that he had been a sailor, but, though there was nothing in his manner or his trim, sturdy figure that suggested the seafarer, one might have guessed as much from his books and from the fact that the ablest of them were all of sailors and the sea. He was the son of an Essex clergyman, and left home to serve for eight years aboard ship. . . . [Many] of his recollections of those eight years have gone to make the characters and incidents and scenery of his stories.

One novel of his, **"The Night Land,"** which appeared in 1912, turns altogether aside from the sea and might almost seem to have presaged, in some dim fashion, the coming of the Great War. He ranked it as his highest achievement and owned he was disappointed that it was not generally regarded as such. The story is told in quaint, archaic language; is by turns grim, idyllic and touched with supernatural horror; it unfolds a romance of the far future when, in the last days of the world, the powers of evil are grown so assertive, so almost all-conquering that the civilized remnant of the human race seeks refuge in an enormous and impregnable pyramid, building their city tier above tier within it, while all around this Last Redoubt stretches immeasurably the menacing Night Land peopled with primeval and loathsome material monsters and dreadful immaterial things of the spirit world banded together to destroy the soul of mankind. It is a strikingly original piece of work, giving full scope to Hope Hodgson's sombre imaginative power and his peculiar flair for the weirdly horrible and the hauntingly mysterious. But it does not grip and hold one as do those three earlier novels that, for all their uncanniness, wear an air of everyday realism and never lose touch with the normal elements of actual earthly life.

He introduced some of his verse into his last book of short stories, **"Captain Gault,"** which came out a few months before his death; but most of what he wrote in this kind is here published [in **"The Calling of the Sea"**] for the first time. And in his poems, as in his prose, it is the mystery, the strength, the cruelty, the grimness and sadness of the sea that most potently appeal to him. He visions it as a House of Storms, a Hall of Thunders; calm at times, but with such a calm as one sees

> When some fierce beast veils anger in its breast,

or raging and heaving and roaring tumultuously as though through its tortured waves

> Some frightful Thing climbed growling from cold depths.

For him the voices of the sea are the sighing or calling of its multitudinous dead, and there are lines in which he hints that one day he, too, will be called down to them; but that was not the death he was to die. (pp. 4-5)

It is hard to think of him as dead, he was so vigorously and intensely alive. That vigour and intensity of life pulses and burns in everything he has written; and I think he will still be living in, at least, those three of his novels when we who knew and loved him are passed from remembrance. In the world of letters he had only half fulfilled his promise, but in the larger world of men he left no promise unfulfilled. . . . (p. 6)

A. St. John Adcock, in an introduction to The Calling of the Sea *by William Hope Hodgson, Selwyn & Blount, 1920, pp. 3-6.*

H. P. LOVECRAFT (essay date 1927)

[Lovecraft is considered one of the foremost modern authors of supernatural horror fiction, as well as one of the most notable critics within that field. Lovecraft was well versed in the history of Gothic writing, and his Supernatural Horror in Literature, *which is excerpted below, is one of the earliest and most comprehensive studies of this genre. Discussing both major and minor works, from the myths of antiquity to pulp adventures of the modern era, this study provides a rationale for the functions of and motivations behind fictional works of supernatural horror. Lovecraft argues that the most successful specimens of the form inspire in the reader a sense of liberation, along with horrific revulsion, through fictional violations of the laws of the natural world. From the opening statement—"the oldest and strongest emotion of mankind is fear"—to its concluding question—"who shall declare the dark theme a handicap?"—Lovecraft in* Supernatural Horror in Literature *examines this genre as an "essential branch of human expression." In the following excerpt, Lovecraft finds that* The House on the Borderland *is "perhaps the greatest of all Mr. Hodgson's works." He further finds that Hodgson's fiction benefits from his familiarity with the sea and with seafaring.]*

Of rather uneven stylistic quality, but vast occasional power in its suggestion of lurking worlds and beings behind the ordinary surface of life, is the work of William Hope Hodgson, known today far less than it deserves to be. Despite a tendency toward conventionally sentimental conceptions of the universe, and of man's relation to it and to his fellows, Mr. Hodgson is perhaps second only to Algernon Blackwood in his serious treatment of unreality. Few can equal him in adumbrating the nearness of nameless forces and monstrous besieging entities through casual hints and insignificant details, or in conveying feelings of the spectral and the abnormal in connection with regions or buildings.

In ***The Boats of the Glen Carrig*** . . . we are shown a variety of malign marvels and accursed unknown lands as encountered by the survivors of a sunken ship. The brooding menace in the earlier parts of the book is impossible to surpass, though a letdown in the direction of ordinary romance and adventure occurs toward the end. An inaccurate and pseudo-romantic attempt to reproduce eighteenth-century prose detracts from the general effect, but the really profound nautical erudition everywhere displayed is a compensating factor.

The House on the Borderland . . .—perhaps the greatest of all Mr. Hodgson's works—tells of a lonely and evilly regarded house in Ireland which forms a focus for hideous otherworld forces and sustains a siege by blasphemous hybrid anomalies from a hidden abyss below. The wanderings of the Narrator's spirit through limitless light-years of cosmic space and Kalpas of eternity, and its witnessing of the solar system's final destruction, constitute something almost unique in standard literature. And everywhere there is manifest the author's power to suggest vague, ambushed horrors in natural scenery. But for a few touches of commonplace sentimentality this book would be a classic of the first water.

The Ghost Pirates . . . , regarded by Mr. Hodgson as rounding out a trilogy with the two previously mentioned works, is a powerful account of a doomed and haunted ship on its last voyage, and of the terrible sea-devils (of quasi-human aspect, and perhaps the spirits of bygone buccaneers) that besiege it and finally drag it down to an unknown fate. With its command of maritime knowledge, and its clever selection of hints and incidents suggestive of latent horrors in nature, this book at times reaches enviable peaks of power.

The Night Land . . . is a long-extended (538 pp.) tale of the earth's infinitely remote future—billions of billions of years ahead, after the death of the sun. It is told in a rather clumsy fashion, as the dreams of a man in the seventeenth century, whose mind merges with its own future incarnation; and is seriously marred by painful verboseness, repetitiousness, artificial and nauseously sticky romantic sentimentality, and an attempt at archaic language even more grotesque and absurd than that in ***Glen Carrig.***

Allowing for all its faults, it is yet one of the most potent pieces of macabre imagination ever written. The picture of a night-black, dead planet, with the remains of the human race concentrated in a stupendously vast mental pyramid and besieged by monstrous, hybrid, and altogether unknown forces of the darkness, is something that no reader can ever forget. Shapes and entities of an altogether non-human and inconceivable sort—the prowlers of the black, man-forsaken, and unexplored world outside the pyramid—are *suggested* and *partly* described with ineffable potency; while the night-land landscape with its chasms and slopes and dying volcanism takes on an almost sentient terror beneath the author's touch.

Midway in the book the central figure ventures outside the pyramid on a quest through death-haunted realms untrod by man for millions of years—and in his slow, minutely described, day-by-day progress over unthinkable leagues of immemorial blackness there is a sense of cosmic alienage, breathless mystery, and terrified expectancy unrivalled in the whole range of literature. The last quarter of the book drags woefully, but fails to spoil the tremendous power of the whole.

Mr. Hodgson's later volume, ***Carnacki, the Ghost-Finder,*** consists of several longish short stories published many years before in magazines. In quality it falls conspicuously below the level of the other books. We here find a more or less conventional stock figure of the "infallible detective" type—the progeny of M. Dupin and Sherlock Holmes, and the close kin of Algernon Blackwood's John Silence—moving through scenes and events badly marred by an atmosphere of professional "occultism." A few of the episodes, however, are of undeniable power, and afford glimpses of the peculiar genius characteristic of the author. (pp. 395-97)

H. P. Lovecraft, "Supernatural Horror in Literature" (1927), in his Dagon and Other Macabre Tales, *edited by August Derleth (copyright 1965, by August Derleth; reprinted by permission of Arkham House Publishers, Inc.), Arkham House, 1965, pp. 347-413.**

CLARK ASHTON SMITH (essay date 1944)

[*Smith was the author of horror and fantastic fiction noted for its lush and intricate prose style (reflecting his work as a poet of the nineteenth-century Decadent mold), and for its narrative perspectives that both reject and transcend the normal course of human affairs. His expertise was in the interplanetary or fantastic tale which allowed for the unrestrained, and invariably nightmarish, use of his artistic imagination. In the following excerpt, Smith offers qualified praise of Hodgson's abilities as an author of fantastic fiction.*]

Among those fiction writers who have elected to deal with the shadowlands and borderlands of human existence, William Hope Hodgson surely merits a place with the very few that inform their treatment of such themes with a sense of authenticity. His writing itself, as Mr. Lovecraft justly says [see excerpt above, 1927], is far from equal in stylistic merit: but it would be impossible to withhold the rank of master from an author who has achieved so authoritatively, in volume after volume, a quality that one might term the realism of the unreal. In some ways, Hodgson's work is no doubt most readily comparable to that of Algernon Blackwood. But I am not sure that even Blackwood has managed to intimate a feeling of such profound and pervasive familiarity with the occult as one finds in ***The House on the Borderland.*** Hideous phantoms and unknown monsters from the nightward gulf are adumbrated in all their terror, with no dispelling of their native mystery; and surely such things could be described only by a seer who has dwelt overlong on the perilous verges and has peered too deeply into the regions veiled by invisibility from normal sight.

However, ***The House on the Borderland,*** though probably the most sustained and least faulty of Hodgson's volumes, is far from being his most unique achievement. In all literature, there are few works so sheerly remarkable, so purely creative, as ***The Night Land.*** Whatever faults this book may possess, however inordinate its length may seem, it impresses the reader as being the ultimate saga of a perishing cosmos, the last epic of a world beleaguered by eternal night and by the unvisageable spawn of darkness. Only a great poet could have conceived and written this story; and it is perhaps not illegitimate to wonder how much of actual prophecy may have been mingled with the poesy.

The books above mentioned are, in my opinion, Mr. Hodgson's masterpieces. However, the first portion of ***The Boats of the "Glen Carrig"*** maintains a comparable level of imaginative power; and one regrets that the lost mariners should have escaped so soon from the malign and mysterious dimension into which they were carried. One must also accord a more than formal praise to ***The Ghost Pirates,*** which is really one of the few successful long stories dealing with the phantasmal. Its rout of ghastly and persistent specters will follow the reader long after they have seized the haunted ship!

It is to be hoped that work of such unusual power will eventually win the attention and fame to which it is entitled. (pp. 46-7)

Clark Ashton Smith, "In Appreciation of William Hope Hodgson" (originally published in The Reader and Collector, *June, 1944), in his* Planets and Dimensions: Collected Essays of Clark Ashton Smith, *edited by Charles K. Wolfe, Mirage Press, 1973, pp. 46-7.*

B. V. WINEBAUM (essay date 1946)

[*Winebaum remarks upon Hodgson's ability to sustain horror and interest through the length of a novel, a point which is also noted by Lin Carter (see excerpt below, 1971). Winebaum concurs with H. P. Lovecraft (see excerpt above, 1927) and C. S. Lewis (see Additional Bibliography) that the love interest in* The Night Land *seriously flaws the novel.*]

[William Hope Hodgson] has retained a certain following among experts of the horror story, who claim that his ability to sustain horror and interest (beyond the ordinary length of the nominal magazine novelette) distinguishes him from many in the field. Unimpressed with even extraordinary endurance, I was pleasantly surprised by the cleanness of his prose, though a word of critical horror must be expressed for the liberties of diction he has taken in **"The Night Land."**

Of the four [novels in **"The House on the Borderland and Other Novels," "The Night Land"**] is about three times the longest, and though it may rank highest as a work of pure imagination, the middle section, in which the hero searches endlessly for his true love, is far too long, the adventures repetitively similar, and the love affair offensively cloying. My favorites . . . are **"The Boats of the 'Glen Carrig'"** and **"The Ghost Pirates."** These two are sea stories. Here too is horror, but presented squarely in relation to the mechanics of ordinary life, and doubly effective in making fast the points of terror.

B. V. Winebaum, "Four-Decker Horror Special," in The New York Times Book Review *(copyright © 1946 by The New York Times Company; reprinted by permission), September 15, 1946, p. 20.*

SID BIRCHBY (essay date 1964)

[In the following excerpt, Birchby discusses sexual symbolism in Hodgson's works.]

The House on the Borderland was first published in 1908 and shows certain affinities with H. G. Wells's "Time Machine." There is a time-travel episode, for instance, in which the hero notes the passage of day and night as "a sort of gigantic ponderous flicker," a convention familiar to most readers of time-travel stories. (p. 70)

There are pseudo-scientific footnotes to the text, which in a plonking way mirror those found in Wells, e.g., "I can only suppose that the time of the Earth's yearly journey had ceased to bear its present relative proportion to the period of the Sun's rotation." Such footnotes remained an accepted writer's device in science-fiction until well into the 1930's.

But behind the facade of straight science-fiction is a story told by Hodgson alone. Its hero, identified only as "The Recluse," lives in a lonely house in Western Ireland. This house, for no very clear reasons, is under siege by weird creatures which emerge from a nearby ravine. In mid-plot the Recluse finds himself making an apocalyptic trip into the future. From this he learns that the monsters have always existed underground, and always will until the remote age when the dead Earth falls into the Sun. He returns to the present and to his doom. The story ends as the creatures burst into his study.

The sense of nemesis brooding over the house is competently done, and looks backwards to Poe and forwards to Lovecraft. But where Poe's necrophily would have coloured the narrative, or Lovecraft's penchant for the degradation of Man, Hodgson lays on a wash of courtly romance. True to the idiom it is a Hopeless Romance; no more than two sketchy encounters with a Soul-mate while time-travelling, plus a certain amount of breast-beating and cries of "Shall we never meet again?" It could easily be discounted as standard literary practice at Hodgson's level and in his day, and of no special importance in understanding the work. Yet in the light of certain sexual symbols appearing in the story it is indeed, like the impassive iceberg, the only visible fraction of a submerged giant.

The besieging creatures are pallid swine-like things prowling through the bushes like the transformed lovers of Circe, yet as savage as those other symbols of erotic lust, the Gadarene swine. They are linked with images of carnality, foulness, and female genitalia: their home is "in the bowels of the world" and they pour out through a pit which mysteriously enlarges itself: "The side of the Pit appeared to have collapsed, forming a deep V-shaped cleft. In the angle of the V was a great hole, not unlike an arched doorway." We learn that through this hole the monsters emerge. Gradually the Pit fills with water and overflows into caverns under the House itself. The final end of the House is to collapse into the Pit.

Physical love is an animal thing, foul and all-engulfing. No good will come of sexual intercourse, only the savage lusts of the swine (whose speech is described as similar to human speech but "glutinous and sticky"). The True Love spurns physical contact:

> She came over swiftly and touched me and it was as though Heaven had opened. Yet when I reached out my hands to her, she put me from her with tenderly stern hands, and I was abashed.

The Recluse meets her first as he stands upon the shore of an immense and silent sea, which she tells him is called "The Sea of Sleep." It is in fact the womb-image, from which she emerges in "a bubble of white foam floating up out of the depths." Overhead, reiterating the symbolism, was "a stupendous globe of pale fire, that swam a little above the far horizon, and shed a foam-like light above the quiet waters."

The true love is virginal as a new-born babe, and is glimpsed only in sleep. Or she is as impregnable as a Sleeping Princess.

Only once again does he meet her. It is after the end of the Solar System, and he sees "a boundless river of softly shimmering globes." He is impelled towards one of them: "Then I slid through into the interior without experiencing the least resistance." Would that the return to the womb were always so easy! Once inside the globe, he recognises his surroundings. He is again by the Sea of Sleep, and sure enough his loved one is there. With this wealth of imagery, can we any longer doubt her identity? (pp. 70-1)

Sid Birchby, "Sexual Symbolism in W. H. Hodgson," in Riverside Quarterly *(© 1964 by Leland Sapiro), Vol. 1, No. 2, November, 1964, pp. 70-1.*

LIN CARTER (essay date 1971)

[Carter, a noted author and critic in the fields of supernatural horror and sword-and-sorcery fiction, provides critical commentary along with an extensive publication history of Hodgson's first novel in his introduction to The Boats of the "Glen Carrig." *The following excerpt from that introduction discusses Hodgson's most significant achievements.]*

The greatness of William Hope Hodgson lies, I would say, in two factors. In the first place, most of the masters of the macabre tale—Bierce, Machen, Poe, Lovecraft, Chambers, Blackwood, Dunsany, James, Le Fanu—worked best in short story length. While they occasionally attempted the novel of supernatural terror, their finest work lay in the short story. *Dracula* towers alone, in my estimation, as virtually the only masterpiece of horror ever written in novel length.

The reason for this preference of the short story over the novel as the medium for superior supernatural fiction is not difficult to understand. The horror tale is primarily one of mood, of suggestive atmosphere; this tenuous mood of terror is very difficult to sustain, and usually is sustained best at short length. Even so mighty a master as Poe could not keep up this mood at novel-length; his *Narrative of Arthur Gordon Pym* is generally considered a failure. But Hodgson, a brilliant artist of the supernatural short story, is every bit as good when working in the novel; and therefore he is almost alone in the field. (*Dracula*, the best example I know of the horror novel, is really abominably written; it succeeds only through the novelty and dramatic power of its conception.)

Hodgson's second claim to fame lies in his use of the sea. To my taste, no other writer in history has so wonderfully and perfectly captured the mystery and strangeness, the awe and terror and beauty of that illimitable waste of waters which conceals three quarters of our planet. In this respect, Hodgson comes very close to challenging the supremacy of the great Joseph Conrad; so very close, in fact, that I cannot make up my mind which of the two authors more powerfully suggests the haunting strangeness and wonder of the sea and its mysteries.

It is now a quarter of a century since ***The Boats of the "Glen Carrig"*** was included in that Arkham House omnibus edition of Hodgson's novels. . . . It is time this extraordinary and deeply moving book was brought into print again. (pp. x-xi)

The novel is now 64 years old, but its power, simplicity and dreamlike mood have not aged. I doubt if a novel as unique and well-crafted as this will ever again be permitted to lapse into obscurity. (p. xii)

Lin Carter, "Introduction: Strange Odyssey" (introduction copyright © 1971 by Lin Carter; reprinted by permission of Ballantine Books, a division of Random House, Inc.), in The Boats of the "Glen Carrig" *by William Hope Hodgson, Ballantine, 1971, pp. vii-xii.*

LIN CARTER (essay date 1972)

[*Like B. V. Winebaum and H. P. Lovecraft (see excerpts above, 1927 and 1946) and C. S. Lewis (see Additional Bibliography), Carter criticizes the stylistic and conceptual flaws of Hodgson's* The Night Land, *while praising its imaginative force.*]

For much of his forty-three years of life, William Hope Hodgson had sailed the seas. From the texture of his experiences he wrought stories of the sea and its mysteries which are without parallel in all of our literature. Not Joseph Conrad—not even Herman Melville—has captured with such depth and insight the strangeness and beauty and haunting terror of the mighty oceans. All too few books came from Hodgson's marvelous hand before a German shell cut short his life and robbed the world of a talent that promised a brilliant literary career.

One of the best of these books [is] ***The Boats of the "Glen Carrig."*** . . . But . . . the finest of them all [is] ***The Night Land***. . . . (pp. vii-viii)

There is no doubt in my mind that ***The Night Land*** is one of the oddest and most unique novels ever written.

It is the strangest mingling of beauty and wonder and darkness and terror ever set down in one novel.

It virtually defies classification.

Since most of the story takes place in the very far distant future when the sun has gone out and the earth is wrapped in unending darkness, you could call it science fiction.

But since the mood and setting are of overwhelming weirdness and mystery and awe of the unknown, you could equally well label it a novel of supernatural horror.

And yet again, in that it concerns itself with an heroic quest through a strange world of marvels largely left unexplained, you might consider it epic fantasy.

To be honest, it is all three forms of fantasy at once. And it is also a love story, a novel of character revelation, a dream, a nightmare, and a parable.

The Night Land has had a powerful influence on the fantasy genre. Lovecraft praised it in most fulsome terms in his famous survey of the field of weird fiction, *Supernatural Horror in Literature* [see excerpt above, 1927]. . . . (pp. x-xi)

C. S. Lewis, another admirer of this remarkable novel, noted that it bore certain flaws—the maudlin love-dialogue scenes, for example [see Additional Bibliography]. These scenes occur only in the second half of this very long novel, but they are Victorian sentimentality at its nadir of taste and, in the opinion of many readers (myself among them), they severely injure the cumulative power and movement of the story. . . .

This magnificent novel, now sixty years old, has aged very little, despite its High Victorian prose. Like most fine antiques of genuine craftsmanship and artistry, the years have but added a patina to its luster. (p. xii)

Lin Carter, "The Last Redoubt" (introduction copyright © 1972 by Lin Carter; reprinted by permission of Ballantine Books, a division of Random House, Inc.), in The Night Land *by William Hope Hodgson, Ballantine, 1972, pp. vii-xii.*

SAM MOSKOWITZ (essay date 1973)

[*Moskowitz, a science fiction and fantasy critic, editor, and author, provides a lengthy biographical and critical study of Hodgson in the following excerpt. First magazine publications of many of Hodgson's short stories and nonfiction articles are cited.*]

The supreme master of imaginative horror in science fiction was William Hope Hodgson and his *tour de force* was the apocalyptic novel ***The Night Land***. . . . (p. 9)

The 200,000 word epic is written in a "seventeenth century style," which William Hope Hodgson may have invented. It is artificial, contrived, repetitious and awkward. The introductory portions are both tedious and absurd as they relate the background of the 17th century storyteller. With the shift to The Last Redoubt in that world at the end of time, that same impossible style succeeds in painting a canvas of that milieu with awesome literary strokes, inspired by imaginative genius. Possibly no other writer has written fiction which succeeds in sustaining a mood of true horror over so long a work as had William Hope Hodgson. The sense of horror never falters, the fascination never slackens, and the subject matter never sickens. (pp. 12-13)

The Night Land is an awkward, sprawling, and in places mawkish novel, but in the words of H. P. Lovecraft: "Allowing for all its faults, it is [yet] one of the most potent pieces of macabre imagination ever written" [see excerpt above, 1927].

The travel of the young hero across the berserk terrain of a world that has forgotten its past and has no tomorrow is an unforgettable odyssey into nightmare. Rarely has an author conveyed to the reader a landscape so alien as that in ***The Night Land.*** This is no grown-up *Wizard of Oz* where the strange encounters thrill, amaze and delight, but never become real. Every obstacle and menace encountered is so ominous and formidable that the reader is never certain for a page that the story will not end in tragedy. (pp. 13-14)

The title of [Hodgson's first] novel was ***The Boats of the "Glen Carrig,"*** written in an 18th century manner that presaged his experiment in writing ***The Night Land*** in a 17th century style. To give the novel the flavor of the 18th century, Hodgson added the lengthy sub-title **"Being an account of their Adventure in the Strange Places of the Earth, after the foundering of the good ship Glen Carrig through striking upon a hidden rock in the unknown seas to the Southward. As told by John Winterstraw, Gent., to his son James Winterstraw, in the year 1757, and by him committed very properly and legibly to manuscript."** It was issued October, 1907. The book was dedicated to Hodgson's mother in the form of ***Madre Mia,*** a poem written by Hodgson. . . . (pp. 47-8)

The novel opens when the crew of the unfortunate Glen Carrig have been five days in their life boats when they sight land. Sailing up a creek, they confront a dreary vista of mud flats, with stagnant pools of water, bereft of life except for a strange group of trees. . . . (p. 48)

In searching for springwater, they find what appears to be a bird growing out of one of the trees, which were themselves as soft as mushrooms. Another tree has its branches wrapped around it and through them there peers a brown human face that was literally part of the trunk. On the other side of the face is a face like a woman's. The bosun begins to cut at the tree, and blood oozes from it and it begins to yowl. All the other trees start to quiver. The great cabbage-like protuberances on the end of the branches turn red and stretch towards the bosun.

The men hack their way back to their boat and row out to sea. (pp. 49-50)

This sequence could very easily be a short story in itself. In fact, it appears that initially Hodgson intended to make his story a sort of an Odyssey, never having written a novel before, but found he had a novelist's capability and did not need the device. (p. 50)

Critical success was immediate. (p. 52)

Literally no unfavorable reviews have yet been discovered. From the beginning William Hope Hodgson was regarded as a literary find, with a craftsmanship that approached genius.

At this very time, the story that was to be his greatest, most reprinted masterpiece, ***The Voice in the Night,*** appeared in the November, 1907 issue of *The Blue Book Magazine*. A ship becalmed in the Northern Pacific is hailed by a man in a small boat rowing towards them. It is night, and there is a mist about, but he will not approach closer if there is any light. He begs for food from the ship for him and "a lady" on a nearby island. He refused to permit himself or the woman to be taken aboard. When food is floated out to him in a box, he takes it and leaves, to return three hours later to tell a bizarre story.

As a young man, he and his fiancee, deserted on a sinking ship after a storm, make their way to an island. There is a ship in the harbor covered with a strange fungus. It grows so persistently that even carbolic cannot keep it away for more than twenty-four hours. The island is covered with it, except for certain stretches of ground where it will not grow. Their food runs out and fish are hard to come by. Odd bits of the fungus begin to grow on them. One day, he catches the woman eating it. Not too long afterward, a huge piece of fungus in roughly human shape detaches itself from the mass and rubs the stuff across his lips. He consumes it in great quantities, almost ecstatically. Day by day he and his fiancee gradually turn into one mound of fungus. They try to slow down the process by eating anything but the grey mass around them. They know they must never return to civilization, because they might infect all mankind.

His story told, there is a dip of the oar and with a "God bless you! Good-bye!" the boat moves away. As it does so, a stray beam from the rising sun is flung across the sea and one of the men aboard the ship writes: "Indistinctly, I saw something nodding between the oars. I thought of a sponge—a great, grey nodding sponge—. The oars continued to play. They were grey—as was the boat—and my eyes searched a moment vainly for the conjunction of hand and oar."

Probably never has such shuddering horror been transmitted in words so gentle, so soft as in this short story. (pp. 53-5)

Almost simultaneous with the publication of ***A Voice in the Night*** appeared one of the most remarkable personal features ever written and photographed by a writer, ***Through the Vortex of a Cyclone.*** While sailing out of San Francisco on the four-masted barque, *Golconda,* in the capacity of Second Mate, William Hope Hodgson, with the cooperation of the First Mate and the Captain, took some of the most extraordinary photographs of a cyclone up to his time. These were night shots, taken no later than 1899, and included superb pictures of stalk lightning, the actual complete funnel of the cyclone itself, waves as high as a seven-story building curving down on the barque, hundreds of tons of water sweeping across the decks, and the vessel dipping almost on its side in mountainous seas, and concluding with a view of the sea the "morning after."

These slides would be the subject of Hodgson lectures for many years, and remained so until the end of his life. (p. 56)

Arising from this extraordinary true experience came a short story that for sublime horror festering out of beauty has rarely been equalled, and for a compassionate insight into the psyche of the veteran seaman expressed in prose of near poetry has been matched only by Dylan Thomas' play *Under the Milk Wood Tree*. That story [is] ***The Shamraken Homeward Bounder***. . . . (pp. 58-9)

[***The House on the Borderland*** was] dedicated "To my father, whose feet have tread the lost aeons," and carried a poem of considerable merit, ***Shoon of the Dark***. . . . (p. 60)

Another poem, ***Grief,*** prefaces the book (this was the only method by which Hodgson, who had poetical aspirations, could get his poems into hardcover during his lifetime) and displays, as do many of his poems, an overwhelming obsession with the methods, rhythms and themes of Edgar Allan Poe. (p. 61)

Again reviewers universally praised the book, their comments typified by the October, 1909 *The Bookman* which spoke of "Mr. Hodgson's wonderful qualities of imagination" [see excerpt above, 1909]. In recent times H. P. Lovecraft called it "Perhaps the greatest of all Mr. Hodgson's works . . . but for a few touches of commonplace sentimentality this book would be a classic of the first water'' [see excerpt above, 1927]. (pp. 65-6)

What H. P. Lovecraft and many others admired most in ***The House on the Borderland*** was the mind-freeing pre-Stapledonian probe into the nature of the cosmos; the concept of two central suns, one dead and the other alive and *intelligent.* This segment, despite its imaginative qualities, is the great weakness of the novel, since it is extraneous. As a separate story it would have been brilliant. Only Hodgson's talent for creating an atmosphere of horror at will, and sustaining it in perfect pitch indefinitely, enabled him to pick up the story after the almost fatal intercession and carry it through to a conclusion. (p. 66)

More important in fastening Hodgson's true attitude towards the sea than any other thing he ever wrote, even his critical articles, was the short story ***Out of the Storm,*** placed in *Putnam's Monthly* for February, 1909, which is so emotionally charged that it almost seems a cry of torment from the author. Though fiction, it is virtually a sequel to ***Through the Vortex of a Cyclone*** published in the same magazine.

The story of the last hours of a sinking ship is received in the laboratory of a scientist on his wireless, from a friend of his transmitting aboard the doomed vessel. The sea is called the ''Thing'' throughout. ''I will expose in all its hideous nakedness, the death-side of the sea,'' the transmitter says. As carnage and death mounts, a crescendo is reached with the statement:

> Oh! God art Thou indeed God? Canst Thou sit above and watch calmly that which I have just seen? Nay! Thou art no God! Thou art weak and puny beside this foul THING which Thou didst create in thy lusty youth. It is now God—and I am one of its children. . . . I ignore God; for there is a stronger than He. My God is here, beside me, around me, and will be soon above me. You know what that means. It is merciless. The sea is now all the God there is! That is one of the things I have learnt.
>
> (pp. 67-8)

This story proved an emotional testament beyond all other evidence. Hodgson, whose literary success would be in a large measure based on the impressions he received at sea, actually hated and feared the waters with an intensity that was the passion of his life. In his stories, poems and articles, nothing but fearsome, loathsome horror arises from the sea. There is not in his entire output a bright, cheerful, positive story of sea life. He hated the sea, he hated ships because they sailed upon the sea, he hated the sailors on those ships (tempered with pity), and at times he hated God because He created the sea!

Yet, it was ironical that despite his obvious hatred of the sea, without the experience he received there he would have been considerably poorer in providing grist for the mill of literary creativity. ***The Ghost Pirates*** . . . was a short novel imbued throughout with the lore of the sea. (pp. 68-9)

The skill with which Hodgson conveys the situation that the ship [in ***The Ghost Pirates***] is obviously caught between dimensions, that she is out of touch with reality, and the strange lights cutting across her bows are normal ships she cannot contact, is superlative. The sense of supernatural begins from the first page and mounts steadily for 45,000 words in what may be the longest sustained masterpiece of a mood of horror in the English language. Most great horror stories are short, because the ability of the author to hold the reader in thrall is understandably finite. Those whose length runs beyond the short story or short novelette usually assemble their facts leisurely and bring them all into focus to form a culmination of horror. Hodgson starts on a high note of terror, never falters, never weakens, never digresses, but holds and amplifies it for the entire length of the short novel. (p. 73)

Because of his proclivity towards horror, Hodgson struck upon the notion of an occult detective. (p. 79)

The cardinal weakness of Hodgson's Carnacki series was an almost total lack of visualization of the main character and a story frame for the introduction of the stories so weak that they can only be construed as deliberate pot boilers. It is only in a few of the stories that Hodgson regains integrity in the heat of narration. . . .

[In] ***The Gateway of the Monster,*** [which] ran in the January, 1910 issue of *The Idler,* Carnacki, a youthful detective who utilizes the camera in all his cases, is called in to solve the mystery of a mansion in which the door to ''The Grey Room'' slams every night, without the aid of any apparent human agency. (p. 80)

There are brief moments of suspenseful writing, and it is a bonafide supernatural story, but obviously an ill-concealed pastiche on the genre.

The House Among the Laurels, which appeared in the February issue, takes place in Western Ireland, and starts off like a legitimate ghost story. It is about an old mansion in which two tramps have died. A man with an entire group of villagers who go to test the spooks find blood dripping from the walls, have their giant mastiff mysteriously killed, and finally call in Carnacki. . . . Candles snuff out as they do in ***The Gateway of the Monster,*** but it all turns out to be caused by a group of men who improvise the effects for causes unknown. By this time, if anyone had the slightest doubt that Hodgson was writing spoofs, the flip lines which interpose the piece destroy all pretense.

The Whistling Room in the March issue had its locale in Ireland, too. A room in an old castle is the source of a strange and frightening whistling sound. . . . The story could have been cast as a very effective supernatural yarn, for some of the scenes are excellently done, but Hodgson jokes it up before and aft, curtailing the impact.

The Horse of the Invisible in the April issue dealt with a man who reproduces the sound of a horse galloping as a supernatural phenomenon to frighten a rival suitor, and then upon the moment when his hoax is discovered, the bizarre hoofbeats occur without any assistance from him. The story had possibilities destroyed by the sleight-of-hand wrap-up of events in a hasty, untidy conclusion. (pp. 81-3)

[In] ***The Searcher of the End House,*** the mystery occurs to Carnacki himself, who is living with his mother in a detached cottage villa on the South Coast. (p. 83)

Again, Hodgson, with the introduction of humor almost, but not quite, destroys the story. (p. 85)

[The] final Carnacki story to appear during Hodgson's lifetime [was] ***The Thing Invisible.*** Carnacki is called in to investigate a haunted chapel on an estate in South Kent, where a butler has been stabbed, but not fatally, with ''a peculiar old dagger.'' It is the dagger which is really ''haunted,'' and it is alleged to stab to death any enemy of the family. Carnacki spends a night in the chapel, with camera and gun, but protected by a coat of armor. The dagger, launched by some invisible agency, almost drives itself through the armor, and sends him streaking, galvanized with fear, from the chapel. He discovers, through a clue in the photograph, that the opening of the chancel gate launches the dagger by mechanical means. It has been preset by the aging owner to protect his late wife's jewels which he keeps hidden in the chapel.

Were it not for the planting of false clues, as a non-supernatural mystery this would be the only one of the series not tainted by cynical humor. Its chief merit rests in the superb suspense which Hodgson invests in Carnacki's night vigil in the chapel. (pp. 89-90)

Briefly, Hodgson ventured back into the Sargasso Sea framework with his short story ***The Thing in the Weeds***. . . . The story is ordinary, compared to the more imaginative plots of other of Hodgson's Sargasso adventures, but the handling, the building of horror, the action, and the writing techniques are little short of superb. (pp. 91-2)

Somewhere, somehow, during 1910 and 1911, Hodgson whipped into final shape the 200,000 words of his epic, ***The Night Land.*** It is possible this novel may have been in the works as far back as 1906. . . . In many . . . letters, notes, and interviews there is no question that in ***The Night Land,*** Hodgson laid his greatest hope of fame. (pp. 93-4)

The Night Land is a difficult book to read because of the insipidness of its opening seventeenth century love sequence, its length and small type. Nevertheless, the reviews were astonishingly favorable and perceptive. *The Bookman* for June, 1912, while aware of its weaknesses . . . still carefully acknowledged its strengths [see excerpt above, 1912]. . . . (p. 95)

If we are to speak only in a technical sense, ***The Boats of the "Glen Carrig"*** is Hodgson's best novel. But skillful and literary as that work is, only another outstanding adventure story would have been lost if it had never been published. ***The Night Land*** is an imaginative achievement, standing uniquely alone. Nothing like it had ever been previously written. Fantastic literature specifically would be unquestionably poorer without it. Hodgson was undoubtedly right in regarding it as his supreme achievement. (p. 97)

Men of the Deep Waters . . . [contains] some of his most superlative short stories—***The Derelict, From the Tideless Sea*** (and its sequel), ***The Voice in the Night, The Mystery of the Derelict,*** and ***The Shamraken Homeward-Bounder***—six of the finest horror classics of the sea in all literature. . . . (p. 112)

His book ***Luck of the Strong*** . . . was predominantly made up of adventure stories . . . but was most notable for the inclusion of ***The Stone Ship***. . . . (pp. 113-14)

All of his life William Hope Hodgson had written poetry, ranging in quality from amateurish to excellent. He managed to slip samples of it into many of his books. As a memorial to him after his death, his wife paid to have two books of verse published by Selwyn & Blount in 1920, ***The Calling of the Sea*** and ***The Voice of the Ocean,*** both in editions of 500.

Two other proposed volumes were *More Deorum and Other Poems* and *Spume*. Virtually all of the poems planned for both those volumes are on the subject of death. (p. 116)

Sam Moskowitz, "William Hope Hodgson" ("William Hope Hodgson," biographical essay, copyright © 1973 by Sam Moskowitz; reprinted by permission of the author), in Out of the Storm: Uncollected Fantasies *by William Hope Hodgson, edited by Sam Moskowitz, Donald M. Grant, Publisher, 1975, pp. 9-118.*

DENNIS WHEATLEY (essay date 1975)

[*Wheatley is a prolific and much-translated author of historical thrillers, spy stories, and novels and nonfiction studies of the occult. His* The Devil and All His Works *is considered "a modern textbook on Satanism" by many critics. Between 1974 and 1977 Wheatley edited the "Dennis Wheatley Library of the Occult" series, which included Hodgson's* Carnacki the Ghost-Finder *and* The Ghost Pirates. *Wheatley's introduction to* The Ghost Pirates *is excerpted below.*]

I have always regarded William Hope Hodgson as one of the great masters of occult fiction. [Hodgson's complete works] run only to ten items—five novels, three books of short stories and two slim volumes of poetry. . . . The poems were about the sea, for which Hope Hodgson clearly had a great love.

The Ghost Pirates, as is indicated by the title, also has the sea as its background. Jessop, who tells the story, is an able seaman on one of those big cutters that used to sail round Cape Horn; but he is a man of some education and has passed his Mate's certificate. That he is a superior type to his shipmates is evidenced by his talks with the other occupants of the fo'cas'le whose manner of speech is a brilliant example of using dialogue to convey character.

When the ship has been for a while at sea, strange things begin to happen. During a night watch Jessop thinks he sees the shadowy form of a man who must have come up out of the sea climbing in over the side of the vessel. Young Tammy, an apprentice, also sees things, and they compare notes. (p. 9)

Rigging begins to go slack unaccountably; and the technical terms used so frequently by Hope Hodgson for the complicated tackle of a sailing ship make it clear that he must have spent a considerable time serving in one himself. That they are correct I happen to know as I spent four years of my youth as a cadet in the old three-decker ship-of-the-line H.M.S. Worcester.

These details, and the speech of the rough seamen, add much to the apparent plausibility of the belief that the ship is in danger of a fate which has overtaken numerous others lost at sea in periods of calm weather, disappearing without trace with all hands.

The Second Mate, a decent fellow, becomes aware that something uncanny is occurring. He, Jessop and Tammy consult together and agree that their fears must be kept from the men in the fo'cas'le. But the hands soon have evidence that supernatural powers are attacking the ship. . . . Mutiny is brewing and the crew demand that the Captain shall put them ashore at the nearest port. But the haunted ship is by then almost surrounded by an impenetrable mist. Would she make it or, sailing blind, be dashed to pieces on a rocky coast?

This is a unique story magnificently told. (p. 11)

Dennis Wheatley, "Introduction" (introduction copyright © Dennis Wheatley 1975), in The Ghost Pirates *by William Hope Hodgson, Sphere Books Limited, 1975, pp. 9-11.*

ADDITIONAL BIBLIOGRAPHY

Derleth, August. Foreword to *Men of the Deep Waters,* by William Hope Hodgson, pp. ix-x. Sauk City, Wis.: Arkham House, 1967.

Finds that Hodgson was singularly successful in "evoking the horror and terror of the sea."

Everts, R. Alain. "Some Facts in the Case of William Hope Hodgson: Master of Phantasy, Parts 1 and 2." *Shadow* 3, Nos. 2 and 3 (April, October 1973): 4-11; 7-13.

Noncritical biographical essay employing information gathered from Hodgson's relatives.

Lewis, C. S. "On Science Fiction." In his *On Stories, and Other Essays on Literature,* pp. 55-68. New York: Harcourt Brace Jovanovich, 1982.*

Originally delivered as a lecture at the Cambridge University English Club on 24 November 1955. Lewis praises "the unforgettable sombre splendour of the images" presented in *The Night Land,* but finds the novel is "disfigured by a sentimental and irrelevant erotic interest and by a foolish, and flat archaism of style." The "attempt at archaic language" is also disparaged by H. P. Lovecraft (see excerpt above, 1927).

Sullivan, Jack. "Psychological, Antiquarian, and Cosmic Horror: 1872-1919." In *Horror Literature: A Core Collection and Reference Guide,* edited by Marshall B. Tymn, pp. 230-75. New York: R. R. Bowker, 1981.*

Discusses Hodgson's short stories organized around his Sargasso Sea mythos, finding them to have "superb atmosphere and memorable comic touches." Sullivan also briefly discusses the Carnacki stories and Hodgson's four novels.

Tremayne, Peter. "William Hope Hodgson: His Life and Work." In *Masters of Terror, Volume One: William Hope Hodgson,* edited by Peter Tremayne, pp. 7-14. London: Corgi Books, 1977.

Biographical and critical introduction, including a brief account of Hodgson's life and publication history as well as critical comments about his works.

Ricarda (Octavia) Huch

1864-1947

(Also wrote under pseudonyms of Richard Hugo and R. I. Carda) German novelist, historian, essayist, critic, short story and novella writer, biographer, poet, autobiographer, and dramatist.

Distinguished for her work in many genres, Huch is considered Germany's foremost woman writer of the first half of the twentieth century. While many of her contemporaries followed the literary trend of Naturalism, she adhered to aesthetic principles consistent with Romanticism, combining a poetic sensitivity with lucid prose to create her distinctive style. Today, Huch is best known for her romantic historical novels, which skillfully and imaginatively recreate a panorama of historical events, and for her erudite studies of German history and literature.

The Granger Collection, New York

A native of Brunswick, Huch was among the progeny of an artistically talented patrician family. She was encouraged to pursue a variety of intellectual interests and began writing lyric poetry as a youth. One of the few German women of her generation to attend college, Huch studied history and philosophy at the University of Zurich, Switzerland, because her own country did not allow female university students. Her fond recollections of these student days are recorded in *Frühling in der Schweiz.* In 1892 Huch obtained a doctoral degree in history and worked for several years as a library archivist, then as a schoolteacher. During this time she also published her first volume of poetry, her first novel, and several short stories. Huch was married and divorced twice. With her first husband, an Italian dentist, she lived in the slums of Trieste, which was then part of Austria. There, Huch gathered the experiences which inspired her novel about tenement life, *Aus der Triumphgasse: Lebensskizzen.* Her second marriage was to her cousin Richard Huch, a lawyer. Some critics believe that although their marriage failed, their lifelong love was the inspiration for one of Huch's most popular novels, *Erinnerungen von Ludolf Ursleu dem Jüngeren (Eros Invincible).* Shortly after the turn of the century, as Europe's political strife worsened and war appeared imminent, Huch turned her attention to history. Thereafter she spent the major portion of her career searching the past for moral and philosophical answers that would help to explain the two catastrophic world wars. During the Nazi regime, Huch openly defied National Socialism and resigned her seat in the Academy of Prussian Writers rather than join the newly formed, propagandist Nazi Academy of Writers. Throughout her long career Huch was honored with numerous awards, including honorary degrees, a special citation from the Italian government for her works on Italian history, and, in 1931, the Goethe Prize of Frankfurt.

Critics often divide Huch's literary career into three overlapping phases. The earliest of these periods, occurring in the last decade of the nineteenth century, is characterized by highly imaginative romantic fiction that is often centered around an unconventional passionate love that exceeds human understanding. One of her most important works of this period is *Eros Invincible.* Safely sequestered in a monastery, the narrator, Ludolf Ursleu, relates the decay of his Hanseatic patrician family, whose members sought beauty and love in a world of tragic events and conflicting codes of morality. Favorably compared to classic Greek tragedy, *Eros Invincible* forcefully depicts the ill-fated destinies of its characters, while conveying a profound psychological understanding of their often irrational behavior. With *Aus der Triumph gasse,* set in the slums of Trieste, Huch created a romantic work similar to *Eros Invincible* in its affirmation of life. Critics generally praise Huch for her skillful blend of realistic elements in *Aus der Triumphgasse*—such as her description of the city's squalor—with the work's romantic, sometimes mystical qualities. In addition to her novels, she also wrote numerous short stories, which are collected in *Fra Celeste und andere Erzählungen.* Most critics agree that these works contain some of her best fictional writing and that they demonstrate her proficiency for depicting the mundane aspects of life, often in a humorously ironic manner. Huch's artistry in short fiction is often compared to that of the acknowledged Swiss masters of the short story, Gottfried Keller and Conrad Ferdinand Meyer. During this first literary phase, Huch also wrote *Blütezeit der Romantik* and *Ausbreitung und Verfall der Romantik,* two important volumes of criticism and essays on the history of German Romanticism. These two collections helped establish Huch's reputation as a leading literary academician.

The major works in the middle period of Huch's career explore the historical past in pursuit of an ideal heroism—one that

will reaffirm life in the modern world. The two historical novels, *Die Verteidigung Roms (Defeat)* and *Der Kampf um Rom (Victory)*, published together as *Die Geschichten von Garibaldi (Garibaldi and the New Italy)*, are the best known works of this period. Together they recount the heroic efforts of the Italian patriot Giuseppe Garibaldi to unify the Italian government during the nineteenth century. *Garibaldi and the New Italy* combines history, biography, and fiction to provide a creative, yet accurate account of historical events. Some commentators consider Huch's portrayal of Garibaldi an attempt to create the ideal heroic man, similar to Friedrich Nietzsche's "superman." However, detractors of the two novels maintain that Huch's aggrandizement of Garibaldi overlooks his human passions and foibles, making the patriot a somewhat one-dimensional character by idealizing him. In her trilogy, *Der grosse Krieg in Deutschland,* Huch again combines history and fiction—this time, to chronicle the Thirty Years' War. Although the work adheres to historical detail in a moderately dry, textbook-like manner, it is generally praised for its realistic representation of a society in turmoil, as well as for its philosophical examination of the forces behind the upheaval.

For the most part, Huch devoted the last period of her career to writing nonfictional studies of German history and philosophical essays that conveyed her newly-formed commitment to Lutheran Protestantism. The significant works of this creative phase include *Luthers Glaube: Briefe an einen Freund* and *Entpersönlichung*. The former work, a collection of essays on the religious leader and thinker Martin Luther, is based on Huch's affirmation of Luther's doctrines, while the latter work provides an interpretation of human moral development founded on Huch's analysis of her own character. One of her last literary projects—left unfinished at her death, but later completed as *Der lautlose Aufstand* by Günther Weisenborn—is a series of biographical studies of the German resistance fighters of World War II. This anti-Nazi work expressed Huch's deep love of her homeland, and upon its publication served to increase her reputation as one of Germany's most fervent patriots.

Huch made a significant contribution to German literature. Her romantic fiction served as an influential force in the German Neoromantic movement at the turn of the century, while her essays and criticism reinterpreted the important historical and cultural events of her homeland. In his estimation of Huch's literary artistry, Richard Friedenthal states: "Ricarda Huch may not be read as widely as others are read; she will never be the darling of the lending libraries, or the idol of a school. But she will stand out in the history of German literature, and German cultural history, as a great artist, a strongly personal mind, and as a 'fearless heart'."

(See also *Contemporary Authors,* Vol. 111.)

PRINCIPAL WORKS

Gedichte [as Richard Hugo] (poetry) 1891
Erinnerungen von Ludolf Ursleu dem Jüngeren (novel) 1893
[*Recollections of Ludolf Ursleu the Younger* (abridged edition), 1913-15; also published as *Eros Invincible,* 1931]
Der Mondreigen von Schlaraffis (novella) 1896
Teufeleien (novellas) 1897
Der arme Heinrich (novella) 1899
**Blütezeit der Romantik* (essays and criticism) 1899
Fra Celeste und andere Erzählungen (short stories) 1899
**Ausbreitung und Verfall der Romantik* (essays and criticism) 1902
Aus der Triumphgasse: Lebensskizzen (novel) 1902
Vita somnium breve (novel) 1903; also published as *Michael Unger,* 1909
Von den Königen und der Krone (novel) 1904
Das Judengrab (novella) 1905
***Die Geschichten von Garibaldi.* 2 vols. (novels) 1906-07
[*Garibaldi and the New Italy,* 1928-29]
Der letzte Sommer (novella) 1910
Der grosse Krieg in Deutschland. 3 vols. (novels) 1912-14
Luthers Glaube: Briefe an einen Freund (essays and criticism) 1916
Der Fall Deruga (novel) 1917
[*The Deruga Trial,* 1929]
Entpersönlichung (essays) 1921
Alte und neue Götter (1848): Die Revolution des neunzehnten Jahrunderstsin in Deutschland (history) 1930
Früling in der Schweiz (memoirs) 1938
Herbstfeuer (poetry) 1944
****Der lautlose Aufstand* (biographies) 1953
Gesammelte Schriften (essays, speeches, and autobiography) 1965
Gesammelte Werke. 11 vols. (novels, short stories, novellas, histories, poetry, speeches, essays, and autobiography) 1966-74

*These works were published as *Die Romantik* in 1908.

**This work includes the novels *Die Verteidigung Roms (Defeat)* and *Der Kampf um Rom (Victory).*

***This work was completed by Günther Weisenborn.

OTTO HELLER (essay date 1905)

[*In the following excerpt, Heller discusses the artistry of Huch's novels* Recollections of Ludolf Ursleu the Younger *and* Aus der Triumphgasse.]

It detracts in no wise from the marvelous originality of [Ricarda Huch's] art that it has been influenced by Gottfried Keller and Conrad Ferdinand Meyer, and that it, too, has been electrified by a spark from Nietzsche's wayward genius. The last-mentioned influence is recognized in her favorite heroes. They are the *Lebenskünstler,* the past masters of the art of living, modern Renaissance men and women with a capacity for translating great emotions into action. Huch, at the age of thirty-eight, is the author of fifteen books comprising two metrical plays, two collections of critical essays, a historical study, a book of poems, and nine volumes of fiction. All of these are works of intrinsic value. Her chief title to fame, however, still reposes on ***Erinnerungen von Ludolf Ursleu dem Jüngeren* ("Recollections of Ludolf Ursleu the Younger")**, a book full of the indefinable charm exhaled only by what the French call *une œuvre de longue haleine* [a work requiring time and labor]; one of those rare books, that is to say, which draw the reader into the very mood in which they were conceived and sustain him in it. The novelist whose unerring art has given him supreme power of this sort is Thackeray. By virtue of their temperamental consistency, *Pendennis, Henry Esmond, The Newcomes,* are unsurpassable models. Du Maurier's *Trilby* owes its unquestionable value to close and successful study of those great models. Among living writers, Pierre Loti and Maurice Maeterlinck, by an almost hypnotic power, communicate to the reader their own minor-key temper of mind. Ricarda Huch attains similar effects without the aid of chiaroscuro. At least in ***Ursleu*** and ***Aus der Triumphgasse*** (**"Stories from Triumph Lane"**) she draws in the broad light of her own day. As a rule, however, she makes the color perfection of her picture stand forth more distinctly by incasing it in an artistic frame of chaste design. It is no easy matter to adapt, as Huch has done, the style of an old chronicle to a recital of contemporaneous events. But Huch's vigorous art does not choose the line of least resistance. Altogether she compels the highest admiration for her firm conscientiousness in squaring herself with technical difficulties and exacting from herself heroic tasks. It is characteristic, perhaps, that her most ambitious works are by far her best. Whereas the short stories fall appreciably below the high standard by which her superlative art deserves to be marked, her two master novels, by virtue of their flawless structure, excel even Keller's famous *Der grüne Heinrich* ("Green Henry") and take elevated rank with the lofty achievement of Conrad Ferdinand Meyer's imperishable prose epics.

The **"Memories of Ursleu"** purports to be written in cloistered solitude by the sole representative of a headstrong race whose members, notwithstanding their imperious vital instincts, are doomed to self-destruction by their unbending will. In the unraveling of the plot a most skillful use is made of episode, for the double purpose of enlarging the historical vista and, at the same time, making the private tragedy stand out in bold relief against the general calamity. The action passes in the republic of Hamburg during the cholera epidemic of less than twenty years ago. The plague is not broadly pictured as in Manzoni's *I Promessi Sposi;* rather with the delicate discretion used by Boccaccio in the framing of the *Decamerone*. The "Band of the Holy Life," into which young patricians of both sexes form themselves in order to vindicate amid the surrounding horrors of death the joy of living, serves as a symbol for the chief tenet in Ricarda Huch's philosophy: life is not worth living without the illusions; hence let us cling to the illusions. No need of saying that Ricarda Huch is not a "realist" in the pedantic acceptation of the term. Yet she knows well how to reproduce the *milieu* of the patrician life as well as—in ***Aus der Triumphgasse***—of the slums; and she possesses the highest credential of her art—style. *Le style c'est*—this time—*la femme!* (pp. 287-90)

Otto Heller, "Women Writers of the Twentieth Century," in his Studies in Modern German Literature: Sudermann, Hauptmann, Women Writers of the Nineteenth Century, *Ginn & Company, 1905 (and reprinted by Books for Libraries Press, 1967; distributed by Arno Press, Inc.), pp. 229-95.**

THE AMERICAN REVIEW OF REVIEWS (essay date 1914)

[*In the following excerpt from* The American Review of Reviews, *a journal devoted to synopses of European book reviews, a critical essay in German by Hans Bethge is drawn upon to provide an overview of Huch's career.*]

One of the questions being mooted just now is whether the immediate effect of war upon literature is vivifying or deadening. Will Ricarda Huch, for example, who is rated by both critics and by readers as the most distinguished woman romance writer of Germany, be inspired by the present conflict to make literary use of it as she has of struggles more remote, as in her well-known work, **"The Great German War"**? . . .

Ricarda Huch was the subject of a glowingly enthusiastic sketch in a recent number of *Der Greif* (Stuttgart), by Dr. Hans Bethge, who declares her to be the most important woman writer who has appeared in Germany since the days of the Romantics. . . .

Her first work was **"Evoe,"** a drama of the Italian Renaissance, said to be less a drama than a character picture of the time in dramatic form. It is a mixture of verse and prose, and the speech of the characters is reminiscent of that of Shakespeare's. Shortly afterward her first romance appeared, "the marvelous book, **'Memories of Ludolf Urslev the Younger,'**" which placed her at once in the first rank of living novelists. This work . . . is still considered her finest achievement. . . .

This great novel was followed by some collections of short stories or narratives, in which romance and reality are mingled with much charm, and by a volume of graceful poems, including the most various forms, odes, sonnets, distiches, quatrains, *terzinae*. (p. 751)

Dr. Bethge considers, however, that the lyric accent of Ricarda Huch's narrative prose is more individual and significant than that of her poetry. He finds this quality marked particularly in her second great novel, **"From Out the Street of Triumph,"** which appeared eight years after **"Ludolf Urslev."** He calls it "a profound song of the obscurity of life and death, a mighty melody wherein we catch dread whispers of time and of eternity. . . . In this book occur all the horrors we can conceive of, but they are shown, not in the violent colors customary to romance, but from the view-point of that which is natural, necessary, and humanly obvious; . . . children are murdered, people fall victims to dreadful diseases and death, without the reader's being greatly astonished. . . . Life, which is pitiless, bears all these things in its train."

Like **"Ludolf Urslev"** this book has the narrative form, the story being related by a man whose own life is but slightly connected with it. The location is presumably Trieste. The plot is deeply tragic, the central figure being an old woman, Farfalla, "in whom the practical philosophy of poverty is embodied; a woman who knows all the bitterness of existence and is filled with a gray resignation." The book is said to display an astonishing variety of figures, characters, and types. The critic calls it "an inexhaustible book, which only unremitting labor and love, plus the powers of a genius, could have brought forth." A third novel, **"Vita Somnium Breve,"** appeared a year later, and still later the novels, **"Of Kings and Crowns"** and **"The Conquest of Rome."** The latter is the first of a trilogy built about the figure of Garibaldi. . . .

These words were written before the outbreak of the Great War, and we can but wonder whether the delicate and sensitive instrument of this woman's mind and heart will be able to weave some solemn and significant harmony from the soul-shattering discords which are now rending the very heavens. Only a genius of the first order can cope with such a theme. (p. 752)

"Germany's Greatest Woman Novelist," in The American Review of Reviews, *Vol. L, No. 6, December, 1914, pp. 751-52.*

RUTH SUCKOW (essay date 1928)

[*Suckow discusses* Defeat *as a "representative novel of the classicist ideal in German fiction."*]

"Defeat" might well be chosen as the most thoroughly representative novel of the classicist ideal in German fiction today. The German method of large design and exhaustive treatment, revealed and explained most beautifully by Thomas Mann, is clearly apparent, for Ricarda Huch has taken as her subject the struggle for Italian liberty, and **"Defeat,"** dealing with the leadership and flight of Garibaldi, is followed by **"Victory,"** a story of Solferino. But the character of the design is plainly that of the thorough-going classicist. In fact, this novel, with its largeness of outline and multitude of characters, is much like one of those great battle pieces of painting—grouped men, dying heroes, noble leader and flag over all. Dignity it certainly possesses, dignity of intention and of manner in a certain stern purity of language and what Ludwig Lewisohn has described as an "atmosphere of frugal beauty;" and the simplicity of its ending leaves an effect of nobility. But compared to the historical method of the Norwegian Sigrid Undset, with whom inevitably the German writer *has* been compared, to those novels hot with the immediacy and intensity of intimate human passions to which so-called historical events are only a background, the effect of **"Defeat"** is cold, external and aloof. The noble speeches of the leaders, the deaths of the soldiers, striking a note of exaltation at their best, too frequently have the ring of the patriotic history text for school children. Ricarda Huch executes her epic design with both power and precision; but **"Defeat"** is a novel which commands respect rather than the immediacy of delight. (p. 1255)

Ruth Suckow, "Contemporary German Novels," in The Outlook, *November 28, 1928, pp. 1255-56.**

CLIFTON P. FADIMAN (essay date 1928)

[Fadiman became one of the most prominent American literary critics during the 1930s with his insightful and often caustic book reviews for The Nation *and* The New Yorker *magazines. He also reached a sizeable audience through his work as a radio talk-show host from 1938 to 1948. In the following excerpt, Fadiman notes his objections to Huch's novel about Giuseppe Garibaldi,* Defeat.]

While Ricarda Huch is, as a literary craftswoman, infinitely superior to the purpureal [Stephan] Zeromski, her outlook on the past is at bottom no more moving than his. **"Defeat"** is concerned with Garibaldi's defense of Rome and his ignominious withdrawal before the forces of France in 1849. If [Zeromski's] "Ashes" is chaotic melodrama, **"Defeat"** is a heroic pageant, conceived in Carlylean terms. Confronted with Italy, Ricarda Huch seems to have undergone the same process of mental softening that is observable in her countrymen, Goethe and Winckelmann. When a German crosses the Alps his capacity for detached reflection seems abruptly to desert him and his emotions immediately register high pressure. If there is any political movement that cries out for the judgment of an ironic mind it is the Risorgimento; and if there are any two national heroes who combine the qualities of courage and idealism with those of absurd grandiloquence and sentimental quixotism, they are Garibaldi and Mazzini. But Ricarda Huch remains true to an expiring tradition: Garibaldi and Mazzini are stuck to their pedestals with a heavy Teutonic glue and introduced to us as if they were Achilles and Odysseus. The result of this posturing is comic opera rendered all the more ludicrous by the author's unswerving admiration of her heroes even in their most undignified moments. Ricarda Huch's great historical knowledge and her grave and marmoreal prose cannot atone for her lack of humor and insight. (pp. 692-93)

Clifton P. Fadiman, "Fiction from History," in The Nation, *Vol. CXXVII, No. 3311, December 19, 1928, pp. 692-93.**

EUGENE LOHRKE (essay date 1929)

[Lohrke maintains that, in Victory, *Huch fails to probe the true character of her subject, Giuseppe Garibaldi, and thus presents a narrow, romanticized view of the Italian liberator. He considers Huch's allegiance to Romanticism outdated and the major fault of most of her works.]*

[**"Victory"** the] second volume of Ricarda Huch's study of Garibaldi and the *risorgimento* is, like the first, a series of sketches rather than a painting; a chronicle rather than a novel. It shows a masterful grasp on fact and background, a technique in which the dramatic is given its full value, and an appreciation of the colorful incident. Its aim is to recreate an era; its effect is peculiarly negative.

Many of the defects in Ricarda Huch's two-volume work are characteristic of the movement which she represents. The romantic movement in German literature which passed into its decline in the early years of the nineteenth century, has had sporadic revivals as late as the twentieth. Frau Huch's romanticism fell in the chilly dawn of a new era when the writings of Sudermann and Hauptmann had definitely announced the end of Germany's age of literary innocence. Her attempts to refurbish her narratives with the gallantries of a studied method have a peculiarly dry and evasive quality, like the rustle of autumn leaves over a tomb. Her flourishes and resounding periods are most of all effective as literary exercises; her characterizations are flat; her heroes are foreshortened of even their human significance by her very strenuous effort to set them on a pedestal.

One does not seek to quarrel here with the romantic movement or to dismiss it as any less trivial than the realistic. They are reverse sides of the same coin, which, for the novelist's purposes is or should be, life. But romanticism, by implication as well as definition, must remain the flower of a literature in its youth, of minds groping blindly through encompassing hazes to just as blinding sunlight. In later life it is too much akin to gilding a lilly which is no longer very fragrant. As long as men are human they will be romantic—the present childish faith in science is ample testimony to that. But as long as writers strive to preserve the limitations imposed on them by schools and credos that have been outmoded, they will be dry. And Ricarda Huch's work belongs to an era when externals were first of all important; when gestures flourished and when no one paid any undue attention to what you said as long as you put it nicely.

"Defeat" and **"Victory"** both deal with the career of Garibaldi, the Liberator. They take under consideration two phases of the Italian struggle for unity, in both of which Garibaldi was an active agent. . . .

It is only by reading between the lines of her glowing ineptitudes that one can arrive at an estimate of the man, Garibaldi, and his contributions to Italian unity. Plainly, as Frau Huch says, he was misunderstood. Cavour distrusted him, yet Cavour was clever enough to see that this distrust was not evoked by any blemish in the character of Garibaldi, but by the fact that Garibaldi so plainly misunderstood the world. He was a hero, but there is one side to heroism that is folly, and this Cavour understood. If Frau Huch had made any attempt to understand it we should have had a more sympathetic and penetrating realization of the character of the liberator.

As it is, he is praised in this book, crowned with laurel, saddened but never wisened. The spell of Italy and the past has exercised too vivid a grip on the imagination of the author of **"Defeat"** and **"Victory."** To the sensitive student it is the most powerful glamour that the world provides, for, like an autumn garden, Italy is most of all fragrant of the past. But the aim of the romanticist to set the past on one side of a mountain and the present on the other, is as arid and unfruitful as it is untrue. To the historical novelist as to the historian himself, the present is the only safe index to the past, since the present is the only actuality he knows, and only by knowing the world they live in can men come to discern the truth as apart from the glamour of worlds where other men have lived.

Thus the character of Garibaldi still remains to be created from the solid masonry of fact and the superlative adornment of praise which Ricarda Huch has erected in her two studied books. Her work is monumental—and that is all.

Eugene Lohrke, "Making a Hero Too Heroic," in New York Herald Tribune Books *(© I.H.T. Corporation; reprinted by permission), January 13, 1929, p. 2.*

WILL CUPPY (essay date 1929)

[*Cuppy, who frequently reviewed mystery fiction for the* New York Herald Tribune, *examines Huch's mystery novel* The Deruga Trial.]

In which an eminent author proves herself a slick hand at the kind of detective novel that is probably worthiest in the eyes of Apollo: the tale dealing literately with recognizable humans at a significant crisis, instead of with robots having fits. Whether or not they do these things better in Germany—and they probably do not—it seems fairly clear that **"The Deruga Trial"** is miles ahead of most mysteries on almost any count, a contender for this summer's honors and an engaging novelty for anybody's money.

One's enthusiasm for Ricarda Huch's book is doubtless due, in part, to its almost complete lack of conventional mystery tricks and the absence of that fashionable ingenuity which can bore much more than downright drabness. Ingenious the story is in its larger outlines, but the author depends upon more permanent values—chiefly characterization—to sustain interest in her running account of Dr. Deruga's trial for wife murder. It is with no desire to outlaw such semi-occasionally thrilling items as pearl necklaces, secret passages and haunted teeth that this department recommends the work—but for a change it should be warmly welcomed even by the fanciers of the manic-depressive school.

Will Cuppy, in a review of "The Deruga Trial," in New York Herald Tribune Books *(© I.H.T. Corporation; reprinted by permission), August 11, 1929, p. 11.*

WILLIAM A. DRAKE (essay date 1931)

[*An author and editor, Drake rendered the 1931 translation,* Eros Invincible, *of Huch's first novel,* Erinnerungen von Ludolf Ursleu dem Jüngeren. *In the following excerpt, taken from his introduction to* Eros Invincible, *he appraises Huch's artistic employment of romanticism and offers a concise discussion of the work's plot.*]

[In ***Eros Invincible***] Ricarda Huch, whose spirit is so utterly Greek that her Protestantism merely lends a piquancy to the anachronism, conceives the immortal passion. The present volume contains such a theme as would have served Euripides for a masterpiece. It is a frantic passion that it describes, ruinous and unreasonable, fated to despair, desolating alike to the innocent and to the guilty. Such a love is a conception wholly in the spirit of the past; afar one hears the hoof-beats of the joyous, pitiless goat-god. It has no place in an era whose human relationships are based on calculated whim or rational advantage. Yet, Ricarda Huch does not judge it; she merely records its phenomenal passage, with austere impartiality and reserve.

In ***Entpersönlichung,*** the ingenious semi-philosophical essay which she has provided as a sort of key to her art, Ricarda Huch attempts to explain the enigma of the human personality as it presents itself to her, by showing how the individual is capable, so to speak, of disintegrating his moral structure and reassembling it, in a new and higher arrangement, under the katalysis of a powerful emotional experience or conviction. The essence of Frau Huch's art is in this formula. It is by such analysis that she describes, in her biographical works, the precipitation of genius in the careers of Giuseppe Garibaldi, Federigo Confalonieri, Martin Luther and Mihail Bakunin in spiritual situations comparable to those at which, in her fiction, the characters of Galeide and Ezard Ursleu, Michael Unger and Rosa Sarthorn in ***Vita Somnium Breve,*** Farfalla in ***Aus der Triumphgasse*** and the pathetic Lastari in ***Von den Königen und der Krone*** become artistically significant.

In the art of Ricarda Huch, impartiality approaches a semblance of impassivity; yet we know that she is not impassive, for although the line of her narrative is as unmoved and chaste as a formal report in Heaven upon the doings of a tiresome and contemptible universe, the warm human and ethical sympathies which the artist in her so sternly and rightly represses vibrate behind everything she writes. But she does not fall into the common error of attempting to explain that complex and unfathomable net of contradictions which is the human personality; still less, the tremendous and violent chemistry of human love. (pp. v-vii)

Neither does she attempt to remedy the sad state of things by pointing a moral to her desolate tale; and in this she is unique and heroic. Instead, she dares to glorify a love that is absolutely contrary to all the conventions of man and the persuasions of right reason and to bless those tormented, triumphant lovers "whom one concedes to be right, on whose side one places oneself for no other reason than that Destiny and Nature are on their side."

In the novels of Ricarda Huch, romanticism is assigned to its true employment as an artistic instrument. By its means, the distance between the artist and the theme is so increased as to permit of a comprehensive focus; sharper juxtapositions of the characters are effected, and a veil of fantasy cast over their actions through which the truth becomes more lucid than by any less subtle candor. Thus, beyond the pure romanticism of the plot of the present novel motivating the otherwise strained and incredible gravitations of its characters, we surmise a revelation as deep and mystical as that of Hauptmann's *Der Ketzer von Soana*. Here the monk Ludolf looks back on the panorama of the life he has renounced and although he says: "Be still, my soul, it is past!" the eddies of that dead life, of which he was only a passive spectator, still have the power to reach, trouble and allure him in his Swiss cloister. . . . The words of Sir Walter Raleigh might well stand beneath the colophon of this remarkable book: "O eloquent, just and noble death, whom none could convince, thou hast persuaded!"

This dark tale, so fantastic in its external outlines, is told with a force of emotional emphasis and a subtle architecture of tragic climaxes which compel acquiescence. We are shown characters as "rapt" as Hamlet or Elektra, Klytemnestra or Medea; and we believe in their rapture, not because it is explained, but because it is asserted with imperious conviction. We follow them unquestioning upon their involuntary courses to heaven and hell, because we perceive in their reluctant steps the same inscrutable compulsion which led the Dionysian protagonists on their bloody paths.

And no less omnipotent does this same destiny appear when, elsewhere in Ricarda Huch's fictions, it is completed in the meaner streets of Trieste. In ***Aus der Triumphgasse*** Frau Huch relates the tragedies of a dozen lives which share the squalor of the little street which lends the book its name. Old, wrinkled Farfalla, who drags out her wretched existence so that she may protect her crippled son Riccardo; nor the broken dreamer Riccardo himself; nor the pathetic Antoinetta, who flings her long cherished chastity at the vilest beast of the alley and then dies—these are not the protagonists of this gray narrative. The protagonist is black poverty, the destiny none of these unhappy victims can escape, which, the more bravely they seek to elude its fang, thrusts them the deeper into their misery. Exactly thus, in the narrative of Ludolf Ursleu, the true protagonist is not Galeide or Ezard, but the invincible and persuasive Eros who anciently prepared his maddening feasts not in his marble temples but in the groves without.

Among the woman writers of our epoch, Ricarda Huch easily maintains an altogether unique eminence. She—for she is a seasoned veteran at her craft—was the first considerable novelist of her sex to apprehend and convert to artistic purposes the tremendous resources of the feminine sensibility. When the ***Erinnerungen von Ludolf Ursleu dem Jüngeren*** first appeared, the critics found it incredible that such a novel should have been written by a woman; to us it would seem astounding if any but a woman had written it. ***Eros Invincible*** has been a tremendous success in its time: a classic from its inception. To contemporary German fiction it is what *Of Human Bondage* is to us, or better still, since the dates are more consonant, what *Jude the Obscure* was to our fathers and what it is to us today. As we read it now in its new form, we observe again its extraordinary vitality, its overwhelming majesty and power, the singular clairvoyance of its author in surmising the deepest impulses of lacerated hearts made luminous by the magic of inscrutable passions. To read ***Eros Invincible*** as it must be read—slowly, quietly, savoring each implication to the full—is to know what a tremendous experience a novel can be.

In all the writings of Ricarda Huch, beyond the obvious trappings of romantic situation and treatment, there is an apprehension of something deeper and higher than life itself, which is indeed immanent in life, but which has nothing to do with normal reality. This mysterious presence we have known in German Romanticism since the time of Hoffmann, but it probably has never been so completely—one may say, so systematically—developed as in the novels of Ricarda Huch. It is an intangible quality, yet one both vital and exalted, which lends her fiction the breadth and suggestiveness of poetry and the conviction of Greek tragedy. The last of the great Romantics, the latest survivor of the school of Hoffmann, Tieck and Keller, Ricarda Huch has extended the limits of romantic art into the realm of emotional plausibility, and has devoted it to the vindication of man's infinities. (pp. vii-xi)

William A. Drake, in an introduction to Eros Invincible *by Ricarda Huch, translated by William A. Drake, The Macaulay Company, 1931, pp. v-xi.*

ANGEL FLORES (essay date 1931)

[*In the following excerpt, Flores presents a laudatory appraisal of Huch's most popular work of fiction,* Eros Invincible.]

The heroes and agonists of Greek tragedy were prompted and guided by Fate, a force vaguely called moira, and later known under different names by the Christian and Arabic worlds. Spain almost succumbed under its power, for the Christian-Moorish currents met there and eddied into a devastating maelstrom. Thus the voice of Fate rings in the most serious pages of Spanish literature and in the almost incomprehensible utterances of her mystics. Later, during the French symbolist movement, Fate was converted into a literary formula: Maeterlinck was the high priest and chemist. Only in England, in the novels of Hardy and "The Dynasts" and now in the pages of the German novelist Ricarda Huch, one is able to discern the pristine meaning and inexorable force of Fate and the extrahuman significance of love, of Eros invincible. Ricarda Huch's work stands near the world of Aeschylus and Hardy, not merely for its thematic approximation but because it is intensely alive and contains a dramatic essence extracted from dolorous fibers and lacerating visions. . . .

Ricarda Huch's work is much more than a love story; it is a careful study of a family, of an interesting group tragically disintegrated by Fate. Death hovers over the entire canvas and casts its shadow on most of the characters. However, **"Eros Invincible"** is not one of those lachrymose films imported from Germany (excellent market for very good—and very vile—films), nor one of those well written, morbidly depressing novels (remember Jakob Schaffner's "The Wisdom of Love") so much in fashion among the German literary vanguard. Ricarda Huch's despair is profound, sincere; the dark wind blows from a remote, cosmic source. Even secondary characters, like Flore Lelallen and Gaspard Leroy, are fraught with ultra human radiance, and the Galeide-Exard romance swings amid the classic legends of ancient times, amid the Paolos and Francescas, the Tristans and Isoldes, with uncanny grandeur and majesty.

Angel Flores, "A Tragedy of Love," in New York Herald Tribune Books *(© I.H.T. Corporation; reprinted by permission), March 1, 1931, p. 2.*

THE SATURDAY REVIEW OF LITERATURE **(essay date 1931)**

[*The following excerpt is a review of Huch's collection of historical essays,* Alte und neue Götter.]

[Frau Ricarda Huch's] reputation was really made by her two works on the German Romantic Movement, the **"Blützeit der Romantik,"** and **"Ausbreitung und Verfall der Romantik,"** . . . by her still incomplete prose-epic of the Italian Risorgimento, and by her great historical picture of Germany in the time of the Thirty Years War, the volume entitled **"Der Grosse Krieg und Deutschland,"** which appeared only two years before Germany was engaged in a far greater war than that of which the historian treated. With this book Ricarda Huch's reputation was firmly established, and although a German critic of that time was rather beside the mark in prophesying that her style was of the kind that would prevail in 1920—he did not forsee the rise of Expressionism—he might have added with truth that by that year Ricarda Huch's standing in German literature, already considerable, would be even higher. Now, with her latest work, [**"Alte und Neue Götter,"**] and her reception of the Goethe Prize, she has been acclaimed by the German reviews as one of the foremost living German writers, and in any case the most notable of German women writers of today, numerous though the competent women writers of contemporary Germany are.

A few years ago, after the war, Ricarda Huch wrote a little volume of essays entitled **"Entpersönlichung"**; it dealt with the "de-personalisation" of modern social and political life. At about the same time she wrote a study of the anarchist, Michael Bakunin, in contrast to Karl Marx. Both writings showed her personal point of view, that of the liberal individualist. The rigid centralization that seemed to be the direction in which modern politics were moving filled her with misgiving, and it is no surprise to us to learn that at a very early age she, in sympathy with her mother, conceived a dislike and suspicion of Bismarck. In this latest work of hers, a series of sketches of German politicians from Stein to Bismarck, her early antipathy and her personal political sympathies are easily to be described. **"Alte und Neue Götter"** is, in effect, a brilliant personal study of the forces that influenced the development of Germany after the Napoleonic Wars until the war of 1870. It should not be inferred that the writer has written a thesis; she has no particular case to prove against Bismarck and his work, but as an imaginative writer she cannot disguise her sympathies, and in her delineation—often a truly brilliant delineation—of the outstanding personalities of German political history during the first seventy years of the nineteenth century, it is clear that, for this woman historian, it is the liberal, federal, agrarian ideal of Freiherr von Stein that represents the vanished Paradise, and the modern industrial state, efficient, hard, powerful, but unimaginative, at bottom discontented, that represents the hard fate to which Germany was condemned by the achievement of the "Junker Bismarck."

In between these two extremes there is a remarkable gallery of portraits, above all of the various German revolutionary leaders and their great antagonists. George Herwegh, Georg Büchner, Engels, Marx, Stüve, Max Stirner, Freiligrath—these are portrayed with a practised hand, and against them stand Friedrich Wilhelm the Fourth, Radowitz, Friedrich List. In all these pages of well-documented description of the interplay of political forces and ideas there are many paragraphs of almost startling application to the present day. The chapter on "Grossdeutsch oder Kleindeutsch"—the great and decisive problem for Germany before her unification under Prussia, whether she should include Austria or not—is of great interest now that the "Anschluss" question is so much in the air. The study of the Communist Manifesto illuminates the Bolshevik Revolution, and this latter event is shown to have been, in some sense, foreseen by Radowitz, who towards the end of his life insisted that the withdrawal of moral sanctions from politics would leave power only with the army or the proletariat. The same statesman also held for inevitable the break-up of Austria into her component parts, a process which would hasten the formation of "Mitteleuropa." A general European pact among governments to restrict their armaments to an agreed figure was also regarded by him as a certainty of the future. This was in 1853. And it is of piquant interest to find Freiherr von Stein, in the early part of the century, exclaiming: "We are overpopulated; we have overmanufactured, overproduced, are overfed," and adding: "The aim and object of society is not the greatest possible production of foodstuffs and industrial materials, but the spiritual, moral, and religious ennoblement of man." From this ideal Frau Ricarda Huch clearly feels we have sadly departed, and have been more and more departing since Bismarck's triumph. In the various men whose characters she has sketched, she depicts the growth and fruition of powers which those same men symbolized. It is a work of profound interest for our own day.

"German Women-Historians," in The Saturday Review of Literature, *Vol. VIII, No. 9, September 19, 1931, p. 138.**

ARTHUR ELOESSER (essay date 1931)

[*Eloesser discusses the romantic aspects within several of Huch's works; he especially notes her literary characters—"people who by nature resemble works of art."*]

Ricarda Huch has written a fine book on German Romanticism, [***Die Romantik,***] which gained her recognition as a scholar even among the erudite. But this writer, who has treated the Thirty Years' War and the epic story of Garibaldi in two great series of novels, has not, as a matter of fact, taken any of her subjects from the age of Romanticism, probably because she did not feel it to be a clearly defined period of the past, cut off from the present; while in her novels of modern life she has preserved its attitude because she feels it to be still present in the spirit and working in the blood. Thus Ricarda Huch formed a transition to the neo-Romanticism of the decadent movement, which she had anticipated in her own fashion, though without becoming a partisan either of it or of any other movement. When this authoress, born of an old patrician family of Brunswick, made her first appearance . . . with her ***Erinnerungen von Ludolf Ursleu dem Jüngeren (Recollections of Ludolf Ursleu the Younger),*** she already represented an aristocratic counterblast to the great productive period of naturalism, being a finished stylist who had fully mastered her own style by studying Goethe, Gottfried Keller, and Conrad Ferdinand Meyer. Her characters all belonged to an expiring, languid, highly cultured race which maintained its aesthetic standpoint to the end and was always ready to discuss its own decline. Her dialogue was thoroughly unrealistic; her language scarcely required any purification; but if it did, she effected this by freeing it from the imperfections of halting thought and speech, and purging it of any dross due to its origin in the impromptu—a quality which was carefully cultivated at that time—in order that she might then cast the unalloyed metal of speech in its noblest form, which was no longer to be the common coin of current intercourse. The characters in ***Ludolf Ursleu*** bear such names as Ezard, Gaspard, Lucile, and Galeide, and the complications of their romantic passions make as little concession to the commonplace demands of bourgeois probability as do their names. In the conflict between life and the intelligence the intelligence is victorious, and life is made to expire in beauty. Ricarda Huch's most typical work, a sequel to ***Ludolf Ursleu,*** raised to a higher power, is ***Vita somnium breve (Life is but a Brief Sleep),*** the title of which was afterwards changed to ***Michael Unger.*** The Ungers come of an ancient Hanse family and are in their way a sort of little kings; they represent a rather more progressive type of Buddenbrooks and meet with the usual fate of ancient ruling families, whose last survivors, sated with power and weary of its exercise, abandon their ancient family ties, sometimes to the extent of starting afresh in other spheres and electing to expose themselves to life's unexplored hazards. They have already followed the whole course of decadence, from the old industrious bourgeois life to the phase of aesthetic slackening of activity, accompanied by display. The wanderings of these pilgrims in search of beauty are romantic even though they travel by railway. Relations of friendship and love are formed as they had been in the age of sensibility, rather in the fashion of that widely ramifying circle which included the young Goethe, Lavater, and the Stolbergs, who were athirst for new types and regarded the discovery of new people as a sort of new sport, in which every new find promised a noble enrichment of humanity. Ricarda Huch is a rare phenomenon in German literature, for, thanks to her high breeding and culture, she omitted, as a matter of course, all the lower stages of youthful crudity or lack of finish. She surrounded herself with a set of characters like her own family, and advanced through this series of novels as though through a private portrait-gallery, in which she also acted as guide, never failing to draw attention to each individual beauty of these her kinsfolk—whenever, that is, their ambitious love of display had not already led them to do so on their own account. "Once again I have risen, gleaming like snow, from the black whirlwind, and the moonlight streams down from my arms, stretched out towards you." These characters are as literary as their author and unite to celebrate a perfect festival of language, which seems to wear fancy dress even when it takes place in the present day.

Even before she turned to history for characters on a heroic scale, this craving for magnificence, for people who by nature resemble works of art, was sure to attract Ricarda Huch towards scenes amid which a more splendid type of humanity seems to move, bred in an ancient culture; and the attractions and possibilities were even greater when these people still retained the beauty of primitive wildness as well. The conditions of her own life suggested this point of view to her, when she was living in Trieste, in full view of both the Italian and the Dalmatian coasts of the Adriatic, a region to which Heinrich Mann afterwards followed her, drawn by a similar longing, in his trilogy *Die Göttinnen*. It was among the Dalmatian mountains, which divide East from West, that she laid the scene of the original legend ***Von den Königen und der Krone (Of Kings and the Crown),*** among a pastoral and hunting people still preserving the secret tradition of a royal house that cannot be deposed, even under foreign rule. But the wild, capricious plot, including both Europe and America in its exalted fantasy, never achieved sufficient stability to bring out the force of the fine symbolic idea of the rusty old crown, that outweighs all the prizes of life. Such legends cannot be invented. Daudet's *Les Rois en exil (Kings in Exile)* has its scene laid in the same exotic sphere, but in it the romance arises out of definite historical and political conditions, the satirical treatment of the legend being only of accessory importance. It was her experience at Trieste that provided Ricarda Huch with her masterpiece, when, in her ***Geschichten aus der Triumphgasse (Told round the Triumphal Arch),*** she entered into the life of the poor and drew a wonderful picture, marred by no sociological prepossessions, in which the brilliant and varied hues of rags proudly worn provide a great feast of colour. The little Roman triumphal arch in the decayed quarter of the ancient hill town is absolutely real to us. The chattering little populace that gathers round it to tell one another fanciful tales is more ancient and aristocratic than the merchants and money-changers in the port, upon whom the dwellers in the upper town literally look down from the heights of their antique poverty. These people themselves lead a sort of fairy-tale existence, for ever promising fresh wonders, the great and only possession handed down to them from more ancient civilizations and religions; but they have the childlike pride in their heritage of an ancient race, and this lends them an air of superiority and a noble gait as they walk, clad in rags, among the dirt ennobled by two thousand years. The impression is that of a dream lingering to tell us its own story; and even when they describe sickness, insanity, crime, and moral perversions, the scenes all harmonize in a magical symphony, making this work one of the finest prose poems in German. (pp. 303-07)

Arthur Eloesser, "The Novel about 1900," in his Modern German Literature, *translated by Catherine Alison Phillips (copyright 1933 by Alfred A. Knopf, Inc.; reprinted by permission of the publisher; originally published as* Die Deutsche Literature vom Barock bis zur Gegenwart, *Bruno Cassirer, 1931), Knopf, 1933, pp. 211-307.**

RICHARD FRIEDENTHAL (essay date 1948)

[In the following excerpt, Friedenthal conveys a sense of Huch's personality, while commenting on the three phases of her career.]

Few, very few indeed, of [Ricarda Huch's] books have been translated into English, and few, it must be said, may have any prospect of being translated in the future. Ricarda Huch's style, often harsh and forbidding, and at the same time often romantic and lyrically reckless to a degree rare even in German literature, would make any attempt at rendering extremely difficult. Personally Frau Huch was no less difficult and complex. Although certainly fully aware of her status as one of the foremost German writers and thinkers, she never understood the gentle art of making enemies or friends in literary life—so equally important for the promotion of a writer's fame. . . . There was no Huch-circle, in a country abounding in sects and

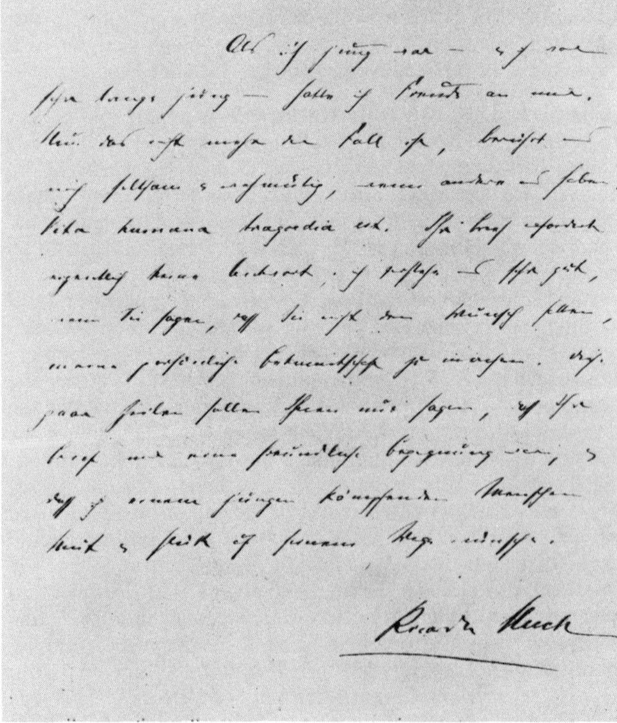

Holograph copy of a letter by Huch. Courtesy of Dr. Riederer-Verlag GmbH.

conglomerations of that kind. There were no Ricardians or Huchites, no faithful apostles or shield-bearers, and the only full biography and appreciation of her work, published about ten years before her death, must have caused her intense embarrassment and discontent by its attempt to claim her for the then reigning ideology. . . . Ricarda Huch neglected even the most harmless and common means of furthering her reputation. There were no letters of recommendations from her, no introductions to books by budding writers, and least of all would she encourage those of her own sex. In fact she encouraged nobody; she discouraged many, if only by her silence.

Nevertheless her fame had grown, year by year, in small and tight annual rings. She was respected, as few were respected, even by her adversaries. And during the last years, after the downfall of the Hitler regime, the octogenarian became the universally venerated representative of the true values of her country, a symbolical figure, indicating in her tireless energy and in the deeply moving power of her last poems the will to live on, and the possibility of a regeneration.

Political considerations enter today into any appreciation of a writer's status in the world of letters. Ricarda Huch undoubtedly owed this last and highest region of her fame largely to her attitude during the years of the spiritual black-out. She had been the first—and, I think, the only—member to resign from her seat in the Academy at the very beginning of the new regime. Her opposition was well known to anybody, and certainly to the respective and numerous authorities who kept her under constant supervision. She never ceased to declare openly her solidarity with the oppressed. She continued to exhort and to forecast the coming catastrophe. . . . [In ***German History***], a sentence from the old Jesuit Scherer, written after the Thirty Years War, fell like a hammer-blow: 'What we Germans are lacking in the highest degree, is joyful courage, and a fearless heart. There has been no lack of big plumes, nor of many-coloured garments, of helmets or basinets . . .' Quotations like these were gallant deeds in those days, coming from a writer living in Berlin, and showed indeed a 'fearless heart'. (pp. 22-3)

A novel dealing with the fall and decline of a patrician family, ***Die Erinnerungen von Ludolf Ursleu dem Jüngeren*** . . . was her first work of full weight, followed by the volumes ***Aus der Triumphgasse,*** set in Trieste, where she was living for a time with her first husband, and ***Vita somnium breve*** (later called ***Michael Unger***). They belong definitely to the history of the 'decadence' of the last years of the nineteenth century, that period that produced more lasting talents than many other epochs which had been regarded as 'sound' and promising. In her short stories—***Der Mondreigen von Schlaraffis, Teufeleien, Seifenblasen***—the influence of the great Swiss writers, Gottfried Keller and C. F. Meyer, was prominent. Ricarda had spent her student's years at Zürich, one of the few universities where at that time women were allowed to study, and her memories ***Frühling in der Schweiz,*** . . . showed her gratitude for those early formative years. Besides her other qualities as poet, novelist, story-teller and writer of historical studies, Ricarda Huch was to some of her friends also one of the first academic women of distinction.

And an academic, or rather semi-academic work, was the book that first won her general recognition: ***Die Blütezeit der Romantik,*** . . . later followed by a second volume on ***Ausbreitung und Verfall der Romantik.*** These volumes are not only a formidable achievement as scholarly studies in a field then not so thoroughly ploughed and harrowed as nowadays, they are a permanent contribution to a subject that will never cease to engage the German mind. Thomas Mann, himself a lifelong struggler with the romantic heritage, as we have seen again with admiration and some consternation in his *Dr. Faustus,* has praised Ricarda Huch, with special reference to these works, on the occasion of her sixtieth birthday. He contrasted her then with Selma Lagerlöf, the great Scandinavian 'teller of tales', as a great 'Schriftstellerin', a word untranslatable in the many connotations it has taken on in the course of a century of controversy between the champions of the conscious and the unconscious in German literary life.

The next phase in her development—there are distinct phases in her life, to the great relief of any biographer or philological observer—was the period of the great chronicles: the 'tales of Garibaldi', and the three volumes on the Thirty Years War, probably her greatest work. Single historical studies on Count Federigo Confalonieri and on Wallenstein accompanied them. The Garibaldi saga is still told with much romantic exuberance. Garibaldi was the Latin hero of her dreams; she will call him 'my lion', and the lion played a great role in her personal imagery. Many of the German writers and poets of that time had a heraldic strain in her mind. 'My eyes want to have their fill in looking at my lion, until his blood tire and his voice expire.' That would sound much better in Italian translation than in English. ***Der grosse Krieg in Deutschland,*** on the other hand, is in many parts almost too austere and even dry. It remains, however, a very great work, painted, or rather embroidered, on a broad canvas. There are unforgettable scenes, highly realistic occasionally like the description of cannibalism in one of the desperately hungry villages, or deeply moving like the last chapter, picturing a little poor community with the old priest who picks up the consecrated bread which had been thrown to the ground, wipes it clean with his sleeve and shares it out to his community and the reckless soldiers. There are many extraordinarily artful tricks of telling a tale in that book. . . . The most significant aspect of these volumes is perhaps the feeling of impending doom they convey. They were published during the first World War, but they gave already then the impression that something even more dreadful might be in store.

The following period saw the three books . . . ***Luther, Entpersönlichung*** and ***The Meaning of Holy Writ.*** They are besides their many beauties and powerfully expressed ideas particularly notable as one of the few emanations of strongly Protestant feeling in German literature, which had, after nearly two centuries of definite predominancy of the Protestant side, swung since the end of the last century to Roman Catholicism . . . , or to secular leanings.

The catalogue of the many remaining works of a long life, spent in indefatigable labour, would sound tedious. There are many more historical studies, on old German towns, the Revolution of 1848; there are monographs on Freiherr von Stein, or on Bakunin—the last book rather a surprise to many of her admirers who had regarded her as a Conservative *pur sang* and counted her as one of the pillars of the group of conservative writers then assembled at Munich, where she was living. Shortly before her death she prepared the material for two volumes on the men and women of the resistance inside Germany against the regime which will eventually be published. Some of the finest poems of her old age are devoted to these men and women, and her song on the devastated country after the catastrophe became to many a hymnic expression of their feelings. . . . (pp. 25-7)

A mere division into periods, however, will give only a very superficial picture of a personality which was always to a rare degree whole and herself. Ricarda Huch may not be read as widely as others are read; she will never be the darling of the lending libraries, or the idol of a school. But she will stand out in the history of German literature, and German cultural history, as a great artist, a strongly personal mind, and as a 'fearless heart' in the sense of the quotation she used in her book on German history, at a time when very few men showed such 'joyful courage' as this woman of nearly eighty. (p. 27)

Richard Friedenthal, "Ricarda Huch," in German Life & Letters, *n.s. Vol. II, No. 1, October, 1948, pp. 22-7.*

AUDREY FLANDREAU (essay date 1950)

[*In the following excerpt, Flandreau provides an insightful study of Huch's novellas.*]

With the exception of ***Der letzte Sommer*** . . . , which readily falls into the form and thought pattern of her novels, Ricarda Huch's earlier Novellen all have for the most part the same essential features. Compared to the novels they are bagatelles. In certain respects one may regard them as resting points between two greater works, down-to-earth moments in which the author stops to catch her breath. The view of the world which they convey is more mocking in its questioning than that conveyed in the novels. The Novellen merely hint at ultimate truths as if in jest.

In the novels, from the highly rhythmic youthful works to the measured epic stream of the historical works, all aspects of the poet's art are subordinated to a certain dynamic direction. Thus the epic moments in these novels do not dissolve in the lyrical rhythm of the author's style, nor do these moments crystallize to such an extent that they exist as independent parts, complete and rounded in themselves. Story (course of action, single episodes, structure), character, and elements of style (rhythm, description, images) are all essentially dramatic in nature; they are there in order that an end may be attained, a problem solved. The course of action attests most clearly to this problematic-dramatic nature of the novels. In each of them a decisive moment, occurring during the course of the story or preceding it, significantly changes the hero's course of life. The action concerns (1) the changes in the spiritual development of the hero which lead to this decisive moment or (2) those stages following it which reveal the hero's struggle to bring his spiritual development to its final culmination or (3) the futile attempt of the hero to overcome the one-sided ego which prevents him from realizing (in certain instances even from striving after) the goal envisaged in the decisive moment. Only in ***Der letzte Sommer*** does the decisive moment itself appear as the outgrowth of a brilliantly warped mind; only in this one novelistic work does the author seek to convey the ideal almost entirely by means of contrast. But even here one senses the hero's longing for some unknown good. Closer examination of these decisive moments discloses that each of them performs the same essential function. Each represents the hero's first conscious step toward love and understanding of the universe, toward an expansion of the single personality through an active exchange with other personalities. In the same way each single event has some bearing on the hero's inner development. It helps reveal his attempt to develop all aspects of his ego—rational, sensuous, and emotional—into a harmonious whole; simultaneously, and beyond this, it helps reveal his striving to unite his ego with the universe through an active, conscious love of those single parts of which the universe consists: human beings, things, and creatures.

Thus in the novels we witness a constant striving for a synthesis of mind and senses in the ego on the one hand, and on the other for a synthesis of this whole with the non-ego, the universe, of which the ego is but one part. Inspired by love, the individual seeks to overcome the confines of his ego by absorbing as much as he can of other beings. This development, which constitutes the dynamic factor in the novels, is later discussed explicitly by the poet in her philosophical works, where she applies such terms as "unconsciousness," "self-consciousness," and "God-consciousness," to the stages of development. In these works she likewise views "God-consciousness"—the state in which ego and universe are united—as that ideal state of being toward which all men, consciously or unconsciously, are striving, as the ultimate goal of human development.

In the Novellen we see the reverse of this ideal: the world not as it is striving to become but as it is, men so unconscious of the ultimate goal of human development that they pursue false, ephemeral goals diametrically opposed to it. We see a world of misunderstanding, confusion, and mistaken identity. Superstition parades under the name of thought; fanaticism and bigotry claim to be signs of deep religious feeling. Self-righteousness passes for piety. Sadism becomes a major ingredient of friendship. Concepts such as greatness and goodness of personality are supplanted by criteria of external beauty and social grace. Shallow self-sufficiency coupled with unlimited self-confidence win their possessor the reputation of personal dignity and, eventually, of holiness, as in the case of Wonnebald Pück, whose brazen self-satisfaction blinds even the more astute. In the world which the Novellen portray love of self is regarded as love of God and might makes right. God's representatives on earth heartily despise each other, and only where deception is added to courage and good will is the good able to outwit the evil. Thus Trud and her lover in ***Teufelei I*** exploit the superstitious fears of their fellow townsmen and disguise themselves as devils in order to remain true to their love for each other. By means of a similar prank the Jew's family in ***Das Judengrab*** outwits the bigoted local priest, who nonetheless continues to believe it is he who has outwitted them. But only rarely is the good able to achieve an active victory. More often, as in the case of Dominik ***(Der Mondreigen von Schlaraffis)*** and Asche ***(Die Maiwiese)***, the good is passive and thus ineffective, the evil shrewdly active. Asche's case offers a striking example. Filled with a lofty longing for the All but unable to translate his feelings into actions, he resolves to reform, not himself, but the world. In certain ways not unlike the novelistic hero Confalonieri, though of considerably lesser stature, Asche disregards the immediate surroundings, confuses his own personal ideals with the common weal and, in the end, sees his reforms lead to wanton folly. In other instances, as that of the innocent prisoner in ***Der Sänger***, chance and circumstance make the fate of the good entirely dependent on the vagaries of the world. To prevail against evil the good must be doubly good; thus the frivolous sector of the population triumphs in ***Der Weltuntergang***, and the pastor, who acts selflessly and nobly, but not always as astutely as he ought to, is plagued to death by the men whom he has persuaded to renounce their wealth. In ***Der Sänger*** the one justice who honestly seeks to perform his duty falls prey to the subtle contrivances of those who wish to curry papal favor and inadvertently aids them in acquitting an unrepentant murderer.

It is thus a world of topsy-turvy values that Ricarda Huch portrays in the Novellen. And this topsy-turviness she aggravates still further by means of a skillful use of ironic effects. The basic confusions of this world are underscored by means of smaller, more specific confusions, absurd juxtapositions, and ridiculous freaks of chance and circumstance. In ***Der Mondreigen von Schlaraffis*** the poet describes with glee the striking similarity between the pastor and the frog with respect to voice and bearing. In ***Der arme Heinrich*** she has an angelic child fall in love with the worldly Heinrich even to the point of desiring to be embraced by him. (pp. 26-8)

But the epic-satirical is only one aspect of Ricarda Huch's art as it reveals itself in the Novellen. Equally important of itself and as a link between novels and Novellen is what one might call the epic-lyrical aspect. The world of concrete reality is depicted not merely in order that the poet may wittily unmask it. Rather the author experiences a personal feeling of warmth toward this world. All living things, imperfect as they are, have a certain magnetic attraction for the poet and certain characters who resemble her. This warm personal element is reflected in the gentle receptiveness and responsiveness of characters like Lux ***(Lebenslauf des heiligen Wonnebald Pück)***, Haduvig ***(Haduvig im Kreuzgang)***, Frau Sälde ***(Der Mondreigen von Schlaraffis)***, and the narrator in ***Teufelei I***. Another aspect of this element is present in the mixture of longing and passive contemplation with which Dominik ***(Der Mondreigen von Schlaraffis)*** regards the world and, particularly, the woman whom he loves. Still another aspect becomes evident in the relation of the narrators in ***Fra Celeste, Die Maiwiese***, and ***Der Weltuntergang*** to the world around them with its lively and impassioned events: amusedly detached and aloof, they are nonetheless inseparably bound, emotionally and physically, to that world. All three aspects become apparent in Ricarda Huch's treatment of the character Heinrich in ***Der arme Heinrich***. Despite his unshakable self-satisfaction and boundless self-confidence, Heinrich exerts a certain charm that is almost irresistible. And, if we examine this figure more closely, we begin to understand the seeming paradox. Neither Heinrich nor his beloved Irmenreich are self-conscious enough to be critical of their own thoughts and deeds or to draw fine distinctions between their ego and the world about them. Sufficient unto themselves, they assume that the rest of the world feels and thinks as they do. Thus Heinrich sees no need to justify Liebheidli's sacrifice and constantly assumes that others experience the same changes of feeling as he does or, if they do not, that they will at least be ready out of love to adapt themselves to him. Like high-spirited animals or children these characters sense that others take delight in their antics and assume this to be their *raison d'être*. It is this very liveliness, this almost utter lack of inhibition, of restraining soul-searching which very often attracts Ricarda Huch to such characters. Not only the naïvely harmonious characters like Frau Sälde, Lux, Haduvig, and Trud, in whom some ethical instinct kindles a love of the universe, but also the one-sided figures who develop one aspect of their being (will, mind, passions) to the exclusion of all other aspects (e.g., Celeste and Marx Grave the Elder) and those whose spiritual development has hardly proceeded beyond the stage of animalistic consciousness (Heinrich and Pück)—all of these characters provide the poet with symbols of life, human beings who indulge in intense living with a minimum of restraint or passive reflection. In adding contrast figures like Dominik and Asche she merely heightens the fascination that the others exert on her, at the same time conveying something of her own shy admiration for the natural forces that operate in such heroes.

Many of these characters have their counterparts in the novels and yet, as we have already seen, there is a world of difference between the novels and the Novellen. Not the world that is, but the world that is to become; not the natural forces with which man is endowed as such, but the end which they serve, the spiritual refining of these natural forces, concerns the poet in her novels. In the Novellen she confines herself to the raw materials. The sheer power of unrestrained instincts fascinates her; the imperfection of the world troubles and yet amuses her. In the shorter works, she is primarily the epic artist, and far less the dramatic artist of the novels. She has paused for brief moments to see the world as it is, to stare in wonderment at the grandeur and the absurdity of life. She does not lose touch with the *epische Grundlage* [''epic foundation''] and try vainly, as do so many of her characters (Celeste, Asche, Dominik; Lasko, Lju, Deruga), to regain this foundation—and with it a feeling of lyrical oneness with the universe—simply by applying dramatic means. That both a dramatic use of irony and a lyrical warmth of feeling nonetheless do attach themselves to this epic world is evidence of the mature artistry of the poet.

Yet in a few of the Novellen Ricarda Huch does succumb entirely to the fascinations of the epic world. Thus in ***Teufelei II***, in writing of a pact with the devil, she assumes and plays the role of a representative of the times, one deeply immersed in medieval superstition and belief, so successfully that despite her playfully ironic intent the reader is likely to see nothing but a conventional devil's tale with sober moral implications. Similarly when Bimbo declares that the thought of becoming a hangman ''had a gruesome sort of fascination'' for him, the reader is tempted to see in these words a hint as to why Ricarda Huch was attracted to the subject matter of ***Aus Bimbos Seelenwanderungen***. Although certain psychological implications (the sadistic father, the masochistic son, the pre-existence of the soul) recall the novel ***Von den Königen und der Krone***, the Novelle, unlike the novel, does not transcend the horror-tale level. In a third Novelle, ***Der neue Heilige*** . . . , the comic effects which chance, circumstance, and opposed character types produce provide the main interest. In three other Novellen, written considerably later in the author's lifetime, both the lyrical undertone and the dramatic dynamism are lacking; external chance and circumstance and the physical basis of human existence play startlingly significant roles. In ***Graf Mark und die Prinzessin von Nassau-Usingen*** . . . an idealistic, youthful passion soon gives way to the mental lassitude and physical corpulence of the ensuing years. The physical gradually assumes control. The plot of ***Weiße Nächte*** . . . is strung along a string of chance occurrences—many of them the result of large-scale political events. In the two main characters one still feels something of the earlier lyrical warmth; but the story lacks inner unity. Neither the grimly playful world of chance nor the inner idealistic world of the two heroes is portrayed with the necessary consistency or intensity. The story of a third character is superimposed on that of the two heroes without good reason. The conclusion does not fully convince and is an anticlimax. In ***Der wiederkehrende Christus*** . . . specific settings and situations combine with bizarre figures and events to produce a grotesque picture of reality. Notably lacking in images, the language in all three of these Novellen frequently resembles journalistic matter-of-factness.

The essential difference in subject matter between Ricarda Huch's novels and Novellen has been pointed out. Another distinction, that should be made in passing at least, concerns essential differences between Ricarda Huch and Gottfried Keller, with whom our poet has often been compared, as if belonging to some mythical Keller school of Novellen writers. In general—and at the risk of oversimplifying—one can localize this difference in the contrast between Huch's irony, which exists on a more active, intellectual plane, and Keller's humor, which is of a more passive, physical nature. Again it is the presence of some dramatic dynamism, however slight, which distinguishes Ricarda Huch. Keller's humor is, in general, *volkstümlich,* down-to-earth, not especially subtle; it draws from an observation of the amusing inconsistencies and incongruities of human behavior, from the essentially human peculiarities of the human being as they become apparent in his everyday behavior, especially from the discrepancy between human dignity and presumption on the one hand and on the other the purely physical bases of human behavior. . . . The human being is constantly reminded of his humble origin and of the limitations placed on him by his physical self. Huch's irony is more subtle and more intellectual. It does not concern itself with the strange interplay of body and spirit in everyday life but rather with the man-made confusions of the mind and spirit—confusions that point less to the physical as a limiting factor and more to the spiritual as limited within itself. This irony exposes not the absurdity of everyday actions but rather the basic confusions in man's thought, the freakish convictions, prejudices, and sophisms which pass for ideals. It shows unmistakably how hard it is for a human being to distinguish between seeming and reality, between ego and non-ego. Ricarda Huch's ironic juxtapositions are not juxtapositions of things which belong to different spheres of human existence but rather of things that absolutely contradict each other; juxtapositions ultimately of good and evil.

Huch's irony is not only more intellectual; it also has more of a romantically whimsical flavor. These characteristics should become apparent if we delve further into the peculiarities of Huch's style and compare them in passing with those of Keller's. The whimsical-romantic flavor of Huch's Novellen appears first of all in the author's choice of subject matter. Thus she writes of characters that stand spatially, temporally, or both, at a distance from herself and her readers: small and isolated villages or princely courts of the present century; cities, towns, and free cities of the sixteenth and seventeenth centuries. And in portraying the confused state of the world she uses the past and the remote as an uncannily distorted mirror of the present; the confusions are the same but they seem all the more striking and grotesque because of the means taken to expose them: the pictures of dark-age superstitions, witchcraft, and ruthless fanaticism. The familiar appears in an unfamiliar garb. Keller achieves the very opposite effect. He makes the familiar more familiar; he calls it by name and robs it of its mask, as in ***Die Leute von Seldwyla,*** whose characters, even in their peculiarities, are typically Swiss. At the same time he selects characters who are a familiar part of any contemporary village scene: comb-makers, tailors, peasant children, and members of the middle class elite—figures, that is, who will conform in most ways to the bourgeois norm. But even in those instances where Keller does depart from this pattern, the end remains essentially the same. Thus the saints' legends unmask the normal human lurking beneath ecclesiastical trappings. (pp. 29-33)

In Huch's Novellen the bourgeois is present only as a foreign principle on the margin; everyday events appear as if in magical disguise; far more important than the vocational and practical aspect of the characters' lives are the workings of their imaginations, their dreams and phantasies. Thus the fear of the devil, the interest in mandrakes, the bewitched cock, the moments of horror on the heath when the fog presses ever nearer like a vampirish phantom, the words and winking eyes of stone statues as heard and observed by Haduvig, and the frog that seems to Dominik to ogle and croak like the pastor. In Huch's Novellen far more often than in Keller's, character, feeling, thought, appearance, and setting are conveyed by means of images which defy the limits of the epic-visual and proceed to the imperceptible essential. Thus a dominant trait of Dominik's character is conveyed in the image of the "toad that is attracted by gleaming objects, ornaments, and precious stones . . . ," his inability to surrender himself to another in the image, "a beastly little devil inside, with claws firmly clutching him. . . ." . . . Synaesthetic effects are especially common to these images—though the visual dominates, there is no sharp distinction between vision, touch, and sound. Reine ***(Die Maiwiese)*** at times appears like "a wave which has become a body"; to hear her speak it is "as if heavy, golden drops of honey glided over one's soul." Aglaia's voice in ***Fra Celeste*** resembles "a small dancing stream of water that plunges down from a towering cliff and leaps foaming from crag to crag." (p. 33)

In all of these images the fantastic element appears either in its more humorous, epic-dramatic or in its more ecstatic, lyrical form or in some whimsical combination of the two. The basic associations are of a sort peculiar to a highly imaginative poet who projects her own lively feelings and warm interest into the object at hand. (p. 34)

[As a writer of descriptive passages] Keller represents the predominantly epic artist who mentions sundry visual details, portraying the whole through many of its parts, and who delights in making lists of separate articles. Thus the lists of foods and of wearing apparel in *Kleider machen Leute,* the finely detailed lists of Züs' treasures and of her compositions, and the list of John Cabys' worldly possessions. Ricarda Huch's descriptions on the other hand are often tempered by lyrical and dramatic undertones. Hence the great selectivity, the emphasis on single features, traits, or gestures which suggest the whole. Eyes and voices, in particular, are often used to convey the essential nature of a personality. . . . Ricarda Huch especially delights in projecting *innere Vorgänge* into images in such a way that an attitude, a state of mind, or an emotion becomes visual without losing any of its immediacy. Because of the fantastic nature of the thought-association it never becomes too visual, too external, too limited to a moment of time. . . . [Of] the attitude of Pück's mother to the ingratiating sort of deception which the son practices on her [she writes]: "At such moments she felt somewhat as if she lay on an ottoman in a pleasant state between sleep and wakefulness so that she perceived sounds and objects only indistinctly, while the fur of a purring cat rubbed against her caressingly."

A magic web likewise veils the external world in Huch's Novellen. We have already alluded to the way in which the poet views the world through the eyes of a highly imaginative child in ***Haduvig im Kreuzgang,*** how Haduvig personifies buildings and statues. A similar sort of personification or more general animation prevails elsewhere where aspects of nature are described. (pp. 34-5)

A characteristic epic feature of Gottfried Keller's which Ricarda Huch in no wise shares and which would be inconsistent with the lyrical-dramatic undertones of her Novellen, her warmly personal and yet whimsically and romantically detached attitude toward her subjects, is Keller's tendency to philosophize and to address the reader by way of comment. Thus Keller occasionally endangers his own role as the—otherwise—omniscient author. He poses questions or suggests possible interpretations in instances where he alone can really be informed. . . . Whereas in Ricarda Huch the distance between author and character or author and reader is bridged over by a fine degree of inner sympathy—as the lyrical undertones of her images reveal—Keller actually widens this distance by his attempts at mediation, by his didactic attitude.

Despite all differences in subject matter between Ricarda Huch's novels and her Novellen a common link may thus be found in the dramatic consciousness and in the lyrical warmth which pervade both genres in varying degrees. Although primarily epic works lacking the dramatic dynamism of the novels, the Novellen are less exclusively epic than the Novellen of Keller. Whether we compare the best of Ricarda Huch's Novellen with Keller's or with the less successful of her own, in either case it becomes abundantly clear how essential this rich fusion of the "three fundamental possibilities of human existence" is to Ricarda Huch's art at its best—whether it be embodied in novel or Novelle. (pp. 35-6)

Audrey Flandreau, "A Study of Ricarda Huch's Novellen with Special Reference to Keller," in The Germanic Review *(copyright 1950 by Helen Dwight Reid Educational Foundation; reprinted by permission of Heldref Publications), Vol. XXV, No. 1, February, 1950, pp. 26-36.*

DOROTHEA BERGER (essay date 1952)

[In the following excerpt, Berger appraises Huch's poetry as one of her lesser accomplishments.]

It is not an accident that Ricarda Huch is known mainly as epic poet and historian. She had no illusions as to her own lyric endowment. Her self-appraisal was sharp and impressive. When a group of her poems was kindly spoken of, she said: "I write poems like these for myself. You might call them little tunes which I play to amuse myself when I'm tired and when nobody else is willing to play for me. When I do that, they seem to me rather pretty."

In her four volumes of verses there are scarcely more than half a dozen poems which can be called perfect, and it may be that there is not one really great lyric poem among them. (p. 245)

In her historical romances, Ricarda Huch has set landmarks for German prose. She has handled multitudes with artistic mastery, in the passionate lyrical music of the Garibaldi romances as well as the impressive objectivity of ***Der Grosse Krieg.*** Her poems are an unimportant incident to her immortal prose achievement, without significance for the history of the German lyric, without a new and original tone. They incorporate no new material, they only repeat melodies often sung before. She was a rich personality, and now and then she achieved beautiful verses, almost always as personal confession, sometimes in the guise of rhymed diary. But in the history of the German lyric she has no place of her own. Her poems do not rank with those of Eichendorff, Mörike, Storm, C. F. Meyer, or, to cite a poet of her own generation, Rilke. Even the form of her poems is casual. Ottave rime, terzine, sonnets, alternate capriciously with the three-foot, four-foot, two-foot lines of the folk songs.

Linguistic slips, expressions that will not quite bear analysis, false images, even errors in grammar are to be found in Ricarda Huch's lyrics as they cannot be found in the works of the great German poets or in her own prose works. . . .

Rhymes are often suggested to Ricarda Huch by mere similarity of sound, as words are suggested to her by purely linguistic association, but she does not always probe deeply into meanings. The poetess is uncertain and artistically immature in her use of the ancient verse-forms. In her well-known poem ***Der Dichter*** a five-foot line has slipped into a series of hexameters, and the poem ends with a completely unjustified pentameter.

There is very little evidence of development of style in Ricarda Huch's lyric production. The themes remain unchanged for decades: pagan joy of living, praise of mainly sensual love, immersion in nature—these themes recur again and again with endless variations. In her late work ***Herbstfeuer,*** she adds resignation to the limitations of age. There is little merit in the ballad-type poems, which never leave the footsteps of Gustav Schwab and Emanuel Geibel. In her beginnings she dropped, apparently without plan or scruple, into the trite tradition in which she had grown up. In her lyric work one hears again and again tones from the choir which was led by Geibel and Paul Heyse. She never left this school, except in infrequent outbursts of the moral passion of which her strong personality was capable. (p. 246)

Ricarda Huch's poems are the personal incidental music of her life, not an enduring element of her work. If she had not written great prose, her lyrics would scarcely merit attention. By now most of her poems have only biographical importance, although a few are lyrical masterpieces. (p. 247)

Dorothea Berger, "The Lyric Poetry of Ricarda Huch," in Books Abroad, *Vol. 26, No. 3, Summer, 1952, pp. 244-47.*

JETHRO BITHELL (essay date 1959)

[Bithell provides one of the more thorough surveys in English of Huch's works.]

In [Ricarda Huch's] case the influence of Conrad Ferdinand Meyer and Gottfried Keller is flagrant, though Goethe's rhythms and syntax may also be distinguished in her nevertheless markedly individualized prose style, which, moreover, extraordinarily supple, adapts itself to the subject and atmosphere of her successive works. Her first novel on a large scale, ***Erinnerungen von Ludolf Ursleu dem Jüngeren*** . . . , lives by reason of its lyrical style with its sad, sated rhythms; it set the model for neo-romantic prose as Hofmannsthal's *Der Tod des Tizian* and *Der Tor und der Tod* set it for verse drama. The story itself is irritatingly decadent; it runs its hectic course in that Dionysian cult of beauty the peril of which was to be shown forth by Thomas Mann's *Tod in Venedig;* there is the familiar ostentation of illicit love as the right of personality. . . . But subconscious forces and the problematic nature of passion are (to the author and the period) the justification; and, since love is fate, there is the same inevitability of seizure as in the tale of Tristan and Isolde. No modern writer handles the mystery of existence more elusively and more poignantly than Ricarda Huch; in this first novel life is fate; in the following novel ***Vita Somnium Breve*** a strong man's will deflects fate by the rejection of the love that fate wills—but to what purpose? As in Thomas Mann's *Buddenbrooks* the main tenor of the Ursleu story is the decay of a Hanseatic patrician family, here in Hamburg, but (since the style is in pointed hostility to the naturalistic formula) without that weaving in of business affairs which makes *Buddenbrooks* as good a commercial novel as Freytag's *Soll und Haben. Buddenbrooks,* by the way, comes eight years later; and it has been suggested that Thomas Mann owes his theme of cultural development inducing incapacity for the boredom of business to this novel of Ricarda Huch's. The story is related by Ludolf Ursleu, who has escaped from the world of such tragic happenings to the peace of the Swiss monastery of Einsiedeln (the framework may have been suggested by E.T.A. Hoffmann's *Die Elixiere des Teufels*): the events he relates, as they pass before him in procession, are thus softened by distance. He is at peace, he muses; but therefore he is dead—for life is the stormy ocean; and where there are no storms of passion, no conflicts of personality, there is no life. The decay of a business firm—Hamburg . . . is again indicated, though Ricarda Huch, true to the romantic formula, does not specify localities—is once again in the background of ***Vita Somnium Breve*** (. . . later rechristened ***Michael Unger***); actually the hero, though as the eldest son of patrician parents he should carry on the firm, throws up his business career to win distinction as a zoologist, and makes frantic efforts to leave his wife for the sake of a woman painter who has physical and mental qualities which his uncongenial wife has not. The wife turns Catholic, and therefore cannot divorce him; but what chains him to her—and here is the grip of the story—is his love for his one child, a son who, as the close of the novel hints, will repay his father's sacrifice of love by being a charming and lively but socially worthless fellow in whom the vigorous old stock will dishonourably die out. To save the boy's fortune the father has returned to business and rescued the firm, brought to the verge of bankruptcy by the brother next in age—artist and poet in an amateur way—who had taken his place at the deserted office desk. The conflict as thus outlined must be common in everyday life; but Ricarda Huch gives it something of the tragic intensity of Racine's *Andromaque,* in which too the theme is the tyranny of child over parent. What gives the novel its value—it must be admitted that many reject it as too hazy, and certainly it is hard to read through—is the slow and careful unfolding of the hero's mental suffering, and the tragic implication of the tale that though duty to family is the paramount consideration it may mean absolute sacrifice of what is best in a man's personality. Certainly what accrues from the sacrifice is treated with a suggestion of irony—and irony (sly, pathetic, or extravagant) is almost half of Ricarda Huch's technique after the Ursleu book; but the main brunt of the theme is surely that a man grows strong by self-mastery. One suspects, too, that a current idea of the time, the doctrine of the Danish philosopher Søren Kierkegaard that a man's character as genius, poet, hero, or saint is made by his *not* getting his girl, may be in the weft of the tale; Ibsen's *Love's Comedy* and *Brand* had familiarized the idea. Michael Unger is man as Ricarda Huch fondly imagines him: the tortured angel, lured by beauty but fettered by duty, to whose problematic lips woman would, if she could, bring the balm of bliss: an utterly romantic and feminine estimation of the male. The woman Michael loves is unconvincing: nothing she says or does has the flash of magic personality; all that is clear is that she is capable and solid and that she is ready to mother her man when he comes to her with his plea—sufficiently hackneyed—of loneliness of spirit. There is attraction for the literary reader in the description of student life in Zurich, that home of *die Internationale,* and still more in two portraits—one obviously of Ernst Haeckel in his conflict with established religion and in his senile eroticism: dismissed from his professorship he takes over Michael's discarded mistress; and the other—quite delightful!—of Stefan George as Aristos, the latest sensation in poetical fashion. . . . From Conrad Ferdinand Meyer Ricarda Huch takes over the device of the *Rahmenerzählung* [*stories within a story*]: Ludolf Ursleu unfolds the saga of the past much as Dante does in the Swiss novelist's *Die Hochzeit des Mönchs;* and in ***Aus der Triumphgasse*** . . . the patrician owner of a medieval mansion (the home of his ancestors), now decayed to a hive of flats, little by little reveals the tangled lives of his tenants and their neighbours in this ancient street of Trieste through which the dark narrow road climbs through a Roman Arch of Triumph—an ironical erection! More fitting were Dante's *Lasciate ogni speranza, voi ch'entrate;* and indeed the Arch and what lies before and behind it is a symbol of life itself: through such a gateway youth climbs, but to the defeat of all hope and to the endless strain and struggle by which all that is human lives. In this street with the illusory name is crowded, like vermin, the scum of the city—cripples, murderers, thieves, and girls who give themselves for bread or passion. At their worst these creatures, as Ricarda Huch shows, with her detached, fondling touch, are intensely human; at their best they may be heroic. Starvation cannot blunt their avid hold on life and may, when the heart is good, give them a ripe humour that lights up even this sordid existence. They are ministered to by a mysterious young priest with a beautiful, sad face: the foster-brother of a murderer and a prostitute who are still close to his heart. In so sad a book humour might not be expected; but it is there—a naughty humour which comes natural to Ricarda Huch as a disciple of Gottfried Keller, as in the story of how the Civic Prize for Virtue is awarded to a girl who is virtuous because her lover is a stoker mostly at sea but who entertains him in bed while her mother and most of the street are on a holy pilgrimage. Ricarda Huch's other novels, except those with themes from history, have hardly more than academic interest. The problem of royalty outworn in a hustling world of business is dreamily approached in ***Von den Königen und der Krone*** . . . : the son of a Slav king, while doctor at a hospital for children, marries the daughter of a German oil magnate. Here, if anywhere, the realism of Thomas Mann's *Königliche Hoheit* was needed; but Ricarda Huch, refining her Romantic fancifulness, lifts earth to the clouds, which will not bear it. ***Der Fall Deruga*** . . . , an experiment in the criminal novel, is painful in the irreality of its realism: a doctor has given his dying wife, at her own request, a sleeping draught, and the court proceedings which the story reports try to bring home the crime to the culprit. Close scrutiny may find a loving care in the characterization of this doctor with an Italian name, but one cannot credit that anywhere a murder could be investigated in so strange a way.

Both the close-packed style of Gottfried Keller and his ironical treatment of religion are closely imitated by Ricarda Huch in a series of short stories whose content varies from tragic or pathetic to quaint or grotesque. Keller had made his game of religion in the Gottmacher's tales in *Der Grüne Heinrich,* and in *Sieben Legenden* (1872) he had transmuted the old Catholic legends of chastity into proof that nothing is closer to the heart of God than the joys of wedlock—His means to His purpose. In ***Der arme Heinrich,*** one of the tales of ***Fra Celeste und andere Erzählungen,*** Ricarda Huch reads the consummation of sexual desire into this physically most absurd of medieval legends. The anti-religious satire, though without coarseness, misses its mark by overstraining probability in ***Der Hahn von Quakenbrück*** . . . : Catholics and Calvinists dispute as to the punishment that should be meted out to the Mayor's cock for laying eggs with scarlet yokes; and in ***Lebenslauf des heiligen Wonnebald Pück*** (in ***Seifenblasen***): an utter fool, a scoundrel and an oozy voluptuary, rises by virtue of his very vices and idiocy to be abbot and bishop, and on his death is canonized because his story is believed that the image of the Virgin in his church has given him Her own jewelled crown—which in sober fact he had stolen to pay for his loose living.

Ricarda Huch breaks new ground as much by her regeneration of the historical novel or *vie romancée* as by her elaboration of a lyrical prose style: she frees it from restrictions of locality and raises it to epic grandeur and timeless significance in [***Die Geschichten von Garibaldi (Die Verteidigung Roms, Der Kampf um Rom, Menschen und Schickesale aus dem Risorgimento,*** and ***Das Leben des Grafen Federigo Confalonieri***]. . . . Typical of the psychological method of her historical tales is the Confalonieri volume: the ripening of a mind in twelve years of imprisonment and the analysis of patriotic idealism provides the interest. Ricarda Huch makes Garibaldi a symbol of genius, isolated (in Thomas Mann's sense) by his own 'difference from the others' (*Anderssein*), prone to excess, and inevitably the tool (as an engineer controls elemental forces) of inferior but calculating minds (Cavour). In her prose epic of the Thirty Years War, ***Der grosse Krieg in Deutschland*** . . . , we have her new conception of historical fiction brought to fruition: in her vision of these vast events—since her aim is to portray not individuals but a whole period with its inner impulses, its mass psychology, its cumulative devastation—she does not bring the great leaders out in stark relief, but lets them take their place (even Gustavus Adolphus and Wallenstein) as actors controlled by the drama rather than controlling it, as scene billows after scene in the ocean of happenings with no ordered beginning and no clear-cut ending.

Her lyric verse [***Gedichte; Neue Gedichte***] . . . modelled as it may be on that of Conrad Ferdinand Meyer, is marked by a somewhat hectic speculative cast rather than by plastic presentation of image and substance. The philosophical staple is that of the prose work: the most insistent idea is that personality should struggle with and wrest from existence the utmost it can bestow—***Alles oder nichts,*** for instance, concentrates the doctrine (essentially that of ***Vita Somnium Breve*** as of other works) in a sonnet. Certain of her poems with a more sentimental appeal have won permanent place in the anthologies, but one doubts whether the bulk of the verse is not superficially imitative or a metrically skilful play with current fancies, though she may give them the ring of intense feeling, as in ***Sehnsucht,*** which owes its poignancy to its Swiss setting. . . . She gets farthest away from traditional moods—and metrically at least her poetry is for the most part wearily traditional—in impressionistic freaks of fancy such as ***Erinnerung***. . . . (pp. 327-32)

A close examination of Ricarda Huch's work would very likely prove that the scholarly elaboration of current ideas which shows in her verse is, rather than original fire of genius, what by the nature of her imitative talent she is best qualified to do. Even the general view of critics that she has a very masculine mind—she certainly has a strong man's capacity for taking infinite pains—needs qualifying by the admission that she has to the full those feminine weaknesses—e.g. worship of man—which make women so delightful to men. At all events any male scholar might be proud of her great mass of critical work. Her literary criticism [***Die Blütezeit der Romantik, Ausbreitung und Verfall der Romantik, Gottfried Keller***] . . . is academically accepted, though rather brilliant than academic; and she even manages to make theology interesting in ***Luthers Glaube***. . . . To her historical work she brings the sound academic training of her Zurich days; it is nevertheless poet's history. Her ***Römisches Reich deutscher Nation*** . . . , in which she traces the cultural and political development of the Empire, did not find favour with Nazi critics because she does not definitely reject the fascination for the German emperors of Rome and all Rome implied. Where she does, perhaps, prepare Nazi ideology is in her philosophical disquisition ***Entpersönlichung*** . . . : she compares the medieval ideal *('heidnisch-christlich-germanisch')* [*'barbarous-Christian-Germanic'*] with the contemporary aim to be as comfortable as possible; in the Middle Ages man strove to complete his personality and to be god-like, but progress has been *'von der Persönlichkeit zur Entpersönlichung'* [*'from personality to the loss of personality'*]. The Germans are less able to resist this rotting of personality because they are no longer racially pure. (pp. 332-33)

Jethro Bithell, "The Women Writers," in his Modern German Literature: 1850-1950 *(copyright © 1959 by Jethro Bithell; reprinted by permission of Methuen & Co. Ltd.), revised edition, Methuen, 1959, pp. 321-45.**

THE TIMES LITERARY SUPPLEMENT (essay date 1965)

[The following excerpt is a short review of Gesammelte Shriften, *a collection of Huch's essays written between 1902 and 1947 on a variety of topics, including literature and history.*]

[Ricarda Huch's] personality and the time in which she lived are only revealed indirectly in the majority of the essays in . . . ***Gesammelte Schriften.*** The particular place of woman in life or literature is implicit in sketches of figures from German Romanticism and in the paper on the Romantics' theory and practice of love and marriage. It is developed further in the careful and sympathetic appraisal of Annette von Droste-Hülshoff. Ricarda Huch's affection for Switzerland is reflected in an evocation of Zurich, and in essays on Gotthelf and Keller, of which the one on Gotthelf is the more substantial. The theme of "German tradition" arouses the author (in 1931) to a reasoned presentation of the case for the Holy Roman Empire and against the absolutism of the princes.

Ricarda Huch's memories of childhood are marked by an early awareness of disagreement with her father's support of the Prussian monarchy, and of her own enthusiasm for freedom. Towards the end of her life she wrote simply and pointedly about war guilt, nationalism and democracy. Perhaps the most vivid and personal piece in this volume is an impression of an air-raid in March, 1945. Here are a directness and spontaneity which are less noticeable in those essays where formality dominates.

"Goethe Prize Ladies," in The Times Literary Supplement *(© Times Newspapers Ltd. (London) 1965; reproduced from* The Times Literary Supplement *by permission), No. 3283, January 28, 1965, p. 69.**

THE TIMES LITERARY SUPPLEMENT (essay date 1970)

[The following excerpt offers a review of volume six of Huch's Gesammelte Werke, *which, for the most part, consists of her collection of critical essays* Die Romantik.]

[Ricarda Huch's ***Gesammelte Werke,*** volume six] is devoted mainly to her study of German Romanticism, the first part of which appeared seventy years ago. . . . Huch's enthusiastic and fluently colourful style introduces the major figures of the first Romantic group in a series of pleasantly readable character-sketches, though today's readers might prefer a drier, terser approach. Literary analysis is subordinated to portraits of personalities and outlines of their main ideas, often accompanied by generous quotations. The brothers Schlegel, then Karoline and Novalis, are initially introduced, while Tieck's early work receives appreciation in the chapters on "the Romantic character", "Romantic books" and "the fairy-tale". The Romantics' relationships with Goethe and Schiller are treated, as are their attitudes to philosophers and painters. When embarking on her survey of the later Romantics, Ricarda Huch finds that they lack the intellectual stature of the earlier group. She has little sympathy with the turning to Catholicism or with the presentation of nationalism in early nineteenth-century Germany. Brentano is found wanting on various counts, and Eichendorff might have been expected to have received more generous appraisal. However, the chapter on E.T.A. Hoffmann is written with keen appreciation.

Some of the shorter essays demonstrate, as does ***Die Romantik*** on occasion, Ricarda Huch's concern for the role of women in German literature. Gottfried Keller is a figure whom she can also approach with sympathy and insight. It may be that Ricarda Huch's literary criticism remains of interest chiefly as revealing a facet of her own personality as a writer, but it is a personality of considerable vitality and forcefulness.

"German Romanticism," in The Times Literary Supplement *(© Times Newspapers Ltd. (London) 1970; reproduced from* The Times Literary Supplement *by permission), No. 3541, January 8, 1970, p. 26.*

ADDITIONAL BIBLIOGRAPHY

Drake, William. "Fiction: *Victory* by Ricarda Huch." *The Bookman,* New York LXIX, No. 2 (April 1929): 199.

Favorable critique of *Victory,* the companion work to Huch's novel *Defeat*. Drake is also the translator of *Eros Invincible,* which is one of the few English translations of Huch's work.

Edinger, Dora. "She Also Bore Witness: Ricarda Huch, 1864-1947." *The American-German Review* XIV, No. 3 (February 1948): 32-3.

Presents a brief biography of and tribute to Huch, as well as a commentary on the literary project Huch had begun shortly before her death. Edinger discusses the "Open Letter" Huch had written to the families of resistance workers and war victims after World War II. She requested documents, letters, and diaries of the war's casualties so that she could compile a book which would be a memorial to those who perished at the hands of the Nazis. For additional comments on Huch's uncompleted work, see Richard Friedenthal's 1948 essay excerpted above.

"Another Woman Pleads for Germany." *The Literary Digest* L, No. 3 (16 January 1915): 99-100.

Largely reprints an early article by Huch in which she defends the German character and refutes "the charges of barbarism hurled at her nation" during World War I.

Lohrke, Eugene. "Mazzini's Defeat." *New York Herald Tribune Books* (16 September 1928): 5.

Negative review of *Defeat* finds Huch's novel "tedious," falling short of literature, and valuable only as a "historical document."

"Garibaldi As the Catspaw of Count Cavour: Ricarda Huch Continues Her Historical Romance of the Unification of Italy." *The New York Times Book Review* (20 January 1929): 6.

Plot summary and review of *Victory,* the sequel novel to Huch's *Defeat.*

"New Books: Fiction." *The Saturday Review of Literature* VII, No. 37 (4 April 1931): 718.

Review of *Eros Invincible,* one of Huch's earliest and most successful works.

Franz Kafka

1883-1924

Austro-Czech novelist, short story writer, and diarist.

The following entry presents criticism of Kafka's story *Die Verwandlung,* first published in 1915 and translated into English in 1937 as *The Metamorphosis*. For a complete discussion of Kafka's career, see *TCLC,* Volumes 1 and 6.

The Bettman Archive, Inc.

***The Metamorphosis* is one of the most frequently analyzed works in literature. This elusive story, which portrays the transformation of Gregor Samsa from a man into an insect, is renowned for its ability to inspire diverse, sometimes mutually exclusive interpretations. While it is not uncommon for criticism of similar insight and conviction to reach dissimilar conclusions on the meaning of a given work, Kafka's narrative has been the focus of a particularly varied body of discussion and judgments. For this reason *The Metamorphosis* has come to be considered one of the central enigmas not only of modern literature but of the literary imagination itself.**

Kafka was born in Prague to financially secure Jewish parents. His father had risen from poverty to success as a businessman, and the family was assimilated into the Czech community by the time of Kafka's birth. Seeking acceptance into the German-speaking élite of Prague, Kafka's father sent Franz to German rather than Czech schools. According to Kafka's biographers, the dichotomy between the German and the Czech communities led to his early feelings of alienation. As the eldest child and only surviving son, Kafka was expected to follow a course in life mapped out for him by his father, but from his childhood he considered himself a disappointment to his authoritarian parent and inadequate when compared with him. His strong mixed feelings about his father were later expressed in his *Brief an den Vater (Letter to His Father)*. Although he was an indifferent student, Kafka earned a degree in law. However, he was unhappy with the prospect of a legal career and took a post with an insurance company, a position which required long hours, making it difficult to pursue his creative endeavors. A year later he obtained a somewhat less demanding job with another insurance firm, leaving him more time to write but requiring frequent business trips of several days duration, a situation analogous to that of Gregor Samsa. Kafka had published nothing, and had destroyed most of what he had previously written, at the time he wrote *The Metamorphosis,* one of the products of a period of intense literary activity which critics have labelled "the breakthrough of 1912." The short story "Das Urteil" ("The Judgement") and the first chapters of the novel *Amerika (America)* were also written at this time. This "veritable burst of 'imaginative' writing," in Mark Spilka's words, was occasioned by Kafka's first meeting with Felice Bauer at the home of his close friend Max Brod. Charles Neider writes that Kafka "experienced an artistic break-through a little more than a month after meeting her, discovering the theme and style characteristic of him." A long and complex relationship developed between Kafka and Bauer. They were twice engaged, but both times Kafka ended the engagement. He wrote Bauer hundreds of letters and implored that she respond as frequently. Bauer's letters were obviously very important to Kafka. According to Evelyn Torton Beck, "Kafka used the hundreds of letters he elicited (indeed coerced) from Felice . . . *as a nourishment for his own writing*." The many letters that passed between them certainly resulted in Kafka's experiencing a hitherto unknown sense of security. These new-found feelings resulted in highly prolific literary activity.

***The Metamorphosis* was composed over a period of three weeks, the greatest amount of time Kafka had yet devoted to a work. His letters to Bauer, and his diary entries concerning *The Metamorphosis,* indicate that although he was substantially satisfied with the story, he felt the ending was seriously flawed. For this he blamed a business trip which had interrupted him just before he completed the story. However, critics note that *The Metamorphosis* is one of the few works for which Kafka actively sought publication, indicating that he must have been sufficiently pleased with the work, since he published little during his lifetime and left instructions that Brod, his friend and literary agent, destroy any unpublished manuscripts left at his death. Kafka submitted the story for magazine publication in 1914 and it appeared in book form a year later. Kafka divided the story into three parts, each headed by a Roman numeral as are the acts of a play or the chapters of a longer work. Many critics have noted the story's threefold construction, demarcated not only by Kafka's numerical headings but also by Gregor's three emergences from his room after the transformation has taken place. Heinz Politzer finds that Gregor's three appearances, which each involve confron-**

tations with different people and conclude with attacks upon Gregor by his father, serve not only to divide the story into segments but also to demonstrate the three primary relationships in Gregor's life: with his employer, his family, and himself.

Critics agree upon little regarding *The Metamorphosis* other than the story's three-part structure and a very basic plot outline: Gregor Samsa works as a traveling salesman, a job he dislikes, to repay a debt incurred by his parents; he oversleeps one morning and awakens to find that he has become a large insect; he and his family attempt to deal in various ways with the change, but gradually the situation becomes intolerable; Gregor ultimately dies, and his relieved family plans for a brighter future. Critics differ widely in their interpretations of such matters as Gregor's precise attitude toward his work, his feelings about his family and their feelings for him, and his sister's motivation in first caring for the transformed Gregor, then neglecting and even turning against him. To what extent elements of the story may be taken as autobiographical is also debated. Some critics point to Kafka's own view of his father as a stern and implacable figure of absolute authority and suggest that the insect Gregor is an apt metaphor for Kafka's own feelings of inadequacy. Other critics dismiss this interpretation as a simplistic reading of an artfully complex story. Even what sort of an insect Gregor has become is the topic of considerable discussion. A few critics, such as Rudolph Binion (see *TCLC*, Vol. 6) and Ruth Tiefenbrun, maintain that no physical change takes place: that Gregor's change is either a mental one (he has become not an insect, but insane), or else that the change is solely in how he is perceived (he shows himself to his family and employer not as an insect but as a sexual deviant). These critics point out that no one in the story has any difficulty recognizing Gregor after the metamorphosis is supposed to have taken place. However, the most common reading of this initial event in the story is typified by Ronald Gray: "The whole story is worked out in terms of Gregor being an insect, and at no point does the reader have the sense of being slyly invited to see more than meets the eye." Walter H. Sokel has confirmed this point, noting that "there is no basis for doubting the physical, objective reality" of the metamorphosis.

Critics who accept the metamorphosis as a fact within the framework of the story interpret it in a variety of ways and attribute it to various causes. Three frequent critical interpretations of Gregor's transformation are that it serves either as retribution, as wish-fulfillment, or as an extended metaphor. Those critics who see the metamorphosis as retribution for an unspecified crime committed by Gregor usually apply comparisons between *The Metamorphosis* and Kafka's posthumously published novel *Der Prozess (The Trial)*, and between Gregor and Josef K., the protagonist of *The Trial*, who never knows the offense for which he is arrested and executed. Critics who see the metamorphosis as a form of wish-fulfillment on Gregor's part find in the text clues indicating that he deeply resented having to support his family. Desiring to be in turn nurtured by them, he becomes a parasite in actual fact. The parasitical nature of Gregor's family and employer is then seen as an ironic foil to the reality of Gregor's parasitic being. Many critics who approach the story in this way believe the primary emphasis of *The Metamorphosis* is not upon Gregor, but on his family, as they abandon their dependence on him and learn to be self-sufficient. One interpretation of the story holds that the title applies more to Gregor's sister Grete than to Gregor: she passes from girlhood to young womanhood during the course of the story. A third interpretation of Gregor's transformation is that it is an extended metaphor, carried from abstract concept to concrete reality: Gregor is thought of as an insect, and thinks of himself as an insect, so he becomes one.

A frequently noted element of the story is the realism of the narrative. *The Metamorphosis* contains only "a single incident foreign to the habits of our world," Paul L. Landsberg writes. "Once this happening is accepted, all the rest of the story develops with a logic, a probability, with what I might even call a banality, characteristic of the most everyday world." Kafka is considered a masterful prose stylist who avoided any touches of ironic whimsicality in dealing with his extremely unrealistic subject matter. *The Metamorphosis*, however, is not without humor. The three lodgers whom the Samsas take in, and the uncouth cleaning woman who ultimately disposes of Gregor, are considered to be among Kafka's finest comic creations. For its technical excellence, as well as for the nightmarish and fascinating nature of the metamorphosis itself, Kafka's story has received a vast amount of attention, and its various problematic features continue to challenge its readers. Stanley Corngold notes that "no single reading of Kafka escapes blindness," but that each new reading of his work encourages the study of the vast body of criticism devoted to it.

(See also *Contemporary Authors*, Vol. 105.)

GUSTAV JANOUCH [CONVERSATION WITH **FRANZ KAFKA**]
(conversation date 1920?)

[*Janouch, the son of a business associate of Kafka, met the writer when his father showed Kafka some of Janouch's poetry. Though Janouch was in his teens and Kafka in his thirties, the two became friends, and often took long walks together through Prague. Janouch made extensive notes of their conversations and later used these to write the book* Conversations with Kafka, *from which the following conversation about* The Metamorphosis *is taken.*]

My friend Alfred Kampf from Altsattel near Falkenau, whose acquaintance I had made in Elbogen, admired Kafka's story ***The Metamorphosis***. He described the author as 'a new, more profound and therefore more significant Edgar Allan Poe'.

During a walk with Franz Kafka on the Altstädter Ring I told him about this new admirer of his, but aroused neither interest nor understanding. On the contrary, Kafka's expression showed that any discussion of his book was distasteful to him. I, however, was filled with a zeal for discoveries, and so I was tactless.

'The hero of the story is called Samsa,' I said. 'It sounds like a cryptogram for Kafka. Five letters in each word. The S in the word Samsa has the same position as the K in the word Kafka. The A . . .'

Kafka interrupted me.

'It is not a cryptogram. Samsa is not merely Kafka, and nothing else. ***The Metamorphosis*** is not a confession, although it is—in a certain sense—an indiscretion.'

'I know nothing about that.'

'Is it perhaps delicate and discreet to talk about the bugs in one's own family?'

'It isn't usual in good society.'

'You see what bad manners I have.'

Kafka smiled. He wished to dismiss the subject. But I did not wish to.

'It seems to me that the distinction between good and bad manners hardly applies here,' I said. '***The Metamorphosis*** is a terrible dream, a terrible conception.'

Kafka stood still.

'The dream reveals the reality, which conception lags behind. That is the horror of life—the terror of art.' (pp. 31-2)

Gustav Janouch, in an excerpt from a conversation with Franz Kafka, in his Conversations with Kafka, *translated by Goronwy Rees (all rights reserved; reprinted by permission of New Directions Publishing Corporation; in Canada by Joan Daves; originally published as his* Gesprache mit Kafka *(copyright © 1968 by Fisher Verlag GmbH, Frankfurt-am Main), S. Fisher, 1968), revised edition, New Directions, 1971, pp. 31-2.*

STEPHEN SPENDER (essay date 1937)

[*Spender is an English man of letters who rose to prominence during the 1930s as a Marxist lyric poet and as an associate of W. H. Auden, Christopher Isherwood, C. Day Lewis, and Louis MacNeice. Like many other artists and intellectuals, Spender became disillusioned with communism after World War II, and though he may still occasionally make use of political and social issues in his work, he is more often concerned with aspects of self-knowledge and depth of personal feeling. Since World War II, Spender's stature as a perceptive literary critic has grown. In the following excerpt, Spender offers an interpretation of* The Metamorphosis *as a nightmare version of a straightforward situation, analogous to the position of a man who discovers he has an incurable disease.*]

Franz Kafka's great allegorical novels have often been compared to "Pilgrim's Progress." But, in fact, they differ from any allegories written before because they do not set up a system of symbols which can easily be recognized as corresponding to some system existing in the real world, nor do they offer any solution, any "moral," as Bunyan does. I believe the fact is that Kafka saw the world much as he describes it in his novels, just as a man who feels himself to be persecuted sees reality fitting into a system, which is really of a spiritual order, to persecute him. . . .

We do, indeed, find that Kafka gives us just such a view of reality as would the victim of persecution. However roundabout it may seem, his approach to reality is direct: he is not building up an allegory in order to illustrate a metaphysic, he is penetrating reality in order to discover a system of truth. How often when reading his fantastic accounts of human behavior we find ourselves exclaiming not "how remotely that corresponds to something in life which we dimly see beyond it," but "how extraordinary, yet how true." (p. 347)

If he had lived, he might have written novels which started off from a goal, instead of these novels which never attain their goal.

"The Metamorphosis" is a strange and terrifying nightmare, the whole plot of which is contained in the first paragraph. "As Gregor Samsa awoke one morning from a troubled dream, he found himself changed in his bed to some monstrous kind of vermin." The story describes, simply and straightforwardly, Gregor's attempts to adapt himself to this change, the attitude to him of his family and his employer, until finally, neglected by them all, he dies. It contains no metaphysical purpose, it is an account, in Kafka's terms, of a given situation in contemporary life: the situation, say, of a bank clerk, on whom his whole family has depended, who wakes up one morning to discover that he is suffering from an incurable disease. (pp. 347-48)

Stephen Spender, "Franz Kafka," in The New Republic *(reprinted by permission of* The New Republic; *©1937 The New Republic, Inc.), Vol. LXXXXII, No. 1195, October 27, 1937, pp. 347-48.*

DESMOND HAWKINS (essay date 1938)

[*In the following excerpted review of the first English translation of* The Metamorphosis, *Hawkins discusses the work as a depiction of the pain of being spiritually or physically alien from the conventions of modern society; for that reason, Gregor's transformation is not as horrific as the reactions of those around him to his condition. Paul L. Landsberg (see excerpt below, 1945) also discusses the story as an example of the alienating effects of social conformity. For a contrasting opinion, see the excerpt below by Norman Friedman (1963), which is a more literal interpretation of the story.*]

All criticism must rightly end with the finger pointing invitingly. A good illustration condones deficiencies of argument, and if out of recently published books I were challenged to select a single example of the short story at its best, it would be ***The Metamorphosis*** by Franz Kafka. . . . Technically, this is as nearly perfect as anyone can hope ever to see. . . . [If Kafka's] symbols were merely substitutive, they would be no more than a cumbersome and pointless code. Kafka's meanings are various, comprising in fact all possible meanings which can be grouped within a single mood. ***The Metamorphosis*** is the story of a man who wakes one morning to find that, *with no diminution of stature,* he has turned into some kind of insect, presumably a cockroach. The peculiar horror of the story, it seems to me, is that instead of dwindling to insect proportion he retains his human dimension. There is a period of terrible comedy while he finds excuses for not leaving his room; then begins the relentless destruction of sentiment by the unalterable fact of his accident; and finally he is stripped even of his dignity as a monster and becomes familiar, dirty, a mere burden to his family. The working-out of this corrosive destruction of the domestic fabric is complete and overwhelming. Kafka misses no effect, no further subtle twist; every implication is crystallized in a haunting and sinister lucidity.

I believe the clue to Kafka's use of fantasy lies in the fact that the ordinary reader can endure horror at this pitch *because* it is touched with the golden light of 'unreality'. Men don't turn into cockroaches, such a thing is scientifically impossible, and therefore we can subdue our shocked sentiments in the act of contemplation. We are not being unfeeling, since after all it is only a fairy-story. We have our excuse as Lamb did with Congreve.

But suppose this unhappy hero were really a lunatic who merely had a delusion that he was a cockroach; or suppose he had some disease which crossed the border into obscenity and wore out the pity and charity of his associates. Suppose him to be a misunderstood man, a cretin, a mediaeval clown, any sort of misfit you like. ***The Metamorphosis*** is the drama of all those men, of all *spiritually alien* men who unwittingly destroy the reassurances of use and conformity and custom. Presented naturally, such a narrative would be dramatically impure, irresolute, obscurely motivated; both author and reader would be tempted towards the sentimental morass of extenuation, nausea, case-pleading, empathic self-pity and a whole clogging mass of extraneous feeling. By transmutation into the objective symbols of fantasy, Kafka carves out the hard structure of fact and magnifies the operation of the drama. The device in itself is simple. Instead of positing some possible kind of man, lunatic, diseased or other, who excites a mood of *strangeness,* Kafka pushes to an artificial limit and produces a man turned cockroach. What distinguishes Kafka from other fantasists in this kind of transmigration is that he does not become whimsical nor even sustainedly fantastic. The one exaggeration is sufficient; from that point the story is developed with a deliberately subdued naturalism. The whole world is normal and commonplace, apart from the single initial accident. And it is *in the normal commonplace behaviour of the world* that the real source of terror lies. Here Kafka transcends the whole group of meanings I have put forward, and passes to the generalized horror of any loss of one's identity in a conventional world of limited probabilities. Fundamentally it is the haunting, brooding fear of the *déraciné,* the unrecognized, the stranger, the one ignorant of local passwords, the inarticulate, the alien, the outcast, the lost man with no antecedents, man in the void, the man without a tribe. In this brief story Kafka explores a whole area of human fear and terror, and analyzes its operation. This is a work of the highest imaginative order, at once terrifying and serenely beautiful. (pp. 506-08)

Desmond Hawkins, in a review of "The Metamorphosis" (reprinted by permission of David Higham Associates Limited, as literary agents for Desmond Hawkins), in The Criterion, *Vol. XVII, No. LXVIII, April, 1938, pp. 506-08.*

PAUL L. LANDSBERG (essay date 1945)

[*Like Desmond Hawkins (see excerpt above, 1938), Landsberg reads* The Metamorphosis *as a parable portraying the power of social conformity to destroy the alien or different individual. Landsberg finds, by extension, that the fate of the transformed Gregor represents the fate of all who cannot accept or conform to traditional social roles, from schizophrenics to religious or racial minorities.*]

Kafka's unique style corresponds to the paradox of his world. His is a world which aims at reality, and in this sense, Kafka could be called a realist. His world wants very much to be real, to resist human imagination and will, to possess its own character, its own causality, and its own habits like the world in which we live. In its strictness and oppressiveness it differs most radically from the popular romantic fairyland, a poetic world which is virtually obedient to the human soul. However, the mere presence of an undeniable realism in his work does not imply that Kafka's world is our everyday one. It is quite evident that it is not at all our own familiar world. Perhaps the reader will even be inclined to range Kafka with whimsical and fantastic writers. But in truth, the transformation suffered by accustomed reality in Kafka's writing is not simply a diminution. Kafka sides with the opposition to all fairytales and escapist literature. His writing treats the question of change—change of a type foreign to our knowledge of reality. To analyze it, we shall discuss the strange story entitled ***Die Verwandlung—The Metamorphosis.*** This story is, in our opinion, completely typical of his art. The nature of the world, if we accept as real the one in which we live, shows a certain coherence in its habits. We are generally quite confident that a certain train or sequence of phenomena will occur, even though previously we have never thought very deeply about the reasons for this sequence. According to our existing yet in general unconscious acquaintance with these habits, we judge reality by its similarity to past, present, and future events. This spiritual tendency existed in humanity and in the individual even prior to the discovery of laws in their proper sense. In the story which Kafka tells us, there is a single incident foreign to the habits of our world, one which shocks our assumed knowledge of it. This occurrence is introduced in its entirety without hesitation or timidity, brutally imposed as an undeniable fact from the very first sentence: "As Gregor Samsa awoke one morning from a troubled dream, he found himself changed in his bed to some monstrous kind of vermin." Once this happening is accepted, all the rest of the story develops with a logic, a probability, with what I might even call a banality, characteristic of the most everyday world. The reactions of the outside world, of Gregor's family and of the other people affected by this phenomenon are extremely true-to-life reactions, almost entirely predictable. They are average reactions, the reactions of anyone. And in a like manner, the feelings and actions of that pitiful commercial traveller, Gregor Samsa himself, when he finds himself thus transformed, are in complete accordance with the perfect mediocrity of his character. The stifling atmosphere of the apartment of a middle-class Prague family, the setting of the story, differs not one iota from that of thousands and thousands of other middle-class apartments. . . . This guise of reality, however, is not strong enough to destroy our rational certitude of its impossibility. Even the existence of consequences so logical and predictable, if we admit their cause, cannot make us forget the absence of an acceptable cause for the cause itself. The conflict which arises in the reader's spirit almost forces him to adhere to the sense of the primary incident, and it is probably only in so adhering that he can approach the mystery hidden under the very clarity of the tale. (pp. 228-30)

According to the habits of the world, and according to the laws which science has discovered, it would be quite impossible for us to awake one morning and find ourselves transformed into a repulsive insect. But in our customary certainty of the identity of our being and world in general, there is just enough of artificiality, enough will, enough fragility so that Kafka's fiction touches an unacknowledged but anguishing reality, nourished from sources deeper than those of rational reflection and scientific knowledge. This is the only way in which such an incident could be validly introduced. It is on awakening "from a troubled dream" that the person in question would discover himself transformed. He would discover his metamorphosis in the miscarrying of his daily expectations and the shattering of his effort to reachieve customary but unconscious continuity.

The metamorphosis of a civilized man into first a coleoptera, perfect example of an instinctive and almost automatic being, and finally into a simple bit of matter, portrays in its successive stages man's instinct for death, the desire for a return to the inorganic of which Freud has shown the power in the human subconscious. All the desires, all the anxiety with which this hidden antagonist upsets the instincts of life are thus evoked by the incident. This nightmare of Gregor Samsa is the expression of a deep and stifled impulse. He can no longer obey his conscious will. . . . It is this satisfaction of pent-up desires that fosters the feeling of culpability which dominates the man who was transformed into a cockroach. He had deserted humanity, and this knowledge fosters his conviction that he must justify himself, and his certainty that he will never be able to do so. In the kingdom of life, the father has right on his side and the son carries in his flesh the rotten apple embedded there by the paternal hand. The culprit instills horror into those who surround him because he calls attention to the universal possibility of the crime. Following an implacable logic, the ignoble death of the culprit and the destruction of his corpse finally intervene as the ultimate deliverance, destroying blame when they destroy the living individual. The return, which could not be halted until it reached the stage of brute matter, close as possible to the unimaginable nothingness, had been achieved. All the world is then relieved, all the world is triumphant, but most of all the fugitive himself. The inevitable struggle between the misfortune of being born and the fault of not wanting to be, the misfortune of being responsible and not wanting to be, has only the saddest solution in Kafka's moral universe.

Our body and our total being are continually in the process of transformation, but we are generally conscious of it only at specified moments. At these times we are brought to the inevitable realization of the anguish of living, the anguish of finding ourselves passengers on a train which we cannot leave and which, infallibly, from change to change, is taking us to the ultimate catastrophe. . . . [There] is yet an oblivion of change in ourselves and our contemporaries which indubitably contains an effort to repress, a subconscious loathing to admit certain things, in the last analysis, a fear of death. There is an agony in change which is the agony of life, of a life eternally pregnant with death. It is this fear which makes us search for and affirm the stable identity of our being through the repetition of our acts, through the constitution of ritual habits. This fear is the secret of a certain bourgeois world, a world where the unchangingness of chattels and ways of life expresses an attempt to deceive the liberating force of life and death. In choosing this very bourgeois world as the setting for his metamorphosis, Kafka frames a revolutionary threat much more disquieting than the usual satire. Imagine the terrible need in such a fundamentally deceitful life. It is manifested in the fear which the metamorphosis of Gregor Samsa awakens in those who surround him, in the ferocious hate which the change irresistibly evokes even in those who previously cherished him and had a thousand reasons for being grateful to this son and exemplary brother. We understand only too well that in essence it is not only a question of defending an honest family against the annoying curiosity of the surrounding world, but also of preserving a world in which these "normal" beings can live free from the fear of possible and universal change and free from the fear of that final, mysterious and unavoidable metamorphosis. This is the true nature of his family's anguish. It is evident at the end of the story. The cockroach dies. The family must get rid of the corpse. The charwoman who had always treated the transformed son as if he were a particle of filth, destroys the remains behind the scenes, to the great relief of the family. Everything returns to order, to the inhuman order in which death is passionately excluded and with it the true life of every person.

The terrible apple which the almost unrecognizing father, himself suddenly transformed by his blue uniform of banking house employee, throws at the back of his poor cockroach of a son, expresses the foolish and inevitable revolt of the likely against the unlikely, of the uniform against the monstrous, of custom against the exceptional, of triviality against the explicit nightmare, of an artificially sweetened, slowed and comfortably falsified life, the life which forgets death, against a true life which progresses resolutely towards the last catastrophe. Besides the psychological resemblance to reality, there is an impression of a truly metaphysical need for this patriarchal act of hostility against a so-degenerated son.

So the metamorphosis, certainly an impossible and unreal incident, is nevertheless charged with a significance which is itself neither arbitrary nor unreal. It is not the caprice of an artist which produces such a symbol. It is the inner force of a poet who sees in this symbol the true mystery hidden deep in the lives of everyone. (pp. 231-33)

Gregor Samsa, this poor man condemned to live his metamorphosis, is morally identical with his former self even as a cockroach. His sweet, timid, and amiable character has not suffered any extraordinary change. Since it is primarily physical, his metamorphosis becomes that much more symbolic. The corporal fact, from the metaphysical point of view, is no more superficial than the psychic fact. The truth of the matter, that we are not only associated with but almost entirely in the power of a corporal existence, is perhaps the most anguishing discovery of our human existence. That this body which is in a certain way "myself" should be subject to all the vicissitudes of a physical world which follows laws apparently having nothing to do with my personal law is an evidence of fatality which not only shocks my pride but wounds my very intimate hope to give at least some sense to my own existence. Our corporeity makes the inhuman world our master. It mocks at our pretended autonomy. The fragility of the identity of our character when a radical physical metamorphosis occurs cruelly shows the fragility of our entire condition. Gregor Samsa as a cockroach, for example, does not believe that he has lost the use of words. He speaks continually, tries to explain and excuse himself, and his arguments seem extremely reasonable to him. But after several minutes he perceives that no one understands him any longer. No one even knows that he is speaking. What he judges to be reasonable language is for the others nothing more than the noise of a disgusting animal. He resembles Kafka's other heroes, refined Talmudists surrounded by corporal beings, superb reasoners in a deaf world. Around Gregor Samsa an abyss has been opened, isolating him from those who were his equals, who still are but do not realize it. This is the way in which a man who becomes insane suffers the awful experience of separation from other men, a radical separation based on misunderstanding. For him reason is no longer reason. One only reasons falsely for others. He makes no faults of logic, for he follows his own logic.

I am reminded in particular of schizophrenia. . . . Kafka's haunted universe calls up spiritual states which would in all likelihood have induced a veritable schizophrenia if art had not conquered them. From this point of view, his tale expresses a possibility of ill health that the author lived through. It is the schizophrenics who are often truly and irrevocably transformed into other people, historical personages, into animals or objects. If Gregor Samsa himself had told his story, it would be the sincere confession of a schizophrenic. By creating this main character and telling his story in the third person, Kafka is liberating himself of an obsession. The poet himself is not a schizophrenic, but in creating his story he defends himself against the human and universal possibility of it which permits comprehension of such an illness.

Beings like ourselves who show only physical manifestations, who, themselves incarnated, only understand when they incarnate their thoughts and feelings, are subject to this type of adventure, but are generally not aware of the danger. Finally, there are even some situations in which the genius or, more simply, the reasoning man finds himself just as isolated among a crowd of his fellow beings, just as incomprehensible, as anguished and as hated as Gregor Samsa. ***The Metamorphosis,*** from the date of its publication, seems to be Kafka's "war book." The transformation into a cockroach can be produced in a thousand ways. To be an exception or in the minority is the original social sin. When in society any group of men characterized by anomalous tastes or racial or social heredity is denounced as "vermin," there will always be one group that from then on will see nothing but the other's rottenness, and another fraction within the scorned group that will think and act as if they had truly been transformed into vermin. Since Kafka was Jewish, he had undoubtedly experienced something of this kind. His recital symbolizes even more validly the situation of a poet of his kind in present society. The fear of those who surround Gregor Samsa is the panicked fear which the presence in a poet's work of the most suppressed secrets will evoke even in a crowd of mediocre people. (pp. 235-36)

Paul L. Landsberg, "Kafka and 'The Metamorphosis'," translated by Caroline Muhlenberg, in Quarterly Review of Literature *(©* Quarterly Review of Literature, *1945, renewed 1973), Vol. II, No. 3, 1945, pp. 228-36.*

PAUL GOODMAN (essay date 1946)

[In his preface to the first American edition of The Metamorphosis, *Goodman finds that Kafka presented in the character of Gregor Samsa a totemic identification of man and beast that represents both Gregor's subconscious conflicts and a desired alter ego. Goodman's interpretation is challenged by William Empson (see excerpt below, 1946); while Charles Neider (see excerpt below, 1948) finds that Goodman neglected many of the widely accepted implications of the concept of the totem.]*

In the simple fables of the ancients, the beasts act like men. In the sentimental animal stories of modern times, the beasts act as themselves, but most often in situations related to men and exemplifying passions and virtues interesting in men. Only the great naturalists study the beasts merely as themselves. There is also a kind of satire in which men act like beasts.

It was the rare gift, and heavy curse, of Kafka to be able to describe his beasts in all these ways at once. This is because he makes an identification of man and beast. Kafka's animals are *totems;* to find the analogy for them we must look in the religion of the primitives, in folklore, and in the animal phobias that haunt the dreams of children.

Now, the totemic identification of beast and man is both symbolical and literal; unless we keep in mind both these aspects, we cannot understand the play and nightmares of children nor the wonderful tales of Kafka. Symbolically the beast is a symptom of unconscious conflicts, mostly those centering round the hostile and castrating father and the son's identification with him; the son's surrender to him; perhaps, most deeply of all, the child himself as the devourer, destroying mother and father both, at the age of his omnipotence—and now he can never make amends! The reader of Kafka is well acquainted with these gnawing, devouring, and bloodsucking little beasts: moles, moths, jackals, mice, and vermin.

But, literally, the beast is in his own person a true friend and communicant, another self. For the primitive, the child, the profound artist like Kafka, the profound sociologist like Kropotkin have not forgotten that there is a community of all life and a continuum of the libido. So in this story of ***The Metamorphosis,*** hearing his sister play the violin, the bug pathetically asks:

> Could it be that he was only an animal, when music moved him so? It seemed to him to open a way toward that unknown nourishment he so longed for.

Now, we know that Kafka himself, the man, abhorred music; it drew round him a wall, he says, it made him "otherwise than free." But Kafka as the animal—yes, even as a loathsome bug!—is laid open to this language of living feeling. Shall we not say that the bug is better, more oneself, than the commercial traveler or the official in the insurance office?

Clearly the literal and symbolical identifications are related: without love of beasts there would not be totemism; without totemism the adult would not return passionately to the beasts for an escape from his ego into nature, freedom, and community. Kafka's beasts are both totems and literal friends; then we see that it is not that an animal is likened to a man, but a man is acting out some animal-identity in himself. I do not mean that man is satirically "reduced" to an animal, for the animal-identity is deeper than the ordinary human being and his behavior, it is nearer to the unknown deity; it is a totem. Likewise the treatment is realistic, the animal acts as itself—often observed with stunning accuracy—but just for this reason it abreacts the human complex, it furnishes a release, because the animal is a literal friend and lover closer to guiltless nature. Again I do not mean that there is a sentimentality of the "happy primitive"; it is an understatement to say that Kafka had a vivid sense of "nature red in tooth and claw"; but there is a release from moral delusions and conventional defenses, a return to living ethics both communal and self-regarding.

One more note that is indispensable for the reader of ***The Metamorphosis:*** in the famous Letter to his Father, Kafka puts in his father's mouth the following remarkable reproach against himself:

> I admit that we are fighting each other, but there are two kinds of fight. There is the knightly battle—and there is the struggle of vermin which not only stings but at the same time preserves itself by sucking the other's blood. Such are you. You are not fit for life, but in order to live in comfort, without worry or self-reproach, you prove that I have taken away your fitness for life and put it all into my pocket.

Kafka did not flee from the reproach, as we others do; he dragged it into the forefront of consciousness. (pp. 5-8)

Paul Goodman, "Preface" (reprinted by permission of the Vanguard Press, Inc.; copyright 1946 by Vanguard Press, Inc.; copyright renewed 1973 by Sally Goodman), in Metamorphosis *by Franz Kafka, translated by A. L. Lloyd, Vanguard Press, 1946, pp. 508.*

WILLIAM EMPSON (essay date 1946)

[In the following excerpt, Empson comments upon Paul Goodman's preface to the first American edition of The Metamorphosis *(see excerpt above, 1946). Empson disagrees with Goodman's belief that the transformation of Gregor reflects a totemic identification with animals; rather, Empson finds that the primary point of the story resides in the kindly human temperament main-*

tained by Gregor Samsa even as he is trapped in the horrifying, undesired body of an insect.]

This brief masterpiece [**"Metamorphosis"**] is so direct, so like a punch on the jaw, that there should be little to say about it. But the introduction and the illustrations of the first American edition are so wrongheaded that they provide employment for a critic. (p. 652)

The introduction [see Paul Goodman excerpt above, 1946] says that Kafka describes animals in all possible ways at once; as in a fable, where they are like men; as having qualities also interesting in men; as themselves, realistically; and as men acting as beasts. "He makes an identification of man and beast. Kafka's animals are *totems*." In accordance with this view, the pictures at the two ends of the book show dogs and pussycats in human poses, and the picture of the monster in the middle, swaggering in white tights, plumes, and a military carapace, might be a society portrait of Lord Byron fighting for the Greeks. . . . Now I think that all this gives an entirely false idea of the story. The point which the story rams home is that the monster is unbearably nauseating, not in the least like a pussycat. The question of what the actual feelings of a man-sized woodlouse would be (he has more legs than a cockroach) is obviously not considered by the author, except perhaps in the one remark that his legs enjoy running. So far from being like *any* animal, for that matter, the sufferer is always human and nearly always high-minded. What he chiefly reminds me of is an elephantiasis case described by a doctor ten or more years ago in a horrible book called "The Elephant Man," who had an even more unbreakable sweetness of temperament in spite of the loathing which his body inspired. The whole story, indeed, might have been told about a real disease, and would only have lost (what is no doubt its chief value) the wild poetry and the sense of the appalling strangeness of the world.

If this is true, you may say, it is very unlike **"The Castle"** and **"The Trial."** I don't deny that the book satisfied the neurotic side of Kafka as well as the mystical one. No doubt the preface is right in quoting the reproach which Kafka supposed his father to give him, that he fought his father like vermin which both sting and suck blood. But though the first idea was a justification of the vermin, that is, the young writer who refused to get a job, the story as it worked out rose entirely away from those foggy troubles and became clear-cut in the sunlight. . . . [It is] part of the Kafka atmosphere that the monster never tries to speak after the first day, though his mother certainly understood one thing he said through the door before she saw him ("he must be ill, even though he denied it this morning"), so that if he had had the courage to go on talking he would have been less completely cut off. Here, you may say, is the wilful defeatism of the usual Kafka; but you can also believe that the man would have acted so within the framework of the story. Indeed, the real Elephant Man, during the years he was with the traveling show, was never spoken to because everyone assumed he was imbecile. It is because the story is so real that the spangles tucked onto it by this edition look so tasteless.

However, there are several minor inconsistencies. For instance, his back is described as a hard carapace onto which this large animal can fall without getting hurt, but his father can throw a "red" (therefore presumably soft) apple which cracks it and makes it fester; no doubt it is the apple of Adam, but one wants the details more convincing. . . . In the other major Kafka books one feels sure the contradictions are intentional, indeed the more baffling they are the more carefully they seem placed; but this is a different kind of story and does not need them. Maybe he could never bear to read over the manuscript. (pp. 652-53)

William Empson, "A Family Monster," in The Nation *(copyright 1946* The Nation *magazine, The Nation Associates, Inc.), Vol. 163, No. 23, December 7, 1946, pp. 652-53.*

CHARLES NEIDER (essay date 1948)

[*Neider is the author of two studies of Kafka:* The Frozen Sea: A Study of Franz Kafka *(1948) and* Kafka: His Mind and Art *(1949). In the following excerpt, he provides a strictly biographical reading of* The Metamorphosis, *finding that Kafka's sense of personal insufficiency before his father is symbolized by Gregor Samsa's domination by his father. Neider mentions Paul Goodman's similar interpretation (see excerpt above, 1946) that the animal figure, or totem, in literature is symbolic of unconscious conflict between a threatening father and the son who identifies with him, but finds that Goodman disregards the Freudian conception of the totem as representing the father and not the son. For a contrasting opinion, see the excerpt below by Norman Friedman (1963), which dismisses the biographical interpretation in favor of a more literal reading of the story.*]

In [***The Metamorphosis***], the most masochistic product of his mature period, Kafka portrays himself as a gigantic bug which plagues a decent family. The autobiographical inferences are inescapable. The affair with F. B. [Felice Bauer] released Kafka's pent up masochism in the form of literary savagery and horror. An important motivation for the length of the novella must have been his creative momentum. This is clear from the essentially weak thematic development and powerful stylistic treatment, as if he were carried off by his literary strength to effects beyond his thematic interest or sincerity.

Gregor Samsa (note the parallelism between *Samsa* and *Kafka*) is an eminently good son; he is, in fact, fanatically good. And he is the economic mainstay of a parasitic family. This is a wish projection of a Kafka depressed by his economic dependence on his father. The tale is full of attacks upon the father. Its strength resides in its fertile invention and its power of empathy. It is not an "amazing story"; it differs from most horror tales because of its core of immediate and personal truth, consisting of the universality of disaster and the fear of the unknown. One feels that the actual transformation is merely symbolic of more real and deadly ones which are ever possible and which haunt even the healthiest and best adjusted of beings. There is implicit everywhere the neurotic's horror of losing control, and there are hints of fear of the lower depths of sleep, night, and dream, and also of existence in death without the release of death—a mythical echo of Tantalus. The illusion of transformation is achieved not only by a sort of bug documentation but also by the behavior of the parents and sister, who never forget that the bug is their Gregor. There are the usual perspicacious psychosomatic implications in Kafka, e.g., the gradual physical degeneration of the family under the impact of disaster, and their regeneration after Gregor's death. A slip on Kafka's part, surprising because of his meticulous care to preserve unity of point of view, is the break near the end of the tale. Kafka might have concluded with Gregor's expiration. He seems, however, to have been unwilling to forgo the opportunity of a few more digs at the family's expense. He lovingly presents them as glorying in their sudden freedom.

A critic, Paul Goodman, has recently written in a preface to ***The Metamorphosis*** that Kafka's animals are totems, and that

Hermann Kafka, Franz's father, who has been called the person after whom Gregor Samsa's father was modeled. Copyright Schocken Books Inc.

the bug in the novella is a totem too [see excerpt above, 1946]. He neglects, however, to consider Freud's contribution to the understanding of totem: the conception of totem as a father symbol. The bug in the novella symbolizes the son, not the father, and therefore cannot be intelligently called a totem. Kafka's symbolism is mythical; in such symbolism, as well as in the symbolism of dreams, children are represented by vermin. It is clear that Kafka used the symbol of the bug to represent the son according to Freudian postulates; also because the notion of bug aptly characterized his sense of worthlessness and parasitism before his father. Goodman fails to use the term *totem* in its original and meaningful context: with the double taboo against killing the totem and against marrying a person of the same totem clan (parracide and incest). Kafka, in an Oedipus relation, probably experienced suppressed and often unconscious parricidal desires; yet in the novella at hand the situation is reversed, and the father is more than once on the verge of infanticide. Reversal, the use of opposites, is a favorite device of Kafka's, one found widely in folklore, in dreams, and in the unconscious mind. Its function is that of censorship.

Gregor's early dilemma is whether or not to recognize the catastrophe. Unable to comprehend it, he withdraws into the known area of his past, complaining, instead of at the transformation, against the details of his former existence. Thus Kafka stresses the mind's inability to adjust before an enormity, while ironically commenting on the importance of the "job" in his world (Gregor is unendingly concerned with his job). Kafka's fixation on the job theme arises from his own necessity to work, at cost to his creative activity. The pervading physical influence of the employer, dramatized in the novella, is a European characteristic more than an American one. It is a feature of a paternalistic, often despotic society, of closed economic frontiers and of slight fluidity between social classes. Gregor's complete transformation, both mental and physical, saves him from realizing the true nature of his tragedy. It is as though the coma of some great illness has overcome him. This mental inadequacy or ignorance is desirable for artistic reasons, for it permits Kafka to tell his story simply and unself-consciously, yet from Gregor's point of view; and it allows him to register the reactions of the family and the manager without unduly delaying the tale's movement with descriptions of Gregor's complicated thoughts and feelings. Gregor's responses are purely behavioristic: he acts as he must in his bug state; every effort is toward self-preservation, this being all that has been left him of the complicated maneuvers of human life. It is part of the strength of Kafka's *tour de force* that it never deviates from its intention, which is a thorough poker-faced documentation of the accomplished fact; while at the same time proceeding at several subterranean levels, such as the Oedipus symbolism and the complex of family relations. Whatever Gregor is, he is totally that: totally the insect, the commercial traveler, the faithful son. He is dedicated to the few roles he may play in life, no matter how minor. It must have afforded Kafka no little pleasure, ambivalent as he was, to write of a character so steadfast in his duty and his conception of his duty. (pp. 45-7)

Charles Neider, "Introduction" (introduction copyright © 1948, copyright renewed © 1975, by Charles Neider; reprinted by permission of the author), in Short Novels of the Masters, *edited by Charles Neider, Holt, Rinehart and Winston, 1948 (and reprinted by Holt, Rinehart and Winston, 1967), pp. 3-51.**

HOWARD FAST (essay date 1950)

[*Fast is an American novelist who was blacklisted during the 1950s for his communist political beliefs. In the following Marxist interpretation of* The Metamorphosis, *Fast differs from most other critics, who find the novel to be an examination of individual powerlessness before the conventions of society. Rather, Fast believes that the work reflects a desire on the part of the ruling classes (whose mouthpiece is Kafka) to make the lower classes equate themselves with insects and thus be less resistant to controls. Fast's interpretation arises from the Marxist belief that literature should present an accurate depiction of objective social reality; for that reason Fast attacks Kafka's use of metaphor. Throughout this essay, Fast uses Kafka's work as a pretext to attack those critics who do not subscribe to his opinion of Marxist ideology. For a more detailed Marxist reading of* The Metamorphosis, *see the excerpt by Walter H. Sokel (1983).*]

Very near the top of what I have, in the past, rather indelicately called the "cultural dung heap of reaction" sits Franz Kafka, one of the major Olympians in that curious shrine the so-called "new critics" and their Trotskyite colleagues have erected. Mr. Kafka is treasured as well as read; in a dozen literary quarterlies and "little" magazines, joss sticks are burned to him, and his stilted prose is exalted as a worthy goal. Worthy or not, that goal is certainly interesting, for in the creation of a shadow world, a world of twisted, tormented mockeries of mankind, Mr. Kafka holds a very high place. It is worth examining the substance of that throne.

Perhaps the most widely read of Kafka's work, here in America, is a tale called ***Metamorphosis,*** which narrates in great detail how a German traveling salesman woke up one morning and discovered that he was a cockroach.

Now, although there is satirical intention in Kafka's tale, he departs from the satirists of the past in the absolute literal presentation of his point. It is much as if, having once proceeded to put down his idea upon paper, he was carried away by a conviction of the reality of the situation he had conceived. (p. 12)

Just this will give you a sense of the horror Kafka evokes in this story, and the evocation of horror is precisely the result of the literal presentation of the situation. Whatever Kafka intended, his product is not satire; satire is a means whereby irony, ridicule, and sarcasm are used to expose tyranny, vice, folly, and stupidity; and thereby satire becomes a shortcut to reality. But in this story, Kafka does not direct himself toward such exposure; he is concerned only with proving that a certain type of human being is so like a cockroach that it is entirely plausible for him to wake up one morning and discover a natural metamorphosis has taken place. And throughout the remainder of the story, with a world of intricate detail concerning the various problems of a man who is a cockroach, Kafka reiterates his thesis.

Horror and nausea are the effects Kafka's tale have on the reader, but what is the purpose? We know that men do not turn into monstrous cockroaches overnight, and we also know that the German petty bourgeois, for all the despicable qualities he may exhibit, is far, far indeed from a cockroach. It was no army of cockroaches that devastated half the civilized world—what then is Kafka's purpose? In his mind, he has performed the equation; man and roach are the same; they are each as worthy as the other; they are each as glorious as the other; they cancel out—and thereby we have the whole miserable philosophy of the "new critics," of the "new poets," of the "avant-garde" of the *Partisan Review*. . . .

But helplessness, disgust, self-loathing, mysticism, and contempt for social action do not arise spontaneously. The equation of man and cockroach is a part of an enormous process on the part of the ruling class which may be quite simply defined as a confusion and distortion of the nature of the objective reality. (p. 13)

Howard Fast, "'The Metamorphosis'" (originally published in his Literature and Reality, *International Publishers, 1950), in* Franz Kafka: An Anthology of Marxist Criticism, *edited and translated by Kenneth Hughes, University Press of New England, 1981, pp. 12-14.*

I. F. PARRY (essay date 1953)

[*Parry provides an extensive comparative reading of* The Metamorphosis *and Nikolai Gogol's* The Nose. *Parry concludes that both stories depict an irrational dream world as a means of conveying the basic dilemmas of human identity.*]

It is soothing to discover that a modern writer like Kafka is really quite old in essence and even in technique. It is a discovery to be matched only by the excitement of finding that a writer of former times, like Gogol, is really modern. Either discovery suggests that the writer in question is here to stay, since he appeals to elements in man which are unchanged and possibly unchangeable. Kafka seems to be in critical disrepute at the moment—perhaps because he has been so intensely overworked as the embodiment of the modern spirit. . . .

But is Kafka so modern? There is a tendency to regard him as a freak among writers, a kind of novelist who could not possibly have happened before. And, some will no doubt hope, may, please God, never happen again. We speak of the Kafka influence as though it were unique. And by Kafka influence we usually mean something extraordinary, grotesque, nightmarish, symbolic of modern frustration. . . .

In Kafka's story ***The Transformation*** Gregor Samsa wakes up in bed one morning to find himself changed into a monstrous cockroach. Yes, extraordinary. But Gregor Samsa is not essentially different from that unfortunate man Kovalev, in Gogol's story, who also wakes up (perhaps not unnaturally) in the same place (bed) and at the same time (early morning) to find that his nose has disappeared overnight, leaving a perfectly smooth patch in the middle of his face. The place and time are significant. For Gregor Samsa and Kovalev are awakening, not from a nightmare, but, reversing the normal process, *into* a nightmare, the nightmare world which is always just below the surface. Instead of finding themselves in the waking world they are in that world of dreams which, so the psychoanalysts tell us, shows us the real truth about ourselves. So they are really finding themselves, for they are in a sphere which is more truthful than the waking world. It is no coincidence that it is just as he is getting out of bed one morning that Joseph K., in Kafka's novel ***The Trial,*** is arrested by strangers on that charge which leads him to his fantastic pursuit of innocence. (p. 141)

The surface writing of both Gogol and Kafka is apparently flat. They love the precise detail, the pedestrian fact. . . . Kafka goes into such detail about the pleats in a man's clothes or the dust that lies thickly on a heap of pictures that it is difficult to believe he is not simply reporting to us on people and places we know well. But this realism is a deceptive surface. Deceptive because pitted with holes, through which we may fall into another and apparently unreal world. But, oddly enough, only the unwary (because unimaginative) can avoid these holes, for they seldom get over the intellectual shock of the initial proposition.

Spinoza starts from self-evident propositions, Gogol and Kafka from propositions which are anything but self-evident. For pure intellect they substitute pure imagination—but go on to develop it as though it were intellect. Given that a man can lose his own nose overnight, given that a man can wake up to find himself transformed into an insect—given these things, the rest follows. But only if these propositions are given, in the sense of being accepted. We must first accept this initial imaginative feat. . . . (p. 142)

Kafka's Gregor Samsa . . . is not independent of his cockroach form, as Kovalev is of his nose, but he too is now really himself. No longer is he the insignificant commercial traveller, the family breadwinner; his new form is the pure expression of his personality. We know that Kafka's work is an expression of fear. All his life he was obsessed with his own father-relationship. He himself was physically puny and, as he considered, a human failure; his father was a gross giant of a man, untroubled by spiritual doubt, who had fought his way up from a miserably impoverished childhood to become a relatively prosperous merchant. (p. 143)

So in the story Samsa/Kafka (who could overlook the clear transliteration?) . . . Samsa/Kafka is the noxious insect, unfit for human life, a pathetic and (some would say) pathological confession of human inadequacy. The human Samsa stands spiritually naked in his insect form. No human conventions shield him from the emotional tensions of the family—father, mother and sister. He has dropped the human mask, and they must take him as he is. The mother and sister almost survive the test, but the father rejects him from the start. The father, who had become economically dependent on his commercial traveller son, is now rejuvenated by the shift of economic importance within the family. With his restoration to the headship of the family he regains his emotional ascendancy; the insect son withers and dies. For this insect does not suck blood; it is a failure even as an insect. It dies because it is dependent—in the last resort dependent on the father. The price of life, to the insect as to man, is personal certainty. This is what Kafka himself did not attain until—ironically enough—the last year of his short life. He is perpetually in that nightmare state where a man is inarticulate when he should speak, and rooted immovably when he knows he must fly from danger. That is the figure that he projects into his stories—the hunter and the hunted, both in one. (p. 144)

But, of course, not everyone will get past the first feeling that these events are impossibilities that remain impossible. And ludicrous and unpleasant impossibilities at that. Who in his right senses can believe in Kovalev's pursuit of his wandering nose? In Gregor Samsa, with that nauseating trail of slime behind him as he crawls over the walls and ceiling of his room? Or in Joseph K., guiltily defending himself against a charge whose nature he does not know and never will know? It's all nonsense, utterly unlike life. But then, Gogol and Kafka might protest, so is life. For life, as we know it, is incomplete. What these authors create is a symbol for the whole of life, including that other realm of consciousness which lies behind appearance. No man, they might argue, *is* in his right senses until he can experience the whole of this reality.

In his essay *Ur-Geräusch (Primal Sound)* Rilke speculates on man's sensory capacities. At present, he says, each of our five senses covers its own sector, which is separate from the others. But, as long as these sense-sectors are separate, there can be no certainty that they cover all that can possibly be experienced. May there not be gaps between them, mysterious chasms in man's perception, spaces of which we are ignorant—not because there is nothing there, but because our sensory capacity is incomplete? It is these gaps in our awareness, Rilke believes, that cause our human anxiety, for we fear the unknown. And it is to these gaps that Gogol and Kafka lead us. They are constantly straining beyond their known boundaries, and this (Rilke holds) is the task of the poet—to extend the boundaries of the individual senses until they meet and coalesce, and the writer is enabled to grasp the whole of the real world with one five-fingered hand of the senses.

Gogol and Kafka and their like plunge into the dark regions, and we follow as best we can—or pull back hastily from the brink, uncharitably scolding them for leaving our firm, rational world. But are we justified in thinking them absurd because irrational? Or should we not recognize that they deliberately abandon the rational world because it is inadequate for them, and they for it? They choose the irrational because they must, and because they know they will find there, as in a dream, the roots of their own human dilemma. And, if we can follow them, we too may find that the non-sensory world is really anything but nonsensical. (p. 145)

I. F. Parry, "Kafka and Gogol," in German Life & Letters, *n.s. Vol. VI, No. 2, January, 1953, pp. 141-45.**

DOUGLAS ANGUS (essay date 1954)

[*Angus combines mythic and biographical elements to interpret* The Metamorphosis *as an inversion of the "Beauty and the Beast" fairy tale, in which a hideously changed person is restored by an unselfish response to an appeal for love. In* The Metamorphosis, *Gregor's thrice-repeated plea for acceptance and understanding is rejected, and he dies.*]

The theory that dream and myth are intimately related, referred to by Freud and elaborated by Jung and associated psychologists, is supported by the curious reappearance in Kafka's surrealistic story **"Metamorphosis"** of certain traits found in folklore. Not only is the story steeped in symbolism, but it is specifically concerned with the metamorphosis of a human being into a lower form of life, an ancient and widely dispersed topic of myth. Then too, the threefold construction of Kafka's story, the thrice repeated appeal for pity, shows how similar the creative process in his mind was to that of the myth maker and balladist. But it is in the specific pattern of the narrative that the most striking similarity to folklore is to be found. Metamorphosis followed by a repeated appeal for love is one of the most wide-spread narrative patterns of myth and ballad, to be found in the "beauty and the beast" and the "loathly lady" tales. Usually in the folklore material the appeal for love, or the symbolic gesture of love, is granted and the magic transformation and marriage follow. With Kafka, however, the masochism that turned his writing into a kind of extended self-torture precluded any such happy solution.

In the search for similarities of psychological meaning it is the "beauty and the beast" tale that offers the more significant parallel. There the beast is masculine, and although Beauty may seem to occupy the center of the stage, being the active agent, the story is really the "beast's" story. . . . In the tale, it will be recalled, a prince, cast through an evil spell into the form of a hideous beast, appeals in the most humble fashion to a beautiful maiden for her love. When the maiden overcomes her repugnance and kisses the beast, the prince regains his human form and marries the girl.

In the tale certain themes are obvious. In the beauty's act of love there is the sentimental and moral concept of love, or rather tender-heartedness, overcoming repugnance; in the prince's marrying her is the commonplace theme of virtue being rewarded. The transformation following the girl's gesture of love expresses a third theme, partially symbolic—the power of love to conquer evil. Not so obvious in meaning are the evil metamorphosis itself and the strangely exaggerated and repeated appeal of the beast for Beauty's love. These latter are the most hauntingly mysterious parts of the tale and are therefore most likely to be the most deeply laden with autobiographical symbols. They are also the two phases of the narrative that are paralleled in Kafka's story. What makes this parallel especially interesting is the fact that the autobiographical meaning of the incidents in Kafka's story can be readily perceived, and thus a hypothesis is presented to elucidate the original autobiographical references in this familiar folklore narrative pattern.

About the general meaning of the metamorphosis in the Kafka story there appears to be no mystery. All our knowledge of Kafka's life and story technique suggests that it is a precipitation in fantasy of his lifelong sense of loneliness and exclusion, of physical inferiority, and of an ingrained hypochondria, references to which in his diaries are too numerous to enumerate. That the entire story is one long, varied and agonized appeal for love is obvious. It is the strangely fawning appeal of the "beast" magnified and elaborated until it absorbs the whole creative impulse. Three times the "black beetle" comes forth to make the symbolic revelation of repulsiveness and the humble appeal for love, and each time he is rewarded with cruelty, derision, or indifference, until finally, when even his kindly sister Greta deserts him, he resorts to the last desperate appeal of the narcissistic neurotic and dies for pity (rationalizing the act as a sacrifice to free his family from the burden of his presence).

The need for affection is the basic psychic hunger. In Kafka's case lack of consistent or reliable sources of affection in childhood seems to have established the narcissistic pattern in conjunction with a morbid sense of physical inferiority, the latter heightened by his complex relationship with his robust and energetic father. The story **"Metamorphosis"** is a symbolistic projection of this psychic pattern. It seems to say, "I am not loved because I am repulsive." In varying degrees the pattern is common to all humanity and so is likely to appear frequently in myth and folklore. What Kafka's neurosis will not permit him to express but the wisdom of the myth comprehends, is that the repulsiveness is really psychic in origin and love could achieve the "magic transformation." (pp. 69-71)

Douglas Angus, "Kafka's 'Metamorphosis' and 'The Beauty and the Beast' Tale," in Journal of English and Germanic Philology *(© 1954 by the Board of Trustees of the University of Illinois), Vol. LIII, No. 1, January, 1954, pp. 69-71.*

WALTER H. SOKEL (essay date 1956)

[*Sokel is the author of* The Writer in Extremis: Expressionism in Twentieth-Century Literature *(1959) in which he examines Kafka's* Metamorphosis *as "an extended metaphor, a metaphoric visualization of an emotional situation, uprooted from any explanatory context." He is also the author of two books on Kafka:* Franz Kafka: Tragik und Ironie, zur Struktur seine Kunst *(1964) and* Franz Kafka *(1966). In the following excerpt Sokel examines the function of the metamorphosis in relation to Gregor's feelings about his employers and his family. He concludes that the metamorphosis both frees Gregor from a hated responsibility and punishes him for this release. For a contrasting opinion, see the excerpt below by Norman Friedman (1963), who disagrees with Freudian interpretations in favor of a more literal reading. In an aside, Sokel likens the transformed Gregor to a cockroach. For a different interpretation of this point, see the excerpt by Vladimir Nabokov in* TCLC, *Volume 6.*]

Günther Anders has pointed out that Kafka's literary uniqueness lies in the fact that he dramatizes conventional figures of speech and endows them with full and consistent detail; his tales act out the implications of metaphors buried in the German idiom. ***Metamorphosis,*** the story of the travelling salesman Gregor Samsa's transformation into a giant species of vermin, is cited as a prominent example. In German usage the appellation "dreckiger Käfer" (dirty bug) denotes a slovenly and unclean individual. Kafka transforms the metaphor into a narrative with a minutely detailed bourgeois setting. (p. 203)

However, to see nothing but an extended metaphor in Kafka's work is not to see enough. The tale is too long, too packed with statements, too rich in meaning to be defined simply as a metaphor, no matter how extended. As a first approach to a formal analysis of Kafka's opus Anders' concept is excellent (Kafka himself is reported to have claimed that the metaphor is the basis of all poetry); as the sole key to his long work it does not suffice. It ignores, for example, the numerous statements in the narrative dealing with the situation of Gregor and his family before the metamorphosis. These alone make for a textual and poetic complexity which overburdens the theory of the single metaphor. . . .

It lies in the nature of Kafka's deeply ambiguous art that no single analysis can completely comprehend his multi-faceted creation. Each can merely be one step toward the explanation of a "mystery," the essence of which can perhaps never be fully resolved. (p. 204)

I propose to raise this question: Does Gregor Samsa's metamorphosis possess a function in the total narrative? Is there a reason for it? The total narrative includes a time before the metamorphosis; it begins with the business failure of Gregor's father and the debt to Gregor's employer contracted at that time. To find an answer to my question it will be necessary to examine the pre-history of the metamorphosis itself, which previous studies have largely ignored, contained in Gregor's musings after he wakes up, specifically his relationship to his firm and to his employer. Also it will be necessary to consider the role of the chief clerk. Finally we must deal with the meaning of the specific insect shape into which Gregor has changed. Mindful of the advice of a number of recent critics to investigators of Kafka's work, this study will "take Kafka at his word"; it will assume, that is, that every statement made by the author "counts" in the context of his work and that a careful scrutiny of the text may reveal his art and a good bit of its "mystery" to us.

Any reader of Kafka's ***Metamorphosis*** must have noted with some surprise that Gregor Samsa, upon waking up to find himself transformed, ponders much more over his job than over his strange misfortune. Appearing to forget what has happened to him, he resents the necessity of getting up and continuing the harried existence of a travelling salesman. Gregor has been intensely dissatisfied with his job; he especially chafes under the lack of respect shown him by his firm and the degrading treatment accorded him by his boss, a tyrant who addresses his employees from a high desk as though he were seated on a throne. We learn from Gregor's reflections that he has nurtured rebellious thoughts about his boss and dreamed of telling him off in a fashion that would send the old man toppling off his high desk, while Gregor would walk out into freedom. However, he has had to inhibit this rebellious wish because of the huge debt which his father owes the employer and which Gregor has to pay off slowly by working for him. He has to continue his hated bondage until the distant day when the debt will be paid. Now he must get up, dress, and catch the early train.

However, the metamorphosis has intervened and made this impossible. It accomplishes, as we can see, in part at least, the goal of Gregor's longed-for rebellion. It sets him free of his odious job. At the same time, it relieves him of having to make a choice between his responsibility to his parents and his yearning to be free. The metamorphosis enables Gregor to become free and stay "innocent," a mere victim of uncontrollable calamity.

The text of the story will shed further light on this function of Gregor's metamorphosis. . . . We note that no sooner does Gregor express the wish that the devil free him of his job than he is reminded of his transformed body. This conjunction endows the figure of speech with a sinister and literal significance. If we substitute "metamorphosis" for "devil" Gregor's wish has actually been granted, for the metamorphosis has surely taken the job from him. . . . But a chill seizes him when he realizes his new form of existence. His shudder is the price exacted for his escape.

Furthermore, we discover through the chief clerk's remarks that shortly before the metamorphosis a crisis has been developing in Gregor's relations with his work. The chief clerk claims that Gregor's efforts have slackened badly and that his sales have diminished to such a point that his job is endangered. The boss even strongly suspects him of having embezzled funds of the firm. Gregor denies the truth of these accusations; but he admits that he has been feeling unwell and should have asked for a sick leave. We see then that Gregor's body was beginning to feel the strain of his work too hard to bear when the metamorphosis occurred, freeing him of any further responsibility.

The question arises whether illness would not have served the same purpose. Indeed there are frequent references to illness in the beginning of the story. . . . But when he considers reporting himself sick, he immediately rejects the idea. The firm never believes in the illness of its employees. . . . Illness, therefore, would still leave him helpless in the company's power. Besides Gregor feels perfectly well physically, after his change, and has a ravenous appetite. The metamorphosis is not sickness. For sickness would not provide a condition vital to Gregor's metamorphosis—the element of retaliation and aggression against the firm.

Gregor's daydream, as we have seen, embraced not only freedom from the job, but also aggressive action against the boss. The metamorphosis realizes this dream of revolt in an oblique, indirect way. To explain this, we must examine the role the chief clerk plays in the story.

The chief clerk comes to the apartment to accuse Gregor of grave neglect of duty and threatens him with dismissal. (pp. 205-07)

What is Gregor's reaction to the chief clerk's coming? First he feels intense anger. Then the thought occurs to him that the chief clerk himself might be changed into a bug some day. . . . There is a parallel between this thought and his former wish of seeing the boss fall down from his high seat. In either case Gregor imagines his superiors humiliated. In one case the desire is openly acknowledged; in the other it is disguised as a possibility imagined, but clearly the fantasy conceals a wish. (pp. 207-08)

When the chief clerk starts his reproaches and threats, Gregor quickly succumbs to fear and pushes his anger out of his consciousness. But his metamorphosis, his horribly changed appearance, has precisely the effect which an outburst of rage on Gregor's part would have; it functions as aggression against the chief clerk. The moment Gregor opens the door and shows himself in his new shape to the chief clerk, the roles of the two are reversed in fact even though Gregor does not recognize this. The chief clerk, who has come to threaten Gregor, now retreats in terror while Gregor, hitherto the poor exploited and despised salesman, drives him out of the apartment so that he leaves his hat and cane behind, tokens of Gregor's triumph. . . .

More important is the fact that the metamorphosis fulfills Gregor's desire for revolt without implicating his conscious mind. The conscious aim of Gregor's pursuit of the chief clerk is not to frighten but to reconcile him. . . . Yet his inadvertent use of the term "pursuit" to describe his advance toward the chief clerk reveals what is actually happening, as does the chief clerk's flight itself. The discrepancy between the actual result of Gregor's action and his own explanation of it has a ludicrous effect upon the reader. It is grotesquely comic to watch the startled chief clerk run away, staring with gaping mouth over his shoulder at the monstrous creature that is relentlessly scuttling after him, while Gregor begs him to stay calm and put in a good word for him at the office. (p. 208)

[It] is less faulty logic than a psychic compromise which lies at the basis of Gregor's self-deception—a compromise between the satisfaction of an aggressively rebellious impulse and a duty-bound conscience that demands submission. The function of the metamorphosis is to allow the compromise. Rebellion proceeds by mere physical phenomena—Gregor's frightening appearance, his misunderstood movements toward the chief clerk, the snapping of his jaws—facts over which his conscious mind has no control. Thus he remains "innocent," the victim of an external calamity which he does not understand. It is Gregor's ignorance of his suppressed anger and hostility toward his superiors that causes him to be surprised at the chief clerk's (and his parents') reactions toward him. He thinks he is animated only by the best intentions; all he wants is to propitiate the chief clerk and return to his job as soon as possible. How deeply he loathes his job and hates his superiors he has forgotten. But the others cannot hear what he tries to tell them; they cannot hear his rationalizations. All they perceive are his appearance and his motions, and these look menacing, and utterly contradict his professed good intentions. What the metamorphosis does is to make Gregor's suppressed desire visible. It turns his inside out, as it were. (Here, of course, we see the technique of expressionism.) His hostility, having erupted, has made his whole body its horrifying manifestation. His conscious mind, of course, does not participate in this eruption, but its rationalizations cannot be communicated to the others. Only the inner truth is there to see for all except Gregor himself. When the chief clerk runs away from him in fright he reacts to Gregor's true wish and, in a way, understands him better than Gregor dares to understand himself. Likewise when Gregor's father reacts to the metamorphosis as though it were a malicious trick of Gregor's, a refusal to do his duty, he is, as our analysis so far has shown, closer to the truth than Gregor and the superficial reader, for whom the catastrophe is an inexplicable blow of fate, a monstrous "accident."

Viewed in this way, the metamorphosis reveals a pattern which Freud has made known to us in his study of accidents. Accidents, says Freud, are often acts springing from motives of which the conscious mind keeps carefully unaware. Accidental injuries are often self-punishment induced by hidden guilt feelings. Accidents in which one person injures another may be caused by unconscious hostility. . . . By the time he wrote ***Metamorphosis*** (November, 1912) Kafka was familiar with the writings of Freud; he alludes to Freud in his diary, in connection with his earlier story ***The Judgment,*** two months before he wrote ***Metamorphosis.*** His familiarity with the world that Freud opened to the Occidental mind does not, of course, mean that he applied Freudian insights deliberately during the composition of his works; everything we know about Kafka's spontaneous mode of creation, especially in the autumn of 1912, would speak against a deliberate, calculating manner of composition. It is something else to suspect that Freudian ideas might have colored the background of his mind and influenced

his spontaneous thinking. At any rate, the remarkable parallelism between the pattern of the metamorphosis and the pattern of many "accidents" described by Freud remains unaffected, whether or not Kafka was aware of it during the writing of his work.

Gregor Samsa's metamorphosis resembles both types of "accidents" described by Freud, those in which a person satisfies his suppressed hostility by "accidentally" hurting someone else, and those in which he hurts himself. So far we have established that Gregor's metamorphosis expresses his secret hostility toward his work and his boss. Now we have to show that it also expresses his guilt and the punishment for this guilt. The metamorphosis clears him of any "official" responsibility for betraying his parents; but it fails to free him of a vague, pervasive sense of guilt toward his family. This sense of guilt manifests itself in a panicky need to prove his innocence, and this need in turn plays a vital part in bringing him to ruin.

When the story begins, the metamorphosis is not complete. Gregor is still able to speak and be understood by his family. . . . He retains a control over his speech that leaves it intelligible and recognizably human. He loses this control after the chief clerk accuses him of indulging in "strange whims" and warns him of losing his job (the very thing Gregor secretly desires). These accusations throw him into a state of "agitation" in which he forgets "everything else" but the desperate need to show his good will and conceal the truth of his situation. Thus he forgets to discipline his voice during his frantic pleading with the chief clerk and his speech is no longer intelligible. The chief clerk tells the flabbergasted parents that what they heard from Gregor's room was "no human voice"; and from then on Gregor loses all possibility of communication and is thrown forever into his terrifying isolation.

Gregor's isolation crowns his metamorphosis. As long as he can be understood, he cannot be a complete insect. To be sure, his mind always remains human; but, after the loss of his voice, his humanity cannot be perceived by his fellow men. It cannot communicate with and act upon them. For the world he has become nothing but an insect although continuing to be a human being for himself. This is, of course, Gregor's agonizing tragedy: that he feels and thinks as a human being while unable to make his humanity felt and known. . . . The nature of the physical transformation . . . makes any attempt to communicate ineffectual—unnoticed or misunderstood; and the mind stays imprisoned, a torturing instrument in a functionless vacuum. . . . [Kafka's] subtle work shows that the hero at least accentuates his tragedy by his panicky urge to conform to what is expected of him, while leaving his real desires unacknowledged even when they work havoc with him. (pp. 209-11)

The same tendency helps bring about his physical destruction in the end. When his angry father pursues him, Gregor, bent on proving his obedience and good intentions, abstains from fleeing up the walls to the ceiling, and so deprives himself of the only advantage his insect shape gives him. Instead he stays on the floor within reach of the father's menacing boots and becomes the easy target of the apples with which his father bombards and cripples him. Gregor never recovers from this wound, and it hastens his death.

From these examples we can now deduce that Gregor's catastrophe is intimately linked to the appeasement both of his own conscience and of his superiors in firm and family. He loses his voice when he seeks to appease the chief clerk; he courts death in seeking to appease his father. Now, it is remarkable that this appeasement has precisely the opposite of the effect it should have. Instead of saving Gregor, it brings him ever closer to destruction. Above all, the examples show us that this ineffectual appeasement of the "superego" tends to accentuate the natural effects of the metamorphosis, namely isolation and helplessness. May we not infer from this that the metamorphosis itself is such a treacherous appeasement of a sense of guilt which in demonstrating innocence and helplessness actually invites punishment and destruction? In order to answer this question let us see what it is exactly that Gregor has been changed into.

Kafka states in the first sentence that Gregor wakes up to find himself changed into a giant kind of vermin ("Ungeziefer"). The term "vermin" holds the key to the double aspect of the metamorphosis. Vermin connotes something parasitic and aggressive, something that lives off human beings and may suck their blood; on the other hand, it connotes something defenseless, something that can be stepped upon and crushed. Gregor's hugeness emphasizes the aggressive aspect. Moreover, at the beginning of the story the reader might be inclined to think of Gregor's new form as that [of] a bedbug. Kafka's famous letter to his father would give support to such a view since Kafka has his father refer to him as a blood-sucking type of vermin, a bedbug or a louse. But later we discover that Gregor does not possess the aggressiveness of the bloodsucking vermin. He does not feed on blood, but on garbage. This diet (as well as the term "Mistkäfer" used by the charwoman and a later reference in Kafka's diary to "the black beetle" of his story) lead one to believe that Gregor is akin to a cockroach, a creature that may nauseate human beings but does not attack them. Offensive in looks, it is defenseless in fact.

The image of the giant cockroach perfectly expresses the two aspects of the metamorphosis, aggression and helplessness, and the order of their importance. The metamorphosis endows Gregor with a terrifying exterior; it causes panic in the chief clerk and makes his mother faint. But at the same time it renders him infinitely more vulnerable than he was in his human form. A foot held up over his head, a chair raised over his back, threaten death. An apple almost kills him. Gregor realizes that, apart from his "frightening appearance," he has no weapons. . . . His menacing appearance is merely appearance, but his helplessness is real. It exposes him to merciless punishment by anyone who, like his father, is eager to exploit it.

Thus the metamorphosis links punishment to aggression, for the very transformation which enables Gregor to drive the chief clerk away renders him helpless in the face of his father's wrath; but punishment, rather than aggression, is its ultimate function. For the father transforms Gregor's victory over the chief clerk into ruinous defeat. He takes over as the chief clerk flees. He seizes the trophy of Gregor's triumph, the chief clerk's cane, left behind in his flight, brandishes it over Gregor's head, and threatens to crush and flatten him with it. Gregor has to cease his movement toward the outside, toward the world and freedom. Under the threat of his furious father he now has to turn back to his room, henceforth the prison in which he will pine away his life in solitary confinement.

In conclusion, it may be said that the metamorphosis would not have occurred in either of these two cases: if Gregor had not nurtured hostility toward his work and his boss, or if he had revolted openly and thrown up his job without regard to his parents. To put it in positive terms: the metamorphosis accommodates Gregor's conflicting needs, the need to rebel, and the need to suffer punishment for this rebellion. Above all, by being an unconscious process, the metamorphosis protects him from self-knowledge. Indeed, one of the most curious facts about it is Gregor's lack of curiosity as to the causes of his change. These causes are something Gregor wishes not to know, something he would prefer to leave buried. Therefore, the metamorphosis appears as an utterly mysterious, inexplicable event. The author, however, by letting us see Gregor's feelings of revolt at the opening of the story (after which they are repressed and extinguished in guilt and fear) has given us a key to the mystery of the metamorphosis. If we make use of this key, Kafka's work seems like the expressionist illustration of an "accident" that is not a true accident according to Freud. To the victim and the superficial observer such a calamity appears a senseless and unforeseeable event, a brute happening bare of meaning. Upon analysis of the victim's life, however, the accident is found to fulfill a function. It comes as the climax of a secret history of hostility and guilt. These combine to erupt in the catastrophe which mutilates and destroys him who has failed to face the turmoil in his soul. (pp. 212-14)

Walter H. Sokel, "Kafka's 'Metamorphosis': Rebellion and Punishment," in Monatshefte *(copyright © 1956 by The Board of Regents of the University of Wisconsin System), Vol. XLVIII, No. 4, April-May, 1956, pp. 203-14.*

ROBERT M. ADAMS (essay date 1958)

[Following a comparison of Kafka's satiric methods with those of Jonathan Swift, Adams discusses the structural and symbolic significance of the triad in the narrative of The Metamorphosis.*]*

Of modern authors, Kafka perhaps comes closest to inhabiting a hall of broken mirrors like Swift's. Although his world is seen, typically, from below the floor rather than from above the horizon, his normal effect is the same: to lacerate, tease, and disquiet the reader. For Swift the human beast is a gibbering baboon, but he looks down on this beast with the calm and lofty eye of a horse; for Kafka the given point of view is that of a dog, a bug, a mouse, an obscure, burrowing, misshapen monster. Both writers use animal imagery to convey their disgust with the human condition; both are expert in the half-serious manipulation of levels of intent and in the use of potential symbolic significances to mask, as well as to reveal, their meaning. Both men stand outside the range of "normal" humanity—the normality is their own conception or misconception, they cannot be sure which—both envy and despise "the others." Both men betray a shuddering horror of domestic intimacy, together with an extraordinary deference before the father-figures of authority; both are extraordinarily nice men with extraordinarily nasty minds. Both are alien and challenging figures, for whom the pure aesthetic effect is a pure aesthetic irrelevance; the sort of freedom in which they are interested is, typically, desperate, frigid, and self-absorbed to the verge of being suicidal. Both employ, as the very structure of their writing, devices of prolonged equivocation; both like to tease the reader with the tricks and traps of numerology.

The central antitheses of Kafka's work are encompassed in the familiar ambiguities of the word "sacred," or, if one prefers anthropological to theological terminology, "taboo." Both words imply among their meanings the notions of "holy" and "accursed," and both meanings are readily convertible. (pp. 168-69)

Kafka's equivocation and ambivalence are qualities both persistent and complex; and the duality of his feeling has sometimes been traced to what Swift would call the brain-maggotry of numerological speculation. For instance, Charles Neider has pointed out Kafka's use of the number two as a symbol of community and solidarity; and one might make even more point out of his play with triads, that is, little groups of three, consisting of one leader and two followers. These patterns certainly occur and perhaps have a vague structural or symbolic significance, for instance, in the famous fable of ***Metamorphosis.*** This is the story, as everyone knows and as the first sentence tells us, of one Gregor Samsa, a commercial traveler, who "awoke one morning from uneasy dreams, and found himself transformed into a gigantic insect." The metamorphosis which so abruptly sets off the story and which animates the hero's later struggles is a symbolic alienation from humanity. Both the alienation and the struggles are expressed in combinations of three which either reject Gregor or offer him a potential status. For instance, his central position in the family before his metamorphosis is evidenced by the fact that he then occupied the central one of three bedrooms. When, after enormous efforts, he emerges from this room for the first time, he encounters a fully formed and hostile triad of authorities: the chief clerk, the father, and the mother confront him directly, two symbols of authority and discipline, one helpless and unconscious figure of revulsion. Meanwhile in the background appear two symbols particularly hopeful for Gregor. The maid runs for a locksmith, the sister for a doctor; and clearly there is room within either grouping for a triad including Gregor. But before help can arrive Gregor has met and been crushed by the triad of his elders. In fainting, in flight, and in rage they testify to the utter revulsion which he inspires; and Gregor is thereby sealed out of the casual, contented fraternity of the well.

That his illness is sexual in nature is suggested by three clues. A picture of impudent salacity hangs on his wall, and his only diversion has been to make with a fretsaw a frame for this pornographic fetish. His erotic memories are either of failure or of furtive, underhanded success—he recalls "a chambermaid in one of the rural hotels, a sweet and fleeting memory, a cashier in a milliner's shop whom he had wooed earnestly but too slowly." His mother refers to an extraordinary streak of docile domesticity in her son: "he never goes out in the evenings; he's been here the last eight evenings and has stayed home every single evening. He just sits there quietly at the table reading a newspaper or looking through railway timetables." He has even made a practice of locking his bedroom door at night. All these touches point toward the sort of sexual failure which is typical of the Kafka protagonist—inversion, withdrawal, fetishism, isolation, and untapped sensuality. And this sort of failure is appropriately symbolized by Gregor's isolation from the number three, the masculine number.

(In the esoteric circles where such things are decided, the masculinity of three, as of odd numbers generally, is an ancient and well-disseminated principle. . . .) (pp. 171-73)

The use of the triad symbol becomes particularly emphatic when Gregor for the second time comes out of his room to claim a position in the human circle. The occasion of this sortie is the cleaning of his room, an act of double significance since it implies both kindness (the room is described as filthy) and condemnation (to remove Gregor's furniture is to deprive him of the memory as well as the hope of humanity). In open defiance of this change Gregor climbs up the wall to his fetish picture and clings there frantically. Enormous outbursts of rage, terror, and confused revulsion result from this act of insubordination. Gregor, sick with remorse and worry, scuttles out of his room and almost at once comes under attack from his father, who, dressed in the uniform of his work and his authority, advances on his insect-son, throwing apples at him. These weapons, literally so trivial and symbolically so heavy, crash upon Gregor with the full weight of his father's once-successful and now-regained sensuality. And they are terribly reinforced as the mother—revived from her faint, disheveled, half-disrobed, and followed by her screaming daughter—rushes out of Gregor's room to reach "a complete union" with the father. The ruin of Gregor Samsa is completed by the formation of this triad, which shuts him out of the very heart of his family. (pp. 173-74)

So menacing is the triad of the family that it seems to be duplicated, if not parodied, in the form of a second triad of lodgers, who arrive at this point to share the unhappy family's quarters. The lodgers are queer in several ways: they seem to occupy but one room and to have brought most of their own furnishings; they are identical in appearance, with full beards, umbrellas, and shabby coats; and they are distinguished only by their position with relation to one another, as the middle lodger, who takes the lead, and the other two, who follow him or repeat what he says.

The nature and function of these lodgers can only be described as puzzling. Their behavior always involves a reversal; their first appearance is just the opposite of their final intent. For example, they are suspicious of the food served them, but soon show satisfaction in it; they wish to hear the sister play on her violin, but are soon bored; learning of Gregor's existence, they threaten the family, but are soon cowed by the father and go off quietly. (pp. 174-75)

There is a phantom quality to the lodgers, who appear and disappear mysteriously; and the constant unexpected reversal of their intentions may perhaps serve to mock Gregor's (and the family's) undue deference to the triad, which has hitherto been order, community, and strength. They have only to be faced firmly and they disappear; thus, if Gregor in the first episode had only faced the menacing triads down instead of submitting to them, he might have triumphed. The inhumanly rigid law which turns out to be no law at all—at least for the person who supposed it applied to him—is a frequent component of Kafka's writing. As for the sister's curious act of hastily making up their beds, it is an act of deference all the more significant if the authority to which she defers is bogus. . . . If the authority of the lodgers is genuine, it is a fitting tribute to the principle of masculine authority, in which Gregor is fatally deficient; if their authority is bogus, her tribute can only confirm Gregor's self-abasing belief in it.

Thus the triad principle has undergone a striking reversal in the course of the fable. At first it was a good and healthy principle from which Gregor was tragically alienated, gradually it was modified by the inevitable cruelty and selfishness of the heatlhy, and at last it appears as a vicious folly. For whether the authority of the lodgers was false in general or only through Gregor's weakness, it is quickly proved false as well as destructive. . . . [The] departure of the malignant triad of lodgers is but a prelude to the loosening of that other malignant triad in which the family has been gripped; and the story ends with the family at leisure, freed from their nightmare by Gregor's death and placidly contemplating a husband for Grete, who will break the whole pattern of triads beyond repair. (pp. 175-77)

[The] protagonist approves and relishes his own abolition, as if by this final humility to ingratiate himself with a superior power. The ending of the story thus emphasizes that reading of the fable according to which Gregor, whose only failing was humility, dies in deference to a bogus deity; and on these terms the triads are mere figments of Gregor's sick mind. On the other hand, the incorporation of threes in the structure of the story itself, as well as the logic of Gregor's early situation, suggests another view of the symbolism, scarcely less plausible. Gregor is indubitably sick, his illness is doubtless an alienation, and three is an eloquent symbol of the health and community from which he is isolated. These two interpretations are wholly incompatible; they are also equally cogent. The conflict between them is heightened by Kafka's occasional use of random threes neither to tell his story nor to satirize it but to tantalize the reader. Thus there appear in the story three servants (cook, maid, and char); it is three o'clock in the morning when Gregor dies; the action of the story takes place over a period of three months. Even if one did not know that teasing the reader was a frequent device of Kafka's, one might suspect it from the thick configuration of threes in ***Metamorphosis,*** their interlocked and layered arrangement, and their occasional complete irrelevance. (p. 177)

Robert M. Adams, "Swift and Kafka: Satiric Incongruity and the Inner Defeat of the Mind," in his Strains of Discord: Studies in Literary Openness *(© 1958 by Cornell University; used by permission of the publisher, Cornell University Press), Cornell University Press, 1958 (and reprinted by Books for Libraries Press, 1971; distributed by Arno Press, Inc., pp. 146-79).**

NORMAN FRIEDMAN (essay date 1963)

[Friedman examines and rejects biographical interpretations of The Metamorphosis *(see the excerpt by Charles Neider, 1948, for a representative example) in favor of a strictly literal reading. Friedman finds that Gregor's transformation serves a valid purpose: it is the only means whereby his family can be freed from their parasitic dependence upon Gregor. This interpretation diverges forcefully from those who believe Gregor's family to be his oppressors. Friedman's interpretation of the story also challenges the psychological approach typified by Walter H. Sokel (see excerpt above, 1956).]*

The problem that teases us in [**"Metamorphosis"**] is how to explain Gregor Samsa's mysterious and disgusting change. Normally, we could attempt to solve such a problem by asking two questions: first, how and why did he become an insect in terms of the probabilities of the action? and second, what are Kafka's reasons for handling it in this way? The first question can usually be answered directly by examining the incidents in the story and their causes, while the second may be answered only indirectly by making inferences about what the author wanted to accomplish in so arranging things.

Now the trouble with this story is that we can never answer the first question, simply because no clues are either stated or implied as to how and why this change came about. (p. 26)

This transformation, then, must be accepted as a *fait accompli,* and so all avenues of explanation regarding the first question are closed. The story, however, deals exclusively with Gregor's and his family's reactions to this change, and it stands to reason that unless we understand the meaning of this change we will fail to understand the meaning of their reactions to it, and hence of the story as a whole. We must rely solely, therefore, on exploring the possible answers to the second question, and here at least two avenues of approach are open to us as we pursue Kafka's motives: the psychological and the artistic. Let us consider them in turn.

The search for psychological causes is the most common approach followed when dealing with this story, and it seeks to find in it an intelligible pattern by building on Kafka's biography, the Freudian hypothesis, and some scheme of literary or archetypal symbolism. Generally speaking, such an interpretation runs along the following lines: We know, to begin with, that Kafka felt inadequate in relation to his efficient and successful father, and therefore he was ambivalent about him, feeling ashamed at not measuring up while at the same time feeling resentful that he had to measure up, and admiring his father and wanting to please him to boot. Since Gregor's father plays a characteristic role in the story, wanting no nonsense from his bug-like son and even wounding him at the end, it seems plausible to attribute to the Samsa situation the factors involved in the Kafka situation (even the names are alike!). Thus Gregor has turned himself into a bug, however unconsciously, in order to spite his father and at the same time to punish himself for being an inadequate son. By becoming something non- or sub-human, he has symbolically allowed his hidden and suppressed self to emerge: his need to escape responsibility, his wish to hurt his father, his desire to express his guilt. (pp. 26-7)

A curious consequence of this kind of interpretation is that it ends by setting us against Gregor's family. Stodgy bourgeois *versus* sensitive artist becomes inevitably the story's formula, just as it is the formula of Kafka's life. Thus the ending, where the family is happily released of its dread burden and looks toward a better and healthier future with renewed hope and strength, has either to be wished away as an artistic mistake or to be read ironically as Kafka's final indictment of a sterile society returning once more to its superficial routines of marriage and work and respectability after an unlooked-for encounter with the profound forces of life and death in the unconscious. (p. 27)

And there are other details of the story which the psychological interpretation fails to explain or has to explain ironically. There is the crucial fact, for instance, that it is not the son who is inadequate, at least to begin with, but rather the father. Gregor has been supporting the family for the past four years, while his father has been lying around the house and growing fat ever since his business failed five years before. Now this could very easily be interpreted as a psychological displacement or inversion, so that inadequate Franz becomes adequate Gregor by way of wish fulfilment. . . . But why, then, does the story proceed to reinstate the father's power over the son by rendering that son incapable of meeting his responsibilities? Can we have it both ways—a Kafka who is symbolically placing himself over his father by means of a story which literally places the father over the son? or who is placing himself beneath his father by means of a story which begins by literally placing the son above the father?

Perhaps the question can be re-phrased in terms of whether we *need* to have it both ways, regardless of whether it is possible. What I want to suggest, in short, is that an answer may be sought within the story itself, regarded as an artistic whole. We can only speculate about the tangled inner forces which impelled Kafka to write such a story, and to write it in such a way, and this speculation can be interesting and valuable. But any answer it may produce regarding the story's meaning is perforce more broad and generic than is necessary, for the significance and function of any given element in that story are in the last analysis to be interpreted only in terms of that story. If such a literal approach fails to provide an answer, then it can only be concluded that there is none. Unless, that is, we are content to accept the story as a dream, and that I am not prepared to do. Certain psychological causes may be uniformly operative throughout an author's lifetime, and yet he may write many different sorts of stories. So we cannot, I believe, settle for a simple explanation of a complex thing: psychological principles are never sufficient when one is asking artistic questions. At best they can point to certain things which the various stories may share in common, and thus are better suited to the study of an author's work as an expression of his personality than to the study of individual stories as works of art. But they cannot by their very nature explain the differences which may obtain among them. And in these differences lies the unique artistic quality of a work.

I do not mean to suggest, however, that we must blind ourselves to symbols when they appear in the story, or to hidden motives, or to our knowledge of family life; I mean only that we must interpret these things in terms of assumptions which are directly relevant to the story, and hypotheses whose ultimate justification lies within the story and its internal relationships. Psychological principles, after all, can and even should be used in the interpretation of the characters'—as distinct from the author's—motives within the framework of the story. Nor do I mean to say that such a literal reading will provide exhaustive and final answers: I mean only that such a reading may supply a sound basis for further inquiry. This is a powerful and mysterious and puzzling story, and it works on us in many ways. It is doubtful whether it can ever be fully explained, but in so far as it is a story it ought to be interpreted as such.

Just what is the story, then, and what is the function of Gregor's transformation in it? The basic problem Kafka set for himself, as I see it, was to show the family gradually freeing itself from its moral dependence upon Gregor, and the solution he hit upon was to turn Gregor into an insect in order to accomplish this. This will take some explaining.

The action is built on two changes: the first is Gregor's gradual deterioration and death, and the second is the family's gradual mobilization and recovery—the two together forming something of an hour-glass pattern. The inciting cause of both changes is, of course, Gregor's unexplained metamorphosis. Its immediate effect is to cut off Gregor from normal life and his family from their sole source of support. This creates in Gregor a pathetic but inevitably frustrated yearning to be recognized, to be understood, to be taken care of, and in his family an opposing disgust and revulsion. This in turn produces in Gregor a selfish unconcern for his family, and in them the need to support themselves combined with an ever-growing desperation as to how to get rid of this monster who was once their son and brother. (The family members, I realize, each react in different ways to his metamorphosis—the mother helplessly, the father tyrannically, and the sister charitably at the outset—but in the end they are united in their resolve to get rid of him.)

Now since we are told nothing about the probabilities of Gregor's change, and cannot therefore interpret it in terms of its causes, perhaps we can interpret it in terms of its effects. Why, to begin with, does his family react so negatively after he becomes a bug? The obvious answer is that he is repulsive. I still think with horror about the insect when I force myself to dwell upon its appearance and movements, although Kafka's manner of treatment softens this horror with pity. And I believe that indeed is part of the point, for the reader sees the story largely from within Gregor's point of view, while the family sees him entirely from without. This means that they are of necessity less sympathetic than we are toward the creature.

But is it not possible, a Freudian might ask, that their hostility toward this bug is in reality a symbolic disguise for their hitherto suppressed hostility toward the son? Surely there is loathing aplenty here, and it is certainly possible within the framework of the story to infer that they have been storing up against him a good deal of resentment for being his parasites. Similarly, it is quite possible to compound the symbol by having it stand for his disguised hatred of them for having to support them. (pp. 28-30)

This is possible, but again I ask whether it is necessary. The only reason for us to postulate a prior mutual resentment between them is our assumption that there must have been bad feeling in such a situation. But the only expressed hostility regarding the circumstances prior to Gregor's change we can find in the story is that which Gregor feels toward his boss, the manager, the other salesmen, and his job itself. He does not blame his family for his hard life as a salesman, nor do they blame him for their dependence on him.

Again, it is possible that Kafka was psychologically unable to confront such hostilities openly, and that this device was a means by which he could deal with them covertly, so that this story is a disguised incest-fantasy, with the bug symbolizing Kafka's suppressed desire to become a child again, and the sister standing cryptically for the mother whom he wishes to wrest from his father. But since such theories postulate a degree of control of the story over the author which I am unable to accept, I would prefer to continue my search for more literal causes. (p. 30)

I reject, on the same grounds, the possibility that the change represents Gregor's desire to escape from his responsibilities. It is true of course that he has been working for four years already and has five or six years to go before his father's debt is paid off; but, disagreeable as he has found his job, there are no expressed signs of any desire on his part to chuck the whole business. The only reason to think so is our assumption that he must want to get out of it. But why choose such a disagreeable way to escape? Is not being a bug even worse than being a travelling salesman? There is surely no pleasure in it for Gregor.

But, says the Freudian, he is also punishing himself: are you so simple-minded as to be unable to see how he can gratify himself and punish himself for this gratification at one and the same time? No one wants to be thought simple-minded, but I wonder whether such a heads-I-win-tails-you-lose assumption covers too many things, and hence fails to be sufficiently clear when applied to a particular case. And besides, why couldn't Gregor have merely developed some psychosomatic ailment and thereby have accomplished his purpose much more effectively? A convenient paralysis of the legs, for example, would have given him enough of an excuse for stopping work while at the same time providing him with enough pain for self-punishment. (pp. 30-1)

But this sort of solution would have hardly suited Kafka's purpose, for then the family would have had to care for him and pity him instead of rejecting him as they do. Robbing the family of their hostility would have robbed Kafka of his story. And that is just the point: not, however, because they have hated him for having been his parasites, but rather because *they* have fallen into a psychosomatic torpor as a result of their dependence on him, and because no other way could be found to bring them out of it.

I reason as follows: Gregor is changed into an insect through no evident fault of his own, nor through any fault of theirs either. It seems to me that Kafka omitted any clues as to the how and why of Gregor's change precisely because he sensed the necessity of preventing the reader from assigning responsibilities in this matter. I believe he wanted us to sympathize with both Gregor and his family—with Gregor, because the story would lose the seriousness of its impact if we were made to feel simply disgust at his transformation; with the family, because without their anguished reaction we would never see for ourselves that Gregor was once human. A moral problem would become for us merely a housecleaning problem. (For the charwoman at the end, remember, it *is* merely a housecleaning problem.) Kafka wants us to sympathize with the family, because we must be prepared for the beneficial transformation they are to undergo: they are about to be released from a trap and we are to feel the force of their rescue as having some positive significance in their lives.

Indeed, if my analysis is correct, it may be that the title refers as much to their change as to his. Some readers have been so moved by Gregor's suffering, however, that they have lost sight of the family's anguish. But recall that Gregor's family do not see this bug as we do. As far as they are concerned, he is no longer their Gregor but a hideous monster with a claim on their affections. (pp. 31-2)

What they *are* accountable for, however, is the torpor into which they have fallen as a result of their dependence on his support. . . . And it is this torpor out of which the shock of Gregor's transformation wakes them, and with that awakening, it seems to me, we can only sympathize. (p. 32)

They have been, in effect, redeemed. The only trouble is that poor Gregor has been sacrificed in the process. Kafka mitigates the pathos of this necessity in two ways: first, he has Gregor get more callous and bug-like in his attitudes as the story progresses (although music retains its power to move him); and second, he has him die peacefully. (pp. 32-3)

Gregor was turned into a bug, then, because there was no other way to free his family from their moral degeneration, and he died because there was no other way to free them for the future. But granted they had to be freed by means of some external agency, it might be objected that Kafka showed poor artistic judgment in choosing so desperate and fantastic an expedient. Consider, however, the alternatives. Had Gregor continued working, they would have continued as his parasites. Had he simply quit his job and left them, they would have been able to blame him and feel sorry for themselves. Had he gotten sick or lame, they would have had to pity him. Had he simply died, they would have been able to feel sorry for themselves. My thesis is that, given the situation, they have to be made to *want* to be free, and the solution Kafka chose was to make Gregor repulsive to them, for only then could they reject him. All avenues of self-defeating escape from their decision are thus closed: blame, pity, remorse—any such emotion would have hindered their desire for freedom. Only by being made to reject him could they be made to want to be free.

It might be further objected that their having to be freed by means of some external agency places Kafka's conception of the situation in a rather poor light. Why were they not capable of rising to the challenge of their lives by drawing upon their own inner resources? Why were they not capable of undergoing an inner change? Why are they worth saving at all, and at so great a cost? The answer lies partly in the fact, I think, that the father and mother are both washed out. . . . The parents simply have no internal resources left, and the sister, just on the threshold of maturity, is too young and inexperienced to expect great things from. They are ordinary people, the victim of a hard life and of a trap they do not know how to get out of. And this, I think, heightens the sympathy we are meant to feel toward them. I doubt, though, whether the parents are in themselves worth saving: it is rather the rescue of the sister which, if anything can justify the cost, explains the sacrifice of Gregor. And that is exactly the note on which Kafka ends. . . . (pp. 33-4)

It was a difficult artistic problem which Kafka set for himself, for he had to retain the reader's sympathy for both parties. Gregor was not to be blamed for turning into a bug, nor was the family to be blamed for rejecting him in this new shape. We were to be made to see both sides and to recognize the inevitable suffering involved in this family convulsion; neither side asked for trouble, but both were caught in a trap not of their own devising. But Gregor has to be destroyed to get them out of it, and the cruelty of this necessity, mitigated or not, cannot be put out of mind. Thus, when the family breathes freely once again at the end, our pleasure is crossed by our knowledge of the price of their redemption. A characteristic aura of Kafkan ambiguity remains as we look back over the whole, for the disagreeable shock of Grete's erotic health when seen in the light of her poor brother's miserable fate, coupled with our memory of the family's miserliness in having withheld some money from his hard-won earnings, of his mother's servile helplessness, and of his father's selfish vanity, prevents us finally from resting content with any simple attribution of sympathy.

The only thing which ultimately allows the story to produce its proper aesthetic satisfaction is our recognition of the fact that of the two possibilities—Gregor continuing on as the sole support of his family, or Gregor being transformed and dying so that they could be reborn—only the second could do any good to any of them. For Gregor was not really alive at all in his role as provider . . . and ironically his continued success in that very role could only have reduced his family further in their moral degradation. Even if he had paid off that impossible debt, they all would have lost in the end—he wasted by overwork and they wallowing in indolence. As it turns out, he paid off the debt after all. (p. 34)

Norman Friedman, "Kafka's 'Metamorphosis': A Literal Reading" (copyright 1963 by Approach; *reprinted from the Approach Collection, by permission of George Arents Research Library for Special Collections at Syracuse University and the author), in* Approach, *No. 49, Fall, 1963, pp. 26-34.*

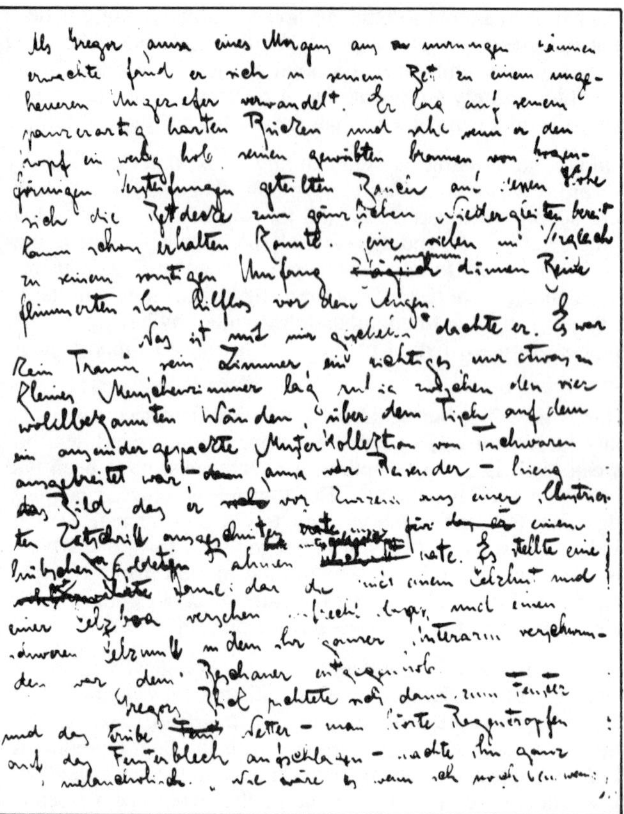

Kafka's original manuscript of the first page of The Metamorphosis. *From* The Complete Stories, *by Franz Kafka. Copyright © 1946, 1947, 1948, 1949, 1954, 1958, 1971 by Schocken Books Inc. Reprinted by permission of Schocken Books Inc.*

ALEXANDER TAYLOR (essay date 1965)

[Taylor finds that Gregor's transformation is an expression of his disenchantment with the structure of his society. However, the transformation also represents the ambivalence of Gregor's position: he yearns to be free, yet is convinced that he is vile because he does not happily fit into the "dehumanizing world of order." For other discussions of The Metamorphosis *as a parable of alienation from society, see the excerpts by Desmond Hawkins (1938) and Paul L. Landsberg (1945).]*

Perhaps the failing of some of the Kafka criticism is the attempt to clarify something that should remain a riddle. ***Metamorphosis*** has certainly had multiple interpretations, many of them prompted by the temptation to lay the corpus of Kafka's works neatly on the psychoanalyst's couch, thus viewing the story as an exercise in masochism or a session in therapy. However, it seems to me that if we look at the story from the viewpoint that it is not Gregor who is sick, but his environment, we will see the story as the reaction of a perceptive individual against a dehumanizing world of order, within which most people are enslaved. . . . [An] indication of the dehumanized world is the father's wearing his bank messenger's uniform at home, where it "began to look dirty despite all the loving care of the mother and sister to keep it clean." The world of order carried into the home destroys the possibility of true human love.

The riddle is Gregor's riddle—how to fulfill himself and simultaneously express his love and understanding among people who react unsympathetically, even violently, against his transformation, and who refuse to recognize his ability to understand them, because they can't understand him. Even more is the riddle Gregor's because he does not understand himself.

The story begins with Gregor's waking; it is a waking in more than one sense, and is therefore represented by his transformation to a giant beetle. Gregor's mind at first refuses to accept this condition even though he senses "it was no dream." He thinks, "What about sleeping a little longer and forgetting all this nonsense?" Then his thoughts turn to his job. It is obvious that he intensely dislikes his work as a travelling salesman . . . , but that on the other hand feels duty bound to continue working until he has saved enough money to pay back his parents' debt to the chief.

Other details of his thoughts, the spineless and stupid porter who checks on him and the insurance doctor who considers "all mankind as perfectly healthy malingerers" emphasize the distrust and suspicion surrounding Gregor and his disgust at this state of affairs.

This disgust stems from Gregor's desire to establish I-thou relationships in a world of I-it or I-she or I-he relationships. [The critic adds in a footnote that "I am using these terms (borrowed from Buber) in a limited sense. I-thou relationships are those of true human affection. I-it are those in which the I uses the person or object as a tool to reach his ends."] In general the people surrounding Gregor do not experience a warm love through a genuine communication, but see each other as objects that are useful or to be used. For instance, the chief clerk is sent to Gregor by the firm because Gregor is not functioning as an object or tool of the firm. (pp. 337-38)

Gregor's relationship to his family previous to his transformation had really become an I-it relationship (further emphasized by the fact that the father had money of his own salted away which he did not use to help pay back his own debt, a debt which kept Gregor in bondage to the firm). . . . Gregor desires desperately to achieve a relation with a "special uprush of warm feeling" but fails to do so in a dehumanized world. It is ironical that his unconscious desire to be his true self destroys his relationship to the two people with whom he most nearly achieved this warm feeling—his mother and his sister.

How do we interpret Gregor's transformation? First, we note that in the beginning Gregor does not consciously will the change, and in fact tries to deny it to himself. Second, Gregor is puzzled about his change, and is constantly questioning himself about it. . . . Third, Gregor yearns passionately for association with the family; he presses his body against the door to catch snatches of family conversation. Fourth, Gregor has always shown almost perverse consideration for the firm and for other members of his family at the expense of his own desires, and immediately after the transformation continues to do so. Fifth, that Gregor, upon waking, is "unusually hungry." And last, Gregor's transformation is a continuing process, initially a retrogression into the natural state of an insect, but later a gradual movement toward self-assertion at the expense of the comfort of others.

The riddle is Gregor's riddle because he is the only one in the story who acknowledges it. It is the riddle of man's existence in his yearning for freedom and self-fulfillment and in the knowledge of his enslavement to the established order.

Let us assume, then, the hypothesis that Gregor's transformation represents a cluster of feelings at the center of which is Gregor's ambivalence—a yearning for freedom from the established order which he does not understand and which he cannot trace back to its original causes, and the feeling that he is as vile as an insect because he does not want to belong to the established order, even though he desires I-thou relationships with individuals in that established order and feels that it is his duty to his family to work within that order. The beetle also represents Gregor's revolt and the established order's revulsion at such a revolt.

So we note that after Gregor's transformation he is "unusually hungry." This hunger theme is developed in much the same way as it is in **"The Hunger Artist"**—neither Gregor nor the hunger artist knows what food will satisfy his hunger, although Gregor gets a glimpse.

Gregor is repulsed by fresh food and eats the decayed foods which are natural to some insects. However, after Gregor defied his mother and sister and was bombarded with apples by his father, his feelings of hunger for love come to his mind and he thinks how they are neglecting him. (pp. 339-40)

So it was naturally not food at all that Gregor needed, but an unknown nourishment that he perceives but faintly when he hears his sister play the violin. . . .

His long day-dream that immediately follows deals with an I-thou relationship with his sister. . . .

It is important here to note that when Gregor saw and heard his sister play, he *followed his impulse* to enter the living room. . . . Thus, Gregor begins to follow his true impulse toward self-fulfillment in an existential reality which denies the world of mechanized and empty but functional public order.

However, the world of order cannot tolerate this monstrosity, and Gregor cannot live in an atmosphere of complete rejection. His sister pronounces sentence. "He must go." (p. 341)

It is interesting that Gregor on then returning to his room is astonished at the distance and wonders how he could have crawled so far into the living room without noticing it. The reader knows the reason—he had been receiving the unknown nourishment that he craved.

Just as **"The Hunger Artist"** ends with the image of the panther with its strong physical existence, unaware of the cage, so ***Metamorphosis*** concludes with the death of the spiritual and the triumph of the unquestioning physical existence in the established order. At the end of the family's journey into the country, Grete "sprang to her feet first and stretched her young body." (pp. 341-42)

Alexander Taylor, "The Waking: The Theme of Kafka's 'Metamorphosis'," in Studies in Short Fiction *(copyright 1965 by Newberry College), Vol. II, No. 4, Summer, 1965, pp. 337-42.*

MARTIN GREENBERG (essay date 1966)

[*Greenberg characterizes Kafka's narration of* The Metamorphosis *as a new kind of storytelling, with the climax coming in the first sentence and the rest of the story serving as resolution. The critic interprets the story not as the unfolding of an action, but of a metaphor: the metamorphosis reveals the true conditions of Gregor's life, which has consisted of self-denial and the denial of love from his family and respect from his employers.*]

The Metamorphosis is peculiar as a narrative in having its climax in the very first sentence: "As Gregor Samsa awoke one morning from uneasy dreams he found himself transformed in his bed into a gigantic insect." The rest of the *novella* falls away from this high point of astonishment in one long expiring sigh, punctuated by three sub-climaxes (the three eruptions of the bug from the bedroom). How is it possible, one may ask, for a story to start at the climax and then merely subside? What kind of story is that? The answer to this question is, I think: a story for which the traditional Aristotelian form of narrative (complication and dénouement) has lost any intrinsic necessity and which has therefore evolved its own peculiar form out of the very matter it seeks to tell. *The Metamorphosis* produces its own form out of itself. The traditional kind of narrative based on the drama of dénouement—on the "unknotting" of complications and the coming to a conclusion—could not serve Kafka because it is just exactly the absence of dénouement and conclusions that is his subject matter. His story is about death, but death that is without dénouement, death that is merely a spiritually inconclusive petering out.

The first sentence of *The Metamorphosis* announces Gregor Samsa's death and the rest of the story is his slow dying. In its movement as an inexorable march toward death it resembles Tolstoy's *Death of Ivan Ilyich*. As Ivan Ilyich struggles against the knowledge of his own death, so does Gregor Samsa. But Tolstoy's work is about death literally and existentially; Kafka's is about death in life. . . . [In] Gregor Samsa's case . . . his life is his death and there is no salvation. For a moment, it is true, near the end of his long dying, while listening to his sister play the violin, he feels "as if the way were opening before him to the unknown nourishment he craved"; but the nourishment remains unknown, he is locked into his room for the last time and he expires.

What Gregor awakens to on the morning of his metamorphosis is the truth of his life. His ordinary consciousness has lied to him about himself; the explosive first sentence pitches him out of the lie of his habitual self-understanding into the nightmare of truth. . . . The poetic of the Kafka story, based on the dream, requires the literal assertion of metaphor; Gregor must literally *be* vermin. This gives Kafka's representation of the subjective reality its convincing vividness. Anything less than metaphor, such as a simile comparing Gregor to vermin, would diminish the reality of what he is trying to represent. Gregor's thinking "What has happened to me? . . . It was no dream," is no contradiction of his metamorphosis' being a dream but a literal-ironical confirmation of it. Of course it is no dream—to the dreamer. The dreamer, while he is dreaming, takes his dream as real; Gregor's thought is therefore literally true to the circumstances in which he finds himself. However, it is also true ironically, since his metamorphosis is indeed no dream (meaning something unreal) but a revelation of the truth.

What, then, is the truth of Gregor's life? There is first of all his soul-destroying job, which keeps him on the move and cuts him off from the possibility of real human associations. . . . Not only is his work lonely and exhausting, it is also degrading. Gregor fails to report to work once in five years and the chief clerk is at his home at a quarter past seven in the morning accusing him of neglect of his business duties, poor work in general and stealing company funds, and threatening him with dismissal. In the guilt-world that Gregor inhabits, his missing his train on this one morning retroactively changes his excellent work record at one stroke into the very opposite. (pp. 69-72)

He has been sacrificing himself by working at his meaningless, degrading job so as to pay off an old debt of his parents' to his employer. . . . But even now, with the truth of his self-betrayal pinning him on his back to his bed, he is unable to claim himself for himself and decide to quit. . . . He pretends that he will get up and resume his old life. He will get dressed "and above all eat his breakfast," after which the "morning's delusions" will infallibly be dissipated. But the human self whose claims he always postponed and continues to postpone, is past being put off, having declared itself negatively by changing him from a human being into an insect. His metamorphosis is a judgment on himself by his defeated humanity. Gregor's humanity has been defeated in his private life as much as in his working life. (p. 72)

For most of the story, Gregor struggles with comic-terrible pathos against the metaphor fastened on him. His first hope is that it is all "nonsense." But he cannot tell; the last thing he knows about is himself. So he works himself into an upright position in order to unlock the door, show himself to the chief clerk and his family and let them decide for him, as he has always let others decide for him. . . . The answer that he gets is his mother's swoon, the chief clerk's hurried departure in silent-movie style, with a loud "Ugh!" and his father's driving him back "pitilessly," with a newspaper and a walking stick that menaces his life, into his room. . . . (p. 73)

This is the first repulse the metamorphosed Gregor suffers in his efforts to re-enter "the human circle." The fact that his voice has altered so that the others can no longer understand what he says, but he can understand them as well as ever, perfectly expresses the pathos of one who is condemned to stand on the outside looking in. Although he must now accept the fact that he has been changed into a monster, he clings to the illusion that his new state is a temporary one. . . . (p. 74)

This, then, is the situation in the Samsa family revealed by the metamorphosis: on the surface, the official sentiments of the parents and the sister toward Gregor, and of Gregor toward them and toward himself; underneath, the horror and disgust, and self-disgust. . . . (p. 78)

Gregor breaks out of his room the first time hoping that his transformation will turn out to be "nonsense"; the second time, in the course of defending at least his hope of returning to his "human past." His third eruption, in Part III, has quite a different aim. The final section of the story discovers a Gregor who tries to dream again, after a long interval, of resuming his old place at the head of the family, but the figures from the past that now appear to him—his boss, the chief clerk, travelling salesmen, a chambermaid ("a sweet and fleeting memory"), and so on—cannot help him, "they were one and all unapproachable and he was glad when they vanished." Defeated, he finally gives up all hope of returning to the human community. Now his existence slopes steeply toward death. The wound in his back, made by the apple his father threw at him in driving Gregor back into his room after his second outbreak, has begun to fester again; his room is now the place in which all the household's dirty old decayed things are thrown, along with Gregor, a dirty old decayed thing; and he has just about stopped eating. (pp. 78-9)

On the last evening of his life, watching from his room the lodgers whom his family have taken in putting away a good supper, he comes to a crucial realization:

> "I'm hungry enough," said Gregor sadly to himself, "but not for that kind of food. How these lodgers are stuffing themselves, and here am I dying of starvation!"

In giving up at last all hope of re-entering the human circle, Gregor finally understands the truth about his life; which is to say he accepts the knowledge of his death, for the truth about his life is his death-in-life by his banishment and self-banishment from the human community. But having finally accepted the truth, having finally bowed to the yoke of the metaphor that he has been trying to shake off, he begins to sense a possibility that exists for him *only* in his outcast state. He is hungry enough, he realizes, but not for the world's fare, "not for that kind of food.'' He feels a hunger that can only be felt in full acceptance of his outcast state. Like Ivan Ilyich when he accepts his death at last and plunges into the black sack's hole, he perceives a glimmer of light; in the degradation, in the utter negativity of his outcastness, he begins to apprehend a positive possibility.

He has already had a hint or two that the meaning of his metamorphosis contains some sort of positive possibility. At the beginning of the story, when he is lying in bed and worrying about not reporting to work, he thinks of saying he is sick, but knows that the sick-insurance doctor will come down on him as a malingerer. ''And would he be so far from wrong on this occasion? Gregor really felt quite well . . . and he was even unusually hungry.'' He has just been changed into a huge bug and he is afraid of pleading sick because he will be accused of malingering! And the accusation would after all be correct because he felt quite well and was even unusually hungry! ''Of course,'' the reader says, ''he means quite well *as an insect*!''—which is a joke, but a joke that points right to the positive meaning of his metamorphosis.

A second hint soon follows. After Gregor unlocks the bedroom door with his jaws and drops down on his legs for the first time, he experiences ''a sense of physical comfort; his legs had firm ground under them; . . . they even strove to carry him forward in whatever direction he chose; and he was inclined to believe that a final relief from all his sufferings was at hand.'' The first meaning here is ironical and comic: Gregor, unable to accept his transformation into a bug and automatically trying to walk like a man, inadvertently falls down on his insect legs and feels an instantaneous sense of comfort which he takes as a promise of future relief from his sufferings—with supreme illogic he derives a hope of release from his animal condition from the very comfort he gets by adapting himself to that condition: so divided is his self-consciousness from his true self. But there is a second meaning, which piles irony upon the irony: *precisely* as a noisome outcast from the human world Gregor feels the possibility of relief, of *final* relief. *Only* as an outcast does he sense the possibility of an ultimate salvation rather than just a restoration of the *status quo*. (pp. 79-80)

Kafka dwells so much in the first part on the horror of Samsa's job that we feel his metamorphosis as something of a liberation, although in the end he is only delivered from the humiliation and death of his job into the humiliation and death of his outcast state.

When Gregor breaks out of his room the third and last time, he is no longer trying to deceive himself about himself and get back to his old life with its illusions about belonging to the human community. He is trying to find that ''final relief'' which lies beyond ''the last earthly frontier,'' a frontier which is to be approached only through exile and solitude. (p. 81)

Both Georg Bendemann [in **''The Judgment''**] and Gregor Samsa die reconciled with their families in a tenderness of self-condemnation. But Georg is sentenced to death by his father; nobody sentences Gregor to his death in life except himself. His ultimate death, however, his death without redemption, is from hunger for the unknown nourishment he needs. What kills Gregor is spiritual starvation. . . .

Although the story does not end with Gregor's death, it is still from his point of view that the last few pages are narrated. The family are of course glad to be freed of the burden and scandal he has been to them but dare not say so openly. (p. 83)

Life triumphs blatantly, not only over Gregor's unlife but over his posthumous irony—[the story's] last lines are entirely without irony. Or if they are ironical it is at Gregor's expense: his moral condemnation of his family here turns into a condemnation of himself. (p. 84)

Is ***The Metamorphosis*** unhealthy art: the artfully prolonged whine of a disaffected neurotic with a submissive ego? Or is it a lament (*Klage*) that is perfect, beautiful, pure? Does Kafka let us down in the end or does he try to lift us up . . .? Doubtless Kafka's critics would find him depressing in any case. Yet in taxing his stories with lack of tension they misunderstand their form and ask them to be what they are not and do not try to be—representations of action. (p. 86)

The Metamorphosis doesn't unfold an action but a metaphor; it is the spelling out of a metaphor. It doesn't end in an Aristotelian dénouement, but draws the metaphor out to its ultimate conclusion which is death. I called the movement of ***The Metamorphosis*** a dying fall. But visual terms serve better than auditory ones. The movement of the story is a seeing more and more: waking up, the metamorphosed Gregor sees his insect belly, then his helplessly waving legs, then his room, cloth samples, picture, alarm clock, furniture, key, living room, family, chief clerk—on and on and on in a relentless march of ever deeper seeing till he sees his own death. Everything he sees is a building stone added to the structure of the metaphor of his banishment from the human circle, capped by the stone of his death. In a story of this kind there is no question of tension or of any of the specifically dramatic qualities: it is a vision.

Of course Gregor Samsa ''can neither dare nor know.'' Neither can Hamlet, his ultimate literary ancestor and the earliest protagonist of the modern plot of doubt and despair in face of the threat of universal meaninglessness. That is just the point of the story: that Gregor can neither dare nor know, neither live in the world nor find the unknown truth he craves. (pp. 86-7)

Martin Greenberg, ''Kafka's 'Metamorphosis' and Modern Spirituality'' (© 1966 by TriQuarterly, *Northwestern University; reprinted by permission of the publisher and the author), in* TriQuarterly, *No. 6, Spring, 1966 (and reprinted as ''Gregor Samsa and Modern Spirituality,'' in his* Kafka: The Terror of Art, *Horizon Press, 1983, pp. 69-91).*

HEINZ POLITZER (essay date 1966)

[In the following study of Gregor's fate and what it portends, Politzer examines in detail Gregor's relationship to his employers, his family, and himself. In his discussion of the Samsa family members, Politzer suggests that the title refers to a metamorphosis in Grete as well as Gregor Samsa.]

The transformation of the commercial traveler Gregor Samsa into an enormous insect is completed in the first sentence of **''The Metamorphosis''** or, rather, before it. Like an analytic tragedy, the story shows but the last stages of the hero's ordeal; yet the crucial element of analytic dramaturgy—the posing of the guilt question and the gradual discovery of its answer—is neglected here. The reader finds himself in the unenviable position of a detective who is confronted by a culprit in safe custody but who is obliged to search for the culprit's guilt (a situation very similar to his attitude toward Joseph K. in ***The Trial***).

To continue the metaphor, the last act of this play is confined to the interplay between the animal and its human opponents, the insect's inglorious end, and the final relief of the humans. This is the only act we see. At least on the surface Gregor's metamorphosis is taken for granted; the question why he was changed is never openly posed. When once drawn into the magic circle of the tale, the reader is forced to accept its premise as unquestionable, a process which is facilitated by the narrator, who continually shuttles back and forth between the world of the transformed and that of the ordinary figures, between suprarealism and realism.

"The Metamorphosis" is unique among Kafka's animal stories in that Gregor is a human in the form of an animal and not an animal who has been humanized. He does not mirror the world of the humans by way of a travesty—as does the ape in **"A Report to an Academy"** or the mouse in **"Josephine the Singer."** Moreover, if he was intended to serve as an allegory of Kafka's own existence, this intention is continuously disturbed by Kafka's insistence on the insect's *being* Gregor in addition to *representing* him. Even in the beginning the shock of the metamorphosis is increased by Gregor's rational reaction to it, and his death cannot fail to remind the reader of Georg Bendemann's submission to the verdict of his father.

The story stands out among Kafka's shorter narratives by being clearly divided into three parts. The first part shows Gregor in his relation to his profession, the second to his family, and the third to himself. This rather schematic structure is not aesthetically disturbing because the three parts are united by Gregor's fate, which is and remains an enigma. In spite of the symmetry and precision of its structure it is basically endless; the actual conclusion is a rather unconvincing addition.

The first part is as strictly limited in time as it is in space (Gregor's room). The alarm clock ticking on his bureau symbolizes the infinite and irrevocable circle of Gregor's professional life as a traveling salesman, to which he has sold himself. . . . The insect's attempt to leave his bed, that is, his gradual awareness of his transformation, is continually accompanied by statements of time. . . . The monstrosity of the scene—an insect preparing for a salesman's trip—is heightened and parodied by the cold mechanism of the passing of time. . . . The General Manager appears. The firm did not allow more than ten minutes before sending out after its missing employee. With uncanny and inhuman regularity, reflected in the incessant ticking of the clock, business moves in to reclaim the fugitive. To escape from the compulsion of his drab and strict job, Gregor may well have changed into an insect during his "agitated dreams" . . . of the past night. **"The Metamorphosis"** then, would be an escapist wish dream come true.

However, Gregor is more than a cog in a capitalistic machine. There is a very human side to his relationship with the firm. His parents once borrowed money from the boss and staked Gregor's services as a guarantee for the sum advanced to them. . . . Nobody can deny that he is a slave, but even slaves are men. If his animal shape were but a dream, then he would have paradoxically sacrificed his humanity in his attempt to escape slavery by his change into an insect.

"The Metamorphosis" is set at the end of one epoch in history and at the beginning of a new one. The boss's personal involvement with his salesman's family bespeaks the still patriarchal attitude of a liberal economic system when at the same time Gregor suffers from the uniformity of life inherent in the organization methods of later capitalism. The employer is both close to the employee and far removed from him. (pp. 65-7)

Obviously Gregor has some reason to complain about his job. At the same time we are given the incidental information that Gregor had been promoted a short while before. Now he is approaching the status of those elevated salesmen whom he envies. . . . Gregor craves success and runs from it at the same time. Thus he circles around in the treadmill of his job, strives forward toward his independence, then turns around to head in the opposite direction as soon as he comes closer to his aim. He is in perpetual motion and yet he does not move from the spot. His professional life is a self-imposed labyrinth. (p. 67)

The second part is characterized by a gradual dissolution of time. The first had lasted one hour, from half-past six to half-past seven in the morning. It was limited by Gregor's awakening at its start and the "deep sleep, more like a swoon than a sleep" . . . to which he succumbs at its end. With another awakening in the dusk of the same fatal day Gregor resumes the wanderings of his body and mind. But now we have left the sphere of everyday; the orderly march of time has been suspended; the alarm clock has vanished from the chest. Twilight fills the room, indefinite adverbs of time like "soon," "later," "daily," blot out the passing of days and nights. . . . [Gregor's] very life is now undergoing a metamorphosis: the distinct rhythm imposed on it by his professional activities has given way to a shapeless vagueness, such as is experienced by prisoners, the sick—and Kafka's bachelor. From now on the story will seem like a parody and refutation of the ideal of the bachelor.

Gregor is both diseased and caged. His sister enters his room "on tiptoe, as if she were visiting an invalid," . . . and he himself calls the time since his transformation an "imprisonment." . . . These phrases point to the interesting contrast that whereas time dissolves, space closes in on him. . . . He is now doubly encased, by his "hard, as it were armor-plated, back" . . . as well as by his room. Both images point back to a preordained solitude.

Nobody can change this solitude any more. The family can only adjust themselves to it and, by so doing, allow us to measure their own humanity. At the beginning of the story the individual members of the Samsa-household were introduced by the insect's reactions to their voices heard from behind his locked door. The mother's voice was "soft," . . . the sister's "low and plaintive," . . . but the father accompanied his summons by knocking with his fist against the door. The mother's softness is Gregor's comfort and the insect's despair. She is the first to catch sight of him after the metamorphosis, and she collapses. (The narrator's evil eye does not fail to notice the black humor of the situation: fainting, she sits down on the coffee table, upsets the coffee pot, and sends the brown flood gushing all over the carpet.) For the rest of the story, however, she appears more and more as her husband's appendage; literally Gregor's mother becomes more and more a Mrs. Samsa (and is mentioned as such in the text).

Among all the figures in the breakthrough stories Mrs. Samsa is most closely modeled after life. Here Kafka has recaptured his own mother's selflessness and the superficiality of her understanding of him. But above all he seems to have suffered from the idea that his mother had surrendered to the father all her love. . . . That Georg Bendemann's mother had to die before **"The Judgment"** begins can now be seen in proper perspective: it was an act of grace as well as of shame.

Compared with Bendemann, Sr., Samsa, Sr., behaves very much like an ordinary being, conditioned and limited by his environment. Wisely Kafka used restraint here, for a realistic reproduction of the father was bound to heighten the contrast between man and animal. The father's aging during the heyday of Gregor's activity, his sudden recovery after the metamorphosis, when it falls upon him to resume his role of provider, and his display of relief after the fate of the insect has been decided are all realized on a thoroughly human plane. His mulishness, his self-assertiveness, and his brusqueness have little in common with old Bendemann's more-than-human stature; they are characteristics he shares with many a *petit bourgeois* father of his generation, which was, we must never forget, still a generation of pre-Freudian parents. There is a great distance between old Bendemann's archaic and unexplained wrath and old Samsa's thoroughly understandable reactions. This distance indicates how far Kafka has succeeded in traveling toward a solid mastery of his craft in a surprisingly short time.

If Samsa, Sr., is more acceptable logically than Bendemann, Sr., he is nevertheless of the same ilk—the family of Kafka fathers. (Even more than Bendemann's, his name resembles the name of Kafka.) Immediately after his metamorphosis Gregor overhears his father explaining the state of the family's finances. . . . It turns out that the resources of the family have not been completely exhausted by old Samsa's bankruptcy; the self-abandonment with which Gregor had applied himself to salesmanship was, to say the least, overdone. Furthermore, the father has set aside certain small sums from Gregor's earnings which have never been fully used up. In other words, he has exploited Gregor's sense of duty, trusting that the son's ingrained submissiveness would prevent him from demanding a clear account. If Gregor's change into an insect was meant to dramatize certain parasitic traits in his character, we realize now that these traits are inherited. (pp. 68-70)

The most complex and decisive character in the Samsa household is the sister, Grete. The assonance between her name and Gregor's is indicative of a deep-rooted familiarity between them. While he was a human, she was the only member of the family with whom he had entertained human relations worthy of the name. After the metamorphosis she is at first the only one to interpret it as Gregor's, and not the family's, misfortune and the first to master her horror and enter the insect's room. Her humaneness seems to be in tune with her artistic talent; she "could play movingly on the violin." . . . Naturally her music is soon forgotten by everybody, including herself, since Gregor's transformation has forced her out into the world of commerce. Like the father, she supports the family now. Thus she serves as a provider to the animal in addition to being his nurse, messenger, interpreter, and an expert in all his dealings with the family. This has given her an undisputed authority in all matters concerning the welfare of her brother and determines her behavior in the first open family crisis.

It is she who has contrived the plan of removing the furniture from Gregor's room. The idea of this change seems to originate in her intuitive understanding of the insect's needs. . . . He clings to the room and its objects as to the last remnants of his identity. However, so great is Gregor's submissiveness and belief in Grete's wisdom that he soon comes to prefer her council to his own predilections and interests. And yet it is his very identity that he endangers by accommodating himself to Grete's design. Soon it turns out that even the mother wants to keep the room in its present state. . . . (p. 71)

In spite of his vacillations Gregor decides to fight for his identity. This struggle is carried out in a very strange way. In the second paragraph of the story we have learned that there hangs in Gregor's room a cheap print of a woman. . . . For the insect, the print becomes the one of his possessions to which he is determined to adhere both physically and metaphorically. He creeps up to the picture and covers it with his body when mother and sister threaten to remove it. (p. 72)

Gregor's defiance precipitates the crisis. We are not surprised to see the mother taking refuge in another of her swoons. The father joins the battle, plunging the insect into an unprecedented panic. He deserts the picture, the image of his love and his identity, and runs before his father, "stopping when he stopped and scuttling forward again when his father made any kind of move. In this way they circled the room several times." Again the image of the circle is chosen as a symbol of the inextricable self-involvement of Gregor's fate. With the consistency that characterizes Kafka's inspiration at its best, he now chooses a round object to put an end once and for all to Gregor's aimless circular wanderings: "It was an apple; a second apple followed immediately; Gregor came to a stop in alarm; there was no point in running on, for his father was determined to bombard him. He had filled his pockets with fruit from the dish on the sideboard." . . . One of the missiles penetrates his armor-plated back and later causes his death by rotting in his body. The deadly bullet appears at first completely unexpected and unrelated to the actual setting of the scene. "It was an apple"; it comes shooting out of the blue, from nowhere or the armory of a whimsically unfathomable fate. Kafka takes his time to establish the provenance of these eerily flying projectiles: only after four main clauses and one dependent clause, running parallel to the victim's gradual recovery from his shock, are we told the origin of these apples in a dish on the sideboard. So cogent, however, is their choice that we never quite wake up to the scurrility of the drama performed before our eyes—the chase of an insect with apples. They seem quite naturally to belong in the imagery of this story; their roundness corresponds with the circles Gregor was running in when they stopped him.

As images these apples are also related to the Tree in the Garden of Eden, Paradise Lost, love, cognition, and sin. These are mere associations, to be sure; yet as such they are meant to turn our glances in the direction of a vague and veiled religious background. . . . (pp. 72-3)

The deathblow Gregor received during this battle was accompanied by another, more subtle, wound. Grete has become a turncoat. From a Good Samaritan, a "sister" in the Christian sense of the word, she has changed into the father's daughter. By taking over his gestures and glances, she has visibly joined forces with him. . . .

The title of the story might apply to Grete with greater justification than to Gregor, for it is her metamorphosis which is developed in the course of the narrative, whereas we have to accept Gregor's as an accomplished fact. More and more she plays herself into the foreground: the end will show her transformation completed, very much to the detriment of the story. (p. 74)

Without Grete's support Gregor succumbs completely to decay. He appears now as "an old dung beetle." . . . This name he is called by the charwoman, who in the meantime has emerged from one of Kafka's limbos, where the social underworld seems to have joined forces with his primal fears to generate a universal nightmare. This "dung beetle" also carries in its back the wound with the rotting apple, which is the symbol of guilt as well as of cognition. Gregor has never been closer to an understanding of his human failure than when he is in the shape of a hurt animal which perishes in its own filth. Deserted by his sister, released from the very last social contacts, he has now the chance to turn inward. Yet he misses even this last opportunity. Whatever attempt at introspection he might have undertaken is thoroughly blocked by his resentment of the others. (pp. 74-5)

We have arrived at the vertex of the story, which, thanks to Kafka's masterful counterpoint, is also the low point in the insect's development. We feel the icy breath of an existence fatally gone astray. The question of Gregor's guilt and the reason for his transformation face us once more. Does his guilt lie in himself, in his possessiveness, of which he remains unaware to his end? . . . Does his guilt consist in his inability to reach beyond himself, in his desire to grasp and digest the "unknown nourishment"? Is this nourishment identical with music? If so, has he been transformed because he had tried to dedicate himself to the unknown by proxy, by sending his sister to the Conservatory instead of attending it himself? Did he want to use her as his emissary to the high unknown? Should he have become a musician, thus partaking of the "unknown nourishment"? Could he have avoided the metamorphosis by renouncing his hated job and embarking on a profession he loved? Would he have found salvation in the pursuit of music? Is music here an image of art in general or of the "art of prayer" in particular, that is, of literature? Is the *ur*-bachelor's paradox repeated in the paradoxical image of a man turned insect? (pp. 77-8)

We have traced this circle through Gregor's human and animal stages. It ends in the state of inanimate matter.

> The rotting apple in his back and the inflamed area around it, all covered with soft dust, already hardly troubled him. He thought of his family with tenderness and love. The decision that he must disappear was one that he held to even more strongly than his sister, if that was possible. In this state of vacant and peaceful meditation he remained until the tower clock struck three in the morning. . . .

Gregor's meditations are not only "peaceful" but "vacant." He agrees to his own demise as he once had submitted to the yoke of his job and, again, to the father's concealment of his savings. (pp. 78-9)

He has not really lived; existence, physical and metaphysical, has moved past him and left no trace. The metamorphosis has failed to change him. He dies, as he lived, a thing. The salesman has been dealing in things; the insect has clung to things; love and music he has craved as if they were things. Resigning himself in his last words to an animal existence, this human being reduces himself to impersonal matter. He does not die, he is put out. The charwoman sweeps "it" away.

Kafka succeeded in creating so complex and inexplicable an image that not even Gregor's "thingness" can be construed as his ultimate guilt. We would moralize unduly if we assumed that his preoccupation with the material side of life has caused his metamorphosis and eventually transformed him into a heap of useless matter. The content of the story contradicts any such moralizing: Gregor is never offered an alternative to his fate. He is given neither a choice between good and evil nor a genuine opportunity to repent or atone for his absorption in the superficial realities of his existence. He is condemned without accusation and judgment, and ultimately he remains in the dark about the reasons of his punishment. He and his readers are forced to accept it unconditionally.

Kafka's story describes the invasion of the material world by a power which resides beyond empirical experience. Empirical experience can only register this invasion and, as the Samsa family tries to do, come to terms with it. . . . [In] Kafka's world only the empirical has limits; the "unusual," the unempirical, is at liberty to transcend these limits wherever and whenever it pleases. It chooses its victims, but the criteria for the choice remain obscure; the selection is grotesquely cruel in its arbitrariness. Why was Gregor Samsa chosen and not one of the three lodgers whom he resembles so closely? No answer is given. Yet in this arbitrariness there is a hidden element of universality. Precisely because Gregor Samsa is an average man, his incredible fate could befall any average man among the readers of this tale. So far does Kafka's skill as a narrator extend that the extraordinary begins to look commonplace.

Because of Gregor Samsa's commonplace character it is difficult to agree to the description of **"The Metamorphosis"** as a fairy tale in reverse, i.e., an "anti-fairy-tale," which shows "the world as it ought not to be." Gregor's craving for his sister, Grete, has not been taken from the old legend of Beauty and the Beast and reprinted here, so to speak, in reflected face. Gregor is no enchanted prince, languishing in the shape of an animal for his redemption. Nor is he the opposite, the legendary pauper, whose sufferings are rewarded by a happy end. The concept of the fairy tale does not apply to him. He is a modest and mediocre salesman who had the misfortune to awake, one morning, in the shape of an insect. There is no tragic plunge from the noble and unique in this transformation. Quite the contrary, the metamorphosis appears consistent and strangely appropriate to Gregor's thoroughly unheroic character. The beast into which this nonhero has been changed remains as nondescript as Gregor was when he still functioned as a human salesman.

Moreover, even if Kafka intended **"The Metamorphosis"** to be an anti-fairy-tale, he would have had to suggest the power which transformed Gregor. Witch or magician, fairy or fate, this power would have had to appear in order to indicate the means by which it could be either placated or exorcised. Furthermore, the outlines of the desired order in the world would have had to become visible if the tale was to be considered an image of "the world as it ought not to be." Such an outline appears indeed in the very last pages of the story, after the insect's death, but it left Kafka, and leaves the attentive reader, dissatisfied. The epilogue of **"The Metamorphosis"** shows the Samsa family on their way to recovering their physical health. But the power which transformed Gregor Samsa is infinitely more than an image of bodily disease. Nowhere does Kafka encourage us to interpret Gregor's insect shape as an expression of his physical or even mental disorder. The principal law of the force which caused his metamorphosis is its incomprehensibility. It can only be described by not being depicted at all. Its image is a blank space yawning amidst the everyday reality of the Samsa household.

The thoroughly negative quality of the transforming power seems to have been imparted to the animal itself. In the first sentence of the original, Gregor is introduced by two negatives as *ungeheures Ungeziefer* ("enormous vermin" . . .). Apart from the repeated negative prefix *un-*, the German word *Ungeziefer,* like its English equivalent, "vermin," is a generic term, a collective noun denoting all sorts of undesirable insects. Kafka never divulges the kind of insect into which Gregor has been transformed, nor does he specify its form and size. In the beginning he is flat like a bedbug, so thin that he can find accommodation under the couch, and yet long enough to reach the door key with his teeth. It would stand to reason that he was changed into precisely that animal which he—and other European salesmen—dreaded most when they entered the dirty and cheap hotels open to them on their route. . . . Whatever vague contours the animal possesses are blurred in the course of the story by the "dust, fluff and hair and remnants of food" . . . which have assembled on its back. When the charwoman finally calls him "an old dung beetle," . . . she does not, as one critic maintains, pronounce an entomological classification, but simply adds an insult to Gregor's fatal injury. By his metamorphosis Gregor Samsa has been turned into an untouchable in the most literal sense of the word.

What Kafka could not describe by words he likewise wished to keep unexplained by pictorial representation. When Kurt Wolff, the publisher, submitted to him a sketch of the title page which showed Gregor as a beetle, Kafka remonstrated: "The insect proper cannot be designed. Not even from far away is it possible to disclose its shape." . . . The *un-*, the dark, the void, are the only designations Kafka could find for the mystery at the center of the tale. Gregor's metamorphosis is the image of his own negative possibilities as well as of the incomprehensibility of the power that changed him into an insect.

The epilogue shows the Samsa family on an excursion into the open country. The insect has been removed, the charwoman dismissed, the triad of lodgers given notice. Nature itself seems to conspire with the rejuvenated Samsas. The trolley in which the family travels alone "was filled with warm sunshine." Sinister past has given way to a future of freedom and light. Now it appears that the prospects of the family are "on closer inspection . . . not at all bad." The tale that had begun with Gregor's "agitated dreams" is ended by "new dreams," in which the parents anticipate a life of petty-bourgeois comfort in an apartment better than the old one, "which Gregor has still selected." Most obvious, however, is Grete's change. The parents are struck by a sudden outburst of vitality, which seems to have changed her into a completely different girl. "In spite of all the sorrow of recent times . . . she had bloomed into a pretty girl with a good figure." . . . Now she is joining the regenerative forces of nature and thereby completes *her* metamorphosis. Precisely because Kafka has devised this end as a counterpoint to Gregor's transformation and precisely because this counterpoint concludes harmoniously, it appears as a somewhat forced adaptation of the now hackneyed antithesis of "art" and "life" to the paradoxical nature of Kafka's new style. But Gregor cannot be accepted as an artist, however frustrated. His metamorphosis is not counterbalanced by Grete's awakening to normalcy, however trivial. Neither the warm sunshine of an early spring day nor the social rehabilitation of a middle-class family nor the successful passing of a young girl's puberty can make us forget the unknown which reached through Gregor into life as it is known to us. So persuasively has Kafka impressed the image of the insect upon reality that the ordinary world itself seems to have changed. After Gregor's metamorphosis Kafka's reality will never be the same. (pp. 79-82)

Heinz Politzer, in his Franz Kafka: Parable and Paradox *(© 1962, copyright © 1966 by Cornell University; used by permission of the publisher, Cornell University Press), revised edition, Cornell University Press, 1966, 398 p.*

RONALD GRAY (essay date 1973)

[In the following biographical discussion, Gray contends that The Metamorphosis *was not intended to be a general allegory on human nature and society but rather an examination of several dilemmas in Kafka's life. Gray concludes that, through the transformation and death of Gregor, Kafka was portraying several elements of his own character that he sought to change or destroy.]*

Kafka was usually reluctant to have anything he had written published, and this remained true of **'The Metamorphosis':** he declined [the publisher] Kurt Wolff's invitation to send it to him in April 1913, perhaps because Kafka intended it for a book planned long before, to be entitled 'Sons'. He did, however, send it in 1914 to the novelist Robert Musil, who accepted it for the *Neue Rundschau,* where it would have appeared but for opposition from the conservative management. And in the following year he came as near as he ever did come to urging a publisher to print a work of his, saying he was 'particularly concerned' to see publication. Considering Kafka's normal hesitancy, this suggests a strong feeling that the story came up to his expectations.

The formal excellence is striking enough in itself. Whereas very many of the stories are incomplete (including a large number of fragmentary beginnings in the diary, not normally printed in collections of the stories as such), or rambling and repetitive, **'The Metamorphosis'** shows all the signs that Kafka was able both to portray his own situation and to achieve artistic mastery over it. That this is Kafka's situation, as he saw it, need not be doubted. He himself comments on the similarity between the name Samsa and his own, noting that this time he has come closer than he did in the case of Bendemann [see Kafka excerpt in *TCLC,* Vol. 6, p. 219]. The parents and the sister correspond closely to his view of his family. . . . It remains, of course, a projection from his own circumstances as much as any autobiographical subject in a novel does. The distinctive feature is the device by which Kafka omits all the repetitive doubts, the neurotic self-circlings, packing them all into the one image of the transformation, and viewing that as though from the outside. The transformation is at first sight incomprehensible, without some experience of it through Kafka's diaries. Yet it remains the obvious and most compelling image for his condition, as he saw it, and there is no symbolism about it, or rather the metaphorical element seems so slight, so ordinary, so much a matter of everyday speech that one scarcely wants to translate when Gregor discovers himself to be 'ein Ungeziefer' (a word which means 'vermin', rather than 'insect'). Gregor is, as one says, a louse. Nor does Kafka allow the comfort which might come from the expectation that the whole affair is a dream from which there will be an awakening. Exceptionally, there is no quality of dreams in this nightmare. Kafka insists on what the reader knows to be a physical impossibility, even though the general idea is common enough, because that is the only way that the full weight of his meaning can be conveyed, without overloading the story with the minutiae of self-recrimination. The conviction of being verminous is given full statement, once and for all, on the first page, and the rest becomes a matter of working out the practical details so that the truth comes home in concrete form.

This conviction is not the conviction of humanity at large, nor does the story ever make it out to be so; the implications exist for Gregor alone, and the rest of the characters are far from thinking themselves or being vermin. (pp. 83-5)

The whole story is worked out in terms of Gregor being an insect, and at no point does the reader have the sense of being slyly invited to see more than meets the eye. There are no enigmas in the dialogue, to be resolved (as in **'The Judgement'**) only by reference to Kafka's own life; though his life is latently present throughout, it is independent of the story and allows it to proceed without hindrance. At times in Kafka's writing he suggests compassion through some artificial device, as he does in **'A Hunger-Artist'.** In **'The Metamorphosis'** there are no devices, and the compassion is felt in the writing. (p. 86)

[A] paradoxical mood characterises the moment of Gregor's death; not in itself, for the description here has nothing ironical or melodramatic, but in its context, in the events which follow immediately on it. Left alone in his room with the apple festering on him, he feels his strength ebb. . . .

> He thought again of his family with affection and love. His feeling that he had to vanish from the face of the earth was, if possible, stronger than his sister's. In this state of vacant, peaceful contemplation he remained, until the tower clock struck three in the morning. . . .

There is no such moment as this anywhere else in Kafka, no such calm recognition of what was a reality of his own condition. He is convinced here that Gregor must disappear from the face of the earth, and the conviction has no resentment in it, nor has it any expectation of Gregor's being rewarded by some dialectical reversal of fortunes. . . . Considering the savagery with which **'In the Penal Colony'** describes a death without prospect of benefit, the calm of **'The Metamorphosis'** is surprising. On the other hand, it is not a passage to which one can do more than assent. There is no other way out for Gregor, it is true, so far as one can see from the story. Yet 'vacant, peaceful contemplation' is not particularly admirable, and the general sense is of a feeble rather than a serene calm.

It is not a calm proudly presented for inspection. As soon as Gregor's death has passed, Kafka allows the charwoman, one of his best comic creations, to burst in. The reaction she shows is inhuman if one still regards Gregor as a human being. But that is the point: for the charwoman Gregor is not a human being; he is an insect and always has been. In allowing her to show such indifference Kafka does, it is true, indicate that the attempt of the sister at bridging the gap between herself and Gregor is vain. The story has this utterly pessimistic note, so far as Gregor is concerned, but the reader who finds this assertion of a human being's unloveableness unbearable may have to see that it is also ineluctable. Gregor must vanish, and the charwoman is chosen to say so. . . . (pp. 87-9)

This is still not the end of Kafka's comment. . . . There remains the final scene when, Gregor being dead, the family is at last free of him and decides, since it is springtime, to take a tram-ride for an excursion into the country. The last sentences have some of Kafka's best cadences as well as his fullest vision. . . . This is Kafka most fully in possession of himself as a writer. The verminous self must go: it has no hold on life, and no destiny but extinction. On the other hand, the brave new world now emerges, not unsatirised: the parents are still slightly uniform and symmetrical, and such good intentions as they may have are coloured by the half-conscious, and presumably calculating glances they exchange, their minds half-fixed on what advantages a suitor may bring. But the story does end with that glimpse of a woman ready for love and marriage; there are subtleties and simplicities here of a human order. (pp. 90-1)

In **'The Metamorphosis'** [Kafka] had seen his own existence as though from outside, in its relation with other lives, and though there was always another self which watched this self, he had recognised the need for this self to die. It was a personal affair, and he made no more of it than that, in this story. Had he realised the implications, he might never have written in the same vein again.

Within a short while, however, the conviction that his own state could represent a universal fact of existence entered his consciousness, and the stories he wrote after this are given a more general symbolic value. (pp. 91-2)

Ronald Gray, in his Franz Kafka *(© Cambridge University Press 1973), Cambridge at the University Press, 1973, 220 p.*

RUTH TIEFENBRUN (essay date 1973)

[Tiefenbrun provides one of the rare interpretations of The Metamorphosis *which posits that no physical change has taken place (for another, see the excerpt by Rudolph Binion in* TCLC, *Vol. 6). Maintaining that "Gregor could not have changed in his outer appearance because he was recognized immediately by everyone in his environment," Tiefenbrun theorizes that Gregor revealed himself not as an insect but as a homosexual, and also attributes homosexuality to Kafka.]*

Kafka identified himself with Gregor Samsa in a conversation with Gustav Janouch and confessed that he had been indiscreet in writing about the "bed bugs" in his family [see excerpt above, 1953]. (p. 111)

Kafka had told Janouch the whole truth, but, in his inimitable fashion, he had contrived to make the truth incomprehensible. What Kafka was really saying was that Gregor was "not merely Kafka" as the world knew Kafka; Gregor represented the homosexual aspect of Kafka which had always been concealed from the eyes of the world. **"The Metamorphosis"** was not a confession because Kafka had never completely exposed himself in his true image and had no intention of removing his mask. But Gregor's metamorphosis was not a dream; it was a reality. Gregor/Kafka had literally been transformed from a man who had appeared to be heterosexual into a homosexual; therefore metaphorically he had become a vermin in the eyes of his fellowmen. The "horror" and "terror" of Kafka's life were that he feared that he, like Gregor, might one day, because of some "chance forgetting of self" . . . , expose himself to the world in his true image. He would then be characterized as a vermin and would suffer the fate of Gregor.

The monstrous vermin which emerged from Gregor's room was only a metaphor. This was evidenced by the fact that Kafka refused to permit his publisher to make any graphic representation of this insect. . . . That Gregor had not really been transformed into a vermin is obvious—no one had the slightest difficulty in recognizing him. However, all of Gregor's viewers were unanimous at one point: they all considered him no better than "some sort of vermin." (pp. 111-12)

Kafka had indicated that Gregor was a homosexual in the fourth paragraph of this story by means of his secret code. When Gregor awakened on the morning of his transformation, he felt an itching area on his belly; he "identified the itching place which was surrounded by many small white spots" and drew his leg back quickly in pain. Gregor's latent disease had erupted. His wound had broken open, and he could no longer control his incestuous and homosexual drives. (p. 113)

"The Metamorphosis" is the story of Gregor, the homosexual who had suppressed his deviant sexual drives for many years and had lived a sham life because he wanted to save his family from disgrace. He had been living as a recluse by compulsion; once this compulsion had been overcome by forces beyond his control, he had awakened to find himself a parasite. Gregor had taken one step out of the circle in which he had encapsulated himself in "some distraction, some fright, some astonishment, some fatigue." Due to fatigue and stresses, reflected by his uneasy dreams, he had overslept. He had not heard the alarm that had been his inexorable warden in his former existence and had always awakened him in time for him to make the elaborate preparations he needed to mask himself so that he could face the world. Gregor had awakened to a nightmare. His disguises had permanently disappeared, and he was forced to face the world in his true image.

In his characterization of Gregor, Kafka observes himself through the eyes of his world and reports with uncompromising realism what would have happened if he removed his mask and appeared in his true image. The gallows humor of this story is the protective clowning and self-mockery of gifted humorists of all harrassed minority groups. Kafka knew that if he were to expose himself, he would be subjected to harrassment, persecution, and self-righteous brutality. Exposure would mean the loss of his job, his reputation, and his social position. His family would suffer. . . . (p. 114)

Kafka achieved a triumph in this story by creating a new technique of mystification. Simply by creating a metaphor and treating it as though it were a literal fact, Kafka ensnared his readers so that it became impossible for anyone to think of Gregor except as some species of vermin. Even those exegetists who knew that Gregor was not really a beetle reacted to Gregor as if he were a noxious insect. They could not react otherwise because they were subliminally conditioned by Kafka's endless elaborations of Gregor's exhausting and exhaustive efforts to adjust himself to his new image. Kafka's contrapuntal treatment of his "vermin" image escaped the scrutiny of all of his explicators. Everyone took it for granted that Gregor had literally become "incomprehensible," that he had literally become "inhuman."

Kafka contrived to get his readers to react to Gregor as if he were a vermin by presenting him from the viewpoint of his society's bias. The reader accepted the verdict of Gregor's microcosm and took it for granted that he was loathsome, indecent, offensive, mentally sick, insolent, and an animal. No one thought of questioning the unjust law which had transformed Gregor into a monstrous vermin. Gregor had been alienated from his family and had been hypocritical in his relations with them both before and after his metamorphosis, but he loved his family and had proved his love by many years of self-sacrifice. Kafka makes it clear in this story that the dehumanized Gregor is infinitely more human and humane than his self-righteous, sadistic father; his dissembling, two-faced mother; and his play-acting, obstinate sister.

When Gregor awoke on the morning of his metamorphosis, he was profoundly disturbed, but he was not unduly surprised. He knew there was nothing incredible about his transformation: "something like what had happened to him today might some day happen to the chief clerk; one really could not deny that it was possible." . . . He also knew that he was not being punished for some crime that he had committed. He had been no great hero, but he had done nothing wrong. His only crime was that he had been ready to sacrifice his entire youth by annihilating his true self in order to save his family from disgrace.

The black humor and bitter irony in this story derives from the literal translation of Kafka's metaphor. For example, when Gregor first presented himself to the world in his true image, he stood erect in the posture of a man. After he had observed the horror on the face of the chief clerk, Gregor knew that his job was at stake and that he would literally become a parasite if he could not win over the chief clerk and persuade him to let him keep his job. Gregor's onerous job had assumed an entirely different aspect when he realized his metamorphosis was irrevocable. It had come to symbolize his passport into the circle of humanity. When he literally crawled toward the chief clerk to appeal for his job, he relinquished his human posture because he knew that henceforth he would have to grovel as a homosexual at the feet of employers to obtain a position. Tongue in cheek, Kafka described Gregor's joy when he realized that forever after he would be able to survive only by crawling before other men. Gregor could not have changed in his outer appearance because he was recognized immediately by everyone in his environment. He had the same body, the same character, and the same speech that he had had before his transformation; nevertheless he had suddenly become incomprehensible to all of humanity. An unbridgeable gap had suddenly appeared between Gregor and his fellowmen because he was a homosexual. . . . Gregor understood clearly all of the people in his world; he had become incomprehensible because his culture regarded him as an animal.

The Satanic fairy-tale test which Gregor imposed upon humanity, when he decided to open the door and present himself in his true image, was perverse only because Gregor knew that it was doomed to failure. Gregor had decided to put humanity to a truly world-redeeming test because he had no other choice: his whole future depended upon it. Gregor's impassioned plea to keep his job fell on deaf ears. No sooner did the chief clerk realize that Gregor was a homosexual than he rushed to leave the apartment as if "driven by some invisible steady pressure." There was no reason why he should have remained: homosexuals were patently unemployable. The Chaplinesque humor in this episode is derived from Kafka's contrapuntal treatment of his metaphor.

The varied reactions of Gregor's world to his image epitomized the reactions of various segments of Kafka's society to the concept of a homosexual. The chief clerk was nervous, horrified, and violently disgusted. The cook was simply terrified. . . . The sixteen-year-old servant girl, who had the "courage" to remain, was afraid that Gregor might attack her and begged to be allowed to keep the kitchen door locked. . . . She remained hidden behind the locked door until she was dismissed and replaced by a dowdy charwoman who came in mornings and evenings to do the heavy cleaning. (pp. 114-17)

This old crone opened Gregor's door daily just to take a look at him. (p. 117)

When Gregor, covered with filth and grime, trailing particles of decayed food, insolently intruded on the chamber-music concert, he was first observed by the middle lodger, who smilingly drew the attention of his friends to Gregor then carefully scrutinized him again. The reaction of the lodgers to Gregor was similar to that of the charwoman. They found him more entertaining than the concert and looked at him with curiosity and amusement. They became quite angry when Mr. Samsa frantically tried to shoo them back to their bedroom, meanwhile trying to block their view of Gregor. . . .

[After Gregor's death, the lodgers] go into Gregor's room. They stood around in Gregor's room, hands inside the pockets of their shabby coats, paying their last respects to Gregor. They were taken aback when Mr. Samsa ordered them to leave instantly. (p. 118)

Thus had the circle of humanity passed judgment on Gregor. He had been viewed with horror, fear, loathing, disgust, condescending scorn, crude amusement, and lustful curiosity. He had lost his job, and his family had been threatened with legal harassment. It was left to the family circle to administer the *coup de grâce*.

When Gregor made his debut into society, his father, who had clenched his fist, looking fiercely at Gregor, restrained his self-righteous brutality because the chief clerk was still in the room. His fury dissolved into tears of self-pity: his family had suffered a terrible disgrace and misfortune. After the chief clerk rushed from the room, and it was clear that Gregor had lost his job, the father's only concern was to conceal his son who had brought the family to a state of utmost degradation. Stamping his foot and flourishing his stick, Gregor's father pitilessly drove him back into his room, "hissing and crying 'Shoo!' like a savage." The shouting and hissing noises sounded to Gregor "no longer like the voice of one single father"; it was the hissing, booing, and raging condemnation of all the authority figures in the universe. (p. 119)

Original cover design for the first German edition of Kafka's The Metamorphosis. *From* Kafka in der Kunst, *by Wolfgang Rothe. Reproduced by permission of Belser Verlag, Stuttgart.*

[Mr. Samsa's later attack on Gregor is] an opportunity of giving vent to his self-righteous sadism. (p. 123)

The "angry and exultant" father advanced with "a grim visage towards Gregor. . . . But Gregor could not risk standing up to him, aware as he had been from the very first day of his new life that his father believed only the severest measures suitable for dealing with him." . . . The father chased his son around the room several times until Gregor began to grow breathless. Suddenly Mr. Samsa picked up an apple from the dining room table and hurled it at Gregor. Gregor stopped short in panic. One apple followed another, each discharged with increasing force and speed until one landed right into his back, sinking in. (pp. 123-24)

Gregor, who had been lying nailed to the spot where he had been crucified by his father, with a last conscious look saw his mother (whose clothing had been loosened by his sister during her swoon) rush into the room in her underclothes (followed by her screaming daughter) dropping her petticoats one by one as she ran to her husband embracing him and pleading for her son's life. This act is Mrs. Samsa's sole claim to humanity in regard to Gregor in this story. Unfortunately for Gregor, the rescue team of his mother and sister had arrived too late. Mr. Samsa had inflicted a fatal wound upon Gregor.

It is the opinion of this explicator that, in the episode just described, Kafka tried to convey to the reader that Mr. Samsa symbolically cast his son out of Paradise by bombarding him with apples from the tree of knowledge. (p. 124)

Throughout his life, Kafka remained full of shame and guilt because he was forced by his culture to lead a "sham life." In **"The Metamorphosis,"** Kafka demonstrates what would have happened to him if he had dared to expose himself—if he had dared to eat of the "tree of life." Only normal men, who could eat of the tree of life with impunity, remained in Paradise. (p. 125)

"The Metamorphosis" is a punitive fantasy in which Kafka depicted the "bed bugs" in his family. The parasitic family, who had exploited their self-sacrificing son, got their comeuppance when Gregor appeared in his true image and became a parasite. The ending is indeed imperfect and unconvincing. (pp. 134-35)

Ruth Tiefenbrun, in her Moment of Torment: An Interpretation of Franz Kafka's Short Stories *(copyright © 1973 by Southern Illinois University Press; reprinted by permission of Southern Illinois University Press), Southern Illinois University Press, 1973, 160 p.*

MENO SPANN (essay date 1976)

[*In a discussion of the presentation of alienation in* The Metamorphosis, *Spann stresses the irony of the fact that Gregor Sam-*

sa's family and business associates display far more parasitic traits than the metamorphosized Gregor.]

"Die Verwandlung" offers the worst example of the disagreement among Kafka's critics as to the moral qualities of his characters. Strangely enough, nobody mentions the patent fact that the people surrounding the metamorphosed Gregor are the real vermin while he begins to rise even before his misfortune. His "uneasy dreams" are the beginning of his development from a timid nothing of a man believing in spurious values to a true human being. There is a gathering of vermin in Gregor's firm. . . .

The worst insect among the vermin in the story is, however, the parasitical father. Although he knew how his son loathed his employment with the firm to whose principal old Samsa owed money, he never told him that he had saved enough from his bankruptcy and from Gregor's earnings, so that Gregor might have ended his debtor's slave work years earlier than would have been possible under the present conditions.

Among the "real" vermin, Gregor's sister is the only exception, at least during the first weeks after his metamorphosis, when she lovingly experiments with food until she knows what her unfortunate brother likes to eat; but then she begins to neglect him more and more. At the same time, Gregor loses his appetite and hardly touches his food any longer. . . . Finally the parents have taken three lodgers into the house, Chaplinesque characters whom he watches while they are eating. (p. 67)

The vulgarity of [Gregor's] former life has disappeared, and the food the three roomers are eating with such audible gusto is no longer just food but a symbol of all that pleases and nourishes them as human beings. Gregor can no longer be satisfied with the "grub" of their lives and the lives of those like them, as he had been before. The unbridgeable gap between him and people like these becomes clear when his sister plays the violin before them. Since the dullards cannot understand the serious music she has chosen, they boorishly show their contempt for this kind of entertainment, although the young girl reveals all her devotion to music in the way she plays. . . .

Gregor's inner needs are increased by her playing. His humiliation is approaching its end, his suffering has raised him to a truly human level, and, for the first time since his metamorphosis, he has good reason to doubt the justice of his frightful degradation. The question in which he expresses his doubt is essential to the understanding of the story: "War er ein Tier, da ihn Musik so ergriff?" ("Could he really be an animal since music touched him so?") The use of the conjunction *da* with adversative force is very rare, and most German, and almost all English, critics understood it in its usual causal function, many of them having to rely on the two English translations in which *da* is also rendered as a causal particle. Nevertheless the commentators succeeded to wrest a meaning from the sibylline rhetorical question: "Was he an animal, that music had such an effect upon him?" [The critic adds in a footnote that "This is the form in which the sentence is usually quoted"]. (p. 68)

One lone commentator [Paul Goodman] gives the correct translation, but then rules out the doubt in Gregor's question and asserts, correcting him: "On the contrary, it is just when he is an animal that music moves him: The totem is the deeper and better self" [see Additional Bibliography]. (p. 69)

Kafka critics cannot agree on the evaluation of his characters. It seems the misunderstood "decisive sentence" has caused many to overlook Gregor's continuous rise toward the level of a truly "human" being even though his monstrous shape remains the same. That rise began before the metamorphosis took place, his uneasy dreams were caused by his inner unhappiness, which preceded his misfortune and gradually led him to crave the true food for his inner man. It is hard to see how the villains of the piece, the firm's porter, its president, its manager, and, most of all, the egotistic father, could have been missed as the true vermin in the story. . . . (p. 71)

And what does this story mean? Of course, like any true work of literary art, it means more than its abstract scheme, that is, the development of a human being from a subhuman level, which is acceptable to the people of his world, to a superior level in a form unacceptable to them and to him, and from which only death can free him. Its meaning is expressed in the words which the author, not the critic, has chosen. The commentator can only help the reader to a closer understanding of motives and images and can clear up philological difficulties. He may do the close reading the works of an author like Kafka require if intellectual obstacles threaten to hinder the understanding of mood and feeling which an older writer like Kafka offers.

The reader himself must feel the humor in the scene where the chief clerk fills the well of the staircase with his shout of fear, while the bug man, rushing toward him on his many thin legs, only wants to excuse his unavoidable tardiness before his superior. The skilled reader, and the one who wants moral edification, will enjoy, each in his own way, the paradox that the "normal" people around Gregor are the vermin while he increasingly becomes a true human being in spite of his monstrous shape. The senile and yet tyrannical father, the Chaplinesque lodgers, the tough maid, the slimy manager as well as the "invisible" characters—the employer at his high desk, the vicious porter, spying at the railroad station—all delight the reader who does not mind enjoying realistically but masterfully presented characters. Gregor's dissatisfaction is indirectly, but for that reason very powerfully, expressed by Kafka. It is not a social or political accusation, but the realization that it is very difficult to find in life the "food" which lifts the inner man above the banality of existence. The temptation is great to blame our modern times for being particularly hostile to the inner man and his hunger, but such cultural criticism is not Kafka's intention, as he had said himself. (p. 73)

Meno Spann, in his Franz Kafka *(copyright © 1976 by Twayne Publishers; reprinted with the permission of Twayne Publishers, a Division of G. K. Hall & Co., Boston), Twayne, 1976, 205 p.*

JOHN UPDIKE (essay date 1983)

[*Considered a perceptive observer of the human condition and an extraordinary stylist, Updike is one of America's most distinguished men of letters. Best known for such novels as* Rabbit Run *(1960),* Rabbit Redux *(1971), and* Rabbit Is Rich *(1981), he is a chronicler of life in Protestant, middle-class America. Against this setting and in concurrence with his interpretation of the thought of Søren Kierkegaard and of Karl Barth, Updike presents people searching for meaning in their lives while facing the painful awareness of their mortality and basic powerlessness. A contributor of literary reviews to various periodicals, he has frequently written the "Books" column in* The New Yorker *since 1955. In the following excerpt, Updike discusses Kafka's life and works, examining* The Metamorphosis *in relation to both.*]

The century since Franz Kafka was born has been marked by the idea of "modernism"—a self-consciousness new among centuries, a consciousness of being new. Sixty years after his death, Kafka epitomizes one aspect of this modern mind-set: a sensation of anxiety and shame whose center cannot be located and therefore cannot be placated; a sense of an infinite difficulty within things, impeding every step; a sensitivity acute beyond usefulness, as if the nervous system, flayed of its old hide of social usage and religious belief, must record every touch as pain. In Kafka's peculiar and highly original case, this dreadful quality is mixed with immense tenderness, oddly good humor, and a certain severe and reassuring formality. The combination makes him an artist; but rarely can an artist have struggled against greater inner resistance and more sincere diffidence as to the worth of his art.

Of his fiction, Kafka committed to publication during his lifetime only a slender sheaf of mostly very short stories—the longest of them, **"The Metamorphosis,"** a mere fifty pages, and a handful of the others as much as five thousand words. He published six slim volumes, four of them single stories, from 1913 to 1919, and was working on the proofs of a seventh in the sanatorium where he died, on June 3, 1924, of tuberculosis, exactly one month short of his forty-first birthday. Among his papers after his death were found several notes addressed to his closest friend and most faithful admirer, Max Brod. One of them stated:

> Of all my writings the only books that can stand are these: **"The Judgment," "The Stoker," "Metamorphosis," "Penal Colony," "Country Doctor,"** and the short story: **"Hunger-Artist."** . . . When I say that those five books and the short story can stand, I do not mean that I wish them to be reprinted and handed down to posterity. On the contrary, should they disappear altogether that would please me best. Only, since they do exist, I do not wish to hinder anyone who may want to, from keeping them.

The little canon that Kafka reluctantly granted posterity would indeed stand; **"The Metamorphosis"** alone would assure him a place in world literature, though undoubtedly a less prominent place than he enjoys thanks to the mass of his posthumously published novels, tales, parables, aphorisms, and letters. (p. 121)

Kafka dated his own maturity as a writer from the long night of September 22-23, 1912, in which he wrote **"The Judgment"** at a single, eight-hour sitting. . . . Soon after its composition, he wrote, in a few weeks, **"The Metamorphosis,"** an indubitable masterpiece. It begins with a fantastic premise, whereas in **"The Judgment"** events become fantastic. Its monstrous premise—that Gregor Samsa has been turned overnight into a gigantic insect—established in the first sentence, **"The Metamorphosis"** unfolds with a beautiful naturalness and a classic economy. It takes place in three acts: three times the metamorphosed hero ventures out of his room, with tumultuous results. The members of his family—rather simpler than Kafka's own, which had three sisters—dispose themselves around the central horror with a touching as well as an amusing plausibility. The father's fury, roused in defense of the fragile mother, stems directly from the action and inflicts a psychic wound gruesomely objectified in the rotting apple Gregor carries in his back; the evolutions of the sister, Grete, from shock to distasteful ministration to a certain sulky possessiveness and finally to exasperated indifference are beautifully sketched, with not a stroke too much. The terrible but terribly human tale ends with Grete's own metamorphosis, into a comely young woman. In a strange way, this great story resembles a great story of the nineteenth century, Tolstoy's "The Death of Ivan Ilyich;" in both a hitherto normal man lies hideously, suddenly stricken in the midst of a family whose irritated banal daily existence flows around him. The abyss within life is revealed, but also life itself.

What kind of insect is Gregor? Considerable paper has been wasted on this question. Popular belief calls him a cockroach, which would be appropriate for a city apartment; and the creature's retiring nature and sleazy dietary preferences would seem to fit. But, as Vladimir Nabokov, who knew his entomology, pointed out [see *TCLC*, Vol. 6] . . . , Gregor is too broad and convex to be a cockroach. The charwoman calls him a "dung beetle" (*Mistkäfer*), but, Nabokov said, "it is obvious that the good woman is adding the epithet only to be friendly." Interestingly, Eduard Raban of **"Wedding Preparations"** daydreams, walking along, "As I lie in bed I assume the shape of a big beetle, a stag beetle or a cockchafer, I think." Gregor Samsa, awaking, sees "numerous legs, which were pitifully thin compared to the rest of his bulk." If "numerous" is more than six, he must be a centipede—not a member of the Insecta class at all. From evidence in the story, he is brown in color and about as long as the distance between a doorknob and the floor; he is broader than half a door. He has a voice at first, "but with a persistent horrible twittering squeak behind it like an undertone," which disappears as the story progresses. His jaws don't work as ours do, but he has eyelids, nostrils, and a neck. He is, in short, impossible to picture except when the author wants to evoke him, to bump the reader up against some astounding, poignant new aspect of Gregor's embodiment. The strange physical discomfort noted in the earlier work is here given its perfect allegorical envelope. . . . When **"The Metamorphosis"** was to be published as a book, in 1915, Kafka, fearful that the cover illustrator "might be proposing to draw the insect itself," wrote the publisher, "Not that, please not that! . . . The insect itself cannot be depicted. It cannot even be shown from a distance." He suggested instead a scene of the family in the apartment with a locked door, or a door open and giving on darkness. Any theatrical or cinematic version of the story must founder on this point of external representation: a concrete image of the insect would be too distracting and shut off sympathy; such a version would lack the very heart of comedy and pathos which beats in the unsteady area between objective and subjective where Gregor's insect and human selves swayingly struggle. Still half asleep, he notes his extraordinary condition yet persists in remembering and trying to fulfill his duties as a travelling salesman and the mainstay of this household. Later, relegated by the family to the shadows of a room turned storage closet, he responds to violin music and creeps forward, covered with dust and trailing remnants of food, to claim his sister's love. Such scenes could not be done except with words. In this age that lives and dies by the visual, **"The Metamorphosis"** stands as a narrative absolutely literary, able to exist only where language and the mind's hazy wealth of imagery intersect.

"The Metamorphosis" stands also as a gateway to the world Kafka created after it. His themes and manner were now all in place. His mastery of official pomposity—the dialect of documents and men talking business—shows itself here for the first time, in the speeches of the chief clerk. Music will again be felt, by mice and dogs, as an overwhelming emanation in

Kafka's later fables—a theme whose other side is the extreme sensitivity to noise, and the longing for unblemished silence, that Kafka shared with his hero in **"The Burrow."** Gregor's death scene, and Kafka's death wish, return in **"A Hunger Artist"**—the saddest, I think, of Kafka's stories, written by a dying man who was increasingly less sanguine (his correspondence reveals) about dying. (pp. 124-29)

John Updike, "Reflections: Kafka's Short Stories" (© 1983 by John Updike), in The New Yorker, *Vol. LIX, No. 12, May 9, 1983, pp. 121-26/29-33.*

WALTER H. SOKEL (essay date 1983)

[*In the following excerpt, Sokel provides complementary Marxist and mythic interpretations of* The Metamorphosis. *Discussing the economic situation depicted in* The Metamorphosis *in Marxist terms, Sokel explains that Gregor Samsa's death can be seen to support Marxist theory even as it demonstrates the mythic pattern of the scapegoat who dies after assuming the collective guilt of the community.*]

Kafka's uniqueness as a narrative author lies, among other things, in the literalness with which the metaphors buried in linguistic usage come alive and are enacted in the scenes he presents. . . . By the appellation "vermin," linguistic usage designates the lowest form of human self-contempt. Seeing himself as vermin, and being treated as such by his business and family, the travelling salesman Gregor Samsa literally turns into vermin.

Kafka's narratives enact not only the metaphors hidden in ordinary speech, but also ideas crucial in the history of thought. ***The Metamorphosis*** is a striking example. Gregor Samsa's transformation into vermin presents self-alienation in a literal way, not merely a customary metaphor become fictional fact. The travelling salesman wakes up one morning and cannot recognize himself. Seeing himself as a gigantic specimen of vermin, he finds himself in a fundamental sense estranged from himself. No manner more drastic could illustrate the alienation of a consciousness from its own being than Gregor Samsa's startled and startling awakening. (p. 485)

Gregor had been estranged from himself in his all-consuming work even before he finds himself literally estranged from his bodily being. Gregor had found his work unbearable. He had longed for nothing more passionately than to leave his job, after telling the head of his firm his true opinion of this job. Gregor's profound self-alienation corresponds, with uncanny precision, to Marx's definition of the "externalization" of work under capitalism:

> his work is *external* to the worker, i.e., it does not form part of his essential being so that instead of feeling well in his work, he feels unhappy, instead of developing his free physical and mental energy, he abuses his body and ruins his mind. . . .
>
> (p. 486)

Gregor Samsa's professional activity has obviously been such purely instrumental work, external to himself, imposed upon him by the necessity of bailing out his bankrupt family, supporting them, and paying back his parents' debt to the boss of his firm. It is not only joyless and uncreative, it is totally determined by needs external to itself and Gregor. Freedom of creativeness—according to Marx the essence of truly human labor—finds an outlet in Samsa's life, prior to his metamorphosis, only in the carpentry in which he indulges in free evenings. Parenthetically we might recall that Kafka himself hated his bureaucrat's desk job because it served as a mere means to a purpose totally extrinsic to itself, namely a relatively short work day, and found by contrast genuine satisfaction in carpentering and gardening, activities chosen for their own sake, which, like writing, united creativeness with the satisfaction of inner needs.

Compared to accusations of his office work found in his autobiographical documents, Kafka's story, ***The Metamorphosis,*** "systematizes," as it were, the Marxist factor, not by conscious design, of course, but by virtue of the astonishing parallelism in the point of view, particularly the presentation of self-alienation. Gregor's sole reason for enduring the hated position, the need to pay his parents' "debt" to his boss, drastically highlights the doubly extrinsic purpose of Gregor's work. For not only is his labor alien to his true desires, but its sole purpose, its fruit—the salary or commission that it affords him—does not even belong to him. Gregor's toil does not serve his own existence. It is not his own *Lebensmittel,* to use Marx's term—if left to himself, he would have quit long before—it belongs to and serves another.

This other is Gregor's father. He is the non-working beneficiary and exploiter of Gregor's labor. The product of this labor is the money which Gregor brings home. This money belongs to the other who does not work himself, but enjoys and disposes of the fruits of Gregor's work: "the money which Gregor had brought home every month—he himself had kept only a few pennies to himself—had not been used up completely and had accrued to form a small *capital*" (. . . Italics mine). Gregor's father had expropriated the "surplus value" of Gregor's labor and formed with it his—to be sure, very modest—"capital." Gregor's relationship to his father thus represents an exact paradigm of the worker's exploitation by his capitalist employer, as described by Marx. (pp. 486-87)

[What] we shall consider now is Kafka's ***The Metamorphosis*** as the telling of a myth, for the mythic dimension relates to the Marxist one the way a picture frame relates to the picture which it contains and transcends, at one and the same time. In order to recognize this relationship, we shall have to consider the *mythos* of ***The Metamorphosis.*** I use the term "mythos" in the Aristotelian sense as the whole chain of fictive events in their chronological as distinct from their narrated order.

The initial point of the mythos is not Gregor's transformation, but the business failure of Gregor's father five years before. This failure led to the contracting of the burdensome debt to the head of Gregor's firm. Thus the mythos begins with a family's cataclysmic fall into adversity through the fault of the father, more precisely the parents, since the text speaks of "die Schuld der Eltern" and only afterward of "die Schuld des Vaters." The German word *Schuld* signifies debt, guilt, and causative fault. This triple meaning is crucial to the understanding of Kafka's mythos. If understood in the sense of debt, the *Schuld* of Gregor's parents belongs to socio-economic quotidian reality. If understood in the two other senses, *Schuld* belongs to a framework of moral and religious values. The text's repeated use of the singular *Schuld* in contrast to the more customary plural *Schulden* for debt provides a subliminally effective counterpoint to the obvious surface meaning of the word.

This subliminal allusion to guilt receives corroboration from the position of "die Schuld der Eltern" ("the guilt of the parents") at the initial point of the narrative mythos. This position creates a subtle analogy to the fall of mankind as told in Genesis. (p. 488)

The son of these guilty parents—Gregor—has to assume their guilt and pay it off "by the sweat of his countenance" (to quote Genesis), by his self-consuming drudgery for his parents' creditor. In the allusive context established by the semantic ambiguity of *Schuld*, Gregor's profoundly alienated existence prior to his metamorphosis establishes the parallel to man's fate after the expulsion from paradise. Like the children of Adam and Eve, Gregor through his sonship in the flesh has been condemned to a perennial debtor's existence. The two semantic realms of *Schuld*—debt and guilt—converge in the fateful consequence of the father's debt. With it, the father surrendered his family to a world in which the exploitation of man by man holds infernal sway. The world to which the father's failing has handed over his family is ruled by the principles of capitalist economics. In this world, the family ceases to be a family in the original and ideal sense of a community in which the bonds of blood—the *Blutkreis* to which Kafka in discussing **"The Judgment"** accords his highest respect—and natural affection prevail. Instead the family falls victim to the egotistical principle of *gegenseitige Übervorteilung* (mutual defrauding) in which Marx saw the governing principle of human life under capitalism.

Precisely because of his self-sacrifice in assuming his father's debt, Gregor rises to power as the breadwinner in his family and threatens to displace his father as the head of the household. This process reverses itself with Gregor's metamorphosis. Gregor's self-inflicted debasement entails his father's rejuvenation and return to power. These successive displacements—first the father's, then the son's—which find their parallel in Grete's ambiguous liberation through her brother's fall, have their contrastive complements in the parasitic exploitation of the winners by the losers. Before Gregor's metamorphosis, the father was the parasite. After the metamorphosis, the son assumes this role.

A world is shown in which the enjoyment of advantages by the one has to be purchased at the cost of the other. This is the world in a fallen state. Gregor's initial self-sacrifice through work whips up his pride in his ability to support his family in style. . . . But his self-surrender to his work causes a twofold alienation. Inwardly he remains estranged from his work because it is the kind of labor that cannot satisfy a human being. Outwardly his rise to power in the family overshadows the other members and results in their alienation from him. . . . Long before his metamorphosis, Gregor and his family have lived coldly and incommunicatively side by side.

The metamorphosis reveals this alienation in its essence as *den völligen Verlust des Menschen* ("the total dehumanization of man") in which Marx saw the ultimate fate of man under capitalism. But it has another and ultimately more important function. Through it Gregor ceases to treat the *Schuld* of his parents as a debt that can be paid back by work, and assumes the *Schuld* in its deeper meaning. He no longer tries to pay back the *Schuld;* he incorporates it. With his incarnation he raises the narrative mythos from its socio-economic to its mythic meaning.

That Gregor's metamorphosis literally incarnates guilt becomes apparent first of all by the fact that his immediate reaction to his transformation is a guilty conscience. He has missed the hour of his work and feels guilty for it. He feels guilty for having plunged his family into misfortune. He is ashamed. He seeks to hide, to make himself invisible. But even apart from all subjectively felt or morally accountable guilt, guilt becomes evident in him objectively. For his transformation into vermin entails the crassest form of parasitic exploitation, a perfect turning of the tables on his family. His metamorphosis compels them to work for him and in his place. Because of him they will henceforth be "overlooked and overtired," . . . condemned to suffer the fate of "paupers." To be sure, his father's bankruptcy five years before had condemned Gregor to an exploited existence. But by his metamorphosis, Gregor himself turns into an arch exploiter, the archetypal parasite which vermin represents. His very appearance as *ungeheueres Ungeziefer* is emblematic and flaunts a gigantic form of parasitism. Even as Gregor's subsequent daydream of declaring his love to his sister constitutes a gruesome parody of bourgeois-sentimental courtship, so his vermin existence as such embodies exploitation as the essence of human relations. By embodying parasitism in his shape, Gregor objectifies the guilt of his entire society. This guilt had originally shown itself in his father when he secretly cheated his son and furtively put aside his son's earnings to form "a modest capital." Reversing their roles, the son now becomes exploitation in its most honest, clearly visible form. . . . Gregor literally becomes what his father had committed in stealthily performed acts.

In the narrative mythos of Kafka's tale, the metamorphosis literally takes the place of the father's debt. The text mentions a debt only for the prehistory of ***The Metamorphosis,*** as a flashback in Gregor's memory. In the action which the reader witnesses, the debt plays no role. The text never mentions it again. It seems that Gregor's *Schreckgestalt,* his new terrifying shape, which the first morning after his awakening had chased away the deputy of the firm, has thereby also cancelled the parents' debt. In place of it, Gregor himself has become "the misfortune" of the Samsa family.

Later, the father wounds Gregor with an apple which rots and festers in Gregor's flesh. This apple functions not only as a renewed allusion to "the guilt of first parents"; it also signifies the function of Gregor's metamorphosis as the literal incorporation of his father's guilt. Gregor, mortally hurt by the blind "rage" of his father, has obviously become his father's victim in the concluding section of the story. Yet this final violation of the son by the father only repeats in a transparent way Gregor's initial victimization. In the beginning, Gregor had to assume his father's debt and thus become its victim. At that time *Schuld* has been understood in the economic and juridical meaning of debt. By his metamorphosis Gregor incorporates this *Schuld* and transforms it from a legal-contractual concept into its full and profound meaning as the concretely visible form of alienated life. Parenthetically one might say that the *Schuld* which the father bequeathes to the son is in the last analysis life itself. The "rotting apple in the flesh" not only causes, but also embodies Gregor's protracted dying. This seems to suggest that the original "guilt of the parents" was the dubious "gift" of physical existence. This reading would connect ***The Metamorphosis*** with numerous other works by Kafka and with the spirit of his aphorisms.

In contrast to his father, Gregor does not incur guilt; he is guilt. His incarnation of guilt corresponds to Christ's incarnation of God in man, in one sense only. Like Christ, Gregor takes the cross upon himself to erase "the guilt of the parents." But in contrast to Christ, Gregor does not merely assume suffering by his fellow creatures; he also assumes their guilt. Since he has made guilt identical with himself, he must liberate the world, i.e., his family, from himself.

"The guilt of the parents" showed itself as indebtedness. It constituted capitulation to the world in its capitalist makeup. In strict consequence, economic determination inserts itself now into the myth as Kafka presents it. This insertion can be understood in socio-cultural and, indeed, Marxist categories. The plot inserted into the mythic events depicts a classic case of the proletarianization of a petty-bourgeois household. . . . In regard to the socio-economic world of exploited labor, Gregor, by the horrible paradox that is his metamorphosis, is now the only "free" member of the family, the only one who does not have to labor and let himself be exploited by the world outside.

The family's proletarianization reaches its nadir when it has to yield the control over its household to the three lodgers. According to Marx, as capitalism increasingly absorbs all pre-capitalistic forms of human life, "the contrast between natural and social existence becomes progressively more extreme." In Kafka's tale, the displacement of the "natural," traditional head of the family, the father, by the three strangers exemplifies the development described by Marx. The three lodgers assume the dominant place in the household merely by virtue of their paying power. Kafka's plot mimetically conforms to and expresses Marx's observation of the historic change from blood kinship to money as the determining element in all human relationships. ***The Metamorphosis*** shows how the basis of power, even within the "natural" unit of the family, slips from blood, age, and sex, the foundations of the father's dominance, to money which makes the unrelated strangers the rulers of the family. The family forfeits its autonomy even within its own walls. Of course, even prior to this loss, the family's independence had been appearance only since the father's debt to Gregor's firm had handed it over to the tyranny of the business world, represented by the creditor's firm. The lodgers' invasion of the household and their assumption of absolute control over it thus, in Marx's words, only "brings to a head" . . . what had been inherent in the family's enslavement to the capitalist world through the father's original guilt.

Since his metamorphosis, however, Gregor must assume the blame for this state of affairs. He alone now appears to be the cause of the whole "misfortune" of his family—unique as it is "in the entire circle of their relatives and acquaintances." . . . He is guilty in a manner which lifts his "guilt" completely out of the sphere in which a socio-economic interpretation could still be relevant. To be sure, in consequence of its economic impoverishment, the family disintegrates as a natural community. So far the analogy to Marx's world view holds. However, the limits of such an analogy are reached as soon as we realize that the ultimate cause of this proletarianization is a circumstance that transcends the observable laws of nature. In the midst of an environment which otherwise seems to be wholly determined by socio-economic factors, Gregor's metamorphosis supplies the evidence of something inexplicable in, and therefore transcendent of, the terms of that *Weltbild*. (pp. 488-92)

In the microscopic society of his petty-bourgeois household, Gregor Samsa plays the same role that the proletariat, in Marx's vision, performs in the macroscopic social and universal society of the bourgeois-capitalist system.

The analogy between Gregor and the proletariat becomes clearer when we realize that Gregor's metamorphosis is bound up with "guilt" in a two-fold way. The "guilt of the parents" is embodied *in* him; but it is also perpetrated *on* him. Insofar as his vermin appearance is the incarnation of parasitic selfishness, their guilt is embodied in him. However, insofar as he serves as the butt of the injustice and cruelty of his family, insofar as he suffers their total neglect and withdrawal of love, their guilt is perpetrated on him. As the unrecognized member of his family, Gregor corresponds to that universal victim of the capitalist order—the proletariat.

Gregor also exercises its eschatological function as the liberator and savior of his society. The "notorious crime" of society diagnosed by Marx as the surrender of man to inhumanity is embodied in the hero of Kafka's tale much more literally even than in the hero of Marx's view of history. Like the proletariat for Marx, Gregor bears in his family "radical chains." His existence, like the proletariat's, represents "the universal sorrows" of mankind. "No particular injustice," but "injustice as such" is committed against him. His very being, like that of the proletariat, proclaims "the total loss of humanity"—a loss that in his case manifests itself of course in its most literal meaning. Finally, like the proletariat in Marx's eschatological view of history, Gregor can regain his own humanity only by the liberation of his whole community.

However, in sharp contrast to Marx, the optimistic "synthesis" of self-liberation and liberation of all others is totally lacking in Kafka's world. Marx's proletariat redeems itself by redeeming mankind. In Kafka, liberation can be achieved only by the total sacrifice, the self-eradication of the scapegoat. Only by vanishing completely can Gregor save his family and himself.

While Marx's messianic view of the proletariat represents a secularized version of the Judaeo-Christian eschatology, the mythic dimension of Kafka's tale contradicts the latter. In the Christian version of the scapegoat myth, the savior's self-sacrifice is merely temporary. He arises again and takes the redeemed with him to eternal bliss. Kafka's myth follows the more primitive and universal "transference" myth. . . . In ***The Metamorphosis***, "the guilt of the parents" has been transferred to Gregor. He is the scapegoat on whom the refuse, the filth, the "sin," of the whole community is deposited. This transference appears in him not only physically and externally as when the *Unrat* of the whole apartment is thrown into his room. It also shows itself inwardly as the—temporary—reprehensible and shocking deterioration of Gregor's character makes clear.

What remains for Gregor to do is to recognize that it is his role and mission "to bear away forever . . . the accumulated misfortunes and sins" of his family by removing himself in whom they are incarnated. In this lies the inner meaning of his metamorphosis which his sister's words make clear to him. "His opinion that he must disappear was if anything even more decided than his sister's." . . . (pp. 492-93)

He literally carries out the "turning," the spatial "return" "back into his room" . . . that transposes ***The Metamorphosis*** from its economically determined foreground plot into the mythic frame from which it had issued. Hitherto intent on breaking out and returning to power, influence, love, and life, Gregor now withdraws forever into his room, into himself. He gives himself up to death by which he liberates not only the world from himself, but more importantly for Kafka, himself from the world.

The death of Gregor Samsa is self-imposed in the literal sense that it occurs only after the consent of the "hero." Gregor carries out the death sentence on himself that his sister, as the representative of the family and of life, has pronounced against him. He executes it by virtue of what can only be considered psychic power. He kills himself simply by his will—resembling in this respect Kleist's *Penthesilea*. His will is to obey the "law" which has chosen him for sacrifice so that his family can live free of *Schuld,* and the formulation of this will is immediately followed by its fulfillment—Gregor's death. It is a sacrificial death for the family of whom he thinks "with tenderness and love." . . . (p. 494)

Kafka's definition of the writer's relationship to mankind applies to Gregor's role in the deliverance of his family:

> The writer is the scapegoat of humanity; he allows human beings to enjoy sin guiltlessly, almost guiltlessly.

In this sense, and in this sense alone, the mythos of ***The Metamorphosis*** describes a myth of literature. Gregor allows his family, as the writer allows humanity, to enjoy their guilt guiltlessly, which does *not* mean that he restores to them their innocence. They remain guilty, but they can now enjoy the fruits of this guilt without being held accountable. For the scapegoat who embodies their conscience makes them free of it. (p. 495)

Walter H. Sokel, "From Marx to Myth: The Structure and Function of Self-Alienation in Kafka's 'Metamorphosis'," in The Literary Review *(copyright © 1983 by Fairleigh Dickinson University), Vol. 26, No. 4, Summer, 1983, pp. 485-95.*

ADDITIONAL BIBLIOGRAPHY

Angress, R. K. "Kafka and Sacher-Masoch: A Note on *The Metamorphosis.*" *Modern Language Notes (German Issue)* 85, No. 5 (October 1970): 745-46.

Posits a connection between the photograph of a woman in furs hanging on Gregor Samsa's bedroom wall and Leopold von Sacher-Masoch's famous piece of Austrian fin-de-siécle pornography *Venus im Pelz (Venus in Furs).*

Barnes, Hazel E. "Myth and Human Experience." *The Classical Journal* 51, No. 3 (December 1955): 121-27.

Interprets *The Metamorphosis* in terms of classic Greek myth.

Beck, Evelyn Torton. "Kafka's Traffic in Women: Gender, Power, and Sexuality." *The Literary Review* 26, No. 4 (Summer 1983): 565-76.

Feminist interpretation of Kafka's principal works and characters. Both Gregor and his father are interpreted as attempting to disrupt any alliance between Grete and Frau Samsa in *The Metamorphosis.*

Cantrell, Carol Helmstetter. "*The Metamorphosis:* Kafka's Study of a Family." *Modern Fiction Studies* 23, No. 4 (Winter 1977-78): 578-86.

Discusses *The Metamorphosis* as "a strange story about an ordinary family" and analyses the Samsas in the light of the studies by existential psychiatrist R. D. Laing: *The Divided Self: An Existential Study in Sanity and Madness* (1965), *The Politics of the Family and Other Essays* (1971), and *Sanity, Madness, and the Family* (1970).

Cox, Harvey. "Kafka East, Kafka West." *The Commonweal* LXXX, No. 20 (4 September 1964): 596-600.

States that Kafka's work represents a serious challenge to the Christian doctrine of salvation and the social salvationism of Marxists.

Daemmrich, Horst S. "The Infernal Fairy Tale: Inversion of Archetypal Motifs in Modern European Literature." *Mosaic* V, No. 3 (Spring 1972): 85-95.*

Discusses spiritual rebirth as a classic fairy tale motif. Daemmrich finds several modern European literary works, including *The Metamorphosis,* to be based upon an inversion of this motif.

Emrich, Wilhelm. *Franz Kafka: A Critical Study of His Writings.* New York: Frederick Ungar Publishing Co., 1968, 561 p.

One of the most comprehensive studies of Kafka's works.

Hayman, Ronald. *Kafka: A Biography.* New York: Oxford University Press, 1982, 349 p.

Most complete biography.

Holland, Norman N. "Realism and Unrealism in Kafka's *Metamorphosis.*" *Modern Fiction Studies* 4, No. 2 (Summer 1958): 143-50.

Advocates reading *The Metamorphosis* with a focus upon the realistic and naturalistic plot elements in order to reduce the danger of viewing the metamorphosis as a biographical symbol representing Kafka's feelings about his relationship to his father. Holland finds job, employer, and employee relations, and not family relations, to be central to the story.

Jofen, Jean. *"Metamorphosis." The American Imago* 55, No. 4 (Winter 1978): 347-56.

Biographical interpretation of *The Metamorphosis.* Jofen assumes that all father or authority figures in Kafka's fiction represent Kafka's own father, and that relationships between authority figures and subordinates mirror Kafka's relationship with his father.

The Literary Review 26, No. 4 (Summer 1983): 477-593.

Special issue devoted to Kafka studies in the year of his centenary. Included are essays by Walter H. Sokel (see excerpt above, 1983), Evelyn Torton Beck, Stanley Corngold, Richard T. Gray, Ruth V. Gross, Philip Grundlehner, Roman Karst, and Ralf R. Nicolai.

Luke, F. D. "The Metamorphosis." In *Franz Kafka Today,* edited by Angel Flores and Homer Swander, pp. 25-44. Madison: University of Wisconsin Press, 1958.

Concurs with the many biographical interpretations of the story, such as that of Jean Jofen (see Additional Bibliography) and Charles Neider (see excerpt above, 1948). Luke calls the story a "punishment fantasy associated with an extremely primitive father-image."

Madden, William A. "A Myth of Mediation: Kafka's *Metamorphosis.*" *Thought* XXVI, No. 101 (Summer 1951): 246-66.

Finds that "Franz Kafka's relationship with his family and society is the real theme of *The Metamorphosis,*" as do Charles Neider (see excerpt above, 1948), Heinz Politzer (see excerpt above, 1966), Carol Helmstetter Cantrell (see Additional Bibliography), and Normal Friedman (see Additional Bibliography). Madden stresses Kafka's use of realism in *The Metamorphosis,* and his efforts to present, if not facts, at least "a real situation."

Pascal, Roy. "The Impersonal Narrator in the Early Tales." In his *Kafka's Narrators: A Study of His Stories and Sketches,* pp. 21-59. London: Cambridge University Press, 1982.

Discussion of Kafka's narrative technique and his use of an impersonal but not omniscient narrator in his earliest stories, including *The Metamorphosis.*

Rolleston, James. "*The Metamorphosis.*" In his *Kafka's Narrative Theatre,* pp. 52-68. University Park: Pennsylvania State University Press, 1974.

Disagrees with the common critical comparisons of *The Metamorphosis* with *Das Urteil (The Judgment).* Rolleston finds *The Metamorphosis* to be a continuation and a further development of themes from *The Judgment.*

Spilka, Mark. "Kafka's Sources for *The Metamorphosis.*" *Comparative Literature* XI, No. 4 (Fall 1959): 289-307.

Cites Leo Tolstoy, Charles Dickens, and Nikolai Gogol as some significant influences upon Kafka's writing of *The Metamorphosis.*

———. *Dickens and Kafka: A Mutual Interpretation*. Bloomington: Indiana University Press, 1963, 315 p.

Examines similarities in the lives and major works of Charles Dickens and Kafka.

Tauber, Herbert. "The Metamorphosis." In his *Franz Kafka: An Interpretation of His Works*, pp. 18-26. 1948. Reprint. Port Washington, N.Y.: Kennikat Press, 1968.

Discusses Gregor's metamorphosis as an expression of the character's "feeling of alienation from the world around him," in an interpretation similar to that of Alexander Taylor (see excerpt above, 1965).

Wolkenfeld, Suzanne. "Christian Symbolism in Kafka's *The Metamorphosis*." *Studies in Short Fiction* X, No. 2 (Spring 1973): 205-07.

Finds in the first part of *The Metamorphosis* "certain parallels between Gregor and Christ that are later developed as an ironic parody."

(Prince) Giuseppe (Maria Fabrizio) Tomasi di Lampedusa

1896-1957

Italian novelist, short story writer, autobiographer, and essayist.

Lampedusa was the author of *Il gattopardo (The Leopard)*, the most popular twentieth-century Italian novel. Written by the previously unpublished Sicilian prince during the last two years of his life, published posthumously, and based on facts drawn from his family history, *The Leopard* is at once a colorful historical novel and a moving testimony of the author's tragic vision of life, narrating the decline of a noble Sicilian family as, by necessity, it embraces the vulgar, social-climbing *nouveau riche* who rose to power after the fall of the Bourbon monarchy during the mid-nineteenth century. Like *The Leopard, Racconti* (partially translated as *Two Stories and a Memory*)—a collection of memoirs, a short story, and a portion of an unfinished novel, which together form Lampedusa's only other major work—explores the author's recurrent theme of the inevitability of change and death.

Courtesy of Gioacchino Lanza Tomasi

Lampedusa was descended from a wealthy family that counted among their forebears some of the major grandees of Spain and Sicily since the sixteenth century, when the Tomasi were named princes of Lampedusa, a small island south of Sicily. The family's enormous fortune began to decline in the 1800s, when there were passed a succession of laws designed to break up the large Sicilian estates. The first of the Tomasi to be seriously affected by these laws were the heirs of Don Giulio Maria Fabrizio, himself the author's great-grandfather and the inspiration for the novel's Don Fabrizio di Salina, called "The Leopard." After the death of Don Giulio, the Tomasi fortune was poorly administered and much of it was lost. Giuseppe Tomasi, the last Prince of Lampedusa, was born in Palermo, where he spent his childhood amid much less luxury than his forebears had enjoyed. As a young man he served as an officer in the Italian artillery during World War I. Captured by the Austrians and held in prison camp in Hungary, Lampedusa escaped and, disguised, made his way back to Italy, where he remained in the national army until 1921. He spent much of the rest of his life traveling in Europe, reading widely in world literature, and attempting to restore his family estate. When the Lampedusa palace in Palermo was bombed and looted by Allied troops during World War II, the Prince fell into a deep state of bitterness and nostalgic depression from which he did not recover for many years. In 1955, at the suggestion of his wife, Lampedusa began writing as a form of therapy. All of his published and unpublished work was written during the eighteen months before his death in 1957.

Within a year of Lampedusa's death, *The Leopard* was accepted for publication by the firm of Giangiacomo Feltrinelli, who had earlier discovered and published Boris Pasternak's *Doktor Zhivago (Doctor Zhivago)*. Set, like Pasternak's novel, in a period of national revolution and social readjustment, *The Leopard* concerns the Risorgimento (the movement for the unification of the Italian states) and its effects on Sicilian life, as perceived by the shrewd, sensual astronomer and mathematician Don Fabrizio, Prince of Salina. During the course of the novel Don Fabrizio watches with a sense of bitter approval as his heir and favorite nephew, Tancredi, joins the anti-Bourbon rebels of Giuseppe Garibaldi, and later as he courts and marries Angelica, the beautiful but grasping and ignorant daughter of a rising, middle-class politician. The Prince sees his own class inexorably displaced by the unpolished new regime, a change that is paralleled by Don Fabrizio's own declining vitality as compared with the strong ambitions and sexual passion of Tancredi and Angelica. Don Fabrizio comes to realize that life's only constants are its vanity, its fleetingness, and change: that "even fixed stars are only so in appearance." A sense of death and impending death pervades *The Leopard,* from the opening line, "Nunc et in hora mortis nostrae" ("Now and in the hour of our death"), through the recurring image of a disemboweled Royalist soldier discovered by the Prince in the palace garden, to the novel's end, when the last memento of the long-dead Fabrizio—the moth-eaten, stuffed body of his favorite hunting dog—is at last thrown on the rubbish heap. Don Fabrizio's—and Lampedusa's—attitude toward death and toward humanity is touchingly revealed in a hunting scene when, having shot a rabbit, the Prince contemplates the mortally wounded creature: "Don Fabrizio found himself stared at by big black eyes soon overlaid by a glaucous veil; they were looking at him with no reproof, but full of tortured amazement at the whole order of things; the velvety ears were already cold, the vigorous paws contracting in rhythm, still-living symbol of useless flight; the animal had

died tortured by anxious hopes of salvation, imagining it could still escape when it was already caught, just like so many human beings. While sympathetic fingers were still stroking that poor snout, the animal gave a last quiver and died." At another point, while sourly watching *nouveau-riche* couples dancing at a ball, "Don Fabrizio felt his heart thaw; his disgust gave way to compassion for all these ephemeral beings out to enjoy the tiny ray of light granted them between two shades, before the cradle, after the last spasms. How could one inveigh against those sure to die?" Lampedusa's vision, as revealed in *The Leopard* and in the later *Two Stories and a Memory,* is one of accepting change and death as necessary parts of life.

Upon its appearance in 1958, *The Leopard* was an immediate popular success—a publishing phenomenon which itself came to be known as "il caso Lampedusa"—as well as the source of a lively critical debate in Europe. While the novel was widely hailed as a minor masterpiece, some influential critics, motivated primarily by religious and political ideology, attacked *The Leopard:* conservative critics objected to the languid decadence portrayed therein, leftists perceived it as merely the nostalgic pinings of a dispossessed aristocrat, and both deplored the author's fatalism. The Neorealist Italian novelist Alberto Moravia dismissed *The Leopard* as "a goodish minor novel," while France's major communist poet, Louis Aragon, astounded the left by pronouncing the novel "one of the great books of this century, one of the great books of all time." Critics note the work's elaborate, allusive style—which has no equivalent in the prosaically spare literature of postwar Italy—and its omniscient narrative voice, which tells of the past, present, and future of Don Fabrizio's family. Lampedusa's essay "Lezioni su Stendhal" is today considered to be of crucial importance in understanding *The Leopard.* "Lezioni" is a detailed, appreciative interpretation of Stendhal's fiction and an analysis of his narrative technique that reveals Lampedusa as a scholar who was well acquainted with the subjective, Jamesian tradition of literary criticism. *The Leopard,* with its melding of historical drama and Lampedusa's personal philosophy as projected in the work's central character, is, thus, often seen as a work written in the tradition of Stendhal's *La Chartreuse de Parme (The Charterhouse of Parma)* and *Le Rouge et le noir (The Red and the Black).* In this matter critics have also noted the influence of Marcel Proust, while Lampedusa's widow has claimed that Leo Tolstoy was her husband's chief literary influence.

Among the short works collected in *Two Stories and a Memory,* "Lighea" ("The Professor and the Mermaid") is considered the most important. Like *The Leopard,* "The Professor and the Mermaid"—a supernatural tale that was inspired by a reading of H. G. Wells's *The Sea Lady*—is concerned with transience and death. But as well crafted as are this story and the memoirs recorded in *Two Stories and a Memory,* Lampedusa's fame continues to rest on *The Leopard,* a novel which has been widely translated and which continues to attract many readers and provoke much critical discussion.

(See also *Contemporary Authors,* Vol. 111.)

PRINCIPAL WORKS

Il gattopardo (novel) 1958
[*The Leopard,* 1960]
"Lezioni su Stendhal" (essay) 1959; published in journal *Paragone*
Racconti (short stories and memoirs) 1961
[*Two Stories and a Memory* (partial translation), 1962]

MARC SLONIM (essay date 1960)

[Slonim was a Russian-born American critic who wrote extensively on European literature. In the following excerpt, he offers a favorable review of the English translation of The Leopard.*]*

The Italian, French and German press call this book a miracle. If there are such things as miracles in literature, **"The Leopard"** comes, indeed, quite close to being one. . . .

From a conventional point of view **"The Leopard"** has no unity of narrative, its story is too simple, its plot is almost nonexistent, and its few characters are not explored in depth. The first four chapters present episodes from the life of Prince Salina, a Sicilian patrician, descendant of a long line of feudal lords; the fifth chapter relates how Father Pirrone, a Jesuit and Salina's chaplain, smoothed out a domestic mess among his rustic relatives; the final chapters tell of a ball, of the death of Prince Salina and the old age of Salina's daughter.

Yet these flashes, which some conservative critics have found fragmentary, have an inner coherence that makes them into a novel. First of all, they turn on a particular moment of Sicilian life—the landing in 1860 of Garibaldi's Red Shirts, which brought about the downfall of the Bourbon monarchy and led to the union of Sicily with the newly formed kingdom of Italy. Secondly, these events are seen through the eyes of Prince Salina, and this extraordinary personage is the hero of the book and dominates the stage even when he is not physically present. (p. 1)

The novelty in Lampedusa's novel is that this social change was portrayed from the point of view of the condemned class, but with a spirit of comprehension and benevolence. **"The Leopard"** is openly anti-Romantic, and its poetry does not derive from flights of religious exaltation or pallid joys of humility. Those who are interested in Italian history and especially in the fate of Sicily will find many instructive passages here. But descriptive scenes and historical material serve in Lampedusa's book only as a means for emphasizing a vision of man and existence that has nothing to do with historical veracity or bright panoramas of the past.

Moreover the whole style of **"The Leopard"** is entirely different from the inventory-like list of particulars and the long-winded narrative of nineteenth-century realistic literature. Those who contend that the popularity of the book is due to the fact that it has the traditional contours of a good yarn, miss its compactness, brevity and constant use of significant trait and symbolic image instead of itemized description—in short, all that makes it a modern novel in structure and manner of writing. And it is also subtly modern in its spirit.

It is quite probable that Lampedusa drew his main character, Prince Salina, from his paternal great grandfather; but it is also quite obvious that he gave him his own traits, thus accomplishing a curious fusion of imagination and self expression, of historical exposition and psychological confession. In the figure of Salina, the author created a memorable, full-blooded individual portrait, but he used it to convey his own philosophy of life.

The main feature of this vigorous specimen of virility and autocracy is his ambivalence. Placed at the watershed of two eras, he belongs to one organically but understands the other intellectually. Like all of us today, like anyone in a time of change and crisis, he is torn by his inner contradictions. Moreover he experiences the rift between lust and intelligence, between reason and impulses, between flesh and spirit. He observes Christian rites, and goes to mass daily, but the mass is celebrated in the drawing room of his palace, which is decorated with nude goddesses fleeing from eager pursuers.

At a time when fiction portrays instincts and physiological reactions with such an insistence that one begins to wonder whether human beings are capable of any other activities except violence and mating, it is refreshing to find a book in which the hero is not ashamed of his intellectual aspirations and of his general ideas. **"The Leopard"** is written by a highly civilized man whose intelligence illuminates the pages of his novel without ever making them arid or specious.

On the contrary, his art is not only intelligent, but also lively and delicate. His characters are portrayed with such colorful vividness, his scenes are so consistently full of life, that one wonders how he can maintain the significant strokes, the poetic diction, the firm craft through such a variety of pictures and situations.

The American translation, on the whole satisfactory, does not always render the brilliance and sophistication of the author's style and its happy merging of dry irony with subtle poetic feeling. It is true that to achieve his artistic aim Lampedusa used devices that belong more to Flaubert or Stendhal than to the modern fiction of symbolic allusions and surrealistic constructions. But its spirit of inner struggle and frustrated humanity, of social ambivalence and spiritual thirst is that of our times, and the genius of its author and the thrill it gives the reader are probably for all time. (pp. 1, 24)

Marc Slonim, "As New Winds Swept an Old Island," in The New York Times Book Review *(copyright © 1960 by The New York Times Company; reprinted by permission), May 1, 1960, pp. 1, 24.*

FRANK KERMODE (essay date 1960)

[Kermode is an English critic whose career combines modern critical methods with expert traditional scholarship, particularly in his work on Shakespeare. In his critical discussions of modern literature, Kermode has embraced many of the conceptions of structuralism and phenomenology. Kermode characterizes all human knowledge as poetic, or fictive: constructed by humans and affected by the perceptual and emotional limitations of human consciousness. Because perceptions of life and the world change, so does human knowledge and the meaning attached to things and events. Thus, there is no single fixed reality over time. Similarly, for Kermode, a work of art has no single fixed meaning, but a multiplicity of possible interpretations. In fact, the best of modern writing is constructed so that it invites a variety of interpretations, all of which depend upon the sensibility of the reader. Kermode believes his critical writings exist to stimulate thought, to offer possible interpretations, but not to fix a single meaning to a work of art. True or "classic" literature, to Kermode, is thus a constantly reinterpreted living text, "complex and indeterminate enough to allow us our necessary pluralities." In the following excerpt, Kermode turns from a review of Allen Tate's novel The Fathers *to favorably appraise* The Leopard, *noting similarities between the two works in plot and theme.]*

The Leopard is . . . a deeply meditated book, extremely original and possessing an archaic harshness of feeling, more alien and more ancient than the civilized calm of *The Fathers*. It is, however, a less consistently well made work; there are one or two sermons, points where the exposition of ideas gets the better of the total figuration of the image; there is also an episode (Father Pirrone's intervention in a peasant marriage dispute) which makes a relevant point but which adheres much more loosely to the main body of the novel than anything Tate would permit. It is also, of course, an aristocratic novel, but with a very different heritage from that of *The Fathers*. If it has the brilliant intelligence of Stendhal it has also something of his superior carelessness. But only a little; it is a work entirely worthy of that master (whose admiration for Ariosto Lampedusa evidently shared) and it is also in many ways a work of this century. The coincidence of theme with Tate's is remarkable. A Southern world is changed by soldiers from the North; but now the South is Sicily and the soldiers Garibaldi's. The time (1860) is the same. The theme—the break-up of a civilization—is the same, though what is lost here is, for all its power, a world of death. And at a level not far below the surface the theme of ***The Leopard*** is death, the conditions under which men as well as societies long for it. (pp. 136-37)

The languor and the violence of this more desperate South is beautifully conveyed; the book is held in the grip of its opening sentence—*Nunc et in hora mortis nostrae [Now and in the hour of our death]*—throughout. Always associated with this knowledge of death are the Prince's love of the undisturbed stars, and a pervasive sensuality made civil by easy autocratic wit. The wit of Lampedusa is equal to the demands of a crucial dinner-party; and in describing the sensuality of Tancredi's wooing in the great house at Donnafugata—a new-style courtship stained with the dead dust of centuries—he achieves something absolutely original, a kind of erotic fugue. Lampedusa's talent was clearly enormous; Mr. Colquhoun's translation has immense resource; and the book is, as it stands in English, worthy of all the admiration that it has received. The civilization that ends with Salina is greater and darker than Major Buchan's [in *The Fathers*]; and Lampedusa has got its presence into his book, which therefore is a bigger book than Tate's. There is nothing that a Major Buchan can do which has the sheer historical weight of significance that Salina's dealings with the Jesuit, in part submissive, in part insulting—as when he makes the priest help to dry his magnificent and recently sinning body—have as a natural right. Yet of the two books Mr. Tate's is the more perfect. It cannot be more than once or twice in a lifetime that a critic might have on his table, at the same time, two new novels of such rare quality. (pp. 138-39)

Frank Kermode, "Old Orders Changing" (© 1960 by Encounter Ltd.; reprinted by permission of the publisher and author), in Encounter, *Vol. XV, No. 2, August, 1960 (and reprinted as "Old Orders Changing (Allen Tate and Giuseppe de Lampedusa)," in his* Puzzles and Epiphanies: Essays and Reviews, 1958-1961, *Routledge & Kegan Paul, 1962, pp. 131-39).**

E. M. FORSTER (essay date 1962)

[Forster was a prominent English novelist, critic, and essayist whose works reflect his liberal humanism. His most celebrated novel, A Passage to India *(1924), is a complex examination of personal relationships amid the conflicts of the modern world. Although some of Forster's critical essays have been called naive in their literary assessments, his discussion of fictional techniques in his* Aspects of the Novel *is regarded as a minor classic of literary criticism. After praising* The Leopard *in a review written upon the novel's appearance in English (see Additional Bibliography), Forster contributed the following laudatory introduc-*

tion to Two Stories and a Memory. *Of particular interest is the critic's thematic comparison of Lampedusa's* "The Professor and the Mermaid" *with his own short story* "The Song of the Siren."]

This prefatory note is a meditation rather than an introduction. Prince Giuseppe di Lampedusa has meant so much to me that I find it impossible to present him formally. His great novel, ***The Leopard (Il Gattopardo),*** has certainly enlarged my life—an unusual experience for a life which is well on in its eighties. Reading and rereading it has made me realize how many ways there are of being alive, how many doors there are, close to one, which someone else's touch may open. (p. 13)

So it is a great pleasure to be connected with this volume [***Two Stories and a Memory (Racconti)***] (an excellent translation) and an austerer pleasure to announce that it is not a second masterpiece. How could it be? Leopards do not hang on every bush. It contains three items greatly differing in their character: an autobiography, a short story, and the opening chapter of an unwritten novel.

The autobiography—**"Places of My Infancy"**—is exquisite. It begins vaguely and unchronologically, and then, as the infant matures and observes the passage of time and the varieties of place, it coalesces, and gives an imaginative account of two houses which reappear still more imaginatively in ***The Leopard.*** There is the Palermo palace, figuring in both works. There is the country palace in western Sicily, Santa Margherita Belice, whose fictional counterpart is Donnafugata. Donnafugata has the lovelier name, is the more difficult to reach, has the sweeter peaches, the more dubious recesses; Santa Margherita is the unchallenged and unchangeable possession of a child. (p. 14)

And now for the most remarkable of the three items—the story entitled **"The Professor and the Mermaid."** It particularly interests me for the reason that, thirty years previously, I too wrote a story about a Siren. I don't know whether he ever read mine—he does refer to something analogous but it is by H. G. Wells and the reference is unfavorable. He and I certainly have points in common as well as points of contrast. I too located my Siren in Sicily, and in waters as glorious as I could contrive. But I kept her under the waters—a decency he makes no effort to imitate. Mine was cosmic, and was to stay hidden until ritually summoned, when she would rise to the surface, sing, destroy silence, primness, and cruelty, and save the world. His Siren is not cosmic; she is personal, and here she shows her superior sense. She gives her body to a number of young men, all of whom are beautiful. She explains to them that she never kills anyone, nor does she, but no one who has once loved her can love anyone else, so they all end up either as suicides or as university professors. Her name is Lighea. She is the daughter not of Mnemosyne, not of Urania, but of Calliope.

It is an exquisite fantasy and a sustained one: mine was short. We shared one other point in common, which I must mention here: we are both of us out of date on the subject of sea. We assumed, as did the Greeks before us, that the sea was untamable and eternal and that strength could drown in it and beauty sport in it forever. Here we underestimated the mightiness of Man, who now dominates the sea as never before and is infecting its depths with atomic waste. Will Man also succeed in poisoning the solar system? It is possible: generals are already likely to meet on the moon. What Man probably won't effect—and here I am getting back to ***The Leopard***—is the distintegration of the outer galaxies. How soothing, in that grand novel, are the astronomical passages where the hero, who has wasted his Sicilian day, repairs to his telescope, and looks up through the Sicilian night at the stars. What a release to the human spirit in its struggle against human possessiveness! There is nothing comparable to this in the Siren story, though I catch an echo of it in "the enchantment of certain summer nights within sight of Castellamare Bay, when stars are mirrored in the sleeping sea and the spirit of anyone lying back among the lentisks is lost in a vortex of sky"; *"mentre il corpo, teso e all'erta, tema l'avvicinarsi dei demoni."* The beauty of the Italian here defies translation, so I quote the original, and the last word in it, *demoni,* is certainly one which everyone can apprehend.

The third item, **"The Blind Kittens,"** is less magical. It is the opening chapter of an unfinished novel which was to deal with the Newest Rich of 1900, the gross and grasping Ibba family. In ***The Leopard,*** a generation earlier, we encountered the New Rich in the persons of the fairly presentable Sedàra family. But the Ibbas are peasants who are unpresentable and have no wish to be presented. They stumble blindly into a world which they cannot understand but are capable of damaging. The scene closes before it has been disclosed, but one of them (we are told) will become an eminent Fascist.

That ends my meditation. Those who have read ***The Leopard*** will not need it. Those who have not yet read ***The Leopard*** may here be introduced to a great contemporary Italian novelist. (pp. 15-17)

> *E. M. Forster, in an introduction to* Two Stories and a Memory *by Giuseppe di Lampedusa, translated by Archibald Colquhoun (copyright © 1962 by William Collins Sons & Co., Ltd., and Pantheon Books, Inc.; reprinted by permission of Pantheon Books, a Division of Random House, Inc.), Collins, 1962, Pantheon Books, 1962, pp. 13-17.*

STANLEY G. ESKIN (essay date 1962)

[*In the following excerpt, Eskin traces Lampedusa's recurrent use of animal imagery in* The Leopard.]

From the title to the very last sentence, describing the destruction of a stuffed dog, Lampedusa in ***Il Gattopardo*** uses animal images of all sorts to convey his themes. . . .

The comparison of men to animals in literature—which is mostly what we mean by "animal imagery"—may be divided into two general categories. One category is the use of animals to symbolize particular human traits. Thus Machiavelli recommends that the Prince cultivate the characteristics of the lion and of the fox, and Montaigne, borrowing from Plutarch, punctures human vanity by enumerating all the qualities in which various animals show themselves superior to men. The second category is reductive and usually involves the notion of bestiality: animals are symbols of the lower attributes of man to which he may sink, or simply of man's physical nature to which he may become enthralled, if reason, will, spirit or intellect fail him. (p. 189)

Lampedusa makes use of both of these categories of animal imagery in ***Il Gattopardo.*** Since one aspect of the novel is the glorification of the aristocratic spirit, certain animals are used to symbolize the virtues of the aristocracy and the deficiencies of its enemies. Don Fabrizio, Prince of Salina, is the chief, perhaps the sole, repository of what is best in the aristocracy: its integrity, its self-possession, its disinterestedness. The beautiful and princely Gattopardo—the cheetah (not a leopard)—represented on the Salina coat of arms, symbolizes Fabrizio's noble spirit. This is a direct metaphor that imposes itself throughout the book; Fabrizio *is* the Gattopardo, stalking proudly and majestically through his feudal domains now in social upheaval. . . . If a cheetah should prove an insufficient association, Fabrizio's character is related several times to the traditional king of the beasts, and is labelled "leonino." (pp. 189-90)

The admirable side of the aristocratic spirit is not only represented in the inherent qualities of these noble animals, but is further emphasized in the contrast of these animals with other baser animals symbolizing the rising new classes. About to negotiate with the up-and-coming capitalist Don Calogero, Fabrizio feels himself a Gattopardo stalking a jackal. . . . The jackals, of course, are winning, and the irony of his metaphor does not escape Fabrizio. But this does not affect the relative values implicit in the two animals, the confrontation of which cannot but leave the Gattopardo in higher esteem than the jackal. As Fabrizio explains later to the Piedmontese emissary Chevalley, Sicily will remain static for a long time but when it changes, it will change for the worse, for the jackals and hyenas will take over. . . . (p. 190)

Jackals and hyenas are not the only animals in contrast with the aristocratic lions and cheetahs. The deplorable qualities of the bourgeois spirit—its acquisitiveness, selfishness, narrowness and crudeness—are embodied in Don Calogero and symbolized by a series of undistinguished animals with which he is associated. When Don Calogero is compared to an Elephant, the awkwardness of that animal is no doubt meant as a contrast to the gracefulness of the Gattopardo. . . . Elsewhere Don Calogero is a bat . . . ; for him, the art of conversation is more like a dog fight . . . ; when Fabrizio has to discuss matrimonial questions with him, this is like swallowing a toad . . . ; and, much later, at the Ponteleone ball, Don Calogero and his kind remind Fabrizio of crows in search of carrion. . . . (pp. 190-91)

The ant hill which Fabrizio observes while hunting in the hills of Donnafugata provides an implicit assertion of the superiority of the aristocratic spirit by a metaphorical demonstration of the paltriness of the opposing spirit. On the one hand we have the lonely, proud, essentially disinterested hunt: the lithe Gattopardo stalking his prey. On the other hand we have the ants, symbols of greed, pettiness and mediocrity. . . . The ant hill is the new order which is about to overwhelm the aristocratic spirit, and that the identification should not escape us, Fabrizio himself associated [the ants] with the plebiscite that has already introduced the new order.

However, ***Il Gattopardo*** is by no means a simple-minded exaltation of aristocratic virtues in contrast with plebeian worthlessness. The real interest in the novel lies in the ambivalence of Fabrizi's attitude toward the class which he so eminently represents, an ambivalence which is of course the author's. Aristocratic virtues may shine when placed in contrast with certain bourgeois traits, but left to themselves, these virtues tend to tarnish. Self-possession can turn into arrogance, pride into vanity, disinterestedness into frivolity, refinement into morbidity, and stability into stagnation. Fabrizio exemplifies the best of aristocratic culture, but it is interesting that the aristocrats toward whom he feels closest are precisely those who reject their own class, like his eldest son, who has left Sicily to become an English businessman, and his Garibaldian nephew Tancredi.

Fabrizio's paradoxical attitude (which takes many forms in the novel) is his response to the complex mixture of strengths and weaknesses in the upper classes. The strength of the aristocratic spirit is the basic aspect of the novel because it is demonstrated by its hero, while the weaknesses are revealed through ironic counterpoints in which animal images play a significant role. The animal imagery here is primarily in the second category mentioned, in which the basic notion is that of bestiality, of elements in man which debase or weaken him. The movement of this image pattern is reductive: the aristocracy is subjected to a series of animal metaphors and symbols tending to undermine its status.

The association with other animals is as debasing to the aristocracy as its association with the Gattopardo is elevating. Fabrizio, for example, in respect to his affair with a mistress in Palermo, considers himself "un porco, e niente altro" ["a pig, and nothing else"], and recalls a previous Parisian mistress who used to call him "mon chat" ["my cat"] and "mon singe blond" ["my blond monkey"]. . . . The episode is slight, but there is a certain suggestion of decadence and moral flippancy which is accentuated by these metaphors. Again, Tancredi courting Angelica is compared to a cat . . . , and, later, arriving from Naples in a storm, he describes himself as "innamorato come un gatto, ma anche bagnato come un ranocchio, sudicio come un cane sperso, e affamato come un lupo" ["as in love as a cat, but also wet as a frog, filthy as a lost dog, and hungry as a wolf"]. . . . His ironic and incidental self-deprecation functions in fact, in a minor way, to deprecate his whole class. Elsewhere, the aristocracy in general is compared to sheep about to be shorn. . . . To be sure, this is in Don Calogero's eyes, but his view is not altogether wrong, and while the image might evoke pity it is certainly reductive in respect to the aristocracy's accustomed status.

But the most elaborate reductive treatment of this sort is executed not by Don Calogero but by Fabrizio himself at the Ponteleone ball. It is both his virtue and (for the sake of his peace of mind) his misfortune to be the arch-critic of his own class. As he wanders about this Proustian gathering of the Sicilian upper-crust, he becomes more and more appalled at their ugliness, insipidity and frivolity. There are a few beautiful women among them, but they are like swans in a pond full of frogs. . . . Indeed, this whole party, after a while, gives him the impression of a zoo, and all the chattering women seem monkeys to him, about to start swinging by their tails from the chandeliers, exhibiting their behinds and throwing nut shells at the guests. . . . A few pages later his sardonic mood has abated, and his scorn has changed to pity. But the stature of the aristocracy is hardly rehabilitated. . . . From silly and annoying apes these poor aristocrats have become cattle being led to slaughter. It is of them, the dying class, no doubt, that we are meant to be reminded a little later when Fabrizio, having decided to walk home, first muses on the serene detachment of his beloved stars, but then is shocked back into the world of earth, flesh and death by a passing cart loaded with recently slaughtered cattle. . . . (pp. 191-93)

The cats and monkeys and cattle associated with the aristocracy suggest its creatural weaknesses, its folly, and its perishability. The Gattopardo, of course, is another matter, and serves not to demean but to enhance the aristocracy. And yet the image of the Gattopardo itself is not immune from the reductive process. There is a stone Gattopardo in bas relief at Rampinzèri, but one of its legs has been knocked off. . . . Since the stance of the Gattopardo on the coat of arms is always described as "dancing," this mutilation has a particular force. Again, the Gattopardo may have been used to knocking over obstacles with his paws, but those paws are weakened by the thorns which are Tancredi's middle-class marriage. . . . And Fabrizio, nearing the end of his life, considers himself "un Gattopardo in pessima forma" ["a leopard in very bad shape"]. . . . This might be taken simply as a Stoical acceptance of his personal condition if it did not apply only too well to the situation of his class.

The animal imagery in ***Il Gattopardo*** helps to symbolize an aristocratic culture deserving, simultaneously and paradoxically, our contempt and our esteem. The novel opens and closes with animal images suggesting this theme. In the opening scene, the drawing room where the daily rosary is said is described in great detail. Among the frescoes, mostly of pagan deities, we find, on the one hand, an exotic scene of monkeys chasing parrots, and, on the other, the coat of arms with the Gattopardo. . . . This seems to suggest both the basic eminence of the aristocratic spirit, and the decadent frivolity which is one of its corruptions. At the end of the novel, Lampedusa describes the half insane life of Fabrizio's three daughters. Among their mementos of the past is a stuffed effigy of Fabrizio's faithful old dog Bendicò. But even stuffed, the poor animal is falling apart and is finally thrown away. For an instant, as he flies out the window, he takes the shape of the dancing Gattopardo. . . . Then he falls on the garbage heap and disintegrates into a heap of dust. A proud and noble jungle animal, momentarily reconstructed, but which is really an old stuffed dog about to become a heap of dust: this is a concise enough symbol of the principal theme of ***Il Gattopardo.*** (pp. 193-94)

Stanley G. Eskin, "Animal Imagery in 'Il Gattopardo'," in Italica, *Vol. XXXIX, September, 1962, pp. 189-94.*

V. S. PRITCHETT (essay date 1962)

[Pritchett is a highly esteemed English novelist, short story writer, and critic. He is considered one of the modern masters of the short story whose work is a subtle blend of realistic detail and psychological revelation. Pritchett is also considered one of the world's most respected and well-read literary critics. He writes in the conversational tone of the familiar essay, a method by which he approaches literature from the viewpoint of a lettered but not overly scholarly reader. A twentieth-century successor to such early nineteenth-century essayist-critics as William Hazlitt and Charles Lamb, Pritchett employs much the same critical method: his own experience, judgment, and sense of literary art are emphasized, as opposed to a codified critical doctrine derived from a school of psychological or philosophical speculation. His criticism is often described as fair, reliable, and insightful. In the following essay, Pritchett favorably reviews Two Stories and a Memory, *noting affinities between the works of Lampedusa and Stendhal.]*

Three short pieces of writing [***Two Stories and a Memory***] by the author of ***The Leopard*** have come to light: a broken-off memoir of his childhood, a short story and the chapter of a novel that was to tell the story of the new rich who were already gnawing at the estates of the Sicilian aristocracy in the Leopard's lifetime. Nothing is added to Prince di Lampedusa's reputation, but the rough fragments are marked by his serene sculptural hand. Even ***The Leopard*** had the air of being the surviving shell of a once massive classical edifice—as if the Prince had felt, as a matter of noblesse oblige, the necessity of avoiding the ennui of great designs. In his introduction to the present volume E. M. Forster calls ***The Leopard*** 'one of the great lonely books', and, in the fragments, there is still the suggestion of a mind rapt in a private past that has melted away and yet is to the author as clear and strong as stone. From Mr Archibald Colquhoun, the excellent translator, come more glimpses of the Prince's strange, self-contained and stoical life. The Prince comes so marvellously close to the people and scenes he describes because he conveys, in the manner of classical artists, the hard gleam of inaccessibility that makes human beings and nature itself seem final and alone.

The same quality is in the Stendhal of *Henri Brulard,* a book that greatly influenced the Prince. In the memoir about his childhood in the great Lampedusa palaces there is the admired directness. The senses are alert; one is physically *there;* there is no emotional blur. Journeys from one palace to another were difficult and slow. The family arrived, broiled by the Sicilian heat, choked and whitened in the dust. The boy ran off on arrival to take possession of these vast houses, their corridors, drawing-rooms and terraces, as if they were a kingdom. It is hard to describe happiness but for him it was total because, perhaps, of his talent for active solitude. From Stendhal, the author learned that fact is so generally obscured by our habits as to have the power of rarity if we stop to put it down. The fact of the Sicilian light or heat, for example is not lost in rhetoric, but is noticed in the changes from room to room and hour to hour. Similarly, human beings are caught, seriously or comically, as their lives hang in the pauses of living, when they are at their most solid. They are seen—and this is brought out by the chapter of his projected novel—in two ways: as they obstinately are and as they exist in the fantasies, rumours and half-truths that are told by the neighbours. The Prince had the art of evoking a whole circle of people when he was, apparently, describing only one person. If this novel had come to anything—and perhaps more may be discovered—it would have conveyed, as it was his gift to do, that the past was once the latest minute of a concrete present. The harking-back would have been nominal; as in ***The Leopard,*** he would have recovered whole and living days. His mind was as timeless as the recording angel's. One feels he would have treated the angel courteously, but with sufficient distance, as an indispensable little man on his estate.

The Prince was insistent on records: one owes a record to the future and it is a form of debt an aristocracy invariably recognizes, in fact regards as capital. He has astonished Italians as well as ourselves by his recovering of an unsuspected Sicilian past, indeed it has been embarrassing in some quarters, and at this time above all, to have a masterpiece whose subject was the nobility. The short fable called ***The Professor and the Siren*** shows him in a different light. An old Greek scholar, obscene, irascible and learned in talk, but absolutely continent in life, eventually tells a disreputable young man about his only love affair. It is an hallucination of learning: he had once been passionately loved by a creature out of the sea who convinced him she was the daughter of Calliope. It is a primitive salt-water love affair, carnal and exalting, with here and there a touch of the grotesque. The libidinous scholar goes gravely to his death and we have read a tale about the imagination that never once ceases to be tangible and deeply sensual. For the professor's one sexual experience is none the less grave for having left him with a comical and dubious taste for the sea urchin—or possibly cause and effect must be reversed. If the story is looser and rougher in surface than the Prince's best manner, the opening pages are an object-lesson in the art of evoking indelicate scenes by oblique methods. He spent most of his life reading and had learned everything from the masters before, alas so late, he wrote himself. (pp. 455-56)

V. S. Pritchett, "Loneliness of the Leopard," in New Statesman *(© 1962 The Statesman & Nation Publishing Co. Ltd.), Vol. LXIV, No. 1647, October 5, 1962, pp. 455-56.*

GIAN-PAOLO BIASIN (essay date 1963)

[Biasin's essay, excerpted below, examines the similar, intertwined themes of love and death in The Leopard *and* The Professor and the Mermaid. *Biasin's is one of the few English-language essays on Lampedusa's short fiction.]*

The publication of Giuseppe Tomasi di Lampedusa's short story ***Lighea*** has somewhat puzzled readers and critics, who have not been quite able to reconcile its light fantasy with the serious and realistic tone of ***Il Gattopardo.*** In fact ***Lighea*** seems, at first sight, only a delightful fable. Young Paolo Corbera, the last descendant of Prince Fabrizio Salina, tells how he met the old senator and famed professor Rosario La Ciura, author of *Uomini e dèi,* in a Turinese *caffé* which is described as "una specie di Ade" ["a kind of Hades"]. The old senator scorns his young friend for his sordid love affairs, and, the night before sailing for Portugal aboard the *Rex* to attend a humanistic congress, he tells the astonished Paolo Corbera about the unforgettable love affair he had with the siren Lighea, an immortal being, in the Sicilian sea in 1887, when he was "un giovane dio" ["a young god"]: the memory of that love made it impossible for him ever to make love to an imperfect human creature. Two days later, the newspapers report that Senator La Ciura has fallen off the ship in the Tyrrenian sea, and that his body has not been found; the apparent mystery of his death is left unresolved.

A closer examination, however, will show that despite its unusual subject ***Lighea*** derives directly from ***Il Gattopardo*** and is almost the *reductio ad absurdum* of its principal theme. . . . The novel communicates a sense of disgust directed toward physical decay and death; but death is not only the necessary condition and the result of the annihilation of the self in the universe, it is also a "vita eterna" glimpsed most often through the eyes of the eros. The short story repeats and concludes that theme, focusing it in the emblematic figure of the siren which seems the more fantastic for the realistic light in which it is cast.

In order to understand the precise relationship between ***Il Gattopardo*** and ***Lighea,*** in order to underline their continuity, we shall first analyze the development of the novel's theme and then consider the way in which that theme is modulated in the short story. It will be seen that the dialectic of death and love is unfolded and made manifest in both works through Tomasi di Lampedusa's imagery.

Few authors sum up their novels so emblematically as he does in the opening lines of ***Il Gattopardo***. . . . (pp. 31-2)

The novel begins with an ending. The word "death" stands out from the beginning, scanned as it is by the rhythmical pauses of the prayer, solemnized by the Latin, and rendered universal by the adjective: *in hora mortis nostrae*. Furthermore, it is linked and juxtaposed to the present *nunc*—which is actually the past, May 1860, the month and year of the ominous landing of Garibaldi in Sicily—by a simple conjunction which is here equally ominous. A few lines later, the word "death" is repeated, and this time it is linked to the present "amore" through "verginità," a flippant Sicilian touch, since virginity implies both an end and a beginning—the end of physical integrity and the beginning of the decay of the flesh: Artemis, the virgin goddess, will be recalled later in a serene hunting scene; Concetta, the spinster, will be the focus of the last desolate pages of the novel. The mention of "i Misteri Gloriosi e Dolorosi" ["the Glorious and the Sorrowful Mysteries"] seems deliberately to underscore a dichotomy, for the "Misteri" are usually recited separately, but are here joined in a single synoptic moment which foreshadows all that is to come.

Death is the well-spring of Tomasi di Lampedusa's poetical inspiration, at once the ontological problem and that problem's solution. There is a polarity in the very meaning of the word: on one hand, death as the inevitable consummation of man's destiny, made of sorrow and love; on the other, death as the sublimation of man's love, whereby he is transferred from decay and time into perfection and eternity. Thus, death is the point of departure but also the point of arrival of the narrative. Death and love are "i fiori d'oro" ["the golden flowers"] which permeate the atmosphere of the novel with their baroque scent; they are the Thanatos and the Eros of the "Olimpo palermitano" ["Palermitan Olympus"] whose Zeus is Prince Fabrizio Salina.

Images of death, examined for the moment only in one of its meanings, permeate the descriptions of places, landscapes, persons and objects. (pp. 32-3)

[But these] images, in fact, illustrate only one aspect of the ontological problem, which can be fully understood only by passing to a consideration of its other pole. Death, as is so often the case, is dialectically opposed and therefore intimately related to love. Eros in the work of Tomasi di Lampedusa presents us with a contrast of images, some of which are light and serene, some full of pleasure and sensually interwoven with death, thus providing us with a *chiaroscuro* composite.

Practically all the characters of ***Il Gattopardo*** are sooner or later seen in a sensual light. First, of course, there is the Prince, followed by Angelica and Tancredi, with their beautiful names that echo Tasso's melancholy. Here we need only mention one detail: a few hours before his death, the Prince notices "Angelica con la seta del corpetto ben tesa dai seni maturi" ["Angelica with silken bodice tight over mature breasts"]. (pp. 37-8)

[When at last the dying Prince is approached by the mysterious woman in brown,] Thanatos has met Eros, in a delicate and powerful scene. Thanatos *is* Eros, for here death is perfection; we can at the same time understand the almost metaphysical disgust, the detachment of the Prince from brute reality and from history, which are dirty and limited, and the delightful appreciation he has for the good things of life. Only now we can fully understand the mocking attitude of the Prince toward his corpse and toward that of the unknown soldier, and at the same time understand his compassion, his moving tenderness for his fellow men: the former descends from the heights of his unreachable ideal, the latter comes from his earthly reality. The mocking attitude is at the same time his reflection of the absolute (before which a corpse is at most only a necessary toll) and his reaction to the contingent (which, like the corpse, is spit upon). The compassion is his reflection of the contingent (which is, after all, the only sure *datum* granted to men) and his reaction to the absolute (which appears too unattainable, at times, even to him).

Perhaps, he wonders, the beautiful things of life, the few moments of grace, the few happy hours he has had, are really nothing but a reflection, an anticipation of death: "Ma queste ore potevano davvero essere collocate nell'attivo della vita? Non erano forse un'elargizione anticipata delle beatitudini mortuarie? Non importava, c'erano state'' [''Could those latter hours be really put down to the credit side of life? Were they not some sort of anticipatory gift of the beatitudes of death? It didn't matter, they had existed'']. The stoicism of the ancient, the resignation of the Christian, the wisdom of the old, the inner balance of the aristocrat, all converge in the supreme pessimism of the Prince—a pessimism which is at the same time personal and historical, involving his own life, his social class, the movement itself of history. His death is the symbolic death of the whole social class he epitomizes; it will be interesting to recall the emblematic figure of the stuffed Bendicò taking for a moment the shape of the ''Gattopardo'' during its last flight out of the window: ''si sarebbe potuto vedere danzare nell'aria un quadrupede dai lunghi baffi, e l'anteriore destro alzato sembrava imprecare'' [''in the air one could have seen dancing a quadruped with long whiskers, and its right foreleg seemed to be raised in imprecation'']. The verb ''imprecare,'' tempered by ''sembrava,'' is the only sign of impotent bitterness toward an unavoidable destiny; for the rest, the movement of history is actually immobility, or at least an imperceptible decay, with the Sedaras replacing the Salinas in the positions of power, only to be replaced in their turn after a few generations by descendants who will be worse than they were. But the final results, specially in the face of eternity, will be inexorably the same. The Prince, because he is so imbued with death, lives more consciously and intensely than the others; by the same token, he sees death in history too, but he understands history with a detached clarity which is denied to those who are unaware—an understanding which is in itself an act of love, even if it is a disdainful love. The description of the plebiscite and of its aftermath, analyzed earlier, is indicative of his position. (pp. 43-4)

As was said at the beginning of this article, [Tomasi di Lampedusa's] achievement is to be considered not only in ***Il Gattopardo,*** which has been analyzed so far, but also in ***Lighea,*** toward which we must finally turn our attention. Between the novel and the short story there is a correspondence which does not seem to be casual: La Ciura, Corbera and Lighea correspond respectively, in a sense, to the Prince, Tancredi and Angelica. La Ciura is another ''Gattopardo'' who treats Corbera (Tancredi) with a sort of rough tenderness: Lighea is the sublimation of the imperfect but so dear Angelica, or, if one prefers, Angelica is the nearest possible approximation of the immortal Lighea. Both the novel and the short story, then, deal with a glorious past which cannot be revived. Both envisage an immortal future which cannot be described, and which can be reached only through ''death.'' In dying, the Prince meets his emblematic ''creatura bramata da sempre'' [''creature forever yearned for'']; by plunging into the Tyrrenian sea, Senator La Ciura meets his emblematic Lighea.

Indeed, the story of the siren seems distilled from the story of the Prince: in the process it has become lighter, more serene. In it there is Glory rather than Sorrow: decay, disgust and material death are subdued and almost obliterated, while joy, eros and immortality are dominant. In fact, only the end of the story, with the images of the ''relics'' left by Senator La Ciura and particularly of his books which ''vanno imputridendo lentamente'' [''are slowly rotting away''], recalls the atmosphere of the closing sentence of ***Il Gattopardo*** (''Poi tutto trovò pace in un mucchietto di polvere livida'' [''Then all found peace in a heap of livid dust'']), but without its poignancy: one notices the present tense of the verb in the former quotation, as contrasted to the past absolute of the latter. The ''insolente distacco'' [''insolent detachment''] with which Senator La Ciura treats Corbera is also noticeable; while reading the newspaper, he comments upon the most stupid news with repeated disdainful spitting, which he himself calls ''simbolico e altamente culturale'' [''symbolic and of high cultural content''] and which is different from that of Russo ''non proprio addosso ma assai vicino alla salma'' [''not right on, but very near the body''] of the soldier in the garden. (p. 47)

The story is imbued with the serenity of ancient Greece, shining with beautiful images of both sensuality and marine landscapes—no darkness or disgust at all, here. In fact the sea, which had accompanied the passing away of the Prince, here is said to give ''morte insieme all'immortalità'' [''death together with immortality''] and is the visual catalyser of most of the descriptions. (p. 48)

The light and the eros pervading the [descriptions of the sea] are interwoven and concentrated in the image of the siren Lighea, who is at the same time sensual and spiritual, a bestial creature and an immortal being. . . . (p. 49)

The description [of Lighea], centered on the senses of sight, smell and hearing, is a beautiful combination of precise realistic elements (from ''il volto liscio di una sedicenne emergeva dal mare'' [''a smooth sixteen-year-old face emerging from the sea''] down to ''infantilmente gridava nettandosi i denti con la lingua'' [''she let out childish cries as she cleaned her teeth with her tongue'']) and of suggestive fantastic ones: besides the insistence on such words as ''magico'' [''magic''] and ''sortilegio'' [''sorcery''] one notices the vagueness of the dividing line between the animal and the human, the human and the spiritual, the sea and Lighea: she seems, at times, to be one with the sea, as in the description of her voice. But above all, the emblematic values of the description deserve consideration; Lighea embodies ''una quasi bestiale gioia di vivere, una quasi divina letizia'' [''an almost animal joy, an almost divine delight in existence'']—more than just sensuality or beauty. The pleasure she promises is higher than the flesh; it is an untouched, primeval purity. Sensuality is just a vehicle for her appeal, it is only the most evident way in which it is manifested: it is not by chance that the sea underscores it by partaking of it: ''si abbandonava al sole e fremeva di piacere'' [''abandoned to the sun and quivering with pleasure'']. Finally, Lighea's seemingly cruel act of eating a live fish has a symbolic meaning: ''il sangue le rigava is mento'' [''the blood flowed in lines down her chin''], but afterwards the prey ''veniva ributtata dietro le sue spalle, e, maculandola di rosso, affondava nell'acqua'' [''would be flung over her shoulder and sink, tainting red the water''] of the sea, which gives death and immortality. Lighea says of herself (in ancient Greek, since she is ''figlia di Calliope'' [''daughter of Calliope''], as her name would suggest): . . . .

> [I am everything because I am simply the current of life, with its detail eliminated; I am immortal because in me every death meets, from that of the fish just now to that of Zeus, and conjoined in me they turn again into a life that is no longer individual and determined but of Pan and so free. . . . I have loved you; and remember that when you are tired, when you can drag on no longer, you have only to lean over the sea and call me; I will always be there, because I am everywhere, and your thirst for sleep will be assuaged.]

In saying so, Lighea not only explains the reason why Senator La Ciura has jumped off the *Rex* (unlike the "merluzzo di dianzi" ["fish just now"], he does not need to pay the toll of blood in order to be mingled in the universe); she also clarifies, by making it explicit ("vita" ["life"]), the longing for immortality of the Prince (the mention of Zeus, while appropriate literally, seems a deliberate suggestion).

Indeed, the siren Lighea realizes the synthesis between Thanatos and Eros in its purest, most serene and Olympian form. Her story is a magic *divertissement,* a delightful tale whose symbolic meaning poetically reaffirms the ontological solution and the ethos of the Prince—Giuseppe Tomasi di Lampedusa. (pp. 49-50)

Gian-Paolo Biasin, "The Prince and the Siren," in MLN *(© copyright 1963 by The Johns Hopkins University Press), Vol. 78, No. 1, January, 1963, pp. 31-50.*

JEFFREY MEYERS (essay date 1965)

[In the following excerpt Meyers provides an insightful study of Lampedusa's use of recurrent and static symbols in The Leopard.*]*

The Leopard is a richly symbolic novel from the first scene during the Rosary to the final moment when the carcass of Bendicò is flung out the window. The symbols form two categories: there are those which emerge and disappear only to be found later in a somewhat varied form, like a pattern of dolphins leaping through the sea. These may be called *recurrent* symbols, which only grow to their fullest meaning toward the end of the book, and through their very expansion advance the theme of the novel. Through repetition and variation they function also as leitmotifs and thereby effect a structural unity. The eviscerated soldier, the stars, Sicily itself, and Bendicò are recurrent symbols, woven like threads into the fabric and texture of Lampedusa's art.

The second mode of symbols are used more conventionally; they occur and evoke a higher meaning only once. But these *static* symbols often appear in an expanded moment which allows their meanings to reverberate through the novel and foreshadow the future. Prophecy is used structurally to link the present with the future and to give an air of predestined inevitability to important actions. The most successful symbols in this group are the series of *objets d'art* which illustrate and prophesy the love of Tancredi and Angelica. (pp. 50-1)

The most famous art object in the novel is the glorious and sensual fountain of Amphitrite at Donnafugata that emanated the Keatsian "promise of pleasure that would never turn to pain" ("Forever wilt thou love and she be fair"). "Perched on an islet in the middle of the round basin, modelled by a crude but sensual hand, a vigorous smiling Neptune was embracing a willing Amphitrite."

According to the myth, Poseidon desired the sea goddess Amphitrite and sent a dolphin to look for her. When the dolphin brought her to Poseidon he married her, and as a reward, placed the dolphin among the constellations. This symbolic fountain, where Sedàra later spies Tancredi kissing Angelica, not only reflects the sensual nature of their love in the goddess whose wet navel gleams in the sun, but more importantly reveals the role of the Prince in the marriage. He is the dolphin, associated with the constellations, who is degraded to the role of Pandaro. Acting on the instructions in Tancredi's letter, he "swallows the toad" and completes the loathesome negotiations with Sedàra, in whose symbolical white tie and tails Fabrizio "saw Revolution." When the Prince is on his deathbed and the illusions about Tancredi's marriage have long since been shattered, he thinks once more of the delicious fountain and fears the grotesque metamorphosis it might suffer if sold to satisfy the debased pleasure of the bourgeoisie.

A series of art objects continue to reflect the love of Tancredi and Angelica and "the instincts lying dormant in the house" as these uncertain sensualists pursue each other through Donnafugata, that "mysterious and intricate labyrinth" which suggests Daedalus, King Minos, and the legend of how Ariadne saved Theseus from the Cretan minotaur (Sedàra). Donnafugata itself symbolizes the legacy of the decayed aristocracy to the young lovers who wander through its vastness "like the explorers of the New World," seeking to salvage something for the future. Behind the elegance and grandeur of its facade, a false front with no substance supporting it, were the ruined, empty, crumbling, and forgotten rooms. Donnafugata is foreshadowed in the first section by the huge desk in the Prince's office "with dozens of drawers, recesses, hollows, and folding shelves . . . decorated like a stage set, full of unexpected, uneven surfaces, and secret drawers."

In one of the secret rooms of Donnafugata Angelica "had hidden behind an enormous picture propped on the floor, and for a short time *Arturo Corbera at the Siege of Antioch* formed a protection for the girl's hopeful anxiety."

Tancredi is named after the Crusader and Prince of Antioch who played an important role in the capture of the city, which was overrun by the Turks in 1094. After an ineffectual siege of seven months, a force of 300,000 Crusaders stormed the city with the help of a traitor in 1098. Once in possession they were soon overtaken by disease and famine. This painting symbolizes the courtship of Tancredi who lays siege to the alien fortress of Angelica, and only wins her after the timely intervention of the Leopard, who betrays his daughter and his class.

Tancredi, Prince of Antioch, is also one of the principal heroes of Tasso's *Gerusalemme Liberata,* whose subject is the First Crusade; just as Angelica is one of the main heroines of Ariosto's *Orlando Furioso.* Tasso's Tancredi has many qualities of Castiglione's *Il Cortegiano,* with his noble heart and graceful manners, his courtesy and generosity. . . . But he is best known in the poem for his agonizing passions and romantic adventures. Ariosto's Angelica, a beautiful but selfish pagan, is a strong contrast to the passionate paladin Tancredi. All men fall in love with her, but she loves no one, not even the great hero Orlando. Finally she marries a simple soldier, Medoro, whom she finds wounded on the battlefield and nurses to health.

Tasso presents a triangle of lovers: Erminia loves Tancredi who loves Clorinda. The tender and helpless Erminia falls in love with Tancredi when he besieges Antioch, takes her prisoner, and treats her chivalrously. Completely overcome by her passion, she is unable to hide it. All this, of course, is reflected in ***The Leopard,*** for Concetta loves Tancredi who loves Angelica. And Concetta, unable to contain her feelings, confides them to Father Pirrone, who then tells the Prince.

The two lovers are surrounded at Donnafugata by other works of art that seem to encourage their "game full of charm and risk," their licentious desires in the decrepit rooms. Like Angelica "a shepherdess [is seen] glancing down consenting from some obliterated fresco"; and they find on the fireplaces "delicate intricate little marble intaglios, with naked figures in paroxysms." (This too evokes the "mad pursuit," the "struggle to escape," and the "wild ecstasy" of Keats' Grecian Urn). Even the accidental music of the *Carnival of Venice* to which "they kissed in rhythm" evokes at once the festivity and sensual outbursts of the present, and the hint of Lenten austerities (their marriage which "even erotically was no success") that must inevitably follow. Exotic Venice of fabled splendor, the most profligate of cities, the very seat of all dissoluteness, is the perfect setting for passionate abandon.

This mixture of passion and denial within a religious context leads the lovers to the climax of these scenes, the most intense and lyrical in the novel. In a secret apartment they find whips of bull's muscle, which of course are male symbols, but are afraid of themselves, leave the room immediately, and kiss as if in expiation. The following day they enter the apartment of the Saint-Duke who with the Blessed Corberà, foundress of the Convent that Fabrizio and Tancredi visit, represents the severe religious traditions of the Salina family. This time they find another whip, used by the Saint-Duke to scourge himself and redeem the earth with his blood, for "in his holy exaltation it must have seemed that only through this expiatory baptism could the earth really become his."

But his descendant Tancredi is a different sort of man, and finds his redemption through Angelica's beauty and her father's money. The religious traditions are embodied in Concetta whose indifference to Caviaghi, her ice-cold hands, and her denial of the flesh contrast strongly with Angelica's passion; and symbolize that Lombardy and Sicily can never be truly united. Ironically, Concetta becomes like the nuns in Tancredi's fictive convent—virginal, isolated, and afraid.

After Angelica prostrates herself and kisses the feet of the enormous and ghastly crucified Christ in the room of the Saint-Duke, Tancredi bites her lip in a rough kiss and draws blood. Angelica assumes the traditional posture of Mary Magdalene, and her fascinating mixture of sinfulness, holiness, and beauty, as if to pay for her sins before she commits them. He scourges himself by a degrading marriage to the woman he calls his whip, and offers her blood, not his own, for atonement. The family has changed considerably in the last two hundred years.

A few days later the lovers enter the most dangerous room with its "neat rolled-up mattress which would spread out again at a mere touch of the hand," like a Sicilian stiletto. That morning Angelica had said, "I'm your novice," offering herself for sexual rather than religious initiation. In the afternoon "already the woman had surrendered, already the male was about to overrun the man, when the Church bell clanged almost straight down on their prone bodies, adding its own throb to the others," and preventing the long-desired consummation. The religious traditions have sounded their final echoes. Tancredi is neither the scourging Saint, nor the predatory Prince who at least takes women when he wants them.

Symbolic paintings also illuminate the character of Fabrizio and prophesy his future, as do references to literature. When Garibaldi's General visits the Prince after the successful landing at Marsala, he substitutes a neutral *Pool of Bethesda* for the portrait of Ferdinand II which hangs in the drawing room.

John v. 2-9 says "there is in Jerusalem a pool called Bethesda around which lay a multitude of invalids blind, lame, and paralyzed." Jesus found a sick man there and said "Rise, take up your pallet and walk;" and the man was healed. The invaders picture themselves as Jesus, coming like Chevalley to cure and heal the Sicilians; and Sedarà is their grotesque John the Baptist, for "whenever he passed secret groups were formed, to prepare the way for those that were to come." The Prince, "with his sensibility to presages and symbols," knows too well that the aristocracy is "blind, lame, and paralyzed." (pp. 52-7)

Literature is the last art that is used symbolically, and three important references appear in ***The Leopard.*** (p. 58)

[Of these, the most] significant instance of the symbolic use of literature in the novel, occurs when Don Fabrizio quotes [from Baudelaire's "Un Voyage a Cythère"] as he leaves his mistress Marianina. . . . "Un Voyage a Cythère" describes the poet's futile quest for an Eldorado on the island where Aphrodite was supposed to have emerged from the sea, and where a famous temple was erected in her honor. His illusions are quickly destroyed when he finds a hanged man whose sexual organs have been torn out by birds of prey as punishment for his sexual excesses. The poet then identifies himself with the man on the gibbet, and realizes that the allegory is directed towards himself. He prays, in the last lines, for the strength and courage to accept his debased self.

The poem symbolizes the conflict in the Leopard between his intellectual and sensual, his heavenly and earthly, his spiritual and fleshly quests. His inability to dispel illusion and face reality, and to reconcile the strivings of his soul and body, are the core of the Prince's weakness. Thus, the lamentations and self-denunciations.

Here again Lampedusa uses symbols to explain the present as well as to reveal the future, thus forming a structural and a thematic effect. In Donnafugata, when Tancredi and Angelica are described as "two lovers embarked for Cythera on a ship made of dark and sunny rooms," the Baudelaire poem is immediately invoked, and we understand at the height of their lyrical love that their hopes for happiness will be disappointed. The sunny rooms are the present, the dark ones the future.

Another static symbol associated with the fountain of Amphitrite and the two lovers is that of the foreign peaches . . . which Fabrizio observes with Tancredi. "The graft with German cuttings, made two years ago, had succeeded perfectly; [the fruit] was big, velvety, luscious-looking; yellowish, with a faint flush of rosy pink on the cheeks." The Prince remarks, "They seem quite ripe . . . [and are] products of love, of coupling."

Unlike the Paul Neyron roses which had been "enfeebled by the strong if languid pull of the Sicilian earth," the grafted peaches thrive and prosper. The difference is that the French roses were planted directly in the Sicilian earth that has always been (passively) hostile to alien elements; while the German peach cuttings were grafted to Sicilian stems. Like his uncle, Tancredi also has German strains in his blood, and the material fruits of his marriage to Angelica are symbolized in the grafted peaches, just as their sensual desire is reflected in the "shameless naked flesh" of the fountain.

When Tancredi steals the peaches, with their "aphrodisiac and seductive properties," from his uncle and carries them to Angelica, whom they seem to resemble, he performs a symbolical marriage ceremony. "He sidestepped a sword-waving urchin [The Revolution], carefully avoided a urinating mule [Don Calogero], and reached the Sedàra's door." The Revolution and Angelica's father are the two dangerous elements which Tancredi must accept and adjust to if the "graft" to Angelica is to take place. Tancredi recognizes this when he says paradoxically, "if we want things to stay as they are, things will have to change." But Tancredi's symbolic stroll also parallels the one Fabrizio took through the *bordello* district of Palermo to reach Marianina's house. It represents yet another stage in the decline of the aristocracy; an ordeal by urine to reach the lower classes.

Here again Falconieri is like Tasso's Tancredi who, in the wood enchanted by devils, boldly leaps through the flames and is unharmed. When storms and clouds follow, he ignores them, and they disappear. Nevertheless, Tancredi, like the Crusader, is doomed to a frustrated, anxious, and unhappy love, and for the same reason. The love of both heroes is unsanctified: the paladin loves a pagan, Falconeri loves a peasant. (pp. 59-62)

The last of the major static symbols (there are numerous minor ones), are also social and political and concern the Plebescite and the Prince's talk with Don Ciccio. When Mayor Sedàra appears on the balcony of the town hall to announce the results of the fraudulent Plebescite, he is flanked by two ushers and carries a "lighted candelabra which the wind blew out at once." On that night the light that the invaders intended to bring to Sicily was symbolically extinguished by the dirty wind, and a new-born babe, good faith, was killed at Donnafugata. (pp. 62-3)

Many of the numerous death images in the novel, and not only the violent ones, converge with a powerful effect in the symphonic scene when Fabrizio himself gives himself to the Woman in Brown, "the creature forever yearned for". A poor doctor is called to the Prince from the slum quarter near by, where he had been an "important witness of a thousand wretched death agonies" such as the one Fabrizio saw on the way to the ball. The little bell with the Last Sacraments rings for him as it did for that other dying man. The Leopard scrutinizes himself in the mirror and regrets that he cannot "die with his own face on," and remembers the blood-daubed soldier for the last time. He re-enacts in a less sanitary and aesthetic way the *Death of a Just Man,* and hears his own death rattle like that of parched Sicily vainly awaiting rain.

The symbolic meaning of the stars in ***The Leopard*** explains Fabrizio's death-wish; illustrates the major theme of change—real and illusory; and at the same time emphasizes the cyclical structure of the novel, for as the Prince is needlessly told at the ball, "fixed stars are only so in appearance." Their eternal movement, but almost always within the limits of predictable laws, symbolizes the idea of permanence in transience, changing as they always do, and yet not changing.

The godlike Leopard feels a strong affinity for these wise bodies that are frequently named after gods; for he tells Chevalley Sicilians are gods and are perfect, and he also attributes these qualities to his skyey companions. He mistakenly believes he has "lordship over both human beings and their works," and is revived by gazing at the swimming stars which he feels are always "docile to his calculations."

The Prince constantly seeks escape from reality: in sensuality with Marianina, in hunting with Don Ciccio, and in the stars with Father Pirrone. He calls astronomy his morphia, his path to sleep and forgetfulness; he merges into its tranquil harmony and lives the "life of the spirit in its most sublimated moments." The stars symbolize to him "the intangible, the unattainable. . . . They are the only truly disinterested, the only really trustworthy creatures." And as he dies he considers the "abstract calculations and the pursuit of the unreachable" among the few happy hours of his life. At the final "crashing of the sea" it is his faithful Venus which leads him out of life.

Lampedusa uses the static symbol of the well at Donnafugata to elucidate one aspect of the more complex recurrent symbol of Sicily. On the outskirts of Donnafugata the Salina family pause at a deep well that "mutely offered its various services: as swimming pool, drinking trough, prison, or cemetery. It slaked thirst, spread typhus, guarded the kidnapped, and hid the corpses of both animals and men till they were reduced to the smoothness of anonymous skeletons." This well symbolizes the dual and ambiguous nature of Sicily. It sustains internal contradictions, and is unconcerned that decomposing corpses lie at the bottom of the life-giving water. Death and life, corpses and prisoners, typhus and water, are wantonly and inextricably mixed, like the descendants of Byzantine, Berber, and Spanish invaders; or like the symbolical culmination of violence and piety of the liturgical poison in the Communion wine.

The well is also democratic and therefore politically *au courant,* for it reduces all men to an equalitarian anonymity. Later in the book Chevalley pities the Prince and the common people: "all were equal, at bottom, all were comrades in misfortune segregated in the same well." The Plebiscite in which the Prince, no different from the others, has only one vote, also emphasizes this most recent political levelling. The Prince is well aware of his lineage and social position, but when he speaks to Chevalley as a Sicilian he places himself aloft with the others and states flatly, "*we* are old . . . *we* are gods."

Like the stars, Sicily too symbolizes the theme of permanence in transience, and emphasizes the cyclical structure of the novel which supports this theme. The cyclical pattern is also stressed by the daily Rosary which begins and concludes the first section; Father Pirrone's arrangement of his niece's marriage that repeats in a cruder way the Prince's negotiations with Sedàra; and the final scene in the chapel which echoes the opening Rosary. Even [the dog] Bendicò emphasizes the cyclical pattern, for he rushes into the Rosary room as the novel opens and is thrown out the window as it concludes. The Sicilian landscape "knows no mean between sensuous slackness and hellish drought" and oscillates eternally between these two disastrous conditions. These changes, though extreme, inevitably follow a seasonal pattern. Sicily, the scene of numerous invasions and conquests, is ultimately indifferent and unchanged. It is a constant and eternal stage upon which the changing scenes of history are performed; the stars look down with their perennial certitude and illuminate this stage. Sicily, like the stars, is irredeemable. (pp. 64-7)

The sun is the true ruler of Sicily, and it is no benevolent despot or tottering Bourbon. The extreme sunlight is blinding; it does not enable one to see clearly, but rather prevents clear vision. At the death of the Prince the sun pitilessly straddled and lashed the city and the man, hastening his death. The vehemence of the light produces a voluptuous torpor, a languorous immobility, a hankering for oblivion and for the release of death. Most significant of all, it produces and enforces a sense of futility and an obsessive fatalism which causes the Leopard to watch "the ruin of his own class and his own inheritance, without ever making, still less wanting to make, any move toward saving it."

Like the stars and like Sicily itself, Bendicò symbolizes for the Prince something unchanging, constant, and faithful in a world of flux and turmoil. Rubbing the dog's big head Fabrizio says, "you Bendicò, are a bit like them, like the stars, happily incomprehensible, incapable of producing anxiety." Bendicò, whose name is short for "good-of-heart," stands for unquestioned loyalty and humble compliance with the wishes of his master. Fabrizio thinks of Marianina, who can refuse him nothing, as "a kind of Bendicò in a silk petticoat." Bendicò means the same to the spinster Concetta, even when he is dead and embalmed, a heap of moth-eaten fur and nest of spiderwebs, like her unused trousseau. She refused "to detach herself from the only memory of her past which aroused no distressing sensations."

The literary model for the dead Bendicò is Loulou, the parrot of the old maidservant Félicité in Flaubert's "A Simple Heart." "Though he was not a corpse, the worms had begun to devour the dead bird; one of his wings was broken, and the stuffing was coming out of his body. But Félicité kissed Loulou's forehead, and pressed him against her cheek . . . when Félicité woke up, she could see him in the dawn's light, and [like Concetta] she would recall painlessly and peacefully the old days." Both Bendicò and Loulou are adored household pets whose mistresses continue to be strongly attached to them for many years after their death, even though they are hideously decomposed. And both works conclude with the metamorphosis of the animal into another image which reveals something important about the illusions of their owners.

Bendicò's realistic approach to things and instinctive good sense is symbolized when he warns the Leopard at three crucial stages of the family's decline. These warnings are merely noted by the perceptive Prince, but not heeded. In the second scene of the novel Fabrizio sits "merely watching the desolation wrought by Bendicò in the flower beds," and remarks, "How human!" Here the dog is symbolically warning the fatalistic Fabrizio of the destruction and disasters of war, and the rapacity of Sedàra's class who will rape the Prince's lands. Bendicò's second warning comes when the enthusiastic Salina family greets the newly engaged Angelica. "Only Bendicò, in contrast to his usual sociability, growled away in the back of his throat." Finally, when the Leopard is speaking to Chevally, Bendicò crawls into the room and falls asleep, failing to hear the wise Northern words just as his master does. (This device is later repeated when the herbalist falls asleep while Father Pirrone is explaining the political situation to him. But Pirrone, like Chevalley, keeps on talking.)

Father Pirrone, who is compared to a sheep dog, symbolically warns the Salinas in much the same way on two occasions. When Tancredi is courting Angelica and kissing her hand, the priest meditates over the Biblical stories of Delilah, Judith, and Esther, three women who betrayed famous and powerful men. When Fabrizio is contracting with Sedàra, Pirrone notices the falling barometer and predicts "bad weather ahead."

The warnings of Bendicò and Father Pirrone are ignored, and at the end of the novel the last of the Salina's illusions are destroyed, for only in the Church had they maintained their preeminence. The relics are cleared out of the family chapel by the priest-technician, who symbolizes the secularization of the Church just as the increasing gullibility of the spinster sisters represents the increasing piety of the aristocracy. Then Concetta's "inner emptiness was total . . . even poor Bendicò was hinting at bitter memories." As the faithful dog, the last relic, is flung through the window "his form recomposed itself for an instant; in the air could have seen dancing a quadruped with long whiskers, and its right foreleg seemed to be raised in imprecation. Then all found peace in a little heap of livid dust."

Bendicò forms the image of the Leopard over the solid but sagging door near the deep well of Donnafugata which "pranced in spite of legs broken off by flung stones," just as Loulou becomes an image of the Holy Ghost to the dying Félicité who "thought she saw in the opening heavens a gigantic parrot, hovering above her head." In the dust heap Bendicò symbolizes the end of all tradition, beliefs, position, and power of the once-great family. The Prince himself says that "the significance of a noble family lies entirely in its traditions, that is in its vital memories." The embodiment of these vital memories, Bendicò and at the same time Prince Fabrizio, is now cast out, and only the "inner emptiness" remains. (pp. 67-70)

Jeffrey Meyers, "Symbol and Structure in 'The Leopard'," in Italian Quarterly *(copyright © 1965 by* Italian Quarterly*), Vol. 9, Nos. 34 & 35, Summer-Fall, 1965, pp. 50-70.*

EDMUND WILSON (essay date 1966)

[*Wilson, considered America's foremost man of letters in the twentieth century, wrote widely on cultural, historical, and literary matters, authoring several seminal critical studies. He is often credited with bringing an international perspective to American letters through his widely read discussions of European literature. Perhaps Wilson's greatest contributions to American literature were his tireless promotion of writers of the 1920s, 1930s, and 1940s, and his essays introducing the best of modern literature to the general reader. In the following excerpt, Wilson records his impressions of* The Leopard *and* The Professor and the Mermaid, *works read during the critic's tour of Paris, Rome, and Budapest in 1963 and 1964.*]

In Paris, we had seen the film of Lampedusa's ***Il Gattopardo (The Leopard)***. I thought it one of the best that have ever been made. It was like a nineteenth-century novel—vast sequences of inter-family relations and a ball that must last half an hour—and so long that it was thought impossible for the English-speaking countries, where it was ruined, I am told, by cutting. But when I read the book in Rome, I found that its effect was different. ***Il Gattopardo*** is not like a nineteenth-century novel. It goes by much more quickly than the film and is told with an ironic tone that in the film is entirely lacking. Lampedusa's writing is full of witty phrase and color. It belongs to the end of the century of Huysmans and D'Annunzio, both of whom, although their subjects are so different from one another, it manages to suggest at moments. There are also little patches of Proust. The rich *pasta* served at the family dinner and the festive refreshments at the ball are described with a splendor of language which is rarely expended on food but which is in keeping with all the rest of Lampedusa's half-nostalgic, half-humorous picture of a declining but still feudal princely family in Sicily in the sixties of the last century. (p. 391)

Now, one of the great distinctions of ***Il Gattopardo*** is that it could not have been produced by a "pro." Lampedusa, who has written to please himself and has not given a thought to the public, does none of the things that a pro would do. In the year after the author's death, the manuscript was sent by a friend to Feltrinelli, the publisher of *Doctor Zhivago,* who had the good taste to appreciate it. In 1959, it won the Strega Award, the most important Italian prize for literature. (p. 393)

Feltrinelli a few years later published a volume of Lampedusa's miscellanies—***Racconti*** [***Two Stories and a Memory***]—collected from among his papers. All the pieces in this book are interesting. The first is a fragment of a sequel to follow ***Il Gattopardo.*** The drama of ***Il Gattopardo*** hinges mainly on the decision of the Prince's nephew—who has become a supporter of Garibaldi—to marry the daughter of the Mayor, a handsome girl who comes of peasant stock but has been sent to school in Florence. Her manners, even so, from the point of view of the family, are likely to give them the shudders, but the boy is infatuated by her beauty, and she will bring him a considerable dowry. The Prince dislikes this alliance but he sees it through with princely dignity. (His dancing with the girl at the ball is one of the great scenes of the picture.) He cannot help being aware that his class is being supplanted. And in the sequel, this *dégringolade* is seen to have gone a good deal further. The rising power in Palermo is now a very low-class *mezzadro*—that is, a kind of sharecropper—who is gradually getting into his hands a good deal of the nobles' property. Beside him, the Mayor's family look almost distinguished. . . . This is all very like the ascendancy of Faulkner's unspeakable Snopeses.

There are also memories of childhood, which deal with the town house and the country mansion already described in the novel, but here in a quite different way, as seen through the eyes of a child. . . . [These] memories are done with the brilliance and love of an unfailingly first-rate writer and make one regret and wonder that Lampedusa had not recognized his métier.

One regrets and wonders even more when one encounters the long short story ***Lighea,*** which was the last thing Lampedusa wrote. This story seems to me a masterpiece. It is so beautifully built up and written that it is impossible to give any real idea of it by attempting to summarize it. (pp. 394-96)

Edmund Wilson, "Notes from a European Diary, 1963-1964: Rome" (originally published in The New Yorker, *Vol. XLII, No. 14, May 28, 1966), in his* Europe without Baedeker *(reprinted by permission of Farrar, Straus and Giroux, Inc.; copyright © 1947, 1966 by Edmund Wilson), second edition, Farrar, Straus and Giroux, 1966, pp. 389-417.**

ANDOR GOMME (essay date 1967)

[In the following excerpt, Gomme examines Lampedusa's use of irony in The Leopard, *noting the author's frequently unsuccessful employment of the device.]*

The Leopard was written in less than a year. But Lampedusa had pondered the idea of the novel for twenty-five years before writing it; and he wrote almost nothing else: the literary preoccupation of a quarter of a century has gone into one quite short book. We are not surprised, therefore, to find it written with immense artfulness. Its surface shows it to be one of the most deliberately and methodically calculated novels ever written. Whether or not one enjoys this preciseness of calculation depends to a large extent on one's reaction to the ends to which it is put; for of course it does not exist in isolation. I believe that it is in fact inseparable from the whole attitude of mind with which the author views his subject, and that an examination of his technique is the clearest and most direct way to discover where one stands in relation to the novel and its intentions.

This technique has extreme visibility: the calculation is there for the most casual reader to see. The following two illustrations show the method at its most characteristic. Ferdinand, the last but one Bourbon king of Naples has just died, and the Bourbon kingdom is about to be overthrown by the Garibaldini, who have landed in Sicily and have just been joined by Tancredi, the Prince's favourite nephew, with whom his daughter Concetta is in love. The Prince himself, though a representative of the old order, looks ambiguously on both the personal and political aspects of the situation, but he loves Tancredi:

> One of his glasses was still half-full of marsala. He raised it, glanced round the family, gazed for a second into Concetta's blue eyes, then said: "To the health of our Tancredi". He drank his wine at a gulp. The initials F. D. [Ferdinandus dedit] which before had stood out clearly on the golden colour of the full glass, were no longer visible. . . .

It is as if we had the author himself at our elbow. "Look", he says, "I have made a symbol of the passing of the monarchy, which I thus carefully link with the personal issues at the heart of the book. Note the device well. None of my observations is random".

Less explicit in its purpose, but having a characteristic elementary pedantry is the occasion when the Prince's carriage, on the way to a grand ball, is stopped by the little procession of a priest and his acolytes carrying the Last Sacrament. The message is clear: "do not forget that death is always present, even among your revels". But there is more to it than this, for a dozen pages later the memory of this little event provides the Prince with the occasion for meditation on the universal fate sooner or later to descend on all those at the ball, now so forgetful of all but their immediate enjoyment. Every smallest item of meaning must be used to the utmost.

The technique, such as it is, becomes in such cases visible to the point of slickness; one's complaint is not that the effect is too precisely calculated but that it is too easily achieved, for we have the sense that events are being manipulated for a special purpose which, as presented, they do not justify, and which is in itself perhaps undignified or even trivial. It would be unfair to suggest that such technical tricks form the staple writing of the novel. But there are enough of them to make one ask what we think of a novelist who thus so openly calls attention to the cleverness of his own calculation. (pp. 23-4)

The obvious name for the attitude that pervades ***The Leopard*** is irony. But "irony" is a word which has been used to describe so many different things that it seems necessary to define more closely what is required of it in any given instance. Here a contrast may be handy—a representative piece of George Eliot's irony, from the account of Sir James Chettan in Chapter 2 of *Middlemarch:*

> As to the excessive religiousness alleged against Miss Brooke, he had a very indefinite notion of what it consisted in, and thought that it would die out with marriage. In short, he felt himself to be in love in the right place, and was ready to endure a great deal of predominance, which, after all, a man could always put down when he liked. Sir James had no idea that he should ever like to put down the predominance of this handsome girl, in whose cleverness he delighted. Why not? A man's mind—what there is of it—has always the advantages of being masculine—as the smallest birch-tree is of a higher kind than the most soaring palm—and even his ignorance is of a sounder quality. Sir James might not have originated this estimate; but a kind Providence furnishes the limpest personality with a little gum or starch in the form of tradition.

This a relatively simple example. Its great virtue is the precision with which it defines a certain kind of masculine stupidity and at the same time makes perfectly clear the author's view of it. We know exactly where we stand; and for this the relatively "straight" description of Miss Brooke which makes such patent nonsense of Sir James's idea of her is essential. For George Eliot's mode is not habitually ironic: she reserves her irony for the treatment of special features for which it is appropriate. Here it is attractive in showing up Chettam for a fool just because she is quite unironic in defining the conditions against which his assumptions and ignorance can be judged. Furthermore there is complete detachment in her view of Chettam—her irony is reserved, indeed, for just those aspects of life where she *can* be fully detached from any complicating involvement: it is never intermixed with a nostalgia, which is then "corrected" by ironic comment. Of course it is unthinkable that a George Eliot should feel nostalgically toward a Sir James Chettam. But that is the point—she knows just when irony *is* the appropriate mode to adopt, the most conclusive and delicate way of placing a character or viewpoint.

Lampedusa by contrast *is* habitually ironic. But since it is humanly impossible to be totally detached from everything that surrounds one, the irony is rarely frank and clear in intention as it is with George Eliot. The description of the passing of the Last Sacrament . . . is a case in point:

> there was a faint tinkle and round the corner appeared a priest bearing a ciborium with the Blessed Sacrament; behind, a young acolyte held over him a white canopy embroidered in gold; in front another bore a big lighted candle in his left hand and in his right a little silver bell which he was shaking with obvious enjoyment. These were the Last Sacraments; in one of those barred houses someone was in a death agony. Don Fabrizio got out and knelt on the pavement, the ladies made the sign of the Cross, the tinkling faded into the alleys tumbling down towards San Giacomo, and the barouche, its occupants burdened with a salutary warning, set off again towards its destination, now close by. . . .

The little episode has a certain piquant charm. We can well believe that the choirboy would enjoy shaking his bell and his sense of the importance of his function. It is entirely characteristic of Lampedusa that he should make a point of this seeming contradiction of the solemnity of the occasion. And Don Fabrizio—the Prince himself—is often ironic to the point of scepticism about the practices of his religion. Yet there can be no doubt that at the same time his gesture of kneeling before the Sacrament is to be seen as a sincere expression of humility on the part of both Don Fabrizio and his author. It has nevertheless been clouded by the slight mockery in the observation of the acolyte, so that we cannot take altogether seriously the Prince's solemn thoughts about the universality of death. Furthermore the whole device of placing the episode in the way of the approach to an unparalleled display of the riches of this world suggests an impurity of intention masquerading as worldly wisdom or breadth of mind: the irony is preconceived and determines the perception too completely.

In ***The Leopard*** therefore, an ironical mode does not normally mean a complete detachment from the object of the irony. Neither certain people nor particular themes are treated consistently in this respect. But the case of the Prince is a special one; for there is an identification between this character and his author so close that at times it is hardly possible to tell them apart. Consequently the Prince's own mode of reflexion is also characteristically ironic. Even the agonies of life must be regarded in such a way as to leave room for a mocking smile, for a quick withdrawal from any commitment to a too definite expression of feeling. Hence the basis of judgment through the novel, though centred on the Prince, shifts continually; and neither the author nor his protagonist emerges as a figure of moral authority. There is throughout a refusal to make judgments except on grounds of expediency (the one unforgivable offence is stupidity); and those who protest against this habit are regarded as at best mistaken and at worst feeble-minded.

The admiration for irony as a habitual viewpoint and approach to life is most explicit in the Prince's relations with Tancredi, whose "sympathy was all the more precious for being ironic": it is this which makes the link between uncle and nephew so close. When Tancredi is in Naples he writes to request his uncle in Sicily to plead his cause with the beautiful daughter of the nouveau-riche mayor of the town where the Prince's country palace stands:

> Tancredi let himself go on to long considerations of the expediency, nay the necessity of unions between families such as the Falconeri and the Sedàra (once he even dared write "the House of Sedàra") being encouraged in order to bring new blood into old families, and also to level out classes, one of the aims of the current political movement in Italy. This was the only part of the letter that Don Fabrizio read with any pleasure; and not just because it confirmed his own previsions and crowned him with the laurel of a prophet, but also (it would be harsh to say "above all") because the style, full of subdued irony, magically evoked his nephew's face; the jesting nasal tone, the sly sparkling mockery of his blue eyes, the maliciously polite smile. When he realized that this little Jacobin sally was written out on exactly one sheet of paper so that if he wanted he could let others read the letter while subtracting this revolutionary chapter, his admiration for Tancredi's tact knew no bounds. . . .

This is moderately amusing; its most notable feature is surely the root of the Prince's admiration for his nephew: the style of the letter is an epitome of that of the Prince's own meditations and indeed of the whole book—a style which is, like Tancredi's, compounded of mockery and slyness never far from malice. Tancredi's "tact" amounts to no more than an agreement between the two men that they both know that his motives are anything but pure, that the words intended for public reception are at least partly bogus, that his inability even for a moment to "drive from his mind and heart the image of the Signorina Angelica" is at least partly the result of a shrewd calculation of the advantages of an alliance with her father's money, and further that even the Jacobin opinions are themselves merely expedients—a mockery of the principles on which the Risorgimento was supposed to have been built. All is mockery; and the one thing, which, in the nature of the novel's outlook, cannot be the subject of it is the irony itself. The outlook, that is, has its self-defence built in: he who dares to call it ignoble runs the risk of being mocked in his turn.

The habit of irony has led Lampedusa to be extremely unself-critical in indulging his facility for superficial effects which may amuse momentarily but become most tiresome when they set a general rule. Slick generalizations and comparisons abound. The tone sometimes lapses into facetiousness; which may turn sour and cynical, without seriously offering any new understanding: reading ***The Leopard*** is often like watching a clever but malevolent child; for the habit of mind which so readily assumes a trivially mocking appearance is an immature one. It implies a contempt for life more radical, though not more intelligent, than that of Flaubert, with whom Lampedusa has much in common. Lawrence said of Flaubert that he stood away from life as from a leprosy. This could not possibly be said of Lampedusa: he knows that life holds no danger of infection for him, for basically life is not interesting enough to be taken seriously; and Lampedusa is in fact not seriously interested in it.

If this were all, ***The Leopard*** could be laid aside as having little more than anthropological interest for the serious reader. But Lampedusa's ironic habit cannot be altogether fairly summed up as one of shallow mockery. It has, beneath the cynical surface, a serious and a distinctive outlook; and even if the purpose turns out to be one we dislike, I believe that it is a refinement of attitudes so prevalent in our time that it would be foolish simply to ignore it. If Lampedusa's irony too often reminds one of Laforgue, his conscious aims at least are fundamentally anti-romantic; and the nostalgia that is nevertheless so evident in much of his book comes less from an attempted compromise with what he satirizes, than because Lampedusa is, like so many cynics, easily given to sentimentality.

The choice of period for the main action of the novel is singularly well calculated to demonstrate how well placed—we are to feel—is Lampedusa's ironic detachment. It is the period of the height of "Byronic" romanticism in Italy, whose exponent in the novel is the fatuous Count Cavriaghi. There can be no escaping how Lampedusa regards him: he is a silly child, indeed something of a caricature. And Lampedusa stresses the one-sidedness of the romanticism which Cavriaghi represents. The love-affair between Tancredi and Angelica is sensual, even passionate; but it is described in curiously dispassionate terms. Angelica herself, cultivated beauty though she is, is linked to a sordid present and a brutal past; and Tancredi's wooing of her gets its share of ironic scrutiny. One of the most fantastic pieces of description in the book is of his walk to the Sedàra house on the day after he has first met Angelica.

> He had changed his clothes; he was no longer in brown as at the convent, but in Prussian blue, "my seduction colour" as he himself called it. In one hand he held a cane with an enamel handle (doutless the one bearing the Unicorn of the Falconeri and their motto *Semper purus*) and he was walking with cat-like tread, as if taking care not to get his shoes dusty. Ten paces behind him followed a lackey carrying a tasselled box containing a dozen yellow peaches with pink cheeks. He sidestepped a sword-waving urchin, avoided a urinating mule, and reached the Sedàra's door.

The total effect here is not likely to be to everyone's taste. But the verbal calculation is masterly. Every word tells, the contrast between the clothes appropriate for a visit to a convent (at which, significantly, he has been spurned in a fit of jealous meanness by Concetta) and those for a seduction (though it turns out—ironically, of course—so very differently); the invocation of the family motto; the theft of the peaches which the Prince and Tancredi had, before Angelica's appearance, looked forward to eating en famille; above all the intensely anti-romantic detail of the urinating mule expertly placed just at the moment of arrival at Angelica's door. Love has to live not only with the everyday, but with an everyday which is grubby and even sordid: the cultivated, the complete, man knows how to sidestep the one as delicately as he advances in the other. It is a matter of breeding to be decently aware of all circumstantial detail even at the moment of passion.

But the period of the novel is also that of the Risorgimento, which provides the ground for the principal actions. And the Risorgimento has meant for later writers a glamourizing of war, with its heroically tiny band of Garibaldini, led by a romantically unorthodox leader. Consequently, to counteract any tendencies to simple-mindedness in the reader, we are given a smell of the nastiness of war at the very start of the book, when the Prince, enjoying the rich but decadent scents of his garden, remembers a very different scent of a few weeks earlier:

> He remembered the nausea diffused throughout the entire villa by certain sweetish odours before their cause was traced: the corpse of a young soldier of the Fifth Regiment of Sharpshooters who had been wounded in the skirmish with the rebels at San Lorenzo and come up there to die, all alone, under a lemon tree. They had found him lying face downwards in the thick clover, his face covered in blood and vomit, crawling with ants, his nails dug into the soil; a pile of purplish intestines had formed a puddle under his bandoleer. . . .

It is curious how little of horror this manages to convey. The impression is less of shock at the lonely wretchedness of such a death than of the author's thrill at his demonstration that he is not afraid of such details, and will indeed insist on them. Death becomes the occasion for mockery, as the soldier's corpse is turned into a puppet and his once-living organs into stuffing. The effect is surely rather cheap, but the episode is intended as a serious reminder of what may be involved in the flickering bonfires lit by the rebels each night on the hills:

> They seemed like lights that burn in sick-rooms during the final nights. . . .

They surely seem so only to one bent on finding a neat moral in each detail.

In all this one may feel the irony chiefly as a determination to keep a balance of a sort, to avoid any degree of sentimental special pleading. It becomes more sinister in the treatment of the political outcome of the Risorgimento, the movement which meant change, a revolution leading to democracy and an end to the corruption of the Bourbon state—a movement of high hopes which are corrupted from the very start. "If we want things to stay as they are, things must change", Tancredi slyly observes. . . . But Lampedusa insists that things stay as they are in more ways than one: the real victor of the revolution that brings no change is Don Calogero Sedàra, the shrewd, self-seeking demagogue, who is too entirely innocent of principle to be capable of cynicism, which implies the rejection of principle. It is Don Calogero, mayor of the town, who manipulates the votes in the referendum, in order to make a show of unanimity but also a demonstration of power: "Voters, 515; Voting, 512; Yes, 512; No, zero". (pp. 24-30)

At this moment, in the passionate reaction of Don Ciccio, the Prince's hunting companion, comes the most moving passage in the book; and it is significant that, though the overall moral of the passage is ironic, Don Ciccio's speech and the Prince's reflexions on it are given quite straight and are the more powerful for the contrast.

> "I, Excellency, voted 'no'. 'No', a hundred times 'no'. I know what you told me: necessity, unity, expediency, you may be right; I know nothing of politics. Such things I leave to others. But Ciccio Tumeo is a man of honour, . . . and I don't forget favours done me! Those swine in the Town Hall just swallowed up my opinion, chewed it and then spat it out transformed as they wanted. I said black and they made me say white! The one time when I could say what I thought, that bloodsucker Sedàra went and annulled it, behaved as if I'd never existed, as if I were simply nothing" . . .
>
> At this point calm descended on Don Fabrizio, who had finally solved the enigma; now he knew who had been killed at Donnafugata, at a hundred other places, in the course of that night of foul wind: a new-born babe: good faith; just the very child who should have been cared for most, whose strengthening would have justified all the silly vandalisms. Don Ciccio's negative vote, fifty similar votes at Donnafugata, a hundred thousand "no's" in the whole kingdom, would have had no effect on the result, would have made it, in fact, if anything more significant; and this maiming of souls would have been avoided. . . .

There is something theatrical in the personification of "good faith". But here, as nowhere else in ***The Leopard,*** is the ring of something wholeheartedly believed in. Wholeheartedness is the quality most of all lacking in Lampedusa's world; and for this reason the reader is less moved than he should be by the picture of a world which "cannot" change in substance. There is corruption at the heart of the new regime, because the heart is always corrupted. This is only not a message of despair, because of the breeding which allows one to look on it with good-natured but supercilious cynicism.

If the irony which issues in the generalization that it is hopeless to do anything seems somewhat childish, it is sinister in its effect on the well-intentioned and (within limits) public-spirited. Later the Prince *is* given the chance of becoming a direct and wholesome influence in the new state, when he is invited to become a member of the Senate. He refuses, and the explanation of the refusal is basically that he is a Sicilian, and that Sicilians object to engaging in deliberate action at all. . . . (Nevertheless he seriously proposes Don Calogero instead of himself, as one who has more of the qualities needed in the Senate, though he knows full well what Sedàra's qualities are.)

At this stage Lampedusa seems to be making a special case of Sicily: as the Prince explains at length, Sicily is not like other places. It is poor, squalid and corrupt, but—uniquely—it does not want to improve. Sicily only wants to sleep, "a sleep like the end of all things". It is not for an outsider, a northerner, to comment on the accuracy of this picture of Sicily and the Sicilians. But it is worth remarking that the general impression is not close to that of Verga, to whom one naturally turns for comparison. Lawrence thought Verga occasionally had his thumb in the pan on the side of misery: his Sicily is certainly squalid. But it is not sleepy. *Mastro-Don Gesualdo* is full of busy, ant-like activity. There is nothing lofty, certainly no disdainful remoteness; the aristocrats grub around as much as anyone else. The dirt, the wet, the decay are in fact much more real in Verga than in ***The Leopard,*** where one usually has the sense of their being talked about rather than actually experienced. In Lampedusa one looks at the squalid scene from a decently remote upper-floor window; in Verga one wades.

Lampedusa's vision of Sicily is nonetheless the natural counterpart of his (or the Prince's) obsession with decay and death. Just as the sordid is the everlasting accompaniment of the romantic, so there is no growth without simultaneous decay; and the only way to keep things presentably alive is through the continual grafting of new blood. The Prince himself had a German mother, and only the influence of the analytic north gives him the power to recognize the "languid pull" of Sicily, though he is too much of a Sicilian to be able to escape it. The peaches are grafted from German cuttings, and for the time being they have taken perfectly. But so did the roses which, earlier, the Prince had brought from Paris: now they too have become languid, cabbagey: like the earth to which they have succumbed. They too are submitting to the Sicilian longing for death; and it is no accident that their scent merges in the Prince's thoughts with the smell of the soldier's corpse. In Palermo, there is "a sense of death which not even the frenzied Sicilian light could ever manage to disperse". (pp. 30-1)

The pull of death is not simply recorded by the Prince; he is himself a Sicilian and, as the longing for death is part of Lampedusa's Sicily, yields himself to it more and more as the book progresses and he grows older. Yet the thought of *others'* death "disturbs" him—not the physical details, but the fact of mortality itself. In his rather clumsily stage-managed meditation on death the Prince finds his disgust giving way to compassion for the "ephemeral beings out to enjoy the tiny ray of light granted them between two shades, before the cradle, after the last spasms". . . . There is a certain melodramatic coarseness about this; and we are not surprised to find it leading to a softening of the sharp edges which had previously distinguished the Prince's powers of judgment (notice the effect, in its context, of the word "ephemeral"), so that he can now sentimentally identify himself with others whom he had previously mocked and despised: "only by them could he be understood". The phrase implies a contrast, but there is nothing really there to provide it, and the extent of the "understanding" is minimal. As if further to insist on the sentimental nature of this relaxation, it is followed by a glimpse of the eyes of Don Calogero going "liquid and gentle" at the "beatific" prospect of a rise in the price of Sicilian cheese. The softening must be retracted at once, contradicted by the ironic observation of those with whom the Prince must make "common cause", with whom he is "at his ease"—a cynical dismissal of a feeling not worth having in the first place, which completely devalues the acceptance of common mortality which has just been handed out and which is reduced to the level of at best resignation, giving no impetus to creation in life; it is an "acceptance" of death which implies the evasion of responsibilities in life. Just as we have seen the Prince evading them before, we now meet the generalization intended to justify the evasion.

The Prince's attitude to the prospect of his own death is very different. This calms him as much as he is disturbed by the death of others. Yet the calm takes a remarkably morbid form at the same time as it constitutes another refusal to face up to what death actually is. He thinks of his body after death:

> A pity corpses could not be hung up by the neck in the crypt and then watched slowly mummifying; he would have looked magnificent, big and tall as he was, terrifying girls by the set smile on his sandpaper face, by his long, long white nankeen trousers. . . .

It is noteworthy that this apparent dwelling on the physical details actually pushes away the fact of death from the front of his (and perhaps the reader's) consciousness: there is something childish and factitious about it, as one can recognize by comparing it with Claudio's vision of death in *Measure for Measure:*

> Ay, but to die, and go we know not where,
> To lie in cold obstruction, and to rot,
> This sensible warm motion, to become
> A kneaded clod; and the delighted spirit
> To bathe in fiery floods, or to reside
> In thrilling regions of thick-ribbed ice . . .

This is looking terrified into the face of death; the Prince's bit of Grand Guignol simply makes a puppet show of it.

When death does finally come to him we see it again dressed up and muffled, though to the quick glance there is relish in the Prince's looking forward to it. Death is a feast, which he will not spoil by anticipation:

> He did feel sleepy; but he found that to give way to drowsiness now would be as absurd as eating a slice of cake immediately before a longed-for banquet. He smiled. "I've always been a wise gourmet". . . .

There is, it seems to me, something cheap in this image, which is one that only a man on the point of death might possibly have the right to make for himself. But for the Sicilian Prince, what is longed for is a new and special kind of sensual experience which has to be described in the metaphors which naturally suggest themselves from his sensual life. Finally, in the most sensual image of all, death is a young woman—the one "eternally yearned for", who now, "chaste but ready to be taken", appears miraculously within his grasp. The observed details have an almost aphrodisiac quality—"she insinuated a little suede-gloved hand between one elbow and another of the mourners" . . . ; but their effect is profoundly distracting. The suede glove does away with death and brings before us a real young woman; and if there is acceptance here, it is of something very different from what I suppose most people believe they will have to face. It is not even death seen in the sensual terms which hang over the whole book; it is simply a substitution of one thing, for another which is too terrible to describe or to face. I do not find this a brave death.

"Disillusion, boredom, all the rest". The phrase slips easily into the Prince's mind as he looks back over his life. It is the casual reference to "the rest" which is so disturbing. We have all known disappointment and boredom, for much of which we are ourselves responsible. But "the rest" . . . One hardly knows what to do with the word, so shamelessly general as it is. Its effect here is to throw more emphasis on to the two phrases which precede it, and on to the pathetic human situation in which the Prince, and all of us, poor victims of life's mockery, must endure the hollowness of it all—the theme on which both the Prince's life and the book end. He sums up his life thus:

> "I'm seventy-three years old, and all in all I may have lived, really lived, a total of two . . . three at the most". And the pains, the boredom, how long had they been? Useless to try and make himself count those; the whole of the rest; seventy years. . . .

This is in itself a bored and hopeless gesture; but its true atmosphere of despair is only felt when one takes into account the details of the years that have been "really lived". These too the Prince sums up, "the credit side" of his life—a series of fragments ranging from his delight in Tancredi, through friendships with dogs to "a few minutes of compunction at the convent amid odours of musk and sweetmeats". . . . Even at the moments of compunction, it is striking that the smell of musk and sweetmeats is what is most strongly remembered. Like Tancredi, the Prince has spent his time "manoeuvring among the difficulties of life"—which present him now only with a memory of "aesthetic pleasures". So the sensual catalogue goes on, passing "moments of satisfaction when he had made some biting reply to a fool" to "the exquisite sensation of a few fine silk cravats". . . . There are, it is true, some offerings of a superficially intellectual sort. Yet even these amount to no more than scraps of egotistic self-satisfaction, always given their colour by the aesthetic dilettantism which seems to provide the only standard recognized by the Prince or his author. What sort of life can be made out of bits and pieces like these? or out of an attitude which estimates life in terms of such? No wonder seventy seventy-thirds of it is boredom; for it is an existence without purpose, whose only coherence comes from the fundamentally cowardly irony with which every event and action is viewed.

The hopelessness and cynicism of this moral attitude (if it deserves the name) are still further emphasized in the epilogue, with its picture of three decaying and quarrelsome spinsters and their pathetic collection of bogus religious relics. Even the pathos of Concetta, Tancredi's youthful sweetheart, now living out her agony among relics of her own past which she dare not look at, must be given its ironic twist as she discovers in old age that it was her rash pride which had put Tancredi off for ever. Concetta is the only person in the book who ever discovers a personal responsibility for her own situation—a realisation, surely, that is normally deeply painful. Yet here all she loses is "the solace of being able to blame her own unhappiness on others". . . . If the implication that she is, hence, even worse off than before seems a poor kind of morality to live on, its egoism and immaturity are entirely consistent with the tone throughout the book. Even suffering is a mockery; all life is a mockery; and they only will live through with a sense of dignity and decorum who will treat it mockingly. Nowhere is there real compassion. The understanding of the human situation—"an understanding the more precious for being ironic"—is superficial in proportion as it is ironic. It is the expression of a blunted sensibility masking a refusal to face "the difficulties of life"; as for the opportunities, they are nowhere. Like much irony, this is in fact a form of self-conceit, which insists on seeing the world as part of one's own very limited self. It is for this reason that the Prince is so soothed by the thought of his own death, in that "his own death meant in the first place that of the whole world". (pp. 32-5)

Death is to be welcomed as a kind of triumph over the rest of the world. It is always present in life; for death, like life, is part of universal decay: the same sensual terms will do for both; and the book ends with an image that combines the two, as mockingly gruesome as any before. The sensuality of decay has literally the last word, as the long-embalmed but now moth-eaten carcase of a dog is finally thrown out:

> During the flight down from the window its form recomposed itself for an instant; in the air there seemed to be dancing a quadruped with long whiskers, its right foreleg raised in imprecation. Then all found peace in a heap of livid dust. . . .

It is the perfect ending to the book; and the attitude to life that calculates such an effect is intensely—deliberately—unwholesome. Yet even here a little more must be said. As a portrait, a revelation, it does, uncannily, carry conviction; and what saves ***The Leopard*** from being merely horrible or merely cynical, is the intensity of certain visions—the smell and the heat of Sicily, the unchanging stillness which broods over and eats into all, the sense of the compelling conditions under which certain lives must be led. As for my own life, I cannot believe it to be compelled towards the total attitude of the book by any set of conditions which I can conceive. But then I am no Sicilian. ***The Leopard*** makes me shudder, but not with a sense of coming face to face with dreadful reality. Reality is always somewhere else. The book's power to shock comes from the passionate intensity of its surrender to the illusion that its world in some way represents that in which the rest of us live. (p. 35)

Andor Gomme, "Irony and 'The Leopard'" (reprinted by permission of the author), in The Oxford Review, *No. 6, September 29, 1967, pp. 23-35.*

Don Giulio Maria Fabrizio Tomasi, Prince of Lampedusa, the man on whom Lampedusa modeled his character The Leopard. Courtesy of Gioacchino Lanza Tomasi.

RICHARD F. KUHNS (lecture date 1968)

[*An American educator and essayist, Kuhns is the author of one of the most important studies of* The Leopard. *In the following excerpt from that essay, Kuhns closely examines Lampedusa's novel as a work not on death, but on dying, and relates* The Leopard *to Stendhal's* The Charterhouse of Parma.]

Despite our literary preoccupation with violence and death, it is extraordinary in this day to find a novel about dying. Art, or what passes as art, can readily depict the contortions of death; it can only through much greater effort and with a more delicate hand present the living of life as a preparation for death—to present death not as a terminal event, the sudden, unexpected ending of a life, but the dominant theme lived throughout a life. . . . Death demands but a rhetoric; dying an aesthetic and a philosophy. (p. 95)

When we do encounter philosophical novels in our time, they are usually "novels of ideas" in a didactic sense; but the work I discuss here is, I believe, a philosophical novel concerned principally with the theme of death, yet it is *not* a novel of ideas in the didactic sense. Rather, it assumes as a foundation, without being explicit about this, the political vision of Plato and the psychological insight of Freud. The mind that produced ***The Leopard*** was aware of the dangers within historical narration due to the change modernity has wrought in the power of narrative art. Modernity suspects all portrayals of the past as mere expressive discharges of the present, rooted in private and cultural psychic needs. Questions of truth in art are considered irrelevant largely because we have come to accept, unquestioningly, an expressive theory of art in the place of the imitative or mimetic theory of art, within the logic of which truth could be defended as an artistic value.

But what are we to make, given our assumption of the expressive theory of art, of a novel in which the hero himself exhibits the complexities of a man accepting the changes of modernity, yet perpetuating in his private concerns the traditional attitudes of the past towards death? The writer in this case is clearly taking the problem of modernity and death as a subject for reflection, and even dares to suggest in this setting that truth may be an object of his story.

The protagonist of ***The Leopard,*** Don Fabrizio, Prince of Salina, is a Sicilian aristocrat, yet a man of revolutionary involvement for he is born into the *ancien regime* and compelled to live through the Risorgimento of the nineteenth century. He is witness to the several kinds of government men frame for themselves and the many character types for whom they function poorly and well. In himself he sees the sorrowfully impotent man of passion and the joyously effective man of intellect. Yet neither aspect of himself can stay in the assurance of its proper place any more than the governments of decadent Bourbons and progressive Garibaldini can convince us of the right and better order. For both in the self and in the polity, these sides exist; now one, now the other has ascendency, which is to say overcomes the other only to be overcome in its turn. So considered, this novel could be called a representation of the relativity of all patterns of self and state which we try, forever unsuccessfully, to structurally coerce with ideas and actions.

Although the story is told in the specific terms of Italy's consolidation under Garibaldini and King Victor Emmanuel, yet it is a universal—and therefore artful—presentation of interdependent realities: self and polity. In these terms, it is a novel which expresses an insight of the ancient world and the earliest literature we have from Greece. Because of the close dependence of self and polity in their ambivalences, the story must be told with an emphasis on shifting values. This is fictionally realized through the technique of shifting viewpoints, but without systematic perspective. Thus, it is not told with flashback, nor with chapters moving successively from one character to another—all this being far too artificial for the realities Lampedusa wishes to convey. Rather, it is told from an unusually omniscient present, *our* present of about 1959-1961, yet a present fully aware of the past both in its contemporaneous manifestation—how the past was in its presentness to those experiencing it—and in its pastness to ourselves who can only tell stories about it. The past is therefore permeated by a thoroughly twentieth century mind, and events are never without their relevant towardness to the present, while the present (*our* present, that is, as readers now) is always shown to be reminiscent of a pattern or duplication in the past.

In this way a tale of Sicily in the nineteenth century can mention the names of Freud, Eisenstein, the year 1960, the Second World War, and can indulge in novelistic editorials such as this: "it should not be forgotten that romanticism was then at high noon." . . . The impression achieved is of a reality in which there is no crucial past or present, but rather all events participate in a tenseless world made by art. And yet, we come into this possibility of timelessness through the temporal unfolding of a story.

Timelessness confronts the self, phenomenologically, in the expectation of death. The novel sounds this preoccupation, as if a perpetual tolling, in the opening words: "*Nunc et in hora mortis nostrae. Amen.*" As if closing this parenthesis, the death of Don Fabrizio concludes the main action of the novel; yet the book does not end there, but continues with a brief account of the survivors. This simple coda, once a trite novelistic device to tie up all the loose ends, becomes here a structural contribution to a central theme: Just as the shifting temporal perspective of the omniscient narrator establishes the timelessness of life lived through generations, so the survivors' thoughts and actions give us a shocking realization of what an individual death means. We are forced to look upon the Prince's death ultimately in the way we regard the death of any individual, including the death of the reader himself. For an individual death is always survived by the awareness of others even though its suffocation cuts off all events for the one who dies. From one point of view, therefore, death is a finality; from another, it is but a succeeded event. This is true in the world of literature as it is true in life. (pp. 97-9)

Lampedusa's treatment of time determines the kind of novel he writes; he has removed any possibility of tragedy in the traditional sense. That is to say, the tragedy of *reversal* and *recognition,* in which necessity is realized by means of a plot with a beginning, middle, and end, has been deemed inappropriate precisely because in this case the work is a *historical* novel in the best sense, i.e., in the sense explained above of a novel that takes the self and the polity as mutually interacting. For the tragedy of reversal and recognition, inevitability must be realized in the actions of the hero; in ***The Leopard*** it exists for the hero, to be sure, not in his actions, but rather in the principles of nature and of history. The Prince's expanding awareness of inevitable cosmic and historical processes constitutes a central theme of the novel. This, then, I suggest, is a tragedy, but not a tragedy of reversal and recognition; it is rather a tragedy of suffering. (pp. 99-100)

The tragedy of suffering, or, as I prefer to call it, the tragedy of endurance and decline, exhibits inevitability in a different way from the tragedy of complex action. The inevitability derives from forces clearly distinct from the protagonist's will and intention, and therefore a distinctive literary form is allowable—perhaps the literary form is *required* by plot structure. One of the liberties this kind of plot permits is to be found in the coda at the end of the novel in which we learn what happens after the Prince's death. This structural peculiarity is a function of the tragic subject. (p. 100)

The tragedy of endurance and decline has its rules and its limitations just as does the tragedy of reversal and recognition. One of its problems is to show that the suffering self is a function of a larger order, which I will call the political; thus the subject of the tragedy of suffering, most broadly stated, is the relation of soul states to history. Their interdependence is one of the themes of ***The Leopard.*** Beneath the accidents of time, there is a constancy of the self in its forms and developmental phases, just as there is a constancy in the forms and progressions of the state. Here the state is Sicily, whose spirit survives in all the political orders impressed upon her.

Lampedusa's technique for bringing together the self and the state is the great house of Donnafugata, which stands at once as ancestral and intimately personal history for the Prince. Through the house this novel establishes parities of self and reality which define what the characters are. Donnafugata, its hidden rooms revealing the inner lives of past generations, especially their religious and erotic sufferings, its muteness symbolizing the inevitability of death, first establishes parity between the Prince and the generations of his family; secondly, between the family and the history of the state of Sicily; finally, Donnafugata is the link between the human and the governing rhythm of the cosmic order.

From the observatory of his house, the Prince searches for the source of order and inevitability in the stars. The flux of daily experience hides the orders of life from us, but when we recognize heavenly constancies we begin to suspect, as the Prince does, that all of nature, including our own seemingly chaotic experience, is orderly and ultimately understandable as well. The heavens he studies with scientific detachment help him to see himself; yet his awareness of an analogy between the cosmic order and human life does not lead him to postulate a Dantean universe presided over by a personal eminence; rather, it leads him to reaffirm the order of life that Sicily and his family seem naturally to foster, an order of totemic scientific naturalism indigenous to the pagan past. (pp. 100-01)

Out of the pagan past the Prince of Salina plucks his armorial identity, a totem beast boastfully representing those qualities the Prince would find in himself, ruthlessness, power, and wiliness. None of the Prince's fellow "beasts" has his nobility, and none who come after him can command the esteem he enjoys. (p. 101)

[The] identification with animals is not simply a metaphorical issue in the book; it grows out of a natural condition of life in the tradition the Prince represents, for he lives close to the wild animals he both nurtures and hunts. . . . (p. 102)

The dying rabbit is at least offered a moment of compassion, but what of the men everywhere dying for the King, or for the new Italy? Don Fabrizio recalls that a dead soldier was found in the garden of his house in Palermo. The mutilated body fills him with disgust and anxiety: "But the image of that gutted corpse often recurred, as if asking to be given peace in the only possible way the Prince could give it: by justifying the last agony on grounds of general necessity." . . . The Prince can give no such justification in the terms that come lightly to the lips of his contemporaries: one dies for the King, an ideal, for duty. Dying is more mysterious than that, and it is his search after the mystery of death which leads Don Fabrizio on his daily hunt. For hunting and star-gazing are like activities inquiring into the ways of nature. Hunting, as Machiavelli points out, is the physical counterpart to the mind's search for understanding.

On his hunting expeditions the Prince is accompanied by his dog Bendicò, a central "character" of the story, for Bendicò opens the book and closes it. He brings life and vigor into the deadening routine of prayers; he is the last image of the Salina house. . . . Bendicò's end simply reaffirms a quality of animal life that allows the novel to treat its central theme of death the more fully, for in their dumbness animals are like death, and in their closeness to us they are a sometimes comforting, more often disquieting, reminder of our own mortality. (pp. 102-03)

Because Bendicò is an animal, lives in a bestial time parenthesis, the author can use him to make ironic comments on the relation of a living form to its fate. Bendicò, in grotesque literalness, survives death—indeed he remains with the House of Salina long after the Prince is gone, but the dog's presence is a stuffed one, and his end but trash.

Bendicò helps us to see another aspect of our lives more clearly: In Sicily particularly, because of its ambivalence of pagan and modern, the human finds it hard to realize and assert itself above the animal conditions of life. No matter how civilized a man may be—the Prince is, among his family and his countrymen, most civilized—what is human in him must suffer the coercion of the bestial.

One way to cope with this force in the self is to exercise one's animal compulsion in adversary relationships; but the Prince cannot find one among his peers able to meet his physical and intellectual powers. Therefore he is lonely, forced to pit himself against the only forces that at all come up to him: rude nature and death. The Leopard has not the objects of prey upon which to exercise his potency; on an island of fowls and jackals, he is alone. His physical and intellectual powers untested, the Prince lives as if the ordinary world is vulgar and witless. The best he can do is sharpen his manners on his family and his yokel tenants; his intellect seeks its match in the totally otherworldly pursuit of astronomy. The consequence for the Prince is sad, and herein lies one of the grounds for asserting that this is a tragedy of suffering. In both manners and intellect, the Prince is less impressive and developed than he might be were there a social and intellectual world worthy of his talents.

The Prince cannot help but misunderstand himself in this setting, and the story makes clear the extent to which the man Don Fabrizio is misled, almost distorted, one might say, by the impoverishment of his realm. When two British naval officers ask Don Fabrizio what the Garibaldini hope to accomplish, he answers (in English): "They are coming to teach us good manners, but they won't succeed, because we are gods."

The Prince's comment on himself is at once true and filled with misunderstanding, for he has indeed manners and a godlike mien, but they are absolutely of no account in affecting political events. His misapprehension follows from his belief that a man ought not care to affect events, that the best for an individual is understanding. And yet his purpose in understanding is, covertly, to be able to control events. The Prince is not aware, but we are aware, of the manifest and latent wishes he expresses.

Manifestly, the Prince has his escape and his superior in the heavens, for they in their simple intelligibility and might are worthy of a person's total yielding of himself. . . . The escape and pleasure afforded by astronomical calculation, the feeling of power derived from observing the stars "docile to his calculations, just the contrary to human beings," is an activity of sublimation very like death. (pp. 103-05)

Yet the stars are not wholly independent of human affairs; there must be a meaningful relationship between human caprice and cosmic order. The fact of a mirroring is suggested in the names of two women—the Prince's wife, Stella, and Tancredi's fiancée, Angelica. The astronomical order is somehow linked with the sensual world of love. Love and death are related, and to discover how they are related is the truth pursued by the Prince.

Crudely stated, the answer the Prince finds is that death unites the woman of earthly longing with the woman of heavenly aspiration, the two Aphrodites of whom Plato speaks in the *Symposium*. In terms of the life of the Prince, this means that in death he is able at last to unite sensuality and intellect, (the seemingly contradictory aspects of the self) with the apparent inconsistency of feminine qualities, for women are at once attractive and troublesome, promising peace but bringing more often restlessness and dissatisfaction. Only in death does a woman fulfill the promise of peaceful sensuality. In the treatment of this difficult theme Lampedusa combines two traditions, one Romantically poetic, the other introspectively psychological. Romantically, the theme finds its purest expression in Keat's "Bright Star," which brings love, death, and heavenly power into one grand gratification completing and closing a life. . . . I believe it is this poetic statement which best opens up to us the meaning of Don Fabrizio's final vision, the moving description of which closes Chapter 7.

Yet this is not the source of Lampedusa's theme, for the treatment he accords it is obviously dependent upon another, far less poetic inquiry, part of Freud's speculation on love and death. The final revelation of the Prince's character grows out of a somewhat unsatisfactory, but deeply insightful essay written by Freud in 1913, "The Theme of the Three Caskets." Here Freud explores a recurrent literary situation: the choice by a man of one of three women. Examples are to be found in myth (e.g. Paris' choice of Aphrodite), in fairy tales, and in literature, especially in Shakespeare's *The Merchant of Venice* and *King Lear*. In all the examples cited by Freud, one pattern emerges: The fairest, the truest, the most desirable is the youngest. Yet choosing her and possessing her is fraught with difficulties. Success in settling the selection brings with it apparent happiness, but often death as well. The significance Freud finds in the theme is that it unites the preoccupation of men with love and death through depicting the three women in the life of every man, the mother, the mistress, and finally the woman who receives him at the end of his life, death or "Mother Earth." That the third is represented as the most desirable is a displacement; i.e., the successful suitor *chooses* the beautiful one because in this way the ugly inevitability of death is transformed into the freely chosen gratification of one's most intimate desires.

Lampedusa has self-consciously provided another literary instance of this theme, and yet has done it without forcing the didactic issue because the symbolism works within the world constructed and the characters' relationship to one another. That I trace the theme in this way does not imply I find the treatment artificial or superimposed gratuitously upon the story. Rather, the life and death of Don Fabrizio allows an alliance with an ancient and recurring literary subject because his life is defined by an ideological ambience peculiar to Sicily in whose past and present, in whose social and political affairs, we see the violent efforts to cope with an essentially pagan antiquity. It is against the pagan tradition and its conflict with Christianity that the Prince's relationship to women must be seen. (pp. 105-07)

Every woman the Prince encounters—including his mistress, Mariannina—is something of a travesty on what he seeks among the stars and in his house. Only the one who comes for him at death realizes the perfect mating he longs for. That he happily departs with her is proof of his having lived as a pagan with the object of dying well. But much of his life was devoted to the proud, defensive belief that women of Christian charity might protect him and save him from death as if he were a child and they his mother.

This illusion of protection is sustained by his proprietary attitude towards the nuns of Donnafugata. Once a year, coincident with his return to his ancestral house, he visits the convent, access to which is allowed only to him and the King of Naples, a privilege of which "he was both jealous and proud." Towards the nuns, his feelings are those of a child toward the inviolable and consoling mother. They complete the trinity of women in the Prince's life, and indirectly suggest that King and Prince, i.e. father and son, share access to the mother.

His deeply complex involvement with woman, so carefully drawn in the novel, is contrasted with the cavalier, violating behavior of Tancredi who, we are told, was party to an assault on a convent. The Prince is shocked at this, not only because it is ungentlemanly, but also because it disturbs the delicate weighting of pagan and Christian so necessary to the preservation of Sicily. The Prince defends a tradition that depends upon the ambiguity of pagan and Christian conflict; Tancredi announces the new politics of revolutionary freedom. Tancredi's violations extend further than that, however, for he, with his fiancée, Angelica, makes an assault on the Prince's deepest self, the family past of the Salinas. Together the lovers penetrate the most secret rooms and corridors of Donnafugata, discovering hints of licentious perversions which excite their passion. The ancient house preserves the family unconscious; Tancredi would expose to light what has so far remained hidden. In this, his attempt at love, as in politics, he would deny ambiguity and complexity, seeking for the explicitly direct in libidinous expression. Therefore he and Angelica can find in their explorations no cease to their physical craving. And, indeed, the omniscient author tells us that they will never find satisfaction in love. But this is a way of saying, also, that the revolutionaries cannot create a world fit for men of possible greatness, like the Prince.

That he does have greatness near him is suggested by the fact that he can consider the new revolutionary state without feeling it denies *him*. He can examine the claims of the Garibaldini because they promise resolution of conflict; but he sees through the unreality of such a longing and naive social program. Yet *his* sense of political reality allows him to see that the new order must be given its place, just as paganism had to yield a place to the naivetés of Catholicism. Acceptance, however, is not acquiescence, and in this the Prince exhibits greatness of soul. (pp. 108-09)

The Prince is able to accept the modern renovation, just as, at some distant time, an ancestor of his was able to accept the proclaimed regeneration of Christianity. The Prince inherited from that compromise his duties to the church, which he meets in full; he supports Father Pirrone as his confessor and spiritual guide, but without conviction; and for his part Father Pirrone recognizes the ultimate hopelessness of his effort to "save" the Prince. He sees that the Prince belongs to "a class difficult to suppress because it's in continual renewal and because if needs be it can die well, that is it can throw out a seed at the moment of death." (p. 110)

The Prince and the Priest are each effective in his own world, guiding their families, settling disputes, acting as lawmakers. But between them there can be only the tie of a modest friendship, which survives the strained relationship of sponsor and spiritual adviser. Whatever conflicts there are between the first and second estates have been mitigated by years of living together. Yet that cannot survive the Risorgimento, which will strike at the foundation not only of the nobility springing from the pagan world, but also at the church. To preserve itself after the Risorgimento, the nobility must become allied with the new monied class, as Tancredi does with Angelica, joining the Salinas to the Calogeros; and the church must become bureaucratic. Each lapses into its more primitive self: the family of Salina into erotic paganism, venerating false relics and dubious paintings in a hideously decorated chapel; the church into smug literalism. Under the scrutiny of a young priest, trained in the Vatican School of Paleography, the relics collected by the surviving daughters of the Prince are declared fakes.

But the meddlesome interest of the church in the private devotions of the Salinas is not hurtful to the three old princesses; the effect of social change is seen in the personal suffering it causes. More disturbing than the enforced renovation and reconsecration of the chapel is the past that the censure awakens for Concetta, who so long ago hoped to marry Tancredi.

The concluding chapter of the book, taking place twenty-two years after the death of the Prince, carries us back to the vital moments of a family, now no more than dim memories distorted by wishes and unfulfilled desires. A dominant purpose of the story is here realized; for we see the impotence of the past in setting an enduring pattern for the future, yet recognize the staying power and print of the past on the reflections and memories of the individuals who have lived through. (pp. 110-11)

The key to understanding changes such as the Risorgimento is in the nature of the persons who submitted and suffered. Yet they elude us unless they can be given life in art. Of the many art forms in which this possibility might be realized, the so-called historical novel is peculiar for it permits a revivifying that no other literary form can realize, the reciprocal relationship of the self and the state, or, in Plato's terms, the interdependence of souls and constitutions. History, Lampedusa wants us to see, is a succession of soul-states.

This theme, repeated again and again in the scenes of encounter between the Prince and those who act or would act in the political world, leads inevitably to the conclusion drawn by the Prince: There is no political role for him, because his person and the new state cannot be coordinate. When he is asked to serve as a Senator, the Prince declares his incompetence and, as he talks, breaks the cross upon the little model of St. Peter's, a gesture that conveys the impotence of an institution as a coordinate decline to his own. In historical terms, there is never the perishing of a self without the perishing of a political counterpart; never the passing of an institution without the destruction of persons. The era of manners has come to an end. We begin to see how much is contained in that single term *manners*. But the polity and soul-type to succeed is already on the scene, in the persons of Tancredi and Angelica. They shall be politically potent, the story seems to say, in proportion as they are impotent between themselves, while in the life of the Prince, political power is directly related to his success in intimate relationships. (p. 112)

Ordinarily, what we think of as the historical novel reconstructs history as events; it is a form of melodrama. But the historical novel realized in its capacity as a way to understand human action, is far different, recreating the historical by means of the personal. This is the great discovery of Stendhal, and the reason why, I believe, ***The Leopard*** is so close to *The Charterhouse of Parma* in its emphasis not only on the essential subjectivity of historical events, but in its theory of how the past is to be recaptured.

In ***The Leopard,*** then, the changes that occurred in Sicily, to which we give the empty name *Risorgimento,* begin to take on the qualities of persons, and the events which we think of as "historical" are seen to be reorganizations of personal qualities—if we want to be Platonic, we say that one soul-type is succeeded by another soul-type.

This treatment of change is brought out clearly in Chapter 6, "Going to a Ball," for here two generations meet and are seen in their stark contrast: fading ancestral tradition succeeded by waxing revolutionary progress. . . . [The scene] is not only unreal to the Prince ["The crowd of dancers, among whom he could count so many near to him in blood if not in heart, began to seem unreal, made up of that material from which are woven lapsed memories, more elusive than the stuff of disturbing dreams"], but it suddenly becomes shockingly anachronistic to us:

> From the ceiling the gods, reclining on gilded couches, gazed down smiling and inexorable as a summer sky. They thought themselves eternal; but a bomb manufactured in Pittsburgh, Pennsylvania, was to prove the contrary in 1943.
> (pp. 113-14)

Lampedusa here has worked another trick of historical omniscience which takes ***The Leopard*** beyond anything Stendhal would have thought appropriate, although we may find the innovation in poor taste. The point, I think, is to force upon us the radical nature of the political and psychic change which occurred in the proper time of historical narration, by jumping its limitations to our own violence, our own passively accepted destruction. We are the descendants of those unlovely creatures upon whom the Prince looks with disgust.

The revulsion the Prince feels, and presumably the revulsion we may feel towards ourselves as we recognize ourselves, is soothed by the consolation of human mortality. The Prince recalls the little procession, seen on the way to the ball, of a priest and an acolyte, ringing the bell of death as they go to bestow the Last Sacrament on a dying man. All will come to this. At the thought the Prince is calmed, for, "when all was said and done, his own death would in the first place mean that of the whole world." . . . The death of a man is always, whatever the political condition of his day, the end of the world.

Is the Prince's death any more a finality now, now that his family in his form shall not survive? Is not every Duke of Salina the last one, in his death? However much the Duke loves Donnafugata, it disappears with him, though the residue of dusty rooms, so intimately searched by Tancredi and Angelica, will yield up their obscene impressions to others. Whatever Donnafugata is to the Prince, we see that it is far different to his heirs. To each the past is possessed in the exploration of it, but to each, what is apprehended differs. This is the hard necessity of death: that the world ends with oneself, that the seeming permanence of history is an illusion. When the Prince recognizes this—and the novel exhibits to us his coming to this recognition—he is, as much as any man ever is, ready for death.

Within the flux of social change, the Prince discerns a necessity as hard as that of the heavens; his awareness of the unpredictable necessity of the earthly is joined to his awe in the predictable necessity of the heavens. Heretofore, the Prince has regarded the heavens as peculiarly "his" realm, for we are told, "In his mind, now, pride and mathematical analysis were so linked as to give him an illusion that the stars obeyed his calculations too (as in fact they seemed to be doing) . . .". . . . (pp. 114-15)

While he has lived with the happy illusion that somehow the stars obey him, though he knows they do not, he has until recently lived with the belief that the terrestrial order does obey him, for he is the Prince whose domains are his by immemorial right. However, where he is supposed in fact to govern he is least puissant. Growing old, approaching death, he realizes that the earthly realm is no more his to rule in accordance with his will than the heavenly; both obey laws beyond human desire. The Prince ends his life more keenly, self-consciously aware of the necessities in both earth and heaven.

It is this recognition which brings him before us as possibly a tragic figure. Although not tragic in the sense of the hero of reversal and recognition, he is tragic in the sense already stated, of that kind of tragedy we find more often—the tragedy of suffering. Pathos marks every aspect of the Prince's actions, for he is aloof, remote, removed: Events are known through his reaction to them rather than through an effort to define the events themselves. Of course, this is part of Lampedusa's commitment to a vision of history that makes reversal and recognition in the historical context beyond the novel's grasp. What comes thereby centrally within the novel's grasp is the subject of dying.

The necessity of death enters the Prince's awareness with his realization that he commands little, and is subject to the necessity of unpredictable forces. The bond of affection which the Prince would have forged with other persons is never possible for him; rather his affect is directed to nature, to animals, and to his own end. In this simple sense a tragedy of reversal and recognition is irrelevant to the story because, as Aristotle noted, that requires two persons between whom there is a bond of love or hate. ***The Leopard,*** in its concentration on dying, forges the bond of affect between the hero and those impersonal, nonhuman aspects of reality to which he, like all living things, must succumb.

In this sense, then, it seems to me appropriate to speak of ***The Leopard*** as a philosophical novel, for its concerns are the relationship between human actions and nature. If this is a theme which has an established genre, as I believe it does, then we can evaluate Plato's comment in the *Laws* to the effect that philosophers would necessarily make the best tragedians; they might be writers of pathetic tragedy, but they could not sustain the vision of a Sophocles.

The necessities that make the Prince a hero of tragic suffering are not nobly met with by the other characters, who fall far below the Prince. Tancredi might have been a political leader, were he not lazy and passive, content with conferred power in a new order. Angelica might die for love, were she not sensually self-conscious, incapable of giving herself to another. Concetta might have realized the Salina potentiality for fineness, if she were not dominated by the past; she lives her life with the stuffed carcass of Bendicò in her room, preserving around her the false memories of having been wronged. Too late she realizes that "there had been no enemies, just one single adversary, herself; her future had been killed by her own impudence, by the rash Salina pride." . . . She has had no time to live life because she has been unable to face death.

Only in the Prince is the man of contemplation strong enough not to be overwhelmed by the demands of scientific observation, and the man of natural appetite not overwhelmed by religious asceticism. These are characteristics that make him pathetically fit for the endurance of suffering. Unlike the hero of conventional tragedy, the pathetic hero must have a stability and inner power to persevere that sets him apart from other fragile persons, and from the weight of events. Pagan and empiricistic by nature, autocratic and domineering by fortune of birth, the Prince is able to cultivate manners. Thus protected, he can come to know himself. There is here a "moral" as urgent as that we associate with the more shocking tragedy of reversal and recognition.

The proper mis-en-scène of the tragedy of suffering is history, and it may be that the historical novel is the only genre to perpetuate this tragic possibility. Whether this be so or not, the tragedy of suffering in historical contexts such as those of ***The Leopard*** shows us important truths about the past and the future as it relates to our lives. (pp. 115-17)

The corollary to Freud's assertion that in literature we still find people who know how to die, is that in literature we may learn something of our death. In ***The Leopard*** we are presented with the fact that life is but a moment, "the tiny ray of light granted . . . between two shades, before the cradle, after the last spasms." (p. 117)

This is a banal truth, to which all would assent, but the literary work in which the statement appears is at once a consolation and a shock; for through it we vault the blinding urgencies of our actual present to inhabit, for a moment, the wider necessities of the past and future of the Salina house. We see in the Prince's life the spindle of necessity and the consequences of choice. This vision, which lasts only as long as the book, cannot endure the importunate moments of everyday life. Back in our time-coerced lives where the future threatens, we lose the value of death because we fear it, while in the novel that denies the usual temporal order, we see that to deny time is to make death a part of life and thereby to confer upon life the only survival possible. This is to render life art-like, and that Lampedusa has done. In this way the literary arts survive modernity, which dealt an almost fatal blow to story in denying the stable truthfulness of the past. (pp. 117-18)

Richard F. Kuhns, "Modernity and Death: 'The Leopard'" (originally a lecture delivered at the meeting of the William Alanson White Society on March 6, 1968), in Contemporary Psychoanalysis *(© by the William Alanson White Psychoanalytic Society and the William Alanson White Institute of Psychiatry Psychoanalysis and Psychology, 1969), Vol. 5, No. 2, Spring, 1969, pp. 95-119.*

TOM O'NEILL (essay date 1970)

[*In the following excerpt O'Neill compares and contrasts* The Leopard *with Federico De Roberto's novel* I vicerè (The Viceroys), *a novel which, like Lampedusa's, portrays an aristocratic Sicilian family in decline. O'Neill finds the primary theme of* The Leopard *to be death and its proper relation to life.*]

Il Gattopardo, at first sight, presents many similarities with *I Vicerè*. Both novels take place in the same crucially important period of Italian history—the years of Unification; both are concerned with the presentation of a noble Sicilian family and both are concerned with the attempts of that family to preserve the "integrity" of their class against the oncoming tide of social reform.

It is especially in the attempts of both families to rough ride the tide of social change that most critics have seen the strongest similarities between the two novels and yet, to look more closely, it is precisely here that is to be seen the gulf that separates them.

The De Roberto novel, in addition to being the story of the destruction of a noble family through base motivations, is also, as has been said, an attempt to save that family from destruction in the social upheavals that resulted from Unification and what is more, it is a *successful* attempt, or more precisely, the protagonist of this attempt, Consalvo, thinks it is so. His meeting with his aunt Ferdinanda who has so obstinately upheld the "purity" of the race throughout the novel, is more than revealing for it shows that Consalvo, like every other member of his family, has his eyes either fixed on the past or firmly fixed in the present, and if they are turned to the future, it is a future which merely reflects or rather repeats the past, one in which, thanks to the unchanging nature of History, the *status quo* of his family has remained essentially intact. . . . (pp. 172-73)

Il Gattopardo is also an attempt to save a noble family and it too in its way may be judged a successful attempt since Tancredi weds the beautiful Angelica, thus adding wealth to his family name—that wealth so necessary for success in the modern world,—and what is more, by uniting the noble Falconeri family to the rich but plebeian Sedara family, he too, like Consalvo, saves his family from destruction in the social upheaval resultant on the Risorgimento.

But, unlike *I Vicerè*, ***Il Gattopardo*** does not end with Tancredi's belief that he has saved his family from destruction. By the end of the novel Tancredi is long since dead, nor, in spite of the attractiveness of his character, had he balked large in it. The protagonist is not Tancredi but his *zione* ["old uncle"], don Fabrizio, and if for a moment he fondly imagines that the actions of Tancredi in courting the Revolutionaries will stop the march of History, it is not characteristic of him. (p. 173)

[In others of the book's passages,] don Fabrizio is more than conscious that any success will be limited in time because of the futility of reacting against Destiny. (p. 174)

It is the lack of consciousness of the eventual futility of his political actions that restricts Consalvo's view and which also keeps De Roberto's novel within the well-defined bounds of a particular literary genre, namely the historical novel. It is a *consciousness* of the futility of action that takes ***Il Gattopardo*** beyond the realms of the historical novel. History in Lampedusa's novel is an integral part of the novel but it does not constitute the only or, indeed, the main theme. It is merely part of a larger and truer theme, that of *death.*

This aspect of ***Il Gattopardo*** has, naturally, not failed to attract the attention of many readers. . . . The *leit-motif* of death which runs through the book from the opening prayers, the garden with its "aspetto cimiteriale" ["air of a cemetery"] and the body of the young soldier, to the "senso di morte che neppure la frenetica luce siciliana riusciva a disperdere" ["sense of death which not even the vibrant Sicilian light could ever manage to disperse"] which hangs over Palermo, to the beautiful chapter on the Prince's death and the final "mucchietto di polvere livida" ["heap of livid dust"] which closes the book, has seemed to many the very essence of the book and consequently they have defined it as a Decadent novel.

To define the novel as Decadent, however, to classify it as purely a "corteggiamento della morte" ["courtship with death"] is singularly to fail to realise that don Fabrizio, just as he has an ambivalent attitude towards his class, also has an ambivalent attitude towards death. This attitude (*sui generis,* the ambivalence at the basis of Petrarch's *Canzoniere*), if on the one hand it produces a desire for death, a longing for eternity, symbolised in the love he has for astronomy and the desire he has for communion with the stars, produces on the other hand an abhorrence of death because it destroys life which even with all its limitations still attracts him so. That this is so is made perfectly clear from the meditations of the Prince at the ball at Palazzo Ponteleone as he watches Tancredi and Angelica dancing. The young couple, in the flower of youth, unaware of what the future holds for them . . . contrast painfully with the Prince and it is from this contrast and the consciousness of it that there is born in him that "compassione per tutti questi effimeri esseri" ["compassion for all these ephemeral beings"] which leads him to conclude: "Non era lecito odiare altro che l'eternità" ["Nothing could be decently hated except eternity"]. . . . (pp. 174-75)

It is this legitimate hatred of eternity that produces in Lampedusa that "sentimento profondamente caritativo" ["profound sense of charity"] that Montale attributed to him and it is precisely this charity towards his fellow men that separates him from De Roberto who would have dwelt on the "calcoli" ["self-interests"], the "mire segrete" ["secret aims"], the "non limpide ambizioni" ["murky ambitions"] which Lampedusa, through the meditations of don Fabrizio, recognises in both Tancredi and Angelica and, indeed, in human nature in general, but which he does not dwell upon. . . . (p. 175)

"Art," as Pasternak said in *Doctor Zhivago,* "has two constant, two unending preoccupations: it is always meditating upon death and it is always thereby producing life" and it is in this concern with *life,* heightened by the consciousness of death, and in the portrayal of that life that Lampedusa differs so greatly from De Roberto.

The author of *I Vicerè* is concerned with painting a huge, detailed canvass of a *whole* family whereas Lampedusa's novel evolves essentially round *one* member of a family, the *pater familias,* don Fabrizio, but even if we limit our attention in De Roberto to the head of the family, Giacomo, whose essential features are all to be found in varying degrees in the other characters, and compare him to Fabrizio, this in itself will be sufficient to illustrate the totally different approach to life and its depiction in both novels.

In Giacomo there are two predominant traits. There is a deep rooted desire which he has in common with the other members of his immediate family, to undo all that his mother, donna Teresa, has obliged him to do against his wishes—an authoritarian trait in his mother which he himself also manifests, perhaps nowhere more so than when on his death bed, he disinherits his son Consalvo, in favour of his daughter, Teresa, because of his son's unwillingness to marry. (pp. 175-76)

Along with this desire to undo the wishes of his dead mother and, in several ways, linked with it, there is also the boundless desire to amass material goods. (p. 177)

How much of this selfish, wrangling and, in many ways, bitter man is to be found in don Fabrizio? The picture presented of him in the early pages of the book—for example, in the scene at dinner—would seem to be not inappropriate as a description of Giacomo, namely, a "temperamento autoritario" ["imperious temperament"], but the tyrannical Prince of the First Chapter changes in the Second Chapter—just as the original time sequence changed—to the "uomo paternalistico e lungomirante" ["far-sighted, paternalistic man"] who stalks the pages of the rest of the novel. There is undoubtedly a very deep pessimistic streak in don Fabrizio but it is considerably muted by his "fondamentale bonomia" ["fundamental good nature"] which does not separate him or isolate him from other men but rather unites him to them.

So too, just as he is paternalistic rather than authoritarian, he is also, unlike Giacomo, conscious of the futility of amassing goods. (p. 178)

But perhaps the greatest difference between the two men is to be seen not in this or that individual characteristic of their personalities but rather in their complete outlook on life. What is lacking in Giacomo and what is so evident in Fabrizio is that sense of *otium,* in its original meaning, that Guido Piovene (in *La Stampa,* 8 febbraio 1959) attributed to ***Il Gattopardo,*** that "aristocratic culture deserving simultaneously and paradoxically our contempt and our esteem." This innate quality that don Fabrizio has *in fact* and not, like Giacomo, merely *in name,* is, perhaps, ironically, best perceived by don Calogero Sedara, the father of Angelica, who senses in the Prince "una forza di attrazione differente in tono, ma simile in intensità, a quella del giovane Falconeri" ["a strength of attraction different in tinge, but similar in intensity, to young Falconeri's"], and who realises, in his own rough way, that an educated man "non è altro che qualcheduno che elimina le manifestazioni piú sgradevoli di tanta parte della condizione umana e che esercita una specie di profittevole altruismo" ["is only someone who eliminates the unpleasant aspects of so much of the human condition and exercises a kind of profitable altruism"]. . . . (pp. 178-79)

The difference between the two heads of family is essentially the difference between the families themselves. The Uzedas . . . are corrupt, bitter, wrangling, vicious and degenerate and it is these qualities that dictate the often vicious and violent scenes in the book—for example, the confrontation between donna Ferdinanda, ever intent on upholding the "purity" of the family tradition, and her niece, Lucrezia, who, through her intended marriage with the young bourgeois lawyer, Benedetto Giuliente, would inevitably compromise it. It is these same qualities in the Uzedas that also dictate the bitter, biting sarcasm of the author.

The Salinas, on the other hand, are noble because gentle—in its philological sense from *gens*—and deserving in many respects of our admiration. It is this admiration on the part of the author too that dictates the gentle irony of the novel—an irony implying participation and understanding on his part—as well as the nostalgia with which he portrays their life. (p. 179)

The reason for this, to my mind, is that Lampedusa is concerned with the *last* of a great family. He, Lampedusa, like don Fabrizio, realises only too well that degeneration will come—witness his, Fabrizio's, consciousness of it as he lies dying in a hotel room, far from all that means so much to him—but it does not interest him, it is not the subject of his book.

In De Roberto's novel, the last of the Francalanzas, the principessa Teresa, is dead at the beginning of the story and the author is taken up in his novel with what happens *after* the death of the last, true Francalanza.

I Vicerè is a great novel *of its kind* which enthrals and holds the reader's attention to the very last. So too is ***Il Gattopardo,*** but for essentially different reasons, for the beauty and dignity portrayed therein, not of death but, as Henry James would have put it, of man going down fighting. If life, in Lampedusa's novel, is a Leopardian "rischio di morte" ["dangerous risk"], its presentation—as in Leopardi—is greatly heightened because of this. What is essentially lacking in *I Vicerè,* but not in ***Il Gattopardo,*** is *dignity*. It is this portrayal of the dignity of man—essentially the dignity of the author himself—that makes Lampedusa's novel a masterpiece, a book that offers pleasure and stimulation reading after reading, a book that transcends its period and its author, a book, in short, which has those qualities of *poliedricità* ["many-sidedness"] which Lampedusa attributed to Stendhal. . . . (p. 180)

Tom O'Neill, "Lampedusa and De Roberto," in Italica, *Vol. 47, No. 2, Summer, 1970, pp. 170-82.**

OLGA RAGUSA (essay date 1976)

[*In an abstract that summarizes the essay from which the following excerpt is taken, Ragusa explains that Lampedusa's article* "Lezioni su Stendhal" *contains "an analysis of narrative technique that is important to a study of the formal aspects of . . .* Il gattopardo, *aspects that were obscured by ideological criticism of the work and by the impact of the* nouveau roman *as against the lack of impact of the Jamesian tradition on critical opinion at the time. Information on the book's conception, composition, and publication coincides with the clues in the* "Lezioni" *to show that* Gattopardo *is the work of a craftsman fully conscious of his narrative strategy, that chapters 5 and 8 are skillfully integrated parts of a whole, and that Concetta (with Lucia of* I promessi sposi *and Mena of* I Malavoglia, *one of the great understated "heroines" of Italian literature) must be placed next to the novel's giant protagonist as the object of Lampedusa's particular attention and strategy."*]

In the flood of critical appraisals that followed the publication of ***Il gattopardo*** in 1958, surprisingly scant attention was paid to Lampedusa's analysis of the work of a fellow novelist, Stendhal. His lectures on Stendhal, part of a series of "lessons" he held privately for a small group of students and friends in Palermo, were published while the ***Gattopardo*** controversy was still at its fiercest. Yet they engaged the attention only of Louis Aragon, who made use of them in an article for *Les Lettres françaises*. . . . A few months later, Aragon's remarks were made the subject of illuminating comment in a survey of French criticism of ***Il gattopardo,*** one of several articles defending the novel to appear in 1959-60 in Luigi Russo's leftist review *Belfagor*. The writer of that article came to the conclusion that Aragon's was the only *truly critical analysis* of ***Il gattopardo*** to have come out in France. (p. 1)

Lampedusa deals with the whole of Stendhal's production, convinced that all Stendhal's works, including the so-called minor ones, bear the mark of an exceptional personality, a personality able to give new life even to what appeared to be outworn and no longer valid genres. Thus he describes *Les Promenades dans Rome* as a unique travel book that ranks as a literary work of art and *De l'amour* as an extraordinary "physiologie" that belongs with the best in literature. But . . . if this attention reveals Lampedusa's thorough acquaintance with the corpus of Stendhal's work, it is to the two masterpieces that he devotes the substance and particular acumen of his analysis. *Le Rouge et le noir* and *La Chartreuse de Parme* are presented first together as "works of absolute first rank" . . . and are then discussed separately under the section heading "L'Heure des cuirassiers." . . . Since this study is concerned mainly not with Lampedusa as critic of Stendhal but with Lampedusa as novelist, I propose to focus only on those passages of **"Lezioni su Stendhal"** in which he formulates general rules of narrative technique and applies them to Stendhal or where he uses Stendhal as a point of departure to discuss the art of fiction.

In light of the kind of criticism to which ***Il gattopardo*** was later subjected, Lampedusa's single most significant statement comes at the very beginning of the essay, when he writes that Stendhal's two masterpieces possess a quality that the minor works for all their excellence do not. That quality is manysidedness (*poliedricità*), the distinguishing feature of works of absolute first rank. For, Lampedusa says, if *Le Rouge* and *La Chartreuse* can from one point of view be considered (1) historical novels, they can also be considered (2) the "lyrical" outpouring of their author's sentiments, (3) psychological case studies, (4) lessons in a certain kind of morality, and (5) models of the most difficult of styles, the style of extreme conciseness (*estrema abbreviazione*). Let us discuss each of these points.

Inasmuch as ***Il gattopardo*** was generally recognized to be first and foremost a historical novel, we should note the meaning Lampedusa gives to the term. He ignores Scott and the novel of archeological reconstruction of the past altogether. Instead, he speaks of "novels that have become historical for us," that portray objectively (*oggettivazione*) a period that was contemporary for their author but has become so remote for the reader that he can know it only through art. (pp. 5-6)

We can treat the next three points as a unit. Lampedusa connects the lyrical quality of Stendhal's work, his psychological penetration, and the ethical doctrine that his novels imply and others of his works openly display with Stendhal's sense of himself and with the projection of that self into his fictional creations. Thus, Sorel is the man the ambitious Stendhal actually was; del Dongo, the noble, wealthy, beloved man he would have wished to be. Through both, Stendhal speaks directly; that is, lyrically. The other characters, those who are neither the author himself nor stand-ins for him, are given life not so much by his feelings as by his intelligence: Stendhal's much-admired psychological knowledge. The Epicurean, hedonistic ethic that paradoxically attributes greater satisfaction to the pursuit of pleasure than to its attainment and enjoyment impels Stendhal's characters as it impelled him. These points, though Lampedusa does not present them as such, might be summarized as his comment on the autobiographical aspects of Stendhal's novels.

This leaves us with the fifth point: Stendhal's style, the "mortar that binds together the different stones and assures the durability of the edifice." . . . It is here that we encounter the first unmistakable sign that Lampedusa's reading of Stendhal is that of the craftsman or potential craftsman interested in the writing of fiction. His reading is not simply that of the enthusiastic reader who finds himself extraordinarily well attuned to a favorite writer's portrayal of experience, nor is it that of the cultivated and educated reader who is at home in the critical literature that deals with his subject. Lampedusa makes a point of separating himself from the average reader, whose main concern in a novel is plot. He specifically warns that Stendhal's works must be read with the proper attention and not merely to find out what happens in the story. He does not fix his gaze on the world created by Stendhal—though that world is completely "real" to him, as witness his rounded views of the characters Julien and Fabrice, Mme de Rênal and Sanseverina, of the "twin figures" of M. de Rênal and Count Mosca, the "absurd and attractive" Ferrante Palla, the "wooden" General Fabio Conti, the "myriad mean priests and plotters" (the descriptive epithets are all Lampedusa's). Rather, his attention is on Stendhal in the act of creating that world. And just as he emphasized Stendhal's involvement in his characters, playing down his much vaunted objectivity, so he now chooses as the perspective from which to examine his style not the traditional view of the "style du Code Civil" but Jean Prévost's "style de l'improvisateur." (pp. 7-8)

When Lampedusa returns to the subject of the two novels the second time in **"Lezioni,"** . . . he moves at once to place the discussion within a broader frame of reference. He no longer focuses on the characteristics of Stendhal's works (the five points just considered) but on the more general questions of narrative technique. While the earlier set of remarks is therefore useful as a key to the affinities that draw ***Il gattopardo*** and the novels of Stendhal together, . . . this second set serves to confirm the impression of technical control, of conscious craftsmanship . . . that accompanies a careful reading of the novel. Lampedusa's "reading" of Stendhal and his acquaintance with the tools for critical analysis of narrative technique converge to throw the formal—as against the ideological—aspects of ***Il gattopardo*** into strong relief. . . .

Lampedusa starts out by recognizing the uselessness of repeating praise of Stendhal's gifts as a poet, a psychologist, and an "evoker" of milieus. . . . But if there is little point in repeating what has already been said and about which there is general agreement, he continues, there is every reason for turning to the why (*il perchè*) of Stendhal's greatness—for examining, that is, his technique of expression. "In art," Lampedusa states axiomatically, "the possibility of communicating is everything." . . . And again later: "In art the 'technique of execution' is everything, for the artist is nothing more than a fellow (*tizio*) who knows how to express himself." . . . In the case of the novel the specific problems of expression are (1) the treatment of time, (2) the concretization of the narrative situation (*concretizzare la narrazione*), (3) the suggestion of milieu, and (4) the treatment of dialogue. Although Lampedusa lists the problems in this order, he does not discuss them thus. For as soon as he is forced to touch upon (5) the position of the narrator, it becomes obvious that the central and crucial consideration, the pivot around which all else revolves, is "point of view," a term he does not use but a concept he describes perceptively and at length. (pp. 9-10)

Lampedusa warns that passing time must be suggested or alluded to incidentally, almost secretly (*di sfuggita e quasi di nascosto*), for time in a novel is not the time of a "train schedule," . . . and that first-person narrative in which the protagonist also knows the inner life of other characters is fraught with dangers that only a genius like Proust can brave with impunity. As for Stendhal, he "chose the quickest and proudest way: to simplify, we may call it the way of having God tell the story. In the garb of a deity, Stendhal knows the most hidden thoughts of every character, pointing them out to the reader who shares in his omniscience. Stendhal leaves nothing in shadow, except what he chooses not to say in order to heighten the emotion." . . . (p. 10)

The remaining three technical problems dealing with expression are concerned essentially with the concretization of the action, with turning theme into plot. Here Lampedusa's most significant remark has to do with the treatment of dialogue. In Stendhal, he points out, "there is not one instance of a famous dialogue." . . . This he attributes to the fact that Stendhal avoided the "error of so many novelists (including some of the greatest!) who reveal a character's inner life through what he says." In real life, Lampedusa continues, "verbal revelation" almost never occurs: we understand people through "their actions, their glances, their stammering, the entwining of their fingers, their silences or their sudden speech, the color of their cheeks, the rhythm of their step." . . . Thus, Lampedusa illustrates, Stendhal reports not Julien's words in refusing to marry Elisa, but their gist. This permits him to interject his own implied comments so as "to rectify what has been said," to unmask the intention that words so often hide or misrepresent—"words which are always the chaste or impudent masks of a person's inmost being." . . . (pp. 10-11)

The relatively few passages from Lampedusa's **"Lezioni su Stendhal"** on which I have based these remarks were selected for the strong light they shed on Lampedusa's conscious art in ***Il gattopardo*** and have been rearranged in such a way as to form a kind of statement on the poetics of the novel. (p. 11)

I shall single out two problem areas [in ***Il gattopardo***] to which critics have returned time and again: the relevance or discrepancy of chapter 5, and the significance, appropriateness, or incongruence of chapter 8. Though ultimately the judgments made depend on one's view of the overall form or structure of the work, these two chapters present sufficiently differentiated problems to permit us to consider them as separate and independent case studies. Because it is more closely and obviously related to the novel's ideological content, chapter 5 has received the greater share of attention. Chapter 8, instead, has been rapidly dismissed as an unfortunate afterthought on the part of the author, who was presumably torn between a biographically centered and a cyclical concept of the historical novel.

Chapter 5 is the first chapter of the novel in which the prince does not occupy center stage. . . . At its end, when Father Pirrone returns to Palermo, the hierarchy is reestablished and the prince again becomes the major god of his household.

During the two-day visit to his native village, however, Father Pirrone is given the opportunity to talk and act on his own initiative: his reflections on the political changes taking place echo the prince's colloquy with Chevalley; his arrangement of a marriage for his niece parallels the prince's "swallowing of a toad" in the latter's negotiations for the marriage of Tancredi. Father Pirrone's visit marks an anniversary, that of his father's death fifteen years before. Lampedusa's retrospective look at the priest's family background—something he had not been able to do when the character was first introduced—is thus deftly justified, and the introductory pages in which don Gaetano's business activities and Father Pirrone's childhood and youth are rapidly recalled show no signs of artifice or strain.

The sense of the unchanging continuity of life and of the momentary surface disturbance brought by the recent "liberation" of Sicily (chapter 5 is dated February 1861, a mere three months after the preceding one) is expressed by two "objective correlatives," mirror images of identical objects that function in the prince's milieu: the dog Romeo, "great-great-grandson" of a dog that had romped with the boy Saverio, and the tricolor cockade that Father Pirrone's nephew Carmelo "had had the bad taste" of putting in his cap as a sign of rejoicing. The chapter forms a diptych: Father Pirrone answers the old herbalist's question about the reactions of the nobility to the revolution that is undermining its privileges; and Father Pirrone smoothes over a revengeful seduction and one brother's "dirty trick" on another, by convincing his sister to give her daughter the proper dowry. With understated irony, Lampedusa reduces Father Pirrone's audience to one sleeping man, no doubt intending to show thereby that truth can be revealed only when there is no chance of its being heard. . . . More overtly, Lampedusa calls attention to the parallelism between the love antics of the rustics Angelina and Santino and Angelica's and Tancredi's retracing of the stops on the *carte du tendre*, by remarking on the residue of unpleasant impressions that his visit has left in Father Pirrone: "that brutal love affair whose culmination had come during Saint Martin's Summer (November 1860 was also the time of Angelica's and Tancredi's exploration of the abandoned rooms at Donnafugata), that miserable half of an almond grove grabbed back by means of a premeditated courtship, showed him the rustic, sordid side of other happenings that he had recently witnessed." . . . But before we reach this explicit statement at the very end of the chapter, the sophisticated reader has been free to draw his own conclusions from the careful balancing of mood and event, of characters and comments. (pp. 14-15)

[Chapter 5 is one of] two chapters that were not part of the original manuscript read by Bassani. Bassani came upon the chapter later, in the [author's] longhand version, and decided to use it in spite of the objection [of Lampedusa's wife]. "I found that it was essential to the structure of the novel. This sort of descent to hell is a fundamental clue to understanding Fabrizio and Sicily," he was quoted as saying in the 1970 interview. The princess, instead, would have preferred to keep the chapter, together with the scene of the ball, to which she had herself called Bassani's attention, for inclusion in a possible publication of Lampedusa's shorter pieces. But she may of course also have been influenced by what Lanza Tomasi remembers of Lampedusa's own hesitation about the chapter, which displeased him because, contrary to his usual practice, it was "explicit" rather than "implicit", providing a kind of "gloss" to the prince's behavior rather than permitting it to express itself simply through the narration of events. . . . It is interesting to note once again that Lampedusa's judgment as reported here is based on a consideration of technique, on an awareness of the importance of the choice of point of view in storytelling. But it is equally interesting to note that he seems to have shared with Bassani, at this point at least, the conviction that the prince is after all the one and only center of the novel.

Simonetta Salvestroni, whose two articles in *Filologia e letteratura* and whose full-length study of Lampedusa are among the few really perceptive discussions of ***Il gattopardo,*** advances a different hypothesis, and buttresses it with a rare, if not unique, reference to **"Lezioni su Stendhal."** . . . By asking herself how Lampedusa succeeded in giving movement and complexity to what is essentially a static situation, she discovered elements of a thoroughly worked-out pattern in which scenes of bitterness and pessimism alternate with others which mark a recovery of serenity. Chapter 5 thus counterbalances the taste of ashes left by the prince's encounter with Chevalley at the end of chapter 4, and lightens the atmosphere before the depressing observations in chapter 6 on the decline of his class and on the inevitable sinking of all men into old age and death, made by the prince during the festivities at the ball of the Ponteleones. The passage which she quotes from **"Lezioni su Stendhal"** reads as follows: "But in the course of a novel, especially if it is composed of tense psychological probing and of a hurried action, moments of pause must be provided for the reader. Obviously, it always takes less time to read a novel than to write it, and even if the author does not feel the need to pause for himself, he must not forget that the reader needs it. If the reader fails to find these oases in which to rest, he will close the book at the least appropriate moment and reopen it when the accumulated energy has evaporated. Every great author of long works has provided these breathing spaces." . . . (pp. 15-16)

Thus, for Simonetta Salvestroni chapter 5 is not only a pendant to and a parody of the main story but also a break in the narrative, a determined turning away from the main character and the lesser characters disposed about him in the guise of satellites. Or to put it in Lampedusa's own terms, chapter 5 is a major device for the expansion of narrative time, for creating what he called "*rallentamenti nel ritmo della narrazione.*"

These, then, are some of the thematic and formal reasons that can be adduced to support the idea that chapter 5 is an integral part of the novel and that Lampedusa might perhaps have changed parts of it but would not have abandoned it altogether. . . . Of course, these reasons become apparent only after we discard the preconceived notion that the unity of ***Il gattopardo*** depends on the continuous presence of the protagonist on stage. How deeply rooted this notion is (a notion the title of the book itself does not help dispel) can be seen in the fact that although chapter 6 was, like chapter 5, an afterthought, and felt by Bassani to be stylistically inferior to the rest of the novel, it was never seriously considered *de trop:* the presence of the prince was enough to mute any nascent negative impressions. And yet, not only the book's original tripartite plan and the report that Lampedusa once planned to call it *Ultime luci* . . . ("Last Lights," a theatrical, cinematic allusion that would not have been inappropriate, although far less economical and striking than **"The Leopard"**) but especially its inclusion of another chapter that does without the prince—these facts should have alerted the critics that they might possibly have overlooked something.

Chapter 8 takes place twenty-seven years after the death of the prince and fifty after the opening pages of the book. Of the Salina family only the girls survive: Carolina, Caterina, Concetta, and Chiara, their married sister in Naples, of whom there had been no mention earlier. Angelica, too, whose forty-year marriage to Tancredi "had erased all traces of the Donnafugata accent and manners," . . . is in her seventies. Like chapter 5, chapter 8 moves between two main episodes: the official inspection of the private chapel at Villa Salina, in accordance with the new regulations of the Papal Curia, and the visit to Concetta of Tassoni, erstwhile comrade-in-arms of Tancredi and now an aged senator. Like chapter 5 but with greater force of impact, chapter 8 ends with the new experiences of the two days (13-14 May) whose events it recounts echoing through the psyche of its protagonist, this time however with the grand conclusiveness of the final chords of a heroic symphony. The word *Fine,* centered on the last page of the 1957 manuscript, is corroboration of the *completo* we read on the title page. In omitting the word, the English edition respects a publisher's sensitivity to the quaintness of its use in a modern novel but betrays Lampedusa's own intention of emphasizing the fully conscious aspect of his technique of composition.

If chapter 5 is in some respects, as we have seen, an anniversary chapter, chapter 8 is almost exclusively so. There is first of all and most obviously the celebration being planned to mark the 1860 conquest, or liberation, of Palermo. It is an occasion for which visitors are expected to arrive from all parts of Italy and in which the Salina's are to participate in an official capacity. Angelica is a member of the Board of Patrons, and the young Fabrizio will march down Via Libertà in frock coat as part of the parade. "Don't you think that's a first-rate idea? A Salina will render homage to Garibaldi. It will be a fusion of the old and new Sicily," Angelica says to Concetta, . . . thus underlining for the last time one of the principal public themes of the novel.

Equally obvious is the parallelism of the dates, May 1860 and May 1910, that stand at the beginning of the first and last chapters respectively: not only do they state the fifty-year lapse, but none of the other six chapters takes place in the month of May. A closer look reveals that the day of the month corresponds as well. In chapter 1, which is filled with allusions to the beleaguered state of Sicily between the uprising of 4 April in Palermo and Garibaldi's landing at Marsala on 11 May, the precise date 13 May appears in the course of a landscape description made from the vantage point of the prince's observatory. . . . It is stated incidentally, almost in passing. . . . In chapter 8 we find the precise date 14 May spelled out during the description of the cardinal's visit to the Salina household to make arrangements for the required examination of the relics. . . . As in chapter 1, the date enteres surreptitiously and elusively while the reader's attention is engaged elsewhere.

What is particularly significant about 13-14 May, however, is that it is not the date of the fall of Palermo (27 May, presumably the day for which the celebrations to commemorate the exploits of Garibaldi's Thousand are being planned) but a date with a private meaning in the history of the Salina family. Yet the proximity of the two dates and Lampedusa's skilful interweaving and blending of references to historical and individual destiny muddy the waters sufficiently to make the novel's concealment or disclosure of meaning entirely dependent on the reader's capacity of penetration. And this in spite of the fact that there is a moment in the account of Tassoni's visit to Concetta at which the author intervenes with his own statement of the perspective from which the episode should be read. Of Concetta's youthful love for Tancredi, Lampedusa writes at this point: "But as someone who recovered from smallpox fifty years before still bears the marks of the illness upon his face although he may have forgotten its pain, so she bore in her present tormented life the scars of her by now historical disappointment, historical indeed to the point that *its fiftieth anniversary* was now being officially celebrated" (. . . italics mine).

For chapter 8 is Concetta's chapter. Just as Father Pirrone was finally allowed to speak and act on his own in chapter 5, so in chapter 8 is the spotlight finally and unequivocally on the prince's daughter. That she has become both an unappealing and a pathetic figure, "fat and imposing in her stiff black moiré . . . with contemptuous eyes and an expression of resentment above her nose," . . . must not blind us to this fact. In spite of the fanfare of political celebrations and in spite of the feeling of nausea Lampedusa so ably imparts to the reader through his reflection on the fate of the Church, religion, and taste in the Italy of democracy, . . . this is the great "family" chapter of the book, the point at which the historical novel most clearly makes way for the deep psychological insights of the bourgeois novel. It is the chapter of leave-taking, the enforced discarding of the objects of a naive and superstitious piety that clutter the Salina chapel, and the voluntary rejection of the "mummified memories" . . . that make Concetta's room a place of torture to her. At the end, when "the little heap of moth-eaten fur" . . . that had been Bendicò forty-five years before, turns from "the only memory of [Concetta's] past that did not awaken painful feelings in her" . . . to the only thing left in the utter emptying out of all her feelings . . . still capable of evoking a shadow of uneasiness in her, and she orders it thrown out, we have truly reached that "end of everything" we had not reached at the prince's deathbed. Thus, Concetta and not Tancredi, nor yet the blooming Angelica, is revealed to be the figure most closely related to the prince and second in importance only to him for a full explication of the novel's meaning.

And indeed, in retrospect, it becomes obvious that in spite of the central group—the giant prince; the gay, self-affirming, opportunistic Tancredi; the opulently beautiful and confident Angelica—in whom the fictional elements of the story find expression, Concetta has actually never been far from Lampedusa's focus of interest. With repeated insistence but at the same time extraordinary discreetness he has directed the reader's attention to her time and again.

She appears first in chapter 1, with what will become characteristic understatement, when in the course of a flashback her father remembers an audience granted him by Ferdinand II: the king's godchild, she is the only one of the prince's offspring to be mentioned by name. . . . Her second appearance in chapter 1 is at the Salinas' midday table: the prince surmises that she is anxious about Tancredi, who has just left to join the invaders, and Lampedusa quotes him as thinking, "They would make a fine couple. But I fear Tancredi will have to aim higher, by which of course I mean lower." . . . (pp. 17-20)

Against the background of the prince's rediscovery of the perennially unchanged attractions of Donnafugata and his perception of some alas! altered social and economic circumstances, chapters 2 and 3 recount his betrayal of his daughter in favor of Angelica and Concetta's own double rejection of Tancredi: the first time at the dinner table when he tells a vulgar soldier's tale about the forcing of a convent . . . , the second during the Salinas' visit to the Convent of the Holy Spirit. . . . Concetta's realization of what has happened fails to reach the level of consciousness at this point, but in the final paragraph of chapter 3, when she is the only one who does not look up when her father crosses the girls' sitting room and she does not *hear* "the vigorous, rapid steps that announce his arrival thirty feet away," . . . Lampedusa has created one of those "accentuated silences intended to make the attentive reader prick up his ears," a silence which surely places this episode next to Manzoni's "La sventurata rispose" and Stendhal's "Aucune résistance ne fut opposée," cited in **"Lezioni su Stendhal"** as instances of quasi-miraculous understatement.

The many pages devoted in chapter 4 to Chevalley's visit to Donnafugata and those that follow Tancredi and Angelica in their voyage of erotic discovery through the maze of used and abandoned apartments of the palace—these pages have diverted all critical attention from the rest of the chapter. The public themes of the historical novel, which reach their acme in the long monologue in which the prince rejects the Piedmontese envoy's invitation to participate in the new government of united Italy by becoming a member of its senate, and the love theme of the romance, whose high point of optimistic life-affirmation is placed in the *hortus conclusus* of a magic place where time stands still, have overshadowed other aspects of the story being told. The chapter, which takes place only one month after the preceding one, shows the situation that has crystallized after Angelica's engagement to Tancredi. Remorseful over his abandonment of Concetta, Tancredi brings a young fellow officer, the Lombard Cavriaghi, on a visit to Donnafugata: he hopes that Concetta may follow his own example and let self-interest and common sense rule her heart. But Concetta is deaf to Cavriaghi's wooing: "she looked at the sentimental little count with icy eyes, in whose depths one could even read a bit of contempt." . . . (p. 20)

It is no surprise then to find Concetta again in chapter 7, unmarried and forty. . . . Already on the way toward assuming the position of leadership in the family ("hegemony," Lampedusa calls it not without a touch of irony), a position which will later earn her the nickname of "La Grande Catherine" from one of her nephews . . . , it is she who has accompanied her father to consult a specialist in Naples and it is she who insists that a priest be called to his deathbed. In the prince's balance sheet of his life, in which the "happy moments" are no more than "golden specks" on the "immense ash-heap of liabilities," . . . Concetta figures as having provided him with the satisfaction of having one day discovered her beauty and character to be those of "a true Salina." . . . But with another deft, almost imperceptible touch, Lampedusa notes what it cost her to be a true Salina: she is the only one of those gathered at the prince's bedside—his son Francesco Paolo, his daughter Carolina, Tancredi, and Fabrizietto, but *not* Angelica—who does not weep. . . . It is a step in that process of petrification of feeling that had begun with the repeated numbing "transitions from a secret, warm world to an open, frozen one" . . . and that had made it possible for her to live with the pain of the double betrayal of her father and Tancredi. . . .

Thus chapter 8, which has been judged by most critics as the application of an unimaginative and overworked device for finishing off the novel by calling attention to its cyclical aspect, is the celebration of that member of the Salina family who has been most obviously sacrificed to the inexorable laws of historical development which, according to sound naturalistic doctrine, entrust the future to the "fittest." Beside the prince, oversized protagonist whose physical presence and philosophical reflections fill the pages until his death, Lampedusa has placed a quiet, cruelly overshadowed figure whose inner life actually explodes in the space he has created around her. The final chapter recapitulates her story, as Senator Tassoni unwittingly brings her a message from the long-since-dead Tancredi, "transmitted across that morass of time the dead can so rarely ford." . . . And together with the recapitulation comes also the interpretation: in rapid succession, insights born of depth psychology show Concetta that "there had been no enemies, but one single adversary, herself." . . . Throughout, Lampedusa's sympathy, which in the course of the novel had so often been on the prince's side, is unmistakably on Concetta's: hers is the story of "the desperate." . . . That she may not be every reader's idea of a "heroine" is quite another matter: neither Lucia in *I promessi sposi* nor Mena in *I Malavoglia,* the other two great understated heroines of Italian literature, has had a particularly good press.

At the end of **"Lezioni su Stendhal"** Lampedusa turns for a last time to a comparative evaluation of Stendhal's two masterpieces. He remarks wryly that his listeners were troubled by his having at one time singled out *Le Rouge et le noir* for the highest praise, while he had more recently assigned that place of preeminence to *La Chartreuse:* "it is true that I changed my mind. My irrepressible historiographical tendencies had misled me; as an aesthetic document of an historical period *Le Rouge et le noir* is of greater merit. From a lyrical, artistic, and human point of view it is *La Chartreuse* that excels." . . . These two aspects of the type of novel with which Lampedusa was concerned, aspects which find their separate and equal embodiment in his view of Stendhal's two masterpieces, are the inseparable poles around which his own ***Il gattopardo*** finds its unity. (pp. 20-2)

Olga Ragusa, "Stendhal, Tomasi di Lampedusa, and the Novel," in Comparative Literature Studies *(© 1973 by The Board of Trustees of the University of Illinois; reprinted by permission), Vol. X, No. 3, September, 1973 (and reprinted in a slightly different form in her* Narrative and Drama: Essays in Modern Italian Literature from Verga to Pasolini, *Mouton, 1976, pp. 1-34).**

JOHN GATT-RUTTER (essay date 1978)

[*In the following excerpt Gatt-Rutter examines Lampedusa's sense of history in* The Leopard, *as well as the narrative problems arising from the author's historiographical tendency.*]

> When philosophy paints its gloomy picture a form of life has grown old. It cannot be rejuvenated by the gloomy picture, but only understood. Only when dusk starts to fall does the owl of Minerva spread its wings and fly.

Hegel's words could have been written of ***Il gattopardo.*** There can hardly be a literary work, even a historical novel, so steeped in historicism or a novelist, since Scott, with such 'insopprimibili tendenze storiografiche' ['insuppressible historiographical tendency'], in the deepest and broadest sense, as Lampedusa. No novelist has shown with such sophisticated awareness and precision, and with such a tragic sense of human betrayal and self-betrayal, the shifts of class supremacy and the changing forms and methods of economic, political and social control. A Hegelian 'Cunning of Reason' (or a Marxian 'development in the relations of production and exchange') uses people to make history, but not as they would like to make it. History itself, not the Zeus-like Prince Fabrizio Salina, is the protagonist of ***Il gattopardo,*** as it is in any true historical novel. The book's chapter-titles are dates.

It may indeed appear that history provides the background rather than the foreground of the novel, even though the events themselves—the passing of the Bourbon Kingdom of the Two Sicilies—seal the tomb of eight hundred years of feudalism. True, we witness no battles. We do not meet Garibaldi. The 'action' of the school history-books is merely reported as hearsay. Fabrizio keeps out of it. But he cannot keep out of history. He in fact makes the historic decisions, even when he thinks he is abstaining from history. He advises the people of Donnafugata to vote for Unification; he arranges for Tancredi to marry the wealthy, beautiful but plebeian Angelica rather than his daughter Concetta, who is as fond of Tancredi as he is of her, and thus gives away what is left of his family's future; in the famous meeting with Chevalley, he turns down the offer of a seat on the new Senate and recommends Angelica's father, Sedàra, instead. He has power, which he abdicates. Fabrizio, described as the most intelligent member of his class, 'stava a contemplare la rovina del proprio ceto e del proprio patrimonio senza avere nessuna attività ed ancora minor voglia di porvi riparo' . . . ['looked on at the ruin of his own class and his own birthright without doing anything and with even less inclination to stem the tide']. (pp. 25-6)

Most critics—*gattopardeschi* or *anti-gattopardeschi*—have rather naively lifted out Fabrizio's extemporised statement to Chevalley of his 'philosophy' of geographical and social determinism and Sicilian immobility as if it were *the* philosophy of the book, of the author, and of history itself. Chevalley's own presence contradicts this. So does the figure of the self-made man, Sedàra, with whom the future lies; and Fabrizio contradicts himself, on the subject of Sicilian inertia, by proposing Sedàra's name, rather than his own, for the Senate. It is clear that what Fabrizio says of Sicily is only true of himself and most of his class. It is not even true of the whole of his class, as his nephew Tancredi proves, not to mention Fabrizio's own son, Giovanni, who has escaped to be a coal-merchant's clerk in London.

It is a paradox of Lampedusa's art (and not of his alone), and perhaps its main weakness, that misinterpretation of his book should be at one and the same time a tribute to his skill in making a living character of Fabrizio and a token of his failure to put Fabrizio into clear perspective. The paradox makes itself evident in the book's unresolved technical difficulties, which arise from the problem of reconciling the method of narrating by 'point of view' or 'interior monologue' (Lampedusa uses this latter term himself in his ***Lezioni su Stendhal***) with that of 'omniscience' ('il metodo di far narrare la storia da Dio' ['the method of having the story told by God'], to quote the same source).

Fabrizio's 'point of view' does not extend over the whole novel. It is not even absolute and continuous in those sections which it covers. Yet such is the power of the characterisation that Fabrizio's presence tends to fill the whole novel and overwhelm it, and his brilliance almost conceals his incompetence.

Lampedusa attempts to keep his protagonist within bounds by the use of an omniscience which is not that of God but that of history. He fails largely because of the fascinating complexity of his character: Fabrizio frequently anticipates (if only by the chance shifts of his reflective intelligence) both the future course of history and history's judgment of himself and his times—just as frequently as he mistakes both; he also frequently anticipates the author's, or the reader's, moral judgments of him. . . . It is the omniscience of Lampedusa's historical hindsight that explicitly steps in to correct the false perspective that Fabrizio is shortly to put before Chevalley:

> Don Fabrizio non poteva saperlo allora, ma una buona parte della neghittosità, dell'acquiescenza per la quale durante i decenni seguenti si doveva vituperare la gente del Mezzogiorno, ebbe la propria origine nello stupido annullamento della prima espressione di libertà che a questi si fosse mai presentata. . . . [Don Fabrizio could not have known it at the time, but a good part of the inertia, the servility for which the people of the South were to be reviled during the ensuing decades, had its origins in the senseless annulment of the first expression of liberty which opportunity had ever allowed them.]

This frequently clumsy intrusion of the historian upon the narrator is one of the least artistically successful of a number of devices which Lampedusa uses to establish a critical detachment of the reader from his protagonist—devices which, in Brechtian terms, might be called *Verfremdungseffekten*. Most notable of these are the chapters which revolve around other 'centres of consciousness'—Padre Pirrone's in the fifth chapter and Concetta's in the last. The extended time-span of the novel also emphasises the irony of history.

Still, these devices only emphasise what is already discernible through Fabrizio's own 'interior monologues': his bullying of his family and dependents; his weakness for Tancredi and Angelica; his neglect of his affairs; his betrayal of his family, of the values he purports to stand for, of himself, to one of the men he despises most. The crumbling of his estate and his class—so splendidly and discreetly suggested throughout the novel by the significant interplay of concrete details—is made by him to appear to himself and the reader as the inexorable work of Time and Death, as part of the deterministic, naturalistic rise and fall of civilisations, while all along he makes or avoids decisions which, within their measure of freedom (and, for a Sicilian Prince in 1860, it is a considerable one), help to determine the specific features of a political system. He *chooses* to fulfil the economic determinism advocated by the new capitalist hegemony represented by Sedàra.

And this brings us back to the present. For many have seen the parallel between the Risorgimento, with its unfulfilled promise, and the Resistance and its equally disappointing fruits. Numerous allusions suggest such a parallelism in the novel, and the emphasis on clerical influence in the final chapter is only too pointed.

'Se vogliamo che tutto rimanga come è, bisogna che tutto cambi.' ['If we want everything to stay as it is, everything has to change.'] Tancredi's paradox, which subtends the whole novel and could well be the historical judgment of the novel, beyond the intentions of its protagonists, cuts with both edges. Like Pareto's and Mosca's analyses of ruling groups, which the whole novel so closely echoes, it demystifies the historical transmission of power. (pp. 26-9)

John Gatt-Rutter, "Giuseppe Tomasi di Lampedusa's 'Il gattopardo': The Owl of Minerva," in his Writers and Politics in Modern Italy *(copyright © 1978 John Gatt-Rutter; Holmes & Meier Publishers, Inc., New York, reprinted by permission), Holmes & Meier, 1978, pp. 25-9.*

SERGIO PACIFICI (essay date 1979)

[*In the following excerpt Pacifici offers a general discussion of the primary elements of* The Leopard, *focusing on the novel's recurrent theme of the nobility of death.*]

By all standards, ***Il Gattopardo* [*The Leopard*]** . . . surely ranks as one of the most extraordinary and written-about novels to have appeared in post-World War II Italy. . . . [It] is also one of the most controversial books of fiction to have been published in Italy during the last one hundred years. The polemics sparked by ***The Leopard*** split the literary establishment in diametrically opposed factions, exalting the work as one of the most important, meaningful, and beautifully written in recent times, or condemning it for a variety of sins, usually as reactionary, fraudulent, structurally and stylistically archtraditional in an era of experimentation and openness. (p. 68)

What is ***The Leopard*** about? Is it history, autobiography, or fiction? Like many novels, it is a little of all three: but the three elements have been masterfully blended so as to give some rare insights into the nature of change and death. Life is a constant exposure to change—human, political, intellectual, historical—and in this respect the changes, which are the very elements of the fabric of existence, and as such part of life as well as of our preparation for death. Lampedusa is exceptional in feeling, and giving form to the preoccupation with death. To create a believable world in which his synthesis can be dramatically shown, rather than intellectually discussed, he takes us back a full century, to a delicate and central moment of the history of modern Italy and of the Salinas, a respected and powerful Sicilian family. (pp. 71-2)

The plot of ***The Leopard*** is unusually simple, a fact that has led more than one critic to complain that the book is very static. On the surface at least, the work would appear to be a historical novel: it is, after all, set in the 1860s, at the end of the *Risorgimento,* chronologically developed, and told from the vantage point of the actual date of the publication of the work, a point that permits the author to enjoy considerable detachment and insight. But the impression soon proves to be wrong, as we perceive that what we are going to get is not the reconstruction of a pivotal period in modern Italian history, but an interpretation of how those historical events have affected the characters in the story and, by implication, the entire nation. The changes about to take place are numerous and far-reaching; the very title of the book suggests, in an oblique manner, the irony of the situation: a "*gattopardo*" is a cheetah, or a crossbreed of lion and panther. But the prince is no longer the fast, sly, powerful and much-feared killer of the jungle: in point of fact, he is about to be dislodged by the jackals and the hyenas, two animals that came to symbolize the new rich that are making their entrance on the political scene, and take complete charge of the leadership.

The "*gattopardo,*" in short, is an "old" man watching history run its course without his being able to determine in any significant way the direction it will take. Hardly a "positive" hero, he is a skeptic who holds few illusions about life, and actually prepares himself for death which alone can free man from the suffering life compels him to endure. The only way open to him, if he is to preserve at least a measure of the power and influence he and his family have always enjoyed is by the alliance, through marriage, of his nephew Tancredi with Angelica—a union which is not without its share of irony. It is Don Fabrizio, born of a mixed marriage (a Sicilian father and a German mother) who lays the groundwork for the union of Tancredi (also the offspring of a mixed marriage) with Angelica. No one can predict, of course, how successful any human scheme will be. An intimation of this stance is found early in the novel, when the prince, in his daily visit to his garden, is attracted by a "somewhat crude," strong offense to his nose: "The Paul Neyron roses, whose cuttings he had himself bought in Paris, had degenerated; first stimulated and then enfeebled by the strong if languid pull of Sicilian earth, burned by apocalyptic Julies, they had changed into things like flesh-colored cabbages, obscene and distilling a dense, almost indecent, scent which no French horticulturist would have dared hope for." The comment might seem innocent: but when we complete our reading of the book, we realize how pointedly ironic (like so much of the novel) it is: the Sicilian soil (or Sicily itself) is not often receptive to flowers (or customs and ways of life) imported from the mainland. This notwithstanding, the marriage represents a chance worth taking, if for no other reason than that there are few other alternatives.

Alas, just as the marriage of the two lovely young people means a further thinning down of aristocratic blood, the "purity" of the Salinas is further weakened by Tancredi's unavoidable alliance with the forces of the national government. And, in a way, this is what the book is about—at least, in part. In the face of sweeping changes, just how does the ruling class adjust to the new facts? "If we want things to stay as they are," proclaims Tancredi at one point, "things must change," an observation that reflects accurately the scheming and turmoil of the 1860s and the decades that followed the realization of political unification. Indeed, it is precisely Tancredi's inventiveness, his determination not to allow himself to be drowned by the tempest of the *Risorgimento,* and his pragmatism, that attract the affection and faith of the prince in his nephew. . . . (pp. 73-4)

The impelling necessity to find ways to preserve the status quo, springs not only from an understandable desire to retain the family's influence, but also from a deep-seated conviction that Sicilians (or, for that matter, Southerners in general) do not really want any change, a thesis many Italian critics rejected outright. The prince's own skepticism toward the whole issue of change is symbolically depicted through his love of the stars and his impatience with the realities of everyday existence. A dedicated astronomer of an aristocratic sensitivity, he would like nothing less than to believe in the absolute permanence of the cosmos. As a serious scientist and mathematician, he knows that changes do occur in the "fixed stars," but such changes cannot be detected by the naked human eye as they occur over a time span measurable in terms of thousands or millions of years, thus justifying what is aptly called "permanence in transience." The prince's only hope is that all the changes in the sociopolitical order of the South will proceed at the same rate of speed as the stars'. (p. 75)

I think it is vital to point out that it is not change per se that the prince fears, but the futility of change that generally comes too slowly to be truly effective in molding the temperament of a large segment of the population. The prince's actions reveal his philosophical consistency: cognizant of the necessity of change, he goes no further than arranging the marriage of Tancredi and Angelica, which ultimately means little or nothing in the standing and fortune of the family. As a matter of fact, despite the prince's willingness to change the economic and personal relationships that have long prevailed between himself and his tenant farmers, we are given to see the apathy and incompetence the ruling class shows in its efforts to come to grips with the conditions of the new times.

The novel's interest in reality, in the world of objects, tangible things, and people, balances what is the other pervasive theme of the story, Fabrizio's love with death, carefully interwoven with his healthy sensuality. The insistence on death is evident from the words that open the book: *"Nunc et in hora mortis nostrae. Amen,"* and the final scene, in which the prince's faithful dog Bendicò, properly stuffed and preserved with other relics of the family, is thrown out of the window, "flung into a corner of the courtyard visited every day by the dustman."

The slow, agonizing death of a political order that for centuries shaped the quality of life in the *Mezzogiorno* is revealed through numerous, striking images of the death of people, animals, and nature. Indeed, in one way or another, the author manages to keep death prominently before us, particularly in the first part of the book: "Enclosed between three walls and a side of the house, [the garden's] seclusion gave it the air of a cemetery." "The real problem," so reasons the prince when thinking about the uncertain political situation, "is how to go on living this life of the spirit in its most sublime moments, those moments that are most like death." Death constantly haunts the prince, particularly when violence is its cause. What repels him in particular, however, is not the philosophical question of death, which his religious faith has enabled him to accept with a certain amount of serenity, but its visible horror, as when the body of a dead Royalist soldier is found in his garden, "his face covered in blood and vomit, his nails dug into the soil, crawling with ants," or the gruesome sight of a rabbit, killed during a hunting event with his accountant Ciccio Ferrata, or the open wagon, "stacked with bulls killed shortly before at the slaughterhouse, already quartered and exhibiting their intimate mechanism with the shamelessness of death," the prince sees as he returns from the ball in honor of Tancredi and his fiancée, Angelica.

While a great era is slowly dying around him, the prince is himself preparing for his own death. That he esteemed and loved few people is implicit in his attitudes and behavior. He is, however, consoled by the understanding that it is the fact of human mortality that serves to redress the mistakes we commit while we live, and teaches us to be more forgiving toward the failings of society as well as of the individual. With death, comes the end of all those illusions that give us mortals a reason for enduring the suffering life so generously bestowed upon us. "Growing old," notes Richard Kuhns in a brilliant essay on "Modernity and Death" in ***The Leopard,*** "approaching death, he [the prince] realizes that the earthly realm is no more his to rule in accordance with his will than the heavenly; both obey laws beyond human desire. The Prince ends his life more keenly, self-consciously aware of the necessities in both earth and heaven."

Ultimately, the novel, through its various characters, addresses itself to the question of fulfillment, a problem that must take into account the sufferings man must endure in his quest on earth. And here the picture becomes very clear indeed: no one has really attained the best he or she could and should have attained by reasons of his preparation, character, circumstances: Tancredi accepts the role granted him by the new government; Angelica turns out to be too absorbed in herself to be capable of giving of herself; Concetta, sacrificed by her father when her genuine love for Tancredi is brushed aside, is condemned to live a spinster; Stella, the prince's wife, is constantly excluded from any meaningful feeling, while her two other daughters live out their existence without ever being touched by love, marriage and a family; even the prince, for all his sensitivity, intelligence, power and so-called wisdom, takes one last glance at all the years he has lived, at all the things—good, bad or indifferent—he has done, and attempts to draw "a general balance sheet of his whole life, trying to sort out of the immense ash-heap of liabilities the golden flecks of happy moments. These were: two weeks before his marriage, six weeks after; half an hour when Paolo was born, when he felt proud of having prolonged by a twig the Salina tree (the pride had been misplaced, he knew that now, but there had been some genuine self-respect in it); a few talks with Giovanni before the latter vanished (a few monologues, if the truth were told, during which he had thought to find in the boy a kindred mind); and in many hours in the observatory, absorbed in abstract calculations and the pursuit of the unreachable. Could those latter hours be really put down to the credit of life? Were they not some sort of anticipatory gift of the beatitudes of death? It didn't matter, they had existed."

With these words, the prince sums up his entire existence, leaving us with the distinct awareness that little, if indeed anything, is changed by man's actions. They are far from encouraging words, just as the vision of life they express is anything but positive. His notions are not the ones we are likely to entertain and agree with. Taking issue with the prince's view of history, Andor Gomme comments: "There is corruption at the heart of the new regime because the heart is always corrupted. This is not only a message of despair, because of the breeding which allows one to look on it with good natured but supercilious cynicism" [see excerpt above, 1967]. Unquestionably, the novel by Giuseppe Tomasi di Lampedusa is pessimistic in the extreme. Perhaps, as Furio Felcini suggests, we ought to see the novel as a kind of metaphysical correlative of Lampedusa's own existence, lived in full knowledge that there would be no heir to carry on the illustrious family name. I prefer seeing it as a book whose very conception and creation was an affirmation of life, and as a brave and rare acceptance of the nobility of death. (pp. 76-8)

Sergio Pacifici, "The 'Southern' Novel," in his The Modern Italian Novel from Pea to Moravia *(copyright © 1979 by Southern Illinois University Press; reprinted by permission of Southern Illinois University Press), Southern Illinois University Press, 1979, pp. 47-78.**

ADDITIONAL BIBLIOGRAPHY

Barzini, Luigi. "Quest for a Lost Master." *The Reporter* 25, No. 4 (14 September 1961): 43-5.

An insightful biographical and critical essay, written after a visit in Palermo with Lampedusa's widow and uncle.

Brown, Calvin S. "Parallel Incidents in Émile Zola and Tomasi di Lampedusa." *Comparative Literature* XV, No. 3 (Summer 1963): 193-202.

Examines two episodes found in *The Leopard* which share affinities with two episodes in Zola's *La faute de l'abbé Mouret (Albine; or, The Abbe's Temptation)*, and concludes that there is strong evidence that Zola's work influenced Lampedusa.

Colquhoun, Archibald. "Lampedusa in Sicily: The Lair of the Leopard." *The Atlantic Monthly* 211, No. 2 (February 1963): 91-3, 98-110.

The most detailed biographical essay available in English. The critic, general editor of the Oxford Library of Italian Classics, translated Lampedusa's works into English.

Ehrenstein, David. "Leopard Redux." *Film Comment* 19, No. 5 (September-October 1983): 16-18.

Discusses Luchino Visconti's 1963 film adaptation of *The Leopard,* which stars Burt Lancaster as Don Fabrizio, Claudia Cardinale as Angelica, and Alain Delon as Tancredi. Ehrenstein offers high praise for Visconti's film, calling it "a rich orchestration of the novelistic and theatrical, full-bodied as Tolstoy, precise as Proust, held together by a vision of space and time as lucid as the screen has known."

Evans, Arthur, and Evans, Catherine. "'Salina e svelto': The Symbolism of Change in *Il gattopardo.*" *Wisconsin Studies in Contemporary Literature* 4, No. 3 (Autumn 1963): 298-304.

Examines the theme of spiritual and physical degeneration in *The Leopard.*

Fletcher, John. "Lampedusa." In his *New Directions in Literature: Critical Approaches to a Contemporary Phenomenon,* pp. 86-90. London: Calder and Boyars, 1968.

Examines the recurrent topic of death in *The Leopard.* Fletcher concludes that Lampedusa shares in "the disillusioned world-weariness of contemporary Italian literature, such as [Alberto] Moravia has rendered so familiar. And yet Lampedusa is a greater artist than Moravia. He stands with the film-director [Michelangelo] Antonioni, fully in the world class; he has left us one novel, but it is a masterpiece."

Forster, E. M. "The Prince's Tale," *The Spectator* 205, No. 6881 (13 May 1960); 702.

A favorable review of *The Leopard,* called by the critic a "noble book." Forster also wrote the introduction to *Two Stories and a Memory* [see excerpt above, 1962].

Gilbert, John. "The Metamorphosis of the Gods in *Il gattopardo.*" *MLN* 81, No. 2 (January 1966): 22-32.

Examines the theme of the degeneration and passing of traditional values in *The Leopard.*

Jonas, Ilsedore B. "Tomasi di Lampedusa (1896-1957)." In her *Thomas Mann and Italy,* translated by Betty Crouse, pp. 121-24. University: University of Alabama Press, 1979.

Addresses the question of Mann's literary influence on Lampedusa. Jonas concludes that "unquestionably, similarities and parallels can be established in connection with Thomas Mann and Lampedusa, which however probably rest more on their mutual literary models—the great tradition of the Russian and French novel of the nineteenth century—than on a direct influence of Thomas Mann on the Sicilian author."

Nolan, David. "Lampedusa's *The Leopard.*" *Studies* LV, No. 220 (Winter 1966): 403-14.

An excellent general essay on *The Leopard.* Nolan's study examines the fame of Lampedusa's novel, its subject and theme, its technique and characterization, its indebtedness to the influence of Stendhal and Leo Tolstoy, and the recurrent concern with death and the need to accept death as a necessary part of life.

Pritchett, V. S. "A Sicilian Novel." *New Statesman* LIX, No. 1522 (14 May 1960): 721-22.

Favorably reviews *The Leopard.* Pritchett states that in his novel Lampedusa "has taken everything from Stendhal except his coldness and abruptness."

(Harry) Sinclair Lewis

1885-1951

(Also wrote under pseudonym of Tom Graham) American novelist, short story writer, essayist, critic, dramatist, journalist, and poet.

The Granger Collection, New York

One of the foremost American novelists of the 1920s, Lewis is regarded as the author of some of the most effective satires in American literature. Along with the noted critic and essayist H. L. Mencken, he vengefully attacked the dullness, the smug provincialism, and the socially enforced conformity of the American middle class. Lewis's fame rests upon five satiric novels published during the 1920s: *Main Street, Babbitt, Arrowsmith, Elmer Gantry,* and *Dodsworth.* In these works, he created grotesque yet disturbingly recognizable caricatures of middle-class Americans with a skill for which he is often likened to Charles Dickens. In 1930 Lewis was awarded the Nobel Prize in literature, becoming the first American to be so honored.

Lewis was born in the small town of Sauk Centre, Minnesota, and was raised to follow the traditions of his middle-class, Protestant home town. As scholars have observed, throughout his early life Lewis was torn between two conflicting desires. The first was to conform to the standards of sameness, of respectability, and of financial advancement as prescribed by his family and by the town. Opposing this desire to be a "Regular Guy" was Lewis's need to acknowledge his own nonconformist nature and ambitions: his agnosticism, his literary inclinations, and his general rebellion against the village's preference for unquestioning adherence to established standards of thought, faith, and aesthetics. After writing news stories and working at various odd jobs in the offices of Sauk Centre's two newspapers during his teens, Lewis—to the townsfolks' disapproval—left the Midwest to attend a university in the East. During his years at Yale, which were frequently interspersed with travel and temporary employment, he read voraciously and published a number of light stories and poems. For a time Lewis worked as the furnaceman at Upton Sinclair's Helicon Hall, a socialist communal experiment in Englewood, New Jersey, and then went on to graduate from Yale in 1908. He married writer Grace Hegger and drifted about America for the next few years, writing and selling short stories to *The Saturday Evening Post* and other popular journals. A prolific writer with an abundant imagination, Lewis even sold ideas for stories to novelist Jack London during London's final years.

For the most part, Lewis's early short stories and novels reflect what the author termed the "Sauk-Centricities" of his own nature; they are conventional, optimistic, lightly humorous, and were written for a middle-class audience. Of Lewis's apprentice fiction, critics generally cite two works that foreshadow the skill and themes of the author's novels of the 1920s: *The Job,* a novel that evidences traces of harsh realism as it tells of a small-town woman's struggle for success as a businesswoman in a large city; and the story "I'm a Stranger Here Myself," which narrates the adventures of a smug, narrow-minded Midwestern couple who condescend to leave "God's Country" for a vacation in Florida. These works marked the first significant sign of Lewis's discontent with writing about what William Dean Howells termed "the more smiling aspects of life, which are the more American." In 1920 Lewis published *Main Street,* the novel he had long intended to write in revolt against the sentimental myth of the American small town.

With *Main Street* Lewis assumed the leadership of the movement known as "the revolt from the village" in American literature, culminating a tradition begun by Mark Twain, Harold Frederic, Edgar Lee Masters, and Sherwood Anderson, among others. The partly autobiographical novel portrays the frustrations of Carol Kennicott's idealistic crusades to bring elements of liveliness and culture to her new husband's home town of Gopher Prairie, Minnesota, an ugly little settlement populated by an appalling collection of blustering, inarticulate oafs and prying, vicious shrews. To *Main Street*'s early readers and critics, the work was perceived as a damning indictment of traditional nineteenth-century values, which were completely unacceptable to the jaded, sophisticated climate of the Jazz Age. The new generation, fresh from witnessing the mechanized mass-slaughter of World War I, was ready for literature that would reflect its rejection of genteel optimism, hidebound nationalism, and traditional religion, and it embraced Lewis's next two novels as it had earlier embraced *Main Street.* Of Lewis's five major satires, *Babbitt* and *Arrowsmith* are widely considered his most accomplished works. In *Babbitt,* Lewis

skewered the loud, hypocritical American businessman as well as members of America's public service organizations and booster clubs, with their endless, vapid speeches and inane rituals. In the character of businessman George F. Babbitt, Lewis created a literary archetype equal in stature to Mark Twain's Huckleberry Finn. *Arrowsmith* tells of the battles of a humanitarian scientist to conduct medical research against the beckoning forces of fame, commercialism, and material comforts. Widely acclaimed as one of America's most significant voices of the postwar era, Lewis won the 1926 Pulitzer Prize in fiction for *Arrowsmith,* but refused to accept the award, claiming that it was intended only for champions of American wholesomeness. Evidence from Lewis's letters suggests that another, less idealistic reason for his refusal was his anger that Edith Wharton's *The Age of Innocence* had been chosen over *Main Street* as winner of the 1921 Pulitzer Prize.

In 1927 storms of both protest and of acclamation erupted at the appearance of Lewis's "preacher novel," *Elmer Gantry.* An all-out attack on Fundamentalist Protestantism as practiced by such flamboyant evangelists as Billy Sunday and Aimee Semple McPherson, the book was praised by Mencken and several other major critics as a fair-minded exposé that revealed the essential fraudulence of Christianity and the gullibility of its adherents. The majority of critics, however, have joined Walter Lippmann in judging *Elmer Gantry* to be a deeply flawed novel, one in which Lewis's satiric intent is crushed beneath his hatred of the faith he had rejected as a young man. A year after the publication of this, the weakest but most controversial of his five major novels, Lewis, who had divorced his first wife, married the distinguished journalist Dorothy Thompson. Thompson was a major influence on Lewis's work and thought for the rest of his life. In 1930 the couple traveled to Stockholm, where Lewis received the Nobel Prize for his literary achievement. In his now-famous acceptance speech, Lewis blasted the entire American literary tradition up until roughly his own era, and then hailed the rising new generation of the nation's writers, praising Ernest Hemingway, John Dos Passos, Thomas Wolfe, and several others. Lewis's own artistic stature had reached its zenith with the appearance in 1929 of *Dodsworth,* a novel in which a harried, disillusioned American businessman seeks peace of mind through travel in Europe. Considered one of the best of Lewis's satires, *Dodsworth* nonetheless marked the end of his preeminence as a major novelist; he never again wrote with the skill and power exhibited in his landmark satires of the 1920s.

Critics continue to speculate about the reasons for Lewis's literary decline during the last two decades of his life. Of all the theories offered, from his failure to complete a proposed novel on American labor to the possibility of his having strained to compete professionally with his wife, it is fairly certain that the Great Depression had the most blighting effect on his talent; for with much of the American middle class jobless and impoverished, Lewis lost both his reading audience and the target of his satiric jibes. During the rest of his career, Lewis periodically lectured, taught university writing courses, contributed book reviews to various magazines, and turned out a succession of relatively undistinguished novels. Among these, three contain traces of the early satiric skill and have received more favorable critical treatment than the others: they are *It Can't Happen Here,* which documents a plausible fascist takeover of America from within; *Cass Timberlane,* a broadside aimed at the institution of marriage; and *Kingsblood Royal,* which attacks racial bigotry. Lewis was living in Italy, where he had just completed *World So Wide*—a novel that resurrects businessman Sam Dodsworth of the author's earlier work—when he died of heart disease, in 1951.

A common concern among critics of Lewis's work is the ambivalent attitude expressed throughout the author's mature fiction toward the American middle class. In a recurrently cited example, Carol Kennicott of *Main Street* is alternately depicted as a sensitive, intelligent woman and as a pretentious, naive whiner. Her husband Will is likewise portrayed as at once a bellicose lout and as a practical, warm, and loving man. Speaking of *Main Street* in a conversation with Charles Breasted, Lewis acknowledged his longstanding love/hate relationship with small-town America, admitting that Carol is a portrait of himself: "always groping for something she isn't capable of attaining, always dissatisfied, always restlessly straining to see what lies just over the horizon, intolerant of her surroundings, yet lacking any clearly defined vision of what she really wants to do or to be." Lewis's lack of a clear vision of life and his impatient nature are often noted as crucial to understanding the weakness of his fiction: the occasionally shrill tone, the sometimes overly harsh exaggerations of society's foibles, and the bleak outlook that remains even after the fooleries of the "booboisie" are exposed. In praise of Lewis's ability, critics note his superb skill at caricaturing and mimicking the appearance and speech of the common American. And although Lewis's work is not today the subject of extensive critical discussion, in the author's time he performed the role of American gadfly with a power unequalled except by Thomas Paine, Mark Twain, and H. L. Mencken, according to critic Sheldon Norman Grebstein. His five major satires not only introduced such definitive terms as "Main Street," "Babbitt," and "Babbittry" into common usage, but they also paved the way for much of the self-critical realistic fiction of mid-century American literature. As Lewis's biographer, Mark Schorer, has written: "In any strict literary sense, he was not a great writer, but without his writing one cannot imagine modern American literature."

(See also *TCLC*, Vol. 4; *Contemporary Authors*, Vol. 104; *Dictionary of Literary Biography*, Vol. 9: *American Novelists, 1910-1945;* and *Dictionary of Literary Biography Documentary Series*, Vol. 1.)

PRINCIPAL WORKS

Hike and the Aeroplane [as Tom Graham] (novel) 1912
Our Mr. Wrenn: The Romantic Adventures of a Gentle Man (novel) 1914
The Trail of the Hawk: A Comedy of the Seriousness of Life (novel) 1915
The Job (novel) 1917
Free Air (novel) 1919
Main Street: The Story of Carol Kennicott (novel) 1920
Babbitt (novel) 1922
Arrowsmith (novel) 1925; also published as *Martin Arrowsmith,* 1925
Mantrap (novel) 1926
Elmer Gantry (novel) 1927
The Man Who Knew Coolidge: Being the Soul of Lowell Schmaltz, Constructive and Nordic Citizen (novel) 1928
Cheap and Contented Labor: The Picture of a Southern Mill Town in 1929 (essay) 1929
Dodsworth (novel) 1929
Ann Vickers (novel) 1933
Work of Art (novel) 1934

It Can't Happen Here (novel) 1935
Jayhawker [with Lloyd Lewis] (drama) 1935
Selected Short Stories of Sinclair Lewis (short stories) 1935
The Prodigal Parents (novel) 1938
Bethel Merriday (novel) 1940
Gideon Planish (novel) 1943
Cass Timberlane (novel) 1945
Kingsblood Royal (novel) 1947
The God-Seeker (novel) 1949
World So Wide (novel) 1951
From Main Street to Stockholm: Letters of Sinclair Lewis, 1919-1930 (letters) 1952
The Man from Main Street: Selected Essays and Other Writings, 1904-1950 (essays and criticism) 1953

[R. D. TOWNSEND] (essay date 1914)

[*Townsend favorably reviews the first novel of Lewis's literary apprenticeship,* Our Mr. Wrenn, *and cites Lewis as a promising new author.*]

[**"Our Mr. Wrenn"** is] a promising story by a new writer. At times it reminds one of Mr. H. G. Wells when in his younger writing days he described the life of a draper's assistant, at times of O. Henry because Mr. Lewis has the knack of making New York in its ordinarily humdrum aspects alive and interesting. There is no imitation, however. Mr. Lewis has his own methods of realism, and there is more than a hint of the romantic disposition underneath the outwardly commonplace nature of "our Mr. Wrenn." Constructively the story is unsatisfactory, but it certainly arouses attention—and expectation also.

[*R. D. Townsend*], *in a review of "Our Mr. Wrenn," in* The Outlook, *May 2, 1914, p. 46.*

W. D. HOWELLS (letter date 1916)

[*Howells was the chief progenitor of American Realism and the most influential American literary critic during the late nineteenth century. He was the author of nearly three dozen novels, few of which are read today. Despite his eclipse, he stands as one of the major literary figures of the nineteenth century: he successfully weaned American literature away from the sentimental romanticism of its infancy, earning the popular sobriquet "the Dean of American Letters." Four years before his death, Howells was introduced to Lewis in St. Augustine, Florida, where each was vacationing. At their meeting, Lewis presented Howells with a copy of his latest novel,* The Trail of the Hawk. *Shortly thereafter, Howells sent Lewis the following letter praising the younger writer's work. Less than fifteen years after their meeting, in his famous Nobel acceptance speech, Lewis attacked Howells as a writer who held "the code of a pious old maid whose greatest delight was to have tea at the vicarage."*]

Dear Mr. Lewis:

I did not like your boy [the protagonist of ***The Trail of the Hawk***] in the beginning; I thought him overdone; and so dropped the book for a while. Today I took it up and read about the flying, from the mob scene in California to the end of the flying at New Haven. It was all good, BETTER, BEST. The go was full of throbs, and the people real and palpable. I am awfully glad of it. Now I shall keep on to the end—I hope.

W. D. Howells, in a letter to Sinclair Lewis on February 11, 1916 (reprinted by permission of William W. Howells on behalf of the William Dean Howells Estate), in Sinclair Lewis: An American Life *by Mark Schorer, McGraw-Hill Book Company Inc., 1961, p. 231.*

SINCLAIR LEWIS (letter date 1920)

[*Writing to his publisher shortly after the appearance of* Main Street, *Lewis delineates the character of George F. Babbitt, the protagonist of his yet-unwritten next novel. Lewis compares Babbitt to Will and Carol Kennicott, the principal characters in* Main Street.]

Dear Alf:

[Babbitt] is ambitious, very much so, but "ambition" gives an idea of a man who climbs very high, whereas Babbitt never becomes more than a ten-thousand-a-year real estate man. He is the typical T[ired] B[usiness] M[an], the man you hear drooling in the Pullman smoker; but having once so seen him, I want utterly to develop him so that he will seem not just typical but an individual. I want the novel to be the G[reat] A[merican] N[ovel] in so far as it crystallizes and makes real the Average Capable American. No one has done it, I think; no one has even *touched* it except Booth Tarkington in *Turmoil* and *Magnificent Ambersons;* and he romanticizes away all bigness. Babbitt is a little like Will Kennicott but bigger, with a bigger field to work on, more sensations, more perceptions. . . . He is all of us Americans at 46, prosperous but worried, wanting—passionately—to seize something more than motor cars and a house *before it's too late*. Yet, utterly unlike Carol, it never even occurs to him that he might live in Europe, might like poetry, might be a senator; he is content to live and work in the city of Zenith, which is, as everybody knows, the best little ole city in the world. But he would like for once the flare of romantic love, the satisfaction of having left a mark on the city, and a let-up in his constant warring on competitors, and when his beloved friend Riesling commits suicide, he suddenly says, "Oh hell, what's the use of the cautious labor to which I've given everything"—only for a little while is he discontented, though. . . . I want to make Babbitt big in his realness, in his relation to all of us, not in the least exceptional, yet dramatic, passionate, struggling. (p. 59)

Sinclair Lewis, in a letter to Alfred Harcourt on December 28, 1920, in his From Main Street to Stockholm: Letters of Sinclair Lewis, 1919-1930, *edited by Harrison Smith (copyright, 1952, and renewed 1980 by the Executors of the Estate of Sinclair Lewis; reprinted by permission of the Executors of the Estate of Sinclair Lewis), Harcourt, Brace and Company, 1952, pp. 59-60.*

H. L. MENCKEN (essay date 1921)

[*From the era of World War I until the early years of the Great Depression, Mencken was one of the most influential figures in American letters. His strongly individualistic, irreverent outlook on life and his vigorous, invective-charged writing style helped establish the iconoclastic spirit of the Jazz Age and significantly shaped the direction of American literature. As a social and literary critic—the roles for which he is best known—Mencken was the scourge of evangelical Christianity, public service organi-*

zations, literary censorship, boosterism, provincialism, democracy, all advocates of personal or social improvement, and every other facet of American life that he perceived as humbug. In his literary criticism, Mencken encouraged American writers to shun the anglophilic, moralistic bent of the nineteenth century and to practice Realism. He was an outspoken champion of the works of Theodore Dreiser, Sherwood Anderson, F. Scott Fitzgerald, and Lewis. Mencken's first contact with Lewis was in 1916, when the latter's short story "I'm a Stranger Here Myself" *was submitted for publication in* The Smart Set, *a literary magazine co-edited by Mencken and George Jean Nathan. According to Nathan, four years after the story's appearance Lewis was introduced to himself and to Mencken at the New York apartment of T. R. Smith, managing editor of* The Century. *Intoxicated and boisterous, Lewis proceeded to wrap an arm around the neck of each* Smart Set *editor and bellow in the ear of each that he had recently written "the gottdamn best book of its kind that this here gottdamn country has had and don't you guys forget it! I'm a-telling you! . . . Just wait till you read the gottdamn thing. You've got a treat coming, Georgie and Hank, and don't you boys make no mistake about that!" Enduring Lewis's self-endorsing uproar for more than a half hour, Mencken and Nathan fled Smith's apartment at the first opportunity for the haven of a nearby bar, where Mencken groaned, "Of all the idiots I've ever laid eyes on, that fellow is the worst!" Three days later, Nathan received a letter from Mencken, which read, in part: "Dear George: Grab hold of the bar rail, steady yourself, for a terrible shock! I've just read the advance sheets of the book of that* Lump *we met at Schmidt's and, by God he has done the job! It's a genuinely excellent piece of work. Get it as soon as you can and take a look." Shortly thereafter, Mencken wrote the following glowing review of Lewis's novel,* Main Street. *Throughout the 1920s, Mencken praised Lewis's books as resounding indictments of America's provincial stupidity.*]

Authors with their pockets full of best-seller money are bitten by high ambition, and strive heroically to scramble out of the literary Cloaca Maxima. Now and then one of them succeeds, bursting suddenly into the light of the good red sun with the foul liquors of the depths still streaming from him, like a prisoner loosed from some obscene dungeon. . . . A few months ago I recorded the case of Zona Gale, emerging from her stew of glad books with *Miss Lulu Bett*. Now comes another fugitive, his face blanched by years in the hulks, but his eyes alight with high purpose. His name is Sinclair Lewis, and the work he offers is a novel called ***Main Street***. . . .

This ***Main Street*** I commend to your polite attention. It is, in brief, good stuff. It presents characters that are genuinely human, and not only genuinely human but also authentically American; it carries them through a series of transactions that are all interesting and plausible; it exhibits those transactions thoughtfully and acutely, in the light of the social and cultural forces underlying them; it is well written, and full of a sharp sense of comedy, and rich in observation, and competently designed. Superficially, the story of a man and his wife in a small Minnesota town, it is actually the typical story of the American family—that is, of the family in its first stage, before husband and wife have become lost in father and mother. The average American wife, I daresay, does not come quite so close to downright revolt as Carol Kennicott, but that is the only exaggeration, and we may well overlook it. Otherwise, she and her Will are triumphs of the national normalcy—she with her vague stirrings, her unintelligible yearnings, her clumsy gropings, and he with his magnificent obtuseness, his childish belief in meaningless phrases, his intellectual deafness and nearsightedness, his pathetic inability to comprehend the turmoil that goes on within her. Here is the essential tragedy of American life, and if not the tragedy, then at least the sardonic farce; the disparate cultural development of male and female, the great strangeness that lies between husband and wife when they begin to function as members of society. The men, sweating at their sordid concerns, have given the women leisure, and out of that leisure the women have fashioned disquieting discontents. To Will Kennicott, as to most other normal American males, life remains simple; do your work, care for your family, buy your Liberty Bonds, root for your home team, help to build up your lodge, venerate the flag. But to Carol it is far more complex and challenging. She has become aware of forces that her husband is wholly unable to comprehend, and that she herself can comprehend only in a dim and muddled way. The ideas of the great world press upon her, confusing her and making her uneasy. She is flustered by strange heresies, by romantic personalities, by exotic images of beauty. To Kennicott she is flighty, illogical, ungrateful for the benefits that he and God have heaped upon her. To her he is dull, narrow, ignoble.

Mr. Lewis depicts the resultant struggle with great penetration. He is far too intelligent to take sides—to turn the thing into a mere harangue against one or the other. Above all, he is too intelligent to take the side of Carol, as nine novelists out of ten would have done. He sees clearly what is too often not seen—that her superior culture is, after all, chiefly bogus—that the oafish Kennicott, in more ways than one, is actually better than she is. Her war upon his Philistinism is carried on with essentially Philistine weapons. Her dream of converting a Minnesota prairie town into a sort of Long Island suburb, with overtones of Greenwich Village and the Harvard campus, is quite as absurd as his dream of converting it into a second Minneapolis, with overtones of Gary, Ind., and Paterson, N.J. When their conflict is made concrete and dramatic by the entrance of a *tertium quid,* the hollowness of her whole case is at once made apparent, for this *tertium quid* is a Swedish trousers-presser who becomes a moving-picture actor. It seems to me that the irony here is delicate and delicious. This, then, is the end-product of the Maeterlinck complex! Needless to say, Carol lacks the courage to decamp with her Scandinavian. Instead, she descends to sheer banality. That is, she departs for Washington, becomes a war-worker, and rubs noses with the suffragettes. In the end, it goes without saying, she returns to Gopher Prairie and the hearth-stone of her Will. The fellow is at least honest. He offers her no ignominious compromise. She comes back under the old rules, and is presently nursing a baby. Thus the true idealism of the Republic, the idealism of its Chambers of Commerce, its Knights of Pythias, its Rotary Clubs and its National Defense Leagues, for which Washington froze at Valley Forge and Our Boys died at Château-Thierry—thus this genuine and unpolluted article conquers the phoney idealism of Nietzsche, Edward W. Bok, Dunsany, George Bernard Shaw, Margaret Anderson, Mrs. Margaret Sanger, Percy Mackaye and the I.W.W.

But the mere story, after all, is nothing; the virtue of the book lies in its packed and brilliant detail. It is an attempt, not to solve the American cultural problem, but simply to depict with great care a group of typical Americans. This attempt is extraordinarily successful. The figures often remain in the flat; the author is quite unable to get that poignancy into them which Dreiser manages so superbly; one seldom sees into them very deeply or feels with them very keenly. But in their externals, at all events, they are done with uncommon skill. In particular, Mr. Lewis represents their speech vividly and accurately. It would be hard to find a false note in the dialogue, and it would be impossible to exceed the verisimilitude of the various extracts from the Gopher Prairie paper, or of the sermon by a Methodist dervish in the Gopher Prairie Wesleyan cathedral, or of a speech by a boomer at a banquet of the Chamber of Commerce. Here Mr. Lewis lays on with obvious malice, but always he keeps within the bounds of probability, always his realism holds up. It is, as I have said, good stuff. I have read no more genuinely amusing novel for a long while. (pp. 279-82)

H. L. Mencken, "Sinclair Lewis: The Story of An American Family" (originally published as "Consolation—I—An American Novel," in The Smart Set, *Vol. LXIV, No. 1, January, 1921), in his* H. L. Mencken's "Smart Set" Criticism, *edited by William H. Nolte (copyright © 1968 by Cornell University; used by permission of the publisher, Cornell University Press), Cornell University Press, 1968, pp. 279-82.*

MAY SINCLAIR (essay date 1922)

[*Sinclair was one of the earliest authors to incorporate the theories of modern psychology into her fiction. In novels such as* The Divine Fire *(1904),* The Three Sisters *(1914), and* Mary Olivier *(1919) she utilized the psychoanalytic concepts of Sigmund Freud to explore the subtle consequences of sexual sublimation. In the following review of* Babbitt, *Sinclair hails the novel as a much better work than* Main Street.]

In **"Main Street"** Mr. Sinclair Lewis wrote the history of a highly complex organism, the street that stood for the little Middle-Western town, the Middle-Western town that stood for every provincial town in the United States: a town that was Everytown and yet itself, given in all its raw, reeking individuality. The characters in **"Main Street"** are not merely individual men and women, they are cells in that organism, that thing of habits, of shrewd eternal instincts, which is more powerful than they, which resists and conquers and absorbs the foreign elements that invade it. **"Main Street"** is the story of the revolt of an individual and her defeat by the community. Its heroine is a crude and pretentious enthusiast for "culture" sick with discontent. Moved by a feverish loathing of her environment, she tries to reform Main Street, to impose on it her own moth-like passion for artificial light, to lead it onward and upward. And Main Street, adamant in its solidarity, and completely satisfied with itself, refuses to be led and enlightened. By sheer inertia it crushes the fluttering devotee of the ideal. In the earlier novel the protagonist is Main Street, the community. Mr. Sinclair Lewis's presentation of the conflict is inimitable. But in the nature of the case the interest is scattered, and the book lacks a certain concentration and unity. It is like his description of Main Street, where every house stands out, distinct and vivid, where you smell the ash-heaps in every back yard, but the reader is left to gather these details together, to join house to house down the long vista, as best he may. He is given no clear massive image of Main Street as a whole.

In his last novel, **"Babbitt,"** Mr. Sinclair Lewis triumphs precisely where in **"Main Street"** he failed. By fixing attention firmly on one superb central figure he has achieved an admirable effect of unity and concentration. Not once in all his 401 close-packed pages does your gaze wander, or desire to wander, from the personality of George F. Babbitt (of the Babbitt-Thompson Realty Company). You are rapt, fascinated, from the moment when you find him waking in the sleeping porch of his house at Floral Heights to that final moment of sorrowful insight when he sees himself as he is. You have the complete, brilliant portrait of a man. You know what he does and his gesture in doing it; what he says, with every trick of speech, every tone and accent; what he thinks and feels, openly and secretly. Nothing is hidden from you, nothing is left mysterious and unaccounted for. Mr. Sinclair Lewis has done his work with a remorseless and unfaltering skill. (p. 1)

It is a very remarkable achievement to have made such a thing as Babbitt so lovable and so alive that you watch him with a continuous thrill of pleasurable excitement. Mr. Sinclair Lewis's method of presenting him is masterly, and in the highest sense creative because it is synthetic. He does not dissect and analyze his subject, but exhibits him all of a piece in a whole skin, yet under such powerful X-rays that the organism is transparent; you see all its articulated internal machinery at work. Never for a moment do you detect the clever hand of the surgeon with his scalpel. Not once does so much as the shadow of Mr. Sinclair Lewis come between you and Babbitt. In his hands Babbitt becomes stupendous and significant.

The minor characters have not perhaps the solidity and richness of the persons of **"Main Street,"** because in **"Main Street"** the protagonist is the community, and all the cast are principals, significant members of the group. Here the minor characters are important only in their relation to the central figure, but (with the exception of one fantastic caricature, the poet, Chum Frink) each one of them is drawn with the same devout reverence for reality; each is alive and whole in its own skin. . . . If reality is the supreme test, Mr. Sinclair Lewis's novel is a great work of art.

And it is an advance on its predecessor in style, construction and technique. One might say it would have as many readers but that "popularity" is a mysterious and unpredictable quality. For though nobody will recognize himself in George F. Babbitt, everybody will recognize somebody else. Here, as in **"Main Street,"** Mr. Sinclair Lewis has hidden the profound and deterrent irony of his intention under the straightforward innocence and simplicity of his tale. (p. 11)

May Sinclair, "The Man from Main Street," in The New York Times Book Review *(copyright © 1922 by The New York Times Company; reprinted by permission), September 24, 1922, pp. 1, 11.*

STUART P. SHERMAN (essay date 1925)

[*Sherman was for many years considered one of America's most conservative literary critics. During the early twentieth century he was influenced by New Humanism (or Neo-Humanism), a literary movement which maintained that the aesthetic quality of any literary work must be subordinate to its support of traditional moral values. During ten years of service as a literary critic at* The Nation, *Sherman established himself as a champion of the long-entrenched Anglo-Saxon, genteel tradition in American letters and as a bitter enemy of literary Naturalism and its proponents. Theodore Dreiser and his chief defender, H. L. Mencken, were Sherman's special targets during the World War I era, as Sherman perceived the Naturalism they espoused to be a life-denying cultural product of America's enemy, Germany. During the 1920s, Sherman became the editor of the book review section of the* New York Herald Tribune, *a move that coincided with a distinct liberalization of his hitherto staunch critical tastes; in the last years of his life, he even praised his old enemies Dreiser and Mencken. In the following review, Sherman applauds* Arrowsmith *as a far better novel than both* Main Street *and* Babbitt.]

"Main Street" and **"Babbitt"** raised the question whether Mr. Lewis was anything but a satirist, rudely blurting out his boredom at the humdrum and vulgarity of our great heroic middle class—a humdrum and a vulgarity which many people consider it the part of good citizenship to accept and silently to endure as in the order of nature. . . .

Sooner or later, I surmised, his faculty of admiration would crave release and exercise, and then we should have a new sort of book to talk about. (p. 1)

[**"Arrowsmith"**] is winged with derision on one side, but with admiration on the other. It is a book with a butt, but it is also a book with a hero, with several heroes, and it is a far better book than **"Babbitt."** Before I say anything more about that I request permission to depose that I am not under any oath or obligation to applaud each of Mr. Lewis's novels more loudly than the last.

"Main Street" immediately captivated me with the rich, pungent odor of new tilled soil, with the Hogarthian vigor of its caricatures, its exuberance of comic perception. But **"Babbitt,"** which the general cry of reviewers hailed as superior to its predecessor, I thought less intensely and vividly conceived than **"Main Street"**—the character drawing less sharp and memorable, the entire social picture inadequately lighted.

"Main Street" had in the way of material civilization, led to Zenith. But where should we go from there? To New York? Mr. Lewis did not even suggest New York—though of course it is the Mahomet's Paradise at the end of **"Main Street."** He rang down the curtain, leaving us with a sense that nothing was to be gained by going anywhere from Zenith—in any of the directions toward which its inhabitants were headed.

Now, the sense that life must be lived but that life is not, in any direction, worth while is a futile sense. It is not worth talking about. No great work of art with which I am acquainted communicates as the ultimate gist of its message the sense of futility. Even a beautiful and *ineffectual* angel beating *in the void* its luminous wings *in vain* has at least been beautiful and luminous. But Mr. George F. Babbitt's wings were neither luminous nor beautiful, and he was ineffectual. All that prevents Mr. Babbitt from being utterly depressing is his restlessness. That is something, but not much.

A social historian who planned an American *comédie humaine*—a social historian whose intelligence moved at the ordinary tempo, would obviously have attempted in his next book to enter the territory of Mrs. Wharton. Perhaps Mr. Lewis has not adequately observed that territory. I do not know. There are several chapters in the latter part of **"Arrowsmith"** which suggest that he has glanced into it but that he grew tired of its futility before he got there, and was unwilling, even for the duration of one novel, to seem seeking a way out of the humdrum and vacuity of American life through the inanities of our fashionable "leisure class."

At any rate, in **"Arrowsmith"** Mr. Lewis turns from the small town and the big town, which he has treated, and from "Society," which he has not treated, to a profession which runs through all the social strata; he turns his satire upon the medical profession and upon institutions for scientific research. The titular hero's career takes him from the bottom to the top. (pp. 1-2)

The book is long but the narrative is not prolix. It goes straight, hard and fast from the opening paragraph to the last, with the earnest fullness of a writer who is dealing with a superabundance of very rich material, yet with marvelous syncopations and abridgments, and in a style of almost telegraphic succinctness. Each of its eight or nine scenes is firmly constituted, impregnated with its proper colors and odors, peopled with the men and women appropriate to it, busy with the talk, action and passion that belong to it.

The language employed by the characters is that used in the United States of America. The medical students and the professors; the rival country doctors; the Nautilus board of health and its political friends and enemies and their wives; the suave money-making Chicago surgeons; the McGurk Institute, with its inter-departmental jealousies, its fussy, pompous director, and the ladies of means and social position who peep in on the experiments and patronize the experimenters and occasionally carry off a promising one in a limousine and marry him—each of these groups authentically buzzes and hums and fusses about one of the scenes of Martin's labors, using its own highly flavored lingo, ranging from medical college slang through the Walt Whitman poetry of the Nautilus board of health to the elaborate technicalities of bacteriological research.

I suppose there is more science and scientific talk in **"Arrowsmith"** than in any other novel that has hitherto appeared in the world. Some persons, I hear, think there is more than the populace will stand. I think not. Consider those feelers of the public pulse, the newspapers; consider their radio sections. Science as Mr. Lewis handles it is hot with the latest master-passion of this age. He himself is the son of a country doctor, and some of his medical knowledge came to him with his bread and milk. He accounts for his bacteriological lore in a dedication to Dr. Paul H. De Kruif, his companion on the cruise in which he acquired his West Indian isle. With all explanations made, the amount of his special information is astonishing. Still more astonishing, the special information nowhere clutters the story: it is all at work. . . .

I suppose valiant and angry penmen will rise to accuse Mr. Lewis of gross injustice and libelous caricature in showing up the medical colleges, the medical profession and the institutions for research. For my part, I was surprised at his moderation when I began to consider the number of shocking and true "revelations" which he might have made but did not make. His account of the obstacles encountered by Martin is not sensational. There is nothing in this book of the fanatical and inflammatory "muckraker" or scandalmonger. The sum of his satire consists in the suggestion that the advancement of science, though much prated about in America, is a long way from being the first interest in the quarters of its professed friends. The average doctor, the average teacher, the average researcher, such is Martin's discovery, is not burning with "a hard, gem-like flame," but with a very dull, smoky flame, fanned by pecuniary need, pecuniary greed, humanitarian sympathy, social fear, social aspiration and lust for applause and publicity. . . .

Babbittry with the grave bedside manner of Medicine; Babbittry with the austere uplifted countenance of Science.

It is not a jot worse there than anywhere else—in art, or letters, for example. The satire cuts into the quick of human nature.

There is only one way out. It runs through fire. If there is fire enough within, that doesn't matter.

"Arrowsmith" is hot with the authentic fire in which art and science are purified. (p. 2)

Stuart P. Sherman, "A Way Out: Sinclair Lewis Discovers a Hero," in New York Herald Tribune Books

(© I.H.T. Corporation; reprinted by permission), March 8, 1925, pp. 1-2.

WALTER LIPPMANN (essay date 1927)

[Throughout much of the twentieth century, Lippmann was considered the dean of American political journalists. He began his career as an investigative reporter for Lincoln Steffens's Everybody's Magazine *and later helped found the liberal* New Republic *in 1914, serving for several years as associate editor and literary critic. During the 1920s, the focus of his interests swung from literature to politics, and he worked as editor and political writer for various major American periodicals for the rest of his life. In the following extremely insightful discussion of Lewis's career, Lippmann concludes that Lewis cannot differentiate between genuine evil and human ignorance; thus, Lewis attacks both with equal vigor, which forces the reader to question the validity of the attack and makes mere caricatures of figures that should have been great satirical characters. While Lewis believes himself to be speaking from above the vulgarities of American life, Lippmann finds that he is guilty of a variant form of the very bigotry, intolerance, and misguided provincialism that he attacks.]*

The career of Mr. Lewis is usually divided into two periods: an earlier in which he wrote popular fiction without much success, and a later, beginning with **"Main Street,"** in which he tried only to please himself and had a huge success. Roughly speaking, this second period began with the inauguration of Warren Harding. Mr. Lewis has continued to flourish under Calvin Coolidge.

This is not, I imagine, a mere coincidence. The election of 1920 marked the close of that period of democratic idealism and of optimism about the perfectibility of American society, which began in its modern phase with Bryan, was expressed for a while by Roosevelt, and culminated in the exaltation and the spiritual disaster under Wilson. By 1920 the American people were thoroughly weary of their old faith that happiness could be found by public work, and very dubious about the wisdom of the people. They had found out that the problem of living is deeper and more complex than they had been accustomed to think it was. They had, moreover, become rich. They were ready for an examination of themselves.

Mr. Lewis was in a position to supply the demand. (pp. 71-2)

It so happened that the personal mood of Sinclair Lewis suited exactly the mood of a very large part of the American people. Very quickly he became a national figure. **"Main Street," "Babbitt,"** and, in a certain measure, **"Arrowsmith,"** became source books for the new prejudices and rubber stamps with which we of the Harding-Coolidge era examined ourselves.

Although we are all endowed with eyes, few of us see very well. We see what we are accustomed to see, and what we are told to see. . . . As a mere matter of economy in time and trouble, we demand simple and apparently universal stereotypes with which to see the world.

Mr. Lewis has an extraordinary talent for inventing stereotypes. This talent is uninhibited, for he is wholly without that radical skepticism which might make a man of equal, or even greater, genius hesitate at substituting new prejudices for old. "This is America," he says in an italicized foreword; "this Main Street is the continuation of Main Streets everywhere." Now a writer without this dogmatism of the practical man, and with a greater instinct for reality, could not have written these words. He would have remembered that the world is not so simple. But what he would have gained in truthfulness, he would have lost in influence. He would probably not have induced a large part of the nation to adopt his line of stereotypes as a practical convenience for daily use along with the telephone, the radio, the syndicated newspaper, and similar mechanical contrivances for communicating with other men. (pp. 72-4)

Because of Mr. Lewis's success in fixing the conception of Main Street, it is now very difficult to see any particular Main Street with an innocent eye. A Babbitt is no longer a man; he is a prejudice.

The art of creating these prejudices consists, in Mr. Lewis's case, of an ability to assemble in one picture a collection of extraordinarily neat imitations of lifelike details. Had his gift been in a different medium he could have manufactured wax flowers that would make a man with hay fever sneeze; he could have crowed so much like a rooster that the hens would palpitate. He has a photo-and phonographic memory with an irresistible gift of mimicry. But since his business is the creation of types rather than of living characters, he does not photograph and mimic individuals. Babbitt is not a man; he is assembled out of many actual Babbitts. The effect is at once lifelike and weird. As with an almost perfect scarecrow the thing is so much like life that it nearly lives. Yet it is altogether dead. It is like an anatomical model of an average man, a purely theoretical concept which has no actual existence. For in any living man the average qualities are always found in some unique combination.

But just because Mr. Lewis's creations are composed of skillful imitations of details, they are extraordinarily successful as stereotypes. The Babbitt pattern covers no actual Babbitt perfectly, but it covers so many details in so many Babbitts that it is highly serviceable for practical purposes. The veracity in detail is so striking that there is no disposition to question the verity of the whole.

It is not going too far to say that Mr. Lewis has imposed his conception of America on a very considerable part of the reading and writing public. To-day they see what he has selected out of the whole vast scene. Now Mr. Lewis is a reformer. He does not assemble his collection of details with the disinterested desire to hold a mirror up to nature. He wishes to destroy what he dislikes and to put something better in its place; he is rarely relieved of an overpowering compulsion to make or break something. Yet this particular zeal is no necessary part of his great talent for mimicry. For he might conceivably have loved life more than his own purposes, and have written a human comedy. Or he might have felt that sense of their destiny which makes all human creatures tragic. Or he might have been filled with a feeling for the mystery that enshrouds so temporary a thing as man, and then he would have confessed that after you have studied their behavior no matter how accurately from the outside, there is much in all human souls that remains to be known. But Mr. Lewis is not a great artist. He has a great skill. He himself is a practical man with the practical man's illusion that by bending truth to your purposes, you can make life better.

There was a moment, I think, when Mr. Lewis was tempted to use his talent with that serene disinterestedness by which alone wisdom comes. I refer to that passage in one of the early chapters of **"Main Street"** when for the first time Mr. Lewis describes Main Street. Until I reread the book recently I had forgotten that in this early stage Mr. Lewis presents the reader with two quite contrasting versions of the same scene. One is the version we all remember, a dull, fly-specked, timidly gaudy spectacle of human vacuity. The other version, which he soon allows the reader to forget, is romantic, exciting, and full or promise. There is no doubt that at this juncture Mr. Lewis meant to say: What you see in Main Street will depend on what you are; it all depends on who is looking at it. In order to emphasize this notion he gives you first the Main Street which Carol Kennicott sees on her first walk in Gopher Prairie, and then immediately following the identical aspects of Main Street as seen by Bea Sorenson who is just off a lonely farm.

Carol is a comparatively sophisticated person; at least she does not belong to the prairies but to a town which with "its garden-sheltered streets and aisles of elms is white and green New England reborn." Carol, moreover, came from a cultivated home with a "brown library" in which she "absorbed" Balzac and Rabelais and Thoreau and Max Mueller. It might reasonably be objected, I know, that Carol never absorbed anything, let alone such heady stuff as Rabelais. But what Mr. Lewis meant to say is plain enough. It is that Carol came from a background which predisposed her to dislike the raw ugliness of Main Street civilization. And having said that, he introduced Bea by way of contrast and justice to show how delightful Main Street would look to a peasant mind.

"It chanced that Carol Kennicott and Bea Sorenson were viewing Main Street at the same time." Carol looks through the fly-specked windows of the Minniemashie House and sees only the row of rickety chairs with the brass cuspidors; Bea is thrilled by the swell traveling man in there—probably been to Chicago lots of times. At Dyer's drug store Carol sees a greasy marble soda fountain with an electric lamp of red and green and curdled-yellow mosaic shade; to Bea the soda fountain is all lovely marble with the biggest shade you ever saw—all different kinds of colored glass stuck together."

There is a humility in this passage which might have become the seed of a much richer wisdom than his regular practice exhibits. Here for a moment Mr. Lewis used his gift without self-righteousness. Here in this interlude he was willing to show some courtesy to the souls of other people. He was willing even to admit that their feelings are authentic. In this mood, had he been able to retain it, he might have risen above the irritations of his time and his clique, have given even the devil his due, and become the creator of a great American comedy of manners instead of the mere inventor of new prejudices.

But to have done that he would have had to care more about human beings than about his own attitude toward them. Apparently that was impossible for him. He cannot for long detach himself from the notion that what Sinclair Lewis feels about Main Street, about Babbittry, about the Protestant churches is of primary importance. What he feels would have more importance if he had great insight as well as great sight, if he had fine taste instead of sharp distastes, if he had salient intuition as to what moves people as well as an astounding memory of how they look to him when they move. Then his figures might have come alive, and been something more than a synthetic mass of detail which serves as the butt for the uncritical, rebellious yearning of the author.

Had he a real interest in character, and not such a preoccupation with behavior, he would have expressed his view of the world through all his characters, and not merely through one mouthpiece. He would have given you Main Street through Dr. Kennicott and Bea and Vida and Percy Bresnahan, instead of giving you Kennicott, Bea, Vida, and Bresnahan through Carol. For that young woman staggers under the burden of the weighty message she is forced to carry. "There—she meditated—is the newest empire of the world; the Northern Middle West . . . an empire which feeds a quarter of the world—yet its work is merely begun. They are pioneers, these sweaty wayfarers, for all their telephones and bank accounts and automatic pianos and coöperative leagues. And for all its fat richness, theirs is a pioneer land. What is its future? she wondered."

She meditated! She wondered! Did she really, or did Sinclair Lewis? I ask the question in no captious spirit. This uncertainty as to who is talking and who is seeing the detail he reports pervades all of Mr. Lewis's books, and prevents him from achieving that "more conscious life" for which Carol yearns in phrases that are borrowed from H. G. Wells. When Mr. Lewis described Bea's walk on Main Street, he remembered for a moment what he usually forgets, that a more conscious life is one in which a man is conscious not only of what he sees, but of the prejudices with which he sees it.

Though he is absorbed in his own vision of things, Mr. Lewis is curiously unaware of himself. He is aware only of the object out there. Carol, Babbitt, Arrowsmith and Frank Shallard have sharp eyes but vague spirits. Mr. Lewis is sophisticated enough to realize how they flounder about, and he laughs at them. But this laughter is not comic, it is protective. It is a gesture of defense by a man who knows that some mature reader, say Mr. Mencken, is going to laugh, and it is better to laugh first. It is not the carefree laughter of a man who is detached from the rather adolescent rebellion which he is describing. On the contrary, he is absorbed by it. Underneath their sardonic and brutal tone, these novels are extraordinarily earnest and striving. **"Main Street," "Babbitt"** and **"Arrowsmith"** are stories of an individual who is trying to reform the world, or to find salvation by escaping it. (pp. 74-80)

Dr. Arrowsmith is the only one who may have found what he wanted. He has fled from the barbarians and their gauds, he has left "a soft bed for a shanty bunk in order to be pure. For he had perceived the horror of the shrieking, bawdy thing called Success." (p. 81)

Arrowsmith is saved by embracing the religion of science. But for Carol and for Babbitt and for Shallard there is no religion available which they can embrace, and therefore, there is no salvation. Mr. Lewis knew what to do with Arrowsmith. For there is an ideal in science to which a modern man can give himself and find peace. But there is no ideal for Carol or Babbitt. They would not be helped by "believing in" science, no matter how devoutly. Only Arrowsmith who can do scientific work can be saved by it. Only Arrowsmith finds a god to love whom no man can possess and no man can cajole.

This is the point of Mr. Lewis's greatest insight into the human predicament. There is an unconscious pathos about it, for obviously the religion which Arrowsmith embraces, ascetic, disinterested, purified, is for Mr. Lewis like some fine mystery seen at a distance. That there might be a path of salvation like it for his ordinary characters, though in other ways, is too difficult for him to believe. It would be hard for me to believe. But it would have been possible to put the rebellion of Carol and the yearning of Babbitt in the perspective of an understanding of how, as Spinoza says, all things excellent are as difficult as they are rare. They might have failed, but their failure would have been measured against a spiritual insight as fine as Arrowsmith's. Then at least the author would have understood the failure of his characters to understand themselves.

That degree of insight Mr. Lewis does not attain. He can report what he sees; having known about the religion of science, he was able to report it in Arrowsmith. But in Carol and in Babbitt he was projecting only his own spirit, and when he attempts to make it articulate, he becomes literary and fumbling: "It was mystery which Carol had most lacked in Gopher Prairie . . . where there were no secret gates opening upon moors over which one might walk by moss-deadened paths to strange, high adventures in an ancient garden." Babbitt escapes from Zenith only when he is asleep, when he is drunk, and vicariously when his son tells the family to go to the devil. For Carol and Babbitt are worldlings, and for the worldling there is no personal salvation. He must either conquer the world and remake it, though in that he will almost surely fail, or he must escape into his dreams.

The America of Mr. Lewis is dominated by the prosperous descendants of the Puritan pioneers. He has fixed them at a moment when they have lost the civilized traditions their ancestors brought from Europe, and are groping to find new ways of life. Carol is the daughter of a New Englander who went west taking with him an English culture. In Carol that culture is little more than a dim memory of a more fastidious society; it merely confuses her when she tries to live by it in Gopher Prairie. Babbitt is the descendant of a pioneer; he is completely stripped of all association with an ordered and civilized life. He has no manners, no coherent code of morals, no religion, no piety, no patriotism, no knowledge of truth and no love of beauty. He is almost completely decivilized, if by civilization you mean an understanding of what is good, better and best in the satisfaction of desire, and a knowledge of the customs, the arts, and the objects which can give these satisfactions.

Carol and Babbitt inherit the culture of the pioneers who were preoccupied with the business of establishing themselves in a new world. But for them there is no wilderness to subdue, there are no Indians to fight, they have houses and sanitation and incomes. They have the leisure to be troubled; for they really have very little to do. They have nothing to do which exhausts them sufficiently to distract them when they ask themselves: What is it all about? Is it worth while? Their ancestors came as emigrants, and they divested themselves for the voyage of that burden of ancient customs which, with all its oppressions, made life a rite, and gave it shape and significance. For Carol and Babbitt this European heritage has been liquidated until all that remains of it is a series of prohibitions called morality, and a habit of church attendance without a god they adore or an ideal of holiness with which they can commune. Their religion has become a creed which they do not understand; it has ceased to be, as it was in Catholic Europe, or even in theocratic New England, a way of life, a channel of their hopes, an order with meaning. They are creatures of the passing moment who are vaguely unhappy in a boring and senseless existence that is without dignity, without grace, without purpose. They are driven by they know not what compulsions, they are ungoverned and yet unfree, the sap of life does not reach them, their taproots having been cut. In that great transplantation of peoples which has made America, not many have as yet struck down deep into the nourishing earth. And those who have not are only dimly alive, like Carol, like Babbitt, who are weedy and struggling to bloom.

The "splendid indefinite freedoms" for which Carol yearns are an emancipation from the frayed remnants of the heritage her Yankee forefathers brought with them to America. That stern culture nerved the pioneers to hardship. It merely makes Carol nervous. She will, however, soon be free of this bondage. In the big city, where her creator has preceded her, she will be bothered no longer. She will be a free metropolitan spirit, like Mr. Lewis, free to do anything, free to disbelieve, free to scorn her past, free to be free.

The prophet of this metropolitan spirit, toward which Carol reaches out, is Mr. Mencken. Now Mr. Mencken is a true metropolitan. Mr. Lewis is a half-baked metropolitan. He has just arrived in the big city. He has the new sophistication of one who is bursting to write to the folks back home and let them know what tremendous fellows we are who live in the great capitals. There is more than a touch of the ex-naif in Mr. Lewis, not a little of the snobbery of the newly arrived. For he has as yet none of the radical skepticism of the true metropolitan. His iconoclasm is merely a way of being cocksure that the household gods of Gopher Prairie are a joke. There is no evidence in his writing that he knows or cares much about the good things which the world city contains, as Mr. Mencken does with his German music, his fine sense of learning, and his taste for speculation about genus homo apart from his manifestations on Main Street. Mr. Lewis is proud to belong to the great city, he enjoys the freedom from the Main Street tabus. But he is as restless in the big city as he is in Gopher Prairie. Unlike Mr. Mencken who is quite comfortable, happy, and well settled, as he shells the outer barbarians from his fastness at Baltimore, Mr. Lewis is forever running about the world and giving out interviews about how Main Street is to be found everywhere. He is probably right for he takes it with him wherever he goes.

The terrible judgments which he pronounces upon the provincial civilization of America flow from the bitterness of a revolted provincial. Mr. Mencken is savage at times, but there is a disinfectant on his battle-ax, because he is in no way turned morbidly in upon himself. Mr. Mencken is not a revolted Puritan. He is a happy mixture of German gemuethlichkeit and Maryland cavalier. But Mr. Lewis is still so enmeshed with the thing he is fighting that he can never quite strike at it gallantly and with a light heart. He is too much a part of the revolt he describes ever for long to understand it. That, it seems to me, is why he cannot distinguish between a sample of human ignorance and the deepseated evil which is part of this world. Everything is in the foreground and in the same focus, ugly furniture and hypocrisy, dull talk and greed, silly mannerisms and treachery. This makes his books so monotonously clever. He will take the trouble to be as minutely devastating about poor Babbitt's fondness for a trick cigarette lighter as about the villainies of Elmer Gantry. He puts everything in the same perspective, because he has no perspective. Like Carol, he is annoyed by almost everything he sees in the provinces, and all his annoyances are about equally unpleasant to him.

For he is still in that phase of rebellion where the struggle to get free is all-absorbing. Of the struggle that comes after, of the infinitely subtler and more bewildering problems of mature men, he has written nothing, and not, I think, thought much. It cannot be an accident that in his whole picture gallery there is not the portrait of one wholly mature personality, of one man or woman who has either found his way in the new world, or knows clearly why he has not. There are such personalities in America, and Mr. Lewis is not a writer who tells less than he knows, or would fail to draw such a character if he had ever actually realized his existence. But Mr. Lewis's characters are all adolescent, and they express an adolescent rebellion.

Mr. Lewis's revolt against the Puritan civilization had of course to include an attack on the evangelical churches. "That small pasty-white Baptist Church had been the center of all his emotions, aside from hell-raising, hunger, sleepiness, and love. . . . He had, in fact, got everything from the Church and Sunday School, except, perhaps any longing whatever for decency and kindness and reason." This is Mr. Lewis's conclusion at the beginning of **"Elmer Gantry,"** and the rest of the book is a sockdologer to prove it.

Had Mr. Lewis followed the pattern of the earlier novels he would have taken as his theme the struggle of an increasingly liberal clergyman to square his real faith with his creed. He would have made a clerical Arrowsmith. There is, in fact, such a character in the book, Frank Shallard, who symbolizes the central confusion of the churches. But Mr. Lewis merely sketches him in, and then lynches him with the help of the Ku Klux Klan. He was not greatly interested in Shallard. His hatred of the Protestant churches was too hot for any patient and sympathetic interest in the men who are somewhat vaguely trying to make organized religion suit the needs and doubts of modern men. He is not conscious as yet that somewhere in the ferment of religious discussion, Carol and Babbitt will have to find an equivalent for the salvation which Arrowsmith achieves. All that, which is after all the main question, Mr. Lewis ignores completely. For his central character he has chosen an absolute villain. And so **"Elmer Gantry,"** instead of being the story of a fundamentalist like Babbitt beset by doubts, or of a liberal like Carol, who has more impulse than direction, the book is a synthesis of all the villainies, short of murder, which the most villainous villain could commit.

Elmer Gantry is not, however, the portrait of a villain as such. It is the study of a fundamentalist clergyman in the United States, portrayed as utterly evil in order to injure the fundamentalists. The calumny is elaborate and deliberate. Mr. Lewis hates fundamentalists, and in his hatred he describes them as villains. This was, I believe, a most intolerant thing to do. It is intellectually of a piece with the sort of propaganda which says that John Smith is an atheist, and that he beats his wife; that Jones is a radical, and that he cheats at cards; that Robinson is a free trader, and that he robs the till.

Mr. Lewis is a maker of stereotypes. He had successfully fixed his versions of Main Street and of Babbittry on the American mind. Then, quite unscrupulously, it seems to me, he set out to stereotype the fundamentalist as an Elmer Gantry. His method was his old device of assembling details, but in his choice of details he was interested only in those which were utterly damning. It is as if he had gone to the clipping files of an atheist society, pored over the considerable collection of reports about preachers "arrested for selling fake stock, for seducing fourteen-year-old girls in orphanages under their care, for arson, for murder" . . . and out of this material had then concocted the portrait of a clergyman. This is a stock method of the propagandist, and one of the least admirable. There is no truth in it. There is no human dignity in it. It is utterly irrational. If it succeeds it merely creates new prejudices for old, and if it fails it leaves a nasty smell behind it.

I have seen **"Elmer Gantry"** described as the greatest blow ever struck in America at religious hypocrisy. It may be a great blow. It may, for all I know, be another "Uncle Tom's Cabin." But it is none the less a foul blow, and I do not think the cause of "decency, kindness and reason," which Mr. Lewis espouses . . . , is greatly helped by adapting toward fundamentalists the essential spirit of the Ku Klux Klan. The practice of describing your opponent as a criminal ought to be reserved for low disordered minds with white sheets over their heads. A novelist who pretends to be writing in behalf of a civilized life ought not himself to behave like a barbarian.

The animating spirit of **"Elmer Gantry"** is the bigotry of the anti-religious, a bigotry which is clever but as blind as any other. Were it not that the discussion of religion seems always to stir up exceptional passions, the quality of this book might well alarm Mr. Lewis's friends. For until he wrote it, he had his hatred under control. **"Main Street"** is a rather sentimental book at bottom. **"Babbitt"** is pervaded by an almost serene kindliness. **"Arrowsmith"** reaches moments of spiritual understanding. But **"Elmer Gantry"** is written with a compulsion to malice as if the author could hardly hold himself. The industriousness of his hatred is extraordinary. He gives himself to an abandoned fury which is fascinating as a mere spectacle of sustained ferocity. You say to yourself: What endurance! What voluptuous delight this fellow takes in beating and kicking this effigy, and then beating him and kicking him again! If only he keeps it up, the sawdust in Gantry will be spilled all over the ground!

For in **"Elmer Gantry"** the revolted Puritan has become fanatical. The book is a witch-burning to make an atheist holiday.

There has been some curiosity as to what Mr. Lewis would tackle next. Bets have been laid, I hear, on the politician, the editor, the lawyer, the professor, the business executive. It is a fairly important question because Mr. Lewis is a very important man. But what interests me is whether Mr. Lewis will reach maturity, or remain arrested in his adolescent rebellion. After **"Arrowsmith"** one would have said that he was beginning to be free of that shapeless irritation and yearning which Carol Kennicott typifies. But after **"Elmer Gantry"** one cannot be so sure. The hatreds are turned inward, as if the effort to escape had failed and become morbid. There is some sort of crisis in this astonishing career, which is not yet resolved. (pp. 81-92)

Walter Lippmann, "Sinclair Lewis," in his Men of Destiny *(reprinted with permission of Macmillan Publishing Company; copyright 1927 and renewed 1955, by Walter Lippmann), Macmillan, 1927, pp. 71-92.*

CONSTANT READER [PSEUDONYM of DOROTHY PARKER] (essay date 1928)

[*A critic noted for her caustic wit, Parker offers a scathing review of* The Man Who Knew Coolidge.]

I have, at the moment, a friend who is trying to make a lady out of me, and the first step in the uphill climb has been the gaining of my promise to keep from employing certain words. So I can't tell you that I think **"The Man Who Knew Coolidge,"** whether regarded as an entertainment, a portrait, a contribution to American letters, or as all three, is rotten. I could say that if I could use the word "rotten," but I can't use the word "rotten." . . .

But I can say—and, if you don't mind, I will—that I think Mr. Lewis's latest work is as heavy-handed, clumsy, and dishonest a burlesque as it has been my misfortune to see in years. . . . (p. 106)

It seems to me that **"The Man Who Knew Coolidge"** is Babbitt broadened by a mile, and Babbitt, Lord knows, was never instanced as an exercise in the subtle. Mr. Lewis is no longer the reporter; he has become the parodist. Doubtless it is all very well to sacrifice honesty and accuracy for the sake of comic effect, but when the comic effect doesn't come off, then where are you? Well, of course you are, and a pretty uncomfortable place to be, too.

I have been one who has for years marched under a banner inscribed "Sinclair Lewis for Pope." I think he is of vast importance. To my mind **"Main Street"** and **"Babbitt"** are invaluable historical documents. It seems to me that **"Arrowsmith"** belongs with the few American novels that have real magnificence. And **"Elmer Gantry"**—well, they say it's great. I never told anybody this in my life before, and please, for Heaven's sake, don't get it around; but I couldn't read **"Elmer Gantry."** I simply could not read it. (pp. 106-07)

But I am not a bit ashamed to admit my inability to finish **"The Man Who Knew Coolidge."** . . . It is to me, because of its deliberate untruth, an outrageously irritating book. It is not caricature; it is absolute misrepresentation. I hold not even the briefest brief for the Babbittry, but there was never any one as bad as Mr. Lewis's hundred-per-cent American, Lowell Schmaltz. The more I think of it, the madder I get. I am in a fair way towards getting on into what is locally known as "one of those spells of hers."

I wish I could say "rotten." You don't know how much I need to say it. (p. 107)

Constant Reader [pseudonym of Dorothy Parker], "Mr. Lewis Lays It On with a Trowel," in The New Yorker *(© 1928, renewed 1955, by The New Yorker Magazine, Inc.), Vol. IV, No. 7, April 7, 1928, pp. 106-07.*

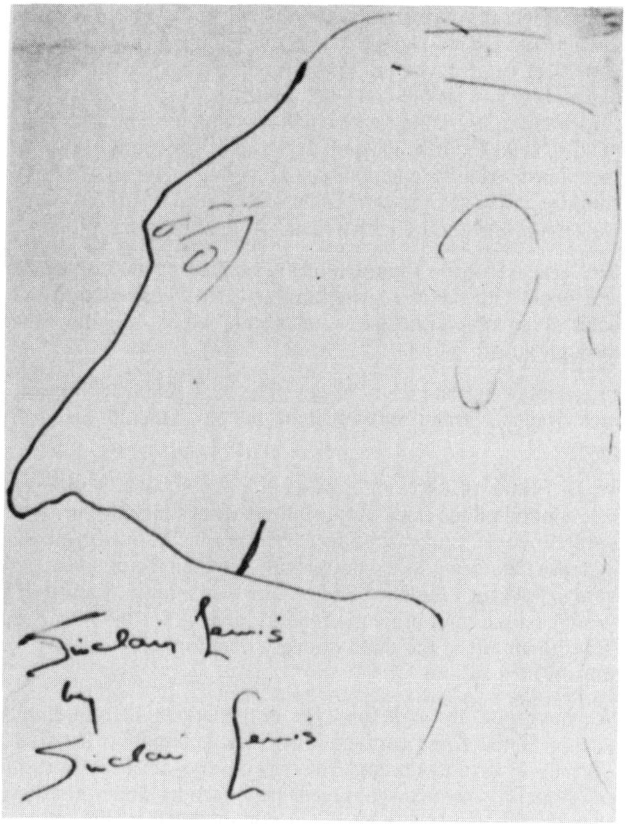

A self-portrait by Lewis drawn in the mid-1930's. Papers of Carl Van Doren, Princeton University Library.

SHERWOOD ANDERSON (essay date 1930)

[Anderson was one of the most original and influential early twentieth-century American writers. He was among the first American authors to explore the effects of the unconscious upon human life. Anderson's "hunger to see beneath the surface of lives" was best expressed in the collection of bittersweet short stories which form the classic Winesburg, Ohio *(1919). This, his most important book, exhibits the author's characteristically simple, unornamented prose style and his personal vision, which combined a sense of wonder at the potential beauty of life with despair over its tragic aspects. Anderson's style and outlook were influential in shaping the work of Ernest Hemingway, William Faulkner, Thomas Wolfe, John Steinbeck, and other American authors. Much of Anderson's own writing was influenced by the work of D. H. Lawrence, Gertrude Stein, and his close friend Theodore Dreiser. Both Anderson and Lewis have long been called leaders in American literature's "revolt from the village." But although Anderson examined in his fiction the troubled, darker aspects of provincial existence, he saw the small town as an admirable feature of American life. In a letter to editor John Hall Wheelock of Charles Scribner's Sons, Anderson indicated that the unnamed writer discussed in the excerpt below, an attacker of the American small town and labor practices, is Lewis. In another letter, Anderson wrote of the following essay that "you will find in it what I think is a true criticism, not only of Lewis, but of the whole modern Mencken, hard-boiled attitude. It takes strength to be tender, and these men haven't strength. It is too easy to attack individuals."]*

It is with an odd feeling of futility that a man interested in modern industry, sensing something of its possibilities, moved by the strength and power of its marching stride through the world contemplates the attitude taken toward it by so many of our modern American writers. To be quite in line now a man should be quite hopeless of everything American and surely America is industrial. There the factories are. They are everywhere. They have crept out through the Middle West. They are invading town after town of the South. (p. 7)

The attitude toward the factories and industrialism is too much like the present popular attitude toward the American small town.

We all remember that, a few years ago, there was published here a certain very popular novel [***Main Street***] built about an American small town. It has been read all over the world. It has made a certain definite fixed picture of life in the American small town in innumerable minds.

It is because I am interested in labor and industry as I am in the small town that I speak of this matter. It is because a particular book brought to a kind of focus a general attitude here toward all American small towns and all life in American small towns.

So there it was. The book came into my hands on a certain summer afternoon. I got it at a book store one day several years ago (the windows were piled full of them) and went with it in my hand to a certain house. I sat down in a room in the house and began to read.

There is no doubt the book was done with a certain skill. As I read, people passed before me in its pages and when I lifted my eyes certain living people, seen through a window, passed before me along the streets of the town I was in. In the pages of the book held in my hand that day people were living their lives. I remember yet the peculiar feeling of disdain the lives of these people gave me. I had myself always been a small-town man. On the whole I like the people I have found in American small towns and have many friends among them. I like to hang about the court houses of small towns, go to ball games there, go fishing with small-town men in the spring and hunting with them in the fall. I like to go to county fairs and the Fourth of July celebration. At night, when the moon is shining, I like to get with some small-town man and take a walk with him on a country road, preferably in the hills.

But let us return to the town of the book. I haven't a copy of that book with me as I sit writing of it but I remember a man back of an ugly little house on a side street, shaking ashes through an ash sifter.

I remember hot and dusty places. The air is filled with heavy, rank smells. I remember pretentious people, mentally dishonest people.

When I think of the book town people are always, it seems to me, spitting on the floor. Rotarians are always making speeches. I smell people's unwashed feet. I do not mean to suggest that all these details are in the book, but what I am trying to suggest here is the effect the book had on one man's mind. I am trying to suggest the kind of memories and feelings for the American small town left in the mind of every man to whom I have ever spoken of this book.

We have got, through this type of American literature, this picture of the American small town. It abounds in Rotarians who are always Rotarians. They are always absurdly boastful and hopeful, never discouraged, never tender about anything or anybody, never human. I am not saying that this kind of writer has worked with this end in view. I am telling what has happened. They have made for us towns in which no grass ever grows. Grapes and apples never ripen there. There are no spring rains. They are towns to which no ball teams ever come, no circus parade. I am convinced that, to a large extent, the success of books, written in this tone, is due to just that quality in them that arouses people's contempt. There is that streak in all of us. We all adore hating something, having contempt for something. It makes us feel big and superior.

And how does this concern the field of labor?

I have seen recently a sample of what can be done in the field of Southern industry. A certain well-known and very popular writer recently issued a small book [***Cheap and Contented Labor***] about the cotton mills. As I understand the matter the writer went to a town in the South in the employ of a certain newspaper syndicate. There was a terrible situation there. Certain people, mill hands, were fighting for better working conditions in the mill. They wanted, of course, better wages and shorter hours. A strike was called.

The strike was called at night when the night shift was on and the workers, men and women who had left the mill, gathered about the mill gate. This was in the early morning, in the gray dawn. The strikers at the mill gate tried to stop the workers of the day shift from passing through the gate. The sheriff, with his deputies, had been called.

A struggle started and five or six workers were killed. It is said they were all shot in the back as they were fleeing from the scene. It is about this incident that the story of Southern industry, as told in the booklet, is built.

It is a booklet that sets forth the wrongs of labor, and I have no quarrel with that. It attacks certain people, mill managers, a certain merchant and others. Let these people look out for themselves. All the usual stage figures, so commonly used nowadays in writing of the small town, are in this town. There are, of course, the Kiwanians and the Rotarians. There are bullies swaggering through the streets.

It is like so many of this kind of books and magazine articles. You can't quarrel with its facts, only it does not tell enough facts. This sort of thing is no doubt good reporting of certain phases of life now in all American towns and, in particular, of our industrial towns. It is good reporting of certain phases of life now in towns and cities all over the industrial world.

It is good reporting and it is to my mind very bad reporting. There are too many bullies, too many Kiwanians.

For example, in the description of the Southern town to which I refer, there is a lot of space devoted to a certain lady stock-holder of the mill. We are given a quick, sketchy picture of the woman. She, it seems, is a maiden lady who sits, I presume in a great house, somewhere in a distant city, and receives dividend checks. From time to time she is presumed to issue orders. The screws are put to the little mill girls of the South at her command. It is this kind of writing that seems to be all nonsense, and that is at the bottom of the harm such ink-slinging can do. (pp. 7-9)

I am protesting against an unbalanced view of modern industrial life. I protest against the point of view that sees nothing in the small town but Rotarians and boosters, that sees nothing in industry but devils and martyrs, that does not see people as people, realizing that we are all caught in a strange new kind of life. (p. 10)

Let us return for a moment to the American small town. A moment ago I spoke of a certain book, taken as a type, that has created a certain impression. We have to presume that any writer, writing thus of life in American small towns, getting small-town life so, got his impression from the small town from which he himself came. He must have seen his home town as an ugly place and so all towns became ugly to him. The conclusion seems inevitable. . . .

There is a young painter living in the city of New York. He works there at night in a stockbroker's office. When he is not too tired he tries to paint in his room during the day. Once, by chance, I saw a painting of his. I bought the painting. I own it now. . . .

He was a young painter who, having no money and wanting to paint in the daytime, worked at night. He dreamed of a day coming when he would not be tired. "Perhaps I will really paint a little then," he said. . . .

He spoke of many things and among others of a country from which he had come as a young boy, and to which he hopes some day to return. "I want to go back there," he said. "I want to paint there."

He spoke of river valleys and of creeks at the edge of his native town. It was an American town. He said willows grew along the creek. He spoke of white farmhouses seen through trees, of white farmhouses clinging to the sides of hills.

"There is something to paint there," he said. "If I ever get money enough I'll go back there and I'll stay there."

"It is a lovely town," he said, and I speak of this young man here because, by an odd chance, my young painter came from the very town from which had come the writer mentioned above who, we must conclude, by the way in which he has written of the American small town, has hated it so. (p. 11)

Sherwood Anderson, "Cotton Mill" (copyright, 1930, by Charles Scribner's Sons, and renewed 1957 by Eleanor Copenhauer Anderson; reprinted by permission of Harold Ober Associates Incorporated), in Scribner's Magazine, *Vol. LXXXVIII, No. 1, July, 1930, pp. 1-11.*

JAMES BRANCH CABELL (essay date 1930)

[Cabell's novels, which combine extremes of lavish romance and degraded reality, idealistic fantasy and jaded disillusionment, are among the outstanding oddities in American fiction. His most enduring achievement, The Biography of Manuel *(1904-29), belongs to a tradition of fantasy literature that includes Edmund Spenser's* The Faerie Queene *(1590-96) and Jonathan Swift's* Gulliver's Travels *(1726).* Beyond Life *(1919), an important collection of literary criticism which was written to introduce the* Biography, *outlines the literary and philosophic concepts that serve as its foundation. Cabell adhered to a special definition of fiction which allowed him to portray glorified adventures beyond mundane reality without falsifying what he saw as the harsh truths of existence: the suffering of life, the emptiness of death, and a permanent alienation at the core of even the most intimate human relations. Cabell's most important later criticism appears in* Some of Us *(1930), a defense of several contemporary writers—including Elinor Wylie, Ellen Glasgow, and Joseph Hergesheimer—against the trend of Neo-Humanist criticism, which demanded the subservience of art to moral and social issues. In the following excerpt from* Some of Us, *Cabell praises Lewis as the creator of exaggerated literary types and likens him, in this respect, to Charles Dickens.]*

I perceive some merit in Sinclair Lewis, even though I fail to detect it upon the grounds usually advanced. People who ought to know a great deal better will tell you that Sinclair Lewis has portrayed many aspects of our American life. In fact, when ***Babbitt*** and ***Main Street*** were but lately included in the library presented to President Herbert C. Hoover, it was upon the tactless ground, as stated by one of the selectors, that "the reading of them will help a man to understand the temperament of the American people." I put aside the ineluctable inference—as being an over-blunt if unintentional criticism of our first British President's conduct in office,—and I remark merely that I do not think the statement itself is true.

I shall come back to that. Meanwhile, in whatsoever milieu, Mr. Lewis throughout the deceased 'twenties dealt incessantly with one single problem: whether or not it is better to do that which seems expected? As long ago as in the autumn of 1920, in ***Main Street,*** the question was raised whether Carol Kennicott should or should not conform to what Gopher Prairie expected? The question was given perhaps its most nearly classic form in ***Babbitt,*** wherein the protagonist fidgets before this problem, of conforming or of not conforming, in connection with well-nigh all departments of life as it is led in Zenith the Zip City. Then Mr. Lewis turned to the especial variant of the same problem as it concerns the scientist, in ***Arrowsmith;*** in ***Elmer Gantry*** he brought the minister of the gospel face to face with this problem; and finally, in 1929, he confronted Sam Dodsworth with the problem (already touched upon in ***Mantrap***) of conforming or of not conforming to that which seemed expected in—of all avocations—the pursuit of pleasure. (pp. 61-2)

Mr. Lewis does not ever answer [the] question outright: but he does very insistently compel his readers to cast about for an answer. Time and again Sinclair Lewis has exalted the bravery if not precisely the wisdom of individualism by the roundabout method of depicting the conformist. There is, he has discovered, a great deal of humbug and stupidity and viciousness going about masked as the correct thing to do in every walk of life as life speeds in Winnemac, the home of manly men and of womanly women and of other Regular Guys. And Mr. Lewis portrays with loving abhorrence superb monsters, now and then a bit suggestive of human beings, who make the very best (in an entirely utilitarian sense) of this humbug and of this stupidity and of this viciousness, to enhance their own moral standing and bank accounts.

I said, he portrays. Yet Sinclair Lewis is far too opulently gifted to have to plagiarize his manly men and his womanly women from the life about him. He has turned instead—compelled it may be by those freakish planets which ruled over the date of his birth,—to commemorate a more striking race, [that of Charles Dickens]. (p. 63)

In every book by Dickens the backbone of all is optimism and a fixed faith that by-and-by justice and candor will prevail. (p. 65)

The doctrine of Mr. Lewis would seem to run quite the other way. In book after book he has presented one or another individualist at least as truly heroic as ever was young Martin Chuzzlewit, and an individualist who, in opposing the solicitations of the elvish burghers of Winnemac, remains theoretically in the right, but who ends as a rule in material ruin and who ends always in defeat. I shall not labor this point, because Mr. Lewis himself does not make much of it. He does but indicate, by sketching lightly the career of a Frank Shallard or of a Max Gottleib, the truism that in Winnemac as elsewhere the opponent of any communal folly is in for a bad time of it. These adventurers find that the old recipe, of not conforming to that which the goblins urge them to do, is of no least avail to deliver them from the goblins of Winnemac. Instead, the Rev. Dr. Elmer Gantry and the Honorable Almus Pickerbaugh are with them to the very end, in some not unfriendly bewilderment as to why the poor mutt should have opposed the *mores* of Winnemac when he could so easily have made use of these fantasies to enhance his moral standing and his bank account.

This is a tragedy, I repeat, which Mr. Lewis does but indicate. His real interest turns other-whither as though bewitched by the quaintness of the commonplace. It remains fascinated by the conformist and by the droll ways of his goblin flourishing (wherein timidity turns to sound money and lies become limousines) at the cost of intellectual and spiritual ruin. The individualist is lost in a world made over-safe for democracy; and the conformist becomes not worth saving. That is the doctrine which informs all the derisive apologues Sinclair Lewis has fetched out of Winnemac. That is, in one sense, the powder which speeds his every shot at our polity. In another sense it is the powder disguised in the succulent jam of his caricatures.

So it has been throughout the ten years since Mr. Lewis first toyed with his pet problem in Gopher Prairie. He then told us, with a mendacity which time and his later books have coöperated to expose, that Gopher Prairie was a small town in Minnesota. We all know now that Gopher Prairie—like Zenith and Monarch and Sparta and Banjo Crossing, and like every other place that Mr. Lewis has written about since 1920,—is a portion of the grotesque and yet always rather sinister, strange goblin land of Winnemac.

I delight in Winnemac and in all its citizenry: yet it is, as I have suggested, with very much the same pleasure I derive from Dickens. That pleasure is, to the one side, somewhat the pleasure I get from the "Mr. and Mrs." cartoons in the Sunday paper and from Amos and Andy over the radio, and (to the other side) from a great deal of Molière and Swift and Aristophanes and Lucian,—the pleasure, that is, of seeing a minim of reality exaggerated into Brobdingnagian incredibility. There is apparent in each that single grain of truth which has budded, through more or less skilled and patient gardening, into this gaudy efflorescence of the impossible. The seed explains the flowering: but it is the flowering which counts, and which charms. So when I hear Sinclair Lewis classed as a "realist," it is with something of the same wonderment in which I have heard that he lives, along with Messrs. Dreiser and Cabell and Anderson, in a never lifting atmosphere of despair and frustration. (pp. 66-9)

If you can believe in the "realism" of Sinclair Lewis it will give you a great deal more of comfort than does any other "realism." For my part, I can but protest that I very heartily enjoy his books without any more believing in Almus Pickerbaugh and Elmer Gantry and the other hobgoblins as persons whom one may hope to encounter in our imperfect world than I can believe (after any such literal fashion) in Joe and Vi, or in Jefferson Brick and Colonel Diver, or, for that matter, in Bottom and Caliban.

Meanwhile if, as one hears freely nowadays, Sinclair Lewis is obsolescent, and his books are doomed, the trouble is not merely that the United States is due to lose one of its most interesting commonwealths, in the State of Winnemac. For one really wonders what in the world is to be done about George Follansbee Babbitt? Just eight years ago this Babbitt emigrated from 401 pages of a novel into the racial consciousness of mankind. He is one of those satisfying large symbols which at long intervals some author hits upon, and which promptly take on a life that is not confined to the books wherein they first figured. Babbitt is in train, I think, to become one of those myths which rove forever through the irrational Marches of Antan, and about which writers not yet born will weave their own pet stories as inevitably as writers will continue to concern themselves with Faust and Don Juan and the Brown God Pan. (pp. 69-71)

James Branch Cabell, "Goblins in Winnemac" (originally published as "A Note As to Sinclair Lewis," in American Mercury, *Vol. XX, No. 80, August, 1930), in his* Some of Us: An Essay in Epitaphs *(copyright, 1930, renewed 1958, by James Branch Cabell; reprinted by permission of the Literary Estate of James Branch Cabell), Robert M. McBride & Company, 1930, pp. 59-73.*

CONSTANCE ROURKE (essay date 1931)

[*Rourke was a pioneer in the field of American cultural history. Her reputation was established by her* American Humor: A Study of the National Character *(1931), which is still widely read. The work advances Rourke's opposition to such critics as Van Wyck Brooks and T. S. Eliot, who asserted that America had no cultural traditions other than those it had imported from Europe. Rourke theorized that an American cultural tradition indeed exists, and that it is based on humor. The findings presented in* American Humor *and in Rourke's later* The Roots of American Culture *(1942) were a major factor in leading Brooks and other critics to reassess and revise their previously held opinions of America as a cultural wasteland. In the following excerpt, Rourke traces Lewis's satiric technique to an earlier tradition in American literature, that of the fable.*]

With one exception none of those definitive novelists have appeared who make an aspect of contemporary life their own and leave it with the color of their imagination upon it forever afterward.

The exception of course is Sinclair Lewis; he possesses the copious touch; and people of the present day fill his pages. Yet with all his grasp of an immediate life, Lewis remains within the older American tradition; he is primarily a fabulist. In ***Main Street*** he stresses his intention at the outset.

> On a hill by the Mississippi where Chippewas had camped two generations ago, a girl stood in relief against the cornflower blue of Northern sky. She saw no Indians now; she saw flour-mills and the blinking windows of skyscrapers in Minneapolis and St. Paul. . . . A breeze which had crossed a thousand miles of wheatlands bellied her taffeta skirt in a line so graceful, so full of animation and moving beauty, that the heart of a chance watcher on the lower road tightened to wistfulness over her quality of suspended freedom. . . . The days of pioneering, of lassies in sunbonnets, and bears killed with axes in piney clearings, are deader now than Camelot; and a rebellious girl is the spirit of that bewildered empire called the American Middlewest.

Even occasional digressions from immediate circumstance in ***Main Street*** have the fabulous touch, like the wind that blows a thousand miles, or the eras of history brought to bear upon the Kennicott's courtship. Later in the book Lewis changes his definition of the pioneer, declaring that the farmers—"those sweaty wayfarers"—whose lands surround Gopher Prairie and stretch into the farther distance, are pioneers, "for all their telephones and bank-accounts and automatic pianos and co-operative leagues." In the end Gopher Prairie itself takes on aspects of a pioneer existence, half shaped, inarticulate, pressed against an uncertain void. Then once again the theme enlarges, and Main Street becomes a national street, its existence a pervasive American existence.

This is that highly circumstantial fable-making which had been a characteristic American gift; and the prevailing tone is one which had appeared within the whole line of American fabulists, particularly those of the frontier. The material is prosaic, the mood at bottom romantic; gusto infuses the whole, with an air of discovery. Even the derision is not a new note; this had appeared again and again in American attitudes toward American life, and is part of the enduring native self-consciousness; it is seen here, as before, in a close tie with the comic. Lewis uses homely metaphors that might have been spoken by Yankee Hill, describing "an old farmer, solid, wholesome, but not clean—his face like a potato fresh from the earth." The familiar biting understatement appears, and the inflation; the western strain is as strong in Lewis as the Yankee. "She sat down as though it were a gymnasium exercise." "He was always consulting John Flickerbaugh, who handled more real estate than law, and more law than justice." The American gift for comic mimicry seems concentrated in Lewis, and his people seem to possess the unfailing native passion for the monologue: flood-gates of their talk are opened at a touch. Sights, sounds, the look of things and of people, as well as speech, are crowded against one another with tireless fluency. Nothing halts this movement in ***Main Street;*** nothing halts the cumulative intention; episode is piled on episode. The movement lengthens, and finally becomes in the large flow sagalike. The outcome is to portray the generic; the human situation steadily diminishes in force. At the beginning it is clear that the division between Carol and Kennicott is emotional, not civic: but the human circumstance is pushed aside by an urgent intention to reveal a comprehensive aspect of American life. The preoccupation is the familiar social preoccupation.

Lewis displays a detachment which never belonged to the early fabulists. Babbitt's shrewd traction dealings are seen with an appraising eye instead of with that exhilaration by which earlier artists had been carried away, viewing similar triumphs. An unmitigated nationalism is slit by the same penetrative view; and that primitive desire for cohesion which had risen strongly through early comedy is shown to have become the crudest of mass instincts. Lewis turns his abundant fables into critiques and challenges, but the transcendent effect is the traditional effect: the American portrait, a comic portrait once more, has been drawn in amplitude. Babbitt takes a place beside the archetypal Yankee; and for the first time an archetypal native scene is drawn in Main Street. The response too has been the habitual response. Bitterly as the direct seizure of American life has been resented, it has offered the portrait; the mirror was upheld, and the American with his invincible curiosity about himself could not fail to gaze therein.

There is a sense in which Lewis may be considered the first American novelist. In his unflagging absorption of detail and his grasp of the life about him he suggests Defoe; and it may be that like Defoe in England he will prove to have opened a way for the development of the novel in America. The impact of his scrutiny lies all about; the American scene and the American character can never slide back into the undifferentiated state of an earlier view. (pp. 283-86)

Constance Rourke, "Round Up," in her American Humor: A Study of the National Character *(copyright 1931 by Harcourt Brace Jovanovich, Inc.; renewed 1959 by Alice D. Fore; reprinted by permission of the publisher), Harcourt Brace Jovanovich, 1931, pp. 266-303.**

GRANVILLE HICKS (essay date 1935)

[*In 1933 Hicks published his famous study* The Great Tradition: An Interpretation of American Literature since the Civil War *and quickly established himself as the foremost advocate of Marxist critical thought in America. Throughout the 1930s, he argued for a more socially engaged brand of literature and severely criticized those writers, such as Henry James, Mark Twain, and Edith Wharton, who he believed failed to confront the realities of their society and, instead, took refuge in their own work. Hicks was shocked by the effects of the Great Depression and believed that events demanded a new commitment on the part of writers to clearly understand and express their times. In Marxist terms, this meant that all American artists should comprehend the growth of capitalism and its negative side effects, such as war, periodic depressions, and the exploitation and alienation of the working class. Thus the question Hicks posed was always the same: to what degree did an artist come to terms with the economic condition of the time and the social consequences of those conditions. What he sought from American literature was an extremely critical examination of the capitalist system itself and its inherently repressive nature. After 1939, Hicks sharply denounced communist ideology, which he called a "hopelessly narrow way of judging literature," and in his later years adopted a less ideological posture in critical matters. In the following excerpt from* The Great Tradition, *Hicks examines what he perceives as the strengths and weaknesses of Lewis's vision and work.*]

In Sinclair Lewis we have to reckon with a different kind of talent, neither Dreiser's massiveness nor Anderson's penetration. Lewis is the shrewd reporter, armed with the skepticism and frankness of his generation, the shrewd reporter with a chip on his shoulder. For six years he wrote books in which he gave free play neither to his powers of observation nor to his acute exasperation with his complacent contemporaries. ***Main Street*** . . . he wrote deliberately, as a foreword shows, to expose "our comfortable tradition and sure faith," to "betray himself as an alien cynic," and to "distress the citizens by speculating whether there may not be other faiths." Its success pointed to the existence of other persons not quite convinced that "Main Street is the climax of civilization."

Once he had abandoned himself to his temperament and his talents, Lewis took his place among the recorders of the contemporary scene. With systematic zeal he has described the small town, the prosperous mid-western city, and the great metropolis, and he has written of business, medicine, the church, and social work. If what one wants is the detailed, accurate record of the way people live, Lewis is the most satisfying of our authors. What Carol Kennicott saw in Gopher Prairie might be seen in thousands of American communities; the day in Babbitt's life that Lewis so minutely records has been duplicated in the lives of tens of thousands of small business men; it is to the keeping of such doctors as Martin Arrowsmith met in Wheatsylvania, Nautilus, and the McGurk Institute that our lives are entrusted. About the middle stratum of the population, the moderately prosperous professional and business men, Lewis has written with a keenness of eye and an alertness of ear that any novelist might envy him.

In the books of these three authors we have the best that the middle generation has contributed to the study of the contemporary scene. They have brought our literature closer to the center of American life, and we can rejoice in Dreiser's strength, Lewis's shrewdness, and Anderson's sensitivity. But can we be satisfied with their work? We are grieved, of course, by such things as Dreiser's clumsiness, Anderson's frequent obscurity, Lewis's reliance on mimicry; but these are superficial faults, lamentable but chiefly significant as symptoms of more serious failures. Dreiser seems always to be heavily stalking some secret that constantly eludes him. The brilliant flash of Anderson's imagination illuminates a tiny spot in a black night of mystery. Lewis's amusing chatter fails to conceal his blind helplessness. (pp. 230-31)

Sinclair Lewis, though he became interested in socialism many years ago, has not joined Dreiser and Anderson in endorsing the Communist Party. In ***Ann Vickers*** the heroine recognizes a certain validity in the communist position, but she is irritated by the fanaticism of a party member she knows, and in any case her life is too full for her to limit herself to a particular program. Lewis is rather like her. In his own way he perfectly illustrates the middle-class contradiction. . . . The side of him that secretly sympathizes with Will Kennicott and George Babbitt lends authority to his portraits, and the side of him that damns them gives his books their salt.

Criticism and satire imply the conception of a better way of life. Lewis knows what he would like to destroy—provincialism, complacency, hypocrisy, intellectual timidity, and similar faults—but he has only the vaguest idea of what kind of society he would like to see in existence. Carol Kennicott's attempts to reform Gopher Prairie are not only futile; they reveal standards almost as inadequate as those of the villagers. George Babbitt's only guides, as he goes along the path of revolt, are the old-fashioned liberalism of Seneca Doane and the dull bohemianism of the Bunch. Beside Elmer Gantry's foul hypocrisy Lewis can place only the weak modernism of Frank Shallard and the sentimental piety of Father Pengilly; he is as incapable of revealing the strength of the church as he is of expounding the nature of honest, intelligent atheism. Dodsworth returns from Europe, freed from subservience to both the narrow American idea of success and the narrow European idea of culture; and he returns to build better houses—an experiment in constructive capitalism in which Jack London's Elam Harnish had already anticipated him. Ann Vickers, who wants a career and has one, finds happiness in a man and a baby. The man, Judge Dolphin, seems to be Lewis's ideal, a straight-shooting he-man who plays the game; and he is one of the few characters in Lewis's books that are completely unconvincing. Only once, in all his novels, has Lewis succeeded in creating a worthy antagonist to the myriad of petty-minded men he has described: in ***Arrowsmith*** Max Gottlieb's devotion to pure science is both convincing and admirable.

Arrowsmith is Lewis's strongest and most unified novel. In ***Main Street*** and ***Babbitt*** he showed his keenness of eye and ear and his sharpness of tongue; but the very effectiveness of his satire compelled him to speak in positive as well as negative terms, and in ***Arrowsmith*** he succeeded in doing so. Lewis's discovery of the scientific method as a possible alternative to the confusion of the age was, as has been noted, characteristic of the middle generation. And for the moment his assumptions worked. But pure science operates in too narrow a field to provide a theory and an attitude for a social critic, and Lewis could not establish the relevance of science to his own interests. He was thus forced back into his old confusion, and his superficiality became increasingly apparent. ***Elmer Gantry, Dodsworth,*** and ***Ann Vickers*** are inferior to ***Main Street, Babbitt,*** and ***Arrowsmith. Ann Vickers*** not only is less unified than ***Arrowsmith,*** which in its general outlines it resembles; it shows less interest in the characteristic details of American life and is less convincing in the handling of detail; its satire is diffused, and Lewis's old power of indignation is felt only in the description of Copperhead Gap Penitentiary; the ending is a peculiarly painful confession of surrender to standards the satirist has pretended to scorn. Lewis's virtues were never enough, and he is losing those virtues.

Not only is the absence of adequate comprehension itself a weakness in the work of Dreiser, Anderson, and Lewis; it accounts for many of their other faults. . . . Lewis, acute as he is in noting revealing mannerisms and tricks of speech, has only created two or three rounded personalities.

However, with all their faults, these three writers are far more important than Mrs. Wharton, Miss Cather, Hergesheimer, and Cabell. Not only have they achieved more; their failures have more significance for the future of American literature than the successes of the others. Their work was a natural development of the tendencies of the muckrakers. Less concerned with specific reforms, they had the same interest in the dominant tendencies of American life. And they made real advances over the muckrakers: they ended the tyranny of boarding school standards; they substituted the fresh, natural speech of the people for the language of books; they created a certain number of convincing and representative men and women. The novel grew in their hands, but the great central problem—emphasized by the failures of all the realists from Howells on—was left unsolved. (pp. 234-37)

Granville Hicks, "Two Roads," in his The Great Tradition: An Interpretation of American Literature since the Civil War, *revised edition, The Macmillan Company, 1935, pp. 207-56.**

ANTHONY WEST (essay date 1951)

[West is the author of several novels—some of them fictionally detailing his own life as the son of illustrious parents, Rebecca West and H. G. Wells—that are concerned with the moral, social, psychological, and political disruptions of the twentieth century. As a critic he has written a study of D. H. Lawrence in addition to his many reviews published in various magazines. In the following essay, West surveys Lewis's career and praises the novels written during the 1920s, deeming them a worthy testament to Lewis's skill.]

It is almost impossible to look back, at this moment, to the splendid ten-year run of Sinclair Lewis's talent, beginning with **"Free Air,"** in 1919, including **"Main Street," "Babbitt," "Arrowsmith," "Mantrap," "Elmer Gantry,"** and **"The Man Who Knew Coolidge,"** and ending with **"Dodsworth,"** in 1929. The agonizing self-parodies that came later, such as **"Cass Timberlane"** and **"Kingsblood Royal,"** with their intensification of all the small defects found in his finest work—the absurd names given to characters, the ear no longer attuned to the common speech, the grotesque interior monologues, and the fumbling intimacies between men and women—form an impassable barrier. In the early thirties, Lewis either ran out of or ran out on ideas about character and personality, and started basing his books on issues of a near-political nature, leaving matters of art for matters more properly the concern of the day's newspapers. There is a certain amount of truth in the purist theory that journalism is essentially concerned with the facts of particular situations, while art is concerned with the facts that relate a wide variety of situations. Babbitt's political cowardice sprang out of his dishonest and hesitant way of life, and Lewis's picture of his way of life gave many people a look at themselves in a mirror. Neil and Vestal Kingsblood were marionettes carved out to fit an issue, ticketed casually with some more or less human characteristics, and jerked into action that illustrated an abstract and unfelt idea about the impropriety of racial discrimination and segregation. It was bad art and, since none of the facts were true of any particular situation, worthless journalism. All his last ten novels have this dead unreality about them, and in the next ten years they are going to vanish quietly away. When they are gone, the eight books of his best period will come back, with their vitality, their knowledge of people, and their vivid creation of a time and a mental atmosphere. They were a real contribution to a wholly American literature, and to America's understanding of itself. When they stand by themselves, there will no longer be any mystery about how Sinclair Lewis got his reputation or his Nobel Prize. (pp. 114, 117)

Anthony West, "The Party Again," in The New Yorker *(© 1951, renewed 1979, by The New Yorker Magazine, Inc.), Vol. XXVII, April 28, 1951, pp. 113-14, 117.**

ORVILLE PRESCOTT (essay date 1952)

[Prescott was the daily literary critic for The New York Times *from 1942 to 1966. His major critical work is* In My Opinion:

An Inquiry into the Contemporary Novel *(1952). In the following excerpt from that work, he disparages the last novels of Lewis's career, but indicates that the major satires of the 1920s will continue to bear testimony to Lewis's great skill.*]

That Sinclair Lewis' last five novels are sadly inferior to the great ones he wrote in the 1920s cannot detract from the importance of his life achievement. From 1920 and the publication of ***Main Street*** until his death in 1951 this redheaded man with his deeply furrowed forehead, his freckled, haggard face, his pale-blue eyes and manner of desperate high tension, meant American literature to much of the world. His books were widely read wherever people read books at all. His passionate feeling for his native land—a white-hot compound of fierce affection and raging hatred for its vulgarities, hypocrisies and general lack of perfection—caused many of his books to be misunderstood. For seldom have they portrayed typical Americans, as many Europeans and too many Americans thought that they did.

Rather, they concentrated the distilled essence of some aspect of America and magnified it, exaggerated it, interpreted it and explained it until the nation and the world had new myths which would never be forgotten. So, as Paul Bunyan means lumberjacks and Uncle Tom slavery, George F. Babbitt has come to mean a familiar type of American businessman.

In the great books which made him famous, ***Main Street, Babbitt, Arrowsmith*** and ***Dodsworth,*** Lewis wrote with such intensity and vigor, such rampaging high spirits and satiric wit that he soared triumphantly over his own limitations, his two-dimensional characters and the repetitious exaggeration of his mocking dialogue. He was a true creator, an artist who could impose his vision of his fellow men on much of the world and make his elementary characters seem brilliantly true and more than life-sized. It was a great achievement. The former pulp-magazine editor from Sauk Center, Minnesota, had more substantial qualifications for the Nobel Prize in literature than any of the other Americans who also have won that accolade.

But the novels which Lewis wrote in the last decade of his life were either pale imitations of his earlier work or venomous outbursts of hatred and melodrama. They made a dreary conclusion to a great career. It is always a melancholy spectacle when a richly gifted writer exhausts his material or his creative abilities and continues to write anyway because writing is his life and he cannot stop while life endures. Sinclair Lewis' last five novels were: ***Gideon Planish, Cass Timberlane, Kingsblood Royal, The God-Seeker*** and ***World So Wide.*** Three of these were limp and soggy, but comparatively harmless, examples of Lewis in decline. Two, and they were much the most popular, were neurotic cries of hate.

The inoffensive ones require little comment. ***Gideon Planish*** was the best of the three, a moderately lively blast at the uplift racket, philanthropic foundations, pressure groups and money-raising combines. . . . Lewis was as angry and brutally sarcastic when he wrote ***Gideon Planish*** as at any time in his career. But somehow his heavy artillery sounded like popguns and his sanctimonious and hypocritical hero remained dull and insipid.

The God-Seeker was Lewis' only historical novel, the story of a Presbyterian mission to the Sioux Indians and the early days of the city of St. Paul. . . . As a novel by Sinclair Lewis ***The God-Seeker*** is flat, dull and third-rate. Even as one of hundreds of historical novels about the American frontier published at about the same time it is mediocre.

World So Wide, his last and twenty-second novel, tells of a young man's search for knowledge of his true self in travel and in historical and artistic scholarship. In a way it reflects Lewis' own lifelong pursuit of happiness and the meaning of life, the quest which made him a restless and lonely wanderer, always moving on from one home to another, destined in the end to die, like so many other literary exiles, in Rome. If Lewis had turned his stony glare inward on his own tormented mind and written an autobiography he could have produced an important and psychologically fascinating work. But he preferred to write of a young widower discovering the bloody splendor of Italy's spectacular past, wavering between love for two rather wooden and ridiculous young women. ***World So Wide*** contains flashes of the old Lewis satiric gusto, but not many. On the whole it is dull and superficial.

In ***Cass Timberlane*** and ***Kingsblood Royal*** Lewis seemed to turn on the American citizens, whom he had formerly loved while he chastised them, in a fit of contemptuous rage. Satire was replaced by denunciation, understanding by spite. Prejudice and sour bad temper ran riot. The two books were not only inferior as fiction, they were cruelly unjust caricatures of American life.

Cass Timberlane is a novel about marriage, about one marriage in particular and a dozen others in general. The particular one is between a middle-aged judge, a decent, likable man something like Sam Dodsworth, and Jinny, a pretty, vivacious, selfish, stupid, unfaithful girl of twenty-one. . . . The story of the ups and downs of their unhappy marriage is routine and undistinguished fare intermittently brightened by Lewis' photographic eye for the surface details of American life, by outbursts of savage wit and even by surprising interludes of whimsy and pathos. But, since a marriage with a twenty-year age difference between the contracted parties is not typical, Lewis set down his ideas on American marriage in general in a series of portrait sketches of other couples in Cass's and Jinny's circle of friends.

These comprise as ghastly a set of grossly exaggerated caricatures as Lewis could imagine. Nearly all the marriages are bitterly unhappy; the happy ones are between near idiots. Snobs, boors, drunkards, lechers, weaklings, selfish and contemptible women, vile and repulsive men, the married couples of ***Cass Timberlane*** draw out their sordid and petty lives in boredom and futility, occasionally enlivened by cheap and nasty adulteries. Through long stretches of this curious book the prevailing emotion seems to be pure hatred of men and women as such. The satire is gross and malicious, the cards wickedly stacked. There isn't one honorable, intelligent, loyal and affectionate couple in the whole book to relieve the monotony of blighted lives.

Somehow, somewhere, Lewis had lost his sense of balance and proportion. Divorce statistics prove that unhappy marriages are common; one eye half open is enough to find evidence that the world is not inhabited solely by the virtuous and noble. If Lewis had confined his attention to one unsavory marriage, or to three or four, all would have been well. But when he deliberately wrote of more than a dozen miserable marriages and included not one good one in the lot he passed the boundaries of reasonable satire. For artistic verisimilitude he should have remembered that, as it takes all kinds of people to make a world, so it takes all kinds of marriages to make that general abstraction, marriage. ***Cass Timberlane*** is so vicious a diatribe that it is neither good fiction nor effective satire.

When Lewis said of ***Kingsblood Royal*** that "the story itself is the important thing" he was either willfully obtuse or even more sarcastic than usual. For the story of ***Kingsblood Royal*** is the crudest sort of melodrama, artificial and wildly unconvincing. The only important thing about this book is its significance as Lewis' contribution to the mounting tide of protest against race discrimination. But even as propaganda for social and economic justice for Negroes, ***Kingsblood Royal*** is inferior. Lewis protested much too much.

In his desire to strike a blow in a good cause and in his hatred of injustice Lewis painted his canvas solely in blacks and whites and bloody reds, piled caricature on top of exaggeration, and populated his scene with a fantastic collection of detestable human skunks. His incredible plot, with his conventional hero discovering that he is one thirty-secondth Negro and his consequent involvement in persecution and riots, is an insult to credibility. How so experienced a writer with so wide an acquaintance of men and life and books could have committed this monstrosity passes all understanding. Lewis seemed to have fared beyond the realms of observation, humor, satire and artistic fiction into the dark outer marches of scurrilous propaganda.

The novels which have most effectively dramatized the Negro's plight as a second-class citizen have made their points by arousing sympathy for unhappy people without making monsters out of other people, equally human, who accept the inequalities of segregation and discrimination customary in their social culture. . . . The crux of the race problem is that the misfortunes of others rarely matter much to most people.

In ***Kingsblood Royal*** Lewis ignored such considerations and portrayed his hero's former friends as gibbering Nazis, ardent believers in every slander ever circulated against Negroes, and even argumentatively convinced that Negroes "would be a damn sight better off under slavery."

It just didn't wash. The Negro-baiters of ***Kingsblood Royal*** are as unreal and unrepresentative as the husbands and wives of ***Cass Timberlane,*** and Lewis hated them with equal gusto. Race prejudice undoubtedly flourishes in Minnesota as well as in Georgia, but it varies from person to person in the degree of its virulence and all the prejudiced are not monsters. Lewis, by abandoning all restraint in his plea for tolerance, did more to increase the world's excess of hate than he did to diminish it. His warm feeling for average Americans had degenerated into irrational contempt. Sinclair Lewis' last two really popular books were completely unworthy of the author of ***Arrowsmith.***

And such lapses are inevitable, for writers cannot be expected to maintain unfailing standards of excellence. Even Shakespeare wrote *Cymbeline* as well as *Hamlet*. . . . Writers are not judged by the average of their total output, but by their maximum achievements. (pp. 52-8)

Orville Prescott, "Squandered Talents: Lewis, Steinbeck, Hemingway, O'Hara," in his In My Opinion: An Inquiry into the Contemporary Novel *(© 1942, 1943, 1944, 1945, 1946, 1947, 1948, 1949, 1950, 1951 by The New York Times Company; copyright, 1952, by Orville Prescott; used by permission of the publisher, The Bobbs-Merrill Company, Inc.), Bobbs-Merrill, 1952, pp. 50-74.*

MARK SCHORER (essay date 1969)

[*Schorer was a noted American critic and the author of the definitive biography of Lewis. In his often anthologized essay* "Technique As Discovery," *Schorer put forth the argument that fiction deserves the same scrutiny, the same close attention to diction and metaphor, that the New Critics had been lavishing on poetry. He determined that fiction viewed only with respect to content was not art at all, but experience. For Schorer, only when individuals examine "achieved content," or form, do they speak of art, and consequently, speak as critics. Schorer also argued that the difference between content and art is "technique," and that the study of technique demonstrates how fictional form discovers and evaluates meaning, meaning that is often not intended by the author. The author of many essays on Lewis's work, Schorer closely examines the compositional technique of* Babbitt *in the following excerpt.*]

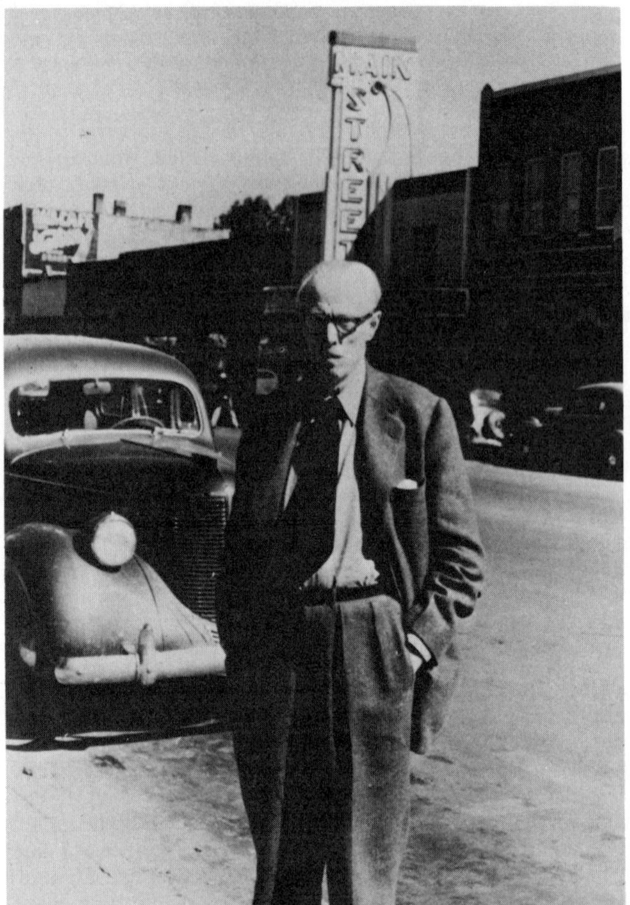

Lewis in Sauk Centre, Minnesota (1948). The Granger Collection, New York.

It has been fashionable since some time before his death in 1951 to say that Sinclair Lewis' fiction has nothing now to say to Americans, and nothing to say any longer that is centrally relevant to American life. Americans no longer talk like Lewis' characters, it is asserted, if indeed they ever did. Sinclair Lewis is dead! To the bulk of his twenty-one novels and to almost the entire mass of his shorter fiction, the charge is probably applicable enough, but to three or four or possibly even five novels, above all, to ***Babbitt,*** it is not. (p. 105)

Main Street was published in 1920. This story about the sluggish backwaters of American village life was published in the year that officially announced American village life to have become a backwater. The 1920 census showed that at some point between 1915 and that year American society had crossed a line from what had been a rural to what had become an urban society. Sometime between those years, the old majority of farmers and villagers had become the minority, and the residents of cities comprised the new majority. ***Babbitt*** opens in April 1920. It is concerned not only with the new urban society but also with certain new urban attitudes that attach to American commercial culture: the idea of "boosting," for example, that aggressive promotion of special civic interests that finally finds its apotheosis in our enormous system of Public Relations; and that idea of business "service" to the community, which bears the same relationship to the actual practices of commercialism as the idea of "the white man's burden" bears to the actualities of imperialism and colonialism. Yet it shows us, too, how the residents of Zenith, booming the city, profess still much of the rural faith of their fathers, and how from this conflict between old and newer attitudes proceed frustration, guilt, despair of a watered kind, at last emptiness. (pp. 107-08)

Babbitt is a satiric prelude to a decade of dizzying and often mindless economic expansion, the epic of our "boom" years, and it remains today the major documentation in literature of American business culture in general. We can no longer say, as Woodrow Wilson said in 1900, that "The history of a nation is only the history of its villages written large." By 1920, we substitute for *village* the name of *Zenith.*

As we see Zenith looming beyond Gopher Prairie, so we see Gopher Prairie still in the process of receding in Zenith. On the first page "the mist took pity on the fretted structures of earlier generations: the Post Office with its shingle-tortured mansard, the red brick minarets of hulking old houses. . . ." There is the explicit contrast between Babbitt and his father-in-law, Henry Thompson, between "the old-fashioned, lean Yankee, rugged, traditional stage type of American business man, and Babbitt, the plump, smooth, efficient, up-to-the-minute and otherwise perfected modern." The ironic limitations of this contrast are underlined in the discussion of small towns at the Babbitts' first dinner party in the novel, when the talk of the whole company, consisting of the emptiest banalities and comprising a pure parody of any interchange that could be called conversation, laments the absence of meaningful conversation and "culture" in the "hick towns" that Chum Frink, "a Famous Poet and a distinguished advertising agent," has just been touring.

Physically, the culture has become predominantly urban; but psychologically it is in large part still stubbornly rural, perhaps even more profoundly provincial than before. . . . [The] whole aim of the documentation of ***Babbitt*** is to demonstrate that with the cultural shift, the slavery of the individual has become even more rigid, that freedom exists only in impossibly infantile, whimpering dreams.

I have twice used the word *documentation,* and quite intentionally. ***Babbitt*** is the first of Lewis' novels that rests on what was henceforth to be his characteristic method of "research." His preceding five novels had shown traces of similar "research," but now it becomes nearly systematic. He established a *pied-à-terre* ["base of operations"] at the Queen City Club in Cincinnati, Ohio, and if Zenith is modeled on any one city, it is this one. Here he consolidated his researches, and his gray notebooks were already fat with his notation.

The method involved a series of steps. First, he chose a subject and a "field" within it to be mastered—not, as for most novelists, a character situation or a mere theme, but a social area (a sub-class within the middle class) that could be studied and "worked up"—in this instance, the world of the small businessman and within that, real estate. Then, armed with his notebooks, he mingled with the kind of people that the fiction would mainly concern. In Pullman cars and smokers, in the lobbies of side-street hotels, in athletic clubs, in a hundred junky streets he watched and listened, and then meticulously copied into his notebooks whole catalogs of expressions drawn from the American lingo, elaborate lists of proper names, every kind of physical detail. Once his story was determined, he drew intricately detailed maps, and maps not only of the city in which the story was set but of the houses in which his actions would take place, floor plans with furniture precisely located, streets and the kind and color of dogs that walked on them. Once his chief characters were settled upon, he wrote out full biographies of all of them. From this body of material, he would then write out a summary of his story, and from this, a much more extended "plan," as he called it, with every scene sketched in, the whole sometimes nearly as long as the book that would come from it. A first draft would then follow, usually much longer than the final version, and then a long process of revision and cutting, and at last the publishable text. (pp. 109-10)

The immediate result is not surprising even though the ultimate effect may be. The immediate result is a fictional approximation of the social anthropologist's field report. A year after the publication of ***Babbitt,*** when asked about its origins, Lewis said that all he could remember was that the original name of the protagonist was Pumphrey and that "I planned to make the whole novel 24 hours in his life, from alarm clock to alarm clock. The rest came more or less unconsciously." . . . The name *Pumphrey* remained as that of a minor character—"Professor Joseph K. Pumphrey, owner of the Riteway Business College and instructor in Public Speaking, Business English, Scenario Writing, and Commercial Law"—and the original structural conception remained in the first seven chapters, in which we do indeed follow George Babbitt from dreaming sleep to dreaming sleep. But that is only one-fourth of the whole novel.

The remainder, twenty-seven chapters, did not come about "unconsciously," as their obviously planned substance makes very clear. They are, rather than "unconscious," a quite highly conscious, indeed systematic series of set pieces, each with its own topic, and all together giving us an almost punctilious analysis of the sociology of American commercial culture and middle-class life. Over halfway through the novel, mingling with these set pieces, the first of three "plots" begins.

These twenty-seven chapters could well have carried, in the convention of earlier fiction, subject titles. Chapters Eight and Nine, in which the Babbitts entertain at dinner in their Floral Heights house, could have been called Domestic Manners of the Americans. The next two chapters might have been headed Marital Relations and Pullman Car Customs. Chapter Twelve is about Leisure: baseball, golf, the movies, bridge, motoring. Chapter Thirteen takes up the phenomenon of the annual Trade Association Convention and, since it ends with some adult but immature louts in a brothel, Juvenile Delinquency. Chapter Fourteen has to do with Political and Professional Oratory, and Fifteen, with Class Structure. The next two chapters devote themselves to Religion, and Eighteen, to Family Relations. The first of the three separate "plots" begins in the next chapter, Nineteen, and delaying discussion of these for a moment, we may observe that the general topics remaining are the weekly Service Club Lunch, the Bachelor, the Barber Shop, Labor

Relations, the Speakeasy, and "Crank" Religion. It is a very thorough canvassing of an entire milieu, and its nearly anthropological intention is made evident in such a sentence as "Now this was the manner of obtaining alcohol under the reign of righteousness and prohibition," the sentence that introduces Babbitt's visit to a bootlegger.

If the canvas that these pieces comprise is surprisingly complete, their ordering is nevertheless quite haphazard. They might have been presented in almost any other sequence, and that is because there is no genuine plot or coherent, causative march of dramatic events from beginning to end and that would necessarily have determined their order. Their fragmentariness is in part overcome by the fact that it is the single figure of Babbitt who moves through all of them in the course of his mounting discontent, revolt, his retreat and relapse into resignation. (pp. 111-12)

It is Babbitt's tragedy that he can never be anything but Babbitt, even though he has a glimmering recognition of what it is about being Babbitt that he does not always like. . . . The terror and loneliness that he feels in his brief taste of freedom (and that freedom itself consists largely of a very "mechanical" bit of adultery) arise from the fact that when he is free he is nothing at all. His only self is the self that exists solely within the circle of conformity.

Since the publication of ***Babbitt,*** everyone has learned that conformity is the great price that our predominantly commercial culture exacts of American life. But when ***Babbitt*** was published, this was its revelation to Americans, and this was likewise how the novel differed from all novels about business that had been published before it.

American literature had a rich if brief tradition of the business novel. Henry James, William Dean Howells, Charles and Frank Norris, Jack London, David Graham Phillips, Robert Herrick, Upton Sinclair, Edith Wharton, Theodore Dreiser, Ernest Poole, Booth Tarkington—all these writers and others as well had been concerned with the businessman, and after James and Howells, only Tarkington was to find in him any of the old, perdurable American virtues. Business was synonymous with ethical corruption; the world of business was savagely competitive, brutally aggressive, murderous. The motivation of the businessman was power, money, social prestige, in that order. But the businessman in all this fiction was the tycoon, the powerful manufacturer, the vast speculator, the fabulous financier, the monarch of enormous enterprises, the arch-individual responsible only to himself. He was the equivalent in the developing industrial world of the old, aggressively independent frontiersman. And his concern was with production, if only of more money from money.

After the First World War and our shift to an urban culture, the tycoon may still have been the most colorful and dramatic figure in the business myth, but he was no longer by any means the characteristic figure, and ***Babbitt*** discovers that difference. If George F. Babbitt has vague hankerings after the old frontier independence, his incompetence in that role is made plain enough by his ridiculous vacation excursions into Maine. His is the shriveled office world of the small businessman, and more particularly, of the small middleman. If his morals are no better, his defections are anything but spectacular: a little cheating in a deal, a little lie to one's wife, a little stealthy fornication that one pretends did not occur. Not in the least resembling the autocratic individualist, he is always the compromising conformist. No producer himself, his success depends on public relations. He does not rule; he "joins" to be safe. He boosts and boasts with his fellows, sings and cheers and prays with the throng, derides all difference, denounces all dissent—and all to climb with the crowd. With the supremacy of public relations, he abolishes human relations. And finally, therefore, without at all knowing it, he abolishes all but a wretched remnant of his own humanity.

All this Sinclair Lewis' novel gave back to a culture that was just becoming aware that it would not be able to tolerate what it was in the process of making itself. And his novel did it with a difference. The older novels, generally speaking, were solemn or grandly melodramatic denunciations of monstrous figures of aggressive evil. ***Babbitt*** was raucously satirical of a crowd of ninnies and buffoons who, if they were vindictive and petty, were also absurd. Yet, along with all that, Babbitt himself was pathetic. How could the novel possibly have failed? It did not. It was one of the greatest international successes in all publishing history.

The European response was unadulterated delight: this was the way—crass, materialistic, complacent, chauvinistic—that Europe had always known America to be, and now an American had made the confession to the world. In the United States the response was, understandably, more diluted. Among those who were either unimpressed or outraged, there was, however, a small complaint on the score of the deficiencies of ***Babbitt*** as a novel. No one, for example, observed the slack structure, or the repetitiousness of point in the long series of sociological demonstrations. Edith Wharton, in her letter of congratulations to Lewis, did recognize that he seemed to depend on an excess of slang, on nearly endless imitation of midwestern garrulity; but this did not bother others. Had anyone complained, for example, that in his use of public addresses of one sort or another, Lewis' pleasure in mimicry threatened to carry him far beyond the demands of his fiction, it could have been pointed out that here is a very integral part of his satire. Elocution is an old American institution, and a windy, mindless rhetoric has been of its essence, as the oratory at the conventions of either of our chief political parties still painfully reminds us. Lewis' use of elocution adds a swelling note to the already loud *blat-blat* of the public voice that roars and rattles through the novel, and if Lewis lets Babbitt admire Chan Mott because he "can make a good talk even when he hasn't got a doggone thing to say," he is also making an observation on the empty and noisy restlessness of American life.

It was not generally the writing, nor even Lewis' satiric exposure of American commercial culture in itself that disturbed those readers who were disturbed, but rather their failure to find in the novel anything beyond this grossness. With George Santayana, who was otherwise impressed by the novel, they saw "no suggestion of the direction . . . in which salvation may come." The complaint was to say of Lewis, in effect, what Lewis had himself said of Babbitt, that he was "without a canon [of value] which would enable him to speak with authority." If Babbitt, with his faint sense that the values of excellence, joy, passion, wisdom, do indeed exist somewhere, but had not the slightest notion of how to pursue them, did Sinclair Lewis?

It became a commonplace to say of Lewis that he was himself too much a George F. Babbitt to lift his sights to values beyond Babbitt's own. In many ways the charge is just. But Lewis is different from Babbitt in one supreme way: he *observed* him, and Babbitt had not been observed before; thus he *created* him; and Babbitt endures in our literature as in our life, where

Sinclair Lewis enabled all of us to see him for the first and for an enduring time.

He endures with a special kind of solidity and vitality. He is so inexhaustibly *there*. This achievement obviously derives from Lewis' technique. That mass of social notation that we have remarked, notation that Lewis pursued with all the naturalist's compulsiveness, is yet, in the end, not at all a naturalistic performance. It shares rather in the realm of what today we call Pop Art. Take any very mundane item from our daily lives—a Campbell's Soup can, for example; observe it in the most exact and even microscopic detail; then enlarge it; then repeat it over and over in the monotonous design; and at last something *not* naturalistic but rather grotesque and even monstrous emerges, and something in the end much more substantial than the absurdity from which it is constructed.

It was this quality that Constance Rourke had in mind in 1931 [see excerpt above] when she singled Lewis out among his contemporaries: "With one exception none of those definitive novelists have appeared who make an aspect of contemporary life their own and leave it with the color of their imagination upon it forever afterward. The exception of course is Sinclair Lewis. . . ." The term *novelist* in the usual sense was not quite right for him. She gave him, and we do still, the larger title: *fabulist*. (pp. 113-16)

Mark Schorer, "Sinclair Lewis: 'Babbitt'," in Landmarks of American Writing, *edited by Hennig Cohen (© 1969 by Basic Books, Inc., Publishers; reprinted by permission of the publisher), Basic Books, 1969 (and reprinted in* The Merrill Studies in "Babbitt," *edited by Martin Light, Charles E. Merrill Publishing Company, 1971, pp. 105-16).*

ANTHONY CHANNELL HILFER (essay date 1969)

[*Hilfer offers a close textual and thematic analysis of* Main Street *and* Babbitt, *viewing each as an indictment of small-town values.*]

Many critics see ***Main Street*** and Lewis' other novels only as sociological and historical events: superficial and intrinsically valueless reflections of a widespread discontent with old values. Lewis is attacked for the very faults his fiction satirizes: the banality and Babbittry that he does, in truth, partially share with his characters. Lewis lacks very obviously the psychological penetration and the subjective sensibility that modern criticism does well to value. His characters are, it is true, all surface, no depth, but Lewis' talent lies precisely in the incisiveness and suggestiveness of his delineations of the social surface, his unmasking of the dominant middle class. As a sociological satirist, Lewis deserves critical attention and respect.

Lewis' best novels are sociological in content and, to a large extent, in form. Mark Schorer notes, "With Lewis, the subject, the social section, always came first; systematic research, sometimes conducted by research assistants and carrying Lewis himself into 'the field' like any cultural anthropologist, followed; the story came last, devised to carry home and usually limping under the burden of data." Lewis conceived of novels in sociological terms. ***Main Street*** is a fictional study of the small town, ***Babbitt*** is a study of the "businessman," later novels deal with a social worker (***Ann Vickers***), with organized "philanthropy" (***Gideon Planish***), and the "race problem" (***Kingsblood Royal***). The structure of his novels is often sociological. The first seven chapters of ***Babbitt,*** for instance, are based on the businessman's day—a standard sociological method—followed by twenty-seven chapters built around sociological topics that reflect various aspects of bourgeois manners and mores. Finally, the intended and actual importance of ***Main Street*** and ***Babbitt*** is as cultural critiques.

Lewis even makes half-hearted efforts toward the fairness and objectivity that sociologists strive for, but Lewis is not fair and not objective; like Mencken he uses sociology as a satirical weapon. In one sense, Gopher Prairie and Babbitt are sociological ideal types. The most general and essential qualities of small towns and of businessmen are abstracted and then put together in the concrete image of the ideal type: Gopher Prairie is the typical town; Babbitt, the archetypal businessman. But the image is stacked, and tendentious; the portraits are caricatures. (pp. 158-59)

Main Street is a sociological caricature unmasking the small town. (p. 160)

In sociological manner, Lewis attacks false stereotypes of the small town. The stereotype of the hick town populated by comic farmers with whiskers is, Lewis notes, forty years out of date. The 1920 small town differs from the city mostly in negative terms: it has the same standardized products but with less a variety, the same social and political orthodoxies but with less dissent. The more popular stereotype is that "the American village remains the one sure abode of friendship, honesty, and clean sweet marriageable girls." To this favorable stereotype, Lewis opposes his caricature: Gopher Prairie, a sketch unifying the physiognomy of the town into a single expression of mechanical and fatuous dullness.

The ideas behind Lewis' image come from several sources. Like Van Wyck Brooks, Lewis was what might be termed an aesthetic socialist in the tradition of Ruskin and Morris. The physical ugliness of the village, from this point of view, reflects its dearth of spiritual values. Church, school, and post office are all shabby, but the bank is an "ionic temple of marble. Pure, exquisite, solitary." . . . Lewis overrates bank architecture, but the spiritual stature of finance as contrasted to church and state is clearly established. As an aesthetic socialist, Lewis blames the ugliness of the town on its lack of a guiding and unifying spiritual ideal—the *sine qua non* of all great architecture in the view of the Victorian culture critics. In Brooksian fashion, Lewis blames the hangover of pioneer values for the "planlessness, the flimsy temporariness of the buildings." . . . The town is a frontier outpost that has lost its vigor and its contact with nature without gaining culture.

Main Street also has the Brooksian buried life, though treated with gross and clumsy clichés. The Vida Sherwin of ***Main Street*** is an unintentional parody of Masters and Anderson: "She lived an engrossed useful life, and seemed as cool and simple as an apple. But secretly she was creeping among fears, longing, and guilt. She knew what it was, but she dared not name it. She hated even the sound of the word "sex." (pp. 161-62)

Lewis did not have to have read Brooks to pick up such ideas. They were in the air though Brooks was their most influential exponent. Such is the case with Thorstein Veblen, as well, but it is hard to believe Lewis' later claim that he had never read Veblen. ***The Job,*** an earlier novel, seems to reflect Veblen, as do ***Main Street*** and ***Babbitt.*** At any rate, Lewis' characters read Veblen: Carol Kennicott and Miles Bjornstam are Veblen readers. . . . When Carol decides that the most properly subversive thing she could do would be "asking people to define their jobs," . . . she is talking Veblen's language. Much of Veblen's writings consist of vituperative redefinitions of economic functions which unmask the merchant class as exploitative and parasitic. Lewis makes it clear that Gopher Prairie lives off the farmers whom the town despises, overcharges, and cheats.

The central influence on ***Main Street,*** as later on ***Babbitt*** and ***Elmer Gantry,*** was H. L. Mencken. For what most bothers Carol is not the ugliness of the town, not its injustice, but the soul-destroying intellectual conformity that leads to a pervasive and inescapable dullness.

Percy Boynton has commented that the reader has difficulty remembering individual characters by the end of the book. The characters are indistinguishable because, though some are kinder or better-natured, they all think in the same clichés. The sociology of the book is Mencken's and Sumner's: the group mind thinks in stock formulas and is controlled by group conventions. (pp. 162-63)

The townspeople completely lack the sympathetic and the critical imagination. They are as unable to conceive of the possibility of anyone outside their own class having a mind or emotions as they are to conceive of the possibility that any value of the in-group might be wrong. They are in mental prisons, able to see the world only through the narrow slits of self-interest and accepted ideas. In such a world, critical thought cannot exist, and conversation consists either of the ritual chanting of orthodoxies or of gossip about personalities. As for personality, the villagers discuss it at the lowest level of superficiality. Someone's personality is forever fixed and tagged by some ancient joke or scandal about him or by some peculiarity of manner or physique.

This anatomy of provincialism still holds fairly true: provincial people are closed-minded and unable to cope with objective thought. Worse yet, they really believe in the mythology of the small town: that it is decent, moral, democratic, honest, God's own country, etc. This is what most irritates Lewis' heroine, Carol Kennicott. The villagers have faith in their superiority to the undemocratic East, but in reality the town is a "sterile oligarchy." . . . The final straw for Carol is the town's boosting campaign: "she could, she asserted, endure a shabby but modest town; the town shabby but egomaniac she could not endure." . . . Like most satirists Lewis was less irritated by the dreariness of his targets than by their complacent pride in their dreariness. His satire is an attack on the pride of what seemed to be a village civilization newly inflated to a world power. . . . (pp. 163-64)

Lewis, then, exaggerates the actual power of the American small town but not its mythic significance. He attacks widespread American provincialism at its symbolic source. The popularity of ***Main Street*** is not hard to account for; the myth it deflates was—like all combinations of pride, hypocrisy, smugness, and meanness—ripe for unmasking and a vast amount of irritation was released by the public exposure of what everyone really knew.

Lewis' anatomy of provincialism is accurate but it is also old hat. No one is likely to be surprised by anything in ***Main Street.*** Lewis has become so assimilated as to become almost obsolescent. This could not happen to an author who *renders* human experience, but ***Main Street*** is largely editorial; we are told about, rather than shown, the town. Its gossips and dullards never come to life even in their deadness so that the weakest passages in the novel are those in which Lewis has dialogue or action. Even at the level of abstract editorializing, Lewis' ideas are trite and obvious. His exposure of small towns never cuts to the bone as Mark Twain's often does. There is a more intense vision of human meanness in two or three passages of "The Man That Corrupted Hadleyburg" than in all of Lewis' overstuffed novel.

Lewis' banal style is another element contributing to the loss of favor his writings have suffered. He should, however, be granted the virtues of his vices: his personal superficiality is mirrored in his style, but so is his intense nervous vitality; his writing is thin but electric.

Even 1920 readers were irritated by Carol Kennicott, though many thought Lewis intended her to seem ridiculous. Some modern readers like to suppose, conversely, that Lewis has no idea of his heroine's defects; Lewis is properly shown up by such a reading. In fact, not only Lewis but Carol herself is aware of her faults. The pattern of the book is made up of her self-assertions followed by her self-doubtings. She thoroughly realizes the absurdity of many of her ideas, and Lewis' irony can hardly be doubted in his descriptions of her belief in a "rather vaguely conceived sweetness and light" . . . or of her desire to "conquer the world—almost entirely for the world's own good." . . . Nevertheless, Lewis does overrate his heroine and in some ways he is reflected in her. He overrates her, however, not through failing to realize her silliness but because of his indulgence toward it. He did not expect as much from a heroine as most readers do. (Perhaps the reader's irritation is slightly priggish, for that matter.) Some critics seemed to feel that Carol should be content with Gopher Prairie simply because she herself was no genius but that is to miss the point of the book. Carol does not condemn the ignorance of Gopher Prairie so much as its complacency in ignorance nor its stupidity so much as its resistance to knowledge. Carol has the one quality Lewis most admires: she wants to know, she stays loose, she refuses to renounce her freedom to criticize and to wonder. This is what gives her a life in the novel which the other characters, fixed in their provincial orthodoxies, lack.

Freedom is, in fact, the main theme of Lewis' novels. At the beginning of ***Main Street,*** we find Carol in an attitude of "suspended freedom." . . . Since freedom was the one and only thing that Lewis really believed in, freedom can only exist in suspension; an absolute conviction enslaves. When someone asked Lewis if Carol were a self-portrait, he replied: "Yes . . . Carol is 'Red' Lewis: always groping for something she isn't capable of attaining, always dissatisfied, always restlessly straining to see what lies just over the horizon, intolerant of her surroundings, yet lacking any clearly defined vision of what she really wants to do or be." This commitment to a rootless and indefinable freedom is the key to Lewis' writings and career, the essential quality responsible for his success and failure. Lewis is nervous and alive, a man on the move, but he never gets anywhere. He is free to go but where to?

As far as the theme of freedom goes, ***Babbitt*** is a mere rewriting of ***Main Street*** though far superior in technique. In ***Babbitt,*** the protagonist is at the center of the world Lewis is attacking rather than on the periphery, illustrating the absurdities that Carol merely editorializes. Carol sees Gopher Prairie from the outside whereas Babbitt is the archetype of Zenith.

Zenith is something more than Gopher Prairie. As Lewis' unpublished introduction to ***Babbitt*** makes clear, Zenith is meant to represent the typical, small, boom city, a relatively unexploited literary subject. . . . (pp. 165-68)

Zenith is between the large city and the small village in more aspects than merely size. Gopher Prairie aspires to reach the heights of Zenith, but in all too many ways Zenith is merely a monstrously enlarged Gopher Prairie. Zenith is an anomaly: physically it is a city, but spiritually it is still a small town. . . . This along with the usual freedom-conformity conflict is the essential theme of ***Babbitt:*** the anomalous relationship of the American businessman with his small-town mass mind to the vastly powerful urban-industrial complex that he rules without understanding. It is a fictional variation on the themes of Thorstein Veblen's *The Theory of Business Enterprise* and a fictional anticipation of Ortega y Gasset's *The Revolt of the Masses*.

Lewis' image of the businessman and his relation to his culture begins in the early pages of ***Babbitt*** with a Veblen-like comparison of industrial power and the businessmen who take credit for it. Zenith at dawn is described in a passage emphasizing what Lewis believes to be the beauty and majesty of industrial power. The essential joke in the book is established with the description of the man who lives in "a city built—it seemed—for giants." . . . (pp. 168-69)

The businessman as baby is the dominant image that runs throughout ***Babbitt.*** The name itself suggests part of the image: Babbitt = baby, babble. Moreover, in addition to the details given in the quoted passage which establish the image of a baby—the pink head, the baby plumpness, the helpless hand—there are the later touches of Babbitt's "baby-blue pajamas," . . . his childishly petulant face, . . . and "the sleeveless dimity B.V.D. undershirt, in which he resembled a small boy humorlessly wearing a cheesecloth tabard at a civic pageant." . . . In this last image, Babbitt is less the baby than the pre-adolescent, but nowhere in the book does he seem to have wandered very far from the border of puberty. Even his wife is an indulgent mother, "as sexless as an anemic nun." . . . She calls him "Georgie boy." . . . (p. 169)

Babbitt does have sexual fantasies about a "fairy child," but if the fairy child sometimes seems to be a dream substitute for a flapper, at other times she is a childish playmate and sometimes, like Myra Babbitt, a mother. . . . Even the fantasies expressive of Babbitt's "buried life" are adolescent.

Babbitt's world, like that of any small boy, is ruled by rituals of speech and behavior. The more commonplace the action, the more of a ritual it becomes. Even having the car filled with gasoline is a "rite." . . . Driving the car is both a rite and a game: "Babbitt . . . devoted himself to the game of beating trolley cars to the corner: a spurt, a tail-chase, nervous speeding between the huge yellow side of the trolley and the jagged row of parked motors, shooting past just as the trolley stopped—a rare game and valiant." . . .

Babbitt's relation then to the complex technological world around him is that of a baby surrounded by shiny toys. His small-town mind is quite as incapable of understanding the scientific principles underlying his world as Theron Ware's was to cope with the new theology. Babbitt's car, for instance, is a private fighter plane, a virility-substitute. Babbitt lives in a world of meaningless gadgetry, a world typified by the worship rather than the understanding of machinery. . . . (p. 170)

In a strange reversal of Kant, machines rather than people are regarded as ends in themselves, as with the electric cigar lighter that Babbitt buys: "It was a pretty thing, a nickeled cylinder with an almost silvery socket, to be attached to the dashboard of his car. It was not only, as the placard on the counter observed, 'a dandy little refinement, lending the last touch of class to a gentleman's auto,' but a priceless time-saver. By freeing him from halting the car to light a match, it would in a month or two easily save ten minutes." . . . The lighter is similar to Babbitt's own business function: he too is expensive, decorative, and modern but not very useful. As the small-towners of ***Main Street*** have a parasitic relationship with the farmers, so is Babbitt a mere parasite of modern industry.

The bathroom is the supreme architectural accomplishment of Babbitt's culture. At the end of his working day, we see Babbitt, "plump, smooth, pink," reverting unashamedly to babyhood in the bathtub. . . . The porcelain tub, the nickel taps, and the tiled walls of Babbitt's bathroom symbolize a civilization that is typified by all that is antiseptic, cellophane-wrapped, and standardized: a civilization separated from nature and inimical to human nature. (pp. 170-71)

The main difference between Zenith and Gopher Prairie, and between Babbitt and Doctor Kennicott, is just this predominance of the machine and the hygenic. (p. 171)

Zenith is merely a Gopher Prairie enlarged, mechanized, and cleaned up; Babbitt and his friends merely small-towners who are better dressed, closer shaved, slicker, and running on faster though equally mechanical rhythms. These men have graduated to the machine age only in the most superficial manner; their relation to the machine is merely that of superstitious worship and mindless, uncomprehending imitation. Essentially they are small-towners, mass minds, babies lost in a world of machines.

The world of Lewis' novel is machine made. It is characterized by images of glittering surfaces, meaningless hustle and bustle, inescapable noise, and standardized people. At times, Babbitt himself seems merely a mechanical cog in this world-machine, as, indeed, he imagines himself: "He felt superior and powerful, like a shuttle of polished steel darting in a vast machine." . . . Babbitt's very name has a mechanistic as well as babyish association: babbitt metal is an antifriction alloy used for bearings. Yet Babbitt, other-directed though he is, does not always avoid friction nor is he forever content as a cog in a machine. Babbitt is humanized not only by his childishness but also by a pathetic attempt at rebellion. . . . His buried emotional life attempts to assert itself.

A very unsatisfactory and abortive rebellion it is. Babbitt manages to make a brief escape to the Maine woods in an attempt to find solace in nature, in the manner of Thoreau, who was a central influence on Lewis' writing. Thoreau's influence shows in Babbitt's curious choice of the Maine woods as a refuge rather than the nearer wilds of Minnesota or Michigan; in Babbitt's realization that he is living "a life of barren heartiness" with its echo of "lives of quiet desperation"; and in the pervasive presence of a set of values in opposition to those of Babbitt's world—an organic, natural, inward existence, fronting the essential truths of life. Far from becoming transformed into a Midwestern Thoreau, Babbitt turns out to be a babe in the woods. He conceives of nature in terms of the childish adventure story and the motion picture: "Moccasins—sixgun—frontier town—gamblers—sleep under the stars—be a regular man." . . . Babbitt, corrupted by his culture, lacks the inner quietude, the ability to absorb experience without its being thrust upon him. Thoreau was able to discover nature by freeing his mind from the petty encumbrances of a busy and unimportant civilization. Babbitt, however, as a victim of the machine age "could never run away from Zenith and family and office, because in his own brain he bore the office and the family and every street and disquiet and illusion of Zenith." . . . If Thomas Wolfe could not go home again, Babbitt could never leave.

At home in Zenith, Babbitt's ineffectual rebellion continues. He becomes a liberal for a while on no better grounds than a conversation with a lawyer. He has an affair. But these efforts are merely impotent attempts to escape the vague dissatisfaction that haunts him throughout the novel. He has dim intimations of what he wants to escape from but no idea of what he wants to escape to. He cannot escape from his world of standardized and mechanical thought for he has nothing with which to replace it. In fact, he has no real alternative, for he is trapped not by outer circumstances so much as his own conditioned and inert mind.

Eventually, the near-fatal illness of Babbitt's wife allows him, rather gratefully, to return to the comfortable world of stereotypes and expected responses, free from the insupportable requirements of freedom. Accompanying his wife to the hospital, he burns his hand on the radiator. His wife immediately assumes her accustomed role and he his. . . . (pp. 172-74)

Still Babbitt does not wholly succumb. He keeps the spark of freedom alive by defending his son's elopement with a girl who is the embodiment of Babbitt's own wished-for fairy child. It is no accident that this ending is an almost exact repetition of ***Main Street:*** the unequipped rebel finally succumbs but with an inner defiance and hopes for a younger generation. Both novels begin well but begin to get a bit dull when it becomes apparent that neither the characters nor the plot is really going anywhere and that both are condemned to circle back to their starting point, with nothing gained and much energy lost. Lewis' own dilemma is exactly mirrored. Although his life was, in a sense, a continual flight from Sauk Center, he was never able to transcend the limiting dichotomies bequeathed him by his background. He has only two basic characters: the conformist and the nonconformist, the latter symbiotically dependent on the former since his only energy is in rejection. Even this rejection cannot become an absolute and transcendent gesture since total rejection would demand a reflexive conviction—and Lewis has none to offer.

It is questionable as to whether the actual limitations of freedom in American society are as strong as Lewis represents them to be in his novels. Genuinely critical thought may run into obstacles anywhere, but Lewis exaggerates the strength of the obstacles and the weakness of the rebels. Lewis himself, after all, was a successful rebel; he made rebellion pay to the extent that he even became honored in his own country, Sauk Center's "favorite son." But such success is denied his main characters as if to indicate his own apparent freedom was illusory. Lewis would likely defend himself on realistic grounds. When Floyd Dell complained that ***Main Street*** was too one-sided, not fairly representing the presence and strength of nonconformist elements, Lewis replied that Gopher Prairie was a much smaller town than the more mixed Port Royal of Dell's *Moon-Calf.* Similarly, a real estate man might find it difficult to be unorthodox, whereas a lawyer (like the liberal Senaca Doane, a minor character in ***Babbitt)*** has more leeway. The truth is that Lewis simply cannot imagine freedom within the social structure of America.

Moreover, Lewis cannot make up his mind about another of the major conflicts that runs through the novel, that of the mechanization of life. On the one hand, Babbitt and his cohorts are judged for having failed to measure up to the romantic possibilities of an industrial-technological world. They are in the wrong for not being adequately attuned to the machine world they live in. They are small-towners and provincials in their inability to truly comprehend the rich possibilities of a technological world. On the other hand, one of the key indictments against the Babbitt-world, just as against the Main Street world, is its mechanism, and Lewis indicts this in the traditional organic *vs.* mechanical formula of the Victorian culture critics (not to mention Van Wyck Brooks). Here the complaint is that the small-town mind is *too* mechanistic, too willing to submit to merely mechanical rhythms. If Lewis had any notion of how to reconcile these contradictions, it is not apparent in ***Babbitt.*** (pp. 175-76)

Anthony Channell Hilfer, "Sinclair Lewis: Caricaturist of the Village Mind," in his The Revolt from the Village: 1915-1930 *(copyright © 1969 by The University of North Carolina Press), University of North Carolina Press, 1969, pp. 158-76.*

C. HUGH HOLMAN (essay date 1973)

[*Holman was an American detective novelist and literary scholar whose critical works focus predominantly on the fiction of Southern writers, particularly Ellen Glasgow, William Faulkner, Flannery O'Connor, and Thomas Wolfe. He edited several notable collections of Wolfe's writings, including* The Short Novels of Thomas Wolfe *(1961) and* The Letters of Thomas Wolfe to His Mother *(1968). In the following excerpt, Holman discusses Lewis's skill and technique as a satirist.*]

Sinclair Lewis, America's first Nobel laureate in literature, was the summation and epitome of the satiric and comic reaction to what he labeled the "Village Virus." Indeed, the Nobel citation read: "The 1930 Nobel Prize in Literature is awarded to Sinclair Lewis for his powerful and vivid art of description and his ability to use wit and humor in the creation of original characters." . . . In the 1920's he turned his attention back to the country of his childhood and adolescence and produced five novels that, despite a number of obvious weaknesses, seem to have a secure place in our national literature. These novels are ***Main Street,*** a satiric portrait of a small town huddled on the Great Plains; ***Babbitt,*** a portrait of a representative businessman in a typical small city in the Middle West; ***Arrowsmith,*** a portrait of the scientist as saint, of a physician pursuing truth with unselfish and absolute commitment, and an attack on the society that tries to inhibit and pervert his search; ***Elmer Gantry,*** a savagely comic portrait of a dishonest and insincere minister and of the world in which he works; and ***Dodsworth,*** a mellower satire, this time of Americans seeking culture in Europe. He was to produce ten more novels before his death in 1951, but none of them had the energy, vitality, and originality of the five that established his fame and, in fact, said just about all that he had to say of a world that he both loved and mocked for its painful inadequacies. Yet most of the novels published after ***Dodsworth*** remained grounded in the life of the Middle West, were couched in the language of the earlier works, and maintained many of the same attitudes, although mellowed by time, of his earlier years.

Lewis was originally taken as a realist, partly because his great power of mimicry gave an apparent authenticity to the speech of his characters and partly because the massive research which he did in getting the surface details of the daily lives of his people precisely right cast an air of great accuracy over the world he represented. But Sinclair Lewis was really a satirist and a humorist, and in his use of the devices and methods of the satirist and humorist lie both his greatest strengths and his chief weaknesses.

As a humorist he belongs clearly in the tradition of Yankee humor, that of the shrewd and knowing peddler or the cracker-box philosopher. For the most important person in Lewis's best work is Lewis himself. It is he who sees with great clarity, describes with deflating directness, mocks, sneers at, condemns. Everywhere in his novels—and particularly in ***Main Street*** and ***Babbitt***—the reader is listening to the narrator-novelist and indeed is being invited to share with him his sense of the incongruity and falseness of the world being described. Thus the novels become extended comic and satiric essays, with narrative exempla to illustrate and underscore the points. The most common posture of the narrator is that of detached observer and sardonic critic. The characters are seen from the outside, their words checked against their deeds, their actions presented mockingly. When we enter their thoughts, it is seldom to explore them as fully realized characters but rather to pinpoint a motive or make ridiculous an aspiration or dream. For example, when Carol Kennicott, in ***Main Street,*** is putting out plants in a park near the railroad station, Lewis says: "Passengers looking from trains saw her as a village woman of fading prettiness, incorruptible virtue, and no abnormalities . . . and all the while she saw herself running garlanded through the streets of Babylon." Certainly the interior glimpse is not intended to make an exploration of psychological depths but to deflate and to mock. The original plan of ***Babbitt*** was that it should represent a typical day in the life of a typical businessman. That plan still survives in the first seven chapters, one-fourth of the total book, and it is only after this eventless and typical day that the casual plot of Babbitt's futile efforts at rebellion get underway. Lewis's statement about Elmer Gantry is not unusual: "He had been sitting with a Bible and an evening paper in his lap, reading one of them." Nor is the description of Gantry praying in the pulpit of his church: "He turned to include the choir, and for the first time he saw that there was a new singer, a girl with charming ankles and lively eyes, with whom he would certainly have to become well acquainted. But the thought was so swift that it did not interrupt the paean of his prayer." No, Lewis is not drawing extended psychographs of people; he is exhibiting specimens as though they were insects in a display case, and when he penetrates their skin it is primarily to make them squirm.

This narrator is superior to his subjects. In the five big novels he presents only two characters who are treated with full sympathy, Martin Arrowsmith and Sam Dodsworth, and one, Carol Kennicott of ***Main Street,*** whom he likes but frequently mocks. The superiority he feels toward his people is based on his greater knowledge and his distance from them but, most important of all, it is based on his moral sense. To find the standard against which to measure these people in establishing this judgment of their morality, Lewis looks toward the past. He finds it in the sturdy pioneers, whom he often celebrates. ***Main Street*** begins: "On a hill by the Mississippi where Chippewas camped two generations ago. . . ." And it goes on to say, "The days of pioneering, of lassies in sunbonnets, and bears killed with axes in piney clearings, are deader now than Camelot; and a rebellious girl is the spirit of that bewildered empire called the American Middlewest." ***Arrowsmith*** opens with the protagonist's great-grandmother, as a girl of fourteen, driving a wagon in the Ohio wilderness in the face of great adversity. It is what the towns and cities, the practices of business and the conventions of so-called polite society do to these pioneer virtues that Lewis is attacking, and it is the individualism and rugged independence which the pioneers exemplify to him whose passing he laments. It is little wonder that that most antisocial of American individualists, Henry David Thoreau, should have been one of his ideals.

This narrator is brash and even outrageous in his style. He flings at his satiric target not merely the customary satiric methods, but he brightens and sharpens his writing with vigorous metaphors. In ***Elmer Gantry*** he describes the workers in the "Charity Organization Society" as being "as efficient and as tender as vermin-exterminators," and he says of a saloon that "it had the delicacy of a mining camp minus its vigor." In ***Main Street*** he says that the people at a party "sat up with gaiety as with a corpse." (pp. 267-70)

Lewis is a satirist above all other things. While satire is often comic, its object is not to evoke mere laughter but laughter for a corrective purpose. It always has a target, an object which it attacks, such as pretense, falsity, deception, arrogance; and this target is held up to ridicule by the satirist's unmasking it. The satirist's vision is ultimately that of the cold-eyed realist, who penetrates shams and pretenses to reveal the truth. The simplest kind of satire is invective—that is, forthright and abusive language directed against a target so that it makes a sudden revelation of a damaging truth. Another kind of direct satire is exaggeration, by which the good characteristics are reduced and the evil or ridiculous ones are increased. Indirect satire whereby characters render themselves ridiculous by their actions and their speech is more subtle. Lewis as a satirist is usually direct and blunt. His favorite devices are invective and caricature, and in his role of unabashed and self-conscious narrator he can apply these methods directly.

His invective can be devastating. He wrote of small-town ladies as "creamy-skinned fair women, smeared with grease and chalk, gorgeous in the skins of beasts and the bloody feathers of slain birds, playing bridge with puffy pink-nailed jeweled fingers, women who after much expenditure of labor and bad temper still grotesquely resemble their own flatulent lap-dogs." He described a group of small-town citizens as a "Sunday-afternoon mob staring at monkeys in the Zoo, poking fingers and making faces and giggling at the resentment of the more dignified race." He described Gantry as being like his watch, "large, thick, shiny, with a near-gold case," and declared, "He was born to be a senator. He never said anything important, and he always said it sonorously." (p. 271)

Of course, this kind of invective leads very directly to caricature, in which the bad is exaggerated and the good reduced. For example Carol in ***Main Street*** went calling on Mrs. Lyman Cass, and Lewis wrote that she

> pounced on . . . the hook-nosed consort of the owner of the floor-mill. Mrs. Cass's parlor belonged to the crammed-Victorian school. . . . It was furnished on two principles: First, everything must resemble something else. A rocker had a back like a lyre, a near-leather seat imitating tufted cloth, and arms like Scotch Presbyterian lions; with knobs, scrolls, shields, and spear-points on unexpected portions of the chair. The second principle of the crammed-Victorian school was that every inch of the interior must be filled with useless objects.

Lewis then gives a detailed and hilarious listing of the contents of the parlor. The intention and the result is caricature.

Another kind of exaggeration results from a literal-minded reductio ad absurdum, as in the assertion that "the Maker of a universe with stars a hundred thousand light-years apart was interested, furious, and very personal about it if a small boy played baseball on Sunday afternoon.'' Lewis is a master of this kind of literal statement for satiric ends, as in ''In the spring of '18 he was one of the most courageous defenders of the Midwest against the imminent invasion of the Germans.'' (p. 272)

One of the qualities of Lewis's work that is difficult to describe or analyze is the way in which he can take the speech of his people, weave it into a monologue or an address, and make of it a severe indictment of the speaker, and yet appear at no point to be exaggerating the normal talk of such men. . . . As Edgar Johnson has observed, ''Burlesque there is in Lewis, but when we try to put a finger on it, in Babbitt's speech before the Real Estate Board, Luke Dawson's opinions on labor unions, or 'Old Jud's' Y.M.C.A. evangelism, it is embarrassingly apt to melt away and turn into realism. Mainly it is a matter of proportion rather than detail.'' (p. 273)

Lewis holds the Middle Western world up to Juvenalian laughter, points with unmistakable directness to its weaknesses and errors, and, as satirists have always done, seems to hope that seeing itself in the steel mirror of his description will make it repent and improve. Sometimes what he has to say is blunt and direct. In ***Main Street*** he declares of the small town:

> It is an unimaginatively standardized background, a sluggishness of speech and manners, a rigid ruling of the spirit by the desire to appear respectable. It is contentment . . . the contentment of the quiet dead, who are scornful of the living for their restless walking. It is negation canonized as the one positive virtue. It is the prohibition of happiness. It is slavery self-sought and self-defended. It is dullness made God.
>
> A savorless people, gulping tasteless food, and sitting afterward, coatless, and thoughtless, in rocking-chairs prickly with inane decorations, listening to mechanical music, saying mechanical things about the excellence of Ford automobiles, and viewing themselves as the greatest race in the world.

Here the outrage and anger are not masked, the comic cushion is not present. The point of view that leads the narrator through his long attack on the people of the books is present in red-faced anger. But such direct statement is unusual in Lewis.

Even at his most solemn moments, wit and the comic spirit usually cloak his rage. In a statement that is almost a declaration of faith for Lewis, he describes Martin Arrowsmith as preaching to himself ''the loyalty of dissent, the faith of being very doubtful, the gospel of not bawling gospels, the wisdom of admitting the probable ignorance of one's self and of everybody else, and the energetic acceleration of a Movement for going very slow.'' In that series of witty paradoxes on a most serious subject Lewis is very much himself. If the paradox undercuts a little the seriousness of the portrait of Martin Arrowsmith, it enhances the role that Lewis the narrator wants to play. If his form is nearer essay than fiction, if his laughter is more embittered and angry than exuberant or outgoing, if his view of men and institutions is that of Juvenal and not Horace—that is merely another way of saying that he is of the Middle West and its towns and Main Streets, and while satiric laughter is an anodyne for what he feels there, he wants it to be more than an analgesic; he wants it to be a specific for the disease that causes the pain. If, as Mark Schorer has said, ''he gave us a vigorous, perhaps a unique thrust into the imagination of ourselves,'' he intended the thrust to be therapeutic. If it has not been, then we are the poorer for its failure. (pp. 273-74)

C. Hugh Holman, ''Anodyne for the Village Virus,'' in The Comic Imagination in American Literature, *edited by Louis D. Rubin, Jr. (reprinted by permission of Louis D. Rubin, Jr.), Rutgers University Press, 1973, pp. 263-74.*

MARTIN LIGHT (essay date 1975)

[Light traces the quixotic vision found throughout Lewis's mature fiction, examining Carol Kennicott and several other major characters as sympathetic but foolish reformers who are defeated in the quest for a better world.]

Professor Lowry Nelson, Jr., points to ''the trajectory of great fiction indebted to Cervantes from . . . Henry Fielding's *Tom Jones* to Stendhal's *The Red and the Black,* Gustave Flaubert's *Madame Bovary,* Herman Melville's *Moby Dick,* and Mark Twain's *Huckleberry Finn,* to mention only a few notable instances.'' To these novels we may add Lewis's ***Main Street*** and ***Arrowsmith***—and, ultimately, the whole body of his fiction, weak novels included. Important attempts to purge us of romanticism took place in the 1920s in the work of writers that Lewis knew well. . . . Dreiser's *An American Tragedy* shows us Clyde Griffiths, who, driven by the inspiration of an Arabic evil genie, had committed murder and had been electrocuted in the testing and breaking of his illusions. But Sinclair Lewis's Arrowsmith, another character within [a] cluster of great novels published during that remarkable season of 1925 and 1926, was allowed to shape a survival; though defeated in his attempts to test his antitoxin under the most romantic, unmethodical conditions spun from his own fantasizing mind, he is allowed to withdraw to a shack in the woods, later, it is implied, to return to society, as he chooses, with his work accomplished.

Arrowsmith survives because he possesses the eternal optimism of the romanticist. The kind of romanticist who schools himself on sentimental novels, who sees himself as riding forth to conquer, and who finds a world that is more the projection of his illusions than the result of a sense of reality is called a quixote. The quixote has enduring hope, is blind to defeat, and walks down paths and into adventures of his own making. (pp. 2-3)

Professor Richard Predmore lists three elements of the quixotic world: ''literature, which is an all-pervasive presence and source of illusions; adventures, which arise from the clash between illusions and reality; and enchantment, which serves to defend illusions against inhospitable reality.'' Applying a modification of this formula to Sinclair Lewis and the characters of his fiction, we will study them in terms of the way books create the imaginations of those who read them, in terms of the mission to redress wrongs in the community, and in terms of the need to romanticize or transform reality; in other words, we will study reading, adventure, and enchantment in Lewis and his characters.

Sinclair Lewis possessed the quixotic imagination, and many of his characters, who read, venture, and fancy, as he did, are inheritors of his vision. In him opposing emotions ran deep, yet surfaced quickly. Perhaps volatility goes hand-in-hand with the impulse to create a body of fiction that searches out and breaks stereotypes apart, pillories injustices, and exposes those beliefs we loosely call "myths" about the American way of living and the American character. In Lewis, the classic struggle between illusion and reality is particularly fierce—for Lewis's enemies were both the illusions he discovered in the world and the illusions his nature invented. He fought the illusions the world offered and struggled to understand the illusions his mind and emotions brought forth.

As a result, impudence, flamboyance, and audacity, at one extreme, and gloom, despair, and carelessness, at the other, characterize Lewis's books. Mark Schorer and others record Lewis's exuberant performances, deep angers, rantings, drunkenness, tasteless practical jokes, and contrition—the emotionalism of a distraught quixote who finds outlet in audacious gestures.

Lewis stubbornly adhered to a few romantic ideas, personified in his books by yearners, rebels, and builders. His central characters are the pioneer, the doctor, the scientist, the businessman, and the feminist. The appeal of his best fiction lies in the opposition between his idealistic protagonists and an array of fools, charlatans, and scoundrels—evangelists, editorialists, pseudo-artists, cultists, and boosters. (p. 4)

[Lewis] is something beyond a realist. It may be closer to the truth to nominate him, as Constance Rourke proposed [see excerpt above, 1931] and Mark Schorer recently seconded [see excerpt above, 1969], a "fabulist." He had been labelled "journalist," "photographer," "realist," and "satirist." Some of these labels were offered, I think, to suggest that he was a literalist and that he lacked "imagination." However, he counterbalanced his literalness not only with imagination but with "fancy." *Fancy* is a term he often used himself (both when speaking in his own voice and when speaking through the voices of his characters). Still innocent and still assembling an inner world which they hope they will find in the outer one, his young, idealistic, and adventuring characters fancy; they fancy the long-ago, the far-away, and the exotic. Nevertheless, they, and others of his figures whom the plot puts in their path, "observe"—that is, they examine and document reality. But his fancy is the symptom of his quixotism. He is the quixote who projects his inner world upon the external experience, while reality hammers at him for attention. Fancy drew him as much as observation did. Though he delighted in fancy, he was often suspicious of it; it is a trivial, whimsical attribute, but he thought it could be converted to good use.

Many of Lewis's characters are full of fancy, yet his heroes and heroines will waken to an awareness of reality. (p. 6)

Here let me call one of Lewis's characters forward to exemplify the way quixotism functions in his work. It is the protagonist of ***Main Street,*** young Carol Milford (soon to be Carol Kennicott), who had fed her imagination on "village-improvement" (pictures of "greens and garden-walls in France"), who had, at the banks of the Mississippi, "listened to its fables about the wide land of yellow waters and bleached buffalo bones to the West," and who had thought of "Southern levees and singing darkies" and palm trees and river steamers and Dakota chiefs; she stands on the High Bridge across the Mississippi and sees Yang-tse villages below. She fancies turning "a prairie town into Georgian houses and Japanese bungalows." Her conversation, we are told, is some modern equivalent of that of Elaine and Sir Launcelot. Her mind is filled by images of "elsewhere." Yet her plan is to create a hometown that will fulfill her vision. She articulates her ambitions by saying, "I'll get my hands on one of these prairie towns and make it beautiful." Soon this quixotic girl meets that other American prototype, the practical man. Doctor Kennicott, courting Carol in St. Paul, attempts to persuade her to come to Gopher Prairie with him by showing her a dozen snapshots of the town. The pictures are "streaky." But her fanciful vision overcomes the reality of the photographs. At first she can see only "trees, shrubbery, a porch indistinct in leafy shadows." But she creates what she wants to see and exclaims over the lakes, bluffs, ducks, and fishermen, and then a "clumsy log cabin chinked with mud, . . . a sagging woman . . . a baby bedraggled." Moved by his love, Kennicott deceives her: "Just look at that baby's eyes, look how he's begging—." She answers in self-delusion: "Oh, it would be sweet to help him—." What follows is four hundred pages of lessons in how to see and what to believe, lessons regrettably never firmly learned. Lewis's books are attempts at correct viewing. The whole life's work is the study of illusions and realities. Lewis, having begun with a vacuous and misleading set of illusions, makes us witness, down through the years, the same ritual encounter between illusion and reality. He repeatedly brings his illusions before us and then destroys them. And he cries out both for what is lost and against the agents of betrayal. Fortunately, he can also surround the ritual in comedy, and the comedy pleases us.

Lewis's flaws of style and some of his puerile notions will remain a problem for every reader. But perhaps one way to approach his novels is this: He was a great talker. He began as an admirer of a bad "literary" language, but he learned the uses of common speech. He employed the comic potential of the vernacular to expose the boosters and hypocrites he saw in American life. As T. K. Whipple so well put it, he stalked the enemy like a Red Indian. He was a demon of anger toward waste and cruelty. Yet he was sympathetic and could give in to a whimsical imagination, which sought solace in places governed by a romanticized chivalric code. He began his career as a journalist and publicist, and perhaps always thought in terms of giant typography, headlines, billboards. There is amplitude in his best books, and if he is read for size—for his large quixotic vision—then his faults, in his best books at least, accordingly diminish. (pp. 9-10)

Let us return to Carol Kennicott of ***Main Street,*** who is so central to Lewis's work. . . . Let us consider the problem of "Winky Poo"—that is, the question as to whether Lewis saw, at the time he was writing, the foolishness of Carol's standards of art and reform, as exemplified in the party she holds for her friends at which she asks them to costume themselves in Chinese hats and she appears before them in an Oriental robe, exclaiming, "The Princess Winky Poo salutes her court!" . . . Looking at "Main Street's Been Paved" in the *Nation* four years after publication of the novel, we can see that Lewis made Carol the victim of his own changing attitudes. But *she* is frozen forever in her book, doomed to reenact her life at any reader's cue, exposing her misjudgments, while Lewis moves on in insight. When he conceived of her, he and she looked out upon the world from very nearly the same point of view, side by side. Her way of looking—through Arcady and the Yang-tse—was still his own, and her Chinese costume was an objectification of her quixotic vision, an objectification she thought innocent enough. I think Lewis at first believed it to be harmless, too; her Chinese party need not be a model of all parties, but it was a harmless indulgence of a fanciful interest, and, beyond that, a plausible escape from Gopher Prairie. Arcady and the Yang-tse were ways of enchanting the village scene, transforming it from liver-colored clapboards and bloodreeking meatstore windows to something imaginatively engaging, and of making connections between "home" and the exotic "elsewhere" of older times, far-off places, and her literary heritage. He was gathering hints that Carol's view was foolish. Later he became convinced that it was so. Then he placed her at a distance from himself, as he had done often before with cults and fads.

The fanciful vision, which dominates each protagonist through Arrowsmith, remains present, is a problem, and becomes a source of nostalgic sympathy in later heroes, especially in Dodsworth and Cass Timberlane. What one discovers is that the fanciful vision has been shifted, for the most part, away from the heroes, so that no later hero quite has it entirely. For instance, it was shifted, in bitterness yet therapeutically, I think, to Ora Weagle, a figure of contempt, and then to innumerable minor characters. Nonetheless, some element of fancy invariably remains throughout Lewis's work. Thus, in ***Ann Vickers*** it appears in Ann's fantasies about her aborted child, whom she calls "Pride," in the man who seduces her, who must be that out-moded villain the New York Jew, and in her lover Judge Dolphin, who is so big as to be above the law. It is also present in ***Dodsworth*** in a figure like Nande or in ***Timberlane*** and ***Kingsblood*** in Sweeney Fishberg.

Lewis attempted to convert to good use the quixotic impulses he had by making fanciful ascriptions the method of creating largeness of character; the extremes, in fact the contradictions, of behavior led to the "fabulous" figures that Constance Rourke saw in Lewis's books and appropriately named. Lewis converted his fancy to Münchausen-like ends—to tall tales—which thereby gave his people "folkloristic" or "mythic" features. . . . Perry Miller thought Lewis "in love with mythological and typological creations like Micawber and Gradgrind." By "mythic" I suggest that Lewis casts over his characters an aura of knighthood and medieval romance and sets them forth on a quest, for example, and by "folkloristic" I suggest that he connects his types to American pioneers, to confidence men, to orators and braggarts. Occasionally he gives a character (like Hawk Ericson, Arrowsmith, Kingsblood, or Aaron Gadd, for instance) such elements of the traditional hero as uncertain parentage, a mentor, a shadowy co-worker, a period of wandering, and a final withdrawal from society. In a way that one can only admire for its audacity, Lewis even measures Dodsworth and Cornplow against his own archetypal creation called "Babbitt" (whose name *had* entered the lexicon, after all)—Dodsworth was *not* a babbitt, we are told, though Cornplow had been a babbitt throughout all history.

A lot of Lewis's flamboyant maneuvering is a substitute for style and thought. The novels do not show evidence that Lewis worried over the full implications of "style," though as a parodist he was attentive to corruptions of language. Corruptions of language correspond to the corruptions of society, and Lewis can be said to have followed Cervantes and Mark Twain in his effort to expunge such evil.

Although Wells, Lewis's mentor, expended effort and wordage on argument, it was Wells's early, less didactic books that Lewis liked. From these Lewis did pick up some ideas about progress, socialism, ethics, and religion, which he made use of. But these ideas have a quixotic naïveté about them as they are enunciated by Professor Fraser, or by Hawk Ericson, or by Gottlieb, Arrowsmith, Dodsworth, Ann Vickers, and Cass Timberlane. One thing Lewis does when he wishes to make use of "ideas" is to satirize the stupidity of a character who has garbled them.

Still, what Wells did for Lewis in 1910 to 1915 Lewis needed to have done again for him after 1930—that is, he needed a stimulus; he especially needed new ways of seeing and conceptualizing. He approached the ensuing years, however, by further exploiting his satire and his character types. Through the influence of Dorothy Thompson, his sense of justice was stirred. He attacked prisons in ***Ann Vickers,*** although prisons were not the central problem of the time. He attacked native fascism and communism in ***It Can't Happen Here*** and ***The Prodigal Parents;*** in both books, however, he blunted his attacks by employing gross cleverness and using as protagonists his "little men." He turned from the excesses of the right and left, but he did so in the name of nothing which would enrich his own work. One might desire some better motive for social criticism than the motive he gives to an unidentified young man in ***Gideon Planish*** who has been listening to a power-hungry propagandist who "attacked Fascism so hysterically, and with such a suggestion that he was the one lone anti-Hitler, that I almost found myself beginning to be pro-Fascist, anti-Semite, anti-Chinese, anti-feminist, anti-socialized-medicine, anti everything I had always believed in." . . . Because one perceives the foolishness in an advocate of one point of view one need not run to the opposite extreme. To do so was characteristic of Lewis, however. It is the perverse attitude of the village atheist, of the bad boy of letters, of the quixote, yet it has done Lewis the disservice of drawing from some critics the charge that he had no standards, that he cannot imagine any protagonist capable of a sustained struggle, and that he created no truly individual character to resist social types, though Carol Kennicott, Sam Dodsworth, and Cass Timberlane belie that judgment.

A sense of life as tragic might have enabled him to surmount uncertainties and inconsistencies by looking above the characters in some overall view of human nature; he might have moved beyond 1930, the year of the prize, toward new achievements. But Lewis did not have such a view, and if my interpretation of Lewis's career is correct, it was the thin air of the culture at the turn of the century and the temptations and illusions of fancies and cults which deprived him of it. He freed himself in part from these, but they returned to weaken his later work.

He lacked a framework for belief, whether it be humanism, socialism, modern psychology, or religion. Of course, to have been a doctrinaire socialist, for example, would have been an error for him, yet Lewis's ideas on politics or economy were ill-defined. Perhaps with a remark about a minor figure, Mamie Magen, in his third novel, ***The Job,*** he came closest to stating what his social goal was—the advent of a "scientific era": "Mamie Magen was a socialist who believed that the capitalists with their profit-sharing and search for improved methods of production were as sincere in desiring the scientific era as were the most burning socialists." . . . Such a statement muddles definitions and illuminates little; yet it is so warmly attributed to an admired character as to suggest that the author agrees. (pp. 134-37)

One will always remember a number of effective scenes in Lewis's books: Carol walking down Main Street for the first time; the episodes during Babbitt's day—at the breakfast table, in the office, at the club; the parties in ***Main Street*** and in ***Babbitt;*** Babbitt's speech before the Real Estate Board; Vergil Gunch and his friends stalking Babbitt during his rebellion: Paul and Zilla Riesling quarreling; the petty Tozers of Wheatsylvania in ***Arrowsmith;*** the visit to Pickerbaugh's family; Gottlieb's sad defeats; the beating of Frank Shallard; Elmer Gantry's hollow triumph; Dodsworth's lonely clumping from place to place; the prisons in ***Ann Vickers.*** Lewis's novels get their shape from a patterning of characters along a biographical storyline: the hero, his mentor or friend, the rebel, the gallery of portraits of the professional circle, the choices between at least two kinds of women, and the regular reappearance of Lewis's satiric virtuoso orators.

Beyond the brilliance of satire, there should be aspects of characterization which suggest deeper meanings. Lewis certainly intended these, as his preoccupation with the idea of the God-seeker would indicate ("the quest of scientists after God" in ***Arrowsmith,*** the God-seeking motive behind the proposed labor novel, *Neighbor,* and even the notion that Myron Weagle serves God through humane management of an inn). Furthermore, Lewis's insistence that he was interested in both the typicality and the individuality of his characters and locales suggests that he was trying to understand and explain America in breadth and in detail. Yet it must be acknowledged that Lewis's quixotic heroes show a weakness of ultimate definition that prevents them from evoking the admiration that we have for Gavin Stevens, let us say, in Faulkner's *The Town* and *The Mansion.*

Lewis pictured an America of false beliefs and of material strength. The men who created material America could be justifiably proud of their achievement, yet they might well yearn for an enrichment in their lives which could come with a larger sense of purpose, if only they didn't consider economics the sole motivation and end of their work. Thus in Lewis the American hero would be a fusion of the builder and the man of culture, who does his job and pays his debts responsibly, yet reads, views art, discusses ideas. The western wind blowing clear for him may clean away corruption, dullness, and bewilderment.

In his portraiture, Lewis exposed the failings of the babbitts, men of small spirit who all too sadly seemed to him to be the most characteristic of Americans. More than them, however, he hated fakers and pretenders: bohemian wasters, trivial sophisticates of the city, and charlatans in education, art, religion, and government. He directed his satire against domineering women, but he sympathized deeply with exploited women who rebel against enslavement at home or in menial jobs. He cried out against poverty, prejudice, materialism, and shallow education. He was outraged by stupidity. He felt that the cause of the world's troubles was lack of the use of reason; on the contrary, the use of reason could cure the world. He could build quite a powerful outrage against injustices, and this outrage animated his best scenes. Therein many of his people suffer memorably.

Lewis accomplished a great deal in his writing career. As America's first Nobel Prize winner in literature, he became for Europe the symbol of America's coming of age. He was a leader on best-seller lists in the United States; he was a spokesman in quarrels with the Old Gang; he helped destroy one picture of the small town and substitute another; he attacked various abuses; his name was better known by the general public than that of any other writer in the twenties, when his rejection of the Pulitzer Prize, the reception of ***Elmer Gantry,*** and the Nobel Award caused sensations, as the *New York Times* for those years testifies. He had many champions who have called him the finest writer of his time. If that judgment goes too far, yet it must be recognized that he worked notably toward portraying an America in which values of trust and honor might be understood more clearly. (pp. 137-39)

Martin Light, in his The Quixotic Vision of Sinclair Lewis *(© 1975 by the Purdue Research Foundation, West Lafayette, IN 47907; reprinted with permission), Purdue University Press, 1975, 162 p.*

DAVID D. ANDERSON (essay date 1981)

[Anderson is the founder of the Society for the Study of Midwestern Literature. He has written critical studies of such figures as William Jennings Bryan, Brand Whitlock, Robert Ingersoll, and Louis Bromfield, as well as several important works on Sherwood Anderson. In the following excerpt, Anderson praises Lewis as a writer who revealed remarkable insight into the middle-class American mind.]

When Sinclair Lewis stood before the Swedish Academy and distinguished guests on December 12, 1930, as the first American to win the Nobel Prize in Literature, he was, although he was unaware of it, at the end of the second phase of his career and at the beginning of the third, the period that was to continue to his death, to the detriment of his literary reputation. The first phase, from ***Our Mr. Wrenn*** of 1914 through ***Free Air*** (1919), was essentially that of Lewis's apprenticeship, the period during which he discovered a major theme that was to dominate his best work under the guise of satire, that is, that dull people are, in spite of—or perhaps because of—their dullness and the shallowness of the world in which they live, essentially likeable, even good.

During the second phase, extending from ***Main Street*** in 1920 to ***Dodsworth*** in 1929, with the single lapse of ***Mantrap*** . . . , Lewis created his best work as he earned the reputation that brought him wealth, notoriety, and the Nobel Prize. (p. 14)

Throughout his career and even yet Lewis remains the great paradoxical figure in our literary history. As early as 1922, in an essay in the *New Republic* [see Additional Bibliography], Sherwood Anderson wrote that "The texture of the prose written by Mr. Lewis gives me but faint joy and I cannot escape the conviction that for some reason Lewis has himself found but little joy, either in life among us or in his own effort to channel his reactions to our life into prose . . . one has the feeling that Lewis never laughs at all, that he is in an odd way too serious about something to laugh." More succinctly, on page 813 of his definitive 814-page biography of Lewis [see Additional Bibliography], Mark Schorer comments that "He was one of the worst writers in modern American literature. . . ." Yet, in spite of his flaws as a writer, in spite of our condescension toward his work, in spite of our refusal to give his works serious critical appraisal, we not only do not ignore him, but we cannot. As Schorer goes on to point out, we cannot imagine modern American literature without him.

We cannot, I think, for reasons that are psychological, sociological, and historical rather than literary—qualities that, I suspect, are the source of his continued popularity as well as the reasons why he was selected to be the first American to receive the Nobel Prize for literature. Unable to define the tragic dimensions of human life, incapable of expressing joy or revealing, even in moments, the subjective life, the inner life, of his people in spite of his sometimes grudging affection for them, he did, nevertheless, provide fleeting, distorted, but frightening moments of insight into ourselves, into the reality of our lives, and into the myths by which we live.

Lewis was a product of the Midwest as it reached maturity, as it became Middle America, the mainstream that has given focus to American life in this century, and it is this Middle America that is not only the substance of the works—***Main Street, Babbitt, Arrowsmith, Elmer Gantry, Dodsworth***—that we remember when we speak of Lewis, but it is also the substance of those glimpses of ourselves that fascinate and frighten us. In this sense, Lewis was, perhaps, the democratic literatus out of the West for whom Walt Whitman called, but he was not the voice for which Whitman listened.

Nevertheless, Whitman and certainly Mark Twain would recognize Lewis's people—or more properly his character-types—as they appear in the best of his works, those of the 1920's (before he absorbed Dorothy Thompson's passion for justice, to the detriment of his work in the 1930's and '40's). His people are of the American past, the mythic, folkloric past of the Old West and the nineteenth century; they are the confidence man—Elmer Gantry; the hero—Arrowsmith; the uncertain seeker after an ambiguous fulfillment—Babbitt; the braggart—Lowell Schmaltz, the man who knew Coolidge; the helpless romantic—Dodsworth; the reformer—Carol Kennicott—all of them caught up in an age that distorted their weaknesses and perverted their strengths, the age of Gopher Prairie and Zenith, of prosperity, prohibition, and the culmination of the American myth of success, the age Lewis describes in the opening of ***Main Street***. . . . (pp. 15-16)

In the nineteenth century each of Lewis's people would have been larger than life; in the twentieth, the age of the bewildered empire, Gopher Prairie, Zenith, and values defined and perpetuated by place and by things have become Lewis's gargantuan reality. (p. 17)

[None] of Lewis's people, including Arrowsmith, is large enough to manipulate the new America as the con men, the braggarts, the heroes, the romantics of the nineteenth century had been able to manipulate the old. It is not the nightmare of Faulkner's Popeye, of grotesque horror, but the nightmare of the ordinary, of a world larger and more materially successful than life, more spiritually bankrupt than we can imagine.

Contrary to too many popular—and critical—conclusions, Lewis's people, limited in perception as they often are, are never the enemy; Lewis was eminently capable of creating a fool or a knave but never a villain. Beneath the veneer of satire, of exaggeration, of sophistication, of vulgarity, Lewis's people, limited in the breadth and depth of their lives, are innocently corrupt, insignificantly rebellious, ultimately defeated, each of them low-keyed but real. Out of all of them, from Carol Kennicott to Sam Dodsworth, only Martin Arrowsmith and Lowell Schmaltz survive emotionally and psychologically, Arrowsmith because he rejects all but the god that he serves, Schmaltz because he is a fool. Not incidentally, however, Arrowsmith endures as an authentic American hero at the cost of his humanity; he must, unlike Carol Kennicott, George Babbitt, Elmer Gantry, and Sam Dodsworth, make his own separate, lonely peace. For the others—Carol, who asserts that she may not have fought the good fight but she has kept the faith, for Babbitt, who insists that the bright new world is his son's, for Gantry, whose new-found faith is marred by a glimpse of charming ankles and lively eyes, for Dodsworth, whose happiness is so complete that he did not yearn for Fran for two whole days, there is only a moment of self-realization, a shadowlike acceptance of personal defeat.

For each of Lewis's protagonists except the new American hero, survival is possible, re-admission to the institutions that govern the new America and reward its members is readily available, but only at the price of two of the three premises that marked the beginning of the search for American fulfillment. Life, a materially successful life, is theirs at the cost of their liberty and the sacrifice of whatever potential happiness they no longer pursue.

For Lewis's women—and no adequate study of Lewis's women has yet been undertaken—whether protagonist or secondary character, whether Carol Kennicott, Leora Arrowsmith, or Cleo Gantry, the price is identical in kind but greater in degree: if his men are captured by a social system and value structure that they can neither understand nor overcome, his women are enslaved by the conventional role of women as well as the structure of the society in which they live. His women, protagonists or secondary characters, career women or housewives, seekers after direct or vicarious fulfillment, are limited not only by the flaws of insight and judgement imposed on them by their environment, but they are limited by the peculiarly female roles imposed on them by biology as well. Just as Carol Kennicott returns pregnant to home and hearth, defeated and unfulfilled, Leora Arrowsmith goes quietly and loyally to her grave, and Cleo Gantry and Lulu Bains surrender to the godhead manifested in the Rev. Elmer Gantry. Even the later Ann Vickers, who had confidently declared her independence of convention, finds her properly subservient role as woman. . . . (pp. 17-18)

In a sense, perhaps, all of Lewis's people, male or female, protagonists or secondary characters, deserve the ignominy of their surrender, conscious or not, to the forces of convention, but not because they are mean-spirited or small-spirited, although many of them are. Lewis's people are intensely if two-dimensionally human, likeable in their humanity, even in a sense admirable in their weaknesses. Lewis's people live their lives as tragicomic players reading lines they don't understand in a play that baffles them before a set that overwhelms them. But they go on, in determined dignity, to the end that life has written for them. They are members of what Lewis has described as the "cranky, hysterical, brave, mass-timorous, hard-minded, imaginative Chosen Race, the Americans," those, he adds, whose history for nearly a century can best be read in the long sequence of catalogues issued by Sears, Roebuck and Company.

Lewis recognized early what his critics have yet to perceive but his readers note intuitively: that his works are neither poetry nor drama; they are history, sociology, psychology. They are not the reality of Howells's real grasshopper but the reality of the monograph, the field study, or the case history. The substance of his work, then, is not the "fearless exposure of humbuggery," as one of his early critics commented, nor is it the result of his "Satirist's hard eye and the romancer's soft heart," as a more recent critic insists; it is the nightmare of mass society, of material values, of carefully-assigned roles to players who know their lines but not their parts, and the terror is not that of standardization; it is that of inevitable depersonalization and dehumanization. Lewis's people seek God in their dreams, their work, themselves, but they find instead that they are trapped not only by time, place, and circumstances, but by their very humanity.

Lewis's people accept the reality imposed on them and survive, but Lewis—and here he is at his best—perceives the nightmare, the terror of survival after surrender. Each of his authentic American types—and I think that perhaps this is the reason why Lewis's people are types rather than fully developed individuals—is both product and victim of his or her environment, beset and imprisoned by hypocrisy, narrowness, greed, and prejudice not only from without but from within, and the new beginnings, the happy endings, the escapes that appear to become possible for his people are, Lewis makes clear, compounded of cosmic irony, acceptance, and self-delusion.

Lewis prided himself on the faithfulness with which he reproduced and exaggerated the America he knew, that of the forty years of his active writing career, and because he gave free rein to his gift of mimicry, it has become a critical cliche to insist that he is out of date, that the America of the teens, twenties, thirties, and forties has long vanished, that today, as Geoffrey Moore comments, the bankers and lawyers of Gopher Prairie have been to Yale, the storekeepers to the state university, and, of course, three generations of Midwestern males—and some females—have experienced government-sponsored junkets to virtually every part of the world.

The implication of these observations is clear: that today Lewis merits little more than a footnote in literary history. But the bankers and lawyers have read Lewis at Yale and the shopkeepers at State as part of their new sophistication and learning, and ***Main Street*** and ***Babbitt*** were published by the thousands in Armed Forces Editions during World War II and read by many on those government-sponsored tours of Europe, Africa, the South Pacific, and the Far East. And in spite of the apparent or alleged transformation of American society, these new generations of readers continue to recognize, if not themselves, certainly their contemporaries, their families, perhaps even their professors. They recognize, too, that Lewis's world, beneath its veneer of contemporaneity, is their world, that Babbitt's "carrying on" is today's "lifestyle," that the Good Citizen's League and the Booster's Club are only a generation removed from the Old Newsboys, the Downtown Coaches Club, and the Chamber of Commerce, that the Elks, Rotary, and the Lions clubs are with us yet, perhaps more democratic but no more imaginative than in 1924. And Lewis was spared the Reverend Jerry Falwell, the Moral Majority, and the spectre of an actor in the White House, an actor whose favorite predecessor is Calvin Coolidge. To point to Lewis's shortcomings as a writer is to ignore the accuracy with which he defined our lives and our world as we enter the last decades of the twentieth century.

Lewis was not a great writer, nor perhaps was he good enough to win the Nobel Prize in literature—although the political and social dimensions of that award often outweigh literary considerations. But the best of his works, those that have added words to our language, those that give us greater insight into the moral shortcomings of our times and ourselves, those that define the victimization of the individual in a world of mass vulgarity, deserve better of us than we have been willing to give. (pp. 19-21)

David D. Anderson, "Sinclair Lewis and the Nobel Prize," in MidAmerica *(copyright 1981 by The Society for the Study of Midwestern Literature), Vol. VIII, 1981, pp. 9-21.*

ADDITIONAL BIBLIOGRAPHY

Anderson, Sherwood. "Four American Impressions (Gertrude Stein, Paul Rosenfeld, Ring Lardner, Sinclair Lewis)." In his *Sherwood Anderson's Notebook,* pp. 47-58. New York: Boni & Liveright, 1926.*

Attacks what Anderson considered the unrealistic joylessness of Lewis's satiric novels. (This essay originally appeared in *The New Republic* in 1922.)

Benét, William Rose. "The Earlier Lewis." *The Saturday Review of Literature* X, No. 27 (20 January 1934): 421-22.

Benét's reminiscences of his friend Lewis, which provide interesting insights into Lewis's love for the very people he satirized.

Bucco, Martin. "The Serialized Novels of Sinclair Lewis." *Western American Literature* IV, No. 1 (Spring 1969): 29-37.

Examines the differences between the early serialized versions of Lewis's novels and the later hardcover editions.

Bunge, Nancy L. "The Midwestern Novel: Walt Whitman Transplanted." *The Old Northwest* 3, No. 3 (September 1977): 275-87.*

Examines similarities in the vision and literary aim of Sherwood Anderson, Ernest Hemingway, Saul Bellow, and Lewis.

Conroy, Stephen S. "Sinclair Lewis's Sociological Imagination." *American Literature* 42, No. 3 (November 1970): 348-62.

A study of Lewis's great novels of the 1920s from a sociological perspective.

Derleth, August. "Sinclair Lewis." In his *Three Literary Men: A Memoir of Sinclair Lewis, Sherwood Anderson, Edgar Lee Masters,* pp. 7-28. New York: Candlelight Press, 1963.

Recounts interesting biographical anecdotes drawn from Derleth's several meetings with Lewis.

Ford, Ford Madox. "Fiction: *Dodsworth.*" *The Bookman,* New York LXIV, No. 2 (April 1929): 191-92.

A laudatory review of *Dodsworth.*

Fyvel, T. R. "Martin Arrowsmith and His Habitat." *The New Republic* 133, No. 3 (18 July 1955): 16-18.

Assesses Lewis's skill as a satirist of the middle class.

Griffin, Robert J., ed. *Twentieth Century Interpretations of "Arrowsmith."* Englewood Cliffs, N.J.: Prentice-Hall, 1968, 119 p.

Reprints twenty-two important essays on *Arrowsmith* by such prominent critics as Stuart P. Sherman, Carl Van Doren, and Joseph Wood Krutch.

Hoffman, Frederick J. "The Text: Sinclair Lewis's *Babbitt.*" In his *The Twenties: American Writing in the Postwar Decade,* rev. ed., pp. 408-15. New York: Free Press, 1949.

A general essay on *Babbitt* and close examination of the work's central character.

Hollis, C. Carroll. "Sinclair Lewis: Reviver of Character." in *Fifty Years of the American Novel: A Christian Appraisal,* edited by Harold C. Gardner, S.J., pp. 89-106. New York: Charles Scribner's Sons, 1952.

An essay which examines Lewis's strength as a creator of Theophrastian characters rather than as a writer of novels.

Light, Martin, ed. *The Merrill Studies in "Babbitt."* Columbus: Charles E. Merrill Publishing Co., 1971, 116 p.

Reprints many important essays on *Babbitt* by such noted critics as Upton Sinclair, Maxwell Geismar, and Sheldon Norman Grebstein.

Maglin, Nan Bauer. "Women in Three Sinclair Lewis Novels." *The Massachusetts Review* XIV, No. 4 (Autumn 1973): 783-801.

Examines the female principals in *The Job, Ann Vickers,* and *Main Street* as creations Lewis used to explore the choices of and pressures on women in the early part of the twentieth century.

Millgate, Michael. "Sinclair Lewis and the Obscure Hero." *Studi Americani* 8 (1962): 111-27.

Examines the main characters in several of Lewis's novels.

O'Connor, Richard. *Sinclair Lewis.* New York: McGraw-Hill Book Co., 1971, 144 p.

A useful work of biography and criticism that provides a moderately detailed survey of Lewis's life, his books, and their critical reception.

Schorer, Mark. "Sinclair Lewis and His Critics." In his *The World We Imagine: Selected Essays,* pp. 183-94. New York: Farrar, Straus and Giroux, 1948.

An interesting survey of Lewis's critical reception throughout his career.

——. *Sinclair Lewis: An American Life*. New York: McGraw-Hill Book Co., 1961, 867 p.

The definitive biography.

Sherman, Stuart P. *The Significance of Sinclair Lewis*. 1922. Reprint. Freeport, N.Y.: Books for Libraries Press, 1971, 20 p.

Discusses Lewis's first seven novels, responds to critics of Lewis's satirical method, and provides an interesting comparison of Lewis and Gustave Flaubert as chroniclers of provincial life.

Thompson, Dorothy. "The Boy and Man from Sauk Centre." *The Atlantic Monthly* 206, No. 5 (November 1960): 39-48.

A short biography of Lewis by his second wife, containing interesting insights into the man, his descendants, and his forebears.

Van Doren, Carl. *Sinclair Lewis: A Biographical Sketch*. Garden City, N.Y.: Doubleday, Doran & Co., 1933, 205 p.

An enthusiastic biographical and critical essay which includes bibliography of Lewis's writings to-date.

H(enry) L(ouis) Mencken

1880-1956

(Also wrote under pseudonyms of Owen Hatteras, George Weems Peregoy, Raoul della Torre, Herbert Winslow Archer, Francis Clegg Thompson, Irving S. Watson, Harriet Morgan, Janet Jefferson, William Fink, Marie de Verdi, Pierre d'Aubigy, Amelia Hatteras, and The Ringmaster, among many others) American essayist, critic, journalist, autobiographer, dramatist, short story writer, and poet.

The Bettmann Archive, Inc.

From the era of World War I until the early years of the Great Depression, Mencken was one of the most influential figures in American letters. His strongly individualistic, irreverent outlook on life and his vigorous, invective-charged writing style helped establish the iconoclastic spirit of the Jazz Age and significantly shaped the direction of American literature. As a social and literary critic—the roles for which he is best known—Mencken was the scourge of evangelical Christianity, public service organizations, boosterism, democracy, politicians, all advocates of personal or social improvement, the genteel tradition in American literature, and every other facet of American life that he perceived as humbug. In his literary criticism, Mencken encouraged American writers to shun the anglophilic, moralistic bent of the nineteenth century and to practice realism. His critical writings introduced and promoted the works of such authors as Theodore Dreiser, Sherwood Anderson, and Sinclair Lewis, while mocking the fiction of William Dean Howells, Henry James, and a host of lesser artists who had been supplanted by the "new realists." A master of satiric attack and one who awakened a nation to the low cultural standards and provincial stupidity of the species he classified as *boobus Americanus,* Mencken was at once one of the most admired and most thoroughly hated men of his time.

Mencken was born into a middle-class German-American family in Baltimore, where he lived all of his life. Although expected to join his father in the tobacco industry, Mencken was more interested in literature and writing. Joining the staff of the Baltimore *Herald* at the age of nineteen, he worked successfully at every job in the newspaper's office, attaining the editorship shortly before the paper's demise (through no fault of his own) in 1906. During his years at the *Herald* Mencken also published a collection of jaunty, Kiplingesque poetry (of which he was, in later years, greatly embarrassed), as well as the more respectable *George Bernard Shaw: His Plays,* the first book ever published on Shaw's drama. After the Baltimore *Herald* folded, the young writer began working for the city's Sunpapers news service, and for the rest of his career Mencken wrote for the morning *Sun* and *The Evening Sun.* But newspaper work did not completely fulfill his ambitions, and by 1908 Mencken was seeking a wider audience. That year was marked by two key events in his life: the publication of his *The Philosophy of Friedrich Nietzsche* and his initial meeting with George Jean Nathan. Nietzsche has been cited by critics as one of Mencken's foremost influences, and although Mencken misinterpreted much of the German philosopher's thought, he did share with Nietzsche the belief that reckless iconoclasm is necessary to bring about cultural change. This idea, as well as a deep disgust at the state of contemporary American life and art, were shared by George Jean Nathan, whom Mencken met in 1908 in the New York offices of *The Smart Set* magazine, where each had come seeking work as drama critic and literary critic, respectively. Their immediate friendship and shared vision led to a renowned partnership that lasted for nearly twenty years. At *The Smart Set,* each developed his characteristically vivid, biting critical style and found a podium from which to assail the low standards of American literature and theater. According to Philip Wagner, "with high spirits, total confidence in their own judgments, and a torrent of brilliant invective, they laid about them, bashing heads, pulling down idols, puncturing inflated pomposity, infuriating the sources of conventional wisdom, sweeping away the rubbish that then passed for literature and drama." Acquiring the magazine's joint-editorship in 1914, Mencken and Nathan attracted new, sophisticated contributors to its pages and transformed *The Smart Set* from a moderately literary scandal magazine into a respectable forum of realistic fiction. During his long association with Nathan, Mencken conducted much of the necessary talent-hunting, editing, writing, and business correspondence from his home in Baltimore, periodically joining his partner in New York for consultation. Concurrent with his early career at *The Smart Set,* Mencken conducted a regular column, "The Free Lance," in *The Evening Sun,* in which he brought his satiric skill to bear on local and national politics and contemporary culture. Informed with impertinent humor, liveliness, and withering contempt for sham or "buncombe," Mencken's editorials became an influential and much-read feature in the region of Baltimore and Washington. But World War I brought an end to "The Free Lance" and to the hitherto promising fortunes of *The Smart Set.*

During the years of war before American military involvement, a period of growing anti-German sentiment in the United States, Mencken—a man fiercely proud of his ethnic heritage and a writer whose essays were sprinkled with German expressions—was vilified in the press as a "Hun" sympathizer. "The Free Lance" was discontinued by the editorial directive of *The Evening Sun,* while *The Smart Set* suffered through declining sales and contributions, with Mencken and Nathan forced to write much of the magazine's copy under any of several dozen pseudonyms. Faced with a fading journalistic career, Mencken devoted his skill to a long-considered linguistic study, which appeared in 1919 as *The American Language.* The work was an immediate popular and critical success and is recognized today as an important early examination of the gradual development of the American language from its colonial origins into a distinctly original form of expression. *The American Language* as well as *Prejudices: First Series* were highly praised and are considered among the most significant books published in 1919. *Prejudices,* the first of a series of six such volumes of essays, reprints a selection of Mencken's cocky "blasts and bravos" from various periodicals. The book heralded the disenchanted, joyfully defiant spirit of the postwar generation, and with its publication Mencken was quickly recognized, with F. Scott Fitzgerald and Sinclair Lewis, as one of the chief commentators on contemporary American culture. This recognition led to the rejuvenation of *The Smart Set,* in which Mencken promoted the works of Anderson, Fitzgerald, Dreiser, Lewis, and other realists. But Mencken and Nathan were tiring of the constraints set by the magazine's somewhat tawdry physical appearance and history, and each desired a freer hand at all stages of the editorial and production process. With the financial backing of publisher Alfred A. Knopf, Mencken and Nathan left *The Smart Set* and founded *The American Mercury* in 1924. Embraced by the nation's college students and sophisticated "flaming youth," the new magazine immediately became one of the most widely read and influential periodicals of the era, rivalled only by Harold Ross's *New Yorker* and Henry Seidel Canby's *Saturday Review of Literature.* Its stance was mockingly sceptical of established American values, and it included some of the best writing of the 1920s. But the partnership of the two coeditors ended soon after the *Mercury* was launched, as Nathan wanted the periodical to be primarily a review of the arts, while Mencken sought to create in the *Mercury* a journal of social and political opinion. Unable to resolve their differences, Nathan resigned his position and Mencken became sole editor of the magazine.

Mencken reached the height of his influence and notoriety during the mid-1920s. By then, his 1920 essay "The Sahara of the Bozart," an attack on the paucity of *beaux arts* in the South, had successfully angered and then goaded many Southern writers to shun the sentimental sword-and-cape literature of long tradition and to experiment with realism. His news coverage of the Scopes "Monkey Trial" of 1925 was nationally syndicated, and he played a minor role in bringing about the dramatic concluding confrontation between attorneys Clarence Darrow and William Jennings Bryan, having previously advised Darrow that the best defense of schoolteacher John Scopes would be to "make a fool out of Bryan." When Bryan died shortly before the trial ended, Mencken published a mocking elegy, "In Memoriam: W.J.B.," which is considered a masterpiece of humorous wit. Mencken's columns in *The American Mercury* and in other journals either outraged or delighted much of America: in each case, the "Sage of Baltimore's" writings were avidly read and his views widely quoted. But the Wall Street Crash of 1929 and the ensuing Great Depression ended Mencken's popularity, for with much of America's workforce suddenly jobless and living in poverty, his jibes at American backwardness ceased to amuse. His outspoken opposition to President Franklin Roosevelt's New Deal and his disparagement of people who benefited from the various national relief programs increased his growing unpopularity. Discouraged, Mencken resigned from *The American Mercury* in 1933, and for the rest of the decade he devoted most of his skill to newspaper work. In the 1940s, Mencken rose once again to popularity with three nostalgic autobiographical books—*Happy Days: 1880-1892, Newspaper Days: 1899-1906,* and *Heathen Days: 1890-1936*—and with two lengthy supplements to *The American Language.* Shortly after completing coverage for the Baltimore *Sun* of the 1948 Presidential election, Mencken fell victim to a massive stroke that left him unable to read or write for the last eight years of his life.

In a brief article for *The Bookman,* Mencken wrote: "All of my work, barring a few obvious burlesques, is based upon three fundamental ideas. 1. That knowledge is better than ignorance; 2. That it is better to tell the truth than to lie; and 3. That it is better to be free than to be a slave." A man who was renowned or feared during his lifetime as a would-be destroyer of established American culture, Mencken nonetheless adhered to fairly conventional American ideals; essentially a libertarian, he believed in limited government, an aristocracy of the intellect, free expression of thought and action, and the right of the individual to live free from legally enforced moral coercion. In conjunction with these beliefs were Mencken's atheism and absurdist view of existence. Like Mark Twain's Mysterious Stranger, he held that laughter and unbridled fun were the only appropriate responses to life; he once wrote to Burton Rascoe: "My notion is that all the larger human problems are insoluble, and that life is quite meaningless—a spectacle without purpose or moral. I detest all efforts to read a moral into it." Hence the mutual contempt that existed between Mencken and society's potential reformers or "wowsers" as he often called them. Believing morality and art to be mutually exclusive, Mencken championed opposition to didactic literature and literary censorship, both of which he considered products of America's genteel nineteenth-century heritage. He attacked the defenders of the old order in "Puritanism As a Literary Force," which is included in his *A Book of Prefaces* and is considered one of the seminal essays in modern literary criticism. This assault on mass-tastes and moralistic literature reflects, in part, Mencken's view of his fellow Americans as a collection of gullible, self-centered fools who cling to religion and democratic government for some degree of purpose and security. The follies of American life—whether in religion, art, or politics—fascinated Mencken, who once admitted: "I love my country as a small boy loves a circus."

Stung by his ridicule, Mencken's victims often flared back at their attacker. William Allen White wrote: "With a pig's eyes that never look up, with a pig's snout that loves muck, with a pig's brain that knows only the sty, and a pig's squeal that cries only when he is hurt, he sometimes opens his pig's mouth, tusked and ugly, and lets out the voice of God, railing at the whitewash that covers the manure about his habitat." This

critical bouquet delighted Mencken, who collected excerpts from the most pointed critical attacks against himself and published them in *Menckeniana: A Schimpflexikon*. The collection, which includes critical comments ranging from the semiliterate ragings of Ku Klux Klansmen to the polished polemics of Rebecca West, is itself indicative of one of Mencken's self-acknowledged attributes: his closed-mindedness. To Mencken, all hostile critics of his work were dolts; all Southerners and small-town residents were sentimental, ignorant louts; every Protestant minister was the prototype of Sinclair Lewis's infamous Elmer Gantry; and in general, every American male "goes to rest every night with the uneasy feeling that there is a burglar under the bed, and he gets up every morning with a sickening fear that his underwear has been stolen." Mencken's strongly held prejudices are central to his weaknesses as a critic of life and literature; for a time he failed to recognize American alarm at the rise of nazism during the 1930s as anything but the Germanophobia of the nation's yokels, and he long believed that the Depression was a hoax and that Roosevelt's New Deal was a plot to plunder the honest worker's bank account for the benefit of the lazy. As a literary critic, he sometimes exhibited the same flaw he ascribed to Howells, who was so "busy in the sideshows, he didn't see the elephants go by"; although Mencken recognized many important new writers, he also doggedly praised several poor ones, and failed to recognize such prominent contemporaries as Virginia Woolf, William Faulkner, and Thomas Wolfe.

But as Upton Sinclair has observed of Mencken, "You don't argue with Niagara, and you don't interrupt a circus." Despite his failings, Mencken is widely acknowledged to have written perhaps the most forceful, humorous, and convincing polemics in twentieth-century American literature, to have elevated the standards of American thought and letters, and to have invigorated the writing style of his contemporaries and successors. Among the writers who most influenced Mencken were T. H. Huxley, whose work taught him the importance of clarity and simple sentence structure; Mark Twain, who demonstrated the value of sly humor in confronting and exposing human folly; and Edward Kingsbury, editorial writer of the New York *Sun*, whose work taught him "that good sense was at the bottom of all good writing." Mencken was also indebted to Ambrose Bierce, with whom he shared contempt for the "common herd," and to Nietzsche, Shaw, and James Gibbons Huneker, who shaped his belief in the importance of scepticism, iconoclasm, and reaching the "civilized minority." Mencken's accomplishment has been summarized by Philip Wagner, his successor as editor of *The Evening Sun*, as follows: "As a slashing and wonderfully comic critic of American life and institutions he attained for a time a stature and influence such as no other American writer has ever known."

(See also *Contemporary Authors*, Vol. 105 and *Dictionary of Literary Biography*, Vol. 11: *American Humorists, 1800-1950*.)

PRINCIPAL WORKS

Ventures into Verse (poetry) 1903
George Bernard Shaw: His Plays (criticism) 1905
The Philosophy of Friedrich Nietzsche (essay) 1908
A Book of Burlesques (essays) 1916
A Book of Prefaces (essays and criticism) 1917
In Defense of Women (essay) 1918
The American Language (nonfiction) 1919
Prejudices: First Series (essays and criticism) 1919
Prejudices: Second Series (essays and criticism) 1920
Prejudices: Third Series (essays and criticism) 1922
Prejudices: Fourth Series (essays and criticism) 1924
Notes on Democracy (essay) 1926
Prejudices: Fifth Series (essays and criticism) 1926
Prejudices: Sixth Series (essays and criticism) 1927
Menckeniana: A Schimpflexikon [editor] (criticism) 1928
Treatise on the Gods (essay) 1930
Treatise on Right and Wrong (essay) 1934
**Happy Days: 1880-1892* (autobiography) 1940
**Newspaper Days: 1899-1906* (autobiography) 1941
**Heathen Days: 1890-1936* (autobiography) 1943
The American Language: Supplement One (nonfiction) 1945
The American Language: Supplement Two (nonfiction) 1948
A Mencken Chrestomathy (essays and criticism) 1949
The Vintage Mencken (essays) 1955
Minority Report: H. L. Mencken's Notebooks (notebooks) 1956
The Bathtub Hoax and Other Blasts and Bravos from the "Chicago Tribune" (essays) 1958
Letters (letters) 1961
H. L. Mencken's "Smart Set" Criticism (criticism) 1968

*These works were published as *The Days of H. L. Mencken* in 1947.

***THE NATION* (essay date 1906)**

[*In the following excerpt, an anonymous reviewer offers a negative appraisal of Mencken's* George Bernard Shaw: His Plays, *finding it to be composed of little more than synopses of Shaw's dramas.*]

Mr. Mencken, in this brief volume of about one hundred pages, [**'George Bernard Shaw: His Plays'**], attempts to do for Mr. Shaw what was done for Ibsen in the 'Quintessence of Ibsenism,' years ago. But it not so easy to write a Quintessence of Shavianism unless one is ready, as Mr. Shaw was in his tract, to go all the way with one's subject, or even further, and to wring the quintessence out of him. This Mr. Mencken cannot do. What made the 'Quintessence' valuable was the peculiar equipment of Mr. Shaw for the task, just as George Meredith's 'Idea of Comedy' has become a classic because he himself was a master of the comic spirit. But the writer of the present volume does little more than give us a résumé of the plays and novels. The book is, in fact, intended for those who, after seeing a performance of "Man and Superman," are disinclined for the exertion of reading those plays that are not now being presented on the stage. The truth is, that the time has not yet arrived for a book on Mr. Shaw. . . .

It is not easy to interpret the plays of a playwright with a purpose. . . . [Mr. Mencken] rather describes than interprets, and his book will no doubt find grateful readers among Mr. Shaw's American audiences. What he means when he tells the playgoer that "Man and Superman" is "in purpose one with the 'Odyssey,'" we cannot imagine, for we had always thought that there was a purpose in the play, and there is none in the 'Odyssey,' save to delight the weary. Mr. Mencken says of "The Devil's Disciple" that, among the religious, only "a man given to constant self-analysis—the 999th man in the thousand" could appreciate it. This is probably an echo of Mr. Shaw's one realist in a thousand in the 'Quintessence.' But he was, of course, the thousandth man, not the 999th.

Mr. Mencken's English is rather too colloquial for elegance. "When Darwin bobbed up," "A young woman of money," "oldster" (a horrid analogous formation), are a few of his faults of style. Nor can we admire the tone of the biographical note. It is not in good taste to drag in a man's relatives as evidence of his private circumstances—at any rate, not until he is dead and has been handed over to his biographers for dissection. (p. 104)

A review of "George Bernard Shaw: His Plays," in The Nation, *Vol. LXXXII, No. 2118, February 1, 1906, pp. 103-04.*

STUART P. SHERMAN (essay date 1917)

[*Sherman was for many years considered one of America's most conservative literary critics. During the early twentieth century, he was influenced by the New Humanism, a literary movement whose members subscribed to the belief that the aesthetic quality of any literary work must be subordinate to its support of traditional moral values. During his years as a literary critic at* The Nation, *Sherman established himself as a champion of the long-entrenched Anglo-Saxon, genteel tradition in American letters and as a bitter enemy of literary Naturalism and its proponents. Theodore Dreiser and his chief defender, H. L. Mencken, were Sherman's special targets during the World War I era, as Sherman perceived the Naturalism they espoused to be a life-denying cultural product of America's enemy, Germany. During the 1920s, Sherman became the editor of the book review section of the* New York Herald Tribune, *a move that coincided with a distinct liberalization of his hitherto staunch critical tastes; in the last years of his life, he even praised his old enemies Dreiser and Mencken. In the following excerpt from an essay written during the war years, Sherman attacks Mencken's* A Book of Prefaces.]

Mr. Mencken is not at all satisfied with life or literature in America, for he is a lover of the beautiful. We have nowadays no beautiful literature in this country, with the possible exception of Mr. Dreiser's novels; nor do we seem in a fair way to produce anything aesthetically gratifying. . . . For a competent historical account of our national anaesthesia one should turn, Mr. Mencken assures us, to a translation, from some foreign tongue—we cannot guess which—by Dr. Leon Kellner. Thus one readily perceives [in **"A Book of Prefaces"**] that Mr. Mencken's introductions to Conrad, Dreiser, and Huneker and his discourse on **"Puritanism as a Literary Force"** are of the first importance to all listeners for the soft breath and finer spirit of letters. (p. 593)

As Mr. Mencken conceives the aesthetic ministry, there is nothing in the world more dispassionate, disinterested, freer from moral, religious, or political significance. The "typical American critic," to be sure, is a pestilent and dangerous fellow; he is a Puritan; he is obsessed by nonaesthetic ideas; he is ever bent on giving instruction in the sphere of conduct; he is always talking about politics and morals. But, Mr. Mencken assures us, "criticism, as the average American 'intellectual' understands it, is what a Frenchman, a German, or a Russian would call donkeyism." Now, though Mr. Mencken is not a German, he has an open mind. One may even say that he has a "roomy" mind. And by that token he is quite certainly not a typical American critic. We imagine that he may fairly be taken as a representative of the high European critical outlook over "beautiful letters"—as he loves to call such finely sensitive work as that of Mr. Dreiser. He does not wander over the wide field of conduct with a birth rod; he simply perceives and feels and interprets the soul of loveliness in art—to use his own expressive phrase, he beats a drum for beauty.

One who does not fix firmly in mind Mr. Mencken's theoretical *Standpunkt* is likely to be somewhat confused by his practice. The careless and cursory reader of these *belles pages* of his will probably not, it is true, be impressed with their aesthetic purity and serenity, not at first. One's first impression, indeed, is that Mr. Mencken has as many moral and political irons in the fire as the "typical American critic"—the poor native whose blood is not so richly tinctured with Saxon, Bavarian, and Hessian elements. He has a dozen non-aesthetic standards which he incessantly employs in the judgment of books and authors. He has a "philosophical theory," "politics," "social ideas," "ideas of education," and "moral convictions," with all which a piece of literature has to square, if it is to please him. These general ideas he treats by no means as trifles; he thrusts them into one's face with peculiar emphasis and insistence. So that presently one begins to suspect that his quarrel with American criticism is not so much in behalf of beauty as in behalf of a *Kultur* which has been too inhospitably received by such of his fellow-citizens as look to another *Stammvater* than his. Of course, the true explanation is that Mr. Mencken's culture-propaganda is what a drummer (for *das Schöne*) would call his "side-line." Beauty is the main burden of his pack.

Though Mr. Mencken's *Kultur* is not German, it reminds one faintly of the German variety as described by Professor Eucken in October, 1914: "Our German Kultur has, in its unique depth, something shrinking and severe; it does not obtrude itself, or readily yield itself up; it must be earnestly sought after and lovingly assimilated from within. This love was lacking in our neighbors; wherefore they easily came to look upon us with the eyes of hatred." Mr. Mencken's culture is like this in that one must love it ere it will seem worthy of one's love. For example, his fundamental philosophical idea is, that "human life is a seeking without finding, that its purpose is impenetrable, that joy and sorrow are alike meaningless." Then there are his political notions. The good Mr. Knopf—the good and helpful Mr. Knopf—tells us that in politics our lover of beautiful letters is "an extreme Federalist." We had divined that. Mr. Mencken himself shrinkingly betrays the fact that he considers the hopes and professions of democracy as silly and idle sentimentality. Then there are his social ideas: he is for a somewhat severe male aristocracy; he firmly points out "how vastly the rôle of women has been exaggerated, how little they amount to in the authentic struggle of man." Then there are his educational ideas. The useful Mr. Knopf informs us that Mr. Mencken "attended no university." We had divined that also. Does he not explicitly declare that "college professors, alas, never learn anything"? Does he not steadily harp on "the bombastic half-knowledge of a school teacher"? Does he not note as a sign of Mr. Huneker's critical decadence the fact that he has spoken civilly of a Princeton professor? Does he not scornfully remark, "*I* could be a professor if I would"? Then there are his moral convictions. He is anti-Christian. He is for the *Herrenmoral* and against the "Sklavmoral that besets all of us of English speech." He holds with Blake that "the lust of the goat is also to the glory of God." Finally there are his national and racial feelings and convictions. He holds that the Americans are an "upstart people," and that "formalism is the hall-mark of the national culture." He holds that the Anglo-Saxon civilization excels all others as a prolific mother of quacks and mountebanks. Mr. Mencken's continuous tirade against everything respectable in American morals, against everything characteristic of American society, and against everything and everybody distinguished in American scholarship and letters, is not precisely and strictly *aesthetic* criticism; indeed, an unsympathetic person might say that it is not criticism at all, but mere scurrility and blackguardism. His continous laudation of a Teutonic-Oriental pessimism and nihilism in philosophy, of anti-democratic politics, of the subjection and contempt of women, of the *Herrenmoral,* and of anything but Anglo-Saxon civilization, is not precisely and strictly *aesthetic* criticism; an unsympathetic person might call it infatuated propagandism. But, of course, all these things are properly to be regarded as but the *obiter dicta* of a quiet drummer for beauty.

Still, for the aesthetic critic, it is a pleasure to turn from Mr. Mencken's somewhat polemical general ideas to the man himself as revealed by the subtle and finely woven garment of his style. Though not a German, Mr. Mencken has a beautiful style; and though he could be a professor if he would, he has a learned style. To his erudition let stand as witnesses the numberless choice words calculated to send the vulgar reader to a dictionary: "multipara," "chandala," "lamaseries," "coryza," "lagniappe," "umbilicarii," "Treuga Dei," "swamis," "gemaras," "munyonic," "glycosuria." This is clearly the vocabulary of an artist and a scholar. As an additional sign of his erudition, consider his discovery that Mr. Dreiser "stems" from the Greeks; also his three-line quotation from a Greek dramatist—in the original Greek. To prove the beauty of his phrasing and his general literary feeling, one has but to open the book and dip in anywhere. Here, in Dryden's words, is "God's plenty." How gently he touches the decline of religious faith in New England; "the old God of Plymouth Rock, as practically conceived, is now scarcely worse than the average jail warden or Italian pardone." How nobly he lays to rest the moral faith of our fathers: "the huggermugger morality of timorous, whining unintelligent and unimaginative men—envy turned into law, cowardice sanctified, stupidity made noble, Puritanism." How adequately he interprets the spirit of our emancipators: "The thing that worried the more ecstatic Abolitionists was their sneaking sense of responsibility, the fear that they themselves were flouting the fire by letting slavery go." What a felicitous image of Emerson!—"a diligent drinker from German spigots"; alas, poor Emerson, he left the German taproom too soon, and so remained a "dilettante" all his life. And here are jewels three words long that on the forefinger of Belles Lettres will sparkle forever: . . . the "calm superior numskullery that was Victorian," "eminent excoriators of the Rum Demon," "the intolerable prudishness and dirtymindedness of Puritanism"—"one ingests a horse-doctor's dose of words, but fails to acquire any illumination."

The sheer verbal loveliness of writing like this can never pass away. It is the writing of a sensitive intellectual aristocrat. It has the quality and tone of high breeding. It is the flower and fragrance of a noble and elevated mind that dwells habitually with beauty. Does not one breathe a sigh of relief as one escapes from the ruck and muck of American "culture" into the clear and spacious atmosphere of genuine aesthetic criticism? If, by exchanging our American set of standards for his "European" set, we could learn to write as Mr. Mencken does, why do we hesitate? Well, as a matter of fact, there is already a brave little band of sophomores in criticism who do not hesitate. These humming Ephemera are mostly preserved in the pure amber of Mr. Mencken's prose. At everything accepted as finely and soundly American, swift fly the pebbles, out gushes the corrosive vapor of a *discriminating* abuse. The prospect for beautiful letters in America is visibly brightening. (pp. 593-94)

Stuart P. Sherman, "Beautifying American Literature," in The Nation, *Vol. CV, No. 2735, November 29, 1917, pp. 593-94.*

BRANDER MATTHEWS (essay date 1919)

[An American critic, playwright, and novelist, Matthews wrote extensively on world drama and served for a quarter century at Columbia as professor of dramatic literature, becoming the first to hold such a position at any American university. Matthews was also a founding member and president of the National Institute of Arts and Letters. Matthews, whose criticism is both witty and informative, has been called "perhaps the last of the gentlemanly school of critics and essayists" in America. In the following excerpt, he favorably reviews The American Language.*]*

[A leading American scholar recently] declared that he was shocked and grieved and saddened by the many evidences he had noticed that our speech in America was no longer conforming to the conventions of our kin across the sea in the little island where English had come to its maturity. He even went so far as to suggest that our English here in America was deteriorating and degenerating, as Greek had declined after it had entered on its decadence in the Hellenistic period, when the centre of Greek civilization had migrated across the "tideless dolorous, inland sea" from Athens to Alexandria.

And now comes H. L. Mencken, armed at all points, to maintain the same contention, not whimsically, like the American humorist, and not dolefully, like the American critic, but unhesitatingly and joyfully. He holds that the tongue which we speak on this side of the Western Ocean is no longer English, but is now American. . . .

[Mr. Mencken's ***The American Language***] is interesting and useful; it is a book to be taken seriously; it is a book well planned, well proportioned, well documented, and well written. As I read its pages with both pleasure and profit I was reminded of an anecdote. Emerson once lent a translation of Plato to one of his rustic neighbors at Concord; and when the Yankee farmer returned it he did this with this characteristic remark: "I see Plato has a good many of my idees!" As I lingered over Mr. Mencken's successive and suggestive chapters I discovered that he had a good many of my ideas and that I had a good many of his ideas. I suppose that the foundation of my assertion that Mr. Mencken's book is useful and interesting is to be found in the fact that I agree with many of his opinions. . . .

Everybody knows that there are a host of divergences between the English language as it is now spoken in the British Isles and as it is now spoken in the United States, differences of intonation, of pronunciation, of vocabulary, and even of grammar; but nobody has ever marshaled this host as amply, as logically, or as impressively as Mr. Mencken has done. (p. 157)

Mr. Mencken is rejoiced by the vitality, the vigor, the freshness of the American language, and he looks forward to a time when the foremost American authors will cast off all allegiance to the traditions of the language as these came into being in England. Yet he has to regret that he can see no sign of any new departure in the writings of these foremost authors. Walt Whitman and Mark Twain and Mr. Howells are devoid of any colonial subservience to British standards, but what they wrote is still English and English of an indisputable purity. Even Mr. Mencken's own book is written in what he would call English and not in what he would call American. (p. 164)

I find I cannot quit Mr. Mencken without a little faultfinding. He avoids the violent vituperation which used to characterize linguistic debate; but he is not always so courteous as he might be toward the predecessors with whom he does not agree. He mentions the American Academy of Arts and Letters only to sneer at "the gifted philologs of that sanhedrin." He speaks slightingly of the late Thomas Raynesford Lounsbury, who deserved well of all linguistic inquirers; and he adds injury to insult by calling him Thomas S. Lounsbury. And he terms the writer of this review "a pundit." What have I ever done to deserve this stigma? (p. 170)

Brander Matthews, "Developing the American from the English Language," in The New York Times Book Review *(copyright © 1919 by The New York Times Company; reprinted by permission), March 30, 1919, pp. 157, 164, 170.*

A[LDOUS] L. H[UXLEY] (essay date 1920)

[*Known primarily for his dystopian novel* Brave New World, *Huxley was a British-American man of letters noted for his novels of ideas. The grandson of noted Darwinist T. H. Huxley and the brother of scientist Julian Huxley, he was interested in many fields of knowledge; daring conceptions of science, philosophy, and religion are woven throughout his fiction. Continually searching for an escape from the ambivalence of modern life, Huxley sought a sense of spiritual renewal and a clarification of his artistic vision through the use of hallucinogenic drugs, an experience explored in one of his best known later works,* The Doors of Perception *(1954). He praises Mencken in the following excerpted review of* Prejudices: First Series.]

[In **"Prejudices: First Series,"**] Mr. Mencken turns a pair of very civilized eyes on the extraordinary and fantastic spectacle which is contemporary American life. It passes before him, a circus parade—vast ponderous elephants, lions, shy gazelles, apes, performing horses—and he comments upon it, laughingly, in that brilliant, masterfully vulgar style of which he knows the strange secret. All the animals interest him, graceful and ugly alike, noble and repulsive; but by preference he lingers, fascinated no doubt by the fabulous grotesqueness of their swollen shapes, among the solemn mammoths of stupidity, mountain-bodied and mouse-brained, slow-moving, prehistoric. They exist everywhere, these monsters; but it is surely in America that they reach their greatest growth. Puritanism there swells into Comstockism; our harmless little European uplift becomes a sinister, rapacious philanthropic beast; religions pullulate, strange and improbable as the saurians of the Mesozoic age. Mr. Mencken contemplates them with a civilized man's astonishment and horror, then sets his pen in rest and charges upon them. His pen is sharp, his aim unerring, and the punctured monsters collapse with a dolorous whistling of escaping gas. It is a wonderful display. Admiring his skill, one thinks of what Dryden said of himself in his Essay on Satire: "There is still a vast difference between the slovenly butchering of a man and the fineness of a stroke that separates the head from the body and leaves it standing in its place. A man may be capable, as Jack Ketch's wife said of his servant, of a plain piece of work, a bare hanging; but to make a malefactor die sweetly was only belonging to her husband." Mr. Mencken is a worthy apprentice of this great Jack Ketch of literature. Of all his performances, perhaps the most brilliantly conducted is his execution of Professor Doctor Thorstein Veblen, author of "The Theory of the Leisure Class" and "The Higher Learning in America." Professor Veblen is almost too good to be true. He is a Great Thinker who teaches us that we have lawns round our houses because we are "the descendants of a pastoral people inhabiting a region with a humid climate," and that we do not keep cows on these lawns "because a herd of cattle so pointedly suggests thrift and economy," and we, being members of the Leisured Class, have a feudal contempt for thrift. Mr. Mencken, it may be imagined, deals with Veblenism as it deserves; but when one has laughed over Veblen and the other monsters at which he goes a-tilting, one begins to wonder whether, after all, the thing is not too easy. The monsters of America are so undisguisedly monstrous that it is not hard to recognize them and with a hunter's eye to mark out their vulnerable spots. But here in Europe the monstrosity of the dragons is not always quite so obvious. They appear in distinguished traditional shapes, in lions' skins, or winged with the plumes of eagles. The eye must be sharp indeed that can detect at a glance the true nature of the beasts. We should like to see if Mr. Mencken's critical gift served him as well as an older, more intellectually sophisticated world, where the circus parade of life and letters, though perhaps equally grotesque, is grotesque in a different way from the transatlantic spectacle. In any case, we should welcome his appearance among us here; for we have sore need of critics who hate humbug, who are not afraid of putting out their tongues at pretentiousness however noble an aspect it may wear, who do not mind being vulgar at need, and who, finally, know not only how to make us think, but how to make us laugh as well.

A[ldous] L. H[uxley], "American Criticism," in The Athenaeum, *No. 4679, January 2, 1920, p. 10.**

H. L. MENCKEN (letter date 1920?)

[*In the following excerpt from a revealing letter to Burton Rascoe, a literary critic and editor of several periodicals, Mencken discusses the influences on his work, his professional vision, and the similarity of his writings to those of George Jean Nathan.*]

I believe, and have often argued, that the battle of ideas should be international—that is idiotic to expect any one country to offer hospitality to every imaginable sort of man. I do not fit into the United States very well. My skepticism is intolerably offensive to the normal American man; only the man under strong foreign influences sees anything in it save a gross immorality. (p. 184)

[Nathan and I] are constantly accused of imitating each other. This is absurd. No two men could possibly be more unlike, in style and thought. Nathan detests philosophical questions, and particularly political questions; he sees life purely as idiotic spectacle. I delight in such questions, though I reject all solutions. Nathan aims at a very complex style; I aim at the greatest possible lucidity. Our point of contact is our common revulsion from American sentimentality. We are both essentially foreigners. But he is more French than anything else, and I am more German than anything else. We work together amicably because we are both lonely, and need some support. He dislikes the ***American Language*** book because it is full of facts, and has never read it. I dislike his interest in the theatre, which seems to me to be an intellectual hogpen. But we come together on several essentials, e.g. our common disinclination to know authors or to belong to literary coteries, our lack of national feeling, and (perhaps most important) our similar attitudes toward money, religion, women, etc. . . . Both of us detest martyrs of all sorts. (p. 185)

I have never consciously imitated any man save the anonymous editorial writer of the New York Sun. The man who made a critic of me was Robert I. Carter, an old New York Herald man, then managing editor of the Baltimore Herald, and my boss (circa 1912). He taught me a lot, but particularly one thing—that the first desideratum in criticism is to be *interesting*. . . . Next to Carter, I learned most from Percival Pollard—

particularly the value, to a critic, of concentrating on a few men. Pollard used Ambrose Bierce; I used Dreiser. I seldom read criticism. The work of such men as [W. C. Brownell, Paul Elmer More, Stuart P. Sherman], etc. seems to me to be simply silly—a dull emission of the obviously untrue.

I believe that the public likes criticism only in so far as it is a good show, which means only in so far as it is bellicose. The crowd is always with the prosecution. Hence, when I have to praise a writer, I usually do it by attacking his enemies. And when I say the crowd I mean all men. My own crowd is very small and probably somewhat superior, but it likes rough-house just as much as a crowd around a bulletin board. All the favorable notices of ***Prejudices*** show an obvious delight in my onslaughts on Cobb, Veblen, Howells, Hamlin Garland, Sydnor Harrison, Shaw, etc. Such doings, of course, involve reprisals. I am myself attacked with great vigor. . . . But such attacks do not annoy me. I am skeptic enough to believe that some other fellow's notions of honor may be quite as sound as my own. Moreover, there is always a certain amount of truth in every attack, however dishonest.

I have no superstitions about critical honor. I lean toward men I like and away from men I dislike. The calm, Judicial judgment makes me laugh. It is a symptom of a delusion of infallibility. I am often wrong. My prejudices are innumerable, and often idiotic. My aim is not to determine facts, but to function freely and pleasantly—as Nietzsche used to say, to dance with arms and legs.

All of my work hangs together, once the main ideas under it are discerned. Those ideas are chiefly of a skeptical character. I believe that nothing is unconditionally true, and hence I am opposed to every statement of positive truth and to every man who states it. Such men seem to me to be either idiots or scoundrels. To one category or the other belong all theologians, professors, editorial writers, right-thinkers, etc. I am against patriotism because it demands the acceptance of propositions that are obviously imbecile, e.g., that an American Presbyterian is the equal of Ludendorff. I am against democracy for the same reason: it rests upon lunacy. To me democracy seems to be founded upon the inferior man's envy of his superior—of the man who is having a better time. This is also the origin of Puritanism. I detest all such things. I acknowledge that many men are my superiors, and always defer to them. In such a country as the United States, of course, few such men are to be encountered. Hence my foreignness: most of the men I respect are foreigners. But this is not my fault. I'd be glad to respect Americans if they were respectable. (pp. 186-87)

I detest men who meanly admire mean things, e.g., fellows who think that Rockefeller is a great man. I also detest poltroons—that is, men who seek unfair advantages in combat. In my gladiatorial days on the Baltimore Sun I never attacked a single man who was without means of hitting back. (p. 187)

As I say, all my work hangs together. Whether it appears to be burlesque, or serious criticism, or mere casual controversy, it is always directed against one thing: unwarranted pretension. It always seeks to expose a false pretense, to blow up a wobbly axiom, to uncover a sham virtue. My experience of the world teaches me that the best people are those who make no profession of being good—that all who do, absolutely without exception, are frauds. . . .

My weapon is adapted to the enemy and the fight. Sometimes I try to spoof them, and sometimes I use a club. But the end is always the same. I have no general aim save this—that is, I do not aspire to set up any doctrine of my own. Few doctrines seem to me to be worth fighting for. I can't understand the martyr. Far from going to the stake for a Great Truth, I wouldn't even miss a meal for it. My notion is that all the larger human problems are insoluble, and that life is quite meaningless—a spectacle without purpose or moral. I detest all efforts to read a moral into it. I do not write because I want to make converts. In point of fact, I seldom make one—and then it is embarrassing. I write because the business amuses me. It is the best of sports. (p. 188)

My style of writing is chiefly grounded upon an early enthusiasm for Huxley, the greatest of all masters of orderly exposition. He taught me the importance of giving to every argument a simple structure. As for the fancy work on the surface, it comes chiefly from an anonymous editorial writer in the New York Sun, circa 1900. He taught me the value of apt phrases. My vocabulary is pretty large; it probably runs to 25,000 words. It represents much labor. I am constantly expanding it. I believe that a good phrase is better than a Great Truth—which is usually buncombe. I delight in argument, not because I want to convince, but because argument itself is an end. (p. 189)

All my criticism is, at bottom, a criticism of ideas, not of mere books. But ideas—i.e., the follies and imbecilities of men—interest me. Blowing them up is the noblest of human occupations. (pp. 189-90)

H. L. Mencken, in a letter to Burton Rascoe in Summer, 1920? in his Letters of H. L. Mencken, *edited by Guy J. Forgue (copyright © 1961 by Alfred A. Knopf, Inc.; all rights reserved; reprinted by permission of Alfred A. Knopf, Inc.), Knopf, 1961, pp. 184-90.*

GEORGE JEAN NATHAN (essay date 1920)

[Nathan has been called the most learned and influential drama critic the United States has yet produced. During the early decades of the twentieth century he was greatly responsible for shifting the emphasis of the American theater from light entertainment to serious drama, introducing audiences and producers to the work of Eugene O'Neill, Henrik Ibsen, and Bernard Shaw, among others. With Mencken, Nathan belonged to an iconoclastic school of American critics who attacked the vulgarity of accepted ideas and sought to bring a new level of sophistication to American culture, which they found provincial and backward. Throughout his career, Nathan shared with Mencken a gift for stinging invective and verbal adroitness, as well as total confidence in his own judgments. In the following excerpt, he expresses his admiration for Mencken's honesty as a man and as a critic.]

I respect [Mencken] and am his friend, because he is one of the very few Americans I know who is entirely free of cheapness, toadyism and hypocrisy. In close association with him for more than twelve years, I have yet to catch him in a lie against himself, or in a compromise with his established faiths. (pp. 34-5)

Perhaps no man has ever been more accurately mirrored by his writings than this man. He has never, so far as I know, written a single line that he hasn't believed. He has never sold a single adjective—and there have been times when opulent temptations have dangled before him. And on certain of these occasions he could have used the money. There may be times when he is wrong and when his opinions are biased—I believed that there are not a few such times—yet if he is wrong, he is wrong honestly, and if he is biased, he neither knows it in his own mind nor feels it in his own heart. He is the best fighter

I have ever met. And he is the fairest, the cleanest, and the most relentless.

But does he accept himself with forefinger to temple, with professorial wrinkles, as an Uplifting Force, a Tonic Influence? Not on your ball-room socks! No critic has ever snickered at him as loudly and effectively as he snickers at himself. "What do you think of your new book?" I usually ask him when he has finished one. And his reply generally is, "It's got some good stuff in it—and a lot of cheese. What the hell's the use of writing such a book, anyway? My next one . . ."

Life to him is a sort of Luna Park, and he gets the same sort of innocent, idiotic fun out of it. . . . His work, which so clearly reflects him spiritually, represents him equally clearly in helpless revolt against his corporeal self.

This, a snapshot of Henry Mencken, for ever applying the slapstick to his own competence, constantly sceptical of his own talents, and ever trying vainly to run away from the pleasure that his temperament rebelliously mocks. I am happy to know him, for knowing him has made the world a gayer place and work a more diverting pastime. I am glad to be his partner, his collaborator, his co-editor, his drinking companion, and his friend. For after all these many years of our friendship and professional alliance, there is only one thing that I can hold against him. For ten years he has worn the damndest looking overcoat that I've ever seen. (pp. 35-6)

George Jean Nathan, "On H. L. Mencken," in The Borzoi 1920: Being a Sort of Record of Five Years' Publishing, *edited by Alfred A. Knopf (copyright 1920 renewed 1947, by Alfred A. Knopf, Inc.; reprinted by permission of the publisher), Knopf, 1920, pp. 34-6.*

F. SCOTT FITZGERALD (essay date 1921)

[*The author of such American classics as* The Great Gatsby *(1925) and* Tender is the Night *(1934), Fitzgerald was the spokesman for the Jazz Age, America's decade of prosperity, excess, and abandon, which began soon after the end of World War I and ended with the 1929 Wall Street Crash. The novels and stories for which he is best known examine an entire generation's search for the elusive American dream of wealth and happiness. Mencken played a significant role in launching Fitzgerald's professional career, having published several of the younger writer's stories in* The Smart Set *and favorably reviewing his first novel,* This Side of Paradise, *in the same journal. In the following excerpted review, Fitzgerald praises Mencken's* Prejudices: Second Series.]

The incomparable Mencken will, I fear, meet the fate of Aristides. He will be exiled because one is tired of hearing his praises sung. (p. 79)

Of the essays in the [**"Prejudices: Second Series"**] the best is the autopsy on the still damp bones of Roosevelt. In the hands of Mencken Roosevelt becomes almost a figure of Greek tragedy; more, he becomes alive and loses some of that stuffiness that of late has become attached to all 100% Americans. Not only is the essay most illuminating but its style is a return to Mencken's best manner, the style of **"Prefaces"**, with the soft pedal on his amazing chord of adjectives and a tendency to invent new similes instead of refurbishing his amusing but somewhat overworked old ones.

Except for the section on American aristocracy there is little new in the first essay **"The National Letters":** an abundance of wit and a dozen ideas that within the past year and under his own deft hand have become bromides. The Knights of Pythias, Right Thinkers, On Building Universities, Methodists,

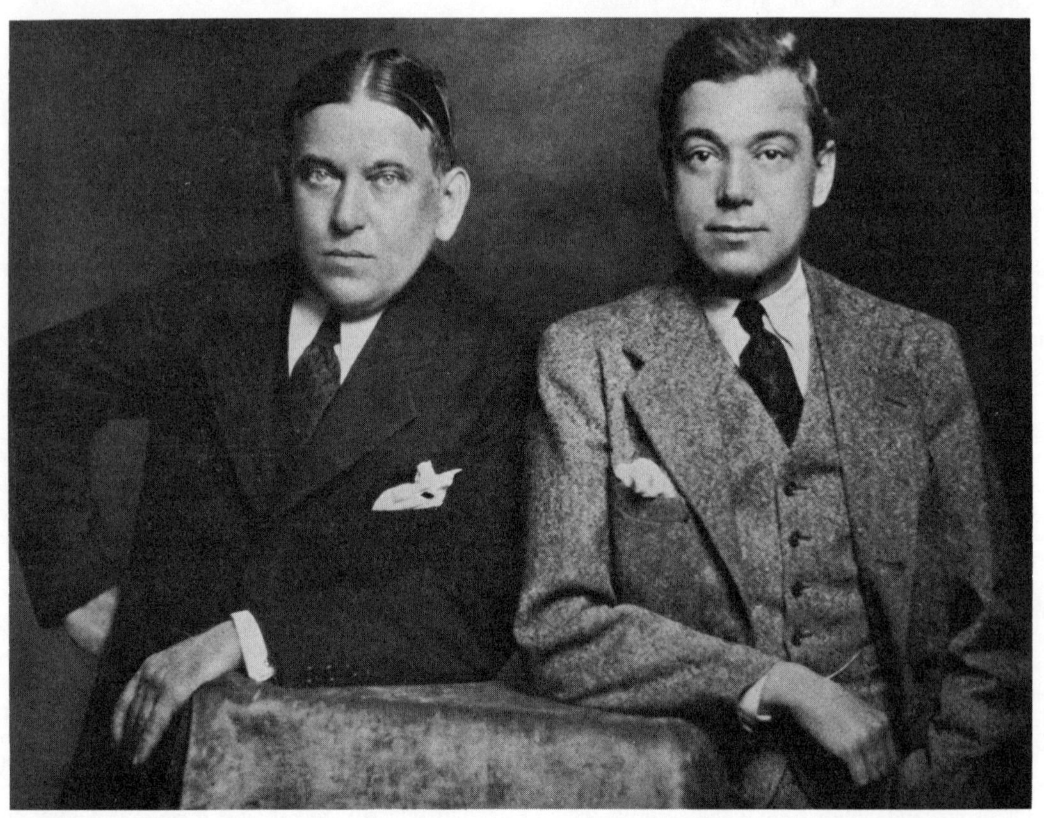

Mencken and George Jean Nathan (1928). The Granger Collection, New York.

as well as the corps of journeyman critics and popular novelists come in for their usual bumping, this varied with unexpected tolerance toward "The Saturday Evening Post" and even a half grudging mention of Booth Tarkington. Better than any of this comment, valid and vastly entertaining as it is, would be a second **"Book of Prefaces"** say on Edith Wharton, Cabell, Woodrow Wilson—and Mencken himself. But the section of the essay devoted to the Cultural Background rises to brilliant analysis. Here again he is thinking slowly, he is on comparatively fresh ground, he brings the force of his clarity and invention to bear on the subject—passes beyond his function as a critic of the arts and becomes a reversed Cato of a civilization.

In **"The Sahara of Bozart"** the dam breaks, devastating Georgia, Carolina, Mississippi, and Company. The first trickle of this overflow appeared in the preface to **"The American Credo"**; here it reaches such a state of invective that one pictures all the region south of Mason-Dixon to be peopled by moron Catilines. The ending is gentle—too gentle, the gentleness of ennui.

To continue in the grand manner of a catalogue: **"The Divine Afflatus"** deals with the question of inspiration and the lack of it, an old and sad problem to the man who has done creative work. **"Examination of a Popular Virtue"** runs to eight pages of whimsical excellence—a consideration of ingratitude decided at length with absurd but mellow justice. **"Exeunt Omnes"**, which concerns the menace of death, I choose to compare with a previous **"Discussion"** of the same subject in **"A Book of Burlesques"**. The comparison is only in that the former piece, which I am told Mencken fatuously considers one of his best, is a hacked out, glued together bit of foolery, as good, say, as an early essay of Mark Twain's, while this **"Exeunt Omnes"**, which follows it by several years, is smooth, brilliant, apparently jointless. To my best recollection it is the most microscopical examination of this particular mote on the sun that I have ever come across.

Follows a four paragraph exposition of the platitude that much music loving is an affectation and further paragraphs depreciating opera as a form. As to the **"Music of Tomorrow"** the present reviewer's ignorance must keep him silent, but in **"Tempo di Valse"** Mencken, the modern, becomes Victorian by insisting that what people are tired of is more exciting than what they have just learned to do. If his idea of modern dancing is derived from watching men who learned it circa thirty-five, toiling interminably around the jostled four square feet of a cabaret, he is justified; but I see no reason why the "Bouncing Shimmee" efficiently performed is not as amusing and as graceful and certainly as difficult as any waltz ever attempted. The section continues with the condemnation of a musician named Hadley, an ingenious attempt to preserve a portrait of Dreiser, and a satisfactory devastation of the acting profession.

In **"The Cult of Hope"** he defends his and "Dr. Nathan's" attitude toward constructive criticism—most entertainingly—but the next section **"The Dry Millennium"**, patchworked from the Ripetizione Generale, consists of general repetitions of theses in his previous books. **"An Appendix on a Tender Theme"** contains his more recent speculations on women, eked out with passages from "The Smart Set."

An excellent book! Like Max Beerbohm, Mencken's work is inevitably distinguished. But now and then one wonders—granted that, solidly, book by book, he has built up a literary reputation most to be envied of any American, granted also that he has done more for the national letters than any man alive, one is yet inclined to regret a success so complete. What will he do now? (pp. 79-81)

F. Scott Fitzgerald, "The Baltimore Anti-Christ" (reprinted by permission of Harold Ober Associates Incorporated; copyright, 1921, by George H. Doran Company), in The Bookman, *New York, Vol. LIII, No. 1, March, 1921, pp. 79-81.*

EDMUND WILSON, JR. (essay date 1921)

[Wilson, America's foremost man of letters in the twentieth century, wrote widely on cultural, historical, and literary matters, including several seminal critical studies. He is often credited with bringing an international perspective to American letters through his widely-read discussions of European literature. Wilson was allied to no critical school: however, several dominant concerns serve as guiding motifs throughout his work. He invariably examined the social and historical implications of a work of literature, particularly literature's significance as "an attempt to give meaning to our experience" and its value for the improvement of humanity. Although he was not a moralist, his criticism displays a deep concern with moral values. Another constant was his discussion of a work of literature as a revelation of its author's personality. However, though Wilson examined the historical and psychological implications of a work of literature, he rarely did so at the expense of a discussion of its literary qualities. Perhaps Wilson's greatest contributions to American literature were his tireless promotion of writers of the 1920s, 1930s, and 1940s, and his essays introducing the best of modern literature to the general reader. In the following excerpt, written early in his career, Wilson provides an astute study of Mencken's outlook, stressing his cynicism and the influence of Friedrich Nietzsche on Mencken's thought.]

The striking things about Mencken's mind are its ruthlessness and its rigidity. It has all the courage in the world in a country where courage is rare. He has even had the fearlessness to avoid the respectable and the wholesome; those two devils which so often betray in the end even the most intelligent of Americans. He fought outspokenly against optimism, Puritanism and democratic ineptitude, at a time when they had but few foes. It is well to remember, now that these qualities have become stock reproaches among the intelligentsia, that it was Mencken who began the crusade against them at a lonely and disregarded post and that we owe to him much of the disfavor into which they have recently fallen,—and also that it was Mencken who first championed the kind of American literary activity of which we have now become proudest. But the activity of his mind is curiously cramped by its extreme inflexibility. In the first place, as a critic, he is not what is called "sympathetic." His criticisms deal but little with people from their own point of view: he simply brings the other man's statements and reactions to the bar of his own dogma and, having judged them by that measure, proceeds to accept or reject them. Though one of the fairest of critics, he is one of the least pliant.

In the second place, in spite of his scepticism and his frequent exhortations to hold one's opinions lightly, he himself has been conspicuous for seizing upon simple dogmas and sticking to them with fierce tenacity. When he is arguing his case against democracy or Christianity, he reminds one rather of Bishop Manning or Dr. Straton than of Renan or Anatole France. The true sceptics like Renan or France see both the truth and weakness of every case; they put themselves in the place of people who believe differently from themselves and finally come to sympathize with them,—almost, to accept their point of view. But Mencken, once having got his teeth into an idea, can never be induced to drop it, and will only shake his head and growl when somebody tries to tempt him with something else.

Thus, in 1908, when he published his admirable book on Nietzsche, he had reached a certain set of conclusions upon society and ethics. Humanity, he had come to believe, is divided into two classes: the masters and the slaves. The masters are able and courageous men who do whatever they like and are not restrained by any scruples save those that promote their own interest; the slaves are a race of wretched underlings, stupid, superstitious and untrustworthy, who have no rights and no raison d'être except to be exploited by the masters. To talk of equality and fraternity is the most fatuous of nonsense: there is as much difference in kind between the masters and the slaves as there is between men and animals.

Therefore, Christianity is false because it asserts that all souls are worth saving and democracy is a mistake because it emancipates the slaves and tries to make them the masters. It is absurd to try to correct the evolutionary process which would allow the fittest to survive and the weaklings and fools to go under. "I am," Mr. Mencken has said, "against the under dog every time." But things are getting more and more democratic and consequently worse and worse. What we need is an enlightened aristocracy to take charge of society. But there has never been any such aristocracy and we are certainly not going to produce one. In the meantime, one can but curse the mob and die at one's post. (pp. 10-11)

Mencken has been upholding these theories without modification since 1908 at least. He has cherished them through the European war and through the industrial war that has followed it. (Quite recently they have led him into the absurdity of asserting that it would have been a good thing for America if the war had continued longer, because this would have stamped out "hundreds of thousands of the relatively unfit." The men who were left at the end of the war in the French and German armies, were, he adds "very superior men.") And, in consequence, it seems to me that he has cut himself off in an intellectual cul-de-sac.

He has much to say to America that is of the first usefulness and importance: he has no peer in the brilliance and effectiveness of his onslaught upon political ignorance and corruption, upon Y.M.C.A.'ism and popular morality, upon the cheapness and sordidness of current ideals. But, though the moral strength which gives him courage is drawn partly from his Nietzschean principles, these principles so close his horizon as to render his social criticism rather sterile. In the matters of politics and society he can do nothing but denounce. He has taken up a position in which it is impossible that any development should please him. He detests the present state of affairs, but he disbelieves in liberalism and radicalism, and any change in their directions would presumably only make him detest the world more. He really hates repression and injustice, but he has long ago repudiated the idea of human rights to freedom and justice and he consequently cannot come out as their champion.

There have, however,been a few signs of late that he feels his old house too small: in his recent discussion of Mr. Chafee's book on free speech, he reached a pitch of righteous indignation at which he has scarcely been seen before. "In those two years," he cried, "all the laborious work of a century and a half—toward the free and honest administration of fair laws, the dealing of plain justice between man and man, the protection of the weak and helpless, the safeguarding of free assemblage and free speech—was ruthlessly undone." This is obviously in direct contradiction to the faith he has previously professed. What has one who is "against the under dog every time" to do with "the protection of the weak and helpless"? He has told us again and again that we should let the weak and helpless perish.

The truth is that in the last few years Mencken has entered so far into the national intellectual life that it has become impossible for him to maintain his old opinions quite intact: he has begun to worry and hope with the American people in the throes of their democratic experiment. I know that this is a terrible statement; it is as if one should say that the Pope had begun to worry and hope with the western world in its attempt to shake off creed; but I honestly believe it is true. This phenomenon seemed to make its appearance toward the last page of ***The American Language;*** and if it does not come to bulk yet larger we shall have one of our strongest men still fighting with one arm tied behind his back.

So much for the critic; but what of the evangelist and artist? For Mencken, in spite of all his professions of realistic resignation, is actually a militant idealist. Most Americans—even of fine standards—have long ago resigned themselves to the cheapness and ugliness of America, but Mencken has never resigned himself. He has never ceased to regard his native country with wounded and outraged eyes. The shabby politics, the childish books, the factories turning out wooden nut-megs have never lost their power to offend him. At this late date, he is, I suppose, almost the only man in the country who still expects American novelists to be artists and American politicians gentlemen.

And his expression of his resentment is by no means temperate or aloof. It is righteous indignation of the most violent sort. His denunciations are as ferocious as those of Tertullian or Billy Sunday. It is in purpose rather than in method that he differs from these great divines. (See especially his excommunication of the professors in the essay on **"The National Letters."**) In his exhortations to disobey the rules of the current American morality he has shown himself as noisy and as bitter as any other Puritan preacher.

And this brings us to what is perhaps, after all, the most important thing about Mencken, the thing which gives him his enormous importance in American literature today: it is the fact that here we have a genuine artist and man of first-rate education and intelligence who is thoroughly familiar with, even thoroughly saturated with, the common life. The rule has been heretofore for men of superior intelligence, like Henry Adams and Henry James, to shrink so far from the common life that, in a country where there was practically nothing else, they had almost no material to work on, and for men who were part of the general society, like Mark Twain, to be handicapped by Philistinism and illiteracy; but in the case of Mencken we have Puritanism and American manners in a position to criticize itself. For in his attitude toward all the things with which Puritanism is supposed to deal Mencken is thoroughly American and thoroughly Puritan. If he were what he exhorts us to be in regard to the amenities and the pleasures he would never rage so much about them. His sermons would be unintelligible, I should think, to a Frenchman or an Italian. Nobody but a man steeped in Puritanism could have so much to say about love and yet never convey any idea of its beauties or delights; poor Aphrodite, usually identified in his pages with the whore and the bawdy-house, wears as unalluring a face as she does in the utterances of any Y.M.C.A. lecturer; no one else would confine himself to a harsh abuse, on principle, of the people who have outlawed love. . . . Horace or Anatole France, who really represent the sort of civilization which Mencken admires, would never be so acutely conscious of the problems of love and art and wine; they would take them easily for granted and enjoy them as a matter of course. But Mencken, who was born an American, with the truculent argumentative mind of the Puritan, can never enjoy them as a matter of course, as even some Americans can do, but must call down all the dark thunders of logic to defend them, like any Milton or Luther.

And he is saturated with the thought and aspect of modern commercial America. He is, we feel, in spite of everything, in the long run most at home there; are we not told that once, when walking in Paris in the spring, he was annoyed by the absence of a first-class drug-store? Instead of taking refuge among remote literatures, like Mr. Cabell and Mr. Pound, he makes his poetry of the democratic life which absorbs and infuriates him. He takes the slang of the common man and makes fine prose of it. He has studied the habits and ideas and language of the common run of his countrymen with a close first-hand observation and an unflagging interest. And he has succeeded in doing with the common life what nobody else has done,—(at least with any authentic stamp of literary distinction): he has taken it in all its coarseness and angularity and compelled it to dance a ballet, in which the Odd Fellow, the stockbroker, the Y.M.C.A. Secretary, the Knight of Pythias, the academic critic, the Methodist evangelical, the lecturer at Chautauquas, the charlatan politician, the Vice Crusader, the Department of Justice, the star-spangled army officer,—and the man who reveres all these, with all his properties and settings: the derby hat, the cheap cigar, the shaving soap advertisement, the popular novel, the cuspidor, the stein of prohibition beer, the drug store, the patent medicine, the American Legion button,—join hands and perform, to the strains of a sombre but ribald music, which ranges from genial boisterousness to morose and cynical brooding. (pp. 11-12)

Is not Mencken's gloomy catalogue as much the poetry of modern America as Walt Whitman's was of the early Republic? When the States were fresh and new and their people were hardy pioneers, we had a great poet, from whose pages the youth and wonder of that world can reach us forever; and now that that air is soured with industry and those pioneers have become respectable citizens dwelling hideously ugly towns and devoted to sordid ideals, we have had a great satirist to arouse us against the tragic spectacle we have become. For Mencken is the civilized consciousness of modern America, its learning, its intelligence and its taste, realizing the grossness of its manners and mind and crying out in horror and chagrin. (p. 13)

Edmund Wilson, Jr., "H. L. Mencken" (reprinted by permission of the Literary Estate of Edmund Wilson and Farrar, Straus and Giroux, Inc.), in The New Republic, *Vol. XXVII, No. 339, June 1, 1921, pp. 10-13.*

THEODORE DREISER (letter date 1922)

[Considered among America's foremost novelists, Dreiser was one of the principal American exponents of literary Naturalism. He is known primarily for his novels Sister Carrie *(1901),* An American Tragedy *(1926), and the Frank Cowperwood trilogy (1912-47), in each of which the author combined his vision of life as a meaningless series of chemical reactions and animal impulses with a sense of sentimentality and pity for humanity's lot. Deeply concerned with the human condition but contemptuous of traditional social, political, and religious remedies, Dreiser associated for many years with the American socialist and communist movements, an interest reflected in much of his writing after 1925. Mencken and Dreiser were longtime friends; as a magazine editor, Dreiser helped Mencken secure work at* The Smart Set, *and Mencken soon became one of Dreiser's most outspoken and supportive critics. In the following excerpt from a letter to Mencken, Dreiser warmly appraises* Prejudices: Third Series.]

Dear Mencken:

Yes, I received ***Prejudices III*** & read in it several hours[.] Such things as **"Spangled Men," "Memorial Service," "Five Men at Random"** and **"Advice to Young Men"**—or a part of it—I had read before. I like such things as **"On Being an American," "Huneker,"** your defense of the critic as an artist, and **"The Novel."** All of the stuff is really vastly entertaining[.] You always muster a brisk and refreshing style & brisk and refreshing thoughts. That the people you openly attack in **"On Being an American"** don't retaliate is a marvel to me. I assume that your aim is to goad them into action.

In regard to the critic as artist—you never were a critic really. You have as you say—a definite point of view & a philosophy & you have used the critical role to put it over[.] Your comments on life have always been vastly more diverting to me than your more intensive comment on books. I notice the freer brush strokes the moment you set forth your direct observations on men & things. (pp. 405-06)

Theodore Dreiser, in a letter to H. L. Mencken on December 6, 1922, in his Letters of Theodore Dreiser: A Selection, Vol. 2, *edited by Robert H. Elias (© 1959 by the Trustees of the University of Pennsylvania), University of Pennsylvania Press, 1959, pp. 405-06.*

JOSEPH CONRAD (letter date 1922)

[Conrad is considered an innovator of novel structure as well as one of the finest stylists of modern English literature. His novels are complex moral and psychological examinations of the ambiguities of good and evil. Conrad was one of the few authors deeply admired by Mencken. In the following excerpt from a letter to George J. Keating, which was written with an eye to a recent article on Conrad by the American critic, Conrad offers guarded praise of Mencken's abilities.]

Mencken's vigour is astonishing. It is like an electric current. In all he writes there is a crackle of blue sparks like those one sees in a dynamo house amongst revolving masses of metal that give you a sense of enormous hidden power. For that is what he has. Dynamic power. When he takes up a man he snatches him away and fashions him into something that (in my case) he is pleased with—luckily for me, because had I not pleased him he would have torn me limb from limb. Whereas as it is he exalts me almost above the stars. It makes me giddy. But who could quarrel with such generosity, such vibrating sympathy and with a mind so intensely alive? What, however, surprises me is that a personality so genuine in its sensations, so independent in judgment, should now and then condescend to mere parrot talk; for his harping on my Slavonism is only that. I wonder what meaning he attaches to the word? Does he mean by it primitive natures fashioned by a Byzantine theological conception of life, with an inclination to perverted mysticism? Then it cannot possibly apply to me. Racially I belong to a group which has historically a political past, with a Western Roman culture derived at first from Italy and then from France;

and a rather Southern temperament; an outpost of Westernism with a Roman tradition, situated between Slavo-Tartar Byzantine barbarism on one side and the German tribes on the other; resisting both influences desperately and still remaining true to itself to this very day. . . . Mencken might have given me the credit of being just an individual somewhat out of the common, instead of ramming me into a category, which proceeding, anyhow, is an exploded superstition.

This outburst is provoked, of course, by dear Mencken's amazing article about me, so many-sided, so brilliant and so warm-hearted. For that man of a really ruthless mind, pitiless to all shams and common formulas, has a great generosity. My debt of gratitude to him has been growing for years, and I am glad I have lived long enough to read the latest contribution. It's enough to scare anyone into the most self-searching mood. It is difficult to believe that one has deserved all that. So that is how I appear to Mencken! Well, so be it.

What more could anyone expect! (pp. 288-90)

Joseph Conrad, in a letter to George T. Keating on December 14, 1922, in Joseph Conrad: Life and Letters, Vol. II *by G. Jean-Aubry (copyright © 1926, renewed 1954, by Doubleday & Company, Inc.; reprinted by permission of Doubleday & Company, Inc.), Doubleday, 1927, pp. 288-90.*

Cover of the November, 1923, issue of The Smart Set. *Reproduced by permission of Enoch Pratt Free Library, in accordance with the will of H. L. Mencken.*

FRANK HARRIS (essay date 1923)

[*Harris was a highly controversial editor, critic, and biographer who is best known as the author of a maliciously inaccurate biography of Oscar Wilde, a dubious life of Bernard Shaw, and a massive autobiography that portrays Edwardian life primarily as a background for Harris's near-Olympian sexual adventures. A man frequently referred to in colorfully insulting terms by major critics, he was by most accounts a remarkable liar and braggart, traits which deeply color the quality of his works and their critical reception. His greatest accomplishments were achieved as editor of* The Fortnightly Review, Pearson's Magazine, *the* Evening News, *and* The Saturday Review. *As editor of* The Saturday Review *he helped launch the careers of Shaw and H. G. Wells, hiring them as drama critic and literary critic, respectively, during the mid-1890s. Shaw later wrote that Harris "had no quality of editorship except the supreme one of knowing good work from bad, and not being afraid of it." Harris's fame as a critic rests primarily upon his five-volume* Contemporary Portraits *(1915-30), which contain essays marked by the author's characteristically vigorous style and patronizing tone. In the following discussion of the first two books of* Prejudices, *Harris questions several of Mencken's literary judgments and finds Mencken's strength to be mainly in political commentary. Interestingly, less than a year after this essay appeared, Mencken and Nathan launched* The American Mercury, *in which Mencken concerned himself with mainly social and political matters rather than literary criticism.*]

Mencken is a publicist of the first class; he deals victoriously with the best writers of his time, and in still more masterly fashion with the political guides and governors. No position can daunt him; no puffing hoodwink; he will see for himself, and state what he sees without fear or favour. Only one or two journalists of this calibre are given to any country in a single generation; he ranks with the Lemaitres and the Shaws, above the Garvins and the Bennetts.

What, now, are his blind spots and shortcomings? His judgment of poetry . . . is worse than weak; he treats "The Jungle" of Upton Sinclair as a mere compilation; he swears by all his gods that no propagandist book can be a work of art, forgetting the "Don Quixote" of Cervantes, and "War and Peace" and "Anna Karenina" of Tolstoi; and, worst of all, he praises Mark Twain as a great writer: "a greater artist than Emerson or Poe or Whitman"; his "Huckleberry Finn," he asserts, is a masterpiece, and his "Mysterious Stranger" can never die.

Well, time and again I have given it as my mature conviction that Mark Twain is not among even the second-rate writers. But Mencken's assertions force me to face the issue once more. . . . [My] readers can decide whether or not I judge righteous judgment.

But between Mencken and myself the agreements are far more numerous and infinitely more important than the points of difference. (pp. 152-53)

To say that Mencken is the best critic in the United States is less than his due; he is one of the best critics in English. In his absorption in criticism alone, and in a certain masculine abruptness and careless piquancy of style, he reminds me often of Hazlitt, one of the few critics who belong to literature. In regard to creative work, especially to stories and plays, his judgment is often at fault, and always leaves a good deal to be desired; but in dealing with politicians and political issues, how sane he is, how brave, how honest, how surely he finds the fitting word, the blistering epithet! And what a delight it is to hear this bold strong voice in the unholy din of sycophants and of the hirelings' praise and blame which makes the American press the vilest in Christendom! And kindly Mencken is, too; kindly as only the honest can afford to be; full of the milk of human kindness for all those who choose the upward way. (p. 154)

Frank Harris, "H. L. Mencken, Critic" (originally published in a different form in Pearson's Magazine, *Vol. 46, No. 11, May, 1921), in his* Contemporary Portraits, fourth series *(copyright, 1923, by Brentano's, Inc., and renewed 1951 by the Literary Estate of Frank Harris; all rights reserved; reprinted by permission of the Literary Estate of Frank Harris), Brentano's, 1923, pp. 143-54.*

ERNEST BOYD (essay date 1925)

[An Irish-American writer and translator, Boyd was a prominent literary critic known for his erudite, honest, and often satirical critiques. In the candidly wrought essays which form his important studies of Irish literature, Ireland's Literary Renaissance *(1916) and* The Contemporary Dramas of Ireland *(1917), Boyd evaluated Irish literary works apart from English literature. He was also a respected translator, especially of French and German works, and his* Studies in Ten Literatures *(1925) demonstrates his knowledge of modern literature. His* H. L. Mencken *(1925) was the first book-length study of Mencken, and—though extremely sympathetic to its subject—is still of high value as a critical source. In the following excerpt from that work, Boyd posits that Mencken's concern with freedom of thought and of expression is the connecting link between his contrasting editorial roles at* The Smart Set *and* The American Mercury. *Boyd also discusses Mencken's music criticism, his* Book of Burlesques, The American Language, *and his iconoclastic individualism.]*

[Mr. Mencken] has hinted that his function as a literary critic has been fully discharged. "I moved steadily from practical journalism, with its dabblings in politics, economics and so on, towards purely esthetic concerns, chiefly literature and music, but of late I have felt a strong pull in the other direction, and what interests me chiefly to-day is what may be called public psychology, *i.e.*, the nature of the ideas that the larger masses of men hold, and the processes whereby they reach them. If I do any serious writing hereafter, it will be in that field." The founding of *The American Mercury* in 1924, showed the new trend of Mr. Mencken's interests, for *belles-lettres* have been relegated to the background, and both his editorials and his critical articles have been concerned with ideas rather than with pure literature.

While he undoubtedly owes his fame largely to his work as a literary critic, H. L. Mencken's gradual abandonment of this field is not surprising. Had conditions in 1908 been what they are to-day, it is open to doubt whether he would have turned his energies in that direction at all. What attracted him was the opportunity, the necessity, for a struggle with the forces that were stifling the growth of art and literature in this country, rather than any desire to impose a theory of criticism. His actual conception of the critic's function has always been self-contradictory, and his doctrinal pronouncements have been destructively analyzed and severely criticized from the most varied standpoints, from the Crocean J. E. Spingarn to the Marxian V. F. Calverton. All the remains constant is his practice, which has been to insist upon freedom for the artist, upon such conditions as alone can ensure the recognition of creative originality.

The only art which Mr. Mencken has viewed without regard for its intellectual content, is music. Here, and here only, does his writing become emotional; at times, sentimental. The creator of music stands highest in his scale of artistic values, and to music alone he has responded with his whole being, revealing himself, of course, as the great conservative that he really is. He is as contemptuous of jazz and musical comedy as a Paul Elmer More might be of George Ade, and his preferences, Brahms, Bach, Beethoven, Schumann, Haydn, have their equivalent in the predilection of the college professors for the authors of the Five-foot Bookshelf.

As a humorist of the first rank, H. L. Mencken has not yet received his due. He combines that essential element in American humor, grotesque exaggeration, with an intellectual quality which is absent from almost all authors popularly regarded as humourous. ***A Book of Burlesques*** is as thoroughly American as anything of Mark Twain's, but it lacks his incurable vulgarity and cheap philistinism, as it is free from the sheer puerility which renders the popular American funny man so intolerable to the uninitiated. Here one does not find "ancient and infantile wheezes, as flat to the taste as so many crystals of hyposulphite of soda," to quote his own description of a widely acclaimed humorist of to-day. Mr. Mencken's humor is informed by a genuine comic spirit, which has just that tang of intelligence whose absence explains the ephemeral reputations of most writers in the depressing limbo reserved for the professional humorists of yesteryear. Both his sense of humor and his instinctive love of patient pedantry are revealed in the portentous tome, ***The American Language,*** which "grew out of a satirical article on American grammar, written for the Baltimore *Evening Sun* in 1910 or thereabout." His reward was ample when the inevitable agitation stirred the minds of the Colonials, and one of them described this study of the vulgar tongue as "a wedge to split asunder the two great English-speaking peoples." Whether one accept or reject the theory based upon this voluminous evidence of the existence of an American vulgate, it is obviously unnecessary to accuse Mr. Mencken of having invented that tongue. The Americanism surely antedates even the reign of this Anti-Christ, and all that he can properly be charged with is having expended a vast amount of time, learning and research in tracing its growth and development. His versions of the Gettysburg address and the Declaration of Independence in the vernacular are masterpieces of Menckenian satire.

This book, to conclude, is typical of H. L. Mencken and all his works. Whatever his ostensible subject, in whichever one of the varied fields of his varied and restless activity, his method and aim are the same. He chose his objective at the outset of his career and he has never deviated from it. A born individualist and iconoclast, his multifarious criticism has tended to strike in all directions at such beliefs, superstitions, laws and conventions as threaten the growth of free personality. When Nietzsche and Ibsen and Shaw could be effectively employed to clear the ground of social and political rubble, he used them. Theodore Dreiser served as a standard under which he could honorably call the intelligent to arms against the defenders of inert tradition. The American language was simply one amongst a host of other phenomena, positive and negative, to which attention must be called, if these was to be any realistic conception of the actual America of to-day as distinct from that of the dreams of New England.

Mr. Mencken, for all that his enemies may say, has shown throughout his lifetime a more consistent and exclusive concern for purely American problems than any other public figure in this country above the level of a politician. He has contrived to escape most of the temptations which beset men of his type, once they have caught the public ear, because, as he once said, "the difference between a moral man and a man of honor is that the latter regrets discreditable act, even when it has worked and he has not been caught." If his judgments sometimes confirm the philistines in their contempt for art which they do not understand, and if his pragmatic dogma concerning the ease and importance of achieving material success adds further weight to the prevailing mercantilism—these things are not due to any deliberate attempt on his part to play down to the facile prejudices of his audience. They come, as has been shown, from the deep-seated and natural identity of his fundamental philosophy with that of his national environment.

"Of a piece with the absurd pedagogical demand for so-called constructive criticism is the doctrine that an iconoclast is a hollow and evil fellow unless he prove his case. Why, indeed, should he prove it? Doesn't he prove enough when he proves by his blasphemy that this or that idol is defectively convincing—that at least *one* visitor to the shrine is left full of doubts? . . . The pedant and the priest have always been the most expert logicians—and the most diligent disseminators of nonsense and worse. The liberation of the human mind has never been furthered by such learned dunderheads; it has been furthered by gay fellows who heaved dead cats into sanctuaries and then went roistering down the highways of the world, proving to all men that doubt, after all, was safe—that the god in the sanctuary was finite in his power, and hence a fraud."

From one who declares himself "wholly devoid of public spirit or moral purpose" this may be taken as a confession of faith. It clarifies the purpose behind all the wit, humor, boisterous gayety and mocking laughter, which H. L. Mencken invests his criticism of American life. "One horse-laugh is worth ten thousand syllogisms," he says, and we remember that Swift and Voltaire still live to prove it. "The only thing I respect is intellectual honesty, of which, of course, intellectual courage is a necessary part. A Socialist who goes to jail for his opinions seems to me a much finer man than the judge who sends him there, though I disagree with all the ideas of the Socialist and agree with some of those of the judge." Thus the American libertarian joins hands with his eighteenth-century French forbear who said: "I am opposed to every one of your beliefs but will uphold to the end your right to express them." (pp. 80-6)

Ernest Boyd, in his H. L. Mencken *(copyright, 1925, by Robert M. McBride & Co.; reprinted by permission of The American Play Company, Inc.), McBride, 1925, 89 p.*

UPTON SINCLAIR (essay date 1927)

[*An American novelist, dramatist, journalist, and essayist, Sinclair was a prolific writer who is most famous for* The Jungle *(1906), a novel that portrays the unjust labor practices, filth, and horrifying conditions of Chicago's meat-processing industry, and which prompted passage of the Pure Food and Drug Act of 1906. A lifelong, outspoken socialist, Sinclair addressed the excesses of capitalist society in most of his works and demanded, in his critical theory, the subservience of art to social change. Although most of his fiction is dismissed in the United States for its obtrusive didacticism, Sinclair is one of America's most-read authors outside of North America, his works being particularly popular in the Soviet Union. Mencken loathed socialists and reformers; not surprisingly, he and Sinclair were longstanding antagonists. In the following excerpted review Sinclair, who was often the victim of Mencken's sarcastic wit, attacks his foe's journalistic excesses and his* Notes on Democracy.]

Mencken is in a Berserk rage against stupidity, dullness and sham; he is a whole army, horse, foot, artillery, aviation and general staff all in one, mobilized in a war upon his enemies. He has a spy bureau all over the country, which collects for him illustrations of the absurdities of democracy, and he sorts them out by states, and once a month they appear between the arsenical green covers [of *The American Mercury*], and once a year they make a book, "Americana". . . . [He] is a new-style crusader, a Christian Anti-Christ, a tireless propagandist of no-propaganda. (p. 255)

He lashes with his powerful language the stupidities of bureaucrats and the knaveries of politicians. He declares that government is "the common enemy of all well-disposed, industrious and decent men". I protest to him that this is a rather sweeping statement; for example, our government distributes *The American Mercury*. He replies that the government doesn't want to distribute the *Mercury*, and wouldn't if it could help it. But that is obviously no reply; the fact is that the government does distribute the *Mercury*, on precisely the same terms as all other magazines. I cite the fact that it issues many postal orders for five dollars each, which Mencken's magazine collects. He replies that the government loses most of these orders. I cite the fact that the government will save his house if it catches fire, and he answers that fire departments are so inefficient that most fires burn out.

These statements illustrate an unfortunate weakness of our great libertarian crusader, he has very little regard for facts; all he is thinking about is to amuse and startle. He once made a funny newspaper article about me as the man who has believed more things than any other man alive; he managed to compile a plausible list, by including a number of things which I don't believe and never did; also, a number of things which all sensible men believe—including Mencken himself if you could pin him down; and finally, a few things which I believe because I have investigated them, and which Mencken disbelieves because he is ignorant about them.

For example, fasting. I have published a book setting forth the fact that fasting will cure many diseases. Mencken has never fasted, and has never read a book on the subject—I managed in our correspondence to bring out that fact. . . . [The] effect of fasting is rejuvenation—which is exactly what I have been asserting for sixteen years. But did Mencken verify his facts before compiling his list of Sinclair absurdities? No indeed.

Again, I was rebuked in Mencken's review of "Mammonart", for having suggested an identity in the fundamental ideas of Jesus and Nietzsche. That seemed to Mencken the height of absurdity; but he did not give his readers the words I had quoted from Jesus and Nietzsche, which are in substance identical. My friend Haldeman-Julius came forward to rebuke me for disputing with such a Nietzsche authority as Mencken; but Mencken's study of Nietzsche bears the date 1908, while you will find in my "Journal of Arthur Stirling", published in 1903, a complete statement of Nietzsche's philosophy.

Liberty, says Mencken. So let me quote him a few words from his great master. "Art thou such a one that can escape a yoke? Free from what? What is that to Zarathustra! Clear shall your eye tell me: free *to* what?" And that is the time when Mencken's eye becomes clouded. The darling and idol of the young intelligenzia has no message to give them, except that they are free to do what they please—which they interpret to mean that they are to get drunk, and read elegant pornography, and mock at the stupidities and blunders of people with less expensive educations. . . . For the present, that is all that is required; that is the mood of the time. But some day the time spirit will change; America will realize that its problems really have to be solved, and that will take serious study of exploitation and wage slavery, of co-operation and the democratic control of industry—matters concerning which Mencken is as ignorant as any Babbitt-boob.

There lies on my desk his new book [***Notes on Democracy***], an onslaught upon democracy. In the fly leaf he has written: "Upton Sinclair, to make him yell!" And perhaps this is yelling—judge for yourself. My friend Mencken has made the discovery that the masses of the people are inferior to himself; but that was known to every French marquis of the *ancien régime*.

We agree that we want the wise and competent in power; the question is, how are they to get there? The principle of hereditary aristocracy has been given a long trial, and Mencken omits to tell us where in history's roll of wars and intrigues and assassinations he finds the ideal state. At present we have a government based on the right of active and enterprising capital to have its own way; under this system *The American Mercury* has built up a hundred thousand circulation, and the popular editor is not nearly so discontented as he talks. But meantime the masses of labor see themselves disinherited and dispossessed, and the rumble of their protest grows audible. Sooner or later my friend Mencken will have to face these new facts, and choose between the bloody reaction of Fascism and the new dawn of industrial brotherhood. (pp. 255-56)

Upton Sinclair, "Mr. Mencken Calls on Me," in The Bookman, *New York, Vol. LXVI, No. 3, November, 1927, pp. 254-57.*

WALTER LIPPMANN (essay date 1927)

[*Throughout much of the twentieth century, Lippmann was considered the "dean" of American political journalists. He began his career as an investigative reporter for Lincoln Steffens's* Everybody's Magazine *and in 1914 helped found the leftist* New Republic, *serving for several years as associate editor and literary critic. During the 1920s the focus of his interests shifted from literature to politics, and he worked as editor and political writer for various major American periodicals for the rest of his life. In the following excerpt, Lippmann provides a balanced review of* Notes on Democracy *and cites Mencken's abuse as a tonic for the betterment of its victims.*]

Here in two hundred pages [***Notes on Democracy***] is Mr. Mencken's philosophy. Here are the premises of that gargantuan attack upon the habits of the American nation which has made Mr. Mencken the most powerful personal influence on this whole generation of educated people. I say personal influence, for one thing this book makes clear, and that is that the man is bigger than his ideas.

If you subtract from this book the personality of H. L. Mencken, if you attempt to restate his ideas in simple, unexcited prose, there remains only a collection of trite and somewhat confused ideas. To discuss it as one might discuss the ideas of first-rate thinkers like Russell, Dewey, Whitehead, or Santayana would be to destroy the book and to miss its importance. Though it purports to be the outline of a social philosophy, it is really the highly rhetorical expression of a mood which has often in the past and may again in the future be translated into thought. In the best sense of the word the book is sub-rational: it is addressed to those vital preferences which lie deeper than coherent thinking.

The most important political books are often of this sort. Rousseau's *Social Contract* and Tom Paine's *Rights of Man* were far inferior as works of the mind to the best thought of the eighteenth century, but they exerted an incalculably great influence because they altered men's prejudices. Mr. Mencken's book is of the same sort. The democratic phase which began in the eighteenth century has about run its course. Its assumptions no longer explain the facts of the modern world and its ideals are no longer congenial to modern men. There is now taking place a radical change of attitude not merely toward parliamentary government but toward the whole conception of popular sovereignty and majority rule. (pp. 61-2)

In the United States Mr. Mencken's is the most powerful voice announcing the change. The effect of his tremendous polemic is to destroy, by rendering it ridiculous and unfashionable, the democratic tradition of the American pioneers. This attack on the divine right of demos is an almost exact equivalent of the earlier attacks on the kings, the nobles, and the priests. He strikes at the sovereign power, which in America to-day consists of the evangelical churches in the small communities, the proletarian masses in the cities, and the organized smaller business men everywhere. The Baptist and Methodist sects, the city mobs, and the Chamber of Commerce are in power. They are the villains of the piece. Mr. Mencken does not argue with them. He lays violent hands upon them in the conviction, probably correct, that you accomplish results quicker by making your opponent's back teeth rattle than by laboriously addressing his reason. Mr. Mencken, moreover, being an old newspaper man, has rather strong notions about the capacity of mankind to reason. He knows that the established scheme is not supported by reason but by prejudice, prestige, and reverence, and that a good joke is more devastating than a sound argument. He is an eminently practical journalist, and so he devotes himself to dogmatic and explosive vituperation. The effect is a massacre of sacred cows, a holocaust of idols, and the poor boobs are no longer on their knees.

Mr. Mencken is so effective just because his appeal is not from mind to mind but from viscera to viscera. If you analyze his arguments you destroy their effect. You cannot take them in detail and examine their implications. You have to judge him totally, roughly, approximately, without definition, as you would a barrage of artillery, for the general destruction rather than for the accuracy of the individual shots. He presents an experience, and if he gets you, he gets you not by reasoned conviction, but by a conversion which you may or may not be able to dress up later as a philosophy. If he succeeds with you, he implants in you a sense of sin, and then he revives you with grace, and disposes you to a new and somewhat fierce pride in a non-gregarious excellence.

One example will show what happens if you pause to analyze his ideas. The thesis of this whole book is that we must cease to be governed by "the inferior four-fifths of mankind." Here surely is a concept which a thinker would have paused to define. Mr. Mencken never does define it, and, what is more, he quite evidently has no clear idea of what he means. Sometimes he seems to think that the difference between the inferior four-fifths and the superior one-fifth is the difference between the "haves" and the "have nots." At other times he seems to think it is the difference between the swells and the nobodies, between the well born and those who come "out of the gutter." At other times he abandons these worldly distinctions and talks and thinks about "free spirits," a spiritual élite, who have no relation either to income or to a family tree. This vagueness as to whether the superior one-fifth are the Prussian Junkers or the Pittsburgh millionaires, or the people who can appreciate Bach and Beethoven, persists throughout the book.

This confusion is due, I think, to the fact that he is an outraged sentimentalist. Fate and his own curiosity have made him a connoisseur of human ignorance. Most educated men are so preoccupied with what they conceive to be the best thought in the field of their interest, that they ignore the follies of uneducated men. . . . But Mr. Mencken is overwhelmingly preoccupied with popular culture. He collects examples of it. He goes into a rage about it. He cares so much about it that he cannot detach himself from it. And he measures it not by relative standards, but by the standards which most educated men reserve for a culture of the first order. He succeeds, of course, in establishing a *reductio ad absurdum* of the shibboleths of liberals. That is worth doing. But it is well to know what you are doing, and when Mr. Mencken measures the culture of the mass by the cultural standards of the élite, he is not throwing any real light on the modern problem. He is merely smashing a delusion by means of an effective rhetorical device.

I doubt, however, if he is aware that he is using a rhetorical device. When he measures the popular culture by the standards of the élite, the humor is all on the surface. The undertone is earnest and intensely sincere. One feels that Mr. Mencken is deeply outraged because he does not live in a world where all men love truth and excellence and honor. I feel it because I detect in this book many signs of yearning for the good old days. When Mr. Mencken refers to feudalism, to kings, to the Prussian aristocracy, to any ordered society of the ancient régime, he adopts a different tone of voice. I don't mean to say that he talks like an *émigré* or like a writer for the *Action Française,* but it is evident to me that his revolt against modern democratic society exhausts his realism, and that the historic alternatives are touched for him with a romantic glamour. The older aristocratic societies exist only in his imagination; they are idealized sufficiently to inhibit that drastic plainness of perception which he applies to the democratic society all about him.

The chief weakness of the book, as a book of ideas, arises out of this naïve contrast in Mr. Mencken's mind between the sordid reality he knows and the splendid society he imagines. He never seems to have grasped the truth that the thing he hates is the direct result of the thing he most admires. This modern democracy meddling in great affairs could not be what it is but for that freedom of thought which Mr. Mencken, to his everlasting credit, cares more about than about anything else. It is freedom of speech and freedom of thought which have made all questions popular questions. What sense is there then in shouting on one page for a party of "liberty," and on another bewailing the hideous consequences? The old aristocracies which Mr. Mencken admires did not delude themselves with any nonsense about liberty. They reserved what liberty there was for a privileged élite, knowing perfectly well that if you granted liberty to every one you would have sooner or later everything that Mr. Mencken deplores. But he seems to think that you can have a privileged, ordered, aristocratic society with complete liberty of speech. That is as thoroughgoing a piece of utopian sentimentalism as anything could be. You might as well proclaim yourself a Roman Catholic and then ask that excerpts from *The American Mercury* and the works of Charles Darwin be read from the altar on the first Sunday of each month. If Mr. Mencken really wishes an aristocracy he will have to give up liberty as he understands it; and if he wishes liberty he will have to resign himself to hearing *homo boobiens* speak his mind.

What Mr. Mencken desires is in substance the distinction, the sense of honor, the chivalry, and the competence of an ideal aristocracy combined with the liberty of an ideal democracy. This is an excellent wish, but like most attempts to make the best of both worlds, it results in an evasion of the problem. The main difficulty in democratic society arises out of the increasing practice of liberty. The destruction of authority, of moral values, of cultural standards is the result of using the liberty which has been won during the last three or four centuries. Mr. Mencken is foremost among those who cry for more liberty, and who use that liberty to destroy what is left of the older tradition. I do not quarrel with him for that. But I am amazed that he does not see how fundamentally the spiritual disorder he fights against is the effect of that régime of liberty he fights for. Because he fails to see that, I think he claims too much when he says that he is engaged in a diagnosis of the democratic disease. He has merely described with great emphasis the awful pain it gives him.

In the net result these confusions of thought are a small matter. It is no crime not to be a philosopher. What Mr. Mencken has created is a personal force in American life which has an extraordinarily cleansing and vitalizing effect. . . . His humor is so full of animal well-being that he acts upon his public like an elixir. The wounds he inflicts heal quickly. His blows have the clean brutality of a natural phenomenon. They are directed by a warm and violent but an unusually healthy mind which is not divided, as most minds are, by envy and fear and ambition and anxiety. When you can explain the heightening effect of a spirited horse, of a swift athlete, of a dancer really in control of his own body, when you can explain why watching them you feel more alive yourself, you can explain the quality of his influence.

For this reason the Mencken manner can be parodied, but the effect is ludicrous when it is imitated. The same prejudices and the same tricks of phrase employed by others are usually cheap and often nasty. I never feel that in Mr. Mencken himself even when he calls quite harmless people cockroaches and lice. I do not care greatly for phrases like that. They seem to me like spitting on the carpet to emphasize an argument. They are signs that Mr. Mencken writes too much and has occasionally to reach for the effect without working for it. I think he is sometimes lazy, and when he is lazy he is often unfair, not in the grand manner but in the small manner. And yet his wounds are clean wounds and they do not fester. I know, because I have fragments of his shellfire in my own skin. The man is admirable. He writes terribly unjust tirades, and yet I know of nobody who writes for his living who will stay up so late or get up so early to untangle an injustice. He often violates not merely good taste according to the genteel tradition, but that superior kind of good taste according to which a man refuses to hurt those who cannot defend themselves.

Nevertheless I feel certain that in so far as he has influenced the tone of public controversy he has elevated it. The Mencken attack is always a frontal attack. It is always explicit. The charge is all there. He does not leave the worst unsaid. He says it. And when you have encountered him, you do not have to wonder whether you are going to be stabbed in the back when you start to leave and are thinking of something else.

I have not written this as a eulogy, but as an explanation which to me at least answers the question why Henry L. Mencken is as popular as he is in a country in which he professes to dislike most of the population. I lay it to the subtle but none the less sure sense of those who read him that here is nothing sinister that smells of decay, but that on the contrary this holy terror from Baltimore is splendidly and exultantly and contagiously alive. He calls you a swine and an imbecile, and he increases your will to live. (pp. 62-70)

Walter Lippmann, "H. L. Mencken" (originally published in a slightly different form in The Saturday Review of Literature, *Vol. III, No. 20, December 11, 1926), in his* Men of Destiny *(reprinted with permission of Macmillan Publishing Company; copyright 1927 and renewed 1955, by Walter Lippmann), Macmillan, 1927, pp. 61-70.*

IRVING BABBITT (essay date 1928)

[With Paul Elmer More, Babbitt was one of the founders of the New Humanism (or neo-humanism) movement that arose during the twentieth-century's second decade. The New Humanists were strict moralists who adhered to traditional conservative values in reaction to an age of scientific and artistic self-expression. In regard to literature, they believed that the aesthetic qualities of a work of art should be subordinate to its moral and ethical purpose. They were particularly opposed to Naturalism, which they believed accentuated the animal nature of humans, and to any literature, such as Romanticism, that broke with established classical tradition. Besides Babbitt and More, other prominent New Humanists included Norman Foerster and T. S. Eliot, although the latter's conversion to Christianity angered Babbitt, whose concept of humanism substituted faith in humanity for faith in God. The author of several books propounding his philosophy, Babbitt was more a theorist than a literary critic; most of the New Humanist criticism was written by More, Eliot, and—until the mid-1920s—Stuart P. Sherman. Babbitt was, not surprisingly, the frequent target of Mencken's barbs. In the following excerpt reprinted from the February 1928 issue of The Forum, *Babbitt attacks certain of his antagonist's critical theories which were revealed in an earlier issue of the same journal.]*

H. L. MENCKEN trying to think of more things that annoy him.

Caricature of Mencken by Gene Markey (1923). The Granger Collection, New York.

[Most] persons nowadays aspire to be not critical but creative. We have not merely creative poets and novelists, but creative readers and listeners and dancers. Lately a form of creativeness has appeared that may in time swallow up all the others—creative salesmanship. The critic himself has caught the contagion and also aspires to be creative. He is supposed to become so when he receives from the creation of another, conceived as pure temperamental overflow, so vivid an impression that, when passed through his temperament, it issues forth as a fresh creation. What is eliminated in both critic and creator is any standard that is set above temperament and that therefore might interfere with their eagerness to get themselves expressed.

This notion of criticism as self-expression is important for our present subject, for it has been adopted by the writer who is, according to the last edition of the *Encyclopaedia Britannica*, "the greatest critical force in America"—Mr. H. L. Mencken. "The critic is first and last," says Mr. Mencken, "simply trying to express himself; he is trying to achieve thereby for his own inner ego the grateful feeling of a function performed, a tension relieved, a katharsis attained which Wagner achieved when he wrote *Die Walküre*, and a hen achieves every time she lays an egg." This creative self-expression, as practiced by himself and others, has, according to Mr. Mencken, led to a salutary stirring up of the stagnant pool of American letters. . . . (pp. 112-13)

But it may be that criticism is something more than Mr. Mencken would have us believe, more in short than a squabble between Bohemians, each eager to capture the attention of the public for his brand of self-expression. To reduce criticism indeed to the satisfaction of a temperamental urge, to the uttering of one's gustos and disgustos (in Mr. Mencken's case chiefly the latter) is to run counter to the very etymology of the word which implies discrimination and judgment. The best one would anticipate from a writer like Mr. Mencken, possessing an unusual verbal virtuosity and at the same time temperamentally irresponsible, is superior intellectual vaudeville. One must grant him, however, certain genuine critical virtues—for example, a power of shrewd observation within rather narrow limits. Yet the total effect of his writing is nearer to intellectual vaudeville than to serious criticism. (p. 113)

[Behind Mr. Mencken's] pleas for more constructiveness it is usually easy to detect the voice of the booster. A critic who did not get beyond a correct diagnosis of existing evils might be very helpful. If Mr. Mencken has fallen short of being such a diagnostician, the failure is due not to his excess of severity but to his lack of discrimination.

The standards with reference to which men have discriminated in the past have been largely traditional. The outstanding fact of the present period, on the other hand, has been the weakening of traditional standards. An emergency has arisen not unlike that with which Socrates sought to cope in ancient Athens. Anyone who is untraditional and seeks at the same time to be discriminating must also necessarily own Socrates as his master. As is well known, Socrates sought above all to be discriminating in his use of general terms. (p. 114)

It is, therefore, unfortunate that at a time like the present, which plainly calls for a Socrates, we should instead have got a Mencken. One may take as an example of Mr. Mencken's failure to discriminate adequately, his attitude toward the term that for several generations past has been governing the imagination of multitudes—democracy. His view of democracy is simply that of Rousseau turned upside down, and nothing, as has been remarked, resembles a hollow so much as a swelling. A distinction of which he has failed to recognize the importance is that between a direct or unlimited and a constitutional democracy. In the latter we probably have the best thing in the world. The former, on the other hand, as all thinkers of any penetration from Plato and Aristotle down have perceived, leads to the loss of liberty and finally to the rise of some form of despotism. The two conceptions of democracy involve not merely incompatible views of government but ultimately of human nature. The desire of the constitutional democrat for institutions that act as checks on the immediate will of the people implies a similar dualism in the individual—a higher self that acts restrictively on his ordinary and impulsive self. The partisan of unlimited democracy on the other hand is an idealist in the sense that the term assumed in connection with the so-called romantic movement. His faith in the people is closely related to the doctrine of natural goodness proclaimed by the sentimentalists of the eighteenth century and itself marking an extreme recoil from the dogma of total depravity. The doctrine of natural goodness favors the free temperamental expansion that I have already noticed in speaking of the creative critic.

It is of the utmost importance, however, if one is to understand Mr. Mencken, to discriminate between two types of temperamentalist—the soft and sentimental type, who cherishes various "ideals," and the hard, or Nietzschean type, who piques himself on being realistic. As a matter of fact, if one sees in the escape from traditional controls merely an opportunity to live temperamentally, it would seem advantageous to pass promptly from the idealistic to the Nietzschean phase, sparing oneself as many as possible of the intermediary disillusions. It is at all events undeniable that the rise of Menckenism has been marked by a certain collapse of romantic idealism in the political field and elsewhere. The numerous disillusions that have supervened upon the War have provided a favoring atmosphere.

The symptoms of Menckenism are familiar: a certain hardness and smartness and disposition to rail at everything that, rightly or wrongly, is established and respected; a tendency to identify the real with what Mr. Mencken terms "the cold and clammy facts" and to assume that the only alternative to facing these facts is to fade away into sheer romantic unreality. These and similar traits are becoming so widely diffused that, whatever one's opinion of Mr. Mencken as a writer and thinker, one must grant him representativeness. He is a chief prophet at present of those who deem themselves emancipated but who are, according to Mr. Brownell, merely unbuttoned.

The crucial point in any case is one's attitude toward the principle of control. Those who stand for this principle in any form or degree are dismissed by the emancipated as reactionaries or, still graver reproach, as Puritans. Mr. Mencken would have us believe that the historical Puritan was not even sincere in his moral rigorism, but was given to "lamentable transactions with loose women and fiery jugs." This may serve as a sample of the assertions, picturesquely indiscriminate, by which a writer wins immediate notoriety at the expense of his permanent reputation. (pp. 114-16)

If the Protestant Church is at present threatened with bankruptcy, it is not because it has produced an occasional Elmer Gantry. The true reproach it has incurred is that, in its drift toward modernism, it has lost its grip not merely on certain dogmas but, simultaneously, on the facts of human nature. It has failed above all to carry over in some modern and critical form the truth of a dogma that unfortunately receives much support from these facts—the dogma of original sin. At first sight Mr. Mencken would appear to have a conviction of evil—when, for example, he reduces democracy in its essential aspect to a "combat between jackals and jackasses"—that establishes at least one bond between him and the austere Christian.

The appearance, however, is deceptive. The Christian is conscious above all of the "old Adam" in himself: hence his humility. The effect of Mr. Mencken's writing, on the other hand, is to produce pride rather than humility, a pride ultimately based on flattery. The reader, especially the young and callow reader, identifies himself imaginatively with Mr. Mencken and conceives of himself as a sort of morose and sardonic divinity surveying from some superior altitude an immeasurable expanse of "boobs." This attitude will not seem especially novel to anyone who has traced the modern movement. One is reminded in particular of Flaubert, who showed a diligence in collecting bourgeois imbecilities comparable to that displayed by Mr. Mencken in his *Americana*. Flaubert's discovery that one does not add to one's happiness in this way would no doubt be dismissed by Mr. Mencken as irrelevant, for he has told us that he does not believe in happiness. Another discovery of Flaubert's may seem to him more worthy of consideration. "By dint of railing at idiots," Flaubert reports, "one runs the risk of becoming idiotic oneself." (pp. 117-18)

Irving Babbitt, "The Critic and American Life," in The Forum, *Vol. LXXIX, No. 2, February, 1928 (and reprinted in* Modern Writers at Work, *edited by Josephine K. Piercy, The Macmillan Company, 1930, pp. 111-30.)**

G. K. CHESTERTON (essay date 1929)

[*Regarded as one of England's premier men of letters during the first half of the twentieth century, Chesterton is best known today as a colorful* bon vivant, *a witty essayist, and creator of the Father Brown mysteries and the fantasy* The Man Who Was Thursday. *Much of Chesterton's work reveals his childlike* joie de vivre *and reflects his pronounced Anglican and, later, Roman Catholic beliefs. His essays are characterized by their humor, frequent use of paradox, and chatty, rambling structure. In the following excerpt, Chesterton examines several seeming inconsistencies in Mencken's critical theory.*]

I heartily admire Mr. Mencken, not only for his vivacity and wit, but for his vehemence and sometimes for his violence. I warmly applaud him for his scorn and detestation of Service; and I think he was stating a historical fact when he said, as quoted in *The Forum:* "When a gang of real estate agents, bond salesmen, and automobile dealers gets together to sob for Service, it takes no Freudian to surmise that someone is about to be swindled." I do not see why he should not call a spade a spade and a swindler a swindler. I do not blame him for using vulgar words for vulgar things. But I do remark upon two ways in which the fact of his philosophy's being negative makes his criticism almost shallow. First of all, it is obvious that such a satire is entirely meaningless unless swindling is a sin. And it is equally obvious that we are instantly swallowed up in the abysses of "moralism" and "religionism," if it is a sin. And the second point, if less obvious, is equally important—that his healthy instinct against greasy hypocrisy does not really enlighten him about the heart of that hypocrisy.

What is the matter with the cult of Service is that, like so many modern notions, it is an idolatry of the intermediate, to the oblivion of the ultimate. It is like the jargon of the idiots who talk about Efficiency without any criticism of Effect. . . . There is a sense in serving God, and an even more disputed sense in serving man; but there is no sense in serving Service. (p. 66)

Two other characteristic passages from Mr. Mencken . . . will serve to show more sharply this curious sense in which he misses his own point. On the one hand, he appears to state most positively the purely personal and subjective nature of criticism; he makes it individual and almost irresponsible. "The critic is first and last simply trying to express himself; he is trying to achieve thereby for his own inner ego the grateful feeling of a function performed, a tension relieved, a katharsis attained, which Wagner achieved when he wrote *Die Walküre*, and a hen achieves every time she lays an egg." That is all consistent enough as far as it goes; but unfortunately Mr. Mencken appears to go on to something quite inconsistent with it. According to the quotation, he afterward bursts into a song of triumph because there is now in America not only criticism but controversy. "To-day for the first time in years there is strife in American criticism . . . ears are bitten off, noses are bloodied. There are wallops both above and below the belt."

Now, there may be something in his case for controversy; but it is quite inconsistent with his case for creative self-expression. If the critic produces the criticism *only* to please himself, it is entirely irrelevant that it does not please somebody else. The somebody else has a perfect right to say the exact opposite to please himself, and be perfectly satisfied with himself. But they cannot controvert because they cannot compare. They cannot compare because there is no common standard of comparison. Neither I nor anybody else can have a controversy about literature with Mr. Mencken, because there is no way of criticizing the criticism, except by asking whether the critic is satisfied. And there the debate ends, at the beginning, for nobody can doubt that Mr. Mencken is satisfied. (pp. 66-7)

G. K. Chesterton, "The Skeptic As a Critic," in The Forum *(copyright, 1929, by Events Publishing Company, Inc.; reprinted by permission of Current History, Inc.), Vol. LXXXI, No. 2, February, 1929, pp. 65-9.**

WILLIAM SAROYAN (essay date 1929)

[*Saroyan was a popular American novelist, dramatist, and short story writer whose works are noted for their optimistic spirit and celebration of the common individual. He is best known for the story collection* The Daring Young Man on the Flying Trapeze *(1934) and the drama* The Time of Your Life *(1939). In the following excerpt, Saroyan hotly attacks Mencken, George Jean Nathan, and Emanuel Haldeman-Julius for what he considers their destructiveness, shrillness, and prejudice.*]

There are evidently people in America who imagine they are becoming beautifully civilized merely because they laugh at things Babbitt is supposed to be worshipping, but really isn't. . . . And it must be a most singularly uncivilized audience, composed mostly of the type of people who find it highly gratifying to assume they belong to the sophisticated minority and who suppose themselves not to be Babbitts. They are the ones who want to be among the few with sense enough to laugh at things. Things like God and Coolidge and Virtue. It never occurs to them, apparently, that such laughter is neither wholesome nor pleasant. In fact, that it is not laughter at all, but is sneering and snickering, and a thing of no good to the soul.

The point is: It would be perfectly fine for these people to laugh at the Deity and the President were it not for the fact that in jeering one Deity they are worshipping another, which is very bad business.

And so we find that if a person of this type reads for instance, that it is Mr. Mencken's honest opinion that God is a charlatan and a foreigner, he immediately takes just that for granted, quits his God, and commences worshipping Mr. Mencken instead. This is an uncivilized thing for a person to do. It is a thing only intellectual Babbitts do. A person who doesn't believe in a God certainly has no business worshipping a mere man. It is twice as intelligent for a person to worship himself than to worship another man. That is why Mencken, Nathan, and Haldeman-Julius are only twice as intelligent as their humble worshippers.

In view of the fact that no one else cares for the job, I, myself, shall try to give these three gentlemen a regular, old-fashioned horse-laugh. . . .

In the first place all three of these critics are unreasonably intolerant in almost everything they write, and more or less prejudiced as well. (p. 77)

Henry Louis Mencken . . . is undoubtedly a very clever gentleman and [one] who will never be forgotten for founding and editing (and how?) one of the most civilized magazines the world has ever known. It would seem by the way, that the reason a great number of young fellows have nothing to say against Mr. Mencken is because they want to get their names on the pages of his *Mercury* and spend all their energy and time in that occupation, impossible as it is.

There can be no denying that, at first, there was a delightful charm in his hilariously impish maneuvers and his agreeable jargon. It must have been a rare pleasure for many of his nature, who lacked his ability and fearlessness, to watch him as he went through life making faces at everything most people were afraid to make faces at. But today that old charm of Mr. Mencken is dead, or at least fast dying. Let me explain.

It was either Mr. Mencken, himself, or his good friend, Mr. Nathan, who remarked in the pages of the *Mercury* that it would be quite idiotic for anyone to suppose George Gershwin's Rhapsody In Blue, for example, could be enjoyed if it were played twice in one evening or twice in one week or even twice in one month. And yet Mr. Mencken does not notice that his rhapsody has been played so many times in the same manner and with so little variation that familiar listeners know both the tune and the technique by heart.

His habit of calling all things by their proper names (even if he must resort to German to remain within the bounds of propriety) and of making fun of the things his nature cannot help making fun of, is highly entertaining to most readers, until, of course, they find they have read too much of him. His ***Prejudices*** have been admirably named in order to protect anything written therein, but in the handling of his subjects he does not seem to remember that he is actually prejudiced; and he makes the mistake of taking himself very seriously, which is probably the only thing he does take seriously. His generalizations often annoy the reader who is not fond of unfounded statements, even if they do very often sound really clever.

When it became evident that Mr. Mencken was 100 per cent against everything and everybody except probably a few things such as George Jean Nathan, a large following delighted in his attitude of healthy boyishness and those who did not, or could not, imitate him in writing, imitated him in their private lives. This was just another case of one more God slowly but surely making his man in his own image.

A little later when it was observed that the same things were being said in the same old unnecessarily boisterous manner, a few readers began to yawn and drop him and turn to, say, Dr. Frank Crane, who is in exactly the same business as Mr. Mencken, only on a larger scale. For, whereas Mr. Mencken has ten readers, Dr. Crane has eleven. And Daniel DeFoe fourteen.

Mr. Mencken has become more or less mature and so when he writes of the younger generation he very often gets things twisted because he cannot very well write from personal experience, he having been a boy when the parents of the younger generation were yet unacquainted, let alone married. Although he writes considerable about youth he actually knows very little about the boys who are commencing to shave regularly every Tuesday and Saturday mornings, and the girls who are gradually getting plump.

He has, in a very recent editorial, mentioned that the young man of about twenty invariably seeks an ideal in some living person who is supposed to be honorable, only to discover that the person is nothing more nor less than a fraud. And he adds that the fact that a great person is a fraud bothers the young man and he is quite puzzled and upset over the truth. Nothing could be further from the fact. The young person who seeks an ideal very seldom turns to one now living, but goes instead to ideals of which he can be certain. He goes to names which have become established. That is, if he is looking for ideals at all, which is rather unlikely, Mr. Mencken is certainly suddenly oddly optimistic if he supposes modern youth is ambitious enough to seek such things as honorable, and half-decent ideals. I have observed that the young fellows think most of salesmanship and stocks and bonds and that ideals can be damned. (pp. 77-8)

Whatever Mr. Mencken writes he is careful that it entertains and it usually *does,* especially if one has not read too much of him. And there are always enough young people who are maturing each year to whom a morsel of Mencken is as a gift from heaven, when it happens to be the very first morsel. It is too bad that Mr. Mencken is intolerant for that is as much a sin as cruelty. (p. 78)

[Mencken, Nathan, and Haldeman-Julius] pursue the uncivilized method of exposing shams and idiocies by pointing them out directly instead of carefully and quietly reporting them in the manner of Anatole France. The latter has undoubtedly done more with his pleasant writings to murder superstition, ignorance, cruelty and intolerance than these three gentlemen combined. But that is saying nothing that might injure these gentlemen, for it will be considerable time before the world will see another Anatole France. Of course, this unrefined method of pointing out superstitions and idiocies is probably entertaining if written by a Mencken or a Nathan. It is however too harsh for the person who is ignorant and superstitious, to see it as the author does, and for that reason, the ignorant remains ignorant and the uncivilized remain uncivilized.

As before stated, there is certainly a lack of intelligent tolerance in these critics, which is regrettable, for what good is a critic who cannot see two sides to every question?

These men are much too prejudiced. So much so that they cannot give such persons and things as the following a half-way decent hearing, but continually dismiss them with gestures of disgust: Eddie Guest, Los Angeles, James Oliver Curwood, moving pictures, idiots, Billy Sunday, song and dance men, English literature, Democracy, Gertrude Atherton, politicians, psychoanalysts, prohibition, Rotary, censors, love, William Randolph Hearst, and God.

But on the other hand they worship and endlessly praise anything they prefer. Thus Mr. Mencken bows his head humbly to medicine, Mr. Nathan to pretty legs and fair faces, and Mr. Haldeman-Julius to himself.

Today it is popularly believed that of these three critics Mr. Mencken is the greatest, with Mr. Nathan a close second. And in the vague and dim distance Mr. Haldeman-Julius is also noticed, but in no wise connected with the other two gentlemen, who are, if not actually, brothers, at least so by adoption and preference.

But they are an intolerant group of men and intolerance is a terrible sin, punishable, at least, with horse laughing and nose thumbing.

Is it any wonder then, when the supposedly sophisticated publications of the land are given to so much unnecessary breast beating on the one hand over trivialities and to an unending haw-haw of a horse laugh at ignorance on the other hand, that more and more people are burying themselves in the pages of such things as *The Saturday Evening Post, The Ladies' Home Journal,* and The Holy Bible? (pp. 92-3)

William Saroyan, "The American Clowns of Criticism—," in Overland Monthly and Out West Magazine, *Vol. 87, No. 3, March, 1929, pp. 77-8, 92-3.**

WYNDHAM LEWIS (essay date 1929)

[*Together with T. S. Eliot, Ezra Pound, and T. E. Hulme, Lewis was instrumental in establishing the anti-Romantic movement in literature during the first decades of the twentieth century. He also emerged as a leader of the Vorticist movement founded by Pound. Although its principles are vague, critical consensus holds that Vorticism is related to Imagism in poetry and to Cubism in painting, and that one of its primary characteristics is a belief in the total impersonality of art, achieved by fragmenting and reordering the elements of experience into a new and more meaningful synthesis. Pound and Lewis established the short-lived but now-famous periodical* Blast *to give the movement a voice and a rallying point. Lewis's savage, satiric fiction has been compared to the work of Jonathan Swift and Alexander Pope. His best-known novel,* The Apes of God *(1930), is a long and aggressive satire on the cultural life of England in the 1920s. Some critics believe he will eventually be ranked with Eliot, Pound, and James Joyce as one of the most fascinating, controversial, and influential writers of the early twentieth century. In the following excerpt, Lewis discusses Mencken's role as a scourge of American dullness and stupidity. Lewis especially cites* "Americana," *a monthly feature in* The American Mercury, *as influential in creating an "inferiority complex" in the educated person;* "Americana" *was also ably described by Upton Sinclair (see excerpt above, 1927).*]

The once proud, boastful, super-optimistic American of the United States has become just a White 'man-in-the-street' with a pronounced 'inferiority complex.' (I speak of the educated, or book-reading, American.) This fact, or something like it, is patent to anybody who has followed american thought of late and had opportunities of meeting a good many Americans. (p. 113)

The toning-down of the American is coeval, I suppose, to give it a fairly exact convenient date, with the activities of Mr. Mencken. I do not of course mean that this great transformation has been effected by the editor of the *American Mercury*. But the *Americana* of that writer is not calculated to inspire a very acute sense of self-respect in the american bosom: and certainly attacks by Mr. Mencken upon the traditional american conceit must have been a powerful factor in bringing to the surface this gradual sensation of insecurity, the habit of self-criticism, the dissatisfaction, to which I am alluding. At the present moment this has grown, it would seem, into what is actually an 'inferiority complex.' Or that is how the situation presents itself to me.

That the influence of Mr. Mencken, both in his own writings and through his disciple Mr. Sinclair Lewis, is of a popular, rather than an intellectual, order is true. But we are concerned here with the wider general discouragement and disillusion of the large book-reading mass of a prosperous modern democracy: so that does not affect our statement. (pp. 113-14)

It would not be an exaggeration . . . to say that *Americana* is making a present to the White American of a formidable and full-fledged 'inferiority complex,' that is, in so far as he is the widely-advertised, popular focus of all the disillusioned thought of the post-war Western mind in the United States.

Parallel with this, many writers of american nationality are busy providing the Negro, the Mexican Indian, the Asiatic Settler, and indeed anybody and everybody who is not a *pur sang* White, of the original american-european stock, with a 'superiority complex.' (p. 117)

At this point I had better make clear what I suppose is Mr. Mencken's position in this racial turning of the tables, and that of those associated with him in these revolutionary enterprises. Mr. Mencken, let us say, became more and more impressed with the futility of the machinery of Democracy, which he was able to observe in full and indecent operation all round him, in the rich and exaggerated american scene. It showed itself capable of idiocies of unequalled dimensions. The Poor White showed how unable he was to defend himself against his interfering rulers, of whatever shade of race or politics. The Rich White was not a specially high type of magnate, and he manipulated his power with a sickly unction of cordiality and righteousness that gave the intelligent american patriot (such as Mr. Mencken) a violent nausea, and every sort of misgiving for the future of american life. This violent nausea translated itself into violent acts of criticism and persiflage. The more truly patriotic, the more disgusted he would be.

I am not acquainted with Mr. Mencken; but that, as a description of what has brought about his famous critical attacks, would, I suppose, be generally accepted by educated Americans. In any case he has convicted the American Democracy (mainly out of its own mouth, in his *Americana,* which are extracts from newspapers, handbills, advertisements, etc.) of surprising stupidities. Generalizing from this body of evidence, he concludes that such a form of Democracy as has developed in America is fundamentally bad and absurd.

Passing on from the general statement to my private view of the matter, I do not see how any one surveying the evidence Mr. Mencken has collected could deny that a radical change of some sort was to be desired for this great key-nation of the modern world. (pp. 118-19)

It must be admitted, in general criticism of these documents, that another sort of patriot than this earnest, clever, germanic editor could easily throw doubt on their value and significance. Perhaps the most useful way of considering them would be to approach them from the standpoint of this hypothetic patriot, of another persuasion. Their very qualities, even, will be best brought out by this method. I will proceed to do this. But by adopting this procedure I wish to make it clear that I would not minimize the great debt of America to Mr. Mencken, or to Sinclair Lewis, for holding up their hostile mirrors.

In the first place, then, it could be said that the *Americana* consist mostly of ridicule of religious emotionality. But all religion, looked at with the uninterested eye of the outsider, or from the exclusively secular or scientific standpoint, lends itself to ridicule. For instance, to the Anglo-Saxon of two centuries ago, the religious 'superstitions' of every race whatever, except the Anglo-Saxon, provided much amusement. . . . And, of course, his laughter increased his self-esteem.

From this point of view, Mr. Mencken's *Americana* is merely the Anglo-Saxon at *his* devotions being laughed at, in his turn. (pp. 127-28)

[It] is more than half of the matter of Mr. Mencken's book, and the richest and funniest portion. (p. 129)

Really these collections called *Americana* throw a more interesting light upon the people who are amused and delighted (apparently) by them, than they do upon the people whom ostensibly they are supposed to hold up to ridicule. As you read them you are inclined rather to glance aside and survey your *fellow-readers,* and to wonder what variety of snobbery, or superiority complex, has brought together this large 'reading-public.'

The critic of these collections, again, would have occasion often to object that things quoted as solemn statements were evidently intended to be jokes. They are not usually very good jokes. They look, in fact, as though they had been specially concocted to catch Mencken's eye. (p. 130)

Then a great number of the extracts have reference to the absurdity of Prohibition. Prohibition is, of course, a joke played upon the American People of a very perfect kind. (p. 132)

The War provides some *Americana* fun, as well. But the War is another joke, like Prohibition, that has been played on all of us without exception. So, *people who live in glass houses,* etc. (p. 133)

And here we have to note another feature of the *Americana:* namely, that many of them are designed to turn the tables upon the 'Allied' war-propagandist. Mr. Mencken, being of german origin, naturally resented that propaganda, and, in the heat and folly of the moment, its frequent unfairness. But such material for a turning-of-the-tables of this sort could be found in any community. It is merely the tale of general human stupidity. And, of course, the Germans did destroy an irreplaceable work of art, and would have destroyed others had they been able.—This undercurrent of nationalist passion in Mr. Mencken, it would be claimed, weakens his criticism.

When he says that there have been rumours of the suppression of his paper, he refers to the american police as *Polizei*. He refers to the 'goose-stepping' habits of the american masses.

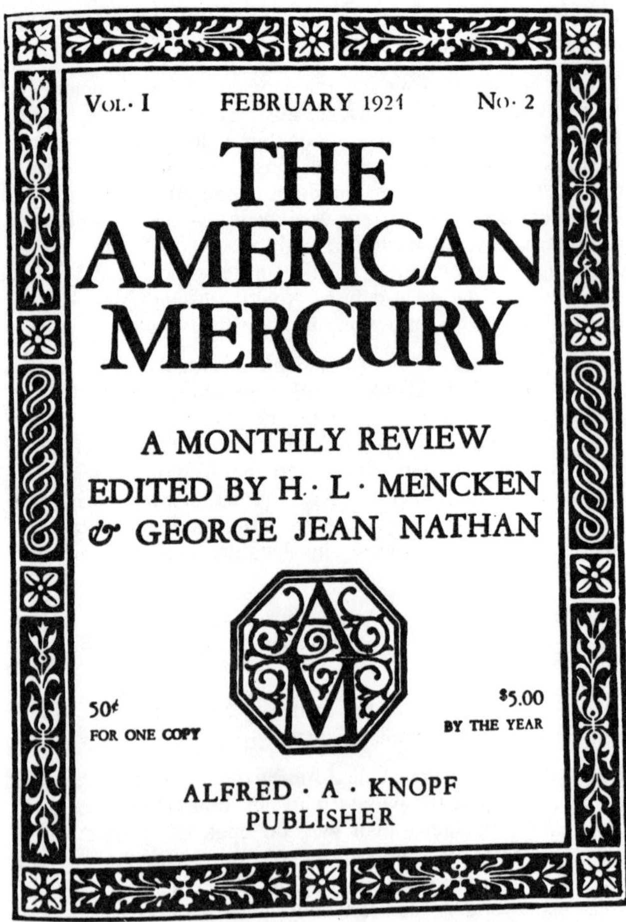

Cover of the second number of The American Mercury, *which included works by Eugene O'Neill, Sherwood Anderson, and James M. Cain. Reproduced by permission of the Enoch Pratt Free Library, in accordance with the will of H. L. Mencken.*

So he rubs it in. If he had conveyed that Americans were mesmerized and drilled without this familiar war-time tag of *Polizei,* the effect would have been stronger. But Mr. Mencken is, I should say, a very honest man, and he has strong feelings.

Kentucky should be a good state for Mr. Mencken. If you refer to *Americana,* 1925, you can fairly take that as an example. But it is surprising how little he gets out of it to his purpose. Of course, there is the usual extravagant Salvation Army language quoted. But that vernacular of provincial religion is rather engaging than otherwise, and an example of extreme high-spirits on the part of very simple folk indeed—whose principal offence seems to be that they do not want their kind to intermarry with Negroes, and that they believe in the hebrew sacred books so deeply that they object to people teaching that men are descended from monkeys, instead of having been created along with monkeys and all other things, all in one simultaneous Fiat. (pp. 134-35)

The first of these two arch-offences I regard as a substantial virtue; the bitter contempt directed upon the second by many people I do not share: so all this part of *Menckeniana* I find dull or pointless. (p. 135)

The more I go into it, and proceed to give effect to my idea of finding an *answer* to Mencken, the more I find I should agree with the other sort of american patriot rather than with Mr. Mencken. But still there remains Mr. Mencken's great service in stirring the pot round, and that with honesty, it seems, and not with malice. Also, in straining every nerve to find fault—if only in that—he has done good. For he has demonstrated the *limits* of average imbecility, as well as its extent: he has done the worst that can be done, and it actually is not so impressive as all that. He has even revealed many unsuspected virtues in the 'moron of the Backward States.' (p. 137)

Wyndham Lewis, "Romanticism and Complexes" (originally published in part in a somewhat different form in The Enemy, *No. 2, September, 1928), in his* Paleface: The Philosophy of the "Melting-Pot" *(reprinted by permission of The Wyndham Lewis Memorial Trust), Chatto & Windus, 1929 (and reprinted by Scholarly Press, Inc., 1971), pp. 113-48.**

JAMES BRANCH CABELL (essay date 1930)

[*Combining extremes of lavish romance and degraded reality, idealistic fantasy and jaded disillusionment, Cabell was one of the outstanding oddities in American fiction. His most enduring achievement,* The Biography of Manuel *(1904-29), belongs to a tradition of fantasy literature that includes Edmund Spenser's* The Faerie Queene *and Jonathan Swift's* Gulliver's Travels. Beyond Life *(1919), an important collection of literary criticism that was written to introduce the* Biography, *outlines the literary and philosophic concepts that serve as its foundation. Cabell adhered to a special definition of fiction which allowed him to portray glorified adventures beyond mundane reality without falsifying what he saw as the harsh truths of existence: the suffering of life, the emptiness of death, and a permanent alienation at the core of even the most intimate human relations. Cabell's most important later criticism appears in* Some of Us *(1930), a defense of several contemporary writers—including Elinor Wylie, Ellen Glasgow, and Joseph Hergesheimer—against the trend of Neo-humanist criticism, which demanded the subservience of art to moral and social issues. In the following excerpt, Cabell praises* Treatise on the Gods *as an illumination of religious fraud.*]

Mencken is one of the very few indisputably great men now living. He is a force which endures and which will endure for a long while. He is that force which has reshaped all the present world of American letters, the force from which, more prevalently than from any other origin, has sprung the cosmogony of that limited but not unimportant world.

He is an inestimable force, . . . a force somewhere between electricity and influenza. For electricity brings power and speed. It begets a clear, if not always a genial, lighting of dark places. It does not, perhaps, build; but it devastates readily. It is brisk; whatsoever else it may lack, it is never lacking in animation. It retains always the power to shock.

Just such a force came out of Baltimore, some fifteen years ago, into the then peaceful and wholly barren field of American letters. Just such a force, I submit, has convulsed and changed that field throughout—a field which it still dominates. Not everybody, to be sure, enjoyed the invasion; many of us are made uneasy by thunder storms; but without these thunder storms the field might well have remained barren. (pp. 108-09)

To the other side of my analogue you may note that, for the more immediately concerned, influenza is the most agreeable of house guests. To have influenza is, to my not inconsiderable experience, pleasant. Between aspirin and whisky, the patient is kept in a comfortable glow, wherein a recumbently regarded universe seems droll, and no obligations nor calamities appear imminent nor of real importance. It is only the convalescence which costs—that damnable and that so long-drawn-out aftermath of post-influenzal depression, wherein all is a vague paining, and worthlessness seems omnipresent. The superb glow of Mencken also has had its sad aftermath, in the form of very many disciples whom one can but describe as the debunkers, the Menckenoids. (p. 110)

I would here dwell only upon the fact that Mr. Mencken's gravest literary offences have been his admirers. All through the 'twenties he demoralized the village press and most college magazines with disciples who had taken his notions quite seriously. That is an error which Mr. Mencken himself has always avoided.

He has avoided any such naïveté with an artfulness and a shrewd humor and a very vast commonsense which now for fifteen years have made the man as immeasurably inimitable as he is entertaining. Indeed, I suspect the real secret of that never-flagging entertainingness to be the fact that the writer also has been entertained, and has at no moment been obsessed, by the notions with which he is playing. They may or they may not be true. Who knows?—well, not the right thinkers, in any case, nor the old maids, male and female. Meanwhile Mr. H. L. Mencken himself does know, at least, that these droll notions are amusing to play with. And meanwhile also his pleasure and his gusto prove to the reader as titillating as electricity and as infectious as influenza. (pp. 111-12)

[The] entertainment has never flagged. Mr. Mencken puts forth with the vigor of a perpetual April.

Even his very latest book, ***Treatise on the Gods,*** as completed in 1929, is most excellent Mencken. In many ways, indeed, this shrewd and robustious volume epitomizes all Mencken handsomely. He has graduated *cum laude* from the 'twenties with this long thesis upon religion. . . . (p. 113)

Now, as a professed churchman, with some real faith and with a great many duplex envelopes for 1930 still left to show for it, I may well deplore the manner in which this theme is approached by Mr. Mencken. His approach is the approach favored always by the zealous infidel, and very often, as in this case, by the convinced agnostic; it is the same approach which has caused so much of the wit of Voltaire to appear trivial in its dusty irrelevance: for Mr. Mencken also approaches religion rationally. To me, I admit, that seems futile, since if religion be founded upon any truth whatsoever, that truth is self-confessedly not amenable to human reason; and the mere rationalist in his approach is thus foredoomed to find nothing. Or perhaps I might better put it that the rationalist, when he applies his common-sense to religion, reminds me somewhat of a man attempting to measure distances with a thermometer; his measuring instrument is an excellent measurer in its own way, and in its proper field, but he happens to be misapplying it.

This much of protest I owe to my faith. I owe with equal fairness to Mr. Mencken the statement that I enjoyed his ***Treatise on the Gods*** tremendously. If in his attempts to dispose of religion my misguided friend has never found religion, nor even apprehended its nature, he has missed few of its parasites: and with every one of them he has diverted himself, and me also, consumedly. For the rest, Mr. Mencken's always admirable prose style now that the 'twenties have ended seems to be, if a little subdued, far more adroit than ever. And I question if any person writing at any time, or within any known civic limits, has ever hit upon a manner of writing better suited to convey to his readers, precisely and lucidly and memorably, whatsoever Mr. Mencken wills to convey. Mr. Mencken has evolved his own medium, in a language which no one else has written: his imitators have over well proved to us that no one else can handle this medium: but he, the incomparable, he controls it perfectly. (pp. 113-15)

James Branch Cabell, "Dreams on Cosmogony" (originally published in New York Herald Tribune Books, *April 13, 1930), in his* Some of Us: An Essay in Epitaphs *(copyright, 1930, renewed 1958, by James Branch Cabell; reprinted by permission of the Literary Estate of James Branch Cabell), Robert M. McBride & Company, 1930, pp. 105-18.*

C.E.M. JOAD (essay date 1934)

[*Joad was a minor English philosopher and the author of three dozen books, most of which address questions of ethics, religion, and human nature. He became popular and widely-known in England during World War II through his participation in the B.B.C. panel-show "Brains Trust." Through the radio program and his written works, Joad espoused a philosophy based on rationalism, pacifism, and distrust of modern science for its role in industrializing and standardizing society. In the following excerpt, he finds Mencken's* Treatise on Right and Wrong *to be unfair in its attack on Christianity and on other systematic moral philosophies.*]

It is possible to write amusingly about morality. La Rochefoucauld did it; so did Gratian, in that undeservedly neglected book *The Art of Worldly Wisdom.* It is also possible to write dully, albeit profoundly, about morality. Kant did it, so did Mill, so did Sidgwick. When the two qualities of amusingness and depth are combined, when a moralist is also a wit, we get a Shaw or a Swift. The highest excellence of ethical writing consists, in fact, in the author's ability to make righteousness readable.

Judged by any of these standards Mr. Mencken's [***Treatise on Right and Wrong***] cannot be rated very high. It is facetious without humour (it is not, I submit, very funny to have "astonished" Jewish friends "more than once" by assuring them that they were "perfectly free under Yahweh to dine upon June bugs," or to describe contemporary Protestant clergymen in the United States as "those sorry bounders of God") and serious without scholarship (it is not true that Descartes revolted against Christian dogma; on the contrary, at the very first signs of trouble, he toed the line of theological orthodoxy with painful zeal); it is not very righteous, and, for my part, I do not find it very readable. The book is described by its author as a companion volume to his ***Treatise on the Gods***. . . . Mr. Mencken does not, he says, think that there is any necessary connexion between religion and ethics; but for some reason or other they do, he finds, happen to have been associated rather frequently in history, and his investigation of Gods has led him naturally on to an examination of morals. However, he seems to find it hard to leave the Gods behind, since at least three-quarters of the present book is about religious rather than about ethical beliefs and customs.

Treatise on Right and Wrong is neither history nor philosophy; it neither tells us systematically what men have believed and how they have behaved, nor what, on the author's view, they ought to have believed and how they ought to have behaved. In fact Mr. Mencken confesses to "a great dislike for metaphysics" and takes credit for his deliberate refusal to "define such concepts as right and wrong, good and evil, moral and immoral, sin and virtue!'' Nevertheless, he indulges in metaphysical discussions of such matters as free will, and, in spite of his avowed ignorance of the meaning of morals, does not hesitate to pass frequent moral judgements. Where Christians are concerned, these judgements are almost uniformly harsh. Mr. Mencken tells us that his object is to criticize ''as amiably as possible the theories hatched by other men, either on their own motion or under inspiration from the powers and principalities of the air.'' The sentiment shows a becoming condescension; but if the following—a fairly typical passage—is the best Mr. Mencken can do in the way of amiability, I can only conclude that he has either lamentably failed to carry out his intention, or that he is a singularly unamiable man.—''Its'' (Christianity's) ''moral system remains an easy and grateful refuge for the weak and sick, the stupid and the misinformed, the confiding and the irresolute, but there is little in it to attract men and women who are intelligent and enterprising, and do not fear remote gaseous and preposterous Gods, and have a proper respect for the dignity of man.''

For the rest Mr. Mencken is concerned to ''set forth a few common facts,'' apparently in the belief that ethics can be ranked among the sciences, and that it is high time that somebody, in the name of scientific ethics, undertook the task of cataloguing the beliefs and behaviour of men, especially primitive men, whom Mr. Mencken delights ethically to honour. Anthropologists and sociologists who spend their time, or so one had supposed, in compiling precisely such a catalogue, appear to have studied and written in vain. Or perhaps they are too systematic for Mr. Mencken, whose selection of facts for insertion appears to have been dictated by no principle other than that of the accident of his reading and interest. Thus we learn that all ''property save a few trinkets has been taken away from'' contemporary Russians; that in contemporary Germany ''the reigning powers have come to terms with ecclesiastical authority''; . . . and so on. Mr. Mencken believes that the five fundamental prohibitions which are to be found in every moral system are ''murder, theft, trespass, adultery and false witness.'' It is high time that he added uncharitableness. (pp. 530, 532)

C.E.M. Joad, ''Ethical Fireworks,'' in The Spectator *(© 1934 by* The Spectator; *reprinted by permission of* The Spectator*), Vol. 153, No. 5546, October 12, 1934, pp. 530, 532.*

V. S. PRITCHETT (essay date 1940)

[*Pritchett is a highly esteemed English novelist, short story writer, and critic. A twentieth-century successor to such early nineteenth-century essayist-critics as William Hazlitt and Charles Lamb, Pritchett employs much the same critical method: his own experience, judgment, and sense of literary art, rather than a codified critical doctrine derived from a school of psychological or philosophical speculation. His criticism is often described as fair, reliable, and insightful. In the following excerpt, he praises Mencken's* Happy Days.]

Most people who can write at all write well about their early childhood. The material is ''made'' already, for a child lives in a world of incredibly small things and dramatically large cones. . . . Adolescence is the difficulty, the time when the savage is converted, civilised, exploited by traders and missionaries, comes out in pimple politics and has sudden collapses into apathy or riot. That emergent period is always too near us and indeed so often is carried on into what is called maturity, that the average autobiography breaks down between 13 and 20. It might be better—and there is, after all, an awful glut of early childhoods in contemporary literature—if writers decided to face the real difficulty and began their autobiographies at their 13th year.

Mr. H. L. Mencken is one of the confirmed de-bunkers who has ended by creating a special bunk of his own: caustic and facetious common sense. He has cautiously kept to the first dozen years of savagery. He is, of course, a sentimentalist and ***Happy Days*** has the cheerful brutality and elaborate periphrasis of the Mark Twain tradition. He and his brothers, like another generation of Huck Finns and Tom Sawyers, ''infest'' the respectable Baltimore of the eighties, are rapped into shape by their German American schoolmasters, put in their place by their German grandfather, join gangs, escape from cops, overeat, indulge the pestilential curiosity of small boys. ''A larva of the bourgeoisie'' he opposes the sentimentalities and hard luck stories of left wing autobiography with the traditional and sardonic humours of ''the tough American boy'' school of writing. He is the credulous if healthy young puppy living in a world of wonderful cranks and he assumes in his studies—''First Steps in Divinity,'' ''Recreations of a Reactionary,'' ''Cops and their Ways''—the air of anthropological satire. This humour is the natural successor to the kind which goes in for describing trivialities in long words, the nasal humour of the sarcastic schoolmaster. (p. 584)

V. S. Pritchett, ''Themselves,'' in The New Statesman & Nation *(© 1940 The Statesman & Nation Publishing Co. Ltd.), Vol. 20, No. 511, December 7, 1940, pp. 584-85.**

ALFRED KAZIN (essay date 1942)

[*A highly respected American literary critic, Kazin is best known for his essay collections* The Inmost Leaf *(1955) and* Contemporaries *(1962), and particularly for* On Native Grounds *(1942), a study of American prose writing since the era of William Dean Howells. Having studied the works of ''the critics who were the best writers—from Sainte-Beuve and Matthew Arnold to Edmund Wilson and Van Wyck Brooks'' as an aid to his own critical understanding, Kazin has found that ''criticism focussed many—if by no means all—of my own urges as a writer: to show literature as a deed in human history, and to find in each writer the uniqueness of the gift, of the essential vision, through which I hoped to penetrate into the mystery and sacredness of the individual soul.'' In the following excerpt from an essay which attempts to define Mencken's role in twentieth-century American literature, Kazin acknowledges the Baltimorean's frequent excesses and unfairness, but stresses the vivifying effect he exercised on American writing.*]

At a time when the seriousness of a profound moralist like Paul Elmer More seemed utterly remote from anything the new writers understood; when an enemy of modern literature like Irving Babbitt could say nothing better of them than that they were the ill-begotten children of Rousseau; when a Stuart Sherman thought of Dreiser only as a ''barbaric naturalist,'' and declaimed pompously that the Younger Generation was following ''alien guides,'' that ''Beauty has a heart full of service,'' Mencken seemed one of the few guides to a necessary culture and civilization. At any other time, it may be, Mencken would have been almost an affront; later, as he proved with all his familiar energy, he could be as tedious and inflexible an old fogy as any he had once demolished. But if Mencken had never lived, it would have taken a whole army of assorted philosophers, monologists, editors, and patrons of the new writing to make up for him. As it was, he not only rallied all the young writers together and imposed his skepticism upon the new generation, but also brought a new and uproarious gift for high comedy into a literature that had never been too quick to laugh. He was just the oracle the new literature had prepared for itself, the total of the wisdom it was ready to receive; and it was not entirely his fault if, at a time when the loudest noise made the brightest satire and the most boisterous prose recorded the most direct hits, Mencken proved that one could be "a civilizing influence" by writing like a clown.

Mencken belonged so resplendently to the twenties that it is sometimes fancied that he came in with them. The twenties came to him. Much as the thirties passed him by because he did not prove equal to them—was there ever an American writer who seemed to belong so squarely to one period in time?—he was in the prewar years a remotely satiric figure who propounded more than the times were prepared to understand. As a newspaperman from his earliest days, he was taught in the school of Huneker, Percival Pollard, and Vance Thompson, a school not so much of newspapermen as of the bright new esthetic of the nineties which found its shrines in Ibsen, Nietzsche, Wagner, and Shaw. Everything that has been characteristic of Mencken except the scholarly curiosity displayed in ***The American Language*** was learned in that school; there were times when the monotone of his rasping skepticism suggested that he had learned nothing else. There he absorbed and improved upon his facile style; there he picked up the learning—too often only the marks of learning—that marked the esthetic newspaperman of the period; a learning characterized by its flashing eagerness, its naïve addiction to tags and titles and appropriate quotations from the Latin or the German, its sharp wit and occasional penetration and theatrical superficiality.

What Mencken learned chiefly from the fin-de-siècle mind, however, was a superior contempt for the native culture and manners. . . . As a writer he was a dilettante, and in his revolt against the provincial he believed himself a connoisseur. The sexual emancipation that was one of the main props of the renascence of the nineties gave him an added contempt for native American inhibitions; the greater resolution and intellectual distinction of European revolutionaries even provoked a final disgust with the plodding social reformers at home. But Mencken went far beyond Huneker in his contempt for social rebels. For him Marx was always the "philosopher out of the gutter," and Debs was "poor old Debs." Of others in his day one could say that they found Debs's rhetoric soggy because they had been dazzled by Shaw or moved by the nobility of Jean Jaurès; in the brilliance of the European revolutionary tradition, so characteristically European and so pleasingly intellectual, they had found the necessary excuse for their indifference to social problems at home. Mencken needed no excuse. There was a fatal want of generosity in his mind from the first, and his writing was finally corrupted by it.

The gay satire of the American scene that runs all through Mencken's first writings, and which is marked in his editing of the *Smart Set,* was a significantly theatrical revulsion against the American as a type. There was never in it the mark of that quarrel with something one loves that distinguished the best criticism before the war or the humanity and tenderness of postwar rebels like Anderson and Fitzgerald. Entering into critical journalism at a time when traditionalists and insurrectionists divided the field between them, Mencken began, almost experimentally, with a gay and mocking irresponsibility; and the irresponsibility worked so well that it entered into his constitutional habits as a writer. By 1919, when the ***Prejudices*** began to appear, this irresponsibility was no longer a trick; it was a facile and pyrotechnical dogmatism which persuaded Mencken himself as easily as it persuaded callow undergraduates in search of a cultural standard. . . . The times demanded a certain violence of expression and exasperation, and Mencken's appreciation of his sudden notoriety satisfied that demand and encouraged it. If he had not written so brilliantly and recklessly, he would not have been fully understood; but there was no need at the time to know that many of his ideas were cynical improvisations designed to startle and shock. He was an irrepressible force, a stimulant, an introduction to wisdom; when he roared, it was enough to roar with him.

With gay confidence Mencken was thus able to say anything he liked, and he usually did. The American was a lumpish peasant, an oaf, a barbarian in the most elementary matters. His culture was a monstrosity, his manners absurd and indecent, his courage a fiction, his instincts generally revolting. His literature, at best second-rate but usually impossibly mediocre and pretentious, was riddled by impostors, snoopers, and poseurs, dictated to by fakers, criticized by nincompoops, and read chiefly by fools. If there had ever been anything good in it, it had been speedily throttled, since the one thing Americans feared above all else was truth; the worst of it was always ceremoniously glorified. The American was neither a tragic nor a humble figure; he was merely an object of amusement, a figure out of caricature whose struggles for culture were vain, whose heroes were absurd, and whose sufferings were mere drool. To put it gently, he was hopelessly bourgeois, provincial, hypocritical, cowardly, and stupid. Only the lowest representatives of the racial stocks of Europe had congregated to produce him. Everything he possessed was borrowed from the worst of Europe; everything he aped defiled the best of it.

In his own way Mencken thus illustrated perfectly the passage from the America of Randolph Bourne to the postwar America in which he glittered; but it was not entirely his doing. For if he capitalized on the twenties as the period of the Great Silliness, with its profligacy, its vice-snooping in literature, its oil scandals and shady politics, the decade made good use of him. It raised him from a newspaper Petrouchka to the dignity of a social critic; his mockery was prophecy, his very delivery—and what a delivery it was!—became a fashion, and his scorn was almost a benediction. By prodigious skill he managed to insult everyone except his readers. He flattered them by kindling a sense of disgust; his ferocious attacks on Babbittry implied that his readers were all Superior Citizens; his very recklessness was intoxicating. (pp. 198-201)

Under such a stimulus Mencken's craving to say the unexpected, as Louis Kronenberger put it, proved stronger than his integrity against saying what was untrue. What he believed and what his readers wanted to be told were soon indistinguishable; his work became a series of circus tricks, a perpetual search for some new object of middle-class culture to belabor and some new habit or caprice of *Homo Americanus* to ridicule. There were no longer divergent American types and patterns; there was only a strange, fur-bearing, highly unpleasant animal entitled the American. (p. 202)

Mencken's technique was simple: he inverted conventional prejudices. To a Protestant America, he proclaimed himself a Nietzschean; to a moral America, an atheist; to the Anti-Saloon League mind, a devotee of the fine art of drinking; to a provincial America, a citizen of the world. *His* sphere was that of scholarship, of good manners, and the European graces. It did not matter then that his scholarship, with the exception of his works on language, was as pedestrian as it was showy, or that the translator of Nietzsche and the great apostle of German culture was not a very trustworthy guide to German. Nor did it matter that his scorn for poetry was the manly bigotry of the locker room, or that his conception of the esthetic life, which saw in every great artist the cynicism of La Rochefoucauld, the devotion of Flaubert, the manners of a Hollywood duke, and the liberalism of Metternich, was monstrous in its frivolity and ignorance. Mencken was Civilization Incarnate. Every Babbitt read him gleefully and pronounced his neighbor a Babbitt. Every intellectual blushed for the idiocies of the Bible Belt, and thought Cabell's prose the height of elegance. Good citizens who had forgotten Bryan's significance in the days before he became the absurd figure at the monkey trial thought Mencken's ridicule of him the last work in political sophistication. Under the whip of Mencken's raillery people generally saw the world's folly in their Congressman, the world's wisdom in their scorn of him.

Fortunately, Mencken so parodied the best aspirations of criticism that his most egregious utterances seemed the work of a vigorous comic spirit. What could be more appropriate, in a day when Carol Kennicott dreamed of literary noblemen in velvet jackets and Hergesheimer's butlers came out of the *Almanach de Gotha,* than Mencken's call for an aristocracy? The *Uebermensch* sat on the white steps of Baltimore and invoked the spirits of Dante, Machiavelli, Voltaire, Beethoven, and General von Ludendorff, to come and make America inhabitable. It was to be a community of the rich, the witty, assorted magazine editors, George Jean Nathan, and those who could remember drinking at least one quart of genuine Pilsener. The arbiter elegantiarum was suddenly transformed into a Prussian Junker with a taste for Havelock Ellis. What could be more amusing than an "aristocratic" principle that was fully as provincial as the antics of the "booboisie" Mencken loved to bait, or as romantic and incoherent as Babbitt's search for the dream girl?

Occasionally, of course, Mencken was not amusing at all, and his loose tongue got in his way, as when he said of Altgeld that "his error consisted in taking the college yells of democracy seriously." And it was significant that one of the cruelest things he ever wrote, his essay on Bryan, was probably the most brilliant. But who in Mencken's heyday could seriously resent a writer who so joyously declared that there was no real poverty in the United States; or that public schools were a drag on the community; or "that the ignorant should be permitted to spawn *ad libitum* that there may be a steady supply of slaves"; or that war was an admirable institution, and capital punishment an edifying one?

Mencken's gaiety was the secret of his charm, and his charm was everything. He seemed so brilliantly alive, so superb a service toward the advancement of taste and civilization, that it would have been churlish to oppose him. In a young and growing modern literature which believed that the revolt against gentility was all, Mencken's scorn for the Henry Van Dykes and his long fight for Dreiser were extremely important. In a culture aching for emancipation from the Prohibition mind, from vulgarity and provincialism and conventionality, Mencken was a source of light and strength. What did it matter that he was an eccentric and willful critic who celebrated bad writers and cried down good ones simply because it suited his sense of fun to do so? What did it matter that he said as many false things about established writers simply because they were established as he could say true and urgent things about writers waiting to be heard? What did it matter that he was not always a sound guide to culture, that he frequently proved himself cheap and cruel, that his pronouncements on art and music and books were not always wise and witty, but frequently glib and malicious? He was the great cultural emancipator, the conqueror of Philistia, the prophet and leader of all those who had been given their emancipation and were now prepared to live by it. (pp. 202-04)

Alfred Kazin, "The Postwar Scene," in his On Native Grounds: An Interpretation of Modern American Prose Literature *(copyright © 1942, 1970 by Alfred Kazin; reprinted by permission of Harcourt Brace Jovanovich, Inc.), Reynal & Hitchcock, 1942, pp. 189-204.**

MALCOLM COWLEY (essay date 1943)

[Cowley has made several valuable contributions to contemporary letters through his editions of important American authors (Nathaniel Hawthorne, Walt Whitman, Ernest Hemingway, William Faulkner, and F. Scott Fitzgerald), his writings as a literary critic for The New Republic, *and, above all, his chronicles and criticism of modern American literature. Cowley's literary criticism does not attempt a systematic philosophical view of life and art, nor is it representative of a neatly defined school of critical thought, but rather focuses on works—particularly those of "lost generation" writers—that he believes personal experience has qualified him to explicate and that he considers worthy of public appreciation. The critical approach Cowley follows is undogmatic and is characterized by a willingness to view a work from whatever perspective—social, historical, aesthetic—that the work itself seems to demand for its illumination. In the following excerpt, Cowley attacks what he perceives as Mencken's middle-class smugness and social-Darwinist bent.]*

In describing his childhood, H. L. Mencken devotes several pages to his discovery of "Huckleberry Finn," which he calls "probably the most stupendous event of my whole life. . . . If I undertook to tell you the effect it had upon me my talk would sound frantic, and even delirious." . . .

After reading his three books of memoirs, you feel that Mark Twain must have been the decisive influence in forming both his style and his literary picture of himself. All his life he has been, not a Connecticut Yankee but something quite similar, a Baltimore bourgeois at the court of ideas, eager to strip them of their romantic armor. All his life he has been rephrasing and modernizing the rather innocent bitterness of Mark Twain's later years. And there must have been times when he regarded himself as another Huck Finn—the bad boy at Sunday school, the bad boy at political conventions, the bad boy of literary criticism and highbrow magazines. If that is the case, however, you have to imagine that Huck was really the son of Judge Thatcher, and that no matter how many jokes he played or how many stretchers he told, he never really defied the standards of the owning classes. This was a Huck Finn who came home for supper every night and slept in his own bed.

Grown old, he likes to boast of his brass-bound and copper-riveted conservatism. (p. 321)

One of his bourgeois traits is what he calls "a kind of caginess that has dissuaded me, at all stages of my life, from attempting enterprises clearly beyond my power." Another trait derived partly from his background but more from within himself is a strict honesty that is not confined to financial matters. There were times when he could have sold just a little of his independence or just a few of his personal convictions for very stiff prices, but he always refused these offers even when they were disguised as opportunities to improve the world. The master shoemaker stuck to his last.

Still another of the bourgeois traits he reveals is contempt and even hatred for all the people living on the wrong side of the tracks. He is very funny on the subject of their faults and misfortunes, but after a while the reader tires of his humor and begins to feel that there is too much gleeful malice in his stories of the Negroes beaten over the head and skilled workingmen arrested because it was time to paint and repair the city jail. In his newspaper days, he rather enjoyed being present at hangings—"I found the work light and instructive," he says, without bothering to pretend that he pitied the men who were dying. It is not that Mencken is cruel by temperament. When he was editing *The American Mercury* there were dozens of stories about his kindness to young writers, and everybody knows that he is devoted to his friends. He seems to feel, however, that only the bourgeoisie is authentically human. The rest of mankind belongs to a subhuman species whose members can best be described as bucks and wenches, black-amoors, apes, simians, anthropoids and stumblebums. These are some of Mencken's favorite words, and his use of them reveals a defect that is not so much of the heart as of the imagination. He simply cannot believe that people outside the middle classes are worth the trouble of trying to understand them.

If anybody wonders why he seems a much smaller figure than Mark Twain, and less important in the history of American letters, I think we are not far from the answer. Except in point of imagination, Mencken comes close to his earliest model and sometimes even surpasses him. He is much more at home in the world of ideas than Mark Twain ever learned to be. He never makes Twain's enormous blunders in taste—not because his own taste is extremely good, but because it is always on the same level. He is a marvelous story-teller, even when he hasn't much of a story to tell, as in several chapters of his latest book. His style is one that other writers admire and hundreds of them used to imitate. They never did more than a botched job, because the original was completely suited to his own personality—picturesque, clear, self-satisfied and never attempting anything beyond its power. It reduces the universe to something within four walls—something simple, boisterous, but not disorderly—let us say a middle-class Munich beerhall in the good days of Wilhelm II. Mark Twain always sweeps you outside; and the raft floats down the river into the mist; and each village it passes is a separate world, full of the human misery, cowardice and kindness that Mencken claims to despise.

Indeed, if he had written "Huckleberry Finn," it would have been a very different book. Huck himself, coming from a shiftless family, could scarcely have been the principal character. Nigger Jim would merely have been a stupid, good-natured blackamoor. The real heroes would have been the King and the Duke, who royally defrauded the yokels on both banks of the river, and thereby proved Mencken's thesis about human rascality. The book would have ended with both of them preparing for greater exploits in Washington. It would have made a hilarious story, but no little boy would have read it word by word and have found at the end that his life had been forever transformed. (pp. 321-22)

Malcolm Cowley, "Mencken and Mark Twain" (© 1943 The New Republic, Inc., and renewed 1970 by Malcolm Cowley; reprinted by permission of the author), in The New Republic, *Vol. 108, No. 10, March 8, 1943, pp. 321-22.**

RICHARD WRIGHT (essay date 1945)

[*Wright is considered one of the most esteemed spokespersons for the oppressed black American of the late 1930s and 1940s. His earliest fiction,* Uncle Tom's Children *(1938), portrayed the violent mechanics of Southern racial bigotry with moving realism, and a later novel* Native Son *(1940), a violent tale of the terror of racism, was one of the most controversial books of its time.* Black Boy *(1945), which tells of the author's childhood and youth in Mississippi, is widely considered one of America's most eloquent and effective protest autobiographies. In the following excerpt from* Black Boy, *Wright recounts his first encounter with the books of a major American author. Having read in a local newspaper that a certain H. L. Mencken was of no worth as a writer or as a man, Wright recognized Mencken as a fellow outcast and enemy of the white South. Having never read any of Mencken's works, Wright checked out two of his books at a library, using a forged note and the library card of a sympathetic white friend. The following excerpt records Wright's initial impressions and the impact of Mencken's work upon his life.*]

A block away from the library I opened one of the books and read a title: ***A Book of Prefaces.*** I was nearing my nineteenth birthday and I did not know how to pronounce the word "preface." I thumbed the pages and saw strange words and strange names. I shook my head, disappointed. I looked at the other book; it was called ***Prejudices.*** I knew what that word meant; I had heard it all my life. And right off I was on guard against Mencken's books. Why would a man want to call a book ***Prejudices***? The word was so stained with all my memories of racial hate that I could not conceive of anybody using it for a title. Perhaps I had made a mistake about Mencken? A man who had prejudices must be wrong. (p. 271)

That night in my rented room, while letting the hot water run over my can of pork and beans in the sink, I opened ***A Book of Prefaces*** and began to read. I was jarred and shocked by the style, the clear, clean, sweeping sentences. Why did he write like that? And how did one write like that? I pictured the man as a raging demon, slashing with his pen, consumed with hate, denouncing everything American, extolling everything European or German, laughing at the weaknesses of people, mocking God, authority. What was this? I stood up, trying to realize what reality lay behind the meaning of the words . . . Yes, this man was fighting, fighting with words. He was using words as a weapon, using them as one would use a club. Could words be weapons? Well, yes, for here they were. Then, maybe, perhaps. I could use them as a weapon? No. It frightened me. I read on and what amazed me was not what he said, but how on earth anybody had the courage to say it.

Occasionally I glanced up to reassure myself that I was alone in the room. Who were these men about whom Mencken was talking so passionately? Who was Anatole France? Joseph Conrad? . . . Baudelaire, Edgar Lee Masters, Stendhal, Turgenev, Huneker, Nietzsche, and scores of others? Were these men real? Did they exist or had they existed? And how did one pronounce their names?

I ran across many words whose meanings I did not know, and I either looked them up in a dictionary or, before I had a chance to do that, encountered the word in a context that made its meaning clear. But what strange world was this? I concluded the book with the conviction that I had somehow overlooked something terribly important in life. I had once tried to write, had once reveled in feeling, had let my crude imagination roam, but the impulse to dream had been slowly beaten out of me by experience. Now it surged up again and I hungered for books, new ways of looking and seeing. It was not a matter of believing or disbelieving what I read, but of feeling something new, of being affected by something that made the look of the world different. (pp. 271-73)

Richard Wright, in a chapter in his Black Boy: A Record of Childhood and Youth *('Black Boy'. copyright 1937, 1942, 1944, 1945 by Richard Wright; reprinted by permission of Harper & Row, Publishers, Inc.), Harper & Brothers, 1945 (and reprinted by Harper & Row, 1964, pp. 267-77).**

VAN WYCK BROOKS (essay date 1952)

[Brooks is noted chiefly for his biographical and critical studies of such writers as Mark Twain, Henry James, and Ralph Waldo Emerson, and for his influential commentary on the history of American literature. His career can be neatly divided into two distinct periods: the first, from 1908 to 1925, dealt primarily with the negative impact of European Puritanism on the development of artistic genius in America. Brooks argued that the puritan conscience in the United States, carried over from Europe, produced an unhealthy dichotomy in American writers and resulted in a literature split between stark realism and what he called "vaporous idealism." During this early period, Brooks believed that America had no culture of its own, and that American literature relied almost exclusively on its European heritage. After 1925 and his study of Emerson, Brooks radically altered his view of American literary history. He began to see much in America's past as unique and artistically valuable, and he called for a return in literary endeavors to the positive values of Emerson, as opposed to the modern pessimism of such writers as T. S. Eliot and James Joyce. Despite the radical difference in these two critical approaches, one element remains constant throughout Brooks's career, namely his concern with the reciprocal relationship between the writer and society. In the following excerpt, Brooks examines Mencken's role as a liberator of American art from its conservative, Anglo-Saxon roots.]

[During the jazz age,] Mencken played a decisive part in stabbing a flabby society wide awake, in shaking up the American spirit and rousing it out of its lethargy of optimistic fatuity and dull conventions. Mencken's astringent realism seared its adiposity, its provincial self-satisfaction and romantic moonshine, and, reintroducing acrimony into American criticism, he harrowed the ground for the literature and art of the future. As he said, all the benefits that he had ever got from critics had come from those who gave him a "hearty slating," for this led him to examine his ideas, shelve them when he found holes in them and set about hatching others that were better; and was he not right in saying that literature thrives best in an atmosphere of strife? Poe had introduced this three generations before at the dawn of the so-called American Renaissance, and what it really meant was that literary and aesthetic matters were felt to be worth the trouble of a *mêlée* and a combat. Mencken was hardly a literary critic, for his mind was devoid of the feminine traits this type must have in order to be effective. He was a social critic and a literary showman who had taken lessons from Macaulay, as well as from Nietzsche, Huneker and Bierce, and he fought with all his masculine force against the elements in American society that impeded the creative life and stifled its growth. A transatlantic Attila, with his own Teutonic fury, a coarse mind that had undertaken a literary spadesman's work, he accomplished a task that only a coarse mind could do. He was concerned with "numbers," the big Philistine public that blocked his way and that he attacked with his humour and his rude common sense,—the "Texas Taines," the "policemen of letters," the rural fundamentalists, the "Ku Klux Kritics" that battened in the solid South. In their fear of the new literature that he was fostering, the "cow-state John the Baptists" and their colleagues and supporters were as thoroughly American as the Knights of Pythias or chewing-gum, or Diamond Jim Brady, or Billy Sunday; and, defending what they called the sewage of the mental slums of Chicago and New York, he set the new realistic literature squarely on its feet. (pp. 465-66)

Mencken was a humorist, a more pungent successor of Artemus Ward, no longer the country showman but the man of the city, and he conveyed an infectious feeling of the spectacle of life in America as a monstrous county fair or museum of freaks. Then he had the pride of craftsmanship that betokened the genuine artist in words, and, "naturally monkish," for all his worldly cynicism, he had much, after all, in common with the professors. His work on ***The American Language*** showed this in time. He esteemed the man who devoted himself to a subject with hard diligence, the man who put poverty and a shelf of books above evenings of jazz or profiteering; and in all these and other ways he stimulated writers, especially those who appeared after the first world war. If, as he said, these younger writers had a "new-found elasticity," together with a "glowing delight in the spectacle before them,"—a vigorous naive self-consciousness and sense of aliveness,—it was partly owing to the influence of Mencken himself. He had seen an exhilarating prospect for American letters, as he put it in one of his essays, in the exhaustion of Europe.

Still later, after the jazz age passed, when he had become an institution, Mencken's limitations and faults were more generally apparent. It was evident that he had the vaguest of literary standards, that there were no fixed stars in his literary firmament such as sea-faring critics must have in order to sail. In music, with which he was more at home,—conventional as his taste there was, for he hated the "musical felonies" of Ravel and Stravinsky,—he never wavered in his devotion to the "lovely music of Haydn and Mozart" and even went so far as to call Beethoven "noble." This was a word he would never have connected with a writer, for he saw in Dante the "elaborate jocosity" of a satire on the "Christian hocus-pocus" and in *Romeo and Juliet* he found only "tinpot heroics." He called Greek tragedy an "unparalleled bore," he spoke of the "weakness for poetry" as "another hoary relic from the adolescence of the race," and, describing philosophy as "largely moonshine and wind-music," he referred to "metaphysics, which is to say, nonsense." He had no literary scale of values or he could scarcely have spoken of the "harsh Calvinistic fables of Hawthorne" or of Emerson as "an importer of stale German elixirs"; he could never have described Howells as a "placid conformist" because he was indifferent to the "surge of passion" or called Robert Frost a "Whittier without the whiskers." He was so undiscriminating that he spoke of Gertrude Atherton in the same breath with Sarah Orne Jewett, and "Prof. Dr. William James," when Mencken finished speaking of him, was virtually indistinguishable from Orison Swett Marden. He was apt enough when he referred to Veblen's "vast kitchen-midden of discordant and raucous polysyllables," but this did not exhaust the subject of the "geyser of pishposh" even in the matter of style, and his dispraise of American critics lost much of its convincingness when he praised the third-rate Austrian Leon Kellner. Then what was one to say of the absence in him of the sentiment of reverence and the "shudder of awe,"—"humanity's highest faculty," as Goethe called it,—the recognition of certain realities of a spiritual kind upon which all human values are ultimately based? That Mencken really lacked this one saw in his treatment of Bernard Shaw, his early master and one of his early heroes, who became for him the "ulster Polonius" in 1914, nine years after Shaw had been the subject of his first prose book. Mencken retained so little respect for the man he had admired so much that he said it was Shaw's life-work to "announce the obvious in terms of the scandalous." Mencken remained a child in this region of feeling. (pp. 467-69)

Mencken once observed himself that his "essential trouble" was that he was "devoid of what are called spiritual gifts." This was an actual trouble indeed, for without these "gifts" one lacks the scale, in the literary and human spheres alike, by which one distinguishes the ephemeral and the small from the great. Mencken's realistic note was admirable and useful, as one saw in his book, for instance, ***In Defence of Women,***—women as the logical practical sex, aesthetically responsible, wary, discreet, in distinction from the vainglorious sex to which he belonged. He was as shrewd as Benjamin Franklin there and in other books, the ***Treatise on Right and Wrong*** and the ***Treatise on the Gods,***—in which he admitted the reality of a kind of "progress,"—but elsewhere his arid rationalism blended with a hedonism that was quite without spirituality and completely fatalistic. It was this tendency of his that blossomed in the jazz age in which so many writers were influenced by him, an age that also inherited the thinking of William Graham Sumner with his contempt for the idealism and "illusions" of the past. That life no longer had a purpose was the belief of millions then for whom the bootlegger became a national hero, and, while man was a "bad monkey" for many a scientific mind, others embraced the despair of Eliot's "waste land." Shakespeare's man, "glorious in reason, infinite in faculty," had been dethroned, and Melville's "man noble and sparkling,"—where now was he? He had been supplanted by Mencken's man, the "king dupe of the cosmos," the "yokel *par excellence*," the "booby." Much of Mencken's humour was based upon these denigrations of the "boob" man, "brother to the lowly ass," whose pretensions he delighted in undoing, and his disdain of democracy followed from this low view of human nature that struck the note of the fiction of the nineteen-twenties. If he saw democracy as "the art and science of running the circus from the monkey-cage," was it not precisely because he saw men as monkeys and because their continued existence in the world was therefore so inconsequential that one had no reason to assure and facilitate it? Inevitably, from this point of view, philanthropy, socialism, pacifism, like the notion of educability, were sentimental, while Mencken's opposition to birth-control was deadlier even than his attacks on most of the other aspects of the democratic process. He said the ignorant should be "permitted to spawn *ad libitum* that there may be a steady supply of slaves." For the rest, he was convinced that the war between the haves and the have-nots was an affair of "envy pure and simple."

With all his reactionary cynicism, Mencken was a liberator who opened paths for writers and made straight their way by turning many of their obstacles into laughing-stocks, but his campaign against democracy lost any glamour it might have had when Hitler murdered seven million Poles and Jews. While much that Mencken said was true, the inevitable answer was that all other forms of government had proved to be worse, that democracy, as Whitman put it, was the only safe system; and, when virtually every thinking German was only too happy to escape to America, Mencken's assaults on the country lost much of their force. Time broke the lance of the "literary uhlan," as the German-American societies had called him, and the critic who had said, "Most of the men I respect are foreigners," ceased to be a spokesman for the "mongrel and inferior" Yankees. It was almost forgotten that he had performed a major work of criticism in giving the *coup de grâce* to the colonial tradition, while, by fully recognizing the new interracial point of view, he contributed to the nationalizing of American letters. (pp. 470-71)

As for the question of colonialism,—still a live issue in 1920,—this was soon to be settled, thanks partly to him; and perhaps it could have been settled only by a critic of recent immigrant stock whose mind was entirely detached from the English tradition. Mencken's solution of the question was in certain ways unfortunate precisely because of this and all it implied, but he performed an invaluable work in helping to establish the interracial American literature of the future. Mencken had observed that the distrust of Dreiser was very largely racial,—he was felt to be sinister because he was not Anglo-Saxon; and it pleased him to point out how many of the new novelists and poets might be regarded as sinister for the same reason. But, he remarked, the "old easy domination of the 'Anglo-Saxon'" was rapidly passing,—the nation was becoming "transnational," as Randolph Bourne put it,—and what was the use of attempting to restore, as Stuart P. Sherman wished to do, the Anglo-Saxon tradition in American letters? Mencken was right in saying that this was a "demand for supine conformity," for, in fact, the *restoration* of this tradition was by no means the relevant or desirable thing. What was important was the *recognition* of it, the reëstablishing of a living relation between the future and the past, the sense of which, for a number of reasons, had been lost. Mencken was the last man to reëstablish this relation, for, having no inherited knowledge of the American past, he was even antagonistic to its main stream of feeling. He was "frankly against the Anglo-Saxon," and this led to a confusion he shared with others, especially during the first world war, when the issue of "colonialism" was confounded with the issue of "England." One could never tell how far "pro-German" American writers were opposed to colonialism because of this hostility to England. But to fight to "throw off the yoke of England's intellectual despotism,"—in the melodramatic phrase of Mencken's friend Wright,—to settle this age-old question was a service to the country; and in order to exalt the new "foreign" strains in the American literary world it was natural enough to depreciate the Anglo-Saxon. The trouble was that Mencken carried this to impossible lengths, and he indulged in grotesque misstatements regarding New England, especially, that a serious critic should have been ashamed to utter. One wonders what the proud "founding fathers,"—or Governor Winthrop or William Byrd,—would have said to his remark about the first English settlers, that they were "the botched and unfit"; and what was anyone to say to his statement that "New England has never shown the slightest sign of a genuine enthusiasm for ideas"? In **"Puritanism as a Literary Force,** he said that the literature of the years 1831-1861,—the times of Emerson, Melville, Thoreau and Hawthorne,—was the "work of women and admittedly second-rate men." It was by assertions of this kind that he "liquidated the American past," as certain of his admirers praised him for doing, and this was anything but a service to the country or its writers. But that one could impute these feats to him was a proof of the force of Mencken's mind, and one could leave the balance to be redressed by others. (pp. 472-74)

Van Wyck Brooks, "Mencken in Baltimore," in his The Confident Years: 1885-1915 *(copyright, 1952, by Van Wyck Brooks; copyright renewed 1980 by Gladys Brooks; reprinted by permission of the pub-*

lisher, E. P. Dutton, Inc.), Dutton, 1952, pp. 455-74.

JAMES T. FARRELL (essay date 1954)

[Farrell was an American novelist, short story writer, and critic who is best known for his grim Studs Lonigan trilogy, a series of novels which examines the life of a working class Chicago man. Influenced primarily by the author's own Irish-Catholic upbringing in Chicago's rough South Side, and by the writings of Theodore Dreiser, Marcel Proust, and James Joyce, Farrell's fiction is a Naturalistic, angry portrait of urban life. His literature explores—from a compassionate, moralistic viewpoint—the problems spawned of poverty, circumstance, and spiritual sterility. Farrell has written: "I am concerned in my fiction with the patterns of American destinies and with presenting the manner in which they unfold in our times. My approach to my material can be suggested by a motto of Spinoza which I have quoted on more than one occasion: 'Not to weep or laugh, but to understand.'" In the following general discussion of Mencken's work, Farrell emphasizes the timeless freshness of his writings.]

Mencken's contribution to the liberation of American literature from hypocrisy and Victorian stuffiness is not so highly regarded now as it should be. But those of us who were young in the twenties remember. How eagerly we waited every month for that green-covered magazine, the *American Mercury*! How avidly we read him! To us he was a spokesman, a liberator, a voice speaking out in the name of truth, honesty, and sincerity in literature.

His writings were admittedly full of prejudices. He was conservative in his political views, often criticizing and lampooning the excesses of democracy. (p. 44)

Mencken believed that men were not born biologically equal, and that there was an hereditary basis for the superior man. He spoke for what he considered to be the civilized minority of superior men. These were aristocratic because of innate capacity and talent. Few of them, according to him, ever became politicians—almost all of whom, to him, were frauds and mountebanks. But artists were to be included in the superior and civilized minority.

Today, the piously liberal may decry Mencken as the Fundamentalists once did. If they do so, they err. America needed a critic like Mencken. The American liberals needed such a critic, too. Is his phrase "the kept idealists of the New Republic" forgotten? There was an essential soundness in his attacks on bigness in government. We are threatened by bigness in life, and thoughtful men today are concerned with the fate of liberty in an era in which bigness seems inescapable.

I think Mencken was often wrong: he oversimplified. But the values of his criticism cannot be underestimated. It is especially those in the liberal group who need to be flayed by such a critic. Mencken is today especially worth reading from this standpoint. For the key to Mencken's thought is to be found in his libertarianism. He believed in complete liberty. He was of the opinion that government was becoming more centralized and more bureaucratized and that, with this process, liberty could well be doomed. He saw encroachments on the liberty of the individual from all sides. The institutions of society in general, and of democracy in particular, were threatening the liberty of the individual. And liberty meant, more than anything else, liberty of thought. He took the privilege of this liberty in his own writings. Like or dislike them, agree or disagree with them, one cannot fail but be struck by their honesty and vigor. (pp. 44-5)

What sounded true and valid in the twenties seemed excessive after the onset of the Great Depression. Individualism, which Mencken so ardently championed, was more seriously endangered by economic misery. Mencken failed to see the significance of the New Deal, and likewise the need for a growth of unions. He was right about the danger of bigness. But the conditions of our world impose this on our society. Government must now be big for the many or for the few. The world has changed since Mencken's heyday. He was a prophet predicting that change, and he prepared many to meet it. Thus, though he was at times extravagant, he was never irrelevant. No voice of liberty is ever irrelevant. (pp. 47-8)

[If] one examines his judgments, one will find that he was a sound critic of fiction. . . . To realize that Mencken was a man with a profound sense of and respect for literature, one need only go back, say, to his essay ***The Late Mr. Wells.*** His distinctions there between the best and the worst of Wells are clear, sharp, and to the point. He saw clearly the difference between a great artist like Conrad, and a skilled craftsman such as Arnold Bennett. Mencken himself became a figure around whom there were many fashionable imitators. The literary world was full of Menckenians. But he was not himself a man of fashions. He was a literary critic who knew what he liked and who stated his likes frankly, clearly, forcefully, and with intelligence and feeling. His likes ran mainly along the line of realistic fiction, but realism was not a fetish to him. He looked for works that were grounded in reality and that had something to say about the condition and nature of man. Whatever he himself might write about "*boobus Americanus*" in the flesh, when he read of him in a novel, Mencken showed a power of empathy. He was able to feel and to convey how a writer captured a sense of a man. He saw literature in terms of characters. He did not regard a novel as good unless the characters were real. He insisted the characters be plausible and lifelike, and that they act, think, and feel like human beings rather than stereotypes. (pp. 48-9)

Mencken's ideas on criticism diverged sharply from those of many of his contemporaries. He believed that basically the critic was himself an artist. He held that just as the writer uses the material of life as a means of expression, so does the critic. Books provide a means for the critic to practice self-expression. In this attitude he was close to James Gibbons Huneker, whom he admired, and, with George Jean Nathan, he was a follower of Huneker, who was one of the first to bring to America a taste for the great art of the Continent. (p. 51)

[Civilized] enjoyments, freedom, and a new vision were what a new generation sought. The old success myth and the Horatio Alger legend were being rejected. In colleges all over America, boys and girls wanted something newer and freer. Mencken became a voice expressing what that was. In this sense, he was a voice of his times.

And as a voice of the times, he made revolt and protest fun. He was a great satirist and humorist. (p. 53)

He lambasted right, left, and center, and everything fell before his original onslaught of words. Some of this is interesting today only because it is so well-written. Other writings, on the Prohibition era, for instance, have only an historical interest. But practically everything he wrote is remarkable for its style. You will always come upon a neologism, a vivid phrase, a sharp sentence, a tirade of words which pour out and reveal an amazing capacity to handle the American language.

Mencken is one of the masters of American prose. He will live as such.

In the forties, Mencken retired from journalism. He devoted himself to writing three autobiographical works now collected in one volume, ***The Days of H. L. Mencken.*** This is composed of the three single volumes, ***Happy Days, Newspaper Days,*** and ***Heathen Days.*** They recount Mencken's childhood experiences, his early career as a newspaperman, and a number of experiences of his later years. He declares in one preface that the books are reasonably accurate but that there are some stretchers in them. He re-creates a sense of the old Baltimore in which he grew up, his parents, his family, his teachers, the odd characters in the neighborhood. He does the same for the newspapermen and others he met in his first years as a reporter and editor. This work is one of the most charming of modern American autobiographical works. (p. 55)

The Republic has not been the same since H. L. Mencken sat down to his typewriter and began pouring it out. To use a phrase he liked, H. L. Mencken has been a man and a writer of the first chop. (p. 57)

James T. Farrell, "Dr. Mencken: Criticus Americanus" (copyright © 1954, renewed 1982, by James T. Farrell; reprinted by permission of the Literary Estate of James T. Farrell), in New World Writing: Sixth Mentor Selection, *The New American Library, 1954 (and reprinted in* Reflections at Fifty and Other Essays *by James T. Farrell, The Vanguard Press, Inc., 1954, pp. 42-57).*

IRVING HOWE (essay date 1956)

[*A longtime editor of the leftist magazine* Dissent *and a regular contributor to* The New Republic, *Howe is one of America's most highly respected literary critics and social historians. He has been a socialist since the 1930s, and his criticism is frequently informed by a liberal social viewpoint. Howe is widely praised for what F. R. Dulles has termed his "knowledgeable understanding, critical acumen and forthright candor." Howe has written: "My work has fallen into two fields: social history and literary criticism. I have tried to strike a balance between the social and the literary; to fructify one with the other; yet not to confuse one with the other. Though I believe in the social approach to literature, it seems to me peculiarly open to misuse; it requires particular delicacy and care." In contrast to the many critics who dismiss Mencken's excesses in light of his role as a liberator of thought and expression, Howe, in the following excerpted review of* Minority Report: H. L. Mencken's Notebooks, *takes issue with what he considers Mencken's pettiness, humorlessness, and repetitiveness.*]

No obligation is more destructive to the aging writer—yet none more honorable—than the feeling that, come fashions as they may and intellectual revolutions as they must, he will continue to write as in his youth, bitterly loyal to the public image he had created of and for himself, aware that only by its smudged contours can he be remembered at all. For self-imitation and then self-parody is the fate of almost every writer. . . .

To the painful end H. L. Mencken was determined to remain the Mencken everyone knew. The script had changed, the cast had died, the whole theatre had burned down; yet there he was, still performing his usual act, this Baltimore iconoclast who simmered with contempt for "the blowsy vacuity which marks so much of the so-called thinking of mankind." (p. 17)

Like an orator making speeches in his bedroom, Mencken keeps driving his hard-and-ready opinions into his notebooks. . . . Philosophy? "It consists very largely of one philosopher arguing that all others are jackasses." The American workers? "The more skilled men in the CIO automobile union settled toward one side and *the mere human mules* toward the other." [My emphasis—I.H.] And the Orientals? "The Hindus, save when they have been denaturized by Western influences, are actually barbarians. . . ."

What is so depressing here is that Mencken actually believed this bilge, it was the offspring of his heart, he was never more serious than when everyone thought he was merely carrying on. Yet it is clear that he was also a highly intelligent man. He could write that "man, in the last analysis, is intrinsically unconsolable" and "moral certainty is always a sign of cultural inferiority." These are very fine: they conform to the modest requirement that even epigrams be true. But the need to be Mencken finally destroyed him; in the thirties and forties it would have destroyed anyone.

It has become a commonplace of literary history that Mencken was an emancipator who helped free American writing from gentility and American manners from provinciality; and this is true, or at least true enough to make it worth saying. But it is also true that whenever we fall back upon a writer's "historical importance" and try to assert his value in terms of what was peculiarly local to his time, it is probably due to an uneasy awareness that his voice no longer reaches us. In the recent efforts to "revive" Mencken it has been customary to speak of the need for a similar figure in our own time. To be sure; nothing could be more useful than a cultural leader who would outrage our genteel and conformist literary world. But the whole point is that Mencken, even at his best, would no longer be adequate, he could no longer affect our cultural life, for in whatever ways we have regressed since the twenties—and we *have* regressed—it is unlikely that we can again respond to the carnival Nietzschianism that was the essence of his thought.

The mind one sees at work in [***Minority Report: H. L. Mencken's Notebooks***] is neither interesting nor supple; it is a shrewd brassy mind, infatuated with its own display and cosy with its own assurance. The thought and the writing are characterized by a pitiful narrowness of spirit, an iconoclasm as rigid and lifeless as the academic humanism of Irving Babbitt, once Mencken's great enemy. Mencken's mind lacked pliability, a readiness to lie open and listen; he had little of the true critic's gift for exposing himself to the thought of others; and above all, he lacked ordinary relaxed affection, simple generosity. . . . The Mencken who claimed to care only for the select few, who spoke in the name of cosmopolitanism and *Kultur* and superior beer, finally came to seem another in the long line of provincial American intellectuals, with their homespun cynicism, their cracker-barrel "philosophy," their unfocussed and burgeoning resentments, their distrust of the life of the mind.

Having written this much I called a stop, for I know how easy and tempting it is to batter down yesterday's household gods. Surely there is more to Mencken? And so I have gone back to his books, sampling here and there, and can say with pleasure, Yes there *is* more, though not quite as much as his admirers claim.

At his best Mencken was a superb reporter, a first-rate entertainer, and this particularly when he found a subject or occasion outside of himself. . . . [His essay on] Dreiser is marvellous, a classic of our cultural history, though less as evidence of Mencken's critical gift, which was small and uncertain, than as evidence of the close kinship he could establish with a few of his contemporaries. The pieces on Wilson and Harding, the fine sketch of Valentino, the murderously unjust but brilliant obituary of William Jennings Bryan, the extremely funny eulogy of Coolidge ("He had no ideas, and he was not a nuisance")—such writings are still worth turning back to, and they should have a long life as useful contrasts to the increasingly adulatory tone of American historiography. Alistair Cooke, whose paper-back Mencken is very good if only because it reduces him to properly modest proportions, strikes exactly the right note when he speaks of Mencken as "a humorist by instinct and a superb craftsman by temperament." Humorist and craftsman he certainly was, but also a humorist who could be singularly humorless and cheap. (pp. 17-18)

Irving Howe, "A Comedian Playing Hamlet," in The New Republic *(reprinted by permission of* The New Republic; © *1956 The New Republic, Inc.), Vol. 134, No. 21, May 21, 1956, pp. 17-18.*

PHILIP WAGNER (essay date 1966)

[*In the following excerpt, Wagner, Mencken's successor as editor of* The Evening Sun, *surveys Mencken's career, notes several major characteristics of his writings, and judges which works by Mencken are most likely to endure.*]

From the beginning [of his newspaper career, Mencken] did not limit his writing to daily journalism, prodigious though his output for the *Herald* was. He began experimenting with verse, and selling it. He was a "stringer" providing features for out-of-town papers. He became a fabricator of short stories for most of the popular magazines of the day—formula fiction loaded with blood and thunder, done by the yard and showing small trace of the style we think of as Mencken's. . . .

The hack period began to recede, and in 1905 he published his "first real book," as he called it, ***George Bernard Shaw: His Plays*** (he preferred not to count a little book of rather dreadful verse that too much fuss was later made about simply because copies were rare: the poetic muse kept clear of him always). This essay offered the first intimations of the Mencken style and his formidable critical capacity, immature though they were. (p. 11)

Mencken reporting the Republican National Convention (1936). Reproduced by permission of the Enoch Pratt Free Library, in accordance with the will of H. L. Mencken.

Three years later he published his ***Philosophy of Friedrich Nietzsche,*** a better book and still very much worth the reading. William Manchester, in *Disturber of the Peace,* best of the several Mencken biographies and studies, says, "The subject . . . was Mencken's Nietzsche, not Nietzsche's Nietzsche. There is a difference." It is probably a better guide to Mencken than to Nietzsche, to the extraordinary toughness and stiffness of his mind beneath its lively movement at the surface. (p. 12)

A chance encounter with Theodore Dreiser, then a magazine editor, led [Mencken] to another chance encounter with George Jean Nathan; and out of that all-day meeting of two men as unlike as two could be, yet so surprisingly alike in their disgust with contemporary life and letters, there came a partnership that lasted better than two decades. The inspiration of the partnership was a magazine of dubious reputation, the *Smart Set,* which was about to undergo one of its rejuvenations, or reincarnations. Mencken had been invited to do a monthly full-length piece for it on books, Nathan to do dramatic criticism. The result was something like a volcanic eruption. The shallow standards and appalling inanity of most American writing and the theater of the early years of this century were the targets of both. With high spirits, total confidence in their own judgments, and a torrent of brilliant invective, they laid about them, bashing heads, pulling down idols, puncturing inflated pomposity, infuriating the sources of conventional wisdom, sweeping away the rubbish that then passed for literature and drama. Prodigous labor was required, and it was a bravura performance. (pp. 12-13)

The *Smart Set* was a tour de force, a gale of fresh air across the campuses, a serial spoof, bellwether of a new generation, an object of delighted devotion. (p. 14)

So things went for Mencken in the years before World War I, exuberantly, as he juggled two careers: those of a literary critic of rapidly growing stature and of a newspaper columnist knowing no bounds except those of libel and common prudence. There was no time for larger works, though these had begun to gestate in his mind; and the only thing that appeared between hard covers was his priceless little drama without words, ***The Artist, a Drama without Words*** . . . , which was later reprinted in his ***A Book of Burlesques***. . . . (pp. 15-16)

The war years were years of misery for Mencken, carrying the brand of pro-Germanism though his loyalty as a çitizen was never in real doubt. He was left with no means but his private correspondence for venting his opinions. He solved the problem—that is to say, the problem of one who must write but is constrained on all sides—by plunging into his linguistic project, ***The American Language,*** which had been simmering gently for a long time. The conclusion of this landmark work was being written, appropriately, as the war ended. It was a critical and popular triumph when published a year later, in 1919. The impression it made on the new college generation especially, by its style, its humor and its lightly worn scholarship, was tremendous. That same year saw also the publication of the first volume in the series of ***Prejudices,*** consisting of reprints from the *Smart Set,* the *Evening Sun,* and some other sources. (p. 17)

[The] Mencken Period had begun. He offered what the times needed: a clearinghouse for the cynicism and discontents of the postwar years and a lash for their excesses wielded with alternating scorn and high good humor. . . . And yet even as he reached the peak of his influence as a critic of letters he began to move out of this role and into criticism of the American mores. This was not a new role for him, of course, but it now got far more emphasis: the truth is that imaginative writing was beginning to bore him. His work for the *Evening Sun* reflected this—it ran more and more to political and social commentary. His ***Prejudices*** books reflected this too, the first of these being devoted almost entirely to writers and writing—what he called beautiful letters and the bozart—and the last containing hardly anything relating to current writing. The change in his interests was reflected also in the *Smart Set,* where increasingly he tacked away from literature and toward life, in spite of Nathan's persistence in the old course. (p. 18)

Nathan the complete aesthete, absorbed as always in the theater, was cold to that "show"—the excesses and absurdities of the jazz age—which so dazzled and delighted Mencken as a theme for writing.

This is really what ended that long partnership. Though Mencken had no conscious intention of neglecting the arts he wanted the emphasis placed on American life—to him, the American comedy. . . . He hankered for a "swell" review, to be Brahmin in its typographical dress if not in its contents. Knopf stood ready to back such a review, and indeed had proposed it and offered to finance it, and so, after a sufficiency of preliminary planning and wrangling, the *American Mercury* got its name, the *Smart Set* was published for the last time in December 1923, and in January 1924 the new critical review appeared in its Garamond typeface and ultra-dignified green cover. The Mencken orbit was moving toward its apogee, and the reception of the *Mercury* far exceeded the expectations of the three principals, in circulation and in acclaim. (p. 19)

Mencken himself did but one book from the ground up, so to speak, during . . . the latter half of the twenties. That was not a success: his ***Notes on Democracy***. . . . Even that one was mainly a rewriting job based on previously published material. (p. 21)

The magazine itself began to show evidence of strain, of stridency. Mencken's commentaries on books continued, and at length, but there was a forced quality in much of this now, and they tended to turn into lectures on his special brand of sociology. (p. 22)

In 1929, Mencken completed the second of his trilogy treating formally of politics, religion, and morals: his ***Treatise on the Gods***. . . . As [Huntington] Cairns remarks, he had plowed new land when he wrote ***The American Language,*** which was in every sense an original work, in subject as well as treatment. Religion was another matter, a preoccupation of powerful minds since the dawn of human consciousness, the most thoroughly worked field of all: small room here for originality. What he could do, and did, was to restate the materialist-rationalist position as so thoroughly developed in the nineteenth century by Huxley and others, but in contemporary terms, bringing to bear the abundant new material of psychology and the study of human institutions. He saw the religious motive as a prudent form of hedging against the terrors of the unknown, and organized religion as an elaborate tool for bamboozling and manipulating the credulous masses, a tool of government really. There was not a trace of the mystic in him, and while acknowledging the genuineness of the mystical experience he looked upon it as one of the puzzles not yet worked out by scientific means. . . . Anathema to the conventionally religious, his ***Treatise on the Gods*** is nevertheless a storehouse of learning and curious information; and it has ample helpings of the characteristic Mencken audacity and wit. (pp. 22-3)

In the meantime other troubles of a worldly and professional kind had been piling up on him. As the times had embraced him following World War I, so now with the crash and the onset of the Great Depression they were ready to reject him. . . . To his readers he ceased abruptly to be a champion of the individual and herald of freedom and became an arch-reactionary—this without changing his position one iota. His newspaper polemics seemed suddenly and oddly out of date. . . . One does not write easily in the face of a situation like that; and Mencken's writing showed it. The familiar refrains turned stale, the variations were no longer amusing. (p. 25)

The third of his trilogy on politics, religion, and morals, the ***Treatise on Right and Wrong*** . . . , got a critical mauling and had a poor sale—a far poorer sale than the same book would have had, certainly, ten years before, for it is highly readable still. (p. 26)

[He] plunged into the work of rewriting, enlarging, and in many ways reshaping ***The American Language*** for its fourth edition. This was published in 1936. The reception of it proved that whatever may have happened to his standing as a publicist, in this other field it was secure. Supplement I and Supplement II, massive works and complete in themselves, came along in due course. . . . (p. 27)

More surprising was the way he opened an entirely new lode. Those who knew Mencken well knew how false was the impression of his personality that his no-quarter polemical writing gave. That was his battle dress. To be sure it was not exactly a mask, since he loved the give and take of public controversy. But it did conceal a much more complicated personality through which ran a broad stream of sentiment and warm humanity. . . . Now, disarmed as a controversialist, he yielded to it in his writing. He turned to the recollection of his childhood in the Baltimore of another day, that childhood for which he had no regrets, in a series of sketches written for the *New Yorker* magazine. They were by turns rollicking, mordant, warmhearted, and nostalgic; and they were greeted with surprise and delight. These were brought together in his book called ***Happy Days,*** published in 1940. (pp. 27-8)

There followed in 1941 a second volume, ***Newspaper Days.*** This second group of autobiographical sketches, covering his first years of newspaper life in Baltimore, he described as "mainly true, but with occasional stretchers," and he commended them to the understanding sort of reader who, in Charles Lamb's phrase, felt no call to take "everything perversely in the absolute and literal sense." Absolutely and literally true they certainly were not, as for example his deathless story of "A Girl from Red Lion, P.A." They were better than that: they caught and preserved the smells and flavor and temper of an era. . . . He did one more book of reminiscences, ***Heathen Days*** . . . , which made pleasant enough reading and did well but lacked the perfect autumnal quality of its predecessors, and called quits on this enterprise.

Mencken was coming to the end of his days as a writer. There was his book of quotations, fruit of a lifetime of clipping and marking and note-saving, and a very different thing from Bartlett's. It was published in 1940 as ***A New Dictionary of Quotations.*** His ***Christmas Story,*** a brief bit of mellow buffoonery on a sardonic theme, was published in 1946. (pp. 28-9)

[In 1948] he was taken by the thrombosis that ended his career with such terrible finality. One last book had occupied him toward the end of his writing years: a book of aphorisms and short statements culled from his notes. The manuscript, completed and ready for the printer, was found some years later and was published as ***Minority Report: H. L. Mencken's Notebooks*** following his death in 1956. (p. 29)

Of stylistic characteristics peculiar to him, there were many. I mention four.

One of these was his belief that the function of criticism—coming ahead even of the discovery of the true and the beautiful—was to be interesting. He never forgot the man on the receiving end: the reader. Always before him as he wrote was the vision of a reader who might fall into a doze with a book, one of his, in his lap; or of the newspaper reader who might pause for a moment over what he had written, yawn, and move on to the next column.

Corollary to this was the care he took to be always on the offensive. He had discovered early that what the public likes is a fight. His first purpose being to catch and hold the interest of the reader, he always charged. This made for difficulties if in all honesty he was compelled to bestow praise. But he had a way around that, too. "When I have to praise a writer, I always do it by attacking his enemies."

Another was his constant resort to the *reductio ad absurdum*, which as James Farrell says he often handled not only cleverly but even brilliantly. The object was to make his victim a butt of ridicule. Here he was most plainly Mark Twain's disciple, who saw laughter as the one really effective weapon of an honest man in an imperfect and on the whole inattentive world. Other weapons might, with time and diligence, make some impression on humbug, but as Mark Twain said, "only laughter can blow it to rags and atoms at a blast."

The fourth was the care with which he placed his readers, those he wanted to persuade, on his side in any argument. He wrote, as he never tired of assuring his readers, for "the nobility and gentry," for "the truly civilized minority." Anyone taking the trouble to read him could therefore consider himself complimented. (pp. 33-4)

Mencken has been spared, fortunately, the deadly Collected Edition which abandons discrimination for comprehensiveness and which serves as a tombstone for so many writers whose work, in part, might otherwise live. As a newspaperman he wrote most of the time for the moment; but as Alistair Cooke quite properly insists there is a great deal of life, maybe immortality, in a fair bit of that stuff. The thing to do is to let time winnow it. (p. 43)

Of his formal treatises—his ***Notes on Democracy, A Treatise on the Gods,*** and ***A Treatise on Right and Wrong***—what is likely to be the verdict? He obviously put great store by them as a distillation of his views on the three abiding human preoccupations, with politics (or the art of living together without too much trouble) and with religion and morals (together, the art of living with oneself). But neither as a corpus nor individually can they really be called successful. The first, as suggested already, is badly organized, undisciplined, and shrill despite many a penetrating and cathartic paragraph. It overstates. It leaves the reader, shall we say, not quite persuaded. Its leading ideas are set forth better anyway in his posthumous ***Minority Report,*** a book which will continue to appeal to readers with a taste for the aphoristic form, and in his journalism, where they are illuminated by concrete issues and people. As for ***A Treatise on the Gods*** and ***A Treatise on Right and Wrong,*** both smell too strongly of the lamp, which is to say that they seem somehow concocted. The reading that went into them was extraordinarily wide. They contain much curious information. But Mencken's concern to make them *interesting,* to "fetch" the reader, seems inappropriate to what at bottom were intended as sober and deadly serious treatises. One is left with the conviction, again, that his leading ideas were better put by the thinkers from whom he absorbed them, that he added relatively little of his own beyond the form of the statement, that in any case they are far better stated in his topical writing and that he is not at his best in the sustained development of ideas. Mencken was simply not a systematist.

The one exception to that generalization is his great ***The American Language.*** And it is not hard to see why. Here Mencken the stylist, Mencken the word-juggler, is at work investigating the raw materials of his own great talent and constant preoccupation. He is studying his native tongue, his own means of communication—its origin, its evolution, the springs that feed it, its marvelous suppleness and fluidity. The theme needed systematic exploration, for it had never been given this before; and it took a man sensitive to every nuance of speech and writing to do it. Mencken was that man; and his fascination as well as his supreme capacity for the task shows through as it does nowhere in the three efforts at systematization mentioned above.

Yet ***The American Language*** comes up against another fate. It deals with a living and changing thing. . . . The original ***American Language*** will live as a period piece, a monumental work of scholarship fixing the language as of its time, like a still shot from a film, and full of wit and wisdom. But the title shows signs of developing a life of its own, like Bartlett, Webster, Roget, and even Fanny Farmer.

If we leave out this singular case, the surest candidates for immortality seem to be his ***Happy Days*** and ***Newspaper Days,*** redolent of a life that is gone yet no more to be forgotten than the Wild West, and done in a style ripened and purged of excess, a style that as Cooke says is "flexible, fancy-free, ribald, and always beautifully lucid; a native product unlike any other style in the language." Those books and the best of his "transient" work: they are the essential Mencken. They are what he gave to our literature which time is least likely to tarnish or erode. (pp. 44-5)

Philip Wagner, in his H. L. Mencken *(American Writers Pamphlet No. 62; © 1966, University of Minnesota), University of Minnesota Press, Minneapolis, 1966, 48 p.*

MAURICE M. LaBELLE (essay date 1970)

[In the following excerpt from The Philosophy of Friedrich Nietzsche, *La Belle seeks to demonstrate that Mencken failed to understand Nietzsche's concepts, concluding that he used the work as a vehicle to present his own ideas. "Thus," writes La Belle in an abstract that prefaces the following essay, "Mencken was not significantly influenced by Nietzsche but was interested in Nietzsche's conclusion that iconoclasm is necessary to allow man to build a better world."]*

H. L. Mencken devoted most of his life to ripping apart American religions, attitudes, and goals in order to expose what he considered to be the hypocrisy and stupidity of the beliefs and believers. Some students of Mencken's life and thought attribute many of his concepts to his study of Friedrich Nietzsche . . . whom Mencken avidly read when in his late teens. Mencken was so impressed by and interested in Nietzsche's thoughts that he took considerable time from his newspaper work to read many of Nietzsche's books and to publish an explication of some of them in ***The Philosophy of Friedrich Nietzsche,*** in 1908. Mencken admitted in 1913 that the aim of the work had been "to make Nietzsche comprehensible to the general reader," and one can admire this goal, especially since Mencken was severely limited by the lack of scholarship on Nietzsche. (p. 43)

Mencken begins his book with a brief and frequently vague biographical sketch, and almost immediately he faces one of the foremost problems in any presentation and understanding of Nietzsche's life and thought, that is, the question of his sanity. . . . The problem is about the validity of Nietzsche's thought: Can his ideas be taken seriously when they might very well be the product of a diseased mind? Such a question can be a tremendous hindrance to an understanding and appreciation of Nietzsche's works, and it must be met and countered. Mencken does so in a very effective way when he explains that "a man's reasoning is to be judged, not by his physical condition, but by its own ingenuity and accuracy. If a raving maniac says that twice two make four, it is just as true as it would be if Pope Pius X or any other undoubtedly sane man were to maintain it. Judged in this way Nietzsche's philosophy is very far from insane . . .". (p. 44)

Mencken's presentation then moves on to Nietzsche's first book, *The Birth of Tragedy* . . . , and to the question which Nietzsche attempts to answer there. The question is stated in the preface to the 1886 edition. Mencken accurately summarizes it as: ". . . why [was it] that the ancient Greeks, who were an efficient and vigourous people, living in a green and sunny land, should so delight in gloomy tragedies?" . . . Nietzsche's answer is based on the interaction of two forces, which he named after the gods Apollo and Dionysus.

Mencken correctly sees that Apollo was the god of art . . . , music, poetry, and oratory, and that "under his beneficent sway the Greeks became a race of artists and acquired all the refinement and culture that this implies" . . . , but this generalization does not include a discussion of Nietzsche's concepts of Apollonianism and Dionysianism. (pp. 44-5)

The struggle between Apollo and Dionysus is essential to Nietzsche's thesis, but Mencken shows little awareness of the depth and subtlety of Nietzsche's thinking. He does see the existence of the contest between the two forces, but his statement that "this conflict was the essence of Greek tragedy" . . . needs further elaboration and clarification. Mencken's generalization is essentially correct. . . .

While Mencken saw that many of the ideas in *The Birth of Tragedy* influenced a great deal of Nietzsche's subsequent thought, he did not recognize the extent of Nietzsche's achievement. *The Birth of Tragedy* is more than an interpretation of the Greek view of human existence; it is also a tool to stimulate the reader to contemplate his or her own nature, to recognize that the self is too vast to be understood, to establish an effective and workable relationship between the individual and ultimate reality, and to evaluate cultures, actions, and people. (p. 46)

The limitations of Mencken's understanding of Nietzsche are also shown in his treatment of *Thus Spoke Zarathustra*. As one would expect, his attention focuses upon the *Übermensch* (superman) concept, and he correctly sees that the superman is governed by his will to power (the instinct to live), which demands that the individual focus his attention on reality, himself, others, and his environment, and not speculate on such meaningless and unanswerable problems as why the world exists. While it is true that the superman is more keenly aware of the need to live than others, I question whether one can correctly conclude that the superman's senses, his ability to know the external world, "will give him absolute knowledge about everything that exists on earth," including knowing "exactly *how* a tubercle bacillus attacks the lung tissue . . . *how* the blood fights the bacillus, and . . . *how* to interfere in this battle in such a manner that the blood shall be invariably victorious. In a word, he will be the possessor of exact and complete knowledge regarding the working of all the benign and malignant forces in the world about him." . . . Mencken has overextended the concept of the superman and has presented an erroneous picture of one of Nietzsche's greatest ideas, because Nietzsche never asserted that the superman will have total knowledge and the ability to intervene in such bodily functions as the battle between a bacillus and the antibodies.

Mencken compounds his error when he mistakenly concludes that Nietzsche's idea was to create an aristocracy which regards "the proletariat merely as a conglomeration of draft animals made to be driven, enslaved and exploited." . . . Admittedly, Nietzsche has very little love for the herd, as the section "Of the Rabble" amply demonstrates, but Zarathustra repeatedly says that he loves mankind and is bringing them a gift: freedom of thought and action, means of self-fulfillment, and enjoyment of life and self. This is hardly the attitude of an aristocrat and tyrant, but Mencken correctly sees that Nietzsche's admiration for the superman makes him anything but a democrat.

Mencken had a great deal of difficulty trying to comprehend Nietzsche's doctrine of eternal recurrence, which he interprets as "a cosmic year, corresponding, in some fashion, to the terrestrial year. Man, who has sprung from the elements, will rise into superman, and perhaps infinitely beyond, and then, in the end, by catastrophe or slow decline, he will be resolved into the primary elements again, and the whole process will begin anew." . . . [Mencken] errs in his application of this doctrine to the concept of the superman because, as Nietzsche states in "Of Voluntary Death" in *Thus Spoke Zarathustra,* the superman must die at the right time, that is, when he is at the zenith of his life.

Mencken does not appreciate the importance of the doctrine of eternal recurrence to the body of Nietzsche's thought, and he goes so far as to conclude that "it would have been better for his philosophy and for his repute as an intelligent thinker had he never sought to elucidate it." . . . Admittedly, the idea of eternal repetition seems strange; nevertheless, it is invaluable to Nietzsche because it removes any sense of order or purpose from the universe; God is dead. The doctrine is a key part of Nietzsche's concept of morality; it invests all of human thought and action with supreme importance, since they will exist forever. Nietzsche's injunction is that the individual should so conduct himself or herself, both in action and thought, that he or she will not be afraid or ashamed to have these manifestations of themselves last eternally. Mencken incorrectly concludes that this doctrine is pessimistic . . . ; in fact, Nietzsche has constructed a very useful and optimistic theory which seeks to free people and allow them to live unencumbered by fear and dogma. (pp. 46-8)

At best, Mencken's knowledge of Nietzsche was superficial, and while he was genuinely interested in Nietzsche's concepts, he was unable to remove his own thinking and attitudes from his presentation. As a result, his study is largely a platform from which his own ideas were expounded. Peter Buitenhuis concurs in this conclusion when he says that Mencken "found in Nietzsche the anti-Christianity, the contempt for the herd and the respect for the superman that reflected his own bias. He rejected, however, at least for his own purposes, Nietzsche's metaphysics and circling speculative thinking." Thus, Mencken was not really influenced by Nietzsche but found in him a kindred spirit. This similarity is vividly seen in Mencken's conclusion about Nietsche, and his words there . . . might very well serve as his own epitaph: "Such was his mission, as he conceived it: to attack error wherever he found it. It is only by such iconoclasm and proselyting that humanity can be helped." (p. 49)

Maurice M. LaBelle, "H. L. Mencken's Comprehension of Friedrich Nietzsche," in Comparative Literature Studies *(© 1970 by The Board of Trustees of the University of Illinois), Vol. VII, No. 1, March, 1970, pp. 43-9.*

DOUGLAS C. STENERSON (essay date 1971)

[An American critic and educator with a special interest in Mencken and his era, Stenerson was guest lecturer at the annual Mencken birthday celebration at Baltimore's Enoch Pratt Free Library in 1971, the same year in which he published his H. L. Mencken: Iconoclast from Baltimore. *In the following excerpt from the conclusion to that work, Stenerson offers an informative overview of Mencken's critical theory, examining the influence of his critical forebears and discussing his most important contributions to American culture.]*

Despite the changes which transformed America during Mencken's lifetime, his basic attitudes remained much the same in his maturity as they had been in his youth. His wide-ranging interests, the soundness of his information on many issues, and the common sense with which he treated them were offset, to a considerable extent, by his failure to see any need for modifying his premises. He was no more capable of renouncing the dogmas of "scientism" and social Darwinism, even though they were outmoded by the twenties, than the more sincere of the Fundamentalists he derided were able to renounce theirs. In an age when scientists were developing the theory of relativity and psychologists were exploring the power in human affairs of the instincts and the unconscious mind, his faith in the mechanistic science and the rationalism of the late nineteenth century was itself naive. His opinions on such topics as mysticism and psychical research, though expressed pungently and amusingly, reflect a corresponding naiveté.

Although he delighted in commenting on literature, music, economic and political issues, the social sciences, and the natural sciences, he was not an original or a systematic thinker in any of these fields. His prejudices were the themes of his art, not the building blocks of a coherent system of thought. When viewed as the materials of his art, his ideas take on a unity of mood and emotion generated by the vigor of his style and by the intensity of his commitment to certain values, especially those he associated with the truth-seeker and the gentleman. Scrutinized as the materials of a philosophy, his ideas are baffling in their ambiguity. Just as we think we have grasped the quintessential Mencken, another and contradictory phase of his thought emerges. His theoretical determinism is at odds with his faith in individual initiative, his libertarianism, and his belief that the small group of truth-seekers can bring about at least a limited kind of progress. His social and political views range from conservatism in the manner of William Graham Sumner, at one extreme, to Jeffersonian liberalism and distrust of all government, at the other. On the purportedly scientific ground that Negroes are far behind the whites in the process of evolution, he stereotypes them unfavorably, but he is quick to praise individual Negroes who have vitality and talent. Similarly, he condemns farmers as "Puritans" who want to impose Prohibition and other restraints on city people, but he sees that the struggles and problems of farmers can make moving subject matter for fiction. Politically, despite many shrewd hits and insights, he proved himself as utopian as any of the liberals or radicals to whom he applied that label. He called upon the United States to "invent" a genuine aristocracy, but failed to explain how she could do so.

He professed to be a skeptic even about his own beliefs, but he did not subject them to a truly skeptical analysis. Nevertheless, he had certain qualities which tended to counterbalance his rigid adherence to his prejudices and the contrarieties inherent in them. To begin with, he had a temperamental distrust of all systems and system-makers, and he made no pretence of being consistent except in the matter of expressing forthrightly the opinions which seemed to him most relevant to a particular topic at a particular time. He also had the ability to laugh at himself as well as at others. As an expert in controversy, he welcomed attacks on himself, partly because they showed that his thrusts had gone home, partly because he defended everyone's right to have his say, and partly because he felt that destructive criticism, even of his own work, was much more stimulating than acclaim. "I have learned more from attacks than from praise," he once told Dreiser.

In even the most vicious of them there is a touch or two of plausibility. There is always something embarrassing about unqualified praise. A man knows, down in his heart, that he doesn't deserve it. When he sees all his petty bluffs and affectations accepted seriously, the sole result is to make him lose respect for the victim.

As this statement suggests, Mencken was embarrassed whenever he converted an opponent to his way of thinking. Dogmatic as he was about his own opinions, he admitted the right of others to maintain conflicting views. He admired spunk and spark wherever he discerned them, even though they were present in people whose ideas he detested. In the case of individuals whose integrity as artists he respected, he acknowledged that, if his advice was at variance with their own best insights, they should reject it. . . . (pp. 225-27)

If it were not for Mencken's provincial origins, the dissonant traditions to which he was exposed, and the tensions and ambivalences in his thought, his career might have taken an entirely different direction. Without the stimulus from these sources, he would probably not have entered into that half affectionate, half exasperated, quarrel with America which furnished his major theme and helped create his national reputation. A remark he made about Theodore Roosevelt applied with equal force to himself: "Life fascinated him, and he knew how to make his own doings fascinating to others." His youthful writings reveal two impulses that coalesced and shaped his mature work as artist and critic. The first was the impulse to lash out at the institutions, individuals, and values which he saw as forcing into conformity potential truth-seekers and artists (or members of any other dissident minority). The second was the impulse toward self-expression—"to give outward and objective form to ideas that bubble inwardly and have a fascinating lure.''

In championing the rights and freedoms of an intellectual or artistic minority against the cramping effects of the culture of the majority, Mencken was, of course, by no means unique. In this respect, he belonged in a major tradition in American letters, represented in the nineteenth century by such diverse figures as John Randolph of Roanoke, James Fenimore Cooper, Emerson, Thoreau, Melville, Emily Dickinson, Mark Twain, and Ambrose Bierce, and in the twentieth by many of the authors for whom Mencken had a kindred feeling, including John Macy, Van Wyke Brooks, Dreiser, Ring Lardner, and Sinclair Lewis.

When compared with his contemporaries, Mencken is remarkable, first, for the extent to which his concern with all aspects of the national culture dominated his consciousness and, second, for the great flow of energy he poured into his iconoclasm. The tensions implicit in his ambivalent attitudes toward the American scene provided much of this motive power. On the one hand, he sensed in the ''gorgeous and prodigal'' manifestations of American culture a vitality matching his own. On the other, he was moved to indignation by the discrepancy between the realities he observed about him and his vision of the kind of art, ethics, and personal behavior a society composed exclusively of truth-seekers and artists would produce. Caught up in this process of mutual attraction and repulsion, he developed an omnivorous appetite for all phases of the national life and letters. His iconoclasm, despite his disclaimers, had some reformist overtones, but it took the form mainly of such negative emotions as scorn and humorous disdain for whatever conflicted with his conception of what should be.

A minor paradox here is that, like most iconoclasts and satirists, he would have been extremely unhappy in his own version of Utopia. . . .

Mencken—with nothing in American economics, politics, society, criticism, or art to react against—would have lost his chief joy and main motive as an artist-journalist. His orientation developed out of ''an aesthetic of aggression''—an awareness ''that stimulation comes only by opposition.'' He described his mission in life as ''the tracking down of quacks of all sorts, and the appreciative exhibition of their multifarious tricks to catch coneys.'' Of his own writing, he said, ''It always seeks to expose a false pretence, to blow up a wobbly axiom, to uncover a sham virtue.'' . . . (pp. 227-29)

Literary journalism was the main workshop in which the writers of Mencken's generation studied their craft. In wanting to develop an individual style capable of dramatizing his impressions, Mencken was like many of his colleagues with literary interests. With that aim in mind, he carefully pondered the essays of Thomas Huxley, whose ability to deal lucidly with difficult subjects he never ceased to admire. At various times, he took as his models the works of Thackeray, Kipling, Shaw, O. Henry, Mark Twain, Ambrose Bierce, and George Ade. His style inevitably reflected both the strengths and weaknesses of the kind of training he received in the hurly-burly of daily journalism. The *New York Sun* . . . helped him to learn to see the life about him and to interpret it vividly, much as novelist like Crane, Norris, and Dreiser had learned to do during their newspaper experience. The *New York Sun* editorials also encouraged him to attack those he regarded as frauds and mountebanks, but to bring good sense and good humor to the process. The same paper had its bad effects ''because,'' as he commented many years afterward, ''it showed a considerable artificiality of style, and made me over-estimate the value of smart phrases.'' He never completely succeeded in suppressing the impulse to use the smart phrase rather than one more apt or just. Another part of his apprenticeship was learning to write quickly and copiously in order to meet deadlines—a virtue in a newspaper writer but not necessarily in a literary or social critic.

His newspaper experience left an indelible mark on his personal attitudes. Throughout his working life, he cherished his concept of newspapermen, especially those he had known in his youth, as a privileged group who observed the human comedy from the front row and could say pretty much what they pleased about it, providing they had a style which would attract as well as startle readers. He looked upon himself as a newspaperman before all else, with magazine editing and literary criticism in second place.

As illustrated by his reviewing for *The Smart Set,* literary journalism had still another significance: it was the major channel through which the spirit of the moral and literary revolt of the nineties was transmitted to the twenties. With his efforts sometimes paralleling and sometimes differing from those of bohemian critics like Huneker and Pollard, he exerted a major influence in bringing about the transition between the two periods. The fixity with which he held to his basic premises accentuates the fact that the eighties and nineties, not the twenties, shaped his attitudes. Through denunciation and ridicule similar to those in the more extreme of the little magazines of the nineties, he publicized the dangers of literary commercialism and defied the genteel tradition, with its insistence that American letters should be predominantly ''Anglo-Saxon,'' optimistic, and morally uplifting. By discussing and urging his audience to read authors like Ibsen and Shaw, Pinero and Wilde, Sudermann and Hauptmann, Zola and Wells, Mark Twain and Norris, Crane and Dreiser, he helped popularize the idea that art and artists are important and that one function of art may legitimately be to question accepted axioms and standards. In these ways he assisted in creating a climate of opinion which once again made a moderate degree of revolt possible. By attacking hypocrisy, puritanism, philistinism, and censorship, and pointing out the need for a new national ethic, he suggested the form the moral rebellion might take and what it might seek to accomplish. By stressing the tradition of Norris, Crane, and Dreiser and calling on American writers to challenge the shibboleths of the native culture and deal realistically or satirically with the life they knew, he indicated the goals he hoped the literary uprising would attain. (pp. 229-30)

No matter how much understanding is brought to bear upon a study of Mencken, he will always remain a controversial figure. Because of the wide range of his interests, the tensions and contradictions in his thought, his intermingling of humor with contentiousness and dogmatism, and the multiplicity of roles he assumed as journalist, literary critic, social and political commentator, and scholar, he inevitably invites a wide range of responses. Those who dismiss him as a ''mere'' journalist or a third-rate disciple of Shaw and Nietzsche greatly underestimate his importance, while those who rank him with Swift and Voltaire probably unduly exaggerate it. . . . [It] is fair to ask one final question: what were his most enduring contributions to American culture?

On balance, the two aspects of his work which seem most durable are his libertarianism—his affirmation of the right to dissent—and the gusto and artistry with which he expresses it.

The evils he attacked on behalf of "common decency" take different forms today than they did in the twenties, but they still exist, as they have in every age. While recognizing that many of his principles were basically conservative and that those he brought to his iconoclastic mission were not fully thought out, one may yet hope that America will continue to produce rebels as determined and able as he. Although he often indulged in stereotyping and namecalling, he usually did so with a characteristic humor which warned the reader not to be completely taken in. By and large, his weapons were those he urged the young southerners to wield in their fight against the old tradition—the "weapons of sound information, of common sense, of good taste, of lively wit, of ready humor." His style conveys his delight in combat, his sense of exhilaration at "dancing with arms and legs" in defiance of the multitude. "The unimaginative and ignoble man," he maintained, "likes the grayness, as a worm likes the dark; he wants to be made secure in his wallow; he craves certainties to protect him—a simple and gross religion, safety for his precious money, no wild ideas to craze his wife, Prohibition, the rope for agitators, no bawdy twanging of lyres. It is the business of the artist to blast his contentment with the sounds of joy." At his best, Mencken performed this function supremely well. The "bawdy twanging" of his own lyre is his legacy to America. (pp. 234-35)

Douglas C. Stenerson, in his H. L. Mencken: Iconoclast from Baltimore *(reprinted by permission of The University of Chicago Press and the author; © 1971 by The University of Chicago), University of Chicago Press, 1971, 287 p.*

KURT VONNEGUT, JR. (essay date 1976)

[*Vonnegut is an American writer of darkly comic fiction that reflects his essential compassion for humanity and his complete pessimism. He rose to prominence during the 1960s with such works as* Mother Night *(1961),* Cat's Cradle *(1963), and* Slaughterhouse Five *(1969), which is considered his best novel to-date. His novels and short stories, which frequently contain elements of science fiction, satirize human stupidity, short-sightedness, and brutality, assailing in particular humanity's tendency towards warfare and the worship of automation. Vonnegut is considered by some critics to be, in outlook and style, a direct literary descendent of Mark Twain. In the following excerpt, Vonnegut briefly compares the lives and works of Twain and Mencken.*]

A single modern American writer has seemed on occasion like a true son of Twain to me. He is the late Henry Louis Mencken . . . , who, like Twain, grew up in a border state, had a technical background, was not a college graduate, and who was taught to write by newspaper men.

All these shared circumstances tended to make both men irreverent about so-called spiritual matters and conventional patriotism, I think. But their most admirable similarity was their genius for perceiving and exploiting the American language's peculiar powers to surprise and amuse. If a writer does not have such genius, and it is rare, then he cannot be a true follower of Mark Twain.

Mencken's masterpiece, incidentally, is a scholarly work entitled, simply enough, ***The American Language.*** (p. xiv)

Mencken's reputation does not continue to bloom as Twain's does. Little about Twain's work seems dated now, save for his pre-Freudian innocence about sexual matters, which only makes him more beguiling. But a lot of Mencken seems narrowly and crankily political now.

And he wrote no fiction. Fiction just might have done for Mencken what it did for Twain—just might have given his often outrageous prejudices the semblance of being universal. (pp. xiv-xv)

Kurt Vonnegut, Jr., "Opening Remarks," in The Unabridged Mark Twain *by Mark Twain, edited by Lawrence Teacher (copyright © 1976 Running Press; reprinted by permission of Running Press, Philadelphia), Running Press, 1976, pp. xi-xv.**

ALISTAIR COOKE (essay date 1980)

[*Cooke is known and respected worldwide as one of the most perceptive and eloquent popular interpreters of American life and history. English by birth and an American citizen since 1941, Cooke began his journalistic career in America, first as a correspondent for* The Times *of London and later as chief U.S. correspondent for* The Guardian, *a position he held for 24 years. Since 1938 he has also delivered a weekly broadcast for the B.B.C., "Letter from America." Cooke is best known to Americans for his award-winning television series "America: A Personal History of the United States," upon which is based his popular book* Alistair Cooke's America. *Cooke was a friend of Mencken and edited* The Vintage Mencken, *a collection of the "Sage of Baltimore's" most notable essays. In the following excerpt, Cooke writes of the technique and style that made Mencken a major force in American letters.*]

When Mencken published the parent volume of ***The American Language,*** he unwittingly gave a fillip to the sagging chauvinism of his countrymen in the collapse of the Coolidge prosperity. He seemed to be saying that even if the economy, which had been vaunted throughout the 1920s as a uniquely self-sustaining system, had gone the way of all other previous economies, it was time to assert that the United States had developed, in three hundred years, a language that was not a variant dialect of the mother tongue but a separate offshoot more inventive and vigorous than its parent. (p. 84)

Mencken did not defend his new thesis (about the strong viability of American) by quoting—so far as I can discover—any of the new vernacular writers who had come up since he unloosed his first blast against the genteel tradition in 1920. It is curious that he should have admitted to ***The American Language*** barely a mention of Sinclair Lewis, James M. Cain, James T. Farrell, Theodore Dreiser, or the other new young realists that he had encouraged and launched in the *Smart Set* and the *American Mercury*.

But there was no contradiction between his bemoaning the "marshmallow gentility" of American literature in 1920 and his apparent salute in 1930 to the arrival of a native literature independent of the literary Establishment of England. The strictures of . . . [dissenting] English critics were based in a misunderstanding of Mencken's thesis, which was about *language,* not the literature that might one day grow from it. The whole of ***The American Language*** is a prolonged demonstration of the fact that the Americans, in a three-hundred-year experience of a new landscape, new crops, new climates, a new society, and the melding of many immigrant languages and ways of life, had developed institutions, foods, habits, relationships that coined thousands of new nouns, adjectives, and—in their speech—even new syntactical forms. It was, in fact, a new dialect at least as different from British English as the language of Brazil is different from that of Portugal or the Spanish of

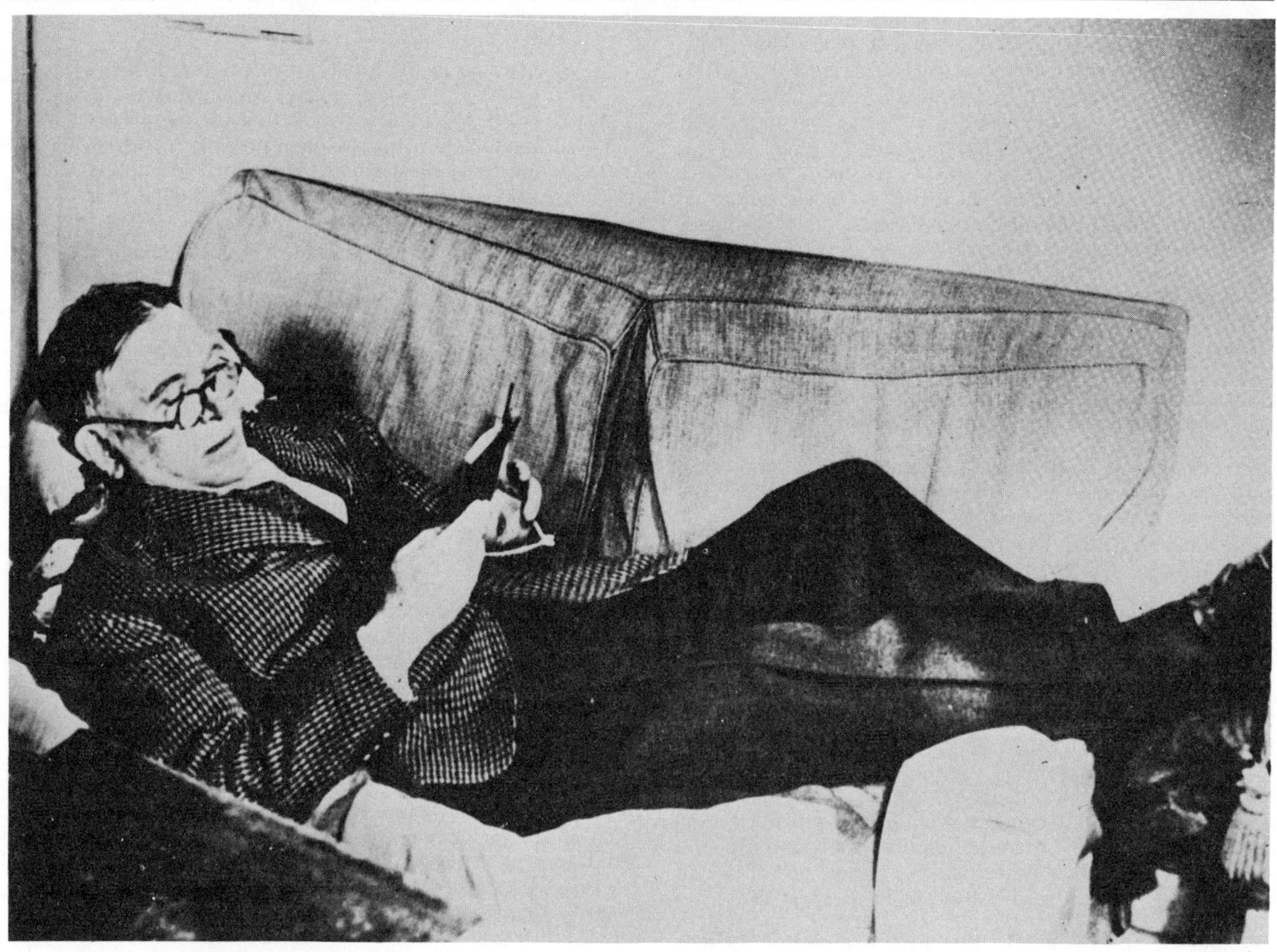

Mencken at home (1942). Reproduced by permission of the Enoch Pratt Free Library, in accordance with the will of H. L. Mencken.

Mexico from that of Spain. But Mencken pushed his argument too far in his frequent assertions that American English was altogether more robust and virile than the English of England. (pp. 85-6)

The truth is that till the day he died, Mencken's own style, while it may be more pungent and outrageous than that of his English contemporaries, is hardly different in any particular of vocabulary, syntax, or cadence from that of the prevailing English models. Indeed, it often struck his English contemporaries as being rather behind their time, a powerful and verbose variation on the invective style of Bernard Shaw.

Consider, for instance, the language of Mencken's first and most famous blast at the condition of American literature in his 1920 essay **"The National Letters,"** published in the second series of ***Prejudices***. . . . Apart from the mention of such institutions as the Knights of Pythias and the *Saturday Evening Post,* there is practically nothing here to indicate that we are reading an American, and not an English, critic. "Technic" for technique and "toward" for towards are tiny giveaways. "When one proceeds from such agencies and externals" could be Emerson. The verbosity, which English critics complained of when Mencken was published in England in the 1920s, takes the form of an accumulation of almost tautological adjectives. Shaw, for instance, could never have written: "In all that mass of suave and often highly diverting writing there is no visible movement toward a distinguished and singular excellence, a signal national quality, a ripe and stimulating flavor." He would most likely have pared it down to: "In all that mass of often highly diverting writing there is no sign of a distinctive American character."

Mencken was in his fortieth year when he wrote this passage. And in a year or two he would be in his early prime. I doubt he would ever again write anything so sustained which failed to give off a single vivid analogy, or some outlandishly funny simile, or some other hint that we were in the presence of an original. Toward the end of his life, he had this to say about his early apprenticeship: "My early writing was pretty bad, and it always makes me uncomfortable, on looking into an old clipping-book, to remember that this or that piece was regarded as well done at the time it was written . . . my model in those days was the old New York *Sun,* and especially its editorial page. This model was both good and bad—good because it taught me that good sense was at the bottom of all good writing, but bad because it showed a considerable artificiality of style, and made me overestimate the value of smart phrases."

He is talking, of course, of his earliest newspaper writing. But the same, and more, may be said about his early books, on Nietzsche and Shaw. For a time, his prose, whenever it was concerned with ideas rather than with reported events, was an earnest, almost a sweating, parody of iconoclasts both dead and alive that he particularly admired: Macaulay, Shaw, Nietzsche, worst of all Ambrose Bierce. A great deal of his first volume of ***Prejudices*** . . . is heavy going. Of course, it has already achieved command of a diverse and thoroughly disciplined vocabulary and it has great driving force. But it is the energy of a railway engine and not yet that of a racehorse spanking along down the stretch. It cries for drastic editing. It didn't get it only, I suppose, because Mencken was obviously superior to his rivals in invective writing.

It will be obvious by now what this essay is about and what it is not. I am not discussing Mencken's incomparable three volumes on ***The American Language*** but his handling of the English language: what it was that made him the first master craftsman of American journalism in the twentieth century; what makes him still, in a word, inimitable.

The key to his originality lies, I think, not in his chronological growth, in the time when pieces were written, so much as in the sort of piece he was writing. Compare, for example . . . , **"The National Letters"** with his overnight obituary of William Jennings Bryan written in 1925. . . . (pp. 86-91)

[The latter] is as highly wrought as his lament for the National Letters, and I imagine that a few years later he would have shed such sophomoric jocosities as *Musca domestica* (for housefly) and *Homo neandertalensis* (for Neanderthal man). But it is alive with metaphors and images that could have been written by nobody but Mencken: "with coo and bellow," "the bilge of idealism," "wives . . . fecund as the shad," "winding his horn," "the cockney gallery," "debauched by the refinements of the toilet," "cocks crowing on the dunghill." And his picture of an Old Testament primitive is wonderfully reinforced by such Biblical echoes as "the powers and principalities of the air" and "since Johann fell to Herod's ax."

The main thing to notice is that this was a piece written in haste to a deadline. It was a condition that may have left Mencken no time to suppress or moderate the strain of cruelty in him, but it testifies to a characteristic of the best journalists: the heat of the deadline fires their truest talents, galvanizes their wits, as the leisure of a plotted essay can never do. (p. 93)

I can imagine, for another instance, Mencken sitting down some time to deplore the vulgarity, the sentimentality and the narcissism of the motion-picture industry. He expressed his loathing of what we now call show business in many an acid aside. But nothing he wrote on the subject has the force, the persuasiveness and—I might add—the touching simplicity, of his account of a dinner with Rudolph Valentino a week or so before the latter's fatal illness. . . . I am saying, I think, that Mencken was only a second-rate philosopher when he came to do a set piece, but that he was a wiser and a better writer as a journalist, and as such an original. Like all originals, he was a bad master. By which I mean that he is a dangerous model for authors of lesser talent. (pp. 95-9)

Throughout the 1920s Mencken reveled in his talent, but he reveled just as much, I believe, in the propagandist role that he assigned to himself, which was simplified by his worshipers into that of a Daniel come to judgment, and was twisted even more by the general public into the role of a radical public scold. The fireworks of this reputation bedazzled his public and blinded it to what was best in him as a writer. I have tried to clarify this point elsewhere (in my preface to the collection called ***The Vintage Mencken***) and since I cannot say it better, I will beg pardon for quoting the gist of it again:

> What has stood the test of time and the exhaustion of the Mencken cult is not, it seems to me, his orderly essays on religion or his healthy but noisy crusade against the genteel tradition; it is his passing reflections on the sex uproar of the twenties; his reports of political conventions and the (Dayton) evolution trial; an evening with Valentino, the memory of a minor revolution in Cuba . . . indeed, much of what book-writers with one foot already in obscurity call 'transient' journalism. The one prepared indictment that keeps its clarion freshness through the years is that against the plutocracy. This may be because every time the United States is launched on a new prosperity, the plutocrats take to the bridge again to dictate our values while the country-club guests reappear to set the tone of our sea-going manners. . . . Looking over the whole range of his work today, we can see that if he was overrated in his day as a thinker . . . he was vastly under rated as a humorist with one deadly sensible eye on the behavior of the human animal. He helped along this misconception by constantly reminding people that he was 'a critic of ideas,' which was true only as the ideas were made flesh. He was, in fact, a humorist by instinct and a superb craftsman by temperament."
>
> (pp. 100-01)

[All] humorists—before they develop a craft—must have a character trait to work on. In Mencken, this was a gift for maintaining a sweet temper at the precise moment that his victim—especially during a public argument—was beginning to fly off the handle. (pp. 104-05)

Mencken made [his victims] ridiculous and did it in good temper, as if their absurdity were subject, some other time, to mathematical proof. In other words, the secret of his best and most characteristic invective is the control of his blood pressure. In his later work, the control is invisible, and what we have, instead of ringing, if merry, denunciation, is a kind of irony so rounded that it appears to be almost a species of tribute. We forget, if we ever knew, that Mencken never ceased to work on his writing and, as he grew older, purified it very strikingly. Compare the rolling derision of his obituary on Bryan with his obituary on Coolidge written in 1933. . . . Even glanced at on the page, this looks much less dense than Mencken's earlier writing. The sentences are shorter. There are few double adjectives. The subject hits the verbs at once without subsidiary qualifications. The mood turns easily on familiar idioms and connectives. It works up not to a peroration but a simple, blank epitaph. To my mind, it is a more memorable piece of writing than the Bryan obituary, for all its majestic drum-rolling and its funny fury.

It will be plain from this . . . , I think, that a man who is honing the grammar of a phrase, and carefully steering the cadence of a sentence, is going to hit his target with more devilish precision than a man who explodes at his enemies through bloodshot prose. The calm choice of a single epithet in Mencken can persuade us into believing a palpable untruth. Witness his—frankly ridiculous—remark on why he does not believe in democracy. "No doubt," he wrote, with mock simplicity, "my distaste for democracy is . . . like every other human prejudice, due to an inner lack. In this case it is very probably my incapacity for envy. . . . In the face of another man's good fortune, I am as inert as a curb broker before Johann Sebastian Bach." In one sentence, Rockefeller's millions have been earned at the expense of an ear for music, and the stock exchange is consigned to the stupid ward of a mental hospital. All because of the cool choice of the word "inert." (pp. 105-07)

Intellectual clowns are wits, and Mencken could certainly be witty. But he was also, and I maintain more remarkably, a humorist, and all humorists are professional mountebanks. They instinctively (when they are good) and deliberately (when they are bad) adopt an attitude toward the facts of life that is more naive than that of their audience. This puts the audience in a superior frame of mind, which is the proper frame for the agreeable form of compassion known as laughter. However, the laughter would remain in its pure state of pity if the humorist were really naive. He is, in fact, sharper than his audience. But the successful technique of humor demands that he should throw furtive hints of intelligence to his readers, as if they were his only allies in a world of oafs. The circuit of flattery is now complete. The audience begins by chuckling at the simpleness of the writer and goes on to laugh in triumph at the sudden discovery that they and he alone form a secret society of mockers at the great mass of men. (pp. 107-08)

[Mencken's] most effective personal technique is one that combines an affected naiveté with the pose of a conscientious reporter of absurd events. He used this brilliantly at presidential conventions, where he employed a portentous vocabulary on people who, in life, took themselves portentously but whom Mencken turns into comic characters. (p. 110)

So what we have unveiled at the end is a humorist in the classic American tradition, about halfway between Mark Twain and Woody Allen. Aside from his tribute to the lasting effect on him of *Huckleberry Finn,* Mencken has left us almost nothing about the writers who excited him to imitation, apart from his aforementioned early apeings of Shaw and Nietzsche and Bierce. But on the last page of the last book he published (***Minority Report***) he has something revealing to say about an early idol, to whom he reverted in later life:

> I am still convinced that the prose of Thomas Henry Huxley was the best produced by an Englishman in the Nineteenth Century. He always put clarity first. . . . The imbeciles who have printed acres of comment on my books have seldom noticed the chief character of my style. It is that I write with almost scientific precision—that my meaning is never obscure. The ignorant have often complained that my vocabulary is beyond them, but that is simply because my ideas cover a wider range than theirs do. Once they have consulted the dictionary they always know exactly what I intend to say. I am as far as any writer can get from the muffled sonorities of, say, John Dewey.
>
> (pp. 112-13)

[There] is enough in his own pronouncement of T. H. Huxley as a model, and the abundant witness of his later work (his autobiographical masterpiece, ***Happy Days,*** especially) to show that Mencken himself moved toward a similar ideal of what he took to be good writing. (p. 113)

Alistair Cooke, "Mencken and the English Language," in On Mencken, *edited by John Dorsey (copyright © 1980 by Alfred A. Knopf, Inc.; reprinted by permission of the publisher), Knopf, 1980, pp. 84-113.*

JAMES J. KILPATRICK (essay date 1981)

[In the following excerpt, Kilpatrick—a nationally syndicated political columnist and one of Mencken's heirs in his propensity for clever invective, pugnaciousness, and political conservatism—discusses Mencken's style. Kilpatrick's essay was originally a speech delivered at the Mencken Memorial Lecture, which was held at the Enoch Pratt Free Library in Baltimore on September 12, 1981—the 101st anniversary of Mencken's birth.

What ails so many writers, [Mencken] said, "is not defective technical equipment but a defective natural equipment. They write badly simply because they cannot think clearly. They cannot think clearly because they lack the brains. . . . What is in the head infallibly oozes out of the nub of the pen. If it is sparkling Burgundy, the writing is full of life and charm. If it is mush, the writing is mush too." . . .

Mencken's main point, in brief, is that "style cannot go beyond the ideas which lie at the heart of it. If they are clear, it too will be clear. If they are held passionately, it will be eloquent."

None of us here this afternoon will doubt that Mencken had ideas. He had ideas about men, women, senators, and Southerners. He had ideas about beer and Beethoven, crime and punishment, medicine, economics, theology, literature, and poetry. Except for a couple of pieces on the prize fight between Dempsey and Carpentier—both of them lame efforts—his ***Chrestomathy*** reflects no ideas on sport. I suspect he had little interest in the games men play. But he had ideas on everything else.

The question before the house is, how did Mencken express these ideas? What can we list among the elements of his style? What made his writing so distinctive that no informed reader could fail to identify Mencken's authorship after reading fifty to one hundred words of his prose? (p. 3)

Mencken himself disclosed the key to his style in his lovely essay on **"The Critical Process,"** in the third ***Prejudices*** of 1922. Here he spoke of "the almost universal human susceptibility to messianic delusions," and he delivered himself of a line I have quoted a hundred times. Most of us yield to what he termed "the irresistible tendency of practically every man, once he finds a crowd in front of him, to strut and to roll his eyes."

I suggest to you that in the exercise of that tendency, we find the very essence of the Mencken style. He was full of bluster, bravado, and bombast. He delighted, as they say, in showing off befo' God. For Mencken, writing for the Sunpapers was like playing the Palace; he was the Eddie Foy, Jimmy Durante, and W. C. Fields of journalism, juggling words, twirling rhetorical canes, winding up his pieces with a spectacular buck and wing. He wrote with a twinkle in his eye. As Pegler observed, Mencken was a smart-ass.

But Pegler's modifying superlative went to the heart of the matter. Mencken, he said, was the *smartest* smart-ass he had ever known. If there had been nothing more to Mencken's writing that bluster, bravado, and bombast, we would not be celebrating his work today. Underlying the vaudeville was the discipline that marks every great entertainer. At bottom were the ideas—the original, outrageous, provocative, enchanting ideas that bubbled incessantly within him. And with the ideas were the means to express them—the prodigious vocabulary, the vast reading in different fields, the tools that he fashioned from his insatiable curiosity about men and institutions.

Thus equipped, Mencken put his belly to the typewriter. I think he provides an exception to Dr. Johnson's maxim that no one but a blockhead ever wrote, except for money. This was seldom Mencken's motive. Neither was his motive to teach. The motive of a critic, he said, "is not the motive of the pedagogue, but the motive of the artist." (p. 4)

All of us will recall Mencken's long association with Dreiser, whose novels he regularly reviewed. But was he engaged in reviewing the ideas of Mr. Dreiser? Not at all. "My motive," he said, "well known to Mr. Dreiser himself and to everyone else who knew me as intimately as he did, was simply and solely to sort out and give coherence to the ideas of Mr. Mencken, and to discharge them with a flourish, and maybe with a phrase of pretty song into the dense fog that blanketed the Republic."

For Mencken, his role was "first and last, simply trying to express himself." He was trying "to arrest and challenge a sufficient body of readers, to make them pay attention to him, to impress them with the charm and novelty of his ideas, to provoke them into an agreeable (or shocked) awareness of him." Such a critic, he said, "is trying to achieve thereby for his own inner ego the grateful feeling of a function performed, a tension relieved, a *katharsis* attained which Wagner achieved when he wrote 'Die Walküre,' and a hen achieves every time she lays an egg." (pp. 4-5)

In the expression of [his] ideas, Mencken devised tricks of style as distinctive as the trills of Mozart and the chords of Debussy. You can no more miss his touch than you can miss the hand of Strauss behind a waltz.

In a mood of mockery—a mood in which he spent much of his professional life—Mencken was addicted to the satirical honorific. It was "Dr." Hoover and "Dr. Harding," "the late Calvin Coolidge, L.L.D." and "The Hon. A. Mitchell Palmer." The extravagances of parliamentary speech were perfectly suited to the Menckenian satire. The more he laid on the titles of respect, the more he winged his targets. (p. 5)

Looking at Mencken's style in the fashion of a graphologist, charting the downstrokes and curlicues of penmanship, we also would note the dog-Latin thrown in for effect. In an obituary on William Jennings Bryan, Mencken noted that the deceased had a little-noted skill. Bryan could catch flies bare-handed. He was, said Mencken, "the most sedulous flycatcher in American history, and in many ways the most successful." But Bryan's quarry, of course, "was not *Musca domestica* but *Homo neandertalensis*." Mencken invented the genus, or perhaps the species, of *Homo cooligensis*. He invented *Homo boobiens* and *Boobus americanus*. Writing on evolution, he felt compelled to identify the organ grinder's monkey as *Cebus capichinus*. To the fundamentalists, Clarence Darrow was not merely a chimpanzee; he is a pig (*Sus scrofa*), a jackal (*Canis aureus*), and a rat (*Mus rattus*). There were times, as I say, that our hero loved to show off befo' God.

A part of the Mencken style lies in the use of grand and sweeping exaggerations. One manifestation may be found in Macaulay's omniscient schoolboy, born again.

> The female sex, as everyone knows, has a great talent for martyrdom.
>
> Everyone knows how the right to free speech has been invaded.

(pp. 5-6)

What everyone knows—everyone who knows Mencken, that is—is that Dr. Mencken was a great kidder.

He was also a man of great enthusiasms and almost infinite antipathies. His flowers and weeds could not be classified botanically as annuals. They were perennials; they came up every year—enthusiasm for Dreiser, for *Huckleberry Finn,* for the symphonies and string quartets of Beethoven, for honest beer. His antipathies were more extensive—so extensive that they became elements of his style. Mencken had much in common with that peer made famous by Johnson, the Dear Bathurst who was a man to his very heart's content: "He hated a fool, and he hated a rogue, and he hated a whig; he was a very good hater." Mencken's fundamentally cheerful nature made him immune from actual *hatred,* but a list of his targets could go on and on.

At random, culled from every tenth page of the ***Chrestomathy,*** Mencken took aim upon politicians, bishops, Holy Rollers, Christian Scientists, Methodists, Baptists, Presbyterians, and evangelicals of high and low degree. He belabored Comstocks, chiropractors, prohibitionists, chautauqua orators, charity mongers, drive managers, YMCA secretaries, executive secretaries, town boomers, Rotarians, Kiwanians, Boomers, and Elks. He scorned bank presidents, tin roofers, delicatessen dealers, retired bookkeepers, nose and throat specialists, railroad purchasing agents, and the National Association of Teachers of English.

More broadly, the Menckenian blunderbuss sprayed powder and shot upon fools, yokels, half-wits, ignoramuses, dunderheads, scoundrels, lunatics, morons, rogues, charlatans, mountebanks, imbeciles, barbarians, vagabonds, clowns, fanatics, idiots, bunglers, hacks, quacks, and wowsers. He especially loathed the wowser. "We are run by wowsers," he complained, "and wowser is an Australian word that I hereby formally nominate for inclusion in the American language. What does it mean? It means precisely what you think of inevitably when you hear it. A wowser is a wowser. He bears a divine commission to regulate and improve the rest of us. He knows exactly what is best for us. He is what E. W. Howe calls a Good Man. So long as you and I are sinful he can't sleep. So long as we are happy he is after us."

Mencken had favorite words. We all have them, but he fondled a few beauties as if he were collecting coins or stamps. He was seldom content to say of an idea, a speech, or a book that the thing was inferior. No. It was balderdash, it was rubbish, it was bilge. He doted on *brummagem,* which the OED traces to 1691 as a form of counterfeit goods made in Birmingham. And if an offensive item were not brummagem, it was bogus, it was nonsense, it was buncombe, it was sham. As for honest goods, he hailed them with whoops and hosannahs.

I am running out of steam, and would touch upon only one or two more characteristics of the Mencken style. Except when he sought deliberately to slow the pace of his rush of ideas, he stuck with active verbs and avoided the passive voice. He wrote of the postwar Socialists who recanted their Marxism, saw a great light, "and began to bawl and sob for the flag." He sympathized with the thousands of young Kansas conscripts who were "yanked from the plow and the manure fork."

Curiously, his writing relied little upon metaphor or simile. In a hundred pages I found few really notable examples. His comparisons tended toward self-deprecation: "I knew little more about Havelock Ellis, as a man, than I knew about the Grand Lama of Tibet.'' And again, ''I have no more talent for music than a cow.'' And though Mencken's reading was astoundingly eclectic in poetry, drama, and the classics, I note few allusions or quotations to buttress or adorn his prose. Out of the few days of casual reading that preceded my remarks this afternoon, I recall only a passing reference to Hamlet's ''pale cast of thought.'' Mencken needed no injections of manufactured soda; he foamed and bubbled on his own.

But at one technique of writing, our Sage excelled. He was a master of what is known in the editorial writing trade as the cracker, or the sting—the final sentence in an essay. . . . It is the last word, often a one-syllable word possessed of a diphthong or a long vowel, or with one of those glottal phonemes that go off with the finality of a mouse trap. Such sentences have the beauty of a perfect fast ball, centering in the catcher's mitt with an absolutely satisfying smack.

I think of Mencken's lecture at Columbia in 1940, which ended with a recounting of the cynical admonition of a long-time observer of Washington politics. '' 'In politics,' he said, 'man must learn to rise above principle.' Then he drove it in. 'When the water reaches the upper deck,' he said, 'follow the rats.' '' (pp. 6-7)

There are twenty chapters in ***Happy Days.*** Only four of them slide polysyllabically to an end. Others end with such snaps as *God, heat, mop, out, indeed, games, gone,* and *end.* You find the same technique in ***Heathen Days.*** Observe, if you will, how Mencken fashioned the final paragraph of his hilarious account of the night his music club set out to play the symphonies of Beethoven: ''If we actually played the eight symphonies, then no other group of Tonkünstler has ever done it. And if we only tried, then no one else has ever tried.'' . . .

One more thought. Mencken had an intuitive—and doubtless a highly cultivated—sense of cadence. . . . In the final sentence of his piece in ***Newspaper Days,*** remarking his irritation at having to wait in ticket lines: ''It seems to me an intolerable affront, not ON-ly TO my PRI-vate POMP and CIR-cum-STANCE, but AL-so TO the HON-or OF the FOURTH es-TATE.'' Pure iambic, and deliberately so. (p. 8)

If Bierce was ''the first man to lay about him with complete gusto,'' Mencken was certainly the second. He too had no more discretion than a runaway locomotive, and this afternoon we toast his roguish and venerable shade for the pleasure of his prose. . . .

He left us not only his serious works in philology and religion, and not only the most delightful autobiographical memoirs in American literature, but something more besides. He left us the crash of glass in the china shop of brummagem ideas. He left us the better and wiser for the healthy skepticism of his life and work. There was, he acknowledged, a ''certain ribaldry'' in his writings, but he never apologized for it. . . .

If much of his writing was vaudeville, it was great vaudeville. He left us laughing. In the gathering gloom of our vanishing century, who could ask for anything more? (p. 10)

James J. Kilpatrick, ''The Writer Mencken'' (reprinted by permission of the author; originally a lecture delivered at the Enoch Pratt Free Library on September 12, 1981), in Menckeniana, *No. 79, Fall, 1981, pp. 2-10.*

ADDITIONAL BIBLIOGRAPHY

Babcock, C. Merton. ''Mark Twain, Mencken, and 'The Higher Goofyism'.'' *American Quarterly* XVI, No. 4 (Winter 1964): 587-94.*
Compares the humor and vision of Mencken and Twain.

Bode, Carl. *Mencken.* Carbondale and Edwardsville: Southern Illinois University Press, 1969, 452 p.
Detailed and complete biography of Mencken.

Chesterton, G. K. ''On Mr. Mencken and Fundamentalism.'' In his *All Is Grist: A Book of Essays,* pp. 58-64. New York: Dodd, Mead and Co., 1932.
Jibes at Mencken's prejudices in the field of science.

——. ''Nothing to Shout About.'' *The Listener* XII, No. 307 (28 November 1934): 921.*
A lighthearted review which dismisses Mencken's *Treatise on Right and Wrong* as the work of an intellectual pretender. Chesterton writes: ''This is an excellent book to be recommended to all intelligent and instructed readers; partly because intelligent and instructed readers will not believe a word of it.''

Cooke, Alistair. ''An Introduction to H. L. Mencken.'' In *The Vintage Mencken,* by H. L. Mencken, edited by Alistair Cooke, pp. v-xii. New York: Vintage Books, 1955.
A short, valuable biographical and critical summary of Mencken's life and work.

——. ''H. L. Mencken: The Public and the Private Face.'' In his *Six Men,* pp. 83-117. New York: Alfred A. Knopf, 1977.
Personal reminiscences which recount, in part, Mencken's humorous antics at the 1948 Progressive Party convention.

Cowley, Malcolm. ''Mencken: The Former Fugleman.'' In his *Think Back on Us . . . A Contemporary Chronicle of the 1930s,* edited by Henry Dan Piper, pp. 70-4. Carbondale and Edwardsville: Southern Illinois University Press, 1967.
Reprints a 1934 essay attacking Mencken as an anti-Semite and an antilabor bigot.

Dorsey, John, ed. *On Mencken.* New York: Alfred A. Knopf, 1980, 313 p.
A collection of critical and biographical essays by several noted critics, including Huntington Cairns, William H. Nolte, Carl Bode, and Alistair Cooke (see excerpt above, 1980). Compiled for the Mencken centennial, the essays are interspersed with selections from Mencken's own writings.

Farrell, James T. ''Personal Memories of H. L. Mencken.'' *The New Leader* XXXIX, No. 7 (13 February 1956):7.
A sad, thoughtful tribute to Mencken.

Fitzgerald, F. Scott. ''How to Waste Material: A Note on My Generation.'' *The Bookman,* New York LXIII, No. 3 (May 1926): 262-65.*
Cites Mencken as one of the writers responsible for what Fitzgerald perceives as a stagnant period in American fiction, when critics ''manufactured enthusiasm when each new mass of raw data was dumped on the literary platform—mistaking incoherence for vitality, chaos for vitality.'' While praising Mencken as the one who ''has done more for American letters than any man alive,'' Fitzgerald disparaged his influence on other, less perceptive critics, a group he describes as ''a family of hammer and tongs men—insensitive, suspicious of glamour, preoccupied exclusively with the external, the contemptible, the 'national' and the drab, whose style was a debasement of [Mencken's] least effective manner and who, like glib children, played continually with his themes in his maternal shadow.''

Geismar, Maxwell. ''H. L. Mencken: On the Dock.'' In his *The Last of the Provincials: The American Novel, 1915-1925,* pp. 3-66. London: Secker & Warburg, 1947.
A balanced, important biographical and critical examination of Mencken's life and work, and of his effect on American culture.

Hobson, Fred C. *Serpent in Eden: H. L. Mencken and the South.* Baton Rouge: Louisiana State University Press, 1974.

Examines the effect of Mencken's essay "The Sahara of the Bozart" on the development of Southern literature. As part of his exposition, Hobson reprints some of the more inflammable quotations from *Menckeniana: A Schimpflexikon* as well as many excerpts from Mencken's correspondence.

Kemler, Edgar. *The Irreverent Mr. Mencken.* Boston: Little, Brown and Co., 1950, 317 p.

A useful critical portrait of Mencken.

Manchester, William. *Disturber of the Peace: The Life of H. L. Mencken.* New York: Harper & Brothers Publishers, 1950, 336 p.

The authorized biography.

Martin, Edward A. "H. L. Mencken's Poetry." *Texas Studies in Literature and Language* VI, No. 3 (Autumn 1964): 346-53.

Examines Mencken's poetic sensibility as revealed in *Ventures into Verse* and in the syntax of his prose.

Nathan, George Jean. "H. L. Mencken." In his *The World of George Jean Nathan,* edited by Charles Angoff, pp. 43-66. New York: Alfred A. Knopf, 1952.

Humorous reminiscences by Mencken's longtime partner. The essay reprints several letters by Mencken and Nathan, each to the other.

——. "The Happiest Days of H. L. Mencken." In *The Armchair "Esquire,"* edited by Arnold Gingrich and L. Rust Hills, pp. 340-49. New York: G. P. Putnam's Sons, 1958.

Further reminiscences by Mencken's friend. Of particular interest is an account of the initial meeting of Mencken and Nathan with Sinclair Lewis on the eve of *Main Street*'s publication.

Nolte, William H. "GBS and HLM." *Southwest Review* XLIX, No. 2 (Spring 1964): 163-73.

Compares and contrasts the thought of Mencken and Shaw, and examines the evolution of Mencken's critical opinion of the Irish dramatist.

Scruggs, Charles. *The Sage in Harlem: H. L. Mencken and the Black Writers of the 1920s.* Baltimore: Johns Hopkins University Press, 1984, 213 p.

Demonstrates "how Mencken, through the example of his own work, his power as editor of the *American Mercury,* and his passionate dedication to literary quality, was able to nurture the developing talents of black authors from James Weldon Johnson to Richard Wright."

Sherman, Stuart. "H. L. Mencken As Liberator." In his *Critical Woodcuts,* pp. 235-43. New York: Charles Scribner's Sons, 1926.

A critical attack on Mencken's thought as revealed in *Prejudices: Fourth Series.*

Sinclair, Upton. "A Letter." In *New World Writing, Eighth Mentor Selection,* pp. 280-81. New York: New American Library, 1955.

An open letter to James T. Farrell, written in response to his earlier essay in *New World Writing* (see excerpt above, 1927). Sinclair attacks Farrell for reviving "Mencken's rubbish" and for "causing thousands of young readers, who do not know Mencken's technique, to think of me as a boob."

Untermeyer, Louis. "The Bad Boy of Baltimore." In his *From Another World: The Autobiography of Louis Untermeyer,* pp. 184-205. New York: Harcourt, Brace and Co., 1939.

Interesting reminiscences by one of Mencken's friends.

West, Rebecca. "In Defense of the Democratic Idea." *New York Herald Tribune Books* (14 November 1926): 4.

An astute critical rebuttal of Mencken's premises in *Notes on Democracy.*

Williams, W.H.A. *H. L. Mencken.* Boston: Twayne Publishers, 1977, 179 p.

A helpful, well-organized biographical and critical study.

Wilson, Edmund. "Talking United States." In his *The Shores of Light: A Literary Chronicle of the Twenties and Thirties,* pp. 630-39. New York: Farrar, Straus and Young, 1952.

Reviews the fourth edition of *The American Language* and the work's *First Supplement.*

Marcel Proust

1871-1922

French novelist, critic, essayist, translator, short story writer, and poet.

Pictorial Parade Inc.

Proust's multivolume novel *À la recherche du temps perdu (Remembrance of Things Past)* is among literature's works of highest genius. Renowned for its artistic construction, this masterpiece is often appreciated for presenting within one work a social historian's chronicle of turn-of-the-century Paris society, a philosopher's reflections on the nature of time and consciousness, and a psychologist's insight into a tangled network of personalities. Despite the fact that Proust drew almost exclusively upon a narrow range of characters from the upper classes for his novel, the work has been widely praised by readers and critics for conveying a profound view of all human existence.

Proust was born at Auteuil, which in part served as a model for Combray in *Remembrance of Things Past.* His childhood was a sheltered but for the most part comfortably idyllic one. In 1880, however, he suffered his first attack of asthma, one of many chronic maladies that affected the acutely sensitive Proust. But his uncertain health did not interrupt his formal education at the Lycée Condorcet, where he was a major contributor to the class magazine, or his attendance at the École des Sciences Politiques, where he studied under Henri Bergson. Neither did his condition keep him from a year of military service, which he recalled as one of the happiest periods of his life. Some of Proust's commentators suggest that although he genuinely suffered from ill health, he sometimes exaggerated it to diminish others' expectations of him. As a young man he moved in the complex society of salon matrons, aristocrats, and the literati, distinguishing himself as an entertaining wit with a talent for mimicking others' speech and mannerisms. Particularly applauded were his imitations of Count Robert de Montesquiou, whose flamboyant personality provided some of the character traits for the pederast Baron de Charlus in *Remembrance of Things Past.*

In the mid-1890s Proust was chiefly known as a contributor of short prose works to various Paris reviews. These pieces, collected in *Les plaisirs et les jours (Pleasures and Days, and Other Writings),* are often described as precious, though in retrospect they have gained value as examples of Proust's earliest experiments with the themes and techniques of his major work. Likewise *Jean Santeuil,* Proust's first attempt at extended fiction, served as a rehearsal for many of the characters and scenes in *Remembrance of Things Past* while lacking, in Martin Turnell's phrase, the "richness and complexity" of the later novel. Similarly, a number of critics have noted that in *Jean Santeuil* Proust did not utilize the perspective of a first person narrator, which in *Remembrance of Things Past* becomes a unifying device for a vast and complicated scenario.

Proust's most important early work is to be found in the critical writings of *Contre Sainte-Beuve (By Way of Sainte-Beuve),* where he describes a personal view of literature contrary to the doctrines of the nineteenth-century critic. Whereas C.A. Sainte-Beuve failed to make a distinction between the writer's life and his work, Proust contended that a work of literature offers a perspective unique to itself, independent of its author's biography. Walter A. Straus explains that Proust was a critic who looked "deeply into the writer's creative personality, discerning the writer's special vision and his method of re-creating this vision in terms of literature." This concern with a special vision achieved through art became one of the basic precepts of the work that occupied Proust for the remainder of his life.

Remembrance of Things Past originally appeared in seven volumes, three of which were not published until after Proust's death in 1922. Proust never finished revising these final volumes, and they retain inconsistencies in plot and occasional uncharacteristic abridgements in the narrative where Proust did not get an opportunity to elaborate on incidents in his usual fashion. *Du côté de chez Swann (Swann's Way),* the first volume of *Remembrance of Things Past,* was published in 1913. Like the other volumes in the series, it is a complete novel in itself. However, it also introduces the many themes and motifs—such as memory, jealous love, social ambition, sexual inversion, and the importance of art—that are developed at length in later volumes. In the second volume, *A l'ombre des jeunes filles en fleurs (Within a Budding Grove),* the narrator Marcel describes his youthful love for Gilberte Swann. This love, as Wallace Fowlie has observed, is not based on "the satisfaction of the senses," but entirely on " the proliferation of the lover's imagination," with the result that Marcel is utterly deceived regarding Gilberte's wanton nature. Such unresolvable and often tragic conflicts between imagination and reality are characteristic of Proustian love.

The third volume of *Remembrance of Things Past, Le côté de Guermantes (The Guermantes Way),* won the Prix Goncourt, a national literary prize for young authors, in 1920, and brought Proust international recognition. In *The Guermantes Way,* Proust introduced his most masterfully drawn character, the Baron de Charlus. The elegant Baron is the apotheosis of the French aristocracy as portrayed by Proust in *Remembrance of Things Past;* Charlus's moral corruption and eventual fall parallel the degeneracy and decline of his class. In *The Guermantes Way,* Proust also ironically examined the phenomenon of social ambition, and the disillusionment that often accompanies the achievement of one's social goals. *Sodome et Gommorrhe (Cities of the Plain)* explores the theme of homosexuality and corruption. In the novel, sexual inversion, as it is revealed in such unlikely individuals as Charlus and Robert de Saint-Loup, becomes a symbol for the hidden but pervasive evils that afflict society, rendering it shallow, ineffectual, and decadent. Proust also discusses his theory of memory in an important prelude to the second half of this volume, entitled "Les intermittances du coeur" ("The Intermittances of the Heart"). *La prisonière (The Captive)* and *La fugitive (The Sweet Cheat Gone),* the fifth and sixth volumes of the series, were not included in Proust's original plan for *Remembrance of Things Past,* and some critics now believe that events in Proust's personal life led him to expand the scheme of his novel to include the story of Albertine with the themes of jealous love and deception. *Le temps retrouvé (Time Regained),* the final volume of the work, successfully ties together all of the novel's recurrent themes and motifs. In *Time Regained,* Marcel realizes that memory is the key to the meaning of the past that he has been seeking, and that art has the ability to redeem experience from disillusionment, deception, and the decay of time. The themes which were touched upon throughout the novel are here given full expression. *Remembrance of Things Past* concludes with Marcel's discovery of his own artistic vocation, and his determination to recover his past by writing a novel based on his life.

The title of *À la recherche du temps perdu* is often rendered more literally as *In Search of Lost Time* to emphasize the conscious pursuit by the narrator of past selves which have been altered over the years, and for the original qualities of experiences which are effaced by normal memory. For the narrator there are two means of recapturing a former stage of one's life: either through the consciously willed effort of "voluntary memory," or through the unwilled and unexpected outpouring of "involuntary memory." The first yields only limited and deceptive impressions of the past, while the second creates a vivid and faithful recollection. In the absence of religion, memory becomes a vehicle of transcending the annihilation by time and death of all things known in one's life. Sensation, sensibility, and intuition are the keys to the world of lost time, and as such supercede the laws of reason, in Proust's view of experience. Another source of triumph over the frustrations of human existence is that of art, which allows viewpoints not possible in mundane experience. Among life's major frustrations are the unstable nature of personal identity and the deceptive quality of private truths subsequently revealed as illusion. Proust used various devices to convey his sense of confusion and disillusionment to the reader of *Remembrance of Things Past.* Most notable among them was his deliberate misrepresentation of certain characters, such as Albertine and Monsieur Vinteuil. Proust allowed Marcel, and consequently the reader, to perceive these characters in a way that is ultimately shown to be false, and contrary to their true natures. Albertine, in particular, dramatically embodies Proust's ideas about the confusing and elusive nature of identity. Critics have long regarded her as one of the most enigmatic characters in all of literature. Although the narrator's relationship with her provides the subject matter for two volumes of *Remembrance of Things Past,* the mystery that surrounds her is never penetrated by Marcel or by the reader. For this reason, she perfectly illustrates Proust's theory that the experience of love is utterly subjective: based entirely in the imagination of the lover, and not, as is commonly thought, on the character of the beloved. Thus, in Proust's view, even romantic love is subject to the "intermittances of the heart," which transform seemingly durable emotions into occasional phenomena without continuity.

Although today the brilliance of Proust's achievement is seldom disputed, in the past his novel was frequently the subject of critical controversy. Its almost overwhelming length and sprawling structure, combined with Proust's reticular and highly original prose style has occasionally led critics to assert that Proust's aesthetic was actually a rationalization of his artistic weakness: his inability to select and reject material. Proust constantly disputed such statements, maintaining that the novel had to be considered as a whole in order for its structure, which is based on the musical leit-motif, to become apparent. One of the most important issues in Proust criticism is the role of Marcel as protagonist and narrator of *Remembrance of Things Past,* and his relationship to Proust himself. Briefly, there is strong evidence for both identifying Proust with Marcel and for isolating the two, and some critics' readings of the novel are more autobiographical than those of others. Perhaps the firmest ground for likening Proust with Marcel is their mutual struggle to realize themselves as artists, with each making art the highest value in their lives. The search for lost time ends in the disillusioned abandonment of life and in an affirmative recreation of life as a work of art.

(See also *TCLC,* Vol. 7 and *Contemporary Authors,* Vol. 104.)

PRINCIPAL WORKS

Les plaisirs et les jours (short stories, sketches, poetry, and criticism) 1896
[*Pleasures and Regrets,* 1948; also translated as *Pleasures and Days, and Other Writings,* 1957]
Portraits de peintres (poetry) 1896
**Du côté de chez Swann* (novel) 1913
[*Swann's Way,* 1922]
**A l'ombre des jeunes filles en fleurs* (novel) 1919
[*Within a Budding Grove,* 1924]
Pastiches et mélanges (parodies and essays) 1919
**Le côté de Guermantes* (novel) 1920
[*The Guermantes Way,* 1924]
**Sodome et Gommorrhe* (novel) 1922
[*Cities of the Plain,* 1927]
**La prisonnière* (novel) 1923
[*The Captive,* 1929]
**La fugitive* (novel) 1925
[*The Sweet Cheat Gone,* 1930; also published as *The Fugitive,* 1981, in *Remembrance of Things Past*]

**Le temps retrouvé* (novel) 1927
[*The Past Recaptured,* 1931; also published as *Time Regained,* 1970]
Oeuvres complètes de Marcel Proust. 10 vols. (novels, criticism, short stories, sketches, poetry, parodies, and essays) 1929-36
Correspondance générale de Marcel Proust (letters) 1930
Letters of Marcel Proust (letters) 1949
Jean Santeuil (unfinished novel) 1952
[*Jean Santeuil,* 1955]
Correspondance avec sa mère: 1887-1905 (letters) 1953
[*Letters to his Mother* (partial translation), 1956]
Contre Sainte-Beuve (criticism) 1954
[*By Way of Sainte-Beuve,* 1958]
***À la recherche du temps perdu.* 3 vols. (novel) 1954
[*Remembrance of Things Past.* 3 vols., 1981]
Marcel Proust et Jacques Rivière: Correspondance, 1914-1922 (letters) 1955
Lettres à Reynaldo Hahn (letters) 1956
Choix de lettres (letters) 1965
Lettres retrouvées (letters) 1966
Marcel Proust: Selected Letters 1880-1903 (letters) 1983

*These works were published as *À la recherche du temps perdu* in *Oeuvres complètes de Marcel Proust* in 1929-36.

**This edition of *À la recherche du temps perdu,* compiled by Pierre Clarac and André Ferré for Biblioteque de la Pleiade, is a corrected edition based on Proust's own notes and galley corrections. It is now considered the standard edition and is the text on which Terence Kilmartin's 1981 revised translation of the novel is based.

MARCEL PROUST (letter date 1912)

[*In the following excerpt, Proust discusses the themes of* Swann's Way *and briefly explains his theory of involuntary memory.*]

Du côté de chez Swann is the fragment of a novel, which will have as general title ***A la recherche du temps perdu.*** I should have liked to have published it as a single whole, but it would have been too long. They no longer publish works in several volumes. There are novelists, on the other hand, who envisage a brief plot with few characters. That is not my conception of the novel. There is a plane geometry and a geometry of space. And so for me the novel is not only plane psychology but psychology in space and time. That invisible substance, time, I try to isolate. But in order to do this it was essential that the experience be continuous. I hope that by the end of my book what I have tried to do will be understandable; some unimportant little event will show that time has passed and it will take on that beauty certain pictures have, enhanced by the passage of the years.

Then, like a city which, while the train pursues its winding course, seems to be first on our right, then on our left, the varying aspects the same character will have assumed to such a degree that they will have made him seem like successive and different characters, will project—but only in that one way—the sensation of time passed. Such characters will later reveal themselves as different from what they were in the present, different from what one believes them to be, a circumstance which, indeed, occurs frequently enough in life.

But not only the same characters who reappear under varying aspects, in the course of this work as in certain of Balzac's cycles, but there is one continuous character. From that point of view my book will perhaps be like an attempt at a sequence of novels of the unconscious. They are not Bergsonian novels, for my work is dominated by a distinction which not only doesn't figure in Bergson's philosophy but which is even contradicted by it.

Voluntary memory, which is above all the memory of the intelligence end of the eyes, gives us only the surface of the past without the truth; but when an odor, a taste, rediscovered under entirely different circumstances evoke for us, in spite of ourselves, the past, we sense how different is this past from the one we thought we remembered and which our voluntary memory was painting like a bad painter using false colors. Even in this first volume the character who narrates, who calls himself "I" (and who is not I) will suddenly rediscover forgotten years, gardens, people in the taste of a sip of tea in which he found a piece of a *madeleine;* doubtless he remembers them anyway, but without color and shapes. I have been able to make him tell how as in the little Japanese game of dipping into water compressed bits of paper which, as soon as they are immersed in the bowl, open up, twist around and become flowers and people, so all the flowers of his garden, the good folk of the village, their little houses and the church and all of Combray and its environs—everything that takes on form and solidity has come, city and garden, out of his cup of tea.

I believe that it is involuntary memories practically altogether that the artist should call for the primary subject matter of his work. First, just because they are involuntary, because they take shape of their own accord, inspired by the resemblance to an identical minute, they alone have the stamp of authenticity. Then they bring things back to us in an exact proportion of memory and of forgetting. And finally, as they make us savor the same sensation under wholly different circumstances, they free it from all context, they give us the extratemporal essence. Moreover, Chateaubriand and Baudelaire practised this method. My novel is not a work of ratiocination; its least elements have been supplied by my sensibility; first I perceived them in my own depths without understanding them, and I had as much trouble converting them into something intelligible as if they had been as foreign to the sphere of the intelligence as a motif in music.

Style is in no way an embellishment, as certain people think, it is not even a question of technique; it is, like color with certain painters, a quality of vision, a revelation of a private universe which each one of us sees and which is not seen by others. The pleasure an artist gives us is to make us know an additional universe. How, under these conditions, do certain writers declare that they try not to have a style? I don't understand it. (pp. 225-28)

Marcel Proust, in a letter to Antoine Bibesco in November ? 1912, in his Letters of Marcel Proust, *edited and translated by Mina Curtiss (copyright 1949 by Random House Inc.; and renewed 1976 by Mina Curtiss; reprinted by permission of Mina Curtiss), Random House, 1949, pp. 225-28.*

J. MIDDLETON MURRY (essay date 1922)

[*In the following review of* Swann's Way, *the first volume of the English translation of* Remembrance of Things Past, *Murry discusses Proust's prose style and his vision of the past.*]

It is customary to declare, and theoretically it is true, that a translation cannot possibly be as good as the original. Either it is a colorless copy, or a re-creation by another mind, and therefore a different thing. Most theoretical axioms concerning the arts are occasionally confuted by practice. Mr. Moncrieff has confuted this one. His translation [of **"Swann's Way"**] does seem as good as his original. Of course, this is an English opinion; but a French opinion would carry no greater weight. No one can know two languages well enough to pronounce absolutely upon a translation which reaches this standard of excellence. Perhaps, however, it would be less controversial (though the practical meaning would be the same) to say that no English reader will get more out of reading **"Du Côté de chez Swann"** in French than he will out of reading **"Swann's Way"** in English.

That is a very unusual thing. Many of Anatole France's books have been well translated into English; but something quite essential is lacking in the English version—the gliding, insinuating rhythm of his prose, above all. And some such sense of loss is general even in the best translation. In the case of **"Swann's Way"** we are not conscious of it. That is due, in a large part, to Mr. Moncrieff, but not wholly. He could not have made the same success with "Le Petit Pierre." Indeed, what interests us most in his triumph with **"Du Côté de chez Swann"** is the accidental light it throws upon the nature and quality of M. Proust's work.

Mr. Moncrieff has demonstrated that the qualities of M. Proust's work at its best—for his best is to be found in **"Swann"**—can be transferred almost entire into another language. It is the completeness of the transference which is astonishing. Any universal author, any author who is concerned with the large issues of human life, can be transferred, to some extent, from one language to another. Shakespeare can be transferred into French; but hardly more than a skeleton of Shakespeare survives the passage. His qualities of detail, his close-knit imagery, the whole habit of sensuous perception by which he instinctively articulates his thought—the flesh and blood itself, we might say, is dissolved. But M. Proust's qualities of detail survive. It will be said: Shakespeare was a poet. The objection is of value if we are sure that it is because of his poetic qualities that Shakespeare cannot be transferred; and if we remember that a host of prose-writers stand under the same disability—Carlyle and Hardy in English, Hugo and Anatole France in French, for example.

If we take "poetic qualities" in this large sense as certain qualities of detail and texture which may be possessed both by writers of prose and writers of verse, and which are so peculiar that they prevent these writers from being adequately transferred from their own language to another, we may say that M. Proust is curiously lacking in them; but we have still to determine what they are. It is easier, by regarding M. Proust's work more closely, to decide what they are not. Consider, for instance, the fact that M. Proust, quite as much as any poet, and far more than most writers of prose, abounds in metaphors and similes. Mr. Moncrieff has no difficulty in rendering them perfectly; for they belong, almost without exception, to this kind:—

> As a surgical patient, by means of a local anaesthetic, can look on with a clear consciousness while an operation is being performed upon him and yet feel nothing, I could repeat to myself some favorite lines, or watch my grandfather attempting to talk to Swann about the Duc d'Audiffret-Pasquier, without being able to kindle any emotion from one or amusement from the other.

They are almost always detailed and expanded analogies, and the resemblances are generally taken from the same kind of experience. M. Proust hardly ever illuminates the mental by means of the physical: he compares, with the precision of the scientific psychologist (more precisely than most scientific psychologists), one mental condition with another, artificially induced, or with some mechanical process of applied science. It would be worth while to count the number of times he makes use of the analogy of the camera to elucidate some complicated emotional process.

In other words, M. Proust's method is intellectual and analytical to an extreme degree. He defines and dissects far more often than he presents; and since the methods of intellectual analysis are the same for all men, since he deliberately excludes to the utmost of his power all emotional suggestion of language, he can be transferred almost bodily into another language. His long and complicated French sentences are not a bit longer or more complicated in English; they are just the same. Because he is often difficult in French, we had imagined, illogically and unthinkingly, that he was difficult to translate. He deals with a complex, fluid, and difficult material, but in so far as he is successful in dealing with it, he abolishes its difficulty. He is a historian and a scientist much more than a creator; he chronicles, on a scale never attempted before, but by methods which, in spite of their apparent novelty, are really familiar, the growth of a modern consciousness.

We have no intention, in saying this, of diminishing M. Proust's genius. The capacity for analysis on this scale and of this exactness is just as rare as any other kind of genius. And, in any case, a description of this kind is only large and general; it applies only to the predominant bias of M. Proust's work. His methods are intellectual, his results very often are not. So, in this first volume of his prodigious narrative more than in any other, the minuteness of his analysis does not dissipate, but rather seems to intensify, the actual living quality of the experience to which it is applied. We never lose the wood for the trees: on the contrary, we can see and enjoy the wood more fully because we know and understand its elements. In the later volumes, however, this complete enjoyment becomes more fitful; it is only at moments (such as the death of the Grandmother; or the episode in the latest section called "Les Intermittences du Coeur") that the quality of the experience recorded seems to return and compel its dissected elements into a unity once more. The scientific and historical value of M. Proust's work is invariable; its artistic value, its power of making us directly feel as well as understand its truth, varies strangely from volume to volume.

We incline to believe that M. Proust is an artist more by accident than design. If it could be rigorously applied, his method would tend to diminish steadily, and finally to abolish altogether, the possibility of the emotional compulsion which is vital to art. But M. Proust cannot apply his method rigorously. The data vanish. Even if his memory is (as it probably is) incomparably more perfect and more practised than the ordinary memory, he forgets. He can remember of the distant past only that which was in some way significant; not even he can drag the insignificant out of oblivion. And the remoter the past with which he tries to grapple, the more thoroughly has the unconscious work of elimination been performed. His first volume is his best. There are wonderful things in them all;

nevertheless, as his narrative winds its way through adolescence and approaches his adult consciousness, we are aware that the proportion of significance (that is, of literature) to the whole is steadily decreasing. The method never varies; but the quality of the material supplied to it does. M. Proust has begun to remember too much—too much from the point of view of those who approach his work as literature, never more than enough for those who regard it as a masterpiece of psychological history.

This, we believe, is how the author himself, in the main, regards it. That is, in the precise meaning of the phrase, its *raison d'être*. Its literary value is largely accidental. M. Proust is "out for" truth; literature, also, is "out for" truth: but they are not the same kinds of truth, and it merely happens that M. Proust, in looking for the one, sometimes presents us with the other. In that, however, he does not essentially differ from other writers of his scope. They achieve literature often because they have something else in mind. (pp. 124-25)

J. Middleton Murry, "Proust in Translation," in The Nation and The Athenaeum, *Vol. XXXII, No. 3, October 21, 1922, pp. 124-25.*

JOSEPH WOOD KRUTCH (essay date 1930)

[Krutch is widely regarded as one of America's most respected literary and drama critics. A conservative and idealistic thinker, he was a consistent proponent of human dignity and the preeminence of literary art. His literary criticism is characterized by such concerns: in The Modern Temper *(1929) he argued that because scientific thought has denied human worth, tragedy had become obsolete, and in* The Measure of Man *(1954) he attacked modern culture for depriving humanity of the sense of individual responsibility necessary for making important decisions in an increasingly complex age. In the following excerpt, Krutch discusses the artistic nature of* Remembrance of Things Past *and concludes that the greatest strengths of the work are found in Proust's masterful portrayal of character, his dissection of all types of social ritual, and his examination of the nature and effects of passing time on human beings and society.]*

To enter the first volume of [Proust's] great romance is to find oneself plunged immediately into an unfamiliar world whose strangeness is more than a mere strangeness of scene. For however remote the persons and the places may be, it is not so much their remoteness which is responsible for the sense of novelty as it is the angle from which they are regarded. Seen through Proust's eyes, the most familiar people and the most ordinary events would take on an aspect of unfamiliarity. He notes the things not usually noted and stresses the things not usually stressed. Only the sensations which ordinarily seem too fleeting to be recorded are set down, only the distinctions which seem ordinarily too intangible to be defined are noted, and only the pleasures so tenuous as to be ordinarily not counted are considered real enough to make life worth living. Everything is measured by some sense of values as unusual as it is consistent and by the simple but summary process of redefining the adjective "important" a whole new world is created.

Indeed it would hardly be an exaggeration to say that he writes as though he had never read the works of his predecessors; as though he were not even aware of the preoccupations and the enthusiasms which made up their world. Yet he was, as a matter of fact, rather more widely read than novelists are accustomed to be both in the literature of his own and in that of other countries. . . . He had a secret of his own—a magic formula which alone could give meaning to life—but that formula was one which it took many years to discover and the results of a merciless discipline to apply. (pp. 254-56)

No work of literature could possibly illustrate more perfectly than does **"Remembrance of Things Past"** the characteristics of what Nietzsche called Apollonian art. It takes no sides and though it makes many thousand distinctions it pronounces no judgments which are other than purely relative. Curiously aloof and curiously undynamic, it never for a moment seems to consider life as anything which could (or should) be acted upon. In it events have all of the inevitability and something of the intangibility characteristic of a dream. (pp. 256-57)

What then among so many excellences, is the virtue which is peculiarly Proust's? Though there is not in the entire novel a page which is not immediately recognizable as undoubtedly his, he seems (while we are under the spell of his consistency) to possess all the qualities which a novelist should have. One thinks of this fragment or that; one calls to mind a subtle page of reverie followed by a brilliantly dramatic scene. And one is tempted to commit the monstrous error which some have been guilty of, the error of praising **"Remembrance of Things Past"** as a brilliant miscellany, as a scrap book of purple passages. Indeed, even though we reject this error, it seems hardly possible to escape the necessity of writing a series of essays devoted to this or that aspect of his work.

One such essay would, for instance, be concerned with the contrast just discussed between Proust as a master of the subjective and Proust as the creator of brilliantly observed characters. Another would consider the construction of his interminably evolving sentences which, despite the oddness of the impression at first created, are soon found both to emit a delicious music of their own and to follow with an amazing suppleness all the delicate contours of his thought. A third would attempt to define that moral attitude, or rather that lack of a moral attitude, which results from an all-enveloping aestheticism—an aestheticism which is as far as possible removed from that characteristic of "decadent" literature and which arises out of Proust's remarkable sensitiveness to all phenomena, coupled with his power of accepting *pro tem* the premises of any philosophy of life when it is necessary to do so for the purpose of understanding his characters.

Passing then to his treatment of various themes or subject matters, one would have to consider his treatment of love and jealousy. And in connection with the former one would have to note especially a masterly synthesis of apparently incompatible elements, for Proust achieved a kind of romanticism —succeeded at least in attributing a very high value to love— while coldly dismissing most of the illusions which are commonly called upon to support romanticism. (pp. 304-05)

Proust (or the narrator) never fails, even in the midst of his own unhappy passion, to dissociate the ideas of love and of permanence, to compare his attitude towards this or that with what the attitude is destined to be "when I shall have ceased to love Albertine." Indeed one might say that Proustian love shows no trace of any of the elements which usually accompany and which are, perhaps, usually thought necessary to romantic love. For it is not only the ideas of objective reality and of permanence which are absent; one notes also that his Love has neither reticence nor selflessness since he is as ready to analyse even the most intimate of its sensual aspects as he finds it frankly unnecessary to make any pretence of a primary concern with the happiness of the beloved. And yet not one of the least of the charms of the novel is the fact that in it one discovers once more the possibility of Love as a serious theme in a novel which remains, nevertheless, wholly modern in its freedom from the shabbier of romantic delusions. Proustian love, despite all that is left out of it, has a power to torture and to absorb which cannot belong to sense, simple and unadorned. To the making of it has gone (besides sense) only sentiment, but it has become, nevertheless, something marvellously elaborate and well-nigh unique in literature.

And finally, in this series of imaginary essays, there would have to be one devoted to a consideration of Proust's interest in formal society, to his passionate absorption in the details of etiquette; for that interest is undoubtedly responsible for one of the most striking peculiarities of the book, even though it has not been sufficiently noted that he is hardly more delighted by the traditions which determine the conduct of the Queen of Naples than he is by the fact that the servants in his mother's household have traditions of their own—among which is a sort of poetically real deafness to any bell which may be rung during the sacred period of their repast.

Something has already been said concerning one of the possible reasons for this interest in formal society. It has already been explained that Proust was attracted to it by the glamour of historic names whose possessors seemed, by virtue of the very fact that they bore them, to be lifted above time, and that, besides, he was fascinated by the idea (so imperfectly realized in any actual society) of manners as a technique of gentleness. Yet it would, no doubt, be necessary in such an essay as we are imagining to defend him against the charge (sometimes made) of being a snob—to point out that, on the one hand, his interest in humble people is no less conspicuous than his interest in great ones and that, on the other hand, he certainly did not hesitate to represent most of his aristocrats as stupid, vulgar, and dull, even though, it may be conceded, he never ceased to wonder that they could be so. (pp. 305-07)

But to turn now from the consideration of such aspects of his work to the unity which embraces all these details. What is **"Remembrance of Things Past"** *about*? One may say, of course, that it is the autobiography of an imaginary personage whose life and whose character bear many striking resemblances to the life and character of Proust himself—that it describes the development of that person's sensibility, carries him through his strange love affair with the mysterious Albertine, and ends with the Great Enlightenment which made it possible for him to see all his experiences under the form of a work of art. With equal truth it might be maintained that this autobiographical form is no more than a thread, that the real story of which all the separate stories are a part is the story of the rise and fall of certain social groups; that (in a technical sense) the main catastrophe is brought about by the gradual decay of those social standards typified by the traditions of the Guermantes group, and that to it are related various minor catastrophes of a similar sort—the disappearance of "the faithful" from Madame Verdurin's second-rate salon and the dissolution both of M. de Charlus' integrity and of Berma's fame. (pp. 308-09)

Proust had believed in the forms of politeness and, like the forms under which *noblesse oblige* pretends to find expression, they too become most often only a technique of cruelty.

Thus in one sense it might be said that the story of **"Remembrance of Things Past"** is the story of the narrator's disillusion with certain things upon which he had rested his faith in the possibility of a beautiful life—that he had believed in both politeness (which is the means by which ordinary people express their good will) and in the promptings of that sense of *noblesse oblige* (which leads the great to even larger gestures of benevolence)—that he had believed in them only to discover how, for the most part, they exist only as hideous counterfeits.

But quitting temporarily—and in the middle—this effort to extract the meaning of the novel, let us turn for a moment to the consideration of its form. It has already been remarked that the order of its events is not the order of time because to emphasize the relationship which exists between merely simultaneous events evidently seemed to Proust to obscure the more significant relationships which unite situations separated by days, by months, or by years. But to say this is not to explain the form adopted, which is, as a matter of fact, not likely to be appreciated unless the volumes of the novel are read consecutively and which, indeed, can hardly be grasped in all its complicated perfection until the first volumes are reread with the last still in mind.

Proust himself, it will be remembered, spoke of the various *themes* whose full significance would not be clear until, in the later volumes, they had begun to combine; and this remark of his gives the key to his method, for it is, as a matter of fact, not unlike the method of an elaborate musical composition. One may, if one likes, study it first in some small unit like the first volume—much as one might begin to study the structure of a symphony by considering the first movement alone. (pp. 310-11)

The motifs appear one by one. It would be possible to go through the work and to note, as one would note in a symphony, that at this point or that each one of the themes—love, taste, manners, etc.—is introduced for the first time merely in passing before it is returned to again and again for more and more complete development. In **"Swann's Way,"** for example, the slight, apparently purposeless incident centring about the daughter of Vinteuil serves to suggest the theme of homosexuality later so elaborately treated and, though probably no reader who did not turn back would realize the fact, the very first pages of the whole work hint at most of the major themes. Thus the escape from Time is alluded to on page three where it is immediately followed by the incident of the magic lantern, which, as the first work of art introduced, serves to suggest the technique by which Time is to be transcended. And one result of this arrangement is to make the novel in another respect like a piece of music, for of it may be said, more truly even than of most great novels, that the second reading is more rewarding than the first. To know what is coming does not detract from the pleasure—is indeed necessary to the full enjoyment of it—since each incident is, like a musical theme, only enriched by a knowledge of the variations to follow.

This original and perfected form has its own self-justifying beauties, but to consider the intention which determined its choice is to be led back again to that obsession with Time whose influence is discoverable in every detail of Proust's work and which gives it its unity. Thanks to the method which disregards chronology he was able to bring together, for purposes of contrast or comparison, widely separated periods or—as he said in a sentence previously quoted in its context—to show men as monstrous creatures straddling between the distant past and the present. Moreover it was necessary for his purpose to do just this because the full horror of Time had to be revealed in order that the miraculous joy which comes through the escape from it might be properly appreciated.

Thus the commonplace fact that faces grow old and characters change becomes, for him, something to be analysed with a fascinated terror. When, for example, he is describing, in the second volume of **"Within a Budding Grove,"** the impression made upon him by a group of beautiful girls he cannot refrain from adding: "Alas! in the freshest flower it is possible to discern those just perceptible signs which to the instructed mind indicate already what will be, by the desiccation or fructification of the flesh which is today in bloom, the ultimate form, immutable and already predestinate, of the autumnal seed." . . . (pp. 312-14)

But this change in faces is only trivially important in comparison with that change which takes place in character—the change which, as he realized at the fateful reception given by the Guermantes, makes men into creatures totally different from what they were. Hence it came at last to seem to him that it was folly to speak of Albertine, of de Charlus, of himself even, as though any one of them were an entity maintaining its identity while time flowed past; and he realized that if his novel was to attain the full significance which he wished, it must manage somehow, not only to attain timelessness itself, but also to suggest the triumph of Time over the persons and the experiences which the novel alone could rescue. For the most essential distinction between art and experience is exactly that the former is changeless while the latter flows.

Antiquities and history were beautiful to him, not because they had been subjected to the ravages of Time, but because of the impression which they gave of having achieved at least a partial triumph over it. Time itself is the enemy of all beauty because Time produces change and it becomes an aid to the discovery of beauty only when, if the expression be permitted, it is pluperfect—only when, that is to say, all the changes which it can produce seem, as in the historical and the antique they do, to be already complete; only when the pattern of which they are a part has been unrolled so that it can be seen as the whole it had not yet come to be while it was still unrolling.

Proust's problem as an artist was, then, the problem of finding the means of rescuing something from the flux, of establishing in the eternity of art the experiences which he had undergone or observed. But how was this to be accomplished? What was the bridge between the two realms? There was memory of course, and memory seems to the uninitiated the only enemy of Time. It alone seems to link what we are to what we were and it gives a false sense of continuity to our lives. Through its aid the days that are passed may be recovered after a fashion. But memory collects rather than joins together, and what it gives us is a bag of detached and dissimilar fragments. The aggregate of them is the thing which we ordinarily call ourselves, but it remains only an aggregate, not a meaningful whole. Hence though merely to remember in the ordinary fashion is generally the last expedient of the man who feels himself dissolving in the eternal flux, this mere memory leaves him aware that it preserves only the detritus of himself out of the common ruin into which the passions and purposes of one moment are thrown by the next.

From the dilemma presented by the fact that memory reveals its impotence at the same time that it seems the only instrument which we possess, Proust was rescued by the Great Enlightenment—by the discovery that for him there was possible a kind of memory not identical with the ordinary sort: a vision of the eternity in which even the most completely forgotten experience had already taken its place. This vision was mystical and hence, by very definition, not to be explained in any terms except its own; but it cannot be repeated too often that in it lies the meaning of the novel, every detail of which it controls. And if we cannot analyse further a thing ultimate in its own nature, we can at least note the quality which it bestows, can at least ask how it determines the impression produced by the work which it dominates.

In the first place it gives to **"Remembrance of Things Past"** that curiously detached and passionless character which the novel preserves even when passion is being so brilliantly described. Doubtless it had enabled Proust himself to achieve that complete substitution of contemplation for will which he had begun to find necessary just as soon as he realized how little active he could expect to be; and as a result of this fact it enabled him to write a work so cool, so calm, and so pure that its artistic perfection is never disturbed by anything which seems to arise in a mere human being whose impartiality can be disturbed as—occasionally at least—that of most writers is, by the private passions or desires of a man.

In the second place it furnished him with his particular means of achieving an effect which every really great work of art must in some manner produce: it supplied him with a point of view from which even calamitous events could be seen as no longer actually painful. Always aware of the whole of which any incident is a part, he can, in his novel, calmly accept his own sufferings as well as the sufferings of others because it is the pattern of which they are a part, rather than either the pleasure or the pain of the moment, of which he is most acutely aware; and by thus seeing the passing events of time as part of a static eternity in which the end is simultaneous with the beginning, he achieves that indifference which is not the indifference of the insensitive but the indifference of the gods.

Events become, even as he recounts them, already a part of legend and thus life is magically transmuted into art. He himself, as well as M. Swann and M. de Charlus, are no longer mere human beings but analagous to the figures painted upon the slides of the little magic lantern which had fascinated him so long ago. Their suffering and their wickedness have now ceased to have any significance except as parts of a formal design. . . . (pp. 314-17)

Very diverse opinions have been expressed concerning the rank which ought to be accorded to Proust as a novelist, and when such matters are discussed it is as well not to enter into dispute. But perhaps it is, on the contrary, worth while remarking that at least he very perfectly realized the conception of the artist which was formulated by his philosophical master, Bergson.

The latter, it will be remembered, held that artistic vision is distinguished from ordinary vision by the fact that it manages to escape from the effects of habit and to see a thing itself rather than the conventionalization of it with which we happen to be most familiar. The artist, discarding everything except his own sensations and his own mind, is actually far less influenced by other works of art—which is the same thing as to say by the conventions established by others—than even the most inartistic of men; for the latter, without being aware of the fact, is a slave to such conventions as have filtered down to him. Hence the artist, combining sensations afresh with the aid of nothing except his own intelligence, is enabled to conceive of them as forming patterns hitherto unrecognized and to make others see them under forms totally new.

And whatever other qualities Proust may or may not have, one can hardly deny him his freshness of vision which makes his novel very unlike any other. . . . The result is the creation of a strange new world. Perhaps we recognize its elements even though we have not ever before been consciously aware of their existence; but the whole which they compose is new. We enter the pages of **"Remembrance of Things Past"** as we might enter a realm totally unfamiliar, and before we are aware of the fact we have closed a door behind us, forgetting the standards and the conventions of familiar life as completely as we forget its personages. For the world which the novel reveals is more than merely strange; it is also so consistent, so self-sustaining, and so logically complete that we are never by any reference led back to the other world of our ordinary concerns. (pp. 320-22)

[Great] works are so rare and so precious that it is hardly worth while to reject one of them merely because it is not of the *genre* which we expected. **"Remembrance of Things Past"** is Proust's *Apologia Pro Vita Sua,* and if the life which it defends seems to us a very odd one, at least the defence is successful and Proust in his novel has achieved certain qualities (like charm, and order, and peace) which seemed to have departed forever from modern literature. His world has definitely taken its place in the not very long list of those possible worlds which art creates; de Charlus, Saint-Loup, the Duchesse de Guermantes, Françoise, and Madame Verdurin have definitely taken their places in the not very long list of characters who are more real than reality. Something—both in the particular sense defined by Proust and in the more general sense in which the phrase is applicable to all great literature—has been rescued from Time. It is not often that that can be said. (pp. 327-28)

Joseph Wood Krutch, "Marcel Proust," in his Five Masters: A Study in the Mutations of the Novel *(copyright 1930, copyright renewed © 1958, by Joseph Wood Krutch), Jonathan Cape & Harrison Smith, 1930, pp. 251-328.*

DANE BETTMAN (essay date 1932)

[In the following excerpt, Bettman discusses Proust's intentions for Remembrance of Things Past *and concludes that Proust succeeded at each of his three objectives: to seek out the essence of life and time; to justify life; and to convey his vision to his readers. In his analysis, Bettman provides a detailed explication of Proust's thought regarding the nature of time, personality, and memory.]*

One suspects that in the case of most masterpieces, theories are either read in after the fact, or else that the author succeeds in spite of them—as Flaubert did, by being a romanticist against his will.

It is startling, therefore, to find that one of the most important of modern novels, both in itself and for its influence, was constructed according to a theory which it fulfills as precisely as a building corresponds to its blueprints. Much has been written concerning the elaborate structure and implied philosophy of ***A La Recherche du Temps Perdu.*** Yet many writers seem to ignore what many readers have not yet discovered: that Proust himself has said the last word. Just as our old arithmetic carried an answer in the back of the book, so ***Le Temps Retrouve [The Past Recaptured]*** holds the solution to many questions which rise on the long, long road between ***[Du Côté de chez Swann] Swann's Way*** and the end of the series. In this final volume Proust develops at length the ideas which were responsible for the particular form and flavor of ***A La Recherche du Temps Perdu,*** and he states his own case more effectively than all those who have written about him. As he sets forth his articles of faith with his own almost weird mixture of the specific and the general, he leaves no doubt but that his practice fulfills his preachings to the letter. Where it triumphs,

Proust in military service (1890). The Granger Collection, New York.

they triumph, and its shortcomings—with one exception—are theirs.

Hints of his theories are dropped throughout the work. But a thorough exposition comes only at the end, forming a climax to the pilgrimage which has continued almost unperceived from the very outset. Without an appreciation of this crowning position and of the dramatic value it imparts to them, one can hardly appreciate the theories themselves. Fundamentally, the quest which led in their direction was that of every individual: the way that is the right way for him. Specifically, in this instance, it involves the history of Proust's relation with the art and craft of literature.

When we think of the stories that emerge from this novel, like repoussé designs against an equally precious background, we think of Swann and Odette, of Marcel and Albertine, of the Baron and Morel. But there is another story, as definitely formed as these amid what appears (deceptively) to be the general formlessness. It starts at the beginning and runs throughout the book, though it only emerges at the end. It is the romance of the writer and his muse. Not only are its outlines definitely shaped. They follow a scheme which in itself is actually banal: the time-worn pattern of misunderstanding, estrangement and final reconciliation between heaven-mated affinities.

For years the narrator—whose artistic development at least we may identify with the author's—flirted with his lady literature, always intending to settle down with her when health and social pleasures should permit. At last he found that she was not what he thought her. She was deceptive, untrue to life. He made the discovery through the brothers Goncourt, who also caused him to be bitterly disappointed in his own ability to look, to listen, to record as they did. He determined to leave her forever, and kept his vow until a chance event brought him round to a new conception of his mistress and his rôle opposite her. The successive adjustments are as dramatic as actual events in a romance, and the final reconciliation dominates all the other romances of ***A La Recherche du Temps Perdu.***

This reconciliation occurred only after the narrator had spent long years in a secluded sanitorium. When he finally returned to Paris, determined to put away all thoughts of a career, his dejection was as profound as his resolve to give himself over henceforth to social pleasures—"since I now knew that I could expect to attain nothing more." At the same time he felt that he had lost the most precious thing in life, that though he should go on even for a hundred years, even without the illness which had always beset him, it would be a lorn existence, devoid of happiness.

"But it is sometimes at the moment when everything seems lost that the warning arrives which is able to save us." Just when he was most dejected came revelation, from beneath his very feet. As he was about to enter the house where he would once more greet his old friends and plunge into the frivolous whirl from which there was no longer any reason to preserve himself, he happened to step on two uneven paving stones. At once "all my discouragement vanished before the same happiness which at various periods of my life had been given me. . . ." Always this sudden access of bliss had swept over him when some sensation of the present recalled a period of the past. The whole of ***Swann's Way*** unwinds from two such experiences, one when he dips a little cake, a *madeleine,* into his cup of tea, and its flavor recalls a whole epoch of his life with all the sights, sounds, emotions, that formed an aura about it. Now again "as at the moment when I tasted the *madeleine,* all disquietude about the future, all intellectual doubt, were dissipated." He remained "to the mirth of the innumerable crowd of coachmen, teetering as I had done a moment ago, one foot on the higher paving block, the other on the lower one." Each time he moved he lost the sensation; but if he placed his foot in exactly the right position on the uneven stones, "again the dazzling and indistinct vision swept me, as if it said: 'Seize me in flight if you have the power, and try to solve the enigma of the bliss I offer you.'"

This time it was not enough to identify the feeling itself as reminiscent of a certain afternoon in Venice. He determined to discover why such images should give him "moments endowed with a joy equal to a certainty, and sufficient without other proofs to make death indifferent." In pursuing the analysis he found his message and his vocation.

He realized, first of all, that the essential emotion had been the same in eating the *madeleine,* in teetering on the paving stones, or in any of the similar moments which occurred. "The purely physical difference was in the images evoked." He realized too that he enjoyed the reminiscence far more than the actual experience. Often the moments, so glorious in their brief duration, were the recall of a time which actually bored him. It was as if the past returned "disencumbered of all that was imperfect in exterior perception."

Nor was the self who relished these moments his everyday self, but an intermittent being, nourished on essences. "In them alone it found its subsistence, its delight. It languished under observation of the present where the senses are not able to bring it that [essential quality], under consideration of a past parched for it by the intelligence, under the expectation of a future which the will constructs with fragments of the present. . . . But let a noise, an odor, already heard and formerly breathed, be so again, at once in the present and in the past, real without being actual, ideal without being abstract, immediately the permanent essence of things, normally hidden, is liberated, and our true self . . . wakes up, bestirs itself as it receives the celestial nourishment. . . . A moment set free from the order of time has created in us, in order to feel it, a man set free from the laws of time."

This intermittent self was not a new idea to him. It had, years earlier, explained the difference between his type of observation and the Goncourts'. But then he had viewed it as a disqualification. For even in the moments when it "set itself joyously in pursuit" this intermittent person "looked and listened, but only at a certain depth so that observation didn't profit thereby. . . . What interested me was not what [people] wanted to say but the manner in which they said it in so far as it revealed their character or their idiosyncrasies; or rather, it was an object which had always been the especial end of my research because it gave me a specific pleasure, the point which was common to one thing and to another." Herein is implied the whole of his philosophy: its academic and hedonistic qualities, its passionate preoccupation with the hidden ranges of consciousness and the universal elements in trivial experience.

Considering further, he realized that this "specific pleasure" was for him "the only one which was fruitful and true" and he resolved to spend the rest of his days pursuing it. "I had now decided to devote myself to contemplating the essence of things, to capture it, but how?" Since the essential is the very stuff of art, he realized that despite his former decision to the contrary, he had unconsciously determined to create a work of art. Proving, perhaps, his own contention that "genius is only instinct." Because his instinct was for writing, his work would assume that form. The book which he thus decides to write is the one which ends with his decision to begin writing it.

Those moments in which the memory set free "fragments of existence underlying time" were always brought about by a likeness between sensations experienced now and formerly. Though the present was always victor in that clash, the conquered always appeared more beautiful, and he vainly tried to hold it. But one respect in which associative memory differs from voluntary recall, is that it cannot be prolonged. Asking himself why these moments always seemed so much more beautiful than the present, so that "the true paradise is that which is lost", he concluded that reality fell short because "my imagination which was my sole organ for enjoying beauty was not able to apply itself by virtue of the ineluctable law which decrees that one can only imagine what is absent. And behold how suddenly, by a marvelous expedient of nature which makes a sensation occur at once in the past, permitting my imagination to enjoy it, and in the present where the actual rousing of my sense . . . added to the dreams of imagination that of which they are normally deprived, the idea of existence, . . . my being was permitted to . . . transfix—during a flash—that which it never understands: a little time in a pure state."

Looking back over the disappointments of his life, he realized that they were "but the varied aspect taken by our inability to realize ourselves in material enjoyment, in real action." He concluded that his ecstatic moments had a reality far deeper than immediate sensual perception or even than that specious impression we give ourselves when we voluntarily try to remember. As illustration he compares the ease with which Swann in after years could allude to his love for Odette, and the spasm of pain he betrayed when the musical phrase which to him represented that dead love, brought back its days in their essence. Deliberate recall, he maintains, being founded on cold intellect, brings back a "memory without truth rather than something which, common both to the past and the present, is more essential than either of them." The only way to enjoy these truer realities is to "know them more completely, there where they are to be found, that is to say, within [oneself] . . . to render them clear, down to their very depths." To this end one must, as in fact Proust did, close "ears and eyes to the external world."

But it would be a mistake to regard his work as written for the sake of *reminiscence*. It is based on reminiscence, because to him that was the most obvious way of approaching the reality which begins when one fixes "the point common to one thing and to another." The end of his search was the essential. In the case of memory, the essence was of time, and time, as Mr. Clive Bell has said, is the true hero of the book, with the subconscious for heroine. "It was this notion of incorporate time . . . that I had now the intention of putting so strongly into relief in my work . . . I should here describe men, even if that made them resemble monstrous beings, as occupying in time a considerable place, unlike that very limited one which is reserved for them in space, a place . . . prolonged without end, since like giants buried in the years they touch at the same instant such distant epochs lived by them . . . in Time." So definite was this idea of man's place in time that when he met the daughter of a former sweetheart he saw her "tall figure measuring that distance I had not wished to see . . . formed of the very years I had lost."

His moments of vision, however, were not always connected with time. Sometimes "they were impressions of a new truth . . . which I was trying to discover by efforts of the same sort as those one makes in order to recall something, as if our most beautiful ideas were like airs of music which 'come back' to us without our ever having heard them before, and which we force ourselves to listen to and to transcribe." He remembers "with pleasure because that showed me I was already the same" that even as a child he had fixed before his mind some image which commanded his attention, "a cloud, a triangle, a bell tower, a flower, a pebble, thinking that there was perhaps under those appearances something quite different which I ought to try to discover, a thought which they translated after the manner of those hieroglyphic characters which one thinks represent only material things."

It is here that the work of Proust takes wings. Not when he proceeds, as he often does, to generalize falsely from his own bias. That habit of his is revealed in his very language, which will change during one sentence from the first person singular, which with him is apt to be singular indeed, to the first person plural, embracing all mankind. In a sense his whole book may be said to issue from such a false generalization, since few will subscribe to his worship of the moment re-lived. He soars highest when he projects himself by means of his minute and colossal imagination; particularly when he finds a universal tragi-comedy in a gesture which appears trivial until his exhaustive analysis makes us endow it with enough volume to accommodate its complexity. The Baron de Charlus bows to a lady, and the phenomena of illness, age, snobbery, fidelity, sweep past us with murmuring overtones and rustling undertones. It is significant that these universalizations which flash across his pages as if by accident appeared to the writer, as to the reader, the *raison d'être* of his work.

With utter naiveté this sophisticate Proust extolls his universal verities as the end and the alleviation of life. His fervent instinct, balked of an orthodox God to worship, finds outlet here. An eternal truth, bounded by a nutshell and king of infinite space, to him represents salvation. And once it has been revealed, he never falters from the piety which he avows in the very terms we associate with religious experience.

One of the prime verities implied in his discussion of memory, but rising to an identity of its own, is the unreality of objective fact. The objective is there no doubt, but it does not exist for us. For us there is only the elusive resultant of the interplay between our psychic history, our present emotional state, and the qualities with which for one reason or another, we imbue a person or thing. The external world, like our internal being, is constantly changing. Since ourself, a personality in flux, or rather a series of personalities linked in a chain of experience, must react to an equal flux, the consequence is an instability which finds its physical counterpart only in the realm of relativity, and its philosophical equivalent in the writings of Bergson. To mirror this condition in a novel, one must prepare "a hundred masks to attach to a single visage, were it only according to the eyes which see it and the sense in which they read its features, and for the same eyes according to the hope or the fear or on the contrary, the love and the habit which over so many years hid the alterations of age."

People will persist, he complains, in seeking objective truth, an absolute medical diagnosis, a simple right or wrong in the Dreyfus affair, a yes-or-no answer to whether their mistress is false. Yet insight will tell them that truth lies as much in the eye which beholds and the mind which ponders as in the conditions envisaged. When it comes to emotion, Proust goes so far as to claim for individual love and even for national hatred, a reality far more durable than that of the objects to which they may be temporarily attached.

The perceptions of such verities as these "could not but make me rejoice, since it is the truth, the truth suspected by everyone, which I was to try to reveal." This rejoicing is potent to assuage and to compensate the grief of any particular experience, once it has reached the stage where the victim is able to generalize. "Ideas are medicines which can be substituted for griefs." Moreover, unhappiness itself is to be prized, "even though it ends by killing", for that is "the only way in which certain ideas first enter us." Except possibly in the case of rare genius, it is only in times of grief that our thoughts, roused as by a storm, ascend to a level where we can perceive them. Perhaps this conviction is in itself a compensation for Proust's belief that most experience leads to pain—especially love, which to him is conceivable only in conjunction with jealousy. Every love he depicts is of this type, and here is one instance of his generalizing from the particular. Yet of the type he depicts, his analysis is probably the most complete ever written, and like the studies of Freud, has much to reveal concerning more normal processes.

Finally, he finds in grief a spur as well as a source of material. "Imagination and thought are excellent machines, but it is grief that sets them in motion." Not during its ascendancy, but in the respite that follows internal storm, grief pricks us on to labor. That is, if we are artists. Otherwise all our pain goes for nought; it will not even bring the insight which is its balm and compensation. Those who are not creative must depend on the writer whose work "is only a kind of optical instrument which he offers to the reader" enabling him "to discern what without this book he might not have seen."

It comes to pass, then, that every experience of the artist's life can be transmuted into the gold which is his currency, and that the people who love him or hurt him or casually brush against him serve only as models for the general truths he must portray in order to make his life seem precious to himself.

It takes many instances to build up the knowledge which will enable us to generalize, and Proust himself indicates that even a very long experience may not be a very wide one. Each vital episode holds the prognostication of those to come, being stamped indelibly by the essential self which endures through all our transmutations. We need not fear, however, that a multitude of instances will be lacking. "Those who pose for happiness have not many sittings to give us, but those who pose for grief will grant frequent appointments in that studio . . . which is the interior of ourselves." Far from regretting this fact, he urges us to welcome suffering. "Let us tear apart our bodies, since each new piece that is detached comes, this time luminous and legible, to add to our work, to complete it."

Looking over his life in the light of his new revelation, he saw it as an unmitigated training for the work he now projected. "Each least episode had given a lesson in idealism", profitting him today by proving the unreliability of mere substance. As if to satisfy those who cavill at his emphasis on sexual inversion, he points out that this "idealism is illustrated even more aptly by inverted than by normal love." It shows that "it is not to people we should attach ourselves, it is not people who actually exist . . . but ideas." Therefore "the writer must not be offended if the invert gives to his heroine a masculine countenance. . . . If M. de Charlus had not given to the 'infidèle' over whom Musset wept in the Nuit d'Octobre or in the Souvenir, the countenance of Morel"—a youth the Baron loved—"he would neither have wept nor understood."

The term 'idealism' may ring strangely on the ears of those who have considered Proust an exponent of something quite different. True, he used it in the philosophical rather than the moral sense. But neither meaning is inapplicable to his work, which viewed in its entirety, represents a man's pilgrimage toward what for him constitutes the good life. An author who depicts a man's honesty leading him through cities of the plain and primrose paths, through the darkness of doubt and the winds of despair, to final reunion with his very self, has a right to call himself and to be called, idealist.

These "lessons in idealism" carried over from life into literature, indicating the fallacy of "the literature vaunted realistic" which ends by warping our own perceptions so that we mistake appearance for truths, forgetting that reality which is "half in the object and half in ourselves." He goes further, insisting that for the true literary masterpiece one is not free to choose his subject matter. We do not create works of art, we discover them, when we discover "what ought to be most precious and normally remains forever unknown, our true life, reality as we have felt it. . . . The book with characters traced, not drawn by us" although it be "most painful of all to inscribe, is also the only one which reality has dictated to us." This book, in which the writer is really a translator, reveals the truth that "begins when the author will take two different objects, establish their relationship . . . extract their essence, reuniting both in a metaphor in order to release them from the contingencies of time, and will couple them by the indescribable bond of an alliance of words."

Since Proust's style has been so berated and so lauded, it is worth examining further what he has to say on the subject. That he found in metaphor something more vital than mere rhetorical adornment is obvious from the foregoing passage, and also from his statement that by constantly changing comparisons he explained, *and understood,* himself better. The boldness, the bulk, the dogged thoroughness of his similes, vindicates them from the charge of preciosity. Whether his comparison be drawn from science or art, history or daily observation, it is no facile picture, but the clear image which results when the scales of habit are patiently scraped from the eye. He will not be deterred by fear of uncouth novelty, of triteness, or of repetition. (Of course where a whole sentence or even paragraph is repeated, one attributes it to a flaw in editing, due to the circumstances under which the later volumes were published.) Because he shunned the "speed acquired by habit" the reading of his book moves so slowly that his tempo, like his figures of speech, has become an earmark. Whether that be viewed as virtue or fault is an individual and for the moment an irrelevant matter; it is deliberate, and it is Proust.

Both his literary criticism and his habits of work proved him extremely sensitive to beauty of word and rhythm. Yet he rigorously subordinated symmetry to sense. "In my anxiety that my sentences should exactly reproduce what I seemed to have detected in my mind, and in my fear of their not turning out 'true to life' I had no time to ask myself whether what I was writing would be pleasant to read." Style was a very special problem with Proust, since the matter of his contribution lay precisely in the manner of its presentation. Although for this reason, manner may appear to outweigh matter in his work, it is essential to realize that he evolved his medium by concentrating, not on the means of expression, but on the meaning he wished to express. His final word on the relationship of expression and conception would in itself be clue to his whole theory of art and of life. "Style for the writer as for the painter is a question, not of technique, but of vision. It is the revaluation which would be impossible by direct and conscious methods of the qualitative difference which there is in the way the world appears to us, a difference which, if there were not art, would remain the eternal secret of each one." Therein, he implies, lies the real escape offered by art; not an escape from physical milieu, by reading of princes if one be a pauper, and of Hottentots if one be a Parisian, but a participation in those various worlds of which one is offered to us by each original artist. It is an escape, moreover, which is at the same time a home-coming; for every true work of art lights up unknown places within ourselves as well as outside.

The emphasis on this boon of escape suggests a greater regard for his audience than Proust actually felt. He scorned alike the common man, the critic, the social butterfly, the "feeble and sterile connoisseur." He did hail, however, that rare reader who vivifies a work until his appreciation becomes almost creative. But—"how many are there in twenty years?" There are always those who resent a writer's disdain for the public, particularly when to an unfamiliar form is added what certain wholesome temperaments term Proust's morbid egocentricity. They charge that he makes a cult of his own reactions, that he lived with his head turned over his shoulder and his finger on his own pulse. From this point of view, self indulgence is seen even in the literary style which leads the reader so active a chase through mazy sentences and towering similes.

But if he contemplated his own experience like a mystic who forgets the world about him to plunge his speculations in a blade of grass, it must be remembered that the mystic sees a universe reflected in that tiny green spear. Proust found a universality in the fragment of a cookie melting on his tongue. He complained that even his admirers congratulated him "on having so successfully used the microscope, when I had on the contrary used a telescope." As a matter of fact, his great gift lay in combining the lense of one with the scope of the other.

Proust, like most artists, cheerfully admitted self-realization as the prime motive for his work. But in the last analysis, he insists, all fruitful altruism is merely egoism made utilizable for others. What he sought was not public acclaim, nor catharsis by self-expression, but the joy of performing a task whose difficulties were outweighed only by the ardor with which he approached it, and which would benefit the reader as well as himself. In writing this book, which to him was the only one worth writing, he avowed a triple purpose. (1) He was to seek out the essence of things, that world of prototypes which is approached by the fragmentary events of human life; to capture incorporate time and so for a moment lay hands on eternity; to track down universal verities and so transmute pain into joy. (2) By doing this, he was to justify life to himself—more than justify, to make it precious and fruitful. (3) Finally, he was to offer "an optical instrument whereby the reader could more truly read himself" at the same time that he opened up the vision of another soul's universe, thus providing the only true escape through literature.

All these marks he has hit so accurately that his novel must be reckoned, not only as a rare creation, but also as a rare fulfillment of its own design. He has, as he said he must do, perfected a new medium which in its thematic development, and reiteration, its evocation of overtones and undertones, its gradual building up of concepts too elusive for mere words, suggests music more than literature. With infinite labor, with rigid concentration, he actually did, as he said he must, "prepare his book minutely, with perpetual regroupings of forces, as for an offensive, support it like a fatigue, accept it like a rule, construct it like a cathedral, follow it like a regimen, conquer it like an obstacle, subdue it like a friendship, nourish it like an infant, create it like a world, without overlooking those mysteries which probably have their explanation only in other worlds, and the presentiment of which is what moves us most in life and in art." (pp. 229-40)

Dane Bettman, "Marcel Proust Explains Himself," in The Sewanee Review *(reprinted by permission of the editor; published 1932 by The University of the South), Vol. XL, No. 2, Spring, 1932, pp. 229-40.*

HAAKON M. CHEVALIER (essay date 1932)

[*Chevalier is an American educator, author, and translator; in the following excerpt he reviews* The Past Recaptured *and contends, contrary to Proust's assertion that the structure of* Remembrance of Things Past *would become clear when the final volume appeared, that the novel is completely without structure. Chevalier maintains that Proust's aesthetic was a "rationalization of his weakness, of his inability to control his material, to select and reject." Nonetheless, Chevalier believes Proust's masterpiece to be among the great literary productions of the century. For a contrasting discussion of the success of Proust's designs, see the excerpt by Dane Bettman (1932).*]

When his readers complained that his long novel, which began to appear in 1913, was formless and discursive, Marcel Proust begged them to delay their judgment till the publication of the last volume (which came only in 1927), when it would appear that the whole was "rigorously constructed," and "the last page of **'The Past Recaptured'** would close exactly on the first of **'Swann.'**" I am among those who upon the reading of this last volume remain unconvinced.

A great part of the volume is concerned with the author's recurring meditations upon his art. From the first page there is established the mood of half-conscious reverie which is Proust's special domain, in which events, characters, places and ideas flow into each other, losing their sharp outlines without losing their identity, and images have the peculiar elasticity of objects seen through stirred water. A careful reading fails to reveal more than a feeble thread of association linking these together, save at long intervals when, as with a jolt, the author seems to remember that he must get on with his subject. The subject is, as the title announces, the recapture of the past—or more exactly, how the narrator stumbles upon the secret which enables him to write a book in which his past will live again, more richly than it did in actuality, so that all his life will seem to have been merely a necessary prelude to the writing of this work.

In the first short chapter the narrator, beset by his growing illness, spends an indefinite period of several years, up to 1916, in the sanitarium at Tansonville. Characteristically, the passage of these years takes up only half of the chapter, the last half being given over to an incident occupying but a few hours, in which the reading of a fragment of the Journal of the Goncourt brothers leads to important meditations upon the relations of literature to life.

The next chapter gives a brilliant picture of wartime Paris. The author evokes admirably the feverish, abnormal atmosphere, the curious modifications of character which patriotism induces, the extraordinary distortions of fact as recorded in the press, the elasticity of minds that can continue for four years confidently to believe that the War will be over within a week. The War breaks down social barriers. The slow process of infiltration which Proust has described as wearing away the protective layers separating the social strata over the fifty-year period covered by the novel is tremendously accelerated. The widowed Odette Swann has married the Comte de Forcheville. Mme. Verdurin becomes a social dictator. Saint-Loup, in a sense regenerated by the War, enters the service and is killed in action. The Baron de Charlus, Proust's most remarkable creation, holds the center of the stage in this chapter. His vices, his opinions, are discussed at great length, and the progress of the War is reflected through his eyes. With the same scrupulous detachment, without any modification of tone, Proust describes on the one hand his rapid progress in his increasingly sordid vices and the consequent disintegration of his whole personality and, on the other, the fine workings of his sensitive intellect, the delicacy and courage of his judgment of people and situations, the admirable sanity of his attitude towards the War.

The third and last chapter, "The Princesse de Guermantes Receives," brilliantly caps the whole novel. Here, as in the last act of an eighteenth-century play, all the surviving actors reappear for the last time. And here all the forces set into motion in the course of the preceding volumes reach their climax. For the fusion of the various social classes that has been in progress is now complete, and a new distribution of ranks has completely superseded that which obtained when the narrator, as a boy, first dreamed of the Guermantes, "that mysterious race with piercing eyes and birdlike beaks, that pink, golden, unapproachable race."

The time is long after the War. The scene is the drawing-room of the Princesse de Guermantes. The people are, most of them, grotesquely old; indeed, by strict chronology, both the Princesse and Odette—now the mistress of the Duc de Guermantes—would be in their nineties. The narrator observes the ravages of Time upon the faces that he sees. All these people, who have lived empty or vicious lives, are sinking into tragedy, and their old age is hideous. The low have been raised to high position, but they derive no pleasure from their success. Those who were at the top have lost their inviolability. Some, like Charlus, have sunk to the lowest depths. The Duchesse de Guermantes—the "purest" of the Guermantes—is "thought to be a *déclassée*." Every life is a failure. Upon each of them Time has exercised its destructive hand. And in this last chapter, which fills more than half the entire book, the author achieves a grandiose sense of eternal flux, of an inexorable movement that carries with it not only people but places, systems and civilizations, that constantly alters the aspects and relationships of things. And the individuals themselves also change: at no two moments of their lives are they the same.

Time, then, the author concludes, from all he has observed over a period that seems to him immeasurably long, is the great enemy of human happiness. Is there no way to escape its tyranny? Is there no way to preserve human values? This poignant question forms one of the basic themes of the entire novel. During the Princesse de Guermantes' reception, the narrator makes his great discovery: art can rescue what is best in human experience. On that day, a series of sensations, like the sound of a spoon against a teacup, the feeling of starchy stiffness of a napkin, cause certain moments of his past, now liberated from Time, to live again for him with greater vividness than in their original actuality and to arouse in him a kind of felicity with which nothing else in his life can compare. The scenes thus recreated are just the ones he has vainly attempted in the past to describe in writing, the ones which have caused him so much discouragement that on this very morning he had definitely abandoned the prospect of a literary career. From the discovery of this psychological phenomenon he elaborates his whole esthetic. The artist, he concludes, must proceed in this same manner. It is useless for him to try consciously to achieve an effect. The result will be a lifeless presentation of facts which do not correspond to any reality perceptible to the imagination. He must wait upon these accidental sensations that shall revive for him the totality of an experience.

There is, of course, more to this "credo" than I am here able to expound; and it is impossible adequately to discuss its merits. The essential, if not revolutionary, truth which it embodies is that the artist must not copy what he sees but record what he feels. He himself—not his subject matter, not his reader—is the measure of his art. This is the essential difference between "realistic" art and that which Proust proposes to practise. The realist attempts to reproduce as accurately as possible that which he sees. Proust attempts to make the reader *participate* in his own experience. What this means is that the reader must enter into the processes of the writer in order to have the experience. Since Proust's processes are highly exceptional, this is difficult, if not impossible, for most readers.

The ideal reader of Proust's novel is Proust. And the only way to read him is to keep one's eye, not on the characters and incidents and scenes which he projects, but on the processes of his mind. It is this mind, its extraordinary activity, its lapses, its hallucinations, its uncanny insights, the strange creatures given forth by it, which forms the principal interest of the book. It is useless, for instance, to try to picture a face that he describes. He will not draw it for you, he will give you practically nothing to go by. He will tell you that it looks like an aquarium, or a garden, or a fruit. His descriptive technique consists almost entirely of metaphor. These creatures do, amazingly, live for the reader; but they live as monsters. They are vivid, but fantastic, like creatures in a dream. Everything is improbable, strained. The characters are exaggerated, distorted; many of them lack any unity of personality. The events have no sequence or coherence. There is no distinction drawn between what is important and what is trivial. Yet in that extraordinary fluid atmosphere which inundates Proust's world, which distorts, magnifies or minimizes objects at the author's will, disbelief is completely suspended: the triumph of art is complete. But the reader must remain completely docile in order to preserve the spell. He must follow the image as it slowly winds through the intricate convolutions of the author's brain, as it becomes modified, as it stumbles against an obstacle which in turn sets a whole new process into motion.

Convinced that he was obeying eternal laws in the composition of his work, he was in fact obeying only the laws of his own extraordinary but afflicted temperament. As his work grew, its structure assumed for him a kind of mystic inevitability. It was "The Work" for which he was made. He was invested with a sacred responsibility. "I felt myself pregnant with the work which I was carrying within me, like some precious and fragile object which had been entrusted to me and which I desired to transmit intact to the other persons for whom it was destined." And so the monster grew. And as it grew it came to assume that rightness and that "obscure necessity" which religions have for their believers.

What strikes us as we read is that Proust is not master of his subject. He is its slave. That long, formless, yet in many ways so superb novel, is in a poignant sense a defeat. It betrays, in the large, a complete absence of will power before the work of art considered as a whole. Proust is powerless to conceive, to create, a structure. He cannot control, except as it flows through his hands, the mass of material that covers his pages like a lava. His esthetic is a rationalization of his weakness, of his inability to control his material, to select and reject.

Yet all these reservations—which I feel to be valid—completely fall in the presence of the work itself. For in spite of them (or because of them, if you will) the book, in its voluminous, disconcerting, afflicted entirety, has a strength, a wholeness, a vital richness with which no other literary production of our century can compare. It has the strength of seemingly inexhaustible resources of imagination utilized in the creation of its fictive world. It has the wholeness of a life's experience deeply lived and assimilated, so that all the reality of the author's inner self could be poured into his work. And the complex picture of society which it projects has a richness of ideas and images which, even though they are those of a sick man, are sufficient to illuminate what seems to us, in our limited sense of things permanent, the whole experience of a generation. (pp. 157-58)

Haakon M. Chevalier, "Proust: The Final Chapter," in The New Republic *(reprinted by permission of* The New Republic; *© 1932 The New Republic, Inc.), Vol. LXXII, No. 929, September 21, 1932, pp. 157-58.*

HARRY LEVIN (essay date 1948)

[*In the following excerpt Levin, an American scholar and literary critic, traces the prototypes of many of the characters in* Remembrance of Things Past *back to Proust's earliest work,* Pleasures and Days.]

Originally published in 1896, when Proust was 25, [***Pleasures and Regrets***] comprises a sequence of stories and sketches which date back as far as his twentieth year. . . .

These were gathered together . . . and luxuriously printed at the author's expense. Lacking confidence in the intrinsic appeal of his text, he embellished it with chic accessories: flower-illustrations by Madeleine Lemaire, musical settings by Reynaldo Hahn, preface by Anatole France [see *TCLC*, Vol. 7, p. 518]. The latter, which is included in the present translation, seemed at the time no more than a polite gesture. Rereading it today, we can credit the older writer with prophetic insight into a talent destined to surpass his own. For **"The Remembrance of Things Past"** not only returned the compliment with its masterly portrait of Bergotte. It also lived up to the comparison between Proust's subject-matter and the orchidaceous atmosphere of a hothouse, between his method and the newly discovered X-ray.

Any contemporary reader could have noted that these prose poems and Italianate chronicles—with their echoes from Flaubert and Stendhal, their overtones of Laforgue and Barbey d'Aurevilly—were the writing of a clever young man. What France discerned, in their very precocity, was a profound sense of the world's old age. Seeking to characterize his protégé, he balanced two equally far-fetched epithets against each other: "a depraved Bernardin de Saint-Pierre" and "a guileless Petronius." The resulting impression is aptly Proustian in its mingling of idyllic innocence and decadent experience, in the interplay between "Paul and Virginia" the "The Satyricon." Proust's mature work is kept perennially fresh by its nostalgia for childhood. His youthful book is already overcast by the consciousness of worldly corruption.

His own words, addressed to another, apply to himself: "Almost before you were a man, you were a man of letters." In the direction of his thought, as well as the derivation of his technique, the child was father to the man. His unique perception of seascapes and landmarks, regional names and personal relics and associated memories, the smell of hawthorns and the suffocations of asthma, is as evident in his early fragments as in his later novel. Here, as later, music is the leitmotif of love. In two of these brief episodes, as in the long-drawn-out romance of Albertine, jealousy ends and oblivion begins with an equestrian accident. In none are the lovers happy, except when watching the sleep of the beloved.

We are thus permitted to follow Proust as he sketches out his crucial situations and rehearses his principal characters. He describes a dinner party presided over by a hostess whom he will immortalize as Madame Verdurin. He details the genealogy of another lady, half bird and half goddess, to be better known as the Duchesse de Guermantes. Four of his weak-willed protagonists trace an autobiographical pattern: the child who demands, and subsequently profanes, the sanction of its mother's goodnight kiss. The very first scene, like the last, is characteristically set at the deathbed of a young man. And the bitter lesson in worldliness, which M. Swann would not learn until the end of his leisurely career, is foresuffered by the dying Viscount of Sylvania.

The fundamental plight, for Proust's characters, is the paradox of solitude in the midst of society. It is not surprising to find him quoting frequently from Emerson. Another favorite source of quotation is "The Imitation of Christ," which often counterweights his frivolous album leaves. Snobbery, which lends a kind of poetic glamour to his material, is undercut by guilt, remorse and regret. "The pleasures of the evening sadden the morning." This comment of Thomas à Kempis illuminates the English title, **"Pleasures and Regrets."** The French title, **"Pleasures and Days,"** is a debonair evocation of Hesiod's "Work and Days." The narrator's role is that of the diner-out sauntering homeward, detaching himself from a series of fashionable occasions, retrospectively weighing his pleasures against his regrets.

In comparison with the vast fresco of **"The Remembrance of Things Past"**—to use another Proustian metaphor—**"Pleasures and Regrets"** is a delicately painted fan. It is fascinating to observe, through such different media, the same persisting figures and attitudes. Between the two works lay the one political event in which Proust actively participated, the Dreyfus Affair. Meanwhile, too, under the tutelage of John Ruskin, he came to recognize the dynamic relationship between art and morality. After that decade of extended apprenticeship, when his mother died, he was ready to withdraw from the world and write his masterpiece. But that was neither a sudden decision nor an inspired afterthought. It was the logical completion of a train of ideas which had long been germinating.

Harry Levin, "Proust's First-Published Writings," in The New York Times Book Review *(copyright © 1948 by The New York Times Company; reprinted by permission), August 1, 1948, p. 3.*

HAROLD MARCH (essay date 1948)

[*In the following excerpt, March discusses the many fluctuations in Proust's literary reputation since his death, and then attempts to enumerate the stylistic and thematic strengths and weaknesses of* Remembrance of Things Past.]

Although there has always been a great diversity of opinion about the value of Proust's work, it is possible to distinguish since his death successive trends, alternately favorable and unfavorable. (p. 240)

On the whole the nineteen-twenties marked the high point of Proust's prestige. The difficulty and complexity of his work, and comparisons made between him and Bergson, Einstein, and Freud, combined to make him a shibboleth among the intelligentsia. He was a fad with literary and esthetic snobs, and in wider circles his name was mentioned with a respect that was unhampered by sound knowledge. Obviously mere complexity is no valid criterion of worth, and the comparison with Bergson, although true enough in some respects, has been greatly overemphasized. The bracketing of Proust with Einstein was chiefly done by people who knew nothing of Einstein and little of Proust. It was enough that some critics (beginning with Camille Vettard, who really did have some preliminary qualifications for speaking of Einstein) had mentioned the two together for the word to be busily repeated among the bright young moderns. Whether or not there was any useful connection between a principle of astro-physics and a reputed point of view on truth and morals, did not matter; the magic word "relativity" was enough—"everything was relative."

Another magic word, "the subconscious," connected Proust and Freud, although here—Freud being much more accessible to the layman than Einstein—the comparison had a better chance of validity. Freud dealt with the subconscious, the unconscious, and the id; Proust dealt, it was generally said, with the subconscious, although his word was really *l'inconscient,* the unconscious. But there is nothing Freudian in Proust's point of view or terminology, and not the slightest indication that he was personally acquainted with Freud's work. The grounds on which he referred, in his Bois interview and subsequently, to his work being "a series of novels of the unconscious" were the phenomena of forgetting and remembering. We note, he claimed (and here he crossed Bergson's path), what our reasoning minds consider to have possible future or present utility. Such items may drop out of our mind, but can be recalled by an effort of the voluntary memory, or occasionally by accident through the organic memory. But we *unconsciously* note a host of other items which we can scarcely speak of forgetting because they never occupied the focus of attention, but which may rise to the surface, intact and powerful, through the involuntary memory. In these ideas there is no hint of repressions, the id, the censor, moral tumors, or their cure by analysis; nor does sex play any rôle.

Of course there are numerous small ways in which Proust touches on Freud's domain. Something like the id is evoked by Proust's allusions to "visceral depths" and "primitive existences" to which one descends in sleep; human conduct is of course subconsciously motivated; various associational elements in memory and thinking are observed. And finally, but quite unconsciously, Proust presented in the character of Marcel (and himself) a beautiful Freudian case, complete with mother fixation, father rivalry, fantasy, perversion, neurosis, dreams, repressions—practically everything the most confirmed Freudian could ask for. But he was merely giving a personal history; he had no idea of writing a Freudian novel. (pp. 241-42)

[Proust's] prestige of the twenties had unsound foundations, and when the new decadence was succeeded by the inevitable new moral earnestness, it went into a long decline. True, Proust was now much better understood, as several well-informed and intelligent studies testified; but to offset this advantage to his reputation came new attacks on his character and personality. How could so evil a tree, it was argued, bring forth good fruit? Proust was a decadent, a weak-willed homosexual neurotic; it was high time he and all he stood for were forgotten. The publication, in 1930, of the first volume of his collected correspondence, the letters to Montesquiou, showed his obsequiousness in its most unpleasant light, and aided in the depreciation. Then came Professor Feuillerat's attempt to demonstrate that Proust's poetic mysticism was an early phase of his thought, disavowed by the skeptical and pessimistic Proust that came into being during the war. Feuillerat professed a guarded respect for the later Proust, and one was left with the impression that if there was anything of worth in him it was to be found in his later phase; the rest was mere naïve nonsense, an infirmity of childhood which he had thrown off like the measles.

The net result was that by the late thirties implacable opponents of Proust took heart; clearly he was on his way out, and some even declared that he was already dead.

"Forever dead? Who shall say?" Proust's words about the death and possible survival of Bergotte are applicable to the fate of his own work, which shows a disconcerting tendency to return to life. No sooner has the dust of the supposedly ultimate battle settled, than new readers, indifferent to his annihilation, discover him and sing his praises. A new world war has made the society Proust described seem more remote than ever; and yet during it, as in the first war, and before the days of his unwholesome notoriety, he acquired admirers.

It is time to drop attack and defense and, without evasion or concealment, but also without idolatry, to take Proust for what he is. The continued vitality of his work shows that he cannot be shrugged off as a mere abnormal phenomenon, of passing historical interest; but his weaknesses as a man and as an artist are written into his work, and must also be recognized.

The immense length of ***A la Recherche du temps perdu*** is not justified by the maintenance of a uniform standard of excellence. Parts of it are masterly; other parts, merely dull. There are confusions, irrelevances, inadvertent repetitions; and the frequent complexity of the style imposes on the reader a burden of attention not always warranted by the effect produced.

As a realistic panorama of society the novel is far inferior in scope to Balzac's *Comédie humaine,* to which it is occasionally compared. Proust's limited world is largely made up of decaying aristocrats, wealthy bourgeois, and servants. Within these limits he has given us some unforgettable portraits, but they remain fictional creations; living, indeed, with a monstrous vitality of their own, but seldom convincing us that they are representative. It is impossible to believe that people are, literally, such as Proust represents them—at least in any large numbers; in particular we cannot accept his estimate of the prevalence of homosexuality. And his hordes of characters remain aggregations of individuals; one does not feel them to constitute a society.

As a psychologist Proust must unquestionably be ranked very high, and yet even here he is one-sided. He in inclined to attribute to everyone his own peculiarities, weaknesses, and limitations. There is more in love, for example, or in friendship, than he seems prepared to admit.

The only way to take Proust is on his own terms. The mere fact that he wrote a very long novel containing a large number of characters is insufficient reason for judging him on the same standards as one would judge Balzac. His characters, his viewpoint, and his psychology are of a very special kind; within the limits of his domain he is supreme.

The singularity of Proust's viewpoint, and of much of his power, results in large part from the combination in him of the poet and the analyst. Poetry, obviously, is much more than a matter of rhythm; it is a way of seeing. And Proust saw like a poet. He was not content with surface resemblances and disparities; he always struggled to get at the "profound, authentic impression," and to relate it to something else. It was in this relating to something else, this effort to classify and to explain, that the analyst in him came into play.

But a part of Proust's special savor comes also from his invalidism and neuroticism. His world is that of the man in bed, seen at one remove, and this fact is his strength and his weakness. Imagination and memory play larger rôles than in the case of a more normal writer. He remembers and he imagines slights, deceptions, tricks; he projects his idiosyncrasies beyond his cork-lined walls and fastens them on to others. But from his claustration, too, he drew his extraordinary acuity of vision and the rich quality of his memory. "Never," he wrote, long before he could realize how fully the statement was to apply to himself, "was Noah able to see the world so well as from the Ark."

His great achievement as a psychologist is his description of himself. No one, not even Stendhal, has told himself so fully; and no one has probed more patiently and more exhaustively into the dark corners of the neurotic personality. To do this, it was not enough to be himself the neurotic introvert; he needed, and he had, a remarkable power of detachment and a strong analytic talent. The result is that from his own highly special psychology he was able to extract general truth.

But social panorama, character creation, style, psychology—all these aspects of Proust's individuality acquire significance only in relation to his basic philosophy, his report on experience. Here what Proust has to say sifts down to this: there are two worlds, one the world of time, where necessity, illusion, suffering, change, decay, and death are the law; the other the world of eternity, where there is freedom, beauty, and peace. Normal experience is in the world of time, but glimpses of the other world may be given in moments of contemplation or through accidents of involuntary memory. It is the function of art to develop these insights and to use them for the illumination of life in the world of time.

That there is a relation between this message and the ideas of other writers seems clear enough. Like Schopenhauer, whom he read and admired, Proust believed that in the world of ordinary experience illusion was inescapable, desire insatiable and always frustrated, and happiness impossible; like him he asserted the possibility of rising above ordinary experience in contemplation; like him he believed that the function of art was not to describe superficial appearances but to penetrate to the world of Platonic Idea. Unlike Schopenhauer, who believed that this superior insight was attainable only in proportion to the surrender of individuality, Proust clung to a faith in an irreducible minimum of personality in artist or seer.

Proust's sense of the continuing past has often and with some justice been compared to Bergson's idea of duration. There is also a resemblance to be noted between Bergsonian intuition—instinctive apprehension and reason fused into a higher instrument of knowing—and Proust's moments of contemplation. Yet here Bergson is nearer to Schopenhauer's fusion of will and idea than he is to Proust, in whom emotional apprehension and reason appear rather to play successive and complementary rôles.

It is also evident that contemplation, whether in Proust or Schopenhauer, is psychologically much the same experience as the one described under the same name by mystics of various times and places. But the very word "mysticism" has the unfortunate effect of awakening obstinate ready-made attitudes of hostility or of veneration. To the favorably disposed the mystic is one who has risen above ordinary humanity and seen into immortal Reality; to the hostile, he is a self-deluded hysteric. We are not concerned (nor was Proust) with the experiences of supermen or of a lunatic fringe; we simply want to know whether there is a faculty, latent in all and developed in some, whereby may be apprehended a transcendent Reality which, as Proust puts it, "is simply our life, true life . . . the life which, in a sense, dwells at every instant in all men, and not in the artist alone." There is, as we have seen, strong evidence that Proust had experiences of involuntary memory and of contemplation, and that the philosophy expounded in his novel was not to him mere literary capital, but a personal view of the world and a way of life. What we need is evidence outside of speculative philosophies which Proust read and which colored his thinking, independent evidence tending to show that resemblances between Proust and this or that other writer are due, not to borrowings or "influences," but to the fact they are talking about the same thing.

Involuntary memory—the resurgence of the past through the repetition of a sensation—is a fairly common experience, though few have had it with the intensity of Proust. Somewhat less common, but still familiar, is the sudden feeling that around us, at this place and in this moment, there is something real, beautiful, important, and permanent, if we could but shake off preoccupation with our personal concerns, open our eyes, and see it. But we can go farther than such vague appeals to the possible experience of the reader.

It happens that there exists a document so situated in time that the possibility of literary influence is virtually excluded. *With the Door Open,* by the Danish novelist J. Anker Larsen, was first published in 1926, after the death of Proust, whose ideas were consequently unaffected by it, and before the publication of ***Le Temps retrouvé,*** so that Larsen was in the highest degree unlikely to have had a clear idea of Proust's philosophy. Furthermore, *With the Door Open* is not a novel, but a simple and patently honest autobiographical record. Describing . . . [a] series of what he calls "lightning flashes," Larsen says: . . .

> I walked and walked, until I found myself standing in front of a dyke by the wood. As I glanced at it, there was a flash of lightning. . . . It was a dyke by one of the fields belonging to the estate where I was born. I actually saw it. That is to say, at that moment I did not distinguish between this dyke and the old one, between my present ego and the one of the past. The two phenomena were *simultaneous and one*. . . . Suddenly a change occurred. I saw another dyke by another field at home—with the same feeling of present experience. . . .
>
> Now it was quite evident that this dyke resembled the others just as much as any other dyke. . . . No, the similarity did not lie outside of myself, in what I was looking at, but within myself, in the manner of my perception. I had succeeded in seeing this dyke *honestly and straightforwardly* with the eyes which were my birthright. The profound joy of reality filled me; my own inner condition opened out, and became one with all the homogeneous conditions. It was not a question of remembrance, but of a state of being. I did not miss the old dykes, for they were present.

Larsen's "lightning flashes" were accompanied by a joy so intense that he could not remain indifferent to it; but as soon as the joy passed into conscious enjoyment, the moment ended. Gradually he learned to rest in the moment, to be content with being, without self-conscious feeling. The result was that he became able to a certain extent to control the experience. He could look upon a road in the usual way, and then see it freed from space and time. "If I looked at the Holte road . . . it *opened* itself out, and I *saw within it* the road to Rudköbing."

Finally he reached what he calls his first "meeting with Eternity," an experience that seems to be a heightening and prolonging of the "lightning flash," but without the image from the past. He confesses himself unable adequately to describe it, but his few halting words are enough to identify it as full mystic experience. He concludes, "That was my first actual meeting with Reality; because such is the real life: a Now which *is* and a Now which *happens*. There is no beginning and no end. I cannot say anything more about this Now. I sat in my garden, but there was no place in the world where I was not."

It is scarcely necessary to enlarge on the extraordinary likeness between the experiences of the Danish author and those of Proust: the resurgence of the past with such vividness that it competes with the present; the sense of freedom, joy, and escape from time; the idea that in contemplation an object "opens," and reveals its true nature; the feeling that life as lived at other times than such moments is futile and meaningless; the description of transcendent Reality as the true life and the eternal Now. Proust and Larsen are talking about the same experience.

But clearly Larsen carried it farther than Proust, who did not get beyond the unpredictable and uncontrolled "flash." Yet for literary purposes the advantage is not wholly with Larsen. Such a novel as his *Philosopher's Stone* is at once too esoteric and too explicit: the sense of the other world is so strong that this one loses its reality. Larsen lacks the colossal humor, the horror, the subtle analysis of Proust's relentless probing into ordinary human experience. ***A la Recherche du temps perdu*** has neither the serenity of assured spiritual achievement nor the unrelieved pessimism of the cynical materialist; what it does give is a somber panorama of time lit by flashes of eternity. (pp. 243-50)

Harold March, in his The Two Worlds of Marcel Proust *(copyright 1948 University of Pennsylvania Press, and renewed 1975 by Harold March), University of Pennsylvania Press, 1948, 276 p.*

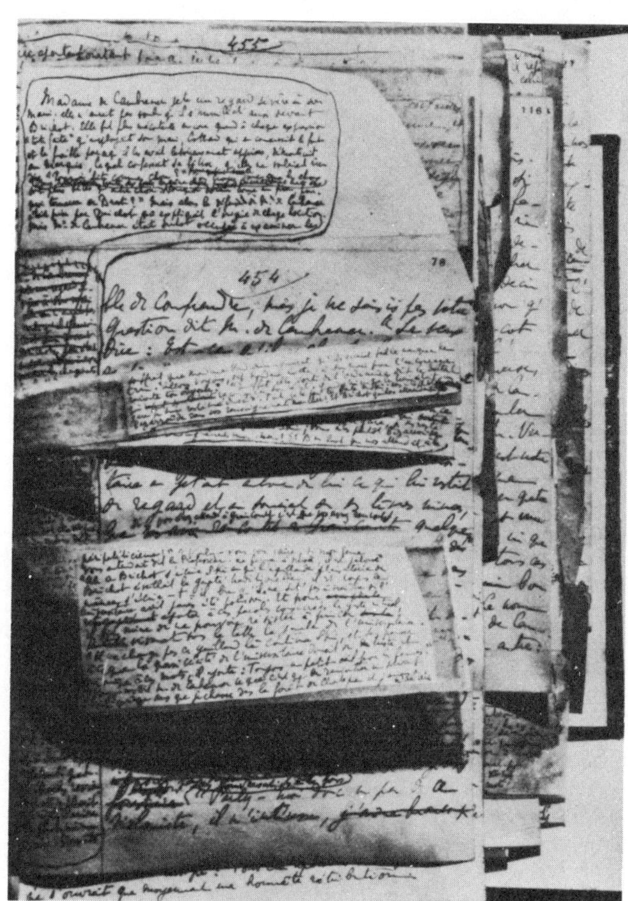

Manuscript pages from Proust's Sodom et Gomorrhe. *When the margins were full, Proust would attach small strips of paper with corrections and additions. Bibliotheque Nationale, Paris.*

MILTON HINDUS (essay date 1954)

[*In the following excerpt, Hindus compares Proust's style and characterizations in* Jean Santeuil *and* Remembrance of Things Past *and concludes that they are very similar; in the process, he illuminates many of the stylistic and thematic concerns of* Remembrance of Things Past. *Hindus feels that the chief difference between the earlier and the later work is the more skillful manner in which plot is manipulated in* Remembrance of Things Past.]

As a result of the discovery of ***Jean Santeuil,*** there is now a bridge to cover the gap between ***Les Plaisirs et les jours*** and ***A la recherche du temps perdu.*** There had been till now an astonishing, unaccountable leap from the immaturity of the first work to the mastery of the last. With nothing to stand in between them, the differences were an obvious invitation to romantic conjectures, for not only did it seem that the writer had managed to raise himself by his own bootstraps into greatness, but that he had done so all at once. ***Jean Santeuil*** supplies the necessary link, and we now see the development from the earlier to the later Proust as a gradual, evolutionary process, much less exciting and dramatic but also much more natural. The long foreground of Proust's accomplishment is at last securely established.

It is instructive to look at the evolution of Proust's faculties as a creative artist in terms of the categories of Aristotle's *Poetics*. Aristotle called the management of *plot* the most important element in dramatic composition, and he subordinated to it the ability to create character, the command over languge, and the other elements that enter into literary composition. The philosopher said, furthermore (and it is one of his amazingly fruitful observations), that it may be observed among the dramatists that mastery with regard to the drawing of character precedes mastery with regard to the satisfactory management of the plot, which generally awaits the growth of the writer's abilities. This fine distinction is fully confirmed by the development which we find in Proust, it seems to me. The principal difference between ***Jean Santeuil*** and ***A la recherche du temps perdu*** lies in the management of the plot found in the latter work and entirely absent from the former.

So far as the ability to animate his characters is concerned, Proust's talents must certainly be judged notable in the earlier work. What is absent there is the ability to put his characters into any real and long-drawn-out relations with each other. It is the pattern of these interrelationships that creates the conviction of the passage of time in the later novel, and with the passage of time the changes which the characters undergo. ***Jean Santeuil,*** on the other hand, can only by the widest latitude of criticism and with the utmost courtesy of definition be called a novel at all. It lacks entirely that organic unity and logic which seem inherent in the concept of this literary form. The difference is not such as exists between the episodic type of story and one with a more tightly knit development, because even in the episodic type the writer must create a coherent sense of movement or progress in the steps of his fable. ***Jean Santeuil*** does not manage to convey this movement to the reader. It is nothing more than a bundle of charming sketches revolving for the most part around the same characters. These characters do not seem to be going anywhere in particular. We are *told* that they grow old, for example, but we do not really believe it, because the author has not as yet the skill to create the illusion by imitating the slow and subtle changes by which age shows itself.

This skill of the full-fledged novelist Proust was to achieve in a pre-eminent degree later on. The delicate functioning of the connective tissues in his masterpiece is something to consider, and this smoothes over the deep changes in character, so that they carry conviction to the reader and are accepted without difficulty. Proust's gifts in ***Jean Santeuil*** are still mostly hidden in the cocoon, and the result is a work which possesses about as much organic connectedness as a bag full of beautiful marbles. The chapters individually are filled with lovely impressions, but we fail to see why any one of them should precede or follow any other. As a book, it is without beginning, middle, or end. Its sequences seem to be entirely fortuitous. Necessity here is not a compelling and unbreakable chain but only the slenderest of threads.

In his later life, Proust used to refer to his "architectural labors" ("travaux d'architecte") upon ***A la recherche du temps perdu.*** The phrase is instructive. What Aristotle means by the term plot is indeed the work of an "architect" of literary form. In the earlier work there is little evidence of long-range, planned construction, and successful articulation of separate parts. Everything seems largely improvised, and though a plan seems to lurk somewhere in the back of the author's mind as a potentiality of his material, it is all pretty vague, indefinite, and unrealized.

What we have then in ***Jean Santeuil*** is a gathering of the writer's forces and a marshaling of his materials, which are as yet not subjected to the proper discipline and order. The experienced reader of Proust will take pleasure in discovering the germs of many later developments in his work. As a trivial example, in the description of the novelist C. in ***Jean Santeuil***—"Occasionally he would remove his pince-nez, wipe his forehead, and run his hand through his reddish hair which was just beginning to be touched with gray"—the reader of ***Remembrance of Things Past*** is reminded of Swann's hair and of one of his most characteristic gestures. When Proust tells us that Jean regularly attended the courtroom sessions of the trial of Zola which grew out of the Dreyfus Case and that he took sandwiches along with him, we recall the transposition of this into a similar anecdote told about the character Bloch in the later novel. Sometimes both a minor character and incident are lifted bodily from the earlier composition. This is the case with the Bonapartist Prince de Borodino, whose name and traits remain unchanged in both books. Jean's memory of a happier time in love is reawakened by a theme of music in the same way as Swann's is. And Jean's cross-examination of his mistress becomes Swann's of Odette with little change. . . . Present also is a premonition of one of the most powerful scenes involving the jealousy of Swann—the scene in which he believes that he has at last surprised the perfidious Odette in a room at night with her guilty lover, only to find at the last moment, after intolerable suspense, that he has mistaken the lighted shutters of another house on the same street for those of the windows of her room.

All these scenes and characters are virtually unchanged, and yet the forceful effect which they have in the later book is lacking in the earlier one. The force is lacking because the arrangement of materials in the two books is different. This seems to be clear proof that the power of a character or an episode is not inherent in itself alone but is dependent on its precise place in the composition of which it is a part. No better argument exists for the importance of form in art. I remember once hearing a dance critic say that art without form would be like soup on a flat plate—"there just wouldn't be any soup." Something of the kind may be said of ***Jean Santeuil.*** There are many nourishing qualities in this earlier book of Proust, but he has not yet devised the receptacle from which the reader might imbibe its effect with pleasure.

A legitimate extension of Aristotle's remarks about plot and character and the degree of maturity in the writer necessary to mastering each one is that some of the other elements of composition which he mentions—thought and diction—may be mastered by the writer even before he has solved the problems of character and plot. Certainly this proves to be so with Proust whose ***Les Plaisirs et les jours,*** earlier in date of composition than either ***Jean Santeuil*** or ***A la recherche du temps perdu,*** is inferior to both of these with regard to characterization and storytelling. Only a certain sweetness of style, a music of words, and an aphoristic ability are to be found in all the works of Proust from first to last. He visibly mounts from one rung of the ladder of composition to the next, beginning with a harmonious style and proceeding from mastery of character drawing to the command of plot construction. Style is his native endowment. It is his starting point. Everything else comes to him slowly through hard work. (pp. 3-8)

It would be tempting to believe that for anyone who still remained to be convinced of the euphony of Proust's style the discovery of ***Jean Santeuil*** should definitely settle the question. But this temptation must be resisted if only because of the reflection that a man who has not been pleased by the harmonies of Proust's prose before this time is hardly likely to hear what the lovers of his style hear not only in ***Jean Santeuil*** but throughout his work.

It is not inconceivable, indeed, that a writer may be great because of the predominant power of other more important elements of literary composition and be notoriously deficient in his feeling for words and their arrangement, as is said to be the case with the journalistic sloppiness of Dostoyevsky's Russian and as is manifestly the case with the boorish awkwardness of Dreiser's English. One of the chief beauties of Proust to me, however, is his style in French, and whoever does not read him in the original must, I feel, be necessarily deprived of an important element, the absence of which helps to highlight some other aspect—Proust's thought, his characters, his story. In French, the latter elements are combined with a vivacity of language which at times almost puts them in shadow and always manages to keep them in their place. (pp. 21-2)

To me the overall merit of Proust's style is defined by the phenomenally close adherence of the flowing robe of his language to the body of feeling which I sense underneath. The twisted shapes often found in his expression must seem willful to those who do not see in these shapes the outward and accurate renditions of something below the language itself. But to those who sympathetically follow the hidden movements, the fidelity of the imitations in the draperies above will seem wondrous. Proust's language is like some very soft, very clinging, very bright and precious material, which betrays by its glancing lights and spreading shadows the faintest stirring of the sensitivities. It is like sea water troubled by a nervous shimmer of light, whether because it is blown by the wind or heaved up by some pressure it is difficult to say. We only know that it seems continually filled with brilliant flashes of excitement and is never for a moment still. (pp. 23-4)

The feelings of the reader glide over the periods of Proust's prose without awareness of any difference between sound and sense. Proper words in proper places was the phrase with which Jonathan Swift, himself a magnificent stylist, tried to catch the essence of what must ultimately remain a private experience because it is enclosed within each reader's own sensibility. This sort of thing defies logical definition and lends itself, if at all, only to sensible appeals based upon similar experiences.

The intimate clasp between ideas and words, the closeness of their touch and adherence to each other, has always been the measure of good style. And the gift of Proust as a stylist, if I attempt for a moment to fix its sensuous quality as it comes through to me, is that his words have the genius of following the shifting contours of his feelings with the immediacy with which the edge of darkness closes in upon the twitching and tremblings, the slidings and leapings of a flame.

This is the reaction of a reader to so large a mass of the work that it cannot be satisfactorily illustrated through isolated quotations, though it is the most important recommendation of his style. In a sense, this *is* the style of a writer's *whole* work. Fortunately there are other elements of style which do not resist supplying concrete examples. One of these elements is the felicitous comparison which shoots up in the text of a brilliant firework of simile or metaphor, supplied by that eye for resemblances which from the most ancient times has been recognized as the prime sign of poetic genius. By the quality of their metaphors, the quality of poets is made known as by an abbreviated symbol. From this point of view, ***Jean Santeuil*** supplies the most impressive confirmations of the poetic powers of Proust. When he speaks of "those moments of profound illumination in whcih the mind descends into the depths of things and lights them up like the sun going down into the sea," he not only supplies us with a beautiful example of simile but states its function very clearly and exactly. For it is the perception of true analogies underneath superficial differences and true differences underneath superficial analogies that enables the poet, by means of his figures of speech, to penetrate into the deeps of reality.

Proust realized the rarity of the inspiration which resulted in really memorable metaphors and when he discovered them he hoarded them very carefully for use later on. The most telltale sign in ***Jean Santeuil*** is the presence of certain striking figures of speech immediately recognizable to the reader of Proust's masterpiece.

Occasionally a simile is drawn out by Proust to almost epic length, concealing a shock of surprise in its very tail which none but he seems capable of inventing. . . . (pp. 24-6)

Wit is always accompanied by rapidity of association, which, whether it has come after long preparation or without any warning, completes its arc more quickly than we have been quite able to follow. He's there before we know it. It is the speed of the sally not the seriousness of its subject which makes us smile when Proust tells us that a man with cancer is like one who unexpectedly possesses "an inner life."

And as a final example of his metaphorical genius as it was expressed in his earlier work, it is worthwhile considering how the feelings and limitless fancies of elementary school days are recaptured in single figure depicting a classroom to which the teacher suddenly returns after being away for a little while: "The pupils—who were still parading fearlessly on top of the rows of desks like sailors on a boat, clambering the beams or balancing precariously between two planks, amidst noises as numerous and deafening as the sounds of the winds, the rigging and the sea—rushed back to their seats in a split second."

There is another element of Proust's style that seems adequately demonstrable and this is the quality and conciseness of his early aphorisms. Here, too, quickness of association is essential, and yet it is something more than mere cleverness which results: "We trust ourselves to love as we do to life without taking account of the nothingness of either one." And it is Proust at his best who remarks of love in ***Jean Santeuil:*** "What we call our power over things is perhaps nothing more than our lack of demands upon them. One must be in love in order to know that one is not loved in return. When one is no longer in love, one is always certain of being sufficiently loved."

The short, sharp observation from his newly discovered work, "Life is never pretty except at a distance," is good enough to justify the observation of Mauriac about the work of Proust: "What a collection of admirable maxims could one not extract from this book for the profit of busy people." (pp. 26-7)

It is style which communicates first the news to our nerve ends that a writer whom we have never read before is sending out his message on the wave length of our own sensibility. The other qualities of literature, being strained through the meshes of our intellect, take more time to make themselves felt by us. It is the immediate, overpowering fragrance of personality present in the style which overpowers the sensitive reader, throws him "into a sort of stupor," makes him vibrate in sympathy with the writer, and convinces him that he is on "the frontiers of an unknown country." But style, just to the degree that it is calculated to cause the strongest initial impression on the delicately attuned aesthetic response, escapes the notice of less gifted readers and those with grosser sensibilities, who are invariably more interested in penetrating first *what* a writer has to say rather than being aware of *how* he is saying it. These readers are not aware that the two considerations, though in some sense separate, are also intimately joined together and that one may be a clue to the other. Missing the significance of one may mean missing the significance of both. That seems to have been for a long time what happened to Proust. People who were insensitive to the distinction of his style were also unaware of the importance of what he had to say through his style about art and life. When the more sensitive had shown the way to Proust's value as a writer, many who had not perceived this to begin with came to respond to his work through the power of suggestion and imitation, and these latecomers, not feeling the inner reason which had given rise to the fashion in the first place and responding only to the grosser features of the work visible to those who read as they run, the sensational subject matter, the portrayal of society, and so on, are probably responsible, either through indifference or through active sponsorship, for the pernicious myth that Proust is a writer primarily of content and that he is negligible as a stylist. (pp. 28-9)

[It] is interesting to see in . . . [*Jean Santeuil*] those central themes which were destined for much fuller exposition and development later. For example, the idea expressed in this passage: "That sense of exaltation which compels us to offer up beautiful words to achieve some interested object is precisely the contrary of the literary spirit which is forced to express exactly what the writer feels. From which difference undoubtedly springs the antagonism between art and life." Art here is conceived of as the refuge, the sanctuary from an affected and insincere world. Art offers the sole possibility of an escape from tormenting reality.

To the eye grown accustomed to the finer shadings of Proust's meaning and to a mind knowing something about Proust's intellectual influences, the source of this antagonism between art and life is contained for us in the single word "interested" in the preceding passage. The trouble with the actions of life is that they are necessarily *interested* actions, which find their motivations and consequences in the present, the immediate past, or the immediate future. Art, on the other hand, takes for itself the subject and the object of eternity. It can draw its material from the remote past and address itself to the most distant future. Art is, whenever it is genuine and truly deserving of its name, *disinterested*. And this distinction, furthermore, is the same as that drawn by the philosopher [who influenced] . . . Proust so greatly—namely, Schopenhauer. Life for Proust, too, is the restless expression of the unceasingly striving will, and only in art do we manage briefly for a moment to transcend this will, whose principal characteristic is its changeableness, and manage to reach a more secure and permanent ground of judgment. (pp. 29-30)

Life is the subject of art, but to grasp its meaning we must first stand aside from it and rid ourselves of the distortion which our will introduces between our experience and our understanding. The tonality of disillusion is as strong in the earlier Proust as it is in the later one. He saw through the deceptions of desire, and the terms in which he tells us how he saw through them suggests that his formulation was helped substantially by the German philosopher:

> Why indeed torment ourselves because we do not have what we have desired. For in the course of their perpetual revolutions these things will inevitably end by coming to us. Circumstances change, and what we have once desired we always end by having. Yet circumstances change less quickly than do our own hearts, and if we always end by having what we desire, it is only when we desire it no longer.

With such an attitude to both life and art, it is not surprising that we find in ***Jean Santeuil,*** as we are to find several times in ***A la recherche du temps perdu,*** an artist who puts the value of art so far above that of life that the latter appears to him much less precious than do those thoughts which he is able to transpose into his work. The theme of the self-sacrificing artist is foreshadowed as soon as the value of the will is negated. The novelist Bergotte, created by the later Proust, who, in a vision as he is dying, sees life and art in two opposite scales before him and regrets that he has too often sacrificed the permanent joys of one for the ephemera of the other, is clearly germinating in the character of Santeuil, whom Proust describes as follows:

> The various thoughts which he loved to set down seemed to him much more important than himself, to the extent that he was always dreaming, found himself good for nothing if for several days they did not appear in his brain, and when he had them nearly all written down he no longer saw any serious inconvenience in the idea of dying and was entirely resigned to it.

Also in ***Jean Santeuil*** is the most important point in Proust's psychology of love—namely, that love is essentially a subjective phenomenon and that the overwhelming attraction which the object of our desire exercises upon us is created by our desire itself rather than by its object. This theme, stated in bare abstraction in the earlier book, is destined to be the basis of innumerable ingenious variations later on.

The advice of Proust . . . that if we would understand society and its motions we must first of all descend into the depths of the individual psyche has its counterpart in ***Jean Santeuil*** in the observation that history is composed of exactly the same stuff as our petty lives.

And, finally, the central motif of Proust's most mature reflections on morality is beautifully expressed in his appeal for kindness and universal toleration found in his recently uncovered work: "We cannot draw near to the most abandoned creatures without recognizing in them the images of men. And the sympathy we feel for their humanity compels our tolerance of their perversity."

The imaginative development of these themes is, of course, only barely suggested in the earlier work, and certainly the lack is felt of that coherence, order, and "architecture" which is Proust's glory in his maturity, but his basic thoughts remain largely unchanged. ***Jean Santeuil*** holds many novel delights but few real surprises for those who have mastered the materials of which ***A la recherche du temps perdu*** is composed. (pp. 31-2)

Milton Hindus, in an introduction to his The Proustian Vision, *Columbia University Press, 1954, pp. 3-32.*

PAMELA HANSFORD JOHNSON (essay date 1971)

[*Johnson is a noted English novelist who has written a book on Proust, and prepared several radio programs dealing with his works. Her own works have been described in Proustian fashion as "social novels, closely tied to a particular time and place and social milieu," in which "time and memory are integral parts of the action." In the following excerpt, Johnson discusses* Remembrance of Things Past *as the story of a quest that ends triumphantly.*]

It has been held by those who have read it imperfectly that ***A la Recherche du temps perdu*** is a depressing book. Nothing could be further from the truth. The ending tells of a great discovery, of major significance to the artist: that Time the destroyer can be overcome by its preservation through art, and that, through art, no matter what our fate has been, not a sorrow nor a joy, a triumph or a tragedy, need be irretrievably lost, but may be written or painted or sung into art itself to be preserved for ever in its first freshness and dew.

In the Fitzwilliam Museum at Cambridge, there is a painting by Ruysdael, a view of Amsterdam from the river Amstel. It expresses not a single afternoon hundreds of years ago, but a particular, selected moment in that afternoon. It has been raining—the fields glisten with rain in the pallid light—and it will rain again. The tender and sallow sun, streaming through a sky patched with black cloud and cineraria blue, touches a few sails on the river: soon they will be shadowed again. It is an interim between storms. This painting is the essence of ***Le Temps retrouvé:*** so it was once, in the artist's recording eye and so it will ever be, netted, captured, the moment for ever sparkling, outside of Time because Time has been conquered.

A la Recherche du temps perdu concerns the anxieties of Time. Once there was a great passion. Where is it now? Drowned in oblivion. Once there was a beautiful woman. Where is her beauty now?

'On [the cheeks] for instance, of Madame de Guermantes, in many respects so little changed and yet composite now like a bar of nougat, I could distinguish traces here and there of verdigris, a small pink patch of fragmentary shell-work, and a little growth of an undefinable character, smaller than a mistletoe berry and less transparent than a glass bead.'

Where, now, is Oriane, duchesse de Guermantes, blonde, bird-nosed and lovely, repository of the essence of the family wit? We have just seen her at the beginning of decay. Yet she remains for ever still young, still sparkling, still malicious—with her electric eyes—in the pages of Marcel Proust, never to age.

Once there was a great composer, made to suffer torments through his lesbian daughter, laid in an obscure grave followed only by a few neighbours and by Monsieur Swann in his black top hat. Where are his few joys, his many sorrows, now? In his music, sublimely preserved. In his sonata, with its leitmotif for the love of Swann and Odette, of Marcel and Albertine, and above all in his superb septet, resuscitated from odd scraps of paper by the devoted labours of his daughter and her friend. Vinteuil and his whole life live in his music. (p. 195)

As, in some people, memory is awakened by a scent—say, of wallflowers or of hay—so [Proust] has been awakened by the memories of taste, sound, texture, by the stumble on the uneven paving-stone. And all these experiences are magical because they are *outside of Time*—free from it, free to come and to go, to inspire, or to rest in non-recognition. Outside of Time entirely, and therefore infinitely potent.

Here, I think, Proust has been a little specious. The single experience of this sort—most of us have known it, and it has gone deep into the springs of self-knowledge. But to know a series of such experiences, during the course of a single afternoon—this is to speak of miracles, and it is in our own self-knowledge to determine that such miracles come far less frequently to most of us than to Proust's Marcel.

In all, an unforgettable afternoon, bearing the keys not only to Time past but to Time to come. It is a little hard for us to believe in it, hard for us to credit that we are not being subjected to the trickery of genius. Perhaps we are. I suspect it is so. But it is a wonderful, glittering trick, the unlocking of the secret of a novel a million words long. Without it, there could have been no more than despair, the despair of a wasted life. So much time wasted on the social ladder, wasted on a long and tormenting love which ended in death and, worse, oblivion. So much heartache, headache, the ache of the bones, and to no purpose. But here is the purpose. This is what all of it, from the most trivial to the most sublime, from the most ridiculous to the most delicate and sore, was all about. To few of us it is given to sense such a purpose: but to the artist, perhaps, yes. (pp. 198-99)

What was the secret of the series of recognitions which had caused Marcel such joy and had even banished the fear of death?

This is the key-passage.

> . . . another inquiry demanded my attention most imperiously, the inquiry . . . into the cause of this felicity which I had just experienced, into the character of the certitude with which it imposed itself. And this cause I began to divine as I compared these diverse happy impressions, diverse yet with this in common, that I experienced them at the present moment and at the same time in the context of a different moment, so that the past was made to encroach upon the present and I was made to doubt whether I was in the one or the other. The truth surely was that the being within me which had enjoyed these impressions, had enjoyed them because they had in them something that was common to a day long past and to now, because in some way they were extra-temporal, and this being made its appearance only when, through one of these identifications of the present with the past, it was likely to find itself in the one and only medium in which it could exist and enjoy the essence of things, that is to say: outside time. This explained why it was that my anxiety on the subject of my death had ceased at the moment when I had unconsciously recognized the taste of the little madeleine, since the being which at that moment I had been was an extra-temporal being and therefore unalarmed by the vicissitudes of the future. This being had only come to me, only manifested itself outside of activity and immediate enjoyment, on those rare occasions when the miracle of an analogy had made me escape from the present. And only this being had the power to perform that task which had always defeated the efforts of my memory and my intellect, the power to make me discover days that were long past, the Time that was Lost.

This passage explains Proust's challenge to Sainte-Beuve that instinct must be rated higher than intellect—though Proust himself was a man of the most formidable intellect. It links, too, with the famous 'flash-back', *Un Amour de Swann*, near the beginning of the entire work. (pp. 199-200)

The scheme of the entire novel is circular. Marcel's childhood home lay between his two favourite walks, Swann's way, and the Guermantes's way. The two ways seem irreconcilable: yet Gilberte, Swann's child, marries that most enchanting of Guermantes, Robert de Saint-Loup, and Odette becomes the duke's mistress in his old age. And, linking the ways for ever, Gilberte at the Princess's final party presents to Marcel her lovely young daughter—Robert's child. (pp. 200-01)

She is like the diamond drop which completes the necklace, the jewel gleaming with the numberless refractions of Time Past. She is yet too young for the tarnishings of change, and so Marcel sees her now as he had seen her parents in youth, shining with the same almost-forgotten radiance.

Marcel's world has changed, radically: the result of the Dreyfus case, which brought about so many extraordinary social mutations, and of the Great War, which threw up Madame Verdurin and Albertine's vulgar aunt, Madame Bontemps, to the pinnacle of busybody wartime society. 'The Faubourg St. Germain was like some senile dowager now, who replies only with timid smiles to the insolent servants who invade her drawing-rooms, drink her orangeade, present their mistresses to her.'

Madame Verdurin, the exhibitionist *salonnière,* who was nevertheless possessed of an unfailing instinct for the arts, is the reigning hostess over the Faubourg these days, since Oriane, duchesse de Guermantes, has long ago lost interest in Society. Ironically enough, she has frittered away her position by taking a Verdurin-like interest in poets, musicians and painters. Oriane is old now: and she startles Marcel by claiming him as her 'oldest friend'. Can it possibly be that he, too, is old? Yes it can. (Though in fact, according to such chronology as can be drawn from the book, he is no more than fifty years of age.) Her claim—for was he not the nervous young cit so awed by her invitations?—shocks him, certainly; but not for long. The parade of physical degeneration has lost the power to frighten him. He has, at last, work to do.

> If at least, Time enough were allotted to me to accomplish my work, I would not fail to mark it with the seal of Time, the idea of which imposed itself upon me with so much force today, and I would therein describe men, if need be, as monsters occupying a place in Time infinitely more important than the restricted one reserved for them in space, a place, on the contrary, prolonged immeasureably since, simultaneously touching widely separated years and the distant periods they have lived through—between which so many days have ranged themselves—they stand like giants, immersed in Time.

This is the way the book ends. It ends in a glory of decision, born out of the triumph over Time. For me, it is the greatest ending of any novel ever written. It has to be borne in mind that the true title of the work, in English, is not ***Remembrance of Things Past,*** the poor choice of a great translator and misleading: it is, *In Search of Lost Time*. It is the story of a great quest which actually succeeds. Thomas Wolfe strove to make communication in 'the incommunicable prison of this earth'. He failed, and felt he had failed. Proust communicates the way in which we may recover and fix, as under a glass, the whole of our lives.

The analogous 'recognitions' are contributions to the entire structure. Another contribution is the phenomenon of the *false recognition*—things are not what they at first seem. This idea Proust took from his master, Dostoievski. At first sight, the baron de Charlus appears to Marcel as a shady character, perhaps an hotel detective watching for thieves or for dubious couples. Marcel believes Madame de Villeparisis to be the greatest among great ladies, though in the eyes of Society (though not of her own family circle) she has been declassed by marriage and by *louche* behaviour in her youth. The 'little band of girls' on the *plage* at Balbec might possibly be the juvenile mistresses of racing cyclists. Impressions form, are dissolved, reform into other and stranger shapes. All things seem inconstant as the sea itself, which is one of the book's most powerful symbols, and at the core of them all is the smiling or sullen Albertine, herself mutable as the sea, in her being the vast disturbing secrecies of love. Albertine, the arcane, the temptress and tormentor, never to be recovered in her essential truth (if truth is in her at all), upon whose memory, after she is dead, the Narrator conducts a hideous autopsy. Here Marcel was perhaps less fortunate than Swann, for once, who, when passionate love had died, could see Odette as she really was without ceasing to support and encourage her. She was essentially commonplace. As Proust says, life had given her some good parts, but she could not play them. At the final party where, in her paint and dye, she still looks much as she ever did, we are given a flash-forward to her in senility, mumbling, nervous, almost stone deaf. This is one of those blows Proust deals us when we are least expecting them.

But for Marcel himself, the artist both intuitive and highly conscious, there is the splendid 'happy ending' which turns the whole work into a Divine Comedy. We have been with him in the earthly Paradise of childhood and Combray, walking between the hedges of pink and white hawthorn, crying out—'Zut! Zut!' in a vain struggle to express the beauty of a cloud shadow upon water: have been with him through the Vanity Fair of society, to Sodom and Gomorrah, the Cities of the Plain, down to the ninth circle of Hell: have been with him through purgatory (the discovery of oblivion after love and death) to the heaven of the personal discovery: no less than this—*what the whole of a life is for*. We have made this journey (less dreadful than Dante's for it is rich in humour) step by step to the revelation of Beatrice—in this case, the revelation that there is no death. Marcel comes at the end to his Beatrice, not a girl, but a divine assurance. (pp. 201-03)

Apart from the device of the recognitions (madeleine, paving-stone, spoon, napkin) there are no tricks of time in this book. It is, with the exception of the flashback, *Un Amour de Swann* (in which almost every major theme of the entire work is stated), a straightforward narrative by chronological progression. From the beginning, it gives the effect of a search, of a young boy setting forth into the great world in quest of—what? At first he hardly knows. This is not the fashionable problem of the search for identity: Marcel is fully cognisant of who he is, and his roots are deep in society. After a while he believes that he has a vocation for writing, but all he manages to produce is an article for *Le Figaro*. (This runs counter to the life of the author who, before achieving ***A la Recherche,*** wrote, and suppressed, a prentice novel of nine hundred manuscript pages, ***Jean Santeuil,*** and the wonderful critical essays, a trial of strength for the great work to come, which were later gathered together under the title ***Contre Sainte-Beuve.*** The old idea of Proust wasting years in dilettantism and social climbing has now been dispelled.) It is not until late in the book that he realizes the object of his search, which is nothing less than that for Time itself. It is, despite its length and complexity, a wonderfully lucid novel, and the climax, when it comes, is brought about by a display of marvellous intellectual force and clarity.

Not a depressing book. Essentially it is, as has been said, a 'young man's book', full of the excitements, joys, discoveries and despairs of youth, sparkling with humour and irony. If it contains much tragedy, if friendship comes to seem an illusion, love a delusion, if beautiful men and women are degraded by, often made almost ridiculous by, age and the propinquity of death, all this is *used* for the final purpose, as if the writer were carrying back from the well of Time a vessel filled to the brim with dancing water, of which he will not spill a single drop. The work is shaped like Vinteuil's septet, which culminates in a strong-beating shock of pure joy, an analogy made clear by Proust as his novel progresses and the septet grows slowly out of scraps of almost unreadable paper lovingly hoarded and transcribed by the two young women who broke the composer's heart.

A la Recherche comes to an ending entirely affirmative, far more so than Molly Bloom's ecstatic but capricious 'Yes, I will, Yes'. ***Le Temps retrouvé*** is the title of the final volume. It could have been the title of the entire book.

Of all very great writers, Proust was the most avid in the search for affirmation. Himself a man of considerable moral courage, he took it upon himself to find answers. There is no sign of such searching in the preliminary sketch, ***Jean Santeuil*** which . . . is lacking in direction. This is, however, a most interesting book, shedding light upon what Proust was like before he took the tremendous moral grasp upon himself from which ***A la Recherche*** resulted. The 'snobbery' of which he has so often been accused was certainly present—ragingly present—in parts of ***Jean Santeuil:*** but recognizing this, he learned to *use* it for quite determined purposes, to make it work for him through his new-found irony.

I have said elsewhere that what makes the great work so morally tough is that behind Marcel, the Narrator, we sense a 'second Marcel', mocking, critical, undeceived. There is no 'second Jean' in ***Jean Santeuil.*** Proust learned how to make fine metal out of his own faults, even when he could not entirely overcome them. He turned his writing itself into a tremendous moral exercise: as Marcel grows up from the coxcomberies of adolescence to the wisdom of middle age, so Proust grows with him. ***A la Recherche*** is by no means a fully autobiographical novel, yet the writer and his book are curiously at one. We never know Marcel's surname, but in our hearts we cannot stop believing that it was Proust.

He was a stern moralist, sometimes almost too stern. Homosexual himself, he still thinks of homosexuality as a vice, and its men and women accursed upon the Plain. The truth was that, unlike Gide, he did not love his own condition and wished that it had been otherwise with him, as once it might have been. Yet the archetype homosexual, the baron de Charlus, is drawn with charity and humour, even when he sinks low enough to become a habitué of Jupien's brothel. It is part of Proust's genius that he can make this incident seem funny and even a little touching: in other hands it might have seemed disgusting, and no more than that.

The only major character in the book from whom he withholds charity is Morel, the violinist whom the Baron loves. There is an odd failure here: there are even times when Morel seems to be set apart from this particular work like a fragment of a painting which has escaped varnishing. We believe in him as an artist, but is is hard to credit that there is really nothing else to be said for him. He remains an ungrateful, deceitful scoundrel in a world where men and women may be sacred monsters steeped in Time, but are never—what shall one call it?—mingy. One cannot believe that Morel will ever grow to the status of splendid monstrosity with the years.

I do not claim that ***A la Recherche du temps perdu*** is a totally perfect book: but, because of its intellectual force and its use of the intuitions, it is a great one, certainly the greatest of this century. It is also a very strange and original novel, which yields more and more with every re-reading. For me, it is impossible to close it without a sense of exhilaration, and perhaps with a touch of regret that the taste of the madeleine may never come to one's own salvation. (pp. 203-05)

Pamela Hansford Johnson, "Triumph over Time," in Marcel Proust, 1871-1922: A Centenary Volume, *edited by Peter Quennell (copyright © 1971 by George Weidenfeld and Nicolson Limited), Weidenfeld and Nicolson, 1971, pp. 195-205.*

JOHN STURROCK (essay date 1981)

[In 1981 a revised English translation of Remembrance of Things Past, *by Terence Kilmartin, was published. This publication was significant, for it was an improvement upon the only available English language edition of one of the primary masterpieces of twentieth-century literature. In the following excerpt, Sturrock discusses the reasons for Kilmartin's revisions and offers high, though tempered, praise for the completed work.]*

In the spring of 1920 Marcel Proust was fretting because the good 'Gaston' (Gallimard, his post-war publisher) had been unforgivably slow in arranging for translations of his now successful novel to be started. In the past 12 months ***Du Côté de chez Swann*** had been published for a second time (the little-noticed earlier edition was in 1913) and ***A l'Ombre des Jeunes Filles en Fleurs*** for the first time; and Proust had, strangely, won the Prix Goncourt, a corrupt award which he had wanted but which generally goes to works of uncomplicated mediocrity. There should, he thought, have been foreign editions pending of these first instalments of ***A la Recherche du Temps Perdu,*** and an English edition mattered most of all. English was a language which Proust knew and had read in; with help, he had translated his dear Ruskin into French. His sense of symmetry, if not of justice, called now for his own deeply Ruskinian work to be turned into English, and if nothing had so far been done the fault must be Gaston's because the English themselves were hugely enthusiastic about it: there had, he promised Jacques Rivière, been 'eight or nine articles in the *Times* alone'.

This was a wild exaggeration born of the real neglect which the novelist was then feeling. He had, however, an advocate on the *Times* who was quite unknown to him: a Scottish infantry officer, lately demobbed, who was well connected but unfortunate enough to have been appointed private secretary to the bizarre Lord Northcliffe. C. K. Scott-Moncrieff had been keeping up with the books that were being read in Paris, and had been led by the Goncourt prize to Marcel Proust. Indeed, he had already written to J. C. Squire, that hub of the literary journalistic world, to see if he couldn't now make something of his discovery. . . .

[Squire] didn't bite; nor did any London publisher. But Scott-Moncrieff was inspired and convinced and began his translation just the same, without waiting until he had been given the commission. Quickly, and understandably, he came to find Proust more to his taste than Lord Northcliffe, and Combray more interesting than Printing House Square: he resigned from the *Times* to work at them full-time. He found a publisher, Messrs Chatto and Windus, who in 1922 brought out the two volumes of ***Swann's Way,*** so inaugurating the single largest, most distinctive and most venerated work of translation into English of this century.

Literary translators rarely make a name for themselves, save among their own kind. They are hired dependents of the authors whom they translate. If Scott-Moncrieff stands alone among the translators of the 20th century, then that is very much Proust's doing: their names go together. In fact, however, it was translating that Scott-Moncrieff loved, not Proust. He did not start by translating Proust, nor only translate Proust once he had come together with him. His first translations were of *Beowulf* and the *Chanson de Roland,* whose gory, impetuous verses were an odd preparation for the coiled introspections of ***Swann's Way***. . . . During breaks from ***A la Recherche,*** Scott-Moncrieff took refuge in the altogether shorter and more urgent sentences of Stendhal, and in the plays of Pirandello. If he was drawn so greatly to Proust this may have been for technical rather than temperamental reasons, for he was not, by all accounts, a Proust-like man: but the awesome elaboration of Proust's style, and the effortless precision of his mind, offered an ultimate test of the examinee's powers.

We are naturally suspicious when a translator acquires a name, as Scott-Moncrieff did, because translation, to be good, must be self-effacing. If the translator blocks our view of the original, he exceeds his brief. The great masters of literary translation of the past did just that, of course: Urquhart, Florio, Burton, FitzGerald set themselves up to be conspicuous intermediaries and not mere transparencies. The languid but superior FitzGerald saw no virtue in sticking too closely to what old Khayyam had written: 'It is an amusement to me to take what liberties I like with these Persians, who (as I think) are not Poets enough to frighten one from such excursions.'

But famous or not, Scott-Moncrieff was not of this piratical company. He was a genuine translator, unfailingly respectful of the text before him. There is a serious and consistent difference of tone between his English and Proust's French, as we shall see, but that does not invalidate what one salutes as a prodigious effort of translation, incomparably resourceful in its vocabulary, fiercely attentive to the logic of Proust's sometimes interminable periods, beautifully even in its style over a length of a million words. (Scott-Moncrieff did not live to finish it—it was completed, rather clumsily, by Sydney Schiff.) ***A la Recherche*** found an English translator worthy of it, and at once: it did not have to wait, as so commanding a masterpiece might expect to wait, to be matched with someone who had the understanding, the fluency and the stamina to overcome it.

Given the splendour of Scott-Moncrieff's translation, why now should his first publisher be bringing out ***Remembrance of Things Past*** in a revised version? There are two reasons. One is that since the 1920s the French text of the novel has changed; the second is that there were things wrong with Scott-Moncrieff which a long stint of quiet and informed editing could finally put right. Terence Kilmartin has thus altered the original translation in two ways: changing it where changes in the French text determined changes in the English one, and improving it where Scott-Moncrieff was found to have nodded or been carried away. This is hard and public-spirited work, admirably carried through—Scott-Moncrieff benefits on every page from Kilmartin's remedial attentions. ***Remembrance of Things Past*** is now, for sure, in its definitive state. (p. 14)

What every Proustian, and every Scott-Moncrieffian, will most want to know about this revision, however, is why, where and how Kilmartin has edited the original wording even though the French remains the same. He has made many hundreds of changes, mostly very small, a word or two at a time, to what Scott-Moncrieff wrote. He has proceeded carefully and worked sensitively. Almost every change that I came upon, in a prolonged sampling of four separate volumes of the novel, I thought to be a clear success for the reviser over the revised. There are chances that Kilmartin has missed, whether through diffidence or fatigue: but he has taken as many as he could humanly have been asked to. This is a better because truer edition of ***Remembrance of Things Past*** than the earlier one.

What Kilmartin has done to Scott-Moncrieff is the thing which one knew—or to be truthful, since I have never before stopped to compare at length the English with the French—which one had been told needed doing: he has sobered him down. SM (as he must from here on become) is too mannered to be quite faithful to Proust, too bellettristic, seeing invitations to poetry where Proust offers only the most dauntingly exact prose. He cannot suppress his own undeveloped taste for the pretty phrase, and anyone coming to Scott-Moncrieff's English straight from a page of Proust's rigorous French gets a feeling of alienation and of slight impatience with a translator so ingenious and painstaking who spurns settling for the plain answer even though plainness is so obviously wanted.

It is the innumerable and uncalled-for preciosities, therefore, that Kilmartin has hunted down, and substituted with something more suitably prosaic. The substitutions are mostly slight in themselves but their general effect is thoroughly salutary. Some examples: Pr(oust)'s flatly descriptive *où l'eau bleuit* turns in the too excitable hands of SM into 'where the water glows with a blue lurking fire', which K(ilmartin) now reduces once again to 'glows blue'—though even 'glows' might be criticised as overdoing it, when *bleuit* means no more than '*shows* blue'; Pr *comme le jour quand le soir tombe* becomes SM 'like the day when night gathers', and K 'like the daylight when night falls'; Pr *qu'il n'avait pas la place d'honneur* becomes SM 'who was not set in the post of honour', and K 'who did not have the place of honour'; Pr *s'expatrier* becomes SM 'remove to another place', and K 'move elsewhere'; Pr *dévote* becomes SM 'instinct with piety', and K 'devout'; Pr *en rapport avec* becomes SM 'in some degree of harmony with', and K 'in keeping with'; Pr *orageux et doux* becomes SM 'dear tempestuous', and K 'delightful stormy'.

In such modest but necessary doses has Scott-Moncrieff's heightened prose been subdued. In rare instances he has been allowed to get away with his embellishments, and on other rare occasions Kilmartin has succumbed to embellishments of his own: Pr *si innombrablement fleuri* gives SM 'so countlessly blossomed', and K 'so multitudinously aflower' which is scarcely better; *donnant à la journée quelque chose de douleureux* gives SM 'had given the day a sorrowful aspect', and K 'infused the day with a certain poignancy', where 'infused' and 'poignancy' are out of key with Proust's matter-of-fact psychological notation, which might best read 'giving the day a certain sadness'.

Kilmartin finds more work to do in the later volumes of the novel. Scott-Moncrieff's health may not have been as weak as Proust's was but it was not good during the later 1920s and could not in his case, unlike the novelist's, be compensated for by a fanatical, unresting will to complete what would be his own cenotaph. Scott-Moncrieff was living moreover in Italy, somewhat isolated from the language into which he was translating, which can be risky for a translator. In the second half of ***Remembrance of Things Past*** he finds it hard at times to break sufficiently free from Proust's admittedly enthralling syntax, and clings wearily to the clause-structure of the original. Kilmartin has done some patient and convincing rearrangement in these cases, where the need for it is glaring. (pp. 14-15)

Kilmartin scores further in the matter of colloquialisms, at which few translators are talented. They come a good deal into ***A la Recherche*** as enclitic marks on the diction of certain characters, at once identifying and humiliating them, since it is perfectly clear that the novelist himself holds a higher idea of language than they do. SM is ill at ease with the barbed vulgarities of the Verdurin circle, for instance, and the fact that he translates the word *cénacle* in their connection as 'symposium', so endowing those catty gatherings with an unmerited classical sheen, makes one wonder whether he actually thought them so very bad. Mme. Verdurin's favourite young pianist is said by SM, where Pr uses the transitive verb *enfonçait,* to 'leave both Planté and Rubinstein "sitting"', which is downright eccentric on the part of both translator and speaker, when the words Mme. Verdurin is given to speak should surely show her to be both ridiculous and possessive: K's 'licked both Planté and Rubinstein hollow' is just about right. SM, indeed, remains culpably deaf to the effects of 'indirect free speech'. Still amidst the Verdurins, he turns Pr's *si ça lui chantait,* which is artfully slangy, into the insipid 'if he felt inclined,' which does not sound like reported speech at all: K again catches the tone ideally with 'if the spirit moved him'—Verduring-talk if ever I heard it. It is more excusable that our honourable Old Wykhamist should falter when faced with Proust's open indelicacies: a woman who in the French *se soulage* is said by SM to be 'doing something', but in K to be 'relieving herself'; while another salty character who exults in the thought *je puisse un peu les emmerder* has to make do in SM with the hyphened 'I can s-t on them,' though K now naturally gives us the full four letters. As, finally, for SM's actual howlers, these too seem to have been regularly caught, but it would be unjust to linger over them because they were, in my sampling, extremely few and surely inadvertent rather than ignorant.

What I shall linger on, however, is a major change which remains unmade: that of the English title for Proust's great work. ***Remembrance of Things Past*** is an improper title, long familiar to English readers but dispensable—it is not much used as a title, since most people, I fancy, talk of the novel as simply 'Proust'. Scott-Moncrieff was being particularly arty and self-indulgent when he chose it, and Proust himself protested against it in a letter he wrote to his English translator only weeks before he died. The French title he had first wanted for his novel was no more than *'Le Temps Perdu',* though he had come to accept the longer ***A la Recherche du Temps Perdu.*** But by rendering that as ***Remembrance of Things Past*** Scott-Moncrieff had missed the 'deliberate amphibology' of the title. 'Time Lost' at the beginning was to be balanced against 'Time Regained' at the end: the vast architectural scheme of the whole, which could not be understood except as a saving progression from desolation to triumph, was embodied in the title. Scott-Moncrieff should have looked to Milton for his English equivalent and not, as he did, to Shakespeare. (p. 15)

John Sturrock, "Proust Regained" (appears here by permission of the London Review of Books *and the author), in* London Review of Books, *March 19 to April 1, 1981, pp. 14-15.*

RICHARD HOWARD (essay date 1981)

[Howard is a Pulitzer Prize winning American poet and critic. However, he is best known as the preeminent contemporary translator of French literature and the person most responsible for introducing contemporary French literature to American readers. In the following review of Terence Kilmartin's revised translation of Remembrance of Things Past, *Howard relates the history of Proust's publications and of the various translations of Proust's major work. In his discussion of Kilmartin's translation, Howard finds much to praise but expresses a few points of reservation.]*

Sixty years after Proust's death, we may read him decently in English, and only now. As has been said of Chartres Cathedral—with which Proust's vast work has so many acknowledged analogies—gratitude is the only appropriate response. Books have their fates; the fate of Proust's was ill-starred. Hence to understand the value of [Terence Kilmartin's] revision of the first English translation of his great novel, even to understand the reason for its existence, requires a glance at the circumstances of Proust's publishing history.

In 1896, at the age of 25 and at his own expense, Proust brought out his first book, **"Les Plaisirs et les Jours."** Embellished or, as we would say, burdened with a preface by Anatole France, with illustrations by Madeleine Lemaire, and even with music by Reynaldo Hahn, this collection of stories, whatever its prophetic virtues, must have seemed an effete business to Parisian literary circles, for when in 1913 (he was 42) Proust tried to find a publisher for the first volume of what was to be his great novel, he failed. After four rejections, he decided to pay Bernard Grasset to bring out what we call **"Swann's Way,"** the first volume of **"A la Recherche du Temps Perdu" ("In Search of Lost Time").**

But in the intervening years, Proust's uncertainties had been fruitful. Between 1898 and 1904 he had filled many notebooks with an enormous autobiographical novel, **"Jean Santeuil,"** written straight off and never corrected by its author, who made no effort to publish it. In 1906, Proust had his room at 102 Boulevard Haussmann in Paris lined with cork to insulate himself and his asthma from the city's encroachments. In 1907, apparently, an initial conception of his novel occurred to him, and he began composition. And in 1908, after publishing translations (Ruskin), criticism, and parodies (the finest in all French literature), he began work on **"Contre Sainte-Beuve,"** a study in literary criticism which is also an intermediate version of his novel. This work, too, was unknown in Proust's lifetime. In 1909, Proust withdrew from "the world" (or at least from the reciprocal existence of healthy persons) to dedicate himself to the final draft of his novel, of which the first volume was completed by 1910, unknown to anyone but his friend Reynaldo Hahn.

Though a second volume of the novel was set up in type in 1914 and fragments of it appeared in periodicals, the First World War delayed publication (it won the Prix Goncourt in 1919, when it was published), and Proust took advantage of this interval to reconsider the scale of his novel. (I shall return to this reconsideration of scale, but first I must finish this vexed history.) The remaining eight years of Proust's life (he died in 1922, at the age of 51) were spent dilating the original half-million words to more than a million and a quarter. The last three sections of the novel had not yet been published at the time of Proust's death, and indeed he was still correcting typescript on his deathbed. Margins of proof and typescript were covered with handwritten corrections and insertions, often overflowing onto additional sheets pasted to the galleys or to each other to form long scrolls. The unraveling and deciphering of these additions became the intricate task of the editors, Pierre Clarac and André Ferré, of the three-volume Pléiade edition undertaken at the request of Proust's heirs in 1954.

In the 1920's the retired English military officer C. K. Scott Moncrieff began translating Proust's book—and completed the first 11 volumes of the 12-volume English edition. Proust was aware of the inception of this project, and suspicious. Yet he did not forbid the translator's choice of a tag from Shakespeare's Sonnet 30 as the overall English title of his work,

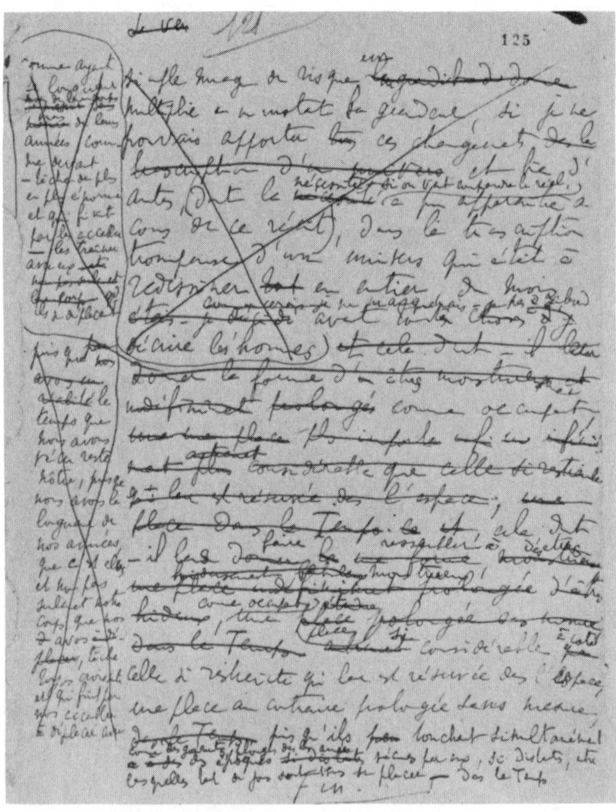

Manuscript of the last page of Proust's Á la recherche du temps perdu. *Bibliotheque Nationale, Paris.*

however unrelated it was to the explicit significance of the French words. But Proust died in 1922 (the year Pirandello's play "Six Characters in Search of an Author" was published in English, confirming that theme of the search which was to mark modern letters from "Ulysses," published that same year, to "Waiting for Godot" in 1951), and Scott Moncrieff himself died in 1930. The final and fulfilling volume was translated by "Stephen Hudson" (Sidney Schiff) in England and by Frederick Blossom in America as **"The Past Recaptured"**; a third and superior version of this crucial text, **"Time Regained,"** was made by Andreas Mayor and published in 1970. Indeed, Mayor was to have done a new translation of the entire work, but his death made necessary a different enterprise—the one for which we may be so grateful to Terence Kilmartin today.

Before discussing the old translation and the ameliorations of it which this revision affords, I must suggest something of Proust's attitude toward the composition of his work—an attitude responsible for the difficulties and discrepancies which have belatedly occasioned Mr. Kilmartin's undertaking. In **"The Captive"** Proust's narrator speaks with notable ambivalence of how markedly certain great works of music and literature "partake of that quality of being . . . , always incomplete, which is the characteristic of all the great works of the nineteenth century . . . whose greatest writers . . . , watching themselves work as though they were at once workman and judge, derived from this self-contemplation a new form of beauty, . . . imposing on it a retroactive unity, a grandeur which it does not possess."

The reference here is explicitly to Baudelaire and to Wagner, but we must take note that Proust is suggesting an attitude toward his own "unity, his own architecture" which is one of radical modernism. He is saying that unity and completeness are to be—deliberately—subverted on the structural level in favor of a different sense of wholeness, one to be found, or created, on the level of verbal immediacy (hence the hypertrophic dilation in the manuscripts), on the level of language itself, between invention and style, between writing and rhetoric.

Such a notion makes any focused view of his work particularly dependent, when we read a translation, on the right connections or the useful differentiations of even the tiniest details, on displacements of word order or alterations of morphological signposts of the most recondite kind. Finished but incomplete, Proust's work requires of us—readers and translators alike—an attention to details of linguistic creation we never granted to narrative prose, to "the novel," before (an attention we find similarly required of us in works of Joyce and Beckett, however): a sign of literary transformation to which the translator must dutifully, must drastically attend.

The Scott Moncrieff translation, based on the muddled and incomplete text which was all he had to work from, is embalmed among us as—well, semi-classical. (One recalls E. M. Forster's praise of it in "Aspects of the Novel.") I disagree with this widespread but careless approval, and would seek out any excuse to dislodge the thing from such status. The text is frequently erroneous, almost always at odds with the temper of Proust's prose: Where the original is infallibly immediate and alive, Scott Moncrieff sounds, to me, stale and dated. And this is only in part because all translations date; as Mr. Kilmartin himself points out, "Proust's style is essentially natural and unaffected, whereas Scott Moncrieff's prose tends to the purple and the precious. . . ." When Kilmartin remarks of his predecessor that he has obscured the sense and falsified the tone, he speaks only justice, though it is a justice masked as a compliment: "I hope I have preserved the undoubted felicity of Scott Moncrieff while doing the fullest possible justice to Proust." The only justice to be done to Proust must derive from doubts about Scott Moncrieff; fortunately Mr. Kilmartin has had them.

Within the limits of his corrective enterprise, Mr. Kilmartin has done a conscientious and illuminating job. I can barely imagine the skills—beyond the dreams of dentistry—which such a labor of reconstruction must have demanded. (pp. 7, 36)

Major and minor, Mr. Kilmartin's revisions occur almost sentence by sentence, always with great pertinacity. What afforded mere puzzlement in Scott Moncrieff is now discerned to be mere precision in Proust. For instance, describing an artist's particular activity, Proust refers to his motive for making a specific choice as "en choisissant une expression ou en faisant un rapprochement," which Scott Moncrieff renders or misrenders "when they choose an expression or start a friendship." Mr. Kilmartin removes that oddity of artists' starting friendships by putting the phrase right: "when they choose an expression or draw a parallel." And in addition to such clarification, Mr. Kilmartin has translated as addenda many of the passages found in the appendix of the Pléiade edition. He also offers at the end of each huge volume a valuable thematic synopsis, as well as a limited but extremely useful series of notes to explain literary and historical references—and inconsistencies—which occur throughout the text. Thirty notes for each thousand pages of a work published half a century ago is a modest enough apparatus, but an immediately helpful one, and I believe all new readers of Proust in English are in an inestimably advantageous position compared with their predecessors.

Mr. Kilmartin, almost apologetic about this urgently needed enterprise, refers to the Scott Moncrieff translation as "almost a masterpiece in its own right," a judgment I believe to be critically, if not criminally mistaken. In any case, Mr. Kilmartin is not mistaken about his revisions, which are all for the better if not for the best.

Why not? The discrepancy between better and best (between, that is, the genuine visionary contribution of an entirely new translation and the revisionary patchwork of these astute corrections) is corollary to the decision to retain the Shakespearean title instead of using the Proustian one. Readers will recall the late Vladimir Nabokov's irritation with this perversity, and one must so far agree with him as to note that the original title of Proust's work *means something*—means, in fact, what Proust meant the work itself to mean, a significance altogether absent from the lovely phrase from the Sonnets. The search, the pursuit, the quest for an eventual repossession of "lost time" is so much more of an evangelical action, a crusade, indeed, than the passive notion of "remembrance" can suggest that the book must suffer from its English title.

Thus, if there is any cavil to be registered about this extraordinary venture—so important that I can only wonder it has not been attempted sooner, and can only rejoice that it has been so brilliantly effected at last—it is precisely the partial nature of its achievement. As we know from the late Andreas Mayor's version of the final volume—which has been retained, with some "minor emendations"—a new translation is a new writing. But at least we now have a proper instrument for any future reading—in English—of an old writing, Proust's transfiguring realization of experience, which I believe to be the greatest in all fiction. (pp. 37-8)

Richard Howard, "Proust Re-Englished," in The New York Times Book Review *(copyright © 1981 by The New York Times Company; reprinted by permission), May 3, 1981, pp. 7, 36-8.*

V. S. PRITCHETT (essay date 1981)

[*Pritchett is highly esteemed as a novelist, short story writer, and critic. He is considered one of the modern masters of the short story, and his work is a subtle blend of realistic detail and psychological revelation. Pritchett is also considered one of the world's most respected and well-read literary critics. He writes in the conversational tone of the familiar essay, a method by which he approaches literature from the viewpoint of a lettered but not overly scholarly reader. A twentieth-century successor to such early nineteenth-century essayist-critics as William Hazlitt and Charles Lamb, Pritchett employs much the same critical method: his own experience, judgment, and sense of literary art are emphasized, as opposed to a codified critical doctrine derived from a school of psychological or philosophical speculation. His criticism is often described as fair, reliable, and insightful. In the following excerpt, Pritchett reviews the Kilmartin revision of* Remembrance of Things Past, *then discusses the artistic purpose of the work and the manner in which the novel echoes the work of Honoré de Balzac and the tales of* The Arabian Nights.]

Scott Moncrieff's translation of Proust's **"A la Recherche du Temps Perdu"** is a period masterpiece of that dangerous transposing art. So luminous and fervid does it still seem to us that it is even lazily said to rival the original, by those who did not find the French all that difficult as they skated over the surface but then gave up. Of course, we know that no translation can be a perfect mirror, but we did feel rather dished when the Pléiade edition showed us that Scott Moncrieff had been obliged to work from what has been called the "abominable" early *Nouvelle Revue Française* text, which Proust was still covering with revisions on a Balzacian scale when he died, in 1922. Scott Moncrieff died in 1930, and did not get as far as the grand disillusioned peroration of **"Le Temps Retrouvé,"** which was translated first by Stephen Hudson and later by Andreas Mayor. Not until 1954 did the patient Pléiade scholars complete their work, adding two hundred pages of explanatory notes and a long addendum of doubtful passages—for Proust was notoriously a writer who fed afterthoughts in from the scraps of paper scattered on his bed in the cork-lined room. Now, from the Pléiade edition, Terence Kilmartin has completed years of dedicated revision of Scott Moncrieff and a slightly emended Mayor, and we have **"Remembrance of Things Past"** in three handsome volumes. . . . In the third volume, there are often considerable rearrangements. One change of title is certainly better: **"The Fugitive,"** which Scott Moncrieff had rather archly called **"The Sweet Cheat Gone."** Mr. Kilmartin is a remarkably sensitive mediator. He has certainly been loyal to both Proust and his translator, and has not tinkered for tinkering's sake in the interests of pedantry. "'Loyal" is his own word, and it fits his labors: he has not killed Scott Moncrieff's tune, though he recognizes it belongs to its generation. (p. 186)

Scott Moncrieff had the great advantage of belonging to Proust's time. Its accents were in his ears. Intellectually, society was sententious and cosmopolitan, and as the crackup approached its artists broke into experiment and the reëxamination of tradition. Proust admired Balzac but was, on a different impulse, rewriting him. Among English writers, he turned to Ruskin, George Eliot, and Thomas Hardy. But Proust is a mingling of aesthete, surgeon, moralist, and scientist as he bursts traditional forms and the novelist himself becomes the novelist-as-hero of a critical exploration. He is seen in the act of clearing his mind for a novel that will never get written. He absorbs his characters into his own haze, as we do in autobiography. Rereading him now, after half a century, one also has the impression of being at the self-indulgent beginning of nonlinear writing—of which there has been a lot since, but none so crystalline. His reflections create an inland sea in which his people disappear into the hollows of the short waves and then reappear, excitingly changed for a moment, only to disappear once more. Very few of us now, except the professors and the saints of leisure, can have read him steadily from beginning to end in one long go; yet his gift is such that we can pick him up anywhere and be at once in his power—perhaps because his method is directed to floating small fleets of tales on the sea of speculation. One can begin anywhere, as one can with Gibbon as a moralist, or with the author of "The Arabian Nights" as an enchanter who mingles intellect with the shameless intrigues and passions taken for granted. And, like these writers, Proust is wide open to parody, and sometimes parodies himself.

For the reviewer who dutifully searches the new text in order to test the reordering of passages, the task is a nightmare—in fact, impossible. Despite the notes and a valuable synopsis of each section, one wanders like a fidgeting angler, trying three or four French and English ponds, tormented by both the big and the little fishes that will not tell him where they are hiding. We need a team of readers moving from version to version and reading aloud as, book in hand, we try to catch the differences. Ah, here's a bite, we may say: "Well-respected by all and sundry" runs more easily than "well-respected on all sides,'' which sounds like Albertine putting on public airs. Scott Moncrieff's ''paschal season'' sounds like one of his Gallicisms, though the new ''Eastertide'' is rather arty High Church English. ''Prodigiously intimidating,'' a voguish extravagance heard among Bloomsbury Proustians—say, Lytton Strachey—in the twenties and thirties, is better than the prim Victorian ''alarming.'' One gives up fishing for such small fry, and Scott Moncrieff's style still keeps its beguiling throb.

Yet what about that style? Scott Moncrieff has indeed been accused of raising the tone of the text, but Mr. Kilmartin points out that he kept extraordinarily close to the words, syntax, and rhythms of Proust's manner; there is little, if any, of paraphrasing, packaging, or the shortcut. The common criticism, Mr. Kilmartin says, is ''that his prose tends to the purple and the precious—or that this is how he interpreted the tone of the original: whereas the truth is that, complicated, dense, overloaded though it often is, Proust's style is essentially natural and unaffected, quite free of preciosity, archaism, or self-conscious elegance.'' Scott Moncrieff will say, for example, that Françoise sees her body too eloquently as being dropped ''like a stone into the hollow of the tomb'' when she imagines herself dying neglected (incidentally, echoing one of Mr. Pecksniff's pet phrases). Mr. Kilmartin is surely better with his ''like a stone into a hole in the ground,'' which is plain peasant talk.

The other criticism, Mr. Kilmartin goes on, is a defect of a virtue:

> In his efforts to reproduce the structure of those elaborate sentences with their spiralling subordinate clauses, not only does he sometimes lose the thread but he wrenches his syntax into oddly un-English shapes: a whiff of Gallicism clings to some of the longer periods, obscuring the sense and falsifying the tone. A corollary to this is a tendency to translate French idioms and turns of phrase literally, thus making them sound weirder, more outlandish, than they would to a French reader.

As for the purple and the precious, one has to say that a translator is likely to be affected by the ''going'' prose of his period. In Scott Moncrieff's time, *le mot juste*—as found in George Moore, for example—was often the poetic or exotic word. It is exceedingly difficult to find an English correlative of the precisions of French rhetoric—which seems to us extravagant, whereas it is sharply and formally contrived. One thinks of the French as being the *exalté* lawyers of the passions, in their analyses of them. Then, the English title **''Remembrance of Things Past''** evokes a drifting into the twilight of recollection; the French **''A la Recherche du Temps Perdu''** is intellectual—it defines the search for an exact recovery of what has been obscured by the memory of memory, and is a scientific expedition, an analysis of evidence, started off by involuntary memory. Again, Proust was sensitive to the ''style'' of each of his people; personal, social, and moral history lay in the variety of these styles. In the famous description of the hawthorn hedge in blossom, he is at once poetic and botanical yet feels the earthy infection of the senses. No symbol was more rooted in pagan nature, of which we are a part.

In the prolonged utterance in **''Time Regained''** on the nature of the book, as he clears his mind in the act of writing he says:

> Through art alone are we able to emerge from ourselves, to know what another person sees of a universe which is not the same as our own and of which, without art, the landscapes would remain as unknown to us as those that may exist in the moon. Thanks to art, instead of seeing one world only, our own, we see that world multiply itself and we have at our disposal as many worlds as there are original artists.

And, again, there is the essential moralist and student of manners:

> Our vanity, our passions, our spirit of imitation, our abstract intelligence, our habits have long been at work, and it is the task of art to undo this work of theirs, making us travel back in the direction from which we have come to the depths where what has really existed lies unknown within us.

Such a view (he mockingly says) M. de Norpois ''would have called a dilettante's pastime,'' whereas ''it is our passions which draw the outline of our books, the ensuing intervals of repose which write them.'' So his people change and become richer as they reappear and as the hidden impulses are drawn out by his irony. Legrandin, at first sight, is a harmless comic example of preciosity in his speeches; but it is shown that his affectations have a pathetic and, ultimately, a heartless hypocritical aspect. His mellifluousness is a disguise. When Legrandin warns the narrator against the ''Cimmerian'' influences of the Balbec country on a youthful mind and pretends he has no connections in the region, he is trying to prevent the youth from discovering he has an unpresentable poor relation there. Legrandin is a snob, but he is a failed snob, wounded because he, in his turn, has been snubbed by the Guermantes. Proust compares Legrandin's torments as a snob to the martyrdom of Saint Sebastian, and his skill in hiding his motives to the cunning of a Machiavelli: the fantasy outdoes Legrandin. Proust's mock-heroics are devastating. But when he begins one of his innumerable asides, starting with the famous ''Just as in,'' we know we are going to get a course in music, literature, painting, and sculpture. Is he, too, a high-flier on these Ruskinian tours? No; he is an excited, encyclopedic talker who has been trained in the salons and knows how to be competitive when it comes to being *''instruit.''* Sometimes he seems to parody his own manner (which, of course, a Legrandin would be unable to do), as in the later mock-heroic dismissal of ''the Young Ladies of the Telephone . . . the Vigilant Virgins . . . the Danaïds of the unseen who incessantly empty and fill and transmit to one another the urns of sound . . . the umbrageous priestesses of the Invisible,'' but at the point where the flight begins to sound a shade *de haut en bas,* and even facetious, he is saved by going off into a serious divagation on the relation of nostalgia to distance and on the pain of hearing the voice of a loved one without seeing the face. That face—especially Albertine's—may be telling lies. So may his. On the subject of lies, he is a metaphysician. (pp. 186, 190-92)

But I think still more of ''The Arabian Nights'' and Balzac. There is an element of adventure in the serpentine and magical expeditions of Proust's mind; his long sentences are indeed like the circling journeys of a snake. If the end is never in sight, a continuing expectation relieves the intellectual strain. Open these volumes anywhere and one is on the move, compelled by the feverishness of his egoism; the fever accentuates his clearheadedness and his sight. He is an invalid making insistent demands. Every place or person becomes more than itself, even when he ''sees through.'' And yet he is putting an order on his sensations. He is always present in his observations of people, never self-effacing. He has, of course, a good deal of the martinet in him, particularly in his relations with young women, who are in part young men: "Look, I have idealized you. Now I see through you, but in seeing through I enhance you. I have returned you, imperfect as you are, to the world to which I have shown you belonging. Now we break. It is interesting to remember the time when I began to forget you"—so he seems to be saying. The only loved women are his grandmother and his mother, who will reappear years after their deaths in his life-giving memory. But the lasting love—the love of the artist for his creation—is really Françoise, the servant, whose mind and language he mocks, and whose simple and often perverse opinions he treasures as a sort of grand national monument. Françoise is a statue for the Louvre. The "Arabian Nights" side of his genius gives the whole novel the cruel, proverbial, yet fantastic strain of a fairy tale, with Charlus acting the stentorian monster and Mme. de Guermantes the Fairy Queen.

The Balzac derivation is plain in the recurring characters, in the panorama of a society that is always out and about—but it excepts the working class. It must also be said that tradesmen are few. From pimps to duchesses, everyone is "going on." (There were few workers in Balzac also.) Proust has Balzac's fascination with status, professions, and class, his belief in categories, his eye for greed, obsession, lust, high pleasures and low, and, above all, his universal curiosity. There is some bothering mysticism. In Proust, this is not Balzac's animal magnetic fluid but the magnetism of time flowing through his people. He has not Balzac's obsession with *getting* money, but he takes for granted that love must be bought, that money is indispensable to the fulfillment of love. The system is felt to be normal. He is a mocker of ambition and is almost hardheaded in his judgments. He admires Saint-Loup's courage in war but faces the fact that men of honor may be privately corrupted.

As Proust said when he wrote about Balzac in **"Contre Sainte-Beuve,"** the great difference is that Balzac has the style of a coarse feeder and of one who collects the dossier and lays down the law; his metaphors, Proust complained, are like posters that have no real connection with what he is describing. Proust sought to make his metaphors arise from the scene and multiply its significance. Why, for example, are those telephone operators "Vigilant Virgins"? Because they can listen to your intimate conversations. "Umbrageous" because they work and listen in hiding. Read life *is* hidden. But the key to the difference between Balzac and Proust is Balzac's famous "That is why. . . ." Balzac explains Paris, the provinces, etc. He is a fact fetishist. The novelist must *not* explain, and Proust never does: he expands by suggestion, by reflection on parallels to the incidents or thoughts he has first put down. A work of art "brings back" life as it runs rife in nature. He was once congratulated for using a microscope on his people. He replied that what he used was not a microscope but a telescope, which brought the distant nearer and into focus, for time distances every moment of our lives at every tick of the clock. . . . There is none of Balzac's romantic melodrama in Proust or in his view of his period. The voice is never raised, and the word "time," with which the book ends, has a knell in it—the melancholy of requiem. (pp. 192-94)

V. S. Pritchett, "Proust" (copyright © 1981 by V. S. Pritchett; reprinted by permission of Literistic, Ltd.), in The New Yorker, *Vol. LVII, No. 34, October 12, 1981, pp. 186, 190-94.*

J. M. COCKING (essay date 1982)

[Cocking is a prominent Proust scholar. In the following excerpt he discusses the thematic preoccupations and personal concerns exhibited in Proust's correspondence.]

There was a time when Proust's biographers and critics were on the defensive about his letters, aware as they were of the unprepossessing image those letters might conjure up. Philip Kolb's work in editing and presenting them, pursued with hardly a break over nearly half a century, has changed all that and revealed the wealth and variety of interests to be found there.

Proust's letters began to be known to the reading public in the late 1920s and the '30s; first, a few at a time, in the memoirs published by people he cultivated, or in periodicals; then, from 1930 onwards, in the old edition of the ***Correspondance générale.*** The first collected volume . . . , which revealed all the then known letters of Proust to Robert de Montesquiou-Fezensac, did very little for Proust's reputation as a correspondent. As a one-sided view of the relationship, it was like incense burning for a god; and, thought Proust's more serious readers, a dubious god. Montesquiou was known to the literary public as the model for des Esseintes, in Huysmans's novel *À rebours,* and for the Baron de Charlus, in ***À la recherche du temps perdu:*** the two images combined to reflect the essence of decadent aristocracy, arrogance, and vice. Montesquiou himself was little read in the '30s, and known only vaguely as a third-rate poet. So Proust the letter-writer made his first great impression as an uncritical and shameless snob, flattering his way to the social summits.

When the second volume of the ***Correspondance générale*** came out, in the following year, the situation was not much improved in the eyes of Proust's critics. Letters to another aristocrat, the Comtesse de Noailles; thus, unbounded flattery of another minor poet—second-rate rather than third, perhaps, but no great shakes. And little attention was paid to Proust's essay on Anna de Noailles's *Les Éblouissements* (1907), printed in the same volume as the letters, since it seemed to follow the same sort of pattern as the letters themselves. The letters in the four remaining volumes, which appeared from 1932 to 1936—miscellaneous, often superficially socializing—did not reassure Proust's admirers; even his friendliest critics felt obliged to draw a distinction between the man and the writer, the personality and the genius.

This, of course, was a distinction more than suggested by Proust himself in his novel, in the passages dealing with the nature of literary vocation, and it was a theme he had worked out pretty thoroughly in an unpublished work, now in print as ***Contre Saint-Beuve.*** He was bothered by what he judged to be his own moral shortcomings and anxious to keep the notion of art on a high spiritual level with the artist as a man of almost religious insight. Art, he reiterated, is life transformed, and the artist is separated from the man by the success of his metamorphosis. Style, he believed, is not a clever way of saying things but a quality of vision. He virtually gave his critics leave, therefore, to apologize for his letters and keep them well apart from his creative writing.

Philip Kolb was the first to see that Proust's letters were of more than trivial interest. As early as 1938 he spotted references to unknown writings that Proust was working at between 1895 and 1900, thought of then as the novelist's idle years; he was proved right in 1952, when the drafts of Proust's unpublished story of Jean Santeuil were revealed to the public. More important, Kolb set to work on the letters as they were then published—dated inaccurately or not at all, arranged in approximate and often improbable sequence—and played the ingenious detective. (pp. xix-xx)

The definitive edition is full of all kinds of interest. With everything properly dated and in order, and with the intercalation of a good many replies from Proust's correspondents, often for the first time in print, the letters now look very different and reveal a very different Proust and a different set of human relationships. The bridges between the man and the artist are discernibly there, in spite of Proust's attempt to demolish them; not only are some of the raw materials of the novel well in evidence, in the recorded substance of characters and events, but something of the sensibility and intellectual power that went into the making of the novel is to be seen growing and groping in the letters. In spite of the neurosis and egotism, there is a tremendous deal of common sense, wisdom, and even morality. The letters are still a far cry from the novel, of course; art is art. They show why the novel lacks what it does: an understanding of some kinds of human relationships. But they also help us to see its virtues more roundly and more clearly.

The inclusion in the full edition of many of Montesquiou's replies, for instance, makes him and his relationship with Proust look quite different. . . . In these newly revealed letters, Montesquiou tells Proust a few home truths that can raise an appreciative smile in the reader. . . . And when Proust praises Montesquiou for his virtues as an aesthete and a poet, there is beneath the unction a serious and acutely analytical set of observations that may be applied less truly to Montesquiou than to Proust himself. Proust is never quite blinded by his own pretences, even when desire to please can seem to get the better of his judgement or, hypocritically, to cover his genuine judgements with a veneer. . . . (pp. xx-xxi)

Sometimes we find Proust writing in a deliberately affected style, such as he will attribute to characters in his novels. . . . A great many other passages which at first sight seem to be extravagant exercises in free fantasy or improbably strenuous hyperbole, often designed to please and flatter the recipient of the letter but proliferating into verbal self-indulgence, we can now, with our clearer idea of what Proust was trying to write, see as experiment and a flexing of linguistic muscle. The experiment is not only in the actual use of words and images but in thought, always subtle and often far-reaching, about the nature of language, the function of imagery, and the concept of literary style and meaning.

Such thought is to be found especially in the letters after 1904 to Anna de Noailles about her writing, where Proust's analysis of the poet's effects is leading him towards his own techniques for generating the kind of poetic aura, of magic and the light that never was, that every one of his readers has marvelled at in the first section of his novel, the evocation of Combray. But within the present selection [***Marcel Proust: Selected Letters (1880-1903)***] there is plenty of evidence of Proust's attempts to analyse and understand his spontaneous responses to literature, music, and painting. . . . (p. xxi)

The two sides of Proust's mind are perceptible throughout—sensitive responses and penetrating analyses. In [a letter to] Suzette Lemaire [dated 25 or 26 September 1894]: 'I have never written a *line* for the pleasure of writing, but only to express something that struck my heart or my imagination'; exaggeration, perhaps, but essentially true. In [a letter to Reynaldo Hahn dated 18 January 1895] he is 'drunk with reading Emerson', but not thereby prevented from going off to hear one of the teachers at the Lycée Condorcet defend his thesis on 'The Modern City and the Metaphysics of Sociology'. In [another letter to Reynaldo Hahn dated May 1895] he is sorting his impressions of Wagner, whose music, like Anna de Noailles's poetry, is to stimulate his thinking about aesthetic effects. But the most striking passage about music is in [a letter to Suzette Lemaire dated 20 May 1895], which defines Proust's position within the Romantic world of nineteenth-century aesthetics. His mysticism of music marks him as a typical transcendentalist, and puts him close to the Symbolists. Yet he is a transcendentalist without belief in any definable metaphysical transcendence. His mystery is inherent in a particular kind of *human* meaning. And he utterly rejected the obscurity of style that some Symbolists cultivated. His own style is difficult until it becomes familiar, but it is never obscure. And he is a classical observer of manners as well as a Romantic prose-poet.

No less interesting are Proust's earliest attempts to size himself up, to pick out the reasons for some of his reactions to life, to look at himself objectively and sometimes through the eyes of his family and friends. Montesquiou sees through him as a valetudinarian; his relatives, and particularly his grandparents—as in the case of Jean Santeuil—see through him as one who takes too much pleasure in his own sensibility. . . . But among those who know him, even the friends who mock what they came to label 'Proustification', criticism and disapproval are for the most part offset by affection and admiration.

Particularly interesting are the letters about his own homosexuality, which appeared for the first time in Kolb's definitive edition. The mixture of guilt and resolute enjoyment of his particular kind of sensuality is obvious from the start, as is the awareness of how it would look if people knew, the adoption of poses to prevent them knowing, the intermittent defiance of outside opinion. This complexity of attitude was to give rise to some uncertainty in the theses about homosexuality in the novel, but also to a richness in the portrayal of a variety of homosexual psychologies. . . . Defending himself in the latter to Daniel Halévy, Proust writes: 'My ethical beliefs allow me to regard the pleasures of the senses as a splendid thing.' Later, writing when in Brittany with Reynaldo Hahn about his character Jean Santeuil, he evoked not only the strong sensory stimulus of seaweed and cider apples but 'sweet and impotent kisses, arms tight-knit in embraces and legs twined round legs, caresses which intensify the silence'. When guilt evaporates, sensuality becomes lyricism; and this is one of the driving forces of Proust's most poetically effective prose.

For years he hesitated between what might roughly be called a Romantic and a Classical image of himself as a potential author. What often worried him was the difficulty of ordering and systematizing his experience, whether of knowledge or of lyrical feeling. He feared his own dilettantism. [In a letter to Charles Grandjean dated 13 November 1893] he says his intellectual development was arrested when he left school and that his writings 'have been the products solely of imagination and sensibility, the two ignorant Muses which require no cultivation'. He still has the illusion, he goes on, that he 'might have been something else, which is comforting and sad and undoubtedly an illusion'. By no means an illusion, however. Intellectual development, for Proust, was to be not systematic philosophizing or anything of the kind, but a continual sharpening of his powers of insight and of independent but value-dominated judgement. (pp. xxii-xxiii)

Holograph copy of a letter by Proust. Reproduced by permission of Librarie Plon.

Altogether, then, the letters are neither trivial nor, in the witness they bear to so many features of *la belle époque,* merely picturesque. But there *is* plenty of local colour, and a pronounced period flavour. . . . [A letter to Mme. de Brantes dated 23 October 1894 was written] with gold ink on violet paper; not without some practical inconvenience, as the letter itself reveals: 'But I shall tell you about it some day or write about it with more convenient ink.' Brittany must have seemed a delightfully primitive contrast to life in Paris; there Proust found it impossible to buy paper of any kind, and wrote whole sections of the ***Jean Santeuil*** drafts on the backs of old letters, bills, any odds and ends of paper he could lay hands on. And so he wrote to Robert de Billy in September 1895 . . . on the backs of two visiting cards, and promised more when he could find paper to write on.

In the early years of the new century we note his increasing involvement with friends in a social class above his own, with feelings that range from warm friendship to the equivalent, in the case of Bertrand de Fénelon, of passionate love; and reactions from the friends in question can awaken in Proust irritation, resentment, and even rebellion if their behaviour towards him carries any implication that they consider him socially inferior, or are mocking his hypersensitive and eccentric ways. Outside these emotional subtleties and complexities there is his admiration for their aristocratic manners, and his obvious enjoyment, though from the sidelines, of their high-spirited and often arrogant behaviour.

His observation of their ways and of his own reactions is meticulous; and, on a grander scale, so is his observation of groups and classes. For instance he writes to Reynaldo Hahn [on 15 November 1895] about a dinner party at the Daudets . . . and records generalizations about the differences between aristocrats and middle-class intellectuals that will be at the root of a number of fictional situations in his novel. The aristocrats are sensitive, intelligent, and accomplished in the exercise of their one art, which is graciousness; in almost every other respect they are gross and stupid. The intellectuals are not only socially insensitive but strangely blinkered within their own sphere of literature. The former are fascinating and eventually disappointing; the latter are exasperating. The Daudets, moreover, are anti-Semitic—particularly disturbing to Proust's sense of loyalty to his mother's side of the family. This dinner party, in November 1895, took place of course before the Dreyfus Affair became critical and brought so much anti-Semitism into the open. Proust seems to have swallowed what he must in the way of private humiliation and resentment; later he joined the vocal Dreyfusards and found the moral courage to protest against Montesquiou's anti-Jewish witticisms and to declare his own ancestry. But it was in the novel that he took his full revenge. portraying the Dreyfus Affair through the absurd prejudices of the anti-Dreyfusard faction.

Apart from his comments on class reactions to the Affair, where the interest is sociological in very general terms but not specifically political, there is not much historical reference in the novel; nor is there much to be found in the letters in this selection. He sometimes comments on day-to-day events as any intelligent reader of *Le Figaro* might do. But there is no sign of awareness of the major political changes in the Third Republic: the definitive political victory of the bourgeoisie, the increased influence of the financiers and the industrialists, the establishment of Radicalism as the majority political attitude, with lip-service to the Revolution and the Nation, hostility to aristocracy, Church, and Army, and real interest in wealth and material prosperity. Unlike Balzac, Proust is not much interested in the economic mechanisms of social change, only in the repercussions of such change on social groupings, conventions, and rituals. Until, it must be said, political moves awaken his aesthetic sense because they threaten what he takes to be the bases of the French cultural edifice he respects and loves. When, under the minister Émile Combes, the law of 1901 against the religious orders was strictly enforced, depriving them of the right to teach in France, Proust saw clearly that Radical anti-clericalism was changing the 'feel' of French life, and wrote a vigorous protest . . . to his friend Georges de Lauris, who had defended the government's measures.

In all such matters—the Panama scandal, the Dreyfus Affair, the 'affaire des fiches'—Proust is placed rather like Jean Santeuil in the passages about the scandal involving Charles Marie: portrayed as a criminal but a close friend of the family. Proust's family was socially involved with a good many political eminences—with the President of the Republic, Félix Faure, for instance, at the time when Faure felt obliged to refuse to acknowledge that a political error had been made over Dreyfus. Proust had therefore a dual perspective on many contemporary events, and it was only with the passage of time, with reflection on these events in the isolation of his cork-lined room, and with the maturing of his judgements, that detachment took precedence over the automatic assumptions arising out of personal familiarities and of the spontaneous identification in his early life with middle-class wealth, comfort, and cosiness.

The sequential and exactly dated order of the letters in Philip Kolb's full edition helps the reader to follow Proust through his successive efforts to write a novel about Jean Santeuil between 1895 and 1900; to plan a better kind of novel after abandoning this first attempt, but without making further headway; to please his mother by translating Ruskin even when enthusiasm waned and the devoted service of the disciple degenerated into rather grudging hackwork. The most exciting references to Proust's developing sense of vocation come in letters later than those included here. But in many ways these earlier letters reveal what Proust was later to call the 'fundamental notes' of a personality, on which the subsequent music of a human sensibility is based. Their interest is varied and subtle, and in Ralph Manheim's excellent translation they are suitably stylish and agreeable to read as well as faithful to the original French. (pp. xxiii-xxv)

J. M. Cocking, "Introduction" (1982; copyright © 1983 J. M. Cocking; reprinted by permission of Doubleday & Company, Inc.; in Canada by William Collins Sons & Co. Ltd.), in Marcel Proust: Selected Letters [1880-1903], *edited by Philip Kolb, translated by Ralph Manheim, Doubleday, 1983, pp. xix-xxv.*

JOHN WEIGHTMAN (essay date 1983)

[*In the following excerpt Weightman reviews a recent compilation of Proust's letters in English translation.*]

Proust is that rare phenomenon, a French writer almost fully acclimatized in the English-speaking world, so that **"Remembrance of Things Past"** (in C. Scott Moncrieff's translation, now excellently revised by Terence Kilmartin) is as familiar to us as, or perhaps even more familiar than, James Joyce's "Ulysses." But **"Marcel Proust: Selected Letters (1880-1903)"** is the first opportunity the English-langugage reader has had to assess Proust as a letter writer, apart from the excerpts from his correspondence quoted in biographies or critical works. In France, as it happens, even his greatest admirers have never made high claims for the letters contained in the early fragmentary editions, and some have even expressed dismay at the apparent gap between the genius who wrote the novel and the garrulous neurotic who penned so many excitable notes to friends and acquaintances.

Perhaps this is why the great labor of assembling and editing the often undated texts was taken on by an American enthusiast, Philip Kolb, who, with admirable devotion, has made it his life's work to resuscitate Proust, the letter writer, in every possible detail. The process is not yet complete, but the nine volumes so far published in French constitute a sort of epistolary autobiography of great psychological interest. From the first three volumes, Mr. Kolb has extracted for translation into English a representative selection, showing us Proust as he was from the ages of 9 to 32, during the long, uncertain, preparatory period before the idea of his great book clarified in his mind and he withdrew from the world to devote himself to literary composition. . . .

In introducing the selection, the distinguished English Proustian, J. M. Cocking, draws attention to the mixture of acute sensibility and analytical intelligence to be found in many of these letters in spite of their quirkiness, and he argues that the exaggerations, the preciosity and the outrageous flattery stood as literary exercises: Proust, he says, is flexing the linguistic muscles he will need for the great work. About this second point, I am not altogether convinced. As I read the letters, they seem to prove that, at least as a boy and a young man, Proust *was* in fact, most of the time, a mother-fixated, fluttery, hysterical, effeminate, obsequious, self-centered, snobbish person, a victim of his nerves, and so delicate that he would have been complete crushed by life had he not had first a protective family and then a large private income. We find him, even at the age of 31, presenting a two-week separation from his parents as an excruciating experience.

The miracle was that, inside this bundle of neuroses or this mass of psychosomatic tensions, which is expressed in letters crammed with fussy detail, was a strong, impartial mind demanding, as it were, to be let out, and which, when it did assert itself, was capable of great objective wisdom. The difference between the letters and **"Remembrance of Things Past"** is that, in the novel, the objectification is almost—if not quite—complete, whereas in the letters it is still very spasmodic. Perhaps, as has been suggested, Proust had to wait for the death of his mother before the umbilical cord would be cut; only then would he retire from life to build his immense imaginative structure that was both a consummation and a living tomb.

Now, of course, we read the letters with hindsight and inevitably find many signs of his future genius. For instance, in his teens, Proust complains during a holiday of the tedium of the surrounding society and says that he is searching the countryside "for the grain of poetry indispensable for existence"—the poetry he would express, or invent, so memorably at a later stage.

It is also clear that, if he gravitated to the aristocracy, this was because he mistakenly thought it entirely poetic, although he was not long deceived. Even during his most fashionable period, he was a social butterfly with a sting, whose obsequious letters often have more than a hint of ironical impertinence. He may enthuse hypocritically about second-rate literature for tactical reasons, then suddenly produce a brilliant fragment of critical appraisal—as when he explains the beauties of a poem by Mallarmé, and comments that Alphonse Daudet is "simplistic in his intelligence" since he thinks that Mallarmé "is fooling the public." Although the musician Reynaldo Hahn was one of his closest friends, and he genuinely admired him, he explains with perfect lucidity why Hahn was temperamentally incapable of really appreciating Beethoven.

It is only on the sexual question that the letters are ambiguous or self-contradictory (as, indeed, is to some extent also the case with the novel), as if Proust never fully made up his mind whether homosexuality was good, bad or indifferent, or where exactly his own preferences lay. . . . The only certainty is that he never had a totally successful affair with anyone of either sex. A sad comment on page 337 forecasts the erotic bleakness of **"Remembrance of Things Past"**: "I know that shared loves exist. But, alas, I do not know their secret."

John Weightman, "Proust before He Built His Monument," in The New York Times Book Review *(copyright © 1983 by The New York Times Company; reprinted by permission), May 29, 1983, p. 5.*

ADDITIONAL BIBLIOGRAPHY

Adams, Robert M. "A Clear View of Combray." *The Times Literary Supplement,* No. 4080 (12 June 1981): 667.

Review of the new translation of *Remembrance of Things Past* by Terence Kilmartin. The reviewer finds many interesting points of comparison between the Kilmartin text and the old Scott Moncrieff translation.

Alden, Douglas W. *Marcel Proust and His French Critics.* Los Angeles: Lymanhouse, 1940, 259 p.

Record of Proust's critical reputation in France to 1940, with a bibliography of French-language criticism arranged by country of origin.

———. "'Jean Santeuil'." *Saturday Review* XXXIX, No. 7 (8 February 1956): 14-15.

Review of Proust's *Jean Santeuil.* Alden discusses the merits of Proust's first novel and examines the probable reasons for Proust's abandonment of it before completion.

Auchincloss, Louis. "Proust's Picture of Society." *The Partisan Review* XXVII, No. 4 (1960): 690-701.

Discussion of Proust's characterizations of French aristocrats. Auchincloss is an American novelist and lawyer whose novels focus on characters from the upper echelons of society.

Barker, Richard H. *Marcel Proust: A Biography.* New York: Criterion Books, 1958, 373 p.

Biographical and critical study. Barker focuses on the interrelationship of Proust's two lives as a socialite and as a writer.

Bersani, Leo. *Marcel Proust: The Fictions of Life and Art.* New York: Oxford University Press, 1965, 269 p.

Psychological study. Bersani examines the conflict between the objective world and subjective reality as delineated by Proust in *Remembrance of Things Past.*

Bree, Germaine. "New Trends in Proust Criticism." *Symposium* V, No. 1 (May 1951): 62-71.

Analysis of various trends in Proust criticism. Bree examines the critical standing of *Remembrance of Things Past* twenty-five years after the death of Proust.

Cocking, J. M. *Proust.* New Haven: Yale University Press, 1956, 80 p.

Illustrates the manner in which Proust's style and aesthetic ideas evolved as he wrote *Pleasures and Days* and *Jean Santeuil,* and reached their full development in *Remembrance of Things Past.*

Corn, Alfred. "Time to Read Proust." *The Hudson Review* XXXV, No. 2 (Summer 1982): 298-305.

Discussion of Terence Kilmartin's revised translation of *Remembrance of Things Past.* Corn believes Kilmartin's translation is adequate, but points out many inconsistencies or inadequacies of translation.

Daiches, David. "Father of Swann." *The New Republic* 120, No. 18 (2 May 1949): 22-3.

Review of *The Letters of Marcel Proust,* edited and translated by Mina Curtiss. Daiches concludes that although these letters were ostensibly selected specifically to shed light on the composition of *Remembrance of Things Past,* they actually reveal little about the novel and much about Proust's personality.

Ellis, Havelock. "In Search of Proust." In his *From Rousseau to Proust,* pp. 363-96. Cambridge, Mass.: Riverside Press, 1935.*

Psychological study. Ellis's book focuses on writers whom he believes have brought about spiritual revolutions by altering the ways in which humans perceive themselves.

Green, F. C. *The Mind of Proust: A Detailed Interpretation of "A la recherche du temps perdu."* Cambridge: Cambridge University Press, 1949, 546 p.

Book by book analysis of Proust's novel. Green's study takes particular note of Proust's use of recurring themes and motifs.

Hughes, Edward J. *Marcel Proust: A Study in the Quality of Awareness.* New York: Cambridge University Press, 1983, 212 p.

Study of Proust's attempts to convey various examples of individual consciousness in his fiction. Hughes argues that Proust successfully reproduced states of consciousness ranging from the extreme self-awareness of the narrator of *A la recherche du temps perdu,* to "the faint glimpses of consciousness" experienced by Françoise.

Kilmartin, Terence. *A Reader's Guide to "Remembrance of Things Past."* New York: Random House, 1983, 256 p.

Includes synopsis of plot, themes, and characters of the novel.

Kopp, Richard L. *Marcel Proust As a Social Critic.* Rutherford, N.J.: Fairleigh Dickinson University Press, 1971, 230 p.

Discussion of Proust's social views. Kopp disputes the commonly held critical belief that Proust was an impartial observer of society.

Rivers, J. E. *Proust and the Art of Love.* New York: Columbia University Press, 1980, 327 p.

Psychological and sociological study of Proust's attitudes toward love, sex, and homosexuality as they are manifested in his writings. Rivers also provides an excellent description of the social climate in Europe at the time that Proust was working on *Remembrance of Things Past.*

Rogers, B. G. *Proust's Narrative Techniques.* Geneva: Librairie Droz, 1965, 214 p.

Discussion of Proust's literary techniques in *A la recherche du temps perdu.*

Sansom, William. *Proust and His World.* London: Thames and Hudson, 1973, 128 p.

Introduction to the social and historical background of Proust's period. This is a straightforward and richly illustrated book that reveals the autobiographical sources of Proust's major characters without confusing the reader with a plethora of names.

Shattuck, Roger. "Kilmartin's Way." *The New York Review of Books* XXVII, No. II (25 June 1981): 16-20.

Review by a prominent Proust scholar of the Terence Kilmartin translation of *Remembrance of Things Past*. Unlike many other critics, Shattuck finds that C. K. Scott-Moncrieff's translation works remarkably well, but believes that many of Kilmartin's alterations enhance the work. However, he also points out what he considers to be errors in Kilmartin's work and concludes that this is still not a "definitive" translation.

Spagnoli, John J. *The Social Attitude of Marcel Proust*. New York: Publications of the Institute of French Studies, Columbia University, 1936, 174 p.

Examination of Proust's social attitudes. Spagnoli believes that one may infer much about Proust's beliefs regarding various social issues through a careful reading of his novel.

Rudolf(us Josephus Laurentius) Steiner

1861-1925

Austrian philosopher, critic, essayist, dramatist, autobiographer, nonfiction writer, and poet.

Rudolf Steiner Publications/Garber Communications, Inc.

Steiner was the founder of Anthroposophy, one of the most important modern schools of spiritual and philosophical thought. This system of belief derives almost wholly from Steiner's own perceptions of the supersensible, or spiritual realm, and the interrelationship between this realm and the sense-perceived, or physical world. As explained by Steiner, the universe is essentially spiritual and not physical in nature, and a belief in the objective reality of the supersensible realm and its influence upon the physical world is central to Anthroposophical thought. Anthroposophists believe a direct apprehension of spiritual reality can be experienced inwardly through the development of psychic organs of spiritual perception. Steiner sought in Anthroposophy to expound "ideas that would point to the spiritual in the way scientific ideas point to the physical," and defined Anthroposophy as "a path of knowledge to guide the Spiritual in the human being to the Spiritual in the universe."

Steiner was born to Austrian parents in Kraljevec, a small village lying on the border of Hungary and Croatia. Following his primary school education, he attended a secondary school in Weiner-Neustadt with a curriculum emphasizing the sciences. Upon graduation Steiner went on to the Technical Institute of Vienna, where he augmented his scientific training with extensive readings of classical literature. Steiner's family was unable to offer him much financial assistance, and he supported himself by working as a tutor during his years at the Technical Institute. In his autobiography, Steiner recounts that the course of instruction he imparted to his young charges helped him fill the gaps in his own early education. Steiner was intrigued by his studies of Wolfgang von Goethe's scientific writings, and he achieved some prominence as a Goethe scholar. In 1889 he was invited to edit Goethe's natural science writings as part of the Standard Edition of Goethe's works then being prepared at the Weimar Goethe Archive. This massive editorial project occupied Steiner for seven years. During this time, he further developed the powers of clairvoyance which he believed had been transmitted to him through a previous incarnation and had been active in him since the age of nine. In his autobiography, Steiner wrote that "during my time in Weimar I did not feel inclined to speak directly about my experience of the spiritual world, even to those whom I knew intimately."

On concluding his duties at Weimar, Steiner obtained the editorship of *Das Magazin für Litteratur,* a literary magazine published in Berlin. He wrote drama reviews and became involved in adapting literary works for the stage. A growing desire to share his spiritual experiences led Steiner to a brief association with the Theosophical Society. As Secretary General of the German branch of the Society, Steiner began touring Europe to lecture on spiritual matters. His career as a lecturer was to occupy much of his time thereafter and it is estimated that he delivered some six thousand lectures during his lifetime. However, Steiner did not adhere strictly to Theosophic doctrine. For example, Theosophy is based upon ancient Eastern religions, which Steiner regarded as valuable but incomplete systems of spiritual development. His views and those of the Theosophists were largely in accord, however, until 1913, when Annie Besant, then president of the Theosophical Society, presented a young Indian boy as the new incarnation of Jesus Christ. Steiner could not accept this claim, which he felt trivialized the significance of Christ, whose life he saw as the central event in the spiritual history of humankind. He broke with Theosophy and founded the Anthroposophical Society in 1913. Steiner acknowledged a connection between the two groups when he wrote that "the nucleus of what later became the Anthroposophical Society was formed within the framework of the Theosophical Society."

Steiner's activities leading up to and following the formation of the Anthroposophical Society can be examined in three stages. From approximately 1901 until 1909 Steiner set forth in such works as *Die Philosophie der Freiheit (The Philosophy of Spiritual Activity)* what would later become the founding tenets of Anthroposophy. During Steiner's first stage of activity, extensive lecture tours took much of his time as he expounded his beliefs.

The years 1910 to 1917 saw Steiner's practical application of Anthroposophical thought to various branches of the arts and sciences, including drama, dance, education, agriculture, ar-

chitecture, and medicine. Also during these years, construction was started on the Goetheanum in Dornach, Switzerland. This structure was designed by Steiner to serve as a focal point for the movement and as a "school for spiritual science." It was a matter of pride for Steiner that throughout the years of World War I, Anthroposophists from virtually all of the warring nations continued to work together to construct the Goetheanum. Architects characterize the structure as stylistically unclassifiable, though clearly influenced by architectural Expressionism, and liken the Goetheanum to a huge piece of open sculpture. The structure stood until 1922, when it was destroyed by fire. Steiner immediately began designing a second Goetheanum of poured concrete. Not completed until after his death, this building was one of the first major structures built using reinforced concrete as a plastic building material.

During the period from 1910 to 1917, Steiner also wrote, produced, and directed four "Mystery Plays" which embody Anthroposophical thought—*Die Pforte der Einweihung (The Portal of Initiation), Die Prüfung der Seele (The Soul's Probation), Der Hüter der Schwelle (The Guardian of the Threshold)* and *Der Seelen Erwachen (The Soul's Awakening)*. Paul Marshall Allen writes that with these plays Steiner "created a new access to the spirit in artistic form." Presentation of each of the dramas takes an entire day. They contain little dramatic action and are difficult for non-Anthroposophists to comprehend. Performers for the most part stand motionless and deliver lengthy speeches in a cadenced monotone. Actors appear who represent various spiritual aspects of a character and, as each play progresses, one performer may enact many different states of being and several incarnations of one character. Hermon Ould has criticized Steiner's use of drama to convey a spiritual message, noting that "it is possible that these four plays enshrine a great philosophy of life; but that does not warrant the author in using a medium for which he has no aptitude."

From 1918 until his death in 1925, Steiner continued to lecture and teach, concentrating upon relaying his perceptions of the spiritual world to his followers. During this period he established the first of the Rudolf Steiner Schools, which have become known as the Waldorf Schools because the first was sponsored by the Stuttgart Waldorf cigaret factory to serve the families of its workers. The Steiner method of teaching incorporated Anthroposophical beliefs, focusing on holistic education rather than rote memorization of unrelated facts. During this period Steiner and his wife also developed the art of Eurythmy, or visual speech, a highly stylized dance form in which motions represent sounds.

Steiner's many books serve to expound his Anthroposophical ideas. Probably the most comprehensive of his works is *The Philosophy of Spiritual Activity,* in which he presents an introduction to his "science of the spirit." Steiner subtitled the work "Results of Introspective Observations according to the Method of Natural Science," indicating Anthroposophy's professed scientific, logical approach to the spiritual realm. In *The Philosophy of Spiritual Activity* Steiner endeavored to show that this realm lies not beyond but within the physical world, and that it is "possible for the personal individual self of man to penetrate the world's spiritual reality" whereas other systems of belief allow only a hypothetical view of the spiritual realm, rather than an actual experience of it. Steiner's own experience of this realm was attained by means of conscious will and intellectual discipline rather than mystical influence. In his autobiography he wrote: "I never approached the spiritual sphere through mystical feelings, but always through crystal-clear concepts." From a starting point of pure thought, Steiner believed that an individual could develop latent faculties that would enable the perception of an objective spiritual reality. This reality is one to which humanity once belonged prior to the existence of other forms of organic life and in isolation from them. Possessing a "soul-spirit," human beings follow a spiritual destiny separate from the strictly material processes of the natural world. Steiner himself considered *The Philosophy of Spiritual Activity* to be his most important work and the one which would most likely endure. Allen writes that this work "is intended—as Steiner intended all his writings—to *awaken* in the reader a new experience of the world of ideas, to arouse in him an inner activity, enabling him to come to grips with some of the most fundamental questions anyone can ask."

Today Anthroposophy remains a somewhat obscure system of beliefs, and the name of Steiner relatively unknown to the general public. However, there has long existed a serious interest in Steiner's thought among artists and intellectuals, including the Russian Symbolist writers, Franz Kafka, Albert Schweitzer, Owen Barfield, and Saul Bellow. Aspects of Anthroposophical thought have become widespread, perhaps most notably in the Waldorf Schools which are now established in many countries. Anthroposophy is for its adherents not only a formal system of beliefs but an all-inclusive way of life, and Steiner is esteemed by Anthroposophists and non-Anthroposophists alike for the high moral and ethical quality of his teachings.

(See also *Contemporary Authors,* Vol. 107.)

*PRINCIPAL WORKS

Grundlinien einer Erkenntnistheorie der Goetheschen Weltanschauung (philosophical treatise) 1886
[*The Theory of Knowledge Implicit in Goethe's World Conception,* 1940]
Die Philosophie der Freiheit (philosophical treatise) 1894; also published as *Die Philosophie der Freiheit* [revised and enlarged edition], 1918
[*The Philosophy of Freedom,* 1916; also published as *The Philosophy of Spiritual Activity* (revised and enlarged edition), 1980]
Friedrich Nietzsche: Ein Kampfer gegen seine Zeit (criticism) 1895
[*Friedrich Nietzsche: Fighter for Freedom,* 1960]
Goethes Weltanschauung (philosophical treatise) 1897; also published as *Goethes Weltanschauung* [revised and enlarged edition], 1918
[*Goethe's Conception of the World,* 1928]
Die Mystik im Aufgange des neuzeitlichen Geisteslebens und ihr Vehältnis zu modernen Weltanschauungen (essays) 1901
[*Mystics of the Renaissance and Their Relation to Modern Thought,* 1911; also published as *Mysticism and Modern Thought,* 1928; and *Mysticism at the Dawn of the Modern Age,* 1960]
Welt- und Lebensanschauungen im 19. Jahrhundert. (philosophical treatise) 1901; also published as *Die Rätsel der Philosophie* [enlarged edition], 1914
Das Christentum als mystische Tatsache (philosophical treatise) 1902; also published as *Das Christentum als mystische Tatsache und die Mysterien des Altertums* [revised and enlarged edition], 1910
[*Christianity as Mystical Fact and the Mysteries of Antiquity,* 1914; also published as *Christianity as*

Mystical Fact and the Mysteries of Antiquity (revised and enlarged edition), 1961]
Aus der Akasha-Chronik (nonfiction) 1904; published in the journal *Lucifer-Gnosis*
[*The Submerged Continents of Atlantis and Lemuria: Their History and Civilization,* 1911; also published as *Cosmic Memory: Prehistory of Earth and Man,* 1959]
Theosophie (nonfiction) 1904; also published as *Theosophie* [revised edition], 1922
[*Theosophy: An Introduction to the Supersensible Knowledge of the World and the Destiny of Man,* 1910; also published as *Theosophy: An Introduction to the Supersensible World and the Destination of Man* (revised edition), 1946]
Wie erlangt man Erkenntnisse der höheren Welten? (philosophical treatise) 1904; published in the journal *Lucifer-Gnosis;* also published as *Wie erlangt man Erkenntnisse der hoheren Welten?* [revised and enlarged edition], 1918
[*The Way of Initiation: or, How to Attain Knowledge of the Higher Worlds,* 1908; also published as *Knowledge of the Higher Worlds and Its Attainment* (revised and enlarged edition), 1923]
***Initiation and Its Results: A Sequel to "The Way of Initiation"* (philosophical treatise) 1909
Die Geheimwissenschaft im Umriss (philosophical treatise) 1910
[*An Outline of Occult Science,* 1914]
Die Pforte der Einweihung (drama) 1910
[*The Portal of Initiation* published in *Four Mystery Plays,* 1920]
Die Prüfung der Seele (drama) 1911
[*The Soul's Probation* published in *Four Mystery Plays,* 1920]
Der Hüter der Schwelle (drama) 1912
[*The Guardian of the Threshold* published in *Four Mystery Plays,* 1920]
Der Seelen Erwachen (drama) 1913
[*The Soul's Awakening* published in *Four Mystery Plays,* 1920]
Four Mystery Plays (drama) 1920
Anthroposophie: Eine Einfuhrung in die Anthroposophische Weltanschauung (lectures) 1924
[*Anthroposophy: An Introduction,* 1931]
Anthroposophie Leitsätze (philosophical treatise) 1925
[*Anthroposophical Leading Thoughts,* 1927]
Mein Lebensgang (autobiography) 1925
[*The Story of My Life,* 1928; also published as *The Course of My Life* (revised edition), 1951; and *Rudolf Steiner: An Autobiography* (revised edition), 1977]
Eurythmie als sichtbare Sprache (lectures) 1927
[*Eurythmy as Visible Speech,* 1931]
Die Kunst der Rezitation und Deklamation (lectures) 1929
[*Art in the Light of Mystery Wisdom,* 1935]
Bauformen als Kultur- und Weltempfindungagedanken (philosophical treatise) 1934
[*Architectural Forms Considered as the Thoughts of Culture and World-Perception,* 1935]
Grenzen der Naturerkenntnis (lectures) 1969
[*The Boundaries of Natural Science,* 1983]

*The following is a select bibliography from among the hundreds of titles by Steiner that have appeared in German and in English translation. Many of Steiner's works were published posthumously and are in the form of brief pamphlets or lectures transcribed from his unrevised notes.

**This work was published with *The Way of Initiation; or, How to Attain Knowledge of the Higher Worlds* as *Knowledge of the Higher Worlds and Its Attainment* in 1923.

THE BOOKMAN, LONDON (essay date 1910)

[*The following review of* Initiation and Its Results *gives a general outline of the occult subjects Steiner is concerned with in this work.*]

In these days when the doctrine of a future life and of the possibility of communication between the material and spiritual worlds has won a (more or less) qualified assent even in scientific circles, it is only to be expected that the literature of the subject should show signs of considerable expansion both from within and without. . . . [In] the little volume by the German occultist, Dr. Rudolf Steiner [***Initiation and Its Results***] . . . , we approach the matter from the standpoint of the advanced Theosophist. Here we behold the psychic expert, equipped with what the student is invited to accept as occult knowledge and not merely hypothesis and experiment. Small as it is, the book traverses a large territory, quite unexplored by the ordinary mind. We have a description of the "astral centres"—those organs of the astral, or super-physical, body which are known to Oriental occultists as "chakras"; the constitution of the "etheric body" (the term "etheric," by the way, is admittedly a misnomer, scientifically speaking, but is employed for convenience); the dream life; the three states of consciousness; together with some impressive deliverances concerning the higher spiritual evolution of man. Whatever may be thought of these dicta, there is no denying the high ethical quality of the teaching. . . . Although the volume, as already indicated, is designed for those who have made some advance in occult studies, it is not without passages likely to prove interesting and suggestive even to the tyro in such matters. Much of the book is taken up with a consideration of the changes and development of the psychical organs—the "lotus-flowers" as Dr. Steiner calls them—necessary to bring the initiate into close contact with superphysical realms of existence. These lotus-flowers of the soul are no mere poetical figures of speech to the occultist, for we learn of "the twelve-petalled lotus which lies in the region of the heart," and of "the six-petalled lotus" whereby communication is gained with beings who are native to the higher worlds. Needless to say this is likely to prove caviare to the general, and the book's true function is obviously to serve as a guide to well-grounded students of occultism ambitious to become "adepts." To such, without necessarily endorsing all its conclusions, we cordially commend it. . . . (pp. 199-200)

A review of "Initiation and Its Results," in The Bookman, *London, Vol. XXXVII, No. 220, January, 1910, pp. 199-200.*

FRANZ KAFKA (diary date 1911)

[*Kafka is best known as the author of* The Metamorphosis *(1915) and* The Trial *(1925), two seminal works of modern literature. The following excerpt is taken from Kafka's diaries and is a rambling account of his impressions of Steiner gathered from Theosophical lectures, things he heard about Steiner, and a meeting between the two men.*]

March 26. Theosophic lectures by Dr. Rudolph Steiner, Berlin. Rhetorical effect: Comfortable discussion of the objections of opponents, the listener is astonished at this strong opposition, further development and praise of these objections, the listener becomes worried, complete immersion in these objections as though there were nothing else, the listener now considers any refutation as completely impossible and is more than satisfied with a cursory description of the possibility of a defense.

Continual looking at the palm of the extended hand.—Omission of the period. In general, the spoken sentence starts off from the speaker with its initial capital letter, curves in its course, as far as it can, out to the audience, and returns with the period to the speaker. But if the period is omitted then the sentence, no longer held in check, falls upon the listener immediately with full force. (p. 54)

In the Vienna lodge there is a theosophist, sixty-five years old, strong as a giant, a great drinker formerly, and a blockhead, who constantly believes and constantly has doubts. It is supposed to have been very funny when once, during a congress in Budapest, at a dinner on the Blocksberg one moonlit evening, Dr. Steiner unexpectedly joined the company; in fear he hid behind a beer barrel with his beer mug (although Dr. Steiner would not have been angered by it).

He is, perhaps, not the greatest contemporary psychic scholar, but he alone has been assigned the task of uniting theosophy and science. And that is why he knows everything too. Once a botanist came to his native village, a great master of the occult. He enlightened him.

That I would look up Dr. Steiner was interpreted to me by the lady as the beginning of recollection. The lady's doctor, when the first signs of influenza appeared in her, asked Dr. Steiner for a remedy, prescribed this for the lady and restored her to health with it immediately. A French woman said goodbye to him with "Au revoir." Behind her back he shook his head. In two months she died. A similar case in Munich. A Munich doctor cures people with colors decided upon by Dr. Steiner. He also sends invalids to the picture gallery with instructions to concentrate for half an hour or longer before a certain painting.

End of the Atlantic world, lemuroid destruction, and now through egoism. We live in a period of decision. The efforts of Dr. Steiner will succeed if only the Ahrimanian forces do not get the upper hand.

He eats two liters of emulsion of almonds and fruits that grow in the air.

He communicates with his absent disciples by means of thought-forms which he transmits to them without bothering further about them after they are generated. But they soon wear out and he must replace them. (pp. 56-7)

Mrs. F.: "I have a poor memory." Dr. St.: "Eat no eggs."

In his room I try to show my humility, which I cannot feel, by seeking out a ridiculous place for my hat, I lay it down on a small wooden stand for lacing boots. Table in the middle, I sit facing the window, he on the left side of the table. On the table papers with a few drawings which recall those of the lectures dealing with occult physiology. An issue of the *Annalen für Naturphilosophie* topped a small pile of the books which seemed to be lying about in other places as well. However, you cannot look around because he keeps trying to hold you with his glance. But if for a moment he does not, then you must watch for the return of his glance. He begins with a few disconnected sentences: So you are Dr. Kafka? Have you been interested in theosophy long?

But I push on with my prepared address: I feel that a great part of my being is striving toward theosophy, but at the same time I have the greatest fear of it. That is to say, I am afraid it will result in a new confusion which would be very bad for me, because even my present unhappiness consists only of confusion. (p. 58)

He listened very attentively without apparently looking at me at all, entirely devoted to my words. He nodded from time to time, which he seems to consider an aid to strict concentration. At first a quiet head cold disturbed him, his nose ran, he kept working his handkerchief deep into his nose, one finger at each nostril. (p. 59)

Franz Kafka, "The Urban World" and "My Visit to Dr. Steiner," diary entries of 1911, in his The Diaries of Franz Kafka: 1910-1913, *edited by Max Brod, translated by Joseph Kresh (reprinted by permission of Schocken Books Inc.; copyright © 1948, by Schocken Books Inc.; copyright © renewed 1975 by Schocken Books, Inc.), Schocken Books, 1948, pp. 47-57, 57-63.**

THE NATION **(essay date 1912)**

[*The following review of* Mystics of the Renaissance and Their Relation to Modern Thought *is devoted to a discussion of panpsychism—the concept that both the natural and the human worlds are constituted of a spiritual as well as a material aspect. The reviewer explains that Steiner "holds that nature is entirely material, and that spirit is to be found only in man."*]

[***Mystics of the Renaissance and Their Relation to Modern Thought***] is an excellent little work excellently translated by a competent English mystic, Bertram Keightley. It puts in brief compass and in popular form the scattered schools from Meister Eckhart to Boehme and Silesius; it gives clear and simple expositions of that which has not been accounted clear and simple. Avoiding the problems of remote sources or over-technical explanations, the author, by his sympathetic insight, has made friends even with that difficult trio—the Friends of God, Tauler, Suso, and Ruysbroeck. An engaging feature of the book is the endeavor to make mysticism a living doctrine. The problems raised by the men of the interior or hidden life are shown to be those of present and somewhat public discussion. Such are the problems of panpsychism, of the evolution of spirit, of the subjectivity of sensations, of the validity of inferential knowledge.

In this connection Steiner takes a unique position: he hopes that one may be a faithful adherent of the scientific conception of the world and yet be able to seek out those paths to the soul along which mysticism, rationally understood, must lead. Previous to these lectures, delivered at the Theosophical Library in Berlin, he had described his view of the world, which had no thought of driving out the spirit because it beholds nature as Darwin and Haeckel beheld it. There lies no contradiction, he explains, in the fact of saturating one's self with the knowledge of the most recent natural science, and at the same time treading the path which Jacob Boehme and Angelus Silesius have sought.

Is this conclusion valid? Is there no contradiction between mysticism and modernism? The first problem attacked is that of panpsychism, or the vitalizing of nature. Here it is held to be false to ascribe to a plant a soul which is supposed to be only remotely analogous to that of man, for man does not grasp nature by peopling it from within himself with arbitrarily assumed entities, but by accepting and valuing it as it is, as nature. This is a definite thesis. But it may be asked whether panpsychism is not a supplement, or rather an intermediate step to mystic pantheism. By analogy the modern thinker infers a logical possibility of an ensouling of all nature; the mystic assumes this by the direct awareness of the inner light. Panpsychism admits a dualism, matter infused with spirit; mysticism favors a monism, spurns matter, shuts its eye to the physical. Now, if panpsychism be a logical inference or supplement to the physical, there arise three steps or stages in knowledge—physical, logical, mystical. As Tauler has put it: "Man is just as if he were three men—his animal man as he is according to the senses, then his rational man, and lastly his highest, godlike man. The one is the outer, animal, sensuous man; the other is the inner, understanding man, with his understanding and reasoning powers; the third man is spirit." The master is here clearer and more comprehensive than the interpreter. The third man is above the first, but the second is not thereby precluded. Steiner, however, constantly disparages the second stage because the inferred panpsychism leads to the conceit of anthropomorphism, since, as he asserts, the false materialists and the false idealists confuse the sensibly-natural with the spiritual.

We take this criticism to mean that panpsychism runs the risk of blocking the advance into the truly spiritual. As the ensouling of nature it gives rise to two groups of thinkers, both over-satisfied with the position they have attained. There are no longer mere materialists, for they have more or less idealized matter. Nor are there pure idealists, for the physical universe is necessary for the embodiment of the spirit—without matter there can be no incarnation of form. In a word, panpsychism may be a half-way house to mysticism, but it has become so comfortably furnished, so filled with modern improvements, that it tempts many to linger there. To the true pilgrim on the path of pure spirituality there is the harder road, the *via negativa* of asceticism and renunciation, seldom travelled by the modernist.

And panpsychism runs the further risk of anthropomorphizing nature, of injecting into it a purposiveness conceived after human notions of design. In this point Steiner should agree with a panpsychist like Paulsen, who expressly disavows cosmic design after the manner of man, and suggests that nature has a life of its own, running alongside human life, yet not to be expressed in terms of the latter. The author at this juncture is evidently attacking an older type of thought, the Fichtean philosophy, which would inject into nature the creative ideas of the individual. The discussion raised is extremely interesting to the irenecist, for the difference between the two interpretations seems largely one of emphasis. Steiner emphasizes the subjective, and easily shows that the individual's self-inspired teleology is false. Paulsen emphasizes the objective, and from Haeckel himself offers illuminating inferences as to the existence of a world-soul in even the lowest forms of matter.

This reconciliation does not occur to the author. He holds that nature is entirely material, and that spirit is to be found only in man; this is the entity that connects us with the entire world, this the inner illumination that lights up all reality at once. For the evolution of this spirit he points for corroboration to nineteenth-century thought. Eckhart and Tauler, Boehme and Silesius, he explains, would needs feel the deepest satisfaction in contemplating this natural science which no longer sees in nature any being that is like unto the human soul, that no longer makes the organic forms to be created by a man-like God, but follows up their development in the sense-world according to "purely natural forms." If this be mysticism, it is unlike the mysticism alleged to exist in recent expositions of creative evolution. Steiner denies that any creative thought ruled in the forthcoming of the spirit in the organism, and yet admits that spirit as perceivable is a result of evolution, and that upon lower levels of evolution such spirit must not be sought for. It is difficult to see how such an evolution took place unless one call in the aid of some vital impetus, some psychic factor. Steiner's exposition may accord with the crude dualism of primitive Darwinism, where nature was regarded as purely material and man as its intellectual observer; it hardly accords with the Neo-Aristotelianism of the Bergsonians with their appeal to the internal perfecting principle. Indeed, this entire work gives an unusual, if not an unwarranted, exposition of mysticism. That doctrine has generally been thought of as tending towards monism, "the unfoldment of the Root-Being" as leading to a unitary view of the cosmos. But if that unfoldment be confined to man, and nature be put to one side as barely material, the resulting system is an ill-balanced dualism. It is the fallacy of taking the part for the whole to say that, if we experience the spirit in ourselves, then we have no need of such in external nature.

This haling of the world-soul out of the body of nature is our chief criticism of this stimulating work. Minor criticisms concern including among the mystics of the Renaissance such an early writer as Eckhart. Again, it is somewhat forced to assert that Paracelsus in his "astral" phenomena recognizes an intermediate stage between the purely physical and the properly spiritual or soul-phenomena, and thus anticipates the scientific conceptions of the sub-conscious. This is an aberration of the so-called New Thought, a false hypostatizing of the dream life, as if it were a separate existence and not a state of partial decentralization. In this connection the writer inadvertently contradicts his previous view of nature as merely material, man as solely spiritual. Connecting with this "astral" region all the phenomena belonging to hypnotism and suggestion, he asks if in the latter we are not compelled to recognize an interaction between human beings, which points to some connection or relation between beings in nature, which is normally hidden by the higher activity of the mind. From this starting-point one may indeed reach an understanding of what Paracelsus meant by the "astral" body, but such an interpretation is that of a discredited disciple of Paracelsus—Mesmer, that believer in "beamy spirits which stream forth invisibly." We have not space to discuss other anticipations of modern thought discovered among these worthies, but there are interesting expositions of such topics as the subjectivity of sensation under Valentine Weigel, and the validity of inferential knowledge under Nicholas of Cusa. (pp. 169-70)

"A Study of Mysticism," in The Nation, *Vol. XCV, No. 2460, August 22, 1912, pp. 169-70.*

HERMON OULD (essay date 1922)

[While not denying the possibility of a valid spiritual philosophy expressed in Steiner's four Mystery Plays, *Ould finds Steiner unable to utilize the medium of the drama to expound his ideas.*

For other examinations of Steiner's dramatic works, see the excerpts by Richard Rosenheim (1952), Adam Bittleston (1956), Hans Pusch (1972), and Robb Creese (1978).]

I find myself in possession of ***Four Mystery Plays,*** by Rudolf Steiner. Their titles are ***The Portal of Initiation, The Soul's Probation, The Guardian of the Threshold,*** and ***The Soul's Awakening;*** they contain 560 pages and are published by Messrs. G. P. Putnam & Sons. I give all these details so that anybody whose interest has been quickened by this man, whose power to influence many hundreds of thousands of people cannot be doubted, may try to get to the heart of his teaching by reading these plays. I repeat: "Try." I have tried, perseveringly, and have failed, abjectly.

A preface tells us that Dr. Steiner's habit is to write a play whilst the rehearsals are actually in progress, finishing it a few days before the first public performance. Only the greatest of dramatists could adopt such a method of working and succeed; and however great a thinker Dr. Steiner may be, it is quite certain that he is a very poor playwright. These four plays have practically no form at all. They are a series of dialogues, with interpolated verses, in which it is possible that some occult idea is exhaustively developed; but, since the drama form was chosen, and since the plays were written for performance in a theatre, one is justified in judging them according to the criteria which govern the art of the theatre.

The Prelude is in prose, and two women, employing exactly the same characterless idiom, express themselves. . . . (pp. 447-48)

It is possible that these four plays enshrine a great philosophy of life; but that does not warrant the author in using a medium for which he has no aptitude. (p. 448)

Hermon Ould, "Caviare," in The English Review, *Vol. XXXIV, May, 1922, pp. 447-53.**

RUDOLF STEINER (essay date 1923-25)

[*In the following excerpt, Steiner explains that* The Philosophy of Spiritual Activity *represents his efforts to express his perceptions of the spiritual world. The Weimar period Steiner mentions refers to the years 1889 through 1896, during which he worked as one of the editors of the standard edition of Wolfgang von Goethe's works, which was prepared at Weimar from the mid-1880s until the late 1890s.*]

[In] my writings I had to find forms of expression for my inner perception. It is not possible to find at once new expressions for something unfamiliar to the reader. I had to choose either the formulation usual in science, or that of mystically-inclined writers. The difficulties connected with the latter seemed insuperable.

I came to the conclusion that the ideas expressing scientific knowledge are full of inner reality, even if this reality is chiefly thought of in a materialistic sense. I sought to formulate ideas that would point to the spiritual in the way scientific ideas point to the physical. It would enable me to retain a conceptual character for what I had to say, which was not possible with a mystical formulation. The latter does not point to any *objective reality outside* man. It describes only inner, subjective experiences. I had no wish to describe human experiences; I wished to point to the fact that through spiritual organs of perception an objective spiritual world is revealed *within* man. Out of these considerations I formulated the ideas which later became my ***Philosophy of Spiritual Activity.*** When I formulated these ideas I had no wish to be overcome by a mystical mood, although it was clear to me that the ultimate experience of what is revealed through ideas within the inner being of the soul will be of the same character as the inner perception of the mystic. (p. 154)

My ***Philosophie der Freiheit,*** **Philosophy of Freedom** (Spiritual Activity) is based upon an inner experience of human consciousness. An experience of freedom *practiced* through the will, *experienced* in feeling, *recognized* through thinking. But to attain this experience, thinking must not have lost its inner life.

When I worked on my ***Philosophie der Freiheit,*** **Philosophy of Spiritual Activity** it was my constant care, as I presented my thoughts, to remain fully awake within all their ramifications. This gives to thoughts the mystical quality of sight, but sight that resembles seeing in the sense world. Once this inner experience has been gained, no contradiction exists between the cognition of nature and the cognition of the spirit. One sees the latter as a metamorphosed continuation of the former.

Thus I could later write on the title page of my ***Philosophie der Freiheit,*** **Philosophy of Spiritual Activity,** "Results of Introspective Observations According to the Method of Natural Science." For if the method of natural science is faithfully adhered to in regard to the spirit, it leads to cognition in this sphere also. (pp. 158-59)

I came to know many a person's outlook on the world and life during my Weimar-period. . . . This was partly because I was in constant, direct contact with people who were discussing these matters; and also, in those days it was just people of philosophical interests who passed through Weimar.

I was then at an age when by inclination one turns intensively toward one's surroundings, seeking to establish a firm connection with external life. For me, various views and philosophies were an aspect of that external life. I now realized how little I had really participated in the external world up to then. Whenever I withdrew from animated social life I became aware, particularly at this period, that really the only world I had been familiar with so far was the spiritual world I inwardly beheld. I found it easy to establish a connection with that world. And I began to realize how very difficult it had been for me during childhood and youth to relate myself to the outer world through the senses. I had always found it difficult to commit to memory external data that has to be assimilated, for example in the study of science. I had to observe natural objects repeatedly in order to be able to identify them and to know their scientific classification. The external world really appeared to me somewhat shadow-like or picture-like. It moved past me like pictures, whereas my relationship with the spiritual always had the character of concrete reality.

I felt this more particularly during the early 'nineties in Weimar. I was then adding the final touches to my ***Philosophy of Spiritual Activity.*** In writing this book I felt I was setting down the thoughts given me by the spiritual world up to my thirtieth year. What I had received from the external world was experienced merely as a stimulus.

This stimulus I experienced in particular when I shared in the lively discussions in Weimar about world-views. I had to enter into the way of thinking and feeling of others, but they did not enter into the content of my inner life. I experienced their outlook and thoughts, but the spiritual reality within me could not unite with what I thus experienced. My innermost being had always to remain within itself. My inner world was really separated from the outer world as if by a thin wall.

Thus inwardly I lived in a world that bordered upon the outer world; it was as if I had to cross a threshold when I wanted to have intercourse with the outer world. I was continually sharing in lively discussions but in order to have them I had each time, as it were, to go through a door. This made me feel that I was paying a visit every time I participated in the outer world. It did not prevent me from devoting my interest to the person I was "visiting." Indeed I felt very much at home while on such a visit.

This was my experience with people and also with their outlook. (pp. 205-06)

I immersed myself in the most contrasting world-views: in those based on science as well as in those based on idealism and in many shades of both. I felt a need to enter into them all, to be orientated in them, but they threw no light into my spiritual world. They were phenomena I met, not realities with which I could live.

It was during these impressions that I came into direct contact with world-views like those of Haeckel and Nietzsche. I recognized their relative justification. It was therefore not possible for me to say about either that this is right, or that is wrong. I could have done so only if I had felt what they expressed as alien to myself. But I did not find the one more alien than the other; for while I could feel "at home" in *all* world-views, I was truly at home only in the spiritual world I directly perceived.

Thus described it may appear as if fundamentally everything was a matter of indifference to me. But that was by no means the case. What I experienced was something very different. The reason I was able to participate fully in the views of others was because I did not alienate myself from them by bringing my own views and feelings into the judgment at once. (p. 207)

It was always the same in those days. I had to come to terms with everything that concerned my spiritual perception entirely alone. I lived in the spiritual world; not one among all the people I knew followed me there. My social life consisted in excursions into the world of others. And I loved these excursions. (p. 214)

Such was my "loneliness" in Weimar where I led such an active social life. I did not hold it against people that they condemned me to loneliness in this way. Indeed, I perceived that unconsciously many felt a deep need of a world view which could penetrate to the source of existence. I could sense that many men were troubled by the prevailing way of thinking, which appeared so reliable just because it was concerned only with the immediately obvious. "The material world is the *entire* world," was the outlook of this thinking. And it was believed that there was no other choice, that one *had* to regard this way of thinking as correct. Thus all feelings were suppressed that might arise in the soul suggesting that it was *impossible* to regard it as correct. This fact threw light upon many things in my spiritual environment. This was the time when I gave the final form to my ***Philosophy of Spiritual Activity,*** the content of which had lived within me for a long time. (pp. 214-15)

I tried to show in my book that nothing *unknowable* lies *behind* the sense-world, but that *within* it is the spiritual world. And I tried to show that man's idea-world has its existence within that spiritual world. Therefore, the true reality of the sense-world remains hidden from human consciousness *only* for *as long as* man is merely engaged in sense-perception. When to the experience of sense-perception is added the experience of ideas, then the consciousness experiences the sense-world in its objective reality. Cognition is not a portrayal of some unknowable entity; to cognize is to enter into that entity. The advance from the unessential external aspect of the sense-world to its essential inner reality is a step that takes place *within* consciousness. Thus, the sense-world is semblance (phenomenon) only for so long as man's consciousness has not penetrated it fully.

Thus the sense-world is in truth spiritual, and the human soul lives within this recognized spiritual world by widening the consciousness to encompass it. The goal of cognition, of knowledge, is the conscious *experience* of the spiritual world before which everything ultimately resolves into spirit.

Against phenomenalism I put spiritual reality. (pp. 215-16)

Thus, there was set over against my search for the spirit through a widening of consciousness the view that "spirit" is found directly only in the form of man's mental pictures; apart from them one can approach the spirit only *hypothetically*. Fundamentally this was the view of the age into which my ***Philosophy of Spiritual Activity*** had to be introduced. According to this view man's experience of spirit had shrunk, had become merely an experience of mental pictures, and from these no path could be found to a real (objective) world of spirit.

I wanted to show that within the subjective experience of mental pictures the objective spirit shines forth and can become the actual content of consciousness; Eduard von Hartmann held against me that in the way I explain matters I remain within the *semblance* of what is sense-perceptible, that I fail to speak of objective reality at all. (pp. 216-17)

[What] is the foundation of ethical individualism in my ***Philosophy of Spiritual Activity***? It is the fact that I saw the center of the soul's life in complete union with the world of spirit. I attempted to present matters so that an apparent difficulty, disturbing to many, would resolve itself! Namely, the view that in order to cognize, the soul—or the "I"—must *differentiate* itself from what is cognized, and therefore, cannot unite with it. Yet this differentiation is also possible when the soul, as it were, swings like a pendulum, back and forth between self-reflection and being-at-one-with a spiritual reality. The soul becomes "unconscious" when it penetrates objective spirit, but brings, in self-reflection, the complete reality over into consciousness.

Thus, as it is possible for the personal individual self of man to penetrate the world's spiritual reality, it can also experience the sphere of moral impulses within that reality. Morality becomes a revelation of the spiritual world *within* man's individuality; his consciousness, now widened to encompass the spirit, penetrates to a direct perception of what is thus revealed. What impels man to a moral action is his experience of the world of spirit through the revelation of that world within his soul. This experience takes place within the personal individuality of man. To experience oneself in reciprocal intercourse with the spiritual world through a moral action, is to experience *freedom*. For the spiritual content does not act within the soul of necessity, but in such a way that man himself must develop the activity which impels him to receive the spiritual.

One of the aims in writing the ***Philosophy of Spiritual Activity*** was to point to the fact that in its true reality the sense-world is spiritual, and that as a being of soul, man lives and moves in spiritual reality when he gains true knowledge of the sense-world. A second aim was to show that the moral world is a sphere which is approached in freedom, for its existence lights up for man when he experiences the spiritual world consciously. Thus man's moral nature must be sought in his entirely personal conscious union with the ethical impulses of the world of spirit. I experienced the two parts of my ***Philosophy of Spiritual Activity*** as a spiritual organism, as a true unity. . . . (pp. 217-18)

My inner experiences at that time determined the way I formulated the ideas of the book. Through my direct experience and perception of the spiritual world the sense-world was revealed to me as spiritual, and I wished to create a science of nature in which the spirit is acknowledged. Through direct perception of the human soul in self-knowledge the moral sphere lights up within the soul as an entirely individual experience.

Thus the ideas of my book are formulated directly out of spiritual experience. The book represents above all an Anthroposophy which is orientated toward the sense-world and toward man as he stands within that world with his entirely individual moral nature.

During the first chapter of my life I was destined to experience the riddle of the universe as it faced modern science; in my ***Philosophy of Spiritual Activity*** I formulated the ideas demanded of me through this experience. My further task could only be an attempt to formulate ideas for the spiritual world itself.

The knowledge man receives from outside through sense observation I presented in my book as the human soul's inner anthroposophical experience of the spirit. That I did not, as yet, use the term "Anthroposophy" was due to the fact that my first inclination was always to formulate ideas rather than a terminology. Now I stood before the task of formulating ideas that would present the human soul's experience of the spiritual world itself.

My life between the age of thirty and forty was filled with intense inner struggle for such ideas. During the greater part of this period I was destined to be occupied externally with things that were related to my inner life in such a way that the latter could not find expression. (pp. 218-19)

Before I began to be active in the Theosophical Society . . . , I drafted my book (in two volumes), [***Welt- und Lebensanschauung im 19. Jahrhundert***] ***Conceptions of the World and of Life in the Nineteenth Century.*** Since its second edition this book has been published in an enlarged edition to include a survey of the philosophic development from the time of Greece until the nineteenth century, under the title, [***Die Rätsel der Philosophie***] ***Riddles of Philosophy.*** (p. 350)

The substance of the book had occupied me for a very long time. My study of world-views had a personal starting-point in Goethe. The contrast I have described between Goethe's thinking and Kantian philosophy, and also the new philosophic trends appearing at the turn of the eighteenth and nineteenth century with Fichte, Schelling and Hegel, all this represented to me the beginning of a new epoch in philosophy. . . . Thus the philosophic development of the nineteenth century appeared to me as a well-defined totality, and I gladly seized the opportunity to describe it.

Looking back, this book appears to me symptomatic of my inner way. Contrary to the belief held by many, I have not gone through a series of contradictions. If that were the case I would willingly admit it. But it is not true of my spiritual path. I advanced from one stage to the next by adding new insight to what I had previously attained. And I made a particularly important discovery in the spiritual realm soon after I had finished my book, ***Conceptions of the World and of Life in the Nineteenth Century.***

In this connection I would stress that I never approached the spiritual sphere through mystical feelings, but always through crystal-clear concepts. My conscious experience of concepts and ideas led me through the world of ideas into spiritual reality.

Only after I had worked out in the content of ***Conceptions of the World and of Life in the Nineteenth Century*** did I gain insight, through imaginative perception, into the *full reality* of the evolution of organic life from primeval times to the present.

While actually working on the book I had in mind the scientific view of evolution as presented by Darwin. This to me was merely a description of the sequence of physical events in nature. Within this sequence I recognized *spiritual impulses* at work, as Goethe visualized them in his ideas on metamorphosis.

Thus the natural sequence of stages in evolution, as presented scientifically by Haeckel, I never thought of as ruled by mechanical and organic laws alone; I saw them as stages through which the spirit leads organic development from the simplest to the most complex, right up to man. I saw in Darwinism a kind of thinking that approaches that of Goethe but remains behind the latter.

All this was still at the stage of ideas I had *worked out*. Only later did I reach imaginative insight. And only then did I learn that in primeval times there were present, within the spiritual reality of the earth, *Beings* of a quite different order from the simple organisms. And I recognized that the soul-spirit aspect of man's being is older than all other living beings; that to attain his present physical form he had to "dismember" himself from a World-Being encompassing *him* and all other organic beings. Thus the beings below man have fallen away from his evolution; he did not develop from them, but he left them behind, severing them from himself, so his physical form could attain the image of his spiritual form. Man was a macrocosmic being comprising the rest of the earthly world; he became a microcosmos by throwing off all the rest; this spiritual insight I gained only during the first years of the new century.

This knowledge therefore could not yet influence me while I wrote ***Conceptions of the World and of Life in the Nineteenth Century.*** I purposely wrote the second volume so that Darwinism and Haeckelism in a *spiritualized form*—seen in the light of Goethe's world-conception—become a starting-point for penetrating deeper into the world-riddle.

Later, when I prepared the second edition, I had attained the further imaginative insight into the full reality of evolution as described above. I did not alter the approach I had adopted in the first edition, an approach that illustrates what *thinking—even without spiritual perception*—can reach, but I found it necessary to make slight changes in the forms of expression. This necessity arose partly because the composition was entirely different now that the book contained a survey of the philosophic development as a whole, and partly because, by the time this second edition appeared I had already published an exposition of my further insight into the full reality of organic evolution.

But the final form in which my ***Riddles of Philosophy*** appears is not based upon a merely subjective view-point retained from a certain stage of my spiritual development; it is justified on *purely objective* grounds. Namely this: When *thinking itself* is experienced as a spiritual reality *it cannot* depict organic evolution otherwise than as presented in my book. It will be seen that the very next step must be taken through spiritual perception.

Thus my book is an objective presentation of the preanthroposophical insight that has to be reached and thoroughly experienced before it is possible to rise to the higher stage. The person who is striving to reach the spiritual world with clarity of thought, and not merely through a nebulous mysticism must attain this insight as a stage on the path to higher cognition. Therefore, a description of what is attained through this insight is something the striving person needs as a preliminary stage before reaching the higher stage.

To me Haeckel was someone who had the courage to approach science from a standpoint that reckons with thinking as a reality, whereas the rest of the world of science excluded thinking, allowing only for the results of sense-observation. I deeply appreciated in Haeckel that he put value on *creative* thinking in exploring reality. For this reason I dedicated my book to him although its content—even in its first form—did not at all agree with his views. But Haeckel was simply not of a philosophic mind. He approached philosophy as a layman. Therefore I considered the attacks quite unjustified which the philosophers let rain down upon him like a hailstorm. I dedicated my book to Haeckel in opposition to them, just as I had written the essay, ***Haeckel und seine Gegner,*** **Haeckel and his Opponents** for the same reason. Haeckel based his explanation of biological facts upon the reality of thinking, in complete ignorance of all philosophical argument; he was attacked upon philosophical grounds that were quite foreign to him. I am certain he never understood what it was the philosophers demanded of him. (pp. 351-54)

Instead of criticizing such blindness as Haeckel's with dead philosophies, it would have been better to acknowledge the inability of the age to experience the spirit, and attempt to kindle the spiritual spark where a foundation was offered: in biological research.

This was the insight I had reached. And this was the basis upon which I wrote ***Conceptions of the World and of Life in the Nineteenth Century.*** (p. 355)

It was my task to create a basis for Anthroposophy through a thinking as objective as scientific thinking that does not stop short at merely registering the sense-perceptible facts, but advances to comprehensive knowledge. Whatever I presented in the field of learning and philosophy or, in connection with Goethe's ideas, in the field of science, is open to discussion. One may doubt its degree of correctness, but it is in the fullest sense scientifically objective.

Through this objective cognition, free of mystical feeling, I transmitted my experience of the spiritual world. In my books [***Die Mystik im Aufgange des neuzeitlichen geisteslebens und ihr Vehältnis zu modernen Weltanschauung***] ***Mysticism at the Dawn of the Modern Age*** and [***Das Christentum als Mystische Tatsache***] ***Christianity as Mystical Fact,*** Mysticism is carried over into this *objective* cognition. More especially is the structure of my book ***Theosophy*** an example of this. Every stage is based upon direct spiritual perception. . . . A plant without its blossom is not experienced in its entirety: the physical world is not experienced in its entirety if one does not rise from the sense-perceptible to the spiritual aspect.

Thus it was not my goal to *place beside* science a merely subjective sphere, but to continue science objectively as Anthroposophy. That this goal should at first be misunderstood was inevitable. Science was considered complete as it was, and one saw no *need* to advance to the sphere of Anthroposophy; there was no inclination to bring life into the scientific ideas to enable them to grasp the spirit. People were held in bondage by the thought-habits developed in the second half of the nineteenth century. (pp. 358-59)

Rudolf Steiner, in extracts from his autobiography written between December 9, 1923 and April 5, 1925, in his Rudolf Steiner: An Autobiography, *edited by Paul M. Allen, translated by Rita Stebbing (copyright © 1977 by Rudolf Steiner Publications; reprinted by permission of Rudolf Steiner Publications, Blauvelt, NY; originally published as* Mein Lebensgang, *Rudolf Steiner-Nachlassverwaltung, seventh edition, 1961), Steiner, 1977, 541 p.*

KENNETH D. MACKENZIE (essay date 1925)

[*In the following excerpt, Mackenzie discusses the importance in Steiner's thought of joining the science of the physical world with a science of the spiritual world.*]

A keen student of modern science, for which he had not only interest but profound respect, [Dr. Rudolph Steiner] was, nevertheless, the founder of a "higher science" in which the world of Spirit, or, as most people would call it, of "mind," takes a rôle of chief importance. Just as religious teaching avoids the facts of science, and scientific research evades all questions of religion, Steiner's "Science" provides a bridge between them. This bridge, he maintained, is to be sought for and found in "self-knowledge," the command, "Know thyself," being at the root of all human advancement. Later on, at the invitation of the Theosophical Society, he became their General Secretary for Germany, but differing too widely from the Oriental tenets held by Mrs. Besant to enable him to conform his teachings of Christianity with hers he, with many other members of that branch, was cast out from the Theosophical Society, only to continue his work, however, under the title of "Anthroposophy" at Dornach. Very little of a personal nature has ever appeared about him, he was so entirely an expression of his work. (p. 772)

Steiner's outlook on humanity was based on the understanding and belief that it has evolved and is being developed from a spiritual and not a material origin. Therein his science, recognised over a considerable portion of Europe, if not yet in England except by a comparative few, is directly opposed to the usual scientific theory that the organic springs from the inorganic, for he held and taught that all material physical manifestations are the results of spiritual impulses. . . . [Steiner] steadily maintained for thirty years by word and pen that the physical sciences, although the greatest achievement of the human mind during the centuries since the thirteenth, are quite misled in believing that their methods constitute the *sole* way by which human beings can arrive at a knowledge of truth. He taught consistently and with profound earnestness, with utter sincerity and assurance, that every human being is endowed with germinal spiritual organs for direct perception of truth, and that these can be developed, once we realise their existence, by methods of mental and ethical discipline, which coincide absolutely with sane scientific conceptions, and with the deepest ethical teachings of Christ. By these methods, so ably set forth in several of his works, notably in ***The Way of Initiation,*** mankind can study and investigate spiritual facts as thoroughly and as accurately as modern science now does in regard to physical research with the various appliances as its disposal. This psychic faculty he developed within himself to an extent unequalled, perhaps, by any mystic of Occidental origin, as his works show; for it was his belief that "It is in the Soul that the meaning of the Universe is revealed." He felt that humanity has now arrived at a crucial stage when it is of the utmost importance that thought should be directed in a far higher degree towards the spiritual, and less toward the material world. In this belief there are many who will agree absolutely with him.

Now, though teaching for over thirty years man's capacity for direct knowledge of spiritual reality, Steiner was greatly opposed to "Spiritualism" as generally understood, and the use of mediums; warning always that mediums are misusing their own personalities, and that resort to them is harmful to other persons. He has written a great deal, and lectured still more, on Life after Death. To the writer it seems that Steiner considered "Spiritualism" in the manner usually studied to be more "materialistic" than "spiritual," a word which from his point of view may, perhaps, be more accurately expressed by "mental-moral." Life with those who are "dead" was to him very much what life is with those who are "alive," still together and unseparated, seeing that whilst in the flesh we are also in spirit, and when we are dead we are altogether in spirit and not in matter at all. By that it seems he wished us to realise that contact with the dead must be a spiritual or "mental-moral" contact, and in no way a material one, which to a certain extent is what is obtained through the use of mediums.

But to those who know the immense difficulty that exists of awakening in the generality of people the truth and reality of an after-life existence, the purely psychic methods of Steiner would appear infeasible and inadequate if conviction is to be forced upon the average pre-biassed intellect. Very few, indeed, would attempt to qualify themselves for intuitional knowledge, and fewer still would succeed in so doing. A more forcible and emphatic system is necessary if conviction of the truth is to be gained, for the generality of mankind can only receive such truths through their normal senses, not through that "Inward Light," which is the real awakener of the soul to what is spiritual whilst it is in the body. Consequently, Steiner's higher method of enlightenment appeals but to few. The true facts of the case, unknown to most people, are that two divergent streams of occultism exist, one favouring what might be termed "materialistic" methods appealing to the physical senses, and the other strongly opposing these. Dr. Steiner belonged to the latter stream. (pp. 773-74)

Kenneth D. Mackenzie, "Rudolf Steiner," in Contemporary Review, *Vol. CXXVII, June, 1925, pp. 772-76.*

MARIE STEINER (essay date 1935)

[*Marie Steiner was the wife of Rudolf Steiner. In the following introduction to* Art in the Light of Mystery Wisdom, *she discusses the three spheres of human experience—art, science, and religion—and notes that Steiner's teachings seek to reunite these three paths.*]

The impulses of regeneration given to mankind in this series of lectures **"Art in the Light of Mystery Wisdom"** will only be understood by those who are able to assimilate the nature of spiritual science fully in such a way that for them the concreteness of the spiritual world, its richness of form and being, has become a self-evident fact. Rudolf Steiner, fully equipped with the most modern scientific methods and with the utmost singleness of thought, has brought the reality of the spiritual world close to his contemporaries and has shown them how the ego of mankind is placed at the focal point of the development of consciousness and how mankind must grasp this ego with full knowledge. One path towards the grasping of the ego in the fullness of life's experience, but also in sun-filled contemplation, is the path of art. It is one of the healthiest and most revealing and most direct; it was the last to leave its source in the temple of mystery wisdom and has not been so quickly buried as has the path of religion by the passion of the church for power or the path of science by the rigidity of thought born out of the materialistic age. For these three paths once more to find each other, for art, science and religion once more to unite and intermingle—it was for this that Rudolf Steiner worked among us. He turned his fullest attention to each of these paths; in their living synthesis he saw the salvation of mankind. They . . . must again be brought together and re-united through the knowledge of their undivided spiritual origin.

Man must now awaken within himself a knowledge of this living and essential union. This he can do in complete freedom through careful investigation and practice if he does not timidly close his being in the face of superior and as yet unknown powers, if he does not bow before the restraining influence of the church nor before the authority of dogmatic science. The stages along the path have been revealed to man under the wise and entirely impersonal guidance of one who knows it and who, in conformity with the demands of our time, has not appealed to the human craving for submission and devotion but only to men's capacity for knowledge. (pp. 7-8)

Through words, pictures and deeds Rudolf Steiner summoned human beings to wakefulness in each of [the] three spheres. He has created works that give art a new orientation. He has delivered it from rigidity and brought movement into it; he has restored life to what had been strangled. (p. 9)

Marie Steiner, "Introduction" (1935), in Art in the Light of Mystery Wisdom: A Collection of Eight Lectures *by Rudolf Steiner, translated by Johanna Collis, Rudolf Steiner Press, 1970, pp. 7-12.*

POWELL SPRING (essay date 1943)

[*In the following excerpt, Spring stresses that the basis of Anthroposophy is not to give humankind easy answers to spiritual questions, but rather to teach people how to find these answers for themselves. Spring writes that in* The Philosophy of Spiritual Activity *Steiner put forth "the ultimate philosophy."*]

There are many who have probably not heard his name, but in 500 years the world will know very well who Rudolf Steiner was. Humanity being on the wrong track in so many fields today, a truly superhuman effort was needed to prevent utter ultimate chaos. The natural sciences, philosophy, sociology, economics and education, religion, the drama, painting, sculp-

Statuten der anthroposophischen Gesellschaft.

1. Die anthroposophische Gesellschaft soll eine Vereinigung von Menschen sein, die das seelische Leben im einzelnen Menschen und in der menschlichen Gemeinschaft auf der Grundlage einer wahren Erkenntnis der geistigen Welt pflegen wollen.

2. Den Grundstock dieser Gesellschaft bilden die in der Weihnachtszeit 1923 am Goetheanum in Dornach versammelten Persönlichkeiten, sowie diejenigen Einzelnen oder zu Gruppen gehörigen, in deren Auftrag sie erschienen sind. Sie sind von der Anschauung durchdrungen, dass es gegenwärtig eine wirkliche Wissenschaft von der geistigen Welt schon giebt und dass der heutigen Civilisation die Pflege einer solchen Wissenschaft fehlt. Die anthroposophische Gesellschaft soll diese Pflege zu ihrer Aufgabe haben. Sie wird diese Aufgabe so zu lösen versuchen, dass sie die im Goetheanum zu Dornach gepflegte anthroposophische Geisteswissenschaft mit ihren Ergebnissen für die Brüderlichkeit im menschlichen Zusammenleben, für das moralische und religiöse, sowie für das künstlerische und Allgemein-Geistige im Menschenwesen zum Mittelpunkte ihrer Bestrebungen macht.

3. Die als Grundstock der Gesellschaft in Dornach versammelten Persönlichkeiten erkennen zustimmend die Anschauung der Goetheanum-Leitung in Bezug auf das Folgende an: Die im Goetheanum gepflegte Anthroposophie führt zu Ergebnissen, die jedem Menschen ohne Unterschied der Nation, des Standes, der Religion als Anregung für das geistige Leben dienen können. Sie kann zu einem wirklich auf brüderliche Liebe aufgebauten sozialen Leben führen. Ihre Aneignung als Lebensgrundlage ist nicht an einen wissenschaftlichen Bildungsgrad gebunden, sondern nur an das unbefangene Menschenwesen. Ihre Forschung und die sachgemäße Beurteilung ihrer Forschungsergebnisse unterliegt aber der geisteswissenschaftlichen Schulung, die stufenweise zu erlangen ist. Diese Ergebnisse sind auf ihre Art so exact wie die Ergebnisse

Holograph copy of an essay by Steiner. Rudolf Steiner Publications/Garber Communications, Inc.

ture and architecture owe him leads that groups of research students in all countries of the world are diligently making fruitful. His archives contain untold riches. Rudolf Steiner established Human Science for all time. May the world learn his message through the medium of hard thinking, rather than through the bitter experience ever attendant upon ignorance.

Best of all, Rudolf Steiner personally demonstrated that species of moral knighthood which Americans so ungrudgingly admire and which alone can save the world. Thanks to him we can now see the problems of human development in the light of wisely guided cultural epochs descending meaningfully, and in a very gradually ascending curve of individual evolution. His teaching has been carefully protected against dilettantism and a cheap dissemination of half-truths. Beyond a half dozen introductory works, Rudolf Steiner's books are intelligible only on a basis of these. In short, not the telling of these truths was his chief aim, but to teach us how to find them ourselves. A species of higher logic must be acquired. Difficult as it is to penetrate into these gold mines of information and intellectual impulse our effort is repaid a thousandfold. These matters are stated not in a moment of enthusiasm, but in the light of deep and diligent study. The world has lived horizontally as it were. We must now add the vertical dimension of depth in our study of life's problems. We will never improve the world until we have improved man. (pp. 5-7)

Human Science, taking man in his entirety, is logically subdivided into Anthropology and Anthroposophy. The former deals in the main with the physical aspects of human nature and human evolution. Anthroposophy emphasizes the spiritual aspects, by which are meant thought, emotion and impulse, together with the development of certain latent organs of perception inherent in man. A knowledge of Anthroposophy is indispensable if we wish to understand the unceasing interplay between physical and spiritual factors in human nature. Anthroposophy has, without question, thrown more light upon current problems in the world than any philosophic theory or medical and psychological findings have done in modern times. (p. 8)

Rudolf Steiner in **"The Philosophy of Spiritual Activity"** has written the ultimate philosophy—the philosophy to end philosophies, as it were. It is he who first demonstrated the energizing and activating power of higher knowledge which is indeed the sole source of energy that can create a better world out of the one now in its death throes. (p. 16)

In the final analysis we cannot but conclude after careful study that the ultimate philosophy—the quotient of all preceding systems of thought—is found in Human Science as presented to the world by Rudolf Steiner, a pathway to valid cognition. He has hewn a pathway which every serious student may follow. It is a pathway obviously intended by Providence for the western mind. Eastern philosophies were not wrong, but they have had their day in human evolution. To warm them up and serve them anew is bound to remain fruitless for the very simple reason that man in his spiritual makeup and mental processes is differently constituted than formerly.

Every phase of life both in man and nature requires what we may call *deeper insight,* if we wish to fathom its real significance. Our five senses can not yield what we here call *deeper insight,* if we wish to fathom its real significance. Our five senses can yield us Knowledge useful in a limited sense. . . . Wisdom always implies supersensible experience of a sort. Nothing remains "occult" once we have learned to enter its recesses with the clear sight of intelligent awareness. . . . Spiritual law is no less adamant than is physical law. It is a knowledge of the proper interweaving of both, which yields us the results we all crave. Freudian so-called psycho-analysis has never dealt with the supersensible facts of life unless it be through inadvertence. Freud dwelt upon physical factors insofar as they affected spiritual life. While he believed that we should attempt to "control" these physical factors as much as possible, he did not tell us how this can be done. It remained for Human Science to enter into a full understanding of the spirit in the rôle of molder of character. (pp. 17-19)

Powell Spring, in a foreword and an introduction to his Essays on Human Science, *The Orange Press, 1943, pp. 1-7, 8-20.**

RICHARD ROSENHEIM (essay date 1952)

[*Rosenheim offers a favorable evaluation of the spiritual insight conveyed in Steiner's* Mystery Plays. *Rosenheim also claims artistic merit for the plays, which he indicates is only perceptible to spiritual adepts. For other analyses of the* Mystery Plays, *see the excerpts by Hermon Ould (1922), Adam Bittleston (1956), Hans Pusch (1972), and Robb Creese (1978).*]

Rudolf Steiner produced the first part of a *Mystery Tetralogy* in Munich, completed during the fateful three years preceding the First World War. They bore the titles:

"The Portal of Initiation"
"The Soul's Probation."
"The Guardian of the Threshold"
"The Soul's Awakening"

Represented by unskilled laymen-players on a poorly equipped stage, their magic power took a lasting hold on those who were able to at least guess what they had seen and heard. The rest was silence, laughter or damnation. Dogmatic! Doctrinaire! A symbolic Allegory! A play for reading, not for hearing! No stock phrase of quick-witted criticism was left out in ripping apart what was not wanted because it was feared. But the ***Four Mystery Dramas*** survived two World Wars and two world-shaking revolutions, in spite of all that had been said about them and against them. (p. 269)

In his ***Four Mystery Dramas,*** Rudolf Steiner presents in four subsequent stages the spiritual and psychic crises of a group of people who under the guidance of a great initiate try to gain access to the higher secrets of creation. In them a worldwide problem of our time is reflected from the inner growth of seventeen different people, bound together merely by intensive striving for a common goal.

Coming from various spheres of life, they have gathered around a man by the name of *Benedictus,* who leads his pupils to a concrete understanding of the world and of themselves according to the principles of modern Christian initiation. At the center of his teachings stands *the doctrine of Reincarnation and Karma,* illuminated by a fundamentally new revelation regarding the resurrection of Christ Jesus whose return in non-physical form he prophesies as near at hand. His most advanced disciple, *Maria,* a nobleminded woman of highly developed spiritual power, devotes herself with the purified motherly and sisterly passion of another Beatrice to the task of guiding the painter, *Johannes Thomasius,* in his new way of radical inner metamorphosis. But the fiery young artist, still strongly fettered to the world of sensual appearance, soon realizes that it is much more the woman than the spirit friend he loves in her. From that a painful dual crisis starts to rift apart his ego. (pp. 271-72)

[Maria] is led by Benedictus upon a new and higher stage of transformation by beholding transformation. There she learns that what impedes the orderly fulfillment of her mission by Thomasius is *unexpiated guilt committed in a former incarnation.* Because not only theirs, the karmic ways of all the followers of Benedictus were linked together in preceding former lives on earth. What all of them do for another or suffer from another can only be comprised aright and set aright through conscious deliberate acceptance of *the law of karmic equity and sanction.* There are three mighty powers of the supersensory world, *Christ, Lucifer and Ahriman,* incessantly warring for the guidance of humanity, supported by a host of lower spirit-soul-and elemental beings of angelic or demonic nature; and from their intercrossing interference there results a load of tests and trials for everyone. . . . (p. 272)

[With] the same powerful summons of creative imagination employed by Goethe when he wrote the Second Part of "Faust," Rudolf Steiner in the Second Part of the Four Mysteries, goes on to show how, in the souls of the leading characters, the past arises from the darkness of forgetting, in order that each of them may find the healing strength for right transition from the present into future. (pp. 272-73)

Descriptive comments and circumscriptive allusions are but poorly adequate means for suggesting the wealth of new insight into the dark riddles of creation Rudolf Steiner as the first in our days has ventured to dramatize in his Four Mysteries. When first performed on stage, what they demanded in respect to artistic as well as spiritual qualification could only be responded to by an enthusiastic group of men and women transported first hand into the final purpose of the author. But having dedicated themselves for more than two decades to their chosen task, the *actors' group at the Goetheanum* today has grown already to a very remarkable degree of maturity in both regards. Until the beginning and right after the close of World War II, thousands of visitors from near and far came by to see the annual *Great Festivals in Dornach, Switzerland.* On the free soil of a free country the lofty idea, so gloriously inaugurated in Weimar and so forcefully advanced in Bayreuth, had become a historical fact: the establishment of a genuine Mystery Center of Art in modern times. If history permits its undisturbed continuance, the modern Drama, I believe, one day will draw the decisive impulse for its vigorous rejuvenation from the Festival Hill at Dornach. For there was born anew what once stood as god-mother at the cradle of all human culture as the sacred unity of Art, Religion and Wisdom. (pp. 273-74)

Richard Rosenheim, "Art at the Threshold of Two Worlds: Rebirth of Mystery Dramatics in the XX Century," in his The Eternal Drama: A Comprehensive Treatise on the Syngenetic History of Humanity, Dramatics, and Theatre *(copyright, 1952, by Philosophical Library), Philosophical Library, 1952, pp. 269-78.**

A. P. SHEPHERD (essay date 1954)

[The following excerpt, taken from Shepherd's book-length study of Steiner's life and works, discusses Steiner's Anthroposophical career from the turn of the century until his death.]

To his revelation of the objective reality of the supersensible world and of its relation to sense-perceived phenomena, and his explanation of the origin and destiny of man and all that flows from it, Steiner gave the name "Anthroposophy". The significance of this name is that the secret of the universe is expressed in and discoverable by an understanding of the real nature of man. If Anthroposophy is true it supplies the answer to the present human dilemma. It extends the horizons of knowledge, it integrates the material with the spiritual, it resolves the dualism of science and religion, it restores dignity and significance to human life, it justifies the assumption of human instinct and of religion as to the eternal importance of the individual, and it disproves any political or social system that is based upon a materialistic conception of life or of history. Nothing could be more important than that mankind, and especially the leaders of human thought, should study and examine it.

It must be admitted, however, that there are considerable difficulties in the way of such study. The first difficulty is Steiner's statement that his teaching is based upon his immediate and direct perception of supersensible realities, that are not perceptible to the ordinary man. *Ipso facto,* the truth of this claim cannot be scientifically proved or disproved at the level of physical consciousness. There are other considerations, however, to be borne in mind. In the first place, if it is true, as Sir James Jeans says, that any real extension of knowledge waits upon the evolution or development of further senses of perception, we must not be surprised that, if anyone speaks out of the possession of such senses, we are not able directly to test the experience which he relates. Moreover, Steiner declares that the organs of supersensible perception, which in him, as in some other men and women, were already highly developed, are organs which in all of us await development, and he gives detailed instructions as to how this may in full consciousness be taken in hand. (pp. 25-6)

There were . . . [for Steiner] three types of knowledge. In the first place there was the ordinary intellectual apprehension of the sense-world. Then there was the direct apprehension of spirit-realities experienced inwardly in pure thinking, a knowledge that transcended thought, but arose out of it. . . . [Finally] there was this new knowledge of the spirit-realities expressed in the sense-world, derived from direct meditation on sense-phenomena.

This new knowledge was not arrived at out of penetrating logical thought; indeed, in the meditation through which it was reached, every activity of mind and body had to be stilled. It was as if one sat silently before the facts of the world of sense-experience, until the eyes of the spirit were opened to their secrets. And yet the meditation was of the nature of thought. It was not a logical activity, that analysed the sense-phenomenon in order to arrive at the mechanism of its physical being, or the ultimate rudiments of its material substance. It was a concentration upon the phenomenon as it is manifest to the senses, *in its complete form,* in an endeavour to penetrate to the ideal realities of form or colour or growth or consciousness, expressed in it. It was a concentration that demanded the awareness of the whole being of the observer, his feeling and will no less than his thinking, and it awoke in him deeper faculties of perception. It was still *thought* that was leading him on to the world of spirit, but in the process thought itself was transformed into a higher form of perception. This was a knowledge which led to wider fields of spirit discovery than Steiner had ever reached before. Each object of sense-experience became a doorway into the world of spirit, not only manifest in the visible phenomenon, but actively at work in it, informing and upholding it.

This new method of penetrating into the reality of the universe, revealed all the more clearly to Steiner the fundamental error in the then widely-accepted atomistic method of natural-scientific investigation. Both natural and spiritual science were based on an intensive study of sense-phenomena, but the natural scientist relied too much upon logical analysis and experimental hypothesis. Having accumulated all the evidence offered by the perception of his physical sense, and having reduced it, by logical analysis, to its ultimate component elements, he concluded that the task of observation was now over, and proceeded to fashion, out of his observation and analysis, a hypothetical explanation or world-picture based on that evidence. In most cases the world-picture transcended the evidence, and propounded as realities what were only thought-fantasies. The answers to all these riddles, Steiner perceived, was not to be found in thought-speculation, but in the phenomena themselves. They could, however, only be discovered by this concentrated meditative thinking, and in that sense man himself holds the key to the secrets of nature. In such concentrated meditation, human thinking is brought into awareness of the creative activity of thought that lies behind the world of Nature.

More and more clearly could Steiner see that the error of the natural-scientific world-outlook was entirely bound up with *its false idea of matter*. (pp. 53-4)

The deeper Steiner penetrated into direct experience of the spirit-realities expressed in the world, the wider seemed the gulf which separated him from the thought of his day. It seemed impossible to bridge it. It appeared to him as though all the forces of darkness were massed against the revelation of the spirit. In face of them he felt that he could no longer remain silent about the truths, of which he was aware. (p. 55)

Rudolf Steiner's work of spreading the knowledge of spiritual science fell into three stages. The first twelve years of the century were spent in the development of his own esoteric knowledge and in imparting and expounding it. The next six years were spent in laying the foundation of a movement which would ensure that his work would go on after his death. In the last six years of his life—post-war years of intense political and social crisis—he was actively engaged in applying spiritual science to all kinds of human activity.

In his autobiography Steiner reveals that the first ten years of the century were a time when the facts and being of the spirit-world came more and more intimately into his direct experience. By regular, concentrated meditation his powers of spirit-perception developed, through the stages which he describes as Imagination, Inspiration and Intuition. . . . The first stage gives knowledge of the spiritual background of our physical life and of the world in which we live. The second stage opens the way into the purely supersensible world, giving understanding of its conditions and of the beings who inhabit it, and of their relation to the physical world. The third stage is one in which a man is able to act himself as an inhabitant of the spiritual world, and to have intercourse with those to be found in it.

The knowledge derived from these levels of higher consciousness falls into three categories: the knowledge of the supersensible nature and significance of the physical phenomena that are the field of inquiry of Natural Science; the knowledge of the inter-relation of the physical and spiritual in the being of man, both in his earthly existence and in the spirit-world; and finally the recovery of the whole past of mankind, reaching back into ages far behind human history or even earthly existence. The development of these categories of knowledge is manifest in the books which Steiner produced in the first years of the century, ***How to obtain knowledge of the Higher Worlds,*** and ***Theosophy;*** the latter a specific account of man's earthly and spiritual existences and the relationship between them. Although the subject-matter is unfamiliar and not easy to grasp at once, one cannot fail to notice the factual way in which it is presented. The two books which he had produced previously point to the importance to him of the Christian revelation which had come to him at the turn of the century. These were ***Mysticism in Relation to the Modern World-Conception*** and ***Christianity as Mystical Fact.*** To these were added a few years later his remarkable courses of lectures on the four Gospels and on the Apocalypse. (pp. 63-4)

Except in name and constitution, there was nothing new about the Anthroposophical Society [which met as such for the first time in February of 1913]. It was a direct continuance of the work and teaching of Rudolf Steiner since 1900, and of the life of the German Section of the Theosophical Society. The name itself Steiner had used frequently in his teaching. . . . Various definitions of it are given and perhaps no one definition would contain its whole meaning. The word "sophia" always denotes the divine wisdom, and "Anthroposophy" indicates that this wisdom is to be found in the knowledge of the true being of man and of his relation to the universe. There is also the further connotation that, whereas formerly the divine wisdom was imparted by the divine world itself to man, now man himself, by divine grace, must transmute his earth-born thinking to the higher level of divine wisdom, by the true understanding of himself.

The Society was formed, not merely as an association of Steiner's supporters, but as a living movement of the spirit, which sought to awaken in mankind new powers of spiritual perception, and also to apply, to all departments of human life and thought, the spiritual outlook and understanding which had been given by Rudolf Steiner out of his own super-sensory perception. (p. 73)

Rudolf Steiner had brought the whole of his super-sensible understanding of the evolution of the Universe and Man into one volume, under the title ***An Outline of Occult Science.*** In the same year he wrote ***The Portal of Initiation,*** the first of a series of four modern mystery plays, written one by one in subsequent years. These plays represented the process of Initiation to Higher Knowledge among a group of people in modern life. The plays were produced year by year at the annual meeting of the German Section, a very important part of the teaching of Rudolf Steiner. (p. 74)

With the coming of peace and the social upheavals consequent in Europe [following World War I], Rudolf Steiner came forward with an entirely new approach to social and political problems, based on the three-fold nature of Man. His book ***The Threefold Social Order*** . . . created a great impression in Germany and was soon translated into many languages. (p. 75)

[There] were developed, in the light of Spiritual Science, all forms of art and of dramatic representation, particularly in connection with the Mystery Plays. There was also evolved the new art of movement called ''Eurhythmy'', which had been devised by Rudolf Steiner and developed by Marie von Sievers (now Marie Steiner). Eurhythmy is an art which expresses in movement the same spiritual forces which are expressed in speech and music. Although as an art it is yet in its beginning, Steiner reveals that in its full development it will be the expression of a level of spiritual evolution, towards which humanity is moving, but which still lies far ahead. Already it has proved to be of great curative and educational value. (pp. 76-7)

In [his] last years . . . , as a factual and non-contentious answer to attack and criticisms, [Steiner] set forth what he describes simply as ***The Story of My Life.*** He was not able to complete it. On March 30th, 1925, he died. (p. 78)

In these important spheres of knowledge . . . , Science, History, Religion, Art, Psychology, and Ethics, Spiritual Science sheds new light upon the conclusions of modern thought, and, in doing so, it deepens and unifies them. It thereby establishes a claim to the serious and unprejudiced consideration of all thoughtful people, and especially of those who are the leaders of thought. (p. 164)

The whole theme of Steiner's book, ***Christianity as Mystical Fact,*** is that in Jesus Christ the hidden ritual of the ancient Mysteries was openly enacted, in an actual historical life. (p. 170)

The path which is offered by Spiritual Science is that of direct, clear, conscious spiritual knowledge, evolved by an intensification of true scientific thinking, prepared for by a real moral preparation, and leading, not to a materialised vision of spiritual reality, but to the development of the higher organs of the human organism, by means of which spirit-reality can be perceived and understood in its own proper environment. To reject Spiritual Science is to leave uncontrolled the evil occult movements of our day, and to refuse the enlightenment and certainty which is offered to religion. In these days when men's minds are absorbed in their scientific achievements, it is more than ever important to be able to read the spiritual signs of the times. (p. 173)

Anthroposophy is essentially not a mere world-concept to be argued about. It is a Movement seeking to penetrate with spirit understanding the whole of human thought and activity. As Rudolf Steiner expresses it in one of his lectures, ''Anthroposophy wishes knowledge everywhere to flow into life, to give knowledge in a form which can help, wherever help is needed in the affairs of life.'' . . . [The] practical expressions of Anthroposophy have widely expanded in recent years, both in this country and in Europe; indeed, many people's knowledge of Anthroposophy is entirely limited to its expression in such activities, educational, therapeutic or agricultural.

Now, however attractive and convincing these activities may be, they will never lead to a true understanding of Anthroposophy itself, unless the central spiritual principles underlying them are understood. On many occasions Rudolf Steiner stressed this fact. (p. 174)

The serous student of Anthroposophy . . . will find himself confronted, almost from the start, with difficulties which challenge his perseverance and sincerity of purpose. The first difficulty is in the nature of the subject itself. Spiritual Science reveals facts of which, in his normal consciousness, he is unaware. Moreover, this revelation is based upon the clairvoyant perception of Rudolf Steiner, the factual reality of which he cannot directly prove or disprove. (pp. 205-06)

At the commencement of this study the natural reaction of our logical thinking will be to suspect these unfamiliar facts and to marshal arguments against them. On the assumptions of ordinary thinking this is not difficult to do, as every student of Anthroposophy has found for himself in the early stages of his study. It was the experience of the author of this book that, at his first reading of ***The Philosophy of Spiritual Activity,*** the margin of almost every page was heavily scored with logical and philosophical queries and objections. At the next reading half of them were deleted, and in subsequent reading they have almost all disappeared.

The facts that Spiritual Science reveals lie in a different level of consciousness from that in which our normal logical reasoning works, and they are related to elements in our own being of which we are unconscious. But if the facts imparted to us are not immediately rejected, if we give them unprejudiced consideration, they will awaken a response in those deeper levels of our being, and we become aware of this in the growing perception that the facts present us with a more complete and comprehensible picture of ourselves and our environment than we possessed before. This feeling, if allowed to live and deepen in us, grows into a rational understanding of the truths of Spiritual Science.

A mere hurried reading of the presentation of Rudolf Steiner's teaching, can only result—in self-defence—in a sceptical rejection of it. Only the willingness of the student to read thoughtfully, and to think over again and again, without prejudice, difficult or startling statements, and to allow them, meanwhile, to work upon his mind, will enable him to arrive at an apprehension of Anthroposophy. (pp. 206-07)

A. P. Shepherd, in his A Scientist of the Invisible: An Introduction to the Life and Work of Rudolf Steiner *(reprinted by permission of the Literary Estate of A. P. Shepherd), Hodder and Stoughton, 1954, 221 p.*

ADAM BITTLESTON (essay date 1956)

[In a discussion of Steiner's Mystery Plays, *Bittleston points out some elements common to Steiner's first play,* The Portal of Initiation, *and Wolfgang von Goethe's fairy tale* "The Green Snake and the Beautiful Lily." *For more studies of the* Mystery Plays, *see the excerpts by Hermon Ould (1922), Richard Rosenheim (1952), Hans Pusch (1972), and Robb Creese (1978).]*

Every summer from 1910 to 1913 Rudolf Steiner wrote and produced a new play at one of the theatres in Munich, the four dramas forming a continuous series. Very few of the actors had professional experience; they were men and women with widely varying occupations and backgrounds brought together by their common interest in spiritual knowledge. Music, scenery, costumes—all had to be devised and prepared by this limited circle of people. The audiences too consisted of those taking part in the summer congresses at which Rudolf Steiner and others lectured; there were no public performances. This was not in order to keep the plays secret; they were printed and published at the same time, and were available to anyone. But there would then have been no wide interest in seeing such plays; their original intention was to lead those who had a general, theoretical understanding of Rudolf Steiner's teaching into a more practical grasp of it. He knew that the time would come when a much wider interest would exist.

The four plays deal with the same chief characters; men and women of the beginning of the twentieth century, all in some way concerned with the development of inner capacities of knowledge beyond those provided by the senses and by our ordinary thinking. The plays show the many difficulties they have to encounter in themselves and with each other. Often events are shown which are not happening in the physical world, but are experienced by the participants on another level of consciousness.

When the first play was performed, those who knew Goethe's fairy tale ["The Green Snake and the Beautiful Lily"] could see that there was a remarkable correspondence between them. Every character of the story, and almost every event, in some way reappears. What in Goethe has the universality of a myth, in the play is worked out among particular earthly human beings, at a particular, critical time in human history. Story and play continually illumine each other. The relationship was not only to be inferred from the text; details of Rudolf Steiner's production often emphasised it.

Yet to say that he had retold the fairy story in a modern and dramatic form would be an over-simplification. Goethe and Rudolf Steiner drew in these works upon the same spiritual realities. In their struggle to reconcile the eternal and the temporal within themselves, with the help of conscious perception of facts and being beyond the range of the everyday senses, they had passed through many experiences which made them akin. Rudolf Steiner did not *depend* upon Goethe, or on any of the many mystics and teachers of earlier times to whom he often referred. But he was thankful to be able to show that much of the knowledge, which seemed so completely strange and incomprehensible to many of his contemporaries, was in harmony with the spiritual discoveries achieved in earlier times. (pp. 32-4)

Adam Bittleston, "Introduction to 'The Portal of Initiation'," in The Portal of Initiation: A Rosicrucian Mystery Drama *by Rudolf Steiner, translated by Adam Bittleston (copyright © 1961, 1981 by Rudolf Steiner Publications; reprinted by permission of Rudolf Steiner Publications, Blauvelt, NY; originally published as* Die Pforte der Einweihung (Initiation), Ein Rosenkreuzermysterium durch Rudolf Steiner, *ninth edition, Verlag der Rudolf Steiner-Nachlassverwaltung, 1956), revised edition, Steinerbooks, 1981, pp. 29-42.*

PAUL MARSHALL ALLEN (essay date 1959)

[In the following excerpt, Allen describes Cosmic Memory: Prehistory of Earth and Man *as "the first written expression" of Steiner's personal perceptions of the spiritual world.]*

A full evaluation of what Rudolf Steiner accomplished for the good of mankind in so many directions can come about only when one comprehends the ideas which motivated him. He expressed these in his writings. . . . Taken together, these written works comprise the body of knowledge to which Steiner gave the name, the science of the spirit, or Anthroposophy. (p. 16)

Many of the thoughts expressed in [***Cosmic Memory: Prehistory of Earth and Man***] may at first appear startling, even fantastic in their implications. Yet when the prospect of space travel, as well as modern developments in technology, psychology, medicine and philosophy challenge our entire understanding of life and the nature of the living, strangeness as such should be no valid reason for the serious reader to turn away from a book of this kind. For example, while the word "occult" or "supersensible" may have undesirable connotations for many, current developments are fast bringing re-examination of knowledge previously shunned by conventional research. The challenge of the atomic age has made serious re-evaluation of all knowledge imperative, and it is recognized that no single area of that knowledge can be left out of consideration. (pp. 16-17)

On the other hand, a further problem arises as a result of Steiner's conviction regarding the purpose for which a book dealing with the science of the spirit is designed. This involves the *form* of the book as against its content. Steiner stressed repeatedly that a book on the science of the spirit does not exist only for the purpose of conveying information to the reader. With painstaking effort, he elaborated his books in such a manner that while the reader receives certain information from the pages, he also experiences a kind of *awakening* of spiritual life within himself. (p. 17)

The essays contained in [***Cosmic Memory: Prehistory of Earth and Man***] occupy a significant place in the life-work of Rudolf Steiner. They are his first written expression of a cosmology resulting from that spiritual perception which he described as "a fully conscious standing-within the spiritual world." In his autobiography he refers to the early years of the present century as the time when, "Out of the experience of the spiritual world in general developed specific details of knowledge." . . . Steiner has stated that from his early childhood he knew the reality of the spiritual world because he could experience this spiritual world directly. However, only after nearly forty years was it possible for him to transmit to others concrete, detailed information regarding this spiritual world.

As they appear in the present essays, these "specific details" touch upon processes and events of extraordinary sweep and magnitude. They include essential elements of man's prehistory and early history, and shed light upon the evolutionary development of our earth. Published now for the first time in America, just a century after Darwin's *Origin of the Species* began its tranformation of man's view of himself and of his environment, these essays clarify and complement the pioneer work of the great English scientist.

Rudolf Steiner shows that the insoluble link between man and cosmos is the fundamental basis of evolution. As man has participated in the development of the world we know today, so his achievements are directly connected with the ultimate destiny of the universe. In his hands rests the freedom to shape the future course of creation. Knowledge of his exalted origins and of the path he followed in forfeiting divine direction for the attainment of his present self-dependent freedom, are indispensable if man is to evolve a future worthy of a responsible human being.

This book appears now because of its particular significance at a moment when imperative and grave decisions are being made in the interests of the future of mankind. (pp. 18-19)

Paul Marshall Allen, "Introduction: Rudolf Steiner, the Man and His Work," in Cosmic Memory: Prehistory of Earth and Man *by Rudolf Steiner, translated by Karl E. Zimmer (copyright © 1959 by Rudolf Steiner Publications, Inc.; reprinted by permission of Rudolf Steiner Publications, Blauvelt, NY), Steiner, 1959 (and reprinted by Harper & Row, Publishers, 1981), pp. 9-19.*

PAUL MARSHALL ALLEN (essay date 1960)

[In the following excerpt, Allen provides an introduction to Steiner's Mysticism at the Dawn of the Modern Age.*]*

Mysticism at the Dawn of the Modern Age is a fruit of Steiner's lecturing activity. (p. 11)

The term *mysticism,* as Steiner uses it in this book, is a further development of what Goethe indicated in his aphoristic description of mysticism in relation to poetry and philosophy. "Poetry," said Goethe, "points to the riddles of nature, and tries to solve them by means of the image. Philosophy directs itself to the riddles of reason, and attempts to solve them by means of the word. Mysticism considers the riddles of both nature and reason, and seeks to solve them through both word and image."

This book is significant in the life-work of Rudolf Steiner because it is a first result of his decision to speak out in a direction not immediately apparent in his earlier, more philosophical writings, mentioned above. Here—particularly in Steiner's Introduction—is to be found a vitally fundamental exposition of the science of the spirit, embracing the path of spiritual knowledge suited to the needs and capacities of modern men and women. This subject occupied Steiner increasingly during the whole of the first quarter of this present century, and to it he devoted his entire talents as lecturer and writer.

Rudolf Steiner indicated that [***Mysticism at the Dawn of the Modern Age***] is not intended to be a history of mysticism. It deals with a problem that had occupied him for decades, and which today has become a cardinal concern of all mankind: the impact of modern scientific thinking upon the experiences of man's inner, spiritual life. In the conflict between reason and revelation which reached its climax in the nineteenth century, but which had its origins in much earlier times, Steiner saw the seed of a still greater conflict to come, a conflict which involves humanity's struggle against the sub-human in modern technical developments. (pp. 12-13)

In [***Mysticism at the Dawn of the Modern Age***] Steiner tells how eleven men [Meister (Johannes) Eckhart, Johannes Tauler, Heinrich Suso, Jan von Ruysbroeck, Nicolas Chyrpffs, Henry Cornelius, Theophrastus Bombast von Hohenheim (Paracelsus), Valentine Weigel, Jacob Boehme, (Philip) Giordano Bruno, and Johannes Scheffler], whose lives bridge the four centuries from the Gothic time to the mid-seventeenth century, solved the conflict between their inner spiritual perceptions and the world of individual freedom, invention, and discovery then coming to birth. He explains the positive contribution of their ideas to an understanding and preservation of the humanity of modern men and women in face of contemporary events. (p. 13)

Paul Marshall Allen, "About the Author, the People and the Background of This Book," in Mysticism at the Dawn of the Modern Age *by Rudolf Steiner, translated by Karl E. Zimmer (copyright © 1960 by Rudolf Steiner Publications, Inc.; reprinted by permission of Rudolf Steiner Publications, Blauvelt, NY), Steiner, 1960, pp. 9-96.*

REV. ALFRED HEIDENREICH (essay date 1961)

[In the following excerpt, Heidenreich distinguishes Steiner's philosophy and methods of spiritual advancement from those of Eastern mysticism and provides an overview of Steiner's achievement, particularly as an exemplar of Christian thought.]

It is a plain fact that in some form or other spiritual knowledge has existed throughout the ages. Secret wisdom has never been absent from human history. But in Steiner it assumed a totally new form. In order to appreciate this revolutionary novelty, we must first have a picture of the old form.

The faculty of spiritual perception and secret wisdom is obtained through certain organs in the "subtle body" of man, to borrow a convenient term from Eastern Indian medicine. In Sanscrit these organs are called *"chakrams,"* generally translated into English as "lotus flowers." They fulfil a function in the "subtle body" similar to our senses in the physical body. They are usually dormant today, but can be awakened. We can disregard for the moment the rites of Initiation which were employed in the Mystery Temples of the ancient world, and confine ourselves to the survival of more general methods which today are still practised in many parts of the world. They all have one thing in common: they operate through the vegetative system in man, through bodily posture, through the control of breathing, through physical or mental exercises which work upon the solar plexus and the sympathetic nervous system. (pp. 22-3)

Steiner broke with all this. He began to operate from the opposite pole of the human organism, from pure thought. Thought—ordinary human thought—even if it is brilliant and positive, is at first something very weak. It does not possess the life, say, of our breathing, let alone the powerful life of our pulsating blood. It is—shall we say—flat, without substance; it is really lifeless. It is "pale thought," as Shakespeare called it.

This relative lifelessness of our thoughts is providential, however. If the living thoughts filling the Universe were to enter our consciousness just as they are, we would faint. If the living idea in every created thing simply jumped into our consciousness with all its native force, it would blot us out. Fortunately, our cerebro-spinal system exerts a kind of resistance in the process; it functions like a resistor in an electric circuit; it is a sort of transformer, reducing the violence of reality to such a degree that our mind can tolerate it and register it. However, as a result, we see only the shadows of reality on the back wall of our Platonic cave, not reality itself.

Now one of the magic words in Steiner's philosophy with which he attempts to break this spell, is *''Erkraftung des Denkens.''* It means putting force, life into thinking, through thinking, within thinking. All his basic philosophic works, notably the ***Philosophy of Spiritual Activity,*** and many of his exercises, are directed to this purpose. If they are followed, sooner or later the moment arrives when thinking becomes *leibfrei,* i.e. independent of the bodily instrument, when it works itself free from the cerebro-spinal system.

This is at first a most disturbing experience. . . . The sheer power of cosmic thought is such that at first one loses one's identity. And perhaps one *would* lose it for good, if it were not for a fact which now emerges from the hidden mysteries of Christianity. One does not finally lose one's identity because He Himself has walked the waves and extended a helping hand to Peter who ventured out prematurely. Gradually the waves seem to calm down, and a condition ensues which Steiner expresses in a wonderful phrase: ''Thinking itself becomes a body which draws into itself as its soul the Spirit of the Universe.''

This is a stage which, broadly speaking, Steiner had attained. . . . Now he made a discovery which was not known to him before. He discovered that this ''living thinking'' could awaken the *chakrams* from ''above,'' just as in the old way they could be stimulated from ''below.'' Thought which at first in the normal and natural psychosomatic process ''died'' on the place of the skull, but which through systematic exercises had risen again to the level of cosmic reality, could now impart life to the dormant organs of spiritual perception which have been implanted into man by Him who created him in His image. From about the turn of the century Steiner began to pursue this path with ever greater determination, and gradually developed the three forms of Higher Knowledge which he called Imagination: a *higher seeing* of the spiritual world in revealing images; Inspiration: a *higher hearing* of the spiritual world, through which it reveals its creative forces and its creative order; Intuition: the stage at which an *intuitive penetration* into the sphere of Spiritual Beings becomes possible.

With these unfolding powers Steiner now developed up to his death in 1925, in twenty-five momentous years, that truly vast and awe-inspiring body of spiritual and practical knowledge to which he gave the name ''Anthroposophy.'' . . . Anthroposophy literally means wisdom of man or the wisdom concerning man, but in his later years Steiner himself interpreted it on occasion as ''an adequate consciousness of being human.'' In this interpretation the moral achievement of Steiner's work, his mission, his message to a bewildered humanity which has lost ''an adequate consciousness of being human,'' to which Man has become ''the Unknown,'' is summed up. This monumental work lies before us today—and is waiting to be fully discovered by our Age—in some 170 books and in the published transcripts of nearly 6,000 lectures.

Three characteristic stages can be observed in Steiner's anthroposophical period. In a lecture given at the headquarters of the German Anthroposophical Society at Stuttgart (on February 6, 1923) he himself described these stages. Stage one (approximately 1901-1909): to lay the foundation for a Science of the Spirit within Western Civilization, with its center in the Mystery of Golgotha, as opposed to the purely traditional handing down of ancient oriental wisdom which is common to other organizations such as the Theosophical Society. Stage two (approximately 1910-1917): the application of the anthroposophical Science of the Spirit to various branches of Science, Art and practical life. As one of the milestones for the beginning of this second stage Steiner mentions the building of the Goetheanum, that architectural wonder (since destroyed by fire) in which his work as an artist had found its culmination. Stage three (approximately 1917-1925): first-hand descriptions of the spiritual world. During these twenty-five years of anthroposophical activity, Steiner's biography is identical with the history of the Anthroposophical Movement. His personal life is entirely dedicated to and absorbed in the life of his work.

It was during the last of the three phases that Steiner's prodigious achievements in so many fields of life began to inspire a number of his students and followers to practical foundations. Best known today are perhaps the Rudolf Steiner Schools for boys and girls, which have been founded in many countries and in which his concept of the true human being is the wellspring of all educational methods and activities. . . . A separate branch are the Institutes for Curative Education which have sprung up both in Europe and Overseas, and whose activities have been immensely beneficial to the ever increasing number of physically and mentally handicapped children and adults. Steiner's contributions to medical research and to medicine in general are used by a steadily growing number of doctors all over the world, and his indications are tested and followed up in a number of research centers and clinics. Another blessing for humanity flowed from his method of Biodynamic Agriculture, by which he was able to add to the basic principles of organic husbandry just those extras which, if rightly used, can greatly increase both fertility and quality without those chemical stimulants which in the long run poison both the soil and its products.

In the field of Art there is hardly an area he did not touch with the magic wand of creative originality. The second Goetheanum which replaced the first one destroyed by fire shows the massive use of reinforced concrete as a plastic material for architecture a generation before this use was attempted by others. Steiner's direct and indirect influence on modern painting with the symphonic use of color, on sculpture, on glass-engraving, on metal work and other visual arts is too far-reaching for anyone even to attempt to describe in condensed form. Students and graduates of the Steiner schools for Eurythmy and for Dramatic Art have performed before enthusiastic audiences in the cultural centers of the world, ably directed by Marie Steiner, his wife.

To those who have been attracted to this present publication [***Christianity as Mystical Fact and the Mysteries of Antiquity***] by its title and its reference to Christianity, it will be of particular interest to hear that among those foundations which came into being during the last phase of Steiner's anthroposophical work was a Movement for Religious Renewal, formed by a body of Christian ministers, students and other young pioneers who had found in Rudolf Steiner ''a man sent from God,'' able to show the way to a true reconciliation of faith and knowledge, of religion and science. This Movement is known today as ''The Christian Community'' and has centers in many cities in the Old and New World. Apart from the inestimable help this Movement received from him in theological and pastoral matters, Rudolf Steiner was instrumental in mediating for this Movement a complete spiritual rebirth of the Christian Sacraments for the modern age and a renewal of the Christian priestly office.

Christianity as Mystical Fact and the Mysteries of Antiquity holds a special place in the story of his remarkable and dedicated life. The book contains the substance of a series of lectures Rudolf Steiner gave in the winter of 1901-1902. . . . (pp. 23-9)

After [Steiner's] lectures on the mystics which was something of a prelude, ***Christianity as Mystical Fact*** now ushered in a new period in the understanding of the basic facts of Christianity as well as in Steiner's own life.

Compared with the free flow of spiritual teaching on Christianity offered by Steiner in his later works, the book may appear somewhat tentative and even reticent in its style. But it contains as in a nutshell all the essential new elements he was able to develop and unfold so masterfully in his later years.

Steiner considered the phrase "Mystical *Fact*" in the title to be very important. "I did not intend simply to describe the mystical content of Christianity," he says in his autobiography. "I attempted to show that in the ancient Mysteries cult-images were given of cosmic events, which occurred later on the field of actual history in the Mystery of Golgotha as a *Fact* transplanted from the cosmos into the earth." (p. 29)

Rev. Alfred Heidenreich, in an introduction to Christianity As Mystical Fact and the Mysteries of Antiquity *by Rudolf Steiner, translated by E. A. Frommer, Gabrielle Hess, and Peter Kändler (copyright © 1961 by Rudolf Steiner Publications; reprinted by permission of Rudolf Steiner Publications, Blauvelt, NY), Steinerbooks, 1961, pp. 15-33.*

ILSE MEISSNER REESE (essay date 1965)

[*In the following excerpt, Reese discusses the architectural qualities of the Goetheanum.*]

[The] monumental masses which, from a distance, appear to be part of the limestone crags of the Jura Mountains near Basel, Switzerland, reveal themselves at close range as the reinforced concrete shells of an unusual collection of man-made structures. The most dominant of these buildings houses the headquarters of a philosophical organization known as the Anthroposophical Society, and its affiliated School of Spiritual Science. The Goetheanum, as this headquarters is officially named, derives its name from the German poet Goethe, whose philosophy—a somewhat unique combination of mysticism and pragmatism—formed the basis and the inspiration of the philosophy of the society's founder and mentor, Rudolf Steiner.

As a structure, the Goetheanum has always fascinated the design-conscious, and with the resurgence of interest in Art Nouveau and architectural expressionism, it has in recent years been subjected to closer scrutiny. Stylistically, the building, begun in 1923, is unclassifiable. . . .

Whether judged in terms of the 20's or the 60's, the Goetheanum is without doubt one of the purest examples of expressionist architecture, for seldom has a structure been designed more specifically to express, to interpret, to reflect a way of life, a philosophy. Although this philosophy, like the architecture, defies definition, the intent of anthroposophy, according to Steiner, is to reveal a "logic of life" through Goethe's observations of the natural sciences. It was Steiner's hope that, through his writings and through the school, he might both nurture and further develop the work begun by the poet-philosopher. (The school, incidentally, encompasses departments of speech and music; plastic arts; medicine, with its own clinic; natural sciences, with laboratories for biology, physics, and agriculture; mathematics and astronomy; and belles lettres.) Accordingly, Steiner insisted that the architecture, in all its details, derive from the same impulses, the same sources as the anthroposophic philosophy.

That this unification of thought, architecture, and function was realized is largely due to the fact that one man, Rudolf Steiner, evolved the philosophy, designed the building, and, as leader of the society, guided the activities the completed building would house. Steiner delivered many lectures, wrote four dramas, designed costumes and scenery, and certainly had these activities in mind when designing the main interior space. With few exceptions—Wright's Taliesin West, for example—architects rarely have the opportunity to exercise such absolute control over form and function.

Interestingly enough, Steiner was not an architect and had had no professional training. His approach was entirely intuitive. To him, architectural forms were organic growths undergoing the same metamorphoses as plant and animal life. His goal was "to imbue forms with life," to establish "a harmony of supporting and downward-bearing forces" and to achieve a balanced "counterpoint of concave and convex architectonic forms." The static, geometric structures of previous generations, he felt, were not adequate to express his new Spiritual Science. . . . [The first Goetheanum]—a vast hollow wood sculpture of rare design interest—was destroyed by fire soon after its completion in 1922. Reinforced concrete was therefore the logical choice for the second Goetheanum, not only because of its fire-resistive qualities but mostly for its plastic possibilities. These Steiner explored to the fullest with the help of a study model of clay, which served as the guide for the erection of the wooden forms into which the concrete was poured. "Let us try to feel how one thing is connected with another," he said again and again to his followers, and, in demonstrating this thesis in terms of architecture, he revealed a rare intuitive talent that many trained architects would envy. (p. 146)

Ilse Meissner Reese, "Steiner's Goetheanum at Dornach," in Progressive Architecture *(copyright 1965, Reinhold Publishing Corp.; reprinted from the September, 1965, issue of* Progressive Architecture*), Vol. XLVI, No. 9, September, 1965, pp. 146-53.*

ALBERT SCHWEITZER (essay date 1966)

[*Schweitzer held degrees in medicine, theology, and music, and was the author of several significant theological studies as well as a standard biography of J. S. Bach, when he decided to devote his life "to the direct service of humanity." He established a hospital at Lambarene in central Africa and worked there for the rest of his life. Schweitzer was Principal of the Theological College of St. Thomas in Strassbourg at the time of his meeting with Steiner, which was brought about through a mutual acquaintance with Theosophical leader Annie Besant. The following excerpt details Schweitzer's recollections of his meeting with Steiner.*]

My meeting with Rudolf Steiner took place on the occasion of a Theosophical Conference in Strassburg. If I am not mistaken, it was either 1902 or 1903. Annie Besant, with whom I had become acquainted through friends in Strassburg, introduced us to each other.

Rudolf Steiner entered at that time into connection with the Theosophical Society, not so much because he shared its convictions as because he expected the possibility of finding among its members those who would have interest and understanding for the spiritual truths which he had to present.

I knew that he had occupied himself in Weimar with the study of Goethe. . . .

I arranged matters so that we were neighbors at table for the conference meal.

From the outset, the conversation developed in such a way that he was the speaker and I the one who listened and put questions.

The conversation turned quite naturally—even before we had finished our soup—to his studies in Weimar about Goethe and to Goethe's world conception. I became immediately aware that my neighbor possessed extensive knowledge in the field of the natural sciences. What was a great surprise to me was that he spoke of the crucial importance of recognizing the far-reaching significance of Goethe's knowledge of nature. . . .

My table companion saw that he had an attentive listener at his side. He held the floor. We forgot that we were at dinner.

In the afternoon we stood about together, paying little heed to what was going on in the theosophical meeting.

When the conversation turned to Plato I was better able to keep up. But also here Steiner astonished me by drawing attention to hidden insights whose significance had not yet been rightly understood and appreciated. (p. 13)

And then something remarkable occurred. One of us—I no longer remember which—came to speak of the spiritual decline of our culture as the fundamental, yet unheeded, problem of our time. With this we learned that we were both preoccupied with the same question. Neither had anticipated this of the other.

A lively discussion then ensued. Each of us discovered from the other that we had set ourselves the same life task, to strive for the awakening of that true culture which would be enlivened and penetrated by the ideal of humanity, and to guide and hold men to the goal of becoming truly intelligent, thinking beings.

In the awareness of our community of interest, we took leave of one another. Destiny did not bring us a second meeting, but the consciousness of our common striving remained. Each of us followed the other's activity in later life.

It was not granted me to take part in the lofty flight of thought of Rudolf Steiner's spiritual science. I know, however, that he carried many with him in his thought and made new men out of them. Outstanding achievements in many fields have been accomplished by his pupils.

I have continued to follow the life and work of Rudolf Steiner with heartfelt participation: his achievements up to the first World War; the problems and needs which the war brought with it; the courageous efforts to bring order into the confusion of the post-war years by means of the presentation of the ideas of the threefold nature of the social organism; the successful establishment of the Goetheanum in Dornach, where the world of his thought found its home; the pain which its destruction by fire brought him in the night of New Year's Eve 1922 to 1923; the courage with which he pursued its rebuilding, and, at last, the greatness of soul which he maintained in his untiring teaching and creative work during the suffering of the final months which he spent on earth. (pp. 13-14)

In my meeting with him, his countenance with its wonderful eyes made an unforgettable impression upon me. (p. 14)

Albert Schweitzer, "My Meeting with Rudolf Steiner," in Journal for Anthroposophy, *No. 4, Autumn, 1966, pp. 13-14.*

DENNIS SHARP (essay date 1966)

[In the following excerpt, Sharp discusses some general tendencies in Steiner's architecture.]

An analysis of the architecture of Expressionism, particularly in its most self-conscious and enigmatic phase, would not be complete without reference to the work of Rudolf Steiner.

Although Steiner's architectural ideas and so-called 'aesthetic laws' were developed before the time of the exaggerated and vigorous postwar ideas of the Berlin circle, his completed buildings were an important contribution to the romantic stream within the Modern Movement. In time, Steiner's work is contemporary with that of the Amsterdam 'phantasts', but totally different in spirit.

Rudolf Steiner . . . , philosopher, Goethe scholar and occultist, was not a trained architect. But he did design buildings, discourse on the merits of a new style in architecture, and gather around himself craftsmen and artists to interpret his own ideas on the way architecture should develop. In many ways he was a modern *Uomo Universale,* around whom all disciplines are brought together as part of a way of life. Like the Renaissance masters he awarded architecture the pride of first place among the arts. He brought to the study of architecture and aesthetics a knowledge of mathematics, history and literature, as well as an experimental knowledge of philosophy and science. It is impossible to divorce Steiner's views on architecture from his attitude to other aspects of life. This makes the study of his aesthetic views even more difficult to understand because as a philosopher he was free to invent his own vocabulary and symbolic ideas. (p. 145)

In the years just before the turn of the century Steiner was attracted into the artistic and cultural circles of Berlin. . . . (p. 146)

While in Berlin and involved in the pre-Expressionist circles Steiner consolidated his own ideas into what he termed a 'spiritual science'. In 1902, at the age of forty-one, he became the leader of the German section of the Theosophical Society. Later he and his followers gradually broke away from that movement to form provisionally, in 1912, the first Anthroposophical Society. This movement of Anthroposophy took its name from the literal derivation of the Greek words, *Anthropos*—man, *Sophos*—wise, the wisdom of mankind. Man was placed in this concept, at the centre of all perceptions: 'Anthroposophy,' Steiner wrote in 1925, 'is the path of knowledge to guide the Spiritual in the human being to the Spiritual in the Universe. It arises as a need of the heart, of the life of feeling: and it can only be justified inasmuch as it can satisfy this inner need.' (pp. 146-47)

Anthroposophy was an occult sect, based largely on Christian teaching. It was typical of the many strong, pseudo-religious sects prevalent in the German atmosphere of Expressionism. Undoubtedly, it has been far more successful than its many, now extinct, sister cults. This is mainly because Steiner was himself a powerful and unique individual. In some ways he was akin—although never one himself—to the Expressionists; he embodied their zeal and revolutionary spirit in a deeply spiritual way. Almost apostolically he sought to create a new order, relating man and the world to a perception of rhythms of time. . . .

This mystical approach extended into the world of Steiner's architecture. (p. 147)

Steiner was a spiritual romantic who was inspired by the sensuous forms to be found in nature. In using these forms he appointed some a symbolic purpose and lent to others a static quality. Many of the forms he used and invented had a powerful erotic quality (or perhaps were unconscious fertility symbols), indicating, no doubt, his sympathy with nature. A similar tendency towards this kind of eroticism in art forms can be clearly seen in the religious and symbolic sculptures of primitive societies, and significantly Steiner talks at length in his lecture of 1914 to which he gave the title **'True Aesthetic Laws of Form',** of the 'atavistic clairvoyance' that was an attribute of primitive man. 'Many of the forms to be found in primitive art can only be understood when we realize that they were the outcome of this primordial clairvoyant consciousness.' By adapting these forms to his own philosophy Steiner was trying to imply the eternal validity of such forms.

Steiner's excursion into architecture began almost by accident, and quite late in his career. He had decorated a number of columns of an interior for a convention in Frankfurt and was approached by two mathematician/engineers about his seriousness as a designer and architect. This eventually led him to take his ideas further with a design for a temple type structure for a site in Munich. However, his application to erect the structure was later turned down by the Kaiser himself, as the site was opposite a well-known church and the law as it existed did not allow two religious buildings in close proximity. With his regard for, and background knowledge of, Goethe's work it seemed only appropriate that the main centre of the newly founded society should be named the 'Goetheanum'. This centre, 'a free high school for spiritual science', was finally established at Dornach, near Basel, in Switzerland. This was in 1913 and the building then erected, Goetheanum I, . . . was Steiner's major architectural work. The second Goetheanum, built to replace the first which was destroyed by fire on New Year's Eve, 1922-3, was opened in 1928, three years after Steiner's death. It remains incomplete. (pp. 147-48)

The first Goetheanum. Rudolf Steiner Publications/Garber Communications, Inc.

Steiner commanded a form language peculiarly his own. He married his sense of movement to the second characteristic of sculptural form, so that the buildings are moulded *en masse* and made to appear almost pliable. This can be seen more clearly in the house Steiner designed for himself and in the second Goetheanum, where the maquette for the project, made by Steiner out of Harbutt's red plasticine, is in the form of a jelly mould. This sculptural quality, and indeed the whole architecture of man was, for Steiner, 'the result of the interplay of earthly and cosmic forces'. Steiner's metaphysical ideas permeated this architecture of the soul. 'Architecture stands on the earth in a central position. ''A spiritual being'' on one hand, inspiring mankind; on the other a solid structure of brick or concrete serving a sensible earthly purpose.'

Metamorphosis of form is the characteristic, culled from the writings and lectures, that is most commonly associated with Steiner's sculptural and architectural work. (p. 148)

Metamorphosis by definition suggests a natural change, a transformation that has occurred by an inner, natural action, and as such is a type of change that cannot ever take place in an art so rigid as architecture. Steiner was in fact trying to create an environment in which the sum of the smaller, unrelated parts of a building would add up to a common, harmonious whole 'image', an idea common to the postwar Expressionist architects in Germany (i.e. Häring's idea of *Gestalt-werk*).

Steiner has an even closer connection with the Berlin Utopians in that his notion, that a building should be a living organism, comes very close to the ideas propounded by Hermann Finsterlin in his numerous drawings and articles on architectural form. But whereas Finsterlin presented an architecture in which the spaces themselves, the glands, had an organic validity, Steiner saw this organic quality in the surface area and structure of each building. 'The wall is not merely wall, it is living, just like a living organism that allows elevations and depressions to grow out of itself.' Out of these walls the details of the building grow with a life of their own, as part of one organism: '. . . inside our building we shall find one plastic form, a continuous relief sculpture on the capitals, plinths, architraves. They grow out of the wall, and the wall is their basis, their soil, without which they could not exist.'

Undoubtedly with the first Goetheanum, he achieved his aim. The site for the building was on a ridge of one of the smaller foothills of the Jura mountain range, overlooking the city of Basel. Its outward shape was a strong contrast to the undulating countryside. During the period the building was being constructed, Steiner spoke of the new style in architecture saying that the present task was 'to translate the static, geometric structure of previous architectural forms into an organic dynamic method of designing and shaping'. (p. 151)

Steiner's architecture is really open sculpture; huge pieces of sculpture in which people move and have a new sense of being. This is what he intended. It is not sculptural building in the sense that Mendelsohn or Le Corbusier referred to in their equation of architecture with the magnificent play of light on form. It is rather an environment above and around which the primary spaces are created to invoke the response of the Spirit in man. With Steiner the interior was all important. Whether the spaces he actually created internally are totally satisfactory as 'architectural spaces' is another question. For him they were 'soul spaces' in which there was an important distinction between *real space*, which remains external to man, and *soul space* in which spiritual events, interior to man, were realized. (pp. 152-54)

Within ten years of its erection the first vast Temple of Spiritual Science was reduced to ashes. Almost immediately out of the conflagration arose a new and even more dynamic structure, Goetheanum II (begun in 1925), known affectionately to the adherents of Steiner's movement as The Building. This time it was more firmly constructed in reinforced concrete. Chronologically the two buildings indicate Steiner's progress as an architect. The experimental nature of the first building and the almost blind groping for the expression of new aesthetic laws gave way to the imposing sculptural mass of the second. (p. 156)

Dennis Sharp, "Rudolf Steiner and the Way to a New Style in Architecture," in his Modern Architecture and Expressionism *(copyright © 1966 by Dennis Sharp; all rights reserved; reprinted by permission of the author), Longmans, 1966 (and reprinted by George Braziller, 1967), pp. 145-65.*

OWEN BARFIELD (essay date 1966)

[Barfield is an English novelist, critic, and philosopher. As his parents were "freethinkers," Barfield was raised a religious agnostic, but as an adult he became a Christian as well as a follower of Anthroposophy. Barfield has written several works, fiction and nonfiction, based on Anthroposophical teachings. For a discussion of Steiner's influence on Barfield's thought, see the excerpt below by Patrick Grant (1982). In the following excerpt from his Romanticism Comes of Age, *Barfield provides a summary of Steiner's concept of pure thought as a means of attaining objective knowledge of a spiritual level of being.]*

It was Rudolf Steiner's view that many philosophical errors have arisen from the fact that philosophers have been too ready to enquire what we can know and what we cannot know, without first enquiring what we mean by 'knowing'. This was, above all, the omission which he sought to rectify and it may be said that his own philosophy is primarily an epistemology, a theory of knowledge. Why is it so important that we should grasp the true nature of thinking? Because thinking is the 'instrument of knowledge'. A philosopher starting out to construct a true theory of knowledge must start, if he is faithful to his calling, from the very beginning. If we start from any assumptions at all—astronomical or historical assumptions, for instance, or assumptions about the part played by the brain and the nerves or sense-organs in the process of knowledge—we are clearly not starting from zero. We are starting from something on which cognitive activity has already been expended. The same remark applies if we start from the 'ego', or 'consciousness', or 'the mind', or by raising the question whether there is such an entity as the mind, or from the experience of a 'normal observer'. Only if we start from thinking itself, no such objection can be made. For thinking is the very first possible move we can make in the direction from ignorance towards knowledge. We cannot think about the world, or about anything at all, without thinking.

Thus, by way of example, it follows from the former of the two axioms that thinking is anterior even to the elementary distinction between subject and object. Thinking

> produces these two concepts just as it produces all others. When, therefore, I, as thinking subject, refer a concept to an object, we must not regard this reference as something purely subjective. It is not the subject, but thinking, which makes the reference. The subject does not think because it is a subject, rather it conceives itself to be a subject because it can think. The activity performed by man as a thinking being is thus not merely subjective. Rather it is neither subjective nor objective; it transcends both these concepts. I ought never to say that I, as an individual subject, think, but rather that I, as subject, exist myself by the grace of thinking. Thinking is thus an element which leads me beyond myself and relates me to objects. At the same time it separates me from them, inasmuch as it sets me, as subject, over against them.
>
> It is just this which constitutes the double nature of man. His thinking embraces himself and the rest of the world. But by this same act of thinking he determines himself also as an individual, in contrast with the objective world.

If, however, I owe my separate existence, as subject, to 'the grace of thinking', yet something else besides thinking is required to bring this separate existence about. This brings us to the other primary element with which any theory of knowledge must deal, namely perception. Unlike my thoughts, my perceptions are private and personal to me, inasmuch as they depend on my point of observation and my separate physical organism. It is the perceptual element in the totality of my experience which thinking makes use of, as the means, to bring about my subjectivity—that is, my separate existence apart from nature and apart from my fellow human beings.

This important, and from one point of view startling, proposition requires a little further consideration. It is startling because we are accustomed to accept precisely the *perceptual* element in our experience—the evidence, as we say, of our senses—as constituting the 'public' world that is common to all mankind; while we contrast with this the 'private', inner world of our thoughts. This is justifiable enough in the ordinary loose use of language, but how carefully we must distinguish under the strict discipline of an epistemological enquiry! It is just here that the difference between 'thought' (as the product of the act) and 'thinking', the act itself, is relevant. For if it is *pure* thinking, disentangled from all perception, to which we are directing our attention, then, as we have seen, it is precisely this which is *not* private and personal to ourselves. And again, if it is pure perception, disentangled from all thinking, to which we are directing our attention, then it is precisely this which *is* private and personal to ourselves. Thus, it is not perception alone which can ever put us in touch with the solid, public, objective world, but only the percept mixed with thinking. (pp. 244-46)

Concepts and percepts are, for Steiner, the bricks out of which the whole edifice of human knowledge is constructed; and the *pure* concept and the *pure* percept are accordingly the only elements on which an adequate *theory* of knowledge can be based. (p. 246)

A good deal has been said already of the nature of the concept. We must now ask what Steiner meant by 'percept'. But let it first be made clear (in view of what has just been said on the topic of 'subjectivity') what he did *not* mean. He did not mean anything in the nature of a subjective representation; he did not mean the same thing as perception. *Esse est percipi* ["To be is to be perceived''] was no part of his doctrine. 'It is not,' he writes, 'the process of perception, but the object of this process, which I call the "percept".' And again: '"objective" means that which, for perception, presents itself as external to the perceiving subject.' What *are* subjective, on the other hand, are the after-images of those determined percepts, which remain in the mind when actual perception has ceased. These he called *Ideen*—ideas; and it is these which are the principal source of error and illusion, and the cause why the 'public' world-picture is by no means necessarily also an 'objective' one. The pure concept of a triangle is one and the same in your mind and mine—not so the perceptual trappings, which may have stuck, as it were, to the concept, left there by particular representations of triangles on particular blackboards.

Just as the concept unavoidably presents itself to us as the product of our own activity, so the percept unavoidably presents itself as *not* the product of our own activity. Indeed, that is almost its definition. The percept is all *that* in the totality of our experience which is *not* the product of our activity. It may, for that reason and to that extent, be properly described as 'given':

> What then is a percept? This question, asked in this general way, is absurd. A percept occurs always as a perfectly determinate, concrete content. This content is immediately given and is completely contained in the given. The only question we can ask concerning the given content is, what it is apart from perception, that is, what it is for thinking. The question concerning the 'what' of a percept can, therefore, only refer to the conceptual intuition which corresponds to the percept.

Here it will be necessary to say something of Steiner's concept of 'the Given', which plays such an important part in his epistemology. We find that he uses the word in two different ways. William James, writing on man's experience of time, adopted from E. R. Clay that useful term 'the specious present'. By analogy with this use—once more introducing a piece of terminology not employed by Steiner himself—we will call his 'given', in the first sense, 'the specious Given'. It is simply what we actually find, of any description whatever, when we look around us in the world. What we find, that is, at the point in our lives when we first decide to tackle the problem of knowledge (not, therefore, at the breast or in the cradle). We have made up our minds about the true nature of the instrument called thought. The next step is to apply our thinking for the general purpose of acquiring knowledge. And clearly we must start where we actually find ourselves. We have no right to start with assumptions of any sort. We have certainly no right to pretend that we start from some imaginary state of mind, such as a man might have who had perceptions but as yet no thoughts—the 'blooming, buzzing confusion' of which William James also wrote. Whatever preceded the starting-point must, *to begin with,* be taken for granted. What we are actually surrounded by is a world of phenomena, both outer and inner—trees, houses, books, theories, pains, pleasures, dreams, hallucinations and what you will—some parts of which present themselves as connected or related wholes, while others are as yet unconnected and unrelated.

How, asked Steiner in his doctorial Thesis ***Wahrheit und Wissenschaft,*** do we start out upon the business of *knowing* about all this? We have to discover a bridge that leads from the picture of the world as given to the picture of it which our cognitive activity unfolds:

> Somewhere in the Given, we must discover the spot where we can get to work, where something homogeneous to cognition meets us . . . If there is to be knowledge, everything depends on there being, somewhere within the Given, a field in which our cognitive activity does not merely presuppose the Given, but is at work in the very heart of the Given itself.

This spot, or field, is the activity of thinking. At all points and at every moment it keeps inserting us, as it were, into the very texture of the Given. Out for a walk, we hear a sudden whirring noise, which 'means' nothing to us; a moment later a partridge rises from the hedge near at hand. The concept of cause and effect arises in us to unite the two percepts and at once becomes part of the Given. Next time we heard the whirring noise, it carries its meaning within it.

And now, what proved such a disadvantage when our problem was to *notice* the act of thinking, to be *aware* of it—namely, the fact that we 'enjoy' thinking and do not 'contemplate' it, *because thinking is so much our own activity (so much our very self in action)*—now this becomes the very stamp upon its passport to utility. For the problem of knowledge is always how to relate the knower to the known. What has the phenomenal world got to *do* with me, the observing outsider? Why should there, and how can there, be a link between them called truth, or knowledge? Well, it seems there is one point where the two incompatibles coalesce; one point where 'the object of observation is qualitatively identical with the activity directed upon it.' And that point is, precisely, the activity of thinking.

Now if we reason back a little from the example of the whirring noise and the partridge, we at once have it brought home to us that the specious Given is positively full of such conceptual determinations. This applies even to that part of the specious Given which we call 'sense-data'. We owe it to our concepts that we perceive a world of shapes, forms, 'things' at all. 'The picture of the world with which we begin philosophical reflection,' wrote Steiner in *Truth and Science,*

> is already qualified by predicates which are the results solely of the act of knowing. We have no right to accept these predicates without question. On the contrary, we must carefully extract them from out of the world-picture, in order that it may appear in its purity without any admixture due to the process of cognition.

This brings us to his other use of the term 'given'—according to which it coincides with the pure percept, prior to all conceptual determinations whatsoever—to that element in experience which is *wholly* perceptual. Let us call it here the 'net Given'. It is important to be clear that the Given is never actually experienced 'net'. Thus, the net Given is something which a philosopher is concerned with, not as knower, but as epistemologist. This is a distinction Positivism fails to observe. Certainly we are not entitled to build up a picture of the world by starting from James's 'blooming, buzzing confusion'—a thing we never experience. But that is not to say that we *are* entitled to treat the specious Given (i.e. the world as normally experienced) as though it were the same as the net Given. We arrive at the concept of the net Given, not empirically, but by analysis. We may say of it (as James said of what he called the 'real', in contrast to the 'specious', present): 'Reflection leads us to the conclusion that it must exist, but that it *does* exist can never be a part of our immediate experience.'

To seek to limit the *theory* of knowledge by applying to it, for instance, the principle of verification is like seeking to use a well-cooked meal, not for eating, but as material for making pots and pans; or like hunting for your spectacles with the help of those very spectacles which are already (you have forgotten) lodged on your nose. (pp. 247-51)

If we are determined to eliminate all subjectivity and to be uncompromisingly empirical, if we insist on verifying from experience at all points, from the very start onwards, our only course is to find some way of penetrating with full consciousness into that unconscious no-man's-land (or should one say 'every-man's-land'?) which lies between the net Given and the specious Given. This is the realm where thinking performs the function of Coleridge's 'primary imagination', or what Susanne Langer calls 'formulation'. It is, incidentally, the realm where language is born.

It is obvious that this penetration cannot be effected with only the techniques and disciplines which science has so far developed. Instrument after instrument of ever greater precision and power is invented and applied, but, for our purpose, *the mind itself* must be treated as an instrument and *its* precision and power systematically augmented. It follows from all that has been said of the relation between thinking and perceiving that the strengthened thinking to which the discipline inculcated by Steiner is directed, must also result in widening the field of *perception* or *observation* themselves (as those words are ordinarily understood). This aspect he deals with in his Introductions to Geothe's scientific writings and in his short treatise ***Grundlinien einer Erkenntnistheorie der Goetheschen Weltanschauung*** which, together with the two books previously referred to in this article, contain the fundamental principles underlying Rudolf Steiner's concept of mind.

Moreover, since thinking is at one and the same time the activity of man himself *and* his only guarantee of objectivity, we have no right to assume that sense-perception is the indispensable witness to reality. Thinking is—and strengthened thinking will be aware of itself as being—that factor in man 'through which he inserts himself spiritually into reality'. It will make direct contact with reality somewhat in the manner we normally attribute to perception and if, on the one hand, it is 'an active process taking place in the human mind', on the other hand it will be 'a perception mediated by no sense-organ . . . a perception in which the percipient is himself active, and a self-activity which is at the same time perceived.'

It is with the detailed results, both of that enhanced faculty of observation and of these purely spiritual perceptions, that so large a part of Steiner's books and lectures are concerned. But long before he began to bring them before the public, he had laid, in purely philosophical form, the epistemological foundation on which his investigations were based, and it is this foundation we have briefly tried to sketch here. (pp. 253-54)

Owen Barfield, "Rudolf Steiner's Concept of Mind," in his Romanticism Comes of Age *(© 1966 by the Rudolf Steiner Press; © 1966 by Owen Barfield), revised edition, Rudolf Steiner Press, 1966 (and reprinted by Wesleyan University Press, 1967), pp. 241-54.*

REX RAAB, ARNE KLINGBORG and ÅKE FANT (essay date 1972)

[In the following excerpt from Eloquent Concrete, *a detailed history of Steiner's ventures into architecture, the authors provide information on the practical as well as theoretical aspects of the design and construction of the Goetheanums I and II, along with other structures conceived by Steiner. This book was first published in Switzerland in 1972.]*

The founder of the Goetheanum particularly emphasized that it is important to apply contemporary materials in the right way. And concrete, which has to undergo so many mechanically-induced processes and chemical transformations before it is *in situ* and has set, is precisely such a material. A spirited connoisseur of architectural matters, Erich Schwebsch, would wax enthusiastic about these processes when he showed that the raw materials needed to produce cement—lime and clay—must pass through the four stages of the elementary states, that used to be termed earth, water, air and fire. "Thanks to cement, man himself can make a stone!" he would exclaim. By using this new building material in place of an "old, conventional" one (which would be inappropriate or even false for producing a plastic continuity of surface), it must be so totally transformed that it again harmonizes with what is living and creating. This could not happen of itself since such a material is divorced from life and growth or indeed from the whole of nature. Hence the attempt must be made to approach the living, creative process in another way, bringing forth appropriate new shapes from the very source. This can only be done out of insight and artistic sensitivity.

Thus Rudolf Steiner was happy that this material could be used at least for the substructure of the first Goetheanum, as well as for the separate "Heizhaus" belonging to it, which housed the central heating and electrical plant. (pp. 113-14)

In the "Heizhaus" (central heating plant), Steiner, as an architect, was able for the first time to tackle the design of an all-concrete building. At that time, he often referred to concrete as an unresponsive material: "It is remarkably difficult to evolve concrete buildings of a suitable and genuinely artistic character, and the solution to this problem is very demanding." To develop appropriate forms for concrete and convert them into organic shapes in the round, Rudolf Steiner executed wax models to which his collaborators could refer. He favoured this procedure on good grounds.

If we are to show how a seemingly dumb and unresponsive material like concrete can be made to speak, how it can become eloquent, it seems justified to quote in detail Rudolf Steiner's relevant remarks. In Berlin, early in 1914, in connection with the colony evolving in Dornach, he explained:

> As a second building which has already found a definite form, we must consider the 'Heizhaus'. This structure certainly had to be conceived in the contemporary material, in reinforced concrete. The problem presented was how to execute its soaring chimney which, if it were done in the ordinary way, would certainly be an atrocity; how, too, to bring it architecturally into relationship with the main structure in a suitable building material. From the little model and the drawing you will see how an attempt has been made to find the right architectural form. When it is finally erected, especially when the furnaces are in use—for the smoke is included in the architectural concept!—then, despite its prosaic purpose, an appropriate beauty of form will perhaps be felt through the fact that the function of the building comes to real exprssion through it, that the form

> is not determined by the customary attitude to utility buildings, but that an aesthetic modelling has taken place out of the inner nature of the task. In linking the two little domes with an adjoining mass that is shaped differently in the different directions and culminates in the chimney in 'leaflike' forms (one member compared them to ears)—through all these forms it should be possible for us to experience that even a building serving the modern purpose of central heating (the Johannesbau or Goetheanum and its neighbouring premises will be heated from here), that even such a building can be given an aesthetically satisfying form. In a case like this it is necessary first of all to be fully acquainted with the purpose and content of the building.

Seven years later, in a lantern lecture held in Berne, it is said of the same building:

> We were really forced to design it according to the intractable nature of concrete; and true to aesthetic law and artistic feeling, we had to say to ourselves: here the starting point is the necessary heating and lighting technology. Here is the nut, around which the shell has to be built, that will draw off the smoke. This principle of 'nutshell building', if I may use this trivial expression, is carried out consistently. And whoever feels critical should consider what would otherwise have come about if the attempt had not been made—even if it is perhaps not wholly successful. There would be a towering red chimney in its place!

Then follows the significant remark:

> Basically a utility building has to be created by first of all acquiring the essential feeling for the material, and then by developing the shell out of the given purpose.

(pp. 115-17)

The second Goetheanum. Rudolf Steiner Publications/Garber Communications, Inc.

Thus this building reveals its secret to the beholder, as its creator hoped it would. An "appropriate beauty" has indeed come into being through finding a truly honest though not unimaginative shell for technical processes—combustion in the boiler, circulation in the piping, the rising and even branching of smoke, the transformation of electric current. This distinct expression was also necessary to enable an unencumbered architectural development of the main building, which was to be released from just those forces represented in the heating plant.

Here a principle is at work which deserves imitation. (p. 122)

Rex Raab, Arne Klingborg, and Åke Fant, in their Eloquent Concrete: How Rudolf Steiner Employed Reinforced Concrete *(copyright (text) Rudolf Steiner Press, London 1979), Rudolf Steiner Press, 1979, 180 p.*

HANS PUSCH (essay date 1972)

[*Pusch, who with Ruth Pusch translated* The Portal of Initiation, *notes the difficulties of rendering in English the "mobility and transparency" of Steiner's language. For other discussions of the* Mystery Plays, *see the excerpts by Hermon Ould (1922), Richard Rosenheim (1952), Adam Bittleston (1956), and Robb Creese (1978).*]

[The] vitality with which the thoughts behind the words are expressed, and the rhythmical flow of the line [of ***The Portal of Initiation,*** are] characteristic of Rudolf Steiner's dramatic style. Many almost insurmountable obstacles arise for the translator through the freedom of sentence construction in the German text which leads often to ambiguity. Difficulties come also from Rudolf Steiner's creation of new words, words that are in harmony with the spirit of the German language. He thus gives the spoken word a mobility and transparency through which spirit realities can reveal themselves. The English language rarely allows this kind of spiritualization. But the speaker or the reader, reading aloud, can achieve much by the way he speaks the lines: he has to put them into motion, by having the last word of the sentence in mind already at the start. Such a mobility gives the listener the opportunity to grasp quickly and clearly the underlying thought. This penetration to the vividly moving thought is the best a translation can achieve. (p. 3)

Hans Pusch, "Introduction" (1972), in The Portal of Initiation: A Rosicrucian Mystery through Rudolf Steiner *by Rudolf Steiner, translated by Ruth Pusch and Hans Pusch (© Steiner Book Centre 1973), Steiner, 1973, pp. 3-4.*

ROBB CREESE (essay date 1978)

[*Creese provides a detailed examination of the meaning of various elements of the performance of Steiner's* Mystery Plays, *including the significance of certain Eurythmic movements, costume colors, spoken sounds, and lighting effects. For other studies of the* Mystery Plays, *see the excerpts by Hermon Ould (1922), Richard Rosenheim (1952), Adam Bittleston (1956), and Hans Pusch (1972).*]

Between 1909 and 1913 the German section of the Theosophical Society held annual conventions in Munich. Part of the festival was the production of plays that were pertinent to spiritual science. It was Rudolf Steiner who gave the impulse for dramatic performances. His four "Mystery Dramas" were written for the Theosophical conventions. He wrote plays only when he knew that they were about to go into rehearsal in Munich, and each was in production for about two months. . . .

The four Mystery Dramas are titled [***Die Pforte der Einweihung (The Portal of Initiation), Die Prüfung der Seele (The Soul's Probation), Der Hüter der Schwelle (The Guardian of the Threshold),*** and ***Der Seelen Erwachen (The Soul's Awakening)***]. . . . Rudolph Steiner wrote, directed, designed and supervised the productions. (p. 46)

Each of the four plays was finished just a couple days before they opened. In the middle of the night Steiner called out for messengers to carry the manuscript pages to the printers. Scripts were literally still wet from the press when the actors got their parts. They barely had time to memorize the lines of the final scenes. The completed scripts were on sale two days before the performances premiered.

The Mystery Dramas were not well received in Munich. Many things confused the audiences. Each play took all day to perform with one break in the middle of the day. Characters in the dramas appeared in different incarnations and in different spiritual states of being. The performance style was highly conventionalized and the words were recited very slowly and rhythmically. Richard Rosenheim wrote in *The Eternal Drama* that spectators who were inwardly aware of occult science were deeply moved by the plays [see excerpt above, 1952]. Others laughed at the performers and many were silent. The reviews condemned the plays as dogmatic and too doctrinaire to be performed.

But Theosophists of Europe continued to attend the plays. The crowds were growing too large by 1913 for the rented theatres, and there were no lecture rooms that could hold all the participants for the two-week lecture series Rudolf Steiner gave to accompany the dramas. (p. 47)

All art springs from spiritual sources, Rudolf Steiner believed. He set up a hierarchy of art forms. Each one flows from a different interaction within the being of Man. . . . Architecture is a manifestation of the laws of the first member of the human being, the physical body. Sculpture begins in the second member, the ether body, and flows into the physical body. (p. 50)

The next higher member of the human being Steiner called the spirit-self. If the spirit-self's laws are brought down into the ego, there is poetry and drama. One further form can be envisioned, one that will only come to full maturity in the future: when impulses of the life-spirit are brought into the spirit-self, that art will be realized. . . .

The interaction among the members of the human being and the art forms were summarized by Rudolf Steiner in this way:

Physical body	
	Architecture
Etheric body	
	Sculpture
Astral body	
	Painting
Ego	
	Music
Spirit-self	
	Poetry (speech and drama)
Life-spirit	
	Eurythmy

Eurythmy is an art form that involves the visualization of human speech with the body. It is an integral part of any Anthroposophical performance in Dornach or elsewhere, as it is used to present nonmaterial spirit-beings. (p. 51)

The Mystery Dramas are rarely performed outside Anthroposophical circles. They were never intended for entertainment of society. They cannot be fully understood with the intellect. They can be described, but their full impact is felt only by an audience with an active, well-developed inner life. Steiner addressed the situation in the prolog to ***The Portal of Initiation.*** This scene is in prose, unlike the rest of the play, and it presents a realistic setting. It is a conversation between Sophia, presumably an Anthroposophist, and her friend, Estella.

Estella wants to go to a new social drama, *The Uprooted,* but Sophia must attend a performance being given by her society the same night. Estella feels Sophia and her circle are arrogant and without social conscience. She resents their "empty triteness" and their lack of feeling for their fellow men. Moreover, the society's plays seem nothing more than very old-fashioned, didactic allegories. There are no real people, only symbolical events.

Sophia counters that the new social theatre is poverty-stricken since its primary concern is materialism. It cannot reach the source of all life. She tells Estella that she and her theatre can only deal with the spirit in intellectual terms, the "thought-aspect" of the spirit. But Sophia believes her own theatre can bring together spontaneity and conscious spiritual activity. And she is proud that her performances can use unsophisticated sources without robbing them of their originality and richness.

Estella remarks that, still, she seeks enrichment through the challenges of plays like *The Uprooted.* By studying society's problems through theatre, she hopes to learn how to solve them. Sophia answers that dreams of justice for all can only come once Mankind can connect "reality" with deeper inner feelings of the spirit. (p. 52)

Rudolf Steiner utterly renounced naturalism in all the arts. In his nineteen lectures on speech and drama in 1924, he called the new writers of the turn of the century "idealists who stood on their heads—instead of walking on their feet." They looked for truth in stage routines and stage mechanism, but they could not find it. "Art they had not," Steiner declared, "style they had not, so they introduced naturalism; that was the best they could do." In naturalism, style cannot exist, he contended. It paralyzes artistic forms. Instead, Steiner called for a new theatre that harked back to the ancient Mysteries. His last words to the 1924 gathering of theatre artists were these:

> When the right shaping and moulding of speech is revealed through correct gesture within the frame of the correct scene on the stage, the spirit living in the drama will manifest itself as soul from the stage.

Steiner's emphasis on speech is better understood when we know how he viewed the origins of theatre.

The first phase of drama, Rudolf Steiner believed, presented only the performance of the Word, through which men could still feel God. Through music, painting, sculpture, and poetry, God was made to appear before the audience. In the second phase of drama, Mankind took the stage itself as it represented divine beings. In the third phase, Mankind switched to portraying itself on stage, and its inner experiences were stylized for performance.

Steiner eulogized the ancient drama as the "framework" for the appearance of the gods. . . . Steiner did not speak symbolically. He believed that the ancient audience literally perceived not merely ideas but the presence created by the words and rhythms. . . . The ancient audience felt itself moved to a supersensible world. And that was the intention. (p. 53)

The innermost soul could be revealed in *words*. But if words were held back, they would translate themselves then, and only then, into *gestures*. The words came first. Through this deep reverence for the spoken word, Steiner developed his performances in both drama and eurhythmy. Both are based on speech.

Actors or eurythmists who tune into the higher consciousness of sound must forget themselves. Steiner called for the "human being who lives in speech" to be heard by the audience. "The spectator will then instinctively perceive around the actor an aura; as he listens to the formed speech, he will see before him the auric contours," Steiner said in Lecture 10 in 1924. The performer cannot, therefore, present a "naturalistic" character because he or she is not the same as in everyday life. In naturalism the supersensible world is only a shadow. But in Anthroposophical performance the participants perceive what the senses tell them, and they feel the spirit underneath. (pp. 54-5)

Steiner quite consciously used sounds of words in the writing of his plays. Since vowels and consonants emerged from different sources, they could be used in different ways to describe characters. Vowels, which arise from the astral body deep inside the inner being, and which flow into the ether body, are the revealers of soul states. Consonants, on the other hand, flow from the astral body into the ego. They have a more direct interaction with the senses and are more closely tied to objects. (p. 55)

Speech has come a long way from its original meaning. Through centuries of soul-burdening materialism, language has become locked into signifying physical things. It has lost its innate powers. Steiner hoped to restore inner power to words in the dramas. He stated that in the four plays he attempted to lead sounds back into their rhythmical, musical, plastic birthright lost long ago.

We know specifically how Steiner felt about the use of sounds in three speeches from ***Portal of Initiation***. In the seventh scene the three soul forces of Maria speak: Philia, Luna, and Astrid. Steiner wanted the sounds of this scene to express the spirituality of the ancient languages. Philia is the character who "lives purely in the vocalic-spiritual element." The consonants are in the speech only to remind the audience that this is speech, not song. . . . Astrid is the bridge between Philia and Luna. Astrid is thus a mixture of vowels and consonants. . . . In the third character, according to Steiner, "we encounter weight," for while the speech is still vocalic, it begins to become quite consonantal in Luna's speech. . . . (pp. 56-7)

The whole scene lives "preeminently in the vocalic which leads one away from the physical world and takes one into the realm of spirit." . . . In performance such speeches are recited very slowly with strong emphasis on the vowel sounds.

The iambic rhythm of this scene is also intended to take the audience away from the physical into the spiritual. Much of the verse of all four plays is written in iambs. Steiner indicated that iambic lines should be spoken slowly, quietly, and gently for their effect to be felt. . . .

Different sounds have different spiritual impacts, however. Steiner classifies four categories of sounds by their effects upon the soul. First, there are the "blown sounds" (as indicated by the German letters *h, ch, i, sch, s, f,* and *w*), which allow the audience to *hear* the intoning of the sound. The "impact sounds" (*d, t, b, p, q, k, m,* and *n*) allow the audience to *see* the sound. The one "vibrating sound," the German *r*, is *felt in the arms and hands*. The "wave sound," the *l*, is *felt* also, this time *in the legs and feet*. (p. 57)

Eurythmy became a vital part of Anthroposophical performances of the Mystery Dramas. . . .

Eurythmy is used to represent nonhuman beings and supersensible soul states. Generally speaking, spirit characters appear on stage performing eurythmy forms as their lines are recited slowly offstage. (p. 62)

Eurythmy forms can be described, but it must be kept in mind that Rudolf Steiner warned they could not be understood intellectually. They must be experienced inwardly. Their nature is cosmic, and the feeling one gets in a performance is that for the speeches spoken no other movements are possible. They are in no way arbitrary movements. The etheric body rises out of the movements. It is the life force that, like lightning in the sky, never stands still. It is impossible to capture it motionless—in thought.

Sound is, of course, the basis for all the movements, which, in Steiner's words, "express their very essence exactly the same as is expressed by the sounds themselves as they are breathed into the air." If the shape that is made in the air by a sound could be frozen, one could see a gesture. These air gestures are taken into the body to present the visible sounds of eurythmy. The movement primarily affects the hands and the arms. The reason is, of course, spiritual. The feet and legs tie Mankind to the earth, and in the feet is expressed the principle that human suffering is drawn from the weight of the earth. On the other hand, the joy and freedom of the spirit expresses itself in the arms and hands, which reveal the life of the soul.

Each sound brings to the spirit a specific inner feeling. No matter what language one speaks, allowing for slight variations of sound from language to language, sounds always mean the same things. The materialistic expression of language is only the veneer that distracts us from the soul states we are capable of perceiving. As was mentioned above, the vowel expresses inner feelings and the consonants are imitations of the outside world. The vowel is spiritual while the consonant is material. Moreover, the Dionysian vowels, *a, i,* and *o,* are especially expressive of the feelings within the soul.

The vowels can be described by the inner states they represent. When *a* is spoken, speakers send out a part of their being: the feeling of wonder. Whenever a person speaks the sound *a* in a word, the feeling of wonder is expressed. The *e* sound expresses the fact that something has happened to the speaker, but he or she has confronted it and resisted.

The vowel *i* is the simple assertion of self. *O* is similar to *a* in the wonder it expresses, but at the same time *o* means that the speaker is in an intelligent relationship to the thing that evokes wonder. And *u* chills the soul. It is the opposite of the *i* sound, for *u* means the speaker is pulling back rather than asserting selfhood.

The consonants are more solid. (pp. 62-3)

Some consonants are very mysterious. For example, the German *w* (English *v*) expresses the need to move. It expresses the feeling of a nomad's tent or a shelter in the forest. Its nomadic quality makes it a favorite letter for alliteration, Steiner believed. The *s* sound is understood only when one can "penetrate the inmost nature of another being." And *f* speaks of wisdom. (p. 64)

Since eurythmy is visible speech, remember that each sound is represented by a specific movement. Each one seeks to express physically what the sound expresses audibly. The German sounds, as Steiner described their meanings for both drama and eurythmy, are summarized this way:

a wonder, amazement; admiration.
b to wrap around, to envelop, to house.
c, z the quality of lightness.
d to indicate; ponderousness, gravity.
e to be affected by something and to withstand it.
f *thou* knowest that I am.
g an inner strengthening of the self.
h rapture, delight.
i the assertion of self; joy, curiosity.
k mastered by the spirit.
l matter overcome by form.
m to be in agreement; imitation plus understanding.
n contempt, disdain.
o wonder in an intelligent relationship to something; sympathy.
r rolling, revolving; inner excitement.
s penetration of the inmost nature of another being.
sch disappearing, moving out of sight.
t the streaming downward of forces from above.
u becoming stiffened or chilled; anxiety.
v low spirits.
w to seek moving shelter.

The meaning of these sounds is meant to be taken literally. Steiner believed that they were true meanings and that in former ages all speech reflected these qualities rather than materialistic meanings. To the critics who said that the various languages had different words for things, Steiner answered that there is no conflict. For example, the Germans speak of the head as *Kopf;* the sounds express the roundness of the head. On the other hand, the Italian word, *testa,* expresses the idea that the head sits atop the shoulders and speaks. If the spirit behind the Italian culture had wished to express the roundness of the head, they also would use the word *Kopf.*

By combining the meanings of sounds, one discovers the true meaning of words. (pp. 64-5)

The specific movements prescribed for the soul states expressed by the vowels can be described briefly. The *a* is expressed by stretching both arms outward, as if grasping for something in two different directions. The muscles are stretched. Steiner felt the *a* should be expressed as quickly as possible after the sound that preceded it. The idea the performer must hold is that he is being created, determined by the cosmos—from two different directions.

The *e* gesture is the touching together of two limbs. The performer must feel that something has just been withstood. In the body, two crossed lines are formed. There are several variations. The arms or legs may be crossed, or one finger may touch another. And one may even get the right feeling if one crosses the eyes, consciously crossing the two lines of vision of the right and left eyes.

The *i* also forces action in two different directions, but, as opposed to the *a,* the energy goes from the center outward, away from the performer. The energy begins inside the heart and flows out through the arm, both arms, or through the legs. The *i* is expressed in the eyes when a performer consciously looks more through one eye than the other. The one active eye and the one passive eye give the feeling of *i.*

For *o,* the arms are very rounded throughout the movement, and they are kept flexible. "In *o,*" Steiner taught, "we have the movement whereby the world experiences something through man himself, for in this movement man lays hold of something belonging to the outer world." ***(Eurythmy as Visible Speech.)***

And for *u,* the arms are held close together or against the body. The legs are held together tightly to express *u.*

Gestures for a couple of consonants can be mentioned. The *d* sound expresses a raying outward and is a pointing gesture. The feeling is "*there* is something; *there* is something else." But there must be a certain harmony with the two arms; one must definitely reach a certain point before the other. The arm that moves first moves to its position more quickly. The movement for *g* expresses the warding off of everything that is external, a protective gesture.

Eurythmy can express things other than sounds—punctuation and mood, for example. Punctuation can be physicalized by a quiet pause and frozen gesture. The movement for the exclamation point, comma, or question mark may be inserted among the sounds. Usually the movement of a sentence is continuous, but moods such as devotion, liveliness, mirth, inwardness, and lovableness have standardized forms. Devotion, expressed with arms close to the body, bent upward from the elbows, could be used in a poem or dramatic passage. The gesture is used before and after the recitation. Or, in a very devout piece, before and after each verse. (p. 65)

The movement pattern made on the stage expresses soul states. The three categories—namely, thinking, feeling, and willing—are represented respectively by straight lines, curved and straight lines mixed, and curved lines only. In ***The Guardian of the Threshold*** in Dornach, the character Ahriman moves through a pattern of only straight lines in scene six. . . . As the embodiment of intellect, his movement shows absolutely definite thought. In the same scene, Lucifer moves only in curved lines, the luciferic force of self-will. A combination of straight lines and curved lines is used in Dornach in the second scene of ***The Soul's Awakening*** for the feeling passage of the gnomes. (p. 66)

A performance of Steiner's eurythmyc communication. Rudolf Steiner Publications/Garber Communications, Inc.

Eurythmy was a great breakthrough for the performance of Steiner's dramas. The presentation of supersensible beings was very important to him. He felt the spirits, gnomes, sylphs, soul forces, and other beings presented themselves as convincingly to the soul as physical beings presented themselves to the senses.

One must not take the spirit beings in Steiner's work to be symbols or allegories. Steiner sternly warned his audience about this in program notes. Spirits are every bit as real as the human beings in the play. The main difference is that onstage spirits are necessarily performed by real human beings. Eurythmy allowed the pure spirit more freedom on the stage.

Psychic events are presented in the plays—what goes on in Johannes' meditations, for example—but even these do not present symbolical scenes. (p. 67)

Steiner has ideas about how to act emotions on the stage. In directing actors, he first presented a spiritual explanation behind a mood. He then presented a specific, but simple, mental state to induce the right spirit state. The feeling then was to transform the body and the face of the performer: these physical expressions are cataloged. Steiner called them "mimes." Anthroposophical performers understand their emotions at a high level of consciousness.

Rudolf Steiner's prescription for weeping is an example. He explained what is behind weeping, how to induce the proper weeping mood, and then how the weeping manifests itself into the weeping mime. When Mankind cries, the ether body puts a painful hold on the physical body. The soul tries to counterbalance the force of the ether body's grip by reinforcing the astral body (which is connected with the liquid part of the being). So the shedding of tears is a relief of the painful restriction.

To induce the same state in the theatre, the actor of course begins with sound. He must hold his attention on the sound *a*. With a full feeling for *a*, as learned in eurythmy and speech training, the performer can concentrate on what *a* does to the eyes, the nose, the face, and the body. Once the awareness is complete, the performer puts a few drops of water on the face, and there is weeping. "Yes," Rudolf Steiner explained, "it will then be weeping; no need at all for real tears to well up from within."

The other mimes call for the same priming by sounds and then bringing the induced feeling into the eyes. A few examples:

Laughter:	concentrate on the sounds *o e o e o e*.
Attention:	hold inside the sounds *a a a*.
Surprise:	hold eyes wide open, intone sound *i i i;* then stop; the feeling is moved to the eyes for "dumbfounded amazement."
Terror:	hold eyes closed; intone *u*, and stop; carry the feeling to the eyes. . . .

These mimes are not learned from the outside in. First one must have a firm grasp on the inner meanings of the sounds.

Steiner sometimes worked with actors to begin from taste sensations to perform characters. Carrying a vinegar taste, for example, induces a sour face. Wormwood tastes and sugary tastes bring out resentment or cringing flattery, respectively. Steiner said that in the ancient Mysteries performers literally ingested vinegar or wormwood to perform these feelings. (pp. 70-1)

Color is exceedingly important in Rudolf Steiner's concepts of theatre. . . . To Steiner, all theatrical style depends on color and lighting. Line and form are of little importance. Steiner's sets tended to negate walls in favor of colored surfaces for the play of light. . . .

In both eurythmy and drama, colors assist the audience in seeing the true nature of sounds. Lighting in eurythmy performances is specifically keyed to the predominant sound in the passage. The colors also help the performers feel the sounds. Steiner charts the colors of the vowels:

a	blue violet
e	greenish yellow
i	red-yellow-orange
o	reddish yellow
u	blue green

(p. 72)

In eurythmy, a basic dress is worn with one or two veils added, usually of different colors. The veil expresses the aura. Its fluid movements take one's attention away from the physical body and emphasize the formed speech.

Movement and feeling are related by color. The color of the dress relates to the color of the veil(s) in this way:

$$\frac{\text{dress color}}{\text{veil color}} :: \frac{\text{movement}}{\text{feeling}}$$

(p. 73)

In the Mystery Dramas, characters in their human forms generally wear everyday costumes. Spirits wear dresses and flowing veils. . . .

Light plays upon the colors of the sets and costumes. The color of the set expresses the overall mood (and sounds) of the scene. Lighting changes indicate the changing moods of the characters. Lighting indicates internal states; painting shows external moods. Those who have seen a performance in Dornach stress that no photograph can capture the excitement of the constantly changing lighting effects on the vivid colors of the sets. Steiner urged caution in these changes, however, stating that, for example, if one has a violet set, one must be very careful when a character's mood changes to scarlet. An inharmonious effect must be avoided. (p. 74)

Robb Creese, "Anthroposophical Performance," in The Drama Review *(copyright © 1978,* The Drama Review; *reprinted by permission of MIT Press), Vol. 22, No. 2, June, 1978, pp. 45-74.*

PATRICK GRANT (essay date 1982)

[In the following excerpt, Grant examines the influence of Steiner's thought on Owen Barfield, an English novelist, critic, and philosopher who is also a longstanding follower of Anthroposophy. For a discussion by Barfield of Steiner's ideas, see the excerpt dated 1966.]

Owen Barfield insists on his debt to Rudolf Steiner, and regrets that people are prejudiced against Anthroposophy. It is probably fair to say that those of Barfield's readers who have not come to him through Steiner do proceed more reluctantly to Anthroposophy than Barfield would like. There are, however, good reasons to take the disciple's advice and read the master: first, anyone interested in Barfield is likely to be intrigued and instructed by Steiner's development of many questions with which Barfield also deals; second, reading Steiner can help us to appreciate not only similarities, but differences, and thereby clarify the special character of the disciple's thinking.

The fact that Barfield is a sensitive literary critic and an accomplished Coleridge scholar has of course served to deflect attention from his Anthroposophy. It is tempting, even, to view the interest in Steiner rather as one views Yeats's interest in the Order of the Golden Dawn, and to interpret it as the eccentric formal underpinning for an imaginative achievement which is more considerable than the ideas from which it is built. An obvious rejoinder is that Barfield is not known mainly as a poet; in reading him we encounter *arguments,* the end point of which is, simply, the Anthroposophical truth. Still, the dialogue between the man of English letters and the Anthroposophist cannot be put aside altogether; the fact remains that Barfield's play of imagination and skill as an essayist do make him interesting to readers who will not persist with ***Occult Science, an Outline.*** On the one hand it seems we must stop short of saying Anthroposophy is not a central concern; on the other, that all Barfield's virtue emanates from the master.

A possible middle-of-the-road solution might suggest that Barfield popularises ideas which in their original form are too difficult for most readers. Yet here again the question presses: what does a populariser *do* to the original? What did Paul do to Jesus, Shakespeare to Cinthio? The very plea, for instance, which Barfield makes for open-mindedness to Anthroposophy can show how difficult it is to strike a right balance on this question of derivation and originality. In the introduction to *Romanticism Comes of Age* Barfield calls explicitly for an end to prejudice against Steiner, and in *Unancestral Voice* Flume the scientist, Burgeon the spokesman, and the wonderful Meggid, who visits him with instruction and insight, repeatedly keep before us the value of thinking "without prejudice." One might feel that in *Unancestral Voice* Barfield continues to call attention to people's unfairness to Anthroposophy, the same unfairness which he specifically regrets in *Romanticism Comes of Age*.

Brief acquaintance with Steiner's writings, however, reveals that "openmindedness" is a virtue he especially values, and he means by it the "integrity of thought with which Natural Science is imbued," . . . a principle which he holds basic to the "method" itself of occult science. It is difficult, here, to separate or even clearly distinguish Barfield's special pleading *for* Steiner (whose ideas need to be approached with an open mind) from direct promulgation *of* Steiner (for whom openmindedness is a kind of mental training). Nor is the point incidental, for Barfield has much to say in *What Coleridge Thought* . . . on the value of a genuinely methodical approach to nature based on true scientific spirit. Barfield and Steiner, in short, share a conviction that the achievements of the scientific revolution can assist us in entering the realms of spirit. The "occultist knows," says Steiner, "that he can found no science without the integrity of thought with which Natural Science is imbued." . . . Beneath a superficially innocuous gesture for tolerance we can thus detect an extensive foundation of shared thought.

So it is with a good number of Barfield's leading ideas: even when they appear as the speculations of an unprejudiced mind engaged in open enquiry, they can be found indebted to Anthroposophical teachings. For instance, Barfield and Steiner agree that in ancient times human consciousness was different, and we need to re-imagine the condition of past thought to know how the human mind experienced the world as spiritually vibrant and filled with a soul-life which we have grown gradually accustomed to locating within the human head. "When man received impressions from supersensible worlds in olden time," writes Steiner, "they felt like forces influencing and impelling him from an external spiritual world": for the primitive mind, writes Barfield, "there stands behind the phenomena, *and on the other side of them from me,* a represented which is of the same nature as me." Both men are concerned alike to impress on us that humanity in "olden times" experienced the world full of spirit akin to humanity's own spiritual nature. Of course, such participatory experience is unself-conscious, and with the growth and development of the human ego comes an increasing separation from nature.

There were, we learn, three periods of special importance in the evolution of ego: the moment at which the Christian era began, the scientific revolution of the seventeenth century, and the Romantic movement. The first is important, Steiner says, as the "center of gravity," the moment at which the true direction of man's evolution is revealed to man himself. The Mystery of Golgotha shows that through the death of the body, spirit lives, and we discover the "true inner content" of our human story. With Christ, the human ego is reborn, achieving autonomy, but to a proportionate degree becoming shut off from direct participation in the worlds of soul and spirit. . . . However, ego thereby is prepared to set out on the immense task of spiritualising, by its own experiences and achievements, the outer world itself. . . . Barfield frequently repeats this line of argument, insisting, for instance, that Christianity has enabled us to speak the word "I" in a uniquely authentic and responsible manner: "Had Christ not come to earth, individual human beings would never have been able to utter the word 'I' at all."

Barfield agrees also with Steiner that vestiges of the old 'participatory' consciousness remained in the thinking of the Middle Ages, but were banished with the rise of critical philosophy. The scientific revolution resulted, says Barfield, in a change in our " 'reality principle' or common sense, or what you will." By this, he means that the polarity of subject and object achieved a high degree of clarity, that nature was disenchanted by the critical gaze of the rationalists and empiricists, and objects were held real insofar as they were found 'hard' and measurable. Natural science, as Steiner puts it, "has banished from the field of sensible phenomena all that does not pertain thereto but is to be found only in man's inner being." In effecting this result, science has promoted the evolution of human consciousness to a point where the development now ought to precipitate a "backlash into perception of spirit," and, thereby, lead to "a methodical development of authentic inner experience."

Steiner teaches that in the story of such a development the Eighth Ecumenical Council of Constantinople played a significant and unfortunate part. By promulgating the doctrine that man consists of soul and body, the Council dangerously modified an age-old teaching that human beings are constituted of body, soul and spirit. A consequent insistence, in Western theology, on the body-soul duality encouraged an eventual, debilitating rationalist preoccupation with the dualism of mind and matter. The *tertium quid,* spirit, necessary to explain nature's transformation and man's interpenetration with nature was suppressed. This theory is echoed also in Barfield, as is another highly particular idea of Steiner's, namely that the 1870s marked a crucial phase in the influence of the Archangel Michael upon human evolution in contention with the opposed but insiduously co-operative forces of Lucifer and Ahriman.

Finally, Steiner began his career as a distinguished student and editor of Goethe, and in Romanticism found an appreciation of how, through imagination, the dichotomy of subject and object is to be overcome. Barfield retains Steiner's interest in Goethe, and has supplemented it with a study of Coleridge. But in Steiner alone among the authors he has read, says Barfield, there is a clear indication of how Romanticism must develop. In the very apprehension of the process of imagination as a means of overcoming the dichotomy of soul and body, the mind is beckoned to examine, systematically and clearly, its own spiritual, purely noetic activity.

How then are we to assess what Barfield *adds* to Steiner, if, as we now claim, the indebtedness is extensive and deep? First, it is important to point out that Barfield did not begin as an Anthroposophist, but had gone some way in exploring his own ideas on the evolution of consciousness before he encountered Steiner. The main lines of the story are clear in a lecture on "The Origin of Language": Barfield's distinctive interest in metaphor, lyric poetry, and the immaterial origins of language had arisen independently of Anthroposophy, in which he became interested in 1921 or 1922. For "quite a long time," Barfield tells us, the "two processes" (of developing his own ideas and of exploring Anthroposophy) "went on side by side," working upon one another, yet distinct. Consequently, despite the indebtedness to Steiner of a book like *Saving the Appearances,* Barfield says it is "not an exposition of Anthroposophy, and because there is so much of the Subject's own in it, the full extent of its indebtedness is very likely not apparent. . . . The two are so inextricably mixed." One thing Barfield adds to Steiner is, therefore, simply the fact of an independent reflection on connections between lyric poetry and the evolution of language, and this leads to a second point, namely that Barfield is preoccupied with certain aspects of Anthroposophy more than with others. For instance, he all but ignores Steiner's social and educational theory and concentrates on teachings which lie on the border between philosophy and psychology. He is interested, as we see, in the evolution of consciousness, but concentrates on its historical phase rather than, for instance, on the 'Akashic records' which Steiner describes as revealed to spiritual perception, and which tell, among other things, of three incarnations of planet earth, of its development through embodiments designated as Saturn, Sun, and Moon, before arriving at its present phase, preceding the future Vulcan evolution.

A further difference which almost immediately strikes the reader who compares these two authors is the fact that Steiner is characteristically clear, explicit, and assertive at points where Barfield is not. Thinking should be "strong and vigorous and to the point," Steiner says, and his writing strives for the requisite "wakefulness." He recalls, for instance, an inaugural lecture by a famous professor of literature and history, which concluded with the words "You see, gentlemen, I have led you into a forest of question marks." Steiner reflects: "I pictured it to myself: a forest of question marks? Just think: a forest of *question marks*!" The Professor's metaphor is evasive and obscure; by contrast, on hard questions Steiner is prepared to stand and be counted, and rarely fails to give an answer, even, at times, with dumbfounding explicitness. The human head, we are told, is "a transformed animal shape": it is the oldest part of the human body, and the rest of the human organism was added "at a time when the simultaneous development of the animals occurred." Seen from spirit land, "a red stone is experienced with a greenish and a green stone with a reddish hue." At a certain phase of evolution the physical body is "intermingled with a portion of the retarded Saturn nature, and here the activity of the Fire Spirits is at work. In what the Fire Spirits achieve in this retarded Saturn nature, we have to recognise the forerunners of the present-day sense organs of Earth men."

It is not my purpose to call in question the content of such assertions, or to underestimate Steiner's stylistic range, only to confirm that, characteristically, as the founder of Anthroposophy for which he makes direct claims, he confronts us in this direct manner, even when his assertions challenge common sense. This is not to say he does not often write with compelling insight and real depth of understanding: indeed, coming to terms with antinomous responses—sceptical and enthusiastic—within one's self is the major challenge in reading him. Where, then, does one draw the line between assertion and suggestion? Characteristically, Steiner does not fudge.

With Barfield it is otherwise: he fudges all the time, and he does so as a literary man might be expected to, through metaphor and the subtle effects of language and structure. When Barfield presents us with challenging ideas, he tantalises common sense in order to do so. He prefers not to assault it directly in Steiner's fashion, because he does not share Steiner's direct intuition of the particular geography of the spirit world, and he tends, as we have seen, to avoid those aspects of Steiner's teaching which seem insufficiently anchored in ordinary experience. In short, Barfield frequently relies on effects akin to the "forest of question marks" which Steiner abjured in the learned professor. The sensibility which early appreciated the "wonder" and "strangeness" of poetic diction did not afterwards relinquish its fine-tuned responsiveness. In his introduction to *The Case for Anthroposophy,* Barfield admires "effective precision," but calls also for "requisite finesse," . . . and through this latter quality especially emerges what is distinctive in his writing. (pp. 113-17)

Not surprisingly, the work in which Barfield addresses a non-Anthroposophical audience and yet expresses the widest variety of Anthroposophical ideas, is also the work where he is most plainly a literary practitioner. In *Unancestral Voice* the protagonist is Burgeon, who is visited by the Meggid, servant of the Archangel Michael, and instructed, through a series of encounters and arguments with various characters, in the truths of Anthroposophy. It is not hard to see that Burgeon is Barfield's spokesman, and not too much to claim that the Meggid speaks with the wisdom of Steiner. Nonetheless, Barfield does address us indirectly, and we participate in Burgeon's journey towards higher understanding through a series of arguments on such subjects as teenage vandalism, the penal system, D. H. Lawrence, Buddhism, historiography, and particle physics. Because the fictive structure is preserved, Anthroposophical teachings on Arhiman, Gabriel and Michael, on thinking without physical support, the developments of the 1870s, and the Council of Constantinople are allowed to surface for our consideration, carefully placed in the dialogue so that our suspension of disbelief is encouraged while we are drawn, with Burgeon, to reflect on the boundaries of thinking and on what is implied by our encounter with them.

And yet, the fiction is not *quite* granted autonomy. The work of a sixteenth-century Rabbi, Joseph Karo, lawyer and mystic, is picked up by Burgeon who discovers there the record, in diary form, of a series of visitations from a figure called the "Maggid." The historical curiosity of Karo's account, claiming to be an *actual* venture in experience, helps to build a bridge (as Barfield intends it should) between the fiction of

Unancestral Voice and the world of fact. We are thereby discouraged from dismissing all this as just made up. The technique of course is also Plato's, who deploys the legendary, dead Socrates in much the same fashion. So too the numerous whimsical connections, delivered especially by the Meggid, receive their full flavour when we acknowledge how closely behind Burgeon stands Barfield, wryly aware of his own problems as an author: "Do not interrupt. Listen;" . . . "Come, said the Meggid, *you* are not blind, but only ignorant;" . . . "Whatever else I may accuse you of," says Chevalier, "it won't be of being a bore;" . . . "At this point he [Burgeon] realised he was going too fast;" . . . "He knew he could not speak of this without the risk of being avoided as a crank or a lunatic." . . . Such remarks combine good humour with perception of the difficulties involved in giving voice to challenging ideas. Fiction is one way of negotiating the difficulties, but we must be aware that fiction is a means to an end. Our initial resistance to bar assertion, however, *can* be undermined imaginatively, and by the encounter with a quality of thinking which we respect for its learning, its awareness of human problems both current and perennial, its good sense and clarity, as well as for its literary accomplishment and ability to lead us to the edges of thought and thereby to the possibility of some direct experience of spiritual life. Barfield's skill resides in such a combination of effects, combined with a special tact in knowing where to stop: of how to accommodate his reading of Steiner to matters of current concern without activating anti-Anthroposophical prejudice. In so doing, Barfield is Steiner's most discerning disciple, but in the discernment lies a quality distinctively his own. It consists in part in a most teasing deficiency combined with a most provocative suggestion that he knows, and we can find out for ourselves, how that deficiency is to be repaired. Such deficiency, we might reflect, is an inherent characteristic of the beautiful: that in which we delight, but which draws us on. (pp. 122-23)

Patrick Grant, "The Quality of Thinking: Owen Barfield As Literary Man and Anthroposophist," in VII: An Anglo-American Literary Review *(© published by Wheaton College, Illinois, March, 1982), Vol. 3, March, 1982, pp. 113-23.*

SAUL BELLOW (essay date 1983)

[Recipient of the Noble Prize in literature in 1976, Bellow is one of the most prominent figures in contemporary American fiction. Among his most celebrated novels are The Adventures of Augie March *(1953),* Herzog *(1964), and* Humboldt's Gift *(1975). Bellow's stature is due to his supreme achievement as an artist who upholds the traditional moral values of humanism and literary conventions of Realism, thus opposing the trend toward a modern literature that is nihilistic in temperament and experimental by conscious design. Two of Bellow's most esteemed qualities as an author are his profound facility for humor and a narrative realism which, in the words of critic Allen Guttman, "reproduces in written language the excited, disorderly buzz and bloom of life itself." Critics find that novels such as* Augie March *and* Herzog *advance a basically affirmative sense of life and a belief in human dignity, attitudes that at the same time are thoroughly grounded in the complex and disturbing realities of the modern world. While recognizing the same world that many modern authors take for granted as declining and evil, Bellow has produced a body of work based on the possibility that "there may be truths on the side of life." In his novel* Humboldt's Gift *Bellow presented aspects of Steiner's teachings. The following excerpt is taken from his introduction to a translation of a volume of lectures by Steiner.]*

The audience attending this series of lectures [***The Boundaries of Natural Science***] in 1920 was at once informed by Steiner that he proposed to consider the connections between natural science and social renewal.

Everyone agrees, he says, that such a renewal requires a renewal of our thinking (one must remember that he was speaking of the groping and soul-searching that followed the great and terrible war of 1914-18), yet not everyone "imagines something clear and distinct when speaking in this way."

Steiner then sketches rapidly the effects of the scientific world-view on the modern social order. Scientific progress has made us very confident of our analytical powers. Inanimate nature, we are educated to believe, will eventually become transparently intelligible. It will yield all its secrets under scientific examination, and we will be able to describe it with mathematical lucidity. After we have conquered the inorganic we will proceed to master the organic world by the same means.

The path of scientific progress however has not been uniformly smooth. Steiner reminds us that by the end of the 19th century doubts concerning the origins of scientific knowledge had arisen within the scientific community itself, and in a famous and controversial lecture the physiologist Du Bois Reymond asked the question, How does consciousness arise out of material processes? What is the source of the consciousness with which we examine the outer world? To this Du Bois Reymond answers, *Ignorabimus*—we shall never know.

In this *Ignorabimus* Steiner finds a parallel to an earlier development, that of medieval Scholasticism. Scholastic thinking had made its way to the limits of the supersensible world. Modern natural science has also reached a limit. This limit is delineated by two concepts: "matter"—which is everywhere assumed to be within the sensory realm but nowhere actually to be found—and consciousness, which is assumed to originate within the same world, "although no one can comprehend how." Can we fathom the fact of consciousness with explanations conceived in observing external nature? Steiner argues that we cannot. He suggests that scientific research is entangling itself in a web, and that only outside this web can we find the real world. The great victories of science have subdued our minds. We accept the all pervading scientific method. It has transformed the earth. Nevertheless it seems incapable of understanding its own deepest sources. Scientific method as we of the modern world define it can bring us only to the *Ignorabimus* because it is powerless to explain the consciousness that directs it. In our study of nature, and by means of our concept of matter, we have made everything very clear, but this clarity does not give us Man. Him we have lost. And the lucidity to which we owe our great successes in the study of the external world is rejected by consciousness itself. For in the depths of consciousness there lies a will, and this will revolts when lucid science tries to "think" Man as it thinks external nature.

To conclude from this that Steiner is "anti-science" would be a great mistake. To him science is a necessary, indeed indispensable stage in the development of the human spirit. The scientific examination of the external world awakens consciousness to clear concepts and it is by means of clear conceptual thinking that we become fully human. Spiritual development requires a full understanding of pure thought, and pure thought is thought devoid of sensory impressions. "Countless philosophers have expounded the view that pure thinking does not exist, but is bound to contain traces, however diluted, of sense perception. A strong impression is left that philosophers who maintain this have never really studied mathematics, or gone into the difference between analytical and empirical physics,'' Steiner writes. Mathematical thought is thought detached from the sense world, and as it is entirely based upon rules of reason that are universal it offers spiritual communion to mankind, as well as a union with reality. It is moreover a *free* activity. Spiritual training, says Steiner, reveals it to be not only sense-free but also brain-free. The operations of thought are directed by spiritual powers. Pure thinking leads to the discovery of freedom and leads us to the realm of spirit. And Steiner tells us explicitly that out of sense-free thinking ''there can flow impulses to moral action. . . . One experiences pure spirit by observing, by actually observing how moral forces flow into sense-free thinking.'' This is something very different from mystical experience, for it is a result of spiritual training, of a sort of scientific discipline through which we discover more organs of knowledge than are available to those who limit themselves, as modern philosophers do, to scientific orthodoxy and to ordinary consciousness. (pp. vii-ix)

[Steiner] is a modern thinker. What distinguishes him from most others is his refusal to stop at what he calls ''the boundary of the material world.'' And how does one pass beyond this boundary? By a discipline that takes us from ordinary consciousness and familiarizes us with consciousness of another kind, by finding the path that leads us into Imagination. ''It is possible to pursue this path in a way consonant with Western life,'' he writes, ''if we attempt to surrender ourselves completely to the world of outer phenomena, so that we allow them to work upon us without thinking about them, but still perceiving them. In ordinary waking life, you will agree, we are constantly perceiving, but actually in the very process of doing so we are continually saturating our percepts with concepts; in scientific thinking we interweave percepts and concepts entirely systematically, building up systems of concepts. . . . One can become capable of such acute inner activity that one can exclude and suppress conceptual thinking from the process of perception and surrender oneself to bare percepts.'' This is not a depreciation of thought. Rather, it releases the imagination. One ''acquires a potent psychic force 'when one is able' to absorb the external world free from concepts.'' Steiner says, ''Man is given over to the external world continually, from birth onwards. Nowadays this giving-over of oneself to the external world is held to be nothing but abstract perception or abstract cognition. This is not so. We are surrounded by a world of color, sound and warmth and by all kinds of sensory impressions.'' The cosmos communicates with us also through color, sound and warmth. ''Warmth is something other than warmth; light something other than light in the physical sense; sound is something other than physical sound. Through our sensory impressions we are conscious only of what I would term external sound and external color. And when we surrender ourselves to nature we do not encounter the ether-waves, atoms and so on of which modern physics and physiology dream; rather, it is spiritual forces that are at work, forces that fashion us between birth and death into what we are as human beings.'' I have thought it best not to interpose myself but to allow Steiner to speak for himself, for he is more than a thinker, he is an initiate and only he is able to communicate what he has experienced. The human mind, he tells us, must learn to will pure thinking, but it must learn also how to set conceptual thinking aside and to live within the phenomena. (pp. xi-xii)

Saul Bellow, in a foreword to The Boundaries of Natural Science *by Rudolf Steiner, translated by Frederick Amrine and Konrad Oberhuber (copyright © 1983 by Anthroposophic Press), Anthroposophic Press, 1983, pp. vii-xiii.*

ADDITIONAL BIBLIOGRAPHY

Adams, David. ''Architecture and Metamorphosis: The Buildings of Rudolf Steiner.'' *ReVision* 6, No. 2 (Fall 1983): 48-55.

Technical disquisition on the architectural features and the philosophic ideas contributing to the structure of both the first and second Goetheanum.

Allen, Paul Marshall. Foreword to *The Philosophy of Spiritual Activity: Fundamentals of a Modern View of the World,* by Rudolf Steiner, translated by Rita Stebbing, pp. 7-10. Blauvelt, N.Y.: Steinerbooks, 1980.

Introduction to Steiner's *The Philosophy of Spiritual Activity,* stating that the book's intended purpose is ''to *awaken* in the reader a new experience of the world of ideas.''

Belyi, Andrei. *Anthroposophy and Russia.* Translated by Linda Maloney. New York: St. George Publications, 1983, 43 p.

Originally published in the German periodical *Die Drei* in July and August of 1922. Russian poet and novelist Bely, a devout follower of Steiner, finds in Anthroposophy the hope and promise of a new Russian culture.

Harwood, A. C. ''Rudolph Steiner Schools.'' In *Education and Philosophy,* edited by George Z. F. Bereday and Joseph A. Lauwerys, pp. 483-90. Yonkers-on-Hudson, N.Y.: World Book Co., 1957.

Describes the methods of the Rudolph Steiner (Waldorf) schools.

Hemleben, Johannes. *Rudolf Steiner: A Documentary Biography.* Surrey: Henry Goulden, 1975, 176 p.

Biography employing lengthy quotations from Steiner's autobiography. Hemleben reproduces many photographs and manuscript pages.

Kotzsch, Ronald E. ''The Legacy of Rudolf Steiner.'' *East-West Journal* 14, No. 3 (March 1984): 66-71.

Provides an introduction to the range of Steiner's accomplishments and briefly outlines a history of the Anthroposophical movement.

Landau, Rom. ''Occult Truth: Rudolph Steiner'' and ''The Testament of Rudolph Steiner.'' In his *God Is My Adventure,* pp. 45-83, pp. 312-41. London: Ivor Nicholson and Watson, 1935.

Provides biographical information and anecdotes about Steiner, focusing on his spiritual development. The second chapter cited examines the author's investigation of Anthroposophical methods of agriculture, medicine, education, and art.

Lehrs, Ernst. *Man or Matter: Introduction to a Spiritual Understanding of Nature on the Basis of Goethe's Method of Training Observation and Thought.* London: Faber and Faber, 1951, 378 p.*

Recounts in the introduction to the book how the author became acquainted with and inspired by Rudolf Steiner. Mention is made throughout the book of Steiner.

Pehnt, Wolfgang. ''The Architecture of Rudolf Steiner.'' In his *Expressionist Architecture,* pp. 137-48. New York: Praeger Press, 1973.

Technical examination of Steiner's architecture.

Wachsmuth, Guenther. *The Life and Work of Rudolf Steiner.* Rev. ed. Translated by Olin D. Wannamaker and Reginald E. Raab. 1955. Reprint. Blauvelt, N.Y.: Steinerbooks, 594 p.

Biography examining in depth the last twenty-five years of Steiner's life. This biography is characterized by the translator as ''of inestimable value'' to ''all who will wish seriously to acquaint themselves with one of the most notable personalities of the modern world.''

Thomas (Clayton) Wolfe

1900-1938

American novelist, short story and novella writer, essayist, dramatist, and poet.

Wolfe is considered one of the foremost American novelists of the twentieth century. In his four major novels—*Look Homeward, Angel; Of Time and the River; The Web and the Rock;* and *You Can't Go Home Again*—he took the facts of his own life and wove them into an epic celebration of the struggle of the lonely, sensitive, and artistic individual to find spiritual fulfillment in America. Containing intense and lyrical portrayals of life in both rural and urban America, Wolfe's novels are often compared to the poetry of Walt Whitman and are critically perceived as forming a single *künstlerroman,* evoking the spiritual isolation of an artist's progress toward personal and professional maturity.

Wolfe was born in Asheville, a city located in the mountains of North Carolina. His parents, who separated when Wolfe was a young boy, served as the models for some of his most intriguing characters and are considered to have been powerful influences on Wolfe's psychologically troubled adult life. His mother, the owner of a boarding house, was a devout, possessive woman who coddled Wolfe throughout his childhood, while his father was an insensitive, gregarious, hard-drinking stonecutter whose every emotion was expressed in an exaggerated manner. Extremely well read in world literature and considered a bright student, Wolfe, at the age of sixteen, entered the University of North Carolina, where he developed an interest in drama and prepared for a career as a playwright. Upon graduation Wolfe continued his education at Harvard, writing and producing plays as a member of George Pierce Baker's famous 47 Workshop, and studying English under John Livingston Lowes, a key influence. Lowes, who was at the time at work on his important critical study of Samuel Taylor Coleridge, *The Road to Xanadu,* propounded his thesis to his students that great literature is produced by the subconscious fusion of the author's literary influences, personal experiences, and imagination. Embracing Lowes's theory, Wolfe spent many hours at the Harvard library attempting to read every important work of world literature. After receiving a master's degree in 1922, he accepted a teaching post at New York University with the hope of having his plays accepted for production on Broadway. Unsuccessful in this endeavor and wearied by teaching, Wolfe resigned his position in 1925, determined to live entirely by his writing. Shortly after reaching this decision Wolfe met Aline Bernstein, a New York stage designer and a woman who became central to his personal life and career. During their five-year relationship, Bernstein provided Wolfe with the emotional and financial support that enabled him to write his first and what many critics consider his best novel, *Look Homeward, Angel.*

The acceptance of *Look Homeward, Angel* in 1928 by editor Maxwell E. Perkins of Charles Scribner's Sons initiated one of the most controversial editor-author relationships of the century. Confronted by the many reams of manuscript that formed the sprawling first draft of Wolfe's novel, Perkins—who had worked for several years with such major American authors as F. Scott Fitzgerald and Ernest Hemingway—recognized Wolfe as a literary genius, but as a genius unable to discern essential material from the inessential, and lacking the editorial self-discipline necessary to shape his work into cohesive, publishable form. With Wolfe's reluctant cooperation, the manuscript of "O Lost!" (as the work was at first titled) was extensively cut, and the resulting autobiographical novel was published in 1929 to wide popular and critical acclaim. In the persona of Eugene Gant, a sensitive young man from the mountain city of Altamont, Wolfe traced his own life story in *Look Homeward, Angel,* introducing his Wordsworthian vision of life as a lonely search for "a stone, a leaf, an unfound door": a sign that will rewaken his subconscious and reveal a world of fulfilling joy and purpose left behind at birth. Like all of Wolfe's novels, *Look Homeward, Angel* possesses an epic quality—every thought, feeling, and action is depicted as of monumental importance—and an all-encompassing empathy for humanity, inspired by the author's own attempts to read all, sense all, and experience all. In his 1930 Nobel acceptance speech, recognizing Wolfe as a significant new American author, Sinclair Lewis praised *Look Homeward, Angel* as a novel "worthy to be compared with the best in our literary production, a gargantuan creature with great gusto of life." Awash in lavish description, *Look Homeward, Angel* is narrated in a variety of styles ranging from Elizabethan lyricism to modern satiric rhetoric and stream of consciousness. The various styles

The Granger Collection, New York

reveal the influence upon Wolfe of many authors, notably Coleridge, William Wordsworth, Sherwood Anderson, and James Joyce.

After several years of directionless uncertainty, during which he was troubled by the highly emotional breakup of his relationship with Bernstein and moved to doubt his own abilities by the few unfavorable reviews of *Look Homeward, Angel,* Wolfe conceived of a multi-volume novel series titled "The October Fair," in which Eugene's story and that of his family would continue. His theme of the loneliness of the individual was expanded to include what he considered a universal quest: the search for a spiritual father, or "someone who can help you, save you, ease the burden for you." This theme, stemming from Wolfe's estrangement from his own father, surfaced in the turbulent, myth-ridden *Of Time and the River,* a massive novel that was culled by Perkins from several crates of manuscript composed and collected by the author during several years of intense creative activity. *Of Time and the River,* the second novel concerning Eugene Gant as well as the first (and, as it turned out, the last) segment of "The October Fair," was greeted with mixed reviews upon its appearance in 1935. While many critics admired the sheer power of Wolfe's novel, many by this time had come to object to Wolfe's self-obsessed epic stance, the thinly disguised autobiographical cast of his novels, and the increasing intrusion of the author's voice in the narrative. One critical essay in particular, Bernard DeVoto's "Genius Is Not Enough," infuriated Wolfe, as the critic accused him of utter dependence upon Perkins and "the assembly line at Scribner's" to give form to his lengthy novels. "For five years the artist pours out words 'like burning lava from a volcano'—with little or no idea what their purpose is, which book they belong in, what the relation of part to part is, what is organic and what is irrelevant, or what emphasis or coloration in the completed work of art is being served by the job at hand. Then Mr. Perkins decides these questions," wrote DeVoto, adding: "Worse still, the artist goes on writing till Mr. Perkins tells him the novel is finished." Stung by such criticism and recognizing that relations with Perkins had grown increasingly strained (due in great measure to Wolfe's suspicion that Perkins was a literary "conservative" who, like many critics, was trying to destroy his career), Wolfe left Scribner's in 1937, intent on proving to the critics—the "literary rubbish of sniffers, whiffers, and puny, poisonous apes" as he called them—that he was an artist dependent upon no one. Working now with editor Edward C. Aswell of Harper and Brothers, Wolfe announced the abandonment of his autobiographical mode and set to work on an "objective" novel. Writing of his business relationship with Aswell while thinking of the editor who had launched his career, Wolfe noted to a friend: "I think it's going to turn out to be a wonderful experience. . . . However, I am still a little sad about the past." But, he added, "You can't go home again, can you?"

In 1938 Wolfe left New York, his home since the early 1920s, for a tour of the western United States, leaving Aswell with a mass of manuscript consisting of all of his recent writings as well as portions deleted from his first two novels. While in the West, Wolfe contracted pneumonia, aggravating a long-dormant tubercular condition which led to his death shortly before his thirty-eighth birthday. After Wolfe's death his manuscript was honed by Aswell to form two complete novels and the fragment *The Hills Beyond,* a work considered of much less importance than the other two. Published in 1939 and 1940 respectively, *The Web and the Rock* and *You Can't Go Home Again* exhibit little evidence of Wolfe's promised progression to objectivity, although they do contain a powerful, more mature retelling of Wolfe's life story, with Eugene Gant now in the guise of George "Monk" Webber, and with Aline Bernstein appearing in the character of Esther Jack: the course of their love affair is one of the highlights of the two companion novels. In *The Web and the Rock* and *You Can't Go Home Again* Wolfe's artistic scope expanded from the individual's quest for fulfillment to include social concerns such as the ominous rise of the Nazis in Germany, an event witnessed by Wolfe while traveling in Europe during the 1930s. Through a letter from Webber to editor Foxhall Edwards (Maxwell Perkins) in *You Can't Go Home Again,* Wolfe explained his outlook on life, writing: "Man was born to live, to suffer and die, and what befalls him is a tragic lot. There is no denying this in the final end. *But we must, dear Fox, deny it all along the way.*"

Aswell spoke for many critics when he stated that Wolfe "really wrote only one book, and that runs to some 4,000 printed pages comprising the total of his works. The individual titles that bear his name are only so many numbered volumes of this master book. The parts should be thought of as having been brought out separately merely for convenience." Together the four complete novels trace Wolfe's own beginnings in an isolated mountaintop city, his college days, and his struggles to succeed as a writer, while some of his short stories and *The Hills Beyond* tell of Wolfe's ancestry as far back as the early nineteenth century. His autobiographical fiction reveals—as does the story of his alternately affectionate and cruel relationship with Bernstein and with Perkins—a man torn between the desire for intensely close communion with others and the impersonal drive to painfully distance himself from those closest to him: to assert his sense of spiritual independence in order to experience as much as he could of American life and culture. In each of his works of fiction Wolfe strove, in part, to capture and bring to life a portion of America as he had experienced it, relating the vastness of the country to the vastness of his artistic ambition.

While some critics see in Wolfe's work the high-flown artiness of an eternal adolescent—one who continually, in his life and work, cast himself in the role of a tragic martyr to the cause of Art—others contend, as Wolfe himself had written of his father, that "though a man's work may be as full of flaws as a Swiss cheese it will somehow continue to endure if only it has fire." Most critics today concur with C. Hugh Holman, who wrote that "however flawed as novels and imperfect as art his books may be, Thomas Wolfe's works constitute a major and remarkably successful effort to write his autobiography as that of a representative American and to embody in the record of his time and deeds on this earth a vision of the nature and the hope of his democratic land." Writing of Wolfe's service to American literature, Perkins stated the still-prevalent view that Wolfe "knew to the uttermost meaning the literature of other lands and that they were not the literature of America. He knew that the light and color of America were different; that the smells and sounds, its people, and all the structure and dimensions of our continent were unlike anything before. It was with this that he was struggling, and it was that struggle alone that, in a large sense, governed all he did. How long his books may last as such, no one can say, but the trail he has blazed is now open forever."

(See also *TCLC,* Vol. 4; *Contemporary Authors,* Vol. 104; *Dictionary of Literary Biography,* Vol. 9: *American Novelists, 1910-1945;* and *Dictionary of Literary Biography Documentary Series,* Vol. 3.)

PRINCIPAL WORKS

The Return of Buck Gavin (drama) 1919
The Mountains (drama) 1921
Welcome to Our City (drama) 1923
Look Homeward, Angel: A Story of the Buried Life (novel) 1929
From Death to Morning (short stories) 1935
Of Time and the River: A Legend of a Man's Hunger in His Youth (novel) 1935
The Story of a Novel (essay) 1936
The Face of a Nation (poetry) 1939
The Web and the Rock (novel) 1939
You Can't Go Home Again (novel) 1940
The Hills Beyond (short stories, sketches, and unfinished novel) 1941
A Stone, a Leaf, a Door (poetry) 1945
Mannerhouse (drama) 1948
The Letters of Thomas Wolfe (letters) 1956
The Short Novels of Thomas Wolfe (novellas) 1961
The Autobiography of an American Novelist (essays) 1983
Beyond Love and Loyalty: The Letters of Thomas Wolfe and Elizabeth Nowell (letters) 1983
My Other Loneliness: Letters of Thomas Wolfe and Aline Bernstein (letters) 1983

MARGARET WALLACE (essay date 1929)

[*In the following excerpted review, Wallace praises* Look Homeward, Angel *as a masterful novel.*]

[**"Look Homeward, Angel"**] is a novel of the sort one is too seldom privileged to welcome. It is a book of great drive and vigor, of profound originality, of rich and variant color. Its material is the material of every-day life, its scene is a small provincial Southern city, its characters are the ordinary persons who come and go in our daily lives. Yet the color of the book is not borrowed; it is native and essential. Mr. Wolfe has a very great gift—the ability to find in simple events and in humble, unpromising lives the whole meaning and poetry of human existence. He reveals to us facets of observation and depths of reality hitherto unsuspected, but he does so without outraging our notions of truth and order. His revelations do not startle. We come upon them, instead, with an almost electric sense of recognition. The plot, if the book can be said to have a plot at all, is at once too simple and too elaborate to relate in synopsis. **"Look Homeward, Angel"** is a chronicle of a large family, the Gants of Altamont, over a period of twenty years. In particular, it is the chronicle of Eugene Gant, the youngest son, who entered the world in 1900. . . . Eugene Gant grew from childhood into an awkward and rather withdrawn adolescence, hedged about by the turbulent lives of his family and singularly lonely in the midst of them. Indeed, each of the Gants was lonely in a separate fashion. Mr. Wolfe, in searching among them for the key to their hidden lives, comes upon no unifying fact save that of isolation.

Through the book like the theme of a symphony runs the note of loneliness and of a groping, defeated search for an answer to the riddle of eternal solitude. . . .

"Look Homeward, Angel" is as interesting and powerful a book as has ever been made out of the drab circumstances of provincial American life. It is at once enormously sensuous, full of the joy and gusto of life, and shrinkingly sensitive, torn with revulsion and disgust. Mr. Wolfe's style is sprawling, fecund, subtly rhythmic and amazingly vital. He twists language masterfully to his own uses, heeding neither the decency of a word nor its licensed existence, so long as he secures his sought for and instantaneous effect. Assuredly, this is a book to be savored slowly and reread, and the final decision upon it, in all probability, rests with another generation than ours.

Margaret Wallace, "A Novel of Provincial American Life," in The New York Times Book Review *(copyright © 1929 by The New York Times Company; reprinted by permission), October 27, 1929, p. 7.*

MALCOLM COWLEY (essay date 1935)

[*Cowley has made several valuable contributions to contemporary letters with his editions of important American authors (Nathaniel Hawthorne, Walt Whitman, Ernest Hemingway, William Faulkner, F. Scott Fitzgerald), his writings as a literary critic for* The New Republic, *and, above all, for his chronicles and criticism of modern American literature. Cowley's literary criticism does not attempt a systematic philosophical view of life and art, nor is it representative of a neatly defined school of critical thought, but rather focuses on works—particularly those of "lost generaion" writers—that he believes personal experience has qualified him to explicate and that he considers worthy of public appreciation. The critical approach Cowley follows is undogmatic and is characterized by a willingness to view a work from whatever perspective—social, historical, aesthetic—that the work itself seems to demand for its illumination. In the following excerpt, Cowley reviews* Of Time and the River, *finding it an ambitious novel with tremendous strengths as well as tremendous weaknesses.*]

I have just read Thomas Wolfe's new novel [**"Of Time and the River"**] all of the 912 big, solidly printed pages, almost every one of the 450,000 words, and, like a traveler returning safely from Outer Mongolia, I am eager to record what I heard and saw during forty days in the wilderness. It isn't so much a book review I should like to write as a topographical description of the regions newly explored, with a list of deserts and oases.

I have to report that the good passages in the novel are, first of all, the picture of Uncle Bascom Pentland, originally published by itself and now partly deprived of its effectiveness through being sawed and mortised into another framework, but still grotesque and vastly appealing; then the description of the little people in Professor Hatcher's course in dramatic writing; then the burlesque adventures of Oswald Ten Eyck in search of food and fame; then the death of old Oliver Gant, a tremendous Dostoevskian scene; then the comedy of Abe Jones, the melodrama of the consumptive cuckold, the tragedy of the Coulson family at Oxford; then the disintegration of Francis Starwick, whom I knew at college under his own name, and whose story is long enough to form a good novel in itself; then finally the train ride to Orléans and the episode of the old humbug countess. Together these scenes compose at least a third of the book, and they are extraordinarily strong and living. Thomas Wolfe at his best is the only contemporary American writer who can be mentioned in the same breath with Dickens and Dostoevsky. But the trouble is that the best passages are scattered, that they occur without logic or pattern, except the biographical pattern of the hero's life, and they lack the cumulative effect, the slow tightening of emotions to an intolerable pitch, that one finds in great novels like "The Possessed."

I have to report that the bad passages are about as numerous and as extensive in area as the good ones. There is the description of Eugene Gant's vast aloneness at Harvard, there are Eugene's reveries about time and death and the ever flowing mysterious river of life, there is his drunken police-station brawl in South Carolina, there are his anxieties as a teacher and his European musings on the lonely American soul. In particular there are the beginning of the book, in which he flees like Orestes into the North, and the end, in which he returns to set his Antæus feet on native soil. And, just as the good parts of the novel are massively and overwhelmingly good, so too the bad parts are Brobdingnagianly bad, are possibly worse than anything that any other reputable American novelist has permitted himself to publish.

The good and the bad can both be expressed in a general statement. When Wolfe is writing about people that his hero loved or hated or merely observed with delighted curiosity, then he writes with real vigor and with an astonishing sense of character; he writes clear, swinging prose. But when he is dealing with the hero, Eugene Gant, he almost always overwrites; he repeats himself, grows dithyrambic, shouts and sings in blank verse, scatters his adjectives like a charge of rock-salt from a ten-gauge shotgun. He is prayerful and solemn; all his grand wild humor is hidden away. One could scarcely say that **"Of Time and the River"** becomes a bad novel whenever the hero appears on the scene, for he is always there; but the author's style goes flabby as soon as attention is taken away from the outside world and concentrated on the hero's yearning and hungering soul.

The truth is that although Eugene Gant has many individual and warmly human traits, they scarcely add up into a character. He is not anyone that we should immeditely recognize in the street, like his father or his Uncle Bascom Pentland. Rather than being a person, he is a proud abstraction, "a legend of man's hunger in his youth," and his actions are magnified to such an extent that they cease to resemble those of ordinary young men. . . . If he received a polite letter of rejection, he was not merely downhearted: no, "he stood there in the hallway . . . his face convulsed and livid, his limbs trembling with rage, his bowels and his heart sick and trembling with a hideous gray nausea of hopelessness and despair, his throat choking with an intolerable anguish of resentment and wrong." Then, when he began to write once more, "the words were wrung out of him in a kind of bloody sweat, they poured out of his fingertips, spat out of his snarling throat like writhing snakes: he wrote them with his heart, his brain, his sweat, his guts." He is Goethe giving birth to Werther, he is Orestes in flight before the Furies, he is Young Faustus, Telemachus, Jason, he is Antæus seeking his own life-restoring soil—and at the same time . . . he is unmistakably Thomas Wolfe himself, and there are at least two occasions, on pages 186 and 466, where the author refers to Eugene in the first person singular.

"Of Time and the River" might have been a better book if the author had spoken in the first person from beginning to end. It seems to me that frank autobiography is a safer form than the disguised autobiographical novel. When the writer says "I felt this" and "I did that," he is forced, paradoxically, to look at himself from the outside. There are common rules of courtesy that compel him to moderate his boasts, to speak as one person among others, even to invent a character for himself. On the other hand, if he speaks of "me" under the guise of "him," all his acts are made conveniently impersonal. He is encouraged to regard himself, not as a character among others, but rather as a unique and all-embracing principle—in youth as the universal Boy, in manhood as the universal Poet. He is tempted to exhibit and magnify and admire his own adventures, till perhaps he reaches the point of wondering how he could ever "find a word to speak the joy, the pain, the grandeur bursting in the great vine of his heart, swelling like a huge grape in his throat—mad, sweet, wild, intolerable with all the mystery, loneliness, wild secret joy, and death, the ever returning and renewing fruitfulness of earth." In other words, he reaches the point of writing like a God-intoxicated ninny.

Such are the reports and ideas that I carried back from my forty days in the wilderness. This book of Thomas Wolfe's is better and worse than I have dared to say—richer, shriller, more exasperating. Cut down by half, it would be twice as good. Strangely, in the midst of its gigantic faults, it gives you the idea that Wolfe might and could write a novel that was great beyond question. But he will not write it until he chooses some other theme and some other hero than a young Faustus and Orestes squeezing out his blood, his sweat, his guts and not enough of his brains to produce the fabulous great American novel. (pp. 163-64)

Malcolm Cowley, "The Forty Days of Thomas Wolfe" (© 1935 The New Republic, Inc., and renewed 1963 by Malcolm Cowley; reprinted by permission of the author), in The New Republic, *Vol. LXXXII, No. 1059, March 20, 1935, pp. 163-64.*

F. SCOTT FITZGERALD (letter date 1935)

[The author of such American classics as The Great Gatsby *(1925) and* Tender is the Night *(1934), Fitzgerald was the spokesman for the Jazz Age, America's decade of prosperity, excess, and abandon, which began soon after the end of World War I and ended with the 1929 Wall Street Crash. The novels and stories for which he is best known examine an entire generation's search for the elusive American dream of wealth and happiness. In the following excerpt from a letter to Maxwell Perkins, Fitzgerald candidly assesses Wolfe's talent, discussing the weaknesses of the short story* "Circus at Dawn."]

Dear Max:

Reading Tom Wolfe's story [**"Circus at Dawn"**] in the current *Modern Monthly* makes me wish he was the sort of person you could talk to about his stuff. It has all his faults and virtues. It seems to me that with any sense of humor he could see the Dreiserian absurdities of how the circus people "ate the cod, bass, mackerel, halibut, clams and oysters of the New England coast, the terrapin of Maryland, the fat beeves, porks and cereals of the middle west" etc. etc. down to "the pink meated lobsters that grope their way along the sea-floors of America." And then (after one of his fine paragraphs which sounds a note to be expanded later) he remarks that they leave nothing behind except "the droppings of the camel and the elephant in Illinois." A few pages further on his redundance ruined some paragraphs . . . that might have been gorgeous. I sympathize with his use of repetition, of Joyce-like words, endless metaphor, but I wish he could have seen the disgust in Edmund Wilson's face when I once tried to interpolate part of a rhymed sonnet in the middle of a novel, disguised as prose. How he can put side by side such a mess as "With chitterling tricker fast-fluttering skirrs of sound the palmy honied birderies came" and such fine phrases as "tongue-trilling chirrs, plum-bellied smoothness, sweet lucidity" I don't know. He who has such

Wolfe in a Brooklyn apartment with the manuscript of Of Time and the River *(1935). Thomas Wolfe Collection, Pack Memorial Library, Asheville, NC.*

infinite power of suggestion and delicacy has absolutely no right to glut people on whole meals of caviar. I hope to Christ he isn't taking all these emasculated paeans to his vitality seriously. I'd hate to see such an exquisite talent turn into one of those muscle-bound and useless giants seen in a circus. Athletes have got to learn their games; they shouldn't just be content to tense their muscles, and if they do they suddenly find when called upon to bring off a necessary effect they are simply liable to hurl the shot into the crowd and not break any records at all. The metaphor is mixed but I think you will understand what I mean, and that he would too—save for his tendency to almost feminine horror if he thinks anyone is going to lay hands on his precious talent. I think his lack of humility is his most difficult characteristic, a lack oddly enough which I associate only with second or third rate writers. He was badly taught by bad teachers and now he hates learning.

There is another side of him that I find myself doubting, but this is something that no one could ever teach or tell him. His lack of feeling other people's passions, the lyrical value of Eugene Gant's love affair with the universe—is that going to last through a whole saga? God, I wish he could discipline himself and really plan a novel. (pp. 220-21)

F. Scott Fitzgerald, in a letter to Maxwell Perkins on April 17, 1935, in his The Letters of F. Scott Fitzgerald, *edited by Andrew Turnbull (copyright © 1963 Frances Scott Fitzgerald Lanahan; reprinted with permission of Charles Scribner's Sons), Charles Scribner's Sons, 1963 (and reprinted in* Dear Scott/ Dear Max: The Fitzgerald-Perkins Correspondence, *edited by John Kuehl and Jackson R. Bryer, Charles Scribner's Sons, 1971, pp. 220-22).*

THOMAS WOLFE (essay date 1935)

[*In the following excerpt from his important essay* The Story of a Novel, *Wolfe discusses his artistic vision and its reflection in the novel* Look Homeward, Angel.]

I was surprised not only by the kind of response [***Look Homeward, Angel***] had with the critics and the general public, I was most of all surprised with the response it had in my native town. . . . For months the town seethed with a fury of resentment which I had not believed possible. (p. 18)

[For] the first time I learned [a] lesson which every young writer has got to learn. And that lesson is the naked, blazing power of print. At that time it was for me a bewildering and almost overwhelming situation. My joy at the success my book had won was mixed with bitter chagrin at its reception in my native town. And yet I think I learned something from that experience, too. For the first time I was forced to consider squarely this problem: where does the material of an artist come from? What are the proper uses of that material, and how far must his freedom in the use of that material be controlled by his responsibility as a member of society? This is a difficult problem, and I have by no means come to the bottom of it yet. Perhaps I never shall, but . . . I have done much thinking and arrived at certain conclusions.

My book was what is often referred to as an autobiographical novel. I protested against this term in a preface to the book upon the grounds that any serious work of creation is of necessity autobiographical and that few more autobiographical works than *Gulliver's Travels* have ever been written. (pp. 19-20)

But I also believe now that the young writer is often led through inexperience to a use of the materials of life which are, perhaps, somewhat too naked and direct for the purpose of a work of art. The thing a young writer is likely to do is to confuse the limits between actuality and reality. He tends unconsciously to describe an event in such a way because it actually happened that way, and from an artistic point of view, I can now see that this is wrong. It is not, for example, important that one remembers a beautiful woman of easy virtue as having come from the state of Kentucky in the year 1907. She could perfectly well have come from Idaho or Texas or Nova Scotia. The important thing really is only to express as well as possible the character and quality of the beautiful woman of easy virtue. (p. 21)

Everything in a work of art is changed and transfigured by the personality of the artist. And as far as my own first book is concerned, I can truthfully say that I do not believe that there is a single page of it that is true to fact. And from this circumstance, also, I learned another curious thing about writing. For although my book was not true to fact, it was true to the general experience of the town I came from and I hope, of course, to the general experience of all men living. (p. 22)

The life of the artist at any epoch of man's history has not been an easy one. And here in America, it has often seemed to me, it may well be the hardest life that man has ever known. . . . [I am speaking] in the concrete terms of the artist's actual experience, of the nature of the physical task before him. It seems to me that the task is one whose physical proportions are vaster and more difficult here than in any other nation on the earth. It is not merely that in the cultures of Europe and of the Orient the American artist can find no antecedent scheme, no structural plan, no body of tradition that can give his work the validity and truth that it must have. It is not merely that he must make somehow a new tradition for himself, derived from his own life and from the enormous space and energy of American life, the structure of his own design; it is not merely that he is confronted by these problems; it is even more than this, that the labor of a complete and whole articulation, the discovery of an entire universe and of a complete language, is the task that lies before him.

Such is the nature of the struggle to which henceforth our lives must be devoted. Out of the billion forms of America, out of the savage violence and the dense complexity of all its swarming life; from the unique and single substance of this land and life of ours, must we draw the power and energy of our own life, the articulation of our speech, the substance of our art.

For here it seems to me in hard and honest ways like these we may find the tongue, the language, and the conscience that as men and artists we have got to have. Here, too, perhaps, must we who have no more than what we have, who know no more than what we know, who are no more than what we are, find our America. Here, at this present hour and moment of my life, I seek for mine. (pp. 91-3)

Thomas Wolfe, in his The Story of a Novel *(copyright, 1935, by The Saturday Review Company, Inc.; copyright, 1936, by Charles Scribner's Sons and renewed 1964 by Paul Gitlin, Administrator C.T.A. of the Literary Estate of Thomas Wolfe; reprinted by permission of Charles Scribner's Sons; originally published as "The Story of a Novel," "The Story of a Novel: II," and "The Story of a Novel: III," in* The Saturday Review of Literature, *Vol. XIII, Nos. 7, 8 and 9, December 14, 21, and 28, 1935), Charles Scribner's Sons, 1936, 93 p.*

BERNARD DeVOTO (essay date 1940)

[*An editor of* The Saturday Review of Literature *and longtime contributor to* Harper's Magazine, *DeVoto was a highly controversial literary critic and historian. A man whose thought enraged much of America's literary establishment during the 1930s and 1940s, he was frequently motivated by anger at authors he considered ignorant of American life and history. As a critic, he admired mastery of form and psychological subtlety in literature. His own work is characterized by its scholarly thoroughness and by its vigorous, infectious style. Shortly after Wolfe's* The Story of a Novel *was serialized in* The Saturday Review of Literature *in late 1935, DeVoto contributed to that periodical his famous essay* "Genius Is Not Enough" *(see* TCLC, *Vol. 4), a critical attack on the Byronic grandiosity of Wolfe's novels and on his close working relationship with Maxwell Perkins. Wolfe, acutely sensitive to the least adverse criticism of his works, was infuriated and his confidence severely shaken by DeVoto's article, which triggered the souring and, finally, the termination of his relationship with Perkins and with Charles Scribner's Sons. In the following excerpted review of* The Web and the Rock—*a novel written during Wolfe's association with Harper and Brothers's editor Edward C. Aswell—DeVoto perceives the novel as further evidence of Wolfe's failure as an artist.*]

Even more than Thomas Wolfe's earlier novels, ***The Web and the Rock*** is a collaboration between author and publisher. The first half of it reads as if it had been written to the publisher's specifications in order to support the second half, and the second half was admittedly assembled by the publishers from a larger bulk. This arbitrary organization makes criticism reluctant, and reluctance is increased by Mr. Wolfe's death and his tragic unfulfillment. But that unfulfillment is the one important problem that criticism must discuss in relating him to the fiction of his time.

For ***The Web and the Rock*** confirms what ***Of Time and the River*** had already established: that the intensity of Wolfe's desire to make fiction out of his experience was not matched by his ability, that the fury which drove him could not be disciplined into art, and that apart from fury he had only a commonplace endowment as a novelist. ***Look Homeward, Angel,*** his first novel, manifested an intermittent and fragmentary ability to realize the vision in fiction. That was his promise. But in ***Of Time and the River*** both vision and realization had diminished; they were swamped in fury and bad prose. That diminution is progressive in ***The Web and the Rock,*** which in the last third abandons all other objectives and becomes merely a documentation of insanity that seldom troubles to assume the appearance of fiction. It is clear that Wolfe could never have overcome the forces of disintegration; they had already defeated him. The memory of his promise and the tragedy of his defeat will remain. He will go down in our literature as a tormented soul, like Herman Melville, whose books will provide psychology and literary scholarship something of the same attractive hunting ground that Melville's do. But they are much less important than Melville's and their failure is much less mysterious. And regret for an artist's failure to attain greatness has never yet made a work of art great.

It is true of many novelists, perhaps of most novelists except first-rate ones, that they can make the childhood of imagined characters more real than their maturity. The probable reason is that the novelists' own childhood was more real to them than maturity—that minor fiction is frequently a form of infantile fixation. The best parts of Wolfe's work are nearly all to be found in the boyhood of Eugene Gant and of the George Webber who is distinguished from Eugene only by name. It is there that frenzy most often forges the objective symbols of fiction and becomes a drama of human experience, of people living with one another in a world where events occur. It is a child's world, however, and Wolfe never gets out of it. . . . What he gives us is a child's-eye view. He was a giant, but he was a giant child.

His violent emotions, the ether in which his books exist, are simple, superficial, and in the end empty. He had an eager, loving recognition of many facets of American life. He understood, as more sophisticated novelists sometimes fail to understand, that baseball and fishing, livery stables and boys' gangs, the Dempsey-Firpo fight and small-town superstitions, are important to Americans. But he could not tell what their importance is; their significance always turns out to be that of something that is said to or felt by a child. The inability does not matter when George Webber is frightened by the cruelty of other boys,—it is right that a boy's terror shall be, in one of his favorite adjectives, nameless,—but it is paralyzing when the adult George Webber falls in love with an adult woman. This love affair is the exclusive occupation of the second half of ***The Web and the Rock;*** it extends through more than three hundred pages; it is, in words, the most tortured love affair rolling through his finger tips, and know the ~~[illegible]~~ instant ~~[illegible]~~ that he finds the combination to unlock the safe) - and that by making this rotation with ~~my~~ his hand, ~~in space, I~~ he would find the lost dimension of that secret world, and instantly step through the door that ~~I~~ he had opened.

And ~~I~~ he had ~~as well a thousand spells and~~ other chants and incantations that would make that world reveal itself to ~~me~~ him. Thus, for a period of ten years or more, ~~I~~ he had a spell for almost everything ~~I~~ he did. ~~I~~ He would hold ~~my~~ his breath along a certain block, or take four breaths in pounding down the hill from school, or touch each cement block upon a wall ~~of cement blocks with my finger~~ as ~~I~~ he went past, ~~the wall~~, and touch each of the end-blocks where the steps went up two times, and if ~~I~~ he failed to touch them twice, go back and touch the whole wall over from the start.

~~At night, I said my prayers in rhymes of four - for "four", "eight", "sixteen", "thirty-two", were somehow the key numbers in my arithmetic of sorcery. I would say my one set prayer at night in chants of four times four, until all the words and meanings of the prayer (which I had composed myself with four times four in mind) were lost, and all that I would follow would be the rhythm and the number of the chant, muttered so rapidly that the prayer was just a rapid blur but muttered always sixteen times.~~

~~And if I failed to do this, or doubted I had got the proper count, then I could not sleep or rest after I got into bed, and would get up instantly, and go down upon my knees again, no matter how cold or raw the weather was, no matter how I felt, and would not pause until I did the full count to my satisfaction, with another sixteen thrown in as penalty.~~

Typescript of a page from Wolfe's The Web and the Rock *including corrections by Edward Aswell. By permission of the Houghton Library, Harvard University.*

our fiction contains. But it does not press through words to experience, it never comes alive. (pp. 69-70)

They do not live—and that is the failure of Wolfe's work. Nor does the failure result solely from the immaturity of his understanding; he had other, equally fatal insufficiencies. He was a solipsist; no experience but his own was real. Like Eugene Gant, George Webber sees terrible things happen to other people. But they are terrible because they cause terror in Webber, not because other people suffer. Wolfe has said repeatedly that his drive was to absorb the world and then reproduce it; but he does not absorb the world, he only confuses it with his own world-hunger; and he does not reproduce the world, but only his own frenzy. (p. 70)

And the catalogue is not yet complete, for he was under the further handicap that he could not impose on the material that obsessed him the elementary forms of fiction. He could tell us that life is dread, that life is fury, that the world is beautiful and terrible, that men are passionate and terrified and preyed on by longing and despair, that America is many-voiced and billion-footed. They are not new nor particularly penetrating messages, they are essentially an adolescent rhetoric, but the intensity with which they are announced might have given them importance if they had been forged into drama. But they are only infrequently and imperfectly raised from rhetorical assertion into a realization of people whose lives are engaged with one another. He tells us many times about some never understood evil in Southern life; the very repetition shows that he had some idea which one may associate with William Faulkner's mystical but nevertheless dramatized vision, but it is only in an occasional passage that a Negro goes berserk or the poor-white boys draw knives. The rest is rhapsodic language, not experience. He tells us equally often about an evil in the life of the metropolis; the very repetition shows that he had some idea which one may associate with James Farrell's slums, but it is never wrought into such a drama as Studs Lonigan's wasting life. It remains a statement, many pages long and made through a megaphone, that George Webber walked in the city and felt bad about it.

Is there much to him besides frenzy? If you strain out the whirling agony of words unshaped in character, whose exact designation is cyclothymia, there is left nothing that would distinguish him from scores of mediocre novelists. He is fury and little more. Now the representation of fury is a proper occupation for fiction in our era; but it is not representation that we get from him, it is pure fury untransformed. His books are its conduits, not a significant form imposed on it by art, not its projection in human life. . . .

[One] need only turn from ***The Web and the Rock*** to *The Grapes of Wrath*. Steinbeck is always a novelist in a way that Wolfe is only briefly and incompletely. Fiction is for him the thing happening to the people he is writing about; in Wolfe's book the thing seldom happens—it is announced, described, chanted, yelled, trumpeted, but not realized. A page of Steinbeck is, to use a dramatist's word, *scene:* people saying and doing and feeling things in the world of experience. A page of Wolfe is typically Wolfe himself gloating or mourning in private about something which he tells us has happened, something which he usually neglects to make happen, something furthermore which usually has no bearing on the people of his book. But fiction is the people of the book and what happens to them. So in the outcome the Joads break one's heart, while George Webber and his mistress and his sinister enemies leave one untouched. The tragedy attributed to Webber by assertion is, in outline, quite as harrowing as that of the Joads, but it remains an assertion; it is not realized in fiction as theirs is, and so it is without power.

Wolfe's life was tragic, but it would be unfortunate if his death should create the myth that a great artist died unfulfilled. Admirers of his books who are now working at such a myth are doing a disservice to young writers and the future of our fiction. He had intensity, a great vehemence, a splendid dedication to his work, and till this last book a noble, affirmative belief in the worth of life. All those qualities should be praised and will remain an inspiration to novelists. But he found no way to focus his intensity, he never developed enough craftsmanship to work his private world into fiction, his ideas and perceptions remained those of a child, and he had little to say about human experience. The torment he lived was pitiful, but his books are a disintegration. Praise of them is a betrayal of literature. For fiction is an art: it must begin by shaping the raw stuff that is without shape and by suffusing it with life; it has no meaning, nor even existence, except as it contrives to make imaginary people seem alive and what happens to them seem important. (p. 71)

Bernard DeVoto, "American Novels: 1939" (copyright © 1940, renewed 1967, by The Atlantic Monthly Company, Boston, MA; reprinted by permission of Mrs. Bernard DeVoto), in The Atlantic Monthly, *Vol. 165, No. 1, January, 1940, pp. 66-74.**

BURTON RASCOE (essay date 1940)

[*In the following excerpt, Rascoe praises* You Can't Go Home Again *as a novel that marks the apex of Wolfe's rise to artistic maturity.*]

Wolfe achieved maturity just before he died. He left a posthumous manuscript entitled ***You Can't Go Home Again.*** It showed that long before Tom Wolfe died he had begun to see and feel and think like a grown-up man and not like an exuberant but depressed, angered and inhibited adolescent, at once arrogant toward and afraid of the world and its people, as he had shown himself to be in his magnificent but almost childishly crude and faulty novels, ***Look Homeward, Angel*** and ***Of Time and the River.***

In ***You Can't Go Home Again,*** Wolfe is no longer the voluminously and repetitiously articulate Pantagruel of Asheville, North Carolina, ex-instructor in English at New York University, who aspired to write, instead of teaching, English, pouring out millions of unedited and even uncorrelated words about the people and the scenes he had known, and displaying on nearly every page the peculiar terror of his heart—sometimes by arrogantly glorifying this terror which was of his own gigantic size; and yet, again, pathetically resenting his abnormal heft and stature.

Forgetting his gigantism, sometimes, Wolfe would turn on the faucet of the immense reservoir of his memory; there would come bucketfuls of impressions—homely street and domestic scenes, caricatures, personal slights, personal victories, portraits of communities, of individuals, depictions of feuds, hates, loves, ambitions, jealousies, achievements, vanities and defeats. Some of these were superb, beautiful; all reflected boundless energy. Some were the mere talkativeness of a nervously tortured man, of a man who had read too much and aspired too much, a man who wished to get away from a reality and from memories of a reality which were hateful to him, a man who was eager to feel and to experience but who was harassed by a tick in the mind which prevented him from feeling at all, except in the chill recording of his writer's brain—not the heart; a man who had energy, thirst, appetite, curiosity, but who did not, until he was in his thirties, begin to deduce the simplest truths about life which any tobacco auctioneer, tobacco farmer, or Negro roustabout in the Asheville market knows with only a few years of adult experience. In the manuscript Thomas Wolfe left to be published after his death, he had become adult enough to draw some age-old truths about life—truths as old and as valid as the mightiest of those in all great literature, from the Old Testament to Mark Twain—and to express these truths with humility, clarity, force, beauty and originality. (pp. 493-94)

Burton Rascoe, "Wolfe, Farrell, and Hemingway," in American Mercury, *Vol. LI, No. 204, December, 1940, pp. 493-98.**

THOMAS LYLE COLLINS (essay date 1942)

[*In the following excerpt, Collins applies a fourfold test to Wolfe's accomplishment, attempting to determine if Wolfe can be considered the author of the Great American Novel.*]

[The] appearance of Thomas Wolfe may have been an event of the utmost significance in the history of American literature: certainly, at least, his power of description and narration is unexcelled in the entire range of our literature. There is even a possibility that future generations will come to regard him as the author of The Great American Novel which we have so long awaited. Let us then take this popular phrase, The Great American Novel, as a four-unit yardstick to measure him; for in these four words lie the four main problems which the modern critic encounters in the novel. These four critical problems, in their respective order, are: *the problem of scope, the problem of greatness, the problem of significance,* and *the problem of form.* By this standard perhaps we may be able to decide how nearly Wolfe's novels approach the ideal of The Great American Novel. (p. 489)

The Problem of Greatness: True greatness, in the strictest sense of the word, always implies a certain transcendency, an ability to rise above the particular circumstance or experience to its more universal implications. This is precisely the quality which distinguishes Wolfe from his lesser contemporaries. This is precisely why the sentimental Mr. Steinbeck, although he is a more disciplined craftsman, is a less great novelist. Wolfe had a sort of super-vision which enabled him to see people in their several artistic dimensions. He found some people, such as the Simpsons, tremendously funny, and he shared with us his belly-laugh over them—but then he penetrated beyond the comic surface to the pathetic essence. He found the Pierces to be quite wonderful—for a while he thought he had discovered the "lane-end into heaven"—but then, rising above them, he saw beyond the cloud of glory which hid them and looked upon the weariness and decay which possessed them. He was completely taken in by the magic of Starwick's glamour, but he eventually saw through it. He was enraptured by Paris "sophistication", but he eventually saw through it. This is the key to Wolfe's genius, this ability to transcend his own experiences, and once having done so, to look back upon it all and write of it with power and clarity, flooding the scene with the rich light of his own personality. (pp. 495-96)

Wolfe's general theme is somewhat reminiscent of Wordsworth's *Odes on Intimations of Immortality* in that it is suggestive of the passage containing the lines "trailing clouds of glory do we come." On the title page of ***Look Homeward, Angel,*** Wolfe quotes this sentence from Tarr and McMurry—"At one time the earth was probably a white-hot sphere like the sun." Then the prefatory poem which follows explains in a measure both the quotation and the theme of the book. . . . (p. 496)

From this we may extract a brutally prosaïc statement of Wolfe's theme: all through life we are searching for some sign—"a stone, a leaf, a door"—which will open up to us the universe of perfection and enchantment which we feel vaguely to have left behind us when we were born. The implication is that our souls have been torn from this enchanted heaven and imprisoned in corporeal frames here on earth. A spiritually necessary unity is wanting, for we are unable to communicate with our fellow-prisoners. Monads have no windows: "we seek the great forgotten language . . ."

Or: Wolfe notes a discrepancy between the ideal world and the real, the former figuratively represented by the sun, the latter by "this most weary unbright cinder", the earth.

Or: Wolfe believes, in a non-Christian sense, in Original Sin. We are born into the damnation of spiritual isolation, and must achieve grace by ending that isolation. (pp. 496-97)

At the heart of Wolfe's novels is an essential paradox which does not become apparent until Eugene's visit to England: it is that there is a door, there is a way to feel at home on the earth, there is a secret room—but though when you're outside you want in, when you're inside you want out! Tradition-less

America is on the outside and wants in; traditional England is on the inside and wants out. (p. 497)

All his life Eugene had been seeking "an unfound door". The English had found a door; had they found *the* door? He found the answer when, upon his departure, Edith Coulson told him—

> We shall remember you. . . And I hope you think of us sometime—back here, buried, lost, in all the fog and rain and ruin of England. How good it must be to know that you are young in a very young country—where nothing that you did yesterday matters very much. How wonderful it must be to know that none of the failure of the past can pull you down—that there will always be another day for you—a new beginning. I wonder if you Americans will ever know how fortunate you are. . .

The answer is, then, that life without meaning is far better and more preferable than life with certainty and security, for the latter results in death-in-life, which Wolfe views with abhorrence in all his novels.

This paradox of man accounts for Eugene's fascination with Jewish people. Wolfe bestows upon them a symbolic rôle because they alone were at home on the earth without being enmeshed by it. They are not beset by death-in-life because their certainty is the true one—the certainty of Ecclesiastes, the certainty of pain and folly and useless endeavor. (pp. 497-98)

But the two principal symbols are love and death, for they are the only things that will end the spiritual isolation of the soul. In the great poem which prefaces ***Of Time and the River,*** these symbols are presented, symbols which are expanded throughout the novel. . . . (p. 498)

The other symbols now unfold to us with greater ease. Gant's father stands for his spiritual, certain past, a past to which he can never return for certainty. This symbol may have been derived from the Bloom-Dedalus relationship in James Joyce's *Ulysses,* particularly since Wolfe is self-admittedly indebted to Joyce. His brother Ben is the symbol for all men who cannot speak or give a sign of brotherhood. The Simpsons are the millions of lonely families in America "huddled below immense and timeless skies". In Starwick, Eugene found the unfound door: Francis could order a spaghetti dinner and make it sound like a royal banquet—thus the great shock when Eugene's illusions about Starwick crumbled. Eugene's mad desire to read all the books ever written is due to his hunger to see out over the walls of his soul into the outside world. The trains rushing through America are symbols of America itself—violent, splendid, powerful, blindly rushing through the night. The night is also symbolic of America, and the lonely men who huddle about the streetlamps and in the lighted lunchrooms late at night take on a transcendent meaning.

It is this unity of the soul and the body of Wolfe's novels, this synthesis of the universal and the particular, which is the chief contributor to his greatness. The worlds of great artists are always complete. Homer's world was complete, as was Dante's, Shakespeare's, Goethe's. In other words, to put it crudely, they have an answer for everything. These artists, although they never lost sight of men, looked beyond and saw a vision of Man, eternal and immutable. Wolfe's *Weltanschauung* displays this same combination of completeness and accuracy, and therefore, in many ways, ranks him accordingly.

The Problem of Significance: The American reading public, made acutely self-critical by Mr. Mencken et al. during the Twenties, is very message-conscious in their reading of novels. What is the author's theme? What suggestion does he have to make in his novel for the political, economic, sociological, or cultural improvement of the nation? . . . I think this accounts in part, at least, for the hesitant reception of Wolfe's novels by the American critics. For Wolfe seemed much more concerned with his own personal problems than with the problems of America. This is why ***You Can't Go Home Again*** was greeted with such sighs of satisfaction, for at last Wolfe had become "significant".

I have already spoken of Wolfe's central theme of spiritual isolation. Its universal nature is apparent. Its particular application is that while it is true in varying degree for men of all time and place, it is most true for Americans of the present day. We *are* "like blind sucks and sea-valves and the eyeless crawls that grope along the forest of the sea's great floor . . ." Our poverty of tradition, our blind materialism, our barrenness of middle-class life could not be described better. One does not have to read ***You Can't Go Home Again*** to find "significance". There is significance a-plenty in Wolfe's first three novels if one will but read carefully some of the passages of "dark substance" therein.

And Wolfe for the most part avoids the sentimental fallacy of ascribing our evils to institutions. With a dim but perceptible certainty he sees that the fault lies not outside but inside, deep within the heart of man.

In ***You Can't Go Home Again*** this implied belief becomes explicit. In his conclusion, called "Credo", he says "I think the enemy is single selfishness and compulsive greed." In the chapters called "Boom Town" and "The Company" he lashes out viciously at this single selfishness and compulsive greed. And in the chapter, "Piggy Logan's Circus", he achieves an effect of strange and gripping horror of a decadent aristocracy which will watch for hours the morbidly pointless antics of a giggling moron.

In regard to Wolfe's position in our national literature, I think it is safe to say that he stands, and will stand, very close to the top. For in his novels he caught that strange and unique combination of brilliant hope and black despair which is the quintessence of the American spirit.

The Problem of Form: The form of Wolfe's novels is enough to give any critic a nightmare. At first reading they seem to be little more than miscellaneous collections of autobiographical anecdotes and personal observations. But after complete reading and thoughtful contemplation, the nature of his literary form begins to emerge in one's mind.

First, however, a satisfactory definition of form must be found. (pp. 499-501)

Kenneth Burke has a practical and useful definition of form which will serve in this case. He says that "form is the creation of an appetite in the mind of the auditor, and the adequate satisfying of that appetite."

Applying this definition to Wolfe's works, I find three basic and interdependent forms. They are, in the order of excellence, the episode, the complete work, and the novel.

Sometimes these episodes, such as the one about the Simpsons, are very short. Sometimes, as in "The Child by Tiger" in ***The Web and the Rock*** and "The World That Jack Built" in ***You***

Can't Go Home Again, they are as long as a short novel. In the latter instance, they are subdivided into sub-episodes, and sub-sub-episodes, each one creating an appetite in the mind of the reader, and satisfying that appetite adequately; each one having a surprising singleness and intensity of effect. The sub-episodes which go to make up a complete episode do not always observe a time or place sequence; instead, Wolfe sketches in a detail here, makes a few strokes there, until finally the whole picture is completed. (pp. 501-02)

The second basic form, Wolfe's complete work of four novels, contains a spiritual evolution in which may be found the beginning of a conflict, the body of a conflict, and the resolution, elements of a form which should satisfy the most reactionary of critics. The beginning of the conflict is contained in ***Look Homeward, Angel,*** in which a boy of energy and ambition finds himself buried in a world of pettiness and animosity and meaninglessness, and determines to escape into the outside world, where he may seek glory and love and meaning. (p. 502)

Of Time and the River and ***The Web and the Rock*** constitute the body of the conflict. In the first he escapes into the world, and his interests and passions diverge in a thousand different directions in his Faustian search for glory and love and meaning. In the latter his passion strikes a lens and is focussed and concentrated in his love for Esther Jack. The lens is then shattered, and the last volume, ***You Can't Go Home Again,*** contains a desperate race between death and meaning. The last lines he wrote present his premonition of death and his triumphant reaffirmation of a spiritual idealism. . . . (p. 503)

The form of each novel, then, since it is so loose, is only important as a phase of Gant-Webber's spiritual evolution, and as a frame for Wolfe's episodic structure; it has no inherent and self-sufficient form to speak of. But Thomas Wolfe, genius that he was, had that inevitable instinct for form which served him twice where it failed him once.

The Problem of Scope: Wolfe wrote *great* American novels, he wrote great *American* novels, and, loosely speaking, he wrote great American *novels*. But he fails to measure up in the fourth respect: he did not write *the* great American novel. Contained in the phrase is the implication that the novel should summarize and epitomize the promise of America's becoming one of the great ages of man, just as Homer's *Iliad* epitomizes the heroic age of Greece, Dante's *Divine Comedy* the medieval age, and Shakespeare's plays the English Renaissance. This is virtually impossible. There are so many forces of disunity and skepticism present in present-day America that a novel, or even a series of novels, could not bring them all together into a coherent and comprehensible pattern. Homer and Shakespeare and Dante stand far above us because they stand at the peak of a high and mighty structure erected by men of great talent and culture, all working together. There was little in the modern world for Wolfe to stand on.

Also, Wolfe was not of the artistic temper to write such a work. The author of The Great American Novel must be dramatic and omnipresent; Thomas Wolfe was lyrical and unipresent. For him there was only one world and he was at the center of it.

But his third and gravest limitation was his genius: it was the tragic flaw, a flaw of which he was only too conscious. "Genius is not enough", sneers Mr. De Voto [see *TCLC,* Vol. 4]. On the contrary, the genius of Thomas Wolfe was too much. He was driven by a restlessness which kept him from achieving that cool perfection which often comes easy to lesser men. (pp. 503-04)

Thomas Lyle Collins, "Thomas Wolfe," in The Sewanee Review *(reprinted by permission of the editor; published 1942 by The University of the South), Vol. L, No. 4, Fall, 1942, pp. 487-504.*

MONROE M. STEARNS (essay date 1945)

[In the following excerpt, Stearns traces the strong influence of Samuel Taylor Coleridge and William Wordsworth on Wolfe's metaphysical vision.]

There are three stages through which the artist passes on his journey toward personal adjustment to the world. The first is his idea of God as a void, especially conspicuous in America because of the prevalence of the old frontier attitude toward any of the forms of art. The second stage is the idea of God as the enemy. The first produces in the artist the sense of being an orphan and an outcast; the second produces the sense of being a rebel. Wolfe gives signs of having reached the second stage only at the close of his career. The third stage, that of God the friend, representing complete assimilation into the world and adjustment with it, he never attained.

Deep-seated in the hypersensitive organism of the artist is his relationship with his mother. Perhaps in the process of Wolfe's growth no period was so hazardous to the child's emotional stability as the period of weaning. This is the point at which the physical relationship of the child with his mother is severed and lost. . . . If the weaning period is tactfully and intelligently managed, the shock of having to sustain himself is lessened for the infant; but, should the opposite obtain, the child experiences a frantic sense of rejection and abandonment.

In the case of Thomas Wolfe, his accurately autobiographical novels, his letters, and his mother's own words serve as indisputable evidence of this experience. Wolfe's descriptions of his mother are perfect. In real life she has the same pursing lips, the same gestures, and the same speech. . . . In ***Look Homeward, Angel*** she is represented as so engrossed in her speculations with real estate and money-making that her family become a nuisance and a hindrance rather than a vital concern. Not only would this attitude produce a psychological feeling of rejection on her youngest child through her lack of motherly empathy and her inability to see the world from the child's point of view, but the fact that she refused to wean Thomas until he was three and a half years old would make that process far more difficult than if it had been accomplished when the child was an infant. It caused a spiritual wound from which he never recovered. (pp. 194-95)

The hopeless rejection of Wolfe by his mother caused him later to regard all the women he was to love as food-producers. In real life, for example, Elinor in ***Of Time and the River*** is an experienced and accomplished cook who studied cookery in France with a leading chef. Esther Jack, of the last two novels, also holds her power over George Webber-Wolfe by her succulent dishes. Her prototype is a woman so fond of cooking that her idea of relaxation is to go into her kitchen and prepare Sunday lunch for twenty or thirty guests. Food and its consumption figure in Wolfe's novels more often than any other pleasure.

After this rejection, what next can the child do? Gathering its energies into itself, it loves itself. In normal cases, however, this solution is unsatisfactory, and a counterreaction takes place.

Having rejected its mother, the child now rejects itself. The possibility remains, nevertheless, of a relationship with the father, who in the home and the family symbolizes God in the universe. (p. 195)

William Oliver Wolfe, however, was a socially irresponsible man, both actually and as he is represented in the novels of his son. He was a semioutcast, and Thomas Wolfe's identification of himself with him tended to make the author even more of an outcast than he had already felt himself to be. The introductory paragraphs of ***Look Homeward, Angel*** . . . are primarily concerned with the mother, but the intention includes the father and the search for him as well. (pp. 195-96)

The rejection of the child by his family and the repulsion caused by his environment are likely to release themselves in a story that takes the form of a pilgrimage or odyssey. It is thus no coincidence that one of the chapters in ***Of Time and the River*** is entitled "Telemachus," and another, "Jason's Voyage." This is perhaps the simplest of Wolfe's symbols.

Long before Wolfe had embarked on his semifictionalized autobiography, he had found the secret of releasing his feelings of rejection and revulsion, and he had found it in the metaphysical Wordsworth and Coleridge. . . . In Coleridge, Wolfe found the means of expression by which he could sublimate his feelings. The subjective writer finds a perfect model in the figure of the Romantic genius, and out of the books in which he finds him he remembers and uses that material which also exists in himself and which relates to his own problems. (pp. 196-97)

There is a passage in ***Look Homeward, Angel*** in which the young Eugene Gant-Wolfe looked up misty-eyed in the growing dark from the last page of a sensational novel and concluded: "Yes, this was as it should be. This was what he would have done." . . . The escape from reality which the child enjoyed was the seed of the power Wolfe possessed of making himself one with whatever person he was reading or writing about. Furthermore, both boys were petted by one of their brothers: Coleridge, by his brother George; Wolfe, by the famous Ben. Both apotheosized this brother. . . .

Wolfe wrote to his mother in 1927: "Strangers we were born alone into a strange world. We live in it, as Ben did alone and strange, and we are without ever knowing anyone." In 1926 he had written: "In our family Ben was the stranger until his death—I suppose I'm the other one." The dithyrambic rhapsodies of Eugene over Ben in Wolfe's novel expand these statements and raise them into poetry of a higher order than [the lines of Coleridge's "To the Rev. George Coleridge"]. Coleridge taught Wolfe how to see and how to feel and how to express what he saw and felt. (p. 197)

It was through [his] familiarity with Wordsworth that Wolfe found one path to his escape. A thorough familiarity it was, and another identification of himself with his author-model. When in Book III of *The Prelude* Wordsworth writes of his eye

> Which, from a tree, a stone, a withered leaf,
> To the broad ocean and the azure heavens
> Spangled with kindred multitudes of stars
> Could find no surface where its power might sleep;

Wolfe recognized the similarity of the poet's emotion to his own and appropriated Wordsworth's phrase for his own motto of "a stone, a leaf, a door," by which he could express the psychological pains of birth. The loss of relationship with his protector-mother is symbolized for Wolfe in Wordsworth's nostalgia for that spiritual home whence comes the soul trailing its clouds of glory. Life thus became to Wolfe a penance for the sin of having been born and having left that apocalyptic world of Plato, Plotinus, Wordsworth, and Coleridge, in which the soul knows its true nature and is free.

When Wolfe was to continue the tale of his life, Wordsworth also helped him. Again Wolfe shows his intimacy with the poet's less familiar lines, and the key to ***Of Time and the River*** is the last of Wordsworth's sonnet sequence. *The River Duddon*. At the beginning of the "Telemachus" section of this novel Wolfe writes of himself: "His father was dead and now it seemed to him that he had never found him. His father was dead, and yet he sought him everywhere." And the rest of the novel has as its theme [the lines of Wordsworth's sonnet "After-Thought"]. (p. 198)

The point of view of the professional metaphysician is different from that of the artist; the artist treats metaphysics as being helpful to life. Thus the definite subjectivity of Wolfe's personality brought the other world away from a distinct existence into one continually interwoven with his own. The very use that he makes of physical metaphors demonstrates his willingness to see this world on a physical level. He accepts the symbolism of the world and nature as Wordsworth and Coleridge did. He does not—and perhaps cannot—impersonalize his problems, as might a Catholic writer, through priest or character sublimation.

Without a knowledge of the total environment of an author, his intention cannot be completely understood, nor can the entire meaning of his communications be perceived. The terms Wolfe uses in recurring refrains are symbols of other things than their direct referents. Thus "home" is not only the Asheville boarding-house of Wolfe's childhood or a prenatal uterine existence; the word is also used in the Wordsworthian sense for God. The search for a father becomes, as well, a search for God. The "door" is the entrance both back to the protective maternal womb and to the heaven from which, in the Platonic doctrine, we in our essence come. The "stone, leaf, door" refrain symbolizes not only the pain of birth but also those tokens (like Wordsworth's rainbow, rose, tree, and pansy) which remind the mortal of his immortal nature. The "lost and by the wind-grieved ghost" corresponds to the sense of the pre-existence of the soul, which vanishes as the individual advances in material time down the river of corporeal existence. (pp. 198-99)

The events and the spirit of Wolfe's own lifetime correspond rather closely to those of the period of Wordsworth and Coleridge. As they lamented the materialism, the skepticism, the regimentation, and the conservatism of their day, and put their faith in the elemental goodness and spiritual inheritance of the individual man, so Wolfe's higher purpose is to lead America out of the confusion and disillusionment of the years following the oubreak of the first World War. His father-search becomes universalized in the common quest for a substitute for the autocratic character of the home—with the father as autocrat—which was then disappearing. Motivated by the same complexes, Wolfe uses the same methods that his poets did in rescuing his generation from the futility of its existence. As they were a link between an old world and a new one, so Wolfe, in following them, becomes a bridge from our world of the past to a new future, and thus he takes his place in the great stream of Anglo-Saxon thought and literature, which has stressed democracy since the time of *Beowulf*.

Thomas Wolfe preaches a return to the natural man, exalts the dignity and beauty of human nature, reaffirms man's divinity and purpose, and restores to his readers thereby a sense of their own value and importance. Like all tragedy, the tragedy of Wolfe's life as he records it purifies and restores the ideals of his readers which else would languish for want of sufficient illustration. (p. 199)

Monroe M. Stearns, "The Metaphysics of Thomas Wolfe," in College English, *Vol. 6, No. 4, January, 1945, pp. 193-99.*

PAMELA HANSFORD JOHNSON (essay date 1948)

[*Johnson's* Hungry Gulliver *was the first book-length critical study of Wolfe's works. In the following excerpt, she offers a general appraisal of Wolfe's accomplishment and posits reasons for the appeal of his books to the young.*]

It is no accident that ***Look Homeward, Angel*** is the most clear-sighted of [Wolfe's] novels. Born into the lower middle-class life of a small mountain town, he pictured the familiar world with an objectivity altogether remarkable. The farther he journeyed from Asheville the more baffled he became, and the less sure of himself. When he left the mountains he discovered that he could not go home again, and for the rest of his life was haunted by the sense of being a wanderer and adrift. He was lost in the city and in the foreign lands; in 1929 the whole world of his most intimate experience came to an end, and he never came to terms with the new one. In his loneliness he was America herself, America of the nineteen-twenties: huge, young, aggressive, unfound, like an adolescent at a grownup party, and he looked with desire and awe upon the future. He managed to "greet the unseen with a cheer," proclaiming his certainties, thundering his reassurances; but he was never again as confident of himself as Eugene had been when he spoke with Ben's ghost beneath the stone angel. . . .

With all his gigantic faults, his prolixity, his ranting, his stupefying absurdities, Wolfe is incomparably the most significant figure in three decades of American literature. His egotism arises from a profound desire to analyse the nature of his own being, not from a passion to display himself to others. He is the egotist unconscious of an audience. . . . Wolfe is labouring upon a mental excavation that engages his entire attention; he would no sooner make a concession to an interruptor than a surgeon would break off in the middle of trepanning to look out of the window at a Salvation Army band. . . .

He never acquired "poise." His later work displays even more sharply than his earlier books the defiance that comes of being uncertain. His antagonism towards modern European culture sprang from worshipful envy of its long ancestry. By his references to "fancy" writing, he means the oversophisticated writing of the intellectual who believes fundamentally that his learning has made him superior to the common man; and this is a peculiarly European outlook. Wolfe felt that the foundations of an American literature were still being laid; and he therefore resented the writer whose ease arises out of a conviction that he is simply continuing, and adorning, a tradition. The youthfulness of his country weighed heavily upon Wolfe; he thought of America *culturally* as the brilliant but underprivileged board school boy matched against the university man of Europe—a boy who, because of his very disadvantages, must work twice as hard and succeed three times as brilliantly. . . .

He never acquired "professionalism." He never learned to trim his work, polish it, or play safe with it. . . . He wrote because he wished to communicate something that seemed to him inexpressibly urgent; nothing else mattered. This is why his books carry so powerful a sense of his personality; they are the most intimate writings, the most naked and the most trustful, of this generation. He set out in search of an impossible ideal—to communicate that which is incommunicable. He ended with a philosophy that is little more than a few vague conclusions and a few verifications. What he did achieve was a finished portrait of the artist as a young man, and within this man the portrait of a continent. "The whole thing's there—it really *is*." (pp. 154-57)

The most striking feature of the Gant-Webber novels is their youthfulness. They do, indeed, look outward upon the future as a boy looks out in fear and terrifying hope upon his manhood. Their sincerity is a boy's sincerity, and their confidence is that friendliness which is offered to all men only before experience has brought common sense and distrust, balance and corruption. . . .

When ***Look Homeward, Angel,*** was first published in England, it was the young people who greeted it with excitement and with that curious uprush of personal affection which upon rare occasion greets the author of a novel that has come upon certain

Wolfe at the time of the composition of Of Time and the River. *Photograph by Robert Disraeli.*

hidden springs in the wilderness of the reader's desire. Young men and women between seventeen and twenty-three years of age felt that in some obscure way Wolfe was their spokesman; perhaps, after all, he had managed to send out some message from the incommunicable prison. His lyricism was the expression of their own longing to put into words the wonder and strangeness of coming out of childhood. The Laura James idyll which, to the mature critic, shows Wolfe at his weakest, to the adolescent represented love as he most deeply wished to find it. The boy who felt himself in any way restrained or subjected by his parents was moved by Eugene's protest to his family after the fight with Luke and Ben; this, thought the boy, is what *I* should like to have said, if only I could have found the words. The optimism towards the future, *despite the gainsaying of a dead man,* encouraged the young reader to feel himself Promethean, capable of defying not only those set in authority over him by reason of kinship, age and experience, but of defying also the supernatural authority—God and the voice of the Prophets. Wolfe gave to the young man a conviction that whatever might be the defeat of others, his own future would be straight and shining as the path of the sun across the sea.

He is American as Whitman was American, and like Whitman realises the *earliness* of the time at which he speaks. Although he cannot claim, as Whitman could, to be among the pioneers, he does believe himself in the company of those who follow after them to develop the ore and oil of a new continent. His tremendous pride, the pride that vented itself in hostility towards the friends of Esther Jack, towards the English, and towards the publishers "Rawng and Wright," is counteracted by an even greater joy in being young, in being uncertain, of sitting down with the primer and learning the world from the beginning as once he learned new languages. Alone among the writers of his generation he understands that the indigenous culture of his country today is as young as England's was when Chaucer struck open the great way of modern English letters, and that the spaces of her future are unbounded. (p. 164)

Pamela Hansford Johnson, in her Hungry Gulliver *(copyright © 1948 Charles Scribner's Sons, and renewed 1975; copyright © 1963 Pamela Hansford Johnson; by kind permission of Curtis Brown on behalf of the Estate of Pamela Hansford Johnson), Charles Scribner's Sons, 1948 (and reprinted as* The Art of Thomas Wolfe, *Charles Scribner's Sons, 1963, 170 p.).*

[WALLACE STEGNER] (essay date 1950)

[In the following excerpt Stegner, a highly respected American man of letters, closely examines Wolfe's short story "The Lost Boy."]

The writings of Thomas Wolfe, whatever their other virtues, are not usually notable for the strictness of their form. At any length Wolfe was large and loose; his talents were antipathetic to the concentration and control by which the short story has always been marked. But **"The Lost Boy"** is something of an exception. It is large enough and loose enough, but it does have an unmistakable form, which arises immediately and inevitably out of the intention and is inseparable from it.

"The Lost Boy" has within it most of what Thomas Wolfe made his total message. It has the haunting evocation of the past, the preoccupation with Time, the irreparable loneliness of the individual, the constant solipsistic attempt to convert the remembered into the real. The characteristic search for the father is apparently not here, but the search for the brother which is the subject of this story is so closely related as to seem a part of Wolfe's extraordinary longing to project himself backward toward someone loved and respected and envied and lost. And the style and manner are Wolfe's typical manner; the form the story takes does not hinder his incantatory flow of words.

Wolfe was a magician, a witch doctor, drawing upon the same profundities of awe and ecstasy and fear which primitive religions and magic and superstition draw upon. His writing impulse was very often directed toward the laying of ghosts, the evoking of spirits, the making of medicine to confound restricting Time, the exorcism of evil, the ritual expiation of sin. It is entirely appropriate that the form of this story should be very close to that of a primitive or superstitious ritual. The story is as surely an act of healing as a Navajo Yehbetzai, as much a superstitious rite as the calling up of a spirit at a séance. It has the same compulsive, ritualistic, gradual accretion of excitement toward the point of the ghost's appearance. It observes rules older than literary criticism and taboos embedded in the subconscious of the race. This is a very sub-surface story; it comes close to being pure necromancy. Story and ritual are one; the form is utterly compulsive, though perhaps largely unconscious.

It does not begin like an exercise in voodoo, but like one of Wolfe's hymns to Time. In the beginning Wolfe evokes the Square in all its concreteness, from the dry whisking of the tails of the firehorses to the catalogue of implements in the hardware store window. Here is Grover, the lost boy, before he was lost; here is Grover "caught upon a point of Time." Grover is real in a real place, but the Square is more than a square, Grover is a child who is more than a child. There is a quality of trance: the returning plume of the fountain, the returning winds of April, the streetcars that go and come, the chanting of the strong repetitious rhetoric and the sonority of recurrent sounds put a magic on this Square even at its most real. Grover's birthmark is a mark of difference and perhaps of doom. And we cannot miss the heightening of everything, from Grover's gravity to old Gant's Old-Testament potency as the Father. Gant is all but God. It is not accidental that he works at an altarlike bench among half-formed shapes of angels and that he strikes awe into Grover. Neither is it accident that Grover prays to him and that Gant in a godlike rage seizes him by the hand and goes to enforce justice upon old twisted Crocker. The father leaves an absence in the story because after the first section he is not mentioned again. His absence is like the absence of Grover. He duplicates and parallels that tantalizing ghost.

There are magic words in this story with magic powers to evoke. "St. Louis" and "the Fair" are two of them. It will be observed that the story follows a course from the Square where Grover's real life was, through Indiana to St. Louis, to the street called King's Highway, to the house where the family lived during the summer of the Fair, and finally to the room where Grover died. There is a progression from the more general to the more particular, a constant working closer to the point of mystery. But at the same time there is progression of another kind. This story fades and sharpens, comes and goes, like the fountain plume and the streetcars, and like the memory that recreates the past and sees it fade again, but it always works closer and closer toward the mystery of Grover, the mystery of Time, the thing which is being summoned and the thing which has been lost. As it comes closer it grows on tension; its climax, surely, will be the dramatic appearance of this ghost, the dramatic revelation of mystery.

But the spell moves slowly. The lost boy must be built up bit by bit. First his mother and then his sister bear testimony about him, recreating him in quality and feature. Their testimony is like that of mourners at a funeral of one much loved: they have fixed the dead in their minds so that he cannot entirely disappear or be entirely lost. Through the mother, as the family travels down through Indiana to St. Louis and the Fair, we see Grover from one side. Through the sister, less sentimental, more touched with questionings, more moved by irrecoverable loss, we see him from another, and we follow him through the St. Louis summer to his death.

For the sister the Past is dead, the things they were and dreamed as children are dead, there is a kind of horror in thinking of how sad and lonely is the gap between Then and Now, and a sharper compulsion to cling to it and linger over it and understand it. Through the sister's part of the story we have come closer to the place of magic, and we have come much closer to Grover, for at the heart of her recollection is the photograph. There is his veritable face; there are the faces of all of them as they were—caught and petrified unchanged, but strange, almost unbelievable. Wolfe makes the same use of the photograph that a medicine man might make of nail parings or hair cuttings or gathered-up footprints in the mud: the possession of this picture gives us a power, by associative magic, over Grover's spirit.

And in both these witnesses note the hypnotic mumbling of the spell—the words and images that will roll Time back and restore the lost, or seem to for a moment. . . . (pp. 178-81)

Over and over the images are recalled, the words of magic repeated. In section four the story begins to tighten toward its climactic moment. It has here the same trancelike repetitions, the same bewitched enslavement to memory, and it insists more upon the supernatural. In Eugene's childhood King's Highway had been "a kind of road that wound from magic out of some dim and haunted land," but he finds it now a common street, and his compulsive return toward the core of the mystery is delayed and made irritable by the contrasts between what he remembers and what really is. Finding the street, the house, the steps, he pauses and looks back "as if the street were Time," and waits "for a word, for a door to open, for the child to come."

But neither the dead nor the child that he himself once was can be recalled so easily. He knows he is close to them. He feels how it is all the same "except for absence, the stained light of absence in the afternoon, and the child who had once sat there, waiting on the stairs." It is as tantalizing as a séance where the ghost is coy. (pp. 181-82)

And suddenly he is evoked and present and palpable. The witch doctor has made the Past real by naming its every particle, chanting and cataloguing the memories it is made of. Now he brings up the ghost by the same "name" magic. "Say *Grover!*" the ghost is saying. "No—not Gova—*Grover!* Say it!"

Among many primitive tribes the name is a secret revealed to none, for fear strength and life will be exposed with it. Among organizations as various as street gangs and Catholic sisterhoods the spiritual or special self has its special name. Among the ancient Irish it was a capital crime to put a man by name into a poem, for both poem and name were potent with magic and power could be got over anyone so be-spelled. It is the name that reveals Grover briefly and brings him up from the dark cellar of Time. It is as if, if only the child Eugene could say the name right, Grover might now literally appear. But this attempt to cross between Forever and Now is never more than half successful. The closest we get to Grover's quiet ghost is his little brother's lisping "Gova."

But this is enough. Wolfe's magic, like Eugene's, invokes the ghost briefly and holds him a moment before he fades. The ghost that troubled Eugene, the rival that he loved and half envied, is laid and quieted. The man sick with Time is healed, the voodoo spell is finished, the spirit has spoken its cryptic word and departed. (pp. 182-83)

When the ghost has been summoned and held briefly and allowed to fade, the story is over. Ritual and story are one, with one shape. What suspense the story has is the suspense of the growing, circling, nearing incantation. Its climax is the moment of confrontation. Its peculiar emotional power comes from the chanting, the repetition, the ceremonial performances, the magical tampering with Time, the sure touching of symbols that lie deep among the sources of all superstition and all religion, above all by the anguished invocation of the dead. No one who has lived at all with his dead can be left entirely unmoved by this.

Not a line of this story, not a trick in it, could have been learned from any generalization about the shaping of fiction. The shape this story takes it takes by a process of transplantation, associated images and ideas being moved from one category of thought to another. A formal ritual becomes a formal fiction by what William James calls "similar association." Material and form are so nearly one that they can never be effectively separated. (p. 183)

[Wallace Stegner], "Thomas Wolfe, 'The Lost Boy': Analysis," in The Writer's Art: A Collection of Short Stories, *Wallace Stegner, Richard Scowcroft, Boris Ilyin, eds. (copyright 1950 by D. C. Heath and Company), Heath, 1950, pp. 178-83.*

LOUIS UNTERMEYER (essay date 1955)

[A poet during his early career, Untermeyer is better known as an anthologist of poetry and short fiction, an editor, and a master parodist. Horace Gregory and Marya Zaturenska have noted that Untermeyer was "the first to recognize the importance of the anthology in voicing a critical survey of his chosen field." Notable among his anthologies are Modern American Poetry *(1919), and* The Book of Living Verse *(1931). Untermeyer was also a contributing editor to* The Liberator *and* The Seven Arts, *and served as poetry editor of* The American Mercury *from 1934 to 1937. In the following excerpt he surveys Wolfe's career.]*

Thomas Wolfe was the epitome of gigantic need and illimitable excess, a symbol of the "enormous space and energy of American life," its rawness and richness, its frenetic successes and stupendous failures. The man who might have stood for the portrait of the magnified American hero—a shaggy black-haired, burning-eyed, six-foot-six Paul Bunyan, a craftsman who built everything on a monstrous scale—was vulnerable to the least murmur of criticism, tormented by the passing of time, and fearful of loneliness and the sense of being lost. Nothing ever conceived in America, except by Whitman, vibrated with so exuberant and desperate a craving for life—*all* of life, experienced simultaneously and on every level-as the four novels of the writer who died before he had lived thirty-eight years. (p. 726)

Writing came easily—often too easily—to Wolfe. Words flowed from him freely, inexhaustibly, furiously, as though they had been held back too long, sudden freshets released and rushing uncontrollably out of orderly channels. At twenty the river which was to carry him in full flood was taking an uncertain course, but it was already beginning to rise. New plays were written, were praised, but were always rejected. Everyone was impressed with Wolfe's dramas, but no one wanted to produce them. (p. 727)

He had already begun to think of a kind of novel when he went abroad for a year. Forced to resume teaching, he returned, ran away again, and, in the fall of 1926, found himself in London. Alone, and in a foreign country, he began his book. Back in New York, after two and a half years more of teaching all day and writing all night, he finished it. "The book took hold of me and possessed me," he wrote in his revealing quasi-diary, ***The Story of a Novel.*** "In a way, I think it shaped itself. Like every young man, I was strongly under the influence of writers I admired. One of the chief writers at that time was Mr. James Joyce with his book *Ulysses*. The book that I was writing was much influenced, I believe, by his own book, and yet the powerful energy and fire of my own youth played over and, I think, possessed it all. Like Mr. Joyce, I wrote about things that I had known, the immediate life and experience that had been familiar to me in my childhood. Unlike Mr. Joyce, I had no literary experience. I had never had anything published before." . . . (pp. 727-28)

The work, finally called ***Look Homeward, Angel,*** was published a few days after his twenty-ninth birthday. Wolfe had worried that he had exposed himself—"the awful, utter nakedness of print, that thing which is for all of us so namelessly akin to shame came closer day by day"—and he was relieved when most of the critics hailed the book with surprised superlatives. He was, however, unprepared for the howls of outrage which arose from his home town. He was irrevocably hurt when he heard that the book had been denounced from the pulpits and reviled on street corners. (p. 728)

Six months after publication, his book went so well that he was able to resign from the faculty of New York University and, assisted by an award of a Guggenheim Fellowship, go abroad again. In Paris he felt a great wave of homesickness and, in "the almost intolerable effort of memory and desire," recreated and enlarged the entire progress of his life. The past came back to him "loaded with electricity, pregnant, crested, with a kind of hurricane violence." He says that the second book was not really written; it wrote him. It was to be called *The October Fair,* but the onrushing memories bore him along on a "torrential and ungovernable flood," and he decided on the inevitable title ***Of Time and the River.*** (p. 729)

He wanted to cram into it detail upon detail, to reproduce in its entirety "the full flood and fabric of a scene in life itself." There was always something more, he felt, that needed desperately to be said, something to be added to the thousands of pages in the packing case. . . . In March, 1935, after the author had worked on the continuation of his (or Eugene Gant's) story for almost six years, ***Of Time and the River*** appeared. (p. 730)

Although the next two novels continue the saga of the writer's life the four books are actually one book, one towering autobiography—Wolfe now calls his hero George Webber. . . . Except for the arbitrary distortions, Webber remains Gant and, with a somewhat toughened manner, Wolfe.

In ***The Web and the Rock*** and ***You Can't Go Home Again,*** both of which were published posthumously, the character of Gant-Webber-Wolfe changes only insofar as any man changes with age and experience. He is ambivalent, pitiful, perverse, sometimes even paranoiac, but always aware of his weaknesses; he analyzes his compulsive rages and ramping inconsistencies, balancing self-pity with self-mockery. Always he is something more than himself. He is (or meant to be) not only the ambivalent American artist but the symbol of America itself, intransigent and contradictory, looking to Europe for escape and inspiration and, at the same time, repudiating the past, denying any heritage but our own. . . . (p. 731)

Wolfe's faults are so obvious that it was all too easy for the critics to belabor them. The faults are part of his excess: the disorganized gusto, the fierce energy that will not be beaten into form, the confusion of philosophy and feeling, the contradiction between social consciousness and the failure to do anything about it. (p. 732)

It is not enough to say that Wolfe is great in spite of his faults; the exaggerations, the wild monologs, the overextended raptures must be accepted as integrated and inseparable parts of the man. The pared concision, the brusque epigram was not for him. Wolfe luxuriated in length; he had to have great expanses to stretch himself. . . . One must also grant Wolfe's inability to distinguish between eloquence and verbosity, letting rhetoric slide into rant; his personal and general jealousies; his mixed envy and hatred of the well-to-do sophisticates, especially the Jews, the intellectuals, "the liberated princelings"; his incredible total recall which, superficially like Proust's, was without Proust's magic power of revelation. Properly balanced, the defects are minor blemishes when weighed against Wolfe's major accomplishments: the inexhaustible vitality—only in Rabelais and Joyce is there a swifter spate of words, a more joyful use of speech—the exuberant optimism; the enigmatic but noble summaries, the salutations to his native soil, a country compounded of "nameless fear and of soaring conviction, of brutal, empty, naked, bleak, corrosive ugliness, and of beauty so lovely and so overwhelming that the tongue is stopped by it, and the language for it has not yet been uttered." (pp. 732-33)

Wolfe tried too hard and stretched himself too far for perfection, but perfection was scarcely his aim. His furious desire to outreach time and space was bound to fail. But, as William Faulkner, Wolfe's fellow-Southerner and in many ways his opposite, contended, "Wolfe made the best failure because he had tried hardest to say the most . . . He was willing to throw away style, coherence, all the rules of preciseness, to try to put all the experience of the human heart on the head of a pin, as it were" [see *TCLC,* Vol. 4]. (p. 733)

I'd rather be a poet than anything else in the world." [Wolfe once] cried. "God! What I wouldn't give to be one!" Two posthumous volumes—***The Face of a Nation,*** a collection of poetical passages from his writings, and ***A Stone, A Leaf, A Door,*** segments of his prose rearranged as verse—prove that Wolfe not only wrote prose-poetry but that Wolfe was a poet who happened to use the medium of prose. He mistakenly thought that he was not a poet because he put the emphasis on conventional form and refused to believe that his sprawling lines could attain the art he most admired. Nevertheless, the beat of ecstatic life, the rise and fall of tidal emotions, and the restless flow of the river of time are held in Wolfe's rhythmical, strongly cadenced lines. In no prose and only in a small body of verse has there been expressed a greater sense of urgency, of unhappy adolescence and its insatiable desires, of loving kindness and unexpected cruelty, the wanderings of the human spirit. (p. 734)

Louis Untermeyer, "Thomas Wolfe [1900-1938]," in his Makers of the Modern World: The Lives of Ninety-Two Writers, Artists, Scientists, Statesmen, Inventors, Philosophers, Composers, and Other Creators Who Formed the Pattern of Our Century *(copyright © 1955 by Louis Untermeyer; renewed © 1983 by Bryna Ivens Untermeyer; all rights reserved; reprinted by permission of Simon & Schuster, Inc.), Simon & Schuster, 1955, pp. 726-35.*

WRIGHT MORRIS (essay date 1958)

[Morris, an American Midwestern novelist, discusses Wolfe's acquisition of experience and its transformation into fiction by comparing Wolfe to hungry Gulliver among the Lilliputians: each has an enormous appetite, consumes much, but is never filled.]

> Didn't Hemingway say this in effect: if Tom Wolfe ever learns to separate what he gets from books from what he gets from life, he will be an original. —"Notebooks"
> F. Scott Fitzgerald

If Tom Wolfe ever learned, he left no evidence of it. He never learned to separate what he got from books from what he got from life. His appetite wouldn't let him. A glutton for life, he actually died of impoverishment. He bolted both life and literature in such a manner he failed to get real nourishment from either. . . . Slabs of raw life were reduced to crates of raw manuscript. The figure of Wolfe, a piece of manuscript in hand, standing beside a bulging crate of typewritten paper, convincingly symbolizes our raw-material myth and attests to our belief in it. Both the size of the man and the size of the crate are in *scale*.

No greater paradox could be imagined than this raw young giant, a glutton for life, whose experience, in substance, was essentially vicarious. He got it from books. He gives it back to us in books. His lyrical rhetoric and his sober narration—the full range, that is, of his style—derives from his reading, and his reading, like his living, was something he bolted.

If literature is your life—the artist's life—it, too, must be processed by your imagination. It must be transformed, as raw material is transformed, before it is possessed. In this transformation there is a destructive element. The artist must destroy, in this act of possession, a part of what he loves. In passing it on, through his own achievement, he leaves it different from what he found. It is the element of difference, not sameness, that testifies to his right of possession. But it is the element of sameness—transference rather than transformation—that we find in Wolfe. Described as the Walt Whitman of novelists, here is what he does, how he echoes Whitman:

> Oh, there are women in the East—and new lands, morning, and a shining city! There are forgotten fume-flaws of bright smoke above Manhattan, the forest of masts about the crowded isle, the proud cleavages of departing ships, the soaring web, the wing-like swoop and joy of the great bridge, and men with derby hats who come across the bridge to greet us—come brothers, let us go to find them all. For the huge murmur of the city's million-footed life, far, bee-like, drowsy, strange as time, has come to haunt our ears with all its golden prophecy of joy and triumph, fortune, happiness, and love such as no men before have ever known. Oh brothers. . . .

This is meant to be an invocation. What we have is a man with his eyes closed, his pores open, whipping himself into a state of intoxication with what is left of *another* man's observations. The rhetorical flow, lyrical in intent, is unable to keep up with the flow of the emotion, the verbal surge of clichés, of scenic props, to the winded anticlimax of

> the men with derby hats who come across the bridge to greet us—come brothers, let us go to find them all.

The pathetic irrelevance of his touch is central to the flow of fantasy. Rather than Whitman's artifacts, closely and lovingly observed, we have a river of clichés, nouns and soaring adjectives. This giant from the hills may be in love with life, but he woos her with books. It is through another man's eyes that he looks, and it is another man's language that he uses. Life might well ask him, as Priscilla did John Alden, to speak for himself. The presence of raw material, real, raw, bleeding life—the one thing that Wolfe believed he got his big hands on—is precisely what is absent from his work. He begins and he ends with raw-material clichés. (pp. 147-50)

In a letter to Fitzgerald—frequently cited to show Wolfe's superior vitality and passion—Wolfe made this confession:

> . . . one of my besetting sins, whether you know it or not, is lack of confidence in what I do.

It was a sound intuition. He *knew,* but he did not know *what* he knew. It was a *feeling* he had, but like all of his feelings it remained unexamined, one of his frequent apprehensions, his premonitions of disorder and early sorrow that increased, rather than calmed, his romantic agony. In his effort to both release, and control his muse, he had two styles. Samples of his "release," usually referred to as lyrical flights, I have quoted. In contrast to the lyrical flight is sober, dispassionate, narrative.

> It would have been evident to an observer that of the four people who were standing together at one end of the platform three—the two women and the boy—were connected by the relationship of blood.

This is "control." It is also unintentional parody. Max Beerbohm might have coined it to take care of the great *traditional* novel. Wolfe assumes the stance, he clears his throat, but the voice that issues from his mouth is not his own, and the words fall into unconscious parody. The shades of Thackeray and Trollope, in this prose, were not connected by the relationship of blood. (pp. 150-51)

He believed in doing nothing—as Faulkner reminds us—short of the impossible. The existence of the legend of Paul Bunyan may have given young Tom Wolfe something to shoot at, but in many ways he overshot the mark. The word prodigious—in energy, in scale, in talent, in ambition, and in failure—is the word that most happily characterizes the pilgrimage. For

Wolfe made one. He made one for all of us. Although his song is a song of himself—a choric forest murmur to the lyric Walt Whitman—his hunger, insatiable as it was, was still too small. It is the continent itself that seeks to speak in the bellow of Wolfe. Everything observable, desirable, and, on certain rare occasions, even conceivable is thrown into the hopper of his hunger and—*bolted*. Nothing, absolutely *nothing*, is left on the table. We see only where his elbows leaned, and the crumbs he dropped.

What we observe in Wolfe—if we care to observe him—is how a man *eats*. As we watch him eat his very appetite grows; he bolts his food, he reaches for more, and in the very act of gorging himself he starves to death. It is a vivid and appalling projection of our buried life. We want to grasp life whole, grasp it raw and bleeding, and then gulp it while it's hot. Sometimes we do. But the results are not what we were led to expect. Our appetite, rather than being diminished, has increased. In living out this dream of our buried lives—in living it up, as we would now describe it—Wolfe threw himself into the bonfire all of us had built. His identification with the myth, with its attendant exaltations, and, as the fire began to die, with the usual premonitions, took on the nature of a public purge and sacrifice. These premonitions of death are self-induced; an infinite craving finds its resolution in a craving for the infinite. In his prodigious effort, in his prodigious failure, was our success. (pp. 151-53)

The continent too big for one man to tame it, the story too big for one man to tell it, the manuscript too big for one crate to hold it, one man to shape it—this myth of too-muchness received its classic affirmation in the figure of Wolfe. In identifying himself, lavishly, with the malady that masquerdes as a virtue, he lived to the hilt the illusion that is fatal to both the man and the artist. The impotence of *material*, raw or otherwise, receives its widest advertising in his mammoth showcase—almost everything is there but the imagined thing, and all of it bigger than life. The sight of all these objects generated in Wolfe sentiments and sensations of a literary nature, and on occasion, unknowingly, he was moved to something like creative activity. But *that* sensation, singularly unfamiliar, and smacking unmistakably of *self*-control, and self-denial, was the one sensation that he deeply distrusted, distrusted intuitively one might say. That sort of thing led him away from *himself*, and where, if anywhere, did that lead?

He didn't know, and he put off, deliberately, every chance to find out. His artistic solution was to write the same book over and over again, each time in the hope that this time the spirit would inhabit it, each time in the hope that his chronic self-doubt would stop tormenting him. The chorus of praise, world-wide, did not console or beguile him. After all, he *knew*. He knew better than those who hailed his failure as a success. As a martyr to our greed, our insatiable lust for life, which makes life itself an anticlimax, Wolfe is such proof as we need that appetite and raw material are not enough. They are where art begins, but to begin at all calls for the tools of technique.

Loneliness, as a theme of adolescence, rather than aloneness, a condition of man, is what the reader finds in Wolfe and what will asure his continued popularity. It is idle to speak of Wolfe's defects as a writer, since it is precisely the defects that we find immortal. In them, on a cineramic scale, we see ourselves. Wolfe's impressive powers of description persuaded him, as it does most of his readers, that imaginative power of an impressive range was being exercised. On the evidence the contrary is the case, description takes the place of imagination, and an excess of description, a rhetoric of hyperbole, take the place of imaginative passion.

His book—for it is all one book—offers us the extraordinary spectacle, both haunting and appalling, of the artist as a cannibal. An insatiable hunger, like an insatiable desire, is not the sign of life, but of impotence. Impotence, indeed, is part of the romantic agony. If one desires what one cannot have, if one must do what cannot be done, the agony in the garden is one of self-induced impotence. It is Wolfe's tragic distinction to have suffered his agony for us all. (pp. 153-55)

Wright Morris, "The Function of Appetite: 'Thomas Wolfe'" (1958), in his The Territory Ahead *(copyright © 1957, © 1958, © 1961 by Wright Morris; copyright © 1957 by The Macmillan Company; all rights reserved; reprinted by permission of the author), Atheneum, 1963, pp. 147-55.*

CYRIL CONNOLLY (essay date 1958)

[*Connolly was an English novelist and critic who reviewed books for the* New Statesman, The Observer *and* The Sunday Times *from 1927 until his death in 1974. Considered a remarkably hard-to-please critic, he was the founding editor of the respected literary monthly* Horizon *(1939-1950). In the following excerpt from a review of* Selected Letters of Thomas Wolfe, *Connolly finds Wolfe to have been a fascinating but deeply flawed writer whose career was marred by his own self-obsession.*]

'I have at last discovered my own America, I believe I have found my language. I think I know my way. And I shall wreak out my vision of this life, this way, this world, and this America, to the top of my bent and to the height of my ability but with an unswerving devotion, integrity and purity of purpose that shall not be menaced, altered or weakened by anyone.'

Admittedly Thomas Wolfe is writing to his publisher, and they are gluttons for verbal beefcake, but the language is strangely like Hitler's. Why bring in America always? And who are these enemies who wish to menace, alter or weaken him? Right first time. The critics.

Not the critics one values, the constructive who praise but the sterile, the dead—the Hemingways, Fadimans, etc., who find fault. Expatriates! Waste-landers! 'Their idea of helping you is to kick you in the face.' . . . And so they are all put into the gaschamber of Thomas Wolfe's novels.

I should like to say more about these novels for they belong to my youth and I remember them coming out as one remembers the sullen explosions from a quarry. . . . (pp. 308-09)

This time I have really tried to read one and I can say with all my heart: this man is not a novelist; he is an obsessional neurotic with a gift for words who should write only about himself and who cannot create other people. He is the Benjamin Robert Haydon of American literature beside whom Dreiser is a dainty Benvenuto Cellini. He is hypnotised by the growth of his own personality and by the search for a spiritual father, a hormone who will accelerate the manic urge still further.

To be looking for a father is a wonderful excuse for dropping people, and Wolfe took advantage of this to the full. Although the climax in his short life seems to have been the 'break with Scribners' or the shedding of the faithful pilot, Maxwell Perkins, my own experience as a much-dropped, deposed, dethroned, decapitated father figure, a wandering Wotan, is that the father invariably does the dropping first in so far as he senses the mist of total obscurity or the hideous alpine glow of success that is gathering round his prodigy and I think that Maxwell Perkins must have failed to conceal his apprehension, both as a publisher and a friend, about the ponderous, paranoid, turgid flow of the Wolfe novels as the lonely giant, at grips with his enormous task of holding back absolutely nothing, emerged from solitude, every few minutes, to complain about some utterly unimportant word or criticism or well-meant piece of advice. 'I don't think he *consciously* wants me to fail or come to grief,' wrote Wolfe, 'but it's almost as if *unconsciously*, by some kind of *wishful* desire, he wants me to come to grief, as a kind of sop to his pride and his unyielding conviction that he is right in everything.'

Intimate, impressive and exemplary as was his relationship with Perkins, it was thereby doomed. . . . (pp. 309-10)

The king of father-chasers and prince of autobiographers was Joyce, and this similarity of purpose (fulfilment of genius through finding of father) united Wolfe to the great exile, with fatal detriment to his style. These echoes are apparent throughout ***Look Homeward, Angel,*** which mews with self-pity and Celtic twilight. (p. 310)

The high spirits, clowning and parodying, the scenes of broken-down family life are Joycean too. I have said I do not think Wolfe was a genius, nor am I sure he was a novelist; but in these ***Selected Letters*** he stands out as a fascinating writer. In his letters he could permit his egotism full rein. He made copies of his best letters or else did not send them or else got them back; he gloried in the fluent medium.

As he was a large and violent young man things were constantly happening to him. There was a terrible beating-up in Munich, an encounter with Joyce on the battlefield of Waterloo. The editor of the letters does not seem aware that the account of the 'musey-room' at Waterloo forms one of the key passages of *Finnegans Wake,* and that Wolfe (chagrined at not being recognised) was present at one of the most fortunate fertilisations of modern literature.

Inexcusable I find the omission, in the edition prepared for this country, of Wolfe's most interesting letter (unsent naturally), in which he describes at great length a devastating encounter with Scott Fitzgerald at the Ritz in Paris in 1930. Here this huge, ramshackle, shy, deep, good, suspicious and resentful young man, who looks like a genius and has nothing but talent, meets the older but not very fatherly little dandy, drunk and at the height of his success, who tries to launch Wolfe on Franco-American society. 'Every writer,' Fitzgerald tells him, 'is a social climber.' Wolfe rebuts the charge splendidly, but it is, all the same, in the little man from Princeton for all his snobbery and air of talent that the genius resides. Their subsequent Zola-Flaubert arguments are all coloured by this episode.

Suppose Wolfe had lived (for his death was inadvertent): at his present age (fifty-seven) he would have been an enormous figure in American literature. His driving energy, his egotism, the basic strength and rightness of his values both as an artist and a man would have seared away the blindness and the rhetoric; he would have come to terms with his persecution mania for he could never have dried up or become a spent ranter.

His prose would have been worthy of the poetical force beneath it, his absurd rocketry about great America, decadent Europe and so on been chastened by failures—the bull blundering about after critics' capes would have learnt wisdom. He would have been the Whitman of the Beat Generation, of course—and of many others—instead of the Thinking Bull. 'Why is it that we are burnt out to an empty shell by the time we are forty. . . . Is it because we take a young man of talent—a young man proud of spirit, and a thirst for glory, and full with the urge to make his life prevail—praise him up to the skies at first, and then press in upon him from all sides with cynics' eyes and scornful faces, asking him if he can *ever do it again* or is done for, finished?' (pp. 310-12)

Cyril Connolly, "Thomas Wolfe" (1958; copyright © 1958 by Cyril Connolly; reprinted by permission of the Literary Estate of Cyril Connolly), in his Previous Convictions, *Hamish Hamilton, 1963, pp. 308-12.*

RICHARD S. KENNEDY (essay date 1962)

[*Kennedy is an American critic and biographer whose sensitive and insightful lives of Thomas Wolfe and E. E. Cummings are highly acclaimed. Since the 1970s he has edited and published several collections of Wolfe's previously uncollected writings, and he is currently at work on studies of Robert Browning, Thomas Hardy, and of twentieth-century American fiction. In the following excerpt from* The Window of Memory: The Literary Career of Thomas Wolfe, *Kennedy surveys Wolfe's career as a dramatist, which began at the University of North Carolina.*]

[Among] the various [campus] organizations to which [Wolfe] belonged, only one had a direct bearing on his career, The Carolina Playmakers, supervised by Professor Frederick Koch. (p. 46)

Wolfe enrolled in Koch's courses in dramatic composition for two years, but apparently he never worked very hard at his writing. Paul Green recalls that Wolfe would always wait until the night before an assignment was due, stay up all night writing his one-act play, and come to class hollow-eyed and unshaven to read the result. His mountaineer play, **"The Return of Buck Gavin,"** which was enacted in the first Playmakers program, spring, 1919, was composed in this fashion. Wolfe dashed off the play in three hours one rainy evening after seeing a newspaper item in the *Grand Forks* [*North Dakota*] *Herald* reporting the capture of Patrick Lavein, a Texas outlaw, in a Chicago tenement. His gift for mimicry made the mountain dialogue an easy matter, but the play was poor, even for a student effort. (p. 47)

[During his two years with the Playmakers, Wolfe] was introduced to a writing method that he later used in his significant work. Frederick Koch (who had adopted the idea from Professor [George Pierce] Baker) urged all his students to use the materials of their own experience in their writing. Later, Wolfe realized that his plays at Chapel Hill were bad because they were false. As he said, he knew all about boarding houses, but he wrote about bootlegging mountaineers. He did not turn to his real experience until his later years at Harvard. (pp. 48-9)

At Harvard, not only did Thomas Wolfe soak himself in the great literature of the world but, during this time, he made the all-important decision to become a professional writer. His prolific writing career began in Professor George Pierce Baker's 47 Workshop, where he turned out ***Welcome to Our City,*** his first creditable literary production. Moreover, living alone, far from home and familiar surroundings, he began to formulate ideas about writing and about the life of the artist that were to have far-reaching effects on his future. (p. 59)

Still, it was not until he had absorbed the enthusiasm of the older students that he thought of becoming a professional playwright. He dared to think so just after he had written his first play, **"The Mountains,"** a one-act revision of a script begun in North Carolina: "For the first time, it occurs to me that writing may be taken seriously—separated from home I realize that it is not a remote thing for me—that it is a very present thing—Life begins to have [shape?] in spite of the welter of events and reading."

"The Mountains," which Wolfe had begun writing in Chapel Hill, is a folk play in which people say "hit ain't" and "that air," and as a folk play it follows, supposedly, the theory of realism that he began to practice at Harvard and developed further for his autobiographical novels. In a paper written for Professor Greenough in the spring of 1921, Wolfe had this to say about the folk plays of the Chapel Hill group: "The promise of such a movement in which the material is based on the author's own experience and observation and more than that, perhaps grows out of his very life, cannot be under-estimated. From such stuff as this drama is made!"

The plot of **"The Mountains,"** however, does not make use of Wolfe's life but only of the mountain region around Asheville. A young Carolina doctor returns from medical school to take up his father's practice in his native region, for he intends to care for the needs of the poor mountain folk. On the day of his return, a long-standing family feud breaks out, and in spite of his former resolve to hold aloof from old quarrels, he goes out with his rifle to join his kinfolk as the curtain falls. Baker liked the play and promised to include it in the next year's program. It was presented first in a trial performance on January 25, 1921, in the Workshop Rehearsal Room along with three other one-act plays. After revision it was included in the regular program of the Workshop performances, October 21 and 22, 1921, as one of three one-act plays, with John Mason Brown as the old doctor and Dorothy Sands as his daughter. Since the dialogue was over-wordy and there was very little action, the play was a miserable failure. (pp. 71-2)

Wolfe had come upon the idea for his new play [***Welcome to Our City***] about a year previous to its final production. In June, 1922, when he had gone home for the first time in two years, he found that Asheville had changed. The boom years had come. In a letter to Mrs. Roberts that fall, he thundered out his complaint:

> Coming home this last time I have gathered enough additional material to write a new play,—the second fusillade of the battle. This thing I had thought naive and simple is as old and as evil as hell; there is a spirit of world-old evil that broods about us, with all the subtle sophistication of Satan. Greed, greed, greed,—deliberate, crafty, motivated—masking under the guise of civic associations for municipal betterment. The disgusting spectacle of thousands of industrious and accomplished liars, engaged in the mutual and systematic pursuit of their profession, salting their editorials and sermons and advertisements with the religious and philosophic platitudes of Dr. Frank Crane, Edgar A. Guest, and the American Magazine.

This was the situation that set him writing "Niggertown," the play in ten scenes which was produced by the Workshop on May 11 and 12, 1923, under the title ***Welcome to Our City.*** This work, covering the life of a Southern town, tells the story of a real-estate group who, together with civic authorities, contrive to buy up all the property in the centrally located Negro district of the town. They plan, after evicting all the tenants, to tear down the old property in order to build a new white residential section. When the Negro group resists eviction, a minor race riot breaks out, and the militia comes to restore order. Since Wolfe tries to picture a cross section of the town life, much of the dialogue does not pertain to the central action, but with the exception of the last scene the play reads very well.

Wolfe employs a variety of techniques (even including stylized pantomime) as the play ranges in mood from broad comedy to the tragedy of the death of the Negro leader. His characters include all classes and ages, both colored and white. Here, too, he brings in for the first time some of the "humorous" characters, in the Jonson-Smollett-Dickens tradition, that he was to draw with such success in his novels. His satire has many targets: Southern politics, backward universities, evangelical preachers, small-town boosters, provincial little theatre groups, and even short-sighted humanitarians. (pp. 77-8)

Welcome to Our City, as produced in Agassiz Theater in May, 1923, was one of the most spectacular productions ever undertaken by the Workshop. It made use of seven different arrangements of a unit set and had a cast of forty-four people, with thirty-one speaking parts (Wolfe himself put on blackface to take part in the crowd scenes). The performances were very exciting; yet the play was not a complete success. It was original in its presentation of several strata of town life and in its forthright treatment of race relations; but some of the scenes extraneous to the main action were far too lengthy for their purpose. The chief fault, however, was that the moral positions of the antagonists—Rutledge, the white leader, and Johnson, the Negro leader—were not clear, probably because Wolfe's views on the race question were not clear in his own mind. . . . As a piece of writing, the play was the best work Wolfe had done: the characters were the first life-like creatures he had ever drawn. But he had also used real-life models for the first time. One of the guests in the audience, Miss Laura Plonk from Asheville, was astounded as the plot unfolded. After the show, she rushed backstage to Dorothy Sands to exlaim with horror, "I know every person in the play!" (p. 80)

Whereas ***Welcome to Our City*** is a happy product of Professor Baker's training and Wolfe's keen observation of life in his home town, ***Mannerhouse*** is a combination of all the unfortunate influences of the 47 Workshop and Wolfe's own faults in judgment. As a piece of dramaturgy, it illustrates what can happen to a young writer with great natural powers, who, having studied world drama and having been impressed by professorial commentary, tries to imitate modes of drama he is unfitted to write. It also illustrates Wolfe's tendency to throw everything in the pot together, thinking that if a few added ingredients improve the dish, a whole cupboardful will make an even better mixture. (pp. 90-1)

In its final version ***Mannerhouse*** presents the conflicting loyalties of a young man, Eugene Ramsay, during the Civil War, the decline of an aristocratic Southern family, and the passing of a romantic way of life. (p. 91)

[Wolfe] gives Eugene dark mutterings in the manner of the Elizabethan malcontent, continually stripping away appearances (" . . . just as all wars are the most terrible, so are all nations the greatest and most powerful; all armies the bravest;

and all women the most beautiful and virtuous. Major, everything has grown so great we must prepare for changes''). Besides innumerable Shakespearean allusions, he includes a scene in which Eugene, Hamlet-like, harshly rejects his Ophelia. He employs Ibsen's device of giving symbolic significance to a phrase which, early in the play, has been tossed out innocently (for example, the punch line to Eugene's fish story, ''The rivers are flowing backward''). Of course, Wolfe's use of the techniques or the ideas of other dramatists does not in itself make the play faulty. But when they are tumbled together, when they are introduced inappropriately, or when they contribute a false, contrived color to the action, belief in the author's sincerity is inevitably impaired.

But the chief difficulty with the play came about because Wolfe altered the theme while the writing was in progress. He had begun with an attack on Southern aristocracy, then changed to a preachment of 'a sincere belief in men and masters,'' and finally arrived at a compromise position; as he told Alice Lewisohn when he submitted the play to the Neighborhood Playhouse, ''even in its fierce burlesquing of old romanticism, it defends the thing it attacks.'' As a result, the gross improbability of Eugene's abrupt shifts in attitude are more disturbing than his mouthing of meaningless paradoxes (''I have lost something in the sun. I cannot find it—there is no moon''). It is desirable to have complexity in character, but here is only confusion. Wolfe had become absorbed with Eugene's dilemma, but he still retained the early plot about the sale of the land.

Yet there is, as Wolfe said, good stuff in it. The prologue, the building of the house in colonial times, is thrilling and significant. Later, peeping out of the rubbish of romantic posturing, there are occasional scenes that bring the play to life. (pp. 91-2)

Artistically, ***Mannerhouse*** is not a step forward from the achievement of ***Welcome to Our City***. Although Wolfe never felt the play was a total failure, he returned to the successful method of the earlier play, a reshuffling of characters and events in the life that he knew from close observation, when he began to write prose narrative. However, if we examine ***Mannerhouse*** for marks of Wolfe's development from 1923 to 1925, there are features that merit comment. First of all, it offers another criticism of urban and industrial civilization, a theme which recurs continually in Wolfe's work. Second, in this play Wolfe makes his first attempt to deal with the problem of reality (''Then, which of us is the ghost? Perhaps we live when we believe, we dream,'' says Eugene), a problem he later would treat in ***Look Homeward, Angel***, using Plato's idea of the prenatal life. Finally, ***Mannerhouse*** contains the first real manifestations of Wolfe's later prose eloquence. Although the linguistic calisthenics throughout the work occur, for the most part, at the expense of appropriateness, they are replaced occasionally by a highly charged rhythmic style, full of the devices of poetry. An example is the concluding stage direction of the prologue: ''A wind blows through the pines. All the million-noted little creatures of the night have come to life and are singing now in a vast, low chorus: a weird ululation which seems to continue and prolong the deep chant of the savages; which seems to hold in it the myriad voices of their demons.''

In the realm of social ideas, Wolfe was still under the influence of the anti-democratic writings of Carlyle and Mencken. He expreses these ideas through the character of General Ramsay, who in the end wins Eugene to his own belief in the established order of the South. (p. 93)

This, then, was the play Wolfe was chafing to complete while he was crushed under the load of freshman themes in 1924. ''Never have I wanted to write as I do now,'' he told Billy Polk. ''It is a crude hunger of the spirit. And never have I had less time for writing.'' As a remedy, he determined to go to Europe in September with the remainder of his year's pay, hoping he could accomplish enough work to support himself without teaching. (pp. 93-4)

Wolfe wanted the grand tour, he wanted to extend his observation to the European continent; then perhaps new work would shape itself. (p. 94)

Richard S. Kennedy, in his The Window of Memory: The Literary Career of Thomas Wolfe *(copyright © 1962 by The University of North Carolina Press), University of North Carolina Press, 1962, 461 p.*

EDWARD A. BLOOM (essay date 1964)

[In the following excerpt, Bloom offers a close analysis of one of Wolfe's most famous short stories, ''Only the Dead Know Brooklyn.''*]*

Until the concluding paragraphs, [**''Only the Dead Know Brooklyn''**] has what might be taken for a clear enough literal meaning. That is, we read a rather amusing account of an experience in Brooklyn, a well-tried subject. But the literal, we discover, does not carry us very far. What does simple paraphrase reveal? A stranger in Brooklyn looking for a location asks some natives for directions. None can agree on the location or a way of getting there, and they quarrel among themselves. . . .

It is then that the truculent first-person narrator takes over, tries to guide the stranger and fails. But at the same time he has the irrepressible curiosity of the legendary Brooklynite, and pumps the stranger to discover his motives. The narrator learns—to his intense surprise—that the unnamed stranger habitually wanders around Brooklyn with a map, looking for places that have pleasant-sounding names. Suddenly, without forewarning, the stranger asks the narrator (also unnamed) whether he can swim, and whether he has ever seen a drowning. The story ends on this puzzling note and the narrator, with justification, considers the incident one of some lunacy. For such peculiar things simply do not happen in Brooklyn.

Before we consider the actual meaning, point, or significance of the story, let us look at the fundamental details of technique. (p. 269)

Although we may choose to identify Wolfe with the stranger, the author at no time exposes his private personality. Rather, he permits two unidentified characters to carry the entire emotional and intellectual burden. The feeling of the story thus becomes fairly complex, even ambivalent. The stranger evokes a mood of wistfulness and sympathy. We can appreciate the esthetic hunger which drives him. Simultaneously, though we respect his yearning, we wonder whether the discovery is ever as rich as the anticipation. These are emotional details implied in the dialogue between protagonist and antagonist. The antithesis of the stranger is the narrator—commonplace, literal, irascible, and yet kindly. He intensifies a feeling of futility because of his banal repudiation of the search for beauty. The mood, then, combines sadness and frustration with provincial humor and unresolved optimism for the stranger's success. (pp. 269-70)

By subtle means the author is able to assert his attitude toward the reader. First he warns us in the title that only the dead know Brooklyn. Then he draws attention to normal impatience with idealistic, impractical quests such as the stranger's. Consequently, Wolfe implies the confusion and crudity of the vast area in which the search takes place. Toward this end he relies upon the aimless arguments of the anonymous speakers, who are like disembodied voices representative of ordinary mankind. Contrasting with this disorder is the map to which the stranger refers throughout the story. Presumably a symbol of order and stability, this manmade device is hopelessly misleading. Wolfe appears to say that the individual really has nothing material to guide him in his groping for values; only innate desire can direct him toward knowledge and beauty, which cannot be charted on a map: note the random (if esthetically motivated) manner in which the stranger selects the places he will visit.

Looking for an ultimate truth which he cannot readily isolate, he nevertheless persists. Each new place that he visits may provide him with the insight he seeks, so he must continue to roam about. Indeed, to cease striving, to endure the atrophy of the sense of wonder and inquiry—as the narrator has done—is to perish. Once the stranger hits upon the notion of drowning, it becomes a disturbing metaphor to connote human failure. The word "drowning" offers a significant clue to the tone of the story, because as a form of suffocation, drowning can be incorporeal as well as physical. The literal-minded narrator responds to the stranger as though he were talking about physical death. But the latter is not concerned here with physical death, only with that other death, the wasting away of the spirit. Although the stranger's attitude must be inferred, the inference follows logically from his consistent inattention to mundane matters. While the narrator returns to his world of actuality, the stranger pursues his ineffable search. In Brooklyn, where physical drowning is an impractical feat, the stranger consults his map and contemplates another kind of smothering. From his depiction of these men at cross-purposes, Wolfe has established tone in a twofold way: 1) to show us the aimlessness and inner bankruptcy of ordinary life; 2) to admonish and warn us against surrendering to spiritual and esthetic indifference.

Tone and mood are closely bound in with theme. The search for order, beauty, and individuality, it is suggested, may indeed be fruitless but must never be abandoned. Striving for positive values, one must also contend with ugliness and ignorance, for the good and the bad coexist. Yet that there can be no guarantee of success is implied in the ironical title. The dead are those who, like the narrator, have physically survived the material confusion and stifling effects of existence. Their survival, however, has depended upon an unquestioning attitude, one that is antithetical to the ultimate truth sought by the stranger. If people like the narrator are alive physically, the stranger's questions appear to disclose, they are dead spiritually. They know Brooklyn—which is life—only on the confused surface, and fragmentarily at that. The stranger, therefore, is left with a riddle of the disparity between material appearance and its hidden meaning. His own resolution of the riddle is left unstated, but we may assume that he will continue his search for answers.

Against the very real backdrop of Brooklyn, the atmosphere is paradoxically hazy and unrealistic. It emerges as a pervasive feeling of futility and impersonality—possibly an overwhelming challenge to individualism. Wolfe withholds names from his characters, who—as in allegory—are representative of society, of everyman. The conflict is not between flesh-and-blood people but between concepts: the restless individual search for the bluebird and the passivity of the acceptance. The struggle is one between a broad idea of absorptive materialism and threatened ideals. The surface humor of the dialect turns to bitter realization through our awareness of the complete absence of humor in the situation. There is, indeed, a sense of tragedy, enlarged by the blindness of the narrator to his own loss of individuality.

Except for superficial details, everything in this story is implicit. Wolfe does not tell us through any direct means the exact nature of the problem with which he is concerned. Nor does he develop his characters explicitly. Everything must come out through dialogue or through the rational process of the narrator's puzzlement. Only by inference do we discover Wolfe's allegorical intention of representing Brooklyn as modern confused society which suffocates individuality. By inference also we recognize that for most people this state of suffocation is acceptable, while those who resist are stigmatized as outsiders and eccentrics. (pp. 270-72)

Edward A. Bloom, "Critical Commentary On 'Only the Dead Know Brooklyn'," in his The Order of Fiction: An Introduction *(copyright © 1964 by the Odyssey Press, Inc.; used by permission of the author and The Bobbs-Merrill Company, Inc.), Odyssey Press, 1964 (and reprinted in* Thomas Wolfe: Three Decades of Criticism, *edited by Leslie A. Field, New York University Press, 1968, pp. 269-72).*

PASCHAL REEVES (essay date 1965)

[Reeves is the respected author and editor of many critical works on Wolfe's career. In the following excerpt he offers a close study of the character Esther Jack (from The Web and the Rock*) and traces similarities to her real-life counterpart, Aline Bernstein.]*

Esther Jack is not only one of Wolfe's greatest character creations but she is undoubtedly one of the most versatile heroines in literature. Seldom in the annals of amour have greater demands been made on mortal woman or have been more willingly and fully met by her. When Wolfe wrote in exultation of Esther "in all the world there was no one like her," . . . his romantic praise embodies a literal truth that would be difficult to dispute. Surely the ghosts of many women from Helen of Troy to Jennie Gerhardt must have curtsied to Esther Jack. For Esther the lover is cast in the hexamerous role of mistress, cook, mentor, patron, mother, and muse, all of which combine into a tripartite ministration to the heart, body, and spirit of George Webber. While each of these roles is important to the lonely, frustrated young man in the million-footed city, to George Webber the aspiring author that of muse is a paramount one. To Webber, however, even a muse has a dual function: she is both a source of inspiration and a fountainhead of information. Esther readily fills this dichotomous office.

Esther's vitality and enthusiasm provide a powerful stimulus to George's smoldering literary aspirations, and her own artistic temperament proves to be a catalytic agent to his latent powers. Certainly Esther functioned in her other capacities also to make possible the literary upsurge in George Webber and to direct it to fruition. She brought to the wild young man, who was about to be engulfed by the city, the love and certitude that he desperately needed. Her firm belief in a Carlylean doctrine of work aided her in bringing order to the chaos of George's life and setting him upon a regular schedule of work that would in time yield results. And spiritual succor was augmented by financial subsidization. But all of this important aid would have been ineffectual had not the creative fire in Webber been fanned to a consuming flame. Whether this artistic impetus was accomplished largely by her own competent craftsmanship, her deep understanding of and sympathy for the whole artistic process, or her loyal and oft articulated belief in George's ability is not revealed. It may have been a combination of these and other factors, but the important thing is that under Esther's aegis Webber did conceive and execute his novel *Home to Our Mountains*. In the primary function of muse Esther played no small part.

Likewise the secondary function of muse was equally well performed by Esther. In Webber's ardent quest for fictive material he found in her a rich source, and he mined the lode with the relentlessness of a forty-niner who discovered gold. This drawing on Esther for literary material is overtly described in ***The Web and the Rock***. . . . His method is that of a hostile lawyer cross-examining a witness: "He would go for her with ceaseless questions until she was bewildered and worn out; then he would come pounding back at her again." . . . This technique . . . produced the desired results: "In that way he kept after her, prying, probing, questioning about everything she told him, until at last he got from her the picture of her lost and vanished years." . . . If Esther became an exhausted muse, it is not surprising, because of Webber's efforts to squeeze her dry of literary material.

There is, moreover, yet another important service which Esther rendered in her role of muse. A fiction writer may write upon one or more of three ascending levels of experience. The first level is that of the experience of the author himself, the material which his own life provides him. The second level is the experience of others, that which the author learns through observation and investigation. The third level, and the one generally conceded to be the highest, is that of pure creation, the working of the author's imagination. (pp. 280-82)

Writing on the first level, an author runs the risk of producing autobiography rather than fiction. Since Webber wrote *Home to Our Mountains* on the first level, that is the very trap into which he fell. This is not to maintain that fictionalized autobiography is inartistic *per se;* it may be artistry of a high quality as is exemplified by the works of Proust and D. H. Lawrence. But until autobiographical fiction becomes a recognized and accepted genre, Webber will of course be deprecated by some critics for his persistence in writing *Home to Our Mountains* largely on the first level. However, Webber was not doomed to continue writing mostly on the first level, because Esther added a tertiary function to the role of muse. Not only did she provide Webber with fresh literary material but her zest for it enabled him to use the material with confidence and to break through his self-limiting barrier. Thus she aided him in progressing from the first to the second level, thereby greatly extending his range as a writer and adding a new dimension to his work.

Esther Jack's contributions to George Webber's literary achievements indeed are many. But in supplying a source of inspiration, furnishing fictive material, and assisting him to rise to the second level of fiction writing, she was in a very real sense George Webber's muse.

But what of Thomas Wolfe?

The temptation is always strong to make a hundred percent carryover from Wolfe's fiction to his own life, and to read into his fiction a literalness that he did not intend and indeed is, in many instances, just *not* present. This distinction—the difference between actuality and the fictional treatment of actuality—is one of the difficult problems confronting serious Wolfe scholarship, and the problem arises from the fact that in some instances there is practically no distinction at all while in others it is very great.

In the relationship between Thomas Wolfe and Aline Bernstein there are many obvious parallels to the George Webber-Esther Jack story. When Wolfe met Mrs. Bernstein in 1925, he was a frustrated playwright still trying to peddle his plays. If he had possessed the playwriting ability he at that time thought he had, she could have been a very great asset to him because her knowledge of the theater was truly extensive. But his attempt to write plays was, as he was later to say in his Purdue Speech, "not only wrong—it was as fantastically wrong as anything could be." While all of the reasons for his shift from drama to fiction writing are not entirely clear, it is true that this shift was made during the period of his closest association with Mrs. Bernstein and she encouraged him fully in it. Mrs. Bernstein's great faith in Wolfe's talents was unwavering and her trust was undergirded with financial support that enabled him to devote his full time to writing for long periods. It is undeniable that during her tenure ***Look Homeward, Angel*** was conceived, written, and published. (pp. 282-83)

Though Wolfe returned time and time again to his own life to structure his work, actually he did some of his best writing using other people's experiences as fictive material. **"Chickamauga,"** one of his best stories, is based on the experiences of his great-uncle, John Westall, who was ninety-five when he related them to Wolfe in the spring of 1937. His Joycean gem, **"The Web of Earth,"** is based on his mother's reminiscences. His unfinished novel ***The Hills Beyond*** is replete with similar examples. During the last three years of his life Wolfe wrote much more frequently on the second level and his work profited accordingly.

From 1925 to 1930 the greatest single influence on the life of Thomas Wolfe was Aline Bernstein. After his return from Europe in 1931 the romance was virtually over; there were painful confrontations and a few brief reconciliations after that, but the period of great intimacy had passed. Even though Wolfe burrowed into Brooklyn to escape her, he could never banish her completely from his mind; the powerful memories were stirred anew when he wrote or reworked the love story. Hence Aline Bernstein not only fulfilled a multi-role function in the life of Wolfe during a crucial period but she continued to hover over his literary material in spirit after their estrangement. It is no wonder, therefore, that when he developed the character Esther Jack he portrayed Esther, among other things, as George Webber's muse. Perhaps this is another of those instances in Wolfe's writing where a distinction between actuality and its fictional treatment does not exist, or if it does exist, that distinction is minimal. (pp. 284-85)

Paschal Reeves, "Thomas Wolfe: Notes on Three Characters," in Modern Fiction Studies *(© 1965 by Purdue Research Foundation, West Lafayette, IN 47907; reprinted with permission), Vol. XI, No. 3, Autumn, 1965, pp. 275-85.*

ALFRED KAZIN (essay date 1968)

[*A highly respected American literary critic, Kazin is best known for his essay collections* The Inmost Leaf *(1955) and* Contem-

poraries (1962), and particularly for On Native Grounds *(1942), a study of American prose writing since the era of William Dean Howells. Having studied the works of "the critics who were the best writers—from Sainte-Beuve and Matthew Arnold to Edmund Wilson and Van Wyck Brooks" as an aid to his own critical understanding, Kazin has found that "criticism focussed many—if by no means all—of my own urges as a writer: to show literature as a deed in human history, and to find in each writer the uniqueness of the gift, of the essential vision, through which I hoped to penetrate into the mystery and sacredness of the individual soul." In the following excerpt, Kazin deems Wolfe's works tediously self-centered, repetitious, and unreal.]*

Reading Thomas Wolfe today is like listening to a seedy, insanely garrulous old man who can never stop explaining each yellowed old photo in the family album. Everyone has seen those photographs and heard the stories for so long! . . .

Who cares? Who, any longer, can take in the maddening repetition and elongation of so much self-centered emotion? Emotion which we outsiders have had to endure over and again, first because Thomas Wolfe had an experience, then because Thomas Wolfe wrote about it, then because Thomas Wolfe described what it was like having this writing published, then because Thomas Wolfe had affairs with women who were moved by Thomas Wolfe's experience of *talking* about *writing* about being *published*. By now the Wolfe family saga, the Thomas Wolfe literary saga, the Thomas Wolfe publishing saga, the Thomas Wolfe computer saga about eating and drinking and copulating and reading 3.7 million times more than anybody else, have all become as boring as those other synthetic American myths about Paul Bunyan and Davy Crockett and George Washington and Mike Fink. (p. 1)

[Wolfe] only lived a great American novel: he did not write one. He is different from [other famous American] novelists in one important particular that may explain why his books have faded like old family snapshots. Despite all the legends about "young Gulliver's up from the Carolina mountains, despite all the pages he created of his resemblance to the great heroes and myth-makers of the past, Thomas Wolfe has never been real as an individual mind, real as everything about Mark Twain's mind or Fitzgerald's mind is real to us. . . . Under all those mountains of words, all that huffing and puffing, the mad days and nights of writing, the devotion of Maxwell Perkins, the devotion of Aline Bernstein, the idolatry felt by so many young men who alone read him today with the old exultancy, Wolfe remains a cipher, a cartoon of the Great American Effort, his features as smoothly heroic as Li'l Abner's.

The essential fact about Wolfe, I think, is the doomed "o lost!" quality—the sense of his own abysmal freakishness and loneliness, and thus unreality to himself—that from the beginning contracted his life around this tight center of fear and loss and internal dismay. (pp. 1, 3)

[The] extraordinary visibility of being six-foot-six, a deep unsatisfiable homesickness pervades Wolfe's writing, and gives it the pathos and longing that by now uselessly bombard our senses, for the emotion has been too insistent, too undifferentiated, to impress us any longer. . . .

[Wolfe's] lack of feeling for other people, the peculiarly harsh and always external description of others as interfering with Eugene Gant-George Webber's "destiny," . . . makes [***Look Homeward, Angel***] boring now—it is the anguished need to see, cover and describe everything as an instrument of power, the humorless literary confounding of everything into the same importance. What Wolfe's admirers have always praised him for is his "power," his gift of shaping and extending an anecdote, the briefest possible experience, to make single, strong, vibrant scenes. But this quality of powerfully imposing himself upon any and all experiences is what finally makes Wolfe unreal to us, as it made him unreal to himself—there was always the sotto voce of whispering dismay to return to, the *o lost!* theme that recurs in his work. Too-Soft Wolfe and Too-Hard Wolfe: he no longer knew, after a certain point, whether he was suffering his life or mastering it by endless writing. It is this that made him treat as raw material even the people he had loved. . . .

[He] seems to have felt about them all as he felt about a page in his books—something to get through. . . . [One] feels amazement about Wolfe's life, because it was always like a "story"—which may explain why his books now read as if they were the experiences not of a single man, not of *this* man, whoever he was, but of all the characters in all the books he had ever read. (p. 3)

Alfred Kazin, in a review of "Thomas Wolfe," in Book World—The Washington Post *(© 1968 Postrib Corp.; reprinted by permission of* Chicago Tribune *and* The Washington Post*), January 28, 1968, pp. 1, 3.*

JOSEPH R. MILLICHAP (essay date 1973)

[In the following excerpt, Millichap posits that the loose structure of Look Homeward, Angel *is entirely appropriate to the genre of the apprentice-novel, and that Wolfe's symbolism is likewise appropriate to the work's title and epitaph: to unify "the complexities in the themes of self-discovery, self-realization, and self-expression."]*

Wolfe, like Joyce, produced a special variant of the development novel, the *Künstlerroman,* the story of an artist's growth to maturity. This particular form became more important than the larger genre, the *Bildungsroman,* in the twentieth century, as the artist became more and more isolated from the bourgeois community. The young writer found it exceedingly difficult to adjust to middle-class "reality," and his story became a struggle toward finding his individual uniqueness. The spiritual paralysis of Dublin or the suffocating boosterism and democratic mediocrity of Asheville engendered the same reaction in the artist; he had to discover, realize, and express a selfhood separate from his time and environment. These are Wolfe's themes; his narrative is structured by the growth of a central personality to a creative self-realization. The forms presented by the traditional *Bildungsroman* and *Künstlerroman* and the particular symbols created by Wolfe's imagination combine, in ***Look Homeward, Angel,*** into a complex but unified work of art.

The New Criticism has always insisted that style is organic with structure; therefore Wolfe's prose has been deprecated without a full understanding of his rhetorical stance. Although the obvious power in Wolfe's words affects even an unfriendly reader of the novel, many of its New Critical detractors have avoided their responsibilities by inventing some special category for Wolfe's poetic prose. John Peale Bishop provides an example in his famous attack: "He [Wolfe] achieved probably the utmost intensity of which incoherent writing is capable."

Criticism of this sort has not adequately dealt with point-of-view in the novel. For the narrator of ***Look Homeward, Angel*** is not Thomas Wolfe; rather, Eugene Gant relates his own history in the tradition of the modern confessional novel. The prose poem which prefaces the narrative perfectly unifies the novel's patterns of imagery because it is a product of Eugene's effusive imagination. After the lush, romantic vision of his future which emerged from his dialogue with the ghost of Ben, Eugene creates the prose poem and the narrative, including Chapter 40. The overall tone of the novel will not allow an ironic reading of Eugene's vision of himself in that final chapter; however, the New Critics insisted that it must be read ironically; otherwise, Wolfe is celebrating a Romantic fool. Eugene is no fool, no *poseur,* no artistic dandy. The novel itself, which his older, wiser voice narrates, serves as the proof of his self-prophecies. Point-of-view and style are integral with the thematic insistence on self-discovery, self-realization, and self-expression.

This identification of voice and character might seem to identify Wolfe and young Gant, but the character is easily differentiated from his creator. . . . [Much] of Wolfe's most significant experience is excluded from or changed in the novel, and much of young Gant's is invented. . . . Like Joyce's Stephen Dedalus, Eugene exaggerates the isolated, posturing side of a young artist's personality. Lonelier, more eccentric, more self-concerned than Stephen, Eugene is the prototypical adolescent hero. His romanticism, his soulfulness, his intuition all make him the perfect central character for a *Künstlerroman.*

The narrative patterns presented in Eugene's development serve to structure Wolfe's thematic purpose of self-realization. Beginning the family history before Eugene's birth, Wolfe depicts the hereditary factors which partially form the individual self; in the later parts of the novel Eugene struggles to reconcile his heritage from the past and his growing individuality, with each stage in his development involving a further separation of himself from his family and his younger self. Like his father before him, Eugene hungers for voyages, and each of his journeys finds him further estranged from his family. In Part One, the sojourn in St. Louis separates him from his father; the trip to Charleston in Part Two cuts his ties with his mother; his summer at Norfolk breaks definitively his dependence on Ben, his older brother and surrogate father, and hence on his family in general. Ben's death then releases Eugene for the final voyage out of the family and the town forever.

Several tripartite elements in Eugene's education correspond to the three journeys, with each division of the novel covering a part of his formal education—primary, secondary, university. Though at each level his increased academic knowledge widens the separation from his family, his more informal education in life is the germination of his real growth toward self-realization. As in *Portrait,* the young man learns of hypocrisy and bullying in that perfect embryo of society, school. Eugene's inner self develops through an increasing knowledge of death, of sex, of work, and of language and literature. His understanding of how death isolates the self in a final separation from others progresses through Grover's death in Part One, the death of Lily in Part Two, and Ben's death in Part Three. His sexual insights grow from the sniggering revelations of Otto Krause in Chapter 8 to Justin Roper's risqué ballads in Chapter 17, to his painful initiation at the Exeter bawdyhouse in Chapter 29. His "pure" infatuations keep pace, developing from Mrs. Selbourne, to Margaret Leonard, to Laura James, all of whom are mother surrogates. He experiences the reality of labor and its multiple rewards. . . . (pp. 296-98)

Language and literature are the most important parts of both his formal and informal educations. . . . At each stage [of his education] he understands more about the power for self-expression inherent in words. Speechlessly, the young artist constantly searches for the password which will open the last door into the heaven of self-realization. All of these carefully paralleled events in Eugene's life unify the seemingly disparate profusion of the narrative in ordered patterns of self-discovery, self-realization, and self-expression.

The patterns of imagery create a correlative unity in Wolfe's material. The major image patterns all first appear in the prose-poem. . . . [There,] words and phrases, images and concepts are interwoven with Wolfe's narrative threads to create a design depicting the search for self-realization. The universalized mother, father and brother become the particularized Eliza, W.O., and Ben. The concepts of loss, exile, and isolation are illustrated constantly in Eugene's young life. The words ring through the narrative like poetic refrains, the phrases echo like magical incantations.

The most often emphasized images—the stone, the leaf, and the door—are all analagous to "the lost lane-end into heaven." They provide keys to the realization of the self, something which Eugene feels that he has once possessed and must possess again. The Platonic and Romantic implications of this idea, particularly the connection with Wordsworth's "Immortality Ode" have been remarked by several scholars. Lionel Trilling's well known essay on the psychosexual aspects of the "Immortality Ode" also presents a clue to Wolfe's meaning. In particular, the door seems a psychological symbol which connects "heaven" with the womb, but Wolfe's romantic emphasis on pre-natal harmony and knowledge has caused considerable misunderstanding of ***Look Homeward, Angel.*** For example, Leslie Fiedler deems the novel a failure because Eugene Gant "remains a great panting blubbering hulk of an adolescent, who can age but not grow up . . . a lonely child, who wants really only to recapture his lost, unknowable Mother." This reaction ignores the implications for later life inherent in the concept of a pre-natal harmony; if this wholeness existed once, it can be achieved again. In fact, this is exactly what self-discovery and self-realization imply in the individual life. Wolfe's novel assumes this attitude toward such preconscious knowledge. (pp. 298-99)

The leaf and the stone are more difficult to interpret, but various studies of psychological symbolism in dreams, particularly those of C. G. Jung, suggest some distinct possibilities. The leaf represents organic life and the annual rebirth of organic nature which, in turn, symbolizes the cyclic movement of the self from preconscious to conscious knowledge; here, the leaf contains the promise of continuing life and growth, as it preserves this meaning in many religious systems, for example, the Judeo-Christian "Tree of Life." Eugene's vision of Ben's immortality confirms such a reading. . . .

The inorganic stone traditionally stands for the self in its eternal solidity, immortality, and unalterable selfhood. Jung recognized the universal significance of the stone in his studies of Christianity (Christ as the cornerstone, Peter as the rock) and of alchemy, where the philosopher's stone or *lapis* represented the unification of conscious and unconscious knowledge, the key to all discoveries. The use of stones as grave markers rests on a primitive sense of the unity of self, even in death. Gravestones are also the most obvious analogue in the narrative of the general image from the prose poem. The senior Gant finds his self-identity working in stone, but fails to achieve the complete expression and fulfillment of this identity in the creation of a stone angel, his goal since childhood. (p. 300)

W. O. Gant's angels, both the uncreated ideal figures and the purchased, imperfect actualities which fill his porch, form the

Maxwell Perkins. The Thomas Wolfe Collection of Alexander D. Wainwright, the Princeton University Library.

nexus of the novel's two most important groups of imagery. Set off from the "stone, leaf, door" pattern, associated images of angels and ghosts are also crucial to the theme of self-realization. Wolfe uses ghosts not in the traditional sense of the restless spirits of the dead, but to denote the images of the individual as he has existed in the past. . . . The lost and wind-grieved ghost haunts the novel from the prose-poem to Chapter 40; its equation with past images of self, especially of the lost, pre-natal harmony, clarifies the self-realization theme. The individual must understand and absorb what has been in the past in order to discover his full identity and purpose in the future. The angel, a perfected spiritual being, symbolized this future realization of the self. W. O. Gant cannot attain it, so he sells his angel; Ben attains a distorted version of it in his "dark angel"; Eugene attains it fully by voyaging into the world and by writing the novel itself. The miraculous movement of the stone angels in Chapter 40 confirms the success of Eugene's endeavor; Ben, angel-like, has revealed the meaning of the search, and Eugene stands ready to begin his final great voyage both out to the world and into the self.

This conception of the angel may appear unique at first glance, but Wolfe probably derived his angelology from the popular traditions of American Protestantism. (pp. 300-01)

John Milton, who provided Wolfe with his novel's title, might also have presented an adaptable angelology. Milton's concept of angels as corporeal beings who could eat, drink, and copulate brought them closer to human reality, though they remained a distinct grouping, above man on the hierarchical scale. Wolfe undoubtedly combined Milton's literary use of angels with the religious beliefs of his Asheville background. Much has been made of the fact that Wolfe added the present title to the novel long after it was finished. Yet Wolfe knew "Lycidas" from memory, and four allusions to the poem can be found among the poetic echoes in Chapter 24. His choice of a phrase from this poem as his new title for the book is more than fortuitous; it is a perfect indication of the novel's theme, and it provides an allusive key to the meaning of his major image pattern. ***Look Homeward, Angel*** is Wolfe's "Lycidas," his apprentice work which proves his mastery of craft and his personal maturity. More important, as for the shepherd-poet in "Lycidas," the narrative marks the beginning of self-expression for Eugene. He also sees in the death of a beloved friend and guide the full terror and beauty of the human condition; when he can understand and accept this death, when he can order it in literary form, he then will be ready to assume his place in the world. In both works the cyclic rebirth of nature, symbolized by the leaf, provides solace for the mourner and promises continuing life, even for the dead.

In the words of Wolfe's title, the shepherd-poet calls on the Archangel Michael, guardian of St. Michael's Mount in Cornwall, to turn his sentinel gaze homeward and find the drowned body of Lycidas. Eugene, if he will be an angel, must look homeward or inward to find self-realization. In a sense, he finds himself while searching for the lost Ben, but Ben, like Lycidas, becomes a guiding spirit, the "genius" of the shores of self, bearing the message of self-discovery to Eugene.

A careful analysis of Wolfe's symbolic use of imagery in ***Look Homeward, Angel*** confirms the narrative patterns of the typical *Künstlerroman,* while the intricate symbolism centered on the angel affirms the self-discovery, self-realization, and self-expression of the central character. Eugene's inner life, presented in the imagery, correlates perfectly with his outer life, presented in the narrative, to form a unified whole. Imagery, narrative, symbolism, and theme combine in Wolfe's first book to make it the finest example of the development novel in American literature. (p. 302)

Joseph R. Millichap, "Narrative Structure and Symbolic Imagery in 'Look Homeward, Angel'," in The Southern Humanities Review *(copyright 1973 by Auburn University), Vol. VII, No. 3, Spring, 1973, pp. 295-303.*

C. HUGH HOLMAN (essay date 1975)

[Holman was an American detective novelist and literary scholar whose critical works focus predominantly on the fiction of Southern writers, particularly Ellen Glasgow, William Faulkner, Flannery O'Connor, and Thomas Wolfe. He edited several notable collections of Wolfe's writings, including The Short Novels of Thomas Wolfe *(1961) and* The Letters of Thomas Wolfe to His Mother *(1968). In the following excerpt, Holman discusses Wolfe's novels as epic works.]*

To look at Wolfe's "book" as an attempt at an American epic helps us see what he is about and appreciate at least some of the causes for his successes and his failures. He felt a compulsive need to "sing America." As he expressed it in 1936: "I have at last discovered my own America. . . . And I shall wreak out my vision of this life, this way, this world and this America, to the top of my bent, to the height of my ability, but with an unswerving devotion, integrity and purity of purpose that shall not be menaced, altered or weakened by any one." In addition to this epic urge, the nature and content of his work was shaped by the quality of his personal experience, by the influence of John Livingston Lowes's theory of the imagination, and by the special way in which he wrote. Out of the interactions of these things with his powerful rhetoric and his dramatic talent came a body of writing which corresponds with remarkable accuracy to the special shapes and tensions of the American epic.

His brief life was successively pastoral, provincial, urban, national, and international; and it embraced a great range of experience. (pp. 161-62)

As he moved through these stages, Wolfe was formatively influenced in his concept of art and the artist by John Livingston Lowes's theories of the functioning of the creative imagination. He studied under Lowes while Lowes was writing his justly famous study of Coleridge, *The Road to Xanadu,* and heard Lowes read chapters of this new book to his classes. . . . Lowes's theory greatly encouraged Wolfe's innate epic impulse, for he believed that an artist stored experiences of all kinds—physical, emotional, intellectual, and vicarious—in his "deep well of unconscious cerebration," and that there, in the fullness of time, "the shaping power of the imagination" worked upon it to create an ordered cosmos out of this teeming and fecund chaos. Lowes said: "The imagination never operates in a vacuum. Its stuff is always fact of some order, somehow experienced; its product is that fact transmuted. I am not forgetting that facts may swamp imagination, and remain unassimilated and untransformed." At another place he said: "For the Road to Xanadu, as we have traced it, is the road of the human spirit, and the imagination voyaging through chaos and reducing it to clarity and order is the symbol of all the quests which lend glory to our dust. . . . For the work of the creators is the mastery and transmutation and reordering into shapes of beauty of the given universe within us and without us." Wolfe added to these ideas a conviction that "*conscious* interests and efforts at all times" are working in the making of art from the matter in the "deep well of unconscious cerebration." Thus Lowes's ideas, together with certain of his cadences and phrases, encouraged Wolfe's frantic attempt to "stockpile" experience of all kinds, with the intention of later drawing consciously upon it for the materials of his art.

Out of his commitment to this view of the imagination probably came at least the sanction if not the full impulse for Wolfe's effort to engulf all experience. . . . Few writers have ever immersed themselves in the turbulent stream of experience more thoroughly than Wolfe; few writers have tried to touch more segments of America and know them with greater sensory surety.

In addition to this passion for experience, Wolfe had too a sensibility and a memory unusual in their power to recall odors, sounds, colors, shapes, and the feel of things with great precision. When these qualities were combined with his hunger for experience, Wolfe possessed a subject matter appropriate to the ambition of an epic poet, and he could, with some justification, feel that his experience approached that of everyman-in-America's and was thus a subject adequate to describe the democratic protagonist.

Wolfe's method of working, too, yielded itself quite easily to the attempt at a modern epic. With a remarkable ear for speech and eye for physical detail and with an equally keen sense of character and of dramatic action, Wolfe as person encountered experiences which seem to have come to him in relatively short and self-contained units. Many of these units are self-sufficient short stories and short novels—both forms in which he did excellent work. It is when these short stories and short novels become the materials of the long narratives that they begin to lose much of their objectivity and dramatic intensity. Even in ***Look Homeward, Angel,*** frequently and accurately called his most unified work, the individual episodes exist so independently that many can be extracted and published as self-contained units—short stories—without doing violence to their fundamental meaning. The satiric portrait of Professor Hatcher's playwriting course in ***Of Time and the River*** is a unified piece that is broken into four separate parts. The picture of Abraham Jones, a detailed character study in the same novel, is also fragmented into three parts. The posthumously published novels were assembled by Edward Aswell and, therefore, the unity or the fragmentary character of their episodes cannot be directly attributed to Wolfe. However, some of their finest parts originally appeared as self-contained units in magazines; for example, "The Child by Tiger" in ***The Web and the Rock,*** "Boom Town," "The Party at Jack's," and "'I Have a Thing to Tell You'" in ***You Can't Go Home Again.***

Wolfe's method seemingly was to write these episodes with much of the objectivity of an observer, and then later to fit them into the experience of the observer. Hence they play a part not unlike the long and varied vicarious experiences of Walt Whitman in *Song of Myself.* Such a method is not a very fruitful one for the novel, but for the epic it is reasonably workable. If we can consider the novel, at least in its "well-made" examples, to be not unlike Aristotle's tragedy, we may use Aristotle to gain for the epic a liberty from these binding restrictions of plot, consistency, and causation to which the tragedy—and some forms of the novel—is subject. Indeed, although it is highly questionable that Wolfe ever sought or relied upon authority for his artistic methods, Aristotle's discussion of the structure of the epic is almost a discussion of Wolfe's method in his "book." Aristotle says: "Epic poetry has, however, a great—a special—capacity for enlarging its dimensions." Distinguishing between a controling action and episodes, he says: "Thus the story of the *Odyssey* can be stated briefly. A certain man is absent from home for many years; he is jealously watched by Poseidon and left desolate. Meanwhile his home is in a wretched plight—suitors are wasting his substance and plotting against his son. At length, tempest-tossed, he himself arrives; he makes certain persons acquainted with him; he attacks the suitors with his own hand and is himself preserved while he destroys them. This is the essence of the plot; the rest is episode." Indeed, Aristotle asserts, "The epic imitation has less unity [than tragedy has] . . . the poem is composed out of several actions." Such a definition applied to Wolfe's "book" would find in its controlling action—that is, "the essence of its plot"—the experiences of Wolfe (under the guises of Eugene Gant and George Webber) as he moved from childhood and "the meadows of sensation" through adolescence to maturity in his search for identity as an American. The rest are "episodes," events which, however real to those who participate in them, are significant in the making of this American primarily in what they teach him about the difficulty of being a democratic man on this continent. The search aims at bringing him self-knowledge, but as he matures it aims increasingly at bringing him a definition of the representative aspects of his national being. As his life was an outward movement, so are his books outward movements. From the absorption in the self, he moves to an absorption in society. The road from ***Look Homeward, Angel*** to ***You Can't Go Home Again*** is the trail of the epic impulse. From the baby's contemplation of its own toe, Wolfe moves to the serious portrayal of the social world, but always in terms of how that world registers on his own consciousness and becomes a part of his experience as a representative American.

Eugene Gant was a person of whom Wolfe could say that, as a boy, "He did not want to reform the world, or to make it a better place to live in." He came finally to see, even in those he loved "his vision of the grand America . . . the structure of that enchanted life of which every American has dreamed . . . a world distilled of our own blood and earth, and qualified by all our million lights and weathers, and we know that it will be noble, intolerably strange and lovely, when we find it." And before his career was to reach its untimely end, he was to be able to take his reader to the place "where the hackles of the Rocky Mountains blaze in the blank and naked radiance of the moon" and bid him "make your resting stool upon the highest peak" and from that vantage point survey the vast and lonely sweep of continent to east and west. And to find in a Negro boy in the Chicago slums, in a young baseball player in "the clay-baked outfields down in Georgia," and in an intense and studious Jewish boy in "the East-Side Ghetto of Manhattan" the essence of his native land and the symbols of its grand design and promise. Thus he can declare: "So, then, to every man his chance—to every man, regardless of his birth, his shining, golden opportunity—to every man the right to live, to work, to be himself, and to become whatever thing his manhood and his vision can combine to make him—this, seeker, is the promise of America."

However flawed as novels and imperfect as art his books may be, Thomas Wolfe's works constitute a major and remarkably successful effort to write his autobiography as that of a representative American and to embody in the record of his time and deeds on this earth a vision of the nature and the hope of his democratic land. (pp. 162-67)

C. Hugh Holman, "The Epic Impulse" (originally published in a slightly different form as "The American Epic Impulse and Thomas Wolfe," in Literatur und Sprache der Verinigten Staaten: Aufsätze zu Ehren von Hans Galinsky, *edited by Hans Helmcke & others, Carl Winter Universitätsverlag, 1969) in his* The Loneliness at the Core: Studies in Thomas Wolfe *(reprinted by permission of Louisiana State University Press; copyright © 1975 by Louisiana State University Press), Louisiana State University Press, 1975, pp. 155-67.*

JAMES BOYER (essay date 1982)

[In the following excerpt, Boyer surveys Wolfe's short stories, offering evidence that his later stories demonstrate a progressing artistic maturity: "in dramatizing rather than telling, in careful plotting, in building characters with significant internal conflicts, and in using imagery to reinforce theme."]

John Halberstadt's *Yale Review* article on Thomas Wolfe [see Additional Bibliography] revived a criticism of Wolfe's work that has persisted ever since Bernard DeVoto wrote his scorching critical review of Wolfe's ***Story of a Novel*** in 1936. Not surprisingly, Halberstadt quotes a later DeVoto statement to establish a frame for his current argument: "You are manifestly and, if you will excuse me, absurdly wrong," DeVoto wrote to Struthers Bert in 1950, "when you say that I created 'the legend of the Wolfe who couldn't write without Papa Perkins.' It is no legend but a fact so widely established that I wonder you have missed it that at any rate he did not produce novels without Perkins' and later Ed Aswell's symbiotic editing." The gist of Halberstadt's charge in this recent article is that Aswell did indeed overedit the posthumous Wolfe novels, that in fact he went so far beyond the ordinary role of editor in order to create a structure in those books that while "the words . . . , most of them anyway—were written by Wolfe . . . , the books were made by Aswell. He was the dominant contributor to the books that bore Wolfe's name . . ."

It is not my purpose here to contend with Halberstadt; Richard Kennedy in *The Window of Memory* did a careful job of assessing what Aswell had done and why. Yet while Halberstadt's conclusions about Wolfe's work are overstated and extreme, it is true that those three posthumous novels contain an amalgam of Wolfe's early and late writing, making it difficult to assess his development as a writer through them. Thus even friendly critics tend to generalize about Wolfe and all of his work; Wolfe the eternal adolescent; Wolfe the giant of insatiable appetite; Wolfe the writer of formless autobiography.

It is possible to overcome some of this confusion on Wolfe's handling of formal matters, a confusion produced by the novels, if we turn to Wolfe's magazine stories, thirty-eight of which were published before his death in 1938. By examining this considerable body of work, we can see some important directions Wolfe's fiction was taking—specifically his increasing ability to control plot, character and conflict.

Objections, of course, can be raised here too. Elizabeth Nowell, Wolfe's agent for magazine publications, played a significant role in the production of Wolfe's short stories. . . . Nowell encouraged Wolfe's development in the form, but the significant changes in the products of the late period are clearly attributable to Wolfe himself.

One might also object, if we are making assertions about development, that while Wolfe revised stories before publication, he didn't write them in the order in which they were published. And this is true. But it is possible through information available in the Wisdom Collection at Harvard to date the writing of most stories, so that one can attribute particular characteristics in the writing to a particular time period in his career. It is these changing characteristics that I should like to consider in the following paper. What we shall find is that Wolfe was moving toward more conventional fiction, with plots more carefully organized, characters whose internal conflicts form the core of those plots, and imagery that supports and unifies.

In examining these magazine publications, it will be convenient to divide Wolfe's stories into three groups: those stories published between 1932-1934, most of them before Elizabeth Nowell became his agent; those published in 1935, many of which were republished with some alteration in ***From Death to Morning;*** and those published between 1936 and his death in 1938. Significant formal distinctions divide these three groups of stories.

One feature of the early stories, which begin to appear in *Scribner's Magazine* in 1932, is their length. Of the five published before 1934, only **"The Train and the City"** runs under 20,000 words. (It is about 10,000.) Wolfe had given up on writing drama in part because of the demands of that genre for concision; he was at this point unwilling to shorten works to make them more attractive to magazines. Indeed, after the middle period where many of the stories are quite short, he returns to fuller development in his best stories of the final period.

Some of the length of these early stories results from the use of long lyric passages elaborating major Wolfe themes—spring in the city, death as a brother, loneliness as a friend, America as a land of promise. While these passages contain some vivid images and personifications and employ a rhythmic, verse-like prose, they interrupt the narrative element of the story. Wolfe was reluctant to reduce them, since they were a distinctive feature of his style that brought praise from some critics. Only by the very end of 1934 does he begin to use such passages as separate magazine pieces or as carefully limited and balanced components, a practice he continues thereafter.

This early emphasis on theme and lyric refrain often results in a casual handling of the narrative element in the story. **"The Four Lost Men"** begins with a father, a son, and boarders on the porch of a boarding house in a small Southern town, discussing the beginning of World War I and earlier wars; but the setting and event are forgotten as the story moves to a lyrical vision of four lost Presidents and never returns to the porch and the people on it. In **"The Train and the City,"** the narrator's trip out from and back to the city, including the well-known passage where the two trains race, is overbalanced by paragraph after paragraph of lyric tribute to spring and to the American people. The only carefully controlled plots of the early period are found in **"The Sun and the Rain,"** where a simple chronology provides sufficient structure, and **"The Web of Earth,"** which is carefully wrought like the late stories but exceptional because of the controlling voice of the old woman who narrates.

Characters in these early stories tend to be static rather than dynamic; often they represent something significant, but that something is a set idea little dependent on the action of the story. In the manner of Dickens, characters are identified by peculiar mannerisms rather than internal conflicts. What we remember about Bascom Hawke, in spite of a very long story that gives much of his life in summary, are his facial grimaces and "snuffling laugh"; his weakness and resignation, which in the end of the story are contrasted with the exuberance of the young narrator, come to the reader as a surprise. (pp. 31-4)

Short, then, on conventional plot structure and characters in conflict, many of these early stories are structured with simple contrast—hopeful youth and resigned age, or "wandering" and "earth again" or violent death and quiet death—rather than conflict. Elaboration in such stories is often accomplished through multiple illustration: all three of the 1933 stories (**"Death the Proud Brother," "The Train and the City,"** and **"No Door"**), as well as **"The Face of the War,"** written then but published later, are composed of a series of unrelated events, each illustrating the same themes.

Finally, many of these early stories have passages that mean little to the stories themselves but relate in some significant way to Wolfe's big books. Delia Hawke's interest in the burial of her husband's first wife is simply perplexing in **"Boomtown,"** as are the references to Esther Jack in **"Death the Proud Brother."** If one has read the novels, he recognizes the loss suffered when these episodes are removed from the larger context. By contrast the later stories often lose some of their meaning and effect when they are forced into the framework of the larger novel. Clearly, at this stage in his career, Wolfe had much to learn about story writing.

By the latter half of 1934, however, Wolfe was publishing stories very different from those described above, and the changes become more striking in 1935. Much of the change at this time results not from the writing process but from the selection process. Elizabeth Nowell, who had begun to work with Wolfe's fiction while part of Max Lieber's Agency in 1934, now opened her own agency, with Wolfe as her best-known client. During this period she played an increasingly important role in selecting suitable materials from the manuscripts and in suggesting ways to shorten them and strengthen them for use as stories. (pp. 34-5)

Even more consistently than in the earlier period, these 1935-36 stories are episodes cut from the larger work. Richard Kennedy calls them "captured fugitives," as indeed they are, many of them having come from the ***Of Time and the River*** manuscript. . . . Stories like **"Cottage by the Tracks"** or **"Bums at Sunset"** represent units complete in themselves which were to have functioned in the novel to illustrate various themes or facets of the national character. (pp. 35-6)

Of the twelve 1935 stories, most of which reappear in ***From Death to Morning,*** ten have fewer than 6,000 words. More than half of them present a single event. Emphasis consistently remains on the narrative element. This shift toward a simpler structure undoubtedly reflects Nowell's involvement in the selection. The result is this sequence of stories that make us aware of the diversity in Wolfe's work.

Contrasting with the prevailing serious, lyrical tone of the early stories, we find in these stories a great variety in tone. . . . Stories center on persons other than Eugene Gant—this is true, of course, of stories in the first period, too, but not so apparent in the novels. And we have some stories that demonstrate an increasing capacity in Wolfe, even when he is dealing with his Eugene-George protagonist, for getting outside himself. . . . (p. 36)

Along with varying tone, these stories present a great variety in dialogue. . . . Not only does he use these voices in dialogue; he uses them as narrators of episodes. (pp. 36-7)

Since the stories are short, character development is more limited than in the early period, but it is in some instances more interesting, too. . . . Some plots in these stories, too, show Wolfe's developing concern with structure. (p. 37)

But the finest examples of both plot and character development come a little later. (p. 38)

Wolfe had begun working on a new book, his ***Vision of Spangler's Paul,*** in March of 1936. . . . In a June 1936 letter to Heinz Ledig, his German editor, Wolfe explains his intentions: "The idea as I conceive it is the story of a good man abroad in the world—shall we say the naturally innocent man, the man who sets out in life with his own vision of what life is going to be like, what men and women are going to be like, what he is going to find, and then the story of what he really finds." Wolfe went on to cite *Don Quixote, Candide* and *Gulliver* as models for what he was attempting.

One notes, of course, that this frame is very flexible, allowing Wolfe to use any of his experiences, with the focus remaining on other people and events, the narrator serving simply as story teller and interpreter. Thus, though the 1937 stories are written as separate units and move in very different directions, Wolfe no doubt had a clear notion of how he would eventually incorporate all of them into the major work. Yet his impulse for writing them came from diverse sources rather than a single conception of the "big book," he spent considerable time with Elizabeth Nowell sharpening and shortening them, and they are often more effective as separate units than as parts of the book. And a careful look at them reveals significant changes from the earlier stories in formal matters.

They are longer than the stories of the middle period; two of the best, **"I Have a Thing to Tell You"** and **"The Lost Boy,"** approach the length of **"Bascom Hawke."** But their content remains almost exclusively narrative. Gone are the long lyric passages of the earliest period and the visions of both earlier periods; gone are the expository passages on youth and exuberance.

Wolfe has become more careful, too, in use of images. Description effectively foreshadows and reinforces action or theme. The contrast of the dark forests of Germany, with "their legendary sense of magic and of time," and the shiny German tram, "perfect in its function," gives the first indication in **"I Have a Thing to Tell You"** of the two sides of the German character, its great heritage of art but its preoccupation with a dehumanizing scientific precision. . . . Not only descriptive detail but characters themselves are used to represent or reinforce theme. . . . It is not simply that Wolfe now sees persons, places or things as representational—he had always consciously done that—but he begins now to integrate them more carefully with action and theme to form a unified whole.

More important still, Wolfe is developing characters in conflict, characters who are trying to resolve something. All characters are functional, and the action of the stories brings both character and reader to a point of clarification. Prosser in **"Child by Tiger"** is a complex figure, his orderly exterior undercut by a smoldering anger over his blackness that erupts against everyone, black and white alike. . . . These characters, in their complexity and their reality, rank with the greatest of fictional creations.

The plots of these stories are generally simple, focusing on a few days in time, a crucial event, a single idea. **"I Have a Thing to Tell You"** takes place in one day, with only four important scenes, three of them on the train leaving Germany. (pp. 38-40)

Wolfe's reputation as a writer from whom a stream of undigested experience simply poured is undeserved. As the stories illustrate, his later writing shows genuine improvement in his craft—in dramatizing rather than telling, in careful plotting, in building characters with significant internal conflicts, and in using imagery to reinforce theme. (p. 41)

James Boyer, "The Development of Form in Thomas Wolfe's Short Fiction" (originally a paper read at Harvard University, Cambridge, Massachusetts, on May 8, 1982), in Thomas Wolfe: A Harvard Perspective, *edited by Richard S. Kennedy (copyright © 1983 by Croissant & Company, P.O. Box 282, Athens, Ohio 45701), Croissant, 1983, pp. 31-42.*

DAVID O'ROURKE (essay date 1983)

[*In the following excerpt, O'Rourke examines the theme of lost innocence in* Look Homeward, Angel.]

While there can be little doubt that a loss of innocence takes place in ***Look Homeward, Angel,*** exactly what form that innocence takes and when it is lost, are matters much more open to debate. . . . The lack of a consensus as to what exactly constitutes the loss of innocence, or "paradise," in ***Look Homeward, Angel*** is a serious problem given its dominance in the book and frequent presence in Wolfe's fiction. In this paper, I propose a return to the text for a more detailed treatment of the question. In the process, I think it becomes evident that Thomas Wolfe was a much better craftsman than most critics have hitherto given him credit for being.

The opening poem suggests quite plainly that a fall has taken place: "Naked and alone we came into exile." Man has entered "the unspeakable and incommunicable prison of this earth," having lost the "lane-end into heaven." Given the title of the book, ***Look Homeward, Angel,*** these religious images ought not to be dismissed too quickly. In Chapter I, they are repeated and developed. Oliver Gant becomes the focus of the exile; unable to "wreak something dark and unspeakable in him into cold stone" . . . , to carve a stone angel, Gant begins to both geographically and morally wander. . . . In this fallen state, Gant finds a home in the Reconstruction South "under the attentive eye of a folk still raw with defeat and hostility." . . . Before long, he falls off the wagon and is thought to be at least partly responsible for the death of his new, but tubercular, wife. He curses "at Rebel ways" . . . and soon feels that he too is dying of tuberculosis. Wolfe's next paragraphs become quite significant in view of Gant's proximity to death:

> So, alone and lost again, having found neither order nor establishment in the world, and with the earth cut away from his feet. Oliver resumed his aimless drift along the continent.
>
> (pp. 16-17)

Two major American wars receive treatment in the first chapter of ***Look Homeward, Angel:*** the Civil and the Revolutionary. . . . It is appropriate that the novel should have opened with reference to an important turning-point in the Civil War, for the War itself is representative of a loss of innocence in ***Look Homeward, Angel;*** it is dissension in America, the Garden of Eden, and it is responsible for the fall from paradise to a subsequent exile on earth. The town of Altamont, while described realistically, is a scene out of Dante's *Inferno* on a symbolic level. . . . Like the life of his wife, Cynthia, Gant's exile in the Reconstruction South is brought to a close by tuberculosis. Eliza symbolically dies of the same disease. The lost paradise turns into a metaphorical hell. (pp. 17-18)

Eliza is an appropriate representative of the new, commercial South. Perpetually "pursing" her lips, she is unable to relate to anything except on a materialistic basis. . . . The Pentland religion of acquisition and commercialism spreads as the family multiplies. In a fusion of the myths of lost heaven and lost Eden, Wolfe refers to the Pentland clan as a strange "tribe" . . . coming out of the hills after the Revolution, and increasing in number by "begetting" . . . children. The Biblical allusions are intentional: this is a new race, but demonic compared to anything which has preceded it. It is in this hell that Oliver Gant finds his isolation:

> And as they sat there in the hot little room with its warm odor of mellowing apples, the vast winds howled down from the hills, there was a roaring in the pines, remote and demented, the bare boughs clashed. And as they peeled, or pared, or whittled, their talk slid from its rude jocularity to death and burial: they drawled monotonously, with evil hunger, their gossip of destiny, and of men but newly lain in the earth. And as their talk wore on, and Gant heard the spectre moan of the wind, he was entombed in loss and darkness, and his soul plunged

> downward in the pit of night, for he saw that he must die a stranger—that all, all but these triumphant Pentlands, who banqueted on death—must die. . . .

Apart from a tortured syntax, the technique used in this family portrait of the Pentlands is pure Joycean, and the paragraph would not be out of place in either *Dubliners* or *Ulysses*. . . . It is accepted that Joyce's influence on Wolfe is apparent in varying degrees in the latter's conception of time, use of structure, and employment of narrative and interior monologue techniques, but rarely is a specific instance such as Wolfe's own "Wandering Rocks" episode singled out. It should be remembered that Wolfe admitted to being strongly under the influence of Joyce when writing ***Look Homeward, Angel,*** and even referred to it as his "*Ulysses* book." These cues are important reminders that the text of ***Look Homeward, Angel*** should be approached with a similar expectation of ironic complexity as that which is commonly reserved for any sentence or paragraph written by James Joyce.

The allegory of the South as fallen world and Altamont as hell is continued beyond the first chapter, but to a less elaborate extent. (pp. 18-19)

Not surprisingly, Altamont becomes peopled by a number of devils. The description of a millionaire boarder turns progressively satanic. . . . (p. 19)

It might be noted that the infernal allusions are not always marked by negative connotations. Hell is sometimes used in a Shelleyan or Blakean sense of energy. Altamont is for Eugene not only an oppressive situation, but also "the centre of the earth, the small but dynamic core of all life." . . . The character of Oliver Gant fuses these divergent aspects of Thomas Wolfe's hell; his "fallen" state progressively deteriorates with his residence in Altamont, but he is able to break free under the influence of alcohol to personify all that is vibrant in life. (pp. 20-1)

[The] mountains are representative of time immutable, preexistence either in the Platonic or Biblical sense. It would not be a mistake to emphasize the latter interpretation. The reader is informed, "The wasting helve of the moon rode into heaven over the bulk of the hills." . . . Ben models for Eugene one form of escape: death. After "his lonely adventure on earth," Ben rises in bed "bodilessly"—"as if his resurrection and rebirth had come upon him." . . .

Other escape routes are either illusory or able to offer only temporary relief. (p. 21)

Look Homeward, Angel portrays the traditional pattern of the process of maturity: innocence, experience and, while not as often apparent, one might expect eventually some degree of vision. These stages are manifested in the characters of Oliver and Eugene Gant, father and son, whose lives are intrinsically interwoven with the history of America and the tragedy of the South. As the Civil War marks the end of Oliver's initial stage of maturity, it signals the transition of America from agrarian landscape to Trojan horse of industry and commercialism. Oliver never completely transcends his captivity in the hell of experience, but his prophetic rhetoric indicates a recognition of his condition and serves as some explanation for his Biblical tone.

Because Eugene is severed completely from the pre-Civil War pastoral of America, it is not that surprising that he looks for it in the person of a father in ***Of Time and the River.*** Born into a civilization on wheels but locked into the microcosm of Altamont, he has but one hope of vision: Ben's advice of escape. That he is on his way to Boston by the novel's end indicates possible promise in the city and, perhaps, future of America. (p. 22)

David O'Rourke, "The Lost Paradise of 'Look Homeward, Angel'," in The Thomas Wolfe Review *(© copyright 1983 by The University of Akron), Vol. 7, No. 1, Spring, 1983, pp. 16-23.*

JAMES D. BOYER (essay date 1983)

[In the following excerpt, Boyer examines the ways that Wolfe's stories reveal an increasingly receptive attitude towards the city.]

[Thomas Wolfe] found that he couldn't go home again, or more accurately, that fourteen years of living in New York City had made it his real home.

When he had come to the city in 1925, Wolfe was, of course, as much the provincial as his fictional protagonists, Eugene Gant and George Webber. He had grown up in the mountain country of Asheville, had gone to a rural university in Chapel Hill, and had spent three years cloistered at Harvard. After that, from 1925 until his death in 1938, he made New York his home. He had brought to the city more than the usual number of fears and prejudices. Those fourteen years show a significant change in his feelings toward the city, a growth in understanding and sympathy for its people that is clearly reflected in his writing.

Wolfe's earliest fiction dealing with New York is **"The Train and the City,"** a story published in *Scribner's Magazine* in May 1933, but written in 1930 or earlier. That story reflects deep division in the feelings of his protagonist between what he had anticipated of the city and what he found it to be. In a passage early in the story he pictures the city as he experienced it on a glorious first day of spring when everything came to life. . . . The wonders of that day rekindle in the speaker his childhood vision of the city. . . . (p. 36)

The feelings are, of course, those generalized anticipations of the rural-bred youth heading for the city, a vision more powerful perhaps in the 1920's than now, but still close enough to our own experience to rekindle strong feelings, if only nostalgia.

But a few phrases in those passages—"the blind and brutal stupefaction of the streets" and "the gray flesh of the living dead"—reveal a contrasting response that surfaces in the narrator even as he tries to recapture the childhood vision. This response, a feeling of mistrust and repulsion, deepens as he moves from description of place to description of people: "I saw again," he says, the million faces—the faces dark, dingy, driven, harried, and corrupt, the faces stamped with all the familiar markings of suspicion and mistrust, cunning, contriving, and a hard and stupid cynicism." . . . Though the narrator tries to tie these people in with his vision of wonder over the city, the reader remains unconvinced. Clearly the real city is, for the narrator filled with strange, frightening, unfriendly people.

In another early story, **"Death, the Proud Brother,"** . . . Wolfe gives us further insight into what was wrong with city life; here the city is impersonal, isolating, mechanical, violent. The story is a graphic account of four unrelated city deaths. . . . The tone of the story changes dramatically in the long lyric apostrophe to death, loneliness and sleep that ends it, but that beautiful lyric fails to erase the narrator's angry feelings toward man alive.

This sense of city man as "man swarm"—abrasive, strident, reptilian, vulpine and uncaring—reflects "Wolfe's early response to the city. Characteristic of his writing done before 1932, the response tells us more about his own isolation and defensiveness during that period than about the city, for as he lives in the city over a period of years, especially after his move from Manhattan to Brooklyn in 1931, his angry tone is softened considerably. **"No Door,"** written after that move, shows some beginning steps in that change of feelings. In its opening section, where the narrator is conversing with a pleasant, aesthetic-looking millionaire, it is clearly the wealthy host who is naive about city life and the narrator who understands the real richness of life there. And the city people, as the narrator describes them now, contribute to the richness. Of his landlady in Brooklyn, he explains "what a good and liberal-hearted woman she is: how rough and ready, full of life and energy, how she likes drinking and the fellowship of drinking men, and knows all the rough and seamy sides of life. . . . And ironically, though the overall theme of **"No Door"** has to do with man's inescapable isolation, the narrator appears to be experiencing acceptance and feeling community with these people. **"No Door"** is clearly a turning point.

This changing attitude toward the city and its people is further illustrated in one of Wolfe's simplest and most impressive short stories, **"Only the Dead Know Brooklyn,"** published two years later in 1935. Here one of the city people, a Brooklynite, narrates the story. (pp. 37-8)

The reader, of course, has more understanding of the whole situation than does the narrator. The reader sees that the stranger with the map is trying to absorb the city, to experience everything; he understands that drowning, while not a literal but a metaphorical danger, is a serious danger nonetheless for the stranger. (It is Wolfe's greatest struggle with the protean city.) But the final wisdom in the story is given to the city man, even though he doesn't fully understand the implications of his own words: "It'd take a guy a lifetime to know Brooklyn t'roo and t'roo. An even den, yuh wouldn't know it all." Though the tall stranger in the story hasn't learned yet, Wolfe is clearly learning to curb the insatiable appetite for experience.

The extent to which Wolfe came to identify with the lower classes in the city—in his fiction and in his life—is spelled out in one of the final stories he worked on before his final trip west in 1938 and his death. **"The Party at Jack's"** concerns the other side of the society of the city, the very rich. Wolfe had, of course, come to know personally the ways of the rich through his relationship with Aline Bernstein. She worked as a designer in the theater, but her husband had amassed a fortune as a stockbroker, and through their parties Wolfe came to know a significant circle of the rich and powerful of the city. And for a time he had viewed that life as a glorious goal to reach out for. But through his years of living in Brooklyn, by observing first hand the poverty and deprivation of the poor, he had begun to recognize the injustice and evil of the system that supported Aline's family and others of that privileged class. Having moved from his romantic period to one of great social concern, Wolfe wrote **"The Party at Jack's"** to make clear where he stood. (p. 39)

Characters, events, images—all function in the story to condemn the privileges of the wealthy, the greed and the essential sterility of the upper classes. Wolfe's final statement on the city, it aims its criticism not at the city as such, but at its privileged class. It demonstrates Wolfe's real allegiance to and love for the city people he had been living with.

Though he pictured city man as poor, often the victim, often alienated, he showed a growing compassion for and identification with these people throughout his career. As a result, he was able to write of Brooklyn in summer, "There are so many million doors tonight. There's a door for everyone tonight, all's open to the air, all's interfused tonight . . . and there is something over all tonight, something fused, remote and trembling . . . upon the huge and weaving ocean of the night in Brooklyn." And before that fatal Western trip, he had carefully reinstalled himself in a Manhattan apartment. After his reconciliation with the South, he did come home again, to New York City. (p. 40)

James D. Boyer, "The City in the Short Fiction of Thomas Wolfe," in The Thomas Wolfe Review *(© copyright 1983 by The University of Akron), Vol. 7, No. 2, Fall, 1983, pp. 36-40.*

LESLIE FIELD (essay date 1983)

[*Field is an American educator, editor, and critic who has written extensively on the works of Thomas Wolfe and Bernard Malamud. In the following excerpt, Field discusses Wolfe's* The Autobiography of an American Novelist, *which is composed of* The Story of a Novel *and the essay* "Writing and Living," *originally a speech delivered at Purdue University in 1938.*]

[In ***The Story of a Novel*** and ***Writing and Living,***] brought together in their original form for the first time, Thomas Wolfe's subject is creativity. Of his generation of writers—including Faulkner, Fitzgerald, Hemingway—he alone attempted to explain the creative process of the artist. Here, he shares with his audience that process.

In so doing, Wolfe was like his great nineteenth-century predecessors Mark Twain and Henry James, who also tried to convey how the novelist transmutes experience and mind in creating fiction. His portrayal of the role of the writer both resembled and often went beyond that of his contemporaries. Like Faulkner, he felt compelled to depict his view of the South: black versus white, the Civil War, the pull of the land, Yoknapatawpha. Like Fitzgerald, he wrote of the Lost Generation, the Jazz Age, wealth, the elusiveness of the American dream. He admired Hemingway's creation of the hero, the code of manliness, grace under pressure.

But perhaps Wolfe is really closer to Walt Whitman. Like Whitman, Wolfe was a romantic who moved from a preoccupation with himself to an interest in his family, his friends, his town, his America, and finally the larger, external world. Wolfe explored time, faith, loneliness, and death; isolation, alienation, change, experience; the city versus the country; the North versus the South; the structure of society; the limits of folklore, language, rhetoric, symbolism, humor, satire.

These concerns run through all of Wolfe's fiction, from his first and most famous novel, ***Look Homeward, Angel*** . . . , and his enormously long second book, ***Of Time and the River*** . . . , to his posthumously published books [***The Web and the Rock*** and ***You Can't Go Home Again***]. . . . They also resonate in his collection of short stories ***From Death to Morning*** . . . and in the posthumous ***The Hills Beyond***. . . . (pp. vii-viii)

While these major interests defined Wolfe's life, his belief that writing was a serious craft shaped his art. Through it he planned to encompass and convey his vision of the world. And so in ***The Story of a Novel*** and ***Writing and Living*** Wolfe tried to explain how a writer thinks and then goes about writing. "My conviction is," he said, "that all serious work must be at the bottom autobiographical, and that a man must use the material and experience of his own life if he is to create anything that has substantial value." Late in life Wolfe continued to wrestle with charges that he made excessive use of autobiography in his fiction. In a letter to Elizabeth Nowell, his literary agent, he once summed up his position. As usual he was thinking of facts—in this instance, an address he delivered to students—and his fictional rendering of those facts. He wrote, "That is what I am doing now, transforming . . . material . . . into the terms of poetic and imaginative fact—into the truth of fiction—because it seems to me that is really my essential job." In a word, Wolfe was translating *fact* into what he considered *truth*. (p. viii)

Taken together in their original versions, published here for the first time, ***The Story of a Novel*** and ***Writing and Living*** constitute Thomas Wolfe's major statements about his life and his art. They are similar in many respects. In both he wanted to define the role of the writer in America. In both he emphasized that a writer is a *worker* and must be regarded as such. In both he insisted that there were no easy formulas for writing. In both he also wanted to convey the importance of autobiography to his fiction and how he legitimately used the facts of his life.

But there are also differences. In ***The Story of a Novel*** he was more concerned with discussing the romantic themes he saw as important to his early work: the themes of permanence and change, and man's search for a spiritual father. And he wanted to share with his audience and readers the close editor-author relationship that went into creating ***Of Time and the River.*** In ***Writing and Living*** Wolfe revealed his growth, his movement away from the romantic egocentrism of his youthful period to a new awareness of life outside himself, and his new social consciousness. Now, Wolfe believed that his earlier themes were no longer crucial. He realized that as a beginning writer he had been too narcissistic, too much the sensitive artist divorced from his environment. Late in his short life he saw the need for moving outside himself, for looking at the political, social, and economic world, and for trying to understand it, assimilate it, and somehow bring it into his writing. This, in fact, he attempted in his last novel, ***You Can't Go Home Again.***

Taken together these two essays capture the essence of a writer's life and how it is molded into fiction. They form ***The Autobiography of an American Novelist,*** a significant statement by an important American writer, his candid commentary on his craft. (pp. x-xi)

Leslie Field, in a preface to The Autobiography of an American Novelist *by Thomas Wolfe, edited by Leslie Field (copyright © 1983 by the President and Fellows of Harvard College; excerpted by permission), Cambridge, Mass.: Harvard University Press, 1983, pp. vii-xi.*

ADDITIONAL BIBLIOGRAPHY

Beach, Joseph Warren. "Discovery of Brotherhood." In his *American Fiction: 1920-1940,* pp. 197-215. New York: Macmillan Co., 1941.

A critical examination of *You Can't Go Home Again.* Beach places the book alongside its three predecessors in importance, noting Wolfe's progression from "a Byronic sentimentalist" to "a social-minded realist."

Bowden, Edwin T. "The Mighty Individual." In his *The Dungeon of the Heart: Human Isolation and the American Novel,* pp. 66-102. New York: Macmillan Co., 1961.*

Perceives *Look Homeward, Angel* to be in the tradition of the frontier novel; that is, "a direct exploitation of the American sense of isolation." Bowden finds Wolfe's portrayal of Eugene Gant as the besieged individualist to be poorly done.

Cowley, Malcolm. "Wolfe: Homo Scribens." In his *A Second Flowering: Works and Days of the Lost Generation,* pp. 156-90. New York: Viking Press, 1973.

Studies Wolfe's writing methods, answers critical charges against Wolfe by showing the close link between his outlook and method of composition, and notes the faults and virtues of his work.

Fagin, N. Bryllion. "In Search of an American *Cherry Orchard.*" *The Texas Quarterly* 1, No. 3 (Summer-Autumn 1958): 132-41.*

An exposition of Wolfe's *Mannerhouse* as a drama containing borrowings from Anton Chekhov's *The Cherry Orchard.*

Field, Leslie, ed. *Thomas Wolfe: Three Decades of Criticism.* New York: New York University Press, 1968, 304 p.

A well-chosen collection of critical essays on Wolfe's major themes, his style, and on specific novels and short stories. Included are essays by Paschal Reeves, Oscar Cargill, Louis D. Rubin, Jr., and many others.

Forrey, Robert. "Whitman to Wolfe." *Mainstream* 13, No. 10 (October 1960): 19-27.

Finds Wolfe's writings to be at the end of the American liberal tradition, which dates back to the work of Henry David Thoreau, Herman Melville, and Walt Whitman. The critic finds Wolfe a failure in his attempts to exalt the common individual in his novels.

Geismar, Maxwell. Introduction to *The Portable Thomas Wolfe,* by Thomas Wolfe, edited by Maxwell Geismar, pp. 1-27. New York: Viking Press, 1946.

An excellent introduction to Wolfe's life and career, finding him "one of the most acute and entertaining social commentators of [the 1920s]—and a prime chronicler of the national mind during the decade of the bust and the hangover."

Gilman, Richard. "The Worship of Thomas Wolfe." *The New Republic* 158, No. 8 (24 February 1968): 31-2, 34.

A critical attack on Andrew Turnbull's biography of Wolfe. The critic believes Wolfe's critical reputation to be grossly inflated and sees the novelist as neither an artist nor an important writer.

Halberstadt, John. "The Making of Thomas Wolfe's Posthumous Novels." *The Yale Review* 70, No. 1 (Autumn 1980): 79-94.

Attacks Edward C. Aswell's "creative editing" of Wolfe's posthumous fiction. Halberstadt maintains that "Aswell's editing not only violated the spirit (if not the letter) of Wolfe's contract with Harper and Brothers, but also fundamentally changed the character of Wolfe's work." For an opposing view, see the excerpt by James Boyer (1982).

Hesse, Hermann. "Thomas Wolfe (1933)." In his *My Belief: Essays on Life and Art,* edited by Theodore Ziolkowski, translated by Denver Lindley, pp. 346-49. New York: Farrar, Straus and Giroux, 1974.

A favorable review and synopsis of *Look Homeward, Angel.* Hesse concludes that Wolfe's novel is "the most powerful piece of fiction from present-day America that I know of."

Holman, C. Hugh. *Thomas Wolfe.* University of Minnesota Pamphlets on American Writers, edited by William Van O'Connor, Allen Tate, Leonard Unger, and Robert Penn Warren, no. 6. Minneapolis: University of Minnesota Press, 1960, 47 p.

A brief biographical and critical introduction to Wolfe's life and work.

Kussy, Bella. "The Vitalist Trend and Thomas Wolfe." *The Sewanee Review* L, No. 3 (July-September 1942): 306-24.

An essay which finds Wolfe's novels steeped in vitalist beliefs: the doctrine of life as an all-pervading force or presence not bound by physical limitations. The works and thought of Walt Whitman, Friedrich Nietzsche, and Adolf Hitler are also discussed, and their own vitalist ideas are compared and contrasted with those of Wolfe.

McElderry, B. R., Jr. *Thomas Wolfe*. New York: Twayne Publishers, 1964, 207 p.

A brief biography and critical appraisal of Wolfe, examining his use of autobiographical material and finding the claim exaggerated which accuses him of uncreative use of that material. Wolfe is also favorably compared to Mark Twain.

Powell, W. Allen. "Thomas Wolfe's Phoenix Nest: The Plays of Thomas Wolfe As Related to His Fiction." *The Markham Review* 2, No. 6 (May 1971): 104-10.

Identifies elements of Wolfe's novels that originally appeared in his dramas.

Reeves, Paschal. *Thomas Wolfe's Albatross: Race and Nationality in America*. Athens: University of Georgia Press, 1968, 160 p.

Examines the attitudes held by Wolfe towards various ethnic minorities, including blacks, Jews, and American Indians.

———, ed. *The Merrill Studies in "Look Homeward, Angel."* Columbus: Charles E. Merrill Publishing Co., 1970, 155 p.

A collection of reviews and essays on Wolfe's first novel. Contributors include Stringfellow Barr, Floyd C. Watkins, and Maxwell Geismar, among many others.

———, ed. *Thomas Wolfe and the Glass of Time*. Athens: University of Georgia Press, 1971, 166 p.

Papers on Wolfe and his art, originally read at the first South Atlantic Graduate English (SAGE) symposium. Contributors include Richard S. Kennedy, Richard Walser, C. Hugh Holman, Ladell Payne, Paschal Reeves, and Fred Wolfe, the author's brother.

Rothman, Nathan L. "Thomas Wolfe and James Joyce: A Study in Literary Influence." In *A Southern Vanguard: The John Peale Bishop Memorial Volume,* edited by Allen Tate, pp. 52-77. New York: Prentice-Hall, 1947.

An important essay on Wolfe's great debt to Joyce. The critic cites many instances of Joycean influence in Wolfe's work and finds Eugene Gant to be the "twin" of Stephen Dedalus.

Rubin, Larry. "Thomas Wolfe and the Lost Paradise." *Modern Fiction Studies* XI, No. 3 (Autumn 1965): 250-58.

Traces the theme of man as an exile from paradise through Wolfe's four novels. The critic contends that most of the major motifs of those novels spring from this main theme.

Rubin, Louis D., Jr. *Thomas Wolfe: The Weather of His Youth*. Baton Rouge: Louisiana State University Press, 1955, 183 p.

A critical appraisal by one of the nation's foremost Wolfe scholars. Rubin examines Wolfe's use of time and autobiography in his novels, highlighting the author's dedication to his craft.

Schoenberger, Franz. "Wolfe's Genius Seen Afresh: A European Recounts His Discovery of an Eloquent Voice of the New World." *The New York Times Book Review* (4 August 1946): 1, 25.

Laudatory appraisal of Wolfe by a German emigrant. The critic finds Wolfe's impressions of Germany's nazism in *You Can't Go Home Again* to be superior to the reports of American news correspondents writing from that country during the prewar era.

Snyder, William U. *Thomas Wolfe: Ulysses and Narcissus*. Athens: Ohio University Press, 1971, 234 p.

A detailed psychoanalytic biography of Wolfe which concludes that he "can be classified as a psycho-neurotic with severe labile and cyclical emotional features."

Steele, Richard. *Thomas Wolfe: A Study in Psychoanalytic Criticism*. Philadelphia: Dorrance & Co., 1976, 214 p.

A psychoanalytic study of Wolfe's works, examining the narcissism, racism, sense of alienation, and other aspects found in them.

Turnbull, Andrew. *Thomas Wolfe*. New York: Charles Scribner's Sons, 1967, 374 p.

The most complete biography of Wolfe to date.

Walser, Richard, ed. *The Enigma of Thomas Wolfe: Biographical and Critical Selections*. Cambridge: Harvard University Press, 1953, 313 p.

A collection of essays on Wolfe's life and work, containing important critical comments by his editors, Margaret Church, W. P. Albrecht, and others.

Watkins, Floyd C. *Thomas Wolfe's Characters: Portraits from Life*. Norman: University of Oklahoma Press, 1957, 194 p.

Identifies the actual persons, places, and events fictionalized in Wolfe's works.

Appendix

THE EXCERPTS IN TCLC, VOLUME 13, WERE REPRINTED FROM THE FOLLOWING PERIODICALS:

American Mercury
The American Review of Reviews
The American Scandinavian Review
Appeal to Reason
Approach
The Athenaeum
The Atlantic Monthly
Australian Journal of French Studies
The Bookman, *London*
The Bookman, *New York*
Books Abroad
Book World—The Washington Post
Brecht Heute/Brecht Today
Canadian Literature
Catholic World
College English
Commentary
Commonweal
Comparative Drama
Comparative Literature
Comparative Literature Studies
Contemporary Drama
Contemporary Literature
Contemporary Psychoanalysis
Contemporary Review
The Criterion
The Drama Magazine
The Drama Review
Educational Theatre Journal
The Egoist
Encounter
The English Review
Essays on Canadian Writing
The Forum
The Freeman
French Studies
The Germanic Review
German Life & Letters
Harper's Weekly
The Hudson Review
The Illustrated Weekly of India
The International Fiction Review
The Italian Quarterly
Italica
Journal for Anthroposophy
Journal of English and Germanic Philology
Krasnaya Gazeta
The Literary Review
The Little Review
London Review of Books
The Massachusetts Review
Menckeniana
Mecure de France
MidAmerica
MLN
Modern Drama
Modern Fiction Studies
Modern Language Quarterly
The Modern Language Review
Modern Poetry Studies
Monatshefte
MOSAIC
The Nation
The Nation and the Athenaeum
The New Republic
New Statesman
The New Statesman & Nation
The New Yorker
New York Herald Tribune Books
The New York Review of Books
The New York Times
The New York Times Book Review
Nineteenth-Century Fiction
Oeuvres et opinions
The Outlook
Overland Monthly and Out West Magazine
The Oxford Review
Partisan Review
Pravda
Progressive Architecture
The Quarterly Journal of Speech
Quarterly Review of Literature
The Reader and Collector
Renascence
Research in African Literatures
Riverside Quarterly
The Saturday Review of Literature
Scandinavian Studies
Scribner's Magazine
Scrutiny
VII: An Anglo-American Literary Review
The Sewanee Review
Slavic Review
The Smart Set
The Southern Humanities Review
The Spectator
Studies in Short Fiction
The Thomas Wolfe Review
The Times Literary Supplement
TriQuarterly
University of Toronto Quarterly
Wascana Review
Western Humanities Review
World Literature Today
The Yale Review

THE EXCERPTS IN TCLC, VOLUME 13, WERE REPRINTED FROM THE FOLLOWING BOOKS:

Adams, Robert Martin. Strains of Discord: Studies in Literary Openness. *Cornell University Press, 1958, Books for Libraries Press, 1971.*

Adams, Robert Martin. AfterJoyce: Studies in Fiction after "Ulysses." *Oxford University Press, 1977.*

Adcock, A. St. John. Introduction to The Calling of the Sea, *by William Hope Hodgson. Selwyn & Blount, 1920.*

Allen, Paul Marshall. Introduction to Cosmic Memory: Prehistory of Earth and Man, *by Rudolph Steiner. Translated by Karl E. Zimmer. Steiner, 1959, Harper & Row, 1981.*

Babbitt, Irving. Modern Writers at Work. *Edited by Josephine K. Piercy. Macmillan, 1930.*

Babel, Isaac. Isaac Babel: The Lonely Years 1925-1939. *Edited by Nathalie Babel. Translated by Andrew R. MacAndrew and Max Hayward. Farrar, Straus and Giroux, 1964.*

Barfield, Owen. Romanticism Comes of Age. *Rev. ed. Rudolf Steiner Press, 1966, Wesleyan University Press, 1967.*

Bauland, Peter. The Hooded Eagle: Modern German Drama on the New York Stage. *Syracuse University Press, 1968.*

Bellow, Saul. Foreword to The Boundaries of Natural Science, *by Rudolf Steiner. Translated by Frederick Amrine and Konrad Oberhuber. Anthroposophic Press, 1983.*

Bennett, D. M. Anthony Comstock, His Career of Cruelty and Crime: A Chapter from "The Champions of the Church." *D. M. Bennett, 1878, Da Capo Press, 1971.*

Bentley, Eric. The Brecht Commentaries: 1943-1980. *Grove Press, 1981.*

Bentley, Eric. Introduction to Seven Plays, *by Bertolt Brecht. Edited by Eric Bentley. Grove Press, 1961.*

Bertaux, Félix. A Panorama of German Literature: From 1871 to 1931. *Translated by John J. Trounstine. McGraw-Hill, 1935, Cooper Square Publishers, 1970.*

Birnbaum, Marianna D. Introduction to The Magician's Garden, and Other Stories, *by Géza Csáth. Edited by Marianna D. Birnbaum. Translated by Jascha Kessler and Charlotte Rogers. Columbia University Press, 1980.*

Bithell, Jethro. Modern German Literature: 1850-1950. *Rev. ed. Methuen, 1959.*

Bittleston, Adam. Introduction to The Portal of Initiation: A Rosicrucian Mystery Drama, *by Rudolf Steiner. Translated by Adam Bittleston. Rev. ed. Steinerbooks, 1981.*

Bloom, Edward A. The Order of Fiction: An Introduction. *Odyssey Press, 1964.*

Boyd, Ernest. H. L. Mencken. *McBride, 1925.*

Bradbury, Malcolm, and McFarlane, James, eds. Modernism: 1890-1930. *Penquin, 1974, Harvester Press, 1978.*

Brecht, Bertolt. Plays, Vol. I. *Translated by Desmond I. Vesey. Methuen, 1960.*

Bremner, Robert. Introduction to Traps for the Young, *by Anthony Comstock. Belknap Press, 1967.*

Brod, Max, ed. The Diaries of Franz Kafka: 1910-1913. *Edited by Max Brod. Translated by Joseph Kresh. Schocken, 1948.*

Brooks, Van Wyck. The Confident Years: 1885-1915. *Dutton, 1952.*

Brown, Edward J. Russian Literature Since the Revolution. *Rev. ed. Harvard University Press, 1982.*

Brown, Edward J., ed. Major Soviet Writers: Essays in Criticism. *Oxford University Press, 1973.*

Buckley, J. M. Introduction to Traps for the Young, *by Anthony Comstock. Funk & Wagnalls, 1883, Belknap Press, 1967.*

Cabell, James Branch. Some of Us: An Essay in Epitaphs. *McBride, 1930.*

Canetti, Elias. The Torch in My Ear. *Translated by Joachim Neugroschel. Farrar, Straus and Giroux, 1982.*

Carter, Angela. Introduction to Opium, and Other Stories, *by Géza Csáth. Edited by Marianna D. Birnbaum. Translated by Jascha Kessler and Charlotte Rogers. Penguin, 1983.*

Carter, Lin. Introduction to The Boats of the "Glen Carrig," *by William Hope Hodgson. Ballantine, 1971.*

Carter, Lin. Introduction to The Night Land, *by William Hope Hodgson. Ballantine, 1972.*

Cocking, J. M. Introduction to Marcel Proust: Selected Letters, 1880-1903, *by Marcel Proust. Edited by Philip Kolb. Translated by Ralph Manheim. Doubleday, 1983.*

Cohen, Hennig, ed. Landmarks of American Writing. *Edited by Hennig Cohen. Basic Books, 1969.*

Comstock, Anthony. Traps for the Young. *Funk & Wagnalls, 1883, Belknap Press, 1967.*

Connolly, Cyril. Previous Convictions. *Hamish Hamilton, 1963.*

Conrad, Joseph. Joseph Conrad: Life and Letters, Vol. II. *Edited by G. Jean-Aubry. Doubleday, 1927.*

Cook, Bruce. Brecht in Exile. *Holt, Rinehart and Winston, 1983.*

Cooke, Alistair. On Mencken. *Edited by John Dorsey. Knopf, 1980.*

Davis, Elmer. By Elmer Davis. *Bobbs-Merrill, 1964.*

Dell, Floyd. Women As World Builders: Studies in Modern Feminism. *Forbes, 1913.*

Demetz, Peter, ed. Brecht: A Collection of Critical Essays. *Prentice-Hall, 1962.*

Drake, William A. Introduction to Eros Invincible, *by Ricarda Huch. Translated by William A. Drake. Macauley, 1931.*

Dreiser, Theodore. Letters of Theodore Dreiser: A Selection, Vol. 2. *Edited by Robert H. Elias. University of Pennsylvania Press, 1959.*

Drinnon, Richard. Rebel in Paradise: A Biography of Emma Goldman. *University of Chicago Press, 1961.*

Edel, Leon. Introduction to We'll to the Woods No More, *by Édouard Dujardin. Translated by Stuart Gilbert. New Directions, 1958.*

Eloesser, Arthur. Modern German Literature. *Translated by Catherine Alison Phillips, Knopf, 1933.*

Erlich, Victor, ed. Twentieth-Century Russian Literary Criticism. *Yale University Press, 1975.*

Ewen, Frederic. Bertolt Brecht: His Life, His Art, and His Times. *Citadel Press, 1967.*

Farrell, James T. Fifty and Other Essays. *Vanguard Press, 1954.*

Fast, Howard. Literature and Reality. *International Publishers, 1950.*

Field, Leslie A., ed. Thomas Wolfe: Three Decades of Criticism. *New York University Press, 1968.*

Field, Leslie. Preface to The Autobiography of an American Novelist, *by Thomas Wolfe. Edited by Leslie Field. Harvard University Press, 1983.*

Fitzgerald, F. Scott. The Letters of F. Scott Fitzgerald. *Edited by Andrew Turnbull. Scribner's, 1963.*

Forster, E. M. Introduction to Two Stories and a Memory, *by Giuseppe Tomasi di Lampedusa. Translated by Archibald Colquhoun. Collins, 1962, Pantheon, 1962.*

Frank, Waldo. In the American Jungle: 1925-1936. *Farrar & Rinehart, 1937.*

Garneau, Saint-Denys. Journal. *Translated by John Glassco. McClelland and Stewart, 1962.*

Gatt-Rutter, John. Writers and Politics in Modern Italy. *Holmes & Meier, 1978.*

Ghosh, Shibdas. An Evaluation of Saratchandra. *Sachin Banerjee, 1977.*

Glassco, John. Introduction to Complete Poems of Saint Denys Garneau, *by Saint Denys Garneau. Translated by John Glassco. Oberon Press, 1975.*

Goodman, Paul. Preface to Metamorphosis, *by Franz Kafka. Translated by A. L. Lloyd. Vanguard Press, 1946.*

Grass, Günter. Preface to A People Betrayed: November 1918, a German Revolution, *by Alfred Döblin. Translated by John E. Woods. Fromm, 1983.*

Gray, Ronald. Franz Kafka. *Cambridge University Press, 1973.*

Grossvogel, David I. The Self-Conscious Stage in Modern French Drama. *Columbia University Press, 1958.*

Guerard, Albert J. Conrad the Novelist. *Harvard University Press, 1966.*

Guerard, Albert J. Introduction to "Heart of Darkness" and "The Secret Sharer," *by Joseph Conrad. New American Library, 1950.*

Hallett, Richard. Isaac Babel. *Bradda, 1972, Ungar, 1973.*

Harris, Frank. Contemporary Portraits, fourth series. *Brentano's, 1923.*

Harwood, A. C. Education and Philosophy. *Edited by George Z. F. Bereday and Joseph A. Lauwerys. World, 1957.*

Hassan, Ihab. The Dismemberment of Orpheus: Toward a Postmodern Literature. *2d ed. University of Wisconsin Press, 1982.*

Havel, Hippolyte. Anarchism, and Other Essays, *by Emma Goldman. Mother Earth Publishing Association, 1910.*

Heidenreich, Rev. Alfred. Introduction to Christianity as Mystical Fact and the Mysteries of Antiquity, *by Rudolf Steiner. Translated by E. A. Frommer, Gabvielle Hess, and Peter Kändler. Steinerbooks, 1961.*

Heller, Otto. Studies in Modern German Literature: Sudermann, Hauptmann, Women Writers of the Nineteenth Century. *Ginn, 1905, Books for Libraries Press, 1967.*

Helstein, Nadia. Preface to Red Cavalry, *by I. Babel. Translated by Nadia Helstein. Knopf, 1929.*

Hicks, Granville. The Great Tradition: An Interpretation of American Literature since the Civil War. *Rev. ed. Macmillan, 1935.*

Hilfer, Anthony Channell. The Revolt from the Village: 1915-1930. *University of North Carolina Press, 1969.*

Hill, Claude. Bertolt Brecht. *Twayne, 1975.*

Hindus, Milton. The Proustian Vision. *Columbia University Press, 1954.*

Holman, C. Hugh. The Comic Imagination in American Literature. *Edited by Louis D. Rubin, Jr. Rutgers University Press, 1973.*

Holman, C. Hugh. The Loneliness at the Core: Studies in Thomas Wolfe. *Louisiana State University Press, 1975.*

Hughes, Kenneth, ed. Franz Kafka: An Anthology of Marxist Criticism. *Translated by Kenneth Hughes. University Press of New England, 1981.*

Innes, Christopher. Holy Theatre: Ritual and the Avant Garde. *Cambridge University Press, 1981.*

Ishill, Joseph. Emma Goldman: A Challenging Rebel. *Translated by Herman Frank. Oriole Press, 1957.*

Janouch, Gustav. Conversations with Kafka. *Translated by Goronwy Rees. Rev. ed. New Directions, 1971.*

Johnson, Pamela Hansford. Hungry Gulliver. *Scribner's, 1948.*

Johnson, Pamela Hansford. The Art of Thomas Wolfe. *Scribner's, 1963.*

Karl, Frederick R. A Reader's Guide to Joseph Conrad. *Rev. ed. Farrar, Straus and Giroux, 1969.*

Kazin, Alfred. On Native Grounds: An Interpretation of Modern American Prose Literature. *Reynal & Hitchcock, 1942.*

Kennedy, Richard S. The Window of Memory: The Literary Career of Thomas Wolfe. *University of North Carolina Press, 1962.*

Kennedy, Richard S., ed. Thomas Wolfe: A Harvard Perspective. *Croissant, 1983.*

Kermode, Frank. Puzzles and Epiphanies: Essays and Reviews, 1958-1961. *Routledge & Kegan Paul, 1962.*

Knopf, Alfred A., ed. The Borzoi 1920: Being a Sort of Record of Five Years' Publishing. *Knopf, 1920.*

Kort, Wolfgang. Alfred Döblin. *Twayne, 1974.*

Krutch, Joseph Wood. Five Masters: A Study in the Mutations of the Novel. *Cape & Smith, 1930.*

Kuehl, John, and Bryer, Jackson R., eds. Dear Scott/Dear Max: The Fitzgerald-Perkins Correspondence. *Scribner's, 1971.*

Kumarappa, Bharatan, ed. The Indian Literatures of Today: A Symposium. *International Book House, 1947.*

Leavis, F. R. The Great Tradition: George Eliot, Henry James, Joseph Conrad. *New York University Press, 1963.*

Lewis, Wyndham. Paleface: The Philosophy of the "Melting-Pot." *Chatto & Windus, 1929, Scholarly Press, 1971.*

Light, Martin. The Quixotic Vision of Sinclair Lewis. *Purdue University Press, 1975.*

Light, Martin, ed. The Merrill Studies in "Babbitt." *Merrill, 1971.*

Lippmann, Walter. Men of Destiny. *Macmillan, 1927.*

Lovecraft, H. P. Dagon, and Other Macabre Tales. *Edited by August Derleth. Arkham House, 1965.*

Lowenthal, Leo. Literature and the Image of Man: Sociological Studies of the European Drama and Novel, 1600-1900. *Beacon Press, 1957.*

Lynn, Kenneth S. Visions of America: Eleven Literary Historical Essays. *Greenwood Press, 1973.*

Lyons, Charles R. Bertolt Brecht: The Despair and the Polemic. *Southern Illinois University Press, 1968.*

Mansfield, Katherine. Novels and Novelists. *Edited by J. Middleton Murry. Knopf, 1930.*

March, Harold. The Two Worlds of Marcel Proust. *University of Pennsylvania Press, 1948.*

Mencken, H. L. A Book of Prefaces. *Knopf, 1924.*

Mencken, H. L. H. L. Mencken's "Smart Set" Criticism. *Edited by William H. Nolte. Cornell University Press, 1968.*

Miller, Henry. Letters to Anaïs Nin. *Edited by Gunther Stuhlmann. Putnam's, 1965.*

Morris, Lloyd. Postscript to Yesterday: America, the Last Fifty Years. *Random House, 1947.*

Morris, Wright. The Territory Ahead. *Atheneum, 1963.*

Moser, Thomas. Joseph Conrad: Achievement and Decline. *Harvard University Press, 1957.*

Moskowitz, Sam. Preface to Out of the Storm: Uncollected Fantasies, *by William Hope Hodgson. Edited by Sam Moskowitz. Grant, 1975.*

Mukhopadhyay, Manik, ed. The Golden Book of Saratchandra: A Centenary Commemorative Volume. *All Bengal Sarat Centenary Committee, 1977.*

Naravane, Vishwanath S. Sarat Chandra Chatterji: An Introduction to His Life and Work. *Macmillan, 1976.*

Nathan, George Jean. The Theatre Book of the Year, 1947-1948: A Record and an Interpretation. *Knopf, 1948.*

Neider, Charles. Introduction to Short Novels of the Masters. *Edited by Charles Neider. Holt, Rinehart and Winston, 1967.*

O'Higgins, Harvey, and Reede, Edward H. The American Mind in Action. *Harper, 1924.*

Pacifici, Sergio. The Modern Italian Novel from Pea to Moravia. *Southern Illinois University Press, 1979.*

Politzer, Heinz. Parable and Paradox. *Rev. ed. Cornell University Press, 1966.*

Prescott, Orville. In My Opinion: An Inquiry into the Contemporary Novel. *Bobbs-Merrill, 1952.*

Proust, Marcel. Letters of Marcel Proust. *Edited and translated by Mina Curtiss. Random House, 1949.*

Pusch, Hans. Introduction to The Portal of Initiation: A Rosicrucian Mystery through Rudolf Steiner, *by Rudolf Steiner. Translated by Ruth Pusch and Hans Pusch. Steinerbooks, 1973.*

Quennell, Peter, ed. Marcel Proust, 1871-1922: A Centenary Volume. *Weidenfeld and Nicolson, 1971.*

Raab, Rex; Klingbord, Arne; and Fant, Åke. Eloquent Concrete: How Rudolf Steiner Employed Reinforced Concrete. *Rudolf Steiner Press, 1979.*

Ragusa, Olga. Narrative and Drama: Essays in Modern Italian Literature from Verga to Pasolini. *Mouton, 1976.*

Rathburn, Robert C., and Steinman, Martin, Jr., eds. From Jane Austen to Joseph Conrad: Essays Collected in Memory of James T. Hillhouse. *University of Minnesota Press, 1958.*

Rosenheim, Richard. The Eternal Drama: A Comprehensive Treatise on the Syngenetic History of Humanity, Dramatics, and Theatre. *Philosophical Library, 1952.*

Rourke, Constance. American Humor: A Study of the National Character. *Harcourt Brace Jovanovich, 1931.*

Roy, Dilip Kumar. Preface to The Deliverance, *by Sarat Chandra Chattopadhyaya. Rev. ed. Edited by Sri Aurobindo. Translated by Dilip Kumar Roy. Vora, 1944.*

Schorer, Mark. Sinclair Lewis: An American Life. *McGraw-Hill, 1961.*

Sharp, Dennis. Modern Architecture and Expressionism. *Longmans, 1966, Braziller, 1967.*

Shaw, Bernard. Bernard Shaw: Collected Letters, 1898-1910. *Edited by Dan H. Laurence. Reinhardt, 1972.*

Shepherd, A. P. A Scientist of the Indivisible: An Introduction to the Life and Work of Rudolf Steiner. *Hodder and Stoughton, 1954.*

Smith, Clark Ashton. Planets and Dimensions: Collected Essays of Clark Ashton Smith. *Edited by Charles K. Wolfe. Miragé Press, 1973.*

Spalek, John M., and Bell, Robert F., eds. Exile: The Writer's Experience. *University of North Carolina Press, 1982.*

Spann, Meno. Franz Kafka. *Twayne, 1976.*

Spender, Dale, ed. Feminist Theorists: Three Centuries of Key Women Thinkers. *Pantheon, 1983.*

Stegner, Wallace; Scowcroft, Richard; and Ilyin, Boris, eds. The Writer's Art: A Collection of Short Stories. *Heath, 1950.*

Steiner, Marie. Introduction to Art in the Light of Mystery Wisdom: A Collection of Eight Lectures, *by Rudolf Steiner. Translated by Johanna Collis. Rudolf Steiner Press, 1970.*

Steiner, Rudolf. Rudolf Steiner: An Autobiography. *Edited by Paul M. Allen. Translated by Rita Stebbing. Steiner, 1977.*

Stenerson, Douglas. H. L. Mencken: Iconoclast from Baltimore. *University of Chicago Press, 1971.*

Struve, Gleb. Russian Literature under Lenin and Stalin: 1917-1953. *University of Oklahoma Press, 1971.*

Styan, J. L. Modern Drama in Theory and Practice: Expressionism and Epic Theatre, Vol. 3. *Cambridge University Press, 1981.*

Tagore, Rabindranath. Preface to The Deliverance, *by Sarat Chandra Chattopadhyaya. Rev. ed. Translated by Dilip Kumar Roy. Vora, 1944.*

Tiefenbrun, Ruth. Moment of Torment: An Interpretation of Franz Kafka's Short Stories. *Southern Illinois University Press, 1973.*

Tougas, Gerard. History of French-Canadian Literature. *2d ed. Translated by Alta Lind Cook. Ryerson Press, 1966.*

Untermeyer, Louis. Makers of the Modern World: The Lives of Ninety-two Writers, Artists, Scientists, Statesmen, Inventors, Philosophers, Composers, and Other Creators Who Formed the Pattern of Our Century. *Simon & Schuster, 1955.*

Updike, John. Hugging the Shore: Essays and Criticism. *Knopf, 1983.*

Vonnegut, Kurt, Jr. Foreword to The Unabridged Mark Twain, *by Mark Twain. Edited by Lawrence Teacher. Running Press, 1976.*

Wagner, Philip. H. L. Mencken. *University of Minnesota Press, 1966.*

Watt, Ian. Conrad in the Nineteenth Century. *University of California Press, 1979.*

Watts, Cedric. Conrad's ''Heart of Darkness'': A Critical and Contextual Discussion. *Mursia International, 1977.*

Weideli, Walter. The Art of Bertolt Brecht. *Translated by Daniel Russell. New York University Press, 1963.*

West, Rebecca. Introduction to My Disillusionment in Russia, *by Emma Goldman. Daniel, 1925.*

Wheatley, Dennis. Introduction to The Ghost Pirates, *by William Hope Hodgson. Sphere, 1975.*

Wilson, Edmund. Europe without Baedecker. *2d ed. Farrar, Straus and Giroux, 1966.*

Wright, Richard. Black Boy: A Record of Childhood and Youth. *Harper, 1945.*

Yeats, W. B. Autobiographies. *Macmillan, 1955.*

Ziolkowski, Theodore. Dimensions of the Modern Novel: German Texts and European Contexts. *Princeton University Press, 1969.*

Cumulative Index to Authors

This index lists all author entries in the Gale Literary Criticism Series and includes cross-references to other Gale sources. References in the index are identified as follows:

AITN: *Authors in the News*, Volumes 1-2
CA: *Contemporary Authors* (original series), Volumes 1-111
CANR: *Contemporary Authors New Revision Series*, Volumes 1-11
CAP: *Contemporary Authors Permanent Series*, Volumes 1-2
CA-R: *Contemporary Authors* (revised editions), Volumes 1-44
CLC: *Contemporary Literary Criticism*, Volumes 1-29
CLR: *Children's Literature Review*, Volumes 1-6
DLB: *Dictionary of Literary Biography*, Volumes 1-26
DLB-DS: *Dictionary of Literary Biography Documentary Series*, Volumes 1-4
DLB-Y: *Dictionary of Literary Biography Yearbook*, Volumes 1980-1982
LC: *Literature Criticism from 1400 to 1800*, Volume 1
NCLC: *Nineteenth-Century Literature Criticism*, Volumes 1-6
SATA: *Something about the Author*, Volumes 1-34
TCLC: *Twentieth-Century Literary Criticism*, Volumes 1-13
YABC: *Yesterday's Authors of Books for Children*, Volumes 1-2

A. E. 1867-1935 .... **TCLC 3, 10**
See also Russell, George William
See also DLB 19

Abé, Kōbō 1924- .... **CLC 8, 22**
See also CA 65-68

Abell, Kjeld 1901-1961 .... **CLC 15**
See also obituary CA 111

Abish, Walter 1931- .... **CLC 22**
See also CA 101

Abrahams, Peter (Henry) 1919- ..... **CLC 4**
See also CA 57-60

Abrams, M(eyer) H(oward)
1912- .... **CLC 24**
See also CA 57-60

Abse, Dannie 1923- .... **CLC 7, 29**
See also CANR 4
See also CA 53-56

Achebe, Chinua
1930- .... **CLC 1, 3, 5, 7, 11, 26**
See also CANR 6
See also CA 1-4R

Acorn, Milton 1923- .... **CLC 15**
See also CA 103
See also AITN 2

Adamov, Arthur 1908-1970 ..... **CLC 4, 25**
See also CAP 2
See also CA 17-18
See also obituary CA 25-28R

Adams, Alice (Boyd) 1926- ...... **CLC 6, 13**
See also CA 81-84

Adams, Douglas (Noel) 1952- .... **CLC 27**
See also CA 106

Adams, Henry (Brooks)
1838-1918 .... **TCLC 4**
See also CA 104
See also DLB 12

Adams, Richard (George)
1920- .... **CLC 4, 5, 18**
See also CANR 3
See also CA 49-52
See also SATA 7
See also AITN 1, 2

Adamson, Joy(-Friederike Victoria)
1910-1980 .... **CLC 17**
See also CA 69-72
See also obituary CA 93-96
See also SATA 11
See also obituary SATA 22

Adler, Renata 1938- .... **CLC 8**
See also CANR 5
See also CA 49-52

Ady, Endre 1877-1919 .... **TCLC 11**
See also CA 107

Agee, James 1909-1955 .... **TCLC 1**
See also CA 108
See also DLB 2, 26
See also AITN 1

Agnon, S(hmuel) Y(osef Halevi)
1888-1970 .... **CLC 4, 8, 14**
See also CAP 2
See also CA 17-18
See also obituary CA 25-28R

Ai 1947- .... **CLC 4, 14**
See also CA 85-88

Aiken, Conrad (Potter)
1899-1973 .... **CLC 1, 3, 5, 10**
See also CANR 4
See also CA 5-8R
See also obituary CA 45-48
See also SATA 3, 30
See also DLB 9

Ajar, Emile 1914-1980
See Gary, Romain

Akhmatova, Anna
1888-1966 .... **CLC 11, 25**
See also CAP 1
See also CA 19-20
See also obituary CA 25-28R

Aksakov, Sergei Timofeyvich
1791-1859 .... **NCLC 2**

Aksenov, Vasily (Pavlovich)
1932- .... **CLC 22**
See also CA 53-56

Aksyonov, Vasily (Pavlovich) 1932-
See Aksenov, Vasily (Pavlovich)

Alain-Fournier 1886-1914 .... **TCLC 6**
See also CA 104

Alarcón, Pedro Antonio de
1833-1891 .... **NCLC 1**

Albee, Edward (Franklin III)
1928- ..... **CLC 1, 2, 3, 5, 9, 11, 13, 25**
See also CANR 8
See also CA 5-8R
See also DLB 7
See also AITN 1

Alberti, Rafael 1902- .... **CLC 7**
See also CA 85-88

Alcott, Amos Bronson
1799-1888 .... **NCLC 1**
See also DLB 1

Alcott, Louisa May 1832-1888 ..... **NCLC 6**
See also CLR 1
See also YABC 1
See also DLB 1

Aldiss, Brian (Wilson) 1925- .... **CLC 5, 14**
See also CANR 5
See also CA 5-8R
See also SATA 34
See also DLB 14

Aleichem, Sholom 1859-1916...... **TCLC 1**
See also CA 104

Aleixandre, Vicente 1898- .... **CLC 9**
See also CA 85-88

Alepoudelis, Odysseus 1911-
See Elytis, Odysseus

Algren, Nelson 1909-1981 ...... **CLC 4, 10**
See also CA 13-16R
See also obituary CA 103
See also DLB 9
See also DLB-Y 81, 82

Allen, Heywood 1935-
See Allen, Woody
See also CA 33-36R

Allen, Woody 1935-.............. **CLC 16**
See also Allen, Heywood

Allingham, Margery (Louise)
1904-1966.................... **CLC 19**
See also CANR 4
See also CA 5-8R
See also obituary CA 25-28R

Allston, Washington
1779-1843.................. **NCLC 2**
See also DLB 1

Almedingen, E. M. 1898-1971...... **CLC 12**
See also Almedingen, Martha Edith von

Almedingen, Martha Edith von 1898-1971
See Almedingen, E. M.
See also CANR 1
See also CA 1-4R
See also SATA 3

Alonso, Dámaso 1898-............. **CLC 14**
See also CA 110

Alta 1942-....................... **CLC 19**
See also CA 57-60

Alther, Lisa 1944-................. **CLC 7**
See also CA 65-68

Altman, Robert 1925-............. **CLC 16**
See also CA 73-76

Alvarez, A(lfred) 1929-......... **CLC 5, 13**
See also CANR 3
See also CA 1-4R
See also DLB 14

Amado, Jorge 1912- .... **CLC 13**
See also CA 77-80

Ambler, Eric 1909-........... **CLC 4, 6, 9**
See also CANR 7
See also CA 9-12R

Amichai, Yehuda 1924- .... **CLC 9, 22**
See also CA 85-88

Amiel, Henri Frédéric
1821-1881................... **NCLC 4**

Amis, Kingsley (William)
1922-............ **CLC 1, 2, 3, 5, 8, 13**
See also CANR 8
See also CA 9-12R
See also DLB 15
See also AITN 2

Amis, Martin 1949-............. **CLC 4, 9**
See also CANR 8
See also CA 65-68
See also DLB 14

Ammons, A(rchie) R(andolph)
1926-............ **CLC 2, 3, 5, 8, 9, 25**
See also CANR 6
See also CA 9-12R
See also DLB 5
See also AITN 1

Anand, Mulk Raj 1905- .... **CLC 23**
See also CA 65-68

Anaya, Rudolfo A(lfonso)
1937-........................ **CLC 23**
See also CANR 1
See also CA 45-48

Anderson, Jon (Victor) 1940- .... **CLC 9**
See also CA 25-28R

Anderson, Lindsay 1923-.......... **CLC 20**

Anderson, Maxwell 1888-1959 .... **TCLC 2**
See also CA 105
See also DLB 7

Anderson, Poul (William)
1926-........................ **CLC 15**
See also CANR 2
See also CA 1-4R
See also DLB 8

Anderson, Robert (Woodruff)
1917-........................ **CLC 23**
See also CA 21-24R
See also DLB 7
See also AITN 1

Anderson, Roberta Joan 1943-
See Mitchell, Joni

Anderson, Sherwood
1876-1941................ **TCLC 1, 10**
See also CA 104
See also DLB 4, 9
See also DLB-DS 1

Andrade, Carlos Drummond de
1902-........................ **CLC 18**

Andrews, Cicily Fairfield 1892-1983
See West, Rebecca

Andreyev, Leonid (Nikolaevich)
1871-1919.................. **TCLC 3**
See also CA 104

Andrézel, Pierre 1885-1962
See Dinesen, Isak
See also Blixen, Karen (Christentze Dinesen)

Andrić, Ivo 1892-1975 .... **CLC 8**
See also CA 81-84
See also obituary CA 57-60

Angelique, Pierre 1897-1962
See Bataille, Georges

Angell, Roger 1920-............... **CLC 26**
See also CA 57-60

Angelou, Maya 1928- .... **CLC 12**
See also CA 65-68

Anouilh, Jean (Marie Lucien Pierre)
1910-................. **CLC 1, 3, 8, 13**
See also CA 17-20R

Anthony, Florence 1947-
See Ai

Antoninus, Brother 1912-
See Everson, William (Oliver)

Antonioni, Michelangelo 1912- ..... **CLC 20**
See also CA 73-76

Antschel, Paul 1920-1970
See Celan, Paul
See also CA 85-88

Apollinaire, Guillaume
1880-1918................ **TCLC 3, 8**
See also CA 104

Appelfeld, Aharon 1932- .... **CLC 23**

Apple, Max (Isaac) 1941-........... **CLC 9**
See also CA 81-84

Aquin, Hubert 1929-1977.......... **CLC 15**
See also CA 105

Aragon, Louis 1897-1982....... **CLC 3, 22**
See also CA 69-72
See also obituary CA 108

Arbuthnot, John 1667-1735.......... **LC 1**

Archer, Jeffrey (Howard)
1940-........................ **CLC 28**
See also CA 77-80

Archer, Jules 1915-............... **CLC 12**
See also CANR 6
See also CA 9-12R
See also SATA 4

Arden, John 1930-.......... **CLC 6, 13, 15**
See also CA 13-16R
See also DLB 13

Arguedas, José María
1911-1969................ **CLC 10, 18**
See also CA 89-92

Armah, Ayi Kwei 1939- .... **CLC 5**
See also CA 61-64

Armatrading, Joan 1950-.......... **CLC 17**

Arnim, Achim von 1781-1831 ..... **NCLC 5**

Arnold, Matthew 1822-1888 ...... **NCLC 6**

Arnow, Harriette (Louisa Simpson)
1908-................... **CLC 2, 7, 18**
See also CA 9-12R
See also DLB 6

Arp, Jean 1887-1966............... **CLC 5**
See also CA 81-84
See also obituary CA 25-28R

Arquette, Lois S(teinmetz)
See Duncan (Steinmetz Arquette), Lois
See also SATA 1

Arrabal, Fernando 1932- ..... **CLC 2, 9, 18**
See also CA 9-12R

Artaud, Antonin 1896-1948....... **TCLC 3**
See also CA 104

Arthur, Ruth M(abel)
1905-1979.................... **CLC 12**
See also CANR 4
See also CA 9-12R
See also obituary CA 85-88
See also SATA 7
See also obituary SATA 26

Arundel, Honor (Morfydd)
1919-1973.................... **CLC 17**
See also CAP 2
See also CA 21-22
See also obituary CA 41-44R
See also SATA 4
See also obituary SATA 24

Asch, Sholem 1880-1957.......... **TCLC 3**
See also CA 105

Ashbery, John (Lawrence)
1927-..... **CLC 2, 3, 4, 6, 9, 13, 15, 25**
See also CANR 9
See also CA 5-8R
See also DLB 5
See also DLB-Y 81

Ashton-Warner, Sylvia (Constance)
1908-........................ **CLC 19**
See also CA 69-72

Asimov, Isaac
1920- . . . . **CLC 1, 3, 9, 19, 26**
See also CANR 2
See also CA 1-4R
See also SATA 1, 26
See also DLB 8

Asturias, Miguel Ángel
1899-1974 . . . . **CLC 3, 8, 13**
See also CAP 2
See also CA 25-28
See also obituary CA 49-52

Atheling, William, Jr. 1921-1975
See Blish, James (Benjamin)

Atherton, Gertrude (Franklin Horn)
1857-1948 . . . . **TCLC 2**
See also CA 104
See also DLB 9

Atwood, Margaret (Eleanor)
1939- . . . . **CLC 2, 3, 4, 8, 13, 15, 25**
See also CANR 3
See also CA 49-52

Auchincloss, Louis (Stanton)
1917- . . . . **CLC 4, 6, 9, 18**
See also CANR 6
See also CA 1-4R
See also DLB 2
See also DLB-Y 80

Auden, W(ystan) H(ugh)
1907-1973 . . . . **CLC 1, 2, 3, 4, 6, 9, 11, 14**
See also CANR 5
See also CA 9-12R
See also obituary CA 45-48
See also DLB 10, 20

Austen, Jane 1775-1817 . . . . **NCLC 1**

Avison, Margaret 1918- . . . . **CLC 2, 4**
See also CA 17-20R

Ayckbourn, Alan 1939- . . . . **CLC 5, 8, 18**
See also CA 21-24R
See also DLB 13

Aymé, Marcel (Andre)
1902-1967 . . . . **CLC 11**
See also CA 89-92

Ayrton, Michael 1921-1975 . . . . **CLC 7**
See also CANR 9
See also CA 5-8R
See also obituary CA 61-64

Azorín 1874-1967 . . . . **CLC 11**
See also Martínez Ruiz, José

Azuela, Mariano 1873-1952 . . . . **TCLC 3**
See also CA 104

"Bab" 1836-1911
See Gilbert, (Sir) W(illiam) S(chwenck)

Babel, Isaak (Emmanuilovich)
1894-1941 . . . . **TCLC 2, 13**
See also CA 104

Bacchelli, Riccardo 1891- . . . . **CLC 19**
See also CA 29-32R

Bach, Richard (David) 1936- . . . . **CLC 14**
See also CA 9-12R
See also SATA 13
See also AITN 1

Bagnold, Enid 1889-1981 . . . . **CLC 25**
See also CANR 5
See also CA 5-8R
See also obituary CA 103
See also SATA 1, 25
See also DLB 13

Bagryana, Elisaveta 1893- . . . . **CLC 10**

Baillie, Joanna 1762-1851 . . . . **NCLC 2**

Bainbridge, Beryl
1933- . . . . **CLC 4, 5, 8, 10, 14, 18, 22**
See also CA 21-24R
See also DLB 14

Baker, Elliott 1922- . . . . **CLC 8**
See also CANR 2
See also CA 45-48

Bakshi, Ralph 1938- . . . . **CLC 26**

Baldwin, James (Arthur)
1924- . . . . . . **CLC 1, 2, 3, 4, 5, 8, 13, 15, 17**
See also CANR 3
See also CA 1-4R
See also SATA 9
See also DLB 2, 7

Ballard, J(ames) G(raham)
1930- . . . . **CLC 3, 6, 14**
See also CA 5-8R
See also DLB 14

Balmont, Konstantin Dmitriyevich
1867-1943 . . . . **TCLC 11**
See also CA 109

Balzac, Honoré de 1799-1850 . . . . . **NCLC 5**

Bambara, Toni Cade . . . . **CLC 19**
See also CA 29-32R

Banks, Lynne Reid 1929- . . . . **CLC 23**
See also Reid Banks, Lynne

Baraka, Imamu Amiri
1934- . . . . **CLC 2, 3, 5, 10, 14**
See also Jones, (Everett) LeRoi
See also DLB 5, 7, 16

Barbey d'Aurevilly, Jules Amédée
1808-1889 . . . . **NCLC 1**

Barbusse, Henri 1873-1935 . . . . **TCLC 5**
See also CA 105

Barfoot, Joan 1946- . . . . **CLC 18**
See also CA 105

Baring, Maurice 1874-1945 . . . . **TCLC 8**
See also CA 105

Barker, George (Granville)
1913- . . . . **CLC 8**
See also CANR 7
See also CA 9-12R
See also DLB 20

Barnes, Djuna
1892-1982 . . . . **CLC 3, 4, 8, 11, 29**
See also CA 9-12R
See also obituary CA 107
See also DLB 4, 9

Barnes, Peter 1931- . . . . **CLC 5**
See also CA 65-68
See also DLB 13

Baroja (y Nessi), Pío
1872-1956 . . . . **TCLC 8**
See also CA 104

Barondess, Sue K(aufman) 1926-1977
See Kaufman, Sue
See also CANR 1
See also CA 1-4R
See also obituary CA 69-72

Barrett, William (Christopher)
1913- . . . . **CLC 27**
See also CANR 11
See also CA 13-16R

Barrie, (Sir) J(ames) M(atthew)
1860-1937 . . . . **TCLC 2**
See also CA 104
See also YABC 1
See also DLB 10

Barry, Philip (James Quinn)
1896-1949 . . . . **TCLC 11**
See also CA 109
See also DLB 7

Barth, John (Simmons)
1930- . . . . . . **CLC 1, 2, 3, 5, 7, 9, 10, 14, 27**
See also CANR 5
See also CA 1-4R
See also DLB 2
See also AITN 1, 2

Barthelme, Donald
1931- . . . . . . **CLC 1, 2, 3, 5, 6, 8, 13, 23**
See also CA 21-24R
See also SATA 7
See also DLB 2
See also DLB-Y 80

Barthes, Roland 1915-1980 . . . . **CLC 24**
See also obituary CA 97-100

Bassani, Giorgio 1916- . . . . **CLC 9**
See also CA 65-68

Bataille, Georges 1897-1962 . . . . **CLC 29**
See also CA 101
See also obituary CA 89-92

Baudelaire, Charles
1821-1867 . . . . **NCLC 6**

Baum, L(yman) Frank
1856-1919 . . . . **TCLC 7**
See also CA 108
See also SATA 18
See also DLB 22

Baumbach, Jonathan 1933- . . . . . **CLC 6, 23**
See also CA 13-16R
See also DLB-Y 80

Baxter, James K(eir)
1926-1972 . . . . **CLC 14**
See also CA 77-80

Bayer, Sylvia 1909-1981
See Glassco, John

Beagle, Peter S(oyer) 1939- . . . . **CLC 7**
See also CANR 4
See also CA 9-12R
See also DLB-Y 80

Beardsley, Aubrey 1872-1898 . . . . . **NCLC 6**

Beattie, Ann 1947- . . . . **CLC 8, 13, 18**
See also CA 81-84
See also DLB-Y 82

Beauvoir, Simone de
1908- . . . . **CLC 1, 2, 4, 8, 14**
See also CA 9-12R

Becker, Jurek 1937- . . . . **CLC 7, 19**
See also CA 85-88

Becker, Walter 1950-
See Becker, Walter and Fagen, Donald

Becker, Walter 1950- and **Fagen, Donald**
1948- . . . . **CLC 26**

Beckett, Samuel (Barclay)
1906- . . . . . . **CLC 1, 2, 3, 4, 6, 9, 10, 11, 14, 18, 29**
See also CA 5-8R
See also DLB 13, 15

Beckman, Gunnel 1910- . . . . **CLC 26**
See also CA 33-36R
See also SATA 6

Becque, Henri 1837-1899 . . . . **NCLC 3**

Beddoes, Thomas Lovell
1803-1849 . . . . **NCLC 3**

Beecher, John 1904-1980 . . . . **CLC 6**
See also CANR 8
See also CA 5-8R
See also obituary CA 105
See also AITN 1

Beerbohm, (Sir Henry) Max(imilian)
1872-1956 . . . . **TCLC 1**
See also CA 104

Behan, Brendan
1923-1964 . . . . **CLC 1, 8, 11, 15**
See also CA 73-76
See also DLB 13

Behn, Aphra 1640?-1689 . . . . **LC 1**

Belasco, David 1853-1931 . . . . **TCLC 3**
See also CA 104
See also DLB 7

Belcheva, Elisaveta 1893-
See Bagryana, Elisaveta

Belinski, Vissarion Grigoryevich
1811-1848 . . . . **NCLC 5**

Belitt, Ben 1911- . . . . **CLC 22**
See also CANR 7
See also CA 13-16R
See also DLB 5

Bell, Acton 1820-1849
See Brontë, Anne

Bell, Currer 1816-1855
See Brontë, Charlotte

Bell, Marvin 1937- . . . . **CLC 8**
See also CA 21-24R
See also DLB 5

Bellamy, Edward 1850-1898 . . . . . . **NCLC 4**
See also DLB 12

Belloc, (Joseph) Hilaire (Pierre)
1870-1953 . . . . **TCLC 7**
See also CA 106
See also YABC 1
See also DLB 19

Bellow, Saul
1915- . . . . . **CLC 1, 2, 3, 6, 8, 10, 13, 15, 25**
See also CA 5-8R
See also DLB 2
See also DLB-Y 82
See also DLB-DS 3
See also AITN 2

Belser, Reimond Karel Maria de 1929-
See Ruyslinck, Ward

Bely, Andrey 1880-1934 . . . . **TCLC 7**
See also CA 104

Benary-Isbert, Margot
1889-1979 . . . . **CLC 12**
See also CANR 4
See also CA 5-8R
See also obituary CA 89-92
See also SATA 2
See also obituary SATA 21

Benavente (y Martinez), Jacinto
1866-1954 . . . . **TCLC 3**
See also CA 106

Benchley, Peter (Bradford)
1940- . . . . **CLC 4, 8**
See also CA 17-20R
See also SATA 3
See also AITN 2

Benchley, Robert 1889-1945 . . . . . . **TCLC 1**
See also CA 105
See also DLB 11

Benedikt, Michael 1935- . . . . **CLC 4, 14**
See also CANR 7
See also CA 13-16R
See also DLB 5

Benet, Juan 1927- . . . . **CLC 28**

Benét, Stephen Vincent
1898-1943 . . . . **TCLC 7**
See also CA 104
See also YABC 1
See also DLB 4

Benn, Gottfried 1886-1956 . . . . **TCLC 3**
See also CA 106

Bennett, (Enoch) Arnold
1867-1931 . . . . **TCLC 5**
See also CA 106
See also DLB 10

Bennett, George Harold 1930-
See Bennett, Hal
See also CA 97-100

Bennett, Hal 1930- . . . . **CLC 5**
See also Bennett, George Harold

Bennett, Louise (Simone)
1919- . . . . **CLC 28**
See also Bennett-Coverly, Louise Simone

Bennett-Coverly, Louise Simone 1919-
See Bennett, Louise (Simone)
See also CA 97-100

Benson, Sally 1900-1972 . . . . **CLC 17**
See also CAP 1
See also CA 19-20
See also obituary CA 37-40R
See also SATA 1
See also obituary SATA 27

Bentley, E(dmund) C(lerihew)
1875-1956 . . . . **TCLC 12**
See also CA 108

Bentley, Eric (Russell) 1916- . . . . **CLC 24**
See also CANR 6
See also CA 5-8R

Berger, John (Peter) 1926- . . . . . . **CLC 2, 19**
See also CA 81-84
See also DLB 14

Berger, Melvin (H.) 1927- . . . . **CLC 12**
See also CANR 4
See also CA 5-8R
See also SATA 5

Berger, Thomas (Louis)
1924- . . . . **CLC 3, 5, 8, 11, 18**
See also CANR 5
See also CA 1-4R
See also DLB 2
See also DLB-Y 80

Bergman, (Ernst) Ingmar
1918- . . . . **CLC 16**
See also CA 81-84

Bergstein, Eleanor 1938- . . . . **CLC 4**
See also CANR 5
See also CA 53-56

Bernanos, (Paul Louis) Georges
1888-1948 . . . . **TCLC 3**
See also CA 104

Bernhard, Thomas 1931- . . . . **CLC 3**
See also CA 85-88

Berrigan, Daniel J. 1921- . . . . **CLC 4**
See also CANR 11
See also CA 33-36R
See also DLB 5

Berry, Chuck 1926- . . . . **CLC 17**

Berry, Wendell (Erdman)
1934- . . . . **CLC 4, 6, 8, 27**
See also CA 73-76
See also DLB 5, 6
See also AITN 1

Berryman, John
1914-1972 . . . . . **CLC 1, 2, 3, 4, 6, 8, 10, 13, 25**
See also CAP 1
See also CA 15-16
See also obituary CA 33-36R

Bertolucci, Bernardo 1940- . . . . **CLC 16**
See also CA 106

Besant, Annie (Wood)
1847-1933 . . . . **TCLC 9**
See also CA 105

Bessie, Alvah 1904- . . . . **CLC 23**
See also CANR 2
See also CA 5-8R
See also DLB 26

Beti, Mongo 1932- . . . . **CLC 27**

Betjeman, John 1906- . . . . **CLC 2, 6, 10**
See also CA 9-12R
See also DLB 20

Betti, Ugo 1892-1953 . . . . **TCLC 5**
See also CA 104

Betts, Doris (Waugh)
1932- . . . . **CLC 3, 6, 28**
See also CANR 9
See also CA 13-16R
See also DLB-Y 82

Bienek, Horst 1930- . . . . **CLC 7, 11**
See also CA 73-76

Bierce, Ambrose (Gwinett)
1842-1914? . . . . **TCLC 1, 7**
See also CA 104
See also DLB 11, 12, 23

Bioy Casares, Adolfo
1914- . . . . **CLC 4, 8, 13**
See also CA 29-32R

Bird, Robert Montgomery
1806-1854 . . . . **NCLC 1**

Birdwell, Cleo 1936-
See DeLillo, Don

Birney (Alfred) Earle
1904- . . . . **CLC 1, 4, 6, 11**
See also CANR 5
See also CA 1-4R

Bishop, Elizabeth
1911-1979 . . . . **CLC 1, 4, 9, 13, 15**
See also CA 5-8R
See also obituary CA 89-92
See also obituary SATA 24
See also DLB 5

Bishop, John 1935- . . . . **CLC 10**
See also CA 105

Bissett, Bill 1939-.................CLC 18
See also CA 69-72

Biyidi, Alexandre 1932-
See Beti, Mongo

Bjørnson, Bjørnstjerne (Martinius)
1832-1910................... TCLC 7
See also CA 104

Blackburn, Paul 1926-1971 ....CLC 9
See also CA 81-84
See also obituary CA 33-36R
See also DLB 16
See also DLB-Y 81

Blackmur, R(ichard) P(almer)
1904-1965................. CLC 2, 24
See also CAP 1
See also CA 11-12
See also obituary CA 25-28R

Blackwood, Algernon (Henry)
1869-1951................... TCLC 5
See also CA 105

Blackwood, Caroline 1931- ...... CLC 6, 9
See also CA 85-88
See also DLB 14

Blair, Eric Arthur 1903-1950
See Orwell, George

Blais, Marie-Claire
1939-............. CLC 2, 4, 6, 13, 22
See also CA 21-24R

Blaise, Clark 1940- ....CLC 29
See also CANR 5
See also CA 53-56R
See also AITN 2

Blake, Nicholas 1904-1972
See Day Lewis, C(ecil)

Blasco Ibáñez, Vicente
1867-1928.................. TCLC 12
See also CA 110

Blatty, William Peter 1928-.........CLC 2
See also CANR 9
See also CA 5-8R

Blish, James (Benjamin)
1921-1975....................CLC 14
See also CANR 3
See also CA 1-4R
See also obituary CA 57-60
See also DLB 8

Blixen, Karen (Christentze Dinesen)
1885-1962
See Dinesen, Isak
See also CAP 2
See also CA 25-28

Blok, Aleksandr (Aleksandrovich)
1880-1921................... TCLC 5
See also CA 104

Bloom, Harold 1930-..............CLC 24
See also CA 13-16R

Blume, Judy (Sussman Kitchens)
1938-........................CLC 12
See also CLR 2
See also CA 29-32R
See also SATA 2, 31

Blunden, Edmund (Charles)
1896-1974.....................CLC 2
See also CAP 2
See also CA 17-18
See also obituary CA 45-48
See also DLB 20

Bly, Robert 1926- ..... CLC 1, 2, 5, 10, 15
See also CA 5-8R
See also DLB 5

Bødker, Cecil 1927-...............CLC 21
See also CA 73-76
See also SATA 14

Boell, Heinrich (Theodor) 1917-
See Böll, Heinrich
See also CA 21-24R

Bogan, Louise 1897-1970 ....CLC 4
See also CA 73-76
See also obituary CA 25-28R

Bogarde, Dirk 1921- ....CLC 19
See also Van Den Bogarde, Derek (Jules Gaspard Ulric) Niven
See also DLB 14

Böll, Heinrich (Theodor)
1917-........... CLC 2, 3, 6, 9, 11, 15
See also Boell, Heinrich (Theodor)

Bolt, Robert (Oxton) 1924- ....CLC 14
See also CA 17-20R
See also DLB 13

Bond, Edward 1934-......CLC 4, 6, 13, 23
See also CA 25-28R
See also DLB 13

Bonham, Frank 1914-.............CLC 12
See also CANR 4
See also CA 9-12R
See also SATA 1

Bonnefoy, Yves 1923-.......... CLC 9, 15
See also CA 85-88

Bontemps, Arna (Wendell)
1902-1973................. CLC 1, 18
See also CLR 6
See also CANR 4
See also CA 1-4R
See also obituary CA 41-44R
See also SATA 2
See also obituary SATA 24

Booth, Martin 1944- ....CLC 13
See also CA 93-96

Booth, Philip 1925- ....CLC 23
See also CANR 5
See also CA 5-8R
See also DLB-Y 82

Booth, Wayne C(layson) 1921- .....CLC 24
See also CANR 3
See also CA 1-4R

Borchert, Wolfgang 1921-1947 .... TCLC 5
See also CA 104

Borges, Jorge Luis
1899-.......CLC 1, 2, 3, 4, 6, 8, 9, 10, 13, 19
See also CA 21-24R

Borowski, Tadeusz 1922-1951 ..... TCLC 9
See also CA 106

Bourget, Paul (Charles Joseph)
1852-1935.................. TCLC 12
See also CA 107

Bourjaily, Vance (Nye) 1922-........CLC 8
See also CANR 2
See also CA 1-4R
See also DLB 2

Bowen, Elizabeth (Dorothea Cole)
1899-1973...... CLC 1, 3, 6, 11, 15, 22
See also CAP 2
See also CA 17-18
See also obituary CA 41-44R
See also DLB 15

Bowering, George 1935-...........CLC 15
See also CANR 10
See also CA 21-24R

Bowers, Edgar 1924-...............CLC 9
See also CA 5-8R
See also DLB 5

Bowie, David 1947-...............CLC 17
See also Jones, David Robert

Bowles, Jane (Sydney)
1917-1973.....................CLC 3
See also CAP 2
See also CA 19-20
See also obituary CA 41-44R

Bowles, Paul (Frederick)
1910-................... CLC 1, 2, 19
See also CANR 1
See also CA 1-4R
See also DLB 5, 6

Boyd, William 1952-..............CLC 28

Boyle, Kay 1903-............ CLC 1, 5, 19
See also CA 13-16R
See also DLB 4, 9

Boyle, Patrick.....................CLC 19

Bradbury, Edward P. 1939-
See Moorcock, Michael

Bradbury, Ray (Douglas)
1920-................CLC 1, 3, 10, 15
See also CANR 2
See also CA 1-4R
See also SATA 11
See also DLB 2, 8
See also AITN 1, 2

Bradley, David (Henry), Jr.
1950-.........................CLC 23
See also CA 104

Bragg, Melvyn 1939-..............CLC 10
See also CANR 10
See also CA 57-60
See also DLB 14

Braine, John (Gerard) 1922-..... CLC 1, 3
See also CANR 1
See also CA 1-4R
See also DLB 15

Brancati, Vitaliano
1907-1954.................. TCLC 12
See also CA 109

Brand, Millen 1906-1980 ....CLC 7
See also CA 21-24R
See also obituary CA 97-100

Brandes, Georg (Morris Cohen)
1842-1927.................. TCLC 10
See also CA 105

Branley, Franklyn M(ansfield)
1915-........................CLC 21
See also CA 33-36R
See also SATA 4

Brathwaite, Edward 1930-.........CLC 11
See also CANR 11
See also CA 25-28R

Brautigan, Richard 1935- .... **CLC 1, 3, 5, 9, 12**
See also CA 53-56
See also DLB 2, 5
See also DLB-Y 80

Brecht, (Eugen) Bertolt (Friedrich) 1898-1956 .... **TCLC 1, 6, 13**
See also CA 104

Brennan, Maeve 1917- .... **CLC 5**
See also CA 81-84

Brentano, Clemens (Maria) 1778-1842 .... **NCLC 1**

Breslin, James (E.) 1930-
See Breslin, Jimmy
See also CA 73-76

Breslin, Jimmy 1930- .... **CLC 4**
See also Breslin, James (E.)
See also AITN 1

Bresson, Robert 1907- .... **CLC 16**
See also CA 110

Breton, André 1896-1966 ..... **CLC 2, 9, 15**
See also CAP 2
See also CA 19-20
See also obituary CA 25-28R

Breytenbach, Breyten 1939- .... **CLC 23**

Bridgers, Sue Ellen 1942- .... **CLC 26**
See also CANR 11
See also CA 65-68
See also SATA 22

Bridges, Robert 1844-1930 .... **TCLC 1**
See also CA 104
See also DLB 19

Bridie, James 1888-1951 .... **TCLC 3**
See also CA 104
See also DLB 10

Brink, André (Philippus) 1935- ..... **CLC 18**
See also CA 104

Brinsmead, H(esba) F(ay) 1922- .... **CLC 21**
See also CANR 10
See also CA 21-24R
See also SATA 18

Brittain, Vera (Mary) 1893?-1970 .... **CLC 23**
See also CAP 1
See also CA 15-16
See also obituary CA 25-28R

Brodsky, Iosif Alexandrovich 1940-
See Brodsky, Joseph
See also CA 41-44R
See also AITN 1

Brodsky, Joseph 1940- .... **CLC 4, 6, 13**
See also Brodsky, Iosif Alexandrovich

Brodsky, Michael (Mark) 1948- .... **CLC 19**
See also CA 102

Bromell, Henry 1947- .... **CLC 5**
See also CANR 9
See also CA 53-56

Bromfield, Louis (Brucker) 1896-1956 .... **TCLC 11**
See also CA 107
See also DLB 4, 9

Broner, E(sther) M(asserman) 1930- .... **CLC 19**
See also CANR 8
See also CA 17-20R

Bronk, William 1918- .... **CLC 10**
See also CA 89-92

Brontë, Anne 1820-1849 .... **NCLC 4**
See also DLB 21

Brontë, Charlotte 1816-1855 ...... **NCLC 3**
See also DLB 21

Brooke, Henry 1703?-1783 .... **LC 1**

Brooke, Rupert (Chawner) 1887-1915 .... **TCLC 2, 7**
See also CA 104
See also DLB 19

Brooks, Cleanth 1906- .... **CLC 24**
See also CA 17-20R

Brooks, Gwendolyn 1917- .... **CLC 1, 2, 4, 5, 15**
See also CANR 1
See also CA 1-4R
See also SATA 6
See also DLB 5
See also AITN 1

Brooks, Mel 1926- .... **CLC 12**
See also CA 65-68
See also DLB 26

Brooks, Van Wyck 1886-1963 ...... **CLC 29**
See also CANR 6
See also CA 1-4R

Brophy, Brigid (Antonia) 1929- .... **CLC 6, 11, 29**
See also CA 5-8R
See also DLB 14

Brosman, Catharine Savage 1934- .... **CLC 9**
See also CA 61-64

Broughton, T(homas) Alan 1936- .... **CLC 19**
See also CANR 2
See also CA 45-48

Broumas, Olga 1949- .... **CLC 10**
See also CA 85-88

Brown, Dee (Alexander) 1908- ..... **CLC 18**
See also CANR 11
See also CA 13-16R
See also SATA 5
See also DLB-Y 80

Brown, George Mackay 1921- .... **CLC 5**
See also CA 21-24R
See also DLB 14

Brown, Rita Mae 1944- .... **CLC 18**
See also CANR 2, 11
See also CA 45-48

Brown, Sterling A(llen) 1901- .... **CLC 1, 23**
See also CA 85-88

Brown, William Wells 1816?-1884 .... **NCLC 2**
See also DLB 3

Browne, Jackson 1950- .... **CLC 21**

Browning, Elizabeth Barrett 1806-1861 .... **NCLC 1**

Browning, Tod 1882-1962 .... **CLC 16**

Bruce, Lenny 1925-1966 .... **CLC 21**
See also Schneider, Leonard Alfred

Brunner, John (Kilian Houston) 1934- .... **CLC 8, 10**
See also CANR 2
See also CA 1-4R

Bryan, C(ourtlandt) D(ixon) B(arnes) 1936- .... **CLC 29**
See also CA 73-76

Bryant, William Cullen 1794-1878 .... **NCLC 6**
See also DLB 3

Bryusov, Valery (Yakovlevich) 1873-1924 .... **TCLC 10**
See also CA 107

Buchheim, Lothar-Günther 1918- .... **CLC 6**
See also CA 85-88

Buck, Pearl S(ydenstricker) 1892-1973 .... **CLC 7, 11, 18**
See also CANR 1
See also CA 1-4R
See also obituary CA 41-44R
See also SATA 1, 25
See also DLB 9
See also AITN 1

Buckler, Ernest 1908- .... **CLC 13**
See also CAP 1
See also CA 11-12

Buckley, William F(rank), Jr. 1925- .... **CLC 7, 18**
See also CANR 1
See also CA 1-4R
See also DLB-Y 80
See also AITN 1

Buechner, (Carl) Frederick 1926- .... **CLC 2, 4, 6, 9**
See also CANR 11
See also CA 13-16R
See also DLB-Y 80

Buell, John (Edward) 1927- .... **CLC 10**
See also CA 1-4R

Buero Vallejo, Antonio 1916- ...... **CLC 15**
See also CA 106

Bukowski, Charles 1920- ...... **CLC 2, 5, 9**
See also CA 17-20R
See also DLB 5

Bulgakov, Mikhail (Afanas'evich) 1891-1940 .... **TCLC 2**
See also CA 105

Bullins, Ed 1935- .... **CLC 1, 5, 7**
See also CA 49-52
See also DLB 7

Bulwer-Lytton, (Lord) Edward (George Earle Lytton) 1803-1873 .... **NCLC 1**
See also SATA 23
See also DLB 21

Bunin, Ivan (Alexeyevich) 1870-1953 .... **TCLC 6**
See also CA 104

Bunting, Basil 1900- .... **CLC 10**
See also CANR 7
See also CA 53-56
See also DLB 20

Buñuel, Luis 1900- .... **CLC 16**
See also CA 101
See also obituary CA 110

Burgess, Anthony 1917- ..... **CLC 1, 2, 4, 5, 8, 10, 13, 15, 22**
See also Wilson, John (Anthony) Burgess
See also DLB 14
See also AITN 1

Burke, Kenneth (Duva) 1897- .... **CLC 2, 24**
See also CA 5-8R

Burns, Tex 1908?-
See L'Amour, Louis (Dearborn)

Burnshaw, Stanley 1906- .... **CLC 3, 13**
See also CA 9-12R

Burr, Anne 1937- .... **CLC 6**
See also CA 25-28R

Burroughs, Edgar Rice 1875-1950 .... **TCLC 2**
See also CA 104
See also DLB 8

Burroughs, William S(eward) 1914- .... **CLC 1, 2, 5, 15, 22**
See also CA 9-12R
See also DLB 2, 8, 16
See also DLB-Y 81
See also AITN 2

Busch, Frederick 1941- .... **CLC 7, 10, 18**
See also CA 33-36R
See also DLB 6

Butler, Samuel 1835-1902 .... **TCLC 1**
See also CA 104
See also DLB 18

Butor, Michel (Marie François) 1926- .... **CLC 1, 3, 8, 11, 15**
See also CA 9-12R

Byatt, A(ntonia) S(usan Drabble) 1936- .... **CLC 19**
See also CA 13-16R
See also DLB 14

Byrne, David 1953?- .... **CLC 26**

Byrne, John Keyes 1926-
See Leonard, Hugh
See also CA 102

Byron, George Gordon (Noel), Lord Byron 1788-1824 .... **NCLC 2**

Cabell, James Branch 1879-1958 .... **TCLC 6**
See also CA 105
See also DLB 9

Cable, George Washington 1844-1925 .... **TCLC 4**
See also CA 104
See also DLB 12

Cabrera Infante, G(uillermo) 1929- .... **CLC 5, 25**
See also CA 85-88

Cain, G. 1929-
See Cabrera Infante, G(uillermo)

Cain, James M(allahan) 1892-1977 .... **CLC 3, 11, 28**
See also CANR 8
See also CA 17-20R
See also obituary CA 73-76
See also AITN 1

Caldwell, Erskine 1903- .... **CLC 1, 8, 14**
See also CANR 2
See also CA 1-4R
See also DLB 9
See also AITN 1

Caldwell, (Janet Miriam) Taylor (Holland) 1900- .... **CLC 2, 28**
See also CANR 5
See also CA 5-8R

Calisher, Hortense 1911- .... **CLC 2, 4, 8**
See also CANR 1
See also CA 1-4R
See also DLB 2

Callaghan, Morley (Edward) 1903- .... **CLC 3, 14**
See also CA 9-12R

Calvino, Italo 1923- .... **CLC 5, 8, 11, 22**
See also CA 85-88

Campbell, (Ignatius) Roy (Dunnachie) 1901-1957 .... **TCLC 5**
See also CA 104
See also DLB 20

Campbell, (William) Wilfred 1861-1918 .... **TCLC 9**
See also CA 106

Camus, Albert 1913-1960 .... **CLC 1, 2, 4, 9, 11, 14**
See also CA 89-92

Canby, Vincent 1924- .... **CLC 13**
See also CA 81-84

Canetti, Elias 1905- .... **CLC 3, 14, 25**
See also CA 21-24R

Cape, Judith 1916-
See Page, P(atricia) K(athleen)

Čapek, Karel 1890-1938 .... **TCLC 6**
See also CA 104

Capote, Truman 1924- .... **CLC 1, 3, 8, 13, 19**
See also CA 5-8R
See also DLB 2
See also DLB-Y 80

Capra, Frank 1897- .... **CLC 16**
See also CA 61-64

Carey, Ernestine Gilbreth 1908-
See Gilbreth, Frank B(unker), Jr. and Carey, Ernestine Gilbreth
See also CA 5-8R
See also SATA 2

Carleton, William 1794-1869 .... **NCLC 3**

Carman, (William) Bliss 1861-1929 .... **TCLC 7**
See also CA 104

Carpentier (y Valmont), Alejo 1904-1980 .... **CLC 8, 11**
See also CANR 11
See also CA 65-68
See also obituary CA 97-100

Carr, John Dickson 1906-1977 .... **CLC 3**
See also CANR 3
See also CA 49-52
See also obituary CA 69-72

Carrier, Roch 1937- .... **CLC 13**

Carroll, Lewis 1832-1898 .... **NCLC 2**
See also CLR 2
See also YABC 2
See also DLB 18

Carroll, Paul Vincent 1900-1968 .... **CLC 10**
See also CA 9-12R
See also obituary CA 25-28R
See also DLB 10

Carruth, Hayden 1921- .... **CLC 4, 7, 10, 18**
See also CANR 4
See also CA 9-12R
See also DLB 5

Carter, Angela 1940- .... **CLC 5**
See also CA 53-56
See also DLB 14

Carver, Raymond 1938- .... **CLC 22**
See also CA 33-36R

Cary, (Arthur) Joyce 1888-1957 .... **TCLC 1**
See also CA 104
See also DLB 15

Casares, Adolfo Bioy 1914-
See Bioy Casares, Adolfo

Casey, John 1880-1964
See O'Casey, Sean

Casey, Michael 1947- .... **CLC 2**
See also CA 65-68
See also DLB 5

Casey, Warren 1935-
See Jacobs, Jim and Casey, Warren
See also CA 101

Cassavetes, John 1929- .... **CLC 20**
See also CA 85-88

Cassill, R(onald) V(erlin) 1919- .... **CLC 4, 23**
See also CANR 7
See also CA 9-12R
See also DLB 6

Cassity, (Allen) Turner 1929- .... **CLC 6**
See also CANR 11
See also CA 17-20R

Castaneda, Carlos 1935?- .... **CLC 12**
See also CA 25-28R

Castro, Rosalía de 1837-1885 .... **NCLC 3**

Cather, Willa (Sibert) 1873-1947 .... **TCLC 1, 11**
See also CA 104
See also SATA 30
See also DLB 9
See also DLB-DS 1

Causley, Charles (Stanley) 1917- .... **CLC 7**
See also CANR 5
See also CA 9-12R
See also SATA 3

Caute, (John) David 1936- .... **CLC 29**
See also CANR 1
See also CA 1-4R
See also DLB 14

Cavafy, C(onstantine) P(eter) 1863-1933 .... **TCLC 2, 7**
See also CA 104

Cavanna, Betty 1909- .... **CLC 12**
See also CANR 6
See also CA 9-12R
See also SATA 1, 30

Cayrol, Jean 1911- .... **CLC 11**
See also CA 89-92

Cela, Camilo José 1916- .... **CLC 4, 13**
See also CA 21-24R

Celan, Paul 1920-1970 .... **CLC 10, 19**
See also Antschel, Paul

Céline, Louis-Ferdinand 1894-1961 .... **CLC 1, 3, 4, 7, 9, 15**
See also Destouches, Louis Ferdinand

Cendrars, Blaise 1887-1961 .... **CLC 18**
See also Sauser-Hall, Frédéric

Césaire, Aimé (Fernand) 1913- .....CLC 19
See also CA 65-68

Chabrol, Claude 1930- ....CLC 16
See also CA 110

Challans, Mary 1905-1983
See Renault, Mary
See also CA 81-84
See also obituary CA 111
See also SATA 23

Chambers, James 1948-
See Cliff, Jimmy

Chandler, Raymond
1888-1959.................TCLC 1, 7
See also CA 104

Chaplin, Charles (Spencer)
1889-1977....................CLC 16
See also CA 81-84
See also obituary CA 73-76

Chapman, Graham 1941?-
See Monty Python

Chapman, John Jay
1862-1933................... TCLC 7
See also CA 104

Char, René (Emile)
1907-...................CLC 9, 11, 14
See also CA 13-16R

Charyn, Jerome 1937- ....CLC 5, 8, 18
See also CANR 7
See also CA 5-8R

Chase, Mary Ellen 1887-1973.......CLC 2
See also CAP 1
See also CA 15-16
See also obituary CA 41-44R
See also SATA 10

Chateaubriand, François René de
1768-1848................... NCLC 3

Chatterji, Saratchandra
1876-1938.................. TCLC 13
See also CA 109

Chatwin, (Charles) Bruce
1940-........................CLC 28
See also CA 85-88

Chayefsky, Paddy 1923-1981.......CLC 23
See also CA 9-12R
See also obituary CA 104
See also DLB 7
See also DLB-Y 81

Chayefsky, Sidney 1923-1981
See Chayefsky, Paddy

Cheever, John
1912-1982......CLC 3, 7, 8, 11, 15, 25
See also CANR 5
See also CA 5-8R
See also obituary CA 106
See also DLB 2
See also DLB-Y 80, 82

Cheever, Susan 1943- ....CLC 18
See also CA 103
See also DLB-Y 82

Chekhov, Anton (Pavlovich)
1860-1904................TCLC 3, 10
See also CA 104

Chernyshevsky, Nikolay Gavrilovich
1828-1889................... NCLC 1

Chesnutt, Charles Waddell
1858-1932................... TCLC 5
See also CA 106
See also DLB 12

Chesterton, G(ilbert) K(eith)
1874-1936.................TCLC 1, 6
See also CA 104
See also SATA 27
See also DLB 10, 19

Ch'ien Chung-shu 1910-...........CLC 22

Child, Lydia Maria 1802-1880 .... NCLC 6
See also DLB 1

Child, Philip 1898-1978 ....CLC 19
See also CAP 1
See also CA 13-14

Childress, Alice 1920-......... CLC 12, 15
See also CANR 3
See also CA 45-48
See also SATA 7
See also DLB 7

Chitty, (Sir) Thomas Willes 1926-
See Hinde, Thomas
See also CA 5-8R

Chomette, René 1898-1981
See Clair, René
See also obituary CA 103

Chopin, Kate (O'Flaherty)
1851-1904................... TCLC 5
See also CA 104
See also DLB 12

Christie, Agatha (Mary Clarissa)
1890-1976.............CLC 1, 6, 8, 12
See also CANR 10
See also CA 17-20R
See also obituary CA 61-64
See also DLB 13
See also AITN 1, 2

Christie, (Ann) Philippa 1920-
See Pearce, (Ann) Philippa
See also CANR 4

Ciardi, John (Anthony) 1916- ......CLC 10
See also CANR 5
See also CA 5-8R
See also SATA 1
See also DLB 5

Cimino, Michael 1943?- ....CLC 16
See also CA 105

Clair, René 1898-1981 ....CLC 20
See also Chomette, René

Clark, (Robert) Brian 1932- ....CLC 29
See also CA 41-44R

Clark, Eleanor 1913-........... CLC 5, 19
See also CA 9-12R
See also DLB 6

Clark, Mavis Thorpe 1912?- ....CLC 12
See also CANR 8
See also CA 57-60
See also SATA 8

Clark, Walter Van Tilburg
1909-1971....................CLC 28
See also CA 9-12R
See also obituary CA 33-36R
See also SATA 8
See also DLB 9

Clarke, Arthur C(harles)
1917-................CLC 1, 4, 13, 18
See also CANR 2
See also CA 1-4R
See also SATA 13

Clarke, Austin 1896-1974........ CLC 6, 9
See also CAP 2
See also CA 29-32
See also obituary CA 49-52
See also DLB 10, 20

Clarke, Austin C(hesterfield)
1934-.........................CLC 8
See also CA 25-28R

Clarke, Shirley 1925- ....CLC 16

Claudel, Paul (Louis Charles Marie)
1868-1955................TCLC 2, 10
See also CA 104

Clavell, James (duMaresq)
1924-..................... CLC 6, 25
See also CA 25-28R

Cleese, John 1939-
See Monty Python

Clemens, Samuel Langhorne 1835-1910
See Twain, Mark
See also CA 104
See also YABC 2
See also DLB 11, 12, 23

Cliff, Jimmy 1948-................CLC 21

Clifton, Lucille 1936- ....CLC 19
See also CLR 5
See also CANR 2
See also CA 49-52
See also SATA 20
See also DLB 5

Clutha, Janet Paterson Frame 1924-
See Frame (Clutha), Janet (Paterson)
See also CANR 2
See also CA 1-4R

Coburn, D(onald) L(ee) 1938-......CLC 10
See also CA 89-92

Cocteau, Jean (Maurice Eugene Clement)
1889-1963............CLC 1, 8, 15, 16
See also CAP 2
See also CA 25-28

Coetzee, J(ohn) M. 1940-..........CLC 23
See also CA 77-80

Cohen, Arthur A(llen) 1928- ....CLC 7
See also CANR 1
See also CA 1-4R

Cohen, Leonard (Norman)
1934-.........................CLC 3
See also CA 21-24R

Cohen, Matt 1942-................CLC 19
See also CA 61-64

Colette (Sidonie-Gabrielle)
1873-1954................. TCLC 1, 5
See also CA 104

Collins, Hunt 1926-
See Hunter, Evan

Collins, (William) Wilkie
1824-1889................... NCLC 1
See also DLB 18

Colman, George 1909-1981
See Glassco, John

Colum, Padraic 1881-1972 . . . . **CLC 28**
See also CA 73-76
See also obituary CA 33-36R
See also SATA 15
See also DLB 19

Colvin, James 1939-
See Moorcock, Michael

Colwin, Laurie 1945- . . . . **CLC 5, 13, 23**
See also CA 89-92
See also DLB-Y 80

Comfort, Alex(ander) 1920- . . . . **CLC 7**
See also CANR 1
See also CA 1-4R

Compton-Burnett, Ivy
1892-1969 . . . . **CLC 1, 3, 10, 15**
See also CANR 4
See also CA 1-4R
See also obituary CA 25-28R

Comstock, Anthony
1844-1915 . . . . **TCLC 13**
See also CA 110

Condon, Robert (Thomas)
1915- . . . . **CLC 4, 6, 8, 10**
See also CANR 2
See also CA 1-4R

Connell, Evan S(helby), Jr.
1924- . . . . **CLC 4, 6**
See also CANR 2
See also CA 1-4R
See also DLB 2
See also DLB-Y 81

Connelly, Marc(us Cook)
1890-1980 . . . . **CLC 7**
See also CA 85-88
See also obituary CA 102
See also obituary SATA 25
See also DLB 7
See also DLB-Y 80

Conrad, Joseph
1857-1924 . . . . **TCLC 1, 6, 13**
See also CA 104
See also SATA 27
See also DLB 10

Constant (de Rebecque), (Henri) Benjamin
1767-1830 . . . . **NCLC 6**

Cook, Robin 1940- . . . . **CLC 14**
See also CA 108, 111

Cooke, John Esten 1830-1886 . . . . . **NCLC 5**
See also DLB 3

Cooper, James Fenimore
1789-1851 . . . . **NCLC 1**
See also SATA 19
See also DLB 3

Coover, Robert (Lowell)
1932- . . . . **CLC 3, 7, 15**
See also CANR 3
See also CA 45-48
See also DLB 2
See also DLB-Y 81

Copeland, Stewart (Armstrong) 1952-
See The Police

Coppard, A(lfred) E(dgar)
1878-1957 . . . . **TCLC 5**
See also YABC 1

Coppola, Francis Ford 1939- . . . . **CLC 16**
See also CA 77-80

Corcoran, Barbara 1911- . . . . **CLC 17**
See also CANR 11
See also CA 21-24R
See also SATA 3

Corman, Cid 1924- . . . . **CLC 9**
See also Corman, Sidney
See also DLB 5

Corman, Sidney 1924-
See Corman, Cid
See also CA 85-88

Cormier, Robert (Edmund)
1925- . . . . **CLC 12**
See also CANR 5
See also CA 1-4R
See also SATA 10

Cornwell, David (John Moore) 1931-
See le Carré, John
See also CA 5-8R

Corso, (Nunzio) Gregory
1930- . . . . **CLC 1, 11**
See also CA 5-8R
See also DLB 5, 16

Cortázar, Julio
1914- . . . . **CLC 2, 3, 5, 10, 13, 15**
See also CA 21-24R

Corvo, Baron 1860-1913
See Rolfe, Frederick (William Serafino Austin Lewis Mary)

Ćosić, Dobrica 1921- . . . . **CLC 14**

Costello, Elvis 1955- . . . . **CLC 21**

Coward, Nöel (Pierce)
1899-1973 . . . . **CLC 1, 9, 29**
See also CAP 2
See also CA 17-18
See also obituary CA 41-44R
See also DLB 10
See also AITN 1

Cox, William Trevor 1928-
See Trevor, William
See also CANR 4
See also CA 9-12R

Cozzens, James Gould
1903-1978 . . . . **CLC 1, 4, 11**
See also CA 9-12R
See also obituary CA 81-84
See also DLB 9
See also DLB-DS 2

Crane, (Harold) Hart
1899-1932 . . . . **TCLC 2, 5**
See also CA 104
See also DLB 4

Crane, R(onald) S(almon)
1886-1967 . . . . **CLC 27**
See also CA 85-88

Crane, Stephen 1871-1900 . . . . **TCLC 11**
See also DLB 12
See also YABC 2

Craven, Margaret 1901-1980 . . . . **CLC 17**
See also CA 103

Crayencour, Marguerite de 1913-
See Yourcenar, Marguerite

Creasey, John 1908-1973 . . . . **CLC 11**
See also CANR 8
See also CA 5-8R
See also obituary CA 41-44R

Crébillon, Claude Prosper Jolyot de (fils)
1707-1777 . . . . **LC 1**

Creeley, Robert (White)
1926- . . . . **CLC 1, 2, 4, 8, 11, 15**
See also CA 1-4R
See also DLB 5, 16

Crews, Harry 1935- . . . . **CLC 6, 23**
See also CA 25-28R
See also DLB 6
See also AITN 1

Crichton, (John) Michael
1942- . . . . **CLC 2, 6**
See also CA 25-28R
See also SATA 9
See also DLB-Y 81
See also AITN 2

Crispin, Edmund 1921-1978 . . . . **CLC 22**
See also Montgomery, Robert Bruce

Cristofer, Michael 1946- . . . . **CLC 28**
See also CA 110
See also DLB 7

Cross, Amanda 1926-
See Heilbrun, Carolyn G(old)

Crowley, Aleister 1875-1947 . . . . . . **TCLC 7**
See also CA 104

Crumb, Robert 1943- . . . . **CLC 17**
See also CA 106

Cryer, Gretchen 1936?- . . . . **CLC 21**

Csáth, Géza 1887-1919 . . . . **TCLC 13**
See also CA 111

Cullen, Countee 1903-1946 . . . . **TCLC 4**
See also CA 108
See also SATA 18
See also DLB 4

Cummings, E(dward) E(stlin)
1894-1962 . . . . **CLC 1, 3, 8, 12, 15**
See also CA 73-76
See also DLB 4

Cunningham, J(ames) V(incent)
1911- . . . . **CLC 3**
See also CANR 1
See also CA 1-4R
See also DLB 5

Cunningham, Julia (Woolfolk)
1916- . . . . **CLC 12**
See also CANR 4
See also CA 9-12R
See also SATA 1, 26

Dąbrowska, Maria (Szumska)
1889-1965 . . . . **CLC 15**
See also CA 106

Dahl, Roald 1916- . . . . **CLC 1, 6, 18**
See also CLR 1
See also CANR 6
See also CA 1-4R
See also SATA 1, 26

Dahlberg, Edward
1900-1977 . . . . **CLC 1, 7, 14**
See also CA 9-12R
See also obituary CA 69-72

Daly, Maureen 1921- . . . . **CLC 17**
See also McGivern, Maureen Daly
See also SATA 2

Dannay, Frederic 1905-1982
See Queen, Ellery
See also CANR 1
See also CA 1-4R
See also obituary CA 107

D'Annunzio, Gabriele 1863-1938 .... **TCLC 6**
See also CA 104

Danziger, Paula 1944- .... **CLC 21**
See also SATA 30

Darío, Rubén 1867-1916 .... **TCLC 4**
See also CA 104

Darley, George 1795-1846 .... **NCLC 2**

Daryush, Elizabeth 1887-1977 .... **CLC 6, 19**
See also CANR 3
See also CA 49-52
See also DLB 20

Daudet, (Louis Marie) Alphonse 1840-1897 .... **NCLC 1**

Davenport, Guy (Mattison), Jr. 1927- .... **CLC 6, 14**
See also CA 33-36R

Davidson, Donald (Grady) 1893-1968 .... **CLC 2, 13, 19**
See also CANR 4
See also CA 5-8R
See also obituary CA 25-28R

Davidson, Sara 1943- .... **CLC 9**
See also CA 81-84

Davie, Donald (Alfred) 1922- .... **CLC 5, 8, 10**
See also CANR 1
See also CA 1-4R

Davies, Ray(mond Douglas) 1944- .... **CLC 21**

Davies, Rhys 1903-1978 .... **CLC 23**
See also CANR 4
See also CA 9-12R
See also obituary CA 81-84

Davies, (William) Robertson 1913- .... **CLC 2, 7, 13, 25**
See also CA 33-36R

Davies, W(illiam) H(enry) 1871-1940 .... **TCLC 5**
See also CA 104
See also DLB 19

Davis, Rebecca (Blaine) Harding 1831-1910 .... **TCLC 6**
See also CA 104

Davison, Frank Dalby 1893-1970 .... **CLC 15**

Davison, Peter 1928- .... **CLC 28**
See also CANR 3
See also CA 9-12R
See also DLB 5

Davys, Mary 1674-1732 .... **LC 1**

Dawson, Fielding 1930- .... **CLC 6**
See also CA 85-88

Day, Thomas 1748-1789 .... **LC 1**
See also YABC 1

Day Lewis, C(ecil) 1904-1972 .... **CLC 1, 6, 10**
See also CAP 1
See also CA 15-16
See also obituary CA 33-36R
See also DLB 15, 20

Dazai Osamu 1909-1948 .... **TCLC 11**
See also Tsushima Shūji

Defoe, Daniel 1660?-1731 .... **LC 1**
See also SATA 22

De Hartog, Jan 1914- .... **CLC 19**
See also CANR 1
See also CA 1-4R

Deighton, Len 1929- .... **CLC 4, 7, 22**
See also CA 9-12R

De la Mare, Walter (John) 1873-1956 .... **TCLC 4**
See also CA 110
See also SATA 16
See also DLB 19

Delaney, Shelagh 1939- .... **CLC 29**
See also CA 17-20R
See also DLB 13

Delany, Samuel R(ay, Jr.) 1942- .... **CLC 8, 14**
See also CA 81-84
See also DLB 8

De la Roche, Mazo 1885-1961 .... **CLC 14**
See also CA 85-88

Delbanco, Nicholas (Franklin) 1942- .... **CLC 6, 13**
See also CA 17-20R
See also DLB 6

Delibes (Setien), Miguel 1920- .... **CLC 8, 18**
See also CANR 1
See also CA 45-48

DeLillo, Don 1936- .... **CLC 8, 10, 13**
See also CA 81-84
See also DLB 6

De Lisser, H(erbert) G(eorge) 1878-1944 .... **TCLC 12**
See also CA 109

Deloria, Vine (Victor), Jr. 1933- .... **CLC 21**
See also CANR 5
See also CA 53-56
See also SATA 21

Del Vecchio, John M(ichael) 1947- .... **CLC 29**
See also CA 110

Dennis, Nigel (Forbes) 1912- .... **CLC 8**
See also CA 25-28R
See also DLB 13, 15

De Palma, Brian 1940- .... **CLC 20**
See also CA 109

De Quincey, Thomas 1785-1859 .... **NCLC 4**

Deren, Eleanora 1908-1961
See Deren, Maya
See also CA 111

Deren, Maya 1908-1961 .... **CLC 16**
See also Deren, Eleanora

Derrida, Jacques 1930- .... **CLC 24**

Desai, Anita 1937- .... **CLC 19**
See also CA 81-84

De Saint-Luc, Jean 1909-1981
See Glassco, John

De Sica, Vittorio 1902-1974 .... **CLC 20**

Destouches, Louis Ferdinand 1894-1961
See Céline, Louis-Ferdinand
See also CA 85-88

Deutsch, Babette 1895-1982 .... **CLC 18**
See also CANR 4
See also CA 1-4R
See also obituary CA 108
See also SATA 1
See also obituary SATA 33

De Vries, Peter 1910- .... **CLC 1, 2, 3, 7, 10, 28**
See also CA 17-20R
See also DLB 6
See also DLB-Y 82

Dick, Philip K(indred) 1928-1982 .... **CLC 10**
See also CANR 2
See also CA 49-52
See also obituary CA 106
See also DLB 8

Dickens, Charles 1812-1870 .... **NCLC 3**
See also SATA 15
See also DLB 21

Dickey, James (Lafayette) 1923- .... **CLC 1, 2, 4, 7, 10, 15**
See also CANR 10
See also CA 9-12R
See also DLB 5
See also DLB-Y 82
See also AITN 1, 2

Dickey, William 1928- .... **CLC 3, 28**
See also CA 9-12R
See also DLB 5

Dickinson, Peter 1927- .... **CLC 12**
See also CA 41-44R
See also SATA 5

Didion, Joan 1934- .... **CLC 1, 3, 8, 14**
See also CA 5-8R
See also DLB 2
See also DLB-Y 81
See also AITN 1

Dillard, Annie 1945- .... **CLC 9**
See also CANR 3
See also CA 49-52
See also SATA 10
See also DLB-Y 80

Dillard, R(ichard) H(enry) W(ilde) 1937- .... **CLC 5**
See also CANR 10
See also CA 21-24R
See also DLB 5

Dillon, Eilis 1920- .... **CLC 17**
See also CANR 4
See also CA 9-12R
See also SATA 2

Dinesen, Isak 1885-1962 .... **CLC 10, 29**
See also Blixen, Karen (Christentze Dinesen)

Disch, Thomas M(ichael) 1940- .... **CLC 7**
See also CA 21-24R
See also DLB 8

Disraeli, Benjamin 1804-1881 .... **NCLC 2**
See also DLB 21

Dixon, Paige 1911-
See Corcoran, Barbara

Döblin, Alfred 1878-1957 .... **TCLC 13**
See also CA 110

Dobrolyubov, Nikolai Alexandrovich 1836-1861 .... **NCLC 5**

Doctorow, E(dgar) L(aurence) 1931- . . . . **CLC 6, 11, 15, 18**
See also CANR 2
See also CA 45-48
See also DLB 2
See also DLB-Y 80
See also AITN 2

Dodgson, Charles Lutwidge 1832-1898
See Carroll, Lewis

Donleavy, J(ames) P(atrick) 1926- . . . . **CLC 1, 4, 6, 10**
See also CA 9-12R
See also DLB 6
See also AITN 2

Donoso, José 1924- . . . . **CLC 4, 8, 11**
See also CA 81-84

Doolittle, Hilda 1886-1961
See H(ilda) D(oolittle)
See also CA 97-100
See also DLB 4

Dorn, Ed(ward Merton) 1929- . . . . **CLC 10, 18**
See also CA 93-96
See also DLB 5

Dos Passos, John (Roderigo) 1896-1970 . . . . . . **CLC 1, 4, 8, 11, 15, 25**
See also CANR 3
See also CA 1-4R
See also obituary CA 29-32R
See also DLB 4, 9
See also DLB-DS 1

Dostoevski, Fedor Mikhailovich 1821-1881 . . . . **NCLC 2**

Dourado, (Waldomiro Freitas) Autran 1926- . . . . **CLC 23**
See also CA 25-28R

Dowson, Ernest (Christopher) 1867-1900 . . . . **TCLC 4**
See also CA 105
See also DLB 19

Doyle, (Sir) Arthur Conan 1859-1930 . . . . **TCLC 7**
See also CA 104
See also SATA 24
See also DLB 18

Dr. A 1933-
See Silverstein, Alvin and Virginia B(arbara Opshelor) Silverstein

Drabble, Margaret 1939- . . . . **CLC 2, 3, 5, 8, 10, 22**
See also CA 13-16R
See also DLB 14

Dreiser, Theodore (Herman Albert) 1871-1945 . . . . **TCLC 10**
See also CA 106
See also DLB 9, 12
See also DLB-DS 1

Drexler, Rosalyn 1926- . . . . **CLC 2, 6**
See also CA 81-84

Dreyer, Carl Theodor 1889-1968 . . . . **CLC 16**

Droste-Hülshoff, Annette Freiin von 1797-1848 . . . . **NCLC 3**

Drummond de Andrade, Carlos 1902-
See Andrade, Carlos Drummond de

Duberman, Martin 1930- . . . . **CLC 8**
See also CANR 2
See also CA 1-4R

Du Bois, W(illiam) E(dward) B(urghardt) 1868-1963 . . . . **CLC 1, 2, 13**
See also CA 85-88

Dubus, Andre 1936- . . . . **CLC 13**
See also CA 21-24R

Duclos, Charles Pinot 1704-1772 . . . . . **LC 1**

Dudek, Louis 1918- . . . . **CLC 11, 19**
See also CANR 1
See also CA 45-48

Dudevant, Amandine Aurore Lucile Dupin 1804-1876
See Sand, George

Dugan, Alan 1923- . . . . **CLC 2, 6**
See also CA 81-84
See also DLB 5

Duhamel, Georges 1884-1966 . . . . **CLC 8**
See also CA 81-84
See also obituary CA 25-28R

Dujardin, Édouard (Émile Louis) 1861-1949 . . . . **TCLC 13**
See also CA 109

Duke, Raoul 1939-
See Thompson, Hunter S(tockton)

Dumas, Henry (L.) 1934-1968 . . . . **CLC 6**
See also CA 85-88

Du Maurier, Daphne 1907- . . . . . **CLC 6, 11**
See also CANR 6
See also CA 5-8R
See also SATA 27

Dunbar, Paul Laurence 1872-1906 . . . . **TCLC 2, 12**
See also CA 104
See also SATA 34

Duncan (Steinmetz Arquette), Lois 1934- . . . . **CLC 26**
See also CANR 2
See also CA 1-4R
See also SATA 1
See also Arquette, Lois S(teinmetz)

Duncan, Robert 1919- . . . . **CLC 1, 2, 4, 7, 15**
See also CA 9-12R
See also DLB 5, 16

Dunlap, William 1766-1839 . . . . **NCLC 2**

Dunn, Douglas (Eaglesham) 1942- . . . . **CLC 6**
See also CANR 2
See also CA 45-48

Dunne, John Gregory 1932- . . . . **CLC 28**
See also CA 25-28R
See also DLB-Y 80

Dunsany, Lord (Edward John Moreton Drax Plunkett) 1878-1957 . . . . **TCLC 2**
See also CA 104
See also DLB 10

Durang, Christopher (Ferdinand) 1949- . . . . **CLC 27**
See also CA 105

Duras, Marguerite 1914- . . . . **CLC 3, 6, 11, 20**
See also CA 25-28R

Durrell, Lawrence (George) 1912- . . . . **CLC 1, 4, 6, 8, 13, 27**
See also CA 9-12R
See also DLB 15

Dürrenmatt, Friedrich 1921- . . . . **CLC 1, 4, 8, 11, 15**
See also CA 17-20R

Dylan, Bob 1941- . . . . **CLC 3, 4, 6, 12**
See also CA 41-44R
See also DLB 16

Eastlake, William (Derry) 1917- . . . . . **CLC 8**
See also CANR 5
See also CA 5-8R
See also DLB 6

Eberhart, Richard 1904- . . . . **CLC 3, 11, 19**
See also CANR 2
See also CA 1-4R

Echegaray (y Eizaguirre), José (María Waldo) 1832-1916 . . . . **TCLC 4**
See also CA 104

Eckert, Allan W. 1931- . . . . **CLC 17**
See also CA 13-16R
See also SATA 27, 29

Eco, Umberto 1932- . . . . **CLC 28**
See also CA 77-80

Edel, (Joseph) Leon 1907- . . . . **CLC 29**
See also CANR 1
See also CA 1-4R

Edgeworth, Maria 1767-1849 . . . . . **NCLC 1**
See also SATA 21

Edmonds, Helen (Woods) 1904-1968
See Kavan, Anna
See also CA 5-8R
See also obituary CA 25-28R

Edson, Russell 1905- . . . . **CLC 13**
See also CA 33-36R

Edwards, G(erald) B(asil) 1899-1976 . . . . **CLC 25**
See also obituary CA 110

Ehle, John (Marsden, Jr.) 1925- . . . . **CLC 27**
See also CA 9-12R

Ehrenbourg, Ilya (Grigoryevich) 1891-1967
See Ehrenburg, Ilya (Grigoryevich)

Ehrenburg, Ilya (Grigoryevich) 1891-1967 . . . . **CLC 18**
See also CA 102
See also obituary CA 25-28R

Eich, Günter 1907-1971 . . . . **CLC 15**
See also CA 111
See also obituary CA 93-96

Eigner, Larry 1927- . . . . **CLC 9**
See also Eigner, Laurence (Joel)
See also DLB 5

Eigner, Laurence (Joel) 1927-
See Eigner, Larry
See also CANR 6
See also CA 9-12R

Eiseley, Loren (Corey) 1907-1977 . . . . **CLC 7**
See also CANR 6
See also CA 1-4R
See also obituary CA 73-76

Ekeloef, Gunnar (Bengt) 1907-1968
See Ekelöf, Gunnar (Bengt)
See also obituary CA 25-28R

Ekelöf, Gunnar (Bengt) 1907-1968 . . . . **CLC 27**
See also Ekeloef, Gunnar (Bengt)

Ekwensi, Cyprian (Odiatu Duaka) 1921- . . . . **CLC 4**
See also CA 29-32R

Eliade, Mircea 1907- . . . . **CLC 19**
See also CA 65-68

Eliot, George 1819-1880 . . . . **NCLC 4**
See also DLB 21

Eliot, T(homas) S(tearns) 1888-1965 . . . . **CLC 1, 2, 3, 6, 9, 10, 13, 15, 24**
See also CA 5-8R
See also obituary CA 25-28R
See also DLB 7, 10

Elkin, Stanley L(awrence) 1930- . . . . **CLC 4, 6, 9, 14, 27**
See also CANR 8
See also CA 9-12R
See also DLB 2
See also DLB-Y 80

Elliott, George P(aul) 1918-1980 . . . . **CLC 2**
See also CANR 2
See also CA 1-4R
See also obituary CA 97-100

Ellis, A. E. . . . . **CLC 7**

Ellison, Harlan 1934- . . . . **CLC 1, 13**
See also CANR 5
See also CA 5-8R
See also DLB 8

Ellison, Ralph (Waldo) 1914- . . . . **CLC 1, 3, 11**
See also CA 9-12R
See also DLB 2

Elman, Richard 1934- . . . . **CLC 19**
See also CA 17-20R

Éluard, Paul 1895-1952 . . . . **TCLC 7**
See also CA 104

Elvin, Anne Katharine Stevenson 1933-
See Stevenson, Anne
See also CA 17-20R

Elytis, Odysseus 1911- . . . . **CLC 15**
See also CA 102

Emecheta, (Florence Onye) Buchi 1944- . . . . **CLC 14**
See also CA 81-84

Emerson, Ralph Waldo 1803-1882 . . . . **NCLC 1**
See also DLB 1

Empson, William 1906- . . . . **CLC 3, 8, 19**
See also CA 17-20R
See also DLB 20

Endo, Shusaku 1923- . . . . **CLC 7, 14, 19**
See also CA 29-32R

Enright, D(ennis) J(oseph) 1920- . . . . **CLC 4, 8**
See also CANR 1
See also CA 1-4R
See also SATA 25

Ephron, Nora 1941- . . . . **CLC 17**
See also CA 65-68
See also AITN 2

Epstein, Daniel Mark 1948- . . . . **CLC 7**
See also CANR 2
See also CA 49-52

Epstein, Jacob 1956- . . . . **CLC 19**

Epstein, Leslie 1938- . . . . **CLC 27**
See also CA 73-76

Erdman, Paul E(mil) 1932- . . . . **CLC 25**
See also CA 61-64
See also AITN 1

Erenburg, Ilya (Grigoryevich) 1891-1967
See Ehrenburg, Ilya (Grigoryevich)

Eseki, Bruno 1919-
See Mphahlele, Ezekiel

Esenin, Sergei (Aleksandrovich) 1895-1925 . . . . **TCLC 4**
See also CA 104

Eshleman, Clayton 1935- . . . . **CLC 7**
See also CA 33-36R
See also DLB 5

Espriu, Salvador 1913- . . . . **CLC 9**

Evans, Marian
See Eliot, George

Evans, Mary Ann
See Eliot, George

Evarts, Esther 1900-1972
See Benson, Sally

Everson, R(onald) G(ilmour) 1903- . . . . **CLC 27**
See also CA 17-20R

Everson, William (Oliver) 1912- . . . . **CLC 1, 5, 14**
See also CA 9-12R
See also DLB 5, 16

Evtushenko, Evgenii (Aleksandrovich) 1933-
See Yevtushenko, Yevgeny

Ewart, Gavin (Buchanan) 1916- . . . . **CLC 13**
See also CA 89-92

Ewers, Hanns Heinz 1871-1943 . . . . **TCLC 12**
See also CA 109

Ewing, Frederick R. 1918-
See Sturgeon, Theodore (Hamilton)

Exley, Frederick (Earl) 1929- . . . . **CLC 6, 11**
See also CA 81-84
See also DLB-Y 81
See also AITN 2

Fagen, Donald 1948-
See Becker, Walter and Fagen, Donald

Fagen, Donald 1948- and **Becker, Walter** 1950-
See Becker, Walter and Fagen, Donald

Fair, Ronald L. 1932- . . . . **CLC 18**
See also CA 69-72

Fallaci, Oriana 1930- . . . . **CLC 11**
See also CA 77-80

Fargue, Léon-Paul 1876-1947 . . . . **TCLC 11**
See also CA 109

Farigoule, Louis 1885-1972
See Romains, Jules

Fariña, Richard 1937?-1966 . . . . **CLC 9**
See also CA 81-84
See also obituary CA 25-28R

Farley, Walter 1915- . . . . **CLC 17**
See also CANR 8
See also CA 17-20R
See also SATA 2
See also DLB 22

Farmer, Philip José 1918- . . . . **CLC 1, 19**
See also CANR 4
See also CA 1-4R
See also DLB 8

Farrell, J(ames) G(ordon) 1935-1979 . . . . **CLC 6**
See also CA 73-76
See also obituary CA 89-92
See also DLB 14

Farrell, James T(homas) 1904-1979 . . . . **CLC 1, 4, 8, 11**
See also CANR 9
See also CA 5-8R
See also obituary CA 89-92
See also DLB 4, 9
See also DLB-DS 2

Fassbinder, Rainer Werner 1946-1982 . . . . **CLC 20**
See also CA 93-96
See also obituary CA 106

Fast, Howard (Melvin) 1914- . . . . **CLC 23**
See also CANR 1
See also CA 1-4R
See also SATA 7
See also DLB 9

Faulkner, William (Cuthbert) 1897-1962 . . . . **CLC 1, 3, 6, 8, 9, 11, 14, 18, 28**
See also CA 81-84
See also DLB 9, 11
See also DLB-DS 2
See also AITN 1

Fauset, Jessie Redmon 1884?-1961 . . . . **CLC 19**
See also CA 109

Faust, Irvin 1924- . . . . **CLC 8**
See also CA 33-36R
See also DLB 2
See also DLB-Y 80

Federman, Raymond 1928- . . . . **CLC 6**
See also CANR 10
See also CA 17-20R
See also DLB-Y 80

Feiffer, Jules 1929- . . . . **CLC 2, 8**
See also CA 17-20R
See also SATA 8
See also DLB 7

Feldman, Irving (Mordecai) 1928- . . . . **CLC 7**
See also CANR 1
See also CA 1-4R

Fellini, Federico 1920- . . . . **CLC 16**
See also CA 65-68

Felsen, Gregor 1916-
See Felsen, Henry Gregor

Felsen, Henry Gregor 1916- . . . . **CLC 17**
See also CANR 1
See also CA 1-4R
See also SATA 1

Ferber, Edna 1887-1968 . . . . **CLC 18**
See also CA 5-8R
See also obituary CA 25-28R
See also SATA 7
See also DLB 9
See also AITN 1

Ferlinghetti, Lawrence (Monsanto) 1919?- . . . . **CLC 2, 6, 10, 27**
See also CANR 3
See also CA 5-8R
See also DLB 5, 16

Feuchtwanger, Lion 1884-1958 . . . . **TCLC 3**
See also CA 104

Fiedler, Leslie A(aron) 1917- . . . . **CLC 4, 13, 24**
See also CANR 7
See also CA 9-12R

Field, Eugene 1850-1895 . . . . **NCLC 3**
See also SATA 16
See also DLB 21

Fielding, Henry 1707-1754 . . . . **LC 1**

Fielding, Sarah 1710-1768 . . . . **LC 1**

Finch, Robert (Duer Claydon) 1900- . . . . **CLC 18**
See also CANR 9
See also CA 57-60

Findley, Timothy 1930- . . . . **CLC 27**
See also CA 25-28R

Fink, Janis 1951-
See Ian, Janis

Firbank, (Arthur Annesley) Ronald 1886-1926 . . . . **TCLC 1**
See also CA 104

Firbank, Louis 1944-
See Reed, Lou

Fisher, Roy 1930- . . . . **CLC 25**
See also CA 81-84

Fisher, Rudolph 1897-1934 . . . . . . **TCLC 11**
See also CA 107

Fisher, Vardis (Alvero) 1895-1968 . . . . **CLC 7**
See also CA 5-8R
See also obituary CA 25-28R
See also DLB 9

Fitzgerald, F(rancis) Scott (Key) 1896-1940 . . . . **TCLC 1, 6**
See also CA 110
See also DLB 4, 9
See also DLB-Y 81
See also DLB-DS 1
See also AITN 1

Fitzgerald, Penelope 1916- . . . . **CLC 19**
See also CA 85-88
See also DLB 14

FitzGerald, Robert D(avid) 1902- . . . . **CLC 19**
See also CA 17-20R

Flanagan, Thomas (James Bonner) 1923- . . . . **CLC 25**
See also CA 108
See also DLB-Y 80

Flaubert, Gustave 1821-1880 . . . . . . **NCLC 2**

Fleming, Ian (Lancaster) 1908-1964 . . . . **CLC 3**
See also CA 5-8R
See also SATA 9

Follett, Ken(neth Martin) 1949- . . . . **CLC 18**
See also CA 81-84
See also DLB-Y 81

Forbes, Esther 1891-1967 . . . . **CLC 12**
See also CAP 1
See also CA 13-14
See also obituary CA 25-28R
See also DLB 22
See also SATA 2

Forché, Carolyn 1950- . . . . **CLC 25**
See also CA 109
See also DLB 5

Ford, Ford Madox 1873-1939 . . . . . **TCLC 1**
See also CA 104

Ford, John 1895-1973 . . . . **CLC 16**
See also obituary CA 45-48

Forman, James D(ouglas) 1932- . . . . **CLC 21**
See also CANR 4
See also CA 9-12R
See also SATA 8, 21

Forrest, Leon 1937- . . . . **CLC 4**
See also CA 89-92

Forster, E(dward) M(organ) 1879-1970 . . . . **CLC 1, 2, 3, 4, 9, 10, 13, 15, 22**
See also CAP 1
See also CA 13-14
See also obituary CA 25-28R

Forsyth, Frederick 1938- . . . . **CLC 2, 5**
See also CA 85-88

Fosse, Bob 1925- . . . . **CLC 20**
See also CA 110

Fouqué, Friedrich (Heinrich Karl) de La Motte 1777-1843 . . . . **NCLC 2**

Fournier, Pierre 1916- . . . . **CLC 11**
See also CA 89-92

Fowles, John 1926- . . . . . . **CLC 1, 2, 3, 4, 6, 9, 10, 15**
See also CA 5-8R
See also SATA 22
See also DLB 14

Fox, Paula 1923- . . . . **CLC 2, 8**
See also CLR 1
See also CA 73-76
See also SATA 17

Fox, William Price (Jr.) 1926- . . . . . . **CLC 22**
See also CANR 11
See also CA 17-20R
See also DLB 2
See also DLB-Y 81

Frame (Clutha), Janet (Paterson) 1924- . . . . **CLC 2, 3, 6, 22**
See also Clutha, Janet Paterson Frame

France, Anatole 1844-1924 . . . . **TCLC 9**
See also CA 106

Francis, Dick 1920- . . . . **CLC 2, 22**
See also CANR 9
See also CA 5-8R

Francis, Robert (Churchill) 1901- . . . . **CLC 15**
See also CANR 1
See also CA 1-4R

Franklin, (Stella Maria Sarah) Miles 1879-1954 . . . . **TCLC 9**
See also CA 104

Fraser, George MacDonald 1925- . . . . **CLC 7**
See also CANR 2
See also CA 45-48

Frayn, Michael 1933- . . . . **CLC 3, 7**
See also CA 5-8R
See also DLB 13, 14

Freeman, Douglas Southall 1886-1953 . . . . **TCLC 11**
See also CA 109
See also DLB 17

Freeman, Mary (Eleanor) Wilkins 1852-1930 . . . . **TCLC 9**
See also CA 106
See also DLB 12

French, Marilyn 1929- . . . . **CLC 10, 18**
See also CANR 3
See also CA 69-72

Freneau, Philip Morin 1752-1832 . . . . **NCLC 1**

Friedman, B(ernard) H(arper) 1926- . . . . **CLC 7**
See also CANR 3
See also CA 1-4R

Friedman, Bruce Jay 1930- . . . . . . **CLC 3, 5**
See also CA 9-12R
See also DLB 2

Friel, Brian 1929- . . . . **CLC 5**
See also CA 21-24R
See also DLB 13

Friis-Baastad, Babbis (Ellinor) 1921-1970 . . . . **CLC 12**
See also CA 17-20R
See also SATA 7

Frisch, Max (Rudolf) 1911- . . . . **CLC 3, 9, 14, 18**
See also CA 85-88

Frost, Robert (Lee) 1874-1963 . . . . . . **CLC 1, 3, 4, 9, 10, 13, 15, 26**
See also CA 89-92
See also SATA 14

Fry, Christopher 1907- . . . . . . **CLC 2, 10, 14**
See also CANR 9
See also CA 17-20R
See also DLB 13

Frye, (Herman) Northrop 1912- . . . . **CLC 24**
See also CANR 8
See also CA 5-8R

Fuchs, Daniel 1909- . . . . **CLC 8, 22**
See also CA 81-84
See also DLB 9, 26

Fuentes, Carlos 1928- . . . . **CLC 3, 8, 10, 13, 22**
See also CANR 10
See also CA 69-72
See also AITN 2

Fugard, Athol 1932- . . . . . . **CLC 5, 9, 14, 25**
See also CA 85-88

Fuller, Charles (H., Jr.) 1939- . . . . . **CLC 25**
See also CA 108

Fuller, (Sarah) Margaret 1810-1850 . . . . **NCLC 5**
See also DLB 1
See also Ossoli, Sarah Margaret (Fuller marchesa d')

Fuller, Roy (Broadbent) 1912- . . . . **CLC 4, 28**
See also CA 5-8R
See also DLB 15, 20

Gadda, Carlo Emilio 1893-1973 .... **CLC 11**
See also CA 89-92

Gaddis, William 1922- .... **CLC 1, 3, 6, 8, 10, 19**
See also CA 17-20R
See also DLB 2

Gaines, Ernest J. 1933- ..... **CLC 3, 11, 18**
See also CANR 6
See also CA 9-12R
See also DLB 2
See also DLB-Y 80
See also AITN 1

Gale, Zona 1874-1938 .... **TCLC 7**
See also CA 105
See also DLB 9

Gallagher, Tess 1943- .... **CLC 18**
See also CA 106

Gallant, Mavis 1922- .... **CLC 7, 18**
See also CA 69-72

Gallant, Roy A(rthur) 1924- .... **CLC 17**
See also CANR 4
See also CA 5-8R
See also SATA 4

Gallico, Paul (William) 1897-1976 .... **CLC 2**
See also CA 5-8R
See also obituary CA 69-72
See also SATA 13
See also DLB 9
See also AITN 1

Galsworthy, John 1867-1933 ...... **TCLC 1**
See also CA 104
See also DLB 10

Galt, John 1779-1839 .... **NCLC 1**

Gann, Ernest K(ellogg) 1910- ...... **CLC 23**
See also CANR 1
See also CA 1-4R
See also AITN 1

García Lorca, Federico 1899-1936 .... **TCLC 1, 7**
See also CA 104

García Márquez, Gabriel 1928- .... **CLC 2, 3, 8, 10, 15, 27**
See also CANR 10
See also CA 33-36R

Gardner, John (Champlin, Jr.) 1933-1982 .... **CLC 2, 3, 5, 7, 8, 10, 18, 28**
See also CA 65-68
See also obituary CA 107
See also obituary SATA 31
See also DLB 2
See also DLB-Y 82
See also AITN 1

Garfield, Leon 1921- .... **CLC 12**
See also CA 17-20R
See also SATA 1, 32

Garland, (Hannibal) Hamlin 1860-1940 .... **TCLC 3**
See also CA 104
See also DLB 12

Garneau, Hector (de) Saint Denys 1912-1943 .... **TCLC 13**
See also CA 111

Garner, Alan 1935- .... **CLC 17**
See also CA 73-76
See also SATA 18

Garner, Hugh 1913-1979 .... **CLC 13**
See also CA 69-72

Garnett, David 1892-1981 .... **CLC 3**
See also CA 5-8R
See also obituary CA 103

Garrett, George (Palmer) 1929- .... **CLC 3, 11**
See also CANR 1
See also CA 1-4R
See also DLB 2, 5

Garrigue, Jean 1914-1972 .... **CLC 2, 8**
See also CA 5-8R
See also obituary CA 37-40R

Gary, Romain 1914-1980 .... **CLC 25**
See also Kacew, Romain

Gascar, Pierre 1916-
See Fournier, Pierre

Gaskell, Elizabeth Cleghorn 1810-1865 .... **NCLC 5**
See also DLB 21

Gass, William H(oward) 1924- .... **CLC 1, 2, 8, 11, 15**
See also CA 17-20R
See also DLB 2

Gautier, Théophile 1811-1872 ..... **NCLC 1**

Gaye, Marvin 1939-1984 .... **CLC 26**

Gee, Maurice (Gough) 1931- .... **CLC 29**
See also CA 97-100

Gelbart, Larry (Simon) 1923- ...... **CLC 21**
See also CA 73-76

Gelber, Jack 1932- .... **CLC 1, 6, 14**
See also CANR 2
See also CA 1-4R
See also DLB 7

Gellhorn, Martha (Ellis) 1908- ..... **CLC 14**
See also CA 77-80
See also DLB-Y 82

Genet, Jean 1910- ..... **CLC 1, 2, 5, 10, 14**
See also CA 13-16R

Gent, Peter 1942- .... **CLC 29**
See also CA 89-92
See also DLB-Y 82
See also AITN 1

George, Stefan (Anton) 1868-1933 .... **TCLC 2**
See also CA 104

Gerhardi, William (Alexander) 1895-1977
See Gerhardie, William (Alexander)

Gerhardie, William (Alexander) 1895-1977 .... **CLC 5**
See also CA 25-28R
See also obituary CA 73-76

Gessner, Friedrike Victoria 1910-1980
See Adamson, Joy(-Friederike Victoria)

Ghelderode, Michel de 1898-1962 .... **CLC 6, 11**
See also CA 85-88

Ghiselin, Brewster 1903- .... **CLC 23**
See also CA 13-16R

Giacosa, Giuseppe 1847-1906 ..... **TCLC 7**
See also CA 104

Gibbon, Lewis Grassic 1901-1935 .... **TCLC 4**
See also Mitchell, James Leslie

Gibran, (Gibran) Kahlil 1883-1931 .... **TCLC 1, 9**
See also CA 104

Gibson, William 1914- .... **CLC 23**
See also CANR 9
See also CA 9-12R
See also DLB 7

Gide, André (Paul Guillaume) 1869-1951 .... **TCLC 5, 12**
See also CA 104

Gilbert, (Sir) W(illiam) S(chwenck) 1836-1911 .... **TCLC 3**
See also CA 104

Gilbreth, Ernestine 1908-
See Carey, Ernestine Gilbreth

Gilbreth, Frank B(unker), Jr. 1911-
See Gilbreth, Frank B(unker), Jr. and Carey, Ernestine Gilbreth
See also CA 9-12R
See also SATA 2

Gilbreth, Frank B(unker), Jr. 1911- and **Carey, Ernestine Gilbreth** 1908- .... **CLC 17**

Gilliam, Terry (Vance) 1940-
See Monty Python
See also CA 108

Gilliatt, Penelope (Ann Douglass) 1932- .... **CLC 2, 10, 13**
See also CA 13-16R
See also DLB 14
See also AITN 2

Gilman, Charlotte (Anna) Perkins (Stetson) 1860-1935 .... **TCLC 9**
See also CA 106

Gilroy, Frank D(aniel) 1925- .... **CLC 2**
See also CA 81-84
See also DLB 7

Ginsberg, Allen 1926- .... **CLC 1, 2, 3, 4, 6, 13**
See also CANR 2
See also CA 1-4R
See also DLB 5, 16
See also AITN 1

Ginzburg, Natalia 1916- .... **CLC 5, 11**
See also CA 85-88

Giono, Jean 1895-1970 .... **CLC 4, 11**
See also CANR 2
See also CA 45-48
See also obituary CA 29-32R

Giovanni, Nikki 1943- .... **CLC 2, 4, 19**
See also CLR 6
See also CA 29-32R
See also SATA 24
See also DLB 5
See also AITN 1

Giovene, Andrea 1904- .... **CLC 7**
See also CA 85-88

Giraudoux, (Hippolyte) Jean 1882-1944 .... **TCLC 2, 7**
See also CA 104

Gironella, José María 1917- .... **CLC 11**
See also CA 101

Gissing, George (Robert) 1857-1903 .... **TCLC 3**
See also CA 105
See also DLB 18

Glanville, Brian (Lester) 1931- . . . . . . **CLC 6**
See also CANR 3
See also CA 5-8R
See also DLB 15

Glasgow, Ellen (Anderson Gholson)
1873?-1945 . . . . **TCLC 2, 7**
See also CA 104
See also DLB 9, 12

Glassco, John 1909-1981 . . . . **CLC 9**
See also CA 13-16R
See also obituary CA 102

Glissant, Edouard 1928- . . . . **CLC 10**

Glück, Louise 1943- . . . . **CLC 7, 22**
See also CA 33-36R
See also DLB 5

Godard, Jean-Luc 1930- . . . . **CLC 20**
See also CA 93-96

Godwin, Gail 1937- . . . . **CLC 5, 8, 22**
See also CA 29-32R
See also DLB 6

Goethe, Johann Wolfgang von
1749-1832 . . . . **NCLC 4**

Gogol, Nikolai (Vasilyevich)
1809-1852 . . . . **NCLC 5**

Gökçeli, Yasar Kemal 1923-
See Kemal, Yashar

Gold, Herbert 1924- . . . . **CLC 4, 7, 14**
See also CA 9-12R
See also DLB 2
See also DLB-Y 81

Goldbarth, Albert 1948- . . . . **CLC 5**
See also CANR 6
See also CA 53-56

Golding, William (Gerald)
1911- . . . . **CLC 1, 2, 3, 8, 10, 17, 27**
See also CA 5-8R
See also DLB 15

Goldman, Emma 1869-1940 . . . . . **TCLC 13**
See also CA 110

Goldman, William (W.) 1931- . . . . **CLC 1**
See also CA 9-12R

Goldmann, Lucien 1913-1970 . . . . . . **CLC 24**
See also CAP 2
See also CA 25-28

Gombrowicz, Witold
1904-1969 . . . . **CLC 4, 7, 11**
See also CAP 2
See also CA 19-20
See also obituary CA 25-28R

Gómez de la Serna, Ramón
1888-1963 . . . . **CLC 9**

Goncharov, Ivan Alexandrovich
1812-1891 . . . . **NCLC 1**

Goodman, Paul
1911-1972 . . . . **CLC 1, 2, 4, 7**
See also CAP 2
See also CA 19-20
See also obituary CA 37-40R

Gordimer, Nadine
1923- . . . . **CLC 3, 5, 7, 10, 18**
See also CANR 3
See also CA 5-8R

Gordon, Caroline
1895-1981 . . . . **CLC 6, 13, 29**
See also CAP 1
See also CA 11-12
See also obituary CA 103
See also DLB 4, 9
See also DLB-Y 81

Gordon, Mary (Catherine)
1949- . . . . **CLC 13, 22**
See also CA 102
See also DLB 6
See also DLB-Y 81

Gordon, Sol 1923- . . . . **CLC 26**
See also CANR 4
See also CA 53-56
See also SATA 11

Gordone, Charles 1925- . . . . **CLC 1, 4**
See also CA 93-96
See also DLB 7

Gorenko, Anna Andreyevna 1889?-1966
See Akhmatova, Anna

Gorky, Maxim 1868-1936 . . . . **TCLC 8**
See also CA 105

Goryan, Sirak 1908-1981
See Saroyan, William

Gotlieb, Phyllis (Fay Bloom)
1926- . . . . **CLC 18**
See also CANR 7
See also CA 13-16R

Gould, Lois 1938?- . . . . **CLC 4, 10**
See also CA 77-80

Goyen, (Charles) William
1915-1983 . . . . **CLC 5, 8, 14**
See also CANR 6
See also CA 5-8R
See also obituary CA 110
See also DLB 2
See also AITN 2

Goytisolo, Juan 1931- . . . . **CLC 5, 10, 23**
See also CA 85-88

Grabbe, Christian Dietrich
1801-1836 . . . . **NCLC 2**

Gracq, Julien 1910- . . . . **CLC 11**

Grade, Chaim 1910-1982 . . . . **CLC 10**
See also CA 93-96
See also obituary CA 107

Graham W(illiam) S(ydney)
1918- . . . . **CLC 29**
See also CA 73-76
See also DLB 20

Graham, Winston (Mawdsley)
1910- . . . . **CLC 23**
See also CANR 2
See also CA 49-52

Granville-Barker, Harley
1877-1946 . . . . **TCLC 2**
See also CA 104

Grass, Günter (Wilhelm)
1927- . . . . **CLC 1, 2, 4, 6, 11, 15, 22**
See also CA 13-16R

Grau, Shirley Ann 1929- . . . . **CLC 4, 9**
See also CA 89-92
See also DLB 2
See also AITN 2

Graves, Robert 1895- . . . . . . **CLC 1, 2, 6, 11**
See also CANR 5
See also CA 5-8R
See also DLB 20

Gray, Amlin 1946- . . . . **CLC 29**

Gray, Francine du Plessix
1930- . . . . **CLC 22**
See also CANR 11
See also CA 61-64

Gray, Simon 1936- . . . . **CLC 9, 14**
See also CA 21-24R
See also DLB 13
See also AITN 1

Greeley, Andrew M(oran)
1928- . . . . **CLC 28**
See also CANR 7
See also CA 5-8R

Green, Hannah 1932- . . . . **CLC 3**
See also Greenberg, Joanne
See also CA 73-76

Green, Henry 1905-1974 . . . . **CLC 2, 13**
See also Yorke, Henry Vincent
See also DLB 15

Green, Julien (Hartridge)
1900- . . . . **CLC 3, 11**
See also CA 21-24R
See also DLB 4

Greenberg, Ivan 1908-1973
See Rahv, Philip
See also CA 85-88

Greenberg, Joanne (Goldenberg)
1932- . . . . **CLC 7**
See also Green, Hannah
See also CA 5-8R
See also SATA 25

Greene, Gael . . . . **CLC 8**
See also CANR 10
See also CA 13-16R

Greene, Graham
1904- . . . . **CLC 1, 3, 6, 9, 14, 18, 27**
See also CA 13-16R
See also SATA 20
See also DLB 13, 15
See also AITN 2

Gregor, Arthur 1923- . . . . **CLC 9**
See also CANR 11
See also CA 25-28R

Gregory, Lady (Isabella Augusta Persse)
1852-1932 . . . . **TCLC 1**
See also CA 104
See also DLB 10

Greve, Felix Paul Berthold Friedrich
1879-1948
See Grove, Frederick Philip
See also CA 104

Grey, (Pearl) Zane
1872?-1939 . . . . **TCLC 6**
See also CA 104
See also DLB 9

Grieg, (Johan) Nordahl (Brun)
1902-1943 . . . . **TCLC 10**
See also CA 107

Grieve, C(hristopher) M(urray) 1892-1978
See MacDiarmid, Hugh
See also CA 5-8R
See also obituary CA 85-88

Griffiths, Trevor 1935-............CLC 13
See also CA 97-100
See also DLB 13

Grigson, Geoffrey (Edward Harvey) 1905-..........................CLC 7
See also CA 25-28R

Grillparzer, Franz 1791-1872..... NCLC 1

Grimm, Jakob (Ludwig) Karl 1785-1863
See Grimm, Jakob (Ludwig) Karl and Grimm, Wilhelm Karl

Grimm, Jakob (Ludwig) Karl 1785-1863 and **Grimm, Wilhelm Karl** 1786-1859.................. NCLC 3
See also SATA 22

Grimm, Wilhelm Karl 1786-1859
See Grimm, Jakob (Ludwig) Karl and Grimm, Wilhelm Karl

Grimm, Wilhelm Karl 1786-1859 and **Grimm, Jakob (Ludwig) Karl** 1785-1863
See Grimm, Jakob (Ludwig) Karl and Grimm, Wilhelm Karl

Grove, Frederick Philip 1879-1948................... TCLC 4
See also Greve, Felix Paul Berthold Friedrich

Grumbach, Doris (Isaac) 1918-.................... CLC 13, 22
See also CANR 9
See also CA 5-8R

Grundtvig, Nicolai Frederik Severin 1783-1872.................. NCLC 1

Guare, John 1938-.......... CLC 8, 14, 29
See also CA 73-76
See also DLB 7

Gudjonsson, Halldór Kiljan 1902-
See Laxness, Halldór (Kiljan)
See also CA 103

Guest, Judith 1936-................CLC 8
See also CA 77-80

Guillén, Jorge 1893-..............CLC 11
See also CA 89-92

Gunn, Bill 1934-..................CLC 5
See also Gunn, William Harrison

Gunn, Thom(son William) 1926-.................. CLC 3, 6, 18
See also CANR 9
See also CA 17-20R

Gunn, William Harrison 1934-
See Gunn, Bill
See also CA 13-16R
See also AITN 1

Guthrie, A(lfred) B(ertram), Jr. 1901-........................CLC 23
See also CA 57-60
See also DLB 6

Guy, Rosa (Cuthbert) 1928-........CLC 26
See also CA 17-20R
See also SATA 14

Haavikko, Paavo (Juhani) 1931-........................CLC 18
See also CA 106

Hacker, Marilyn 1942-....... CLC 5, 9, 23
See also CA 77-80

Haggard, (Sir) H(enry) Rider 1856-1925................. TCLC 11
See also CA 108
See also SATA 16

Haig-Brown, Roderick L(angmere) 1908-1976...................CLC 21
See also CANR 4
See also CA 5-8R
See also obituary CA 69-72
See also SATA 12

Hailey, Arthur 1920-...............CLC 5
See also CANR 2
See also CA 1-4R
See also DLB-Y 82
See also AITN 2

Haley, Alex (Palmer) 1921-..... CLC 8, 12
See also CA 77-80

Hall, Donald (Andrew, Jr.) 1928-...................... CLC 1, 3
See also CANR 2
See also CA 5-8R
See also SATA 23
See also DLB 5

Hall, (Marguerite) Radclyffe 1886-1943.................. TCLC 12

Halpern, Daniel 1945-.............CLC 14
See also CA 33-36R

Hamburger, Michael (Peter Leopold) 1924-..................... CLC 5, 14
See also CANR 2
See also CA 5-8R

Hamill, Pete 1935-................CLC 10
See also CA 25-28R

Hamilton, Edmond 1904-1977.......CLC 1
See also CANR 3
See also CA 1-4R
See also DLB 8

Hamilton, Gail 1911-
See Corcoran, Barbara

Hamilton, Mollie 1909?-
See Kaye, M(ary) M(argaret)

Hamilton, Virginia 1936-..........CLC 26
See also CLR 1
See also CA 25-28R
See also SATA 4

Hammett, (Samuel) Dashiell 1894-1961............CLC 3, 5, 10, 19
See also CA 81-84
See also AITN 1

Hammon, Jupiter 1711?-1800?................ NCLC 5

Hamner, Earl (Henry), Jr. 1923-........................CLC 12
See also CA 73-76
See also DLB 6
See also AITN 2

Hampton, Christopher (James) 1946-.........................CLC 4
See also CA 25-28R
See also DLB 13

Hamsun, Knut 1859-1952........ TCLC 2
See also CA 104

Handke, Peter 1942-...... CLC 5, 8, 10, 15
See also CA 77-80

Hanley, James 1901-....... CLC 3, 5, 8, 13
See also CA 73-76

Hannah, Barry 1942-.............CLC 23
See also CA 108, 110
See also DLB 6

Hansberry, Lorraine 1930-1965....................CLC 17
See also CA 109
See also obituary CA 25-28R
See also DLB 7
See also AITN 2

Hanson, Kenneth O(stlin) 1922-........................CLC 13
See also CANR 7
See also CA 53-56

Hardwick, Elizabeth 1916-.........CLC 13
See also CANR 3
See also CA 5-8R
See also DLB 6

Hardy, Thomas 1840-1928..... TCLC 4, 10
See also CA 104
See also SATA 25
See also DLB 18, 19

Hare, David 1947-................CLC 29
See also CA 97-100
See also DLB 13

Harper, Michael S(teven) 1938-..................... CLC 7, 22
See also CA 33-36R

Harris, Christie (Lucy Irwin) 1907-........................CLC 12
See also CANR 6
See also CA 5-8R
See also SATA 6

Harris, Joel Chandler 1848-1908.................. TCLC 2
See also CA 104
See also YABC 1
See also DLB 11, 23

Harris, John (Wyndham Parkes Lucas) Beynon 1903-1969
See Wyndham, John
See also CA 102
See also obituary CA 89-92

Harris, MacDonald 1921-...........CLC 9
See also Heiney, Donald (William)

Harris, Mark 1922-...............CLC 19
See also CANR 2
See also CA 5-8R
See also DLB 2
See also DLB-Y 80

Harris, (Theodore) Wilson 1921-........................CLC 25
See also CANR 11
See also CA 65-68

Harrison, James (Thomas) 1937-
See Harrison, Jim
See also CANR 8
See also CA 13-16R

Harrison, Jim 1937-........... CLC 6, 14
See also Harrison, James
See also DLB-Y 82

Harte, (Francis) Bret(t) 1836?-1902................. TCLC 1
See also CA 104
See also SATA 26
See also DLB 12

Hartley, L(eslie) P(oles) 1895-1972 .... **CLC 2, 22**
See also CA 45-48
See also obituary CA 37-40R
See also DLB 15

Hartman, Geoffrey H. 1929- .... **CLC 27**

Hašek, Jaroslav (Matej Frantisek) 1883-1923 .... **TCLC 4**
See also CA 104

Hass, Robert 1941- .... **CLC 18**
See also CA 111

Hauptmann, Gerhart (Johann Robert) 1862-1946 .... **TCLC 4**
See also CA 104

Havel, Václav 1936- .... **CLC 25**
See also CA 104

Hawkes, John (Clendennin Burne, Jr.) 1925- .... **CLC 1, 2, 3, 4, 7, 9, 14, 15, 27**
See also CANR 2
See also CA 1-4R
See also DLB 2
See also DLB-Y 80

Hawthorne, Nathaniel 1804-1864 .... **NCLC 2**
See also SATA 2
See also DLB 1

Hayden, Robert (Earl) 1913-1980 .... **CLC 5, 9, 14**
See also CA 69-72
See also obituary CA 97-100
See also SATA 19
See also obituary SATA 26
See also DLB 5

Haywood, Eliza (Fowler) 1693?-1756 .... **LC 1**

Hazzard, Shirley 1931- .... **CLC 18**
See also CANR 4
See also CA 9-12R
See also DLB-Y 82

H(ilda) D(oolittle) 1886-1961 .... **CLC 3, 8, 14**
See also Doolittle, Hilda

Head, Bessie 1937- .... **CLC 25**
See also CA 29-32R

Heaney, Seamus 1939- .... **CLC 5, 7, 14, 25**
See also CA 85-88

Hearn, (Patricio) Lafcadio (Tessima Carlos) 1850-1904 .... **TCLC 9**
See also CA 105
See also DLB 12

Heat Moon, William Least 1939- .... **CLC 29**

Hébert, Anne 1916- .... **CLC 4, 13, 29**
See also CA 85-88

Hecht, Anthony (Evan) 1923- .... **CLC 8, 13, 19**
See also CANR 6
See also CA 9-12R
See also DLB 5

Hecht, Ben 1894-1964 .... **CLC 8**
See also CA 85-88
See also DLB 7, 9, 25, 26

Heidegger, Martin 1889-1976 .... **CLC 24**
See also CA 81-84
See also obituary CA 65-68

Heidenstam, (Karl Gustaf) Verner von 1859-1940 .... **TCLC 5**
See also CA 104

Heifner, Jack 1946- .... **CLC 11**
See also CA 105

Heilbrun, Carolyn G(old) 1926- .... **CLC 25**
See also CANR 1
See also CA 45-48

Heine, Harry 1797-1856
See Heine, Heinrich

Heine, Heinrich 1797-1856 .... **NCLC 4**

Heiney, Donald (William) 1921-
See Harris, MacDonald
See also CANR 3
See also CA 1-4R

Heinlein, Robert A(nson) 1907- .... **CLC 1, 3, 8, 14, 26**
See also CANR 1
See also CA 1-4R
See also SATA 9
See also DLB 8

Heller, Joseph 1923- .... **CLC 1, 3, 5, 8, 11**
See also CANR 8
See also CA 5-8R
See also DLB 2
See also DLB-Y 80
See also AITN 1

Hellman, Lillian (Florence) 1906- .... **CLC 2, 4, 8, 14, 18**
See also CA 13-16R
See also DLB 7
See also AITN 1, 2

Helprin, Mark 1947- .... **CLC 7, 10, 22**
See also CA 81-84

Hemingway, Ernest 1899-1961 .... **CLC 1, 3, 6, 8, 10, 13, 19**
See also CA 77-80
See also DLB 4, 9
See also DLB-Y 81
See also DLB-DS 1
See also AITN 2

Henley, Beth 1952- .... **CLC 23**
See also Henley, Elizabeth Becker

Henley, Elizabeth Becker 1952-
See Henley, Beth
See also CA 107

Henley, William Ernest 1849-1903 .... **TCLC 8**
See also CA 105
See also DLB 19

Hennissart, Martha
See Lathen, Emma
See also CA 85-88

Henry, O. 1862-1909? .... **TCLC 1**
See also Porter, William Sydney
See also YABC 2

Hentoff, Nat(han Irving) 1925- .... **CLC 26**
See also CLR 1
See also CANR 5
See also CA 1-4R
See also SATA 27

Heppenstall, (John) Rayner 1911-1981 .... **CLC 10**
See also CA 1-4R
See also obituary CA 103

Herbert, Frank (Patrick) 1920- .... **CLC 12, 23**
See also CANR 5
See also CA 53-56
See also SATA 9
See also DLB 8

Herbert, Zbigniew 1924- .... **CLC 9**
See also CA 89-92

Hergesheimer, Joseph 1880-1954 .... **TCLC 11**
See also CA 109
See also DLB 9

Herlagñez, Pablo de 1844-1896
See Verlaine, Paul (Marie)

Herlihy, James Leo 1927- .... **CLC 6**
See also CANR 2
See also CA 1-4R

Herriot, James 1916- .... **CLC 12**
See also Wight, James Alfred

Hersey, John (Richard) 1914- .... **CLC 1, 2, 7, 9**
See also CA 17-20R
See also SATA 25
See also DLB 6

Herzog, Werner 1942- .... **CLC 16**
See also CA 89-92

Hesse, Hermann 1877-1962 .... **CLC 1, 2, 3, 6, 11, 17, 25**
See also CAP 2
See also CA 17-18

Heyen, William 1940- .... **CLC 13, 18**
See also CA 33-36R
See also DLB 5

Heyerdahl, Thor 1914- .... **CLC 26**
See also CANR 5
See also CA 5-8R
See also SATA 2

Heym, Georg (Theodor Franz Arthur) 1887-1912 .... **TCLC 9**
See also CA 106

Heyse, Paul (Johann Ludwig von) 1830-1914 .... **TCLC 8**
See also CA 104

Hibbert, Eleanor (Burford) 1906- .... **CLC 7**
See also CANR 9
See also CA 17-20R
See also SATA 2

Higgins, George V(incent) 1939- .... **CLC 4, 7, 10, 18**
See also CA 77-80
See also DLB 2
See also DLB-Y 81

Highsmith, (Mary) Patricia 1921- .... **CLC 2, 4, 14**
See also CANR 1
See also CA 1-4R

Highwater, Jamake 1942- .... **CLC 12**
See also CANR 10
See also CA 65-68
See also SATA 30, 32

Hill, Geoffrey 1932- .... **CLC 5, 8, 18**
See also CA 81-84

Hill, George Roy 1922- .... **CLC 26**

Hill, Susan B. 1942- .... **CLC 4**
See also CA 33-36R
See also DLB 14

Hilliard, Noel (Harvey) 1929- ...... **CLC 15**
See also CANR 7
See also CA 9-12R

Himes, Chester (Bomar) 1909- .... **CLC 2, 4, 7, 18**
See also CA 25-28R
See also DLB 2

Hinde, Thomas 1926- .... **CLC 6, 11**
See also Chitty, (Sir) Thomas Willes

Hine, (William) Daryl 1936- .... **CLC 15**
See also CANR 1
See also CA 1-4R

Hippius (Merezhkovsky), Zinaida (Nikolayevna) 1869-1945 ..... **TCLC 9**
See also CA 106

Hiraoka, Kimitake 1925-1970
See Mishima, Yukio
See also CA 97-100
See also obituary CA 29-32R

Hitchcock, (Sir) Alfred (Joseph) 1899-1980 .... **CLC 16**
See also obituary CA 97-100
See also SATA 27
See also obituary SATA 24

Hoagland, Edward 1932- .... **CLC 28**
See also CANR 2
See also CA 1-4R
See also DLB 6

Hoban, Russell C(onwell) 1925- .... **CLC 7, 25**
See also CLR 3
See also CA 5-8R
See also SATA 1

Hobson, Laura Z(ametkin) 1900- .... **CLC 7, 25**
See also CA 17-20R

Hochhuth, Rolf 1931- .... **CLC 4, 11, 18**
See also CA 5-8R

Hochman, Sandra 1936- .... **CLC 3, 8**
See also CA 5-8R
See also DLB 5

Hocking, Mary (Eunice) 1921- ..... **CLC 13**
See also CA 101

Hodgins, Jack 1938- .... **CLC 23**
See also CA 93-96

Hodgson, William Hope 1877-1918 .... **TCLC 13**
See also CA 111

Hoffman, Daniel (Gerard) 1923- .... **CLC 6, 13, 23**
See also CANR 4
See also CA 1-4R
See also DLB 5

Hoffman, Stanley 1944- .... **CLC 5**
See also CA 77-80

Hoffmann, Ernst Theodor Amadeus 1776-1822 .... **NCLC 2**
See also SATA 27

Hofmannsthal, Hugo (Laurenz August Hofmann Edler) von 1874-1929 .... **TCLC 11**
See also CA 106

Hogg, James 1770-1835 .... **NCLC 4**

Holden, Ursula 1921- .... **CLC 18**
See also CA 101

Holland, Isabelle 1920- .... **CLC 21**
See also CANR 10
See also CA 21-24R
See also SATA 8

Holland, Marcus 1900-
See Caldwell, (Janet Miriam) Taylor (Holland)

Hollander, John 1929- ..... **CLC 2, 5, 8, 14**
See also CANR 1
See also CA 1-4R
See also SATA 13
See also DLB 5

Hollis, Jim 1916-
See Summers, Hollis (Spurgeon, Jr.)

Holt, Victoria 1906-
See Hibbert, Eleanor (Burford)

Holub, Miroslav 1923- .... **CLC 4**
See also CA 21-24R

Hood, Hugh (John Blagdon) 1928- .... **CLC 15, 28**
See also CANR 1
See also CA 49-52

Hope, A(lec) D(erwent) 1907- .... **CLC 3**
See also CA 21-24R

Hopkins, John (Richard) 1931- ...... **CLC 4**
See also CA 85-88

Horgan, Paul 1903- .... **CLC 9**
See also CANR 9
See also CA 13-16R
See also SATA 13

Horwitz, Julius 1920- .... **CLC 14**
See also CA 9-12R

Household, Geoffrey (Edward West) 1900- .... **CLC 11**
See also CA 77-80
See also SATA 14

Housman, A(lfred) E(dward) 1859-1936 .... **TCLC 1, 10**
See also CA 104
See also DLB 19

Housman, Laurence 1865-1959 .... **TCLC 7**
See also CA 106
See also SATA 25
See also DLB 10

Howard, Elizabeth Jane 1923- .... **CLC 7, 29**
See also CANR 8
See also CA 5-8R

Howard, Maureen 1930- .... **CLC 5, 14**
See also CA 53-56

Howard, Richard 1929- .... **CLC 7, 10**
See also CA 85-88
See also DLB 5
See also AITN 1

Howard, Robert E(rvin) 1906-1936 .... **TCLC 8**
See also CA 105

Howells, William Dean 1837-1920 .... **TCLC 7**
See also CA 104
See also DLB 12

Howes, Barbara 1914- .... **CLC 15**
See also CA 9-12R
See also SATA 5

Hrabal, Bohumil 1914- .... **CLC 13**
See also CA 106

Huch, Ricarda (Octavia) 1864-1947 .... **TCLC 13**
See also CA 111

Hueffer, Ford Madox 1873-1939
See Ford, Ford Madox

Hughes, (James) Langston 1902-1967 .... **CLC 1, 5, 10, 15**
See also CANR 1
See also CA 1-4R
See also obituary CA 25-28R
See also SATA 4, 33
See also DLB 4, 7

Hughes, Richard (Arthur Warren) 1900-1976 .... **CLC 1, 11**
See also CANR 4
See also CA 5-8R
See also obituary CA 65-68
See also SATA 8
See also obituary SATA 25
See also DLB 15

Hughes, Ted 1930- .... **CLC 2, 4, 9, 14**
See also CLR 3
See also CANR 1
See also CA 1-4R
See also SATA 27

Hugo, Richard F(ranklin) 1923-1982 .... **CLC 6, 18**
See also CANR 3
See also CA 49-52
See also obituary CA 108
See also DLB 5

Hugo, Victor Marie 1802-1885 .... **NCLC 3**

Hunt, E(verette) Howard (Jr.) 1918- .... **CLC 3**
See also CANR 2
See also CA 45-48
See also AITN 1

Hunt, (James Henry) Leigh 1784-1859 .... **NCLC 1**

Hunter, Evan 1926- .... **CLC 1**
See also CANR 5
See also CA 5-8R
See also SATA 25
See also DLB-Y 82

Hunter, Mollie (Maureen McIlwraith) 1922- .... **CLC 21**
See also McIlwraith, Maureen Mollie Hunter

Hurston, Zora Neale 1901-1960 ..... **CLC 7**
See also CA 85-88

Huston, John (Marcellus) 1906- .... **CLC 20**
See also CA 73-76
See also DLB 26

Huxley, Aldous (Leonard) 1894-1963 .... **CLC 1, 3, 4, 5, 8, 11, 18**
See also CA 85-88

Huysmans, Joris-Karl 1848-1907 .... **TCLC 7**
See also CA 104

Hyde, Margaret O(ldroyd) 1917- .... **CLC 21**
See also CANR 1
See also CA 1-4R
See also SATA 1

Ian, Janis 1951- .... **CLC 21**
See also CA 105

Ibsen, Henrik (Johan) 1828-1906 .... **TCLC 2, 8**
See also CA 104

Ibuse, Masuji 1898- .... **CLC 22**

Ichikawa, Kon 1915- .... **CLC 20**

Idle, Eric 1941?-
See Monty Python

Ignatow, David 1914- .... **CLC 4, 7, 14**
See also CA 9-12R
See also DLB 5

Immermann, Karl (Lebrecht) 1796-1840 .... **NCLC 4**

Inge, William (Motter) 1913-1973 .... **CLC 1, 8, 19**
See also CA 9-12R
See also DLB 7

Innaurato, Albert 1948- .... **CLC 21**

Innes, Michael 1906-
See Stewart, J(ohn) I(nnes) M(ackintosh)

Ionesco, Eugène 1912- .... **CLC 1, 4, 6, 9, 11, 15**
See also CA 9-12R
See also SATA 7

Irving, John (Winslow) 1942- .... **CLC 13, 23**
See also CA 25-28R
See also DLB 6
See also DLB-Y 82

Irving, Washington 1783-1859 .... **NCLC 2**
See also YABC 2
See also DLB 3, 11

Isherwood, Christopher (William Bradshaw) 1904- .... **CLC 1, 9, 11, 14**
See also CA 13-16R
See also DLB 15

Ishiguro, Kazuo 1954?- .... **CLC 27**

Ivask, Ivar (Vidrik) 1927- .... **CLC 14**
See also CA 37-40R

Jackson, Jesse 1908-1983 .... **CLC 12**
See also obituary CA 109
See also CA 25-28R
See also SATA 2, 29

Jackson, Laura (Riding) 1901-
See Riding, Laura
See also CA 65-68

Jackson, Shirley 1919-1965 .... **CLC 11**
See also CANR 4
See also CA 1-4R
See also obituary CA 25-28R
See also SATA 2
See also DLB 6

Jacob, (Cyprien) Max 1876-1944 .... **TCLC 6**
See also CA 104

Jacobs, Jim 1942-
See Jacobs, Jim and Casey, Warren
See also CA 97-100

Jacobs, Jim 1942- and **Casey, Warren** 1935- .... **CLC 12**

Jacobson, Dan 1929- .... **CLC 4, 14**
See also CANR 2
See also CA 1-4R
See also DLB 14

Jagger, Mick 1944-
See Jagger, Mick and Richard, Keith

Jagger, Mick 1944- and **Richard, Keith** 1943- .... **CLC 17**

Jakes, John (William) 1932- .... **CLC 29**
See also CANR 10
See also CA 57-60

James, Henry (Jr.) 1843-1916 .... **TCLC 2, 11**
See also CA 104
See also DLB 12

James, M(ontague) R(hodes) 1862-1936 .... **TCLC 6**
See also CA 104

James, P(hyllis) D(orothy) 1920- .... **CLC 18**
See also CA 21-24R

Jarrell, Randall 1914-1965 .... **CLC 1, 2, 6, 9, 13**
See also CLR 6
See also CANR 6
See also CA 5-8R
See also obituary CA 25-28R
See also SATA 7

Jarry, Alfred 1873-1907 .... **TCLC 2**
See also CA 104

Jeffers, (John) Robinson 1887-1962 .... **CLC 2, 3, 11, 15**
See also CA 85-88

Jellicoe, (Patricia) Ann 1927- .... **CLC 27**
See also CA 85-88
See also DLB 13

Jennings, Elizabeth (Joan) 1926- .... **CLC 5, 14**
See also CANR 8
See also CA 61-64

Jennings, Waylon 1937- .... **CLC 21**

Jerrold, Douglas 1803-1857 .... **NCLC 2**

Jewett, Sarah Orne 1849-1909 .... **TCLC 1**
See also CA 108
See also SATA 15
See also DLB 12

Jhabvala, Ruth Prawer 1927- .... **CLC 4, 8, 29**
See also CANR 2
See also CA 1-4R

Jiles, Paulette 1943- .... **CLC 13**
See also CA 101

Jiménez (Mantecón), Juan Ramón 1881-1958 .... **TCLC 4**
See also CA 104

Joel, Billy 1949- .... **CLC 26**
See also Joel, William Martin

Joel, William Martin 1949-
See Joel, Billy
See also CA 108

Johnson, B(ryan) S(tanley William) 1933-1973 .... **CLC 6, 9**
See also CANR 9
See also CA 9-12R
See also obituary CA 53-56
See also DLB 14

Johnson, Charles 1948- .... **CLC 7**

Johnson, Diane 1934- .... **CLC 5, 13**
See also CA 41-44R
See also DLB-Y 80

Johnson, Eyvind (Olof Verner) 1900-1976 .... **CLC 14**
See also CA 73-76
See also obituary CA 69-72

Johnson, James Weldon 1871-1938 .... **TCLC 3**
See also CA 104
See also SATA 31

Johnson, Marguerita 1928-
See Angelou, Maya

Johnson, Pamela Hansford 1912-1981 .... **CLC 1, 7, 27**
See also CANR 2
See also CA 1-4R
See also obituary CA 104
See also DLB 15

Johnson, Uwe 1934- .... **CLC 5, 10, 15**
See also CANR 1
See also CA 1-4R

Johnston, Jennifer 1930- .... **CLC 7**
See also CA 85-88
See also DLB 14

Jones, D(ouglas) G(ordon) 1929- .... **CLC 10**
See also CA 29-32R

Jones, David 1895-1974 .... **CLC 2, 4, 7, 13**
See also CA 9-12R
See also obituary CA 53-56
See also DLB 20

Jones, David Robert 1947-
See Bowie, David
See also CA 103

Jones, Diana Wynne 1934- .... **CLC 26**
See also CANR 4
See also CA 49-52
See also SATA 9

Jones, Gayl 1949- .... **CLC 6, 9**
See also CA 77-80

Jones, James 1921-1977 ...... **CLC 1, 3, 10**
See also CANR 6
See also CA 1-4R
See also obituary CA 69-72
See also DLB 2
See also AITN 1, 2

Jones, (Everett) LeRoi 1934- .... **CLC 1**
See also Baraka, Imamu Amiri
See also CA 21-24R

Jones, Madison (Percy, Jr.) 1925- .... **CLC 4**
See also CANR 7
See also CA 13-16R

Jones, Mervyn 1922- .... **CLC 10**
See also CANR 1
See also CA 45-48

Jones, Preston 1936-1979 .... **CLC 10**
See also CA 73-76
See also obituary CA 89-92
See also DLB 7

Jones, Robert F(rancis) 1934- .... **CLC 7**
See also CANR 2
See also CA 49-52

Jones, Terry 1942?-
See Monty Python

Jong, Erica 1942- .... **CLC 4, 6, 8, 18**
See also CA 73-76
See also DLB 2, 5
See also AITN 1

Jordan, June 1936- ....CLC 5, 11, 23
See also CA 33-36R
See also SATA 4

Josipovici, G(abriel) 1940- ....CLC 6
See also CA 37-40R
See also DLB 14

Joyce, James (Augustine Aloysius) 1882-1941 ....TCLC 3, 8
See also CA 104
See also DLB 10, 19

Just, Ward S(wift) 1935- .... CLC 4, 27
See also CA 25-28R

Justice, Donald (Rodney) 1925- .... CLC 6, 19
See also CA 5-8R

Kacew, Romain 1914-1980
See Gary, Romain
See also CA 108
See also obituary CA 102

Kacewgary, Romain 1914-1980
See Gary, Romain

Kafka, Franz 1883-1924 ....TCLC 2, 6, 13
See also CA 105

Kaiser, (Friedrich Karl) Georg 1878-1945 .... TCLC 9
See also CA 106

Kallman, Chester (Simon) 1921-1975 ....CLC 2
See also CANR 3
See also CA 45-48
See also obituary CA 53-56

Kaminsky, Melvin 1926-
See Brooks, Mel

Kane, Paul 1941-
See Simon, Paul

Kanin, Garson 1912- ....CLC 22
See also CANR 7
See also CA 5-8R
See also DLB 7
See also AITN 1

Kaniuk, Yoram 1930- ....CLC 19

Kantor, MacKinlay 1904-1977 ......CLC 7
See also CA 61-64
See also obituary CA 73-76
See also DLB 9

Karamzin, Nikolai Mikhailovich 1766-1826 .... NCLC 3

Karapánou, Margaríta 1946- ....CLC 13
See also CA 101

Kassef, Romain 1914-1980
See Gary, Romain

Kaufman, Sue 1926-1977 .... CLC 3, 8
See also Barondess, Sue K(aufman)

Kavan, Anna 1904-1968 .... CLC 5, 13
See also Edmonds, Helen (Woods)
See also CANR 6

Kavanagh, Patrick (Joseph) 1905-1967 ....CLC 22
See also CA 25-28R
See also DLB 15, 20

Kawabata, Yasunari 1899-1972 ....CLC 2, 5, 9, 18
See also CA 93-96
See also obituary CA 33-36R

Kaye, M(ary) M(argaret) 1909?- ....CLC 28
See also CA 89-92

Kaye, Mollie 1909?-
See Kaye, M(ary) M(argaret)

Kazan, Elia 1909- .... CLC 6, 16
See also CA 21-24R

Kazantzakis, Nikos 1885?-1957 ....TCLC 2, 5
See also CA 105

Keaton, Buster 1895-1966 ....CLC 20

Keaton, Joseph Francis 1895-1966
See Keaton, Buster

Keller, Gottfried 1819-1890 .... NCLC 2

Kelley, William Melvin 1937- ......CLC 22
See also CA 77-80

Kellogg, Marjorie 1922- ....CLC 2
See also CA 81-84

Kemal, Yashar 1922- .... CLC 14, 29
See also CA 89-92

Kemelman, Harry 1908- ....CLC 2
See also CANR 6
See also CA 9-12R
See also AITN 1

Keneally, Thomas (Michael) 1935- ....CLC 5, 8, 10, 14, 19, 27
See also CANR 10
See also CA 85-88

Kennedy, John Pendleton 1795-1870 .... NCLC 2
See also DLB 3

Kennedy, Joseph Charles 1929-
See Kennedy, X. J.
See also CANR 4
See also CA 1-4R
See also SATA 14

Kennedy, William 1928- .... CLC 6, 28
See also CA 85-88

Kennedy, X. J. 1929- ....CLC 8
See also Kennedy, Joseph Charles
See also DLB 5

Kerouac, Jack 1922-1969 .... CLC 1, 2, 3, 5, 14, 29
See also Kerouac, Jean-Louis Lebrid de
See also DLB 2, 16
See also DLB-DS 3

Kerouac, Jean-Louis Lebrid de 1922-1969
See Kerouac, Jack
See also CA 5-8R
See also obituary CA 25-28R
See also AITN 1

Kerr, Jean 1923- ....CLC 22
See also CANR 7
See also CA 5-8R

Kerr, M. E. 1927- ....CLC 12
See also Meaker, Marijane

Kerrigan, (Thomas) Anthony 1918- .... CLC 4, 6
See also CANR 4
See also CA 49-52

Kesey, Ken (Elton) 1935- ....CLC 1, 3, 6, 11
See also CA 1-4R
See also DLB 2, 16

Kessler, Jascha (Frederick) 1929- ....CLC 4
See also CANR 8
See also CA 17-20R

Kettelkamp, Larry 1933- ....CLC 12
See also CA 29-32R
See also SATA 2

Kherdian, David 1931- .... CLC 6, 9
See also CA 21-24R
See also SATA 16

Kielland, Alexander (Lange) 1849-1906 .... TCLC 5
See also CA 104

Kiely, Benedict 1919- ....CLC 23
See also CANR 2
See also CA 1-4R
See also DLB 15

Kienzle, William X(avier) 1928- ....CLC 25
See also CANR 9
See also CA 93-96

Killens, John Oliver 1916- ....CLC 10
See also CA 77-80

King, Francis (Henry) 1923- ....CLC 8
See also CANR 1
See also CA 1-4R
See also DLB 15

King, Stephen (Edwin) 1947- .... CLC 12, 26
See also CANR 1
See also CA 61-64
See also SATA 9
See also DLB-Y 80

Kingman, (Mary) Lee 1919- ....CLC 17
See also Natti, (Mary) Lee
See also CA 5-8R
See also SATA 1

Kingston, Maxine Hong 1940- .... CLC 12, 19
See also CA 69-72
See also DLB-Y 80

Kinnell, Galway 1927- .... CLC 1, 2, 3, 5, 13, 29
See also CANR 10
See also CA 9-12R
See also DLB 5

Kinsella, Thomas 1928- .... CLC 4, 19
See also CA 17-20R

Kinsella, W(illiam) P(atrick) 1935- ....CLC 27
See also CA 97-100

Kipling, (Joseph) Rudyard 1865-1936 .... TCLC 8
See also CA 105
See also YABC 2
See also DLB 19

Kirkup, James 1927- ....CLC 1
See also CANR 2
See also CA 1-4R
See also SATA 12

Kirkwood, James 1930- ....CLC 9
See also CANR 6
See also CA 1-4R
See also AITN 2

Kizer, Carolyn (Ashley) 1925- ......CLC 15
See also CA 65-68
See also DLB 5

Klein, A(braham) M(oses) 1909-1972 .... **CLC 19**
See also CA 101
See also obituary CA 37-40R

Kleist, Heinrich von 1777-1811 .... **NCLC 2**

Klinger, Friedrich Maximilian von 1752-1831 .... **NCLC 1**

Knebel, Fletcher 1911- .... **CLC 14**
See also CANR 1
See also CA 1-4R
See also AITN 1

Knowles, John 1926- .... **CLC 1, 4, 10, 26**
See also CA 17-20R
See also SATA 8
See also DLB 6

Koch, Kenneth 1925- .... **CLC 5, 8**
See also CANR 6
See also CA 1-4R
See also DLB 5

Koestler, Arthur 1905-1983 .... **CLC 1, 3, 6, 8, 15**
See also CANR 1
See also CA 1-4R
See also obituary CA 109

Kohout, Pavel 1928- .... **CLC 13**
See also CANR 3
See also CA 45-48

Konrád, György 1933- .... **CLC 4, 10**
See also CA 85-88

Konwicki, Tadeusz 1926- .... **CLC 8, 28**
See also CA 101

Kopit, Arthur (Lee) 1937- .... **CLC 1, 18**
See also CA 81-84
See also DLB 7
See also AITN 1

Kops, Bernard 1926- .... **CLC 4**
See also CA 5-8R
See also DLB 13

Kornbluth, C(yril) M. 1923-1958 .... **TCLC 8**
See also CA 105
See also DLB 8

Kosinski, Jerzy (Nikodem) 1933- .... **CLC 1, 2, 3, 6, 10, 15**
See also CANR 9
See also CA 17-20R
See also DLB 2
See also DLB-Y 82

Kostelanetz, Richard (Cory) 1940- .... **CLC 28**
See also CA 13-16R

Kotlowitz, Robert 1924- .... **CLC 4**
See also CA 33-36R

Kotzwinkle, William 1938- .... **CLC 5, 14**
See also CLR 6
See also CANR 3
See also CA 45-48
See also SATA 24

Kozol, Jonathan 1936- .... **CLC 17**
See also CA 61-64

Krasiński, Zygmunt 1812-1859 .... **NCLC 4**

Kraus, Karl 1874-1936 .... **TCLC 5**
See also CA 104

Kristofferson, Kris 1936- .... **CLC 26**
See also CA 104

Krleža, Miroslav 1893-1981 .... **CLC 8**
See also CA 97-100
See also obituary CA 105

Kroetsch, Robert 1927- .... **CLC 5, 23**
See also CANR 8
See also CA 17-20R

Krotkov, Yuri 1917- .... **CLC 19**
See also CA 102

Krumgold, Joseph (Quincy) 1908-1980 .... **CLC 12**
See also CANR 7
See also CA 9-12R
See also obituary CA 101
See also SATA 1
See also obituary SATA 23

Krutch, Joseph Wood 1893-1970 .... **CLC 24**
See also CANR 4
See also CA 1-4R
See also obituary CA 25-28R

Krylov, Ivan Andreevich 1768?-1844 .... **NCLC 1**

Kubrick, Stanley 1928- .... **CLC 16**
See also CA 81-84
See also DLB 26

Kumin, Maxine (Winokur) 1925- .... **CLC 5, 13, 28**
See also CANR 1
See also CA 1-4R
See also SATA 12
See also DLB 5
See also AITN 2

Kundera, Milan 1929- .... **CLC 4, 9, 19**
See also CA 85-88

Kunitz, Stanley J(asspon) 1905- .... **CLC 6, 11, 14**
See also CA 41-44R

Kunze, Reiner 1933- .... **CLC 10**
See also CA 93-96

Kuprin, Aleksandr (Ivanovich) 1870-1938 .... **TCLC 5**
See also CA 104

Kurosawa, Akira 1910- .... **CLC 16**
See also CA 101

Kuttner, Henry 1915-1958 .... **TCLC 10**
See also CA 107
See also DLB 8

Kuzma, Greg 1944- .... **CLC 7**
See also CA 33-36R

Labrunie, Gérard 1808-1855
See Nerval, Gérard de

Laclos, Pierre Ambroise François Choderlos de 1741-1803 .... **NCLC 4**

Laforgue, Jules 1860-1887 .... **NCLC 5**

Lagerkvist, Pär (Fabian) 1891-1974 .... **CLC 7, 10, 13**
See also CA 85-88
See also obituary CA 49-52

Lagerlöf, Selma (Ottiliana Lovisa) 1858-1940 .... **TCLC 4**
See also CA 108
See also SATA 15

La Guma, (Justin) Alex(ander) 1925- .... **CLC 19**
See also CA 49-52

Lamming, George (William) 1927- .... **CLC 2, 4**
See also CA 85-88

LaMoore, Louis Dearborn 1908?-
See L'Amour, Louis (Dearborn)

L'Amour, Louis (Dearborn) 1908- .... **CLC 25**
See also CANR 3
See also CA 1-4R
See also DLB-Y 80
See also AITN 2

Lampedusa, (Prince) Giuseppe (Maria Fabrizio) Tomasi di 1896-1957 .... **TCLC 13**
See also CA 111

Landis, John 1950- .... **CLC 26**

Landolfi, Tommaso 1908- .... **CLC 11**

Landwirth, Heinz 1927-
See Lind, Jakov
See also CANR 7

Lane, Patrick 1939- .... **CLC 25**
See also CA 97-100

Lang, Fritz 1890-1976 .... **CLC 20**
See also CA 77-80
See also obituary CA 69-72

Lanier, Sidney 1842-1881 .... **NCLC 6**
See also SATA 18

Larbaud, Valéry 1881-1957 .... **TCLC 9**
See also CA 106

Lardner, Ring(gold Wilmer) 1885-1933 .... **TCLC 2**
See also CA 104
See also DLB 11, 25

Larkin, Philip (Arthur) 1922- .... **CLC 3, 5, 8, 9, 13, 18**
See also CA 5-8R

Latham, Jean Lee 1902- .... **CLC 12**
See also CANR 7
See also CA 5-8R
See also SATA 2
See also AITN 1

Lathen, Emma .... **CLC 2**
See also Hennissart, Martha
See also Latsis, Mary J(ane)

Latsis, Mary J(ane)
See Lathen, Emma
See also CA 85-88

Lattimore, Richmond (Alexander) 1906- .... **CLC 3**
See also CANR 1
See also CA 1-4R

Laurence, (Jean) Margaret (Wemyss) 1926- .... **CLC 3, 6, 13**
See also CA 5-8R

Lavin, Mary 1912- .... **CLC 4, 18**
See also CA 9-12R
See also DLB 15

Lawrence, D(avid) H(erbert) 1885-1930 .... **TCLC 2, 9**
See also CA 104
See also DLB 10, 19

Laxness, Halldór (Kiljan) 1902- .... **CLC 25**
See also Gudjonsson, Halldór Kiljan

Laye, Camara 1928-1980 .... **CLC 4**
See also CA 85-88
See also obituary CA 97-100

Layton, Irving (Peter) 1912- .... **CLC 2, 15**
See also CANR 2
See also CA 1-4R

Leacock, Stephen (Butler)
1869-1944 .... **TCLC 2**
See also CA 104

Lear, Edward 1812-1888 .... **NCLC 3**
See also CLR 1
See also SATA 18

Lear, Norman (Milton) 1922- ...... **CLC 12**
See also CA 73-76

Leavis, F(rank) R(aymond)
1895-1978 .... **CLC 24**
See also CA 21-24R
See also obituary CA 77-80

Lebowitz, Fran 1951?- .... **CLC 11**
See also CA 81-84

Le Carré, John
1931- .... **CLC 3, 5, 9, 15, 28**
See also Cornwell, David (John Moore)

Leduc, Violette 1907-1972 .... **CLC 22**
See also CAP 1
See also CA 13-14
See also obituary CA 33-36R

Lee, Don L. 1942- .... **CLC 2**
See also Madhubuti, Haki R.
See also CA 73-76

Lee, (Nelle) Harper 1926- .... **CLC 12**
See also CA 13-16R
See also SATA 11
See also DLB 6

Lee, Manfred B(ennington) 1905-1971
See Queen, Ellery
See also CANR 2
See also CA 1-4R
See also obituary CA 29-32R

Lee, Stan 1922- .... **CLC 17**
See also CA 108, 111

Lee, Vernon 1856-1935 .... **TCLC 5**
See also Paget, Violet

Leet, Judith 1935- .... **CLC 11**

Leffland, Ella 1931- .... **CLC 19**
See also CA 29-32R

Léger, (Marie-Rene) Alexis Saint-Léger
1887-1975
See Perse, St.-John
See also CA 13-16R
See also obituary CA 61-64

Le Guin, Ursula K(roeber)
1929- .... **CLC 8, 13, 22**
See also CLR 3
See also CANR 9
See also CA 21-24R
See also SATA 4
See also DLB 8
See also AITN 1

Lehmann, Rosamond (Nina)
1901- .... **CLC 5**
See also CANR 8
See also CA 77-80
See also DLB 15

Leiber, Fritz (Reuter, Jr.)
1910- .... **CLC 25**
See also CANR 2
See also CA 45-48
See also DLB 8

Leithauser, Brad 1953- .... **CLC 27**
See also CA 107

Lelchuk, Alan 1938- .... **CLC 5**
See also CANR 1
See also CA 45-48

Lem, Stanislaw 1921- .... **CLC 8, 15**
See also CA 105

L'Engle, Madeleine 1918- .... **CLC 12**
See also CLR 1
See also CANR 3
See also CA 1-4R
See also SATA 1, 27
See also AITN 2

Lennon, John (Ono) 1940-1980
See Lennon, John (Ono) and McCartney, Paul
See also CA 102

Lennon, John (Ono) 1940-1980 and **McCartney, Paul** 1942- .... **CLC 12**

Lenz, Siegfried 1926- .... **CLC 27**
See also CA 89-92

Leonard, Elmore 1925- .... **CLC 28**
See also CA 81-84
See also AITN 1

Leonard, Hugh 1926- .... **CLC 19**
See also Byrne, John Keyes
See also DLB 13

Lerman, Eleanor 1952- .... **CLC 9**
See also CA 85-88

Lermontov, Mikhail Yuryevich
1814-1841 .... **NCLC 5**

Lessing, Doris (May)
1919- .... **CLC 1, 2, 3, 6, 10, 15, 22**
See also CA 9-12R
See also DLB 15

Lester, Richard 1932- .... **CLC 20**

Levertov, Denise
1923- .... **CLC 1, 2, 3, 5, 8, 15, 28**
See also CANR 3
See also CA 1-4R
See also DLB 5

Levin, Ira 1929- .... **CLC 3, 6**
See also CA 21-24R

Levin, Meyer 1905-1981 .... **CLC 7**
See also CA 9-12R
See also obituary CA 104
See also SATA 21
See also obituary SATA 27
See also DLB 9
See also DLB-Y 81
See also AITN 1

Levine, Philip 1928- .... **CLC 2, 4, 5, 9, 14**
See also CANR 9
See also CA 9-12R
See also DLB 5

Levitin, Sonia 1934- .... **CLC 17**
See also CA 29-32R
See also SATA 4

Lewis, Alun 1915-1944 .... **TCLC 3**
See also CA 104
See also DLB 20

Lewis, C(ecil) Day 1904-1972
See Day Lewis, C(ecil)

Lewis, C(live) S(taples)
1898-1963 .... **CLC 1, 3, 6, 14, 27**
See also CLR 3
See also CA 81-84
See also SATA 13
See also DLB 15

Lewis, (Harry) Sinclair
1885-1951 .... **TCLC 4, 13**
See also CA 104
See also DLB 9
See also DLB-DS 1

Lewis, (Percy) Wyndham
1882?-1957 .... **TCLC 2, 9**
See also CA 104
See also DLB 15

Lezama Lima, José
1910-1976 .... **CLC 4, 10**
See also CA 77-80

Li Fei-kan 1904-
See Pa Chin
See also CA 105

Lie, Jonas (Lauritz Idemil)
1833-1908 .... **TCLC 5**

Lieber, Joel 1936-1971 .... **CLC 6**
See also CA 73-76
See also obituary CA 29-32R

Lieber, Stanley Martin 1922-
See Lee, Stan

Lieberman, Laurence (James)
1935- .... **CLC 4**
See also CANR 8
See also CA 17-20R

Lightfoot, Gordon 1938- .... **CLC 26**
See also CA 109

Lima, José Lezama 1910-1976
See Lezama Lima, José

Lind, Jakov 1927- .... **CLC 1, 2, 4, 27**
See also Landwirth, Heinz
See also CA 9-12R

Lipsyte, Robert (Michael)
1938- .... **CLC 21**
See also CANR 8
See also CA 17-20R
See also SATA 5

Livesay, Dorothy 1909- .... **CLC 4, 15**
See also CA 25-28R
See also AITN 2

Llewellyn, Richard 1906- .... **CLC 7**
See also Llewellyn Lloyd, Richard (Dafydd Vyvyan)
See also DLB 15

Llewellyn Lloyd, Richard (Dafydd Vyvyan)
1906-
See Llewellyn, Richard
See also CANR 7
See also CA 53-56
See also obituary CA 111
See also SATA 11

Llosa, Mario Vargas 1936-
See Vargas Llosa, Mario

Lloyd, Richard Llewellyn 1906-
See Llewellyn, Richard

Lockhart, John Gibson
1794-1854 .... **NCLC 6**

Logan, John 1923-.................CLC 5
See also CA 77-80
See also DLB 5

London, Jack 1876-1916 .... TCLC 9
See also London, John Griffith
See also SATA 18
See also DLB 8, 12
See also AITN 2

London, John Griffith 1876-1916
See London, Jack
See also CA 110

Long, Emmett 1925-
See Leonard, Elmore

Longfellow, Henry Wadsworth
1807-1882.................. NCLC 2
See also SATA 19
See also DLB 1

Longley, Michael 1939-............CLC 29
See also CA 102

Lopate, Phillip 1943-..............CLC 29
See also CA 97-100
See also DLB-Y 80

Lord, Bette Bao 1938-.............CLC 23
See also CA 107

Lorde, Audre 1934-...............CLC 18
See also CA 25-28R

Loti, Pierre 1850-1923 .... TCLC 11
See also Viaud, (Louis Marie) Julien

Lovecraft, H(oward) P(hillips)
1890-1937.................. TCLC 4
See also CA 104

Lowell, Amy 1874-1925 .... TCLC 1, 8
See also CA 104

Lowell, James Russell
1819-1891.................. NCLC 2
See also DLB 1, 11

Lowell, Robert (Traill Spence, Jr.)
1917-1977...... CLC 1, 2, 3, 4, 5, 8, 9, 11, 15
See also CA 9-12R
See also obituary CA 73-76
See also DLB 5

Lowndes, Marie (Adelaide Belloc)
1868-1947.................. TCLC 12
See also CA 107

Lowry, (Clarence) Malcolm
1909-1957.................. TCLC 6
See also CA 105
See also DLB 15

Loy, Mina 1882-1966 ....CLC 28
See also DLB 4

Lucas, George 1944-..............CLC 16
See also CA 77-80

Lucas, Victoria 1932-1963
See Plath, Sylvia

Ludlum, Robert 1927- ....CLC 22
See also CA 33-36R
See also DLB-Y 82

Ludwig, Otto 1813-1865.......... NCLC 4

Lu Hsün 1881-1936............. TCLC 3

Lukács, Georg 1885-1971..........CLC 24
See also Lukács, György

Lukács, György 1885-1971
See Lukács, Georg
See also CA 101
See also obituary CA 29-32R

Lurie, Alison 1926- .... CLC 4, 5, 18
See also CANR 2
See also CA 1-4R
See also DLB 2

Luzi, Mario 1914-................CLC 13
See also CANR 9
See also CA 61-64

Lytle, Andrew (Nelson) 1902- ......CLC 22
See also CA 9-12R
See also DLB 6

Lytton, Edward Bulwer 1803-1873
See Bulwer-Lytton, (Lord) Edward (George Earle Lytton)

Maas, Peter 1929-................CLC 29
See also CA 93-96

Macaulay, (Dame Emile) Rose
1881-1958.................. TCLC 7
See also CA 104

MacBeth, George (Mann)
1932-.................... CLC 2, 5, 9
See also CA 25-28R
See also SATA 4

MacDiarmid, Hugh
1892-1978............CLC 2, 4, 11, 19
See also Grieve, C(hristopher) M(urray)
See also DLB 20

Macdonald, Cynthia 1928-..... CLC 13, 19
See also CANR 4
See also CA 49-52

MacDonald, George
1824-1905.................. TCLC 9
See also CA 106
See also SATA 33
See also DLB 18

MacDonald, John D(ann)
1916-.................... CLC 3, 27
See also CANR 1
See also CA 1-4R
See also DLB 8

Macdonald, Ross
1915-.................CLC 1, 2, 3, 14
See also Millar, Kenneth

MacEwen, Gwendolyn 1941-.......CLC 13
See also CANR 7
See also CA 9-12R

Machado (y Ruiz), Antonio
1875-1939.................. TCLC 3
See also CA 104

Machado de Assis, (Joaquim Maria)
1839-1908................. TCLC 10
See also CA 107

Machen, Arthur (Llewellyn Jones)
1863-1947.................. TCLC 4
See also CA 104

MacInnes, Colin 1914-1976..... CLC 4, 23
See also CA 69-72
See also obituary CA 65-68
See also DLB 14

MacInnes, Helen 1907-............CLC 27
See also CANR 1
See also CA 1-4R
See also SATA 22

Mackenzie, (Edward Montague) Compton
1883-1972...................CLC 18
See also CAP 2
See also CA 21-22
See also obituary CA 37-40R

MacLean, Alistair (Stuart)
1922-.................... CLC 3, 13
See also CA 57-60
See also SATA 23

MacLeish, Archibald
1892-1982............... CLC 3, 8, 14
See also CA 9-12R
See also obituary CA 106
See also DLB 4, 7
See also DLB-Y 82

MacLennan, (John) Hugh
1907-.................... CLC 2, 14
See also CA 5-8R

MacNeice, (Frederick) Louis
1907-1963............... CLC 1, 4, 10
See also CA 85-88
See also DLB 10, 20

Macpherson, (Jean) Jay 1931-......CLC 14
See also CA 5-8R

Macumber, Mari 1896-1966
See Sandoz, Mari (Susette)

Madden, (Jerry) David
1933-.................... CLC 5, 15
See also CANR 4
See also CA 1-4R
See also DLB 6

Madhubuti, Haki R. 1942-..........CLC 6
See also Lee, Don L.
See also DLB 5

Maeterlinck, Maurice
1862-1949.................. TCLC 3
See also CA 104

Mahon, Derek 1941-..............CLC 27

Mailer, Norman
1923-......CLC 1, 2, 3, 4, 5, 8, 11, 14, 28
See also CA 9-12R
See also DLB 2, 16
See also DLB-Y 80
See also DLB-DS 3
See also AITN 2

Mais, Roger 1905-1955........... TCLC 8
See also CA 105

Major, Clarence 1936- .... CLC 3, 19
See also CA 21-24R

Major, Kevin 1949-...............CLC 26
See also CA 97-100
See also SATA 32

Malamud, Bernard
1914-......CLC 1, 2, 3, 5, 8, 9, 11, 18, 27
See also CA 5-8R
See also DLB 2
See also DLB-Y 80

Mallarmé, Stéphane
1842-1898.................. NCLC 4

Mallet-Joris, Françoise 1930-.......CLC 11
See also CA 65-68

Maloff, Saul 1922-.................CLC 5
See also CA 33-36R

Malouf, David 1934-..............CLC 28

Malraux, (Georges-) André
1901-1976......... CLC 1, 4, 9, 13, 15
See also CAP 2
See also CA 21-24R
See also obituary CA 69-72

Malzberg, Barry N. 1939- .... CLC 7
See also CA 61-64
See also DLB 8

Mamet, David 1947- .... CLC 9, 15
See also CA 81-84
See also DLB 7

Mamoulian, Rouben 1898- .... CLC 16
See also CA 25-28R

Mandelstam, Osip (Emilievich) 1891?-1938? .... TCLC 2, 6
See also CA 104

Manley, Mary Delariviere ?-1724 ..... LC 1

Mann, (Luiz) Heinrich 1871-1950 .... TCLC 9
See also CA 106

Mann, Thomas 1875-1955 ...... TCLC 2, 8
See also CA 104

Manning, Olivia 1915-1980 ..... CLC 5, 19
See also CA 5-8R
See also obituary CA 101

Mano, D. Keith 1942- .... CLC 2, 10
See also CA 25-28R
See also DLB 6

Mansfield, Katherine 1888-1923 .... TCLC 2, 8
See also CA 104

Marcel, Gabriel (Honore) 1889-1973 .... CLC 15
See also CA 102
See also obituary CA 45-48

Marchbanks, Samuel 1913-
See Davies, (William) Robertson

Marinetti, F(ilippo) T(ommaso) 1876-1944 .... TCLC 10
See also CA 107

Markandaya, Kamala (Purnaiya) 1924- .... CLC 8
See also Taylor, Kamala (Purnaiya)

Markfield, Wallace (Arthur) 1926- .... CLC 8
See also CA 69-72
See also DLB 2

Markham, Robert 1922-
See Amis, Kingsley (William)

Marks, J. 1942-
See Highwater, Jamake

Marley, Bob 1945-1981 .... CLC 17
See also Marley, Robert Nesta

Marley, Robert Nesta 1945-1981
See Marley, Bob
See also CA 107
See also obituary CA 103

Marquand, John P(hillips) 1893-1960 .... CLC 2, 10
See also CA 85-88
See also DLB 9

Márquez, Gabriel García 1928-
See García Márquez, Gabriel

Marquis, Don(ald Robert Perry) 1878-1937 .... TCLC 7
See also CA 104
See also DLB 11, 25

Marryat, Frederick 1792-1848 .... NCLC 3
See also DLB 21

Marsh, (Edith) Ngaio 1899-1982 .... CLC 7
See also CANR 6
See also CA 9-12R

Marshall, Garry 1935?- .... CLC 17
See also CA 111

Marshall, Paule 1929- .... CLC 27
See also CA 77-80

Marsten, Richard 1926-
See Hunter, Evan

Martínez Ruiz, José 1874-1967
See Azorín
See also CA 93-96

Martínez Sierra, Gregorio 1881-1947
See Martínez Sierra, Gregorio and Martínez Sierra, María (de la O'LeJárraga)
See also CA 104

Martínez Sierra, Gregorio 1881-1947 and **Martínez Sierra, María (de la O'LeJárraga)** 1880?-1974 .... TCLC 6

Martínez Sierra, María (de la O'LeJárraga) 1880?-1974
See Martínez Sierra, Gregorio and Martínez Sierra, María (de la O'LeJárraga)

Martínez Sierra, María (de la O'LeJárraga) 1880?-1974 and **Martínez Sierra, Gregorio** 1881-1947
See Martínez Sierra, Gregorio and Martínez Sierra, María (de la O'LeJárraga)

Martinson, Harry (Edmund) 1904-1978 .... CLC 14
See also CA 77-80

Masefield, John (Edward) 1878-1967 .... CLC 11
See also CAP 2
See also CA 19-20
See also obituary CA 25-28R
See also SATA 19
See also DLB 10, 19

Mason, Bobbie Ann 1940- .... CLC 28
See also CANR 11
See also CA 53-56

Masters, Edgar Lee 1868?-1950 .... TCLC 2
See also CA 104

Mathews, Harry 1930- .... CLC 6
See also CA 21-24R

Matthias, John (Edward) 1941- ...... CLC 9
See also CA 33-36R

Matthiessen, Peter 1927- ..... CLC 5, 7, 11
See also CA 9-12R
See also SATA 27
See also DLB 6

Maturin, Charles Robert 1780?-1824 .... NCLC 6

Matute, Ana María 1925- .... CLC 11
See also CA 89-92

Maugham, W(illiam) Somerset 1874-1965 .... CLC 1, 11, 15
See also CA 5-8R
See also obituary CA 25-28R
See also DLB 10

Maupassant, (Henri René Albert) Guy de 1850-1893 .... NCLC 1

Mauriac, Claude 1914- .... CLC 9
See also CA 89-92

Mauriac, François (Charles) 1885-1970 .... CLC 4, 9
See also CAP 2
See also CA 25-28

Maxwell, William (Keepers, Jr.) 1908- .... CLC 19
See also CA 93-96
See also DLB-Y 80

May, Elaine 1932- .... CLC 16

Mayakovsky, Vladimir (Vladimirovich) 1893-1930 .... TCLC 4
See also CA 104

Maynard, Joyce 1953- .... CLC 23
See also CA 111

Mayne, William (James Carter) 1928- .... CLC 12
See also CA 9-12R
See also SATA 6

Mayo, Jim 1908?-
See L'Amour, Louis (Dearborn)

Maysles, Albert 1926-
See Maysles, Albert and Maysles, David
See also CA 29-32R

Maysles, Albert 1926- and **Maysles, David** 1932- .... CLC 16

Maysles, David 1932-
See Maysles, Albert and Maysles, David

Mazer, Norma Fox 1931- .... CLC 26
See also CA 69-72
See also SATA 24

McBain, Ed 1926-
See Hunter, Evan

McCaffrey, Anne 1926- .... CLC 17
See also CA 25-28R
See also SATA 8
See also DLB 8
See also AITN 2

McCarthy, Cormac 1933- .... CLC 4
See also CANR 10
See also CA 13-16R
See also DLB 6

McCarthy, Mary (Therese) 1912- .... CLC 1, 3, 5, 14, 24
See also CA 5-8R
See also DLB 2
See also DLB-Y 81

McCartney, Paul 1942-
See Lennon, John (Ono) and McCartney, Paul

McClure, Michael 1932- .... CLC 6, 10
See also CA 21-24R
See also DLB 16

McCourt, James 1941- .... CLC 5
See also CA 57-60

McCrae, John 1872-1918 .... TCLC 12

McCullers, (Lula) Carson 1917-1967 .... CLC 1, 4, 10, 12
See also CA 5-8R
See also obituary CA 25-28R
See also SATA 27
See also DLB 2, 7

McCullough, Colleen 1938?- .... CLC 27
See also CA 81-84

McElroy, Joseph 1930- .... CLC 5
See also CA 17-20R

McEwan, Ian 1948-............... **CLC 13**
See also CA 61-64
See also DLB 14

McGahern, John 1935-.......... **CLC 5, 9**
See also CA 17-20R
See also DLB 14

McGinley, Phyllis 1905-1978....... **CLC 14**
See also CA 9-12R
See also obituary CA 77-80
See also SATA 2
See also obituary SATA 24
See also DLB 11

McGivern, Maureen Daly 1921-
See Daly, Maureen
See also CA 9-12R

McGrath, Thomas 1916- .... **CLC 28**
See also CANR 6
See also CA 9-12R

McGuane, Thomas (Francis III)
1939-.................... **CLC 3, 7, 18**
See also CANR 5
See also CA 49-52
See also DLB 2
See also DLB-Y 80
See also AITN 2

McHale, Tom 1941-1982 .... **CLC 3, 5**
See also CA 77-80
See also obituary CA 106
See also AITN 1

McIlwraith, Maureen Mollie Hunter 1922-
See Hunter, Mollie
See also CA 29-32R
See also SATA 2

McIntyre, Vonda N(eel) 1948-...... **CLC 18**
See also CA 81-84

McKay, Claude 1889-1948........ **TCLC 7**
See also CA 104
See also DLB 4

McKuen, Rod 1933- .... **CLC 1, 3**
See also CA 41-44R
See also AITN 1

McManus, Declan Patrick 1955-
See Costello, Elvis

McMurtry, Larry (Jeff)
1936-............. **CLC 2, 3, 7, 11, 27**
See also CA 5-8R
See also DLB 2
See also DLB-Y 80
See also AITN 2

McNally, Terrence 1939- .... **CLC 4, 7**
See also CANR 2
See also CA 45-48
See also DLB 7

McPherson, James Alan 1943- ..... **CLC 19**
See also CA 25-28R

Meaker, Marijane 1927-
See Kerr, M. E.
See also CA 107
See also SATA 20

Medoff, Mark (Howard)
1940-..................... **CLC 6, 23**
See also CANR 5
See also CA 53-56
See also DLB 7
See also AITN 1

Megged, Aharon 1920-............. **CLC 9**
See also CANR 1
See also CA 49-52

Meltzer, Milton 1915-............. **CLC 26**
See also CA 13-16R
See also SATA 1

Melville, Herman 1819-1891 ...... **NCLC 3**
See also DLB 3

Mencken, H(enry) L(ouis)
1880-1956.................. **TCLC 13**
See also CA 105
See also DLB 11

Mercer, David 1928-1980........... **CLC 5**
See also CA 9-12R
See also obituary CA 102
See also DLB 13

Meredith, William (Morris)
1919-.................. **CLC 4, 13, 22**
See also CANR 6
See also CA 9-12R
See also DLB 5

Mérimée, Prosper 1803-1870...... **NCLC 6**

Merrill, James (Ingram)
1926-........... **CLC 2, 3, 6, 8, 13, 18**
See also CANR 10
See also CA 13-16R
See also DLB 5

Merton, Thomas (James)
1915-1968............... **CLC 1, 3, 11**
See also CA 5-8R
See also obituary CA 25-28R
See also DLB-Y 81

Merwin, W(illiam) S(tanley)
1927-.........**CLC 1, 2, 3, 5, 8, 13, 18**
See also CA 13-16R
See also DLB 5

Mew, Charlotte (Mary)
1870-1928................... **TCLC 8**
See also CA 105
See also DLB 19

Mewshaw, Michael 1943-........... **CLC 9**
See also CANR 7
See also CA 53-56
See also DLB-Y 80

Meynell, Alice (Christiana Gertrude Thompson) 1847-1922 .... **TCLC 6**
See also CA 104
See also DLB 19

Michaels, Leonard 1933- .... **CLC 6, 25**
See also CA 61-64

Michaux, Henri 1899-.......... **CLC 8, 19**
See also CA 85-88

Michener, James A(lbert)
1907-................**CLC 1, 5, 11, 29**
See also CA 5-8R
See also DLB 6
See also AITN 1

Mickiewicz, Adam 1798-1855 ..... **NCLC 3**

Middleton, Christopher 1926-...... **CLC 13**
See also CA 13-16R

Middleton, Stanley 1919-........... **CLC 7**
See also CA 25-28R
See also DLB 14

Miguéis, José Rodrigues 1901- ..... **CLC 10**

Miles, Josephine 1911-....... **CLC 1, 2, 14**
See also CANR 2
See also CA 1-4R

Millar, Kenneth 1915-1983
See Macdonald, Ross
See also CA 9-12R
See also obituary CA 110
See also DLB 2

Millay, Edna St. Vincent
1892-1950................... **TCLC 4**
See also CA 104

Miller, Arthur
1915-.......... **CLC 1, 2, 6, 10, 15, 26**
See also CANR 2
See also CA 1-4R
See also DLB 7
See also AITN 1

Miller, Henry (Valentine)
1891-1980.......... **CLC 1, 2, 4, 9, 14**
See also CA 9-12R
See also obituary CA 97-100
See also DLB 4, 9
See also DLB-Y 80

Miller, Jason 1939?-............... **CLC 2**
See also CA 73-76
See also DLB 7
See also AITN 1

Miller, Walter M(ichael), Jr.
1923-......................... **CLC 4**
See also CA 85-88
See also DLB 8

Millhauser, Steven 1943- .... **CLC 21**
See also CA 108, 110, 111
See also DLB 2

Milne, A(lan) A(lexander)
1882-1956................... **TCLC 6**
See also CLR 1
See also CA 104
See also YABC 1
See also DLB 10

Miłosz, Czesław 1911-....... **CLC 5, 11, 22**
See also CA 81-84

Miró (Ferrer), Gabriel (Francisco Víctor)
1879-1930................... **TCLC 5**
See also CA 104

Mishima, Yukio
1925-1970.......... **CLC 2, 4, 6, 9, 27**
See also Hiraoka, Kimitake

Mistral, Gabriela 1889-1957 ...... **TCLC 2**
See also CA 104

Mitchell, James Leslie 1901-1935
See Gibbon, Lewis Grassic
See also CA 104
See also DLB 15

Mitchell, Joni 1943-............... **CLC 12**

Mitchell (Marsh), Margaret (Munnerlyn)
1900-1949.................. **TCLC 11**
See also CA 109
See also DLB 9

Mitchell, W(illiam) O(rmond)
1914-......................... **CLC 25**
See also CA 77-80

Mitford, Mary Russell
1787-1855................... **NCLC 4**

Modiano, Patrick (Jean) 1945- ..... **CLC 18**
See also CA 85-88

Mohr, Nicholasa 1935-............ **CLC 12**
See also CANR 1
See also CA 49-52
See also SATA 8

Mojtabai, A(nn) G(race) 1938- . . . . CLC 5, 9, 15, 29
See also CA 85-88

Momaday, N(avarre) Scott 1934- . . . . CLC 2, 19
See also CA 25-28R
See also SATA 30

Monroe, Harriet 1860-1936 . . . . TCLC 12
See also CA 109

Montague, John (Patrick) 1929- . . . . CLC 13
See also CANR 9
See also CA 9-12R

Montale, Eugenio 1896-1981 . . . . CLC 7, 9, 18
See also CA 17-20R
See also obituary CA 104

Montgomery, Marion (H., Jr.) 1925- . . . . CLC 7
See also CANR 3
See also CA 1-4R
See also DLB 6
See also AITN 1

Montgomery, Robert Bruce 1921-1978
See Crispin, Edmund
See also CA 104

Montherlant, Henri (Milon) de 1896-1972 . . . . CLC 8, 19
See also CA 85-88
See also obituary CA 37-40R

Monty Python . . . . CLC 21

Mooney, Ted 1951- . . . . CLC 25

Moorcock, Michael (John) 1939- . . . . CLC 5, 27
See also CANR 2
See also CA 45-48
See also DLB 14

Moore, Brian 1921- . . . . CLC 1, 3, 5, 7, 8, 19
See also CANR 1
See also CA 1-4R

Moore, George (Augustus) 1852-1933 . . . . TCLC 7
See also CA 104
See also DLB 10, 18

Moore, Marianne (Craig) 1887-1972 . . . . CLC 1, 2, 4, 8, 10, 13, 19
See also CANR 3
See also CA 1-4R
See also obituary CA 33-36R
See also SATA 20

Moore, Thomas 1779-1852 . . . . NCLC 6

Morante, Elsa 1918- . . . . CLC 8
See also CA 85-88

Moravia, Alberto 1907- . . . . CLC 2, 7, 11, 18, 27
See also Pincherle, Alberto

Morgan, Berry 1919- . . . . CLC 6
See also CA 49-52
See also DLB 6

Morgan, Frederick 1922- . . . . CLC 23
See also CA 17-20R

Morgan, Robin 1941- . . . . CLC 2
See also CA 69-72

Morgenstern, Christian (Otto Josef Wolfgang) 1871-1914 . . . . TCLC 8
See also CA 105

Morris, Steveland Judkins 1950-
See Wonder, Stevie
See also CA 111

Morris, William 1834-1896 . . . . NCLC 4
See also DLB 18

Morris, Wright 1910- . . . . CLC 1, 3, 7, 18
See also CA 9-12R
See also DLB 2
See also DLB-Y 81

Morrison, James Douglas 1943-1971
See Morrison, Jim
See also CA 73-76

Morrison, Jim 1943-1971 . . . . CLC 17
See also Morrison, James Douglas

Morrison, Toni 1931- . . . . CLC 4, 10, 22
See also CA 29-32R
See also DLB 6
See also DLB-Y 81

Morrison, Van 1945- . . . . CLC 21

Mortimer, John (Clifford) 1923- . . . . CLC 28
See also CA 13-16R
See also DLB 13

Mortimer, Penelope (Ruth) 1918- . . . . CLC 5
See also CA 57-60

Moss, Howard 1922- . . . . CLC 7, 14
See also CANR 1
See also CA 1-4R
See also DLB 5

Motley, Willard (Francis) 1912-1965 . . . . CLC 18
See also obituary CA 106

Mott, Michael (Charles Alston) 1930- . . . . CLC 15
See also CANR 7
See also CA 5-8R

Mowat, Farley 1921- . . . . CLC 26
See also CANR 4
See also CA 1-4R
See also SATA 3

Mphahlele, Es'kia 1919-
See Mphahlele, Ezekiel

Mphahlele, Ezekiel 1919- . . . . CLC 25
See also CA 81-84

Mrożek, Sławomir 1930- . . . . CLC 3, 13
See also CA 13-16R

Mueller, Lisel 1924- . . . . CLC 13
See also CA 93-96

Muir, Edwin 1887-1959 . . . . TCLC 2
See also CA 104
See also DLB 20

Mull, Martin 1943- . . . . CLC 17
See also CA 105

Munro, Alice 1931- . . . . CLC 6, 10, 19
See also CA 33-36R
See also SATA 29
See also AITN 2

Munro, H(ector) H(ugh) 1870-1916
See Saki
See also CA 104

Murdoch, (Jean) Iris 1919- . . . . CLC 1, 2, 3, 4, 6, 8, 11, 15, 22
See also CANR 8
See also CA 13-16R
See also DLB 14

Musgrave, Susan 1951- . . . . CLC 13
See also CA 69-72

Musil, Robert (Edler von) 1880-1942 . . . . TCLC 12
See also CA 109

Nabokov, Vladimir (Vladimirovich) 1899-1977 . . . . CLC 1, 2, 3, 6, 8, 11, 15, 23
See also CA 5-8R
See also obituary CA 69-72
See also DLB 2
See also DLB-Y 80
See also DLB-DS 3

Nagy, László 1925- . . . . CLC 7

Naipaul, V(idiadhar) S(urajprasad) 1932- . . . . CLC 4, 7, 9, 13, 18
See also CANR 1
See also CA 1-4R

Nakos, Ioulia 1899?-
See Nakos, Lilika

Nakos, Lilika 1899?- . . . . CLC 29

Nakou, Lilika 1899?-
See Nakos, Lilika

Narayan, R(asipuram) K(rishnaswami) 1907- . . . . CLC 7, 28
See also CA 81-84

Nash, (Fredric) Ogden 1902-1971 . . . . CLC 23
See also CAP 1
See also CA 13-14
See also obituary CA 29-32R
See also SATA 2
See also DLB 11

Natsume, Sōseki 1867-1916 . . . . TCLC 2, 10
See also CA 104

Natti, (Mary) Lee 1919-
See Kingman, (Mary) Lee
See also CANR 2

Naylor, Gloria 1950- . . . . CLC 28
See also CA 107

Nelson, Willie 1933- . . . . CLC 17
See also CA 107

Nemerov, Howard 1920- . . . . CLC 2, 6, 9
See also CANR 1
See also CA 1-4R
See also DLB 5, 6

Neruda, Pablo 1904-1973 . . . . CLC 1, 2, 5, 7, 9, 28
See also CAP 2
See also CA 19-20
See also obituary CA 45-48

Nerval, Gérard de 1808-1855 . . . . NCLC 1

Nervo, (José) Amado (Ruiz de) 1870-1919 . . . . TCLC 11
See also CA 109

Neufeld, John (Arthur) 1938- . . . . CLC 17
See also CANR 11
See also CA 25-28R
See also SATA 6

Neville, Emily Cheney 1919- .... **CLC 12**
See also CANR 3
See also CA 5-8R
See also SATA 1

Newbound, Bernard Slade 1930-
See Slade, Bernard
See also CA 81-84

Newby, P(ercy) H(oward) 1918- .... **CLC 2, 13**
See also CA 5-8R
See also DLB 15

Newlove, Donald 1928- .... **CLC 6**
See also CA 29-32R

Newlove, John (Herbert) 1938- ..... **CLC 14**
See also CANR 9
See also CA 21-24R

Newman, Charles 1938- .... **CLC 2, 8**
See also CA 21-24R

Newman, Edwin (Harold) 1919- .... **CLC 14**
See also CANR 5
See also CA 69-72
See also AITN 1

Ngugi, James (Thiong'o) 1938- .... **CLC 3, 7**
See also Wa Thiong'o, Ngugi
See also CA 81-84

Ngugi Wa Thiong'o 1938-
See Ngugi, James
See Wa Thiong'o, Ngugi

Nichol, B(arne) P(hillip) 1944- ...... **CLC 18**
See also CA 53-56

Nichols, Peter 1927- .... **CLC 5**
See also CA 104
See also DLB 13

Niedecker, Lorine 1903-1970 .... **CLC 10**
See also CAP 2
See also CA 25-28

Nietzsche, Friedrich (Wilhelm) 1844-1900 .... **TCLC 10**
See also CA 107

Nightingale, Anne Redmon 1943-
See Redmon (Nightingale), Anne
See also CA 103

Nin, Anaïs 1903-1977 .... **CLC 1, 4, 8, 11, 14**
See also CA 13-16R
See also obituary CA 69-72
See also DLB 2, 4
See also AITN 2

Nissenson, Hugh 1933- .... **CLC 4, 9**
See also CA 17-20R

Niven, Larry 1938- .... **CLC 8**
See also Niven, Laurence Van Cott
See also DLB 8

Niven, Laurence Van Cott 1938-
See Niven, Larry
See also CA 21-24R

Nixon, Agnes Eckhardt 1927- ...... **CLC 21**
See also CA 110

Norman, Marsha 1947- .... **CLC 28**
See also CA 105

Norris, Leslie 1921- .... **CLC 14**
See also CAP 1
See also CA 11-12

North, Andrew 1912-
See Norton, Andre

North, Christopher 1785-1854
See Wilson, John

Norton, Alice Mary 1912-
See Norton, Andre
See also CANR 2
See also CA 1-4R
See also SATA 1

Norton, Andre 1912- .... **CLC 12**
See also DLB 8

Nossack, Hans Erich 1901-1978 ..... **CLC 6**
See also CA 93-96
See also obituary CA 85-88

Nova, Craig 1945- .... **CLC 7**
See also CANR 2
See also CA 45-48

Nowlan, Alden (Albert) 1933- ...... **CLC 15**
See also CANR 5
See also CA 9-12R

Noyes, Alfred 1880-1958 .... **TCLC 7**
See also CA 104
See also DLB 20

Nye, Robert 1939- .... **CLC 13**
See also CA 33-36R
See also SATA 6
See also DLB 14

Nyro, Laura 1947- .... **CLC 17**

Oates, Joyce Carol 1938- ..... **CLC 1, 2, 3, 6, 9, 11, 15, 19**
See also CA 5-8R
See also DLB 2, 5
See also DLB-Y 81
See also AITN 1

O'Brien, Darcy 1939- .... **CLC 11**
See also CANR 8
See also CA 21-24R

O'Brien, Edna 1932- .... **CLC 3, 5, 8, 13**
See also CANR 6
See also CA 1-4R
See also DLB 14

O'Brien, Flann 1911-1966 .... **CLC 1, 4, 5, 7, 10**
See also O Nuallain, Brian

O'Brien, Richard 19?- .... **CLC 17**

O'Brien, Tim 1946- .... **CLC 7, 19**
See also CA 85-88
See also DLB-Y 80

O'Casey, Sean 1880-1964 .... **CLC 1, 5, 9, 11, 15**
See also CA 89-92
See also DLB 10

Ochs, Phil 1940-1976 .... **CLC 17**
See also obituary CA 65-68

O'Connor, Edwin (Greene) 1918-1968 .... **CLC 14**
See also CA 93-96
See also obituary CA 25-28R

O'Connor, (Mary) Flannery 1925-1964 ...... **CLC 1, 2, 3, 6, 10, 13, 15, 21**
See also CANR 3
See also CA 1-4R
See also DLB 2
See also DLB-Y 80

O'Connor, Frank 1903-1966 .... **CLC 14, 23**
See also O'Donovan, Michael (John)

Odets, Clifford 1906-1963 ...... **CLC 2, 28**
See also CA 85-88
See also DLB 7, 26

O'Donovan, Michael (John) 1903-1966
See O'Connor, Frank
See also CA 93-96

Ōe, Kenzaburō 1935- .... **CLC 10**
See also CA 97-100

O'Faolain, Julia .... **CLC 6, 19**
See also CA 81-84
See also DLB 14

O'Faoláin, Seán 1900- .... **CLC 1, 7, 14**
See also CA 61-64
See also DLB 15

O'Flaherty, Liam 1896- .... **CLC 5**
See also CA 101

O'Grady, Standish (James) 1846-1928 .... **TCLC 5**
See also CA 104

O'Hara, Frank 1926-1966 .... **CLC 2, 5, 13**
See also CA 9-12R
See also obituary CA 25-28R
See also DLB 5, 16

O'Hara, John (Henry) 1905-1970 .... **CLC 1, 2, 3, 6, 11**
See also CA 5-8R
See also obituary CA 25-28R
See also DLB 9
See also DLB-DS 2

Okigbo, Christopher (Ifenayichukwu) 1932-1967 .... **CLC 25**
See also CA 77-80

Olesha, Yuri (Karlovich) 1899-1960 .... **CLC 8**
See also CA 85-88

Oliver, Mary 1935- .... **CLC 19**
See also CANR 9
See also CA 21-24R
See also DLB 5

Olivier, (Baron) Laurence 1907- .... **CLC 20**
See also CA 111

Olsen, Tillie 1913- .... **CLC 4, 13**
See also CANR 1
See also CA 1-4R
See also DLB-Y 80

Olson, Charles (John) 1910-1970 .... **CLC 1, 2, 5, 6, 9, 11, 29**
See also CAP 1
See also CA 15-16
See also obituary CA 25-28R
See also DLB 5, 16

Olson, Theodore 1937-
See Olson, Toby

Olson, Toby 1937- .... **CLC 28**
See also CANR 9
See also CA 65-68

Ondaatje, (Philip) Michael 1943- .... **CLC 14, 29**
See also CA 77-80

O'Neill, Eugene (Gladstone) 1888-1953 .... TCLC 1, 6
See also CA 110
See also AITN 1
See also DLB 7

Onetti, Juan Carlos 1909- ...... CLC 7, 10
See also CA 85-88

O'Nolan, Brian 1911-1966
See O'Brien, Flann

O Nuallain, Brian 1911-1966
See O'Brien, Flann
See also CAP 2
See also CA 21-22
See also obituary CA 25-28R

Oppen, George 1908- .... CLC 7, 13
See also CANR 8
See also CA 13-16R
See also DLB 5

Orlovitz, Gil 1918-1973 .... CLC 22
See also CA 77-80
See also obituary CA 45-48
See also DLB 2, 5

Ortega y Gasset, José 1883-1955 .... TCLC 9
See also CA 106

Orton, Joe 1933?-1967 .... CLC 4, 13
See also Orton, John Kingsley
See also DLB 13

Orton, John Kingsley 1933?-1967
See Orton, Joe
See also CA 85-88

Orwell, George 1903-1950 ...... TCLC 2, 6
See also CA 104
See also SATA 29
See also DLB 15

Osborne, John (James) 1929- .... CLC 1, 2, 5, 11
See also CA 13-16R
See also DLB 13

Osceola 1885-1962
See Dinesen, Isak
See also Blixen, Karen (Christentze Dinesen)

Oshima, Nagisa 1932- .... CLC 20

Ossoli, Sarah Margaret (Fuller marchesa d') 1810-1850
See Fuller, (Sarah) Margaret
See also SATA 25

Otero, Blas de 1916- .... CLC 11
See also CA 89-92

Owen, Wilfred (Edward Salter) 1893-1918 .... TCLC 5
See also CA 104
See also DLB 20

Owens, Rochelle 1936- .... CLC 8
See also CA 17-20R

Owl, Sebastian 1939-
See Thompson, Hunter S(tockton)

Oz, Amos 1939- .... CLC 5, 8, 11, 27
See also CA 53-56

Ozick, Cynthia 1928- .... CLC 3, 7, 28
See also CA 17-20R
See also DLB-Y 82

Ozu, Yasujiro 1903-1963 .... CLC 16

Pa Chin 1904- .... CLC 18
See also Li Fei-kan

Pack, Robert 1929- .... CLC 13
See also CANR 3
See also CA 1-4R
See also DLB 5

Padgett, Lewis 1915-1958
See Kuttner, Henry

Page, Jimmy 1944-
See Page, Jimmy and Plant, Robert

Page, Jimmy 1944- and **Plant, Robert** 1948- .... CLC 12

Page, P(atricia) K(athleen) 1916- .... CLC 7, 18
See also CANR 4
See also CA 53-56

Paget, Violet 1856-1935
See Lee, Vernon
See also CA 104

Palamas, Kostes 1859-1943 .... TCLC 5
See also CA 105

Palazzeschi, Aldo 1885-1974 .... CLC 11
See also CA 89-92
See also obituary CA 53-56

Paley, Grace 1922- .... CLC 4, 6
See also CA 25-28R
See also AITN 1

Palin, Michael 1943-
See Monty Python
See also CA 107

Pancake, Breece Dexter 1952-1979
See Pancake, Breece D'J

Pancake, Breece D'J 1952-1979 .... CLC 29
See also obituary CA 109

Parker, Dorothy (Rothschild) 1893-1967 .... CLC 15
See also CAP 2
See also CA 19-20
See also obituary CA 25-28R
See also DLB 11

Parker, Robert B(rown) 1932- ...... CLC 27
See also CANR 1
See also CA 49-52

Parks, Gordon (Alexander Buchanan) 1912- .... CLC 1, 16
See also CA 41-44R
See also SATA 8
See also AITN 2

Parra, Nicanor 1914- .... CLC 2
See also CA 85-88

Pasolini, Pier Paolo 1922-1975 ..... CLC 20
See also CA 93-96
See also obituary CA 61-64

Pasternak, Boris 1890-1960 .... CLC 7, 10, 18

Pastan, Linda (Olenik) 1932- .... CLC 27
See also CA 61-64
See also DLB 5

Patchen, Kenneth 1911-1972 .... CLC 1, 2, 18
See also CANR 3
See also CA 1-4R
See also obituary CA 33-36R
See also DLB 16

Paterson, Katherine (Womeldorf) 1932- .... CLC 12
See also CA 21-24R
See also SATA 13

Paton, Alan (Stewart) 1903- .... CLC 4, 10, 25
See also CAP 1
See also CA 15-16
See also SATA 11

Paulding, James Kirke 1778-1860 .... NCLC 2
See also DLB 3

Pavese, Cesare 1908-1950 .... TCLC 3
See also CA 104

Payne, Alan 1932-
See Jakes, John (William)

Paz, Octavio 1914- ..... CLC 3, 4, 6, 10, 19
See also CA 73-76

Peake, Mervyn 1911-1968 .... CLC 7
See also CANR 3
See also CA 5-8R
See also obituary CA 25-28R
See also SATA 23
See also DLB 15

Pearce, (Ann) Philippa 1920- .... CLC 21
See also Christie, (Ann) Philippa
See also CA 5-8R
See also SATA 1

Pearl, Eric 1934-
See Elman, Richard

Peck, John 1941- .... CLC 3
See also CANR 3
See also CA 49-52

Peck, Richard 1934- .... CLC 21
See also CA 85-88
See also SATA 18

Peck, Robert Newton 1928- .... CLC 17
See also CA 81-84
See also SATA 21

Peckinpah, (David) Sam(uel) 1925- .... CLC 20
See also CA 109

Péguy, Charles (Pierre) 1873-1914 .... TCLC 10
See also CA 107

Percy, Walker 1916- .... CLC 2, 3, 6, 8, 14, 18
See also CANR 1
See also CA 1-4R
See also DLB 2
See also DLB-Y 80

Perelman, S(idney) J(oseph) 1904-1979 .... CLC 3, 5, 9, 15, 23
See also CA 73-76
See also obituary CA 89-92
See also DLB 11
See also AITN 1, 2

Perse, St.-John 1887-1975 ...... CLC 4, 11
See also Léger, (Marie-Rene) Alexis Saint-Léger

Pesetsky, Bette 1932- .... CLC 28

Peters, Robert L(ouis) 1924- .... CLC 7
See also CA 13-16R

Petrakis, Harry Mark 1923- .... CLC 3
See also CANR 4
See also CA 9-12R

Petry, Ann (Lane) 1912- ...... CLC 1, 7, 18
See also CANR 4
See also CA 5-8R
See also SATA 5

Phillips, Jayne Anne 1952- . . . . **CLC 15**
See also CA 101
See also DLB-Y 80

Phillips, Robert (Schaeffer)
1938- . . . . **CLC 28**
See also CANR 8
See also CA 17-20R

Piccolo, Lucio 1901-1969 . . . . **CLC 13**
See also CA 97-100

Piercy, Marge
1936- . . . . **CLC 3, 6, 14, 18, 27**
See also CA 21-24R

Pincherle, Alberto 1907-
See Moravia, Alberto
See also CA 25-28R

Pinero, Miguel (Gomez) 1947?- . . . . . . **CLC 4**
See also CA 61-64

Pinget, Robert 1919- . . . . **CLC 7, 13**
See also CA 85-88

Pinsky, Robert 1940- . . . . **CLC 9, 19**
See also CA 29-32R
See also DLB-Y 82

Pinter, Harold
1930- . . . . **CLC 1, 3, 6, 9, 11, 15, 27**
See also CA 5-8R
See also DLB 13

Pirandello, Luigi 1867-1936 . . . . **TCLC 4**
See also CA 104

Pirsig, Robert M(aynard)
1928- . . . . **CLC 4, 6**
See also CA 53-56

Plaidy, Jean 1906-
See Hibbert, Eleanor (Burford)

Plant, Robert 1948-
See Page, Jimmy and Plant, Robert

Plante, David 1940- . . . . **CLC 7, 23**
See also CA 37-40R

Plath, Sylvia
1932-1963 . . . . **CLC 1, 2, 3, 5, 9, 11, 14, 17**
See also CAP 2
See also CA 19-20
See also DLB 5, 6

Platt, Kin 1911- . . . . **CLC 26**
See also CA 17-20R
See also SATA 21

Plomer, William (Charles Franklin)
1903-1973 . . . . **CLC 4, 8**
See also CAP 2
See also CA 21-22
See also SATA 24
See also DLB 20

Poe, Edgar Allan 1809-1849 . . . . . . **NCLC 1**
See also SATA 23
See also DLB 3

Pohl, Frederik 1919- . . . . **CLC 18**
See also CANR 11
See also CA 61-64
See also SATA 24
See also DLB 8

Poirier, Louis 1910-
See Gracq, Julien

Poitier, Sidney 1924?- . . . . **CLC 26**

Polanski, Roman 1933- . . . . **CLC 16**
See also CA 77-80

Police, The . . . . **CLC 26**

Pollitt, Katha 1949- . . . . **CLC 28**

Pomerance, Bernard 1940- . . . . **CLC 13**
See also CA 101

Ponge, Francis (Jean Gaston Alfred)
1899- . . . . **CLC 6, 18**
See also CA 85-88

Poole, Josephine 1933- . . . . **CLC 17**
See also CANR 10
See also CA 21-24R
See also SATA 5

Popa, Vasko 1922- . . . . **CLC 19**

Porter, Katherine Anne
1890-1980 . . . . . **CLC 1, 3, 7, 10, 13, 15, 27**
See also CANR 1
See also CA 1-4R
See also obituary CA 101
See also obituary SATA 23
See also DLB 4, 9
See also DLB-Y 80
See also AITN 2

Porter, Peter (Neville Frederick)
1929- . . . . **CLC 5, 13**
See also CA 85-88

Porter, William Sydney 1862-1909?
See Henry, O.
See also CA 104
See also YABC 2
See also DLB 12

Potok, Chaim 1929- . . . . **CLC 2, 7, 14, 26**
See also CA 17-20R
See also SATA 33
See also AITN 1, 2

Pound, Ezra (Loomis)
1885-1972 . . . . . **CLC 1, 2, 3, 4, 5, 7, 10, 13, 18**
See also CA 5-8R
See also obituary CA 37-40R
See also DLB 4

Powell, Anthony (Dymoke)
1905- . . . . **CLC 1, 3, 7, 9, 10**
See also CANR 1
See also CA 1-4R
See also DLB 15

Powers, J(ames) F(arl)
1917- . . . . **CLC 1, 4, 8**
See also CANR 2
See also CA 1-4R

Pownall, David 1938- . . . . **CLC 10**
See also CA 89-92
See also DLB 14

Powys, John Cowper
1872-1963 . . . . **CLC 7, 9, 15**
See also CA 85-88
See also DLB 15

Powys, T(heodore) F(rancis)
1875-1953 . . . . **TCLC 9**
See also CA 106

Pratt, E(dwin) J(ohn)
1883-1964 . . . . **CLC 19**
See also obituary CA 93-96

Preussler, Otfried 1923- . . . . **CLC 17**
See also CA 77-80
See also SATA 24

Prévert, Jacques (Henri Marie)
1900-1977 . . . . **CLC 15**
See also CA 77-80
See also obituary CA 69-72
See also obituary SATA 30

Prévost, Abbé (Antoine Francois)
1697-1763 . . . . **LC 1**

Price, (Edward) Reynolds
1933- . . . . **CLC 3, 6, 13**
See also CANR 1
See also CA 1-4R
See also DLB 2

Price, Richard 1949- . . . . **CLC 6, 12**
See also CANR 3
See also CA 49-52
See also DLB-Y 81

Priestley, J(ohn) B(oynton)
1894- . . . . **CLC 2, 5, 9**
See also CA 9-12R
See also DLB 10

Prince, F(rank) T(empleton)
1912- . . . . **CLC 22**
See also CA 101
See also DLB 20

Pritchett, V(ictor) S(awdon)
1900- . . . . **CLC 5, 13, 15**
See also CA 61-64
See also DLB 15

Procaccino, Michael 1946-
See Cristofer, Michael

Prokosch, Frederic 1908- . . . . **CLC 4**
See also CA 73-76

Proust, Marcel 1871-1922 . . . . . **TCLC 7, 13**
See also CA 104

Pryor, Richard 1940- . . . . **CLC 26**

Puig, Manuel 1932- . . . . **CLC 3, 5, 10, 28**
See also CANR 2
See also CA 45-48

Purdy, A(lfred) W(ellington)
1918- . . . . **CLC 3, 6, 14**
See also CA 81-84

Purdy, James (Amos)
1923- . . . . **CLC 2, 4, 10, 28**
See also CA 33-36R
See also DLB 2

Pushkin, Alexander (Sergeyevich)
1799-1837 . . . . **NCLC 3**

Puzo, Mario 1920- . . . . **CLC 1, 2, 6**
See also CANR 4
See also CA 65-68
See also DLB 6

Pym, Barbara (Mary Crampton)
1913-1980 . . . . **CLC 13, 19**
See also CAP 1
See also CA 13-14
See also obituary CA 97-100
See also DLB 14

Pynchon, Thomas
1937- . . . . **CLC 2, 3, 6, 9, 11, 18**
See also CA 17-20R
See also DLB 2

Quasimodo, Salvatore
1901-1968 . . . . **CLC 10**
See also CAP 1
See also CA 15-16
See also obituary CA 25-28R

Queen, Ellery 1905-1982 .... **CLC 3, 11**
See also Dannay, Frederic
See also Lee, Manfred B(ennington)

Queneau, Raymond
1903-1976 .... **CLC 2, 5, 10**
See also CA 77-80
See also obituary CA 69-72

Quin, Ann (Marie) 1936-1973 .... **CLC 6**
See also CA 9-12R
See also obituary CA 45-48
See also DLB 14

Quinn, Simon 1942-
See Smith, Martin Cruz

Quoirez, Françoise 1935-
See Sagan, Françoise
See also CANR 6
See also CA 49-52

Rabe, David (William) 1940- ..... **CLC 4, 8**
See also CA 85-88
See also DLB 7

Radcliffe, Ann (Ward)
1764-1823 .... **NCLC 6**

Rado, James 1939-
See Ragni, Gerome and Rado, James
See also CA 105

Radomski, James 1932-
See Rado, James

Radvanyi, Netty Reiling 1900-1983
See Seghers, Anna
See also CA 85-88
See also obituary CA 110

Ragni, Gerome 1942-
See Ragni, Gerome and Rado, James
See also CA 105

Ragni, Gerome 1942- and **Rado, James**
1939- .... **CLC 17**

Rahv, Philip 1908-1973 .... **CLC 24**
See also Greenberg, Ivan

Raine, Kathleen (Jessie) 1908- .... **CLC 7**
See also CA 85-88
See also DLB 20

Rand, Ayn 1905-1982 .... **CLC 3**
See also CA 13-16R
See also obituary CA 105

Randall, Dudley (Felker) 1914- ...... **CLC 1**
See also CA 25-28R

Ransom, John Crowe
1888-1974 .... **CLC 2, 4, 5, 11, 24**
See also CANR 6
See also CA 5-8R
See also obituary CA 49-52

Rao, Raja 1909- .... **CLC 25**
See also CA 73-76

Raphael, Frederic (Michael)
1931- .... **CLC 2, 14**
See also CANR 1
See also CA 1-4R
See also DLB 14

Rattigan, Terence (Mervyn)
1911-1977 .... **CLC 7**
See also CA 85-88
See also obituary CA 73-76
See also DLB 13

Raven, Simon (Arthur Noel)
1927- .... **CLC 14**
See also CA 81-84

Rawlings, Marjorie Kinnan
1896-1953 .... **TCLC 4**
See also CA 104
See also YABC 1
See also DLB 9, 22

Ray, Satyajit 1921- .... **CLC 16**

Read, Herbert (Edward)
1893-1968 .... **CLC 4**
See also CA 85-88
See also obituary CA 25-28R
See also DLB 20

Read, Piers Paul 1941- ...... **CLC 4, 10, 25**
See also CA 21-24R
See also SATA 21
See also DLB 14

Reade, Charles 1814-1884 .... **NCLC 2**
See also DLB 21

Reaney, James 1926- .... **CLC 13**
See also CA 41-44R

Rechy, John (Francisco)
1934- .... **CLC 1, 7, 14, 18**
See also CANR 6
See also CA 5-8R
See also DLB-Y 82

Redgrove, Peter (William)
1932- .... **CLC 6**
See also CANR 3
See also CA 1-4R

Redmon (Nightingale), Anne
1943- .... **CLC 22**
See also Nightingale, Anne Redmon

Reed, Ishmael 1938- .... **CLC 2, 3, 5, 6, 13**
See also CA 21-24R
See also DLB 2, 5

Reed, John (Silas) 1887-1920...... **TCLC 9**
See also CA 106

Reed, Lou 1944- .... **CLC 21**

Reid Banks, Lynne 1929-
See Banks, Lynne Reid
See also CANR 6
See also CA 1-4R
See also SATA 22

Reiner, Max 1900-
See Caldwell, (Janet Miriam) Taylor (Holland)

Remark, Erich Paul 1898-1970
See Remarque, Erich Maria

Remarque, Erich Maria
1898-1970 .... **CLC 21**
See also CA 77-80
See also obituary CA 29-32R

Renault, Mary 1905- .... **CLC 3, 11, 17**
See also Challans, Mary

Rendell, Ruth 1930- .... **CLC 28**
See also CA 109

Renoir, Jean 1894-1979 .... **CLC 20**
See also obituary CA 85-88

Resnais, Alain 1922- .... **CLC 16**

Rexroth, Kenneth
1905-1982 .... **CLC 1, 2, 6, 11, 22**
See also CA 5-8R
See also obituary CA 107
See also DLB 16
See also DLB-Y 82

Reyes y Basoalto, Ricardo Eliecer Neftali
1904-1973
See Neruda, Pablo

Reymont, Wladyslaw Stanislaw
1867-1925 .... **TCLC 5**
See also CA 104

Reynolds, Jonathan 1942?- .... **CLC 6**
See also CA 65-68

Reznikoff, Charles 1894-1976 .... **CLC 9**
See also CAP 2
See also CA 33-36
See also obituary CA 61-64

Rezzori, Gregor von 1914- .... **CLC 25**

Rhys, Jean
1894-1979 .... **CLC 2, 4, 6, 14, 19**
See also CA 25-28R
See also obituary CA 85-88

Ribeiro, João Ubaldo (Osorio Pimentel)
1941- .... **CLC 10**
See also CA 81-84

Ribman, Ronald (Burt) 1932- .... **CLC 7**
See also CA 21-24R

Rice, Elmer 1892-1967 .... **CLC 7**
See also CAP 2
See also CA 21-22
See also obituary CA 25-28R
See also DLB 4, 7

Rice, Tim 1944-
See Rice, Tim and Webber, Andrew Lloyd
See also CA 103

Rice, Tim 1944- and **Webber, Andrew Lloyd** 1948- .... **CLC 21**

Rich, Adrienne (Cecile)
1929- .... **CLC 3, 6, 7, 11, 18**
See also CA 9-12R
See also DLB 5

Richard, Keith 1943-
See Jagger, Mick and Richard, Keith

Richards, I(vor) A(rmstrong)
1893-1979 .... **CLC 14, 24**
See also CA 41-44R
See also obituary CA 89-92

Richards, Keith 1943-
See Richard, Keith
See also CA 107

Richardson, Dorothy (Miller)
1873-1957 .... **TCLC 3**
See also CA 104

Richardson, Ethel 1870-1946
See Richardson, Henry Handel
See also CA 105

Richardson, Henry Handel
1870-1946 .... **TCLC 4**
See also Ethel Richardson

Richardson, Samuel 1689-1761 .... **LC 1**

Richler, Mordecai
1931- .... **CLC 3, 5, 9, 13, 18**
See also CA 65-68
See also SATA 27
See also AITN 1

Riding, Laura 1901- .... **CLC 3, 7**
See also Jackson, Laura (Riding)

Riefenstahl, Berta Helene Amalia 1902-
See Riefenstahl, Leni
See also CA 108

Riefenstahl, Leni 1902- . . . . **CLC 16**
See also Riefenstahl, Berta Helene Amalia

Rilke, Rainer Maria
1875-1926 . . . . **TCLC 1, 6**
See also CA 104

Rimbaud, (Jean Nicolas) Arthur
1854-1891 . . . . **NCLC 4**

Ritsos, Yannis 1909- . . . . **CLC 6, 13, 29**
See also CA 77-80

Rivers, Conrad Kent 1933-1968 . . . . . **CLC 1**
See also CA 85-88

Robbe-Grillet, Alain
1922- . . . . **CLC 1, 2, 4, 6, 8, 10, 14**
See also CA 9-12R

Robbins, Harold 1916- . . . . **CLC 5**
See also CA 73-76

Robbins, Thomas Eugene 1936-
See Robbins, Tom
See also CA 81-84

Robbins, Tom 1936- . . . . **CLC 9**
See also Robbins, Thomas Eugene
See also DLB-Y 80

Robbins, Trina 1938- . . . . **CLC 21**

Roberts, (Sir) Charles G(eorge) D(ouglas)
1860-1943 . . . . **TCLC 8**
See also CA 105

Roberts, Kate 1891- . . . . **CLC 15**
See also CA 107

Roberts, Keith (John Kingston)
1935- . . . . **CLC 14**
See also CA 25-28R

Robinson, Edwin Arlington
1869-1935 . . . . **TCLC 5**
See also CA 104

Robinson, Jill 1936- . . . . **CLC 10**
See also CA 102

Robinson, Marilynne 1944- . . . . **CLC 25**

Robinson, Smokey 1940- . . . . **CLC 21**

Robinson, William 1940-
See Robinson, Smokey

Roddenberry, Gene 1921- . . . . **CLC 17**

Rodgers, Mary 1931- . . . . **CLC 12**
See also CANR 8
See also CA 49-52
See also SATA 8

Rodgers, W(illiam) R(obert)
1909-1969 . . . . **CLC 7**
See also CA 85-88
See also DLB 20

Rodriguez, Claudio 1934- . . . . **CLC 10**

Roethke, Theodore (Huebner)
1908-1963 . . . . **CLC 1, 3, 8, 11, 19**
See also CA 81-84
See also DLB 5

Rogers, Sam 1943-
See Shepard, Sam

Rogers, Will(iam Penn Adair)
1879-1935 . . . . **TCLC 8**
See also CA 105
See also DLB 11

Rogin, Gilbert 1929- . . . . **CLC 18**
See also CA 65-68

Rohmer, Eric 1920- . . . . **CLC 16**

Roiphe, Anne (Richardson)
1935- . . . . **CLC 3, 9**
See also CA 89-92
See also DLB-Y 80

Rolfe, Frederick (William Serafino Austin Lewis Mary) 1860-1913 . . . . . **TCLC 12**
See also CA 107

Romains, Jules 1885-1972 . . . . **CLC 7**
See also CA 85-88

Rooke, Leon 1934- . . . . **CLC 25**
See also CA 25-28R

Rosa, João Guimarães
1908-1967 . . . . **CLC 23**
See also obituary CA 89-92

Rosenberg, Isaac 1890-1918 . . . . . . **TCLC 12**
See also CA 107
See also DLB 20

Rosenblatt, Joe 1933- . . . . **CLC 15**
See also Rosenblatt, Joseph
See also AITN 2

Rosenblatt, Joseph 1933-
See Rosenblatt, Joe
See also CA 89-92

Rosenthal, M(acha) L(ouis)
1917- . . . . **CLC 28**
See also CANR 4
See also CA 1-4R
See also DLB 5

Ross, (James) Sinclair 1908- . . . . **CLC 13**
See also CA 73-76

Rossetti, Christina Georgina
1830-1894 . . . . **NCLC 2**
See also SATA 20

Rossetti, Dante Gabriel
1828-1882 . . . . **NCLC 4**

Rossetti, Gabriel Charles Dante 1828-1882
See Rossetti, Dante Gabriel

Rossner, Judith (Perelman)
1935- . . . . **CLC 6, 9, 29**
See also CA 17-20R
See also DLB 6
See also AITN 2

Rostand, Edmond (Eugène Alexis)
1868-1918 . . . . **TCLC 6**
See also CA 104

Roth, Henry 1906- . . . . **CLC 2, 6, 11**
See also CAP 1
See also CA 11-12

Roth, Philip (Milton)
1933- . . . . . . **CLC 1, 2, 3, 4, 6, 9, 15, 22**
See also CANR 1
See also CA 1-4R
See also DLB 2
See also DLB-Y 82

Rothenberg, Jerome 1931- . . . . **CLC 6**
See also CANR 1
See also CA 45-48
See also DLB 5

Rourke, Constance (Mayfield)
1885-1941 . . . . **TCLC 12**
See also CA 107
See also YABC 1

Rovit, Earl (Herbert) 1927- . . . . **CLC 7**
See also CA 5-8R

Rowson, Susanna Haswell
1762-1824 . . . . **NCLC 5**

Roy, Gabrielle 1909-1983 . . . . . . **CLC 10, 14**
See also CANR 5
See also CA 53-56
See also obituary CA 110

Różewicz, Tadeusz 1921- . . . . **CLC 9, 23**
See also CA 108

Ruark, Gibbons 1941- . . . . **CLC 3**
See also CA 33-36R

Rubens, Bernice 1927- . . . . **CLC 19**
See also CA 25-28R
See also DLB 14

Rudkin, (James) David 1936- . . . . . . **CLC 14**
See also CA 89-92
See also DLB 13

Rudnik, Raphael 1933- . . . . **CLC 7**
See also CA 29-32R

Ruiz, José Martínez 1874-1967
See Azorín

Rukeyser, Muriel
1913-1980 . . . . **CLC 6, 10, 15, 27**
See also CA 5-8R
See also obituary CA 93-96
See also obituary SATA 22

Rule, Jane (Vance) 1931- . . . . **CLC 27**
See also CA 25-28R

Rulfo, Juan 1918- . . . . **CLC 8**
See also CA 85-88

Runyon, Damon 1880-1946 . . . . . . **TCLC 10**
See also CA 107
See also DLB 11

Rushdie, (Ahmed) Salman
1947- . . . . **CLC 23**
See also CA 108, 111

Rushforth, Peter (Scott) 1945- . . . . . . **CLC 19**
See also CA 101

Russ, Joanna 1937- . . . . **CLC 15**
See also CANR 11
See also CA 25-28R
See also DLB 8

Russell, George William 1867-1935
See A. E.
See also CA 104

Russell, (Henry) Ken(neth Alfred)
1927- . . . . **CLC 16**
See also CA 105

Ruyslinck, Ward 1929- . . . . **CLC 14**

Ryan, Cornelius (John)
1920-1974 . . . . **CLC 7**
See also CA 69-72
See also obituary CA 53-56

Rybakov, Anatoli 1911?- . . . . **CLC 23**

Ryga, George 1932- . . . . **CLC 14**
See also CA 101

Sabato, Ernesto 1911- . . . . **CLC 10, 23**
See also CA 97-100

Sachs, Nelly 1891-1970 . . . . **CLC 14**
See also CAP 2
See also CA 17-18
See also obituary CA 25-28R

Sackler, Howard (Oliver)
1929-1982 . . . . **CLC 14**
See also CA 61-64
See also obituary CA 108
See also DLB 7

Sade, Donatien Alphonse François, Comte de
1740-1814 . . . . **NCLC 3**

Sadoff, Ira 1945- .... **CLC 9**
See also CANR 5
See also CA 53-56

Safire, William 1929- .... **CLC 10**
See also CA 17-20R

Sagan, Françoise 1935- ..... **CLC 3, 6, 9, 17**
See also Quoirez, Françoise

Sainte-Beuve, Charles Augustin
1804-1869 .... **NCLC 5**

Sainte-Marie, Beverly 1941-
See Sainte-Marie, Buffy
See also CA 107

Sainte-Marie, Buffy 1941- .... **CLC 17**
See also Sainte-Marie, Beverly

Saint-Exupéry, Antoine (Jean Baptiste Marie Roger) de 1900-1944 .... **TCLC 2**
See also CA 108
See also SATA 20

Saki 1870-1916 .... **TCLC 3**
See also Munro, H(ector) H(ugh)

Salama, Hannu 1936- .... **CLC 18**

Salamanca, J(ack) R(ichard)
1922- .... **CLC 4, 15**
See also CA 25-28R

Salinger, J(erome) D(avid)
1919- .... **CLC 1, 3, 8, 12**
See also CA 5-8R
See also DLB 2

Salter, James 1925- .... **CLC 7**
See also CA 73-76

Saltus, Edgar (Evertson)
1855-1921 .... **TCLC 8**
See also CA 105

Samarakis, Antonis 1919- .... **CLC 5**
See also CA 25-28R

Sánchez, Luis Rafael 1936- .... **CLC 23**

Sanchez, Sonia 1934- .... **CLC 5**
See also CA 33-36R
See also SATA 22

Sand, George 1804-1876 .... **NCLC 2**

Sandburg, Carl (August)
1878-1967 .... **CLC 1, 4, 10, 15**
See also CA 5-8R
See also obituary CA 25-28R
See also SATA 8
See also DLB 17

Sandoz, Mari (Susette)
1896-1966 .... **CLC 28**
See also CA 1-4R
See also obituary CA 25-28R
See also SATA 5
See also DLB 9

Saner, Reg(inald Anthony)
1931- .... **CLC 9**
See also CA 65-68

Sansom, William 1912-1976 ...... **CLC 2, 6**
See also CA 5-8R
See also obituary CA 65-68

Santos, Bienvenido N(uqui)
1911- .... **CLC 22**
See also CA 101

Sarduy, Severo 1937- .... **CLC 6**
See also CA 89-92

Saroyan, William
1908-1981 .... **CLC 1, 8, 10, 29**
See also CA 5-8R
See also obituary CA 103
See also SATA 23
See also obituary SATA 24
See also DLB 7, 9
See also DLB-Y 81

Sarraute, Nathalie
1902- .... **CLC 1, 2, 4, 8, 10, 29**
See also CA 9-12R

Sarton, (Eleanor) May
1912- .... **CLC 4, 14**
See also CANR 1
See also CA 1-4R
See also DLB-Y 81

Sartre, Jean-Paul
1905-1980 ...... **CLC 1, 4, 7, 9, 13, 18, 24**
See also CA 9-12R
See also obituary CA 97-100

Saura, Carlos 1932- .... **CLC 20**

Sauser-Hall, Frédéric-Louis 1887-1961
See Cendrars, Blaise
See also CA 102
See also obituary CA 93-96

Sayers, Dorothy L(eigh)
1893-1957 .... **TCLC 2**
See also CA 104
See also DLB 10

Sayles, John (Thomas)
1950- .... **CLC 7, 10, 14**
See also CA 57-60

Schaeffer, Susan Fromberg
1941- .... **CLC 6, 11, 22**
See also CA 49-52
See also SATA 22

Schevill, James (Erwin) 1920- .... **CLC 7**
See also CA 5-8R

Schisgal, Murray (Joseph)
1926- .... **CLC 6**
See also CA 21-24R

Schneider, Leonard Alfred 1925-1966
See Bruce, Lenny
See also CA 89-92

Schnitzler, Arthur 1862-1931 ..... **TCLC 4**
See also CA 104

Schorer, Mark 1908-1977 .... **CLC 9**
See also CANR 7
See also CA 5-8R
See also obituary CA 73-76

Schrader, Paul (Joseph) 1946- ...... **CLC 26**
See also CA 37-40R

Schreiner (Cronwright), Olive (Emilie Albertina) 1855-1920 .... **TCLC 9**
See also CA 105
See also DLB 18

Schulberg, Budd (Wilson) 1914- ..... **CLC 7**
See also CA 25-28R
See also DLB 6
See also DLB-Y 81

Schulz, Bruno 1892-1942 .... **TCLC 5**

Schulz, Charles M(onroe)
1922- .... **CLC 12**
See also CANR 6
See also CA 9-12R
See also SATA 10

Schuyler, James (Marcus)
1923- .... **CLC 5, 23**
See also CA 101
See also DLB 5

Schwartz, Delmore
1913-1966 .... **CLC 2, 4, 10**
See also CAP 2
See also CA 17-18
See also obituary CA 25-28R

Schwarz-Bart, André 1928- ...... **CLC 2, 4**
See also CA 89-92

Schwarz-Bart, Simone 1938- .... **CLC 7**
See also CA 97-100

Sciascia, Leonardo 1921- .... **CLC 8, 9**
See also CA 85-88

Scoppettone, Sandra 1936- .... **CLC 26**
See also CA 5-8R
See also SATA 9

Scorsese, Martin 1942- .... **CLC 20**
See also CA 110

Scotland, Jay 1932-
See Jakes, John (William)

Scott, Duncan Campbell
1862-1947 .... **TCLC 6**
See also CA 104

Scott, F(rancis) R(eginald)
1899- .... **CLC 22**
See also CA 101

Scott, Paul (Mark) 1920-1978 .... **CLC 9**
See also CA 81-84
See also obituary CA 77-80
See also DLB 14

Seare, Nicholas 1925-
See Trevanian
See also Whitaker, Rodney

Seelye, John 1931- .... **CLC 7**
See also CA 97-100

Seferiades, Giorgos Stylianou 1900-1971
See Seferis, George
See also CANR 5
See also CA 5-8R
See also obituary CA 33-36R

Seferis, George 1900-1971 ...... **CLC 5, 11**
See also Seferiades, Giorgos Stylianou

Segal, Erich (Wolf) 1937- .... **CLC 3, 10**
See also CA 25-28R

Seghers, Anna 1900- .... **CLC 7**
See Radvanyi, Netty

Seidel, Frederick (Lewis) 1936- ..... **CLC 18**
See also CANR 8
See also CA 13-16R

Selby, Hubert, Jr.
1928- .... **CLC 1, 2, 4, 8**
See also CA 13-16R
See also DLB 2

Sender, Ramón (José)
1902-1982 .... **CLC 8**
See also CANR 8
See also CA 5-8R
See also obituary CA 105

Seton, Cynthia Propper
1926-1982 .... **CLC 27**
See also CANR-7
See also CA 5-8R
See also obituary CA 108

Settle, Mary Lee 1918- . . . . **CLC 19**
See also CA 89-92
See also DLB 6

Sexton, Anne (Harvey)
1928-1974 . . . . **CLC 2, 4, 6, 8, 10, 15**
See also CANR 3
See also CA 1-4R
See also obituary CA 53-56
See also SATA 10
See also DLB 5

Shaara, Michael (Joseph)
1929- . . . . **CLC 15**
See also CA 102
See also AITN 1

Shaffer, Anthony 1926- . . . . **CLC 19**
See also CA 110
See also DLB 13

Shaffer, Peter (Levin)
1926- . . . . **CLC 5, 14, 18**
See also CA 25-28R
See also DLB 13

Shalamov, Varlam (Tikhonovich)
1907?-1982 . . . . **CLC 18**
See also obituary CA 105

Shamlu, Ahmad 1925- . . . . **CLC 10**

Shange, Ntozake 1948- . . . . **CLC 8, 25**
See also CA 85-88

Shapiro, Karl (Jay) 1913- . . . . . **CLC 4, 8, 15**
See also CANR 1
See also CA 1-4R

Shaw, (George) Bernard
1856-1950 . . . . **TCLC 3, 6**
See also CA 104, 109
See also DLB 10

Shaw, Irwin 1913- . . . . **CLC 7, 23**
See also CA 13-16R
See also DLB 6
See also AITN 1

Shaw, Robert 1927-1978 . . . . **CLC 5**
See also CANR 4
See also CA 1-4R
See also obituary CA 81-84
See also DLB 13, 14
See also AITN 1

Sheed, Wilfrid (John Joseph)
1930- . . . . **CLC 2, 4, 10**
See also CA 65-68
See also DLB 6

Shepard, Sam 1943- . . . . **CLC 4, 6, 17**
See also CA 69-72
See also DLB 7

Sheridan, Richard Brinsley
1751-1816 . . . . **NCLC 5**

Sherman, Martin . . . . **CLC 19**

Sherwin, Judith Johnson
1936- . . . . **CLC 7, 15**
See also CA 25-28R

Sherwood, Robert E(mmet)
1896-1955 . . . . **TCLC 3**
See also CA 104
See also DLB 7, 26

Shiel, M(atthew) P(hipps)
1865-1947 . . . . **TCLC 8**
See also CA 106

Shimazaki, Tōson 1872-1943 . . . . . . **TCLC 5**
See also CA 105

Sholokhov, Mikhail (Aleksandrovich)
1905- . . . . **CLC 7, 15**
See also CA 101

Shreve, Susan Richards 1939- . . . . . . **CLC 23**
See also CANR 5
See also CA 49-52

Shulman, Alix Kates 1932- . . . . . . **CLC 2, 10**
See also CA 29-32R
See also SATA 7

Shuster, Joe 1914-
See Siegel, Jerome and Shuster, Joe

Shuttle, Penelope (Diane) 1947- . . . . . . **CLC 7**
See also CA 93-96
See also DLB 14

Siegel, Jerome 1914-
See Siegel, Jerome and Shuster, Joe

Siegel, Jerome 1914- and **Shuster, Joe**
1914- . . . . **CLC 21**

Sienkiewicz, Henryk (Adam Aleksander Pius)
1846-1916 . . . . **TCLC 3**
See also CA 104

Sigal, Clancy 1926- . . . . **CLC 7**
See also CA 1-4R

Silkin, Jon 1930- . . . . **CLC 2, 6**
See also CA 5-8R

Silko, Leslie Marmon 1948- . . . . **CLC 23**

Sillanpää, Franz Eemil
1888-1964 . . . . **CLC 19**
See also obituary CA 93-96

Sillitoe, Alan 1928- . . . . **CLC 1, 3, 6, 10, 19**
See also CANR 8
See also CA 9-12R
See also DLB 14
See also AITN 1

Silone, Ignazio 1900-1978 . . . . **CLC 4**
See also CAP 2
See also CA 25-28
See also obituary CA 81-84

Silver, Joan Micklin 1935- . . . . **CLC 20**

Silverberg, Robert 1935- . . . . **CLC 7**
See also CANR 1
See also CA 1-4R
See also SATA 13
See also DLB 8

Silverstein, Alvin 1933-
See Silverstein, Alvin and Silverstein, Virginia B(arbara Opshelor)
See also CANR 2
See also CA 49-52
See also SATA 8

Silverstein, Alvin 1933- and **Silverstein, Virginia B(arbara Opshelor)**
1937- . . . . **CLC 17**

Silverstein, Virginia B(arbara Opshelor)
1937-
See Silverstein, Alvin and Silverstein, Virginia B(arbara Opshelor)
See also CANR 2
See also CA 49-52
See also SATA 8

Simak, Clifford D(onald) 1904- . . . . . . **CLC 1**
See also CANR 1
See also CA 1-4R
See also DLB 8

Simenon, Georges (Jacques Christian)
1903- . . . . **CLC 1, 2, 3, 8, 18**
See also CA 85-88

Simic, Charles 1938- . . . . **CLC 6, 9, 22**
See also CA 29-32R

Simms, William Gilmore
1806-1870 . . . . **NCLC 3**
See also DLB 3

Simon, Carly 1945- . . . . **CLC 26**
See also CA 105

Simon, Claude 1913- . . . . **CLC 4, 9, 15**
See also CA 89-92

Simon, (Marvin) Neil 1927- . . . . . **CLC 6, 11**
See also CA 21-24R
See also DLB 7
See also AITN 1

Simon, Paul 1941- . . . . **CLC 17**

Simpson, Louis (Aston Marantz)
1923- . . . . **CLC 4, 7, 9**
See also CANR 1
See also CA 1-4R
See also DLB 5

Simpson, N(orman) F(rederick)
1919- . . . . **CLC 29**
See also CA 11-14R
See also DLB 13

Sinclair, Andrew (Annandale)
1935- . . . . **CLC 2, 14**
See also CA 9-12R
See also DLB 14

Sinclair, May 1865?-1946 . . . . . . **TCLC 3, 11**
See also CA 104

Sinclair, Upton (Beall)
1878-1968 . . . . **CLC 1, 11, 15**
See also CANR 7
See also CA 5-8R
See also obituary 25-28R
See also SATA 9
See also DLB 9

Singer, Isaac Bashevis
1904- . . . . **CLC 1, 3, 6, 9, 11, 15, 23**
See also CLR 1
See also CANR 1
See also CA 1-4R
See also SATA 3, 27
See also DLB 6
See also AITN 1, 2

Singh, Khushwant 1915- . . . . **CLC 11**
See also CANR 6
See also CA 9-12R

Sinyavsky, Andrei (Donatevich)
1925- . . . . **CLC 8**
See also CA 85-88

Sissman, L(ouis) E(dward)
1928-1976 . . . . **CLC 9, 18**
See also CA 21-24R
See also obituary CA 65-68
See also DLB 5

Sisson, C(harles) H(ubert) 1914- . . . . . **CLC 8**
See also CANR 3
See also CA 1-4R

Sitwell, (Dame) Edith
1887-1964 . . . . **CLC 2, 9**
See also CA 9-12R
See also DLB 20

Sjoewall, Maj 1935-
See Wahlöö, Per
See also CA 65-68

Sjöwall, Maj 1935-
See Wahlöö, Per

Skelton, Robin 1925- .... CLC 13
See also CA 5-8R
See also AITN 2

Skolimowski, Jerzy 1938- .... CLC 20

Skolimowski, Yurek 1938-
See Skolimowski, Jerzy

Škvorecký, Josef (Victor)
1924- .... CLC 15
See also CANR 10
See also CA 61-64

Slade, Bernard 1930- .... CLC 11
See also Newbound, Bernard Slade

Slaughter, Frank G(ill) 1908- ...... CLC 29
See also CANR 5
See also CA 5-8R
See also AITN 2

Slavitt, David (R.) 1935- .... CLC 5, 14
See also CA 21-24R
See also DLB 5, 6

Slesinger, Tess 1905-1945 .... TCLC 10
See also CA 107

Slessor, Kenneth 1901-1971 .... CLC 14
See also CA 102
See also obituary CA 89-92

Smith, A(rthur) J(ames) M(arshall)
1902-1980 .... CLC 15
See also CANR 4
See also CA 1-4R
See also obituary CA 102

Smith, Betty (Wehner)
1896-1972 .... CLC 19
See also CA 5-8R
See also obituary CA 33-36R
See also SATA 6
See also DLB-Y 82

Smith, Dave 1942- .... CLC 22
See also Smith, David (Jeddie)
See also DLB 5

Smith, David (Jeddie) 1942-
See Smith, Dave
See also CANR 1
See also CA 49-52

Smith, Florence Margaret 1902-1971
See Smith, Stevie
See also CAP 2
See also CA 17-18
See also obituary CA 29-32R

Smith, Lee 1944- .... CLC 25

Smith, Martin Cruz 1942- .... CLC 25
See also CANR 6
See also CA 85-88

Smith, Martin William 1942-
See Smith, Martin Cruz

Smith, Patti 1946- .... CLC 12
See also CA 93-96

Smith, Sara Mahala Redway 1900-1972
See Benson, Sally

Smith, Stevie 1902-1971 ...... CLC 3, 8, 25
See also Smith, Florence Margaret
See also DLB 20

Smith, William Jay 1918- .... CLC 6
See also CA 5-8R
See also SATA 2
See also DLB 5

Snodgrass, W(illiam) D(e Witt)
1926- .... CLC 2, 6, 10, 18
See also CANR 6
See also CA 1-4R
See also DLB 5

Snow, C(harles) P(ercy)
1905-1980 .... CLC 1, 4, 6, 9, 13, 19
See also CA 5-8R
See also obituary CA 101
See also DLB 15

Snyder, Gary 1930- .... CLC 1, 2, 5, 9
See also CA 17-20R
See also DLB 5, 16

Snyder, Zilpha Keatley 1927- ...... CLC 17
See also CA 9-12R
See also SATA 1, 28

Sokolov, Raymond 1941- .... CLC 7
See also CA 85-88

Sologub, Fyodor 1863-1927 .... TCLC 9
See also CA 104

Solwoska, Mara 1929-
See French, Marilyn

Solzhenitsyn, Aleksandr I(sayevich)
1918- ..... CLC 1, 2, 4, 7, 9, 10, 18, 26
See also CA 69-72
See also AITN 1

Sommer, Scott 1951- .... CLC 25
See also CA 106

Sontag, Susan 1933- ...... CLC 1, 2, 10, 13
See also CA 17-20R
See also DLB 2

Sorrentino, Gilbert
1929- .... CLC 3, 7, 14, 22
See also CA 77-80
See also DLB 5
See also DLB-Y 80

Souster, (Holmes) Raymond
1921- .... CLC 5, 14
See also CA 13-16R

Southern, Terry 1926- .... CLC 7
See also CANR 1
See also CA 1-4R
See also DLB 2

Soyinka, Wole 1934- .... CLC 3, 5, 14
See also CA 13-16R

Spacks, Barry 1931- .... CLC 14
See also CA 29-32R

Spark, Muriel (Sarah)
1918- .... CLC 2, 3, 5, 8, 13, 18
See also CA 5-8R
See also DLB 15

Spencer, Elizabeth 1921- .... CLC 22
See also CA 13-16R
See also SATA 14
See also DLB 6

Spender, Stephen (Harold)
1909- .... CLC 1, 2, 5, 10
See also CA 9-12R
See also DLB 20

Spicer, Jack 1925-1965 .... CLC 8, 18
See also CA 85-88
See also DLB 5, 16

Spielberg, Peter 1929- .... CLC 6
See also CANR 4
See also CA 5-8R
See also DLB-Y 81

Spielberg, Steven 1947- .... CLC 20
See also CA 77-80
See also SATA 32

Spillane, Frank Morrison 1918-
See Spillane, Mickey
See also CA 25-28R

Spillane, Mickey 1918- .... CLC 3, 13
See also Spillane, Frank Morrison

Spivack, Kathleen (Romola Drucker)
1938- .... CLC 6
See also CA 49-52

Springsteen, Bruce 1949- .... CLC 17
See also CA 111

Staël-Holstein, Anne Louise Germaine Necker, Baronne de
1766-1817 .... NCLC 3

Stafford, Jean 1915-1979 ..... CLC 4, 7, 19
See also CANR 3
See also CA 1-4R
See also obituary CA 85-88
See also obituary SATA 22
See also DLB 2

Stafford, William (Edgar)
1914- .... CLC 4, 7, 29
See also CANR 5
See also CA 5-8R
See also DLB 5

Stanton, Maura 1946- .... CLC 9
See also CA 89-92

Stead, Christina (Ellen)
1902-1983 .... CLC 2, 5, 8
See also CA 13-16R
See also obituary CA 109

Stegner, Wallace (Earle) 1909- ...... CLC 9
See also CANR 1
See also CA 1-4R
See also DLB 9
See also AITN 1

Stein, Gertrude 1874-1946 ...... TCLC 1, 6
See also CA 104
See also DLB 4

Steinbeck, John (Ernst)
1902-1968 .... CLC 1, 5, 9, 13, 21
See also CANR 1
See also CA 1-4R
See also obituary CA 25-28R
See also SATA 9
See also DLB 7, 9
See also DLB-DS 2

Steiner, George 1929- .... CLC 24
See also CA 73-76

Steiner, Rudolf(us Josephus Laurentius)
1861-1925 .... TCLC 13
See also CA 107

Stephens, James 1882?-1950 ...... TCLC 4
See also CA 104
See also DLB 19

Steptoe, Lydia 1892-1982
See Barnes, Djuna

Stern, Richard G(ustave) 1928- ...... CLC 4
See also CANR 1
See also CA 1-4R

Sternberg, Jonas 1894-1969
See Sternberg, Josef von

Sternberg, Josef von
1894-1969 .... CLC 20
See also CA 81-84

Sternheim, (William Adolf) Carl 1878-1942 .... TCLC 8
See also CA 105

Stevens, Wallace 1879-1955 .... TCLC 3, 12
See also CA 104

Stevenson, Anne (Katharine) 1933- .... CLC 7
See also Elvin, Anne Katharine Stevenson
See also CANR 9

Stevenson, Robert Louis 1850-1894 .... NCLC 5
See also YABC 2
See also DLB 18

Stewart, J(ohn) I(nnes) M(ackintosh) 1906- .... CLC 7, 14
See also CA 85-88

Stewart, Mary (Florence Elinor) 1916- .... CLC 7
See also CANR 1
See also CA 1-4R
See also SATA 12

Stewart, Will 1908-
See Williamson, Jack

Sting 1951-
See The Police

Stitt, Milan 1941- .... CLC 29
See also CA 69-72

Stoker, Bram (Abraham) 1847-1912 .... TCLC 8
See also CA 105
See also SATA 29

Stolz, Mary (Slattery) 1920- .... CLC 12
See also CA 5-8R
See also SATA 10
See also AITN 1

Stone, Irving 1903- .... CLC 7
See also CANR 1
See also CA 1-4R
See also SATA 3
See also AITN 1

Stone, Robert 1937?- .... CLC 5, 23
See also CA 85-88

Stoppard, Tom 1937- .... CLC 1, 3, 4, 5, 8, 15, 29
See also CA 81-84
See also DLB 13

Storey, David (Malcolm) 1933- .... CLC 2, 4, 5, 8
See also CA 81-84
See also DLB 13, 14

Storm, Hyemeyohsts 1935- .... CLC 3
See also CA 81-84

Storm, (Hans) Theodor (Woldsen) 1817-1888 .... NCLC 1

Storni, Alfonsina 1892-1938 .... TCLC 5
See also CA 104

Stout, Rex (Todhunter) 1886-1975 .... CLC 3
See also CA 61-64
See also AITN 2

Stow, (Julian) Randolph 1935- .... CLC 23
See also CA 13-16R

Stowe, Harriet (Elizabeth) Beecher 1811-1896 .... NCLC 3
See also YABC 1
See also DLB 1, 12

Strachey, (Giles) Lytton 1880-1932 .... TCLC 12

Strand, Mark 1934- .... CLC 6, 18
See also CA 21-24R
See also DLB 5

Straub, Peter (Francis) 1943- .... CLC 28
See also CA 85-88

Strauss, Botho 1944- .... CLC 22

Straussler, Tomas 1937-
See Stoppard, Tom

Streatfeild, Noel 1897- .... CLC 21
See also CA 81-84
See also SATA 20

Stribling, T(homas) S(igismund) 1881-1965 .... CLC 23
See also obituary CA 107
See also DLB 9

Strindberg, (Johan) August 1849-1912 .... TCLC 1, 8
See also CA 104

Strugatskii, Arkadii (Natanovich) 1925-
See Strugatskii, Arkadii (Natanovich) and Strugatskii, Boris (Natanovich)
See also CA 106

Strugatskii, Arkadii (Natanovich) 1925- and **Strugatskii, Boris (Natanovich)** 1933- .... CLC 27

Strugatskii, Boris (Natanovich) 1933-
See Strugatskii, Arkadii (Natanovich) and Strugatskii, Boris (Natanovich)
See also CA 106

Strugatskii, Boris (Natanovich) 1933- and **Strugatskii, Arkadii (Natanovich)** 1925-
See Strugatskii, Arkadii (Natanovich) and Strugatskii, Boris (Natanovich)

Stuart, (Hilton) Jesse 1907- .... CLC 1, 8, 11, 14
See also CA 5-8R
See also SATA 2
See also DLB 9

Sturgeon, Theodore (Hamilton) 1918- .... CLC 22
See also CA 81-84
See also DLB 8

Styron, William 1925- .... CLC 1, 3, 5, 11, 15
See also CANR 6
See also CA 5-8R
See also DLB 2
See also DLB-Y 80

Sue, Eugène 1804-1857 .... NCLC 1

Sukenick, Ronald 1932- .... CLC 3, 4, 6
See also CA 25-28R
See also DLB-Y 81

Suknaski, Andrew 1942- .... CLC 19
See also CA 101

Summers, Andrew James 1942-
See The Police

Summers, Andy 1942-
See The Police

Summers, Hollis (Spurgeon, Jr.) 1916- .... CLC 10
See also CANR 3
See also CA 5-8R
See also DLB 6

Sumner, Gordon Matthew 1951-
See The Police

Susann, Jacqueline 1921-1974 .... CLC 3
See also CA 65-68
See also obituary CA 53-56
See also AITN 1

Sutcliff, Rosemary 1920- .... CLC 26
See also CLR 1
See also CA 5-8R
See also SATA 6

Sutro, Alfred 1863-1933 .... TCLC 6
See also CA 105
See also DLB 10

Sutton, Henry 1935-
See Slavitt, David (R.)

Svevo, Italo 1861-1928 .... TCLC 2
See also CA 104

Swados, Elizabeth 1951- .... CLC 12
See also CA 97-100

Swados, Harvey 1920-1972 .... CLC 5
See also CANR 6
See also CA 5-8R
See also obituary CA 37-40R
See also DLB 2

Swenson, May 1919- .... CLC 4, 14
See also CA 5-8R
See also SATA 15
See also DLB 5

Swift, Jonathan 1667-1745 .... LC 1
See also SATA 19

Swinburne, Algernon Charles 1837-1909 .... TCLC 8
See also CA 105

Symons, Arthur (William) 1865-1945 .... TCLC 11
See also CA 107
See also DLB 19

Symons, Julian (Gustave) 1912- .... CLC 2, 14
See also CANR 3
See also CA 49-52

Synge, (Edmund) John Millington 1871-1909 .... TCLC 6
See also CA 104
See also DLB 10, 19

Tabori, George 1914- .... CLC 19
See also CANR 4
See also CA 49-52

Tagore, (Sir) Rabindranath 1861-1941 .... TCLC 3
See also CA 104

Tamayo y Baus, Manuel 1829-1898 .... NCLC 1

Tanizaki, Jun'ichirō 1886-1965 .... CLC 8, 14, 28
See also CA 93-96
See also obituary CA 25-28R

Tarkington, (Newton) Booth 1869-1946 .... TCLC 9
See also CA 110
See also SATA 17
See also DLB 9

Tate, (John Orley) Allen 1899-1979 .... CLC 2, 4, 6, 9, 11, 14, 24
See also CA 5-8R
See also obituary CA 85-88
See also DLB 4

Tate, James 1943- .... **CLC 2, 6, 25**
See also CA 21-24R
See also DLB 5

Tavel, Ronald 1940- .... **CLC 6**
See also CA 21-24R

Taylor, C(ecil) P(hillip)
1929-1981 .... **CLC 27**
See also CA 25-28R
See also obituary CA 105

Taylor, Eleanor Ross 1920- .... **CLC 5**
See also CA 81-84

Taylor, Elizabeth
1912-1975 .... **CLC 2, 4, 29**
See also CANR 9
See also CA 13-16R
See also SATA 13

Taylor, Kamala (Purnaiya) 1924-
See Markandaya, Kamala (Purnaiya)
See also CA 77-80

Taylor, Mildred D(elois) .... **CLC 21**
See also CA 85-88
See also SATA 15

Taylor, Peter (Hillsman)
1917- .... **CLC 1, 4, 18**
See also CANR 9
See also CA 13-16R
See also DLB-Y 81

Taylor, Robert Lewis 1912- .... **CLC 14**
See also CANR 3
See also CA 1-4R
See also SATA 10

Teasdale, Sara 1884-1933 .... **TCLC 4**
See also CA 104
See also SATA 32

Tegnér, Esaias 1782-1846 .... **NCLC 2**

Teilhard de Chardin, (Marie Joseph) Pierre
1881-1955 .... **TCLC 9**
See also CA 105

Tennant, Emma 1937- .... **CLC 13**
See also CANR 10
See also CA 65-68
See also DLB 14

Terry, Megan 1932- .... **CLC 19**
See also CA 77-80
See also DLB 7

Tertz, Abram 1925-
See Sinyavsky, Andrei (Donatevich)

Thackeray, William Makepeace
1811-1863 .... **NCLC 5**
See also SATA 23
See also DLB 21

Thelwell, Michael (Miles)
1939- .... **CLC 22**
See also CA 101

Theroux, Alexander (Louis)
1939- .... **CLC 2, 25**
See also CA 85-88

Theroux, Paul
1941- .... **CLC 5, 8, 11, 15, 28**
See also CA 33-36R
See also DLB 2

Thiele, Colin (Milton) 1920- .... **CLC 17**
See also CA 29-32R
See also SATA 14

Thomas, Audrey (Callahan)
1935- .... **CLC 7, 13**
See also CA 21-24R
See also AITN 2

Thomas, D(onald) M(ichael)
1935- .... **CLC 13, 22**
See also CA 61-64

Thomas, Dylan 1914-1953 ...... **TCLC 1, 8**
See also CA 104
See also DLB 13, 20

Thomas, Edward (Philip)
1878-1917 .... **TCLC 10**
See also CA 106
See also DLB 19

Thomas, John Peter 1928-
See Thomas, Piri

Thomas, Piri 1928- .... **CLC 17**
See also CA 73-76

Thomas, R(onald) S(tuart)
1913- .... **CLC 6, 13**
See also CA 89-92

Thompson, Francis (Joseph)
1859-1907 .... **TCLC 4**
See also CA 104
See also DLB 19

Thompson, Hunter S(tockton)
1939- .... **CLC 9, 17**
See also CA 17-20R

Thurber, James (Grover)
1894-1961 .... **CLC 5, 11, 25**
See also CA 73-76
See also SATA 13
See also DLB 4, 11, 22

Thurman, Wallace 1902-1934 ..... **TCLC 6**
See also CA 104

Tieck, (Johann) Ludwig
1773-1853 .... **NCLC 5**

Tillinghast, Richard 1940- .... **CLC 29**
See also CA 29-32R

Tindall, Gillian 1938- .... **CLC 7**
See also CANR 11
See also CA 21-24R

Tolkien, J(ohn) R(onald) R(euel)
1892-1973 .... **CLC 1, 2, 3, 8, 12**
See also CAP 2
See also CA 17-18
See also obituary CA 45-48
See also SATA 2, 32
See also obituary SATA 24
See also DLB 15
See also AITN 1

Toller, Ernst 1893-1939 .... **TCLC 10**
See also CA 107

Tolstoy, (Count) Leo (Lev Nikolaevich)
1828-1910 .... **TCLC 4, 11**
See also CA 104
See also SATA 26

Tomlin, Lily 1939- .... **CLC 17**

Tomlin, Mary Jean 1939-
See Tomlin, Lily

Tomlinson, (Alfred) Charles
1927- .... **CLC 2, 4, 6, 13**
See also CA 5-8R

Toole, John Kennedy
1937-1969 .... **CLC 19**
See also CA 104
See also DLB-Y 81

Toomer, Jean
1894-1967 .... **CLC 1, 4, 13, 22**
See also CA 85-88

Tournier, Michel 1924- .... **CLC 6, 23**
See also CANR 3
See also CA 49-52
See also SATA 23

Townshend, Peter (Dennis Blandford)
1945- .... **CLC 17**
See also CA 107

Trakl, Georg 1887-1914 .... **TCLC 5**
See also CA 104

Traven, B. 1890-1969 .... **CLC 8, 11**
See also CAP 2
See also CA 19-20
See also obituary CA 25-28R
See also DLB 9

Tremblay, Michel 1942- .... **CLC 29**

Trevanian 1925- .... **CLC 29**
See also Whitaker, Rodney
See also CA 108

Trevor, William
1928- .... **CLC 7, 9, 14, 25**
See also Cox, William Trevor
See also DLB 14

Trilling, Lionel
1905-1975 .... **CLC 9, 11, 24**
See also CANR 10
See also CA 9-12R
See also obituary CA 61-64

Trogdon, William 1939-
See Heat Moon, William Least

Trollope, Anthony 1815-1882 ..... **NCLC 6**
See also SATA 22
See also DLB 21

Troyat, Henri 1911- .... **CLC 23**
See also CANR 2
See also CA 45-48

Trudeau, G(arretson) B(eekman) 1948-
See Trudeau, Garry
See also CA 81-84

Trudeau, Garry 1948- .... **CLC 12**
See also Trudeau, G(arretson) B(eekman)
See also AITN 2

Truffaut, François 1932- .... **CLC 20**
See also CA 81-84

Trumbo, Dalton 1905-1976 .... **CLC 19**
See also CANR 10
See also CA 21-24R
See also obituary CA 69-72
See also DLB 26

Tryon, Thomas 1926- .... **CLC 3, 11**
See also CA 29-32R
See also AITN 1

Ts'ao Hsuëh-ch'in 1715?-1763 .... **LC 1**

Tshushima Shūji 1909-1948
See Dazai Osamu
See also CA 107

Tunis, John R(oberts)
1889-1975 .... **CLC 12**
See also CA 61-64
See also SATA 30
See also DLB 22

Turco, Lewis (Putnam) 1934- ...... **CLC 11**
See also CA 13-16R

Tutuola, Amos 1920-........CLC 5, 14, 29
See also CA 9-12R

Twain, Mark 1835-1910.......TCLC 6, 12
See also Clemens, Samuel Langhorne

Tyler, Anne 1941-.......CLC 7, 11, 18, 28
See also CANR 11
See also CA 9-12R
See also SATA 7
See also DLB 6
See also DLB-Y 82

Tyler, Royall 1757-1826..........NCLC 3

Tynan (Hinkson), Katharine
1861-1931...................TCLC 3
See also CA 104

Unamuno (y Jugo), Miguel de
1864-1936................TCLC 2, 9
See also CA 104

Underwood, Miles 1909-1981
See Glassco, John

Undset, Sigrid 1882-1949.........TCLC 3
See also CA 104

Ungaretti, Giuseppe
1888-1970..............CLC 7, 11, 15
See also CAP 2
See also CA 19-20
See also obituary CA 25-28R

Updike, John (Hoyer)
1932-......CLC 1, 2, 3, 5, 7, 9, 13, 15, 23
See also CANR 4
See also CA 1-4R
See also DLB 2, 5
See also DLB-Y 80, 82
See also DLB-DS 3

Uris, Leon (Marcus) 1924-..........CLC 7
See also CANR 1
See also CA 1-4R
See also AITN 1, 2

Ustinov, Peter (Alexander)
1921-.........................CLC 1
See also CA 13-16R
See also DLB 13
See also AITN 1

Vaculík, Ludvík 1926-.............CLC 7
See also CA 53-56

Valera (y Acalá-Galiano), Juan
1824-1905..................TCLC 10
See also CA 106

Valéry, Paul (Ambroise Toussaint Jules)
1871-1945...................TCLC 4
See also CA 104

Valle-Inclán (y Montenegro), Ramón (María) del 1866-1936..............TCLC 5
See also CA 106

Vallejo, César (Abraham)
1892-1938..................TCLC 3
See also CA 105

Van Den Bogarde, Derek (Jules Gaspard Ulric) Niven 1921-
See Bogarde, Dirk
See also CA 77-80

Van der Post, Laurens (Jan)
1906-.........................CLC 5
See also CA 5-8R

Van Doren, Mark
1894-1972.................CLC 6, 10
See also CANR 3
See also CA 1-4R
See also obituary CA 37-40R

Van Druten, John (William)
1901-1957..................TCLC 2
See also CA 104
See also DLB 10

Van Duyn, Mona 1921-.........CLC 3, 7
See also CANR 7
See also CA 9-12R
See also DLB 5

Van Itallie, Jean-Claude 1936-......CLC 3
See also CANR 1
See also CA 45-48
See also DLB 7

Van Peebles, Melvin 1932-......CLC 2, 20
See also CA 85-88

Van Vogt, A(lfred) E(lton)
1912-.........................CLC 1
See also CA 21-24R
See also SATA 14
See also DLB 8

Varda, Agnès 1928-...............CLC 16

Vargas Llosa, (Jorge) Mario (Pedro)
1936-.............CLC 3, 6, 9, 10, 15
See also CA 73-76

Vassilikos, Vassilis 1933-........CLC 4, 8
See also CA 81-84

Verga, Giovanni 1840-1922.......TCLC 3
See also CA 104

Verhaeren, Émile (Adolphe Gustave)
1855-1916..................TCLC 12
See also CA 109

Verlaine, Paul (Marie)
1844-1896...................NCLC 2

Verne, Jules (Gabriel)
1828-1905...................TCLC 6
See also CA 110
See also SATA 21

Vian, Boris 1920-1959...........TCLC 9
See also CA 106

Viaud, (Louis Marie) Julien 1850-1923
See Loti, Pierre
See also CA 107

Vicker, Angus 1916-
See Felsen, Henry Gregor

Vidal, Gore
1925-...........CLC 2, 4, 6, 8, 10, 22
See also CA 5-8R
See also DLB 6
See also AITN 1

Viereck, Peter (Robert Edwin)
1916-.........................CLC 4
See also CANR 1
See also CA 1-4R
See also DLB 5

Villiers de l'Isle Adam, Jean Marie Mathias Philippe Auguste, Comte de,
1838-1889...................NCLC 3

Visconti, Luchino 1906-1976.......CLC 16
See also CA 81-84
See also obituary CA 65-68

Vittorini, Elio 1908-1966.....CLC 6, 9, 14
See also obituary CA 25-28R

Vliet, R(ussell) G. 1929-...........CLC 22
See also CA 37-40R

Voinovich, Vladimir (Nikolaevich)
1932-........................CLC 10
See also CA 81-84

Vonnegut, Kurt, Jr.
1922-......CLC 1, 2, 3, 4, 5, 8, 12, 22
See also CANR 1
See also CA 1-4R
See also DLB 2, 8
See also DLB-Y 80
See also DLB-DS 3
See also AITN 1

Voznesensky, Andrei 1933-.....CLC 1, 15
See also CA 89-92

Waddington, Miriam 1917-........CLC 28
See also CA 21-24R

Wagman, Fredrica 1937-...........CLC 7
See also CA 97-100

Wagoner, David (Russell)
1926-...................CLC 3, 5, 15
See also CANR 2
See also CA 1-4R
See also SATA 14
See also DLB 5

Wahlöö, Per 1926-1975............CLC 7
See also CA 61-64

Wain, John (Barrington)
1925-..................CLC 2, 11, 15
See also CA 5-8R
See also DLB 15

Wajda, Andrzej 1926-.............CLC 16
See also CA 102

Wakefield, Dan 1932-..............CLC 7
See also CA 21-24R

Wakoski, Diane
1937-..............CLC 2, 4, 7, 9, 11
See also CANR 9
See also CA 13-16R
See also DLB 5

Walcott, Derek (Alton)
1930-............CLC 2, 4, 9, 14, 25
See also CA 89-92
See also DLB-Y 81

Waldman, Anne 1945-.............CLC 7
See also CA 37-40R
See also DLB 16

Waldo, Edward Hamilton 1918-
See Sturgeon, Theodore (Hamilton)

Walker, Alice
1944-.............CLC 5, 6, 9, 19, 27
See also CANR 9
See also CA 37-40R
See also SATA 31
See also DLB 6

Walker, David Harry 1911-........CLC 14
See also CANR 1
See also CA 1-4R
See also SATA 8

Walker, Joseph A. 1935-..........CLC 19
See also CA 89-92

Walker, Margaret (Abigail)
1915-.......................CLC 1, 6
See also CA 73-76

Walker, Ted 1934-................CLC 13
See also CA 21-24R

Wallace, Irving 1916- .... **CLC 7, 13**
See also CANR 1
See also CA 1-4R
See also AITN 1

Wallant, Edward Lewis 1926-1962 .... **CLC 5, 10**
See also CA 1-4R
See also DLB 2

Walpole, (Sir) Hugh (Seymour) 1884-1941 .... **TCLC 5**
See also CA 104

Walser, Martin 1927- .... **CLC 27**
See also CANR 8
See also CA 57-60

Wambaugh, Joseph (Aloysius, Jr.) 1937- .... **CLC 3, 18**
See also CA 33-36R
See also DLB 6
See also AITN 1

Ward, Douglas Turner 1930- .... **CLC 19**
See also CA 81-84
See also DLB 7

Warhol, Andy 1928- .... **CLC 20**
See also CA 89-92

Warner, Francis (Robert le Plastrier) 1937- .... **CLC 14**
See also CANR 11
See also CA 53-56

Warner, Sylvia Townsend 1893-1978 .... **CLC 7, 19**
See also CA 61-64
See also obituary CA 77-80

Warren, Robert Penn 1905- .... **CLC 1, 4, 6, 8, 10, 13, 18**
See also CANR 10
See also CA 13-16R
See also DLB 2
See also DLB-Y 80
See also AITN 1

Washington, Booker T(aliaferro) 1856-1915 .... **TCLC 10**
See also SATA 28

Wassermann, Jakob 1873-1934 .... **TCLC 6**
See also CA 104

Wa Thiong'o, Ngugi 1938- .... **CLC 13**
See also Ngugi, James (Thiong'o)

Waugh, Auberon (Alexander) 1939- .... **CLC 7**
See also CANR 6
See also CA 45-48
See also DLB 14

Waugh, Evelyn (Arthur St. John) 1903-1966 ...... **CLC 1, 3, 8, 13, 19, 27**
See also CA 85-88
See also obituary CA 25-28R
See also DLB 15

Waugh, Harriet 1944- .... **CLC 6**
See also CA 85-88

Webb, Charles (Richard) 1939- ...... **CLC 7**
See also CA 25-28R

Webb, James H(enry), Jr. 1946- .... **CLC 22**
See also CA 81-84

Webb, Phyllis 1927- .... **CLC 18**
See also CA 104

Webber, Andrew Lloyd 1948-
See Rice, Tim and Webber, Andrew Lloyd

Weber, Lenora Mattingly 1895-1971 .... **CLC 12**
See also CAP 1
See also CA 19-20
See also obituary CA 29-32R
See also SATA 2
See also obituary SATA 26

Wedekind, (Benjamin) Frank(lin) 1864-1918 .... **TCLC 7**
See also CA 104

Weidman, Jerome 1913- .... **CLC 7**
See also CANR 1
See also CA 1-4R
See also AITN 2

Weir, Peter 1944- .... **CLC 20**

Weiss, Peter (Ulrich) 1916-1982 .... **CLC 3, 15**
See also CANR 3
See also CA 45-48
See also obituary CA 106

Weiss, Theodore (Russell) 1916- .... **CLC 3, 8, 14**
See also CA 9-12R
See also DLB 5

Welch, James 1940- .... **CLC 6, 14**
See also CA 85-88

Weldon, Fay 1933- .... **CLC 6, 9, 11, 19**
See also CA 21-24R
See also DLB 14

Wellek, René 1903- .... **CLC 28**
See also CANR 8
See also CA 5-8R

Weller, Michael 1942- .... **CLC 10**
See also CA 85-88

Weller, Paul 1958- .... **CLC 26**

Welles, (George) Orson 1915- ...... **CLC 20**
See also CA 93-96

Wells, H(erbert) G(eorge) 1866-1946 .... **TCLC 6, 12**
See also CA 110
See also SATA 20

Wells, Rosemary .... **CLC 12**
See also CA 85-88
See also SATA 18

Welty, Eudora 1909- .... **CLC 1, 2, 5, 14, 22**
See also CA 9-12R
See also DLB 2

Werfel, Franz (V.) 1890-1945 ..... **TCLC 8**
See also CA 104

Wergeland, Henrik Arnold 1808-1845 .... **NCLC 5**

Wertmüller, Lina 1928- .... **CLC 16**
See also CA 97-100

Wescott, Glenway 1901- .... **CLC 13**
See also CA 13-16R
See also DLB 4, 9

Wesker, Arnold 1932- .... **CLC 3, 5**
See also CANR 1
See also CA 1-4R
See also DLB 13

Wesley, Richard (Errol) 1945- .... **CLC 7**
See also CA 57-60

West, Jessamyn 1907- .... **CLC 7, 17**
See also CA 9-12R
See also DLB 6

West, Morris L(anglo) 1916- .... **CLC 6**
See also CA 5-8R

West, Nathanael 1903?-1940 ...... **TCLC 1**
See also CA 104
See also DLB 4, 9

West, Paul 1930- .... **CLC 7, 14**
See also CA 13-16R
See also DLB 14

West, Rebecca 1892-1983 .... **CLC 7, 9**
See also obituary CA 109
See also CA 5-8R

Westall, Robert (Atkinson) 1929- .... **CLC 17**
See also CA 69-72
See also SATA 23

Westlake, Donald E(dwin) 1933- .... **CLC 7**
See also CA 17-20R

Whalen, Philip 1923- .... **CLC 6, 29**
See also CANR 5
See also CA 9-12R
See also DLB 16

Wharton, Edith (Newbold Jones) 1862-1937 .... **TCLC 3, 9**
See also CA 104
See also DLB 4, 9, 12

Wharton, William 1925- .... **CLC 18**
See also CA 93-96
See also DLB-Y 80

Wheelock, John Hall 1886-1978 .... **CLC 14**
See also CA 13-16R
See also obituary CA 77-80

Whitaker, Rodney 1925-
See Trevanian
See also CA 29-32R

White, E(lwyn) B(rooks) 1899- ..... **CLC 10**
See also CLR 1
See also CA 13-16R
See also SATA 2, 29
See also DLB 11, 22
See also AITN 2

White, Edmund III 1940- .... **CLC 27**
See also CANR 3
See also CA 45-48

White, Patrick (Victor Martindale) 1912- .... **CLC 3, 4, 5, 7, 9, 18**
See also CA 81-84

Whitehead, E(dward) A(nthony) 1933- .... **CLC 5**
See also CA 65-68

Whitman, Walt 1819-1892 .... **NCLC 4**
See also SATA 20
See also DLB 3

Whittemore, (Edward) Reed (Jr.) 1919- .... **CLC 4**
See also CANR 4
See also CA 9-12R
See also DLB 5

Wicker, Thomas Grey 1926-
See Wicker, Tom
See also CA 65-68

Wicker, Tom 1926- .... **CLC 7**
See also Wicker, Thomas Grey

Wideman, J(ohn) E(dgar) 1941- ..... **CLC 5**
See also CA 85-88

Wiebe, Rudy (H.) 1934- ..... **CLC 6, 11, 14**
See also CA 37-40R

Wieners, John 1934- .... **CLC 7**
See also CA 13-16R
See also DLB 16

Wiesel, Elie(zer) 1928- .... **CLC 3, 5, 11**
See also CANR 8
See also CA 5-8R
See also AITN 1

Wight, James Alfred 1916-
See Herriot, James
See also CA 77-80

Wilbur, Richard (Purdy)
1921- .... **CLC 3, 6, 9, 14**
See also CANR 2
See also CA 1-4R
See also SATA 9
See also DLB 5

Wild, Peter 1940-................. **CLC 14**
See also CA 37-40R
See also DLB 5

Wilde, Oscar (Fingal O'Flahertie Wills)
1855-1900................. **TCLC 1, 8**
See also CA 104
See also SATA 24
See also DLB 10, 19

Wilder, Billy 1906- .... **CLC 20**
See also Wilder, Samuel
See also DLB 26

Wilder, Samuel 1906-
See Wilder, Billy
See also CA 89-92

Wilder, Thornton (Niven)
1897-1975......... **CLC 1, 5, 6, 10, 15**
See also CA 13-16R
See also obituary CA 61-64
See also DLB 4, 7, 9
See also AITN 2

Wilhelm, Kate 1928-............... **CLC 7**
See also CA 37-40R
See also DLB 8

Willard, Nancy 1936- .... **CLC 7**
See also CLR 5
See also CANR 10
See also CA 89-92
See also SATA 30
See also DLB 5

Williams, Charles (Walter Stansby)
1886-1945................ **TCLC 1, 11**
See also CA 104

Williams, (George) Emlyn
1905-........................ **CLC 15**
See also CA 104
See also DLB 10

Williams, John A(lfred)
1925-..................... **CLC 5, 13**
See also CANR 6
See also CA 53-56
See also DLB 2

Williams, Jonathan (Chamberlain)
1929-........................ **CLC 13**
See also CANR 8
See also CA 9-12R
See also DLB 5

Williams, Paulette 1948-
See Shange, Ntozake

Williams, Tennessee
1914-1983....... **CLC 1, 2, 5, 7, 8, 11, 15, 19**
See also CA 5-8R
See also obituary CA 108
See also DLB 7
See also DLB-DS 4
See also AITN 1, 2

Williams, Thomas (Alonzo)
1926-........................ **CLC 14**
See also CANR 2
See also CA 1-4R

Williams, William Carlos
1883-1963....... **CLC 1, 2, 5, 9, 13, 22**
See also CA 89-92
See also DLB 4, 16

Williamson, Jack 1908-............ **CLC 29**
See also CA 17-20R
See also DLB 8

Willingham, Calder (Baynard, Jr.)
1922-........................ **CLC 5**
See also CANR 3
See also CA 5-8R
See also DLB 2

Wilson, Angus (Frank Johnstone)
1913-................. **CLC 2, 3, 5, 25**
See also CA 5-8R
See also DLB 15

Wilson, Brian 1942- .... **CLC 12**

Wilson, Colin 1931-............ **CLC 3, 14**
See also CANR 1
See also CA 1-4R
See also DLB 14

Wilson, Edmund
1895-1972.......... **CLC 1, 2, 3, 8, 24**
See also CANR 1
See also CA 1-4R
See also obituary CA 37-40R

Wilson, Ethel Davis (Bryant)
1888-1980.................... **CLC 13**
See also CA 102

Wilson, John 1785-1854.......... **NCLC 5**

Wilson, John (Anthony) Burgess 1917-
See Burgess, Anthony
See also CANR 2
See also CA 1-4R

Wilson, Lanford 1937- .... **CLC 7, 14**
See also CA 17-20R
See also DLB 7

Wilson, Robert (M.) 1944-....... **CLC 7, 9**
See also CANR 2
See also CA 49-52

Wilson, Sloan 1920-............... **CLC 29**
See also CANR 1
See also CA 1-4R

Winters, (Arthur) Yvor
1900-1968.................. **CLC 4, 8**
See also CAP 1
See also CA 11-12
See also obituary CA 25-28R

Wiseman, Frederick 1930-......... **CLC 20**

Witkiewicz, Stanislaw Ignacy
1885-1939................... **TCLC 8**
See also CA 105

Wittig, Monique 1935?- .... **CLC 22**

Wittlin, Joseph 1896-1976 .... **CLC 25**
See also Wittlin, Józef

Wittlin, Józef 1896-1976
See Wittlin, Joseph
See also CANR 3
See also CA 49-52
See also obituary CA 65-68

Wodehouse, P(elham) G(renville)
1881-1975......... **CLC 1, 2, 5, 10, 22**
See also CANR 3
See also CA 45-48
See also obituary CA 57-60
See also SATA 22
See also AITN 2

Woiwode, Larry (Alfred)
1941-..................... **CLC 6, 10**
See also CA 73-76
See also DLB 6

Wojciechowska, Maia (Teresa)
1927-........................ **CLC 26**
See also CLR 1
See also CANR 4
See also CA 9-12R
See also SATA 1, 28

Wolf, Christa 1929-........... **CLC 14, 29**
See also CA 85-88

Wolfe, Gene (Rodman) 1931- ...... **CLC 25**
See also CANR 6
See also CA 57-60
See also DLB 8

Wolfe, Thomas (Clayton)
1900-1938................ **TCLC 4, 13**
See also CA 104
See also DLB 9
See also DLB-DS 2

Wolfe, Thomas Kennerly, Jr. 1931-
See Wolfe, Tom
See also CANR 9
See also CA 13-16R

Wolfe, Tom 1931- ....**CLC 1, 2, 9, 15**
See also Wolfe, Thomas Kennerly, Jr.
See also AITN 2

Wolitzer, Hilma 1930-............. **CLC 17**
See also CA 65-68
See also SATA 31

Wonder, Stevie 1950- .... **CLC 12**
See also Morris, Steveland Judkins

Wong, Jade Snow 1922-........... **CLC 17**
See also CA 109

Woodcott, Keith 1934-
See Brunner, John (Kilian Houston)

Woolf, (Adeline) Virginia
1882-1941................. **TCLC 1, 5**
See also CA 104

Woollcott, Alexander (Humphreys)
1887-1943.................. **TCLC 5**
See also CA 105

Wouk, Herman 1915- .... **CLC 1, 9**
See also CANR 6
See also CA 5-8R
See also DLB-Y 82

Wright, Charles 1935- ...... **CLC 6, 13, 28**
See also CA 29-32R
See also DLB-Y 82

Wright, James (Arlington) 1927-1980............**CLC 3, 5, 10, 28**
See also CANR 4
See also CA 49-52
See also obituary CA 97-100
See also DLB 5
See also AITN 2

Wright, Judith 1915-..............**CLC 11**
See also CA 13-16R
See also SATA 14

Wright, Richard (Nathaniel) 1908-1960.......**CLC 1, 3, 4, 9, 14, 21**
See also CA 108
See also DLB-DS 2

Wright, Richard B(ruce) 1937-......**CLC 6**
See also CA 85-88

Wurlitzer, Rudolph 1938?-..................**CLC 2, 4, 15**
See also CA 85-88

Wylie (Benét), Elinor (Morton Hoyt) 1885-1928...................**TCLC 8**
See also CA 105
See also DLB 9

Wyndham, John 1903-1969........**CLC 19**
See also Harris, John (Wyndham Parkes Lucas) Beynon

Yanovsky, Vassily S(emenovich) 1906-.....................**CLC 2, 18**
See also CA 97-100

Yates, Richard 1926-.........**CLC 7, 8, 23**
See also CANR 10
See also CA 5-8R
See also DLB 2
See also DLB-Y 81

Yeats, William Butler 1865-1939................**TCLC 1, 11**
See also CANR 10
See also CA 104
See also DLB 10, 19

Yehoshua, Abraham B. 1936-......**CLC 13**
See also CA 33-36R

Yerby, Frank G(arvin) 1916-...................**CLC 1, 7, 22**
See also CA 9-12R

Yevtushenko, Yevgeny (Aleksandrovich) 1933-................**CLC 1, 3, 13, 26**
See also CA 81-84

Yglesias, Helen 1915- ....**CLC 7, 22**
See also CA 37-40R

Yorke, Henry Vincent 1905-1974
See Green, Henry
See also CA 85-88
See also obituary CA 49-52

Young, Al 1939-..................**CLC 19**
See also CA 29-32R

Young, Andrew 1885-1971..........**CLC 5**
See also CANR 7
See also CA 5-8R

Young, Neil 1945-................**CLC 17**

Yourcenar, Marguerite 1913-......**CLC 19**
See also CA 69-72

Yurick, Sol 1925-..................**CLC 6**
See also CA 13-16R

Zamyatin, Yevgeny Ivanovich 1884-1937...................**TCLC 8**
See also CA 105

Zappa, Francis Vincent, Jr. 1940-
See Zappa, Frank
See also CA 108

Zappa, Frank 1940- ....**CLC 17**
See also Zappa, Francis Vincent, Jr.

Zaturenska, Marya 1902-1982.................**CLC 6, 11**
See also CA 13-16R
See also obituary CA 105

Zelazny, Roger 1937- ....**CLC 21**
See also CA 21-24R
See also DLB 8

Zimmerman, Robert 1941-
See Dylan, Bob

Zindel, Paul 1936-.............**CLC 6, 26**
See also CLR 3
See also CA 73-76
See also SATA 16
See also DLB 7

Zinoviev, Alexander 1922-.........**CLC 19**

Zola, Émile 1840-1902 ....**TCLC 1, 6**
See also CA 104

Zorrilla y Moral, José 1817-1893...................**NCLC 6**

Zuckmayer, Carl 1896-1977 ....**CLC 18**
See also CA 69-72

Zukofsky, Louis 1904-1978.......**CLC 1, 2, 4, 7, 11, 18**
See also CA 9-12R
See also obituary CA 77-80
See also DLB 5

Cumulative Index to Nationalities

AMERICAN
Adams, Henry **4**
Agee, James **1**
Anderson, Maxwell **2**
Anderson, Sherwood **1, 10**
Atherton, Gertrude **2**
Barry, Philip **11**
Baum, L. Frank **7**
Belasco, David **3**
Benchley, Robert **1**
Benét, Stephen Vincent **7**
Bierce, Ambrose **1, 7**
Bromfield, Louis **11**
Burroughs, Edgar Rice **2**
Cabell, James Branch **6**
Cable, George Washington **4**
Cather, Willa **1, 11**
Chandler, Raymond **1, 7**
Chapman, John Jay **7**
Chesnutt, Charles Waddell **5**
Chopin, Kate **5**
Comstock, Anthony **13**
Crane, Hart **2, 5**
Crane, Stephen **11**
Crawford, F. Marion **10**
Cullen, Countee **4**
Davis, Rebecca Harding **6**
Dreiser, Theodore **10**
Dunbar, Paul Laurence **2, 12**
Fisher, Rudolph **11**
Fitzgerald, F. Scott **1, 6**
Freeman, Douglas Southall **11**
Freeman, Mary Wilkins **9**
Gale, Zona **7**
Garland, Hamlin **3**
Gilman, Charlotte Perkins **9**
Glasgow, Ellen **2, 7**
Goldman, Emma **13**
Grey, Zane **6**
Harris, Joel Chandler **2**
Harte, Bret **1**
Hearn, Lafcadio **9**
Henry, O. **1**
Hergesheimer, Joseph **11**
Howard, Robert E. **8**
Howells, William Dean **7**
James, Henry **2, 11**
Jewett, Sarah Orne **1**
Johnson, James Weldon **3**
Kornbluth, C. M. **8**
Kuttner, Henry **10**
Lardner, Ring **2**
Lewis, Sinclair **4, 13**
London, Jack **9**
Lovecraft, H. P. **4**
Lowell, Amy **1, 8**
Marquis, Don **7**
Masters, Edgar Lee **2**
McKay, Claude **7**
Mencken, H. L. **13**
Millay, Edna St. Vincent **4**
Mitchell, Margaret **11**
Monroe, Harriet **12**
O'Neill, Eugene **1, 6**
Rawlings, Majorie Kinnan **4**
Reed, John **9**
Robinson, Edwin Arlington **5**
Rogers, Will **8**
Rourke, Constance **12**
Runyon, Damon **10**
Saltus, Edgar **8**
Sherwood, Robert E. **3**
Slesinger, Tess **10**
Stein, Gertrude **1, 6**
Stevens, Wallace **3, 12**
Tarkington, Booth **9**
Teasdale, Sara **4**
Thurman, Wallace **6**
Twain, Mark **6, 12**
Washington, Booker T. **10**
West, Nathanael **1**
Wharton, Edith **3, 9**
Wolfe, Thomas **4, 13**
Woollcott, Alexander **5**
Wylie, Elinor **8**

ARGENTINIAN
Storni, Alfonsina **5**

AUSTRALIAN
Franklin, Miles **7**
Richardson, Henry Handel **4**

AUSTRIAN
Hofmannsthal, Hugo von **11**
Kafka, Franz **2, 6, 13**
Kraus, Karl **5**
Musil, Robert **12**
Schnitzler, Arthur **4**
Steiner, Rudolf **13**
Trakl, Georg **5**
Werfel, Franz **8**

BELGIAN
Maeterlinck, Maurice **3**
Verhaeren, Émile **12**

BRAZILIAN
Machado de Assis, Joaquim Maria **10**

CANADIAN
Campbell, Wilfred **9**
Carman, Bliss **7**
Garneau, Hector Saint-Denys **13**
Grove, Frederick Philip **4**
Leacock, Stephen **2**
McCrae, John **12**
Roberts, Charles G. D. **8**
Scott, Duncan Campbell **6**

CHILEAN
Mistral, Gabriela **2**

CHINESE
Lu Hsün **3**

CZECHOSLOVAKIAN
Capek, Karel **6**
Hašek, Jaroslav **4**

DANISH
Brandes, Georg **10**

ENGLISH
Baring, Maurice **8**
Besant, Annie **9**
Beerbohm, Max **1**
Belloc, Hilaire **7**
Bennett, Arnold **5**
Bentley, E. C. **12**
Blackwood, Algernon **5**
Bridges, Robert **1**
Brooke, Rupert **2, 7**
Butler, Samuel **1**
Chesterton, G. K. **1, 6**
Conrad, Joseph **1, 6, 13**
Coppard, A. E. **5**
Crowley, Aleister **7**
De la Mare, Walter **4**
Dowson, Ernest **4**
Doyle, Arthur Conan **7**
Firbank, Ronald **1**
Ford, Ford Madox **1**
Galsworthy, John **1**

Gilbert, W. S. **3**
Gissing, George **3**
Granville-Barker, Harley **2**
Haggard, H. Rider **11**
Hall, Radclyffe **12**
Hardy, Thomas **4, 10**
Henley, William Ernest **8**
Hodgson, William Hope **13**
Housman, A. E. **1, 10**
Housman, Laurence **7**
James, M. R. **6**
Kipling, Rudyard **8**
Lawrence, D. H. **2, 9**
Lee, Vernon **5**
Lewis, Wyndham **2, 9**
Lowndes, Marie Belloc **12**
Lowry, Malcolm **6**
Macaulay, Rose **7**
Mew, Charlotte **8**
Meynell, Alice **6**
Milne, A. A. **6**
Noyes, Alfred **7**
Orwell, George **2, 6**
Owen, Wilfred **5**
Powys, T. F. **9**
Richardson, Dorothy **3**
Rolfe, Frederick **12**
Rosenberg, Isaac **12**
Saki **3**
Sayers, Dorothy L. **2**
Shiel, M. P. **8**
Sinclair, May **3, 11**
Strachey, Lytton **12**
Sutro, Alfred **6**
Swinburne, Algernon Charles **8**
Symons, Arthur **11**
Thomas, Edward **10**
Thompson, Francis **4**
Van Druten, John **2**
Walpole, Hugh **5**
Wells, H. G. **6, 12**
Williams, Charles **1, 11**
Woolf, Virginia **1, 5**

FRENCH
Alain-Fournier **6**
Apollinaire, Guillaume **3, 8**
Artaud, Antonin **3**
Barbusse, Henri **5**
Bernanos, Georges **3**
Bourget, Paul **12**
Claudel, Paul **2, 10**
Colette **1, 5**
Dujardin, Édouard **13**
Éluard, Paul **7**
Fargue, Léon-Paul **11**
France, Anatole **9**
Gide, André **5, 12**
Giraudoux, Jean **2, 7**
Huysmans, Joris-Karl **7**
Jacob, Max **6**
Jarry, Alfred **2**
Larbaud, Valéry **9**
Loti, Pierre **11**
Péguy, Charles **10**
Proust, Marcel **7, 13**
Rostand, Edmond **6**
Saint-Exupéry, Antoine de **2**
Teilhard de Chardin, Pierre **9**
Valéry, Paul **4**
Verne, Jules **6**
Vian, Boris **9**
Zola, Émile **1, 6**

GERMAN
Benn, Gottfried **3**
Borchert, Wolfgang **5**
Brecht, Bertolt **1, 6, 13**
Döblin, Alfred **13**
Ewers, Hanns Heinz **12**
Feuchtwanger, Lion **3**
George, Stefan **2**
Hauptmann, Gerhart **4**
Heym, Georg **9**
Heyse, Paul **8**
Huch, Ricarda **13**
Kaiser, Georg **9**
Mann, Heinrich **9**
Mann, Thomas **2, 8**
Morgenstern, Christian **8**
Nietzsche, Friedrich **10**
Rilke, Rainer Maria **1, 6**
Sternheim, Carl **8**
Toller, Ernst **10**
Wassermann, Jakob **6**
Wedekind, Frank **7**

GREEK
Cafavy, C. P. **2, 7**
Kazantzakis, Nikos **2, 5**
Palamas, Kostes **5**

HUNGARIAN
Ady, Endre **11**
Csáth, Géza **13**

INDIAN
Chatterji, Saratchandra **13**
Tagore, Rabindranath **3**

IRISH
A. E. **3, 10**
Cary, Joyce **1**
Dunsany, Lord **2**
Gregory, Lady **1**
Joyce, James **3, 8**
Moore, George **7**
O'Grady, Standish **5**
Shaw, Bernard **3, 9**
Stephens, James **4**
Stoker, Bram **8**
Synge, J. M. **6**
Tynan, Katharine **3**
Wilde, Oscar **1, 8**
Yeats, William Butler **1, 11**

ITALIAN
Betti, Ugo **5**
Brancati, Vitaliano **12**
D'Annunzio, Gabriel **6**
Giacosa, Giuseppe **7**
Lampedusa, Giuseppe Tomasi di **13**
Marinetti, F. T. **10**
Pavese, Cesare **3**
Pirandello, Luigi **4**
Svevo, Italo **2**
Verga, Giovanni **3**

JAMAICAN
De Lisser, H. G. **12**
Mais, Roger **8**

JAPANESE
Dazai, Osamu **11**
Natsume, Sōseki **2, 10**
Shimazaki, Tōson **5**

LEBANESE
Gibran, Kahlil **1, 9**

MEXICAN
Azuela, Mariano **3**
Nervo, Amado **11**

NEW ZEALAND
Mansfield, Katherine **2, 8**

NICARAGUAN
Darío, Rubén **4**

NORWEGIAN
Bjørnson, Bjørnstjerne **7**
Grieg, Nordhal **10**
Hamsun, Knut **2**
Ibsen, Henrik **2, 8**
Kielland, Alexander **5**
Lie, Jonas **5**
Undset, Sigrid **3**

PERUVIAN
Vallejo, César **3**

POLISH
Borowski, Tadeusz **9**
Reymont, Wladyslaw Stanislaw **5**
Schulz, Bruno **5**
Sienkiewitz, Henryk **3**
Witkiewicz, Stanislaw Ignacy **8**

RUSSIAN
Andreyev, Leonid **3**
Babel, Isaak **2, 13**
Balmont, Konstantin Dmitriyevich **11**
Bely, Andrey **7**
Blok, Aleksandr **5**
Bryusov, Valery **10**
Bulgakov, Mikhail **2**
Bunin, Ivan **6**
Chekhov, Anton **3, 10**
Esenin, Sergei **4**
Gorky, Maxim **8**
Hippius, Zinaida **9**
Kuprin, Aleksandr **5**
Mandelstam, Osip **2, 6**
Mayakovsky, Vladimir **4**
Sologub, Fyodor **9**
Tolstoy, Leo **4, 11**
Tsvetaeva, Marina **7**
Zamyatin, Yevgeny Ivanovich **8**

SCOTTISH
Barrie, J. M. **2**
Bridie, James **3**
Gibbon, Lewis Grassic **4**
MacDonald, George **9**
Muir, Edwin **2**

SOUTH AFRICAN
Campbell, Roy **5**
Schreiner, Olive **9**

SPANISH
Baroja, Pío **8**
Benavente, Jacinto **3**
Blasco Ibáñez, Vicente **12**
Echegaray, José **4**
García Lorca, Federico **1, 7**
Jiménez, Juan Ramón **4**
Machado, Antonio **3**
Martínez Sierra, Gregorio **6**
Miró, Gabriel **5**
Ortega y Gasset, José **9**
Unamuno, Miguel de **2, 9**
Valera, Juan **10**
Valle-Inclán, Ramón del **5**

SWEDISH
Heidenstam, Verner von **5**
Lagerlöf, Selma **4**
Strindberg, August **1, 8**

SWISS
Spitteler, Carl **12**

WELSH
Davies, W. H. **5**
Lewis, Alun **3**
Machen, Arthur **4**
Thomas, Dylan **1, 8**

YIDDISH
Aleichem, Sholom **1**
Asch, Sholem **3**

Cumulative Index to Critics

A. E.
See also **Russell, George William**
Standish O'Grady **5**:348, 349
James Stephens **4**:407
Leo Tolstoy **4**:459
Katharine Tynan **3**:505
William Butler Yeats **11**:516

Aaron, Daniel
Nathanael West **1**:485

Abbott, Lyman
Booker T. Washington **10**:522

Abcarian, Richard
Sherwood Anderson **1**:59

Abel, Lionel
Bertolt Brecht **1**:109
Henrik Ibsen **2**:232

Abercrombie, Lascelles
Thomas Hardy **4**:153

Abrams, Ivan B.
Sholom Aleichem **1**:24

Abramson, Doris E.
Rudolph Fisher **11**:207
Wallace Thurman **6**:449

Abril, Xavier
César Vallejo **3**:526

Achebe, Chinua
Joseph Conrad **13**:130

Adams, Henry
William Dean Howells **7**:363
Mark Twain **12**:428

Adams, J. Donald
Theodore Dreiser **10**:177
F. Scott Fitzgerald **1**:239

Adams, Marion
Gottfried Benn **3**:111

Adams, Phoebe-Lou
Malcolm Lowry **6**:237

Adams, Robert M.
Gabriele D'Annunzio **6**:140
Franz Kafka **13**:268
Tess Slesinger **10**:441

Adams, Robert Martin
Alfred Döblin **13**:179
James Joyce **3**:273

Adams, Samuel Hopkins
Alexander Woollcott **5**:524

Adams, Walter S.
Thomas Wolfe **4**:506

Adcock, A. St. John
Wilfred Campbell **9**:31
O. Henry **1**:347
Joseph Hergesheimer **11**:274
William Hope Hodgson **13**:230
Bernard Shaw **3**:386

Adell, Alberto
Ramón del Valle-Inclán **5**:484

Adereth, M.
Charles Péguy **10**:413

Adrian, John
Paul Heyse **8**:123

Ady, Endre
Endre Ady **11**:12

Aguirre, Ángel Manuel
Juan Ramón Jiménez **4**:223

Aguinaga, Carlos Blanco
Miguel de Unamuno **2**:561

Aiken, Conrad
Sherwood Anderson **1**:37
Robert Bridges **1**:127
James Branch Cabell **6**:62
Walter de la Mare **4**:71
F. Scott Fitzgerald **1**:237
John Galsworthy **1**:296
Federico García Lorca **1**:308
Thomas Hardy **4**:155
Joseph Hergesheimer **11**:262
A. E. Housman **10**:241
Henry James **11**:329
D. H. Lawrence **2**:344
Wyndham Lewis **9**:236
Edgar Lee Masters **2**:460
Harriet Monroe **12**:216
Eugene O'Neill **1**:383
Charles Péguy **10**:415
Dorothy Richardson **3**:349
Rainer Maria Rilke **1**:414
Edwin Arlington Robinson **5**:403
Gertrude Stein **6**:406
Dylan Thomas **1**:466
H. G. Wells **12**:499
Virginia Woolf **1**:529

Aiken, Henry David
Friedrich Nietzsche **10**:383

Akhsharumov, N. D.
Leo Tolstoy **4**:446

Alcott, Louisa May
Rebecca Harding Davis **6**:148

Aldington, Richard
Oscar Wilde **1**:499

Aldiss, Brian W.
Henry Kuttner **10**:271
Jules Verne **6**:497

Aldridge, John
F. Scott Fitzgerald **1**:246

Alexander, Holmes
Margaret Mitchell **11**:373

Alexandrova, Vera
Sergei Esenin **4**:113

Allen, Clifford
Radclyffe Hall **12**:190

Allen, Paul
Hanns Heinz Ewers **12**:135

Allen, Paul Marshall
Rudolf Steiner **13**:447, 448
Jakob Wassermann **6**:520

Allen, Walter
Arnold Bennett **5**:40
Wyndham Lewis **2**:394
Dorothy Richardson **3**:358

Allison, J. E.
Heinrich Mann **9**:331

Alpers, Antony
Katherine Mansfield **8**:291

Alpert, Hollis
O. Henry **1**:350

Alsen, Eberhard
Hamlin Garland **3**:200

Altrocchi, Rudolph
Gabriele D'Annunzio **6**:135

Alvarez, A.
Hart Crane **2**:118
Thomas Hardy **10**:221
D. H. Lawrence **2**:364
Wallace Stevens **3**:454
William Butler Yeats **1**:564

Alworth, E. Paul
Will Rogers **8**:336

Amann, Clarence A.
James Weldon Johnson **3**:247

Amis, Kingsley
G. K. Chesterton **1**:185
C. M. Kornbluth **8**:213
Jules Verne **6**:493

Ammons, Elizabeth
Edith Wharton **9**:552

Amoia, Alba della Fazia
Edmond Rostand **6**:381

Amon, Frank
D. H. Lawrence **9**:220

Anders, Gunther
Franz Kafka **2**:302

Anderson, David D.
Sherwood Anderson **1**:52
Louis Bromfield **11**:85, 87
Sinclair Lewis **13**:351

Anderson, Frederick
Mark Twain **12**:445

Anderson, Isaac
Raymond Chandler **7**:167
Rudolph Fisher **11**:204

Anderson, Margaret C.
Anthony Comstock **13**:90
Emma Goldman **13**:210

Anderson, Maxwell
Sherwood Anderson **10**:31
Vicente Blasco Ibáñez **12**:32
Joseph Hergesheimer **11**:261
Edna St. Vincent Millay **4**:306

Anderson, Quentin
Willa Cather **1**:163

Anderson, Sherwood
Sherwood Anderson **10**:31
Stephen Crane **11**:133
Theodore Dreiser **10**:169
Sinclair Lewis **13**:333
Gertrude Stein **6**:407
Mark Twain **6**:459

Andreas, Osborn
Henry James **11**:330

Andrews, William L.
Charles Waddel Chesnutt **5**:136

Angenot, Marc
Jules Verne **6**:501

Angus, Douglas
Franz Kafka **13**:264

Annenkov, P. V.
Leo Tolstoy **4**:444

Anouilh, Jean
Jean Giraudoux **7**:320

Anthony, Edward
Don Marquis **7**:443

Anthony, G. F. Penn
Pierre Teilhard de Chardin **9**:501

Antoninus, Brother
Hart Crane **2**:119

Appignanesi, Lisa
Robert Musil **12**:257

Aptheker, Herbert
Booker T. Washington **10**:530

Aquilar, Helene J.F. de
Federico García Lorca **7**:302

Aragon, Louis
Paul Éluard **7**:249

Aratari, Anthony
Federico García Lorca **1**:316

Arce de Vazquez, Margot
Gabriela Mistral **2**:477

Archer, William
Bliss Carman **7**:135
W. S. Gilbert **3**:207
A. E. Housman **10**:239
Laurence Housman **7**:352
Henrik Ibsen **2**:224
Selma Lagerlöf **4**:229
Alice Meynell **6**:294
Duncan Campbell Scott **6**:385
Arthur Symons **11**:428
Francis Thompson **4**:434
Mark Twain **12**:427
William Butler Yeats **11**:510

Arden, Eugene
Paul Laurence Dunbar **12**:113

Arendt, Hannah
Bertolt Brecht **1**:114
Franz Kafka **2**:301

Arms, George
Kate Chopin **5**:149

Armstrong, Martin
Katherine Mansfield **2**:446

Arner, Robert D.
Kate Chopin **5**:155

Arnold, Matthew
Leo Tolstoy **11**:458

Aron, Albert W.
Jakob Wassermann **6**:509

Arrowsmith, William
Cesare Pavese **3**:334
Dylan Thomas **1**:468

Arvin, Newton
Henry Adams **4**:12

Ashbery, John
Gertrude Stein **1**:442

Ashworth, Arthur
Miles Franklin **7**:264

Aswell, Edward C.
Thomas Wolfe **4**:515

Atheling, William Jr.
See also **Blish, James**
Henry Kuttner **10**:266

Atherton, Gertrude
Ambrose Bierce **7**:88
May Sinclair **3**:434

Atkins, Elizabeth
Edna St. Vincent Millay **4**:311

Atkins, John
Walter de la Mare **4**:75
George Orwell **6**:341

Atkinson, Brooks
Rudolph Fisher **11**:204

Atlas, James
Gertrude Stein **1**:442
Thomas Wolfe **4**:538

Atlas, Marilyn Judith
Sherwood Anderson **10**:54

Attebery, Brian
L. Frank Baum **7**:25

Atterbury, Rev. Anson P.
Annie Besant **9**:13

Auchincloss, Louis
Paul Bourget **12**:72
Willa Cather **1**:164
Ellen Glasgow **2**:188
Henry James **2**:275
Sarah Orne Jewett **1**:367
Edith Wharton **3**:570

Auden, W. H.
Max Beerbohm **1**:72
Hilaire Belloc **7**:41
C. P. Cavafy **2**:90
Raymond Chandler **7**:168
G. K. Chesterton **1**:184, 186
Walter de la Mare **4**:81
Hugo von Hofmannsthal **11**:310
A. E. Housman **1**:358
Rudyard Kipling **8**:189
George MacDonald **9**:295
George Orwell **2**:512
Rainer Maria Rilke **6**:359
Frederick Rolfe **12**:268
Bernard Shaw **3**:389
Paul Valéry **4**:499
Nathanael West **1**:480
Oscar Wilde **1**:504, 507
Charles Williams **1**:516
Virginia Woolf **1**:546
William Butler Yeats **1**:562

Austin, Henry
Charlotte Gilman **9**:96

Austin, James C.
Rebecca Harding Davis **6**:151

Avseenko, V. G.
Leo Tolstoy **4**:446

Azorín
Ramón del Valle-Inclán **5**:479

Bab, Julius
Alfred Döblin **13**:158

Babbitt, Irving
H. L. Mencken **13**:371

Babel, Isaac
Isaac Babel **13**:17

Bacon, Leonard
Alexander Woollcott **5**:522

Bailey, Joseph W.
Arthur Schnitzler **4**:391

Bailey, Mabel Driscoll
Maxwell Anderson **2**:7

Baird, James
Wallace Stevens **3**:471

Baker, Carlos
Sherwood Anderson **1**:64
Edwin Muir **2**:483

Baker, George P.
Philip Barry **11**:45

Baker, Houston A., Jr.
Countee Cullen **4**:52
Paul Laurence Dunbar **12**:128
Booker T. Washington **10**:533

Baker, I. L.
E. C. Bentley **12**:16

Balakian, Anna
Guillaume Apollinaire **8**:19
Paul Claudel **10**:131
Paul Éluard **7**:257

Baldwin, Charles C.
Louis Bromfield **11**:71
Booth Tarkington **9**:458

Baldwin, Richard E.
Charles Waddell Chesnutt **5**:135

Baldwin, Roger N.
Emma Goldman **13**:216

Ball, Robert Hamilton
David Belasco **3**:88

Balmforth, Ramsden
Laurence Housman **7**:355

Balogh, Eva S.
Emma Goldman **13**:223

Baltrušaitis, Jurgis
Émile Verhaeren **12**:467

Bander, Elaine
Dorothy L. Sayers **2**:537

Bandyopadhyay, Manik
Saratchandra Chatterji **13**:83

Bangerter, Lowell A.
Hugo von Hofmannsthal **11**:311

Banks, Nancy Huston
William Butler Yeats Charles Waddell Chesnutt **5**:130

Bannister, Winifred
James Bridie **3**:134

Barbour, Ian G.
Pierre Teilhard de Chardin **9**:488

Barbusse, Henri
Henri Barbusse **5**:14

Barclay, Glen St John
H. Rider Haggard **11**:252
H. P. Lovecraft **4**:273
Bram Stoker **8**:399

Barea, Arturo
Miguel de Unamuno **2**:559

Barea, Ilsa
Miguel de Unamuno **2**:559

Bareham, Terence
Malcolm Lowry **6**:251

Barfield, Owen
Rudolf Steiner **13**:453

Baring, Maurice
Maurice Baring **8**:32
Hilaire Belloc **7**:32
Anton Chekhov **3**:145
Anatole France **9**:40
W. S. Gilbert **3**:211
Saki **3**:363
Leo Tolstoy **11**:459

Barker, Dudley
G. K. Chesterton **6**:101

Barker, Frank Granville
Joseph Conrad **1**:219

Barker, John
H. G. Wells **12**:515

Barker, Murl G.
Fyodor Sologub **9**:445

Barksdale, Richard K.
Claude McKay **7**:466

Barnard, Ellsworth
Edwin Arlington Robinson **5**:411

Barnard, Marjorie
Miles Franklin **7**:270

Barnes, Clive
August Strindberg **8**:420

Barnstone, Willis
C. P. Cavafy **7**:163
Edgar Lee Masters **2**:472

Barrett, Francis X.
Wallace Thurman **6**:450

Barrett, William
F. Scott Fitzgerald **1**:246
Friedrich Nietzsche **10**:378

Barrow, Leo L.
Pío Baroja **8**:57
Machado de Assis **10**:293

Barthes, Roland
Bertolt Brecht **1**:102
Pierre Loti **11**:363
Jules Verne **6**:491

Bartkovich, Jeffrey
Maxim Gorky **8**:89

Barzun, Jacques
E. C. Bentley **12**:20
Raymond Chandler **7**:171, 176
John Jay Chapman **7**:195
Malcolm Lowry **6**:236
Friedrich Nietzsche **10**:371
Bernard Shaw **3**:398

Basdekis, Demetrios
Miguel de Unamuno **2**:566

Baskervill, William Malone
George Washington Cable **4**:24
Joel Chandler Harris **2**:209

Baskett, Sam S.
Jack London **9**:267

Bates, H. E.
A. E. Coppard **5**:179
Radclyffe Hall **12**:188
Thomas Hardy **4**:161
Katherine Mansfield **8**:278

Bates, Scott
Guillaume Apollinaire **3**:37

Baudouin, Charles
Carl Spitteler **12**:335
Émile Verhaeren **12**:472

Baugh, Edward
Arthur Symons **11**:445

Bauland, Peter
Bertolt Brecht **13**:58
Gerhart Hauptmann **4**:209

Baum, L. Frank
L. Frank Baum **7**:12, 15

Baxandall, Lee
Bertolt Brecht **1**:119

Bayerschmidt, Carl F.
Sigrid Undset **3**:525

Bayley, John
Thomas Hardy **4**:177
Bruno Schulz **5**:427
Virginia Woolf **1**:550

Beach, Joseph Warren
Joseph Conrad **1**:199
Theodore Dreiser **10**:175
Thomas Hardy **4**:154
James Joyce **3**:257
D. H. Lawrence **2**:350
Hugh Walpole **5**:498
Edith Wharton **3**:562
Émile Zola **1**:588

Beals, Carleton
Mariano Azuela **3**:74

Beaumont, E. M.
Paul Claudel **10**:132

Beckelman, June
Paul Claudel **2**:104

Becker, May Lamberton
Marie Belloc Lowndes **12**:203

Beckett, Samuel
James Joyce **3**:255
Marcel Proust **7**:525

Beckley, Richard
Carl Sternheim **8**:371
Ernst Toller **10**:486

Bédé, Jean-Albert
Émile Zola **1**:596

Bedient, Calvin
D. H. Lawrence **2**:370

Beebe, Maurice
James Joyce **8**:163

Beer, Thomas
Stephen Crane **11**:131
T. F. Powys **9**:362

Beerbohm, Max
Maurice Baring **8**:31
J. M. Barrie **2**:39
Joseph Conrad **1**:195
F. Marion Crawford **10**:144
Arthur Conan Doyle **7**:217
José Echegaray **4**:98
John Galsworthy **1**:301
W. S. Gilbert **3**:209
Maxim Gorky **8**:70
Harley Granville-Barker **2**:192
William Ernest Henley **8**:99
Laurence Housman **7**:353
Henrik Ibsen **8**:143
Rudyard Kipling **8**:180
Edmond Rostand **6**:372, 376
Bernard Shaw **3**:378
Lytton Strachey **12**:404
Alfred Sutro **6**:419, 420
Arthur Symons **11**:429
John Millington Synge **6**:425

Beharriell, S. Ross
Stephen Leacock **2**:382

Behrman, S. N.
Robert E. Sherwood **3**:414

Beicken, Peter U.
Franz Kafka **2**:309

Bell, Aubrey F. G.
Juan Ramón Jiménez **4**:212
Gregorio Martinez Sierra and
Maria Martinez Sierra **6**:278

Bell, Clive
Marcel Proust **7**:521

Bell, David F.
Alfred Jarry **2**:286

Bellman, Samuel I.
Marjorie Kinnan Rawlings
4:365
Constance Rourke **12**:330

Belloc, Hilaire
Maurice Baring **8**:34
G. K. Chesterton **1**:178
H. G. Wells **6**:530; **12**:490

Bellow, Saul
Sholom Aleichem **1**:23
James Joyce **8**:168
Rudolf Steiner **13**:463

Bellquist, John Eric
August Strindberg **8**:418

Bely, Andrey
Zinaida Hippius **9**:154

Benamou, Michel
Wallace Stevens **3**:457

Benavente, Jacinto
Ramón del Valle-Inclán **5**:479

Bender, Bert
Kate Chopin **5**:157

Benet, Mary Kathleen
Colette **5**:171

Benét, Stephen Vincent
Stephen Vincent Benét **7**:69
Douglas Southall Freeman
11:217, 220
Margaret Mitchell **11**:371
Constance Rourke **12**:317
Elinor Wylie **8**:526

Benét, William Rose
Hart Crane **5**:185
F. Scott Fitzgerald **1**:236
Alfred Noyes **7**:505
Elinor Wylie **8**:526

Benjamin, Walter
Marcel Proust **7**:538

Benn, Gottfried
Friedrich Nietzsche **10**:371

Bennett, Arnold
Maurice Baring **8**:31
Joseph Conrad **1**:196
Theodore Dreiser **10**:172
Anatole France **9**:44
John Galsworthy **1**:292
George Gissing **3**:223
Joris-Karl Huysmans **7**:408
Olive Schreiner **9**:396
H. G. Wells **12**:487

Bennett, Charles A.
John Millington Synge **6**:427

Bennett, D.R.M.
Anthony Comstock **13**:86

Bennett, E. K.
Paul Heyse **8**:120

Benoit, Leroy J.
Paul Éluard **7**:247

Bensen, Alice R.
Rose Macaulay **7**:430

Benson, Eugene
Gabriele D'Annunzio **6**:127

Benson, Ruth Crego
Leo Tolstoy **4**:481

Benstock, Bernard
James Joyce **8**:165

Bentley, C. F.
Bram Stoker **8**:388

Bentley, D.M.R.
Wilfred Campbell **9**:33
Bliss Carman **7**:149

Bentley, E. C.
E. C. Bentley **12**:15
Damon Runyon **10**:423

Bentley, Eric
Stephen Vincent Benét **7**:78
Bertolt Brecht **1**:98, 99; **6**:40;
13:47
James Bridie **3**:134
Anton Chekhov **3**:156
Federico García Lorca **1**:310
Henrik Ibsen **2**:225
Friedrich Nietzsche **10**:377
Eugene O'Neill **1**:392
Luigi Pirandello **4**:337, 340
August Strindberg **1**:446
Frank Wedekind **7**:578
Oscar Wilde **1**:499
William Butler Yeats **1**:562

Berendsohn, Walter A.
Selma Lagerlöf **4**:231

Beresford, J. D.
Dorothy Richardson **3**:349

Bereza, Henryk
Bruno Schulz **5**:421

Berger, Dorothea
Ricarda Huch **13**:251

Berger, Harold L.
C. M. Kornbluth **8**:218

Bergin, Thomas Goddard
Giovanni Verga **3**:540

Bergon, Frank
Stephen Crane **11**:161

Bergonzi, Bernard
Hilaire Belloc **7**:39
Rupert Brooke **7**:127
G. K. Chesterton **1**:180
Ford Madox Ford **1**:289
John Galsworthy **1**:302
Wyndham Lewis **9**:250
Wilfred Owen **5**:371
Isaac Rosenberg **12**:301
H. G. Wells **6**:541

Berkman, Sylvia
Katherine Mansfield **2**:452

Berlin, Isaiah
Osip Mandelstam **6**:259
Leo Tolstoy **4**:463

Berman, Paul
Emma Goldman **13**:223
John Reed **9**:390

Bermel, Albert
Guillaume Apollinaire **8**:22
Antonin Artaud **3**:61

Bernhard, Svea
Verner von Heidenstam **5**:250

Bernstein, Melvin H.
John Jay Chapman **7**:198

Berryman, John
Isaak Babel **2**:36
Stephen Crane **11**:139
F. Scott Fitzgerald **1**:240
Ring Lardner **2**:334
Dylan Thomas **8**:449
William Butler Yeats **11**:513

Bersani, Leo
D. H. Lawrence **2**:374

Bertaux, Felix
Alfred Döblin **13**:160
Heinrich Mann **9**:316
Jakob Wassermann **6**:512

Berthoff, Warner
Ambrose Bierce **1**:94
Willa Cather **1**:165
Gertrude Stein **1**:434

Bertocci, Angelo P.
Charles Péguy **10**:417

Besant, Annie
Annie Besant **9**:12

Best, Alan
Frank Wedekind **7**:590

Besterman, Theodore
Annie Besant **9**:17

Bettany, F. G.
Arnold Bennett **5**:22

Bettinson, Christopher
André Gide **5**:244

Bettman, Dane
Marcel Proust **13**:406

Beucler, André
Léon-Paul Fargue **11**:198

Bevington, Helen
Laurence Housman **7**:360

Bewley, Marius
F. Scott Fitzgerald **1**:260
Isaac Rosenberg **12**:304
Wallace Stevens **3**:450

Beyer, Harald
Bjørnstjerne, Bjørnson **7**:112
Nordahl Grieg **10**:207
Alexander Kielland **5**:279

Bhattacharya, Bhabani
Rabindranath Tagore **3**:494

Bhattacharyya, Birendra Kumar
Saratchandra Chatterji **13**:78

Biagi, Shirley
Tess Slesinger **10**:444

Biasin, Gian-Paolo
Giuseppe Tomasi di Lampedusa **13**:296

Bien, Peter
C. P. Cavafy **2**:91
Nikos Kazantzakis **2**:315, 321, **5**:268

Bier, Jesse
Ambrose Bierce **1**:96

Bierce, Ambrose
William Dean Howells **7**:367
Jack London **9**:254

Bierstadt, Edward Hale
Lord Dunsany **2**:138

Bigelow, Gordon E.
Marjorie Kinnan Rawlings **4**:362

Bilton, Peter
Saki **3**:372

Binion, Rudolph
Franz Kafka **6**:221

Birchby, Sid
William Hope Hodgson **13**:233

Birmingham, George A.
John Millington Synge **6**:425

Birnbaum, Marianna D.
Géza Csáth **13**:146

Birnbaum, Martin
Arthur Schnitzler **4**:385

Birrell, Francis
Alfred Sutro **6**:422

Bishop, Charles
Christian Morgenstern **8**:308

Bishop, Ferman
Sarah Orne Jewett **1**:365

Bishop, John Peale
Sherwood Anderson **10**:33
Stephen Vincent Benét **7**:69
F. Scott Fitzgerald **6**:160
A. E. Housman **10**:245
Margaret Mitchell **11**:371
Thomas Wolfe **4**:511

Bithell, Jethro
Ricarda Huch **13**:251
Christian Morgenstern **8**:307
Émile Verhaeren **12**:463

Bittleston, Adam
Rudolf Steiner **13**:447

Björkman, Edwin
Selma Lagerlöf **4**:229
Maurice Maeterlinck **3**:323
Władysław Stanisław Reymont **5**:391
Arthur Schnitzler **4**:388
Sigrid Undset **3**:510
Edith Wharton **3**:556

Bjørnson, Bjørnstjerne
Georg Brandes **10**:59
Jonas Lie **5**:325

Blackmur, R. P.
Henry Adams **4**:9
Samuel Butler **1**:135
Hart Crane **2**:113
Thomas Hardy **4**:165
Henry James **2**:252, 258, 263
D. H. Lawrence **2**:351
Wyndham Lewis **9**:235
Thomas Mann **2**:421
Edwin Muir **2**:484
Wallace Stevens **3**:445
Leo Tolstoy **4**:471
William Butler Yeats **1**:565

Blair, Walter
Robert Benchley **1**:77, 79
Will Rogers **8**:333
Mark Twain **6**:463

Blake, Caesar R.
Dorothy Richardson **3**:355

Blake, George
J. M. Barrie **2**:46

Blake, Nicholas
See also **Day Lewis, C.**
E. C. Bentley **12**:15

Blake, Patricia
Vladimir Mayakovsky **4**:298

Blake, Warren Barton
Lafcadio Hearn **9**:123

Blankenagel, John C.
Jakob Wassermann **6**:513, 517

Blankner, Frederick V.
Luigi Pirandello **4**:330

Bleiler, E. F.
Algernon Blackwood **5**:77
Arthur Conan Doyle **7**:237
M. R. James **6**:211
H. P. Lovecraft **4**:271

Bligh, John
A. E. Housman **10**:262

Blish, James
See also **Atheling, William Jr.**
Henry Kuttner **10**:270

Blissett, William
Thomas Mann **2**:428

Bloch, Adèle
Nikos Kazantzakis **2**:319

Blok, Alexander
Fyodor Sologub **9**:440

Bloom, Edward A.
Willa Cather **11**:103
Thomas Wolfe **13**:484

Bloom, Harold
Isaac Rosenberg **12**:309
Wallace Stevens **3**:476
Oscar Wilde **8**:498
William Butler Yeats **11**:529

Bloom, Lillian D.
Willa Cather **11**:103

Bloom, Robert
H. G. Wells **6**:548

Bluestein, Gene
Constance Rourke **12**:324

Blunden, Allan
Georg Heym **9**:149

Blunden, Edmund
Robert Bridges **1**:128
W. H. Davies **5**:202
Wilfred Owen **5**:360

Blunt, Wilfrid Scawen
Charlotte Mew **8**:295

Boas, Guy
Lytton Strachey **12**:401

Boatwright, James
Margaret Mitchell **11**:381

Bodelsen, C. A.
Rudyard Kipling **8**:202

Bodenheim, Maxwell
Eugene O'Neill **1**:382

Bogan, Louise
Colette **1**:190
Paul Éluard **7**:244
Federico García Lorca **1**:308
James Joyce **3**:261
Edwin Arlington Robinson **5**:410
Wallace Stevens **12**:359
Sara Teasdale **4**:427

Bogard, Carley Rees
Kate Chopin **5**:158

Bohn, Willard
Guillaume Apollinaire **8**:25

Bóka, László
Endre Ady **11**:19

Bold, Alan
Wyndham Lewis **2**:397

Boll, Theophilus E. M.
May Sinclair **3**:440

Bond, Tonette L.
Ellen Glasgow **7**:344

Bondanella, Peter E.
Italo Svevo **2**:553

Bone, Robert A.
Charles Waddell Chesnutt **5**:133
Countee Cullen **4**:49
Paul Laurence Dunbar **2**:131; **12**:117
Rudolph Fisher **11**:208
James Weldon Johnson **3**:242
Claude McKay **7**:458
Wallace Thurman **6**:449

Bonheim, Helmut
James Joyce **3**:277

Bonnell, Peter H.
Aleksandr Kuprin **5**:301

Bonnerjea, René
Endre Ady **11**:14

Bonwit, Marianne
Wolfgang Borchert **5**:102

Böök, Fredrik
Verner von Heidenstam **5**:251

Booker, John Manning
Henri Barbusse **5**:13

Booth, Wayne C.
Anatole France **9**:54

Borelli, Mary
Ramón del Valle-Inclán **5**:476

Borges, Jorge Luis
G. K. Chesterton **1**:181
Friedrich Nietzsche **10**:385
Bernard Shaw **9**:420
H. G. Wells **6**:545
Oscar Wilde **1**:498

Borland, Hal
Louis Bromfield **11**:81

Borras, F. M.
Maxim Gorky **8**:85

Borrello, Alfred
H. G. Wells **6**:545

Bort, Barry D.
Sherwood Anderson **10**:50

Bose, Buddhadeva
Rabindranath Tagore **3**:495

Bosmajian, Hamida
Tadeusz Borowski **9**:23

Bottome, Phyllis
Olive Schreiner **9**:395

Bouché, H. P.
Léon-Paul Fargue **11**:201

Bouraoui, H. A.
Georges Bernanos **3**:128

Bourget, Paul
Joris-Karl Huysmans **7**:403

Bourne, Randolph
George Washington Cable **4**:25
Dorothy Richardson **3**:346
H. G. Wells **12**:495

Bovary, Claude
Willa Cather **1**:151

Bowen, Elizabeth
Rose Macaulay **7**:424
Katherine Mansfield **8**:279
Henry Handel Richardson **4**:374

Bowie, Malcolm
Paul Éluard **7**:258

Bowra, C. M.
Guillaume Apollinaire **3**:34
Aleksandr Blok **5**:85
C. P. Cavafy **2**:87
Federico García Lorca **1**:309
Stefan George **2**:150
Vladimir Mayakovsky **4**:293
Rainer Maria Rilke **1**:409, 414
Algernon Charles Swinburne **8**:435
Paul Valéry **4**:490
William Butler Yeats **1**:560

Boxill, Anthony
H. G. de Lisser **12**:99

Boyd, Ernest A.
A. E. **3**:3
Lord Dunsany **2**:136
Thomas Hardy **10**:217
H. L. Mencken **13**:367
Standish O'Grady **5**:349
Władysław Stanisław Reymont **5**:392
Gregorio Martínez Sierra and María Martínez Sierra **6**:278
Carl Spitteler **12**:336
Lytton Strachey **12**:397
Katharine Tynan **3**:504
Miguel de Unamuno **9**:512

Boyd, Ian
G. K. Chesterton **6**:103

Boyd, Thomas
John Reed **9**:383

Boyer, James
Thomas Wolfe **13**:491, 494

Boyesen, Hjalmar Hjorth
Bjørnstjerne Bjørnson **7**:100
Georg Brandes **10**:60
George Washington Cable **4**:23
Alexander Kielland **5**:275
Jonas Lie **5**:324
Friedrich Nietzsche **10**:358

Boynton, H. W.
Marie Belloc Lowndes **12**:202
Don Marquis **7**:434

Boynton, Percy H.
Sherwood Anderson **1**:38
Ambrose Bierce **1**:84
Lafcadio Hearn **9**:126
Sinclair Lewis **4**:247
Booth Tarkington **9**:457

Brachfeld, Georges I.
André Gide **5**:234

Bradbrook, M. C.
Henrik Ibsen **2**:238

Bradbury, Malcolm
Malcolm Lowry **6**:249
Virginia Woolf **1**:546

Bradbury, Ray
L. Frank Baum **7**:20
Edgar Rice Burroughs **2**:86
Henry Kuttner **10**:271

Bragdon, Claude
Kahlil Gibran **1**:326

Bragman, Louis J.
Arthur Symons **11**:436

Braithwaite, William Stanley
Countee Cullen **4**:44
Claude McKay **7**:455
Sara Teasdale **4**:424

Branch, Douglas
Zane Grey **6**:179

Brand, Alice Glarden
Mary Wilkins Freeman **9**:77

Brandes, Georg
Bjørnstjerne Bjørnson **7**:101
Paul Heyse **8**:113
Henrik Ibsen **2**:218
Friedrich Nietzsche **10**:356
Émile Verhaeren **12**:458

Brathwaite, Edward [Kamau]
Roger Mais **8**:246

Bratsas, Dorothy
Amado Nervo **11**:404

Braun, Lucille V.
Miguel de Unamuno **2**:570

Braun, Wilhelm
Robert Musil **12**:239

Brawley, Benjamin
Countee Cullen **4**:41
Paul Laurence Dunbar **12**:106
Claude McKay **7**:457

Braybrooke, Neville
George Orwell **2**:498

Braybrooke, Patrick
J. M. Barrie **2**:43
Alfred Noyes **7**:513
Katharine Tynan **3**:505
Hugh Walpole **5**:497
H. G. Wells **6**:531

Brazil, John
Jack London **9**:280

Brecht, Bertolt
Bernard Shaw **9**:418

Brée, Germaine
Georges Bernanos **3**:119
André Gide **5**:221; **12**:165
Jean Giraudoux **2**:162
Marcel Proust **7**:529

Brégy, Katharine
Ernest Dowson **4**:87
Katharine Tynan **3**:503

Bremner, Robert
Anthony Comstock **13**:95

Brenan, Gerald
Juan Ramón Jiménez **4**:213

Brennan, Joseph Payne
H. P. Lovecraft **4**:270

Brennan, Joseph X.
Edith Wharton **3**:568

Brenner, Rica
Alfred Noyes **7**:512

Bresky, Dushan
Anatole France **9**:52

Bresnahan, Roger J.
Booker T. Washington **10**:541

Breunig, Leroy C.
Guillaume Apollinaire **3**:42; **8**:16

Brewster, Dorothy
Emma Goldman **13**:216
Virginia Woolf **1**:531

Briggs, A.D.P.
Leo Tolstoy **4**:482

Briggs, Julia
Algernon Blackwood **5**:78
M. R. James **6**:211
Vernon Lee **5**:320

Brinnin, John Malcolm
Gertrude Stein **1**:431
Dylan Thomas **1**:473

Bristol, Evelyn
Konstantin Dmitriyevich Balmont **11**:42
Fyodor Sologub **9**:443

Britten, Florence Haxton
Stephen Vincent Benét **7**:73
Alfred Döblin **13**:158

Brittin, Norman A.
Edna St. Vincent Millay **4**:318

Broadus, Edmund Kemper
Robert Bridges **1**:125

Brockway, James
O. Henry **1**:352

Brod, Max
Franz Kafka **2**:304

Brodie, A. H.
John McCrae **12**:209

Brodin, Pierre
Pierre Loti **11**:361

Bronowski, Jacob
Pierre Teilhard de Chardin **9**:488
A. E. Housman **10**:243

Brook, Stephen
Radclyffe Hall **12**:197

Brooks, Cleanth
Ivan Bunin **6**:47
F. Scott Fitzgerald **6**:163
A. E. Housman **1**:355; **10**:249
William Butler Yeats **1**:571; **11**:517

Brooks, Van Wyck
Ambrose Bierce **1**:89
Willa Cather **1**:160
F. Marion Crawford **10**:152
Emma Goldman **13**:219
Bret Harte **1**:342
O. Henry **1**:350
Henry James **11**:324
Vernon Lee **5**:311
Jack London **9**:262
Amy Lowell **8**:231
H. L. Mencken **13**:382
Constance Rourke **12**:317
Edgar Salt:317
us **8**:351
Gertrude Stein **1**:430
Booth Tarkington **9**:462
Mark Twain **6**:461

Brophy, Brigid
Colette **1**:192
Ronald Firbank **1**:229
Thomas Hardy **10**:223
Francis Thompson **4**:441

Brosman, Catherine Savage
Alain-Fournier **6**:22

Brotherston, Gordon
Rubén Darío **4**:68

Broun, Heywood
Damon Runyon **10**:422
Booth Tarkington **9**:454

Brouta, Julius
Jacinto Benavente **3**:93

Brown, Clarence
Osip Mandelstam **2**:401; **6**:260, 262

Brown, Daniel R.
Sinclair Lewis **4**:261
Nathanael West **1**:491

Brown, E. K.
Duncan Campbell Scott **6**:389
Bliss Carman **7**:144
Willa Cather **11**:99
Thomas Wolfe **4**:514

Brown, Edward J.
Isaac Babel **13**:39

Brown, G. G.
Gabriel Miró **5**:339

Brown, Ivor
Lewis Grassic Gibbon **4**:122
Alfred Sutro **6**:422

Brown, J. F.
Aleister Crowley **7**:211

Brown, John L.
Valéry Larbaud **9**:205

Brown, John Mason
Philip Barry **11**:48
Anton Chekhov **10**:103
Eugene O'Neill **1**:394
Bernard Shaw **9**:419
Robert E. Sherwood **3**:416
John Van Druten **2**:573, 575
Alexander Woollcott **5**:525

Brown, Leonard
Harriet Monroe **12**:219

Brown, Malcolm
George Moore **7**:486

Brown, Morrison
Louis Bromfield **11**:81

Brown, Sterling
Charles Waddell Chesnutt **5**:132
Paul Laurence Dunbar **12**:109, 110
Rudolph Fisher **11**:205
James Weldon Johnson **3**:241
Wallace Thurman **6**:447

Brown, Stuart Gerry
John Jay Chapman **7**:192

Brownstein, Michael
Max Jacob **6**:203

Broyde, Steven
Osip Mandelstam **6**:267

Bruckner, D.J.R.
Charles Williams **11**:502

Bruehl, Charles P.
Georges Bernanos **3**:117

Bruffee, Kenneth A.
Joseph Conrad **13**:122

Bruford, W. H.
Anton Chekhov **10**:107

Brushwood, John S.
Amado Nervo **11**:403

Brustein, Robert
Antonin Artaud **3**:50
Bertolt Brecht **1**:111
Henrik Ibsen **8**:149
Eugene O'Neill **1**:400
Luigi Pirandello **4**:345
Bernard Shaw **3**:404
August Strindberg **1**:451

Bryant, Joseph G.
Paul Laurence Dunbar **12**:104

Bryusov, Valery
Konstantin Dmitriyevich Balmont **11**:29

Buber, Martin
Franz Kafka **2**:295

Buchan, A. M.
Sarah Orne Jewett **1**:363

Buchanan, Robert
Rudyard Kipling **8**:178
Algernon Charles Swinburne **8**:423

Buck, Philo M., Jr.
Henrik Ibsen **2**:224
Jack London **9**:254
Eugene O'Neill **1**:388
Émile Zola **1**:588

Buckley, J. M.
Anthony Comstock **13**:87

Buckley, Jerome Hamilton
William Ernest Henley **8**:104

Buckley, Vincent
Henry Handel Richardson **4**:377

Budd, Louis J.
William Dean Howells **7**:380
Mark Twain **6**:473
Thomas Wolfe **4**:525

Büdel, Oscar
Luigi Pirandello **4**:351

Budyonny, Semyon
Isaac Babel **13**:14

Bump, Jerome
D. H. Lawrence **9**:229

Bunin, Ivan
Ivan Bunin **6**:44
Aleksandr Kuprin **5**:298

Buning, M.
T. F. Powys **9**:375

Burbank, Rex
Sherwood Anderson **1**:55

Burch, Charles Eaton
Paul Laurence Dunbar **12**:105

Burdett, Osbert
Alice Meynell **6**:300

Burgess, Anthony
C. P. Cavafy **7**:162
John Galsworthy **1**:305
James Joyce **8**:164

Burgess, C. F.
Joseph Conrad **13**:121

Burke, Kenneth
Gertrude Stein **1**:425

Burkhart, Charles
George Moore **7**:493

Burnshaw, Stanley
Rainer Maria Rilke **1**:418

Burpee, Lawrence J.
Wilfred Campbell **9**:29

Burroughs, John
Charles G. D. Roberts **8**:315

Büscher, Gustav
Friedrich Nietzsche **10**:368

Bush, Douglas
Robert Bridges **1**:130

Bush, William
Georges Bernanos **3**:127

Butcher, Philip
George Washington Cable **4**:29

Butler, E. M.
Rainer Maria Rilke **6**:360
Carl Spitteler **12**:342

Butor, Michel
Guillaume Apollinaire **3**:37

Buttel, Robert
Wallace Stevens **12**:384

Butter, Peter H.
Edwin Muir **2**:486
Francis Thompson **4**:439

Butts, Mary
M. R. James **6**:206

Byalik, Boris
Maxim Gorky **8**:87

Byrne, J. Patrick
A. E. **10**:17

Cabell, James Branch
James Branch Cabell **6**:61
Theodore Dreiser **10**:173
Ellen Glasgow **7**:337
Joseph Hergesheimer **11**:265
Sinclair Lewis **13**:335
H. L. Mencken **13**:376
Booth Tarkington **9**:454
Elinor Wylie **8**:523

Cady, Edwin H.
Stephen Crane **11**:163
William Dean Howells **7**:381

Cahan, Abraham
Sholem Asch **3**:65
Anton Chekhov **10**:100

Cahill, Daniel J.
Harriet Monroe **12**:224

Cairns, Christopher
Ugo Betti **5**:66

Calder, Jenni
George Orwell **2**:509

Calder-Marshall, Arthur
Louis Bromfield **11**:79
Wyndham Lewis **2**:384

Caldwell, Erskine
Louis Bromfield **11**:77

Caldwell, Helen
Machado de Assis **10**:297

Calisher, Hortense
Henry James **2**:274

Calista, Donald J.
Booker T. Washington **10**:528

Callan, Richard J.
Machado de Assis **10**:289

Calvin, Judith S.
Jean Giraudoux **7**:321

Cambon, Glauco
Hart Crane **2**:121
Gabriele D'Annunzio **6**:139

Cammell, Charles Richard
Aleister Crowley **7**:205

Campbell, Ian
Lewis Grassic Gibbon **4**:129, 130

Campbell, Joseph
James Joyce **3**:261

Campbell, Roy
Federico García Lorca **1**:311

Campbell, T. M.
Gerhart Hauptmann **4**:198

Camus, Albert
Franz Kafka **2**:297
Friedrich Nietzsche **10**:375

Canario, John W.
Joseph Conrad **13**:124

Canby, Henry Seidel
Gertrude Atherton **2**:15
Stephen Vincent Benét **7**:71
F. Scott Fitzgerald **1**:235
Joseph Hergesheimer **11**:267
John Millington Synge **6**:430
Mark Twain **6**:470

Cancalon, Elaine D.
Alain-Fournier **6**:24

Canetti, Elias
Isaac Babel **13**:35
Franz Kafka **6**:222

Cantor, Jay
William Butler Yeats **11**:539

Cantwell, Robert
Kate Chopin **5**:147

Capetanakis, Demetrios
Stefan George **2**:148

Cappon, James
Bliss Carman **7**:141

Carden, Patricia
Isaak Babel **2**:23, 25

Cargill, Oscar
Sherwood Anderson **1**:41
Sholem Asch **3**:68
James Branch Cabell **6**:69
F. Scott Fitzgerald **1**:239
Henry James **2**:269
George Moore **7**:483
Eugene O'Neill **1**:387
Bernard Shaw **3**:388
Gertrude Stein **1**:427
August Strindberg **1**:445
Sara Teasdale **4**:428
Émile Zola **1**:589

Carman, Bliss
Charles G. D. Roberts **8**:314

Carmer, Carl
Philip Barry **11**:47

Carner, Mosco
Guiseppe Giacosa **7**:313

Caron, James E.
Mark Twain **12**:449

Carpenter, Humphrey
Charles Williams **11**:497

Carpenter, Margaret Haley
Sara Teasdale **4**:429

Carpenter, William H.
Alexander Kielland **5**:277

Carr, John Dickson
Raymond Chandler **1**:169

Carr, W. I.
T. F. Powys **9**:373

Carrington, C. E.
Rudyard Kipling **8**:195

Carroll, Lewis
George MacDonald **9**:287

Carruth, Hayden
Edwin Muir **2**:484
William Butler Yeats **1**:575

Carter, Angela
Géza Csáth **13**:152

Carter, Eunice Hunton
Wallace Thurman **6**:446

Carter, Lawson A.
Émile Zola **6**:567

Carter, Lin
William Hope Hodgson **13**:233, 234
Henry Kuttner **10**:271

Carus, Paul
Friedrich Nietzsche **10**:363

Cary, Lucian
Joseph Hergesheimer **11**:260

Cary, Richard
Sarah Orne Jewett **1**:365
Vernon Lee **5**:313

Casey, T. J.
Georg Trakl **5**:460

Cassidy, John A.
Algernon Charles Swinburne **8**:438

Cassity, Turner
James Agee **1**:12

Cather, Willa
Kate Chopin **5**:142
Stephen Crane **11**:134
Sarah Orne Jewett **1**:361
Thomas Mann **2**:417
Katherine Mansfield **2**:450

Cavaliero, Glen
T. F. Powys **9**:375
Charles Williams **11**:499

Caws, Mary Ann
Paul Éluard **7**:255

Cecchetti, Giovanni
Giovanni Verga **3**:546

Cecil, David
Max Beerbohm **1**:71
Walter de la Mare **4**:80
W. S. Gilbert **3**:213
Virginia Woolf **5**:508

Cerf, Bennett
O. Henry **1**:350

Cevasco, G. A.
Joris-Karl Huysmans **7**:416

Chakravarty, Amiya
Thomas Hardy **4**:163

Chamberlain, John
Charles Waddell Chesnutt **5**:131
Claude McKay **7**:456
Tess Slesinger **10**:439
Thomas Wolfe **4**:506

Chambers, Edmund K.
Alice Meynell **6**:293

Champigny, Robert
Alain-Fournier **6**:14

Chandler, Frank W.
José Echegaray **4**:102
Guiseppe Giacosa **7**:312

Chandler, Raymond
Raymond Chandler **7**:167, 168
A. A. Milne **6**:311

Chapman, C. A.
Jaroslav Hasek **4**:181

Chapman, Edward M.
Sarah Orne Jewett **1**:360

Chapman, Esther
H. G. de Lisser **12**:95

Chapman, John Jay
G. K. Chesterton **1**:177

Chapman, Raymond
Samuel Butler **1**:138

Chapman, Robert T.
Wyndham Lewis **9**:241

Chase, Richard
George Washington Cable **4**:27

Chatterton, Wayne
Alexander Woollcott **5**:526

Chattopadhyay, Saratchandra
Saratchandra Chatterji **13**:73

Chaudhuri, Nirad C.
Rudyard Kipling **8**:197

Chekhov, Anton Pavlovich
See also **Tchekhov, Anton**
Leo Tolstoy **4**:449

Chernyshevsky, N. G.
Leo Tolstoy **4**:444

Chesnutt, Charles W.
Booker T. Washington **10**:515

Chesterton, Cecil
Hilaire Belloc **7**:31

Chesterton, G. K.
Maurice Baring **8**:37
Hilaire Belloc **7**:37
Paul Claudel **10**:124
Aleister Crowley **7**:203, 204
Walter de la Mare **4**:75
Arthur Conan Doyle **7**:217
Theodore Dreiser **10**:173
Anatole France **9**:45
Bret Harte **1**:339
William Ernest Henley **8**:100
Henrik Ibsen **2**:221
Rudyard Kipling **8**:181
George MacDonald **9**:289
H. L. Mencken **13**:372
Alice Meynell **6**:295
George Moore **7**:475
Bernard Shaw **3**:380; **9**:413
Francis Thompson **4**:439
Leo Tolstoy **4**:452
Mark Twain **12**:428
H. G. Wells **6**:524; **12**:503

Chevalier, Haakon M.
Marcel Proust **13**:410

Chevalley, Abel
May Sinclair **3**:439

Chiari, Joseph
Paul Claudel **2**:103
Paul Éluard **7**:250
Edmond Rostand **6**:380

Chiaromonte, Nicola
Luigi Pirandello **4**:353

Childs, Herbert Ellsworth
Edgar Lee Masters **2**:466

Chisolm, Lawrence W.
Lu Hsün **3**:298

Christian, R. F.
Leo Tolstoy **4**:470; **11**:474

Chukovsky, Korney
Vladimir Mayakovsky **4**:288

Church, Dan M.
Alfred Jarry **2**:281

Church, Richard
Maurice Baring **8**:36
Laurence Housman **7**:357

Churchill, Kenneth
F. Marion Crawford **10**:157
Frederick Rolfe **12**:283

Ciancio, Ralph
Sherwood Anderson **1**:64

Ciardi, John
Roy Campbell **5**:122
Edna St. Vincent Millay **4**:316

Ciecierska, Joanna
T. F. Powys **9**:377

Ciholas, Karin Nordenhaug
André Gide **5**:241

Cioran, E. M.
Leo Tolstoy **11**:471
Paul Valéry **4**:500

Cioran, Samuel D.
Andrey Bely **7**:57

Cismaru, Alfred
Boris Vian **9**:533

Clark, Barrett H.
Maxwell Anderson **2**:1
Booth Tarkington **9**:461

Clark, Earl John
James Joyce **3**:278

Clark, Emily
Joseph Hergesheimer **11**:273

Clark, Tom
Damon Runyon **10**:434

Clarke, Arthur C.
Jules Verne **6**:492

Clarke, H. A.
Charlotte Gilman **9**:98

Clarke, Helen A.
Bliss Carman **7**:134

Claudel, Paul
Paul Claudel **10**:120

Cleman, John
George Washington Cable **4**:36

Clemens, S. L.
See also **Twain, Mark**
Mark Twain **6**:454; **12**:426

Clements, Clyde C., Jr.
Thomas Wolfe **4**:533

Clever, Glenn
Duncan Campbell Scott **6**:398, 400

Closs, August
Stefan George **2**:149
Christian Morgenstern **8**:305

Clurman, Harold
Bertolt Brecht **1**:108, 109, 115, 122; **13**:51
Henrik Ibsen **8**:152
Eugene O'Neill **1**:395

Cobb, Carl W.
Antonio Machado **3**:311

Coblentz, Stanton A.
Sinclair Lewis **4**:246

Cock, Albert A.
Francis Thompson **4**:436

Cocking, J. M.
Marcel Proust **13**:427

Cockshut, A.O.J.
Radclyffe Hall **12**:196
Thomas Hardy **10**:229
Algernon Charles Swinburne **8**:442

Cocteau, Jean
Colette **5**:163
Paul Valéry **4**:493

Coffman, Stanley K., Jr.
Hart Crane **5**:187

Cogswell, Fred
Duncan Campbell Scott **6**:399

Cohen, Arthur A.
Osip Mandelstam **2**:406

Cohen, J. M.
Georg Trakl **5**:460

Cohen, Joseph
Isaac Rosenberg **12**:295

Cohen, M. A.
Bertolt Brecht **13**:60

Cohen, Morton
H. Rider Haggard **11**:243

Cohen, Robert
Jean Giraudoux **2**:167

Cohn, Ruby
Bertolt Brecht **1**:116; **13**:59

Colbron, Grace Isabel
Algernon Blackwood **5**:70

Colby, Elbridge
F. Marion Crawford **10**:147

Colby, Frank Moore
Gabriele D'Annunzio **6**:130
Rudyard Kipling **8**:180

Colby, Vineta
Vernon Lee **5**:316

Cole, Leo R.
Juan Ramón Jiménez **4**:220

Coleman, Charles W.
Lafcadio Hearn **9**:118

Collier, Eugenia W.
James Weldon Johnson **3**:242

Collier, S. J.
Max Jacob **6**:191

Collignon, Jean
André Gide **12**:151

Collin, W. E.
Hector Saint-Denys Garneau **13**:196

Collins, Christopher
Yevgeny Ivanovich Zamyatin **8**:557

Collins, Harold R.
Joseph Conrad **13**:104

Collins, Joseph
Edna St. Vincent Millay **4**:309
Booth Tarkington **9**:459

Collins, Thomas Lyle
Thomas Wolfe **13**:472

Colombo, J. R.
Malcolm Lowry **6**:237

Colum, Padraic
A. E. **3**:6; **10**:13
Lord Dunsany **2**:142
Kahlil Gibran **1**:328
Lady Gregory **1**:333
George Moore **7**:478
Edna St. Vincent Millay **4**:306
James Stephens **4**:414

Colvert, James B.
Stephen Crane **11**:146

Combs, Robert
Hart Crane **2**:125

Comeau, Paul
Willa Cather **11**:113

Comerchero, Victor
Nathanael West **1**:482

Commager, Henry Steele
Henry Adams **4**:6
Stephen Vincent Benét **7**:75
Willa Cather **1**:155
F. Scott Fitzgerald **1**:245

Comstock, Anthony
Anthony Comstock **13**:88

Connell, Allison
Valéry Larbaud **9**:204

Connolly, Cyril
Nordahl Grieg **10**:205
A. E. Housman **1**:354
James Joyce **3**:276
D. H. Lawrence **2**:369
Gertrude Stein **1**:434
Thomas Wolfe **13**:481

Connolly, Francis X.
Willa Cather **1**:156

Connolly, Julian W.
Ivan Bunin **6**:58

Conquest, Robert
Charles Williams **11**:490

Conrad, Joseph
Joseph Conrad **6**:112
Stephen Crane **11**:132
Anatole France **9**:43
Henry James **2**:245
H. L. Mencken **13**:365
Marcel Proust **7**:520

Hugh Walpole **5**:495
H. G Wells **6**:523

Constable, W. G.
Wyndham Lewis **9**:234

Cook, Bruce
Raymond Chandler **1**:175
Bertolt Brecht **13**:67

Cooke, Alistair
H. L. Mencken **13**:392
Will Rogers **8**:334

Cooke, Judy
May Sinclair **11**:421

Cooke, Michael G.
H. G. de Lisser **12**:98

Coombes, H.
T. F. Powys **9**:371
Edward Thomas **10**:458

Cooper, Frederic Taber
See also **Winter, Calvin**
Gertrude Atherton **2**:13
Arnold Bennett **5**:23
Willa Cather **11**:92
F. Marion Crawford **10**:146
Theodore Dreiser **10**:164
Anatole France **9**:41
Zona Gale **7**:277
Ellen Glasgow **2**:175; **7**:332
Zane Grey **6**:176
Jack London **9**:253
Marie Belloc Lowndes **12**:201, 202
May Sinclair **11**:408

Cope, Jackson I.
James Joyce **8**:169

Corbett, Edward P. J.
Margaret Mitchell **11**:375

Cordle, Thomas
André Gide **5**:222

Corke, Hilary
Charlotte Mew **8**:298

Corkery, Daniel
John Millington Synge **6**:432

Corn, Alfred
Andrey Bely **7**:66
Wallace Stevens **12**:385

Cornford, Frances
Rupert Brooke **7**:123

Correa, Gustavo
Federico García Lorca **7**:294

Corrigan, Matthew
Malcolm Lowry **6**:244

Corrigan, Robert W.
Bertolt Brecht **1**:119
Federico García Lorca **1**:324
Henrik Ibsen **2**:239
Gregorio Martínez Sierra and María Martínez Sierra **6**:284

Cortissoz, Royal
Hamlin Garland **3**:190

Cosman, Max
Joyce Cary **1**:141

Costa, Richard Haver
Malcolm Lowry **6**:246

Costello, Peter
Jules Verne **6**:499

Costich, Julia F.
Antonin Artaud **3**:62

Cournos, John
Fyodor Sologub **9**:434

Coustillas, Pierre
George Gissing **3**:236

Coward, Noël
Saki **3**:373

Cowley, Malcolm
Sherwood Anderson **1**:51
Guillaume Apollinaire **3**:33
Henri Barbusse **5**:13
A. E. Coppard **5**:176
Hart Crane **2**:117
Theodore Dreiser **10**:179
F. Scott Fitzgerald **1**:238, 272; **6**:166
Lafcadio Hearn **9**:130
Amy Lowell **1**:371, 378
Katherine Mansfield **2**:445
H. L. Mencken **13**:380
Margaret Mitchell **11**:372
Arthur Schnitzler **4**:392
H. G. Wells **12**:502
Thomas Wolfe **13**:467
Virginia Woolf **1**:533

Cox, C. B.
Joseph Conrad **1**:218

Cox, James M.
Booker T. Washington **10**:538

Cox, James Trammell
Ford Madox Ford **1**:286

Cox, Oliver C.
Booker T. Washington **10**:526

Coxe, Louis O.
Edith Wharton **3**:567

Coxhead, Elizabeth
Lady Gregory **1**:335

Craig, G. Dundas
Rubén Darío **4**:63
Amado Nervo **11**:395

Craige, Betty Jean
Federico García Lorca **7**:297

Crane, Hart
Sherwood Anderson **10**:32
Hart Crane **5**:184

Crane, Stephen
Stephen Crane **11**:123

Crankshaw, Edward
Jakob Wassermann **6**:511

Crawford, F. Marion
F. Marion Crawford **10**:141

Crawford, John
Will Rogers **8**:332

Crawford, John W.
Émile Verhaeren **12**:472

Crawford, Virginia M.
Joris-Karl Huysmans **7**:407
Edmond Rostand **6**:373

Creary, Jean
Roger Mais **8**:241

Creelman, James
Booker T. Washington **10**:514

Creese, Robb
Rudolf Steiner **13**:456

Crews, Frederick C.
Joseph Conrad **1**:216
Henry James **11**:332

Crispin, Edmund
C. M. Kornbluth **8**:217

Crites
See also **Eliot, T. S.**
Bernard Shaw **9**:417

Croce, Arlene
Eugene O'Neill **1**:404

Croce, Benedetto
Émile Zola **1**:588

Cross, Richard K.
Malcolm Lowry **6**:253

Cross, Wilbur
Arnold Bennett **5**:33
John Galsworthy **1**:297

Crowley, Aleister
James Branch Cabell **6**:65
Aleister Crowley **7**:205, 208

Cruse, Harold
James Weldon Johnson **3**:246
Booker T. Washington **10**:531

Cuénot, Claude
Pierre Teilhard de Chardin **9**:481

Cullen, Countee
James Weldon Johnson **3**:240

Cunliffe, John W.
A. E. Housman **1**:354

Cunningham, J. V.
Wallace Stevens **3**:454

Cuppy, Will
Raymond Chandler **7**:167
Ricarda Huch **13**:243
Marie Belloc Lowndes **12**:203

Currey, R. N.
Alun Lewis **3**:289

Curry, Steven S.
André Gide **12**:180

Curti, Merle
Booker T. Washington **10**:523

Curtis, Penelope
Anton Chekhov **3**:170

Curtius, Ernst Robert
José Ortega y Gasset **9**:339

Cushman, Keith
Ernest Dowson **4**:93

Dabney, Virginius
Douglas Southall Freeman **11**:224
Ellen Glasgow **7**:337

Daemmrich, Horst S.
Thomas Mann **2**:441

Dahlberg, Edward
Sherwood Anderson **1**:56
F. Scott Fitzgerald **1**:256

Dahlie, Hallvard
Nordahl Grieg **10**:211

Daiches, David
Willa Cather **1**:157
Joseph Conrad **1**:211
A. E. Housman **1**:355
James Joyce **3**:258
Katherine Mansfield **2**:449
Wilfred Owen **5**:362
Isaac Rosenberg **12**:291
Dylan Thomas **1**:469
Virginia Woolf **1**:539
William Butler Yeats **1**:558

Daleski, H. M.
Joseph Conrad **1**:220

Dalphin, Marcia
A. A. Milne **6**:309

Damon, S. Foster
Amy Lowell **1**:374

Dane, Clemence
Hugh Walpole **5**:497

Daniel, John
Henri Barbusse **5**:16

Daniels, Jonathan
Marjorie Kinnan Rawlings **4**:359

Danielson, Larry W.
Selma Lagerlöf **4**:242

Danto, Arthur C.
Friedrich Nietzsche **10**:382

Darío, Rubén
F. T. Marinetti **10**:310

Darrow, Clarence
Theodore Dreiser **10**:171

Darton, F. J. Harvey
Arnold Bennett **5**:25

Dathorne, Oscar R.
Roger Mais **8**:244

Dauner, Louise
Joel Chandler Harris **2**:212

Davenport, Basil
Lewis Grassic Gibbon **4**:120, 121

Daviau, Donald G.
Hugo von Hofmannsthal **11**:307
Karl Kraus **5**:282

Davidow, Mary C.
Charlotte Mew **8**:299

Davidson, Donald
Louis Bromfield **11**:76
Joseph Conrad **6**:114
Harriet Monroe **12**:218

Davie, Donald
D. H. Lawrence **2**:373
Wallace Stevens **3**:449

Davies, A. Emil
Laurence Housman **7**:354

Davies, Barrie
Wilfred Campbell **9**:33

Davies, J. C.
André Gide **5**:237

Davies, John
Alun Lewis **3**:289

Davies, Margaret
Colette **5**:165

Davies, Norman
Isaac Babel **13**:28

Davies, Robertson
Stephen Leacock **2**:381

Davies, Ruth
Leonid Andreyev **3**:27
Anton Chekhov **3**:168

Davis, Arthur P.
Countee Cullen **4**:44
Rudolph Fisher **11**:207
Wallace Thurman **6**:450

Davis, Beatrice
Miles Franklin **7**:267

Davis, Cynthia
Dylan Thomas **1**:475

Davis, Elmer
Anthony Comstock **13**:94

Davis, Richard Harding
Stephen Crane **11**:124

Davis, Robert Bernard
A. E. **10**:20

Davis, Robert Murray
F. Scott Fitzgerald **6**:167
Katherine Mansfield **8**:282

Davis, Oswald H.
Arnold Bennett **5**:45

Davison, Edward
A. E. **10**:16
Robert Bridges **1**:125
Walter de la Mare **4**:74
Alfred Noyes **7**:507
Saki **3**:365

Day, A. Grove
Vicente Blasco Ibáñez **12**:48

Day, Douglas
Malcolm Lowry **6**:241, 247

Day Lewis, C.
See also **Blake, Nicholas**
Wilfred Owen **5**:368
Dylan Thomas **8**:450
Edward Thomas **10**:456

D'Costa, Jean
Roger Mais **8**:247

Dean, James L.
William Dean Howells **7**:394

Debicki, Andrew P.
César Vallejo **3**:530

De Bosschere, Jean
May Sinclair **3**:437

De Camp, L. Sprague
Robert E. Howard **8**:130

De Casseres, Benjamin
Pierre Loti **11**:356
Arthur Symons **11**:430

De Castris, A. L.
Luigi Pirandello **4**:342

Decavalles, A.
C. P. Cavafy **7**:162

Decker, Donald M.
Machado de Assis **10**:290

DeCoster, Cyrus
Juan Valera **10**:507

De Fornaro, Sofia
Giuseppe Giacosa **7**:305

Degler, Carl N.
Charlotte Gilman **9**:103

Dehon, Claire L.
Émile Verhaeren **12**:479

DeKoven, Marianne
Gertrude Stein **6**:415

De la Mare, Walter
Rupert Brooke **2**:53
Edward Thomas **10**:451

Delany, Paul
Katherine Mansfield **8**:286

De la Selva, Salomón
Rubén Darío **4**:55

Dell, Floyd
Charlotte Gilman **9**:100
Emma Goldman **13**:209
Olive Schreiner **9**:395

De Loss, John
Anthony Comstock **13**:97

Dennis, Scott A.
William Dean Howells **7**:397

De Onis, Federico
Pío Baroja **8**:47

De Ónis, Harriet
Mariano Azuela **3**:80

Derleth, August
Zona Gale **7**:282
H. P. Lovecraft **4**:266

De Selincourt, E.
Robert Bridges **1**:129

Desmond, Shaw
Lord Dunsany **2**:143

Des Pres, Terrence
Bertolt Brecht **6**:38

Deutsch, Babette
Stephen Vincent Benét **7**:69
A. E. Coppard **5**:177
Hart Crane **5**:186
Countee Cullen **4**:40
Charlotte Mew **8**:299
Edna St. Vincent Millay **4**:311
Christian Morgenstern **8**:304
Wilfred Owen **5**:365
Edwin Arlington Robinson **5**:413
Sara Teasdale **4**:426, 427

Deutsch, Leonard J.
Rudolph Fisher **11**:211

Deutscher, Isaac
George Orwell **2**:500

Devlin, John
Vicente Blasco Ibáñez **12**:45

DeVoto, Bernard
Douglas Southall Freeman **11**:221
Don Marquis **7**:440
Margaret Mitchell **11**:374
Eugene O'Neill **6**:328
Mark Twain **6**:465
Thomas Wolfe **4**:509; **13**:470

Dick, Kay
Colette **1**:192

Dick, Susan
George Moore **7**:495

Dickey, James
Stephen Crane **11**:159
Edwin Arlington Robinson **5**:414

Dickinson, Patric
Charlotte Mew **8**:297

Dickman, Adolphe-Jacques
André Gide **5**:213

Dickson, Lovat
Radclyffe Hall **12**:194

Didier, Pierre
Georges Bernanos **3**:117

Dilla, Geraldine P.
Émile Verhaeren **12**:470

Dillon, E. J.
Maxim Gorky **8**:69

Dimnet, Ernest
T. F. Powys **9**:363

Dimock, Edward C., Jr.
Rabindranath Tagore **3**:493

Disch, Thomas M.
Rose Macaulay **7**:432

D'Itri, Patricia Ward
Damon Runyon **10**:435

Dobie, Ann B.
Gerhart Hauptmann **4**:207

Dobrée, Bonamy
Rudyard Kipling **8**:204
D. H. Lawrence **2**:345

Dobson, A.
Miguel de Unamuno **2**:569

Dobzhansky, Theodosius
Pierre Teilhard de Chardin **9**:489

Doggett, Frank
Wallace Stevens **3**:469; **12**:384

Dombroski, Robert
Vitaliano Brancati **12**:83, 90

Donceel, Joseph F., S.J.
Pierre Teilhard de Chardin **9**:487

Donchin, Georgette
Valery Bryusov **10**:81
Maxim Gorky **8**:92

Donnelly, John
Leo Tolstoy **11**:476

Donnelly, Mabel Collins
George Gissing **3**:233

Donoghue, Denis
Malcolm Lowry **6**:239
George MacDonald **9**:301
Eugene O'Neill **1**:404
Dorothy L. Sayers **2**:533
Wallace Stevens **3**:473
William Butler Yeats **1**:580

Dorosz, Kristofer
Malcolm Lowry **6**:251

Dos Passos, John
Pío Baroja **8**:48
Jacinto Benavente **3**:96
Vicente Blasco Ibáñez **12**:36
F. Scott Fitzgerald **1**:240
Miguel de Unamuno **9**:512

Dostoievsky, F. M.
Leo Tolstoy **4**:447

Doud, Robert E.
Pierre Teilhard de Chardin **9**:505

Douglas, Alfred
Oscar Wilde **8**:491, 495

Douglas, Frances
Gabriel Miró **5**:337
Gregorio Martinez Sierra and Maria Martinez Sierra **6**:276

Downer, Alan S.
Harley Granville-Barker **2**:195
Eugene O'Neill **1**:393

Downey, Fairfax
Rebecca Harding Davis **6**:150

Downs, Brian W.
Bjørnstjerne Bjørnson **7**:115
Henrik Ibsen **8**:146
August Strindberg **8**:408

Doyle, Arthur Conan
Rudyard Kipling **8**:182

Drake, Robert
Saki **3**:367, 368

Drake, Robert Y., Jr.
Margaret Mitchell **11**:376

Drake, William A.
Karel Čapek **6**:38
Ricarda Huch **13**:243
Georg Kaiser **9**:172
Charles Péguy **10**:404
Carl Sternheim **8**:368
Ramón del Valle-Inclán **5**:474
Jakob Wassermann **6**:509

Draper, Ronald P.
D. H. Lawrence **9**:222

Drayton, Arthur D.
Claude McKay **7**:463

Dreiser, Theodore
Sherwood Anderson **10**:41
Stephen Crane **11**:126
Theodore Dreiser **10**:173
H. L. Mencken **13**:365
Mark Twain **12**:436

Drew, Elizabeth
Arnold Bennett **5**:31
Joseph Conrad **1**:212
James Joyce **3**:276
D. H. Lawrence **2**:368
Saki **3**:366

Drinkwater, John
Rupert Brooke **7**:121
William Ernest Henley **8**:101
Amy Lowell **8**:227
Alice Meynell **6**:298

Drinnon, Richard
Emma Goldman **13**:220

Driver, Tom F.
Eugene O'Neill **1**:397

DuBois, W. E. Burghardt
Rudolph Fisher **11**:204
Claude McKay **7**:455
Wallace Thurman **6**:446
Booker T. Washington **10**:520

Ducharme, Edward
Elinor Wylie **8**:535

Duclaux, Mary
Charles Péguy **10**:403

Duffey, Bernard
Sherwood Anderson **1**:46

Duffin, Henry Charles
Walter de la Mare **4**:78

Duke, Maurice
James Branch Cabell **6**:78

Dukes, Ashley
Karel Capek **6**:81
Anton Chekhov **3**:147
Gerhart Hauptmann **4**:195
Hugo von Hofmannsthal **11**:291
Georg Kaiser **9**:172
A. A. Milne **6**:307
Arthur Schnitzler **4**:390
Leo Tolstoy **4**:453
Bernard Shaw **3**:381
Ernst Toller **10**:475
Frank Wedekind **7**:575

Dukore, Bernard F.
Ernst Toller **10**:488
Stanisław Ignacy Witkiewicz **8**:512

Dunbar, Olivia Howard
Alice Meynell **6**:296

Dunleavy, Janet Egleston
George Moore **7**:497

Dupee, F. W.
Henry James **2**:274

Durant, Ariel
James Joyce **8**:167

Durant, Will
James Joyce **8**:167

Dusenbury, Winifred L.
Robert E. Sherwood **3**:414

Dust, Patrick, H.
José Ortega y Gasset **9**:351

Duus, Louise
Rebecca Harding Davis **6**:155

Dyboski, Roman
Władysław Stanisław Reymont **5**:392
Henryk Sienkiewicz **3**:425

Dyrenforth, Harald O.
Georg Brandes **10**:67

Dyson, A. E.
F. Scott Fitzgerald **1**:252
Oscar Wilde **1**:504

Eagle, Solomon
See also **Squire, J. C.**
Maurice Baring **8**:32
D. H. Lawrence **9**:212
F. T. Marinetti **10**:315

Eagleson, Harvey
Dorothy Richardson **3**:352

Eaker, J. Gordon
John Galsworthy **1**:300

Eakin, Paul John
Sarah Orne Jewett **1**:368

Eames, Ninetta
Jack London **9**:253

Early, L. R.
Charles G. D. Roberts **8**:327

Eastman, Max
Stephen Vincent Benét **7**:72
John Reed **9**:384
Yevgeny Ivanovich Zamyatin **8**:545

Eaton, G. D.
Pío Baroja **8**:50

Eaton, Walter Prichard
David Belasco **3**:87

Eberhart, Richard
Edwin Muir **2**:481
Wallace Stevens **3**:475

Eble, Kenneth
Kate Chopin **5**:147

Echegaray, José
José Echegaray **4**:97

Eckstein, George
Tadeusz Borowski **9**:22

Economou, George
C. P. Cavafy **7**:164

Edel, Leon
Willa Cather **1**:161
Édouard Dujardin **13**:185
Ford Madox Ford **1**:287
Henry James **2**:271, 274
Dorothy Richardson **3**:354
Lytton Strachey **12**:417
Dylan Thomas **1**:473
Virginia Woolf **1**:540

Edgar, Pelham
Sherwood Anderson **1**:40
Bliss Carman **7**:145
Henry James **11**:325
Charles G. D. Roberts **8**:318
Duncan Campbell Scott **6**:386
Virginia Woolf **1**:530

Edman, Irwin
A. E. **3**:5

Edmonds, Dale
Malcolm Lowry **6**:240

Edwards, George Clifton
Maxim Gorky **8**:68

Edwards, Gwynne
Federico García Lorca **7**:300

Eggleston, Wilfrid
Frederick Philip Grove **4**:137

Eglinton, John
A. E. **3**:6; **10**:18

Ehre, Milton
Isaac Babel **13**:36
Valery Bryusov **10**:96
Yevgeny Ivanovich Zamyatin **8**:558

Eikenbaum, Boris
Leo Tolstoy **4**:456; **11**:461

Ekström, Kjell
George Washington Cable **4**:27

Elder, Donald
Ring Lardner **2**:335

Eldershaw, M. Barnard
Henry Handel Richardson **4**:373

Elimimian, Isaac
Oscar Wilde **8**:502

Eliot, T. S.
See also **Crites**
Henry Adams **4**:5
Gottfried Benn **3**:105
Arthur Conan Doyle **7**:218
Thomas Hardy **4**:161
Henry James **2**:250
James Joyce **3**:252
Rudyard Kipling **8**:190
D. H. Lawrence **9**:219
Wyndham Lewis **9**:234
Edwin Muir **2**:487
Edmond Rostand **6**:378
May Sinclair **11**:410
Algernon Charles Swinburne **8**:429
Arthur Symons **11**:439
Mark Twain **6**:468
Paul Valéry **4**:495
H. G. Wells **12**:504
Charles Williams **11**:485
William Butler Yeats **1**:557

Ellin, Stanley
Rudolph Fisher **11**:207

Elliot, Walter
James Bridie **3**:134

Elliott, George P.
Edgar Rice Burroughs **2**:76
Raymond Chandler **1**:169
George Orwell **6**:346

Ellis, Havelock
Alain-Fournier **6**:12
Vicente Blasco Ibáñez **12**:29
Paul Bourget **12**:57
Miles Franklin **7**:264
Radclyffe Hall **12**:184
Thomas Hardy **4**:147
Joris-Karl Huysmans **7**:404
Olive Schreiner **9**:395
Miguel de Unamuno **9**:508
Juan Valera **10**:499
H. G. Wells **12**:488
Émile Zola **6**:560

Ellis, Keith
Machado de Assis **10**:286

Ellis-Fermor, Una
John Millington Synge **6**:438

Ellmann, Mary
Colette **1**:193

Ellmann, Richard
James Joyce **3**:267; **8**:171
Wallace Stevens **12**:363
Italo Svevo **2**:550
Arthur Symons **11**:444
Oscar Wilde **1**:506; **8**:497
William Butler Yeats **1**:572

Eloesser, Arthur
Ricarda Huch **13**:245
Carl Spitteler **12**:341
Carl Sternheim **8**:369
Jakob Wassermann **6**:510
Frank Wedekind **7**:577

Elsworth, John
Andrey Bely **7**:58

Emery, Clark
Dylan Thomas **8**:454

Empson, William
Franz Kafka **13**:260

Emrich, Wilhelm
Franz Kafka **2**:309

Enck, John J.
Wallace Stevens **12**:370

Eng, Steve
Robert E. Howard **8**:137

Engel, Edwin A.
Eugene O'Neill **1**:399

Engle, Paul
Stephen Vincent Benét **7**:75

Englekirk, John Eugene
Mariano Azuela **3**:75, 79
Amado Nervo **11**:394

Enright, D. J.
Bertolt Brecht **1**:121
Rupert Brooke **7**:129
Aleister Crowley **7**:207
Knut Hamsun **2**:208
D. H. Lawrence **2**:371
Thomas Mann **2**:427
Georg Trakl **5**:461

Eoff, Sherman H.
Pío Baroja **8**:54
Vicente Blasco Ibáñez **12**:44
Juan Valera **10**:504

Epstein, Perle S.
Malcolm Lowry **6**:242

Erickson, John D.
Joris-Karl Huysmans **7**:414

Ericson, Edward E., Jr.
Mikhail Bulgakov **2**:69

Erlich, Victor
Aleksandr Blok **5**:94
Valery Bryusov **10**:88

Erskine, John
Lafcadio Hearn **9**:123

Ervine, St. John G.
A. E. **10**:15
G. K. Chesterton **1**:178
John Galsworthy **1**:293
Bernard Shaw **3**:385
William Butler Yeats **1**:552

Erwin, John F., Jr.
Paul Claudel **2**:108

Eshleman, Clayton
César Vallejo **3**:527

Eskin, Stanley G.
Giuseppi Tomasi di Lampedusa **13**:293

Esslin, Martin
Antonin Artaud **3**:59
Bertolt Brecht **1**:102, 117
Henrik Ibsen **2**:237
Alfred Jarry **2**:285
Luigi Pirandello **4**:352
Arthur Schnitzler **4**:401
Boris Vian **9**:530
Frank Wedekind **7**:588
Stanisław Ignacy Witkiewicz **8**:511

Etō, Jun
Sōseki Natsume **2**:492

Etulain, Richard W.
Zane Grey **6**:182
George MacDonald **9**:281

Evans, Calvin
Maurice Maeterlinck **3**:330

Evans, I. O.
Jules Verne **6**:494

Evans, Ifor
George MacDonald **9**:300

Evans, Robert O.
Joseph Conrad **13**:110

Ewart, Gavin
E. C. Bentley **12**:24

Ewen, Frederic
Bertolt Brecht **13**:52

Ewers, John K.
Miles Franklin **7**:267

Fabrizi, Benedetto
Valéry Larbaud **9**:201

Fackler, Herbert V.
A. E. **3**:12

Fadiman, Clifton P.
Ambrose Bierce **1**:87
Louis Bromfield **11**:76
Willa Cather **11**:94
Joseph Hergesheimer **11**:276
Ricarda Huch **13**:242
Ring Lardner **2**:328
Marie Belloc Lowndes **12**:204
T. F. Powys **9**:360
May Sinclair **11**:412
Leo Tolstoy **4**:466; **11**:466
Thomas Wolfe **4**:513

Fagin, N. Bryllion
Anton Chekhov **3**:151

Fain, John Tyree
Joseph Hergesheimer **11**:278

Fairchild, Hoxie Neale
Charlotte Mew **8**:299
Alice Meynell **6**:302
Charles Williams **1**:521

Falen, James E.
Isaak Babel **2**:32

Falk, Doris V.
Eugene O'Neill **6**:332

Fallis, Richard
Standish O'Grady **5**:357

Fanger, Donald
Mikhail Bulgakov **2**:64

Fant, Åke
Rudolf Steiner **13**:455

Farber, Manny
James Agee **1**:6

Fargue, Léon-Paul
Léon-Paul Fargue **11**:199

Farnsworth, Robert M.
Charles Waddell Chesnutt **5**:134

Farrar, John
Robert Benchley **1**:77

Farrell, James T.
Sherwood Anderson **1**:45
Anton Chekhov **10**:104
Theodore Dreiser **10**:180
Jack London **9**:262
H. L. Mencken **13**:384
Leo Tolstoy **4**:461

Farren, Robert
John Millington Synge **6**:435

Farrison, W. Edward
Booker T. Washington **10**:524

Farrow, Anthony
George Moore **7**:498

Farson, Daniel
Bram Stoker **8**:394

Farwell, Marilyn R.
Virginia Woolf **1**:549

Fast, Howard
Franz Kafka **13**:262

Faulhaber, Uwe Karl
Lion Feuchtwanger **3**:184

Faulkner, William
Sherwood Anderson **1**:45; **10**:35
Mark Twain **6**:471
Thomas Wolfe **4**:521

Fauset, Jessie
Countee Cullen **4**:40

Feder, Lillian
Joseph Conrad **13**:106
William Butler Yeats **1**:583

Feger, Lois
Willa Cather **11**:105

Feibleman, James
Will Rogers **8**:332

Feld, Ross
Guillaume Apollinaire **8**:27

Fender, Stephen
Eugene O'Neill **6**:337

Fennimore, Keith J.
Booth Tarkington **9**:473

Ferenczi, László
Endre Ady **11**:24

Fergusson, Francis
Anton Chekhov **3**:158
Federica García Lorca **1**:315
James Joyce **3**:262
D. H. Lawrence **2**:351
Robert E. Sherwood **3**:413
Paul Valéry **4**:496

Ferlinghetti, Lawrence
John Reed **9**:388

Festa-McCormick, Diana
Andrey Bely **7**:65

Feuchtwanger, Lion
Lion Feuchtwangter **3**:178, 180
Frank Wedekind **7**:578

Feuerlight, Ignace
Thomas Mann **8**:260

Fickert, Kurt J.
Wolfgang Borchert **5**:110

Ficowski, Jerzy
Bruno Schulz **5**:425

Fiedler, Leslie A.
James Agee **1**:1
Ronald Firbank **1**:228
F. Scott Fitzgerald **1**:249, 263
Jaroslav Hasek **4**:181
Nikos Kazantzakis **5**:260
Margaret Mitchell **11**:385
Cesare Pavese **3**:335
Mark Twain **6**:467; **12**:439
Nathanael West **1**:485

Field, Andrew
Fyodor Sologub **9**:437, 438

Field, Frank
Henri Barbusse **5**:17

Field, Leslie
Thomas Wolfe **13**:495

Field, Louise Maunsell
Algernon Blackwood **5**:71
Vicente Blasco Ibáñez **12**:36
F. Scott Fitzgerald **1**:235

Field, Norma Moore
Sōseki Natsume **10**:338

Fife, Robert Herndon
Georg Brandes **10**:63

Figgis, Darrell
A. E. **3**:4

Figh, Margaret Gillis
Marjorie Kinnan Rawlings **4**:362

Firkins, Oscar W.
William Dean Howells **7**:372
Edgar Lee Masters **2**:463
Sara Teasdale **4**:425

First, Ruth
Olive Schreiner **9**:405

Fishtine, Edith
Juan Valera **10**:503

Fitzgerald, F. Scott
Sherwood Anderson **10**:34
Ring Lardner **2**:330
H. L. Mencken **13**:362
Thomas Wolfe **13**:468

Fitzgibbon, Constantine
Dylan Thomas **1**:474

Fitzmaurice-Kelly, James
Vicente Blasco Ibáñez **12**:35
Juan Valera **10**:498

Flanagan, John T.
Edgar Lee Masters **2**:468

Flandreau, Audrey
Ricarda Huch **13**:248

Flanner, Hildegarde
Edna St. Vincent Millay **4**:313

Flanner, Janet
Colette **1**:192

Flatin, Kjetil A.
Alexander Kielland **5**:279

Flaubert, Gustave
Leo Tolstoy **4**:448

Flautz, John T.
Edgar Rice Burroughs **2**:81

Flay, Joseph C.
Nikos Kazantzakis **2**:319

Fleming, Robert E.
James Weldon Johnson **3**:247

Fletcher, Ian
Arthur Symons **11**:450

Fletcher, John Gould
William Ernest Henley **8**:106
Amy Lowell **1**:370

Flexner, Eleanor
Philip Barry **11**:55
Robert E. Sherwood **3**:410

Flint, F. Cudworth
Amy Lowell **1**:379

Flint, R. W.
James Agee **1**:7
F. T. Marinetti **10**:320
Cesare Pavese **3**:340

Flora, Joseph M.
William Ernest Henley **8**:107

Flores, Angel
Ricarda Huch **13**:244

Fogelquist, Donald F.
Juan Ramón Jiménez **4**:224

Folsom, James K.
Hamlin Garland **3**:199
Zane Grey **6**:180

Foltin, Lore B.
Arthur Schnitzler **4**:401
Franz Werfel **8**:482

Forbes, Helen Cady
A. A. Milne **6**:307, 309

Ford, Ford Madox
Joseph Conrad **1**:202
Stephen Crane **11**:135
John Galsworthy **1**:299
Henry James **2**:245
H. G. Wells **6**:532

Ford, Julia Ellsworth
A. E. **3**:1

Forman, Henry James
Kahlil Gibran **1**:327
O. Henry **1**:347

Forster, E. M.
Samuel Butler **1**:136
C. P. Cavafy **2**:87; **7**:154
Joseph Conrad **1**:196
Gabriele D'Annunzio **6**:134
Ronald Firbank **1**:225
Anatole France **9**:48
André Gide **12**:151
Thomas Hardy **4**:156
Henrik Ibsen **2**:221
Henry James **2**:252
Giuseppe Tomasi di Lampedusa **13**:292
George Orwell **6**:340
Marcel Proust **7**:523
Lytton Strachey **12**:406
Rabindranath Tagore **3**:484
Leo Tolstoy **4**:457
Edith Wharton **9**:543
Virginia Woolf **1**:527, 533; **5**:506

Fortebus, Thos.
Maurice Maeterlinck **3**:318

Foster, Edward
Mary Wilkins Freeman **9**:68

Foster, George Burman
Friedrich Nietzsche **10**:366

Foster, John Wilson
A. E. **10**:23

Foster, Richard
F. Scott Fitzgerald **1**:264, 267
William Dean Howells **7**:384

Fowlie, Wallace
Guillaume Apollinaire **3**:35
Antonin Artaud **3**:47
Paul Claudel **2**:103; **10**:125
Paul Éluard **7**:246
Léon-Paul Fargue **11**:200
André Gide **5**:233
Jean Giraudoux **2**:159
Max Jacob **6**:193
Charles Péguy **10**:409
Marcel Proust **7**:543
Paul Valéry **4**:492

Fox, W. H.
Franz Werfel **8**:478

Fox-Genovese, Elizabeth
Margaret Mitchell **11**:389

Fraiberg, Selma
Franz Kafka **2**:299

France, Anatole
Paul Bourget **12**:58, 59
Pierre Loti **11**:354
Marcel Proust **7**:518

Franco, Jean
Ramón del Valle-Inclán **5**:477
César Vallejo **3**:534

Frank, Bruno
Thomas Mann **8**:253

Frank, Joseph
José Ortega y Gasset **9**:348

Frank, Waldo
Mariano Azuela **3**:75
Hart Crane **2**:112
Theodore Dreiser **10**:170
Emma Goldman **13**:217
Jack London **9**:258
Machado de Assis **10**:283

Frankenberg, Lloyd
James Stephens **4**:414

Franklin, Miles
Miles Franklin **7**:266

Franz, Thomas R.
Ramón del Valle-Inclán **5**:489

Fraser, G. S.
Roy Campbell **5**:118, 121
Wallace Stevens **3**:451
Dylan Thomas **1**:472
Oscar Wilde **1**:505
William Butler Yeats **1**:563

Fraser, Howard M.
Rubén Darío **4**:67

Freccero, John
Italo Svevo **2**:543

Freedley, George
Lady Gregory **1**:335

Freedman, Morris
Federico García Lorca **1**:324
Luigi Pirandello **4**:344

Freeman, Douglas Southall
Lytton Strachey **12**:406

Freeman, John
Robert Bridges **1**:124
Joseph Conrad **1**:196
Maurice Maeterlinck **3**:326
George Moore **7**:477
Bernard Shaw **3**:384
Edward Thomas **10**:450

Freeman, Kathleen
Katherine Mansfield **2**:447

Freeman, Mary
D. H. Lawrence **2**:358

Freeman, Mary E. Wilkins
Mary Wilkins Freeman **9**:64

French, Donald G.
John McCrae **12**:208

French, Warren
Hamlin Garland **3**:203

Frenz, Horst
Georg Kaiser **9**:175

Freud, Sigmund
Arthur Schnitzler **4**:391
Lytton Strachey **12**:397

Friar, Kimon
C. P. Cavafy **7**:155
Nikos Kazantzakis **2**:311

Friedenthal, Richard
Ricarda Huch **13**:246

Friedman, Alan
Joseph Conrad **1**:215

Friedman, Lawrence J.
Booker T. Washington **10**:535

Friedman, Melvin
Édouard Dujardin **13**:189
Valéry Larbaud **9**:199

Friedman, Norman
Franz Kafka **13**:269

Friedman, Thomas
Rudolph Fisher **11**:210

Friedrich, Otto
Ring Lardner **2**:340

Frierson, William C.
Rose Macaulay **7**:424
George Moore **7**:484
May Sinclair **11**:412

Frohock, W. M.
James Agee **1**:2
F. Scott Fitzgerald **1**:253
Thomas Wolfe **4**:522

Frost, Robert
Edwin Arlington Robinson **5**:406
Edward Thomas **10**:452

Fruchter, Moses Joseph
Georg Kaiser **9**:173

Frye, Northrop
Bliss Carman **7**:147
Frederick Philip Grove **4**:135
Wyndham Lewis **9**:238
Charles G. D. Roberts **8**:319
Wallace Stevens **3**:452
Charles Williams **11**:488

Frynta, Emanuel
Jaroslav Hašek **4**:183

Fuchs, Daniel
Wallace Stevens **3**:462

Fuller, Edmund
Sholem Asch **3**:68
James Joyce **3**:271
Nikos Kazantzakis **5**:259
Charles Williams **1**:522

Fuller, Henry Blake
Louis Bromfield **11**:74
Hanns Heinz Ewers **12**:134
William Dean Howells **7**:364

Fuller, Roy
Thomas Hardy **4**:176

Furbank, P. N.
G. K. Chesterton **1**:186
Italo Svevo **2**:547

Furness, Edna Lue
Alfonsina Storni **5**:446

Fussell, D. H.
Thomas Hardy **10**:232

Fussell, Edwin
Sherwood Anderson **1**:51
F. Scott Fitzgerald **1**:248

Fussell, Paul
John McCrae **12**:211

Gagey, Edmond M.
Eugene O'Neill **6**:329

Gaillard, Dawson
Margaret Mitchell **11**:382

Gaines, Francis Pendleton
Joel Chandler Harris **2**:210

Galassi, Frank S.
Stanisław Ignacy Witkiewicz **8**:515

Gale, Zona
Zona Gale **7**:278
Charlotte Gilman **9**:101

Galloway, David D.
Nathanael West **1**:481

Galsworthy, John
Anton Chekhov **10**:102
Joseph Conrad **1**:199
Anatole France **9**:47
Leo Tolstoy **4**:457

Gamble, George
Edgar Saltus **8**:343

Ganz, Arthur
Jean Giraudoux **2**:173

García Lorca, Federico
Rubén Darío **4**:63

Gardner, Martin
L. Frank Baum **7**:19

Gardner, May
Gregorio Martinez Sierra and Maria Martinez Sierra **6**:279

Gardner, Monica M.
Henryk Sienkiewicz **3**:425

Garis, Robert
Boris Vian **9**:529

Garland, Hamlin
Stephen Crane **11**:121
Zona Gale **7**:281
Zane Grey **6**:180

Garneau, Saint-Denys
Hector Saint-Denys Garneau **13**:194, 195

Garnett, Constance
Leo Tolstoy **4**:450

Garnett, David
Virginia Woolf **1**:526

Garnett, Edward
Roy Campbell **5**:115
Anton Chekhov **3**:152
Joseph Conrad **1**:198
Stephen Crane **11**:126
Sarah Orne Jewett **1**:359
D. H. Lawrence **2**:343
Leo Tolstoy **4**:450

Garrigue, Jean
Dylan Thomas **1**:471

Garten, F.
Gerhart Hauptmann **4**:203, 205

Garvey, Marcus
Booker T. Washington **10**:522

Gascoigne, Bamber
Eugene O'Neill **1**:403

Gascoyne, David
Ernst Toller **10**:478

Gass, William H.
Bertolt Brecht **6**:33
Colette **5**:172
Malcolm Lowry **6**:244
Marcel Proust **7**:549
Gertrude Stein **1**:438
Paul Valéry **4**:502

Gassner, John
Maxwell Anderson **2**:3
Philip Barry **11**:60
Bertolt Brecht **1**:100
Anton Chekhov **3**:167
Jean Giraudoux **2**:160
Lady Gregory **1**:334
Federico García Lorca **7**:294
Eugene O'Neill **1**:389
August Strindberg **1**:460
John Van Druten **2**:576
Oscar Wilde **1**:498

Gates, Norman T.
William Ernest Henley **8**:109

Gatt-Rutter, John
Giuseppe Tomasi di Lampedusa **13**:318

Gayle, Addison, Jr.
Paul Laurence Dunbar **12**:121

Geddes, Gary
Duncan Campbell Scott **6**:395

Geduld, Harry M.
J. M. Barrie **2**:47

Geismar, Maxwell
Sherwood Anderson **1**:50
Willa Cather **1**:153
F. Scott Fitzgerald **1**:244
Ellen Glasgow **2**:179
Henry James **11**:335
Ring Lardner **2**:330, 339
Sinclair Lewis **4**:253
Jack London **9**:263

Gekle, William Francis
Arthur Machen **4**:280

Gelfant, Blanche H.
Margaret Mitchell **11**:386

Genette, Gerard
Marcel Proust **7**:550

Genovese, Eugene D.
Booker T. Washington **10**:529

George, Ralph W.
Sholem Asch **3**:69

George, W. L.
Edgar Saltus **8**:349

Gerber, Helmut E.
George Moore **7**:489

Gerber, Philip L.
Theodore Dreiser **10**:190

Gerhardi, William
Anton Chekhov **3**:153

Gerould, Daniel
Ernst Toller **10**:488
Stanisław Ignacy Witkiewicz **8**:510, 512

Gerould, Gordon Hall
F. Marion Crawford **10**:152

Gersh, Gabriel
Lytton Strachey **12**:412

Gershman, Herbert S.
Paul Éluard **7**:254

Gerson, Villiers
C. M. Kornbluth **8**:213

Getlein, Frank
Machado de Assis **10**:283

Getsi, Lucia
Georg Trakl **5**:464

Ghiselin, Brewster
James Joyce **3**:266

Ghose, Sisirkumar
Rabindranath Tagore **3**:486

Ghosh, Shibdas
Saratchandra Chatterji **13**:76

Gibbon, Monk
A. E. **3**:7

Gibbons, Stella
H. Rider Haggard **11**:243

Gibbs, Wolcott
Robert Benchley **1**:78
John Van Druten **2**:574

Gibson, Anne L.
Boris Vian **9**:537

Gibson, Robert
Alain-Fournier **6**:25

Gibson, William M.
William Dean Howells **7**:391

Gide, André
Paul Bourget **12**:66
Paul Claudel **10**:120
Jean Giraudoux **7**:317
Henry James **11**:328
Charles Péguy **10**:401
Marcel Proust **7**:525
Antoine de Saint-Exupéry **2**:515
Oscar Wilde **1**:501

Giergielewicz, Mieczyslaw
Henryk Sienkiewicz **3**:430

Gifford, Henry
Osip Mandelstam **2**:409; **6**:269

Gignilliat, John L.
Douglas Southall Freeman **11**:231

Gilbert, Mary E.
Hugo von Hofmannsthal **11**:303

Gilbert, Sandra M.
D. H. Lawrence **9**:224

Gilbert, Stuart
Algernon Blackwood **5**:73
James Joyce **3**:265

Giles, James R.
Claude McKay **7**:470

Gilkes, Michael
H. G. de Lisser **12**:99

Gill, Brendan
Eugene O'Neill **1**:407

Gillen, Charles H.
Saki **3**:373

Gillespie, Diane F.
May Sinclair **11**:417

Gilman, Charlotte Perkins
Charlotte Gilman **9**:102

Gilman, Richard
Sholom Aleichem **1**:26
Bertolt Brecht **1**:121
Anton Chekhov **3**:173
Henrik Ibsen **2**:233
Eugene O'Neill **1**:399
Bernard Shaw **3**:402
August Strindberg **1**:461
Italo Svevo **2**:546

Gindin, James
F. Scott Fitzgerald **1**:265
Virginia Woolf **1**:544

Gingrich, Arnold
F. Scott Fitzgerald **1**:238

Ginzburg, Lidija
Osip Mandelstam **2**:407

Ginzburg, Natalia
Cesare Pavese **3**:337

Giovanni, Nikki
Paul Laurence Dunbar **12**:124

Gippius, Zinaida
Fyodor Sologub **9**:433

Gittleman, Sol
Carl Sternheim **8**:378
Frank Wedekind **7**:583

Gladstone, W. E.
Annie Besant **9**:14

Glasgow, Ellen
Ellen Glasgow **7**:336
Joseph Hergesheimer **11**:269

Glassco, John
Hector Saint-Denys Garneau **13**:202

Gloster, Hugh M.
Rudolph Fisher **11**:205
James Weldon Johnson **3**:242
Wallace Thurman **6**:448

Goble, Danney
Zane Grey **6**:184

Godwin, A. H.
W. S. Gilbert **3**:211

Godwin, Murray
Damon Runyon **10**:422

Goetz, T. H.
Paul Bourget **12**:75

Gogarty, Oliver St. John
Lord Dunsany **2**:144
Oscar Wilde **1**:501

Goist, Park Dixon
Zona Gale **7**:287
Booth Tarkington **9**:474

Gold, Herbert
Sherwood Anderson **1**:49

Gold, Joseph
Charles G. D. Roberts **8**:322

Goldberg, Isaac
Sholem Asch **3**:65
Jacinto Benavente **3**:97
Vicente Blasco Ibáñez **12**:31
Rubén Darío **4**:59
Machado de Assis **10**:278
Amado Nervo **11**:393

Goldberg, S. L.
James Joyce **8**:160

Golden, Bruce
Ford Madox Ford **1**:285

Golding, William
Jules Verne **6**:492

Goldman, Emma
Emma Goldman **13**:211, 212

Goldsmith, Ulrich K.
Stefan George **2**:154

Golffing, Francis
Gottfried Benn **3**:104
C. P. Cavafy **7**:155

Gomme, Andor
Giuseppe Tomasi di Lampedusa **13**:302

Goodman, Paul
Franz Kafka **13**:260

Gordon, Ambrose, Jr.
Ford Madox Ford **1**:280, 286

Gordon, Caroline
James Joyce **3**:266

Gordon, Ian A.
Katherine Mansfield **2**:456; **8**:281

Gordon, Jan B.
Arthur Symons **11**:447

Gorky, Maxim
Leonid Andreyev **3**:25
Isaac Babel **13**:15
Anton Chekhov **3**:145
Sergei Esenin **4**:107

Gorman, Herbert S.
Sholem Asch **3**:66
Katharine Tynan **3**:504

Gosse, Edmund
Bjørnstjerne Bjørnson **7**:105
Paul Claudel **10**:122
Anatole France **9**:42
André Gide **5**:213
Thomas Hardy **4**:149
Henrik Ibsen **8**:141
Henry James **11**:321
Jonas Lie **5**:323
Pierre Loti **11**:354
George Moore **7**:478
Henryk Sienkiewicz **3**:421
Lytton Strachey **12**:391
Émile Zola **1**:585

Gottlieb, Annie
Tess Slesinger **10**:442

Gould, George M.
Lafcadio Hearn **9**:120

Gould, Gerald
May Sinclair **3**:438

Gould, Jean
Amy Lowell **8**:234

Gourmont, Remy de
André Gide **12**:142
Joris-Karl Huysmans **7**:412
Émile Verhaeren **12**:458

Grabowski, Zbigniew A.
Stanisław Ignacy Witkiewicz **8**:506

Graham, Eleanor
A. A. Milne **6**:313

Graham, Kenneth
Henry James **11**:342

Graham, Stephen
Valery Bryusov **10**:78
Aleksandr Kuprin **5**:296

Gramont, Sanche de
Antonin Artaud **3**:54

Grandgent, Charles Hall
John Jay Chapman **7**:187

Grant, Patrick
Rudolf Steiner **13**:460

Granville-Barker, Harley
Laurence Housman **7**:355

Granville-Barker, Helen
Gregorio Martínez Sierra and María Martínez Sierra **6**:275

Grass, Günter
Alfred Döblin **13**:180

Grattan, C. Hartley
Ambrose Bierce **1**:85
Jack London **9**:259
H. G. Wells **12**:500

Graver, Lawrence
Ronald Firbank **1**:232

Graves, Robert
Samuel Butler **1**:134
Alun Lewis **3**:284
George Moore **7**:488

Gray, Donald P.
Pierre Teilhard de Chardin **9**:495

Gray, J. M.
Arthur Symons **11**:426

Gray, James
Edna St. Vincent Millay **4**:318

Gray, Ronald D.
Bertolt Brecht **6**:35
Franz Kafka **6**:222; **13**:279

Gray, Simon
Tadeusz Borowski **9**:20

Gray, Thomas A.
Elinor Wylie **8**:532

Grayburn, William Frazer
Rebecca Harding Davis **6**:152

Grebstein, Sheldon Norman
Sinclair Lewis **4**:256

Green, Benny
Damon Runyon **10**:434

Green, Dorothy
Henry Handel Richardson **4**:380

Green, Ellin
Laurence Housman **7**:360

Green, Julian
Charles Péguy **10**:406

Green, Martin
Dorothy L. Sayers **2**:532

Greenberg, Clement
Bertolt Brecht **1**:97

Greenberg, Martin
Franz Kafka **13**:273

Greene, Anne
James Bridie **3**:139

Greene, Graham
George Bernanos **3**:126
Louis Bromfield **11**:78
Samuel Butler **1**:135
Ford Madox Ford **1**:282
Henry James **2**:256
Dorothy Richardson **3**:353
Frederick Rolfe **12**:270
Saki **3**:366
Hugh Walpole **5**:501
H. G. Wells **12**:505

Greene, Naomi
Antonin Artaud **3**:54

Greenslet, Ferris
Ernest Dowson **4**:85
Lafcadio Hearn **9**:121

Gregg, Richard A.
Yevgeny Ivanovich Zamyatin **8**:549

Gregor, Ian
Thomas Hardy **4**:170
D. H. Lawrence **9**:216
Oscar Wilde **1**:505

Gregory, Alyse
Sherwood Anderson **1**:36
Paul Valéry **4**:487

Gregory, Horace
Sherwood Anderson **10**:43
Vernon Lee **5**:318
Amy Lowell **1**:378
Harriet Monroe **12**:221

Grey, Zane
Zane Grey **6**:177

Griffith, John
Stephen Vincent Benét **7**:82

Griffith, Marlene
Ford Madox Ford **1**:284

Griffiths, Richard
Paul Claudel **2**:105

Grigson, Geoffrey
Wyndham Lewis **2**:386
A. A. Milne **6**:319
Dylan Thomas **1**:467; **8**:462

Grimm, Clyde L.
Mark Twain **12**:446

Gross, Harvey
Thomas Mann **8**:264

Gross, John
William Ernest Henley **8**:106

Gross, Seymour L.
Ivan Bunin **6**:52

Gross, Theodore L.
F. Scott Fitzgerald **1**:269
Booker T. Washington **10**:532

Grosshut, F. S.
Lion Feuchtwanger **3**:178

Grossman, Joan Delaney
Valery Bryusov **10**:95

Grossman, Manual L.
Alfred Jarry **2**:284

Grossman, William L.
Machado de Assis **10**:282, 288

Grossvogel, David I.
Guillaume Apollinaire **8**:13
Bertolt Brecht **1**:106

Grubbs, Henry A.
Alfred Jarry **2**:278

Gruening, Martha
Wallace Thurman **6**:447

Grummann, Paul H.
Gerhart Hauptmann **4**:197

Guerard, Albert J.
Joseph Conrad **6**:115; **13**:103, 104
André Gide **5**:224
Thomas Hardy **4**:171

Guest, Boyd
Mark Twain **12**:438

Guha-Thakurta, P.
Rabindranath Tagore **3**:485

Guicharnaud, Jacques
Paul Claudel **2**:104

Guillen, Claudio
Juan Ramón Jiménez **4**:214

Guiton, Margaret
Georges Bernanos **3**:119

Gullace, Giovanni
Gabrielle D'Annunzio **6**:136

Gullason, Thomas A.
Stephen Crane **11**:148

Gullón, Ricardo
Miguel de Unamuno **9**:516
Ramón del Valle-Inclán **5**:482

Gumilev, Nikolai
Konstantin Dmitriyevich Balmont **11**:30
Andrey Bely **7**:46
Valery Bryusov **10**:77

Gunn, James
Henry Kuttner **10**:272

Gunn, Peter
Vernon Lee **5**:313

Gunther, John
Arthur Machen **4**:279

Günther, Werner
Carl Spitteler **12**:349

Gurko, Leo
Sinclair Lewis **4**:251

Gurko, Miriam
Sinclair Lewis **4**:251

Gustafson, Alrik
Bjørnstjerne Bjørnson **7**:111
Nordahl Grieg **10**:206
Knut Hamsun **2**:205
Verner von Heidenstam **5**:253
Selma Lagerlöf **4**:236
Jonas Lie **5**:325
August Strindberg **1**:448
Sigrid Undset **3**:516

Guthrie, William Norman
Gerhart Hauptmann **4**:192

Gwynn, Stephen
Henri Barbusse **5**:11
W. H. Davies **5**:198

Haber, Edythe C.
Mikhail Bulgakov **2**:71

Haber, Tom Burns
A. E. Housman **10**:258

Hackett, Francis
Henri Barbusse **5**:12
O. Henry **1**:349

Hadfield, Alice Mary
Charles Williams **1**:516

Hadgraft, Cecil
Miles Franklin **7**:268

Haggard, H. Rider
H. Rider Haggard **11**:242

Haight, Gordon
Marie Belloc Lowndes **12**:204

Hakutani, Yoshinobu
Theodore Dreiser **10**:197

Hale, Edward Everett, Jr.
John Jay Chapman **7**:186
Edmond Rostand **6**:376

Hall, J. C.
Edwin Muir **2**:483

Hall, James
Joyce Cary **1**:142

Hall, Robert A., Jr.
W. S. Gilbert **3**:213

Hall, Trevor H.
Arthur Conan Doyle **7**:228

Hall, Wayne E.
A. E. **10**:26
George Moore **7**:499

Hallett, Richard
Isaac Babel **13**:29

Halline, Allan G.
Maxwell Anderson **2**:5

Halls, W. D.
Maurice Maeterlinck **3**:328

Halperin, John
Lytton Strachey **12**:418

Halpern, Joseph
Joris-Karl Huysmans **7**:417

Haman, Aleš
Karel Čapek **6**:90

Hamblen, Abigail Ann
Mary Wilkins Freeman **9**:71

Hamburger, Michael
Gottfried Benn **3**:105
Hugo von Hofmannsthal **11**:305
Georg Trakl **5**:457

Hamilton, Clayton
Alfred Sutro **6**:420
Leo Tolstoy **4**:453
Alexander Woollcott **5**:520

Hamilton, G. Rostrevor
Alice Meynell **6**:302

Hammelmann, H. A.
Hugo von Hofmannsthal **11**:299

Hammond, Josephine
Lord Dunsany **2**:142

Hampshire, Stuart N.
Oscar Wilde **8**:498

Hanan, Patrick
Lu Hsün **3**:300

Hankin, Cherry
Katherine Mansfield **2**:458

Hankin, St. John
Oscar Wilde **1**:495

Hanna, Suhail Ibn-Salim
Kahlil Gibran **9**:85

Hannum, Hunter G.
Arthur Schnitzler **4**:398

Hansen, Harry
Sherwood Anderson **1**:37

Hanser, Richard
Karl Kraus **5**:287

Hapgood, Hutchins
Emma Goldman **13**:208

Hardaway, R. Travis
Heinrich Mann **9**:319

Harding, D. W.
Isaac Rosenberg **12**:287

Hardison, Felicia
Ramón del Valle-Inclán **5**:480

Hardwick, Elizabeth
Henrik Ibsen **2**:240
Leo Tolstoy **4**:480

Hardy, Evelyn
Thomas Hardy **10**:220

Hardy, Thomas
Thomas Hardy **4**:152; **10**:216

Hare, Humphrey
Algernon Charles Swinburne **8**:436

Harkins, William E.
Karel Čapek **6**:87, 88

Harlan, Louis R.
Booker T. Washington **10**:532

Harman, H. E.
Joel Chandler Harris **2**:210
John McCrae **12**:208

Harper, Allanah
Léon-Paul Fargue **11**:197

Harris, Austin
Francis Thompson **4**:437

Harris, Frank
Paul Bourget **12**:65
Lord Dunsany **2**:142
H. L. Mencken **13**:366
Oscar Wilde **1**:508

Harris, William J.
Stephen Vincent Benét **7**:84

Harrison, Barbara Grizzuti
Dorothy L. Sayers **2**:536

Harrison, John R.
Wyndham Lewis **9**:240

Harrison, Stanley R.
Hamlin Garland **3**:202

Hart, Francis Russell
George MacDonald **9**:308

Hart, James D.
Margaret Mitchell **11**:374

Hart, Jeffrey
F. Scott Fitzgerald **1**:274

Hart, Pierre
Andrey Bely **7**:55

Hart, Pierre R.
Mikhail Bulgakov **2**:67

Hart, Walter Morris
Rudyard Kipling **8**:182

Harte, Bret
Mark Twain **6**:453

Hartley, L. P.
Marie Belloc Lowndes **12**:202
Saki **3**:364

Hartnett, Edith
Joris-Karl Huysmans **7**:417

Harwell, Richard
Douglas Southall Freeman **11**:230

Hasley, Louis
Don Marquis **7**:446

Hassall, Christopher
Rupert Brooke **2**:56; **7**:124

Hassan, Ihab
Franz Kafka **2**:306
Edwin Muir **2**:485

Hastings, Michael
Rupert Brooke **7**:128

Hastings, R.
Gabriele D'Annunzio **6**:141

Hatfield, Henry
Thomas Mann **2**:435
Robert Musil **12**:255

Hathaway, R. H.
Bliss Carman **7**:136

Hatvary, George Egon
James Stephens **4**:412

Hatzantonis, Emmanuel
Nikos Kazantzakis **5**:260

Havel, Hippolyte
Emma Goldman **13**:208

Hawi, Khalil S.
Kahlil Gibran **9**:87

Hawk, Affable
See also **MacCarthy, Desmond**
Marcel Proust **7**:520

Hawkins, Desmond
Franz Kafka **13**:257

Haycraft, Howard
E. C. Bentley **12**:18
Dorothy L. Sayers **2**:529

Hayes, Richard
James Agee **1**:4
Colette **5**:163

Haynes, Reneé
Hilaire Belloc **7**:38

Haynes, Roslynn D.
H. G. Wells **6**:553

Hays, H. R.
Robert E. Howard **8**:129

Hays, Michael
Carl Sternheim **8**:381

Hayward, Max
Marina Tsvetaeva **7**:565

Hazo, Samuel
Hart Crane **2**:119
Wilfred Owen **5**:366

Heaney, Seamus
William Butler Yeats **11**:532

Heard, Gerald
Kahlil Gibran **1**:328

Hearn, Lafcadio
Bjørnsterne Bjørnson **7**:108
Paul Bourget **12**:57
Anatole France **9**:39
Pierre Loti **11**:351
Leo Tolstoy **4**:455
Émile Zola **6**:559

Hebblethwaite, Peter, S.J.
Georges Bernanos **3**:122

Hecht, Ben
Sholom Aleichem **1**:22

Hedges, Elaine R.
Charlotte Gilman **9**:105

Heermance, J. Noel
Charles Waddell Chesnutt **5**:137

Heidegger, Martin
Friedrich Nietzsche **10**:380
Georg Trakl **5**:459

Heidenreich, Rev. Alfred
Rudolf Steiner **13**:448

Heilburn, Carolyn
Dorothy L. Sayers **2**:535

Heiney, Donald
Cesare Pavese **3**:341
Boris Vian **9**:536

Heller, Erich
Franz Kafka **6**:225
Karl Kraus **5**:288
Thomas Mann **2**:442
Rainer Maria Rilke **1**:419

Heller, Otto
Gerhart Hauptmann **4**:193
Ricarda Huch **13**:240
August Strindberg **1**:443

Hellersberg-Wendriner, Anna
Thomas Mann **8**:257

Hemingway, Ernest
Sherwood Anderson **10**:35
Joseph Conrad **6**:113
Stephen Crane **11**:143
Marie Belloc Lowndes **12**:205
Mark Twain **6**:463

Hemmings, F.W.J.
Émile Zola **6**:561, 570

Henderson, Alice Corbin
Edgar Lee Masters **2**:460

Henderson, Archibald
John Galsworthy **1**:295
Harley Granville-Barker **2**:193
Maurice Maeterlinck **3**:322
Bernard Shaw **3**:382
August Strindberg **1**:444
Mark Twain **6**:458
Oscar Wilde **1**:496

Henderson, Harry III
John Reed **9**:386

Henderson, Philip
Algernon Charles Swinburne **8**:441

Hendricks, Frances Kellam
Mariano Azuela **3**:79

Henighan, Tom
Edgar Rice Burroughs **2**:83

Henkle, Roger B.
Wyndham Lewis **9**:248

Henley, William Ernest
H. Rider Haggard **11**:238
Mark Twain **12**:426
Oscar Wilde **8**:490

Henn, Thomas Rice
A. E. **10**:18

Hennelly, Mark M., Jr.
Bram Stoker **8**:395

Henshaw, N. W.
W. S. Gilbert **3**:216

Heppenstall, Rayner
Paul Claudel **2**:99

Hergesheimer, Joseph
Gabriele D'Annunzio **6**:131
Joseph Hergesheimer **11**:261
Hugh Walpole **5**:494

Herrick, Robert
Henri Barbusse **5**:12

Herron, Ima Honaker
Zona Gale **7**:281

Heseltine, Harry
Miles Franklin **7**:273

Hesford, Walter
Rebecca Harding Davis **6**:156

Hesse, Hermann
André Gide **12**:143, 160
José Ortega y Gasset **9**:337
Rainer Maria Rilke **1**:409
Rabindranath Tagore **3**:493

Hewett-Thayer, Harvey W.
Gerhart Hauptmann **4**:199

Hewitt, Douglas
Joseph Conrad **6**:122

Heymann, C. David
Amy Lowell **8**:235

Hibberd, Dominic
Wilfred Owen **5**:372

Hibberd, J. L.
Frank Wedekind **7**:590

Hicks, Granville
Henry Adams **4**:6
Sherwood Anderson **10**:40
George Washington Cable **4**:26
Willa Cather **11**:96
Theodore Dreiser **10**:176
Ford Madox Ford **1**:275
George Gissing **3**:230
William Dean Howells **7**:375
Henry James **2**:255
Sarah Orne Jewett **1**:362
Sinclair Lewis **13**:337
Jack London **9**:260
George Moore **7**:495
Eugene O'Neill **1**:385
John Reed **9**:383
Franz Werfel **8**:467
Oscar Wilde **1**:497

Higginbotham, Virginia
Federico García Lorca **7**:296

Higgins, F. R.
William Butler Yeats **1**:556

Higgins, Ian
Émile Verhaeren **12**:476

Higgins, James
César Vallejo **3**:531

Highet, Gilbert
A. E. Housman **1**:357
James Joyce **3**:264
Carl Spitteler **12**:343

Highsmith, James Milton
Ambrose Bierce **7**:92

Hilfer, Anthony Channell
Zona Gale **7**:286
Sinclair Lewis **13**:343

Hill, Claude
Bertolt Brecht **13**:64
Arthur Schnitzler **4**:397
Frank Wedekind **7**:579

Hill, Hamlin L.
Don Marquis **7**:442

Hillyer, Robert
Kahlil Gibran **1**:327; **9**:84

Hilton, Ian
Gottfried Benn **3**:109

Hind, Charles Lewis
G. K. Chesterton **1**:177
Laurence Housman **7**:353

Hinden, Michael
Friedrich Nietzsche **10**:396

Hindus, Milton
F. Scott Fitzgerald **1**:243
Marcel Proust **13**:415

Hingley, Ronald
Anton Chekhov **3**:165

Hinton, Norman D.
Hart Crane **5**:194

Hively, Evelyn T. Helmick
Elinor Wylie **8**:531

Hobman, D. L.
Olive Schreiner **9**:397

Hobson, J. A.
Olive Schreiner **9**:394

Hochfield, George
Henry Adams **4**:16

Hockey, Lawrence
W. H. Davies **5**:208

Hodson, W. L.
Marcel Proust **7**:538

Hofacker, Erich P.
Christian Morgenstern **8**:309

Hoffman, Charles G.
Joyce Cary **1**:143

Hoffman, Daniel
Edwin Muir **2**:488

Hoffman, Frederick J.
Sherwood Anderson **1**:48, 53
Willa Cather **1**:159, 161
Hart Crane **2**:117
F. Scott Fitzgerald **1**:255, 256
James Joyce **3**:263
Franz Kafka **2**:293
D. H. Lawrence **2**:354
Thomas Mann **2**:420
Gertrude Stein **1**:432

Hofmannsthal, Hugo von
Hugo von Hofmannsthal **11**:290
Eugene O'Neill **6**:325

Hogan, Robert
Bernard Shaw **9**:422

Hoggart, Richard
George Orwell **2**:506

Holbrook, David
Dylan Thomas **8**:452

Holdheim, William W.
André Gide **5**:230

Holl, Karl
Gerhart Hauptmann **4**:196

Hollingdale, R. J.
Thomas Mann **8**:266
Friedrich Nietzsche **10**:387

Hollis, Christopher
George Orwell **2**:502

Holloway, John
Wyndham Lewis **2**:393

Holman, C. Hugh
Ellen Glasgow **7**:348
Sinclair Lewis **13**:346
Thomas Wolfe **4**:526, 528; **13**:489

Holmes, H. H.
C. M. Kornbluth **8**:212

Holmes, John Haynes
Kahlil Gibran **9**:82

Holroyd, Michael
Lytton Strachey **12**:413

Holroyd, Stuart
Rainer Maria Rilke **1**:416
Dylan Thomas **1**:470
William Butler Yeats **1**:564

Honig, Edwin
Federico García Lorca **1**:318

Hooker, Jeremy
Edward Thomas **10**:460

Hope, A. D.
Henry Handel Richardson **4**:376

Hope, John
Booker T. Washington **10**:515

Hopkins, Kenneth
Walter de la Mare **4**:81

Hopkins, Mary Alden
Anthony Comstock **13**:90

Horgan, Paul
Maurice Baring **8**:40

Hough, Graham
Wallace Stevens **3**:457

Houston, Ralph
Alun Lewis **3**:287

Hovey, Richard B.
John Jay Chapman **7**:196, 200

Howard, Richard
Marcel Proust **13**:423

Howard, Robert E.
Robert E. Howard **8**:128

Howarth, Herbert
A. E. **3**:8
Ford Madox Ford **1**:291
James Joyce **3**:270

Howe, Irving
Sholom Aleichem **1**:23, 26
Sherwood Anderson **1**:43
Isaac Babel **13**:19
Theodore Dreiser **10**:187
George Gissing **3**:235
Sarah Orne Jewett **1**:364
Rudyard Kipling **8**:207
Sinclair Lewis **4**:256
H. L. Mencken **13**:385
George Orwell **2**:512
Luigi Pirandello **4**:341
Isaac Rosenberg **12**:306
Wallace Stevens **3**:464
Leo Tolstoy **4**:472
Edith Wharton **3**:574
Émile Zola **1**:595

Howe, M. A. DeWolfe
John Jay Chapman **7**:189

Howe, Marquerite
José Ortega y Gasset **9**:350

Howe, P. P.
John Millington Synge **6**:428

Howell, Elmo
George Washington Cable **4**:34

Howells, Bernard
Paul Claudel **2**:106

Howells, William Dean
Bjørnsterne Bjørnson **7**:105
Vicente Blasco Ibáñez **12**:33
George Washington Cable **4**:25
Charles Waddell Chesnutt **5**:130
Stephen Crane **11**:126
Paul Laurence Dunbar **2**:127; **12**:103
Mary Wilkins Freeman **9**:60
Hamlin Garland **3**:190
Charlotte Gilman **9**:101
Thomas Hardy **4**:150
William Dean Howells **7**:368
Henrik Ibsen **2**:218
Henry James **11**:319
Sinclair Lewis **13**:325
Booth Tarkington **9**:452
Leo Tolstoy **4**:450
Mark Twain **6**:456; **12**:424
Juan Valera **10**:497
Giovanni Verga **3**:538
Booker T. Washington **10**:516
Edith Wharton **9**:54
Émile Zola **1**:586

Hsia, T. A.
Lu Hsün **3**:296

Hsueh-Feng, Feng
Lu Hsün **3**:295

Hubbard, Elbert
Edgar Saltus **8**:344

Hubben, William
Franz Kafka **2**:296

Hueffer, Ford Madox
See **Ford, Ford Madox**

Hueffer, Oliver Madox
Jack London **9**:256

Huffman, Claire Licari
Vitaliano Brancati **12**:86

Huggins, Nathan Irvin
Claude McKay **7**:465

Hughes, Glenn
David Belasco **3**:88

Hughes, Helen Sard
May Sinclair **3**:440

Hughes, Langston
Wallace Thurman **6**:447
Mark Twain **6**:474

Hughes, Merritt Y.
Luigi Pirandello **4**:329

Hughes, Riley
F. Scott Fitzgerald **1**:247

Hughes, Ted
Wilfred Owen **5**:370

Hulbert, Ann
W. H. Davies **5**:210

Hume, Robert A.
Henry Adams **4**:10

Humphries, Rolfe
Federico García Lorca **1**:309
Lady Gregory **1**:334

Huneker, James
Georg Brandes **10**:63
Maxim Gorky **8**:71
Lafcadio Hearn **9**:124
Joris-Karl Huysmans **7**:411
Henrik Ibsen **2**:222
Maurice Maeterlinck **3**:319
Friedrich Nietzsche **10**:361
Bernard Shaw **3**:381
Leo Tolstoy **4**:453
Edith Wharton **9**:541

Hunt, Elizabeth R.
José Echegaray **4**:99

Hunt, Peter R.
G. K. Chesterton **6**:107

Hunter, William
T. F. Powys **9**:364

Huntington, Christopher
Alfred Döblin **13**:163

Hutchison, Percy
Marjorie Kinnan Rawlings **4**:360

Hutchinson, Percy A.
Alfred Noyes **7**:506

Hutman, Norma Louise
Antonio Machado **3**:311

Hutton, Richard Holt
H. G. Wells **6**:523

Huxley, Aldous
Ernest Dowson **4**:86
Maxim Gorky **8**:76
D. H. Lawrence **2**:352
Katherine Mansfield **2**:447
H. L. Mencken **13**:360
Edward Thomas **10**:453
Émile Verhaeren **12**:470

Huxley, Julian
Pierre Teilhard de Chardin **9**:479

Huysmans, J. K.
Joris-Karl Huysmans **7**:409

Hyde, Fillmore
Kahlil Gibran **1**:325

Hyde, Lawrence
Dorothy Richardson **3**:348

Hyman, Frieda Clark
Isaac Rosenberg **12**:292

Hyman, Stanley Edgar
F. Scott Fitzgrald **1**:263
Constance Rourke **12**:320

Hynes, Samuel
G. K. Chesterton **1**:183
Joseph Conrad **1**:213
Ford Madox Ford **1**:278
Thomas Hardy **4**:168

Hytier, Jean
André Gide **5**:214

Iggers, Wilma Abeles
Karl Kraus **5**:285

Ilie, Paul
Miguel de Unamuno **2**:565

Illiano, Antonio
Ugo Betti **5**:65

Innes, Christopher
Paul Claudel **10**:134

Ireland, G. W.
André Gide **12**:176

Iribarne, Louis
Stanisław Ignacy Witkiewicz **8**:516

Iron, Ralph
See also **Schreiner, Olive**
Olive Schreiner **9**:393

Irvine, William
Bernard Shaw **3**:394

Irwin, W. R.
Rose Macaulay **7**:425
Charles Williams **1**:523

Isaacs, Edith J. R.
Robert E. Sherwood **3**:411

Isherwood, Christopher
Arthur Conan Doyle **7**:228
H. G. Wells **12**:506

Isitt, Yvonne
Robert Musil **12**:244

Isola, Pietro
Gabriele D'Annunzio **6**:130

Jack, Peter Monro
Federico García Lorca **1**:307
Lewis Grassic Gibbon **4**:121

Jackson, Blyden
Countee Cullen **4**:51

Jackson, David
James Agee **1**:16

Jackson, Holbrook
Maurice Maeterlinck **3**:322

Jackson, Robert Louis
Aleksandr Kuprin **5**:298

Jackson, Rosemary
George MacDonald **9**:310
Bram Stoker **8**:402

Jacob, Max
Max Jacob **6**:190

Jacobson, Dan
Olive Schreiner **9**:402

Jaffe, Don
Don Marquis **7**:450

Jahn, Werner
Lion Feuchtwanger **3**:183

Jakobson, Roman
Vladimir Mayakovsky **4**:291

Jaloux, Edmond
Valéry Larbaud **9**:196

James, Clive
Arthur Conan Doyle **7**:232

James, Henry
Paul Bourget **12**:64
Rupert Brooke **2**:51; **7**:120, 121
John Jay Chapman **7**:185
Joseph Conrad **6**:113
F. Marion Crawford **10**:139
George Gissing **3**:221
Thomas Hardy **4**:156
William Dean Howells **7**:365
Henrik Ibsen **2**:218
Henry James **2**:244
Pierre Loti **11**:352
Edmond Rostand **6**:375
Hugh Walpole **5**:492
H. G. Wells **6**:525, 526; **12**:493

Edith Wharton **3**:555, 557
Émile Zola **1**:586

James, M. R.
M. R. James **6**:206

Jameson, Fredric
Raymond Chandler **7**:170
Wyndham Lewis **9**:247

Jameson, Storm
Jacinto Benavente **3**:95
Walter de la Mare **4**:71
José Echegaray **4**:100

Janeway, Elizabeth
Joyce Cary **1**:140

Janouch, Gustav
Alfred Döblin **13**:158
Franz Kafka **13**:256

Janson, Kristofer
Bjørnstjerne, Bjørnson **7**:101

Jarrell, Randall
Ellen Glasgow **7**:334
A. E. Housman **10**:242
Rudyard Kipling **8**:201
Walter de la Mare **4**:79
Wallace Stevens **3**:449

Jaspers, Karl
Friedrich Nietzsche **10**:370

Jean-Aubry, G.
Edmond Rostand **6**:377

Jennings, Elizabeth
Wallace Stevens **3**:459

Jerrold, Walter
Alfred Noyes **7**:508

Jiménez, Juan Ramón
Antonio Machado **3**:306

Joad, C.E.M.
Samuel Butler **1**:134
H. L. Mencken **13**:377

Johannesson, Eric O.
Selma Lagerlöf **4**:241

John, Alun
Alun Lewis **3**:291

Johns, Marilyn
August Strindberg **8**:416

Johnson, Abby Arthur
Harriet Monroe **12**:225

Johnson, Diane
Colette **5**:173

Johnson, James Weldon
Countee Cullen **4**:41
Paul Laurence Dunbar **12**:105
Claude McKay **7**:456

Johnson, Lionel
Rudyard Kipling **8**:176
William Butler Yeats **11**:507

Johnson, Pamela Hansford
Marcel Proust **13**:418

Johnson, R. Brimley
Rose Macaulay **7**:421
May Sinclair **3**:435

Johnson, Robert Underwood
George Washington Cable **4**:26

Johnson, Roberta
Gabriel Miró **5**:342

Johnson, Talmage C.
Kahlil Gibran **9**:83

Johnson, Walter
August Strindberg **8**:417

Joll, James
F. T. Marinetti **10**:316

Jones, D. G.
Bliss Carman **7**:149
Charles G. D. Roberts **8**:325

Jones, Ernest
Ronald Firbank **1**:225

Jones, Frank
Stephen Vincent Benét **7**:75

Jones, G. P.
Frederick Rolfe **12**:279

Jones, John Bush
W. S. Gilbert **3**:215

Jones, Llewellyn
Joseph Hergesheimer **11**:274

Jones, P. Mansell
Émile Verhaeren **12**:474

Jones, Robert A.
Frank Wedekind **7**:587

Jones, Sonia
Alfonsina Storni **5**:451

Jong, Erica
Colette **1**:193, 194

Jordy, William H.
Henry Adams **4**:13

Josephson, Matthew
Lafcadio Hearn **9**:128

Josipovici, Gabriel
Bruno Schulz **5**:427

Joyce, James
Henrik Ibsen **2**:219
Bernard Shaw **3**:381
Oscar Wilde **1**:494

Juhnke, Janet
L. Frank Baum **7**:23

Jullian, Philipe
Gabriele D'Annunzio **6**:143
Oscar Wilde **8**:496

Jung, C. G.
James Joyce **3**:257

Jung, Claire
George Heym **9**:145

Jussem-Wilson, N.
Charles Péguy **10**:410

Justice, Donald
A. E. Housman **1**:357

Justus, James H.
Joseph Hergesheimer **11**:282
Katherine Mansfield **8**:283

Kafka, Franz
Endre Ady **11**:12
Alfred Döblin **13**:158
Franz Kafka **6**:219; **13**:256
Christian Morgenstern **8**:304
Rudolf Steiner **13**:435
Franz Werfel **8**:466

Kahler, Erich
Franz Werfel **8**:471

Kahn, Coppélia
Rebecca Harding Davis **6**:155

Kahn, Lothar
Lion Feuchtwanger **3**:183, 187

Kaiser, Ernst
Robert Musil **12**:232

Kallet, Marilyn
Paul Éluard **7**:260

Kallich, Martin
Lytton Strachey **12**:409

Kam, Rose Salberg
Joseph Conrad **1**:220

Kanfer, Stefan
Kahlil Gibran **1**:329

Kaplan, Sydney Janet
Dorothy Richardson **3**:359
May Sinclair **11**:414

Karl, Frederick R.
Joyce Cary **1**:146
Joseph Conrad **6**:117; **13**:126
George Orwell **6**:349

Karlinsky, Simon
Zinaida Hippius **9**:168
Marina Tsvetaeva **7**:559

Kauffman, Stanley
James Agee **1**:5

Kaufmann, R. J.
August Strindberg **1**:454

Kaufmann, Walter
Friedrich Nietzsche **10**:391

Kaun, Alexander S.
Leonid Andreyev **3**:21
Georg Brandes **10**:62
Sergei Esenin **4**:110

Kayden, Eugene M.
Leonid Andreyev **3**:20

Kayser, Wolfgang
Hanns Heinz Ewers **12**:136
Christian Morgenstern **8**:306

Kazin, Alfred
James Agee **1**:4
Sholom Aleichem **1**:25
Sherwood Anderson **1**:47; **10**:41
James Branch Cabell **6**:69
Willa Cather **11**:98
John Jay Chapman **7**:194
Stephen Crane **11**:136
Theodore Dreiser **10**:184
Édouard Dujardin **13**:183
F. Scott Fitzgerald **1**:250
Hamlin Garland **3**:195
André Gide **12**:164
Ellen Glasgow **2**:176
Maxim Gorky **8**:82
Joseph Hergesheimer **11**:278
William Dean Howells **7**:378
James Joyce **3**:259
Franz Kafka **2**:296
D. H. Lawrence **2**:365
Sinclair Lewis **4**:250
Jack London **9**:261
Rose Macaulay **7**:423
Thomas Mann **8**:272
H. L. Mencken **13**:378
Marcel Proust **7**:532
Constance Rourke **12**:319
Gertrude Stein **1**:431
H. G. Wells **12**:508
Edith Wharton **3**:565
Thomas Wolfe **4**:516; **13**:486
Elinor Wylie **8**:530

Keefer, L. B.
Gerhart Hauptmann **4**:199

Keeley, Edmund
C. P. Cavafy **2**:93, 94

Keene, Donald
Dazai Osamu **11**:173
Toson Shimazaki **5**:433

Keith, W. J.
Charles G. D. Roberts **8**:323
Edward Thomas **10**:465

Kejzlarov́, Ingeborg
Joseph Hergesheimer **11**:284

Kelly, H. A., S.J.
Édouard Dujardin **13**:187

Kelly, Robert Glynn
Dorothy Richardson **3**:353

Kemelman, H. G.
Eugene O'Neill **6**:326

Keniston, R. H.
Vicente Blasco Ibáñez **12**:28

Kennedy, Andrew K.
Bernard Shaw **3**:406

Kennedy, Edwin J. Jr.
Virginia Woolf **5**:517

Kennedy, Eileen **7**:274

Kennedy, P. C.
Virginia Woolf **5**:506

Kennedy, Richard S.
Thomas Wolfe **13**:482

Kennedy, Ruth Lee
José Echegaray **4**:100

Kennelly, Brendan
George Moore **7**:491

Kenner, Hugh
Roy Campbell **5**:120
F. Scott Fitzgerald **1**:273
Ford Madox Ford **1**:278
James Joyce **3**:268
Wyndham Lewis **2**:388, 389
Wallace Stevens **3**:474
William Butler Yeats **1**:566

Kent, George E.
Claude McKay **7**:467

Kenworthy, B. J.
Georg Kaiser **9**:179

Kercheville, F. M.
Rubén Darío **4**:62

Keresztury, Dezső
Endre Ady **11**:22

Kermode, Frank
Ernest Dowson **4**:90
Giuseppe Tomasi di Lampedusa **13**:292
D. H. Lawrence **2**:372
Robert Musil **12**:251
Wallace Stevens **3**:458
Arthur Symons **11**:442

Kerrigan, Anthony
Pío Baroja **8**:53
Miguel de Unamuno **2**:568

Kestner, Joseph
Antoine de Saint-Exupéry **2**:523

Kettle, Arnold
Arnold Bennett **5**:48
Joyce Cary **1**:141
Joseph Conrad **1**:206
John Galsworthy **1**:301
Henry James **2**:264

Keylor, William R.
Charles Péguy **10**:416

Khodasevich, Vladislaw
Valery Bryusov **10**:79
Zinaida Hippius **9**:155

Kidder, Rushworth M.
Dylan Thomas **8**:458

Kiddle, Lawrence B.
Mariano Azuela **3**:75

Kilmer, Joyce
Lafcadio Hearn **9**:125
Don Marquis **7**:434
Rabindranath Tagore **3**:482
Sara Teasdale **4**:424

Kilpatrick, James J.
H. L. Mencken **13**:395

Kimball, Sidney Fiske
Henry Adams **4**:4

Kinahan, Frank
F. Scott Fitzgerald **1**:267

Kindilien, Carlin T.
Hamlin Garland **3**:197

King, C. D.
Édouard Dujardin **13**:183

King, Edmund L.
Gabriel Miró **5**:345

King, Henry Safford
Paul Heyse **8**:121

King, J. Marin
Marina Tsvetaeva **7**:570

King, Jonathan
Henri Barbusse **5**:18

King, Martin Luther, Jr.
Booker T. Washington **10**:530

Kinnaird, Clark
Damon Runyon **10**:428

Kipling, Rudyard
H. Rider Haggard **11**:241

Kirby, Michael
F. T. Marinetti **10**:317

Kirkconnell, Watson
Endre Ady **11**:13

Klarmann, Adolf D.
Wolfgang Borchert **5**:103
Franz Werfel **8**:472

Klinck, Carl F.
Wilfred Campbell **9**:31

Klingborg, Arne
Rudolf Steiner **13**:455

Klotz, Martin B.
Isaak Babel **2**:31

Knapp, Bettina L.
Antonin Artaud **3**:52
Paul Claudel **10**:134
Maurice Maeterlinck **3**:331

Knaust, Rebecca
Guiseppe Giacosa **7**:315

Knecht, Loring D.
André Gide **12**:172

Knickerbocker, Conrad
Malcolm Lowry **6**:238

Knight, Damon
C. M. Kornbluth **8**:216
Henry Kuttner **10**:269

Knight, G. Wilson
Oscar Wilde **1**:503

Knight, Max
Christian Morgenstern **8**:308

Knister, Raymond
Duncan Campbell Scott **6**:385

Knodel, Arthur
Pierre Teilhard de Chardin **9**:478

Knowlton, Edgar C., Jr.
Vicente Blasco Ibáñez **12**:48

Knox, Ronald A.
Maurice Baring **8**:37
G. K. Chesterton **6**:99

Kobler, J. F.
Katherine Mansfield **8**:289

Koch, Stephen
Antonin Artaud **3**:51

Koestler, Arthur
George Orwell **2**:498

Koht, Halvdan
Nordahl Grieg **10**:205

Kolb, Philip
Marcel Proust **7**:547

Königsberg, I.
Alfred Jarry **2**:283

Korg, Jacob
George Gissing **3**:235

Kornbluth, C. M.
C. M. Kornbluth **8**:213

Kort, Wolfgang
Alfred Döblin **13**:173

Kosove, Joan Pataky
Maurice Maeterlinck **3**:330

Kossman, Rudolf R.
Henry James **11**:338

Kostelanetz, Richard
Gertrude Stein **6**:414

Kostka, Edmund
Heinrich Mann **9**:329

Kott, Jan
Tadeusz Borowski **9**:23
Stanisław Ignacy Witkiewicz **8**:507

Kramer, Leonie
Henry Handel Richardson **4**:380

Kramer, Victor A.
James Agee **1**:16

Krans, Horatio Sheafe
William Butler Yeats **11**:512

Kraus, Michael
Douglas Southall Freeman **11**:224

Kreuter, Gretchen
F. Scott Fitzgerald **1**:252

Kreuter Kent
F. Scott Fitzgerald **1**:252

Kreymborg, Alfred
Edgar Lee Masters **2**:465
Thomas Wolfe **4**:518

Kridl, Manfred
Władysław Stanisław Reymont **5**:393
Henryk Sienkiewicz **3**:429

Krige, Uys
Olive Schreiner **9**:397

Krispyn, Egbert
Georg Heym **9**:145
Carl Sternheim **8**:374

Kronenberger, Louis
Henry Adams **4**:6
Max Beerbohm **1**:67
Vicente Blasco Ibáñez **12**:40
W. H. Davies **5**:204
Ronald Firbank **1**:225
Jean Giraudoux **7**:317
Franz Werfel **8**:468
Virginia Woolf **5**:507
Alexander Woollcott **5**:523

Krook, Dorothea
Henry James **2**:272

Kroth, Anya M.
Marina Tsvetaeva **7**:567

Krutch, Joseph Wood
Maxwell Anderson **2**:6
Philip Barry **11**:46
Louis Bromfield **11**:78
Ivan Bunin **6**:44
Anton Chekhov **10**:105
Colette **1**:192
Zona Gale **7**:280
Ellen Glasgow **7**:335
Joseph Hergesheimer **11**:270
Henrik Ibsen **2**:230
Sinclair Lewis **4**:255
Rose Macaulay **7**:423
Arthur Machen **4**:277
Eugene O'Neill **1**:396
Marcel Proust **13**:403
Władysław Stanisław Reymont **5**:390
Frederick Rolfe **12**:267
Constance Rourke **12**:318
Bernard Shaw **3**:397
Robert E. Sherwood **3**:412
May Sinclair **3**:438; **11**:411
August Strindberg **1**:450
Oscar Wilde **1**:502
Jakob Wassermann **6**:508
Alexander Woollcott **5**:521

Krzyzanowski, Jerzy R.
Władysław Stanisław Reymont **5**:395
Stanisław Ignacy Witkiewicz **8**:509

Kuhns, Richard F.
Giuseppe Tomasi di Lampedusa **13**:307

Kunst, Arthur E.
Lafcadio Hearn **9**:135

Kurrick, Maire Jaanus
Georg Trakl **5**:466

Kustow, Michael
Bertolt Brecht **1**:122

Kuttner, Henry
Henry Kuttner **10**:265

Kwiat, Joseph J.
Stephen Crane **11**:142
Theodore Dreiser **10**:200

LaBelle, Maurice M.
H. L. Mencken **13**:388

Labor, Earle
Jack London **9**:272

Laffitte, Sophie
Anton Chekov **10**:111

Lafourcade, Georges
Arnold Bennett **5**:38

La France, Marston
Stephen Crane **11**:156

Lagerkvist, Pär
August Strindberg **1**:456

Lagerroth, Erland
Selma Lagerlöf **4**:241

Lago, Mary M.
Rabindranath Tagore **3**:498, 499

Lakshin, Vladimir
Mikhail Bulgakov **2**:73

Lalou, René
Valéry Larbaud **9**:196

Lambasa, Frank
Franz Werfel **8**:474

Lambert, J. W.
John Galsworthy **1**:304
Saki **3**:369

Lamm, Martin
Federico García Lorca **1**:314
August Strindberg **1**:444

Lampan, Archibald
Charles G. D. Roberts **8**:313

Landis, Joseph C.
Sholem Asch **3**:70

Landsberg, Paul L.
Franz Kafka **13**:258

Lane, Ann J.
Charlotte Gilman **9**:108, 112

Lane, Lauriat, Jr.
Mark Twain **12**:441

Lang, Andrew
Anatole France **9**:44
H. Rider Haggard **11**:237
Rudyard Kipling **8**:176
George MacDonald **9**:288
Mark Twain **12**:427
Émile Zola **6**:559

Lang, Cecil Y.
Charles Swinburne **8**:439

Langbaum, Robert
Thomas Hardy **10**:233

Lange, Victor
Georg Kaiser **9**:184

Langer, Lawrence L.
Tadeusz Borowski **9**:25

Lapp, John C.
Émile Zola **6**:568

Lardner, John
Damon Runyon **10**:427

Larsen, Erling
James Agee **1**:16

Larsen, Hanna Astrup
Knut Hamsun **2**:202
Selma Lagerlöf **4**:234
Sigrid Undset **3**:511

Larson, Harold
Bjørnstjerne Bjørnson **7**:109

Laski, Marghanita
Radclyffe Hall **12**:192

Last, R. W.
Georg Kaiser **9**:185

Lauterbach, Charles E.
W. S. Gilbert **3**:212

Lavrin, Janko
Leonid Andreyev **3**:26
Andrey Bely **7**:49
Aleksandr Blok **5**:98
Sergei Esenin **4**:110
Maxim Gorky **8**:76
Knut Hamsun **2**:203
Fyodor Sologub **9**:436

Lawler, James R.
Paul Claudel **2**:109

Lawrence, D. H.
Thomas Hardy **4**:162
D. H. Lawrence **9**:217
F. T. Marinetti **10**:314
Frederick Rolfe **12**:268
Giovanni Verga **3**:539, 543
H. G. Wells **6**:529

Lawrence, Margaret
Radclyffe Hall **12**:189
Rose Macaulay **7**:423

Lawrence, Thomas Edward
Charlotte Mew **8**:296

Lawry, Jon S.
Sherwood Anderson **10**:46

Lawson, Henry
Miles Franklin **7**:264

Lawson, John Howard
Robert E. Sherwood **3**:410

Lawson, Richard H.
Edith Wharton **3**:579

Lawson, Robb
Algernon Blackwood **5**:70

Lawson, Victor
Paul Laurence Dunbar **12**:110

Layton, Susan
Yevgeny Ivanovich Zamyatin **8**:555

Lea, Henry A.
Franz Werfel **8**:481

Leach, Henry Goddard
Selma Lagerlöf **4**:230

Leacock, Stephen
O. Henry **1**:346
Mark Twain **12**:434

Leal, Luis
Mariano Azuela **3**:80

Leary, Lewis
Kate Chopin **5**:150
Lafcadio Hearn **9**:134
Mark Twain **6**:475

Leaska, Mitchell A.
Virginia Woolf **5**:512

Leavis, F. R.
Joseph Conrad **1**:204; **13**:102
Thomas Hardy **4**:164
Henry James **2**:262
D. H. Lawrence **2**:360
Isaac Rosenberg **12**:290
Edward Thomas **10**:454
Leo Tolstoy **11**:473

Leavis, Q. D.
Dorothy L. Sayers **2**:528
Edith Wharton **3**:564

Leblanc-Maeterlinck, Georgette
Maurice Maeterlinck **3**:320

Lebowitz, Naomi
Italo Svevo **2**:554

Lederman, Marie Jean
Katherine Mansfield **2**:456

Lednicki, Waclaw
Henryk Sienkiewicz **3**:427

Leduc, Renato
John Reed **9**:386

Lee, Alice
Isaak Babel **2**:23

Lee, Lynn
Don Marquis **7**:450

Le Gallienne, Richard
Rudyard Kipling **8**:179
Don Marquis **7**:435
Alfred Noyes **7**:504
Arthur Symons **11**:426

Leggett, B. J.
A. E. Housman **10**:259

Legh-Jones, J.
Guillaume Apollinaire **3**:40

Lehan, Richard
F. Scott Fitzgerald **1**:267
Ford Madox Ford **1**:287

Lehmann, John
Rupert Brooke **7**:129
Lewis Grassic Gibbon **4**:121
Alun Lewis **3**:287
Edward Thomas **10**:455
Virginia Woolf **1**:538

Lehnert, Herbert
Georg Heym **9**:151

Leiber, Fritz, Jr.
Robert E. Howard **8**:130
H. P. Lovecraft **4**:267

Leibowitz, Herbert A.
Hart Crane **2**:122

Lemaitre, Georges
André Gide **5**:216
Jean Giraudoux **2**:169

Lemaître, Jules
Paul Bourget **12**:65
Anatole France **9**:46
Pierre Loti **11**:357

LeMoyne, Jean
Hector Saint-Denys Garneau **13**:197

Lenin, Nikolai
See also **Lenin, V. I.**
Vladimir Mayakovsky **4**:289

Lenin, V. I.
See also **Lenin, Nikolai**
John Reed **9**:382
Leo Tolstoy **4**:452

Lentricchia, Frank
Wallace Stevens **12**:374

Leon, Derrick
Marcel Proust **7**:527

Lerner, Michael G.
Pierre Loti **11**:368
Boris Vian **9**:535

LeSage, Laurent
Jean Giraudoux **2**:163

Leslie, Shane
Frederick Rolfe **12**:266

Lessing, Doris
A. E. Coppard **5**:181
Olive Schreiner **9**:400

Lessing, Otto
Heinrich Mann **9**:314

Levey, Michael
Thomas Hardy **10**:223
Francis Thompson **4**:441

Levin, Harry
James Joyce **3**:272
José Ortega y Gasset **9**:339
Charles Péguy **10**:407
Marcel Proust **7**:540; **13**:412
Émile Zola **6**:566

Levine, Robert T.
Franz Kafka **6**:229

Levitt, Morton P.
Nikos Kazantzakis **2**:318

Levy, Babette May
Mary Wilkins Freeman **9**:67

Levy, Diane Wolfe
Anatole France **9**:57

Levy, Karen D.
Alain-Fournier **6**:28

Levy, Kurt L.
Mariano Azuela **3**:82

Lewis, Allan
Maxim Gorky **8**:88
Federico García Lorca **7**:296

Lewis, C. S.
G. K. Chesterton **6**:99
H. Rider Haggard **11**:246
Rudyard Kipling **8**:192
George MacDonald **9**:293
George Orwell **2**:501
H. G. Wells **12**:496
Charles Williams **1**:511; **11**:485

Lewis, Charlton M.
Francis Thompson **4**:437

Lewis, Peter
Charlotte Gilman **9**:115

Lewis, R. W. B.
Joseph Conrad **1**:210
Hart Crane **5**:191
F. Scott Fitzgerald **1**:245
Henry James **2**:267
Edith Wharton **3**:575; **9**:546

Lewis, Sinclair
Sherwood Anderson **10**:34
Willa Cather **1**:151
Theodore Dreiser **10**:164
Hamlin Garland **3**:194
Joseph Hergesheimer **11**:260
William Dean Howells **7**:374
Sinclair Lewis **13**:325

Lewis, Theophilus
Wallace Thurman **6**:445

Lewis, Wyndham
Sherwood Anderson **10**:38
James Joyce **3**:253
H. L. Mencken **13**:374

Lewisohn, Adèle
Hanns Heinz Ewers **12**:133

Lewisohn, Ludwig
A. E. Coppard **5**:176
Zona Gale **7**:278
John Galsworthy **1**:295
Gerhart Hauptmann **4**:197
William Dean Howells **7**:374
Georg Kaiser **9**:171
Luigi Pirandello **4**:327
Rainer Maria Rilke **1**:408
Ernst Toller **10**:475

Leys, Gwen
Radclyffe Hall **12**:189

Lid, R. W.
Raymond Chandler **7**:168

Liddell, Robert
C. P. Cavafy **7**:152

Liddiard, Jean
Isaac Rosenberg **12**:308

Light, James F.
Nathanael West **1**:486

Light, Martin
Sinclair Lewis **13**:348

Lima, Robert
Federico García Lorca **1**:321
Ramón del Valle-Inclán **5**:485

Lindbergh, Anne Morrow
Antoine de Saint-Exupéry **2**:516

Lindenberger, Herbert
Georg Trakl **5**:462

Linklater, Eric
James Bridie **3**:131

Linn, Rolf N.
Heinrich Mann **9**:320

Lippman, Monroe
Philip Barry **11**:61

Lippmann, Walter
Sinclair Lewis **13**:329
Amy Lowell **8**:223
H. L. Mencken **13**:369
John Reed **9**:381

Liptzin, Sol
Arthur Schnitzler **4**:393

Liszt, Franz
Friedrich Nietzsche **10**:353

Littell, Robert
Ambrose Bierce **1**:83

Little, Roger
Guillaume Apollinaire **3**:45

Littlefield, Hazel
Lord Dunsany **2**:145

Littlefield, Henry M.
L. Frank Baum **7**:17

Littlejohn, David
F. Scott Fitzgerald **1**:254

Livingston, Dennis
C. M. Kornbluth **8**:217

Livingstone, Angela
Marina Tsvetaeva **7**:563

Livingstone, L.
Miguel de Unamuno **2**:558

Lloyd-Jones, Hugh
Friedrich Nietzsche **10**:385

Lo Cicero, Donald
Paul Heyse **8**:122

Locke, Frederick W.
Alain-Fournier **6**:17

Lockerbie, S. I.
Max Jacob **6**:197

Lockert, Lacy
Henryk Sienkiewicz **3**:423

Locklin, Gerald
Nathanael West **1**:489

Lockwood, William J.
Rose Macaulay **7**:428

Lodge, David
Maurice Baring **8**:38
G. K. Chesterton **1**:181
Gertrude Stein **1**:442

Lodge, Oliver
Alfred Noyes **7**:506

Loftus, Richard J.
A. E. **3**:9
James Stephens **4**:415

Logan, J. D.
John McCrae **12**:208
Charles G. D. Roberts **8**:315

Loggins, Vernon
Paul Laurence Dunbar **12**:107
Amy Lowell **1**:378
Gertrude Stein **1**:427

Lohner, Edgar
Gottfried Benn **3**:104

Lohrke, Eugene
Ricarda Huch **13**:242

London, Jack
Jack London **9**:256

Longaker, Mark
Ernest Dowson **4**:89

Longford, Elizabeth
Arthur Conan Doyle **7**:232

Longhurst, C. A.
Miguel de Unamuno **9**:523

Loomis, Emerson Robert
Bertolt Brecht **6**:30

Lott, Robert E.
Juan Valera **10**:506

Loram, Ian C.
Georg Kaiser **9**:177

Love, Debra Harper
Miguel de Unamuno **9**:522

Lovecraft, H. P.
Ambrose Bierce **7**:90
Algernon Blackwood **5**:72
F. Marion Crawford **10**:149
William Hope Hodgson **13**:231
Robert E. Howard **8**:129
M. R. James **6**:206
M. P. Shiel **8**:359
Bram Stoker **8**:386

Loveman, Samuel
Ambrose Bierce **7**:89

Lovett, Robert Morss
Sherwood Anderson **1**:35, 37, 41
Radclyffe Hall **12**:186
May Sinclair **3**:435, 440
Edith Wharton **3**:559

Loving, Pierre
Carl Sternheim **8**:367
Ernst Toller **10**:476

Lowell, Amy
Stephen Crane **11**:129
Amy Lowell **8**:223
Edgar Lee Masters **2**:462
Edwin Arlington Robinson **5**:401
Émile Verhaeren **12**:465

Lowell, James Russell
William Dean Howells **7**:363
Algernon Charles Swinburne **8**:425

Lowell, Robert
Wallace Stevens **3**:448

Lowes, John Livingston
Amy Lowell **8**:226

Lowry, Malcolm
Malcolm Lowry **6**:235

Lubbock, Percy
Henry James **11**:322
Leo Tolstoy **4**:454
Edith Wharton **3**:557

Lucas, Frank L.
Rupert Brooke **7**:123
Roy Campbell **5**:116
W. H. Davies **5**:202
A. E. Housman **10**:240
Isaac Rosenberg **12**:287
Algernon Charles Swinburne **8**:434

Lucas, John
Arnold Bennett **5**:50

Luciani, Vincent
Guiseppe Giacosa **7**:313

Lucie-Smith, Edward
Paul Claudel **2**:107

Lüdeke, H.
Elinor Wylie **8**:527

Luft, David S.
Robert Musil **12**:261

Lukács, Georg
Endre Ady **11**:23
Lion Feuchtwanger **3**:179
Maxim Gorky **8**:77
Heinrich Mann **9**:318
Thomas Mann **2**:419
Leo Tolstoy **4**:462

Lukashevich, Olga
Bruno Schulz **5**:422

Luker, Nicholas
Aleksandr Kuprin **5**:303

Lumley, Frederick
James Bridie **3**:137
Jean Giraudoux **2**:157

Lundquist, James
Theodore Dreiser **10**:193
Sinclair Lewis **4**:261

Lundwall, Sam J.
C. M. Kornbluth **8**:218

Lupoff, Richard A.
Edgar Rice Burroughs **2**:77

Luquiens, Frederick Bliss
Henry Adams **4**:5

Lurie, Alison
A. A. Milne **6**:320

Luyben, Helen L.
James Bridie **3**:140

Lyell, William, Jr.
Lu Hsün **3**:302

Lynd, Robert
John Millington Synge **6**:431

Lynes, Carlos, Jr.
André Gide **12**:147

Lyngstad, Sverre
Jonas Lie **5**:330

Lynn, Kenneth S.
Theodore Dreiser **10**:181
Emma Goldman **13**:222
Constance Rourke **12**:323
Mark Twain **6**:482

Lyon, Melvin
Henry Adams **4**:19

Lyons, Charles R.
Bertolt Brecht **13**:55

Lyons, Phyllis I.
Dazai Osamu **11**:190

Lytton, The Earl of
A. E. **10**:12

Mabbott, T. O.
H. P. Lovecraft **4**:265

MacAdam, Alfred J.
Machado de Assis **10**:303

MacAndrew, Andrew R.
Aleksandr Kuprin **5**:299

Macaree, David
Lewis Grassic Gibbon **4**:124

MacArthur, James
Bram Stoker **8**:385

MacCampbell, Donald
T. F. Powys **9**:367

MacCarthy, Desmond
See also **Hawk, Affable**
Paul Claudel **10**:122
Radclyffe Hall **12**:186
Vernon Lee **5**:312
Gregorio Martínez Sierra and María Martínez Sierra **6**:281
Gertrude Stein **6**:403
August Strindberg **8**:407
Ernst Toller **10**:476

MacClintock, Lander
Guiseppe Giacosa **7**:308
Luigi Pirandello **4**:338

MacDiarmid, Hugh
Lewis Grassic Gibbon **4**:122

Macdonald, Dwight
James Agee **1**:7
George Orwell **2**:505

MacDonald, George
George MacDonald **9**:288

MacDonald, Greville
George MacDonald **9**:291

Macdonald, Ian R.
Gabriel Miró **5**:342

MacGillivray, Royce
Bram Stoker **8**:390

Machen, Arthur
Mary Wilkins Freeman **9**:66

Mackail, J. W.
Maurice Maeterlinck **3**:317

MacKay, L. A.
Bliss Carman **7**:144

Mackenzie, Compton
Joseph Conrad **1**:201
John Galsworthy **1**:298

MacKenzie, Kenneth D.
Rudolf Steiner **13**:441

Mackridge, Peter
Nikos Kazantzakis **5**:272

Maclaren, Hamish
A. E. Coppard **5**:177

Maclaren-Ross, J.
M. P. Shiel **8**:363

Maclean, H.
Carl Sternheim **8**:374

MacLean, Hugh N.
John Millington Synge **6**:437

MacLeish, Archibald
Amy Lowell **1**:373
Elinor Wylie **8**:522
William Butler Yeats **1**:560

MacNeice, Louis
George MacDonald **9**:298
Dylan Thomas **8**:449
William Butler Yeats **11**:521

MacShane, Frank
Raymond Chandler **7**:172

Madariaga, Salvador de
Pío Baroja **8**:49
Gabriel Miró **5**:334
Miguel de Unamuno **9**:508
Ramón del Valle-Inclán **5**:471

Madeleva, Sister M.
Edna St. Vincent Millay **4**:309

Madison, Charles A.
Sholom Aleichem **1**:28
Sholem Asch **3**:70

Magalaner, Marvin
Katherine Mansfield **2**:454

Magarshack, David
Anton Chekhov **3**:161

Magny, Claude-Edmonde
Franz Kafka **2**:292

Maguire, Robert A.
Andrey Bely **7**:62

Mahlendorf, Ursula R.
Georg Heym **9**:142

Mahony, Patrick
Maurice Maeterlinck **3**:328

Mallarmé, Stéphane
Émile Verhaeren **12**:457
Émile Zola **6**:558

Mallinson, Jean
Charles G. D. Roberts **8**:326

Malmstad, John E.
Andrey Bely **7**:62

Malone, Andrew W.
Lord Dunsany **2**:143

Malone, Dumas
Douglas Southall Freeman **11**:223, 225

Mandelstam, Nadezhda
Osip Mandelstam **2**:403; **6**:265

Manganiello, Dominic
Guiseppe Giacosa **7**:314

Mangione, Jerre
Hanns Heinz Ewers **12**:136

Mankin, Paul A.
Ugo Betti **5**:57
Jean Giraudoux **2**:172

Manley, Norman Washington
Roger Mais **8**:241

Mann, Erika
Thomas Mann **8**:254

Mann, Heinrich
Heinrich Mann **9**:316

Mann, Klaus
Thomas Mann **8**:254

Mann, Thomas
Anton Chekhov **3**:160
Joseph Conrad **1**:200
Franz Kafka **2**:291
Heinrich Mann **9**:322
Thomas Mann **8**:256
Friedrich Nietzsche **10**:373
Bernard Shaw **3**:396
Leo Tolstoy **4**:459
Frank Wedekind **7**:576
Oscar Wilde **1**:503

Manning, Clarence Augustus
Sergei Esenin **4**:108

Mansfield, Katherine
John Galsworthy **1**:293
H. Rider Haggard **11**:242
Joseph Hergesheimer **11**:262
Jack London **9**:258
Rose Macaulay **7**:421
George Moore **7**:476
Dorothy Richardson **3**:347
Hugh Walpole **5**:492
Edith Wharton **3**:558

Manship, J. P.
Paul Claudel **10**:129

Marble, Annie Russell
Verner von Heidenstam **5**:253
Władysław Stanisław Reymont **5**:391

March, George
Thomas Mann **2**:412

March, Harold
André Gide **12**:160
Marcel Proust **13**:412

Marcotte, Gilles
Hector Saint-Denys Garneau **13**:99

Marcus, Jane
Olive Schreiner **9**:404

Marcus, Phillip L.
Standish O'Grady **5**:354

Marcus, Roxanne B.
Juan Valera **10**:509

Marcus, Steven
Isaac Babel **13**:20
O. Henry **1**:351

Marder, Herbert
Isaak Babel **2**:30

Marias, Julian
José Ortega y Gasset **9**:346
Miguel de Unamuno **2**:563

Marinetti, F. T.
F. T. Marinetti **10**:309, 312

Marker, Lise-Lone
David Belasco **3**:90

Markert, Lawrence W.
Arthur Symons **11**:453

Markish, Simon
Isaac Babel **13**:31

Markov, Vladimir
Konstantin Dmitriyevich Balmont **11**:35

Marks, Elaine
Colette **5**:164

Markus, Liselotte
Anatole France **9**:51

Marlow, Norman
A. E. Housman **10**:254, 261

Marquerie, Alfredo
Jacinto Benavente **3**:101

Marquis, Don
Don Marquis **7**:438

Marrow, Arminel
Guillaume Apollinaire **8**:17

Marsden, Kenneth
Thomas Hardy **10**:223

Marsh, E.
Rupert Brooke **2**:50

Marsh, Fred T.
Damon Runyon **10**:424

Marshall, Margaret
James Bridie **3**:132

Martin, Edward A.
Don Marquis **7**:448

Martin, Jay
Hamlin Garland **3**:200

Martin, Ronald E.
Joseph Hergesheimer **11**:279

Marx, Leo
F. Scott Fitzgerald **6**:172

Masing-Delic, Irene
Valery Bryusov **10**:91

Maskaleris, Thanasis
Kostes Palamas **5**:382

Maslenikov, Oleg A.
Konstantin Dmitriyevich Balmont **11**:32
Hilaire Belloc **7**:49
Zinaida Hippius **9**:155

Mason, Eudo C.
Rainer Maria Rilke **6**:364

Mason, Lawrence
Robert Benchley **1**:76

Masson, David I.
C. M. Kornbluth **8**:221

Masters, Edgar Lee
Theodore Dreiser **10**:164
Harriet Monroe **12**:215

Materer, Timothy
Wyndham Lewis **9**:243

Mathew, Ray
Miles Franklin **7**:269

Mathews, Jackson
Paul Valéry **4**:492

Mathewson, Rufus W., Jr.
Maxim Gorky **8**:90

Mathewson, Ruth
Raymond Chandler **1**:176

Matich, Olga
Zinaida Hippius **9**:164, 165

Matsui, Sakuko
Sōseki Natsume **10**:331

Matthews, Brander
James Weldon Johnson **3**:239
H. L. Mencken **13**:359
Mark Twain **6**:454

Matthews, J. H.
Paul Éluard **7**:253

Matthews, John F.
Bernard Shaw **3**:405

Matthews, T. S.
James Agee **1**:9

Matthiessen, Francis Otto
Mary Wilkins Freeman **9**:66
Henry James **2**:259
Sarah Orne Jewett **1**:362

Maude, Aylmer
Leo Tolstoy **4**:458

Maugham, W. Somerset
Arnold Bennett **5**:34
Aleister Crowley **7**:207
Rudyard Kipling **8**:193
H. G. Wells **12**:507

Mauriac, François
Jean Giraudoux **7**:321

Maurice, Arthur Bartlett
Arthur Conan Doyle **7**:216

Maurois, André
Paul Claudel **10**:124
Antoine de Saint-Exupéry **2**:516
Anatole France **9**:49
André Gide **12**:171
Rudyard Kipling **8**:186
D. H. Lawrence **9**:218
Katherine Mansfield **8**:277
Marcel Proust **7**:530
Lytton Strachey **12**:402

Mautner, Franz H.
Karl Kraus **5**:292

Maxwell, William
Samuel Butler **1**:138

May, Frederick
Luigi Pirandello **4**:349

May, Georges
Jean Giraudoux **2**:156

May, Rollo
Friedrich Nietzsche **10**:389

Mayne, Richard
Wyndham Lewis **2**:398

McArthur, Peter
Stephen Leacock **2**:377

McCarthy, Justin Huntly
August Strindberg **8**:406

McCarthy, Mary
Henrik Ibsen **2**:230
Eugene O'Neill **1**:389, 393
John Van Druten **2**:575

McCarthy, Patrick
Alice Meynell **6**:303

McClellan, Edwin
Sōseki Natsume **2**:490; **10**:330, 338
Tōson Shimazaki **5**:434

McClintock, James I.
Jack London **9**:273

McComas, J. Francis
C. M. Kornbluth **8**:212
Henry Kuttner **10**:265

McCormick, John
Sherwood Anderson **1**:62
F. Scott Fitzgerald **1**:270

McCourt, Edward A.
Rupert Brooke **2**:55

McDonald, E. Cordel
José Ortega y Gasset **9**:344

McDowell, D.
Boris Vian **9**:537

McDowell, Frederick P. W.
Ellen Glasgow **2**:185

McDowell, Margaret B.
Edith Wharton **3**:578

McElderry, Bruce R., Jr.
Max Beerbohm **1**:73
Thomas Wolfe **4**:522

McElrath, Joseph R., Jr.
Mary Wilkins Freeman **9**:78

McFarland, Timothy
Géza Csáth **13**:151

McFarlane, Brian
Henry Handel Richardson **4**:381

McFarlane, James Walter
Bjørnstjerne, Bjørnson **7**:113
Georg Brandes **10**:73
Knut Hamsun **2**:206
Jonas Lie **5**:330
Sigrid Undset **3**:525

McFate, Patricia
Ford Madox Ford **1**:285
James Stephens **4**:418

McGreivey, John C.
Hamlin Garland **3**:204

McHaffie, Margaret
Carl Spitteler **12**:345, 352

McKay, D. F.
Dylan Thomas **1**:475

McKee, Mary J.
Edna St. Vincent Millay **4**:317

McKeon, Joseph T.
Antone de Saint-Exupéry **2**:526

McKilligan, K. M.
Édouard Dujardin **13**:189

McKitrick, Eric
Edgar Saltus **8**:350

McLaughlin, Ann L.
Katherine Mansfield **2**:456

McLean, Andrew M.
Alfred Döblin **13**:171

McLean, Robert C.
Ambrose Bierce **7**:94

McLeod, Addison
Guiseppe, Giacosa **7**:305

McLouth, Lawrence A.
Paul Heyse **8**:118

McLuhan, Herbert Marshall
Wyndham Lewis **2**:387
G. K. Chesterton **6**:107

McMichael, Barbara
Charles Williams **11**:493

McMillin, A. B.
Aleksandr Kuprin **5**:300

McMurray, William
William Dean Howells **7**:390

McVay, Gordon
Sergei Esenin **4**:117

McWilliam, G. H.
Ugo Betti **5**:55, 59, 61

Mechem, Rose Mary
Bertolt Brecht **1**:121

Medina, Jeremy T.
Vicente Blasco Ibáñez **12**:50

Meeker, Richard K.
Ellen Glasgow **7**:342

Meier, August
Booker T. Washington **10**:527

Meixner, John A.
Ford Madox Ford **1**:283

Melcher, Edith
Paul Claudel **10**:128

Mencken, H. L.
Sherwood Anderson **10**:37
Ambrose Bierce **1**:85; **7**:90
James Branch Cabell **6**:66
Willa Cather **11**:92
Anthony Comstock **13**:92, 93
Joseph Conrad **1**:197; **13**:101
Stephen Crane **11**:129
Theodore Dreiser **10**:163, 168, 178
F. Scott Fitzgerald **6**:159
Anatole France **9**:45
Douglas Southall Freeman **11**:220
Hamlin Garland **3**:191
Ellen Glasgow **7**:333
Emma Goldman **13**:214
H. Rider Haggard **11**:241
Joseph Hergesheimer **11**:274
William Dean Howells **7**:369
Henry James **2**:151
Ring Lardner **2**:328
Sinclair Lewis **4**:246; **13**:325
Jack London **9**:257
Marie Belloc Lowndes **12**:200
H. L. Mencken **13**:360
José Ortega y Gasset **9**:337
Edgar Saltus **8**:349
Bernard Shaw **3**:378; **9**:415
August Strindberg **8**:406
Mark Twain **6**:459; **12**:429
H. G. Wells **6**:528; **12**:497
Edith Wharton **9**:54

Menes, Bonnie
Arthur Conan Doyle **7**:240

Merchant, W. Moelwyn
Bertolt Brecht **1**:113

Mercier, Vivian
Édouard Dujardin **13**:188
Standish O'Grady **5**:353
James Stephens **4**:411

Meredith, G. E.
F. Marion Crawford **10**:139

Meredith, George
Alice Meynell **6**:293

Merrill, James
C. P. Cavafy **7**:162

Merwin, W. S.
Edwin Muir **2**:482

Meserve, Walter J.
Philip Barry **11**:65
William Dean Howells **7**:386
Robert E. Sherwood **3**:417

Mesher, David R.
Sherwood Anderson **10**:52

Meyerhoff, Hans
Robert Musil **12**:237

Meyers, Jeffrey
Giuseppe Tomasi di Lampedusa **13**:298
Robert Musil **12**:260
George Orwell **6**:350

Mezei, Kathy
Hector Saint-Denys Garneau **13**:204

Michael, D.P.M.
Arthur Machen **4**:285

Michaels, Leonard
Raymond Chandler **1**:175

Michaud, Regis
Léon-Paul Fargue **11**:194
André Gide **12**:143
Max Jacob **6**:191

Michelson, Bruce
Mark Twain **6**:485

Michie, James A.
James Bridie **3**:142

Mickelson, Anne Z.
Thomas Hardy **4**:176

Mikes, George
Stephen Leacock **2**:379

Miles, David H.
Hugo von Hofmannsthal **11**:310

Miles, Hamish
Arthur Machen **4**:278

Millay, Edna St. Vincent
Elinor Wylie **8**:521

Miller, Arthur M.
Ambrose Bierce **7**:91

Miller, Henry
James Joyce **3**:272
D. H. Lawrence **2**:366
Marcel Proust **7**:526
Jakob Wassermann **6**:519

Miller, J. Hillis
Joseph Conrad **1**:213
Thomas Hardy **4**:174
Wallace Stevens **3**:468
Dylan Thomas **1**:474
William Butler Yeats **1**:575

Miller, James E., Jr.
Willa Cather **1**:167
F. Scott Fitzgerald **1**:257

Miller, Perry
Douglas Southall Freeman **11**:223

Miller, Richard F.
Henry Adams **4**:11

Miller, Walter James
Jules Verne **6**:498

Miller, William Lee
Robert Benchley **1**:79

Millichap, Joseph R.
Thomas Wolfe **13**:487

Milligan, E. E.
Antoine de Saint-Exupéry **2**:519

Millner, Curtis
Pío Baroja **8**:64

Mills, Gordon
Jack London **9**:275

Mills, Ralph J., Jr.
W. H. Davies **5**:207

Milne, A. A.
A. A. Milne **6**:311
Saki **3**:363

Milne, Gordon
Edith Wharton **9**:549

Miłosz, Czesław
Tadeusz Borowski **9**:22
Joseph Conrad **1**:207

Miner, Earl
Lafcadio Hearn **9**:131
Dazai Osamu **11**:172

Mirsky, D. S.
Leonid Andreyev **3**:27
Isaac Babel **13**:13
Konstantin Dmitriyevich Balmont **11**:32
Andrey Bely **7**:47
Aleksandr Blok **5**:83
Valery Bryusov **10**:80
Anton Chekhov **3**:154
Sergei Esenin **4**:111
Maxim Gorky **8**:73
Zinaida Hippius **9**:155
Aleksandr Kuprin **5**:298
Fyodor Sologub **9**:435
Lytton Strachey **12**:393
Leo Tolstoy **11**:462, 464
Marina Tsvetaeva **7**:556
Yevgeny Ivanovich Zamyatin **8**:543

Mitchell, Bonner
Antoine de Saint-Exupéry **2**:521

Mitchell, David
F. T. Marinetti **10**:321

Mitchell, Julian
Aleister Crowley **7**:207

Miyoshi, Masao
Sōseki Natsume **2**:494
Dazai Osamu **11**:177

Mizener, Arthur
F. Scott Fitzgerald **1**:241, 261
Thomas Hardy **10**:218

Mochulsky, Konstantin
Andrey Bely **7**:53

Moers, Ellen
F. Scott Fitzgerald **1**:254

Moestrup, Jørn
Luigi Pirandello **4**:353

Molina, Roderick A., O.F.M.
Amado Nervo **11**:400

Mollinger, Robert N.
Wallace Stevens **12**:381

Molnar, Thomas
Georges Bernanos **3**:118

Monahan, Michael
Gabriele D'Annunzio **6**:132

Monas, Sidney
Andrey Bely **7**:53
Osip Mandelstam **2**:404; **6**:267

Mondelli, Rudolph J.
Paul Bourget **12**:69

Monkhouse, Cosmo
Vernon Lee **5**:309

Monkshood, G. F.
Edgar Saltus **8**:343

Monod, G.
Anatole France **9**:38

Monro, Harold
Charlotte Mew **8**:295, 297

Monroe, Harriet
Stephen Vincent Benét **7**:73
Robert Bridges **1**:127
Hart Crane **5**:184
Thomas Hardy **4**:157
Amy Lowell **8**:229
Edgar Lee Masters **2**:462
John McCrae **12**:208
Edna St. Vincent Millay **4**:307
John Reed **9**:382
Edwin Arlington Robinson **5**:405
May Sinclair **11**:410
Wallace Stevens **12**:356
Sara Teasdale **4**:427

Monroe, N. Elizabeth
Selma Lagerlöf **4**:239
Sigrid Undset **3**:520

Montague, C. E.
John Millington Synge **6**:426

Moody, A. D.
Virginia Woolf **5**:509

Mooney, Harry J., Jr.
Leo Tolstoy **4**:477

Moore, Marianne
Laurence Housman **7**:355
Wallace Stevens **3**:446

Moore, Raylyn
L. Frank Baum **7**:21

Moore, Virginia
Charlotte Mew **8**:297
Alice Meynell **6**:301

Moorman, Charles
Charles Williams **1**:519

Mora, José Ferrater
Miguel de Unamuno **2**:560

Moran, Carlos Alberto
Raymond Chandler **1**:174

Moran, John C.
F. Marion Crawford **10**:157

More, Paul Elmer
James Branch Cabell **6**:66
Lafcadio Hearn **9**:119
Friedrich Nietzsche **10**:361
José Ortega y Gasset **9**:335
Arthur Symons **11**:430

Moreland, David Allison
Jack London **9**:282

Morgan, A. E.
Harley Granville-Barker **2**:194

Morgan, Bayard Quincy
Christian Morgenstern **8**:304
Arthur Schnitzler **4**:386

Morgan, Charles
George Moore **7**:481

Morgan, Edwin
Edwin Muir **2**:489

Morgan, Florence A. H.
Charles Waddell Chesnutt **5**:129

Morgan, H. Wayne
Hart Crane **2**:122
Hamlin Garland **3**:198

Morgan, John H.
Pierre Teilhard de Chardin **9**:504

Morita, James R.
Tōson Shimazaki **5**:438

Morley, Christopher
Arthur Conan Doyle **7**:219
Don Marquis **7**:434, 439
Saki **3**:365

Morley, S. Griswold
Rubén Darío **4**:57

Morris, Irene
Georg Trakl **5**:456

Morris, Lloyd
Sherwood Anderson **1**:42
Willa Cather **1**:12
F. Scott Fitzgerald **1**:244
Emma Goldman **13**:219
O. Henry **1**:349
Eugene O'Neill **1**:391
Marjorie Kinnan Rawlings **4**:361
Edwin Arlington Robinson **5**:405
Franz Werfel **8**:466

Morris, Wright
F. Scott Fitzgerald **1**:251
Thomas Wolfe **13**:480

Morrow, Carolyn
Antonio Machado **3**:306

Morsberger, Robert E.
Edgar Rice Burroughs **2**:85

Morse, A. Reynolds
M. P. Shiel **8**:360

Morse, J. Mitchell
James Joyce **3**:272

Morse, Samuel French
Wallace Stevens **3**:477

Mortensen, Brita M. E.
August Strindberg **8**:408

Mortimer, Raymond
Marie Belloc Lowndes **12**:204
Lytton Strachey **12**:392

Morton, J. B.
Hilaire Belloc **7**:37

Moseley, Edwin M.
F. Scott Fitzgerald **1**:264

Moser, Thomas
Joseph Conrad **1**:208; **13**:113

Moses, Montrose J.
Philip Barry **11**:54
David Belasco **3**:85

Mosig, Dirk
H. P. Lovecraft **4**:272

Moskowitz, Sam
Arthur Conan Doyle **7**:224
William Hope Hodgson **13**:234
Henry Kuttner **10**:266
M. P. Shiel **8**:361

Moss, Howard
Anton Chekhov **3**:175

Motion, Andrew
Edward Thomas **10**:464

Mott, Frank Luther
Zane Grey **6**:180

Muchnic, Helen
Andrey Bely **7**:61
Aleksandr Blok **5**:93
Mikhail Bulgakov **2**:65
Maxim Gorky **8**:78
Vladimir Mayakovsky **4**:296
Yevgeny Ivanovich Zamyatin **8**:551

Muddiman, Bernard
Duncan Campbell Scott **6**:396

Mudrick, Marvin
Joseph Conrad **13**:119
D. H. Lawrence **2**:366
Wyndham Lewis **2**:386
Frederick Rolfe **12**:271
Bernard Shaw **3**:402

Mueller, Dennis
Lion Feuchtwanger **3**:185

Mueller, Gustave
Carl Spitteler **12**:343

Muir, Edwin
Joseph Conrad **1**:198
Thomas Hardy **4**:173
Hugo von Hofmannsthal **11**:295
Franz Kafka **6**:219
Marie Belloc Lowndes **12**:203
Lytton Strachey **12**:396
Virginia Woolf **1**:527, **5**:507

Muirhead, James F.
Carl Spitteler **12**:340

Muller, Herbert J.
Thomas Wolfe **4**:519

Mumford, Lewis
Heinrich Mann **9**:318

Munro, Ian S.
Lewis Grassic Gibbon **4**:126

Munro, John M.
Arthur Symons **11**:450

Munson, Gorham B.
Hart Crane **2**:111
Edgar Saltus **8**:347
Wallace Stevens **3**:445
Émile Zola **1**:590

Murch, A. E.
E. C. Bentley **12**:17
Cesare Pavese **3**:340
Dorothy L. Sayers **2**:531

Murfin, Ross C.
Algernon Charles Swinburne **8**:445

Murray, Edward
F. Scott Fitzgerald **1**:272

Murray, Les
Isaac Rosenberg **12**:312

Murry, John Middleton
Ivan Bunin **6**:43
Anton Chekhov **3**:150
Paul Claudel **10**:121
Anatole France **9**:45
George Gissing **3**:233
Aleksandr Kuprin **5**:296
D. H. Lawrence **2**:346; **9**:214, 215
Katherine Mansfield **2**:451; **8**:281
Wilfred Owen **5**:359
Marcel Proust **13**:401
Edward Thomas **10**:451
Hugh Walpole **5**:493

Muzzey, Annie L.
Charlotte Gilman **9**:99

Myers, David
Carl Sternheim **8**:377

Myers, Doris T.
Charles Williams **11**:496

Nabokov, Vladimir
See also **Sirin, Vladimir**
Andrey Bely **7**:55
James Joyce **8**:158
Franz Kafka **6**:230
Marcel Proust **7**:552

Nadel, Ira Bruce
Lytton Strachey **12**:420

Naess, Harald S.
Nordahl Grieg **10**:208

Naff, William E.
Tōson Shimazaki **5**:441

Nagel, James
Stephen Crane **11**:166

Nagy, Moses M.
Paul Claudel **2**:109

Naimy, Mikhail
Kahlil Gibran **9**:82

Naimy, N.
Kahlil Gibran **9**:90

Naipaul, V. S.
Joyce Cary **1**:142

Naravane, Vishwanath S.
Saratchandra Chatterji **13**:74

Naremore, James
Virginia Woolf **5**:514

Nash, Berta
Arthur Machen **4**:284

Nassar, Eugene Paul
Kahlil Gibran **9**:93

Natan, Alex
Carl Sternheim **8**:370
Frank Wedekind **7**:580

Nathan, George Jean
Philip Barry **11**:58
David Belasco **3**:87
Jacinto Benavente **3**:96
Ugo Betti **5**:54
Ambrose Bierce **1**:87
Bertolt Brecht **13**:43
James Bridie **3**:132
Karel Čapek **6**:87
H. L. Mencken **13**:361
A. A. Milne **6**:306
Eugene O'Neill **1**:386
Luigi Pirandello **4**:331
Bernard Shaw **3**:387
John Van Druten **2**:573
Franz Werfel **8**:469
Oscar Wilde **1**:500
Alexander Woolcott **5**:520

Neale-Silva, Eduardo
César Vallejo **3**:529

Neff, Rebeccah Kinnamon
May Sinclair **11**:419

Neider, Charles
Franz Kafka **13**:261

Nejdefors-Frisk, Sonya
George Moore **7**:486

Nelson, Donald F.
Wolfgang Borchert **5**:112

Nelson, Lowry, Jr.
Italo Svevo **2**:539

Nemerov, Howard
James Joyce **3**:280
Thomas Mann **2**:431
Wallace Stevens **3**:453

Nemes, Graciela P.
Juan Ramón Jiménez **4**:215

Nersoyan, H. J.
André Gide **12**:174

Neruda, Pablo
Rubén Darío **4**:63

Nettelbeck, C. W.
Georges Bernanos **3**:124

Nevius, Blake
Edith Wharton **3**:566

Newberry, Wilma
José Echegaray **4**:104

Newcombe, Josephine M.
Leonid Andreyev **3**:29

Newton, Nancy A.
Antonio Machado **3**:314

Nevins, Allan
Ring Lardner **2**:327

Nicholls, Roger A.
Heinrich Mann **9**:322

Nichols, Wallace B.
Alfred Noyes **7**:508

Nicoll, Allardyce
Maurice Baring **8**:33
Henrik Ibsen **2**:228
Eugene O'Neill **1**:391
Bernard Shaw **3**:395
August Strindberg **1**:450

Nietzsche, Friedrich
Friedrich Nietzsche **10**:354
August Strindberg **8**:405

Niger, Shmuel
Sholom Aleichem **1**:20

Nilsson, Nils Ake
Osip Mandelstam **6**:257

Nin, Anaïs
D. H. Lawrence **2**:348

Nissenson, Hugh
Ivan Bunin **6**:54

Noble, David W.
F. Scott Fitzgerald **1**:264

Nock, Albert J.
Bret Harte **1**:341

Nolin, Bertil
Georg Brandes **10**:71

Nordau, Max
Friedrich Nietzsche **10**:357

Nordon, Pierre
Arthur Conan Doyle **7**:226

Noreng, Harald
Bjørnstjerne Bjørnson **7**:114

Norman, Henry
F. Marion Crawford **10**:138
Olive Schreiner **9**:393

Normand, Guessler
Henri Barbusse **5**:19

Norris, Frank
Stephen Crane **11**:123

Norris, Margot
James Joyce **3**:281

Novak, Barbara
A. A. Milne **6**:313

Noyes, Alfred
William Ernest Henley **8**:103
Algernon Charles Swinburne **8**:431

Noyes, Henry
Alfred Noyes **7**:515

Nozick, Martin
Miguel de Unamuno **2**:568

Nugent, Robert
Paul Éluard **7**:257

Nye, Russel
L. Frank Baum **7**:15
Zane Grey **6**:182

Oates, Joyce Carol
Géza Csáth **13**:149
Henry James **11**:340
Thomas Mann **2**:441
Virginia Woolf **1**:540
William Butler Yeats **1**:582

O'Brien, James
Dazai Osamu **11**:180

O'Brien, Justin
André Gide **12**:157
Valéry Larbaud **9**:197
Marcel Proust **7**:528

O'Casey, Sean
Bernard Shaw **3**:399

O'Connor, Frank
A. E. **3**:8
Anton Chekhov **3**:161
A. E. Coppard **5**:180
Lady Gregory **1**:336
Thomas Hardy **4**:168
James Stephens **4**:416

O'Connor, Patricia Walker
Gregorio Martínez Sierra and María Martínez Sierra **6**:282, 284

O'Connor, William Van
Joyce Cary **1**:145
Wallace Stevens **3**:464
Mark Twain **12**:443

O'Conor, Norreys Jepson
Standish O'Grady **5**:353

O'Donnell, J. P.
Bertolt Brecht **1**:116

O'Faolain, Sean
A. E. **3**:8
George Moore **7**:482
Leo Tolstoy **4**:461

O'Hagan, Thomas
John Millington Synge **6**:431

O'Hara, John
Robert Benchley **1**:78

Ohlin, Peter H.
James Agee **1**:10

Okeke-Ezigbo, Emeka
Paul Laurence Dunbar **12**:127

Olgin, Moissaye J.
Leonid Andreyev **3**:21
Konstantin Dmitriyevich Balmont **11**:31
Aleksandr Kuprin **5**:297

Oliphant, Margaret
Thomas Hardy **4**:150

Oliver, Edith
Maxim Gorky **8**:93

Olivero, Federico
Émile Verhaeren **12**:460

Olsen, Tillie
Rebecca Harding Davis **6**:153

Olson, Elder
Dylan Thomas **1**:470

Olson, Paul R.
Juan Ramón Jiménez **4**:218

Olson, Stanley
Elinor Wylie **8**:537

O'Neill, Eugene
Mark Twain **12**:439

O'Neill, Tom
Giuseppe Tomasi di Lampedusa **13**:312

Orage, A. R.
A. E. **10**:14
Ernest Dowson **4**:87

O'Reilly, Robert F.
André Gide **12**:168

O'Rell, Max
Paul Bourget **12**:64

Ornstein, Robert
F. Scott Fitzgerald **1**:250

O'Rourke, David
Thomas Wolfe **13**:493

Ortega y Gasset, José
José Ortega y Gasset **9**:334
Marcel Proust **7**:536
Ramón del Valle-Inclán **5**:479

Ortiz-Vargas, A.
Gabriela Mistral **2**:475

Orwell, George
D. H. Lawrence **2**:354
Jules Verne **6**:491
H. G. Wells **6**:533

Osborne, Charles
Thomas Hardy **10**:223
Francis Thompson **4**:411

O'Sheel, Shaemas
Lady Gregory **1**:333

Ossar, Michael
Ernst Toller **10**:491

O'Sullivan, Susan
Gabriel Miró **5**:337

Oswald, Victor A., Jr.
Hugo von Hofmannsthal **11**:297

Ouida
F. Marion Crawford **10**:140

Ouimette, Victor
José Ortega y Gasset **9**:354

Ould, Hermon
Rudolf Steiner **13**:437

Overmyer, Janet
Saki **3**:371

Ozick, Cynthia
Bruno Schulz **5**:424

Pacey, Desmond
Bliss Carman **7**:145
Frederick Philip Grove **4**:140
Charles G. D. Roberts **8**:319
Duncan Campbell Scott **6**:393

Pachmuss, Temira
Zinaida Hippius **9**:160, 166
Franz Werfel **8**:475

Pacifici, Sergio
Vitaliano Brancati **12**:90
Giuseppe Tomasi di Lampedusa **13**:320
Giovanni Verga **3**:545

Pack, Robert
Wallace Stevens **3**:455

Painter, George D.
Marcel Proust **7**:537

Pal, Bepin Chandra
Annie Besant **9**:15

Palamari, Demetra
Émile Zola **6**:569

Palamas, Kostes
Kostes Palamas **5**:377

Palmer, Nettie
Henry Handel Richardson **4**:375

Panek, LeRoy
E. C. Bentley **12**:22

Paolucci, Anne
Luigi Pirandello **4**:356

Parker, Alexander A.
Miguel de Unamuno **2**:565

Parker, Dorothy
See also **Reader, Constant**
Theodore Dreiser **10**:174

Parker, H. T.
Karl Čapek **6**:82

Parks, Edd Winfield
Edna St. Vincent Millay **4**:310

Parrington, Vernon Louis
James Branch Cabell **6**:63
Hamlin Garland **3**:193

Parrot, Louis
Paul Éluard **7**:249

Parrott, Cecil
Jaroslav Hašek **4**:189

Parry, I. F.
Franz Kafka **13**:263

Parry, Idris
Rainer Maria Rilke **1**:422

Parry, M.
Antoine de Saint-Exupéry **2**:524

Parsons, Ian
Isaac Rosenberg **12**:310

Pasternak, Boris
Vladimir Mayakovsky **4**:298
Marina Tsvetaeva **7**:558

Pater, Walter
Arthur Symons **11**:426
Oscar Wilde **1**:495

Patmore, Coventry
Alice Meynell **6**:290
Francis Thompson **4**:433
Juan Valera **10**:498

Patrick, Walton R.
Ring Lardner **2**:338

Patt, Beatrice P.
Pío Baroja **8**:60

Pattee, Fred Lewis
Gertrude Atherton **2**:17
Kate Chopin **5**:144
Rebecca Harding Davis **6**:150
Mary Wilkins Freeman **9**:65
Bret Harte **1**:340
Lafcadio Hearn **9**:127
O. Henry **1**:348
Edith Wharton **3**:560

Patterson, Rodney L.
Konstantin Dmitriyevich Balmont **11**:39

Patteson, Richard F.
H. Rider Haggard **11**:249

Pattison, Walter T.
Juan Ramón Jiménez **4**:212

Paul, David
Alain-Fournier **6**:12

Paul, Sherman
John Jay Chapman **7**:197

Pavese, Cesare
Edgar Lee Masters **2**:473

Payne, William Morton
Arnold Bennett **5**:22
Bjørnstjerne Bjørnson **7**:109
Georg Brandes **10**:61
Wilfred Campbell **9**:29
Arthur Conan Doyle **7**:216
Mary Wilkins Freeman **9**:61
Ellen Glasgow **7**:332
Zane Grey **6**:177
Selma Lagerlöf **4**:229
Harriet Monroe **12**:214, 215
Duncan Campbell Scott **6**:385
Leo Tolstoy **4**:449
Edith Wharton **3**:551

Paz, Octavio
Guillaume Apollinaire **3**:44
Rubén Darío **4**:64
Amado Nervo **11**:402

Peabody, A. P.
George MacDonald **9**:288

Peacock, Ronald
Hugo von Hofmannsthal **11**:295
Henrik Ibsen **2**:227
Georg Kaiser **9**:176
Bernard Shaw **3**:389
William Butler Yeats **1**:561

Pearsall, Robert Brainard
Rupert Brooke **2**:58

Pearsall, Ronald
Arthur Conan Doyle **7**:236

Pearson, Hesketh
Arthur Conan Doyle **7**:221
Bernard Shaw **3**:395

Pearson, Norman Holmes
Sherwood Anderson **1**:42

Peck, Harry Thurston
Charlotte Gilman **9**:97
William Dean Howells **7**:367
Joris-Karl Huysmans **7**:407
Edith Wharton **3**:551

Peckham, Morse
Edgar Saltus **8**:355
Algernon Charles Swinburne **8**:440

Peers, E. Allison
Rubén Darío **4**:64
José Echegaray **4**:103

Péguy, Charles
Charles Péguy **10**:401

Pehrson, Elsa
Selma Lagerlöf **4**:240

Pellizzi, Camillo
Eugene O'Neill **6**:327

Peña, Carlos González
Amado Nervo **11**:402

Pendo, Stephen
Raymond Chandler **7**:174

Penzoldt, Peter
Algernon Blackwood **5**:74
F. Marion Crawford **10**:153
M. R. James **6**:208
H. P. Lovecraft **4**:269

Perkins, George
William Dean Howells **7**:395

Perkins, Maxwell E.
F. Scott Fitzgerald **6**:159
Douglas Southall Freeman **11**:219
Thomas Wolfe **4**:518

Perkins, Michael
Guillaume Apollinaire **8**:25

Perlmutter, Elizabeth P.
Edna St. Vincent Millay **4**:321

Perosa, Sergio
Frederick Rolfe **12**:273

Perry, Henry Ten Eyck
W. S. Gilbert **3**:212

Persky, Serge
Leonid Andreyev **3**:17

Person, Leland S., Jr.
F. Scott Fitzgerald **6**:164

Peters, H. F.
Rainer Maria Rilke **6**:363

Peterson, Dale E.
Vladimir Mayakovsky **4**:300

Peyre, Henri
Paul Claudell **2**:100
Colette **5**:170
Paul Éluard **7**:252
André Gide **5**:219, 227
Marcel Proust **7**:548

Pfohl, Russell
Italo Svevo **2**:542

Phelan, Kappo
Bertolt Brecht **13**:43
Federico García Lorca **1**:309

Phelps, Arthur L.
Frederick Philip Grove **4**:132

Phelps, William Lyon
Sherwood Anderson **10**:31
Leonid Andreyev **3**:16
Maurice Baring **8**:33
J. M. Barrie **2**:40
Bjørnstjerne Bjørnson **7**:107
Rupert Brooke **7**:122
Anton Chekhov **3**:146
Stephen Crane **11**:130
Theodore Dreiser **10**:172
Zona Gale **7**:280
Maxim Gorky **8**:71
O. Henry **1**:346
Paul Heyse **8**:119
William Dean Howells **7**:371
Aleksandr Kuprin **5**:296
Jack London **9**:256
Amy Lowell **8**:224
Harriet Monroe **12**:217
Alfred Noyes **7**:502
Bernard Shaw **3**:384
Henryk Sienkiewicz **3**:422
May Sinclair **3**:433; **11**:410
Fyodor Sologub **9**:435
Lytton Strachey **12**:392
Booth Tarkington **9**:453
H. G. Wells **12**:494
Edith Wharton **3**:557

Phillips, Klaus
Rainer Maria Rilke **6**:369

Phillips, Rachel
Alfonsina Storni **5**:447

Philmus, Robert M.
H. G. Wells **12**:511

Phoutrides, Aristides E.
Kostes Palamas **5**:378

Pickford, John
Wolfgang Borchert **5**:112

Pickman, Hester
Rainer Maria Rilke **6**:357

Picon, Gaëtan
André Gide **5**:218

Pierce, Lorne
Frederick Philip Grove **4**:136
Charles G. D. Roberts **8**:318

Pike, Burton
Robert Musil **12**:241

Pikoulis, John
Alun Lewis **3**:291

Pilkington, John, Jr.
F. Marion Crawford **10**:154

Pinchin, Jane Lagoudis
C. P. Cavafy **2**:98

Pinkerton, Jan
Wallace Stevens **3**:474

Pinsker, Sanford
Sholom Aleichem **1**:30

Pinto, Vivian De Sola
William Ernest Henley **8**:106
A. E. Housman **1**:358
D. H. Lawrence **2**:367
William Butler Yeats **11**:526

Pirandello, Luigi
Bernard Shaw **9**:416
Giovanni Verga **3**:542

Pisarev, Dmitri
Leo Tolstoy **4**:466

Piscator, Erwin
Ernst Toller **10**:488

Pitcher, Harvey
Anton Chekhov **3**:172

Pitt, Valerie
Charles Williams **11**:492

Pittock, Malcolm
Ernst Toller **10**:489

Pizer, Donald
Stephen Crane **11**:152
Hamlin Garland **3**:197, 198
William Dean Howells **7**:385

Plant, Richard
Arthur Schnitzler **4**:395

Plomer, William
Lewis Grassic Gibbon **4**:120
George Gissing **3**:231

Podhoretz, Norman
Sholom Aleichem **1**:23
John Millington Synge **6**:436
Nathanael West **1**:478

Poggioli, Renato
Isaak Babel **2**:20
Konstantin Dmitriyevich Balmont **11**:33
Aleksandr Blok **5**:90
Valery Bryusov **10**:86
Ivan Bunin **6**:49
C. P. Cavafy **7**:158
Sergei Esenin **4**:112
Zinaida Hippius **9**:158
Osip Mandelstam **2**:400
Vladimir Mayakovsky **4**:299
Fyodor Sologub **9**:436
Marina Tsvetaeva **7**:558

Pohl, Frederik
C. M. Kornbluth **8**:215, 221

Politis, Linos
Kostes Palamas **5**:384

Politzer, Heinz
Bertolt Brecht **6**:31
Franz Kafka **13**:275
Arthur Schnitzler **4**:400
Franz Werfel **8**:471

Pollard, Percival
Kate Chopin **5**:143
Rainer Maria Rilke **6**:357
Edgar Saltus **8**:345
Arthur Schnitzler **4**:385
Frank Wedekind **7**:574

Pollock, John
A. A. Milne **6**:306

Poncé, Juan García
Robert Musil **12**:254

Ponomareff, Constantin V.
Sergei Esenin **4**:116

Popper, Hans
Wolfgang Borchert **5**:108

Porter, Katherine Anne
Max Beerbohm **1**:69
Willa Cather **1**:160
Colette **1**:191
Ford Madox Ford **1**:277
D. H. Lawrence **2**:367
Katherine Mansfield **2**:450
Gertrude Stein **1**:428
Virginia Woolf **1**:534

Porter, Laurence M.
Guillaume Apollinaire **8**:18

Porter, Richard N.
Ivan Bunin **6**:55

Porter, Thomas E.
Eugene O'Neill **1**:404

Poster, William
H. P. Lovecraft **4**:265

Potoker, Edward Martin
Ronald Firbank **1**:230

Poulakidas, Andreas K.
Nikos Kazantzakis **2**:320

Poulet, George
Marcel Proust **7**:541

Pound, Ezra
W. H. Davies **5**:199
Thomas Hardy **4**:174
Henry James **2**:249
James Joyce **3**:252
Wyndham Lewis **2**:386
Harriet Monroe **12**:219, 220
Algernon Charles Swinburne **8**:429
Rabindranath Tagore **3**:481

Povey, John
Roy Campbell **5**:126

Powell, Anthony
George Orwell **2513**

Powell, Kerry
Arthur Symons **11**:452

Powell, Lawrence Clark
Gertrude Atherton **2**:18
Raymond Chandler **1**:172

Powys, John Cowper
Edgar Lee Masters **2**:464
T. F. Powys **9**:361
Dorothy Richardson **3**:350

Praz, Mario
Luigi Pirandello **4**:326

Predmore, Michael P.
Juan Ramón Jiménez **4**:221, 225

Prescott, Orville
Joyce Cary **1**:141
Sinclair Lewis **13**:338

Preston, Harriet Waters
Vernon Lee **5**:309

Prevelakis, Pandelis
Nikos Kazantzakis **2**:313

Price, Lucien
John Jay Chapman **7**:188

Price, Martin
Joyce Cary **1**:141

Price, Nancy
Lord Dunsany **2**:144

Priestley, J. B.
J. M. Barrie **2**:45
Arnold Bennett **5**:29
James Bridie **3**:137
Walter de la Mare **4**:72
Anatole France **9**:51
Henrik Ibsen **2**:231
Stephen Leacock **2**:380
Sinclair Lewis **4**:255
August Strindberg **1**:451
Hugh Walpole **5**:495
William Butler Yeats **1**:567
Émile Zola **1**:594

Primeau, Ronald
Countee Cullen **4**:52

Pringle, Mary Beth
Charlotte Gilman **9**:110

Pritchard, William H.
Edwin Arlington Robinson **5**:417

Pritchett, V. S.
Isaac Babel **13**:26
Maurice Baring **8**:33
Arnold Bennett **5**:44
Samuel Butler **1**:136, 137
Karel Čapek **6**:86
Anton Chekhov **3**:155
Joseph Conrad **1**:203, 206
Stephen Crane **11**:150
Ronald Firbank **1**:229
Anatole France **9**:50
George Gissing **3**:232
H. Rider Haggard **11**:256
Radclyffe Hall **12**:191
Thomas Hardy **4**:165
Giuseppe Tomasi di Lampedusa **13**:295
D. H. Lawrence **2**:355
Wyndham Lewis **2**:387
Machado de Assis **10**:306
Katherine Mansfield **2**:451
H. L. Mencken **13**:378
Robert Musil **12**:247
George Orwell **2**:497
Marcel Proust **13**:425
Dorothy Richardson **3**:358
Saki **3**:366
Bruno Schulz **5**:425
Lytton Strachey **12**:400
John Millington Synge **6**:434
Giovanni Verga **3**:545
H. G. Wells **6**:534
Edith Wharton **9**:545
Émile Zola **1**:594

Proffer, Carl R.
Aleksandr Kuprin **5**:301

Proust, Marcel
Marcel Proust **13**:401
Leo Tolstoy **4**:466

Prusek, Jaroslav
Lu Hsün **3**:299

Pryce-Jones, Alan
Alain-Fournier **6**:18
Bertolt Brecht **1**:107
Robert Musil **12**:238

Puckett, Hugh W.
Robert Musil **12**:235

Punter, David
Ambrose Bierce **7**:98

Purdom, C. B.
Harley Granville-Barker **2**:196

Purser, John Thibaut
Ivan Bunin **6**:47

Pusch, Hans
Rudolf Steiner **13**:456

Putnam, Samuel
Machado de Assis **10**:281

Pyatkovsky, A. Ya.
Leo Tolstoy **4**:445

Pyne-Timothy, Helen
Claude McKay **7**:468

Quennell, Peter
Radclyffe Hall **12**:188

Quiller-Couch, Arthur
George Moore **7**:474

Quinn, Arthur Hobson
James Branch Cabell **6**:67
F. Marion Crawford **10**:149
Rebecca Harding Davis **6**:150
Joel Chandler Harris **2**:210
Bret Harte **1**:342

Quinn, Sister M. Bernetta, O.S.F.
Wallace Stevens **12**:360

Quinn, Vincent
Hart Crane **5**:188

Raab, Rex
Rudolf Steiner **13**:455

Rabinovich, Isaiah
Sholom Aleichem **1**:29

Rabinowitz, Peter J.
Raymond Chandler **7**:177

Rabinowitz, Stanley J.
Fyodor Sologub **9**:447

Rabkin, Eric S.
George MacDonald **9**:307

Ragusa, Olga
Giuseppe Tomasi di Lampedusa **13**:314

Ragussis, Michael
D. H. Lawrence **2**:373

Rahv, Philip
Franz Kafka **2**:289
George Orwell **6**:340
Tess Slesinger **10**:439
Leo Tolstoy **11**:468
Virginia Woolf **5**:509

Raknes, Ola
Jonas Lie **5**:325

Raleigh, John Henry
F. Scott Fitzgerald **1**:251
Eugene O'Neill **6**:335

Ralston, W.R.S.
Leo Tolstoy **4**:447

Ramchand, Kenneth
H. G. de Lisser **12**:95, 96
Roger Mais **8**:243
Claude McKay **7**:464

Ramsey, Warren
Guillaume Apollinaire **3**:36
Paul Valéry **4**:493

Randall, John H., III
Willa Cather **11**:101

Rankin, Daniel S.
Kate Chopin **5**:144

Ransom, John Crowe
Thomas Hardy **4**:164
Edna St. Vincent Millay **4**:314
Wallace Stevens **12**:366
Edith Wharton **3**:563

Ransome, Arthur
Oscar Wilde **8**:492

Raper, J. R.
Ellen Glasgow **2**:189; **7**:345

Rapin, René
Willa Cather **11**:

Rascoe, Burton
Zane Grey **6**:180
Don Marquis **7**:455
Thomas Wolfe **13**:472

Raven, Charles E.
Pierre Teilhard de Chardin **9**:486

Raven, Simon
Joyce Cary **1**:142

Rawson, Judy
F. T. Marinetti **10**:324

Ray, Gordon N.
H. G. Wells **6**:540

Ray, Robert J.
Ford Madox Ford **1**:285

Rayfield, Donald
Anton Chekhov **10**:114
Osip Mandelstam **6**:266

Read, Herbert
Robert Bridges **1**:126
George Moore **7**:479

Reck, Rima Drell
Georges Bernanos **3**:121

Reader, Constant
See also **Parker, Dorothy**
Sinclair Lewis **13**:332

Redding, J. Saunders
Charles Waddell Chesnutt **5**:132
Countee Cullen **4**:42
Paul Laurence Dunbar **2**:128; **12**:113
James Weldon Johnson **3**:241

Reding, Katherine
Vicente Blasco Ibáñez **12**:38

Redman, Ben Ray
Georges Bernanos **3**:116
Georg Brandes **10**:64

Reed, F. A.
Nikos Kazantzakis **5**:267

Reed, John
John Reed **9**:381

Reed, John R.
H. G. Wells **6**:551

Reese, Ilse Meissner
Rudolf Steiner **13**:450

Reeve, F. D.
Aleksandr Blok **5**:88
Fyodor Sologub **9**:441

Reeves, Paschal
Thomas Wolfe **13**:485

Rehder, R. M.
Thomas Hardy **4**:177

Reichert, Herbert W.
Robert Musil **12**:248

Reid, James H.
Alfred Döblin **13**:164

Reid, John T.
Pío Baroja **8**:51

Reilly, John H.
Jean Giraudoux **7**:324

Reilly, Joseph J.
Maurice Baring **8**:34
Kate Chopin **5**:146
Alice Meynell **6**:300

Reinert, Otto
August Strindberg **1**:458

Reis, Richard H.
George MacDonald **9**:304

Reiss, H. S.
Arthur Schnitzler **4**:394

Reményi, Joseph
Endre Ady **11**:15

Repplier, Agnes
Laurence Housman **7**:358
Alice Meynell **6**:295

Revell, Peter
Paul Laurence Dunbar **12**:125

Revitt, Paul J.
W. S. Gilbert **3**:215

Rexroth, Kenneth
Roy Campbell **5**:124
Anton Chekhov **10**:110
Arthur Conan Doyle **7**:229
Ford Madox Ford **1**:290
Lafcadio Hearn **9**:138
Wallace Stevens **3**:459
H. G. Wells **12**:508

Reynolds, Barbara
E. C. Bentley **12**:20

Rhodenizer, V. B.
John McCrae **12**:209

Rhodes, Anthony
Gabriele D'Annunzio **6**:137

Rhodes, S. A.
Guillaume Apollinaire **8**:12
Léon-Paul Fargue **11**:194

Rhys, Brian
Henri Barbusse **5**:14

Rhys, Ernest
Rabindranath Tagore **3**:483

Ribbans, Geoffrey
Miguel de Unamuno **2**:564

Rice, Martin P.
Valery Bryusov **10**:94

Rice, Wallace
Harriet Monroe **12**:215

Rich, Amy C.
Zona Gale **7**:277

Richards, D. J.
Yevgeny Ivanovich Zamyatin **8**:546

Richards, I. A.
George Moore **7**:494

Richardson, Jack
Eugene O'Neill **1**:406

Richardson, Maurice
M. R. James **6**:209
Bram Stoker **8**:386

Richey, Elinor
Gertrude Atherton **2**:18

Richler, Mordecai
Jack London **9**:269

Richman, Robert
Edward Thomas **10**:468

Ricks, Christopher
A. E. Housman **10**:257

Riddel, Joseph N.
Wallace Stevens **3**:466

Rideout, Walter B.
Sherwood Anderson **1**:54; **10**:47

Ridge, George Ross
Joris-Karl Huysmans **7**:413
Émile Zola **6**:565

Ridge, Lola
Henri Barbusse **5**:13

Riemer, Svend
Damon Runyon **10**:425

Riewald, J. G.
Max Beerbohm **1**:69

Riley, Anthony W.
Alfred Döblin **13**:177
Frederick Philip Grove **4**:142, 144

Rilke, Rainer Maria
Thomas Mann **8**:252

Rimanelli, Giose
Cesare Pavese **3**:339

Rimer, J. Thomas
Sōseki Natsume **10**:341
Dazai Osamu **11**:188

Ringe, Donald A.
George Washington Cable **4**:35

Rinsler, Norma
Guillaume Apollinaire **8**:21

Río, Amelia A. de del
Miguel de Unamuno **9**:513

Río, Ángel del
Federico García Lorca **7**:291
Miguel de Unamuno **9**:513

Ritchie, J. M.
Gottfried Benn **3**:113
Georg Kaiser **9**:189
Carl Spitteler **12**:345
Carl Sternheim **8**:375

Rittenhouse, Jessie B.
Edna St. Vincent Millay **4**:305
Sara Teasdale **4**:425

Rizzo, Gino
Ugo Betti **5**:57, 62

Roback, A. A.
Sholem Asch **3**:67

Robb, Nesca A.
A. E. Housman **10**:249

Roberts, Charles G. D.
Bliss Carman **7**:136
Charles G. D. Roberts **8**:315

Roberts, David
Heinrich Mann **9**:326

Roberts, R. Ellis
Ernst Toller **10**:478

Roberts, S. C.
Arthur Conan Doyle **7**:223

Roberts, W. Adolphe
H. G. de Lisser **12**:95

Robertson, J. G.
Henry Handel Richardson **4**:371
Carl Spitteler **12**:347

Robinson, Christopher
Kostes Palamas **5**:385

Robinson, Henry Morton
James Joyce **3**:261

Robinson, Lennox
Lady Gregory **1**:333

Robinson, W. R.
Edwin Arlington Robinson **5**:416

Robinson, William H., Jr.
Rudolph Fisher **11**:206

Robson, W. W.
G. K. Chesterton **1**:188

Rodgers, Lise
Hart Crane **5**:194

Roditi, Edouard
Oscar Wilde **1**:500

Rodrigue, Elizabeth M.
André Gide **12**:146

Rogers, Timothy
Rupert Brooke **2**:57

Rogers, W. G.
Gertrude Stein **1**:429

Rogers, Will, Jr.
Will Rogers **8**:340

Roggendorf, Joseph
Tōson Shimazaki **5**:430

Rohrmoser, Günter
Bertolt Brecht **13**:44

Rolland, Romain
Carl Spitteler **12**:336

Rolleston, James L.
Franz Werfel **8**:482

Rollins, Peter C.
Will Rogers **8**:338

Ronald, Ann
Zane Grey **6**:185

Ronay, Gabriel
Hanns Heinz Ewers **12**:137

Roosevelt, Theodore
H. Rider Haggard **11**:241

Roppolo, Joseph Patrick
Philip Barry **11**:63

Rose, Marilyn Gaddis
Katharine Tynan **3**:506

Rose, Mark
Henry Kuttner **10**:276
Jules Verne **6**:504

Rose, Shirley
Dorothy Richardson **3**:358

Rosen, Norma
Rebecca Harding Davis **6**:154

Rosenbaum, Belle
Margaret Mitchell **11**:373

Rosenbaum, Sidonia Carmen
Gabriela Mistral **2**:476
Alfonsina Storni **5**:444

Rosenberg, Harold
James Weldon Johnson **3**:241

Rosenberg, Isaac
Isaac Rosenberg **12**:286, 287

Rosenberg, Samuel
Arthur Conan Doyle **7**:230

Rosenblatt, Roger
John Millington Synge **6**:442

Rosenfeld, Paul
Sherwood Anderson **1**:34

Rosenheim, Richard
Rudolf Steiner **13**:443

Rosenstone, Robert A.
John Reed **9**:388

Rosenthal, M. L.
César Vallejo **3**:529
William Butler Yeats **1**:567; **11**:533

Rosenthal, Michael
Joyce Cary **1**:147

Rosenthal, Raymond
Isaac Babel **13**:17
Leo Tolstoy **4**:469
Giovanni Verga **3**:544

Ross, Alan
Nathanael West **1**:478

Ross, Stephen M.
James Weldon Johnson **3**:249

Rosten, Norman
Stephen Vincent Benét **7**:77

Rostropowicz, Joanna
Bruno Schulz **5**:424

Roth, Philip
Géza Csáth **13**:154

Roth, Phyllis A.
Bram Stoker **8**:396

Rourke, Constance Mayfield
Zona Gale **7**:277
Sinclair Lewis **13**:336

Rouse, Blair
Ellen Glasgow **7**:339

Routley, Erik
E. C. Bentley **12**:19

Rowe, Anne
Lafcadio Hearn **9**:138

Rowse, A. L.
Alun Lewis **3**:285

Roy, Dilip Kumar
Saratchandra Chatteji **13**:73

Rozhdestvensky, Vsevolod
Sergei Esenin **4**:113

Rubens, Philip M.
Ambrose Bierce **7**:95

Rubin, Joan Shelley
Constance Rourke **12**:327

Rubin, Louis D., Jr.
George Washington Cable **4**:32
Countee Cullen **4**:51
Ellen Glasgow **2**:184
Thomas Wolfe **4**:536

Rudwin, Maximilian J.
Paul Heyse **8**:119

Ruehlen, Petroula Kephala
C. P. Cavafy **2**:92

Ruhm, Herbert
Raymond Chandler **1**:171

Ruihley, Glenn Richard
Amy Lowell **8**:232

Rule, Jane
Radclyffe Hall **12**:192
Gertrude Stein **6**:413

Rumbold, Richard
Antoine de Saint-Exupéry **2**:518

Runciman, James
H. Rider Haggard **11**:239

Runyon, Damon
Damon Runyon **10**:425

Runyon, Damon, Jr.
Damon Runyon **10**:429

Russell, Bertrand
Joseph Conrad **1**:207
Henrik Ibsen **2**:231
Friedrich Nietzsche **10**:373
Bernard Shaw **3**:400
May Sinclair **3**:436
H. G. Wells **6**:538

Russell, D. C.
Raymond Chandler **1**:168

Russell, Frances Theresa
Edith Wharton **3**:561

Russell, Francis
Gertrude Stein **6**:410

Russell, George William
See also **A. E.**
Kahlil Gibran **1**:327

Ryan, Don
Hanns Heinz Ewers **12**:134

Ryf, Robert S.
Joseph Conrad **1**:218

Sachs, Murray
Anatole France **9**:54

Sackville-West, Edward
Joseph Conrad **1**:204
Stefan George **2**:147
Henry James **2**:261
Émile Zola **1**:589

Sackville-West, V.
Hilaire Belloc **7**:36
Selma Lagerlöf **4**:230

Saddlemyer, Ann
Lady Gregory **1**:336

Sadleir, Michael
Alfred Döblin **13**:159

Sadler, Glenn Edward
George MacDonald **9**:303
Charles Williams **11**:495

Sagar, Keith
D. H. Lawrence **2**:371

St. Martin, Hardie
Antonio Machado **3**:307

Saintsbury, George
H. Rider Haggard **11**:237
Juan Valera **10**:497
Émile Zola **6**:560

Sale, Roger
L. Frank Baum **7**:24
Ford Madox Ford **1**:288
A. A. Milne **6**:321

Salinas, Pedro
Ramón del Valle-Inclán **5**:476

Salmon, Eric
Ugo Betti **5**:63

Salmonson, Jessica Amanda
Robert E. Howard **8**:137

Sampley, Arthur M.
Maxwell Anderson **2**:6

Samuel, Maurice
Sholom Aleichem **1**:21

Samuel, Richard
Carl Sternheim **8**:369

Samuels, Ernest
Henry Adams **4**:15

Sanchez, Roberto G.
Jacinto Benavente **3**:100

Sandburg, Carl
See also **Sandburg, Charles A.**
Stephen Vincent Benét **7**:77
Douglas Southall Freeman **11**:219
Jack London **9**:254
Harriet Monroe **12**:216
Robert E. Sherwood **3**:412

Sandburg, Charles A.
See also **Sandburg, Carl**
Jack London **9**:254

Sanders, Charles Richard
Lytton Strachey **12**:408

Sanders, Ivan
Géza Csáth **13**:151

Sanders, Scott
D. H. Lawrence **9**:225

Sandison, Alan
H. Rider Haggard **11**:248

Sandwell, B. K.
Frederick Philip Grove **4**:135

San Juan, E., Jr.
André Gide **5**:232

Sankrityayan, Kamala
Saratchandra Chatteji **13**:79

Santas, Joan Foster
Ellen Glasgow **2**:186

Santayana, George
Friedrich Nietzsche **10**:364
Marcel Proust **7**:523

Sapir, Edward
A. E. Housman **1**:353

Sargent, Daniel
Charles Péguy **10**:405

Saroyan, William
H. L. Mencken **13**:373

Sartre, Jean-Paul
Jean Giraudoux **7**:318

Sarvan, C. P.
Joseph Conrad **13**:141

Sassoon, Siegfried
Wilfred Owen **5**:358
Isaac Rosenberg **12**:290

Saul, George Brandon
A. E. Coppard **5**:178, 181
Lord Dunsany **2**:145
James Stephens **4**:416
Sara Teasdale **4**:428

Saunders, Thomas
Frederick Philip Grove **4**:137

Saurat, Denis
Pierre Loti **11**:360

Savage, D. S.
F. Scott Fitzgerald **1**:248

Savage, George
David Belasco **3**:88

Saveth, Edward N.
Henry Adams **4**:14

Sayers, Dorothy L.
Arthur Conan Doyle **7**:219
Charles Williams **11**:486

Sayers, Raymond S.
Machado de Assis **10**:284

Scalia, S. E.
Vitaliano Brancati **12**:80

Scannell, Vernon
Edward Thomas **10**:459

Scarborough, Dorothy
Arthur Machen **4**:277

Scarfe, Francis
Dylan Thomas **1**:465

Schacht, Richard
Friedrich Nietzsche **10**:386

Scheffauer, Herman George
Ernst Toller **10**:474

Scheick, William J.
H. G. Wells **12**:513

Schevill, James
Eugene O'Neill **1**:405

Schickel, Richard
Raymond Chandler **1**:170

Schier, Donald
Alain-Fournier **6**:14

Schlegel, Dorothy B.
James Branch Cabell **6**:72

Schlesinger, Arthur M., Jr.
George Orwell **2**:497

Schlochower, Harry
Thomas Mann **2**:413

Schlueter, Paul
Arthur Schnitzler **4**:403

Schmidt, Michael
Walter de la Mare **4**:82
Charlotte Mew **8**:301

Schmitt, Hans
Charles Péguy **10**:407

Schneider, Daniel J.
Henry James **11**:344
Wallace Stevens **12**:379

Schneider, Judith Morganroth
Max Jacob **6**:201

Schneider, Sister Lucy
Willa Cather **1**:165

Schöpp-Schilling, Beate
Charlotte Gilman **9**:107

Schorer, Mark
Sherwood Anderson **1**:60
F. Scott Fitzgerald **1**:239
Ford Madox Ford **1**:277
Sinclair Lewis **4**:259; **13**:340
Malcolm Lowry **6**:236
Gertrude Stein **1**:437
H. G. Wells **6**:535
Thomas Wolfe **4**:521

Schreiner, Olive
See also **Iron, Ralph**
Olive Schreiner **9**:393

Schubert, P. Z.
Jaroslav Hašek **4**:189

Schultz, Robert
Joseph Conrad **6**:123

Schultze, Sydney
Leo Tolstoy **11**:478

Schumacher, Ernst
Bertolt Brecht **13**:53

Schürer, Ernst
Georg Kaiser **9**:190

Schwartz, Delmore
Ring Lardner **2**:334
Edna St. Vincent Millay **4**:314
Wallace Stevens **3**:451
William Butler Yeats **1**:556

Schwartz, Kessel
Antonio Machado **3**:309

Schwartz, William Leonard
Amy Lowell **8**:228

Schwarz, Egon
Hugo von Hofmannsthal **11**:306

Schweitzer, Albert
Rudolf Steiner **13**:450

Schweitzer, Darrell
Robert E. Howard **8**:133
H. P. Lovecraft **4**:274

Scott, Ann
Olive Schreiner **9**:405

Scott, Dixon
George Bernard Shaw **3**:382

Scott, J. A.
Ugo Betti **5**:54

Scott, J. D.
André Gide **5**:217

Scott, Kenneth W.
Zane Grey **6**:181

Scott, Nathan A., Jr.
D. H. Lawrence **2**:357

Scott, Winfield Townley
H. P. Lovecraft **4**:265
Amy Lowell **8**:230
Edna St. Vincent Millay **4**:315
Booth Tarkington **9**:472

Scott-Craig, T.S.K.
A. E. Housman **10**:248

Scott-James, R. A.
Lytton Strachey **12**:407

Scrimgeour, Gary J.
F. Scott Fitzgerald **1**:262
John Galsworthy **1**:303

Seaton, Jerome F.
Lu Hsün **3**:300

Seccombe, Thomas
George Gissing **3**:223

Secor, Walter Todd
Paul Bourget **12**:67

Sedgewick, G. G.
Stephen Leacock **2**:378

Sedgewick, Henry Dwight
Edith Wharton **3**:551

Sedgwick, H. D., Jr.
Gabriele D'Annunzio **6**:129

Seeley, Carol
Paul Éluard **7**:245

Seelye, John D.
Booth Tarkington **9**:470
Mark Twain **12**:451

Seferis, George
C. P. Cavafy **7**:159

Segall, Brenda
Rubén Darío **4**:66

Segel, Harold B.
Leonid Andreyev **3**:29
Aleksandr Blok **5**:99
Zinaida Hippius **9**:167
Vladimir Mayakovsky **4**:301

Sehmsdorf, Henning K.
Bjørnstjerne Bjørnson **7**:117

Seib, Kenneth
James Agee **1**:12
Dylan Thomas **8**:462

Seidensticker, Edward G.
Dazai Osamu **11**:171

Seidlin, Oskar
Georg Brandes **10**:64
Gerhart Hauptmann **4**:201
Thomas Mann **2**:423

Seldes, Gilbert
Max Beerbohm **1**:66
F. Scott Fitzgerald **1**:237
Ring Lardner **2**:333
Eugene O'Neill **1**:383

Seltzer, Alvin J.
Joyce Cary **1**:149
Joseph Conrad **1**:219
Franz Kafka **6**:224
Virginia Woolf **1**:548

Seltzer, Thomas
Leonid Andreyev **3**:18

Sendak, Maurice
George MacDonald **9**:300

Sender, Ramon
Federico García Lorca **1**:317

Senf, Carol A.
Bram Stoker **8**:400

Sergeant, Howard
Roy Campbell **5**:122
Wilfred Owen **5**:365

Setchkarev, V.
Valery Bryusov **10**:83

Sewell, Elizabeth
Paul Valéry **4**:494

Seyersted, Per
Kate Chopin **5**:150

Seymour, Alan
Antonin Artaud **3**:49

Seymour-Smith, Martin
Wyndham Lewis **2**:396

Shafer, Robert
James Stephens **4**:408

Shain, Charles E.
F. Scott Fitzgerald **1**:259; **6**:161

Shane, Alex M.
Yevgeny Ivanovich Zamyatin **8**:551

Shanks, Edward
M. P. Shiel **8**:360

Shapiro, Karl
Dylan Thomas **1**:476
William Butler Yeats **1**:568

Sharistanian, Janet
Tess Slesinger **10**:446

Sharp, Dennis
Rudolf Steiner **13**:451

Sharp, Francis Michael
Georg Heym **9**:150

Sharp, William
Bliss Carman **7**:133

Shattuck, Roger
Guillaume Apollinaire **3**:33
Antonin Artaud **3**:59
Alfred Jarry **2**:278, 283
Marcel Proust **7**:542
Paul Valéry **4**:501

Shaw, Bernard
Maurice Baring **8**:31
David Belasco **3**:84
Hilaire Belloc **7**:36
Samuel Butler **1**:136
G. K. Chesterton **6**:97
Anthony Comstock **13**:88
W. H. Davies **5**:198
José Echegaray **4**:96
William Ernest Henley **8**:98
William Dean Howells **7**:367
Henrik Ibsen **2**:220; **8**:143
Henry James **11**:318
Friedrich Nietzsche **10**:360
Edmond Rostand **6**:372
Bernard Shaw **9**:410
Mark Twain **12**:432
Leo Tolstoy **11**:465
H. G. Wells **12**:489
Oscar Wilde **8**:489

Shaw, Donald L.
Pío Baroja **8**:56
José Echegaray **4**:105

Shaw, Irwin
Bertolt Brecht **13**:43

Shaw, Leroy R.
Georg Kaiser **9**:187

Shaw, Priscilla Washburn
Paul Valéry **4**:498

Shaw, Vivian
F. Scott Fitzgerald **1**:236

Sheean, Vincent
Sinclair Lewis **4**:252

Sheed, Wilfrid
G. K. Chesterton **1**:182

Shenker, Israel
E. C. Bentley **12**:25

Shepard, Odell
Bliss Carman **7**:137
Alexander Woollcott **5**:523

Shepherd, A. P.
Rudolf Steiner **13**:444

Sherman, Stuart P.
Arnold Bennett **5**:27
Louis Bromfield **11**:72
Theodore Dreiser **10**:165
Sinclair Lewis **13**:327
Pierre Loti **11**:359
Don Marquis **7**:437
H. L. Mencken **13**:358

Sherrard, Philip
C. P. Cavafy **7**:155

Sherwood, Margaret
Marie Belloc Lowndes **12**:200

Sherwood, Robert Emmet
Philip Barry **11**:58
Robert Sherwood **3**:409

Shestov, Lev
Anton Chekhov **3**:147
Leo Tolstoy **4**:478

Shiel, M. P.
M. P. Shiel **8**:360

Shivers, Albert S.
Maxwell Anderson **2**:9

Short, Clarice
James Stephens **4**:413

Showalter, Elaine
Dorothy Richardson **3**:360
Olive Schreiner **9**:403

Shreffler, Philip A.
H. P. Lovecraft **4**:272

Shulman, Alix Kates
Emma Goldman **13**:224

Shumaker, Wayne
George Moore **7**:495

Shuman, R. Baird
Robert E. Sherwood **3**:414

Shuttleworth, Martin
Henri Barbusse **5**:16

Sibley, Agnes
Charles Williams **11**:498

Sichel, Walter
W. S. Gilbert **3**:209

Sidney-Fryer, Donald
Ambrose Bierce **7**:96

Sievers, W. David
Philip Barry **11**:58

Silk, Dennis
Isaac Rosenberg **12**:298

Silver, Arnold
Bernard Shaw **9**:426

Silvi, Margherita M.
Vitaliano Brancati **12**:80

Silz, Walter
Paul Heyse **8**:122

Simmons, Ernest J.
Konstantin Dmitriyevich Balmont **11**:32
Leo Tolstoy **4**:473

Simon, Anne
F. T. Marinetti **10**:315

Simon, John
Henrik Ibsen **2**:232
Bernard Shaw **3**:405

Simon, John Kenneth
Valéry Larbaud **9**:202

Simonson, Harold P.
Zona Gale **7**:284

Simpson, Donald H.
Lytton Strachey **12**:415

Simpson, Lesley Byrd
Mariano Azuela **3**:79

Sinclair, May
Sinclair Lewis **13**:327
Dorothy Richardson **3**:345
Edwin Arlington Robinson **5**:400

Sinclair, Upton
Sherwood Anderson **10**:37
Vicente Blasco Ibáñez **12**:34
Emma Goldman **13**:213
Joseph Hergesheimer **11**:272
Jack London **9**:256
H. L. Mencken **13**:368
Mark Twain **12**:433
H. G. Wells **12**:492

Sinden, Margaret
Gerhart Hauptmann **4**:201

Singer, Armand E.
Paul Bourget **12**:73

Singer, Isaac B.
Bruno Schulz **5**:420, 426

Singh, Amritjit
Wallace Thurman **6**:450

Singh, Bhupal
Rudyard Kipling **8**:184

Sinyavsky, Andrey
Isaac Babel **13**:24

Sirin, Vladimir
See also **Nabokov, Vladimir**
Rupert Brooke **2**:54

Sisson, C. H.
Edward Thomas **10**:468

Sitwell, Edith
W. H. Davies **5**:203
A. E. Housman **10**:240
D. H. Lawrence **2**:369
Gertrude Stein **6**:403
William Butler Yeats **1**:555

Sitwell, Sir Osbert
Ronald Firbank **1**:227
Alfred Noyes **7**:514

Sizemore, Christine W.
Franz Kafka **6**:227

Skaggs, Merrill Maguire
Willa Cather **11**:115

Skelton, Isabel
Frederick Philip Grove **4**:133

Skelton, Robin
John Millington Synge **6**:439

Skinner, B. F.
Gertrude Stein **6**:404

Skinner, Richard Dana
Philip Barry **11**:51
Wallace Thurman **6**:445
Alexander Woollcott **5**:522

Slate, Tom
Edgar Rice Burroughs **2**:82

Slater, Candace
César Vallejo **3**:534

Slesinger, Tess
Tess Slesinger **10**:440

Slochower, Harry
Sholem Asch **3**:67
Alfred Döblin **13**:162
Heinrich Mann **9**:317
Arthur Schnitzler **4**:393
Ernst Toller **10**:483
Sigrid Undset **3**:515
Franz Werfel **8**:469

Slonim, Marc
Isaak Babel **2**:37
Konstantin Dmitriyevich Balmont **11**:33
Andrey Bely **7**:52
Aleksandr Blok **5**:87
Ivan Bunin **6**:51
Maxim Gorky **8**:79
Giuseppe Tomasi di Lampedusa **13**:291
Marina Tsvetaeva **7**:557, 566

Smertinko, Johan J.
Sholem Asch **3**:65

Smith, A.J.M.
Duncan Campbell Scott **6**:390

Smith, Clark Ashton
William Hope Hodgson **13**:232

Smith, George N.
Booker T. Washington **10**:514

Smith, Grover
Ford Madox Ford **1**:288

Smith, Harrison
Joyce Cary **1**:141
Heinrich Mann **9**:315

Smith, Hazel Littlefield
See **Littlefield, Hazel**

Smith, Henry James
O. Henry **1**:345

Smith, Henry Nash
Theodore Dreiser **10**:190
Mark Twain **6**:478

Smith, Hugh Allison
Edmond Rostand **6**:379

Smith, Maxwell A.
Antoine de Saint-Exupéry **2**:520

Smith, Nora Archibald
José Echegaray **4**:98

Smith, R. B.
Pierre Teilhard de Chardin **9**:500

Smith, Robert A.
Claude McKay **7**:457

Smith, Rowland
Roy Campbell **5**:125
Wyndham Lewis **2**:399

Smith, Stanley Astredo
Guiseppe Giacosa **7**:306, 312

Smith, Verity
Ramón del Valle-Inclán **5**:487

Smith, Virginia Llewellyn
Anton Chekhov **10**:112

Smith, William Jay
Valéry Larbaud **9**:200

Smith, Winifred
Arthur Schnitzler **4**:387

Smuts, J. C.
Olive Schreiner **9**:396

Snell, George
Ambrose Bierce **1**:88

Snider, Clifton
Virginia Woolf **5**:516

Snodgrass, Chris
Oscar Wilde **1**:509

Snodgrass, W. D.
Gottfried Benn **3**:108

Snow, C. P.
Ronald Firbank **1**:227

Sochen, June
Zona Gale **7**:286

Sokel, Walter H.
Gottfried Benn **3**:107
Georg Heym **9**:142
Franz Kafka **2**:305; **13**:265, 285
Georg Kaiser **9**:182, 183
Robert Musil **12**:253
Carl Sternheim **8**:369, 370
Ernst Toller **10**:485
Frank Wedekind **7**:579
Franz Werfel **8**:473

Sologub, Fyodor
Fyodor Sologub **9**:432

Solomon, Eric
Stephen Crane **11**:154

Solovyov, Vladimir
Valery Bryusov **10**:77

Sonnerfeld, Albert
Georges Bernanos **3**:120, 123

Sontag, Susan
Antonin Artaud **3**:56
Cesare Pavese **3**:338

Sorensen, Otto M.
Bertolt Brecht **13**:50

Sorley, Charles Hamilton
Rupert Brooke **7**:120

Soskin, William
Marjorie Kinnan Rawlings **4**:360

Southerington, F. R.
Thomas Hardy **10**:225

Southworth, James Granville
Hart Crane **2**:117
Thomas Hardy **4**:166
Elinor Wylie **8**:530

Spacks, Patricia Meyer
Charles Williams **1**:524

Spalek, John M.
Franz Werfel **8**:482

Spalter, Max
Karl Kraus **5**:283

Spangler, George M.
Kate Chopin **5**:154

Spann, Meno
Franz Kafka **13**:282

Spanos, William V.
Dorothy L. Sayers **2**:534

Speaight, Robert
Pierre Teilhard de Chardin **9**:491

Spear, Allan H.
James Weldon Johnson **3**:246

Spears, Monroe K.
Hart Crane **2**:119

Spector, Ivar
Leonid Andreyev **3**:25

Speir, Jerry
Raymond Chandler **7**:179

Spell, Jefferson Rea
Mariano Azuela **3**:76

Spencer, Benjamin T.
Sherwood Anderson **1**:61

Spencer, Theodore
William Butler Yeats **1**:554

Spender, Natasha
Raymond Chandler **1**:176

Spender, Stephen
Wolfgang Borchert **5**:106
Robert Bridges **1**:131
C. P. Cavafy **2**:93
Henry James **2**:253
James Joyce **3**:277
Franz Kafka **13**:257
D. H. Lawrence **2**:369
Wyndham Lewis **2**:385
Malcolm Lowry **6**:238
Wilfred Owen **5**:361
Bernard Shaw **3**:393
Dylan Thomas **8**:451
Charles Williams **11**:484
William Butler Yeats **1**:555

Sperber, Murray
George Orwell **6**:353

Spettigue, Douglas O.
Frederick Philip Grove **4**:138, 143, 144

Spiller, Robert E.
Henry Adams **4**:11
Hamlin Garland **3**:195

Spitteler, Carl
Carl Spitteler **12**:334

Spivey, Ted R.
Oscar Wilde **8**:501

Sprague, Claire
Edgar Saltus **8**:352
Virginia Woolf **1**:545

Sprague, Rosemary
Sara Teasdale **4**:431

Spring, Powell
Rudolf Steiner **13**:442

Squire, J. C.
See also **Eagle, Solomon**
Maurice Baring **8**:32
Robert Bridges **1**:125
G. K. Chesterton **6**:97
W. H. Davies **5**:201
Walter de la Mare **4**:72
A. E. Housman **1**:353
D. H. Lawrence **9**:212
Katherine Mansfield **8**:275
Alice Meynell **6**:297
Bernard Shaw **3**:385
William Butler Yeats **1**:553

Stafford, Jean
Anthony Comstock **13**:96

Stafford, John
Joel Chandler Harris **2**:211

Stahl, E. L.
Rainer Maria Rilke **1**:411

Stallman, Robert Wooster
Stephen Crane **11**:137

Stamm, Rudolf
Eugene O'Neill **1**:390

Stanford, Derek
Alfred Noyes **7**:515
Arthur Symons **11**:446
Dylan Thomas **8**:455

Stanford, W. B.
Nikos Kazantzakis **2**:314

Stanislavski, Constantin
Anton Chekhov **10**:101

Stansbury, Milton H.
Jean Giraudoux **2**:155

Stanton, Edward F.
Federico García Lorca **7**:298

Starkie, Enid
André Gide **12**:163

Starkie, Walter
Jacinto Benavente **3**:97
Vicente Blasco Ibáñez **12**:40
Federico García Lorca **1**:317
Gregorio Martinez Sierra and Maria Martinez Sierra **6**:277

Starr, Nathan Comfort
Charles Williams **11**:488

Starrett, Vincent
Ambrose Bierce **7**:89
Arthur Conan Doyle **7**:220
Arthur Machen **4**:278

Stavrou, C. N.
Nikos Kazantzakis **5**:261

Stearns, Harold
John Reed **9**:382

Stearns, Monroe M.
Thomas Wolfe **13**:474

Steele, Elizabeth
Hugh Walpole **5**:502

Steen, Marguerite
Hugh Walpole **5**:499

Steene, Birgitta
August Strindberg **8**:413

Stegner, Wallace
Willa Cather **1**:167
Bret Harte **1**:343
Thomas Wolfe **13**:477

Stein, Allen F.
Ring Lardner **2**:340

Stein, Gertrude
Henry James **2**:261

Stein, Paul
Jack London **9**:278

Steiner, George
Ford Madox Ford **1**:288
Henrik Ibsen **8**:148
Leo Tolstoy **4**:467

Steiner, Marie
Rudolf Steiner **13**:442

Steiner, Rudolf
Friedrich Nietzsche **10**:358
Rudolf Steiner **13**:438

Steinmann, Martin Jr.
T. F. Powys **9**:369

Stempel, Daniel
Lafcadio Hearn **9**:129

Stender-Petersen, Adolph
Władysław Stanisław Reymont **5**:390

Stenerson, Douglas C.
H. L. Mencken **13**:390

Stephen, James Kenneth
H. Rider Haggard **11**:240

Stephens, Donald
Bliss Carman **7**:147

Stephens, James
A. E. **10**:17
William Butler Yeats **11**:525

Stephensen, P. R.
Aleister Crowley **7**:210

Sterling, George
Ambrose Bierce **7**:88, 91

Stern, Alfred
José Ortega y Gasset **9**:341

Stern, Guy
Bertolt Brecht **13**:62

Stern, J. P.
Jaroslav Hašek **4**:186
Thomas Mann **2**:438
Friedrich Nietzsche **10**:394
Rainer Maria Rilke **1**:424

Stern, Philip Van Doren
Arthur Machen **4**:279

Stevens, Wallace
Harriet Monroe **12**:220
Wallace Stevens **12**:357
Paul Valéry **4**:494

Stevenson, Lionel
Gertrude Atherton **2**:16
John McCrae **12**:209
M. P. Shiel **8**:364
May Sinclair **11**:412

Stewart, Allegra
Gertrude Stein **1**:434

Stewart, Donald Ogden
Robert Benchley **1**:78

Stewart, J.I.M.
James Joyce **3**:274
Rudyard Kipling **8**:197
D. H. Lawrence **2**:368
William Butler Yeats **1**:569

Stewart, Lady Margaret
Antoine de Saint-Exupéry **2**:518

Stine, Peter
Franz Kafka **6**:232

Stirling, Monica
Colette **1**:191

Stock, Irvin
André Gide **12**:154

Stock, Michael O. P.
Pierre Teilhard de Chardin **9**:484

Stone, Albert E., Jr.
Mark Twain **6**:471

Stone, Geoffrey
Roy Campbell **5**:117
Oscar Wilde **8**:499

Stonesifer, Richard J.
W. H. Davies **5**:205

Storer, Edward
Luigi Pirandello **4**:325

Stork, Charles Wharton
Sigrid Undset **3**:511
Verner von Heidenstam **5**:248, 249, 256
Hugo von Hofmannsthal **11**:294

Stouck, David
Willa Cather **11**:107, 112
Sarah Orne Jewett **1**:369

Stout, Joseph A., Jr.
Will Rogers **8**:338

Strachey, James
Lytton Strachey **12**:407

Strachey, John
George Orwell **2**:505

Strachey, Lytton
Thomas Hardy **4**:154
Lytton Strachey **12**:391

Strakhov, Nikolai N.
Leo Tolstoy **4**:449

Strakhovsky, Leonid I.
Osip Mandelstam **6**:257

Strauss, Harold
Jakob Wassermann **6**:512

Strauss, Walter A.
Marcel Proust **7**:533

Stream, George G.
Ugo Betti **5**:63

Strier, Richard
Hart Crane **2**:125

Strindberg, August
Friedrich Nietzsche **10**:353

Strizhevskaya, L
Saratchandra Chatterji **13**:81

Strong, Kenneth
Toson Shimazaki **5**:440

Strong, L.A.G.
Lewis Grassic Gibbon **4**:120
Radclyffe Hall **12**:188
Hugh Walpole **5**:501

Stroud, Parry
Stephen Vincent Benét **7**:78

Struc, Roman S.
Fyodor Sologub **9**:444

Struve, Gleb
Isaac Babel **13**:27
Mikhail Bulgakov **2**:63, 65
Ivan Bunin **6**:44
Maxim Gorky **8**:75
Yevgeny Ivanovich Zamyatin **8**:545

Stuart, John
John Reed **9**:384

Stubbs, Marcia C.
Alain-Fournier **6**:15

Stuckey, W. J.
Margaret Mitchell **11**:377
Marjorie Kinnan Rawlings **4**:365

Sturgeon, Mary C.
James Stephens **4**:409

Sturrock, John
Marcel Proust **13**:421

Sturtevant, Albert Morey
Alexander Kielland **5**:278

Styan, J. L.
Bertolt Brecht **13**:67
Georg Kaiser **9**:193

Styron, William
Thomas Wolfe **4**:535

Suckow, Ruth
Ricarda Huch **13**:241

Sukenick, Ronald
Wallace Stevens **12**:372

Sullivan, Jack
Algernon Blackwood **5**:78
Hanns Heinz Ewers **12**:139
M. R. James **6**:214

Sullivan, Kevin
Lady Gregory **1**:335
Oscar Wilde **1**:507

Summer, Ed
Robert E. Howard **8**:138

Summers, Montague
Bram Stoker **8**:385

Sussex, Ronald
Émile Verhaeren **12**:473

Sutherland, Donald
Gertrude Stein **6**:407

Sutherland, Ronald
Frederick Philip Grove **4**:140

Sutton, Graham
Harley Granville-Barker **2**:195
A. A. Milne **6**:308
Alfred Sutro **6**:421

Sutton, Max Keith
W. S. Gilbert **3**:217

Suvin, Darko
Karel Čapek **6**:930
H. G. Wells **12**:510
Yevgeny Ivanovich Zamyatin **8**:554

Swain, J. O.
Vicente Blasco Ibáñez **12**:43

Swales, Martin
Thomas Mann **8**:268
Arthur Schnitzler **4**:402

Swallow, Alan
Hart Crane **2**:116

Swan, Michael
Max Beerbohm **1**:71

Swann, Thomas Burnett
Ernest Dowson **4**:90
A. A. Milne **6**:315

Swanson, Roy Arthur
Kostes Palamas **5**:382

Sweetser, Wesley D.
Arthur Machen **4**:282

Swinburne, Algernon Charles
Algernon Charles Swinburne **8**:424

Swinnerton, Frank
Hilaire Belloc **7**:40
Arnold Bennett **5**:43
Robert Bridges **1**:130
Joseph Conrad **1**:201
Ford Madox Ford **1**:277
John Galsworthy **1**:298
George Gissing **3**:226
Wyndham Lewis **9**:237
Rose Macaulay **7**:426
Charlotte Mew **8**:298
A. A. Milne **6**:310
George Moore **7**:480
Wilfred Owen **5**:360
Dorothy Richardson **3**:352
Dorothy L. Sayers **2**:527
Bernard Shaw **3**:388
James Stephens **4**:411
H. G. Wells **6**:536
Virginia Woolf **1**:532

Sykes, Christopher
Frederick Rolfe **12**:272

Sykes, W. J.
Duncan Campbell Scott **6**:387

Symes, Gordon
Alun Lewis **3**:286

Symonds, John
Aleister Crowley **7**:211

Symonds, John Addington
Vernon Lee **5**:309
Algernon Charles Swinburne **8**:426

Symons, A.J.A.
Frederick Rolfe **12**:269

Symons, Arthur
Gabriele D'Annunzio **6**:128
Ernest Dowson **4**:85
Thomas Hardy **4**:154
William Ernest Henley **8**:97
Joris-Karl Huysmans **7**:410
Alfred Jarry **2**:277
James Joyce **8**:158
Maurice Maeterlinck **3**:327
George Moore **7**:474
Edgar Saltus **8**:348
Olive Schreiner **9**:393
Arthur Symons **11**:427
Sara Teasdale **4**:423
Émile Verhaeren **12**:468
William Butler Yeats **11**:509

Symons, Julian
E. C. Bentley **12**:18
Raymond Chandler **1**:173; **7**:175
Arthur Conan Doyle **7**:238

Szabolcsi, Miklós
Endre Ady **11**:21

Szczesny, Gerhard
Bertolt Brecht **6**:32

Tagore, Rabindranath
Saratchandra Chatterji **13**:72

Taine, H.
Friedrich Nietzsche **10**:353

Talamantes, Florence
Alfonsina Storni **5**:446

Tanner, Tony
Jack London **9**:269
George MacDonald **9**:297

Tarkington, Booth
Booth Tarkington **9**:462
Mark Twain **12**:437

Tarn, Adam
Stanisław Ignacy Witkiewicz **8**:508

Tarrant, Desmond
James Branch Cabell **6**:76
Theodore Dreiser **10**:196

Tate, Allen
Stephen Vincent Benét **7**:70
Roy Campbell **5**:117
Hart Crane **2**:114, 117
Douglas Southall Freeman **11**:222
Edwin Muir **2**:481
Edwin Arlington Robinson **5**:405
Charles Williams **11**:484
William Butler Yeats **11**:523

Taubman, Jane Adelman
Marina Tsvetaeva **7**:566

Taylor, A.J.P.
John Reed **9**:390

Taylor, Alexander
Franz Kafka **13**:272

Taylor, Colleen M.
Bruno Schulz **5**:423

Taylor, Desmond Shaw
Lady Gregory **1**:338

Taylor, Martin C.
Gabriela Mistral **2**:480

Taylor, Una
Maurice Maeterlinck **3**:324

Taylor, Wendell Hertig
E. C. Bentley **12**:20

Tchekhov, Anton
See also **Chekhov, Anton Pavlovich**
Maxim Gorky **8**:67, 68

Tchukovsky, K.
Valery Bryusov **10**:78

Teilhard de Chardin, Pierre
Pierre Teilhard de Chardin **9**:477

Temple, Ruth Zabriskie
Arthur Symons **11**:440

Tenenbaum, Louis
Vitaliano Brancati **12**:80, 82
Cesare Pavese **3**:337

Tennyson, Alfred
Algernon Charles Swinburne **8**:423

Terras, Victor
Isaak Babel **2**:21
Osip Mandelstam **2**:402; **6**:262

Terwilliger, Thomas
Hanns Heinz Ewers **12**:135

Test, George A.
Karel Čapek **6**:92

Thale, Jerome
Joseph Conrad **13**:108

Thau, Annette
Max Jacob **6**:195, 199

Theis, O. F.
Frank Wedekind **7**:576

Thomas, David
Henrik Ibsen **8**:154

Thomas, Dylan
Wilfred Owen **5**:363
Dylan Thomas **8**:451

Thomas, Lawrence
André Gide **5**:219

Thomas, R. George
Edward Thomas **10**:463

Thompson, Charles Miner
Mary Wilkins Freeman **9**:61

Thompson, Edward J.
Rabindranath Tagore **3**:484, 490

Thompson, Ewa M.
Aleksandr Blok **5**:97

Thompson, Francis
Bliss Carman **7**:133
Gabriele D'Annunzio **6**:128
Ernest Dowson **4**:90
A. E. Housman **10**:238
Alice Meynell **6**:291
Algernon Charles Swinburne **8**:428
William Butler Yeats **11**:508

Thompson, William Irwin
A. E. **3**:12

Thomson, H. Douglas
E. C. Bentley **12**:13

Thomson, Paul van Kuykendall
Francis Thompson **4**:440

Thorp, Willard
Sherwood Anderson **1**:52

Thuente, Mary Helen
William Butler Yeats **11**:537

Thurber, James
L. Frank Baum **7**:14
Robert Benchley **1**:80

Thurley, Geoffrey
Sergei Esenin **4**:114

Thurman, Wallace
Countee Cullen **4**:41
Claude McKay **7**:456

Thurston, Henry W.
Henry Adams **4**:4

Tiefenbrun, Ruth
Franz Kafka **13**:280

Tietjens, Eunice
Willa Cather **11**:93

Tikhonov, Nikolay
Sergei Esenin **4**:113

Tilles, Solomon H.
Rubén Darío **4**:65

Tillotson, Geoffrey
Ernest Dowson **4**:88

Tillyard, E.M.W.
Joseph Conrad **1**:209
James Joyce **3**:269

Timberlake Craig
David Belasco **3**:89

Timms, Edward
Karl Kraus **5**:291

Tindall, Gillian
George Gissing **3**:237

Tindall, William York
Joseph Conrad **13**:117
D. H. Lawrence **2**:356
Wallace Stevens **3**:460
William Butler Yeats **1**:578

Titche, Leon L., Jr.
Alfred Döblin **13**:169
Robert Musil **12**:250

Titiev, Janice Geasler
Alfonsina Storni **5**:450

Tobin, Patricia
James Joyce **3**:278

Toksvig, Signe
Sigrid Undset **3**:510

Tolkien, J.R.R.
Charles Williams **11**:493

Toller, Ernst
Ernst Toller **10**:479

Tolstoy, Leo
Leonid Andreyev **3**:16

Tolton, C.D.E.
André Gide **5**:243

Tomlin, E.W.F.
Wyndham Lewis **2**:391

Topping, Gary
Zane Grey **6**:183, 186

Toth, Susan Allen
Mary Wilkins Freeman **9**:74

Tougas, Gerard
Hector Saint-Denys Garneau **13**:200

Toumanova, Nina Andronikova
Anton Chekhov **3**:155

Townsend, R. D.
Vicente Blasco Ibáñez **12**:38
Sinclair Lewis **13**:325

Towson, M. R.
Gottfried Benn **3**:110

Toynbee, Philip
André Gide **5**:228
James Joyce **3**:264

Traschen, Isadore
Thomas Mann **2**:436

Treece, Henry
Dylan Thomas **1**:467

Tremper, Ellen
A. A. Milne **6**:320

Trend, J. B.
Antonio Machado **3**:305

Trensky, Paul I.
Karel Čapek **6**:90

Trent, William P.
Edwin Arlington Robinson **5**:400
F. Marion Crawford **10**:142

Trickett, Rachel
Dorothy Richardson **3**:355

Trilling, Lionel
Willa Cather **1**:162
Eugene O'Neill **1**:402
George Orwell **2**:499

Trombly, Albert Edmund
W. H. Davies **5**:200

Trotsky, Leon
Andrey Bely **7**:46
Aleksandr Blok **5**:83
Maxim Gorky **8**:75
Zinaida Hippius **9**:154
Jack London **9**:260
Vladimir Mayakovsky **4**:289
Frank Wedekind **7**:589

Trotter, William Monroe
Booker T. Washington **10**:517

Troy, William
James Joyce **3**:259
Virginia Woolf **1**:534

Trueblood, Charles K.
John Galsworthy **1**:296

Tsvetaeva, Marina
Valery Bryusov **10**:79

Tucker, Carll
Eugene O'Neill **1**:407

Tuell, Anne Kimball
Alice Meynell **6**:297

Tull, J. F., Jr.
Miguel de Unamuno **9**:517

Turgenev, Ivan
Leo Tolstoy **4**:448, 460

Turk, F. A.
Pierre Teilhard de Chardin **9**:497

Turnell, Martin
Alain-Fournier **6**:19
Guillaume Apollinaire **3**:40
Paul Claudel **10**:130

Turner, Arlin
George Washington Cable **4**:28

Turner, Darwin T.
Countee Cullen **4**:49
Paul Laurence Dunbar **2**:129
Joel Chandler Harris **2**:216

Turner, Henry M.
Booker T. Washington **10**:518

Turner, Matthew Freke
Mark Twain **12**:425

Turner, Sheila
Kahlil Gibran **1**:328

Turpin, Waters E.
Rudolph Fisher **11**:206

Turquet-Milnes, G.
Paul Valéry **4**:490

Turrell, Charles Alfred
Gregorio Martinez Sierra and Maria Martinez Sierra **6**:273

Twain, Mark
See also **Clemens, S. L.**
Paul Bourget **12**:61
William Dean Howells **7**:368

Tyler, Robert L.
Arthur Machen **4**:281

Tynan, Katherine
Rose Macaulay **7**:421
William Butler Yeats **11**:506

Tynan, Kenneth
Bertolt Brecht **1**:102

Tytell, John
Frederick Rolfe **12**:277

Ueda, Makoto
Sōseki Natsume **2**:495
Dazai Osamu **11**:185

Ullmann, Christiane
Paul Heyse **8**:123

Ullmann, Stephen
Alain-Fournier **6**:19

Umphrey, George W.
Rubén Darío **4**:58
Amado Nervo **11**:398

Underhill, John Garrett
Jacinto Benavente **3**:93, 95
Gregorio Martinez Sierra and Maria Martinez Sierra **6**:273

Undset, Sigrid
D. H. Lawrence **2**:353

Unterecker, John
Hart Crane **2**:123

Untermeyer, Louis
W. H. Davies **5**:205
Lion Feuchtwanger **3**:178
F. Scott Fitzgerald **1**:250
Amy Lowell **1**:371
Edna St. Vincent Millay **4**:307
Wallace Stevens **12**:376
Sara Teasdale **4**:425, 426
Thomas Wolfe **13**:478

Updike, John
James Agee **1**:6
Max Beerbohm **1**:71, 72
Franz Kafka **13**:283
Sōseki Natsume **10**:347
Bruno Schulz **5**:428

Urban, G. R.
Stefan George **2**:152

Ureña, Pedro Henriquez
Rubén Darío **4**:56

Uroff, M. D.
Hart Crane **2**:124

Usmiani, Renate
Gerhart Hauptmann **4**:208

Valency, Maurice
Anton Chekhov **3**:163
Jean Giraudoux **7**:327

Valera, Juan
Juan Valera **10**:495

Vallery-Radot, Robert
Charles Péguy **10**:403

Van Doren, Carl
James Branch Cabell **6**:64
Willa Cather **1**:150
F. Scott Fitzgerald **1**:236
Zona Gale **7**:279
John Galsworthy **1**:300

Hamlin Garland **3**:192
Joseph Hergesheimer **11**:263
Ring Lardner **2**:326
Don Marquis **7**:436
Edgar Lee Masters **2**:461
Edna St. Vincent Millay **4**:308
Gertrude Stein **1**:427
Booth Tarkington **9**:455
Mark Twain **12**:430
Elinor Wylie **8**:525

Van Doren, Mark
John Galsworthy **1**:300
Thomas Hardy **4**:167
Thomas Mann **2**:425
Luigi Pirandello **4**:333
Constance Rourke **12**:316
Sara Teasdale **4**:425
Miguel de Unamuno **9**:512

Van Ghent, Dorothy
Henry James **11**:331
Dazai Osamu **11**:172

Van Horne, John
Jacinto Benavente **3**:94

Van Kranendonk, A. G.
Katherine Mansfield **2**:448
T. F. Powys **9**:368

Van Nostrand, Albert
Booth Tarkington **9**:464

Van Vechten, Carl
Gertrude Atherton **2**:15
Countee Cullen **4**:39
Ronald Firbank **1**:224
James Weldon Johnson **3**:240
Edgar Saltus **8**:346
M. P. Shiel **8**:359
Elinor Wylie **8**:524

Vass, George, S. J.
Pierre Teilhard de Chardin **9**:483

Vedder, Henry C.
George Washington Cable **4**:24

Vendler, Helen Hennessy
Wallace Stevens **12**:377
William Butler Yeats **1**:570

Ventura, L. D.
Guiseppe Giacosa **7**:305

Verne, Jules
Jules Verne **6**:490
H. G. Wells **6**:524

Verschoyle, Derek
Malcolm Lowry **6**:235

Versluys, Kristiaan
Émile Verhaeren **12**:482

Vessey, David
Arthur Machen **4**:286

Vezér, Erzsébet
Endre Ady **11**:26

Vial, Fernand
Paul Claudel **2**:102

Vidal, Gore
L. Frank Baum **7**:21
Edgar Rice Burroughs **2**:76
F. Scott Fitzgerald **6**:167
Bernard Shaw **9**:420
Edith Wharton **9**:551

Vigar, Penelope
Thomas Hardy **4**:174

Vigliemo, V. H.
Sōseki Natsume **10**:333

Vigneault, Robert
Hector Saint-Denys Garneau **13**:204

Villaseñon, José Sánchez, S. J.
José Ortega y Gasset **9**:338

Vinde, Victor
Sigrid Undset **3**:513

Virgillo, Carmelo
Machado de Assis **10**:295

Vitins, Ieva
Anton Chekhov **10**:115

Vittorini, Domenico
Gabriele D'Annunzio **6**:132
Luigi Pirandello **4**:331, 333

Vlach, Robert
Jaroslav Hašek **4**:181

Voelker, Joseph C.
D. H. Lawrence **9**:227

Vogt Gapp, Samuel
George Gissing **3**:229

Völker, Klaus
Bertolt Brecht **6**:34

Volpe, Edmond L.
Nathanael West **1**:479

Von Hofmannsthal, Hugo
Arthur Schnitzler **4**:392

Von Mohrenschildt, D. S.
Valery Bryusov **10**:81

Vonnegut, Kurt, Jr
H. L. Mencken **13**:392
Mark Twain **6**:482

Voronskij, Aleksandr
Isaac Babel **13**:12

Voronsky, A. K.
Yevgeny Ivanovich Zamyatin **8**:541

Vortriede, Werner
Georg Heym **9**:163

Voss, Arthur
Bret Harte **1**:344
O. Henry **1**:351

Wadlington, Warwick
Nathanael West **1**:489

Wadsworth, Frank W.
Ugo Betti **5**:56

Wadsworth, Philip A.
Antoine de Saint-Exupéry **2**:516

Wagenknecht, Edward
L. Frank Baum **7**:13
Walter de la Mare **4**:77
Ellen Glasgow **2**:178
Henry James **11**:346
Katherine Mansfield **2**:447
Margaret Mitchell **11**:375

Waggoner, Hyatt Howe
Edwin Arlington Robinson **5**:409

Wagner, Geoffrey
Lewis Grassic Gibbon **4**:123
Wyndham Lewis **2**:391

Wagner, Jean
Countee Cullen **4**:46
Paul Laurence Dunbar **12**:114
James Weldon Johnson **3**:243
Claude McKay **7**:459
Damon Runyon **10**:430

Wagner, Philip
H. L. Mencken **13**:386

Wagstaff, Christopher
F. T. Marinetti **10**:321

Wahr, F. B.
Gerhart Hauptmann **4**:200

Wain, John
Arnold Bennett **5**:47
George Orwell **6**:343
Dylan Thomas **1**:471

Wake, Clive
Pierre Loti **11**:364

Walbrook, H. M.
J. M. Barrie **2**:42

Walcutt, Charles Child
Sherwood Anderson **1**:48
Stephen Crane **11**:143
Hamlin Garland **3**:196

Wald, Alan M.
Tess Slesinger **10**:442

Walkley, A. B.
Harley Granville-Barker **2**:192

Wallace, Margaret
Thomas Wolfe **13**:467

Wallace, William
George Moore **7**:473

Walpole, Hugh
James Branch Cabell **6**:63
F. Marion Crawford **10**:147
Joseph Hergesheimer **11**:269

Walser, Richard
Thomas Wolfe **4**:530

Walsh, Chad
Charles Williams **11**:487

Walsh, William
Katherine Mansfield **2**:453

Walter, Elisabeth
Hugo von Hofmannsthal **11**:293

Walters, Jennifer
Boris Vian **9**:531

Walters, Ray
Robert E. Howard **8**:133

Walton, Edith H.
Tess Slesinger **10**:440

Walton, Geoffrey
Edith Wharton **9**:548

Ward, A. C.
Rupert Brooke **7**:125
George Gissing **3**:233

Ward, J. A.
Henry James **11**:336

Ward, J. P.
Edward Thomas **10**:461

Ward, Susan
Jack London **9**:276

Wardropper, Bruce W.
Antonio Machado **3**:309

Ware, Martin
Duncan Campbell Scott **6**:399

Warncke, Wayne
George Orwell **6**:346

Warner, Beverley E.
Edgar Saltus **8**:342

Warner, Rex
C. P. Cavafy **7**:153

Warren, Austin
Henry Adams **4**:19
M. R. James **6**:210
Franz Kafka **2**:295

Warren, L. A.
Jacinto Benavente **3**:99
Gregorio Martinez Sierra and Maria Martinez Sierra **6**:280
Juan Valera **10**:501
Ramón del Valle-Inclán **5**:476

Warren, Robert Penn
Ivan Bunin **6**:47
Joseph Conrad **1**:205
Mark Twain **6**:480; **12**:448
Franz Werfel **8**:469
Thomas Wolfe **4**:507

Washington, Booker T.
Booker T. Washington **10**:513, 519

Wasson, Richard
Bram Stoker **8**:387

Waters, Brian
W. H. Davies **5**:205

Watkins, Floyd C.
Margaret Mitchell **11**:379
Thomas Wolfe **4**:524

Watson, Barbara Bellow
Bernard Shaw **3**:402

Watson, E. H. Lacon
Edgar Rice Burroughs **2**:75

Watson, George
Alice Meynell **6**:303

Watson, Harold
Paul Claudel **2**:108

Watson, William
William Butler Yeats **11**:507

Watt, Ian
Joseph Conrad **13**:134

Watters, R. E.
Stephen Leacock **2**:381

Watts, Cedric
Joseph Conrad **13**:132

Watts, Emily Stipes
Elinor Wylie **8**:536

Watts, Harold H.
Maxwell Anderson **2**:4
Ugo Betti **5**:65

Watts, Theodore
See also **Watts-Dunton, Theodore**
Algernon Charles Swinburne **8**:426

Watts-Dunton, Theodore
See also **Watts, Theodore**
Theodore Dreiser **10**:163

Waugh, Arthur
Robert Bridges **1**:128
Rupert Brooke **2**:54
Samuel Butler **1**:133
D. H. Lawrence **2**:344
Arthur Symons **11**:433

Waugh, Evelyn
H. G. Wells **12**:503

Way, Brian
F. Scott Fitzgerald **6**:168

Weales, Gerald
James Bridie **3**:138
Harley Granville-Barker **2**:199
Laurence Housman **7**:358
Dorothy L. Sayers **2**:531
Charles Williams **1**:521

Webb, Charles Henry
Mark Twain **6**:453

Webb, Howard W., Jr.
Ring Lardner **2**:336

Weber, Brom
Sherwood Anderson **1**:56
Hart Crane **2**:115

Webster, Harvey Curtis
Countee Cullen **4**:43
Thomas Hardy **4**:166

Webster, Wentworth
José Echegaray **4**:97

Weideli, Walter
Bertolt Brecht **13**:48

Weidle, Wladimir
Paul Claudel **10**:126

Weigand, Hermann J.
Gerhart Hauptmann **4**:202
Henrik Ibsen **8**:144
Thomas Mann **2**:414

Weightman, John
Colette **5**:170
Marcel Proust **13**:430

Weil, Irwin
Maxim Gorky **8**:83

Weimar, Karl S.
Wolfgang Borchert **5**:106
Bertolt Brecht **13**:50

Weinstein, Arnold L.
Joseph Conrad **1**:219
Ford Madox Ford **1**:290
James Joyce **3**:279
Franz Kafka **2**:308

Weinstein, Bernard
Stephen Crane **11**:159

Weinstein, Norman
Gertrude Stein **1**:439

Weintraub, Stanley
Bernard Shaw **3**:400

Weir, Charles, Jr.
F. Scott Fitzgerald **1**:239

Weiss, Beno
Italo Svevo **2**:552

Weisstein, Ulrich
Heinrich Mann **9**:323

Welby, T. Earle
Algernon Charles Swinburne **8**:432
Arthur Symons **11**:434

Welland, Dennis
Wilfred Owen **5**:373

Wellek, René
Georg Brandes **10**:69
Karel Čapek **6**:84
William Dean Howells **7**:388
Henry James **2**:268

Wellman, Esther Turner
Amado Nervo **11**:396

Wells, Arvin B.
James Branch Cabell **6**:73

Wells, H. G.
Hilaire Belloc **7**:34
Arnold Bennett **5**:23
Stephen Crane **11**:124
George Gissing **3**:222
Henry James **2**:247
James Joyce **3**:252
Rudyard Kipling **8**:184
Dorothy Richardson **3**:345
Bernard Shaw **9**:419
Jules Verne **6**:491
Booker T. Washington **10**:518
H. G. Wells **6**:531; **12**:492

Wells, Henry W.
Stephen Vincent Benét **7**:76
Wallace Stevens **12**:369

Wellwarth, G. E.
Antonin Artaud **3**:48
Alfred Jarry **2**:280

Welty, Eudora
Willa Cather **11**:110

Wertheim, Albert
Philip Barry **11**:68

Wescott, Glenway
F. Scott Fitzgerald **6**:160
Thomas Mann **8**:258

West, Anthony
Joyce Cary **1**:142
Machado de Assis **10**:286
Nikos Kazantzakis **5**:259
Sinclair Lewis **13**:338
Robert Musil **12**:236
George Orwell **2**:504
H. G. Wells **6**:538

West, Donald
C. M. Kornbluth **8**:219

West, Geoffrey
Arnold Bennett **5**:35
Annie Besant **9**:16

West, Paul
José Ortega y Gasset **9**:343

West, Rebecca
Sherwood Anderson **1**:39
Maurice Baring **8**:32
Arnold Bennett **5**:32
Willa Cather **1**:153
Colette **1**:191
Ford Madox Ford **1**:275
Emma Goldman **13**:215
Radclyffe Hall **12**:187
Henry James **2**:248
Franz Kafka **2**:298
Wyndham Lewis **2**:397
Katherine Mansfield **8**:275
Olive Schreiner **9**:394
May Sinclair **3**:436
H. G. Wells **6**:525; **12**:493
Edith Wharton **9**:542
Virginia Woolf **1**:530

Westbrook, Perry D.
Mary Wilkins Freeman **9**:72

Wexelblatt, Robert
Leo Tolstoy **11**:476

Weygandt, Cornelius
A. E. **3**:2
George Moore **7**:476
James Stephens **4**:410
Edward Thomas **10**:454

Weyhaupt, Angela Evonne
Stanisław Ignacy Witkiewicz **8**:514

Wharton, Edith
F. Marion Crawford **10**:145
F. Scott Fitzgerald **6**:160
Marcel Proust **7**:520
Edith Wharton **9**:543

Wharton, Lewis
John McCrae **12**:208

Wheatley, Dennis
William Hope Hodgson **13**:237

Wheatley, Elizabeth D.
Arnold Bennett **5**:36

Wheelwright, John
Federico García Lorca **1**:307

Whipple, T. K.
Sherwood Anderson **1**:39
Willa Cather **1**:151
Zane Grey **6**:178
Sinclair Lewis **4**:248
Eugene O'Neill **1**:384

White, David
José Ortega y Gasset **9**:342

White, E. B.
Louis Bromfield **11**:79
Don Marquis **7**:441

White, Gertrude M.
Hilaire Belloc **7**:42

White, Greenough
Bliss Carman **7**:134
Francis Thompson **4**:434

White, Ray Lewis
Sherwood Anderson **1**:58

Whittemore, Reed
Joseph Conrad **1**:212
Bernard Shaw **3**:401

Whittock, Trevor
Bernard Shaw **9**:423

Wiggins, Robert A.
Ambrose Bierce **1**:90

Wilbur, Richard
A. E. Housman **10**:256

Wilcox, Earl
Jack London **9**:271

Wilde, Oscar
William Ernest Henley **8**:96
Rudyard Kipling **8**:175
Algernon Charles Swinburne **8**:427
Oscar Wilde **8**:488
William Butler Yeats **11**:507

Wilden, Anthony
Italo Svevo **2**:550

Wildiers, N. M.
Pierre Teilhard de Chardin **9**:493

Wilkins, Eithne
Robert Musil **12**:232

Wilkins, Ernest Hatch
Gabriele D'Annunzio **6**:136

Wilkinson, Louis U.
T. F. Powys **9**:359

Wilkinson, Marguerite
Charlotte Mew **8**:295

Wilks, Ronald
Maxim Gorky **8**:83

Will, Frederic
Nikos Kazantzakis **5**:264
Kostes Palamas **5**:381-82

Willard, Nancy
Rainer Maria Rilke **1**:421

Williams, C. E.
Robert Musil **12**:258

Williams, Charles
E. C. Bentley **12**:14

Williams, Cratis D.
Sherwood Anderson **1**:55

Williams, Ellen
Harriet Monroe **12**:223

Williams, Harold
W. H. Davies **5**:200
Harley Granville-Barker **2**:193
Laurence Housman **7**:353
Katharine Tynan **3**:504

Williams, John Stuart
Alun Lewis **3**:288

Williams, Kenny J.
Paul Laurence Dunbar **12**:119

Williams, Orlo
Luigi Pirandello **4**:327

Williams, Raymond
Bertolt Brecht **1**:105; **13**:66
George Orwell **6**:348
August Strindberg **1**:457; **8**:411
Ernst Toller **10**:484

Williams, Rhys W.
Carl Sternheim **8**:379

Williams, T. Harry
Douglas Southall Freeman **11**:227

Williams, William Carlos
Federico García Lorca **7**:290
Wallace Stevens **3**:451

Williams-Ellis, A.
Charlotte Mew **8**:296

Williamson, Audrey
James Bridie **3**:133

Williamson, Hugh Ross
Alfred Sutro **6**:423

Williamson, Karina
Roger Mais **8**:240, 250

Willibrand, William Anthony
Ernst Toller **10**:480

Willoughby, L. A.
Christian Morgenstern **8**:304

Willson, A. Leslie
Wolfgang Borchert **5**:110

Wilson, Angus
Arnold Bennett **5**:43
Samuel Butler **1**:137
Rudyard Kipling **8**:205
Bernard Shaw **3**:398
Émile Zola **1**:591

Wilson, Clotilde
Machado de Assis **10**:281

Wilson, Colin
Henri Barbusse **5**:14
Arthur Conan Doyle **7**:233
F. Scott Fitzgerald **1**:251
M. R. James **6**:210
Nikos Kazantzakis **2**:317
H. P. Lovecraft **4**:270
Rainer Maria Rilke **1**:417
Bernard Shaw **3**:400; **9**:425
August Strindberg **8**:411

Wilson, Daniel J.
Zane Grey **6**:186

Wilson, Donald
André Gide **5**:240

Wilson, Edmund
Henry Adams **4**:13
Maxwell Anderson **2**:3
Sherwood Anderson **1**:35, 50
Maurice Baring **8**:43
Philip Barry **11**:46, 51
Max Beerbohm **1**:68, 73
Robert Benchley **1**:76
Ambrose Bierce **1**:89
Louis Bromfield **11**:80
Samuel Butler **1**:134
James Branch Cabell **6**:70
George Washington Cable **4**:29
Willa Cather **1**:152
John Jay Chapman **7**:187, 190
Anton Chekhov **3**:159
Kate Chopin **5**:148
Hart Crane **5**:185
Arthur Conan Doyle **7**:222
Theodore Dreiser **10**:178
Ronald Firbank **1**:226, 228
F. Scott Fitzgerald **1**:233; **6**:159
Anatole France **9**:48
A. E. Housman **10**:252
James Weldon Johnson **3**:240
James Joyce **3**:256, 260
Franz Kafka **2**:294
Rudyard Kipling **8**:187
Giuseppe Tomasi di Lampedusa **13**:301
Ring Lardner **2**:325
D. H. Lawrence **2**:345
H. P. Lovecraft **4**:268
H. L. Mencken **13**:363
Edna St. Vincent Millay **4**:317
Marcel Proust **7**:524
Dorothy L. Sayers **2**:530
Bernard Shaw **3**:391, 396
Gertrude Stein **1**:426; **6**:404
Wallace Stevens **3**:444
Lytton Strachey **12**:398
Algernon Charles Swinburne **8**:443
Leo Tolstoy **4**:480
Paul Valéry **4**:487
H. G. Wells **12**:500
Edith Wharton **3**:558, 579; **9**:544
Elinor Wylie **8**:523
William Butler Yeats **1**:554

Wilson, H. Schütz
Émile Zola **6**:558

Winchell, Walter
Damon Runyon **10**:423

Winebaum, B. V.
William Hope Hodgson **13**:232

Wing, George Gordon
César Vallejo **3**:527

Winkler, R.O.C.
Franz Kafka **2**:288

Winner, Anthony
Anton Chekhov **10**:116
Joris-Karl Huysmans **7**:415

Winship, George P., Jr.
Charles Williams **1**:523

Winsnes, A. H.
Sigrid Undset **3**:521

Winter, Calvin
See also **Cooper, Frederic Taber**
Edith Wharton **3**:553

Winter, William
David Belasco **3**:86
Paul Heyse **8**:118

Winterich, John T.
Will Rogers **8**:334

Winters, Yvor
Henry Adams **4**:8
Hart Crane **2**:112
Robert Bridges **1**:131
Henry James **2**:257
Edwin Arlington Robinson **5**:407
Wallace Stevens **3**:447

Wirth, Andrzej
Tadeusz Borowski **9**:20

Wisse, Ruth R.
Sholom Aleichem **1**:32

Wister, Owen
John Jay Chapman **7**:189

Witkiewicz, Stanisław Ignacy
Stanisław Ignacy Witkiewicz **8**:505

Witte, W.
Christian Morgenstern **8**:305

Wittig, Kurt
Lewis Grassic Gibbon

Wolf, Leonard
Bram Stoker **8**:392

Wolfe, Bernard
Joel Chandler Harris **2**:214

Wolfe, Bertram D.
John Reed **9**:385

Wolfe, Deborah Cannon Partridge
Booker T. Washington **10**:544

Wolfe, Thomas
Thomas Wolfe **4**:510; **13**:469

Wolff, Cynthia Griffin
Kate Chopin **5**:156

Wolff, Robert Lee
George MacDonald **9**:296

Wood, Clement
Edgar Lee Masters **2**:464

Woodburn, John
Thomas Wolfe **4**:521

Woodcock, George
Alain-Fournier **6**:23
Wyndham Lewis **2**:395
Malcolm Lowry **6**:236
George Orwell **2**:508
Oscar Wilde **1**:502

Woodford, Arthur B.
Charlotte Gilman **9**:98

Woodress, James
Booth Tarkington **9**:466

Woodring, Carl
Virginia Woolf **1**:542

Woodruff, Bertram L.
Countee Cullen **4**:42

Woodruff, Stuart C.
Ambrose Bierce **1**:92

Woodson, C. G.
Douglas Southall Freeman **11**:221

Woodward, James B.
Leonid Andreyev **3**:27
Aleksandr Blok **5**:96
Ivan Bunin **6**:56

Woolf, D.
Giovanni Verga **3**:546

Woolf, Leonard S.
Hilaire Belloc **7**:33
Anton Chekhov **3**:149
Radclyffe Hall **12**:185
Amy Lowell **8**:225
Constance Rourke **12**:316
Mark Twain **6**:460
H. G. Wells **12**:498

Woolf, Virginia
Hilaire Belloc **7**:34
Arnold Bennett **5**:28
Rupert Brooke **2**:53
Anton Chekhov **10**:101
Joseph Conrad **1**:198
George Gissing **3**:228
Thomas Hardy **4**:160
Henry James **2**:251
Ring Lardner **2**:326
D. H. Lawrence **9**:213
Sinclair Lewis **4**:247
Katherine Mansfield **8**:276
George Moore **7**:483
Dorothy Richardson **3**:347
Olive Schreiner **9**:395
Lytton Strachey **12**:403
Leo Tolstoy **4**:456
H. G. Wells **6**:527; **12**:496

Woollcott, Alexander
Theodore Dreiser **10**:170
Zona Gale **7**:278
Eugene O'Neill **1**:381
Bernard Shaw **3**:387

Worsley, T. C.
James Bridie **3**:133

Worster, W. W.
Knut Hamsun **2**:201

Wright, Charles
Frederick Rolfe **12**:277

Wright, Richard
H. L. Mencken **13**:381

Wright, Walter F.
Arnold Bennett **5**:49

Wycherley, H. Alan
F. Scott Fitzgerald **1**:261

Wyers, Frances
Miguel de Unamuno **9**:520

Wyndham, Francis
Philip Barry **11**:67

Wyndham, George
Stephen Crane **11**:121

Yamanouchi, Hisaaki
Sōseki Natsume **10**:343

Yarmolinsky, Avrahm
Christian Morgenstern **8**:304

Yates, May
George Gissing **3**:224

Yates, Norris W.
Robert Benchley **1**:80
Don Marquis **7**:443
Will Rogers **8**:334

Yatron, Michael
Edgar Lee Masters **2**:470

Ybarra, T. R.
Vicente Blasco Ibáñez **12**:35

Yeats, William Butler
A. E. **3**:5; **10**:12, 16
Robert Bridges **1**:123
Ernest Dowson **4**:87
Lord Dunsany **2**:135
Lady Gregory **1**:331
William Ernest Henley **8**:101
George Moore **7**:482
Standish O'Grady **5**:347
Wilfred Owen **5**:362
Bernard Shaw **9**:412
Arthur Symons **11**:427
John Millington Synge **6**:425
Rabindranath Tagore **3**:501
Katharine Tynan **3**:502
Oscar Wilde **8**:490
Elinor Wylie **8**:527
William Butler Yeats **11**:515

York, Lamar
Marjorie Kinnan Rawlings **4**:367

Yoshie, Okazaki
Sōseki Natsume **10**:328

Young, Alfred
Booker T. Washington **10**:536

Young, Beatrice
Anatole France **9**:51

Young, Douglas F.
Lewis Grassic Gibbon **4**:126

Young, Howard T.
Federico García Lorca **1**:321
Juan Ramón Jiménez **4**:216
Antonio Machado **3**:307
Miguel de Unamuno **2**:562

Young, Kenneth
H. G. Wells **6**:547

Young, Stark
David Belasco **3**:89
Louis Bromfield **11**:75
Federico García Lorca **7**:290
Eugene O'Neill **1**:385; **6**:324
Luigi Pirandello **4**:327

Bernard Shaw **3**:390
Robert E. Sherwood **3**:410
Gregorio Martínez Sierra and María Martínez Sierra **6**:281
Franz Werfel **8**:467

Youngberg, Karin
G. K. Chesterton **6**:105

Yourcenar, Marguerite
Thomas Mann **2**:433

Yu, Beongcheon
Lafcadio Hearn **9**:133
Sōseki Natsume **2**:493; **10**:336

Yuill, W. E.
Lion Feuchtwanger **3**:181, 186
Heinrich Mann **9**:324

Yutang, Lin
Lu Hsün **3**:294

Zabel, Morton Dauwen
Stephen Vincent Benét **7**:74
Joseph Conrad **1**:202
A. E. Coppard **5**:177
A. E. Housman **10**:247
James Joyce **3**:255
Harriet Monroe **12**:222
Wallace Stevens **12**:355

Zamyatin, Yevgeny
Andrey Bely **7**:48
Anatole France **9**:47
Yevgeny Ivanovich Zamyatin **8**:543

Zangwill, Israel
H. G. Wells **12**:487

Zaturenska, Marya
Amy Lowell **1**:378
Harriet Monroe **12**:221
Sara Teasdale **4**:430

Zavalishin, Vyacheslav
Mikhail Bulgakov **2**:64

Zegger, Hrisey Dimitrakis
May Sinclair **3**:441

Ziff, Larzer
Ambrose Bierce **1**:94
John Jay Chapman **7**:199
Kate Chopin **5**:148
F. Marion Crawford **10**:156
Hamlin Garland **3**:199
Sarah Orne Jewett **1**:368

Zilboorg, Gregory
Yevgeny Ivanovich Zamyatin **8**:542

Zimmerman, Dorothy
Virginia Woolf **1**:543

Zinman, Toby Silverman
Katherine Mansfield **2**:457

Ziolkowski, Theodore
Alfred Döblin **13**:166
Rainer Maria Rilke **6**:366

Zlobin, Vladimir
Zinaida Hippius **9**:158

Zohn, Harry
Karl Kraus **5**:290

Zola, Émile
Joris-Karl Huysmans **7**:403

Zorn, Marilyn
Katherine Mansfield **8**:288

Zweig, Stefan
Maxim Gorky **8**:74
Thomas Mann **2**:418
Friedrich Nietzsche **10**:365
Leo Tolstoy **4**:458
Émile Verhaeren **12**:459